THE
COMPLETE WORKS OF
WILLIAM
SHAKESPEARE

Oxford University Press, Amen House, London E.C. 4

GLASGOW NEW YORK TORONTO MELBOURNE WELLINGTON
BOMBAY CALCUTTA MADRAS CAPE TOWN

Geoffrey Cumberlege, Publisher to the University

THE
COMPLETE WORKS OF
WILLIAM
SHAKESPEARE

Edited with a Glossary by

W. J. CRAIG, M.A.
Trinity College, Dublin

GEOFFREY CUMBERLEGE
OXFORD UNIVERSITY PRESS
London   New York   Toronto

This edition of Shakespeare's Works was first published in 1905, and reprinted in 1905, 1907, 1909, 1911, 1913, 1914, 1916, 1919, 1922, 1924, 1926, 1928, 1930, 1935, and 1942. In 1943 the book was re-set and published in its present form and was reprinted in 1945, 1947, 1950, and 1952

PRINTED IN GREAT BRITAIN

PREFACE

THERE is no proof that Shakespeare personally superintended the printing of any of his plays. Although sixteen came separately from the press in small quarto volumes during his lifetime, many, if not all, of these were published without the consent or supervision of the author from copies often surreptitiously obtained from the playhouse. At the time of Shakespeare's death in 1616, no less than twenty-one plays remained in manuscript. Six years later, in 1622, one of these, 'Othello', was issued to the public in quarto. It was not until 1623 that Shakespeare's actor friends, John Heming and Henry Condell, brought together the previously printed and unprinted dramas of which they knew him to be the author, and published them in a folio volume in order 'to keep' (as they wrote) 'the memory of so worthy a friend and fellow alive'. Thirty-six plays were thus claimed for Shakespeare. The thirty-seventh, 'Pericles', had been first printed separately in quarto in 1609, but was not added to the collection until the third folio appeared in 1664.

The text alike of the first folio and the quartos was doubtless supplied by playhouse copies which often embodied the ill-conditioned interpolations and alterations of actors and theatrical managers. As a rule the editors of 1623 followed where they could the text of the quartos, but in a few cases they unwisely had recourse to less correct copies. Moreover, the printers of both Elizabeth's and James I's reigns were very liable to typographical error, and they introduced much that is unintelligible into the original editions of Shakespeare's works. But in the absence of Shakespeare's manuscripts, the seventeen early quartos and the folio of 1623 jointly present, despite defect of copyist and printer, the sole authorized version of the Shakespearian text. From that version I have only ventured to deviate where it seemed to me that the carelessness of either copyist or printer deprived a word or sentence wholly of meaning. Editors of Shakespeare have sometimes denounced as corrupt and have partially altered passages which owe their difficulty of interpretation to the presence of some word or phrase rare in Shakespeare's day and long since obsolete. It has been my endeavour to avoid this danger. I have only adopted a change after convincing myself that the characteristics of Shakespeare's vocabulary or literary style failed to justify the original reading.

For the uncertain orthography of the old editions I have substituted the recognized orthography of the present day. But metrical considerations occasionally render the retention of the older spelling necessary, and I have deemed it desirable to adhere to the older forms of a few words which modern orthography has practically shaped anew. The punctuation has been thoroughly revised, and, to increase facilities of reference, I have numbered the lines at shorter intervals than have been adopted hitherto.

In seeking to emend corrupt passages I have carefully considered the suggestions of my many predecessors, and from few of those who have already laboured in the field of textual criticism have I failed to derive some enlightenment. Of the older editors, Theobald, whose edition of Shakespeare appeared in 1733, and Capell, whose edition appeared in 1768, have proved most helpful. Among more modern editions I am chiefly indebted to the work of Delius, Dyce, and the Cambridge editors. A very few of the emendations which I have adopted are now introduced into the text for the first time. My thanks are due to my friend Mr. P. A. Daniel for many useful suggestions.

I have appended a short glossary, which I trust will adequately explain the meaning of the obsolete words which Shakespeare employed.

W. J. CRAIG.

1894.

CONTENTS

CONTENTS

POEMS

THE TEMPEST

DRAMATIS PERSONÆ

ALONSO, King of Naples.
SEBASTIAN, his Brother.
PROSPERO, the right Duke of Milan.
ANTONIO, his Brother, the usurping Duke of Milan.
FERDINAND, Son to the King of Naples.
GONZALO, an honest old Counsellor.
ADRIAN, } Lords.
FRANCISCO, }
CALIBAN, a savage and deformed Slave.
TRINCULO, a Jester.

STEPHANO, a drunken Butler.
Master of a Ship, Boatswain, Mariners.
MIRANDA, Daughter to Prospero.
ARIEL, an airy Spirit.
IRIS, }
CERES, }
JUNO, } presented by Spirits.
Nymphs, }
Reapers, }
Other Spirits attending on Prospero.

SCENE.—*The Sea, with a Ship; afterwards an Island.*

ACT I

SCENE I.—*On a Ship at Sea. A tempestuous noise of thunder and lightning heard.*

Enter a Shipmaster *and a* Boatswain *severally.*

Mast. Boatswain!
Boats. Here, master: what cheer?
Mast. Good, speak to the mariners: fall to't yarely, or we run ourselves aground: bestir, bestir.   [*Exit.*

Enter Mariners.

Boats. Heigh, my hearts! cheerly, cheerly, my hearts! yare, yare! Take in the topsail. Tend to the master's whistle.—Blow, till thou burst thy wind, if room enough!   9

Enter ALONSO, SEBASTIAN, ANTONIO, FERDINAND, GONZALO, *and others.*

Alon. Good boatswain, have care. Where's the master? Play the men.
Boats. I pray now, keep below.   12
Ant. Where is the master, boson?
Boats. Do you not hear him? You mar our labour: keep your cabins: you do assist the storm.   16
Gon. Nay, good, be patient.
Boats. When the sea is. Hence! What cares these roarers for the name of king? To cabin: silence! trouble us not.   20
Gon. Good, yet remember whom thou hast aboard.   22
Boats. None that I more love than myself. You are a counsellor: if you can command these elements to silence, and work the peace of the present, we will not hand a rope more; use your authority: if you cannot, give thanks you have lived so long, and make yourself ready in your cabin for the mischance of the hour, if it so hap.—Cheerly, good hearts!—Out of our way, I say.   [*Exit.*
Gon. I have great comfort from this fellow: methinks he hath no drowning mark upon him; his complexion is perfect gallows. Stand fast, good Fate, to his hanging! make the rope of his destiny our cable, for our own doth little advantage! If he be not born to be hanged, our case is miserable.   [*Exeunt.*

Re-enter Boatswain.

Boats. Down with the topmast! yare! lower, lower! Bring her to try with main-course. [*A cry within.*] A plague upon this howling! they are louder than the weather, or our office.— 42

Re-enter SEBASTIAN, ANTONIO, *and* GONZALO.
Yet again? what do you here? Shall we give o'er, and drown? Have you a mind to sink?
Seb. A pox o' your throat, you bawling, blasphemous, incharitable dog!
Boats. Work you, then.   47
Ant. Hang, cur, hang! you whoreson, insolent noisemaker, we are less afraid to be drowned than thou art.
Gon. I'll warrant him for drowning; though the ship were no stronger than a nutshell, and as leaky as an unstanched wench.   53
Boats. Lay her a-hold, a-hold! Set her two courses; off to sea again; lay her off.

Enter Mariners, *wet.*
Mar. All lost! to prayers, to prayers! all lost!   [*Exeunt.*
Boats. What, must our mouths be cold? 58
Gon. The king and prince at prayers! let us assist them,
For our case is as theirs.
Seb.   I am out of patience. 60
Ant. We are merely cheated of our lives by drunkards.—
This wide-chapp'd rascal,—would thou might'st lie drowning,
The washing of ten tides!
Gon.   He'll be hang'd yet,
Though every drop of water swear against it, 64
And gape at wid'st to glut him.
[*A confused noise within,*—'Mercy on us!'—
'We split, we split!'—'Farewell, my wife and children!'—
'Farewell, brother!'—'We split, we split, we split!'   67
Ant. Let's all sink wi' the king.   [*Exit.*
Seb. Let's take leave of him.   [*Exit.*
Gon. Now would I give a thousand furlongs of sea for an acre of barren ground; long heath, brown furze, any thing. The wills above be done! but I would fain die a dry death. [*Exit.*

SCENE II. *The Island: before the Cell of*
PROSPERO.

Enter PROSPERO *and* MIRANDA.

Mira. If by your art, my dearest father, you
  have
Put the wild waters in this roar, allay them.
The sky, it seems, would pour down stinking
  pitch,   3
But that the sea, mounting to th' welkin's cheek,
Dashes the fire out. O! I have suffer'd
With those that I saw suffer: a brave vessel,
Who had, no doubt, some noble creatures in her,
Dash'd all to pieces. O! the cry did knock   8
Against my very heart. Poor souls, they perish'd.
Had I been any god of power, I would
Have sunk the sea within the earth, or e'er   11
It should the good ship so have swallow'd and
The fraughting souls within her.
Pro.   Be collected:
No more amazement. Tell your piteous heart
There's no harm done.
Mira.   O, woe the day!
Pro.   No harm.
I have done nothing but in care of thee,— 16
Of thee, my dear one! thee, my daughter!—who
Art ignorant of what thou art, nought knowing
Of whence I am: nor that I am more better
Than Prospero, master of a full poor cell, 20
And thy no greater father.
Mira.   More to know
Did never meddle with my thoughts.
Pro.   'Tis time
I should inform thee further. Lend thy hand,
And pluck my magic garment from me.—So: 24
    [*Lays down his mantle.*
Lie there, my art.—Wipe thou thine eyes; have
  comfort.
The direful spectacle of the wrack, which touch'd
The very virtue of compassion in thee,
I have with such provision in mine art 28
So safely order'd, that there is no soul—
No, not so much perdition as an hair,
Betid to any creature in the vessel
Which thou heard'st cry, which thou saw'st
  sink. Sit down;   32
For thou must now know further.
Mira.   You have often
Begun to tell me what I am, but stopp'd,
And left me to a bootless inquisition,
Concluding, 'Stay; not yet.'
Pro.   The hour's now come, 36
The very minute bids thee ope thine ear;
Obey and be attentive. Canst thou remember
A time before we came unto this cell?
I do not think thou canst, for then thou wast
  not   40
Out three years old.
Mira.   Certainly, sir, I can.
Pro. By what? by any other house or person?
Of anything the image tell me, that
Hath kept with thy remembrance.
Mira.   'Tis far off; 44
And rather like a dream than an assurance
That my remembrance warrants. Had I not
Four or five women once that tended me?

Pro. Thou hadst, and more, Miranda. But
  how is it   48
That this lives in thy mind? What seest thou else
In the dark backward and abysm of time?
If thou remember'st aught ere thou cam'st here,
How thou cam'st here, thou may'st.
Mira.   But that I do not. 52
Pro. Twelve year since, Miranda, twelve year
  since,
Thy father was the Duke of Milan and
A prince of power.
Mira.   Sir, are not you my father?
Pro. Thy mother was a piece of virtue, and
She said thou wast my daughter; and thy father
Was Duke of Milan, and his only heir 58
A princess,—no worse issued.
Mira.   O, the heavens!
What foul play had we that we came from
  thence?   60
Or blessed was't we did?
Pro.   Both, both, my girl:
By foul play, as thou say'st, were we heav'd
  thence;
But blessedly holp hither.
Mira.   O! my heart bleeds
To think o' the teen that I have turn'd you to,
Which is from my remembrance. Please you,
  further.   65
Pro. My brother and thy uncle, call'd An-
  tonio,—
I pray thee, mark me,—that a brother should
Be so perfidious!—he whom next thyself, 68
Of all the world I lov'd, and to him put
The manage of my state; as at that time,
Through all the signiories it was the first, 71
And Prospero the prime duke; being so reputed
In dignity, and for the liberal arts,
Without a parallel: those being all my study,
The government I cast upon my brother,
And to my state grew stranger, being trans-
  ported   76
And rapt in secret studies. Thy false uncle—
Dost thou attend me?
Mira.   Sir, most heedfully.
Pro. Being once perfected how to grant suits,
How to deny them, who t'advance, and who 80
To trash for over-topping; new created
The creatures that were mine, I say, or chang'd
  'em,
Or else new form'd 'em: having both the key
Of officer and office, set all hearts i' the state 84
To what tune pleas'd his ear; that now he was
The ivy which had hid my princely trunk,
And suck'd my verdure out on't.—Thou at-
  tend'st not.
Mira. O, good sir! I do.
Pro.   I pray thee, mark me. 88
I, thus neglecting worldly ends, all dedicated
To closeness and the bettering of my mind
With that, which, but by being so retir'd, 91
O'erpriz'd all popular rate, in my false brother
Awak'd an evil nature; and my trust,
Like a good parent, did beget of him
A falsehood in its contrary as great 95
As my trust was; which had, indeed no limit,
A confidence sans bound. He being thus lorded,

Not only with what my revenue yielded,
But what my power might else exact,—like one,
Who having, into truth, by telling of it,   100
Made such a sinner of his memory,
To credit his own lie,—he did believe
He was indeed the duke; out o' the substitution,
And executing th' outward face of royalty,   104
With all prerogative:—Hence his ambition
growing,—
Dost thou hear?
    Mira. Your tale, sir, would cure deafness.
    Pro. To have no screen between this part he
play'd
And him he play'd it for, he needs will be   108
Absolute Milan. Me, poor man,—my library
Was dukedom large enough: of temporal royalties
He thinks me now incapable; confederates,—
So dry he was for sway,—wi' the king of Naples
To give him annual tribute, do him homage;
Subject his coronet to his crown, and bend
The dukedom, yet unbow'd,—alas, poor Milan!—
To most ignoble stooping.
    Mira. O the heavens!   116
    Pro. Mark his condition and the event; then
tell me
If this might be a brother.
    Mira. I should sin
To think but nobly of my grandmother:
Good wombs have borne bad sons.
    Pro. Now the condition.   120
This King of Naples, being an enemy
To me inveterate, hearkens my brother's suit;
Which was, that he, in lieu o' the premises
Of homage and I know not how much tribute,
Should presently extirpate me and mine   125
Out of the dukedom, and confer fair Milan,
With all the honours on my brother: whereon,
A treacherous army levied, one midnight   128
Fated to the purpose did Antonio open
The gates of Milan; and, i' the dead of darkness,
The ministers for the purpose hurried thence
Me and thy crying self.
    Mira. Alack, for pity!   132
I, not rememb'ring how I cried out then,
Will cry it o'er again: it is a hint,
That wrings mine eyes to 't.
    Pro. Hear a little further,
And then I'll bring thee to the present business
Which now 's upon us; without the which this
story   137
Were most impertinent.
    Mira. Wherefore did they not
That hour destroy us?
    Pro. Well demanded, wench:
My tale provokes that question. Dear, they
durst not,   140
So dear the love my people bore me, nor set
A mark so bloody on the business; but
With colours fairer painted their foul ends.
In few, they hurried us aboard a bark,   144
Bore us some leagues to sea; where they prepar'd
A rotten carcass of a boat, not rigg'd,
Nor tackle, sail, nor mast; the very rats
Instinctively have quit it: there they hoist us,
To cry to the sea that roar'd to us; to sigh   149

To the winds whose pity, sighing back again,
Did us but loving wrong.
    Mira. Alack! what trouble
Was I then to you!
    Pro. O, a cherubin   152
Thou wast, that did preserve me! Thou didst
smile,
Infused with a fortitude from heaven,
When I have deck'd the sea with drops full salt,
Under my burden groan'd; which rais'd in me
An undergoing stomach, to bear up   157
Against what should ensue.
    Mira. How came we ashore?
    Pro. By Providence divine.   159
Some food we had and some fresh water that
A noble Neapolitan, Gonzalo,
Out of his charity,—who being then appointed
Master of this design,—did give us; with   163
Rich garments, linens, stuffs, and necessaries,
Which since have steaded much; so, of his
gentleness,
Knowing I lov'd my books, he furnish'd me,
From mine own library with volumes that
I prize above my dukedom.
    Mira. Would I might   168
But ever see that man!
    Pro. Now I arise:—
              [*Resumes his mantle.*
Sit still, and hear the last of our sea-sorrow.
Here in this island we arriv'd; and here
Have I, thy schoolmaster, made thee more profit
Than other princes can, that have more time
For vainer hours and tutors not so careful.
    Mira. Heavens thank you for 't! And now, I
pray you, sir,—
For still 'tis beating in my mind,—your
reason   176
For raising this sea-storm?
    Pro. Know thus far forth.
By accident most strange, bountiful Fortune,
Now my dear lady, hath mine enemies
Brought to this shore; and by my prescience   180
I find my zenith doth depend upon
A most auspicious star, whose influence
If now I court not but omit, my fortunes
Will ever after droop. Here cease more questions;   184
Thou art inclin'd to sleep; 'tis a good dulness,
And give it way;—I know thou canst not
choose.—   [MIRANDA *sleeps.*
Come away, servant, come! I'm ready now.
Approach, my Ariel! come!   188

Enter ARIEL.

    Ari. All hail, great master! grave sir, hail!
I come
To answer thy best pleasure; be 't to fly,
To swim, to dive into the fire, to ride   191
On the curl'd clouds: to thy strong bidding task
Ariel and all his quality.
    Pro. Hast thou, spirit,
Perform'd to point the tempest that I bade
thee?
    Ari. To every article.
I boarded the king's ship; now on the beak,   196
Now in the waist, the deck, in every cabin,

I flam'd amazement: sometime I'd divide
And burn in many places; on the topmast,
The yards, and boresprit, would I flame dis-
tinctly, 200
Then meet, and join: Jove's lightnings, the
precursors
O' the dreadful thunder-claps, more momentary
And sight-outrunning were not: the fire and
cracks
Of sulphurous roaring the most mighty Neptune
Seem to besiege and make his bold waves
tremble, 205
Yea, his dread trident shake.
Pro. My brave spirit!
Who was so firm, so constant, that this coil
Would not infect his reason?
Ari. Not a soul 208
But felt a fever of the mad and play'd
Some tricks of desperation. All but mariners,
Plunged in the foaming brine and quit the
vessel,
Then all a-fire with me: the king's son, Fer-
dinand, 212
With hair up-staring,—then like reeds, not
hair,—
Was the first man that leap'd; cried, 'Hell is
empty,
And all the devils are here.'
Pro. Why, that's my spirit!
But was not this nigh shore?
Ari. Close by, my master. 216
Pro. But are they, Ariel, safe?
Ari. Not a hair perish'd;
On their sustaining garments not a blemish,
But fresher than before: and, as thou bad'st
me,
In troops I have dispers'd them 'bout the isle.
The king's son have I landed by himself; 221
Whom I left cooling of the air with sighs
In an odd angle of the isle and sitting,
His arms in this sad knot.
Pro. Of the king's ship 224
The mariners, say how thou hast dispos'd,
And all the rest o' the fleet.
Ari. Safely in harbour
Is the king's ship; in the deep nook, where once
Thou call'dst me up at midnight to fetch dew
From the still-vex'd Bermoothes; there she's
hid:
The mariners all under hatches stow'd; 230
Who, with a charm join'd to their suffer'd
labour,
I have left asleep: and for the rest o' the fleet
Which I dispers'd, they all have met again,
And are upon the Mediterranean flote,
Bound sadly home for Naples,
Supposing that they saw the king's ship
wrack'd, 236
And his great person perish.
Pro. Ariel, thy charge
Exactly is perform'd: but there's more work:
What is the time o' th' day?
Ari. Past the mid season.
Pro. At least two glasses. The time 'twixt
six and now 240
Must by us both be spent most preciously.

Ari. Is there more toil? Since thou dost
give me pains,
Let me remember thee what thou hast promis'd
Which is not yet perform'd me.
Pro. How now! moody? 244
What is 't thou canst demand?
Ari. My liberty.
Pro. Before the time be out? no more!
Ari. I prithee
Remember, I have done thee worthy service;
Told thee no lies, made no mistakings, serv'd
Without or grudge or grumblings: thou didst
promise 249
To bate me a full year.
Pro. Dost thou forget
From what a torment I did free thee?
Ari. No.
Pro. Thou dost; and think'st it much to
tread the ooze 252
Of the salt deep,
To run upon the sharp wind of the north,
To do me business in the veins o' th' earth
When it is bak'd with frost.
Ari. I do not, sir. 256
Pro. Thou liest, malignant thing! Hast thou
forgot
The foul witch Sycorax, who with age and envy
Was grown into a hoop? hast thou forgot her?
Ari. No, sir.
Pro. Thou hast. Where was she
born? speak; tell me. 260
Ari. Sir, in Argier.
Pro. O! was she so? I must,
Once in a month, recount what thou hast been,
Which thou forget'st. This damn'd witch,
Sycorax, 263
For mischiefs manifold and sorceries terrible
To enter human hearing, from Argier,
Thou know'st, was banish'd: for one thing she
did
They would not take her life. Is not this true?
Ari. Ay, sir. 268
Pro. This blue-ey'd hag was hither brought
with child
And here was left by the sailors. Thou, my
slave,
As thou report'st thyself, wast then her servant:
And, for thou wast a spirit too delicate 272
To act her earthy and abhorr'd commands,
Refusing her grand hests, she did confine thee,
By help of her more potent ministers,
And in her most unmitigable rage, 276
Into a cloven pine; within which rift
Imprison'd, thou didst painfully remain
A dozen years; within which space she died
And left thee there, where thou didst vent thy
groans 280
As fast as mill-wheels strike. Then was this
island,—
Save for the son that she did litter here,
A freckled whelp hag-born,—not honour'd with
A human shape.
Ari. Yes; Caliban her son. 284
Pro. Dull thing, I say so; he that Caliban,
Whom now I keep in service. Thou best know'st
What torment I did find thee in; thy groans

Did make wolves howl and penetrate the breasts
Of ever-angry bears: it was a torment   289
To lay upon the damn'd, which Sycorax
Could not again undo; it was mine art,
When I arriv'd and heard thee, that made gape
The pine, and let thee out.
    Ari.   I thank thee, master.
    Pro. If thou more murmur'st, I will rend an
oak
And peg thee in his knotty entrails till
Thou hast howl'd away twelve winters.
    Ari.   Pardon, master;   296
I will be correspondent to command,
And do my spiriting gently.
    Pro.   Do so; and after two days
I will discharge thee.
    Ari.   That's my noble master!
What shall I do? say what? what shall I do?
    Pro. Go make thyself like a nymph of the
sea: be subject   301
To no sight but thine and mine; invisible
To every eyeball else. Go, take this shape,
And hither come in 't: go, hence with dili-
gence!   [*Exit* ARIEL.
Awake, dear heart, awake! thou hast slept well;
Awake!
    Mira. [*Waking.*] The strangeness of your
story put
Heaviness in me.
    Pro.   Shake it off. Come on;
We'll visit Caliban my slave, who never   308
Yields us kind answer.
    Mira.   'Tis a villain, sir,
I do not love to look on.
    Pro.   But, as 'tis,
We cannot miss him: he does make our fire,
Fetch in our wood; and serves in offices   312
That profit us.—What ho! slave! Caliban!
Thou earth, thou! speak.
    Cal. [*Within.*] There's wood enough within.
    Pro. Come forth, I say; there's other busi-
ness for thee:
Come, thou tortoise! when?   316

Re-enter ARIEL, *like a water-nymph.*

Fine apparition! My quaint Ariel,
Hark in thine ear.
    Ari.   My lord, it shall be done. [*Exit.*
    Pro. Thou poisonous slave, got by the devil
himself
Upon thy wicked dam, come forth!   320

Enter CALIBAN.

    Cal. As wicked dew as e'er my mother
brush'd
With raven's feather from unwholesome fen
Drop on you both! a south-west blow on ye,
And blister you all o'er!   324
    Pro. For this, be sure, to-night thou shalt
have cramps,
Side-stitches that shall pen thy breath up; urchins
Shall forth at vast of night, that they may
work
All exercise on thee: thou shalt be pinch'd   328

As thick as honeycomb, each pinch more
stinging
Than bees that made them.
    Cal.   I must eat my dinner.
This island's mine, by Sycorax my mother,
Which thou tak'st from me. When thou camest
first,   332
Thou strok'dst me, and mad'st much of me;
wouldst give me
Water with berries in 't; and teach me how
To name the bigger light, and how the less,
That burn by day and night: and then I lov'd
thee   336
And show'd thee all the qualities o' th' isle,
The fresh springs, brine-pits, barren place, and
fertile.
Cursed be I that did so!—All the charms
Of Sycorax, toads, beetles, bats, light on you!
For I am all the subjects that you have,   341
Which first was mine own king; and here you
sty me
In this hard rock, whiles you do keep from me
The rest o' th' island.
    Pro.   Thou most lying slave,   344
Whom stripes may move, not kindness! I have
us'd thee,
Filth as thou art, with human care; and lodg'd
thee
In mine own cell, till thou didst seek to violate
The honour of my child.   348
    Cal. Oh ho! Oh ho!—would it had been done!
Thou didst prevent me; I had peopled else
This isle with Calibans.
    Pro.   Abhorred slave,
Which any print of goodness will not take,   352
Being capable of all ill! I pitied thee,
Took pains to make thee speak, taught thee each
hour
One thing or other: when thou didst not, savage,
Know thine own meaning, but wouldst gabble
like   356
A thing most brutish, I endow'd thy purposes
With words that made them known: but thy
vile race,
Though thou didst learn, had that in 't which
good natures
Could not abide to be with; therefore wast thou
Deservedly confin'd into this rock,   361
Who hadst deserv'd more than a prison.
    Cal. You taught me language; and my profit
on 't   363
Is, I know how to curse: the red plague rid you,
For learning me your language!
    Pro.   Hag-seed, hence!
Fetch us in fuel; and be quick, thou 'rt best,
To answer other business. Shrug'st thou, malice?
If thou neglect'st, or dost unwillingly   368
What I command, I'll rack thee with old cramps,
Fill all thy bones with aches; make thee roar,
That beasts shall tremble at thy din.
    Cal.   No, pray thee!—
[*Aside.*] I must obey: his art is of such power,
It would control my dam's god, Setebos,   373
And make a vassal of him.
    Pro.   So, slave; hence!
               [*Exit* CALIBAN,

Re-enter ARIEL *invisible, playing and singing;*
FERDINAND *following.*

ARIEL'S SONG.

Come unto these yellow sands,
   And then take hands:
Curtsied when you have, and kiss'd,—   376
   The wild waves whist,—
Foot it featly here and there;
And, sweet sprites, the burden bear.
   Hark! hark!   380
      [*Burden:* Bow, wow, *dispersedly.*
   The watch-dogs bark:
      [*Burden:* Bow, wow, *dispersedly.*
   Hark, hark! I hear
The strain of strutting Chanticleer
      [*Cry,* Cock-a-diddle-dow.   384

Fer. Where should this music be? i' th' air,
   or th' earth?
It sounds no more;—and sure, it waits upon
Some god o' th' island. Sitting on a bank,
Weeping again the king my father's wrack,   388
This music crept by me upon the waters,
Allaying both their fury, and my passion,
With its sweet air: thence I have follow'd it,—
Or it hath drawn me rather,—but 'tis gone.   392
No, it begins again.

ARIEL *sings.*

Full fathom five thy father lies:
   Of his bones are coral made:
Those are pearls that were his eyes:
   Nothing of him that doth fade,   396
But doth suffer a sea-change
Into something rich and strange.
Sea-nymphs hourly ring his knell:
      [*Burden:* ding-dong.   400
Hark! now I hear them,—ding-dong, bell.

Fer. The ditty does remember my drown'd
   father.
This is no mortal business, nor no sound
That the earth owes:—I hear it now above me.
Pro. The fringed curtains of thine eye ad-
   vance,   405
And say what thou seest yond.
Mira.   What is't? a spirit?
Lord, how it looks about! Believe me, sir,
It carries a brave form:—but 'tis a spirit.   408
Pro. No, wench; it eats and sleeps, and hath
   such senses
As we have, such; this gallant which thou
   see'st,
Was in the wrack; and, but he's something
   stain'd
With grief,—that's beauty's canker,—thou
   might'st call him   412
A goodly person: he hath lost his fellows
And strays about to find 'em.
Mira.   I might call him
A thing divine; for nothing natural
I ever saw so noble.
Pro. [*Aside.*] It goes on, I see,   416
As my soul prompts it.—Spirit, fine spirit! I'll
   free thee
Within two days for this.
Fer.   Most sure, the goddess
On whom these airs attend!—Vouchsafe, my
   prayer
May know if you remain upon this island;   420

And that you will some good instruction give
How I may bear me here: my prime request,
Which I do last pronounce, is,—O you won-
   der!—
If you be maid or no?
Mira.   No wonder, sir;   424
But certainly a maid.
Fer.   My language! heavens!—
I am the best of them that speak this speech,
Were I but where 'tis spoken.
Pro.   How! the best?
What wert thou, if the King of Naples heard
   thee?   428
Fer. A single thing, as I am now, that
   wonders
To hear thee speak of Naples. He does hear me;
And, that he does, I weep: myself am Naples,
Who with mine eyes,—ne'er since at ebb,—be-
   held
The king, my father wrack'd.
Mira.   Alack, for mercy!
Fer. Yes, faith, and all his lords; the Duke
   of Milan,   434
And his brave son being twain.
Pro.   [*Aside.*] The Duke of Milan,
And his more braver daughter could control
   thee,
If now 'twere fit to do 't.—At the first sight   437
      [*Aside.*]
They have changed eyes:—delicate Ariel,
I'll set thee free for this!—[*To* FER.] A word,
   good sir;
I fear you have done yourself some wrong: a
   word.   440
Mira. [*Aside.*] Why speaks my father so
   ungently? This
Is the third man that e'er I saw; the first
That e'er I sigh'd for: pity move my father
To be inclin'd my way!
Fer.   [*Aside.*] O! if a virgin,   444
And your affection not gone forth, I'll make you
The Queen of Naples.
Pro.   Soft, sir! one word more—
[*Aside.*] They are both in either's powers: but
   this swift business
I must uneasy make, lest too light winning   448
Make the prize light.—[*To* FER.] One word
   more: I charge thee
That thou attend me. Thou dost here usurp
The name thou ow'st not; and hast put thyself
Upon this island as a spy, to win it   452
From me, the lord on 't.
Fer.   No, as I am a man.
Mira. There's nothing ill can dwell in such
   a temple:
If the ill spirit have so fair a house,
Good things will strive to dwell with 't.
Pro.   [*To* FER.] Follow me.—   456
[*To* MIRA.] Speak not you for him; he's a
   traitor.—[*To* FER.] Come;
I'll manacle thy neck and feet together:
Sea-water shalt thou drink; thy food shall be
The fresh-brook muscles, wither'd roots and
   husks   460
Wherein the acorn cradled. Follow.
Fer.   No;

I will resist such entertainment till
Mine enemy has more power.

[*He draws, and is charmed from moving.*
　　　Mira.　　　　　　　　　O dear father!
Make not too rash a trial of him, for　464
He's gentle, and not fearful.
　　　　　　　　　　　Pro.　　　　What! I say,
My foot my tutor?—Put thy sword up, traitor;
Who mak'st a show, but dar'st not strike, thy
　　conscience
Is so possess'd with guilt: come from thy ward,
For I can here disarm thee with this stick　469
And make thy weapon drop.
　　　Mira.　　　　　　Beseech you, father!
　　　Pro. Hence! hang not on my garments.
　　　Mira.　　　　　　　　Sir, have pity!
I'll be his surety.
　　　Pro.　　　　Silence! one word more　472
Shall make me chide thee, if not hate thee.
　　What!
An advocate for an impostor? hush!
Thou think'st there is no more such shapes as he,
Having seen but him and Caliban: foolish
　　wench!　　　　　　　　　　　　　476
To the most of men this is a Caliban
And they to him are angels.
　　　Mira.　　　　　　My affections
Are then most humble; I have no ambition
To see a goodlier man.
　　　Pro.　　　[*To* FER.] Come on; obey:　480
Thy nerves are in their infancy again,
And have no vigour in them.
　　　Fer.　　　　　　So they are:
My spirits, as in a dream, are all bound up.
My father's loss, the weakness which I feel,　484
The wrack of all my friends, or this man's
　　threats,
To whom I am subdued, are but light to me,
Might I but through my prison once a day
Behold this maid: all corners else o' th' earth
Let liberty make use of; space enough　489
Have I in such a prison.
　　　Pro. [*Aside.*] It works.—[*To* FER.] Come on.—
Thou hast done well, fine Ariel!—[*To* FER.]
　　Follow me.—
[*To* ARIEL.] Hark, what thou else shalt do me.
　　　Mira.　　　　　Be of comfort;　492
My father's of a better nature, sir,
Than he appears by speech: this is unwonted,
Which now came from him.
　　　Pro.　　　　Thou shalt be as free
As mountain winds; but then exactly do　496
All points of my command.
　　　Ari.　　　　　　To the syllable.
　　　Pro. [*To* FER.] Come, follow.—Speak not for
　　him.　　　　　　　　　　　　[*Exeunt.*

ACT II

SCENE I.—*Another Part of the Island.*

Enter ALONSO, SEBASTIAN, ANTONIO, GONZALO,
　ADRIAN, FRANCISCO, *and others.*

　　　Gon. Beseech you, sir, be merry: you have
　　cause,
So have we all, of joy; for our escape
Is much beyond our loss. Our hint of woe

Is common: every day some sailor's wife,　4
The masters of some merchant and the mer-
　chant,
Have just our theme of woe; but for the miracle,
I mean our preservation, few in millions
Can speak like us: then wisely, good sir, weigh
Our sorrow with our comfort.
　　　Alon.　　　　　Prithee, peace. 9
　　　Seb. He receives comfort like cold porridge.
　　　Ant. The visitor will not give him o'er so.
　　　Seb. Look, he's winding up the watch of his
wit; by and by it will strike.　　　　13
　　　Gon. Sir,—
　　　Seb. One: tell.
　　　Gon. When every grief is entertain'd that's
　offer'd,　　　　　　　　　　　16
Comes to the entertainer—
　　　Seb. A dollar.
　　　Gon. Dolour comes to him, indeed: you have
spoken truer than you purposed.　　　20
　　　Seb. You have taken it wiselier than I meant
you should.
　　　Gon. Therefore, my lord,—
　　　Ant. Fie, what a spendthrift is he of his
tongue!　　　　　　　　　　　25
　　　Alon. I prithee, spare.
　　　Gon. Well, I have done: but yet—
　　　Seb. He will be talking.　　　　28
　　　Ant. Which, of he or Adrian, for a good
wager, first begins to crow?
　　　Seb. The old cock.
　　　Ant. The cockerel.　　　　　32
　　　Seb. Done. The wager?
　　　Ant. A laughter.
　　　Seb. A match!
　　　Adr. Though this island seem to be desert,—
　　　Seb. Ha, ha, ha! So you're paid.
　　　Adr. Uninhabitable, and almost inacces-
sible,—
　　　Seb. Yet—
　　　Adr. Yet—
　　　Ant. He could not miss it.
　　　Adr. It must needs be of subtle, tender, and
delicate temperance.
　　　Ant. Temperance was a delicate wench.　45
　　　Seb. Ay, and a subtle; as he most learnedly
delivered.
　　　Adr. The air breathes upon us here most
sweetly.　　　　　　　　　　　49
　　　Seb. As if it had lungs, and rotten ones.
　　　Ant. Or as 'twere perfumed by a fen.
　　　Gon. Here is everything advantageous to life.
　　　Ant. True; save means to live.　　53
　　　Seb. Of that there's none, or little.
　　　Gon. How lush and lusty the grass looks!
how green!　　　　　　　　　56
　　　Ant. The ground indeed is tawny.
　　　Seb. With an eye of green in't.
　　　Ant. He misses not much.
　　　Seb. No; he doth but mistake the truth
totally.　　　　　　　　　　　61
　　　Gon. But the rarity of it is,—which is indeed
almost beyond credit,—
　　　Seb. As many vouch'd rarities are.　64
　　　Gon. That our garments, being, as they were,
drenched in the sea, hold notwithstanding their

freshness and glosses; being rather new-dyed
than stain'd with salt water.   68

Ant. If but one of his pockets could speak,
would it not say he lies?

Seb. Ay, or very falsely pocket up his report.

Gon. Methinks, our garments are now as fresh
as when we put them on first in Afric, at the
marriage of the king's fair daughter Claribel to
the King of Tunis.   75

Seb. 'Twas a sweet marriage, and we prosper
well in our return.

Adr. Tunis was never graced before with
such a paragon to their queen.

Gon. Not since widow Dido's time.   80

Ant. Widow! a pox o' that! How came that
widow in? Widow Dido!

Seb. What if he had said, widower Æneas
too? Good Lord, how you take it!   84

Adr. Widow Dido, said you? you make me
study of that: she was of Carthage, not of Tunis.

Gon. This Tunis, sir, was Carthage.

Adr. Carthage?   88

Gon. I assure you, Carthage.

Ant. His word is more than the miraculous
harp.

Seb. He hath rais'd the wall, and houses too.

Ant. What impossible matter will he make
easy next?

Seb. I think he will carry this island home in
his pocket, and give it his son for an apple.   96

Ant. And, sowing the kernels of it in the sea,
bring forth more islands.

Alon. Ay?

Ant. Why, in good time.   100

Gon. [*To* ALON.] Sir, we were talking that
our garments seem now as fresh as when we
were at Tunis at the marriage of your daughter,
who is now queen.   104

Ant. And the rarest that e'er came there.

Seb. Bate, I beseech you, widow Dido.

Ant. O! widow Dido; ay, widow Dido.

Gon. Is not, sir, my doublet as fresh as the
first day I wore it? I mean, in a sort.   109

Ant. That sort was well fish'd for.

Gon. When I wore it at your daughter's
marriage?   112

Alon. You cram these words into mine ears,
against
The stomach of my sense. Would I had never
Married my daughter there! for, coming thence,
My son is lost; and, in my rate, she too,   116
Who is so far from Italy remov'd,
I ne'er again shall see her. O thou, mine heir
Of Naples and of Milan! what strange fish
Hath made his meal on thee?

Fran.   Sir, he may live: 120
I saw him beat the surges under him,
And ride upon their backs: he trod the water,
Whose enmity he flung aside, and breasted
The surge most swoln that met him: his bold
head   124
'Bove the contentious waves he kept, and oar'd
Himself with his good arms in lusty stroke
To the shore, that o'er his wave-worn basis bow'd,
As stooping to relieve him. I not doubt   128
He came alive to land.

Alon.   No, no; he's gone.

Seb. Sir, you may thank yourself for this
great loss,
That would not bless our Europe with your
daughter,
But rather lose her to an African;   132
Where she at least is banish'd from your eye,
Who hath cause to wet the grief on't.

Alon.   Prithee, peace.

Seb. You were kneel'd to and importun'd
otherwise
By all of us; and the fair soul herself   136
Weigh'd between loathness and obedience, at
Which end o' the beam should bow. We have
lost your son,
I fear, for ever: Milan and Naples have
More widows in them of this business' making,
Than we bring men to comfort them: the
fault's   141
Your own.

Alon. So is the dearest of the loss.

Gon. My lord Sebastian,
The truth you speak doth lack some gentle-
ness
And time to speak it in; you rub the sore,   145
When you should bring the plaster.

Seb.   Very well.

Ant. And most chirurgeonly.

Gon. It is foul weather in us all, good sir,   148
When you are cloudy.

Seb.   Foul weather?

Ant.   Very foul.

Gon. Had I plantation of this isle, my lord,—

Ant. He'd sow't with nettle-seed.

Seb.   Or docks, or mallows.

Gon. And were the king on't, what would
I do?

Seb. 'Scape being drunk for want of wine. 153

Gon. I' the commonwealth I would by con-
traries
Execute all things; for no kind of traffic
Would I admit; no name of magistrate;   156
Letters should not be known; riches, poverty,
And use of service, none; contract, succession,
Bourn, bound of land, tilth, vineyard, none;
No use of metal, corn, or wine, or oil;   160
No occupation; all men idle, all;
And women too, but innocent and pure;
No sovereignty,—

Seb.   Yet he would be king on't.

Ant. The latter end of his commonwealth
forgets the beginning.   165

Gon. All things in common nature should
produce
Without sweat or endeavour: treason, felony,
Sword, pike, knife, gun, or need of any engine,
Would I not have; but nature should bring
forth,   169
Of its own kind, all foison, all abundance,
To feed my innocent people.

Seb. No marrying 'mong his subjects?   172

Ant. None, man; all idle; whores and knaves.

Gon. I would with such perfection govern, sir,
To excel the golden age.

Seb.   Save his majesty!

Ant. Long live Gonzalo!

Gon.   And,—do you mark me, sir? 176

Alon. Prithee, no more: thou dost talk nothing to me.

Gon. I do well believe your highness; and did it to minister occasion to these gentlemen, who are of such sensible and nimble lungs that they always use to laugh at nothing.

Ant. 'Twas you we laugh'd at.   183

Gon. Who in this kind of merry fooling am nothing to you; so you may continue and laugh at nothing still.

Ant. What a blow was there given!

Seb. An it had not fallen flat-long.   188

Gon. You are gentlemen of brave mettle: you would lift the moon out of her sphere, if she would continue in it five weeks without changing.   192

Enter ARIEL, *invisible, playing solemn music.*

Seb. We would so, and then go a-bat-fowling.

Ant. Nay, good my lord, be not angry.

Gon. No, I warrant you; I will not adventure my discretion so weakly. Will you laugh me asleep, for I am very heavy?   197

Ant. Go sleep, and hear us.

      [*All sleep but* ALON., SEB., *and* ANT.

Alon. What! all so soon asleep! I wish mine eyes

Would, with themselves, shut up my thoughts: I find   200

They are inclin'd to do so.

Seb.   Please you, sir,

Do not omit the heavy offer of it:

It seldom visits sorrow; when it doth

It is a comforter.

Ant.   We two, my lord, 204

Will guard your person while you take your rest,

And watch your safety.

Alon.   Thank you. Wondrous heavy.

      [ALONSO *sleeps. Exit* ARIEL.

Seb. What a strange drowsiness possesses them!

Ant. It is the quality o' the climate.

Seb.   Why 208

Doth it not then our eyelids sink? I find not

Myself dispos'd to sleep.

Ant.   Nor I: my spirits are nimble.

They fell together all, as by consent;

They dropp'd, as by a thunder-stroke. What might,   212

Worthy Sebastian? O! what might?—No more:—

And yet methinks I see it in thy face,

What thou should'st be. The occasion speaks thee; and

My strong imagination sees a crown   216

Dropping upon thy head.

Seb.   What! art thou waking?

Ant. Do you not hear me speak?

Seb.   I do; and surely,

It is a sleepy language, and thou speak'st

Out of thy sleep. What is it thou didst say? 220

This is a strange repose, to be asleep

With eyes wide open; standing, speaking, moving,

And yet so fast asleep.

Ant.   Noble Sebastian, 223

Thou let'st thy fortune sleep—die rather; wink'st

Whiles thou art waking.

Seb.   Thou dost snore distinctly:

There's meaning in thy snores.

Ant. I am more serious than my custom: you

Must be so too, if heed me; which to do   228

Trebles thee o'er.

Seb.   Well; I am standing water.

Ant. I'll teach you how to flow.

Seb.   Do so: to ebb,

Hereditary sloth instructs me.

Ant.   O!   231

If you but knew how you the purpose cherish

Whiles thus you mock it! how, in stripping it,

You more invest it! Ebbing men, indeed,

Most often do so near the bottom run

By their own fear or sloth.

Seb.   Prithee, say on: 236

The setting of thine eye and cheek proclaim

A matter from thee, and a birth indeed

Which throes thee much to yield.

Ant.   Thus, sir:

Although this lord of weak remembrance, this

Who shall be of as little memory   241

When he is earth'd, hath here almost persuaded,—

For he's a spirit of persuasion, only

Professes to persuade,—the king, his son's alive,

'Tis as impossible that he's undrown'd   245

As he that sleeps here swims.

Seb.   I have no hope

That he's undrown'd.

Ant.   O! out of that 'no hope'

What great hope have you! no hope that way is

Another way so high a hope that even   249

Ambition cannot pierce a wink beyond,

But doubts discovery there. Will you grant with me

That Ferdinand is drown'd?

Seb.   He's gone.

Ant.   Then tell me 252

Who's the next heir of Naples?

Seb.   Claribel.

Ant. She that is Queen of Tunis; she that dwells

Ten leagues beyond man's life; she that from Naples

Can have no note, unless the sun were post— 256

The man i' th' moon's too slow—till new-born chins

Be rough and razorable: she that, from whom?

We all were sea-swallow'd, though some cast again,

And by that destiny to perform an act   260

Whereof what's past is prologue, what to come

In yours and my discharge.

Seb.   What stuff is this!—How say you?

'Tis true my brother's daughter's Queen of Tunis;

So is she heir of Naples; 'twixt which regions

There is some space.

Ant.   A space whose every cubit

Seems to cry out, 'How shall that Claribel 266

Measure us back to Naples?—Keep in Tunis,

And let Sebastian wake!'—Say, this were death

That now hath seiz'd them; why, they were no worse

Than now they are. There be that can rule
  Naples
As well as he that sleeps; lords that can prate
As amply and unnecessarily   272
As this Gonzalo; I myself could make
A chough of as deep chat. O, that you bore
The mind that I do! what a sleep were this
For your advancement! Do you understand
  me?
  Seb. Methinks I do.
  Ant.   And how does your content
Tender your own good fortune?
  Seb.   I remember 278
You did supplant your brother Prospero.
  Ant.   True:
And look how well my garments sit upon me;
Much feater than before; my brother's servants
Were then my fellows; now they are my men.
  Seb. But, for your conscience,— 283
  Ant. Ay, sir; where lies that? if it were a kibe,
'Twould put me to my slipper; but I feel not
This deity in my bosom: twenty consciences,
That stand 'twixt me and Milan, candied be they,
And melt ere they molest! Here lies your
  brother, 288
No better than the earth he lies upon,
If he were that which now he's like, that's dead;
Whom I, with this obedient steel,—three inches
  of it,—
Can lay to bed for ever; whiles you, doing thus,
To the perpetual wink for aye might put 293
This ancient morsel, this Sir Prudence, who
Should not upbraid our course. For all the rest,
They'll take suggestion as a cat laps milk; 296
They'll tell the clock to any business that
We say befits the hour.
  Seb.   Thy case, dear friend,
Shall be my precedent: as thou got'st Milan,
I'll come by Naples. Draw thy sword: one stroke
Shall free thee from the tribute which thou pay'st,
And I the king shall love thee.
  Ant.   Draw together;
And when I rear my hand, do you the like, 303
To fall it on Gonzalo.
  Seb. O! but one word. [*They converse apart.*

    Music. Re-enter ARIEL, *invisible.*

  Ari. My master through his art foresees the
  danger
That you, his friend, are in; and sends me forth—
For else his project dies—to keep thee living.
        [*Sings in* GONZALO'S *ear.*
    While you here do snoring lie, 308
    Open-ey'd Conspiracy
      His time doth take.
    If of life you keep a care,
    Shake off slumber, and beware: 312
      Awake! awake!
  Ant. Then let us both be sudden.
  Gon.   Now, good angels
Preserve the king!   [*They wake.*
  Alon. Why, how now! ho, awake! Why are
  you drawn? 316
Wherefore this ghastly looking?
  Gon.   What's the matter?
  Seb. Whiles we stood here securing your
  repose,

Even now, we heard a hollow burst of bellowing
Like bulls, or rather lions; did 't not wake you?
It struck mine ear most terribly.
  Alon.   I heard nothing.
  Ant. O! 'twas a din to fright a monster's ear,
To make an earthquake: sure it was the roar
Of a whole herd of lions.
  Alon.   Heard you this, Gonzalo? 324
  Gon. Upon mine honour, sir, I heard a
  humming,
And that a strange one too, which did awake me.
I shak'd you, sir, and cry'd; as mine eyes open'd,
I saw their weapons drawn:—there was a noise,
That's verily. 'Tis best we stand upon our guard,
Or that we quit this place: let's draw our
  weapons.
  Alon. Lead off this ground, and let's make
  further search
For my poor son. 332
  Gon. Heavens keep him from these beasts!
For he is, sure, i' the island.
  Alon.   Lead away. [*Exit with the others.*
  Ari. Prospero my lord shall know what I
  have done:
So, king, go safely on to seek thy son.   [*Exit.*

  SCENE II.—*Another Part of the Island.*

  Enter CALIBAN, *with a burden of wood.*
    A noise of thunder heard.

  Cal. All the infections that the sun sucks up
From bogs, fens, flats, on Prosper fall, and make
  him
By inch-meal a disease! His spirits hear me,
And yet I needs must curse. But they'll nor
  pinch,
Fright me with urchin-shows, pitch me i' the
  mire,
Nor lead me, like a firebrand, in the dark
Out of my way, unless he bid 'em; but
For every trifle are they set upon me: 8
Sometime like apes, that mow and chatter at me
And after bite me; then like hedge-hogs, which
Lie tumbling in my bare-foot way and mount
Their pricks at my foot-fall; sometime am I 12
All wound with adders, who with cloven tongues
Do hiss me into madness.—

      Enter TRINCULO.
            Lo now! lo!
Here comes a spirit of his, and to torment me
For bringing wood in slowly: I'll fall flat; 16
Perchance he will not mind me.
  Trin. Here's neither bush nor shrub to bear
off any weather at all, and another storm brew-
ing; I hear it sing i' the wind: yond same black
cloud, yond huge one, looks like a foul bombard
that would shed his liquor. If it should thunder
as it did before, I know not where to hide my
head: yond same cloud cannot choose but fall
by pailfuls.—What have we here? a man or a
fish? Dead or alive? A fish: he smells like a
fish; a very ancient and fish-like smell; a kind
of not of the newest Poor-John. A strange fish!
Were I in England now,—as once I was,—and
had but this fish painted, not a holiday fool there

but would give a piece of silver: there would this monster make a man; any strange beast there makes a man. When they will not give a doit to relieve a lame beggar, they will lay out ten to see a dead Indian. Legg'd like a man! and his fins like arms! Warm, o' my troth! I do now let loose my opinion, hold it no longer; this is no fish, but an islander, that hath lately suffered by a thunderbolt. [*Thunder.*] Alas! the storm is come again: my best way is to creep under his gaberdine; there is no other shelter hereabout: misery acquaints a man with strange bedfellows. I will here shroud till the dregs of the storm be past.   44

Enter STEPHANO, *singing; a bottle in his hand.*

Ste. I shall no more to sea, to sea,
                 Here shall I die a-shore:—

This is a very scurvy tune to sing at a man's funeral:
Well, here's my comfort.   [*Drinks.*

The master, the swabber, the boatswain and I,   49
         The gunner and his mate,
Lov'd Mall, Meg, and Marian and Margery,
         But none of us car'd for Kate;   52
For she had a tongue with a tang,
         Would cry to a sailor, 'Go hang!'
She lov'd not the savour of tar nor of pitch,
Yet a tailor might scratch her where-e'er she did itch:
         Then to sea, boys, and let her go hang. 57

This is a scurvy tune too: but here's my comfort.   [*Drinks.*
Cal. Do not torment me: O!
Ste. What's the matter? Have we devils here? Do you put tricks upon us with savages and men of Ind! Ha! I have not 'scaped drowning, to be afeard now of your four legs; for it hath been said, As proper a man as ever went on four legs cannot make him give ground: and it shall be said so again while Stephano breathes at's nostrils.
Cal. The spirit torments me: O!   68
Ste. This is some monster of the isle with four legs, who hath got, as I take it, an ague. Where the devil should he learn our language? I will give him some relief, if it be but for that: if I can recover him and keep him tame and get to Naples with him, he's a present for any emperor that ever trod on neat's-leather.   75
Cal. Do not torment me, prithee: I'll bring my wood home faster.
Ste. He's in his fit now and does not talk after the wisest. He shall taste of my bottle: if he have never drunk wine afore it will go near to remove his fit. If I can recover him, and keep him tame, I will not take too much for him: he shall pay for him that hath him, and that soundly.   84
Cal. Thou dost me yet but little hurt; thou wilt anon, I know it by thy trembling: now Prosper works upon thee.   87
Ste. Come on your ways: open your mouth; here is that which will give language to you, cat. Open your mouth: this will shake your shaking, I can tell you, and that soundly [*gives* CALIBAN

drink]: you cannot tell who's your friend; open your chaps again.
Trin. I should know that voice: it should be—but he is drowned, and these are devils. O! defend me.   96
Ste. Four legs and two voices; a most delicate monster! His forward voice now is to speak well of his friend; his backward voice is to utter foul speeches, and to detract. If all the wine in my bottle will recover him, I will help his ague. Come. Amen! I will pour some in thy other mouth.
Trin. Stephano!   104
Ste. Doth thy other mouth call me? Mercy! mercy! This is a devil, and no monster: I will leave him; I have no long spoon.
Trin. Stephano!—if thou beest Stephano, touch me, and speak to me; for I am Trinculo: —be not afeard—thy good friend Trinculo. 110
Ste. If thou beest Trinculo, come forth. I'll pull thee by the lesser legs: if any be Trinculo's legs, these are they. Thou art very Trinculo indeed! How cam'st thou to be the siege of this moon-calf? Can he vent Trinculos?   115
Trin. I took him to be killed with a thunder-stroke. But art thou not drowned, Stephano? I hope now thou art not drowned. Is the storm overblown? I hid me under the dead moon-calf's gaberdine for fear of the storm. And art thou living, Stephano? O Stephano! two Nea-politans 'scaped!   122
Ste. Prithee, do not turn me about: my stomach is not constant.
Cal. [*Aside.*] These be fine things an if they be not sprites.
That's a brave god and bears celestial liquor: I will kneel to him.   127
Ste. How didst thou 'scape? How cam'st thou hither? swear by this bottle, how thou cam'st hither. I escaped upon a butt of sack, which the sailors heaved overboard, by this bottle! which I made of the bark of a tree with mine own hands, since I was cast ashore. 133
Cal. I'll swear upon that bottle, to be thy true subject; for the liquor is not earthly.
Ste. Here: swear then, how thou escapedst.
Trin. Swam ashore, man, like a duck: I can swim like a duck, I'll be sworn.   138
Ste. Here, kiss the book [*gives* TRINCULO *drink*]. Though thou canst swim like a duck, thou art made like a goose.   141
Trin. O Stephano! hast any more of this?
Ste. The whole butt, man: my cellar is in a rock by the seaside, where my wine is hid. How now, moon-calf! how does thine ague?   146
Cal. Hast thou not dropped from heaven?
Ste. Out o' the moon, I do assure thee: I was the man in the moon, when time was.
Cal. I have seen thee in her, and I do adore thee; my mistress showed me thee, and thy dog, and thy bush.   152
Ste. Come, swear to that; kiss the book; I will furnish it anon with new contents; swear.
Trin. By this good light, this is a very shallow monster.—I afeard of him!—a very weak mon-

ster.—The man i' the moon! a most poor credulous monster!—Well drawn, monster, in good
sooth.

Cal. I'll show thee every fertile inch o' the
island; 160
And I will kiss thy foot. I prithee, be my god.

Trin. By this light, a most perfidious and
drunken monster: when his god's asleep, he'll
rob his bottle. 164

Cal. I'll kiss thy foot: I'll swear myself thy
subject.

Ste. Come on then; down, and swear.

Trin. I shall laugh myself to death at this
puppy-headed monster. A most scurvy monster! I could find in my heart to beat him,— 169

Ste. Come, kiss.

Trin. But that the poor monster's in drink:
an abominable monster! 172

Cal. I'll shew thee the best springs; I'll pluck
thee berries;
I'll fish for thee, and get thee wood enough.
A plague upon the tyrant that I serve!
I'll bear him no more sticks, but follow thee,
Thou wondrous man. 177

Trin. A most ridiculous monster, to make a
wonder of a poor drunkard!

Cal. I prithee, let me bring thee where crabs
grow; 180
And I with my long nails will dig thee pig-nuts;
Show thee a jay's nest and instruct thee how
To snare the nimble marmozet; I'll bring thee
To clust'ring filberts, and sometimes I'll get thee
Young scamels from the rock. Wilt thou go
with me? 185

Ste. I prithee now, lead the way, without any
more talking.—Trinculo, the king and all our
company else being drowned, we will inherit
here.—Here; bear my bottle.—Fellow Trinculo,
we'll fill him by and by again. 190

Cal. Farewell, master; farewell, farewell,

[*Sings drunkenly.*

Trin. A howling monster, a drunken monster.

Cal. No more dams I'll make for fish;
　Nor fetch in firing
At requiring,
Nor scrape trenchering, nor wash dish; 196
　'Ban, 'Ban, Ca—Caliban,
　Has a new master—Get a new man.

Freedom, high-day! high-day, freedom! freedom! high-day, freedom! 200

Ste. O brave monster! lead the way. [*Exeunt.*

ACT III

SCENE I.—*Before* PROSPERO'S *Cell.*

Enter FERDINAND, *bearing a log.*

Fer. There be some sports are painful, and
their labour
Delight in them sets off: some kinds of baseness
Are nobly undergone, and most poor matters
Point to rich ends. This my mean task 4
Would be as heavy to me as odious; but
The mistress which I serve quickens what's dead
And makes my labours pleasures: O! she is 7
Ten times more gentle than her father's crabbed,

And he's compos'd of harshness. I must remove
Some thousands of these logs and pile them up,
Upon a sore injunction: my sweet mistress
Weeps when she sees me work, and says such
baseness 12
Had never like executor. I forget:
But these sweet thoughts do even refresh my
labours,
Most busiest when I do it.

Enter MIRANDA; *and* PROSPERO *behind.*

Mira.　　　　　Alas! now, pray you,
Work not so hard: I would the lightning had 16
Burnt up those logs that you are enjoin'd to
pile!
Pray, set it down and rest you: when this burns,
'Twill weep for having wearied you. My father
Is hard at study; pray now, rest yourself: 20
He's safe for these three hours.

Fer.　　　　　O most dear mistress,
The sun will set, before I shall discharge
What I must strive to do.

Mira.　　　　　If you'll sit down,
I'll bear your logs the while. Pray, give me
that; 24
I'll carry it to the pile.

Fer.　　　　　No, precious creature;
I had rather crack my sinews, break my back,
Than you should such dishonour undergo,
While I sit lazy by.

Mira.　　　　　It would become me 28
As well as it does you: and I should do it
With much more ease; for my good will is to it,
And yours it is against.

Pro. [*Aside.*] Poor worm! thou art infected:
This visitation shows it.

Mira.　　　　　You look wearily. 32

Fer. No, noble mistress; 'tis fresh morning
with me
When you are by at night. I do beseech you—
Chiefly that I might set it in my prayers—
What is your name?

Mira.　　　　　Miranda.—O my father! 36
I have broke your hest to say so.

Fer.　　　　　Admir'd Miranda!
Indeed, the top of admiration! worth
What's dearest to the world! Full many a lady
I have ey'd with best regard, and many a time 40
The harmony of their tongues hath into bondage
Brought my too diligent ear: for several virtues
Have I lik'd several women; never any
With so full soul but some defect in her 44
Did quarrel with the noblest grace she ow'd,
And put it to the foil: but you, O you!
So perfect and so peerless, are created
Of every creature's best.

Mira.　　　　　I do not know 48
One of my sex; no woman's face remember,
Save, from my glass, mine own; nor have I seen
More that I may call men than you, good friend,
And my dear father: how features are abroad, 52
I am skill-less of; but, by my modesty,—
The jewel in my dower,—I would not wish
Any companion in the world but you;
Nor can imagination form a shape, 56
Besides yourself, to like of. But I prattle

Something too wildly and my father's precepts
I therein do forget.

Fer.   I am in my condition
A prince, Miranda; I do think, a king;— 60
I would not so!—and would no more en-
    dure
This wooden slavery than to suffer
The flesh-fly blow my mouth.—Hear my soul
    speak:—
The very instant that I saw you did   64
My heart fly to your service; there resides,
To make me slave to it; and for your sake
Am I this patient log-man.

Mira.   Do you love me?

Fer. O heaven! O earth! bear witness to this
    sound,   68
And crown what I profess with kind event
If I speak true: if hollowly, invert
What best is boded me to mischief! I,
Beyond all limit of what else i' the world, 72
Do love, prize, honour you.

Mira.   I am a fool
To weep at what I am glad of.

Pro.   [*Aside.*] Fair encounter
Of two most rare affections! Heavens rain
    grace
On that which breeds between them!

Fer.   Wherefore weep you? 76

Mira. At mine unworthiness, that dare not
    offer
What I desire to give; and much less take
What I shall die to want. But this is trifling;
And all the more it seeks to hide itself   80
The bigger bulk it shows. Hence, bashful cun-
    ning!
And prompt me, plain and holy innocence!
I am your wife, if you will marry me;
If not, I'll die your maid: to be your fellow 84
You may deny me; but I'll be your servant
Whether you will or no.

Fer.   My mistress, dearest;
And I thus humble ever.

Mira.   My husband then?

Fer. Ay, with a heart as willing   88
As bondage e'er of freedom: here's my hand.

Mira. And mine, with my heart in't: and
    now farewell
Till half an hour hence.

Fer.   A thousand thousand!
            [*Exeunt* FER. *and* MIR. *severally.*

Pro. So glad of this as they, I cannot be, 92
Who are surpris'd withal; but my rejoicing
At nothing can be more. I'll to my book;
For yet, ere supper time, must I perform
Much business appertaining.   [*Exit.*

SCENE II.—*Another Part of the Island.*
Enter CALIBAN, *with a bottle,* STEPHANO, *and*
    TRINCULO.

Ste. Tell me not:—when the butt is out, we
will drink water; not a drop before: therefore
bear up, and board 'em.—Servant-monster, drink
to me.   4

Trin. Servant-monster! the folly of this
island! They say there's but five upon this isle:
we are three of them; if th' other two be brained
like us, the state totters.   8

Ste. Drink, servant-monster, when I bid thee:
thy eyes are almost set in thy head.

Trin. Where should they be set else? he
were a brave monster indeed, if they were set
in his tail.   13

Ste. My man-monster hath drowned his tongue
in sack: for my part, the sea cannot drown
me; I swam, ere I could recover the shore, five-
and-thirty leagues, off and on, by this light.
Thou shalt be my lieutenant, monster, or my
standard.   19

Trin. Your lieutenant, if you list; he's no
standard.

Ste. We'll not run, Monsieur monster.

Trin. Nor go neither: but you'll lie, like
dogs; and yet say nothing neither.   24

Ste. Moon-calf, speak once in thy life, if thou
beest a good moon-calf.

Cal. How does thy honour? Let me lick thy
shoe. I'll not serve him, he is not valiant. 28

Trin. Thou liest, most ignorant monster:
I am in case to justle a constable. Why, thou
deboshed fish thou, was there ever a man a
coward that hath drunk so much sack as I
to-day? Wilt thou tell a monstrous lie, being
but half a fish and half a monster?

Cal. Lo, how he mocks me! wilt thou let
him, my lord?   36

Trin. 'Lord' quoth he!—that a monster
should be such a natural!

Cal. Lo, lo, again! bite him to death, I
prithee.   40

Ste. Trinculo, keep a good tongue in your
head: if you prove a mutineer, the next tree!
The poor monster's my subject, and he shall
not suffer indignity.   44

Cal. I thank my noble lord. Wilt thou be
pleas'd
To hearken once again the suit I made thee?

Ste. Marry, will I; kneel, and repeat it: I will
stand, and so shall Trinculo.   48

Enter ARIEL, *invisible.*

Cal. As I told thee before, I am subject to a
tyrant, a sorcerer, that by his cunning hath
cheated me of the island.

Ari. Thou liest.   52

Cal. Thou liest, thou jesting monkey thou;
I would my valiant master would destroy thee;
I do not lie.

Ste. Trinculo, if you trouble him any more in
his tale, by this hand, I will supplant some of
your teeth.   58

Trin. Why, I said nothing.

Ste. Mum then and no more.—[*To* CALI-
BAN.] Proceed.

Cal. I say, by sorcery he got this isle;
From me he got it: if thy greatness will,
Revenge it on him,—for, I know, thou dar'st;
But this thing dare not,—   65

Ste. That's most certain.

Cal. Thou shalt be lord of it and I'll serve
    thee.

Ste. How now shall this be compassed? Canst
thou bring me to the party?   69
   Cal. Yea, yea, my lord: I'll yield him thee
asleep,
Where thou may'st knock a nail into his head.
   Ari. Thou liest; thou canst not.   72
   Cal. What a pied ninny's this! Thou scurvy
patch!—
I do beseech thy greatness, give him blows,
And take his bottle from him: when that's
gone
He shall drink nought but brine; for I'll not
show him   76
Where the quick freshes are.
   Ste. Trinculo, run into no further danger: in-
terrupt the monster one word further, and, by
this hand, I'll turn my mercy out o' doors and
make a stock-fish of thee.   81
   Trin. Why, what did I? I did nothing. I'll
go further off.
   Ste. Didst thou not say he lied?   84
   Ari. Thou liest.
   Ste. Do I so? take thou that. [*Strikes* TRIN.]
As you like this, give me the lie another time.
   Trin. I did not give thee the lie:—Out
o' your wits and hearing too?—A pox o' your
bottle! this can sack and drinking do.—A mur-
rain on your monster, and the devil take your
fingers!   92
   Cal. Ha, ha, ha!
   Ste. Now, forward with your tale.—Prithee
stand further off.
   Cal. Beat him enough: after a little time 96
I'll beat him too.
   Ste.   Stand further.—Come, proceed.
   Cal. Why, as I told thee, 'tis a custom with
him
I' the afternoon to sleep: there thou may'st
brain him,
Having first seiz'd his books; or with a log 100
Batter his skull, or paunch him with a stake,
Or cut his wezand with his knife. Remember
First to possess his books; for without them
He's but a sot, as I am, nor hath not   104
One spirit to command: they all do hate him
As rootedly as I. Burn but his books;
He has brave utensils,—for so he calls them,—
Which, when he has a house, he'll deck withal:
And that most deeply to consider is   109
The beauty of his daughter; he himself
Calls her a nonpareil: I never saw a woman,
But only Sycorax my dam and she;   112
But she as far surpasseth Sycorax
As great'st does least.
   Ste.   Is it so brave a lass?
   Cal. Ay, lord; she will become thy bed, I
warrant,
And bring thee forth brave brood.   116
   Ste. Monster, I will kill this man: his daugh-
ter and I will be king and queen,—save our
graces! and Trinculo and thyself shall be vice-
roys. Dost thou like the plot, Trinculo?   120
   Trin. Excellent.
   Ste. Give me thy hand: I am sorry I beat
thee; but, while thou livest, keep a good tongue
in thy head.   124

   Cal. Within this half hour will he be asleep;
Wilt thou destroy him then?
   Ste.   Ay, on mine honour.
   Ari. This will I tell my master.
   Cal. Thou mak'st me merry: I am full of
pleasure.   128
Let us be jocund: will you troll the catch
You taught me but while-ere?
   Ste. At thy request, monster, I will do reason,
any reason: Come on, Trinculo, let us sing. 132
                        [*Sings.*

Flout 'em, and scout 'em; and scout 'em, and
   flout 'em;
Thought is free.

   Cal. That's not the tune.
    [ARIEL *plays the tune on a Tabor and Pipe.*
   Ste. What is this same?   136
   Trin. This is the tune of our catch, played by
the picture of Nobody.
   Ste. If thou beest a man, show thyself in thy
likeness: if thou beest a devil, take't as thou
list.   141
   Trin. O, forgive me my sins!
   Ste. He that dies pays all debts: I defy thee.
—Mercy upon us!   144
   Cal. Art thou afeard?
   Ste. No, monster, not I.
   Cal. Be not afeard: the isle is full of noises,
Sounds and sweet airs, that give delight, and
hurt not.   148
Sometimes a thousand twangling instruments
Will hum about mine ears; and sometime voices,
That, if I then had wak'd after long sleep,
Will make me sleep again: and then, in dreaming,
The clouds methought would open and show
riches   153
Ready to drop upon me; that, when I wak'd
I cried to dream again.
   Ste. This will prove a brave kingdom to me,
where I shall have my music for nothing.
   Cal. When Prospero is destroyed.
   Ste. That shall be by and by: I remember
the story.   160
   Trin. The sound is going away: let's follow
it, and after do our work.
   Ste. Lead, monster; we'll follow.—I would I
could see this taborer! he lays it on. Wilt come?
   Trin. I'll follow, Stephano.   [*Exeunt.*

SCENE III.—*Another Part of the Island.*

Enter ALONSO, SEBASTIAN, ANTONIO, GONZALO,
   ADRIAN, FRANCISCO, *and others.*

   Gon. By'r lakin, I can go no further, sir;
My old bones ache: here's a maze trod indeed,
Through forth-rights, and meanders! by your
patience,
I needs must rest me.
   Alon.   Old lord, I cannot blame thee, 4
Who am myself attach'd with weariness,
To the dulling of my spirits: sit down, and rest.
Even here I will put off my hope, and keep it
No longer for my flatterer: he is drown'd   8
Whom thus we stray to find; and the sea mocks
Our frustrate search on land. Well, let him go.

Ant. [*Aside to* SEB.] I am right glad that he's
so out of hope.
Do not, for one repulse, forego the purpose 12
That you resolv'd to effect.
  Seb.   [*Aside to* ANT.] The next advantage
Will we take throughly.
  Ant.   [*Aside to* SEB.] Let it be to-night;
For, now they are oppress'd with travel, they
Will not, nor cannot, use such vigilance   16
As when they are fresh.
  Seb. [*Aside to* ANT.] I say to-night: no more.

Solemn and strange music; and PROSPERO
*above, invisible. Enter below several strange
Shapes, bringing in a banquet: they dance
about it with gentle actions of salutation;
and, inviting the King, &c., to eat, they
depart.*

  Alon. What harmony is this? my good
friends, hark!
  Gon. Marvellous sweet music!
  Alon. Give us kind keepers, heavens! What
were these?   20
  Seb. A living drollery. Now I will believe
That there are unicorns; that in Arabia
There is one tree, the phœnix' throne; one
phœnix
At this hour reigning there.
  Ant.   I'll believe both; 24
And what does else want credit, come to me,
And I'll be sworn 'tis true: travellers ne'er did lie,
Though fools at home condemn them.
  Gon.   If in Naples
I should report this now, would they believe me?
If I should say I saw such islanders,—   29
For, certes, these are people of the island,—
Who, though they are of monstrous shape, yet,
note,
Their manners are more gentle-kind than of 32
Our human generation you shall find
Many, nay, almost any.
  Pro.   [*Aside.*] Honest lord,
Thou hast said well; for some of you there
present
Are worse than devils.
  Alon.   I cannot too much muse, 36
Such shapes, such gesture, and such sound,
expressing,—
Although they want the use of tongue,—a kind
Of excellent dumb discourse.
  Pro.   [*Aside.*] Praise in departing.
  Fran. They vanish'd strangely.
  Seb.   No matter, since 40
They have left their viands behind; for we have
stomachs.—
Will't please you to taste of what is here?
  Alon.   Not I.
  Gon. Faith, sir, you need not fear. When we
were boys,
Who would believe that there were moun-
taineers   44
Dew-lapp'd like bulls, whose throats had hang-
ing at them
Wallets of flesh? or that there were such men
Whose heads stood in their breasts? which now
we find

Each putter-out of five for one will bring us 48
Good warrant of.
  Alon.   I will stand to and feed,
Although my last; no matter, since I feel
The best is past.—Brother, my lord the duke,
Stand to and do as we.   52

Thunder and lightning. Enter ARIEL *like a
harpy; claps his wings upon the table; and,
with a quaint device, the banquet vanishes.*

  Ari. You are three men of sin, whom Destiny—
That hath to instrument this lower world
And what is in't,—the never-surfeited sea 55
Hath caused to belch up you; and on this island
Where man doth not inhabit; you 'mongst men
Being most unfit to live. I have made you mad;
  [*Seeing* ALON., SEB., *&c., draw their swords.*
And even with such-like valour men hang and
drown
Their proper selves. You fools! I and my
fellows   60
Are ministers of fate: the elements
Of whom your swords are temper'd, may as well
Wound the loud winds, or with bemock'd-at
stabs
Kill the still-closing waters, as diminish   64
One dowle that's in my plume; my fellow-
ministers
Are like invulnerable. If you could hurt,
Your swords are now too massy for your strengths,
And will not be uplifted. But, remember,— 68
For that's my business to you,—that you three
From Milan did supplant good Prospero;
Expos'd unto the sea, which hath requit it,
Him and his innocent child: for which foul
deed   72
The powers, delaying, not forgetting, have
Incens'd the seas and shores, yea, all the crea-
tures,
Against your peace. Thee of thy son, Alonso,
They have bereft; and do pronounce, by me, 76
Lingering perdition,—worse than any death
Can be at once,—shall step by step attend
You and your ways; whose wraths to guard
you from—   79
Which here in this most desolate isle, else falls
Upon your heads,—is nothing but heart-sorrow
And a clear life ensuing.

*He vanishes in thunder: then, to soft music,
enter the Shapes again, and dance with mocks
and mows, and carry out the table.*

  Pro. [*Aside.*] Bravely the figure of this harpy
hast thou
Perform'd, my Ariel; a grace it had, devouring:
Of my instruction hast thou nothing bated 85
In what thou hadst to say: so, with good life
And observation strange, my meaner ministers
Their several kinds have done. My high charms
work,   88
And these mine enemies are all knit up
In their distractions: they now are in my power;
And in these fits I leave them, while I visit
Young Ferdinand,—whom they suppose is
drown'd,—   92
And his and mine lov'd darling. [*Exit above.*

Gon. I' the name of something holy, sir, why
    stand you
In this strange stare?
    Alon.   O, it is monstrous! monstrous!
Methought the billows spoke and told me of it;
The winds did sing it to me; and the thunder,
That deep and dreadful organ-pipe, pronounc'd
The name of Prosper: it did bass my trespass.
Therefore my son i' th' ooze is bedded; and 100
I'll seek him deeper than e'er plummet sounded,
And with him there lie mudded.   [*Exit.*
    Seb.   But one fiend at a time,
I'll fight their legions o'er.
    Ant.   I'll be thy second.
                 [*Exeunt* SEB. *and* ANT.
    Gon. All three of them are desperate; their
    great guilt,   104
Like poison given to work a great time after,
Now 'gins to bite the spirits.—I do beseech you
That are of suppler joints, follow them swiftly
And hinder them from what this ecstasy   108
May now provoke them to.
    Adr.   Follow, I pray you. [*Exeunt.*

ACT IV

SCENE I.—*Before* PROSPERO'S *Cell.*

Enter PROSPERO, FERDINAND, *and* MIRANDA.

Pro. If I have too austerely punish'd you,
Your compensation makes amends; for I
Have given you here a thrid of mine own life,
Or that for which I live; whom once again   4
I tender to thy hand: all thy vexations
Were but my trials of thy love, and thou
Hast strangely stood the test: here, afore
    Heaven,
I ratify this my rich gift. O Ferdinand!   8
Do not smile at me that I boast her off,
For thou shalt find she will outstrip all praise,
And make it halt behind her.
    Fer.   I do believe it
Against an oracle.   12
    Pro. Then, as my gift and thine own acquisi-
    tion
Worthily purchas'd, take my daughter: but
If thou dost break her virgin knot before
All sanctimonious ceremonies may   16
With full and holy rite be minister'd,
No sweet aspersion shall the heavens let fall
To make this contract grow; but barren hate,
Sour-ey'd disdain and discord shall bestrew 20
The union of your bed with weeds so loathly
That you shall hate it both: therefore take heed,
As Hymen's lamps shall light you.
    Fer.   As I hope
For quiet days, fair issue and long life,   24
With such love as 'tis now, the murkiest den,
The most opportune place, the strong'st sug-
    gestion
Our worser genius can, shall never melt
Mine honour into lust, to take away   28
The edge of that day's celebration
When I shall think, or Phœbus' steeds are
    founder'd,
Or Night kept chain'd below.

    Pro.   Fairly spoke.
Sit then, and talk with her, she is thine own.
What, Ariel! my industrious servant Ariel! 33

Enter ARIEL.

Ari. What would my potent master? here
    I am.
    Pro. Thou and thy meaner fellows your last
    service
Did worthily perform; and I must use you 36
In such another trick. Go bring the rabble,
O'er whom I give thee power, here to this place:
Incite them to quick motion; for I must
Bestow upon the eyes of this young couple   40
Some vanity of mine art: it is my promise,
And they expect it from me.
    Ari.   Presently?
    Pro. Ay, with a twink.
    Ari. Before you can say, 'Come,' and 'Go,' 44
And breathe twice; and cry, 'so, so,'
Each one, tripping on his toe,
Will be here with mop and mow.
Do you love me, master? no?   48
    Pro. Dearly, my delicate Ariel. Do not ap-
    proach
Till thou dost hear me call.
    Ari.   Well, I conceive. [*Exit.*
    Pro. Look, thou be true; do not give dalliance
Too much the rein: the strongest oaths are
    straw   52
To the fire i' the blood: be more abstemious,
Or else good night your vow!
    Fer.   I warrant you, sir;
The white-cold virgin snow upon my heart
Abates the ardour of my liver.
    Pro.   Well.—   56
Now come, my Ariel! bring a corollary,
Rather than want a spirit: appear, and pertly.
No tongue! all eyes! be silent.   [*Soft music.*

A Masque. Enter IRIS.

Iris. Ceres, most bounteous lady, thy rich
    leas   60
Of wheat, rye, barley, vetches, oats, and peas;
Thy turfy mountains, where live nibbling sheep,
And flat meads thatch'd with stover, them to
    keep;
Thy banks with pioned and twilled brims,   64
Which spongy April at thy hest betrims,
To make cold nymphs chaste crowns; and thy
    broom groves,
Whose shadow the dismissed bachelor loves,
Being lass-lorn; thy pole-clipt vineyard;   68
And thy sea-marge, sterile and rocky-hard,
Where thou thyself dost air: the queen o' the sky,
Whose watery arch and messenger am I,
Bids thee leave these; and with her sovereign
    grace,   72
Here on this grass-plot, in this very place,
To come and sport: her peacocks fly amain:
Approach, rich Ceres, her to entertain.

Enter CERES.

Cer. Hail, many-colour'd messenger, that
    ne'er   76
Dost disobey the wife of Jupiter;

Who with thy saffron wings upon my flowers
Diffusest honey-drops, refreshing showers:
And with each end of thy blue bow dost crown
My bosky acres, and my unshrubb'd down, 81
Rich scarf to my proud earth; why hath thy
  queen
Summon'd me hither, to this short-grass'd
  green?
  Iris. A contract of true love to celebrate, 84
And some donation freely to estate
On the bless'd lovers.
  Cer.   Tell me, heavenly bow,
If Venus or her son, as thou dost know,
Do now attend the queen? since they did plot
The means that dusky Dis my daughter got, 89
Her and her blind boy's scandal'd company
I have forsworn.
  Iris.   Of her society
Be not afraid; I met her deity   92
Cutting the clouds towards Paphos and her son
Dove-drawn with her. Here thought they to
  have done
Some wanton charm upon this man and maid,
Whose vows are, that no bed-rite shall be paid
Till Hymen's torch be lighted; but in vain: 97
Mars's hot minion is return'd again;
Her waspish-headed son has broke his arrows,
Swears he will shoot no more, but play with
  sparrows,   100
And be a boy right out.
  Cer.   Highest queen of state,
Great Juno comes; I know her by her gait.

Enter JUNO.

  Jun. How does my bounteous sister? Go
  with me
To bless this twain, that they may prosperous
  be,   104
And honour'd in their issue.

SONG.

  Jun. Honour, riches, marriage-blessing,
       Long continuance, and increasing,
       Hourly joys be still upon you!   108
       Juno sings her blessings on you.

  Cer. Earth's increase, foison plenty.
       Barns and garners never empty:
       Vines, with clust'ring bunches growing; 112
       Plants with goodly burden bowing;
       Spring come to you at the farthest
       In the very end of harvest!
       Scarcity and want shall shun you; 116
       Ceres' blessing so is on you.

  Fer. This is a most majestic vision, and
Harmonious charmingly: May I be bold
To think these spirits?
  Pro.   Spirits, which by mine art 120
I have from their confines call'd to enact
My present fancies.
  Fer.   Let me live here ever:
So rare a wonder'd father and a wise,
Makes this place Paradise.
       [JUNO *and* CERES *whisper, and send*
           IRIS *on employment.*
  Pro.   Sweet, now, silence! 124
Juno and Ceres whisper seriously,

There's something else to do: hush, and be mute,
Or else our spell is marr'd.
  Iris. You nymphs, call'd Naiades, of the
  windring brooks,   128
With your sedg'd crowns, and ever-harmless
  looks,
Leave your crisp channels, and on this green
  land
Answer your summons: Juno does command.
Come, temperate nymphs, and help to celebrate
A contract of true love: be not too late. 133

Enter certain Nymphs.

You sun-burn'd sicklemen, of August weary,
Come hither from the furrow, and be merry:
Make holiday: your rye-straw hats put on, 136
And these fresh nymphs encounter every one
In country footing.

Enter certain Reapers, *properly habited: they
  join with the* Nymphs *in a graceful dance;
  towards the end whereof* PROSPERO *starts
  suddenly, and speaks; after which, to a
  strange, hollow, and confused noise, they
  heavily vanish.*

  Pro. [*Aside.*] I had forgot that foul con-
    spiracy
Of the beast Caliban, and his confederates 140
Against my life: the minute of their plot
Is almost come.—[*To the* Spirits.] Well done!
  avoid; no more!
  Fer. This is strange: your father's in some
    passion
That works him strongly.
  Mira.   Never till this day 144
Saw I him touch'd with anger so distemper'd.
  Pro. You do look, my son, in a mov'd sort,
As if you were dismay'd: be cheerful, sir:
Our revels now are ended. These our actors, 148
As I foretold you, were all spirits and
Are melted into air, into thin air:
And, like the baseless fabric of this vision,
The cloud-capp'd towers, the gorgeous palaces,
The solemn temples, the great globe itself, 153
Yea, all which it inherit, shall dissolve
And, like this insubstantial pageant faded,
Leave not a rack behind. We are such stuff 156
As dreams are made on, and our little life
Is rounded with a sleep.—Sir, I am vex'd:
Bear with my weakness; my old brain is troubled.
Be not disturb'd with my infirmity.   160
If you be pleas'd, retire into my cell
And there repose: a turn or two I'll walk,
To still my beating mind.
  Fer. Mira.   We wish your peace.
                            [*Exeunt.*
  Pro. Come with a thought!—[*To them.*] I
    thank thee: Ariel, come!   164

Enter ARIEL.

  Ari. Thy thoughts I cleave to. What's thy
    pleasure?
  Pro.   Spirit,
We must prepare to meet with Caliban.
  Ari. Ay, my commander; when I presented
    Ceres,

I thought to have told thee of it; but I fear'd 168
Lest I might anger thee.

Pro. Say again, where didst thou leave these
varlets?

Ari. I told you, sir, they were red-hot with
drinking;
So full of valour that they smote the air 172
For breathing in their faces; beat the ground
For kissing of their feet; yet always bending
Towards their project. Then I beat my tabor;
At which, like unback'd colts, they prick'd their
ears, 176
Advanc'd their eyelids, lifted up their noses
As they smelt music: so I charm'd their ears
That, calf-like, they my lowing follow'd through
Tooth'd briers, sharp furzes, pricking goss and
thorns, 180
Which enter'd their frail shins: at last I left
them
I' the filthy-mantled pool beyond your cell,
There dancing up to the chins, that the foul
lake
O'erstunk their feet.

Pro. This was well done, my bird. 184
Thy shape invisible retain thou still:
The trumpery in my house, go bring it hither,
For stale to catch these thieves.

Ari. I go, I go. [*Exit.*

Pro. A devil, a born devil, on whose nature
Nurture can never stick; on whom my pains, 189
Humanely taken, are all lost, quite lost;
And as with age his body uglier grows,
So his mind cankers. I will plague them all, 192
Even to roaring.

Re-enter ARIEL, *loaden with glistering
apparel, &c.*

Come, hang them on this line.

PROSPERO *and* ARIEL *remain invisible. Enter*
CALIBAN, STEPHANO, *and* TRINCULO, *all wet.*

Cal. Pray you, tread softly, that the blind
mole may not
Hear a foot fall: we now are near his cell. 195

Ste. Monster, your fairy, which you say is a
harmless fairy, has done little better than played
the Jack with us.

Trin. Monster, I do smell all horse-piss; at
which my nose is in great indignation. 200

Ste. So is mine.—Do you hear, monster? If I
should take a displeasure against you, look you,—

Trin. Thou wert but a lost monster.

Cal. Good my lord, give me thy favour still:
Be patient, for the prize I'll bring thee to 205
Shall hoodwink this mischance: therefore speak
softly;
All's hush'd as midnight yet.

Trin. Ay, but to lose our bottles in the
pool,— 209

Ste. There is not only disgrace and dishonour
in that, monster, but an infinite loss.

Trin. That's more to me than my wetting:
yet this is your harmless fairy, monster. 213

Ste. I will fetch off my bottle, though I be
o'er ears for my labour.

Cal. Prithee, my king, be quiet. Seest thou
here, 216
This is the mouth o' the cell: no noise, and
enter.
Do that good mischief, which may make this
island
Thine own for ever, and I, thy Caliban,
For aye thy foot-licker. 220

Ste. Give me thy hand: I do begin to have
bloody thoughts.

Trin. O king Stephano! O peer! O worthy
Stephano! look, what a wardrobe here is for
thee! 225

Cal. Let it alone, thou fool; it is but trash.

Trin. O, ho, monster! we know what belongs
to a frippery.—O king Stephano! 228

Ste. Put off that gown, Trinculo; by this
hand, I'll have that gown.

Trin. Thy grace shall have it.

Cal. The dropsy drown this fool! what do
you mean 232
To dote thus on such luggage? Let's along,
And do the murder first: if he awake,
From toe to crown he'll fill our skins with
pinches;
Make us strange stuff. 236

Ste. Be you quiet, monster.—Mistress line, is
not this my jerkin? Now is the jerkin under the
line: now, jerkin, you are like to lose your hair
and prove a bald jerkin. 240

Trin. Do, do: we steal by line and level,
an't like your grace.

Ste. I thank thee for that jest; here's a garment for't: wit shall not go unrewarded while I
am king of this country: 'Steal by line and
level,' is an excellent pass of pate; there's another garment for't. 247

Trin. Monster, come, put some lime upon
your fingers, and away with the rest.

Cal. I will have none on't: we shall lose our
time,
And all be turn'd to barnacles, or to apes 252
With foreheads villanous low.

Ste. Monster, lay-to your fingers: help to bear
this away where my hogshead of wine is, or I'll
turn you out of my kingdom. Go to; carry this.

Trin. And this. 256

Ste. Ay, and this.

A noise of hunters heard. Enter divers Spirits,
in shape of hounds, and hunt them about;
PROSPERO *and* ARIEL *setting them on.*

Pro. Hey, Mountain, hey!

Ari. Silver! there it goes, Silver!

Pro. Fury, Fury! there, Tyrant, there! hark,
hark! 260

[CAL., STE., *and* TRIN. *are driven out.*

Go, charge my goblins that they grind their
joints
With dry convulsions; shorten up their sinews
With aged cramps, and more pinch-spotted
make them
Than pard, or cat o' mountain.

Ari. Hark! they roar. 264

Pro. Let them be hunted soundly. At this
hour

Lie at my mercy all mine enemies:
Shortly shall all my labours end, and thou
Shalt have the air at freedom: for a little,   268
Follow, and do me service.   [*Exeunt.*

ACT V

SCENE I.—*Before the Cell of* PROSPERO.

Enter PROSPERO *in his magic robes; and* ARIEL.

Pro. Now does my project gather to a head:
My charms crack not; my spirits obey, and time
Goes upright with his carriage. How's the day?
Ari. On the sixth hour; at which time, my
lord,   4
You said our work should cease.
Pro.   I did say so,
When first I rais'd the tempest. Say, my spirit,
How fares the king and 's followers?
Ari.   Confin'd together
In the same fashion as you gave in charge;   8
Just as you left them: all prisoners, sir,
In the line-grove which weather-fends your cell;
They cannot budge till your release. The king,
His brother, and yours, abide all three dis-
tracted,   12
And the remainder mourning over them,
Brimful of sorrow and dismay; but chiefly
Him, that you term'd, sir, 'The good old lord
Gonzalo:'
His tears run down his beard, like winter's drops
From eaves of reeds; your charm so strongly
works them,   17
That if you now beheld them, your affections
Would become tender.
Pro.   Dost thou think so, spirit?
Ari. Mine would, sir, were I human.
Pro.   And mine shall.   20
Hast thou, which art but air, a touch, a feeling
Of their afflictions, and shall not myself,
One of their kind, that relish all as sharply,
Passion as they, be kindlier mov'd than thou
art?   24
Though with their high wrongs I am struck to
the quick,
Yet with my nobler reason 'gainst my fury
Do I take part: the rarer action is
In virtue than in vengeance: they being peni-
tent,   28
The sole drift of my purpose doth extend
Not a frown further. Go, release them, Ariel.
My charms I'll break, their senses I'll restore,
And they shall be themselves.
Ari.   I'll fetch them, sir. [*Exit.*
Pro. Ye elves of hills, brooks, standing lakes,
and groves;   33
And ye, that on the sands with printless foot
Do chase the ebbing Neptune and do fly him
When he comes back; you demi-puppets, that 36
By moonshine do the green sour ringlets make
Whereof the ewe not bites; and you, whose
pastime
Is to make midnight mushrooms; that rejoice
To hear the solemn curfew; by whose aid,— 40
Weak masters though ye be—I have bedimm'd

The noontide sun, call'd forth the mutinous
winds,
And 'twixt the green sea and the azur'd vault
Set roaring war: to the dread-rattling thunder 44
Have I given fire and rifted Jove's stout oak
With his own bolt: the strong-bas'd promontory
Have I made shake; and by the spurs pluck'd
up
The pine and cedar: graves at my command 48
Have wak'd their sleepers, op'd, and let them
forth
By my so potent art. But this rough magic
I here abjure; and, when I have requir'd
Some heavenly music,—which even now I do,—
To work mine end upon their senses that   53
This airy charm is for, I'll break my staff,
Bury it certain fathoms in the earth,
And, deeper than did ever plummet sound, 56
I'll drown my book.   [*Solemn music.*

Re-enter ARIEL: *after him,* ALONSO, *with a
frantic gesture, attended by* GONZALO; SEBAS-
TIAN *and* ANTONIO *in like manner, attended by*
ADRIAN *and* FRANCISCO: *they all enter the
circle which* PROSPERO *had made, and there
stand charmed; which* PROSPERO *observing,
speaks.*

A solemn air and the best comforter
To an unsettled fancy, cure thy brains,
Now useless, boil'd within thy skull! There
stand,   60
For you are spell-stopp'd.
Holy Gonzalo, honourable man,
Mine eyes, even sociable to the show of thine,
Fall fellowly drops. The charm dissolves apace;
And as the morning steals upon the night, 65
Melting the darkness, so their rising senses
Begin to chase the ignorant fumes that mantle
Their clearer reason.—O good Gonzalo!   68
My true preserver, and a loyal sir
To him thou follow'st, I will pay thy graces
Home, both in word and deed.—Most cruelly
Didst thou, Alonso, use me and my daughter: 72
Thy brother was a furtherer in the act;—
Thou'rt pinch'd for't now, Sebastian.—Flesh
and blood,
You, brother mine, that entertain'd ambition,
Expell'd remorse and nature; who, with Se-
bastian,—   76
Whose inward pinches therefore are most
strong,—
Would here have kill'd your king; I do forgive
thee,
Unnatural though thou art!—Their under-
standing
Begins to swell, and the approaching tide   80
Will shortly fill the reasonable shores
That now lie foul and muddy. Not one of
them
That yet looks on me, or would know me.—
Ariel,
Fetch me the hat and rapier in my cell:— 84
    [*Exit* ARIEL.
I will discase me, and myself present,
As I was sometime Milan.—Quickly, spirit;
Thou shalt ere long be free.

ARIEL *re-enters, singing, and helps to attire*
PROSPERO.

Ari. Where the bee sucks, there suck I   88
  In a cowslip's bell I lie;
  There I couch when owls do cry.
  On the bat's back I do fly
  After summer merrily: 92
  Merrily, merrily shall I live now
  Under the blossom that hangs on the bough.

Pro. Why, that's my dainty Ariel! I shall
  miss thee;
But yet thou shalt have freedom;—so, so, so.—
To the king's ship, invisible as thou art: 97
There shalt thou find the mariners asleep
Under the hatches; the master and the boat-
  swain
Being awake, enforce them to this place,   100
And presently, I prithee.
  Ari. I drink the air before me, and return
Or e'er your pulse twice beat.   [*Exit.*
  Gon. All torment, trouble, wonder, and
  amazement   104
Inhabits here: some heavenly power guide us
Out of this fearful country!
  Pro.   Behold, sir king,
The wronged Duke of Milan, Prospero.
For more assurance that a living prince   108
Does now speak to thee, I embrace thy body;
And to thee and thy company I bid
A hearty welcome.
  Alon.   Whe'r thou beest he or no,
Or some enchanted trifle to abuse me,   112
As late I have been, I not know: thy pulse
Beats, as of flesh and blood; and, since I saw
  thee,
Th' affliction of my mind amends, with which,
I fear, a madness held me: this must crave,—
An if this be at all—a most strange story.   117
Thy dukedom I resign, and do entreat
Thou pardon me my wrongs.—But how should
  Prospero
Be living, and be here?
  Pro.   First, noble friend, 120
Let me embrace thine age; whose honour can-
  not
Be measur'd, or confin'd.
  Gon.   Whether this be,
Or be not, I'll not swear.
  Pro.   You do yet taste
Some subtilties o' the isle, that will not let you
Believe things certain.—Welcome! my friends
  all:—   125
[*Aside to* SEB. *and* ANT.] But you, my brace of
  lords, were I so minded,
I here could pluck his highness' frown upon
  you,
And justify you traitors: at this time   128
I will tell no tales.
  Seb.   [*Aside.*] The devil speaks in him.
  Pro.   No.
For you, most wicked sir, whom to call brother
Would even infect my mouth, I do forgive
Thy rankest fault; all of them; and require 132
My dukedom of thee, which, perforce, I know,
Thou must restore.
  Alon.   If thou beest Prospero,

Give us particulars of thy preservation;
How thou hast met us here, who three hours
  since   136
Were wrack'd upon this shore; where I have
  lost,—
How sharp the point of this remembrance is!—
My dear son Ferdinand.
  Pro.   I am woe for't, sir.
  Alon. Irreparable is the loss, and patience
Says it is past her cure.
  Pro.   I rather think   141
You have not sought her help; of whose soft
  grace,
For the like loss I have her sovereign aid,
And rest myself content.
  Alon.   You the like loss! 144
  Pro. As great to me, as late; and, supportable
To make the dear loss, have I means much
  weaker
Than you may call to comfort you, for I
Have lost my daughter.
  Alon.   A daughter? 148
O heavens! that they were living both in Naples,
The king and queen there! that they were, I wish
Myself were mudded in that oozy bed
Where my son lies. When did you lose your
  daughter?   152
  Pro. In this last tempest. I perceive, these
  lords
At this encounter do so much admire
That they devour their reason, and scarce think
Their eyes do offices of truth, their words 156
Are natural breath: but, howsoe'r you have
Been justled from your senses, know for certain
That I am Prospero and that very duke
Which was thrust forth of Milan; who most
  strangely   160
Upon this shore, where you were wrack'd, was
  landed,
To be the lord on't. No more yet of this;
For 'tis a chronicle of day by day,
Not a relation for a breakfast nor   164
Befitting this first meeting. Welcome, sir;
This cell's my court: here have I few attendants
And subjects none abroad: pray you, look in.
My dukedom since you have given me again, 168
I will requite you with as good a thing;
At least bring forth a wonder, to content ye
As much as me my dukedom.

The entrance of the Cell opens, and discovers
FERDINAND *and* MIRANDA *playing at chess.*

  Mira. Sweet lord, you play me false.
  Fer.   No, my dearest love, 172
I would not for the world.
  Mira. Yes, for a score of kingdoms you should
  wrangle,
And I would call it fair play.
  Alon.   If this prove
A vision of the island, one dear son 176
Shall I twice lose.
  Seb.   A most high miracle!
  Fer. Though the seas threaten, they are merci-
  ful:
I have curs'd them without cause.
                  [*Kneels to* ALON.

Alon.　　　　　Now, all the blessings
Of a glad father compass thee about!　180
Arise, and say how thou cam'st here.
Mira.　　　　　O, wonder!
How many goodly creatures are there here!
How beauteous mankind is! O brave new world,
That has such people in 't!
Pro.　　　　　'Tis new to thee.　184
Alon. What is this maid, with whom thou
wast at play?
Your eld'st acquaintance cannot be three hours:
Is she the goddess that hath sever'd us,
And brought us thus together?
Fer.　　　　　Sir, she is mortal;　188
But by immortal Providence she's mine;
I chose her when I could not ask my father
For his advice, nor thought I had one. She
Is daughter to this famous Duke of Milan,　192
Of whom so often I have heard renown,
But never saw before; of whom I have
Receiv'd a second life; and second father
This lady makes him to me.
Alon.　　　　　I am hers:　196
But O! how oddly will it sound that I
Must ask my child forgiveness!
Pro.　　　　　There, sir, stop:
Let us not burden our remembrances
With a heaviness that's gone.
Gon.　　　　　I have inly wept,　200
Or should have spoke ere this. Look down, you
gods,
And on this couple drop a blessed crown;
For it is you that have chalk'd forth the way
Which brought us hither!
Alon.　　　　　I say, Amen, Gonzalo!　204
Gon. Was Milan thrust from Milan, that his
issue
Should become kings of Naples? O, rejoice
Beyond a common joy, and set it down
With gold on lasting pillars. In one voyage　208
Did Claribel her husband find at Tunis,
And Ferdinand, her brother, found a wife
Where he himself was lost; Prospero his duke-
dom
In a poor isle; and all of us ourselves,　212
When no man was his own.
Alon. [*To* FER. *and* MIRA.] Give me your
hands:
Let grief and sorrow still embrace his heart
That doth not wish you joy!
Gon.　　　　　Be it so: Amen!

Re-enter ARIEL, *with the* Master *and* Boatswain
amazedly following.

O look, sir! look, sir! here are more of us.　216
I prophesied, if a gallows were on land,
This fellow could not drown.—Now, blas-
phemy,
That swear'st grace o'erboard, not an oath on
shore?
Hast thou no mouth by land? What is the news?
Boats. The best news is that we have safely
found
Our king and company: the next, our ship,—　221
Which but three glasses since we gave out
split,—

Is tight and yare and bravely rigg'd as when
We first put out to sea.
Ari. [*Aside to* PRO.] Sir, all this service　225
Have I done since I went.
Pro. [*Aside to* ARI.] My tricksy spirit!
Alon. These are not natural events; they
strengthen
From strange to stranger.—Say, how came you
hither?　228
Boats. If I did think, sir, I were well awake,
I'd strive to tell you. We were dead of sleep,
And,—how we know not,—all clapp'd under
hatches,
Where, but even now, with strange and several
noises　232
Of roaring, shrieking, howling, jingling chains,
And mo diversity of sounds, all horrible,
We were awak'd; straightway, at liberty:
Where we, in all her trim, freshly beheld　236
Our royal, good, and gallant ship; our master
Capering to eye her: on a trice, so please you,
Even in a dream, were we divided from them,
And were brought moping hither.
Ari. [*Aside to* PRO.] Was't well done?　240
Pro. [*Aside to* ARI.] Bravely, my diligence!
Thou shalt be free.
Alon. This is as strange a maze as e'er men
trod;
And there is in this business more than nature
Was ever conduct of: some oracle　244
Must rectify our knowledge.
Pro.　　　　　Sir, my liege,
Do not infest your mind with beating on
The strangeness of this business: at pick'd
leisure
Which shall be shortly, single I'll resolve you,—
Which to you shall seem probable,—of every
These happen'd accidents; till when, be cheerful,
And think of each thing well.—[*Aside to* ARI.]
Come hither, spirit;
Set Caliban and his companions free;　252
Untie the spell. [*Exit* ARI.] How fares my
gracious sir?
There are yet missing of your company
Some few odd lads that you remember not.

Re-enter ARIEL, *driving in* CALIBAN, STEPHANO,
and TRINCULO, *in their stolen apparel.*

Ste. Every man shift for all the rest, and let
no man take care for himself, for all is but
fortune.—Coragio! bully-monster, Coragio!
Trin. If these be true spies which I wear in
my head, here's a goodly sight.　260
Cal. O Setebos! these be brave spirits, indeed.
How fine my master is! I am afraid
He will chastise me.
Seb.　　　　　Ha, ha!
What things are these, my lord Antonio?　264
Will money buy them?
Ant.　　　　　Very like; one of them
Is a plain fish, and, no doubt, marketable.
Pro. Mark but the badges of these men, my
lords,
Then say, if they be true.—This mis-shapen
knave,—　258
His mother was a witch; and one so strong

That could control the moon, make flows and
  ebbs,
And deal in her command without her power.
These three have robb'd me; and this demi-
  devil,—   272
For he's a bastard one,—had plotted with them
To take my life: two of these fellows you
Must know and own; this thing of darkness I
Acknowledge mine.
  Cal.   I shall be pinch'd to death. 276
  Alon. Is not this Stephano, my drunken
    butler?
  Seb. He is drunk now: where had he wine?
  Alon. And Trinculo is reeling-ripe: where
    should they
Find this grand liquor that hath gilded them?
How cam'st thou in this pickle?   281
  Trin. I have been in such a pickle since I
saw you last that, I fear me, will never out of
my bones: I shall not fear fly-blowing.   284
  Seb. Why, how now, Stephano!
  Ste. O! touch me not: I am not Stephano,
but a cramp.
  Pro. You'd be king of the isle, sirrah?
  Ste. I should have been a sore one then.   288
  Alon. This is a strange thing as e'er I look'd
on.   [*Pointing to* CAL.
  Pro. He is as disproportion'd in his manners
As in his shape.—Go, sirrah, to my cell;
Take with you your companions: as you look
To have my pardon, trim it handsomely.   293
  Cal. Ay, that I will; and I'll be wise here-
    after,
And seek for grace. What a thrice-doudle ass
Was I, to take this drunkard for a god,   295
And worship this dull fool!
  Pro.   Go to; away!
  Alon. Hence, and bestow your luggage where
    you found it.
  Seb. Or stole it, rather.
            [*Exeunt* CAL., STE., *and* TRIN.
  Pro. Sir, I invite your highness and your
    train   300

To my poor cell, where you shall take your rest
For this one night; which—part of it—I'll waste
With such discourse as, I not doubt, shall make it
Go quick away; the story of my life   304
And the particular accidents gone by
Since I came to this isle: and in the morn
I'll bring you to your ship, and so to Naples,
Where I have hope to see the nuptial   308
Of these our dear-beloved solemniz'd;
And thence retire me to my Milan, where
Every third thought shall be my grave.
  Alon.   I long
To hear the story of your life, which must   312
Take the ear strangely.
  Pro.   I'll deliver all;
And promise you calm seas, auspicious gales
And sail so expeditious that shall catch
Your royal fleet far off.—[*Aside to* ARI.] My
    Ariel, chick,   316
That is thy charge: then to the elements
Be free, and fare thou well!—Please you, draw
    near.   [*Exeunt.*

EPILOGUE

Spoken by PROSPERO.

Now my charms are all o'erthrown,
And what strength I have's mine own;
Which is most faint: now, 'tis true,
I must be here confin'd by you,   4
Or sent to Naples. Let me not,
Since I have my dukedom got
And pardon'd the deceiver, dwell
In this bare island by your spell;   8
But release me from my bands
With the help of your good hands.
Gentle breath of yours my sails
Must fill, or else my project fails,   12
Which was to please. Now I want
Spirits to enforce, art to enchant;
And my ending is despair,
Unless I be reliev'd by prayer,   16
Which pierces so that it assaults
Mercy itself and frees all faults.
As you from crimes would pardon'd be,
Let your indulgence set me free.   20

THE TWO GENTLEMEN OF VERONA

DRAMATIS PERSONÆ

DUKE OF MILAN, Father to Silvia.
VALENTINE,} the Two Gentlemen.
PROTEUS,
ANTONIO, Father to Proteus.
THURIO, a foolish rival to Valentine.
EGLAMOUR, Agent for Silvia, in her escape.
SPEED, a clownish Servant to Valentine.
LAUNCE, the like to Proteus.

PANTHINO, Servant to Antonio.
HOST, where Julia lodges in Milan.
OUTLAWS with Valentine.

JULIA, beloved of Proteus.
SILVIA, beloved of Valentine.
LUCETTA, waiting woman to Julia.
Servants, Musicians.

SCENE.—*Verona; Milan; and the frontiers of Mantua.*

ACT I

SCENE I.—*Verona. An open place.*

Enter VALENTINE *and* PROTEUS.

Val. Cease to persuade, my loving Proteus:
Home-keeping youth have ever homely wits.
Were 't not affection chains thy tender days
To the sweet glances of thy honour'd love,   4
I rather would entreat thy company
To see the wonders of the world abroad
Than, living dully sluggardiz'd at home,
Wear out thy youth with shapeless idleness.   8
But since thou lov'st, love still, and thrive
   therein,
Even as I would when I to love begin.
   Pro. Wilt thou be gone? Sweet Valentine,
   adieu!
Think on thy Proteus, when thou haply seest   12
Some rare note-worthy object in thy travel:
Wish me partaker in thy happiness
When thou dost meet good hap; and in thy
   danger,
If ever danger do environ thee,   16
Commend thy grievance to my holy prayers,
For I will be thy beadsman, Valentine.
   Val. And on a love-book pray for my success?
   Pro. Upon some book I love I'll pray for
   thee.   20
   Val. That's on some shallow story of deep
   love,
How young Leander cross'd the Hellespont.
   Pro. That's a deep story of a deeper love;
For he was more than over shoes in love.   24
   Val. 'Tis true; for you are over boots in love,
And yet you never swum the Hellespont.
   Pro. Over the boots? nay, give me not the
   boots.
   Val. No, I will not, for it boots thee not.
   Pro.   What?   28
   Val. To be in love, where scorn is bought
   with groans;
Coy looks with heart-sore sighs; one fading
   moment's mirth
With twenty watchful, weary, tedious nights:
If haply won, perhaps a hapless gain;   32
If lost, why then a grievous labour won:
However, but a folly bought with wit,
Or else a wit by folly vanquished.
   Pro. So, by ycur circumstance, you call me
   fool.   36

Val. So, by your circumstance, I fear you'll
   prove.
   Pro. 'Tis love you cavil at: I am not Love.
   Val. Love is your master, for he masters you;
And he that is so yoked by a fool,   40
Methinks, should not be chronicled for wise.
   Pro. Yet writers say, as in the sweetest bud
The eating canker dwells, so eating love
Inhabits in the finest wits of all.   44
   Val. And writers say, as the most forward
   bud
Is eaten by the canker ere it blow,
Even so by love the young and tender wit
Is turned to folly; blasting in the bud,   48
Losing his verdure even in the prime,
And all the fair effects of future hopes.
But wherefore waste I time to counsel thee
That art a votary to fond desire?   52
Once more adieu! my father at the road
Expects my coming, there to see me shipp'd.
   Pro. And thither will I bring thee, Valentine.
   Val. Sweet Proteus, no; now let us take our
   leave.   56
To Milan let me hear from thee by letters
Of thy success in love, and what news else
Betideth here in absence of thy friend;
And I likewise will visit thee with mine.   60
   Pro. All happiness bechance to thee in
   Milan!
   Val. As much to you at home! and so, fare-
   well.   [*Exit.*
   Pro. He after honour hunts, I after love:
He leaves his friends to dignify them more;   64
I leave myself, my friends and all, for love.
Thou, Julia, thou hast metamorphos'd me;—
Made me neglect my studies, lose my time,
War with good counsel, set the world at nought;
Made wit with musing weak, heart sick with
   thought.   69

Enter SPEED.

   Speed. Sir Proteus, save you! Saw you my
   master?
   Pro. But now he parted hence, to embark for
   Milan.
   Speed. Twenty to one, then, he is shipp'd
   already,   72
And I have play'd the sheep, in losing him.
   Pro. Indeed, a sheep doth very often stray,
An if the shepherd be a while away.

Speed. You conclude that my master is a
shepherd, then, and I a sheep?   77
Pro. I do.
Speed. Why then my horns are his horns,
whether I wake or sleep.   80
Pro. A silly answer, and fitting well a sheep.
Speed. This proves me still a sheep.
Pro. True, and thy master a shepherd.
Speed. Nay, that I can deny by a circum-
stance.   85
Pro. It shall go hard but I'll prove it by
another.
Speed. The shepherd seeks the sheep, and
not the sheep the shepherd; but I seek my
master, and my master seeks not me: therefore
I am no sheep.   91
Pro. The sheep for fodder follow the shepherd, the shepherd for food follows not the
sheep; thou for wages followest thy master,
thy master for wages follows not thee: therefore
thou art a sheep.   96
Speed. Such another proof will make me cry
'baa.'
Pro. But, dost thou hear? gavest thou my
letter to Julia?   100
Speed. Ay, sir: I, a lost mutton, gave your
letter to her, a laced mutton; and she, a laced
mutton, gave me, a lost mutton, nothing for my
labour.   104
Pro. Here's too small a pasture for such
store of muttons.
Speed. If the ground be overcharged, you
were best stick her.   108
Pro. Nay, in that you are astray; 'twere best
pound you.
Speed. Nay, sir, less than a pound shall serve
me for carrying your letter.   112
Pro. You mistake: I mean the pound,—a
pinfold.
Speed. From a pound to a pin? fold it over
and over,
'Tis threefold too little for carrying a letter to
your lover.   116
Pro. But what said she? [SPEED *nods.*] Did
she nod?
Speed. Ay.
Pro. Nod, ay? why, that's noddy.   120
Speed. You mistook, sir: I say she did nod;
and you ask me if she did nod; and I say, Ay.
Pro. And that set together is—noddy.
Speed. Now you have taken the pains to set
it together, take it for your pains.   125
Pro. No, no; you shall have it for bearing
the letter.
Speed. Well, I perceive I must be fain to bear
with you.   129
Pro. Why, sir, how do you bear with me?
Speed. Marry, sir, the letter very orderly;
having nothing but the word 'noddy' for my
pains.   133
Pro. Beshrew me, but you have a quick wit.
Speed. And yet it cannot overtake your
slow purse.   136
Pro. Come, come; open the matter in brief:
what said she?

Speed. Open your purse, that the money and
the matter may be both at once delivered.   140
Pro. Well, sir, here is for your pains [*giving
him money*]. What said she?
Speed. Truly, sir, I think you'll hardly win her.
Pro. Why? couldst thou perceive so much
from her?   145
Speed. Sir, I could perceive nothing at all
from her; no, not so much as a ducat for
delivering your letter. And being so hard to
me that brought your mind, I fear she'll prove
as hard to you in telling your mind. Give her
no token but stones, for she's as hard as steel.
Pro. What! said she nothing?   152
Speed. No, not so much as 'Take this for
thy pains.' To testify your bounty, I thank you,
you have testerned me; in requital whereof,
henceforth carry your letters yourself. And so,
sir, I'll commend you to my master.   157
Pro. Go, go, be gone, to save your ship from
wrack;
Which cannot perish, having thee aboard,
Being destin'd to a drier death on shore.—   160
                  [*Exit* SPEED.
I must go send some better messenger:
I fear my Julia would not deign my lines,
Receiving them from such a worthless post.   163
                       [*Exit.*

SCENE II.—*The Same. The Garden of* JULIA'S
House.

Enter JULIA *and* LUCETTA.

Jul. But say, Lucetta, now we are alone,
Wouldst thou then counsel me to fall in love?
Luc. Ay, madam, so you stumble not un-
heedfully.
Jul. Of all the fair resort of gentlemen   4
That every day with parle encounter me,
In thy opinion which is worthiest love?
Luc. Please you repeat their names, I'll
show my mind
According to my shallow simple skill.   8
Jul. What think'st thou of the fair Sir Egla-
mour?
Luc. As of a knight well-spoken, neat and
fine;
But, were I you, he never should be mine.   11
Jul. What think'st thou of the rich Mercatio?
Luc. Well of his wealth; but of himself, so so.
Jul. What think'st thou of the gentle Proteus?
Luc. Lord, Lord! to see what folly reigns in
us!
Jul. How now! what means this passion at
his name?   16
Luc. Pardon, dear madam; 'tis a passing
shame
That I, unworthy body as I am,
Should censure thus on lovely gentlemen.
Jul. Why not on Proteus, as of all the rest?
Luc. Then thus,—of many good I think him
best.   21
Jul. Your reason?
Luc. I have no other but a woman's reason:
I think him so because I think him so.   24

Jul. And wouldst thou have me cast my love on him?

Luc. Ay, if you thought your love not cast away.

Jul. Why, he, of all the rest hath never mov'd me.

Luc. Yet he of all the rest, I think, best loves ye.   28

Jul. His little speaking shows his love but small.

Luc. Fire that's closest kept burns most of all.

Jul. They do not love that do not show their love.

Luc. O! they love least that let men know their love.   32

Jul. I would I knew his mind.

Luc.   Peruse this paper, madam.
                                                        [*Gives a letter.*

Jul. 'To Julia.'—Say from whom?

Luc.   That the contents will show.

Jul. Say, say, who gave it thee?

Luc. Sir Valentine's page, and sent, I think, from Proteus.   36

He would have given it you, but I, being in the way,

Did in your name receive it; pardon the fault, I pray.

Jul. Now, by my modesty, a goodly broker!

Dare you presume to harbour wanton lines?   40

To whisper and conspire against my youth?

Now, trust me, 'tis an office of great worth

And you an officer fit for the place.

There, take the paper: see it be return'd;   44

Or else return no more into my sight.

Luc. To plead for love deserves more fee than hate.

Jul. Will ye be gone?

Luc.   That you may ruminate. [*Exit.*

Jul. And yet I would I had o'erlook'd the letter.   48

It were a shame to call her back again

And pray her to a fault for which I chid her.

What fool is she, that knows I am a maid,

And would not force the letter to my view!   52

Since maids, in modesty, say 'No' to that

Which they would have the profferer construe 'Ay.'

Fie, fie! how wayward is this foolish love

That, like a testy babe, will scratch the nurse   56

And presently all humbled kiss the rod!

How churlishly I chid Lucetta hence,

When willingly I would have had her here:

How angerly I taught my brow to frown,   60

When inward joy enforc'd my heart to smile.

My penance is, to call Lucetta back

And ask remission for my folly past.

What ho! Lucetta!

Re-enter LUCETTA.

Luc.   What would your ladyship?   64

Jul. Is it near dinner-time?

Luc.   I would it were;

That you might kill your stomach on your meat

And not upon your maid.

Jul. What is't that you took up so gingerly?

Luc. Nothing.   69

Jul. Why didst thou stoop, then?

Luc.   To take a paper up

That I let fall.

Jul.   And is that paper nothing?

Luc. Nothing concerning me.   72

Jul. Then let it lie for those that it concerns.

Luc. Madam, it will not lie where it concerns,

Unless it have a false interpreter.

Jul. Some love of yours hath writ to you in rime.   76

Luc. That I might sing it, madam, to a tune:

Give me a note: your ladyship can set.

Jul. As little by such toys as may be possible;

Best sing it to the tune of 'Light o' Love.'   80

Luc. It is too heavy for so light a tune.

Jul. Heavy! belike it hath some burden, then?

Luc. Ay; and melodious were it, would you sing it.

Jul. And why not you?

Luc.   I cannot reach so high.   84

Jul. Let's see your song. [*Taking the letter.*]

How now, minion!

Luc. Keep tune there still, so you will sing it out:

And yet methinks, I do not like this tune.

Jul. You do not?

Luc.   No, madam; it is too sharp.   88

Jul. You, minion, are too saucy.

Luc. Nay, now you are too flat

And mar the concord with too harsh a descant:

There wanteth but a mean to fill your song.   92

Jul. The mean is drown'd with your unruly bass.

Luc. Indeed, I bid the base for Proteus.

Jul. This babble shall not henceforth trouble me.

Here is a coil with protestation!—   96
                                                        [*Tears the letter.*

Go, get you gone, and let the papers lie:

You would be fingering them, to anger me.

Luc. She makes it strange; but she would be best pleas'd

To be so anger'd with another letter.   [*Exit.*

Jul. Nay, would I were so anger'd with the same!   101

O hateful hands, to tear such loving words!

Injurious wasps, to feed on such sweet honey

And kill the bees that yield it with your stings!

I'll kiss each several paper for amends.   105

Look, here is writ 'kind Julia:' unkind Julia!

As in revenge of thy ingratitude,

I throw thy name against the bruising stones,

Trampling contemptuously on thy disdain.   109

And here is writ 'love-wounded Proteus:'

Poor wounded name! my bosom, as a bed

Shall lodge thee till thy wound be throughly heal'd;   112

And thus I search it with a sovereign kiss.

But twice or thrice was 'Proteus' written down:

Be calm, good wind, blow not a word away

Till I have found each letter in the letter,   116

Except mine own name; that some whirlwind bear

Unto a ragged, fearful-hanging rock,

And throw it thence into the raging sea!
Lo! here in one line is his name twice writ, 120
'Poor forlorn Proteus, passionate Proteus,
To the sweet Julia':—that I'll tear away;
And yet I will not, sith so prettily
He couples it to his complaining names: 124
Thus will I fold them one upon another:
Now kiss, embrace, contend, do what you will.

Re-enter LUCETTA.

Luc. Madam,
Dinner is ready, and your father stays. 128
Jul. Well, let us go.
Luc. What! shall these papers lie like tell-
tales here?
Jul. If you respect them, best to take them up.
Luc. Nay, I was taken up for laying them
down; 132
Yet here they shall not lie, for catching cold.
Jul. I see you have a month's mind to them.
Luc. Ay, madam, you may say what sights
you see;
I see things too, although you judge I wink. 136
Jul. Come, come; will't please you go?
[*Exeunt.*

SCENE III.—*The Same. A Room in* ANTONIO'S
House.

Enter ANTONIO *and* PANTHINO.

Ant. Tell me, Panthino, what sad talk was
that
Wherewith my brother held you in the cloister?
Pant. 'Twas of his nephew Proteus, your son.
Ant. Why, what of him?
Pant. He wonder'd that your lordship 4
Would suffer him to spend his youth at home,
While other men, of slender reputation,
Put forth their sons to seek preferment out:
Some to the wars, to try their fortune there; 8
Some to discover islands far away;
Some to the studious universities.
For any or for all these exercises
He said that Proteus your son was meet, 12
And did request me to importune you
To let him spend his time no more at home,
Which would be great impeachment to his age,
In having known no travel in his youth. 16
Ant. Nor need'st thou much importune me
to that
Whereon this month I have been hammering.
I have consider'd well his loss of time,
And how he cannot be a perfect man, 20
Not being tried and tutor'd in the world:
Experience is by industry achiev'd
And perfected by the swift course of time.
Then tell me, whither were I best to send him?
Pant. I think your lordship is not ignorant
How his companion, youthful Valentine, 26
Attends the emperor in his royal court.
Ant. I know it well. 28
Pant. 'Twere good, I think, your lordship
sent him thither:
There shall he practise tilts and tournaments,
Hear sweet discourse, converse with noblemen,
And be in eye of every exercise 32
Worthy his youth and nobleness of birth.

Ant. I like thy counsel; well hast thou
advis'd:
And that thou mayst perceive how well I like it
The execution of it shall make known. 36
Even with the speediest expedition
I will dispatch him to the emperor's court.
Pant. To-morrow, may it please you, Don
Alphonso
With other gentlemen of good esteem, 40
Are journeying to salute the emperor
And to commend their service to his will.
Ant. Good company; with them shall Proteus
go; 43
And in good time:—now will we break with him.

Enter PROTEUS.

Pro. Sweet love! sweet lines! sweet life!
Here is her hand, the agent of her heart;
Here is her oath for love, her honour's pawn.
O! that our fathers would applaud our loves, 48
To seal our happiness with their consents!
O heavenly Julia!
Ant. How now! what letter are you reading
there?
Pro. May't please your lordship, 'tis a word
or two 52
Of commendations sent from Valentine,
Deliver'd by a friend that came from him.
Ant. Lend me the letter; let me see what
news.
Pro. There is no news, my lord; but that he
writes 56
How happily he lives, how well belov'd
And daily graced by the emperor;
Wishing me with him, partner of his fortune.
Ant. And how stand you affected to his wish?
Pro. As one relying on your lordship's will 61
And not depending on his friendly wish.
Ant. My will is something sorted with his wish.
Muse not that I thus suddenly proceed; 64
For what I will, I will, and there an end.
I am resolv'd that thou shalt spend some time
With Valentinus in the emperor's court:
What maintenance he from his friends receives,
Like exhibition thou shalt have from me. 69
To-morrow be in readiness to go:
Excuse it not, for I am peremptory.
Pro. My lord, I cannot be so soon provided:
Please you, deliberate a day or two. 73
Ant. Look, what thou want'st shall be sent
after thee:
No more of stay; to-morrow thou must go.
Come on, Panthino: you shall be employ'd 76
To hasten on his expedition.
[*Exeunt* ANTONIO *and* PANTHINO.
Pro. Thus have I shunn'd the fire for fear of
burning,
And drench'd me in the sea, where I am drown'd.
I fear'd to show my father Julia's letter, 80
Lest he should take exceptions to my love;
And with the vantage of mine own excuse
Hath he excepted most against my love.
O! how this spring of love resembleth 84
The uncertain glory of an April day,
Which now shows all the beauty of the sun,
And by and by a cloud takes all away!

Re-enter PANTHINO.

Pant. Sir Proteus, your father calls for you:
He is in haste; therefore, I pray you, go.   89
Pro. Why, this it is: my heart accords thereto,
And yet a thousand times it answers, 'no.'
                                 [*Exeunt.*

ACT II

SCENE I.—*Milan. A Room in the* DUKE'S
Palace.

Enter VALENTINE *and* SPEED.

Speed. Sir, your glove.   [*Offering a glove.*
Val.   Not mine; my gloves are on.
Speed. Why, then this may be yours, for this
   is but one.
Val. Ha! let me see: ay, give it me, it's mine:
Sweet ornament that decks a thing divine!   4
Ah Silvia! Silvia!
Speed. [*Calling.*] Madam Silvia! Madam
Silvia!
Val. How now, sirrah?
Speed. She is not within hearing, sir.
Val. Why, sir, who bade you call her?
Speed. Your worship, sir; or else I mistook.
Val. Well, you'll still be too forward.   12
Speed. And yet I was last chidden for being
too slow.
Val. Go to, sir. Tell me, do you know
Madam Silvia?   16
Speed. She that your worship loves?
Val. Why, how know you that I am in love?
Speed. Marry, by these special marks: first,
you have learned, like Sir Proteus, to wreathe
your arms, like a malecontent; to relish a love-
song, like a robin-redbreast; to walk alone, like
one that had the pestilence; to sigh, like a
schoolboy that had lost his A B C; to weep, like
a young wench that had buried her grandam;
to fast, like one that takes diet; to watch, like
one that fears robbing; to speak puling, like a
beggar at Hallowmas. You were wont, when
you laughed, to crow like a cock; when you
walked, to walk like one of the lions; when you
fasted, it was presently after dinner; when you
looked sadly, it was for want of money: and now
you are metamorphosed with a mistress, that,
when I look on you, I can hardly think you my
master.
Val. Are all these things perceived in me?   36
Speed. They are all perceived without ye.
Val. Without me? they cannot.
Speed. Without you? nay, that's certain;
for, without you were so simple, none else would:
but you are so without these follies, that these
follies are within you and shine through you
like the water in an urinal, that not an eye that
sees you but is a physician to comment on your
malady.   45
Val. But tell me, dost thou know my lady
Silvia?
Speed. She that you gaze on so as she sits at
supper?   49
Val. Hast thou observed that? even she, I
mean.

Speed. Why, sir, I know her not.   52
Val. Dost thou know her by my gazing on
her, and yet knowest her not?
Speed. Is she not hard-favoured, sir?
Val. Not so fair, boy, as well-favoured.   56
Speed. Sir, I know that well enough.
Val. What dost thou know?
Speed. That she is not so fair, as, of you, well-
favoured.   60
Val. I mean that her beauty is exquisite,
but her favour infinite.
Speed. That's because the one is painted
and the other out of all count.   64
Val. How painted? and how out of count?
Speed. Marry, sir, so painted to make her
fair, that no man counts of her beauty.
Val. How esteemest thou me? I account of
her beauty.   69
Speed. You never saw her since she was
deformed.
Val. How long hath she been deformed?   72
Speed. Ever since you loved her.
Val. I have loved her ever since I saw her,
and still I see her beautiful.
Speed. If you love her you cannot see her.   76
Val. Why?
Speed. Because Love is blind. O! that you
had mine eyes; or your own eyes had the lights
they were wont to have when you chid at Sir
Proteus for going ungartered!   81
Val. What should I see then?
Speed. Your own present folly and her pass-
ing deformity: for he, being in love, could not
see to garter his hose; and you, being in love,
cannot see to put on your hose.   86
Val. Belike, boy, then, you are in love; for
last morning you could not see to wipe my
shoes.
Speed. True, sir; I was in love with my
bed. I thank you, you swinged me for my love,
which makes me the bolder to chide you for
yours.   93
Val. In conclusion, I stand affected to her.
Speed. I would you were set, so your affection would cease.   96
Val. Last night she enjoined me to write
some lines to one she loves.
Speed. And have you?
Val. I have.   100
Speed. Are they not lamely writ?
Val. No, boy, but as well as I can do them.
Peace! here she comes.

Enter SILVIA.

Speed. [*Aside.*] O excellent motion! O exceeding puppet! now will he interpret to her.
Val. Madam and mistress, a thousand good
morrows.   107
Speed. [*Aside.*] O! give ye good even: here's
a million of manners.
Sil. Sir Valentine and servant, to you two
thousand.
Speed. [*Aside.*] He should give her interest,
and she gives it him.
Val. As you enjoin'd me, I have writ your
   letter

Unto the secret nameless friend of yours;
Which I was much unwilling to proceed in 116
But for my duty to your ladyship. [*Gives a letter.*
Sil. I thank you, gentle servant. 'Tis very
clerkly done.
Val. Now, trust me, madam, it came hardly
off;   120
For, being ignorant to whom it goes
I writ at random, very doubtfully.
Sil. Perchance you think too much of so
much pains?
Val. No, madam; so it stead you, I will write,
Please you command, a thousand times as much.
And yet—   126
Sil. A pretty period! Well, I guess the sequel;
And yet I will not name it; and yet I care not;
And yet take this again; and yet I thank you,
Meaning henceforth to trouble you no more. 130
Speed. [*Aside.*] And yet you will; and yet
another yet.
Val. What means your ladyship? do you not
like it?   132
Sil. Yes, yes: the lines are very quaintly writ,
But since unwillingly, take them again:
Nay, take them.   [*Gives back the letter.*
Val.   Madam, they are for you.
Sil. Ay, ay; you writ them, sir, at my request,
But I will none of them; they are for you. 137
I would have had them writ more movingly.
Val. Please you, I'll write your ladyship
another.
Sil. And when it's writ, for my sake read it
over: 140
And if it please you, so; if not, why, so.
Val. If it please me, madam, what then?
Sil. Why, if it please you, take it for your
labour: 143
And so, good morrow, servant.   [*Exit.*
Speed. O jest unseen, inscrutable, invisible,
As a nose on a man's face, or a weathercock on
a steeple!
My master sues to her, and she hath taught her
suitor,
He being her pupil, to become her tutor. 148
O excellent device! was there ever heard a better,
That my master, being scribe, to himself should
write the letter?
Val. How now, sir! what are you reasoning
with yourself?
Speed. Nay, I was riming: 'tis you that have
the reason.   152
Val. To do what?
Speed. To be a spokesman from Madam
Silvia.
Val. To whom?
Speed. To yourself. Why, she wooes you by
a figure.   156
Val. What figure?
Speed. By a letter, I should say.
Val. Why, she hath not writ to me?
Speed. What need she, when she hath made
you write to yourself? Why, do you not perceive
the jest?   162
Val. No, believe me.
Speed. No believing you, indeed, sir. But did
you perceive her earnest?

Val. She gave me none, except an angry word.
Speed. Why, she hath given you a letter.
Val. That's the letter I writ to her friend. 168
Speed. And that letter hath she delivered, and
there an end.
Val. I would it were no worse.
Speed. I'll warrant you, 'tis as well: 172
'For often have you writ to her, and she, in
modesty,
Or else for want of idle time, could not again
reply;
Or fearing else some messenger that might her
mind discover,
Herself hath taught her love himself to write
unto her lover.'   176
All this I speak in print, for in print I found it.
Why muse you, sir? 'tis dinner-time.
Val. I have dined.   179
Speed. Ay, but hearken, sir: though the
chameleon Love can feed on the air, I am one
that am nourished by my victuals and would
fain have meat. O! be not like your mistress;
be moved, be moved.   [*Exeunt.*

SCENE II.—*Verona. A Room in* JULIA'S *House.*

Enter PROTEUS *and* JULIA.

Pro. Have patience, gentle Julia.
Jul. I must, where is no remedy.
Pro. When possibly I can, I will return.
Jul. If you turn not, you will return the
sooner.   4
Keep this remembrance for thy Julia's sake.
          [*Gives him a ring.*
Pro. Why, then, we'll make exchange: here,
take you this.   [*Gives her another.*
Jul. And seal the bargain with a holy kiss.
Pro. Here is my hand for my true constancy;
And when that hour o'erslips me in the day 9
Wherein I sigh not, Julia, for thy sake,
The next ensuing hour some foul mischance
Torment me for my love's forgetfulness!   12
My father stays my coming; answer not.
The tide is now: nay, not thy tide of tears;
That tide will stay me longer than I should.
Julia farewell.   [*Exit* JULIA.
          What! gone without a word? 16
Ay, so true love should do: it cannot speak;
For truth hath better deeds than words to
grace it.

Enter PANTHINO.

Pant. Sir Proteus, you are stay'd for.
Pro.   Go; I come, I come.
Alas! this parting strikes poor lovers dumb. 20
          [*Exeunt.*

SCENE III.—*The Same. A Street.*

Enter LAUNCE, *leading a dog.*

Launce. Nay, 'twill be this hour ere I have done
weeping: all the kind of the Launces have this
very fault. I have received my proportion, like the
prodigious son, and am going with Sir Proteus

to the imperial's court. I think Crab my dog be the sourest-natured dog that lives: my mother weeping, my father wailing, my sister crying, our maid howling, our cat wringing her hands, and all our house in a great perplexity, yet did not this cruel-hearted cur shed one tear. He is a stone, a very pebble stone, and has no more pity in him than a dog; a Jew would have wept to have seen our parting: why, my grandam, having no eyes, look you, wept herself blind at my parting. Nay, I'll show you the manner of it. This shoe is my father; no, this left shoe is my father: no, no, this left shoe is my mother; nay, that cannot be so neither:—yes, it is so; it is so; it hath the worser sole. This shoe, with the hole in, is my mother, and this my father. A vengeance on't! there 'tis: now, sir, this staff is my sister; for, look you, she is as white as a lily and as small as a wand: this hat is Nan, our maid: I am the dog; no, the dog is himself, and I am the dog,—O! the dog is me, and I am myself: ay, so, so. Now come I to my father; 'Father, your blessing;' now should not the shoe speak a word for weeping: now should I kiss my father; well, he weeps on. Now come I to my mother;—O, that she could speak now like a wood woman! Well, I kiss her; why, there 'tis; here's my mother's breath up and down. Now come I to my sister; mark the moan she makes: Now the dog all this while sheds not a tear nor speaks a word; but see how I lay the dust with my tears.   36

Enter PANTHINO.

Pant. Launce, away, away, aboard! thy master is shipped, and thou art to post after with oars. What's the matter? why weepest thou, man? Away, ass! you'll lose the tide if you tarry any longer.   41

Launce. It is no matter if the tied were lost; for it is the unkindest tied that ever any man tied.

Pant. What's the unkindest tide?   44

Launce. Why, he that's tied here, Crab, my dog.

Pant. Tut, man, I mean thou'lt lose the flood; and, in losing the flood, lose thy voyage, and, in losing thy voyage, lose thy master; and, in losing thy master, lose thy service; and, in losing thy service,—Why dost thou stop my mouth?   52

Launce. For fear thou shouldst lose thy tongue.

Pant. Where should I lose my tongue?

Launce. In thy tale.   56

Pant. In thy tail!

Launce. Lose the tide, and the voyage, and the master, and the service, and the tied! Why, man, if the river were dry, I am able to fill it with my tears; if the wind were down, I could drive the boat with my sighs.

Pant. Come, come away, man; I was sent to call thee.   64

Launce. Sir, call me what thou darest.

Pant. Wilt thou go?

Launce. Well, I will go.   *[Exeunt.*

SCENE IV.—*Milan. A Room in the* DUKE'S *Palace.*

Enter VALENTINE, SILVIA, THURIO, *and* SPEED.

Sil. Servant!

Val. Mistress?

Speed. Master, Sir Thurio frowns on you.

Val. Ay, boy, it's for love.   4

Speed. Not of you.

Val. Of my mistress, then.

Speed. 'Twere good you knock'd him.

Sil. Servant, you are sad.   8

Val. Indeed, madam, I seem so.

Thu. Seem you that you are not?

Val. Haply I do.

Thu. So do counterfeits.   12

Val. So do you.

Thu. What seem I that I am not?

Val. Wise.

Thu. What instance of the contrary?   16

Val. Your folly.

Thu. And how quote you my folly?

Val. I quote it in your jerkin.

Thu. My jerkin is a doublet.   20

Val. Well, then, I'll double your folly.

Thu. How?

Sil. What, angry, Sir Thurio! do you change colour?   24

Val. Give him leave, madam; he is a kind of chameleon.

Thu. That hath more mind to feed on your blood than live in your air.   28

Val. You have said, sir.

Thu. Ay, sir, and done too, for this time.

Val. I know it well, sir: you always end ere you begin.   32

Sil. A fine volley of words, gentlemen, and quickly shot off.

Val. 'Tis indeed, madam; we thank the giver.   36

Sil. Who is that, servant?

Val. Yourself, sweet lady; for you gave the fire. Sir Thurio borrows his wit from your ladyship's looks, and spends what he borrows kindly in your company.   41

Thu. Sir, if you spend word for word with me, I shall make your wit bankrupt.

Val. I know it well, sir: you have an exchequer of words, and, I think, no other treasure to give your followers; for it appears by their bare liveries that they live by your bare words.

Sil. No more, gentlemen, no more. Here comes my father.

Enter DUKE.

Duke. Now, daughter Silvia, you are hard beset.
Sir Valentine, your father's in good health:
What say you to a letter from your friends   52
Of much good news?

Val.   My lord, I will be thankful
To any happy messenger from thence.

Duke. Know ye Don Antonio, your countryman?

Val. Ay, my good lord; I know the gentleman   56

To be of worth and worthy estimation,
And not without desert so well reputed.
   Duke. Hath he not a son?
   Val. Ay, my good lord; a son that well
     deserves   60
The honour and regard of such a father.
   Duke. You know him well?
   Val. I know him as myself; for from our
     infancy
We have convers'd and spent our hours to-
     gether: 64
And though myself have been an idle truant,
Omitting the sweet benefit of time
To clothe mine age with angel-like perfection,
Yet hath Sir Proteus,—for that's his name,— 68
Made use and fair advantage of his days:
His years but young, but his experience old;
His head unmellow'd, but his judgment ripe;
And, in a word,—for far behind his worth 72
Come all the praises that I now bestow,—
He is complete in feature and in mind
With all good grace to grace a gentleman.
   Duke. Beshrew me, sir, but if he make this
     good,   76
He is as worthy for an empress' love
As meet to be an emperor's counsellor.
Well, sir, this gentleman is come to me
With commendation from great potentates; 80
And here he means to spend his time awhile:
I think, 'tis no unwelcome news to you.
   Val. Should I have wish'd a thing, it had
     been he.
   Duke. Welcome him then according to his
     worth.   84
Silvia, I speak to you; and you, Sir Thurio:—
For Valentine, I need not cite him to it.
I'll send him hither to you presently.   [*Exit.*
   Val. This is the gentleman I told your lady-
     ship   88
Had come along with me, but that his mistress
Did hold his eyes lock'd in her crystal looks.
   Sil. Belike that now she hath enfranchis'd
     them
Upon some other pawn for fealty.   92
   Val. Nay, sure, I think she holds them
     prisoners still.
   Sil. Nay, then he should be blind; and, being
     blind,
How could he see his way to seek out you?
   Val. Why, lady, Love hath twenty pairs of
     eyes.
   Thu. They say that Love hath not an eye
     at all.   97
   Val. To see such lovers, Thurio, as your-
     self:
Upon a homely object Love can wink.
   Sil. Have done, have done. Here comes the
     gentleman.   100

Enter PROTEUS.

   Val. Welcome, dear Proteus! Mistress, I be-
     seech you,
Confirm his welcome with some special favour.
   Sil. His worth is warrant for his welcome
     hither,   103
If this be he you oft have wish'd to hear from.

   Val. Mistress, it is: sweet lady, entertain him
To be my fellow-servant to your ladyship.
   Sil. Too low a mistress for so high a servant.
   Pro. Not so, sweet lady; but too mean a
     servant   108
To have a look of such a worthy mistress.
   Val. Leave off discourse of disability:
Sweet lady, entertain him for your servant.
   Pro. My duty will I boast of, nothing else. 112
   Sil. And duty never yet did want his meed.
Servant, you are welcome to a worthless mis-
     tress.
   Pro. I'll die on him that says so but yourself.
   Sil. That you are welcome?
   Pro.   That you are worthless. 116

Enter a Servant.

   Ser. Madam, my lord your father would
     speak with you.
   Sil. I wait upon his pleasure. [*Exit* Servant.]
     Come, Sir Thurio,
Go with me. Once more, new servant, welcome:
I'll leave you to confer of home-affairs; 120
When you have done, we look to hear from you.
   Pro. We'll both attend upon your ladyship.
     [*Exeunt* SILVIA, THURIO, *and* SPEED.
   Val. Now, tell me, how do all from whence
     you came?
   Pro. Your friends are well and have them
     much commended.   124
   Val. And how do yours?
   Pro.   I left them all in health.
   Val. How does your lady and how thrives
     your love?
   Pro. My tales of love were wont to weary you;
I know you joy not in a love-discourse.   128
   Val. Ay, Proteus, but that life is alter'd now:
I have done penance for contemning love;
Whose high imperious thoughts have punish'd
     me
With bitter fasts, with penitential groans, 132
With nightly tears and daily heart-sore sighs;
For, in revenge of my contempt of love,
Love hath chas'd sleep from my enthralled eyes,
And made them watchers of mine own heart's
     sorrow.   136
O, gentle Proteus! Love's a mighty lord,
And hath so humbled me as I confess,
There is no woe to his correction,
Nor to his service no such joy on earth.   140
Now no discourse, except it be of love;
Now can I break my fast, dine, sup and sleep,
Upon the very naked name of love.
   Pro. Enough; I read your fortune in your eye.
Was this the idol that you worship so? 145
   Val. Even she; and is she not a heavenly
     saint?
   Pro. No; but she is an earthly paragon.
   Val. Call her divine.
   Pro.   I will not flatter her. 148
   Val. O! flatter me, for love delights in
     praises.
   Pro. When I was sick you gave me bitter pills,
And I must minister the like to you.
   Val. Then speak the truth by her; if not
     divine,   152

Yet let her be a principality,
Sovereign to all the creatures on the earth.
Pro. Except my mistress.
Val.   Sweet, except not any,
Except thou wilt except against my love. 156
Pro. Have I not reason to prefer mine own?
Val. And I will help thee to prefer her too:
She shall be dignified with this high honour,—
To bear my lady's train, lest the base earth 160
Should from her vesture chance to steal a kiss,
And, of so great a favour growing proud,
Disdain to root the summer-swelling flower,
And make rough winter everlastingly.   164
Pro. Why, Valentine, what braggardism is
this?
Val. Pardon me, Proteus: all I can is nothing
To her whose worth makes other worthies
nothing.
She is alone.
Pro.   Then, let her alone.   168
Val. Not for the world: why, man, she is
mine own,
And I as rich in having such a jewel
As twenty seas, if all their sand were pearl,
The water nectar, and the rocks pure gold. 172
Forgive me that I do not dream on thee,
Because thou see'st me dote upon my love.
My foolish rival, that her father likes
Only for his possessions are so huge,   176
Is gone with her along, and I must after,
For love, thou know'st, is full of jealousy.
Pro. But she loves you?
Val. Ay, and we are betroth'd: nay, more,
our marriage-hour,   180
With all the cunning manner of our flight,
Determin'd of: how I must climb her window,
The ladder made of cords, and all the means
Plotted and 'greed on for my happiness. 184
Good Proteus, go with me to my chamber,
In these affairs to aid me with thy counsel.
Pro. Go on before; I shall inquire you forth:
I must unto the road, to disembark   188
Some necessaries that I needs must use,
And then I'll presently attend you.
Val. Will you make haste?
Pro. I will.   [*Exit* VALENTINE.
Even as one heat another heat expels,   193
Or as one nail by strength drives out another,
So the remembrance of my former love
Is by a newer object quite forgotten.   196
Is it mine eye, or Valentinus' praise,
Her true perfection, or my false transgression,
That makes me reasonless to reason thus?
She's fair; and so is Julia that I love,— 200
That I did love, for now my love is thaw'd,
Which, like a waxen image 'gainst a fire,
Bears no impression of the thing it was.
Methinks my zeal to Valentine is cold,   204
And that I love him not as I was wont:
O! but I love his lady too-too much;
And that's the reason I love him so little.
How shall I dote on her with more advice, 208
That thus without advice begin to love her?
'Tis but her picture I have yet beheld,
And that hath dazzled my reason's light;
But when I look on her perfections,   212

There is no reason but I shall be blind.
If I can check my erring love, I will;
If not, to compass her I'll use my skill. [*Exit.*

SCENE V.—*The Same. A Street.*

Enter SPEED *and* LAUNCE.

Speed. Launce! by mine honesty, welcome to
Milan!
Launce. Forswear not thyself, sweet youth,
for I am not welcome. I reckon this always
that a man is never undone till he be hanged;
nor never welcome to a place till some certain
shot be paid and the hostess say, 'Welcome!' 7
Speed. Come on, you madcap, I'll to the
alehouse with you presently; where, for one
shot of five pence, thou shalt have five thousand
welcomes. But, sirrah, how did thy master part
with Madam Julia?   12
Launce. Marry, after they closed in earnest,
they parted very fairly in jest.
Speed. But shall she marry him?
Launce. No.   16
Speed. How then? Shall he marry her?
Launce. No, neither.
Speed. What, are they broken?
Launce. No, they are both as whole as a fish.
Speed. Why then, how stands the matter
with them?
Launce. Marry, thus; when it stands well
with him, it stands well with her.   24
Speed. What an ass art thou! I understand
thee not.
Launce. What a block art thou, that thou
canst not! My staff understands me.   28
Speed. What thou sayest?
Launce. Ay, and what I do too: look thee,
I'll but lean, and my staff understands me.
Speed. It stands under thee, indeed.   32
Launce. Why, stand-under and under-stand
is all one.
Speed. But tell me true, will't be a match?
Launce. Ask my dog: if he say ay, it will;
if he say no, it will; if he shake his tail and say
nothing, it will.
Speed. The conclusion is, then, that it will.
Launce. Thou shalt never get such a secret
from me but by a parable.   41
Speed. 'Tis well that I get it so. But, Launce,
how sayest thou, that my master is become a
notable lover?   44
Launce. I never knew him otherwise.
Speed. Than how?
Launce. A notable lubber, as thou reportest
him to be.   48
Speed. Why, thou whoreson ass, thou mis-
takest me.
Launce. Why, fool, I meant not thee; I meant
thy master.   52
Speed. I tell thee, my master is become a hot
lover.
Launce. Why, I tell thee, I care not though
he burn himself in love. If thou wilt go with
me to the alehouse so; if not, thou art a
Hebrew, a Jew, and not worth the name of a
Christian.

Speed. Why?   60
Launce. Because thou hast not so much
charity in thee as to go to the ale with a
Christian. Wilt thou go?
Speed. At thy service.   [*Exeunt.*

SCENE VI.—*The Same. A Room in the* DUKE'S
Palace.

Enter PROTEUS.

Pro. To leave my Julia, shall I be forsworn;
To love fair Silvia, shall I be forsworn;
To wrong my friend, I shall be much forsworn;
And even that power which gave me first my
    oath   4
Provokes me to this threefold perjury:
Love bade me swear, and Love bids me for-
    swear.
O sweet-suggesting Love! if thou hast sinn'd,
Teach me, thy tempted subject, to excuse it. 8
At first I did adore a twinkling star,
But now I worship a celestial sun.
Unheedful vows may heedfully be broken;
And he wants wit that wants resolved will 12
To learn his wit to exchange the bad for better.
Fie, fie, unreverend tongue! to call her bad,
Whose sovereignty so oft thou hast preferr'd
With twenty thousand soul-confirming oaths.
I cannot leave to love, and yet I do;   17
But there I leave to love where I should love.
Julia I lose and Valentine I lose:
If I keep them, I needs must lose myself;   20
If I lose them, thus find I by their loss,
For Valentine, myself; for Julia, Silvia.
I to myself am dearer than a friend,
For love is still most precious in itself;   24
And Silvia—witness heaven that made her
    fair!—
Shows Julia but a swarthy Ethiope.
I will forget that Julia is alive,
Remembering that my love to her is dead;   28
And Valentine I'll hold an enemy,
Aiming at Silvia as a sweeter friend.
I cannot now prove constant to myself
Without some treachery us'd to Valentine: 32
This night he meaneth with a corded ladder
To climb celestial Silvia's chamber-window,
Myself in counsel, his competitor.
Now presently, I'll give her father notice   36
Of their disguising and pretended flight;
Who, all enrag'd, will banish Valentine;
For Thurio, he intends, shall wed his daughter;
But, Valentine being gone, I'll quickly cross, 40
By some sly trick blunt Thurio's dull pro-
    ceeding.
Love, lend me wings to make my purpose swift,
As thou hast lent me wit to plot this drift!
                                          [*Exit.*

SCENE VII.—*Verona. A Room in* JULIA'S
House.

Enter JULIA *and* LUCETTA.

Jul. Counsel, Lucetta; gentle girl, assist me:
And e'en in kind love I do conjure thee,
Who art the table wherein all my thoughts
Are visibly character'd and engrav'd,   4
To lesson me and tell me some good mean
How, with my honour, I may undertake
A journey to my loving Proteus.
Luc. Alas! the way is wearisome and long. 8
Jul. A true-devoted pilgrim is not weary
To measure kingdoms with his feeble steps;
Much less shall she that hath Love's wings to fly.
And when the flight is made to one so dear,   12
Of such divine perfection, as Sir Proteus.
Luc. Better forbear till Proteus make return.
Jul. O! know'st thou not his looks are my
    soul's food?
Pity the dearth that I have pined in,   16
By longing for that food so long a time.
Didst thou but know the inly touch of love,
Thou wouldst as soon go kindle fire with snow
As seek to quench the fire of love with words. 20
Luc. I do not seek to quench your love's hot
    fire,
But qualify the fire's extreme rage,
Lest it should burn above the bounds of reason.
Jul. The more thou damm'st it up, the more
    it burns.   24
The current that with gentle murmur glides,
Thou know'st, being stopp'd, impatiently doth
    rage;
But when his fair course is not hindered,
He makes sweet music with th' enamell'd stones,
Giving a gentle kiss to every sedge   29
He overtaketh in his pilgrimage;
And so by many winding nooks he strays
With willing sport, to the wild ocean.   32
Then let me go and hinder not my course:
I'll be as patient as a gentle stream
And make a pastime of each weary step,
Till the last step have brought me to my love; 36
And there I'll rest, as after much turmoil
A blessed soul doth in Elysium.
Luc. But in what habit will you go along?
Jul. Not like a woman; for I would prevent
The loose encounters of lascivious men.   41
Gentle Lucetta, fit me with such weeds
As may beseem some well-reputed page.
Luc. Why, then, your ladyship must cut your
    hair.   44
Jul. No, girl; I'll knit it up in silken strings
With twenty odd-conceited true-love knots:
To be fantastic may become a youth
Of greater time than I shall show to be.   48
Luc. What fashion, madam, shall I make
    your breeches?
Jul. That fits as well as 'Tell me, good my lord,
What compass will you wear your farthingale?'
Why, even what fashion thou best lik'st, Lu-
    cetta.   52
Luc. You must needs have them with a
    cod-piece, madam.
Jul. Out, out, Lucetta! that will be ill-
    favour'd.
Luc. A round hose, madam, now's not worth
    a pin,
Unless you have a cod-piece to stick pins on. 56
Jul. Lucetta, as thou lov'st me, let me have
What thou think'st meet and is most mannerly.
But tell me, wench, how will the world repute me

For undertaking so unstaid a journey?   60
I fear me, it will make me scandaliz'd.
   Luc. If you think so, then stay at home and
go not.
   Jul. Nay, that I will not.
   Luc. Then never dream on infamy, but go. 64
If Proteus like your journey when you come,
No matter who's displeas'd when you are gone.
I fear me, he will scarce be pleas'd withal.
   Jul. That is the least, Lucetta, of my fear: 68
A thousand oaths, an ocean of his tears,
And instances of infinite love
Warrant me welcome to my Proteus.   71
   Luc. All these are servants to deceitful men.
   Jul. Base men, that use them to so base effect;
But truer stars did govern Proteus' birth:
His words are bonds, his oaths are oracles,
His love sincere, his thoughts immaculate, 76
His tears pure messengers sent from his heart,
His heart as far from fraud as heaven from earth.
   Luc. Pray heaven he prove so when you
come to him!
   Jul. Now, as thou lov'st me, do him not that
wrong   80
To bear a hard opinion of his truth:
Only deserve my love by loving him,
And presently go with me to my chamber,
To take a note of what I stand in need of   84
To furnish me upon my longing journey.
All that is mine I leave at thy dispose,
My goods, my lands, my reputation;
Only, in lieu thereof, dispatch me hence.   88
Come, answer not, but to it presently!
I am impatient of my tarriance.   [*Exeunt.*

ACT III

Scene I.—*Milan. An anteroom in the
DUKE'S Palace.*

Enter DUKE, THURIO, and PROTEUS.

   Duke. Sir Thurio, give us leave, I pray,
awhile;
We have some secrets to confer about.
                            [*Exit THURIO.*
Now tell me, Proteus, what's your will with me?
   Pro. My gracious lord, that which I would
discover   4
The law of friendship bids me to conceal;
But when I call to mind your gracious favours
Done to me, undeserving as I am,
My duty pricks me on to utter that   8
Which else no worldly good should draw from
me.
Know, worthy prince, Sir Valentine, my friend,
This night intends to steal away your daughter;
Myself am one made privy to the plot.   12
I know you have determin'd to bestow her
On Thurio, whom your gentle daughter hates;
And should she thus be stol'n away from you
It would be much vexation to your age.   16
Thus, for my duty's sake, I rather chose
To cross my friend in his intended drift,
Than, by concealing it, heap on your head
A pack of sorrows which would press you down,
Being unprevented, to your timeless grave.   21

   Duke. Proteus, I thank thee for thine honest
care,
Which to requite, command me while I live.
This love of theirs myself have often seen, 24
Haply, when they have judg'd me fast asleep,
And oftentimes have purpos'd to forbid
Sir Valentine her company and my court;
But fearing lest my jealous aim might err   28
And so unworthily disgrace the man,—
A rashness that I ever yet have shunn'd,—
I gave him gentle looks, thereby to find
That which thyself hast now disclos'd to me. 32
And, that thou mayst perceive my fear of this,
Knowing that tender youth is soon suggested,
I nightly lodge her in an upper tower,
The key whereof myself have ever kept;   36
And thence she cannot be convey'd away.
   Pro. Know, noble lord, they have devis'd a
mean
How he her chamber-window will ascend
And with a corded ladder fetch her down;   40
For which the youthful lover now is gone
And this way comes he with it presently;
Where, if it please you, you may intercept him.
But, good my lord, do it so cunningly   44
That my discovery be not aimed at;
For love of you, not hate unto my friend,
Hath made me publisher of this pretence.
   Duke. Upon mine honour, he shall never
know   48
That I had any light from thee of this.
   Pro. Adieu, my lord: Sir Valentine is com-
ing.   [*Exit.*

Enter VALENTINE.

   Duke. Sir Valentine, whither away so fast?
   Val. Please it your Grace, there is a mes-
senger   52
That stays to bear my letters to my friends,
And I am going to deliver them.
   Duke. Be they of much import?
   Val. The tenour of them doth but signify 56
My health and happy being at your court.
   Duke. Nay then, no matter: stay with me
awhile;
I am to break with thee of some affairs
That touch me near, wherein thou must be
secret.   60
'Tis not unknown to thee that I have sought
To match my friend Sir Thurio to my daughter.
   Val. I know it well, my lord; and sure, the
match
Were rich and honourable; besides, the gentle-
man   64
Is full of virtue, bounty, worth, and qualities
Beseeming such a wife as your fair daughter.
Cannot your Grace win her to fancy him?
   Duke. No, trust me: she is peevish, sullen,
froward,   68
Proud, disobedient, stubborn, lacking duty;
Neither regarding that she is my child,
Nor fearing me as if I were her father:
And, may I say to thee, this pride of hers,   72
Upon advice, hath drawn my love from her;
And, where I thought the remnant of mine
age

Should have been cherish'd by her child-like
duty,
I now am full resolv'd to take a wife 76
And turn her out to who will take her in:
Then let her beauty be her wedding-dower,
For me and my possessions she esteems not.
Val. What would your Grace have me to do
in this? 80
Duke. There is a lady of Verona here,
Whom I affect; but she is nice and coy
And nought esteems my aged eloquence:
Now therefore, would I have thee to my tutor,
For long agone I have forgot to court; 85
Besides, the fashion of the time is chang'd,
How and which way I may bestow myself
To be regarded in her sun-bright eye. 88
Val. Win her with gifts, if she respect not
words:
Dumb jewels often in their silent kind
More than quick words do move a woman's
mind.
Duke. But she did scorn a present that I
sent her. 92
Val. A woman sometime scorns what best
contents her.
Send her another; never give her o'er,
For scorn at first makes after-love the more.
If she do frown, 'tis not in hate of you, 96
But rather to beget more love in you;
If she do chide, 'tis not to have you gone;
For why the fools are mad if left alone.
Take no repulse, whatever she doth say; 100
For, 'get you gone,' she doth not mean, 'away!'
Flatter and praise, commend, extol their graces;
Though ne'er so black, say they have angels'
faces.
That man that hath a tongue, I say, is no
man, 104
If with his tongue he cannot win a woman.
Duke. But she I mean is promis'd by her
friends
Unto a youthful gentleman of worth,
And kept severely from resort of men, 108
That no man hath access by day to her.
Val. Why then, I would resort to her by
night.
Duke. Ay, but the doors be lock'd and keys
kept safe,
That no man hath recourse to her by night. 112
Val. What lets but one may enter at her
window?
Duke. Her chamber is aloft, far from the
ground,
And built so shelving that one cannot climb it
Without apparent hazard of his life. 116
Val. Why then, a ladder quaintly made of
cords,
To cast up, with a pair of anchoring hooks,
Would serve to scale another Hero's tower,
So bold Leander would adventure it. 120
Duke. Now, as thou art a gentleman of blood,
Advise me where I may have such a ladder.
Val. When would you use it? pray, sir, tell
me that.
Duke. This very night; for Love is like a
child, 124

That longs for every thing that he can come by.
Val. By seven o'clock I'll get you such a
ladder.
Duke. But hark thee; I will go to her alone:
How shall I best convey the ladder thither? 128
Val. It will be light, my lord, that you may
bear it
Under a cloak that is of any length.
Duke. A cloak as long as thine will serve the
turn?
Val. Ay, my good lord.
Duke. Then let me see thy cloak: 132
I'll get me one of such another length.
Val. Why, any cloak will serve the turn, my
lord.
Duke. How shall I fashion me to wear a
cloak?
I pray thee, let me feel thy cloak upon me. 136
[*Pulls open* VALENTINE'S *cloak.*
What letter is this same? What's here?—*To
Silvia!*
And here an engine fit for my proceeding!
I'll be so bold to break the seal for once.

My thoughts do harbour with my Silvia nightly; 140
And slaves they are to me that send them flying:
O! could their master come and go as lightly,
Himself would lodge where senseless they are lying!
My herald thoughts in thy pure bosom rest them;
While I, their king, that thither them importune,
Do curse the grace that with such grace hath bless'd them,
Because myself do want my servants' fortune:
I curse myself, for they are sent by me, 148
That they should harbour where their lord would be.

What's here?

Silvia, this night I will enfranchise thee.

'Tis so; and here's the ladder for the purpose.
Why, Phaethon,—for thou art Merops' son,—
Wilt thou aspire to guide the heavenly car
And with thy daring folly burn the world?
Wilt thou reach stars, because they shine on
thee? 156
Go, base intruder! overweening slave!
Bestow thy fawning smiles on equal mates,
And think my patience, more than thy desert,
Is privilege for thy departure hence. 160
Thank me for this than for all the favours
Which all too much I have bestow'd on thee.
But if thou linger in my territories
Longer than swiftest expedition 164
Will give thee time to leave our royal court,
By heaven! my wrath shall far exceed the love
I ever bore my daughter or thyself.
Be gone! I will not hear thy vain excuse; 168
But, as thou lov'st thy life, make speed from
hence. [*Exit.*
Val. And why not death rather than living
torment?
To die is to be banish'd from myself;
And Silvia is myself: banish'd from her 172
Is self from self,—a deadly banishment!
What light is light, if Silvia be not seen?
What joy is joy, if Silvia be not by?
Unless it be to think that she is by 176
And feed upon the shadow of perfection.
Except I be by Silvia in the night,

There is no music in the nightingale;
Unless I look on Silvia in the day,   180
There is no day for me to look upon.
She is my essence; and I leave to be,
If I be not by her fair influence
Foster'd, illumin'd, cherish'd, kept alive.   184
I fly not death, to fly his deadly doom:
Tarry I here, I but attend on death;
But, fly I hence, I fly away from life.

     Enter PROTEUS *and* LAUNCE.

Pro. Run, boy; run, run, and seek him out.
Launce. Soho! soho!   189
Pro. What seest thou?
Launce. Him we go to find: there's not a
hair on's head but 'tis a Valentine.   192
Pro. Valentine?
Val. No.
Pro. Who then? his spirit?
Val. Neither.   196
Pro. What then?
Val. Nothing.
Launce. Can nothing speak? Master, shall I
strike?   200
Pro. Who would'st thou strike?
Launce. Nothing.
Pro. Villain, forbear.
Launce. Why, sir, I'll strike nothing: I pray
you,—   204
Pro. Sirrah, I say, forbear.—Friend Valen-
tine, a word.
Val. My ears are stopp'd and cannot hear
good news,
So much of bad already hath possess'd them.
Pro. Then in dumb silence will I bury mine,
For they are harsh, untuneable and bad.   209
Val. Is Silvia dead?
Pro. No, Valentine.
Val. No Valentine, indeed, for sacred Silvia!
Hath she forsworn me?   213
Pro. No, Valentine.
Val. No Valentine, if Silvia have forsworn
me!
What is your news?   216
Launce. Sir, there is a proclamation that you
are vanished.
Pro. That thou art banished, O, that's the
news,
From hence, from Silvia, and from me thy friend.
Val. O, I have fed upon this woe already,   220
And now excess of it will make me surfeit.
Doth Silvia know that I am banished?
Pro. Ay, ay; and she hath offer'd to the
doom—   223
Which, unrevers'd, stands in effectual force—
A sea of melting pearl, which some call tears;
Those at her father's churlish feet she tender'd;
With them, upon her knees, her humble self;
Wringing her hands, whose whiteness so be-
came them   228
As if but now they waxed pale for woe:
But neither bended knees, pure hands held
up,
Sad sighs, deep groans, nor silver-shedding tears,
Could penetrate her uncompassionate sire;   232
But Valentine, if he be ta'en, must die.

Besides, her intercession chaf'd him so,
When she for thy repeal was suppliant,
That to close prison he commanded her,   236
With many bitter threats of biding there.
Val. No more; unless the next word that
thou speak'st
Have some malignant power upon my life:
If so, I pray thee, breathe it in mine ear,   240
As ending anthem of my endless dolour.
Pro. Cease to lament for that thou canst not
help,
And study help for that which thou lament'st.
Time is the nurse and breeder of all good.   244
Here if thou stay, thou canst not see thy love;
Besides, thy staying will abridge thy life.
Hope is a lover's staff; walk hence with that
And manage it against despairing thoughts.   248
Thy letters may be here, though thou art hence;
Which, being writ to me, shall be deliver'd
Even in the milk-white bosom of thy love.
The time now serves not to expostulate: 252
Come, I'll convey thee through the city-gate,
And, ere I part with thee, confer at large
Of all that may concern thy love-affairs.
As thou lov'st Silvia, though not for thyself,   256
Regard thy danger, and along with me!
Val. I pray thee, Launce, and if thou seest
my boy,
Bid him make haste and meet me at the
North-gate.
Pro. Go, sirrah, find him out. Come, Valen-
tine.   260
Val. O my dear Silvia! hapless Valentine!
     [*Exeunt* VALENTINE *and* PROTEUS.
Launce. I am but a fool, look you; and yet I
have the wit to think my master is a kind of a
knave: but that's all one, if he be but one knave.
He lives not now that knows me to be in love:
yet I am in love; but a team of horse shall
not pluck that from me, nor who 'tis I love; and
yet 'tis a woman; but what woman, I will not
tell myself; and yet 'tis a milkmaid; yet 'tis
not a maid, for she hath had gossips; yet 'tis a
maid, for she is her master's maid, and serves
for wages. She hath more qualities than a
water-spaniel,—which is much in a bare
Christian. [*Pulling out a paper.*] Here is the
catelog of her condition. *Imprimis, She
can fetch and carry.* Why, a horse can do no
more: nay, a horse cannot fetch, but only carry;
therefore, is she better than a jade. *Item, She
can milk;* look you, a sweet virtue in a maid
with clean hands.   280

     Enter SPEED.

Speed. How now, Signior Launce! what news
with your mastership?
Launce. With my master's ship? why, it is
at sea.   284
Speed. Well, your old vice still; mistake the
word. What news, then, in your paper?
Launce. The blackest news that ever thou
heardest.   288
Speed. Why, man, how black?
Launce. Why, as black as ink.
Speed. Let me read them.

Launce. Fie on thee, jolthead! thou canst not read.   293

Speed. Thou liest; I can.

Launce. I will try thee. Tell me this: who begot thee?   296

Speed. Marry, the son of my grandfather.

Launce. O, illiterate loiterer! it was the son of thy grandmother. This proves that thou canst not read.   300

Speed. Come, fool, come: try me in thy paper.

Launce. There; and Saint Nicholas be thy speed!   304

Speed. Imprimis, She can milk.

Launce. Ay, that she can.

Speed. Item, She brews good ale.

Launce. And thereof comes the proverb, 'Blessing of your heart, you brew good ale.' 309

Speed. Item, She can sew.

Launce. That's as much as to say, Can she so?   312

Speed. Item, She can knit.

Launce. What need a man care for a stock with a wench, when she can knit him a stock?

Speed. Item, She can wash and scour.   316

Launce. A special virtue; for then she need not be washed and scoured.

Speed. Item, She can spin.

Launce. Then may I set the world on wheels, when she can spin for her living.   321

Speed. Item, She hath many nameless virtues.

Launce. That's as much as to say, bastard virtues; that, indeed, know not their fathers, and therefore have no names.

Speed. Here follow her vices.

Launce. Close at the heels of her virtues. 328

Speed. Item, She is not to be kissed fasting, in respect of her breath.

Launce. Well, that fault may be mended with a breakfast. Read on.   332

Speed. Item, She hath a sweet mouth.

Launce. That makes amends for her sour breath.

Speed. Item, She doth talk in her sleep. 336

Launce. It's no matter for that, so she sleep not in her talk.

Speed. Item, She is slow in words.

Launce. O villain, that set this down among her vices! To be slow in words is a woman's only virtue: I pray thee, out with't, and place it for her chief virtue.

Speed. Item, She is proud.   344

Launce. Out with that too: it was Eve's legacy, and cannot be ta'en from her.

Speed. Item, She hath no teeth.

Launce. I care not for that neither, because I love crusts.   349

Speed. Item, She is curst.

Launce. Well; the best is, she hath no teeth to bite.   352

Speed. Item, She will often praise her liquor.

Launce. If her liquor be good, she shall: if she will not, I will; for good things should be praised.   356

Speed. Item, She is too liberal.

Launce. Of her tongue she cannot, for that's writ down she is slow of: of her purse she shall not, for that I'll keep shut: now, of another thing she may, and that cannot I help. Well, proceed.

Speed. Item, She hath more hair than wit, and more faults than hairs, and more wealth than faults.   365

Launce. Stop there; I'll have her: she was mine, and not mine, twice or thrice in that last article. Rehearse that once more.   368

Speed. Item, She hath more hair than wit.—

Launce. More hair than wit it may be; I'll prove it: the cover of the salt hides the salt, and therefore it is more than the salt; the hair that covers the wit is more than the wit, for the greater hides the less. What's next?

Speed. And more faults than hairs.—   376

Launce. That's monstrous! O, that that were out!

Speed. And more wealth than faults.

Launce. Why, that word makes the faults gracious. Well, I'll have her; and if it be a match, as nothing is impossible,—

Speed. What then?

Launce. Why, then will I tell thee,—that thy master stays for thee at the North-gate.   385

Speed. For me?

Launce. For thee! ay; who art thou? he hath stayed for a better man than thee.   388

Speed. And must I go to him?

Launce. Thou must run to him, for thou hast stayed so long that going will scarce serve the turn.   392

Speed. Why didst not tell me sooner? pox of your love-letters!   [*Exit.*

Launce. Now will he be swing'd for reading my letter. An unmannerly slave, that will thrust himself into secrets. I'll after, to rejoice in the boy's correction.   [*Exit.*

SCENE II.—*The Same. A Room in the* DUKE'S *Palace.*

Enter DUKE *and* THURIO.

Duke. Sir Thurio, fear not but that she will love you,

Now Valentine is banish'd from her sight.

Thu. Since his exile she hath despis'd me most,

Forsworn my company and rail'd at me,   4

That I am desperate of obtaining her.

Duke. This weak impress of love is as a figure

Trenched in ice, which with an hour's heat

Dissolves to water and doth lose his form.   8

A little time will melt her frozen thoughts,

And worthless Valentine shall be forgot.

Enter PROTEUS.

How now, Sir Proteus! Is your countryman

According to our proclamation gone?   12

Pro. Gone, my good lord.

Duke. My daughter takes his going grievously.

Pro. A little time, my lord, will kill that grief.

Duke. So I believe; but Thurio thinks not so.
Proteus, the good conceit I hold of thee,— 17
For thou hast shown some sign of good desert,—
Makes me the better to confer with thee.
  Pro. Longer than I prove loyal to your Grace
Let me not live to look upon your Grace. 21
  Duke. Thou know'st how willingly I would
effect
The match between Sir Thurio and my daughter.
  Pro. I do, my lord. 24
  Duke. And also, I think, thou art not
ignorant
How she opposes her against my will.
  Pro. She did, my lord, when Valentine was
here.
  Duke. Ay, and perversely she persevers so. 28
What might we do to make the girl forget
The love of Valentine, and love Sir Thurio?
  Pro. The best way is to slander Valentine
With falsehood, cowardice, and poor descent,
Three things that women highly hold in hate.
  Duke. Ay, but she'll think that it is spoke
in hate.
  Pro. Ay, if his enemy deliver it:
Therefore it must with circumstance be spoken
By one whom she esteemeth as his friend. 37
  Duke. Then you must undertake to slander
him.
  Pro. And that, my lord, I shall be loath to do:
'Tis an ill office for a gentleman, 40
Especially against his very friend.
  Duke. Where your good word cannot advan-
tage him,
Your slander never can endamage him;
Therefore the office is indifferent, 44
Being entreated to it by your friend.
  Pro. You have prevail'd, my lord. If I can
do it,
By aught that I can speak in his dispraise,
She shall not long continue love to him. 48
But say this weed her love from Valentine,
It follows not that she will love Sir Thurio.
  Thu. Therefore, as you unwind her love from
him,
Lest it should ravel and be good to none, 52
You must provide to bottom it on me;
Which must be done by praising me as much
As you in worth dispraise Sir Valentine.
  Duke. And, Proteus, we dare trust you in
this kind, 56
Because we know, on Valentine's report,
You are already Love's firm votary
And cannot soon revolt and change your mind.
Upon this warrant shall you have access 60
Where you with Silvia may confer at large;
For she is lumpish, heavy, melancholy,
And, for your friend's sake, will be glad of you;
Where you may temper her, by your persuasion
To hate young Valentine and love my friend. 65
  Pro. As much as I can do I will effect.
But you, Sir Thurio, are not sharp enough;
You must lay lime to tangle her desires 68
By wailful sonnets, whose composed rimes
Should be full-fraught with serviceable vows.
  Duke. Ay,
Much is the force of heaven-bred poesy. 72

  Pro. Say that upon the altar of her beauty
You sacrifice your tears, your sighs, your heart.
Write till your ink be dry, and with your tears
Moist it again, and frame some feeling line 76
That may discover such integrity:
For Orpheus' lute was strung with poets' sinews,
Whose golden touch could soften steel and
stones,
Make tigers tame and huge leviathans 80
Forsake unsounded deeps to dance on sands.
After your dire-lamenting elegies,
Visit by night your lady's chamber-window
With some sweet consort: to their instruments
Tune a deploring dump; the night's dead silence
Will well become such sweet-complaining griev-
ance.
This, or else nothing, will inherit her.
  Duke. This discipline shows thou hast been
in love. 88
  Thu. And thy advice this night I'll put in
practice.
Therefore, sweet Proteus, my direction-giver,
Let us into the city presently
To sort some gentlemen well skill'd in music. 92
I have a sonnet that will serve the turn
To give the onset to thy good advice.
  Duke. About it, gentlemen!
  Pro. We'll wait upon your grace till after-
supper, 96
And afterward determine our proceedings.
  Duke. Even now about it! I will pardon
you. [*Exeunt.*

ACT IV

SCENE I.—*A Forest between Milan and Verona.*

    Enter certain Outlaws.

  First Out. Fellows, stand fast; I see a passenger.
  Sec. Out. If there be ten, shrink not, but
down with 'em.

    Enter VALENTINE *and* SPEED.

  Third Out. Stand, sir, and throw us that you
have about ye;
If not, we'll make you sit and rifle you. 4
  Speed. Sir, we are undone: these are the
villains
That all the travellers do fear so much.
  Val. My friends,—
  First Out. That's not so, sir; we are your
enemies. 8
  Sec. Out. Peace! we'll hear him.
  Third Out. Ay, by my beard, will we, for he
is a proper man.
  Val. Then know, that I have little wealth to
lose.
A man I am cross'd with adversity: 12
My riches are these poor habiliments,
Of which if you should here disfurnish me,
You take the sum and substance that I have.
  Sec. Out. Whither travel you? 16
  Val. To Verona.
  First Out. Whence came you?
  Val. From Milan.

Third Out. Have you long sojourn'd there?
Val. Some sixteen months; and longer might
  have stay'd   21
If crooked fortune had not thwarted me.
  Sec. Out. What! were you banish'd thence?
  Val. I was.   24
  Sec. Out. For what offence?
  Val. For that which now torments me to
  rehearse.
I kill'd a man, whose death I much repent;
But yet I slew him manfully, in fight,   28
Without false vantage or base treachery.
  First Out. Why, ne'er repent it, if it were
  done so.
But were you banish'd for so small a fault?
  Val. I was, and held me glad of such a doom.
  Sec. Out. Have you the tongues?   33
  Val. My youthful travel therein made me
  happy,
Or else I often had been miserable.
  Third Out. By the bare scalp of Robin Hood's
  fat friar,   36
This fellow were a king for our wild faction!
  First Out. We'll have him: Sirs, a word.
  Speed. Master, be one of them;
It is an honourable kind of thievery.   40
  Val. Peace, villain!
  Sec. Out. Tell us this: have you anything to
  take to?
  Val. Nothing, but my fortune.
  Third Out. Know then, that some of us are
  gentlemen,   44
Such as the fury of ungovern'd youth
Thrust from the company of awful men:
Myself was from Verona banished
For practising to steal away a lady,   48
An heir, and near allied unto the duke.
  Sec. Out. And I from Mantua, for a gentle-
  man,
Who, in my mood, I stabb'd unto the heart.
  First Out. And I for such like petty crimes
  as these.   52
But to the purpose; for we cite our faults,
That they may hold excus'd our lawless lives;
And, partly, seeing you are beautified
With goodly shape, and by your own report 56
A linguist, and a man of such perfection
As we do in our quality much want—
  Sec. Out. Indeed, because you are a banish'd
  man,
Therefore, above the rest, we parley to you. 60
Are you content to be our general?
To make a virtue of necessity
And live, as we do, in this wilderness?
  Third Out. What say'st thou? wilt thou be
  of our consort?   64
Say 'ay,' and be the captain of us all:
We'll do thee homage and be rul'd by thee,
Love thee as our commander and our king.
  First Out. But if thou scorn our courtesy,
  thou diest.   68
  Sec. Out. Thou shalt not live to brag what we
  have offer'd.
  Val. I take your offer and will live with you,
Provided that you do no outrages
On silly women, or poor passengers.   72

  Third Out. No; we detest such vile, base
  practices.
Come, go with us; we'll bring thee to our crews,
And show thee all the treasure we have got,
Which, with ourselves, all rest at thy dispose. 76
                    [*Exeunt.*

SCENE II.—*Milan. The Court of the* DUKE'S
Palace.

Enter PROTEUS.

  Pro. Already have I been false to Valentine,
And now I must be as unjust to Thurio.
Under the colour of commending him,
I have access my own love to prefer: 4
But Silvia is too fair, too true, too holy,
To be corrupted with my worthless gifts.
When I protest true loyalty to her,
She twits me with my falsehood to my friend;
When to her beauty I commend my vows,   9
She bids me think how I have been forsworn
In breaking faith with Julia whom I lov'd:
And notwithstanding all her sudden quips, 12
The least whereof would quell a lover's hope,
Yet, spaniel-like, the more she spurns my love,
The more it grows, and fawneth on her still.
But here comes Thurio: now must we to her
  window,   16
And give some evening music to her ear.

Enter THURIO, *and* Musicians.

  Thu. How now, Sir Proteus! are you crept
  before us?
  Pro. Ay, gentle Thurio; for you know that
  love
Will creep in service where it cannot go.   20
  Thu. Ay; but I hope, sir, that you love not
  here.
  Pro. Sir, but I do; or else I would be hence.
  Thu. Who? Silvia?
  Pro. Ay, Silvia, for your sake.   24
  Thu. I thank you for your own. Now, gentle-
  men,
Let's tune, and to it lustily a while.

Enter Host *and* JULIA *behind.* JULIA *in boy's
clothes.*

  Host. Now, my young guest, methinks you're
allycholly: I pray you, why is it?   28
  Jul. Marry, mine host, because I cannot be
merry.
  Host. Come, we'll have you merry. I'll bring
you where you shall hear music and see the
gentleman that you asked for.   33
  Jul. But shall I hear him speak?
  Host. Ay, that you shall.
  Jul. That will be music.   [*Music plays.*
  Host. Hark! hark!   37
  Jul. Is he among these?
  Host. Ay; but peace! let's hear 'em.

SONG

Who is Silvia? what is she,   40
  That all our swains commend her?
Holy, fair, and wise is she;
  The heaven such grace did lend her,
  That she might admired be.   44

Is she kind as she is fair?
  For beauty lives with kindness:
Love doth to her eyes repair,
  To help him of his blindness;
And, being help'd, inhabits there.   48

Then to Silvia let us sing,
  That Silvia is excelling;
She excels each mortal thing   52
  Upon the dull earth dwelling;
To her let us garlands bring.

Host. How now! are you sadder than you
were before? How do you, man? the music likes
you not.   57
Jul. You mistake; the musician likes me not.
Host. Why, my pretty youth?
Jul. He plays false, father.   60
Host. How? out of tune on the strings?
Jul. Not so; but yet so false that he grieves
my very heart-strings.
Host. You have a quick ear.   64
Jul. Ay; I would I were deaf; it makes me
have a slow heart.
Host. I perceive you delight not in music.
Jul. Not a whit,—when it jars so.   68
Host. Hark! what fine change is in the music!
Jul. Ay, that change is the spite.
Host. You would have them always play but
one thing?   72
Jul. I would always have one play but one
thing.
But, host, doth this Sir Proteus that we talk on
Often resort unto this gentlewoman?
Host. I will tell you what Launce, his man,
told me: he lov'd her out of all nick.   77
Jul. Where is Launce?
Host. Gone to seek his dog; which, to-morrow,
by his master's command, he must carry for a
present to his lady.   81
Jul. Peace! stand aside: the company parts.
Pro. Sir Thurio, fear not you: I will so plead
That you shall say my cunning drift excels. 84
Thu. Where meet we?
Pro. At Saint Gregory's well.
Thu. Farewell.

    [*Exeunt* THURIO *and* Musicians.

Enter SILVIA *above, at her window.*

Pro. Madam, good even to your ladyship. 88
Sil. I thank you for your music, gentlemen.
Who is that that spake?
Pro. One, lady, if you knew his pure heart's
  truth,
You would quickly learn to know him by his
  voice.   92
Sil. Sir Proteus, as I take it.
Pro. Sir Proteus, gentle lady, and your ser-
  vant.
Sil. What is your will?
Pro.   That I may compass yours.
Sil. You have your wish; my will is even this: 97
That presently you hie you home to bed.
Thou subtle, perjur'd, false, disloyal man!
Think'st thou I am so shallow, so conceitless, 100
To be seduced by thy flattery,
That hast deceiv'd so many with thy vows?
Return, return, and make thy love amends.

For me, by this pale queen of night I swear,
I am so far from granting thy request   104
That I despise thee for thy wrongful suit,
And by and by intend to chide myself
Even for this time I spend in talking to thee.
Pro. I grant, sweet love, that I did love a lady;
But she is dead.
Jul. [*Aside.*] 'Twere false, if I should speak it;
For I am sure she is not buried.
Sil. Say that she be; yet Valentine thy friend
Survives; to whom, thyself art witness   112
I am betroth'd: and art thou not asham'd
To wrong him with thy importunacy?
Pro. I likewise hear that Valentine is dead.
Sil. And so suppose am I; for in his grave,
Assure thyself my love is buried.   117
Pro. Sweet lady, let me rake it from the earth.
Sil. Go to thy lady's grave and call hers thence;
Or, at the least, in hers sepulchre thine. 120
Jul. [*Aside.*] He heard not that.
Pro. Madam, if your heart be so obdurate,
Vouchsafe me yet your picture for my love,
The picture that is hanging in your chamber:
To that I'll speak, to that I'll sigh and weep;
For since the substance of your perfect self
Is else devoted, I am but a shadow,
And to your shadow will I make true love. 128
Jul. [*Aside.*] If 'twere a substance, you would,
  sure, deceive it,
And make it but a shadow, as I am.
Sil. I am very loath to be your idol, sir;
But, since your falsehood shall become you well
To worship shadows and adore false shapes, 133
Send to me in the morning and I'll send it.
And so, good rest.
Pro.   As wretches have o'er night
That wait for execution in the morn.   136

    [*Exeunt* PROTEUS, *and* SILVIA, *above.*

Jul. Host, will you go?
Host. By my halidom, I was fast asleep.
Jul. Pray you, where lies Sir Proteus?
Host. Marry, at my house. Trust me, I think
'tis almost day.   141
Jul. Not so; but it hath been the longest
  night
That e'er I watch'd and the most heaviest.

    [*Exeunt.*

SCENE III.—*The Same.*

Enter EGLAMOUR.

Egl. This is the hour that Madam Silvia
Entreated me to call, and know her mind:
There's some great matter she'd employ me in.
Madam, Madam!

Enter SILVIA *above, at her window.*

Sil. Who calls?
Egl.   Your servant, and your friend; 4
One that attends your ladyship's command.
Sil. Sir Eglamour, a thousand times good
  morrow.
Egl. As many, worthy lady, to yourself.
According to your ladyship's impose,   8
I am thus early come to know what service
It is your pleasure to command me in.
Sil. O Eglamour, thou art a gentleman—

Think not I flatter, for I swear I do not— 12
Valiant, wise, remorseful, well-accomplish'd.
Thou art not ignorant what dear good will
I bear unto the banish'd Valentine,
Now how my father would enforce me marry 16
Vain Thurio, whom my very soul abhors.
Thyself hast lov'd; and I have heard thee say
No grief did ever come so near thy heart
As when thy lady and thy true love died, 20
Upon whose grave thou vow'dst pure chastity.
Sir Eglamour, I would to Valentine,
To Mantua, where, I hear he makes abode;
And, for the ways are dangerous to pass, 24
I do desire thy worthy company,
Upon whose faith and honour I repose.
Urge not my father's anger, Eglamour,
But think upon my grief, a lady's grief, 28
And on the justice of my flying hence,
To keep me from a most unholy match,
Which heaven and fortune still rewards with
plagues.
I do desire thee, even from a heart 32
As full of sorrows as the sea of sands,
To bear me company and go with me:
If not, to hide what I have said to thee,
That I may venture to depart alone. 36
   Egl. Madam, I pity much your grievances;
Which since I know they virtuously are plac'd,
I give consent to go along with you,
Recking as little what betideth me 40
As much I wish all good befortune you.
When will you go?
   Sil.   This evening coming.
   Egl. Where shall I meet you?
   Sil.   At Friar Patrick's cell,
Where I intend holy confession. 44
   Egl. I will not fail your ladyship.
Good morrow, gentle lady.
   Sil. Good morrow, kind Sir Eglamour.
                  [Exeunt severally.

Scene IV.—*The Same.*

Enter LAUNCE *with his dog.*

   Launce. When a man's servant shall play the
cur with him, look you, it goes hard; one that
I brought up of a puppy; one that I saved from
drowning, when three or four of his blind brothers and sisters went to it. I have taught him,
even as one would say precisely, 'Thus would I
teach a dog.' I was sent to deliver him as a
present to Mistress Silvia from my master, and
I came no sooner into the dining-chamber but
he steps me to her trencher and steals her
capon's leg. O! 'tis a foul thing when a cur
cannot keep himself in all companies. I would
have, as one should say, one that takes upon
him to be a dog indeed, to be, as it were, a dog
at all things. If I had not had more wit than
he, to take a fault upon me that he did, I think
verily he had been hanged for't: sure as I live,
he had suffered for't: you shall judge. He thrusts
me himself into the company of three or four
gentleman-like dogs under the duke's table: he
had not been there—bless the mark—a pissing-

while, but all the chamber smelt him. 'Out with
the dog!' says one; 'What cur is that?' says
another; 'Whip him out,' says the third; 'Hang
him up,' says the duke. I, having been acquainted
with the smell before, knew it was Crab, and
goes me to the fellow that whips the dogs:
'Friend,' quoth I, 'you mean to whip the dog?'
'Ay, marry, do I,' quoth he. 'You do him the
more wrong,' quoth I; ''twas I did the thing you
wot of.' He makes me no more ado, but whips
me out of the chamber. How many masters
would do this for his servant? Nay, I'll be
sworn, I have sat in the stocks for puddings he
hath stolen, otherwise he had been executed;
I have stood on the pillory for geese he hath
killed, otherwise he had suffered for't; thou
thinkest not of this now. Nay, I remember the
trick you served me when I took my leave of
Madam Silvia: did not I bid thee still mark me
and do as I do? When didst thou see me heave
up my leg and make water against a gentlewoman's farthingale? Didst thou ever see me
do such a trick? 44

Enter PROTEUS, *and* JULIA *in boy's clothes.*

   Pro. Sebastian is thy name? I like thee well
And will employ thee in some service presently.
   Jul. In what you please: I will do what I can.
   Pro. I hope thou wilt. [*To* LAUNCE.] How
    now, you whoreson peasant! 48
Where have you been these two days loitering?
   Launce. Marry, sir, I carried Mistress Silvia
the dog you bade me.
   Pro. And what says she to my little jewel? 52
   Launce. Marry, she says, your dog was a cur,
and tells you, currish thanks is good enough for
such a present.
   Pro. But she received my dog? 56
   Launce. No, indeed, did she not: here have I
brought him back again.
   Pro. What! didst thou offer her this from me?
   Launce. Ay, sir: the other squirrel was stolen
from me by the hangman boys in the market-
place; and then I offered her mine own, who is
a dog as big as ten of yours, and therefore the
gift the greater. 64
   Pro. Go, get thee hence, and find my dog
    again,
Or ne'er return again into my sight.
Away, I say! Stay'st thou to vex me here?
A slave that still an end turns me to shame. 68
                  [Exit LAUNCE.
Sebastian, I have entertained thee
Partly, that I have need of such a youth,
That can with some discretion do my business,
For 't is no trusting to yond foolish lout; 72
But chiefly for thy face and thy behaviour,
Which, if my augury deceive me not,
Witness good bringing up, fortune, and truth:
Therefore, know thou, for this I entertain thee.
Go presently, and take this ring with thee. 77
Deliver it to Madam Silvia:
She lov'd me well deliver'd it to me.
   Jul. It seems, you lov'd not her, to leave her
    token. 80
She's dead, belike?

Pro.   Not so: I think, she lives.
Jul. Alas!
Pro. Why dost thou cry 'alas?'
Jul.   I cannot choose
But pity her.   84
Pro. Wherefore should'st thou pity her?
Jul. Because methinks that she lov'd you as
well
As you do love your lady Silvia.
She dreams on him that has forgot her love; 88
You dote on her, that cares not for your love.
'Tis pity, love should be so contrary;
And thinking on it makes me cry, 'alas!'
Pro. Well, well, give her that ring and there-
withal   92
This letter: that's her chamber. Tell my lady
I claim the promise for her heavenly picture.
Your message done, hie home unto my chamber,
Where thou shalt find me sad and solitary. [*Exit.*
Jul. How many women would do such a
message?   97
Alas, poor Proteus! thou hast entertain'd
A fox to be the shepherd of thy lambs.
Alas, poor fool! why do I pity him
That with his very heart despiseth me?   100
Because he loves her, he despiseth me;
Because I love him, I must pity him.
This ring I gave him when he parted from me,
To bind him to remember my good will;
And now am I—unhappy messenger—   105
To plead for that which I would not obtain,
To carry that which I would have refus'd,   108
To praise his faith which I would have dispraís'd.
I am my master's true-confirmed love,
But cannot be true servant to my master,
Unless I prove false traitor to myself.   112
Yet will I woo for him; but yet so coldly
As heaven it knows, I would not have him speed.

Enter SILVIA, *attended.*

Gentlewoman, good day! I pray you, be my
mean
To bring me where to speak with Madam Silvia.
Sil. What would you with her, if that I be she?
Jul. If you be she, I do entreat your patience
To hear me speak the message I am sent on.
Sil. From whom?   120
Jul. From my master, Sir Proteus, madam.
Sil. O! he sends you for a picture?
Jul. Ay, madam.
Sil. Ursula, bring my picture there.   124
                          [*A picture brought.*
Go, give your master this: tell him from me,
One Julia, that his changing thoughts forget,
Would better fit his chamber than this shadow.
Jul. Madam, please you peruse this letter.—
Pardon me, madam, I have unadvis'd   129
Deliver'd you a paper that I should not:
This is the letter to your ladyship.
Sil. I pray thee, let me look on that again.
Jul. It may not be: good madam, pardon me.
Sil. There, hold.
I will not look upon your master's lines:
I know, they are stuff'd with protestations   136
And full of new-found oaths, which he will break
As easily as I do tear his paper.

Jul. Madam, he sends your ladyship this
ring.
Sil. The more shame for him that he sends
it me;   140
For, I have heard him say a thousand times,
His Julia gave it him at his departure.
Though his false finger have profan'd the ring,
Mine shall not do his Julia so much wrong. 144
Jul. She thanks you.
Sil. What say'st thou?
Jul. I thank you, madam, that you tender
her.
Poor gentlewoman! my master wrongs her
much.   148
Sil. Dost thou know her?
Jul. Almost as well as I do know myself:
To think upon her woes, I do protest
That I have wept a hundred several times.   152
Sil. Belike, she thinks, that Proteus hath for-
sook her.
Jul. I think she doth, and that's her cause
of sorrow.
Sil. Is she not passing fair?   155
Jul. She hath been fairer, madam, than she is.
When she did think my master lov'd her well,
She, in my judgment, was as fair as you;
But since she did neglect her looking-glass
And threw her sun-expelling mask away,   160
The air hath starv'd the roses in her cheeks
And pinch'd the lily-tincture of her face,
That now she is become as black as I.
Sil. How tall was she?   164
Jul. About my stature; for, at Pentecost,
When all our pageants of delight were play'd,
Our youth got me to play the woman's part,
And I was trimm'd in Madam Julia's gown,   168
Which served me as fit, by all men's judgments,
As if the garment had been made for me:
Therefore I know she is about my height.
And at that time I made her weep agood;   172
For I did play a lamentable part.
Madam, 'twas Ariadne passioning
For Theseus' perjury and unjust flight;
Which I so lively acted with my tears   176
That my poor mistress, moved therewithal,
Wept bitterly, and would I might be dead
If I in thought felt not her very sorrow!
Sil. She is beholding to thee, gentle youth.—
Alas, poor lady, desolate and left!   181
I weep myself to think upon thy words.
Here, youth, there is my purse: I give thee this
For thy sweet mistress' sake, because thou lov'st
her.   184
Farewell.
Jul. And she shall thank you for't, if e'er you
know her.—[*Exit* SILVIA, *with* Attendants.
A virtuous gentlewoman, mild and beautiful.
I hope my master's suit will be but cold,   188
Since she respects my mistress' love so much.
Alas, how love can trifle with itself!
Here is her picture: let me see; I think,
If I had such a tire, this face of mine   192
Were full as lovely as is this of hers;
And yet the painter flatter'd her a little,
Unless I flatter with myself too much.
Her hair is auburn, mine is perfect yellow: 196

If that be all the difference in his love
I'll get me such a colour'd periwig.
Her eyes are grey as glass, and so are mine:
Ay, but her forehead's low, and mine's as high.
What should it be that he respects in her   200
But I can make respective in myself,
If this fond Love were not a blinded god?
Come, shadow, come, and take this shadow up,
For 'tis thy rival. O thou senseless form!
Thou shalt be worshipp'd, kiss'd, lov'd, and
    ador'd,   205
And, were there sense in his idolatry,
My substance should be statue in thy stead.
I'll use thee kindly for thy mistress' sake,
That us'd me so; or else, by Jove I vow,
I should have scratch'd out your unseeing eyes,
To make my master out of love with thee. [*Exit.*]

ACT V

Scene I.—*Milan. An Abbey.*

Enter EGLAMOUR.

Egl. The sun begins to gild the western sky,
And now it is about the very hour
That Silvia at Friar Patrick's cell should meet
me.
She will not fail; for lovers break not hours, 4
Unless it be to come before their time,
So much they spur their expedition.
See, where she comes.

Enter SILVIA.

                        Lady, a happy evening!
Sil. Amen, amen! go on, good Eglamour, 8
Out at the postern by the abbey-wall.
I fear I am attended by some spies.
Egl. Fear not: the forest is not three leagues
off;
If we recover that, we're sure enough. [*Exeunt.*]

Scene II.—*The Same. A Room in the*
DUKE'S *Palace.*

Enter THURIO, PROTEUS, *and* JULIA.

Thu. Sir Proteus, what says Silvia to my suit?
Pro. O, sir, I find her milder than she was;
And yet she takes exceptions at your person.
Thu. What! that my leg is too long?   4
Pro. No, that it is too little.
Thu. I'll wear a boot to make it somewhat
rounder.
Jul. [*Aside.*] But love will not be spurr'd to
what it loathes.
Thu. What says she to my face?   8
Pro. She says it is a fair one.
Thu. Nay then, the wanton lies; my face is
black.
Pro. But pearls are fair, and the old saying is,
'Black men are pearls in beauteous ladies' eyes.'
Jul. [*Aside.*] 'Tis true, such pearls as put out
ladies' eyes;   13
For I had rather wink than look on them.
Thu. How likes she my discourse?
Pro. Ill, when you talk of war.   16

Thu. But well, when I discourse of love and
peace?
Jul. [*Aside.*] But better, indeed, when you
hold your peace.
Thu. What says she to my valour?
Pro. O, sir, she makes no doubt of that. 20
Jul. [*Aside.*] She needs not, when she knows
it cowardice.
Thu. What says she to my birth?
Pro. That you are well deriv'd.
Jul. [*Aside.*] True; from a gentleman to a
fool.   24
Thu. Considers she my possessions?
Pro. O, ay; and pities them.
Thu. Wherefore?
Jul. [*Aside.*] That such an ass should owe
them.   28
Pro. That they are out by lease.
Jul. Here comes the duke.

Enter DUKE.

Duke. How now, Sir Proteus! how now,
Thurio!
Which of you saw Sir Eglamour of late?   32
Thu. Not I.
Pro.   Nor I.
Duke.   Saw you my daughter?
Pro.   Neither.
Duke. Why then,
She's fled unto that peasant Valentine,
And Eglamour is in her company.   36
'Tis true; for Friar Laurence met them both,
As he in penance wander'd through the forest;
Him he knew well, and guess'd that it was she,
But, being mask'd, he was not sure of it; 40
Besides, she did intend confession
At Patrick's cell this even, and there she was
not.
These likelihoods confirm her flight from hence.
Therefore, I pray you, stand not to discourse, 44
But mount you presently and meet with me
Upon the rising of the mountain-foot,
That leads towards Mantua, whither they are
fled.
Dispatch, sweet gentlemen, and follow me.
                                        [*Exit.*]
Thu. Why, this it is to be a peevish girl,
That flies her fortune when it follows her. 50
I'll after, more to be reveng'd on Eglamour
Than for the love of reckless Silvia. [*Exit.*]
Pro. And I will follow, more for Silvia's love
Than hate of Eglamour that goes with her.
                                        [*Exit.*]
Jul. And I will follow, more to cross that love
Than hate for Silvia that is gone for love. [*Exit.*]

Scene III.—*Frontiers of Mantua. The Forest.*

Enter Outlaws *with* SILVIA.

First Out. Come, come,
Be patient; we must bring you to our captain.
Sil. A thousand more mischances than this
one
Have learn'd me how to brook this patiently. 4
Second Out. Come, bring her away.

First Out. Where is the gentleman that was
with her?
Third Out. Being nimble-footed, he hath
outrun us;
But Moyses and Valerius follow him.   8
Go thou with her to the west end of the wood;
There is our captain. We'll follow him that's
fled:
The thicket is beset; he cannot 'scape.
    [*Exeunt all except the First* Outlaw
                    and SILVIA.
First Out. Come, I must bring you to our
captain's cave.   12
Fear not; he bears an honourable mind,
And will not use a woman lawlessly.
Sil. O Valentine! this I endure for thee.
                    [*Exeunt.*

SCENE IV.—*Another Part of the Forest.*

Enter VALENTINE.

Val. How use doth breed a habit in a man!
This shadowy desert, unfrequented woods,
I better brook than flourishing peopled towns.
Here can I sit alone, unseen of any,   4
And to the nightingale's complaining notes
Tune my distresses and record my woes.
O thou that dost inhabit in my breast,
Leave not the mansion so long tenantless   8
Lest, growing ruinous, the building fall
And leave no memory of what it was!
Repair me with thy presence, Silvia!   11
Thou gentle nymph, cherish thy forlorn swain!
                    [*Noise within.*
What halloing and what stir is this to-day?
These are my mates, that make their wills their
law,
Have some unhappy passenger in chase.
They love me well; yet I have much to do 16
To keep them from uncivil outrages.
Withdraw thee, Valentine: who's this comes
here?   [*Steps aside.*

Enter PROTEUS, SILVIA, *and* JULIA.

Pro. Madam, this service I have done for
you—
Though you respect not aught your servant
doth—   20
To hazard life and rescue you from him
That would have forc'd your honour and your
love.
Vouchsafe me, for my meed, but one fair look;
A smaller boon than this I cannot beg,   24
And less than this, I am sure, you cannot give.
Val. [*Aside.*] How like a dream is this I see
and hear!
Love, lend me patience to forbear awhile.
Sil. O, miserable, unhappy that I am!   28
Pro. Unhappy were you, madam, ere I came;
But by my coming I have made you happy.
Sil. By thy approach thou mak'st me most
unhappy.
Jul. [*Aside.*] And me, when he approacheth
to your presence.   32
Sil. Had I been seized by a hungry lion,

I would have been a breakfast to the beast,
Rather than have false Proteus rescue me.
O! heaven be judge how I love Valentine, 36
Whose life's as tender to me as my soul,
And full as much—for more there cannot be—
I do detest false perjur'd Proteus.
Therefore be gone, solicit me no more.   40
Pro. What dangerous action, stood it next
to death,
Would I not undergo for one calm look!
O, 'tis the curse in love, and still approv'd,
When women cannot love where they're be-
lov'd!   44
Sil. When Proteus cannot love where he's
belov'd.
Read over Julia's heart, thy first best love,
For whose dear sake thou didst then rend thy
faith
Into a thousand oaths; and all those oaths 48
Descended into perjury to love me.
Thou hast no faith left now, unless thou'dst two,
And that's far worse than none: better have
none
Than plural faith which is too much by one. 52
Thou counterfeit to thy true friend!
Pro.   In love
Who respects friend?
Sil.   All men but Proteus.
Pro. Nay, if the gentle spirit of moving words
Can no way change you to a milder form, 56
I'll woo you like a soldier, at arms' end,
And love you 'gainst the nature of love,—
force ye.
Sil. O heaven!
Pro.   I'll force thee yield to my desire.
Val. [*Coming forward.*] Ruffian, let go that
rude uncivil touch;   60
Thou friend of an ill fashion!
Pro.   Valentine!
Val. Thou common friend, that's without
faith or love!
For such is a friend now—treacherous man!
Thou hast beguil'd my hopes; naught but mine
eye   64
Could have persuaded me. Now I dare not say
I have one friend alive: thou wouldst disprove
me.
Who should be trusted now, when one's right
hand
Is perjur'd to the bosom? Proteus,   68
I am sorry I must never trust thee more,
But count the world a stranger for thy sake.
The private wound is deep'st. O time most
curst!
'Mongst all foes that a friend should be the
worst!
Pro. My shame and guilt confound me. 73
Forgive me, Valentine. If hearty sorrow
Be a sufficient ransom for offence,
I tender 't here: I do as truly suffer   76
As e'er I did commit.
Val.   Then, I am paid;
And once again I do receive thee honest.
Who by repentance is not satisfied
Is nor of heaven, nor earth; for these are pleas'd.
By penitence the Eternal's wrath's appeas'd: 81

And, that my love may appear plain and free,
All that was mine in Silvia I give thee.
  Jul. O me unhappy!   [*Swoons.*
  Pro. Look to the boy. 85
  Val. Why, boy! why, wag! how now! what's
the matter?
Look up; speak.
  Jul. O good sir, my master charg'd me 88
To deliver a ring to Madam Silvia,
Which out of my neglect was never done.
  Pro. Where is that ring, boy?
  Jul.   Here 'tis: this is it. [*Gives a ring.*
  Pro. How! let me see. 92
Why, this is the ring I gave to Julia.
  Jul. O, cry you mercy, sir; I have mistook:
This is the ring you sent to Silvia.
                [*Shows another ring.*
  Pro. But how cam'st thou by this ring? 96
At my depart I gave this unto Julia.
  Jul. And Julia herself did give it me;
And Julia herself hath brought it hither.
  Pro. How! Julia! 100
  Jul. Behold her that gave aim to all thy oaths,
And entertain'd them deeply in her heart:
How oft hast thou with perjury cleft the root!
O Proteus! let this habit make thee blush. 104
Be thou asham'd that I have took upon me
Such an immodest raiment; if shame live
In a disguise of love.
It is the lesser blot, modesty finds, 108
Women to change their shapes than men their
minds.
  Pro. Than men their minds! 'tis true. O
heaven! were man
But constant, he were perfect: that one error
Fills him with faults; makes him run through
all the sins: 112
Inconstancy falls off ere it begins.
What is in Silvia's face, but I may spy
More fresh in Julia's with a constant eye?
  Val. Come, come, a hand from either. 116
Let me be blest to make this happy close:
'Twere pity two such friends should be long
foes.
  Pro. Bear witness, heaven, I have my wish,
for ever.
  Jul. And I mine. 120

Enter Outlaws *with* DUKE *and* THURIO.

  Out. A prize! a prize! a prize!
  Val. Forbear, forbear, I say; it is my lord
the duke.
Your Grace is welcome to a man disgrac'd,
Banished Valentine.
  Duke.   Sir Valentine! 124
  Thu. Yonder is Silvia; and Silvia's mine.

  Val. Thurio, give back, or else embrace thy
death;
Come not within the measure of my wrath;
Do not name Silvia thine; if once again, 128
Verona shall not hold thee. Here she stands;
Take but possession of her with a touch;
I dare thee but to breathe upon my love.
  Thu. Sir Valentine, I care not for her, I. 132
I hold him but a fool that will endanger
His body for a girl that loves him not:
I claim her not, and therefore she is thine. 135
  Duke. The more degenerate and base art
thou,
To make such means for her as thou hast done,
And leave her on such slight conditions.
Now, by the honour of my ancestry,
I do applaud thy spirit, Valentine, 140
And think thee worthy of an empress' love.
Know then, I here forget all former griefs,
Cancel all grudge, repeal thee home again,
Plead a new state in thy unrivall'd merit, 144
To which I thus subscribe: Sir Valentine,
Thou art a gentleman and well deriv'd;
Take thou thy Silvia, for thou hast deserv'd her.
  Val. I thank your Grace; the gift hath made
me happy. 148
I now beseech you, for your daughter's sake,
To grant one boon that I shall ask of you.
  Duke. I grant it, for thine own, whate'er it be.
  Val. These banish'd men, that I have kept
withal 152
Are men endu'd with worthy qualities:
Forgive them what they have committed here,
And let them be recall'd from their exile.
They are reformed, civil, full of good, 156
And fit for great emloyment, worthy lord.
  Duke. Thou hast prevail'd; I pardon them,
and thee:
Dispose of them as thou know'st their deserts.
Come, let us go: we will include all jars 160
With triumphs, mirth, and rare solemnity.
  Val. And as we walk along, I dare be bold
With our discourse to make your Grace to smile.
What think you of this page, my lord? 164
  Duke. I think the boy hath grace in him: he
blushes.
  Val. I warrant you, my lord, more grace
than boy.
  Duke. What mean you by that saying?
  Val. Please you, I'll tell you as we pass along,
That you will wonder what hath fortuned. 169
Come, Proteus; 'tis your penance, but to hear
The story of your loves discovered:
That done, our day of marriage shall be yours;
One feast, one house, one mutual happiness. 173
                      [*Exeunt.*

THE MERRY WIVES OF WINDSOR

DRAMATIS PERSONÆ

SIR JOHN FALSTAFF.
FENTON, a young Gentleman.
SHALLOW, a Country Justice.
SLENDER, Cousin to Shallow.
FORD,
PAGE, } two Gentlemen dwelling at Windsor.
WILLIAM PAGE, a Boy, Son to Page.
SIR HUGH EVANS, a Welsh Parson.
DOCTOR CAIUS, a French Physician.
HOST of the Garter Inn.
BARDOLPH, PISTOL, NYM, Followers of Falstaff.

ROBIN, Page to Falstaff.
SIMPLE, Servant to Slender.
RUGBY, Servant to Doctor Caius.

MISTRESS FORD.
MISTRESS PAGE.
ANNE PAGE, her Daughter, in love with Fenton.
MISTRESS QUICKLY, Servant to Doctor Caius.

Servants to Page, Ford, &c.

SCENE.—*Windsor; and the Neighbourhood.*

ACT I

SCENE I.—*Windsor. Before* PAGE'S *House.*

Enter JUSTICE SHALLOW, SLENDER, *and* SIR HUGH EVANS.

Shal. Sir Hugh, persuade me not; I will make a Star-chamber matter of it; if he were twenty Sir John Falstaffs he shall not abuse Robert Shallow, esquire. 4

Slen. In the county of Gloster, justice of peace, and *coram*.

Shal. Ay, cousin Slender, and *cust-alorum*.

Slen. Ay, and *rato-lorum* too; and a gentleman born, Master Parson; who writes himself *armigero*, in any bill, warrant, quittance, or obligation,—*armigero*. 11

Shal. Ay, that I do; and have done any time these three hundred years.

Slen. All his successors gone before him hath done 't; and all his ancestors that come after him may: they may give the dozen while luces in their coat. 17

Shal. It is an old coat.

Eva. The dozen white louses do become an old coat well; it agrees well, *passant;* it is a familiar beast to man, and signifies love. 21

Shal. The luce is the fresh fish; the salt fish is an old coat.

Slen. I may quarter, coz? 24

Shal. You may, by marrying.

Eva. It is marring indeed, if he quarter it.

Shal. Not a whit.

Eva. Yes, py'r lady; if he has a quarter of your coat, there is but three skirts for yourself, in my simple conjectures: but that is all one. If Sir John Falstaff have committed disparagements unto you, I am of the Church, and will be glad to do my benevolence to make atonements and compromises between you. 34

Shal. The Council shall hear it; it is a riot.

Eva. It is not meet the Council hear a riot; there is no fear of Got in a riot. The Council, look you, shall desire to hear the fear of Got, and not to hear a riot; take your vizaments in that.

Shal. Ha! o' my life, if I were young again, the sword should end it. 41

Eva. It is petter that friends is the sword, and end it; and there is also another device in my prain, which, peradventure, prings goot discretions with it. There is Anne Page, which is daughter to Master Thomas Page, which is pretty virginity.

Slen. Mistress Anne Page? She has brown hair, and speaks small like a woman. 49

Eva. It is that fery person for all the orld, as just as you will desire; and seven hundred pounds of moneys, and gold and silver, is her grandsire, upon his death's-bed,—Got deliver to a joyful resurrections!—give, when she is able to overtake seventeen years old. It were a goot motion if we leave our pribbles and prabbles, and desire a marriage between Master Abraham and Mistress Anne Page.

Shal. Did her grandsire leave her seven hundred pound? 60

Eva. Ay, and her father is make her a petter penny.

Shal. I know the young gentlewoman; she has good gifts. 64

Eva. Seven hundred pounds and possibilities is goot gifts.

Shal. Well, let us see honest Master Page. Is Falstaff there? 68

Eva. Shall I tell you a lie? I do despise a liar as I do despise one that is false; or as I despise one that is not true. The knight, Sir John, is there; and, I beseech you, be ruled by your well-willers. I will peat the door for Master Page. [*Knocks.*] What, hoa! Got pless your house here!

Page. [*Within.*] Who's there? 76

Eva. Here is Got's plessing, and your friend, and Justice Shallow; and here young Master Slender, that peradventures shall tell you another tale, if matters grow to your likings. 80

Enter PAGE.

Page. I am glad to see your worships well. I thank you for my venison, Master Shallow.

Shal. Master Page, I am glad to see you: much good do it your good heart! I wished your venison better; it was ill killed. How doth good

Mistress Page?—and I thank you always with
my heart, la! with my heart.
  Page. Sir, I thank you. 88
  Shal. Sir, I thank you; by yea and no, I do.
  Page. I am glad to see you, good Master
Slender.
  Slen. How does your fallow greyhound, sir?
I heard say he was outrun on Cotsall. 93
  Page. It could not be judged, sir.
  Slen. You'll not confess, you'll not confess.
  Shal. That he will not: 'tis your fault, 'tis
your fault. 'Tis a good dog. 97
  Page. A cur, sir.
  Shal. Sir, he's a good dog, and a fair dog;
can there be more said? he is good and fair.
Is Sir John Falstaff here? 101
  Page. Sir, he is within; and I would I could
do a good office between you.
  Eva. It is spoke as a Christians ought to speak.
  Shal. He hath wronged me, Master Page. 105
  Page. Sir, he doth in some sort confess it.
  Shal. If it be confessed, it is not redressed:
is not that so, Master Page? He hath wronged
me; indeed, he hath;—at a word, he hath,—be-
lieve me: Robert Shallow, esquire, saith, he is
wronged.
  Page. Here comes Sir John. 112

Enter SIR JOHN FALSTAFF, BARDOLPH, NYM,
and PISTOL.

  Fal. Now, Master Shallow, you'll complain
of me to the king?
  Shal. Knight, you have beaten my men, killed
my deer, and broke open my lodge. 116
  Fal. But not kissed your keeper's daughter?
  Shal. Tut, a pin! this shall be answered.
  Fal. I will answer it straight: I have done
all this. That is now answered. 120
  Shal. The Council shall know this.
  Fal. 'Twere better for you if it were known
in counsel: you'll be laughed at.
  Eva. Pauca verba, Sir John; goot worts. 124
  Fal. Good worts! good cabbage. Slender, I
broke your head: what matter have you against
me?
  Slen. Marry, sir, I have matter in my head
against you; and against your cony-catching
rascals, Bardolph, Nym, and Pistol. They car-
ried me to the tavern, and made me drunk, and
afterwards picked my pocket. 132
  Bard. You Banbury cheese!
  Slen. Ay, it is no matter.
  Pist. How now, Mephistophilus!
  Slen. Ay, it is no matter. 136
  Nym. Slice, I say! pauca, pauca; slice!
that's my humour.
  Slen. Where's Simple, my man? can you tell,
cousin? 140
  Eva. Peace, I pray you. Now let us understand: there is three umpires in this matter, as
I understand; that is—Master Page, *fidelicet*,
Master Page; and there is myself, *fidelicet*, my-
self; and the three party is, lastly and finally,
mine host of the Garter.
  Page. We three, to hear it and end it between
them. 148

  Eva. Fery goot: I will make a prief of it in
my note-book; and we will afterwards ork upon
the cause with as great discreetly as we can.
  Fal. Pistol! 152
  Pist. He hears with ears.
  Eva. The tevil and his tam! what phrase is
this, 'He hears with ear?' Why, it is affectations.
  Fal. Pistol, did you pick Master Slender's
purse? 157
  Slen. Ay, by these gloves, did he,—or I would
I might never come in mine own great chamber
again else,—of seven groats in mill-sixpences,
and two Edward shovel-boards, that cost me two
shilling and two pence a-piece of Yead Miller, by
these gloves.
  Fal. Is this true, Pistol? 164
  Eva. No; it is false, if it is a pick-purse.
  Pist. Ha, thou mountain foreigner!—Sir John
    and master mine,
I combat challenge of this latten bilbo.
Word of denial in thy labras here! 168
Word of denial: froth and scum, thou liest.
  Slen. By these gloves, then, 'twas he.
  Nym. Be avised, sir, and pass good humours.
I will say, 'marry trap,' with you, if you run the
nuthook's humour on me: that is the very note
of it. 174
  Slen. By this hat, then, he in the red face had
it; for though I cannot remember what I did
when you made me drunk, yet I am not altoge-
ther an ass. 178
  Fal. What say you, Scarlet and John?
  Bard. Why, sir, for my part, I say, the gentleman had drunk himself out of his five sentences.
  Eva. It is his 'five senses;' fie, what the ignorance is! 183
  Bard. And being fap, sir, was, as they say,
cashier'd; and so conclusions pass'd the careires.
  Slen. Ay, you spake in Latin then too; but
'tis no matter. I'll ne'er be drunk whilst I live
again, but in honest, civil, godly company, for
this trick: if I be drunk, I'll be drunk with those
that have the fear of God, and not with drunken
knaves. 191
  Eva. So Got udge me, that is a virtuous mind.
  Fal. You hear all these matters denied, gentlemen; you hear it. 194

Enter ANNE PAGE, *with Wine;* MISTRESS FORD
and MISTRESS PAGE.

  Page. Nay, daughter, carry the wine in; we'll
drink within.   [*Exit* ANNE PAGE.
  Slen. O heaven! this is Mistress Anne Page.
  Page. How now, Mistress Ford!
  Fal. Mistress Ford, by my troth, you are very
well met: by your leave, good mistress. 200
    [*Kissing her.*
  Page. Wife, bid these gentlemen welcome.
Come, we have a hot venison pasty to dinner:
come, gentlemen, I hope we shall drink down all
unkindness. 204
    [*Exeunt all but* SHALLOW, SLENDER,
      and EVANS.
  Slen. I had rather than forty shillings I had
my Book of Songs and Sonnets here.

Enter SIMPLE.

How now, Simple! Where have you been? I must wait on myself, must I? You have not the Book of Riddles about you, have you?   209

Sim. Book of Riddles! why, did you not lend it to Alice Shortcake upon All-Hallowmas last, a fortnight afore Michaelmas?   212

Shal. Come, coz; come, coz; we stay for you. A word with you, coz; marry, this, coz: there is, as 'twere a tender, a kind of tender, made afar off by Sir Hugh here: do you understand me?   216

Slen. Ay, sir, you shall find me reasonable: if it be so, I shall do that that is reason.

Shal. Nay, but understand me.

Slen. So I do, sir.   220

Eva. Give ear to his motions, Master Slender: I will description the matter to you, if you pe capacity of it.

Slen. Nay, I will do as my cousin Shallow says. I pray you pardon me; he's a justice of peace in his country, simple though I stand here.

Eva. But that is not the question; the question is concerning your marriage.   228

Shal. Ay, there's the point, sir.

Eva. Marry, is it, the very point of it; to Mistress Anne Page.

Slen. Why, if it be so, I will marry her upon any reasonable demands.   233

Eva. But can you affection the 'oman? Let us command to know that of your mouth or of your lips; for divers philosophers hold that the lips is parcel of the mouth: therefore, precisely, can you carry your good will to the maid?   239

Shal. Cousin Abraham Slender, can you love her?

Slen. I hope, sir, I will do as it shall become one that would do reason.   243

Eva. Nay, Got's lords and his ladies! you must speak possitable, if you can carry her your desires towards her.

Shal. That you must. Will you, upon good dowry, marry her?   248

Slen. I will do a greater thing than that, upon your request, cousin, in any reason.

Shal. Nay, conceive me, conceive me, sweet coz: what I do, is to pleasure you, coz. Can you love the maid?   253

Slen. I will marry her, sir, at your request; but if there be no great love in the beginning, yet heaven may decrease it upon better acquaintance, when we are married and have more occasion to know one another: I hope, upon familiarity will grow more contempt: but if you say, 'Marry her,' I will marry her; that I am freely dissolved, and dissolutely.   261

Eva. It is a fery discretion answer; save, the faul is in the ort 'dissolutely:' the ort is, according to our meaning, 'resolutely.' His meaning is goot.

Shal. Ay, I think my cousin meant well.

Slen. Ay, or else I would I might be hanged, la!   268

Shal. Here comes fair Mistress Anne.

Re-enter ANNE PAGE.

Would I were young for your sake, Mistress Anne.

Anne. The dinner is on the table; my father desires your worships' company.   273

Shal. I will wait on him, fair Mistress Anne.

Eva. Od's plessed will! I will not be absence at the grace.   276

[*Exeunt* SHALLOW *and* EVANS.

Anne. Will't please your worship to come in, sir?

Slen. No, I thank you, forsooth, heartily; I am very well.   280

Anne. The dinner attends you, sir.

Slen. I am not a-hungry, I thank you forsooth. Go, sirrah, for all you are my man, go wait upon my cousin Shallow. [*Exit* SIMPLE.] A justice of peace sometime may be beholding to his friend for a man. I keep but three men and a boy yet, till my mother be dead; but what though? yet I live like a poor gentleman born.   289

Anne. I may not go in without your worship: they will not sit till you come.

Slen. I' faith, I'll eat nothing; I thank you as much as though I did.

Anne. I pray you, sir, walk in.   294

Slen. I had rather walk here, I thank you. I bruised my shin th' other day with playing at sword and dagger with a master of fence; three veneys for a dish of stewed prunes;—and, by my troth, I cannot abide the smell of hot meat since. Why do your dogs bark so? be there bears i' the town?   301

Anne. I think there are, sir; I heard them talked of.

Slen. I love the sport well; but I shall as soon quarrel at it as any man in England. You are afraid, if you see the bear loose, are you not?

Anne. Ay, indeed, sir.   308

Slen. That's meat and drink to me, now: I have seen Sackerson loose twenty times, and have taken him by the chain; but, I warrant you, the women have so cried and shrieked at it, that it passed: but women, indeed, cannot abide 'em; they are very ill-favoured rough things.   315

Re-enter PAGE.

Page. Come, gentle Master Slender, come; we stay for you.

Slen. I'll eat nothing, I thank you, sir.

Page. By cock and pie, you shall not choose, sir! come, come.   320

Slen. Nay, pray you, lead the way.

Page. Come on, sir.

Slen. Mistress Anne, yourself shall go first.

Anne. Not I, sir; pray you, keep on.   324

Slen. Truly, I will not go first: truly, la! I will not do you that wrong.

Anne. I pray you, sir.

Slen. I'll rather be unmannerly than troublesome. You do yourself wrong, indeed, la!   329

[*Exeunt.*

SCENE II.—*The Same.*

Enter SIR HUGH EVANS *and* SIMPLE.

Eva. Go your ways, and ask of Doctor Caius' house, which is the way: and there dwells one Mistress Quickly, which is in the manner of his nurse, or his try nurse, or his cook, or his laundry, his washer, and his wringer.   5

Sim. Well, sir.

Eva. Nay, it is petter yet. Give her this letter; for it is a 'oman that altogether 's acquaintance with Mistress Anne Page: and the letter is, to desire and require her to solicit your master's desires to Mistress Anne Page. I pray you, be gone: I will make an end of my dinner; there 's pippins and seese to come.   13
[*Exeunt.*

SCENE III.—*A Room in the Garter Inn.*

Enter FALSTAFF, HOST, BARDOLPH, NYM, PISTOL, *and* ROBIN.

Fal. Mine host of the Garter!

Host. What says my bully-rook? Speak scholarly and wisely.

Fal. Truly, mine host, I must turn away some of my followers.   5

Host. Discard, bully Hercules; cashier: let them wag; trot, trot.

Fal. I sit at ten pounds a week.   8

Host. Thou'rt an emperor, Cæsar, Keisar, and Pheezar. I will entertain Bardolph; he shall draw, he shall tap: said I well, bully Hector?   12

Fal. Do so, good mine host.

Host. I have spoke; let him follow. [*To* BARD.] Let me see thee froth and lime: I am at a word; follow.   [*Exit.*

Fal. Bardolph, follow him. A tapster is a good trade: an old cloak makes a new jerkin; a withered serving-man, a fresh tapster. Go; adieu.

Bard. It is a life that I have desired. I will thrive.   20

Pist. O base Hungarian wight! wilt thou the spigot wield?   [*Exit* BARD.

Nym. He was gotten in drink; is not the humour conceited?   24

Fal. I am glad I am so acquit of this tinderbox; his thefts were too open; his filching was like an unskilful singer; he kept not time.

Nym. The good humour is to steal at a minim's rest.   29

Pist. 'Convey,' the wise it call. 'Steal!' foh! a fico for the phrase!

Fal. Well, sirs, I am almost out at heels.   32

Pist. Why, then, let kibes ensue.

Fal. There is no remedy; I must cony-catch, I must shift.

Pist. Young ravens must have food.   36

Fal. Which of you know Ford of this town?

Pist. I ken the wight: he is of substance good.

Fal. My honest lads, I will tell you what I am about.   41

Pist. Two yards, and more.

Fal. No quips now, Pistol! Indeed, I am in the waist two yards about; but I am now about no waste; I am about thrift. Briefly, I do mean to make love to Ford's wife: I spy entertainment in her; she discourses, she carves, she gives the leer of invitation: I can construe the action of her familiar style; and the hardest voice of her behaviour, to be Englished rightly, is, 'I am Sir John Falstaff's.'   51

Pist. He hath studied her well, and translated her well, out of honesty into English.

Nym. The anchor is deep: will that humour pass?

Fal. Now, the report goes she has all the rule of her husband's purse; he hath a legion of angels.

Pist. As many devils entertain, and 'To her, boy,' say I.   60

Nym. The humour rises; it is good: humour me the angels.

Fal. I have writ me here a letter to her; and here another to Page's wife, who even now gave me good eyes too, examined my parts with most judicious œilliades: sometimes the beam of her view gilded my foot, sometimes my portly belly.

Pist. Then did the sun on dunghill shine.   68

Nym. I thank thee for that humour.

Fal. O! she did so course o'er my exteriors with such a greedy intention, that the appetite of her eye did seem to scorch me up like a burning-glass. Here's another letter to her: she bears the purse too; she is a region in Guiana, all gold and bounty. I will be 'cheator to them both, and they shall be exchequers to me: they shall be my East and West Indies, and I will trade to them both. Go bear thou this letter to Mistress Page; and thou this to Mistress Ford. We will thrive, lads, we will thrive.   80

Pist. Shall I Sir Pandarus of Troy become, And by my side wear steel? then, Lucifer take all!

Nym. I will run no base humour: here, take the humour-letter. I will keep the haviour of reputation.   85

Fal. [*To* ROBIN.] Hold, sirrah, bear you these letters tightly:
Sail like my pinnace to these golden shores.
Rogues, hence! avaunt! vanish like hailstones, go;
Trudge, plod away o' the hoof; seek shelter, pack!
Falstaff will learn the humour of this age,
French thrift, you rogues: myself and skirted page.   [*Exeunt* FALSTAFF *and* ROBIN.

Pist. Let vultures gripe thy guts! for gourd and fullam holds,   92
And high and low beguile the rich and poor.
Tester I'll have in pouch when thou shalt lack,
Base Phrygian Turk!

Nym. I have operations in my head, which be humours of revenge.   97

Pist. Wilt thou revenge?

Nym. By welkin and her star!

Pist. With wit or steel?   100

Nym. With both the humours, I:
I will discuss the humour of this love to Page.

Pist. And I to Ford shall eke unfold
    How Falstaff, varlet vile,   104
His dove will prove, his gold will hold,
And his soft couch defile.

Nym. My humour shall not cool: I will
incense Page to deal with poison; I will possess
him with yellowness, for the revolt of mine is
dangerous: that is my true humour.   110

Pist. Thou art the Mars of malcontents: I
second thee; troop on.   *[Exeunt.*

SCENE IV.—*A Room in* DOCTOR CAIUS's *House.*

Enter MISTRESS QUICKLY *and* SIMPLE.

Quick. What, John Rugby!—

Enter RUGBY.

I pray thee, go to the casement, and see if you
can see my master, Master Doctor Caius, coming: if he do, i' faith, and find anybody in the
house, here will be an old abusing of God's
patience and the king's English.   6

Rug. I'll go watch.

Quick. Go; and we'll have a posset for't soon
at night, in faith, at the latter end of a sea-coal
fire. *[Exit* RUGBY.] An honest, willing, kind
fellow, as ever servant shall come in house
withal; and, I warrant you, no tell-tale, nor
no breed-bate: his worst fault is, that he is
given to prayer; he is something peevish that
way, but nobody but has his fault; but let that
pass. Peter Simple you say your name is? 16

Sim. Ay, for fault of a better.

Quick. And Master Slender's your master?

Sim. Ay, forsooth.

Quick. Does he not wear a great round beard
like a glover's paring-knife?   21

Sim. No, forsooth: he hath but a little whey-
face, with a little yellow beard—a cane-coloured
beard.   24

Quick. A softly-sprighted man, is he not?

Sim. Ay, forsooth; but he is as tall a man of
his hands as any is between this and his head:
he hath fought with a warrener.   28

Quick. How say you?—O! I should remember
him: does he not hold up his head, as it were,
and strut in his gait?

Sim. Yes, indeed, does he.   32

Quick. Well, heaven send Anne Page no
worse fortune! Tell Master Parson Evans I will
do what I can for your master: Anne is a good
girl, and I wish—   36

Re-enter RUGBY.

Rug. Out, alas! here comes my master.

Quick. We shall all be shent. Run in here,
good young man; go into this closet. *[Shuts* SIM-
PLE *in the closet.]* He will not stay long. What,
John Rugby! John, what, John, I say! Go, John,
go inquire for my master; I doubt he be not
well, that he comes not home. *[Exit* RUGBY.]
[Sings.]

    'And down, down, adown-a,' &c.   44

Enter DOCTOR CAIUS.

Caius. Vat is you sing? I do not like dese
toys. Pray you, go and vetch me in my closet
une boitine verde; a box, a green-a box: do intend vat I speak? a green-a box.   48

Quick. Ay, forsooth; I'll fetch it you. *[Aside.]*
I am glad he went not in himself: if he had found
the young man, he would have been horn-mad.

Caius. Fe, fe, fe, fe! ma foi, il fait fort
chaud. Je m'en vais à la cour,—la grande
affaire.   54

Quick. Is it this, sir?

Caius. Oui; mettez le au mon pocket; dé-
pêchez, quickly.—Vere is dat knave Rugby?

Quick. What, John Rugby! John!   58

Re-enter RUGBY.

Rug. Here, sir.

Caius. You are John Rugby, and you are
Jack Rugby: come, take-a your rapier, and
come after my heel to de court.

Rug. 'Tis ready, sir, here in the porch.   63

Caius. By my trot, I tarry too long.—Od's
me! *Qu'ay j'oublié?* dere is some simples in my
closet, dat I vill not for de varld I shall leave
behind.   67

Quick. *[Aside.]* Ay me! he'll find the young
man there, and be mad.

Caius. O diable! diable! vat is in my closet?
—Villain! larron! *[Pulling* SIMPLE *out.]* Rugby,
my rapier!   72

Quick. Good master, be content.

Caius. Verefore shall I be content-a?

Quick. The young man is an honest man.

Caius. Vat shall de honest man do in my
closet? dere is no honest man dat shall come in
my closet.   78

Quick. I beseech you, be not so phlegmatic.
Hear the truth of it: he came of an errand to
me from Parson Hugh.   81

Caius. Vell.

Sim. Ay, forsooth, to desire her to—

Quick. Peace, I pray you.   84

Caius. Peace-a your tongue!—Speak-a your
tale.

Sim. To desire this honest gentlewoman, your
maid, to speak a good word to Mistress Anne
Page for my master in the way of marriage. 89

Quick. This is all, indeed, la! but I'll ne'er
put my finger in the fire, and need not.

Caius. Sir Hugh send-a you?—Rugby, *baillez*
me some paper: tarry you a little-a while. 93
                  [Writes.

Quick. I am glad he is so quiet: if he had
been throughly moved, you should have heard
him so loud, and so melancholy. But, notwithstanding, man, I'll do your master what good I
can; and the very yea and the no is, the French
doctor, my master,—I may call him my master,
look you, for I keep his house; and I wash,
wring, brew, bake, scour, dress meat and drink,
make the beds, and do all myself,—   102

Sim. 'Tis a great charge to come under one
body's hand.

Quick. Are you avis'd o' that? you shall find

it a great charge: and to be up early and down late; but notwithstanding,—to tell you in your ear,—I would have no words of it,—my master himself is in love with Mistress Anne Page: but notwithstanding that, I know Anne's mind, that's neither here nor there.   111

Caius. You jack'nape, give-a dis letter to Sir Hugh; by gar, it is a challenge: I vill cut his troat in de Park; and I vill teach a scurvy jack-a-nape priest to meddle or make. You may be gone; it is not good you tarry here: by gar, I vill cut all his two stones; by gar, he shall not have a stone to trow at his dog. [*Exit* SIMPLE.

Quick. Alas! he speaks but for his friend.   119

Caius. It is no matter-a for dat:—do not you tell-a me dat I shall have Anne Page for myself? By gar, I vill kill de Jack priest; and I have appointed mine host of de *Jartiere* to measure our weapon. By gar, I vill myself have Anne Page.

Quick. Sir, the maid loves you, and all shall be well. We must give folks leave to prate: what, the good-jer!   127

Caius. Rugby, come to the court vit me. By gar, if I have not Anne Page, I shall turn your head out of my door. Follow my heels, Rugby.
[*Exeunt* CAIUS *and* RUGBY.

Quick. You shall have An fool's-head of your own. No, I know Anne's mind for that: never a woman in Windsor knows more of Anne's mind than I do; nor can do more than I do with her, I thank heaven.

Fent. [*Within.*] Who's within there? ho!   136

Quick. Who's there, I trow? Come near the house, I pray you.

Enter FENTON.

Fent. How now, good woman! how dost thou?

Quick. The better, that it pleases your good worship to ask.   141

Fent. What news? how does pretty Mistress Anne?

Quick. In truth, sir, and she is pretty, and honest, and gentle; and one that is your friend, I can tell you that by the way; I praise heaven for it.

Fent. Shall I do any good, thinkest thou? Shall I not lose my suit?   149

Quick. Troth, sir, all is in his hands above: but notwithstanding, Master Fenton, I'll be sworn on a book, she loves you. Have not your worship a wart above your eye?   153

Fent. Yes, marry have I; what of that?

Quick. Well, thereby hangs a tale. Good faith, it is such another Nan; but, I detest, an honest maid as ever broke bread: we had an hour's talk of that wart. I shall never laugh but in that maid's company:—but, indeed, she is given too much to allicholy and musing. But for you—well, go to.   161

Fent. Well, I shall see her to-day. Hold, there's money for thee; let me have thy voice in my behalf: if thou seest her before me, commend me.   165

Quick. Will I? i' faith, that we will: and I will tell your worship more of the wart the

next time we have confidence; and of other wooers.   169

Fent. Well, farewell; I am in great haste now.

Quick. Farewell to your worship.—[*Exit* FENTON.] Truly, an honest gentleman: but Anne loves him not; for I know Anne's mind as well as another does. Out upon't! what have I forgot?   [*Exit.*

ACT II

SCENE I.—*Before* PAGE'S *House.*

Enter MISTRESS PAGE, *with a Letter.*

Mrs. Page. What! have I 'scaped love-letters in the holiday-time of my beauty, and am I now a subject for them? Let me see.

Ask me no reason why I love you; for though Love use Reason for his physician, he admits him not for his counsellor. You are not young, no more am I; go to then, there's sympathy; you are merry, so am I; ha! ha! then, there's more sympathy; you love sack, and so do I; would you desire better sympathy? Let it suffice thee, Mistress Page, at the least, if the love of a soldier can suffice, that I love thee. I will not say, pity me,—'tis not a soldier-like phrase; but I say, love me. By me,

> Thine own true knight,
> By day or night,   16
> Or any kind of light,
> With all his might
> For thee to fight,

JOHN FALSTAFF.

What a Herod of Jewry is this! O wicked, wicked world! one that is well-nigh worn to pieces with age, to show himself a young gallant! What an unweighed behaviour hath this Flemish drunkard picked, with the devil's name! out of my conversation, that he dares in this manner assay me? Why, he hath not been thrice in my company! What should I say to him? I was then frugal of my mirth:—heaven forgive me! Why, I'll exhibit a bill in the parliament for the putting down of men. How shall I be revenged on him? for revenged I will be, as sure as his guts are made of puddings.   32

Enter MISTRESS FORD.

Mrs. Ford. Mistress Page! trust me, I was going to your house.

Mrs. Page. And, trust me, I was coming to you. You look very ill.   36

Mrs. Ford. Nay, I'll ne'er believe that: I have to show to the contrary.

Mrs. Page. Faith, but you do, in my mind.

Mrs. Ford. Well, I do then; yet, I say I could show you to the contrary. O, Mistress Page! give me some counsel.   42

Mrs. Page. What's the matter, woman?

Mrs. Ford. O woman, if it were not for one trifling respect, I could come to such honour!   45

Mrs. Page. Hang the trifle, woman; take the honour. What is it?—dispense with trifles;—what is it?   48

Mrs. Ford. If I would but go to hell for an eternal moment or so, I could be knighted.

Mrs. Page. What? thou liest. Sir Alice Ford! These knights will hack; and so thou shouldst not alter the article of thy gentry. 53

Mrs. Ford. We burn daylight: here, read, read; perceive how I might be knighted. I shall think the worse of fat men as long as I have an eye to make difference of men's liking: and yet he would not swear; praised women's modesty; and gave such orderly and well-behaved reproof to all uncomeliness, that I would have sworn his disposition would have gone to the truth of his words; but they do no more adhere and keep place together than the Hundredth Psalm to the tune of 'Green Sleeves.' What tempest, I trow, threw this whale, with so many tuns of oil in his belly, ashore at Windsor? How shall I be revenged on him? I think, the best way were to entertain him with hope, till the wicked fire of lust have melted him in his own grease. Did you ever hear the like? 70

Mrs. Page. Letter for letter, but that the name of Page and Ford differs! To thy great comfort in this mystery of ill opinions, here's the twin brother of thy letter: but let thine inherit first; for, I protest, mine never shall. I warrant, he hath a thousand of these letters, writ with blank space for different names, sure more, and these are of the second edition. He will print them, out of doubt; for he cares not what he puts into the press, when he would put us two: I had rather be a giantess, and lie under Mount Pelion. Well, I will find you twenty lascivious turtles ere one chaste man. 83

Mrs. Ford. Why, this is the very same; the very hand, the very words. What doth he think of us?

Mrs. Page. Nay, I know not: it makes me almost ready to wrangle with mine own honesty. I'll entertain myself like one that I am not acquainted withal; for, sure, unless he know some strain in me, that I know not myself, he would never have boarded me in this fury.

Mrs. Ford. Boarding call you it? I'll be sure to keep him above deck. 93

Mrs. Page. So will I: if he come under my hatches, I'll never to sea again. Let's be revenged on him: let's appoint him a meeting; give him a show of comfort in his suit, and lead him on with a fine-baited delay, till he hath pawned his horses to mine host of the Garter. 99

Mrs. Ford. Nay, I will consent to act any villany against him, that may not sully the chariness of our honesty. O, that my husband saw this letter! it would give eternal food to his jealousy.

Mrs. Page. Why, look, where he comes; and my good man too: he's as far from jealousy, as I am from giving him cause; and that, I hope, is an unmeasurable distance.

Mrs. Ford. You are the happier woman. 108

Mrs. Page. Let's consult together against this greasy knight. Come hither. [*They retire.*

Enter FORD, PISTOL, PAGE, *and* NYM.

Ford. Well, I hope it be not so.

Pist. Hope is a curtal dog in some affairs: 112 Sir John affects thy wife.

Ford. Why, sir, my wife is not young.

Pist. He woos both high and low, both rich and poor,

Both young and old, one with another, Ford. 116

He loves the galimaufry: Ford, perpend.

Ford. Love my wife!

Pist. With liver burning hot: prevent, or go thou,

Like Sir Actæon he, with Ringwood at thy heels.—

O! odious is the name! 121

Ford. What name, sir?

Pist. The horn, I say. Farewell:

Take heed; have open eye, for thieves do foot by night: 124

Take heed, ere summer comes or cuckoo-birds do sing.

Away, sir Corporal Nym!

Believe it, Page; he speaks sense. [*Exit.*

Ford. [*Aside.*] I will be patient: I will find out this. 129

Nym. [*To* PAGE.] And this is true; I like not the humour of lying. He hath wronged me in some humours: I should have borne the humoured letter to her, but I have a sword and it shall bite upon my necessity. He loves your wife; there's the short and the long. My name is Corporal Nym; I speak, and I avouch 'tis true: my name is Nym, and Falstaff loves your wife. Adieu. I love not the humour of bread and cheese; and there's the humour of it. Adieu. [*Exit.*

Page. [*Aside.*] 'The humour of it,' quoth 'a! here's a fellow frights humour out of his wits. 142

Ford. I will seek out Falstaff.

Page. I never heard such a drawling, affecting rogue. 145

Ford. If I do find it: well.

Page. I will not believe such a Cataian, though the priest o' the town commended him for a true man. 149

Ford. 'Twas a good sensible fellow: well.

Page. How now, Meg!

Mrs. Page. Whither go you, George?—Hark you. 153

Mrs. Ford. How now, sweet Frank! why art thou melancholy?

Ford. I melancholy! I am not melancholy. Get you home, go. 157

Mrs. Ford. Faith, thou hast some crotchets in thy head now. Will you go, Mistress Page?

Mrs. Page. Have with you. You'll come to dinner, George? [*Aside to* MRS. FORD.] Look, who comes yonder: she shall be our messenger to this paltry knight.

Mrs. Ford. Trust me, I thought on her: she'll fit it. 165

Enter MISTRESS QUICKLY.

Mrs. Page. You are come to see my daughter Anne?

Quick. Ay, forsooth; and, I pray, how does good Mistress Anne? 169

Mrs. Page. Go in with us, and see: we'd have an hour's talk with you.

[*Exeunt* MISTRESS PAGE, MISTRESS FORD, *and* MISTRESS QUICKLY.

Page. How now, Master Ford!   172
Ford. You heard what this knave told me, did you not?
Page. Yes; and you heard what the other told me?   176
Ford. Do you think there is truth in them?
Page. Hang 'em, slaves! I do not think the knight would offer it: but these that accuse him in his intent towards our wives, are a yoke of his discarded men; very rogues, now they be out of service.
Ford. Were they his men?
Page. Marry, were they.   184
Ford. I like it never the better for that. Does he lie at the Garter?
Page. Ay, marry, does he. If he should intend this voyage towards my wife, I would turn her loose to him; and what he gets more of her than sharp words, let it lie on my head.
Ford. I do not misdoubt my wife, but I would be loath to turn them together. A man may be too confident: I would have nothing 'lie on my head:' I cannot be thus satisfied.   194
Page. Look, where my ranting host of the Garter comes. There is either liquor in his pate or money in his purse when he looks so merrily.—   198

Enter Host and SHALLOW.

How now, mine host!
Host. How now, bully-rook! thou'rt a gentleman. Cavaliero-justice, I say!   201
Shal. I follow, mine host, I follow. Good even and twenty, good Master Page! Master Page, will you go with us? we have sport in hand.   204
Host. Tell him, cavaliero-justice; tell him, bully-rook.
Shal. Sir, there is a fray to be fought between Sir Hugh the Welsh priest and Caius the French doctor.   209
Ford. Good mine host o' the Garter, a word with you.
Host. What sayest thou, my bully-rook?   212
                                    [*They go aside.*
Shal. [*To* PAGE.] Will you go with us to behold it? My merry host hath had the measuring of their weapons, and, I think, hath appointed them contrary places; for, believe me, I hear the parson is no jester. Hark, I will tell you what our sport shall be.   [*They go aside.*
Host. Hast thou no suit against my knight, my guest-cavalier?   220
Ford. None, I protest: but I'll give you a pottle of burnt sack to give me recourse to him and tell him my name is Brook, only for a jest.
Host. My hand, bully: thou shalt have egress and regress; said I well? and thy name shall be Brook. It is a merry knight. Will you go, mynheers?
Shal. Have with you, mine host.   228
Page. I have heard, the Frenchman hath good skill in his rapier.
Shal. Tut, sir! I could have told you more. In these times you stand on distance, your passes, stoccadoes, and I know not what: 'tis the heart, Master Page; 'tis here, 'tis here. I

have seen the time with my long sword I would have made you four tall fellows skip like rats.   236
Host. Here, boys, here, here! shall we wag?
Page. Have with you. I had rather hear them scold than fight.
                        [*Exeunt Host,* SHALLOW, *and* PAGE.
Ford. Though Page be a secure fool, and stands so firmly on his wife's frailty, yet I cannot put off my opinion so easily. She was in his company at Page's house, and what they made there, I know not. Well, I will look further into't; and I have a disguise to sound Falstaff. If I find her honest, I lose not my labour; if she be otherwise, 'tis labour well bestowed. [*Exit.*

SCENE II.—*A Room in the Garter Inn.*

Enter FALSTAFF *and* PISTOL.

Fal. I will not lend thee a penny.
Pist. Why, then the world's mine oyster, Which I with sword will open.
I will retort the sum in equipage.   4
Fal. Not a penny. I have been content, sir, you should lay my countenance to pawn: I have grated upon my good friends for three reprieves for you and your coach-fellow Nym; or else you had looked through the grate, like a geminy of baboons. I am damned in hell for swearing to gentlemen my friends, you were good soldiers and tall fellows; and when Mistress Bridget lost the handle of her fan, I took't upon mine honour thou hadst it not.   14
Pist. Didst thou not share? hadst thou not fifteen pence?
Fal. Reason, you rogue, reason: thinkest thou, I'll endanger my soul gratis? At a word, hang no more about me; I am no gibbet for you: go: a short knife and a throng!—to your manor of Pickt-hatch! go. You'll not bear a letter for me, you rogue!—you stand upon your honour!—Why, thou unconfinable baseness, it is as much as I can do to keep the terms of mine honour precise. I, I, I, myself sometimes, leaving the fear of God on the left hand and hiding mine honour in my necessity, am fain to shuffle, to hedge and to lurch; and yet you, rogue, will ensconce your rags, your cat-a-mountain looks, your red-lattice phrases, and your bold-beating oaths, under the shelter of your honour! You will not do it, you!
Pist. I do relent: what wouldst thou more of man?   32

Enter ROBIN.

Rob. Sir, here's a woman would speak with you.
Fal. Let her approach.

Enter MISTRESS QUICKLY.

Quick. Give your worship good morrow.   36
Fal. Good morrow, good wife.
Quick. Not so, an't please your worship.
Fal. Good maid, then.
Quick. I'll be sworn   40
As my mother was, the first hour I was born.

Fal. I do believe the swearer. What with me?

Quick. Shall I vouchsafe your worship a word or two? 44

Fal. Two thousand, fair woman; and I'll vouchsafe thee the hearing.

Quick. There is one Mistress Ford, sir,—I pray, come a little nearer this ways:—I myself dwell with Master Doctor Caius. 49

Fal. Well, on: Mistress Ford, you say,—

Quick. Your worship says very true:—I pray your worship, come a little nearer this ways. 52

Fal. I warrant thee, nobody hears; mine own people, mine own people.

Quick. Are they so? God bless them, and make them his servants! 56

Fal. Well: Mistress Ford; what of her?

Quick. Why, sir, she's a good creature. Lord, Lord! your worship's a wanton! Well, heaven forgive you, and all of us, I pray! 60

Fal. Mistress Ford; come, Mistress Ford,—

Quick. Marry, this is the short and the long of it. You have brought her into such a canaries as 'tis wonderful: the best courtier of them all, when the court lay at Windsor, could never have brought her to such a canary; yet there has been knights, and lords, and gentlemen, with their coaches, I warrant you, coach after coach, letter after letter, gift after gift; smelling so sweetly—all musk, and so rushling, I warrant you, in silk and gold; and in such alligant terms; and in such wine and sugar of the best and the fairest, that would have won any woman's heart; and, I warrant you, they could never get an eye-wink of her. I had myself twenty angels given me this morning; but I defy all angels, in any such sort, as they say, but in the way of honesty: and, I warrant you, they could never get her so much as sip on a cup with the proudest of them all; and yet there has been earls, nay, which is more, pensioners; but, I warrant you, all is one with her.

Fal. But what says she to me? be brief, my good she-Mercury. 83

Quick. Marry, she hath received your letter; for the which she thanks you a thousand times; and she gives you to notify that her husband will be absence from his house between ten and eleven. 88

Fal. Ten and eleven?

Quick. Ay, forsooth; and then you may come and see the picture, she says, that you wot of: Master Ford, her husband, will be from home. Alas! the sweet woman leads an ill life with him; he's a very jealousy man; she leads a very frampold life with him, good heart.

Fal. Ten and eleven. Woman, commend me to her; I will not fail her. 97

Quick. Why, you say well. But I have another messenger to your worship: Mistress Page hath her hearty commendations to you too: and let me tell you in your ear, she's as fartuous a civil modest wife, and one, I tell you, that will not miss you morning nor evening prayer, as any is in Windsor, whoe'er be the other: and she bade me tell your worship that her husband is seldom from home; but, she hopes there will come a time. I never knew a woman so dote

upon a man: surely, I think you have charms, la; yes, in truth. 109

Fal. Not I, I assure thee: setting the attraction of my good parts aside, I have no other charms.

Quick. Blessing on your heart for 't! 112

Fal. But, I pray thee, tell me this: has Ford's wife and Page's wife acquainted each other how they love me? 115

Quick. That were a jest indeed! they have not so little grace, I hope: that were a trick, indeed! But Mistress Page would desire you to send her your little page, of all loves: her husband has a marvellous infection to the little page; and, truly, Master Page is an honest man. Never a wife in Windsor leads a better life than she does: do what she will, say what she will, take all, pay all, go to bed when she list, rise when she list, all is as she will: and, truly she deserves it; for if there be a kind woman in Windsor, she is one. You must send her your page; no remedy. 128

Fal. Why, I will.

Quick. Nay, but do so, then: and, look you, he may come and go between you both; and in any case have a nay-word, that you may know one another's mind, and the boy never need to understand any thing; for 'tis not good that children should know any wickedness: old folks, you know, have discretion, as they say, and know the world. 137

Fal. Fare thee well: commend me to them both. There's my purse; I am yet thy debtor.—Boy, go along with this woman.—[*Exeunt* MISTRESS QUICKLY *and* ROBIN.] This news distracts me. 142

Pist. This punk is one of Cupid's carriers. Clap on more sails; pursue; up with your fights; Give fire! she is my prize, or ocean whelm them all!   [*Exit.*

Fal. Sayest thou so, old Jack? go thy ways; I'll make more of thy old body than I have done. Will they yet look after thee? Wilt thou, after the expense of so much money, be now a gainer? Good body, I thank thee. Let them say 'tis grossly done; so it be fairly done, no matter. 151

Enter BARDOLPH, *with a cup of Sack.*

Bard. Sir John, there's one Master Brook below would fain speak with you, and be acquainted with you: and hath sent your worship a morning's draught of sack.

Fal. Brook is his name? 156

Bard. Ay, sir.

Fal. Call him in. [*Exit* BARDOLPH.] Such Brooks are welcome to me, that o'erflow such liquor. Ah, ha! Mistress Ford and Mistress Page, have I encompassed you? go to; *via!* 161

Re-enter BARDOLPH, *with* FORD *disguised.*

Ford. Bless you, sir!

Fal. And you, sir; would you speak with me?

Ford. I make bold to press with so little preparation upon you. 165

Fal. You're welcome. What's your will?—Give us leave, drawer.   [*Exit* BARDOLPH.

Ford. Sir, I am a gentleman that have spent much: my name is Brook. 169

Fal. Good Master Brook, I desire more acquaintance of you.

Ford. Good Sir John, I sue for yours: not to charge you; for I must let you understand I think myself in better plight for a lender than you are: the which hath something emboldened me to this unseasoned intrusion; for, they say, if money go before, all ways do lie open. 177

Fal. Money is a good soldier, sir, and will on.

Ford. Troth, and I have a bag of money here troubles me: if you will help to bear it, Sir John, take all, or half, for easing me of the carriage. 183

Fal. Sir, I know not how I may deserve to be your porter.

Ford. I will tell you, sir, if you will give me the hearing.

Fal. Speak, good Master Brook; I shall be glad to be your servant. 189

Ford. Sir, I hear you are a scholar,—I will be brief with you, and you have been a man long known to me, though I had never so good means, as desire, to make myself acquainted with you. I shall discover a thing to you, wherein I must very much lay open mine own imperfection; but, good Sir John, as you have one eye upon my follies, as you hear them unfolded, turn another into the register of your own, that I may pass with a reproof the easier, sith you yourself know how easy it is to be such an offender. 200

Fal. Very well, sir; proceed.

Ford. There is a gentlewoman in this town, her husband's name is Ford.

Fal. Well, sir. 204

Ford. I have long loved her, and, I protest to you, bestowed much on her; followed her with a doting observance; engrossed opportunities to meet her; fee'd every slight occasion that could but niggardly give me sight of her; not only bought many presents to give her, but have given largely to many to know what she would have given. Briefly, I have pursued her as love hath pursued me; which hath been on the wing of all occasions. But whatsoever I have merited, either in my mind or in my means, meed, I am sure, I have received none; unless experience be a jewel that I have purchased at an infinite rate; and that hath taught me to say this,

'Love like a shadow flies when substance love pursues;   220
Pursuing that that flies, and flying what pursues.

Fal. Have you received no promise of satisfaction at her hands?

Ford. Never. 224

Fal. Have you importuned her to such a purpose?

Ford. Never.

Fal. Of what quality was your love, then? 228

Ford. Like a fair house built upon another man's ground; so that I have lost my edifice by mistaking the place where I erected it.

Fal. To what purpose have you unfolded this to me? 233

Ford. When I have told you that, I have told you all. Some say, that though she appear honest to me, yet in other places she enlargeth her mirth so far that there is shrewd construction made of her. Now, Sir John, here is the heart of my purpose: you are a gentleman of excellent breeding, admirable discourse, of great admittance, authentic in your place and person, generally allowed for your many war-like, court-like, and learned preparations.

Fal. O, sir! 244

Ford. Believe it, for you know it. There is money; spend it, spend it; spend more; spend all I have; only give me so much of your time in exchange of it, as to lay an amiable siege to the honesty of this Ford's wife: use your art of wooing, win her to consent to you; if any man may, you may as soon as any. 251

Fal. Would it apply well to the vehemency of your affection, that I should win what you would enjoy? Methinks you prescribe to yourself very preposterously. 255

Ford. O, understand my drift. She dwells so securely on the excellency of her honour, that the folly of my soul dares not present itself: she is too bright to be looked against. Now, could I come to her with any detection in my hand, my desires had instance and argument to commend themselves: I could drive her then from the ward of her purity, her reputation, her marriage-vow, and a thousand other her defences, which now are too-too strongly embattled against me. What say you to't, Sir John? 266

Fal. Master Brook, I will first make bold with your money; next, give me your hand; and last, as I am a gentleman, you shall, if you will, enjoy Ford's wife.

Ford. O good sir!

Fal. I say you shall. 272

Ford. Want no money, Sir John; you shall want none.

Fal. Want no Mistress Ford, Master Brook; you shall want none. I shall be with her, I may tell you, by her own appointment; even as you came in to me, her assistant or go-between parted from me: I say I shall be with her between ten and eleven; for at that time the jealous rascally knave her husband will be forth. Come you to me at night; you shall know how I speed. 283

Ford. I am blest in your acquaintance. Do you know Ford, sir?

Fal. Hang him, poor cuckoldly knave! I know him not. Yet I wrong him, to call him poor: they say the jealous wittolly knave hath masses of money; for the which his wife seems to me well-favoured. I will use her as the key of the cuckoldly rogue's coffer; and there's my harvest-home. 292

Ford. I would you knew Ford, sir, that you might avoid him, if you saw him.

Fal. Hang him, mechanical salt-butter rogue! I will stare him out of his wits; I will awe him with my cudgel: it shall hang like a meteor o'er

the cuckold's horns. Master Brook, thou shalt
know I will predominate over the peasant, and
thou shalt lie with his wife. Come to me soon at
night. Ford's a knave, and I will aggravate his
style; thou, Master Brook, shalt know him for
knave and cuckold. Come to me soon at night.
                                            [*Exit.*
Ford. What a damned Epicurean rascal is
this! My heart is ready to crack with impatience.
Who says this is improvident jealousy? my wife
hath sent to him, the hour is fixed, the match is
made. Would any man have thought this? See
the hell of having a false woman! My bed shall
be abused, my coffers ransacked, my reputation
gnawn at; and I shall not only receive this
villanous wrong, but stand under the adoption
of abominable terms, and by him that does me
this wrong. Terms! names! Amaimon sounds
well; Lucifer, well; Barbason, well; yet they
are devil's additions, the names of fiends: but
Cuckold! Wittol!—Cuckold! the devil himself
hath not such a name. Page is an ass, a secure
ass: he will trust his wife; he will not be jealous.
I will rather trust a Fleming with my butter,
Parson Hugh the Welshman with my cheese, an
Irishman with my aqua-vitæ bottle, or a thief to
walk my ambling gelding, than my wife with herself: then she plots, then she ruminates, then she
devises; and what they think in their hearts
they may effect, they will break their hearts but
they will effect. God be praised for my jealousy! Eleven o'clock the hour: I will prevent
this, detect my wife, be revenged on Falstaff, and
laugh at Page. I will about it; better three
hours too soon than a minute too late. Fie, fie,
fie! cuckold! cuckold! cuckold!   [*Exit.*

SCENE III.—*A Field near Windsor.*

Enter CAIUS *and* RUGBY.

Caius. Jack Rugby!
Rug. Sir?
Caius. Vat is de clock, Jack?
Rug. 'Tis past the hour, sir, that Sir Hugh
promised to meet.   5
Caius. By gar, he has save his soul, dat he is
no come: he has pray his Pible vell, dat he is no
come. By gar, Jack Rugby, he is dead already,
if he be come.   9
Rug. He is wise, sir; he knew your worship
would kill him, if he came.
Caius. By gar, de herring is no dead so as I
vill kill him. Take your rapier, Jack; I vill tell
you how I vill kill him.
Rug. Alas, sir! I cannot fence.
Caius. Villany, take your rapier.   16
Rug. Forbear; here's company.

Enter Host, SHALLOW, SLENDER, *and* PAGE.

Host. Bless thee, bully doctor!
Shal. Save you, Master Doctor Caius!
Page. Now, good Master doctor!   20
Slen. Give you good morrow, sir.
Caius. Vat be all you, one, two, tree, four,
come for?

Host. To see thee fight, to see thee foin, to
see thee traverse; to see thee here, to see thee
there; to see thee pass thy punto, thy stock, thy
reverse, thy distance, thy montant. Is he dead,
my Ethiopian? is he dead, my Francisco? ha,
bully! What says my Æsculapius? my Galen?
my heart of elder? ha! is he dead, bully stale?
is he dead?   31
Caius. By gar, he is de coward Jack priest of
de vorld; he is not show his face.
Host. Thou art a Castilian King Urinal!
Hector of Greece, my boy!   35
Caius. I pray you, bear witness that me have
stay six or seven, two, tree hours for him, and
he is no come.   38
Shal. He is the wiser man, Master doctor:
he is a curer of souls, and you a curer of
bodies; if you should fight, you go against the
hair of your professions. Is it not true, Master
Page?   43
Page. Master Shallow, you have yourself been
a great fighter, though now a man of peace.
Shal. Bodykins, Master Page, though I now
be old and of the peace, if I see a sword out, my
finger itches to make one. Though we are justices and doctors and churchmen, Master Page,
we have some salt of our youth in us; we are
the sons of women, Master Page.   52
Page. 'Tis true, Master Shallow.
Shal. It will be found so, Master Page. Master Doctor Caius, I am come to fetch you home.
I am sworn of the peace: you have showed
yourself a wise physician, and Sir Hugh hath
shown himself a wise and patient churchman.
You must go with me, Master doctor.
Host. Pardon, guest-justice.—A word, Mon-
sieur Mockwater.   60
Caius. Mock-vater! vat is dat?
Host. Mock-water, in our English tongue, is
valour, bully.
Caius. By gar, den, I have as mush mock-
vater as de Englishman.—Scurvy jack-dog
priest! by gar, me vill cut his ears.
Host. He will clapper-claw thee tightly, bully.
Caius. Clapper-de-claw! vat is dat?   68
Host. That is, he will make thee amends.
Caius. By gar, me do look, he shall clapper-
de-claw me; for, by gar, me vill have it.
Host. And I will provoke him to 't, or let him
wag.   73
Caius. Me tank you for dat.
Host. And moreover,—bully, But first, Master
guest, and Master Page, and eke Cavaliero Slen-
der, go you through the town to Frogmore.   77
                                [*Aside to them.*
Page. Sir Hugh is there, is he?
Host. He is there: see what humour he is in;
and I will bring the doctor about by the fields.
Will it do well?   81
Shal. We will do it.
Page, Shal., and Slen. Adieu, good Master
doctor.   [*Exeunt* PAGE, SHAL., *and* SLEN.
Caius. By gar, me vill kill de priest; for he
speak for a jack-an-ape to Anne Page.   86
Host. Let him die. Sheathe thy impatience;
throw cold water on thy choler: go about the

fields with me through Frogmore: I will bring thee where Mistress Anne Page is, at a farm-house a-feasting; and thou shalt woo her. Cried I aim? said I well?

Caius. By gar, me tank you for dat: by gar, I love you; and I shall procure-a you de good guest, de earl, de knight, de lords, de gentlemen, my patients.   96

Host. For the which I will be thy adversary toward Anne Page: said I well?

Caius. By gar, 'tis good; vell said.

Host. Let us wag, then.   100

Caius. Come at my heels, Jack Rugby.
                                                [*Exeunt.*

ACT III

SCENE I.—*A Field near Frogmore.*

Enter SIR HUGH EVANS *and* SIMPLE.

Eva. I pray you now, good Master Slender's serving-man, and friend Simple by your name, which way have you looked for Master Caius, that calls himself doctor of physic?   4

Sim. Marry, sir, the pittie-ward, the park-ward, every way; old Windsor way, and every way but the town way.

Eva. I most fehemently desire you you will also look that way.   9

Sim. I will, sir.   [*Exit.*

Eva. Pless my soul! how full of chollors I am, and trempling of mind! I shall be glad if he have deceived me. How melancholies I am! I will knog his urinals about his knave's costard when I have goot opportunities for the 'ork: pless my soul!   [*Sings.*

> To shallow rivers, to whose falls   17
> Melodious birds sing madrigals;
> There will we make our peds of roses,
> And a thousand fragrant posies.   20
> To shallow—

Mercy on me! I have a great dispositions to cry.
                                                [*Sings.*
> Melodious birds sing madrigals,—
> When as I sat in Pabylon,—   24
> And a thousand vagram posies.
> To shallow,—

Re-enter SIMPLE.

Sim. Yonder he is coming, this way, Sir Hugh.

Eva. He's welcome.   [*Sings.*
> To shallow rivers, to whose falls—   29

Heaven prosper the right!—what weapons is he?

Sim. No weapons, sir. There comes my master, Master Shallow, and another gentleman, from Frogmore, over the stile, this way.   33

Eva. Pray you, give me my gown; or else keep it in your arms.   [*Reads in a book.*

Enter PAGE, SHALLOW, *and* SLENDER.

Shal. How now, Master Parson! Good morrow, good Sir Hugh. Keep a gamester from the dice, and a good student from his book, and it is wonderful.

Slen. [*Aside.*] Ah, sweet Anne Page!   40

Page. Save you, good Sir Hugh!

Eva. Pless you from His mercy sake, all of you!

Shal. What, the sword and the word! do you study them both, Master Parson?   45

Page. And youthful still in your doublet and hose! this raw rheumatic day?

Eva. There is reasons and causes for it.   48

Page. We are come to you to do a good office, Master parson.

Eva. Fery well: what is it?

Page. Yonder is a most reverend gentleman, who, belike having received wrong by some person, is at most odds with his own gravity and patience that ever you saw.   55

Shal. I have lived fourscore years and up-ward; I never heard a man of his place, gravity, and learning, so wide of his own respect.

Eva. What is he?

Page. I think you know him; Master Doctor Caius, the renowned French physician.   61

Eva. Got's will, and his passion of my heart! I had as lief you would tell me of a mess of porridge.   64

Page. Why?

Eva. He has no more knowledge in Hibbo-crates and Galen,—and he is a knave besides; a cowardly knave as you would desires to be acquainted withal.

Page. I warrant you, he's the man should fight with him.

Slen. [*Aside.*] O, sweet Anne Page!   72

Shal. It appears so, by his weapons. Keep them asunder: here comes Doctor Caius.

Enter HOST, CAIUS, *and* RUGBY.

Page. Nay, good Master parson, keep in your weapon.   76

Shal. So do you, good Master doctor.

Host. Disarm them, and let them question: let them keep their limbs whole and hack our English.   80

Caius. I pray you, let-a me speak a word vit your ear: verefore vill you not meet-a me?

Eva. [*Aside to Caius.*] Pray you, use your patience: in good time.   84

Caius. By gar, you are de coward, de Jack dog, John ape.

Eva. [*Aside to Caius.*] Pray you, let us not be laughing-stogs to other men's humours; I desire you in friendship, and I will one way or other make you amends: [*Aloud.*] I will knog your urinals about your knave's cogscomb for missing your meetings and appointments.   92

Caius. Diable!—Jack Rugby,—mine host de Jarretierre,—have I not stay for him to kill him? have I not, at de place I did appoint?

Eva. As I am a Christians soul, now, look you, this is the place appointed: I'll be judgment by mine host of the Garter.

Host. Peace, I say, Gallia and Guallia; French and Welsh, soul-curer and body-curer!   100

Caius. Ay, dat is very good; excellent.

Host. Peace, I say! hear mine host of the Garter. Am I politic? am I subtle? am I a Machiavel? Shall I lose my doctor? no; he gives me the potions and the motions. Shall I lose my parson, my priest, my Sir Hugh? no; he gives me the proverbs and the no-verbs. Give

me thy hand, terrestrial; so;—give me thy hand,
celestial; so. Boys of art, I have deceived you
both; I have directed you to wrong places:
your hearts are mighty, your skins are whole,
and let burnt sack be the issue. Come, lay their
swords to pawn. Follow me, lads of peace;
follow, follow, follow.   114
Shal. Trust me, a mad host!—Follow, gentlemen, follow.
Slen. [*Aside.*] O, sweet Anne Page!
[*Exeunt* SHALLOW, SLENDER, PAGE, *and* Host.
Caius. Ha! do I perceive dat? have you
make-a de sot of us, ha, ha?   119
Eva. This is well; he has made us his vlout-
ing-stog. I desire you that we may be friends
and let us knog our prains together to be revenge
on this same scall, scurvy, cogging companion,
the host of the Garter.   124
Caius. By gar, vit all my heart. He promise
to bring me vere is Anne Page: by gar, he
deceive me too.
Eva. Well, I will smite his noddles. Pray
you, follow.   [*Exeunt.*

Scene II.—*A Street in Windsor.*

Enter MISTRESS PAGE *and* ROBIN.

Mrs. Page. Nay, keep your way, little gallant:
you were wont to be a follower, but now you
are a leader. Whether had you rather lead
mine eyes, or eye your master's heels ?   4
Rob. I had rather, forsooth, go before you
like a man than follow him like a dwarf.
Mrs. Page. O! you are a flattering boy: now
I see you'll be a courtier.   8

Enter FORD.

Ford. Well met, Mistress Page. Whither go
you?
Mrs. Page. Truly, sir, to see your wife: is
she at home?   12
Ford. Ay; and as idle as she may hang together, for want of company. I think, if your
husbands were dead, you two would marry.
Mrs. Page. Be sure of that,—two other
husbands.   17
Ford. Where had you this pretty weather-
cock?
Mrs. Page. I cannot tell what the dickens
his name is my husband had him of. What do
you call your knight's name, sirrah?
Rob. Sir John Falstaff.
Ford. Sir John Falstaff!   24
Mrs. Page. He, he; I can never hit on's
name. There is such a league between my good
man and he! Is your wife at home indeed?
Ford. Indeed she is.   28
Mrs. Page. By your leave, sir: I am sick till
I see her.   [*Exeunt* MISTRESS PAGE *and* ROBIN.
Ford. Has Page any brains? hath he any
eyes? hath he any thinking? Sure, they sleep;
he hath no use of them. Why, this boy will
carry a letter twenty mile, as easy as a cannon
will shoot point-blank twelve score. He pieces
out his wife's inclination; he gives her folly
motion and advantage: and now she's going to

my wife, and Falstaff's boy with her. A man may
hear this shower sing in the wind: and Falstaff's boy with her! Good plots! they are laid;
and our revolted wives share damnation together. Well; I will take him, then torture my
wife, pluck the borrowed veil of modesty from
the so seeming Mistress Page, divulge Page himself for a secure and wilful Actæon; and to
these violent proceedings all my neighbours
shall cry aim. [*Clock strikes.*] The clock gives
me my cue, and my assurance bids me search;
there I shall find Falstaff. I shall be rather
praised for this than mocked; for it is as positive as the earth is firm, that Falstaff is there:
I will go.   52

Enter PAGE, SHALLOW, SLENDER, Host, SIR
HUGH EVANS, CAIUS, *and* RUGBY.

Page, Shal., &c. Well met, Master Ford.
Ford. Trust me, a good knot. I have good
cheer at home; and I pray you all go with me.
Shal. I must excuse myself, Master Ford. 56
Slen. And so must I, sir: we have appointed to
dine with Mistress Anne, and I would not break
with her for more money than I'll speak of.
Shal. We have lingered about a match between Anne Page and my cousin Slender, and
this day we shall have our answer.
Slen. I hope I have your good will, father
Page.   64
Page. You have, Master Slender; I stand
wholly for you: but my wife, Master doctor, is
for you altogether.
Caius. Ay, by gar; and de maid is love-a me:
my nursh-a Quickly tell me so mush.   69
Host. What say you to young Master Fenton?
he capers, he dances, he has eyes of youth, he
writes verses, he speaks holiday, he smells April
and May: he will carry't, he will carry't; 'tis in
his buttons; he will carry't.   74
Page. Not by my consent, I promise you. The
gentleman is of no having: he kept company
with the wild prince and Pointz; he is of too
high a region; he knows too much. No, he
shall not knit a knot in his fortunes with the
finger of my substance: if he take her, let him
take her simply; the wealth I have waits on my
consent, and my consent goes not that way. 82
Ford. I beseech you heartily, some of you go
home with me to dinner: besides your cheer, you
shall have sport; I will show you a monster.
Master doctor, you shall go; so shall you,
Master Page; and you, Sir Hugh.
Shal. Well, fare you well: we shall have the
freer wooing at Master Page's.   89
[*Exeunt* SHALLOW *and* SLENDER.
Caius. Go home, John Rugby; I come anon.
[*Exit* RUGBY.
Host. Farewell, my hearts: I will to my
honest knight Falstaff, and drink canary with
him.   [*Exit* Host.
Ford. [*Aside.*] I think I shall drink in pipe-
wine first with him; I'll make him dance. Will
you go, gentles?   96
All. Have with you to see this monster.
[*Exeunt.*

C

SCENE III.—*A Room in* FORD'S *House.*

Enter MISTRESS FORD *and* MISTRESS PAGE.

Mrs. Ford. What, John! what, Robert!

Mrs. Page. Quickly, quickly:—Is the buck-basket—

Mrs. Ford. I warrant. What, Robin, I say! 4

Enter Servants *with a Basket.*

Mrs. Page. Come, come, come.

Mrs. Ford. Here, set it down.

Mrs. Page. Give your men the charge; we must be brief. 8

Mrs. Ford. Marry, as I told you before, John, and Robert, be ready here hard by in the brew-house; and when I suddenly call you, come forth, and without any pause or staggering, take this basket on your shoulders: that done, trudge with it in all haste, and carry it among the whitsters in Datchet-mead, and there empty it in the muddy ditch, close by the Thames side. 16

Mrs. Page. You will do it?

Mrs. Ford. I have told them over and over; they lack no direction. Be gone, and come when you are called. [*Exeunt* Servants.

Mrs. Page. Here comes little Robin. 21

Enter ROBIN.

Mrs. Ford. How now, my eyas-musket! what news with you?

Rob. My master, Sir John, is come in at your back-door, Mistress Ford, and requests your company.

Mrs. Page. You little Jack-a-Lent, have you been true to us? 28

Rob. Ay, I'll be sworn. My master knows not of your being here, and hath threatened to put me into everlasting liberty if I tell you of it; for he swears he'll turn me away. 32

Mrs. Page. Thou 'rt a good boy; this secrecy of thine shall be a tailor to thee and shall make thee a new doublet and hose. I'll go hide me.

Mrs. Ford. Do so. Go tell thy master I am alone. [*Exit* ROBIN.] Mistress Page, remember you your cue. 38

Mrs. Page. I warrant thee; if I do not act it, hiss me. [*Exit.*

Mrs. Ford. Go to, then: we'll use this unwholesome humidity, this gross watery pumpion; we'll teach him to know turtles from jays. 44

Enter FALSTAFF.

Fal. 'Have I caught my heavenly jewel?' Why, now let me die, for I have lived long enough: this is the period of my ambition: O this blessed hour! 48

Mrs. Ford. O, sweet Sir John!

Fal. Mistress Ford, I cannot cog, I cannot prate, Mistress Ford. Now shall I sin in my wish: I would thy husband were dead. I'll speak it before the best lord, I would make thee my lady.

Mrs. Ford. I your lady, Sir John! alas, I should be a pitiful lady. 56

Fal. Let the court of France show me such another. I see how thine eye would emulate the diamond: thou hast the right arched beauty of the brow that becomes the ship-tire, the tire-valiant, or any tire of Venetian admittance. 61

Mrs. Ford. A plain kerchief, Sir John: my brows become nothing else; nor that well neither. 64

Fal. By the Lord, thou art a traitor to say so: thou wouldst make an absolute courtier; and the firm fixture of thy foot would give an excellent motion to thy gait in a semi-circled farthingale. I see what thou wert, if Fortune thy foe were not, Nature thy friend. Come, thou canst not hide it. 71

Mrs. Ford. Believe me, there 's no such thing in me.

Fal. What made me love thee? let that persuade thee there 's something extraordinary in thee. Come, I cannot cog and say thou art this and that, like a many of these lisping hawthorn-buds, that come like women in men's apparel, and smell like Bucklersbury in simple-time; I cannot; but I love thee; none but thee; and thou deservest it. 81

Mrs. Ford. Do not betray me, sir. I fear you love Mistress Page.

Fal. Thou mightst as well say, I love to walk by the Counter-gate, which is as hateful to me as the reek of a lime-kiln.

Mrs. Ford. Well, heaven knows how I love you; and you shall one day find it. 88

Fal. Keep in that mind; I'll deserve it.

Mrs. Ford. Nay, I must tell you, so you do, or else I could not be in that mind.

Rob. [*Within.*] Mistress Ford! Mistress Ford! here 's Mistress Page at the door, sweating and blowing and looking wildly, and would needs speak with you presently.

Fal. She shall not see me: I will ensconce me behind the arras. 97

Mrs. Ford. Pray you, do so: she 's a very tattling woman. [FALSTAFF *hides himself.*

Re-enter MISTRESS PAGE *and* ROBIN.

What 's the matter? how now! 100

Mrs. Page. O Mistress Ford! what have you done? You 're shamed, you are overthrown, you 're undone for ever!

Mrs. Ford. What 's the matter, good Mistress Page? 105

Mrs. Page. O well-a-day, Mistress Ford! having an honest man to your husband, to give him such cause of suspicion! 108

Mrs. Ford. What cause of suspicion?

Mrs. Page. What cause of suspicion! Out upon you! how am I mistook in you!

Mrs. Ford. Why, alas, what 's the matter? 112

Mrs. Page. Your husband's coming hither, woman, with all the officers of Windsor, to search for a gentleman that he says is here now in the house by your consent, to take an ill advantage of his absence: you are undone. 117

Mrs. Ford. [*Aside.*] Speak louder.—'Tis not so, I hope.

Mrs. Page. Pray heaven it be not so, that you have such a man here! but 'tis most certain your husband's coming with half Windsor at his heels, to search for such a one. I come before to tell you. If you know yourself clear, why, I am glad of it; but if you have a friend here, convey, convey him out. Be not amazed; call all your senses to you: defend your reputation, or bid farewell to your good life for ever.   128

Mrs. Ford. What shall I do?—There is a gentleman, my dear friend; and I fear not mine own shame so much as his peril: I had rather than a thousand pound he were out of the house. 132

Mrs. Page. For shame! never stand 'you had rather' and 'you had rather:' your husband's here at hand; bethink you of some conveyance: in the house you cannot hide him. O, how have you deceived me! Look, here is a basket: if he be of any reasonable stature, he may creep in here; and throw foul linen upon him, as if it were going to bucking: or—it is whiting-time—send him by your two men to Datchet-mead.

Mrs. Ford. He's too big to go in there. What shall I do?   144

Fal. [Coming forward.] Let me see't, let me see't, O, let me see't! I'll in, I'll in. Follow your friend's counsel. I'll in.

Mrs. Page. What, Sir John Falstaff! Are these your letters, knight?   149

Fal. I love thee, and none but thee; help me away: let me creep in here. I'll never—

[*He gets into the basket; they cover him with foul linen.*

Mrs. Page. Help to cover your master, boy. Call your men, Mistress Ford. You dissembling knight!   154

Mrs. Ford. What, John! Robert! John!

[*Exit* ROBIN.

Re-enter Servants.

Go take up these clothes here quickly; where's the cowl-staff? look, how you drumble! carry them to the laundress in Datchet-mead; quickly, come.

Enter FORD, PAGE, CAIUS, *and* SIR HUGH EVANS.

Ford. Pray you, come near: if I suspect without cause, why then make sport at me; then let me be your jest; I deserve it. How now! what goes here? whither bear you this?

Serv. To the laundress, forsooth.   163

Mrs. Ford. Why, what have you to do whither they bear it? You were best meddle with buck-washing.

Ford. Buck! I would I could wash myself of the buck! Buck, buck, buck! Ay, buck; I warrant you, buck; and of the season too, it shall appear. [*Exeunt* Servants *with the basket.*] Gentlemen, I have dreamed to-night; I'll tell you my dream. Here, here, here be my keys: ascend my chambers; search, seek, find out: I'll warrant we'll unkennel the fox. Let me stop this way first. [*Locking the door.*] So, now uncape.

Page. Good Master Ford, be contented: you wrong yourself too much.   177

Ford. True, Master Page. Up, gentlemen; you shall see sport anon: follow me, gentlemen.

[*Exit.*

Eva. This is fery fantastical humours and jealousies.   181

Caius. By gar, 'tis no de fashion of France; it is not jealous in France.

Page. Nay, follow him, gentlemen; see the issue of his search.   185

[*Exeunt* PAGE, CAIUS, *and* EVANS.

Mrs. Page. Is there not a double excellency in this?

Mrs. Ford. I know not which pleases me better; that my husband is deceived, or Sir John.

Mrs. Page. What a taking was he in when your husband asked who was in the basket! 191

Mrs. Ford. I am half afraid he will have need of washing; so throwing him into the water will do him a benefit.

Mrs. Page. Hang him, dishonest rascal! I would all of the same strain were in the same distress.   197

Mrs. Ford. I think my husband hath some special suspicion of Falstaff's being here; for I never saw him so gross in his jealousy till now.

Mrs. Page. I will lay a plot to try that; and we will yet have more tricks with Falstaff: his dissolute disease will scarce obey this medicine.

Mrs. Ford. Shall we send that foolish carrion Mistress Quickly to him, and excuse his throwing into the water; and give him another hope, to betray him to another punishment?   207

Mrs. Page. We will do it: let him be sent for to-morrow, eight o'clock, to have amends. 209

Re-enter FORD, PAGE, CAIUS, *and* SIR HUGH EVANS.

Ford. I cannot find him: may be the knave bragged of that he could not compass.

Mrs. Page. [*Aside to* MRS. FORD.] Heard you that?   213

Mrs. Ford. [*Aside to* MRS. PAGE.] Ay, ay, peace.—You use me well, Master Ford, do you?

Ford. Ay, I do so.   216

Mrs. Ford. Heaven make you better than your thoughts!

Ford. Amen!

Mrs. Page. You do yourself mighty wrong, Master Ford.   221

Ford. Ay, ay; I must bear it.

Eva. If there pe any pody in the house, and in the chambers, and in the coffers, and in the presses, heaven forgive my sins at the day of judgment!   226

Caius. By gar, nor I too, dere is no bodies.

Page. Fie, fie, Master Ford! are you not ashamed? What spirit, what devil suggests this imagination? I would not ha' your distemper in this kind for the wealth of Windsor Castle.

Ford. 'Tis my fault, Master Page: I suffer for it.

Eva. You suffer for a pad conscience: your wife is as honest a 'omans as I will desires among five thousand, and five hundred too.   235

Caius. By gar, I see 'tis an honest woman.

Ford. Well; I promised you a dinner. Come, come, walk in the Park: I pray you, pardon me; I will hereafter make known to you why I have done this. Come, wife; come, Mistress Page. I pray you, pardon me; pray heartily, pardon me.

Page. Let's go in, gentlemen; but, trust me, we'll mock him. I do invite you to-morrow morning to my house to breakfast; after, we'll a-birding together: I have a fine hawk for the bush. Shall it be so? 246

Ford. Any thing.

Eva. If there is one, I shall make two in the company.

Caius. If dere be one or two, I shall make-a de turd.

Ford. Pray you go, Master Page. 252

Eva. I pray you now, remembrance to-morrow on the lousy knave, mine host.

Caius. Dat is good; by gar, vit all my heart.

Eva. A lousy knave! to have his gibes and his mockeries! [*Exeunt.*

SCENE IV.—*A Room in* PAGE'S *House.*

Enter FENTON, ANNE PAGE, *and* MISTRESS QUICKLY. MISTRESS QUICKLY *stands apart.*

Fent. I see I cannot get thy father's love; Therefore no more turn me to him, sweet Nan.

Anne. Alas! how then?

Fent.   Why, thou must be thyself. He doth object, I am too great of birth, 4 And that my state being gall'd with my expense, I seek to heal it only by his wealth. Besides these, other bars he lays before me, My riots past, my wild societies; 8 And tells me 'tis impossible I should love thee but as a property.

Anne. May be he tells you true.

Fent. No, heaven so speed me in my time to come! 12 Albeit I will confess thy father's wealth Was the first motive that I woo'd thee, Anne; Yet, wooing thee, I found thee of more value Than stamps in gold or sums in sealed bags; 16 And 'tis the very riches of thyself That now I aim at.

Anne.   Gentle Master Fenton, Yet seek my father's love; still seek it, sir: If opportunity and humblest suit 20 Cannot attain it, why, then,—hark you hither. [*They converse apart.*

Enter SHALLOW *and* SLENDER.

Shal. Break their talk, Mistress Quickly: my kinsman shall speak for himself.

Slen. I'll make a shaft or a bolt on't. 'Slid, 'tis but venturing. 25

Shal. Be not dismayed.

Slen. No, she shall not dismay me: I care not for that, but that I am afeard. 28

Quick. Hark ye; Master Slender would speak a word with you.

Anne. I come to him. [*Aside.*] This is my father's choice.

O, what a world of vile ill-favour'd faults 32 Looks handsome in three hundred pounds a year!

Quick. And how does good Master Fenton? Pray you, a word with you.

Shal. She's coming; to her, coz. O boy, thou hadst a father! 37

Slen. I had a father, Mistress Anne; my uncle can tell you good jests of him. Pray you, uncle, tell Mistress Anne the jest, how my father stole two geese out of a pen, good uncle. 41

Shal. Mistress Anne, my cousin loves you.

Slen. Ay, that I do; as well as I love any woman in Glostershire. 44

Shal. He will maintain you like a gentle-woman.

Slen. Ay, that I will, come cut and long-tail, under the degree of a squire. 48

Shal. He will make you a hundred and fifty pounds jointure.

Anne. Good Master Shallow, let him woo for himself. 52

Shal. Marry, I thank you for it; I thank you for that good comfort. She calls you, coz: I'll leave you.

Anne. Now, Master Slender. 56

Slen. Now, good Mistress Anne.—

Anne. What is your will? 58

Slen. My will! od's heartlings! that's a pretty jest, indeed! I ne'er made my will yet, I thank heaven; I am not such a sickly creature, I give heaven praise.

Anne. I mean, Master Slender, what would you with me? 64

Slen. Truly, for mine own part, I would little or nothing with you. Your father and my uncle have made motions: if it be my luck, so; if not, happy man be his dole! They can tell you how things go better than I can: you may ask your father; here he comes. 70

Enter PAGE *and* MISTRESS PAGE.

Page. Now, Master Slender: love him, daughter Anne. Why, how now! what does Master Fenton here? You wrong me, sir, thus still to haunt my house: I told you, sir, my daughter is dispos'd of.

Fent. Nay, Master Page, be not impatient.

Mrs. Page. Good Master Fenton, come not to my child. 76

Page. She is no match for you.

Fent. Sir, will you hear me?

Page.   No, good Master Fenton. Come, Master Shallow; come, son Slender, in. Knowing my mind, you wrong me, Master Fenton. 80 [*Exeunt* PAGE, SHALLOW, *and* SLENDER.

Quick. Speak to Mistress Page.

Fent. Good Mistress Page, for that I love your daughter In such a righteous fashion as I do, Perforce, against all checks, rebukes and manners, 84 I must advance the colours of my love And not retire: let me have your good will.

Anne. Good mother, do not marry me to yond fool.

Mrs. Page. I mean it not; I seek you a better husband. 88

Quick. That's my master, Master doctor.

Anne. Alas! I had rather be set quick i' the
earth,
And bowl'd to death with turnips.
Mrs. Page. Come, trouble not yourself. Good
Master Fenton,   92
I will not be your friend nor enemy:
My daughter will I question how she loves you,
And as I find her, so am I affected.
'Till then, farewell, sir: she must needs go in;
Her father will be angry.   97
Fent. Farewell, gentle mistress. Farewell,
Nan.   [*Exeunt* MISTRESS PAGE *and* ANNE.
Quick. This is my doing, now: 'Nay,' said I,
'will you cast away your child on a fool, and a
physician? Look on Master Fenton.' This is
my doing.   102
Fent. I thank thee: and I pray thee, once
to-night
Give my sweet Nan this ring. There's for thy
pains.   104
Quick. Now heaven send thee good fortune!
[*Exit* FENTON.] A kind heart he hath: a woman
would run through fire and water for such a
kind heart. But yet I would my master had
Mistress Anne; or I would Master Slender had
her; or, in sooth, I would Master Fenton had
her. I will do what I can for them all three,
for so I have promised, and I'll be as good as
my word; but speciously for Master Fenton.
Well, I must of another errand to Sir John
Falstaff from my two mistresses: what a beast
am I to slack it!   [*Exit.*

SCENE V.—*A Room in the Garter Inn.*

Enter FALSTAFF *and* BARDOLPH.

Fal. Bardolph, I say,—
Bard. Here, sir.
Fal. Go fetch me a quart of sack; put a
toast in't. [*Exit* BARD.] Have I lived to be
carried in a basket, and to be thrown in the
Thames like a barrow of butcher's offal? Well,
if I be served such another trick, I'll have my
brains ta'en out, and buttered, and give them to
a dog for a new year's gift. The rogues slighted
me into the river with as little remorse as they
would have drowned a blind bitch's puppies,
fifteen i' the litter; and you may know by my
size that I have a kind of alacrity in sinking: if
the bottom were as deep as hell, I should down.
I had been drowned but that the shore was
shelvy and shallow; a death that I abhor, for
the water swells a man, and what a thing should
I have been when I had been swelled! I should
have been a mountain of mummy.   19

Re-enter BARDOLPH, *with the sack.*

Bard. Here's Mistress Quickly, sir, to speak
with you.   21
Fal. Come, let me pour in some sack to the
Thames water, for my belly's as cold as if I had
swallowed snowballs for pills to cool the reins.
Call her in.   25
Bard. Come in, woman.

Enter MISTRESS QUICKLY.

Quick. By your leave. I cry you mercy: give
your worship good morrow.   28
Fal. Take away these chalices. Go brew me
a pottle of sack finely.
Bard. With eggs, sir?
Fal. Simple of itself; I'll no pullet-sperm in
my brewage. [*Exit* BARDOLPH.]—How now! 33
Quick. Marry, sir, I come to your worship
from Mistress Ford.
Fal. Mistress Ford! I have had ford enough;
I was thrown into the ford; I have my belly full
of ford.   38
Quick. Alas the day! good heart, that was
not her fault: she does so take on with her
men; they mistook their erection.   41
Fal. So did I mine, to build upon a foolish
woman's promise.
Quick. Well, she laments, sir, for it, that it
would yearn your heart to see it. Her husband
goes this morning a-birding: she desires you
once more to come to her between eight and
nine. I must carry her word quickly: she'll
make you amends, I warrant you.   49
Fal. Well, I will visit her: tell her so; and
bid her think what a man is: let her consider
his frailty, and then judge of my merit.   52
Quick. I will tell her.
Fal. Do so. Between nine and ten, sayest thou?
Quick. Eight and nine, sir.
Fal. Well, be gone: I will not miss her. 56
Quick. Peace be with you, sir.   [*Exit.*
Fal. I marvel I hear not of Master Brook;
he sent me word to stay within. I like his
money well. O! here he comes.   60

Enter FORD.

Ford. Bless you, sir!
Fal. Now, Master Brook, you come to know
what hath passed between me and Ford's
wife?   64
Ford. That, indeed, Sir John, is my busi-
ness.
Fal. Master Brook, I will not lie to you: I
was at her house the hour she appointed me. 68
Ford. And how sped you, sir?
Fal. Very ill-favouredly, Master Brook.
Ford. How so, sir? did she change her determination?   72
Fal. No, Master Brook; but the peaking
cornuto her husband, Master Brook, dwelling in
a continual 'larum of jealousy, comes me in the
instant of our encounter, after we had embraced,
kissed, protested, and, as it were, spoke the
prologue of our comedy; and at his heels a
rabble of his companions, thither provoked and
instigated by his distemper, and, forsooth, to
search his house for his wife's love.   81
Ford. What! while you were there?
Fal. While I was there.
Ford. And did he search for you, and could
not find you?   85
Fal. You shall hear. As good luck would
have it, comes in one Mistress Page; gives
intelligence of Ford's approach; and in her

invention, and Ford's wife's distraction, they conveyed me into a buck-basket.   90

Ford. A buck-basket!

Fal. By the Lord, a buck-basket! rammed me in with foul shirts and smocks, socks, foul stockings, greasy napkins; that, Master Brook, there was the rankest compound of villanous smell that ever offended nostril.   96

Ford. And how long lay you there?

Fal. Nay, you shall hear, Master Brook, what I have suffered to bring this woman to evil for your good. Being thus crammed in the basket, a couple of Ford's knaves, his hinds, were called forth by their mistress to carry me in the name of foul clothes to Datchet-lane: they took me on their shoulders; met the jealous knave their master in the door, who asked them once or twice what they had in their basket. I quaked for fear lest the lunatic knave would have searched it; but Fate, ordaining he should be a cuckold, held his hand. Well; on went he for a search, and away went I for foul clothes. But mark the sequel, Master Brook: I suffered the pangs of three several deaths: first, an intolerable fright, to be detected with a jealous rotten bell-wether; next, to be compassed, like a good bilbo, in the circumference of a peck, hilt to point, heel to head; and then, to be stopped in, like a strong distillation, with stinking clothes that fretted in their own grease: think of that, a man of my kidney, think of that, that am as subject to heat as butter; a man of continual dissolution and thaw: it was a miracle to 'scape suffocation. And in the height of this bath, when I was more than half stewed in grease, like a Dutch dish, to be thrown into the Thames, and cooled, glowing hot, in that surge, like a horse-shoe; think of that, hissing hot, think of that, Master Brook!   127

Ford. In good sadness, sir, I am sorry that for my sake you have suffered all this. My suit then is desperate; you'll undertake her no more?

Fal. Master Brook, I will be thrown into Etna, as I have been into Thames, ere I will leave her thus. Her husband is this morning gone a-birding: I have received from her another embassy of meeting; 'twixt eight and nine is the hour, Master Brook.   136

Ford. 'Tis past eight already, sir.

Fal. Is it? I will then address me to my appointment. Come to me at your convenient leisure, and you shall know how I speed, and the conclusion shall be crowned with your enjoying her: adieu. You shall have her, Master Brook; Master Brook, you shall cuckold Ford. [*Exit.*

Ford. Hum! ha! is this a vision? is this a dream? do I sleep? Master Ford, awake! awake, Master Ford! there's a hole made in your best coat, Master Ford. This 'tis to be married! this 'tis to have linen and buck-baskets! Well, I will proclaim myself what I am: I will now take the lecher; he is at my house; he cannot 'scape me; 'tis impossible he should; he cannot creep into a half-penny purse, nor into a pepper-box; but, lest the devil that guides him should aid

him, I will search impossible places. Though what I am I cannot avoid, yet to be what I would not, shall not make me tame: if I have horns to make me mad, let the proverb go with me; I'll be horn-mad.   [*Exit.*

ACT IV

SCENE I.—*The Street.*

Enter MISTRESS PAGE, MISTRESS QUICKLY, *and* WILLIAM.

Mrs. Page. Is he at Master Ford's already, thinkest thou?   2

Quick. Sure he is by this, or will be presently; but truly, he is very courageous mad about his throwing into the water. Mistress Ford desires you to come suddenly.   6

Mrs. Page. I'll be with her by and by: I'll but bring my young man here to school. Look, where his master comes; 'tis a playing-day, I see.   10

Enter SIR HUGH EVANS.

How now, Sir Hugh! no school to-day?

Eva. No; Master Slender is get the boys leave to play.   13

Quick. Blessing of his heart!

Mrs. Page. Sir Hugh, my husband says my son profits nothing in the world at his book: I pray you, ask him some questions in his accidence.

Eva. Come hither, William; hold up your head; come.   20

Mrs. Page. Come on, sirrah; hold up your head; answer your master, be not afraid.

Eva. William, how many numbers is in nouns?

Will. Two.   24

Quick. Truly, I thought there had been one number more, because they say, 'Od's nouns.'

Eva. Peace your tattlings! What is *fair*, William?   28

Will. *Pulcher.*

Quick. Polecats! there are fairer things than polecats, sure.

Eva. You are a very simplicity 'oman: I pray you peace. What is *lapis*, William?   33

Will. A stone.

Eva. And what is *a stone*, William?

Will. A pebble.   36

Eva. No, it is *lapis*: I pray you remember in your prain.

Will. *Lapis.*

Eva. That is a good William. What is he, William, that does lend articles?   41

Will. Articles are borrowed of the pronoun, and be thus declined, *Singulariter, nominativo, hic, hæc, hoc.*   44

Eva. *Nominativo, hig, hag, hog;* pray you, mark: *genitivo, hujus.* Well, what is your accusative case?

Will. *Accusativo, hinc.*   48

Eva. I pray you, have your remembrance, child; *accusativo, hung, hang, hog.*

Quick. Hang hog is Latin for bacon, I warrant you.   52

Eva. Leave your prabbles, 'oman. What is the focative case, William?

Will. O *vocativo,* O.

Eva. Remember, William; focative is *caret.*

Quick. And that's a good root.   57

Eva. 'Oman, forbear.

Mrs. Page. Peace!

Eva. What is your genitive case plural, William?   61

Will. Genitive case?

Eva. Ay.

Will. *Genitive, horum, harum, horum.*   64

Quick. Vengeance of Jenny's case! fie on her! Never name her, child, if she be a whore.

Eva. For shame, 'oman!

Quick. You do ill to teach the child such words. He teaches him to hick and to hack, which they'll do fast enough of themselves, and to call 'horum?' fie upon you!   71

Eva. 'Oman, art thou lunatics? hast thou no understandings for thy cases and the numbers and the genders? Thou art as foolish Christian creatures as I would desires.

Mrs. Page. Prithee, hold thy peace.   76

Eva. Show me now, William, some declensions of your pronouns.

Will. Forsooth, I have forgot.

Eva. It is *qui, quæ, quod;* if you forget your *quis,* your *quæs,* and your *quods,* you must be preeches. Go your ways and play; go.

Mrs. Page. He is a better scholar than I thought he was.   84

Eva. He is a good sprag memory. Farewell, Mistress Page.

Mrs. Page. Adieu, good Sir Hugh. [*Exit* SIR HUGH.] Get you home, boy. Come, we stay too long.   [*Exeunt.*

SCENE II.—*A Room in* FORD'S *House.*

Enter FALSTAFF *and* MISTRESS FORD.

Fal. Mistress Ford, your sorrow hath eaten up my sufferance. I see you are obsequious in your love, and I profess requital to a hair's breadth; not only, Mistress Ford, in the simple office of love, but in all the accoutrement, complement and ceremony of it. But are you sure of your husband now?

Mrs. Ford. He's a-birding, sweet Sir John. 8

Mrs. Page. [*Within.*] What ho! gossip Ford! what ho!

Mrs. Ford. Step into the chamber, Sir John.
    [*Exit* FALSTAFF.

Enter MISTRESS PAGE.

Mrs. Page. How now, sweetheart! who's at home besides yourself?   13

Mrs. Ford. Why, none but mine own people.

Mrs. Page. Indeed!

Mrs. Ford. No, certainly.—[*Aside to her.*] Speak louder.   17

Mrs. Page. Truly, I am so glad you have nobody here.

Mrs. Ford. Why?   20

Mrs. Page. Why, woman, your husband is in his old lunes again: he so takes on yonder with my husband; so rails against all married mankind; so curses all Eve's daughters, of what complexion soever; and so buffets himself on the forehead, crying, 'Peer out, peer out!' that any madness I ever yet beheld seemed but tameness, civility and patience, to this his distemper he is in now. I am glad the fat knight is not here.   30

Mrs. Ford. Why, does he talk of him?

Mrs. Page. Of none but him; and swears he was carried out, the last time he searched for him, in a basket: protests to my husband he is now here, and hath drawn him and the rest of their company from their sport, to make another experiment of his suspicion. But I am glad the knight is not here; now he shall see his own foolery.

Mrs. Ford. How near is he, Mistress Page? 40

Mrs. Page. Hard by; at street end; he will be here anon.

Mrs. Ford. I am undone! the knight is here.

Mrs. Page. Why then you are utterly shamed, and he's but a dead man. What a woman are you! Away with him, away with him! better shame than murder.   47

Mrs. Ford. Which way should he go? how should I bestow him? Shall I put him into the basket again?

Re-enter FALSTAFF.

Fal. No, I'll come no more i' the basket. May I not go out ere he come?   52

Mrs. Page. Alas! three of Master Ford's brothers watch the door with pistols, that none shall issue out; otherwise you might slip away ere he came. But what make you here? 56

Fal. What shall I do? I'll creep up into the chimney.

Mrs. Ford. There they always use to discharge their birding-pieces.   60

Mrs. Page. Creep into the kiln-hole.

Fal. Where is it?

Mrs. Ford. He will seek there, on my word. Neither press, coffer, chest, trunk, well, vault, but he hath an abstract for the remembrance of such places, and goes to them by his note: there is no hiding you in the house.

Fal. I'll go out, then.   68

Mrs. Page. If you go out in your own semblance, you die, Sir John. Unless you go out disguised,—

Mrs. Ford. How might we disguise him? 72

Mrs. Page. Alas the day! I know not. There is no woman's gown big enough for him; otherwise, he might put on a hat, a muffler, and a kerchief, and so escape.   76

Fal. Good hearts, devise something: any extremity rather than a mischief.

Mrs. Ford. My maid's aunt, the fat woman of Brainford, has a gown above.   80

Mrs. Page. On my word, it will serve him: she's as big as he is: and there's her thrummed hat and her muffler too. Run up, Sir John.

Mrs. Ford. Go, go, sweet Sir John: Mistress Page and I will look some linen for your head.

Mrs. Page. Quick, quick! we'll come dress you straight; put on the gown the while. 87
    [*Exit* FALSTAFF.

Mrs. Ford. I would my husband would meet him in this shape: he cannot abide the old woman of Brainford; he swears she's a witch; forbade her my house, and hath threatened to beat her.

Mrs. Page. Heaven guide him to thy husband's cudgel, and the devil guide his cudgel afterwards! 94

Mrs. Ford. But is my husband coming?

Mrs. Page. Ay, in good sadness, is he; and talks of the basket too, howsoever he hath had intelligence.

Mrs. Ford. We'll try that; for I'll appoint my men to carry the basket again, to meet him at the door with it, as they did last time. 101

Mrs. Page. Nay, but he'll be here presently: let's go dress him like the witch of Brainford.

Mrs. Ford. I'll first direct my men what they shall do with the basket. Go up; I'll bring linen for him straight. [*Exit.*

Mrs. Page. Hang him, dishonest varlet! we cannot misuse him enough. 108
We'll leave a proof, by that which we will do,
Wives may be merry, and yet honest too:
We do not act that often jest and laugh;
'Tis old, but true, 'Still swine eats all the draff.' [*Exit.*

Re-enter MISTRESS FORD, *with two*
Servants.

Mrs. Ford. Go, sirs, take the basket again on your shoulders: your master is hard at door; if he bid you set it down, obey him. Quickly; dispatch. [*Exit.*

First Serv. Come, come, take it up. 117

Sec. Serv. Pray heaven, it be not full of knight again.

First Serv. I hope not; I had as lief bear so much lead. 121

Enter FORD, PAGE, SHALLOW, CAIUS, *and*
SIR HUGH EVANS.

Ford. Ay, but if it prove true, Master Page, have you any way then to unfool me again? Set down the basket, villains. Somebody call my wife. Youth in a basket! O you panderly rascals! there's a knot, a ging, a pack, a conspiracy against me: now shall the devil be shamed. What, wife, I say! Come, come forth! Behold what honest clothes you send forth to bleaching! 130

Page. Why, this passes! Master Ford, you are not to go loose any longer; you must be pinioned. 133

Eva. Why, this is lunatics! this is mad as a mad dog!

Shal. Indeed, Master Ford, this is not well, indeed. 137

Ford. So say I too, sir.—

Re-enter MISTRESS FORD.

Come hither, Mistress Ford, the honest woman, the modest wife, the virtuous creature, that hath the jealous fool to her husband! I suspect without cause, mistress, do I?

Mrs. Ford. Heaven be my witness, you do, if you suspect me in any dishonesty. 144

Ford. Well said, brazen-face! hold it out. Come forth, sirrah! [*Pulls the clothes out of the basket.*

Page. This passes!

Mrs. Ford. Are you not ashamed? let the clothes alone. 149

Ford. I shall find you anon.

Eva. 'Tis unreasonable. Will you take up your wife's clothes? Come away. 152

Ford. Empty the basket, I say!

Mrs. Ford. Why, man, why?

Ford. Master Page, as I am an honest man, there was one conveyed out of my house yesterday in this basket: why may not he be there again? In my house I am sure he is; my intelligence is true; my jealousy is reasonable. Pluck me out all the linen. 160

Mrs. Ford. If you find a man there he shall die a flea's death.

Page. Here's no man.

Shal. By my fidelity, this is not well, Master Ford; this wrongs you. 165

Eva. Master Ford, you must pray, and not follow the imaginations of your own heart: this is jealousies. 168

Ford. Well, he's not here I seek for.

Page. No, nor nowhere else but in your brain. [*Servants carry away the basket.*

Ford. Help to search my house this one time: if I find not what I seek, show no colour for my extremity; let me for ever be your table-sport; let them say of me, 'As jealous as Ford, that searched a hollow walnut for his wife's leman.' Satisfy me once more; once more search with me. 177

Mrs. Ford. What ho, Mistress Page! come you and the old woman down; my husband will come into the chamber. 180

Ford. Old woman! What old woman's that?

Mrs. Ford. Why, it is my maid's aunt of Brainford. 183

Ford. A witch, a quean, an old cozening quean! Have I not forbid her my house? She comes of errands, does she? We are simple men; we do not know what's brought to pass under the profession of fortune-telling. She works by charms, by spells, by the figure, and such daubery as this is, beyond our element: we know nothing. Come down, you witch, you hag, you; come down, I say! 192

Mrs. Ford. Nay, good, sweet husband! good gentlemen, let him not strike the old woman.

Enter FALSTAFF *in women's clothes, led by*
MISTRESS PAGE.

Mrs. Page. Come, Mother Prat; come, give me your hand. 196

Ford. I'll 'prat' her.—[*Beats him.*] Out of my door, you witch, you rag, you baggage, you polecat, you ronyon! out, out! I'll conjure you, I'll fortune-tell you. [*Exit* FALSTAFF.

Mrs. Page. Are you not ashamed? I think you have killed the poor woman.

Mrs. Ford. Nay, he will do it. 'Tis a goodly credit for you. 204

Ford. Hang her, witch!

Eva. By yea and no, I think the 'oman is a witch indeed: I like not when a 'oman has a great peard; I spy a great peard under her muffler.   209

Ford. Will you follow, gentlemen? I beseech you, follow: see but the issue of my jealousy. If I cry out thus upon no trail, never trust me when I open again.   213

Page. Let's obey his humour a little further. Come, gentlemen.

[*Exeunt* FORD, PAGE, SHALLOW, CAIUS, *and* EVANS.

Mrs. Page. Trust me, he beat him most pitifully.   217

Mrs. Ford. Nay, by the mass, that he did not; he beat him most unpitifully methought.

Mrs. Page. I'll have the cudgel hallowed and hung o'er the altar: it hath done meritorious service.   222

Mrs. Ford. What think you? May we, with the warrant of womanhood and the witness of a good conscience, pursue him with any further revenge?   226

Mrs. Page. The spirit of wantonness is, sure, scared out of him: if the devil have him not in fee-simple, with fine and recovery, he will never, I think, in the way of waste, attempt us again.

Mrs. Ford. Shall we tell our husbands how we have served him?   232

Mrs. Page. Yes, by all means; if it be but to scrape the figures out of your husband's brains. If they can find in their hearts the poor unvirtuous fat knight shall be any further afflicted, we two will still be the ministers.   237

Mrs. Ford. I'll warrant they'll have him publicly shamed, and methinks there would be no period to the jest, should he not be publicly shamed.   241

Mrs. Page. Come, to the forge with it then; shape it: I would not have things cool. [*Exeunt.*

SCENE III.—*A Room in the Garter Inn.*

Enter Host *and* BARDOLPH.

Bard. Sir, the Germans desire to have three of your horses: the duke himself will be to-morrow at court, and they are going to meet him.   3

Host. What duke should that be comes so secretly? I hear not of him in the court. Let me speak with the gentlemen; they speak English?

Bard. Ay, sir; I'll call them to you.   8

Host. They shall have my horses, but I'll make them pay; I'll sauce them: they have had my house a week at command; I have turned away my other guests: they must come off; I'll sauce them. Come.   [*Exeunt.*

SCENE IV.—*A Room in* FORD'S *House.*

Enter PAGE, FORD, MISTRESS PAGE, MISTRESS FORD, *and* SIR HUGH EVANS.

Eva. 'Tis one of the pest discretions of a 'oman as ever I did look upon.

Page. And did he send you both these letters at an instant?   4

Mrs. Page. Within a quarter of an hour.

Ford. Pardon me, wife. Henceforth do what thou wilt;

I rather will suspect the sun with cold
Than thee with wantonness: now doth thy honour stand,   8
In him that was of late an heretic,
As firm as faith.

Page.   'Tis well, 'tis well; no more.
Be not as extreme in submission
As in offence;   12
But let our plot go forward: let our wives
Yet once again, to make us public sport,
Appoint a meeting with this old fat fellow,
Where we may take him and disgrace him for it.

Ford. There is no better way than that they spoke of.   17

Page. How? to send him word they'll meet him in the Park at midnight? Fie, fie! he'll never come.   20

Eva. You say he has been thrown into the rivers, and has been grievously peaten as an old 'oman: methinks there should be terrors in him that he should not come; methinks his flesh is punished, he shall have no desires.   25

Page. So think I too.

Mrs. Ford. Devise but how you'll use him when he comes,
And let us two devise to bring him thither.   28

Mrs. Page. There is an old tale goes that Herne the hunter,
Sometime a keeper here in Windsor forest,
Doth all the winter-time, at still midnight,
Walk round about an oak, with great ragg'd horns;   32
And there he blasts the tree, and takes the cattle,
And makes milch-kine yield blood, and shakes a chain
In a most hideous and dreadful manner:
You have heard of such a spirit, and well you know   36
The superstitious idle-headed eld
Receiv'd and did deliver to our age
This tale of Herne the hunter for a truth.

Page. Why, yet there want not many that do fear   40
In deep of night to walk by this Herne's oak.
But what of this?

Mrs. Ford.   Marry, this is our device;
That Falstaff at that oak shall meet with us,
Disguis'd like Herne with huge horns on his head.   44

Page. Well, let it not be doubted but he'll come,
And in this shape when you have brought him thither,
What shall be done with him? what is your plot?

Mrs. Page. That likewise have we thought upon, and thus: 48
Nan Page my daughter, and my little son,
And three or four more of their growth, we'll dress

Like urchins, ouphs and fairies, green and
  white,
With rounds of waxen tapers on their heads, 52
And rattles in their hands. Upon a sudden,
As Falstaff, she, and I, are newly met,
Let them from forth a sawpit rush at once
With some diffused song: upon their sight, 56
We two in great amazedness will fly:
Then let them all encircle him about,
And, fairy-like, to-pinch the unclean knight;
And ask him why, that hour of fairy revel, 60
In their so sacred paths he dares to tread
In shape profane.
  Mrs. Ford.   And till he tell the truth,
Let the supposed fairies pinch him sound
And burn him with their tapers.
  Mrs. Page.   The truth being known, 64
We'll all present ourselves, dis-horn the spirit,
And mock him home to Windsor.
  Ford.   The children must
Be practis'd well to this, or they'll ne'er do 't.
  Eva. I will teach the children their be-
haviours; and I will be like a jack-an-apes
also, to burn the knight with my taber.
  Ford. That will be excellent. I'll go buy
them vizards.   72
  Mrs. Page. My Nan shall be the queen of all
the fairies,
Finely attired in a robe of white.
  Page. That silk will I go buy:—[*Aside*] and
in that time
Shall Master Slender steal my Nan away, 76
And marry her at Eton. Go, send to Falstaff
straight.
  Ford. Nay, I'll to him again in name of Brook;
He'll tell me all his purpose. Sure, he'll come.
  Mrs. Page. Fear not you that. Go, get us
properties,   80
And tricking for our fairies.
  Eva. Let us about it: it is admirable plea-
sures and fery honest knaveries.
            [*Exeunt* PAGE, FORD, *and* EVANS.
  Mrs. Page. Go, Mistress Ford, 84
Send Quickly to Sir John, to know his mind.
            [*Exit* MISTRESS FORD.
I'll to the doctor: he hath my good will,
And none but he, to marry with Nan Page.
That Slender, though well landed, is an idiot; 88
And him my husband best of all affects:
The doctor is well money'd, and his friends
Potent at court: he, none but he, shall have her,
Though twenty thousand worthier come to
crave her.   [*Exit.*

SCENE V.—*A Room in the Garter Inn.*

Enter Host *and* SIMPLE.

  Host. What wouldst thou have, boor? what,
thick-skin? speak, breathe, discuss; brief, short,
quick, snap.
  Sim. Marry, sir, I come to speak with Sir
John Falstaff from Master Slender.   5
  Host. There's his chamber, his house, his
castle, his standing-bed and truckle-bed: 'tis
painted about with the story of the Prodigal,
fresh and new. Go knock and call: he'll speak
like an Anthropophaginian unto thee: knock,
I say.   11
  Sim. There's an old woman, a fat woman,
gone up into his chamber: I'll be so bold as
stay, sir, till she come down; I come to speak
with her, indeed.   15
  Host. Ha! a fat woman! the knight may be
robbed: I'll call. Bully knight! Bully Sir John!
speak from thy lungs military: art thou there?
it is thine host, thine Ephesian, calls.
  Fal. [*Above.*] How now, mine host!   20
  Host. Here's a Bohemian-Tartar tarries the
coming down of thy fat woman. Let her descend, bully; let her descend; my chambers are
honourable: fie! privacy? fie!   24

Enter FALSTAFF.

  Fal. There was, mine host, an old fat woman
even now with me, but she's gone.
  Sim. Pray you, sir, was't not the wise woman
of Brainford?   28
  Fal. Ay, marry, was it, muscle-shell: what
would you with her?
  Sim. My Master, sir, Master Slender, sent to
her, seeing her go thorough the streets, to know,
sir, whether one Nym, sir, that beguiled him of
a chain, had the chain or no.   34
  Fal. I spake with the old woman about it.
  Sim. And what says she, I pray, sir?   36
  Fal. Marry, she says that the very same man
that beguiled Master Slender of his chain
cozened him of it.
  Sim. I would I could have spoken with the
woman herself: I had other things to have
spoken with her too, from him.
  Fal. What are they? let us know.
  Host. Ay, come; quick.   44
  Sim. I may not conceal them, sir.
  Host. Conceal them, or thou diest.
  Sim. Why, sir, they were nothing but about
Mistress Anne Page; to know if it were my
master's fortune to have her or no.   49
  Fal. 'Tis, 'tis his fortune.
  Sim. What, sir?
  Fal. To have her, or no. Go; say the
woman told me so.   53
  Sim. May I be bold to say so, sir?
  Fal. Ay, Sir Tike; who more bold?
  Sim. I thank your worship: I shall make my
master glad with these tidings.   [*Exit.*
  Host. Thou art clerkly, thou art clerkly, Sir
John. Was there a wise woman with thee? 59
  Fal. Ay, that there was, mine host; one that
hath taught me more wit than ever I learned
before in my life: and I paid nothing for it
neither, but was paid for my learning.   63

Enter BARDOLPH.

  Bard. Out, alas, sir! cozenage, mere cozenage!
  Host. Where be my horses? speak well of
them, varletto.   66
  Bard. Run away, with the cozeners; for so
soon as I came beyond Eton, they threw me off,
from behind one of them, in a slough of mire;

and set spurs and away, like three German
devils, three Doctor Faustuses.　　71

Host. They are gone but to meet the duke,
villain. Do not say they be fled: Germans are
honest men.

Enter SIR HUGH EVANS.

Eva. Where is mine host?

Host. What is the matter, sir?　　76

Eva. Have a care of your entertainments:
there is a friend of mine come to town, tells me,
there is three cozen-germans that has cozened
all the hosts of Readins, of Maidenhead, of
Colebrook, of horses and money. I tell you for
good will, look you: you are wise and full of
gibes and vlouting-stogs, and 'tis not convenient
you should be cozened. Fare you well. [*Exit.*

Enter DOCTOR CAIUS.

Caius. Vere is mine host de Jarteer?　　85

Host. Here, Master doctor, in perplexity and
doubtful dilemma.

Caius. I cannot tell vat is dat; but it is tell-a
me dat you make grand preparation for a duke
de Jamany: by my trot, dere is no duke dat de
court is know to come. I tell you for good vill:
adieu.　　　　　　　　　　　　　　　[*Exit.*

Host. Hue and cry, villain! go. Assist me,
knight; I am undone. Fly, run, hue and cry,
villain! I am undone!　　95

[*Exeunt* Host *and* BARDOLPH.

Fal. I would all the world might be cozened,
for I have been cozened and beaten too. If it
should come to the ear of the court how I have
been transformed, and how my transformation
hath been washed and cudgelled, they would
melt me out of my fat drop by drop, and liquor
fishermen's boots with me: I warrant they
would whip me with their fine wits till I were
as crest-fallen as a dried pear. I never pros-
pered since I forswore myself at primero. Well,
if my wind were but long enough to say my
prayers, I would repent.　　107

Enter MISTRESS QUICKLY.

Now, whence come you?

Quick. From the two parties, forsooth.

Fal. The devil take one party and his dam
the other! and so they shall be both bestowed.
I have suffered more for their sakes, more than
the villanous inconstancy of man's disposition
is able to bear.　　114

Quick. And have not they suffered? Yes, I
warrant; speciously one of them: Mistress Ford,
good heart, is beaten black and blue, that you
cannot see a white spot about her.　　118

Fal. What tellest thou me of black and blue?
I was beaten myself into all the colours of the
rainbow; and I was like to be apprehended for
the witch of Brainford: but that my admirable
dexterity of wit, my counterfeiting the action
of an old woman, delivered me, the knave constable had set me i' the stocks, i' the common
stocks, for a witch.　　126

Quick. Sir, let me speak with you in your
chamber; you shall hear how things go, and, I

warrant, to your content. Here is a letter will
say somewhat. Good hearts! what ado here is
to bring you together! Sure, one of you does
not serve heaven well, that you are so crossed.

Fal. Come up into my chamber. [*Exeunt.*

SCENE VI.—*Another Room in the Garter Inn.*

Enter FENTON *and* Host.

Host. Master Fenton, talk not to me: my
mind is heavy; I will give over all.

Fent. Yet hear me speak. Assist me in my
purpose,
And, as I am a gentleman, I'll give thee　　4
A hundred pound in gold more than your loss.

Host. I will hear you, Master Fenton; and I
will, at the least, keep your counsel.

Fent. From time to time I have acquainted
you　　8
With the dear love I bear to fair Anne Page;
Who mutually hath answer'd my affection,
So far forth as herself might be her chooser,
Even to my wish. I have a letter from her　12
Of such contents as you will wonder at;
The mirth whereof so larded with my matter,
That neither singly can be manifested,
Without the show of both; wherein fat Falstaff　16
Hath a great scare: the image of the jest　17
I'll show you here at large [*Pointing to the
Letter*]. Hark, good mine host:
To-night at Herne's oak, just 'twixt twelve and
one,
Must my sweet Nan present the Fairy Queen;　20
The purpose why, is here: in which disguise,　21
While other jests are something rank on foot,
Her father hath commanded her to slip
Away with Slender, and with him at Eton　24
Immediately to marry: she hath consented:
Now, sir,
Her mother, even strong against that match
And firm for Doctor Caius, hath appointed　28
That he shall likewise shuffle her away,
While other sports are tasking of their minds;
And at the deanery, where a priest attends,
Straight marry her: to this her mother's plot
She, seemingly obedient, likewise hath　33
Made promise to the doctor. Now, thus it
rests:
Her father means she shall be all in white,
And in that habit, when Slender sees his time
To take her by the hand and bid her go,　37
She shall go with him: her mother hath in-
tended,
The better to denote her to the doctor,—
For they must all be mask'd and vizarded—　40
That quaint in green she shall be loose enrob'd,
With ribands pendent, flaring 'bout her head;
And when the doctor spies his vantage ripe,
To pinch her by the hand; and on that token　44
The maid hath given consent to go with him.

Host. Which means she to deceive, father or
mother?

Fent. Both, my good host, to go along with
me:
And here it rests, that you'll procure the vicar

To stay for me at church 'twixt twelve and
one,
And, in the lawful name of marrying, 51
To give our hearts united ceremony.
Host. Well, husband your device; I'll to the
vicar.
Bring you the maid, you shall not lack a
priest.
Fent. So shall I evermore be bound to thee;
Besides, I'll make a present recompense. 56
[*Exeunt.*

ACT V

SCENE I.—*A Room in the Garter Inn.*

Enter FALSTAFF *and* MISTRESS QUICKLY.

Fal. Prithee, no more prattling; go: I'll
hold. This is the third time; I hope good luck
lies in odd numbers. Away! go. They say there
is divinity in odd numbers, either in nativity,
chance or death. Away! 5
Quick. I'll provide you a chain, and I'll do
what I can to get you a pair of horns.
Fal. Away, I say; time wears: hold up your
head, and mince. [*Exit* MISTRESS QUICKLY.

Enter FORD.

How now, Master Brook! Master Brook, the
matter will be known to-night, or never. Be you
in the Park about midnight, at Herne's oak, and
you shall see wonders. 13
Ford. Went you not to her yesterday, sir, as
you told me you had appointed?
Fal. I went to her, Master Brook, as you see,
like a poor old man; but I came from her,
Master Brook, like a poor old woman. That
same knave Ford, her husband, hath the finest
mad devil of jealousy in him, Master Brook, that
ever governed frenzy. I will tell you: he beat
me grievously, in the shape of a woman; for in
the shape of a man, Master Brook, I fear not
Goliath with a weaver's beam, because I know
also life is a shuttle. I am in haste: go along
with me; I'll tell you all, Master Brook. Since
I plucked geese, played truant, and whipped top,
I knew not what it was to be beaten till lately.
Follow me: I'll tell you strange things of this
knave Ford, on whom to-night I will be revenged, and I will deliver his wife into your
hand. Follow. Strange things in hand, Master
Brook! Follow. [*Exeunt.*

SCENE II.—*Windsor Park.*

Enter PAGE, SHALLOW, *and* SLENDER.

Page. Come, come; we'll couch i' the castle-
ditch till we see the light of our fairies. Remember, son Slender, my daughter. 3
Slen. Ay, forsooth; I have spoke with her
and we have a nayword how to know one another. I come to her in white, and cry, 'mum;'
she cries, 'budget;' and by that we know one
another. 8
Shal. That's good too: but what needs either
your 'mum,' or her 'budget?' the white will

decipher her well enough. It hath struck ten
o'clock. 12
Page. The night is dark; light and spirits
will become it well. Heaven prosper our sport!
No man means evil but the devil, and we shall
know him by his horns. Let's away; follow me.
[*Exeunt.*

SCENE III.—*The Street in Windsor.*

Enter MISTRESS PAGE, MISTRESS FORD, *and*
DR. CAIUS.

Mrs. Page. Master Doctor, my daughter is in
green: when you see your time, take her by the
hand, away with her to the deanery, and dispatch it quickly. Go before into the Park: we
two must go together. 5
Caius. I know vat I have to do. Adieu.
Mrs. Page. Fare you well, sir. [*Exit* CAIUS.]
My husband will not rejoice so much at the
abuse of Falstaff, as he will chafe at the doctor's
marrying my daughter: but 'tis no matter; better
a little chiding than a great deal of heart break.
Mrs. Ford. Where is Nan now and her troop
of fairies, and the Welsh devil, Hugh? 13
Mrs. Page. They are all couched in a pit hard
by Herne's oak, with obscured lights; which, at
the very instant of Falstaff's and our meeting,
they will at once display to the night. 17
Mrs. Ford. That cannot choose but amaze
him.
Mrs. Page. If he be not amazed, he will be
mocked; if he be amazed, he will every way be
mocked.
Mrs. Ford. We'll betray him finely.
Mrs. Page. Against such lewdsters and their
lechery, 24
Those that betray them do no treachery.
Mrs. Ford. The hour draws on: to the oak,
to the oak! [*Exeunt.*

SCENE IV.—*Windsor Park.*

Enter SIR HUGH EVANS, *disguised, and others
as Fairies.*

Eva. Trib, trib, fairies: come; and remember
your parts. Be pold, I pray you; follow me into
the pit, and when I give the watch-ords, do as I
pid you. Come, come; trib, trib. [*Exeunt.*

SCENE V.—*Another part of the Park.*

Enter FALSTAFF *disguised as Herne, with a
buck's head on.*

Fal. The Windsor bell hath struck twelve;
the minute draws on. Now, the hot-blooded
gods assist me! Remember, Jove, thou wast a
bull for thy Europa; love set on thy horns. O
powerful love! that, in some respects, makes a
beast a man; in some other, a man a beast. You
were also, Jupiter, a swan for the love of Leda;
O omnipotent love! how near the god drew to
the complexion of a goose! A fault done first in
the form of a beast; O Jove, a beastly fault!
and then another fault in the semblance of a
fowl; think on't, Jove; a foul fault! When gods

have hot backs, what shall poor men do? For
me, I am here a Windsor stag; and the fattest,
I think, i' the forest: send me a cool rut-time,
Jove, or who can blame me to piss my tallow?
Who comes here? my doe?   17

Enter MISTRESS FORD *and* MISTRESS PAGE.

Mrs. Ford. Sir John! art thou there, my deer?
my male deer?
Fal. My doe with the black scut! Let the
sky rain potatoes; let it thunder to the tune of
'Green Sleeves;' hail kissing-comfits and snow
eringoes; let there come a tempest of provocation, I will shelter me here.   *[Embracing her.*
Mrs. Ford. Mistress Page is come with me,
sweetheart.   26
Fal. Divide me like a brib'd buck, each a
haunch: I will keep my sides to myself, my
shoulders for the fellow of this walk, and my
horns I bequeath your husbands. Am I a woodman, ha? Speak I like Herne the hunter?
Why, now is Cupid a child of conscience; he
makes restitution. As I am a true spirit, welcome!   *[Noise within.*
Mrs. Page. Alas! what noise?
Mrs. Ford. Heaven forgive our sins!   36
Fal. What should this be?
Mrs. Ford. }
Mrs. Page. } Away, away!   *[They run off.*
Fal. I think the devil will not have me
damned, lest the oil that is in me should set
hell on fire; he would never else cross me
thus.

Enter SIR HUGH EVANS, *like a Satyr;* PISTOL *as*
Hobgoblin; ANNE PAGE, *as the Fairy Queen,*
attended by her Brother and Others, as Fairies,
with waxen tapers on their heads.

Anne. Fairies, black, grey, green, and white,
You moonshine revellers, and shades of night,
You orphan heirs of fixed destiny,   45
Attend your office and your quality.
Crier Hobgoblin, make the fairy oyes.
Pist. Elves, list your names: silence, you
airy toys!   48
Cricket, to Windsor chimneys shalt thou leap:
Where fires thou find'st unrak'd and hearths
unswept,
There pinch the maids as blue as bilberry:
Our radiant queen hates sluts and sluttery. 52
Fal. They are fairies; he that speaks to them
shall die:
I'll wink and couch: no man their works must
eye.   *[Lies down upon his face.*
Eva. Where's Bede? Go you, and where you
find a maid
That, ere she sleep, has thrice her prayers said,
Rein up the organs of her fantasy,   57
Sleep she as sound as careless infancy;
But those that sleep and think not on their sins,
Pinch them, arms, legs, backs, shoulders, sides,
and shins.   60
Anne. About, about!
Search Windsor castle, elves, within and out:
Strew good luck, ouphs, on every sacred room,

That it may stand till the perpetual doom, 64
In state as wholesome as in state 'tis fit,
Worthy the owner, and the owner it.
The several chairs of order look you scour
With juice of balm and every precious flower: 68
Each fair instalment, coat, and several crest,
With loyal blazon, ever more be blest!
And nightly, meadow-fairies, look you sing,
Like to the Garter's compass, in a ring: 72
The expressure that it bears, green let it be,
More fertile-fresh than all the field to see;
And, *Honi soit qui mal y pense* write
In emerald tufts, flowers purple, blue, and white;
Like sapphire, pearl, and rich embroidery, 77
Buckled below fair knighthood's bending knee:
Fairies use flowers for their charactery.
Away! disperse! But, till 'tis one o'clock, 80
Our dance of custom round about the oak
Of Herne the hunter, let us not forget.
Eva. Pray you, lock hand in hand; your-
selves in order set;
And twenty glow-worms shall our lanthorns be,
To guide our measure round about the tree. 85
But, stay; I smell a man of middle-earth.
Fal. Heavens defend me from that Welsh
fairy, lest he transform me to a piece of cheese!
Pist. Vile worm, thou wast o'erlook'd even
in thy birth.   89
Anne. With trial-fire touch me his finger-end:
If he be chaste, the flame will back descend
And turn him to no pain; but if he start, 92
It is the flesh of a corrupted heart.
Pist. A trial! come.
Eva.   Come, will this wood take fire?
     [They burn him with their tapers.
Fal. Oh, oh, oh!
Anne. Corrupt, corrupt, and tainted in
desire!   96
About him, fairies, sing a scornful rime;
And, as you trip, still pinch him to your time.

SONG

Fie on sinful fantasy!
Fie on lust and luxury!   100
Lust is but a bloody fire,
Kindled with unchaste desire,
Fed in heart, whose flames aspire,
As thoughts do blow them higher and higher. 104
Pinch him, fairies, mutually;
Pinch him for his villany;
Pinch him, and burn him, and turn him about,
Till candles and star-light and moonshine be out. 108

During this song, the Fairies pinch FALSTAFF.
DOCTOR CAIUS *comes one way, and steals*
away a Fairy in green; SLENDER *another*
way, and takes off a Fairy in white; and
FENTON *comes, and steals away* ANNE
PAGE. *A noise of hunting is heard within.*
The Fairies run away. FALSTAFF *pulls*
off his buck's head, and rises.

Enter PAGE, FORD, MISTRESS PAGE *and* MIS-
TRESS FORD. *They lay hold on* FALSTAFF.

Page. Nay, do not fly: I think we have
watch'd you now:
Will none but Herne the hunter serve your turn?

Mrs. Page. I pray you, come, hold up the jest no higher.

Now, good Sir John, how like you Windsor wives?   112

See you these, husband? do not these fair yokes Become the forest better than the town?

Ford. Now sir, who's a cuckold now? Master Brook, Falstaff's a knave, a cuckoldly knave; here are his horns, Master Brook: and, Master Brook, he hath enjoyed nothing of Ford's but his buck-basket, his cudgel, and twenty pounds of money, which must be paid too, Master Brook; his horses are arrested for it, Master Brook.   121

Mrs. Ford. Sir John, we have had ill luck; we could never meet. I will never take you for my love again, but I will always count you my deer.   125

Fal. I do begin to perceive that I am made an ass.

Ford. Ay, and an ox too; both the proofs are extant.   129

Fal. And these are not fairies? I was three or four times in the thought they were not fairies; and yet the guiltiness of my mind, the sudden surprise of my powers, drove the grossness of the foppery into a received belief, in despite of the teeth of all rime and reason, that they were fairies. See now how wit may be made a Jack-a-lent, when 'tis upon ill employment!

Eva. Sir John Falstaff, serve Got, and leave your desires, and fairies will not pinse you.   140

Ford. Well said, fairy Hugh.

Eva. And leave you your jealousies too, I pray you.

Ford. I will never mistrust my wife again, till thou art able to woo her in good English.   145

Fal. Have I laid my brain in the sun and dried it, that it wants matter to prevent so gross o'er-reaching as this? Am I ridden with a Welsh goat too? shall I have a coxcomb of frize? 'Tis time I were choked with a piece of toasted cheese.

Eva. Seese is not goot to give putter: your pelly is all putter.   153

Fal. 'Seese' and 'putter!' have I lived to stand at the taunt of one that makes fritters of English? This is enough to be the decay of lust and late-walking through the realm.   157

Mrs. Page. Why, Sir John, do you think, though we would have thrust virtue out of our hearts by the head and shoulders, and have given ourselves without scruple to hell, that ever the devil could have made you our delight?

Ford. What, a hodge-pudding? a bag of flax?

Mrs. Page. A puffed man?   164

Page. Old, cold, withered, and of intolerable entrails?

Ford. And one that is as slanderous as Satan?

Page. And as poor as Job?   168

Ford. And as wicked as his wife?

Eva. And given to fornications, and to taverns, and sack and wine and metheglins, and to drinkings and swearings and starings, pribbles and prabbles?   173

Fal. Well, I am your theme: you have the start of me; I am dejected; I am not able to answer the Welsh flannel. Ignorance itself is a plummet o'er me: use me as you will.   177

Ford. Marry, sir, we'll bring you to Windsor, to one Master Brook, that you have cozened of money, to whom you should have been a pander: over and above that you have suffered, I think, to repay that money will be a biting affliction.

Mrs. Ford. Nay, husband, let that go to make amends;   183

Forgive that sum, and so we'll all be friends.

Ford. Well, here's my hand: all is forgiven at last.

Page. Yet be cheerful, knight: thou shalt eat a posset to-night at my house; where I will desire thee to laugh at my wife, that now laughs at thee. Tell her, Master Slender hath married her daughter.

Mrs. Page. [*Aside.*] Doctors doubt that: if Anne Page be my daughter, she is, by this Doctor Caius' wife.   193

Enter SLENDER.

Slen. Whoa, ho! ho! father Page!

Page. Son, how now! how now, son! have you dispatched?   196

Slen. Dispatched! I'll make the best in Gloster-shire know on't; would I were hanged, la, else!

Page. Of what, son?   200

Slen. I came yonder at Eton to marry Mistress Anne Page, and she's a great lubberly boy: if it had not been i' the church, I would have swinged him, or he should have swinged me. If I did not think it had been Anne Page, would I might never stir! and 'tis a postmaster's boy.   206

Page. Upon my life, then, you took the wrong.

Slen. What need you tell me that? I think so, when I took a boy for a girl. If I had been married to him, for all he was in woman's apparel, I would not have had him.   211

Page. Why, this is your own folly. Did not I tell you how you should know my daughter by her garments?

Slen. I went to her in white, and cried, 'mum,' and she cried 'budget,' as Anne and I had appointed; and yet it was not Anne, but a postmaster's boy.

Eva. Jeshu! Master Slender, cannot you see put marry poys?   220

Page. O I am vexed at heart: what shall I do?

Mrs. Page. Good George, be not angry: I knew of your purpose; turned my daughter into green; and, indeed, she is now with the doctor at the deanery, and there married.   226

Enter DOCTOR CAIUS.

Caius. Vere is Mistress Page? By gar, I am cozened: I ha' married *un garçon*, a boy; *un paysan*, by gar, a boy; it is not Anne Page: by gar, I am cozened.   230

Mrs. Page. Why, did you not take her in green?

Caius. Ay, by gar, and 'tis a boy: by gar, I'll raise all Windsor.   [*Exit.*

Ford. This is strange. Who hath got the right Anne? 235

Page. My heart misgives me: here comes Master Fenton.

Enter FENTON *and* ANNE PAGE.

How now, Master Fenton!

Anne. Pardon, good father! good my mother, pardon! 240

Page. Now, mistress, how chance you went not with Master Slender?

Mrs. Page. Why went you not with Master doctor, maid? 244

Fent. You do amaze her: hear the truth of it. You would have married her most shamefully, Where there was no proportion held in love. The truth is, she and I, long since contracted, 248 Are now so sure that nothing can dissolve us. The offence is holy that she hath committed, And this deceit loses the name of craft, Of disobedience, or unduteous title, 252 Since therein she doth evitate and shun A thousand irreligious cursed hours,

Which forced marriage would have brought upon her.

Ford. Stand not amaz'd: here is no remedy: In love the heavens themselves do guide the state: 257 Money buys lands, and wives are sold by fate.

Fal. I am glad, though you have ta'en a special stand to strike at me, that your arrow hath glanced. 261

Page. Well, what remedy?—Fenton, heaven give thee joy! What cannot be eschew'd must be embrac'd.

Fal. When night dogs run all sorts of deer are chas'd. 264

Mrs. Page. Well, I will muse no further. Master Fenton, Heaven give you many, many merry days! Good husband, let us every one go home, And laugh this sport o'er by a country fire; 268 Sir John and all.

Ford.   Let it be so. Sir John, To Master Brook you yet shall hold your word; For he to-night shall lie with Mistress Ford. 272
                             [*Exeunt.*

MEASURE FOR MEASURE

DRAMATIS PERSONÆ

VINCENTIO, the Duke.
ANGELO, Lord Deputy in the Duke's absence.
ESCALUS, an Ancient Lord, joined with Angelo in the deputation.
CLAUDIO, a young Gentleman.
LUCIO, a Fantastic.
Two other like Gentlemen.
VARRIUS, a Gentleman attending on the Duke.
PROVOST.
THOMAS, } two Friars.
PETER, }
A Justice.

ELBOW, a simple Constable.
FROTH, a foolish Gentleman.
POMPEY, Tapster to Mistress Overdone.
ABHORSON, an Executioner.
BARNARDINE, a dissolute Prisoner.

ISABELLA, sister to Claudio.
MARIANA, betrothed to Angelo.
JULIET, beloved of Claudio.
FRANCISCA, a Nun.
MISTRESS OVERDONE, a Bawd.

Lords, Officers, Citizens, Boy, and Attendants.

SCENE.—*Vienna.*

ACT I

SCENE I.—*An Apartment in the* DUKE'S *Palace.*

Enter DUKE, ESCALUS, *Lords, and* Attendants.

Duke. Escalus.
Escal. My lord?
Duke. Of government the properties to unfold,
Would seem in me to affect speech and discourse,
Since I am put to know that your own science 5
Exceeds, in that, the lists of all advice
My strength can give you: then no more remains,
But that, to your sufficiency, as your worth is able,
And let them work. The nature of our people, 9
Our city's institutions, and the terms
For common justice, you're as pregnant in,
As art and practice hath enriched any 12
That we remember. There is our commission,
[*Giving it.*
From which we would not have you warp. Call hither,
I say, bid come before us Angelo.
[*Exit an* Attendant.
What figure of us think you he will bear? 16
For you must know, we have with special soul
Elected him our absence to supply,
Lent him our terror, drest him with our love,
And given his deputation all the organs 20
Of our own power: what think you of it?
Escal. If any in Vienna be of worth
To undergo such ample grace and honour,
It is Lord Angelo.
Duke. Look where he comes. 24

Enter ANGELO.

Ang. Always obedient to your Grace's will,
I come to know your pleasure.
Duke. Angelo,
There is a kind of character in thy life,
That, to th' observer doth thy history 28
Fully unfold. Thyself and thy belongings
Are not thine own so proper, as to waste
Thyself upon thy virtues, they on thee.
Heaven doth with us as we with torches do, 32
Not light them for themselves; for if our virtues
Did not go forth of us, 'twere all alike
As if we had them not. Spirits are not finely touch'd
But to fine issues, nor Nature never lends 36
The smallest scruple of her excellence,
But, like a thrifty goddess, she determines
Herself the glory of a creditor,
Both thanks and use. But I do bend my speech
To one that can my part in him advertise; 41
Hold, therefore, Angelo:
[*Tendering his commission.*
In our remove be thou at full ourself;
Mortality and mercy in Vienna 44
Live in thy tongue and heart. Old Escalus,
Though first in question, is thy secondary.
Take thy commission. [*Giving it.*
Ang. Now, good my lord,
Let there be some more test made of my metal,
Before so noble and so great a figure 49
Be stamp'd upon it.
Duke. No more evasion:
We have with a leaven'd and prepared choice
Proceeded to you; therefore take your honours.
Our haste from hence is of so quick condition 53
That it prefers itself, and leaves unquestion'd
Matters of needful value. We shall write to you,
As time and our concernings shall importune, 56
How it goes with us; and do look to know
What doth befall you here. So, fare you well:
To the hopeful execution do I leave you
Of your commissions.
Ang. Yet, give leave, my lord, 60
That we may bring you something on the way.
Duke. My haste may not admit it;
Nor need you, on mine honour, have to do
With any scruple: your scope is as mine own, 64
So to enforce or qualify the laws
As to your soul seems good. Give me your hand;
I'll privily away: I love the people,
But do not like to stage me to their eyes. 68
Though it be well, I do not relish well
Their loud applause and Aves vehement,
Nor do I think the man of safe discretion
That does affect it. Once more, fare you well. 72

Ang. The heavens give safety to your purposes!

Escal. Lead forth and bring you back in happiness!

Duke. I thank you. Fare you well. [*Exit.*

Escal. I shall desire you, sir, to give me leave
To have free speech with you; and it concerns me
To look into the bottom of my place:
A power I have, but of what strength and nature
I am not yet instructed.   80

Ang. 'Tis so with me. Let us withdraw together,
And we may soon our satisfaction have
Touching that point.

Escal.   I'll wait upon your honour.
             [*Exeunt.*

Scene II.—*A Street.*

Enter LUCIO *and two* Gentlemen.

Lucio. If the Duke with the other dukes come not to composition with the King of Hungary, why then, all the dukes fall upon the king.

First Gent. Heaven grant us its peace, but not the King of Hungary's!   5

Second Gent. Amen.

Lucio. Thou concludest like the sanctimonious pirate, that went to sea with the Ten Commandments, but scraped one out of the table.

Second Gent. 'Thou shalt not steal?' 10

Lucio. Ay, that he razed.

First Gent. Why, 'twas a commandment to command the captain and all the rest from their functions: they put forth to steal. There's not a soldier of us all, that, in the thanksgiving before meat, doth relish the petition well that prays for peace.   17

Second Gent. I never heard any soldier dislike it.

Lucio. I believe thee, for I think thou never wast where grace was said.   21

Second Gent. No? a dozen times at least.

First Gent. What, in metre?

Lucio. In any proportion or in any language.

First Gent. I think, or in any religion. 25

Lucio. Ay; why not? Grace is grace, despite of all controversy: as, for example, thou thyself art a wicked villain, despite of all grace. 28

First Gent. Well, there went but a pair of shears between us.

Lucio. I grant; as there may between the lists and the velvet: thou art the list. 32

First Gent. And thou the velvet: thou art good velvet; thou art a three-piled piece, I warrant thee. I had as lief be a list of an English kersey as be piled, as thou art piled, for a French velvet. Do I speak feelingly now? 37

Lucio. I think thou dost; and, indeed, with most painful feeling of thy speech: I will, out of thine own confession, learn to begin thy health; but, whilst I live, forget to drink after thee.

First Gent. I think I have done myself wrong, have I not?   44

Second Gent. Yes, that thou hast, whether thou art tainted or free.

Lucio. Behold, behold, where Madam Mitigation comes! I have purchased as many diseases under her roof as come to—   49

Second Gent. To what, I pray?

Lucio. Judge.

Second Gent. To three thousand dolours a year.   53

First Gent. Ay, and more.

Lucio. A French crown more.

First Gent. Thou art always figuring diseases in me; but thou art full of error: I am sound. 57

Lucio. Nay, not as one would say, healthy; but so sound as things that are hollow: thy bones are hollow; impiety has made a feast of thee.   61

Enter MISTRESS OVERDONE.

First Gent. How now! which of your hips has the most profound sciatica?

Mrs. Ov. Well, well; there's one yonder arrested and carried to prison was worth five thousand of you all.   66

Second Gent. Who's that, I pray thee?

Mrs. Ov. Marry, sir, that's Claudio, Signior Claudio.

First Gent. Claudio to prison! 'tis not so. 70

Mrs. Ov. Nay, but I know 'tis so: I saw him arrested; saw him carried away; and, which is more, within these three days his head to be chopped off.

Lucio. But, after all this fooling, I would not have it so. Art thou sure of this? 76

Mrs. Ov. I am too sure of it; and it is for getting Madam Julietta with child.

Lucio. Believe me, this may be: he promised to meet me two hours since, and he was ever precise in promise-keeping.   81

Second Gent. Besides, you know, it draws something near to the speech we had to such a purpose.   84

First Gent. But most of all, agreeing with the proclamation.

Lucio. Away! let's go learn the truth of it.
    [*Exeunt* LUCIO *and* Gentlemen.

Mrs. Ov. Thus, what with the war, what with the sweat, what with the gallows and what with poverty, I am custom-shrunk.

Enter POMPEY.

How now! what's the news with you?

Pom. Yonder man is carried to prison. 92

Mrs. Ov. Well: what has he done?

Pom. A woman.

Mrs. Ov. But what's his offence?

Pom. Groping for trouts in a peculiar river.

Mrs. Ov. What, is there a maid with child by him?

Pom. No; but there's a woman with maid by him. You have not heard of the proclamation, have you?   101

Mrs. Ov. What proclamation, man?

Pom. All houses of resort in the suburbs of Vienna must be plucked down. 104

Mrs. Ov. And what shall become of those in the city?

Pom. They shall stand for seed: they had gone down too, but that a wise burgher put in for them.   109

Mrs. Ov. But shall all our houses of resort in the suburbs be pulled down?

Pom. To the ground, mistress.   112

Mrs. Ov. Why, here's a change indeed in the commonwealth! What shall become of me?

Pom. Come; fear not you: good counsellors lack no clients: though you change your place, you need not change your trade; I'll be your tapster still. Courage! there will be pity taken on you; you that have worn your eyes almost out in the service, you will be considered.   120

Mrs. Ov. What's to do here, Thomas tapster? Let's withdraw.

Pom. Here comes Signior Claudio, led by the provost to prison; and there's Madam Juliet.
                                        [*Exeunt.*

Enter PROVOST, CLAUDIO, JULIET, *and* Officers.

Claud. Fellow, why dost thou show me thus to the world?
Bear me to prison, where I am committed.

Prov. I do it not in evil disposition,
But from Lord Angelo by special charge.   128

Claud. Thus can the demi-god Authority
Make us pay down for our offence by weight.
The words of heaven; on whom it will, it will;
On whom it will not, so: yet still 'tis just.   132

Re-enter LUCIO *and two Gentlemen.*

Lucio. Why, how now, Claudio! whence comes this restraint?

Claud. From too much liberty, my Lucio, liberty:
As surfeit is the father of much fast,
So every scope by the immoderate use   136
Turns to restraint. Our natures do pursue—
Like rats that ravin down their proper bane,—
A thirsty evil, and when we drink we die.

Lucio. If I could speak so wisely under an arrest, I would send for certain of my creditors. And yet, to say the truth, I had as lief have the foppery of freedom as the morality of imprisonment. What's thy offence, Claudio?   144

Claud. What but to speak of would offend again.

Lucio. What, is't murder?

Claud. No.   148

Lucio. Lechery?

Claud. Call it so.

Prov. Away, sir! you must go.   151

Claud. One word, good friend. Lucio, a word with you.   [*Takes him aside.*

Lucio. A hundred, if they'll do you any good. Is lechery so looked after?

Claud. Thus stands it with me: upon a true contract
I got possession of Julietta's bed: 156
You know the lady; she is fast my wife,
Save that we do the denunciation lack
Of outward order: this we came not to,
Only for propagation of a dower   160
Remaining in the coffer of her friends,
From whom we thought it meet to hide our love
Till time had made them for us. But it chances
The stealth of our most mutual entertainment
With character too gross is writ on Juliet.   165

Lucio. With child, perhaps?

Claud.   Unhappily, even so.
And the new deputy now for the duke,—
Whether it be the fault and glimpse of newness,   168
Or whether that the body public be
A horse whereon the governor doth ride,
Who, newly in the seat, that it may know
He can command, lets it straight feel the spur;
Whether the tyranny be in his place,   173
Or in his eminence that fills it up,
I stagger in:—but this new governor
Awakes me all the enrolled penalties   176
Which have, like unscour'd armour, hung by the wall
So long that nineteen zodiacs have gone round,
And none of them been worn; and, for a name,
Now puts the drowsy and neglected act   180
Freshly on me: 'tis surely for a name.

Lucio. I warrant it is: and thy head stands so tickle on thy shoulders that a milkmaid, if she be in love, may sigh it off. Send after the duke and appeal to him.   185

Claud. I have done so, but he's not to be found.
I prithee, Lucio, do me this kind service.
This day my sister should the cloister enter,   188
And there receive her approbation:
Acquaint her with the danger of my state;
Implore her, in my voice, that she make friends
To the strict deputy; bid herself assay him: 192
I have great hope in that; for in her youth
There is a prone and speechless dialect,
Such as move men; beside, she hath prosperous art
When she will play with reason and discourse,
And well she can persuade.   197

Lucio. I pray she may: as well for the encouragement of the like, which else would stand under grievous imposition, as for the enjoying of thy life, who I would be sorry should be thus foolishly lost at a game of tick-tack. I'll to her.

Claud. I thank you, good friend Lucio.

Lucio. Within two hours.

Claud.   Come, officer, away!
                                        [*Exeunt.*

SCENE III.—*A Monastery.*

Enter DUKE *and* FRIAR THOMAS.

Duke. No, holy father; throw away that thought:
Believe not that the dribbling dart of love
Can pierce a complete bosom. Why I desire thee
To give me secret harbour, hath a purpose   4
More grave and wrinkled than the aims and ends
Of burning youth.

Fri. T.   May your Grace speak of it?

Duke. My holy sir, none better knows than you
How I have ever lov'd the life remov'd,   8
And held in idle price to haunt assemblies
Where youth, and cost, and witless bravery keeps.
I have deliver'd to Lord Angelo—
A man of stricture and firm abstinence—   12
My absolute power and place here in Vienna,

And he supposes me travell'd to Poland;
For so I have strew'd it in the common ear,
And so it is receiv'd.   16
You will demand of me why I do this?
  Fri. T. Gladly, my lord.
  Duke. We have strict statutes and most biting
laws,—
The needful bits and curbs to headstrong
steeds,—   20
Which for this fourteen years we have let sleep;
Even like an o'ergrown lion in a cave,
That goes not out to prey. Now, as fond fathers,
Having bound up the threat'ning twigs of birch,
Only to stick it in their children's sight   25
For terror, not to use, in time the rod
Becomes more mock'd than fear'd; so our de-
crees,
Dead to infliction, to themselves are dead,   28
And liberty plucks justice by the nose;
The baby beats the nurse, and quite athwart
Goes all decorum.
  Fri. T.   It rested in your Grace
T' unloose this tied-up justice when you pleas'd;
And it in you more dreadful would have seem'd
Than in Lord Angelo.
  Duke.   I do fear, too dreadful:
Sith 'twas my fault to give the people scope, 35
'Twould be my tyranny to strike and gall them
For what I bid them do: for we bid this be done,
When evil deeds have their permissive pass
And not the punishment. Therefore, indeed,
my father,
I have on Angelo impos'd the office,   40
Who may, in the ambush of my name, strike
home,
And yet my nature never in the sight
To do it slander. And to behold his sway,   44
I will, as 'twere a brother of your order,
Visit both prince and people: therefore, I
prithee,
Supply me with the habit, and instruct me
How I may formally in person bear me
Like a true friar. Moe reasons for this action
At our more leisure shall I render you;   49
Only, this one: Lord Angelo is precise;
Stands at a guard with envy; scarce confesses
That his blood flows, or that his appetite   52
Is more to bread than stone: hence shall we see,
If power change purpose, what our seemers be.
                            [Exeunt.

SCENE IV.—*A Nunnery.*

Enter ISABELLA *and* FRANCISCA.

  Isab. And have you nuns no further privi-
leges?
  Fran. Are not these large enough?
  Isab. Yes, truly: I speak not as desiring
more,   4
But rather wishing a more strict restraint
Upon the sisterhood, the votarists of Saint Clare.
  Lucio. [*Within.*] Ho! Peace be in this
place!
  Isab. Who's that which calls?
  Fran. It is a man's voice. Gentle Isabella,
Turn you the key, and know his business of him:

You may, I may not; you are yet unsworn. 9
When you have vow'd, you must not speak with
men
But in the presence of the prioress:
Then, if you speak, you must not show your
face,   12
Or, if you show your face, you must not speak.
He calls again; I pray you, answer him. [*Exit.*
  Isab. Peace and prosperity! Who is't that
calls?

Enter LUCIO.

  Lucio. Hail, virgin, if you be, as those cheek-
roses   16
Proclaim you are no less! Can you so stead me
As bring me to the sight of Isabella,
A novice of this place, and the fair sister
To her unhappy brother Claudio?   20
  Isab. Why 'her unhappy brother?' let me ask;
The rather for I now must make you know
I am that Isabella and his sister.
  Lucio. Gentle and fair, your brother kindly
greets you: 24
Not to be weary with you, he's in prison.
  Isab. Woe me! for what?
  Lucio. For that which, if myself might be his
judge,
He should receive his punishment in thanks: 28
He hath got his friend with child.
  Isab. Sir, make me not your story.
  Lucio.   It is true.
I would not, though 'tis my familiar sin
With maids to seem the lapwing and to jest, 32
Tongue far from heart, play with all virgins so:
I hold you as a thing ensky'd and sainted;
By your renouncement an immortal spirit,
And to be talk'd with in sincerity,   36
As with a saint.
  Isab. You do blaspheme the good in mock-
ing me.
  Lucio. Do not believe it. Fewness and truth,
'tis thus:
Your brother and his lover have embrac'd: 40
As those that feed grow full, as blossoming time
That from the seedness the bare fallow brings
To teeming foison, even so her plenteous womb
Expresseth his full tilth and husbandry.   44
  Isab. Some one with child by him? My cousin
Juliet?
  Lucio. Is she your cousin?
  Isab. Adoptedly; as school-maids change
their names
By vain, though apt affection.
  Lucio.   She it is.   48
  Isab. O! let him marry her.
  Lucio.   This is the point.
The duke is very strangely gone from hence;
Bore many gentlemen, myself being one,
In hand and hope of action; but we do learn 52
By those that know the very nerves of state,
His givings out were of an infinite distance
From his true-meant design. Upon his place,
And with full line of his authority,   56
Governs Lord Angelo; a man whose blood
Is very snow-broth; one who never feels

The wanton stings and motions of the sense,
But doth rebate and blunt his natural edge 60
With profits of the mind, study and fast.
He,—to give fear to use and liberty,
Which have for long run by the hideous law,
As mice by lions, hath pick'd out an act, 64
Under whose heavy sense your brother's life
Falls into forfeit: he arrests him on it,
And follows close the rigour of the statute,
To make him an example. All hope is gone, 68
Unless you have the grace by your fair prayer
To soften Angelo; and that's my pith of business
Twixt you and your poor brother.
  Isab. Doth he so seek his life?
  Lucio.   He's censur'd him 72
Already; and, as I hear, the provost hath
A warrant for his execution.
  Isab. Alas! what poor ability's in me
To do him good?
  Lucio.   Assay the power you have. 76
  Isab. My power? alas! I doubt—
  Lucio.   Our doubts are traitors,
And make us lose the good we oft might win,
By fearing to attempt. Go to Lord Angelo,
And let him learn to know, when maidens
    sue, 80
Men give like gods; but when they weep and
    kneel,
All their petitions are as freely theirs
As they themselves would owe them.
  Isab. I'll see what I can do.
  Lucio.   But speedily. 84
  Isab. I will about it straight;
No longer staying but to give the Mother
Notice of my affair. I humbly thank you:
Commend me to my brother; soon at night 88
I'll send him certain word of my success.
  Lucio. I take my leave of you.
  Isab.   Good sir, adieu. [*Exeunt.*

ACT II

SCENE I.—*A Hall in* ANGELO'S *House.*

Enter ANGELO, ESCALUS, *a* Justice, PROVOST,
Officers, *and other* Attendants.

  Ang. We must not make a scarecrow of the
    law,
Setting it up to fear the birds of prey,
And let it keep one shape, till custom make it
Their perch and not their terror.
  Escal.   Ay, but yet 4
Let us be keen and rather cut a little,
Than fall, and bruise to death. Alas! this
    gentleman,
Whom I would save, had a most noble father.
Let but your honour know,— 8
Whom I believe to be most strait in virtue,—
That, in the working of your own affections,
Had time coher'd with place or place with
    wishing,
Or that the resolute acting of your blood 12
Could have attain'd the effect of your own pur-
    pose,

Whether you had not, some time in your life,
Err'd in this point which now you censure him,
And pull'd the law upon you. 16
  Ang. 'Tis one thing to be tempted, Escalus,
Another thing to fall. I not deny,
The jury, passing on the prisoner's life,
May in the sworn twelve have a thief or two 20
Guiltier than him they try; what's open made
    to justice,
That justice seizes: what know the laws
That thieves do pass on thieves? 'Tis very preg-
    nant,
The jewel that we find, we stoop and take it 24
Because we see it; but what we do not see
We tread upon, and never think of it.
You may not so extenuate his offence
For I have had such faults; but rather tell me,
When I, that censure him, do so offend, 29
Let mine own judgment pattern out my death,
And nothing come in partial. Sir, he must die.
  Escal. Be it as your wisdom will.
  Ang.   Where is the provost?
  Prov. Here, if it like your honour.
  Ang.   See that Claudio
Be executed by nine to-morrow morning:
Bring him his confessor, let him be prepar'd;
For that's the utmost of his pilgrimage. 36
            [*Exit* PROVOST.
  Escal. Well, heaven forgive him, and forgive
    us all!
Some rise by sin, and some by virtue fall:
Some run from brakes of ice, and answer none,
And some condemned for a fault alone. 40

Enter ELBOW *and Officers, with* FROTH *and*
POMPEY.

  Elb. Come, bring them away: if these be
good people in a common-weal that do nothing
but use their abuses in common houses, I know
no law: bring them away. 44
  Ang. How now, sir! What's your name, and
what's the matter?
  Elb. If it please your honour, I am the poor
duke's constable, and my name is Elbow: I do
lean upon justice, sir; and do bring in here
before your good honour two notorious benefactors. 51
  Ang. Benefactors! Well; what benefactors
are they? are they not malefactors?
  Elb. If it please your honour, I know not well
what they are; but precise villains they are, that
I am sure of, and void of all profanation in the
world that good Christians ought to have. 57
  Escal. This comes off well: here's a wise
officer.
  Ang. Go to: what quality are they of? Elbow
is your name? why dost thou not speak, Elbow?
  Pom. He cannot, sir: he's out at elbow. 62
  Ang. What are you, sir?
  Elb. He, sir! a tapster, sir; parcel-bawd; one
that serves a bad woman, whose house, sir, was,
as they say, plucked down in the suburbs; and
now she professes a hot-house, which, I think, is
a very ill house too. 68
  Escal. How know you that?

Elb. My wife, sir, whom I detest before heaven and your honour,—

Escal. How! thy wife?   72

Elb. Ay, sir; whom, I thank heaven, is an honest woman,—

Escal. Dost thou detest her therefore?

Elb. I say, sir, I will detest myself also, as well as she, that this house, if it be not a bawd's house, it is pity of her life, for it is a naughty house.   79

Escal. How dost thou know that, constable?

Elb. Marry, sir, by my wife; who, if she had been a woman cardinally given, might have been accused in fornication, adultery, and all uncleanliness there.   84

Escal. By the woman's means?

Elb. Ay, sir, by Mistress Overdone's means; but as she spit in his face, so she defied him.

Pom. Sir, if it please your honour, this is not so.   89

Elb. Prove it before these varlets here, thou honourable man, prove it.

Escal. [*To* ANGELO.] Do you hear how he misplaces?   93

Pom. Sir, she came in, great with child, and longing,—saving your honour's reverence,—for stewed prunes. Sir, we had but two in the house, which at that very distant time stood, as it were, in a fruit-dish, a dish of some three-pence; your honours have seen such dishes; they are not China dishes, but very good dishes.

Escal. Go to, go to: no matter for the dish, sir.

Pom. No, indeed, sir, not of a pin; you are therein in the right: but to the point. As I say, this Mistress Elbow, being, as I say, with child, and being great-bellied, and longing, as I said, for prunes, and having but two in the dish, as I said, Master Froth here, this very man, having eaten the rest, as I said, and, as I say, paying for them very honestly; for, as you know, Master Froth, I could not give you three-pence again.

Froth. No, indeed.   112

Pom. Very well: you being then, if you be re-membered, cracking the stones of the foresaid prunes,—

Froth. Ay, so I did, indeed.   116

Pom. Why, very well: I telling you then, if you be remembered, that such a one and such a one were past cure of the thing you wot of, un-less they kept very good diet, as I told you,—   120

Froth. All this is true.

Pom. Why, very well then.—

Escal. Come, you are a tedious fool: to the purpose. What was done to Elbow's wife, that he hath cause to complain of? Come me to what was done to her.

Pom. Sir, your honour cannot come to that yet.   128

Escal. No, sir, nor I mean it not.

Pom. Sir, but you shall come to it, by your honour's leave. And, I beseech you, look into Master Froth here, sir; a man of fourscore pound a year, whose father died at Hallowmas. Was't not at Hallowmas, Master Froth?   134

Froth. All-hallownd eve.

Pom. Why, very well: I hope here be truths. He, sir, sitting, as I say, in a lower chair, sir; 'twas in the Bunch of Grapes, where indeed, you have a delight to sit, have you not?   139

Froth. I have so, because it is an open room and good for winter.

Pom. Why, very well then: I hope here be truths.

Ang. This will last out a night in Russia,   144 When nights are longest there: I'll take my leave,
And leave you to the hearing of the cause,
Hoping you'll find good cause to whip them all.

Escal. I think no less. Good morrow to your lordship.   [*Exit* ANGELO. Now, sir, come on: what was done to Elbow's wife, once more?

Pom. Once, sir? there was nothing done to her once.   152

Elb. I beseech you, sir, ask him what this man did to my wife.

Pom. I beseech your honour, ask me.

Escal. Well, sir, what did this gentleman to her?   157

Pom. I beseech you, sir, look in this gentle-man's face. Good Master Froth, look upon his honour; 'tis for a good purpose. Doth your honour mark his face?   161

Escal. Ay, sir, very well.

Pom. Nay, I beseech you, mark it well.

Escal. Well, I do so.   164

Pom. Doth your honour see any harm in his face?

Escal. Why, no.

Pom. I'll be supposed upon a book, his face is the worst thing about him. Good, then; if his face be the worst thing about him, how could Master Froth do the constable's wife any harm? I would know that of your honour.   172

Escal. He's in the right. Constable, what say you to it?

Elb. First, an' it like you, the house is a respected house; next, this is a respected fellow, and his mistress is a respected woman.   177

Pom. By this hand, sir, his wife is a more respected person than any of us all.

Elb. Varlet, thou liest: thou liest, wicked varlet. The time is yet to come that she was ever respected with man, woman, or child.   182

Pom. Sir, she was respected with him before he married with her.

Escal. Which is the wiser here? Justice, or Iniquity? Is this true?   186

Elb. O thou caitiff! O thou varlet! O thou wicked Hannibal! I respected with her before I was married to her? If ever I was respected with her, or she with me, let not your worship think me the poor duke's officer. Prove this, thou wicked Hannibal, or I'll have mine action of battery on thee.   193

Escal. If he took you a box o' th' ear, you might have your action of slander too.

Elb. Marry, I thank your good worship for it. What is't your worship's pleasure I shall do with this wicked caitiff?   198

Escal. Truly, officer, because he hath some

offences in him that thou wouldest discover if thou couldst, let him continue in his courses till thou knowest what they are. 202

Elb. Marry, I thank your worship for it. Thou seest, thou wicked varlet, now, what's come upon thee: thou art to continue now, thou varlet, thou art to continue.

Escal. Where were you born, friend?

Froth. Here in Vienna, sir. 208

Escal. Are you of fourscore pounds a year?

Froth. Yes, an 't please you, sir.

Escal. So. [*To* POMPEY.] What trade are you of, sir? 212

Pom. A tapster; a poor widow's tapster.

Escal. Your mistress' name?

Pom. Mistress Overdone.

Escal. Hath she had any more than one husband?

Pom. Nine, sir; Overdone by the last. 218

Escal. Nine!—Come hither to me, Master Froth. Master Froth, I would not have you acquainted with tapsters; they will draw you, Master Froth, and you will hang them. Get you gone, and let me hear no more of you.

Froth. I thank your worship. For mine own part, I never come into any room in a taphouse, but I am drawn in. 226

Escal. Well: no more of it, Master Froth: farewell. [*Exit* FROTH.]—Come you hither to me, Master tapster. What's your name, Master tapster?

Pom. Pompey.

Escal. What else? 232

Pom. Bum, sir.

Escal. Troth, and your bum is the greatest thing about you, so that, in the beastliest sense, you are Pompey the Great. Pompey, you are partly a bawd, Pompey, howsoever you colour it in being a tapster, are you not? come, tell me true: it shall be the better for you. 239

Pom. Truly, sir, I am a poor fellow that would live.

Escal. How would you live, Pompey? by being a bawd? What do you think of the trade, Pompey? is it a lawful trade? 244

Pom. If the law would allow it, sir.

Escal. But the law will not allow it, Pompey; nor it shall not be allowed in Vienna.

Pom. Does your worship mean to geld and splay all the youth of the city?

Escal. No, Pompey. 250

Pom. Truly, sir, in my humble opinion, they will to 't then. If your worship will take order for the drabs and the knaves, you need not to fear the bawds.

Escal. There are pretty orders beginning, I can tell you: it is but heading and hanging. 256

Pom. If you head and hang all that offend that way but for ten year together, you'll be glad to give out a commission for more heads. If this law hold in Vienna ten year, I'll rent the fairest house in it after threepence a bay. If you live to see this come to pass, say, Pompey told you so. 263

Escal. Thank you, good Pompey; and, in requital of your prophecy, hark you: I advise you, let me not find you before me again upon any complaint whatsoever; no, not for dwelling where you do: if I do, Pompey, I shall beat you to your tent, and prove a shrewd Cæsar to you. In plain dealing, Pompey, I shall have you whipt. So, for this time, Pompey, fare you well. 272

Pom. I thank your worship for your good counsel;—[*Aside.*] but I shall follow it as the flesh and fortune shall better determine.

Whip me! No, no; let carman whip his jade; The valiant heart's not whipt out of his trade.

[*Exit.*

Escal. Come hither to me, Master Elbow; come hither. Master constable. How long have you been in this place of constable? 280

Elb. Seven year and a half, sir.

Escal. I thought, by your readiness in the office, you had continued in it some time. You say, seven years together? 284

Elb. And a half, sir.

Escal. Alas! it hath been great pains to you! They do you wrong to put you so oft upon 't. Are there not men in your ward sufficient to serve it? 289

Elb. Faith, sir, few of any wit in such matters. As they are chosen, they are glad to choose me for them: I do it for some piece of money, and go through with all. 293

Escal. Look you bring me in the names of some six or seven, the most sufficient of your parish. 296

Elb. To your worship's house, sir?

Escal. To my house. Fare you well.

[*Exit* ELBOW.

What's o'clock, think you?

Just. Eleven, sir. 300

Escal. I pray you home to dinner with me.

Just. I humbly thank you.

Escal. It grieves me for the death of Claudio; But there is no remedy. 304

Just. Lord Angelo is severe.

Escal. It is but needful:
Mercy is not itself, that oft looks so;
Pardon is still the nurse of second woe.
But yet, poor Claudio! There's no remedy. 308
Come, sir. [*Exeunt.*

SCENE II.—*Another Room in the Same.*

Enter PROVOST *and a* Servant.

Serv. He's hearing of a cause: he will come straight:
I'll tell him of you.

Prov. Pray you, do. [*Exit* Serv.] I'll know
His pleasure; may be he will relent. Alas!
He hath but as offended in a dream: 4
All sects, all ages smack of this vice, and he
To die for it!

Enter ANGELO.

Ang. Now, what's the matter, provost?

Prov. Is it your will Claudio shall die to-morrow?

Ang. Did I not tell thee, yea? hadst thou
    not order?   8
Why dost thou ask again?
  Prov.   Lest I might be too rash.
Under your good correction, I have seen,
When, after execution, Judgment hath
Repented o'er his doom.
  Ang.   Go to; let that be mine: 12
Do you your office, or give up your place,
And you shall well be spar'd.
  Prov.   I crave your honour's pardon.
What shall be done, sir, with the groaning
    Juliet?
She's very near her hour.
  Ang.   Dispose of her   16
To some more fitter place; and that with speed.

Re-enter Servant.

  Serv. Here is the sister of the man condemn'd
Desires access to you.
  Ang.   Hath he a sister?
  Prov. Ay, my good lord; a very virtuous
    maid,   20
And to be shortly of a sisterhood,
If not already.
  Ang.   Well, let her be admitted.
         [*Exit* Servant.
See you the fornicatress be remov'd:
Let her have needful, but not lavish, means; 24
There shall be order for't.

Enter ISABELLA *and* LUCIO.

  Prov.   God save your honour!
         [*Offering to retire.*
  Ang. Stay a little while.—[*To* ISAB.] You're
welcome: what's your will?
  Isab. I am a woful suitor to your honour,
Please but your honour hear me.
  Ang.   Well; what's your suit? 28
  Isab. There is a vice that most I do abhor,
And most desire should meet the blow of justice,
For which I would not plead, but that I must;
For which I must not plead, but that I am   32
At war 'twixt will and will not.
  Ang.   Well; the matter?
  Isab. I have a brother is condemn'd to die:
I do beseech you, let it be his fault,
And not my brother.
  Prov.   [*Aside.*] Heaven give thee moving
    graces!   36
  Ang. Condemn the fault, and not the actor
    of it?
Why, every fault's condemn'd ere it be done.
Mine were the very cipher of a function,
To fine the faults whose fine stands in record, 40
And let go by the actor.
  Isab.   O just, but severe law!
I had a brother, then.—Heaven keep your
    honour!   [*Retiring.*
  Lucio. [*Aside to* ISAB.] Give 't not o'er so:
    to him again, entreat him;
Kneel down before him, hang upon his gown;
You are too cold; if you should need a pin, 45
You could not with more tame a tongue desire it.
To him, I say!
  Isab. Must he needs die?

  Ang.   Maiden, no remedy.
  Isab. Yes; I do think that you might pardon
    him,   49
And neither heaven nor man grieve at the
    mercy.
  Ang. I will not do't.
  Isab.   But can you, if you would?
  Ang. Look, what I will not, that I cannot do.
  Isab. But might you do't, and do the world
    no wrong,   53
If so your heart were touch'd with that remorse
As mine is to him?
  Ang.   He's sentenc'd: 'tis too late.
  Lucio. [*Aside to* ISAB.] You are too cold. 56
  Isab. Too late? why, no; I, that do speak a
    word,
May call it back again. Well, believe this,
No ceremony that to great ones 'longs,
Not the king's crown, nor the deputed sword, 60
The marshal's truncheon, nor the judge's robe,
Become them with one half so good a grace
As mercy does.
If he had been as you, and you as he,   64
You would have slipt like him; but he, like you,
Would not have been so stern.
  Ang.   Pray you, be gone.
  Isab. I would to heaven I had your potency,
And you were Isabel! should it then be thus? 68
No; I would tell what 'twere to be a judge,
And what a prisoner.
  Lucio. [*Aside to* ISAB.] Ay, touch him; there's
    the vein.
  Ang. Your brother is a forfeit of the law,
And you but waste your words.
  Isab.   Alas! alas! 72
Why, all the souls that were were forfeit once;
And He that might the vantage best have took,
Found out the remedy. How would you be,
If He, which is the top of judgment, should 76
But judge you as you are? O! think on that,
And mercy then will breathe within your lips,
Like man new made.
  Ang.   Be you content, fair maid;
It is the law, not I, condemn your brother: 80
Were he my kinsman, brother, or my son,
It should be thus with him: he must die to-
    morrow.
  Isab. To-morrow! O! that's sudden! Spare
    him, spare him!
He's not prepar'd for death. Even for our
    kitchens   84
We kill the fowl of season: shall we serve heaven
With less respect than we do minister
To our gross selves? Good, good my lord, be-
    think you:
Who is it that hath died for this offence?   88
There's many have committed it.
  Lucio.   [*Aside to* ISAB.] Ay, well said.
  Ang. The law hath not been dead, though it
    hath slept:
Those many had not dar'd to do that evil,
If that the first that did th' edict infringe 92
Had answer'd for his deed: now 'tis awake,
Takes note of what is done, and, like a prophet,
Looks in a glass, that shows what future evils,
Either new, or by remissness new-conceiv'd, 96

And so in progress to be hatch'd and born,
Are now to have no successive degrees,
But, ere they live, to end.

Isab.   Yet show some pity.

Ang. I show it most of all when I show justice;
For then I pity those I do not know,   101
Which a dismiss'd offence would after gall,
And do him right, that, answering one foul wrong,
Lives not to act another. Be satisfied: 104
Your brother dies to-morrow: be content.

Isab. So you must be the first that gives this sentence,
And he that suffers. O! it is excellent
To have a giant's strength, but it is tyrannous
To use it like a giant.

Lucio. [*Aside to* ISAB.] That's well said.   109

Isab. Could great men thunder
As Jove himself does, Jove would ne'er be quiet,
For every pelting, petty officer   112
Would use his heaven for thunder; nothing but thunder.
Merciful heaven!
Thou rather with thy sharp and sulphurous bolt
Split'st the unwedgeable and gnarled oak   116
Than the soft myrtle; but man, proud man,
Drest in a little brief authority,
Most ignorant of what he's most assur'd,
His glassy essence, like an angry ape,   120
Plays such fantastic tricks before high heaven
As make the angels weep; who, with our spleens,
Would all themselves laugh mortal.

Lucio. [*Aside to* ISAB.] O, to him, to him, wench! He will relent: 124
He's coming: I perceive 't.

Prov. [*Aside.*] Pray heaven she win him!

Isab. We cannot weigh our brother with ourself:
Great men may jest with saints; 'tis wit in them,
But, in the less foul profanation.   128

Lucio. [*Aside to* ISAB.] Thou'rt in the right, girl: more o' that.

Isab. That in the captain's but a choleric word,
Which in the soldier is flat blasphemy.

Lucio. [*Aside to* ISAB.] Art advis'd o' that? more on't.   132

Ang. Why do you put these sayings upon me?

Isab. Because authority, though it err like others,
Hath yet a kind of medicine in itself,
That skins the vice o' the top. Go to your bosom;
Knock there, and ask your heart what it doth know   137
That's like my brother's fault: if it confess
A natural guiltiness such as is his,
Let it not sound a thought upon your tongue 140
Against my brother's life.

Ang.   She speaks, and 'tis
Such sense that my sense breeds with it. Fare you well.

Isab. Gentle my lord, turn back.

Ang. I will bethink me. Come again to-morrow.   144

Isab. Hark how I'll bribe you. Good my lord, turn back.

Ang. How! bribe me?

Isab. Ay, with such gifts that heaven shall share with you.

Lucio. [*Aside to* ISAB.] You had marr'd all else.   148

Isab. Not with fond sicles of the tested gold,
Or stones whose rates are either rich or poor
As fancy values them; but with true prayers
That shall be up at heaven and enter there 152
Ere sun-rise: prayers from preserved souls,
From fasting maids whose minds are dedicate
To nothing temporal.

Ang.   Well; come to me to-morrow.

Lucio. [*Aside to* ISAB.] Go to; 'tis well: away!

Isab. Heaven keep your honour safe!

Ang.   [*Aside.*] Amen:
For I am that way going to temptation,
Where prayers cross.

Isab.   At what hour to-morrow
Shall I attend your lordship?

Ang.   At any time 'fore noon.   160

Isab. Save your honour!

         [*Exeunt* ISABELLA, LUCIO, *and* PROVOST.

Ang.   From thee; even from thy virtue!
What's this? what's this? Is this her fault or mine?
The tempter or the tempted, who sins most?
Ha!   164
Not she; nor doth she tempt: but it is I,
That, lying by the violet in the sun,
Do as the carrion does, not as the flower,
Corrupt with virtuous season. Can it be 168
That modesty may more betray our sense
Than woman's lightness? Having waste ground enough,
Shall we desire to raze the sanctuary,
And pitch our evils there? O, fie, fie, fie! 172
What dost thou, or what art thou, Angelo?
Dost thou desire her foully for those things
That make her good? O, let her brother live!
Thieves for their robbery have authority 176
When judges steal themselves. What! do I love her,
That I desire to hear her speak again,
And feast upon her eyes? What is 't I dream on?
O cunning enemy, that, to catch a saint, 180
With saints dost bait thy hook! Most dangerous
Is that temptation that doth goad us on
To sin in loving virtue: never could the strumpet,
With all her double vigour, art and nature, 184
Once stir my temper; but this virtuous maid
Subdues me quite. Ever till now,
When men were fond, I smil'd and wonder'd how.   [*Exit.*

SCENE III.—*A Room in a Prison.*

Enter DUKE, *disguised as a friar, and* PROVOST.

Duke. Hail to you, provost! so I think you are.

Prov. I am the provost. What's your will, good friar?

Duke. Bound by my charity and my bless'd order,
I come to visit the afflicted spirits   4

Here in the prison: do me the common right
To let me see them and to make me know
The nature of their crimes, that I may minister
To them accordingly.   8
  Prov. I would do more than that, if more
were needful.
Look, here comes one: a gentlewoman of mine,
Who, falling in the flaws of her own youth,
Hath blister'd her report. She is with child,   12
And he that got it, sentenc'd; a young man
More fit to do another such offence,
Than die for this.

Enter JULIET.

  Duke. When must he die?
  Prov.   As I do think, to-morrow.
[*To* JULIET.] I have provided for you: stay a
    while,   17
And you shall be conducted.
  Duke. Repent you, fair one, of the sin you
    carry?
  Juliet. I do, and bear the shame most pa-
    tiently.   20
  Duke. I'll teach you how you shall arraign
    your conscience,
And try your penitence, if it be sound,
Or hollowly put on.
  Juliet.   I'll gladly learn.   23
  Duke. Love you the man that wrong'd you?
  Juliet. Yes, as I love the woman that wrong'd
    him.
  Duke. So then it seems your most offenceful
    act
Was mutually committed?
  Juliet.   Mutually.
  Duke. Then was your sin of heavier kind than
    his.   28
  Juliet. I do confess it, and repent it, father.
  Duke. 'Tis meet so, daughter: but lest you do
    repent,
As that the sin hath brought you to this shame,
Which sorrow is always toward ourselves, not
    heaven,   32
Showing we would not spare heaven as we love it,
But as we stand in fear,—
  Juliet. I do repent me, as it is an evil,
And take the shame with joy.
  Duke.   There rest.   36
Your partner, as I hear, must die to-morrow,
And I am going with instruction to him.
God's grace go with you! *Benedicite!* [*Exit.*
  Juliet. Must die to-morrow! O injurious love,
That respites me a life, whose very comfort   41
Is still a dying horror!
  Prov.   'Tis pity of him. [*Exeunt.*

SCENE IV.—*A Room in* ANGELO'S *House.*

Enter ANGELO.

  Ang. When I would pray and think, I think
    and pray
To several subjects: heaven hath my empty
    words,
Whilst my invention, hearing not my tongue,
Anchors on Isabel: heaven in my mouth,   4
As if I did but only chew his name,
And in my heart the strong and swelling evil
Of my conception. The state, whereon I studied,
Is like a good thing, being often read,   8
Grown fear'd and tedious; yea, my gravity,
Wherein, let no man hear me, I take pride,
Could I with boot change for an idle plume,
Which the air beats for vain. O place! O form!
How often dost thou with thy case, thy habit, 13
Wrench awe from fools, and tie the wiser souls
To thy false seeming! Blood, thou art blood:
Let's write good angel on the devil's horn,   16
'Tis not the devil's crest.

Enter a Servant.

How now! who's there?
  Serv.   One Isabel, a sister,
Desires access to you.
  Ang.   Teach her the way.
                              [*Exit* Servant.
O heavens!   20
Why does my blood thus muster to my heart,
Making both it unable for itself,
And dispossessing all my other parts
Of necessary fitness?   24
So play the foolish throngs with one that
    swounds;
Come all to help him, and so stop the air
By which he should revive: and even so
The general, subject to a well-wish'd king,   28
Quit their own part, and in obsequious fondness
Crowd to his presence, where their untaught love
Must needs appear offence.

Enter ISABELLA.

How now, fair maid!
  Isab. I am come to know your pleasure.   32
  Ang. That you might know it, would much
    better please me,
Than to demand what 'tis. Your brother cannot
    live.
  Isab. Even so. Heaven keep your honour!
  Ang. Yet may he live awhile; and, it may be,
As long as you or I: yet he must die.   37
  Isab. Under your sentence?
  Ang. Yea.
  Isab. When, I beseech you? that in his re-
    prieve,   40
Longer or shorter, he may be so fitted
That his soul sicken not.
  Ang. Ha! fie, these filthy vices! It were as
    good
To pardon him that hath from nature stolen   44
A man already made, as to remit
Their saucy sweetness that do coin heaven's
    image
In stamps that are forbid: 'tis all as easy
Falsely to take away a life true made,   48
As to put metal in restrained means
To make a false one.
  Isab. 'Tis set down so in heaven, but not in
    earth.
  Ang. Say you so? then I shall pose you
    quickly.   52
Which had you rather, that the most just law
Now took your brother's life; or, to redeem him,

Give up your body to such sweet uncleanness
As she that he hath stain'd?
   Isab.   Sir, believe this, 56
I had rather give my body than my soul.
   Ang. I talk not of your soul. Our compell'd
sins
Stand more for number than for accompt.
   Isab.   How say you?
   Ang. Nay, I'll not warrant that; for I can
speak   60
Against the thing I say. Answer to this:
I, now the voice of the recorded law,
Pronounce a sentence on your brother's life:
Might there not be a charity in sin   64
To save this brother's life?
   Isab.   Please you to do't,
I'll take it as a peril to my soul;
It is no sin at all, but charity.
   Ang. Pleas'd you to do't, at peril of your soul,
Were equal poise of sin and charity.   69
   Isab. That I do beg his life, if it be sin,
Heaven let me bear it! you granting of my suit,
If that be sin, I'll make it my morn prayer 72
To have it added to the faults of mine,
And nothing of your answer.
   Ang.   Nay, but hear me.
Your sense pursues not mine: either you are
   ignorant,
Or seem so craftily; and that's not good. 76
   Isab. Let me be ignorant, and in nothing good,
But graciously to know I am no better.
   Ang. Thus wisdom wishes to appear most
   bright
When it doth tax itself; as these black masks 80
Proclaim an enshield beauty ten times louder
Than beauty could, display'd. But mark me;
To be received plain, I'll speak more gross:
Your brother is to die.   84
   Isab. So.
   Ang. And his offence is so, as it appears,
Accountant to the law upon that pain.
   Isab. True.   88
   Ang. Admit no other way to save his life,—
As I subscribe not that, nor any other,
But in the loss of question,—that you, his sister,
Finding yourself desir'd of such a person, 92
Whose credit with the judge, or own great place,
Could fetch your brother from the manacles
Of the all-building law; and that there were
No earthly mean to save him, but that either 96
You must lay down the treasures of your body
To this suppos'd, or else to let him suffer;
What would you do?
   Isab. As much for my poor brother, as myself:
That is, were I under the terms of death,   101
Th' impression of keen whips I'd wear as rubies,
And strip myself to death, as to a bed
That, longing, have been sick for, ere I'd yield
My body up to shame.
   Ang.   Then must your brother die.
   Isab. And 'twere the cheaper way:
Better it were a brother died at once,
Than that a sister, by redeeming him,   108
Should die for ever.
   Ang. Were not you then as cruel as the sen-
   tence

That you have slander'd so?
   Isab. Ignomy in ransom and free pardon 112
Are of two houses: lawful mercy
Is nothing kin to foul redemption.
   Ang. You seem'd of late to make the law a
   tyrant;
And rather prov'd the sliding of your brother 116
A merriment than a vice.
   Isab. O, pardon me, my lord! it oft falls out,
To have what we would have, we speak not what
   we mean.
I something do excuse the thing I hate,   120
For his advantage that I dearly love.
   Ang. We are all frail.
   Isab.   Else let my brother die,
If not a feodary, but only he
Owe and succeed thy weakness.   124
   Ang. Nay, women are frail too.
   Isab. Ay, as the glasses where they view
   themselves,
Which are as easy broke as they make forms.
Women! Help heaven! men their creation mar
In profiting by them. Nay, call us ten times
   frail,   129
For we are soft as our complexions are,
And credulous to false prints.
   Ang.   I think it well:
And from this testimony of your own sex,— 132
Since I suppose we are made to be no stronger
Than faults may shake our frames,—let me be
   bold;
I do arrest your words. Be that you are,
That is, a woman; if you be more, you're none;
If you be one, as you are well express'd   137
By all external warrants, show it now,
By putting on the destin'd livery.
   Isab. I have no tongue but one: gentle my
   lord,   140
Let me entreat you speak the former language.
   Ang. Plainly conceive, I love you.
   Isab. My brother did love Juliet; and you
   tell me
That he shall die for't.   144
   Ang. He shall not, Isabel, if you give me love.
   Isab. I know your virtue hath a licence in't,
Which seems a little fouler than it is,
To pluck on others.
   Ang.   Believe me, on mine honour,
My words express my purpose.   149
   Isab. Ha! little honour to be much believ'd,
And most pernicious purpose! Seeming, seem-
   ing!
I will proclaim thee, Angelo; look for't: 152
Sign me a present pardon for my brother,
Or with an outstretch'd throat I'll tell the
   world aloud
What man thou art.
   Ang.   Who will believe thee, Isabel?
My unsoil'd name, the austereness of my life, 156
My vouch against you, and my place i' the state,
Will so your accusation overweigh,
That you shall stifle in your own report
And smell of calumny. I have begun;   160
And now I give my sensual race the rein:
Fit thy consent to my sharp appetite;
Lay by all nicety and prolixious blushes,

That banish what they sue for; redeem thy
    brother   164
By yielding up thy body to my will,
Or else he must not only die the death,
But thy unkindness shall his death draw out
To lingering sufferance. Answer me to-morrow,
Or, by the affection that now guides me most,
I'll prove a tyrant to him. As for you,   170
Say what you can, my false o'erweighs your
    true.   [*Exit.*
  Isab. To whom should I complain? Did I
    tell this,   172
Who would believe me? O perilous mouths!
That bear in them one and the self-same tongue,
Either of condemnation or approof,
Bidding the law make curt'sy to their will; 176
Hooking both right and wrong to th' appetite,
To follow as it draws. I'll to my brother:
Though he hath fallen by prompture of the blood,
Yet hath he in them such a mind of honour, 180
That, had he twenty heads to tender down
On twenty bloody blocks, he'd yield them up,
Before his sister should her body stoop
To such abhorr'd pollution.   184
Then, Isabel, live chaste, and, brother, die:
More than our brother is our chastity.
I'll tell him yet of Angelo's request,
And fit his mind to death, for his soul's rest. 188
    [*Exit.*

ACT III

SCENE I.—*A Room in the Prison.*

Enter DUKE, *as a friar,* CLAUDIO, *and* PROVOST.

  Duke. So then you hope of pardon from Lord
    Angelo?
  Claud. The miserable have no other medicine
But only hope:
I have hope to live, and am prepar'd to die. 4
  Duke. Be absolute for death; either death
    or life
Shall thereby be the sweeter. Reason thus with
    life:
If I do lose thee, I do lose a thing
That none but fools would keep: a breath thou
    art,   8
Servile to all the skyey influences,
That dost this habitation, where thou keep'st,
Hourly afflict. Merely, thou art death's fool;
For him thou labour'st by thy flight to shun, 12
And yet run'st toward him still. Thou art not
    noble:
For all th' accommodations that thou bear'st
Are nurs'd by baseness. Thou art by no means
    valiant;
For thou dost fear the soft and tender fork 16
Of a poor worm. Thy best of rest is sleep,
And that thou oft provok'st; yet grossly fear'st
Thy death, which is no more. Thou art not
    thyself;
For thou exist'st on many a thousand grains 20
That issue out of dust. Happy thou art not;
For what thou hast not, still thou striv'st to get,
And what thou hast, forget'st. Thou art not
    certain;
For thy complexion shifts to strange effects, 24

After the moon. If thou art rich, thou'rt poor;
For, like an ass whose back with ingots bows,
Thou bear'st thy heavy riches but a journey,
And death unloads thee. Friend hast thou none;
For thine own bowels, which do call thee sire,
The mere effusion of thy proper loins,
Do curse the gout, serpigo, and the rheum,
For ending thee no sooner. Thou hast nor
    youth nor age;   32
But, as it were, an after-dinner's sleep,
Dreaming on both; for all thy blessed youth
Becomes as aged, and doth beg the alms
Of palsied eld; and when thou art old and rich,
Thou hast neither heat, affection, limb, nor
    beauty,   37
To make thy riches pleasant. What's yet in this
That bears the name of life? Yet in this life
Lie hid moe thousand deaths: yet death we fear,
That makes these odds all even.
  Claud.   I humbly thank you.
To sue to live, I find I seek to die,
And, seeking death, find life: let it come on.
  Isab. [*Within.*] What ho! Peace here; grace
    and good company!   44
  Prov. Who's there? come in: the wish de-
    serves a welcome.
  Duke. Dear sir, ere long I'll visit you again.
  Claud. Most holy sir, I thank you.   47

Enter ISABELLA.

  Is. My business is a word or two with Claudio.
  Prov. And very welcome. Look, signior;
    here's your sister.
  Duke. Provost, a word with you.
  Prov. As many as you please.
  Duke. Bring me to hear them speak, where
    I may be conceal'd.   52
    [*Exeunt* DUKE *and* PROVOST.
  Claud. Now, sister, what's the comfort?
  Isab. Why, as all comforts are; most good,
    most good indeed.
Lord Angelo, having affairs to heaven,
Intends you for his swift ambassador,   56
Where you shall be an everlasting leiger:
Therefore, your best appointment make with
    speed;
To-morrow you set on.
  Claud.   Is there no remedy?
  Isab. None, but such remedy, as to save a
    head   60
To cleave a heart in twain.
  Claud.   But is there any?
  Isab. Yes, brother, you may live:
There is a devilish mercy in the judge,
If you'll implore it, that will free your life, 64
But fetter you till death.
  Claud.   Perpetual durance?
  Isab. Ay, just; perpetual durance, a restraint,
Though all the world's vastidity you had,
To a determin'd scope.
  Claud.   But in what nature? 68
  Isab. In such a one as, you consenting to't,
Would bark your honour from that trunk you
    bear,
And leave you naked.
  Claud.   Let me know the point.

Isab. O, I do fear thee, Claudio; and I quake,
Lest thou a feverous life shouldst entertain, 73
And six or seven winters more respect
Than a perpetual honour. Dar'st thou die?
The sense of death is most in apprehension, 76
And the poor beetle, that we tread upon,
In corporal sufferance finds a pang as great
As when a giant dies.
    Claud.   Why give you me this shame?
Think you I can a resolution fetch   80
From flowery tenderness? If I must die,
I will encounter darkness as a bride,
And hug it in mine arms.
    Isab. There spake my brother: there my
        father's grave   84
Did utter forth a voice. Yes, thou must die:
Thou art too noble to conserve a life
In base appliances. This outward-sainted de-
    puty,
Whose settled visage and deliberate word   88
Nips youth i' the head, and follies doth enmew
As falcon doth the fowl, is yet a devil;
His filth within being cast, he would appear
A pond as deep as hell.
    Claud.   The prenzie Angelo? 92
    Isab. O, 'tis the cunning livery of hell,
The damned'st body to invest and cover
In prenzie guards! Dost thou think, Claudio?
If I would yield him my virginity,   96
Thou mightst be freed.
    Claud.   O heavens! it cannot be.
    Isab. Yes, he would give't thee, from this
        rank offence,
So to offend him still. This night's the time
That I should do what I abhor to name,   100
Or else thou diest to-morrow.
    Claud.   Thou shalt not do't.
    Isab. O! were it but my life,
I'd throw it down for your deliverance
As frankly as a pin.
    Claud.   Thanks, dear Isabel.   104
    Isab. Be ready, Claudio, for your death to-
    morrow.
    Claud. Yes. Has he affections in him,
That thus can make him bite the law by the nose,
When he would force it? Sure, it is no sin; 108
Or of the deadly seven it is the least.
    Isab. Which is the least?
    Claud. If it were damnable, he being so wise,
Why would he for the momentary trick   112
Be perdurably fin'd? O Isabel!
    Isab. What says my brother?
    Claud.   Death is a fearful thing.
    Isab. And shamed life a hateful.
    Claud. Ay, but to die, and go we know not
    where;   116
To lie in cold obstruction and to rot;
This sensible warm motion to become
A kneaded clod; and the delighted spirit
To bathe in fiery floods, or to reside   120
In thrilling region of thick-ribbed ice;
To be imprison'd in the viewless winds,
And blown with restless violence round about
The pendant world; or to be worse than worst
Of those that lawless and incertain thoughts
Imagine howling: 'tis too horrible!

The weariest and most loathed worldly life
That age, ache, penury and imprisonment 128
Can lay on nature is a paradise
To what we fear of death.
    Isab. Alas! alas!
    Claud.   Sweet sister, let me live:
What sin you do to save a brother's life,   132
Nature dispenses with the deed so far
That it becomes a virtue.
    Isab.   O you beast!
O faithless coward! O dishonest wretch!
Wilt thou be made a man out of my vice? 136
Is't not a kind of incest, to take life
From thine own sister's shame? What should
    I think?
Heaven shield my mother play'd my father fair;
For such a warped slip of wilderness   140
Ne'er issu'd from his blood. Take my defiance;
Die, perish! Might but my bending down
Reprieve thee from thy fate, it should proceed.
I'll pray a thousand prayers for thy death, 144
No word to save thee.
    Claud. Nay, hear me, Isabel.
    Isab.   O, fie, fie, fie!
Thy sin's not accidental, but a trade.
Mercy to thee would prove itself a bawd: 148
'Tis best that thou diest quickly.   [*Going.*
    Claud.   O hear me, Isabella.

Re-enter DUKE.

Duke. Vouchsafe a word, young sister, but
    one word.
    Isab. What is your will?   151
    Duke. Might you dispense with your leisure,
I would by and by have some speech with you:
the satisfaction I would require is likewise your
own benefit.
    Isab. I have no superfluous leisure: my stay
must be stolen out of other affairs; but I will
attend you a while.   158
    Duke. [*Aside to* CLAUDIO.] Son, I have over-
heard what hath past between you and your
sister. Angelo had never the purpose to corrupt
her; only he hath made an assay of her virtue
to practise his judgment with the disposition of
natures. She, having the truth of honour in her,
hath made him that gracious denial which he is
most glad to receive: I am confessor to Angelo,
and I know this to be true; therefore prepare
yourself to death. Do not satisfy your resolution
with hopes that are fallible: to-morrow you must
die; go to your knees and make ready.   170
    Claud. Let me ask my sister pardon. I am
so out of love with life that I will sue to be rid
of it.
    Duke. Hold you there: farewell.   174
        [*Exit* CLAUDIO.

Re-enter PROVOST.

Provost, a word with you.
    Prov. What's your will, father?
    Duke. That now you are come, you will be
gone. Leave me awhile with the maid: my mind
promises with my habit no loss shall touch her
by my company.   180
    Prov. In good time.   [*Exit.*

Duke. The hand that hath made you fair hath made you good: the goodness that is cheap in beauty makes beauty brief in goodness; but grace, being the soul of your complexion, shall keep the body of it ever fair. The assault that Angelo hath made to you, fortune hath conveyed to my understanding; and, but that frailty hath examples for his falling, I should wonder at Angelo. How would you do to content this substitute, and to save your brother?   192

Isab. I am now going to resolve him; I had rather my brother die by the law than my son should be unlawfully born. But O, how much is the good duke deceived in Angelo! If ever he return and I can speak to him, I will open my lips in vain, or discover his government. 198

Duke. That shall not be much amiss: yet, as the matter now stands, he will avoid your accusation; 'he made trial of you only.' Therefore, fasten your ear on my advisings: to the love I have in doing good a remedy presents itself. I do make myself believe that you may most uprighteously do a poor wronged lady a merited benefit, redeem your brother from the angry law, do no stain to your own gracious person, and much please the absent duke, if peradventure he shall ever return to have hearing of this business.   210

Isab. Let me hear you speak further. I have spirit to do anything that appears not foul in the truth of my spirit.

Duke. Virtue is bold, and goodness never fearful. Have you not heard speak of Mariana, the sister of Frederick, the great soldier who miscarried at sea?

Isab. I have heard of the lady, and good words went with her name.   219

Duke. She should this Angelo have married; was affianced to her by oath, and the nuptial appointed: between which time of the contract, and limit of the solemnity, her brother Frederick was wracked at sea, having in that perished vessel the dowry of his sister. But mark how heavily this befell to the poor gentlewoman: there she lost a noble and renowned brother, in his love toward her ever most kind and natural; with him the portion and sinew of her fortune, her marriage-dowry; with both, her combinate husband, this well-seeming Angelo.   231

Isab. Can this be so? Did Angelo so leave her?

Duke. Left her in her tears, and dried not one of them with his comfort; swallowed his vows whole, pretending in her discoveries of dishonour: in few, bestowed her on her own lamentation, which she yet wears for his sake; and he, a marble to her tears, is washed with them, but relents not.   239

Isab. What a merit were it in death to take this poor maid from the world! What corruption in this life, that it will let this man live! But how out of this can she avail?   243

Duke. It is a rupture that you may easily heal; and the cure of it not only saves your brother, but keeps you from dishonour in doing it.

Isab. Show me how, good father.   248

Duke. This forenamed maid hath yet in her the continuance of her first affection: his unjust unkindness, that in all reason should have quenched her love, hath, like an impediment in the current, made it more violent and unruly. Go you to Angelo: answer his requiring with a plausible obedience: agree with his demands to the point; only refer yourself to this advantage, first, that your stay with him may not be long, that the time may have all shadow and silence in it, and the place answer to convenience. This being granted in course, and now follows all, we shall advise this wronged maid to stead up your appointment, go in your place; if the encounter acknowledge itself hereafter, it may compel him to her recompense; and here by this is your brother saved, your honour untainted, the poor Mariana advantaged, and the corrupt deputy scaled. The maid will I frame and make fit for his attempt. If you think well to carry this, as you may, the doubleness of the benefit defends the deceit from reproof. What think you of it?   271

Isab. The image of it gives me content already, and I trust it will grow to a most prosperous perfection.

Duke. It lies much in your holding up. Haste you speedily to Angelo: if for this night he entreat you to his bed, give him promise of satisfaction. I will presently to St. Luke's; there, at the moated grange, resides this dejected Mariana: at that place call upon me, and dispatch with Angelo, that it may be quickly. 281

Isab. I thank you for this comfort. Fare you well, good father.   [*Exeunt.*

SCENE II.—*The Street before the Prison.*

Enter DUKE, *as a friar; to him* ELBOW, POMPEY, *and* Officers.

Elb. Nay, if there be no remedy for it, but that you will needs buy and sell men and women like beasts, we shall have all the world drink brown and white bastard.   4

Duke. O heavens! what stuff is here?

Pom. 'Twas never merry world, since, of two usuries, the merriest was put down, and the worser allowed by order of law a furred gown to keep him warm; and furred with fox and lamb skins too, to signify that craft, being richer than innocency, stands for the facing.

Elb. Come your way, sir. Bless you, good father friar.   13

Duke. And you, good brother father. What offence hath this man made you, sir?

Elb. Marry, sir, he hath offended the law: and, sir, we take him to be a thief too, sir; for we have found upon him, sir, a strange picklock, which we have sent to the deputy.

Duke. Fie, sirrah: a bawd, a wicked bawd! 20
The evil that thou causest to be done,
That is thy means to live. Do thou but think
What 'tis to cram a maw or clothe a back
From such a filthy vice: say to thyself,   24

From their abominable and beastly touches
I drink, I eat, array myself, and live.
Canst thou believe thy living is a life,   27
So stinkingly depending? Go mend, go mend.

Pom. Indeed, it does stink in some sort, sir;
but yet, sir, I would prove—

Duke. Nay, if the devil have given thee proofs
for sin,
Thou wilt prove his. Take him to prison,
officer;   32
Correction and instruction must both work
Ere this rude beast will profit.

Elb. He must before the deputy, sir; he has
given him warning. The deputy cannot abide a
whoremaster: if he be a whoremonger, and
comes before him, he were as good go a mile
on his errand.

Duke. That we were all, as some would seem
to be,   40
From our faults, as faults from seeming, free!

Elb. His neck will come to your waist,—a
cord, sir.

Pom. I spy comfort: I cry, bail. Here's a
gentleman and a friend of mine.   45

Enter LUCIO.

Lucio. How now, noble Pompey! What, at
the wheels of Cæsar? Art thou led in triumph?
What, is there none of Pygmalion's images,
newly made woman, to be had now, for putting
the hand in the pocket and extracting it
clutched? What reply? ha? What say'st thou
to this tune, matter and method? Is't not
drowned i' the last rain, ha? What sayest thou
Trot? Is the world as it was, man? Which is the
way? Is it sad, and few words, or how? The
trick of it?   56

Duke. Still thus, and thus, still worse!

Lucio. How doth my dear morsel, thy mistress? Procures she still, ha?

Pom. Troth, sir, she hath eaten up all her
beef, and she is herself in the tub.   61

Lucio. Why, 'tis good; it is the right of it;
it must be so: ever your fresh whore and your
powdered bawd: an unshunned consequence; it
must be so. Art going to prison, Pompey?

Pom. Yes, faith, sir.   66

Lucio. Why, 'tis not amiss, Pompey. Farewell. Go, say I sent thee thither. For debt,
Pompey? or how?   70

Elb. For being a bawd, for being a bawd.

Lucio. Well, then, imprison him. If imprisonment be the due of a bawd, why, 'tis his
right: bawd is he, doubtless, and of antiquity
too; bawd-born. Farewell, good Pompey. Commend me to the prison, Pompey. You will turn
good husband now, Pompey; you will keep the
house.   77

Pom. I hope, sir, your good worship will be
my bail.

Lucio. No, indeed will I not, Pompey; it is
not the wear. I will pray, Pompey, to increase
your bondage: if you take it not patiently, why,
your mettle is the more. Adieu, trusty Pompey.
Bless you, friar.   84

Duke. And you.

Lucio. Does Bridget paint still, Pompey, ha?

Elb. Come your ways, sir; come.

Pom. You will not bail me then, sir?   88

Lucio. Then, Pompey, nor now. What news
abroad, friar? What news?

Elb. Come your ways, sir; come.

Lucio. Go to kennel, Pompey; go.   92
          [*Exeunt* ELBOW, POMPEY *and* Officers.
What news, friar, of the duke?

Duke. I know none. Can you tell me of any?

Lucio. Some say he is with the Emperor of
Russia; other some, he is in Rome: but where
is he, think you?   97

Duke. I know not where; but wheresoever,
I wish him well.

Lucio. It was a mad fantastical trick of him
to steal from the state, and usurp the beggary
he was never born to. Lord Angelo dukes it
well in his absence; he puts transgression to't.

Duke. He does well in't.   104

Lucio. A little more lenity to lechery would
do no harm in him: something too crabbed that
way, friar.

Duke. It is too general a vice, and severity
must cure it.   109

Lucio. Yes, in good sooth, the vice is of a
great kindred; it is well allied; but it is impossible to extirp it quite, friar, till eating and
drinking be put down. They say this Angelo
was not made by man and woman after this
downright way of creation: is it true, think you?

Duke. How should he be made, then?   116

Lucio. Some report a sea-maid spawn'd him;
some that he was begot between two stock-fishes.
But it is certain that when he makes water his
urine is congealed ice; that I know to be true;
and he is a motion generative; that's infallible.

Duke. You are pleasant, sir, and speak apace.

Lucio. Why, what a ruthless thing is this
in him, for the rebellion of a cod-piece to take
away the life of a man! Would the duke that
is absent have done this? Ere he would have
hanged a man for the getting a hundred bastards, he would have paid for the nursing a
thousand: he had some feeling of the sport;
he knew the service, and that instructed him
to mercy.   131

Duke. I never heard the absent duke much
detected for women; he was not inclined
that way.

Lucio. O, sir, you are deceived.

Duke. 'Tis not possible.   136

Lucio. Who? not the duke? yes, your beggar
of fifty, and his use was to put a ducat in her
clack-dish; the duke had crotchets in him. He
would be drunk too; that let me inform you.   140

Duke. You do him wrong, surely.

Lucio. Sir, I was an inward of his. A shy
fellow was the duke; and, I believe I know the
cause of his withdrawing.   144

Duke. What, I prithee, might be the cause?

Lucio. No, pardon; 'tis a secret must be
locked within the teeth and the lips; but this
I can let you understand, the greater file of the
subject held the duke to be wise.

Duke. Wise! why, no question but he was.

Lucio. A very superficial, ignorant, unweighing fellow. 152

Duke. Either this is envy in you, folly, or
mistaking: the very stream of his life and the
business he hath helmed must, upon a warranted
need, give him a better proclamation. Let him
be but testimonied in his own bringings forth,
and he shall appear to the envious a scholar,
a statesman and a soldier. Therefore you speak
unskilfully; or, if your knowledge be more, it is
much darkened in your malice.

Lucio. Sir, I know him, and I love him. 162

Duke. Love talks with better knowledge, and
knowledge with dearer love.

Lucio. Come, sir, I know what I know.

Duke. I can hardly believe that, since you
know not what you speak. But, if ever the duke
return,—as our prayers are he may,—let me
desire you to make your answer before him:
if it be honest you have spoke, you have courage
to maintain it. I am bound to call upon you;
and, I pray you, your name? 172

Lucio. Sir, my name is Lucio, well known to
the duke.

Duke. He shall know you better, sir, if I may
live to report you. 176

Lucio. I fear you not.

Duke. O! you hope the duke will return no
more, or you imagine me too unhurtful an
opposite. But indeed I can do you little harm;
you'll forswear this again.

Lucio. I'll be hanged first: thou art deceived
in me, friar. But no more of this. Canst thou
tell if Claudio die to-morrow or no? 184

Duke. Why should he die, sir?

Lucio. Why? for filling a bottle with a tun-
dish. I would the duke we talk of were returned
again: this ungenitured agent will unpeople the
province with continency; sparrows must not
build in his house-eaves, because they are
lecherous. The duke yet would have dark deeds
darkly answered; he would never bring them
to light: would he were returned! Marry, this
Claudio is condemned for untrussing. Farewell,
good friar; I prithee, pray for me. The duke,
I say to thee again, would eat mutton on Fridays.
He's not past it yet, and I say to thee, he would
mouth with a beggar, though she smelt brown
bread and garlic: say that I said so. Farewell.
[*Exit.*

Duke. No might nor greatness in mortality
Can censure 'scape: back-wounding calumny
The whitest virtue strikes. What king so strong
Can tie the gall up in the slanderous tongue?
But who comes here? 204

Enter ESCALUS, PROVOST, *and* Officers *with*
MISTRESS OVERDONE.

Escal. Go; away with her to prison!

Mrs. Ov. Good my lord, be good to me; your
honour is accounted a merciful man; good my
lord. 208

Escal. Double and treble admonition, and
still forfeit in the same kind? This would make
mercy swear, and play the tyrant.

Prov. A bawd of eleven years' continuance,
may it please your honour. 213

Mrs. Ov. My lord, this is one Lucio's information against me. Mistress Kate Keepdown
was with child by him in the duke's time; he
promised her marriage; his child is a year and
a quarter old, come Philip and Jacob: I have
kept it myself, and see how he goes about to
abuse me! 220

Escal. That fellow is a fellow of much licence:
let him be called before us. Away with her to
prison! Go to; no more words. [*Exeunt* Officers *with* MISTRESS OVERDONE.] Provost, my
brother Angelo will not be altered; Claudio
must die to-morrow. Let him be furnished with
divines, and have all charitable preparation: if
my brother wrought by my pity, it should not
be so with him. 229

Prov. So please you, this friar hath been with
him, and advised him for the entertainment of
death. 232

Escal. Good even, good father.

Duke. Bliss and goodness on you!

Escal. Of whence are you?

Duke. Not of this country, though my chance
is now 236
To use it for my time: I am a brother
Of gracious order, late come from the See,
In special business from his Holiness.

Escal. What news abroad i' the world? 240

Duke. None, but there is so great a fever on
goodness, that the dissolution of it must cure
it: novelty is only in request; and it is as
dangerous to be aged in any kind of course, as
it is virtuous to be constant in any undertaking:
there is scarce truth enough alive to make
societies secure, but security enough to make
fellowships accursed. Much upon this riddle
runs the wisdom of the world. This news is old
enough, yet it is every day's news. I pray you,
sir, of what disposition was the duke? 251

Escal. One that, above all other strifes, con-
tended especially to know himself.

Duke. What pleasure was he given to? 254

Escal. Rather rejoicing to see another merry,
than merry at anything which professed to make
him rejoice: a gentleman of all temperance.
But leave we him to his events, with a prayer
they may prove prosperous; and let me desire
to know how you find Claudio prepared. I am
made to understand, that you have lent him
visitation. 262

Duke. He professes to have received no sinister measure from his judge, but most willingly
humbles himself to the determination of justice;
yet had he framed to himself, by the instruction
of his frailty, many deceiving promises of life,
which I, by my good leisure have discredited to
him, and now is he resolved to die. 269

Escal. You have paid the heavens your
function, and the prisoner the very debt of
your calling. I have laboured for the poor
gentleman to the extremest shore of my modesty; but my brother justice have I found so severe,
that he hath forced me to tell him he is indeed
Justice. 276

Duke. If his own life answer the straitness of
his proceeding, it shall become him well; wherein
if he chance to fail, he hath sentenced himself.

Escal. I am going to visit the prisoner. Fare
you well.   281

Duke. Peace be with you!

     [*Exeunt* ESCALUS *and* PROVOST.

He, who the sword of heaven will bear
Should be as holy as severe;   284
Pattern in himself to know,
Grace to stand, and virtue go;
More nor less to others paying
Than by self offences weighing.   288
Shame to him whose cruel striking
Kills for faults of his own liking!
Twice treble shame on Angelo,
To weed my vice and let his grow!   292
O, what may man within him hide,
Though angel on the outward side!
How many likeness made in crimes,
Making practice on the times,   296
To draw with idle spiders' strings
Most pond'rous and substantial things!
Craft against vice I must apply:
With Angelo to-night shall lie   300
His old betrothed but despis'd:
So disguise shall, by the disguis'd,
Pay with falsehood false exacting,
And perform an old contracting.   [*Exit.*

ACT IV

SCENE I.—*The moated Grange at St. Luke's.*

Enter MARIANA *and a* Boy: Boy *sings.*

Take, O take those lips away,
    That so sweetly were forsworn;
And those eyes, the break of day,
    Lights that do mislead the morn: 4
But my kisses bring again,
             bring again,
Seals of love, but seal'd in vain,
             seal'd in vain.   8

Mari. Break off thy song, and haste thee
quick away:
Here comes a man of comfort, whose advice
Hath often still'd my brawling discontent.

     [*Exit* Boy.

Enter DUKE, *disguised as before.*

I cry you mercy, sir; and well could wish   12
You had not found me here so musical:
Let me excuse me, and believe me so,
My mirth it much displeas'd, but pleas'd my
woe.

Duke. 'Tis good; though music oft hath such
a charm   16
To make bad good, and good provoke to harm.
I pray you tell me, hath anybody inquired for
me here to-day? much upon this time have I
promised here to meet.   20

Mari. You have not been inquired after: I
have sat here all day.

Duke. I do constantly believe you. The time
is come even now. I shall crave your forbearance a little; may be I will call upon you anon,
for some advantage to yourself.

Mari. I am always bound to you.   [*Exit.*

Enter ISABELLA.

Duke. Very well met, and well come.   28
What is the news from this good deputy?

Isab. He hath a garden circummur'd with
brick,
Whose western side is with a vineyard back'd;
And to that vineyard is a planched gate,   32
That makes his opening with this bigger key;
This other doth command a little door
Which from the vineyard to the garden leads;
There have I made my promise   36
Upon the heavy middle of the night
To call upon him.

Duke. But shall you on your knowledge find
this way?

Isab. I have ta'en a due and wary note
upon 't: 40
With whispering and most guilty diligence,
In action all of precept, he did show me
The way twice o'er.

Duke.   Are there no other tokens
Between you 'greed concerning her observance?

Isab. No, none, but only a repair i' the
dark;   45
And that I have possess'd him my most stay
Can be but brief; for I have made him know
I have a servant comes with me along,   48
That stays upon me, whose persuasion is
I come about my brother.

Duke.   'Tis well borne up.
I have not yet made known to Mariana
A word of this. What ho! within! come forth.

Re-enter MARIANA.

I pray you, be acquainted with this maid;   53
She comes to do you good.

Isab.   I do desire the like.

Duke. Do you persuade yourself that I respect you?

Mari. Good friar, I know you do, and oft
have found it.   56

Duke. Take then this your companion by the
hand,
Who hath a story ready for your ear.
I shall attend your leisure: but make haste;
The vaporous night approaches.

Mari.   Will 't please you walk aside? 60

     [*Exeunt* MARIANA *and* ISABELLA.

Duke. O place and greatness! millions of
false eyes
Are stuck upon thee: volumes of report
Run with these false and most contrarious
quests
Upon thy doings: thousand escapes of wit   64
Make thee the father of their idle dream,
And rack thee in their fancies!

Re-enter MARIANA *and* ISABELLA.

         Welcome! How agreed?

Isab. She'll take the enterprise upon her,
father,
If you advise it.

Duke.   It is not my consent,   68
But my entreaty too.
Isab.   Little have you to say
When you depart from him, but, soft and low,
'Remember now my brother.'
Mari.   Fear me not.
Duke. Nor, gentle daughter, fear you not at
all.   72
He is your husband on a pre-contract:
To bring you thus together, 'tis no sin,
Sith that the justice of your title to him
Doth flourish the deceit. Come, let us go: 76
Our corn's to reap, for yet our tithe's to sow.
                                        [*Exeunt.*

SCENE II.—*A Room in the Prison.*

Enter PROVOST *and* POMPEY.

Prov. Come hither, sirrah. Can you cut off
a man's head?
Pom. If the man be a bachelor, sir, I can;
but if he be a married man, he is his wife's head,
and I can never cut off a woman's head.   5
Prov. Come, sir, leave me your snatches, and
yield me a direct answer. To-morrow morning
are to die Claudio and Barnardine. Here is in
our prison a common executioner, who in his
office lacks a helper: if you will take it on you
to assist him, it shall redeem you from your
gyves; if not, you shall have your full time of
imprisonment, and your deliverance with an unpitied whipping, for you have been a notorious
bawd.   15
Pom. Sir, I have been an unlawful bawd time
out of mind; but yet I will be content to be a
lawful hangman. I would be glad to receive
some instruction from my fellow partner.
Prov. What ho, Abhorson! Where's Abhorson, there?   21

Enter ABHORSON.

Abhor. Do you call, sir?
Prov. Sirrah, here's a fellow will help you
to-morrow in your execution. If you think it
meet, compound with him by the year, and let
him abide here with you; if not, use him for the
present, and dismiss him. He cannot plead his
estimation with you; he hath been a bawd.   28
Abhor. A bawd, sir? Fie upon him! he will
discredit our mystery.
Prov. Go to, sir; you weigh equally; a feather
will turn the scale.   [*Exit.*
Pom. Pray, sir, by your good favour—for
surely, sir, a good favour you have, but that you
have a hanging look,—do you call, sir, your
occupation a mystery?   36
Abhor. Ay, sir; a mystery.
Pom. Painting, sir, I have heard say, is a
mystery; and your whores, sir, being members
of my occupation, using painting, do prove my
occupation a mystery: but what mystery there
should be in hanging, if I should be hanged, I
cannot imagine.
Abhor. Sir, it is a mystery.   44
Pom. Proof?
Abhor. Every true man's apparel fits your thief.

Pom. If it be too little for your thief, your
true man thinks it big enough; if it be too big
for your thief, your thief thinks it little enough:
so, every true man's apparel fits your thief. 50

Re-enter PROVOST.

Prov. Are you agreed?
Pom. Sir, I will serve him; for I do find that
your hangman is a more penitent trade than
your bawd, he doth often ask forgiveness.
Prov. You, sirrah, provide your block and
your axe to-morrow four o'clock.   56
Abhor. Come on, bawd; I will instruct thee
in my trade; follow.
Pom. I do desire to learn, sir; and, I hope, if
you have occasion to use me for your own turn,
you shall find me yare; for, truly, sir, for your
kindness I owe you a good turn.
Prov. Call hither Barnardine and Claudio:
            [*Exeunt* POMPEY *and* ABHORSON.
The one has my pity; not a jot the other,   64
Being a murderer, though he were my brother.

Enter CLAUDIO.

Look, here's the warrant, Claudio, for thy
   death:
'Tis now dead midnight, and by eight to-morrow
Thou must be made immortal. Where's Bar-
   nardine?   68
Claud. As fast lock'd up in sleep as guiltless
   labour
When it lies starkly in the traveller's bones;
He will not wake.
Prov.   Who can do good on him?
Well, go; prepare yourself. [*Knocking within.*]
   But hark, what noise?—   72
Heaven give your spirits comfort!—[*Exit* CLAU-
DIO.] By and by.
I hope it is some pardon or reprieve
For the most gentle Claudio.

Enter DUKE, *disguised as before.*
                           Welcome, father.
Duke. The best and wholesom'st spirits of
   the night   76
Envelop you, good provost! Who call'd here
   of late?
Prov. None since the curfew rung.
Duke. Not Isabel?
Prov. No.
Duke.   They will, then, ere 't be long.
Prov. What comfort is for Claudio?   80
Duke. There's some in hope.
Prov.   It is a bitter deputy.
Duke. Not so, not so: his life is parallel'd
Even with the stroke and line of his great justice:
He doth with holy abstinence subdue   84
That in himself which he spurs on his power
To qualify in others: were he meal'd with that
Which he corrects, then were he tyrannous;
But this being so, he's just.—[*Knocking within.*]
   Now are they come.   [*Exit* PROVOST.
This is a gentle provost: seldom when   89
The steeled gaoler is the friend of men.
                              [*Knocking.*

D

How now! What noise? That spirit's possess'd
with haste
That wounds the unsisting postern with these
strokes.   92

Re-enter PROVOST.

Prov. There he must stay until the officer
Arise to let him in; he is call'd up.
Duke. Have you no countermand for Claudio
yet,
But he must die to-morrow?
Prov.   None, sir, none. 96
Duke. As near the dawning, provost, as it is,
You shall hear more ere morning.
Prov.   Happily
You something know; yet, I believe there comes
No countermand: no such example have we. 100
Besides, upon the very siege of justice,
Lord Angelo hath to the public ear
Profess'd the contrary.

Enter a Messenger.

This is his lordship's man.
Duke. And here comes Claudio's pardon. 104
Mes. [*Giving a paper.*] My lord hath sent
you this note; and by me this further charge,
that you swerve not from the smallest article of
it, neither in time, matter, or other circumstance.
Good morrow; for, as I take it, it is almost day.
Prov. I shall obey him.   [*Exit* Messenger.
Duke. [*Aside.*] This is his pardon, purchased
by such sin
For which the pardoner himself is in;   112
Hence hath offence his quick celerity,
When it is borne in high authority.
When vice makes mercy, mercy's so extended,
That for the fault's love is the offender
friended.   116
Now, sir, what news?
Prov. I told you: Lord Angelo, belike thinking me remiss in mine office, awakens me with
this unwonted putting on; methinks strangely,
for he hath not used it before.   121
Duke. Pray you, let's hear.
*Prov. Whatsoever you may hear to the con-
trary, let Claudio be executed by four of the
clock; and, in the afternoon, Barnardine. For
my better satisfaction, let me have Claudio's
head sent me by five. Let this be duly performed; with a thought that more depends on
it than we must yet deliver. Thus fail not to do
your office, as you will answer it at your peril.*
What say you to this, sir?   131
Duke. What is that Barnardine who is to be
executed this afternoon?
Prov. A Bohemian born, but here nursed up
and bred; one that is a prisoner nine years old.
Duke. How came it that the absent duke had
not either delivered him to his liberty or executed him? I have heard it was ever his manner
to do so.   139
Prov. His friends still wrought reprieves for
him; and, indeed, his fact, till now in the government of Lord Angelo, came not to an un-
doubtful proof.
Duke. It is now apparent?   144

Prov. Most manifest, and not denied by himself.
Duke. Hath he borne himself penitently in
prison? How seems he to be touched?
Prov. A man that apprehends death no more
dreadfully but as a drunken sleep; careless, reckless, and fearless of what's past, present, or to
come; insensible of mortality, and desperately
mortal.   152
Duke. He wants advice.
Prov. He will hear none. He hath evermore
had the liberty of the prison: give him leave to
escape hence, he would not: drunk many times
a day, if not many days entirely drunk. We
have very oft awaked him, as if to carry him to
execution, and showed him a seeming warrant
for it: it hath not moved him at all.   160
Duke. More of him anon. There is written
in your brow, provost, honesty and constancy:
if I read it not truly, my ancient skill beguiles
me; but, in the boldness of my cunning I will
lay myself in hazard. Claudio, whom here you
have warrant to execute, is no greater forfeit
to the law than Angelo who hath sentenced
him. To make you understand this in a manifested effect, I crave but four days' respite, for
the which you are to do me both a present and
a dangerous courtesy.
Prov. Pray, sir, in what?   172
Duke. In the delaying death.
Prov. Alack! how may I do it, having the
hour limited, and an express command, under
penalty, to deliver his head in the view of Angelo?
I may make my case as Claudio's to cross this
in the smallest.   178
Duke. By the vow of mine order I warrant
you, if my instructions may be your guide. Let
this Barnardine be this morning executed, and
his head borne to Angelo.
Prov. Angelo hath seen them both, and will
discover the favour.   184
Duke. O! death's a great disguiser, and you
may add to it. Shave the head, and tie the
beard; and say it was the desire of the penitent
to be so bared before his death: you know the
course is common. If anything fall to you upon
this, more than thanks and good fortune, by the
saint whom I profess, I will plead against it
with my life.   192
Prov. Pardon me, good father; it is against
my oath.
Duke. Were you sworn to the duke or to the
deputy?   196
Prov. To him, and to his substitutes.
Duke. You will think you have made no
offence, if the duke avouch the justice of your
dealing?   200
Prov. But what likelihood is in that?
Duke. Not a resemblance, but a certainty.
Yet since I see you fearful, that neither my
coat, integrity, nor persuasion can with ease attempt you, I will go further than I meant, to
pluck all fears out of you. Look you, sir; here is
the hand and seal of the duke: you know the
character, I doubt not, and the signet is not
strange to you.   209
Prov. I know them both.

Duke. The contents of this is the return of the duke: you shall anon over-read it at your pleasure, where you shall find within these two days, he will be here. This is a thing that Angelo knows not, for he this very day receives letters of strange tenour; perchance of the duke's death; perchance, his entering into some monastery; but, by chance, nothing of what is writ. Look, the unfolding star calls up the shepherd. Put not yourself into amazement how these things should be: all difficulties are but easy when they are known. Call your executioner, and off with Barnardine's head: I will give him a present shrift and advise him for a better place. Yet you are amaz'd, but this shall absolutely resolve you. Come away; it is almost clear dawn.   [*Exeunt.*

SCENE III.—*Another Room in the Same.*

Enter POMPEY.

Pom. I am as well acquainted here as I was in our house of profession: one would think it were Mistress Overdone's own house, for here be many of her old customers. First, here's young Master Rash; he's in for a commodity of brown paper and old ginger, nine-score and seventeen pounds, of which he made five marks, ready money: marry, then ginger was not much in request, for the old women were all dead. Then is there here one Master Caper, at the suit of Master Three-pile the mercer, for some four suits of peach-colour'd satin, which now peaches him a beggar. Then have we young Dizy, and young Master Deep-vow, and Master Copperspur, and Master Starve-lackey the rapier and dagger man, and young Drop-heir that kill'd lusty Pudding, and Master Forthlight, the tilter, and brave Master Shoe-tie the great traveller, and wild Half-can that stabbed Pots, and, I think, forty more; all great doers in our trade, and are now 'for the Lord's sake.'   21

Enter ABHORSON.

Abhor. Sirrah, bring Barnardine hither.
Pom. Master Barnardine! you must rise and be hanged, Master Barnardine.   24
Abhor. What ho! Barnardine!
Barnar. [*Within.*] A pox o' your throats! Who makes that noise there? What are you?
Pom. Your friends, sir; the hangman. You must be so good, sir, to rise and be put to death.
Barnar. [*Within.*] Away! you rogue, away! I am sleepy.   32
Abhor. Tell him he must awake, and that quickly too.
Pom. Pray, Master Barnardine, awake till you are executed, and sleep afterwards.   36
Abhor. Go in to him, and fetch him out.
Pom. He is coming, sir, he is coming; I hear his straw rustle.
Abhor. Is the axe upon the block, sirrah? 40
Pom. Very ready, sir.

Enter BARNARDINE.

Barnar. How now, Abhorson! what's the news with you?   43
Abhor. Truly, sir, I would desire you to clap into your prayers; for, look you, the warrant's come.
Barnar. You rogue, I have been drinking all night; I am not fitted for 't.   48
Pom. O, the better, sir; for he that drinks all night, and is hang'd betimes in the morning, may sleep the sounder all the next day.   51
Abhor. Look you, sir; here comes your ghostly father: do we jest now, think you?

Enter DUKE, *disguised as before.*

Duke. Sir, induced by my charity, and hearing how hastily you are to depart, I am come to advise you, comfort you, and pray with you. 56
Barnar. Friar, not I: I have been drinking hard all night, and I will have more time to prepare me, or they shall beat out my brains with billets. I will not consent to die this day, that's certain.   61
Duke. O, sir, you must; and therefore, I beseech you look forward on the journey you shall go.   64
Barnar. I swear I will not die to-day for any man's persuasion.
Duke. But hear you.
Barnar. Not a word: if you have anything to say to me, come to my ward; for thence will not I to day.   [*Exit.*

Enter PROVOST.

Duke. Unfit to live or die. O, gravel heart! After him fellows: bring him to the block. 72
          [*Exeunt* ABHORSON *and* POMPEY.
Prov. Now, sir, how do you find the prisoner?
Duke. A creature unprepar'd, unmeet for death;
And, to transport him in the mind he is
Were damnable.
Prov.   Here in the prison, father, 76
There died this morning of a cruel fever
One Ragozine, a most notorious pirate,
A man of Claudio's years; his beard and head
Just of his colour. What if we do omit 80
This reprobate till he were well inclin'd,
And satisfy the deputy with the visage
Of Ragozine, more like to Claudio?
Duke. O, 'tis an accident that heaven provides!   84
Dispatch it presently: the hour draws on
Prefix'd by Angelo. See this be done,
And sent according to command, whiles I
Persuade this rude wretch willingly to die. 88
Prov. This shall be done, good father, presently.
But Barnardine must die this afternoon:
And how shall we continue Claudio,
To save me from the danger that might come 92
If he were known alive?
Duke.   Let this be done:
Put them in secret holds, both Barnardine and
     Claudio:

Ere twice the sun hath made his journal greeting
To the under generation, you shall find   96
Your safety manifested.

Prov. I am your free dependant.

Duke. Quick, dispatch,
And send the head to Angelo. [*Exit* PROVOST.
Now will I write letters to Angelo,—   101
The provost, he shall bear them,—whose contents
Shall witness to him I am near at home,
And that, by great injunctions, I am bound   104
To enter publicly: him I'll desire
To meet me at the consecrated fount
A league below the city; and from thence,
By cold gradation and well-balanc'd form,   108
We shall proceed with Angelo.

Re-enter PROVOST.

Prov. Here is the head; I'll carry it myself.

Duke. Convenient is it. Make a swift return,
For I would commune with you of such things
That want no ear but yours.

Prov.   I'll make all speed. [*Exit.*

Isab. [*Within.*] Peace, ho, be here!

Duke. The tongue of Isabel. She's come to know
If yet her brother's pardon be come hither;   116
But I will keep her ignorant of her good,
To make her heavenly comforts of despair,
When it is least expected.

Enter ISABELLA.

Isab.   Ho! by your leave.

Duke. Good morning to you, fair and gracious daughter.   120

Isab. The better, given me by so holy a man.
Hath yet the deputy sent my brother's pardon?

Duke. He hath releas'd him, Isabel, from the world:
His head is off and sent to Angelo.   124

Isab. Nay, but it is not so.

Duke. It is no other: show your wisdom, daughter,
In your close patience.   127

Isab. O! I will to him and pluck out his eyes!

Duke. You shall not be admitted to his sight.

Isab. Unhappy Claudio! Wretched Isabel!
Injurious world! Most damned Angelo!

Duke. This nor hurts him nor profits you a jot;   132
Forbear it therefore; give your cause to heaven.
Mark what I say, which you shall find
By every syllable a faithful verity.
The duke comes home to-morrow; nay, dry your eyes: 136
One of our covent, and his confessor,
Gives me this instance: already he hath carried
Notice to Escalus and Angelo,
Who do prepare to meet him at the gates,   140
There to give up their power. If you can, pace your wisdom
In that good path that I would wish it go,
And you shall have your bosom on this wretch,
Grace of the Duke, revenges to your heart,   144
And general honour.

Isab.   I am directed by you.

Duke. This letter then to Friar Peter give;
'Tis that he sent me of the duke's return:
Say, by this token, I desire his company   148
At Mariana's house to-night. Her cause and yours,
I'll perfect him withal, and he shall bring you
Before the duke; and to the head of Angelo
Accuse him home, and home. For my poor self,   152
I am combined by a sacred vow
And shall be absent. Wend you with this letter.
Command these fretting waters from your eyes
With a light heart: trust not my holy order,   156
If I pervert your course. Who's here?

Enter LUCIO.

Lucio. Good even. Friar, where is the provost?

Duke. Not within, sir.   160

Lucio. O pretty Isabella, I am pale at mine heart to see thine eyes so red: thou must be patient. I am fain to dine and sup with water and bran; I dare not for my head fill my belly; one fruitful meal would set me to 't. But they say the duke will be here to-morrow. By my troth, Isabel, I loved thy brother: if the old fantastical duke of dark corners had been at home, he had lived.   [*Exit* ISABELLA.

Duke. Sir, the duke is marvellous little beholding to your reports; but the best is, he lives not in them.   172

Lucio. Friar, thou knowest not the duke so well as I do: he's a better woodman than thou takest him for.

Duke. Well, you'll answer this one day. Fare ye well.   177

Lucio. Nay, tarry; I'll go along with thee: I can tell thee pretty tales of the duke.

Duke. You have told me too many of him already, sir, if they be true; if not true, none were enough.   182

Lucio. I was once before him for getting a wench with child.

Duke. Did you such a thing?

Lucio. Yes, marry, did I; but I was fain to forswear it: they would else have married me to the rotten medlar.   188

Duke. Sir, your company is fairer than honest. Rest you well.

Lucio. By my troth, I'll go with thee to the lane's end. If bawdy talk offend you, we'll have very little of it. Nay, friar, I am a kind of burr; I shall stick.   [*Exeunt.*

SCENE IV.—*A Room in* ANGELO'S *House.*

Enter ANGELO *and* ESCALUS.

Escal. Every letter he hath writ hath disvouched other.

Ang. In most uneven and distracted manner. His actions show much like to madness: pray heaven his wisdom be not tainted! And why meet him at the gates, and redeliver our authorities there?

Escal. I guess not.   8

Ang. And why should we proclaim it in an hour before his entering, that if any crave redress of injustice, they should exhibit their petitions in the street?   12

Escal. He shows his reason for that: to have a dispatch of complaints, and to deliver us from devices hereafter, which shall then have no power to stand against us.   16

Ang. Well, I beseech you, let it be proclaim'd: Betimes i' the morn I'll call you at your house; Give notice to such men of sort and suit As are to meet him.   20

Escal. I shall, sir: fare you well.

Ang. Good night.   [*Exit* ESCALUS.

This deed unshapes me quite, makes me unpregnant And dull to all proceedings. A deflower'd maid, And by an eminent body that enforc'd   25 The law against it! But that her tender shame Will not proclaim against her maiden loss, How might she tongue me! Yet reason dares her no: 28 For my authority bears so credent bulk, That no particular scandal once can touch: But it confounds the breather. He should have liv'd, Save that his riotous youth, with dangerous sense,   32 Might in the times to come have ta'en revenge, By so receiving a dishonour'd life With ransom of such shame. Would yet he had liv'd! Alack! when once our grace we have forgot,   36 Nothing goes right: we would, and we would not.   [*Exit.*

SCENE V.—*Fields without the Town.*

Enter DUKE, *in his own habit, and* FRIAR PETER.

Duke. These letters at fit time deliver me.
    [*Giving letters.*
The provost knows our purpose and our plot. The matter being afoot, keep your instruction, And hold you ever to our special drift,   4 Though sometimes you do blench from this to that, As cause doth minister. Go call at Flavius' house, And tell him where I stay: give the like notice To Valentinus, Rowland, and to Crassus,   8 And bid them bring the trumpets to the gate; But send me Flavius first.

F. Peter. It shall be speeded well. [*Exit.*

Enter VARRIUS.

Duke. I thank thee, Varrius; thou hast made good haste.
Come, we will walk. There's other of our friends Will greet us here anon, my gentle Varrius.   13
    [*Exeunt.*

SCENE VI.—*Street near the City Gate.*

Enter ISABELLA *and* MARIANA.

Isab. To speak so indirectly I am loath: I would say the truth; but to accuse him so, That is your part: yet I'm advis'd to do it; He says, to veil full purpose.

Mari.   Be rul'd by him.   4

Isab. Besides, he tells me that if peradventure He speak against me on the adverse side, I should not think it strange; for 'tis a physic That's bitter to sweet end.   8

Mari. I would, Friar Peter—

Isab.   O, peace! the friar is come.

Enter FRIAR PETER.

F. Peter. Come; I have found you out a stand most fit, Where you may have such vantage on the duke, He shall not pass you. Twice have the trumpets sounded: 12 The generous and gravest citizens Have hent the gates, and very near upon The duke is ent'ring: therefore hence, away!
    [*Exeunt.*

ACT V

SCENE I.—*A public Place near the City Gate.*

MARIANA, *veiled,* ISABELLA, *and* FRIAR PETER, *at their stand. Enter* DUKE, VARRIUS, Lords, ANGELO, ESCALUS, LUCIO, PROVOST, Officers, *and* Citizens *at several doors.*

Duke. My very worthy cousin, fairly met! Our old and faithful friend, we are glad to see you.

Ang. } Happy return be to your royal Grace!
Escal. }

Duke. Many and hearty thankings to you both.   4 We have made inquiry of you; and we hear Such goodness of your justice, that our soul Cannot but yield you forth to public thanks, Forerunning more requital.

Ang. You make my bonds still greater.   8

Duke. O! your desert speaks loud; and I should wrong it, To lock it in the wards of covert bosom, When it deserves, with characters of brass, A forted residence 'gainst the tooth of time   12 And razure of oblivion. Give me your hand, And let the subject see, to make them know That outward courtesies would fain proclaim Favours that keep within. Come, Escalus,   16 You must walk by us on our other hand; And good supporters are you.

FRIAR PETER *and* ISABELLA *come forward.*

F. Peter. Now is your time: speak loud and kneel before him.   19

Isab. Justice, O royal duke! Vail your regard Upon a wrong'd, I'd fain have said, a maid! O worthy prince! dishonour not your eye By throwing it on any other object   23

Till you have heard me in my true complaint
And given me justice, justice, justice, justice!
Duke. Relate your wrongs: in what? by
whom? Be brief;
Here is Lord Angelo, shall give you justice:
Reveal yourself to him.
Isab. O worthy duke! 28
You bid me seek redemption of the devil.
Hear me yourself; for that which I must speak
Must either punish me, not being believ'd,
Or wring redress from you. Hear me, O, hear
me, here! 32
Ang. My lord, her wits, I fear me, are not firm:
She hath been a suitor to me for her brother
Cut off by course of justice,—
Isab. By course of justice!
Ang. And she will speak most bitterly and
strange. 36
Isab. Most strange, but yet most truly, will I
speak.
That Angelo's forsworn, is it not strange?
That Angelo's a murderer, is't not strange?
That Angelo is an adulterous thief, 40
A hypocrite, a virgin-violator;
Is it not strange, and strange?
Duke. Nay, it is ten times strange.
Isab. It is not truer he is Angelo
Than this is all as true as it is strange; 44
Nay, it is ten times true; for truth is truth
To the end of reckoning.
Duke. Away with her! poor soul,
She speaks this in the infirmity of sense.
Isab. O prince, I conjure thee, as thou be-
liev'st 48
There is another comfort than this world,
That thou neglect me not, with that opinion
That I am touch'd with madness. Make not
impossible
That which but seems unlike. 'Tis not im-
possible 52
But one, the wicked'st caitiff on the ground,
May seem as shy, as grave, as just, as absolute
As Angelo; even so may Angelo,
In all his dressings, characts, titles, forms, 56
Be an arch-villain. Believe it, royal prince:
If he be less, he's nothing; but he's more,
Had I more name for badness.
Duke. By mine honesty,
If she be mad,—as I believe no other,— 60
Her madness hath the oddest frame of sense,
Such a dependency of thing on thing,
As e'er I heard in madness.
Isab. O gracious duke!
Harp not on that; nor do not banish reason 64
For inequality; but let your reason serve
To make the truth appear where it seems hid,
And hide the false seems true.
Duke. Many that are not mad
Have, sure, more lack of reason. What would
you say? 68
Isab. I am the sister of one Claudio,
Condemn'd upon the act of fornication
To lose his head; condemn'd by Angelo.
I, in probation of a sisterhood, 72
Was sent to by my brother; one Lucio
As then the messenger,—

Lucio. That's I, an't like your Grace:
I came to her from Claudio, and desir'd her
To try her gracious fortune with Lord Angelo 76
For her poor brother's pardon.
Isab. That's he indeed.
Duke. You were not bid to speak.
Lucio. No, my good lord;
Nor wish'd to hold my peace.
Duke. I wish you now, then;
Pray you, take note of it; and when you
have 80
A business for yourself, pray heaven you then
Be perfect.
Lucio. I warrant your honour.
Duke. The warrant's for yourself: take heed
to it. 84
Isab. This gentleman told somewhat of my
tale,—
Lucio. Right.
Duke. It may be right; but you are in the
wrong
To speak before your time. Proceed.
Isab. I went 88
To this pernicious caitiff deputy.
Duke. That's somewhat madly spoken.
Isab. Pardon it;
The phrase is to the matter.
Duke. Mended again: the matter; proceed.
Isab. In brief, to set the needless pro-
cess by, 93
How I persuaded, how I pray'd, and kneel'd,
How he refell'd me, and how I replied,—
For this was of much length,—the vile con-
clusion 96
I now begin with grief and shame to utter.
He would not, but by gift of my chaste body
To his concupiscible intemperate lust,
Release my brother; and, after much debate-
ment, 100
My sisterly remorse confutes mine honour,
And I did yield to him. But the next morn
betimes,
His purpose surfeiting, he sends a warrant
For my poor brother's head.
Duke. This is most likely! 104
Isab. O, that it were as like as it is true!
Duke. By heaven, fond wretch! thou know'st
not what thou speak'st,
Or else thou art suborn'd against his honour
In hateful practice. First, his integrity 108
Stands without blemish; next, it imports no
reason
That with such vehemency he should pursue
Faults proper to himself: if he had so offended,
He would have weigh'd thy brother by himself,
And not have cut him off. Some one hath set
you on: 113
Confess the truth, and say by whose advice
Thou cam'st here to complain.
Isab. And is this all?
Then, O you blessed ministers above, 116
Keep me in patience; and, with ripen'd time
Unfold the evil which is here wrapt up
In countenance! Heaven shield your Grace
from woe,
As I, thus wrong'd, hence unbelieved go! 120

Duke. I know you'd fain be gone. An officer!
To prison with her! Shall we thus permit
A blasting and a scandalous breath to fall
On him so near us? This needs must be a
practice.   124
Who knew of your intent and coming hither?
Isab. One that I would were here, Friar
Lodowick.
Duke. A ghostly father, belike. Who knows
that Lodowick?
Lucio. My lord, I know him; 'tis a meddling
friar;   128
I do not like the man: had he been lay, my
lord,
For certain words he spake against your Grace
In your retirement, I had swing'd him soundly.
Duke. Words against me! This' a good friar,
belike!   132
And to set on this wretched woman here
Against our substitute! Let this friar be found.
Lucio. But yesternight, my lord, she and
that friar,
I saw them at the prison: a saucy friar,   136
A very scurvy fellow.
F. Peter.   Bless'd be your royal Grace!
I have stood by, my lord, and I have heard
Your royal ear abus'd. First, hath this woman
Most wrongfully accus'd your substitute,   140
Who is as free from touch or soil with her,
As she from one ungot.
Duke.   We did believe no less.
Know you that Friar Lodowick that she
speaks of?
F. Peter. I know him for a man divine and
holy;   144
Not scurvy, nor a temporary meddler,
As he's reported by this gentleman;
And, on my trust, a man that never yet
Did, as he vouches, misreport your Grace.   148
Lucio. My lord, most villanously; believe it.
F. Peter. Well; he in time may come to clear
himself,
But at this instant he is sick, my lord,
Of a strange fever. Upon his mere request,   152
Being come to knowledge that there was com-
plaint
Intended 'gainst Lord Angelo, came I hither,
To speak, as from his mouth, what he doth know
Is true and false; and what he with his oath 156
And all probation will make up full clear,
Whensoever he's convented. First, for this
woman,
To justify this worthy nobleman,
So vulgarly and personally accus'd,   160
Her shall you hear disproved to her eyes,
Till she herself confess it.
Duke.   Good friar, let's hear it.
[ISABELLA *is carried off guarded; and*
MARIANA *comes forward.*
Do you not smile at this, Lord Angelo?—
O heaven, the vanity of wretched fools!   164
Give us some seats. Come, cousin Angelo;
In this I'll be impartial; be you judge
Of your own cause. Is this the witness, friar?
First, let her show her face, and after speak 168

Mari. Pardon, my lord; I will not show my
face
Until my husband bid me.
Duke.   What, are you married?
Mari. No, my lord.
Duke.   Are you a maid?
Mari.   No, my lord.
Duke. A widow, then?
Mari.   Neither, my lord.
Duke.   Why, you
Are nothing, then: neither maid, widow, nor
wife?
Lucio. My lord, she may be a punk; for
many of them are neither maid, widow, nor
wife.   176
Duke. Silence that fellow: I would he had
some cause
To prattle for himself.
Lucio. Well, my lord.
Mari. My lord, I do confess I ne'er was
married;   180
And I confess besides I am no maid:
I have known my husband yet my husband
knows not
That ever he knew me.
Lucio. He was drunk then my lord: it can
be no better.   184
Duke. For the benefit of silence, would thou
wert so too!
Lucio. Well, my lord.
Duke. This is no witness for Lord Angelo.
Mari. Now I come to't, my lord: 188
She that accuses him of fornication,
In self-same manner doth accuse my husband;
And charges him, my lord, with such a time,
When, I'll depose, I had him in mine arms, 192
With all th' effect of love.
Ang. Charges she moe than me?
Mari.   Not that I know.
Duke. No? you say your husband.
Mari. Why, just, my lord, and that is Angelo,
Who thinks he knows that he ne'er knew my
body   197
But knows he thinks that he knows Isabel's.
Ang. This is a strange abuse. Let's see
thy face.
Mari. My husband bids me; now I will
unmask.   [*Unveiling.*
This is that face, thou cruel Angelo,   201
Which once thou swor'st was worth the look-
ing on:
This is the hand which, with a vow'd contract,
Was fast belock'd in thine: this is the body 204
That took away the match from Isabel,
And did supply thee at thy garden-house
In her imagin'd person.
Duke.   Know you this woman?
Lucio. Carnally, she says.
Duke.   Sirrah, no more! 208
Lucio. Enough, my lord.
Ang. My lord, I must confess I know this
woman;
And five years since there was some speech of
marriage   211
Betwixt myself and her, which was broke off,
Partly for that her promised proportions

Came short of composition; but, in chief
For that her reputation was disvalu'd
In levity: since which time of five years   216
I never spake with her, saw her, nor heard from
   her,
Upon my faith and honour.
   Mari.   Noble prince,
As there comes light from heaven and words
   from breath,
As there is sense in truth and truth in virtue,
I am affianc'd this man's wife as strongly   221
As words could make up vows: and, my good
   lord,
But Tuesday night last gone in 's garden-house
He knew me as a wife. As this is true,   224
Let me in safety raise me from my knees
Or else for ever be confixed here,
A marble monument.
   Ang.   I did but smile till now:
Now, good my lord, give me the scope of justice;
My patience here is touch'd. I do perceive   229
These poor informal women are no more
But instruments of some more mightier member
That sets them on. Let me have way, my lord,
To find this practice out.
   Duke.   Ay, with my heart;   233
And punish them unto your height of pleasure.
Thou foolish friar, and thou pernicious woman,
Compact with her that's gone, think'st thou
   thy oaths,   236
Though they would swear down each particular
   saint,
Were testimonies against his worth and credit
That's seal'd in approbation? You, Lord Es-
   calus,
Sit with my cousin; lend him your kind pains
To find out this abuse, whence 'tis deriv'd.   241
There is another friar that set them on;
Let him be sent for.
   F. Peter. Would he were here, my lord;
   for he indeed   244
Hath set the women on to this complaint:
Your provost knows the place where he abides
And he may fetch him.
   Duke. Go do it instantly. [*Exit* PROVOST.
And you, my noble and well-warranted cousin,
Whom it concerns to hear this matter forth,
Do with your injuries as seems you best,   250
In any chastisement: I for awhile will leave
   you;
But stir not you, till you have well determin'd
Upon these slanderers.
   Escal. My lord, we'll do it throughly.—
                              [*Exit* DUKE.
Signior Lucio, did not you say you knew that
Friar Lodowick to be a dishonest person?   256
   Lucio. Cucullus non facit monachum: ho-
nest in nothing, but in his clothes; and one
that hath spoke most villanous speeches of
the duke.   260
   Escal. We shall entreat you to abide here
till he come and enforce them against him. We
shall find this friar a notable fellow.
   Lucio. As any in Vienna, on my word.   264
   Escal. Call that same Isabel here once again:
I would speak with her. [*Exit* an Attendant.]

Pray you, my lord, give me leave to question;
you shall see how I'll handle her.   268
   Lucio. Not better than he, by her own report.
   Escal. Say you?
   Lucio. Marry, sir, I think, if you handled her
privately, she would sooner confess: perchance,
publicly, she'll be ashamed.   273
   Escal. I will go darkly to work with her.
   Lucio. That's the way: for women are light
at midnight.   276

   Re-enter Officers *with* ISABELLA.

   Escal. [*To* ISAB.] Come on, mistress: here's
a gentlewoman denies all that you have said.
   Lucio. My lord, here comes the rascal I spoke
of; here with the provost.   280
   Escal. In very good time: speak not you to
him, till we call upon you.

   Enter DUKE, *disguised as a friar, and*
                    PROVOST.

   Lucio. Mum.   283
   Escal. Come, sir. Did you set these women
on to slander Lord Angelo? they have confessed
you did.
   Duke. 'Tis false.
   Escal. How! know you where you are?   288
   Duke. Respect to your great place! and let
the devil
Be sometime honour'd for his burning throne.
Where is the duke? 'tis he should hear me
   speak.
   Escal. The duke's in us, and we will hear
   you speak: 292
Look you speak justly.
   Duke. Boldly, at least. But, O, poor souls!
Come you to seek the lamb here of the fox?
Good night to your redress! Is the duke
   gone?   296
Then is your cause gone too. The duke's un-
   just,
Thus to retort your manifest appeal,
And put your trial in the villain's mouth
Which here you come to accuse.   300
   Lucio. This is the rascal: this is he I spoke
   of.
   Escal. Why, thou unreverend and unhallow'd
   friar!
Is't not enough thou hast suborn'd these women
To accuse this worthy man, but, in foul mouth,
And in the witness of his proper ear,   305
To call him villain?
And then to glance from him to the duke him-
   self,
To tax him with injustice? take him hence;   308
To the rack with him! We'll touse you joint
   by joint,
But we will know his purpose. What! 'unjust'?
   Duke. Be not so hot; the duke
Dare no more stretch this finger of mine than he
Dare rack his own: his subject am I not,   313
Nor here provincial. My business in this state
Made me a looker-on here in Vienna,
Where I have seen corruption boil and bubble
Till it o'er-run the stew: laws for all faults,   317

But faults so countenanc'd, that the strong
statutes
Stand like the forfeits in a barber's shop,
As much in mock as mark. 320
Escal. Slander to the state! Away with him
to prison!
Ang. What can you vouch against him,
Signior Lucio?
Is this the man that you did tell us of?
Lucio. 'Tis he, my lord. Come hither, good-
man bald-pate: do you know me? 325
Duke. I remember you, sir, by the sound of
your voice: I met you at the prison, in the
absence of the duke. 328
Lucio. O! did you so? And do you remem-
ber what you said of the duke?
Duke. Most notedly, sir.
Lucio. Do you so, sir? And was the duke a
flesh-monger, a fool, and a coward, as you then
reported him to be? 334
Duke. You must, sir, change persons with
me, ere you make that my report: you, indeed,
spoke so of him; and much more, much worse.
Lucio. O thou damnable fellow! Did not I
pluck thee by the nose for thy speeches?
Duke. I protest I love the duke as I love
myself. 340
Ang. Hark how the villain would close now,
after his treasonable abuses!
Escal. Such a fellow is not to be talk'd
withal.
Away with him to prison! Where is the
provost? 344
Away with him to prison! Lay bolts enough on
him, let him speak no more. Away with those
giglots too, and with the other confederate companion! 348
[The PROVOST *lays hands on the* DUKE.
Duke. Stay, sir; stay awhile.
Ang. What! resists he? Help him, Lucio.
Lucio. Come, sir; come, sir; come, sir; foh!
sir. Why, you bald-pated, lying rascal, you
must be hooded, must you? show your knave's
visage, with a pox to you! show your sheep-
biting face, and be hanged an hour! Will't
not off? 356
*[Pulls off the friar's hood, and discovers
the* DUKE.
Duke. Thou art the first knave that e'er
made a duke.
First, provost, let me bail these gentle three.
[To LUCIO.] Sneak not away, sir; for the friar
and you
Must have a word anon. Lay hold on him. 360
Lucio. This may prove worse than hanging.
Duke. [*To* ESCALUS.] What you have spoke
I pardon; sit you down:
We'll borrow place of him. [*To* ANGELO.] Sir,
by your leave.
Hast thou or word, or wit, or impudence, 364
That yet can do thee office? If thou hast,
Rely upon it till my tale be heard,
And hold no longer out.
Ang. O my dread lord!
I should be guiltier than my guiltiness, 368
To think I can be undiscernible

When I perceive your Grace, like power divine,
Hath look'd upon my passes. Then, good prince,
No longer session hold upon my shame, 372
But let my trial be mine own confession:
Immediate sentence then and sequent death
Is all the grace I beg.
Duke. Come hither, Mariana.
Say, wast thou e'er contracted to this woman?
Ang. I was, my lord. 377
Duke. Go take her hence, and marry her
instantly.
Do you the office, friar; which consummate,
Return him here again. Go with him, provost.
[Exeunt ANGELO, MARIANA, FRIAR PETER,
and PROVOST.
Escal. My lord, I am more amaz'd at his
dishonour 381
Than at the strangeness of it.
Duke. Come hither, Isabel.
Your friar is now your prince: as I was then
Advertising and holy to your business, 384
Not changing heart with habit, I am still
Attorney'd at your service.
Isab. O, give me pardon,
That I, your vassal, have employ'd and pain'd
Your unknown sovereignty!
Duke. You are pardon'd, Isabel:
And now, dear maid, be you as free to us. 389
Your brother's death, I know, sits at your heart;
And you may marvel why I obscur'd myself,
Labouring to save his life, and would not rather
Make rash remonstrance of my hidden power
Than let him so be lost. O most kind maid!
It was the swift celerity of his death, 395
Which I did think with slower foot came on,
That brain'd my purpose: but, peace be with
him!
That life is better life, past fearing death,
Than that which lives to fear: make it your
comfort,
So happy is your brother.
Isab. I do, my lord. 400

Re-enter ANGELO, MARIANA, FRIAR PETER,
and PROVOST.

Duke. For this new-married man approach-
ing here,
Whose salt imagination yet hath wrong'd
Your well-defended honour, you must pardon
For Mariana's sake. But as he adjudg'd your
brother,— 404
Being criminal, in double violation
Of sacred chastity, and of promise-breach,
Thereon dependent, for your brother's life,—
The very mercy of the law cries out 408
Most audible, even from his proper tongue,
'An Angelo for Claudio, death for death!'
Haste still pays haste, and leisure answers
leisure,
Like doth quit like, and Measure still for
Measure. 412
Then, Angelo, thy fault's thus manifested,
Which, though thou wouldst deny, denies thee
vantage.
We do condemn thee to the very block

Where Claudio stoop'd to death, and with like
haste.   416
Away with him!
   Mari.   O, my most gracious lord!
I hope you will not mock me with a husband.
   Duke. It is your husband mock'd you with
   a husband.   419
Consenting to the safeguard of your honour,
I thought your marriage fit; else imputation,
For that he knew you, might reproach your life
And choke your good to come. For his pos-
   sessions,
Although by confiscation they are ours,   424
We do instate and widow you withal,
To buy you a better husband.
   Mari.   O my dear lord!
I crave no other, nor no better man.   427
   Duke. Never crave him; we are definitive.
   Mari. [*Kneeling.*] Gentle my liege,—
   Duke.   You do but lose your labour.
Away with him to death! [*To* LUCIO.] Now, sir,
   to you.
   Mari. O my good lord! Sweet Isabel, take
   my part:
Lend me your knees, and, all my life to come,
I'll lend you all my life to do you service.   433
   Duke. Against all sense you do importune
   her:
Should she kneel down in mercy of this fact,
Her brother's ghost his paved bed would break,
And take her hence in horror.
   Mari.   Isabel,   437
Sweet Isabel, do yet but kneel by me:
Hold up your hands, say nothing, I'll speak
   all.   439
They say best men are moulded out of faults,
And, for the most, become much more the better
For being a little bad: so may my husband.
O, Isabel! will you not lend a knee?   443
   Duke. He dies for Claudio's death.
   Isab.   [*Kneeling.*] Most bounteous sir,
Look, if it please you, on this man condemn'd,
As if my brother liv'd. I partly think
A due sincerity govern'd his deeds,
Till he did look on me: since it is so,   448
Let him not die. My brother had but justice,
In that he did the thing for which he died:
For Angelo,
His act did not o'ertake his bad intent;   452
And must be buried but as an intent
That perish'd by the way. Thoughts are no
   subjects;
Intents but merely thoughts.
   Mari.   Merely, my lord.
   Duke. Your suit's unprofitable: stand up, I
   say.   456
I have bethought me of another fault.
Provost, how came it Claudio was beheaded
At an unusual hour?
   Prov.   It was commanded so.
   Duke. Had you a special warrant for the
   deed?   460
   Prov. No, my good lord; it was by private
   message.
   Duke. For which I do discharge you of your
   office:

Give up your keys.
   Prov.   Pardon me, noble lord:
I thought it was a fault, but knew it not,   464
Yet did repent me, after more advice;
For testimony whereof, one in the prison,
That should by private order else have died
I have reserv'd alive.
   Duke.   What's he?
   Prov.   His name is Barnardine.
   Duke. I would thou hadst done so by Claudio.
Go, fetch him hither: let me look upon him.
                  [*Exit* PROVOST.
   Escal. I am sorry, one so learned and so
   wise
As you, Lord Angelo, have still appear'd,   472
Should slip so grossly, both in the heat of blood,
And lack of temper'd judgment afterward.
   Ang. I am sorry that such sorrow I procure;
And so deep sticks it in my penitent heart   476
That I crave death more willingly than mercy:
'Tis my deserving, and I do entreat it.

Re-enter PROVOST, *with* BARNARDINE, CLAUDIO
        muffled, and JULIET.

   Duke. Which is that Barnardine?
   Prov.   This, my lord.
   Duke. There was a friar told me of this man.
Sirrah, thou art said to have a stubborn soul,
That apprehends no further than this world,   482
And squar'st thy life according. Thou'rt con-
   demn'd:
But, for those earthly faults, I quit them all,
And pray thee take this mercy to provide   485
For better times to come. Friar, advise him:
I leave him to your hand.—What muffled
   fellow's that?
   Prov. This is another prisoner that I sav'd,
That should have died when Claudio lost his
   head,   489
As like almost to Claudio as himself.
                [*Unmuffles* CLAUDIO.
   Duke. [*To* ISABELLA.] If he be like your bro-
   ther, for his sake
Is he pardon'd; and, for your lovely sake   492
Give me your hand and say you will be mine,
He is my brother too. But fitter time for that.
By this, Lord Angelo perceives he's safe:
Methinks I see a quickening in his eye.   496
Well, Angelo, your evil quits you well:
Look that you love your wife; her worth worth
   yours.—
I find an apt remission in myself,
And yet here's one in place I cannot pardon.—
[*To* LUCIO.] You, sirrah, that knew me for a
   fool, a coward,   501
One all of luxury, an ass, a madman:
Wherein have I so deserv'd of you,
That you extol me thus?   504
   Lucio. 'Faith, my lord, I spoke it but accord-
ing to the trick. If you will hang me for it, you
may; but I had rather it would please you I
might be whipped.   508
   Duke. Whipp'd first, sir, and hang'd after.
Proclaim it, provost, round about the city,
If any woman's wrong'd by this lewd fellow,—
As I have heard him swear himself there's one

Whom he begot with child, let her appear, 513
And he shall marry her: the nuptial finish'd,
Let him be whipp'd and hang'd.
   Lucio. I beseech your highness, do not marry
me to a whore. Your highness said even now,
I made you a duke: good my lord, do not re-
compense me in making me a cuckold.
   Duke. Upon mine honour, thou shalt marry
her. 520
Thy slanders I forgive; and therewithal
Remit thy other forfeits. Take him to prison,
And see our pleasure herein executed.
   Lucio. Marrying a punk, my lord, is pressing
to death, whipping, and hanging. 525
   Duke. Slandering a prince deserves it.
She, Claudio, that you wrong'd, look you re-
store.

Joy to you, Mariana! love her, Angelo: 528
I have confess'd her and I know her virtue.
Thanks, good friend Escalus, for thy much
goodness:
There's more behind that is more gratulate.
Thanks, provost, for thy care and secrecy; 532
We shall employ thee in a worthier place.
Forgive him, Angelo, that brought you home
The head of Ragozine for Claudio's:
The offence pardons itself. Dear Isabel, 536
I have a motion much imports your good:
Whereto if you'll a willing ear incline,
What's mine is yours, and what is yours is
mine. 539
So, bring us to our palace; where we'll show
What's yet behind, that's meet you all should
know.   [*Exeunt.*

THE COMEDY OF ERRORS

DRAMATIS PERSONÆ

SOLINUS, Duke of Ephesus.
ÆGEON, a Merchant of Syracuse.
ANTIPHOLUS of Ephesus, } Twin Brothers, sons to
ANTIPHOLUS of Syracuse, } Ægeon and Æmilia.
DROMIO of Ephesus, } Twin Brothers, attendants on the
DROMIO of Syracuse, } two Antipholuses.
BALTHAZAR, a Merchant.
ANGELO, a Goldsmith.
Merchant, Friend to Antipholus of Syracuse.

A Second Merchant, to whom Angelo is a debtor.
PINCH, a Schoolmaster and a Conjurer.

ÆMILIA, Wife to Ægeon, an Abbess at Ephesus.
ADRIANA, Wife to Antipholus of Ephesus.
LUCIANA, her Sister.
LUCE, Servant to Adriana.
A Courtezan.

Gaoler, Officers, and other Attendants.

SCENE.—*Ephesus.*

ACT I

SCENE I.—*A Hall in the* DUKE'S *Palace.*

Enter DUKE, ÆGEON, Gaoler, Officers, *and other*
Attendants.

Æge. Proceed, Solinus, to procure my fall,
And by the doom of death end woes and all.
Duke. Merchant of Syracusa, plead no more.
I am not partial to infringe our laws: 4
The enmity and discord which of late
Sprung from the rancorous outrage of your duke
To merchants, our well-dealing countrymen,
Who, wanting guilders to redeem their lives, 8
Have seal'd his rigorous statutes with their
  bloods,
Excludes all pity from our threat'ning looks.
For, since the mortal and intestine jars
'Twixt thy seditious countrymen and us, 12
It hath in solemn synods been decreed,
Both by the Syracusians and ourselves,
T' admit no traffic to our adverse towns:
Nay, more, if any, born at Ephesus 16
Be seen at Syracusian marts and fairs;
Again, if any Syracusian born
Come to the bay of Ephesus, he dies,
His goods confiscate to the duke's dispose; 20
Unless a thousand marks be levied,
To quit the penalty and to ransom him.
Thy substance, valu'd at the highest rate,
Cannot amount unto a hundred marks; 24
Therefore, by law thou art condemn'd to die.
Æge. Yet this my comfort: when your words
  are done,
My woes end likewise with the evening sun.
Duke. Well, Syracusian; say, in brief the
  cause 28
Why thou departedst from thy native home,
And for what cause thou cam'st to Ephesus.
Æge. A heavier task could not have been
  impos'd
Than I to speak my griefs unspeakable; 32
Yet, that the world may witness that my end
Was wrought by nature, not by vile offence,
I'll utter what my sorrow gives me leave.
In Syracusa was I born, and wed 36
Unto a woman, happy but for me,

And by me too, had not our hap been bad.
With her I liv'd in joy: our wealth increas'd
By prosperous voyages I often made 40
To Epidamnum; till my factor's death,
And the great care of goods at random left,
Drew me from kind embracements of my spouse:
From whom my absence was not six months
  old, 44
Before herself,—almost at fainting under
The pleasing punishment that women bear,—
Had made provision for her following me,
And soon and safe arrived where I was. 48
There had she not been long but she became
A joyful mother of two goodly sons;
And, which was strange, the one so like the
  other,
As could not be distinguish'd but by names. 52
That very hour, and in the self-same inn,
A meaner woman was delivered
Of such a burden, male twins, both alike.
Those,—for their parents were exceeding
  poor,— 56
I bought, and brought up to attend my sons.
My wife, not meanly proud of two such boys,
Made daily motions for our home return:
Unwilling I agreed; alas! too soon 60
We came aboard.
A league from Epidamnum had we sail'd,
Before the always-wind-obeying deep
Gave any tragic instance of our harm: 64
But longer did we not retain much hope;
For what obscured light the heavens did grant
Did but convey unto our fearful minds
A doubtful warrant of immediate death; 68
Which, though myself would gladly have em-
  brac'd,
Yet the incessant weepings of my wife,
Weeping before for what she saw must come,
And piteous plainings of the pretty babes, 72
That mourn'd for fashion, ignorant what to fear,
Forc'd me to seek delays for them and me.
And this it was, for other means was none:
The sailors sought for safety by our boat, 76
And left the ship, then sinking-ripe, to us:
My wife, more careful for the latter-born,
Had fasten'd him unto a small spare mast,
Such as seafaring men provide for storms; 80

To him one of the other twins was bound,
Whilst I had been like heedful of the other.
The children thus dispos'd, my wife and I,
Fixing our eyes on whom our care was fix'd, 84
Fasten'd ourselves at either end the mast;
And floating straight, obedient to the stream,
Were carried towards Corinth, as we thought.
At length the sun, gazing upon the earth, 88
Dispers'd those vapours that offended us,
And, by the benefit of his wished light
The seas wax'd calm, and we discovered
Two ships from far making amain to us; 92
Of Corinth that, of Epidaurus this:
But ere they came,—O! let me say no more;
Gather the sequel by that went before.
    Duke. Nay, forward, old man; do not break
    off so; 96
For we may pity, though not pardon thee.
    Æge. O! had the gods done so, I had not
    now
Worthily term'd them merciless to us!
For, ere the ships could meet by twice five
    leagues, 100
We were encounter'd by a mighty rock;
Which being violently borne upon,
Our helpful ship was splitted in the midst;
So that, in this unjust divorce of us 104
Fortune had left to both of us alike
What to delight in, what to sorrow for.
Her part, poor soul! seeming as burdened
With lesser weight, but not with lesser woe, 108
Was carried with more speed before the wind,
And in our sight they three were taken up
By fishermen of Corinth, as we thought.
At length, another ship had seiz'd on us; 112
And, knowing whom it was their hap to save,
Gave healthful welcome to their ship-wrack'd
    guests;
And would have reft the fishers of their prey,
Had not their bark been very slow of sail; 116
And therefore homeward did they bend their
    course.
Thus have you heard me sever'd from my bliss,
That by misfortune was my life prolong'd,
To tell sad stories of my own mishaps. 120
    Duke. And, for the sake of them thou sor-
    rowest for,
Do me the favour to dilate at full
What hath befall'n of them and thee till now.
    Æge. My youngest boy, and yet my eldest
    care, 124
At eighteen years became inquisitive
After his brother; and importun'd me
That his attendant—for his case was like,
Reft of his brother, but retain'd his name— 128
Might bear him company in the quest of him;
Whom whilst I labour'd of a love to see,
I hazarded the loss of whom I lov'd.
Five summers have I spent in furthest Greece,
Roaming clean through the bounds of Asia, 133
And, coasting homeward, came to Ephesus,
Hopeless to find, yet loath to leave unsought
Or that or any place that harbours men. 136
But here must end the story of my life;
And happy were I in my timely death,
Could all my travels warrant me they live.

    Duke. Hapless Ægeon, whom the fates have
    mark'd 140
To bear the extremity of dire mishap!
Now, trust me, were it not against our laws,
Against my crown, my oath, my dignity,
Which princes, would they, may not disannul,
My soul should sue as advocate for thee. 145
But though thou art adjudged to the death
And passed sentence may not be recall'd
But to our honour's great disparagement, 148
Yet will I favour thee in what I can:
Therefore, merchant, I'll limit thee this day
To seek thy life by beneficial help.
Try all the friends thou hast in Ephesus; 152
Beg thou, or borrow, to make up the sum,
And live; if no, then thou art doom'd to die.
Gaoler, take him to thy custody.
    Gaol. I will, my lord. 156
    Æge. Hopeless and helpless doth Ægeon
    wend,
But to procrastinate his lifeless end. [*Exeunt.*

SCENE II.—*The Mart.*

Enter ANTIPHOLUS *of Syracuse*, DROMIO *of*
    Syracuse, *and a Merchant.*

    Mer. Therefore, give out you are of Epidam-
    num,
Lest that your goods too soon be confiscate.
This very day, a Syracusian merchant
Is apprehended for arrival here; 4
And, not being able to buy out his life,
According to the statute of the town
Dies ere the weary sun set in the west.
There is your money that I had to keep. 8
    Ant. S. Go bear it to the Centaur, where we
    host,
And stay there, Dromio, till I come to thee.
Within this hour it will be dinner-time:
Till that, I'll view the manners of the town, 12
Peruse the traders, gaze upon the buildings,
And then return and sleep within mine inn,
For with long travel I am stiff and weary.
Get thee away. 16
    Dro. S. Many a man would take you at your
    word,
And go indeed, having so good a mean. [*Exit.*
    Ant. S. A trusty villain, sir, that very oft,
When I am dull with care and melancholy, 20
Lightens my humour with his merry jests.
What, will you walk with me about the town,
And then go to my inn and dine with me?
    Mer. I am invited, sir, to certain merchants,
Of whom I hope to make much benefit; 25
I crave your pardon. Soon at five o'clock,
Please you, I'll meet with you upon the mart,
And afterward consort you till bed-time: 28
My present business calls me from you now.
    Ant. S. Farewell till then: I will go lose my-
    self,
And wander up and down to view the city.
    Mer. Sir, I commend you to your own con-
    tent. [*Exit.*
    Ant. S. He that commends me to mine own
    content, 33

Commends me to the thing I cannot get.
I to the world am like a drop of water
That in the ocean seeks another drop;   36
Who, falling there to find his fellow forth,
Unseen, inquisitive, confounds himself:
So I, to find a mother and a brother,
In quest of them, unhappy, lose myself.   40

Enter DROMIO *of Ephesus.*

Here comes the almanack of my true date.
What now? How chance thou art return'd so
    soon?
Dro. E. Return'd so soon! rather approach'd
    too late:
The capon burns, the pig falls from the spit,   44
The clock hath strucken twelve upon the bell;
My mistress made it one upon my cheek:
She is so hot because the meat is cold;
The meat is cold because you come not home;
You come not home because you have no
    stomach;   49
You have no stomach, having broke your fast;
But we, that know what 'tis to fast and pray,
Are penitent for your default to-day.   52
Ant. S. Stop in your wind, sir: tell me this,
    I pray:
Where have you left the money that I gave you?
Dro. E. O!—sixpence, that I had o' Wednes-
    day last
To pay the saddler for my mistress' crupper;
The saddler had it, sir; I kept it not.   57
Ant. S. I am not in a sportive humour now.
Tell me, and dally not, where is the money?
We being strangers here, how dar'st thou trust
So great a charge from thine own custody?   61
Dro. E. I pray you, jest, sir, as you sit at
    dinner.
I from my mistress come to you in post;
If I return, I shall be post indeed,   64
For she will score your fault upon my pate.
Methinks your maw, like mine, should be your
    clock
And strike you home without a messenger.
Ant. S. Come, Dromio, come; these jests are
    out of season.   68
Reserve them till a merrier hour than this.
Where is the gold I gave in charge to thee?
Dro. E. To me, sir? why, you gave no gold
    to me.
Ant. S. Come on, sir knave, have done your
    foolishness,   72
And tell me how thou hast dispos'd thy charge.
Dro. E. My charge was but to fetch you from
    the mart
Home to your house, the Phœnix, sir, to dinner:
My mistress and her sister stays for you.   76
Ant. S. Now, as I am a Christian, answer me,
In what safe place you have bestow'd my money;
Or I shall break that merry sconce of yours
That stands on tricks when I am undispos'd.   80
Where is the thousand marks thou hadst of me?
Dro. E. I have some marks of yours upon
    my pate,
Some of my mistress' marks upon my shoulders,
But not a thousand marks between you both.
If I should pay your worship those again,   85

Perchance you will not bear them patiently.
Ant. S. Thy mistress' marks! what mistress,
    slave, hast thou?
Dro. E. Your worship's wife, my mistress at
    the Phœnix;   88
She that doth fast till you come home to dinner,
And prays that you will hie you home to dinner.
Ant. S. What! wilt thou flout me thus unto
    my face,   91
Being forbid? There, take you that, sir knave.
                                        [*Strikes him.*
Dro. E. What mean you, sir? for God's sake,
    hold your hands!
Nay, an you will not, sir, I'll take my heels.
                                              [*Exit.*
Ant. S. Upon my life, by some device or
    other
The villain is o'er-raught of all my money.   96
They say this town is full of cozenage;
As, nimble jugglers that deceive the eye,
Dark-working sorcerers that change the mind,
Soul-killing witches that deform the body,   100
Disguised cheaters, prating mountebanks,
And many such-like liberties of sin:
If it prove so, I will be gone the sooner.
I'll to the Centaur, to go seek this slave: 104
I greatly fear my money is not safe.   [*Exit.*

ACT II

SCENE I.—*The House of* ANTIPHOLUS *of
    Ephesus.*

Enter ADRIANA *and* LUCIANA.

Adr. Neither my husband, nor the slave
    return'd,
That in such haste I sent to seek his master!
Sure, Luciana, it is two o'clock.
Luc. Perhaps some merchant hath invited
    him,   4
And from the mart he's somewhere gone to
    dinner.
Good sister, let us dine and never fret:
A man is master of his liberty: 7
Time is their master: and, when they see time,
They'll go or come: if so, be patient, sister.
Adr. Why should their liberty than ours be
    more?
Luc. Because their business still lies out
    o' door.
Adr. Look, when I serve him so, he takes
    it ill.   12
Luc. O! know he is the bridle of your will.
Adr. There's none but asses will be bridled
    so.
Luc. Why, headstrong liberty is lash'd with
    woe.
There's nothing situate under heaven's eye   16
But hath his bound, in earth, in sea, in sky:
The beasts, the fishes, and the winged fowls,
Are their males' subjects and at their controls.
Men, more divine, the masters of all these,   20
Lords of the wide world, and wild wat'ry seas,
Indu'd with intellectual sense and souls,
Of more pre-eminence than fish and fowls,

Are masters to their females and their lords:
Then, let your will attend on their accords. 25
  Adr. This servitude makes you to keep un-
wed.
  Luc. Not this, but troubles of the marriage-
bed.
  Adr. But, were you wedded, you would bear
some sway. 28
  Luc. Ere I learn love, I'll practise to obey.
  Adr. How if your husband start some other
where?
  Luc. Till he come home again, I would for-
bear.
  Adr. Patience unmov'd! no marvel though
she pause; 32
They can be meek that have no other cause.
A wretched soul, bruis'd with adversity,
We bid be quiet when we hear it cry;
But were we burden'd with like weight of
pain, 36
As much, or more we should ourselves com-
plain:
So thou, that hast no unkind mate to grieve thee,
With urging helpless patience wouldst re-
lieve me:
But if thou live to see like right bereft, 40
This fool-begg'd patience in thee will be left.
  Luc. Well, I will marry one day, but to try.
Here comes your man: now is your husband
nigh.

    Enter DROMIO *of Ephesus.*

  Adr. Say, is your tardy master now at
hand? 44
  Dro. E. Nay, he's at two hands with me, and
that my two ears can witness.
  Adr. Say, didst thou speak with him?
Know'st thou his mind?
  Dro. E. Ay, ay, he told his mind upon mine
ear. 48
Beshrew his hand, I scarce could understand
it.
  Luc. Spake he so doubtfully, thou couldst not
feel his meaning? 51
  Dro. E. Nay, he struck so plainly, I could too
well feel his blows; and withal so doubtfully,
that I could scarce understand them.
  Adr. But say, I prithee, is he coming home?
It seems he hath great care to please his wife. 56
  Dro. E. Why, mistress, sure my master is
horn-mad.
  Adr. Horn-mad, thou villain!
  Dro. E. I mean not cuckold-mad; but, sure,
he is stark mad.
When I desir'd him to come home to dinner, 60
He ask'd me for a thousand marks in gold:
''Tis dinner time,' quoth I; 'my gold!' quoth
he:
'Your meat doth burn,' quoth I; 'my gold!'
quoth he:
'Will you come home?' quoth I: 'my gold!'
quoth he: 64
'Where is the thousand marks I gave thee,
villain?'
'The pig,' quoth I, 'is burn'd;' 'my gold!' quoth
he:

'My mistress, sir,' quoth I: 'hang up thy mis-
tress!
I know not thy mistress: out on thy mistress!'
  Luc. Quoth who? 69
  Dro. E. Quoth my master:
'I know,' quoth he, 'no house, no wife, no mis-
tress.'
So that my errand, due unto my tongue, 72
I thank him, I bear home upon my shoulders;
For, in conclusion, he did beat me there.
  Adr. Go back again, thou slave, and fetch
him home.
  Dro. E. Go back again, and be new beaten
home? 76
For God's sake, send some other messenger.
  Adr. Back, slave, or I will break thy pate
across.
  Dro. E. And he will bless that cross with
other beating:
Between you, I shall have a holy head. 80
  Adr. Hence, prating peasant! fetch thy mas-
ter home.
  Dro. E. Am I so round with you as you with
me,
That like a football you do spurn me thus?
You spurn me hence, and he will spurn me
hither: 84
If I last in this service, you must case me in
leather.   [*Exit.*
  Luc. Fie, how impatience loureth in your
face!
  Adr. His company must do his minions
grace,
Whilst I at home starve for a merry look. 88
Hath homely age the alluring beauty took
From my poor cheek? then, he hath wasted it:
Are my discourses dull? barren my wit?
If voluble and sharp discourse be marr'd, 92
Unkindness blunts it more than marble hard:
Do their gay vestments his affections bait?
That's not my fault; he's master of my state:
What ruins are in me that can be found 96
By him not ruin'd? then is he the ground
Of my defeatures. My decayed fair
A sunny look of his would soon repair;
But, too unruly deer, he breaks the pale 100
And feeds from home: poor I am but his stale.
  Luc. Self-harming jealousy! fie! beat it
hence.
  Adr. Unfeeling fools can with such wrongs
dispense.
I know his eye doth homage otherwhere, 104
Or else what lets it but he would be here?
Sister, you know he promis'd me a chain.
Would that alone, alone he would detain,
So he would keep fair quarter with his bed! 108
I see, the jewel best enamelled
Will lose his beauty; and though gold bides
still
That others touch, yet often touching will
Wear gold; and no man that hath a name, 112
By falsehood and corruption doth it shame.
Since that my beauty cannot please his eye,
I'll weep what's left away, and weeping die.
  Luc. How many fond fools serve mad jea-
lousy!   [*Exeunt.*

SCENE II.—*A public Place.*

Enter ANTIPHOLUS *of Syracuse.*

Ant. S. The gold I gave to Dromio is laid up
Safe at the Centaur; and the heedful slave
Is wander'd forth, in care to seek me out.
By computation, and mine host's report,   4
I could not speak with Dromio since at first
I sent him from the mart. See, here he comes.

Enter DROMIO *of Syracuse.*

How now, sir! is your merry humour alter'd?
As you love strokes, so jest with me again.   8
You know no Centaur? You receiv'd no gold?
Your mistress sent to have me home to dinner?
My house was at the Phœnix? Wast thou mad,
That thus so madly thou didst answer me?   12
  Dro. S. What answer, sir? when spake I such
    a word?
  Ant. S. Even now, even here, not half-an-
    hour since.
  Dro. S. I did not see you since you sent me
    hence,
Home to the Centaur, with the gold you gave
    me.   16
  Ant. S. Villain, thou didst deny the gold's
    receipt,
And told'st me of a mistress and a dinner;
For which, I hope, thou felt'st I was displeas'd.
  Dro. S. I am glad to see you in this merry
    vein: 20
What means this jest? I pray you, master,
    tell me.
  Ant. S. Yea, dost thou jeer, and flout me in
    the teeth?
Think'st thou I jest? Hold, take thou that, and
    that.   [*Beating him.*
  Dro. S. Hold, sir, for God's sake! now your
    jest is earnest: 24
Upon what bargain do you give it me?
  Ant. S. Because that I familiarly sometimes
Do use you for my fool, and chat with you,
Your sauciness will jest upon my love,   28
And make a common of my serious hours.
When the sun shines let foolish gnats make
    sport,
But creep in crannies when he hides his beams.
If you will jest with me, know my aspect,   32
And fashion your demeanour to my looks,
Or I will beat this method in your sconce.
  Dro. S. Sconce, call you it? so you would
leave battering, I had rather have it a head:
an you use these blows long, I must get a sconce
for my head and insconce it too; or else I shall
seek my wit in my shoulders. But, I pray, sir,
why am I beaten?   40
  Ant. S. Dost thou not know?
  Dro. S. Nothing, sir, but that I am beaten.
  Ant. S. Shall I tell you why?
  Dro. S. Ay, sir, and wherefore; for they say
every why hath a wherefore.   45
  Ant. S. Why, first,—for flouting me; and
    then, wherefore,—
For urging it the second time to me.
  Dro. S. Was there ever any man thus beaten
    out of season,   48

When, in the why and the wherefore is neither
    rime nor reason?
Well, sir, I thank you.
  Ant. S. Thank me, sir! for what?
  Dro. S. Marry, sir, for this something that
you gave me for nothing.   53
  Ant. S. I'll make you amends next, to give
you nothing for something. But say, sir, is it
dinner-time?   56
  Dro. S. No, sir: I think the meat wants that
I have.
  Ant. S. In good time, sir; what's that?
  Dro. S. Basting.   60
  Ant. S. Well, sir, then 'twill be dry.
  Dro. S. If it be, sir, I pray you eat none of it.
  Ant. S. Your reason?
  Dro. S. Lest it make you choleric, and pur-
chase me another dry basting.   65
  Ant. S. Well, sir, learn to jest in good time:
there's a time for all things.
  Dro. S. I durst have denied that, before you
were so choleric.   69
  Ant. S. By what rule, sir?
  Dro. S. Marry, sir, by a rule as plain as the
plain bald pate of Father Time himself.   72
  Ant. S. Let's hear it.
  Dro. S. There's no time for a man to recover
his hair that grows bald by nature.
  Ant. S. May he not do it by fine and recovery?   77
  Dro. S. Yes, to pay a fine for a periwig and
recover the lost hair of another man.
  Ant. S. Why is Time such a niggard of hair,
being, as it is, so plentiful an excrement?   81
  Dro. S. Because it is a blessing that he be-
stows on beasts: and what he hath scanted men
in hair, he hath given them in wit.   84
  Ant. S. Why, but there's many a man hath
more hair than wit.
  Dro. S. Not a man of those but he hath the
wit to lose his hair.   88
  Ant. S. Why, thou didst conclude hairy men
plain dealers without wit.
  Dro. S. The plainer dealer, the sooner lost:
yet he loseth it in a kind of jollity.   92
  Ant. S. For what reason?
  Dro. S. For two; and sound ones too.
  Ant. S. Nay, not sound, I pray you.
  Dro. S. Sure ones then.   96
  Ant. S. Nay, not sure, in a thing falsing.
  Dro. S. Certain ones, then.
  Ant. S. Name them.   99
  Dro. S. The one, to save the money that he
spends in tiring; the other, that at dinner they
should not drop in his porridge.
  Ant. S. You would all this time have proved
there is no time for all things.   104
  Dro. S. Marry, and did, sir; namely, no time
to recover hair lost by nature.
  Ant. S. But your reason was not substantial,
why there is no time to recover.   108
  Dro. S. Thus I mend it: Time himself is bald,
and therefore to the world's end will have bald
followers.
  Ant. S. I knew 'twould be a bald conclusion.
But soft! who wafts us yonder?   113

Enter ADRIANA *and* LUCIANA.

Adr. Ay, ay, Antipholus, look strange, and
frown:
Some other mistress hath thy sweet aspects,
I am not Adriana, nor thy wife.   116
The time was once when thou unurg'd wouldst
vow
That never words were music to thine ear,
That never object pleasing in thine eye,
That never touch well welcome to thy hand, 120
That never meat sweet-savour'd in thy taste,
Unless I spake, or look'd, or touch'd, or carv'd
to thee.
How comes it now, my husband, O! how comes
it,
That thou art thus estranged from thyself? 124
Thyself I call it, being strange to me,
That, undividable, incorporate,
Am better than thy dear self's better part.
Ah! do not tear away thyself from me,   128
For know, my love, as easy mayst thou fall
A drop of water in the breaking gulf,
And take unmingled thence that drop again,
Without addition or diminishing,   132
As take from me thyself and not me too.
How dearly would it touch thee to the quick,
Shouldst thou but hear I were licentious,
And that this body, consecrate to thee,   136
By ruffian lust should be contaminate!
Wouldst thou not spit at me and spurn at me,
And hurl the name of husband in my face,
And tear the stain'd skin off my harlot-brow, 140
And from my false hand cut the wedding-ring
And break it with a deep-divorcing vow?
I know thou canst; and therefore, see thou do it.
I am possess'd with an adulterate blot;   144
My blood is mingled with the crime of lust:
For if we two be one and thou play false,
I do digest the poison of thy flesh,
Being strumpeted by thy contagion.   148
Keep then fair league and truce with thy true
bed;
I live unstain'd, thou undishonoured.
Ant. S. Plead you to me, fair dame? I know
you not:
In Ephesus I am but two hours old,   152
As strange unto your town as to your talk;
Who, every word by all my wit being scann'd,
Want wit in all one word to understand.
Luc. Fie, brother: how the world is chang'd
with you!   156
When were you wont to use my sister thus?
She sent for you by Dromio home to dinner.
Ant. S. By Dromio?
Dro. S. By me?   160
Adr. By thee; and this thou didst return
from him,
That he did buffet thee, and in his blows,
Denied my house for his, me for his wife.
Ant. S. Did you converse, sir, with this gentle-
woman?   164
What is the course and drift of your compact?
Dro. S. I, sir? I never saw her till this time.
Ant. S. Villain, thou liest; for even her very
words
Didst thou deliver to me on the mart.   168

Dro. S. I never spake with her in all my life.
Ant. S. How can she thus then, call us by
our names,
Unless it be by inspiration?
Adr. How ill agrees it with your gravity 172
To counterfeit thus grossly with your slave,
Abetting him to thwart me in my mood!
Be it my wrong you are from me exempt,
But wrong not that wrong with a more con-
tempt.   176
Come, I will fasten on this sleeve of thine;
Thou art an elm, my husband, I a vine,
Whose weakness, married to thy stronger state,
Makes me with thy strength to communicate:
If aught possess thee from me, it is dross, 181
Usurping ivy, brier, or idle moss;
Who, all for want of pruning, with intrusion
Infect thy sap and live on thy confusion.   184
Ant. S. To me she speaks; she moves me for
her theme!
What! was I married to her in my dream?
Or sleep I now and think I hear all this?   187
What error drives our eyes and ears amiss?
Until I know this sure uncertainty,
I'll entertain the offer'd fallacy.
Luc. Dromio, go bid the servants spread for
dinner.
Dro. S. O, for my beads! I cross me for a
sinner.   192
This is the fairy land: O! spite of spites.
We talk with goblins, owls, and elvish sprites:
If we obey them not, this will ensue,
They'll suck our breath, or pinch us black and
blue.   196
Luc. Why prat'st thou to thyself and an-
swer'st not?
Dromio, thou drone, thou snail, thou slug, thou
sot!
Dro. S. I am transformed, master, am not I?
Ant. S. I think thou art, in mind, and so am I.
Dro. S. Nay, master, both in mind and in
my shape.   201
Ant. S. Thou hast thine own form.
Dro. S.   No, I am an ape.
Luc. If thou art chang'd to aught, 'tis to an
ass.
Dro. S. 'Tis true; she rides me and I long
for grass.   204
'Tis so, I am an ass; else it could never be
But I should know her as well as she knows me.
Adr. Come, come; no longer will I be a fool,
To put the finger in the eye and weep,   208
Whilst man and master laugh my woes to scorn.
Come, sir, to dinner. Dromio, keep the gate.
Husband, I'll dine above with you to-day,
And shrive you of a thousand idle pranks.   212
Sirrah, if any ask you for your master,
Say he dines forth, and let no creature enter.
Come, sister. Dromio, play the porter well.
Ant. S. [*Aside.*] Am I in earth, in heaven, or
in hell?   216
Sleeping or waking? mad or well-advis'd?
Known unto these, and to myself disguis'd!
I'll say as they say, and persever so,
And in this mist at all adventures go.   220
Dro. S. Master, shall I be porter at the gate?

Adr. Ay; and let none enter, lest I break your pate.
Luc. Come, come, Antipholus; we dine too late. [*Exeunt.*

ACT III

SCENE I.—*Before the House of* ANTIPHOLUS *of Ephesus.*

Enter ANTIPHOLUS *of Ephesus,* DROMIO *of Ephesus,* ANGELO, *and* BALTHAZAR.

Ant. E. Good Signior Angelo, you must excuse us all;
My wife is shrewish when I keep not hours;
Say that I linger'd with you at your shop
To see the making of her carkanet, 4
And that to-morrow you will bring it home.
But here's a villain, that would face me down
He met me on the mart, and that I beat him,
And charg'd him with a thousand marks in gold, 8
And that I did deny my wife and house.
Thou drunkard, thou, what didst thou mean by this?
Dro. E. Say what you will, sir, but I know what I know;
That you beat me at the mart, I have your hand to show: 12
If the skin were parchment and the blows you gave were ink,
Your own handwriting would tell you what I think.
Ant. E. I think thou art an ass.
Dro. E. Marry, so it doth appear
By the wrongs I suffer and the blows I bear.
I should kick, being kick'd; and, being at that pass, 17
You would keep from my heels and beware of an ass.
Ant. E. You are sad, Signior Balthazar: pray God, our cheer
May answer my good will and your good welcome here. 20
Bal. I hold your dainties cheap, sir, and your welcome dear.
Ant. E. O, Signior Balthazar, either at flesh or fish,
A table-full of welcome makes scarce one dainty dish.
Bal. Good meat, sir, is common; that every churl affords. 24
Ant. E. And welcome more common, for that's nothing but words.
Bal. Small cheer and great welcome makes a merry feast.
Ant. E. Ay, to a niggardly host and more sparing guest:
But though my cates be mean, take them in good part; 28
Better cheer may you have, but not with better heart.
But soft! my door is lock'd. Go bid them let us in.
Dro. E. Maud, Bridget, Marian, Cicely, Gillian, Ginn!

Dro. S. [*Within.*] Mome, malt-horse, capon, coxcomb, idiot, patch! 32
Either get thee from the door or sit down at the hatch.
Dost thou conjure for wenches, that thou call'st for such store,
When one is one too many? Go, get thee from the door.
Dro. E. What patch is made our porter?— My master stays in the street. 36
Dro. S. [*Within.*] Let him walk from whence he came, lest he catch cold on's feet.
Ant. E. Who talks within there? ho! open the door.
Dro. S. [*Within.*] Right, sir; I'll tell you when, an you'll tell me wherefore.
Ant. E. Wherefore? for my dinner: I have not din'd to-day. 40
Dro. S. Nor to-day here you must not; come again when you may.
Ant. E. What art thou that keep'st me out from the house I owe?
Dro. S. [*Within.*] The porter for this time, sir, and my name is Dromio.
Dro. E. O villain! thou hast stolen both mine office and my name: 44
The one ne'er got me credit, the other mickle blame.
If thou hadst been Dromio to-day in my place,
Thou wouldst have chang'd thy face for a name, or thy name for an ass.
Luce. [*Within.*] What a coil is there, Dromio! who are those at the gate? 48
Dro. E. Let my master in, Luce.
Luce. [*Within.*] Faith, no; he comes too late; And so tell your master.
Dro. E. O Lord! I must laugh. Have at you with a proverb: Shall I set in my staff?
Luce. [*Within.*] Have at you with another: that's—when? can you tell? 52
Dro. S. [*Within.*] If thy name be call'd Luce, —Luce, thou hast answer'd him well.
Ant. E. Do you hear, you minion? you'll let us in, I trow?
Luce. [*Within.*] I thought to have ask'd you.
Dro. S. [*Within.*] And you said, no.
Dro. E. So come, help: well struck! there was blow for blow. 56
Ant. E. Thou baggage, let me in.
Luce. [*Within.*] Can you tell for whose sake?
Dro. E. Master, knock the door hard.
Luce. [*Within.*] Let him knock till it ache.
Ant. E. You'll cry for this, minion, if I beat the door down.
Luce. [*Within.*] What needs all that, and a pair of stocks in the town? 60
Adr. [*Within.*] Who is that at the door that keeps all this noise?
Dro. S. [*Within.*] By my troth your town is troubled with unruly boys.
Ant. E. Are you there, wife? you might have come before.
Adr. [*Within.*] Your wife, sir knave! go, get you from the door. 64

Dro. E. If you went in pain, master, this
'knave' would go sore.

Ang. Here is neither cheer, sir, nor welcome:
we would fain have either.

Bal. In debating which was best, we shall
part with neither.

Dro. E. They stand at the door, master: bid
them welcome hither.   68

Ant. E. There is something in the wind, that
we cannot get in.

Dro. E. You would say so, master, if your
garments were thin.

Your cake here is warm within; you stand here
in the cold:

It would make a man mad as a buck to be so
bought and sold.   72

Ant. E. Go fetch me something: I'll break
ope the gate.

Dro. S. [*Within.*] Break any breaking here,
and I'll break your knave's pate.

Dro. E. A man may break a word with you,
sir, and words are but wind:

Ay, and break it in your face, so he break it not
behind.   76

Dro. S. [*Within.*] It seems thou wantest
breaking: out upon thee, hind!

Dro. E. Here's too much 'out upon thee!' I
pray thee, let me in.

Dro. S. [*Within.*] Ay, when fowls have no
feathers, and fish have no fin.

Ant. E. Well. I'll break in. Go borrow me
a crow.   80

Dro. E. A crow without feather? Master,
mean you so?

For a fish without a fin, there's a fowl without
a feather:

If a crow help us in, sirrah, we'll pluck a crow
together.

Ant. E. Go get thee gone: fetch me an iron
crow.   84

Bal. Have patience, sir; O! let it not be so;
Herein you war against your reputation,
And draw within the compass of suspect
The unviolated honour of your wife.   88
Once this,—your long experience of her wisdom,
Her sober virtue, years, and modesty,
Plead on her part some cause to you unknown;
And doubt not, sir, but she will well excuse   92
Why at this time the doors are made against
you.

Be rul'd by me: depart in patience,
And let us to the Tiger all to dinner;
And about evening come yourself alone,   96
To know the reason of this strange restraint.
If by strong hand you offer to break in
Now in the stirring passage of the day,
A vulgar comment will be made of it,   100
And that supposed by the common rout
Against your yet ungalled estimation,
That may with foul intrusion enter in
And dwell upon your grave when you are dead;
For slander lives upon succession,   105
For ever housed where it gets possession.

Ant. E. You have prevail'd: I will depart in
quiet,

And, in despite of mirth, mean to be merry. 108

I know a wench of excellent discourse,
Pretty and witty, wild and yet, too, gentle:
There will we dine: this woman that I mean,
My wife,—but, I protest, without desert,—   112
Hath oftentimes upbraided me withal:
To her will we to dinner. [*To* ANGELO.] Get you
home,

And fetch the chain; by this I know 'tis made:
Bring it, I pray you, to the Porpentine;   116
For there's the house: that chain will I bestow,
Be it for nothing but to spite my wife,
Upon mine hostess there. Good sir, make haste.
Since mine own doors refuse to entertain me, 120
I'll knock elsewhere, to see if they'll disdain me.

Ang. I'll meet you at that place some hour
hence.

Ant. E. Do so. This jest shall cost me some
expense.   [*Exeunt.*

SCENE II.—*The Same.*

Enter LUCIANA *and* ANTIPHOLUS *of Syracuse.*

Luc. And may it be that you have quite forgot
A husband's office? Shall, Antipholus,
Even in the spring of love, thy love-springs rot?
Shall love, in building, grow so ruinous?   4
If you did wed my sister for her wealth,
Then, for her wealth's sake use her with more
kindness:
Or, if you like elsewhere, do it by stealth;
Muffle your false love with some show of
blindness;   8
Let not my sister read it in your eye;
Be not thy tongue thy own shame's orator;
Look sweet, speak fair, become disloyalty;
Apparel vice like virtue's harbinger;   12
Bear a fair presence, though your heart be
tainted;
Teach sin the carriage of a holy saint;
Be secret-false: what need she be acquainted?
What simple thief brags of his own attaint?
'Tis double wrong to truant with your bed, 17
And let her read it in thy looks at board:
Shame hath a bastard fame, well managed;
Ill deeds are doubled with an evil word.   20
Alas! poor women, make us but believe,
Being compact of credit, that you love us;
Though others have the arm, show us the sleeve;
We in your motion turn, and you may move
us.   24
Then, gentle brother, get you in again;
Comfort my sister, cheer her, call her wife:
'Tis holy sport to be a little vain,
When the sweet breath of flattery conquers
strife.   28

Ant. S. Sweet mistress,—what your name is
else, I know not,
Nor by what wonder you do hit of mine,—
Less in your knowledge and your grace you
show not
Than our earth's wonder; more than earth
divine.   32
Teach me, dear creature, how to think and
speak:
Lay open to my earthy-gross conceit,

Smother'd in errors, feeble, shallow, weak,
  The folded meaning of your words' deceit. 36
Against my soul's pure truth why labour you
  To make it wander in an unknown field?
Are you a god? would you create me new?
  Transform me then, and to your power I'll
    yield.   40
But if that I am I, then well I know
  Your weeping sister is no wife of mine,
Nor to her bed no homage do I owe:
  Far more, far more, to you do I decline. 44
O! train me not, sweet mermaid, with thy note,
  To drown me in thy sister flood of tears:
Sing, siren, for thyself, and I will dote:
  Spread o'er the silver waves thy golden hairs,
And as a bed I'll take them and there lie; 49
  And, in that glorious supposition think
He gains by death that hath such means to die:
  Let Love, being light, be drowned if she sink!
Luc. What! are you mad, that you do
    reason so?   53
Ant. S. Not mad, but mated; how, I do not
    know.
Luc. It is a fault that springeth from your
    eye.
Ant. S. For gazing on your beams, fair sun,
    being by.   56
Luc. Gaze where you should, and that will
    clear your sight.
Ant. S. As good to wink, sweet love, as look
    on night.
Luc. Why call you me love? call my sister so.
Ant. S. Thy sister's sister.
Luc.   That's my sister.
Ant. S.   No; 60
It is thyself, mine own self's better part;
Mine eye's clear eye, my dear heart's dearer
    heart;
My food, my fortune, and my sweet hope's aim,
My sole earth's heaven, and my heaven's claim,
Luc. All this my sister is, or else should be.
Ant. S. Call thyself sister, sweet, for I aim
    thee.
Thee will I love and with thee lead my life:
Thou hast no husband yet nor I no wife. 68
Give me thy hand.
Luc.   O! soft, sir; hold you still:
I'll fetch my sister, to get her good will. [*Exit.*

  Enter DROMIO *of Syracuse, hastily.*

Ant. S. Why, how now, Dromio! where run'st
thou so fast?   72
Dro. S. Do you know me, sir? am I Dromio?
am I your man? am I myself?
Ant. S. Thou art Dromio, thou art my man,
thou art thyself.   76
Dro. S. I am an ass, I am a woman's man
and besides myself.
Ant. S. What woman's man? and how besides thyself?   80
Dro. S. Marry, sir, besides myself, I am due
to a woman; one that claims me, one that
haunts me, one that will have me.
Ant. S. What claim lays she to thee? 84
Dro. S. Marry, sir, such claim as you would
lay to your horse; and she would have me as

a beast: not that, I being a beast, she would
have me; but that she, being a very beastly
creature, lays claim to me.   89
Ant. S. What is she?
Dro. S. A very reverent body; aye, such a
one as a man may not speak of, without he say,
'Sir-reverence.' I have but lean luck in the
match, and yet is she a wondrous fat marriage.
Ant. S. How dost thou mean a fat marriage?   96
Dro. S. Marry, sir, she's the kitchen-wench,
and all grease; and I know not what use to put
her to but to make a lamp of her and run from
her by her own light. I warrant her rags and
the tallow in them will burn a Poland winter;
if she lives till doomsday, she'll burn a week
longer than the whole world.
Ant. S. What complexion is she of? 104
Dro. S. Swart, like my shoe, but her face
nothing like so clean kept: for why she sweats;
a man may go over shoes in the grime of it.
Ant. S. That's a fault that water will mend.
Dro. S. No, sir, 'tis in grain; Noah's flood
could not do it.   110
Ant. S. What's her name?
Dro. S. Nell, sir; but her name and three
quarters,—that is, an ell and three quarters,—
will not measure her from hip to hip.
Ant. S. Then she bears some breadth? 115
Dro. S. No longer from head to foot than
from hip to hip: she is spherical, like a globe;
I could find out countries in her.
Ant. S. In what part of her body stands
Ireland?   120
Dro. S. Marry, sir, in her buttocks: I found
it out by the bogs.
Ant. S. Where Scotland?
Dro. S. I found it by the barrenness; hard
in the palm of the hand.   125
Ant. S. Where France?
Dro. S. In her forehead; armed and reverted,
making war against her heir.   128
Ant. S. Where England?
Dro. S. I looked for the chalky cliffs, but I
could find no whiteness in them: but I guess it
stood in her chin, by the salt rheum that ran
between France and it.   133
Ant. S. Where Spain?
Dro. S. Faith, I saw not; but I felt it hot in
her breath.   136
Ant. S. Where America, the Indies?
Dro. S. O, sir! upon her nose, all o'er embellished with rubies, carbuncles, sapphires, declining their rich aspect to the hot breath of
Spain, who sent whole armadoes of caracks to
be ballast at her nose.   142
Ant. S. Where stood Belgia, the Netherlands?
Dro. S. O, sir! I did not look so low. To
conclude, this drudge, or diviner, laid claim to
me; call'd me Dromio; swore I was assured to
her; told me what privy marks I had about me,
as the mark of my shoulder, the mole in my
neck, the great wart on my left arm, that I,
amazed, ran from her as a witch.   150
And, I think, if my breast had not been made of
    faith and my heart of steel,

She had transform'd me to a curtal dog and
   made me turn i' the wheel.   152
Ant. S. Go hie thee presently post to the road:
An if the wind blow any way from shore,
I will not harbour in this town to-night:
If any bark put forth, come to the mart,   156
Where I will walk till thou return to me.
If every one knows us and we know none,
'Tis time, I think, to trudge, pack, and be gone.
Dro. S. As from a bear a man would run for
   life,   160
So fly I from her that would be my wife. [*Exit.*
Ant. S. There's none but witches do inhabit
   here,
And therefore 'tis high time that I were hence.
She that doth call me husband, even my soul
Doth for a wife abhor; but her fair sister,   165
Possess'd with such a gentle sovereign grace,
Of such enchanting presence and discourse,
Hath almost made me traitor to myself: 168
But, lest myself be guilty to self-wrong,
I'll stop mine ears against the mermaid's song.

Enter ANGELO.

Ang. Master Antipholus!
Ant. S. Ay, that's my name.   172
Ang. I know it well, sir: lo, here is the chain.
I thought to have ta'en you at the Porpentine;
The chain unfinish'd made me stay thus long.
Ant. S. What is your will that I shall do with
   this?   176
Ang. What please yourself, sir: I have made
   it for you.
Ant. S. Made it for me, sir! I bespoke it
   not.
Ang. Not once, nor twice, but twenty times
   you have.
Go home with it and please your wife withal;
And soon at supper-time I'll visit you,   181
And then receive my money for the chain.
Ant. S. I pray you, sir, receive the money now,
For fear you ne'er see chain nor money more.
Ang. You are a merry man, sir: fare you well.
       [*Exit, leaving the chain.*
Ant. S. What I should think of this, I can-
   not tell:
But this I think, there's no man is so vain
That would refuse so fair an offer'd chain. 188
I see, a man here needs not live by shifts,
When in the streets he meets such golden gifts.
I'll to the mart, and there for Dromio stay:
If any ship put out, then straight away. [*Exit.*

ACT IV

SCENE I.—*A Public Place.*

Enter Second Merchant, ANGELO, *and* an Officer.

Mer. You know since Pentecost the sum is
   due,
And since I have not much importun'd you;
Nor now I had not, but that I am bound
To Persia, and want guilders for my voyage: 4
Therefore make present satisfaction,
Or I'll attach you by this officer.

Ang. Even just the sum that I do owe to you
Is growing to me by Antipholus;   8
And in the instant that I met with you
He had of me a chain: at five o'clock
I shall receive the money for the same.
Pleaseth you walk with me down to his house,
I will discharge my bond, and thank you too. 13

Enter ANTIPHOLUS of Ephesus *and* DROMIO
   of Ephesus *from the Courtezan's.*

Off. That labour may you save: see where
   he comes.
Ant. E. While I go to the goldsmith's house,
   go thou
And buy a rope's end, that I will bestow   16
Among my wife and her confederates,
For locking me out of my doors by day.
But soft! I see the goldsmith. Get thee gone;
Buy thou a rope, and bring it home to me. 20
Dro. E. I buy a thousand pound a year:
   I buy a rope!   [*Exit.*
Ant. E. A man is well holp up that trusts to you:
I promised your presence and the chain;   23
But neither chain nor goldsmith came to me.
Belike you thought our love would last too long,
If it were chain'd together, and therefore came
   not.
Ang. Saving your merry humour, here's the
   note
How much your chain weighs to the utmost
   carat.   28
The fineness of the gold, and chargeful fashion,
Which doth amount to three odd ducats more
Than I stand debted to this gentleman:
I pray you see him presently discharg'd,   32
For he is bound to sea and stays but for it.
Ant. E. I am not furnish'd with the present
   money;
Besides, I have some business in the town.
Good signior, take the stranger to my house, 36
And with you take the chain, and bid my wife
Disburse the sum on the receipt thereof:
Perchance I will be there as soon as you.
Ang. Then, you will bring the chain to her
   yourself?   40
Ant. E. No; bear it with you, lest I come not
   time enough.
Ang. Well, sir, I will. Have you the chain
   about you?
Ant. E. An if I have not, sir, I hope you have,
Or else you may return without your money. 44
Ang. Nay, come, I pray you, sir, give me the
   chain:
Both wind and tide stays for this gentleman,
And I, to blame, have held him here too long.
Ant. E. Good Lord! you use this dalliance
   to excuse   48
Your breach of promise to the Porpentine.
I should have chid you for not bringing it,
But, like a shrew, you first begin to brawl.
Mer. The hour steals on; I pray you, sir,
   dispatch.   52
Ang. You hear how he importunes me: the
   chain!
Ant. E. Why, give it to my wife and fetch
   your money.

Ang. Come, come; you know I gave it you
even now. 55
Either send the chain or send by me some token.
Ant. E. Fie! now you run this humour out
of breath.
Come, where's the chain? I pray you, let me
see it.
Mer. My business cannot brook this dalliance.
Good sir, say whe'r you'll answer me or no: 60
If not, I'll leave him to the officer.
Ant. E. I answer you! what should I answer
you?
Ang. The money that you owe me for the
chain.
Ant. E. I owe you none till I receive the chain.
Ang. You know I gave it you half an hour
since. 65
Ant. E. You gave me none: you wrong me
much to say so.
Ang. You wrong me more, sir, in denying it:
Consider how it stands upon my credit. 68
Mer. Well, officer, arrest him at my suit.
Off. I do;
And charge you in the duke's name to obey me.
Ang. This touches me in reputation. 72
Either consent to pay this sum for me,
Or I attach you by this officer.
Ant. E. Consent to pay thee that I never had!
Arrest me, foolish fellow, if thou dar'st. 76
Ang. Here is thy fee: arrest him, officer.
I would not spare my brother in this case,
If he should scorn me so apparently.
Off. I do arrest you, sir: you hear the suit. 80
Ant. E. I do obey thee till I give thee bail.
But, sirrah, you shall buy this sport as dear
As all the metal in your shop will answer.
Ang. Sir, sir, I shall have law in Ephesus, 84
To your notorious shame, I doubt it not.

Enter DROMIO *of Syracuse.*

Dro. S. Master, there is a bark of Epidamnum
That stays but till her owner comes aboard,
And then she bears away. Our fraughtage, sir,
I have convey'd aboard, and I have bought 89
The oil, the balsamum, and aqua-vitæ.
The ship is in her trim; the merry wind
Blows fair from land; they stay for nought at
all 92
But for their owner, master, and yourself.
Ant. E. How now! a madman! Why, thou
peevish sheep,
What ship of Epidamnum stays for me?
Dro. S. A ship you sent me to, to hire
waftage. 96
Ant. E. Thou drunken slave, I sent thee for
a rope;
And told thee to what purpose, and what end.
Dro. S. You sent me for a rope's end as soon:
You sent me to the bay, sir, for a bark. 100
Ant. E. I will debate this matter at more
leisure,
And teach your ears to list me with more heed.
To Adriana, villain, hie thee straight;
Give her this key, and tell her, in the desk 104
That's cover'd o'er with Turkish tapestry,
There is a purse of ducats: let her send it.

Tell her I am arrested in the street,
And that shall bail me. Hie thee, slave, be gone!
On, officer, to prison till it come. 109
[*Exeunt* Merchant, ANGELO, Officer, *and*
ANTIPHOLUS *of Ephesus.*
Dro. S. To Adriana! that is where we din'd,
Where Dowsabel did claim me for her husband:
She is too big, I hope, for me to compass. 112
Thither I must, although against my will,
For servants must their masters' minds fulfil.
[*Exit.*

SCENE II.—*A Room in the House of*
ANTIPHOLUS *of Ephesus.*

Enter ADRIANA *and* LUCIANA.

Adr. Ah! Luciana, did he tempt thee so?
Mightst thou perceive austerely in his eye
That he did plead in earnest? yea or no?
Look'd he or red or pale? or sad or merrily?
What observation mad'st thou in this case 5
Of his heart's meteors tilting in his face?
Luc. First he denied you had in him no right.
Adr. He meant he did me none; the more
my spite. 8
Luc. Then swore he that he was a stranger
here.
Adr. And true he swore, though yet forsworn
he were.
Luc. Then pleaded I for you.
Adr. And what said he?
Luc. That love I begg'd for you he begg'd
of me. 12
Adr. With what persuasion did he tempt thy
love?
Luc. With words that in an honest suit might
move.
First, he did praise my beauty, then my speech.
Adr. Didst speak him fair?
Luc. Have patience, I beseech.
Adr. I cannot, nor I will not hold me still:
My tongue, though not my heart, shall have
his will.
He is deformed, crooked, old and sere, 19
Ill-fac'd, worse bodied, shapeless every where;
Vicious, ungentle, foolish, blunt, unkind,
Stigmatical in making, worse in mind.
Luc. Who would be jealous then, of such
a one?
No evil lost is wail'd when it is gone. 24
Adr. Ah! but I think him better than I say,
And yet would herein others' eyes were worse.
Far from her nest the lapwing cries away:
My heart prays for him, though my tongue
do curse. 28

Enter DROMIO *of Syracuse.*

Dro. S. Here, go: the desk! the purse! sweet,
now, make haste.
Luc. How hast thou lost thy breath?
Dro. S. By running fast.
Adr. Where is thy master, Dromio? is he
well?
Dro. S. No, he's in Tartar limbo, worse than
hell. 32

A devil in an everlasting garment hath him,
One whose hard heart is button'd up with steel;
A fiend, a fairy, pitiless and rough:
A wolf, nay, worse, a fellow all in buff;   36
A back-friend, a shoulder-clapper, one that
    countermands
The passages of alleys, creeks and narrow lands;
A hound that runs counter and yet draws dry-
    foot well;
One that, before the judgment, carries poor
    souls to hell.   40
Adr. Why, man, what is the matter?
Dro. S. I do not know the matter: he is
'rested on the case.
Adr. What, is he arrested? tell me at whose
suit.
Dro. S. I know not at whose suit he is
arrested well;   44
But he's in a suit of buff which 'rested him, that
    can I tell.
Will you send him, mistress, redemption, the
    money in his desk?
Adr. Go fetch it, sister.—[*Exit* LUCIANA.]
This I wonder at:
That he, unknown to me, should be in debt: 48
Tell me, was he arrested on a band?
Dro. S. Not on a band, but on a stronger
    thing;
A chain, a chain. Do you not hear it ring?
Adr. What, the chain?   52
Dro. S. No, no, the bell: 'tis time that I were
gone:
It was two ere I left him, and now the clock
strikes one.
Adr. The hours come back! that did I never
hear.
Dro. S. O yes; if any hour meet a sergeant,
a' turns back for very fear.   56
Adr. As if Time were in debt! how fondly
dost thou reason!
Dro. S. Time is a very bankrupt, and owes
more than he's worth to season.
Nay, he's a thief too: have you not heard men
say,
That Time comes stealing on by night and
day?   60
If Time be in debt and theft, and a sergeant in
the way,
Hath he not reason to turn back an hour in a
day?

Re-enter LUCIANA.

Adr. Go, Dromio: there's the money, bear it
straight,
And bring thy master home immediately.   64
Come, sister; I am press'd down with conceit;
Conceit, my comfort and my injury. [*Exeunt.*

SCENE III.—*A Public Place.*

Enter ANTIPHOLUS *of Syracuse.*

Ant. S. There's not a man I meet but doth
salute me,
As if I were their well acquainted friend;
And every one doth call me by my name.

Some tender money to me: some invite me;   4
Some other give me thanks for kindnesses;
Some offer me commodities to buy:
Even now a tailor call'd me in his shop
And show'd me silks that he had bought for me,
And therewithal, took measure of my body.   9
Sure these are but imaginary wiles,
And Lapland sorcerers inhabit here.

Enter DROMIO *of Syracuse.*

Dro. S. Master, here's the gold you sent me
for.   12
What! have you got the picture of old Adam
new apparelled?
Ant. S. What gold is this? What Adam dost
thou mean?
Dro. S. Not that Adam that kept the Paradise, but that Adam that keeps the prison: he
that goes in the calf's skin that was killed for the
Prodigal: he that came behind you, sir, like an
evil angel, and bid you forsake your liberty.
Ant. S. I understand thee not.   20
Dro. S. No? why, 'tis a plain case: he that
went, like a base-viol, in a case of leather; the
man, sir, that, when gentlemen are tired, gives
them a fob, and 'rests them; he, sir, that takes
pity on decayed men and gives them suits of
durance; he that sets up his rest to do more
exploits with his mace than a morris-pike.
Ant. S. What, thou meanest an officer?   28
Dro. S. Ay, sir, the sergeant of the band; he
that brings any man to answer it that breaks
his band; one that thinks a man always going
to bed, and says, 'God give you good rest!'   32
Ant. S. Well, sir, there rest in your foolery.
Is there any ship puts forth to-night? may we
be gone?   35
Dro. S. Why, sir, I brought you word an hour
since that the bark Expedition put forth to-
night; and then were you hindered by the
sergeant to tarry for the hoy Delay. Here are
the angels that you sent for to deliver you.   40
Ant. S. The fellow is distract, and so am I;
And here we wander in illusions:
Some blessed power deliver us from hence!

Enter a Courtezan.

Cour. Well met, well met, Master Antipholus.
I see, sir, you have found the goldsmith now: 45
Is that the chain you promis'd me to-day?
Ant. S. Satan, avoid! I charge thee tempt
me not!
Dro. S. Master, is this Mistress Satan?   48
Ant. S. It is the devil.
Dro. S. Nay, she is worse, she is the devil's
dam, and here she comes in the habit of a light
wench: and thereof comes that the wenches say,
'God damn me;' that's as much as to say, 'God
make me a light wench.' It is written, they
appear to men like angels of light: light is an
effect of fire, and fire will burn; *ergo*, light
wenches will burn. Come not near her.   57
Cour. Your man and you are marvellous
merry, sir. Will you go with me? we'll mend
our dinner here.   60

Dro. S. Master, if you do, expect spoon-meat,
so bespeak a long spoon.
Ant. S. Why, Dromio?
Dro. S. Marry, he must have a long spoon
that must eat with the devil. 65
Ant. S. Avoid thee, fiend! what tell'st thou
me of supping?
Thou art, as you are all, a sorceress:
I conjure thee to leave me and be gone. 68
Cour. Give me the ring of mine you had at
dinner,
Or, for my diamond, the chain you promis'd,
And I'll be gone, sir, and not trouble you.
Dro. S. Some devils ask but the parings of
one's nail, 72
A rush, a hair, a drop of blood, a pin,
A nut, a cherry-stone;
But she, more covetous, would have a chain.
Master, be wise: an if you give it her, 76
The devil will shake her chain and fright us
with it.
Cour. I pray you, sir, my ring, or else the
chain:
I hope you do not mean to cheat me so.
Ant. S. Avaunt, thou witch! Come, Dromio,
let us go. 80
Dro. S. 'Fly pride,' says the peacock: mis-
tress, that you know.
[*Exeunt* ANTIPHOLUS *of Syracuse and*
DROMIO *of Syracuse.*
Cour. Now, out of doubt, Antipholus is mad,
Else would he never so demean himself.
A ring he hath of mine worth forty ducats, 84
And for the same he promis'd me a chain:
Both one and other he denies me now.
The reason that I gather he is mad,
Besides this present instance of his rage, 88
Is a mad tale he told to-day at dinner,
Of his own doors being shut against his en-
trance.
Belike his wife, acquainted with his fits,
On purpose shut the doors against his way. 92
My way is now to hie home to his house,
And tell his wife, that, being lunatic,
He rush'd into my house, and took perforce
My ring away. This course I fittest choose, 96
For forty ducats is too much to lose. [*Exit.*

SCENE IV.—*A Street.*
Enter ANTIPHOLUS *of Ephesus and the* Officer.

Ant. E. Fear me not, man; I will not break
away:
I'll give thee, ere I leave thee, so much money,
To warrant thee, as I am 'rested for.
My wife is in a wayward mood to-day, 4
And will not lightly trust the messenger.
That I should be attach'd in Ephesus,
I tell you, 'twill sound harshly in her ears.

Enter DROMIO *of Ephesus with a rope's end.*

Here comes my man: I think he brings the
money. 8
How now, sir! have you that I sent you for?
Dro. E. Here's that, I warrant you, will pay
them all.

Ant. E. But where's the money?
Dro. E. Why, sir, I gave the money for the
rope. 12
Ant. E. Five hundred ducats, villain, for a
rope?
Dro. E. I'll serve you, sir, five hundred at the
rate.
Ant. E. To what end did I bid thee hie thee
home?
Dro. E. To a rope's end, sir; and to that end
am I return'd. 16
Ant. E. And to that end, sir, I will welcome
you. [*Beats him.*
Off. Good sir, be patient.
Dro. E. Nay, 'tis for me to be patient; I am
in adversity.
Off. Good now, hold thy tongue. 20
Dro. E. Nay, rather persuade him to hold his
hands.
Ant. E. Thou whoreson, senseless villain!
Dro. E. I would I were senseless, sir, that I
might not feel your blows. 25
Ant. E. Thou art sensible in nothing but
blows, and so is an ass.
Dro. E. I am an ass indeed; you may prove
it by my long ears. I have served him from the
hour of my nativity to this instant, and have
nothing at his hands for my service but blows.
When I am cold, he heats me with beating;
when I am warm, he cools me with beating;
I am waked with it when I sleep; raised with it
when I sit; driven out of doors with it when I go
from home; welcomed home with it when I
return; nay, I bear it on my shoulders, as a
beggar wont her brat; and, I think, when he
hath lamed me, I shall beg with it from door to
door. 40
Ant. E. Come, go along; my wife is coming
yonder.

Enter ADRIANA, LUCIANA, *the* Courtezan, *and*
PINCH.

Dro. E. Mistress, *respice finem*, respect your
end; or rather, to prophesy like the parrot,
'Beware the rope's end.' 45
Ant. E. Wilt thou still talk? [*Beats him.*
Cour. How say you now? is not your hus-
band mad?
Adr. His incivility confirms no less. 48
Good Doctor Pinch, you are a conjurer;
Establish him in his true sense again,
And I will please you what you will demand.
Luc. Alas! how fiery and how sharp he looks.
Cour. Mark how he trembles in his ecstasy!
Pinch. Give me your hand and let me feel
your pulse.
Ant. E. There is my hand, and let it feel your
ear. [*Strikes him.*
Pinch. I charge thee, Satan, hous'd within
this man, 56
To yield possession to my holy prayers,
And to thy state of darkness hie thee straight:
I conjure thee by all the saints in heaven.
Ant. E. Peace, doting wizard, peace! I am
not mad. 60

Adr. O! that thou wert not, poor distressed soul!

Ant. E. You minion, you, are these your customers?

Did this companion with the saffron face
Revel and feast it at my house to-day,   64
Whilst upon me the guilty doors were shut
And I denied to enter in my house?

Adr. O husband, God doth know you din'd at home;
Where would you had remain'd until this time,
Free from these slanders and this open shame!

Ant. E. Din'd at home! Thou villain, what say'st thou?

Dro. E. Sir, sooth to say, you did not dine at home.

Ant. E. Were not my doors lock'd up and I shut out?   72

Dro. E. Perdy, your doors were lock'd and you shut out.

Ant. E. And did not she herself revile me there?

Dro. E. Sans fable, she herself revil'd you there.

Ant. E. Did not her kitchen-maid rail, taunt, and scorn me?   76

Dro. E. Certes, she did; the kitchen-vestal scorn'd you.

Ant. E. And did not I in rage depart from thence?

Dro. E. In verity you did: my bones bear witness,
That since have felt the vigour of his rage.   80

Adr. Is't good to soothe him in these contraries?

Pinch. It is no shame: the fellow finds his vein,
And, yielding to him humours well his frenzy.

Ant. E. Thou hast suborn'd the goldsmith to arrest me.   84

Adr. Alas! I sent you money to redeem you,
By Dromio here, who came in haste for it.

Dro. E. Money by me! heart and good will you might;
But surely, master, not a rag of money.   88

Ant. E. Went'st not thou to her for a purse of ducats?

Adr. He came to me, and I deliver'd it.

Luc. And I am witness with her that she did.

Dro. E. God and the rope-maker bear me witness   92
That I was sent for nothing but a rope!

Pinch. Mistress, both man and master is possess'd:
I know it by their pale and deadly looks.
They must be bound and laid in some dark room.   96

Ant. E. Say, wherefore didst thou lock me forth to-day?
And why dost thou deny the bag of gold?

Adr. I did not, gentle husband, lock thee forth.

Dro. E. And, gentle master, I receiv'd no gold;   100
But I confess, sir, that we were lock'd out.

Adr. Dissembling villain! thou speak'st false in both.

Ant. E. Dissembling harlot! thou art false in all;
And art confederate with a damned pack   104
To make a loathsome abject scorn of me;
But with these nails I'll pluck out those false eyes
That would behold in me this shameful sport.

Adr. O! bind him, bind him, let him not come near me.   108

Pinch. More company! the fiend is strong within him.

Luc. Ay me! poor man, how pale and wan he looks!

Enter three or four and bind ANTIPHOLUS *of Ephesus.*

Ant. E. What, will you murder me? Thou gaoler, thou,
I am thy prisoner: wilt thou suffer them   112
To make a rescue?

Off.   Masters, let him go:
He is my prisoner, and you shall not have him.

Pinch. Go bind this man, for he is frantic too.
          [*They bind* DROMIO *of Ephesus.*

Adr. What wilt thou do, thou peevish officer?
Hast thou delight to see a wretched man   117
Do outrage and displeasure to himself?

Off. He is my prisoner: if I let him go,
The debt he owes will be requir'd of me.   120

Adr. I will discharge thee ere I go from thee:
Bear me forthwith unto his creditor,
And, knowing how the debt grows, I will pay it.
Good Master doctor, see him safe convey'd   124
Home to my house. O most unhappy day!

Ant. E. O most unhappy strumpet!

Dro. E. Master, I am here enter'd in bond for you.

Ant. E. Out on thee, villain! wherefore dost thou mad me?   128

Dro. E. Will you be bound for nothing? be mad, good master; cry, 'the devil!'

Luc. God help, poor souls! how idly do they talk.

Adr. Go bear him hence. Sister, go you with me.—   132
          [*Exeunt* PINCH *and* Assistants *with* ANTIPHOLUS *of Ephesus and* DROMIO *of Ephesus.*
Say now, whose suit is he arrested at?

Off. One Angelo, a goldsmith; do you know him?

Adr. I know the man. What is the sum he owes?

Off. Two hundred ducats.

Adr.   Say, how grows it due?   136

Off. Due for a chain your husband had of him.

Adr. He did bespeak a chain for me, but had it not.

Cour. When as your husband all in rage, to-day
Came to my house, and took away my ring,—
The ring I saw upon his finger now,—   141
Straight after did I meet him with a chain.

Adr. It may be so, but I did never see it.
Come, gaoler, bring me where the goldsmith is:
I long to know the truth hereof at large.   145

Enter ANTIPHOLUS *of* Syracuse *and* DROMIO *of*
Syracuse, *with rapiers drawn.*

Luc. God, for thy mercy! they are loose
again.
Adr. And come with naked swords. Let's
call more help
To have them bound again.
Off.   Away! they'll kill us.
     [*Exeunt* ADRIANA, LUCIANA, *and* Officer.
Ant. S. I see, these witches are afraid of
swords.   149
Dro. S. She that would be your wife now ran
from you.
Ant. S. Come to the Centaur; fetch our stuff
from thence:
I long that we were safe and sound aboard. 152
Dro. S. Faith, stay here this night, they will
surely do us no harm; you saw they speak us
fair, give us gold: methinks they are such a
gentle nation, that, but for the mountain of mad
flesh that claims marriage of me, I could find in
my heart to stay here still, and turn witch.
Ant. S. I will not stay to-night for all the
town;
Therefore away, to get our stuff aboard. 160
                      [*Exeunt.*

ACT V

SCENE I.—*A Street before an Abbey.*

Enter Merchant *and* ANGELO.

Ang. I am sorry, sir, that I have hinder'd you;
But, I protest, he had the chain of me,
Though most dishonestly he doth deny it.
Mer. How is the man esteem'd here in the
city?   4
Ang. Of very reverend reputation, sir,
Of credit infinite, highly belov'd,
Second to none that lives here in the city:
His word might bear my wealth at any time. 8
Mer. Speak softly: yonder, as I think, he
walks.

Enter ANTIPHOLUS *of* Syracuse *and* DROMIO *of*
Syracuse.

Ang. 'Tis so; and that self chain about his
neck
Which he forswore most monstrously to have.
Good sir, draw near to me, I'll speak to him.
Signior Antipholus, I wonder much   13
That you would put me to this shame and
trouble;
And not without some scandal to yourself,
With circumstance and oaths so to deny   16
This chain which now you wear so openly:
Beside the charge, the shame, imprisonment,
You have done wrong to this my honest friend,
Who, but for staying on our controversy, 20
Had hoisted sail and put to sea to-day.
This chain you had of me; can you deny it?

Ant. S. I think I had: I never did deny it.
Mer. Yes, that you did, sir, and forswore it
too.   24
Ant. S. Who heard me to deny it or for-
swear it?
Mer. These ears of mine, thou know'st, did
hear thee.
Fie on thee, wretch! 'tis pity that thou liv'st
To walk where any honest men resort.   28
Ant. S. Thou art a villain to impeach me
thus:
I'll prove mine honour and mine honesty
Against thee presently, if thou dar'st stand.
Mer. I dare, and do defy thee for a villain. 32
                      [*They draw.*

Enter ADRIANA, LUCIANA, Courtezan, *and*
Others.

Adr. Hold! hurt him not, for God's sake! he
is mad.
Some get within him, take his sword away.
Bind Dromio too, and bear them to my house.
Dro. S. Run, master, run; for God's sake,
take a house!   36
This is some priory: in, or we are spoil'd.
     [*Exeunt* ANTIPHOLUS *of* Syracuse *and*
DROMIO *of* Syracuse *to the Abbey.*

Enter the Abbess.

Abb. Be quiet, people. Wherefore throng
you hither?
Adr. To fetch my poor distracted husband
hence.
Let us come in, that we may bind him fast, 40
And bear him home for his recovery.
Ang. I knew he was not in his perfect wits.
Mer. I am sorry now that I did draw on him.
Abb. How long hath this possession held the
man?   44
Adr. This week he hath been heavy, sour, sad,
And much different from the man he was;
But, till this afternoon his passion
Ne'er brake into extremity of rage.   48
Abb. Hath he not lost much wealth by wrack
of sea?
Buried some dear friend? Hath not else his eye
Stray'd his affection in unlawful love?
A sin prevailing much in youthful men,   52
Who give their eyes the liberty of gazing.
Which of these sorrows is he subject to?
Adr. To none of these, except it be the last;
Namely, some love that drew him oft from
home.   56
Abb. You should for that have reprehended
him.
Adr. Why, so I did.
Abb.   Ay, but not rough enough.
Adr. As roughly as my modesty would let me.
Abb. Haply, in private.
Adr.   And in assemblies too. 60
Abb. Ay, but not enough.
Adr. It was the copy of our conference:
In bed, he slept not for my urging it;
At board, he fed not for my urging it;   64
Alone, it was the subject of my theme;

In company I often glanced it:
Still did I tell him it was vile and bad.

Abb. And thereof came it that the man was
    mad: 68
The venom clamours of a jealous woman
Poison more deadly than a mad dog's tooth.
It seems, his sleeps were hinder'd by thy railing,
And thereof comes it that his head is light. 72
Thou say'st his meat was sauc'd with thy up-
    braidings:
Unquiet meals make ill digestions;
Thereof the raging fire of fever bred:
And what's a fever but a fit of madness? 76
Thou say'st his sports were hinder'd by thy
    brawls:
Sweet recreation barr'd, what doth ensue
But moody moping, and dull melancholy,
Kinsman to grim and comfortless despair, 80
And at her heels a huge infectious troop
Of pale distemperatures and foes to life?
In food, in sport, and life-preserving rest
To be disturb'd, would mad or man or beast: 84
The consequence is then, thy jealous fits
Have scar'd thy husband from the use of wits.

Luc. She never reprehended him but mildly
When he demean'd himself rough, rude, and
    wildly. 88
Why bear you these rebukes and answer not?

Adr. She did betray me to my own reproof.
Good people, enter, and lay hold on him.

Abb. No; not a creature enters in my house.

Adr. Then, let your servants bring my hus-
    band forth. 93

Abb. Neither: he took this place for sanc-
    tuary,
And it shall privilege him from your hands
Till I have brought him to his wits again, 96
Or lose my labour in assaying it.

Adr. I will attend my husband, be his nurse,
Diet his sickness, for it is my office,
And will have no attorney but myself; 100
And therefore let me have him home with me.

Abb. Be patient; for I will not let him stir
Till I have us'd the approved means I have,
With wholesome syrups, drugs, and holy
    prayers, 104
To make of him a formal man again.
It is a branch and parcel of mine oath,
A charitable duty of my order;
Therefore depart and leave him here with me.

Adr. I will not hence and leave my husband
    here; 109
And ill it doth beseem your holiness
To separate the husband and the wife.

Abb. Be quiet, and depart: thou shalt not
    have him. [*Exit.*

Luc. Complain unto the duke of this in-
    dignity. 113

Adr. Come, go: I will fall prostrate at his feet,
And never rise until my tears and prayers
Have won his Grace to come in person hither,
And take perforce my husband from the abbess.

Sec. Mer. By this, I think, the dial points at
    five:
Anon, I'm sure, the duke himself in person
Comes this way to the melancholy vale, 120

The place of death and sorry execution,
Behind the ditches of the abbey here.

Ang. Upon what cause?

Sec. Mer. To see a reverend Syracusian mer-
    chant, 124
Who put unluckily into this bay
Against the laws and statutes of this town,
Beheaded publicly for his offence.

Ang. See where they come: we will behold
    his death. 128

Luc. Kneel to the duke before he pass the
    abbey.

Enter DUKE *attended;* ÆGEON *bare-headed; with
the* Headsman *and other* Officers.

Duke. Yet once again proclaim it publicly,
If any friend will pay the sum for him,
He shall not die; so much we tender him. 132

Adr. Justice, most sacred duke, against the
    abbess!

Duke. She is a virtuous and a reverend lady:
It cannot be that she hath done thee wrong.

Adr. May it please your Grace, Antipholus,
    my husband, 136
Whom I made lord of me and all I had,
At your important letters, this ill day
A most outrageous fit of madness took him,
That desperately he hurried through the street,—
With him his bondman, all as mad as he,— 141
Doing displeasure to the citizens
By rushing in their houses, bearing thence
Rings, jewels, anything his rage did like. 144
Once did I get him bound and sent him home,
Whilst to take order for the wrongs I went
That here and there his fury had committed.
Anon, I wot not by what strong escape, 148
He broke from those that had the guard of him,
And with his mad attendant and himself,
Each one with ireful passion, with drawn swords
Met us again, and, madly bent on us 152
Chas'd us away, till, raising of more aid
We came again to bind them. Then they fled
Into this abbey, whither we pursu'd them;
And here the abbess shuts the gates on us, 156
And will not suffer us to fetch him out,
Nor send him forth that we may bear him hence.
Therefore, most gracious duke, with thy com-
    mand
Let him be brought forth, and borne hence for
    help. 160

Duke. Long since thy husband serv'd me in
    my wars,
And I to thee engag'd a prince's word,
When thou didst make him master of thy bed,
To do him all the grace and good I could. 164
Go, some of you, knock at the abbey gate
And bid the lady abbess come to me.
I will determine this before I stir.

Enter a Servant.

Serv. O mistress, mistress! shift and save
    yourself! 168
My master and his man are both broke loose,
Beaten the maids a-row and bound the doctor,
Whose beard they have sing'd off with brands
    of fire;

And ever as it blaz'd they threw on him   172
Great pails of puddled mire to quench the hair.
My master preaches patience to him, and the
  while
His man with scissors nicks him like a fool;
And sure, unless you send some present help,
Between them they will kill the conjurer.   177
  Adr. Peace, fool! thy master and his man
    are here,
And that is false thou dost report to us.
  Serv. Mistress, upon my life, I tell you true;
I have not breath'd almost, since I did see it.   181
He cries for you and vows, if he can take you,
To scotch your face, and to disfigure you.
                                    [*Cry within.*
Hark, hark! I hear him, mistress: fly, be gone!
  Duke. Come, stand by me; fear nothing.
    Guard with halberds!   185
  Adr. Ay me, it is my husband! Witness you,
That he is borne about invisible:
Even now we hous'd him in the abbey here,   188
And now he's here, past thought of human
    reason.

Enter ANTIPHOLUS *of Ephesus and* DROMIO
        of Ephesus.

  Ant. E. Justice, most gracious duke! O!
    grant me justice,
Ever. for the service that long since I did thee,
When I bestrid thee in the wars and took   192
Deep scars to save thy life; even for the blood
That then I lost for thee, now grant me justice.
  Æge. Unless the fear of death doth make me
    dote,
I see my son Antipholus and Dromio!   196
  Ant. E. Justice, sweet prince, against that
    woman there!
She whom thou gav'st to me to be my wife,
That hath abused and dishonour'd me,
Even in the strength and height of injury!   200
Beyond imagination is the wrong
That she this day hath shameless thrown on me.
  Duke. Discover how, and thou shalt find me
    just.
  Ant. E. This day, great duke, she shut the
    doors upon me,   204
While she with harlots feasted in my house.
  Duke. A grievous fault! Say, woman, didst
    thou so?
  Adr. No, my good lord: myself, he, and my
    sister
To-day did dine together. So befall my soul 208
As this is false he burdens me withal!
  Luc. Ne'er may I look on day, nor sleep on
    night,
But she tells to your highness simple truth!
  Ang. O perjur'd woman! They are both for-
    sworn: 212
In this the madman justly chargeth them!
  Ant. E. My liege, I am advised what I say:
Neither disturb'd with the effect of wine,
Nor heady-rash, provok'd with raging ire,   216
Albeit my wrongs might make one wiser mad.
This woman lock'd me out this day from dinner:
That goldsmith there, were he not pack'd with
    her,

Could witness it, for he was with me then;   220
Who parted with me to go fetch a chain,
Promising to bring it to the Porpentine,
Where Balthazar and I did dine together.
Our dinner done, and he not coming thither, 224
I went to seek him: in the street I met him,
And in his company that gentleman.
There did this perjur'd goldsmith swear me
    down
That I this day of him receiv'd the chain,   228
Which, God he knows, I saw not; for the which
He did arrest me with an officer.
I did obey, and sent my peasant home
For certain ducats: he with none return'd.   232
Then fairly I bespoke the officer
To go in person with me to my house.
By the way we met
My wife, her sister, and a rabble more   236
Of vile confederates: along with them
They brought one Pinch, a hungry lean-fac'd
    villain,
A mere anatomy, a mountebank,
A threadbare juggler, and a fortune-teller, 240
A needy, hollow-ey'd, sharp-looking wretch,
A living-dead man. This pernicious slave,
Forsooth, took on him as a conjurer,
And, gazing in mine eyes, feeling my pulse, 244
And with no face, as 'twere, out-facing me,
Cries out, I was possess'd. Then, altogether
They fell upon me, bound me, bore me thence,
And in a dark and dankish vault at home   248
There left me and my man, both bound to-
    gether;
Till, gnawing with my teeth my bonds in sunder,
I gain'd my freedom, and immediately
Ran hither to your Grace; whom I beseech   252
To give me ample satisfaction
For these deep shames and great indignities.
  Ang. My lord, in truth, thus far I witness
    with him,   255
That he din'd not at home, but was lock'd out.
  Duke. But had he such a chain of thee, or no?
  Ang. He had, my lord; and when he ran in
    here,
These people saw the chain about his neck.
  Sec. Mer. Besides, I will be sworn these ears
    of mine   260
Heard you confess you had the chain of him
After you first forswore it on the mart;
And thereupon I drew my sword on you;
And then you fled into this abbey here,   264
From whence, I think, you are come by miracle.
  Ant. E. I never came within these abbey walls;
Nor ever didst thou draw thy sword on me;
I never saw the chain, so help me heaven!   268
And this is false you burden me withal.
  Duke. Why, what an intricate impeach is
    this!
I think you all have drunk of Circe's cup.
If here you hous'd him, here he would have
    been;   272
If he were mad, he would not plead so coldly;
You say he din'd at home; the goldsmith here
Denies that saying. Sirrah, what say you?
  Dro. E. Sir, he din'd with her there, at the
    Porpentine.   276

Cour. He did, and from my finger snatch'd
    that ring.
Ant. E. 'Tis true, my liege; this ring I had
    of her.
Duke. Saw'st thou him enter at the abbey
    here?
Cour. As sure, my liege, as I do see your
    Grace.   280
Duke. Why, this is strange. Go call the
    abbess hither.   [*Exit an* Attendant.
I think you are all mated or stark mad.
Æge. Most mighty duke, vouchsafe me speak
    a word:
Haply I see a friend will save my life,   284
And pay the sum that may deliver me.
Duke. Speak freely, Syracusian, what thou
    wilt.
Æge. Is not your name, sir, called Antipholus?
And is not that your bondman Dromio?   288
Dro. E. Within this hour I was his bond-
    man, sir;
But he, I thank him, gnaw'd in two my cords:
Now am I Dromio and his man, unbound.
Æge. I am sure you both of you remember
    me.   292
Dro. E. Ourselves we do remember, sir, by
    you;
For lately we were bound, as you are now.
You are not Pinch's patient, are you, sir?
Æge. Why look you strange on me? you
    know me well.   296
Ant. E. I never saw you in my life till now.
Æge. O! grief hath chang'd me since you saw
    me last,
And careful hours, with Time's deformed hand,
Have written strange defeatures in my face: 300
But tell me yet, dost thou not know my voice?
Ant. E. Neither.
Æge. Dromio, nor thou?
Dro. E. No, trust me, sir, not I.   304
Æge. I am sure thou dost.
Dro. E. Ay, sir; but I am sure I do not; and
whatsoever a man denies, you are now bound
to believe him.   308
Æge. Not know my voice! O, time's extremity,
Hast thou so crack'd and splitted my poor
    tongue
In seven short years, that here my only son
Knows not my feeble key of untun'd cares? 312
Though now this grained face of mine be hid
In sap-consuming winter's drizzled snow,
And all the conduits of my blood froze up,
Yet hath my night of life some memory,   316
My wasting lamps some fading glimmer left,
My dull deaf ears a little use to hear:
All these old witnesses, I cannot err,
Tell me thou art my son Antipholus.   320
Ant. E. I never saw my father in my life.
Æge. But seven years since, in Syracusa, boy,
Thou know'st we parted: but perhaps, my son,
Thou sham'st to acknowledge me in misery.
Ant. E. The duke and all that know me in
    the city   325
Can witness with me that it is not so:
I ne'er saw Syracusa in my life.
Duke. I tell thee, Syracusian, twenty years

Have I been patron to Antipholus,   329
During which time he ne'er saw Syracusa.
I see thy age and dangers make thee dote.

Re-enter Abbess, *with* ANTIPHOLUS *of Syracuse
    and* DROMIO *of Syracuse.*

Abb. Most mighty duke, behold a man much
    wrong'd.   [*All gather to see him.*
Adr. I see two husbands, or mine eyes de-
    ceive me!   333
Duke. One of these men is Genius to the
    other;
And so of these: which is the natural man,
And which the spirit? Who deciphers them?
Dro. S. I, sir, am Dromio: command him
    away.   337
Dro. E. I, sir, am Dromio: pray let me stay.
Ant. S. Ægeon art thou not? or else his
    ghost?
Dro. S. O! my old master; who hath bound
    him here?   340
Abb. Whoever bound him, I will loose his
    bonds,
And gain a husband by his liberty.
Speak, old Ægeon, if thou be'st the man
That hadst a wife once call'd Æmilia,   344
That bore thee at a burden two fair sons.
O! if thou be'st the same Ægeon, speak,
And speak unto the same Æmilia!
Æge. If I dream not, thou art Æmilia: 348
If thou art she, tell me where is that son
That floated with thee on the fatal raft?
Abb. By men of Epidamnum, he and I,
And the twin Dromio, all were taken up: 352
But by and by rude fishermen of Corinth
By force took Dromio and my son from them,
And me they left with those of Epidamnum.
What then became of them, I cannot tell;   356
I to this fortune that you see me in.
Duke. Why, here begins his morning story
    right:
These two Antipholus', these two so like,
And these two Dromios, one in semblance,   360
Besides her urging of her wrack at sea;
These are the parents to these children,
Which accidentally are met together.
Antipholus, thou cam'st from Corinth first? 364
Ant. S. No, sir, not I; I came from Syracuse.
Duke. Stay, stand apart; I know not which
    is which.
Ant. E. I came from Corinth, my most
    gracious lord,—
Dro. E. And I with him.   368
Ant. E. Brought to this town by that most
    famous warrior,
Duke Menaphon, your most renowned uncle.
Adr. Which of you two did dine with me
    to-day?
Ant. S. I, gentle mistress.   372
Adr. And are not you my husband?
Ant. E. No; I say nay to that.
Ant. S. And so do I; yet did she call me so
And this fair gentlewoman, her sister here, 376
Did call me brother. [*To* LUCIANA.] What I
    told you then,

I hope I shall have leisure to make good,
If this be not a dream I see and hear.
 Ang. That is the chain, sir, which you had
  of me. 380
 Ant. S. I think it be, sir; I deny it not.
 Ant. E. And you, sir, for this chain arrested
 me.
 Ang. I think I did, sir; I deny it not.
 Adr. I sent you money, sir, to be your bail,
By Dromio; but I think he brought it not. 385
 Dro. E. No, none by me.
 Ant. S. This purse of ducats I receiv'd from
 you,
And Dromio, my man, did bring them me. 388
I see we still did meet each other's man,
And I was ta'en for him, and he for me,
And thereupon these errors are arose.
 Ant. E. These ducats pawn I for my father
 here. 392
 Duke. It shall not need: thy father hath his
 life.
 Cour. Sir, I must have that diamond from
 you.
 Ant. E. There, take it; and much thanks for
 my good cheer.
 Abb. Renowned duke, vouchsafe to take the
 pains 396
To go with us into the abbey here,
And hear at large discoursed all our fortunes;
And all that are assembled in this place,
That by this sympathized one day's error 400
Have suffer'd wrong, go keep us company,
And we shall make full satisfaction.
Thirty-three years have I but gone in travail
Of you, my sons; and, till this present hour 404
My heavy burdens ne'er delivered.
The duke, my husband, and my children both,
And you the calendars of their nativity,
Go to a gossip's feast, and joy with me: 408
After so long grief such festivity!
 Duke. With all my heart I'll gossip at this
 feast.
  [*Exeunt* DUKE, Abbess, ÆGEON, Courtezan,
   Merchant, ANGELO, *and* Attendants.
 Dro. S. Master, shall I fetch your stuff from
 shipboard?
 Ant. E. Dromio, what stuff of mine hast thou
 embark'd? 412
 Dro. S. Your goods that lay at host, sir, in
 the Centaur.
 Ant. S. He speaks to me. I am your master,
 Dromio:
Come, go with us; we'll look to that anon:
Embrace thy brother there; rejoice with him.
  [*Exeunt* ANTIPHOLUS *of Syracuse and*
   ANTIPHOLUS *of Ephesus,* ADRIANA
   and LUCIANA.
 Dro. S. There is a fat friend at your master's
 house, 417
That kitchen'd me 'or you to-day at dinner:
She now shall be my sister, not my wife.
 Dro. E. Methinks you are my glass, and not
 my brother: 420
I see by you I am a sweet-fac'd youth.
Will you walk in to see their gossiping?
 Dro. S. Not I, sir; you are my elder.
 Dro. E. That's a question: how shall we try
 it? 424
 Dro. S. We'll draw cuts for the senior: till
 then lead thou first.
 Dro. E. Nay, then, thus:
We came into the world like brother and brother;
And now let's go hand in hand, not one before
 another.   [*Exeunt.*

MUCH ADO ABOUT NOTHING

DRAMATIS PERSONÆ

DON PEDRO, Prince of Arragon.
DON JOHN, his bastard Brother.
CLAUDIO, a young Lord of Florence.
BENEDICK, a young Lord of Padua.
LEONATO, Governor of Messina.
ANTONIO, his Brother.
BALTHAZAR, Servant to Don Pedro.
BORACHIO, } followers of Don John.
CONRADE, }
DOGBERRY, a Constable.

VERGES, a Headborough.
FRIAR FRANCIS.
A Sexton.
A Boy.

HERO, Daughter to Leonato.
BEATRICE, Niece to Leonato.
MARGARET, } Waiting-gentlewomen attending on Hero.
URSULA, }
Messengers, Watch, Attendants, &c.

SCENE.—*Messina.*

ACT I

SCENE I.—*Before* LEONATO'S *House.*

Enter LEONATO, HERO, BEATRICE *and others,*
with a Messenger.

Leon. I learn in this letter that Don Pedro of
Arragon comes this night to Messina.

Mess. He is very near by this: he was not
three leagues off when I left him.   4

Leon. How many gentlemen have you lost in
this action?

Mess. But few of any sort, and none of name.

Leon. A victory is twice itself when the
achiever brings home full numbers. I find here
that Don Pedro hath bestowed much honour on
a young Florentine called Claudio.   11

Mess. Much deserved on his part and equally
remembered by Don Pedro. He hath borne
himself beyond the promise of his age, doing
in the figure of a lamb the feats of a lion: he
hath indeed better bettered expectation than
you must expect of me to tell you how.   17

Leon. He hath an uncle here in Messina will
be very much glad of it.

Mess. I have already delivered him letters,
and there appears much joy in him; even so
much that joy could not show itself modest
enough without a badge of bitterness.

Leon. Did he break out into tears?   24

Mess. In great measure.

Leon. A kind overflow of kindness. There are
no faces truer than those that are so washed:
how much better is it to weep at joy than to joy
at weeping!   29

Beat. I pray you is Signior Mountanto returned from the wars or no?

Mess. I know none of that name, lady: there
was none such in the army of any sort.   33

Leon. What is he that you ask for, niece?

Hero. My cousin means Signior Benedick of
Padua.   36

Mess. O! he is returned, and as pleasant as
ever he was.

Beat. He set up his bills here in Messina and
challenged Cupid at the flight; and my uncle's

fool, reading the challenge, subscribed for Cupid,
and challenged him at the bird-bolt. I pray
you, how many hath he killed and eaten in these
wars? But how many hath he killed? for, indeed,
I promised to eat all of his killing.   45

Leon. Faith, niece, you tax Signior Benedick
too much; but he'll be meet with you, I doubt
it not.   48

Mess. He hath done good service, lady, in
these wars.

Beat. You had musty victual, and he hath
holp to eat it: he is a very valiant trencher-
man; he hath an excellent stomach.   53

Mess. And a good soldier too, lady.

Beat. And a good soldier to a lady; but
what is he to a lord?   56

Mess. A lord to a lord, a man to a man;
stuffed with all honourable virtues.

Beat. It is so, indeed; he is no less than a
stuffed man; but for the stuffing,—well, we are
all mortal.   61

Leon. You must not, sir, mistake my niece.
There is a kind of merry war betwixt Signior
Benedick and her: they never meet but there's
a skirmish of wit between them.   65

Beat. Alas! he gets nothing by that. In our
last conflict four of his five wits went halting off,
and now is the whole man governed with one!
so that if he have wit enough to keep himself
warm, let him bear it for a difference between
himself and his horse; for it is all the wealth
that he hath left to be known a reasonable
creature. Who is his companion now? He hath
every month a new sworn brother.   74

Mess. Is't possible?

Beat. Very easily possible: he wears his faith
but as the fashion of his hat; it ever changes
with the next block.

Mess. I see, lady, the gentleman is not in
your books.   80

Beat. No; an he were, I would burn my
study. But, I pray you, who is his companion?
Is there no young squarer now that will make a
voyage with him to the devil?   84

Mess. He is most in the company of the right
noble Claudio.

Beat. O Lord! he will hang upon him like a disease: he is sooner caught than the pestilence, and the taker runs presently mad. God help the noble Claudio! if he have caught the Benedick, it will cost him a thousand pound ere a' be cured.   92

Mess. I will hold friends with you, lady.

Beat. Do, good friend.

Leon. You will never run mad, niece.

Beat. No, not till a hot January.   96

Mess. Don Pedro is approached.

Enter DON PEDRO, DON JOHN, CLAUDIO, BENEDICK, BALTHAZAR, *and Others.*

D. Pedro. Good Signior Leonato, you are come to meet your trouble: the fashion of the world is to avoid cost, and you encounter it.   100

Leon. Never came trouble to my house in the likeness of your Grace, for trouble being gone, comfort should remain; but when you depart from me, sorrow abides and happiness takes his leave.   105

D. Pedro. You embrace your charge too willingly. I think this is your daughter.

Leon. Her mother hath many times told me so.   109

Bene. Were you in doubt, sir, that you asked her?

Leon. Signior Benedick, no; for then you were a child.   113

D. Pedro. You have it full, Benedick: we may guess by this what you are, being a man. Truly, the lady fathers herself. Be happy, lady, for you are like an honourable father.   117

Bene. If Signior Leonato be her father, she would not have his head on her shoulders for all Messina, as like him as she is.   120

Beat. I wonder that you will still be talking, Signior Benedick: nobody marks you.

Bene. What! my dear Lady Disdain, are you yet living?   124

Beat. Is it possible Disdain should die while she hath such meet food to feed it as Signior Benedick? Courtesy itself must convert to disdain, if you come in her presence.   128

Bene. Then is courtesy a turncoat. But it is certain I am loved of all ladies, only you excepted; and I would I could find in my heart that I had not a hard heart; for, truly, I love none.   133

Beat. A dear happiness to women: they would else have been troubled with a pernicious suitor. I thank God and my cold blood, I am of your humour for that: I had rather hear my dog bark at a crow than a man swear he loves me.   139

Bene. God keep your ladyship still in that mind; so some gentleman or other shall 'scape a predestinate scratched face.

Beat. Scratching could not make it worse, an 'twere such a face as yours were.   144

Bene. Well, you are a rare parrot-teacher.

Beat. A bird of my tongue is better than a beast of yours.

Bene. I would my horse had the speed of your tongue, and so good a continuer. But keep your way, i' God's name; I have done.

Beat. You always end with a jade's trick: I know you of old.   152

D. Pedro. This is the sum of all, Leonato: Signior Claudio, and Signior Benedick, my dear friend Leonato hath invited you all. I tell him we shall stay here at the least a month, and he heartily prays some occasion may detain us longer: I dare swear he is no hypocrite, but prays from his heart.   159

Leon. If you swear, my lord, you shall not be forsworn. [*To* DON JOHN.] Let me bid you welcome, my lord: being reconciled to the prince your brother, I owe you all duty.

D. John. I thank you: I am not of many words, but I thank you.   165

Leon. Please it your Grace lead on?

D. Pedro. Your hand, Leonato; we will go together.   168

[*Exeunt all but* BENEDICK *and* CLAUDIO.

Claud. Benedick, didst thou note the daughter of Signior Leonato?

Bene. I noted her not; but I looked on her.

Claud. Is she not a modest young lady?   172

Bene. Do you question me, as an honest man should do, for my simple true judgment; or would you have me speak after my custom, as being a professed tyrant to their sex?   176

Claud. No; I pray thee speak in sober judgment.

Bene. Why, i' faith, methinks she's too low for a high praise, too brown for a fair praise, and too little for a great praise: only this commendation I can afford her, that were she other than she is, she were unhandsome, and being no other but as she is, I do not like her.   184

Claud. Thou thinkest I am in sport: I pray thee tell me truly how thou likest her.

Bene. Would you buy her, that you inquire after her?   188

Claud. Can the world buy such a jewel?

Bene. Yea, and a case to put it into. But speak you this with a sad brow, or do you play the flouting Jack, to tell us Cupid is a good hare-finder, and Vulcan a rare carpenter? Come, in what key shall a man take you, to go in the song?

Claud. In mine eye she is the sweetest lady that ever I looked on.   197

Bene. I can see yet without spectacles and I see no such matter: there's her cousin, an she were not possessed with a fury, exceeds her as much in beauty as the first of May doth the last of December. But I hope you have no intent to turn husband, have you?

Claud. I would scarce trust myself, though I had sworn to the contrary, if Hero would be my wife.   206

Bene. Is't come to this, i' faith? Hath not the world one man but he will wear his cap with suspicion? Shall I never see a bachelor of three-score again? Go to, i' faith; an thou wilt needs thrust thy neck into a yoke, wear the print of it, and sigh away Sundays. Look! Don Pedro is returned to seek you.   213

Re-enter DON PEDRO.

D. Pedro. What secret hath held you here, that you followed not to Leonato's?

Bene. I would your Grace would constrain me to tell.   217

D. Pedro. I charge thee on thy allegiance.

Bene. You hear, Count Claudio: I can be secret as a dumb man; I would have you think so; but on my allegiance, mark you this, on my allegiance: he is in love. With who? now that is your Grace's part. Mark how short his answer is: with Hero, Leonato's short daughter.   224

Claud. If this were so, so were it uttered.

Bene. Like the old tale, my lord: 'it is not so, nor 'twas not so; but, indeed, God forbid it should be so.'   228

Claud. If my passion change not shortly, God forbid it should be otherwise.

D. Pedro. Amen, if you love her; for the lady is very well worthy.   232

Claud. You speak this to fetch me in, my lord.

D. Pedro. By my troth, I speak my thought.

Claud. And in faith, my lord, I spoke mine.

Bene. And by my two faiths and troths, my lord, I spoke mine.   237

Claud. That I love her, I feel.

D. Pedro. That she is worthy, I know.

Bene. That I neither feel how she should be loved nor know how she should be worthy, is the opinion that fire cannot melt out of me: I will die in it at the stake.

D. Pedro. Thou wast ever an obstinate heretic in the despite of beauty.   245

Claud. And never could maintain his part but in the force of his will.

Bene. That a woman conceived me, I thank her; that she brought me up, I likewise give her most humble thanks; but that I will have a recheat winded in my forehead, or hang my bugle in an invisible baldrick, all women shall pardon me. Because I will not do them the wrong to mistrust any, I will do myself the right to trust none; and the fine is,—for the which I may go the finer,—I will live a bachelor.   256

D. Pedro. I shall see thee, ere I die, look pale with love.

Bene. With anger, with sickness, or with hunger, my lord; not with love: prove that ever I lose more blood with love than I will get again with drinking, pick out mine eyes with a ballad-maker's pen, and hang me up at the door of a brothel-house for the sign of blind Cupid.   264

D. Pedro. Well, if ever thou dost fall from this faith, thou wilt prove a notable argument.

Bene. If I do, hang me in a bottle like a cat and shoot at me; and he that hits me, let him be clapped on the shoulder, and called Adam.

D. Pedro. Well, as time shall try: 270 'In time the savage bull doth bear the yoke.'

Bene. The savage bull may; but if ever the sensible Benedick bear it, pluck off the bull's horns and set them in my forehead; and let me be vilely painted, and in such great letters as they write, 'Here is good horse to hire,' let them signify under my sign 'Here you may see Benedick the married man.'

Claud. If this should ever happen, thou wouldst be horn-mad.   280

D. Pedro. Nay, if Cupid have not spent all his quiver in Venice, thou wilt quake for this shortly.

Bene. I look for an earthquake too then.

D. Pedro. Well, you will temporize with the hours. In the meantime, good Signior Benedick, repair to Leonato's: commend me to him and tell him I will not fail him at supper; for indeed he hath made great preparation.   288

Bene. I have almost matter enough in me for such an embassage; and so I commit you—

Claud. To the tuition of God: from my house, if I had it,—   292

D. Pedro. The sixth of July: your loving friend, Benedick.

Bene. Nay, mock not, mock not. The body of your discourse is sometime guarded with fragments, and the guards are but slightly basted on neither: ere you flout old ends any further, examine your conscience: and so I leave you.
                                        [*Exit.*

Claud. My liege, your highness now may do me good.   300

D. Pedro. My love is thine to teach: teach it but how,
And thou shalt see how apt it is to learn
Any hard lesson that may do thee good.

Claud. Hath Leonato any son, my lord?   304

D. Pedro. No child but Hero; she's his only heir.
Dost thou affect her, Claudio?

Claud.   O! my lord,
When you went onward on this ended action,
I looked upon her with a soldier's eye,   308
That lik'd, but had a rougher task in hand
Than to drive liking to the name of love;
But now I am return'd, and that war-thoughts
Have left their places vacant, in their rooms 312
Come thronging soft and delicate desires,
All prompting me how fair young Hero is,
Saying, I lik'd her ere I went to wars.

D. Pedro. Thou wilt be like a lover presently,
And tire the hearer with a book of words.   317
If thou dost love fair Hero, cherish it,
And I will break with her, and with her father,
And thou shalt have her. Was't not to this end
That thou began'st to twist so fine a story?   321

Claud. How sweetly do you minister to love,
That know love's grief by his complexion!
But lest my liking might too sudden seem,   324
I would have salv'd it with a longer treatise.

D. Pedro. What need the bridge much broader than the flood?
The fairest grant is the necessity.
Look, what will serve is fit: 'tis once, thou lov'st,
And I will fit thee with the remedy.   329
I know we shall have revelling to-night:
I will assume thy part in some disguise,
And tell fair Hero I am Claudio;   332
And in her bosom I'll unclasp my heart,
And take her hearing prisoner with the force
And strong encounter of my amorous tale:
Then, after to her father will I break;   336
And the conclusion is, she shall be thine.
In practice let us put it presently. [*Exeunt.*

E

SCENE II.—*A Room in* LEONATO'S *House.*

Enter LEONATO *and* ANTONIO, *meeting.*

Leon. How now, brother! Where is my cousin, your son? Hath he provided this music? 3

Ant. He is very busy about it. But, brother, I can tell you strange news that you yet dreamt not of.

Leon. Are they good? 7

Ant. As the event stamps them: but they have a good cover; they show well outward. The prince and Count Claudio, walking in a thick-pleached alley in my orchard, were thus much overheard by a man of mine: the prince discovered to Claudio that he loved my niece your daughter, and meant to acknowledge it this night in a dance; and, if he found her accordant, he meant to take the present time by the top and instantly break with you of it. 17

Leon. Hath the fellow any wit that told you this?

Ant. A good sharp fellow: I will send for him; and question him yourself. 21

Leon. No, no; we will hold it as a dream till it appear itself: but I will acquaint my daughter withal, that she may be the better prepared for an answer, if peradventure this be true. Go you, and tell her of it. [*Several persons cross the stage.*] Cousins, you know what you have to do. O! I cry you mercy, friend; go you with me, and I will use your skill. Good cousin, have a care this busy time. [*Exeunt.*

SCENE III.—*Another Room in* LEONATO'S *House.*

Enter DON JOHN *and* CONRADE.

Con. What the good-year, my lord! why are you thus out of measure sad?

D. John. There is no measure in the occasion that breeds; therefore the sadness is without limit. 5

Con. You should hear reason.

D. John. And when I have heard it, what blessing brings it? 8

Con. If not a present remedy, at least a patient sufferance.

D. John. I wonder that thou, being,—as thou say'st thou art,—born under Saturn, goest about to apply a moral medicine to a mortifying mischief. I cannot hide what I am: I must be sad when I have cause, and smile at no man's jests; eat when I have stomach, and wait for no man's leisure; sleep when I am drowsy, and tend on no man's business; laugh when I am merry, and claw no man in his humour. 19

Con. Yea; but you must not make the full show of this till you may do it without controlment. You have of late stood out against your brother, and he hath ta'en you newly into his grace; where it is impossible you should take true root but by the fair weather that you make yourself: it is needful that you frame the season for your own harvest. 27

D. John. I had rather be a canker in a hedge

than a rose in his grace; and it better fits my blood to be disdained of all than to fashion a carriage to rob love from any: in this, though I cannot be said to be a flattering honest man, it must not be denied but I am a plain-dealing villain. I am trusted with a muzzle and enfranchised with a clog; therefore I have decreed not to sing in my cage. If I had my mouth, I would bite; if I had my liberty, I would do my liking: in the meantime, let me be that I am, and seek not to alter me. 39

Con. Can you make no use of your discontent?

D. John. I make all use of it, for I use it only. Who comes here?

Enter BORACHIO.

What news, Borachio? 43

Bora. I came yonder from a great supper: the prince, your brother, is royally entertained by Leonato; and I can give you intelligence of an intended marriage. 47

D. John. Will it serve for any model to build mischief on? What is he for a fool that betroths himself to unquietness?

Bora. Marry, it is your brother's right hand.

D. John. Who? the most exquisite Claudio?

Bora. Even he. 53

D. John. A proper squire! And who, and who? which way looks he?

Bora. Marry, on Hero, the daughter and heir of Leonato. 57

D. John. A very forward March-chick! How came you to this?

Bora. Being entertained for a perfumer, as I was smoking a musty room, comes me the prince and Claudio, hand in hand, in sad conference: I whipt me behind the arras, and there heard it agreed upon that the prince should woo Hero for himself, and having obtained her, give her to Count Claudio. 66

D. John. Come, come; let us thither: this may prove food to my displeasure. That young start-up hath all the glory of my overthrow: if I can cross him any way, I bless myself every way. You are both sure, and will assist me?

Con. } To the death, my lord. 72
Bora. }

D. John. Let us to the great supper: their cheer is the greater that I am subdued. Would the cook were of my mind! Shall we go prove what's to be done? 76

Bora. We'll wait upon your lordship. [*Exeunt.*

ACT II

SCENE I.—*A Hall in* LEONATO'S *House.*

Enter LEONATO, ANTONIO, HERO, BEATRICE, *and Others.*

Leon. Was not Count John here at supper?

Ant. I saw him not.

Beat. How tartly that gentleman looks! I never can see him but I am heart-burned an hour after. 5

Hero. He is of a very melancholy disposition.

Beat. He were an excellent man that were

made just in the mid-way between him and Benedick: the one is too like an image, and says nothing; and the other too like my lady's eldest son, evermore tattling. 11

Leon. Then half Signior Benedick's tongue in Count John's mouth, and half Count John's melancholy in Signior Benedick's face,—

Beat. With a good leg and a good foot, uncle, and money enough in his purse, such a man would win any woman in the world, if a' could get her good will. 18

Leon. By my troth, niece, thou wilt never get thee a husband, if thou be so shrewd of thy tongue. 21

Ant. In faith, she's too curst.

Beat. Too curst is more than curst: I shall lessen God's sending that way; for it is said, 'God sends a curst cow short horns;' but to a cow too curst he sends none.

Leon. So, by being too curst, God will send you no horns? 28

Beat. Just, if he send me no husband; for the which blessing I am at him upon my knees every morning and evening. Lord! I could not endure a husband with a beard on his face: I had rather lie in the woollen.

Leon. You may light on a husband that hath no beard.

Beat. What should I do with him? dress him in my apparel and make him my waiting-gentle-woman? He that hath a beard is more than a youth, and he that hath no beard is less than a man; and he that is more than a youth is not for me; and he that is less than a man, I am not for him: therefore I will even take sixpence in earnest of the bear-ward, and lead his apes into hell. 44

Leon. Well then, go you into hell?

Beat. No; but to the gate; and there will the devil meet me, like an old cuckold, with horns on his head, and say, 'Get you to heaven, Beatrice, get you to heaven; here's no place for you maids:' so deliver I up my apes, and away to Saint Peter for the heavens; he shows me where the bachelors sit, and there live we as merry as the day is long. 53

Ant. [*To* HERO.] Well, niece, I trust you will be ruled by your father.

Beat. Yes, faith; it is my cousin's duty to make curtsy, and say, 'Father, as it please you:' —but yet for all that, cousin, let him be a handsome fellow, or else make another curtsy, and say, 'Father, as it please me.' 60

Leon. Well, niece, I hope to see you one day fitted with a husband.

Beat. Not till God make men of some other metal than earth. Would it not grieve a woman to be over-mastered with a piece of valiant dust? to make an account of her life to a clod of wayward marl? No, uncle, I'll none: Adam's sons are my brethren; and truly, I hold it a sin to match in my kindred. 69

Leon. Daughter, remember what I told you: if the prince do solicit you in that kind, you know your answer. 72

Beat. The fault will be in the music, cousin,

if you be not wooed in good time: if the prince be too important, tell him there is measure in everything, and so dance out the answer. For, hear me, Hero: wooing, wedding, and repenting, is as a Scotch jig, a measure, and a cinque-pace: the first suit is hot and hasty, like a Scotch jig, and full as fantastical; the wedding, mannerly-modest, as a measure, full of state and ancientry; and then comes Repentance, and, with his bad legs, falls into the cinque-pace faster and faster, till he sink into his grave. 84

Leon. Cousin, you apprehend passing shrewdly.

Beat. I have a good eye, uncle: I can see a church by daylight.

Leon. The revellers are entering, brother: make good room. 89

Enter DON PEDRO, CLAUDIO, BENEDICK, BAL-THAZAR, DON JOHN, BORACHIO, MARGARET, URSULA, *and Others, masked.*

D. Pedro. Lady, will you walk about with your friend? 91

Hero. So you walk softly and look sweetly and say nothing, I am yours for the walk; and especially when I walk away.

D. Pedro. With me in your company?

Hero. I may say so, when I please. 96

D. Pedro. And when please you to say so?

Hero. When I like your favour; for God defend the lute should be like the case!

D. Pedro. My visor is Philemon's roof; within the house is Jove. 101

Hero. Why, then, your visor should be thatch'd.

D. Pedro. Speak low, if you speak love. 104
[*Takes her aside.*

Balth. Well, I would you did like me.

Marg. So would not I, for your own sake; for I have many ill qualities.

Balth. Which is one? 108

Marg. I say my prayers aloud.

Balth. I love you the better; the hearers may cry Amen.

Marg. God match me with a good dancer!

Balth. Amen. 113

Marg. And God keep him out of my sight when the dance is done! Answer, clerk.

Balth. No more words: the clerk is an-swered. 117

Urs. I know you well enough: you are Signior Antonio.

Ant. At a word, I am not. 120

Urs. I know you by the waggling of your head.

Ant. To tell you true, I counterfeit him.

Urs. You could never do him so ill-well, unless you were the very man. Here's his dry hand up and down: you are he, you are he.

Ant. At a word, I am not. 127

Urs. Come, come; do you think I do not know you by your excellent wit? Can virtue hide itself? Go to, mum, you are he: graces will appear, and there's an end. 131

Beat. Will you not tell me who told you so?

Bene. No, you shall pardon me.

Beat. Nor will you not tell me who you are?

Bene. Not now.   135

Beat. That I was disdainful, and that I had my good wit out of the 'Hundred Merry Tales.' Well, this was Signior Benedick that said so.

Bene. What's he?

Beat. I am sure you know him well enough.

Bene. Not I, believe me.   141

Beat. Did he never make you laugh?

Bene. I pray you, what is he?

Beat. Why, he is the prince's jester: a very dull fool; only his gift is in devising impossible slanders: none but libertines delight in him; and the commendation is not in his wit, but in his villany; for he both pleases men and angers them, and then they laugh at him and beat him. I am sure he is in the fleet: I would he had boarded me!   151

Bene. When I know the gentleman, I'll tell him what you say.

Beat. Do, do; he'll but break a comparison or two on me; which, peradventure not marked or not laughed at, strikes him into melancholy; and then there's a partridge wing saved, for the fool will eat no supper that night. [*Music within.*] We must follow the leaders.

Bene. In every good thing.   160

Beat. Nay, if they lead to any ill, I will leave them at the next turning.

[*Dance. Then exeunt all but* DON JOHN, BORACHIO, *and* CLAUDIO.

D. John. Sure my brother is amorous on Hero, and hath withdrawn her father to break with him about it. The ladies follow her and but one visor remains.

Bora. And that is Claudio: I know him by his bearing.   168

D. John. Are you not Signior Benedick?

Claud. You know me well; I am he.

D. John. Signior, you are very near my brother in his love: he is enamoured on Hero; I pray you, dissuade him from her; she is no equal for his birth: you may do the part of an honest man in it.

Claud. How know you he loves her?   176

D. John. I heard him swear his affection.

Bora. So did I too; and he swore he would marry her to-night.

D. John. Come, let us to the banquet.   180

[*Exeunt* DON JOHN *and* BORACHIO.

Claud. Thus answer I in name of Benedick, But hear these ill news with the ears of Claudio. 'Tis certain so; the prince woos for himself. Friendship is constant in all other things   184 Save in the office and affairs of love: Therefore all hearts in love use their own tongues; Let every eye negotiate for itself And trust no agent; for beauty is a witch   188 Against whose charms faith melteth into blood. This is an accident of hourly proof, Which I mistrusted not. Farewell, therefore, Hero!

Re-enter BENEDICK.

Bene. Count Claudio?   192

Claud. Yea, the same.

Bene. Come, will you go with me?

Claud. Whither?   195

Bene. Even to the next willow, about your own business, count. What fashion will you wear the garland of? About your neck, like a usurer's chain? or under your arm, like a lieutenant's scarf? You must wear it one way, for the prince hath got your Hero.   201

Claud. I wish him joy of her.

Bene. Why, that's spoken like an honest drovier: so they sell bullocks. But did you think the prince would have served you thus?   205

Claud. I pray you, leave me.

Bene. Ho! now you strike like the blind man: 'twas the boy that stole your meat, and you'll beat the post.   209

Claud. If it will not be, I'll leave you. [*Exit.*

Bene. Alas! poor hurt fowl. Now will he creep into sedges. But, that my lady Beatrice should know me, and not know me! The prince's fool! Ha! it may be I go under that title because I am merry. Yea, but so I am apt to do myself wrong; I am not so reputed: it is the base though bitter disposition of Beatrice that puts the world into her person, and so gives me out. Well, I'll be revenged as I may.   219

Re-enter DON PEDRO.

D. Pedro. Now, signior, where's the count? Did you see him?

Bene. Troth, my lord, I have played the part of Lady Fame. I found him here as melancholy as a lodge in a warren. I told him, and I think I told him true, that your Grace had got the good will of this young lady; and I offered him my company to a willow tree, either to make him a garland, as being forsaken, or to bind him up a rod, as being worthy to be whipped.   229

D. Pedro. To be whipped! What's his fault?

Bene. The flat transgression of a school-boy, who, being overjoy'd with finding a bird's nest, shows it his companion, and he steals it.   233

D. Pedro. Wilt thou make a trust a transgression? The transgression is in the stealer.

Bene. Yet it had not been amiss the rod had been made, and the garland too; for the garland he might have worn himself, and the rod he might have bestowed on you, who, as I take it, have stolen his bird's nest.   240

D. Pedro. I will but teach them to sing, and restore them to the owner.

Bene. If their singing answer your saying, by my faith, you say honestly.   244

D. Pedro. The Lady Beatrice hath a quarrel to you: the gentleman that danced with her told her she is much wronged by you.

Bene. O! she misused me past the endurance of a block: an oak but with one green leaf on it, would have answered her: my very visor began to assume life and scold with her. She told me, not thinking I had been myself, that I was the prince's jester; that I was duller than a great thaw; huddling jest upon jest with such impossible conveyance upon me, that I stood like a man at a mark, with a whole army shooting at me. She speaks poniards, and every word stabs:

if her breath were as terrible as her terminations, there were no living near her; she would infect to the north star. I would not marry her, though she were endowed with all that Adam had left him before he transgressed: she would have made Hercules have turned spit, yea, and have cleft his club to make the fire too. Come, talk not of her; you shall find her the infernal Ate in good apparel. I would to God some scholar would conjure her, for certainly, while she is here, a man may live as quiet in hell as in a sanctuary; and people sin upon purpose because they would go thither; so, indeed, all disquiet, horror and perturbation follow her. 271

Re-enter CLAUDIO, BEATRICE, HERO, *and*
LEONATO.

D. Pedro. Look! here she comes.

Bene. Will your Grace command me any service to the world's end? I will go on the slightest errand now to the Antipodes that you can devise to send me on; I will fetch you a toothpicker now from the furthest inch of Asia; bring you the length of Prester John's foot; fetch you a hair off the Great Cham's beard; do you any embassage to the Pigmies, rather than hold three words' conference with this harpy. You have no employment for me? 282

D. Pedro. None, but to desire your good company.

Bene. O God, sir, here's a dish I love not: I cannot endure my Lady Tongue. [*Exit.*

D. Pedro. Come, lady, come; you have lost the heart of Signior Benedick. 288

Beat. Indeed, my lord, he lent it me awhile; and I gave him use for it, a double heart for a single one: marry, once before he won it of me with false dice, therefore your Grace may well say I have lost it. 293

D. Pedro. You have put him down, lady, you have put him down.

Beat. So I would not he should do me, my lord, lest I should prove the mother of fools. I have brought Count Claudio, whom you sent me to seek. 299

D. Pedro. Why, how now, count! wherefore are you sad?

Claud. Not sad, my lord.

D. Pedro. How then? Sick?

Claud. Neither, my lord. 304

Beat. The count is neither sad, nor sick, nor merry, nor well; but civil count, civil as an orange, and something of that jealous complexion. 308

D. Pedro. I' faith, lady, I think your blazon to be true; though, I'll be sworn, if he be so, his conceit is false. Here, Claudio, I have wooed in thy name, and fair Hero is won; I have broke with her father, and, his good will obtained; name the day of marriage, and God give thee joy!

Leon. Count, take of me my daughter, and with her my fortunes: his Grace hath made the match, and all grace say Amen to it! 317

Beat. Speak, count, 'tis your cue.

Claud. Silence is the perfectest herald of joy: I were but little happy, if I could say how much.

Lady, as you are mine, I am yours: I give away myself for you and dote upon the exchange. 322

Beat. Speak, cousin; or, if you cannot, stop his mouth with a kiss, and let not him speak neither. 325

D. Pedro. In faith, lady, you have a merry heart.

Beat. Yea, my lord; I thank it, poor fool, it keeps on the windy side of care. My cousin tells him in her ear that he is in her heart. 330

Claud. And so she doth, cousin.

Beat. Good Lord, for alliance! Thus goes every one to the world but I, and I am sunburnt. I may sit in a corner and cry heigh-ho for a husband! 335

D. Pedro. Lady Beatrice, I will get you one.

Beat. I would rather have one of your father's getting. Hath your Grace ne'er a brother like you? Your father got excellent husbands, if a maid could come by them. 340

D. Pedro. Will you have me, lady?

Beat. No, my lord, unless I might have another for working days: your Grace is too costly to wear every day. But, I beseech your Grace, pardon me; I was born to speak all mirth and no matter. 346

D. Pedro. Your silence most offends me, and to be merry best becomes you; for, out of question, you were born in a merry hour.

Beat. No, sure, my lord, my mother cried; but then there was a star danced, and under that was I born. Cousins, God give you joy! 352

Leon. Niece, will you look to those things I told you of?

Beat. I cry you mercy, uncle. By your Grace's pardon. [*Exit.*

D. Pedro. By my troth, a pleasant-spirited lady. 358

Leon. There's little of the melancholy element in her, my lord: she is never sad but when she sleeps; and not ever sad then, for I have heard my daughter say, she hath often dreamed of unhappiness and waked herself with laughing.

D. Pedro. She cannot endure to hear tell of a husband. 365

Leon. O! by no means: she mocks all her wooers out of suit.

D. Pedro. She were an excellent wife for Benedick. 369

Leon. O Lord! my lord, if they were but a week married, they would talk themselves mad.

D. Pedro. Count Claudio, when mean you to go to church? 373

Claud. To-morrow, my lord. Time goes on crutches till love have all his rites.

Leon. Not till Monday, my dear son, which is hence a just seven-night; and a time too brief too, to have all things answer my mind. 378

D. Pedro. Come, you shake the head at so long a breathing; but, I warrant thee, Claudio, the time shall not go dully by us. I will in the interim undertake one of Hercules' labours, which is, to bring Signior Benedick and the Lady Beatrice into a mountain of affection the one with the other. I would fain have it a match; and I doubt not but to fashion it, if you three will but minister such assistance as I shall give you direction.   388

Leon. My lord, I am for you, though it cost me ten nights' watchings.

Claud. And I, my lord.

D. Pedro. And you too, gentle Hero?   392

Hero. I will do any modest office, my lord, to help my cousin to a good husband.

D. Pedro. And Benedick is not the unhopefullest husband that I know. Thus far can I praise him; he is of a noble strain, of approved valour, and confirmed honesty. I will teach you how to humour your cousin, that she shall fall in love with Benedick; and I, with your two helps, will so practise on Benedick that, in despite of his quick wit and his queasy stomach, he shall fall in love with Beatrice. If we can do this, Cupid is no longer an archer: his glory shall be ours, for we are the only love-gods. Go in with me, and I will tell you my drift.   406
[*Exeunt.*

SCENE II.—*Another Room in* LEONATO'S *House.*

Enter DON JOHN *and* BORACHIO.

D. John. It is so; the Count Claudio shall marry the daughter of Leonato.

Bora. Yea, my lord; but I can cross it.   3

D. John. Any bar, any cross, any impediment will be medicinable to me: I am sick in displeasure to him, and whatsoever comes athwart his affection ranges evenly with mine. How canst thou cross this marriage?   8

Bora. Not honestly, my lord; but so covertly that no dishonesty shall appear in me.

D. John. Show me briefly how.   11

Bora. I think I told your lordship, a year since, how much I am in the favour of Margaret, the waiting-gentlewoman to Hero.

D. John. I remember.   15

Bora. I can, at any unseasonable instant of the night, appoint her to look out at her lady's chamber-window.

D. John. What life is in that, to be the death of this marriage?   20

Bora. The poison of that lies in you to temper. Go you to the prince your brother; spare not to tell him, that he hath wronged his honour in marrying the renowned Claudio,—whose estimation do you mightily hold up,—to a contaminated stale, such a one as Hero.   26

D. John. What proof shall I make of that?

Bora. Proof enough to misuse the prince, to vex Claudio, to undo Hero, and kill Leonato. Look you for any other issue?

D. John. Only to despite them, I will endeavour any thing.   32

Bora. Go, then; find me a meet hour to draw Don Pedro and the Count Claudio alone: tell them that you know that Hero loves me; intend a kind of zeal both to the prince and Claudio, as—in love of your brother's honour, who hath made this match, and his friend's reputation, who is thus like to be cozened with the sem-

blance of a maid,—that you have discovered thus. They will scarcely believe this without trial: offer them instances, which shall bear no less likelihood than to see me at her chamber-window, hear me call Margaret Hero; hear Margaret term me Claudio; and bring them to see this the very night before the intended wedding: for in the meantime I will so fashion the matter that Hero shall be absent; and there shall appear such seeming truth of Hero's disloyalty, that jealousy shall be called assurance, and all the preparation overthrown.   51

D. John. Grow this to what adverse issue it can, I will put it in practice. Be cunning in the working this, and thy fee is a thousand ducats.

Bora. Be you constant in the accusation, and my cunning shall not shame me.   57

D. John. I will presently go learn their day of marriage.   [*Exeunt.*

SCENE III.—LEONATO'S *Garden.*

Enter BENEDICK.

Bene. **Boy!**

Enter a Boy.

Boy. Signior?

Bene. In my chamber-window lies a book; bring it hither to me in the orchard.   4

Boy. I am here already, sir.

Bene. I know that; but I would have thee hence, and here again. [*Exit Boy.*] I do much wonder that one man, seeing how much another man is a fool when he dedicates his behaviours to love, will, after he hath laughed at such shallow follies in others, become the argument of his own scorn by falling in love: and such a man is Claudio. I have known, when there was no music with him but the drum and the fife; and now had he rather hear the tabor and the pipe: I have known, when he would have walked ten mile afoot to see a good armour; and now will he lie ten nights awake, carving the fashion of a new doublet. He was wont to speak plain and to the purpose, like an honest man and a soldier; and now is he turned orthographer; his words are a very fantastical banquet, just so many strange dishes. May I be so converted, and see with these eyes? I cannot tell; I think not: I will not be sworn but love may transform me to an oyster; but I'll take my oath on it, till he have made an oyster of me, he shall never make me such a fool. One woman is fair, yet I am well; another is wise, yet I am well; another virtuous, yet I am well; but till all graces be in one woman, one woman shall not come in my grace. Rich she shall be, that's certain; wise, or I'll none; virtuous, or I'll never cheapen her; fair, or I'll never look on her; mild, or come not near me; noble, or not I for an angel; of good discourse, an excellent musician, and her hair shall be of what colour it please God. Ha! the prince and Monsieur Love! I will hide me in the arbour.   [*Withdraws.*

Enter DON PEDRO, LEONATO, *and* CLAUDIO,
followed by BALTHAZAR *and* Musicians.

D. Pedro. Come, shall we hear this music? 40
Claud. Yea, my good lord. How still the
  evening is,
As hush'd on purpose to grace harmony!
D. Pedro. See you where Benedick hath hid
  himself?
Claud. O! very well, my lord: the music
  ended,   44
We'll fit the kid-fox with a penny-worth.
D. Pedro. Come, Balthazar, we'll hear that
  song again.
Balth. O! good my lord, tax not so bad a voice
To slander music any more than once.   48
D. Pedro. It is the witness still of excellency,
To put a strange face on his own perfection.
I pray thee, sing, and let me woo no more.   51
Balth. Because you talk of wooing, I will sing;
Since many a wooer doth commence his suit
To her he thinks not worthy; yet he woos,
Yet will he swear he loves.
D. Pedro.   · Nay, pray thee, come;
Or if thou wilt hold longer argument,   56
Do it in notes.
Balth.   Note this before my notes;
There's not a note of mine that's worth the
  noting.
D. Pedro. Why these are very crotchets that
  he speaks;   59
Notes, notes, forsooth, and nothing! [*Music.*
Bene. Now, divine air! now is his soul ra-
vished! Is it not strange that sheeps' guts should
hale souls out of men's bodies? Well, a horn for
my money, when all's done. — *against music.* 64

BALTHAZAR *sings.*

Sigh no more, ladies, sigh no more,
  Men were deceivers ever;
One foot in sea, and one on shore,
  To one thing constant never.   68
      Then sigh not so,
      But let them go,
    And be you blithe and bonny,
  Converting all your sounds of woe   72
  Into Hey nonny, nonny.

Sing no more ditties, sing no mo
  Of dumps so dull and heavy;
The fraud of men was ever so,   76
  Since summer first was leavy.
      Then sigh not so,
      But let them go,
    And be you blithe and bonny,   80
  Converting all your sounds of woe
  Into Hey nonny, nonny.

D. Pedro. By my troth, a good song.
Balth. And an ill singer, my lord.   84
D. Pedro. Ha, no, no, faith; thou singest well
enough for a shift.
Bene. [*Aside.*] An he had been a dog that should
have howled thus, they would have hanged him;
and I pray God his bad voice bode no mischief.
I had as lief have heard the night-raven, come
what plague could have come after it.   91
D. Pedro. Yea, marry; dost thou hear,

Balthazar? I pray thee, get us some excellent
music, for to-morrow night we would have it at
the Lady Hero's chamber-window.
Balth. The best I can, my lord.   96
D. Pedro. Do so: farewell. [*Exeunt* BALTHA-
ZAR *and* Musicians.] Come hither, Leonato:
what was it you told me of to-day, that your niece
Beatrice was in love with Signior Benedick? 100
Claud. O! ay:—[*Aside to* D. PEDRO.] Stalk
on, stalk on; the fowl sits. I did never think
that lady would have loved any man.   103
Leon. No, nor I neither; but most wonderful
that she should so dote on Signior Benedick,
whom she hath in all outward behaviours
seemed ever to abhor.   107
Bene. [*Aside.*] Is't possible? Sits the wind in
that corner?
Leon. By my troth, my lord, I cannot tell
what to think of it but that she loves him with
an enraged affection: it is past the infinite of
thought.   113
D. Pedro. May be she doth but counterfeit.
Claud. Faith, like enough.
Leon. O God! counterfeit! There was never
counterfeit of passion came so near the life of
passion as she discovers it.
D. Pedro. Why, what effects of passion shows
she?   120
Claud. [*Aside.*] Bait the hook well: this fish
will bite.
Leon. What effects, my lord? She will sit you;
[*To* CLAUDIO.] You heard my daughter tell you
how.   125
Claud. She did, indeed.
D. Pedro. How, how, I pray you? You amaze
me: I would have thought her spirit had been
invincible against all assaults of affection. 129
Leon. I would have sworn it had, my lord;
especially against Benedick.
Bene. [*Aside.*] I should think this a gull, but
that the white-bearded fellow speaks it: knavery
cannot, sure, hide itself in such reverence.
Claud. [*Aside.*] He hath ta'en the infection:
hold it up.   136
D. Pedro. Hath she made her affection known
to Benedick?
Leon. No; and swears she never will: that's
her torment.   140
Claud. 'Tis true, indeed; so your daughter
says: 'Shall I,' says she, 'that have so oft encountered him with scorn, write to him that I
love him?'   144
Leon. This says she now when she is beginning to write to him; for she'll be up twenty
times a night, and there will she sit in her smock
till she have writ a sheet of paper: my daughter
tells us all.   149
Claud. Now you talk of a sheet of paper, I
remember a pretty jest your daughter told us of.
Leon. O! when she had writ it, and was reading it over, she found Benedick and Beatrice between the sheet?
Claud. That.   155
Leon. O! she tore the letter into a thousand
halfpence; railed at herself, that she should be
so immodest to write to one that she knew would

flout her: 'I measure him,' says she, 'by my own spirit; for I should flout him, if he writ to me; yea, though I love him, I should.'   161

Claud. Then down upon her knees she falls, weeps, sobs, beats her heart, tears her hair, prays, curses; 'O sweet Benedick! God give me patience!'   165

Leon. She doth indeed; my daughter says so; and the ecstasy hath so much overborne her, that my daughter is sometimes afeard she will do a desperate outrage to herself. It is very true.

D. Pedro. It were good that Benedick knew of it by some other, if she will not discover it.   172

Claud. To what end? he would but make a sport of it and torment the poor lady worse.

D. Pedro. An he should, it were an alms to hang him. She's an excellent sweet lady, and, out of all suspicion, she is virtuous.   177

Claud. And she is exceeding wise.

D. Pedro. In everything but in loving Benedick.   180

Leon. O! my lord, wisdom and blood combating in so tender a body, we have ten proofs to one that blood hath the victory. I am sorry for her, as I have just cause, being her uncle and her guardian.   185

D. Pedro. I would she had bestowed this dotage on me; I would have daffed all other respects and made her half myself. I pray you, tell Benedick of it, and hear what a' will say. 189

Leon. Were it good, think you?

Claud. Hero thinks surely she will die; for she says she will die if he love her not, and she will die ere she make her love known, and she will die if he woo her, rather than she will bate one breath of her accustomed crossness.   195

D. Pedro. She doth well: if she should make tender of her love, 'tis very possible he'll scorn it; for the man,—as you know all,—hath a contemptible spirit.

Claud. He is a very proper man.   200

D. Pedro. He hath indeed a good outward happiness.

Claud. 'Fore God, and in my mind, very wise.

D. Pedro. He doth indeed show some sparks that are like wit.   205

Leon. And I take him to be valiant.

D. Pedro. As Hector, I assure you: and in the managing of quarrels you may say he is wise; for either he avoids them with great discretion, or undertakes them with a most Christian-like fear.   211

Leon. If he do fear God, a' must necessarily keep peace: if he break the peace, he ought to enter into a quarrel with fear and trembling.

D. Pedro. And so will he do; for the man doth fear God, howsoever it seems not in him by some large jests he will make. Well, I am sorry for your niece. Shall we go seek Benedick, and tell him of her love?   219

Claud. Never tell him, my lord: let her wear it out with good counsel.

Leon. Nay, that's impossible: she may wear her heart out first.   223

D. Pedro. Well, we will hear further of it by your daughter: let it cool the while. I love Benedick well, and I could wish he would modestly examine himself, to see how much he is unworthy to have so good a lady.   228

Leon. My lord, will you walk? dinner is ready.

Claud. [*Aside.*] If he do not dote on her upon this, I will never trust my expectation.   231

D. Pedro. [*Aside.*] Let there be the same net spread for her; and that must your daughter and her gentlewoman carry. The sport will be, when they hold one an opinion of another's dotage, and no such matter: that's the scene that I would see, which will be merely a dumb-show. Let us send her to call him in to dinner.

[*Exeunt* DON PEDRO, CLAUDIO, *and* LEONATO.

Bene. [*Advancing from the arbour.*] This can be no trick: the conference was sadly borne. They have the truth of this from Hero. They seem to pity the lady: it seems, her affections have their full bent. Love me! why, it must be requited. I hear how I am censured: they say I will bear myself proudly, if I perceive the love come from her; they say too that she will rather die than give any sign of affection. I did never think to marry: I must not seem proud: happy are they that hear their detractions, and can put them to mending. They say the lady is fair: 'tis a truth, I can bear them witness; and virtuous: 'tis so, I cannot reprove it; and wise, but for loving me: by my troth, it is no addition to her wit, nor no great argument of her folly, for I will be horribly in love with her. I may chance have some odd quirks and remnants of wit broken on me, because I have railed so long against marriage; but doth not the appetite alter? A man loves the meat in his youth that he cannot endure in his age. Shall quips and sentences and these paper bullets of the brain awe a man from the career of his humour? No; the world must be peopled. When I said I would die a bachelor, I did not think I should live till I were married. Here comes Beatrice. By this day! she's a fair lady: I do spy some marks of love in her.   266

Enter BEATRICE.

Beat. Against my will I am sent to bid you come in to dinner.   268

Bene. Fair Beatrice, I thank you for your pains.

Beat. I took no more pains for those thanks than you take pains to thank me: if it had been painful, I would not have come.   273

Bene. You take pleasure then in the message?

Beat. Yea, just so much as you may take upon a knife's point, and choke a daw withal. You have no stomach, signior: fare you well. [*Exit.*

Bene. Ha! 'Against my will I am sent to bid you come in to dinner,' there's a double meaning in that. 'I took no more pains for those thanks than you took pains to thank me,' that's as much as to say, Any pains that I take for you is as easy as thanks. If I do not take pity of her, I am a villain; if I do not love her, I am a Jew. I will go get her picture. [*Exit.*

ACT III

SCENE I.—LEONATO'S *Garden.*

Enter HERO, MARGARET, *and* URSULA.

Hero. Good Margaret, run thee to the parlour;
There shalt thou find my cousin Beatrice
Proposing with the prince and Claudio:
Whisper her ear, and tell her, I and Ursula   4
Walk in the orchard, and our whole discourse
Is all of her; say that thou overheard'st us,
And bid her steal into the pleached bower,
Where honey-suckles, ripen'd by the sun,   8
Forbid the sun to enter; like favourites,
Made proud by princes, that advance their pride
Against that power that bred it. There will she hide her,
To listen our propose. This is thy office;   12
Bear thee well in it and leave us alone.
Marg. I'll make her come, I warrant you,
presently.   [*Exit.*
Hero. Now, Ursula, when Beatrice doth come,
As we do trace this alley up and down,   16
Our talk must only be of Benedick:
When I do name him, let it be thy part
To praise him more than ever man did merit.
My talk to thee must be how Benedick   20
Is sick in love with Beatrice: of this matter
Is little Cupid's crafty arrow made,
That only wounds by hearsay.

Enter BEATRICE, *behind.*
                    Now begin;
For look where Beatrice, like a lapwing, runs 24
Close by the ground, to hear our conference.
Urs. The pleasant'st angling is to see the fish
Cut with her golden oars the silver stream,
And greedily devour the treacherous bait: 28
So angle we for Beatrice; who even now
Is couched in the woodbine coverture.
Fear you not my part of the dialogue.
Hero. Then go we near her, that her ear lose
nothing   32
Of the false sweet bait that we lay for it.
        [*They advance to the bower.*
No, truly, Ursula, she is too disdainful;
I know her spirits are as coy and wild
As haggerds of the rock.
Urs.   But are you sure   36
That Benedick loves Beatrice so entirely?
Hero. So says the prince, and my new-trothed lord.
Urs. And did they bid you tell her of it, madam?
Hero. They did entreat me to acquaint her
of it;   40
But I persuaded them, if they lov'd Benedick,
To wish him wrestle with affection,
And never to let Beatrice know of it.
Urs. Why did you so? Doth not the gentleman   44
Deserve as full as fortunate a bed
As ever Beatrice shall couch upon?
Hero. O god of love! I know he doth deserve

As much as may be yielded to a man;   48
But nature never fram'd a woman's heart
Of prouder stuff than that of Beatrice;
Disdain and scorn ride sparkling in her eyes,
Misprising what they look on, and her wit   52
Values itself so highly, that to her
All matter else seems weak. She cannot love,
Nor take no shape nor project of affection,
She is so self-endear'd.
Urs.   Sure, I think so;   56
And therefore certainly it were not good
She knew his love, lest she make sport at it.
Hero. Why, you speak truth. I never yet
saw man,   59
How wise, how noble, young, how rarely featur'd,
But she would spell him backward: if fair-fac'd,
She would swear the gentleman should be her
sister;
If black, why, Nature, drawing of an antick,
Made a foul blot; if tall, a lance ill-headed;   64
If low, an agate very vilely cut;
If speaking, why, a vane blown with all winds;
If silent, why, a block moved with none.
So turns she every man the wrong side out,   68
And never gives to truth and virtue that
Which simpleness and merit purchaseth.
Urs. Sure, sure, such carping is not commendable.
Hero. No; not to be so odd and from all
fashions   72
As Beatrice is, cannot be commendable.
But who dare tell her so? If I should speak,
She would mock me into air: O! she would
laugh me
Out of myself, press me to death with wit.   76
Therefore let Benedick, like cover'd fire,
Consume away in sighs, waste inwardly:
It were a better death than die with mocks,
Which is as bad as die with tickling.   80
Urs. Yet tell her of it: hear what she will say.
Hero. No; rather I will go to Benedick,
And counsel him to fight against his passion.
And, truly, I'll devise some honest slanders 84
To stain my cousin with. One doth not know
How much an ill word may empoison liking.
Urs. O! do not do your cousin such a wrong.
She cannot be so much without true judgment,—
Having so swift and excellent a wit   89
As she is priz'd to have,—as to refuse
So rare a gentleman as Signior Benedick.
Hero. He is the only man of Italy,   92
Always excepted my dear Claudio.
Urs. I pray you, be not angry with me, madam,
Speaking my fancy: Signior Benedick,
For shape, for bearing, argument and valour, 96
Goes foremost in report through Italy.
Hero. Indeed, he hath an excellent good
name.
Urs. His excellence did earn it, ere he had it.
When are you married, madam?   100
Hero. Why, every day, to-morrow. Come,
go in:
I'll show thee some attires, and have thy counsel
Which is the best to furnish me to-morrow.
Urs. She's lim'd, I warrant you: we have
caught her, madam.   104

Hero. If it prove so, then loving goes by haps:
Some Cupid kills with arrows, some with traps.
                    [*Exeunt* HERO *and* URSULA.
Beat. [*Advancing.*] What fire is in mine ears?
Can this be true?
Stand I condemn'd for pride and scorn so
    much?   108
Contempt, farewell! and maiden pride, adieu!
No glory lives behind the back of such.
And, Benedick, love on; I will requite thee,
Taming my wild heart to thy loving hand: 112
If thou dost love, my kindness shall incite thee
To bind our loves up in a holy band;
For others say thou dost deserve, and I
Believe it better than reportingly.   [*Exit.*

SCENE II.—*A Room in* LEONATO'S *House.*

Enter DON PEDRO, CLAUDIO, BENEDICK,
        and LEONATO.

D. Pedro. I do but stay till your marriage be
consummate, and then go I toward Arragon.
Claud. I'll bring you thither, my lord, if you'll
vouchsafe me.   4
D. Pedro. Nay, that would be as great a soil
in the new gloss of your marriage, as to show a
child his new coat and forbid him to wear it. I
will only be bold with Benedick for his company;
for, from the crown of his head to the sole of his
foot, he is all mirth: he hath twice or thrice cut
Cupid's bow-string, and the little hangman dare
not shoot at him. He hath a heart as sound as
a bell, and his tongue is the clapper; for what
his heart thinks his tongue speaks.
Bene. Gallants, I am not as I have been.
Leon. So say I: methinks you are sadder. 16
Claud. I hope he be in love.
D. Pedro. Hang him, truant! there's no true
drop of blood in him, to be truly touched with
love. If he be sad, he wants money.   20
Bene. I have the tooth-ache.
D. Pedro. Draw it.
Bene. Hang it.
Claud. You must hang it first, and draw it
afterwards.   25
D. Pedro. What! sigh for the tooth-ache?
Leon. Where is but a humour or a worm?
Bene. Well, every one can master a grief but
he that has it.   29
Claud. Yet say I, he is in love.
D. Pedro. There is no appearance of fancy in
him, unless it be a fancy that he hath to strange
disguises; as, to be a Dutchman to-day, a Frenchman to-morrow, or in the shape of two countries
at once, as a German from the waist downward,
all slops, and a Spaniard from the hip upward,
no doublet. Unless he have a fancy to this
foolery, as it appears he hath, he is no fool for
fancy, as you would have it appear he is.   39
Claud. If he be not in love with some woman,
there is no believing old signs: a' brushes his hat
a mornings; what should that bode?
D. Pedro. Hath any man seen him at the
barber's?   44
Claud. No, but the barber's man hath been

seen with him; and the old ornament of his
cheek hath already stuffed tennis-balls.
Leon. Indeed he looks younger than he did
by the loss of a beard.   4
D. Pedro. Nay, a' rubs himself with civet:
can you smell him out by that?
Claud. That's as much as to say the swee
youth's in love.
D. Pedro. The greatest note of it is his melan
choly.
Claud. And when was he wont to wash hi
face?   — means cosmetics —   5
D. Pedro. Yea, or to paint himself? for th
which, I hear what they say of him.
Claud. Nay, but his jesting spirit; which i
now crept into a lute-string, and new-governe
by stops.
D. Pedro. Indeed, that tells a heavy tale fo
him. Conclude, conclude he is in love.   6
Claud. Nay, but I know who loves him.
D. Pedro. That would I know too: I warrant
one that knows him not.
Claud. Yes, and his ill conditions; and i
despite of all, dies for him.   6
D. Pedro. She shall be buried with her fac
upwards.
Bene. Yet is this no charm for the tooth-ache
Old signior, walk aside with me: I have studie
eight or nine wise words to speak to you, whic
these hobby-horses must not hear.   7
            [*Exeunt* BENEDICK *and* LEONATO
D. Pedro. For my life, to break with hin
about Beatrice.
Claud. 'Tis even so. Hero and Margaret hav
by this played their parts with Beatrice, an
then the two bears will not bite one anothe
when they meet.   8

Enter DON JOHN.

D. John. My lord and brother, God save you
D. Pedro. Good den, brother.
D. John. If your leisure served, I would spea
with you.   8
D. Pedro. In private?
D. John. If it please you; yet Count Claudi
may hear, for what I would speak of concern
him.   8
D. Pedro. What's the matter?
D. John. [*To* CLAUDIO.] Means your lordshi
to be married to-morrow?   9
D. Pedro. You know he does.
D. John. I know not that, when he know
what I know.
Claud. If there be any impediment, I pra
you discover it.   9
D. John. You may think I love you not: le
that appear hereafter, and aim better at me b
that I now will manifest. For my brother,
think he holds you well, and in dearness o
heart hath holp to effect your ensuing marriage
surely suit ill-spent, and labour ill bestowed!
D. Pedro. Why, what's the matter?
D. John. I came hither to tell you; and ci
cumstances shortened,—for she hath been to
long a talking of,—the lady is disloyal.
Claud. Who, Hero?   10

D. John. Even she: Leonato's Hero, your Hero, every man's Hero.

Claud. Disloyal?   111

D. John. The word's too good to paint out her wickedness; I could say, she were worse: think you of a worse title, and I will fit her to it. Wonder not till further warrant: go but with me to-night, you shall see her chamber-window entered, even the night before her wedding-day: if you love her then, to-morrow wed her; but it would better fit your honour to change your mind.   120

Claud. May this be so?

D. Pedro. I will not think it.

D. John. If you dare not trust that you see, confess not that you know. If you will follow me, I will show you enough; and when you have seen more and heard more, proceed accordingly.

Claud. If I see any thing to-night why I should not marry her to-morrow, in the congregation, where I should wed, there will I shame her.

D. Pedro. And, as I wooed for thee to obtain her, I will join with thee to disgrace her.   132

D. John. I will disparage her no further till you are my witnesses: bear it coldly but till midnight, and let the issue show itself.

D. Pedro. O day untowardly turned!   136

Claud. O mischief strangely thwarting!

D. John. O plague right well prevented! So will you say when you have seen the sequel.

                 [*Exeunt.*

SCENE III.—*A Street.*

Enter DOGBERRY *and* VERGES, *with the* Watch.

Dogb. Are you good men and true?

Verg. Yea, or else it were pity but they should suffer salvation, body and soul.

Dogb. Nay, that were a punishment too good for them, if they should have any allegiance in them, being chosen for the prince's watch.

Verg. Well, give them their charge, neighbour Dogberry.   8

Dogb. First, who think you the most desartless man to be constable?

First Watch. Hugh Oatcake, sir, or George Seacoal; for they can write and read.   12

Dogb. Come hither, neighbour Seacoal. God hath blessed you with a good name: to be a well-favoured man is the gift of fortune; but to write and read comes by nature.   16

Sec. Watch. Both which, Master constable,—

Dogb. You have: I knew it would be your answer. Well, for your favour, sir, why, give God thanks, and make no boast of it; and for your writing and reading, let that appear when there is no need of such vanity. You are thought here to be the most senseless and fit man for the constable of the watch; therefore bear you the lanthorn. This is your charge: you shall comprehend all vagrom men; you are to bid any man stand, in the prince's name.

Watch. How, if a' will not stand?   28

Dogb. Why, then, take no note of him, but let him go; and presently call the rest of the watch together, and thank God you are rid of a knave.

Verg. If he will not stand when he is bidden, he is none of the prince's subjects.   33

Dogb. True, and they are to meddle with none but the prince's subjects. You shall also make no noise in the streets: for, for the watch to babble and to talk is most tolerable and not to be endured.

Sec. Watch. We will rather sleep than talk: we know what belongs to a watch.   40

Dogb. Why, you speak like an ancient and most quiet watchman, for I cannot see how sleeping should offend; only have a care that your bills be not stolen. Well, you are to call at all the alehouses, and bid those that are drunk get them to bed.   46

Watch. How if they will not?

Dogb. Why then, let them alone till they are sober: if they make you not then the better answer, you may say they are not the men you took them for.

Watch. Well, sir.   52

Dogb. If you meet a thief, you may suspect him, by virtue of your office, to be no true man; and, for such kind of men, the less you meddle or make with them, why, the more is for your honesty.   57

Sec. Watch. If we know him to be a thief, shall we not lay hands on him?

Dogb. Truly, by your office, you may; but I think they that touch pitch will be defiled. The most peaceable way for you, if you do take a thief, is to let him show himself what he is and steal out of your company.   64

Verg. You have been always called a merciful man, partner.

Dogb. Truly, I would not hang a dog by my will, much more a man who hath any honesty in him.

Verg. If you hear a child cry in the night, you must call to the nurse and bid her still it.

Sec. Watch. How if the nurse be asleep and will not hear us?   72

Dogb. Why, then, depart in peace, and let the child wake her with crying; for the ewe that will not hear her lamb when it baes, will never answer a calf when he bleats.   76

Verg. 'Tis very true.

Dogb. This is the end of the charge. You constable, are to present the prince's own person: if you meet the prince in the night, you may stay him.   81

Verg. Nay, by 'r lady, that I think, a' cannot.

Dogb. Five shillings to one on 't, with any man that knows the statues, he may stay him: marry, not without the prince be willing; for, indeed, the watch ought to offend no man, and it is an offence to stay a man against his will.

Verg. By 'r lady, I think it be so.   88

Dogb. Ha, ah, ha! Well, masters, good night: an there be any matter of weight chances, call up me: keep your fellows' counsels and your own, and good night. Come, neighbour.   92

Sec. Watch. Well, masters, we hear our charge: let us go sit here upon the church-bench till two, and then all go to bed.

Dogb. One word more, honest neighbours. I pray you, watch about Signior Leonato's door; for the wedding being there to-morrow, there is a great coil to-night. Adieu; be vigitant, I beseech you.   [*Exeunt* DOGBERRY *and* VERGES.

Enter BORACHIO *and* CONRADE.

Bora. What, Conrade!   101
Watch. [*Aside.*] Peace! stir not.
Bora. Conrade, I say!
Con. Here, man, I am at thy elbow.   104
Bora. Mass, and my elbow itched; I thought there would a scab follow.
Con. I will owe thee an answer for that; and now forward with thy tale.   108
Bora. Stand thee close then under this penthouse, for it drizzles rain, and I will, like a true drunkard, utter all to thee.
Watch. [*Aside.*] Some treason, masters; yet stand close.   113
Bora. Therefore know, I have earned of Don John a thousand ducats.
Con. Is it possible that any villany should be so dear?   117
Bora. Thou shouldst rather ask if it were possible any villany should be so rich; for when rich villains have need of poor ones, poor ones may make what price they will.   121
Con. I wonder at it.
Bora. That shows thou art unconfirmed. Thou knowest that the fashion of a doublet, or a hat, or a cloak, is nothing to a man.   125
Con. Yes, it is apparel.
Bora. I mean, the fashion.
Con. Yes, the fashion is the fashion.   128
Bora. Tush! I may as well say the fool's the fool. But seest thou not what a deformed thief this fashion is?
Watch. [*Aside.*] I know that Deformed; a' has been a vile thief this seven years; a' goes up and down like a gentleman: I remember his name.   135
Bora. Didst thou not hear somebody?
Con. No: 'twas the vane on the house.
Bora. Seest thou not, I say, what a deformed thief this fashion is? how giddily he turns about all the hot bloods between fourteen and five-and-thirty? sometime fashioning them like Pharaoh's soldiers in the reechy painting; sometime like god Bel's priests in the old church-window; sometime like the shaven Hercules in the smirched worm-eaten tapestry, where his cod-piece seems as massy as his club?   146
Con. All this I see, and I see that the fashion wears out more apparel than the man. But art not thou thyself giddy with the fashion too, that thou hast shifted out of thy tale into telling me of the fashion?   151
Bora. Not so, neither; but know, that I have to-night wooed Margaret, the Lady Hero's gentlewoman, by the name of Hero: she leans me out at her mistress' chamber-window, bids me a thousand times good night,—I tell this tale vilely:—I should first tell thee how the prince, Claudio, and my master, planted and placed and possessed by my master Don John, saw afar off in the orchard this amiable encounter.   160
Con. And thought they Margaret was Hero?
Bora. Two of them did, the prince and Claudio; but the devil my master knew she was Margaret; and partly by his oaths, which first possessed them, partly by the dark night, which did deceive them, but chiefly by my villany, which did confirm any slander that Don John had made, away went Claudio enraged; swore he would meet her, as he was appointed, next morning at the temple, and there, before the whole congregation, shame her with what he saw o'er night, and send her home again without a husband.   173
First Watch. We charge you in the prince's name, stand!
Sec. Watch. Call up the right Master constable. We have here recovered the most dangerous piece of lechery that ever was known in the commonwealth.
First Watch. And one Deformed is one of them: I know him, a' wears a lock.   181
Con. Masters, masters!
Sec. Watch. You'll be made bring Deformed forth, I warrant you.   184
Con. Masters,—
First Watch. Never speak: we charge you let us obey you to go with us.
Bora. We are like to prove a goodly commodity, being taken up of these men's bills.   189
Con. A commodity in question, I warrant you. Come, we'll obey you.   [*Exeunt.*

SCENE IV.—*A Room in* LEONATO'S *House.*

Enter HERO, MARGARET, *and* URSULA.

Hero. Good Ursula, wake my cousin Beatrice, and desire her to rise.
Urs. I will, lady.
Hero. And bid her come hither.
Urs. Well.   [*Exit.*
Marg. Troth, I think your other rabato were better.
Hero. No, pray thee, good Meg, I'll wear this.
Marg. By my troth's not so good; and I warrant your cousin will say so.
Hero. My cousin's a fool, and thou art another: I'll wear none but this.   1.
Marg. I like the new tire within excellently if the hair were a thought browner; and you gown's a most rare fashion, i' faith. I saw the Duchess of Milan's gown that they praise so. 1
Hero. O! that exceeds, they say.
Marg. By my troth's but a night-gown in respect of yours: cloth o' gold, and cuts, and laced with silver, set with pearls, down sleeves side sleeves, and skirts round, underborne with a bluish tinsel; but for a fine, quaint, graceful and excellent fashion, yours is worth ten on't
Hero. God give me joy to wear it! for my heart is exceeding heavy.   2
Marg. 'Twill be heavier soon by the weight o a man.
Hero. Fie upon thee! art not ashamed?   2

Marg. Of what, lady? of speaking honourably? is not marriage honourable in a beggar?
Is not your lord honourable without marriage?
I think you would have me say, 'saving your
reverence, a husband:' an bad thinking do not
wrest true speaking, I'll offend nobody. Is there
any harm in 'the heavier for a husband?' None,
I think, an it be the right husband and the right
wife; otherwise 'tis light, and not heavy: ask
my Lady Beatrice else; here she comes.

Enter BEATRICE.

Hero. Good morrow, coz.
Beat. Good morrow, sweet Hero.   40
Hero. Why, how now! do you speak in the
sick tune?
Beat. I am out of all other tune, methinks.
Marg. Clap's into 'Light o' love;' that goes
without a burden: do you sing it, and I'll dance it.
Beat. Ye light o' love with your heels! then,
if your husband have stables enough, you'll
see he shall lack no barns.   48
Marg. O illegitimate construction! I scorn
that with my heels.
Beat. 'Tis almost five o'clock, cousin; 'tis
time you were ready. By my troth, I am ex-
ceeding ill. Heigh-ho!   53
Marg. For a hawk, a horse, or a husband?
Beat. For the letter that begins them all, H.
Marg. Well, an you be not turned Turk,
there's no more sailing by the star.   57
Beat. What means the fool, trow?
Marg. Nothing I; but God send every one
their heart's desire!   60
Hero. These gloves the count sent me; they
are an excellent perfume.
Beat. I am stuffed, cousin, I cannot smell.
Marg. A maid, and stuffed! there's goodly
catching of cold.   65
Beat. O, God help me! God help me! how
long have you professed apprehension?
Marg. Ever since you left it. Doth not my
wit become me rarely!   69
Beat. It is not seen enough, you should wear
it in your cap. By my troth, I am sick.
Marg. Get you some of this distilled Carduus
Benedictus, and lay it to your heart: it is the
only thing for a qualm.
Hero. There thou prick'st her with a thistle.
Beat. Benedictus! why Benedictus? you have
some moral in this Benedictus.   77
Marg. Moral! no, by my troth, I have no moral
meaning; I meant, plain holy-thistle. You may
think, perchance, that I think you are in love:
nay, by 'r lady, I am not such a fool to think
what I list; nor I list not to think what I can;
nor, indeed, I cannot think, if I would think my
heart out of thinking, that you are in love, or
that you will be in love, or that you can be in
love. Yet Benedick was such another, and now
is he become a man: he swore he would never
marry; and yet now, in despite of his heart, he
eats his meat without grudging: and how you
may be converted, I know not; but methinks
you look with your eyes as other women do.

Beat. What pace is this that thy tongue
keeps?   93
Marg. Not a false gallop.

Re-enter URSULA.

Urs. Madam, withdraw: the prince, the count,
Signior Benedick, Don John, and all the gallants
of the town, are come to fetch you to church. 97
Hero. Help to dress me, good coz, good Meg,
good Ursula.   [*Exeunt.*

SCENE V.—*Another Room in* LEONATO'S *House.*

Enter LEONATO *with* DOGBERRY *and* VERGES.

Leon. What would you with me, honest
neighbour?
Dogb. Marry, sir, I would have some confidence with you, that decerns you nearly.   4
Leon. Brief, I pray you; for you see it is a
busy time with me.
Dogb. Marry, this it is, sir.
Verg. Yes, in truth it is, sir.   8
Leon. What is it, my good friends?
Dogb. Goodman Verges, sir, speaks a little off
the matter: an old man, sir, and his wits are not
so blunt, as, God help, I would desire they were;
but, in faith, honest as the skin between his
brows.
Verg. Yes, I thank God, I am as honest as
any man living, that is an old man and no
honester than I.   17
Dogb. Comparisons are odorous: palabras,
neighbour Verges.
Leon. Neighbours, you are tedious.   20
Dogb. It pleases your worship to say so, but
we are the poor duke's officers; but truly, for
mine own part, if I were as tedious as a king, I
could find in my heart to bestow it all of your
worship.   25
Leon. All thy tediousness on me! ha?
Dogb. Yea, an 't were a thousand pound more
than 'tis; for I hear as good exclamation on
your worship, as of any man in the city, and
though I be but a poor man, I am glad to hear it.
Verg. And so am I.   31
Leon. I would fain know what you have to say.
Verg. Marry, sir, our watch to-night, excepting your worship's presence, ha' ta'en a couple
of as arrant knaves as any in Messina.   35
Dogb. A good old man, sir; he will be talking:
as they say, 'when the age is in, the wit is out.'
God help us! it is a world to see! Well said,
i' faith, neighbour Verges: well, God's a good
man; an two men ride of a horse, one must ride
behind. An honest soul, i' faith, sir; by my
troth he is, as ever broke bread: but God is to be
worshipped: all men are not alike; alas! good
neighbour.   44
Leon. Indeed, neighbour, he comes too short
of you.
Dogb. Gifts that God gives.
Leon. I must leave you.   48
Dogb. One word, sir: our watch, sir, hath indeed comprehended two aspicious persons, and
we would have them this morning examined
before your worship.   52
Leon. Take their examination yourself, and

bring it me: I am now in great haste, as may appear unto you.

Dogb. It shall be suffigance.   56

Leon. Drink some wine ere you go: fare you well.

Enter a Messenger.

Mess. My lord, they stay for you to give your daughter to her husband.   60

Leon. I'll wait upon them: I am ready.

[*Exeunt* LEONATO *and* Messenger.

Dogb. Go, good partner, go, get you to Francis Seacoal; bid him bring his pen and inkhorn to the gaol: we are now to examination these men.

Verg. And we must do it wisely.   65

Dogb. We will spare for no wit, I warrant you; here's that shall drive some of them to a *non-come*: only get the learned writer to set down our excommunication, and meet me at the gaol.   [*Exeunt.*

ACT IV

SCENE I.—*The Inside of a Church.*

Enter DON PEDRO, DON JOHN, LEONATO, FRIAR FRANCIS, CLAUDIO, BENEDICK, HERO, BEATRICE, &c.

Leon. Come, Friar Francis, be brief: only to the plain form of marriage, and you shall recount their particular duties afterwards.

Friar. You come hither, my lord, to marry this lady?   5

Claud. No.

Leon. To be married to her, friar; you come to marry her.   8

Friar. Lady, you come hither to be married to this count?

Hero. I do.   11

Friar. If either of you know any inward impediment, why you should not be conjoined, I charge you, on your souls, to utter it.

Claud. Know you any, Hero?

Hero. None, my lord.   16

Friar. Know you any, count?

Leon. I dare make his answer; none.

Claud. O! what men dare do! what men may do! what men daily do, not knowing what they do!

Bene. How now! Interjections? Why then, some be of laughing, as ah! ha! he!

Claud. Stand thee by, friar. Father, by your leave:

Will you with free and unconstrained soul   24
Give me this maid, your daughter?

Leon. As freely, son, as God did give her me.

Claud. And what have I to give you back whose worth

May counterpoise this rich and precious gift?   28

D. Pedro. Nothing, unless you render her again.

Claud. Sweet prince, you learn me noble thankfulness.

There, Leonato, take her back again:
Give not this rotten orange to your friend;   32
She's but the sign and semblance of her honour.
Behold! how like a maid she blushes here.

O! what authority and show of truth
Can cunning sin cover itself withal.   36
Comes not that blood as modest evidence
To witness simple virtue? Would you not swear,
All you that see her, that she were a maid,
By these exterior shows? But she is none: 40
She knows the heat of a luxurious bed;
Her blush is guiltiness, not modesty.

Leon. What do you mean, my lord?

Claud.   Not to be married,
Not to knit my soul to an approved wanton.   44

Leon. Dear my lord, if you, in your own proof,
Have vanquish'd the resistance of her youth,
And made defeat of her virginity,—

Claud. I know what you would say: if I have known her,   48
You'll say she did embrace me as a husband,
And so extenuate the 'forehand sin:
No, Leonato,
I never tempted her with word too large;   52
But, as a brother to his sister, show'd
Bashful sincerity and comely love.

Hero. And seem'd I ever otherwise to you?

Claud. Out on thee! Seeming! I will write against it: 56
You seem to me as Dian in her orb,
As chaste as is the bud ere it be blown;
But you are more intemperate in your blood
Than Venus, or those pamper'd animals   60
That rage in savage sensuality.

Hero. Is my lord well, that he doth speak so wide?

Leon. Sweet prince, why speak not you?

D. Pedro.   What should I speak?
I stand dishonour'd, that have gone about   64
To link my dear friend to a common stale.

Leon. Are these things spoken, or do I but dream?

D. John. Sir, they are spoken, and these things are true.   68

Bene. This looks not like a nuptial.

Hero.   True! O God!

Claud. Leonato, stand I here?
Is this the prince? Is this the prince's brother?
Is this face Hero's? Are our eyes our own?   72

Leon. All this is so; but what of this, my lord?

Claud. Let me but move one question to your daughter;
And by that fatherly and kindly power
That you have in her, bid her answer truly.   76

Leon. I charge thee do so, as thou art my child.

Hero. O, God defend me! how am I beset!
What kind of catechizing call you this?

Claud. To make you answer truly to your name.   80

Hero. Is it not Hero? Who can blot that name
With any just reproach?

Claud.   Marry, that can Hero:
Hero itself can blot out Hero's virtue.
What man was he talk'd with you yesternight   84
Out at your window, betwixt twelve and one?
Now, if you are a maid, answer to this.

Hero. I talk'd with no man at that hour, my lord.

D. Pedro. Why, then are you no maiden.
Leonato,   88
I am sorry you must hear: upon mine honour,
Myself, my brother, and this grieved count,
Did see her, hear her, at that hour last night,
Talk with a ruffian at her chamber-window;   92
Who hath indeed, most like a liberal villain,
Confess'd the vile encounters they have had
A thousand times in secret.
D. John. Fie, fie! they are not to be nam'd,
my lord,   96
Not to be spoke of;
There is not chastity enough in language
Without offence to utter them. Thus, pretty
lady,
I am sorry for thy much misgovernment.   100
Claud. O Hero! what a Hero hadst thou been,
If half thy outward graces had been plac'd
About thy thoughts and counsels of thy heart!
But fare thee well, most foul, most fair! fare-
well,   104
Thou pure impiety, and impious purity!
For thee I'll lock up all the gates of love,
And on my eyelids shall conjecture hang,
To turn all beauty into thoughts of harm,   108
And never shall it more be gracious.
Leon. Hath no man's dagger here a point
for me?   [HERO *swoons.*
Beat. Why, how now, cousin! wherefore sink
you down?
D. John. Come, let us go. These things,
come thus to light,   112
Smother her spirits up.
[*Exeunt* DON PEDRO, DON JOHN *and* CLAUDIO.
Bene. How doth the lady?
Beat.   Dead, I think! help, uncle!
Hero! why, Hero! Uncle! Signior Benedick!
Friar!   116
Leon. O Fate! take not away thy heavy hand!
Death is the fairest cover for her shame
That may be wish'd for.
Beat.   How now, cousin Hero!
Friar. Have comfort, lady.   120
Leon. Dost thou look up?
Friar.   Yea; wherefore should she not?
Leon. Wherefore! Why, doth not every
earthly thing
Cry shame upon her? Could she here deny
The story that is printed in her blood?   124
Do not live, Hero; do not ope thine eyes;
For, did I think thou wouldst not quickly die,
Thought I thy spirits were stronger than thy
shames,   127
Myself would, on the rearward of reproaches,
Strike at thy life. Griev'd I, I had but one?
Chid I for that at frugal nature's frame?
O! one too much by thee. Why had I one?
Why ever wast thou lovely in mine eyes?   132
Why had I not with charitable hand
Took up a beggar's issue at my gates,
Who smirched thus, and mir'd with infamy,
I might have said, 'No part of it is mine;   136
This shame derives itself from unknown loins?'
But mine, and mine I lov'd, and mine I prais'd,
And mine that I was proud on, mine so much
That I myself was to myself not mine,   140

Valuing of her; why, she—O! she is fallen
Into a pit of ink, that the wide sea
Hath drops too few to wash her clean again,
And salt too little which may season give   144
To her foul-tainted flesh.
Bene.   Sir, sir, be patient.
For my part, I am so attir'd in wonder,
I know not what to say.
Beat. O! on my soul, my cousin is belied!
Bene. Lady, were you her bedfellow last
night?   149
Beat. No, truly, not; although, until last
night,
I have this twelvemonth been her bedfellow.
Leon. Confirm'd, confirm'd! O! that is
stronger made,   152
Which was before barr'd up with ribs of iron.
Would the two princes lie? and Claudio lie,
Who lov'd her so, that, speaking of her foul-
ness,
Wash'd it with tears? Hence from her! let her
die.   156
Friar. Hear me a little;
For I have only been silent so long,
And given way unto this course of fortune,
By noting of the lady: I have mark'd   160
A thousand blushing apparitions
To start into her face; a thousand innocent
shames
In angel whiteness bear away those blushes;
And in her eye there hath appear'd a fire,   164
To burn the errors that these princes hold
Against her maiden truth. Call me a fool;
Trust not my reading nor my observations,
Which with experimental seal doth warrant   168
The tenour of my book; trust not my age,
My reverence, calling, nor divinity,
If this sweet lady lie not guiltless here
Under some biting error.
Leon.   Friar, it cannot be.   172
Thou seest that all the grace that she hath left
Is, that she will not add to her damnation
A sin of perjury: she not denies it.
Why seek'st thou then to cover with excuse   176
That which appears in proper nakedness?
Friar. Lady, what man is he you are ac-
cus'd of?
Hero. They know that do accuse me, I know
none;
If I know more of any man alive   180
Than that which maiden modesty doth warrant,
Let all my sins lack mercy! O, my father!
Prove you that any man with me convers'd
At hours unmeet, or that I yesternight   184
Maintain'd the change of words with any crea-
ture,
Refuse me, hate me, torture me to death.
Friar. There is some strange misprision in
the princes.
Bene. Two of them have the very bent of
honour;   188
And if their wisdoms be misled in this,
The practice of it lives in John the bastard,
Whose spirits toil in frame of villanies.
Leon. I know not. If they speak but truth
of her,   192

These hands shall tear her; if they wrong her
    honour,
The proudest of them shall well hear of it.
Time hath not yet so dried this blood of mine,
Nor age so eat up my invention, 196
Nor fortune made such havoc of my means,
Nor my bad life reft me so much of friends,
But they shall find, awak'd in such a kind,
Both strength of limb and policy of mind, 200
Ability in means and choice of friends,
To quit me of them throughly.
    Friar.   Pause awhile,
And let my counsel sway you in this case.
Your daughter here the princes left for dead; 205
Let her awhile be secretly kept in,
And publish it that she is dead indeed:
Maintain a mourning ostentation;
And on your family's old monument 208
Hang mournful epitaphs and do all rites
That appertain unto a burial.
    Leon. What shall become of this? What will
    this do?
    Friar. Marry, this well carried shall on her
    behalf 212
Change slander to remorse; that is some good:
But not for that dream I on this strange course,
But on this travail look for greater birth.
She dying, as it must be so maintain'd, 216
Upon the instant that she was accus'd,
Shall be lamented, pitied and excus'd
Of every hearer; for it so falls out
That what we have we prize not to the worth
Whiles we enjoy it, but being lack'd and lost,
Why, then we rack the value, then we find 222
The virtue that possession would not show us
Whiles it was ours. So will it fare with Claudio:
When he shall hear she died upon his words,
The idea of her life shall sweetly creep
Into his study of imagination,
And every lovely organ of her life 228
Shall come apparell'd in more precious habit,
More moving-delicate, and full of life
Into the eye and prospect of his soul,
Than when she liv'd indeed: then shall he
    mourn,— 232
If ever love had interest in his liver,—
And wish he had not so accused her,
No, though he thought his accusation true.
Let this be so, and doubt not but success 236
Will fashion the event in better shape
Than I can lay it down in likelihood.
But if all aim but this be levell'd false,
The supposition of the lady's death 240
Will quench the wonder of her infamy:
And if it sort not well, you may conceal her,—
As best befits her wounded reputation,—
In some reclusive and religious life, 244
Out of all eyes, tongues, minds, and injuries.
    Bene. Signior Leonato, let the friar advise
    you:
And though you know my inwardness and love
Is very much unto the prince and Claudio, 248
Yet, by mine honour, I will deal in this
As secretly and justly as your soul
Should with your body.
    Leon.   Being that I flow in grief,

The smallest twine may lead me. 252
    Friar. 'Tis well consented: presently away;
For to strange sores strangely they strain the
    cure.
Come, lady, die to live: this wedding day
Perhaps is but prolong'd: have patience and
    endure. 256
            [*Exeunt* FRIAR, HERO, *and* LEONATO.
    Bene. Lady Beatrice, have you wept all this
while?
    Beat. Yea, and I will weep a while longer.
    Bene. I will not desire that. 260
    Beat. You have no reason; I do it freely.
    Bene. Surely I do believe your fair cousin is
wronged.
    Beat. Ah! how much might the man deserve
of me that would right her. 265
    Bene. Is there any way to show such friend-
ship?
    Beat. A very even way, but no such friend.
    Bene. May a man do it? 269
    Beat. It is a man's office, but not yours.
    Bene. I do love nothing in the world so well
as you: is not that strange? 272
    Beat. As strange as the thing I know not.
It were as possible for me to say I loved nothing
so well as you; but believe me not, and yet I lie
not; I confess nothing, nor I deny nothing. I
am sorry for my cousin. 277
    Bene. By my sword, Beatrice, thou lovest me.
    Beat. Do not swear by it, and eat it.
    Bene. I will swear by it that you love me;
and I will make him eat it that says I love
not you.
    Beat. Will you not eat your word?
    Bene. With no sauce that can be devised to
it. I protest I love thee. 285
    Beat. Why then, God forgive me!
    Bene. What offence, sweet Beatrice?
    Beat. You have stayed me in a happy hour:
I was about to protest I loved you. 289
    Bene. And do it with all thy heart.
    Beat. I love you with so much of my heart
that none is left to protest. 292
    Bene. Come, bid me do anything for thee.
    Beat. Kill Claudio.
    Bene. Ha! not for the wide world.
    Beat. You kill me to deny it. Farewell. 296
    Bene. Tarry, sweet Beatrice.
    Beat. I am gone, though I am here: there is
no love in you: nay, I pray you, let me go.
    Bene. Beatrice,— 300
    Beat. In faith, I will go.
    Bene. We'll be friends first.
    Beat. You dare easier be friends with me
than fight with mine enemy. 304
    Bene. Is Claudio thine enemy?
    Beat. Is he not approved in the height a
villain, that hath slandered, scorned, dishonoured my kinswoman? O! that I were a man.
What! bear her in hand until they come to take
hands, and then, with public accusation, uncovered slander, unmitigated rancour,—O God,
that I were a man! I would eat his heart in the
market-place. 313
    Bene. Hear me, Beatrice,—

Beat. Talk with a man out at a window! a proper saying!   316
Bene. Nay, but Beatrice,—
Beat. Sweet Hero! she is wronged, she is slandered, she is undone.
Bene. Beat—   320
Beat. Princes and counties! Surely, a princely testimony, a goodly Count Comfect; a sweet gallant, surely! O! that I were a man for his sake, or that I had any friend would be a man for my sake! But manhood is melted into curtsies, valour into compliment, and men are only turned into tongue, and trim ones too: he is now as valiant as Hercules, that only tells a lie and swears it. I cannot be a man with wishing, therefore I will die a woman with grieving.
Bene. Tarry, good Beatrice. By this hand, I love thee.   332
Beat. Use it for my love some other way than swearing by it.
Bene. Think you in your soul the Count Claudio hath wronged Hero?   336
Beat. Yea, as sure as I have a thought or a soul.
Bene. Enough! I am engaged, I will challenge him. I will kiss your hand, and so leave you. By this hand, Claudio shall render me a dear account. As you hear of me, so think of me. Go, comfort your cousin: I must say she is dead; and so, farewell.   [*Exeunt.*

SCENE II.—*A Prison.*

Enter DOGBERRY, VERGES, *and* SEXTON, *in gowns; and the* Watch, *with* CONRADE *and* BORACHIO.

Dogb. Is our whole dissembly appeared?
Verg. O! a stool and a cushion for the sexton.
Sexton. Which be the malefactors?   4
Dogb. Marry, that am I and my partner.
Verg. Nay, that's certain: we have the exhibition to examine.   7
Sexton. But which are the offenders that are to be examined? let them come before Master constable.
Dogb. Yea, marry, let them come before me. What is your name, friend?   12
Bora. Borachio.
Dogb. Pray write down Borachio. Yours, sirrah?
Con. I am a gentleman, sir, and my name is Conrade.   17
Dogb. Write down Master gentleman Conrade. Masters, do you serve God?
Con. }
Bora. } Yea, sir, we hope.   20
Dogb. Write down that they hope they serve God: and write God first; for God defend but God should go before such villains! Masters, it is proved already that you are little better than false knaves; and it will go near to be thought so shortly. How answer you for yourselves?   26
Con. Marry, sir, we say we are none.
Dogb. A marvellous witty fellow, I assure

you; but I will go about with him. Come you hither, sirrah; a word in your ear: sir, I say to you, you are false knaves.
Bora. Sir, I say to you we are none.   32
Dogb. Well, stand aside. 'Fore God, they are both in a tale. Have you writ down, that they are none?
Sexton. Master constable, you go not the way to examine: you must call forth the watch that are their accusers.   38
Dogb. Yea, marry, that's the eftest way. Let the watch come forth. Masters, I charge you, in the prince's name, accuse these men.
First Watch. This man said, sir, that Don John, the prince's brother, was a villain.   43
Dogb. Write down Prince John a villain. Why, this is flat perjury, to call a prince's brother villain.
Bora. Master constable,—
Dogb. Pray thee, fellow, peace: I do not like thy look, I promise thee.
Sexton. What heard you him say else?   50
Sec. Watch. Marry, that he had received a thousand ducats of Don John for accusing the Lady Hero wrongfully.
Dogb. Flat burglary as ever was committed.
Verg. Yea, by the mass, that it is.
Sexton. What else, fellow?   56
First Watch. And that Count Claudio did mean, upon his words, to disgrace Hero before the whole assembly, and not marry her.
Dogb. O villain! thou wilt be condemned into everlasting redemption for this.   61
Sexton. What else?
Sec. Watch. This is all.
Sexton. And this is more, masters, than you can deny. Prince John is this morning secretly stolen away: Hero was in this manner accused, in this very manner refused, and, upon the grief of this, suddenly died. Master constable, let these men be bound, and brought to Leonato's: I will go before and show him their examination.   [*Exit.*
Dogb. Come, let them be opinioned.   72
Verg. Let them be in the hands—
Con. Off, coxcomb!
Dogb. God's my life! where's the sexton? let him write down the prince's officer coxcomb. Come, bind them. Thou naughty varlet!   77
Con. Away! you are an ass; you are an ass.
Dogb. Dost thou not suspect my place? Dost thou not suspect my years? O that I were here to write me down an ass! but, masters, remember that I am an ass; though it be not written down, yet forget not that I am an ass. No, thou villain, thou art full of piety, as shall be proved upon thee by good witness. I am a wise fellow; and, which is more, an officer; and, which is more, a householder; and, which is more, as pretty a piece of flesh as any in Messina; and one that knows the law, go to; and a rich fellow enough, go to; and a fellow that hath had losses; and one that hath two gowns, and everything handsome about him. Bring him away. O that I had been writ down an ass!   93
     [*Exeunt.*

ACT V

Enter LEONATO *and* ANTONIO.

Ant. If you go on thus, you will kill yourself;
And 'tis not wisdom thus to second grief
Against yourself.
   Leon.   I pray thee, cease thy counsel,
Which falls into mine ears as profitless   4
As water in a sieve: give not me counsel;
Nor let no comforter delight mine ear
But such a one whose wrongs do suit with mine:
Bring me a father that so lov'd his child,   8
Whose joy of her is overwhelm'd like mine,
And bid him speak of patience;
Measure his woe the length and breadth of mine,
And let it answer every strain for strain,   12
As thus for thus and such a grief for such,
In every lineament, branch, shape, and form:
If such a one will smile, and stroke his beard;
Bid sorrow wag, cry 'hem' when he should groan,   16
Patch grief with proverbs; make misfortune drunk
With candle-wasters; bring him yet to me,
And I of him will gather patience.
But there is no such man; for, brother, men   20
Can counsel and speak comfort to that grief
Which they themselves not feel; but, tasting it,
Their counsel turns to passion, which before
Would give preceptial medicine to rage,   24
Fetter strong madness in a silken thread,
Charm ache with air and agony with words.
No, no; 'tis all men's office to speak patience
To those that wring under the load of sorrow,
But no man's virtue nor sufficiency   29
To be so moral when he shall endure
The like himself. Therefore give me no counsel:
My griefs cry louder than advertisement.   32
   Ant. Therein do men from children nothing differ.
   Leon. I pray thee, peace! I will be flesh and blood;
For there was never yet philosopher
That could endure the toothache patiently,   36
However they have writ the style of gods
And made a push at chance and sufferance.
   Ant. Yet bend not all the harm upon yourself;
Make those that do offend you suffer too.   40
   Leon. There thou speak'st reason: nay, I will do so.
My soul doth tell me Hero is belied;
And that shall Claudio know; so shall the prince,
And all of them that thus dishonour her.   44
   Ant. Here come the prince and Claudio hastily.

Enter DON PEDRO *and* CLAUDIO.

D. Pedro. Good den, good den.
   Claud.   Good day to both of you.
   Leon. Hear you, my lords,—
   D. Pedro.   We have some haste, Leonato.
   Leon. Some haste, my lord! well, fare you well, my lord: 48

Are you so hasty now?—well, all is one.
   D. Pedro. Nay, do not quarrel with us, good old man.
   Ant. If he could right himself with quarrelling,
Some of us would lie low.
   Claud.   Who wrongs him?   52
   Leon. Marry, thou dost wrong me; thou dissembler, thou.
Nay, never lay thy hand upon thy sword;
I fear thee not.
   Claud.   Marry, beshrew my hand,   55
If it should give your age such cause of fear.
In faith, my hand meant nothing to my sword.
   Leon. Tush, tush, man! never fleer and jest at me:
I speak not like a dotard nor a fool,
As, under privilege of age, to brag   60
What I have done being young, or what would do,
Were I not old. Know, Claudio, to thy head,
Thou hast so wrong'd mine innocent child and me
That I am forc'd to lay my reverence by,   64
And, with grey hairs and bruise of many days,
Do challenge thee to trial of a man.
I say thou hast belied mine innocent child:
Thy slander hath gone through and through her heart,   68
And she lies buried with her ancestors;
O! in a tomb where never scandal slept,
Save this of hers, fram'd by thy villany!
   Claud. My villany?
   Leon.   Thine, Claudio; thine, I say.   72
   D. Pedro. You say not right, old man.
   Leon.   My lord, my lord,
I'll prove it on his body, if he dare,
Despite his nice fence and his active practice,
His May of youth and bloom of lustihood.   76
   Claud. Away! I will not have to do with you.
   Leon. Canst thou so daff me? Thou hast kill'd my child;
If thou kill'st me, boy, thou shalt kill a man.
   Ant. He shall kill two of us, and men indeed:
But that's no matter; let him kill one first: 81
Win me and wear me; let him answer me.
Come, follow me, boy; come, sir boy, come, follow me.
Sir boy, I'll whip you from your foining fence;
Nay, as I am a gentleman, I will.   85
   Leon. Brother,—
   Ant. Content yourself. God knows I lov'd my niece;
And she is dead, slander'd to death by villains,
That dare as well answer a man indeed   89
As I dare take a serpent by the tongue.
Boys, apes, braggarts, Jacks, milksops!
   Leon.   Brother Antony,—
   Ant. Hold you content. What, man! I know them, yea,   92
And what they weigh, even to the utmost scruple,
Scrambling, out-facing, fashion-monging boys,
That lie and cog and flout, deprave and slander,
Go antickly, show outward hideousness,   96
And speak off half a dozen dangerous words,

How they might hurt their enemies, if they
    durst;
And this is all!

Leon. But, brother Antony,—
Ant. Come, 'tis no matter: 100
Do not you meddle, let me deal in this.

D. Pedro. Gentlemen both, we will not wake
your patience.
My heart is sorry for your daughter's death;
But, on my honour, she was charg'd with no-
    thing   104
But what was true and very full of proof.

Leon. My lord, my lord—
D. Pedro.   I will not hear you.
Leon.   No?
Come, brother, away. I will be heard.— 107
Ant. And shall, or some of us will smart for
    it.   [*Exeunt* LEONATO *and* ANTONIO.

Enter BENEDICK.

D. Pedro. See, see; here comes the man we
went to seek.
Claud. Now, signior, what news?
Bene. Good day, my lord.   112
D. Pedro. Welcome, signior: you are almost
come to part almost a fray.
Claud. We had like to have had our two
noses snapped off with two old men without
teeth.   117
D. Pedro. Leonato and his brother. What
thinkest thou? Had we fought, I doubt we
should have been too young for them.   120
Bene. In a false quarrel there is no true
valour. I came to seek you both.
Claud. We have been up and down to seek
thee; for we are high-proof melancholy, and
would fain have it beaten away. Wilt thou use
thy wit?   126
Bene. It is in my scabbard; shall I draw it?
D. Pedro. Dost thou wear thy wit by thy
side?
Claud. Never any did so, though very many
have been beside their wit. I will bid thee draw,
as we do the minstrels; draw, to pleasure us. 132
D. Pedro. As I am an honest man, he looks
pale. Art thou sick, or angry?
Claud. What, courage, man! What though
care killed a cat, thou hast mettle enough in
thee to kill care.   137
Bene. Sir, I shall meet your wit in the career,
an you charge it against me. I pray you choose
another subject.   140
Claud. Nay then, give him another staff:
this last was broke cross.
D. Pedro. By this light, he changes more and
more: I think he be angry indeed.   144
Claud. If he be, he knows how to turn his
girdle.
Bene. Shall I speak a word in your ear?
Claud. God bless me from a challenge! 148
Bene. [*Aside to* CLAUDIO.] You are a villain;
I jest not: I will make it good how you dare,
with what you dare, and when you dare. Do me
right, or I will protest your cowardice. You
have killed a sweet lady, and her death shall
fall heavy on you. Let me hear from you.

Claud. Well I will meet you, so I may have
good cheer.   156
D. Pedro. What, a feast, a feast?
Claud. I' faith, I thank him; he hath bid me
to a calf's-head and a capon, the which if I do
not carve most curiously, say my knife's naught.
Shall I not find a woodcock too?   161
Bene. Sir, your wit ambles well; it goes
easily.
D. Pedro. I'll tell thee how Beatrice praised
thy wit the other day. I said, thou hadst a fine
wit. 'True,' says she, 'a fine little one.' 'No,'
said I, 'a great wit.' 'Right,' said she, 'a great
gross one.' 'Nay,' said I, 'a good wit.' 'Just,'
said she, 'it hurts nobody.' 'Nay,' said I, 'the
gentleman is wise.' 'Certain,' said she, 'a wise
gentleman.' 'Nay,' said I, 'he hath the tongues.'
'That I believe,' said she, 'for he swore a thing to
me on Monday night, which he forswore on
Tuesday morning: there's a double tongue;
there's two tongues.' Thus did she, an hour
together, trans-shape thy particular virtues; yet
at last she concluded with a sigh, thou wast the
properest man in Italy.   178
Claud. For the which she wept heartily and
said she cared not.
D. Pedro. Yea, that she did; but yet, for all
that, an if she did not hate him deadly, she
would love him dearly. The old man's daughter
told us all.   184
Claud. All, all; and moreover, God saw him
when he was hid in the garden.
D. Pedro. But when shall we set the savage bull's horns on the sensible Benedick's
head?   189
Claud. Yea, and text underneath, 'Here
dwells Benedick the married man!'
Bene. Fare you well, boy: you know my
mind. I will leave you now to your gossip-like
humour: you break jests as braggarts do their
blades, which, God be thanked, hurt not. My
lord, for your many courtesies I thank you: I must
discontinue your company. Your brother the
bastard is fled from Messina: you have, among
you, killed a sweet and innocent lady. For my
Lord Lack-beard there, he and I shall meet; and
till then, peace be with him.   [*Exit.*
D. Pedro. He is in earnest.
Claud. In most profound earnest; and, I'll
warrant you, for the love of Beatrice.   204
D. Pedro. And hath challenged thee?
Claud. Most sincerely.
D. Pedro. What a pretty thing man is when
he goes in his doublet and hose and leaves off
his wit!   209
Claud. He is then a giant to an ape; but then
is an ape a doctor to such a man.
D. Pedro. But, soft you; let me be: pluck
up, my heart, and be sad! Did he not say my
brother was fled?   214

Enter DOGBERRY, VERGES, *and the* Watch, *with*
CONRADE *and* BORACHIO.

Dogb. Come, you, sir: if justice cannot tame
you, she shall ne'er weigh more reasons in her

balance. Nay, an you be a cursing hypocrite once, you must be looked to.

D. Pedro. How now! two of my brother's men bound! Borachio, one!   220

Claud. Hearken after their offence, my lord.

D. Pedro. Officers, what offence have these men done?

Dogb. Marry, sir, they have committed false report; moreover, they have spoken untruths; secondarily, they are slanders; sixth and lastly, they have belied a lady; thirdly, they have verified unjust things; and to conclude, they are lying knaves.   229

D. Pedro. First, I ask thee what they have done; thirdly, I ask thee what's their offence; sixth and lastly, why they are committed; and, to conclude, what you lay to their charge?

Claud. Rightly reasoned, and in his own division; and, by my troth, there's one meaning well suited.   236

D. Pedro. Who have you offended, masters, that you are thus bound to your answer? this learned constable is too cunning to be understood. What's your offence?   240

Bora. Sweet prince, let me go no further to mine answer: do you hear me, and let this count kill me. I have deceived even your very eyes: what your wisdoms could not discover, these shallow fools have brought to light; who, in the night overheard me confessing to this man how Don John your brother incensed me to slander the Lady Hero; how you were brought into the orchard and saw me court Margaret in Hero's garments; how you disgraced her, when you should marry her. My villany they have upon record; which I had rather seal with my death than repeat over to my shame. The lady is dead upon mine and my master's false accusation; and, briefly, I desire nothing but the reward of a villain.   256

D. Pedro. Runs not this speech like iron through your blood?

Claud. I have drunk poison whiles he utter'd it.

D. Pedro. But did my brother set thee on to this?

Bora. Yea; and paid me richly for the practice of it.   260

D. Pedro. He is compos'd and fram'd of treachery:

And fled he is upon this villany.

Claud. Sweet Hero! now thy image doth appear

In the rare semblance that I lov'd it first.   264

Dogb. Come, bring away the plaintiffs: by this time our sexton hath reformed Signior Leonato of the matter. And masters, do not forget to specify, when time and place shall serve, that I am an ass.   269

Verg. Here, here comes Master Signior Leonato, and the sexton too.

Re-enter LEONATO, ANTONIO, *and the* Sexton.

Leon. Which is the villain? Let me see his eyes,   272

That, when I note another man like him, I may avoid him. Which of these is he?

Bora. If you would know your wronger, look on me.

Leon. Art thou the slave that with thy breath hast kill'd   276

Mine innocent child?

Bora.   Yea, even I alone.

Leon. No, not so, villain; thou beliest thyself:

Here stand a pair of honourable men;

A third is fled, that had a hand in it.   280

I thank you, princes, for my daughter's death:

Record it with your high and worthy deeds.

'Twas bravely done, if you bethink you of it.

Claud. I know not how to pray your patience;   284

Yet I must speak. Choose your revenge yourself;

Impose me to what penance your invention

Can lay upon my sin: yet sinn'd I not

But in mistaking.

D. Pedro.   By my soul, nor I: 288

And yet, to satisfy this good old man,

I would bend under any heavy weight

That he'll enjoin me to.

Leon. I cannot bid you bid my daughter live;   292

That were impossible: but, I pray you both,

Possess the people in Messina here

How innocent she died; and if your love

Can labour aught in sad invention,   296

Hang her an epitaph upon her tomb,

And sing it to her bones: sing it to-night.

To-morrow morning come you to my house,

And since you could not be my son-in-law,   300

Be yet my nephew. My brother hath a daughter,

Almost the copy of my child that's dead,

And she alone is heir to both of us:

Give her the right you should have given her cousin,   304

And so dies my revenge.

Claud.   O noble sir,

Your over-kindness doth wring tears from me!

I do embrace your offer; and dispose

For henceforth of poor Claudio.   308

Leon. To-morrow then I will expect your coming;

To-night I take my leave. This naughty man

Shall face to face be brought to Margaret, 311

Who, I believe, was pack'd in all this wrong,

Hir'd to it by your brother.

Bora.   No, by my soul she was not;

Nor knew not what she did when she spoke to me;

But always hath been just and virtuous

In anything that I do know by her.   316

Dogb. Moreover, sir,—which, indeed, is not under white and black,—this plaintiff here, the offender, did call me ass: I beseech you, let it be remembered in his punishment. And also, the watch heard them talk of one Deformed: they say he wears a key in his ear and a lock hanging by it, and borrows money in God's name, the which he hath used so long and never paid, that now men grow hard-hearted, and will lend nothing for God's sake. Pray you, examine him upon that point.   327

Leon. I thank thee for thy care and honest pains.

Dogb. Your worship speaks like a most thankful and reverend youth, and I praise God for you.   332

Leon. There's for thy pains.

Dogb. God save the foundation!

Leon. Go, I discharge thee of thy prisoner, and I thank thee.   336

Dogb. I leave an arrant knave with your worship; which I beseech your worship to correct yourself, for the example of others. God keep your worship! I wish your worship well; God restore you to health! I humbly give you leave to depart, and if a merry meeting may be wished, God prohibit it! Come, neighbour. 343

[*Exeunt* DOGBERRY *and* VERGES.

Leon. Until to-morrow morning, lords, farewell.

Ant. Farewell, my lords: we look for you to-morrow.

D. Pedro. We will not fail.

Claud.   To-night I'll mourn with Hero.

[*Exeunt* DON PEDRO *and* CLAUDIO.

Leon. [*To the* Watch.] Bring you these fellows on. We'll talk with Margaret,   347
How her acquaintance grew with this lewd fellow.   [*Exeunt.*

SCENE II.—LEONATO'S *Garden.*

Enter BENEDICK *and* MARGARET, *meeting.*

Bene. Pray thee, sweet Mistress Margaret, deserve well at my hands by helping me to the speech of Beatrice.

Marg. Will you then write me a sonnet in praise of my beauty?   5

Bene. In so high a style, Margaret, that no man living shall come over it; for, in most comely truth, thou deservest it.   8

Marg. To have no man come over me! why, shall I always keep below stairs?

Bene. Thy wit is as quick as the greyhound's mouth; it catches.   12

Marg. And yours as blunt as the fencer's foils, which hit, but hurt not.

Bene. A most manly wit, Margaret; it will not hurt a woman: and so, I pray thee, call Beatrice. I give thee the bucklers.   17

Marg. Give us the swords, we have bucklers of our own.

Bene. If you use them, Margaret, you must put in the pikes with a vice; and they are dangerous weapons for maids.

Marg. Well, I will call Beatrice to you, who I think hath legs.   24

Bene. And therefore will come.

[*Exit* MARGARET.

The god of love,
That sits above,
And knows me, and knows me,
How pitiful I deserve,—   28

I mean, in singing; but in loving, Leander the

good swimmer, Troilus the first employer of pandars, and a whole book full of these quondam carpet-mongers, whose names yet run smoothly in the even road of a blank verse, why, they were never so truly turned over and over as my poor self, in love. Marry, I cannot show it in rime; I have tried; I can find out no rime to 'lady' but 'baby,' an innocent rime; for 'scorn,' 'horn,' a hard rime; for 'school,' 'fool,' a babbling rime; very ominous endings: no, I was not born under a riming planet, nor I cannot woo in festival terms.   42

Enter BEATRICE.

Sweet Beatrice, wouldst thou come when I called thee?

Beat. Yea, signior; and depart when you bid me.

Bene. O, stay but till then!   47

Beat. 'Then' is spoken; fare you well now: and yet, ere I go, let me go with that I came for; which is, with knowing what hath passed between you and Claudio.   51

Bene. Only foul words; and thereupon I will kiss thee.

Beat. Foul words is but foul wind, and foul wind is but foul breath, and foul breath is noisome; therefore I will depart unkissed.   56

Bene. Thou hast frighted the word out of his right sense, so forcible is thy wit. But I must tell thee plainly, Claudio undergoes my challenge, and either I must shortly hear from him, or I will subscribe him a coward. And, I pray thee now, tell me, for which of my bad parts didst thou first fall in love with me?   63

Beat. For them all together; which maintained so politic a state of evil that they will not admit any good part to intermingle with them. But for which of my good parts did you first suffer love for me?   68

Bene. 'Suffer love,' a good epithet! I do suffer love indeed, for I love thee against my will.

Beat. In spite of your heart, I think. Alas, poor heart! If you spite it for my sake, I will spite it for yours; for I will never love that which my friend hates.   75

Bene. Thou and I are too wise to woo peaceably.

Beat. It appears not in this confession: there's not one wise man among twenty that will praise himself.   80

Bene. An old, an old instance, Beatrice, that lived in the time of good neighbours. If a man do not erect in this age his own tomb ere he dies, he shall live no longer in monument than the bell rings and the widow weeps.   85

Beat. And how long is that think you?

Bene. Question: why, an hour in clamour and a quarter in rheum: therefore it is most expedient for the wise,—if Don Worm, his conscience, find no impediment to the contrary,—to be the trumpet of his own virtues, as I am to myself. So much for praising myself, who, I myself will bear witness, is praiseworthy. And now tell me, how doth your cousin?

Beat. Very ill.

Bene. And how do you?   96

Beat. Very ill too.

Bene. Serve God, love me, and mend. There will I leave you too, for here comes one in haste.   100

Enter URSULA.

Urs. Madam, you must come to your uncle. Yonder's old coil at home: it is proved, my Lady Hero hath been falsely accused, the prince and Claudio mightily abused; and Don John is the author of all, who is fled and gone. Will you come presently?   106

Beat. Will you go hear this news, signior?

Bene. I will live in thy heart, die in thy lap, and be buried in thy eyes; and moreover I will go with thee to thy uncle's.   [*Exeunt.*

SCENE III.—*The Inside of a Church.*

Enter DON PEDRO, CLAUDIO, *and* Attendants, *with music and tapers.*

Claud. Is this the monument of Leonato?

A Lord. It is, my lord.

Claud. [*Reads from a scroll.*]

Done to death by slanderous tongues
    Was the Hero that here lies: 4
Death, in guerdon of her wrongs,
    Gives her fame which never dies.
So the life that died with shame
    Lives in death with glorious fame.   8

Hang thou there upon the tomb,
    Praising her when I am dumb.
Now, music, sound, and sing your solemn hymn.

SONG

Pardon, goddess of the night,   12
Those that slew thy virgin knight;
For the which, with songs of woe,
Round about her tomb they go.
    Midnight, assist our moan;   16
    Help us to sigh and groan,
    Heavily, heavily:
Graves, yawn and yield your dead,
Till death be uttered,   20
    Heavily, heavily.

Claud. Now, unto thy bones good night!
    Yearly will I do this rite.

D. Pedro. Good morrow, masters: put your torches out.   24
The wolves have prey'd; and look, the gentle day,
Before the wheels of Phœbus, round about
Dapples the drowsy east with spots of grey.
Thanks to you all, and leave us: fare you well.

Claud. Good morrow, masters: each his several way.   29

D. Pedro. Come, let us hence, and put on other weeds;
And then to Leonato's we will go.

Claud. And Hymen now with luckier issue speed's,   32
Than this for whom we render'd up this woe!
    [*Exeunt.*

SCENE IV.—*A Room in* LEONATO'S *House.*

Enter LEONATO, ANTONIO, BENEDICK, BEATRICE, MARGARET, URSULA, FRIAR FRANCIS, *and* HERO.

Friar. Did I not tell you she was innocent?

Leon. So are the prince and Claudio, who accus'd her
Upon the error that you heard debated:
But Margaret was in some fault for this,   4
Although against her will, as it appears
In the true course of all the question.

Ant. Well, I am glad that all things sort so well.

Bene. And so am I, being else by faith enforc'd
To call young Claudio to a reckoning for it.   9

Leon. Well, daughter, and you gentlewomen all,
Withdraw into a chamber by yourselves,
And when I send for you, come hither mask'd:
The prince and Claudio promis'd by this hour
To visit me.   [*Exeunt ladies.*
        You know your office, brother;
You must be father to your brother's daughter,
And give her to young Claudio.   16

Ant. Which I will do with confirm'd countenance.

Bene. Friar, I must entreat your pains, I think.

Friar. To do what, signior?

Bene. To bind me, or undo me; one of them.
Signior Leonato, truth it is, good signior,   21
Your niece regards me with an eye of favour.

Leon. That eye my daughter lent her: 'tis most true.

Bene. And I do with an eye of love requite her.

Leon. The sight whereof I think, you had from me,   25
From Claudio, and the prince. But what's your will?

Bene. Your answer, sir, is enigmatical:
But, for my will, my will is your good will   28
May stand with ours, this day to be conjoin'd
In the state of honourable marriage:
In which, good friar, I shall desire your help.

Leon. My heart is with your liking.

Friar.   And my help.   32
Here come the prince and Claudio.

Enter DON PEDRO and CLAUDIO, with Attendants.

D. Pedro. Good morrow to this fair assembly.

Leon. Good morrow, prince; good morrow, Claudio:
We here attend you. Are you yet determin'd
To-day to marry with my brother's daughter?   37

Claud. I'll hold my mind, were she an Ethiop.

Leon. Call her forth, brother: here's the friar ready.   [*Exit* ANTONIO.

D. Pedro. Good morrow, Benedick. Why, what's the matter,   40
That you have such a February face,
So full of frost, of storm and cloudiness?

Claud. I think he thinks upon the savage bull.
Tush! fear not, man, we'll tip thy horns with gold,   44
And all Europa shall rejoice at thee,

As once Europa did at lusty Jove,
When he would play the noble beast in love.
Bene. Bull Jove, sir, had an amiable low: 48
And some such strange bull leap'd your father's
cow,
And got a calf in that same noble feat,
Much like to you, for you have just his bleat.
Claud. For this I owe you: here come other
reckonings. 52

Re-enter ANTONIO, *with the ladies masked.*

Which is the lady I must seize upon?
Ant. This same is she, and I do give you her.
Claud. Why, then she's mine. Sweet, let me
see your face.
Leon. No, that you shall not, till you take her
hand 56
Before this friar, and swear to marry her.
Claud. Give me your hand: before this holy
friar,
I am your husband, if you like of me.
Hero. And when I liv'd, I was your other
wife: [*Unmasking.*
And when you lov'd, you were my other hus-
band. 61
Claud. Another Hero!
Hero. Nothing certainer:
One Hero died defil'd, but I do live,
And surely as I live, I am a maid. 64
D. Pedro. The former Hero! Hero that is
dead!
Leon. She died, my lord, but whiles her slan-
der liv'd.
Friar. All this amazement can I qualify:
When after that the holy rites are ended, 68
I'll tell you largely of fair Hero's death:
Meantime, let wonder seem familiar,
And to the chapel let us presently.
Bene. Soft and fair, friar. Which is Beatrice?
Beat. [*Unmasking.*] I answer to that name.
What is your will? 73
Bene. Do not you love me?
Beat. Why, no; no more than reason.
Bene. Why, then, your uncle and the prince
and Claudio
Have been deceived; for they swore you did. 76
Beat. Do not you love me?
Bene. Troth, no; no more than reason.
Beat. Why, then, my cousin, Margaret, and
Ursula,
Are much deceiv'd; for they did swear you did.
Bene. They swore that you were almost sick
for me. 80
Beat. They swore that you were well-nigh
dead for me.
Bene. 'Tis no such matter. Then, you do not
love me?
Beat. No, truly, but in friendly recompense.

Leon. Come, cousin, I am sure you love the
gentleman. 84
Claud. And I'll be sworn upon 't that he loves
her;
For here's a paper written in his hand,
A halting sonnet of his own pure brain,
Fashion'd to Beatrice.
Hero. And here's another, 88
Writ in my cousin's hand, stolen from her
pocket,
Containing her affection unto Benedick.
Bene. A miracle! here's our own hands against
our hearts. Come, I will have thee; but, by this
light, I take thee for pity. 93
Beat. I would not deny you; but, by this good
day, I yield upon great persuasion, and partly
to save your life, for I was told you were in a
consumption. 97
Bene. Peace! I will stop your mouth.
[*Kisses her.*
D. Pedro. How dost thou, Benedick, the married man? 100
Bene. I'll tell thee what, prince; a college of
witcrackers cannot flout me out of my humour.
Dost thou think I care for a satire or an epi-
gram? No; if a man will be beaten with brains,
a' shall wear nothing handsome about him. In
brief, since I do purpose to marry, I will think
nothing to any purpose that the world can say
against it; and therefore never flout at me for
what I have said against it, for man is a giddy
thing, and this is my conclusion. For thy part,
Claudio, I did think to have beaten thee; but, in
that thou art like to be my kinsman, live unbruised, and love my cousin. 113
Claud. I had well hoped thou wouldst have
denied Beatrice, that I might have cudgelled
thee out of thy single life, to make thee a double-
dealer; which, out of question, thou wilt be, if
my cousin do not look exceeding narrowly to
thee. 119
Bene. Come, come, we are friends. Let's have
a dance ere we are married, that we may lighten
our own hearts and our wives' heels.
Leon. We'll have dancing afterward.
Bene. First, of my word; therefore play,
music! Prince, thou art sad; get thee a wife,
get thee a wife: there is no staff more reverend
than one tipped with horn. 127

Enter a Messenger.

Mes. My lord, your brother John is ta'en in
flight,
And brought with armed men back to Messina.
Bene. Think not on him till to-morrow: I'll
devise thee brave punishments for him. Strike
up, pipers! [*Dance. Exeunt.*

LOVE'S LABOUR'S LOST

DRAMATIS PERSONÆ

FERDINAND, King of Navarre.
BEROWNE,
LONGAVILLE, } Lords, attending on the King.
DUMAINE,
BOYET,
MARCADE, } Lords, attending on the Princess of France.
DON ADRIANO DE ARMADO, a fantastical Spaniard.
SIR NATHANIEL, a Curate.
HOLOFERNES, a Schoolmaster.
DULL, a Constable.

COSTARD, a Clown.
MOTH, Page to Armado.
A Forester.

The PRINCESS of France.
ROSALINE,
MARIA, } Ladies, attending on the Princess.
KATHARINE,
JAQUENETTA, a country Wench.

Officers and Others, Attendants on the King and Princess.

SCENE.—*Navarre.*

ACT I

SCENE I.—*The* KING OF NAVARRE'S *Park.*

Enter the KING, BEROWNE, LONGAVILLE,
and DUMAINE.

King. Let fame, that all hunt after in their
lives,
Live register'd upon our brazen tombs,
And then grace us in the disgrace of death;
When, spite of cormorant devouring Time, 4
The endeavour of this present breath may buy
That honour which shall bate his scythe's keen
edge,
And make us heirs of all eternity.
Therefore, brave conquerors,—for so you are,
That war against your own affections 9
And the huge army of the world's desires,—
Our late edict shall strongly stand in force:
Navarre shall be the wonder of the world; 12
Our court shall be a little academe,
Still and contemplative in living art.
You three, Berowne, Dumaine, and Longaville,
Have sworn for three years' term to live with me,
My fellow-scholars, and to keep those statutes
That are recorded in this schedule here: 18
Your oaths are pass'd; and now subscribe your
names,
That his own hand may strike his honour down
That violates the smallest branch herein. 21
If you are arm'd to do, as sworn to do,
Subscribe to your deep oaths, and keep it too.
Long. I am resolv'd; 'tis but a three years'
fast: 24
The mind shall banquet, though the body pine:
Fat paunches have lean pates, and dainty bits
Make rich the ribs, but bankrupt quite the wits.
Dum. My loving lord, Dumaine is mortified:
The grosser manner of these world's delights 29
He throws upon the gross world's baser slaves:
To love, to wealth, to pomp, I pine and die;
With all these living in philosophy. 32
Ber. I can but say their protestation over;
So much, dear liege, I have already sworn,
That is, to live and study here three years.
But there are other strict observances; 36
As, not to see a woman in that term,
Which I hope well is not enrolled there:

And one day in a week to touch no food,
And but one meal on every day beside; 40
The which I hope is not enrolled there:
And then, to sleep but three hours in the night,
And not be seen to wink of all the day,—
When I was wont to think no harm all night 44
And make a dark night too of half the day,—
Which I hope well is not enrolled there.
O! these are barren tasks, too hard to keep,
Not to see ladies, study, fast, not sleep. 48
King. Your oath is pass'd to pass away from
these.
Ber. Let me say no, my liege, an if you please.
I only swore to study with your Grace,
And stay here in your court for three years' space.
Long. You swore to that, Berowne, and to
the rest. 53
Ber. By yea and nay, sir, then I swore in jest.
What is the end of study? let me know.
King. Why, that to know which else we
should not know. 56
Ber. Things hid and barr'd, you mean, from
common sense?
King. Ay that is study's god-like recompense.
Ber. Come on then; I will swear to study so,
To know the thing I am forbid to know; 60
As thus: to study where I well may dine,
When I to feast expressly am forbid;
Or study where to meet some mistress fine,
When mistresses from common sense are hid;
Or, having sworn too hard-a-keeping oath, 65
Study to break it, and not break my troth.
If study's gain be thus, and this be so,
Study knows that which yet it doth not know.
Swear me to this, and I will ne'er say no. 69
King. These be the stops that hinder study
quite,
And train our intellects to vain delight.
Ber. Why, all delights are vain; but that
most vain 72
Which, with pain purchas'd doth inherit pain:
As, painfully to pore upon a book,
To seek the light of truth; while truth the while
Doth falsely blind the eyesight of his look: 76
Light seeking light doth light of light beguile:
So, ere you find where light in darkness lies,
Your light grows dark by losing of your eyes.

Study me how to please the eye indeed,   80
   By fixing it upon a fairer eye,
Who dazzling so, that eye shall be his heed,
   And give him light that it was blinded by.
Study is like the heaven's glorious sun,   84
   That will not be deep-search'd with saucy
      looks;
Small have continual plodders ever won,
   Save base authority from others' books.
These earthly godfathers of heaven's lights 88
   That give a name to every fixed star,
Have no more profit of their shining nights
   Than those that walk and wot not what
      they are.
Too much to know is to know nought but
      fame;   92
And every godfather can give a name.
   King. How well he 's read, to reason against
      reading!
   Dum. Proceeded well, to stop all good pro-
      ceeding!
   Long. He weeds the corn, and still lets grow
      the weeding.   96
   Ber. The spring is near, when green geese are
      a-breeding.
   Dum. How follows that?
   Ber.   Fit in his place and time.
   Dum. In reason nothing.
   Ber.   Something then, in rime.
   King. Berowne is like an envious sneaping
      frost   100
That bites the first-born infants of the spring.
   Ber. Well, say I am: why should proud sum-
      mer boast
Before the birds have any cause to sing?
Why should I joy in an abortive birth?   104
   At Christmas I no more desire a rose
Than wish a snow in May's new-fangled mirth;
   But like of each thing that in season grows.
So you, to study now it is too late,   108
Climb o'er the house to unlock the little gate.
   King. Well, sit you out: go home, Berowne:
      adieu!
   Ber. No, my good lord; I have sworn to stay
      with you:
And though I have for barbarism spoke more
   Than for that angel knowledge you can
      say,   113
Yet confident I'll keep to what I swore,
   And bide the penance of each three years' day.
Give me the paper; let me read the same;   116
And to the strict'st decrees I'll write my name.
   King. How well this yielding rescues thee
      from shame!
   Ber. Item, *That no woman shall come with-*
in a mile of my court. Hath this been pro-
claimed?   121
   Long. Four days ago.
   Ber. Let's see the penalty. *On pain of losing*
her tongue. Who devised this penalty?   124
   Long. Marry, that did I.
   Ber.   Sweet lord, and why?
   Long. To fright them hence with that dread
      penalty.
   Ber. A dangerous law against gentility!   127
   Item. *If any man be seen to talk with a wo-*

man within the term of three years, he shall
endure such public shame as the rest of the
court can possibly devise.
This article, my liege, yourself must break; 132
   For well you know here comes in embassy
The French king's daughter with yourself to
      speak—
   A maid of grace and complete majesty—
About surrender up of Aquitaine   136
   To her decrepit, sick, and bed-rid father:
Therefore this article is made in vain,
   Or vainly comes th' admired princess hither.
   King. What say you, lords? why, this was
      quite forgot.   140
   Ber. So study evermore is overshot:
While it doth study to have what it would,
It doth forget to do the thing it should;
And when it hath the thing it hunteth most,
'Tis won as towns with fire; so won, so lost. 145
   King. We must of force dispense with this
      decree;
She must lie here on mere necessity.
   Ber. Necessity will make us all forsworn 148
   Three thousand times within this three years'
      space;
For every man with his affects is born,
   Not by might master'd, but by special grace.
If I break faith this word shall speak for me,
I am forsworn 'on mere necessity.'   153
So to the laws at large I write my name:
                              [*Subscribes.*
   And he that breaks them in the least degree
Stands in attainder of eternal shame: 156
   Suggestions are to others as to me;
But I believe, although I seem so loath,
I am the last that will last keep his oath.
But is there no quick recreation granted?   160
   King. Ay, that there is. Our court, you know,
      is haunted
With a refined traveller of Spain;
   A man in all the world's new fashion planted,
That hath a mint of phrases in his brain; 164
One whom the music of his own vain tongue
   Doth ravish like enchanting harmony;
A man of complements, whom right and wrong
   Have chose as umpire of their mutiny: 168
This child of fancy, that Armado hight,
   For interim to our studies shall relate
In high-born words the worth of many a knight
   From tawny Spain lost in the world's debate.
How you delight, my lords, I know not, I; 173
But, I protest, I love to hear him lie,
And I will use him for my minstrelsy.
   Ber. Armado is a most illustrious wight, 176
A man of fire-new words, fashion's own
      knight.
   Long. Costard the swain and he shall be our
      sport;
And, so to study, three years is but short.

Enter DULL, *with a letter, and* COSTARD.

   Dull. Which is the duke's own person? 180
   Ber. This, fellow. What wouldst?
   Dull. I myself reprehend his own person, for
I am his Grace's tharborough: but I would see
his own person in flesh and blood.   184

Ber. This is he.

Dull. Signior Arm—Arm—commends you. There's villany abroad: this letter will tell you more.   188

Cost. Sir, the contempts thereof are as touching me.

King. A letter from the magnificent Armado.

Ber. How long soever the matter, I hope in God for high words.   193

Long. A high hope for a low heaven: God grant us patience!

Ber. To hear, or forbear laughing?   196

Long. To hear meekly, sir, and to laugh moderately; or to forbear both.

Ber. Well, sir, be it as the style shall give us cause to climb in the merriness.   200

Cost. The matter is to me, sir, as concerning Jaquenetta. The manner of it is, I was taken with the manner.

Ber. In what manner?   204

Cost. In manner and form following, sir; all those three: I was seen with her in the manor-house, sitting with her upon the form, and taken following her into the park; which, put together, is, in manner and form following. Now, sir, for the manner,—it is the manner of a man to speak to a woman, for the form,—in some form.

Ber. For the following, sir?   212

Cost. As it shall follow in my correction; and God defend the right!

King. Will you hear this letter with attention?

Ber. As we would hear an oracle.   216

Cost. Such is the simplicity of man to hearken after the flesh.

King. *Great deputy, the welkin's vicegerent, and sole dominator of Navarre, my soul's earth's God, and body's fostering patron,*   221

Cost. Not a word of Costard yet.

King. *So it is,*—

Cost. It may be so; but if he say it is so, he is, in telling true, but so.—   225

King. Peace!

Cost. Be to me and every man that dares not fight.   228

King. No words!

Cost. Of other men's secrets, I beseech you.

King. *So it is, besieged with sable-coloured melancholy, I did commend the black-oppressing humour to the most wholesome physic of thy health-giving air; and, as I am a gentleman, betook myself to walk. The time when? About the sixth hour; when beasts most graze, birds best peck, and men sit down to that nourishment which is called supper: so much for the time when. Now for the ground which; which, I mean, I walked upon: it is ycleped thy park. Then for the place where; where, I mean, I did encounter that most obscene and preposterous event, that draweth from my snow-white pen the ebon-coloured ink, which here thou viewest, beholdest, surveyest, or seest. But to the place where, it standeth north-north-east and by east from the west corner of thy curious-knotted garden: there did I see that low-spirited swain, that base minnow of thy mirth,—*   249

Cost. Me.

King. *that unlettered small-knowing soul,—*

Cost. Me.   251

King. *that shallow vessel,—*

Cost. Still me.

King. *which, as I remember, hight Costard,—*   256

Cost. O me.

King. *sorted and consorted, contrary to thy established proclaimed edict and continent canon, with—with,—O! with but with this passion to say wherewith,—*

Cost. With a wench.   262

King. *with a child of our grandmother Eve, a female; or, for thy more sweet understanding, a woman. Him, I,—as my ever-esteemed duty pricks me on,—have sent to thee, to receive the meed of punishment, by thy sweet Grace's officer, Antony Dull; a man of good repute, carriage, bearing, and estimation.* 269

Dull. Me, an't please you; I am Antony Dull.

King. *For Jaquenetta,—so is the weaker vessel called which I apprehended with the aforesaid swain,—I keep her as a vessel of thy law's fury; and shall, at the least of thy sweet notice, bring her to trial. Thine, in all compliments of devoted and heart-burning heat of duty,*   276

DON ADRIANO DE ARMADO.

Ber. This is not so well as I looked for, but the best that ever I heard.

King. Ay, the best for the worst. But, sirrah, what say you to this?   280

Cost. Sir, I confess the wench.

King. Did you hear the proclamation?

Cost. I do confess much of the hearing it, but little of the marking of it.   284

King. It was proclaimed a year's imprisonment to be taken with a wench.

Cost. I was taken with none, sir: I was taken with a damosel.   288

King. Well, it was proclaimed 'damosel.'

Cost. This was no damosel neither, sir: she was a virgin.

King. It is so varied too; for it was proclaimed 'virgin.'   293

Cost. If it were, I deny her virginity: I was taken with a maid.

King. This maid will not serve your turn, sir.

Cost. This maid will serve my turn, sir.   297

King. Sir, I will pronounce your sentence: you shall fast a week with bran and water.

Cost. I had rather pray a month with mutton and porridge.   301

King. And Don Armado shall be your keeper. My Lord Berowne, see him deliver'd o'er: And go we, lords, to put in practice that   304 Which each to other hath so strongly sworn.

[*Exeunt* KING, LONGAVILLE, *and* DUMAINE.

Ber. I'll lay my head to any good man's hat, These oaths and laws will prove an idle scorn. Sirrah, come on.   308

Cost. I suffer for the truth, sir: for true it is I was taken with Jaquenetta, and Jaquenetta is a true girl; and therefore welcome the sour cup of prosperity! Affliction may one day smile again; and till then, sit thee down, sorrow! [*Exeunt.*

SCENE II.—*The Same.*

Enter ARMADO *and* MOTH.

Arm. Boy, what sign is it when a man of great spirit grows melancholy?

Moth. A great sign, sir, that he will look sad.

Arm. Why, sadness is one and the self-same thing, dear imp.　5

Moth. No, no; O Lord, sir, no.

Arm. How canst thou part sadness and melancholy, my tender juvenal?　8

Moth. By a familiar demonstration of the working, my tough senior.

Arm. Why tough senior? why tough senior?

Moth. Why tender juvenal? why tender juvenal?　13

Arm. I spoke it, tender juvenal, as a congruent epitheton appertaining to thy young days, which we may nominate tender.　16

Moth. And I, tough senior, as an appertinent title to your old time, which we may name tough.

Arm. Pretty, and apt.

Moth. How mean you, sir? I pretty, and my saying apt? or I apt, and my saying pretty?　21

Arm. Thou pretty, because little.

Moth. Little pretty, because little. Wherefore apt?　24

Arm. And therefore apt, because quick.

Moth. Speak you this in my praise, master?

Arm. In thy condign praise.

Moth. I will praise an eel with the same praise.　29

Arm. What! that an eel is ingenious?

Moth. That an eel is quick.

Arm. I do say thou art quick in answers: thou heatest my blood.　33

Moth. I am answered, sir.

Arm. I love not to be crossed.

Moth. [*Aside.*] He speaks the mere contrary: crosses love not him.　37

Arm. I have promised to study three years with the duke.

Moth. You may do it in an hour, sir.　40

Arm. Impossible.

Moth. How many is one thrice told?

Arm. I am ill at reckoning; it fitteth the spirit of a tapster.　44

Moth. You are a gentleman and a gamester, sir.

Arm. I confess both: they are both the varnish of a complete man.　48

Moth. Then, I am sure you know how much the gross sum of deuce-ace amounts to.

Arm. It doth amount to one more than two.

Moth. Which the base vulgar do call three.

Arm. True.　53

Moth. Why, sir, is this such a piece of study? Now, here's three studied, ere you'll thrice wink; and how easy it is to put 'years' to the word 'three,' and study three years in two words, the dancing horse will tell you.

Arm. A most fine figure!

Moth. To prove you a cipher.　60

Arm. I will hereupon confess I am in love; and as it is base for a soldier to love, so am I in love with a base wench. If drawing my sword against the humour of affection would deliver me from the reprobate thought of it, I would take Desire prisoner, and ransom him to any French courtier for a new devised curtsy. I think scorn to sigh: methinks I should outswear Cupid. Comfort me, boy: what great men have been in love?　70

Moth. Hercules, master.

Arm. Most sweet Hercules! More authority, dear boy, name more; and, sweet my child, let them be men of good repute and carriage.　74

Moth. Samson, master: he was a man of good carriage, great carriage, for he carried the towngates on his back like a porter; and he was in love.

Arm. O well-knit Samson! strong-jointed Samson! I do excel thee in my rapier as much as thou didst me in carrying gates. I am in love too. Who was Samson's love, my dear Moth?

Moth. A woman, master.　82

Arm. Of what complexion?

Moth. Of all the four, or the three, or the two, or one of the four.

Arm. Tell me precisely of what complexion.

Moth. Of the sea-water green, sir.　87

Arm. Is that one of the four complexions?

Moth. As I have read, sir; and the best of them too.　90

Arm. Green indeed is the colour of lovers; but to have a love of that colour, methinks Samson had small reason for it. He surely affected her for her wit.　94

Moth. It was so, sir, for she had a green wit.

Arm. My love is most immaculate white and red.

Moth. Most maculate thoughts, master, are masked under such colours.　99

Arm. Define, define, well-educated infant.

Moth. My father's wit, and my mother's tongue, assist me!

Arm. Sweet invocation of a child; most pretty and pathetical!　104

Moth.　If she be made of white and red,
　　　Her faults will ne'er be known,
　　For blushing cheeks by faults are bred,
　　　And fears by pale white shown:　108
　　Then if she fear, or be to blame,
　　　By this you shall not know,
　　For still her cheeks possess the same
　　　Which native she doth owe.　112

A dangerous rime, master, against the reason of white and red.

Arm. Is there not a ballad, boy, of the King and the Beggar?　116

Moth. The world was very guilty of such a ballad some three ages since; but I think now 'tis not to be found; or, if it were, it would neither serve for the writing nor the tune.　120

Arm. I will have that subject newly writ o'er, that I may example my digression by some mighty precedent. Boy, I do love that country girl that I took in the park with the rational hind Costard: she deserves well.　125

Moth. [*Aside.*] To be whipped; and yet a better love than my master.

Arm. Sing, boy: my spirit grows heavy in love.　129

Moth. And that's great marvel, loving a light wench.

Arm. I say, sing.   132

Moth. Forbear till this company be past.

Enter DULL, COSTARD, *and* JAQUENETTA.

Dull. Sir, the duke's pleasure is, that you keep Costard safe: and you must let him take no delight nor no penance, but a' must fast three days a week. For this damsel, I must keep her at the park; she is allowed for the day-woman. Fare you well.   139

Arm. I do betray myself with blushing. Maid!

Jaq. Man?

Arm. I will visit thee at the lodge.

Jaq. That's hereby.

Arm. I know where it is situate.   144

Jaq. Lord, how wise you are!

Arm. I will tell thee wonders.

Jaq. With that face?

Arm. I love thee.   148

Jaq. So I heard you say.

Arm. And so farewell.

Jaq. Fair weather after you!

Dull. Come, Jaquenetta, away!   152

[*Exeunt* DULL *and* JAQUENETTA.

Arm. Villain, thou shalt fast for thy offences ere thou be pardoned.

Cost. Well, sir, I hope, when I do it, I shall do it on a full stomach.   156

Arm. Thou shalt be heavily punished.

Cost. I am more bound to you than your fellows, for they are but lightly rewarded. 159

Arm. Take away this villain: shut him up.

Moth. Come, you transgressing slave: away!

Cost. Let me not be pent up, sir: I will fast, being loose.   163

Moth. No, sir; that were fast and loose: thou shalt to prison.

Cost. Well, if ever I do see the merry days of desolation that I have seen, some shall see—

Moth. What shall some see?   168

Cost. Nay, nothing, Master Moth, but what they look upon. It is not for prisoners to be too silent in their words; and therefore I will say nothing: I thank God I have as little patience as another man, and therefore I can be quiet.   [*Exeunt* MOTH *and* COSTARD.

Arm. I do affect the very ground, which is base, where her shoe, which is baser, guided by her foot, which is basest, doth tread. I shall be forsworn,—which is a great argument of falsehood,—if I love. And how can that be true love which is falsely attempted? Love is a familiar; Love is a devil: there is no evil angel but Love. Yet was Samson so tempted, and he had an excellent strength; yet was Solomon so seduced, and he had a very good wit. Cupid's butt-shaft is too hard for Hercules' club, and therefore too much odds for a Spaniard's rapier. The first and second clause will not serve my turn; the passado he respects not, the duello he regards not: his disgrace is to be called boy, but his glory is, to subdue men. Adieu, valour! rust, rapier! be still, drum! for your manager is in love; yea, he loveth. Assist me some extemporal god of rime, for I am sure I shall turn sonneter. Devise, wit; write, pen; for I am for whole volumes in folio.   [*Exit*

ACT II

SCENE I.—*The* KING OF NAVARRE'S *Park. A Pavilion and Tents at a distance.*

Enter the PRINCESS *of France,* ROSALINE, MARIA, KATHARINE, BOYET, Lords, *and other* Attendants.

Boyet. Now, madam, summon up your dearest spirits:
Consider whom the king your father sends,
To whom he sends, and what's his embassy:
Yourself, held precious in the world's esteem,
To parley with the sole inheritor
Of all perfections that a man may owe,
Matchless Navarre; the plea of no less weight
Than Aquitaine, a dowry for a queen.   8
Be now as prodigal of all dear grace
As Nature was in making graces dear
When she did starve the general world beside,
And prodigally gave them all to you.   12

Prin. Good Lord Boyet, my beauty, though but mean,
Needs not the painted flourish of your praise:
Beauty is bought by judgment of the eye,
Not utter'd by base sale of chapmen's tongues.
I am less proud to hear you tell my worth 17
Than you much willing to be counted wise
In spending your wit in the praise of mine.
But now to task the tasker: good Boyet,   20
You are not ignorant, all-telling fame
Doth noise abroad, Navarre hath made a vow,
Till painful study shall out-wear three years,
No woman may approach his silent court: 24
Therefore to us seemth it a needful course,
Before we enter his forbidden gates,
To know his pleasure; and in that behalf,
Bold of your worthiness, we single you   28
As our best-moving fair solicitor.
Tell him, the daughter of the King of France,
On serious business, craving quick dispatch,
Importunes personal conference with his Grace.
Haste, signify so much; while we attend,   33
Like humble-visag'd suitors, his high will.

Boyet. Proud of employment, willingly I go.

Prin. All pride is willing pride, and yours is so.   [*Exit* BOYET.
Who are the votaries, my loving lords,   37
That are vow-fellows with this virtuous duke?

First Lord. Lord Longaville is one.

Prin.   Know you the man?

Mar. I know him, madam: at a marriage feast,   40
Between Lord Perigort and the beauteous heir
Of Jacques Falconbridge, solemnized
In Normandy, saw I this Longaville.
A man of sovereign parts he is esteem'd;   44
Well fitted in the arts, glorious in arms:
Nothing becomes him ill that he would well.
The only soil of his fair virtue's gloss,—
If virtue's gloss will stain with any soil,— 48
Is a sharp wit match'd with too blunt a will;

Whose edge hath power to cut, whose will still
wills
It should none spare that come within his power.
Prin. Some merry mocking lord, belike; is 't
so? 52
Mar. They say so most that most his humours
know.
Prin. Such short-liv'd wits do wither as they
grow.
Who are the rest?
Kath. The young Dumaine, a well-accom-
plish'd youth, 56
Of all that virtue love for virtue lov'd:
Most power to do most harm, least knowing ill,
For he hath wit to make an ill shape good,
And shape to win grace though he had no wit.
I saw him at the Duke Alençon's once; 61
And much too little of that good I saw
Is my report to his great worthiness.
Ros. Another of these students at that time
Was there with him, if I have heard a truth: 65
Berowne they call him; but a merrier man,
Within the limit of becoming mirth,
I never spent an hour's talk withal. 68
His eye begets occasion for his wit;
For every object that the one doth catch
The other turns to a mirth-moving jest,
Which his fair tongue, conceit's expositor, 72
Delivers in such apt and gracious words,
That aged ears play truant at his tales,
And younger hearings are quite ravished;
So sweet and voluble is his discourse. 76
Prin. God bless my ladies! are they all in
love,
That every one her own hath garnished
With such bedecking ornaments of praise?
First Lord. Here comes Boyet.

Re-enter BOYET.

Prin. Now, what admittance, lord?
Boyet. Navarre had notice of your fair ap-
proach; 81
And he and his competitors in oath
Were all address'd to meet you, gentle lady,
Before I came. Marry, thus much I have learnt;
He rather means to lodge you in the field, 85
Like one that comes here to besiege his court,
Than seek a dispensation for his oath,
To let you enter his unpeeled house. 88
Here comes Navarre. [*The Ladies mask.*

Enter KING, LONGAVILLE, DUMAINE, BEROWNE,
and Attendants.

King. Fair princess, welcome to the court of
Navarre.
Prin. 'Fair,' I give you back again; and
'welcome' I have not yet: the roof of this court
is too high to be yours, and welcome to the wide
fields too base to be mine.
King. You shall be welcome, madam, to my
court.
Prin. I will be welcome, then: conduct me
thither. 96
King. Hear me, dear lady; I have sworn an
oath.

Prin. Our Lady help my lord! he'll be for-
sworn.
King. Not for the world, fair madam, by my
will.
Prin. Why, will shall break it; will, and no-
thing else. 100
King. Your ladyship is ignorant what it is.
Prin. Were my lord so, his ignorance were
wise,
Where now his knowledge must prove igno-
rance.
I hear your grace hath sworn out house-keeping:
'Tis deadly sin to keep that oath, my lord, 105
And sin to break it.
But pardon me, I am too sudden-bold:
To teach a teacher ill beseemeth me. 108
Vouchsafe to read the purpose of my coming,
And suddenly resolve me in my suit.
[*Gives a paper.*
King. Madam, I will, if suddenly I may.
Prin. You will the sooner that I were away,
For you'll prove perjur'd if you make me
stay. 113
Ber. Did not I dance with you in Brabant
once?
Ros. Did not I dance with you in Brabant
once?
Ber. I know you did.
Ros. How needless was it then 116
To ask the question!
Ber. You must not be so quick.
Ros. 'Tis 'long of you that spur me with such
questions.
Ber. Your wit's too hot, it speeds too fast,
'twill tire.
Ros. Not till it leave the rider in the mire.
Ber. What time o' day? 121
Ros. The hour that fools should ask.
Ber. Now fair befall your mask!
Ros. Fair fall the face it covers! 124
Ber. And send you many lovers!
Ros. Amen, so you be none.
Ber. Nay, then I will be gone. 127
King. Madam, your father here doth intimate
The payment of a hundred thousand crowns;
Being but the one half of an entire sum
Disbursed by my father in his wars.
But say that he, or we,—as neither have,— 132
Receiv'd that sum, yet there remains unpaid
A hundred thousand more; in surety of the
which,
One part of Aquitaine is bound to us,
Although not valu'd to the money's worth. 136
If then the king your father will restore
But that one half which is unsatisfied,
We will give up our right in Aquitaine,
And hold fair friendship with his majesty. 140
But that it seems, he little purposeth,
For here he doth demand to have repaid
A hundred thousand crowns; and not demands,
On payment of a hundred thousand crowns,
To have his title live in Aquitaine; 145
Which we much rather had depart withal,
And have the money by our father lent,
Than Aquitaine, so gelded as it is. 148
Dear princess, were not his requests so far

From reason's yielding, your fair self should
make
A yielding 'gainst some reason in my breast,
And go well satisfied to France again.   152
Prin. You do the king my father too much
wrong
And wrong the reputation of your name,
In so unseeming to confess receipt
Of that which hath so faithfully been paid. 156
King. I do protest I never heard of it;
And if you prove it, I'll repay it back
Or yield up Aquitaine.
Prin.   We arrest your word.
Boyet, you can produce acquittances   160
For such a sum from special officers
Of Charles his father.
King.   Satisfy me so.
Boyet. So please your Grace, the packet is not
come
Where that and other specialties are bound: 164
To-morrow you shall have a sight of them.
King. It shall suffice me: at which interview
All liberal reason I will yield unto.
Meantime, receive such welcome at my hand 168
As honour, without breach of honour, may
Make tender of to thy true worthiness.
You may not come, fair princess, in my gates;
But here without you shall be so receiv'd,   172
As you shall deem yourself lodg'd in my heart,
Though so denied fair harbour in my house.
Your own good thoughts excuse me, and fare-
well:
To-morrow shall we visit you again.   176
Prin. Sweet health and fair desires consort
your Grace!
King. Thy own wish wish I thee in every
place!   [*Exeunt* KING *and his Train.*
Ber. Lady, I will commend you to mine own
heart.
Ros. Pray you, do my commendations; I
would be glad to see it.   180
Ber. I would you heard it groan.
Ros. Is the fool sick?
Ber. Sick at the heart.
Ros. Alack! let it blood.   184
Ber. Would that do it good?
Ros. My physic says, 'ay.'
Ber. Will you prick't with your eye?
Ros. No point, with my knife.   188
Ber. Now, God save thy life!
Ros. And yours from long living!
Ber. I cannot stay thanksgiving. [*Retiring.*
Dum. Sir, I pray you, a word: what lady is
that same?   192
Boyet. The heir of Alençon, Katharine her
name.
Dum. A gallant lady. Monsieur, fare you
well.   [*Exit.*
Long. I beseech you a word: what is she in
the white?
Boyet. A woman sometimes, an you saw her
in the light.   196
Long. Perchance light in the light. I desire
her name.
Boyet. She hath but one for herself; to desire
that, were a shame.

Long. Pray you, sir, whose daughter?
Boyet. Her mother's, I have heard.   200
Long. God's blessing on your beard!
Boyet. Good sir, be not offended.
She is an heir of Falconbridge.
Long. Nay, my choler is ended.   204
She is a most sweet lady.
Boyet. Not unlike, sir; that may be.
                        [*Exit* LONGAVILLE.
Ber. What's her name, in the cap?
Boyet. Rosaline, by good hap.   208
Ber. Is she wedded or no?
Boyet. To her will, sir, or so.
Ber. You are welcome, sir. Adieu.
Boyet. Farewell to me, sir, and welcome to
you.   [*Exit* BEROWNE.—*Ladies unmask.*
Mar. That last is Berowne, the merry mad-
cap lord: 213
Not a word with him but a jest.
Boyet.   And every jest but a word.
Prin. It was well done of you to take him at
his word.
Boyet. I was as willing to grapple, as he was
to board.   216
Mar. Two hot sheeps, marry!
Boyet.   And wherefore not ships?
No sheep, sweet lamb, unless we feed on your
lips.
Mar. You sheep, and I pasture: shall that
finish the jest?
Boyet. So you grant pasture for me.
                        [*Offering to kiss her.*
Mar.   Not so, gentle beast. 220
My lips are no common, though several they be.
Boyet. Belonging to whom?
Mar.   To my fortunes and me.
Prin. Good wits will be jangling; but, gentles,
agree.
This civil war of wits were much better us'd 224
On Navarre and his book-men, for here 'tis
abus'd.
Boyet. If my observation,—which very sel-
dom lies,—
By the heart's still rhetoric disclosed with eyes,
Deceive me not now, Navarre is infected. 228
Prin. With what?
Boyet. With that which we lovers entitle
affected.
Prin. Your reason.
Boyet. Why, all his behaviours did make
their retire   232
To the court of his eye, peeping thorough desire;
His heart, like an agate, with your print im-
press'd,
Proud with his form, in his eye pride express'd:
His tongue, all impatient to speak and not see,
Did stumble with haste in his eyesight to be;
All senses to that sense did make their repair,
To feel only looking on fairest of fair,
Methought all his senses were lock'd in his eye,
As jewels in crystal for some prince to buy; 241
Who, tend'ring their own worth from where they
were glass'd,
Did point you to buy them, along as you pass'd.
His face's own margent did quote such amazes,
That all eyes saw his eyes enchanted with gazes.

'll give you Aquitaine, and all that is his, 246
An' you give him for my sake but one loving
kiss.
Prin. Come to our pavilion: Boyet is dispos'd.
Boyet. But to speak that in words which his
eye hath disclos'd.
only have made a mouth of his eye,
By adding a tongue which I know will not lie.
Ros. Thou art an old love-monger, and
speak'st skilfully.   252
Mar. He is Cupid's grandfather and learns
news of him.
Ros. Then was Venus like her mother, for
her father is but grim.
Boyet. Do you hear, my mad wenches?
Mar.   No.
Boyet.   What, then, do you see?
Ros. Ay, our way to be gone.
Boyet.   You are too hard for me. 256
                    [*Exeunt.*

ACT III

Scene I.—*The* King of Navarre's *Park.*

Enter Armado *and* Moth.

Arm. Warble, child; make passionate my
sense of hearing.
Moth. [*Singing.*] Concolinel,—   3
Arm. Sweet air! Go, tenderness of years;
take this key, give enlargement to the swain,
bring him festinately hither; I must employ him
in a letter to my love.
Moth. Master, will you win your love with a
French brawl?   9
Arm. How meanest thou? brawling in
French?
Moth. No, my complete master; but to jig off
a tune at the tongue's end, canary to it with your
feet, humour it with turning up your eyelids,
sigh a note and sing a note, sometime through
the throat, as if you swallowed love by singing
love, sometime through the nose, as if you snuffed
up love by smelling love; with your hat pent-
house-like o'er the shop of your eyes; with your
arms crossed on your thin belly-doublet like a
rabbit on a spit; or your hands in your pocket
like a man after the old painting; and keep not
too long in one tune, but a snip and away. These
are complements, these are humours, these betray nice wenches, that would be betrayed without these; and make them men of note,—do you
note me?—that most are affected to these. 27
Arm. How hast thou purchased this experience?
Moth. By my penny of observation.
Arm. But O—but O,—
Moth. 'The hobby-horse is forgot.'   32
Arm. Callest thou my love 'hobby-horse?'
Moth. No, master; the hobby-horse is but a
colt, and your love perhaps, a hackney. But
have you forgot your love?   36
Arm. Almost I had.
Moth. Negligent student! learn her by heart.
Arm. By heart, and in heart, boy.

Moth. And out of heart, master: all those
three I will prove.   41
Arm. What wilt thou prove?
Moth. A man, if I live; and this, by, in, and
without, upon the instant: by heart you love
her, because your heart cannot come by her; in
heart you love her, because your heart is in love
with her; and out of heart you love her, being
out of heart that you cannot enjoy her.   48
Arm. I am all these three.
Moth. And three times as much more, and
yet nothing at all.
Arm. Fetch hither the swain: he must carry
me a letter.   53
Moth. A message well sympathized: a horse
to be ambassador for an ass.
Arm. Ha, ha! what sayest thou?   56
Moth. Marry, sir, you must send the ass upon
the horse, for he is very slow-gaited. But I go.
Arm. The way is but short: away!
Moth. As swift as lead, sir.   60
Arm. Thy meaning, pretty ingenious?
Is not lead a metal heavy, dull, and slow?
Moth. *Minime,* honest master; or rather,
master, no.
Arm. I say, lead is slow.
Moth.   You are too swift, sir, to say so:
Is that lead slow which is fir'd from a gun? 65
Arm. Sweet smoke of rhetoric!
He reputes me a cannon; and the bullet, that's
he:
I shoot thee at the swain.
Moth.   Thump then, and I flee. [*Exit.*
Arm. A most acute juvenal; volable and free
of grace!   69
By thy favour, sweet welkin, I must sigh in thy
face:
Most rude melancholy, valour gives thee place.
My herald is return'd.   72

Re-enter Moth *with* Costard.

Moth. A wonder, master! here's a costard
broken in a shin.
Arm. Some enigma, some riddle: come, thy
l'envoy; begin.
Cost. No egma, no riddle, no *l'envoy;* no salve
in the mail, sir. O! sir, plantain, a plain plantain: no *l'envoy,* no *l'envoy:* no salve, sir, but a
plantain.   78
Arm. By virtue, thou enforcest laughter; thy
silly thought, my spleen; the heaving of my
lungs provokes me to ridiculous smiling: O!
pardon me, my stars. Doth the inconsiderate
take salve for *l'envoy,* and the word *l'envoy* for
a salve?   84
Moth. Do the wise think them other? is not
l'envoy a salve?
Arm. No, page: it is an epilogue or discourse,
to make plain
Some obscure precedence that hath tofore been
sain.   88
I will example it:
    The fox, the ape, and the humble-bee
    Were still at odds, being but three.
There's the moral. Now the *l'envoy.*   92

Moth. I will add the *l'envoy.* Say the moral again.

Arm. The fox, the ape, and the humble-bee,
 Were still at odds, being but three. 96

Moth. Until the goose came out of door,
 And stay'd the odds by adding four.
Now will I begin your moral, and do you follow with my *l'envoy.* 100
 The fox, the ape, and the humble-bee,
 Were still at odds, being but three.

Arm. Until the goose came out of door,
 Staying the odds by adding four. 104

Moth. A good *l'envoy,* ending in the goose. Would you desire more?

Cost. The boy hath sold him a bargain, a goose, that's flat.
Sir, your pennyworth is good an your goose be fat. 108
To sell a bargain well is as cunning as fast and loose:
Let me see; a fat *l'envoy*; ay, that's a fat goose.

Arm. Come hither, come hither. How did this argument begin?

Moth. By saying that a costard was broken in a shin. 112
Then call'd you for the *l'envoy.*

Cost. True, and I for a plantain: thus came your argument in;
Then the boy's fat *l'envoy,* the goose that you bought;
And he ended the market. 116

Arm. But tell me; how was there a costard broken in a shin?

Moth. I will tell you sensibly.

Cost. Thou hast no feeling of it, Moth: I will speak the *l'envoy*: 121
I, Costard, running out, that was safely within,
Fell over the threshold and broke my shin.

Arm. We will talk no more of this matter. 124

Cost. Till there be more matter in the shin.

Arm. Sirrah Costard, I will enfranchise thee.

Cost. O! marry me to one Frances: I smell some *l'envoy,* some goose, in this. 128

Arm. By my sweet soul, I mean setting thee at liberty, enfreedoming thy person: thou wert immured, restrained, captivated, bound.

Cost. True, true, and now you will be my purgation and let me loose. 133

Arm. I give thee thy liberty, set thee from durance; and in lieu thereof, impose upon thee nothing but this:—[*Giving a letter.*] Bear this significant to the country maid Jaquenetta. [*Giving money.*] There is remuneration; for the best ward of mine honour is rewarding my dependents. Moth, follow. [*Exit.*

Moth. Like the sequel, I. Signior Costard, adieu. 141

Cost. My sweet ounce of man's flesh! my incony Jew! [*Exit* MOTH.
Now will I look to his remuneration. Remuneration! O! that's the Latin word for three farthings: three farthings, remuneration. 'What's the price of this inkle?' 'One penny.' 'No, I'll give you a remuneration:' why, it carries it. Remuneration! why, it is a fairer name than

French crown. I will never buy and sell out o this word.

Enter BEROWNE.

Ber. O! my good knave Costard, exceedingly well met. 153

Cost. Pray you, sir, how much carnation riband may a man buy for a remuneration?

Ber. What is a remuneration?

Cost. Marry, sir, halfpenny farthing. 156

Ber. Why then, three-farthing-worth of silk

Cost. I thank your worship. God be wi you!

Ber. Stay, slave; I must employ thee: 160
As thou wilt win my favour, good my knave,
Do one thing for me that I shall entreat.

Cost. When would you have it done, sir?

Ber. O, this afternoon. 164

Cost. Well, I will do it, sir! fare you well.

Ber. O, thou knowest not what it is.

Cost. I shall know, sir, when I have done it.

Ber. Why, villain, thou must know first. 168

Cost. I will come to your worship to-morrow morning.

Ber. It must be done this afternoon. Hark, slave, it is but this: 172
The princess comes to hunt here in the park,
And in her train there is a gentle lady;
When tongues speak sweetly, then they name her name,
And Rosaline they call her: ask for her 176
And to her white hand see thou do commend
This seal'd-up counsel. [*Gives him a shilling.*]
There's thy guerdon: go.

Cost. Gardon, O sweet gardon! better than remuneration; a 'leven-pence farthing better.
Most sweet gardon! I will do it, sir, in print.
Gardon! remuneration! [*Exit.*

Ber. And I,—
Forsooth, in love! I, that have been love's whip;
A very beadle to a humorous sigh; 185
A critic, nay, a night-watch constable,
A domineering pedant o'er the boy,
Than whom no mortal so magnificent! 188
This wimpled, whining, purblind, wayward boy,
This senior-junior, giant-dwarf, Dan Cupid;
Regent of love-rimes, lord of folded arms,
The anointed sovereign of sighs and groans, 192
Liege of all loiterers and malecontents,
Dread prince of plackets, king of codpieces,
Sole imperator and great general
Of trotting 'paritors: O my little heart! 196
And I to be a corporal of his field,
And wear his colours like a tumbler's hoop!
What I! I love! I sue! I seek a wife!
A woman that is like a German clock, 200
Still a-repairing, ever out of frame,
And never going aright, being a watch,
But being watch'd that it may still go right!
Nay, to be perjur'd, which is worst of all; 204
And, among three, to love the worst of all;
A wightly wanton with a velvet brow,
With two pitch balls stuck in her face for eyes;
Ay, and, by heaven, one that will do the deed 208
Though Argus were her eunuch and her guard:
And I to sigh for her! to watch for her!

To pray for her! Go to; it is a plague
That Cupid will impose for my neglect   212
Of his almighty dreadful little might.
Well, I will love, write, sigh, pray, sue, and
   groan:
Some men must love my lady, and some Joan.
                          [*Exit.*

ACT IV

SCENE I.—*The* KING OF NAVARRE'S *Park.*

Enter the PRINCESS, ROSALINE, MARIA, KATHA-
RINE, BOYET, Lords, Attendants, *and a*
Forester.

Prin. Was that the king, that spurr'd his
   horse so hard
Against the steep uprising of the hill?
  Boyet. I know not; but I think it was not he.
  Prin. Whoe'er a' was, a' show'd a mounting
   mind.   4
Well, lords, to-day we shall have our dispatch;
On Saturday we will return to France.
Then, forester, my friend, where is the bush
That we must stand and play the murderer in? 8
  For. Hereby, upon the edge of yonder cop-
   pice;
A stand where you may make the fairest shoot.
  Prin. I thank my beauty, I am fair that
   shoot,   11
And thereupon thou speak'st the fairest shoot.
  For. Pardon me, madam, for I meant not so.
  Prin. What, what? first praise me, and again
   say no?
O short-liv'd pride! Not fair? alack for woe!
  For. Yes, madam, fair.
  Prin.   Nay, never paint me now: 16
Where fair is not, praise cannot mend the brow.
Here, good my glass:—[*Gives money.*] Take
  this for telling true:
Fair payment for foul words is more than due.
  For. Nothing but fair is that which you in-
   herit.   20
  Prin. See, see! my beauty will be sav'd by
   merit.
O heresy in fair, fit for these days!
A giving hand, though foul, shall have fair
  praise.
But come, the bow: now mercy goes to kill, 24
And shooting well is then accounted ill.
Thus will I save my credit in the shoot:
Not wounding, pity would not let me do't;
If wounding, then it was to show my skill, 28
That more for praise than purpose meant to
  kill.
And out of question so it is sometimes,
Glory grows guilty of detested crimes,
When, for fame's sake, for praise, an outward
  part,   32
We bend to that the working of the heart;
As I for praise alone now seek to spill
The poor deer's blood, that my heart means no
  ill.
  Boyet. Do not curst wives hold that self-
   sovereignty   36
Only for praise' sake, when they strive to be
Lords o'er their lords?

  Prin. Only for praise; and praise we may
  afford
To any lady that subdues a lord.   40

Enter COSTARD.

  Boyet. Here comes a member of the common-
   wealth.
  Cost. God dig-you-den all! Pray you, which
is the head lady?
  Prin. Thou shalt know her, fellow, by the
rest that have no heads.   45
  Cost. Which is the greatest lady, the highest?
  Prin. The thickest, and the tallest.
  Cost. The thickest, and the tallest! it is so;
truth is truth.   48
An your waist, mistress, were as slender as my
  wit,
One o' these maids' girdles for your waist should
  be fit.
Are not you the chief woman? you are the
  thickest here.
  Prin. What's your will, sir? what's your will?
  Cost. I have a letter from Monsieur Berowne
to one Lady Rosaline.   53
  Prin. O! thy letter, thy letter; he's a good
  friend of mine.
Stand aside, good bearer. Boyet, you can carve;
Break up this capon.
  Boyet.   I am bound to serve. 56
This letter is mistook; it importeth none here:
It is writ to Jaquenetta.
  Prin.   We will read it, I swear.
Break the neck of the wax, and every one give
  ear.
  Boyet. By heaven, *that thou art fair, is most
infallible; true, that thou art beauteous; truth
itself, that thou art lovely. More fairer than
fair, beautiful than beauteous, truer than truth
itself, have commiseration on thy heroical vassal! The magnanimous and most illustrate
king Cophetua set eye upon the pernicious and
indubitate beggar Zenelophon, and he it was
that might rightly say* veni, vidi, vici; *which to
anatomize in the vulgar—O base and obscure
vulgar!—videlicet, he came, saw, and overcame:
he came, one; saw, two; overcame, three. Who
came? the king: Why did he come? to see: Why
did he see? to overcome: To whom came he? to
the beggar: What saw he? the beggar. Whom
overcame he? the beggar. The conclusion is
victory: on whose side? the king's; the captive
is enriched: on whose side? the beggar's. The
catastrophe is a nuptial: on whose side? the
king's, no, on both in one, or one in both. I am
the king, for so stands the comparison; thou
the beggar, for so witnesseth thy lowliness. Shall
I command thy love? I may: Shall I enforce
thy love? I could: Shall I entreat thy love? I
will. What shalt thou exchange for rags? robes;
for titles? titles; for thyself? me. Thus, expecting thy reply, I profane my lips on thy foot,
my eyes on thy picture, and my heart on thy
every part.*   88
    Thine, in the dearest design of Industry,
        DON ADRIANO DE ARMADO.

F

Thus dost thou hear the Nemean lion roar
'Gainst thee, thou lamb, that standest as his
  prey: 92
Submissive fall his princely feet before,
  And he from forage will incline to play.
But if thou strive, poor soul, what art thou
  then?
Food for his rage, repasture for his den. 96

  Prin. What plume of feathers is he that indited this letter?
What vane? what weathercock? did you ever hear better?
  Boyet. I am much deceiv'd but I remember the style.
  Prin. Else your memory is bad, going o'er it erewhile. 100
  Boyet. This Armado is a Spaniard, that keeps here in court;
A phantasime, a Monarcho, and one that makes sport
To the prince and his book-mates.
  Prin.   Thou, fellow, a word.
Who gave thee this letter?
  Cost.   I told you; my lord. 104
  Prin. To whom shouldst thou give it?
  Cost.   From my lord to my lady.
  Prin. From which lord, to which lady?
  Cost. From my lord Berowne, a good master of mine,
To a lady of France, that he call'd Rosaline.
  Prin. Thou hast mistaken his letter. Come, lords, away. 109
Here, sweet, put up this: 'twill be thine another day.   [*Exeunt* PRINCESS *and Train.*
  Boyet. Who is the suitor? who is the suitor?
  Ros.   Shall I teach you to know?
  Boyet. Ay, my continent of beauty.
  Ros.   Why, she that bears the bow.
Finely put off! 113
  Boyet. My lady goes to kill horns; but, if thou marry,
Hang me by the neck if horns that year miscarry.
Finely put on! 116
  Ros. Well then, I am the shooter.
  Boyet.   And who is your deer?
  Ros. If we choose by the horns, yourself: come not near.
Finely put on, indeed!
  Mar. You still wrangle with her, Boyet, and she strikes at the brow. 120
  Boyet. But she herself is hit lower: have I hit her now?
  Ros. Shall I come upon thee with an old saying, that was a man when King Pepin of France was a little boy, as touching the hit it? 124
  Boyet. So may I answer thee with one as old, that was a woman when Queen Guinever of Britain was a little wench, as touching the hit it. 128
  Ros.   *Thou canst not hit it, hit it, hit it,*
      Thou canst not hit it, my good man.
  Boyet.   *An I cannot, cannot, cannot,*
      An I cannot, another can. 132
      [*Exeunt* ROSALINE *and* KATHARINE.

  Cost. By my troth, most pleasant: how both did fit it!
  Mar. A mark marvellous well shot, for they both did hit it.
  Boyet. A mark! O! mark but that mark; a mark, says my lady!
Let the mark have a prick in't, to mete at, if it may be. 136
  Mar. Wide o' the bow hand! i' faith your hand is out.
  Cost. Indeed a' must shoot nearer, or he'll ne'er hit the clout.
  Boyet. An' if my hand be out, then belike your hand is in.
  Cost. Then will she get the upshoot by cleaving the pin. 140
  Mar. Come, come, you talk greasily; your lips grow foul.
  Cost. She's too hard for you at pricks, sir: challenge her to bowl.
  Boyet. I fear too much rubbing. Good night, my good owl.   [*Exeunt* BOYET *and* MARIA.
  Cost. By my soul, a swain! a most simple clown! 144
Lord, lord how the ladies and I have put him down!
O' my troth, most sweet jests! most incony vulgar wit!
When it comes so smoothly off, so obscenely, as it were, so fit,
Armado, o' the one side, O! a most dainty man,
To see him walk before a lady. and to bear her fan! 149
To see him kiss his hand! and how most sweetly a' will swear!
And his page o' t'other side, that handful of wit!
Ah! heavens, it is a most pathetical nit. 152
[*Shouting within.*] Sola, sola!   [*Exit running.*

SCENE II.—*The Same.*

Enter HOLOFERNES, SIR NATHANIEL, *and* DULL.

  Nath. Very reverend sport, truly: and done in the testimony of a good conscience.
  Hol. The deer was, as you know, *sanguis*, in blood; ripe as a pomewater, who now hangeth like a jewel in the ear of *cælo*, the sky, the welkin, the heaven; and anon falleth like a crab on the face of *terra*, the soil, the land, the earth. 7
  Nath. Truly, Master Holofernes, the epithets are sweetly varied, like a scholar at the least: but, sir, I assure ye, it was a buck of the first head.
  Hol. Sir Nathaniel, *haud credo.* 11
  Dull. 'Twas not a *haud credo*; 'twas a pricket.
  Hol. Most barbarous intimation! yet a kind of insinuation, as it were, *in via*, in way, of explication; *facere*, as it were, replication, or, rather, *ostentare*, to show, as it were, his inclination,—after his undressed, unpolished, uneducated, unpruned, untrained, or, rather, unlettered, or, rather est, unconfirmed fashion,—to insert again my *haud credo* for a deer. 20
  Dull. I said the deer was not a *haud credo*; 'twas a pricket.

Hol. Twice sod simplicity, *bis coctus!*
O! thou monster Ignorance, how deformed dost thou look!   24
Nath. Sir, he hath not fed of the dainties that are bred of a book;
he hath not eat paper, as it were; he hath not drunk ink: his intellect is not replenished; he is only an animal, only sensible in the duller parts:
And such barren plants are set before us, that we thankful should be,   29
Which we of taste and feeling are, for those parts that do fructify in us more than he;
For as it would ill become me to be vain, indiscreet, or a fool:
So, were there a patch set on learning, to see him in a school: 32
But, *omne bene*, say I; being of an old Father's mind,
Many can brook the weather that love not the wind.
Dull. You two are book-men: can you tell by your wit,
What was a month old at Cain's birth, that's not five weeks old as yet?   36
Hol. Dictynna, goodman Dull: Dictynna, goodman Dull.
Dull. What is Dictynna?
Nath. A title to Phœbe, to Luna, to the moon.
Hol. The moon was a month old when Adam was no more;   40
And raught not to five weeks when he came to five-score.
The allusion holds in the exchange.
Dull. 'Tis true indeed: the collusion holds in the exchange.
Hol. God comfort thy capacity! I say, the allusion holds in the exchange.   45
Dull. And I say the pollusion holds in the exchange, for the moon is never but a month old; and I say beside that 'twas a pricket that the princess killed.   49
Hol. Sir Nathaniel, will you hear an extemporal epitaph on the death of the deer? and, to humour the ignorant, I have call'd the deer the princess killed, a pricket.   53
Nath. *Perge*, good Master Holofernes, *perge*; so it shall please you to abrogate scurrility.
Hol. I will something affect the letter; for it argues facility.   57
The preyful princess pierc'd and prick'd a pretty pleasing pricket;
Some say a sore; but not a sore, till now made sore with shooting.
The dogs did yell; put L *to sore, then sorel jumps from thicket;*   60
Or pricket, sore, or else sorel; the people fall a hooting.
If sore be sore, then L *to sore makes fifty sores one sorel!*
Of one sore I *a hundred make, by adding but one more* L.
Nath. A rare talent!   64
Dull. [*Aside.*] If a talent be a claw, look how he claws him with a talent.
Hol. This is a gift that I have, simple, simple; a foolish extravagant spirit, full of forms, figures,

shapes, objects, ideas, motions, motions, revolutions: these are begot in the ventricle of memory, nourished in the womb of *pia mater*, and delivered upon the mellowing of occasion. But the gift is good in those in whom it is acute, and I am thankful for it.   74
Nath. Sir, I praise the Lord for you, and so may my parishioners; for their sons are well tutored by you, and their daughters profit very greatly under you: you are a good member of the commonwealth.   79
Hol. Mehercle! if their sons be ingenuous, they shall want no instruction; if their daughters be capable, I will put it to them. But, *vir sapit qui pauca loquitur.* A soul feminine saluteth us.

Enter JAQUENETTA *and* COSTARD.

Jaq. God give you good morrow, Master parson.
Hol. Master parson, *quasi* pers-on. An if one should be pierced, which is the one?
Cost. Marry, Master schoolmaster, he that is likest to a hogshead.   88
Hol. Piercing a hogshead! a good lustre of conceit in a turf of earth; fire enough for a flint, pearl enough for a swine: 'tis pretty; it is well.
Jaq. Good Master parson [*giving a letter to* NATHANIEL], be so good as read me this letter: it was given me by Costard, and sent me from Don Armado: I beseech you, read it.   95
Hol. Fauste, precor gelida quando pecus omne sub umbra Ruminat, and so forth. Ah! good old Mantuan. I may speak of thee as the traveller doth of Venice:
            —*Venetia, Venetia,*   100
            Chi non te vede, non te pretia.
Old Mantuan! old Mantuan! Who understandeth thee not, loves thee not. *Ut, re, sol, la, mi, fa.* Under pardon, sir, what are the contents? or, rather, as Horace says in his—What, my soul, verses?
Nath. Ay, sir, and very learned.
Hol. Let me hear a staff, a stanze, a verse: *lege, domine.*   109

Nath. If love make me forsworn, how shall I swear to love?
Ah! never faith could hold, if not to beauty vow'd;
Though to myself forsworn, to thee I'll faithful prove;
    Those thoughts to me were oaks, to thee like osiers bow'd.   113
Study his bias leaves and makes his book thine eyes,
    Where all those pleasures live that art would comprehend:
If knowledge be the mark, to know thee shall suffice.
    Well learned is that tongue that well can thee commend;   117
All ignorant that soul that sees thee without wonder;
    Which is to me some praise that I thy parts admire.
Thy eye Jove's lightning bears, thy voice his dreadful thunder,   120
    Which, not to anger bent, is music and sweet fire.
Celestial as thou art, O! pardon love this wrong,
That sings heaven's praise with such an earthly tongue!

Hol. You find not the apostrophas, and so miss the accent: let me supervise the canzonet. Here are only numbers ratified; but, for the elegancy, facility, and golden cadence of poesy, *caret.* Ovidius Naso was the man: and why, indeed, Naso, but for smelling out the odoriferous flowers of fancy, the jerks of invention? *Imitari* is nothing; so doth the hound his master, the ape his keeper, the 'tired horse his rider. But, damosella virgin, was this directed to you?

Jaq. Ay, sir; from one Monsieur Berowne, one of the strange queen's lords.   136

Hol. I will overglance the superscript. *To the snow-white hand of the most beauteous Lady Rosaline.* I will look again on the intellect of the letter, for the nomination of the party writing to the person written unto: *Your ladyship's, in all desired employment,* BEROWNE.— Sir Nathaniel, this Berowne is one of the votaries with the king; and here he hath framed a letter to a sequent of the stranger queen's, which, accidentally, or by the way of progression, hath miscarried. Trip and go, my sweet; deliver this paper into the royal hand of the king; it may concern much. Stay not thy compliment; I forgive thy duty: adieu.

Jaq. Good Costard, go with me. Sir, God save your life!   152

Cost. Have with thee, my girl.
          [*Exeunt* COSTARD *and* JAQUENETTA.

Nath. Sir, you have done this in the fear of God, very religiously; and, as a certain Father saith—   156

Hol. Sir, tell not me of the Father; I do fear colourable colours. But to return to the verses: did they please you, Sir Nathaniel?

Nath. Marvellous well for the pen.   160

Hol. I do dine to-day at the father's of a certain pupil of mine; where, if before repast it shall please you to gratify the table with a grace, I will, on my privilege I have with the parents of the foresaid child or pupil, undertake your *ben venuto*; where I will prove those verses to be very unlearned, neither savouring of poetry, wit, nor invention. I beseech your society.   168

Nath. And thank you too; for society—saith the text—is the happiness of life.

Hol. And, certes, the text most infallibly concludes it.—[*To* DULL.] Sir, I do invite you too: you shall not say me nay: *pauca verba.* Away! the gentles are at their game, and we will to our recreation.   [*Exeunt.*

SCENE III.—*The Same.*

Enter BEROWNE, *with a paper.*

Ber. The king he is hunting the deer; I am coursing myself: they have pitched a toil; I am toiling in a pitch,—pitch that defiles: defile! a foul word! Well, sit thee down, sorrow! for so they say the fool said, and so say I, and I the fool: well proved, wit! By the Lord, this love is as mad as Ajax: it kills sheep: it kills me, I a sheep: well proved again o' my side! I will not love; if I do, hang me; i' faith, I will not. O! but her eye,—by this light, but for her eye, I would not love her; yes, for her two eyes. Well, I do nothing in the world but lie, and lie in my throat. By heaven, I do love, and it hath

taught me to rime, and to be melancholy; and here is part of my rime, and here my melancholy. Well, she hath one o' my sonnets already: the clown bore it, the fool sent it, and the lady hath it: sweet clown, sweeter fool, sweetest lady! By the world, I would not care a pin if the other three were in. Here comes one with a paper: God give him grace to groan!   21
          [*Gets up into a tree.*

Enter the KING, *with a paper.*

King. Ah me!

Ber. [*Aside.*] Shot, by heaven! Proceed, sweet Cupid: thou hast thumped him with thy bird-bolt under the left pap. In faith, secrets!

King. So sweet a kiss the golden sun gives not
  To those fresh morning drops upon the rose,   28
As thy eye-beams, when their fresh rays have smote
  The night of dew that on my cheeks down flows:
Nor shines the silver moon one half so bright
  Through the transparent bosom of the deep,   32
As doth thy face through tears of mine give light;
  Thou shin'st in every tear that I do weep:
No drop but as a coach doth carry thee;
  So ridest thou triumphing in my woe.   36
Do but behold the tears that swell in me,
  And they thy glory through my grief will show:
But do not love thyself; then thou wilt keep
  My tears for glasses, and still make me weep.   40
O queen of queens! how far thou dost excel,
No thought can think, nor tongue of mortal tell.

How shall she know my griefs? I'll drop the paper:
Sweet leaves, shade folly. Who is he comes here?   [*Steps aside.*
What, Longaville! and reading! listen, ear.   45

Enter LONGAVILLE, *with a paper.*

Ber. Now, in thy likeness, one more fool appear!

Long. Ay me! I am forsworn.

Ber. Why, he comes in like a perjure, wearing papers.   48

King. In love, I hope: sweet fellowship in shame!

Ber. One drunkard loves another of the name.

Long. Am I the first that have been perjur'd so?

Ber. I could put thee in comfort: not by two that I know: 52
Thou mak'st the triumviry, the corner-cap of society,
The shape of love's Tyburn, that hangs up simplicity.

Long. I fear these stubborn lines lack power to move.
O sweet Maria, empress of my love!   56
These numbers will I tear, and write in prose.

Ber. O! rimes are guards on wanton Cupid's hose:
Disfigure not his slop.

Long.   This same shall go.

Did not the heavenly rhetoric of thine eye,   60
  'Gainst whom the world cannot hold argument,
Persuade my heart to this false perjury?
  Vows for thee broke deserve not punishment.

A woman I forswore; but I will prove,   64
  Thou being a goddess, I forswore not thee
My vow was earthly, thou a heavenly love;
  Thy grace, being gain'd, cures all disgrace in me.
Vows are but breath, and breath a vapour is: 68
  Then thou, fair sun, which on my earth dost shine,
Exhal'st this vapour-vow; in thee it is:
  If broken, then, it is no fault of mine:
If by me broke, what fool is not so wise   72
To lose an oath to win a paradise!

Ber. This is the liver-vein, which makes flesh
  a deity;
A green goose a goddess; pure, pure idolatry.
God amend us, God amend! we are much out
  o' the way.   76
  Long. By whom shall I send this?—Company! stay.   [*Steps aside.*
Ber. All hid, all hid; an old infant play.
Like a demi-god here sit I in the sky,
And wretched fools' secrets heedfully o'er-eye.
More sacks to the mill! O heavens! I have my
  wish.   81

Enter DUMAINE, *with a paper.*

Dumaine transform'd: four woodcocks in a
  dish!
  Dum. O most divine Kate!
  Ber. O most profane coxcomb!   84
  Dum. By heaven, the wonder of a mortal
  eye!
  Ber. By earth, she is but corporal; there you
  lie.
  Dum. Her amber hairs for foul have amber
  quoted.
  Ber. An amber-colour'd raven was well
  noted.   88
  Dum. As upright as the cedar.
  Ber.   Stoop, I say;
Her shoulder is with child.
  Dum.   As fair as day.
  Ber. Ay, as some days; but then no sun must
  shine.
  Dum. O! that I had my wish.
  Long.   And I had mine!   92
  King. And I mine too, good Lord!
  Ber. Amen, so I had mine. Is not that a
  good word?
  Dum. I would forget her; but a fever she
Reigns in my blood, and will remember'd be.   96
  Ber. A fever in your blood! why, then incision
Would let her out in saucers: sweet misprision!
  Dum. Once more I'll read the ode that I
  have writ.
  Ber. Once more I'll mark how love can vary
  wit.   100

Dum. On a day, alack the day!
    Love, whose month is ever May,
    Spied a blossom passing fair
    Playing in the wanton air: 104
    Through the velvet leaves the wind,
    All unseen, 'gan passage find;
    That the lover, sick to death,
    Wish'd himself the heaven's breath.   108
    Air, quoth he, thy cheeks may blow;
    Air, would I might triumph so!
    But alack! my hand is sworn
    Ne'er to pluck thee from thy thorn: 112

    Vow, alack! for youth unmeet,
    Youth so apt to pluck a sweet.
    Do not call it sin in me,
    That I am forsworn for thee;   116
    Thou for whom e'en Jove would swear
    Juno but an Ethiop were;
    And deny himself for Jove,
    Turning mortal for thy love.   120

This will I send, and something else more plain,
That shall express my true love's fasting pain.
O! would the King, Berowne, and Longaville
Were lovers too. Ill, to example ill,   124
Would from my forehead wipe a perjur'd note;
For none offend where all alike do dote.
  Long. [*Advancing.*] Dumaine, thy love is far
  from charity,
That in love's grief desir'st society: 128
You may look pale, but I should blush, I know,
To be o'erheard and taken napping so.
  King. [*Advancing.*] Come, sir, you blush: as
  his your case is such;
You chide at him, offending twice as much: 132
You do not love Maria; Longaville
Did never sonnet for her sake compile,
Nor never lay his wreathed arms athwart
His loving bosom to keep down his heart.   136
I have been closely shrouded in this bush,
And mark'd you both, and for you both did
  blush.
I heard your guilty rimes, observ'd your fashion,
Saw sighs reek from you, noted well your
  passion: 140
Ay me! says one; O Jove! the other cries;
One, her hairs were gold, crystal the other's
  eyes:
[*To* LONGAVILLE.] You would for paradise break
  faith and troth;
[*To* DUMAINE.] And Jove, for your love, would
  infringe an oath.   144
What will Berowne say, when that he shall hear
A faith infringed, which such zeal did swear?
How will he scorn! how will he spend his wit!
How will he triumph, leap and laugh at it!   148
For all the wealth that ever I did see,
I would not have him know so much by me.
  Ber. Now step I forth to whip hypocrisy.
              [*Descends from the tree.*
Ah! good my liege, I pray thee, pardon me: 152
Good heart! what grace hast thou, thus to reprove
These worms for loving, that art most in love?
Your eyes do make no coaches; in your tears
There is no certain princess that appears: 156
You'll not be perjur'd, 'tis a hateful thing:
Tush! none but minstrels like of sonneting.
But are you not asham'd? nay; are you not,
All three of you, to be thus much o'ershot?   160
You found his mote; the king your mote did
  see;
But I a beam do find in each of three.
O! what a scene of foolery have I seen,
Of sighs, of groans, of sorrow, and of teen;   164
O me! with what strict patience have I sat,
To see a king transformed to a gnat;
To see great Hercules whipping a gig,
And profound Solomon to tune a jig,   168

And Nestor play at push-pin with the boys,
And critic Timon laugh at idle toys!
Where lies thy grief? O! tell me, good Dumaine,
And, gentle Longaville, where lies thy pain? 172
And where my liege's? all about the breast:
A caudle, ho!

King.   Too bitter is thy jest.
Are we betray'd thus to thy over-view?

Ber. Not you to me, but I betray'd by you:
I, that am honest; I, that hold it sin   177
To break the vow I am engaged in;
I am betray'd, by keeping company
With men like men, men of inconstancy.   180
When shall you see me write a thing in rime?
Or groan for Joan? or spend a minute's time
In pruning me? When shall you hear that I
Will praise a hand, a foot, a face, an eye,   184
A gait, a state, a brow, a breast, a waist,
A leg, a limb?—

King.   Soft! Whither away so fast?
A true man or a thief that gallops so?   187

Ber. I post from love; good lover, let me go.

Enter JAQUENETTA *and* COSTARD.

Jaq. God bless the king!

King.   What present hast thou there?

Cost. Some certain treason.

King.   What makes treason here?

Cost. Nay, it makes nothing, sir.

King.   If it mar nothing neither,
The treason and you go in peace away together.

Jaq. I beseech your Grace, let this letter be
read: 193
Our parson misdoubts it; 'twas treason, he said.

King. Berowne, read it over—
          [*Giving the letter to him.*
Where hadst thou it?   196

Jaq. Of Costard.

King. Where hadst thou it?

Cost. Of Dun Adramadio, Dun Adramadio.
          [BEROWNE *tears the letter.*

King. How now! what is in you? why dost
thou tear it?   200

Ber. A toy, my liege, a toy: your Grace needs
not fear it.

Long. It did move him to passion, and therefore let's hear it.

Dum. [*Picking up the pieces.*] It is Berowne's
writing, and here is his name.

Ber. [*To* COSTARD.] Ah, you whoreson logger-
head, you were born to do me shame.   204
Guilty, my lord, guilty; I confess, I confess.

King. What?

Ber. That you three fools lack'd me fool to
make up the mess;
He, he, and you, and you my liege, and I,   208
Are pick-purses in love, and we deserve to die.
O! dismiss this audience, and I shall tell you
more.

Dum. Now the number is even.

Ber.   True, true; we are four.
Will these turtles be gone?

King.   Hence, sirs; away!   212

Cost. Walk aside the true folk, and let the
traitors stay.
          [*Exeunt* COSTARD *and* JAQUENETTA.

Ber. Sweet lords, sweet lovers, O! let us em-
brace.
As true we are as flesh and blood can be:
The sea will ebb and flow, heaven show his face;
Young blood doth not obey an old decree: 217
We cannot cross the cause why we were born;
Therefore, of all hands must we be forsworn.

King. What! did these rent lines show some
love of thine?   220

Ber. 'Did they,' quoth you? Who sees the
heavenly Rosaline,
That, like a rude and savage man of Inde,
At the first opening of the gorgeous east,
Bows not his vassal head, and, strucken blind,
Kisses the base ground with obedient breast?
What peremptory eagle-sighted eye
Dares look upon the heaven of her brow,
That is not blinded by her majesty?   228

King. What zeal, what fury hath inspir'd thee
now?
My love, her mistress, is a gracious moon;
She, an attending star, scarce seen a light.

Ber. My eyes are then no eyes, nor I Berowne:
O! but for my love, day would turn to night.
Of all complexions the cull'd sovereignty
Do meet, as at a fair, in her fair cheek;
Where several worthies make one dignity, 236
Where nothing wants that want itself doth seek.
Lend me the flourish of all gentle tongues,—
Fie, painted rhetoric! O! she needs it not:
To things of sale a seller's praise belongs; 240
She passes praise; then praise too short doth
blot.
A wither'd hermit, five-score winters worn,
Might shake off fifty, looking in her eye:
Beauty doth varnish age, as if new-born, 244
And gives the crutch the cradle's infancy.
O! 'tis the sun that maketh all things shine.

King. By heaven, thy love is black as ebony.

Ber. Is ebony like her? O wood divine! 248
A wife of such wood were felicity.
O! who can give an oath? where is a book?
That I may swear beauty doth beauty lack,
If that she learn not of her eye to look: 252
No face is fair that is not full so black.

King. O paradox! Black is the badge of hell,
The hue of dungeons and the scowl of night;
And beauty's crest becomes the heavens well.

Ber. Devils soonest tempt, resembling spirits
of light.   257
O! if in black my lady's brows be deck'd,
It mourns that painting and usurping hair
Should ravish doters with a false aspect; 260
And therefore is she born to make black fair.
Her favour turns the fashion of the days,
For native blood is counted painting now;
And therefore red, that would avoid dispraise,
Paints itself black, to imitate her brow. 265

Dum. To look like her are chimney-sweepers
black.

Long. And since her time are colliers counted
bright.

King. And Ethiops of their sweet complexion
crack.   268

Dum. Dark needs no candles now, for dark
is light.

Ber. Your mistresses dare never come in rain,
For fear their colours should be wash'd away.
King. 'Twere good yours did; for, sir, to tell
you plain,   272
I'll find a fairer face not wash'd to-day.
Ber. I'll prove her fair, or talk till doomsday
here.
King. No devil will fright thee then so much
as she.
Dum. I never knew man hold vile stuff so dear.
Long. Look, here's thy love: [*Showing his
shoe.*] my foot and her face see.   277
Ber. O! if the streets were paved with thine
eyes,
Her feet were much too dainty for such tread.
Dum. O vile! then, as she goes, what upward
lies   280
The street should see as she walk'd over head.
King. But what of this? Are we not all in love?
Ber. Nothing so sure; and thereby all for-
sworn.
King. Then leave this chat; and good Be-
rowne, now prove   284
Our loving lawful, and our faith not torn.
Dum. Ay, marry, there; some flattery for this
evil.
Long. O! some authority how to proceed;
Some tricks, some quillets, how to cheat the
devil.   288
Dum. Some salve for perjury.
Ber.   O, 'tis more than need.
Have at you, then, affection's men-at-arms:
Consider what you first did swear unto,
To fast, to study, and to see no woman;   292
Flat treason 'gainst the kingly state of youth.
Say, can you fast? your stomachs are too young,
And abstinence engenders maladies.
And where that you have vow'd to study, lords,
In that each of you hath forsworn his book, 297
Can you still dream and pore and thereon look?
For when would you, my lord, or you, or you,
Have found the ground of study's excellence
Without the beauty of a woman's face?   301
From women's eyes this doctrine I derive:
They are the ground, the books, the academes,
From whence doth spring the true Promethean
fire.   304
Why, universal plodding poisons up
The nimble spirits in the arteries,
As motion and long-during action tires
The sinewy vigour of the traveller.   308
Now, for not looking on a woman's face,
You have in that forsworn the use of eyes,
And study too, the causer of your vow;
For where is any author in the world   312
Teaches such beauty as a woman's eye?
Learning is but an adjunct to ourself,
And where we are our learning likewise is:
Then when ourselves we see in ladies' eyes, 316
Do we not likewise see our learning there?
O! we have made a vow to study, lords,
And in that vow we have forsworn our books:
For when would you, my liege, or you, or you,
In leaden contemplation have found out   321
Such fiery numbers as the prompting eyes
Of beauty's tutors have enrich'd you with?

Other slow arts entirely keep the brain,   324
And therefore, finding barren practisers,
Scarce show a harvest of their heavy toil;
But love, first learned in a lady's eyes,
Lives not alone immured in the brain,   328
But, with the motion of all elements,
Courses as swift as thought in every power,
And gives to every power a double power,
Above their functions and their offices.   332
It adds a precious seeing to the eye;
A lover's eyes will gaze an eagle blind;
A lover's ear will hear the lowest sound,
When the suspicious head of theft is stopp'd:
Love's feeling is more soft and sensible   337
Than are the tender horns of cockled snails:
Love's tongue proves dainty Bacchus gross in
taste.
For valour, is not Love a Hercules,   340
Still climbing trees in the Hesperides?
Subtle as Sphinx; as sweet and musical
As bright Apollo's lute, strung with his hair;
And when Love speaks, the voice of all the
gods   344
Makes heaven drowsy with the harmony.
Never durst poet touch a pen to write
Until his ink were temper'd with Love's
sighs;
O! then his lines would ravish savage ears,   348
And plant in tyrants mild humility.
From women's eyes this doctrine I derive:
They sparkle still the right Promethean fire;
They are the books, the arts, the academes,   352
That show, contain, and nourish all the world;
Else none at all in aught proves excellent.
Then fools you were these women to forswear,
Or, keeping what is sworn, you will prove
fools.   356
For wisdom's sake, a word that all men love,
Or for love's sake, a word that loves all men,
Or for men's sake, the authors of these women;
Or women's sake, by whom we men are men,   360
Let us once lose our oaths to find ourselves,
Or else we lose ourselves to keep our oaths.
It is religion to be thus forsworn;
For charity itself fulfils the law;   364
And who can sever love from charity?
King. Saint Cupid, then! and, soldiers, to the
field!
Ber. Advance your standards, and upon
them, lords!
Pell-mell, down with them! but be first advis'd,
In conflict that you get the sun of them.   369
Long. Now to plain-dealing; lay these glozes
by;
Shall we resolve to woo these girls of France?
King. And win them too: therefore let us
devise   372
Some entertainment for them in their tents.
Ber. First, from the park let us conduct them
thither;
Then homeward every man attach the hand
Of his fair mistress: in the afternoon   376
We will with some strange pastime solace them,
Such as the shortness of the time can shape;
For revels, dances, masks, and merry hours,
Forerun fair Love, strewing her way with flowers.

King. Away, away! no time shall be omitted,
That will betime, and may by us be fitted.
Ber. Allons! allons! Sow'd cockle reap'd no
    corn;
And justice always whirls in equal measure:
Light wenches may prove plagues to men for-
    sworn;   385
If so, our copper buys no better treasure.
                                               [*Exeunt.*

ACT V

Scene I.—*The* King of Navarre's *Park.*

Enter Holofernes, Sir Nathaniel, *and* Dull.

Hol. Satis quod sufficit.
Nath. I praise God for you, sir: your reasons
at dinner have been sharp and sententious;
pleasant without scurrility, witty without affection, audacious without impudency, learned
without opinion, and strange without heresy. I
did converse this *quondam* day with a companion of the king's, who is intituled, nominated, or called, Don Adriano de Armado.   9
Hol. Novi hominem tanquam te: his humour
is lofty, his discourse peremptory, his tongue
filed, his eye ambitious, his gait majestical, and
his general behaviour vain, ridiculous, and
thrasonical. He is too picked, too spruce, too
affected, too odd, as it were, too peregrinate, as
I may call it.   16
Nath. A most singular and choice epithet.
                                  [*Draws out his table-book.*
Hol. He draweth out the thread of his verbo-
sity finer than the staple of his argument. I
abhor such fanatical phantasimes, such insociable and point-devise companions; such rackers
of orthography, as to speak dout, fine, when he
should say, doubt; det, when he should pronounce, debt,—d, e, b, t, not d, e, t: he clepeth a
calf, cauf; half, hauf; neighbour *vocatur* nebour,
neigh abbreviated ne. This is abhominable,
which he would call abominable,—it insinuateth
me of insanie: *anne intelligis, domine?* To
make frantic, lunatic.   29
Nath. Laus Deo bone intelligo.
Hol. Bone?—bone, for *bene:* Priscian a little
scratched; 'twill serve.   32

Enter Armado, Moth, *and* Costard.

Nath. Videsne quis venit?
Hol. Video, et gaudeo.
Arm. [*To* Moth.] Chirrah!
Hol. Quare Chirrah, not sirrah?   36
Arm. Men of peace, well encountered.
Hol. Most military sir, salutation.
Moth. [*Aside to* Costard.] They have been
at a great feast of languages, and stolen the
scraps.   41
Cost. O! they have lived long on the alms-
basket of words. I marvel thy master hath not
eaten thee for a word; for thou art not so long
by the head as *honorificabilitudinitatibus:* thou
art easier swallowed than a flap-dragon.   46
Moth. Peace! the peal begins.

Arm. [*To* Holofernes.] Monsieur, are you
not lettered?
Moth. Yes, yes; he teaches boys the horn-
book. What is a, b, spelt backward, with the
horn on his head?   52
Hol. Ba, *pueritia*, with a horn added.
Moth. Ba! most silly sheep with a horn. You
hear his learning.
Hol. Quis, *quis*, thou consonant?   56
Moth. The third of the five vowels, if you
repeat them; or the fifth, if I.
Hol. I will repeat them,—a, e, i,—
Moth. The sheep; the other two concludes
it,—o, u.   61
Arm. Now, by the salt wave of the Mediter-
raneum, a sweet touch, a quick venew of wit!
snip, snap, quick and home! it rejoiceth my
intellect: true wit!   65
Moth. Offered by a child to an old man;
which is wit-old.
Hol. What is the figure? what is the figure?
Moth. Horns.   69
Hol. Thou disputest like an infant; go, whip
thy gig.
Moth. Lend me your horn to make one, and
I will whip about your infamy *circum circa.* A
gig of a cuckold's horn.   74
Cost. An I had but one penny in the world,
thou shouldst have it to buy gingerbread. Hold,
there is the very remuneration I had of thy
master, thou halfpenny purse of wit, thou
pigeon-egg of discretion. O! an the heavens were
so pleased that thou wert but my bastard, what
a joyful father wouldst thou make me. Go to;
thou hast it *ad dunghill*, at the fingers' ends, as
they say.   83
Hol. O! I smell false Latin; dunghill for
unguem.
Arm. Arts-man, *præambula:* we will be
singled from the barbarous. Do you not educate
youth at the charge-house on the top of the
mountain?   89
Hol. Or *mons*, the hill.
Arm. At your sweet pleasure, for the moun-
tain.   92
Hol. I do, sans question.
Arm. Sir, it is the king's most sweet pleasure
and affection to congratulate the princess at her
pavilion in the posteriors of this day, which the
rude multitude call the afternoon.   97
Hol. The posterior of the day, most gene-
rous sir, is liable, congruent, and measurable
for the afternoon: the word is well culled,
chose, sweet and apt, I do assure you, sir; I do
assure.   102
Arm. Sir, the king is a noble gentleman, and
my familiar, I do assure ye, very good friend.
For what is inward between us, let it pass: I do
beseech thee, remember thy curtsy; I beseech
thee, apparel thy head: and among other importunate and most serious designs, and of great
import indeed, too, but let that pass: for I must
tell thee, it will please his Grace, by the world,
sometime to lean upon my poor shoulder, and
with his royal finger, thus dally with my excrement, with my mustachio: but, sweet heart, let

hat pass. By the world, I recount no fable:
ome certain special honours it pleaseth his
greatness to impart to Armado, a soldier, a man
of travel, that hath seen the world: but let that
pass. The very all of all is, but, sweet heart, I do
implore secrecy, that the king would have me
present the princess, sweet chuck, with some
delightful ostentation, or show, or pageant, or
antick, or fire-work. Now, understanding that
the curate and your sweet self are good at such
eruptions and sudden breaking out of mirth, as
it were, I have acquainted you withal, to the end
to crave your assistance. 126

Hol. Sir, you shall present before her the
Nine Worthies. Sir Nathaniel, as concerning
some entertainment of time, some show in the
posterior of this day, to be rendered by our
assistance, at the king's command, and this
most gallant, illustrate, and learned gentleman,
before the princess; I say, none so fit as to present the Nine Worthies.

Nath. Where will you find men worthy
enough to present them? 136

Hol. Joshua, yourself; myself, or this gallant
gentleman, Judas Maccabæus; this swain, because of his great limb, or joint, shall pass
Pompey the Great; the page, Hercules,— 140

Arm. Pardon, sir; error: he is not quantity
enough for that Worthy's thumb: he is not so
big as the end of his club.

Hol. Shall I have audience? he shall present
Hercules in minority: his enter and exit shall be
strangling a snake; and I will have an apology
for that purpose. 147

Moth. An excellent device! so, if any of
the audience hiss, you may cry, 'Well done,
Hercules! now thou crushest the snake!' that is
the way to make an offence gracious, though
few have the grace to do it. 152

Arm. For the rest of the Worthies?—

Hol. I will play three myself.

Moth. Thrice-worthy gentleman!

Arm. Shall I tell you a thing? 156

Hol. We attend.

Arm. We will have, if this fadge not, an
antick. I beseech you, follow.

Hol. Via, goodman Dull! thou hast spoken
no word all this while. 161

Dull. Nor understood none neither, sir.

Hol. Allons! we will employ thee.

Dull. I'll make one in a dance, or so; or I
will play the tabor to the Worthies, and let them
dance the hay. 166

Hol. Most dull, honest Dull, to our sport,
away! [*Exeunt.*

SCENE II.—*The same. Before the* PRINCESS'S
Pavilion.

Enter the PRINCESS, KATHARINE, ROSALINE,
and MARIA.

Prin. Sweet hearts, we shall be rich ere we
depart,
If fairings come thus plentifully in:
A lady wall'd about with diamonds!
Look you what I have from the loving king. 4

Ros. Madam, came nothing else along with
that?

Prin. Nothing but this! yes, as much love in
rime
As would be cramm'd up in a sheet of paper,
Writ o' both sides the leaf, margent and all, 8
That he was fain to seal on Cupid's name.

Ros. That was the way to make his godhead
wax;
For he hath been five thousand years a boy.

Kath. Ay, and a shrewd unhappy gallows too.

Ros. You'll ne'er be friends with him: a'
kill'd your sister. 13

Kath. He made her melancholy, sad, and
heavy;
And so she died: had she been light, like you,
Of such a merry, nimble, stirring spirit, 16
She might ha' been a grandam ere she died;
And so may you, for a light heart lives long.

Ros. What's your dark meaning, mouse, of
this light word?

Kath. A light condition in a beauty dark. 20

Ros. We need more light to find your meaning out.

Kath. You'll mar the light by taking it in
snuff;
Therefore, I'll darkly end the argument.

Ros. Look, what you do, you do it still i' the
dark. 24

Kath. So do not you, for you are a light
wench.

Ros. Indeed I weigh not you, and therefore
light.

Kath. You weigh me not. O! that's you
care not for me.

Ros. Great reason; for, 'past cure is still
past care.' 28

Prin. Well bandied both; a set of wit well
play'd.
But Rosaline, you have a favour too:
Who sent it? and what is it?

Ros. I would you knew:
An if my face were but as fair as yours, 32
My favour were as great; be witness this.
Nay, I have verses too, I thank Berowne:
The numbers true; and, were the numb'ring
too,
I were the fairest goddess on the ground: 36
I am compar'd to twenty thousand fairs.
O! he hath drawn my picture in his letter.

Prin. Anything like? 39

Ros. Much in the letters, nothing in the praise.

Prin. Beauteous as ink; a good conclusion.

Kath. Fair as a text B in a copy-book.

Ros. 'Ware pencils! how? let me not die
your debtor,
My red dominical, my golden letter: 44
O, that your face were not so full of O's!

Kath. A pox of that jest! and beshrew all
shrows!

Prin. But what was sent to you from fair
Dumaine?

Kath. Madam, this glove.

Prin. Did he not send you twain? 48

Kath. Yes, madam; and, moreover,
Some thousand verses of a faithful lover:

A huge translation of hypocrisy,
Vilely compil'd, profound simplicity.   52
  Mar. This, and these pearls to me sent
    Longaville:
The letter is too long by half a mile.
  Prin. I think no less. Dost thou not wish in
    heart
The chain were longer and the letter short? 56
  Mar. Ay, or I would these hands might never
    part.
  Prin. We are wise girls to mock our lovers so.
  Ros. They are worse fools to purchase mock-
    ing so.
That same Berowne I'll torture ere I go.   60
O that I knew he were but in by the week!
How I would make him fawn, and beg, and seek,
And wait the season, and observe the times,
And spend his prodigal wits in bootless rimes,
And shape his service wholly to my hests,   65
And make him proud to make me proud that
    jests!
So perttaunt-like would I o'ersway his state
That he should be my fool, and I his fate.   68
  Prin. None are so surely caught, when they
    are catch'd,
As wit turn'd fool: folly, in wisdom hatch'd,
Hath wisdom's warrant and the help of school
And wit's own grace to grace a learned fool. 72
  Ros. The blood of youth burns not with such
    excess
As gravity's revolt to wantonness.
  Mar. Folly in fools bears not so strong a note
As foolery in the wise, when wit doth dote;   76
Since all the power thereof it doth apply
To prove, by wit, worth in simplicity.

Enter BOYET.

  Prin. Here comes Boyet, and mirth is in his
    face.
  Boyet. O! I am stabb'd with laughter. Where's
    her Grace?   80
  Prin. Thy news, Boyet?
  Boyet.   Prepare, madam, prepare!—
Arm, wenches, arm! encounters mounted are
Against your peace: Love doth approach dis-
    guis'd,
Armed in arguments; you'll be surpris'd: 84
Muster your wits; stand in your own defence;
Or hide your heads like cowards, and fly hence.
  Prin. Saint Denis to Saint Cupid! What are
    they
That charge their breath against us? say, scout,
    say.   88
  Boyet. Under the cool shade of a sycamore
I thought to close mine eyes some half an hour,
When, lo! to interrupt my purpos'd rest,
Toward that shade I might behold addrest   92
The king and his companions: warily
I stole into a neighbour thicket by,
And overheard what you shall overhear;
That, by and by, disguis'd they will be here. 96
Their herald is a pretty knavish page,
That well by heart hath conn'd his embassage:
Action and accent did they teach him there;
'Thus must thou speak, and thus thy body bear.'

And ever and anon they made a doubt   10
Presence majestical would put him out;
'For,' quoth the king, 'an angel shalt thou see
Yet fear not thou, but speak audaciously.'   10
The boy replied, 'An angel is not evil;
I should have fear'd her had she been a devil.
With that all laugh'd and clapp'd him on the
    shoulder,
Making the bold wag by their praises bolder. 10
One rubb'd his elbow thus, and fleer'd, and
    swore
A better speech was never spoke before;
Another, with his finger and his thumb,   11
Cry'd 'Via! we will do 't, come what will come;
The third he caper'd and cried, 'All goes well;
The fourth turn'd on the toe, and down he fell.
With that, they all did tumble on the ground,
With such a zealous laughter, so profound,   11
That in this spleen ridiculous appears,
To check their folly, passion's solemn tears.
  Prin. But what, but what, come they to visit
    us?
  Boyet. They do, they do; and are apparell'd
    thus,   12
Like Muscovites or Russians, as I guess.
Their purpose is to parle, to court and dance;
And every one his love-feat will advance
Unto his several mistress, which they'll know
By favours several which they did bestow.   12
  Prin. And will they so? the gallants shall be
    task'd:
For, ladies, we will every one be mask'd,
And not a man of them shall have the grace,
Despite of suit, to see a lady's face.   12
Hold, Rosaline, this favour thou shalt wear,
And then the king will court thee for his dear:
Hold, take thou this, my sweet, and give me
    thine,   13
So shall Berowne take me for Rosaline,
And change you favours too; so shall your loves
Woo contrary, deceiv'd by these removes.
  Ros. Come on, then; wear the favours most
    in sight.   13
  Kath. But in this changing what is your in-
    tent?
  Prin. The effect of my intent is, to cross theirs:
They do it but in mocking merriment;
And mock for mock is only my intent.   14
Their several counsels they unbosom shall
To loves mistook and so be mock'd withal
Upon the next occasion that we meet,
With visages display'd, to talk and greet.   14
  Ros. But shall we dance, if they desire us
    to 't?
  Prin. No, to the death, we will not move a
    foot:
Nor to their penn'd speech render we no grace;
But while 'tis spoke each turn away her face. 14
  Boyet. Why, that contempt will kill the
    speaker's heart, .
And quite divorce his memory from his part.
  Prin. Therefore I do it; and I make no doubt,
The rest will ne'er come in, if he be out.   15
There's no such sport as sport by sport o'er-
    thrown,
To make theirs ours and ours none but our own:

So shall we stay, mocking intended game,
And they, well mock'd, depart away with shame.
                [*Trumpets sound within.*
  Boyet. The trumpet sounds: be mask'd; the
     maskers come.   [*The Ladies mask.*

Enter Blackamoors with music: MOTH; *the* KING,
BEROWNE, LONGAVILLE, *and* DUMAINE *in Russian habits, and masked.*

  Moth. All hail, the richest beauties on the
     earth!
  Boyet. Beauties no richer than rich taffeta.
  Moth. *A holy parcel of the fairest dames,* 160
          [*The Ladies turn their backs to him.*
That ever turn'd their—backs—to mortal views!
  Ber. 'Their eyes,' villain, 'their eyes.'
  Moth. *That ever turn'd their eyes to mortal*
     views!
Out—   164
  Boyet. True; 'out,' indeed.
  Moth. '*Out of your favours, heavenly spirits,*
     vouchsafe
Not to behold'—
  Ber. 'Once to behold,' rogue.   168
  Moth. '*Once to behold with your sun-beamed*
     eyes,
  —*with your sun-beamed eyes'*—
  Boyet. They will not answer to that epithet;
You were best call it 'daughter-beamed eyes.'
  Moth. They do not mark me, and that brings
     me out.   173
  Ber. Is this your perfectness? be gone, you
     rogue!   [*Exit* MOTH.
  Ros. What would these strangers? know their
     minds, Boyet:
If they do speak our language, 'tis our will 176
That some plain man recount their purposes:
Know what they would.
  Boyet. What would you with the princess?
  Ber. Nothing but peace and gentle visitation.
  Ros. What would they, say they?   181
  Boyet. Nothing but peace and gentle visitation.
  Ros. Why, that they have; and bid them so
     be gone.
  Boyet. She says, you have it, and you may
     be gone.   184
  King. Say to her, we have measur'd many
     miles,
To tread a measure with her on this grass.
  Boyet. They say, that they have measur'd
     many a mile,
To tread a measure with you on this grass. 188
  Ros. It is not so. Ask them how many inches
Is in one mile: if they have measur'd many,
The measure then of one is easily told.
  Boyet. If to come hither you have measur'd
     miles,   192
And many miles, the princess bids you tell
How many inches do fill up one mile.
  Ber. Tell her we measure them by weary
     steps.
  Boyet. She hears herself.
  Ros.   How many weary steps,
Of many weary miles you have o'ergone, 197
Are number'd in the travel of one mile?

  Ber. We number nothing that we spend for
     you:
Our duty is so rich, so infinite,   200
That we may do it still without accompt.
Vouchsafe to show the sunshine of your face,
That we, like savages, may worship it.
  Ros. My face is but a moon, and clouded too.
  King. Blessed are clouds, to do as such clouds
     do!   205
Vouchsafe, bright moon, and these thy stars, to
     shine,
Those clouds remov'd, upon our wat'ry eyne.
  Ros. O vain petitioner! beg a greater matter;
Thou now request'st but moonshine in the water.
  King. Then, in our measure but vouchsafe
     one change.   210
Thou bid'st me beg; this begging is not strange.
  Ros. Play, music, then! Nay, you must do
     it soon.   [*Music plays.*
Not yet! no dance! thus change I like the moon.
  King. Will you not dance? How come you
     thus estrang'd?   214
  Ros. You took the moon at full, but now
     she's chang'd.
  King. Yet still she is the moon, and I the man.
The music plays; vouchsafe some motion to it.
  Ros. Our ears vouchsafe it.
  King.   But your legs should do it.
  Ros. Since you are strangers, and come here
     by chance,
We'll not be nice: take hands: we will not
     dance.   220
  King. Why take we hands then?
  Ros.   Only to part friends.
Curtsy, sweet hearts; and so the measure ends.
  King. More measure of this measure: be not
     nice.
  Ros. We can afford no more at such a price.
  King. Prize you yourselves? what buys your
     company?   225
  Ros. Your absence only.
  King.   That can never be.
  Ros. Then cannot we be bought: and so,
     adieu;
Twice to your visor, and half once to you! 228
  King. If you deny to dance, let's hold more
     chat.
  Ros. In private, then.
  King.   I am best pleas'd with that.
                [*They converse apart.*
  Ber. White-handed mistress, one sweet word
     with thee.
  Prin. Honey, and milk, and sugar; there are
     three.   232
  Ber. Nay then, two treys, an if you grow so
     nice,
Metheglin, wort, and malmsey: well run, dice!
There's half a dozen sweets.
  Prin.   Seventh sweet, adieu:
Since you can cog, I'll play no more with you.
  Ber. One word in secret.
  Prin.   Let it not be sweet. 237
  Ber. Thou griev'st my gall.
  Prin.   Gall! bitter.
  Ber.   Therefore meet.
                [*They converse apart.*

Dum. Will you vouchsafe with me to change a word?

Mar. Name it.

Dum.   Fair lady,—

Mar.   Say you so? Fair lord, Take that for your fair lady.

Dum.   Please it you, 241 As much in private, and I'll bid adieu.
          [*They converse apart.*

Kath. What! was your visor made without a tongue?

Long. I know the reason, lady, why you ask.

Kath. O! for your reason; quickly, sir; I long. 245

Long. You have a double tongue within your mask,
And would afford my speechless visor half.

Kath. 'Veal,' quoth the Dutchman. Is not 'veal' a calf? 248

Long. A calf, fair lady!

Kath.   No, a fair lord calf.

Long. Let's part the word.

Kath.   No, I'll not be your half: Take all, and wean it: it may prove an ox.

Long. Look, how you butt yourself in these sharp mocks. 252
Will you give horns, chaste lady? do not so.

Kath. Then die a calf, before your horns do grow.

Long. One word in private with you, ere I die.

Kath. Bleat softly then; the butcher hears you cry.   [*They converse apart.*

Boyet. The tongues of mocking wenches are as keen 257
As is the razor's edge invisible,
Cutting a smaller hair than may be seen,
Above the sense of sense; so sensible 260
Seemeth their conference; their conceits have wings
Fleeter than arrows, bullets, wind, thought, swifter things.

Ros. Not one word more, my maids: break off, break off.

Ber. By heaven, all dry-beaten with pure scoff! 264

King. Farewell, mad wenches: you have simple wits.

Prin. Twenty adieus, my frozen Muscovits.
[*Exeunt* KING, LORDS, Music, *and* Attendants.
Are these the breed of wits so wonder'd at?

Boyet. Tapers they are, with your sweet breaths puff'd out. 268

Ros. Well-liking wits they have; gross, gross; fat, fat.

Prin. O poverty in wit, kingly-poor flout!
Will they not, think you, hang themselves to-night?
Or ever, but in visors, show their faces? 272
This pert Berowne was out of countenance quite.

Ros. O! they were all in lamentable cases.
The king was weeping-ripe for a good word.

Prin. Berowne did swear himself out of all suit. 276

Mar. Dumaine was at my service, and his sword:

'No point,' quoth I: my servant straight wa mute.

Kath. Lord Longaville said, I came o'er hi heart;
And trow you what he call'd me?

Prin.   Qualm, perhaps. 28

Kath. Yes, in good faith.

Prin.   Go, sickness as thou art

Ros. Well, better wits have worn plain statute caps.
But will you hear? the king is my love sworr

Prin. And quick Berowne hath plighted fait to me. 28

Kath. And Longaville was for my service borr

Mar. Dumaine is mine, as sure as bark o tree.

Boyet. Madam, and pretty mistresses, giv ear:
Immediately they will again be here 28
In their own shapes; for it can never be
They will digest this harsh indignity.

Prin. Will they return?

Boyet.   They will, they will, God knows
And leap for joy, though they are lame witl blows: 29
Therefore change favours; and, when they re pair,
Blow like sweet roses in this summer air.

Prin. How blow? how blow? speak to b understood.

Boyet. Fair ladies mask'd, are roses in thei bud: 29
Dismask'd, their damask sweet commixture shown,
Are angels vailing clouds, or roses blown.

Prin. Avaunt perplexity! What shall we d If they return in their own shapes to woo? 30

Ros. Good madam, if by me you'll be advis'd Let's mock them still, as well as known as dis guis'd.
Let us complain to them what fools were here Disguis'd like Muscovites, in shapeless gear; 30
And wonder what they were, and to what en Their shallow shows and prologue vilely penn'd And their rough carriage so ridiculous,
Should be presented at our tent to us. 30

Boyet. Ladies, withdraw: the gallants are a hand.

Prin. Whip to your tents, as roes run ove land.
          [*Exeunt* PRINCESS, ROS., KATH., *and* MARIA

Enter the KING, BEROWNE, LONGAVILLE, *and* DUMAINE *in their proper habits.*

King. Fair sir, God save you! Where is th princess?

Boyet. Gone to her tent. Please it your ma jesty, 31
Command me any service to her thither?

King. That she vouchsafe me audience fo one word.

Boyet. I will; and so will she, I know, my lord.   [*Exit*

Ber. This fellow pecks up wit, as pigeon pease, 31
And utters it again when God doth please:

He is wit's pedlar, and retails his wares
At wakes and wassails, meetings, markets, fairs;
And we that sell by gross, the Lord doth know,
Have not the grace to grace it with such show.
This gallant pins the wenches on his sleeve;
Had he been Adam, he had tempted Eve:
He can carve too, and lisp: why, this is he   324
That kiss'd his hand away in courtesy;
This is the ape of form, monsieur the nice,
That, when he plays at tables, chides the dice
In honourable terms: nay, he can sing   328
A mean most meanly, and in ushering
Mend him who can: the ladies call him, sweet;
The stairs, as he treads on them, kiss his feet.
This is the flower that smiles on every one,   332
To show his teeth as white as whales-bone;
And consciences, that will not die in debt,
Pay him the due of honey-tongu'd Boyet.
  King. A blister on his sweet tongue, with my heart,   336
That put Armado's page out of his part!

Re-enter the PRINCESS, *ushered by* BOYET; ROSA-
LINE, MARIA, KATHARINE, *and Attendants.*

  Ber. See where it comes! Behaviour, what
    wert thou,
Till this man show'd thee? and what art thou
    now?
  King. All hail, sweet madam, and fair time of
    day!   340
  Prin. 'Fair,' in 'all hail,' is foul, as I conceive.
  King. Construe my speeches better, if you may.
  Prin. Then wish me better: I will give you
    leave.   343
  King. We came to visit you, and purpose now
To lead you to our court: vouchsafe it then.
  Prin. This field shall hold me, and so hold your
    vow:
Nor God, nor I, delights in perjur'd men.
  King. Rebuke me not for that which you pro-
    voke: 348
The virtue of your eye must break my oath.
  Prin. You nick-name virtue; vice you should
    have spoke;
For virtue's office never breaks men's troth.
Now, by my maiden honour, yet as pure   352
As the unsullied lily, I protest,
A world of torments though I should endure,
I would not yield to be your house's guest;
So much I hate a breaking cause to be   356
Of heavenly oaths, vow'd with integrity.
  King. O! you have liv'd in desolation here,
Unseen, unvisited, much to our shame.   359
  Prin. Not so, my lord; it is not so, I swear;
We have had pastime here and pleasant game.
A mess of Russians left us but of late.
  King. How, madam! Russians?
  Prin. Ay, in truth, my lord;
Trim gallants, full of courtship and of state.   364
  Ros. Madam, speak true. It is not so, my
    lord:
My lady, to the manner of the days,
In courtesy gives undeserving praise.
We four, indeed, confronted were with four   368
In Russian habit: here they stay'd an hour,
And talk'd apace; and in that hour, my lord,

They did not bless us with one happy word.
I dare not call them fools; but this I think,   372
When they are thirsty, fools would fain have
    drink.
  Ber. This jest is dry to me. Fair gentle sweet,
Your wit makes wise things foolish: when we
    greet,
With eyes best seeing, heaven's fiery eye,   376
By light we lose light: your capacity
Is of that nature that to your huge store
Wise things seem foolish and rich things but
    poor.
  Ros. This proves you wise and rich, for in
    my eye—   380
  Ber. I am a fool, and full of poverty.
  Ros. But that you take what doth to you be-
    long,
It were a fault to snatch words from my tongue.
  Ber. O! I am yours, and all that I possess.
  Ros. All the fool mine?
  Ber.   I cannot give you less.
  Ros. Which of the visors was it that you wore?
  Ber. Where? when? what visor? why de-
    mand you this?
  Ros. There, then, that visor; that superfluous
    case   388
That hid the worse, and show'd the better face.
  King. We are descried: they'll mock us now
    downright.
  Dum. Let us confess, and turn it to a jest.
  Prin. Amaz'd, my lord? Why looks your
    highness sad?   392
  Ros. Help! hold his brows! he'll swound.
Why look you pale?
Sea-sick, I think, coming from Muscovy.
  Ber. Thus pour the stars down plagues for
    perjury.
Can any face of brass hold longer out?—   396
Here stand I, lady; dart thy skill at me;
Bruise me with scorn, confound me with a
    flout;
Thrust thy sharp wit quite through my igno-
    rance;
Cut me to pieces with thy keen conceit;   400
And I will wish thee never more to dance,
Nor never more in Russian habit wait.
O! never will I trust to speeches penn'd,
Nor to the motion of a school-boy's tongue,
Nor never come in visor to my friend,   405
Nor woo in rime, like a blind harper's song,
Taffeta phrases, silken terms precise,
Three-pil'd hyperboles, spruce affectation,
Figures pedantical; these summer flies   409
Have blown me full of maggot ostentation:
I do forswear them; and I here protest,
By this white glove,—how white the hand,
    God knows,—   412
Henceforth my wooing mind shall be express'd
In russet yeas and honest kersey noes:
And, to begin, wench,—so God help me, la!—
My love to thee is sound, sans crack or flaw.   416
  Ros. Sans 'sans,' I pray you.
  Ber.   Yet I have a trick
Of the old rage: bear with me, I am sick;
I'll leave it by degrees. Soft! let us see:
Write, 'Lord have mercy on us' on those three;

They are infected, in their hearts it lies;   421
They have the plague, and caught it of your
    eyes:
These lords are visited; you are not free,
For the Lord's tokens on you do I see.   424
    Prin. No, they are free that gave these tokens
to us.
    Ber. Our states are forfeit: seek not to undo
us.
    Ros. It is not so. For how can this be true,
That you stand forfeit, being those that sue? 428
    Ber. Peace! for I will not have to do with you.
    Ros. Nor shall not, if I do as I intend.
    Ber. Speak for yourselves: my wit is at an
end.
    King. Teach us, sweet madam, for our rude
    transgression   432
Some fair excuse.
    Prin.   The fairest is confession.
Were you not here, but even now, disguis'd?
    King. Madam, I was.
    Prin.   And were you well advis'd?
    King. I was, fair madam.
    Prin.   When you then were here,
What did you whisper in your lady's ear? 437
    King. That more than all the world I did
respect her.
    Prin. When she shall challenge this, you will
reject her.
    King. Upon mine honour, no.
    Prin.   Peace! peace! forbear; 440
Your oath once broke, you force not to for-
swear.
    King. Despise me, when I break this oath of
mine.
    Prin. I will; and therefore keep it. Rosaline,
What did the Russian whisper in your ear? 444
    Ros. Madam, he swore that he did hold me
dear
As precious eyesight, and did value me
Above this world; adding thereto, moreover,
That he would wed me, or else die my lover. 448
    Prin. God give thee joy of him! the noble lord
Most honourably doth uphold his word.
    King. What mean you, madam? by my life,
my troth,
I never swore this lady such an oath.   452
    Ros. By heaven you did; and to confirm it
plain,
You gave me this: but take it, sir, again.
    King. My faith and this the princess I did
give:
I knew her by this jewel on her sleeve.   456
    Prin. Pardon me, sir, this jewel did she wear;
And Lord Berowne, I thank him, is my dear.
What, will you have me, or your pearl again?
    Ber. Neither of either; I remit both twain.
I see the trick on't: here was a consent,   461
Knowing aforehand of our merriment,
To dash it like a Christmas comedy.
Some carry-tale, some please-man, some slight
    zany,   464
Some mumble-news, some trencher-knight,
    some Dick,
That smiles his cheek in years, and knows the
    trick

To make my lady laugh when she's dispos'd,
Told our intents before; which once disclos'd,
The ladies did change favours, and then we, 469
Following the signs, woo'd but the sign of she.
Now, to our perjury to add more terror,
We are again forsworn, in will and error.   472
Much upon this it is: [*To* BOYET.] and might
    not you
Forestall our sport, to make us thus untrue?
Do not you know my lady's foot by the squire,
    And laugh upon the apple of her eye?   476
And stand between her back, sir, and the fire,
    Holding a trencher, jesting merrily?
You put our page out: go, you are allow'd;
Die when you will, a smock shall be your shroud.
You leer upon me, do you? there's an eye   481
Wounds like a leaden sword.
    Boyet.   Full merrily
Hath this brave manage, this career, been run.
    Ber. Lo! he is tilting straight. Peace! I have
done.   484

Enter COSTARD.

Welcome, pure wit! thou partest a fair fray.
    Cost. O Lord, sir, they would know
Whether the three Worthies shall come in or no.
    Ber. What, are there but three?
    Cost.   No, sir; but it is vara fine, 488
For every one pursents three.
    Ber.   And three times thrice is nine.
    Cost. Not so, sir; under correction, sir, I
    hope, it is not so.
You cannot beg us, sir, I can assure you, sir;
    we know what we know:
I hope, sir, three times thrice, sir,—
    Ber.   Is not nine.   492
    Cost. Under correction, sir, we know where-
until it doth amount.
    Ber. By Jove, I always took three threes for
nine.
    Cost. O Lord, sir! it were pity you should get
your living by reckoning, sir.   497
    Ber. How much is it?
    Cost. O Lord, sir! the parties themselves, the
actors, sir, will show whereuntil it doth amount:
for mine own part, I am, as they say, but to par-
fect one man in one poor man, Pompion the
Great, sir.
    Ber. Art thou one of the Worthies?   504
    Cost. It pleased them to think me worthy of
Pompion the Great: for mine own part, I know
not the degree of the Worthy, but I am to stand
for him.   508
    Ber. Go, bid them prepare.
    Cost. We will turn it finely off, sir; we will
    take some care.   [*Exit.*
    King. Berowne, they will shame us; let them
    not approach.
    Ber. We are shame-proof, my lord; and 'tis
    some policy   512
To have one show worse than the king's and
    his company.
    King. I say they shall not come.
    Prin. Nay, my good lord, let me o'errule
    you now.   515
That sport best pleases that doth least know how;

Where zeal strives to content, and the contents
Die in the zeal of those which it presents;
Their form confounded makes most form in
    mirth,
When great things labouring perish in their
    birth.   520
Ber. A right description of our sport, my lord.

Enter ARMADO.

Arm. Anointed, I implore so much expense
of thy royal sweet breath as will utter a brace of
words.   524
    [ARMADO *converses with the* KING, *and
        delivers a paper to him.*
Prin. Doth this man serve God?
Ber. Why ask you?
Prin. He speaks not like a man of God's
making.   527
Arm. That's all one, my fair, sweet, honey
monarch; for, I protest, the schoolmaster is
exceeding fantastical; too-too vain; too-too
vain: but we will put it, as they say, to *fortuna
de la guerra.* I wish you the peace of mind,
most royal couplement!   [*Exit.*
King. Here is like to be a good presence of
Worthies. He presents Hector of Troy; the
swain, Pompey the Great; the parish curate,
Alexander; Armado's page, Hercules; the pe-
dant, Judas Maccabæus:
And if these four Worthies in their first show
    thrive,
These four will change habits and present the
    other five.   540
Ber. There is five in the first show.
King. You are deceived, 'tis not so.
Ber. The pedant, the braggart, the hedge-
priest, the fool, and the boy:—   544
Abate throw at novum, and the whole world
    again
Cannot pick out five such, take each one in his
    vein.
King. The ship is under sail, and here she
    comes amain.

Enter COSTARD *armed, for Pompey.*

Cost. I Pompey am,—
Boyet.   You lie, you are not he.   548
Cost. I Pompey am,—
Boyet.   With libbard's head on knee.
Ber. Well said, old mocker: I must needs be
friends with thee.
Cost. I Pompey am, Pompey surnam'd the
    Big,—
Dum. 'The Great.'   552
Cost. It is 'Great,' sir; Pompey surnam'd
    the Great;
That oft in field, with targe and shield, did make
    my foe to sweat:
And travelling along this coast, I here am come
    by chance,
And lay my arms before the legs of this sweet
    lass of France.   556
If your ladyship would say, 'Thanks, Pompey,'
    I had done.
Prin. Great thanks, great Pompey.

Cost. 'Tis not so much worth; but I hope
I was perfect. I made a little fault in 'Great.'
Ber. My hat to a halfpenny, Pompey proves
the best Worthy.

Enter SIR NATHANIEL *armed, for Alexander.*

Nath. When in the world I liv'd, I was the
    world's commander;
By east, west, north, and south, I spread my
    conquering might: 564
My scutcheon plain declares that I am Alisan-
    der,—
Boyet. Your nose says, no, you are not; for
it stands too right.
Ber. Your nose smells 'no,' in this, most ten-
der-smelling knight.
Prin. The conqueror is dismay'd. Proceed,
good Alexander.   568
Nath. When in the world I liv'd, I was the
    world's commander;—
Boyet. Most true; 'tis right: you were so,
Alisander.
Ber. Pompey the Great,—
Cost. Your servant, and Costard.   572
Ber. Take away the conqueror, take away
Alisander.
Cost. [*To* NATHANIEL.] O! sir, you have overthrown Alisander the conqueror! You will be
scraped out of the painted cloth for this: your
lion, that holds his poll-axe sitting on a close-
stool, will be given to Ajax: he will be the ninth
Worthy. A conqueror, and afeard to speak!
run away for shame, Alisander! [NATHANIEL
retires.] There, an't shall please you: a foolish
mild man; an honest man, look you, and soon
dashed! He is a marvellous good neighbour,
faith, and a very good bowler; but, for Alisander,—alas, you see how 'tis,—a little o'erparted.
But there are Worthies a-coming will speak
their mind in some other sort.
Prin. Stand aside, good Pompey.   588

Enter HOLOFERNES *armed, for Judas; and*
    MOTH *armed, for Hercules.*

Hol. Great Hercules is presented by this imp,
    Whose club kill'd Cerberus, that three-headed
      canis;
And, when he was a babe, a child, a shrimp,
    Thus did he strangle serpents in his manus.
Quoniam, he seemeth in minority,   593
Ergo, I come with this apology.
Keep some state in thy exit, and vanish.—
                      [MOTH *retires.*
Judas I am.—   596
    Dum. A Judas!
    Hol. Not Iscariot, sir.
Judas I am, ycleped Maccabæus.
    Dum. Judas Maccabæus clipt is plain Judas.
    Ber. A kissing traitor. How art thou prov'd
    Judas?   601
    Hol. Judas I am.—
    Dum. The more shame for you, Judas.
    Hol. What mean you, sir?   604
    Boyet. To make Judas hang himself.
    Hol. Begin, sir; you are my elder.

Ber. Well follow'd: Judas was hanged on an elder.

Hol. I will not be put out of countenance. 608

Ber. Because thou hast no face.

Hol. What is this?

Boyet. A cittern-head.

Dum. The head of a bodkin. 612

Ber. A death's face in a ring.

Long. The face of an old Roman coin, scarce seen.

Boyet. The pommel of Cæsar's falchion.

Dum. The carved-bone face on a flask. 616

Ber. Saint George's half-cheek in a brooch.

Dum. Ay, and in a brooch of lead.

Ber. Ay, and worn in the cap of a tooth-drawer.

And now forward; for we have put thee in countenance. 620

Hol. You have put me out of countenance.

Ber. False: we have given thee faces.

Hol. But you have outfaced them all.

Ber. An thou wert a lion, we would do so. 624

Boyet. Therefore, as he is an ass, let him go.

And so adieu, sweet Jude! nay, why dost thou stay?

Dum. For the latter end of his name.

Ber. For the ass to the Jude? give it him:—Jud-as, away! 628

Hol. This is not generous, not gentle, not humble.

Boyet. A light for Monsieur Judas! it grows dark, he may stumble.

Prin. Alas! poor Maccabæus, how hath he been baited.

Enter ARMADO *armed, for Hector.*

Ber. Hide thy head, Achilles: here comes Hector in arms. 633

Dum. Though my mocks come home by me, I will now be merry.

King. Hector was but a Troyan in respect of this. 637

Boyet. But is this Hector?

King. I think Hector was not so clean-timbered. 640

Long. His calf is too big for Hector.

Dum. More calf, certain.

Boyet. No; he is best indued in the small.

Ber. This cannot be Hector. 644

Dum. He's a god or a painter; for he makes faces.

Arm. The armipotent Mars, of lances the almighty,

Gave Hector a gift,— 648

Dum. A gilt nutmeg.

Ber. A lemon.

Long. Stuck with cloves.

Dum. No, cloven. 652

Arm. Peace!

The armipotent Mars, of lances the almighty,

Gave Hector a gift, the heir of Ilion;

A man so breath'd, that certain he would fight ye 656

From morn till night, out of his pavilion.

I am that flower,—

Dum. That mint.

Long. That columbine.

Arm. Sweet Lord Longaville, rein thy tongue.

Long. I must rather give it the rein, for it runs against Hector. 661

Dum. Ay, and Hector's a greyhound.

Arm. The sweet war-man is dead and rotten; sweet chucks, beat not the bones of the buried: when he breathed, he was a man. But I will forward with my device. [*To the* PRINCESS.] Sweet royalty, bestow on me the sense of hearing. 667

Prin. Speak, brave Hector; we are much delighted.

Arm. I do adore thy sweet Grace's slipper.

Boyet. [*Aside to* DUMAINE.] Loves her by the foot. 672

Dum. [*Aside to* BOYET.] He may not by the yard.

Arm. This Hector far surmounted Hannibal,—

Cost. The party is gone; fellow Hector, she is gone; she is two months on her way. 677

Arm. What meanest thou?

Cost. Faith, unless you play the honest Troyan, the poor wench is cast away: she's quick; the child brags in her belly already: 'tis yours.

Arm. Dost thou infamonize me among potentates? Thou shalt die. 683

Cost. Then shall Hector be whipped for Jaquenetta that is quick by him, and hanged for Pompey that is dead by him.

Dum. Most rare Pompey!

Boyet. Renowned Pompey! 688

Ber. Greater than great, great, great, great Pompey! Pompey the Huge!

Dum. Hector trembles.

Ber. Pompey is moved. More Ates, more Ates! stir them on! stir them on! 693

Dum. Hector will challenge him.

Ber. Ay, if a' have no more man's blood in's belly than will sup a flea. 696

Arm. By the north pole, I do challenge thee.

Cost. I will not fight with a pole, like a northern man: I'll slash; I'll do it by the sword. I bepray you, let me borrow my arms again. 701

Dum. Room for the incensed Worthies!

Cost. I'll do it in my shirt.

Dum. Most resolute Pompey! 704

Moth. Master, let me take you a button-hole lower. Do you not see Pompey is uncasing for the combat? What mean you? you will lose your reputation. 708

Arm. Gentlemen and soldiers, pardon me; I will not combat in my shirt.

Dum. You may not deny it; Pompey hath made the challenge. 712

Arm. Sweet bloods, I both may and will.

Ber. What reason have you for't?

Arm. The naked truth of it is, I have no shirt. I go woolward for penance. 716

Boyet. True, and it was enjoined him in Rome for want of linen; since when, I'll be sworn, he wore none but a dish-clout of Jaquenetta's, and that a' wears next his heart for a favour. 720

Enter Monsieur MARCADE, *a Messenger.*

Mar. God save you, madam!

Prin. Welcome, Marcade;

But that thou interrupt'st our merriment.

Mar. I am sorry, madam; for the news I
bring   724
Is heavy in my tongue. The king your father—

Prin. Dead, for my life!

Mar. Even so: my tale is told.

Ber. Worthies, away! The scene begins to
cloud.   729

Arm. For my own part, I breathe free breath.
I have seen the day of wrong through the little
hole of discretion, and I will right myself like a
soldier.   [*Exeunt* Worthies.

King. How fares your majesty?

Prin. Boyet, prepare: I will away to-night.

King. Madam, not so: I do beseech you,
stay.   736

Prin. Prepare, I say. I thank you, gracious
lords,
For all your fair endeavours; and entreat,
Out of a new-sad soul, that you vouchsafe
In your rich wisdom to excuse or hide   740
The liberal opposition of our spirits,
If over-boldly we have borne ourselves
In the converse of breath; your gentleness
Was guilty of it. Farewell, worthy lord!   744
A heavy heart bears not a nimble tongue,
Excuse me so, coming so short of thanks
For my great suit so easily obtain'd.

King. The extreme part of time extremely
forms   748
All causes to the purpose of his speed,
And often, at his very loose, decides
That which long process could not arbitrate:
And though the mourning brow of progeny 752
Forbid the smiling courtesy of love
The holy suit which fain it would convince;
Yet, since love's argument was first on foot,
Let not the cloud of sorrow justle it   756
From what it purpos'd; since, to wail friends lost
Is not so much so wholesome-profitable
As to rejoice at friends but newly found.

Prin. I understand you not: my griefs are
double.   760

Ber. Honest plain words best pierce the ear
of grief;
And by these badges understand the king.
For your fair sakes have we neglected time,
Play'd foul play with our oaths. Your beauty,
ladies,   764
Hath much deform'd us, fashioning our humours
Even to the opposed end of our intents;
And what in us hath seem'd ridiculous,—
As love is full of unbefitting strains;   768
All wanton as a child, skipping and vain;
Form'd by the eye, and, therefore, like the eye,
Full of stray shapes, of habits and of forms,
Varying in subjects, as the eye doth roll   772
To every varied object in his glance:
Which parti-coated presence of loose love
Put on by us, if, in your heavenly eyes,
Have misbecome our oaths and gravities,   776
Those heavenly eyes, that look into these faults,
Suggested us to make. Therefore, ladies,

Our love being yours, the error that love makes
Is likewise yours: we to ourselves prove false,
By being once false for ever to be true   781
To those that make us both,—fair ladies, you:
And even that falsehood, in itself a sin,
Thus purifies itself and turns to grace.   784

Prin. We have receiv'd your letters full of
love;
Your favours, the embassadors of love;
And, in our maiden council, rated them
At courtship, pleasant jest, and courtesy,   788
As bombast and as lining to the time.
But more devout than this in our respects
Have we not been; and therefore met your
loves
In their own fashion, like a merriment.   792

Dum. Our letters, madam, show'd much
more than jest.

Long. So did our looks.

Ros.   We did not quote them so.

King. Now, at the latest minute of the hour,
Grant us your loves.

Prin.   A time, methinks, too short
To make a world-without-end bargain in.   797
No, no, my lord, your Grace is perjur'd much,
Full of dear guiltiness; and therefore this:
If for my love,—as there is no such cause,—   800
You will do aught, this shall you do for me:
Your oath I will not trust; but go with speed
To some forlorn and naked hermitage,
Remote from all the pleasures of the world;   804
There stay, until the twelve celestial signs
Have brought about their annual reckoning.
If this austere insociable life   807
Change not your offer made in heat of blood;
If frosts and fasts, hard lodging and thin weeds,
Nip not the gaudy blossoms of your love,
But that it bear this trial and last love;
Then, at the expiration of the year,   812
Come challenge me, challenge me by these de-
serts,
And, by this virgin palm now kissing thine,
I will be thine; and, till that instant, shut
My woful self up in a mourning house.   816
Raining the tears of lamentation
For the remembrance of my father's death.
If this thou do deny, let our hands part;
Neither intitled in the other's heart.   820

King. If this, or more than this, I would deny,
To flatter up these powers of mine with rest,
The sudden hand of death close up mine eye!
Hence ever then my heart is in thy breast. 824

Ber. And what to me, my love? and what to
me?

Ros. You must be purged too, your sins are
rack'd:
You are attaint with faults and perjury;
Therefore, if you my favour mean to get,   828
A twelvemonth shall you spend, and never rest,
But seek the weary beds of people sick.

Dum. But what to me, my love? but what to
me?

Kath. A wife! A beard, fair health, and
honesty;   832
With three-fold love I wish you all these three.

Dum. O! shall I say, I thank you, gentle wife?

Kath. Not so, my lord. A twelvemonth and
a day
I'll mark no words that smooth-fac'd wooers
say: 836
Come when the king doth to my lady come;
Then, if I have much love, I'll give you some.
Dum. I'll serve thee true and faithfully till
then.
Kath. Yet swear not, lest you be forsworn
again.   840
Long. What says Maria?
Mar.   At the twelvemonth's end
I'll change my black gown for a faithful friend.
Long. I'll stay with patience; but the time is
long.   843
Mar. The liker you; few taller are so young.
Ber. Studies my lady? mistress, look on me.
Behold the window of my heart, mine eye,
What humble suit attends thy answer there;
Impose some service on me for thy love.   848
Ros. Oft have I heard of you, my Lord
Berowne,
Before I saw you, and the world's large tongue
Proclaims you for a man replete with mocks;
Full of comparisons and wounding flouts, 852
Which lie within the mercy of your wit:
To weed this wormwood from your fruitful
brain,
And therewithal to win me, if you please,— 856
Without the which I am not to be won,—
You shall this twelvemonth term, from day to
day,
Visit the speechless sick, and still converse
With groaning wretches; and your task shall be,
With all the fierce endeavour of your wit   861
To enforce the pained impotent to smile.
Ber. To move wild laughter in the throat of
death?
It cannot be; it is impossible: 864
Mirth cannot move a soul in agony.
Ros. Why, that's the way to choke a gibing
spirit,
Whose influence is begot of that loose grace
Which shallow laughing hearers give to fools.
A jest's prosperity lies in the ear   869
Of him that hears it, never in the tongue
Of him that makes it: then, if sickly ears,
Deaf'd with the clamours of their own dear
groans,   872
Will hear your idle scorns, continue them,
And I will have you and that fault withal;
But if they will not, throw away that spirit,
And I shall find you empty of that fault,   876
Right joyful of your reformation.
Ber. A twelvemonth! well, befall what will
befall,
I'll jest a twelvemonth in a hospital.
Prin. [*To the* KING.] Ay, sweet my lord; and
so I take my leave.   880
King. No, madam; we will bring you on your
way.
Ber. Our wooing doth not end like an old
play;
Jack hath not Jill; these ladies' courtesy
Might well have made our sport a comedy. 884

King. Come, sir, it wants a twelvemonth and
a day,
And then 'twill end.
Ber.   That's too long for a play.

Enter ARMADO.

Arm. Sweet majesty, vouchsafe me,—
Prin. Was not that Hector?   888
Dum. The worthy knight of Troy.
Arm. I will kiss thy royal finger, and take
leave. I am a votary; I have vowed to Jaquenetta to hold the plough for her sweet love three
years. But, most esteemed greatness, will you
hear the dialogue that the two learned men have
compiled in praise of the owl and the cuckoo? it
should have followed in the end of our show. 896
King. Call them forth quickly; we will do so.
Arm. Holla! approach.

Re-enter HOLOFERNES, NATHANIEL, MOTH,
        COSTARD, *and others.*

This side is *Hiems*, Winter; this *Ver*, the Spring;
the one maintained by the owl, the other by the
cuckoo. *Ver*, begin.   901

SPRING

I

When daisies pied and violets blue
    And lady-smocks all silver-white
And cuckoo-buds of yellow hue   904
    Do paint the meadows with delight,
The cuckoo then, on every tree,
Mocks married men; for thus sings he,
                        Cuckoo;   908
Cuckoo, cuckoo: O, word of fear,
Unpleasing to a married ear!

II

When shepherds pipe on oaten straws,
    And merry larks are ploughmen's clocks, 912
When turtles tread, and rooks, and daws,
    And maidens bleach their summer smocks,
The cuckoo then, on every tree,
Mocks married men; for thus sings he,   916
                        Cuckoo;
Cuckoo, cuckoo: O, word of fear,
Unpleasing to a married ear!

WINTER

III

When icicles hang by the wall,   920
    And Dick the shepherd blows his nail,
And Tom bears logs into the hall,
    And milk comes frozen home in pail,
When blood is nipp'd, and ways be foul, 924
Then nightly sings the staring owl,
                        Tu-who;
Tu-whit, tu-who—a merry note,
While greasy Joan doth keel the pot.   928

IV

When all aloud the wind doth blow,
    And coughing drowns the parson's saw,
And birds sit brooding in the snow,
    And Marian's nose looks red and raw, 932
When roasted crabs hiss in the bowl,
Then nightly sings the staring owl,
                        Tu-who;
Tu-whit, tu-who—a merry note,   936
While greasy Joan doth keel the pot.

Arm. The words of Mercury are harsh after
the songs of Apollo. You, that way: we, this
way.   [*Exeunt.*

A MIDSUMMER-NIGHT'S DREAM

DRAMATIS PERSONÆ

THESEUS, Duke of Athens.
EGEUS, Father to Hermia.
LYSANDER, } in love with Hermia.
DEMETRIUS,
PHILOSTRATE, Master of the Revels to Theseus.
QUINCE, a Carpenter.
SNUG, a Joiner.
BOTTOM, a Weaver.
FLUTE, a Bellows-mender.
SNOUT, a Tinker.
STARVELING, a Tailor.

HIPPOLYTA, Queen of the Amazons, betrothed to
Theseus.

HERMIA, Daughter to Egeus, in love with Lysander.
HELENA, in love with Demetrius.

OBERON, King of the Fairies.
TITANIA, Queen of the Fairies.
PUCK, or Robin Goodfellow.
PEASE-BLOSSOM, }
COBWEB,   } Fairies.
MOTH,   }
MUSTARD-SEED, }

Other Fairies attending their King and Queen. Attendants on Theseus and Hippolyta.

SCENE.—*Athens, and a Wood near it.*

ACT I

SCENE I.—*Athens. The Palace of* THESEUS.

Enter THESEUS, HIPPOLYTA, PHILOSTRATE,
and Attendants.

The. Now, fair Hippolyta, our nuptial hour
Draws on apace: four happy days bring in
Another moon; but O! methinks how slow
This old moon wanes; she lingers my desires,   4
Like to a step-dame, or a dowager
Long withering out a young man's revenue.
Hip. Four days will quickly steep themselves
  in night;
Four nights will quickly dream away the time;   8
And then the moon, like to a silver bow
New-bent in heaven, shall behold the night
Of our solemnities.
The.   Go, Philostrate,
Stir up the Athenian youth to merriments;   12
Awake the pert and nimble spirit of mirth;
Turn melancholy forth to funerals;
The pale companion is not for our pomp.
                              [*Exit* PHILOSTRATE.
Hippolyta, I woo'd thee with my sword,   16
And won thy love doing thee injuries;
But I will wed thee in another key,
With pomp, with triumph, and with revelling.

Enter EGEUS, HERMIA, LYSANDER, *and*
DEMETRIUS.

Ege. Happy be Theseus, our renowned duke!
The. Thanks, good Egeus: what's the news
  with thee?
Ege. Full of vexation come I, with complaint
Against my child, my daughter Hermia.
Stand forth, Demetrius. My noble lord,   24
This man hath my consent to marry her.
Stand forth, Lysander: and, my gracious duke,
This man hath bewitch'd the bosom of my child;
Thou, thou, Lysander, thou hast given her rimes,
And interchang'd love-tokens with my child;   29
Thou hast by moonlight at her window sung,
With feigning voice, verses of feigning love;

And stol'n the impression of her fantasy   32
With bracelets of thy hair, rings, gawds, con-
  ceits,
Knacks, trifles, nosegays, sweetmeats, messen-
  gers
Of strong prevailment in unharden'd youth;
With cunning hast thou filch'd my daughter's
  heart;   36
Turn'd her obedience, which is due to me,
To stubborn harshness. And, my gracious duke,
Be it so she will not here before your Grace
Consent to marry with Demetrius,   40
I beg the ancient privilege of Athens,
As she is mine, I may dispose of her;
Which shall be either to this gentleman,
Or to her death, according to our law   44
Immediately provided in that case.
The. What say you, Hermia? be advis'd, fair
  maid.
To you, your father should be as a god;
One that compos'd your beauties, yea, and one
To whom you are but as a form in wax   49
By him imprinted, and within his power
To leave the figure or disfigure it.
Demetrius is a worthy gentleman.   52
Her. So is Lysander.
The.   In himself he is;
But, in this kind, wanting your father's voice,
The other must be held the worthier.
Her. I would my father look'd but with my
  eyes.   56
The. Rather your eyes must with his judg-
  ment look.
Her. I do entreat your Grace to pardon me.
I know not by what power I am made bold,
Nor how it may concern my modesty   60
In such a presence here to plead my thoughts;
But I beseech your Grace, that I may know
The worst that may befall me in this case,
If I refuse to wed Demetrius.   64
The. Either to die the death, or to abjure
For ever the society of men.
Therefore, fair Hermia, question your desires;
Know of your youth, examine well your blood,

Whether, if you yield not to your father's choice,
You can endure the livery of a nun,
For aye to be in shady cloister mew'd,
To live a barren sister all your life,   72
Chanting faint hymns to the cold fruitless moon.
Thrice blessed they that master so their blood,
To undergo such maiden pilgrimage;
But earthlier happy is the rose distill'd,   76
Than that which withering on the virgin thorn
Grows, lives, and dies, in single blessedness.
    Her. So will I grow, so live, so die, my lord,
Ere I will yield my virgin patent up   80
Unto his lordship, whose unwished yoke
My soul consents not to give sovereignty.
    The. Take time to pause; and, by the next
new moon,—
The sealing-day betwixt my love and me   84
For everlasting bond of fellowship,—
Upon that day either prepare to die
For disobedience to your father's will,
Or else to wed Demetrius, as he would;   88
Or on Diana's altar to protest
For aye austerity and single life.
    Dem. Relent, sweet Hermia; and, Lysander,
yield
Thy crazed title to my certain right.   92
    Lys. You have her father's love, Demetrius;
Let me have Hermia's: do you marry him.
    Ege. Scornful Lysander! true, he hath my
love,
And what is mine my love shall render him; 96
And she is mine, and all my right of her
I do estate unto Demetrius.
    Lys. I am, my lord, as well deriv'd as he,
As well possess'd; my love is more than his; 100
My fortunes every way as fairly rank'd
If not with vantage, as Demetrius';
And, which is more than all these boasts can be,
I am belov'd of beauteous Hermia.   104
Why should not I then prosecute my right?
Demetrius, I'll avouch it to his head,
Made love to Nedar's daughter, Helena,
And won her soul; and she, sweet lady, dotes,
Devoutly dotes, dotes in idolatry,   109
Upon this spotted and inconstant man.
    The. I must confess that I have heard so
much,
And with Demetrius thought to have spoke
thereof;   112
But, being over-full of self-affairs,
My mind did lose it. But, Demetrius, come;
And come, Egeus; you shall go with me,
I have some private schooling for you both. 116
For you, fair Hermia, look you arm yourself
To fit your fancies to your father's will,
Or else the law of Athens yields you up,
Which by no means we may extenuate,   120
To death, or to a vow of single life.
Come, my Hippolyta: what cheer, my love?
Demetrius and Egeus, go along:
I must employ you in some business   124
Against our nuptial, and confer with you
Of something nearly that concerns yourselves.
    Ege. With duty and desire we follow you.
    [*Exeunt* THESEUS, HIPPOLYTA, EGEUS,
DEMETRIUS, *and Train.*

    Lys. How now, my love! Why is your cheek
so pale?   128
How chance the roses there do fade so fast?
    Her. Belike for want of rain, which I could
well
Beteem them from the tempest of mine eyes.
    Lys. Ay me! for aught that ever I could
read,   132
Could ever hear by tale or history,
The course of true love never did run smooth;
But, either it was different in blood,—
    Her. O cross! too high to be enthrall'd to
low.   136
    Lys. Or else misgraffed in respect of years,—
    Her. O spite! too old to be engag'd to young.
    Lys. Or else it stood upon the choice of
friends,—   139
    Her. O hell! to choose love by another's eye.
    Lys. Or, if there were a sympathy in choice,
War, death, or sickness did lay siege to it,
Making it momentany as a sound,
Swift as a shadow, short as any dream,   144
Brief as the lightning in the collied night,
That, in a spleen, unfolds both heaven and earth,
And ere a man hath power to say, 'Behold!'
The jaws of darkness do devour it up: 148
So quick bright things come to confusion.
    Her. If then true lovers have been ever cross'd,
It stands as an edict in destiny:
Then let us teach our trial patience,   152
Because it is a customary cross,
As due to love as thoughts and dreams and
sighs,
Wishes and tears, poor fancy's followers.
    Lys. A good persuasion: therefore, hear me,
Hermia.   156
I have a widow aunt, a dowager
Of great revenue, and she hath no child:
From Athens is her house remote seven leagues;
And she respects me as her only son.   160
There, gentle Hermia, may I marry thee;
And to that place the sharp Athenian law
Cannot pursue us. If thou lov'st me then,
Steal forth thy father's house to-morrow night,
And in the wood, a league without the town, 165
Where I did meet thee once with Helena,
To do observance to a morn of May,
There will I stay for thee.
    Her.   My good Lysander! 168
I swear to thee by Cupid's strongest bow,
By his best arrow with the golden head,
By the simplicity of Venus' doves,
By that which knitteth souls and prospers loves,
And by that fire which burn'd the Carthage
queen,   173
When the false Troyan under sail was seen,
By all the vows that ever men have broke,— 176
In number more than ever women spoke,—
In that same place thou hast appointed me,
To-morrow truly will I meet with thee.
    Lys. Keep promise, love. Look, here comes
Helena.

Enter HELENA.

    Her. God speed fair Helena! Whither away?
    Hel. Call you me fair? that fair again unsay.

Demetrius loves your fair: O happy fair!
Your eyes are lode-stars! and your tongue's
    sweet air
More tuneable than lark to shepherd's ear, 184
When wheat is green, when hawthorn buds
    appear.
Sickness is catching: O! were favour so,
Yours would I catch, fair Hermia, ere I go;
My ear should catch your voice, my eye your eye,
My tongue should catch your tongue's sweet
    melody.   189
Were the world mine, Demetrius being bated,
The rest I'd give to be to you translated.
O! teach me how you look, and with what art
You sway the motion of Demetrius' heart. 193
    Her. I frown upon him, yet he loves me still.
    Hel. O! that your frowns would teach my
        smiles such skill.
    Her. I give him curses, yet he gives me love.
    Hel. O! that my prayers could such affection
        move.   197
    Her. The more I hate, the more he follows
        me.
    Hel. The more I love, the more he hateth me.
    Her. His folly, Helena, is no fault of mine.
    Hel. None, but your beauty: would that fault
        were mine!   201
    Her. Take comfort: he no more shall see my
        face;
Lysander and myself will fly this place.
Before the time I did Lysander see,   204
Seem'd Athens as a paradise to me:
O! then, what graces in my love do dwell,
That he hath turn'd a heaven unto a hell.
    Lys. Helen, to you our minds we will unfold.
To-morrow night, when Phœbe doth behold
Her silver visage in the wat'ry glass,   210
Decking with liquid pearl the bladed grass,—
A time that lovers' flights doth still conceal,—
Through Athens' gates have we devis'd to steal.
    Her. And in the wood, where often you and I
Upon faint primrose-beds were wont to lie,
Emptying our bosoms of their counsel sweet,
There my Lysander and myself shall meet;   217
And thence from Athens turn away our eyes,
To seek new friends and stranger companies.
Farewell, sweet playfellow: pray thou for us;
And good luck grant thee thy Demetrius!   221
Keep word, Lysander: we must starve our sight
From lovers' food till morrow deep midnight.
    Lys. I will, my Hermia.—[*Exit* HERMIA.]
        Helena, adieu: 224
As you on him, Demetrius dote on you! [*Exit.*
    Hel. How happy some o'er other some can
        be!
Through Athens I am thought as fair as she;
But what of that? Demetrius thinks not so;
He will not know what all but he do know; 229
And as he errs, doting on Hermia's eyes,
So I, admiring of his qualities.
Things base and vile, holding no quantity, 232
Love can transpose to form and dignity.
Love looks not with the eyes, but with the mind,
And therefore is wing'd Cupid painted blind.
Nor hath Love's mind of any judgment taste;
Wings and no eyes figure unheedy haste: 237

And therefore is Love said to be a child,
Because in choice he is so oft beguil'd.
As waggish boys in game themselves forswear,
So the boy Love is perjur'd every where;   241
For ere Demetrius look'd on Hermia's eyne,
He hail'd down oaths that he was only mine;
And when this hail some heat from Hermia felt,
So he dissolv'd, and showers of oaths did melt.
I will go tell him of fair Hermia's flight: 246
Then to the wood will he to-morrow night
Pursue her; and for this intelligence
If I have thanks, it is a dear expense:
But herein mean I to enrich my pain,   250
To have his sight thither and back again. [*Exit.*

SCENE II.—*The Same. A Room in* QUINCE'S
    House.

Enter QUINCE, SNUG, BOTTOM, FLUTE, SNOUT,
    and STARVELING.

    Quin. Is all our company here?
    Bot. You were best to call them generally,
man by man, according to the scrip.
    Quin. Here is the scroll of every man's name,
which is thought fit, through all Athens, to play
in our interlude before the duke and the duchess
on his wedding-day at night.   7
    Bot. First, good Peter Quince, say what the
play treats on; then read the names of the
actors, and so grow to a point.   10
    Quin. Marry, our play is, The most lament-
able comedy, and most cruel death of Pyramus
and Thisby.   13
    Bot. A very good piece of work, I assure you,
and a merry. Now, good Peter Quince, call
forth your actors by the scroll. Masters, spread
yourselves.   17
    Quin. Answer as I call you. Nick Bottom,
the weaver.
    Bot. Ready. Name what part I am for, and
proceed.   21
    Quin. You, Nick Bottom, are set down for
Pyramus.
    Bot. What is Pyramus? a lover, or a tyrant?
    Quin. A lover, that kills himself most gal-
lantly for love.   26
    Bot. That will ask some tears in the true per-
forming of it: if I do it, let the audience look to
their eyes; I will move storms, I will condole
in some measure. To the rest: yet my chief
humour is for a tyrant. I could play Ercles
rarely, or a part to tear a cat in, to make all
split.   33

> The raging rocks
> And shivering shocks
> Shall break the locks   36
>   Of prison gates;
> And Phibbus' car
> Shall shine from far
> And make and mar   40
>   The foolish Fates.

This was lofty! Now name the rest of the
players. This is Ercles' vein, a tyrant's vein; a
lover is more condoling.   44
    Quin. Francis Flute, the bellows-mender.

Flu. Here, Peter Quince.

Quin. You must take Thisby on you. 47

Flu. What is Thisby? a wandering knight?

Quin. It is the lady that Pyramus must love.

Flu. Nay, faith, let not me play a woman; I have a beard coming. 51

Quin. That's all one: you shall play it in a mask, and you may speak as small as you will.

Bot. An I may hide my face, let me play Thisby too. I'll speak in a monstrous little voice, 'Thisne, Thisne!' 'Ah, Pyramus, my lover dear; thy Thisby dear, and lady dear!' 57

Quin. No, no; you must play Pyramus; and Flute, you Thisby.

Bot. Well, proceed. 60

Quin. Robin Starveling, the tailor.

Star. Here, Peter Quince.

Quin. Robin Starveling, you must play Thisby's mother. Tom Snout, the tinker. 64

Snout. Here, Peter Quince.

Quin. You, Pyramus' father; myself, Thisby's father; Snug, the joiner, you the lion's part: and, I hope, here is a play fitted. 68

Snug. Have you the lion's part written? pray you, if it be, give it me, for I am slow of study.

Quin. You may do it extempore, for it is nothing but roaring. 72

Bot. Let me play the lion too. I will roar, that I will do any man's heart good to hear me; I will roar, that I will make the duke say, 'Let him roar again, let him roar again.' 76

Quin. An you should do it too terribly, you would fright the duchess and the ladies, that they would shriek; and that were enough to hang us all. 80

All. That would hang us, every mother's son.

Bot. I grant you, friends, if that you should fright the ladies out of their wits, they would have no more discretion but to hang us; but I will aggravate my voice so that I will roar you as gently as any sucking dove; I will roar you as 'twere any nightingale. 87

Quin. You can play no part but Pyramus; for Pyramus is a sweet-faced man; a proper man, as one shall see in a summer's day; a most lovely, gentleman-like man; therefore, you must needs play Pyramus. 92

Bot. Well, I will undertake it. What beard were I best to play it in?

Quin. Why, what you will.

Bot. I will discharge it in either your straw-colour beard, your orange-tawny beard, your purple-in-grain beard, or your French-crown colour beard, your perfect yellow. 99

Quin. Some of your French crowns have no hair at all, and then you will play bare-faced. But masters, here are your parts; and I am to entreat you, request you, and desire you, to con them by to-morrow night, and meet me in the palace wood, a mile without the town, by moonlight: there will we rehearse; for if we meet in the city, we shall be dogged with company, and our devices known. In the meantime I will draw a bill of properties, such as our play wants. I pray you, fail me not. 110

Bot. We will meet; and there we may re-hearse more obscenely and courageously. Take pains; be perfect; adieu.

Quin. At the duke's oak we meet.

Bot. Enough; hold, or cut bow-strings. 115
[*Exeunt.*

ACT II

SCENE I.—*A Wood near Athens.*

Enter a Fairy *on one side, and* PUCK *on the other.*

Puck. How now, spirit! whither wander you?

Fai. Over hill, over dale,
    Thorough bush, thorough brier,
    Over park, over pale, 4
    Thorough flood, thorough fire,
I do wander every where,
Swifter than the moone's sphere;
And I serve the fairy queen, 8
To dew her orbs upon the green:
The cowslips tall her pensioners be;
In their gold coats spots you see;
Those be rubies, fairy favours, 12
In their freckles live their savours:
I must go seek some dew-drops here,
And hang a pearl in every cowslip's ear.
Farewell, thou lob of spirits: I'll be gone; 16
Our queen and all her elves come here anon.

Puck. The king doth keep his revels here to-night.
Take heed the queen come not within his sight;
For Oberon is passing fell and wrath, 20
Because that she as her attendant hath
A lovely boy, stol'n from an Indian king;
She never had so sweet a changeling;
And jealous Oberon would have the child 24
Knight of his train, to trace the forests wild;
But she, perforce, withholds the loved boy,
Crowns him with flowers, and makes him all her joy.
And now they never meet in grove, or green, 28
By fountain clear, or spangled starlight sheen,
But they do square; that all their elves, for fear,
Creep into acorn-cups and hide them there.

Fai. Either I mistake your shape and making quite, 32
Or else you are that shrewd and knavish sprite
Call'd Robin Goodfellow: are you not he
That frights the maidens of the villagery;
Skim milk, and sometimes labour in the quern,
And bootless make the breathless housewife churn; 37
And sometime make the drink to bear no barm;
Mislead night-wanderers, laughing at their harm?
Those that Hobgoblin call you and sweet Puck,
You do their work, and they shall have good luck: 41
Are you not he?

Puck.   Fairy, thou speak'st aright;
I am that merry wanderer of the night.
I jest to Oberon, and make him smile 44
When I a fat and bean-fed horse beguile,
Neighing in likeness of a filly foal:
And sometime lurk I in a gossip's bowl,

In very likeness of a roasted crab;   48
And, when she drinks, against her lips I bob
And on her wither'd dewlap pour the ale.
The wisest aunt, telling the saddest tale,
Sometime for three-foot stool mistaketh me; 52
Then slip I from her bum, down topples she,
And 'tailor' cries, and falls into a cough;
And then the whole quire hold their hips and
    loff;
And waxen in their mirth, and neeze, and
    swear   56
A merrier hour was never wasted there.
But, room, fairy! here comes Oberon.
Fai. And here my mistress. Would that he
    were gone!

Enter OBERON *from one side, with his Train;*
    and TITANIA *from the other, with hers.*

Obe. Ill met by moonlight, proud Titania. 60
Tita. What! jealous Oberon. Fairies, skip
    hence:
I have forsworn his bed and company.
Obe. Tarry, rash wanton! am not I thy lord?
Tita. Then, I must be thy lady; but I know
When thou hast stol'n away from fairy land, 65
And in the shape of Corin sat all day,
Playing on pipes of corn, and versing love
To amorous Phillida. Why art thou here, 68
Come from the furthest steppe of India?
But that, forsooth, the bouncing Amazon,
Your buskin'd mistress and your warrior love,
To Theseus must be wedded, and you come 72
To give their bed joy and prosperity.
Obe. How canst thou thus for shame, Titania,
Glance at my credit with Hippolyta,
Knowing I know thy love to Theseus? 76
Didst thou not lead him through the glimmer-
    ing night
From Perigouna, whom he ravished?
And make him with fair Ægle break his faith,
With Ariadne, and Antiopa?   80
Tita. These are the forgeries of jealousy:
And never, since the middle summer's spring,
Met we on hill, in dale, forest, or mead,
By paved fountain, or by rushy brook,   84
Or in the beached margent of the sea,
To dance our ringlets to the whistling wind,
But with thy brawls thou hast disturb'd our
    sport.
Therefore the winds, piping to us in vain, 88
As in revenge, have suck'd up from the sea
Contagious fogs; which, falling in the land,
Have every pelting river made so proud
That they have overborne their continents: 92
The ox hath therefore stretch'd his yoke in vain,
The ploughman lost his sweat, and the green corn
Hath rotted ere his youth attain'd a beard:
The fold stands empty in the drowned field, 96
And crows are fatted with the murrion flock;
The nine men's morris is fill'd up with mud,
And the quaint mazes in the wanton green
For lack of tread are undistinguishable: 100
The human mortals want their winter here:
No night is now with hymn or carol blest:
Therefore the moon, the governess of floods,
Pale in her anger, washes all the air,   104

That rheumatic diseases do abound:
And thorough this distemperature we see
The seasons alter: hoary-headed frosts
Fall in the fresh lap of the crimson rose, 108
And on old Hiems' thin and icy crown
An odorous chaplet of sweet summer buds
Is, as in mockery, set. The spring, the summer,
The childing autumn, angry winter, change 112
Their wonted liveries, and the mazed world,
By their increase, now knows not which is which.
And this same progeny of evil comes
From our debate, from our dissension: 116
We are their parents and original.
  Obe. Do you amend it then; it lies in you.
Why should Titania cross her Oberon?
I do but beg a little changeling boy,   120
To be my henchman.
  Tita.   Set your heart at rest;
The fairy land buys not the child of me.
His mother was a votaress of my order:
And, in the spiced Indian air, by night, 124
Full often hath she gossip'd by my side,
And sat with me on Neptune's yellow sands,
Marking the embarked traders on the flood;
When we have laugh'd to see the sails conceive
And grow big-bellied with the wanton wind;
Which she, with pretty and with swimming gait
Following,—her womb then rich with my young
    squire,—
Would imitate, and sail upon the land,   132
To fetch me trifles, and return again,
As from a voyage, rich with merchandise.
But she, being mortal, of that boy did die;
And for her sake I do rear up her boy,   136
And for her sake I will not part with him.
  Obe. How long within this wood intend you
    stay?
  Tita. Perchance, till after Theseus' wedding-
    day.
If you will patiently dance in our round, 140
And see our moonlight revels, go with us;
If not, shun me, and I will spare your haunts.
  Obe. Give me that boy, and I will go with
    thee.
  Tita. Not for thy fairy kingdom. Fairies,
    away!   144
We shall chide downright, if I longer stay.
             [*Exit* TITANIA *with her Train.*
  Obe. Well, go thy way: thou shalt not from
    this grove
Till I torment thee for this injury.
My gentle Puck, come hither. Thou remem-
    ber'st   148
Since once I sat upon a promontory,
And heard a mermaid on a dolphin's back
Uttering such dulcet and harmonious breath,
That the rude sea grew civil at her song, 152
And certain stars shot madly from their spheres
To hear the sea-maid's music.
  Puck.   I remember.
  Obe. That very time I saw, but thou couldst
    not,
Flying between the cold moon and the earth,
Cupid all arm'd: a certain aim he took   157
At a fair vestal throned by the west,
And loos'd his love-shaft smartly from his bow.

As it should pierce a hundred thousand hearts;
But I might see young Cupid's fiery shaft   161
Quench'd in the chaste beams of the wat'ry
    moon,
And the imperial votaress passed on,
In maiden meditation, fancy-free.   164
Yet mark'd I where the bolt of Cupid fell:
It fell upon a little western flower,
Before milk-white, now purple with love's
    wound,
And maidens call it, Love-in-idleness.   168
Fetch me that flower; the herb I show'd thee
    once:
The juice of it on sleeping eyelids laid
Will make or man or woman madly dote
Upon the next live creature that it sees.   172
Fetch me this herb; and be thou here again
Ere the leviathan can swim a league.
    Puck. I'll put a girdle round about the earth
In forty minutes.   [*Exit.*
    Obe.   Having once this juice   176
I'll watch Titania when she is asleep,
And drop the liquor of it in her eyes:
The next thing then she waking looks upon,
Be it on lion, bear, or wolf, or bull,   180
On meddling monkey, or on busy ape,
She shall pursue it with the soul of love:
And ere I take this charm off from her sight,
As I can take it with another herb,   184
I'll make her render up her page to me.
But who comes here? I am invisible,
And I will overhear their conference.

Enter DEMETRIUS, HELENA *following him.*

    Dem. I love thee not, therefore pursue me not.
Where is Lysander and fair Hermia?   189
The one I'll slay, the other slayeth me.
Thou told'st me they were stol'n into this wood;
And here am I, and wood within this wood,   192
Because I cannot meet my Hermia.
Hence! get thee gone, and follow me no more.
    Hel. You draw me, you hard-hearted ada-
    mant;
But yet you draw not iron, for my heart   196
Is true as steel: leave you your power to draw,
And I shall have no power to follow you.
    Dem. Do I entice you? Do I speak you fair?
Or, rather, do I not in plainest truth   200
Tell you I do not nor I cannot love you?
    Hel. And even for that do I love you the more.
I am your spaniel; and, Demetrius,
The more you beat me, I will fawn on you: 204
Use me but as your spaniel, spurn me, strike me,
Neglect me, lose me; only give me leave,
Unworthy as I am, to follow you.
What worser place can I beg in your love,   208
And yet a place of high respect with me,
Than to be used as you use your dog?
    Dem. Tempt not too much the hatred of my
    spirit,
For I am sick when I do look on you.   212
    Hel. And I am sick when I look not on you.
    Dem. You do impeach your modesty too
    much,
To leave the city, and commit yourself
Into the hands of one that loves you not;   216

To trust the opportunity of night
And the ill counsel of a desert place
With the rich worth of your virginity.
    Hel. Your virtue is my privilege: for that   220
It is not night when I do see your face,
Therefore I think I am not in the night;
Nor doth this wood lack worlds of company,
For you in my respect are all the world: 224
Then how can it be said I am alone,
When all the world is here to look on me?
    Dem. I'll run from thee and hide me in the
    brakes,
And leave thee to the mercy of wild beasts.   228
    Hel. The wildest hath not such a heart as you.
Run when you will, the story shall be chang'd;
Apollo flies, and Daphne holds the chase;
The dove pursues the griffin; the mild hind   232
Makes speed to catch the tiger: bootless speed,
When cowardice pursues and valour flies.
    Dem. I will not stay thy questions: let me go;
Or, if thou follow me, do not believe   236
But I shall do thee mischief in the wood.
    Hel. Ay, in the temple, in the town, the field,
You do me mischief. Fie, Demetrius!
Your wrongs do set a scandal on my sex.   240
We cannot fight for love, as men may do;
We should be woo'd and were not made to woo.
    [*Exit* DEMETRIUS.
I'll follow thee and make a heaven of hell,
To die upon the hand I love so well.   [*Exit.*
    Obe. Fare thee well, nymph: ere he do leave
    this grove,   245
Thou shalt fly him, and he shall seek thy love.

Re-enter PUCK.

Hast thou the flower there? Welcome, wanderer.
    Puck. Ay, there it is.
    Obe.   I pray thee, give it me.   248
I know a bank whereon the wild thyme blows,
Where oxlips and the nodding violet grows
Quite over-canopied with luscious woodbine,
With sweet musk-roses, and with eglantine: 252
There sleeps Titania some time of the night,
Lull'd in these flowers with dances and delight;
And there the snake throws her enamell'd skin,
Weed wide enough to wrap a fairy in: 256
And with the juice of this I'll streak her eyes,
And make her full of hateful fantasies.
Take thou some of it, and seek through this
    grove:
A sweet Athenian lady is in love   260
With a disdainful youth: anoint his eyes;
But do it when the next thing he espies
May be the lady. Thou shalt know the man
By the Athenian garments he hath on.   264
Effect it with some care, that he may prove
More fond on her than she upon her love.
And look thou meet me ere the first cock crow.
    Puck. Fear not, my lord, your servant shall
    do so.   [*Exeunt.*

SCENE II.—*Another Part of the Wood.*
    Enter TITANIA, *with her Train.*

    Tita. Come, now a roundel and a fairy song;
Then, for the third of a minute, hence:

ome to kill cankers in the musk-rose buds,
ome war with rere-mice for their leathern
   wings, 4
o make my small elves coats, and some keep
   back
he clamorous owl, that nightly hoots, and
   wonders
t our quaint spirits. Sing me now asleep;
hen to your offices, and let me rest. 8

The Fairies sing.

I

You spotted snakes with double tongue,
   Thorny hedge-hogs, be not seen;
Newts, and blind-worms, do no wrong;
   Come not near our fairy queen. 12
Philomel, with melody,
   Sing in our sweet lullaby;
Lulla, lulla, lullaby; lulla, lulla, lullaby:
   Never harm, 16
   Nor spell, nor charm,
Come our lovely lady nigh;
   So, good night, with lullaby.

II

Weaving spiders come not here; 20
   Hence, you long-legg'd spinners, hence!
Beetles black, approach not near;
   Worm nor snail, do no offence.
   Philomel, with melody, &c. 24

Fai. Hence, away! now all is well.
One aloof stand sentinel.
   [*Exeunt Fairies.* TITANIA *sleeps.*

Enter OBERON, *and squeezes the flower on*
TITANIA'S *eyelids.*

Obe. What thou seest when thou dost wake,
Do it for thy true-love take; 28
Love and languish for his sake:
Be it ounce, or cat, or bear,
Pard, or boar with bristled hair,
In thy eye that shall appear 32
When thou wak'st, it is thy dear.
Wake when some vile thing is near. [*Exit.*

Enter LYSANDER *and* HERMIA.

Lys. Fair love, you faint with wandering in the
   wood;
And to speak troth, I have forgot our way: 36
We'll rest us, Hermia, if you think it good,
And tarry for the comfort of the day.
Her. Be it so, Lysander: find you out a bed,
For I upon this bank will rest my head. 40
Lys. One turf shall serve as pillow for us both;
One heart, one bed, two bosoms, and one troth.
Her. Nay, good Lysander; for my sake, my
   dear,
Lie further off yet, do not lie so near. 44
Lys. O! take the sense, sweet, of my innocence,
Love takes the meaning in love's conference.
I mean that my heart unto yours is knit,
So that but one heart we can make of it; 48
Two bosoms interchained with an oath;
So then two bosoms and a single troth.
Then by your side no bed-room me deny,
For, lying so, Hermia, I do not lie. 52
Her. Lysander riddles very prettily:
Now much beshrew my manners and my pride,
If Hermia meant to say Lysander lied.

But, gentle friend, for love and courtesy 56
Lie further off; in human modesty,
Such separation as may well be said
Becomes a virtuous bachelor and a maid,
So far be distant; and, good night, sweet friend.
Thy love ne'er alter till thy sweet life end! 61
   Lys. Amen, amen, to that fair prayer, say I;
And then end life when I end loyalty!
Here is my bed: sleep give thee all his rest! 64
   Her. With half that wish the wisher's eyes be
   press'd! [*They sleep.*

Enter PUCK.

Puck. Through the forest have I gone,
But Athenian found I none,
On whose eyes I might approve 68
This flower's force in stirring love.
Night and silence! who is here?
Weeds of Athens he doth wear:
This is he, my master said, 72
Despised the Athenian maid;
And here the maiden, sleeping sound,
On the dank and dirty ground.
Pretty soul! she durst not lie 76
Near this lack-love, this kill-courtesy.
   [*Squeezes the flower on* LYSANDER'S
   eyelids.]
Churl, upon thy eyes I throw
All the power this charm doth owe.
When thou wak'st, let love forbid 80
Sleep his seat on thy eyelid:
So awake when I am gone;
For I must now to Oberon. [*Exit.*

Enter DEMETRIUS *and* HELENA, *running.*

Hel. Stay, though thou kill me, sweet Deme-
   trius. 84
Dem. I charge thee, hence, and do not haunt
   me thus.
Hel. O! wilt thou darkling leave me? do
   not so.
Dem. Stay, on thy peril: I alone will go.
   [*Exit* DEMETRIUS.
Hel. O! I am out of breath in this fond chase.
The more my prayer, the lesser is my grace. 89
Happy is Hermia, wheresoe'er she lies;
For she hath blessed and attractive eyes.
How came her eyes so bright? Not with salt
   tears:
If so, my eyes are oftener wash'd than hers. 93
No, no, I am as ugly as a bear;
For beasts that meet me run away for fear;
Therefore no marvel though Demetrius 96
Do, as a monster, fly my presence thus.
What wicked and dissembling glass of mine
Made me compare with Hermia's sphery eyne?
But who is here? Lysander! on the ground! 100
Dead? or asleep? I see no blood, no wound.
Lysander, if you live, good sir, awake.
   Lys. [*Awaking.*] And run through fire I will
   for thy sweet sake.
Transparent Helena! Nature shows art, 104
That through thy bosom makes me see thy heart.
Where is Demetrius? O! how fit a word
Is that vile name to perish on my sword.

Hel. Do not say so, Lysander; say not so.
What though he love your Hermia? Lord!
    what though?   109
Yet Hermia still loves you: then be content.

Lys. Content with Hermia! No: I do repent
The tedious minutes I with her have spent. 112
Not Hermia, but Helena I love:
Who will not change a raven for a dove?
The will of man is by his reason sway'd,
And reason says you are the worthier maid. 116
Things growing are not ripe until their season;
So I, being young, till now ripe not to reason;
And touching now the point of human skill,
Reason becomes the marshal to my will,   120
And leads me to your eyes; where I o'erlook
Love's stories written in love's richest book.

Hel. Wherefore was I to this keen mockery
    born?   123
When at your hands did I deserve this scorn?
Is 't not enough, is 't not enough, young man,
That I did never, no, nor never can,
Deserve a sweet look from Demetrius' eye,
But you must flout my insufficiency?   128
Good troth, you do me wrong, good sooth,
    you do,
In such disdainful manner me to woo.
But fare you well: perforce I must confess
I thought you lord of more true gentleness. 132
O! that a lady of one man refus'd,
Should of another therefore be abus'd. [*Exit.*

Lys. She sees not Hermia. Hermia, sleep
    thou there;
And never mayst thou come Lysander near. 136
For, as a surfeit of the sweetest things
The deepest loathing to the stomach brings;
Or, as the heresies that men do leave
Are hated most of those they did deceive: 140
So thou, my surfeit and my heresy,
Of all be hated, but the most of me!
And, all my powers, address your love and
    might
To honour Helen, and to be her knight. [*Exit.*

Her. [*Awaking.*] Help me, Lysander, help
    me! do thy best   145
To pluck this crawling serpent from my breast.
Ay me, for pity! what a dream was here!
Lysander, look how I do quake with fear: 148
Methought a serpent eat my heart away,
And you sat smiling at his cruel prey.
Lysander! what! remov'd?—Lysander! lord!
What! out of hearing? gone? no sound, no
    word?   152
Alack! where are you? speak, an if you hear;
Speak, of all loves! I swound almost with fear.
No! then I well perceive you are not nigh:
Either death or you I'll find immediately.
                                          [*Exit.*

ACT III

SCENE I.—*A Wood.* TITANIA *lying asleep.*

Enter QUINCE, SNUG, BOTTOM, FLUTE, SNOUT,
    and STARVELING.

Bot. Are we all met?

Quin. Pat, pat; and here 's a marvellous convenient place for our rehearsal. This green plot

shall be our stage, this hawthorn-brake ou
tiring-house; and we will do it in action as we
will do it before the duke.

Bot. Peter Quince,—

Quin. What sayst thou, bully Bottom?

Bot. There are things in this comedy o
Pyramus and Thisby that will never please
First, Pyramus must draw a sword to kill him
self, which the ladies cannot abide. How answe
you that?   1

Snout. By'r lakin, a parlous fear.

Star. I believe we must leave the killing out
when all is done.   1

Bot. Not a whit: I have a device to make al
well. Write me a prologue; and let the prologu
seem to say, we will do no harm with our swords
and that Pyramus is not killed indeed; and
for the more better assurance, tell them that I
Pyramus, am not Pyramus, but Bottom th
weaver: this will put them out of fear.

Quin. Well, we will have such a prologue, an
it shall be written in eight and six.   2

Bot. No, make it two more: let it be writte
in eight and eight.

Snout. Will not the ladies be afeard of th
lion?   2

Star. I fear it, I promise you.

Bot. Masters, you ought to consider wit
yourselves: to bring in,—God shield us!—a lio
among ladies, is a most dreadful thing; for ther
is not a more fearful wild-fowl than your lio
living, and we ought to look to it.

Snout. Therefore, another prologue must te
he is not a lion.   3

Bot. Nay, you must name his name, and ha
his face must be seen through the lion's neck
and he himself must speak through, saying thu
or to the same defect, 'Ladies,' or, 'Fair ladies
'I would wish you,' or, 'I would request you,' o
'I would entreat you, not to fear, not to tremble
my life for yours. If you think I come hither a
a lion, it were pity of my life: no, I am no suc
thing: I am a man as other men are;' and the
indeed let him name his name, and tell the
plainly he is Snug the joiner.   4

Quin. Well, it shall be so. But there is tw
hard things, that is, to bring the moonligh
into a chamber; for, you know, Pyramus an
Thisby meet by moonlight.   5

Snug. Doth the moon shine that night w
play our play?

Bot. A calendar, a calendar! look in th
almanack; find out moonshine, find out moo
shine.   5

Quin. Yes, it doth shine that night.

Bot. Why, then may you leave a casemen
of the great chamber-window, where we pla
open; and the moon may shine in at the cas
ment.   6

Quin. Ay; or else one must come in with
bush of thorns and a lanthorn, and say he com
to disfigure, or to present, the person of Moo
shine. Then, there is another thing: we mu
have a wall in the great chamber; for Pyram
and Thisby, says the story, did talk through th
chink of a wall.

Snug. You can never bring in a wall. What
ay you, Bottom?

Bot. Some man or other must present Wall;
nd let him have some plaster, or some loam, or
ome rough-cast about him, to signify wall; and
et him hold his fingers thus, and through that
ranny shall Pyramus and Thisby whisper. 76

Quin. If that may be, then all is well. Come,
it down, every mother's son, and rehearse your
arts. Pyramus, you begin: when you have
poken your speech, enter into that brake; and
o every one according to his cue. 81

Enter PUCK, *behind.*

Puck. What hempen home-spuns have we
   swaggering here,
o near the cradle of the fairy queen?
Vhat! a play toward; I'll be an auditor; 84
n actor too perhaps, if I see cause.

Quin. Speak, Pyramus.—Thisby, stand forth.
*Bot. Thisby, the flowers have odious savours
   sweet,—*
Quin. Odorous, odorous. 88
Bot.—odours savours sweet:
*So hath thy breath, my dearest Thisby dear.
But hark, a voice! stay thou but here awhile,
And by and by I will to thee appear.* [*Exit.*
Puck. A stranger Pyramus than e'er play'd
   here! [*Exit.*
Flu. Must I speak now?
Quin. Ay, marry, must you; for you must
inderstand, he goes but to see a noise that he
eard, and is to come again. 97
*Flu. Most radiant Pyramus, most lily-white of
   hue,*
Of colour like the red rose on triumphant brier,
Most brisky juvenal, and eke most lovely Jew,
*As true as truest horse that yet would never
   tire,* 101
'll meet thee, Pyramus, at Ninny's tomb.
Quin. 'Ninus' tomb,' man. Why, you must
ot speak that yet; that you answer to Pyra-
nus: you speak all your part at once, cues and
ill. Pyramus, enter: your cue is past; it is
never tire.'
Flu. O!—*As true as truest horse, that yet
   would never tire.* 108

Re-enter PUCK, *and* BOTTOM *with an ass's head.*

Bot. If I were, fair Thisby, I were only
thine.
Quin. O monstrous! O strange! we are
haunted.
Pray, masters! fly, masters!—Help!
   [*Exeunt* Clowns.
Puck. I'll follow you, I'll lead you about a
   round, 112
Through bog, through bush, through brake,
   through brier:
Sometime a horse I'll be, sometime a hound,
   A hog, a headless bear, sometime a fire;
And neigh, and bark, and grunt, and roar, and
   burn, 116
Like horse, hound, hog, bear, fire, at every
   turn. [*Exit.*
Bot. Why do they run away? this is a knavery
of them to make me afeard.

Re-enter SNOUT.

Snout. O Bottom, thou art changed! what do
I see on thee? 121
Bot. What do you see? you see an ass-head
of your own, do you? [*Exit* SNOUT.

Re-enter QUINCE.

Quin. Bless thee, Bottom! bless thee! thou
art translated. [*Exit.*
Bot. I see their knavery: this is to make an
ass of me; to fright me, if they could. But I will
not stir from this place, do what they can: I
will walk up and down here, and I will sing,
that they shall hear I am not afraid.

> The ousel-cock, so black of hue,
>   With orange-tawny bill, 132
> The throstle with his note so true,
>   The wren with little quill.

Tita. [*Awaking.*] What angel wakes me from
my flowery bed? 136

Bot. The finch, the sparrow, and the lark,
>   The plain-song cuckoo gray,
> Whose note full many a man doth mark,
>   And dares not answer, nay; 140

for indeed, who would set his wit to so foolish a
bird? who would give a bird the lie, though he
cry 'cuckoo' never so?
Tita. I pray thee, gentle mortal, sing again:
Mine ear is much enamour'd of thy note; 145
So is mine eye enthralled to thy shape;
And thy fair virtue's force, perforce, doth move
   me,
On the first view, to say, to swear, I love thee.
Bot. Methinks, mistress, you should have
little reason for that: and yet, to say the truth,
reason and love keep little company together
now-a-days. The more the pity, that some
honest neighbours will not make them friends.
Nay, I can gleek upon occasion. 154
Tita. Thou art as wise as thou art beautiful.
Bot. Not so, neither; but if I had wit enough
to get out of this wood, I have enough to serve
mine own turn.
Tita. Out of this wood do not desire to go:
Thou shalt remain here, whe'r thou wilt or no.
I am a spirit of no common rate; 161
The summer still doth tend upon my state;
And I do love thee: therefore, go with me;
I'll give thee fairies to attend on thee, 164
And they shall fetch thee jewels from the deep,
And sing, while thou on pressed flowers dost
   sleep:
And I will purge thy mortal grossness so
That thou shalt like an airy spirit go. 168
Pease-blossom! Cobweb! Moth! and Mustard-
seed!

Enter Four Fairies.

Peas. Ready.
Cob.   And I.
Moth.   And I.
Mus.   And I.
All Four.   Where shall we go?
Tita. Be kind and courteous to this gentle-
man;

Hop in his walks, and gambol in his eyes; 172
Feed him with apricocks and dewberries,
With purple grapes, green figs, and mulberries.
The honey-bags steal from the humble-bees,
And for night-tapers crop their waxen thighs,
And light them at the fiery glow-worm's eyes,
To have my love to bed, and to arise;
And pluck the wings from painted butterflies
To fan the moonbeams from his sleeping eyes:
Nod to him, elves, and do him courtesies. 181
  Peas. Hail, mortal!
  Cob. Hail!
  Moth. Hail!   184
  Mus. Hail!
  Bot. I cry your worships mercy, heartily: I
beseech your worship's name.
  Cob. Cobweb.   188
  Bot. I shall desire you of more acquaintance,
good Master Cobweb: if I cut my finger, I shall
make bold with you. Your name, honest gen-
tleman?   192
  Peas. Pease-blossom.
  Bot. I pray you, commend me to Mistress
Squash, your mother, and to Master Peascod,
your father. Good Master Pease-blossom, I
shall desire you of more acquaintance too.
Your name, I beseech you, sir?   198
  Mus. Mustard-seed.
  Bot. Good Master Mustard-seed, I know your
patience well: that same cowardly, giant-like
ox-beef hath devoured many a gentleman of
your house. I promise you, your kindred hath
made my eyes water ere now. I desire you of
more acquaintance, good Master Mustard-seed.
  Tita. Come, wait upon him; lead him to my
    bower.   206
The moon methinks, looks with a watery eye;
And when she weeps, weeps every little flower,
Lamenting some enforced chastity.
Tie up my love's tongue, bring him silently. 210
                                        [*Exeunt.*

SCENE II.—*Another Part of the Wood.*
              Enter OBERON.

  Obe. I wonder if Titania be awak'd;
Then, what it was that next came in her eye,
Which she must dote on in extremity.
Here comes my messenger.

              Enter PUCK.

                     How now, mad spirit! 4
What night-rule now about this haunted grove?
  Puck. My mistress with a monster is in love.
Near to her close and consecrated bower,
While she was in her dull and sleeping hour, 8
A crew of patches, rude mechanicals,
That work for bread upon Athenian stalls,
Were met together to rehearse a play
Intended for great Theseus' nuptial day. 12
The shallowest thick-skin of that barren sort,
Who Pyramus presented in their sport
Forsook his scene, and enter'd in a brake,
When I did him at this advantage take; 16
An ass's nowl I fixed on his head:
Anon his Thisbe must be answered,

And forth my mimick comes. When they him
    spy,
As wild geese that the creeping fowler eye, 20
Or russet-pated choughs, many in sort,
Rising and cawing at the gun's report,
Sever themselves, and madly sweep the sky;
So, at his sight, away his fellows fly, 2
And, at our stamp, here o'er and o'er one falls
He murder cries, and help from Athens calls
Their sense thus weak, lost with their fears thu
    strong,   2
Made senseless things begin to do them wrong
For briers and thorns at their apparel snatch
Some sleeves, some hats, from yielders all thing
    catch.
I led them on in this distracted fear,
And left sweet Pyramus translated there; 3
When in that moment, so it came to pass,
Titania wak'd and straightway lov'd an ass.
  Obe. This falls out better than I could devise
But hast thou yet latch'd the Athenian's eyes
With the love-juice, as I did bid thee do? 3
  Puck. I took him sleeping,—that is finish'
    too,—
And the Athenian woman by his side;
That, when he wak'd, of force she must be ey'd

        Enter DEMETRIUS *and* HERMIA.

  Obe. Stand close: this is the same Athenian
  Puck. This is the woman; but not this th
    man.
  Dem. O! why rebuke you him that love
    you so?
Lay breath so bitter on your bitter foe. 4
  Her. Now I but chide; but I should use the
    worse,
For thou, I fear, hast given me cause to curse
If thou hast slain Lysander in his sleep,
Being o'er shoes in blood, plunge in knee deep
And kill me too. 4
The sun was not so true unto the day
As he to me. Would he have stol'n away
From sleeping Hermia? I'll believe as soon
This whole earth may be bor'd, and that th
    moon
May through the centre creep, and so displeas
Her brother's noontide with the Antipodes.
It cannot be but thou hast murder'd him; 5
So should a murderer look, so dead, so grim
  Dem. So should the murder'd look, and s
    should I,
Pierc'd through the heart with your ster
    cruelty;
Yet you, the murderer, look as bright, as clea
As yonder Venus in her glimmering sphere. 6
  Her. What's this to my Lysander? wher
    is he?
Ah! good Demetrius, wilt thou give him me
  Dem. I had rather give his carcass to m
    hounds. 6
  Her. Out, dog! out, cur! thou driv'st me pa
    the bounds
Of maiden's patience. Hast thou slain him then
Henceforth be never number'd among men!
O! once tell true, tell true, e'en for my sake; 6
Durst thou have look'd upon him being awak

nd hast thou kill'd him sleeping? O brave
  touch!
'ould not a worm, an adder, do so much?
n adder did it; for with doubler tongue   72
'han thine, thou serpent, never adder stung.

Dem. You spend your passion on a mis-
  pris'd mood:
am not guilty of Lysander's blood,
Jor is he dead, for aught that I can tell.   76

Her. I pray thee, tell me then that he is well.

Dem. An if I could, what should I get therefore?

Her. A privilege never to see me more.
nd from thy hated presence part I so;   80
ee me no more, whe'r he be dead or no.   [*Exit.*

Dem. There is no following her in this fierce
  vein:
Iere therefore for awhile I will remain.
o sorrow's heaviness doth heavier grow   84
or debt that bankrupt sleep doth sorrow owe;
Vhich now in some slight measure it will pay,
' for his tender here I make some stay.
          [*Lies down and sleeps.*

Obe. What hast thou done? thou hast mistaken quite,   88
nd laid the love-juice on some true-love's
  sight:
'f thy misprision must perforce ensue
ome true-love turn'd, and not a false turn'd
  true.

Puck. Then fate o'er-rules, that, one man
  holding troth,   92
million fail, confounding oath on oath.

Obe. About the wood go swifter than the
  wind,
nd Helena of Athens look thou find:
ll fancy-sick she is, and pale of cheer   96
'ith sighs of love, that cost the fresh blood
  dear.
y some illusion see thou bring her here:
ll charm his eyes against she do appear.

Puck. I go, I go; look how I go;   100
wifter than arrow from the Tartar's bow.
          [*Exit.*

Obe. Flower of this purple dye,
  Hit with Cupid's archery,
  Sink in apple of his eye.   104
  When his love he doth espy,
  Let her shine as gloriously
  As the Venus of the sky.
  When thou wak'st, if she be by,   108
  Beg of her for remedy.

Re-enter PUCK.

Puck. Captain of our fairy band,
  Helena is here at hand,
  And the youth, mistook by me,   112
  Pleading for a lover's fee.
  Shall we their fond pageant see?
  Lord, what fools these mortals be!

Obe. Stand aside: the noise they make   116
  Will cause Demetrius to awake.

Puck. Then will two at once woo one;
  That must needs be sport alone;
  And those things do best please me   120
  That befall preposterously.

Enter LYSANDER *and* HELENA.

Lys. Why should you think that I should woo
  in scorn?
Scorn and derision never come in tears:
Look, when I vow, I weep; and vows so born,
  In their nativity all truth appears.   125
How can these things in me seem scorn to you,
Bearing the badge of faith to prove them true?

Hel. You do advance your cunning more and
  more.   128
When truth kills truth, O devilish-holy fray!
These vows are Hermia's: will you give her
  o'er?
Weigh oath with oath, and you will nothing
  weigh:
Your vows, to her and me, put in two scales,
Will even weigh, and both as light as tales.   133

Lys. I had no judgment when to her I swore.

Hel. Nor none, in my mind, now you give
  her o'er.

Lys. Demetrius loves her, and he loves not
  you.   136

Dem. [*Awaking.*] O Helen! goddess, nymph,
  perfect, divine!
To what, my love, shall I compare thine eyne?
Crystal is muddy. O! how ripe in show   139
Thy lips, those kissing cherries, tempting grow;
This pure congealed white, high Taurus' snow,
Fann'd with the eastern wind, turns to a crow
When thou hold'st up thy hand. O! let me
  kiss   143
That princess of pure white, this seal of bliss.

Hel. O spite! O hell! I see you all are bent
To set against me for your merriment:
If you were civil and knew courtesy,
You would not do me thus much injury.   148
Can you not hate me, as I know you do,
But you must join in souls to mock me too?
If you were men, as men you are in show,
You would not use a gentle lady so;   152
To vow, and swear, and superpraise my parts,
When I am sure you hate me with your hearts.
You both are rivals, and love Hermia;
And now both rivals, to mock Helena: 156
A trim exploit, a manly enterprise,
To conjure tears up in a poor maid's eyes
With your derision! none of noble sort
Would so offend a virgin, and extort   160
A poor soul's patience, all to make you sport.

Lys. You are unkind, Demetrius; be not so;
For you love Hermia; this you know I know:
And here, with all good will, with all my heart,
In Hermia's love I yield you up my part;   165
And yours of Helena to me bequeath,
Whom I do love, and will do to my death.

Hel. Never did mockers waste more idle
  breath.

Dem. Lysander, keep thy Hermia; I will
  none:
If e'er I lov'd her, all that love is gone.
My heart with her but as guest-wise sojourn'd,
And now to Helen it is home return'd,   172
There to remain.

Lys.   Helen, it is not so.

Dem. Disparage not the faith thou dost not
  know,

Lest to thy peril thou aby it dear.
Look! where thy love comes: yonder is thy
  dear.   176

Enter HERMIA.

Her. Dark night, that from the eye his func-
  tion takes,
The ear more quick of apprehension makes;
Wherein it doth impair the seeing sense,
It pays the hearing double recompense.   180
Thou art not by mine eye, Lysander, found;
Mine ear, I thank it, brought me to thy sound.
But why unkindly didst thou leave me so?
Lys. Why should he stay, whom love doth
  press to go?   184
Her. What love could press Lysander from
  my side?
Lys. Lysander's love, that would not let him
  bide,
Fair Helena, who more engilds the night
Than all yon fiery oes and eyes of light.   188
Why seek'st thou me? could not this make thee
  know,
The hate I bear thee made me leave thee so?
Her. You speak not as you think: it cannot
  be.
Hel. Lo! she is one of this confederacy.   192
Now I perceive they have conjoin'd all three
To fashion this false sport in spite of me.
Injurious Hermia! most ungrateful maid!
Have you conspir'd, have you with these con-
  triv'd   196
To bait me with this foul derision?
Is all the counsel that we two have shar'd,
The sister-vows, the hours that we have spent,
When we have chid the hasty-footed time   200
For parting us, O! is it all forgot?
All school-days' friendship, childhood inno-
  cence?
We, Hermia, like two artificial gods,   203
Have with our needls created both one flower,
Both on one sampler, sitting on one cushion,
Both warbling of one song, both in one key,
As if our hands, our sides, voices, and minds,
Had been incorporate. So we grew together,
Like to a double cherry, seeming parted,   209
But yet an union in partition;
Two lovely berries moulded on one stem;
So, with two seeming bodies, but one heart;
Two of the first, like coats in heraldry,   213
Due but to one, and crowned with one crest.
And will you rent our ancient love asunder,
To join with men in scorning your poor friend?
It is not friendly, 'tis not maidenly: 217
Our sex, as well as I, may chide you for it,
Though I alone do feel the injury.
Her. I am amazed at your passionate words.
I scorn you not: it seems that you scorn me.
Hel. Have you not set Lysander, as in scorn,
To follow me and praise my eyes and face,
And made your other love, Demetrius,—   224
Who even but now did spurn me with his
  foot,—
To call me goddess, nymph, divine and rare,
Precious, celestial? Wherefore speaks he this
To her he hates? and wherefore doth Lysander

Deny your love, so rich within his soul,   22
And tender me, forsooth, affection,
But by your setting on, by your consent?
What though I be not so in grace as you,   23
So hung upon with love, so fortunate,
But miserable most to love unlov'd?
This you should pity rather than despise.
Her. I understand not what you mean by
  this.   23
Hel. Ay, do, persever, counterfeit sad looks
Make mouths upon me when I turn my back
Wink each at other; hold the sweet jest up:
This sport, well carried, shall be chronicled. 24
If you have any pity, grace, or manners,
You would not make me such an argument.
But, fare ye well: 'tis partly mine own fault,
Which death or absence soon shall remedy.   24
Lys. Stay, gentle Helena! hear my excuse:
My love, my life, my soul, fair Helena!
Hel. O excellent!
Her.   Sweet, do not scorn her so
Dem. If she cannot entreat, I can compel.
Lys. Thou canst compel no more than sh
  entreat: 24
Thy threats have no more strength than he
  weak prayers.
Helen, I love thee; by my life, I do:
I swear by that which I will lose for thee,   25
To prove him false that says I love thee not.
Dem. I say I love thee more than he ca
  do.
Lys. If thou say so, withdraw, and prove i
  too.
Dem. Quick, come!
Her.   Lysander, whereto tends all this
Lys. Away, you Ethiop!
Dem.   No, no, he'll . . . 25
Seem to break loose; take on, as you woul
  follow,
But yet come not: you are a tame man, go!
Lys. [*To* HERMIA.] Hang off, thou cat, tho
  burr! vile thing, let loose,   26
Or I will shake thee from me like a serpent.
Her. Why are you grown so rude? wha
  change is this,
Sweet love,—
Lys.   Thy love! out, tawny Tartar, out
Out, loathed medicine! hated poison, hence!
Her. Do you not jest?
Hel.   Yes, sooth; and so do yo
Lys. Demetrius, I will keep my word wit
  thee.
Dem. I would I had your bond, for I perceiv
A weak bond holds you: I'll not trust you
  word.   26
Lys. What! should I hurt her, strike her, ki
  her dead?
Although I hate her, I'll not harm her so.
Her. What! can you do me greater har
  than hate?
Hate me! wherefore? O me! what news, m
  love?   27
Am not I Hermia? Are not you Lysander?
I am as fair now as I was erewhile.
Since night you lov'd me; yet, since night yo
  left me:

hy, then you left me,—O, the gods forbid!—
earnest, shall I say?
Lys.   Ay, by my life; 277
nd never did desire to see thee more.
herefore be out of hope, of question, doubt;
e certain, nothing truer: 'tis no jest, 280
hat I do hate thee and love Helena.
  Her. O me! you juggler! you canker-blossom!
ou thief of love! what! have you come by
   night
nd stol'n my love's heart from him?
  Hel.   Fine, i' faith!
ave you no modesty, no maiden shame, 285
o touch of bashfulness? What! will you tear
npatient answers from my gentle tongue?
ie, fie! you counterfeit, you puppet you! 288
  Her. Puppet! why, so: ay, that way goes the
   game.
ow I perceive that she hath made compare
etween our statures: she hath urg'd her height;
nd with her personage, her tall personage, 292
er height, forsooth, she hath prevail'd with
  him.
nd are you grown so high in his esteem,
ecause I am so dwarfish and so low?
ow low am I, thou painted maypole? speak;
ow low am I? I am not yet so low 297
ut that my nails can reach unto thine eyes.
  Hel. I pray you, though you mock me,
   gentlemen,
et her not hurt me: I was never curst; 300
have no gift at all in shrewishness;
am a right maid for my cowardice:
et her not strike me. You perhaps may think,
ecause she is something lower than myself, 304
han I can match her.
  Her.   Lower! hark, again.
  Hel. Good Hermia, do not be so bitter with
   me.
evermore did love you, Hermia,
id ever keep your counsels, never wrong'd
  you; 308
ave that, in love unto Demetrius,
told him of your stealth unto this wood.
Ie follow'd you; for love I follow'd him;
ut he hath chid me hence, and threaten'd
  me 312
o strike me, spurn me, nay, to kill me too:
nd now, so you will let me quiet go,
o Athens will I bear my foolish back,
nd follow you no further: let me go: 316
ou see how simple and how fond I am.
  Her. Why, get you gone. Who is't that
   hinders you?
  Hel. A foolish heart, that I leave here behind.
  Her. What! with Lysander?
  Hel.   With Demetrius.
  Lys. Be not afraid: she shall not harm thee,
   Helena. 321
  Dem. No, sir; she shall not, though you take
   her part.
  Hel. O! when she's angry, she is keen and
   shrewd.
he was a vixen when she went to school: 324

And though she be but little, she is fierce.
  Her. 'Little' again! nothing but 'low' and
   'little!'
Why will you suffer her to flout me thus?
Let me come to her.
  Lys.   Get you gone, you dwarf; 328
You minimus, of hindering knot-grass made;
You bead, you acorn!
  Dem.   You are too officious
In her behalf that scorns your services.
Let her alone; speak not of Helena; 332
Take not her part, for, if thou dost intend
Never so little show of love to her,
Thou shalt aby it.
  Lys.   Now she holds me not;
Now follow, if thou dar'st, to try whose right,
Or thine or mine, is most in Helena. 337
  Dem. Follow! nay, I'll go with thee, cheek
   by jole.
        [*Exeunt* LYSANDER *and* DEMETRIUS.
  Her. You, mistress, all this coil is 'long of
   you:
Nay, go not back.
  Hel.   I will not trust you, I, 340
Nor longer stay in your curst company.
Your hands than mine are quicker for a fray,
My legs are longer though, to run away. [*Exit.*
  Her. I am amaz'd, and know not what to
   say. [*Exit.*
  Obe. This is thy negligence: still thou mis-
   tak'st, 345
Or else commit'st thy knaveries wilfully.
  Puck. Believe me, king of shadows, I mis-
   took.
Did not you tell me I should know the man
By the Athenian garments he had on? 349
And so far blameless proves my enterprise,
That I have 'nointed an Athenian's eyes;
And so far am I glad it so did sort, 352
As this their jangling I esteem a sport.
  Obe. Thou see'st these lovers seek a place to
   fight:
Hie therefore, Robin, overcast the night;
The starry welkin cover thou anon 356
With drooping fog as black as Acheron;
And lead these testy rivals so astray,
As one come not within another's way.
Like to Lysander sometime frame thy tongue,
Then stir Demetrius up with bitter wrong; 361
And sometime rail thou like Demetrius;
And from each other look thou lead them thus,
Till o'er their brows death-counterfeiting sleep
With leaden legs and batty wings doth creep:
Then crush this herb into Lysander's eye;
Whose liquor hath this virtuous property, 367
To take from thence all error with his might,
And make his eyeballs roll with wonted sight.
When they next wake, all this derision
Shall seem a dream and fruitless vision;
And back to Athens shall the lovers wend, 372
With league whose date till death shall never end.
Whiles I in this affair do thee employ,
I'll to my queen and beg her Indian boy;
And then I will her charmed eye release 376
From monster's view, and all things shall be
  peace.

Puck. My fairy lord, this must be done with haste,
For night's swift dragons cut the clouds full fast,
And yonder shines Aurora's harbinger;   380
At whose approach, ghosts, wandering here and there,
Troop home to churchyards: damned spirits all,
That in cross-ways and floods have burial,
Already to their wormy beds are gone;   384
For fear lest day should look their shames upon,
They wilfully themselves exile from light,
And must for aye consort with black-brow'd night.
Obe. But we are spirits of another sort.   388
I with the morning's love have oft made sport;
And, like a forester, the groves may tread,
Even till the eastern gate, all fiery-red,   391
Opening on Neptune with fair blessed beams,
Turns into yellow gold his salt green streams.
But, notwithstanding, haste; make no delay:
We may effect this business yet ere day.
                              [*Exit* OBERON.
Puck. Up and down, up and down;   396
   I will lead them up and down:
   I am fear'd in field and town;
   Goblin, lead them up and down.
Here comes one.   400

Re-enter LYSANDER.

Lys. Where art thou, proud Demetrius? speak thou now.
Puck. Here, villain! drawn and ready. Where art thou?
Lys. I will be with thee straight.
Puck.   Follow me, then,
To plainer ground.
         [*Exit* LYSANDER *as following the voice.*

Re-enter DEMETRIUS.

Dem.   Lysander! speak again.   404
Thou runaway, thou coward, art thou fled?
Speak! In some bush? Where dost thou hide thy head?
Puck. Thou coward! art thou bragging to the stars,
Telling the bushes that thou look'st for wars,
And wilt not come? Come, recreant; come, thou child;   409
I'll whip thee with a rod: he is defil'd
That draws a sword on thee.
Dem.   Yea, art thou there?
Puck. Follow my voice: we'll try no manhood here.   [*Exeunt.*

Re-enter LYSANDER.

Lys. He goes before me and still dares me on:
When I come where he calls, then he is gone.
The villain is much lighter-heel'd than I:
I follow'd fast, but faster he did fly;   416
That fallen am I in dark uneven way,
And here will rest me. [*Lies down.*] Come, thou gentle day!

For if but once thou show me thy grey light
I'll find Demetrius and revenge this spite. 42
                                    [*Sleeps*

Re-enter PUCK and DEMETRIUS.

Puck. Ho! ho! ho! Coward, why com'st thou not?
Dem. Abide me, if thou dar'st; for well I wo
Thou runn'st before me, shifting every place,
And dar'st not stand, nor look me in the face.   42
Where art thou now?
Puck.   Come hither: I am here.
Dem. Nay then, thou mock'st me. Thou shalt buy this dear,
If ever I thy face by daylight see: 42
Now, go thy way. Faintness constraineth me
To measure out my length on this cold bed:
By day's approach look to be visited.
                          [*Lies down and sleeps*

Re-enter HELENA.

Hel. O weary night! O long and tediou night,
Abate thy hours! shine, comforts, from the east!   43
That I may back to Athens by daylight,
From these that my poor company detest:
And sleep, that sometimes shuts up sorrow' eye,
Steal me awhile from mine own company.   43
                          [*Lies down and sleeps*
Puck. Yet but three? Come one more;
   Two of both kinds make up four.
   Here she comes, curst and sad:
   Cupid is a knavish lad,   44
   Thus to make poor females mad.

Re-enter HERMIA.

Her. Never so weary, never so in woe,
   Bedabbled with the dew and torn with briers
I can no further crawl, no further go;   44
My legs can keep no pace with my desires.
Here will I rest me till the break of day.
Heavens shield Lysander, if they mean a fray
                          [*Lies down and sleeps*
Puck.   On the ground   44
            Sleep sound:
            I'll apply
            To your eye,
         Gentle lover, remedy.   45
   [*Squeezing the juice on* LYSANDER'S *eyes*
            When thou wak'st,
            Thou tak'st
            True delight
            In the sight   45
         Of thy former lady's eye:
   And the country proverb known,
   That every man should take his own,
   In your waking shall be shown: 46
         Jack shall have Jill;
         Nought shall go ill;
   The man shall have his mare again,
   And all shall be well.   [*Exi*

ACT IV

SCENE I.—*A Wood.* LYSANDER, DEMETRIUS,
HELENA *and* HERMIA *lying asleep.*

Enter TITANIA *and* BOTTOM, *Fairies attending;*
OBERON *behind unseen.*

Tita. Come, sit thee down upon this flowery bed,
  While I thy amiable cheeks do coy,
And stick musk-roses in thy sleek smooth head,
  And kiss thy fair large ears, my gentle joy. 4
Bot. Where's Pease-blossom?
Peas. Ready.
Bot. Scratch my head, Pease-blossom. Where's
Mounsieur Cobweb? 8
Cob. Ready.
Bot. Mounsieur Cobweb, good mounsieur, get
your weapons in your hand, and kill me a red-
hipped humble-bee on the top of a thistle; and,
good mounsieur, bring me the honey-bag. Do
not fret yourself too much in the action, moun-
sieur; and, good mounsieur, have a care the
honey-bag break not; I would be loath to have
you overflown with a honey-bag, signior. Where's
Mounsieur Mustard-seed? 18
Must. Ready.
Bot. Give me your neaf, Mounsieur Mustard-
seed. Pray you, leave your curtsy, good mounsieur.
Must. What's your will? 23
Bot. Nothing, good mounsieur, but to help
Cavalery Cobweb to scratch. I must to the
barber's, mounsieur, for methinks I am marvellous hairy about the face; and I am such a
tender ass, if my hair do but tickle me, I must
scratch. 29
Tita. What, wilt thou hear some music, my
sweet love?
Bot. I have a reasonable good ear in music:
let us have the tongs and the bones. 33
Tita. Or say, sweet love, what thou desir'st
to eat.
Bot. Truly, a peck of provender: I could
munch your good dry oats. Methinks I have
a great desire to a bottle of hay: good hay, sweet
hay, hath no fellow. 39
Tita. I have a venturous fairy that shall seek
The squirrel's hoard, and fetch thee thence new
  nuts.
Bot. I had rather have a handful or two of
dried pease. But, I pray you, let none of your
people stir me: I have an exposition of sleep
come upon me. 45
Tita. Sleep thou, and I will wind thee in my
  arms.
Fairies, be gone, and be all ways away.
                    [*Exeunt Fairies.*
So doth the woodbine the sweet honeysuckle
Gently entwist; the female ivy so 49
Enrings the barky fingers of the elm.
O! how I love thee; how I dote on thee!
                    [*They sleep.*

Enter PUCK.

Obe. [*Advancing.*] Welcome, good Robin.
  See'st thou this sweet sight? 52
Her dotage now I do begin to pity:

For, meeting her of late behind the wood,
Seeking sweet favours for this hateful fool,
I did upbraid her and fall out with her; 56
For she my hairy temples then had rounded
With coronet of fresh and fragrant flowers;
And that same dew, which sometime on the
  buds
Was wont to swell like round and orient
  pearls, 60
Stood now within the pretty flowerets' eyes
Like tears that did their own disgrace bewail.
When I had at my pleasure taunted her,
And she in mild terms begg'd my patience, 64
I then did ask of her her changeling child;
Which straight she gave me, and her fairy
  sent
To bear him to my bower in fairy land.
And now I have the boy, I will undo 68
This hateful imperfection of her eyes:
And, gentle Puck, take this transformed scalp
From off the head of this Athenian swain,
That he, awaking when the other do, 72
May all to Athens back again repair,
And think no more of this night's accidents
But as the fierce vexation of a dream.
But first I will release the fairy queen. 76
    [*Touching her eyes with an herb.*
  Be as thou wast wont to be;
  See as thou wast wont to see:
  Dian's bud o'er Cupid's flower
  Hath such force and blessed power. 80
Now, my Titania; wake you, my sweet queen.
Tita. My Oberon! what visions have I seen!
Methought I was enamour'd of an ass.
Obe. There lies your love.
Tita.   How came these things to pass?
O! how mine eyes do loathe his visage now. 85
Obe. Silence, awhile. Robin, take off this
  head.
Titania, music call; and strike more dead
Than common sleep of all these five the sense.
Tita. Music, ho! music! such as charmeth
  sleep. [*Music.*
Puck. When thou wak'st, with thine own
  fool's eyes peep.
Obe. Sound, music! [*Still, music.*] Come, my
  queen, take hands with me,
And rock the ground whereon these sleepers
  be.
Now thou and I are new in amity, 93
And will to-morrow midnight solemnly
Dance in Duke Theseus' house triumphantly,
And bless it to all fair prosperity. 96
There shall the pairs of faithful lovers be
Wedded, with Theseus, all in jollity.
Puck. Fairy king, attend, and mark:
    I do hear the morning lark. 100
Obe. Then, my queen, in silence sad,
    Trip we after the night's shade;
    We the globe can compass soon,
    Swifter than the wandering moon.
Tita. Come, my lord; and in our flight 105
    Tell me how it came this night
    That I sleeping here was found
    With these mortals on the ground. 108
    [*Exeunt. Horns winded within.*

Enter THESEUS, HIPPOLYTA, EGEUS, *and Train.*

The. Go, one of you, find out the forester;
For now our observation is perform'd;
And since we have the vaward of the day,   111
My love shall hear the music of my hounds.
Uncouple in the western valley; let them go:
Dispatch, I say, and find the forester.
We will, fair queen, up to the mountain's top,
And mark the musical confusion   116
Of hounds and echo in conjunction.

Hip. I was with Hercules and Cadmus once,
When in a wood of Crete they bay'd the bear
With hounds of Sparta: never did I hear   120
Such gallant chiding: for, besides the groves,
The skies, the fountains, every region near
Seem'd all one mutual cry. I never heard
So musical a discord, such sweet thunder.   124

The. My hounds are bred out of the Spartan
    kind,
So flew'd, so sanded; and their heads are hung
With ears that sweep away the morning dew;
Crook-knee'd, and dew-lapp'd like Thessalian
    bulls;   128
Slow in pursuit, but match'd in mouth like
    bells,
Each under each. A cry more tuneable
Was never holla'd to, nor cheer'd with horn,
In Crete, in Sparta, nor in Thessaly: 132
Judge, when you hear. But, soft! what nymphs
    are these?

Ege. My lord, this is my daughter here asleep;
And this, Lysander; this Demetrius is;
This Helena, old Nedar's Helena: 136
I wonder of their being here together.

The. No doubt they rose up early to observe
The rite of May, and, hearing our intent,
Came here in grace of our solemnity.   140
But speak, Egeus, is not this the day
That Hermia should give answer of her choice?

Ege. It is, my lord.

The.   Go, bid the huntsmen wake them with
    their horns.   144

[*Horns and shout within.* LYSANDER, DE-
    METRIUS, HERMIA, *and* HELENA, *wake and
    start up.*

Good morrow, friends. Saint Valentine is past:
Begin these wood-birds but to couple now?

Lys. Pardon, my lord. [*He and the rest kneel.*

The.   I pray you all, stand up.
I know you two are rival enemies: 148
How comes this gentle concord in the world,
That hatred is so far from jealousy,
To sleep by hate, and fear no enmity?

Lys. My lord, I shall reply amazedly,   152
Half sleep, half waking: but as yet, I swear,
I cannot truly say how I came here;
But, as I think,—for truly would I speak,
And now I do bethink me, so it is,—   156
I came with Hermia hither: our intent
Was to be gone from Athens, where we might,
Without the peril of the Athenian law—

Ege. Enough, enough, my lord; you have
    enough: 160
I beg the law, the law, upon his head.
They would have stol'n away; they would,
    Demetrius,

Thereby to have defeated you and me;
You of your wife, and me of my consent,   164
Of my consent that she should be your wife.

Dem. My lord, fair Helen told me of their
    stealth,
Of this their purpose hither, to this wood;
And I in fury hither follow'd them,   168
Fair Helena in fancy following me.
But, my good lord, I wot not by what power,—
But by some power it is,—my love to Hermia,
Melted as doth the snow, seems to me now   172
As the remembrance of an idle gaud
Which in my childhood I did dote upon;
And all the faith, the virtue of my heart,
The object and the pleasure of mine eye,   176
Is only Helena. To her, my lord,
Was I betroth'd ere I saw Hermia:
But, like in sickness, did I loathe this food;
But, as in health, come to my natural taste,
Now do I wish it, love it, long for it,   181
And will for evermore be true to it.

The. Fair lovers, you are fortunately met:
Of this discourse we more will hear anon.   184
Egeus, I will overbear your will,
For in the temple, by and by, with us,
These couples shall eternally be knit:
And, for the morning now is something worn,
Our purpos'd hunting shall be set aside.   189
Away with us, to Athens: three and three,
We'll hold a feast in great solemnity.
Come, Hippolyta.   192

[*Exeunt* THESEUS, HIPPOLYTA, EGEUS,
    and Train.

Dem. These things seem small and un-
    distinguishable,
Like far-off mountains turned into clouds.

Her. Methinks I see these things with parted
    eye,
When everything seems double.

Hel.   So methinks:
And I have found Demetrius, like a jewel,   197
Mine own, and not mine own.

Dem.   Are you sure
That we are awake? It seems to me
That yet we sleep, we dream. Do you not think
The duke was here, and bid us follow him?   201

Her. Yea; and my father.

Hel.   And Hippolyta.

Lys. And he did bid us follow to the temple.

Dem. Why then, we are awake. Let's fol-
    low him;   204
And by the way let us recount our dreams.

[*Exeunt.*

Bot. [*Awaking.*] When my cue comes, call
me, and I will answer: my next is, 'Most fair
Pyramus.' Heigh-ho! Peter Quince! Flute, the
bellows-mender! Snout, the tinker! Starveling!
God's my life! stolen hence, and left me asleep!
I have had a most rare vision. I have had a
dream, past the wit of man to say what dream
it was: man is but an ass, if he go about to expound this dream. Methought I was— there is
no man can tell what. Methought I was—and
methought I had,—but man is but a patched
fool, if he will offer to say what methought I had.
The eye of man hath not heard, the ear of man

hath not seen, man's hand is not able to taste, his tongue to conceive, nor his heart to report, what my dream was. I will get Peter Quince to write a ballad of this dream: it shall be called Bottom's Dream, because it hath no bottom; and I will sing it in the latter end of a play, before the duke: peradventure, to make it the more gracious, I shall sing it at her death. 226
                                                                      [Exit.

SCENE II.—*Athens. A Room in* QUINCE'S *House.*

Enter QUINCE, FLUTE, SNOUT, *and* STARVELING.

Quin. Have you sent to Bottom's house? is he come home yet?

Star. He cannot be heard of. Out of doubt he is transported. 4

Flu. If he come not, then the play is marred: it goes not forward, doth it?

Quin. It is not possible: you have not a man in all Athens able to discharge Pyramus but he. 9

Flu. No; he hath simply the best wit of any handicraft man in Athens.

Quin. Yea, and the best person too; and he is a very paramour for a sweet voice. 13

Flu. You must say, 'paragon:' a paramour is, God bless us! a thing of naught.

Enter SNUG.

Snug. Masters, the duke is coming from the temple, and there is two or three lords and ladies more married: if our sport had gone forward, we had all been made men. 19

Flu. O sweet bully Bottom! Thus hath he lost sixpence a day during his life; he could not have 'scaped sixpence a day: an the duke had not given him sixpence a day for playing Pyramus, I'll be hanged; he would have deserved it: sixpence a day in Pyramus, or nothing. 25

Enter BOTTOM.

Bot. Where are these lads? where are these hearts?

Quin. Bottom! O most courageous day! O most happy hour! 29

Bot. Masters, I am to discourse wonders: but ask me not what; for if I tell you, I am no true Athenian. I will tell you everything, right as it fell out. 33

Quin. Let us hear, sweet Bottom.

Bot. Not a word of me. All that I will tell you is, that the duke hath dined. Get your apparel together, good strings to your beards, new ribbons to your pumps; meet presently at the palace; every man look o'er his part; for the short and the long is, our play is preferred. In any case, let Thisby have clean linen; and let not him that plays the lion pare his nails, for they shall hang out for the lion's claws. And, most dear actors, eat no onions nor garlic, for we are to utter sweet breath, and I do not doubt but to hear them say, it is a sweet comedy. No more words: away! go; away.   [*Exeunt.*

ACT V

SCENE I.—*Athens. An Apartment in the Palace of* THESEUS.

Enter THESEUS, HIPPOLYTA, PHILOSTRATE, Lords, *and* Attendants.

Hip. 'Tis strange, my Theseus, that these lovers speak of.

The. More strange than true. I never may believe
These antique fables, nor these fairy toys.
Lovers and madmen have such seething brains,
Such shaping fantasies, that apprehend   5
More than cool reason ever comprehends.
The lunatic, the lover, and the poet,
Are of imagination all compact: 8
One sees more devils than vast hell can hold,
That is, the madman; the lover, all as frantic,
Sees Helen's beauty in a brow of Egypt:
The poet's eye, in a fine frenzy rolling,   12
Doth glance from heaven to earth, from earth to heaven;
And, as imagination bodies forth
The forms of things unknown, the poet's pen
Turns them to shapes, and gives to airy nothing
A local habitation and a name.   17
Such tricks hath strong imagination,
That, if it would but apprehend some joy,
It comprehends some bringer of that joy: 20
Or in the night, imagining some fear,
How easy is a bush suppos'd a bear!

Hip. But all the story of the night told over,
And all their minds transfigur'd so together, 24
More witnesseth than fancy's images,
And grows to something of great constancy,
But, howsoever, strange and admirable.

The. Here come the lovers, full of joy and mirth.   28

Enter LYSANDER, DEMETRIUS, HERMIA, *and* HELENA.

Joy, gentle friends! joy, and fresh days of love
Accompany your hearts!

Lys.   More than to us
Wait in your royal walks, your board, your bed!

The. Come now; what masques, what dances shall we have,   32
To wear away this long age of three hours
Between our after-supper and bed-time?
Where is our usual manager of mirth?
What revels are in hand? Is there no play, 36
To ease the anguish of a torturing hour?
Call Philostrate.

Philost.   Here, mighty Theseus.

The. Say, what abridgment have you for this evening?
What masque? what music? How shall we beguile   40
The lazy time, if not with some delight?

Philost. There is a brief how many sports are ripe;
Make choice of which your highness will see first.   [*Gives a paper.*

The. The battle with the Centaurs, to be sung   44

By an Athenian eunuch to the harp.
We'll none of that: that have I told my love,
In glory of my kinsman Hercules.
The riot of the tipsy Bacchanals, 48
Tearing the Thracian singer in their rage.
That is an old device; and it was play'd
When I from Thebes came last a conqueror.
The thrice three Muses mourning for the death
Of Learning, late deceas'd in beggary. 53
That is some satire keen and critical,
Not sorting with a nuptial ceremony.
A tedious brief scene of young Pyramus 56
And his love Thisbe; very tragical mirth.
Merry and tragical! tedious and brief!
That is, hot ice and wonderous strange snow.
How shall we find the concord of this discord?
  Philost. A play there is, my lord, some ten
    words long, 61
Which is as brief as I have known a play;
But by ten words, my lord, it is too long,
Which makes it tedious; for in all the play 64
There is not one word apt, one player fitted.
And tragical, my noble lord, it is;
For Pyramus therein doth kill himself.
Which when I saw rehears'd, I must confess, 68
Made mine eyes water; but more merry tears
The passion of loud laughter never shed.
  The. What are they that do play it?
  Philost. Hard-handed men, that work in
    Athens here, 72
Which never labour'd in their minds till now,
And now have toil'd their unbreath'd memories
With this same play, against your nuptial.
  The. And we will hear it.
  Philost. No, my noble lord;
It is not for you: I have heard it over, 77
And it is nothing, nothing in the world;
Unless you can find sport in their intents,
Extremely stretch'd and conn'd with cruel pain,
To do you service.
  The. I will hear that play; 81
For never anything can be amiss,
When simpleness and duty tender it.
Go, bring them in: and take your places, ladies.
                [*Exit* PHILOSTRATE.
  Hip. I love not to see wretchedness o'er-
    charg'd, 85
And duty in his service perishing.
  The. Why, gentle sweet, you shall see no
    such thing.
  Hip. He says they can do nothing in this
    kind. 88
  The. The kinder we, to give them thanks for
    nothing.
Our sport shall be to take what they mistake:
And what poor duty cannot do, noble respect
Takes it in might, not merit. 92
Where I have come, great clerks have purposed
To greet me with premeditated welcomes;
Where I have seen them shiver and look pale,
Make periods in the midst of sentences, 96
Throttle their practis'd accent in their fears,
And, in conclusion, dumbly have broke off,
Not paying me a welcome. Trust me, sweet,
Out of this silence yet I pick'd a welcome; 100
And in the modesty of fearful duty

I read as much as from the rattling tongue
Of saucy and audacious eloquence.
Love, therefore, and tongue-tied simplicity 104
In least speak most, to my capacity.

Re-enter PHILOSTRATE.

  Philost. So please your Grace, the Prologue
    is address'd.
  The. Let him approach.
                [*Flourish of trumpets.*

Enter QUINCE *for the* Prologue.

  Prol. If we offend, it is with our good will. 108
    That you should think, we come not to of-
    fend,
But with good will. To show our simple skill,
    That is the true beginning of our end.
Consider then we come but in despite. 112
    We do not come as minding to content you,
Our true intent is. All for your delight,
    We are not here. That you should here re-
    pent you,
The actors are at hand; and, by their show, 116
You shall know all that you are like to know.
  The. This fellow doth not stand upon points.
  Lys. He hath rid his prologue like a rough
colt; he knows not the stop. A good moral, my
lord: it is not enough to speak, but to speak
true. 122
  Hip. Indeed he hath played on his prologue
like a child on a recorder; a sound, but not in
government.
  The. His speech was like a tangled chain;
nothing impaired, but all disordered. Who is
next? 128

Enter PYRAMUS *and* THISBE, WALL, MOON-
SHINE, *and* LION, *as in dumb show.*

  Prol. Gentles, perchance you wonder at this
    show;
    But wonder on, till truth make all things
    plain.
This man is Pyramus, if you would know;
    This beauteous lady Thisby is, certain. 132
This man, with lime and rough-cast, doth pre-
    sent
    Wall, that vile Wall which did these lovers
    sunder;
And through Wall's chink, poor souls, they are
    content 135
    To whisper, at the which let no man wonder.
This man, with lanthorn, dog, and bush of
    thorn,
    Presenteth Moonshine; for, if you will know,
By moonshine did these lovers think no scorn
    To meet at Ninus' tomb, there, there to
    woo. 140
This grisly beast, which Lion hight by name,
The trusty Thisby, coming first by night,
Did scare away, or rather did affright;
And, as she fled, her mantle she did fall, 144
    Which Lion vile with bloody mouth did stain.
Anon comes Pyramus, sweet youth and tall,
    And finds his trusty Thisby's mantle slain:
Whereat, with blade, with bloody blameful
    blade, 148

He bravely broach'd his boiling bloody breast;
And Thisby, tarrying in mulberry shade,
His dagger drew, and died. For all the rest,
Let Lion, Moonshine, Wall, and lovers twain,
At large discourse, while here they do remain.

[*Exeunt* PROLOGUE, PYRAMUS, THISBE, LION, *and* MOONSHINE.

The. I wonder, if the lion be to speak.

Dem. No wonder, my lord: one lion may, when many asses do.   156

Wall. In this same interlude it doth befall
That I, one Snout by name, present a wall;
And such a wall, as I would have you think,
That had in it a crannied hole or chink,   160
Through which the lovers, Pyramus and Thisby,
Did whisper often very secretly.
This loam, this rough-cast, and this stone doth show
That I am that same wall; the truth is so;   164
And this the cranny, is, right and sinister,
Through which the fearful lovers are to whisper.

The. Would you desire lime and hair to speak better?   168

Dem. It is the wittiest partition that ever I heard discourse, my lord.

The. Pyramus draws near the wall: silence!

Re-enter PYRAMUS.

Pyr. O grim-look'd night! O night with hue so black!   172
O night, which ever art when day is not!
O night! O night! alack, alack, alack!
I fear my Thisby's promise is forgot.
And thou, O wall! O sweet, O lovely wall!   176
That stand'st between her father's ground and mine;
Thou wall, O wall! O sweet, and lovely wall!
Show me thy chink to blink through with mine eyne.   [WALL holds up his fingers.
Thanks, courteous wall: Jove shield thee well for this!   180
But what see I? No Thisby do I see.
O wicked wall! through whom I see no bliss;
Curs'd be thy stones for thus deceiving me!

The. The wall, methinks, being sensible, should curse again.   185

Pyr. No, in truth, sir, he should not. 'Deceiving me,' that's her cue: she is to enter now, and I am to spy her through the wall. You shall see, it will fall pat as I told you. Yonder she comes.

Re-enter THISBE.

This. O wall! full often hast thou heard my moans,
For parting my fair Pyramus and me: 192
My cherry lips have often kiss'd thy stones,
Thy stones with lime and hair knit up in thee.

Pyr. I see a voice: now will I to the chink,
To spy an I can hear my Thisby's face.   196

Thisby!

This. My love! thou art my love, I think.

Pyr. Think what thou wilt, I am thy lover's grace;
And, like Limander, am I trusty still.   200

This. And I like Helen, till the Fates me kill.

Pyr. Not Shafalus to Procrus was so true.

This. As Shafalus to Procrus, I to you.

Pyr. O! kiss me through the hole of this vile wall.   204

This. I kiss the wall's hole, not your lips at all.

Pyr. Wilt thou at Ninny's tomb meet me straightway?

This. 'Tide life, 'tide death, I come without delay.   [*Exeunt* PYRAMUS *and* THISBE.

Wall. Thus have I, Wall, my part discharged so;   208
And, being done, thus Wall away doth go. [*Exit.*

The. Now is the mural down between the two neighbours.

Dem. No remedy, my lord, when walls are so wilful to hear without warning.   213

Hip. This is the silliest stuff that ever I heard.

The. The best in this kind are but shadows, and the worst are no worse, if imagination amend them.   217

Hip. It must be your imagination then, and not theirs.

The. If we imagine no worse of them than they of themselves, they may pass for excellent men. Here come two noble beasts in, a man and a lion.

Re-enter LION *and* MOONSHINE.

Lion. You, ladies, you, whose gentle hearts do fear   224
The smallest monstrous mouse that creeps on floor,
May now perchance both quake and tremble here,
When lion rough in wildest rage doth roar.
Then know that I, one Snug the joiner, am   228
A lion-fell, nor else no lion's dam;
For, if I should as lion come in strife
Into this place, 'twere pity on my life.

The. A very gentle beast, and of a good conscience.   233

Dem. The very best at a beast, my lord, that e'er I saw.

Lys. This lion is a very fox for his valour.

The. True; and a goose for his discretion.   237

Dem. Not so, my lord; for his valour cannot carry his discretion, and the fox carries the goose.   240

The. His discretion, I am sure, cannot carry his valour, for the goose carries not the fox. It is well: leave it to his discretion, and let us listen to the moon.   244

Moon. This lanthorn doth the horned moon present;—

Dem. He should have worn the horns on his head.

The. He is no crescent, and his horns are invisible within the circumference.   249

Moon. This lanthorn doth the horned moon present;
Myself the man i' the moon do seem to be.

The. This is the greatest error of all the rest. The man should be put into the lanthorn: how is it else the man i' the moon?

Dem. He dares not come there for the candle;
for, you see, it is already in snuff.   256

Hip. I am aweary of this moon: would he
would change!

The. It appears, by his small light of discretion, that he is in the wane; but yet, in courtesy,
in all reason, we must stay the time.   261

Lys. Proceed, Moon.

Moon. All that I have to say, is, to tell you
that the lanthorn is the moon; I, the man in
the moon; this thorn-bush, my thorn-bush; and
this dog, my dog.

Dem. Why, all these should be in the lanthorn; for all these are in the moon. But,
silence! here comes Thisbe.   269

Re-enter THISBE.

This. This is old Ninny's tomb. Where is my
love?

Lion. [*Roaring.*] Oh—.   [THISBE *runs off.*
Dem. Well roared, Lion.   272
The. Well run, Thisbe.
Hip. Well shone, Moon. Truly, the moon
shines with a good grace.
    [*The* LION *tears* THISBE'S *mantle, and exit.*
The. Well moused, Lion.   276
Dem. And then came Pyramus.
Lys. And so the lion vanished.

Re-enter PYRAMUS.

Pyr. Sweet moon, I thank thee for thy sunny
    beams;   279
I thank thee, moon, for shining now so bright,
For, by thy gracious, golden, glittering streams,
I trust to taste of truest Thisby's sight.
    But stay, O spite!
    But mark, poor knight,   284
What dreadful dole is here!
    Eyes, do you see?
    How can it be?
O dainty duck! O dear!   288
    Thy mantle good,
    What! stain'd with blood!
Approach, ye Furies fell!
    O Fates, come, come,   292
    Cut thread and thrum;
    Quail, crush, conclude, and quell!
The. This passion, and the death of a dear
friend, would go near to make a man look sad.
Hip. Beshrew my heart, but I pity the man.
Pyr. O! wherefore, Nature, didst thou lions
    frame?
Since lion vile hath here deflower'd my dear!
Which is—no, no—which was the fairest dame
That liv'd, that lov'd, that lik'd, that look'd
    with cheer.   301
    Come tears, confound;
    Out, sword, and wound
The pap of Pyramus: 304
    Ay, that left pap,
    Where heart doth hop:
Thus die I, thus, thus, thus.
    [*Stabs himself.*
    Now am I dead,   308
    Now am I fled;

My soul is in the sky:
    Tongue, lose thy light!
    Moon, take thy flight!   312
        [*Exit* MOONSHINE.
Now die, die, die, die, die.   [*Dies.*
Dem. No die, but an ace, for him; for he is
but one.
Lys. Less than an ace, man, for he is dead;
he is nothing.   317
The. With the help of a surgeon, he might
yet recover, and prove an ass.
Hip. How chance Moonshine is gone before
Thisbe comes back and finds her lover?   321
The. She will find him by starlight. Here
she comes; and her passion ends the play.

Re-enter THISBE.

Hip. Methinks she should not use a long one
for such a Pyramus: I hope she will be brief.
Dem. A mote will turn the balance, which Pyramus, which Thisbe, is the better: he for a man,
God warrant us; she for a woman, God bless us.
Lys. She hath spied him already with those
sweet eyes.
Dem. And thus she moans, *videlicet:—*
This. *Asleep, my love?*   332
    What, dead, my dove?
O Pyramus, arise!
    Speak, speak! Quite dumb?
    Dead, dead! A tomb   336
Must cover thy sweet eyes.
    These lily lips,
    This cherry nose,
These yellow cowslip cheeks,   340
    Are gone, are gone:
    Lovers, make moan!
His eyes were green as leeks.
    O, Sisters Three,   344
    Come, come to me,
With hands as pale as milk;
    Lay them in gore,
    Since you have shore   348
With shears his thread of silk.
    Tongue, not a word:
    Come, trusty sword:
Come, blade, my breast imbrue: 352
    [*Stabs herself.*
    And farewell, friends;
    Thus Thisby ends:
    Adieu, adieu, adieu.   [*Dies.*
The. Moonshine and Lion are left to bury the
dead.   357
Dem. Ay, and Wall too.
Bot. No, I assure you; the wall is down that
parted their fathers. Will it please you to see
the epilogue, or to hear a Bergomask dance
between two of our company?   362
The. No epilogue, I pray you; for your play
needs no excuse. Never excuse; for when the
players are all dead, there need none to be
blamed. Marry, if he that writ it had played
Pyramus, and hanged himself in Thisbe's garter, it would have been a fine tragedy: and
so it is, truly, and very notably discharged.
But come, your Bergomask: let your epilogue
alone.   [*A dance.*

The iron tongue of midnight hath told twelve;
Lovers, to bed; 'tis almost fairy time.   373
I fear we shall out-sleep the coming morn,
As much as we this night have overwatch'd.
This palpable-gross play hath well beguil'd 376
The heavy gait of night. Sweet friends, to bed.
A fortnight hold we this solemnity,
In nightly revels, and new jollity.   [*Exeunt.*

Scene II

Enter PUCK.

Puck. Now the hungry lion roars,
     And the wolf behowls the moon;
Whilst the heavy ploughman snores,
     All with weary task fordone.   4
Now the wasted brands do glow,
     Whilst the screech-owl, screeching loud,
Puts the wretch that lies in woe
     In remembrance of a shroud.   8
Now it is the time of night
     That the graves, all gaping wide,
Every one lets forth his sprite,
     In the church-way paths to glide: 12
And we fairies, that do run
By the triple Hecate's team,
From the presence of the sun,
     Following darkness like a dream,   16
Now are frolic; not a mouse
Shall disturb this hallow'd house:
I am sent with broom before,
To sweep the dust behind the door.   20

Enter OBERON *and* TITANIA, *with their Train.*

Obe. Through the house give glimmering light
     By the dead and drowsy fire;
Every elf and fairy sprite
     Hop as light as bird from brier;   24
And this ditty after me
     Sing and dance it trippingly.
Tita. First, rehearse your song by rote,
     To each word a warbling note: 28

Hand in hand, with fairy grace,
Will we sing, and bless this place.
         [*Song and dance.*
Obe. Now, until the break of day,
Through this house each fairy stray.   32
To the best bride-bed will we,
Which by us shall blessed be;
And the issue there create
Ever shall be fortunate.   36
So shall all the couples three
Ever true in loving be;
And the blots of Nature's hand
Shall not in their issue stand: 40
Never mole, hare-lip, nor scar,
Nor mark prodigious, such as are
Despised in nativity,
Shall upon their children be.   44
With this field-dew consecrate,
Every fairy take his gait,
And each several chamber bless,
Through this palace, with sweet peace; 48
Ever shall in safety rest,
And the owner of it blest.
     Trip away;
     Make no stay;   52
Meet me all by break of day.
   [*Exeunt* OBERON, TITANIA, *and Train.*
Puck. If we shadows have offended,
Think but this, and all is mended,
That you have but slumber'd here   56
While these visions did appear.
And this weak and idle theme,
No more yielding but a dream,
Gentles, do not reprehend: 60
If you pardon, we will mend.
And, as I'm an honest Puck,
If we have unearned luck
Now to 'scape the serpent's tongue,   64
We will make amends ere long;
Else the Puck a liar call:
So, good night unto you all.
Give me your hands, if we be friends, 68
And Robin shall restore amends. [*Exit.*

THE MERCHANT OF VENICE

DRAMATIS PERSONÆ

DUKE OF VENICE.
PRINCE OF MOROCCO,
PRINCE OF ARRAGON, } Suitors to Portia.
ANTONIO, a Merchant of Venice.
BASSANIO, his Friend.
GRATIANO,
SALANIO, } Friends to Antonio and Bassanio.
SALARINO,
LORENZO, in love with Jessica.
SHYLOCK, a rich Jew.
TUBAL, a Jew, his Friend.

LAUNCELOT GOBBO, a Clown, Servant to Shylock.
OLD GOBBO, Father to Launcelot.
LEONARDO, Servant to Bassanio.
BALTHAZAR
STEPHANO, } Servants to Portia.

PORTIA, a rich Heiress.
NERISSA, her Waiting-maid.
JESSICA, Daughter to Shylock.

Magnificoes of Venice, Officers of the Court of Justice,
Gaoler, Servants to Portia, and other Attendants.

SCENE.—*Partly at Venice, and partly at Belmont, the seat of Portia, on the Continent.*

ACT I

SCENE I.—*Venice. A Street.*

Enter ANTONIO, SALARINO, *and* SALANIO.

Ant. In sooth, I know not why I am so sad:
It wearies me; you say it wearies you;
But how I caught it, found it, or came by it,
What stuff 'tis made of, whereof it is born,   4
I am to learn;
And such a want-wit sadness makes of me,
That I have much ado to know myself.
Salar. Your mind is tossing on the ocean;   8
There, where your argosies with portly sail,—
Like signiors and rich burghers on the flood,
Or, as it were, the pageants of the sea,—
Do overpeer the petty traffickers,   12
That curtsy to them, do them reverence,
As they fly by them with their woven wings.
Salan. Believe me, sir, had I such venture forth,
The better part of my affections would   16
Be with my hopes abroad. I should be still
Plucking the grass to know where sits the wind;
Peering in maps for ports, and piers, and roads;
And every object that might make me fear   20
Misfortune to my ventures, out of doubt
Would make me sad.
Salar.   My wind, cooling my broth,
Would blow me to an ague, when I thought
What harm a wind too great might do at sea.   24
I should not see the sandy hour-glass run
But I should think of shallows and of flats,
And see my wealthy Andrew dock'd in sand
Vailing her high-top lower than her ribs   28
To kiss her burial. Should I go to church
And see the holy edifice of stone,
And not bethink me straight of dangerous rocks,
Which touching but my gentle vessel's side   32
Would scatter all her spices on the stream,
Enrobe the roaring waters with my silks;
And, in a word, but even now worth this,
And now worth nothing? Shall I have the thought   36
To think on this, and shall I lack the thought

That such a thing bechanc'd would make me sad?
But tell not me: I know Antonio
Is sad to think upon his merchandise.   40
Ant. Believe me, no: I thank my fortune for it,
My ventures are not in one bottom trusted,
Nor to one place; nor is my whole estate
Upon the fortune of this present year: 44
Therefore, my merchandise makes me not sad.
Salar. Why, then you are in love.
Ant.   Fie, fie!
Salar. Not in love neither? Then let's say you are sad,
Because you are not merry: and 'twere as easy
For you to laugh and leap, and say you are merry,   49
Because you are not sad. Now, by two-headed Janus,
Nature hath fram'd strange fellows in her time:
Some that will evermore peep through their eyes
And laugh like parrots at a bag-piper,   53
And other of such vinegar aspect
That they'll not show their teeth in way of smile,
Though Nestor swear the jest be laughable.   56

Enter BASSANIO, LORENZO, *and* GRATIANO.

Salan. Here comes Bassanio, your most noble kinsman,
Gratiano, and Lorenzo. Fare ye well:
We leave you now with better company.
Salar. I would have stay'd till I had made you merry,   60
If worthier friends had not prevented me.
Ant. Your worth is very dear in my regard.
I take it, your own business calls on you,
And you embrace the occasion to depart.   64
Salar. Good morrow, my good lords.
Bass. Good signiors both, when shall we laugh? say when?
You grow exceeding strange: must it be so?
Salar. We'll make our leisures to attend on yours.   [*Exeunt* SALARINO *and* SALANIO.
Lor. My Lord Bassanio, since you have found Antonio,   69

We too will leave you; but, at dinner-time,
I pray you, have in mind where we must meet.
Bass. I will not fail you.   72
Gra. You look not well, Signior Antonio;
You have too much respect upon the world:
They lose it that do buy it with much care:
Believe me, you are marvellously chang'd. 76
Ant. I hold the world but as the world,
   Gratiano;
A stage where every man must play a part,
And mine a sad one.
Gra.   Let me play the fool:
With mirth and laughter let old wrinkles come,
And let my liver rather heat with wine   81
Than my heart cool with mortifying groans.
Why should a man, whose blood is warm within,
Sit like his grandsire cut in alabaster?   84
Sleep when he wakes, and creep into the jaun-
   dice
By being peevish? I tell thee what, Antonio—
I love thee, and it is my love that speaks—
There are a sort of men whose visages   88
Do cream and mantle like a standing pond,
And do a wilful stillness entertain,
With purpose to be dress'd in an opinion
Of wisdom, gravity, profound conceit;   92
As who should say, 'I am Sir Oracle,
And when I ope my lips let no dog bark!'
O, my Antonio, I do know of these,
That therefore only are reputed wise   96
For saying nothing; when, I am very sure,
If they should speak, would almost damn those
   ears
Which, hearing them, would call their brothers
   fools.
I'll tell thee more of this another time: 100
But fish not, with this melancholy bait,
For this fool-gudgeon, this opinion.
Come, good Lorenzo. Fare ye well awhile:
I'll end my exhortation after dinner.   104
Lor. Well, we will leave you then till dinner-
   time.
I must be one of these same dumb-wise men,
For Gratiano never lets me speak.
Gra. Well, keep me company but two years
   moe,   108
Thou shalt not know the sound of thine own
   tongue.
Ant. Farewell: I'll grow a talker for this gear.
Gra. Thanks, i' faith; for silence is only com-
   mendable
In a neat's tongue dried and a maid not vendible.
   [*Exeunt* GRATIANO *and* LORENZO.
Ant. Is that anything now?   113
Bass. Gratiano speaks an infinite deal of
nothing, more than any man in all Venice. His
reasons are as two grains of wheat hid in two
bushels of chaff: you shall seek all day ere you
find them, and, when you have them, they are
not worth the search.
Ant. Well, tell me now, what lady is the same
To whom you swore a secret pilgrimage, 121
That you to-day promis'd to tell me of?
Bass. 'Tis not unknown to you, Antonio,
How much I have disabled mine estate, 124
By something showing a more swelling port

Than my faint means would grant continuance:
Nor do I now make moan to be abridg'd
From such a noble rate; but my chief care 128
Is, to come fairly off from the great debts
Wherein my time, something too prodigal,
Hath left me gag'd. To you, Antonio,
I owe the most, in money and in love;   132
And from your love I have a warranty
To unburthen all my plots and purposes
How to get clear of all the debts I owe.
Ant. I pray you, good Bassanio, let me know
   it;   136
And if it stand, as you yourself still do,
Within the eye of honour, be assur'd,
My purse, my person, my extremest means,
Lie all unlock'd to your occasions.   140
Bass. In my school-days, when I had lost one
   shaft,
I shot his fellow of the self-same flight
The self-same way with more advised watch,
To find the other forth, and by adventuring both,
I oft found both. I urge this childhood proof,
Because what follows is pure innocence.
I owe you much, and, like a wilful youth,
That which I owe is lost; but if you please 148
To shoot another arrow that self way
Which you did shoot the first, I do not doubt,
As I will watch the aim, or to find both,
Or bring your latter hazard back again, 152
And thankfully rest debtor for the first.
Ant. You know me well, and herein spend
   but time
To wind about my love with circumstance;
And out of doubt you do me now more wrong
In making question of my uttermost   157
Than if you had made waste of all I have:
Then do but say to me what I should do
That in your knowledge may by me be done, 160
And I am prest unto it: therefore speak.
Bass. In Belmont is a lady richly left,
And she is fair, and, fairer than that word,
Of wondrous virtues: sometimes from her eyes
I did receive fair speechless messages: 165
Her name is Portia; nothing undervalu'd
To Cato's daughter, Brutus' Portia.
Nor is the wide world ignorant of her worth, 168
For the four winds blow in from every coast
Renowned suitors; and her sunny locks
Hang on her temples like a golden fleece;
Which makes her seat of Belmont Colchos'
   strond,   172
And many Jasons come in quest of her.
O my Antonio! had I but the means
To hold a rival place with one of them,
I have a mind presages me such thrift,   176
That I should questionless be fortunate.
Ant. Thou knowest that all my fortunes are
   at sea;
Neither have I money, nor commodity
To raise a present sum: therefore go forth; 180
Try what my credit can in Venice do:
That shall be rack'd, even to the uttermost,
To furnish thee to Belmont, to fair Portia.
Go, presently inquire, and so will I,   184
Where money is, and I no question make
To have it of my trust or for my sake. [*Exeunt.*

SCENE II.—*Belmont. A Room in* PORTIA'S *House.*

Enter PORTIA *and* NERISSA.

Por. By my troth, Nerissa, my little body is aweary of this great world.

Ner. You would be, sweet madam, if your miseries were in the same abundance as your good fortunes are: and yet, for aught I see, they are as sick that surfeit with too much as they that starve with nothing. It is no mean happiness therefore, to be seated in the mean: superfluity comes sooner by white hairs, but competency lives longer.   10

Por. Good sentences and well pronounced.

Ner. They would be better if well followed.

Por. If to do were as easy as to know what were good to do, chapels had been churches, and poor men's cottages princes' palaces. It is a good divine that follows his own instructions: I can easier teach twenty what were good to be done, than be one of the twenty to follow mine own teaching. The brain may devise laws for the blood, but a hot temper leaps o'er a cold decree: such a hare is madness the youth, to skip o'er the meshes of good counsel the cripple. But this reasoning is not in the fashion to choose me a husband. O me, the word 'choose!' I may neither choose whom I would nor refuse whom I dislike; so is the will of a living daughter curbed by the will of a dead father. Is it not hard, Nerissa, that I cannot choose one nor refuse none?   29

Ner. Your father was ever virtuous, and holy men at their death have good inspirations; therefore, the lottery that he hath devised in these three chests of gold, silver, and lead, whereof who chooses his meaning chooses you, will, no doubt, never be chosen by any rightly but one who you shall rightly love. But what warmth is there in your affection towards any of these princely suitors that are already come?   38

Por. I pray thee, over-name them, and as thou namest them, I will describe them; and, according to my description, level at my affection.

Ner. First, there is the Neapolitan prince.   42

Por. Ay, that's a colt indeed, for he doth nothing but talk of his horse; and he makes it a great appropriation to his own good parts that he can shoe him himself. I am much afeard my lady his mother played false with a smith.

Ner. Then is there the County Falatine.   48

Por. He doth nothing but frown, as who should say, 'An you will not have me, choose.' He hears merry tales, and smiles not: I fear he will prove the weeping philosopher when he grows old, being so full of unmannerly sadness in his youth. I had rather be married to a death's-head with a bone in his mouth than to either of these. God defend me from these two!

Ner. How say you by the French lord, Monsieur Le Bon?   58

Por. God made him, and therefore let him pass for a man. In truth, I know it is a sin to be a mocker; but, he! why, he hath a horse better than the Neapolitan's, a better bad habit of frowning than the Count Palatine; he is every man in no man; if a throstle sing, he falls straight a-capering; he will fence with his own shadow: if I should marry him, I should marry twenty husbands. If he would despise me, I would forgive him, for if he love me to madness I shall never requite him.   6

Ner. What say you, then, to Falconbridge the young baron of England?

Por. You know I say nothing to him, for he understands not me, nor I him: he hath neither Latin, French, nor Italian; and you will come into the court and swear that I have a poor pennyworth in the English. He is a proper man's picture, but, alas! who can converse with a dumb-show? How oddly he is suited! I think he bought his doublet in Italy, his round hose in France, his bonnet in Germany, and his behaviour every where.   8

Ner. What think you of the Scottish lord, his neighbour?

Por. That he hath a neighbourly charity in him, for he borrowed a box of the ear of the Englishman, and swore he would pay him again when he was able: I think the Frenchman became his surety and sealed under for another.

Ner. How like you the young German, the Duke of Saxony's nephew?   9

Por. Very vilely in the morning, when he is sober, and most vilely in the afternoon, when he is drunk: when he is best, he is a little worse than a man, and when he is worst, he is little better than a beast. An the worst fall that ever fell, I hope I shall make shift to go without him.

Ner. If he should offer to choose, and choose the right casket, you should refuse to perform your father's will, if you should refuse to accept him.   10

Por. Therefore, for fear of the worst, I pray thee, set a deep glass of Rhenish wine on the contrary casket, for, if the devil be within and that temptation without, I know he will choose it. I will do anything, Nerissa, ere I will be married to a sponge.   10

Ner. You need not fear, lady, the having any of these lords: they have acquainted me with their determinations; which is, indeed, to return to their home and to trouble you with no more suit, unless you may be won by some other sort than your father's imposition depending on the caskets.   11

Por. If I live to be as old as Sibylla, I will die as chaste as Diana, unless I be obtained by the manner of my father's will. I am glad this parcel of wooers are so reasonable, for there is not one among them but I dote on his very absence, and I pray God grant them a fair departure.   12

Ner. Do you not remember, lady, in your father's time, a Venetian, a scholar and a soldier, that came hither in the company of the Marquis of Montferrat?   12

Por. Yes, yes: it was Bassanio; as I think, he was so called.

Ner. True, madam: he, of all the men that

ever my foolish eyes looked upon, was the best
deserving a fair lady. 129

Por. I remember him well, and I remember
him worthy of thy praise.

Enter a Servant.

How now! what news? 132

Serv. The four strangers seek for you, madam,
to take their leave; and there is a forerunner
come from a fifth, the Prince of Morocco, who
brings word the prince his master will be here
to-night. 137

Por. If I could bid the fifth welcome with so
good heart as I can bid the other four farewell,
I should be glad of his approach: if he have the
condition of a saint and the complexion of a devil,
I had rather he should shrive me than wive me.
Come, Nerissa. Sirrah, go before. 143
Whiles we shut the gate upon one wooer, another
knocks at the door. [*Exeunt.*

SCENE III.—*Venice. A public Place.*

Enter BASSANIO *and* SHYLOCK.

Shy. Three thousand ducats; well?

Bass. Ay, sir, for three months.

Shy. For three months; well?

Bass. For the which, as I told you, Antonio
shall be bound. 5

Shy. Antonio shall become bound; well?

Bass. May you stead me? Will you pleasure
me? Shall I know your answer? 8

Shy. Three thousand ducats, for three
months, and Antonio bound.

Bass. Your answer to that.

Shy. Antonio is a good man. 12

Bass. Have you heard any imputation to the
contrary?

Shy. Ho, no, no, no, no: my meaning in saying
he is a good man is to have you understand me
that he is sufficient. Yet his means are in supposition: he hath an argosy bound to Tripolis,
another to the Indies; I understand moreover
upon the Rialto, he hath a third at Mexico, a
fourth for England, and other ventures he hath,
squandered abroad. But ships are but boards,
sailors but men: there be land-rats and water-
rats, land-thieves, and water-thieves,—I mean
pirates,—and then there is the peril of waters,
winds, and rocks. The man is, notwithstanding,
sufficient. Three thousand ducats; I think, I
may take his bond. 28

Bass. Be assured you may.

Shy. I will be assured I may; and, that I may
be assured, I will bethink me. May I speak with
Antonio? 32

Bass. If it please you to dine with us.

Shy. Yes, to smell pork; to eat of the habitation which your prophet the Nazarite conjured
the devil into. I will buy with you, sell with you,
talk with you, walk with you, and so following;
but I will not eat with you, drink with you, nor
pray with you. What news on the Rialto? Who
is he comes here? 40

Enter ANTONIO.

Bass. This is Signior Antonio.

Shy. [*Aside.*] How like a fawning publican
he looks!
I hate him for he is a Christian;
But more for that in low simplicity 44
He lends out money gratis, and brings down
The rate of usance here with us in Venice.
If I can catch him once upon the hip,
I will feed fat the ancient grudge I bear him. 48
He hates our sacred nation, and he rails,
Even there where merchants most do congre-
gate,
On me, my bargains, and my well-won thrift,
Which he calls interest. Cursed be my tribe, 52
If I forgive him!

Bass. Shylock, do you hear?

Shy. I am debating of my present store,
And, by the near guess of my memory,
I cannot instantly raise up the gross 56
Of full three thousand ducats. What of that?
Tubal, a wealthy Hebrew of my tribe,
Will furnish me. But soft! how many months
Do you desire? [*To* ANTONIO.] Rest you fair,
good signior; 60
Your worship was the last man in our mouths.

Ant. Shylock, albeit I neither lend nor borrow
By taking nor by giving of excess,
Yet, to supply the ripe wants of my friend, 64
I'll break a custom. [*To* BASSANIO.] Is he yet
possess'd
How much ye would?

Shy. Ay, ay, three thousand ducats.

Ant. And for three months.

Shy. I had forgot; three months; you told
me so. 68
Well then, your bond; and let me see. But hear
you;
Methought you said you neither lend nor borrow
Upon advantage.

Ant. I do never use it.

Shy. When Jacob graz'd his uncle Laban's
sheep,— 72
This Jacob from our holy Abram was,
As his wise mother wrought in his behalf,
The third possessor: ay, he was the third,—

Ant. And what of him? did he take interest?

Shy. No; not take interest; not, as you would
say, 77
Directly interest: mark what Jacob did.
When Laban and himself were compromis'd,
That all the eanlings that were streak'd and
pied 80
Should fall as Jacob's hire, the ewes, being rank,
In end of autumn turned to the rams;
And, when the work of generation was
Between these woolly breeders in the act, 84
The skilful shepherd peel'd me certain wands,
And, in the doing of the deed of kind,
He stuck them up before the fulsome ewes,
Who, then conceiving, did in eaning time 88
Fall parti-colour'd lambs, and those were Jacob's.
This was a way to thrive, and he was blest:
And thrift is blessing, if men steal it not.

Ant. This was a venture, sir, that Jacob
serv'd for; 92

A thing not in his power to bring to pass,
But sway'd and fashion'd by the hand of heaven.
Was this inserted to make interest good?
Or is your gold and silver ewes and rams? 96
Shy. I cannot tell; I make it breed as fast:
But note me, signior.
Ant. Mark you this, Bassanio,
The devil can cite Scripture for his purpose.
An evil soul, producing holy witness, 100
Is like a villain with a smiling cheek,
A goodly apple rotten at the heart.
O, what a goodly outside falsehood hath!
Shy. Three thousand ducats; 'tis a good
round sum. 104
Three months from twelve, then let me see the
rate.
Ant. Well, Shylock, shall we be beholding to
you?
Shy. Signior Antonio, many a time and oft
In the Rialto you have rated me 108
About my moneys and my usances:
Still have I borne it with a patient shrug,
For sufferance is the badge of all our tribe.
You call me misbeliever, cut-throat dog, 112
And spet upon my Jewish gaberdine,
And all for use of that which is mine own.
Well then, it now appears you need my help:
Go to then; you come to me, and you say, 116
'Shylock, we would have moneys:' you say so;
You, that did void your rheum upon my beard,
And foot me as you spurn a stranger cur
Over your threshold: moneys is your suit. 120
What should I say to you? Should I not say,
'Hath a dog money? Is it possible
A cur can lend three thousand ducats?' or
Shall I bend low, and in a bondman's key, 124
With bated breath, and whispering humbleness,
Say this:—
'Fair sir, you spet on me on Wednesday last;
You spurn'd me such a day; another time 128
You call'd me dog; and for these courtesies
I'll lend you thus much moneys?'
Ant. I am as like to call thee so again,
To spet on thee again, to spurn thee too. 132
If thou wilt lend this money, lend it not
As to thy friends,—for when did friendship take
A breed for barren metal of his friend?—
But lend it rather to thine enemy; 136
Who if he break, thou mayst with better face
Exact the penalty.
Shy. Why, look you, how you storm!
I would be friends with you, and have your love,
Forget the shames that you have stain'd me
with, 140
Supply your present wants, and take no doit
Of usance for my moneys, and you'll not hear
me:
This is kind I offer.
Ant. This were kindness.
Shy. This kindness will I show.
Go with me to a notary, seal me there 145
Your single bond; and, in a merry sport,
If you repay me not on such a day,
In such a place, such sum or sums as are 148
Express'd in the condition, let the forfeit
Be nominated for an equal pound

Of your fair flesh, to be cut off and taken
In what part of your body pleaseth me. 15:
Ant. Content, i' faith: I'll seal to such a bond
And say there is much kindness in the Jew.
Bass. You shall not seal to such a bond for
me:
I'll rather dwell in my necessity. 15(
Ant. Why, fear not, man; I will not forfeit it
Within these two months, that's a month before
This bond expires, I do expect return
Of thrice three times the value of this bond. 16c
Shy. O father Abram! what these Christians
are,
Whose own hard dealing teaches them suspect
The thoughts of others. Pray you, tell me this:
If he should break his day, what should I gain
By the exaction of the forfeiture? 165
A pound of man's flesh, taken from a man,
Is not so estimable, profitable neither,
As flesh of muttons, beefs, or goats. I say, 168
To buy his favour, I extend this friendship:
If he will take it, so; if not, adieu;
And, for my love, I pray you wrong me not.
Ant. Yes, Shylock, I will seal unto this bond.
Shy. Then meet me forthwith at the notary's;
Give him direction for this merry bond,
And I will go and purse the ducats straight,
See to my house, left in the fearful guard 176
Of an unthrifty knave, and presently
I will be with you.
Ant. Hie thee, gentle Jew. [*Exit* SHYLOCK.
This Hebrew will turn Christian: he grows kind.
Bass. I like not fair terms and a villain's
mind. 180
Ant. Come on: in this there can be no dis-
may;
My ships come home a month before the day.
[*Exeunt.*

ACT II

SCENE I.—*Belmont. A Room in* PORTIA'S
House.

Flourish of Cornets. Enter the PRINCE OF MO-
ROCCO, *and his Followers;* PORTIA, NERISSA,
and Others of her Train.

Mor. Mislike me not for my complexion,
The shadow'd livery of the burnish'd sun,
To whom I am a neighbour and near bred.
Bring me the fairest creature northward born, 4
Where Phœbus' fire scarce thaws the icicles,
And let us make incision for your love,
To prove whose blood is reddest, his or mine.
I tell thee, lady, this aspect of mine 8
Hath fear'd the valiant: by my love, I swear
The best regarded virgins of our clime
Have lov'd it too: I would not change this hue,
Except to steal your thoughts, my gentle queen.
Por. In terms of choice I am not solely led
By nice direction of a maiden's eyes;
Besides, the lottery of my destiny
Bars me the right of voluntary choosing: 16
But if my father had not scanted me
And hedg'd me by his wit, to yield myself
His wife who wins me by that means I told you,

Yourself, renowned prince, then stood as fair 20
As any comer I have look'd on yet
For my affection.

Mor. Even for that I thank you:
Therefore, I pray you, lead me to the caskets
To try my fortune. By this scimitar,— 24
That slew the Sophy, and a Persian prince
That won three fields of Sultan Solyman,—
I would outstare the sternest eyes that look,
Outbrave the heart most daring on the earth, 28
Pluck the young sucking cubs from the she-bear,
Yea, mock the lion when he roars for prey,
To win thee, lady. But, alas the while!
If Hercules and Lichas play at dice 32
Which is the better man, the greater throw
May turn by fortune from the weaker hand:
So is Alcides beaten by his page;
And so may I, blind fortune leading me, 36
Miss that which one unworthier may attain,
And die with grieving.

Por. You must take your chance;
And either not attempt to choose at all,
Or swear before you choose, if you choose wrong,
Never to speak to lady afterward 41
In way of marriage: therefore be advis'd.

Mor. Nor will not: come, bring me unto my
chance.

Por. First, forward to the temple: after
dinner 44
Your hazard shall be made.

Mor. Good fortune then!
To make me blest or cursed'st among men!
[*Cornets, and exeunt.*

SCENE II.—*Venice. A Street.*

Enter LAUNCELOT GOBBO.

Laun. Certainly my conscience will serve me
to run from this Jew my master. The fiend is
at mine elbow, and tempts me, saying to me,
'Gobbo, Launcelot Gobbo, good Launcelot,' or
'good Gobbo,' or 'good Launcelot Gobbo, use
your legs, take the start, run away.' My conscience says, 'No; take heed, honest Launcelot;
take heed, honest Gobbo;' or, as aforesaid, 'honest
Launcelot Gobbo; do not run; scorn running
with thy heels.' Well, the most courageous fiend
bids me pack: '*Via!*' says the fiend; 'away!'
says the fiend; 'for the heavens, rouse up a brave
mind,' says the fiend, 'and run.' Well, my conscience, hanging about the neck of my heart, says
very wisely to me, 'My honest friend Launcelot,
being an honest man's son,'—or rather an honest
woman's son;—for, indeed, my father did something smack, something grow to, he had a kind
of taste;—well, my conscience says, 'Launcelot,
budge not.' 'Budge,' says the fiend. 'Budge
not,' says my conscience. 'Conscience,' say I,
'you counsel well;' 'fiend,' say I, 'you counsel well:'
to be ruled by my conscience, I should stay with
the Jew my master, who, God bless the mark!
is a kind of devil; and, to run away from the Jew,
I should be ruled by the fiend, who, saving your
reverence, is the devil himself. Certainly, the
Jew is the very devil incarnal; and, in my con-

science, my conscience is but a kind of hard conscience, to offer to counsel me to stay with the
Jew. The fiend gives the more friendly counsel:
I will run, fiend; my heels are at your commandment; I will run. 33

Enter Old GOBBO, *with a basket.*

Gob. Master young man, you; I pray you,
which is the way to Master Jew's?

Laun. [*Aside.*] O heavens! this is my true-
begotten father, who, being more than sand-
blind, high-gravel blind, knows me not: I will
try confusions with him.

Gob. Master young gentleman, I pray you,
which is the way to Master Jew's? 41

Laun. Turn up on your right hand at the
next turning, but, at the next turning of all, on
your left; marry, at the very next turning, turn
of no hand, but turn down indirectly to the Jew's
house.

Gob. By God's sonties, 'twill be a hard way to
hit. Can you tell me whether one Launcelot,
that dwells with him, dwell with him or no? 49

Laun. Talk you of young Master Launcelot?
[*Aside.*] Mark me now; now will I raise the
waters. Talk you of young Master Launcelot?

Gob. No master, sir, but a poor man's son:
his father, though I say it, is an honest, exceeding poor man, and, God be thanked, well to
live. 56

Laun. Well, let his father be what a' will, we
talk of young Master Launcelot.

Gob. Your worship's friend, and Launcelot,
sir. 60

Laun. But I pray you, *ergo*, old man, *ergo*, I beseech you, talk you of young Master Launcelot?

Gob. Of Launcelot, an't please your mastership. 64

Laun. *Ergo*, Master Launcelot. Talk not of
Master Launcelot, father; for the young gentleman,—according to Fates and Destinies and such
odd sayings, the Sisters Three and such branches
of learning,—is, indeed, deceased; or, as you
would say in plain terms, gone to heaven.

Gob. Marry, God forbid! the boy was the very
staff of my age, my very prop. 72

Laun. [*Aside.*] Do I look like a cudgel or a
hovel-post, a staff or a prop? Do you know me,
father?

Gob. Alack the day! I know you not, young
gentleman: but I pray you, tell me, is my boy,—
God rest his soul!—alive or dead?

Laun. Do you not know me, father?

Gob. Alack, sir, I am sand-blind; I know you
not. 81

Laun. Nay, indeed, if you had your eyes,
you might fail of the knowing me: it is a wise
father that knows his own child. Well, old man,
I will tell you news of your son. Give me your
blessing; truth will come to light; murder cannot be hid long; a man's son may, but, in the
end, truth will out. 88

Gob. Pray you, sir, stand up. I am sure you
are not Launcelot, my boy.

Laun. Pray you, let's have no more fooling
about it, but give me your blessing: I am

Launcelot, your boy that was, your son that is, your child that shall be. 94

Gob. I cannot think you are my son.

Laun. I know not what I shall think of that; but I am Launcelot, the Jew's man, and I am sure Margery your wife is my mother. 98

Gob. Her name is Margery, indeed: I'll be sworn, if thou be Launcelot, thou art mine own flesh and blood. Lord worshipped might he be! what a beard hast thou got! thou hast got more hair on thy chin than Dobbin my thill-horse has on his tail. 104

Laun. It should seem then that Dobbin's tail grows backward: I am sure he had more hair on his tail than I have on my face, when I last saw him. 108

Gob. Lord! how art thou changed. How dost thou and thy master agree? I have brought him a present. How 'gree you now?

Laun. Well, well: but, for mine own part, as I have set up my rest to run away, so I will not rest till I have run some ground. My master's a very Jew: give him a present! give him a halter: I am famished in his service; you may tell every finger I have with my ribs. Father, I am glad you are come: give me your present to one Master Bassanio, who, indeed, gives rare new liveries. If I serve not him, I will run as far as God has any ground. O rare fortune! here comes the man: to him, father; for I am a Jew, if I serve the Jew any longer. 123

Enter BASSANIO, *with* LEONARDO, *and other Followers.*

Bass. You may do so; but let it be so hasted that supper be ready at the very furthest by five of the clock. See these letters delivered; put the liveries to making; and desire Gratiano to come anon to my lodging. [*Exit a Servant.*

Laun. To him, father. 129

Gob. God bless your worship!

Bass. Gramercy! wouldst thou aught with me? 132

Gob. Here's my son, sir, a poor boy,—

Laun. Not a poor boy, sir, but the rich Jew's man; that would, sir,—as my father shall specify,— 136

Gob. He hath a great infection, sir, as one would say, to serve—

Laun. Indeed, the short and the long is, I serve the Jew, and have a desire, as my father shall specify,— 141

Gob. His master and he, saving your worship's reverence, are scarce cater-cousins,—

Laun. To be brief, the very truth is that the Jew having done me wrong, doth cause me,— as my father, being, I hope, an old man, shall frutify unto you,— 147

Gob. I have here a dish of doves that I would bestow upon your worship, and my suit is,—

Laun. In very brief, the suit is impertinent to myself, as your worship shall know by this honest old man; and, though I say it, though old man, yet poor man, my father.

Bass. One speak for both. What would you?

Laun. Serve you, sir. 156

Gob. That is the very defect of the matter, sir.

Bass. I know thee well; thou hast obtain'd thy suit:
Shylock thy master spoke with me this day, 160
And hath preferr'd thee, if it be preferment
To leave a rich Jew's service, to become
The follower of so poor a gentleman.

Laun. The old proverb is very well parted between my master Shylock and you, sir: you have the grace of God, sir, and he hath enough.

Bass. Thou speak'st it well. Go, father, with thy son.
Take leave of thy old master, and inquire 168
My lodging out. [*To his followers.*] Give him a livery
More guarded than his fellows': see it done.

Laun. Father, in. I cannot get a service, no; I have ne'er a tongue in my head. Well, [*Looking on his palm.*] if any man in Italy have a fairer table which doth offer to swear upon a book, I shall have good fortune. Go to; here's a simple line of life: here's a small trifle of wives: alas! fifteen wives is nothing: a 'leven widows and nine maids is a simple coming-in for one man; and then to 'scape drowning thrice, and to be in peril of my life with the edge of a feather-bed; here are simple 'scapes. Well, if Fortune be a woman, she's a good wench for this gear. Father, come; I'll take my leave of the Jew in the twinkling of an eye. 184

[*Exeunt* LAUNCELOT *and* Old GOBBO.

Bass. I pray thee, good Leonardo, think on this:
These things being bought, and orderly bestow'd,
Return in haste, for I do feast to-night
My best-esteem'd acquaintance: hie thee, go.

Leon. My best endeavours shall be done herein. 189

Enter GRATIANO.

Gra. Where is your master?

Leon. Yonder, sir, he walks. [*Exit.*

Gra. Signior Bassanio!—

Bass. Gratiano! 192

Gra. I have a suit to you.

Bass. You have obtain'd it.

Gra. You must not deny me: I must go with you to Belmont.

Bass. Why, then you must. But hear thee, Gratiano;
Thou art too wild, too rude and bold of voice; 197
Parts that become thee happily enough,
And in such eyes as ours appear not faults;
But where thou art not known, why, there they show
Something too liberal. Pray thee, take pain 200
To allay with some cold drops of modesty
Thy skipping spirit, lest, through thy wild behaviour,
I be misconstru'd in the place I go to,
And lose my hopes.

Gra. Signior Bassanio, hear me: 204
If I do not put on a sober habit,

Talk with respect, and swear but now and then,
Wear prayer-books in my pocket, look de-
    murely,
Nay more, while grace is saying, hood mine
    eyes   208
Thus with my hat, and sigh, and say 'amen;'
Use all the observance of civility,
Like one well studied in a sad ostent   211
To please his grandam, never trust me more.

Bass. Well, we shall see your bearing.

Gra. Nay, but I bar to-night; you shall not
    gauge me
By what we do to-night.

Bass.   No, that were pity:
I would entreat you rather to put on   216
Your boldest suit of mirth, for we have friends
That purpose merriment. But fare you well:
I have some business.

Gra. And I must to Lorenzo and the rest; 220
But we will visit you at supper-time. [*Exeunt.*

SCENE III.—*The Same. A Room in* SHYLOCK'S
    House.

Enter JESSICA *and* LAUNCELOT.

Jes. I am sorry thou wilt leave my father so:
Our house is hell, and thou, a merry devil,
Didst rob it of some taste of tediousness.
But fare thee well; there is a ducat for thee: 4
And, Launcelot, soon at supper shalt thou see
Lorenzo, who is thy new master's guest:
Give him this letter; do it secretly;
And so farewell: I would not have my father 8
See me in talk with him.

Laun. Adieu! tears exhibit my tongue. Most
beautiful pagan, most sweet Jew! If a Christian
did not play the knave and get thee, I am much
deceived. But, adieu! these foolish drops do
somewhat drown my manly spirit: adieu!

Jes. Farewell, good Launcelot.

                                    [*Exit* LAUNCELOT.
Alack, what heinous sin is it in me   16
To be asham'd to be my father's child!
But though I am a daughter to his blood,
I am not to his manners. O Lorenzo!
If thou keep promise, I shall end this strife, 20
Become a Christian, and thy loving wife. [*Exit.*

SCENE IV.—*The Same. A Street.*

Enter GRATIANO, LORENZO, SALARINO, *and*
    SALANIO.

Lor. Nay, we will slink away in supper-time,
Disguise us at my lodging, and return
All in an hour.

Gra. We have not made good preparation. 4

Salar. We have not spoke us yet of torch-
    bearers.

Salan. 'Tis vile, unless it may be quaintly
    order'd,
And better, in my mind, not undertook.

Lor. 'Tis now but four o'clock: we have two
    hours   8
To furnish us.

Enter LAUNCELOT, *with a letter.*

                Friend Launcelot, what's the news?

Laun. An it shall please you to break up this,
it shall seem to signify.

Lor. I know the hand: in faith, 'tis a fair
hand;
And whiter than the paper it writ on   13
Is the fair hand that writ.

Gra.   Love news, in faith.

Laun. By your leave, sir.

Lor. Whither goest thou?   16

Laun. Marry, sir, to bid my old master, the
Jew, to sup to-night with my new master, the
Christian.

Lor. Hold here, take this: tell gentle Jessica
I will not fail her; speak it privately.   21
Go, gentlemen,   [*Exit* LAUNCELOT.
Will you prepare you for this masque to-night?
I am provided of a torch-bearer.   24

Salar. Ay, marry, I'll be gone about it straight.

Salan. And so will I.

Lor.   Meet me and Gratiano.
At Gratiano's lodging some hour hence.

Salar. 'Tis good we do so.   28
                [*Exeunt* SALARINO *and* SALANIO.

Gra. Was not that letter from fair Jessica?

Lor. I must needs tell thee all. She hath
    directed
How I shall take her from her father's house;
What gold and jewels she is furnish'd with; 32
What page's suit she hath in readiness.
If e'er the Jew her father come to heaven,
It will be for his gentle daughter's sake;
And never dare misfortune cross her foot,   36
Unless she do it under this excuse,
That she is issue to a faithless Jew.
Come, go with me: peruse this as thou goest.
Fair Jessica shall be my torch-bearer. [*Exeunt.*

SCENE V.—*The Same. Before* SHYLOCK'S *House.*

Enter SHYLOCK *and* LAUNCELOT.

Shy. Well, thou shalt see, thy eyes shall be
    thy judge,
The difference of old Shylock and Bassanio:—
What, Jessica!—thou shalt not gormandize,
As thou hast done with me;—What, Jessica!—
And sleep and snore, and rend apparel out— 5
Why, Jessica, I say!

Laun.   Why, Jessica!

Shy. Who bids thee call? I do not bid thee
    call.

Laun. Your worship was wont to tell me that
I could do nothing without bidding.   9

Enter JESSICA.

Jes. Call you? What is your will?

Shy. I am bid forth to supper, Jessica:
There are my keys. But wherefore should I go?
I am not bid for love; they flatter me: 13
But yet I'll go in hate, to feed upon
The prodigal Christian. Jessica, my girl,
Look to my house. I am right loath to go: 16
There is some ill a-brewing towards my rest,
For I did dream of money-bags to-night.

Laun. I beseech you, sir, go: my young
master doth expect your reproach.   20

Shy. So do I his.

Laun. And they have conspired together: I
will not say you shall see a masque; but if you
do, then it was not for nothing that my nose fell
a-bleeding on Black-Monday last, at six o'clock
i' the morning, falling out that year on Ash-
Wednesday was four year in the afternoon.

Shy. What! are there masques? Hear you
me, Jessica: 28

Lock up my doors; and when you hear the
drum,

And the vile squealing of the wry-neck'd fife,

Clamber not you up to the casements then,

Nor thrust your head into the public street   32

To gaze on Christian fools with varnish'd faces,

But stop my house's ears, I mean my casements;

Let not the sound of shallow foppery enter

My sober house. By Jacob's staff I swear   36

I have no mind of feasting forth to-night:

But I will go. Go you before me, sirrah;

Say I will come.

Laun. I will go before, sir. Mistress, look out
at window, for all this;   41

There will come a Christian by,

Will be worth a Jewess' eye.

[*Exit* LAUNCELOT.

Shy. What says that fool of Hagar's offspring,
ha?   44

Jes. His words were, 'Farewell, mistress;'
nothing else.

Shy. The patch is kind enough, but a huge
feeder;

Snail-slow in profit, and he sleeps by day

More than the wild cat: drones hive not with
me;   48

Therefore I part with him, and part with him

To one that I would have him help to waste

His borrow'd purse. Well, Jessica, go in:

Perhaps I will return immediately: 52

Do as I bid you; shut doors after you:

'Fast bind, fast find,'

A proverb never stale in thrifty mind. [*Exit.*

Jes. Farewell; and if my fortune be not crost,

I have a father, you a daughter, lost. [*Exit.*

SCENE VI.—*The Same.*

Enter GRATIANO *and* SALARINO, *masqued.*

Gra. This is the penthouse under which
Lorenzo

Desir'd us to make stand.

Salar.   His hour is almost past.

Gra. And it is marvel he out-dwells his hour,

For lovers ever run before the clock.   4

Salar. O! ten times faster Venus' pigeons fly

To seal love's bonds new-made, than they are
wont

To keep obliged faith unforfeited!

Gra. That ever holds: who riseth from a feast

With that keen appetite that he sits down?   9

Where is the horse that doth untread again

His tedious measures with the unbated fire

That he did pace them first? All things that are,

Are with more spirit chased than enjoy'd.   13

How like a younker or a prodigal

The scarfed bark puts from her native bay,

Hugg'd and embraced by the strumpet wind!   16

How like the prodigal doth she return,

With over-weather'd ribs and ragged sails,

Lean, rent, and beggar'd by the strumpet wind!

Salar. Here comes Lorenzo: more of this
hereafter.   20

Enter LORENZO.

Lor. Sweet friends, your patience for my long
abode;

Not I, but my affairs, have made you wait:

When you shall please to play the thieves for
wives,

I'll watch as long for you then. Approach;   24

Here dwells my father Jew. Ho! who's within?

Enter JESSICA *above, in boy's clothes.*

Jes. Who are you? Tell me, for more certainty,

Albeit I'll swear that I do know your tongue.

Lor. Lorenzo, and thy love.   28

Jes. Lorenzo, certain; and my love indeed,

For whom love I so much? And now who knows

But you, Lorenzo, whether I am yours?

Lor. Heaven and thy thoughts are witness
that thou art.   32

Jes. Here, catch this casket; it is worth the
pains.

I am glad 'tis night, you do not look on me,

For I am much asham'd of my exchange;

But love is blind, and lovers cannot see   36

The pretty follies that themselves commit;

For if they could, Cupid himself would blush

To see me thus transformed to a boy.

Lor. Descend, for you must be my torch-
bearer.   40

Jes. What! must I hold a candle to my
shames?

They in themselves, good sooth, are too-too light.

Why, 'tis an office of discovery, love,

And I should be obscur'd.

Lor.   So are you, sweet,   44

Even in the lovely garnish of a boy.

But come at once;

For the close night doth play the runaway,

And we are stay'd for at Bassanio's feast.   48

Jes. I will make fast the doors, and gild myself

With some more ducats, and be with you
straight.   [*Exit above.*

Gra. Now, by my hood, a Gentile, and no Jew.

Lor. Beshrew me, but I love her heartily;   52

For she is wise, if I can judge of her,

And fair she is, if that mine eyes be true,

And true she is, as she hath prov'd herself;

And therefore, like herself, wise, fair, and true,

Shall she be placed in my constant soul.   57

Enter JESSICA.

What, art thou come? On, gentlemen; away!

Our masquing mates by this time for us stay.

[*Exit with* JESSICA *and* SALARINO.

Enter ANTONIO.

Ant. Who's there?   60
Gra. Signior Antonio!
Ant. Fie, fie, Gratiano! where are all the rest?
is nine o'clock; our friends all stay for you.
o masque to-night: the wind is come about;
assanio presently will go aboard: 65
have sent twenty out to seek for you.
Gra. I am glad on't: I desire no more de-
    light
an to be under sail and gone to-night.   68
                                              [*Exeunt.*

ENE VII.—*Belmont. A Room in* PORTIA'S
    House.

ourish of Cornets. Enter PORTIA, with the
    PRINCE OF MOROCCO, *and their Trains.*

Por. Go, draw aside the curtains, and dis-
    cover
e several caskets to this noble prince.
ow make your choice.
Mor. The first, of gold, which this inscrip-
    tion bears: 4
*ho chooseth me shall gain what many men
    desire.*
e second, silver, which this promise carries:
*ho chooseth me shall get as much as he de-
    serves.*
is third, dull lead, with warning all as blunt:
*ho chooseth me must give and hazard all he
    hath.*   9
ow shall I know if I do choose the right?
Por. The one of them contains my picture,
    prince:
you choose that, then I am yours withal.   12
Mor. Some god direct my judgment! Let
    me see:
vill survey the inscriptions back again:
hat says this leaden casket?
*ho chooseth me must give and hazard all he
    hath.*   16
ust give: For what? for lead? hazard for
    lead?
is casket threatens. Men that hazard all
  it in hope of fair advantages:
golden mind stoops not to shows of dross; 20
 then nor give nor hazard aught for lead.
hat says the silver with her virgin hue?
*ho chooseth me shall get as much as he de-
    serves.*
 much as he deserves! Pause there, Morocco,
d weigh thy value with an even hand.   25
thou be'st rated by thy estimation,
ou dost deserve enough; and yet enough
ay not extend so far as to the lady: 28
d yet to be afeard of my deserving
ere but a weak disabling of myself.
 much as I deserve! Why, that's the lady:
lo in birth deserve her, and in fortunes,   32
 graces, and in qualities of breeding;
 t more than these, in love I do deserve.
hat if I stray'd no further, but chose here?
 t's see once more this saying grav'd in gold: 36
*ho chooseth me shall gain what many men
    desire.*

Why, that's the lady: all the world desires her;
From the four corners of the earth they come,
To kiss this shrine, this mortal-breathing saint:
The Hyrcanian deserts and the vasty wilds 41
Of wide Arabia are as throughfares now
For princes to come view fair Portia:
The watery kingdom, whose ambitious head 44
Spits in the face of heaven, is no bar
To stop the foreign spirits, but they come,
As o'er a brook, to see fair Portia.
One of these three contains her heavenly picture.
Is't like that lead contains her? 'Twere dam-
    nation   49
To think so base a thought: it were too gross
To rib her cerecloth in the obscure grave.
Or shall I think in silver she's immur'd,   52
Being ten times undervalu'd to tried gold?
O sinful thought! Never so rich a gem
Was set in worse than gold. They have in Eng-
    land
A coin that bears the figure of an angel   56
Stamped in gold, but that's insculp'd upon;
But here an angel in a golden bed
Lies all within. Deliver me the key:
Here do I choose, and thrive I as I may!   60
    Por. There, take it, prince; and if my form
    lie there,
Then I am yours.
                        [*He unlocks the golden casket.*
    Mor.   O hell! what have we here?
A carrion Death, within whose empty eye
There is a written scroll. I'll read the writing.

    All that glisters is not gold;   65
    Often have you heard that told:
    Many a man his life hath sold
    But my outside to behold: 68
    Gilded tombs do worms infold.
    Had you been as wise as bold,
    Young in limbs, in judgment old,
    Your answer had not been inscroll'd: 72
    Fare you well; your suit is cold.

Cold, indeed; and labour lost:
Then, farewell, heat, and welcome, frost!
Portia, adieu. I have too griev'd a heart   76
To take a tedious leave: thus losers part.
    [*Exit with his Train. Flourish of Cornets.*
    Por. A gentle riddance. Draw the curtains:
    go.
Let all of his complexion choose me so.
                                              [*Exeunt.*

SCENE VIII.—*Venice. A Street.*

    Enter SALARINO *and* SALANIO.

Salar. Why, man, I saw Bassanio under sail:
With him is Gratiano gone along;
And in their ship I'm sure Lorenzo is not.
    Salan. The villain Jew with outcries rais'd
    the duke,   4
Who went with him to search Bassanio's ship.
    Salar. He came too late, the ship was under
    sail:
But there the duke was given to understand
That in a gondola were seen together   8
Lorenzo and his amorous Jessica.
Besides, Antonio certified the duke
They were not with Bassanio in his ship.

Salan. I never heard a passion so confus'd, 12
So strange, outrageous, and so variable,
As the dog Jew did utter in the streets:
'My daughter! O my ducats! O my daughter!
Fled with a Christian! O my Christian ducats!
Justice! the law! my ducats, and my daughter!
A sealed bag, two sealed bags of ducats,
Of double ducats, stol'n from me by my daugh-
ter!
And jewels! two stones, two rich and precious
stones,   20
Stol'n by my daughter! Justice! find the girl!
She hath the stones upon her, and the ducats.'
Salar. Why, all the boys in Venice follow
him,
Crying, his stones, his daughter, and his ducats.
Salan. Let good Antonio look he keep his
day,   25
Or he shall pay for this.
Salar.   Marry, well remember'd.
I reason'd with a Frenchman yesterday,
Who told me,—in the narrow seas that part 28
The French and English,—there miscarried
A vessel of our country richly fraught.
I thought upon Antonio when he told me,
And wish'd in silence that it were not his.
Salan. You were best to tell Antonio what
you hear;
Yet do not suddenly, for it may grieve him.
Salar. A kinder gentleman treads not the
earth.
I saw Bassanio and Antonio part: 36
Bassanio told him he would make some speed
Of his return: he answer'd 'Do not so;
Slubber not business for my sake, Bassanio,
But stay the very riping of the time;   40
And for the Jew's bond which he hath of me,
Let it not enter in your mind of love:
Be merry, and employ your chiefest thoughts
To courtship and such fair ostents of love   44
As shall conveniently become you there:'
And even there, his eye being big with tears,
Turning his face, he put his hand behind him,
And with affection wondrous sensible   48
He wrung Bassanio's hand; and so they parted.
Salan. I think he only loves the world for
him.
I pray thee, let us go and find him out,
And quicken his embraced heaviness   52
With some delight or other.
Salar.   Do we so.
[*Exeunt.*

SCENE IX.—*Belmont. A Room in* PORTIA'S
House.

Enter NERISSA, *with a* Servitor.

Ner. Quick, quick, I pray thee; draw the
curtain straight:
The Prince of Arragon hath ta'en his oath,
And comes to his election presently.

Flourish of Cornets. Enter the PRINCE OF
ARRAGON, PORTIA, *and their Trains.*

Por. Behold, there stand the caskets, noble
prince: 4

If you choose that wherein I am contain'd,
Straight shall our nuptial rites be solemniz'd
But if you fail, without more speech, my lor
You must be gone from hence immediately.
Ar. I am enjoin'd by oath to observe thr
things:
First, never to unfold to any one
Which casket 'twas I chose; next, if I fail
Of the right casket, never in my life
To woo a maid in way of marriage;
Lastly,
If I do fail in fortune of my choice,
Immediately to leave you and be gone.
Por. To these injunctions every one do
swear
That comes to hazard for my worthless self.
Ar. And so have I address'd me. Fortu
now
To my heart's hope! Gold, silver, and ba
lead.
*Who chooseth me must give and hazard all
hath:*
You shall look fairer, ere I give or hazard.
What says the golden chest? ha! let me see
*Who chooseth me shall gain what many m
desire.*
What many men desire! that 'many' may
meant
By the fool multitude, that choose by show,
Not learning more than the fond eye doth teac
Which pries not to the interior, but, like t
martlet,
Builds in the weather on the outward wall,
Even in the force and road of casualty.
I will not choose what many men desire,
Because I will not jump with common spirits
And rank me with the barbarous multitude.
Why, then to thee, thou silver treasure-hous
Tell me once more what title thou dost bea
*Who chooseth me shall get as much as he
serves.*
And well said too; for who shall go about
To cozen fortune and be honourable
Without the stamp of merit? Let none p
sume
To wear an undeserved dignity.
O! that estates, degrees, and offices
Were not deriv'd corruptly, and that cle
honour
Were purchas'd by the merit of the wearer.
How many then should cover that stand ba
How many be commanded that command;
How much low peasantry would then be glea
From the true seed of honour; and how mu
honour
Pick'd from the chaff and ruin of the times
To be new varnish'd! Well, but to my choi
*Who chooseth me shall get as much as he
serves.*
I will assume desert. Give me a key for thi
And instantly unlock my fortunes here.
[*He opens the silver cask*
Por. Too long a pause for that which y
find there.
Ar. What's here? the portrait of a blink
idiot,

Presenting me a schedule! I will read it.
How much unlike art thou to Portia!　56
How much unlike my hopes and my deservings!
Who chooseth me shall have as much as he deserves.
Did I deserve no more than a fool's head?
Is that my prize? are my deserts no better?　60
　Por. To offend, and judge, are distinct offices,
And of opposed natures.
　Ar.　　　　　What is here?

> The fire seven times tried this:
> Seven times tried that judgment is　64
> That did never choose amiss.
> Some there be that shadows kiss;
> Such have but a shadow's bliss:
> There be fools alive, I wis,　68
> Silver'd o'er; and so was this.
> Take what wife you will to bed,
> I will ever be your head:
> So be gone, sir: you are sped.　72

Still more fool I shall appear
By the time I linger here:
With one fool's head I came to woo,
But I go away with two.　76
Sweet, adieu. I'll keep my oath,
Patiently to bear my wroth.
　　　　　　[*Exit* ARRAGON *with his Train.*
　Por. Thus hath the candle sing'd the moth.
O, these deliberate fools! when they do choose,
They have the wisdom by their wit to lose.　81
　Ner. The ancient saying is no heresy:
'Hanging and wiving goes by destiny.'
　Por. Come, draw the curtain, Nerissa.　84

Enter a Servant.

　Ser. Where is my lady?
　Por.　　　　　Here; what would my lord?
　Ser. Madam, there is alighted at your gate
A young Venetian, one that comes before
To signify the approaching of his lord;　88
From whom he bringeth sensible regreets,
To wit,—besides commends and courteous breath,—
Gifts of rich value. Yet I have not seen
So likely an embassador of love.　92
A day in April never came so sweet,
To show how costly summer was at hand,
As this fore-spurrer comes before his lord.
　Por. No more, I pray thee: I am half afeard
Thou wilt say anon he is some kin to thee, 97
Thou spend'st such high-day wit in praising him.
Come, come, Nerissa; for I long to see
Quick Cupid's post that comes so mannerly. 100
　Ner. Bassanio, lord Love, if thy will it be!
　　　　　　　　　　　[*Exeunt.*

ACT III

SCENE I.—*Venice. A Street.*

Enter SALANIO *and* SALARINO.

　Salan. Now, what news on the Rialto?
　Salar. Why, yet it lives there unchecked that
Antonio hath a ship of rich lading wracked on
the narrow seas; the Goodwins, I think they call
the place; a very dangerous flat, and fatal, where
the carcasses of many a tail ship lie buried, as
they say, if my gossip Report be an honest
woman of her word.　8
　Salan. I would she were as lying a gossip in
that as ever knapped ginger, or made her neighbours believe she wept for the death of a third
husband. But it is true,—without any slips of
prolixity or crossing the plain highway of talk,
—that the good Antonio, the honest Antonio,—
O, that I had a title good enough to keep his
name company!—　16
　Salar. Come, the full stop.
　Salan. Ha! what sayst thou? Why, the end
is, he hath lost a ship.
　Salar. I would it might prove the end of his
losses.　21
　Salan. Let me say 'amen' betimes, lest the
devil cross my prayer, for here he comes in the
likeness of a Jew.　24

Enter SHYLOCK.

How now, Shylock! what news among the
merchants?
　Shy. You knew, none so well, none so well as
you, of my daughter's flight.　28
　Salar. That's certain: I, for my part, knew
the tailor that made the wings she flew withal.
　Salan. And Shylock, for his own part, knew
the bird was fledged; and then it is the complexion of them all to leave the dam.　33
　Shy. She is damned for it.
　Salar. That's certain, if the devil may be her
judge.　36
　Shy. My own flesh and blood to rebel!
　Salan. Out upon it, old carrion! rebels it at
these years?
　Shy. I say my daughter is my flesh and
blood.　41
　Salar. There is more difference between thy
flesh and hers than between jet and ivory; more
between your bloods than there is between red
wine and Rhenish. But tell us, do you hear
whether Antonio have had any loss at sea
or no?　47
　Shy. There I have another bad match: a
bankrupt, a prodigal, who dare scarce show his
head on the Rialto; a beggar, that used to come
so smug upon the mart; let him look to his bond:
he was wont to call me usurer; let him look to
his bond: he was wont to lend money for a
Christian courtesy; let him look to his bond. 54
　Salar. Why, I am sure, if he forfeit thou
wilt not take his flesh: what's that good for?
　Shy. To bait fish withal: if it will feed nothing
else, it will feed my revenge. He hath disgraced
me, and hindered me half a million, laughed at
my losses, mocked at my gains, scorned my
nation, thwarted my bargains, cooled my friends,
heated mine enemies; and what's his reason? I
am a Jew. Hath not a Jew eyes? hath not a
Jew hands, organs, dimensions, senses, affections, passions? fed with the same food, hurt
with the same weapons, subject to the same diseases, healed by the same means, warmed and
cooled by the same winter and summer, as a

Christian is? If you prick us, do we not bleed? if you tickle us, do we not laugh? if you poison us, do we not die? and if you wrong us, shall we not revenge? If we are like you in the rest, we will resemble you in that. If a Jew wrong a Christian, what is his humility? Revenge. If a Christian wrong a Jew, what should his sufferance be by Christian example? Why, revenge. The villany you teach me I will execute, and it shall go hard but I will better the instruction. 78

Enter a Servant.

Serv. Gentlemen, my master Antonio is at his house, and desires to speak with you both.

Salar. We have been up and down to seek him.

Enter TUBAL.

Salan. Here comes another of the tribe: a third cannot be matched, unless the devil himself turn Jew. 85

[*Exeunt* SALANIO, SALARINO *and* Servant.

Shy. How now, Tubal! what news from Genoa? Hast thou found my daughter?

Tub. I often came where I did hear of her, but cannot find her. 89

Shy. Why there, there, there, there! a diamond gone, cost me two thousand ducats in Frankfort! The curse never fell upon our nation till now; I never felt it till now: two thousand ducats in that; and other precious, precious jewels. I would my daughter were dead at my foot, and the jewels in her ear! would she were hearsed at my foot, and the ducats in her coffin! No news of them? Why, so: and I know not what's spent in the search: Why thou—loss upon loss! the thief gone with so much, and so much to find the thief; and no satisfaction, no revenge: nor no ill luck stirring but what lights on my shoulders; no sighs but of my breathing; no tears but of my shedding. 104

Tub. Yes, other men have ill luck too. Antonio, as I heard in Genoa,—

Shy. What, what, what? ill luck, ill luck?

Tub. —hath an argosy cast away, coming from Tripolis. 109

Shy. I thank God! I thank God! Is it true? is it true?

Tub. I spoke with some of the sailors that escaped the wrack. 113

Shy. I thank thee, good Tubal. Good news, good news! ha, ha! Where? in Genoa?

Tub. Your daughter spent in Genoa, as I heard, one night, fourscore ducats. 117

Shy. Thou stick'st a dagger in me: I shall never see my gold again: fourscore ducats at a sitting! fourscore ducats! 120

Tub. There came divers of Antonio's creditors in my company to Venice, that swear he cannot choose but break.

Shy. I am very glad of it: I'll plague him; I'll torture him: I am glad of it. 125

Tub. One of them showed me a ring that he had of your daughter for a monkey.

Shy. Out upon her! Thou torturest me, Tubal: it was my turquoise; I had it of Leah when I was a bachelor: I would not have given it for a wilderness of monkeys.

Tub. But Antonio is certainly undone. 132

Shy. Nay, that's true, that's very true. Go Tubal, fee me an officer; bespeak him a fortnight before. I will have the heart of him, if he forfeit; for, were he out of Venice, I can make what merchandise I will. Go, go, Tubal, and meet me at our synagogue; go, good Tubal; at our synagogue, Tubal. [*Exeunt.*

SCENE II.—*Belmont. A Room in* PORTIA'S *House.*

Enter BASSANIO, PORTIA, GRATIANO, NERISSA, *and* Attendants.

Por. I pray you, tarry: pause a day or two Before you hazard; for, in choosing wrong, I lose your company: therefore, forbear awhile. There's something tells me, but it is not love, I would not lose you; and you know yourself, 5 Hate counsels not in such a quality. But lest you should not understand me well,— And yet a maiden hath no tongue but thought,— I would detain you here some month or two 9 Before you venture for me. I could teach you How to choose right, but I am then forsworn; So will I never be: so may you miss me; 12 But if you do, you'll make me wish a sin, That I had been forsworn. Beshrew your eyes, They have o'erlook'd me and divided me: One half of me is yours, the other half yours, 16 Mine own, I would say; but if mine, then yours, And so all yours. O! these naughty times Put bars between the owners and their rights; And so, though yours, not yours. Prove it so, 20 Let fortune go to hell for it, not I. I speak too long; but 'tis to peise the time, To eke it and to draw it out in length, To stay you from election. 24

Bass.   Let me choose;
For as I am, I live upon the rack.

Por. Upon the rack, Bassanio! then confess What treason there is mingled with your love.

Bass. None but that ugly treason of mistrust, Which makes me fear th' enjoying of my love: There may as well be amity and life 30 'Tween snow and fire, as treason and my love.

Por. Ay, but I fear you speak upon the rack, Where men enforced do speak anything. 33

Bass. Promise me life, and I'll confess the truth.

Por. Well then, confess, and live.

Bass.   'Confess' and 'love' Had been the very sum of my confession: 36 O happy torment, when my torturer Doth teach me answers for deliverance! But let me to my fortune and the caskets.

Por. Away then! I am lock'd in one of them: If you do love me, you will find me out. 41 Nerissa and the rest, stand all aloof. Let music sound while he doth make his choice Then, if he lose, he makes a swan-like end, 4 Fading in music: that the comparison May stand more proper, my eye shall be the stream

And watery death-bed for him. He may win;
And what is music then? then music is   48
Even as the flourish when true subjects bow
To a new-crowned monarch: such it is
As are those dulcet sounds in break of day
That creep into the dreaming bridegroom's ear,
And summon him to marriage. Now he goes, 53
With no less presence, but with much more love,
Than young Alcides, when he did redeem
The virgin tribute paid by howling Troy   56
To the sea-monster: I stand for sacrifice;
The rest aloof are the Dardanian wives,
With bleared visages, come forth to view
The issue of the exploit. Go, Hercules!   60
Live thou, I live: with much, much more dismay
view the fight than thou that mak'st the fray.

[*A Song, whilst* BASSANIO *comments on
        the caskets to himself.*

Tell me where is fancy bred,
Or in the heart or in the head?   64
How begot, how nourished?
        Reply, reply.
It is engender'd in the eyes,
With gazing fed; and fancy dies   68
In the cradle where it lies.
        Let us all ring fancy's knell:
        I'll begin it,—Ding, dong, bell.

All.   Ding, dong, bell.   72

Bass. So may the outward shows be least
themselves:
The world is still deceiv'd with ornament.
In law, what plea so tainted and corrupt
But, being season'd with a gracious voice,   76
Obscures the show of evil? In religion,
What damned error, but some sober brow
Will bless it and approve it with a text,
Hiding the grossness with fair ornament?   80
There is no vice so simple but assumes
Some mark of virtue on his outward parts.
How many cowards, whose hearts are all as false
As stairs of sand, wear yet upon their chins 84
The beards of Hercules and frowning Mars,
Who, inward search d, have livers white as milk;
And these assume but valour's excrement
To render them redoubted! Look on beauty,   88
And you shall see 'tis purchas'd by the weight;
Which therein works a miracle in nature,
Making them lightest that wear most of it:
So are those crisped snaky golden locks   92
Which make such wanton gambols with the
        wind,
Upon supposed fairness, often known
To be the dowry of a second head,
The skull that bred them, in the sepulchre. 96
Thus ornament is but the guiled shore
To a most dangerous sea; the beauteous scarf
Veiling an Indian beauty; in a word,
The seeming truth which cunning times put on
To entrap the wisest. Therefore, thou gaudy
gold,   101
Hard food for Midas, I will none of thee;
Nor none of thee, thou pale and common drudge
Tween man and man: but thou, thou meagre
        lead,   104
Which rather threat'nest than dost promise
        aught,

Thy plainness moves me more than eloquence,
And here choose I: joy be the consequence!
Por. [*Aside.*] How all the other passions fleet
        to air,   108
As doubtful thoughts, and rash-embrac'd de-
        spair,
And shuddering fear, and green-ey'd jealousy.
O love! be moderate; allay thy ecstasy;
In measure rain thy joy; scant this excess; 112
I feel too much thy blessing; make it less,
For fear I surfeit!
Bass.   What find I here?
        [*Opening the leaden casket.*
Fair Portia's counterfeit! What demi-god
Hath come so near creation? Move these eyes?
Or whether, riding on the balls of mine,   117
Seem they in motion? Here are sever'd lips,
Parted with sugar breath: so sweet a bar
Should sunder such sweet friends. Here, in her
        hairs   120
The painter plays the spider, and hath woven
A golden mesh to entrap the hearts of men
Faster than gnats in cobwebs: but her eyes!—
How could he see to do them? having made one,
Methinks it should have power to steal both his
And leave itself unfurnish'd: yet look, how far
The substance of my praise doth wrong this
        shadow
In underprizing it, so far this shadow   128
Doth limp behind the substance. Here's the
        scroll,
The continent and summary of my fortune.

You that choose not by the view,
Chance as fair and choose as true!   132
Since this fortune falls to you,
Be content and seek no new.
If you be well pleas'd with this
And hold your fortune for your bliss,   136
Turn you where your lady is
And claim her with a loving kiss.

A gentle scroll. Fair lady, by your leave;
        [*Kissing her.*
I come by note, to give and to receive.   140
Like one of two contending in a prize,
That thinks he hath done well in people's eyes,
Hearing applause and universal shout,
Giddy in spirit, still gazing in a doubt   144
Whether those peals of praise be his or no;
So, thrice-fair lady, stand I, even so,
As doubtful whether what I see be true,
Until confirm'd, sign'd, ratified by you.   148
Por. You see me, Lord Bassanio, where I
        stand,
Such as I am: though for myself alone
I would not be ambitious in my wish,
To wish myself much better; yet, for you   152
I would be trebled twenty times myself;
A thousand times more fair, ten thousand times
More rich;
That only to stand high in your account,   156
I might in virtues, beauties, livings, friends,
Exceed account: but the full sum of me
Is sum of nothing; which, to term in gross,
Is an unlesson'd girl, unschool'd, unpractis'd;
Happy in this, she is not yet so old   161
But she may learn; happier than this,

She is not bred so dull but she can learn;
Happiest of all is that her gentle spirit   164
Commits itself to yours to be directed,
As from her lord, her governor, her king.
Myself and what is mine to you and yours
Is now converted: but now I was the lord   168
Of this fair mansion, master of my servants,
Queen o'er myself; and even now, but now,
This house, these servants, and this same my-
self   171
Are yours, my lord. I give them with this ring;
Which when you part from, lose, or give away,
Let it presage the ruin of your love,
And be my vantage to exclaim on you.

    Bass. Madam, you have bereft me of all
words,   176
Only my blood speaks to you in my veins;
And there is such confusion in my powers,
As, after some oration fairly spoke
By a beloved prince, there doth appear   180
Among the buzzing pleased multitude;
Where every something, being blent together,
Turns to a wild of nothing, save of joy,
Express'd and not express'd. But when this ring
Parts from this finger, then parts life from
hence: 185
O! then be bold to say Bassanio's dead.

    Ner. My lord and lady, it is now our time,
That have stood by and seen our wishes prosper,
To cry, good joy. Good joy, my lord and lady!

    Gra. My Lord Bassanio and my gentle lady,
I wish you all the joy that you can wish;
For I am sure you can wish none from me: 192
And when your honours mean to solemnize
The bargain of your faith, I do beseech you,
Even at that time I may be married too.

    Bass. With all my heart, so thou canst get a
wife.   196

    Gra. I thank your lordship, you have got me
one.
My eyes, my lord, can look as swift as yours:
You saw the mistress, I beheld the maid;
You lov'd, I lov'd for intermission.   200
No more pertains to me, my lord, than you.
Your fortune stood upon the caskets there,
And so did mine too, as the matter falls;
For wooing here until I sweat again,   204
And swearing till my very roof was dry
With oaths of love, at last, if promise last,
I got a promise of this fair one here   207
To have her love, provided that your fortune
Achiev'd her mistress.

    Por.   Is this true, Nerissa?

    Ner. Madam, it is, so you stand pleas'd withal.

    Bass. And do you, Gratiano, mean good
faith?

    Gra. Yes, faith, my lord.   212

    Bass. Our feast shall be much honour'd in
your marriage.

    Gra. We'll play with them the first boy for a
thousand ducats.

    Ner. What! and stake down?   216

    Gra. No; we shall ne'er win at that sport,
and stake down.
But who comes here? Lorenzo and his infidel?
What! and my old Venetian friend, Salanio? 220

Enter LORENZO, JESSICA, *and* SALANIO.

    Bass. Lorenzo, and Salanio, welcome hither,
If that the youth of my new interest here
Have power to bid you welcome. By your leave
I bid my very friends and countrymen,   22
Sweet Portia, welcome.

    Por.   So do I, my lord:
They are entirely welcome.

    Lor. I thank your honour. For my part, my
lord,
My purpose was not to have seen you here; 22
But meeting with Salanio by the way,
He did entreat me, past all saying nay,
To come with him along.

    Salan.   I did, my lord,
And I have reason for it. Signior Antonio   23
Commends him to you. [*Gives* BASSANIO *a letter*

    Bass.   Ere I ope his letter
I pray you, tell me how my good friend doth

    Salan. Not sick, my lord, unless it be in mind
Nor well, unless in mind: his letter there 23
Will show you his estate.

    Gra. Nerissa, cheer yon stranger; bid he
welcome.
Your hand, Salanio. What's the news from
Venice?
How doth that royal merchant, good Antonio
I know he will be glad of our success;   24
We are the Jasons, we have won the fleece.

    Salan. I would you had won the fleece tha
he hath lost.

    Por. There are some shrewd contents in yo
same paper,   24
That steal the colour from Bassanio's cheek:
Some dear friend dead, else nothing in the worl
Could turn so much the constitution
Of any constant man. What, worse and worse
With leave, Bassanio; I am half yourself,   24
And I must freely have the half of anything
That this same paper brings you.

    Bass.   O sweet Portia
Here are a few of the unpleasant'st words 25
That ever blotted paper. Gentle lady,
When I did first impart my love to you,
I freely told you all the wealth I had
Ran in my veins, I was a gentleman: 25
And then I told you true; and yet, dear lady,
Rating myself at nothing, you shall see
How much I was a braggart. When I told yo
My state was nothing, I should then have tol
you   26
That I was worse than nothing; for, indeed,
I have engag'd myself to a dear friend,
Engag'd my friend to his mere enemy,
To feed my means. Here is a letter, lady; 26
The paper as the body of my friend,
And every word in it a gaping wound,
Issuing life-blood. But is it true, Salanio?
Hath all his ventures fail'd? What, not one hit
From Tripolis, from Mexico, and England, 26
From Lisbon, Barbary, and India?
And not one vessel 'scape the dreadful touch
Of merchant-marring rocks?

    Salan.   Not one, my lord. 27
Besides, it should appear, that if he had
The present money to discharge the Jew,

[SCENE II]

He would not take it. Never did I know
A creature, that did bear the shape of man, 276
So keen and greedy to confound a man.
He plies the duke at morning and at night,
And doth impeach the freedom of the state,
If they deny him justice: twenty merchants, 280
The duke himself, and the magnificoes
Of greatest port, have all persuaded with him;
But none can drive him from the envious plea
Of forfeiture, of justice, and his bond. 284
Jes. When I was with him, I have heard him
swear
To Tubal and to Chus, his countrymen,
That he would rather have Antonio's flesh
Than twenty times the value of the sum 288
That he did owe him; and I know, my lord,
If law, authority, and power deny not,
It will go hard with poor Antonio.
Por. Is it your dear friend that is thus in
trouble? 292
Bass. The dearest friend to me, the kindest
man,
The best-condition'd and unwearied spirit
In doing courtesies, and one in whom
The ancient Roman honour more appears 296
Than any that draws breath in Italy.
Por. What sum owes he the Jew?
Bass. For me, three thousand ducats.
Por. What, no more?
Pay him six thousand, and deface the bond; 300
Double six thousand, and then treble that,
Before a friend of this description
Shall lose a hair thorough Bassanio's fault.
First go with me to church and call me wife, 304
And then away to Venice to your friend;
For never shall you lie by Portia's side
With an unquiet soul. You shall have gold
To pay the petty debt twenty times over: 308
When it is paid, bring your true friend along.
My maid Nerissa and myself meantime,
Will live as maids and widows. Come, away!
For you shall hence upon your wedding-day. 312
Bid your friends welcome, show a merry cheer;
Since you are dear bought, I will love you dear.
But let me hear the letter of your friend. 315

Bass. Sweet Bassanio, my ships have all miscarried, my creditors grow cruel, my estate is very
low, my bond to the Jew is forfeit; and since, in
paying it, it is impossible I should live, all debts
are cleared between you and I, if I might but see
you at my death. Notwithstanding, use your
pleasure: if your love do not persuade you to come,
let not my letter.

Por. O love, dispatch all business, and be
gone! 324
Bass. Since I have your good leave to go away,
I will make haste; but, till I come again,
No bed shall e'er be guilty of my stay,
Nor rest be interposer 'twixt us twain.
[*Exeunt.*

SCENE III.—*Venice. A Street.*

Enter SHYLOCK, SALARINO, ANTONIO, *and* Gaoler.

Shy. Gaoler, look to him: tell not me of
mercy;
This is the fool that lent out money gratis:

Gaoler, look to him.
Ant. Hear me yet, good Shylock.
Shy. I'll have my bond; speak not against
my bond: 4
I have sworn an oath that I will have my bond.
Thou call'dst me dog before thou hadst a cause,
But, since I am a dog, beware my fangs:
The duke shall grant me justice. I do wonder,
Thou naughty gaoler, that thou art so fond 9
To come abroad with him at his request.
Ant. I pray thee, hear me speak.
Shy. I'll have my bond; I will not hear thee
speak: 12
I'll have my bond, and therefore speak no more.
I'll not be made a soft and dull-eyed fool,
To shake the head, relent, and sigh, and yield
To Christian intercessors. Follow not; 16
I'll have no speaking; I will have my bond.
[*Exit.*
Salar. It is the most impenetrable cur
That ever kept with men.
Ant. Let him alone:
I'll follow him no more with bootless prayers.
He seeks my life; his reason well I know. 21
I oft deliver'd from his forfeitures
Many that have at times made moan to me;
Therefore he hates me.
Salar. I am sure the duke 24
Will never grant this forfeiture to hold.
Ant. The duke cannot deny the course of law:
For the commodity that strangers have
With us in Venice, if it be denied, 28
'Twill much impeach the justice of the state;
Since that the trade and profit of the city
Consisteth of all nations. Therefore, go:
These griefs and losses have so bated me, 32
That I shall hardly spare a pound of flesh
To-morrow to my bloody creditor.
Well, gaoler, on. Pray God, Bassanio come
To see me pay his debt, and then I care not! 36
[*Exeunt.*

SCENE IV.—*Belmont. A Room in* PORTIA'S
House.

Enter PORTIA, NERISSA, LORENZO, JESSICA,
and BALTHAZAR.

Lor. Madam, although I speak it in your
presence,
You have a noble and a true conceit
Of god-like amity; which appears most strongly
In bearing thus the absence of your lord. 4
But if you knew to whom you show this honour,
How true a gentleman you send relief,
How dear a lover of my lord your husband,
I know you would be prouder of the work 8
Than customary bounty can enforce you.
Por. I never did repent for doing good,
Nor shall not now: for in companions
That do converse and waste the time together,
Whose souls do bear an equal yoke of love, 13
There must be needs a like proportion
Of lineaments, of manners, and of spirit;
Which makes me think that this Antonio, 16
Being the bosom lover of my lord,

Must needs be like my lord. If it be so,
How little is the cost I have bestow'd
In purchasing the semblance of my soul   20
From out the state of hellish cruelty!
This comes too near the praising of myself;
Therefore, no more of it: hear other things.
Lorenzo, I commit into your hands   24
The husbandry and manage of my house
Until my lord's return: for mine own part,
I have toward heaven breath'd a secret vow
To live in prayer and contemplation,   28
Only attended by Nerissa here,
Until her husband and my lord's return.
There is a monastery two miles off,
And there will we abide. I do desire you   32
Not to deny this imposition,
The which my love and some necessity
Now lays upon you.

    Lor.   Madam, with all my heart:
I shall obey you in all fair commands.   36

    Por. My people do already know my mind,
And will acknowledge you and Jessica
In place of Lord Bassanio and myself.
So fare you well till we shall meet again.   40

    Lor. Fair thoughts and happy hours attend
on you!

    Jes. I wish your ladyship all heart's content.

    Por. I thank you for your wish, and am well
pleas'd
To wish it back on you: fare you well, Jessica.

    [*Exeunt* JESSICA *and* LORENZO.

Now, Balthazar,   45
As I have ever found thee honest-true,
So let me find thee still. Take this same letter,
And use thou all the endeavour of a man   48
In speed to Padua: see thou render this
Into my cousin's hand, Doctor Bellario;
And, look, what notes and garments he doth
    give thee,
Bring them, I pray thee, with imagin'd speed   52
Unto the traject, to the common ferry
Which trades to Venice. Waste no time in words,
But get thee gone: I shall be there before thee.

    Balth. Madam, I go with all convenient speed.
    [*Exit.*

    Por. Come on, Nerissa: I have work in hand
That you yet know not of: we'll see our husbands
Before they think of us.

    Ner.   Shall they see us?

    Por. They shall, Nerissa; but in such a habit
That they shall think we are accomplished   61
With that we lack. I'll hold thee any wager,
When we are both accoutred like young men,
I'll prove the prettier fellow of the two,   64
And wear my dagger with the braver grace,
And speak between the change of man and boy
With a reed voice, and turn two mincing steps
Into a manly stride, and speak of frays   68
Like a fine bragging youth, and tell quaint lies,
How honourable ladies sought my love,
Which I denying, they fell sick and died:
I could not do withal; then I'll repent,   72
And wish, for all that, that I had not kill'd them:
And twenty of these puny lies I'll tell,
That men shall swear I have discontinu'd school
Above a twelvemonth. I have within my mind

A thousand raw tricks of these bragging Jack[
Which I will practise.

    Ner.   Why, shall we turn to men

    Por. Fie, what a question's that,
If thou wert near a lewd interpreter!   8
But come: I'll tell thee all my whole device
When I am in my coach, which stays for us
At the park gate; and therefore haste away,
For we must measure twenty miles to-day.   8
    [*Exeun*

SCENE V.—*The Same. A Garden.*

Enter LAUNCELOT *and* JESSICA.

    Laun. Yes, truly; for, look you, the sins o[
the father are to be laid upon the children; there
fore, I promise you, I fear you. I was alway
plain with you, and so now I speak my agitatio
of the matter: therefore be of good cheer; fo[
truly, I think you are damned. There is but on[
hope in it that can do you any good, and that [
but a kind of bastard hope neither.

    Jes. And what hope is that, I pray thee?

    Laun. Marry, you may partly hope that you[
father got you not, that you are not the Jew[
daughter.

    Jes. That were a kind of bastard hope, i[
deed: so the sins of my mother should be visite[
upon me.

    Laun. Truly then I fear you are damned bot[
by father and mother: thus when I shun Scyll[
your father, I fall into Charybdis, your mothe[
well, you are gone both ways.

    Jes. I shall be saved by my husband; he hat[
made me a Christian.

    Laun. Truly the more to blame he: we wer[
Christians enow before; e'en as many as coul[
well live one by another. This making of Chris
tians will raise the price of hogs: if we grow a[
to be pork-eaters, we shall not shortly have [
rasher on the coals for money.

    Jes. I'll tell my husband, Launcelot, what yo[
say: here he comes.

Enter LORENZO.

    Lor. I shall grow jealous of you shortl[
Launcelot, if you thus get my wife into co[
ners.

    Jes. Nay, you need not fear us, Lorenz[
Launcelot and I are out. He tells me flatl[
there is no mercy for me in heaven, because [
am a Jew's daughter: and he says you are n[
good member of the commonwealth, for, in con
verting Jews to Christians, you raise the price o[
pork.

    Lor. I shall answer that better to the com
monwealth than you can the getting up of th[
negro's belly: the Moor is with child by yo[
Launcelot.

    Laun. It is much that the Moor should b[
more than reason; but if she be less than a[
honest woman, she is indeed more than I too[
her for.

    Lor. How every fool can play upon the word
I think the best grace of wit will shortly tur[
into silence, and discourse grow commendabl[

none only but parrots. Go in, sirrah: bid
em prepare for dinner. 52
Laun. That is done, sir; they have all
•machs.
Lor. Goodly Lord, what a wit-snapper are
u! then bid them prepare dinner. 56
Laun. That is done too, sir; only, 'cover' is
e word.
Lor. Will you cover, then, sir? 59
Laun. Not so, sir, neither; I know my duty.
Lor. Yet more quarrelling with occasion!
ilt thou show the whole wealth of thy wit in
instant? I pray thee, understand a plain man
his plain meaning: go to thy fellows; bid
em cover the table, serve in the meat, and we
ll come in to dinner. 66
Laun. For the table, sir, it shall be served in;
r the meat, sir, it shall be covered; for your
ming in to dinner, sir, why, let it be as hu-
ours and conceits shall govern. [*Exit.*
Lor. O dear discretion, how his words are
suited!
e fool hath planted in his memory 72
a army of good words: and I do know
many fools, that stand in better place,
arnish'd like him, that for a tricksy word
fy the matter. How cheer'st thou, Jessica?
id now, good sweet, say thy opinion; 77
ow dost thou like the Lord Bassanio's wife?
Jes. Past all expressing. It is very meet,
e Lord Bassanio live an upright life, 80
r, having such a blessing in his lady,
finds the joys of heaven here on earth;
id if on earth he do not mean it, then
reason he should never come to heaven. 84
hy, if two gods should play some heavenly
match,
id on the wager lay two earthly women,
id Portia one, there must be something else
wn'd with the other, for the poor rude world
th not her fellow.
Lor. Even such a husband 89
ist thou of me as she is for a wife.
Jes. Nay, but ask my opinion too of that.
Lor. I will anon; first, let us go to dinner. 92
Jes. Nay, let me praise you while I have a
stomach.
Lor. No, pray thee, let it serve for table-talk;
en howsoe'er thou speak'st, 'mong other
things
hall digest it.
Jes. Well, I'll set you forth. [*Exeunt.*

ACT IV

SCENE I.—*Venice. A Court of Justice.*

ter the DUKE: *the* Magnificoes; ANTONIO,
BASSANIO, GRATIANO, SALARINO, SALANIO,
and Others.

Duke. What, is Antonio here?
Ant. Ready, so please your Grace.
Duke. I am sorry for thee: thou art come to
answer
stony adversary, an inhuman wretch 4
icapable of pity, void and empty

From any dram of mercy.
Ant. I have heard
Your Grace hath ta'en great pains to qualify
His rigorous course; but since he stands ob-
durate, 8
And that no lawful means can carry me
Out of his envy's reach, I do oppose
My patience to his fury, and am arm'd
To suffer with a quietness of spirit 12
The very tyranny and rage of his.
Duke. Go one, and call the Jew into the
court.
Salar. He's ready at the door: he comes,
my lord.

Enter SHYLOCK.

Duke. Make room, and let him stand before
our face. 16
Shylock, the world thinks, and I think so too,
That thou but lead'st this fashion of thy malice
To the last hour of act; and then 'tis thought
Thou'lt show thy mercy and remorse more
strange 20
Than is thy strange-apparent cruelty;
And where thou now exact'st the penalty,—
Which is a pound of this poor merchant's
flesh,—
Thou wilt not only loose the forfeiture, 24
But, touch'd with human gentleness and love,
Forgive a moiety of the principal;
Glancing an eye of pity on his losses,
That have of late so huddled on his back, 28
Enow to press a royal merchant down,
And pluck commiseration of his state
From brassy bosoms and rough hearts of flint,
From stubborn Turks and Tartars, never train'd
To offices of tender courtesy. 33
We all expect a gentle answer, Jew.
Shy. I have possess'd your Grace of what I
purpose;
And by our holy Sabbath have I sworn 36
To have the due and forfeit of my bond:
If you deny it, let the danger light
Upon your charter and your city's freedom.
You'll ask me, why I rather choose to have 40
A weight of carrion flesh than to receive
Three thousand ducats: I'll not answer that:
But say it is my humour: is it answer'd?
What if my house be troubled with a rat, 44
And I be pleas'd to give ten thousand ducats
To have it ban'd? What, are you answer'd yet?
Some men there are love not a gaping pig;
Some, that are mad if they behold a cat; 48
And others, when the bagpipe sings i' the nose,
Cannot contain their urine: for affection,
Mistress of passion, sways it to the mood
Of what it likes, or loathes. Now, for your
answer: 52
As there is no firm reason to be render'd,
Why he cannot abide a gaping pig;
Why he, a harmless necessary cat;
Why he, a wauling bagpipe; but of force 56
Must yield to such inevitable shame
As to offend, himself being offended;
So can I give no reason, nor I will not,
More than a lodg'd hate and a certain loathing

I bear Antonio, that I follow thus   61
A losing suit against him. Are you answer'd?
Bass. This is no answer, thou unfeeling man,
To excuse the current of thy cruelty.   64
   Shy. I am not bound to please thee with my
   answer.
   Bass. Do all men kill the things they do not
   love?
   Shy. Hates any man the thing he would not
   kill?
   Bass. Every offence is not a hate at first. 68
   Shy. What! wouldst thou have a serpent
   sting thee twice?
   Ant. I pray you, think you question with the
   Jew:
You may as well go stand upon the beach,
And bid the main flood bate his usual height; 72
You may as well use question with the wolf,
Why he hath made the ewe bleat for the lamb;
You may as well forbid the mountain pines
To wag their high tops, and to make no noise 76
When they are fretted with the gusts of heaven;
You may as well do anything most hard,
As seek to soften that—than which what's
harder?—
His Jewish heart: therefore, I do beseech you,
Make no more offers, use no further means; 81
But with all brief and plain conveniency,
Let me have judgment, and the Jew his will.
   Bass. For thy three thousand ducats here
   is six.   84
   Shy. If every ducat in six thousand ducats
Were in six parts and every part a ducat,
I would not draw them; I would have my bond.
   Duke. How shalt thou hope for mercy, ren-
   dering none?   88
   Shy. What judgment shall I dread, doing no
   wrong?
You have among you many a purchas'd slave,
Which, like your asses and your dogs and mules,
You use in abject and in slavish parts,   92
Because you bought them: shall I say to you,
Let them be free, marry them to your heirs?
Why sweat they under burdens? let their beds
Be made as soft as yours, and let their palates
Be season'd with such viands? You will an-
swer: 97
'The slaves are ours:' so do I answer you:
The pound of flesh which I demand of him,
Is dearly bought; 'tis mine and I will have it.
If you deny me, fie upon your law!   101
There is no force in the decrees of Venice.
I stand for judgment: answer; shall I have it?
   Duke. Upon my power I may dismiss this
   court,   104
Unless Bellario, a learned doctor,
Whom I have sent for to determine this,
Come here to-day.
   Salar.   My lord, here stays without
A messenger with letters from the doctor,   108
New come from Padua.
   Duke. Bring us the letters: call the messenger.
   Bass. Good cheer, Antonio! What, man,
   courage yet!
The Jew shall have my flesh, blood, bones,
and all,   112

Ere thou shalt lose for me one drop of bloo
   Ant. I am a tainted wether of the flock,
Meetest for death: the weakest kind of fru
Drops earliest to the ground; and so let me: 1
You cannot better be employ'd, Bassanio,
Than to live still, and write mine epitaph.

Enter NERISSA, *dressed like a lawyer's clerl*

   Duke. Came you from Padua, from Bellari
   Ner. From both, my lord. Bellario gree
   your Grace.   [*Presents a lette*
   Bass. Why dost thou whet thy knife
   earnestly?
   Shy. To cut the forfeiture from that ban
   rupt there.
   Gra. Not on thy sole, but on thy soul, har
Jew,
Thou mak'st thy knife keen; but no metal ca
No, not the hangman's axe, bear half the kee
ness
Of thy sharp envy. Can no prayers pierce the
   Shy. No, none that thou hast wit enough
   make.
   Gra. O, be thou damn'd, inexecrable dog!
And for thy life let justice be accus'd.
Thou almost mak'st me waver in my faith
To hold opinion with Pythagoras,
That souls of animals infuse themselves
Into the trunks of men: thy currish spirit
Govern'd a wolf, who, hang'd for human slaug
ter,
Even from the gallows did his fell soul flee
And whilst thou lay'st in thy unhallow'd da
Infus'd itself in thee; for thy desires
Are wolfish, bloody, starv'd, and ravenous.
   Shy. Till thou canst rail the seal from off
   bond,
Thou but offend'st thy lungs to speak so lou
Repair thy wit, good youth, or it will fall
To cureless ruin. I stand here for law.
   Duke. This letter from Bellario doth co
   mend
A young and learned doctor to our court.
Where is he?
   Ner.   He attendeth here hard by,
To know your answer, whether you'll adi
him.
   Duke. With all my heart: some three or fo
   of you
Go give him courteous conduct to this plac
Meantime, the court shall hear Bellario's lett

   Clerk. Your Grace shall understand that at
   receipt of your letter I am very sick; but in
   instant that your messenger came, in loving vis
   tion was with me a young doctor of Rome;
   name is Balthazar. I acquainted him with
   cause in controversy between the Jew and Anto
   the merchant: we turned o'er many books to
   ther: he is furnished with my opinion; wh
   bettered with his own learning,—the greatn
   whereof I cannot enough commend,—comes v
   him, at my importunity, to fill up your Gra
   request in my stead. I beseech you, let his
   of years be no impediment to let him lack a
   verend estimation, for I never knew so youn
   body with so old a head. I leave him to y
   gracious acceptance, whose trial shall better p
   lish his commendation.

Duke. You hear the learn'd Bellario, what
  he writes:
ad here, I take it, is the doctor come.

Enter PORTIA, *dressed like a doctor of laws.*

ive me your hand. Came you from old
  Bellario?
Por. I did, my lord.
Duke. You are welcome: take your place.
e you acquainted with the difference   171
at holds this present question in the court?
Por. I am informed throughly of the cause.
hich is the merchant here, and which the
  Jew?
Duke. Antonio and old Shylock, both stand
  forth.
Por. Is your name Shylock?
Shy.   Shylock is my name. 176
Por. Of a strange nature is the suit you
  follow;
t in such rule that the Venetian law
nnot impugn you as you do proceed.
o ANTONIO.] You stand within his danger, do
  you not?   180
Ant. Ay, so he says.
Por.   Do you confess the bond?
Ant. I do.
Por.   Then must the Jew be merciful.
Shy. On what compulsion must I? tell me
  that.
Por. The quality of mercy is not strain'd, 184
droppeth as the gentle rain from heaven
oon the place beneath: it is twice bless'd;
blesseth him that gives and him that takes:
is mightiest in the mightiest; it becomes 188
e throned monarch better than his crown;
s sceptre shows the force of temporal power,
e attribute to awe and majesty,
herein doth sit the dread and fear of kings;
t mercy is above this sceptred sway,   193
is enthroned in the hearts of kings,
is an attribute to God himself,
d earthly power doth then show likest God's
hen mercy seasons justice. Therefore, Jew,
ough justice be thy plea, consider this, 198
at in the course of justice none of us
ould see salvation: we do pray for mercy,
d that same prayer doth teach us all to
  render   201
e deeds of mercy. I have spoke thus much
• mitigate the justice of thy plea,
hich if thou follow, this strict court of Venice
ust needs give sentence 'gainst the merchant
  there.   205
Shy. My deeds upon my head! I crave the
  law,
e penalty and forfeit of my bond.
Por. Is he not able to discharge the money?
Bass. Yes, here I tender it for him in the
  court;   209
ea, twice the sum: if that will not suffice,
vill be bound to pay it ten times o'er,
n forfeit of my hands, my head, my heart. 212
this will not suffice, it must appear
at malice bears down truth. And, I beseech
  you,

Wrest once the law to your authority:
To do a great right, do a little wrong,   216
And curb this cruel devil of his will.
  Por. It must not be. There is no power in
  Venice
Can alter a decree established:
'Twill be recorded for a precedent,   220
And many an error by the same example
Will rush into the state. It cannot be.
  Shy. A Daniel come to judgment! yea, a
  Daniel!
O wise young judge, how I do honour thee! 224
  Por. I pray you, let me look upon the bond.
  Shy. Here 'tis, most reverend doctor; here
  it is.
  Por. Shylock, there's thrice thy money offer'd
  thee.
  Shy. An oath, an oath, I have an oath in
  heaven: 228
Shall I lay perjury upon my soul?
No, not for Venice.
  Por.   Why, this bond is forfeit;
And lawfully by this the Jew may claim
A pound of flesh, to be by him cut off   232
Nearest the merchant's heart. Be merciful:
Take thrice thy money; bid me tear the bond.
  Shy. When it is paid according to the tenour.
It doth appear you are a worthy judge;   236
You know the law, your exposition
Hath been most sound: I charge you by the law,
Whereof you are a well-deserving pillar,
Proceed to judgment: by my soul I swear 240
There is no power in the tongue of man
To alter me. I stay here on my bond.
  Ant. Most heartily I do beseech the court
To give the judgment.
  Por.   Why then, thus it is: 244
You must prepare your bosom for his knife.
  Shy. O noble judge! O excellent young man!
  Por. For, the intent and purpose of the law
Hath full relation to the penalty,   248
Which here appeareth due upon the bond.
  Shy. 'Tis very true! O wise and upright
  judge!
How much more elder art thou than thy looks!
  Por. Therefore lay bare your bosom.
  Shy.   Ay, 'his breast:'
So says the bond:—doth it not, noble judge?—
'Nearest his heart:' those are the very words.
  Por. It is so. Are there balance here to weigh
The flesh?   256
  Shy. I have them ready.
  Por. Have by some surgeon, Shylock, on your
  charge,
To stop his wounds, lest he do bleed to death.
  Shy. Is it so nominated in the bond?   260
  Por. It is not so express'd; but what of that?
'Twere good you do so much for charity.
  Shy. I cannot find it: 'tis not in the bond.
  Por. You, merchant, have you anything to
  say?   264
  Ant. But little: I am arm'd and well prepar'd.
Give me your hand, Bassanio: fare you well!
Grieve not that I am fallen to this for you;
For herein Fortune shows herself more kind 268
Than is her custom: it is still her use

To let the wretched man outlive his wealth,
To view with hollow eye and wrinkled brow
An age of poverty; from which lingering pen-
ance   272
Of such a misery doth she cut me off.
Commend me to your honourable wife:
Tell her the process of Antonio's end;
Say how I lov'd you, speak me fair in death; 276
And, when the tale is told, bid her be judge
Whether Bassanio had not once a love.
Repent not you that you shall lose your friend,
And he repents not that he pays your debt; 280
For if the Jew do cut but deep enough,
I'll pay it instantly with all my heart.
  Bass. Antonio, I am married to a wife
Which is as dear to me as life itself;   284
But life itself, my wife, and all the world,
Are not with me esteem'd above thy life:
I would lose all, ay, sacrifice them all,
Here to this devil, to deliver you.   288
  Por. Your wife would give you little thanks
      for that,
If she were by to hear you make the offer.
  Gra. I have a wife, whom, I protest, I love:
I would she were in heaven, so she could   292
Entreat some power to change this currish Jew.
  Ner. 'Tis well you offer it behind her back;
The wish would make else an unquiet house.
  Shy. These be the Christian husbands! I have
      a daughter;   296
Would any of the stock of Barabbas
Had been her husband rather than a Christian!
We trifle time; I pray thee, pursue sentence.
  Por. A pound of that same merchant's flesh
      is thine: 300
The court awards it, and the law doth give it.
  Shy. Most rightful judge!
  Por. And you must cut this flesh from off his
      breast:
The law allows it, and the court awards it.   304
  Shy. Most learned judge! A sentence! come,
      prepare!
  Por. Tarry a little: there is something else.
This bond doth give thee here no jot of blood;
The words expressly are 'a pound of flesh:' 308
Then take thy bond, take thou thy pound of flesh;
But, in the cutting it, if thou dost shed
One drop of Christian blood, thy lands and
      goods
Are, by the laws of Venice, confiscate   312
Unto the state of Venice.
  Gra. O upright judge! Mark, Jew: O learned
      judge!
  Shy. Is that the law?
  Por.   Thyself shalt see the act;
For, as thou urgest justice, be assur'd   316
Thou shalt have justice, more than thou desir'st.
  Gra. O learned judge! Mark, Jew: a learned
      judge!
  Shy. I take this offer then: pay the bond
      thrice,
And let the Christian go.
  Bass.   Here is the money. 320
  Por. Soft!
The Jew shall have all justice; soft! no haste:—
He shall have nothing but the penalty.

  Gra. O Jew! an upright judge, a learn
      judge!
  Por. Therefore prepare thee to cut off
      flesh.
Shed thou no blood; nor cut thou less, nor mo
But just a pound of flesh: if thou tak'st mo
Or less, than a just pound, be it but so much
As makes it light or heavy in the substance,
Or the division of the twentieth part
Of one poor scruple, nay, if the scale do tu
But in the estimation of a hair,
Thou diest and all thy goods are confiscate.
  Gra. A second Daniel, a Daniel, Jew!
Now, infidel, I have thee on the hip.
  Por. Why doth the Jew pause? take thy f
      feiture.
  Shy. Give me my principal, and let me
  Bass. I have it ready for thee; here it is.
  Por. He hath refus'd it in the open cour
He shall have merely justice, and his bond.
  Gra. A Daniel, still say I; a second Dani
I thank thee, Jew, for teaching me that word
  Shy. Shall I not have barely my principa
  Por. Thou shalt have nothing but the f
      feiture,
To be so taken at thy peril, Jew.
  Shy. Why, then the devil give him good of
I'll stay no longer question.
  Por.   Tarry, Jew:
The law hath yet another hold on you.
It is enacted in the laws of Venice,
If it be prov'd against an alien
That by direct or indirect attempts
He seek the life of any citizen,
The party 'gainst the which he doth contriv
Shall seize one half his goods; the other ha
Comes to the privy coffer of the state;
And the offender's life lies in the mercy
Of the duke only, 'gainst all other voice.
In which predicament, I say, thou stand'st
For it appears by manifest proceeding,
That indirectly and directly too
Thou hast contriv'd against the very life
Of the defendant; and thou hast incurr'd
The danger formerly by me rehears'd.
Down therefore and beg mercy of the duke.
  Gra. Beg that thou mayst have leave to ha
      thyself:
And yet, thy wealth being forfeit to the sta
Thou hast not left the value of a cord;
Therefore thou must be hang'd at the sta
      charge.
  Duke. That thou shalt see the difference
      our spirits,
I pardon thee thy life before thou ask it.
For half thy wealth, it is Antonio's;
The other half comes to the general state,
Which humbleness may drive into a fine.
  Por. Ay, for the state; not for Antonio.
  Shy. Nay, take my life and all; pardon
      that:
You take my house when you do take the pr
That doth sustain my house; you take my
When you do take the means whereby I liv
  Por. What mercy can you render him, A
tonio?

Gra. A halter gratis; nothing else, for God's
sake! 380

Ant. So please my lord the duke, and all the
court,
quit the fine for one half of his goods,
n content; so he will let me have
e other half in use, to render it, 384
on his death, unto the gentleman
at lately stole his daughter:
o things provided more, that, for this favour,
presently become a Christian; 388
e other, that he do record a gift,
re in the court, of all he dies possess'd,
to his son Lorenzo, and his daughter.

Duke. He shall do this, or else I do recant
pardon that I late pronounced here. 393

Por. Art thou contented, Jew? what dost
thou say?

Shy. I am content.

Por.   Clerk, draw a deed of gift.

Shy. I pray you give me leave to go from
hence:
n not well. Send the deed after me, 397
d I will sign it.

Duke.   Get thee gone, but do it.

Gra. In christening thou shalt have two godfathers;
d I been judge, thou shouldst have had ten
more, 400
bring thee to the gallows, not the font.
[*Exit* SHYLOCK.

Duke. Sir, I entreat you home with me to
dinner.

Por. I humbly do desire your Grace of pardon:
ust away this night toward Padua, 404
d it is meet I presently set forth.

Duke. I am sorry that your leisure serves
you not.

tonio, gratify this gentleman,
, in my mind, you are much bound to him.
[*Exeunt* DUKE, Magnificoes, *and Train.*

Bass. Most worthy gentleman, I and my friend
ve by your wisdom been this day acquitted
grievous penalties; in lieu whereof,
ree thousand ducats, due unto the Jew, 412
freely cope your courteous pains withal.

Ant. And stand indebted, over and above,
love and service to you evermore.

Por. He is well paid that is well satisfied; 416
d I, delivering you, am satisfied,
d therein do account myself well paid:
mind was never yet more mercenary.
ray you, know me when we meet again: 420
ish you well, and so I take my leave.

Bass. Dear sir, of force I must attempt you
further:
ke some remembrance of us, as a tribute,
t as a fee. Grant me two things, I pray you,
t to deny me, and to pardon me. 425

Por. You press me far, and therefore I will
yield.
ANT.] Give me your gloves, I'll wear them
for your sake;
BASS.] And, for your love, I'll take this ring
from you. 428

Do not draw back your hand; I'll take no more;
And you in love shall not deny me this.

Bass. This ring, good sir? alas! it is a trifle;
I will not shame myself to give you this. 432

Por. I will have nothing else but only this;
And now methinks I have a mind to it.

Bass. There's more depends on this than on
the value.
The dearest ring in Venice will I give you, 436
And find it out by proclamation:
Only for this, I pray you, pardon me.

Por. I see, sir, you are liberal in offers: 439
You taught me first to beg, and now methinks
You teach me how a beggar should be answer'd.

Bass. Good sir, this ring was given me by my
wife;
And, when she put it on, she made me vow
That I should never sell nor give nor lose it. 444

Por. That 'scuse serves many men to save
their gifts.
An if your wife be not a mad-woman,
And know how well I have deserv'd the ring,
She would not hold out enemy for ever, 448
For giving it to me. Well, peace be with you.
[*Exeunt* PORTIA *and* NERISSA.

Ant. My Lord Bassanio, let him have the
ring:
Let his deservings and my love withal
Be valu'd 'gainst your wife's commandment. 452

Bass. Go, Gratiano; run and overtake him;
Give him the ring, and bring him, if thou canst,
Unto Antonio's house. Away! make haste.
[*Exit* GRATIANO.
Come, you and I will thither presently, 456
And in the morning early will we both
Fly toward Belmont. Come, Antonio. [*Exeunt.*

SCENE II.—*The Same. A Street.*

Enter PORTIA *and* NERISSA.

Por. Inquire the Jew's house out, give him
this deed,
And let him sign it. We'll away to-night,
And be a day before our husbands home:
This deed will be well welcome to Lorenzo. 4

Enter GRATIANO.

Gra. Fair sir, you are well o'erta'en.
My Lord Bassanio upon more advice
Hath sent you here this ring, and doth entreat
Your company at dinner.

Por.   That cannot be: 8
His ring I do accept most thankfully;
And so, I pray you, tell him: furthermore,
I pray you, show my youth old Shylock's house.

Gra. That will I do.

Ner.   Sir, I would speak with you. 12
[*Aside to* PORTIA.] I'll see if I can get my hus-
band's ring,
Which I did make him swear to keep for ever.

Por. Thou mayst, I warrant. We shall have
old swearing
That they did give the rings away to men; 16
But we'll outface them, and outswear them too.

Away! make haste: thou know'st where I will
    tarry.

Ner. Come, good sir, will you show me to
    this house?   [*Exeunt.*

ACT V

Scene I.—*Belmont. The Avenue to* PORTIA'S
House.

Enter LORENZO *and* JESSICA.

Lor. The moon shines bright: in such a night
    as this,
When the sweet wind did gently kiss the trees
And they did make no noise, in such a night
Troilus methinks mounted the Troyan walls, 4
And sigh'd his soul toward the Grecian tents,
Where Cressid lay that night.

Jes.   In such a night
Did Thisbe fearfully o'ertrip the dew,
And saw the lion's shadow ere himself,   8
And ran dismay'd away.

Lor.   In such a night
Stood Dido with a willow in her hand
Upon the wild sea-banks, and waft her love
To come again to Carthage.

Jes.   In such a night 12
Medea gather'd the enchanted herbs
That did renew old Æson.

Lor.   In such a night
Did Jessica steal from the wealthy Jew,
And with an unthrift love did run from Venice,
As far as Belmont.

Jes.   In such a night   17
Did young Lorenzo swear he lov'd her well,
Stealing her soul with many vows of faith,
And ne'er a true one.

Lor.   In such a night   20
Did pretty Jessica, like a little shrew,
Slander her love, and he forgave it her.

Jes. I would out-night you, did no body come;
But, hark! I hear the footing of a man.   24

Enter STEPHANO.

Lor. Who comes so fast in silence of the
    night?

Steph. A friend.

Lor. A friend! what friend? your name, I
    pray you, friend.

Steph. Stephano is my name; and I bring
    word   28
My mistress will before the break of day
Be here at Belmont: she doth stray about
By holy crosses, where she kneels and prays
For happy wedlock hours.

Lor.   Who comes with her? 32

Steph. None, but a holy hermit and her maid.
I pray you, is my master yet return'd?

Lor. He is not, nor we have not heard from
    him.
But go we in, I pray thee, Jessica,   36
And ceremoniously let us prepare
Some welcome for the mistress of the house.

Enter LAUNCELOT.

Laun. Sola, sola! wo ha, ho! sola, sola!
Lor. Who calls?   40

Laun. Sola! did you see Master Lorenz
Master Lorenzo! sola, sola!

Lor. Leave holloaing, man; here.

Laun. Sola! where? where?

Lor. Here.

Laun. Tell him there's a post come from
master, with his horn full of good news:
master will be here ere morning.   [*E*

Lor. Sweet soul, let's in, and there exp
their coming.
And yet no matter; why should we go in?
My friend Stephano, signify, I pray you,
Within the house, your mistress is at hand;
And bring your music forth into the air.
                      [*Exit* STEPHAN

How sweet the moonlight sleeps upon this bar
Here will we sit, and let the sounds of mus
Creep in our ears: soft stillness and the night
Become the touches of sweet harmony.
Sit, Jessica: look, how the floor of heaven
Is thick inlaid with patines of bright gold:
There's not the smallest orb which thou
    hold'st
But in his motion like an angel sings,
Still quiring to the young-eyed cherubins;
Such harmony is in immortal souls;
But, whilst this muddy vesture of decay
Doth grossly close it in, we cannot hear it.

Enter Musicians.

Come, ho! and wake Diana with a hymn!
With sweetest touches pierce your mistress' e
And draw her home with music.   [*Mu*

Jes. I am never merry when I hear sw
    music.

Lor. The reason is, your spirits are attenti
For do but note a wild and wanton herd,
Or race of youthful and unhandled colts,
Fetching mad bounds, bellowing and neigh
    loud,
Which is the hot condition of their blood;
If they but hear perchance a trumpet soun
Or any air of music touch their ears,
You shall perceive them make a mutual sta
Their savage eyes turn'd to a modest gaze
By the sweet power of music: therefore the p
Did feign that Orpheus drew trees, stones, a
    floods;
Since nought so stockish, hard, and full of ra
But music for the time doth change his natu
The man that hath no music in himself,
Nor is not mov'd with concord of sweet soun
Is fit for treasons, stratagems, and spoils;
The motions of his spirit are dull as night,
And his affections dark as Erebus:
Let no such man be trusted. Mark the mus

Enter PORTIA *and* NERISSA, *at a distance.*

Por. That light we see is burning in my h
How far that little candle throws his beams
So shines a good deed in a naughty world.

Ner. When the moon shone, we did not
    the candle.

Por. So doth the greater glory dim the le
A substitute shines brightly as a king
Until a king be by, and then his state

npties itself, as doth an inland brook 96
to the main of waters. Music! hark!

Ner. It is your music, madam, of the house.

Por. Nothing is good, I see, without respect:
ethinks it sounds much sweeter than by day.

Ner. Silence bestows that virtue on it, madam.

Por. The crow doth sing as sweetly as the lark
hen neither is attended, and I think
he nightingale, if she should sing by day, 104
hen every goose is cackling, would be thought
o better a musician than the wren.
ow many things by season season'd are
o their right praise and true perfection! 108
eace, ho! the moon sleeps with Endymion,
nd would not be awak'd! [*Music ceases.*

Lor. That is the voice,
r I am much deceiv'd, of Portia.

Por. He knows me, as the blind man knows
the cuckoo, 112
y the bad voice.

Lor. Dear lady, welcome home.

Por. We have been praying for our husbands'
welfare,
hich speed, we hope, the better for our words.
re they return'd?

Lor. Madam, they are not yet; 116
ut there is come a messenger before,
o signify their coming.

Por. Go in, Nerissa:
ive order to my servants that they take
o note at all of our being absent hence; 120
or you, Lorenzo; Jessica, nor you.
[*A tucket sounds.*

Lor. Your husband is at hand; I hear his
trumpet:
Ve are no tell-tales, madam; fear you not.

Por. This night methinks is but the daylight
sick; 124
looks a little paler: 'tis a day,
uch as the day is when the sun is hid.

Enter BASSANIO, ANTONIO, GRATIANO, *and
their Followers.*

Bass. We should hold day with the Antipodes,
' you would walk in absence of the sun. 128

Por. Let me give light, but let me not be light;
or a light wife doth make a heavy husband,
nd never be Bassanio so for me:
ut God sort all! You are welcome home, my
lord. 132

Bass. I thank you, madam. Give welcome
to my friend:
his is the man, this is Antonio,
o whom I am so infinitely bound.

Por. You should in all sense be much bound
to him, 136
or, as I hear, he was much bound for you.

Ant. No more than I am well acquitted of.

Por. Sir, you are very welcome to our house:
t must appear in other ways than words, 140
herefore I scant this breathing courtesy.

Gra. [*To* NERISSA.] By yonder moon I swear
you do me wrong;
h faith, I gave it to the judge's clerk:
Vould he were gelt that had it, for my part, 144
ince you do take it, love, so much at heart.

Por. A quarrel, ho, already! what's the matter?

Gra. About a hoop of gold, a paltry ring
That she did give me, whose poesy was 148
For all the world like cutlers' poetry
Upon a knife, 'Love me, and leave me not.'

Ner. What talk you of the posy, or the value?
You swore to me, when I did give it you, 152
That you would wear it till your hour of death,
And that it should lie with you in your grave:
Though not for me, yet for your vehement oaths,
You should have been respective and have kept
it. 156
Gave it a judge's clerk! no, God's my judge,
The clerk will ne'er wear hair on's face that
had it.

Gra. He will, an if he live to be a man.

Ner. Ay, if a woman live to be a man. 160

Gra. Now, by this hand, I gave it to a youth,
A kind of boy, a little scrubbed boy,
No higher than thyself, the judge's clerk,
A prating boy, that begg'd it as a fee: 164
I could not for my heart deny it him.

Por. You were to blame,—I must be plain
with you,—
To part so slightly with your wife's first gift;
A thing stuck on with oaths upon your finger,
And riveted so with faith unto your flesh. 169
I gave my love a ring and made him swear
Never to part with it; and here he stands,
I dare be sworn for him he would not leave it
Nor pluck it from his finger for the wealth 173
That the world masters. Now, in faith, Gra-
tiano,
You give your wife too unkind a cause of grief:
An 'twere to me, I should be mad at it. 176

Bass. [*Aside.*] Why, I were best to cut my
left hand off,
And swear I lost the ring defending it.

Gra. My Lord Bassanio gave his ring away
Unto the judge that begg'd it, and indeed 180
Deserv'd it too; and then the boy, his clerk,
That took some pains in writing, he begg'd
mine;
And neither man nor master would take aught
But the two rings.

Por. What ring gave you, my lord? 184
Not that, I hope, that you receiv'd of me.

Bass. If I could add a lie unto a fault,
I would deny it; but you see my finger
Hath not the ring upon it; it is gone. 188

Por. Even so void is your false heart of truth.
By heaven, I will ne'er come in your bed
Until I see the ring.

Ner. Nor I in yours,
Till I again see mine.

Bass. Sweet Portia, 192
If you did know to whom I gave the ring,
If you did know for whom I gave the ring,
And would conceive for what I gave the ring,
And how unwillingly I left the ring, 196
When naught would be accepted but the ring,
You would abate the strength of your dis-
pleasure.

Por. If you had known the virtue of the ring,
Or half her worthiness that gave the ring, 200
Or your own honour to contain the ring,

You would not then have parted with the ring.
What man is there so much unreasonable,
If you had pleas'd to have defended it   204
With any terms of zeal, wanted the modesty
To urge the thing held as a ceremony?
Nerissa teaches me what to believe:
I'll die for 't but some woman had the ring.   208
   Bass. No, by my honour, madam, by my soul,
No woman had it; but a civil doctor,
Which did refuse three thousand ducats of me,
And begg'd the ring, the which I did deny him,
And suffer'd him to go displeas'd away;   213
Even he that did uphold the very life
Of my dear friend. What should I say, sweet
   lady?
I was enforc'd to send it after him;   216
I was beset with shame and courtesy;
My honour would not let ingratitude
So much besmear it. Pardon me, good lady,
For, by these blessed candles of the night,   220
Had you been there, I think you would have
   begg'd
The ring of me to give the worthy doctor.
   Por. Let not that doctor e'er come near my
house.
Since he hath got the jewel that I lov'd,   224
And that which you did swear to keep for me,
I will become as liberal as you;
I'll not deny him anything I have;
No, not my body, nor my husband's bed.   228
Know him I shall, I am well sure of it:
Lie not a night from home; watch me like Argus:
If you do not, if I be left alone,
Now by mine honour, which is yet mine own,   232
I'll have that doctor for my bedfellow.
   Ner. And I his clerk; therefore be well ad-
   vis'd
How you do leave me to mine own protection.
   Gra. Well, do you so: let me not take him,
   then;   236
For if I do, I'll mar the young clerk's pen.
   Ant. I am the unhappy subject of these
   quarrels.
   Por. Sir, grieve not you; you are welcome
   notwithstanding.
   Bass. Portia, forgive me this enforced wrong;
And in the hearing of these many friends,   241
I swear to thee, even by thine own fair eyes,
Wherein I see myself,—
   Por.   Mark you but that!
In both my eyes he doubly sees himself;   244
In each eye, one: swear by your double self,
And there's an oath of credit.
   Bass.   Nay, but hear me:
Pardon this fault, and by my soul I swear
I never more will break an oath with thee.   248
   Ant. I once did lend my body for his wealth,
Which, but for him that had your husband's
   ring,
Had quite miscarried: I dare be bound again,
My soul upon the forfeit, that your lord   252
Will never more break faith advisedly.
   Por. Then you shall be his surety. Give him
   this,
And bid him keep it better than the other.

   Ant. Here, Lord Bassanio; swear to kee
   this ring.   2
   Bass. By heaven! it is the same I gave t
   doctor!
   Por. I had it of him: pardon me, Bassani
For, by this ring, the doctor lay with me.   2
   Ner. And pardon me, my gentle Gratiano
For that same scrubbed boy, the doctor's cler
In lieu of this last night did lie with me.
   Gra. Why, this is like the mending of hig
   ways
In summer, where the ways are fair enough.   2
What! are we cuckolds ere we have deserv'd i
   Por. Speak not so grossly. You are a
   amaz'd:
Here is a letter; read it at your leisure;
It comes from Padua, from Bellario: 2
There you shall find that Portia was the docto
Nerissa, there, her clerk: Lorenzo here
Shall witness I set forth as soon as you
And even but now return'd; I have not yet 2
Enter'd my house. Antonio, you are welcome
And I have better news in store for you
Than you expect: unseal this letter soon;
There you shall find three of your argosies 2
Are richly come to harbour suddenly.
You shall not know by what strange acciden
I chanced on this letter.
   Ant.   I am dumb.
   Bass. Were you the doctor and I knew yo
   not?   28
   Gra. Were you the clerk that is to make m
   cuckold?
   Ner. Ay; but the clerk that never means t
   do it,
Unless he live until he be a man.
   Bass. Sweet doctor, you shall be my bed
   fellow: 28
When I am absent, then, lie with my wife.
   Ant. Sweet lady, you have given me life an
   living;
For here I read for certain that my ships
Are safely come to road.
   Por.   How now, Lorenzo! 28
My clerk hath some good comforts too for you
   Ner. Ay, and I'll give them him without
   fee.
There do I give to you and Jessica,
From the rich Jew, a special deed of gift,   29
After his death, of all he dies possess'd of.
   Lor. Fair ladies, you drop manna in the wa
Of starved people.
   Por.   It is almost morning,
And yet I am sure you are not satisfied   29
Of these events at full. Let us go in;
And charge us there upon inter'gatories,
And we will answer all things faithfully.
   Gra. Let it be so: the first inter'gatory   30
That my Nerissa shall be sworn on is,
Whe'r till the next night she had rather stay,
Or go to bed now, being two hours to day:
But were the day come, I should wish it dark
That I were couching with the doctor's clerk.
Well, while I live I'll fear no other thing   30
So sore as keeping safe Nerissa's ring. [*Exeunt*

AS YOU LIKE IT

DRAMATIS PERSONÆ

DUKE, living in exile.
FREDERICK, his Brother, Usurper of his Dominions.
AMIENS, } Lords attending upon the banished Duke.
JAQUES, }
LE BEAU, a Courtier, attending upon Frederick.
CHARLES, a Wrestler.
OLIVER, }
JAQUES, } Sons of Sir Rowland de Boys.
ORLANDO, }
ADAM, } Servants to Oliver.
DENNIS, }
TOUCHSTONE, a Clown.

SIR OLIVER MARTEXT, a Vicar.
CORIN, } Shepherds.
SILVIUS, }
WILLIAM, a Country Fellow, in love with Audrey.

A person representing Hymen.

ROSALIND, Daughter to the banished Duke.
CELIA, Daughter to Frederick.
PHEBE, a Shepherdess.
AUDREY, a Country Wench.

Lords, Pages, Foresters, and Attendants.

SCENE.—First, OLIVER'S *Orchard near his House; afterwards, in the Usurper's Court, and in the Forest of Arden.*

ACT I

SCENE I.—*An Orchard near* OLIVER'S *House.*

Enter ORLANDO *and* ADAM.

Orl. As I remember, Adam, it was upon this fashion bequeathed me by will but poor a thousand crowns, and, as thou sayest, charged my brother on his blessing, to breed me well: and there begins my sadness. My brother Jaques he keeps at school, and report speaks goldenly of his profit: for my part, he keeps me rustically at home, or, to speak more properly, stays me here at home unkept; for call you that keeping for a gentleman of my birth, that differs not from the stalling of an ox? His horses are bred better; for, besides that they are fair with their feeding, they are taught their manage, and to that end riders dearly hired: but I, his brother, gain nothing under him but growth, for the which his animals on his dunghills are as much bound to him as I. Besides this nothing that he so plentifully gives me, the something that nature gave me, his countenance seems to take from me: he lets me feed with his hinds, bars me the place of a brother, and, as much as in him lies, mines my gentility with my education. This is it, Adam, that grieves me; and the spirit of my father, which I think is within me, begins to mutiny against this servitude. I will no longer endure it, though yet I know no wise remedy how to avoid it. 27

Adam. Yonder comes my master, your brother.

Orl. Go apart, Adam, and thou shalt hear how he will shake me up.

Enter OLIVER.

Oli. Now, sir! what make you here? 31

Orl. Nothing: I am not taught to make anything.

Oli. What mar you then, sir?

Orl. Marry, sir, I am helping you to mar that which God made, a poor unworthy brother of yours, with idleness. 37

Oli. Marry, sir, be better employed, and be naught awhile.

Orl. Shall I keep your hogs, and eat husks with them? What prodigal portion have I spent, that I should come to such penury?

Oli. Know you where you are, sir?

Orl. O! sir, very well: here in your orchard.

Oli. Know you before whom, sir? 45

Orl. Ay, better than he I am before knows me. I know you are my eldest brother; and, in the gentle condition of blood, you should so know me. The courtesy of nations allows you my better, in that you are the first-born; but the same tradition takes not away my blood, were there twenty brothers betwixt us. I have as much of my father in me as you; albeit, I confess, your coming before me is nearer to his reverence.

Oli. What, boy! 56

Orl. Come, come, elder brother, you are too young in this.

Oli. Wilt thou lay hands on me, villain? 59

Orl. I am no villain; I am the youngest son of Sir Rowland de Boys; he was my father, and he is thrice a villain that says such a father begot villains. Wert thou not my brother, I would not take this hand from thy throat till this other had pulled out thy tongue for saying so: thou hast railed on thyself. 66

Adam. [*Coming forward.*] Sweet masters, be patient: for your father's remembrance, be at accord.

Oli. Let me go, I say. 70

Orl. I will not, till I please: you shall hear me. My father charged you in his will to give me good education: you have trained me like a peasant, obscuring and hiding from me all gentleman-like qualities. The spirit of my father grows strong in me, and I will no longer endure it; therefore allow me such exercises as may become a gentleman, or give me the poor allottery my father left me by testament; with that I will go buy my fortunes. 80

H

Oli. And what wilt thou do? beg, when that is spent? Well, sir, get you in: I will not long be troubled with you; you shall have some part of your will: I pray you, leave me.   84

Orl. I will no further offend you than becomes me for my good.

Oli. Get you with him, you old dog.

Adam. Is 'old dog' my reward? Most true, I have lost my teeth in your service. God be with my old master! he would not have spoke such a word.   [*Exeunt* ORLANDO *and* ADAM.

Oli. Is it even so? begin you to grow upon me? I will physic your rankness, and yet give no thousand crowns neither. Holla, Dennis!

Enter DENNIS.

Den. Calls your worship?   95

Oli. Was not Charles the duke's wrestler here to speak with me?

Den. So please you, he is here at the door, and importunes access to you.   99

Oli. Call him in. [*Exit* DENNIS.] 'Twill be a good way; and to-morrow the wrestling is.

Enter CHARLES.

Cha. Good morrow to your worship.   102

Oli. Good Monsieur Charles, what's the new news at the new court?

Cha. There's no news at the court, sir, but the old news: that is, the old duke is banished by his younger brother the new duke; and three or four loving lords have put themselves into voluntary exile with him, whose lands and revenues enrich the new duke; therefore he gives them good leave to wander.   111

Oli. Can you tell if Rosalind, the duke's daughter, be banished with her father?

Cha. O, no; for the duke's daughter, her cousin, so loves her,—being ever from their cradles bred together,—that she would have followed her exile, or have died to stay behind her. She is at the court, and no less beloved of her uncle than his own daughter; and never two ladies loved as they do.   120

Oli. Where will the old duke live?

Cha. They say he is already in the forest of Arden, and a many merry men with him; and there they live like the old Robin Hood of England. They say many young gentlemen flock to him every day, and fleet the time carelessly, as they did in the golden world.

Oli. What, you wrestle to-morrow before the new duke?   129

Cha. Marry, do I, sir; and I came to acquaint you with a matter. I am given, sir, secretly to understand that your younger brother Orlando hath a disposition to come in disguised against me to try a fall. To-morrow, sir, I wrestle for my credit, and he that escapes me without some broken limb shall acquit him well. Your brother is but young and tender; and, for your love, I would be loath to foil him as I must, for my own honour, if he come in: therefore, out of my love to you, I came hither to acquaint you withal, that either you might stay him from his intendment, or brook such disgrace well as he

shall run into, in that it is a thing of his ow search and altogether against my will.   14

Oli. Charles, I thank thee for thy love to me which thou shalt find I will most kindly requit I had myself notice of my brother's purpos herein, and have by underhand means laboure to dissuade him from it, but he is resolute. I tell thee, Charles, it is the stubbornest youn fellow of France; full of ambition, an enviou emulator of every man's good parts, a secr and villanous contriver against me his natur, brother: therefore use thy discretion. I had a lief thou didst break his neck as his finger. An thou wert best look to't; for if thou dost hi any slight disgrace, or if he do not mightil grace himself on thee, he will practise agains thee by poison, entrap thee by some treacherou device, and never leave thee till he hath ta'e thy life by some indirect means or other; fo I assure thee,—and almost with tears I spea it,—there is not one so young and so villanou this day living. I speak but brotherly of him but should I anatomize him to thee as he is, I must blush and weep, and thou must look pa and wonder.   16

Cha. I am heartily glad I came hither to yo If he come to-morrow, I'll give him his payment if ever he go alone again, I'll never wrestle fo prize more; and so God keep your worship!
          [*Exit*

Oli. Farewell, good Charles. Now will I sti this gamester. I hope I shall see an end of him for my soul, yet I know not why, hates nothin more than he. Yet he's gentle, never schoole and yet learned, full of noble device, of all sort enchantingly beloved, and, indeed so much i the heart of the world, and especially of my ow people, who best know him, that I am altogethe misprised. But it shall not be so long; th wrestler shall clear all: nothing remains but tha I kindle the boy thither, which now I'll go about

SCENE II.—*A Lawn before the* DUKE'S *Palace*

Enter ROSALIND and CELIA.

Cel. I pray thee, Rosalind, sweet my coz, b merry.

Ros. Dear Celia, I show more mirth than am mistress of, and would you yet I were mer rier? Unless you could teach me to forget banished father, you must not learn me how t remember any extraordinary pleasure.

Cel. Herein I see thou lovest me not with th full weight that I love thee. If my uncle, th banished father, had banished thy uncle, th duke my father, so thou hadst been still wit me, I could have taught my love to take th father for mine: so wouldst thou, if the trut of thy love to me were so righteously tempere as mine is to thee.   1

Ros. Well, I will forget the condition of m estate, to rejoice in yours.

Cel. You know my father hath no child bu I, nor none is like to have; and, truly, when h

lies, thou shalt be his heir: for what he hath
aken away from thy father perforce, I will
ender thee again in affection; by mine honour,
will; and when I break that oath, let me turn
nonster. Therefore, my sweet Rose, my dear
Rose, be merry. 25

Ros. From henceforth I will, coz, and devise
sports. Let me see; what think you of falling
n love? 28

Cel. Marry, I prithee, do, to make sport
vithal: but love no man in good earnest; nor
no further in sport neither, than with safety of
a pure blush thou mayst in honour come off
again. 33

Ros. What shall be our sport then?

Cel. Let us sit and mock the good housewife
Fortune from her wheel, that her gifts may
henceforth be bestowed equally. 37

Ros. I would we could do so, for her benefits
are mightily misplaced, and the bountiful blind
woman doth most mistake in her gifts to women.

Cel. 'Tis true; for those that she makes fair
she scarce makes honest, and those that she
makes honest she makes very ill-favouredly. 43

Ros. Nay, now thou goest from Fortune's
office to Nature's: Fortune reigns in gifts of
the world, not in the lineaments of Nature.

Enter TOUCHSTONE.

Cel. No? when Nature hath made a fair creature, may she not by Fortune fall into the fire?
Though Nature hath given us wit to flout at
Fortune, hath not Fortune sent in this fool to
cut off the argument? 51

Ros. Indeed, there is Fortune too hard for
Nature, when Fortune makes Nature's natural
the cutter-off of Nature's wit.

Cel. Peradventure this is not Fortune's work
neither, but Nature's; who, perceiving our natural wits too dull to reason of such goddesses,
hath sent this natural for our whetstone: for
always the dulness of the fool is the whetstone
of the wits. How now, wit! whither wander
you? 61

Touch. Mistress, you must come away to
your father.

Cel. Were you made the messenger?

Touch. No, by mine honour; but I was bid
to come for you. 66

Ros. Where learned you that oath, fool?

Touch. Of a certain knight that swore by
his honour they were good pancakes, and swore
by his honour the mustard was naught: now,
I'll stand to it, the pancakes were naught and
the mustard was good, and yet was not the
knight forsworn. 73

Cel. How prove you that, in the great heap
of your knowledge?

Ros. Ay, marry: now unmuzzle your wisdom.

Touch. Stand you both forth now: stroke
your chins, and swear by your beards that I am
a knave. 79

Cel. By our beards, if we had them, thou art.

Touch. By my knavery, if I had it, then I
were; but if you swear by that that is not, you

are not forsworn: no more was this knight,
swearing by his honour, for he never had any;
or if he had, he had sworn it away before ever
he saw those pancakes or that mustard. 86

Cel. Prithee, who is't that thou meanest?

Touch. One that old Frederick, your father,
loves.

Cel. My father's love is enough to honour
him. Enough! speak no more of him; you'll
be whipped for taxation one of these days. 92

Touch. The more pity, that fools may not
speak wisely what wise men do foolishly.

Cel. By my troth, thou sayest true; for since
the little wit that fools have was silenced, the
little foolery that wise men have makes a great
show. Here comes Monsieur Le Beau. 98

Ros. With his mouth full of news.

Cel. Which he will put on us, as pigeons feed
their young.

Ros. Then we shall be news-cramm'd.

Cel. All the better; we shall be more marketable. 104

Enter LE BEAU.

Bon jour, Monsieur Le Beau: what's the news?

Le Beau. Fair princess, you have lost much
good sport.

Cel. Sport! Of what colour? 108

Le Beau. What colour, madam! How shall
I answer you?

Ros. As wit and fortune will.

Touch. Or as the Destinies decree. 112

Cel. Well said: that was laid on with a trowel.

Touch. Nay, if I keep not my rank,—

Ros. Thou losest thy old smell.

Le Beau. You amaze me, ladies: I would
have told you of good wrestling, which you have
lost the sight of. 118

Ros. Yet tell us the manner of the wrestling.

Le Beau. I will tell you the beginning; and,
if it please your ladyships, you may see the end,
for the best is yet to do; and here, where you
are, they are coming to perform it. 123

Cel. Well, the beginning, that is dead and
buried.

Le Beau. There comes an old man and his
three sons,— 127

Cel. I could match this beginning with an
old tale.

Le Beau. Three proper young men, of excellent growth and presence;—

Ros. With bills on their necks, 'Be it known
unto all men by these presents.' 133

Le Beau. The eldest of the three wrestled
with Charles, the duke's wrestler; which Charles
in a moment threw him and broke three of his
ribs, that there is little hope of life in him: so
he served the second, and so the third. Yonder
they lie; the poor old man, their father, making
such pitiful dole over them that all the beholders
take his part with weeping. 141

Ros. Alas!

Touch. But what is the sport, monsieur, that
the ladies have lost? 144

Le Beau. Why, this that I speak of.

Touch. Thus men may grow wiser every day:

it is the first time that ever I heard breaking of ribs was sport for ladies.   148

Cel. Or I, I promise thee.

Ros. But is there any else longs to feel this broken music in his sides? is there yet another dotes upon rib-breaking? Shall we see this wrestling, cousin?   153

Le Beau. You must, if you stay here; for here is the place appointed for the wrestling, and they are ready to perform it.   156

Cel. Yonder, sure, they are coming: let us now stay and see it.

Flourish. Enter DUKE FREDERICK, *Lords,*
ORLANDO, CHARLES, *and* Attendants.

Duke F. Come on: since the youth will not be entreated, his own peril on his forwardness.   161

Ros. Is yonder the man?

Le Beau. Even he, madam.

Cel. Alas! he is too young: yet he looks successfully.   165

Duke F. How now, daughter and cousin! are you crept hither to see the wrestling?

Ros. Ay, my liege, so please you give us leave.   169

Duke F. You will take little delight in it, I can tell you, there is such odds in the man: in pity of the challenger's youth I would fain dissuade him, but he will not be entreated. Speak to him, ladies; see if you can move him.

Cel. Call him hither, good Monsieur Le Beau.

Duke F. Do so: I'll not be by.   176

[DUKE *goes apart.*

Le Beau. Monsieur the challenger, the princes call for you.

Orl. I attend them with all respect and duty.

Ros. Young man, have you challenged Charles the wrestler?   181

Orl. No, fair princess; he is the general challenger: I come but in, as others do, to try with him the strength of my youth.   184

Cel. Young gentleman, your spirits are too bold for your years. You have seen cruel proof of this man's strength: if you saw yourself with your eyes or knew yourself with your judgment, the fear of your adventure would counsel you to a more equal enterprise. We pray you, for your own sake, to embrace your own safety and give over this attempt.   192

Ros. Do, young sir: your reputation shall not therefore be misprised. We will make it our suit to the duke that the wrestling might not go forward.   196

Orl. I beseech you, punish me not with your hard thoughts, wherein I confess me much guilty, to deny so fair and excellent ladies anything. But let your fair eyes and gentle wishes go with me to my trial: wherein if I be foiled, there is but one shamed that was never gracious; if killed, but one dead that is willing to be so. I shall do my friends no wrong, for I have none to lament me; the world no injury, for in it I have nothing; only in the world I fill up a place, which may be better supplied when I have made it empty.   208

Ros. The little strength that I have, I would it were with you.

Cel. And mine, to eke out hers.

Ros. Fare you well. Pray heaven I be deceived in you!   21

Cel. Your heart's desires be with you!

Cha. Come, where is this young gallant that is so desirous to lie with his mother earth? 21

Orl. Ready, sir; but his will hath in it a more modest working.

Duke F. You shall try but one fall.   21

Cha. No, I warrant your Grace, you shall not entreat him to a second, that have so mightily persuaded him from a first.

Orl. You mean to mock me after; you should not have mocked me before: but come your ways.   22

Ros. Now Hercules be thy speed, young man!

Cel. I would I were invisible, to catch the strong fellow by the leg.   22

[CHARLES *and* ORLANDO *wrestle*

Ros. O excellent young man!

Cel. If I had a thunderbolt in mine eye, I can tell who should down.

[CHARLES *is thrown. Shout*

Duke F. No more, no more.   23

Orl. Yes, I beseech your Grace: I am not yet well breathed.

Duke F. How dost thou, Charles?

Le Beau. He cannot speak, my lord.   23

Duke F. Bear him away. What is thy name, young man?   [CHARLES *is borne out*

Orl. Orlando, my liege; the youngest son of Sir Rowland de Boys.   24

Duke F. I would thou hadst been son to some man else:
The world esteem'd thy father honourable,
But I did find him still mine enemy:
Thou shouldst have better pleas'd me with this deed,   24
Hadst thou descended from another house.
But fare thee well; thou art a gallant youth:
I would thou hadst told me of another father

[*Exeunt* DUKE FREDERICK, *Train, and*
LE BEAU

Cel. Were I my father, coz, would I do this?

Orl. I am more proud to be Sir Rowland's son,   24
His youngest son; and would not change that calling,
To be adopted heir to Frederick.

Ros. My father lov'd Sir Rowland as his soul,
And all the world was of my father's mind: 25
Had I before known this young man his son,
I should have given him tears unto entreaties
Ere he should thus have ventur'd.

Cel.   Gentle cousin, 25
Let us go thank him and encourage him:
My father's rough and envious disposition
Sticks me at heart. Sir, you have well deserv'd:
If you do keep your promises in love   26
But justly, as you have exceeded all promise,
Your mistress shall be happy.

Ros.   Gentleman,
[*Giving him a chain from her neck*
Wear this for me, one out of suits with fortune

hat could give more, but that her hand lacks
means. 264
hall we go, coz?
Cel. Ay. Fare you well, fair gentleman.
Orl. Can I not say, I thank you? My better
parts
re all thrown down, and that which here
stands up
s but a quintain, a mere lifeless block. 268
Ros. He calls us back: my pride fell with my
fortunes;
'll ask him what he would. Did you call, sir?
ir, you have wrestled well, and overthrown
Iore than your enemies.
Cel. Will you go, coz? 272
Ros. Have with you. Fare you well.
[*Exeunt* ROSALIND *and* CELIA.
Orl. What passion hangs these weights upon
my tongue?
cannot speak to her, yet she urg'd conference.
) poor Orlando, thou art overthrown! 276
)r Charles or something weaker masters thee.

Re-enter LE BEAU.

Le Beau. Good sir, I do in friendship counsel
you
'o leave this place. Albeit you have deserv'd
Iigh commendation, true applause and love,
'et such is now the duke's condition 281
'hat he misconstrues all that you have done.
he duke is humorous: what he is indeed,
Iore suits you to conceive than I to speak of.
Orl. I thank you, sir; and pray you, tell me
this; 285
/hich of the two was daughter of the duke,
'hat here was at the wrestling?
Le Beau. Neither his daughter, if we judge
by manners: 288
ut yet, indeed the smaller is his daughter:
he other is daughter to the banish'd duke,
.nd here detain'd by her usurping uncle,
'o keep his daughter company; whose loves 292
.re dearer than the natural bond of sisters.
ut I can tell you that of late this duke
Iath ta'en displeasure 'gainst his gentle niece,
irounded upon no other argument 296
ut that the people praise her for her virtues,
.nd pity her for her good father's sake;
.nd, on my life, his malice 'gainst the lady
/ill suddenly break forth. Sir, fare you well:
Iereafter, in a better world than this, 301
shall desire more love and knowledge of you.
Orl. I rest much bounden to you: fare you
well. [*Exit* LE BEAU.
hus must I from the smoke into the smother;
'rom tyrant duke unto a tyrant brother. 305
ut heavenly Rosalind! [*Exit.*

SCENE III.—*A Room in the Palace.*

Enter CELIA *and* ROSALIND.

Cel. Why, cousin! why, Rosalind! Cupid
ave mercy! Not a word?
Ros. Not one to throw at a dog. 3
Cel. No, thy words are too precious to be cast
away upon curs; throw some of them at me;
come, lame me with reasons.
Ros. Then there were two cousins laid up;
when the one should be lamed with reasons and
the other mad without any. 9
Cel. But is all this for your father?
Ros. No, some of it is for my child's father:
O, how full of briers is this working-day world!
Cel. They are but burrs, cousin, thrown upon
thee in holiday foolery: if we walk not in the
trodden paths, our very petticoats will catch
them. 16
Ros. I could shake them off my coat: these
burrs are in my heart.
Cel. Hem them away.
Ros. I would try, if I could cry 'hem,' and
have him. 21
Cel. Come, come; wrestle with thy affections.
Ros. O! they take the part of a better wrestler
than myself! 24
Cel. O, a good wish upon you! you will try in
time, in despite of a fall. But, turning these
jests out of service, let us talk in good earnest:
is it possible, on such a sudden, you should fall
into so strong a liking with old Sir Rowland's
youngest son?
Ros. The duke my father loved his father
dearly. 32
Cel. Doth it therefore ensue that you should
love his son dearly? By this kind of chase, I
should hate him, for my father hated his father
dearly; yet I hate not Orlando. 36
Ros. No, faith, hate him not, for my sake.
Cel. Why should I not? doth he not deserve
well?
Ros. Let me love him for that; and do you
love him, because I do. Look, here comes the
duke. 42
Cel. With his eyes full of anger.

Enter DUKE FREDERICK, *with* Lords.

Duke F. Mistress, dispatch you with your
safest haste, 44
And get you from our court.
Ros. Me, uncle?
Duke F. You, cousin:
Within these ten days if that thou be'st found
So near our public court as twenty miles,
Thou diest for it.
Ros. I do beseech your Grace, 48
Let me the knowledge of my fault bear with me.
If with myself I hold intelligence,
Or have acquaintance with mine own desires,
If that I do not dream or be not frantic,— 52
As I do trust I am not,—then, dear uncle,
Never so much as in a thought unborn
Did I offend your highness.
Duke F. Thus do all traitors:
If their purgation did consist in words, 56
They are as innocent as grace itself:
Let it suffice thee that I trust thee not.
Ros. Yet your mistrust cannot make me a
traitor:
Tell me whereon the likelihood depends. 60
Duke F. Thou art thy father's daughter;
there's enough.

Ros. So was I when your highness took his
dukedom;
So was I when your highness banish'd him.
Treason is not inherited, my lord;   64
Or, if we did derive it from our friends,
What's that to me? my father was no traitor:
Then, good my liege, mistake me not so much
To think my poverty is treacherous.   68
  Cel. Dear sovereign, hear me speak.
  Duke F. Ay, Celia; we stay'd her for your
sake;
Else had she with her father rang'd along.
  Cel. I did not then entreat to have her stay:
It was your pleasure and your own remorse. 73
I was too young that time to value her;
But now I know her: if she be a traitor,
Why so am I; we still have slept together, 76
Rose at an instant, learn'd, play'd, eat together;
And whereso'er we went, like Juno's swans,
Still we went coupled and inseparable.
  Duke F. She is too subtle for thee; and her
smoothness,   80
Her very silence and her patience,
Speak to the people, and they pity her.
Thou art a fool: she robs thee of thy name;
And thou wilt show more bright and seem
more virtuous   84
When she is gone. Then open not thy lips:
Firm and irrevocable is my doom
Which I have pass'd upon her; she is banish'd.
  Cel. Pronounce that sentence then, on me,
my liege;   88
I cannot live out of her company.
  Duke F. You are a fool. You, niece, pro-
vide yourself:
If you outstay the time, upon mine honour,
And in the greatness of my word, you die. 92
        [*Exeunt* DUKE FREDERICK *and* Lords.
  Cel. O my poor Rosalind! whither wilt thou
go?
Wilt thou change fathers? I will give thee mine.
I charge thee, be not thou more griev'd than
I am.
  Ros. I have more cause.
  Cel.   Thou hast not, cousin; 96
Prithee, be cheerful; know'st thou not, the duke
Hath banish'd me, his daughter?
  Ros.   That he hath not.
  Cel. No, hath not? Rosalind lacks then the
love   99
Which teacheth thee that thou and I am one:
Shall we be sunder'd? shall we part, sweet
girl?
No: let my father seek another heir.
Therefore devise with me how we may fly,
Whither to go, and what to bear with us: 104
And do not seek to take your change upon you,
To bear your griefs yourself and leave me out;
For, by this heaven, now at our sorrows pale,
Say what thou canst, I'll go along with thee. 108
  Ros. Why, whither shall we go?
  Cel. To seek my uncle in the forest of Arden.
  Ros. Alas, what danger will it be to us,
Maids as we are, to travel forth so far!   112
Beauty provoketh thieves sooner than gold.
  Cel. I'll put myself in poor and mean attire,

And with a kind of umber smirch my face;
The like do you: so shall we pass along   11
And never stir assailants.
  Ros.   Were it not better
Because that I am more than common tall,
That I did suit me all points like a man?
A gallant curtle-axe upon my thigh,   12
A boar-spear in my hand; and,—in my heart
Lie there what hidden woman's fear there will,-
We'll have a swashing and a martial outside,
As many other mannish cowards have   12
That do outface it with their semblances.
  Cel. What shall I call thee when thou art
man?
  Ros. I'll have no worse a name than Jove'
own page,
And therefore look you call me Ganymede. 12
But what will you be call'd?
  Cel. Something that hath a reference to m
state:
No longer Celia, but Aliena.
  Ros. But, cousin, what if we assay'd t
steal   13
The clownish fool out of your father's court?
Would he not be a comfort to our travel?
  Cel. He'll go along o'er the wide world wit
me;
Leave me alone to woo him. Let's away,   13
And get our jewels and our wealth together,
Devise the fittest time and safest way
To hide us from pursuit that will be made
After my flight. Now go we in content   14
To liberty and not to banishment.   [*Exeun*

ACT II

SCENE I.—*The Forest of Arden.*

Enter DUKE *Senior,* AMIENS, *and other* Lords
            like Foresters.

  Duke S. Now, my co-mates and brothers i
exile,
Hath not old custom made this life more swee
Than that of painted pomp? Are not thes
woods
More free from peril than the envious court?
Here feel we but the penalty of Adam,
The seasons' difference; as, the icy fang
And churlish chiding of the winter's wind,
Which, when it bites and blows upon my body
Even till I shrink with cold, I smile and say
'This is no flattery: these are counsellors
That feelingly persuade me what I am.'
Sweet are the uses of adversity,   1
Which like the toad, ugly and venomous,
Wears yet a precious jewel in his head;
And this our life exempt from public haunt,
Finds tongues in trees, books in the runnin
brooks,   1
Sermons in stones, and good in every thing.
I would not change it.
  Ami.   Happy is your Grace,
That can translate the stubbornness of fortun
Into so quiet and so sweet a style.   2
  Duke S. Come, shall we go and kill us venison?

And yet it irks me, the poor dappled fools,
Being native burghers of this desert city,
Should in their own confines with forked heads
Have their round haunches gor'd.
   First Lord.   Indeed, my lord, 25
The melancholy Jaques grieves at that;
And, in that kind, swears you do more usurp
Than doth your brother that hath banish'd you.
To-day my Lord of Amiens and myself 29
Did steal behind him as he lay along
Under an oak whose antique root peeps out
Upon the brook that brawls along this wood;
To the which place a poor sequester'd stag, 33
That from the hunters' aim had ta'en a hurt,
Did come to languish; and, indeed, my lord,
The wretched animal heav'd forth such groans
That their discharge did stretch his leathern
   coat 37
Almost to bursting, and the big round tears
Cours'd one another down his innocent nose
In piteous chase: and thus the hairy fool, 40
Much marked of the melancholy Jaques,
Stood on the extremest verge of the swift brook,
Augmenting it with tears.
   Duke S.   But what said Jaques?
Did he not moralize this spectacle? 44
   First Lord. O, yes, into a thousand similes.
First, for his weeping into the needless stream;
'Poor deer,' quoth he, 'thou mak'st a testament
As worldlings do, giving thy sum of more 48
To that which had too much:' then, being there
   alone,
Left and abandon'd of his velvet friends;
'Tis right,' quoth he; 'thus misery doth part
The flux of company:' anon, a careless herd, 52
Full of the pasture, jumps along by him
And never stays to greet him; 'Ay,' quoth
   Jaques,
'Sweep on, you fat and greasy citizens;
'Tis just the fashion; wherefore do you look 56
Upon that poor and broken bankrupt there?'
Thus most invectively he pierceth through
The body of the country, city, court,
Yea, and of this our life; swearing that we 60
Are mere usurpers, tyrants, and what's worse,
To fright the animals and to kill them up
In their assign'd and native dwelling-place.
   Duke S. And did you leave him in this con-
   templation? 64
   Sec. Lord. We did, my lord, weeping and
   commenting
Upon the sobbing deer.
   Duke S.   Show me the place.
I love to cope him in these sullen fits,
For then he's full of matter. 68
   Sec. Lord. I'll bring you to him straight.
                              [Exeunt.

SCENE II.—*A Room in the Palace.*

Enter DUKE FREDERICK, Lords, *and* Attendants.

   Duke F. Can it be possible that no man saw
   them?
It cannot be: some villains of my court
Are of consent and sufferance in this.

   First Lord. I cannot hear of any that did see
   her. 4
The ladies, her attendants of her chamber,
Saw her a-bed; and, in the morning early
They found the bed untreasur'd of their mistress.
   Sec. Lord. My lord, the roynish clown, at
   whom so oft 8
Your Grace was wont to laugh, is also missing.
Hisperia, the princess' gentlewoman,
Confesses that she secretly o'erheard
Your daughter and her cousin much commend
The parts and graces of the wrestler 13
That did but lately foil the sinewy Charles;
And she believes, wherever they are gone,
That youth is surely in their company. 16
   Duke F. Send to his brother; fetch that
   gallant hither;
If he be absent, bring his brother to me;
I'll make him find him. Do this suddenly,
And let not search and inquisition quail 20
To bring again these foolish runaways.
                              [Exeunt.

SCENE III.—*Before* OLIVER'S *House.*

Enter ORLANDO *and* ADAM, *meeting.*

   Orl. Who's there?
   Adam. What! my young master? O my
   gentle master!
O my sweet master! O you memory
Of old Sir Rowland! why, what make you here?
Why are you virtuous? Why do people love you?
And wherefore are you gentle, strong, and
   valiant?
Why would you be so fond to overcome
The bony priser of the humorous duke? 8
Your praise is come too swiftly home before you.
Know you not, master, to some kind of men
Their graces serve them but as enemies?
No more do yours: your virtues, gentle master,
Are sanctified and holy traitors to you. 13
O, what a world is this, when what is comely
Envenoms him that bears it!
   Orl. Why, what's the matter?
   Adam.   O unhappy youth!
Come not within these doors; within this roof
The enemy of all your graces lives.
Your brother,—no, no brother; yet the son,—
Yet not the son, I will not call him son 20
Of him I was about to call his father,—
Hath heard your praises, and this night he means
To burn the lodging where you use to lie,
And you within it: if he fail of that, 24
He will have other means to cut you off.
I overheard him and his practices.
This is no place; this house is but a butchery:
Abhor it, fear it, do not enter it. 28
   Orl. Why, whither, Adam, wouldst thou have
   me go?
   Adam. No matter whither, so you come not
   here.
   Orl. What! wouldst thou have me go and beg
   my food?
Or with a base and boisterous sword enforce 32
A thievish living on the common road?

This I must do, or know not what to do:
Yet this I will not do, do how I can;
I rather will subject me to the malice 36
Of a diverted blood and bloody brother.

Adam. But do not so. I have five hundred crowns,
The thrifty hire I sav'd under your father,
Which I did store to be my foster-nurse 40
When service should in my old limbs lie lame,
And unregarded age in corners thrown.
Take that; and He that doth the ravens feed,
Yea, providently caters for the sparrow, 44
Be comfort to my age! Here is the gold;
All this I give you. Let me be your servant:
Though I look old, yet I am strong and lusty:
For in my youth I never did apply 48
Hot and rebellious liquors in my blood,
Nor did not with unbashful forehead woo
The means of weakness and debility;
Therefore my age is as a lusty winter, 52
Frosty, but kindly. Let me go with you;
I'll do the service of a younger man
In all your business and necessities.

Orl. O good old man! how well in thee appears 56
The constant service of the antique world,
When service sweat for duty, not for meed!
Thou art not for the fashion of these times,
Where none will sweat but for promotion, 60
And having that, do choke their service up
Even with the having: it is not so with thee.
But, poor old man, thou prun'st a rotten tree,
That cannot so much as a blossom yield, 64
In lieu of all thy pains and husbandry.
But come thy ways, we'll go along together,
And ere we have thy youthful wages spent,
We'll light upon some settled low content. 68

Adam. Master, go on, and I will follow thee
To the last gasp with truth and loyalty.
From seventeen years till now almost fourscore
Here lived I, but now live here no more. 72
At seventeen years many their fortunes seek;
But at fourscore it is too late a week:
Yet fortune cannot recompense me better
Than to die well and not my master's debtor. 76
[*Exeunt.*

SCENE IV.—*The Forest of Arden.*

Enter ROSALIND *in boy's clothes,* CELIA *dressed
like a shepherdess, and* TOUCHSTONE.

Ros. O Jupiter! how weary are my spirits.
Touch. I care not for my spirits if my legs
were not weary.
Ros. I could find it in my heart to disgrace my
man's apparel and to cry like a woman; but I
must comfort the weaker vessel, as doublet and
hose ought to show itself courageous to petticoat: therefore, courage, good Aliena. 8
Cel. I pray you, bear with me: I cannot go
no further.
Touch. For my part, I had rather bear with
you than bear you; yet I should bear no cross if
I did bear you, for I think you have no money
in your purse. 14
Ros. Well, this is the forest of Arden.

Touch. Ay, now am I in Arden; the more
fool I: when I was at home, I was in a better
place: but travellers must be content.
Ros. Ay, be so, good Touchstone. Look you,
who comes here; a young man and an old in
solemn talk. 21

Enter CORIN *and* SILVIUS.

Cor. That is the way to make her scorn you
still.
Sil. O Corin, that thou knew'st how I do love
her!
Cor. I partly guess, for I have lov'd ere now.
Sil. No, Corin; being old, thou canst not
guess, 25
Though in thy youth thou wast as true a lover
As ever sigh'd upon a midnight pillow:
But if thy love were ever like to mine,— 28
As sure I think did never man love so,—
How many actions most ridiculous
Hast thou been drawn to by thy fantasy? 31
Cor. Into a thousand that I have forgotten.
Sil. O! thou didst then ne'er love so heartily.
If thou remember'st not the slightest folly
That ever love did make thee run into,
Thou hast not lov'd: 36
Or if thou hast not sat as I do now,
Wearing thy hearer with thy mistress' praise,
Thou hast not lov'd:
Or if thou hast not broke from company 40
Abruptly, as my passion now makes me,
Thou hast not lov'd. O Phebe, Phebe, Phebe!
[*Exit.*

Ros. Alas, poor shepherd! searching of thy
wound,
I have by hard adventure found mine own. 44
Touch. And I mine. I remember, when I was
in love I broke my sword upon a stone, and bid
him take that for coming a-night to Jane Smile;
and I remember the kissing of her batler, and
the cow's dugs that her pretty chopped hands
had milked; and I remember the wooing of a
peascod instead of her, from whom I took two
cods, and giving her them again, said with weeping tears, 'Wear these for my sake.' We that are
true lovers run into strange capers; but as all is
mortal in nature, so is all nature in love mortal
in folly. 56
Ros. Thou speakest wiser than thou art ware
of.
Touch. Nay, I shall ne'er be ware of mine own
wit till I break my shins against it. 60
Ros. Jove, Jove! this shepherd's passion
Is much upon my fashion.
Touch. And mine; but it grows something
stale with me. 64
Cel. I pray you, one of you question yond
man,
If he for gold will give us any food:
I faint almost to death.
Touch. Holla, you clown!
Ros. Peace, fool: he's not thy kinsman.
Cor. Who calls? 69
Touch. Your betters, sir.
Cor. Else are they very wretched.
Ros. Peace, I say. Good even to you, friend

Cor. And to you, gentle sir, and to you all.

Ros. I prithee, shepherd, if that love or gold
an in this desert place buy entertainment, 73
ing us where we may rest ourselves and feed.
ere's a young maid with travel much oppress'd,
nd faints for succour.

Cor.   Fair sir, I pity her, 76
nd wish, for her sake more than for mine own,
y fortunes were more able to relieve her;
at I am shepherd to another man,
nd do not shear the fleeces that I graze: 80
y master is of churlish disposition
nd little recks to find the way to heaven
y doing deeds of hospitality.
esides, his cote, his flocks, and bounds of feed
re now on sale; and at our sheepcote now, 85
y reason of his absence, there is nothing
hat you will feed on; but what is, come see,
nd in my voice most welcome shall you be. 88

Ros. What is he that shall buy his flock and
    pasture?

Cor. That young swain that you saw here but
    erewhile,
hat little cares for buying anything.

Ros. I pray thee, if it stand with honesty, 92
uy thou the cottage, pasture, and the flock,
nd thou shalt have to pay for it of us.

Cel. And we will mend thy wages. I like this
    place,
nd willingly could waste my time in it. 96

Cor. Assuredly the thing is to be sold:
o with me: if you like upon report
he soil, the profit, and this kind of life,
will your very faithful feeder be,   100
nd buy it with your gold right suddenly.

                   [Exeunt.

SCENE V.—*Another Part of the Forest.*

Enter AMIENS, JAQUES, *and Others.*

SONG

Ami.
      Under the greenwood tree
      Who loves to lie with me,
      And turn his merry note
      Unto the sweet bird's throat,   4
Come hither, come hither, come hither:
       Here shall he see
       No enemy
    But winter and rough weather.   8

Jaq. More, more, I prithee, more.

Ami. It will make you melancholy, Monsieur
aques.   11

Jaq. I thank it. More! I prithee, more. I
an suck melancholy out of a song as a weasel
ucks eggs. More! I prithee, more.

Ami. My voice is ragged; I know I cannot
lease you.   16

Jaq. I do not desire you to please me; I do
esire you to sing. Come, more; another stanzo:
all you them stanzos?

Ami. What you will, Monsieur Jaques. 20

Jaq. Nay, I care not for their names; they
we me nothing. Will you sing?

Ami. More at your request than to please
yself.   24

Jaq. Well then, if ever I thank any man, I'll thank
you: but that they call compliment is like the encounter of two dog-apes, and when a man thanks
me heartily, methinks I have given him a penny
and he renders me the beggarly thanks. Come,
sing; and you that will not, hold your tongues.

Ami. Well, I'll end the song. Sirs, cover the
while; the duke will drink under this tree. He
hath been all this day to look you.   33

Jaq. And I have been all this day to avoid him.
He is too disputable for my company: I think of
as many matters as he, but I give heaven thanks,
and make no boast of them. Come, warble; come.

SONG

Ami.
    Who doth ambition shun, [*All together here.*
      And loves to live i' the sun,
      Seeking the food he eats,
      And pleas'd with what he gets,   40
Come hither, come hither, come hither:
       Here shall he see
       No enemy   44
    But winter and rough weather.

Jaq. I'll give you a verse to this note, that I
made yesterday in despite of my invention.

Ami. And I'll sing it.   48

Jaq. Thus it goes:

      If it do come to pass
      That any man turn ass,
      Leaving his wealth and ease,   52
      A stubborn will to please,
Ducdame, ducdame, ducdame:
       Here shall he see
       Gross fools as he,   56
    An if he will come to me.

Ami. What's that '*ducdame?*'

Jaq. 'Tis a Greek invocation to call fools into
a circle. I'll go sleep if I can; if I cannot, I'll
rail against all the first-born of Egypt.   61

Ami. And I'll go seek the duke: his banquet
is prepared.   *[Exeunt severally.*

SCENE VI.—*Another Part of the Forest.*

Enter ORLANDO *and* ADAM.

Adam. Dear master, I can go no further: O!
I die for food. Here lie I down, and measure
out my grave. Farewell, kind master.   3

Orl. Why, how now, Adam! no greater heart
in thee? Live a little; comfort a little; cheer
thyself a little. If this uncouth forest yield anything savage, I will either be food for it, or bring
it for food to thee. Thy conceit is nearer death
than thy powers. For my sake be comfortable,
hold death awhile at the arm's end, I will here
be with thee presently, and if I bring thee not
something to eat, I will give thee leave to die;
but if thou diest before I come, thou art a
mocker of my labour. Well said! thou lookest
cheerly, and I'll be with thee quickly. Yet thou
liest in the bleak air: come, I will bear thee to
some shelter, and thou shalt not die for lack of
a dinner, if there live anything in this desert.
Cheerly, good Adam.   *[Exeunt.*

SCENE VII.—*Another Part of the Forest.*

A table set out. Enter DUKE *Senior,* AMIENS,
Lords *like Outlaws.*

Duke S. I think he be transform'd into a
beast,
For I can nowhere find him like a man.
First Lord. My lord, he is but even now gone
hence:
Here was he merry, hearing of a song.   4
Duke S. If he, compact of jars, grow musical,
We shall have shortly discord in the spheres.
Go, seek him: tell him I would speak with him.
First Lord. He saves my labour by his own
approach.   8

Enter JAQUES.

Duke S. Why, how now, monsieur! what a
life is this,
That your poor friends must woo your com-
pany?
What, you look merrily!
Jaq. A fool, a fool! I met a fool i' the forest,
A motley fool; a miserable world!   13
As I do live by food, I met a fool;
Who laid him down and bask'd him in the sun,
And rail'd on Lady Fortune in good terms,   16
In good set terms, and yet a motley fool.
'Good morrow, fool,' quoth I. 'No, sir,' quoth
he,
'Call me not fool till heaven hath sent me
fortune.'
And then he drew a dial from his poke,   20
And, looking on it with lack-lustre eye,
Says very wisely, 'It is ten o'clock;
Thus may we see,' quoth he, 'how the world
wags:
'Tis but an hour ago since it was nine,   24
And after one hour more 'twill be eleven;
And so, from hour to hour we ripe and ripe,
And then from hour to hour we rot and rot,
And thereby hangs a tale.' When I did hear 28
The motley fool thus moral on the time,
My lungs began to crow like chanticleer,
That fools should be so deep-contemplative,
And I did laugh sans intermission   32
An hour by his dial. O noble fool!
A worthy fool! Motley's the only wear.
Duke S. What fool is this?
Jaq. O worthy fool! One that hath been a
courtier,   36
And says, if ladies be but young and fair,
They have the gift to know it; and in his
brain,—
Which is as dry as the remainder biscuit
After a voyage,—he hath strange places
cramm'd   40
With observation, the which he vents
In mangled forms. O that I were a fool!
I am ambitious for a motley coat.
Duke S. Thou shalt have one.
Jaq.   It is my only suit;   44
Provided that you weed your better judgments
Of all opinion that grows rank in them
That I am wise. I must have liberty
Withal, as large a charter as the wind,   48
To blow on whom I please; for so fools have:

And they that are most galled with my folly,
They most must laugh. And why, sir, mu
they so?
The 'why' is plain as way to parish church:
He that a fool doth very wisely hit
Doth very foolishly, although he smart,
Not to seem senseless of the bob; if not,
The wise man's folly is anatomiz'd
Even by the squandering glances of the fool.
Invest me in my motley; give me leave
To speak my mind, and I will through an
through
Cleanse the foul body of th' infected world,
If they will patiently receive my medicine.
Duke S. Fie on thee! I can tell what tho
wouldst do.
Jaq. What, for a counter, would I do, b
good?
Duke S. Most mischievous foul sin, in chi
ing sin:
For thou thyself hast been a libertine,
As sensual as the brutish sting itself;
And all the embossed sores and headed evils
That thou with licence of free foot hast caugh
Wouldst thou disgorge into the general worl
Jaq. Why, who cries out on pride,
That can therein tax any private party?
Doth it not flow as hugely as the sea,
Till that the weary very means do ebb?
What woman in the city do I name,
When that I say the city-woman bears
The cost of princes on unworthy shoulders?
Who can come in and say that I mean her,
When such a one as she such is her neighbou
Or what is he of basest function,
That says his bravery is not on my cost,—
Thinking that I mean him,—but therein suit
His folly to the mettle of my speech?
There then; how then? what then? Let me se
wherein
My tongue hath wrong'd him: if it do him righ
Then he hath wrong'd himself; if he be free,
Why then, my taxing like a wild goose flies,
Unclaim'd of any man. But who comes here

Enter ORLANDO, *with his sword drawn.*

Orl. Forbear, and eat no more.
Jaq.   Why, I have eat none ye
Orl. Nor shalt not, till necessity be serv'd.
Jaq. Of what kind should this cock come of
Duke S. Art thou thus bolden'd, man, by th
distress,
Or else a rude despiser of good manners,
That in civility thou seem'st so empty?
Orl. You touch'd my vein at first: the thorn
point
Of bare distress hath ta'en from me the sho
Of smooth civility; yet I am inland bred
And know some nurture. But forbear, I say
He dies that touches any of this fruit
Till I and my affairs are answered.
Jaq. An you will not be answered with reason
I must die.   10
Duke S. What would you have? Your gentle
ness shall force
More than your force move us to gentleness.

Orl. I almost die for food; and let me have it.

Duke S. Sit down and feed, and welcome to
  our table.   105

Orl. Speak you so gently? Pardon me, I pray
  you:
I thought that all things had been savage here,
And therefore put I on the countenance 108
Of stern commandment. But whate'er you are
That in this desert inaccessible,
Under the shade of melancholy boughs,
Lose and neglect the creeping hours of time; 112
If ever you have look'd on better days,
If ever been where bells have knoll'd to church,
If ever sat at any good man's feast,
If ever from your eyelids wip'd a tear, 116
And know what 'tis to pity, and be pitied,
Let gentleness my strong enforcement be:
In the which hope I blush, and hide my sword.

Duke S. True is it that we have seen better
  days, 120
And have with holy bell been knoll'd to church,
And sat at good men's feasts, and wip'd our
  eyes
Of drops that sacred pity hath engender'd;
And therefore sit you down in gentleness 124
And take upon command what help we have
That to your wanting may be minister'd.

Orl. Then but forbear your food a little while,
Whiles, like a doe, I go to find my fawn 128
And give it food. There is an old poor man,
Who after me hath many a weary step
Limp'd in pure love: till he be first suffic'd,
Oppress'd with two weak evils, age and hunger,
I will not touch a bit.

Duke S.   Go find him out, 133
And we will nothing waste till you return.

Orl. I thank ye; and be bless'd for your good
  comfort!   [*Exit.*

Duke S. Thou seest we are not all alone un-
  happy: 136
This wide and universal theatre
Presents more woful pageants than the scene
Wherein we play in.

Jaq.   All the world's a stage,
And all the men and women merely players:
They have their exits and their entrances; 141
And one man in his time plays many parts,
His acts being seven ages. At first the infant,
Mewling and puking in the nurse's arms. 144
And then the whining school-boy, with his
  satchel,
And shining morning face, creeping like snail
Unwillingly to school. And then the lover,
Sighing like furnace, with a woful ballad 148
Made to his mistress' eyebrow. Then a soldier,
Full of strange oaths, and bearded like the pard,
Jealous in honour, sudden and quick in quarrel,
Seeking the bubble reputation 152
Even in the cannon's mouth. And then the
  justice,
In fair round belly with good capon lin'd,
With eyes severe, and beard of formal cut,
Full of wise saws and modern instances; 156
And so he plays his part. The sixth age shifts
Into the lean and slipper'd pantaloon,
With spectacles on nose and pouch on side, 159

His youthful hose well sav'd, a world too wide
For his shrunk shank; and his big manly voice,
Turning again toward childish treble, pipes
And whistles in his sound. Last scene of all,
That ends this strange eventful history, 164
Is second childishness and mere oblivion,
Sans teeth, sans eyes, sans taste, sans every-
  thing.

Re-enter ORLANDO, *with* ADAM.

Duke S. Welcome. Set down your venerable
  burden,
And let him feed.

Orl.   I thank you most for him. 168

Adam. So had you need:
I scarce can speak to thank you for myself.

Duke S. Welcome; fall to: I will not trouble
  you 171
As yet, to question you about your fortunes.
Give us some music; and, good cousin, sing.

SONG

Ami.   Blow, blow, thou winter wind,
      Thou art not so unkind
         As man's ingratitude; 176
      Thy tooth is not so keen,
      Because thou art not seen,
         Although thy breath be rude.
Heigh-ho! sing, heigh-ho! unto the green holly: 180
Most friendship is feigning, most loving mere folly.
      Then heigh-ho! the holly!
      This life is most jolly.

      Freeze, freeze, thou bitter sky, 184
      That dost not bite so nigh
         As benefits forgot;
      Though thou the waters warp,
      Thy sting is not so sharp 188
         As friend remember'd not.
Heigh-ho! sing, heigh-ho! unto the green holly:
Most friendship is feigning, most loving mere folly.
      Then heigh-ho! the holly! 192
      This life is most jolly.

Duke S. If that you were the good Sir Row-
  land's son,
As you have whisper'd faithfully you were,
And as mine eye doth his effigies witness 196
Most truly limn'd and living in your face,
Be truly welcome hither: I am the duke
That lov'd your father: the residue of your
  fortune,
Go to my cave and tell me. Good old man, 200
Thou art right welcome as thy master is.
Support him by the arm. Give me your hand,
And let me all your fortunes understand.
    [*Exeunt.*

ACT III

SCENE I.—*A Room in the Palace.*

Enter DUKE FREDERICK, OLIVER, Lords, *and*
Attendants.

Duke F. Not seen him since! Sir, sir, that
  cannot be:
But were I not the better part made mercy,
I should not seek an absent argument
Of my revenge, thou present. But look to it: 4
Find out thy brother, wheresoe'er he is:

Seek him with candle; bring him, dead or living,
Within this twelvemonth, or turn thou no more
To seek a living in our territory. 8
Thy lands and all things that thou dost call
 thine
Worth seizure, do we seize into our hands,
Till thou canst quit thee by thy brother's mouth
Of what we think against thee. 12
 Oli. O that your highness knew my heart in
 this!
I never lov'd my brother in my life.
 Duke F. More villain thou. Well, push him
 out of doors;
And let my officers of such a nature 16
Make an extent upon his house and lands.
Do this expediently and turn him going.
 [*Exeunt.*

SCENE II.—*The Forest of Arden.*

Enter ORLANDO, *with a paper.*

Orl. Hang there, my verse, in witness of my
 love:
 And thou, thrice-crowned queen of night,
 survey
With thy chaste eye, from thy pale sphere above,
 Thy huntress' name, that my full life doth
 sway. 4
O Rosalind! these trees shall be my books,
 And in their barks my thoughts I'll character,
That every eye, which in this forest looks,
 Shall see thy virtue witness'd everywhere. 8
Run, run, Orlando: carve on every tree
The fair, the chaste, and unexpressive she.
 [*Exit.*

Enter CORIN *and* TOUCHSTONE.

Cor. And how like you this shepherd's life,
Master Touchstone? 12
 Touch. Truly, shepherd, in respect of itself,
it is a good life; but in respect that it is a shepherd's life, it is naught. In respect that it is
solitary, I like it very well; but in respect that
it is private, it is a very vile life. Now, in respect
it is in the fields, it pleaseth me well; but in
respect it is not in the court, it is tedious. As
it is a spare life, look you, it fits my humour
well; but as there is no more plenty in it, it goes
much against my stomach. Hast any philosophy
in thee, shepherd? 23
 Cor. No more but that I know the more one
sickens the worse at ease he is; and that he that
wants money, means, and content, is without
three good friends; that the property of rain is
to wet, and fire to burn; that good pasture
makes fat sheep, and that a great cause of the
night is lack of the sun; that he that hath
learned no wit by nature nor art may complain of good breeding, or comes of a very dull
kindred. 33
 Touch. Such a one is a natural philosopher.
Wast ever in court, shepherd?
 Cor. No, truly. 36
 Touch. Then thou art damned.
 Cor. Nay, I hope.

Touch. Truly, thou art damned like an ill-
roasted egg, all on one side. 40
 Cor. For not being at court? Your reason.
 Touch. Why, if thou never wast at court, thou
never sawest good manners; if thou never sawest
good manners, then thy manners must be wicked; and wickedness is sin, and sin is damnation.
Thou art in a parlous state, shepherd. 46
 Cor. Not a whit, Touchstone: those that are
good manners at the court, are as ridiculous in
the country as the behaviour of the country is
most mockable at the court. You told me you
salute not at the court, but you kiss your hands;
that courtesy would be uncleanly if courtiers
were shepherds. 53
 Touch. Instance, briefly; come, instance.
 Cor. Why, we are still handling our ewes, and
their fells, you know, are greasy. 56
 Touch. Why, do not your courtier's hands
sweat? and is not the grease of a mutton as
wholesome as the sweat of a man? Shallow,
shallow. A better instance, I say; come. 60
 Cor. Besides, our hands are hard.
 Touch. Your lips will feel them the sooner:
shallow again. A more sounder instance; come.
 Cor. And they are often tarred over with the
surgery of our sheep; and would you have us
kiss tar? The courtier's hands are perfumed
with civet. 67
 Touch. Most shallow man! Thou worms-meat,
in respect of a good piece of flesh, indeed! Learn
of the wise, and perpend: civet is of a baser
birth than tar, the very uncleanly flux of a cat.
Mend the instance, shepherd. 72
 Cor. You have too courtly a wit for me: I'll
rest.
 Touch. Wilt thou rest damned? God help
thee, shallow man! God make incision in thee!
thou art raw. 77
 Cor. Sir, I am a true labourer: I earn that I
eat, get that I wear, owe no man hate, envy no
man's happiness, glad of other men's good, content with my harm; and the greatest of my pride
is to see my ewes graze and my lambs suck. 82
 Touch. That is another simple sin in you, to
bring the ewes and the rams together, and to
offer to get your living by the copulation of
cattle; to be bawd to a bell-wether, and to betray a she-lamb of a twelvemonth to a crooked-
pated, old, cuckoldy ram, out of all reasonable
match. If thou be'st not damned for this, the
devil himself will have no shepherds: I canno
see else how thou shouldst 'scape.
 Cor. Here comes young Master Ganymede
my new mistress's brother. 9

Enter ROSALIND, *reading a paper.*

Ros. From the east to western Ind,
 No jewel is like Rosalind.
 Her worth, being mounted on the wind, 9
 Through all the world bears Rosalind.
 All the pictures fairest lin'd
 Are but black to Rosalind.
 Let no face be kept in mind, 10
 But the fair of Rosalind.

Touch. I'll rime you so, eight years together
dinners and suppers and sleeping hours ex

epted: it is the right butter-women's rank to
market. 105

Ros. Out, fool!

Touch. For a taste:—

> If a hart do lack a hind, 108
> Let him seek out Rosalind.
> If the cat will after kind,
> So be sure will Rosalind.
> Winter-garments must be lin'd, 112
> So must slender Rosalind.
> They that reap must sheaf and bind,
> Then to cart with Rosalind.
> Sweetest nut hath sourest rind, 116
> Such a nut is Rosalind.
> He that sweetest rose will find
> Must find love's prick and Rosalind.

This is the very false gallop of verses: why do
you infect yourself with them? 121

Ros. Peace! you dull fool! I found them on
tree.

Touch. Truly, the tree yields bad fruit. 124

Ros. I'll graff it with you, and then I shall
graff it with a medlar: then it will be the earliest
fruit i' the country; for you'll be rotten ere you
be half ripe, and that's the right virtue of the
medlar. 129

Touch. You have said; but whether wisely or
no, let the forest judge.

Enter CELIA, *reading a paper.*

Ros. Peace! 132
Here comes my sister, reading: stand aside.

Cel. Why should this a desert be?
> For it is unpeopled? No;
> Tongues I'll hang on every tree, 136
> That shall civil sayings show.
> Some, how brief the life of man
> Runs his erring pilgrimage,
> That the stretching of a span 140
> Buckles in his sum of age;
> Some, of violated vows
> 'Twixt the souls of friend and friend:
> But upon the fairest boughs, 144
> Or at every sentence' end,
> Will I Rosalinda write;
> Teaching all that read to know
> The quintessence of every sprite 148
> Heaven would in little show.
> Therefore Heaven Nature charg'd
> That one body should be fill'd
> With all graces wide enlarg'd: 152
> Nature presently distill'd
> Helen's cheek, but not her heart,
> Cleopatra's majesty,
> Atalanta's better part, 156
> Sad Lucretia's modesty.
> Thus Rosalind of many parts
> By heavenly synod was devis'd
> Of many faces, eyes, and hearts, 160
> To have the touches dearest priz'd.
> Heaven would that she these gifts should have,
> And I to live and die her slave.

Ros. O most gentle pulpiter! what tedious
homily of love have you wearied your parishioners withal, and never cried, 'Have patience, good
people!'

Cel. How now! back, friends! Shepherd, go
off a little: go with him, sirrah. 169

Touch. Come, shepherd, let us make an ho-

nourable retreat; though not with bag and baggage, yet with scrip and scrippage. 172
    [*Exeunt* CORIN *and* TOUCHSTONE.

Cel. Didst thou hear these verses?

Ros. O, yes, I heard them all, and more too;
for some of them had in them more feet than
the verses would bear. 176

Cel. That's no matter: the feet might bear
the verses.

Ros. Ay, but the feet were lame, and could
not bear themselves without the verse, and
therefore stood lamely in the verse. 181

Cel. But didst thou hear without wondering,
how thy name should be hanged and carved
upon these trees? 184

Ros. I was seven of the nine days out of the
wonder before you came; for look here what I
found on a palm-tree: I was never so be-rimed
since Pythagoras' time, that I was an Irish rat,
which I can hardly remember. 189

Cel. Trow you who hath done this?

Ros. Is it a man?

Cel. And a chain, that you once wore, about
his neck. Change you colour? 193

Ros. I prithee, who?

Cel. O Lord, Lord! it is a hard matter for
friends to meet; but mountains may be removed
with earthquakes, and so encounter. 197

Ros. Nay, but who is it?

Cel. Is it possible?

Ros. Nay, I prithee now, with most petitionary
vehemence, tell me who it is. 201

Cel. O wonderful, wonderful, and most wonderful wonderful! and yet again wonderful! and
after that, out of all whooping! 204

Ros. Good my complexion! dost thou think,
though I am caparison'd like a man, I have a
doublet and hose in my disposition? One inch
of delay more is a South-sea of discovery; I
prithee, tell me who is it quickly, and speak
apace. I would thou couldst stammer, that thou
mightst pour this concealed man out of thy
mouth, as wine comes out of a narrow-mouth'd
bottle; either too much at once, or none at all.
I prithee, take the cork out of thy mouth, that
I may drink thy tidings.

Cel. So you may put a man in your belly. 216

Ros. Is he of God's making? What manner
of man? Is his head worth a hat, or his chin
worth a beard?

Cel. Nay, he hath but a little beard. 220

Ros. Why, God will send more, if the man
will be thankful. Let me stay the growth of his
beard, if thou delay me not the knowledge of his
chin. 224

Cel. It is young Orlando, that tripped up the
wrestler's heels and your heart both, in an instant.

Ros. Nay, but the devil take mocking: speak,
sad brow and true maid. 228

Cel. I' faith, coz, 'tis he.

Ros. Orlando?

Cel. Orlando.

Ros. Alas the day! what shall I do with my
doublet and hose? What did he when thou
sawest him? What said he? How looked he?
Wherein went he? What makes he here? Did

he ask for me? Where remains he? How parted he with thee, and when shalt thou see him again? Answer me in one word. 238

Cel. You must borrow me Gargantua's mouth first: 'tis a word too great for any mouth of this age's size. To say ay and no to these particulars is more than to answer in a catechism. 242

Ros. But doth he know that I am in this forest and in man's apparel? Looks he as freshly as he did the day he wrestled? 245

Cel. It is as easy to count atomies as to resolve the propositions of a lover; but take a taste of my finding him, and relish it with good observance. I found him under a tree, like a dropped acorn.

Ros. It may well be called Jove's tree, when it drops forth such fruit. 252

Cel. Give me audience, good madam.

Ros. Proceed.

Cel. There lay he, stretch'd along like a wounded knight. 256

Ros. Though it be pity to see such a sight, it well becomes the ground.

Cel. Cry 'holla!' to thy tongue, I prithee; it curvets unseasonably. He was furnish'd like a hunter. 261

Ros. O, ominous! he comes to kill my heart.

Cel. I would sing my song without a burthen: thou bringest me out of tune. 264

Ros. Do you not know I am a woman? when I think, I must speak. Sweet, say on.

Cel. You bring me out. Soft! comes he not here? 268

Ros. 'Tis he: slink by, and note him.

Enter ORLANDO *and* JAQUES.

Jaq. I thank you for your company; but, good faith, I had as lief have been myself alone.

Orl. And so had I; but yet, for fashion' sake, I thank you too for your society. 273

Jaq. God be wi' you: let's meet as little as we can.

Orl. I do desire we may be better strangers.

Jaq. I pray you, mar no more trees with writing love-songs in their barks.

Orl. I pray you mar no more of my verses with reading them ill-favouredly. 280

Jaq. Rosalind is your love's name?

Orl. Yes, just.

Jaq. I do not like her name.

Orl. There was no thought of pleasing you when she was christened. 285

Jaq. What stature is she of?

Orl. Just as high as my heart.

Jaq. You are full of pretty answers. Have you not been acquainted with goldsmiths' wives, and conn'd them out of rings?

Orl. Not so; but I answer you right painted cloth, from whence you have studied your questions. 293

Jaq. You have a nimble wit: I think 'twas made of Atalanta's heels. Will you sit down with me? and we two will rail against our mistress the world, and all our misery. 297

Orl. I will chide no breather in the world but myself, against whom I know most faults.

Jaq. The worst fault you have is to be in love.

Orl. 'Tis a fault I will not change for yo[u]r best virtue. I am weary of you.

Jaq. By my troth, I was seeking for a fo[ol] when I found you.

Orl. He is drowned in the brook: look but [in] and you shall see him.

Jaq. There I shall see mine own figure.

Orl. Which I take to be either a fool or a cipher.

Jaq. I'll tarry no longer with you. Farewe[ll] good Signior Love.

Orl. I am glad of your departure. Adie[u] good Monsieur Melancholy. [*Exit* JAQUE[S]

Ros. I will speak to him like a saucy lacke[y] and under that habit play the knave with hi[m] Do you hear, forester?

Orl. Very well: what would you?

Ros. I pray you, what is't o'clock?

Orl. You should ask me, what time o' da[y] there's no clock in the forest.

Ros. Then there is no true lover in the fores[t] else sighing every minute and groaning eve[ry] hour would detect the lazy foot of Time as we[ll] as a clock.

Orl. And why not the swift foot of Time had not that been as proper?

Ros. By no means, sir. Time travels [in] divers paces with divers persons. I'll tell yo[u] who Time ambles withal, who Time trots witha[l] who Time gallops withal, and who he stan[ds] still withal.

Orl. I prithee, who doth he trot withal?

Ros. Marry, he trots hard with a young ma[n] between the contract of her marriage and th[e] day it is solemnized; if the interim be but se'nnight, Time's pace is so hard that it seem[s] the length of seven year.

Orl. Who ambles Time withal?

Ros. With a priest that lacks Latin, and [a] rich man that hath not the gout; for the on[e] sleeps easily because he cannot study, and th[e] other lives merrily because he feels no pai[n] the one lacking the burden of lean and wast[e]ful learning, the other knowing no burde[n] of heavy tedious penury. These Time amble[s] withal.

Orl. Who doth he gallop withal?

Ros. With a thief to the gallows; for thoug[h] he go as softly as foot can fall he thinks himse[lf] too soon there.

Orl. Who stays it still withal?

Ros. With lawyers in the vacation; for the[y] sleep between term and term, and then they pe[r]ceive not how Time moves.

Orl. Where dwell you, pretty youth?

Ros. With this shepherdess, my sister; her in the skirts of the forest, like fringe upon petticoat.

Orl. Are you native of this place?

Ros. As the cony, that you see dwell wher[e] she is kindled.

Orl. Your accent is something finer than yo[u] could purchase in so removed a dwelling.

Ros. I have been told so of many: but indee[d]

old religious uncle of mine taught me to speak, who was in his youth an inland man; one that knew courtship too well, for there he fell in love. I have heard him read many lectures against it; and I thank God, I am not a woman, to be touched with so many giddy offences as he hath generally taxed their whole sex withal.   373

Orl. Can you remember any of the principal evils that he laid to the charge of women?

Ros. There were none principal; they were all like one another as half-pence are; every one fault seeming monstrous till his fellow fault came to match it.

Orl. I prithee, recount some of them.   380

Ros. No, I will not cast away my physic, but on those that are sick. There is a man haunts the forest, that abuses our young plants with carving 'Rosalind' on their barks; hangs odes upon hawthorns, and elegies on brambles; all, forsooth, deifying the name of Rosalind: if I could meet that fancy-monger, I would give him some good counsel, for he seems to have the quotidian of love upon him.   389

Orl. I am he that is so love-shaked. I pray you, tell me your remedy.

Ros. There is none of my uncle's marks upon you: he taught me how to know a man in love; in which cage of rushes I am sure you are not prisoner.

Orl. What were his marks?   396

Ros. A lean cheek, which you have not; a blue eye and sunken, which you have not; an unquestionable spirit, which you have not: but I pardon you for that, for, simply, your having in beard is a younger brother's revenue. Then, your hose should be ungartered, your bonnet unbanded, your sleeve unbuttoned, your shoe untied, and everything about you demonstrating careless desolation. But you are no such man: you are rather point-device in your accoutrements; as loving yourself than seeming the lover of any other.   409

Orl. Fair youth, I would I could make thee believe I love.

Ros. Me believe it! you may as soon make her that you love believe it; which, I warrant, she is apter to do than to confess she does; that is one of the points in the which women still give the lie to their consciences. But, in good sooth, are you he that hangs the verses on the trees, wherein Rosalind is so admired?

Orl. I swear to thee, youth, by the white hand of Rosalind, I am that he, that unfortunate he.   421

Ros. But are you so much in love as your rimes speak?

Orl. Neither rime nor reason can express how much.   425

Ros. Love is merely a madness, and, I tell you, deserves as well a dark house and a whip as madmen do; and the reason why they are not so punished and cured is, that the lunacy is so ordinary that the whippers are in love too. Yet I profess curing it by counsel.

Orl. Did you ever cure any so?   432

Ros. Yes, one; and in this manner. He was to imagine me his love, his mistress; and I set him every day to woo me: at which time would I, being but a moonish youth, grieve, be effeminate, changeable, longing and liking; proud, fantastical, apish, shallow, inconstant, full of tears, full of smiles, for every passion something, and for no passion truly anything, as boys and women are, for the most part, cattle of this colour; would now like him, now loathe him; then entertain him, then forswear him; now weep for him, then spit at him; that I drave my suitor from his mad humour of love to a living humour of madness, which was, to forswear the full stream of the world, and to live in a nook merely monastic. And thus I cured him; and this way will I take upon me to wash your liver as clean as a sound sheep's heart, that there shall not be one spot of love in 't.

Orl. I would not be cured, youth.   452

Ros. I would cure you, if you would but call me Rosalind, and come every day to my cote and woo me.

Orl. Now, by the faith of my love, I will: tell me where it is.   457

Ros. Go with me to it and I'll show it you; and by the way you shall tell me where in the forest you live. Will you go?   460

Orl. With all my heart, good youth.

Ros. Nay, you must call me Rosalind. Come, sister, will you go?   *[Exeunt.*

SCENE III.—*Another Part of the Forest.*

Enter TOUCHSTONE *and* AUDREY; JAQUES *behind.*

Touch. Come apace, good Audrey: I will fetch up your goats, Audrey. And how, Audrey? am I the man yet? doth my simple feature content you?   4

Aud. Your features! Lord warrant us! what features?

Touch. I am here with thee and thy goats, as the most capricious poet, honest Ovid, was among the Goths.   9

Jaq. [*Aside.*] O knowledge ill-inhabited, worse than Jove in a thatch'd house!

Touch. When a man's verses cannot be understood, nor a man's good wit seconded with the forward child Understanding, it strikes a man more dead than a great reckoning in a little room. Truly, I would the gods had made thee poetical.   17

Aud. I do not know what 'poetical' is. Is it honest in deed and word? Is it a true thing?   20

Touch. No, truly, for the truest poetry is the most feigning; and lovers are given to poetry, and what they swear in poetry may be said as lovers they do feign.   24

Aud. Do you wish then that the gods had made me poetical?

Touch. I do, truly; for thou swearest to me

thou art honest: now, if thou wert a poet, I
might have some hope thou didst feign.   29

Aud. Would you not have me honest?

Touch. No, truly, unless thou wert hard-
favour'd; for honesty coupled to beauty is to
have honey a sauce to sugar.   33

Jaq. [*Aside.*] A material fool.

Aud. Well, I am not fair, and therefore I
pray the gods make me honest.   36

Touch. Truly, and to cast away honesty upon
a foul slut were to put good meat into an unclean dish.

Aud. I am not a slut, though I thank the gods
I am foul.   41

Touch. Well, praised be the gods for thy foulness! sluttishness may come hereafter. But be it
as it may be, I will marry thee; and to that end
I have been with Sir Oliver Martext, the vicar
of the next village, who hath promised to meet
me in this place of the forest, and to couple us.

Jaq. [*Aside.*] I would fain see this meeting.

Aud. Well, the gods give us joy!   49

Touch. Amen. A man may, if he were of a
fearful heart, stagger in this attempt; for here
we have no temple but the wood, no assembly
but horn-beasts. But what though? Courage!
As horns are odious, they are necessary. It is
said, 'many a man knows no end of his goods:'
right; many a man has good horns, and knows
no end of them. Well, that is the dowry of his
wife; 'tis none of his own getting. Horns?
Even so. Poor men alone? No, no; the noblest
deer hath them as huge as the rascal. Is the
single man therefore blessed? No: as a walled
town is more worthier than a village, so is the
forehead of a married man more honourable
than the bare brow of a bachelor; and by how
much defence is better than no skill, by so much
is a horn more precious than to want. Here
comes Sir Oliver.   67

Enter SIR OLIVER MARTEXT.

Sir Oliver Martext, you are well met: will you
dispatch us here under this tree, or shall we go
with you to your chapel?

Sir Oli. Is there none here to give the
woman?   72

Touch. I will not take her on gift of any
man.

Sir Oli. Truly, she must be given, or the marriage is not lawful.   76

Jaq. [*Coming forward.*] Proceed, proceed:
I'll give her.

Touch. Good even, good Master What-ye-
call't: how do you, sir? You are very well met:
God 'ild you for your last company: I am very
glad to see you: even a toy in hand here, sir:
nay, pray be covered.

Jaq. Will you be married, motley?   84

Touch. As the ox hath his bow, sir, the horse
his curb, and the falcon her bells, so man hath
his desires; and as pigeons bill, so wedlock
would be nibbling.   88

Jaq. And will you, being a man of your
breeding, be married under a bush, like a
beggar? Get you to church, and have a good

priest that can tell you what marriage is: th
fellow will but join you together as they jo
wainscot; then one of you will prove a shru
panel, and like green timber, warp, warp.

Touch. [*Aside.*] I am not in the mind bu
were better to be married of him than of a
other: for he is not like to marry me well, a
not being well married, it will be a good excu
for me hereafter to leave my wife.   1

Jaq. Go thou with me, and let me counsel the

Touch. Come, sweet Audrey:
We must be married, or we must live in bawdr
Farewell, good Master Oliver: not   1

O sweet Oliver!
O brave Oliver!
Leave me not behind thee:

but,—   1

Wind away,
Begone, I say,
I will not to wedding with thee.

[*Exeunt* JAQUES, TOUCHSTONE, *and* AUDRE

Sir Oli. 'Tis no matter: ne'er a fantastic
knave of them all shall flout me out of my ca
ing.   [*Ex*

SCENE IV.—*Another Part of the Forest.*

Enter ROSALIND *and* CELIA.

Ros. Never talk to me: I will weep.

Cel. Do, I prithee; but yet have the grace
consider that tears do not become a man.

Ros. But have I not cause to weep?

Cel. As good cause as one would desir
therefore weep.

Ros. His very hair is of the dissembling colou

Cel. Something browner than Judas's; marr
his kisses are Judas's own children.

Ros. I' faith, his hair is of a good colour.

Cel. An excellent colour: your chesnut wa
ever the only colour.

Ros. And his kissing is as full of sanctity a
the touch of holy bread.

Cel. He hath bought a pair of cast lips o
Diana: a nun of winter's sisterhood kisses n
more religiously; the very ice of chastity is in then

Ros. But why did he swear he would com
this morning, and comes not?

Cel. Nay, certainly, there is no truth in hin

Ros. Do you think so?   2

Cel. Yes: I think he is not a pick-purse nor
horse-stealer; but for his verity in love, I d
think him as concave as a covered goblet or
worm-eaten nut.   2

Ros. Not true in love?

Cel. Yes, when he is in; but I think he i
not in.

Ros. You have heard him swear downrigh
he was.

Cel. 'Was' is not 'is:' besides, the oath of
lover is no stronger than the word of a tapster
they are both the confirmers of false reckonings
He attends here in the forest on the duke you
father.

Ros. I met the duke yesterday and had muc

question with him. He asked me of what
parentage I was; I told him, of as good as he;
so he laughed, and let me go. But what talk we
of fathers, when there is such a man as Orlando?

Cel. O, that's a brave man! he writes brave
verses, speaks brave words, swears brave oaths,
and breaks them bravely, quite traverse, athwart
the heart of his lover; as a puisny tilter, that
spurs his horse but on one side, breaks his staff
like a noble goose. But all's brave that youth
mounts and folly guides. Who comes here?

Enter CORIN.

Cor. Mistress and master, you have oft in-
quir'd   48
After the shepherd that complain'd of love,
Who you saw sitting by me on the turf,
Praising the proud disdainful shepherdess
That was his mistress.
Cel.   Well, and what of him? 52
Cor. If you will see a pageant truly play'd,
Between the pale complexion of true love
And the red glow of scorn and proud disdain,
Go hence a little, and I shall conduct you,   56
If you will mark it.
Ros.   O! come, let us remove:
The sight of lovers feedeth those in love.
Bring us to this sight, and you shall say
I'll prove a busy actor in their play. [*Exeunt.*

SCENE V.—*Another Part of the Forest.*

Enter SILVIUS *and* PHEBE.

Sil. Sweet Phebe, do not scorn me; do not,
Phebe:
Say that you love me not, but say not so
In bitterness. The common executioner,
Whose heart the accustom'd sight of death
makes hard,   4
Falls not the axe upon the humbled neck
But first begs pardon: will you sterner be
Than he that dies and lives by bloody drops?

Enter ROSALIND, CELIA, *and* CORIN, *behind.*

Phe. I would not be thy executioner: 8
I fly thee, for I would not injure thee.
Thou tell'st me there is murder in mine eye:
'Tis pretty, sure, and very probable,
That eyes, that are the frail'st and softest
things,   12
Who shut their coward gates on atomies,
Should be call'd tyrants, butchers, murderers!
Now I do frown on thee with all my heart;
And, if mine eyes can wound, now let them kill
thee;   16
Now counterfeit to swound; why now fall down;
Or, if thou canst not, O! for shame, for shame,
Lie not, to say mine eyes are murderers.
Now show the wound mine eye hath made in
thee;   20
Scratch thee but with a pin, and there remains
Some scar of it, lean but upon a rush,
The cicatrice and capable impressure
Thy palm some moment keeps; but now mine
eyes,   24

Which I have darted at thee, hurt thee not,
Nor, I am sure, there is no force in eyes
That can do hurt.
Sil.   O dear Phebe,
If ever,—as that ever may be near,—   28
You meet in some fresh cheek the power of
fancy,
Then shall you know the wounds invisible
That love's keen arrows make.
Phe.   But, till that time
Come not thou near me; and, when that time
comes,   32
Afflict me with thy mocks, pity me not;
As, till that time I shall not pity thee.
Ros. [*Advancing.*] And why, I pray you?
Who might be your mother,
That you insult, exult, and all at once,   36
Over the wretched? What though you have no
beauty,—
As by my faith, I see no more in you
Than without candle may go dark to bed,—
Must you be therefore proud and pitiless?   40
Why, what means this? Why do you look on
me?
I see no more in you than in the ordinary
Of nature's sale-work. Od's my little life!
I think she means to tangle my eyes too.   44
No, faith, proud mistress, hope not after it:
'Tis not your inky brows, your black silk hair,
Your bugle eyeballs, nor your cheek of cream,
That can entame my spirits to your worship.   48
You foolish shepherd, wherefore do you follow
her,
Like foggy south puffing with wind and rain?
You are a thousand times a properer man
Than she a woman: 'tis such fools as you   52
That make the world full of ill-favour'd child-
ren:
'Tis not her glass, but you, that flatters her;
And out of you she sees herself more proper
Than any of her lineaments can show her. 56
But, mistress, know yourself: down on your
knees,
And thank heaven, fasting, for a good man's
love:
For I must tell you friendly in your ear,
Sell when you can; you are not for all markets.
Cry the man mercy; love him; take his offer: 61
Foul is most foul, being foul to be a scoffer.
So take her to thee, shepherd. Fare you well.
Phe. Sweet youth, I pray you, chide a year
together: 64
I had rather hear you chide than this man woo.
Ros. He's fallen in love with her foulness, and
she'll fall in love with my anger. If it be so, as
fast as she answers thee with frowning looks, I'll
sauce her with bitter words. Why look you so
upon me?
Phe. For no ill will I bear you.
Ros. I pray you, do not fall in love with me,
For I am falser than vows made in wine: 73
Besides, I like you not. If you will know my
house,
'Tis at the tuft of olives here hard by.
Will you go, sister? Shepherd, ply her hard. 76
Come, sister. Shepherdess, look on him better,

And be not proud: though all the world could
see,
None could be so abus'd in sight as he.
Come, to our flock.   80
    [Exeunt ROSALIND, CELIA, *and* CORIN.
  Phe. Dead shepherd, now I find thy saw of
    might:
'Who ever lov'd that lov'd not at first sight?'
  Sil. Sweet Phebe,—
  Phe.   Ha! what sayst thou, Silvius?
  Sil. Sweet Phebe, pity me.   84
  Phe. Why, I am sorry for thee, gentle Silvius.
  Sil. Wherever sorrow is, relief would be:
If you do sorrow at my grief in love,
By giving love your sorrow and my grief   88
Were both extermin'd.
  Phe. Thou hast my love: is not that neigh-
    bourly?
  Sil. I would have you.
  Phe.   Why, that were covetousness.
Silvius, the time was that I hated thee;   92
And yet it is not that I bear thee love:
But since that thou canst talk of love so well,
Thy company, which erst was irksome to me,
I will endure, and I'll employ thee too;   96
But do not look for further recompense
Than thine own gladness that thou art employ'd.
  Sil. So holy and so perfect is my love,
And I in such a poverty of grace,   100
That I shall think it a most plenteous crop
To glean the broken ears after the man
That the main harvest reaps: loose now and
    then
A scatter'd smile, and that I'll live upon. 104
  Phe. Know'st thou the youth that spoke to
    me erewhile?
  Sil. Not very well, but I have met him oft;
And he hath bought the cottage and the bounds
That the old carlot once was master of.   108
  Phe. Think not I love him, though I ask for
    him.
'Tis but a peevish boy; yet he talks well;
But what care I for words? yet words do well,
When he that speaks them pleases those that
    hear.   112
It is a pretty youth: not very pretty:
But, sure, he's proud; and yet his pride be-
    comes him:
He'll make a proper man: the best thing in him
Is his complexion; and faster than his tongue
Did make offence his eye did heal it up.   117
He is not very tall; yet for his years he's tall:
His leg is but so so; and yet 'tis well:
There was a pretty redness in his lip,   120
A little riper and more lusty red
Than that mix'd in his cheek; 'twas just the
    difference
Betwixt the constant red and mingled damask.
There be some women, Silvius, had they mark'd
    him   124
In parcels as I did, would have gone near
To fall in love with him; but, for my part,
I love him not nor hate him not; and yet
Have more cause to hate him than to love him:
For what had he to do to chide at me?   129
He said mine eyes were black and my hair black;

And, now I am remember'd, scorn'd at me.
I marvel why I answer'd not again: 132
But that's all one; omittance is no quittance.
I'll write to him a very taunting letter,
And thou shalt bear it: wilt thou, Silvius?
  Sil. Phebe, with all my heart.
  Phe.   I'll write it straight;
The matter's in my head and in my heart:
I will be bitter with him and passing short.
Go with me, Silvius.   *[Exeunt.*

ACT IV

SCENE I.—*The Forest of Arden.*

Enter ROSALIND, CELIA, *and* JAQUES.

  Jaq. I prithee, pretty youth, let me be better
acquainted with thee.
  Ros. They say you are a melancholy fellow.
  Jaq. I am so; I do love it better than laughing.   5
  Ros. Those that are in extremity of either are
abominable fellows, and betray themselves to
every modern censure worse than drunkards.   8
  Jaq. Why, 'tis good to be sad and say nothing.
  Ros. Why, then, 'tis good to be a post.
  Jaq. I have neither the scholar's melancholy,
which is emulation; nor the musician's, which is
fantastical; nor the courtier's, which is proud;
nor the soldier's, which is ambitious; nor the
lawyer's, which is politic; nor the lady's, which is
nice; nor the lover's, which is all these: but it is
a melancholy of mine own, compounded of many
simples, extracted from many objects, and indeed the sundry contemplation of my travels,
which, by often rumination, wraps me in a most
humorous sadness.   21
  Ros. A traveller! By my faith, you have great
reason to be sad. I fear you have sold your own
lands to see other men's; then, to have seen
much and to have nothing, is to have rich eyes
and poor hands.   26
  Jaq. Yes, I have gained my experience.
  Ros. And your experience makes you sad: I
had rather have a fool to make me merry than
experience to make me sad: and to travel for it
too!   32

Enter ORLANDO.

  Orl. Good day, and happiness, dear Rosalind!
  Jaq. Nay then, God be wi' you, an you talk
in blank verse.   *[Exit.*
  Ros. Farewell, Monsieur Traveller: look you
lisp, and wear strange suits, disable all the
benefits of your own country, be out of love with
your nativity, and almost chide God for making
you that countenance you are; or I will scarce
think you have swam in a gondola. Why, how
now, Orlando! where have you been all this
while? You a lover! An you serve me such
another trick, never come in my sight more.
  Orl. My fair Rosalind, I come within an hour
of my promise.   45
  Ros. Break an hour's promise in love! He
that will divide a minute into a thousand parts,

and break but a part of the thousandth part of a minute in the affairs of love, it may be said of him that Cupid hath clapped him o' the shoulder, but I'll warrant him heart-whole.

Orl. Pardon me, dear Rosalind. 52

Ros. Nay, an you be so tardy, come no more in my sight: I had as lief be wooed of a snail.

Orl. Of a snail!

Ros. Ay, of a snail; for though he comes slowly, he carries his house on his head; a better jointure, I think, than you make a woman: besides, he brings his destiny with him.

Orl. What's that? 60

Ros. Why, horns; that such as you are fain to be beholding to your wives for: but he comes armed in his fortune and prevents the slander of his wife. 64

Orl. Virtue is no horn-maker; and my Rosalind is virtuous.

Ros. And I am your Rosalind?

Cel. It pleases him to call you so; but he hath a Rosalind of a better leer than you. 69

Ros. Come, woo me, woo me; for now I am in a holiday humour, and like enough to consent. What would you say to me now, an I were your very very Rosalind? 73

Orl. I would kiss before I spoke.

Ros. Nay, you were better speak first, and when you were gravelled for lack of matter, you might take occasion to kiss. Very good orators, when they are out, they will spit; and for lovers lacking,—God warn us!—matter, the cleanliest shift is to kiss. 80

Orl. How if the kiss be denied?

Ros. Then she puts you to entreaty, and there begins new matter.

Orl. Who could be out, being before his beloved mistress? 85

Ros. Marry, that should you, if I were your mistress; or I should think my honesty ranker than my wit. 88

Orl. What, of my suit?

Ros. Not out of your apparel, and yet out of your suit. Am not I your Rosalind?

Orl. I take some joy to say you are, because I would be talking of her. 93

Ros. Well, in her person I say I will not have you.

Orl. Then in mine own person I die. 96

Ros. No, faith, die by attorney. The poor world is almost six thousand years old, and in all this time there was not any man died in his own person, *videlicet*, in a love-cause. Troilus had his brains dashed out with a Grecian club; yet he did what he could to die before, and he is one of the patterns of love. Leander, he would have lived many a fair year, though Hero had turned nun, if it had not been for a hot midsummer night; for, good youth, he went but forth to wash him in the Hellespont, and being taken with the cramp was drowned; and the foolish coroners of that age found it was 'Hero of Sestos.' But these are all lies: men have died from time to time, and worms have eaten them, but not for love. 112

Orl. I would not have my right Rosalind of this mind; for, I protest, her frown might kill me.

Ros. By this hand, it will not kill a fly. But come, now I will be your Rosalind in a more coming-on disposition; and ask me what you will, I will grant it.

Orl. Then love me, Rosalind. 120

Ros. Yes, faith will I, Fridays and Saturdays and all.

Orl. And wilt thou have me?

Ros. Ay, and twenty such. 124

Orl. What sayest thou?

Ros. Are you not good?

Orl. I hope so.

Ros. Why then, can one desire too much of a good thing?—Come, sister, you shall be the priest and marry us.—Give me your hand, Orlando. What do you say, sister?

Orl. Pray thee, marry us. 132

Cel. I cannot say the words.

Ros. You must begin,—'Will you, Orlando,'—

Cel. Go to.—Will you, Orlando, have to wife this Rosalind? 136

Orl. I will.

Ros. Ay, but when?

Orl. Why now; as fast as she can marry us.

Ros. Then you must say, 'I take thee, Rosalind, for wife.' 141

Orl. I take thee, Rosalind, for wife.

Ros. I might ask you for your commission; but, I do take thee, Orlando, for my husband: there's a girl goes before the priest; and, certainly, a woman's thought runs before her actions.

Orl. So do all thoughts; they are winged. 148

Ros. Now tell me how long you would have her after you have possessed her?

Orl. For ever and a day.

Ros. Say 'a day,' without the 'ever.' No, no, Orlando; men are April when they woo, December when they wed: maids are May when they are maids, but the sky changes when they are wives. I will be more jealous of thee than a Barbary cock-pigeon over his hen; more clamorous than a parrot against rain; more newfangled than an ape; more giddy in my desires than a monkey: I will weep for nothing, like Diana in the fountain, and I will do that when you are disposed to be merry; I will laugh like a hyen, and that when thou art inclined to sleep.

Orl. But will my Rosalind do so? 164

Ros. By my life, she will do as I do.

Orl. O! but she is wise.

Ros. Or else she could not have the wit to do this: the wiser, the waywarder: make the doors upon a woman's wit, and it will out at the casement; shut that, and 'twill out at the key-hole; stop that, 'twill fly with the smoke out at the chimney. 172

Orl. A man that hath a wife with such a wit, he might say, 'Wit, whither wilt?'

Ros. Nay, you might keep that check for it till you met your wife's wit going to your neighbour's bed. 177

Orl. And what wit could wit have to excuse that?

Ros. Marry, to say she came to seek you there. You shall never take her without her answer, unless you take her without her tongue. O! that woman that cannot make her fault her husband's occasion, let her never nurse her child herself, for she will breed it like a fool.   185

Orl. For these two hours, Rosalind, I will leave thee.

Ros. Alas! dear love, I cannot lack thee two hours.   189

Orl. I must attend the duke at dinner: by two o'clock I will be with thee again.

Ros. Ay, go your ways, go your ways; I knew what you would prove, my friends told me as much, and I thought no less: that flattering tongue of yours won me: 'tis but one cast away, and so, come, death! Two o'clock is your hour?

Orl. Ay, sweet Rosalind.   197

Ros. By my troth, and in good earnest, and so God mend me, and by all pretty oaths that are not dangerous, if you break one jot of your promise or come one minute behind your hour, I will think you the most pathetical break-promise, and the most hollow lover, and the most unworthy of her you call Rosalind, that may be chosen out of the gross band of the unfaithful. Therefore, beware my censure, and keep your promise.

Orl. With no less religion than if thou wert indeed my Rosalind: so, adieu.   209

Ros. Well, Time is the old justice that examines all such offenders, and let Time try. Adieu.   [*Exit* ORLANDO.

Cel. You have simply misused our sex in your love-prate: we must have your doublet and hose plucked over your head, and show the world what the bird hath done to her own nest.   216

Ros. O coz, coz, coz, my pretty little coz, that thou didst know how many fathom deep I am in love! But it cannot be sounded: my affection hath an unknown bottom, like the bay of Portugal.

Cel. Or rather, bottomless; that as fast as you pour affection in, it runs out.   222

Ros. No; that same wicked bastard of Venus, that was begot of thought, conceived of spleen, and born of madness, that blind rascally boy that abuses every one's eyes because his own are out, let him be judge how deep I am in love. I'll tell thee, Aliena, I cannot be out of the sight of Orlando: I'll go find a shadow and sigh till he come.   230

Cel. And I'll sleep.   [*Exeunt.*

SCENE II.—*Another Part of the Forest.*

Enter JAQUES, Lords, *and* Foresters.

Jaq. Which is he that killed the deer?

First Lord. Sir, it was I.

Jaq. Let's present him to the duke, like a Roman conqueror, and it would do well to set the deer's horns upon his head for a branch of victory. Have you no song, forester, for this purpose? 6

Second Lord. Yes, sir.

Jaq. Sing it: 'tis no matter how it be in tune so it make noise enough.

SONG

What shall he have that kill'd the deer?
His leather skin and horns to wear.
      Then sing him home.   12

[*The rest shall bear this burden.*

Take thou no scorn to wear the horn;
It was a crest ere thou wast born:
      Thy father's father wore it,
      And thy father bore it: 16
The horn, the horn, the lusty horn
Is not a thing to laugh to scorn.

[*Exeunt.*

SCENE III.—*Another Part of the Forest.*

Enter ROSALIND *and* CELIA.

Ros. How say you now? Is it not past two o'clock? And here much Orlando!

Cel. I warrant you, with pure love and a troubled brain, he hath ta'en his bow and arrows, and is gone forth to sleep. Look, who comes here.

Enter SILVIUS.

Sil. My errand is to you, fair youth.
My gentle Phebe did bid me give you this: 8
                    [*Giving a letter.*
I know not the contents; but, as I guess
By the stern brow and waspish action
Which she did use as she was writing of it,
It bears an angry tenour: pardon me;   12
I am but as a guiltless messenger.

Ros. Patience herself would startle at this letter,
And play the swaggerer: bear this, bear all:
She says I am not fair; that I lack manners; 16
She calls me proud, and that she could not love me
Were man as rare as phœnix. 'Od's my will!
Her love is not the hare that I do hunt:
Why writes she so to me? Well, shepherd, well,
This is a letter of your own device.   21

Sil. No, I protest, I know not the contents:
Phebe did write it.

Ros.   Come, come, you are a fool,
And turn'd into the extremity of love.   24
I saw her hand: she has a leathern hand,
A freestone-colour'd hand; I verily did think
That her old gloves were on, but 'twas her hands:
She has a housewife's hand; but that's no matter: 28
I say she never did invent this letter;
This is a man's invention, and his hand.

Sil. Sure, it is hers.

Ros. Why, 'tis a boisterous and a cruel style,
A style for challengers; why, she defies me, 33
Like Turk to Christian: woman's gentle brain
Could not drop forth such giant-rude invention,
Such Ethiop words, blacker in their effect 36
Than in their countenance. Will you hear the letter?

Sil. So please you, for I never heard it yet;
Yet heard too much of Phebe's cruelty.

Ros. She Phebes me. Mark how the tyrant writes. [*Reads.*] 40

> Art thou god to shepherd turn'd,
> That a maiden's heart hath burn'd?

Can a woman rail thus?

Sil. Call you this railing? 44
Ros. [*reads.*]

> Why, thy godhead laid apart,
> Warr'st thou with a woman's heart?

Did you ever hear such railing?

> Whiles the eye of man did woo me, 48
> That could do no vengeance to me.

Meaning me a beast.

> If the scorn of your bright eyne
> Have power to raise such love in mine, 52
> Alack! in me what strange effect
> Would they work in mild aspect.
> Whiles you chid me, I did love;
> How then might your prayers move! 56
> He that brings this love to thee
> Little knows this love in me;
> And by him seal up thy mind;
> Whether that thy youth and kind 60
> Will the faithful offer take
> Of me and all that I can make;
> Or else by him my love deny,
> And then I'll study how to die. 64

Sil. Call you this chiding?
Cel. Alas, poor shepherd!
Ros. Do you pity him? no, he deserves no pity. Wilt thou love such a woman? What, to make thee an instrument and play false strains upon thee! not to be endured! Well, go your way to her, for I see love hath made thee a tame snake, and say this to her: that if she love me, I charge her to love thee: if she will not, I will never have her, unless thou entreat for her. If you be a true lover, hence, and not a word, for here comes more company. [*Exit* SILVIUS.

Enter OLIVER.

Oli. Good morrow, fair ones. Pray you if you know, 77
Where in the purlieus of this forest stands
A sheepcote fenc'd about with olive-trees?
Cel. West of this place, down in the neighbour bottom: 80
The rank of osiers by the murmuring stream
Left on your right hand brings you to the place.
But at this hour the house doth keep itself;
There's none within. 84
Oli. If that an eye may profit by a tongue,
Then should I know you by description;
Such garments, and such years: 'The boy is fair,
Of female favour, and bestows himself 88
Like a ripe sister: but the woman low,
And browner than her brother.' Are not you
The owner of the house I did inquire for? 91
Cel. It is no boast, being ask'd, to say, we are.
Oli. Orlando doth commend him to you both,
And to that youth he calls his Rosalind
He sends this bloody napkin. Are you he?
Ros. I am: what must we understand by this? 96

Oli. Some of my shame; if you will know of me
What man I am, and how, and why, and where
This handkercher was stain'd.
Cel. I pray you, tell it.
Oli. When last the young Orlando parted from you 100
He left a promise to return again
Within an hour; and, pacing through the forest,
Chewing the food of sweet and bitter fancy,
Lo, what befell! he threw his eye aside, 104
And mark what object did present itself:
Under an oak, whose boughs were moss'd with age,
And high top bald with dry antiquity, 107
A wretched ragged man, o'ergrown with hair,
Lay sleeping on his back: about his neck
A green and gilded snake had wreath'd itself,
Who with her head nimble in threats approach'd
The opening of his mouth; but suddenly, 112
Seeing Orlando, it unlink'd itself,
And with indented glides did slip away
Into a bush; under which bush's shade
A lioness, with udders all drawn dry, 116
Lay couching, head on ground, with catlike watch,
When that the sleeping man should stir; for 'tis
The royal disposition of that beast
To prey on nothing that doth seem as dead: 120
This seen, Orlando did approach the man,
And found it was his brother, his elder brother.
Cel. O! I have heard him speak of that same brother;
And he did render him the most unnatural 124
That liv'd 'mongst men.
Oli. And well he might so do,
For well I know he was unnatural.
Ros. But, to Orlando: did he leave him there,
Food to the suck'd and hungry lioness? 128
Oli. Twice did he turn his back and purpos'd so;
But kindness, nobler ever than revenge,
And nature, stronger than his just occasion,
Made him give battle to the lioness, 132
Who quickly fell before him: in which hurtling
From miserable slumber I awak'd.
Cel. Are you his brother?
Ros. Was it you he rescu'd?
Cel. Was 't you that did so oft contrive to kill him? 136
Oli. 'Twas I; but 'tis not I. I do not shame
To tell you what I was, since my conversion
So sweetly tastes, being the thing I am.
Ros. But, for the bloody napkin?
Oli. By and by.
When from the first to last, betwixt us two, 141
Tears our recountments had most kindly bath'd,
As how I came into that desert place:—
In brief, he led me to the gentle duke, 144
Who gave me fresh array and entertainment,
Committing me unto my brother's love;
Who led me instantly unto his cave,
There stripp'd himself; and here, upon his arm
The lioness had torn some flesh away, 149
Which all this while had bled; and now he fainted,

And cried, in fainting, upon Rosalind.
Brief, I recover'd him, bound up his wound; 152
And, after some small space, being strong at
heart,
He sent me hither, stranger as I am,
To tell this story, that you might excuse
His broken promise; and to give this napkin,
Dy'd in his blood, unto the shepherd youth 157
That he in sport doth call his Rosalind.

Cel. [ROSALIND *swoons*.] Why, how now,
Ganymede! sweet Ganymede!

Oli. Many will swoon when they do look on
blood.   160

Cel. There is more in it. Cousin! Ganymede!

Oli. Look, he recovers.

Ros. I would I were at home.

Cel.   We'll lead you thither.
I pray you, will you take him by the arm? 164

Oli. Be of good cheer, youth. You a man!
You lack a man's heart.

Ros. I do so, I confess it. Ah, sirrah! a body
would think this was well counterfeited. I pray
you, tell your brother how well I counterfeited.
Heigh-ho!

Oli. This was not counterfeit: there is too
great testimony in your complexion that it was
a passion of earnest.   173

Ros. Counterfeit, I assure you.

Oli. Well then, take a good heart and counterfeit to be a man.   176

Ros. So I do; but, i' faith, I should have been
a woman by right.

Cel. Come; you look paler and paler: pray
you, draw homewards. Good sir, go with us. 180

Oli. That will I, for I must bear answer back
How you excuse my brother, Rosalind.

Ros. I shall devise something. But, I pray
you, commend my counterfeiting to him. Will
you go?   [*Exeunt.*

ACT V

SCENE I.—*The Forest of Arden.*

Enter TOUCHSTONE *and* AUDREY.

Touch. We shall find a time, Audrey: patience,
gentle Audrey.

Aud. Faith, the priest was good enough, for
all the old gentleman's saying.   4

Touch. A most wicked Sir Oliver, Audrey; a
most vile Martext. But, Audrey, there is a youth
here in the forest lays claim to you.

Aud. Ay, I know who 'tis: he hath no interest
in me in the world. Here comes the man you
mean.   10

Enter WILLIAM.

Touch. It is meat and drink to me to see a
clown. By my troth, we that have good wits have
much to answer for: we shall be flouting; we
cannot hold.

Will. Good even, Audrey.

Aud. God ye good even, William.   16

Will. And good even to you, sir.

Touch. Good even, gentle friend. Cover thy

head, cover thy head; nay, prithee, be covered.
How old are you, friend?   20

Will. Five-and-twenty, sir.

Touch. A ripe age. Is thy name William?

Will. William, sir.

Touch. A fair name. Wast born i' the forest
here?   25

Will. Ay, sir, I thank God.

Touch. 'Thank God;' a good answer. Art
rich?   28

Will. Faith, sir, so so.

Touch. 'So so,' is good, very good, very excellent good: and yet it is not; it is but so so. Art
thou wise?   32

Will. Ay, sir, I have a pretty wit.

Touch. Why, thou sayest well. I do now remember a saying, 'The fool doth think he is
wise, but the wise man knows himself to be a
fool.' The heathen philosopher, when he had a
desire to eat a grape, would open his lips when
he put it into his mouth; meaning thereby that
grapes were made to eat and lips to open. You
do love this maid?   41

Will. I do, sir.

Touch. Give me your hand. Art thou learned?

Will. No, sir.   44

Touch. Then learn this of me: to have, is to
have; for it is a figure in rhetoric, that drink,
being poured out of a cup into a glass, by filling the one doth empty the other; for all your
writers do consent that *ipse* is he: now, you are
not *ipse*, for I am he.   50

Will. Which he, sir?

Touch. He, sir, that must marry this woman.
Therefore, you clown, abandon,—which is in the
vulgar, leave,—the society,—which in the boorish
is, company,—of this female,—which in the common is, woman; which together is, abandon the
society of this female, or, clown, thou perishest;
or, to thy better understanding, diest; or, to wit,
I kill thee, make thee away, translate thy life
into death, thy liberty into bondage. I will deal
in poison with thee, or in bastinado, or in steel;
I will bandy with thee in faction; I will o'errun
thee with policy; I will kill thee a hundred and
fifty ways: therefore tremble, and depart.   64

Aud. Do, good William.

Will. God rest you merry, sir.   [*Exit.*

Enter CORIN.

Cor. Our master and mistress seek you:
come, away, away!   68

Touch. Trip, Audrey! trip, Audrey! I attend,
I attend.   [*Exeunt.*

SCENE II.—*Another Part of the Forest.*

Enter ORLANDO *and* OLIVER.

Orl. Is't possible that on so little acquaintance you should like her? that, but seeing, you
should love her? and, loving, woo? and, wooing,
she should grant? and will you persever to enjoy
her?   5

Oli. Neither call the giddiness of it in question, the poverty of her, the small acquaintance,

my sudden wooing, nor her sudden consenting; but say with me, I love Aliena; say with her, that she loves me; consent with both, that we may enjoy each other: it shall be to your good; for my father's house and all the revenue that was old Sir Rowland's will I estate upon you, and here live and die a shepherd. 14

Orl. You have my consent. Let your wedding be to-morrow: thither will I invite the duke and all's contented followers. Go you and prepare Aliena; for, look you, here comes my Rosalind.

Enter ROSALIND.

Ros. God save you, brother. 20

Oli. And you, fair sister. [*Exit.*

Ros. O! my dear Orlando, how it grieves me to see thee wear thy heart in a scarf.

Orl. It is my arm. 24

Ros. I thought thy heart had been wounded with the claws of a lion.

Orl. Wounded it is, but with the eyes of a lady. 28

Ros. Did your brother tell you how I counterfeited to swound when he showed me your handkercher?

Orl. Ay, and greater wonders than that. 32

Ros. O! I know where you are. Nay, 'tis true: there was never anything so sudden but the fight of two rams, and Cæsar's thrasonical brag of 'I came, saw, and overcame:' for your brother and my sister no sooner met, but they looked; no sooner looked but they loved; no sooner loved but they sighed; no sooner sighed but they asked one another the reason; no sooner knew the reason but they sought the remedy: and in these degrees have they made a pair of stairs to marriage which they will climb incontinent, or else be incontinent before marriage. They are in the very wrath of love, and they will together: clubs cannot part them. 46

Orl. They shall be married to-morrow, and I will bid the duke to the nuptial. But, O! how bitter a thing it is to look into happiness through another man's eyes. By so much the more shall I to-morrow be at the height of heart-heaviness, by how much I shall think my brother happy in having what he wishes for. 53

Ros. Why then, to-morrow I cannot serve your turn for Rosalind?

Orl. I can live no longer by thinking. 56

Ros. I will weary you then no longer with idle talking. Know of me then,—for now I speak to some purpose,—that I know you are a gentleman of good conceit. I speak not this that you should bear a good opinion of my knowledge, insomuch I say I know you are; neither do I labour for a greater esteem than may in some little measure draw a belief from you, to do yourself good, and not to grace me. Believe then, if you please, that I can do strange things. I have, since I was three years old, conversed with a magician, most profound in his art and yet not damnable. If you do love Rosalind so near the heart as your gesture cries it out, when your brother marries Aliena, shall you marry her:

I know into what straits of fortune she is driven; and it is not impossible to me, if it appear not inconvenient to you, to set her before your eyes to-morrow, human as she is, and without any danger. 76

Orl. Speakest thou in sober meanings?

Ros. By my life, I do; which I tender dearly, though I say I am a magician. Therefore, put you in your best array; bid your friends; for if you will be married to-morrow, you shall; and to Rosalind, if you will. Look, here comes a lover of mine, and a lover of hers.

Enter SILVIUS *and* PHEBE.

Phe. Youth, you have done me much ungentleness, 84
To show the letter that I writ to you.

Ros. I care not if I have: it is my study
To seem despiteful and ungentle to you.
You are there follow'd by a faithful shepherd:
Look upon him, love him; he worships you. 89

Phe. Good shepherd, tell this youth what 'tis to love.

Sil. It is to be all made of sighs and tears;
And so am I for Phebe. 92

Phe. And I for Ganymede.

Orl. And I for Rosalind.

Ros. And I for no woman.

Sil. It is to be all made of faith and service;
And so am I for Phebe. 97

Phe. And I for Ganymede.

Orl. And I for Rosalind.

Ros. And I for no woman. 100

Sil. It is to be all made of fantasy,
All made of passion, and all made of wishes;
All adoration, duty, and observance;
All humbleness, all patience, and impatience;
All purity, all trial, all obeisance; 105
And so am I for Phebe.

Phe. And so am I for Ganymede.

Orl. And so am I for Rosalind. 108

Ros. And so am I for no woman.

Phe. [*To* ROSALIND.] If this be so, why blame you me to love you?

Sil. [*To* PHEBE.] If this be so, why blame you me to love you? 113

Orl. If this be so, why blame you me to love you?

Ros. Why do you speak to, 'Why blame you me to love you?' 117

Orl. To her that is not here, nor doth not hear.

Ros. Pray you, no more of this: 'tis like the howling of Irish wolves against the moon. [*To* SILVIUS.] I will help you, if I can: [*To* PHEBE.] I would love you, if I could. To-morrow meet me all together. [*To* PHEBE.] I will marry you, if ever I marry woman, and I'll be married to-morrow: [*To* ORLANDO.] I will satisfy you, if ever I satisfied man, and you shall be married to-morrow: [*To* SILVIUS.] I will content you, if what pleases you contents you, and you shall be married to-morrow. [*To* ORLANDO.] As you love Rosalind, meet: [*To* SILVIUS.] As you love Phebe, meet: and as I love no woman, I'll meet. So, fare you well: I have left you commands.   134

Sil. I'll not fail, if I live.

Phe. Nor I.

Orl. Nor I.   [*Exeunt.*

SCENE III.—*Another Part of the Forest.*

Enter TOUCHSTONE *and* AUDREY.

Touch. To-morrow is the joyful day, Audrey; to-morrow will we be married.

Aud. I do desire it with all my heart, and I hope it is no dishonest desire to desire to be a woman of the world. Here come two of the banished duke's pages.   6

Enter two Pages.

First Page. Well met, honest gentleman.

Touch. By my troth, well met. Come, sit, sit, and a song.   9

Sec. Page. We are for you: sit i' the middle.

First Page. Shall we clap into 't roundly, without hawking or spitting, or saying we are hoarse, which are the only prologues to a bad voice?

Sec. Page. I' faith, i' faith; and both in a tune, like two gipsies on a horse.   17

SONG

It was a lover and his lass,
    With a hey, and a ho, and a hey nonino,
That o'er the green corn-field did pass,   20
    In the spring time, the only pretty ring time,
    When birds do sing, hey ding a ding, ding;
Sweet lovers love the spring.

Between the acres of the rye,   24
    With a hey, and a ho, and a hey nonino,
These pretty country folks would lie,
    In the spring time, &c.

This carol they began that hour,   28
    With a hey, and a ho, and a hey nonino,
How that a life was but a flower
    In the spring time, &c.

And therefore take the present time,   32
    With a hey, and a ho, and a hey nonino;
For love is crowned with the prime
    In the spring time, &c.

Touch. Truly, young gentlemen, though there was no great matter in the ditty, yet the note was very untuneable.

First Page. You are deceived, sir: we kept time; we lost not our time.   40

Touch. By my troth, yes; I count it but time lost to hear such a foolish song. God be wi' you; and God mend your voices! Come, Audrey.
                                            [*Exeunt.*

SCENE IV.—*Another Part of the Forest.*

Enter DUKE *Senior,* AMIENS, JAQUES, ORLANDO, OLIVER, *and* CELIA.

Duke S. Dost thou believe, Orlando, that the boy
Can do all this that he hath promised?

Orl. I sometimes do believe, and sometimes do not;
As those that fear they hope, and know they fear.   4

Enter ROSALIND, SILVIUS, *and* PHEBE.

Ros. Patience once more, whiles our compact is urg'd.
[*To the* DUKE.] You say, if I bring in your Rosalind,
You will bestow her on Orlando here?

Duke S. That would I, had I kingdoms to give with her.   8

Ros. [*To* ORLANDO.] And you say, you will have her when I bring her?

Orl. That would I, were I of all kingdoms king.

Ros. [*To* PHEBE.] You say, that you'll marry me, if I be willing?

Phe. That will I, should I die the hour after.

Ros. But if you do refuse to marry me,   13
You'll give yourself to this most faithful shepherd?

Phe. So is the bargain.

Ros. [*To* SILVIUS.] You say, that you'll have Phebe, if she will?   16

Sil. Though to have her and death were both one thing.

Ros. I have promis'd to make all this matter even.
Keep you your word, O duke, to give your daughter;
You yours, Orlando, to receive his daughter; 20
Keep your word, Phebe, that you'll marry me,
Or else, refusing me, to wed this shepherd;
Keep your word, Silvius, that you'll marry her,
If she refuse me: and from hence I go,   24
To make these doubts all even.
                      [*Exeunt* ROSALIND *and* CELIA.

Duke S. I do remember in this shepherd boy
Some lively touches of my daughter's favour.

Orl. My lord, the first time that I ever saw him,   28
Methought he was a brother to your daughter;
But, my good lord, this boy is forest-born,
And hath been tutor'd in the rudiments
Of many desperate studies by his uncle,   32
Whom he reports to be a great magician,
Obscured in the circle of this forest.

Enter TOUCHSTONE *and* AUDREY.

Jaq. There is, sure, another flood toward, and these couples are coming to the ark. Here comes a pair of very strange beasts, which in all tongues are called fools.   38

Touch. Salutation and greeting to you all!

Jaq. Good my lord, bid him welcome. This is the motley-minded gentleman that I have so often met in the forest: he hath been a courtier, he swears.   43

Touch. If any man doubt that, let him put me to my purgation. I have trod a measure; I have flattered a lady; I have been politic with my friend, smooth with mine enemy; I have undone three tailors; I have had four quarrels, and like to have fought one.   49

Jaq. And how was that ta'en up?

Touch. Faith, we met, and found the quarrel
as upon the seventh cause. 52

Jaq. How seventh cause? Good my lord,
ke this fellow.

Duke S. I like him very well.

Touch. God 'ild you, sir; I desire you of the
ke. I press in here, sir, amongst the rest of
e country copulatives, to swear, and to forswear,
cording as marriage binds and blood breaks.
poor virgin, sir, an ill-favoured thing, sir, but
ine own: a poor humour of mine, sir, to take
at that no man else will. Rich honesty dwells
ke a miser, sir, in a poor house, as your pearl
your foul oyster. 64

Duke S. By my faith, he is very swift and
ntentious.

Touch. According to the fool's bolt, sir, and
ch dulcet diseases. 68

Jaq. But, for the seventh cause; how did you
id the quarrel on the seventh cause?

Touch. Upon a lie seven times removed:—
ear your body more seeming, Audrey:—as thus,
r. I did dislike the cut of a certain courtier's
eard: he sent me word, if I said his beard was
ot cut well, he was in the mind it was: this is
alled 'the retort courteous.' If I sent him word
gain, it was not well cut, he would send me
ord, he cut it to please himself: this is called
ie 'quip modest.' If again, it was not well cut,
e disabled my judgment: this is called the
eply churlish.' If again, it was not well cut, he
ould answer, I spake not true: this is called
ie 'reproof valiant:' if again, it was not well
it, he would say, I lie: this is called the
ountercheck quarrelsome': and so to the 'lie
rcumstantial,' and the 'lie direct.'

Jaq. And how oft did you say his beard was
ot well cut? 88

Touch. I durst go no further than the 'lie
rcumstantial,' nor he durst not give me the 'lie
irect;' and so we measured swords and parted.

Jaq. Can you nominate in order now the de-
rees of the lie? 93

Touch. O sir, we quarrel in print; by the
ook, as you have books for good manners: I
ill name you the degrees. The first, the 'retort
ourteous;' the second, the 'quip modest;' the
ird, the 'reply churlish;' the fourth, the 're-
roof valiant;' the fifth, the 'countercheck
uarrelsome;' the sixth, the 'lie with circum-
ance;' the seventh, the 'lie direct.' All these
ou may avoid but the lie direct; and you may
void that too, with an 'if.' I knew when seven
istices could not take up a quarrel; but when
ie parties were met themselves, one of them
ought but of an 'if,' as 'If you said so, then I
aid so;' and they shook hands and swore
rothers. Your 'if' is the only peace-maker;
uch virtue in 'if.' 109

Jaq. Is not this a rare fellow, my lord? he's
s good at any thing, and yet a fool.

Duke S. He uses his folly like a stalking-
orse, and under the presentation of that he
hoots his wit.

Enter HYMEN, *leading* ROSALIND *in woman's
clothes, and* CELIA.

Still Music.

Hym. *Then is there mirth in heaven,*
    When earthly things made even 116
        Atone together.
    Good duke, receive thy daughter;
    Hymen from heaven brought her;
        Yea, brought her hither, 120
    That thou mightst join her hand with his,
        Whose heart within her bosom is.

Ros. [*To* DUKE S.] To you I give myself, for
I am yours.

[*To* ORLANDO.] To you I give myself, for I am
yours. 124

Duke S. If there be truth in sight, you are
my daughter.

Orl. If there be truth in sight, you are my
Rosalind.

Phe. If sight and shape be true,
Why then, my love adieu! 128

Ros. [*To* DUKE S.] I'll have no father, if you
be not he.

[*To* ORLANDO.] I'll have no husband, if you be
not he:

[*To* PHEBE.] Nor ne'er wed woman, if you be not
she.

Hym. *Peace, ho! I bar confusion:* 132
    'Tis I must make conclusion
        Of these most strange events:
    Here's eight that must take hands
    To join in Hymen's bands, 136
        If truth holds true contents.

[*To* ORLANDO *and* ROSALIND.] You and
you no cross shall part:

[*To* OLIVER *and* CELIA.] You and you are
heart in heart:

[*To* PHEBE.] You to his love must accord,
Or have a woman to your lord: 141

[*To* TOUCHSTONE *and* AUDREY.] You and
you are sure together,
As the winter to foul weather.
Whiles a wedlock hymn we sing, 144
Feed yourselves with questioning,
That reason wonder may diminish,
How thus we met, and these things finish.

SONG

Wedding is great Juno's crown: 148
    O blessed bond of board and bed!
'Tis Hymen peoples every town;
    High wedlock then be honoured.
Honour, high honour, and renown, 152
To Hymen, god of every town!

Duke S. O my dear niece! welcome thou art
to me:
Even daughter, welcome in no less degree.

Phe. [*To* SILVIUS.] I will not eat my word,
now thou art mine; 156
Thy faith my fancy to thee doth combine.

Enter JAQUES DE BOYS.

Jaq. de B. Let me have audience for a word
or two:
I am the second son of old Sir Rowland,

That bring these tidings to this fair assembly.
Duke Frederick, hearing how that every day 161
Men of great worth resorted to this forest,
Address'd a mighty power, which were on foot
In his own conduct, purposely to take   164
His brother here and put him to the sword:
And to the skirts of this wild wood he came,
Where, meeting with an old religious man,
After some question with him, was converted 168
Both from his enterprise and from the world;
His crown bequeathing to his banish'd brother,
And all their lands restor'd to them again
That were with him exil'd. This to be true, 172
I do engage my life.

   Duke S.   Welcome, young man;
Thou offer'st fairly to thy brothers' wedding:
To one, his lands withheld; and to the other
A land itself at large, a potent dukedom. 176
First, in this forest, let us do those ends
That here were well begun and well begot;
And after, every of this happy number
That have endur'd shrewd days and nights with
   us,   180
Shall share the good of our returned fortune,
According to the measure of their states.
Meantime, forget this new-fall'n dignity,
And fall into our rustic revelry.   184
Play, music! and you, brides and bridegrooms
   all,
With measure heap'd in joy, to the measures fall.

   Jaq. Sir, by your patience. If I heard you
   rightly,
The duke hath put on a religious life,   188
And thrown into neglect the pompous court?

   Jaq. de B. He hath.

   Jaq. To him will I: out of these convertites
There is much matter to be heard and learn'd.
[*To* DUKE S.] You to your former honour I be-
   queath;   193
Your patience and your virtue well deserve it:
[*To* ORLANDO.] You to a love that your true
   faith doth merit:
[*To* OLIVER.] You to your land, and love, and
   great allies: 196

[*To* SILVIUS.] You to a long and well-deserved
   bed:
[*To* TOUCHSTONE.] And you to wrangling; fo
   thy loving voyage
Is but for two months victual'd. So, to you
   pleasures:
I am for other than for dancing measures. 20

   Duke S. Stay, Jaques, stay.

   Jaq. To see no pastime, I: what you woul
   have
I'll stay to know at your abandon'd cave. [*Exi*

   Duke S. Proceed, proceed: we will begi
   these rites,   20
As we do trust they'll end, in true delights.

                        [*A dance. Exeun*

EPILOGUE

SPOKEN BY ROSALIND.

   *It is not the fashion to see the lady th
epilogue; but it is no more unhandsome tha
to see the lord the prologue. If it be true tha
good wine needs no bush, 'tis true that a goo
play needs no epilogue; yet to good wine the
do use good bushes, and good plays prove th
better by the help of good epilogues. What
case am I in then, that am neither a good epi
logue, nor cannot insinuate with you in the be
half of a good play! I am not furnished like
beggar, therefore to beg will not become me: m
way is, to conjure you; and I'll begin with th
women. I charge you, O women! for the lov
you bear to men, to like as much of this play a
please you: and I charge you, O men! for th
love you bear to women,—as I perceive by you
simpering none of you hate them,—that betwee
you and the women, the play may please. If
were a woman I would kiss as many of you a
had beards that pleased me, complexions tha
liked me, and breaths that I defied not; and
I am sure, as many as have good beards, o
good faces, or sweet breaths, will, for my kin
offer, when I make curtsy, bid me farewell.*

                                  [*Exeun*

THE TAMING OF THE SHREW

DRAMATIS PERSONÆ

Lord.
CHRISTOPHER SLY, a Tinker. } Persons in the
Hostess, Page, Players, Huntsmen, and } Induction.
   Servants.
BAPTISTA, a rich Gentleman of Padua.
VINCENTIO, an old Gentleman of Pisa.
LUCENTIO, son to Vincentio; in love with Bianca.
PETRUCHIO, a Gentleman of Verona; Suitor to Katharina.
GREMIO, } Suitors to Bianca.
HORTENSIO, }

TRANIO, } Servants to Lucentio.
BIONDELLO, }
GRUMIO, } Servants to Petruchio.
CURTIS, }
Pedant, set up to personate Vincentio.

KATHARINA, the Shrew, } Daughters to Baptista.
BIANCA, }
Widow.

Tailor, Haberdasher, and Servants attending on Baptista
   and Petruchio.

SCENE.—*Sometimes in Padua; and sometimes in* PETRUCHIO'S *House in the Country.*

INDUCTION

SCENE I.—*Before an Alehouse on a Heath.*

Enter Hostess *and* SLY.

Sly. I'll pheeze you, in faith.
Host. A pair of stocks, you rogue!
Sly. Y'are a baggage: the Slys are no rogues; look in the chronicles; we came in with Richard Conqueror. Therefore, *paucas pallabris;* let the world slide! Sessa!
Host. You will not pay for the glasses you have burst?   8
Sly. No, not a denier. Go by, Jeronimy, go to thy cold bed, and warm thee.
Host. I know my remedy: I must go fetch the third-borough.   [*Exit.*
Sly. Third, or fourth, or fifth borough, I'll answer him by law. I'll not budge an inch, boy: let him come, and kindly.

[*Lies down on the ground, and falls asleep.*

Horns winded. Enter a Lord *from hunting, with* Huntsmen *and* Servants.

Lord. Huntsman, I charge thee, tender well my hounds: 16
Brach Merriman, the poor cur is emboss'd,
And couple Clowder with the deep-mouth'd brach.
Saw'st thou not, boy, how Silver made it good
At the hedge-corner, in the coldest fault?   20
I would not lose the dog for twenty pound.
First Hunt. Why, Bellman is as good as he, my lord;
He cried upon it at the merest loss,
And twice to-day pick'd out the dullest scent:
Trust me, I take him for the better dog.   25
Lord. Thou art a fool: if Echo were as fleet,
I would esteem him worth a dozen such.
But sup them well, and look unto them all: 28
To-morrow I intend to hunt again.
First Hunt. I will, my lord.
Lord. [*Sees* SLY.] What's here? one dead, or drunk? See, doth he breathe?
Sec. Hunt. He breathes, my lord. Were he not warm'd with ale,   32

This were a bed but cold to sleep so soundly.
Lord. O monstrous beast! how like a swine he lies!
Grim death, how foul and loathsome is thine image!
Sirs, I will practise on this drunken man.   36
What think you, if he were convey'd to bed,
Wrapp'd in sweet clothes, rings put upon his fingers,
A most delicious banquet by his bed,
And brave attendants near him when he wakes,
Would not the beggar then forget himself?   41
First Hunt. Believe me, lord, I think he cannot choose.
Sec. Hunt. It would seem strange unto him when he wak'd.
Lord. Even as a flattering dream or worthless fancy.   44
Then take him up and manage well the jest.
Carry him gently to my fairest chamber,
And hang it round with all my wanton pictures;
Balm his foul head in warm distilled waters,   48
And burn sweet wood to make the lodging sweet.
Procure me music ready when he wakes,
To make a dulcet and a heavenly sound;
And if he chance to speak, be ready straight,   52
And with a low submissive reverence
Say, 'What is it your honour will command?'
Let one attend him with a silver basin
Full of rose-water, and bestrew'd with flowers;
Another bear the ewer, the third a diaper,   57
And say, 'Will't please your lordship cool your hands?'
Some one be ready with a costly suit,
And ask him what apparel he will wear;   60
Another tell him of his hounds and horse,
And that his lady mourns at his disease.
Persuade him that he hath been lunatic;
And, when he says he is——say that he dreams,   64
For he is nothing but a mighty lord.
This do, and do it kindly, gentle sirs:
It will be pastime passing excellent,
If it be husbanded with modesty.   68

First Hunt. My lord, I warrant you we will
play our part,
As he shall think, by our true diligence,
He is no less than what we say he is.
Lord. Take him up gently, and to bed with
him, 72
And each one to his office when he wakes.

[SLY *is borne out. A trumpet sounds.*
Sirrah, go see what trumpet 'tis that sounds:

[*Exit* Servant.
Belike, some noble gentleman that means,
Travelling some journey, to repose him here. 76

Re-enter Servant.

How now! who is it?
Serv. An it please your honour,
Players that offer service to your lordship.
Lord. Bid them come near.

Enter Players.

Now, fellows, you are welcome.
Players. We thank your honour. 80
Lord. Do you intend to stay with me to-
night?
A Player. So please your lordship to accept
our duty.
Lord. With all my heart. This fellow I re-
member,
Since once he play'd a farmer's eldest son: 84
'Twas where you woo'd the gentlewoman so
well.
I have forgot your name; but, sure, that part
Was aptly fitted and naturally perform'd.
A Player. I think 'twas Soto that your honour
means. 88
Lord. 'Tis very true: thou didst it excellent.
Well, you are come to me in happy time,
The rather for I have some sport in hand
Wherein your cunning can assist me much. 92
There is a lord will hear you play to-night;
But I am doubtful of your modesties,
Lest, over-eyeing of his odd behaviour,—
For yet his honour never heard a play,— 96
You break into some merry passion
And so offend him; for I tell you, sirs,
If you should smile he grows impatient.
A Player. Fear not, my lord: we can con-
tain ourselves 100
Were he the veriest antick in the world.
Lord. Go, sirrah, take them to the buttery,
And give them friendly welcome every one:
Let them want nothing that my house affords.

[*Exeunt one with the Players.*
Sirrah, go you to Barthol'mew my page, 105
And see him dress'd in all suits like a lady:
That done, conduct him to the drunkard's
chamber;
And call him 'madam,' do him obeisance. 108
Tell him from me,—as he will win my love,—
He bear himself with honourable action,
Such as he hath observ'd in noble ladies
Unto their lords, by them accomplished: 112
Such duty to the drunkard let him do
With soft low tongue and lowly courtesy;
And say, 'What is't your honour will com-
mand,

Wherein your lady and your humble wife 11
May show her duty, and make known he
love?'
And then, with kind embracements, temptin
kisses,
And with declining head into his bosom,
Bid him shed tears, as being overjoy'd 12
To see her noble lord restor'd to health,
Who for this seven years hath esteemed him
No better than a poor and loathsome begga
And if the boy have not a woman's gift 12
To rain a shower of commanded tears,
An onion will do well for such a shift,
Which in a napkin being close convey'd
Shall in despite enforce a watery eye. 12
See this dispatch'd with all the haste thou canst
Anon I'll give thee more instructions.

[*Exit* Servan
I know the boy will well usurp the grace,
Voice, gait, and action of a gentlewoman: 13
I long to hear him call the drunkard husbanc
And how my men will stay themselves fron
laughter
When they do homage to this simple peasan
I'll in to counsel them: haply, my presence 13
May well abate the over merry spleen
Which otherwise would grow into extremes.

[*Exeun*

SCENE II.—*A Bedchamber in the* Lord's *House*
SLY *is discovered in a rich nightgown, wit*
Attendants: *some with apparel, others wit*
basin, ewer, and other appurtenances; an
Lord, *dressed like a servant.*

Sly. For God's sake! a pot of small ale.
First Serv. Will't please your lordship drin}
a cup of sack?
Sec. Serv. Will't please your honour taste o
these conserves?
Third Serv. What raiment will your honou
wear to-day?
Sly. I am Christophero Sly; call not me ho
nour, nor lordship: I ne'er drank sack in m
life; and if you give me any conserves, give m
conserves of beef. Ne'er ask me what raimen
I'll wear, for I have no more doublets tha
backs, no more stockings than legs, nor no mor
shoes than feet: nay, sometime more feet tha
shoes, or such shoes as my toes look throug}
the overleather. 1
Lord. Heaven cease this idle humour in you
honour!
O, that a mighty man, of such descent,
Of such possessions, and so high esteem, 1
Should be infused with so foul a spirit!
Sly. What! would you make me mad? An
not I Christopher Sly, old Sly's son, of Burton
heath; by birth a pedlar, by education a card
maker, by transmutation a bear-herd, and nov
by present profession a tinker? Ask Maria
Hacket, the fat ale-wife of Wincot, if she knov
me not: if she say I am not fourteen pence o
the score for sheer ale, score me up for th
lyingest knave in Christendom. What! I an
not bestraught: here's—

First Serv. O! this it is that makes your lady mourn.   28

Sec. Serv. O! this it is that makes your servants droop.

Lord. Hence comes it that your kindred shuns your house,

As beaten hence by your strange lunacy.

O noble lord, bethink thee of thy birth,   32

Call home thy ancient thoughts from banishment,

And banish hence these abject lowly dreams.

Look how thy servants do attend on thee,

Each in his office ready at thy beck: 36

Wilt thou have music? hark! Apollo plays,

[*Music.*

And twenty caged nightingales do sing:

Or wilt thou sleep? we'll have thee to a couch

Softer and sweeter than the lustful bed   40

On purpose trimm'd up for Semiramis.

Say thou wilt walk, we will bestrew the ground:

Or wilt thou ride? thy horses shall be trapp'd,

Their harness studded all with gold and pearl.

Dost thou love hawking? thou hast hawks will soar   45

Above the morning lark: or wilt thou hunt?

Thy hounds shall make the welkin answer them,

And fetch shrill echoes from the hollow earth. 48

First Serv. Say thou wilt course; thy greyhounds are as swift

As breathed stags, ay, fleeter than the roe.

Sec. Serv. Dost thou love pictures? we will fetch thee straight

Adonis painted by a running brook,   52

And Cytherea all in sedges hid,

Which seem to move and wanton with her breath,

Even as the waving sedges play with wind.

Lord. We'll show thee Io as she was a maid,

And how she was beguiled and surpris'd,   57

As lively painted as the deed was done.

Third Serv. Or Daphne roaming through a thorny wood,

Scratching her legs that one shall swear she bleeds;   60

And at that sight shall sad Apollo weep,

So workmanly the blood and tears are drawn.

Lord. Thou art a lord and nothing but a lord:

Thou hast a lady far more beautiful   64

Than any woman in this waning age.

First Serv. And till the tears that she hath shed for thee

Like envious floods o'er-run her lovely face,

She was the fairest creature in the world;   68

And yet she is inferior to none.

Sly. Am I a lord? and have I such a lady?

Or do I dream? or have I dream'd till now?

I do not sleep; I see, I hear, I speak;   72

I smell sweet savours, and I feel soft things:

Upon my life, I am a lord indeed;

And not a tinker, nor Christophero Sly.

Well, bring our lady hither to our sight;   76

And once again, a pot o' the smallest ale.

Sec. Serv. Will't please your mightiness to wash your hands?

[*Servants present a ewer, basin, and napkin.*

O, how we joy to see your wit restor'd!

O, that once more you knew but what you are!

These fifteen years you have been in a dream, 81

Or, when you wak'd, so wak'd as if you slept.

Sly. These fifteen years! by my fay, a goodly nap.

But did I never speak of all that time?   84

First Serv. O! yes, my lord, but very idle words;

For though you lay here in this goodly chamber,

Yet would you say ye were beaten out of door,

And rail upon the hostess of the house,   88

And say you would present her at the leet,

Because she brought stone jugs and no seal'd quarts.

Sometimes you would call out for Cicely Hacket.

Sly. Ay, the woman's maid of the house.   92

Third Serv. Why, sir, you know no house, nor no such maid,

Nor no such men as you have reckon'd up,

As Stephen Sly, and old John Naps of Greece,

And Peter Turf, and Henry Pimpernell,   96

And twenty more such names and men as these,

Which never were nor no man ever saw.

Sly. Now, Lord be thanked for my good amends!

All. Amen.   100

Sly. I thank thee; thou shalt not lose by it.

Enter the Page, *as a lady, with* Attendants.

Page. How fares my noble lord?

Sly. Marry, I fare well, for here is cheer enough.

Where is my wife?   104

Page. Here, noble lord: what is thy will with her?

Sly. Are you my wife, and will not call me husband?

My men should call me lord: I am your goodman.

Page. My husband and my lord, my lord and husband;   108

I am your wife in all obedience.

Sly. I know it well. What must I call her?

Lord. Madam.

Sly. Al'ce madam, or Joan madam?   112

Lord. Madam, and nothing else: so lords call ladies.

Sly. Madam wife, they say that I have dream'd

And slept above some fifteen year or more.

Page. Ay, and the time seems thirty unto me,

Being all this time abandon'd from your bed. 117

Sly. 'Tis much. Servants, leave me and her alone.

Madam, undress you, and come now to bed.

Page. Thrice noble lord, let me entreat of you

To pardon me yet for a night or two,   121

Or, if not so, until the sun be set:

For your physicians have expressly charg'd,

In peril to incur your former malady,   124

That I should yet absent me from your bed:

I hope this reason stands for my excuse.

Sly. Ay, it stands so, that I may hardly tarry

so long; but I would be loath to fall into my

dreams again: I will therefore tarry, in spite of

the flesh and the blood.

Enter a Servant.

Serv. Your honour's players, hearing your amendment,
Are come to play a pleasant comedy; 132
For so your doctors hold it very meet,
Seeing too much sadness hath congeal'd your blood,
And melancholy is the nurse of frenzy:
Therefore they thought it good you hear a play,
And frame your mind to mirth and merriment,
Which bars a thousand harms and lengthens life.

Sly. Marry, I will; let them play it. Is not a commonty a Christmas gambold or a tumbling-trick? 141

Page. No, my good lord; it is more pleasing stuff.

Sly. What! household stuff?

Page. It is a kind of history. 144

Sly. Well, we'll see't. Come, madam wife, sit by my side,
And let the world slip: we shall ne'er be younger.
[*Flourish.*

ACT I

Scene I.—*Padua. A public Place.*

Enter LUCENTIO *and* TRANIO.

Luc. Tranio, since for the great desire I had
To see fair Padua, nursery of arts,
I am arriv'd for fruitful Lombardy,
The pleasant garden of great Italy; 4
And by my father's love and leave am arm'd
With his good will and thy good company,
My trusty servant well approv'd in all,
Here let us breathe, and haply institute 8
A course of learning and ingenious studies.
Pisa, renowned for grave citizens,
Gave me my being and my father first,
A merchant of great traffic through the world,
Vincentio, come of the Bentivolii. 13
Vincentio's son, brought up in Florence,
It shall become to serve all hopes conceiv'd,
To deck his fortune with his virtuous deeds: 16
And therefore, Tranio, for the time I study,
Virtue and that part of philosophy
Will I apply that treats of happiness
By virtue specially to be achiev'd. 20
Tell me thy mind; for I have Pisa left
And am to Padua come, as he that leaves
A shallow plash to plunge him in the deep,
And with satiety seeks to quench his thirst. 24

Tra. Mi perdonate, gentle master mine,
I am in all affected as yourself,
Glad that you thus continue your resolve
To suck the sweets of sweet philosophy. 28
Only, good master, while we do admire
This virtue and this moral discipline,
Let's be no stoics nor no stocks, I pray;
Or so devote to Aristotle's checks 32
As Ovid be an outcast quite abjur'd.
Balk logic with acquaintance that you have,
And practise rhetoric in your common talk;
Music and poesy use to quicken you;
The mathematics and the metaphysics,
Fall to them as you find your stomach serve you;
No profit grows where is no pleasure ta'en:
In brief, sir, study what you most affect.

Luc. Gramercies, Tranio, well dost thou advise.
If, Biondello, thou wert come ashore,
We could at once put us in readiness,
And take a lodging fit to entertain
Such friends as time in Padua shall beget.
But stay awhile: what company is this?

Tra. Master, some show to welcome us town.

Enter BAPTISTA, KATHARINA, BIANCA, GREMIO *and* HORTENSIO. LUCENTIO *and* TRANIO *star aside.*

Bap. Gentlemen, importune me no furthe
For how I firmly am resolv'd you know;
That is, not to bestow my youngest daughter
Before I have a husband for the elder.
If either of you both love Katharina,
Because I know you well and love you well,
Leave shall you have to court her at your plea sure.

Gre. To cart her rather: she's too rough for me.

There, there, Hortensio, will you any wife?

Kath. [*To* BAPTISTA.] I pray you, sir, is your will
To make a stale of me amongst these mates

Hor. Mates, maid! how mean you that? n mates for you,
Unless you were of gentler, milder mould.

Kath. I' faith, sir, you shall never need fear:
I wis it is not half way to her heart;
But if it were, doubt not her care should be
To comb your noddle with a three-legg'd stoc
And paint your face, and use you like a fool.

Hor. From all such devils, good Lord deliv us!

Gre. And me too, good Lord!

Tra. Hush, master! here is some good pa time toward:
That wench is stark mad or wonderful frowar

Luc. But in the other's silence do I see
Maid's mild behaviour and sobriety.
Peace, Tranio!

Tra. Well said, master; mum! and gaze yo fill.

Bap. Gentlemen, that I may soon make goo
What I have said,—Bianca, get you in:
And let it not displease thee, good Bianca,
For I will love thee ne'er the less, my girl.

Kath. A pretty peat! it is best
Put finger in the eye, an she knew why.

Bian. Sister, content you in my discontent
Sir, to your pleasure humbly I subscribe:
My books and instruments shall be my com pany,
On them to look and practise by myself.

Luc. Hark, Tranio! thou mayst hear Minerv speak.

Hor. Signior Baptista, will you be so strange?
Sorry am I that our good will effects
Bianca's grief.
Gre.   Why will you mew her up,
Signior Baptista, for this fiend of hell,   88
And make her bear the penance of her tongue?
Bap. Gentlemen, content ye; I am resolv'd.
Go in, Bianca.   [*Exit* BIANCA.
And for I know she taketh most delight   92
In music, instruments, and poetry,
Schoolmasters will I keep within my house,
Fit to instruct her youth. If you, Hortensio,
Or Signior Gremio, you, know any such,   96
Prefer them hither; for to cunning men
I will be very kind, and liberal
To mine own children in good bringing up;
And so, farewell. Katharina, you may stay; 100
For I have more to commune with Bianca.
                                        [*Exit.*
Kath. Why, and I trust I may go too; may I
not?
What! shall I be appointed hours, as though,
belike,   103
I knew not what to take, and what to leave?
Ha!   [*Exit.*
Gre. You may go to the devil's dam: your
gifts are so good, here's none will hold you.
Their love is not so great, Hortensio, but we
may blow our nails together, and fast it fairly
out: our cake's dough on both sides. Farewell:
yet, for the love I bear my sweet Bianca, if I
can by any means light on a fit man to teach
her that wherein she delights, I will wish him to
her father.   113
Hor. So will I, Signior Gremio: but a word,
I pray. Though the nature of our quarrel yet
never brooked parle, know now, upon advice, it
toucheth us both,—that we may yet again have
access to our fair mistress and be happy rivals
in Bianca's love,—to labour and effect one
thing specially.   120
Gre. What's that, I pray?
Hor. Marry, sir, to get a husband for her
sister.
Gre. A husband! a devil.   124
Hor. I say, a husband.
Gre. I say, a devil. Thinkest thou, Hortensio,
though her father be very rich, any man is so
very a fool to be married to hell?   128
Hor. Tush, Gremio! though it pass your
patience and mine to endure her loud alarums,
why, man, there be good fellows in the world,
an a man could light on them, would take her
with all faults, and money enough.   133
Gre. I cannot tell; but I had as lief take her
dowry with this condition, to be whipped at the
high-cross every morning.   136
Hor. Faith, as you say, there's small choice
in rotten apples. But, come; since this bar in
law makes us friends, it shall be so far forth
friendly maintained, till by helping Baptista's
eldest daughter to a husband, we set his youngest
free for a husband, and then have to't afresh.
Sweet Bianca! Happy man be his dole! He
that runs fastest gets the ring. How say you,
Signior Gremio?   145

Gre. I am agreed: and would I had given him
the best horse in Padua to begin his wooing,
that would thoroughly woo her, wed her, and
bed her, and rid the house of her. Come on. 149
                    [*Exeunt* GREMIO *and* HORTENSIO.
Tra. I pray, sir, tell me, is it possible
That love should of a sudden take such hold?
Luc. O Tranio! till I found it to be true, 152
I never thought it possible or likely;
But see, while idly I stood looking on,
I found the effect of love in idleness;
And now in plainness do confess to thee, 156
That art to me as secret and as dear
As Anna to the Queen of Carthage was,
Tranio, I burn, I pine, I perish, Tranio,
If I achieve not this young modest girl.   160
Counsel me, Tranio, for I know thou canst:
Assist me, Tranio, for I know thou wilt.
Tra. Master, it is no time to chide you now;
Affection is not rated from the heart: 164
If love have touch'd you, nought remains but so,
Redime te captum, quam queas minimo.
Luc. Gramercies, lad; go forward: this con-
tents: 167
The rest will comfort, for thy counsel's sound.
Tra. Master, you look'd so longly on the
maid,
Perhaps you mark'd not what's the pith of all.
Luc. O yes, I saw sweet beauty in her face,
Such as the daughter of Agenor had,   172
That made great Jove to humble him to her
hand,
When with his knees he kiss'd the Cretan strand.
Tra. Saw you no more? mark'd you not how
her sister
Began to scold and raise up such a storm 176
That mortal ears might hardly endure the din?
Luc. Tranio, I saw her coral lips to move,
And with her breath she did perfume the air;
Sacred and sweet was all I saw in her.   180
Tra. Nay, then, 'tis time to stir him from his
trance.
I pray, awake, sir: if you love the maid,
Bend thoughts and wits to achieve her. Thus it
stands:
Her elder sister is so curst and shrewd,   184
That till the father rids his hands of her,
Master, your love must live a maid at home;
And therefore has he closely mew'd her up, 187
Because she will not be annoy'd with suitors.
Luc. Ah, Tranio, what a cruel father's he!
But art thou not advis'd he took some care
To get her cunning schoolmasters to instruct
her?
Tra. Ay, marry, am I, sir; and now 'tis
plotted.   192
Luc. I have it, Tranio.
Tra.   Master, for my hand,
Both our inventions meet and jump in one.
Luc. Tell me thine first.
Tra.   You will be schoolmaster,
And undertake the teaching of the maid: 196
That's your device.
Luc.   It is: may it be done?
Tra. Not possible; for who shall bear your
part,

And be in Padua here Vincentio's son?
Keep house and ply his book, welcome his
   friends;   200
Visit his countrymen, and banquet them?
  Luc. Basta; content thee; for I have it full.
We have not yet been seen in any house,
Nor can we be distinguish'd by our faces   204
For man, or master: then, it follows thus:
Thou shalt be master, Tranio, in my stead,
Keep house, and port, and servants, as I should:
I will some other be; some Florentine,   208
Some Neapolitan, or meaner man of Pisa.
'Tis hatch'd and shall be so: Tranio, at once
Uncase thee, take my colour'd hat and cloak:
When Biondello comes, he waits on thee; 212
But I will charm him first to keep his tongue.
               [They exchange habits.
  Tra. So had you need.
In brief then, sir, sith it your pleasure is,
And I am tied to be obedient;   216
For so your father charg'd me at our parting,
'Be serviceable to my son,' quoth he,
Although I think 'twas in another sense:
I am content to be Lucentio,   220
Because so well I love Lucentio.
  Luc. Tranio, be so, because Lucentio loves;
And let me be a slave, to achieve that maid
Whose sudden sight hath thrall'd my wounded
   eye.   224
Here comes the rogue.

       Enter BIONDELLO.

       Sirrah, where have you been?
  Bion. Where have I been! Nay, how now!
where are you?
Master, has my fellow Tranio stol'n your
  clothes,
Or you stol'n his? or both? pray, what's the
  news?   228
  Luc. Sirrah, come hither: 'tis no time to jest,
And therefore frame your manners to the time.
Your fellow Tranio, here, to save my life,
Puts my apparel and my countenance on, 232
And I for my escape have put on his;
For in a quarrel since I came ashore
I kill'd a man, and fear I was descried.
Wait you on him, I charge you, as becomes, 236
While I make way from hence to save my life:
You understand me?
  Bion.   I, sir! ne'er a whit.
  Luc. And not a jot of Tranio in your mouth:
Tranio is changed to Lucentio.   240
  Bion. The better for him: would I were so
  too!
  Tra. So would I, faith, boy, to have the next
  wish after,
That Lucentio indeed had Baptista's youngest
  daughter.
But, sirrah, not for my sake, but your master's,
  I advise   244
You use your manners discreetly in all kind of
  companies:
When I am alone, why, then I am Tranio;
But in all places else your master, Lucentio.
  Luc. Tranio, let's go. One thing more rests,
that thyself execute, to make one among these

wooers: if thou ask me why, sufficeth my reasons are both good and weighty.   *[Exeunt.*

     The Presenters above speak.

  First Serv. My lord, you nod; you do not
  mind the play.   252
  Sly. Yes, by Saint Anne, I do. A good matter,
surely: comes there any more of it?
  Page. My lord, 'tis but begun.
  Sly. 'Tis a very excellent piece of work,
madam lady: would 'twere done!   257
               [They sit and mark.

SCENE II.—*The Same. Before* HORTENSIO'S
           House.

   Enter PETRUCHIO *and* GRUMIO.

  Pet. Verona, for awhile I take my leave,
To see my friends in Padua; but, of all
My best beloved and approved friend,
Hortensio; and I trow this is his house.   4
Here, sirrah Grumio; knock, I say.
  Gru. Knock, sir! whom should I knock? is
there any man has rebused your worship?
  Pet. Villain, I say, knock me here soundly. 8
  Gru. Knock you here, sir! why, sir, what am
I, sir, that I should knock you here, sir?
  Pet. Villain, I say, knock me at this gate;
And rap me well, or I'll knock your knave's
  pate.   12
  Gru. My master is grown quarrelsome. I
  should knock you first,
And then I know after who comes by the worst.
  Pet. Will it not be?
Faith, sirrah, an you'll not knock, I'll ring it;
I'll try how you can *sol, fa,* and sing it. 17
         [He wrings GRUMIO *by the ears.*
  Gru. Help, masters, help! my master is mad.
  Pet. Now, knock when I bid you, sirrah
  villain!

       Enter HORTENSIO.

  Hor. How now! what's the matter? My old
friend Grumio! and my good friend Petruchio!
How do you all at Verona?
  Pet. Signior Hortensio, come you to part the
  fray?
Con tutto il cuore ben trovato, may I say. 2
  *Hor. Alla nostra casa ben venuto; molto
honorato signior mio Petruchio.*
Rise, Grumio, rise: we will compound this
  quarrel.
  Gru. Nay, 'tis no matter, sir, what he 'leges in
Latin. If this be not a lawful cause for me to
leave his service, look you, sir, he bid me knock
him and rap him soundly, sir: well, was it fit for
a servant to use his master so; being, perhaps,
for aught I see, two-and-thirty, a pip out?
Whom would to God, I had well knock'd at
  first,
Then had not Grumio come by the worst.
  Pet. A senseless villain! Good Hortensio,
I bade the rascal knock upon your gate,
And could not get him for my heart to do it.
  Gru. Knock at the gate! O heavens! Spak

ou not these words plain, 'Sirrah, knock me
ere, rap me here, knock me well, and knock me
oundly?' And come you now with 'knocking
t the gate?' 43

Pet. Sirrah, be gone, or talk not, I advise you.

Hor. Petruchio, patience; I am Grumio's
pledge. 45

Vhy, this's a heavy chance 'twixt him and you,
our ancient, trusty, pleasant servant Grumio.

And tell me now, sweet friend, what happy gale
Blows you to Padua here from old Verona? 49

Pet. Such wind as scatters young men through
the world
To seek their fortunes further than at home,
Where small experience grows. But in a few, 52
Signior Hortensio, thus it stands with me:
Antonio, my father, is deceas'd,
And I have thrust myself into this maze,
Haply to wive and thrive as best I may. 56
Crowns in my purse I have and goods at home,
And so am come abroad to see the world.

Hor. Petruchio, shall I then come roundly
to thee,
And wish thee to a shrewd ill-favour'd wife? 60
Thou'dst thank me but a little for my counsel;
And yet I'll promise thee she shall be rich,
And very rich: but thou 'rt too much my friend,
And I'll not wish thee to her. 64

Pet. Signior Hortensio, 'twixt such friends
as we,
ew words suffice; and therefore, if thou know
One rich enough to be Petruchio's wife,
As wealth is burden of my wooing dance, 68
Be she as foul as was Florentius' love,
As old as Sibyl, and as curst and shrewd
As Socrates' Xanthippe, or a worse,
She moves me not, or not removes, at least, 72
Affection's edge in me, were she as rough
As are the swelling Adriatic seas:
come to wive it wealthily in Padua;
f wealthily, then happily in Padua. 76

Gru. Nay, look you, sir, he tells you flatly
what his mind is: why, give him gold enough
and marry him to a puppet or an aglet-baby;
or an old trot with ne'er a tooth in her head,
hough she have as many diseases as two-and-
ifty horses: why, nothing comes amiss, so
noney comes withal.

Hor. Petruchio, since we are stepp'd thus
far in, 84
will continue that I broach'd in jest.
can, Petruchio, help thee to a wife
With wealth enough, and young and beauteous,
Brought up as best becomes a gentlewoman: 88
Her only fault,—and that is faults enough,—
s, that she is intolerable curst
And shrewd and froward, so beyond all measure,
That, were my state far worser than it is, 92
I would not wed her for a mine of gold.

Pet. Hortensio, peace! thou know'st not
gold's effect:
Tell me her father's name, and 'tis enough;
For I will board her, though she chide as loud
As thunder when the clouds in autumn crack.

Hor. Her father is Baptista Minola, 98
An affable and courteous gentleman;

Her name is Katharina Minola, 100
Renown'd in Padua for her scolding tongue.

Pet. I know her father, though I know not
her;
And he knew my deceased father well.
I will not sleep, Hortensio, till I see her; 104
And therefore let me be thus bold with you,
To give you over at this first encounter,
Unless you will accompany me thither.

Gru. I pray you, sir, let him go while the
humour lasts. O' my word, an she knew him as
well as I do, she would think scolding would do
little good upon him. She may, perhaps, call
him half a score knaves or so: why, that's
nothing: an he begin once, he'll rail in his rope-
tricks. I'll tell you what, sir, an she stand him
but a little, he will throw a figure in her face,
and so disfigure her with it that she shall have
no more eyes to see withal than a cat. You
know him not, sir.

Hor. Tarry, Petruchio, I must go with thee,
For in Baptista's keep my treasure is: 120
He hath the jewel of my life in hold,
His youngest daughter, beautiful Bianca,
And her withholds from me and other more,
Suitors to her and rivals in my love; 124
Supposing it a thing impossible,
For those defects I have before rehears'd,
That ever Katharina will be woo'd:
Therefore this order hath Baptista ta'en, 128
That none shall have access unto Bianca,
Till Katharine the curst have got a husband.

Gru. Katharine the curst!
A title for a maid of all titles the worst. 132

Hor. Now shall my friend Petruchio do me
grace,
And offer me, disguis'd in sober robes,
To old Baptista as a schoolmaster
Well seen in music, to instruct Bianca; 136
That so I may, by this device, at least
Have leave and leisure to make love to her,
And unsuspected court her by herself.

Gru. Here's no knavery! See, to beguile the
old folks, how the young folks lay their heads
together!

Enter GREMIO, *and* LUCENTIO *disguised, with
books under his arm.*

Master, master, look about you: who goes there,
ha? 144

Hor. Peace, Grumio! 'tis the rival of my
love.

Petruchio, stand by awhile.

Gru. A proper stripling, and an amorous!

Gre. O! very well; I have perus'd the note.
Hark you, sir; I'll have them very fairly bound:
All books of love, see that at any hand,
And see you read no other lectures to her.
You understand me. Over and beside 152
Signior Baptista's liberality,
I'll mend it with a largess. Take your papers
too,
And let me have them very well perfum'd;
For she is sweeter than perfume itself 156
To whom they go to. What will you read to
her?

I

Luc. Whate'er I read to her, I'll plead for
    you,
As for my patron, stand you so assur'd,
As firmly as yourself were still in place;   160
Yea, and perhaps with more successful words
Than you, unless you were a scholar, sir.
    Gre. O! this learning, what a thing it is.
    Gru. O! this woodcock, what an ass it is. 164
    Pet. Peace, sirrah!
    Hor. Grumio, mum! God save you, Signior
    Gremio!
    Gre. And you're well met, Signior Hortensio.
Trow you whither I am going? To Baptista
    Minola.   168
I promis'd to inquire carefully
About a schoolmaster for the fair Bianca;
And, by good fortune, I have lighted well
On this young man; for learning and behaviour
Fit for her turn; well read in poetry   173
And other books, good ones, I warrant ye.
    Hor. 'Tis well: and I have met a gentleman
Hath promis'd me to help me to another,   176
A fine musician to instruct our mistress:
So shall I no whit be behind in duty
To fair Bianca, so belov'd of me.
    Gre. Belov'd of me, and that my deeds shall
    prove.   180
    Gru. [*Aside.*] And that his bags shall prove.
    Hor. Gremio, 'tis now no time to vent our
    love:
Listen to me, and if you speak me fair,
I'll tell you news indifferent good for either. 184
Here is a gentleman whom by chance I met,
Upon agreement from us to his liking,
Will undertake to woo curst Katharine.
Yea, and to marry her, if her dowry please. 188
    Gre. So said, so done, is well.
Hortensio, have you told him all her faults?
    Pet. I know she is an irksome, brawling
    scold:
If that be all, masters, I hear no harm.   192
    Gre. No, sayst me so, friend? What country-
    man?
    Pet. Born in Verona, old Antonio's son:
My father dead, my fortune lives for me;
And I do hope good days and long to see.   196
    Gre. O, sir, such a life, with such a wife, were
    strange!
But if you have a stomach, to't i' God's name:
You shall have me assisting you in all.
But will you woo this wild-cat?
    Pet.   Will I live? 200
    Gru. Will he woo her? ay, or I'll hang her.
    Pet. Why came I hither but to that intent?
Think you a little din can daunt mine ears?
Have I not in my time heard lions roar?   204
Have I not heard the sea, puff'd up with winds,
Rage like an angry boar chafed with sweat?
Have I not heard great ordnance in the field,
And heaven's artillery thunder in the skies? 208
Have I not in a pitched battle heard
Loud 'larums, neighing steeds, and trumpets'
    clang?
And do you tell me of a woman's tongue,
That gives not half so great a blow to hear 212
As will a chestnut in a farmer's fire?

Tush, tush! fear boys with bugs.
    Gru.   [*Aside.*] For he fears none
    Gre. Hortensio, hark:
This gentleman is happily arriv'd,   21
My mind presumes, for his own good and ours
    Hor. I promis'd we would be contributors,
And bear his charge of wooing, whatsoe'er.
    Gre. And so we will, provided that he wi
    her.   22
    Gru. [*Aside.*] I would I were as sure of a goo
    dinner.

Enter TRANIO, *bravely apparelled; and*
    BIONDELLO.

    Tra. Gentlemen, God save you! If I ma
    be bold,
Tell me, I beseech you, which is the readiest wa
To the house of Signior Baptista Minola?   22
    Bion. He that has the two fair daughters
    is't he you mean?
    Tra. Even he, Biondello!
    Gre. Hark you, sir; you mean not her to—
    Tra. Perhaps, him and her, sir: what hav
    you to do?   22
    Pet. Not her that chides, sir, at any hand,
    pray.
    Tra. I love no chiders, sir. Biondello, let'
    away.
    Luc. [*Aside.*] Well begun, Tranio.
    Hor.   Sir, a word ere you go
Are you a suitor to the maid you talk of, ye
    or no?   23
    Tra. And if I be, sir, is it any offence?
    Gre. No; if without more words you will ge
    you hence.
    Tra. Why, sir, I pray, are not the streets a
    free
For me as for you?
    Gre.   But so is not she.   23
    Tra. For what reason, I beseech you?
    Gre. For this reason, if you'll know,
That she's the choice love of Signior Gremio
    Hor. That she's the chosen of Signior Hor
    tensio.   24
    Tra. Softly, my masters! if you be gentle
    men,
Do me this right; hear me with patience.
Baptista is a noble gentleman,
To whom my father is not all unknown;   24
And were his daughter fairer than she is,
She may more suitors have, and me for one.
Fair Leda's daughter had a thousand wooers
Then well one more may fair Bianca have, 24
And so she shall; Lucentio shall make one,
Though Paris came in hope to speed alone.
    Gre. What! this gentleman will out-talk u
    all.
    Luc. Sir, give him head: I know he'll prove
    a jade.   252
    Pet. Hortensio, to what end are all these
    words?
    Hor. Sir, let me be so bold as ask you,
Did you yet ever see Baptista's daughter?
    Tra. No, sir; but hear I do that he hath two,
The one as famous for a scolding tongue   257
As is the other for beauteous modesty.

Pet. Sir, sir, the first's for me; let her go by.
Gre. Yea, leave that labour to great Hercules,
And let it be more than Alcides' twelve.   261
Pet. Sir, understand you this of me in sooth:
The youngest daughter, whom you hearken for,
Her father keeps from all access of suitors, 264
And will not promise her to any man
Until the elder sister first be wed;
The younger then is free, and not before.
Tra. If it be so, sir, that you are the man 268
Must stead us all, and me among the rest;
And if you break the ice, and do this feat,
Achieve the elder, set the younger free
For our access, whose hap shall be to have her
Will not so graceless be to be ingrate.   273
Hor. Sir, you say well, and well you do conceive;
And since you do profess to be a suitor,
You must, as we do, gratify this gentleman, 276
To whom we all rest generally beholding.
Tra. Sir, I shall not be slack: in sign whereof,
Please ye we may contrive this afternoon,
And quaff carouses to our mistress' health, 280
And do as adversaries do in law,
Strive mightily, but eat and drink as friends.
Gru. ⎱ O excellent motion! Fellows, let's be
Bion. ⎰   gone.
Hor. The motion's good indeed, and be it
so:—   284
Petruchio, I shall be your *ben venuto*. [*Exeunt.*

ACT II

SCENE I.—*Padua. A Room in* BAPTISTA'S
House.

Enter KATHARINA *and* BIANCA.

Bian. Good sister, wrong me not, nor wrong
yourself,
To make a bondmaid and a slave of me;
That I disdain: but for these other gawds,
Unbind my hands, I'll pull them off myself, 4
Yea, all my raiment, to my petticoat;
Or what you will command me will I do,
So well I know my duty to my elders.   7
Kath. Of all thy suitors, here I charge thee, tell
Whom thou lov'st best: see thou dissemble not.
Bian. Believe me, sister, of all the men alive
I never yet beheld that special face
Which I could fancy more than any other.   12
Kath. Minion, thou liest. Is't not Hortensio?
Bian. If you affect him, sister, here I swear
I'll plead for you myself, but you shall have him.
Kath. O! then, belike, you fancy riches more:
You will have Gremio to keep you fair.   17
Bian. Is it for him you do envy me so?
Nay, then you jest; and now I well perceive
You have but jested with me all this while: 20
I prithee, sister Kate, untie my hands.
Kath. If that be jest, then all the rest was so.
[*Strikes her.*

Enter BAPTISTA.

Bap. Why, how now, dame! whence grows
this insolence?
Bianca, stand aside. Poor girl! she weeps. 24
Go ply thy needle; meddle not with her.

For shame, thou hilding of a devilish spirit,
Why dost thou wrong her that did ne'er wrong
thee?
When did she cross thee with a bitter word? 28
Kath. Her silence flouts me, and I'll be reveng'd.   [*Flies after* BIANCA.
Bap. What! in my sight? Bianca, get thee in.
[*Exit* BIANCA.
Kath. What! will you not suffer me? Nay,
now I see
She is your treasure, she must have a husband;
I must dance bare-foot on her wedding-day, 33
And, for your love to her, lead apes in hell.
Talk not to me: I will go sit and weep
Till I can find occasion of revenge.   [*Exit.*
Bap. Was ever gentleman thus griev'd as I?
But who comes here?

Enter GREMIO, *with* LUCENTIO *in the habit of a
mean man;* PETRUCHIO, *with* HORTENSIO *as
a Musician; and* TRANIO, *with* BIONDELLO
bearing a lute and books.

Gre. Good morrow, neighbour Baptista.
Bap. Good morrow, neighbour Gremio. God
save you, gentlemen!   41
Pet. And you, good sir. Pray, have you not a
daughter
Call'd Katharina, fair and virtuous?
Bap. I have a daughter, sir, call'd Katharina.
Gre. You are too blunt: go to it orderly. 45
Pet. You wrong me, Signior Gremio: give
me leave.
I am a gentleman of Verona, sir,
That, hearing of her beauty and her wit,   48
Her affability and bashful modesty,
Her wondrous qualities and mild behaviour,
Am bold to show myself a forward guest
Within your house, to make mine eye the witness   52
Of that report which I so oft have heard.
And, for an entrance to my entertainment,
I do present you with a man of mine,
[*Presenting* HORTENSIO.
Cunning in music and the mathematics,   56
To instruct her fully in those sciences,
Whereof I know she is not ignorant.
Accept of him, or else you do me wrong:
His name is Licio, born in Mantua.   60
Bap. You're welcome, sir; and he, for your
good sake.
But for my daughter Katharine, this I know,
She is not for your turn, the more my grief.
Pet. I see you do not mean to part with her,
Or else you like not of my company.   65
Bap. Mistake me not; I speak but as I find.
Whence are you, sir? what may I call your name?
Pet. Petruchio is my name; Antonio's son;
A man well known throughout all Italy.   69
Bap. I know him well: you are welcome for
his sake.
Gre. Saving your tale, Petruchio, I pray,
Let us, that are poor petitioners, speak too. 72
Backare! you are marvellous forward.
Pet. O, pardon me, Signior Gremio; I would
fain be doing.

Gre. I doubt it not, sir; but you will curse
your wooing.
Neighbour, this is a gift very grateful, I am sure
of it. To express the like kindness myself, that
have been more kindly beholding to you than
any, freely give unto you this young scholar,
[*Presenting* LUCENTIO.] that has been long
studying at Rheims; as cunning in Greek,
Latin, and other languages, as the other in
music and mathematics. His name is Cambio;
pray accept his service.   84
Bap. A thousand thanks, Signior Gremio;
welcome, good Cambio.—[*To* TRANIO.] But, gentle
sir, methinks you walk like a stranger: may I be
so bold to know the cause of your coming?   88
Tra. Pardon me, sir, the boldness is mine own,
That, being a stranger in this city here,
Do make myself a suitor to your daughter,
Unto Bianca, fair and virtuous.   92
Nor is your firm resolve unknown to me,
In the preferment of the eldest sister.
This liberty is all that I request,
That, upon knowledge of my parentage,   96
I may have welcome 'mongst the rest that woo,
And free access and favour as the rest:
And, toward the education of your daughters,
I here bestow a simple instrument,   100
And this small packet of Greek and Latin books:
If you accept them, then their worth is great.
Bap. Lucentio is your name, of whence, I
pray?
Tra. Of Pisa, sir; son to Vincentio.   104
Bap. A mighty man of Pisa; by report
I know him well: you are very welcome, sir.
[*To* HORTENSIO.] Take you the lute, [*To* LUCEN-
TIO.] and you the set of books;
You shall go see your pupils presently.   108
Holla, within!

Enter a Servant.

                Sirrah, lead these gentlemen
To my two daughters, and then tell them both
These are their tutors: bid them use them well.
[*Exit* Servant, *with* HORTENSIO, LUCENTIO,
and BIONDELLO.
We will go walk a little in the orchard,   112
And then to dinner. You are passing welcome,
And so I pray you all to think yourselves.
Pet. Signior Baptista, my business asketh
haste,
And every day I cannot come to woo.   116
You knew my father well, and in him me,
Left solely heir to all his lands and goods,
Which I have better'd rather than decreas'd:
Then tell me, if I get your daughter's love, 120
What dowry shall I have with her to wife?
Bap. After my death the one half of my lands,
And in possession twenty thousand crowns.
Pet. And, for that dowry, I'll assure her of
Her widowhood, be it that she survive me, 125
In all my lands and leases whatsoever.
Let specialties be therefore drawn between us,
That covenants may be kept on either hand. 128
Bap. Ay, when the special thing is well ob-
tain'd,
That is, her love; for that is all in all.

Pet. Why, that is nothing; for I tell you,
father,
I am as peremptory as she proud-minded; 132
And where two raging fires meet together
They do consume the thing that feeds their fury:
Though little fire grows great with little wind,
Yet extreme gusts will blow out fire and all; 136
So I to her, and so she yields to me;
For I am rough and woo not like a babe.
Bap. Well mayst thou woo, and happy be
thy speed!
But be thou arm'd for some unhappy words. 140
Pet. Ay, to the proof; as mountains are for
winds,
That shake not, though they blow perpetually.

Re-enter HORTENSIO, *with his head broke.*

Bap. How now, my friend! why dost thou
look so pale?
Hor. For fear, I promise you, if I look pale.
Bap. What, will my daughter prove a good
musician?   145
Hor. I think she'll sooner prove a soldier:
Iron may hold with her, but never lutes.
Bap. Why, then thou canst not break her to
the lute?   148
Hor. Why, no; for she hath broke the lute
to me.
I did but tell her she mistook her frets,
And bow'd her hand to teach her fingering;
When, with a most impatient devilish spirit, 152
'Frets, call you these?' quoth she; 'I'll fume
with them;'
And, with that word, she struck me on the head,
And through the instrument my pate made way;
And there I stood amazed for a while,   156
As on a pillory, looking through the lute;
While she did call me rascal fiddler,
And twangling Jack; with twenty such vile terms
As she had studied to misuse me so.   160
Pet. Now, by the world, it is a lusty wench!
I love her ten times more than e'er I did:
O! how I long to have some chat with her!
Bap. [*To* HORTENSIO.] Well, go with me, and
be not so discomfited: 164
Proceed in practice with my younger daughter;
She's apt to learn, and thankful for good turns.
Signior Petruchio, will you go with us,
Or shall I send my daughter Kate to you? 168
Pet. I pray you do; I will attend her here,
            [*Exeunt* BAPTISTA, GREMIO, TRANIO, *and*
                                                        HORTENSIO.
And woo her with some spirit when she comes.
Say that she rail; why then I'll tell her plain
She sings as sweetly as a nightingale: 172
Say that she frown; I'll say she looks as clear
As morning roses newly wash'd with dew:
Say she be mute and will not speak a word;
Then I'll commend her volubility,   176
And say she uttereth piercing eloquence:
If she do bid me pack; I'll give her thanks,
As though she bid me stay by her a week:
If she deny to wed; I'll crave the day   180
When I shall ask the banns, and when be
married.
But here she comes; and now, Petruchio, speak.

Enter KATHARINA.

Good morrow, Kate; for that's your name, I
    hear.
Kath. Well have you heard, but something
    hard of hearing: 184
They call me Katharine that do talk of me.
    Pet. You lie, in faith; for you are call'd
    plain Kate,
And bonny Kate, and sometimes Kate the curst;
But, Kate, the prettiest Kate in Christendom;
Kate of Kate-Hall, my super-dainty Kate, 189
For dainties are all cates: and therefore, Kate,
Take this of me, Kate of my consolation;
Hearing thy mildness prais'd in every town, 192
Thy virtues spoke of, and thy beauty sounded,—
Yet not so deeply as to thee belongs,—
Myself am mov'd to woo thee for my wife.
    Kath. Mov'd! in good time: let him that
    mov'd you hither   196
Remove you hence. I knew you at the first,
You were a moveable.
    Pet.   Why, what's a moveable?
    Kath. A joint-stool.
    Pet.   Thou hast hit it: come, sit on me.
    Kath. Asses are made to bear, and so are you.
    Pet. Women are made to bear, and so are
    you.   201
    Kath. No such jade as bear you, if me you
    mean.
    Pet. Alas! good Kate, I will not burden thee;
For, knowing thee to be but young and light,—
    Kath. Too light for such a swain as you to
    catch,   205
And yet as heavy as my weight should be.
    Pet. Should be! should buz!
    Kath.   Well ta'en, and like a buzzard.
    Pet. O slow-wing'd turtle! shall a buzzard
    take thee?   208
    Kath. Ay, for a turtle, as he takes a buzzard.
    Pet. Come, come, you wasp; i' faith you are
    too angry.
    Kath. If I be waspish, best beware my sting.
    Pet. My remedy is, then, to pluck it out. 212
    Kath. Ay, if the fool could find it where it lies.
    Pet. Who knows not where a wasp does wear
    his sting?
In his tail.
    Kath. In his tongue.
    Pet.   Whose tongue?
    Kath. Yours, if you talk of tails; and so fare-
    well.   216
    Pet. What! with my tongue in your tail?
    nay, come again.
Good Kate, I am a gentleman.
    Kath.   That I'll try. [*Striking him.*
    Pet. I swear I'll cuff you if you strike again.
    Kath. So may you lose your arms: 220
If you strike me, you are no gentleman;
And if no gentleman, why then no arms.
    Pet. A herald, Kate? O! put me in thy
    books.
    Kath. What is your crest? a coxcomb? 224
    Pet. A combless cock, so Kate will be my hen.
    Kath. No cock of mine; you crow too like a
    craven.

    Pet. Nay, come, Kate, come; you must not
    look so sour.
    Kath. It is my fashion when I see a crab. 228
    Pet. Why, here's no crab, and therefore look
    not sour.
    Kath. There is, there is.
    Pet. Then show it me.
    Kath.   Had I a glass, I would.
    Pet. What, you mean my face?
    Kath.   Well aim'd of such a young one.
    Pet. Now, by Saint George, I am too young
    for you.   233
    Kath. Yet you are wither'd.
    Pet.   'Tis with cares.
    Kath.   I care not.
    Pet. Nay, hear you, Kate: in sooth, you
    'scape not so.
    Kath. I chafe you, if I tarry: let me go. 236
    Pet. No, not a whit: I find you passing gentle.
'Twas told me you were rough and coy and
    sullen,
And now I find report a very liar;
For thou art pleasant, gamesome, passing cour-
    teous,   240
But slow in speech, yet sweet as spring-time
    flowers:
Thou canst not frown, thou canst not look
    askance,
Nor bite the lip, as angry wenches will;
Nor hast thou pleasure to be cross in talk; 244
But thou with mildness entertain'st thy wooers,
With gentle conference, soft and affable.
Why does the world report that Kate doth limp?
O slanderous world! Kate, like the hazel-twig,
Is straight and slender, and as brown in hue 249
As hazel nuts, and sweeter than the kernels.
O! let me see thee walk: thou dost not halt.
    Kath. Go, fool, and whom thou keep'st com-
    mand.   252
    Pet. Did ever Dian so become a grove
As Kate this chamber with her princely gait?
O! be thou Dian, and let her be Kate,
And then let Kate be chaste, and Dian sport-
    ful!
    Kath. Where did you study all this goodly
    speech?   257
    Pet. It is extempore, from my mother-wit.
    Kath. A witty mother! witless else her son.
    Pet. Am I not wise?
    Kath.   Yes; keep you warm. 260
    Pet. Marry, so I mean, sweet Katharine, in
    thy bed:
And therefore, setting all this chat aside,
Thus in plain terms: your father hath consented
That you shall be my wife; your dowry 'greed
    on;   264
And will you, nill you, I will marry you.
Now, Kate, I am a husband for your turn;
For, by this light, whereby I see thy beauty,—
Thy beauty that doth make me like thee well,—
Thou must be married to no man but me: 269
For I am he am born to tame you, Kate;
And bring you from a wild Kate to a Kate
Conformable as other household Kates.   272
Here comes your father: never make denial;
I must and will have Katharine to my wife.

Re-enter BAPTISTA, GREMIO, *and* TRANIO.

Bap. Now, Signior Petruchio, how speed you
    with my daughter?

Pet. How but well, sir? how but well?   276
It were impossible I should speed amiss.

Bap. Why, how now, daughter Katharine! in
    your dumps?

Kath. Call you me daughter? now, I pro-
    mise you
You have show'd a tender fatherly regard,   280
To wish me wed to one half lunatic;
A mad-cap ruffian and a swearing Jack,
That thinks with oaths to face the matter out.

Pet. Father, 'tis thus: yourself and all the
    world,   284
That talk'd of her, have talk'd amiss of her:
If she be curst, it is for policy,
For she's not froward, but modest as the dove;
She is not hot, but temperate as the morn;   288
For patience she will prove a second Grissel,
And Roman Lucrece for her chastity;
And to conclude, we have 'greed so well to-
    gether,
That upon Sunday is the wedding-day.   292

Kath. I'll see thee hang'd on Sunday first.

Gre. Hark, Petruchio: she says she'll see thee
    hang'd first.

Tra. Is this your speeding? nay then, good
    night our part!

Pet. Be patient, gentlemen; I choose her for
    myself: 296
If she and I be pleas'd, what's that to you?
'Tis bargain'd 'twixt us twain, being alone,
That she shall still be curst in company.
I tell you, 'tis incredible to believe   300
How much she loves me: O! the kindest Kate.
She hung about my neck, and kiss on kiss
She vied so fast, protesting oath on oath,
That in a twink she won me to her love.   304
O! you are novices: 'tis a world to see,
How tame, when men and women are alone,
A meacock wretch can make the curstest shrew.
Give me thy hand, Kate: I will unto Venice   308
To buy apparel 'gainst the wedding-day.
Provide the feast, father, and bid the guests;
I will be sure my Katharine shall be fine.

Bap. I know not what to say; but give me
    your hands.   312
God send you joy, Petruchio! 'tis a match.

Gre. }
Tra. } Amen, say we: we will be witnesses.

Pet. Father, and wife, and gentlemen, adieu.
I will to Venice; Sunday comes apace: 316
We will have rings, and things, and fine array;
And, kiss me, Kate, we will be married o' Sun-
    day.

[*Exeunt* PETRUCHIO *and* KATHARINA,
                                severally.

Gre. Was ever match clapp'd up so suddenly?

Bap. Faith, gentlemen, now I play a mer-
    chant's part,   320
And venture madly on a desperate mart.

Tra. 'Twas a commodity lay fretting by you:
'Twill bring you gain, or perish on the seas.

Bap. The gain I seek is, quiet in the match.

Gre. No doubt but he hath got a quiet catch.

But now, Baptista, to your younger daughter:
Now is the day we long have looked for:
I am your neighbour, and was suitor first.   328

Tra. And I am one that love Bianca more
Than words can witness, or your thoughts can
    guess.

Gre. Youngling, thou canst not love so dear
    as I.   331

Tra. Greybeard, thy love doth freeze.

Gre.   But thine doth fry.
Skipper, stand back: 'tis age that nourisheth.

Tra. But youth in ladies' eyes that flourisheth.

Bap. Content you, gentlemen; I'll compound
    this strife:
'Tis deeds must win the prize; and he, of both,
That can assure my daughter greatest dower   337
Shall have my Bianca's love.
Say, Signior Gremio, what can you assure her?

Gre. First, as you know, my house within the
    city   340
Is richly furnished with plate and gold:
Basins and ewers to lave her dainty hands;
My hangings all of Tyrian tapestry;
In ivory coffers I have stuff'd my crowns;   344
In cypress chests my arras counterpoints,
Costly apparel, tents, and canopies,
Fine linen, Turkey cushions boss'd with pearl,
Valance of Venice gold in needle-work,   348
Pewter and brass, and all things that belong
To house or housekeeping: then, at my farm
I have a hundred milch-kine to the pail,
Six score fat oxen standing in my stalls,   352
And all things answerable to this portion.
Myself am struck in years, I must confess;
And if I die to-morrow, this is hers,
If whilst I live she will be only mine.   356

Tra. That 'only' came well in. Sir, list to me:
I am my father's heir and only son:
If I may have your daughter to my wife,
I'll leave her houses three or four as good,   360
Within rich Pisa walls, as any one
Old Signior Gremio has in Padua;
Besides two thousand ducats by the year
Of fruitful land, all of which shall be her
    jointure.   364

What, have I pinch'd you, Signior Gremio?

Gre. Two thousand ducats by the year of land!
My land amounts to not so much in all:
That she shall have; besides an argosy   368
That now is lying in Marseilles' road.
What, have I chok'd you with an argosy?

Tra. Gremio, 'tis known my father hath no
    less   371
Than three great argosies, besides two galliasses,
And twelve tight galleys; these I will assure her,
And twice as much, whate'er thou offer'st next.

Gre. Nay, I have offer'd all, I have no more;   376
And she can have no more than all I have:
If you like me, she shall have me and mine.

Tra. Why, then the maid is mine from all
    the world,
By your firm promise. Gremio is out-vied.

Bap. I must confess your offer is the best;
And, let your father make her the assurance,   382
She is your own; else, you must pardon me:
If you should die before him, where's her dower?

Tra. That's but a cavil: he is old, I young.

Gre. And may not young men die as well as
old?   385

Bap. Well, gentlemen,
I am thus resolv'd. On Sunday next, you know,
My daughter Katharine is to be married: 388
Now, on the Sunday following, shall Bianca
Be bride to you, if you make this assurance;
If not, to Signior Gremio:
And so, I take my leave, and thank you both. 392

Gre. Adieu, good neighbour. [*Exit* BAPTIS-
TA.] Now I fear thee not:
Sirrah young gamester, your father were a fool
To give thee all, and in his waning age
Set foot under thy table. Tut! a toy!   396
An old Italian fox is not so kind, my boy. [*Exit.*

Tra. A vengeance on your crafty wither'd
hide!
Yet I have fac'd it with a card of ten.
'Tis in my head to do my master good: 400
I see no reason, but suppos'd Lucentio
Must get a father, called 'suppos'd Vincentio;'
And that's a wonder: fathers, commonly
Do get their children; but in this case of woo-
ing,   404
A child shall get a sire, if I fail not of my cun-
ning.   [*Exit.*

ACT III

SCENE I.—*Padua. A Room in* BAPTISTA'S
House.

Enter LUCENTIO, HORTENSIO, *and* BIANCA.

Luc. Fiddler, forbear; you grow too forward,
sir:
Have you so soon forgot the entertainment
Her sister Katharine welcom'd you withal?

Hor. But, wrangling pedant, this is   4
The patroness of heavenly harmony:
Then give me leave to have prerogative;
And when in music we have spent an hour,
Your lecture shall have leisure for as much. 8

Luc. Preposterous ass, that never read so far
To know the cause why music was ordain'd!
Was it not to refresh the mind of man
After his studies or his usual pain?   12
Then give me leave to read philosophy,
And while I pause, serve in your harmony.

Hor. Sirrah, I will not bear these braves of
thine.

Bian. Why, gentlemen, you do me double
wrong,   16
To strive for that which resteth in my choice.
I am no breeching scholar in the schools;
I'll not be tied to hours nor 'pointed times,
But learn my lessons as I please myself.   20
And, to cut off all strife, here sit we down:
Take you your instrument, play you the
whiles;
His lecture will be done ere you have tun'd.

Hor. You'll leave his lecture when I am in
tune?   [*Retires.*

Luc. That will be never: tune your instru-
ment.   25

Bian. Where left we last?

Luc. Here, madam:—
    Hic ibat Simois; hic est Sigeia tellus;   28
    Hic steterat Priami regia celsa senis.

Bian. Construe them.

Luc. Hic ibat, as I told you before, *Simois,*
I am Lucentio, *hic est,* son unto Vincentio of
Pisa, *Sigeia tellus,* disguised thus to get your
love; *Hic steterat, Priami,* is my man Tranio, *regia,*
bearing my port, *celsa senis,* that we might beguile the old pantaloon.   37

Hor. [*Returning.*] Madam, my instrument's
in tune.

Bian. Let's hear.—   [HORTENSIO *plays.*
O fie! the treble jars.   40

Luc. Spit in the hole, man, and tune again.

Bian. Now let me see if I can construe it:
Hic ibat Simois, I know you not, *hic est Sigeia
tellus,* I trust you not; *Hic steterat Priami,*
take heed he hear us not, *regia,* presume not;
celsa senis, despair not.

Hor. Madam, 'tis now in tune.

Luc.   All but the base.

Hor. The base is right; 'tis the base knave
that jars.   48
How fiery and forward our pedant is!
[*Aside.*] Now, for my life, the knave doth court
my love:
Pedascule, I'll watch you better yet.

Bian. In time I may believe, yet I mistrust.

Luc. Mistrust it not; for, sure, Æacides   53
Was Ajax, call'd so from his grandfather.

Bian. I must believe my master; else, I pro-
mise you,
I should be arguing still upon that doubt: 56
But let it rest. Now, Licio, to you.
Good masters, take it not unkindly, pray,
That I have been thus pleasant with you both.

Hor. [*To* LUCENTIO.] You may go walk, and
give me leave a while: 60
My lessons make no music in three parts.

Luc. Are you so formal, sir? [*Aside.*] Well,
I must wait,
And watch withal; for, but I be deceiv'd,
Our fine musician groweth amorous.   64

Hor. Madam, before you touch the instru-
ment,
To learn the order of my fingering,
I must begin with rudiments of art;
To teach you gamut in a briefer sort,   68
More pleasant, pithy, and effectual,
Than hath been taught by any of my trade:
And there it is in writing, fairly drawn.

Bian. Why, I am past my gamut long ago. 72

Hor. Yet read the gamut of Hortensio.

Bian.
    '*Gamut*' I am, the ground of all accord,
        '*A re,*' to plead Hortensio's passion;
    '*B mi,*' Bianca, take him for thy lord,   76
        '*C fa ut,*' that loves with all affection:
    '*D sol re,*' one clef, two notes have I:
        '*E la mi,*' show pity, or I die.
Call you this gamut? tut, I like it not: 80
Old fashions please me best; I am not so nice,
To change true rules for odd inventions.

Enter a Servant.

Serv. Mistress, your father prays you leave
  your books,
And help to dress your sister's chamber up: 84
You know to-morrow is the wedding-day.

  Bian. Farewell, sweet masters both: I must
    be gone.   [*Exeunt* BIANCA *and* Servant.
  Luc. Faith, mistress, then I have no cause
    to stay.   [*Exit.*
  Hor. But I have cause to pry into this pe-
    dant: 88
Methinks he looks as though he were in love.
Yet if thy thoughts, Bianca, be so humble
To cast thy wandering eyes on every stale,
Seize thee that list: if once I find thee ranging, 92
Hortensio will be quit with thee by changing.
                                      [*Exit.*

SCENE II.—*The Same. Before* BAPTISTA'S
        House.

Enter BAPTISTA, GREMIO, TRANIO, KATHARINA,
    BIANCA, LUCENTIO, *and* Attendants.

  Bap. [*To* TRANIO.] Signior Lucentio, this is
    the 'pointed day
That Katharine and Petruchio should be mar-
  ried,
And yet we hear not of our son-in-law.
What will be said? what mockery will it be 4
To want the bridegroom when the priest attends
To speak the ceremonial rites of marriage!
What says Lucentio to this shame of ours?

  Kath. No shame but mine: I must, forsooth,
    be forc'd   8
To give my hand oppos'd against my heart
Unto a mad-brain rudesby, full of spleen;
Who woo'd in haste and means to wed at leisure.
I told you, I, he was a frantic fool,   12
Hiding his bitter jests in blunt behaviour;
And to be noted for a merry man,
He'll woo a thousand, 'point the day of mar-
  riage,
Make friends invite, and proclaim the banns; 16
Yet never means to wed where he hath woo'd.
Now must the world point at poor Katharine,
And say, 'Lo! there is mad Petruchio's wife,
If it would please him come and marry her.' 20

  Tra. Patience, good Katharine, and Baptista
    too.
Upon my life, Petruchio means but well,
Whatever fortune stays him from his word:
Though he be blunt, I know him passing wise;
Though he be merry, yet withal he's honest. 25

  Kath. Would Katharine had never seen him
    though!   [*Exit weeping, followed by*
                      BIANCA *and others.*
  Bap. Go, girl: I cannot blame thee now to
    weep,
For such an injury would vex a very saint, 28
Much more a shrew of thy impatient humour.

Enter BIONDELLO.

  Bion. Master, master! news! old news, and
such news as you never heard of!
  Bap. Is it new and old too? how may that
be?   33

  Bion. Why, is it not news to hear of Petru-
chio's coming?
  Bap. Is he come?   36
  Bion. Why, no, sir.
  Bap. What then?
  Bion. He is coming.
  Bap. When will he be here?   40
  Bion. When he stands where I am and sees
you there.
  Tra. But, say, what to thine old news? 43
  Bion. Why, Petruchio is coming, in a new
hat and an old jerkin; a pair of old breeches
thrice turned; a pair of boots that have been
candle-cases, one buckled, another laced; an old
rusty sword ta'en out of the town-armoury, with
a broken hilt, and chapeless; with two broken
points: his horse hipped with an old mothy
saddle and stirrups of no kindred; besides,
possessed with the glanders and like to mose in
the chine; troubled with the lampass, infected
with the fashions, full of windgalls, sped with
spavins, rayed with the yellows, past cure of the
fives, stark spoiled with the staggers, begnawn
with the bots, swayed in the back, and shoulder-
shotten; near-legged before, and with a half-
checked bit, and a head-stall of sheep's leather,
which, being restrained to keep him from stumbling, hath been often burst and now repaired
with knots; one girth six times pieced, and a
woman's crupper of velure, which hath two
letters for her name fairly set down in studs, and
here and there pieced with packthread. 65

  Bap. Who comes with him?
  Bion. O, sir! his lackey, for all the world
caparisoned like the horse; with a linen stock
on one leg and a kersey boot-hose on the other,
gartered with a red and blue list; an old hat,
and the 'humour of forty fancies' pricked in't
for a feather: a monster, a very monster in
apparel, and not like a Christian footboy or a
gentleman's lackey.
  Tra. 'Tis some odd humour pricks him to
    this fashion;
Yet oftentimes he goes but mean-apparell'd. 7
  Bap. I am glad he is come, howsoe'er he
    comes.
  Bion. Why, sir, he comes not.
  Bap. Didst thou not say he comes?
  Bion. Who? that Petruchio came?   8
  Bap. Ay, that Petruchio came.
  Bion. No, sir; I say his horse comes, with
him on his back.
  Bap. Why, that's all one.   8
  Bion. Nay, by Saint Jamy,
      I hold you a penny,
    A horse and a man
      Is more than one,   8
    And yet not many.

Enter PETRUCHIO *and* GRUMIO.

  Pet. Come, where be these gallants? who i
at home?
  Bap. You are welcome, sir.
  Pet.   And yet I come not wel
  Bap. And yet you halt not.

Tra.   Not so well apparell'd 92
s I wish you were.
Pet. Were it better, I should rush in thus.
ut where is Kate? where is my lovely bride?
ow does my father? Gentles, methinks you
     frown: 96
nd wherefore gaze this goodly company,
s if they saw some wondrous monument,
ome comet, or unusual prodigy?
Bap. Why, sir, you know this is your wedding-
     day: 100
irst were we sad, fearing you would not come;
ow sadder, that you come so unprovided.
ie! doff this habit, shame to your estate,
n eye-sore to our solemn festival.   104
Tra. And tell us what occasion of import
ath all so long detain'd you from your wife,
nd sent you hither so unlike yourself?
Pet. Tedious it were to tell, and harsh to hear:
ufficeth, I am come to keep my word,   109
hough in some part enforced to digress;
Vhich, at more leisure, I will so excuse
s you shall well be satisfied withal.   112
ut where is Kate? I stay too long from her:
he morning wears, 'tis time we were at church.
Tra. See not your bride in these unreverent
     robes:
o to my chamber; put on clothes of mine. 116
Pet. Not I, believe me: thus I'll visit her.
Bap. But thus, I trust, you will not marry her.
Pet. Good sooth, even thus; therefore ha'
     done with words:
o me she's married, not unto my clothes. 120
ould I repair what she will wear in me
s I can change these poor accoutrements,
were well for Kate and better for myself.
ut what a fool am I to chat with you   124
Vhen I should bid good morrow to my bride,
nd seal the title with a lovely kiss!
[*Exeunt* PETRUCHIO, GRUMIO, *and* BIONDELLO.
Tra. He hath some meaning in his mad attire.
Ve will persuade him, be it possible,   128
o put on better ere he go to church.
Bap. I'll after him, and see the event of this.
[*Exeunt* BAPTISTA, GREMIO, *and* Attendants.
Tra. But to her love concerneth us to add
er father's liking: which to bring to pass, 132
s I before imparted to your worship,
am to get a man,—whate'er he be
skills not much, we'll fit him to our turn,—
nd he shall be Vincentio of Pisa,   136
nd make assurance here in Padua,
f greater sums than I have promised.
o shall you quietly enjoy your hope,
nd marry sweet Bianca with consent.   140
Luc. Were it not that my fellow school-
     master
oth watch Bianca's steps so narrowly,
were good, methinks, to steal our marriage;
Vhich once perform'd, let all the world say
     no,   144
ll keep mine own, despite of all the world.
Tra. That by degrees we mean to look into,
nd watch our vantage in this business.
Ve'll over-reach the greybeard, Gremio,   148
he narrow-prying father, Minola,

The quaint musician, amorous Licio;
All for my master's sake, Lucentio.

Re-enter GREMIO.

Signior Gremio, came you from the church? 152
     Gre. As willingly as e'er I came from school.
     Tra. And is the bride and bridegroom com-
          ing home?
     Gre. A bridegroom say you? 'Tis a groom
          indeed,   155
A grumbling groom, and that the girl shall find.
     Tra. Curster than she? why, 'tis impossible.
     Gre. Why, he's a devil, a devil, a very fiend.
     Tra. Why, she's a devil, a devil, the devil's
          dam.
     Gre. Tut! she's a lamb, a dove, a fool to him.
I'll tell you, Sir Lucentio: when the priest 161
Should ask, if Katharine should be his wife,
'Ay, by gogs-wouns!' quoth he; and swore so
     loud,
That, all amaz'd, the priest let fall the book; 164
And, as he stoop'd again to take it up,
The mad-brain'd bridegroom took him such a
     cuff
That down fell priest and book and book and
     priest:
'Now take them up,' quoth he, 'if any list.' 168
     Tra. What said the wench when he arose
          again?
     Gre. Trembled and shook; for why he stampt
          and swore,
As if the vicar meant to cozen him.
But after many ceremonies done,   172
He calls for wine: 'A health!' quoth he; as if
He had been aboard, carousing to his mates
After a storm; quaff'd off the muscadel,
And threw the sops all in the sexton's face; 176
Having no other reason
But that his beard grew thin and hungrily,
And seem'd to ask him sops as he was drinking.
This done, he took the bride about the neck, 180
And kiss'd her lips with such a clamorous smack
That at the parting all the church did echo:
And I, seeing this, came thence for very shame;
And after me, I know, the rout is coming.   184
Such a mad marriage never was before.
Hark, hark! I hear the minstrels play. [*Music.*

Re-enter PETRUCHIO, KATHARINA, BIANCA, BAP-
     TISTA, HORTENSIO, GRUMIO, *and* Train.

     Pet. Gentlemen and friends, I thank you for
          your pains:
I know you think to dine with me to-day,   188
And have prepar'd great store of wedding cheer;
But so it is, my haste doth call me hence,
And therefore here I mean to take my leave.
     Bap. Is't possible you will away to-night? 192
     Pet. I must away to-day, before night come.
Make it no wonder: if you knew my business,
You would entreat me rather go than stay.
And, honest company, I thank you all,   196
That have beheld me give away myself
To this most patient, sweet, and virtuous wife.
Dine with my father, drink a health to me,
For I must hence; and farewell to you all.   200

Tra. Let us entreat you stay till after dinner.
Pet. It may not be.
Gre. Let me entreat you.
Pet. It cannot be.
Kath. Let me entreat you.
Pet. I am content.
Kath. Are you content to stay? 204
Pet. I am content you shall entreat me stay,
But yet not stay, entreat me how you can.
Kath. Now, if you love me, stay.
Pet. Grumio, my horse!
Gru. Ay, sir, they be ready: the oats have
eaten the horses. 209
Kath. Nay, then,
Do what thou canst, I will not go to-day;
No, nor to-morrow, nor till I please myself. 212
The door is open, sir, there lies your way;
You may be jogging whiles your boots are green;
For me, I'll not be gone till I please myself.
'Tis like you'll prove a jolly surly groom, 216
That take it on you at the first so roundly.
Pet. O Kate! content thee: prithee, be not
angry.
Kath. I will be angry: what hast thou to do?
Father, be quiet; he shall stay my leisure. 220
Gre. Ay, marry, sir, now it begins to work.
Kath. Gentlemen, forward to the bridal
dinner:
I see a woman may be made a fool,
If she had not a spirit to resist. 224
Pet. They shall go forward, Kate, at thy
command.
Obey the bride, you that attend on her;
Go to the feast, revel and domineer,
Carouse full measure to her maidenhead, 228
Be mad and merry, or go hang yourselves;
But for my bonny Kate, she must with me.
Nay, look not big, nor stamp, nor stare, nor fret;
I will be master of what is mine own. 232
She is my goods, my chattels; she is my house,
My household stuff, my field, my barn,
My horse, my ox, my ass, my anything;
And here she stands, touch her whoever dare;
I'll bring mine action on the proudest he 237
That stops my way in Padua. Grumio,
Draw forth thy weapon, we're beset with
thieves;
Rescue thy mistress, if thou be a man. 240
Fear not, sweet wench; they shall not touch
thee, Kate:
I'll buckler thee against a million.
[*Exeunt* PETRUCHIO, KATHARINA, *and* GRUMIO.
Bap. Nay, let them go, a couple of quiet
ones.
Gre. Went they not quickly I should die
with laughing. 244
Tra. Of all mad matches never was the like.
Luc. Mistress, what's your opinion of your
sister?
Bian. That, being mad herself, she's madly
mated.
Gre. I warrant him, Petruchio is Kated. 248
Bap. Neighbours and friends, though bride
and bridegroom wants
For to supply the places at the table,
You know there wants no junkets at the feast.

Lucentio, you shall supply the bridegroom'
place, 25
And let Bianca take her sister's room.
Tra. Shall sweet Bianca practise how t
bride it?
Bap. She shall, Lucentio. Come, gentlemen
let's go. [*Exeun*

ACT IV

SCENE I.—*A Hall in* PETRUCHIO'S *Country
House.*

Enter GRUMIO.

Gru. Fie, fie, on all tired jades, on all ma
masters, and all foul ways! Was ever man s
beaten? was ever man so rayed? was ever ma
so weary? I am sent before to make a fire, an
they are coming after to warm them. Now
were not I a little pot and soon hot, my ver
lips might freeze to my teeth, my tongue t
the roof of my mouth, my heart in my belly
ere I should come by a fire to thaw me; but I
with blowing the fire, shall warm myself; fo
considering the weather, a taller man than
will take cold. Holla, ho! Curtis. 1

Enter CURTIS.

Curt. Who is that calls so coldly?
Gru. A piece of ice: if thou doubt it, tho
mayst slide from my shoulder to my heel wit
no greater a run but my head and my neck.
fire, good Curtis.
Curt. Is my master and his wife comin
Grumio?
Gru. O! ay, Curtis, ay; and therefore fir
fire; cast on no water.
Curt. Is she so hot a shrew as she's reported
Gru. She was, good Curtis, before this fros
but, thou knowest, winter tames man, woma
and beast; for it hath tamed my old master, an
my new mistress, and myself, fellow Curtis.
Curt. Away, you three-inch-fool! I am n
beast.
Gru. Am I but three inches? why, thy hor
is a foot; and so long am I at the least. B
wilt thou make a fire, or shall I complain o
thee to our mistress, whose hand,—she bein
now at hand,—thou shalt soon feel, to thy col
comfort, for being slow in thy hot office?
Curt. I prithee, good Grumio, tell me, ho
goes the world?
Gru. A cold world, Curtis, in every office b
thine; and therefore, fire. Do thy duty, an
have thy duty, for my master and mistress a
almost frozen to death.
Curt. There's fire ready; and therefore, goc
Grumio, the news?
Gru. Why, 'Jack, boy! ho, boy!' and
much news as thou wilt.
Curt. Come, you are so full of cony-catchin
Gru. Why therefore fire: for I have caug
extreme cold. Where's the cook? is supp
ready, the house trimmed, rushes strewed, co
webs swept; the serving-men in their new fu
tian, their white stockings, and every officer h

edding-garment on? Be the Jacks fair within,
ne Jills fair without, and carpets laid, and
verything in order?   53
Curt. All ready; and therefore, I pray thee,
ews?
Gru. First, know, my horse is tired; my
aster and mistress fallen out.   57
Curt. How?
Gru. Out of their saddles into the dirt; and
ereby hangs a tale.   60
Curt. Let's ha't, good Grumio.
Gru. Lend thine ear.
Curt. Here.
Gru. [*Striking him.*] There.   64
Curt. This is to feel a tale, not to hear a tale.
nd this cuff was but to knock at your ear and
eseech listening. Now I begin: *Imprimis*, we
me down a foul hill, my master riding behind
y mistress,—
Curt. Both of one horse?
Gru. What's that to thee?   72
Curt. Why, a horse.
Gru. Tell thou the tale: but hadst thou not
ossed me thou shouldst have heard how her
orse fell, and she under her horse; thou shouldst
ve heard in how miry a place, how she was be-
oiled: how he left her with the horse upon
er; how he beat me because her horse stum-
ed; how she waded through the dirt to pluck
m off me: how he swore; how she prayed, that
ver prayed before; how I cried; how the horses
n away; how her bridle was burst; how I lost
y crupper; with many things of worthy
emory, which now shall die in oblivion, and
ou return unexperienced to thy grave.
Curt. By this reckoning he is more shrew
an she.   88
Gru. Ay; and that, thou and the proudest of
ou all shall find when he comes home. But
hat talk I of this? Call forth Nathaniel, Joseph,
icholas, Philip, Walter, Sugarsop, and the rest:
t their heads be sleekly combed, their blue coats
ushed, and their garters of an indifferent knit:
t them curtsy with their left legs, and not pre-
me to touch a hair of my master's horsetail
l they kiss their hands. Are they all ready? 97
Curt. They are.
Gru. Call them forth.
Curt. Do you hear? ho! you must meet my
aster to countenance my mistress.   101
Gru. Why, she hath a face of her own.
Curt. Who knows not that?
Gru. Thou, it seems, that callest for company
countenance her.   105
Curt. I call them forth to credit her.
Gru. Why, she comes to borrow nothing of
em.   108

Enter several Servants.

Nath. Welcome home, Grumio!
Phil. How now, Grumio?
Jos. What, Grumio!
Nich. Fellow Grumio!   112
Nath. How now, old lad!
Gru. Welcome, you; how now, you; what,

you; fellow, you; and thus much for greeting.
Now, my spruce companions, is all ready, and
all things neat?   117
Nath. All things is ready. How near is our
master?
Gru. E'en at hand, alighted by this; and
therefore be not,—Cock's passion, silence! I
hear my master.

Enter PETRUCHIO *and* KATHARINA.

Pet. Where be these knaves? What! no man
at door
To hold my stirrup nor to take my horse? 124
Where is Nathaniel, Gregory, Philip?—
All Serv. Here, here, sir; here, sir.
Pet. Here, sir! here, sir! here, sir! here, sir!
You logger-headed and unpolish'd grooms! 128
What, no attendance? no regard? no duty?
Where is the foolish knave I sent before?
Gru. Here, sir; as foolish as I was before.
Pet. You peasant swain! you whoreson malt-
horse drudge!   132
Did I not bid thee meet me in the park,
And bring along these rascal knaves with thee?
Gru. Nathaniel's coat, sir, was not fully made,
And Gabriel's pumps were all unpink'd i' the
heel,   136
There was no link to colour Peter's hat,
And Walter's dagger was not come from sheath-
ing,
There were none fine but Adam, Ralph, and
Gregory;
The rest were ragged, old, and beggarly;   140
Yet, as they are, here are they come to meet you.
Pet. Go, rascals, go, and fetch my supper in.
[*Exeunt some of the* Servants.
Where is the life that late I led?
Where are those—? Sit down, Kate, and wel-
come.   144
Soud, soud, soud, soud!

Re-enter Servants *with supper.*

Why, when, I say?—Nay, good sweet Kate, be
merry.—
Off with my boots, you rogues! you villains!
When?
It was the friar of orders grey,   148
As he forth walked on his way:
Out, you rogue! you pluck my foot awry:
[*Strikes him.*
Take that, and mend the plucking off the other.
Be merry, Kate. Some water, here; what, ho!
Where's my spaniel Troilus? Sirrah, get you
hence   153
And bid my cousin Ferdinand come hither:
[*Exit* Servant.
One, Kate, that you must kiss, and be acquainted
with.
Where are my slippers? Shall I have some
water?   156
Come, Kate, and wash, and welcome heartily.—
[*Servant lets the ewer fall.* PETRUCHIO
strikes him.
You whoreson villain! will you let it fall?
Kath. Patience, I pray you; 'twas a fault un-
willing.

Pet. A whoreson, beetle-headed, flap-ear'd knave! 160
Come, Kate, sit down; I know you have a stomach.
Will you give thanks, sweet Kate, or else shall I?—
What's this? mutton?
First Serv. Ay.
Pet. Who brought it?
First Serv. I.
Pet. 'Tis burnt; and so is all the meat. 164
What dogs are these! Where is the rascal cook?
How durst you, villains, bring it from the dresser,
And serve it thus to me that love it not? 167
[*Throws the meat, &c. at them.*
There, take it to you, trenchers, cups, and all.
You heedless joltheads and unmanner'd slaves!
What! do you grumble? I'll be with you straight.
Kath. I pray you, husband, be not so disquiet:
The meat was well if you were so contented. 172
Pet. I tell thee, Kate, 'twas burnt and dried away;
And I expressly am forbid to touch it,
For it engenders choler, planteth anger;
And better 'twere that both of us did fast, 176
Since, of ourselves, ourselves are choleric,
Than feed it with such over-roasted flesh.
Be patient; to-morrow't shall be mended,
And for this night we'll fast for company: 180
Come, I will bring thee to thy bridal chamber.
[*Exeunt* PETRUCHIO, KATHARINA, *and* CURTIS.
Nath. Peter, didst ever see the like?
Peter. He kills her in her own humour.

Re-enter CURTIS.

Gru. Where is he? 184
Curt. In her chamber, making a sermon of continency to her;
And rails, and swears, and rates, that she, poor soul,
Knows not which way to stand, to look, to speak,
And sits as one new-risen from a dream. 189
Away, away! for he is coming hither. [*Exeunt.*

Re-enter PETRUCHIO.

Pet. Thus have I politicly begun my reign,
And 'tis my hope to end successfully. 192
My falcon now is sharp and passing empty,
And till she stoop she must not be full-gorg'd,
For then she never looks upon her lure.
Another way I have to man my haggard, 196
To make her come and know her keeper's call;
That is, to watch her, as we watch these kites
That bate and beat and will not be obedient.
She eat no meat to-day, nor none shall eat; 200
Last night she slept not, nor to-night she shall not:
As with the meat, some undeserved fault
I'll find about the making of the bed; 203
And here I'll fling the pillow, there the bolster,
This way the coverlet, another way the sheets:
Ay, and amid this hurly I intend
That all is done in reverend care of her;
And in conclusion she shall watch all night: 208
And if she chance to nod I'll rail and brawl,

And with the clamour keep her still awake.
This is a way to kill a wife with kindness;
And thus I'll curb her mad and headstrong humour. 212
He that knows better how to tame a shrew,
Now let him speak: 'tis charity to show. [*Exit.*

SCENE II.—*Padua. Before* BAPTISTA'S *House.*

Enter TRANIO *and* HORTENSIO.

Tra. Is't possible, friend Licio, that Mistress Bianca
Doth fancy any other but Lucentio?
I tell you, sir, she bears me fair in hand.
Hor. Sir, to satisfy you in what I have said, 4
Stand by, and mark the manner of his teaching.
[*They stand aside.*

Enter BIANCA *and* LUCENTIO.

Luc. Now, mistress, profit you in what you read?
Bian. What, master, read you? first resolve me that.
Luc. I read that I profess, the Art to Love. 8
Bian. And may you prove, sir, master of your art!
Luc. While you, sweet dear, prove mistress of my heart. [*They retire*
Hor. Quick proceeders, marry! Now, tell me, I pray,
You that durst swear that your mistress Bianca
Lov'd none in the world so well as Lucentio. 1
Tra. O despiteful love! unconstant womankind!
I tell thee, Licio, this is wonderful.
Hor. Mistake no more: I am not Licio,
Nor a musician, as I seem to be;
But one that scorns to live in this disguise,
For such a one as leaves a gentleman,
And makes a god of such a cullion: 2
Know, sir, that I am call'd Hortensio.
Tra. Signior Hortensio, I have often hear
Of your entire affection to Bianca;
And since mine eyes are witness of her lightness
I will with you, if you be so contented,
Forswear Bianca and her love for ever.
Hor. See, how they kiss and court! Signio Lucentio,
Here is my hand, and here I firmly vow
Never to woo her more; but I do forswear he
As one unworthy all the former favours
That I have fondly flatter'd her withal.
Tra. And here I take the like unfeigned oat
Never to marry with her though she would e treat.
Fie on her! see how beastly she doth court hir
Hor. Would all the world, but he had qui forsworn!
For me, that I may surely keep mine oath,
I will be married to a wealthy widow
Ere three days pass, which hath as long lov'd m
As I have lov'd this proud disdainful hagga
And so farewell, Signior Lucentio.
Kindness in women, not their beauteous look

hall win my love: and so I take my leave,
a resolution as I swore before.

[Exit HORTENSIO. LUCENTIO *and* BIANCA
advance.

Tra. Mistress Bianca, bless you with such
grace 44
s 'longeth to a lover's blessed case!
ay, I have ta'en you napping, gentle love,
nd have forsworn you with Hortensio.

Bian. Tranio, you jest. But have you both
forsworn me? 48

Tra. Mistress, we have.

Luc. Then we are rid of Licio.

Tra. I' faith, he'll have a lusty widow now,
hat shall be woo'd and wedded in a day.

Bian. God give him joy! 52

Tra. Ay, and he'll tame her.

Bian. He says so, Tranio.

Tra. Faith, he is gone unto the taming-school.

Bian. The taming-school! what, is there such
a place?

Tra. Ay, mistress, and Petruchio is the master; 56
hat teacheth tricks eleven and twenty long,
o tame a shrew, and charm her chattering
tongue.

Enter BIONDELLO, *running.*

Bion. O master, master! I have watch'd so
long
hat I'm dog-weary; but at last I spied 60
n ancient angel coming down the hill
ill serve the turn.

Tra. What is he, Biondello?

Bion. Master, a mercatante, or a pedant,
know not what; but formal in apparel, 64
a gait and countenance surely like a father.

Luc. And what of him, Tranio?

Tra. If he be credulous and trust my tale,
l make him glad to seem Vincentio, 68
nd give assurance to Baptista Minola,
s if he were the right Vincentio:
ake in your love, and then let me alone.

[Exeunt LUCENTIO *and* BIANCA.

Enter a Pedant.

Ped. God save you, sir!

Tra. And you, sir! you are welcome.
ravel you far on, or are you at the furthest? 73

Ped. Sir, at the furthest for a week or two;
ut then up further, and as far as Rome;
nd so to Tripoli, if God lend me life. 76

Tra. What countryman, I pray?

Ped. Of Mantua.

Tra. Of Mantua, sir! marry, God forbid!
nd come to Padua, careless of your life?

Ped. My life, sir! how, I pray? for that goes
hard. 80

Tra. 'Tis death for any one in Mantua
o come to Padua. Know you not the cause?
our ships are stay'd at Venice; and the duke,—
or private quarrel 'twixt your duke and him,—
ath publish'd and proclaim'd it openly. 85
is marvel, but that you are but newly come,
ou might have heard it else proclaim'd about.

Ped. Alas, sir! it is worse for me than so; 88

For I have bills for money by exchange
From Florence, and must here deliver them.

Tra. Well, sir, to do you courtesy,
This will I do, and this I will advise you: 92
First, tell me, have you ever been at Pisa?

Ped. Ay, sir, in Pisa have I often been;
Pisa, renowned for grave citizens.

Tra. Among them, know you one Vincentio?

Ped. I know him not, but I have heard of him;
A merchant of incomparable wealth. 98

Tra. He is my father, sir; and, sooth to say,
In countenance somewhat doth resemble you.

Bion. [*Aside.*] As much as an apple doth an
oyster, and all one.

Tra. To save your life in this extremity,
This favour will I do you for his sake; 104
And think it not the worst of all your fortunes
That you are like to Sir Vincentio,
His name and credit shall you undertake,
And in my house shall be friendly lodg'd,
Look that you take upon you as you should! 109
You understand me, sir; so shall you stay
Till you have done your business in the city.
If this be courtesy, sir, accept of it. 112

Ped. O sir, I do; and will repute you ever
The patron of my life and liberty.

Tra. Then go with me to make the matter
good.
This, by the way, I let you understand: 116
My father is here look'd for every day,
To pass assurance of a dower in marriage
'Twixt me and one Baptista's daughter here:
In all these circumstances I'll instruct you. 120
Go with me to clothe you as becomes you.

[Exeunt.

SCENE III.—*A Room in* PETRUCHIO'S *House.*

Enter KATHARINA *and* GRUMIO.

Gru. No, no, forsooth; I dare not, for my life.

Kath. The more my wrong the more his
spite appears.
What, did he marry me to famish me?
Beggars, that come unto my father's door, 4
Upon entreaty have a present alms;
If not, elsewhere they meet with charity:
But I, who never knew how to entreat,
Nor never needed that I should entreat, 8
Am starv'd for meat, giddy for lack of sleep;
With oaths kept waking, and with brawling fed:
And that which spites me more than all these
wants,
He does it under name of perfect love; 12
As who should say, if I should sleep or eat
'Twere deadly sickness, or else present death.
I prithee go and get me some repast;
I care not what, so it be wholesome food. 16

Gru. What say you to a neat's foot?

Kath. 'Tis passing good: I prithee let me
have it.

Gru. I fear it is too choleric a meat.
How say you to a fat tripe finely broil'd? 20

Kath. I like it well: good Grumio, fetch it me.

Gru. I cannot tell; I fear 'tis choleric.
What say you to a piece of beef and mustard?

Kath. A dish that I do love to feed upon. 24

Gru. Ay, but the mustard is too hot a little.

Kath. Why, then the beef, and let the mustard rest.

Gru. Nay, then I will not: you shall have the mustard,

Or else you get no beef of Grumio. 28

Kath. Then both, or one, or anything thou wilt.

Gru. Why then, the mustard without the beef.

Kath. Go, get thee gone, thou false deluding slave, [*Beats him.*

That feed'st me with the very name of meat. 32

Sorrow on thee and all the pack of you,

That triumph thus upon my misery!

Go, get thee gone, I say.

Enter PETRUCHIO *with a dish of meat; and*
HORTENSIO.

Pet. How fares my Kate? What, sweeting, all amort? 36

Hor. Mistress, what cheer?

Kath.   Faith, as cold as can be.

Pet. Pluck up thy spirits; look cheerfully upon me.

Here, love; thou seest how diligent I am,

To dress thy meat myself and bring it thee: 40
[*Sets the dish on a table.*

I am sure, sweet Kate, this kindness merits thanks.

What! not a word? Nay then, thou lov'st it not,

And all my pains is sorted to no proof.

Here, take away this dish.

Kath.   I pray you, let it stand. 44

Pet. The poorest service is repaid with thanks,

And so shall mine, before you touch the meat.

Kath. I thank you, sir.

Hor. Signior Petruchio, fie! you are to blame.

Come, Mistress Kate, I'll bear you company. 49

Pet. [*Aside.*] Eat it up all, Hortensio, if thou lov'st me.

Much good do it unto thy gentle heart!

Kate, eat apace: and now, my honey love, 52

Will we return unto thy father's house,

And revel it as bravely as the best,

With silken coats and caps and golden rings,

With ruffs and cuffs and farthingales and things;

With scarfs and fans and double change of bravery, 57

With amber bracelets, beads and all this knavery.

What! hast thou din'd? The tailor stays thy leisure,

To deck thy body with his ruffling treasure. 60

Enter Tailor.

Come, tailor, let us see these ornaments;

Lay forth the gown.—

Enter Haberdasher.

         What news with you, sir?

Hab. Here is the cap your worship did bespeak.

Pet. Why, this was moulded on a porringer;

A velvet dish: fie, fie! 'tis lewd and filthy: 65

Why, 'tis a cockle or a walnut-shell,

A knack, a toy, a trick, a baby's cap:

Away with it! come, let me have a bigger.

Kath. I'll have no bigger: this doth fit t[he] time,

And gentlewomen wear such caps as these.

Pet. When you are gentle, you shall have o[ne] too;

And not till then.

Hor.   [*Aside.*] That will not be in has[te]

Kath. Why, sir, I trust I may have leave [to] speak,

And speak I will; I am no child, no babe:

Your betters have endur'd me say my mind,

And if you cannot, best you stop your ears.

My tongue will tell the anger of my heart,

Or else my heart, concealing it, will break:

And rather than it shall, I will be free

Even to the uttermost, as I please, in words.

Pet. Why, thou sayst true; it is a paltry ca[p,]

A custard-coffin, a bauble, a silken pie.

I love thee well in that thou lik'st it not.

Kath. Love me or love me not, I like the ca[p,]

And it I will have, or I will have none.
[*Exit* Haberdash[er.

Pet. Thy gown? why, ay: come, tailor, let us see 't.

O mercy, God! what masquing stuff is here[!]

What's this? a sleeve? 'tis like a demi-canno[n:]

What! up and down, carv'd like an apple-ta[rt?]

Here's snip and nip and cut and slish and sla[sh,]

Like to a censer in a barber's shop.

Why, what, i' devil's name, tailor, call'st th[ou] this?

Hor. [*Aside.*] I see, she's like to have neith[er] cap nor gown.

Tai. You bid me make it orderly and we[ll,]

According to the fashion and the time.

Pet. Marry, and did: but if you be [re]member'd,

I did not bid you mar it to the time.

Go, hop me over every kennel home,

For you shall hop without my custom, sir.

I'll none of it: hence! make your best of it. [

Kath. I never saw a better-fashion'd gow[n,]

More quaint, more pleasing, nor more co[m]mendable.

Belike you mean to make a puppet of me.

Pet. Why, true; he means to make a pup[pet] of thee. [

Tai. She says your worship means to ma[ke] a puppet of her.

Pet. O monstrous arrogance! Thou lie[st,] thou thread,

Thou thimble, [

Thou yard, three-quarters, half-yard, quart[er,] nail!

Thou flea, thou nit, thou winter-cricket tho[u!]

Brav'd in mine own house with a skein of threa[d!]

Away! thou rag, thou quantity, thou remna[nt,]

Or I shall so be-mete thee with thy yard

As thou shalt think on prating whilst thou liv['st!]

I tell thee, I, that thou hast marr'd her gown.

Tai. Your worship is deceiv'd: the gown [was] made

Just as my master had direction.

Grumio gave order how it should be done.

Gru. I gave him no order; I gave him the stuff.
Tai. But how did you desire it should be made? 120
Gru. Marry, sir, with needle and thread.
Tai. But did you not request to have it cut?
Gru. Thou hast faced many things.
Tai. I have. 124
Gru. Face not me: thou hast braved many men; brave not me: I will neither be faced nor braved. I say unto thee, I bid thy master cut out the gown; but I did not bid him cut it to pieces: *ergo*, thou liest. 129
Tai. Why, here is the note of the fashion to testify.
Pet. Read it. 132
Gru. The note lies in 's throat if he say I said so.
Tai. *Imprimis*. *A loose-bodied gown.*
Gru. Master, if ever I said loose-bodied gown, sew me in the skirts of it, and beat me to death with a bottom of brown thread. I said, a gown.
Pet. Proceed.
Tai. *With a small compassed cape.*
Gru. I confess the cape. 140
Tai. *With a trunk sleeve.*
Gru. I confess two sleeves.
Tai. *The sleeves curiously cut.*
Pet. Ay, there's the villany. 144
Gru. Error i' the bill, sir; error i' the bill. I commanded the sleeves should be cut out and sewed up again; and that I'll prove upon thee, though thy little finger be armed in a thimble.
Tai. This is true that I say: an I had thee in place where thou shouldst know it. 150
Gru. I am for thee straight: take thou the bill, give me thy mete-yard, and spare not me.
Hor. God-a-mercy, Grumio! then he shall have no odds.
Pet. Well, sir, in brief, the gown is not for me. 156
Gru. You are i' the right, sir; 'tis for my mistress.
Pet. Go, take it up unto thy master's use.
Gru. Villain, not for thy life! take up my mistress' gown for thy master's use! 161
Pet. Why, sir, what's your conceit in that?
Gru. O, sir, the conceit is deeper than you think for.
Take up my mistress' gown to his master's use!
O, fie, fie, fie! 165
Pet. [*Aside.*] Hortensio, say thou wilt see the tailor paid.
[*To* Tailor.] Go take it hence; be gone, and say no more.
Hor. [*Aside to* Tailor.] Tailor, I'll pay thee for thy gown to-morrow: 168
Take no unkindness of his hasty words.
Away! I say; commend me to thy master.
[*Exit* Tailor.
Pet. Well, come, my Kate; we will unto your father's,
Even in these honest mean habiliments. 172
Our purses shall be proud, our garments poor:
For 'tis the mind that makes the body rich;
And as the sun breaks through the darkest clouds,
So honour peereth in the meanest habit. 176

What is the jay more precious than the lark
Because his feathers are more beautiful?
Or is the adder better than the eel
Because his painted skin contents the eye? 180
O, no, good Kate; neither art thou the worse
For this poor furniture and mean array.
If thou account'st it shame, lay it on me;
And therefore frolic: we will hence forthwith,
To feast and sport us at thy father's house. 185
Go, call my men, and let us straight to him;
And bring our horses unto Long-lane end;
There will we mount, and thither walk on foot.
Let's see; I think 'tis now some seven o'clock,
And well we may come there by dinner-time.
Kath. I dare assure you, sir, 'tis almost two;
And 'twill be supper-time ere you come there. 192
Pet. It shall be seven ere I go to horse.
Look, what I speak, or do, or think to do,
You are still crossing it. Sirs, let't alone:
I will not go to-day; and ere I do, 196
It shall be what o'clock I say it is.
Hor. Why, so this gallant will command the sun. [*Exeunt.*

SCENE IV.—*Padua. Before* BAPTISTA'S *House.*

Enter TRANIO, *and the* Pedant *dressed like* VINCENTIO.

Tra. Sir, this is the house: please it you that I call?
Ped. Ay, what else? and, but I be deceived,
Signior Baptista may remember me,
Near twenty years ago, in Genoa, 4
Where we were lodgers at the Pegasus.
Tra. 'Tis well; and hold your own, in any case,
With such austerity as 'longeth to a father.
Ped. I warrant you. But, sir, here comes your boy; 8
'Twere good he were school'd.

Enter BIONDELLO.

Tra. Fear you not him. Sirrah Biondello,
Now do your duty throughly, I advise you:
Imagine 'twere the right Vincentio. 12
Bion. Tut! fear not me.
Tra. But hast thou done thy errand to Baptista?
Bion. I told him that your father was at Venice,
And that you look'd for him this day in Padua.
Tra. Thou'rt a tall fellow: hold thee that to drink. 17
Here comes Baptista. Set your countenance, sir.

Enter BAPTISTA *and* LUCENTIO.

Signior Baptista, you are happily met.
[*To the* Pedant.] Sir, this is the gentleman I told you of: 20
I pray you, stand good father to me now,
Give me Bianca for my patrimony.
Ped. Soft, son!
Sir, by your leave: having come to Padua 24

To gather in some debts, my son Lucentio
Made me acquainted with a weighty cause
Of love between your daughter and himself:
And,—for the good report I hear of you,   28
And for the love he beareth to your daughter,
And she to him,—to stay him not too long,
I am content, in a good father's care,
To have him match'd; and, if you please to like
No worse than I, upon some agreement   33
Me shall you find ready and willing
With one consent to have her so bestow'd;
For curious I cannot be with you,   36
Signior Baptista, of whom I hear so well.
    Bap. Sir, pardon me in what I have to say:
Your plainness and your shortness please me
    well.
Right true it is, your son Lucentio here   40
Doth love my daughter and she loveth him,
Or both dissemble deeply their affections:
And therefore, if you say no more than this,
That like a father you will deal with him   44
And pass my daughter a sufficient dower,
The match is made, and all is done;
Your son shall have my daughter with consent.
    Tra. I thank you, sir. Where, then, do you
    know best   48
We be affied and such assurance ta'en
As shall with either part's agreement stand?
    Bap. Not in my house, Lucentio; for, you
    know,
Pitchers have ears, and I have many servants. 52
Besides, old Gremio is hearkening still,
And happily we might be interrupted.
    Tra. Then at my lodging an it like you:
There doth my father lie, and there this night
We'll pass the business privately and well. 57
Send for your daughter by your servant here;
My boy shall fetch the scrivener presently.
The worst is this, that, at so slender warning, 60
You're like to have a thin and slender pittance.
    Bap. It likes me well. Cambio, hie you
    home,
And bid Bianca make her ready straight;
And, if you will, tell what hath happened: 64
Lucentio's father is arriv'd in Padua,
And how she's like to be Lucentio's wife.
    Luc. I pray the gods she may with all my
    heart!
    Tra. Dally not with the gods, but get thee
    gone.   68
Signior Baptista, shall I lead the way?
Welcome! one mess is like to be your cheer.
Come, sir; we will better it in Pisa.
    Bap. I follow you.   72
        [*Exeunt* TRANIO, Pedant, *and* BAPTISTA.
    Bion. Cambio!
    Luc. What sayst thou, Biondello?
    Bion. You saw my master wink and laugh
upon you?   76
    Luc. Biondello, what of that?
    Bion. Faith, nothing; but he has left me
here behind to expound the meaning or moral
of his signs and tokens.   80
    Luc. I pray thee, moralize them.
    Bion. Then thus. Baptista is safe, talking
with the deceiving father of a deceitful son.

    Luc. And what of him?   8
    Bion. His daughter is to be brought by you
to the supper.
    Luc. And then?
    Bion. The old priest at Saint Luke's churc
is at your command at all hours.   8
    Luc. And what of all this?
    Bion. I cannot tell, expect they are busied
about a counterfeit assurance: take you assurance of her, *cum privilegio ad imprimendun
solum.* To the church! take the priest, clerk
and some sufficient honest witnesses.
If this be not that you look for, I have no mor
    to say,   9
But bid Bianca farewell for ever and a day.
                                    [*Going*
    Luc. Hearest thou, Biondello?
    Bion. I cannot tarry: I knew a wench mar-
ried in an afternoon as she went to the garden
for parsley to stuff a rabbit; and so may you
sir; and so, adieu, sir. My master hath appointed me to go to Saint Luke's, to bid the
priest be ready to come against you come with
your appendix.   [*Exit.
    Luc. I may, and will, if she be so contented
She will be pleas'd; then wherefore should I
    doubt?
Hap what hap may, I'll roundly go about her
It shall go hard if Cambio go without her. 10
                                      [*Exit.

SCENE V.—*A public Road.*

Enter PETRUCHIO, KATHARINA, HORTENSIO,
        and Servants.

    Pet. Come on, i' God's name; once more to-
    ward our father's.
Good Lord, how bright and goodly shines the
    moon!
    Kath. The moon! the sun: it is not moon-
light now.
    Pet. I say it is the moon that shines so bright
    Kath. I know it is the sun that shines so
bright.   5
    Pet. Now, by my mother's son, and that's
    myself,
It shall be moon, or star, or what I list,
Or ere I journey to your father's house.   8
Go one and fetch our horses back again.
Evermore cross'd and cross'd; nothing but
    cross'd!
    Hor. Say as he says, or we shall never go.
    Kath. Forward, I pray, since we have come
    so far,   12
And be it moon, or sun, or what you please.
An if you please to call it a rush-candle,
Henceforth I vow it shall be so for me.
    Pet. I say it is the moon.
    Kath.   I know it is the moon. 16
    Pet. Nay, then you lie; it is the blessed
    sun.
    Kath. Then God be bless'd, it is the blessed
    sun:
But sun it is not when you say it is not,
And the moon changes even as your mind. 20

What you will have it nam'd, even that it is;
And so, it shall be so for Katharine.
Hor. Petruchio, go thy ways; the field is
won.
Pet. Well, forward, forward! thus the bowl
should run,   24
And not unluckily against the bias.
But soft! what company is coming here?

Enter VINCENTIO, *in a travelling dress.*

[*To* VINCENTIO.] Good morrow, gentle mistress:
where away?
Tell me, sweet Kate, and tell me truly too,   28
Hast thou beheld a fresher gentlewoman?
Such war of white and red within her cheeks!
What stars do spangle heaven with such beauty,
As those two eyes become that heavenly face? 32
Fair lovely maid, once more good day to thee.
Sweet Kate, embrace her for her beauty's sake.
Hor. A' will make the man mad, to make a
woman of him.   36
Kath. Young budding virgin, fair and fresh
and sweet,
Whither away, or where is thy abode?
Happy the parents of so fair a child;
Happier the man, whom favourable stars   40
Allot thee for his lovely bed-fellow!
Pet. Why, how now, Kate! I hope thou art
not mad:
This is a man, old, wrinkled, faded, wither'd,
And not a maiden, as thou sayst he is.   44
Kath. Pardon, old father, my mistaking eyes,
That have been so bedazzled with the sun
That everything I look on seemeth green:
Now I perceive thou art a reverend father; 48
Pardon, I pray thee, for my mad mistaking.
Pet. Do, good old grandsire; and withal
make known
Which way thou travellest: if along with us,
We shall be joyful of thy company.   52
Vin. Fair sir, and you my merry mistress,
That with your strange encounter much amaz'd
me,
My name is called Vincentio; my dwelling,
Pisa,
And bound I am to Padua, there to visit   56
A son of mine, which long I have not seen.
Pet. What is his name?
Vin.   Lucentio, gentle sir.
Pet. Happily met; the happier for thy son.
And now by law, as well as reverend age,   60
May entitle thee my loving father:
The sister to my wife, this gentlewoman,
Thy son by this hath married. Wonder not,
Nor be not griev'd: she is of good esteem,   64
Her dowry wealthy, and of worthy birth;
Beside, so qualified as may beseem
The spouse of any noble gentleman.
Let me embrace with old Vincentio;   68
And wander we to see thy honest son,
Who will of thy arrival be full joyous.
Vin. But is this true? or is it else your plea-
sure,
Like pleasant travellers, to break a jest   72
Upon the company you overtake?
Hor. I do assure thee, father, so it is.

Pet. Come, go along, and see the truth
hereof;
For our first merriment hath made thee jealous.
[*Exeunt all but* HORTENSIO.
Hor. Well, Petruchio, this has put me in
heart.   77
Have to my widow! and if she be froward,
Then hast thou taught Hortensio to be unto-
ward.   [*Exit.*

ACT V

SCENE I.—*Padua. Before* LUCENTIO'S *House.*

Enter on one side BIONDELLO, LUCENTIO, *and*
BIANCA; GREMIO *walking on the other side.*

Bion. Softly and swiftly, sir, for the priest is
ready.
Luc. I fly, Biondello: but they may chance
to need thee at home; therefore leave us.   4
Bion. Nay, faith, I'll see the church o' your
back; and then come back to my master as soon
as I can.
[*Exeunt* LUCENTIO, BIANCA, *and* BIONDELLO.
Gre. I marvel Cambio comes not all this
while.   8

Enter PETRUCHIO, KATHARINA, VINCENTIO,
and Attendants.

Pet. Sir, here's the door, this is Lucentio's
house:
My father's bears more toward the market-
place;
Thither must I, and here I leave you, sir.
Vin. You shall not choose but drink before
you go.   12
I think I shall command your welcome here,
And, by all likelihood, some cheer is toward.
[*Knocks.*
Gre. They're busy within; you were best
knock louder.   16

Enter Pedant *above, at a window.*

Ped. What's he that knocks as he would beat
down the gate?
Vin. Is Signior Lucentio within, sir?
Ped. He's within, sir, but not to be spoken
withal.   21
Vin. What if a man bring him a hundred
pound or two, to make merry withal?
Ped. Keep your hundred pounds to yourself:
he shall need none so long as I live.   25
Pet. Nay, I told you your son was well beloved
in Padua. Do you hear, sir? To leave frivolous
circumstances, I pray you, tell Signior Lucentio
that his father is come from Pisa, and is here
at the door to speak with him.
Ped. Thou liest: his father is come from
Padua, and here looking out at the window. 32
Vin. Art thou his father?
Ped. Ay, sir; so his mother says, if I may
believe her.
Pet. [*To* VINCENTIO.] Why, how now, gentleman! why, this is flat knavery, to take upon
you another man's name.
Ped. Lay hands on the villain: I believe, a'

means to cozen somebody in this city under my
countenance.   41

Re-enter BIONDELLO.

Bion. I have seen them in the church together: God send 'em good shipping! But who is
here? mine old master, Vincentio! now we are
undone and brought to nothing.   45
Vin. [*Seeing* BIONDELLO.] Come hither,
crack-hemp.
Bion. I hope I may choose, sir.   48
Vin. Come hither, you rogue. What, have
you forgot me?
Bion. Forgot you! no, sir: I could not forget
you, for I never saw you before in all my life. 52
Vin. What, you notorious villain! didst thou
never see thy master's father, Vincentio?
Bion. What, my old, worshipful old master?
yes, marry, sir: see where he looks out of the
window.   57
Vin. Is't so, indeed?   [*Beats* BIONDELLO.
Bion. Help, help, help! here's a madman
will murder me.   [*Exit.*
Ped. Help, son! help, Signior Baptista! 61
                    [*Exit from the window.*
Pet. Prithee, Kate, let's stand aside, and see
the end of this controversy.   [*They retire.*

Re-enter Pedant *below;* BAPTISTA, TRANIO, *and*
Servants.

Tra. Sir, what are you that offer to beat my
servant?   65
Vin. What am I, sir! nay, what are you,
sir? O immortal gods! O fine villain! A silken
doublet! a velvet hose! a scarlet cloak! and a
copatain hat! O, I am undone! I am undone!
while I play the good husband at home, my son
and my servant spend all at the university.
Tra. How now! what's the matter?   72
Bap. What, is the man lunatic?
Tra. Sir, you seem a sober ancient gentleman
by your habit, but your words show you a madman. Why, sir, what 'cerns it you if I wear pearl
and gold? I thank my good father, I am able to
maintain it.
Vin. Thy father! O villain! he is a sail-
maker in Bergamo.   80
Bap. You mistake, sir, you mistake, sir. Pray,
what do you think is his name?
Vin. His name! as if I knew not his name:
I have brought him up ever since he was three
years old, and his name is Tranio.   85
Ped. Away, away, mad ass! his name is Lucentio; and he is mine only son, and heir to the
lands of me, Signior Vincentio.   88
Vin. Lucentio! O! he hath murdered his
master. Lay hold on him, I charge you in the
duke's name. O my son, my son! tell me, thou
villain, where is my son Lucentio?   92
Tra. Call forth an officer.

Enter one with an Officer.

Carry this mad knave to the gaol. Father Baptista, I charge you see that he be forthcoming.
Vin. Carry me to the gaol!   96

Gre. Stay, officer: he shall not go to priso
Bap. Talk not, Signior Gremio: I say he sh
go to prison.
Gre. Take heed, Signior Baptista, lest you
cony-catched in this business: I dare swear th
is the right Vincentio.
Ped. Swear, if thou darest.
Gre. Nay, I dare not swear it.
Tra. Then thou wert best say, that I am n
Lucentio.
Gre. Yes, I know thee to be Signior Lucenti
Bap. Away with the dotard! to the gaol wi
him!
Vin. Thus strangers may be haled a
abused: O monstrous villain!

Re-enter BIONDELLO, *with* LUCENTIO
and BIANCA.

Bion. O! we are spoiled; and yonder he
deny him, forswear him, or else we are all u
done.
Luc. [*Kneeling.*] Pardon, sweet father.
Vin.   Lives my sweetest so
     [BIONDELLO, TRANIO, *and* Pedant *run o*
Bian. [*Kneeling.*] Pardon, dear father.
Bap.   How hast thou offende
Where is Lucentio?
Luc.   Here's Lucentio,
Right son to the right Vincentio;
That have by marriage made thy daughter mir
While counterfeit supposes blear'd thine ey
Gre. Here's packing, with a witness, to d
ceive us all!
Vin. Where is that damned villain Tranio
That fac'd and brav'd me in this matter so?
Bap. Why, tell me, is not this my Cambi
Bian. Cambio is chang'd into Lucentio.
Luc. Love wrought these miracles. Bianca
love
Made me exchange my state with Tranio,
While he did bear my countenance in the tow
And happily I have arriv'd at last
Unto the wished haven of my bliss.
What Tranio did, myself enforc'd him to;
Then pardon him, sweet father, for my sake
Vin. I'll slit the villain's nose, that wou
have sent me to the gaol.
Bap. [*To* LUCENTIO.] But do you hear, si
Have you married my daughter without askir
my good will?
Vin. Fear not, Baptista; we will content yo
go to: but I will in, to be revenged for th
villany.   [*Ex*
Bap. And I, to sound the depth of th
knavery.   [*Ex*
Luc. Look not pale, Bianca; thy father w
not frown.   [*Exeunt* LUCENTIO *and* BIANC
Gre. My cake is dough; but I'll in amor
the rest,
Out of hope of all, but my share of the feas
                                            [*Ex*

PETRUCHIO *and* KATHARINA *advance.*

Kath. Husband, let's follow, to see the en
of this ado.
Pet. First kiss me, Kate, and we will.

Kath. What! in the midst of the street?
Pet. What! art thou ashamed of me? 152
Kath. No, sir, God forbid; but ashamed to kiss.
Pet. Why, then let's home again. Come, sirrah, let's away.
Kath. Nay, I will give thee a kiss: now pray thee, love, stay.
Pet. Is not this well? Come, my sweet Kate: Better once than never, for never too late. 157
[*Exeunt.*

SCENE II.—*A Room in* LUCENTIO'S *House.*

A Banquet set out. Enter BAPTISTA, VINCENTIO, GREMIO, *the* Pedant, LUCENTIO, BIANCA, PETRUCHIO, KATHARINA, HORTENSIO, *and* Widow. TRANIO, BIONDELLO, GRUMIO, *and Others, attending.*

Luc. At last, though long, our jarring notes agree:
And time it is, when raging war is done,
To smile at 'scapes and perils overblown.
My fair Bianca, bid my father welcome, 4
While I with self-same kindness welcome thine.
Brother Petruchio, sister Katharina,
And thou, Hortensio, with thy loving widow,
Feast with the best, and welcome to my house:
My banquet is to close our stomachs up, 9
After our great good cheer. Pray you, sit down;
For now we sit to chat as well as eat.
[*They sit at table.*
Pet. Nothing but sit and sit, and eat and eat! 12
Bap. Padua affords this kindness, son Petruchio.
Pet. Padua affords nothing but what is kind.
Hor. For both our sakes I would that word were true.
Pet. Now, for my life, Hortensio fears his widow. 16
Wid. Then never trust me, if I be afeard.
Pet. You are very sensible, and yet you miss my sense:
I mean, Hortensio is afeard of you.
Wid. He that is giddy thinks the world turns round. 20
Pet. Roundly replied.
Kath. Mistress, how mean you that?
Wid. Thus I conceive by him.
Pet. Conceives by me! How likes Hortensio that?
Hor. My widow says, thus she conceives her tale. 24
Pet. Very well mended. Kiss him for that, good widow.
Kath. 'He that is giddy thinks the world turns round:'
I pray you, tell me what you meant by that.
Wid. Your husband, being troubled with a shrew, 28
Measures my husband's sorrow by his woe:
And now you know my meaning.
Kath. A very mean meaning.
Wid. Right, I mean you.

Kath. And I am mean, indeed, respecting you. 32
Pet. To her, Kate!
Hor. To her, widow!
Pet. A hundred marks, my Kate does put her down.
Hor. That's my office. 36
Pet. Spoke like an officer: ha' to thee, lad.
[*Drinks to* HORTENSIO.
Bap. How likes Gremio these quick-witted folks?
Gre. Believe me, sir, they butt together well.
Bian. Head and butt! a hasty-witted body
Would say your head and butt were head and horn. 41
Vin. Ay, mistress bride, hath that awaken'd you?
Bian. Ay, but not frighted me; therefore I'll sleep again.
Pet. Nay, that you shall not; since you have begun, 44
Have at you for a bitter jest or two.
Bian. Am I your bird? I mean to shift my bush;
And then pursue me as you draw your bow.
You are welcome all. 48
[*Exeunt* BIANCA, KATHARINA, *and* Widow.
Pet. She hath prevented me. Here, Signior Tranio;
This bird you aim'd at, though you hit her not:
Therefore a health to all that shot and miss'd.
Tra. O sir! Lucentio slipp'd me, like his greyhound, 52
Which runs himself, and catches for his master.
Pet. A good swift simile, but something currish.
Tra. 'Tis well, sir, that you hunted for yourself: 55
'Tis thought your deer does hold you at a bay.
Bap. O ho, Petruchio! Tranio hits you now.
Luc. I thank thee for that gird, good Tranio.
Hor. Confess, confess, hath he not hit you here?
Pet. A' has a little gall'd me, I confess; 60
And, as the jest did glance away from me,
'Tis ten to one it maim'd you two outright.
Bap. Now, in good sadness, son Petruchio,
I think thou hast the veriest shrew of all. 64
Pet. Well, I say no: and therefore, for assurance,
Let's each one send unto his wife;
And he whose wife is most obedient
To come at first when he doth send for her, 68
Shall win the wager which we will propose.
Hor. Content. What is the wager?
Luc.   Twenty crowns.
Pet. Twenty crowns!
I'll venture so much of my hawk or hound, 72
But twenty times so much upon my wife.
Luc. A hundred then.
Hor.   Content.
Pet.   A match! 'tis done.
Hor. Who shall begin?
Luc.   That will I.
Go, Biondello, bid your mistress come to me. 76
Bion. I go.
[*Exit.*

Bap. Son, I will be your half, Bianca comes.
Luc. I'll have no halves; I'll bear it all myself.

Re-enter BIONDELLO.

How now! what news?
Bion.   Sir, my mistress sends you word
That she is busy and she cannot come.   81
Pet. How! she is busy, and she cannot come!
Is that an answer?
Gre.   Ay, and a kind one too:
Pray God, sir, your wife send you not a worse.
Pet. I hope, better.   85
Hor. Sirrah Biondello, go and entreat my wife
To come to me forthwith.   [*Exit* BIONDELLO.
Pet.   O ho! entreat her!
Nay, then she must needs come.
Hor.   I am afraid, sir,   88
Do what you can, yours will not be entreated.

Re-enter BIONDELLO.

Now, where's my wife?
Bion. She says you have some goodly jest in hand:
She will not come: she bids you come to her. 92
Pet. Worse and worse; she will not come! O vile,
Intolerable, not to be endur'd!
Sirrah Grumio, go to your mistress; say,
I command her come to me.   [*Exit* GRUMIO.
Hor.   I know her answer.   96
Pet. What?
Hor. She will not.
Pet. The fouler fortune mine, and there an end.

Re-enter KATHARINA.

Bap. Now, by my holidame, here comes Katharina!   100
Kath. What is your will, sir, that you send for me?
Pet. Where is your sister, and Hortensio's wife?
Kath. They sit conferring by the parlour fire.
Pet. Go, fetch them hither: if they deny to come,   104
Swinge me them soundly forth unto their husbands.
Away, I say, and bring them hither straight.
        [*Exit* KATHARINA.
Luc. Here is a wonder, if you talk of a wonder.
Hor. And so it is. I wonder what it bodes.
Pet. Marry, peace it bodes, and love, and quiet life,   109
An awful rule and right supremacy;
And, to be short, what not that's sweet and happy.
Bap. Now fair befall thee, good Petruchio!
The wager thou hast won; and I will add   113
Unto their losses twenty thousand crowns;
Another dowry to another daughter,
For she is chang'd, as she had never been.   116
Pet. Nay, I will win my wager better yet,
And show more sign of her obedience,
Her new-built virtue and obedience.
See where she comes, and brings your froward wives   120
As prisoners to her womanly persuasion.

Re-enter KATHARINA, *with* BIANCA *and* Widow.

Katharine, that cap of yours becomes you not:
Off with that bauble, throw it under foot.
        [KATHARINA *pulls off her cap, and throws it down.*
Wid. Lord! let me never have a cause to sigh,   124
Till I be brought to such a silly pass!
Bian. Fie! what a foolish duty call you this?
Luc. I would your duty were as foolish too:
The wisdom of your duty, fair Bianca,   128
Hath cost me an hundred crowns since suppertime.
Bian. The more fool you for laying on my duty.
Pet. Katharine, I charge thee, tell these headstrong women
What duty they do owe their lords and husbands.   132
Wid. Come, come, you're mocking: we will have no telling.
Pet. Come on, I say; and first begin with her.
Wid. She shall not.
Pet. I say she shall: and first begin with her.   136
Kath. Fie, fie! unknit that threatening unkind brow,
And dart not scornful glances from those eyes,
To wound thy lord, thy king, thy governor:
It blots thy beauty as frosts do bite the meads,
Confounds thy fame as whirlwinds shake fair buds,   141
And in no sense is meet or amiable.
A woman mov'd is like a fountain troubled,
Muddy, ill-seeming, thick, bereft of beauty; 144
And while it is so, none so dry or thirsty
Will deign to sip or touch one drop of it.
Thy husband is thy lord, thy life, thy keeper,
Thy head, thy sovereign; one that cares for thee,   148
And for thy maintenance commits his body
To painful labour both by sea and land,
To watch the night in storms, the day in cold,
Whilst thou liest warm at home, secure and safe;   152
And craves no other tribute at thy hands
But love, fair looks, and true obedience;
Too little payment for so great a debt.
Such duty as the subject owes the prince,   156
Even such a woman oweth to her husband;
And when she's froward, peevish, sullen, sour,
And not obedient to his honest will,
What is she but a foul contending rebel,   160
And graceless traitor to her loving lord?—
I am asham'd that women are so simple
To offer war where they should kneel for peace,
Or seek for rule, supremacy, and sway,   164
When they are bound to serve, love, and obey.
Why are our bodies soft, and weak, and smooth,
Unapt to toil and trouble in the world,
But that our soft conditions and our hearts 168

Should well agree with our external parts?
Come, come, you froward and unable worms!
My mind hath been as big as one of yours,
My heart as great, my reason haply more, 172
To bandy word for word and frown for frown;
But now I see our lances are but straws,
Our strength as weak, our weakness past com-
 pare,
That seeming to be most which we indeed least
 are. 176
Then vail your stomachs, for it is no boot,
And place your hands below your husband's
 foot:
In token of which duty, if he please,
My hand is ready; may it do him ease. 180
 Pet. Why, there's a wench! Come on, and
 kiss me, Kate.

 Luc. Well, go thy ways, old lad, for thou
 shalt ha't.
 Vin. 'Tis a good hearing when children are
 toward.
 Luc. But a harsh hearing when women are
 froward. 184
 Pet. Come, Kate, we'll to bed.
We three are married, but you two are sped.
'Twas I won the wager, [*To* LUCENTIO.] though
 you hit the white;
And, being a winner, God give you good
 night! 188
   [*Exeunt* PETRUCHIO *and* KATHARINA.
 Hor. Now, go thy ways; thou hast tam'd a
 curst shrew.
 Luc. 'Tis a wonder, by your leave, she will
 be tam'd so.   [*Exeunt.*

ALL'S WELL THAT ENDS WELL

DRAMATIS PERSONÆ

KING OF FRANCE.
DUKE OF FLORENCE.
BERTRAM, Count of Rousillon.
LAFEU, an old Lord.
PAROLLES, a follower of Bertram.
Steward to the Countess of Rousillon.
LAVACHE, a Clown in her household.
A Page.

COUNTESS OF ROUSILLON, Mother to Bertram.
HELENA, a Gentlewoman protected by the Countess.
An Old Widow of Florence.
DIANA, Daughter to the Widow.
VIOLENTA,
MARIANA, } Neighbours and Friends to the Widow.

Lords, Officers, Soldiers, &c., French and Florentine.

SCENE.—*Rousillon, Paris, Florence, Marseilles.*

ACT I

SCENE I.—*Rousillon. A Room in the* COUNTESS'S *Palace.*

Enter BERTRAM, *the* COUNTESS OF ROUSILLON, HELENA, *and* LAFEU, *all in black.*

Count. In delivering my son from me, I bury a second husband.

Ber. And I, in going, madam, weep o'er my father's death anew; but I must attend his majesty's command, to whom I am now in ward, evermore in subjection. 6

Laf. You shall find of the king a husband, madam; you, sir, a father. He that so generally is at all times good, must of necessity hold his virtue to you, whose worthiness would stir it up where it wanted rather than lack it where there is such abundance. 12

Count. What hope is there of his majesty's amendment?

Laf. He hath abandoned his physicians, madam; under whose practices he hath persecuted time with hope, and finds no other advantage in the process but only the losing of hope by time. 19

Count. This young gentlewoman had a father,—O, that 'had!' how sad a passage 'tis!—whose skill was almost as great as his honesty; had it stretched so far, would have made nature immortal, and death should have play for lack of work. Would, for the king's sake, he were living! I think it would be the death of the king's disease. 27

Laf. How called you the man you speak of, madam?

Count. He was famous, sir, in his profession, and it was his great right to be so: Gerard de Narbon. 32

Laf. He was excellent indeed, madam: the king very lately spoke of him admiringly and mourningly. He was skilful enough to have lived still, if knowledge could be set up against mortality. 37

Ber. What is it, my good lord, the king languishes of?

Laf. A fistula, my lord. 40

Ber. I heard not of it before.

Laf. I would it were not notorious. Was this gentlewoman the daughter of Gerard de Narbon? 44

Count. His sole child, my lord; and bequeathed to my overlooking. I have those hopes of her good that her education promises: her dispositions she inherits, which makes fair gifts fairer; for where an unclean mind carries virtuous qualities, there commendations go with pity; they are virtues and traitors too: in her they are the better for their simpleness; she derives her honesty and achieves her goodness. 53

Laf. Your commendations, madam, get from her tears.

Count. 'Tis the best brine a maiden can season her praise in. The remembrance of her father never approaches her heart but the tyranny of her sorrows takes all livelihood from her cheek. No more of this, Helena, go to, no more; lest it be rather thought you affect a sorrow, than have it. 62

Hel. I do affect a sorrow indeed, but I have it too. 64

Laf. Moderate lamentation is the right of the dead, excessive grief the enemy to the living.

Hel. If the living be enemy to the grief, the excess makes it soon mortal. 68

Ber. Madam, I desire your holy wishes.

Laf. How understand we that?

Count. Be thou blest, Bertram; and succeed thy father
In manners, as in shape! thy blood and virtue 72
Contend for empire in thee; and thy goodness
Share with thy birthright! Love all, trust a few,
Do wrong to none: be able for thine enemy
Rather in power than use, and keep thy friend 76
Under thy own life's key: be check'd for silence,
But never tax'd for speech. What heaven more will
That thee may furnish, and my prayers pluck down,
Fall on thy head! Farewell, my lord; 80
'Tis an unseason'd courtier; good my lord,
Advise him.

Laf.   He cannot want the best
That shall attend his love.

Count. Heaven bless him! Farewell, Bertram. [*Exit.*

Ber. [*To* HELENA.] The best wishes that can

e forged in your thoughts be servants to you!
e comfortable to my mother, your mistress,
nd make much of her. 88

Laf. Farewell, pretty lady: you must hold
ne credit of your father.

                 [*Exeunt* BERTRAM *and* LAFEU.

Hel. O! were that all. I think not on my
    father;
nd these great tears grace his remembrance
    more 92
han those I shed for him. What was he like?
have forgot him: my imagination
arries no favour in't but Bertram's.
am undone: there is no living, none, 96
'Bertram be away. It were all one
hat I should love a bright particular star
nd think to wed it, he is so above me:
n his bright radiance and collateral light 100
Must I be comforted, not in his sphere.
The ambition in my love thus plagues itself:
The hind that would be mated by the lion
Must die for love. 'Twas pretty, though a
    plague, 104
o see him every hour; to sit and draw
His arched brows, his hawking eye, his curls,
n our heart's table; heart too capable
Of every line and trick of his sweet favour: 108
But now he's gone, and my idolatrous fancy
Must sanctify his reliques. Who comes here?
One that goes with him: I love him for his sake;
nd yet I know him a notorious liar, 112
Think him a great way fool, solely a coward;
'et these fix'd evils sit so fit in him,
That they take place, when virtue's steely bones
Look bleak in the cold wind: withal, full oft we
    see 116
Cold wisdom waiting on superfluous folly.

        Enter PAROLLES.

Par. Save you, fair queen!
Hel. And you, monarch!
Par. No. 120
Hel. And no.
Par. Are you meditating on virginity?
Hel. Ay. You have some stain of soldier in
ou; let me ask you a question. Man is enemy
o virginity; how may we barricado it against
im? 126
Par. Keep him out.
Hel. But he assails; and our virginity, though
aliant in the defence, yet is weak. Unfold to
s some war-like resistance.
Par. There is none: man, sitting down before
ou, will undermine you and blow you up. 132
Hel. Bless our poor virginity from under-
miners and blowers up! Is there no military
policy, how virgins might blow up men?
Par. Virginity being blown down, man will
quicklier be blown up: marry in blowing him
down again, with the breach yourselves made,
ou lose your city. It is not politic in the commonwealth of nature to preserve virginity. Loss
of virginity is rational increase, and there was
never virgin got till virginity was first lost.
That you were made of is metal to make virgins.

Virginity, by being once lost, may be ten times
found: by being ever kept, it is ever lost. 'Tis
too cold a companion: away witn't!

Hel. I will stand for't a little, though therefore I die a virgin. 148

Par. There's little can be said in't; 'tis
against the rule of nature. To speak on the part
of virginity is to accuse your mothers, which
is most infallible disobedience. He that nangs
himself is a virgin: virginity murders itself, and
should be buried in highways, out of all sanctified limit, as a desperate offendress against nature. Virginity breeds mites, much like a cheese,
consumes itself to the very paring, and so dies
with feeding his own stomach. Besides, virginity
is peevish, proud, idle, made of self-love, which
is the most inhibited sin in the canon. Keep it
not; you cannot choose but lose by't! Out with't!
within the year it will make itself two, which is
a goodly increase, and the principal itself not
much the worse. Away with't! 164

Hel. How might cne do, sir, to lose it to her
own liking?

Par. Let me see: marry, ill, to like him that
ne'er it likes. 'Tis a commodity that will lose
the gloss with lying; the longer kept, the less
worth: off with't, while 'tis vendible; answer the
time of request. Virginity, like an old courtier,
wears her cap out of fashion; richly suited, but
unsuitable: just like the brooch and the toothpick, which wear not now. Your date is better in
your pie and your porridge than in your cheek:
and your virginity, your old virginity, is like one
of our French withered pears; it looks ill, it eats
drily; marry, 'tis a withered pear; it was formerly better; marry, yet 'tis a withered pear.
Will you anything with it? 180

    Hel. Not my virginity yet.
There shall your master have a thousand loves,
A mother, and a mistress, and a friend,
A phœnix, captain, and an enemy, 184
A guide, a goddess, and a sovereign,
A counsellor, a traitress, and a dear;
His humble ambition, proud humility,
His jarring concord, and his discord dulcet, 188
His faith, his sweet disaster; with a world
Of pretty, fond, adoptious christendoms,
That blinking Cupid gossips. Now shall he—
I know not what he shall. God send him well!
The court's a learning-place, and he is one— 193
    Par. What one, i' faith?
    Hel. That I wish well. 'Tis pity—
    Par. What's pity? 196
    Hel. That wishing well had not a body in't,
Which might be felt; that we, the poorer born,
Whose baser stars do shut us up in wishes,
Might with effects of them follow our friends,
And show what we alone must think, which
    never 201
Returns us thanks.

        Enter a Page.

    Page. Monsieur Parolles, my lord calls for
you.   [*Exit.*
    Par. Little Helen, farewell: if I can remem-
ber thee, I will think of thee at court.

Hel. Monsieur Parolles, you were born under a charitable star. 208

Par. Under Mars, I.

Hel. I especially think, under Mars.

Par. Why under Mars?

Hel. The wars have so kept you under that you must needs be born under Mars. 213

Par. When he was predominant.

Hel. When he was retrograde, I think rather.

Par. Why think you so? 216

Hel. You go so much backward when you fight.

Par. That's for advantage.

Hel. So is running away, when fear proposes the safety: but the composition that your valour and fear makes in you is a virtue of a good wing, and I like the wear well. 223

Par. I am so full of businesses I cannot answer thee acutely. I will return perfect courtier; in the which, my instruction shall serve to naturalize thee, so thou wilt be capable of a courtier's counsel, and understand what advice shall thrust upon thee; else thou diest in thine unthankfulness, and thine ignorance makes thee away: farewell. When thou hast leisure, say thy prayers; when thou hast none, remember thy friends. Get thee a good husband, and use him as he uses thee: so, farewell. [*Exit.*

Hel. Our remedies oft in ourselves do lie
Which we ascribe to heaven: the fated sky 236
Gives us free scope; only doth backward pull
Our slow designs when we ourselves are dull.
What power is it which mounts my love so high;
That makes me see, and cannot feed mine eye?
The mightiest space in fortune nature brings 241
To join like likes, and kiss like native things.
Impossible be strange attempts to those
That weigh their pains in sense, and do suppose
What hath been cannot be: who ever strove 245
To show her merit, that did miss her love?
The king's disease,—my project may deceive me,
But my intents are fix'd and will not leave me. [*Exit.*

SCENE II.—*Paris. A Room in the* KING'S *Palace.*

Flourish of Cornets. Enter the KING OF FRANCE, *with letters;* Lords *and Others attending.*

King. The Florentines and Senoys are by the ears;
Have fought with equal fortune, and continue
A braving war.

First Lord. So 'tis reported, sir.

King. Nay, 'tis most credible: we here receive it 4
A certainty, vouch'd from our cousin Austria,
With caution that the Florentine will move us
For speedy aid; wherein our dearest friend
Prejudicates the business, and would seem 8
To have us make denial.

First Lord. His love and wisdom,
Approv'd so to your majesty, may plead
For amplest credence.

King. He hath arm'd our answe
And Florence is denied before he comes: n
Yet, for our gentlemen that mean to see
The Tuscan service, freely have they leave
To stand on either part.

Sec. Lord. It well may serve
A nursery to our gentry, who are sick n
For breathing and exploit.

King. What's he comes here

Enter BERTRAM, LAFEU, *and* PAROLLES.

First Lord. It is the Count Rousillon, m
good lord,
Young Bertram.

King. Youth, thou bear'st thy father's face
Frank nature, rather curious than in haste, 2
Hath well compos'd thee. Thy father's mora parts
Mayst thou inherit too! Welcome to Paris.

Ber. My thanks and duty are your majesty's

King. I would I had that corporal soundnes now, 2
As when thy father and myself in friendship
First tried our soldiership! He did look far
Into the service of the time and was
Disciplèd of the bravest: he lasted long; 2
But on us both did haggish age steal on,
And wore us out of act. It much repairs me
To talk of your good father. In his youth
He had the wit which I can well observe 3
To-day in our young lords; but they may jes
Till their own scorn return to them unnoted
Ere they can hide their levity in honour.
So like a courtier, contempt nor bitterness 3
Were in his pride or sharpness; if they were,
His equal had awak'd them; and his honour,
Clock to itself, knew the true minute when
Exception bid him speak, and at this time 4
His tongue obey'd his hand: who were belov him
He us'd as creatures of another place,
And bow'd his eminent top to their low ranks
Making them proud of his humility, 4
In their poor praise he humbled. Such a ma
Might be a copy to these younger times,
Which, follow'd well, would demonstrate them now
But goers backward.

Ber. His good remembrance, sir, 48
Lies richer in your thoughts than on his tomb
So in approof lives not his epitaph
As in your royal speech.

King. Would I were with him! He would always say,— 52
Methinks I hear him now: his plausive words
He scatter'd not in ears, but grafted them,
To grow there and to bear. 'Let me not live,'—
Thus his good melancholy oft began, 56
On the catastrophe and heel of pastime,
When it was out,—'Let me not live,' quoth he,
'After my flame lacks oil, to be the snuff 59
Of younger spirits, whose apprehensive senses
All but new things disdain; whose judgments are
Mere fathers of their garments; whose constancies

xpire before their fashions.' This he wish'd:
after him, do after him wish too,   64
ince I nor wax nor honey can bring home,
quickly were dissolved from my hive,
o give some labourers room.

Sec. Lord.   You are lov'd, sir;
hey that least lend it you shall lack you first. 68

King. I fill a place, I know't. How long is't,
count,
ince the physician at your father's died?
te was much fam'd.

Ber.   Some six months since, my lord.

King. If he were living, I would try him yet:
end me an arm: the rest have worn me out 73
/ith several applications: nature and sickness
)ebate it at their leisure. Welcome, count;
ly son's no dearer.

Ber.   Thank your majesty. 76

[*Exeunt. Flourish.*

SCENE III.—*Rousillon. A Room in the*
COUNTESS'S *Palace.*

Enter COUNTESS, Steward, *and* Clown.

Count. I will now hear: what say you of this
entlewoman?

Stew. Madam, the care I have had to even
our content, I wish might be found in the
alendar of my past endeavours; for then we
ound our modesty and make foul the clearness
f our deservings, when of ourselves we publish
tem.   8

Count. What does this knave here? Get you
one, sirrah: the complaints I have heard of you
do not all believe: 'tis my slowness that I do
ot; for I know you lack not folly to commit
tem, and have ability enough to make such
naveries yours.

Clo. 'Tis not unknown to you, madam, I am
poor fellow.   16

Count. Well, sir.

Clo. No, madam, 'tis not so well that I am
)or, though many of the rich are damned. But, if
may have your ladyship's good will to go to the
orld, Isbel the woman and I will do as we may.

Count. Wilt thou needs be a beggar?

Clo. I do beg your good will in this case.

Count. In what case?   24

Clo. In Isbel's case and mine own. Service is
o heritage; and I think I shall never have the
lessing of God till I have issue o' my body, for
tey say barnes are blessings.   28

Count. Tell me thy reason why thou wilt
tarry.

Clo. My poor body, madam, requires it: I
m driven on by the flesh; and he must needs
o that the devil drives.   33

Count. Is this all your worship's reason?

Clo. Faith, madam, I have other holy reasons,
tch as they are.   36

Count. May the world know them?

Clo. I have been, madam, a wicked creature,
s you and all flesh and blood are; and, indeed,
do marry that I may repent.   40

Count. Thy marriage, sooner than thy
wickedness.

Clo. I am out o' friends, madam; and I hope
to have friends for my wife's sake.   44

Count. Such friends are thine enemies, knave.

Clo. You're shallow, madam, in great friends;
for the knaves come to do that for me which I
am aweary of. He that ears my land spares my
team, and gives me leave to in the crop: if I be
his cuckold, he's my drudge. He that comforts
my wife is the cherisher of my flesh and blood;
he that cherishes my flesh and blood loves my
flesh and blood; he that loves my flesh and
blood is my friend: *ergo*, he that kisses my wife
is my friend. If men could be contented to be
what they are, there were no fear in marriage;
for young Charbon the puritan, and old Poysam
the papist, howsome'er their hearts are severed
in religion, their heads are both one; they may
joul horns together like any deer i' the herd. 60

Count. Wilt thou ever be a foul-mouthed and
calumnious knave?

Clo. A prophet I, madam; and I speak the
truth the next way: 64

For I the ballad will repeat,
    Which men full true shall find;
Your marriage comes by destiny,
    Your cuckoo sings by kind.   68

Count. Get you gone, sir: I'll talk with you
more anon.

Stew. May it please you, madam, that he bid
Helen come to you: of her I am to speak.   72

Count. Sirrah, tell my gentlewoman I would
speak with her; Helen I mean.

Clo. Was this fair face the cause, quoth she,
    Why were the Grecians sacked Troy?   76
Fond done, done fond,
    Was this King Priam's joy?
With that she sighed as she stood,
With that she sighed as she stood,   80
    And gave this sentence then;
Among nine bad if one be good,
Among nine bad if one be good,
    There's yet one good in ten.   84

Count. What! one good in ten? you corrupt
the song, sirrah.

Clo. One good woman in ten, madam; which
is a purifying o' the song. Would God would
serve the world so all the year! we'd find no
fault with the tithe-woman if I were the parson.
One in ten, quoth a'! An we might have a good
woman born but for every blazing star, or at an
earthquake, 'twould mend the lottery well: a
man may draw his heart out ere a' pluck one.

Count. You'll be gone, sir knave, and do as I
command you!   96

Clo. That man should be at woman's command, and yet no hurt done! Though honesty
be no puritan, yet it will do no hurt; it will wear
the surplice of humility over the black gown of a
big heart. I am going, forsooth: the business is
for Helen to come hither.   [*Exit.*

Count. Well, now.

Stew. I know, madam, you love your gentlewoman entirely.   105

Count. Faith, I do: her father bequeathed her to me; and she herself, without other advantage, may lawfully make title to as much love as she finds: there is more owing her than is paid, and more shall be paid her than she'll demand. 111

Stew. Madam, I was very late more near her than I think she wished me: alone she was, and did communicate to herself her own words to her own ears; she thought, I dare vow for her, they touched not any stranger sense. Her matter was, she loved your son: Fortune, she said, was no goddess, that had put such difference betwixt their two estates; Love no god, that would not extend his might, only where qualities were level; Dian no queen of virgins, that would suffer her poor knight surprised, without rescue in the first assault or ransom afterward. This she delivered in the most bitter touch of sorrow that e'er I heard virgin exclaim in; which I held my duty speedily to acquaint you withal, sithence in the loss that may happen, it concerns you something to know it. 128

Count. You have discharged this honestly: keep it to yourself. Many likelihoods informed me of this before, which hung so tottering in the balance that I could neither believe nor misdoubt. Pray you, leave me: stall this in your bosom; and I thank you for your honest care. I will speak with you further anon. [*Exit* Steward.

Enter HELENA.

Even so it was with me when I was young: 136
If ever we are nature's, these are ours; this thorn
Doth to our rose of youth rightly belong;
Our blood to us, this to our blood is born:
It is the show and seal of nature's truth, 140
Where love's strong passion is impress'd in youth:
By our remembrances of days foregone,
Such were our faults; or then we thought them none.
Her eye is sick on't: I observe her now. 144

Hel. What is your pleasure, madam?
Count. You know, Helen, I am a mother to you.
Hel. Mine honourable mistress.
Count. Nay, a mother: Why not a mother? When I said, 'a mother,' Methought you saw a serpent: what's in 'mother' 149
That you start at it? I say, I am your mother;
And put you in the catalogue of those
That were enwombed mine: 'tis often seen 152
Adoption strives with nature, and choice breeds
A native slip to us from foreign seeds;
You ne'er oppress'd me with a mother's groan,
Yet I express to you a mother's care. 156
God's mercy, maiden! does it curd thy blood
To say I am thy mother? What's the matter,
That this distemper'd messenger of wet,
The many-colour'd Iris, rounds thine eye? 160
Why? that you are my daughter?
Hel. That I am not.

Count. I say, I am your mother.
Hel. Pardon, madam
The Count Rousillon cannot be my brother:
I am from humble, he from honour'd name; 16
No note upon my parents, his all noble:
My master, my dear lord he is; and I
His servant live, and will his vassal die.
He must not be my brother.
Count. Nor I your mother? 16
Hel. You are my mother, madam: woul you were,—
So that my lord your son were not my brother,-
Indeed my mother! or were you both ou mothers,
I care no more for than I do for heaven, 1
So I were not his sister. Can't no other,
But, I your daughter, he must be my brother
Count. Yes, Helen, you might be my daugh ter-in-law:
God shield you mean it not! daughter an mother 17
So strive upon your pulse. What, pale again
My fear hath catch'd your fondness: now see
The mystery of your loneliness, and find
Your salt tears' head: now to all sense 'tis gro
You love my son: invention is asham'd, 1
Against the proclamation of thy passion,
To say thou dost not: therefore tell me true;
But tell me then, 'tis so; for, look, thy cheeks 18
Confess it, th' one to th' other; and thine ey
See it so grossly shown in thy behaviours
That in their kind they speak it: only sin
And hellish obstinacy tie thy tongue, 18
That truth should be suspected. Speak, is't so
If it be so, you have wound a goodly clew;
If it be not, forswear't: howe'er, I charge the
As heaven shall work in me for thine avail, 1
To tell me truly.
Hel. Good madam, pardon me!
Count. Do you love my son?
Hel. Your pardon, noble mistress
Count. Love you my son?
Hel. Do not you love him, madam
Count. Go not about; my love hath in't bond 1
Whereof the world takes note: come, com disclose
The state of your affection, for your passion
Have to the full appeach'd.
Hel. Then, I confess,
Here on my knee, before high heaven an you 2
That before you, and next unto high heaven I love your son.
My friends were poor, but honest; so's my lov
Be not offended, for it hurts not him 2
That he is lov'd of me: I follow him not
By any token of presumptuous suit;
Nor would I have him till I do deserve him
Yet never know how that desert should be. 2
I know I love in vain, strive against hope;
Yet, in this captious and intenible sieve
I still pour in the waters of my love,
And lack not to lose still. Thus, Indian-like, 2
Religious in mine error, I adore

e sun, that looks upon his worshipper,
t knows of him no more. My dearest madam,
t not your hate encounter with my love 216
r loving where you do: but, if yourself,
hose aged honour cites a virtuous youth,
d ever in so true a flame of liking 219
ish chastely and love dearly, that your Dian
as both herself and Love; O! then, give pity
her, whose state is such that cannot choose
t lend and give where she is sure to lose;
at seeks not to find that her search implies,
t, riddle-like, lives sweetly where she dies. 225
Count. Had you not lately an intent, speak truly,
go to Paris?
Hel.   Madam, I had.
Count.   Wherefore? tell true.
Hel. I will tell truth; by grace itself I swear.
u know my father left me some prescriptions
rare and prov'd effects, such as his reading
d manifest experience had collected
r general sovereignty; and that he will'd me
heedfull'st reservation to bestow them, 233
notes whose faculties inclusive were
ore than they were in note. Amongst the rest,
ere is a remedy, approv'd, set down 236
cure the desperate languishings whereof
e king is render'd lost.
Count.   This was your motive
r Paris, was it? speak.
Hel. My lord your son made me to think of this; 240
se Paris, and the medicine, and the king,
d from the conversation of my thoughts
ply been absent then.
Count.   But think you, Helen,
you should tender your supposed aid, 244
would receive it? He and his physicians
e of a mind; he, that they cannot help him,
ey, that they cannot help. How shall they credit
poor unlearned virgin, when the schools, 248
nbowell'd of their doctrine, have left off
e danger to itself?
Hel.   There's something in't,
ore than my father's skill, which was the great'st
his profession, that his good receipt 252
all for my legacy be sanctified
the luckiest stars in heaven: and, would your honour
t give me leave to try success, I'd venture 255
e well-lost life of mine on his Grace's cure,
such a day, and hour.
Count.   Dost thou believe't?
Hel. Ay, madam, knowingly.
Count. Why, Helen, thou shalt have my leave and love,
eans, and attendants, and my loving greetings 260
those of mine in court. I'll stay at home
d pray God's blessing into thy attempt.
gone to-morrow; and be sure of this, 263
hat I can help thee to thou shalt not miss.
                              [*Exeunt.*

ACT II

SCENE I.—*Paris. A Room in the* KING'S *Palace.*

Flourish. Enter the KING, *with divers young* Lords *taking leave for the Florentine war;* BERTRAM, PAROLLES, *and* Attendants.

King. Farewell, young lords: these war-like principles
Do not throw from you: and you, my lords, farewell:
Share the advice betwixt you; if both gain, all 4
The gift doth stretch itself as 'tis receiv'd,
And is enough for both.
First Lord.   'Tis our hope, sir,
After well enter'd soldiers, to return
And find your Grace in health.
King. No, no, it cannot be; and yet my heart
Will not confess he owes the malady 9
That doth my life besiege. Farewell, young lords;
Whether I live or die, be you the sons
Of worthy Frenchmen: let higher Italy— 12
Those bated that inherit but the fall
Of the last monarchy—see that you come
Not to woo honour, but to wed it; when
The bravest questant shrinks, find what you seek 16
That fame may cry you loud: I say, farewell.
Sec. Lord. Health, at your bidding, serve your majesty!
King. Those girls of Italy, take heed of them:
They say, our French lack language to deny 20
If they demand: beware of being captives,
Before you serve.
Both Lords. Our hearts receive your warnings.
King. Farewell. Come hither to me.
                    [*Exit attended.*
First Lord. O my sweet lord, that you will stay behind us! 24
Par. 'Tis not his fault, the spark.
Sec. Lord.   O! 'tis brave wars.
Par. Most admirable: I have seen those wars.
Ber. I am commanded here, and kept a coil with
'Too young,' and 'the next year,' and ''tis too early.' 28
Par. An thy mind stand to't, boy, steal away bravely.
Ber. I shall stay here the forehorse to a smock,
Creaking my shoes on the plain masonry,
Till honour be bought up and no sword worn 32
But one to dance with! By heaven! I'll steal away.
First Lord. There's honour in the theft.
Par.   Commit it, count.
Sec. Lord. I am your accessary; and so farewell.
Ber. I grow to you, and our parting is a tortured body. 37
First Lord. Farewell, captain.
Sec. Lord. Sweet Monsieur Parolles!
Par. Noble heroes, my sword and yours are kin. Good sparks and lustrous, a word, good

metals: you shall find in the regiment of the
Spinii, one Captain Spurio, with his cicatrice,
an emblem of war, here on his sinister cheek: it
was this very sword entrenched it: say to him,
I live, and observe his reports for me.   46
  Sec. Lord. We shall, noble captain.
                                   [*Exeunt* Lords.
  Par. Mars dote on you for his novices!
What will ye do?
  Ber. Stay; the king.   50

Re-enter KING; PAROLLES *and* BERTRAM *retire.*

  Par. Use a more spacious ceremony to the
noble lords; you have restrained yourself within
the list of too cold an adieu: be more expressive
to them; for they wear themselves in the cap of
the time, there do muster true gait, eat, speak,
and move under the influence of the most received star; and though the devil lead the measure, such are to be followed. After them, and
take a more dilated farewell.
  Ber. And I will do so.   60
  Par. Worthy fellows; and like to prove
most sinewy swordmen.
              [*Exeunt* BERTRAM *and* PAROLLES.

Enter LAFEU.

  Laf. [*Kneeling.*] Pardon, my lord, for me
and for my tidings.
  King. I'll fee thee to stand up.   64
  Laf. Then here's a man stands that has
brought his pardon.
I would you had kneel'd, my lord, to ask me
mercy,
And that at my bidding you could so stand up.
  King. I would I had; so I had broke thy pate,
And ask'd thee mercy for't.   69
  Laf. Good faith, across: but, my good lord,
'tis thus;
Will you be cur'd of your infirmity?
  King. No.   72
  Laf. O! will you eat no grapes, my royal fox?
Yes, but you will my noble grapes an if
My royal fox could reach them. I have seen a
medicine
That's able to breathe life into a stone,   76
Quicken a rock, and make you dance canary
With spritely fire and motion; whose simple
touch
Is powerful to araise King Pepin, nay,
To give great Charlemain a pen in's hand   80
And write to her a love-line.
  King.   What 'her' is this?
  Laf. Why, Doctor She. My lord, there's one
arriv'd
If you will see her: now, by my faith and honour,
If seriously I may convey my thoughts   84
In this my light deliverance, I have spoke
With one, that in her sex, her years, profession,
Wisdom, and constancy, hath amaz'd me more
Than I dare blame my weakness. Will you see
her,   88
For that is her demand, and know her business?
That done, laugh well at me.
  King.   Now, good Lafeu
Bring in the admiration, that we with thee

May spend our wonder too, or take off thine
By wond'ring how thou took'st it.
  Laf.   Nay, I'll fit yo
And not be all day neither.   [*Ex*
  King. Thus he his special nothing ever pr
logues.

Re-enter LAFEU, *with* HELENA.

  Laf. Nay, come your ways.
  King. This haste hath wings indee
  Laf. Nay, come your ways;
This is his majesty, say your mind to him:
A traitor you do look like; but such traitors
His majesty seldom fears: I am Cressid's unc
That dare leave two together. Fare you well.)
                                             [*Ex*
  King. Now, fair one, does your busine
follow us?
  Hel. Ay, my good lord.
Gerard de Narbon was my father;   1
In what he did profess well found.
  King.   I knew hi
  Hel. The rather will I spare my praises t
wards him;
Knowing him is enough. On's bed of death
Many receipts he gave me; chiefly one,   1
Which, as the dearest issue of his practice,
And of his old experience the only darling,
He bade me store up as a triple eye,
Safer than mine own two, more dear. I have s
And, hearing your high majesty is touch'd)
With that malignant cause wherein the hono
Of my dear father's gift stands chief in powe
I come to tender it and my appliance,   1
With all bound humbleness.
  King.   We thank you, maide
But may not be so credulous of cure,
When our most learned doctors leave us, a)
The congregated college have concluded   )
That labouring art can never ransom nature
From her inaidable estate; I say we must nc
So stain our judgment, or corrupt our hope,
To prostitute our past-cure malady   1
To empirics, or to dissever so
Our great self and our credit, to esteem
A senseless help when help past sense we dee)
  Hel. My duty then, shall pay me for my pair
I will no more enforce mine office on you;   )
Humbly entreating from your royal thought
A modest one, to bear me back again.
  King. I cannot give thee less, to be cal]
grateful.   )
Thou thought'st to help me, and such than
I give
As one near death to those that wish him liv
But what at full I know, thou know'st no pa
I knowing all my peril, thou no art.   1
  Hel. What I can do can do no hurt to tr}
Since you set up your rest 'gainst remedy.
He that of greatest works is finisher
Oft does them by the weakest minister: 1
So holy writ in babes hath judgment showr
When judges have been babes; great floods ha
flown
From simple sources; and great seas have dr{
When miracles have by the greatest been denie

expectation fails, and most oft there 145
~ere most it promises; and oft it hits
~ere hope is coldest and despair most fits.
King. I must not hear thee: fare thee well,
kind maid. 148
~ pains, not us'd, must by thyself be paid:
~ffers not took reap thanks for their reward.
~el. Inspired merit so by breath is barr'd.
~ not so with Him that all things knows, 152
'tis with us that square our guess by shows;
~ most it is presumption in us when
~ help of heaven we count the act of men.
~r sir, to my endeavours give consent; 156
~heaven, not me, make an experiment.
~n not an impostor that proclaim
~self against the level of mine aim;
~know I think, and think I know most sure, ~
~art is not past power nor you past cure. 161
King. Art thou so confident? Within what
~space
~p'st thou my cure?
~el. The great'st grace lending grace,
~twice the horses of the sun shall bring 164
~ir fiery torcher his diurnal ring,
~twice in murk and occidental damp
~ist Hesperus hath quench'd his sleepy lamp,
~four and twenty times the pilot's glass 168
~th told the thievish minutes how they pass,
~at is infirm from your sound parts shall fly,
~lth shall live free, and sickness freely die.
~ing. Upon thy certainty and confidence
~at dar'st thou venture?
~el. Tax of impudence, 173
~trumpet's boldness, a divulged shame,
~duc'd by odious ballads: my maiden's name
~r'd otherwise; nay worse—if worse—ex-
~tended 176
~h vilest torture let my life be ended.
~ing. Methinks in thee some blessed spirit
~doth speak,
~powerful sound within an organ weak;
~d what impossibility would slay 180
~ommon sense, sense saves another way.
~ life is dear; for all that life can rate
~rth name of life in thee hath estimate;
~th, beauty, wisdom, courage, virtue, all 184
~t happiness and prime can happy call:
~u this to hazard needs must intimate
~l infinite or monstrous desperate.
~et practiser, thy physic I will try, 188
~t ministers thine own death if I die.
~el. If I break time, or flinch in property
~what I spoke, unpitied let me die,
~d well deserv'd. Not helping, death's my
~fee; 192
~, if I help, what do you promise me?
~ing. Make thy demand.
~el. But will you make it even?
~ing. Ay, by my sceptre, and my hopes of
~heaven.
~el. Then shalt thou give me with thy kingly
~hand 196
~at husband in thy power I will command:
~mpted be from me the arrogance
~hoose from forth the royal blood of France,
~low and humble name to propagate 200

With any branch or image of thy state;
But such a one, thy vassal, whom I know
Is free for me to ask, thee to bestow.
King. Here is my hand; the premises ob-
serv'd, 204
Thy will by my performance shall be serv'd:
So make the choice of thy own time, for I,
Thy resolv'd patient, on thee still rely.
More should I question thee, and more I must,
Though more to know could not be more to
trust, 209
From whence thou cam'st, how tended on; but
rest
Unquestion'd welcome and undoubted blest.
Give me some help here, ho! If thou proceed 212
As high as word, my deed shall match thy deed.
[*Flourish. Exeunt.*

SCENE II.—*Rousillon. A Room in the*
COUNTESS'S *Palace.*

Enter COUNTESS *and* Clown.

Count. Come on, sir; I shall now put you to
the height of your breeding.
Clo. I will show myself highly fed and lowly
taught. I know my business is but to the
court. 5
Count. To the court! why what place make
you special, when you put off that with such
contempt? 'But to the court!' 8
Clo. Truly, madam, if God have lent a man
any manners, he may easily put it off at court:
he that cannot make a leg, put off's cap, kiss his
hand, and say nothing, has neither leg, hands,
lip, nor cap; and indeed such a fellow, to say
precisely, were not for the court. But, for me, I
have an answer will serve all men.
Count. Marry, that's a bountiful answer
that fits all questions. 17
Clo. It is like a barber's chair that fits all
buttocks; the pin-buttock, the quatch-buttock,
the brawn-buttock, or any buttock. 20
Count. Will your answer serve fit to all
questions?
Clo. As fit as ten groats is for the hand of an
attorney, as your French crown for your taffeta
punk, as Tib's rush for Tom's forefinger, as a
pancake for Shrove-Tuesday, a morris for May-
day, as the nail to his hole, the cuckold to his
horn, as a scolding quean to a wrangling knave,
as the nun's lip to the friar's mouth; nay, as
the pudding to his skin.
Count. Have you, I say, an answer of such
fitness for all questions? 32
Clo. From below your duke to beneath your
constable, it will fit any question.
Count. It must be an answer of most monstrous size that must fit all demands. 36
Clo. But a trifle neither, in good faith, if the
learned should speak truth of it. Here it is, and
all that belongs to't: ask me if I am a courtier;
it shall do you no harm to learn. 40
Count. To be young again, if we could. I will
be a fool in question, hoping to be the wiser by
your answer. I pray you, sir, are you a courtier? 44

Clo. O Lord, sir! there's a simple putting off. More, more, a hundred of them.

Count. Sir, I am a poor friend of yours, that loves you.   48

Clo. O Lord, sir! Thick, thick, spare not me.

Count. I think, sir, you can eat none of this homely meat.   52

Clo. O Lord, sir! Nay, put me to 't, I warrant you.

Count. You were lately whipped, sir, as I think.   56

Clo. O Lord, sir! Spare not me.

Count. Do you cry, 'O Lord, sir!' at your whipping, and 'Spare not me?' Indeed your 'O Lord, sir!' is very sequent to your whipping: you would answer very well to a whipping, if you were but bound to 't.   62

Clo. I ne'er had worse luck in my life in my 'O Lord, sir!' I see things may serve long, but not serve ever.   65

Count. I play the noble housewife with the time,

To entertain 't so merrily with a fool.

Clo. O Lord, sir! why, there 't serves well again.   68

Count. An end, sir: to your business. Give Helen this,

And urge her to a present answer back:
Commend me to my kinsmen and my son.
This is not much.   72

Clo. Not much commendation to them.

Count. Not much employment for you: you understand me?

Clo. Most fruitfully: I am there before my legs.

Count. Haste you again. [*Exeunt severally.*

SCENE III.—*Paris. A Room in the* KING'S *Palace.*

Enter BERTRAM, LAFEU, *and* PAROLLES.

Laf. They say miracles are past; and we have our philosophical persons, to make modern and familiar, things supernatural and causeless. Hence is it that we make trifles of terrors, ensconcing ourselves into seeming knowledge, when we should submit ourselves to an unknown fear.

Par. Why, 'tis the rarest argument of wonder that hath shot out in our latter times.   8

Ber. And so 'tis.

Laf. To be relinquished of the artists,—

Par. So I say.

Laf. Both of Galen and Paracelsus.   12

Par. So I say.

Laf. Of all the learned and authentic fellows,—

Par. Right; so I say.

Laf. That gave him out incurable,—   16

Par. Why, there 'tis; so say I too.

Laf. Not to be helped,—

Par. Right; as 'twere, a man assured of a—

Laf. Uncertain life, and sure death.   20

Par. Just, you say well: so would I have said.

Laf. I may truly say it is a novelty to world.

Par. It is, indeed: if you will have it showing, you shall read it in—what do you there—

Laf. A showing of a heavenly effect in earthly actor.

Par. That's it I would have said; the v same.

Laf. Why, your dolphin is not lustier: ' me, I speak in respect—

Par. Nay, 'tis strange, 'tis very strange, t is the brief and the tedious of it; and he is most facinorous spirit, that will not ackno ledge it to be the—

Laf. Very hand of heaven—

Par. Ay, so I say.

Laf. In a most weak and debile minis great power, great transcendence: which sho indeed, give us a further use to be made t alone the recovery of the king, as to be ge ally thankful.

Par. I would have said it; you say w Here comes the king.

Enter KING, HELENA, *and* Attendants.

Laf. Lustig, as the Dutchman says: I'll a maid the better, whilst I have a tooth in head. Why, he's able to lead her a coranto

Par. Mort du vinaigre! Is not this Hele

Laf. 'Fore God, I think so.

King. Go, call before me all the lords court.   [*Exit an* Attend

Sit, my preserver, by thy patient's side:
And with this healthful hand, whose banis sense
Thou hast repeal'd, a second time receive
The confirmation of my promised gift,
Which but attends thy naming.

Enter several Lords.

Fair maid, send forth thine eye: this yout parcel
Of noble bachelors stand at my bestowing
O'er whom both sov'reign power and fath voice
I have to use: thy frank election make;
Thou hast power to choose, and they non forsake.

Hel. To each of you one fair and virtu mistress
Fall, when Love please! marry, to each, one.

Laf. I'd give bay Curtal, and his furnitu
My mouth no more were broken than t boys'
And writ as little beard.

King.   Peruse them well
Not one of those but had a noble father.

Hel. Gentlemen,
Heaven hath through me restor'd the kin health.

All. We understand it, and thank hea for you.

Hel. I am a simple maid; and the wealthiest

hat I protest I simply am a maid.

lease it your majesty, I have done already:
he blushes in my cheeks thus whisper me,
We blush, that thou shouldst choose; but, be
   refus'd, 76
et the white death sit on thy cheek for ever;
Ve'll ne'er come there again.'

King.   Make choice; and see,
Vho shuns thy love, shuns all his love in
   me.

Hel. Now, Dian, from thy altar do I fly, 80
nd to imperial Love, that god most high,
Do my sighs stream. Sir, will you hear my suit?

First Lord. And grant it.

Hel.   Thanks, sir; all the rest is mute.

Laf. I had rather be in this choice than
rrow ames-ace for my life. 85

Hel. The honour, sir, that flames in your fair
   eyes,
efore I speak, too threateningly replies:
ove make your fortunes twenty times above 88
ler that so wishes, and her humble love!

Sec. Lord. No better, if you please.

Hel.   My wish receive,
Vhich great Love grant! and so I take my leave.

Laf. Do all they deny her? An they were
ons of mine, I'd have them whipp'd or I would
end them to the Turk to make eunuchs of.

Hel. [*To third Lord.*] Be not afraid that I
   your hand should take;
'll never do you wrong for your own sake: 96
lessing upon your vows! and in your bed
ind fairer fortune, if you ever wed!

Laf. These boys are boys of ice, they'll none
ave her: sure, they are bastards to the Eng-
sh; the French ne'er got 'em. 101

Hel. You are too young, too happy, and too
   good,
o make yourself a son out of my blood.

Fourth Lord. Fair one, I think not so. 104

Laf. There's one grape yet. I am sure thy
ather drunk wine. But if thou be'st not an ass,
am a youth of fourteen: I have known thee
lready. 108

Hel. [*To* BERTRAM.] I dare not say I take you;
   but I give
Me and my service, ever whilst I live,
nto your guiding power. This is the man.

King. Why then, young Bertram, take her;
   she's thy wife. 112

Ber. My wife, my liege! I shall beseech your
   highness
n such a business give me leave to use
he help of mine own eyes.

King.   Know'st thou not, Bertram,
Vhat she has done for me?

Ber.   Yes, my good lord; 116
but never hope to know why I should marry her.

King. Thou know'st she has rais'd me from
   my sickly bed.

Ber. But follows it, my lord, to bring me
   down
Must answer for your raising? I know her well:
he had her breeding at my father's charge. 121
poor physician's daughter my wife! Disdain
ather corrupt me ever!

King. 'Tis only title thou disdain'st in her,
   the which 124
I can build up. Strange is it that our bloods,
Of colour, weight, and heat, pour'd all together,
Would quite confound distinction, yet stand off
In differences so mighty. If she be 128
All that is virtuous, save what thou dislik'st,
A poor physician's daughter, thou dislik'st
Of virtue for the name; but do not so:
From lowest place when virtuous things pro-
   ceed, 132
The place is dignified by the doer's deed:
Where great additions swell's, and virtue none,
It is a dropsied honour. Good alone
Is good without a name: vileness is so: 136
The property by what it is should go,
Not by the title. She is young, wise, fair;
In these to nature she's immediate heir,
And these breed honour: that is honour's scorn
Which challenges itself as honour's born, 141
And is not like the sire: honours thrive
When rather from our acts we them derive
Than our foregoers. The mere word's a slave,
Debosh'd on every tomb, on every grave 145
A lying trophy, and as oft is dumb
Where dust and damn'd oblivion is the tomb
Of honour'd bones indeed. What should be
   said? 148
If thou canst like this creature as a maid,
I can create the rest: virtue and she
Is her own dower; honour and wealth from
   me.

Ber. I cannot love her, nor will strive to do't.

King. Thou wrong'st thyself if thou shouldst
   strive to choose. 153

Hel. That you are well restor'd, my lord, I'm
   glad:
Let the rest go.

King.   My honour's at the stake, which to
   defeat 156
I must produce my power. Here, take her hand,
Proud scornful boy, unworthy this good gift,
That dost in vile misprision shackle up
My love and her desert; thou canst not dream
We, poising us in her defective scale, 161
Shall weigh thee to the beam; that wilt not
   know,
It is in us to plant thine honour where
We please to have it grow. Check thy contempt:
Obey our will, which travails in thy good: 165
Believe not thy disdain, but presently
Do thine own fortunes that obedient right
Which both thy duty owes and our power
   claims; 168
Or I will throw thee from my care for ever
Into the staggers and the careless lapse
Of youth and ignorance; both my revenge and
   hate
Loosing upon thee, in the name of justice, 172
Without all terms of pity. Speak; thine answer.

Ber. Pardon, my gracious lord; for I submit
My fancy to your eyes. When I consider 175
What great creation and what dole of honour
Flies where you bid it, I find that she, which
   late
Was in my nobler thoughts most base, is now

The praised of the king; who, so ennobled,
Is, as 'twere, born so.
  King.   Take her by the hand, 180
And tell her she is thine: to whom I promise
A counterpoise, if not to thy estate
A balance more replete.
  Ber.   I take her hand.
  King. Good fortune and the favour of the
king   184
Smile upon this contract; whose ceremony
Shall seem expedient on the now-born brief,
And be perform'd to-night: the solemn feast
Shall more attend upon the coming space, 188
Expecting absent friends. As thou lov'st her,
Thy love's to me religious; else, does err.
  [*Exeunt* KING, BERTRAM, HELENA, Lords,
                    and Attendants.
  Laf. Do you hear, monsieur? a word with you.
  Par. Your pleasure, sir?   192
  Laf. Your lord and master did well to make
his recantation.
  Par. Recantation! My lord! my master!
  Laf. Ay; is it not a language I speak? 196
  Par. A most harsh one, and not to be under-
stood without bloody succeeding. My master!
  Laf. Are you companion to the Count
Rousillon?   200
  Par. To any count; to all counts; to what is
man.
  Laf. To what is count's man: count's master
is of another style.   204
  Par. You are too old, sir; let it satisfy you,
you are too old.
  Laf. I must tell thee, sirrah, I write man; to
which title age cannot bring thee.   208
  Par. What I dare too well do, I dare not do.
  Laf. I did think thee, for two ordinaries,
to be a pretty wise fellow: thou didst make
tolerable vent of thy travel; it might pass: yet
the scarfs and the bannerets about thee did
manifoldly dissuade me from believing thee a
vessel of too great a burden. I have now found
thee; when I lose thee again, I care not; yet art
thou good for nothing but taking up, and that
thou'rt scarce worth.
  Par. Hadst thou not the privilege of antiquity upon thee,—   220
  Laf. Do not plunge thyself too far in anger,
lest thou hasten thy trial; which if—Lord have
mercy on thee for a hen! So, my good window
of lattice, fare thee well: thy casement I need
not open, for I look through thee. Give me thy
hand.
  Par. My lord, you give me most egregious
indignity.   228
  Laf. Ay, with all my heart; and thou art
worthy of it.
  Par. I have not, my lord, deserved it.
  Laf. Yes, good faith, every dram of it; and I
will not bate thee a scruple.   233
  Par. Well, I shall be wiser.
  Laf. E'en as soon as thou canst, for thou
hast to pull at a smack o' the contrary. If ever
thou be'st bound in thy scarf and beaten, thou
shalt find what it is to be proud of thy bondage.
I have a desire to hold my acquaintance with

thee, or rather my knowledge, that I may say
the default, he is a man I know.   2
  Par. My lord, you do me most insupportab
vexation.
  Laf. I would it were hell-pains for thy sak
and my poor doing eternal: for doing I am pas
as I will by thee, in what motion age will gi
me leave.   [*Ex*
  Par. Well, thou hast a son shall take th
disgrace off me; scurvy, old, filthy, scurvy lor
Well, I must be patient; there is no fettering
authority. I'll beat him, by my life, if I c
meet him with any convenience, an he we
double and double a lord. I'll have no more pi
of his age than I would have of—I'll beat hi
an if I could but meet him again!   2

              Re-enter LAFEU.

  Laf. Sirrah, your lord and master's marrie
there's news for you: you have a new mistre
  Par. I most unfeignedly beseech your lor
ship to make some reservation of your wrong
he is my good lord: whom I serve above is n
master.
  Laf. Who? God?
  Par. Ay, sir.
  Laf. The devil it is that's thy master. Wl
dost thou garter up thy arms o' this fashio
dost make hose of thy sleeves? do other servar
so? Thou wert best set thy lower part where tl
nose stands. By mine honour, if I were but tv
hours younger, I'd beat thee: methinks thou a
a general offence, and every man should be
thee: I think thou wast created for men
breathe themselves upon thee.   2
  Par. This is hard and undeserved measu
my lord.
  Laf. Go to, sir; you were beaten in Italy f
picking a kernel out of a pomegranate; you a
a vagabond and no true traveller: you are mo
saucy with lords and honourable personag
than the heraldry of your birth and virtue giv
you commission. You are not worth anoth
word, else I'd call you knave. I leave you. [*Ex*
  Par. Good, very good; it is so then: goo
very good. Let it be concealed awhile.

           Re-enter BERTRAM.

  Ber. Undone, and forfeited to cares for eve
  Par. What is the matter, sweet heart? 2
  Ber. Although before the solemn priest
have sworn,
I will not bed her.
  Par. What, what, sweet heart?
  Ber. O my Parolles, they have married m
I'll to the Tuscan wars, and never bed her.
  Par. France is a dog-hole, and it no mo
    merits
The tread of a man's foot. To the wars! 2
  Ber. There's letters from my mother: wh
    the import is
I know not yet.
  Par. Ay, that would be known. To the wa
    my boy! to the wars!
He wears his honour in a box, unseen, 2
That hugs his kicky-wicky here at home,

[s]ending his manly marrow in her arms,
[w]hich should sustain the bound and high curvet
[of] Mars's fiery steed.   To other regions!   300
[L]ance is a stable; we that dwell in't jades;
[th]erefore, to the war!
Ber. It shall be so: I'll send her to my house,
[Ac]quaint my mother with my hate to her,   304
[an]d wherefore I am fled; write to the king
[th]at which I durst not speak: his present gift
[Sh]all furnish me to those Italian fields,
[W]here noble fellows strike.   War is no strife 308
[To] the dark house and the detested wife.
Par. Will this capriccio hold in thee? art
   sure?
Ber. Go with me to my chamber, and advise
   me.
[I'll] send her straight away: to-morrow   312
[I'll] to the wars, she to her single sorrow.
Par. Why, these balls bound; there's noise
   in it. 'Tis hard:
[A] young man married is a man that's marr'd:
[Th]erefore away, and leave her bravely; go: 316
[Th]e king has done you wrong: but, hush! 'tis
   so.   [*Exeunt.*

SCENE IV.—*Same.   Another Room in the
   Palace.*

Enter HELENA *and* Clown.

Hel. My mother greets me kindly: is she well?
Clo. She is not well; but yet she has her
[he]alth; she's very merry; but yet she is not
[we]ll: but thanks be given, she's very well, and
[wa]nts nothing i' the world; but yet she is not
[we]ll.
Hel. If she be very well, what does she ail
[th]at she's not very well?   8
Clo. Truly, she's very well indeed, but for
[tw]o things.
Hel. What two things?   11
Clo. One, that she's not in heaven, whither
[Go]d send her quickly! the other, that she's in
[ea]rth, from whence God send her quickly!

Enter PAROLLES.

Par. Bless you, my fortunate lady!
Hel. I hope, sir, I have your good will to
[ha]ve mine own good fortunes.   17
Par. You had my prayers to lead them on;
[an]d to keep them on, have them still.   O! my
[kn]ave, how does my old lady?   20
Clo. So that you had her wrinkles, and I her
[mo]ney, I would she did as you say.
Par. Why, I say nothing.
Clo. Marry, you are the wiser man; for many
[a m]an's tongue shakes out his master's undoing.
[To] say nothing, to do nothing, to know nothing,
[an]d to have nothing, is to be a great part of your
[tit]le; which is within a very little of nothing. 28
Par. Away! thou'rt a knave.
Clo. You should have said, sir, before a knave
[th]ou'rt a knave; that is, before me thou'rt a
[kn]ave: this had been truth, sir.   32
Par. Go to, thou art a witty fool; I have
[fo]und thee.

Clo. Did you find me in yourself, sir? or were
you taught to find me?   The search, sir, was
profitable; and much fool may you find in you,
even to the world's pleasure and the increase of
laughter.
Par. A good knave, i' faith, and well fed.   40
Madam, my lord will go away to-night;
A very serious business calls on him.
The great prerogative and rite of love,
Which, as your due, time claims, he does ac-
   knowledge,   44
But puts it off to a compell'd restraint;
Whose want, and whose delay, is strew'd with
   sweets,
Which they distil now in the curbed time,
To make the coming hour o'erflow with joy,   48
And pleasure drown the brim.
Hel.   What's his will else?
Par. That you will take your instant leave
   o' the king,
And make this haste as your own good proceed-
   ing,
Strengthen'd with what apology you think   52
May make it probable need.
Hel.   What more commands he?
Par. That, having this obtain'd, you presently
Attend his further pleasure.
Hel. In everything I wait upon his will.   56
Par. I shall report it so.
Hel.   I pray you.   Come, sirrah.
   [*Exeunt.*

SCENE V.—*Another Room in the Same.*

Enter LAFEU *and* BERTRAM.

Laf. But I hope your lordship thinks not
him a soldier.
Ber. Yes, my lord, and of very valiant approof.
Laf. You have it from his own deliverance.   4
Ber. And by other warranted testimony.
Laf. Then my dial goes not true: I took this
lark for a bunting.
Ber. I do assure you, my lord, he is very
great in knowledge, and accordingly valiant.   9
Laf. I have then sinned against his experience
and transgressed against his valour; and my
state that way is dangerous, since I cannot yet
find in my heart to repent.   Here he comes; I
pray you, make us friends; I will pursue the
amity.

Enter PAROLLES.

Par. [*To* BERTRAM.] These things shall be
done, sir.   17
Laf. Pray you, sir, who's his tailor?
Par. Sir?
Laf. O! I know him well.   Ay, sir; he, sir, is
a good workman, a very good tailor.   21
Ber. [*Aside to* PAROLLES.] Is she gone to the
king?
Par. She is.   24
Ber. Will she away to-night?
Par. As you'll have her.
Ber. I have writ my letters, casketed my
   treasure,

K

Given orders for our horses; and to-night, 28
When I should take possession of the bride,
End ere I do begin.

Laf. A good traveller is something at the latter end of a dinner; but one that lies three
thirds, and uses a known truth to pass a thousand nothings with, should be once heard and
thrice beaten. God save you, captain. 35

Ber. Is there any unkindness between my
lord and you, monsieur?

Par. I know not how I have deserved to run
into my lord's displeasure. 39

Laf. You have made shift to run into 't, boots
and spurs and all, like him that leaped into the
custard; and out of it you'll run again, rather
than suffer question for your residence.

Ber. It may be you have mistaken him, my
lord. 45

Laf. And shall do so ever, though I took him
at his prayers. Fare you well, my lord; and
believe this of me, there can be no kernel in this
light nut; the soul of this man is his clothes.
Trust him not in matter of heavy consequence;
I have kept of them tame, and know their natures. Farewell, monsieur: I have spoken better
of you than you have or will to deserve at my
hand; but we must do good against evil. [*Exit.*

Par. An idle lord, I swear.

Ber. I think not so. 56

Par. Why, do you not know him?

Ber. Yes, I do know him well; and common
speech
Gives him a worthy pass. Here comes my clog.

Enter HELENA.

Hel. I have, sir, as I was commanded from
you, 60
Spoke with the king, and have procur'd his
leave
For present parting; only, he desires
Some private speech with you.

Ber. I shall obey his will.
You must not marvel, Helen, at my course, 64
Which holds not colour with the time, nor does
The ministration and required office
On my particular: prepar'd I was not
For such a business; therefore am I found 68
So much unsettled. This drives me to entreat
you
That presently you take your way for home;
And rather muse than ask why I entreat you;
For my respects are better than they seem, 72
And my appointments have in them a need
Greater than shows itself at the first view
To you that know them not. This to my mother.
                              [*Giving a letter.*
'Twill be two days ere I shall see you, so 76
I leave you to your wisdom.

Hel.   Sir, I can nothing say,
But that I am your most obedient servant.

Ber. Come, come, no more of that.

Hel.   And ever shall
With true observance seek to eke out that 80
Wherein toward me my homely stars have fail'd
To equal my great fortune.

Ber.   Let that go:
My haste is very great. Farewell: hie home.

Hel. Pray sir, your pardon.

Ber.   Well, what would you sa

Hel. I am not worthy of the wealth I owe,
Nor dare I say 'tis mine, and yet it is;
But, like a timorous thief, most fain would ste
What law does vouch mine own.

Ber.   What would you hav

Hel. Something, and scarce so much: n
thing, indeed.
I would not tell you what I would, my lord:
Faith, yes;
Strangers and foes do sunder, and not kiss.

Ber. I pray you, stay not, but in haste
horse.

Hel. I shall not break your bidding, good n
lord.

Ber. [*To* PAROLLES.] Where are my oth
men, monsieur? [*To* HELENA.] Farewell.
                              [*Exit* HELEN
Go thou toward home; where I will never co
Whilst I can shake my sword or hear the dru
Away! and for our flight.

Par.   Bravely, *coragio!*
                              [*Exeu*

ACT III

SCENE I.—*Florence. A Room in the* DUKE'
Palace.

Flourish. Enter the DUKE, *attended;* t
French Lords, *and* Soldiers.

Duke. So that from point to point now ha
you heard
The fundamental reasons of this war,
Whose great decision hath much blood let fort
And more thirsts after.

First Lord.   Holy seems the quarrel
Upon your Grace's part; black and fearful
On the opposer.

Duke. Therefore we marvel much our cous
France
Would in so just a business shut his bosom
Against our borrowing prayers.

First Lord.   Good my lor
The reasons of our state I cannot yield,
But like a common and an outward man,
That the great figure of a council frames
By self-unable motion: therefore dare not
Say what I think of it, since I have found
Myself in my incertain grounds to fail
As often as I guess'd.

Duke.   Be it his pleasure.

Sec. Lord. But I am sure the younger of o
nature,
That surfeit on their ease, will day by day
Come here for physic.

Duke.   Welcome shall they b
And all the honours that can fly from us
Shall on them settle. You know your plac
well;
When better fall, for your avails they fell.
To-morrow to the field. [*Flourish. Exeur*

SCENE II.—*Rousillon. A Room in the* COUNTESS'S *Palace.*

Enter COUNTESS *and* Clown.

Count. It hath happened all as I would have d it, save that he comes not along with her.
Clo. By my troth, I take my young lord to be very melancholy man. 4
Count. By what observance, I pray you?
Clo. Why, he will look upon his boot and ıg; mend the ruff and sing; ask questions and ıg; pick his teeth and sing. I know a man at had this trick of melancholy sold a goodly anor for a song.
Count. [*Opening a letter.*] Let me see what writes, and when he means to come. 12
Clo. I have no mind to Isbel since I was at ırt. Our old ling and our Isbels o' the country e nothing like your old ling and your Isbels the court: the brains of my Cupid's knocked ıt, and I begin to love, as an old man loves oney, with no stomach.
Count. What have we here? 19
Clo. E'en that you have there. [*Exit.*
Count. I have sent you a daughter-in-law: e hath recovered the king, and undone me. "have wedded her, not bedded her; and sworn make the 'not' eternal. You shall hear I am n away: know it before the report come. If ere be breadth enough in the world, I will hold long distance. My duty to you.
Your unfortunate son, 28
BERTRAM.

ıis is not well: rash and unbridled boy, fly the favours of so good a king! pluck his indignation on thy head 32 the misprising of a maid too virtuous r the contempt of empire!

Re-enter Clown.

Clo. O madam! yonder is heavy news within tween two soldiers and my young lady. 36
Count. What is the matter?
Clo. Nay, there is some comfort in the news, me comfort; your son will not be killed so on as I thought he would. 40
Count. Why should he be killed?
Clo. So say I, madam, if he run away, as I ar he does: the danger is in standing to't; at's the loss of men, though it be the getting children. Here they come will tell you more; r my part, I only hear your son was run away. [*Exit.*

Enter HELENA *and* Gentlemen.

First Gen. Save you, good madam.
Hel. Madam, my lord is gone, for ever gone.
Sec. Gen. Do not say so. 49
Count. Think upon patience. Pray you, gentlemen,
ave felt so many quirks of joy and grief, ıat the first face of neither, on the start, 52 ın woman me unto't: where is my son, I pray you?
Sec. Gen. Madam, he's gone to serve the Duke of Florence:
e met him thitherward; for thence we came,

And, after some dispatch in hand at court, 56 Thither we bend again.
Hel. Look on his letter, madam; here's my passport.
When thou canst get the ring upon my finger, which never shall come off, and show me a child begotten of thy body that I am father to, then call me husband: but in such a 'then' I write a 'never.'
This is a dreadful sentence. 64
Count. Brought you this letter, gentlemen?
First Gen. Ay, madam;
And for the contents' sake are sorry for our pains.
Count. I prithee, lady, have a better cheer; If thou engrossest all the griefs are thine, 68 Thou robb'st me of a moiety: he was my son, But I do wash his name out of my blood, And thou art all my child. Towards Florence is he?
Sec. Gen. Ay, madam.
Count. And to be a soldier? 72
Sec. Gen. Such is his noble purpose; and, believe't,
The duke will lay upon him all the honour That good convenience claims.
Count. Return you thither?
First Gen. Ay, madam, with the swiftest wing of speed. 76
Hel. Till I have no wife, I have nothing in France.
'Tis bitter.
Count. Find you that there?
Hel. Ay, madam.
First Gen. 'Tis but the boldness of his hand, haply, which his heart was not consenting to. 80
Count. Nothing in France until he have no wife!
There's nothing here that is too good for him But only she; and she deserves a lord That twenty such rude boys might tend upon, 84 And call her hourly mistress. Who was with him?
First Gen. A servant only, and a gentleman Which I have some time known.
Count. Parolles, was it not?
First Gen. Ay, my good lady, he. 88
Count. A very tainted fellow, and full of wickedness.
My son corrupts a well-derived nature With his inducement.
First Gen. Indeed, good lady,
The fellow has a deal of that too much, 92 Which holds him much to have.
Count. Y'are welcome, gentlemen.
I will entreat you, when you see my son,
To tell him that his sword can never win 96 The honour that he loses: more I'll entreat you Written to bear along.
Sec. Gen. We serve you, madam,
In that and all your worthiest affairs.
Count. Not so, but as we change our courtesies. Will you draw near? 101
[*Exeunt* COUNTESS *and* Gentlemen.
Hel. 'Till I have no wife, I have nothing in France.'

Nothing in France until he has no wife!
Thou shalt have none, Rousillon, none in
France;   104
Then hast thou all again. Poor lord! is't I
That chase thee from thy country, and expose
Those tender limbs of thine to the event
Of the non-sparing war? and is it I   108
That drive thee from the sportive court, where thou
Wast shot at with fair eyes, to be the mark
Of smoky muskets? O you leaden messengers,
That ride upon the violent speed of fire, 112
Fly with false aim; move the still-piecing air,
That sings with piercing; do not touch my lord!
Whoever shoots at him, I set him there;
Whoever charges on his forward breast,   116
I am the caitiff that do hold him to't;
And, though I kill him not, I am the cause
His death was so effected: better 'twere
I met the ravin lion when he roar'd   120
With sharp constraint of hunger; better 'twere
That all the miseries which nature owes
Were mine at once. No, come thou home,
  Rousillon,
Whence honour but of danger wins a scar,   124
As oft it loses all: I will be gone;
My being here is it that holds thee hence:
Shall I stay here to do't? no, no, although
The air of paradise did fan the house,   128
And angels offic'd all: I will be gone,
That pitiful rumour may report my flight,
To consolate thine ear. Come, night; end, day!
For with the dark, poor thief, I'll steal away. 132
                                        [*Exit.*

SCENE III.—*Florence. Before the* DUKE'S
  Palace.

Flourish. Enter DUKE, BERTRAM, PAROLLES,
  Soldiers. *Drum and Trumpets.*

Duke. The general of our horse thou art;
  and we,
Great in our hope, lay our best love and credence
Upon thy promising fortune.
  Ber.   Sir, it is
A charge too heavy for my strength, but yet 4
We'll strive to bear it for your worthy sake
To the extreme edge of hazard.
  Duke.   Then go thou forth,
And fortune play upon thy prosp'rous helm
As thy auspicious mistress!
  Ber.   This very day,   8
Great Mars, I put myself into thy file:
Make me but like my thoughts, and I shall
  prove
A lover of thy drum, hater of love.   [*Exeunt.*

SCENE IV.—*Rousillon. A Room in the*
  COUNTESS'S *Palace.*

Enter COUNTESS *and* Steward.

Count. Alas! and would you take the letter
  of her?
Might you not know she would do as she has
  done,
By sending me a letter? Read it again.

*Stew. I am Saint Jaques' pilgrim, thither go
    Ambitious love hath so in me offended
That bare-foot plod I the cold ground upon
    With sainted vow my faults to have amend*
Write, write, that from the bloody course of w
    My dearest master, your dear son, may hi
Bless him at home in peace, whilst I from fa
    His name with zealous fervour sanctify:
His taken labours bid him me forgive;
    I, his despiteful Juno, sent him forth
From courtly friends, with camping foes to l
    *Where death and danger dog the heels
      worth:*
He is too good and fair for Death and me;
Whom I myself embrace, to set him free.
  Count. Ah, what sharp stings are in h
  mildest words!
Rinaldo, you did never lack advice so much,
As letting her pass so: had I spoke with her,
I could have well diverted her intents,
Which thus she hath prevented.
  Stew.   Pardon me, mada
If I had given you this at over-night
She might have been o'erta'en; and yet s
  writes,
Pursuit would be but vain.
  Count.   What angel sha
Bless this unworthy husband? he cannot thri
Unless her prayers, whom heaven delights
  hear,
And loves to grant, reprieve him from the wra
Of greatest justice. Write, write, Rinaldo,
To this unworthy husband of his wife;
Let every word weigh heavy of her worth
That he does weigh too light: my greatest gri
Though little he do feel it, set down sharply.
Dispatch the most convenient messenger:
When haply he shall hear that she is gone,
He will return; and hope I may that she,
Hearing so much, will speed her foot again,
Led hither by pure love. Which of them bo
Is dearest to me I have no skill in sense
To make distinction. Provide this messenge
My heart is heavy and mine age is weak;
Grief would have tears, and sorrow bids n
  speak.   [*Exeun*

SCENE V.—*Without the Walls of Florence.*

A tucket afar off. Enter a Widow *of Florenc*
  DIANA, VIOLENTA, MARIANA, *and other* Ci
  zens.

Wid. Nay, come; for if they do approach th
city we shall lose all the sight.
  Dia. They say the French Count has do
most honourable service.
  Wid. It is reported that he has taken the
greatest commander, and that with his ow
hand he slew the duke's brother. We have lo
our labour; they are gone a contrary wa
hark! you may know them by their trumpets.
  Mar. Come; let's return again, and suffic
ourselves with the report of it. Well, Diana, tak
heed of this French earl: the honour of a ma
is her name, and no legacy is so rich as honest

Wid. I have told my neighbour how you have
n solicited by a gentleman his companion. 15
Mar. I know that knave; hang him! one
rolles: a filthy officer he is in those suggestions
the young earl. Beware of them, Diana;
ir promises, enticements, oaths, tokens, and
these engines of lust, are not the things they
under: many a maid hath been seduced by
m; and the misery is, example, that so terrible
ws in the wrack of maidenhood, cannot for all
t dissuade succession, but that they are limed
h the twigs that threaten them. I hope I
ed not to advise you further; but I hope your
n grace will keep you where you are, though
re were no further danger known but the
desty which is so lost. 29
Dia. You shall not need to fear me.
Wid. I hope so. Look, here comes a pilgrim:
now she will lie at my house; thither they
d one another. I'll question her. 33

Enter HELENA *in the dress of a Pilgrim.*

d save you, pilgrim! whither are you bound?
Hel. To Saint Jaques le Grand.
here do the palmers lodge, I do beseech you?
Wid. At the Saint Francis, here beside the
port. 37
Hel. Is this the way?
Wid. Ay, marry, is't. Hark you!
      [*A march afar off.*
ey come this way. If you will tarry, holy
pilgrim,
t till the troops come by, 40
ill conduct you where you shall be lodg'd:
e rather, for I think I know your hostess
ample as myself.
Hel. Is it yourself?
Wid. If you shall please so, pilgrim. 44
Hel. I thank you, and will stay upon your
leisure.
Wid. You came, I think, from France?
Hel. I did so.
Wid. Here you shall see a countryman of
yours
at has done worthy service.
Hel. His name, I pray you. 48
Dia. The Count Rousillon: know you such
a one?
Hel. But by the ear, that hears most nobly of
him;
s face I know not.
Dia. Whatsoe'er he is,
's bravely taken here. He stole from France,
'tis reported, for the king had married him 53
ainst his liking. Think you it is so?
Hel. Ay, surely, mere the truth: I know his
lady.
Dia. There is a gentleman that serves the
count 56
ports but coarsely of her.
Hel. What's his name?
Dia. Monsieur Parolles.
Hel. O! I believe with him,
argument of praise, or to the worth
the great count himself, she is too mean 60
have her name repeated: all her deserving

Is a reserved honesty, and that
I have not heard examin'd.
Dia. Alas, poor lady!
'Tis a hard bondage to become the wife 64
Of a detesting lord.
Wid. Ay, right; good creature, wheresoe'er
she is,
Her heart weighs sadly. This young maid might
do her
A shrewd turn if she pleas'd.
Hel. How do you mean? 68
May be the amorous count solicits her
In the unlawful purpose.
Wid. He does, indeed;
And brokes with all that can in such a suit
Corrupt the tender honour of a maid: 72
But she is arm'd for him and keeps her guard
In honestest defence.
Mar. The gods forbid else!

*Enter, with drum and colours, a party of the
Florentine army,* BERTRAM *and* PAROLLES.

Wid. So, now they come.
That is Antonio, the duke's eldest son; 76
That, Escalus.
Hel. Which is the Frenchman?
Dia. He;
That with the plume: 'tis a most gallant fellow;
I would he lov'd his wife. If he were honester,
He were much goodlier; is't not a handsome
gentleman? 80
Hel. I like him well.
Dia. 'Tis pity he is not honest. Yond's that
same knave
That leads him to these places: were I his lady
I would poison that vile rascal.
Hel. Which is he? 84
Dia. That jack-an-apes with scarfs. Why is
he melancholy?
Hel. Perchance he's hurt i' the battle.
Par. Lose our drum! well. 88
Mar. He's shrewdly vexed at something.
Look, he has spied us.
Wid. Marry, hang you!
Mar. And your courtesy, for a ring-carrier!
      [*Exeunt* BERTRAM, PAROLLES, Officers,
                            and Soldiers.
Wid. The troop is past. Come, pilgrim, I
will bring you 93
Where you shall host: of enjoin'd penitents
There's four or five, to great Saint Jaques bound,
Already at my house.
Hel. I humbly thank you. 96
Please it this matron and this gentle maid
To eat with us to-night, the charge and thanking
Shall be for me; and, to requite you further,
I will bestow some precepts of this virgin 100
Worthy the note.
Both. We'll take your offer kindly.
                              [*Exeunt.*

SCENE VI.—*Camp before Florence.*

Enter BERTRAM *and the two French Lords.*

First Lord. Nay, good my lord, put him
to't: let him have his way.

Sec. Lord. If your lordship find him not a
hilding, hold me no more in your respect. 4
First Lord. On my life, my lord, a bubble.
Ber. Do you think I am so far deceived in him?
First Lord. Believe it, my lord, in mine own
direct knowledge, without any malice, but to
speak of him as my kinsman, he's a most notable
coward, an infinite and endless liar, an hourly
promise-breaker, the owner of no one good quality
worthy your lordship's entertainment. 12
Sec. Lord. It were fit you knew him; lest, reposing too far in his virtue, which he hath not,
he might at some great and trusty business in a
main danger fail you. 16
Ber. I would I knew in what particular action
to try him.
Sec. Lord. None better than to let him fetch
off his drum, which you hear him so confidently
undertake to do. 21
First Lord. I, with a troop of Florentines,
will suddenly surprise him: such I will have
whom I am sure he knows not from the enemy.
We will bind and hoodwink him so, that he shall
suppose no other but that he is carried into the
leaguer of the adversaries, when we bring him to
our own tents. Be but your lordship present at
his examination: if he do not, for the promise
of his life and in the highest compulsion of base
fear, offer to betray you and deliver all the intelligence in his power against you, and that
with the divine forfeit of his soul upon oath,
never trust my judgment in anything. 34
Sec. Lord. O! for the love of laughter, let him
fetch his drum: he says he has a stratagem
for't. When your lordship sees the bottom of
his success in't, and to what metal this counterfeit lump of ore will be melted, if you give him
not John Drum's entertainment, your inclining
cannot be removed. Here he comes. 41
First Lord. O! for the love of laughter, hinder
not the honour of his design: let him fetch off
his drum in any hand. 44

Enter PAROLLES.

Ber. How now, monsieur! this drum sticks
sorely in your disposition.
Sec. Lord. A pox on't! let it go: 'tis but a
drum. 48
Par. 'But a drum!' Is't 'but a drum?' A
drum so lost! There was excellent command, to
charge in with our horse upon our own wings,
and to rend our own soldiers! 52
Sec. Lord. That was not to be blamed in the
command of the service: it was a disaster of war
that Cæsar himself could not have prevented if
he had been there to command. 56
Ber. Well, we cannot greatly condemn our
success: some dishonour we had in the loss of
that drum; but it is not to be recovered.
Par. It might have been recovered. 60
Ber. It might; but it is not now.
Par. It is to be recovered. But that the
merit of service is seldom attributed to the true
and exact performer, I would have that drum or
another, or *hic jacet.* 65
Ber. Why, if you have a stomach to't, monsieur,

if you think your mystery in stratagem can br
this instrument of honour again into its nat
quarter, be magnanimous in the enterprise a
go on; I will grace the attempt for a wor
exploit: if you speed well in it, the duke sh
both speak of it, and extend to you what furth
becomes his greatness, even to the utmost s
lable of your worthiness.
Par. By the hand of a soldier, I will und
take it.
Ber. But you must not now slumber in it.
Par. I'll about it this evening: and I w
presently pen down my dilemmas, encoura
myself in my certainty, put myself into
mortal preparation, and by midnight look
hear further from me.
Ber. May I be bold to acquaint his Grace y
are gone about it?
Par. I know not what the success will
my lord; but the attempt I vow.
Ber. I know thou'rt valiant; and, to the p
sibility of thy soldiership, will subscribe for th
Farewell.
Par. I love not many words. [*Ex*
First Lord. No more than a fish loves wat
Is not this a strange fellow, my lord, that so co
fidently seems to undertake this business, whi
he knows is not to be done; damns himself
do, and dares better be damned than to do't?
Sec. Lord. You do not know him, my lord,
we do: certain it is, that he will steal hims
into a man's favour, and for a week escape
great deal of discoveries; but when you fi
him out you have him ever after.
Ber. Why, do you think he will make no de
at all of this that so seriously he does addre
himself unto?
First Lord. None in the world; but retu
with an invention and clap upon you two
three probable lies. But we have almost e
bossed him, you shall see his fall to-night; fo
indeed, he is not for your lordship's respect.
Sec. Lord. We'll make you some sport w
the fox ere we case him. He was first smok
by the old Lord Lafeu: when his disguise
he is parted, tell me what a sprat you shall f
him; which you shall see this very night.
First Lord. I must go look my twigs:
shall be caught.
Ber. Your brother he shall go along with n
First Lord. As't please your lordship:
leave you. [*Ex*
Ber. Now will I lead you to the house, a
show you
The lass I spoke of.
Sec. Lord. But you say she's honest.
Ber. That's all the fault. I spoke with
but once,
And found her wondrous cold; but I sent
her,
By this same coxcomb that we have i' the win
Tokens and letters which she did re-send;
And this is all I have done. She's a fair creatu
Will you go see her?
Sec. Lord. With all my heart, my lo
[*Exeu*

Scene VII.—*Florence. A Room in the*
Widow's House.

Enter HELENA *and* Widow.

Hel. If you misdoubt me that I am not she,
now not how I shall assure you further,
t I shall lose the grounds I work upon.

Wid. Though my estate be fall'n, I was well
	born,					4
othing acquainted with these businesses;
d would not put my reputation now
any staining act.

Hel.				Nor would I wish you.
st, give me trust, the county is my husband,
d what to your sworn counsel I have spoken
so from word to word; and then you cannot,
' the good aid that I of you shall borrow,
r in bestowing it.

Wid.			I should believe you:	12
r you have show'd me that which well approves
u're great in fortune.

Hel.			Take this purse of gold,
d let me buy your friendly help thus far,
hich I will over-pay and pay again		16
hen I have found it. The county woos your
	daughter,
ys down his wanton siege before her beauty,
esolv'd to carry her: let her in fine consent,
s we'll direct her how 'tis best to bear it.	20
ow, his important blood will nought deny
at she'll demand: a ring the county wears,
at downward hath succeeded in his house
om son to son, some four or five descents	24
nce the first father wore it: this ring he holds
 most rich choice; yet, in his idle fire,
 buy his will, it would not seem too dear,
 owe'er repented after.

Wid.				Now I see		28
e bottom of your purpose.

Hel. You see it lawful then. It is no more,
t that your daughter, ere she seems as won,
esires this ring, appoints him an encounter,	32
 fine, delivers me to fill the time,
erself most chastely absent. After this,
 marry her, I'll add three thousand crowns
 what is past already.

Wid.			I have yielded.	36
struct my daughter how she shall persever,
hat time and place with this deceit so lawful
ay prove coherent. Every night he comes
ith musics of all sorts and songs compos'd	40
 her unworthiness: it nothing steads us
 chide him from our eaves, for he persists
s if his life lay on't.

Hel.			Why then to-night
et us assay our plot; which, if it speed,	44
 wicked meaning in a lawful deed,
nd lawful meaning in a lawful act,
here both not sin, and yet a sinful fact.	47
ut let's about it.			[*Exeunt.*

ACT IV

Scene I.—*Without the Florentine Camp.*

nter First French Lord, *with five or six* Sol-
	diers *in ambush.*

First Lord. He can come no other way but
by this hedge-corner. When you sally upon
him, speak what terrible language you will:
though you understand it not yourselves, no
matter; for we must not seem to understand
him, unless some one among us, whom we must
produce for an interpreter.			7

First Sold. Good captain, let me be the interpreter.

First Lord. Art not acquainted with him?
knows he not thy voice?

First Sold. No, sir, I warrant you.		12

First Lord. But what linsey-woolsey hast
thou to speak to us again?

First Sold. Even such as you speak to me.

First Lord. He must think us some band of
strangers i' the adversary's entertainment. Now,
he hath a smack of all neighbouring languages;
therefore we must every one be a man of his
own fancy, not to know what we speak one to
another; so we seem to know, is to know
straight our purpose: chough's language, gabble
enough, and good enough. As for you, interpreter, you must seem very politic. But couch, ho!
here he comes, to beguile two hours in a sleep,
and then to return and swear the lies he forges. 26

Enter PAROLLES.

Par. Ten o'clock: within these three hours
'twill be time enough to go home. What shall
I say I have done? It must be a very plausive
invention that carries it. They begin to smoke
me, and disgraces have of late knocked too often
at my door. I find my tongue is too foolhardy; but
my heart hath the fear of Mars before it and of
his creatures, not daring the reports of my tongue.

First Lord. This is the first truth that e'er
thine own tongue was guilty of.			36

Par. What the devil should move me to undertake the recovery of this drum, being not ignorant of the impossibility, and knowing I had
no such purpose? I must give myself some hurts
and say I got them in exploit. Yet slight ones
will not carry it: they will say, 'Came you off
with so little?' and great ones I dare not give.
Wherefore, what's the instance? Tongue, I must
put you into a butter-woman's mouth, and buy
myself another of Bajazet's mute, if you prattle
me into these perils.

First Lord. Is it possible he should know
what he is, and be that he is?			49

Par. I would the cutting of my garments
would serve the turn or the breaking of my
Spanish sword.				52

First Lord. We cannot afford you so.

Par. Or the baring of my beard, and to say
it was in stratagem.

First Lord. 'Twould not do.			56

Par. Or to drown my clothes, and say I was
stripped.

First Lord. Hardly serve.

Par. Though I swore I leaped from the
window of the citadel—			61

First Lord. How deep?

Par. Thirty fathom.

First Lord. Three great oaths would scarce
make that be believed.				65

Par. I would I had any drum of the enemy's:
I would swear I recovered it.

First Lord. Thou shalt hear one anon.   68

Par. A drum now of the enemy's!
            [*Alarum within.*

First Lord. Throca movousus, cargo, cargo,
cargo.

All. Cargo, cargo, villianda par corbo, cargo.
            [*They seize and blindfold him.*

Par. O! ransom, ransom! Do not hide mine
eyes.   72

First Sold. Boskos thromuldo boskos.

Par. I know you are the Muskos' regiment;
And I shall lose my life for want of language.
If there be here German, or Dane, low Dutch,   76
Italian, or French, let him speak to me:
I will discover that which shall undo
The Florentine.

First Sold.   Boskos vauvado:
I understand thee, and can speak thy tongue:
Kerelybonto: Sir,   81
Betake thee to thy faith, for seventeen poniards
Are at thy bosom.

Par.   O!

First Sold.   O! pray, pray, pray.
Manka revania dulche.

First Lord.   Oscorbidulchos volivorco.

First Sold. The general is content to spare
thee yet;   85
And, hoodwink'd as thou art, will lead thee on
To gather from thee: haply thou may'st inform
Something to save thy life.

Par.   O! let me live,   88
And all the secrets of our camp I'll show,
Their force, their purposes; nay, I'll speak that
Which you will wonder at.

First Sold.   But wilt thou faithfully?

Par. If I do not, damn me.

First Sold.   Acordo linta.   92
Come on; thou art granted space.
            [*Exit, with* PAROLLES *guarded.*
            A short alarum within.

First Lord. Go, tell the Count Rousillon, and
my brother,
We have caught the woodcock, and will keep
him muffled
Till we do hear from them.

Sec. Sold.   Captain, I will.   96

First Lord. A' will betray us all unto ourselves:
Inform on that.

Sec. Sold.   So I will, sir.

First Lord. Till then, I'll keep him dark and
safely lock'd.   [*Exeunt.*

SCENE II.—*Florence. A Room in the* Widow's
House.

Enter BERTRAM *and* DIANA.

Ber. They told me that your name was
Fontibell.

Dia. No, my good lord, Diana.

Ber.   Titled goddess;
And worth it, with addition! But, fair soul,
In your fine frame hath love no quality?   4

If the quick fire of youth light not your mind,
You are no maiden, but a monument:
When you are dead, you should be such a one
As you are now, for you are cold and stern;
And now you should be as your mother was
When your sweet self was got.

Dia. She then was honest.

Ber.   So should you be.

Dia.   N
My mother did but duty; such, my lord,
As you owe to your wife.

Ber.   No more o' that!
I prithee do not strive against my vows.
I was compell'd to her; but I love thee
By love's own sweet constraint, and will for ev
Do thee all rights of service.

Dia.   Ay, so you serve us
Till we serve you; but when you have our ros
You barely leave our thorns to prick oursel
And mock us with our bareness.

Ber.   How have I sworn!

Dia. 'Tis not the many oaths that make t
truth,
But the plain single vow that is vow'd true.
What is not holy, that we swear not by,
But take the Highest to witness: then, pray yo
tell me,
If I should swear by God's great attributes
I lov'd you dearly, would you believe my oath
When I did love you ill? this has no holding,
To swear by him whom I protest to love,
That I will work against him: therefore yo
oaths
Are words and poor conditions, but unseal'
At least in my opinion.

Ber.   Change it, change
Be not so holy-cruel: love is holy;
And my integrity ne'er knew the crafts
That you do charge men with. Stand no mo
off,
But give thyself unto my sick desires,
Who then recover: say thou art mine, and ev
My love as it begins shall so persevere.

Dia. I see that men make ropes in such
scarr
That we'll forsake ourselves. Give me that rin

Ber. I'll lend it thee, my dear; but have
power
To give it from me.

Dia.   Will you not, my lord?

Ber. It is an honour 'longing to our hous
Bequeathed down from many ancestors,
Which were the greatest obloquy i' the world
In me to lose.

Dia.   Mine honour's such a ring:
My chastity's the jewel of our house,
Bequeathed down from many ancestors,
Which were the greatest obloquy i' the world
In me to lose. Thus your own proper wisdo
Brings in the champion honour on my part
Against your vain assault.

Ber.   Here, take my rin
My house, mine honour, yea, my life, be thine,
And I'll be bid by thee.

Dia. When midnight comes, knock at m
chamber-window:

order take my mother shall not hear.
ow will I charge you in the band of truth, 56
hen you have conquer'd my yet maiden bed,
emain there but an hour, nor speak to me.
y reasons are most strong; and you shall
  know them
hen back again this ring shall be deliver'd: 60
nd on your finger in the night I'll put
nother ring, that what in time proceeds
ay token to the future our past deeds.
dieu, till then; then, fail not. You have won
wife of me, though there my hope be done. 65
Ber. A heaven on earth I have won by wooing thee.   [*Exit.*
Dia. For which live long to thank both
  heaven and me!
ou may so in the end.   68
y mother told me just how he would woo
s if she sat in's heart; she says all men
ave the like oaths: he had sworn to marry
  me
hen his wife's dead; therefore I'll lie with him
hen I am buried. Since Frenchmen are so
  braid,   73
arry that will, I live and die a maid:
nly in this disguise I think't no sin
o cozen him that would unjustly win.   [*Exit.*

SCENE III.—*The Florentine Camp.*

nter the two French Lords, *and two or three*
  Soldiers.

First Lord. You have not given him his
other's letter?
Sec. Lord. I have delivered it an hour since:
ere is something in't that stings his nature,
r on the reading it he changed almost into
other man.
First Lord. He has much worthy blame laid
on him for shaking off so good a wife and so
veet a lady.   9
Sec. Lord. Especially he hath incurred the
erlasting displeasure of the king, who had
en tuned his bounty to sing happiness to him.
will tell you a thing, but you shall let it dwell
rkly with you.
First Lord. When you have spoken it, 'tis
ad, and I am the grave of it.   16
Sec. Lord. He hath perverted a young gentle-
oman here in Florence, of a most chaste re-
wn; and this night he fleshes his will in the
oil of her honour: he hath given her his
onumental ring, and thinks himself made in
e unchaste composition.
First Lord. Now, God delay our rebellion!
  we are ourselves, what things are we!   24
Sec. Lord. Merely our own traitors: and as
the common course of all treasons, we still
e them reveal themselves, till they attain to
eir abhorred ends, so he that in this action
ntrives against his own nobility, in his proper
ream o'erflows himself.   30
First Lord. Is it not most damnable in us,
be trumpeters of our unlawful intents? We
all not then have his company to-night?

Sec. Lord. Not till after midnight, for he is
dieted to his hour.   35
First Lord. That approaches apace: I would
gladly have him see his company anatomized,
that he might take a measure of his own judgments, wherein so curiously he had set this
counterfeit.   40
Sec. Lord. We will not meddle with him till
he come, for his presence must be the whip of
the other.
First Lord. In the meantime what hear you
of these wars?   45
Sec. Lord. I hear there is an overture of peace.
First Lord. Nay, I assure you, a peace concluded.   48
Sec. Lord. What will Count Rousillon do
then? will he travel higher, or return again into
France?
First Lord. I perceive by this demand, you
are not altogether of his council.   53
Sec. Lord. Let it be forbid, sir; so should I
be a great deal of his act.
First Lord. Sir, his wife some two months
since fled from his house: her pretence is a
pilgrimage to Saint Jaques le Grand; which
holy undertaking with most austere sanctimony
she accomplished; and, there residing, the
tenderness of her nature became as a prey to
her grief; in fine, made a groan of her last
breath, and now she sings in heaven.
Sec. Lord. How is this justified?   64
First Lord. The stronger part of it by her
own letters, which make her story true, even to
the point of her death: her death itself, which
could not be her office to say is come, was faithfully confirmed by the rector of the place. 69
Sec. Lord. Hath the count all this intelligence?
First Lord. Ay, and the particular confirmations, point from point, to the full arming of
the verity.   73
Sec. Lord. I am heartily sorry that he'll be
glad of this.
First Lord. How mightily sometimes we
make us comforts of our losses!   77
Sec. Lord. And how mightily some other
times we drown our gain in tears! The great
dignity that his valour hath here acquired for
him shall at home be encountered with a shame
as ample.   82
First Lord. The web of our life is of a mingled
yarn, good and ill together: our virtues would
be proud if our faults whipped them not; and
our crimes would despair if they were not
cherished by our virtues.

Enter a Servant.

How now! where's your master?   88
Serv. He met the duke in the street, sir, of
whom he hath taken a solemn leave: his lordship will next morning for France. The duke hath
offered him letters of commendations to the king.
Sec. Lord. They shall be no more than needful
there, if they were more than they can commend.
First Lord. They cannot be too sweet for the
king's tartness. Here's his lordship now.   96

Enter BERTRAM.

How now, my lord! is't not after midnight?

Ber. I have to-night dispatched sixteen businesses, a month's length a-piece, by an abstract of success: I have conge'd with the duke, done my adieu with his nearest, buried a wife, mourned for her, writ to my lady mother I am returning, entertained my convoy; and between these main parcels of dispatch effected many nicer needs: the last was the greatest, but that I have not ended yet. 106

Sec. Lord. If the business be of any difficulty, and this morning your departure hence, it requires haste of your lordship.

Ber. I mean, the business is not ended, as fearing to hear of it hereafter. But shall we have this dialogue between the fool and the soldier? Come, bring forth this counterfeit model: he has deceived me, like a double-meaning prophesier. 115

Sec. Lord. Bring him forth. [*Exeunt* Soldiers.] Has sat i' the stocks all night, poor gallant knave.

Ber. No matter; his heels have deserved it, in usurping his spurs so long. How does he carry himself? 121

First Lord. I have told your lordship already, the stocks carry him. But to answer you as you would be understood; he weeps like a wench that had shed her milk: he hath confessed himself to Morgan,—whom he supposes to be a friar,—from the time of his remembrance to this very instant disaster of his setting i' the stocks: and what think you he hath confessed?

Ber. Nothing of me, has a'? 130

Sec. Lord. His confession is taken, and it shall be read to his face: if your lordship be in't, as I believe you are, you must have the patience to hear it.

Re-enter Soldiers *with* PAROLLES.

Ber. A plague upon him! muffled! he can say nothing of me: hush! hush! 136

First Lord. Hoodman comes! *Porto tartarossa.*

First Sold. He calls for the tortures: what will you say without 'em? 140

Par. I will confess what I know without constraint: if ye pinch me like a pasty, I can say no more.

First Sold. Bosko chimurcho. 144

First Lord. Boblibindo chicurmurco.

First Sold. You are a merciful general. Our general bids you answer to what I shall ask you out of a note. 148

Par. And truly, as I hope to live.

First Sold. First, demand of him how many horse the duke is strong. What say you to that?

Par. Five or six thousand; but very weak and unserviceable: the troops are all scattered, and the commanders very poor rogues, upon my reputation and credit, and as I hope to live. 155

First Sold. Shall I set down your answer so?

Par. Do: I'll take the sacrament on't, how and which way you will.

Ber. All's one to him. What a past-savi slave is this!

First Lord. You are deceived, my lord: t is Monsieur Parolles, the gallant militarist, that was his own phrase,—that had the wh theorick of war in the knot of his scarf, and practice in the chape of his dagger.

Sec. Lord. I will never trust a man again keeping his sword clean; nor believe he have everything in him by wearing his appa neatly.

First Sold. Well, that's set down.

Par. Five or six thousand horse, I said, will say true,—or thereabouts, set down, for speak truth.

First Lord. He's very near the truth in t

Ber. But I con him no thanks for't, in nature he delivers it.

Par. Poor rogues, I pray you, say.

First Sold. Well, that's set down.

Par. I humbly thank you, sir. A truth' truth; the rogues are marvellous poor.

First Sold. Demand of him, of what stren they are a-foot. What say you to that?

Par. By my troth, sir, if I were to live t present hour, I will tell true. Let me s Spurio, a hundred and fifty; Sebastian, so ma Corambus, so many; Jaques, so many; Guilti Cosmo, Lodowick, and Gratii, two hundred f each; mine own company, Chitopher, Vaumo Bentii, two hundred fifty each: so that muster-file, rotten and sound, upon my amounts not to fifteen thousand poll; half the which dare not shake the snow from off th cassocks, lest they shake themselves to pie

Ber. What shall be done to him?

First Lord. Nothing, but let him have than Demand of him my condition, and what cre I have with the duke.

First Sold. Well, that's set down. *You sh demand of him, whether one Captain Dum be i' the camp, a Frenchman; what his repu tion is with the duke; what his valour, hones and expertness in wars; or whether he think were not possible, with well-weighing sums gold, to corrupt him to a revolt.* What say y to this? what do you know of it?

Par. I beseech you, let me answer to particular of the inter'gatories: demand th singly.

First Sold. Do you know this Captain I main?

Par. I know him: a' was a botcher's 'pr tice in Paris, from whence he was whipped getting the shrieve's fool with child; a du innocent, that could not say him nay.

[DUMAIN *lifts up his ha in ang*

Ber. Nay, by your leave, hold your han though I know his brains are forfeit to the n tile that falls.

First Sold. Well, is this captain in the Du of Florence's camp?

Par. Upon my knowledge he is, and lousy.

First Lord. Nay, look not so upon me; shall hear of your lordship anon.

First Sold. What is his reputation with the uke?   224

Par. The duke knows him for no other but a oor officer of mine, and writ to me this other ay to turn him out o' the band: I think I have is letter in my pocket.   228

First Sold. Marry, we'll search.

Par. In good sadness, I do not know: either is there, or it is upon a file with the duke's ther letters in my tent.   232

First Sold. Here 'tis; here's a paper; shall I ead it to you?

Par. I do not know if it be it or no.

Ber. Our interpreter does it well.   236

First Lord. Excellently.

First Sold. Dian, the count's a fool, and full of gold—

Par. That is not the duke's letter, sir; that an advertisement to a proper maid in Flo-ence, one Diana, to take heed of the allurement f one Count Rousillon, a foolish idle boy, but or all that very ruttish. I pray you, sir, put it p again.   244

First Sold. Nay, I'll read it first, by your avour.

Par. My meaning in't, I protest, was very onest in the behalf of the maid; for I knew ne young count to be a dangerous and lasci-ious boy, who is a whale to virginity, and de-ours up all the fry it finds.

Ber. Damnable both-sides rogue!   252

First Sold. When he swears oaths, bid him drop gold, and take it;

After he scores, he never pays the score:
Half won is match well made; match, and well make it;

He ne'er pays after-debts; take it before, 256
And say a soldier, Dian, told thee this,
Men are to mell with, boys are not to kiss;
For count of this, the count's a fool, I know it,
Who pays before, but not when he does owe it.
Thine, as he vow'd to thee in thine ear, 261

PAROLLES.

Ber. He shall be whipped through the army vith this rime in's forehead.   264

First Lord. This is your devoted friend, sir; ne manifold linguist and the armipotent sol-ier.

Ber. I could endure anything before but a at, and now he's a cat to me.   269

First Sold. I perceive, sir, by our general's ooks, we shall be fain to hang you.

Par. My life, sir, in any case! not that I am fraid to die; but that, my offences being many, would repent out the remainder of nature. et me live, sir, in a dungeon, i' the stocks, or nywhere, so I may live.   276

First Sold. We'll see what may be done, so ou confess freely: therefore, once more to this Captain Dumain. You have answered to his eputation with the duke and to his valour: vhat is his honesty?   281

Par. He will steal, sir, an egg out of a cloister; or rapes and ravishments he parallels Nessus; he professes not keeping of oaths; in breaking

'em he is stronger than Hercules; he will lie, sir, with such volubility, that you would think truth were a fool; drunkenness is his best virtue, for he will be swine-drunk, and in his sleep he does little harm, save to his bed-clothes about him; but they know his conditions, and lay him in straw. I have but little more to say, sir, of his honesty: he has everything that an honest man should not have; what an honest man should have, he has nothing.   294

First Lord. I begin to love him for this.

Ber. For this description of thine honesty? A pox upon him for me! he is more and more a cat.

First Sold. What say you to his expertness in war?   299

Par. Faith, sir, he has led the drum before the English tragedians,—to belie him I will not,—and more of his soldiership I know not; except, in that country, he had the honour to be the officer at a place there called Mile-end, to instruct for the doubling of files: I would do the man what honour I can, but of this I am not certain.   307

First Lord. He hath out-villained villany so far, that the rarity redeems him.

Ber. A pox on him! he's a cat still.

First Sold. His qualities being at this poor price, I need not ask you, if gold will corrupt him to revolt.   313

Par. Sir, for a cardecu he will sell the fee-simple of his salvation, the inheritance of it; and cut the entail from all remainders, and a perpetual succession for it perpetually.   317

First Sold. What's his brother, the other Captain Dumain?

Sec. Lord. Why does he ask him of me?

First Sold. What's he?   321

Par. E'en a crow o' the same nest; not alto-gether so great as the first in goodness, but greater a great deal in evil. He excels his brother for a coward, yet his brother is reputed one of the best that is. In a retreat he out-runs any lackey; marry, in coming on he has the cramp.   328

First Sold. If your life be saved, will you undertake to betray the Florentine?

Par. Ay, and the captain of his horse, Count Rousillon.   332

First Sold. I'll whisper with the general, and know his pleasure.

Par. [*Aside.*] I'll no more drumming; a plague of all drums! Only to seem to deserve well, and to beguile the supposition of that lascivious young boy the count, have I run into this danger. Yet who would have suspected an ambush where I was taken?   340

First Sold. There is no remedy, sir, but you must die. The general says, you, that have so traitorously discovered the secrets of your army, and made such pestiferous reports of men very nobly held, can serve the world for no honest use; therefore you must die. Come, headsman, off with his head.

Par. O Lord, sir, let me live, or let me see my death!   349

First Sold. That shall you, and take your
leave of all your friends.   [*Unmuffling him.*
So, look about you: know you any here? 352
  Ber. Good morrow, noble captain.
  Sec. Lord. God bless you, Captain Parolles.
  First Lord. God save you, noble captain.
  Sec. Lord. Captain, what greeting will you
to my Lord Lafeu? I am for France.   357
  First Lord. Good captain, will you give me a
copy of the sonnet you writ to Diana in behalf of
the Count Rousillon? an I were not a very
coward I'd compel it of you; but fare you well.
                    [*Exeunt* BERTRAM *and* Lords.
  First Sold. You are undone, captain; all but
your scarf; that has a knot on't yet.
  Par. Who cannot be crushed with a plot? 364
  First Sold. If you could find out a country
where but women were that had received so
much shame, you might begin an impudent
nation. Fare ye well, sir; I am for France
too: we shall speak of you there.   [*Exit.*
  Par. Yet am I thankful: if my heart were great
'Twould burst at this. Captain I'll be no more;
But I will eat and drink, and sleep as soft 372
As captain shall: simply the thing I am
Shall make me live. Who knows himself a
    braggart,
Let him fear this; for it will come to pass
That every braggart shall be found an ass. 376
Rust, sword! cool, blushes! and Parolles, live
Safest in shame! being fool'd, by foolery thrive!
There's place and means for every man alive.
I'll after them.   [*Exit.*

SCENE IV.—*Florence. A Room in the*
        Widow's *House.*

Enter HELENA, Widow, *and* DIANA.

  Hel. That you may well perceive I have not
        wrong'd you,
One of the greatest in the Christian world
Shall be my surety; 'fore whose throne 'tis
    needful,
Ere I can perfect mine intents, to kneel.   4
Time was I did him a desired office,
Dear almost as his life; which gratitude
Through flinty Tartar's bosom would peep
    forth,
And answer, thanks. I duly am inform'd   8
His Grace is at Marseilles; to which place
We have convenient convoy. You must know,
I am supposed dead: the army breaking,
My husband hies him home; where, heaven
    aiding,   12
And by the leave of my good lord the king,
We'll be before our welcome.
  Wid.   Gentle madam,
You never had a servant to whose trust
Your business was more welcome.
  Hel.   Nor you, mistress, 16
Ever a friend whose thoughts more truly labour
To recompense your love. Doubt not but
    heaven
Hath brought me up to be your daughter's
    dower,

As it hath fated her to be my motive   2
And helper to a husband. But, O strange men
That can such sweet use make of what they
    hate,
When saucy trusting of the cozen'd thoughts
Defiles the pitchy night: so lust doth play   2
With what it loathes for that which is away.
But more of this hereafter. You, Diana,
Under my poor instructions yet must suffer
Something in my behalf.
  Dia.   Let death and honesty
Go with your impositions, I am yours   2
Upon your will to suffer.
  Hel.   Yet, I pray you:
But with the word the time will bring on sum
    mer,
When briers shall have leaves as well as thorns
And be as sweet as sharp. We must away; 3
Our waggon is prepar'd, and time revives us:
All's well that ends well: still the fine's th
    crown;
Whate'er the course, the end is the renown. 3
                    [*Exeunt*

SCENE V.—*Rousillon. A Room in the*
        COUNTESS'S *Palace.*

Enter COUNTESS, LAFEU, *and* Clown.

  Laf. No, no, no; your son was misled with a
snipt-taffeta fellow there, whose villanous saffron
would have made all the unbaked and dough
youth of a nation in his colour: your daughter
in-law had been alive at this hour, and your son
here at home, more advanced by the king than
by that red-tailed humble-bee I speak of.
  Count. I would I had not known him; it wa
the death of the most virtuous gentlewoman
that ever nature had praise for creating. If she
had partaken of my flesh, and cost me the dearest
groans of a mother, I could not have owed he
a more rooted love.   1
  Laf. 'Twas a good lady, 'twas a good lady
we may pick a thousand salads ere we light on
such another herb.   1
  Clo. Indeed, sir, she was the sweet-marjoram
of the salad, or, rather the herb of grace.
  Laf. They are not salad-herbs, you knave
they are nose-herbs.   2
  Clo. I am no great Nebuchadnezzar, sir;
have not much skill in grass.
  Laf. Whether dost thou profess thyself, a
knave, or a fool?   2
  Clo. A fool, sir, at a woman's service, and a
knave at a man's.
  Laf. Your distinction?
  Clo. I would cozen the man of his wife, and
do his service.   2
  Laf. So you were a knave at his service, in
deed.
  Clo. And I would give his wife my bauble
sir, to do her service.   3
  Laf. I will subscribe for thee, thou art both
knave and fool.
  Clo. At your service.   3
  Laf. No, no, no.

Clo. Why, sir, if I cannot serve you, I can
erve as great a prince as you are.

Laf. Who's that? a Frenchman?   40

Clo. Faith, sir, a' has an English name; but
is phisnomy is more hotter in France than
here.

Laf. What prince is that?   44

Clo. The black prince, sir; *alias*, the prince
f darkness; *alias*, the devil.

Laf. Hold thee, there's my purse. I give thee
not this to suggest thee from thy master thou
alkest of: serve him still.   49

Clo. I am a woodland fellow, sir, that always
oved a great fire; and the master I speak of,
ver keeps a good fire. But, sure, he is the
rince of the world; let his nobility remain in's
ourt. I am for the house with the narrow gate,
which I take to be too little for pomp to enter:
ome that humble themselves may; but the
many will be too chill and tender, and they'll
e for the flowery way that leads to the broad
ate and the great fire.   59

Laf. Go thy ways, I begin to be aweary of
hee; and I tell thee so before, because I would
ot fall out with thee. Go thy ways: let my
orses be well looked to, without any tricks. 63

Clo. If I put any tricks upon 'em, sir, they
hall be jade's tricks, which are their own right
y the law of nature.   [*Exit.*

Laf. A shrewd knave and an unhappy.   67

Count. So he is. My lord that's gone made
imself much sport out of him: by his authority
e remains here, which he thinks is a patent for
his sauciness; and, indeed, he has no pace, but
uns where he will.   72

Laf. I like him well; 'tis not amiss. And I
vas about to tell you, since I heard of the good
ady's death, and that my lord your son was
pon his return home, I moved the king my
naster to speak in the behalf of my daughter;
which, in the minority of them both, his majesty,
ut of a self-gracious remembrance, did first
ropose. His highness hath promised me to do
t; and to stop up the displeasure he hath con-
eived against your son, there is no fitter matter.
How does your ladyship like it?   83

Count. With very much content, my lord;
nd I wish it happily effected.

Laf. His highness comes post from Marseilles,
f as able body as when he numbered thirty: he
vill be here to-morrow, or I am deceived by him
hat in such intelligence hath seldom failed. 89

Count. It rejoices me that I hope I shall see
im ere I die. I have letters that my son will be
ere to-night: I shall beseech your lordship to
emain with me till they meet together.   93

Laf. Madam, I was thinking with what man-
ers I might safely be admitted.

Count. You need but plead your honourable
rivilege.   97

Laf. Lady, of that I have made a bold charter;
ut I thank my God it holds yet.

Re-enter Clown.

Clo. O madam! yonder's my lord your son
vith a patch of velvet on's face: whether there
be a scar under it or no, the velvet knows; but
'tis a goodly patch of velvet. His left cheek is a
cheek of two pile and a half, but his right cheek
is worn bare.   105

Laf. A scar nobly got, or a noble scar, is a
good livery of honour; so belike is that.

Clo. But it is your carbonadoed face.   108

Laf. Let us go see your son, I pray you: I
long to talk with the young noble soldier.

Clo. Faith, there's a dozen of 'em, with delicate fine hats and most courteous feathers, which
bow the head and nod at every man. [*Exeunt.*

ACT V

SCENE I.—*Marseilles. A Street.*

Enter HELENA, Widow, *and* DIANA, *with two
Attendants.*

Hel. But this exceeding posting, day and
   night,
Must wear your spirits low; we cannot help it:
But since you have made the days and nights
   as one,
To wear your gentle limbs in my affairs,   4
Be bold you do so grow in my requital
As nothing can unroot you. In happy time;

Enter a gentle Astringer.

This man may help me to his majesty's ear,
If he would spend his power. God save you, sir.

Gent. And you.   9

Hel. Sir, I have seen you in the court of
   France.

Gent. I have been sometimes there.

Hel. I do presume, sir, that you are not fallen
From the report that goes upon your goodness;
And therefore, goaded with most sharp occa-
   sions,
Which lay nice manners by, I put you to
The use of your own virtues, for the which 16
I shall continue thankful.

Gent.   What's your will?

Hel. That it will please you
To give this poor petition to the king,
And aid me with that store of power you have
To come into his presence.   21

Gent. The king's not here.

Hel.   Not here, sir!

Gent.   Not, indeed:
He hence remov'd last night, and with more
   haste
Than is his use.

Wid.   Lord, how we lose our pains! 24

Hel. All's well that ends well yet,
Though time seems so adverse and means unfit.
I do beseech you, whither is he gone?

Gent. Marry, as I take it, to Rousillon; 28
Whither I am going.

Hel.   I do beseech you, sir,
Since you are like to see the king before me,
Commend the paper to his gracious hand;
Which I presume shall render you no blame 32
But rather make you thank your pains for it.

I will come after you with what good speed
Our means will make us means.
Gent. This I'll do for you.
Hel. And you shall find yourself to be well
thank'd, 36
Whate'er falls more. We must to horse again:
Go, go, provide. [*Exeunt.*

SCENE II.—*Rousillon. The inner Court of the*
COUNTESS'S *Palace.*

Enter Clown *and* PAROLLES.

Par. Good Monsieur Lavache, give my Lord
Lafeu this letter. I have ere now, sir, been better
known to you, when I have held familiarity with
fresher clothes; but I am now, sir, muddied in
Fortune's mood, and smell somewhat strong of
her strong displeasure. 6
Clo. Truly, Fortune's displeasure is but sluttish if it smell so strongly as thou speakest of: I
will henceforth eat no fish of Fortune's butter-
ing. Prithee, allow the wind.
Par. Nay, you need not to stop your nose,
sir: I spake but by a metaphor. 12
Clo. Indeed, sir, if your metaphor stink, I
will stop my nose; or against any man's metaphor. Prithee, get thee further.
Par. Pray you, sir, deliver me this paper. 16
Clo. Foh! prithee, stand away: a paper from
Fortune's close-stool to give to a nobleman!
Look, here he comes himself.

Enter LAFEU.

Here is a purr of Fortune's, sir, or of Fortune's
cat—but not a musk-cat—that has fallen into
the unclean fishpond of her displeasure, and, as
he says, is muddied withal. Pray you, sir, use
the carp as you may, for he looks like a poor,
decayed, ingenious, foolish, rascally knave. I do
pity his distress in my similes of comfort, and
leave him to your lordship. [*Exit.*
Par. My lord, I am a man whom Fortune
hath cruelly scratched. 29
Laf. And what would you have me to do? 'tis
too late to pare her nails now. Wherein have
you played the knave with Fortune that she
should scratch you, who of herself is a good lady,
and would not have knaves thrive long under
her? There's a cardecu for you. Let the justices
make you and Fortune friends; I am for other
business. 37
Par. I beseech your honour to hear me one
single word.
Laf. You beg a single penny more: come,
you shall ha't; save your word. 41
Par. My name, my good lord, is Parolles.
Laf. You beg more than one word then.
Cox my passion! give me your hand. How
does your drum? 45
Par. O, my good lord! you were the first that
found me.
Laf. Was I, in sooth? and I was the first
that lost thee. 49
Par. It lies in you, my lord, to bring me in
some grace, for you did bring me out.

Laf. Out upon thee, knave! dost thou p[ut]
upon me at once both the office of God and t[he]
devil? one brings thee in grace and the oth[er]
brings thee out. [*Trumpets sound.*] The king[']s
coming; I know by his trumpets. Sirrah, i[n]
quire further after me; I had talk of you la[st]
night: though you are a fool and a knave, yo[u]
shall eat: go to, follow.
Par. I praise God for you. [*Exeun[t]*

SCENE III.—*The Same. A Room in the*
COUNTESS'S *Palace.*

Flourish. Enter KING, COUNTESS, LAFEU,
Lords, Gentlemen, Guards, &c.

King. We lost a jewel of her, and our estee[m]
Was made much poorer by it: but your son,
As mad in folly, lack'd the sense to know
Her estimation home.
Count. 'Tis past, my liege;
And I beseech your majesty to make it
Natural rebellion, done i' the blaze of youth;
When oil and fire, too strong for reason's forc[e,]
O'erbears it and burns on.
King. My honour'd lady,
I have forgiven and forgotten all,
Though my revenges were high bent upon hi[m]
And watch'd the time to shoot.
Laf. This I must say,—
But first I beg my pardon,—the young lord
Did to his majesty, his mother, and his lady,
Offence of mighty note, but to himself
The greatest wrong of all: he lost a wife
Whose beauty did astonish the survey
Of richest eyes, whose words all ears took ca[p]-
tive,
Whose dead perfection hearts that scorn'd [to]
serve
Humbly call'd mistress.
King. Praising what is lost
Makes the remembrance dear. Well, call hi[m]
hither;
We are reconcil'd, and the first view shall k[ill]
All repetition. Let him not ask our pardon:
The nature of his great offence is dead,
And deeper than oblivion we do bury
The incensing relics of it: let him approach,
A stranger, no offender; and inform him
So 'tis our will he should.
Gent. I shall, my liege.
[*Exi[t]*
King. What says he to your daughter? hav[e]
you spoke?
Laf. All that he is hath reference to you[r]
highness.
King. Then shall we have a match. I hav[e]
letters sent me,
That set him high in fame.

Enter BERTRAM.

Laf. He looks well on'[t]
King. I am not a day of season,
For thou mayst see a sunshine and a hail
In me at once; but to the brightest beams

istracted clouds give way: so stand thou
  forth;
he time is fair again.
  Ber. My high-repented blames, 36
ear sovereign, pardon to me.
  King. All is whole;
ot one word more of the consumed time.
et's take the instant by the forward top,
or we are old, and on our quick'st decrees 40
he inaudible and noiseless foot of time
teals ere we can effect them. You remember
he daughter of this lord?
  Ber. Admiringly, my liege: 44
t first I stuck my choice upon her, ere my
  heart
urst make too bold a herald of my tongue,
here the impression of mine eye infixing,
ontempt his scornful perspective did lend
  me,
hich warp'd the line of every other favour; 49
corn'd a fair colour, or express'd it stolen;
xtended or contracted all proportions
o a most hideous object: thence it came 52
hat she, whom all men prais'd, and whom
  myself,
ince I have lost, have lov'd, was in mine eye
he dust that did offend it.
  King. Well excus'd:
hat thou didst love her, strikes some scores
  away 56
rom the great compt. But love that comes too
  late,
ike a remorseful pardon slowly carried,
o the great sender turns a sour offence,
rying, 'That's good that's gone.' Our rasher
  faults 60
Make trivial price of serious things we have,
Not knowing them until we know their grave:
Oft our displeasures, to ourselves unjust,
Destroy our friends and after weep their dust: 64
Our own love waking cries to see what's done,
While shameful hate sleeps out the afternoon.
Be this sweet Helen's knell, and now forget
  her.
Send forth your amorous token for fair Maud-
  lin: 68
The main consents are had; and here we'll stay
To see our widower's second marriage-day.
  Count. Which better than the first, O dear
  heaven, bless!
Or, ere they meet, in me, O nature, cesse! 72
  Laf. Come on, my son, in whom my house's
  name
Must be digested, give a favour from you
To sparkle in the spirits of my daughter,
That she may quickly come.
               [*BERTRAM gives a ring.*
            By my old beard, 76
And every hair that's on't, Helen, that's dead,
Was a sweet creature; such a ring as this,
The last that e'er I took her leave at court,
I saw upon her finger.
  Ber. Hers it was not. 80
  King. Now, pray you, let me see it; for mine
  eye,
While I was speaking, oft was fasten'd to't.—

This ring was mine; and, when I gave it Helen,
I bade her, if her fortunes ever stood 84
Necessitied to help, that by this token
I would relieve her. Had you that craft to reave
  her
Of what should stead her most?
  Ber. My gracious sovereign,
Howe'er it pleases you to take it so, 88
The ring was never hers.
  Count. Son, on my life,
I have seen her wear it; and she reckon'd it
At her life's rate.
  Laf. I am sure I saw her wear it.
  Ber. You are deceiv'd, my lord, she never
  saw it: 92
In Florence was it from a casement thrown
  me,
Wrapp'd in a paper, which contain'd the name
Of her that threw it. Noble she was, and thought
I stood engag'd: but when I had subscrib'd 96
To mine own fortune, and inform'd her fully
I could not answer in that course of honour
As she had made the overture, she ceas'd,
In heavy satisfaction, and would never 100
Receive the ring again.
  King. Plutus himself,
That knows the tinct and multiplying medicine,
Hath not in nature's mystery more science
Than I have in this ring: 'twas mine, 'twas
  Helen's, 104
Whoever gave it you. Then, if you know
That you are well acquainted with yourself,
Confess 'twas hers, and by what rough enforce-
  ment
You got it from her. She call'd the saints to
  surety, 108
That she would never put it from her finger
Unless she gave it to yourself in bed,
Where you have never come, or sent it us
Upon her great disaster.
  Ber. She never saw it. 112
  King. Thou speak'st it falsely, as I love mine
  honour;
And mak'st conjectural fears to come into me
Which I would fain shut out. If it should prove
That thou art so inhuman,—'twill not prove
  so;— 116
And yet I know not: thou didst hate her deadly,
And she is dead; which nothing, but to close
Her eyes myself, could win me to believe,
More than to see this ring. Take him away. 120
               [*Guards seize* BERTRAM.
My fore-past proofs, howe'er the matter fall,
Shall tax my fears of little vanity,
Having vainly fear'd too little. Away with him!
We'll sift this matter further.
  Ber. If you shall prove 124
This ring was ever hers, you shall as easy
Prove that I husbanded her bed in Florence,
Where yet she never was. [*Exit guarded.*
  King. I am wrapp'd in dismal thinkings.

Enter the gentle Astringer.

  Gent. Gracious sovereign, 128
Whether I have been to blame or no, I know not:
Here's a petition from a Florentine,

Who hath, for four or five removes come short
To tender it herself. I undertook it,   132
Vanquish'd thereto by the fair grace and speech
Of the poor suppliant, who by this I know
Is here attending: her business looks in her
With an importing visage, and she told me,   136
In a sweet verbal brief, it did concern
Your highness with herself.

    King.   *Upon his many protestations to*
marry me when his wife was dead, I blush
to say it, he won me. Now is the Count Rou-
sillon a widower: his vows are forfeited to me,
and my honour's paid to him. He stole from
Florence, taking no leave, and I follow him to
his country for justice. Grant it me, O king! in
you it best lies; otherwise a seducer flourishes,
and a poor maid is undone.   147
                    DIANA CAPILET.

    Laf. I will buy me a son-in-law in a fair, and
toil for this: I'll none of him.

    King. The heavens have thought well on
thee, Lafeu,
To bring forth this discovery. Seek these
suitors: 152
Go speedily and bring again the count.

    [*Exeunt the gentle* Astringer, *and some*
                      Attendants.

I am afeard the life of Helen, lady,
Was foully snatch'd.

    Count.   Now, justice on the doers!

        Re-enter BERTRAM, *guarded.*

    King. I wonder, sir, sith wives are monsters
to you,   156
And that you fly them as you swear them lordship,
Yet you desire to marry.

   Re-enter the gentle Astringer, *with* Widow
              and DIANA.

             What woman's that?
    Dia. I am, my lord, a wretched Florentine,
Derived from the ancient Capilet: 160
My suit, as I do understand, you know,
And therefore know how far I may be pitied.

    Wid. I am her mother, sir, whose age and
honour
Both suffer under this complaint we bring,   164
And both shall cease, without your remedy.

    King. Come hither, county; do you know
these women?

    Ber. My lord, I neither can nor will deny
But that I know them: do they charge me
further?   168

    Dia. Why do you look so strange upon your
wife?

    Ber. She's none of mine, my lord.

    Dia.   If you shall marry,
You give away this hand, and that is mine;
You give away heaven's vows, and those are
mine;   172
You give away myself, which is known mine;
For I by vow am so embodied yours
That she which marries you must marry me;
Either both or none.   176

    Laf. [*To* BERTRAM.] Your reputation com[es]
too short for my daughter: you are no husba[nd]
for her.

    Ber. My lord, this is a fond and despera[te]
creature,   1[80]
Whom sometime I have laugh'd with: let yo[ur]
highness
Lay a more noble thought upon mine hono[ur]
Than for to think that I would sink it here.

    King. Sir, for my thoughts, you have the[m]
ill to friend,   1[84]
Till your deeds gain them: fairer prove yo[ur]
honour,
Than in my thought it lies.

    Dia.   Good my lord[,]
Ask him upon his oath, if he does think
He had not my virginity.   1[88]

    King. What sayst thou to her?

    Ber.   She's impudent, my lor[d,]
And was a common gamester to the camp.

    Dia. He does me wrong, my lord; if I we[re]
so,
He might have bought me at a common pric[e.]
Do not believe him. O! behold this ring,   1[92]
Whose high respect and rich validity
Did lack a parallel; yet for all that
He gave it to a commoner o' the camp,   1[94]
If I be one.

    Count.   He blushes, and 'tis it:
Of six preceding ancestors, that gem
Conferr'd by testament to the sequent issue,
Hath it been ow'd and worn. This is his wif[e]
That ring's a thousand proofs.

    King.   Methought you said   20[0]
You saw one here in court could witness it.

    Dia. I did, my lord, but loath am to produc[e]
So bad an instrument: his name's Parolles. 2[02]

    Laf. I saw the man to-day, if man he be.

    King. Find him, and bring him hither.
                 [*Exit an* Attendan[t.]

    Ber.   What of him[?]
He's quoted for a most perfidious slave,
With all the spots of the world tax'd and d[e-]
bosh'd,   20[8]
Whose nature sickens but to speak a truth.
Am I or that or this for what he'll utter,
That will speak anything?

    King.   She hath that ring of your[s.]

    Ber. I think she has: certain it is I lik'd he[r,]
And boarded her i' the wanton way of youth. 21[2]
She knew her distance and did angle for me,
Madding my eagerness with her restraint,
As all impediments in fancy's course   21[4]
Are motives of more fancy; and, in fine,
Her infinite cunning, with her modern grace,
Subdued me to her rate: she got the ring,
And I had that which any inferior might   22[0]
At market-price have bought.

    Dia.   I must be patient:
You, that have turn'd off a first so noble wif[e]
May justly diet me. I pray you yet,—
Since you lack virtue I will lose a husband,—22[4]
Send for your ring; I will return it home,
And give me mine again.

    Ber.   I have it not.

    King. What ring was yours, I pray you?

Dia. Sir, much like
he same upon your finger. 228
King. Know you this ring? this ring was his
of late.
Dia. And this was it I gave him, being a-bed.
King. The story then goes false you threw it
him
ut of a casement.
Dia. I have spoke the truth. 232

Re-enter Attendant *with* PAROLLES.

Ber. My lord, I do confess the ring was hers.
King. You boggle shrewdly, every feather
starts you.
s this the man you speak of?
Dia. Ay, my lord.
King. Tell me, sirrah, but tell me true, I
charge you, 236
Iot fearing the displeasure of your master,—
Vhich, on your just proceeding I'll keep off,—
y him and by this woman here what know
you?
Par. So please your majesty, my master hath
een an honourable gentleman: tricks he hath
ad in him, which gentlemen have.
King. Come, come, to the purpose: did he
ove this woman? 244
Par. Faith, sir, he did love her; but how?
King. How, I pray you?
Par. He did love her, sir, as a gentleman
oves a woman. 248
King. How is that?
Par. He loved her, sir, and loved her not.
King. As thou art a knave, and no knave.
Vhat an equivocal companion is this! 252
Par. I am a poor man, and at your majesty's
ommand.
Laf. He is a good drum, my lord, but a
aughty orator. 256
Dia. Do you know he promised me marriage?
Par. Faith, I know more than I'll speak.
King. But wilt thou not speak all thou
nowest? 260
Par. Yes, so please your majesty. I did go
etween them, as I said; but more than that, he
oved her, for, indeed, he was mad for her, and
alked of Satan, and of limbo, and of Furies,
nd I know not what: yet I was in that credit
vith them at that time, that I knew of their
oing to bed, and of other motions, as promising
er marriage, and things which would derive
ne ill will to speak of: therefore I will not
peak what I know. 270
King. Thou hast spoken all already, unless
hou canst say they are married: but thou art
oo fine in thy evidence; therefore stand aside.
his ring, you say, was yours?
Dia. Ay, my good lord.
King. Where did you buy it? or who gave it
you? 276
Dia. It was not given me, nor I did not buy it.
King. Who lent it you?
Dia. It was not lent me neither.
King. Where did you find it, then?
Dia. I found it not.

King. If it were yours by none of all these
ways, 280
How could you give it him?
Dia. I never gave it him.
Laf. This woman's an easy glove, my lord:
she goes off and on at pleasure.
King. This ring was mine: I gave it his first
wife. 284
Dia. It might be yours or hers, for aught I
know.
King. Take her away; I do not like her now.
To prison with her; and away with him.
Unless thou tell'st me where thou hadst this
ring
Thou diest within this hour.
Dia. I'll never tell you. 289
King. Take her away.
Dia. I'll put in bail, my liege.
King. I think thee now some common cus-
tomer.
Dia. By Jove, if ever I knew man, 'twas you.
King. Wherefore hast thou accus'd him all
this while? 293
Dia. Because he's guilty, and he is not guilty.
He knows I am no maid, and he'll swear to't;
I'll swear I am a maid, and he knows not. 296
Great king, I am no strumpet, by my life;
I am either maid, or else this old man's wife.
[*Pointing to* LAFEU.
King. She does abuse our ears: to prison
with her!
Dia. Good mother, fetch my bail. [*Exit
Widow.*] Stay, royal sir; 300
The jeweller that owes the ring is sent for,
And he shall surety me. But for this lord,
Who hath abus'd me, as he knows himself,
Though yet he never harm'd me, here I quit him:
He knows himself my bed he hath defil'd, 305
And at that time he got his wife with child:
Dead though she be, she feels her young one
kick:
So there's my riddle: one that's dead is quick;
And now behold the meaning.

Re-enter Widow, *with* HELENA.

King. Is there no exorcist 309
Beguiles the truer office of mine eyes?
Is't real that I see?
Hel. No, my good lord;
'Tis but the shadow of a wife you see; 312
The name and not the thing.
Ber. Both, both. O! pardon.
Hel. O my good lord! when I was like this
maid,
I found you wondrous kind. There is your ring;
And, look you, here's your letter; this it says:
When from my finger you can get this ring, 317
And are by me with child, &c. This is done:
Will you be mine, now you are doubly won?
Ber. If she, my liege, can make me know
this clearly, 320
I'll love her dearly, ever, ever dearly.
Hel. If it appear not plain, and prove untrue,
Deadly divorce step between me and you!
O! my dear mother; do I see you living? 324

Laf. Mine eyes smell onions; I shall weep
anon. [*To* PAROLLES.] Good Tom Drum, lend
me a handkercher: so, I thank thee. Wait on
me home, I'll make sport with thee: let thy
curtsies alone, they are scurvy ones.   329

    King. Let us from point to point this story
know,
To make the even truth in pleasure flow.
[*To* DIANA.] If thou be'st yet a fresh uncropped
flower,   332
Choose thou thy husband, and I'll pay thy
dower;
For I can guess that by thy honest aid
Thou keptst a wife herself, thyself a maid.
Of that, and all the progress, more and less, 336

Resolvedly more leisure shall express:
All yet seems well; and if it end so meet,
The bitter past, more welcome is the sweet.
                 [Flourish. Exeun

EPILOGUE

Spoken by the KING.

The king's a beggar, now the play is done:
All is well ended if this suit be won
That you express content; which we will pay,
With strife to please you, day exceeding day:
Ours be your patience then, and yours our parts
Your gentle hands lend us, and take our hearts
                         [Exeun

TWELFTH-NIGHT; OR, WHAT YOU WILL

DRAMATIS PERSONÆ

ORSINO, Duke of Illyria.
SEBASTIAN, Brother to Viola.
ANTONIO, a Sea Captain, Friend to Sebastian.
A Sea Captain, Friend to Viola.
VALENTINE, } Gentlemen attending on the Duke.
CURIO, }
SIR TOBY BELCH, Uncle to Olivia.
SIR ANDREW AGUECHEEK.
MALVOLIO, Steward to Olivia.

FABIAN, } Servants to Olivia.
FESTE, a Clown, }

OLIVIA, a rich Countess.
VIOLA, in love with the Duke.
MARIA, Olivia's Woman.

Lords, Priests, Sailors, Officers, Musicians, and other Attendants.

SCENE.—*A City in Illyria; and the Sea-coast near it.*

ACT I

SCENE I.—*A Room in the* DUKE'S *Palace.*

Enter DUKE, CURIO, Lords; Musicians attending.

Duke. If music be the food of love, play on;
Give me excess of it, that, surfeiting,
The appetite may sicken, and so die.
That strain again! it had a dying fall: 4
O! it came o'er my ear like the sweet sound
That breathes upon a bank of violets,
Stealing and giving odour. Enough! no more:
'Tis not so sweet now as it was before. 8
O spirit of love! how quick and fresh art thou,
That, notwithstanding thy capacity
Receiveth as the sea, nought enters there,
Of what validity and pitch soe'er, 12
But falls into abatement and low price,
Even in a minute: so full of shapes is fancy,
That it alone is high fantastical.
Cur. Will you go hunt, my lord?
Duke. What, Curio? 16
Cur. The hart.
Duke. Why, so I do, the noblest that I have.
O! when mine eyes did see Olivia first,
Methought she purg'd the air of pestilence. 20
That instant was I turn'd into a hart,
And my desires, like fell and cruel hounds,
E'er since pursue me.

Enter VALENTINE.

How now! what news from her?
Val. So please my lord, I might not be admitted; 24
But from her handmaid do return this answer:
The element itself, till seven years' heat,
Shall not behold her face at ample view;
But, like a cloistress, she will veiled walk, 28
And water once a day her chamber round
With eye-offending brine: all this, to season
A brother's dead love, which she would keep fresh
And lasting in her sad remembrance. 32
Duke. O! she that hath a heart of that fine frame
To pay this debt of love but to a brother,
How will she love, when the rich golden shaft
Hath kill'd the flock of all affections else 36

That live in her; when liver, brain, and heart,
These sovereign thrones, are all supplied, and fill'd
Her sweet perfections with one self king.
Away before me to sweet beds of flowers; 40
Love-thoughts lie rich when canopied with bowers. [*Exeunt.*

SCENE II.—*The Sea-coast.*

Enter VIOLA, Captain, *and* Sailors.

Vio. What country, friends, is this?
Cap. This is Illyria, lady.
Vio. And what should I do in Illyria?
My brother he is in Elysium.
Perchance he is not drown'd: what think you, sailors? 4
Cap. It is perchance that you yourself were sav'd.
Vio. O my poor brother! and so perchance may he be.
Cap. True, madam: and, to comfort you with chance,
Assure yourself, after our ship did split, 8
When you and those poor number sav'd with you
Hung on our driving boat, I saw your brother,
Most provident in peril, bind himself,—
Courage and hope both teaching him the practice,— 12
To a strong mast that liv'd upon the sea;
Where, like Arion on the dolphin's back,
I saw him hold acquaintance with the waves
So long as I could see.
Vio. For saying so there's gold. 16
Mine own escape unfoldeth to my hope,
Whereto thy speech serves for authority,
The like of him. Know'st thou this country?
Cap. Ay, madam, well; for I was bred and born 20
Not three hours' travel from this very place.
Vio. Who governs here?
Cap. A noble duke, in nature as in name.
Vio. What is his name? 24
Cap. Orsino.
Vio. Orsino! I have heard my father name him:
He was a bachelor then.

Cap. And so is now, or was so very late; 28
For but a month ago I went from hence,
And then 'twas fresh in murmur,—as, you
    know,
What great ones do the less will prattle of,—
That he did seek the love of fair Olivia. 32
    Vio. What's she?
Cap. A virtuous maid, the daughter of a count
That died some twelvemonth since; then leaving
    her
In the protection of his son, her brother, 36
Who shortly also died: for whose dear love,
They say she hath abjur'd the company
And sight of men.
    Vio.   O! that I serv'd that lady,
And might not be deliver'd to the world, 40
Till I had made mine own occasion mellow,
What my estate is.
    Cap.   That were hard to compass,
Because she will admit no kind of suit,
No, not the duke's. 44
    Vio. There is a fair behaviour in thee, captain;
And though that nature with a beauteous wall
Doth oft close in pollution, yet of thee
I will believe thou hast a mind that suits 48
With this thy fair and outward character.
I prithee,—and I'll pay thee bounteously,—
Conceal me what I am, and be my aid
For such disguise as haply shall become 52
The form of my intent. I'll serve this duke:
Thou shalt present me as a eunuch to him:
It may be worth thy pains; for I can sing
And speak to him in many sorts of music 56
That will allow me very worth his service.
What else may hap to time I will commit;
Only shape thou thy silence to my wit.
    Cap. Be you his eunuch, and your mute I'll
    be: 60
When my tongue blabs, then let mine eyes not
    see.
    Vio. I thank thee: lead me on.   [*Exeunt.*

SCENE III.—*A Room in* OLIVIA'S *House.*

Enter SIR TOBY BELCH *and* MARIA.

Sir To. What a plague means my niece, to
take the death of her brother thus? I am sure
care's an enemy to life.
    Mar. By my troth, Sir Toby, you must come
in earlier o' nights: your cousin, my lady, takes
great exceptions to your ill hours. 6
    Sir To. Why, let her except before excepted.
    Mar. Ay, but you must confine yourself
within the modest limits of order.
    Sir To. Confine! I'll confine myself no finer
than I am. These clothes are good enough to
drink in, and so be these boots too: an they be
not, let them hang themselves in their own
straps. 14
    Mar. That quaffing and drinking will undo
you: I heard my lady talk of it yesterday; and
of a foolish knight that you brought in one
night here to be her wooer.
    Sir To. Who? Sir Andrew Aguecheek?
    Mar. Ay, he. 20

Sir To. He's as tall a man as any 's in Illyria
    Mar. What 's that to the purpose?
Sir To. Why, he has three thousand ducat
a year. 2.
Mar. Ay, but he'll have but a year in a
these ducats: he 's a very fool and a prodiga
    Sir To. Fie, that you'll say so! he plays o
the viol-de-gamboys, and speaks three or fou
languages word for word without book, an
hath all the good gifts of nature. 3
Mar. He hath indeed, almost natural; for
besides that he 's a fool, he 's a great quarreller
and but that he hath the gift of a coward to alla
the gust he hath in quarelling, 'tis thougb
among the prudent he would quickly have th
gift of a grave. 3
Sir To. By this hand, they are scoundrels and
subtractors that say so of him. Who are they
Mar. They that add, moreover, he 's drunl
nightly in your company. 4
Sir To. With drinking healths to my niece
I'll drink to her as long as there is a passage i
my throat and drink in Illyria. He 's a cowar
and a coystril, that will not drink to my niec
till his brains turn o' the toe like a parish-top
What, wench! *Castiliano vulgo!* for here come
Sir Andrew Agueface.

Enter SIR ANDREW AGUECHEEK.

Sir And. Sir Toby Belch! how now, Sir Toby
Belch! 4
Sir To. Sweet Sir Andrew!
Sir And. Bless you, fair shrew.
Mar. And you too, sir. 5
Sir To. Accost, Sir Andrew, accost.
Sir And. What 's that?
Sir To. My niece's chambermaid.
Sir And. Good Mistress Accost, I desire
better acquaintance. 5
Mar. My name is Mary, sir.
Sir And. Good Mistress Mary Accost,—
Sir To. You mistake, knight: 'accost' is
front her, board her, woo her, assail her. 6
Sir And. By my troth, I would not under
take her in this company. Is that the meanin
of 'accost'? 6
Mar. Fare you well, gentlemen.
Sir To. An thou let her part so, Sir Andrew
would thou mightst never draw sword again!
Sir And. An you part so, mistress, I would
might never draw sword again. Fair lady, d
you think you have fools in hand? 7
Mar. Sir, I have not you by the hand.
Sir And. Marry, but you shall have; an
here's my hand.
Mar. Now, sir, 'thought is free:' I pray you
bring your hand to the buttery-bar and let i
drink. 7
Sir And. Wherefore, sweetheart? what's you
metaphor?
Mar. It's dry, sir.
Sir And. Why, I think so: I am not such ar
ass but I can keep my hand dry. But what'
your jest?
Mar. A dry jest, sir.
Sir And. Are you full of them? 8.

Mar. Ay, sir, I have them at my fingers' ends:
narry, now I let go your hand, I am barren.
                                        [*Exit.*

Sir To. O knight! thou lackest a cup of
anary: when did I see thee so put down?   88

Sir And. Never in your life, I think; unless
ou see canary put me down. Methinks some-
imes I have no more wit than a Christian or an
rdinary man has; but I am a great eater of
eef, and I believe that does harm to my wit.   93

Sir To. No question.

Sir And. An I thought that, I'd forswear it.
'll ride home to-morrow, Sir Toby.   96

Sir To. Pourquoi, my dear knight?

Sir And. What is '*pourquoi?*' do or not do?
would I had bestowed that time in the tongues
hat I have in fencing, dancing, and bear-bait-
ng. O! had I but followed the arts!   101

Sir To. Then hadst thou had an excellent
ead of hair.

Sir And. Why, would that have mended my
air?   105

Sir To. Past question; for thou seest it will
ot curl by nature.

Sir And. But it becomes me well enough,
oes't not?   109

Sir To. Excellent; it hangs like flax on a
istaff, and I hope to see a housewife take thee
etween her legs, and spin it off.   112

Sir And. Faith, I'll home to-morrow, Sir
'oby: your niece will not be seen; or if she be,
's four to one she'll none of me. The count
imself here hard by woos her.   116

Sir To. She'll none o' the count; she'll not
natch above her degree, neither in estate, years,
or wit; I have heard her swear it. Tut, there's
fe in't, man.   120

Sir And. I'll stay a month longer. I am a
ellow o' the strangest mind i' the world; I de-
ght in masques and revels sometimes altogether.

Sir To. Art thou good at these kickchawses,
night?   125

Sir And. As any man in Illyria, whatsoever
e be, under the degree of my betters: and yet I
vill not compare with an old man.   128

Sir To. What is thy excellence in a galliard,
night?

Sir And. Faith, I can cut a caper.

Sir To. And I can cut the mutton to't.   132

Sir And. And I think I have the back-trick
imply as strong as any man in Illyria.

Sir To. Wherefore are these things hid?
vherefore have these gifts a curtain before 'em?
re they like to take dust, like Mistress Mall's
icture? why dost thou not go to church in a
alliard, and come home in a coranto? My very
valk should be a jig: I would not so much as
nake water but in a sink-a-pace. What dost
hou mean? is it a world to hide virtues in? I
id think, by the excellent constitution of thy
g, it was formed under the star of a galliard. 144

Sir And. Ay, 'tis strong, and it does indifferent
vell in a flame-coloured stock. Shall we set
bout some revels?

Sir To. What shall we do else? were we not
orn under Taurus?   149

Sir And. Taurus! that's sides and heart.

Sir To. No, sir, it is legs and thighs. Let me
see thee caper. Ha! higher: ha, ha! excellent!
                                        [*Exeunt.*

SCENE IV.—*A Room in the* DUKE'S *Palace.*

Enter VALENTINE, *and* VIOLA *in man's attire.*

Val. If the duke continue these favours towards you, Cesario, you are like to be much
advanced: he hath known you but three days,
and already you are no stranger.   4

Vio. You either fear his humour or my negligence, that you call in question the continuance
of his love. Is he inconstant, sir, in his favours?

Val. No, believe me.   8

Vio. I thank you. Here comes the count.

Enter DUKE, CURIO, *and* Attendants.

Duke. Who saw Cesario? ho!

Vio. On your attendance, my lord; here.

Duke. Stand you awhile aloof. Cesario,   12
Thou know'st no less but all; I have unclasp'd
To thee the book even of my secret soul:
Therefore, good youth, address thy gait unto her,
Be not denied access, stand at her doors,   16
And tell them, there thy fixed foot shall grow
Till thou have audience.

Vio.   Sure, my noble lord,
If she be so abandon'd to her sorrow
As it is spoke, she never will admit me.   20

Duke. Be clamorous and leap all civil bounds
Rather than make unprofited return.

Vio. Say I do speak with her, my lord, what
        then?

Duke. O! then unfold the passion of my love;
Surprise her with discourse of my dear faith: 25
It shall become thee well to act my woes;
She will attend it better in thy youth
Than in a nuncio of more grave aspect.   28

Vio. I think not so, my lord.

Duke.   Dear lad, believe it;
For they shall yet belie thy happy years
That say thou art a man: Diana's lip
Is not more smooth and rubious; thy small pipe
Is as the maiden's organ, shrill and sound; 33
And all is semblative a woman's part.
I know thy constellation is right apt
For this affair. Some four or five attend him;
All, if you will; for I myself am best   37
When least in company. Prosper well in this,
And thou shalt live as freely as thy lord,
To call his fortunes thine.

Vio.   I'll do my best   40
To woo your lady: [*Aside*] yet, a barful strife!
Whoe'er I woo, myself would be his wife.
                                        [*Exeunt.*

SCENE V.—*A Room in* OLIVIA'S *House.*

Enter MARIA *and* Clown.

Mar. Nay, either tell me where thou hast
been, or I will not open my lips so wide as a
bristle may enter in way of thy excuse. My
lady will hang thee for thy absence.   4

Clo. Let her hang me: he that is well hanged in this world needs to fear no colours.

Mar. Make that good.

Clo. He shall see none to fear.   8

Mar. A good lenten answer: I can tell thee where that saying was born, of, 'I fear no colours.'

Clo. Where, good Mistress Mary?

Mar. In the wars; and that may you be bold to say in your foolery.   13

Clo. Well, God give them wisdom that have it; and those that are fools, let them use their talents.   16

Mar. Yet you will be hanged for being so long absent; or, to be turned away, is not that as good as a hanging to you?

Clo. Many a good hanging prevents a bad marriage; and, for turning away, let summer bear it out.   22

Mar. You are resolute then?

Clo. Not so, neither; but I am resolved on two points.   25

Mar. That if one break, the other will hold; or, if both break, your gaskins fall.

Clo. Apt, in good faith; very apt. Well, go thy way: if Sir Toby would leave drinking, thou wert as witty a piece of Eve's flesh as any in Illyria.   30

Mar. Peace, you rogue, no more o' that. Here comes my lady: make your excuse wisely, you were best.   [*Exit.*

Clo. Wit, an't be thy will, put me into good fooling! Those wits that think they have thee, do very oft prove fools; and I, that am sure I lack thee, may pass for a wise man: for what says Quinapalus? 'Better a witty fool than a foolish wit.'

Enter OLIVIA *with* MALVOLIO.

God bless thee, lady!   40

Oli. Take the fool away.

Clo. Do you not hear, fellows? Take away the lady.

Oli. Go to, you're a dry fool; I'll no more of you: besides, you grow dishonest.   45

Clo. Two faults, madonna, that drink and good counsel will amend: for give the dry fool drink, then is the fool not dry; bid the dishonest man mend himself: if he mend, he is no longer dishonest; if he cannot, let the botcher mend him. Any thing that's mended is but patched: virtue that transgresses is but patched with sin; and sin that amends is but patched with virtue. If that this simple syllogism will serve, so; if it will not, what remedy? As there is no true cuckold but calamity, so beauty's a flower. The lady bade take away the fool; therefore, I say again, take her away.   58

Oli. Sir, I bade them take away you.

Clo. Misprision in the highest degree! Lady, *cucullus non facit monachum;* that's as much to say as I wear not motley in my brain. Good madonna, give me leave to prove you a fool.

Oli. Can you do it?   64

Clo. Dexteriously, good madonna.

Oli. Make your proof.

Clo. I must catechise you for it, madonna: good my mouse of virtue, answer me.   68

Oli. Well, sir, for want of other idleness, I'll bide your proof.

Clo. Good madonna, why mournest thou?

Oli. Good fool, for my brother's death.   7

Clo. I think his soul is in hell, madonna.

Oli. I know his soul is in heaven, fool.

Clo. The more fool, madonna, to mourn fo your brother's soul being in heaven. Take awa the fool, gentlemen.   7

Oli. What think you of this fool, Malvolio doth he not mend?

Mal. Yes; and shall do, till the pangs o death shake him: infirmity, that decays th wise, doth ever make the better fool.   8

Clo. God send you, sir, a speedy infirmity, fo the better increasing your folly! Sir Toby wi be sworn that I am no fox, but he will not pas his word for two pence that you are no fool.

Oli. How say you to that, Malvolio?   8

Mal. I marvel your ladyship takes delight i such a barren rascal: I saw him put down th other day with an ordinary fool that has no mor brain than a stone. Look you now, he's out o his guard already; unless you laugh and ministe occasion to him, he is gagged. I protest, I tak these wise men, that crow so at these set kind o fools, no better than the fools' zanies.   9

Oli. O! you are sick of self-love, Malvolio and taste with a distempered appetite. To b generous, guiltless, and of free disposition, is t take those things for bird-bolts that you deen cannon-bullets. There is no slander in an al lowed fool, though he do nothing but rail; no no railing in a known discreet man, though h do nothing but reprove.

Clo. Now, Mercury endue thee with leasing for thou speakest well of fools!   10

Re-enter MARIA.

Mar. Madam, there is at the gate a youn gentleman much desires to speak with you.

Oli. From the Count Orsino, is it?   1c

Mar. I know not, madam: 'tis a fair youn man, and well attended.

Oli. Who of my people hold him in delay

Mar. Sir Toby, madam, your kinsman.   11

Oli. Fetch him off, I pray you: he speak nothing but madman. Fie on him! [*Exit* MARIA. Go you, Malvolio: if it be a suit from the count I am sick, or not at home; what you will, t dismiss it. [*Exit* MALVOLIO.] Now you see, sir how your fooling grows old, and people dislike i

Clo. Thou hast spoken for us, madonna, as thy eldest son should be a fool; whose sku Jove cram with brains! for here comes one o thy kin has a most weak *pia mater.*

Enter SIR TOBY BELCH.

Oli. By mine honour, half drunk. What i he at the gate, cousin?   12

Sir To. A gentleman.

Oli. A gentleman! what gentleman?

Sir To. 'Tis a gentleman here,—a plague these pickle herring! How now, sot!   12

Clo. Good Sir Toby.

Oli. Cousin, cousin, how have you come so arly by this lethargy?

Sir To. Lechery! I defy lechery! There's ne at the gate.　　　　133

Clo. Ay, marry, what is he?

Sir To. Let him be the devil, an he will, I are not: give me faith, say I. Well, it's all one.　　　　[*Exit.*

Oli. What's a drunken man like, fool?　137

Clo. Like a drowned man, a fool, and a mad-nan: one draught above heat makes him a ool, the second mads him, and a third drowns im.

Oli. Go thou and seek the crowner, and let im sit o' my coz; for he's in the third degree of drink, he's drowned: go, look after him.　144

Clo. He is but mad yet, madonna; and the ool shall look to the madman.　　　[*Exit.*

Re-enter MALVOLIO.

Mal. Madam, yond young fellow swears he will peak with you. I told him you were sick: he akes on him to understand so much, and there-ore comes to speak with you. I told him you vere asleep: he seems to have a foreknowledge of hat too, and therefore comes to speak with you. What is to be said to him, lady? he's fortified against any denial.　　　　154

Oli. Tell him he shall not speak with me.

Mal. Ha's been told so; and he says, he'll stand at your door like a sheriff's post, and be he supporter to a bench, but he'll speak with you.

Oli. What kind o' man is he?　　160

Mal. Why, of mankind.

Oli. What manner of man?

Mal. Of very ill manner: he'll speak with you, will you or no.　　　　164

Oli. Of what personage and years is he?

Mal. Not yet old enough for a man, nor young enough for a boy; as a squash is before 'tis a peascod, or a codling when 'tis almost an apple: 'tis with him in standing water, between boy and man. He is very well-favoured, and he speaks very shrewishly: one would think his mother's milk were scarce out of him.　172

Oli. Let him approach. Call in my gentle-woman.

Mal. Gentlewoman, my lady calls.　[*Exit.*

Re-enter MARIA.

Oli. Give me my veil: come, throw it o'er my face.　　　　176
We'll once more hear Orsino's embassy.

Enter VIOLA *and* Attendants.

Vio. The honourable lady of the house, which is she?

Oli. Speak to me; I shall answer for her. Your will?　　　　181

Vio. Most radiant, exquisite, and unmatch-able beauty,—I pray you tell me if this be the lady of the house, for I never saw her: I would be loath to cast away my speech; for, besides that it is excellently well penned, I have taken great pains to con it. Good beauties, let me

sustain no scorn; I am very comptible, even to the least sinister usage.　　　189

Oli. Whence came you, sir?

Vio. I can say little more than I have studied, and that question's out of my part. Good gentle one, give me modest assurance if you be the lady of the house, that I may proceed in my speech.

Oli. Are you a comedian?　　195

Vio. No, my profound heart; and yet, by the very fangs of malice I swear I am not that I play. Are you the lady of the house?

Oli. If I do not usurp myself, I am.　199

Vio. Most certain, if you are she, you do usurp yourself; for, what is yours to bestow is not yours to reserve. But this is from my commis-sion: I will on with my speech in your praise, and then show you the heart of my message. 204

Oli. Come to what is important in't: I for-give you the praise.

Vio. Alas! I took great pains to study it, and 'tis poetical.　　　　208

Oli. It is the more like to be feigned: I pray you keep it in. I heard you were saucy at my gates, and allowed your approach rather to wonder at you than to hear you. If you be not mad, be gone; if you have reason, be brief: 'tis not that time of moon with me to make one in so skipping a dialogue.　　　215

Mar. Will you hoist sail, sir? here lies your way.

Vio. No, good swabber; I am to hull here a little longer. Some mollification for your giant, sweet lady.

Oli. Tell me your mind.　　220

Vio. I am a messenger.

Oli. Sure, you have some hideous matter to deliver, when the courtesy of it is so fearful. Speak your office.　　　　224

Vio. It alone concerns your ear. I bring no overture of war, no taxation of homage: I hold the olive in my hand; my words are as full of peace as matter.　　　228

Oli. Yet you began rudely. What are you? what would you?

Vio. The rudeness that hath appear'd in me have I learn'd from my entertainment. What I am, and what I would, are as secret as maiden-head; to your ears, divinity; to any other's, profanation.　　　235

Oli. Give us the place alone: we will hear this divinity.　[*Exit* MARIA *and* Attendants.] Now, sir; what is your text?

Vio. Most sweet lady,—

Oli. A comfortable doctrine, and much may be said of it. Where lies your text?　241

Vio. In Orsino's bosom.

Oli. In his bosom! In what chapter of his bosom?　　　　244

Vio. To answer by the method, in the first of his heart.

Oli. O! I have read it: it is heresy. Have you no more to say?　　　248

Vio. Good madam, let me see your face.

Oli. Have you any commission from your lord to negotiate with my face? you are now out of your text: but we will draw the curtain and show you the picture. [*Unveiling.*] Look you,

sir, such a one I was as this present: is't not
well done?

Vio. Excellently done, if God did all.   256
Oli. 'Tis in grain, sir; 'twill endure wind and
weather.

Vio. 'Tis beauty truly blent, whose red and
white
Nature's own sweet and cunning hand laid on:
Lady, you are the cruell'st she alive,   261
If you will lead these graces to the grave
And leave the world no copy.

Oli. O! sir, I will not be so hard-hearted; I
will give out divers schedules of my beauty: it
shall be inventoried, and every particle and
utensil labelled to my will: as *Item*, Two lips,
indifferent red; *Item*, Two grey eyes, with lids to
them; *Item*, One neck, one chin, and so forth.
Were you sent hither to praise me?

Vio. I see you what you are: you are too
proud;
But, if you were the devil, you are fair.   272
My lord and master loves you: O! such love
Could be but recompens'd, though you were
crown'd
The nonpareil of beauty.

Oli.   How does he love me?
Vio. With adorations, with fertile tears,   276
With groans that thunder love, with sighs of fire.
Oli. Your lord does know my mind; I cannot
love him;
Yet I suppose him virtuous, know him noble,
Of great estate, of fresh and stainless youth;   280
In voices well divulg'd, free, learn'd, and valiant;
And, in dimension and the shape of nature
A gracious person; but yet I cannot love him:
He might have took his answer long ago.   284
Vio. If I did love you in my master's flame,
With such a suffering, such a deadly life,
In your denial I would find no sense;
I would not understand it.

Oli.   Why, what would you?   288
Vio. Make me a willow cabin at your gate,
And call upon my soul within the house;
Write loyal cantons of contemned love,
And sing them loud even in the dead of night;
Holla your name to the reverberate hills,   293
And make the babbling gossip of the air
Cry out, 'Olivia!' O! you should not rest
Between the elements of air and earth,   296
But you should pity me!

Oli. You might do much. What is your
parentage?

Vio. Above my fortune, yet my state is well:
I am a gentleman.

Oli.   Get you to your lord: 300
I cannot love him. Let him send no more,
Unless, perchance, you come to me again,
To tell me how he takes it. Fare you well:
I thank you for your pains: spend this for me.
Vio. I am no fee'd post, lady; keep your
purse: 305
My master, not myself, lacks recompense.
Love make his heart of flint that you shall love,
And let your fervour, like my master's, be   308
Plac'd in contempt! Farewell, fair cruelty.

                    [*Exit.*

Oli. 'What is your parentage?'
'Above my fortunes, yet my state is well:
I am a gentleman.' I'll be sworn thou art: 31
Thy tongue, thy face, thy limbs, actions, an
spirit,
Do give thee five-fold blazon. Not too fast
soft! soft!
Unless the master were the man. How now!
Even so quickly may one catch the plague?   31
Methinks I feel this youth's perfections
With an invisible and subtle stealth
To creep in at mine eyes. Well, let it be.
What, ho! Malvolio!

Re-enter MALVOLIO.

Mal.   Here, madam, at your service.   32
Oli. Run after that same peevish messenger
The county's man: he left this ring behind him
Would I, or not: tell him I'll none of it.
Desire him not to flatter with his lord,   32
Nor hold him up with hopes: I'm not for him.
If that the youth will come this way to-morrow
I'll give him reasons for 't. Hie thee, Malvolio.
Mal. Madam, I will.   [*Exit*
Oli. I do I know not what, and fear to find   32
Mine eye too great a flatterer for my mind.
Fate, show thy force: ourselves we do not owe
What is decreed must be, and be this so! [*Exit*

ACT II

SCENE I.—*The Sea-coast.*

Enter ANTONIO *and* SEBASTIAN.

Ant. Will you stay no longer? nor will you
not that I go with you?

Seb. By your patience, no. My stars shine
darkly over me; the malignancy of my fate
might, perhaps, distemper yours; therefore I
shall crave of you your leave that I may bear
my evils alone. It were a bad recompense for
your love to lay any of them on you.

Ant. Let me yet know of you whither you
are bound.

Seb. No, sooth, sir: my determinate voyage
is mere extravagancy. But I perceive in you so
excellent a touch of modesty that you will not
extort from me what I am willing to keep in;
therefore, it charges me in manners the rather
to express myself. You must know of me then,
Antonio, my name is Sebastian, which I called
Roderigo. My father was that Sebastian of
Messaline, whom I know you have heard of. He
left behind him myself and a sister, both born in
an hour: if the heavens had been pleased, would
we had so ended! but you, sir, altered that; for
some hour before you took me from the breach
of the sea was my sister drowned.   24

Ant. Alas the day!

Seb. A lady, sir, though it was said she much
resembled me, was yet of many accounted beautiful: but, though I could not with such estimable wonder overfar believe that, yet thus far I
will boldly publish her: she bore a mind that
envy could not but call fair. She is drowned

lready, sir, with salt water, though I seem to
rown her remembrance again with more. 33

Ant. Pardon me, sir, your bad entertainment.

Seb. O good Antonio! forgive me your trou-
le! 36

Ant. If you will not murder me for my love,
t me be your servant.

Seb. If you will not undo what you have
one, that is, kill him whom you have recovered,
esire it not. Fare ye well at once: my bosom
; full of kindness; and I am yet so near the
nanners of my mother, that upon the least
ccasion more mine eyes will tell tales of me.
am bound to the Count Orsino's court: fare-
vell. [*Exit.*

Ant. The gentleness of all the gods go with
thee!

have many enemies in Orsino's court, 43
lse would I very shortly see thee there;
3ut, come what may, I do adore thee so,
'hat danger shall seem sport, and I will go.
[*Exit.*

SCENE II.—*A Street.*

Enter VIOLA; MALVOLIO *following.*

Mal. Were not you even now with the
Countess Olivia?

Vio. Even now, sir: on a moderate pace I
ave since arrived but hither. 4

Mal. She returns this ring to you, sir: you
night have saved me my pains, to have taken it
way yourself. She adds, moreover, that you
hould put your lord into a desperate assurance
he will none of him. And one thing more; that
ou be never so hardy to come again in his
iffairs, unless it be to report your lord's taking
of this. Receive it so. 12

Vio. She took the ring of me; I'll none of it.

Mal. Come, sir, you peevishly threw it to
er; and her will is it should be so returned:
f it be worth stooping for, there it lies in your
ye; if not, be it his that finds it. [*Exit.*

Vio. I left no ring with her: what means
this lady!
'ortune forbid my outside have not charm'd
her! 19
3he made good view of me; indeed, so much,
'hat sure methought her eyes had lost her
tongue,
'or she did speak in starts distractedly.
3he loves me, sure; the cunning of her passion
invites me in this churlish messenger. 24
None of my lord's ring! why, he sent her none.
[am the man: if it be so, as 'tis,
Poor lady, she were better love a dream.
Disguise, I see, thou art a wickedness, 28
Wherein the pregnant enemy does much.
How easy is it for the proper-false
in women's waxen hearts to set their forms!
Alas! our frailty is the cause, not we! 32
'or such as we are made of, such we be.
How will this fadge? My master loves her
dearly;
And I, poor monster, fond as much on him;

And she, mistaken, seems to dote on me. 36
What will become of this? As I am man,
My state is desperate for my master's love;
As I am woman,—now alas the day!—
What thriftless sighs shall poor Olivia breathe!
O time! thou must untangle this, not I; 41
It is too hard a knot for me to untie. [*Exit.*

SCENE III.—*A Room in* OLIVIA'S *House.*

Enter SIR TOBY BELCH *and* SIR ANDREW
AGUECHEEK.

Sir To. Approach, Sir Andrew: not to be
a-bed after midnight is to be up betimes; and
diluculo surgere, thou knowest,—

Sir And. Nay, by my troth, I know not; but
I know, to be up late is to be up late. 5

Sir To. A false conclusion: I hate it as an
unfilled can. To be up after midnight and to
go to bed then, is early; so that to go to bed
after midnight is to go to bed betimes. Does
not our life consist of the four elements?

Sir And. Faith, so they say; but, I think, it
rather consists of eating and drinking. 12

Sir To. Thou art a scholar; let us therefore
eat and drink. Marian, I say! a stoup of wine!

Enter Clown.

Sir And. Here comes the fool, i' faith.

Clo. How now, my hearts! Did you never
see the picture of 'we three?' 17

Sir To. Welcome, ass. Now let's have a
catch.

Sir And. By my troth, the fool has an excellent breast. I had rather than forty shillings
I had such a leg, and so sweet a breath to sing,
as the fool has. In sooth, thou wast in very
gracious fooling last night, when thou spokest of
Pigrogromitus, of the Vapians passing the equi-
noctial of Queubus: 'twas very good, i' faith. I
sent thee sixpence for thy leman: hadst it? 27

Clo. I did impetico thy gratillity; for Malvolio's nose is no whipstock: my lady has a
white hand, and the Myrmidons are no bottle-
ale houses.

Sir And. Excellent! Why, this is the best
fooling, when all is done. Now, a song. 33

Sir To. Come on; there is sixpence for you:
let's have a song.

Sir And. There's a testril of me too: if one
knight give a— 37

Clo. Would you have a love-song, or a song
of good life?

Sir To. A love-song, a love-song. 40

Sir And. Ay, ay; I care not for good life.

Clo. O mistress mine! where are you roaming?
O! stay and hear; your true love's coming,
That can sing both high and low. 44
Trip no further, pretty sweeting;
Journeys end in lovers meeting,
Every wise man's son doth know.

Sir And. Excellent good, i' faith. 48
Sir To. Good, good.

Clo. What is love? 'tis not hereafter;
  Present mirth hath present laughter;
  What's to come is still unsure: 52
  In delay there lies no plenty;
  Then come kiss me, sweet and twenty,
  Youth's a stuff will not endure.

Sir And. A mellifluous voice, as I am true
knight.   57
  Sir To. A contagious breath.
  Sir And. Very sweet and contagious, i' faith.
  Sir To. To hear by the nose, it is dulcet in
contagion. But shall we make the welkin dance
indeed? Shall we rouse the night-owl in a catch
that will draw three souls out of one weaver?
shall we do that?   64
  Sir And. An you love me, let's do't: I am
dog at a catch.
  Clo. By'r lady, sir, and some dogs will catch
well.   68
  Sir And. Most certain. Let our catch be,
'Thou knave.'
  Clo. 'Hold thy peace, thou knave,' knight?
I shall be constrain'd in't to call thee knave,
knight.   73
  Sir And. 'Tis not the first time I have con-
strained one to call me knave. Begin, fool: it
begins, 'Hold thy peace.'   76
  Clo. I shall never begin if I hold my peace.
  Sir And. Good, i' faith. Come, begin.
    [*They sing a catch.*

Enter MARIA.

Mar. What a caterwauling do you keep here!
If my lady have not called up her steward Malvolio and bid him turn you out of doors, never
trust me.   82
  Sir To. My lady's a Cataian; we are politi-
cians; Malvolio's a Peg-a-Ramsey, and 'Three
merry men be we.' Am not I consanguineous?
am I not of her blood? Tillyvally, lady!
  There dwelt a man in Babylon, lady, lady!
  Clo. Beshrew me, the knight's in admirable
fooling.   89
  Sir And. Ay, he does well enough if he be
disposed, and so do I too: he does it with a
better grace, but I do it more natural.
  Sir To. O! the twelfth day of December,—
  Mar. For the love o' God, peace!   94

Enter MALVOLIO.

Mal. My masters, are you mad? or what are
you? Have you no wit, manners, nor honesty,
but to gabble like tinkers at this time of night?
Do ye make an alehouse of my lady's house, that
ye squeak out your coziers' catches without any
mitigation or remorse of voice? Is there no respect of place, persons, nor time, in you?   101
  Sir To. We did keep time, sir, in our catches.
Sneck up!
  Mal. Sir Toby, I must be round with you.
My lady bade me tell you, that, though she
harbours you as her kinsman, she's nothing
allied to your disorders. If you can separate
yourself and your misdemeanours, you are welcome to the house; if not, an it would please

you to take leave of her, she is very willing t[o]
bid you farewell.
  *Sir To. Farewell, dear heart, since I mus[t]
    needs be gone.*   1[?]
  Mar. Nay, good Sir Toby.
  *Clo. His eyes do show his days are almo[st]
    done.*
  Mal. Is't even so?
  Sir To. But I will never die.   1[?]
  Clo. Sir Toby, there you lie.
  Mal. This is much credit to you.
  Sir To. Shall I bid him go?
  Clo. What an if you do?   12[?]
  Sir To. Shall I bid him go, and spare not?
  Clo. O! no, no, no, no, you dare not.
  Sir To. 'Out o' time!' Sir, ye lie. Art an[y]
more than a steward? Dost thou think, becaus[e]
thou art virtuous, there shall be no more cake[s]
and ale?
  Clo. Yes, by Saint Anne; and ginger shall b[e]
hot i' the mouth too.   12[?]
  Sir To. Thou'rt i' the right. Go, sir, rub you[r]
chain with crumbs. A stoup of wine, Maria!
  Mal. Mistress Mary, if you prized my lady'[s]
favour at anything more than contempt, yo[u]
would not give means for this uncivil rule: sh[e]
shall know of it, by this hand.   [*Exit*
  Mar. Go shake your ears.   13[?]
  Sir And. 'Twere as good a deed as to drin[k]
when a man's a-hungry, to challenge him th[e]
field, and then to break promise with him an[d]
make a fool of him.
  Sir To. Do't, knight: I'll write thee a chal[-]
lenge; or I'll deliver thy indignation to him b[y]
word of mouth.   14[?]
  Mar. Sweet Sir Toby, be patient for to-night[:]
since the youth of the count's was to-day with
my lady, she is much out of quiet. For Mon[-]
sieur Malvolio, let me alone with him: if I d[o]
not gull him into a nayword, and make him [a]
common recreation, do not think I have wi[t]
enough to lie straight in my bed. I know I ca[n]
do it.
  Sir To. Possess us, possess us, tell us some[-]
thing of him.   15[?]
  Mar. Marry, sir, sometimes he is a kind o[f]
puritan.
  Sir And. O! if I thought that, I'd beat hi[m]
like a dog.   15[?]
  Sir To. What, for being a puritan? thy ex[-]
quisite reason, dear knight?
  Sir And. I have no exquisite reason for't, bu[t]
I have reason good enough.   16[?]
  Mar. The devil a puritan that he is, or any[-]
thing constantly but a time-pleaser; an affec[-]
tioned ass, that cons state without book, and
utters it by great swarths: the best persuade[d]
of himself; so crammed, as he thinks, wit[h]
excellencies, that it is his ground of faith tha[t]
all that look on him love him; and on tha[t]
vice in him will my revenge find notable caus[e]
to work.   16[?]
  Sir To. What wilt thou do?
  Mar. I will drop in his way some obscur[e]
epistles of love; wherein, by the colour of hi[s]
beard, the shape of his leg, the manner of hi[s]

ait, the expressure of his eye, forehead, and
omplexion, he shall find himself most feelingly
personated. I can write very like my lady your
niece; on a forgotten matter we can hardly
make distinction of our hands.

Sir To. Excellent! I smell a device.

Sir And. I have't in my nose too.   180

Sir To. He shall think, by the letters that
thou wilt drop, that they come from my niece,
and that she is in love with him.

Mar. My purpose is, indeed, a horse of that
colour.   185

Sir And. And your horse now would make
him an ass.

Mar. Ass, I doubt not.   188

Sir And. O! 'twill be admirable.

Mar. Sport royal, I warrant you: I know my
physic will work with him. I will plant you two,
and let the fool make a third, where he shall find
the letter: observe his construction of it. For
this night, to bed, and dream on the event.
Farewell.   [*Exit.*

Sir To. Good night, Penthesilea.   196

Sir And. Before me, she's a good wench.

Sir To. She's a beagle, true-bred, and one
that adores me: what o' that?

Sir And. I was adored once too.   200

Sir To. Let's to bed, knight. Thou hadst
need send for more money.

Sir And. If I cannot recover your niece, I
am a foul way out.   204

Sir To. Send for money, knight: if thou hast
her not i' the end, call me cut.

Sir And. If I do not, never trust me, take it
how you will.   208

Sir To. Come, come: I'll go burn some sack;
'tis too late to go to bed now. Come, knight;
come, knight.   [*Exeunt.*

Scene IV.—*A Room in the* Duke's *Palace.*

Enter Duke, Viola, Curio, *and Others.*

Duke. Give me some music. Now, good
    morrow, friends:
Now, good Cesario, but that piece of song,
That old and antique song we heard last night;
Methought it did relieve my passion much,   4
More than light airs and recollected terms
Of these most brisk and giddy-paced times:
Come; but one verse.

Cur. He is not here, so please your lordship,
that should sing it.   9

Duke. Who was it?

Cur. Feste, the jester, my lord; a fool that
the Lady Olivia's father took much delight in.
He is about the house.   13

Duke. Seek him out, and play the tune the
    while.   [*Exit* Curio. *Music.*
Come hither, boy: if ever thou shalt love,
In the sweet pangs of it remember me;   16
For such as I am all true lovers are:
Unstaid and skittish in all motions else
Save in the constant image of the creature
That is belov'd. How dost thou like this
    tune?   20

Vio. It gives a very echo to the seat
Where love is thron'd.

Duke.   Thou dost speak masterly.
My life upon't, young though thou art, thine
    eye
Hath stay'd upon some favour that it loves; 24
Hath it not, boy?

Vio.   A little, by your favour.

Duke. What kind of woman is't?

Vio.   Of your complexion.

Duke. She is not worth thee, then. What
    years, i' faith?

Vio. About your years, my lord.   28

Duke. Too old, by heaven. Let still the
    woman take
An elder than herself, so wears she to him,
So sways she level in her husband's heart:
For, boy, however we do praise ourselves,   32
Our fancies are more giddy and unfirm,
More longing, wavering, sooner lost and worn,
Than women's are.

Vio.   I think it well, my lord.

Duke. Then, let thy love be younger than
    thyself,   36
Or thy affection cannot hold the bent;
For women are as roses, whose fair flower
Being once display'd, doth fall that very hour.

Vio. And so they are: alas, that they are
    so;   40
To die, even when they to perfection grow!

Re-enter Curio *with* Clown.

Duke. O, fellow! come, the song we had last
    night.
Mark it, Cesario; it is old and plain;
The spinsters and the knitters in the sun,   44
And the free maids that weave their thread
    with bones,
Do use to chant it: it is silly sooth,
And dallies with the innocence of love,
Like the old age.   48

Clo. Are you ready, sir?

Duke. Ay; prithee, sing.   [*Music.*

Clo. Come away, come away, death,
    And in sad cypress let me be laid;   52
Fly away, fly away, breath;
    I am slain by a fair cruel maid.
My shroud of white, stuck all with yew,
      O! prepare it.   56
My part of death, no one so true
    Did share it.

Not a flower, not a flower sweet,
    On my black coffin let there be strown;   60
Not a friend, not a friend greet
    My poor corse, where my bones shall be thrown.
A thousand thousand sighs to save,
    Lay me, O! where   64
    Sad true lover never find my grave,
      To weep there.

Duke. There's for thy pains.

Clo. No pains, sir; I take pleasure in singing,
sir.   69

Duke. I'll pay thy pleasure then.

Clo. Truly, sir, and pleasure will be paid, one
time or another.   72

Duke. Give me now leave to leave thee.

Clo. Now, the melancholy god protect thee, and the tailor make thy doublet of changeable taffeta, for thy mind is a very opal! I would have men of such constancy put to sea, that their business might be everything and their intent everywhere; for that's it that always makes a good voyage of nothing. Farewell.   [*Exit.*

Duke. Let all the rest give place.

[*Exeunt* CURIO *and* Attendants.

Once more, Cesario,   81
Get thee to yond same sovereign cruelty:
Tell her, my love, more noble than the world,
Prizes not quantity of dirty lands;   84
The parts that fortune hath bestow'd upon her,
Tell her, I hold as giddily as fortune;
But 'tis that miracle and queen of gems
That nature pranks her in attracts my soul. 88

Vio. But if she cannot love you, sir?

Duke. I cannot be so answer'd.

Vio.   Sooth, but you must.
Say that some lady, as perhaps, there is,
Hath for your love as great a pang of heart 92
As you have for Olivia: you cannot love her;
You tell her so; must she not then be answer'd?

Duke. There is no woman's sides   96
Can bide the beating of so strong a passion
As love doth give my heart; no woman's heart
So big, to hold so much; they lack retention.
Alas! their love may be call'd appetite,
No motion of the liver, but the palate,   100
That suffer surfeit, cloyment, and revolt;
But mine is all as hungry as the sea,
And can digest as much. Make no compare
Between that love a woman can bear me   104
And that I owe Olivia.

Vio.   Ay, but I know,—

Duke. What dost thou know?

Vio.   Too well what love women to men may owe:
In faith, they are as true of heart as we.   108
My father had a daughter lov'd a man,
As it might be, perhaps, were I a woman,
I should your lordship.

Duke.   And what's her history?

Vio. A blank, my lord. She never told her love,   112
But let concealment, like a worm i' the bud,
Feed on her damask cheek: she pin'd in thought,
And with a green and yellow melancholy,
She sat like Patience on a monument,   116
Smiling at grief. Was not this love indeed?
We men may say more, swear more; but indeed
Our shows are more than will, for still we prove
Much in our vows, but little in our love.   120

Duke. But died thy sister of her love, my boy?

Vio. I am all the daughters of my father's house,
And all the brothers too; and yet I know not.
Sir, shall I to this lady?

Duke.   Ay, that's the theme. 124
To her in haste; give her this jewel; say
My love can give no place, bide no denay.

[*Exeunt.*

SCENE V.—OLIVIA'S *Garden.*

Enter SIR TOBY BELCH, SIR ANDREW AGUECHEEK *and* FABIAN.

Sir To. Come thy ways, Signior Fabian.

Fab. Nay, I'll come: if I lose a scruple o' this sport, let me be boiled to death with melancholy.

Sir To. Wouldst thou not be glad to have the niggardly rascally sheep-biter come by some notable shame?

Fab. I would exult, man: you know he brought me out o' favour with my lady about a bear-baiting here.   1

Sir To. To anger him we'll have the bear again; and we will fool him black and blue shall we not, Sir Andrew?   1

Sir And. An we do not, it is pity of our lives.

Sir To. Here comes the little villain.   1

Enter MARIA.

How now, my metal of India!

Mar. Get ye all three into the box-tree Malvolio's coming down this walk: he has been yonder i' the sun practising behaviour to his own shadow this half-hour. Observe him, for the love of mockery; for I know this letter will make a contemplative idiot of him. Close, in the name of jesting! Lie thou there: [*Throws down a letter.*] for here comes the trout that must be caught with tickling.   [*Exit*

Enter MALVOLIO.

Mal. 'Tis but fortune; all is fortune. Maria once told me she did affect me; and I have heard herself come thus near, that should she fancy, it should be one of my complexion. Besides, she uses me with a more exalted respect than anyone else that follows her. What should I think on't?   3

Sir To. Here's an over-weening rogue!

Fab. O, peace! Contemplation makes a rare turkey-cock of him: how he jets under his advanced plumes!   37

Sir And. 'Slight, I could so beat the rogue!

Sir To. Peace! I say.

Mal. To be Count Malvolio!   40

Sir To. Ah, rogue!

Sir And. Pistol him, pistol him.

Sir To. Peace! peace!   43

Mal. There is example for't: the lady of the Strachy married the yeoman of the wardrobe.

Sir And. Fie on him, Jezebel!

Fab. O, peace! now he's deeply in; look how imagination blows him.   49

Mal. Having been three months married to her, sitting in my state,—

Sir To. O! for a stone-bow, to hit him in the eye!   53

Mal. Calling my officers about me, in my branched velvet gown; having come from a day-bed, where I have left Olivia sleeping,—   56

Sir To. Fire and brimstone!

Fab. O, peace! peace!

Mal. And then to have the humour of state:
nd after a demure travel of regard, telling
hem I know my place, as I would they should
o theirs, to ask for my kinsman Toby,—

Sir To. Bolts and shackles!

Fab. O, peace, peace, peace! now, now. 64

Mal. Seven of my people, with an obedient
tart, make out for him. I frown the while; and
erchance wind up my watch, or play with my
–some rich jewel. Toby approaches; curtsies
here to me,—   69

Sir To. Shall this fellow live?

Fab. Though our silence be drawn from us
vith cars, yet peace!   72

Mal. I extend my hand to him thus, quench-
ng my familiar smile with an austere regard of
ontrol,—

Sir To. And does not Toby take you a blow
' the lips then?   77

Mal. Saying, 'Cousin Toby, my fortunes hav-
ng cast me on your niece give me this preroga-
ve of speech,'—   80

Sir To. What, what?

Mal. 'You must amend your drunkenness.'

Sir To. Out, scab!

Fab. Nay, patience, or we break the sinews
f our plot.   85

Mal. 'Besides, you waste the treasure of your
ime with a foolish knight,'—

Sir And. That's me, I warrant you.   88

Mal. 'One Sir Andrew,'—

Sir And. I knew 'twas I; for many do call
he fool.

Mal. [*Seeing the letter.*] What employment
ave we here?   93

Fab. Now is the woodcock near the gin.

Sir To. O, peace! and the spirit of humours
ntimate reading aloud to him!   96

Mal. [*Taking up the letter.*] By my life, this
my lady's hand! these be her very C's, her U's,
nd her T's; and thus makes she her great P's.
t is, in contempt of question, her hand.   100

Sir And. Her C's, her U's, and her T's: why
hat—

Mal. [*Reads.*] *To the unknown beloved, this
nd my good wishes:* her very phrases! By
our leave, wax. Soft! and the impressure her
ucrece, with which she uses to seal: 'tis my
ady. To whom should this be?

Fab. This wins him, liver and all.   108

Mal.   Jove knows I love;
                But who?
          Lips, do not move:
          No man must know.   112

No man must know.' What follows? the num-
ers altered! 'No man must know:' if this
hould be thee, Malvolio!

Sir To. Marry, hang thee, brock!   116

Mal. I may command where I adore;
          But silence, like a Lucrece knife,
          With bloodless stroke my heart doth gore:
          M, O, A, I, doth sway my life.   120

Fab. A fustian riddle!

Sir To. Excellent wench, say I.

Mal. 'M, O, A, I, doth sway my life.' Nay,
but first, let me see, let me see, let me see.   124

Fab. What dish o' poison has she dressed
him!

Sir To. And with what wing the staniel
checks at it!   128

Mal. 'I may command where I adore.' Why,
she may command me: I serve her; she is my
lady. Why, this is evident to any formal capacity; there is no obstruction in this. And the
end, what should that alphabetical position
portend? if I could make that resemble something in me,—Softly!—M, O, A, I,—   135

Sir To. O! ay, make up that: he is now at a
cold scent.

Fab. Sowter will cry upon't, for all this,
though it be as rank as a fox.   139

Mal. M, Malvolio; M, why, that begins my
name.

Fab. Did not I say he would work it out? the
cur is excellent at faults.   143

Mal. M,—But then there is no consonancy
in the sequel; that suffers under probation: A
should follow, but O does.

Fab. And O shall end, I hope.

Sir To. Ay, or I'll cudgel him, and make him
cry, O!   149

Mal. And then I comes behind.

Fab. Ay, an you had any eye behind you,
you might see more detraction at your heels
than fortunes before you.   153

Mal. M, O, A, I; this simulation is not as
the former; and yet, to crush this a little, it
would bow to me, for every one of these letters
are in my name. Soft! here follows prose. 157

If this fall into thy hand, revolve. In my stars
I am above thee; but be not afraid of greatness:
some are born great, some achieve greatness, and
some have greatness thrust upon them. Thy Fates
open their hands; let thy blood and spirit embrace
them; and to inure thyself to what thou art like
to be, cast thy humble slough, and appear fresh.
Be opposite with a kinsman, surly with servants;
let thy tongue tang arguments of state; put thyself
into the trick of singularity. She thus advises thee
that sighs for thee. Remember who commended
thy yellow stockings, and wished to see thee ever
cross-gartered: I say, remember. Go to, thou art
made, if thou desirest to be so; if not, let me see
thee a steward still, the fellow of servants, and not
worthy to touch Fortune's fingers. Farewell. She
that would alter services with thee.   174
                    THE FORTUNATE-UNHAPPY.

Daylight and champian discovers not more:
this is open. I will be proud, I will read politic
authors, I will baffle Sir Toby, I will wash off
gross acquaintance, I will be point-devise the
very man. I do not now fool myself, to let
imagination jade me, for every reason excites to
this, that my lady loves me. She did commend
my yellow stockings of late, she did praise my
leg being cross-gartered; and in this she manifests herself to my love, and, with a kind of
injunction drives me to these habits of her
liking. I thank my stars I am happy. I will
be strange, stout, in yellow stockings, and cross-
gartered, even with the swiftness of putting on.

Jove and my stars be praised! Here is yet a
postscript.   191

> Thou canst not choose but know who I am. If
> thou entertainest my love, let it appear in thy
> smiling; thy smiles become thee well; therefore
> in my presence still smile, dear my sweet, I prithee.

Jove, I thank thee. I will smile: I will do every-
thing that thou wilt have me.   [*Exit.*
   Fab. I will not give my part of this sport
for a pension of thousands to be paid from the
Sophy.   200
   Sir To. I could marry this wench for this
device.
   Sir And. So could I too.
   Sir To. And ask no other dowry with her
but such another jest.   205
   Sir And. Nor I neither.
   Fab. Here comes my noble gull-catcher.

Re-enter MARIA.

   Sir To. Wilt thou set thy foot o' my neck?
   Sir And. Or o' mine either?   209
   Sir To. Shall I play my freedom at tray-trip,
and become thy bond-slave?
   Sir And. I' faith, or I either?   212
   Sir To. Why, thou hast put him in such a
dream, that when the image of it leaves him he
must run mad.
   Mar. Nay, but say true; does it work upon
him?   217
   Sir To. Like aqua-vitæ with a midwife.
   Mar. If you will, then see the fruits of the
sport, mark his first approach before my lady;
he will come to her in yellow stockings, and 'tis a
colour she abhors; and cross-gartered, a fashion
she detests; and he will smile upon her, which
will now be so unsuitable to her disposition,
being addicted to a melancholy as she is, that it
cannot but turn him into a notable contempt.
If you will see it, follow me.   227
   Sir To. To the gates of Tartar, thou most
excellent devil of wit!
   Sir And. I'll make one too.   [*Exeunt.*

ACT III

SCENE I.—OLIVIA'S *Garden.*

Enter VIOLA, *and* Clown *with a tabor.*

   Vio. Save thee, friend, and thy music. Dost
thou live by thy tabor?
   Clo. No, sir, I live by the church.
   Vio. Art thou a churchman?   4
   Clo. No such matter, sir: I do live by the
church; for I do live at my house, and my house
doth stand by the church.
   Vio. So thou mayst say, the king lies by a
beggar, if a beggar dwell near him; or, the
church stands by thy tabor, if thy tabor stand
by the church.   11
   Clo. You have said, sir. To see this age!

A sentence is but a cheveril glove to a good wit
how quickly the wrong side may be turned ou
ward!   1
   Vio. Nay, that's certain: they that dall
nicely with words may quickly make ther
wanton.
   Clo. I would therefore my sister had had n
name, sir.   2
   Vio. Why, man?
   Clo. Why, sir, her name's a word; and t
dally with that word might make my siste
wanton. But indeed, words are very rasca
since bonds disgraced them.   2
   Vio. Thy reason, man?
   Clo. Troth, sir, I can yield you none withou
words; and words are grown so false, I a
loath to prove reason with them.   2
   Vio. I warrant thou art a merry fellow, an
carest for nothing.
   Clo. Not so, sir, I do care for something; bu
in my conscience, sir, I do not care for you
if that be to care for nothing, sir, I would
would make you invisible.
   Vio. Art not thou the Lady Olivia's fool? 3
   Clo. No, indeed, sir; the Lady Olivia has n
folly: she will keep no fool, sir, till she b
married; and fools are as like husbands a
pilchards are to herrings—the husband's th
bigger. I am indeed not her fool, but he
corrupter of words.
   Vio. I saw thee late at the Count Orsino's. 4
   Clo. Foolery, sir, does walk about the or
like the sun; it shines every where. I would b
sorry, sir, but the fool should be as oft wit
your master as with my mistress. I think I sa
your wisdom there.   4
   Vio. Nay, an thou pass upon me, I'll no mo
with thee. Hold, there's sixpence for thee.
                          [*Gives a piece of money*
   Clo. Now Jove, in his next commodity c
hair, send thee a beard!   5
   Vio. By my troth, I'll tell thee, I am almos
sick for one, though I would not have it grov
on my chin. Is thy lady within?
   Clo. [*Pointing to the coin.*] Would not a pai
of these have bred, sir?   5
   Vio. Yes, being kept together and put to use
   Clo. I would play Lord Pandarus of Phrygia
sir, to bring a Cressida to this Troilus.   6
   Vio. I understand you, sir; 'tis well begg'd
   Clo. The matter, I hope, is not great, sir,
begging but a beggar: Cressida was a beggar
My lady is within, sir. I will conster to then
whence you come; who you are and what you
would are out of my welkin; I might say 'ele
ment,' but the word is overworn.   [*Exi*
   Vio. This fellow's wise enough to play th
                                              fool,   6
And to do that well craves a kind of wit:
He must observe their mood on whom he jests
The quality of persons, and the time,
And, like the haggard, check at every feather
That comes before his eye. This is a practice
As full of labour as a wise man's art;   7
For folly that he wisely shows is fit;
But wise men folly-fall'n, quite taint their wit.

Enter SIR TOBY BELCH *and* SIR ANDREW
AGUECHEEK.

Sir To. Save you, gentleman.

Vio. And you, sir.

Sir And. Dieu vous garde, monsieur.

Vio. Et vous aussi; votre serviteur.   80

Sir And. I hope, sir, you are; and I am
yours.

Sir To. Will you encounter the house? my
niece is desirous you should enter, if your trade
be to her.   85

Vio. I am bound to your niece, sir: I mean,
she is the list of my voyage.

Sir To. Taste your legs, sir: put them to
motion.   89

Vio. My legs do better understand me, sir,
than I understand what you mean by bidding
me taste my legs.   92

Sir To. I mean, to go, sir, to enter.

Vio. I will answer you with gait and entrance. But we are prevented.

Enter OLIVIA *and* MARIA.

Most excellent accomplished lady, the heavens
rain odours on you!   97

Sir And. That youth's a rare courtier. 'Rain
odours!' well.

Vio. My matter hath no voice, lady, but to
your own most pregnant and vouchsafed ear.   101

Sir And. 'Odours,' 'pregnant,' and 'vouchsafed.' I'll get 'em all three all ready.

Oli. Let the garden door be shut, and leave
me to my hearing.   105

[*Exeunt* SIR TOBY, SIR ANDREW, *and* MARIA.

Give me your hand, sir.

Vio. My duty, madam, and most humble
service.

Oli. What is your name?   108

Vio. Cesario is your servant's name, fair
princess.

Oli. My servant, sir! 'Twas never merry
world

since lowly feigning was call'd compliment.

You're servant to the Count Orsino, youth. 112

Vio. And he is yours, and his must needs be
yours:

Your servant's servant is your servant, madam.

Oli. For him, I think not on him: for his
thoughts,

Would they were blanks rather than fill'd with
me!   116

Vio. Madam, I come to whet your gentle
thoughts

On his behalf.

Oli.   O! by your leave, I pray you,
bade you never speak again of him:

But, would you undertake another suit,   120
I had rather hear you to solicit that

Than music from the spheres.

Vio. Dear lady,—

Oli. Give me leave, beseech you. I did send,
After the last enchantment you did here,   125
A ring in chase of you: so did I abuse

Myself, my servant, and, I fear me, you:

Under your hard construction must I sit,   128

To force that on you, in a shameful cunning,
Which you knew none of yours: what might
you think?

Have you not set mine honour at the stake,
And baited it with all th' unmuzzled thoughts
That tyrannous heart can think? To one of
your receiving   133

Enough is shown; a cypress, not a bosom,
Hideth my heart. So, let me hear you speak.

Vio. I pity you.   136

Oli. That's a degree to love.

Vio. No, not a grize; for 'tis a vulgar proof
That very oft we pity enemies.

Oli. Why, then methinks 'tis time to smile
again.   140

O world! how apt the poor are to be proud.
If one should be a prey, how much the better
To fall before the lion than the wolf!

[*Clock strikes.*

The clock upbraids me with the waste of time.
Be not afraid, good youth, I will not have
you:

And yet, when wit and youth is come to harvest,
Your wife is like to reap a proper man:
There lies your way, due west.

Vio.   Then westward-ho! 148

Grace and good disposition attend your ladyship!

You'll nothing, madam, to my lord by me?

Oli. Stay:

I prithee, tell me what thou think'st of me. 152

Vio. That you do think you are not what you
are.

Oli. If I think so, I think the same of you.

Vio. Then think you right: I am not what
I am.

Oli. I would you were as I would have you
be!   156

Vio. Would it be better, madam, than I am?
I wish it might, for now I am your fool.

Oli. O! what a deal of scorn looks beautiful

In the contempt and anger of his lip.   160

A murderous guilt shows not itself more
soon

Than love that would seem hid; love's night is
noon.

Cesario, by the roses of the spring,
By maidhood, honour, truth, and every thing,
I love thee so, that, maugre all thy pride,   165
Nor wit nor reason can my passion hide.
Do not extort thy reasons from this clause,
For that I woo, thou therefore hast no cause;
But rather reason thus with reason fetter,   169
Love sought is good, but giv'n unsought is
better.

Vio. By innocence I swear, and by my youth,
I have one heart, one bosom, and one truth, 172
And that no woman has; nor never none
Shall mistress be of it, save I alone.
And so adieu, good madam: never more
Will I my master's tears to you deplore.   176

Oli. Yet come again, for thou perhaps mayst
move

That heart, which now abhors, to like his love.

[*Exeunt.*

SCENE II.—*A Room in* OLIVIA'S *House.*

Enter SIR TOBY BELCH, SIR ANDREW AGUE-
CHEEK, *and* FABIAN.

Sir And. No, faith, I'll not stay a jot longer.

Sir To. Thy reason, dear venom; give thy
reason.

Fab. You must needs yield your reason, Sir
Andrew. 5

Sir And. Marry, I saw your niece do more
favours to the count's serving-man than ever
she bestowed upon me; I saw't i' the orchard. 8

Sir To. Did she see thee the while, old boy?
tell me that.

Sir And. As plain as I see you now.

Fab. This was a great argument of love in
her toward you. 13

Sir And. 'Slight! will you make an ass o'
me?

Fab. I will prove it legitimate, sir, upon the
oaths of judgment and reason. 17

Sir To. And they have been grand-jurymen
since before Noah was a sailor.

Fab. She did show favour to the youth in
your sight only to exasperate you, to awake your
dormouse valour, to put fire in your heart, and
brimstone in your liver. You should then have
accosted her, and with some excellent jests, fire-
new from the mint, you should have banged the
youth into dumbness. This was looked for at
your hand, and this was balked: the double gilt
of this opportunity you let time wash off, and
you are now sailed into the north of my lady's
opinion; where you will hang like an icicle on
a Dutchman's beard, unless you do redeem it
by some laudable attempt, either of valour or
policy. 33

Sir And. An't be any way, it must be with
valour, for policy I hate: I had as lief be a
Brownist as a politician. 36

Sir To. Why, then, build me thy fortunes
upon the basis of valour: challenge me the
count's youth to fight with him; hurt him in
eleven places: my niece shall take note of it;
and assure thyself, there is no love-broker in the
world can more prevail in man's commendation
with woman than report of valour.

Fab. There is no way but this, Sir Andrew. 44

Sir And. Will either of you bear me a challenge to him?

Sir To. Go, write it in a martial hand; be
curst and brief; it is no matter how witty, so
it be eloquent, and full of invention: taunt him
with the licence of ink: if thou thou'st him
some thrice, it shall not be amiss; and as many
lies as will lie in thy sheet of paper, although
the sheet were big enough for the bed of Ware
in England, set 'em down: go, about it. Let
there be gall enough in thy ink, though thou
write with a goose-pen, no matter: about it. 56

Sir And. Where shall I find you?

Sir To. We'll call thee at the *cubiculo:* go.

[*Exit* SIR ANDREW.

Fab. This is a dear manakin to you, Sir
Toby. 60

Sir To. I have been dear to him, lad, som
two thousand strong, or so.

Fab. We shall have a rare letter from him
but you'll not deliver it. 6

Sir To. Never trust me, then; and by a
means stir on the youth to an answer. I thin
oxen and wainropes cannot hale them togethe
For Andrew, if he were opened, and you find s
much blood in his liver as will clog the foot c
a flea, I'll eat the rest of the anatomy.

Fab. And his opposite, the youth, bears i
his visage no great presage of cruelty. 7

Sir To. Look, where the youngest wren c
nine comes.

Enter MARIA.

Mar. If you desire the spleen, and will laug
yourselves into stitches, follow me. Yond gu
Malvolio is turned heathen, a very renegad
for there is no Christian, that means to be save
by believing rightly, can ever believe such in
possible passages of grossness. He's in yello
stockings. 8

Sir To. And cross-gartered?

Mar. Most villanously; like a pedant th
keeps a school i' the church. I have dogged hi
like his murderer. He does obey every point c
the letter that I dropped to betray him: h
does smile his face into more lines than are i
the new map with the augmentation of the Indie
You have not seen such a thing as 'tis; I ca
hardly forbear hurling things at him. I kno
my lady will strike him: if she do, he'll smi
and take't for a great favour. 9

Sir To. Come, bring us, bring us where he i
[*Exeun*

SCENE III.—*A Street.*

Enter SEBASTIAN *and* ANTONIO.

Seb. I would not by my will have trouble
you;
But since you make your pleasure of you
pains,
I will no further chide you.

Ant. I could not stay behind you: my desir
More sharp than filed steel, did spur me forth;
And not all love to see you,—though so muc
As might have drawn one to a longer voyage,-
But jealousy what might befall your travel,
Being skilless in these parts; which to a strange
Unguided and unfriended, often prove
Rough and unhospitable: my willing love,
The rather by these arguments of fear,
Set forth in your pursuit.

Seb. My kind Antonio,
I can no other answer make but thanks,
And thanks, and ever thanks; for oft goo
turns
Are shuffled off with such uncurrent pay:
But, were my worth, as is my conscience, firn
You should find better dealing. What's to do
Shall we go see the reliques of this town?

Ant. To-morrow, sir: best first go see you
lodging.

Seb. I am not weary, and 'tis long to night:
pray you, let us satisfy our eyes
with the memorials and the things of fame
that do renown this city.
Ant.   Would you'd pardon me;
do not without danger walk these streets: 25
nce, in a sea-fight 'gainst the Count his galleys,
did some service; of such note indeed,
that were I ta'en here it would scarce be
answer'd.   28
Seb. Belike you slew great number of his
people?
Ant. The offence is not of such a bloody
nature,
lbeit the quality of the time and quarrel
tight well have given us bloody argument. 32
might have since been answer'd in repaying
what we took from them; which, for traffic's
sake,
lost of our city did: only myself stood out;
or which, if I be lapsed in this place,   36
shall pay dear.
Seb.   Do not then walk too open.
Ant. It doth not fit me. Hold, sir; here's my
purse.
the south suburbs, at the Elephant,
best to lodge: I will bespeak our diet,   40
Whiles you beguile the time and feed your
knowledge
with viewing of the town: there shall you have
me.
Seb. Why I your purse?
Ant. Haply your eye shall light upon some
toy   44
ou have desire to purchase; and your store,
think, is not for idle markets, sir.
Seb. I'll be your purse-bearer and leave you
r an hour.   48
Ant. To the Elephant.
Seb. I do remember.   [*Exeunt.*

SCENE IV.—OLIVIA'S *Garden.*

Enter OLIVIA *and* MARIA.

Oli. I have sent after him: he says he'll come;
ow shall I feast him? what bestow of him?
or youth is bought more oft than begg'd or
borrow'd.
speak too loud.   4
Where is Malvolio? he is sad, and civil,
nd suits well for a servant with my fortunes:
Where is Malvolio?
Mar. He's coming, madam; but in very
range manner. He is sure possess'd, madam. 9
Oli. Why, what's the matter? does he rave?
Mar. No, madam; he does nothing but
nile: your ladyship were best to have some
uard about you if he come, for sure the man
tainted in 's wits.
Oli. Go call him hither.   [*Exit* MARIA.
am as mad as he,   16
sad and merry madness equal be.

Re-enter MARIA, *with* MALVOLIO.

ow now, Malvolio!
Mal. Sweet lady, ho, ho.

Oli. Smil'st thou?   20
I sent for thee upon a sad occasion.
Mal. Sad, lady! I could be sad: this does
make some obstruction in the blood, this cross-
gartering; but what of that? if it please the eye
of one, it is with me as the very true sonnet is,
'Please one and please all.'
Oli. Why, how dost thou, man? what is the
matter with thee?   28
Mal. Not black in my mind, though yellow
in my legs. It did come to his hands, and com-
mands shall be executed: I think we do know
the sweet Roman hand.   32
Oli. Wilt thou go to bed, Malvolio?
Mal. To bed! ay, sweetheart; and I'll come
to thee.
Oli. God comfort thee! Why dost thou smile
so and kiss thy hand so oft?   37
Mar. How do you, Malvolio?
Mal. At your request! Yes; nightingales
answer daws.   40
Mar. Why appear you with this ridiculous
boldness before my lady?
Mal. 'Be not afraid of greatness:' 'Twas
well writ.   44
Oli. What meanest thou by that, Malvolio?
Mal. 'Some are born great,'—
Oli. Ha!
Mal. 'Some achieve greatness,'—   48
Oli. What sayst thou?
Mal. 'And some have greatness thrust upon
them.'
Oli. Heaven restore thee!   52
Mal. 'Remember who commended thy yellow
stockings,'—
Oli. Thy yellow stockings!
Mal. 'And wished to see thee cross-gartered.'
Oli. Cross-gartered!   57
Mal. 'Go to, thou art made, if thou desirest
to be so,'—
Oli. Am I made?   60
Mal. 'If not, let me see thee a servant still.'
Oli. Why, this is very midsummer madness.

Enter Servant.

Ser. Madam, the young gentleman of the
Count Orsino's is returned. I could hardly
entreat him back: he attends your ladyship's
pleasure.   66
Oli. I'll come to him.   [*Exit* Servant.]
Good Maria, let this fellow be looked to.
Where's my cousin Toby? Let some of my
people have a special care of him: I would not
have him miscarry for the half of my dowry. 71
    [*Exeunt* OLIVIA *and* MARIA.
Mal. Oh, ho! do you come near me now?
no worse man than Sir Toby to look to me!
This concurs directly with the letter: she sends
him on purpose, that I may appear stubborn to
him; for she incites me to that in the letter.
'Cast thy humble slough,' says she; 'be opposite
with a kinsman, surly with servants; let thy
tongue tang with arguments of state; put
thyself into the trick of singularity;' and consequently sets down the manner how; as, a sad
face, a reverend carriage, a slow tongue, in the

L

habit of some sir of note, and so forth. I have
limed her; but it is Jove's doing, and Jove make
me thankful! And when she went away now,
'Let this fellow be looked to;' fellow! not Malvolio, nor after my degree, but fellow. Why,
everything adheres together, that no dram of
a scruple, no scruple of a scruple, no obstacle,
no incredulous or unsafe circumstance—What
can be said? Nothing that can be can come
between me and the full prospect of my hopes.
Well, Jove, not I, is the doer of this, and he is
to be thanked. 94

Re-enter MARIA, *with* SIR TOBY BELCH
and FABIAN.

Sir To. Which way is he, in the name of
sanctity? If all the devils in hell be drawn in
little, and Legion himself possess'd him, yet I'll
speak to him.
Fab. Here he is, here he is. How is't with
you, sir? how is't with you, man? 100
Mal. Go off; I discard you: let me enjoy my
private; go off.
Mar. Lo, how hollow the fiend speaks within
him! did not I tell you? Sir Toby, my lady
prays you to have a care of him. 105
Mal. Ah, ha! does she so?
Sir To. Go to, go to: peace! peace! we must
deal gently with him; let me alone. How do
you, Malvolio? how is't with you? What, man!
defy the devil: consider, he's an enemy to mankind.
Mal. Do you know what you say? 112
Mar. La you! an you speak ill of the devil,
how he takes it at heart. Pray God, he be not
bewitched!
Fab. Carry his water to the wise-woman. 116
Mar. Marry, and it shall be done to-morrow
morning, if I live. My lady would not lose him
for more than I'll say.
Mal. How now, mistress! 120
Mar. O Lord!
Sir To. Prithee, hold thy peace; this is not
the way: do you not see you move him? let me
alone with him. 124
Fab. No way but gentleness; gently, gently:
the fiend is rough, and will not be roughly used.
Sir To. Why, how now, my bawcock! how
dost thou, chuck? 128
Mal. Sir!
Sir To. Ay, Biddy, come with me. What,
man! 'tis not for gravity to play at cherry-pit
with Satan: hang him, foul collier! 132
Mar. Get him to say his prayers, good Sir
Toby, get him to pray.
Mal. My prayers, minx!
Mar. No, I warrant you, he will not hear of
godliness. 137
Mal. Go, hang yourselves all! you are idle
shallow things: I am not of your element. You
shall know more hereafter. [*Exit.*
Sir To. Is't possible? 141
Fab. If this were played upon a stage now, I
could condemn it as an improbable fiction
Sir To. His very genius hath taken the infec-
tion of the device, man. 145

Mar. Nay, pursue him now, lest the devi[l]
take air, and taint.
Fab. Why, we shall make him mad indee[d]
Mar. The house will be the quieter.
Sir To. Come, we'll have him in a dark roo[m]
and bound, My niece is already in the beli[ef]
that he's mad: we may carry it thus, for o[ur]
pleasure and his penance, till our very pastim[e]
tired out of breath, prompt us to have mercy [on]
him; at which time we will bring the device [to]
the bar, and crown thee for a finder of madme[n]
But see, but see. 1

Enter SIR ANDREW AGUECHEEK.

Fab. More matter for a May morning.
Sir And. Here's the challenge; read it:
warrant there's vinegar and pepper in't.
Fab. Is't so saucy?
Sir And. Ay, is't, I warrant him: do b[ut]
read.
Sir To. Give me. *Youth, whatsoever th[ou]
art, thou art but a scurvy fellow.*
Fab. Good, and valiant.
Sir To. *Wonder not, nor admire not in t[hy]
mind, why I do call thee so, for I will show th[ee]
no reason for't.*
Fab. A good note, that keeps you from th[e]
blow of the law.
Sir To. *Thou comest to the Lady Olivia, a[nd]
in my sight she uses thee kindly: but thou lie[st]
in thy throat; that is not the matter I challen[ge]
thee for.*
Fab. Very brief, and to exceeding good sen[se]
—less.
Sir To. *I will waylay thee going hom[e]
where, if it be thy chance to kill me,—*
Fab. Good.
Sir To. *Thou killest me like a rogue and [a]
villain.*
Fab. Still you keep o' the windy side of th[e]
law: good.
Sir To. *Fare thee well; and God have merc[y]
upon one of our souls! He may have mercy up[on]
mine, but my hope is better; and so look to th[y]
self. Thy friend, as thou usest him, and th[y]
sworn enemy,*
ANDREW AGUECHEE[K]
If this letter move him not, his legs canno[t]
I'll give't him.
Mar. You may have very fit occasion for['t]
he is now in some commerce with my lady, an[d]
will by and by depart.
Sir To. Go, Sir Andrew: scout me for him a[t]
the corner of the orchard like a bum-baily: s[o]
soon as ever thou seest him, draw; and, as tho[u]
drawest, swear horrible; for it comes to pass o[ft]
that a terrible oath, with a swaggering acce[nt]
sharply twanged off, gives manhood more a[p]
probation than ever proof itself would hav[e]
earned him. Away!
Sir And. Nay, let me alone for swearing. 2[0]
[*Ex[it]*
Sir To. Now will not I deliver his letter: f[or]
the behaviour of the young gentleman gives hi[m]
out to be of good capacity and breeding; h[e]

ployment between his lord and my niece
nfirms no less: therefore this letter, being so
cellently ignorant, will breed no terror in the
uth: he will find it comes from a clodpole.
t, sir, I will deliver his challenge by word of
outh; set upon Aguecheek a notable report of
lour; and drive the gentleman,—as I know
s youth will aptly receive it,—into a most
deous opinion of his rage, skill, fury, and
petuosity. This will so fright them both
at they will kill one another by the look, like
ckatrices.   219

Fab. Here he comes with your niece: give them
y till he take leave, and presently after him.

Sir To. I will meditate the while upon some
rrid message for a challenge.

[*Exeunt* SIR TOBY, FABIAN, *and* MARIA.

Re-enter OLIVIA, *with* VIOLA.

Oli. I have said too much unto a heart of
   stone,   224
d laid mine honour too unchary out:
ere's something in me that reproves my fault,
t such a headstrong potent fault it is
at it but mocks reproof.   228

Vio. With the same haviour that your passion bears
oes on my master's griefs.

Oli. Here; wear this jewel for me, 'tis my
   picture;
efuse it not; it hath no tongue to vex you; 232
nd I beseech you come again to-morrow.
hat shall you ask of me that I'll deny,
hat honour sav'd may upon asking give?

Vio. Nothing but this; your true love for my
   master.   236

Oli. How with mine honour may I give him
   that
hich I have given to you?

Vio.   I will acquit you.

Oli. Well, come again to-morrow: fare thee
   well:
fiend like thee might bear my soul to hell. 240
                                                                 [*Exit.*

Re-enter SIR TOBY BELCH *and* FABIAN.

Sir To. Gentleman, God save thee.

Vio. And you, sir.

Sir To. That defence thou hast, betake thee
't: of what nature the wrongs are thou hast
one him, I know not; but thy intercepter,
ll of despite, bloody as the hunter, attends
ee at the orchard-end. Dismount thy tuck, be
re in thy preparation, for thy assailant is
uick, skilful, and deadly.   249

Vio. You mistake, sir: I am sure no man
ath any quarrel to me: my remembrance is
ry free and clear from any image of offence
one to any man.   253

Sir To. You'll find it otherwise, I assure you:
erefore, if you hold your life at any price, be-
ke you to your guard; for your opposite hath
 him what youth, strength, skill, and wrath,
n furnish man withal.

Vio. I pray you, sir, what is he?   259

Sir To. He is knight dubbed with unhatched
rapier, and on carpet consideration; but he is a
devil in private brawl: souls and bodies hath he
divorced three, and his incensement at this moment is so implacable that satisfaction can be
none but by pangs of death and sepulchre. Hob,
nob, is his word: give't or take't.   266

Vio. I will return again into the house and
desire some conduct of the lady: I am no
fighter. I have heard of some kind of men
that put quarrels purposely on others to taste
their valour; belike this is a man of that quirk.

Sir To. Sir, no; his indignation derives itself
out of a very competent injury: therefore get
you on and give him his desire. Back you shall
not to the house, unless you undertake that with
me which with as much safety you might answer
him: therefore, on, or strip your sword stark
naked; for meddle you must, that's certain, or
forswear to wear iron about you.   279

Vio. This is as uncivil as strange. I beseech
you, do me this courteous office, as to know of
the knight what my offence to him is: it is something of my negligence, nothing of my purpose.

Sir To. I will do so. Signior Fabian, stay
you by this gentleman till my return.   [*Exit.*

Vio. Pray you, sir, do you know of this
matter?   287

Fab. I know the knight is incensed against
you, even to a mortal arbitrement, but nothing
of the circumstance more.

Vio. I beseech you, what manner of man
is he?   292

Fab. Nothing of that wonderful promise, to
read him by his form, as you are like to find him
in the proof of his valour. He is, indeed, sir, the
most skilful, bloody, and fatal opposite that
you could possibly have found in any part of
Illyria. Will you walk towards him? I will
make your peace with him if I can.   299

Vio. I shall be much bound to you for't: I
am one that had rather go with sir priest than
sir knight; I care not who knows so much of
my mettle.   [*Exeunt.*

Re-enter SIR TOBY, *with* SIR ANDREW.

Sir To. Why, man, he's a very devil; I have
not seen such a firago. I had a pass with him,
rapier, scabbard and all, and he gives me the
stuck in with such a mortal motion that it is
inevitable; and on the answer, he pays you as
surely as your feet hit the ground they step on.
They say he has been fencer to the Sophy. 310

Sir And. Pox on't, I'll not meddle with him.

Sir To. Ay, but he will not now be pacified:
Fabian can scarce hold him yonder.   313

Sir And. Plague on't; an I thought he had
been valiant and so cunning in fence I'd have
seen him damned ere I'd have challenged him.
Let him let the matter slip, and I'll give him
my horse, grey Capilet.   318

Sir To. I'll make the motion. Stand here;
make a good show on't: this shall end without
the perdition of souls.—[*Aside.*] Marry, I'll ride
your horse as well as I ride you.

Re-enter FABIAN *and* VIOLA.

[*To* FABIAN.] I have his horse to take up the quarrel. I have persuaded him the youth's a devil. 325

Fab. He is as horribly conceited of him; and pants and looks pale, as if a bear were at his heels. 328

Sir To. There's no remedy, sir: he will fight with you for his oath's sake. Marry, he hath better bethought him of his quarrel, and he finds that now scarce to be worth talking of: therefore draw for the supportance of his vow: he protests he will not hurt you.

Vio. [*Aside.*] Pray God defend me! A little thing would make me tell them how much I lack of a man. 337

Fab. Give ground, if you see him furious.

Sir To. Come, Sir Andrew, there's no remedy: the gentleman will, for his honour's sake, have one bout with you; he cannot by the duello avoid it: but he has promised me, as he is a gentleman and a soldier, he will not hurt you. Come on; to't. 344

Sir And. Pray God, he keep his oath!
                                    [*Draws.*

Vio. I do assure you, 'tis against my will.
                                    [*Draws.*

Enter ANTONIO.

Ant. Put up your sword. If this young gentleman
Have done offence, I take the fault on me: 348
If you offend him, I for him defy you.
                                    [*Drawing.*

Sir To. You, sir! why, what are you?

Ant. One, sir, that for his love dares yet do more
Than you have heard him brag to you he will. 352

Sir To. Nay, if you be an undertaker, I am for you.   [*Draws.*

Fab. O, good sir Toby, hold! here come the officers. 356

Sir To. I'll be with you anon.

Vio. [TO SIR ANDREW.] Pray, sir, put your sword up, if you please.

Sir And. Marry, will I, sir; and, for that I promised you, I'll be as good as my word. He will bear you easily and reins well.

Enter two Officers.

First Off. This is the man; do thy office.

Sec. Off. Antonio, I arrest thee at the suit 364
Of Count Orsino.

Ant.   You do mistake me, sir.

First Off. No, sir, no jot: I know your favour well,
Though now you have no sea-cap on your head.
Take him away: he knows I know him well. 368

Ant. I must obey.—[*To* VIOLA.] This comes with seeking you:
But there's no remedy: I shall answer it.
What will you do, now my necessity
Makes me to ask you for my purse? It grieves me
Much more for what I cannot do for you 373
Than what befalls myself. You stand amaz'd:
But be of comfort.

Sec. Off.   Come, sir, away.

Ant. I must entreat of you some of th money.

Vio. What money, sir?
For the fair kindness you have show'd me her
And part, being prompted by your prese trouble,
Out of my lean and low ability 3
I'll lend you something: my having is not muc
I'll make division of my present with you.
Hold, there is half my coffer.

Ant.   Will you deny me now?
Is't possible that my deserts to you 3
Can lack persuasion? Do not tempt my miser
Lest that it make me so unsound a man
As to upbraid you with those kindnesses
That I have done for you.

Vio.   I know of none; 3
Nor know I you by voice or any feature.
I hate ingratitude more in a man
Than lying, vainness, babbling drunkenness
Or any taint of vice whose strong corruption 3
Inhabits our frail blood.

Ant.   O heavens themselve

Sec. Off. Come, sir: I pray you, go

Ant. Let me speak a little. This youth th you see here
I snatch'd one-half out of the jaws of death, 3
Reliev'd him with such sanctity of love,
And to this image, which methought did promi
Most venerable worth, did I devotion.

First Off. What's that to us? The time go by: away! 4

Ant. But O! how vile an idol proves this go
Thou hast, Sebastian, done good feature sham
In nature there's no blemish but the mind;
None can be call'd deform'd but the unkind: 4
Virtue is beauty, but the beauteous evil
Are empty trunks o'erflourish'd by the devil

First Off. The man grows mad: away wi him! Come, come, sir.

Ant. Lead me on. 4
                    [*Exeunt* Officers *with* ANTONI

Vio. Methinks his words do from such pa sion fly,
That he believes himself; so do not I.
Prove true, imagination, O, prove true,
That I, dear brother, be now ta'en for you! 4

Sir To. Come hither, knight; come hithe
Fabian: we'll whisper o'er a couplet or two most sage saws.

Vio. He nam'd Sebastian: I my brother kno
Yet living in my glass; even such and so 4
In favour was my brother; and he went
Still in this fashion, colour, ornament,
For him I imitate. O! if it prove, 4
Tempests are kind, and salt waves fresh in lov
                                    [*Ex*

Sir To. A very dishonest paltry boy, and mo
a coward than a hare. His dishonesty appea
in leaving his friend here in necessity, and den
ing him; and for his cowardship, ask Fabian. 4

Fab. A coward, a most devout coward, r
ligious in it.

Sir And. 'Slid, I'll after him again and be
him. 4

Sir To. **Do**; cuff him soundly, but never w thy sword.

Sir And. An I do not,—   [*Exit.*

Fab. Come, let's see the event.   433

Sir To. I dare lay any money 'twill be no-ng yet.   [*Exeunt.*

ACT IV

NE I.—*The Street adjoining* OLIVIA'S *House.*

Enter SEBASTIAN *and* Clown.

Clo. Will you make me believe that I am not t for you?

Seb. Go to, go to; thou art a foolish fellow: me be clear of thee.   4

Clo. Well held out, i' faith! No, I do not ow you; nor I am not sent to you by my lady oid you come speak with her; nor your name not Master Cesario; nor this is not my nose ther. Nothing that is so is so.   9

Seb. I prithee, vent thy folly somewhere else: ou know'st not me.

Clo. Vent my folly! He has heard that word ome great man, and now applies it to a fool. nt my folly! I am afraid this great lubber, world, will prove a cockney. I prithee now, gird thy strangeness and tell me what I shall it to my lady. Shall I vent to her that thou coming?

Seb. I prithee, foolish Greek, depart from me: ere's money for thee: if you tarry longer   20 all give worse payment.

Clo. By my troth, thou hast an open hand. ese wise men that give fools money get them-ves a good report after fourteen years' pur-ase.   25

Enter SIR ANDREW.

Sir And. Now, sir, have I met you again? re's for you.   [*Striking* SEBASTIAN.

Seb. Why, there's for thee, and there, and there, and there!   [*Beating* SIR ANDREW. e all the people mad?   29

Enter SIR TOBY *and* FABIAN.

Sir To. Hold, sir, or I'll throw your dagger r the house.

Clo. This will I tell my lady straight. I would t be in some of your coats for twopence. [*Exit.*

Sir To. [*Holding* SEBASTIAN.] Come on, sir: d.   35

Sir And. Nay, let him alone; I'll go another y to work with him: I'll have an action of ttery against him if there be any law in ria. Though I struck him first, yet it's no tter for that.   40

Seb. Let go thy hand.

Sir To. Come, sir, I will not let you go. me, my young soldier, put up your iron: you e well fleshed; come on.   44

Seb. I will be free from thee. [*Disengaging himself.*] What wouldst thou now? thou dar'st tempt me further, draw thy sword.

Sir To. What, what! Nay then, I must have an ounce or two of this malapert blood from you.   *Draws.*

Enter OLIVIA.

Oli. Hold, Toby! on thy life I charge thee, hold!   49

Sir To. Madam!

Oli. Will it be ever thus? Ungracious wretch! Fit for the mountains and the barbarous caves, Where manners ne'er were preach'd. Out of my sight!   53 Be not offended, dear Cesario. Rudesby, be gone!

     [*Exeunt* SIR TOBY, SIR ANDREW, *and* FABIAN.   I prithee, gentle friend, Let thy fair wisdom, not thy passion, sway   56 In this uncivil and unjust extent Against thy peace. Go with me to my house, And hear thou there how many fruitless pranks This ruffian hath botch'd up, that thou thereby Mayst smile at this. Thou shalt not choose but go: 61 Do not deny. Beshrew his soul for me, He started one poor heart of mine in thee.

Seb. What relish is in this? how runs the stream?   64 Or I am mad, or else this is a dream: Let fancy still my sense in Lethe steep; If it be thus to dream, still let me sleep!

Oli. Nay; come, I prithee. Would thou'dst be rul'd by me!   68

Seb. Madam, I will.

Oli.   O! say so, and so be!   [*Exeunt.*

SCENE II.—*A Room in* OLIVIA'S *House.*

Enter MARIA *and* Clown; MALVOLIO *in a dark chamber adjoining.*

Mar. Nay, I prithee, put on this gown and this beard; make him believe thou art Sir Topas the curate: do it quickly; I'll call Sir Toby the whilst.   [*Exit.*

Clo. Well, I'll put it on and I will dissemble myself in't: and I would I were the first that ever dissembled in such a gown. I am not tall enough to become the function well, nor lean enough to be thought a good student; but to be said an honest man and a good housekeeper goes as fairly as to say a careful man and a great scholar. The competitors enter.   12

Enter SIR TOBY BELCH *and* MARIA.

Sir To. God bless thee, Master parson.

Clo. Bonos dies, Sir Toby: for, as the old hermit of Prague, that never saw pen and ink, very wittily said to a niece of King Gorboduc, 'That, that is, is;' so I, being Master parson, am Master parson; for, what is 'that,' but 'that,' and 'is,' but 'is'?

Sir To. To him, Sir Topas.   20

Clo. What ho! I say. Peace in this prison!

Sir To. The knave counterfeits well; a good knave.

Mal. [*Within*]. Who calls there?   24

Clo. Sir Topas, the curate, who comes to visit Malvolio the lunatic.

Mal. Sir Topas, Sir Topas, good Sir Topas, go to my lady.   28

Clo. Out, hyperbolical fiend! how vexest thou this man! Talkest thou nothing but of ladies?

Sir To. Well said, Master Parson.

Mal. [*Within.*] Sir Topas, never was man thus wronged. Good Sir Topas, do not think I am mad: they have laid me here in hideous darkness.   35

Clo. Fie, thou dishonest Satan! I call thee by the most modest terms; for I am one of those gentle ones that will use the devil himself with courtesy. Sayst thou that house is dark?

Mal. As hell, Sir Topas.   40

Clo. Why, it hath bay-windows transparent as barricadoes, and the clerestories toward the south-north are as lustrous as ebony; and yet complainest thou of obstruction?   44

Mal. I am not mad, Sir Topas. I say to you, this house is dark.

Clo. Madman, thou errest: I say, there is no darkness but ignorance, in which thou art more puzzled than the Egyptians in their fog.   49

Mal. I say this house is as dark as ignorance, though ignorance were as dark as hell; and I say, there was never man thus abused. I am no more mad than you are: make the trial of it in any constant question.

Clo. What is the opinion of Pythagoras concerning wild fowl?   56

Mal. That the soul of our grandam might haply inhabit a bird.

Clo. What thinkest thou of his opinion?

Mal. I think nobly of the soul, and no way approve his opinion.   61

Clo. Fare thee well: remain thou still in darkness: thou shalt hold the opinion of Pythagoras ere I will allow of thy wits, and fear to kill a woodcock, lest thou dispossess the soul of thy grandam. Fare thee well.

Mal. Sir Topas! Sir Topas!

Sir To. My most exquisite Sir Topas!   68

Clo. Nay, I am for all waters.

Mar. Thou mightst have done this without thy beard and gown: he sees thee not.

Sir To. To him in thine own voice, and bring me word how thou findest him: I would we were well rid of this knavery. If he may be conveniently delivered, I would he were; for I am now so far in offence with my niece that I cannot pursue with any safety this sport to the up-shot. Come by and by to my chamber.

[*Exeunt* SIR TOBY *and* MARIA.

Clo.   Hey Robin, jolly Robin,
          Tell me how thy lady does.   80

Mal. Fool!

Clo. My lady is unkind, perdy!

Mal. Fool!

Clo. Alas, why is she so?   84

Mal. Fool, I say!

Clo. She loves another.

Who calls, ha?

Mal. Good fool, as ever thou wilt deserve well at my hand, help me to a candle, and pen, ink, and paper. As I am a gentleman, I live to be thankful for 't.

Clo. Master Malvolio!

Mal. Ay, good fool.

Clo. Alas, sir, how fell you beside your wits?

Mal. Fool, there was never man so notously abused: I am as well in my wits, fool thou art.

Clo. But as well? then you are mad inde if you be no better in your wits than a fool.

Mal. They have here propertied me; keep in darkness, send ministers to me, asses! and all they can to face me out of my wits.

Clo. Advise you what you say: the mini is here. Malvolio, Malvolio, thy wits the heav restore! endeavour thyself to sleep, and le thy vain bibble-babble.

Mal. Sir Topas!

Clo. Maintain no words with him, g fellow.—Who, I, sir? not I, sir. God be you, good Sir Topas. Marry, amen. I will, I will.

Mal. Fool, fool, fool, I say!

Clo. Alas, sir, be patient. What say you, I am shent for speaking to you.

Mal. Good fool, help me to some light some paper: I tell thee I am as well in my w as any man in Illyria.

Clo. Well-a-day, that you were, sir!

Mal. By this hand, I am. Good fool, s ink, paper, and light; and convey what I set down to my lady: it shall advantage t more than ever the bearing of letter did.

Clo. I will help you to 't. But tell me t are you not mad indeed? or do you but coun feit?

Mal. Believe me, I am not: I tell t true.

Clo. Nay, I'll ne'er believe a madman ti see his brains. I will fetch you light and pa and ink.

Mal. Fool, I'll requite it in the hig degree: I prithee, be gone.

Clo.   I am gone, sir,
              And anon, sir,
          I'll be with you again,
              In a trice,
              Like to the old Vice,
              Your need to sustain;
          Who with dagger of lath,
          In his rage and his wrath,
              Cries, Ah, ah! to the devil:
          Like a mad lad,
          Pare thy nails, dad;
              Adieu, goodman drivel.

[E

SCENE III.—OLIVIA'S *Garden.*

Enter SEBASTIAN.

Seb. This is the air; that is the glorious s
This pearl she gave me, I do feel 't and see 't
And though 'tis wonder that enwraps me th
Yet 'tis not madness. Where's Antonio th
I could not find him at the Elephant;
Yet there he was, and there I found this cre
That he did range the town to seek me o

His counsel now might do me golden service; 8
or though my soul disputes well with my sense
that this may be some error, but no madness,
Yet doth this accident and flood of fortune
So far exceed all instance, all discourse,   12
That I am ready to distrust mine eyes,
And wrangle with my reason that persuades me
To any other trust but that I am mad
Or else the lady's mad: yet, if 'twere so,   16
She could not sway her house, command her
followers,
Take and give back affairs and their dispatch
With such a smooth, discreet, and stable bearing
As I perceive she does. There's something in 't
That is deceivable. But here the lady comes. 21

Enter OLIVIA *and a* Priest.

Oli. Blame not this haste of mine. If you
mean well,
Now go with me and with this holy man
Into the chantry by; there, before him,   24
And underneath that consecrated roof,
Plight me the full assurance of your faith;
That my most jealous and too doubtful soul
May live at peace. He shall conceal it   28
Whiles you are willing it shall come to note,
What time we will our celebration keep
According to my birth. What do you say?
Seb. I'll follow this good man, and go with
you;   32
And, having sworn truth, ever will be true.
Oli. Then lead the way, good father; and
heavens so shine
That they may fairly note this act of mine!
[*Exeunt.*

ACT V

SCENE I.—*The Street before* OLIVIA'S *House.*
Enter Clown *and* FABIAN.

Fab. Now, as thou lovest me, let me see his
letter.
Clo. Good Master Fabian, grant me another
request.   4
Fab. Anything.
Clo. Do not desire to see this letter.
Fab. This is, to give a dog, and, in recom-
pense desire my dog again.   8

Enter DUKE, VIOLA, CURIO, *and* Attendants.

Duke. Belong you to the Lady Olivia, friends?
Clo. Ay, sir; we are some of her trappings.
Duke. I know thee well: how dost thou, my
good fellow?   12
Clo. Truly, sir, the better for my foes and the
worse for my friends.
Duke. Just the contrary; the better for thy
friends.   16
Clo. No, sir, the worse.
Duke. How can that be?
Clo. Marry, sir, they praise me and make an
ass of me; now my foes tell me plainly I am an
ass: so that by my foes, sir, I profit in the know-
edge of myself, and by my friends I am abused:
so that, conclusions to be as kisses, if your four

negatives make your two affirmatives, why then,
the worse for my friends and the better for my
foes.   26
Duke. Why, this is excellent.
Clo. By my troth, sir, no; though it please
you to be one of my friends.
Duke. Thou shalt not be the worse for me:
there's gold.
Clo. But that it would be double-dealing, sir,
I would you could make it another.   33
Duke. O, you give me ill counsel.
Clo. Put your grace in your pocket, sir, for
this once, and let your flesh and blood obey it. 36
Duke. Well, I will be so much a sinner to be
a double-dealer: there's another.
Clo. Primo, secundo, tertio, is a good play;
and the old saying is, 'the third pays for all:'
the *triplex,* sir, is a good tripping measure; or
the bells of Saint Bennet, sir, may put you in
mind; one, two, three.   43
Duke. You can fool no more money out of
me at this throw: if you will let your lady know
I am here to speak with her, and bring her along
with you, it may awake my bounty further. 47
Clo. Marry, sir, lullaby to your bounty till I
come again. I go, sir; but I would not have you
to think that my desire of having is the sin of
covetousness; but as you say, sir, let your bounty
take a nap, I will awake it anon.   [*Exit.*
Vio. Here comes the man, sir, that did rescue
me.

Enter ANTONIO *and* Officers.

Duke. That face of his I do remember well;
Yet when I saw it last, it was besmear'd   56
As black as Vulcan in the smoke of war.
A bawbling vessel was he captain of,
For shallow draught and hulk unprizable;
With which such scathful grapple did he make
With the most noble bottom of our fleet,   61
That very envy and the tongue of loss
Cried fame and honour on him. What's the
matter?
First Off. Orsino, this is that Antonio   64
That took the Phœnix and her fraught from
Candy;
And this is he that did the Tiger board,
When your young nephew Titus lost his leg.
Here in the streets, desperate of shame and
state,   68
In private brabble did we apprehend him.
Vio. He did me kindness, sir, drew on my
side;
But in conclusion put strange speech upon me:
I know not what 'twas but distraction.   72
Duke. Notable pirate! thou salt-water thief!
What foolish boldness brought thee to their
mercies
Whom thou, in terms so bloody and so dear,
Hast made thine enemies?
Ant.   Orsino, noble sir, 76
Be pleas'd that I shake off these names you give
me:
Antonio never yet was thief or pirate,
Though I confess, on base and ground enough,
Orsino's enemy. A witchcraft drew me hither:

That most ingrateful boy there by your side, 81
From the rude sea's enrag'd and foamy mouth
Did I redeem; a wrack past hope he was:
His life I gave him, and did thereto add   84
My love, without retention or restraint,
All his in dedication; for his sake
Did I expose myself, pure for his love,
Into the danger of this adverse town;   88
Drew to defend him when he was beset:
Where being apprehended, his false cunning,
Not meaning to partake with me in danger,
Taught him to face me out of his acquaint-
  ance,   92
And grew a twenty years removed thing
While one would wink, denied me mine own
  purse,
Which I had recommended to his use
Not half an hour before.
   Vio.   How can this be? 96
   Duke. When came he to this town?
   Ant. To-day, my lord; and for three months
before,—
No interim, not a minute's vacancy,—
Both day and night did we keep company. 100

Enter OLIVIA *and* Attendants.

   Duke. Here comes the countess: now heaven
walks on earth!
But for thee, fellow; fellow, thy words are mad-
  ness:
Three months this youth hath tended upon me;
But more of that anon. Take him aside. 104
   Oli. What would my lord, but that he may
not have,
Wherein Olivia may seem serviceable?
Cesario, you do not keep promise with me.
   Vio. Madam!   108
   Duke. Gracious Olivia.—
   Oli. What do you say, Cesario? Good my
lord,—
   Vio. My lord would speak; my duty hushes
me.
   Oli. If it be aught to the old tune, my lord,
It is as fat and fulsome to mine ear   113
As howling after music.
   Duke.   Still so cruel?
   Oli. Still so constant, lord.
   Duke. What, to perverseness? you uncivil
lady,   116
To whose ingrate and unauspicious altars
My soul the faithfull'st offerings hath breath'd
  out
That e'er devotion tender'd! What shall I do?
   Oli. Even what it please my lord, that shall
become him.   120
   Duke. Why should I not, had I the heart to
do it,
Like to the Egyptian thief at point of death,
Kill what I love? a savage jealousy
That sometimes savours nobly. But hear me
this: 124
Since you to non-regardance cast my faith,
And that I partly know the instrument
That screws me from my true place in your
favour,

Live you, the marble-breasted tyrant still; 12
But this your minion, whom I know you love
And whom, by heaven I swear, I tender dearly
Him will I tear out of that cruel eye,
Where he sits crowned in his master's spite. 13
Come, boy, with me; my thoughts are ripe i
  mischief;
I'll sacrifice the lamb that I do love,
To spite a raven's heart within a dove. [*Goin*
   Vio. And I, most jocund, apt, and willingly
To do you rest, a thousand deaths would die. 13
                                    [*Following*
   Oli. Where goes Cesario?
   Vio.   After him I love
More than I love these eyes, more than my lif
More, by all mores, than e'er I shall love wif
If I do feign, you witnesses above   14
Punish my life for tainting of my love!
   Oli. Ah me, detested! how am I beguil'd!
   Vio. Who does beguile you? who does d
  you wrong?   14
   Oli. Hast thou forgot thyself? Is it so long
Call forth the holy father. [*Exit an Attendan*
   Duke.   [*To* VIOLA.] Come away.
   Oli. Whither, my lord? Cesario, husban
stay.
   Duke. Husband?
   Oli.   Ay, husband: can he that deny? 14
   Duke. Her husband, sirrah?
   Vio.   No, my lord, not I
   Oli. Alas! it is the baseness of thy fear
That makes thee strangle thy propriety.
Fear not, Cesario; take thy fortunes up;   15
Be that thou know'st thou art, and then tho
  art
As great as that thou fear'st.

Enter Priest.

                          O, welcome, father
Father, I charge thee, by thy reverence,
Here to unfold,—though lately we intended 15
To keep in darkness what occasion now
Reveals before 'tis ripe,—what thou dost know
Hath newly pass'd between this youth an
  me.
   Priest. A contract of eternal bond of love, 16
Confirm'd by mutual joinder of your hands,
Attested by the holy close of lips,
Strengthen'd by interchangement of your rings
And all the ceremony of this compact   16
Seal'd in my function, by my testimony:
Since when, my watch hath told me, towar
  my grave
I have travell'd but two hours.
   Duke. O, thou dissembling cub! what wil
  thou be   16
When time hath sow'd a grizzle on thy case?
Or will not else thy craft so quickly grow
That thine own trip shall be thine overthrow
Farewell, and take her; but direct thy feet 17
Where thou and I henceforth may never meet
   Vio. My lord, I do protest,—
   Oli.   O! do not swear:
Hold little faith, though thou hast too muc
  fear.

Enter SIR ANDREW AGUECHEEK, *with his head broken.*

Sir And. For the love of God, a surgeon! and one presently to Sir Toby.   177

Oli. What's the matter?

Sir And. He has broke my head across, and has given Sir Toby a bloody coxcomb too. For the love of God, your help! I had rather than forty pound I were at home.   182

Oli. Who has done this, Sir Andrew?

Sir And. The count's gentleman, one Cesario: we took him for a coward, but he's the very devil incardinate.   186

Duke. My gentleman, Cesario?

Sir And. Od's lifelings! here he is. You broke my head for nothing! and that that I did, I was set on to do't by Sir Toby.

Vio. Why do you speak to me? I never hurt you:

you drew your sword upon me without cause; but I bespake you fair, and hurt you not.   193

Sir And. If a bloody coxcomb be a hurt, you have hurt me: I think you set nothing by a bloody coxcomb. Here comes Sir Toby halting;   197

Enter SIR TOBY BELCH, *drunk, led by the* Clown.

you shall hear more: but if he had not been in drink he would have tickled you othergates than he did.   200

Duke. How now, gentleman! how is't with you?

Sir To. That's all one: he has hurt me, and there's the end on't. Sot, didst see Dick surgeon, sot?   205

Clo. O! he's drunk, Sir Toby, an hour agone: his eyes were set at eight i' the morning.

Sir To. Then he's a rogue, and a passy-measures pavin. I hate a drunken rogue.   209

Oli. Away with him! Who hath made this havoc with them?

Sir And. I'll help you, Sir Toby, because we'll be dressed together.   213

Sir To. Will you help? an ass-head and a coxcomb and a knave, a thin-faced knave, a gull!   216

Oli. Get him to bed, and let his hurt be look'd to.   [*Exeunt* Clown, FABIAN, SIR TOBY, *and* SIR ANDREW.

Enter SEBASTIAN.

Seb. I am sorry, madam, I have hurt your kinsman;

but, had it been the brother of my blood,   220 I must have done no less with wit and safety. You throw a strange regard upon me, and by that

you perceive it hath offended you:

pardon me, sweet one, even for the vows   224 we made each other but so late ago.

Duke. One face, one voice, one habit, and two persons!

a natural perspective, that is, and is not!

Seb. Antonio! O my dear Antonio!   228 how have the hours rack'd and tortur'd me since I have lost thee!

Ant. Sebastian are you?

Seb.   Fear'st thou that, Antonio?

Ant. How have you made division of yourself?   232

An apple cleft in two is not more twin Than these two creatures. Which is Sebastian?

Oli. Most wonderful!

Seb. Do I stand there? I never had a brother;   236

Nor can there be that deity in my nature, Of here and every where. I had a sister, Whom the blind waves and surges have devour'd.

Of charity, what kin are you to me?   240 What countryman? what name? what parentage?

Vio. Of Messaline: Sebastian was my father; Such a Sebastian was my brother too, So went he suited to his watery tomb.   244 If spirits can assume both form and suit You come to fright us.

Seb.   A spirit I am indeed; But am in that dimension grossly clad Which from the womb I did participate.   248 Were you a woman, as the rest goes even, I should my tears let fall upon your cheek, And say, 'Thrice welcome, drowned Viola!'

Vio. My father had a mole upon his brow.

Seb. And so had mine.   253

Vio. And died that day when Viola from her birth

Had number'd thirteen years.

Seb. O! that record is lively in my soul.   256 He finished indeed his mortal act That day that made my sister thirteen years.

Vio. If nothing lets to make us happy both But this my masculine usurp'd attire,   260 Do not embrace me till each circumstance Of place, time, fortune, do cohere and jump That I am Viola: which to confirm, I'll bring you to a captain in this town,   264 Where lie my maiden weeds: by whose gentle help

I was preserv'd to serve this noble count. All the occurrence of my fortune since Hath been between this lady and this lord.   268

Seb. [*To* OLIVIA.] So comes it, lady, you have been mistook:

But nature to her bias drew in that.

You would have been contracted to a maid; Nor are you therein, by my life, deceiv'd,   272 You are betroth'd both to a maid and man.

Duke. Be not amaz'd; right noble is his blood. If this be so, as yet the glass seems true, I shall have share in this most happy wrack.

[*To* VIOLA.] Boy, thou hast said to me a thousand times   277

Thou never shouldst love woman like to me.

Vio. And all those sayings will I over-swear, And all those swearings keep as true in soul   280 As doth that orbed continent the fire That severs day from night.

Duke.   Give me thy hand; And let me see thee in thy woman's weeds.

Vio. The captain that did bring me first on shore   284

Hath my maid's garments: he upon some action
Is now in durance at Malvolio's suit,
A gentleman and follower of my lady's.
   Oli. He shall enlarge him. Fetch Malvolio
   hither.   288
And yet, alas, now I remember me,
They say, poor gentleman, he's much distract.
A most extracting frenzy of mine own
From my remembrance clearly banish'd his. 292

Re-enter Clown *with a letter, and* FABIAN.

How does he, sirrah?
   Clo. Truly, madam, he holds Belzebub at the
stave's end as well as a man in his case may do.
He has here writ a letter to you: I should have
given it to you to-day morning; but as a mad-
man's epistles are no gospels, so it skills not
much when they are delivered.
   Oli. Open it, and read it.   300
   Clo. Look then to be well edified, when the
fool delivers the madman.
   By the Lord, madam,—
   Oli. How now! art thou mad?   304
   Clo. No, madam, I do but read madness: an
your ladyship will have it as it ought to be, you
must allow *vox.*
   Oli. Prithee, read i' thy right wits.   308
   Clo. So I do, madonna; but to read his right
wits is to read thus: therefore perpend, my
princess, and give ear.
   Oli. [*To* FABIAN.] Read it you, sirrah.   312
   *Fab. By the Lord, madam, you wrong me,
and the world shall know it: though you
have put me into darkness, and given your
drunken cousin rule over me, yet have I the
benefit of my senses as well as your ladyship.
I have your own letter that induced me to the
semblance I put on; with the which I doubt not
but to do myself much right, or you much shame.
Think of me as you please. I leave my duty a
little unthought of, and speak out of my injury.*
             THE MADLY-USED *MALVOLIO.*
   Oli. Did he write this?   324
   Clo. Ay, madam.
   Duke. This savours not much of distrac-
tion.
   Oli. See him deliver'd, Fabian; bring him
hither.   [*Exit* FABIAN.
My lord, so please you, these things further
thought on,   328
To think me as well a sister as a wife,
One day shall crown the alliance on't, so please
you,
Here at my house and at my proper cost.
   Duke. Madam, I am most apt to embrace
your offer.   332
[*To* VIOLA.] Your master quits you; and, for
your service done him,
So much against the mettle of your sex,
So far beneath your soft and tender breeding;
And since you call'd me master for so long, 336
Here is my hand: you shall from this time be
Your master's mistress.
   Oli.   A sister! you are she.

Re-enter FABIAN, *with* MALVOLIO.

   Duke. Is this the madman?
   Oli.   Ay, my lord, this sar
How now, Malvolio!
   Mal.   Madam, you have done me wro
Notorious wrong.
   Oli.   Have I, Malvolio? no.
   Mal. Lady, you have. Pray you peruse t
letter.
You must not now deny it is your hand:
Write from it, if you can, in hand or phrase
Or say 'tis not your seal nor your invention:
You can say none of this. Well, grant it th
And tell me, in the modesty of honour,
Why you have given me such clear lights
favour,
Bade me come smiling and cross-garter'd to yo
To put on yellow stockings, and to frown
Upon Sir Toby and the lighter people;
And, acting this in an obedient hope,
Why have you suffer'd me to be imprison'd
Kept in a dark house, visited by the priest,
And made the most notorious geck and gu
That e'er invention play'd on? tell me why.
   Oli. Alas! Malvolio, this is not my writi
Though, I confess, much like the character
But, out of question, 'tis Maria's hand:
And now I do bethink me, it was she
First told me thou wast mad; then cam'st
smiling,
And in such forms which here were presuppo
Upon thee in the letter. Prithee, be conten
This practice hath most shrewdly pass'd up
thee;
But when we know the grounds and authors
it,
Thou shalt be both the plaintiff and the ju
Of thine own cause.
   Fab.   Good madam, hear me spe
And let no quarrel nor no brawl to come
Taint the condition of this present hour,
Which I have wonder'd at. In hope it shall n
Most freely I confess, myself and Toby
Set this device against Malvolio here,
Upon some stubborn and uncourteous par
We had conceiv'd against him. Maria wri
The letter at Sir Toby's great importance;
In recompense whereof he hath married her
How with a sportful malice it was follow'd,
May rather pluck on laughter than reveng
If that the injuries be justly weigh'd
That have on both sides past.
   Oli. Alas, poor fool, how have they baf
thee!
   Clo. Why, 'some are born great, some achi
greatness, and some have greatness thrown up
them.' I was one, sir, in this interlude; one
Topas, sir; but that's all one. 'By the Lo
fool, I am not mad:' But do you rememb
'Madam, why laugh you at such a barren rasc
an you smile not, he's gagged:' and thus
whirligig of time brings in his revenges.
   Mal. I'll be reveng'd on the whole pack
you.   [E
   Oli. He hath been most notoriously abu

Duke. Pursue him, and entreat him to a
   peace;—   392
He hath not told us of the captain yet:
When that is known and golden time convents,
A solemn combination shall be made
Of our dear souls. Meantime, sweet sister, 396
We will not part from hence. Cesario, come;
For so you shall be, while you are a man;
But when in other habits you are seen,
Orsino's mistress, and his fancy's queen.   400
                [*Exeunt all except* Clown.

SONG

Clo.   When that I was and a little tiny boy,
      With hey, ho, the wind and the rain;
    A foolish thing was but a toy,
      For the rain it raineth every day.   404

But when I came to man's estate,
    With hey, ho, the wind and the rain;
'Gainst knaves and thieves men shut their gates,
    For the rain it raineth every day.   408

But when I came, alas! to wive,
    With hey, ho, the wind and the rain;
By swaggering could I never thrive,
    For the rain it raineth every day.   412

But when I came unto my beds,
    With hey, ho, the wind and the rain;
With toss-pots still had drunken heads,
    For the rain it raineth every day.   416

A great while ago the world begun,
    With hey, ho, the wind and the rain;
But that's all one, our play is done,
    And we'll strive to please you every day.   420
                        [*Exit.*

THE WINTER'S TALE

DRAMATIS PERSONÆ

LEONTES, King of Sicilia.
MAMILLIUS, young Prince of Sicilia.
CAMILLO, \
ANTIGONUS, } Lords of Sicilia.
CLEOMENES, |
DION, /
POLIXENES, King of Bohemia.
FLORIZEL, his Son.
ARCHIDAMUS, a Lord of Bohemia.
A Mariner.
A Gaoler.
An old Shepherd, reputed Father of Perdita.
Clown, his Son.
Servant to the old Shepherd.

AUTOLYCUS, a Rogue.

HERMIONE, Queen to Leontes.
PERDITA, Daughter to Leontes and Hermione.
PAULINA, Wife to Antigonus.
EMILIA, a Lady, \ attending the Queen.
Other Ladies, / attending the Queen.
MOPSA, \ Shepherdesses.
DORCAS, / Shepherdesses.

Sicilian Lords and Ladies, Attendants, Guards,
Satyrs, Shepherds, Shepherdesses, &c.

Time, as Chorus.

SCENE.—*Sometimes in Sicilia, sometimes in Bohemia.*

ACT I

SCENE I.—*Sicilia. An Antechamber in* LEONTES' *Palace.*

Enter CAMILLO *and* ARCHIDAMUS.

Arch. If you shall chance, Camillo, to visit
Bohemia, on the like occasion whereon my services are now on foot, you shall see, as I have
said, great difference betwixt our Bohemia and
your Sicilia.   5
Cam. I think, this coming summer, the King
of Sicilia means to pay Bohemia the visitation
which he justly owes him.   8
Arch. Wherein our entertainment shall shame
us we will be justified in our loves: for, indeed,—
Cam. Beseech you,—
Arch. Verily, I speak it in the freedom of my
knowledge: we cannot with such magnificence—
in so rare—I know not what to say. We will give
you sleepy drinks, that your senses, unintelligent
of our insufficience, may, though they cannot
praise us, as little accuse us.   17
Cam. You pay a great deal too dear for
what's given freely.
Arch. Believe me, I speak as my understanding instructs me, and as mine honesty puts it to
utterance.   22
Cam. Sicilia cannot show himself over-kind
to Bohemia. They were trained together in
their childhoods; and there rooted betwixt
them then such an affection which cannot
choose but branch now. Since their more mature dignities and royal necessities made separation of their society, their encounters, though
not personal, have been royally attorneyed with
interchange of gifts, letters, loving embassies;
that they have seemed to be together, though
absent, shook hands, as over a vast, and embraced, as it were, from the ends of opposed
winds. The heavens continue their loves!   35
Arch. I think there is not in the world either
malice or matter to alter it. You have an unspeakable comfort of your young Prince Mamil-

lius: it is a gentleman of the greatest promise
that ever came into my note.   40
Cam. I very well agree with you in the hopes
of him. It is a gallant child; one that indeed
physics the subject, makes old hearts fresh:
they that went on crutches ere he was born
desire yet their life to see him a man.   45
Arch. Would they else be content to die?
Cam. Yes; if there were no other excuse why
they should desire to live.   48
Arch. If the king had no son, they would
desire to live on crutches till he had one.
[*Exeunt.*

SCENE II.—*The Same. A Room of State in the Palace.*

Enter LEONTES, POLIXENES, HERMIONE, MAMIL-
LIUS, CAMILLO, *and* Attendants.

Pol. Nine changes of the watery star have
     been
The shepherd's note since we have left our
     throne
Without a burden: time as long again
Would be fill'd up, my brother, with our thanks;
And yet we should for perpetuity   5
Go hence in debt: and therefore, like a cipher,
Yet standing in rich place, I multiply
With one 'We thank you' many thousands moe
That go before it.
     Leon.   Stay your thanks awhile, 9
And pay them when you part.
     Pol.   Sir, that's to-morrow.
I am question'd by my fears, of what may chance
Or breed upon our absence; that may blow   12
No sneaping winds at home, to make us say,
'This is put forth too truly!' Besides, I have
     stay'd
To tire your royalty.
     Leon.   We are tougher, brother,
Than you can put us to 't.
     Pol.   No longer stay.   16

Leon. One seven-night longer.

Pol.   Very sooth, to-morrow.

Leon. We'll part the time between 's then;
and in that
I'll no gainsaying.

Pol.   Press me not, beseech you, so.
There is no tongue that moves, none, none i' the
world,   20
So soon as yours could win me: so it should now,
Were there necessity in your request, although
'Twere needful I denied it. My affairs
Do even drag me homeward; which to hinder 24
Were in your love a whip to me; my stay
To you a charge and trouble: to save both,
Farewell, our brother.

Leon. Tongue-tied, our queen? speak you.

Her. I had thought, sir, to have held my
peace until   28
You had drawn oaths from him not to stay.
You, sir,
Charge him too coldly: tell him, you are sure
All in Bohemia 's well: this satisfaction
The by-gone day proclaim'd: say this to him, 32
He 's beat from his best ward.

Leon.   Well said, Hermione.

Her. To tell he longs to see his son were
strong;
But let him say so then, and let him go;
But let him swear so, and he shall not stay, 36
We'll thwack him hence with distaffs.

To POLIXENES.] Yet of your royal presence I'll
adventure
The borrow of a week. When at Bohemia
You take my lord, I'll give him my commission
To let him there a month behind the gest   41
Prefix'd for 's parting: yet, good deed, Leontes,
I love thee not a jar o' the clock behind
What lady she her lord. You'll stay?

Pol.   No, madam. 44

Her. Nay, but you will?

Pol.   I may not, verily.

Her. Verily!
You put me off with limber vows; but I,
Though you would seek to unsphere the stars
with oaths,   48
Should yet say, 'Sir, no going.' Verily,
You shall not go: a lady's 'verily' 's
As potent as a lord's. Will you go yet?
Force me to keep you as a prisoner,   52
Not like a guest; so you shall pay your fees
When you depart, and save your thanks. How
say you?
My prisoner, or my guest? by your dread
'verily,'
One of them you shall be.

Pol.   Your guest, then, madam: 56
To be your prisoner should import offending;
Which is for me less easy to commit
Than you to punish.

Her.   Not your gaoler then,
But your kind hostess. Come, I'll question you
Of my lord's tricks and yours when you were
boys: 61
You were pretty lordings then.

Pol.   We were, fair queen,
Two lads that thought there was no more behind

But such a day to-morrow as to-day,   64
And to be boy eternal.

Her. Was not my lord the verier wag o' the
two?

Pol. We were as twinn'd lambs that did frisk
i' the sun,
And bleat the one at the other: what we
chang'd   68
Was innocence for innocence; we knew not
The doctrine of ill-doing, no nor dream'd
That any did. Had we pursu'd that life,
And our weak spirits ne'er been higher rear'd 72
With stronger blood, we should have answer'd
heaven
Boldly, 'not guilty;' the imposition clear'd
Hereditary ours.

Her.   By this we gather
You have tripp'd since.

Pol.   O! my most sacred lady, 76
Temptations have since then been born to 's; for
In those unfledg'd days was my wife a girl;
Your precious self had then not cross'd the eyes
Of my young playfellow.

Her.   Grace to boot! 80
Of this make no conclusion, lest you say
Your queen and I are devils; yet, go on:
The offences we have made you do we'll answer;
If you first sinn'd with us, and that with us 84
You did continue fault, and that you slipp'd not
With any but with us.

Leon.   Is he won yet?

Her. He'll stay, my lord.

Leon.   At my request he would not.
Hermione, my dearest, thou never spok'st 88
To better purpose.

Her.   Never?

Leon.   Never, but once.

Her. What! have I twice said well? when
was 't before?
I prithee tell me; cram 's with praise, and make 's
As fat as tame things: one good deed, dying
tongueless,   92
Slaughters a thousand waiting upon that.
Our praises are our wages: you may ride 's
With one soft kiss a thousand furlongs ere
With spur we heat an acre. But to the goal: 96
My last good deed was to entreat his stay:
What was my first? it has an elder sister,
Or I mistake you: O! would her name were
Grace.
But once before I spoke to the purpose: when?
Nay, let me have 't; I long.

Leon.   Why, that was when
Three crabbed months had sour'd themselves
to death,
Ere I could make thee open thy white hand
And clap thyself my love: then didst thou
utter,   104
'I am yours for ever.'

Her.   'Tis grace indeed.
Why, lo you now, I have spoke to the purpose
twice:
The one for ever earn'd a royal husband,
The other for some while a friend.   108

[*Giving her hand to* POLIXENES.

Leon. [*Aside.*] Too hot, too hot!

To mingle friendship far is mingling bloods.
I have *tremor cordis* on me: my heart dances;
But not for joy; not joy. This entertainment 112
May a free face put on, derive a liberty
From heartiness, from bounty, fertile bosom,
And well become the agent: 't may I grant:
But to be paddling palms and pinching fingers,
As now they are, and making practis'd smiles, 117
As in a looking-glass; and then to sigh, as 'twere
The mort o' the deer; O! that is entertainment
My bosom likes not, nor my brows. Mamillius,
Art thou my boy?
  Mam.   Ay, my good lord.
  Leon.   I' fecks? 121
Why, that's my bawcock. What! hast smutch'd
  thy nose?
They say it is a copy out of mine. Come, captain,
We must be neat; not neat, but cleanly, captain:
And yet the steer, the heifer, and the calf, 125
Are all call'd neat. Still virginalling
Upon my palm! How now, you wanton calf!
Art thou my calf?
  Mam.   Yes, if you will, my lord. 128
  Leon. Thou want'st a rough pash and the
    shoots that I have,
To be full like me: yet they say we are
Almost as like as eggs; women say so,
That will say anything: but were they false 132
As o'er-dy'd blacks, as wind, as waters, false
As dice are to be wish'd by one that fixes
No bourn 'twixt his and mine, yet were it true
To say this boy were like me. Come, sir page,
Look on me with your welkin eye: sweet villain!
Most dear'st! my collop! Can thy dam?—may't
  be?—
Affection! thy intention stabs the centre:
Thou dost make possible things not so held, 140
Communicat'st with dreams;—how can this
  be?—
With what's unreal thou co-active art,
And fellow'st nothing: then, 'tis very credent
Thou mayst co-join with something; and thou
  dost, 144
And that beyond commission, and I find it,
And that to the infection of my brains
And hardening of my brows.
  Pol.   What means Sicilia?
  Her. He something seems unsettled.
  Pol.   How, my lord! 148
What cheer? how is't with you, best brother?
  Her.   You look
As if you held a brow of much distraction:
Are you mov'd, my lord?
  Leon.   No, in good earnest.
How sometimes nature will betray its folly, 152
Its tenderness, and make itself a pastime
To harder bosoms! Looking on the lines
Of my boy's face, methoughts I did recoil
Twenty-three years, and saw myself unbreech'd,
In my green velvet coat, my dagger muzzled,
Lest it should bite its master, and so prove,
As ornaments oft do, too dangerous,
How like, methought, I then was to this kernel,
This squash, this gentleman. Mine honest
  friend, 161
Will you take eggs for money?

  Mam.   No my lord, I'll figh
  Leon. You will? why, happy man be his dol
    My brother,
Are you so fond of your young prince as we 1(
Do seem to be of ours?
  Pol.   If at home, sir,
He's all my exercise, my mirth, my matter,
Now my sworn friend and then mine enemy
My parasite, my soldier, statesman, all: 1(
He makes a July's day short as December,
And with his varying childness cures in me
Thoughts that would thick my blood.
  Leon.   So stands this squi
Offic'd with me. We two will walk, my lord, 1
And leave you to your graver steps. Hermion
How thou lov'st us, show in our brother's we
  come:
Let what is dear in Sicily be cheap:
Next to thyself and my young rover, he's 1
Apparent to my heart.
  Her.   If you would seek us,
We are yours i' the garden: shall's attend yo
  there?
  Leon. To your own bents dispose you: you'
    be found,
Be you beneath the sky.—[*Aside.*] I am anglin
  now, 18
Though you perceive me not how I give line.
Go to, go to!
How she holds up the neb, the bill to him!
And arms her with the boldness of a wife 18
To her allowing husband!
    [*Exeunt* POLIXENES, HERMIONE, *an*
                        Attendants
            Gone already!
Inch-thick, knee-deep, o'er head and ears
  fork'd one!
Go play, boy, play; thy mother plays, and I
Play too, but so disgrac'd a part, whose issue
Will hiss me to my grave: contempt an
  clamour 18
Will be my knell. Go play, boy, play. Ther
  have been,
Or I am much deceiv'd, cuckolds ere now;
And many a man there is even at this presen
Now, while I speak this, holds his wife by th
  arm, 19
That little thinks she has been sluic'd in
  absence,
And his pond fish'd by his next neighbour, b
Sir Smile, his neighbour: nay, there's comfo
  in't, 19
Whiles other men have gates, and those gate
  open'd,
As mine, against their will. Should all despai
That have revolted wives the tenth of man
  kind
Would hang themselves. Physic for't there i
  none; 20
It is a bawdy planet, that will strike
Where 'tis predominant; and 'tis powerfu
  think it,
From east, west, north, and south: be it con
  cluded, 20
No barricado for a belly: know't; 20
It will let in and out the enemy

With bag and baggage. Many a thousand on 's
Have the disease, and feel 't not. How now, boy!
　Mam. I am like you, they say.
　Leon.　　Why, that's some comfort. 208
What! Camillo there?
　Cam. Ay, my good lord.
　Leon. Go play, Mamillius; thou 'rt an honest
　　man.　　　　　　　[*Exit* MAMILLIUS.
Camillo, this great sir will yet stay longer. 212
　Cam. You had much ado to make his anchor
　　hold:
When you cast out, it still came home.
　Leon.　　　　　Didst note it?
　Cam. He would not stay at your petitions;
　　made
His business more material.
　Leon.　　　　Didst perceive it? 216
　Aside.] They're here with me already, whisper-
　　ing, rounding
Sicilia is a so-forth.' 'Tis far gone,
When I shall gust it last. How came 't, Camillo,
That he did stay?
　Cam.　　At the good queen's entreaty. 220
　Leon. At the queen's, be 't: 'good' should be
　　pertinent;
But so it is, it is not. Was this taken
By any understanding pate but thine?
For thy conceit is soaking; will draw in 224
More than the common blocks: not noted, is 't,
But of the finer natures? by some severals
Of head-piece extraordinary? lower messes
Perchance are to this business purblind? say.
　Cam. Business, my lord! I think most under-
　　stand 229
Bohemia stays here longer.
　Leon.　　　　Ha!
　Cam.　　　　Stays here longer.
　Leon. Ay, but why?
　Cam. To satisfy your highness and the en-
　　treaties 232
Of our most gracious mistress.
　Leon.　　　Satisfy!
The entreaties of your mistress! satisfy!
Let that suffice. I have trusted thee, Camillo,
With all the nearest things to my heart, as
　well
My chamber-councils, wherein, priest-like, thou
Hast cleans'd my bosom: I from thee departed
Thy penitent reform'd; but we have been
Deceiv'd in thy integrity, deceiv'd　　240
In that which seems so.
　Cam.　　Be it forbid, my lord!
　Leon. To bide upon 't, thou art not honest; or,
If thou inclin'st that way, thou art a coward,
Which hoxes honesty behind, restraining 244
From course requir'd; or else thou must be
　counted
A servant grafted in my serious trust,
And therein negligent; or else a fool
That seest a game play'd home, the rich stake
　drawn,　　　　　　　　248
And tak'st it all for jest.
　Cam.　　My gracious lord,
I may be negligent, foolish, and fearful;
In every one of these no man is free,
But that his negligence, his folly, fear,　252

Among the infinite doings of the world,
Sometime puts forth. In your affairs, my lord,
If ever I were wilful-negligent,
It was my folly; if industriously　　256
I play'd the fool, it was my negligence,
Not weighing well the end; if ever fearful
To do a thing, where I the issue doubted,
Whereof the execution did cry out　　260
Against the non-performance, 'twas a fear
Which oft infects the wisest: these, my lord,
Are such allow'd infirmities that honesty
Is never free of: but, beseech your Grace, 264
Be plainer with me; let me know my trespass
By its own visage; if I then deny it,
'Tis none of mine.
　Leon.　　Ha' not you seen, Camillo,—
But that's past doubt; you have, or your eye-
　glass　　　　　　　　268
Is thicker than a cuckold's horn,—or heard,—
For to a vision so apparent rumour
Cannot be mute,—or thought,—for cogitation
Resides not in that man that does not think,—
My wife is slippery? If thou wilt confess,— 273
Or else be impudently negative,
To have nor eyes, nor ears, nor thought,—then
　say
My wife's a hobby-horse; deserves a name 276
As rank as any flax-wench that puts to
Before her troth-plight: say 't and justify 't.
　Cam. I would not be a stander-by, to hear
My sovereign mistress clouded so, without 280
My present vengeance taken: 'shrew my heart,
You never spoke what did become you less
Than this; which to reiterate were sin
As deep as that, though true.
　Leon.　　Is whispering nothing? 284
Is leaning cheek to cheek? is meeting noses?
Kissing with inside lip? stopping the career
Of laughter with a sigh?—a note infallible
Of breaking honesty,—horsing foot on foot? 288
Skulking in corners? wishing clocks more swift?
Hours, minutes? noon, midnight? and all eyes
Blind with the pin and web but theirs, theirs
　only,
That would unseen be wicked? is this nothing?
Why, then the world and all that's in 't is no-
　thing;　　　　　　　　293
The covering sky is nothing; Bohemia nothing;
My wife is nothing; nor nothing have these
　nothings,
If this be nothing.
　Cam.　　Good my lord, be cur'd 296
Of this diseas'd opinion, and betimes;
For 'tis most dangerous.
　Leon.　　Say it be, 'tis true.
　Cam. No, no, my lord.
　Leon.　　It is; you lie, you lie:
I say thou liest, Camillo, and I hate thee; 300
Pronounce thee a gross lout, a mindless slave,
Or else a hovering temporizer, that
Canst with thine eyes at once see good and
　evil,
Inclining to them both: were my wife's liver 304
Infected as her life, she would not live
The running of one glass.
　Cam.　　Who does infect her?

Leon. Why, he that wears her like her medal, hanging
About his neck, Bohemia: who, if I   308
Had servants true about me, that bare eyes
To see alike mine honour as their profits,
Their own particular thrifts, they would do that
Which should undo more doing: ay, and thou,
His cup-bearer,—whom I from meaner form   313
Have bench'd and rear'd to worship, who mayst see
Plainly, as heaven sees earth, and earth sees heaven,
How I am galled,—mightst bespice a cup,   316
To give mine enemy a lasting wink;
Which draught to me were cordial.

Cam.   Sir, my lord,
I could do this, and that with no rash potion,
But with a lingering dram that should not work
Maliciously like poison: but I cannot   321
Believe this crack to be in my dread mistress,
So sovereignly being honourable.
I have lov'd thee,—

Leon.   Make that thy question, and go rot!
Dost think I am so muddy, so unsettled,   325
To appoint myself in this vexation; sully
The purity and whiteness of my sheets,
Which to preserve is sleep; which being spotted
Is goads, thorns, nettles, tails of wasps?   329
Give scandal to the blood o' the prince my son,
Who I do think is mine, and love as mine,
Without ripe moving to 't? Would I do this?
Could man so blench?

Cam.   I must believe you, sir: 333
I do; and will fetch off Bohemia for 't;
Provided that when he 's remov'd, your highness   335
Will take again your queen as yours at first,
Even for your son's sake; and thereby for sealing
The injury of tongues in courts and kingdoms
Known and allied to yours.

Leon.   Thou dost advise me
Even so as I mine own course have set down:
I'll give no blemish to her honour, none.   341

Cam. My lord,
Go then; and with a countenance as clear
As friendship wears at feasts, keep with Bohemia,
And with your queen. I am his cupbearer;   345
If from me he have wholesome beverage,
Account me not your servant.

Leon.   This is all:
Do 't, and thou hast the one half of my heart;
Do 't not, thou split'st thine own.

Cam.   I'll do 't, my lord.   349

Leon. I will seem friendly, as thou hast advis'd me.   [*Exit.*

Cam. O miserable lady! But, for me,
What case stand I in? I must be the poisoner
Of good Polixenes; and my ground to do 't   353
Is the obedience to a master; one
Who, in rebellion with himself will have
All that are his so too. To do this deed   356
Promotion follows. If I could find example
Of thousands that had struck anointed kings,
And flourish'd after, I'd not do 't; but since
Nor brass nor stone nor parchment bears not one,   360

Let villany itself forswear 't. I must
Forsake the court: to do 't, or no, is certain
To me a break-neck. Happy star reign now!
Here comes Bohemia.

Re-enter POLIXENES.

Pol.   This is strange: methinks   36
My favour here begins to warp. Not speak?—
Good day, Camillo.

Cam.   Hail, most royal sir!

Pol. What is the news i' the court?

Cam.   None rare, my lord.

Pol. The king hath on him such a countenance   36
As he had lost some province and a region
Lov'd as he loves himself: even now I met him
With customary compliment, when he,
Wafting his eyes to the contrary, and falling   37
A lip of much contempt, speeds from me and
So leaves me to consider what is breeding
That changes thus his manners.

Cam. I dare not know, my lord.   37

Pol. How! dare not! do not! Do you know and dare not
Be intelligent to me? 'Tis thereabouts;
For, to yourself, what you do know, you must
And cannot say you dare not. Good Camillo,
Your chang'd complexions are to me a mirror
Which shows me mine chang'd too; for I must be
A party in this alteration, finding
Myself thus alter'd with 't.

Cam.   There is a sickness   38
Which puts some of us in distemper; but
I cannot name the disease, and it is caught
Of you that yet are well.

Pol.   How! caught of me?
Make me not sighted like the basilisk: 38
I have look'd on thousands, who have sped the better
By my regard, but kill'd none so. Camillo,—
As you are certainly a gentleman, thereto
Clerk-like experienc'd, which no less adorns   39
Our gentry than our parents' noble names,
In whose success we are gentle,—I beseech you,
If you know aught which does behove my knowledge
Thereof to be inform'd, imprison it not   39
In ignorant concealment.

Cam.   I may not answer.

Pol. A sickness caught of me, and yet I well!
I must be answer'd. Dost thou hear, Camillo,
I conjure thee, by all the parts of man   40
Which honour does acknowledge,—whereof the least
Is not this suit of mine,—that thou declare
What incidency thou dost guess of harm
Is creeping toward me; how far off, how near
Which way to be prevented if to be;   40
If not, how best to bear it.

Cam.   Sir, I will tell you;
Since I am charg'd in honour and by him
That I think honourable. Therefore mark my counsel,   40
Which must be even as swiftly follow'd as

mean to utter it, or both yourself and me
Cry 'lost,' and so good night!
Pol.   On, good Camillo.
Cam. I am appointed him to murder you. 412
Pol. By whom, Camillo?
Cam.   By the king.
Pol.   For what?
Cam. He thinks, nay, with all confidence he
    swears,
As he had seen 't or been an instrument
To vice you to 't, that you have touch'd his queen
Forbiddenly.
Pol.   O, then my best blood turn 417
To an infected jelly, and my name
Be yok'd with his that did betray the Best!
Turn then my freshest reputation to   420
A savour, that may strike the dullest nostril
Where I arrive; and my approach be shunn'd,
Nay, hated too, worse than the great'st infec-
    tion
That e'er was heard or read!
Cam.   Swear his thought over
By each particular star in heaven and   425
By all their influences, you may as well
Forbid the sea for to obey the moon
As or by oath remove or counsel shake   428
The fabric of his folly, whose foundation
Is pil'd upon his faith, and will continue
The standing of his body.
Pol.   How should this grow?
Cam. I know not: but I am sure 'tis safer to
Avoid what's grown than question how 'tis
    born.   433
If therefore you dare trust my honesty,
That lies enclosed in this trunk, which you
Shall bear along impawn'd, away to-night! 436
Your followers I will whisper to the business,
And will by twos and threes at several posterns
Clear them o' the city. For myself, I'll put
My fortunes to your service, which are here 440
By this discovery lost. Be not uncertain;
For, by the honour of my parents, I
Have utter'd truth, which, if you seek to prove,
I dare not stand by; nor shall you be safer 444
Than one condemn'd by the king's own mouth,
    thereon
His execution sworn.
Pol.   I do believe thee:
I saw his heart in 's face. Give me thy hand:
Be pilot to me and thy places shall   448
Still neighbour mine. My ships are ready and
My people did expect my hence departure
Two days ago. This jealousy
Is for a precious creature: as she's rare   452
Must it be great, and, as his person's mighty
Must it be violent, and, as he does conceive
He is dishonour'd by a man which ever
Profess'd to him, why, his revenges must   456
In that be made more bitter. Fear o'ershades
    me:
Good expedition be my friend, and comfort
The gracious queen, part of his theme, but no-
    thing
Of his ill-ta'en suspicion! Come, Camillo; 460
I will respect thee as a father if
Thou bear'st my life off hence: let us avoid.

Cam. It is in mine authority to command
The keys of all the posterns: please your high-
    ness   464
To take the urgent hour. Come, sir, away!
                                  [*Exeunt.*

ACT II

SCENE I.—*Sicilia. A Room in the Palace.*

Enter HERMIONE, MAMILLIUS, *and* Ladies.

Her. Take the boy to you: he so troubles me,
'Tis past enduring.
First Lady.   Come, my gracious lord,
Shall I be your playfellow?
Mam.   No, I'll none of you.
First Lady. Why, my sweet lord?   4
Mam. You'll kiss me hard and speak to me
    as if
I were a baby still. I love you better.
Sec. Lady. And why so, my lord?
Mam.   Not for because
Your brows are blacker; yet black brows, they
    say,   8
Become some women best, so that there be not
Too much hair there, but in a semicircle,
Or a half-moon made with a pen.
Sec. Lady.   Who taught you this?
Mam. I learn'd it out of women's faces.
    Pray now,   12
What colour are your eyebrows?
First Lady.   Blue, my lord.
Mam. Nay, that's a mock: I have seen a
    lady's nose
That has been blue, but not her eyebrows.
Sec. Lady.   Hark ye;
The queen your mother rounds apace: we shall
Present our services to a fine new prince   17
One of these days; and then you'd wanton with
    us,
If we would have you.
First Lady.   She is spread of late
Into a goodly bulk: good time encounter her! 20
Her. What wisdom stirs amongst you? Come
    sir, now
I am for you again: pray you, sit by us,
And tell 's a tale.
Mam.   Merry or sad shall 't be?
Her. As merry as you will.
Mam.   A sad tale's best for winter. 24
I have one of sprites and goblins.
Her.   Let's have that, good sir.
Come on, sit down: come on, and do your best
To fright me with your sprites; you're power-
    ful at it.
Mam. There was a man,—
Her.   Nay, come, sit down; then on. 28
Mam. Dwelt by a churchyard. I will tell it
    softly;
Yond crickets shall not hear it.
Her.   Come on then,
And give 't me in mine ear.

Enter LEONTES, ANTIGONUS, Lords, *and Others.*

Leon. Was he met there? his train? Camillo
    with him?   32

First Lord. Behind the tuft of pines I met
them: never
Saw I men scour so on their way: I ey'd them
Even to their ships.
Leon. How blest am I
In my just censure, in my true opinion! 36
Alack, for lesser knowledge! How accurs'd
In being so blest! There may be in the cup
A spider steep'd, and one may drink, depart,
And yet partake no venom, for his knowledge 40
Is not infected; but if one present
The abhorr'd ingredient to his eye, make known
How he hath drunk, he cracks his gorge, his
sides,
With violent hefts. I have drunk, and seen the
spider. 44
Camillo was his help in this, his pandar:
There is a plot against my life, my crown;
All's true that is mistrusted: that false villain
Whom I employ'd was pre-employ'd by him: 48
He has discover'd my design, and I
Remain a pinch'd thing; yea, a very trick
For them to play at will. How came the posterns
So easily open?
First Lord. By his great authority; 52
Which often hath no less prevail'd than so
On your command.
Leon. I know't too well.
[*To* HERMIONE.] Give me the boy: I am glad
you did not nurse him: 55
Though he does bear some signs of me, yet you
Have too much blood in him.
Her. What is this? sport?
Leon. Bear the boy hence; he shall not come
about her;
Away with him!—[*Exit* MAMILLIUS, *attended.*]
and let her sport herself
With that she's big with; for 'tis Polixenes 60
Has made thee swell thus.
Her. But I'd say he had not,
And I'll be sworn you would believe my saying,
Howe'er you lean to the nayward.
Leon. You, my lords,
Look on her, mark her well; be but about 64
To say, 'she is a goodly lady,' and
The justice of your hearts will thereto add
''Tis pity she's not honest, honourable:'
Praise her but for this her without-door form,—
Which, on my faith deserves high speech,—and
straight 69
The shrug, the hum or ha, these petty brands
That calumny doth use,—O, I am out!—
That mercy does, for calumny will sear 72
Virtue itself: these shrugs, these hums and ha's,
When you have said 'she's goodly,' come be-
tween,
Ere you can say 'she's honest.' But be't known,
From him that has most cause to grieve it
should be, 76
She's an adulteress.
Her. Should a villain say so,
The most replenish'd villain in the world,
He were as much more villain: you, my lord,
Do but mistake.
Leon. You have mistook, my lady, 80
Polixenes for Leontes. O thou thing!

Which I'll not call a creature of thy place,
Lest barbarism, making me the precedent,
Should a like language use to all degrees, 8
And mannerly distinguishment leave out
Betwixt the prince and beggar: I have said
She's an adulteress; I have said with whom:
More, she's a traitor, and Camillo is 8
A federary with her, and one that knows
What she should shame to know herself
But with her most vile principal, that she's
A bed-swerver, even as bad as those 9
That vulgars give bold'st titles; ay, and privy
To this their late escape.
Her. No, by my life,
Privy to none of this. How will this grieve yo
When you shall come to clearer knowledge tha
You thus have publish'd me! Gentle my lord, 9
You scarce can right me throughly then to sa
You did mistake.
Leon. No; if I mistake
In those foundations which I build upon, 10
The centre is not big enough to bear
A schoolboy's top. Away with her to prison
He who shall speak for her is afar off guilty
But that he speaks.
Her. There's some ill planet reigns: 10
I must be patient till the heavens look
With an aspect more favourable. Good m
lords,
I am not prone to weeping, as our sex
Commonly are; the want of which vain dew 10
Perchance shall dry your pities; but I have
That honourable grief lodg'd here which burn
Worse than tears drown. Beseech you all, m
lords,
With thoughts so qualified as your charities 11
Shall best instruct you, measure me; and so
The king's will be perform'd!
Leon. [*To the* Guards.] Shall I be heard
Her. Who is't that goes with me? Beseec
your highness,
My women may be with me; for you see 11
My plight requires it. Do not weep, good fools
There is no cause: when you shall know you
mistress
Has deserv'd prison, then abound in tears
As I come out: this action I now go on 12
Is for my better grace. Adieu, my lord:
I never wish'd to see you sorry; now
I trust I shall. My women, come; you hav
leave.
Leon. Go, do our bidding: hence! 12
[*Exeunt* Queen *guarded, and* Ladies
First Lord. Beseech your highness call th
queen again.
Ant. Be certain what you do, sir, lest you
justice
Prove violence: in the which three great one
suffer,
Yourself, your queen, your son.
First Lord. For her, my lord, 12
I dare my life lay down, and will do't, sir,
Please you to accept it,—that the queen is spot
less
I' the eyes of heaven and to you: I mean,
In this which you accuse her.

Ant.   If it prove   132
he's otherwise, I'll keep my stables where
lodge my wife; I'll go in couples with her;
than when I feel and see her no further trust
  her;
for every inch of woman in the world,   136
—y, every dram of woman's flesh is false,
f she be.
  Leon. Hold your peaces!
  First Lord.   Good my lord,—
  Ant. It is for you we speak, not for ourselves.
'ou are abus'd, and by some putter-on   140
hat will be damn'd for't; would I knew the
  villain,
would land-damn him. Be she honour-
  flaw'd,—
have three daughters; the eldest is eleven,
he second and the third, nine and some five; 144
f this prove true, they'll pay for't: by mine
  honour,
'll geld them all; fourteen they shall not see,
'o bring false generations: they are co-heirs;
nd I had rather glib myself than they   148
hould not produce fair issue.
  Leon.   Cease! no more.
'ou smell this business with a sense as cold
s is a dead man's nose; but I do see't and feel't,
s you feel doing thus, and see withal   152
he instruments that feel.
  Ant.   If it be so,
Ve need no grave to bury honesty;
here's not a grain of it the face to sweeten
)f the whole dungy earth.
  Leon.   What! lack I credit? 156
  First Lord. I had rather you did lack than I,
  my lord,
Upon this ground; and more it would content
  me
'o have her honour true than your suspicion,
3e blam'd for't how you might.
  Leon.   Why, what need we 160
Commune with you of this, but rather follow
)ur forceful instigation? Our prerogative
:alls not your counsels, but our natural goodness
mparts this; which if you,—or stupified 164
)r seeming so in skill,—cannot or will not
Relish a truth like us, inform yourselves
Ve need no more of your advice: the matter,
he loss, the gain, the ordering on't, is all 168
'roperly ours.
  Ant.   And I wish, my liege,
'ou had only in your silent judgment tried it,
Vithout more overture.
  Leon.   How could that be?
:ither thou art most ignorant by age,   172
)r thou wert born a fool. Camillo's flight,
dded to their familiarity,
Vhich was as gross as ever touch'd conjecture,
'hat lack'd sight only, nought for approbation
3ut only seeing, all other circumstances   177
Made up to the deed, doth push on this proceeding:
'et, for a greater confirmation,—
'or in an act of this importance 'twere   180

Most piteous to be wild,—I have dispatch'd in
  post
To sacred Delphos, to Apollo's temple,
Cleomenes and Dion, whom you know
Of stuff'd sufficiency. Now, from the oracle 184
They will bring all; whose spiritual counsel had,
Shall stop or spur me. Have I done well?
  First Lord. Well done, my lord.
  Leon. Though I am satisfied and need no
  more   188
Than what I know, yet shall the oracle
Give rest to the minds of others, such as he
Whose ignorant credulity will not
Come up to the truth. So have we thought it
  good   192
From our free person she should be confin'd,
Lest that the treachery of the two fled hence
Be left her to perform. Come, follow us:
We are to speak in public; for this business 196
Will raise us all.
  Ant. [*Aside.*] To laughter, as I take it,
If the good truth were known.   [*Exeunt.*

SCENE II.—*The Same. The outer Room of a
  Prison.*

Enter PAULINA *and* Attendants.

  Paul. The keeper of the prison, call to him;
Let him have knowledge who I am.—[*Exit an
  Attendant.*] Good lady,
No court in Europe is too good for thee;
What dost thou then in prison?

Re-enter Attendant *with the* Gaoler.

                           Now, good sir, 4
You know me, do you not?
  Gaol.   For a worthy lady
And one whom much I honour.
  Paul.   Pray you then,
Conduct me to the queen.
  Gaol. I may not, madam: to the contrary 8
I have express commandment.
  Paul.   Here's ado,
To lock up honesty and honour from
The access of gentle visitors! Is't lawful, pray
  you,
To see her women? any of them? Emilia?   12
  Gaol. So please you, madam,
To put apart these your attendants, I
Shall bring Emilia forth.
  Paul.   I pray now, call her.
Withdraw yourselves.   [*Exeunt* Attendants.
  Gaol.   And madam,   16
I must be present at your conference.
  Paul. Well, be't so, prithee. [*Exit* Gaoler.
Here's such ado to make no stain a stain,
As passes colouring.

Re-enter Gaoler, *with* EMILIA.

                         Dear gentlewoman, 20
How fares our gracious lady?
  Emil. As well as one so great and so forlorn
May hold together. On her frights and griefs,—
Which never tender lady hath borne greater,—
She is something before her time deliver'd. 25

Paul. A boy?

Emil. A daughter; and a goodly babe,
Lusty and like to live: the queen receives
Much comfort in't; says, 'My poor prisoner, 28
I am innocent as you.'

Paul. I dare be sworn:
These dangerous unsafe lunes i' the king, be-
    shrew them!
He must be told on't, and he shall: the office
Becomes a woman best; I'll take't upon me. 32
If I prove honey-mouth'd, let my tongue blister,
And never to my red-look'd anger be
The trumpet any more. Pray you, Emilia,
Commend my best obedience to the queen: 36
If she dares trust me with her little babe,
I'll show it to the king and undertake to be
Her advocate to the loud'st. We do not know
How he may soften at the sight of the child: 40
The silence often of pure innocence
Persuades when speaking fails.

Emil. Most worthy madam,
Your honour and your goodness is so evident
That your free undertaking cannot miss 44
A thriving issue: there is no lady living
So meet for this great errand. Please your lady-
    ship
To visit the next room, I'll presently
Acquaint the queen of your most noble offer, 48
Who but to-day hammer'd of this design,
But durst not tempt a minister of honour,
Lest she should be denied.

Paul. Tell her, Emilia,
I'll use that tongue I have: if wit flow from't 52
As boldness from my bosom, let it not be
    doubted
I shall do good.

Emil. Now be you blest for it!
I'll to the queen. Please you, come something
    nearer.

Gaol. Madam, if't please the queen to send
    the babe, 56
I know not what I shall incur to pass it,
Having no warrant.

Paul. You need not fear it, sir:
The child was prisoner to the womb, and is
By law and process of great nature thence 60
Freed and enfranchis'd; not a party to
The anger of the king, nor guilty of,
If any be, the trespass of the queen.

Gaol. I do believe it. 64

Paul. Do not you fear: upon mine honour, I
Will stand betwixt you and danger. [*Exeunt.*

SCENE III.—*The Same. A Room in the
    Palace.*

Enter LEONTES, ANTIGONUS, Lords, *and other*
    Attendants.

Leon. Nor night, nor day, no rest; it is but
    weakness
To bear the matter thus; mere weakness. If
The cause were not in being,—part o' the cause,
She the adulteress; for the harlot king 4
Is quite beyond mine arm, out of the blank
And level of my brain, plot-proof; but she

I can hook to me: say, that she were gone,
Given to the fire, a moiety of my rest
Might come to me again. Who's there?

First Atten. [*Advancing.*] My lord?

Leon. How does the boy?

First Atten. He took good rest to-night;
'Tis hop'd his sickness is discharg'd.

Leon. To see his nobleness! 1
Conceiving the dishonour of his mother,
He straight declin'd, droop'd, took it deeply,
Fasten'd and fix'd the shame on't in himself,
Threw off his spirit, his appetite, his sleep, 1
And downright languish'd. Leave me solely
    go,
See how he fares. [*Exit* Attendant.]—Fie, fie
    no thought of him;
The very thought of my revenges that way
Recoil upon me: in himself too mighty, 2
And in his parties, his alliance; let him be
Until a time may serve: for present vengeance
Take it on her. Camillo and Polixenes
Laugh at me; make their pastime at my sor-
    row: 2
They should not laugh, if I could reach them, no
Shall be within my power.

Enter PAULINA, *with a* Child.

First Lord. You must not enter

Paul. Nay, rather, good my lords, be second
    to me:
Fear you his tyrannous passion more, alas, 2
Than the queen's life? a gracious innocent soul
More free than he is jealous.

Ant. That's enough.

Sec. Atten. Madam, he hath not slept to-
    night; commanded
None should come at him.

Paul. Not so hot, good sir; 3
I come to bring him sleep. 'Tis such as you,
That creep like shadows by him and do sigh
At each his needless heavings, such as you
Nourish the cause of his waking: I 3
Do come with words as med'cinal as true,
Honest as either, to purge him of that humour
That presses him from sleep.

Leon. What noise there, ho?

Paul. No noise, my lord; but needful confer-
    ence
About some gossips for your highness.

Leon. How! 4
Away with that audacious lady! Antigonus,
I charg'd thee that she should not come about
    me:
I knew she would.

Ant. I told her so, my lord, 4
On your displeasure's peril, and on mine,
She should not visit you.

Leon. What! canst not rule her?

Paul. From all dishonesty he can: in this,
Unless he take the course that you have done,
Commit me for committing honour, trust it, 4
He shall not rule me.

Ant. La you now! you hear:
When she will take the rein I let her run;
But she'll not stumble.

Paul. Good my liege, I come. 5

And I beseech you, hear me, who professes
Myself your loyal servant, your physician,
Your most obedient counsellor, yet that dares
Less appear so in comforting your evils   56
Than such as most seem yours: I say, I come
From your good queen.
  Leon.   Good queen!
  Paul. Good queen, my lord, good queen; I
say, good queen;
And would by combat make her good, so were I
A man, the worst about you.
  Leon.   Force her hence.   61
  Paul. Let him that makes but trifles of his
eyes
First hand me: on mine own accord I'll off;
But first I'll do my errand. The good queen,   64
For she is good, hath brought you forth a
daughter:
Here 'tis; commends it to your blessing.
                [Laying down the Child.
  Leon.   Out!
A mankind witch! Hence with her, out o' door:
A most intelligencing bawd!
  Paul.   Not so;   68
I am as ignorant in that as you
In so entitling me, and no less honest
Than you are mad; which is enough, I'll
warrant,
As this world goes, to pass for honest.
  Leon.   Traitors!   72
Will you not push her out? Give her the
bastard.
To ANTIGONUS.] Thou dotard! thou art woman-
tir'd, unroosted
By thy dame Partlet here. Take up the bastard;
Take't up, I say; give't to thy crone.
  Paul.   For ever   76
Unvenerable be thy hands, if thou
Tak'st up the princess by that forced baseness
Which he has put upon't!
  Leon.   He dreads his wife.
  Paul. So I would you did; then, 'twere past
all doubt,   80
You'd call your children yours.
  Leon.   A nest of traitors!
  Ant. I am none, by this good light.
  Paul.   Nor I; nor any
But one that's here, and that's himself; for he
The sacred honour of himself, his queen's,   84
His hopeful son's, his babe's, betrays to slander,
Whose sting is sharper than the sword's; and
will not,—
For, as the case now stands, it is a curse
He cannot be compell'd to't,—once remove   88
The root of his opinion, which is rotten
As ever oak or stone was sound.
  Leon.   A callat
Of boundless tongue, who late hath beat her
husband
And now baits me! This brat is none of mine;
It is the issue of Polixenes: 93
Hence with it; and, together with the dam
Commit them to the fire!
  Paul.   It is yours;
And, might we lay the old proverb to your
charge,   96

'So like you, 'tis the worse.' Behold, my lords,
Although the print be little, the whole matter
And copy of the father; eye, nose, lip,
The trick of 's frown, his forehead, nay, the
valley,   100
The pretty dimples of his chin and cheek, his
smiles,
The very mould and frame of hand, nail, finger:
And thou, good goddess Nature, which hast
made it
So like to him that got it, if thou hast   104
The ordering of the mind too, 'mongst all
colours
No yellow in't; lest she suspect, as he does,
Her children not her husband's.
  Leon.   A gross hag!
And, lozel, thou art worthy to be hang'd,   108
That wilt not stay her tongue.
  Ant.   Hang all the husbands
That cannot do that feat, you'll leave yourself
Hardly one subject.
  Leon.   Once more, take her hence.
  Paul. A most unworthy and unnatural lord
Can do no more.
  Leon.   I'll ha' thee burn'd.
  Paul.   I care not:
It is a heretic that makes the fire,
Not she which burns in't. I'll not call you
tyrant;
But this most cruel usage of your queen,—   116
Not able to produce more accusation
Than your own weak-hing'd fancy,—something
savours
Of tyranny, and will ignoble make you,
Yea, scandalous to the world.
  Leon.   On your allegiance,   120
Out of the chamber with her! Were I a tyrant,
Where were her life? she durst not call me so
If she did know me one. Away with her!
  Paul. I pray you do not push me; I'll be
gone.   124
Look to your babe, my lord; 'tis yours: Jove
send her
A better guiding spirit! What need these hands?
You, that are thus so tender o'er his follies,
Will never do him good, not one of you.   128
So, so: farewell; we are gone.   [*Exit.*
  Leon. Thou, traitor, hast set on thy wife to
this.
My child! away with't!—even thou, that hast
A heart so tender o'er it, take it hence   132
And see it instantly consum'd with fire:
Even thou and none but thou. Take it up
straight:
Within this hour bring me word 'tis done,—
And by good testimony,—or I'll seize thy life,
With what thou else call'st thine. If thou refuse
And wilt encounter with my wrath, say so;
The bastard brains with these my proper hands
Shall I dash out. Go, take it to the fire;   140
For thou sett'st on thy wife.
  Ant.   I did not, sir:
These lords, my noble fellows, if they please,
Can clear me in't.
  First Lord.   We can, my royal liege,
He is not guilty of her coming hither.   144

Leon. You are liars all.

First Lord. Beseech your highness, give us better credit:

We have always truly serv'd you, and beseech you

So to esteem of us; and on our knees we beg, 148
As recompense of our dear services
Past and to come, that you do change this purpose,
Which being so horrible, so bloody, must
Lead on to some foul issue. We all kneel. 152

Leon. I am a feather for each wind that blows.
Shall I live on to see this bastard kneel
And call me father? Better burn it now
Than curse it then. But, be it; let it live: 156
It shall not neither.—[*To* ANTIGONUS.] You, sir, come you hither;
You that have been so tenderly officious
With Lady Margery, your midwife there,
To save this bastard's life,—for 'tis a bastard,
So sure as thy beard's grey,—what will you adventure 161
To save this brat's life?

Ant. Any thing, my lord,
That my ability may undergo,
And nobleness impose: at least, thus much: 164
I'll pawn the little blood which I have left,
To save the innocent: any thing possible.

Leon. It shall be possible. Swear by this sword
Thou wilt perform my bidding.

Ant. I will, my lord. 168

Leon. Mark and perform it,—seest thou!—for the fail
Of any point in 't shall not only be
Death to thyself, but to thy lewd-tongu'd wife,
Whom for this time we pardon. We enjoin thee,
As thou art liegeman to us, that thou carry 173
This female bastard hence; and that thou bear it
To some remote and desart place quite out
Of our dominions; and that there thou leave it,
Without more mercy, to its own protection, 177
And favour of the climate. As by strange fortune
It came to us, I do in justice charge thee,
On thy soul's peril and thy body's torture, 180
That thou commend it strangely to some place,
Where chance may nurse or end it. Take it up.

Ant. I swear to do this, though a present death
Had been more merciful. Come on, poor babe:
Some powerful spirit instruct the kites and ravens 185
To be thy nurses! Wolves and bears, they say,
Casting their savageness aside have done
Like offices of pity. Sir, be prosperous 188
In more than this deed doth require! And blessing
Against this cruelty fight on thy side,
Poor thing, condemn'd to loss!

[*Exit with the* Child.

Leon. No; I'll not rear
Another's issue.

Enter a Servant.

Serv. Please your highness, posts 192
From those you sent to the oracle are come
An hour since: Cleomenes and Dion,
Being well arriv'd from Delphos, are both landed,
Hasting to the court.

First Lord. So please you, sir, their speed
Hath been beyond account.

Leon. Twenty-three day
They have been absent: 'tis good speed; foretel
The great Apollo suddenly will have 19
The truth of this appear. Prepare you, lords
Summon a session, that we may arraign
Our most disloyal lady; for, as she hath
Been publicly accus'd, so shall she have
A just and open trial. While she lives 20
My heart will be a burden to me. Leave me,
And think upon my bidding.

[*Exeunt*

ACT III

SCENE I.—*A Sea-port in Sicilia.*

Enter CLEOMENES *and* DION.

Cleo. The climate's delicate, the air most sweet,
Fertile the isle, the temple much surpassing
The common praise it bears.

Dion. I shall report,
For most it caught me, the celestial habits,—
Methinks I so should term them,—and the reverence
Of the grave wearers. O, the sacrifice!
How ceremonious, solemn, and unearthly
It was i' the offering!

Cleo. But of all, the burst
And the ear-deafening voice o' the oracle,
Kin to Jove's thunder, so surpris'd my sense,
That I was nothing.

Dion. If the event o' the journey
Prove as successful to the queen,—O, be 't so!—
As it hath been to us rare, pleasant, speedy,
The time is worth the use on 't.

Cleo. Great Apollo
Turn all to the best! These proclamations,
So forcing faults upon Hermione,
I little like.

Dion. The violent carriage of it
Will clear or end the business: when the oracle
Thus by Apollo's great divine seal'd up,
Shall the contents discover, something rare
Even then will rush to knowledge.—Go:—fresh horses!
And gracious be the issue! [*Exeunt*

SCENE II.—*Sicilia. A Court of Justice.*

LEONTES, Lords, *and* Officers.

Leon. This sessions, to our great grief we pronounce,
Even pushes 'gainst our heart: the party tried
The daughter of a king, our wife, and one
Of us too much belov'd. Let us be clear'd
Of being tyrannous, since we so openly
Proceed in justice, which shall have due course
Even to the guilt or the purgation.
Produce the prisoner.

Offi. It is his highness' pleasure that the queen
Appear in person here in court. Silence!

Enter HERMIONE *guarded;* PAULINA *and
Ladies attending.*

Leon. Read the indictment.　　　　　　11

Offi. Hermione, queen to the worthy Leontes, *King of Sicilia, thou art here accused and arraigned of high treason, in committing adultery with Polixenes, King of Bohemia, and conspiring with Camillo to take away the life of our soveraign lord the king, thy royal husband: the pretence whereof being by circumstances partly laid open, thou, Hermione, contrary to the faith and allegiance of a true subject, didst counsel and aid them, for their better safety, to fly away by night.*

Her. Since what I am to say must be but that
Which contradicts my accusation, and　　24
The testimony on my part no other
But what comes from myself, it shall scarce boot me
To say 'Not guilty:' mine integrity
Being counted falsehood, shall, as I express it,
Be so receiv'd. But thus: if powers divine　29
Behold our human actions, as they do,
I doubt not then but innocence shall make
False accusation blush, and tyranny　　32
Tremble at patience. You, my lord, best know,—
Who least will seem to do so,—my past life
Hath been as continent, as chaste, as true,
As I am now unhappy; which is more　　36
Than history can pattern, though devis'd
And play'd to take spectators. For behold me,
A fellow of the royal bed, which owe
A moiety of the throne, a great king's daughter,
The mother to a hopeful prince, here standing
To prate and talk for life and honour 'fore
Who please to come and hear. For life, I prize it
As I weigh grief, which I would spare: for honour,　　44
'Tis a derivative from me to mine,
And only that I stand for. I appeal
To your own conscience, sir, before Polixenes
Came to your court, how I was in your grace,　48
How merited to be so; since he came,
With what encounter so uncurrent I
Have strain'd, to appear thus: if one jot beyond
The bound of honour, or in act or will　52
That way inclining, harden'd be the hearts
Of all that hear me, and my near'st of kin
Cry fie upon my grave!

Leon.　　　　　　　I ne'er heard yet
That any of these bolder vices wanted　　56
Less impudence to gainsay what they did
Than to perform it first.

Her.　　　　　　　That's true enough;
Though 'tis a saying, sir, not due to me.

Leon. You will not own it.

Her.　　　　　　More than mistress of　60
Which comes to me in name of fault, I must not
At all acknowledge. For Polixenes,—
With whom I am accus'd,—I do confess
I lov'd him as in honour he requir'd,　　64
With such a kind of love as might become

A lady like me; with a love even such,
So and no other, as yourself commanded:
Which not to have done I think had been in me
Both disobedience and ingratitude　　69
To you and toward your friend, whose love had spoke,
Even since it could speak, from an infant, freely
That it was yours. Now, for conspiracy,　72
I know not how it tastes, though it be dish'd
For me to try how: all I know of it
Is that Camillo was an honest man;
And why he left your court, the gods themselves,
Wotting no more than I, are ignorant.　　77

Leon. You knew of his departure, as you know
What you have underta'en to do in 's absence.

Her. Sir,　　　　　　80
You speak a language that I understand not:
My life stands in the level of your dreams,
Which I'll lay down.

Leon.　　　　　Your actions are my dreams:
You had a bastard by Polixenes,　　84
And I but dream'd it. As you were past all shame,—
Those of your fact are so,—so past all truth:
Which to deny concerns more than avails; for as
Thy brat hath been cast out, like to itself,　88
No father owning it,—which is, indeed,
More criminal in thee than it,—so thou
Shalt feel our justice, in whose easiest passage
Look for no less than death.

Her.　　　　　Sir, spare your threats: 92
The bug which you would fright me with I seek.
To me can life be no commodity:
The crown and comfort of my life, your favour,
I do give lost; for I do feel it gone,　　96
But know not how it went. My second joy,
And first-fruits of my body, from his presence
I am barr'd, like one infectious. My third comfort,
Starr'd most unluckily, is from my breast, 100
The innocent milk in its most innocent mouth,
Hal'd out to murder: myself on every post
Proclaim'd a strumpet: with immodest hatred
The child-bed privilege denied, which 'longs 104
To women of all fashion: lastly, hurried
Here to this place, i' the open air, before
I have got strength of limit. Now, my liege,
Tell me what blessings I have here alive,　108
That I should fear to die? Therefore proceed.
But yet hear this; mistake me not; no life,
I prize it not a straw:—but for mine honour,
Which I would free, if I shall be condemn'd 112
Upon surmises, all proofs sleeping else
But what your jealousies awake, I tell you
'Tis rigour and not law. Your honours all,
I do refer me to the oracle:　　116
Apollo be my judge!

First Lord.　　　This your request
Is altogether just: therefore, bring forth,
And in Apollo's name, his oracle.

[*Exeunt certain* Officers.

Her. The Emperor of Russia was my father:
O! that he were alive, and here beholding 121
His daughter's trial; that he did but see
The flatness of my misery; yet with eyes
Of pity, not revenge!　　124

Re-enter Officers, *with* CLEOMENES *and* DION.

Offi. You here shall swear upon this sword
of justice,
That you, Cleomenes and Dion, have
Been both at Delphos, and from thence have
brought
This seal'd-up oracle, by the hand deliver'd 128
Of great Apollo's priest, and that since then
You have not dar'd to break the holy seal,
Nor read the secrets in't.

Cleo.)
Dion.)   All this we swear.

Leon. Break up the seals, and read.   132

Offi. Hermione is chaste; Polixenes blameless; Camillo a true subject; Leontes a jealous
tyrant; his innocent babe truly begotten; and
the king shall live without an heir if that which
is lost be not found!   137

Lords. Now blessed be the great Apollo!

Her.   Praised!

Leon. Hast thou read truth?

Offi.   Ay, my lord; even so
As it is here set down.   140

Leon. There is no truth at all i' the oracle:
The sessions shall proceed: this is mere falsehood.

Enter a Servant.

Serv. My lord the king, the king!

Leon.   What is the business?

Serv. O sir! I shall be hated to report it: 144
The prince your son, with mere conceit and
fear
Of the queen's speed, is gone.

Leon.   How! gone!

Serv.   Is dead.

Leon. Apollo's angry; and the heavens
themselves
Do strike at my injustice. [HERMIONE *swoons.*
                           How now, there! 148

Paul. This news is mortal to the queen:—
look down,
And see what death is doing.

Leon.   Take her hence:
Her heart is but o'ercharg'd; she will recover:
I have too much believ'd mine own suspicion:
Beseech you, tenderly apply to her   153
Some remedies for life.—

[*Exeunt* PAULINA, *and* Ladies, *with* HER-
MIONE.
                           Apollo, pardon
My great profaneness 'gainst thine oracle!
I'll reconcile me to Polixenes,   156
New woo my queen, recall the good Camillo,
Whom I proclaim a man of truth, of mercy;
For, being transported by my jealousies
To bloody thoughts and to revenge, I chose 160
Camillo for the minister to poison
My friend Polixenes: which had been done,
But that the good mind of Camillo tardied
My swift command; though I with death and
with   164
Reward did threaten and encourage him,
Not doing it, and being done: he, most humane
And fill'd with honour, to my kingly guest
Unclasp'd my practice, quit his fortunes here, 168

Which you knew great, and to the certain hazard
Of all incertainties himself commended,
No richer than his honour: how he glisters
Thorough my rust! and how his piety   172
Does my deeds make the blacker!

Re-enter PAULINA.

Paul.   Woe the while!
O, cut my lace, lest my heart, cracking it,
Break too!

First Lord. What fit is this, good lady?

Paul. What studied torments, tyrant, hast
for me?   176
What wheels? racks? fires? What flaying? or
what boiling
In leads, or oils? what old or newer torture
Must I receive, whose every word deserves
To taste of thy most worst? Thy tyranny, 180
Together working with thy jealousies,
Fancies too weak for boys, too green and idle
For girls of nine, O! think what they have done,
And then run mad indeed, stark mad; for all 184
Thy by-gone fooleries were but spices of it.
That thou betray'dst Polixenes, 'twas nothing;
That did but show thee of a fool, inconstant
And damnable ingrateful; nor was't much 188
Thou wouldst have poison'd good Camillo's
honour
To have him kill a king; poor trespasses,
More monstrous standing by: whereof I reckon
The casting forth to crows thy baby daughter 192
To be or none or little; though a devil
Would have shed water out of fire ere done't:
Nor is't directly laid to thee, the death
Of the young prince, whose honourable
thoughts,—   196
Thoughts high for one so tender,—cleft the heart
That could conceive a gross and foolish sire
Blemish'd his gracious dam: this is not, no,
Laid to thy answer: but the last,—O lords! 200
When I have said, cry, 'woe!'—the queen, the
queen,
The sweetest, dearest creature's dead, and ven-
geance for't
Not dropp'd down yet.

First Lord.   The higher powers forbid!

Paul. I say she's dead; I'll swear't: if word
nor oath   204
Prevail not, go and see: if you can bring
Tincture or lustre in her lip, her eye,
Heat outwardly, or breath within, I'll serve you
As I would do the gods. But, O thou tyrant! 208
Do not repent these things, for they are heavier
Than all thy woes can stir; therefore betake thee
To nothing but despair. A thousand knees
Ten thousand years together, naked, fasting, 212
Upon a barren mountain, and still winter
In storm perpetual, could not move the gods
To look that way thou wert.

Leon.   Go on, go on;
Thou canst not speak too much: I have deserv'd
All tongues to talk their bitterest.

First Lord.   Say no more: 217
Howe'er the business goes, you have made fault
I' the boldness of your speech.

Paul.   I am sorry for't:

ll faults I make, when I shall come to know
  them,   220
do repent. Alas! I have show'd too much
he rashness of a woman: he is touch'd
o the noble heart. What's gone and what's
  past help
ould be past grief: do not receive affliction 224
t my petition; I beseech you, rather
et me be punish'd, that have minded you
f what you should forget. Now, good my liege,
r, royal sir, forgive a foolish woman: 228
he love I bore your queen,—lo, fool again!—
l speak of her no more, nor of your children;
l not remember you of my own lord,
ho is lost too: take your patience to you, 232
nd I'll say nothing.
  Leon.   Thou didst speak but well,
hen most the truth, which I receive much
  better
han to be pitied of thee. Prithee, bring me
o the dead bodies of my queen and son: 236
he grave shall be for both: upon them shall
he causes of their death appear, unto
ur shame perpetual. Once a day I'll visit
he chapel where they lie, and tears shed there
all be my recreation: so long as nature 241
ill bear up with this exercise, so long
daily vow to use it. Come and lead me
nto these sorrows.   *[Exeunt.*

ENE III.—*Bohemia. A desert Country near
        the Sea.*

Enter ANTIGONUS, *with the* Child; *and a*
      Mariner.

  Ant. Thou art perfect, then, our ship hath
  touch'd upon
he desarts of Bohemia?
  Mar.   Ay, my lord; and fear
e have landed in ill time: the skies look grimly
nd threaten present blusters. In my conscience,   4
he heavens with that we have in hand are
  angry,
nd frown upon's.
  Ant. Their sacred wills be done! Go, get
ook to thy bark: I'll not be long before 8
call upon thee.
  Mar.   Make your best haste, and go not
oo far i' the land: 'tis like to be loud weather;
esides, this place is famous for the creatures
f prey that keep upon't.
  Ant.   Go thou away: 12
ll follow instantly.
  Mar.   I am glad at heart
o be so rid of the business.   *[Exit.*
  Ant.   Come, poor babe:
have heard, but not believ'd, the spirits o' the
  dead
[ay walk again: if such thing be, thy mother 16
ppear'd to me last night, for ne'er was dream
o like a waking. To me comes a creature,
ometimes her head on one side, some another;
never saw a vessel of like sorrow,   20
o fill'd, and so becoming: in pure white robes,

Like very sanctity, she did approach
My cabin where I lay; thrice bow'd before me,
And, gasping to begin some speech, her eyes 24
Became two spouts: the fury spent, anon
Did this break from her: 'Good Antigonus,
Since fate, against thy better disposition,
Hath made thy person for the thrower-out 28
Of my poor babe, according to thine oath,
Places remote enough are in Bohemia,
There weep and leave it crying; and, for the
  babe
Is counted lost for ever, Perdita,   32
I prithee, call't: for this ungentle business,
Put on thee by my lord, thou ne'er shalt see
Thy wife Paulina more:' and so, with shrieks,
She melted into air. Affrighted much,   36
I did in time collect myself, and thought
This was so and no slumber. Dreams are toys;
Yet for this once, yea, superstitiously,
I will be squar'd by this. I do believe   40
Hermione hath suffer'd death; and that
Apollo would, this being indeed the issue
Of King Polixenes, it should here be laid,
Either for life or death, upon the earth 44
Of its right father. Blossom, speed thee well!
              [Laying down Child.
There lie; and there thy character: there these;
              [Laying down a bundle.
Which may, if fortune please, both breed thee,
  pretty,
And still rest thine. The storm begins: poor
  wretch!   48
That for thy mother's fault art thus expos'd
To loss and what may follow. Weep I cannot,
But my heart bleeds, and most accurs'd am I
To be by oath enjoin'd to this. Farewell! 52
The day frowns more and more: thou art like
  to have
A lullaby too rough. I never saw
The heavens so dim by day. A savage clamour!
Well may I get aboard! This is the chase: 56
I am gone for ever.   *[Exit, pursued by a bear.*

        Enter a Shepherd.

  Shep. I would there were no age between
sixteen and three-and-twenty, or that youth
would sleep out the rest; for there is nothing in
the between but getting wenches with child,
wronging the ancientry, stealing, fighting. Hark
you now! Would any but these boiled brains
of nineteen and two-and-twenty hunt this weather? They have scared away two of my best
sheep; which I fear the wolf will sooner find
than the master: if anywhere I have them, 'tis
by the sea-side, browsing of ivy. Good luck,
an't be thy will! what have we here? [*Taking
up the* Child.] Mercy on 's, a barne; a very pretty
barne! A boy or a child, I wonder? A pretty
one; a very pretty one; sure some scape: though
I am not bookish, yet I can read waiting-gentle-
woman in the scape. This has been some
stair-work, some trunk-work, some behind-door-
work; they were warmer that got this than the
poor thing is here. I'll take it up for pity; yet
I'll tarry till my son come; he hollaed but even
now. Whoa, ho, hoa!   79

Enter Clown.

Clo. Hilloa, loa!

Shep. What! art so near? If thou'lt see a
thing to talk on when thou art dead and rotten,
come hither. What ailest thou, man?   83

Clo. I have seen two such sights by sea and
by land! but I am not to say it is a sea, for it is
now the sky: betwixt the firmament and it you
cannot thrust a bodkin's point.

Shep. Why, boy, how is it?   88

Clo. I would you did but see how it chafes,
how it rages, how it takes up the shore! but
that's not to the point. O! the most piteous
cry of the poor souls; sometimes to see 'em,
and not to see 'em; now the ship boring the
moon with her mainmast, and anon swallowed
with yest and froth, as you'd thrust a cork into
a hogshead. And then for the land-service: to
see how the bear tore out his shoulderbone;
how he cried to me for help and said his name
was Antigonus, a nobleman. But to make an
end of the ship: to see how the sea flap-dragoned
it: but, first, how the poor souls roared, and the
sea mocked them; and how the poor gentleman
roared, and the bear mocked him, both roaring
louder than the sea or weather.   104

Shep. Name of mercy! when was this, boy?

Clo. Now, now; I have not winked since I
saw these sights: the men are not yet cold under
water, nor the bear half dined on the gentleman: he's at it now.   109

Shep. Would I had been by, to have helped
the old man!

Clo. I would you had been by the ship's side,
to have helped her: there your charity would
have lacked footing.   114

Shep. Heavy matters! heavy matters! but
look thee here, boy. Now bless thyself: thou
mettest with things dying, I with things new
born. Here's a sight for thee; look thee, a
bearing-cloth for a squire's child! Look thee
here: take up, take up, boy; open't. So, let's
see: it was told me, I should be rich by the
fairies: this is some changeling.—Open't.
What's within, boy?   123

Clo. You're a made old man: if the sins of
your youth are forgiven you, you're well to
live. Gold! all gold!

Shep. This is fairy gold, boy, and 'twill prove
so: up with 't, keep it close: home, home, the
next way. We are lucky, boy; and to be so
still, requires nothing but secrecy. Let my
sheep go. Come, good boy, the next way home.

Clo. Go you the next way with your findings.
I'll go see if the bear be gone from the gentleman, and how much he hath eaten; they are
never curst but when they are hungry. If there
be any of him left, I'll bury it.   136

Shep. That's a good deed. If thou mayst
discern by that which is left of him what he is,
fetch me to the sight of him.

Clo. Marry, will I; and you shall help to put
him i' the ground.   141

Shep. 'Tis a lucky day, boy, and we'll do
good deeds on't.   [*Exeunt.*

ACT IV

Enter Time, *the Chorus.*

Time. I, that please some, try all, both j
     and terror
Of good and bad, that make and unfold error,
Now take upon me, in the name of Time,
To use my wings. Impute it not a crime
To me or my swift passage, that I slide
O'er sixteen years, and leave the growth untri
Of that wide gap; since it is in my power
To o'erthrow law, and in one self-born hour
To plant and o'erwhelm custom. Let me pass
The same I am, ere ancient'st order was
Or what is now receiv'd: I witness to
The times that brought them in; so shall I do
To the freshest things now reigning, and ma
     stale
The glistering of this present, as my tale
Now seems to it. Your patience this allowing,
I turn my glass and give my scene such gro
     ing
As you had slept between. Leontes leaving,—
The effects of his fond jealousies so grieving,
That he shuts up himself,—imagine me,
Gentle spectators, that I now may be
In fair Bohemia; and remember well,
I mention'd a son o' the king's, which Floriz
I now name to you; and with speed so pace
To speak of Perdita, now grown in grace
Equal with wondering: what of her ensues
I list not prophesy; but let Time's news
Be known when 'tis brought forth. A shepher
     daughter,
And what to her adheres, which follows afte
Is th' argument of Time. Of this allow,
If ever you have spent time worse ere now;
If never, yet that Time himself doth say
He wishes earnestly you never may.   [*Ex*

SCENE I.—*Bohemia. A Room in the Palace*
     POLIXENES.

Enter POLIXENES *and* CAMILLO.

Pol. I pray thee, good Camillo, be no m
importunate: 'tis a sickness denying thee ar
thing; a death to grant this.

Cam. It is fifteen years since I saw
country: though I have for the most part be
aired abroad, I desire to lay my bones be
Besides, the penitent king, my master, hath s
for me; to whose feeling sorrows I might
some allay, or I o'erween to think so, which
another spur to my departure.

Pol. As thou lovest me, Camillo, wipe
out the rest of thy services by leaving me no
The need I have of thee thine own goodness h
made: better not to have had thee than thus
want thee. Thou, having made me busines
which none without thee can sufficiently mana
must either stay to execute them thyself or ta
away with thee the very services thou hast do
which if I have not enough considered,—as
much I cannot,—to be more thankful to t
shall be my study, and my profit therein,

leaping friendships. Of that fatal country, Sicilia, prithee speak no more, whose very naming punishes me with the remembrance of that penitent, as thou callest him, and reconciled king, my brother; whose loss of his most precious queen and children are even now to be afresh lamented. Say to me, when sawest thou the Prince Florizel, my son? Kings are no less unhappy, their issue not being gracious, than they are in losing them when they have approved their virtues.

Cam. Sir, it is three days since I saw the prince. What his happier affairs may be, are to me unknown; but I have missingly noted he is of late much retired from court, and is less frequent to his princely exercises than formerly he hath appeared.   37

Pol. I have considered so much, Camillo, and with some care; so far, that I have eyes under my service which look upon his removedness; from whom I have this intelligence, that he is seldom from the house of a most homely shepherd; a man, they say, that from very nothing, and beyond the imagination of his neighbours, is grown into an unspeakable estate.   45

Cam. I have heard, sir, of such a man, who hath a daughter of most rare note: the report of her is extended more than can be thought to begin from such a cottage.   49

Pol. That's likewise part of my intelligence; but I fear, the angle that plucks our son thither. Thou shalt accompany us to the place; where we will, not appearing what we are, have some question with the shepherd; from whose simplicity I think it not uneasy to get the cause of my son's resort thither. Prithee, be my present partner in this business, and lay aside the thoughts of Sicilia.   58

Cam. I willingly obey your command.

Pol. My best Camillo!—We must disguise ourselves.   [*Exeunt.*

SCENE II.—*The Same. A Road near the Shepherd's Cottage.*

Enter AUTOLYCUS, *singing.*

When daffodils begin to peer,
  With heigh! the doxy, over the dale,
Why, then comes in the sweet o' the year;
  For the red blood reigns in the winter's pale.   4

The white sheet bleaching on the hedge,
  With heigh! the sweet birds, O, how they sing!
Doth set my pugging tooth on edge;
  For a quart of ale is a dish for a king.   8

The lark, that tirra-lirra chants,
  With, heigh! with, heigh! the thrush and the jay,
Are summer songs for me and my aunts,
  While we lie tumbling in the hay.   12

I have served Prince Florizel, and in my time wore three-pile; but now I am out of service:

But shall I go mourn for that, my dear?
  The pale moon shines by night;   16
And when I wander here and there,
  I then do most go right.

If tinkers may have leave to live,
  And bear the sow-skin bowget,   20
Then my account I well may give,
  And in the stocks avouch it.

My traffic is sheets; when the kite builds, look to lesser linen. My father named me Autolycus; who being, as I am, littered under Mercury, was likewise a snapper-up of unconsidered trifles. With die and drab I purchased this caparison, and my revenue is the silly cheat. Gallows and knock are too powerful on the highway: beating and hanging are terrors to me: for the life to come, I sleep out the thought of it. A prize! a prize!   32

Enter Clown.

Clo. Let me see: Every 'leven wether tods; every tod yields pound and odd shilling: fifteen hundred shorn, what comes the wool to?

Aut. [*Aside.*] If the springe hold, the cock's mine.   37

Clo. I cannot do 't without compters. Let me see; what am I to buy for our sheep-shearing feast? 'Three pound of sugar; five pound of currants; rice,' what will this sister of mine do with rice? But my father hath made her mistress of the feast, and she lays it on. She hath made me four-and-twenty nosegays for the shearers, three-man song-men all, and very good ones; but they are most of them means and bases: but one puritan amongst them, and he sings psalms to hornpipes. I must have saffron, to colour the warden pies; mace, dates,—none; that's out of my note:—nutmegs seven; a race or two of ginger,—but that I may beg;—four pound of prunes, and as many of raisins o' the sun.   53

Aut. O! that ever I was born!
            [*Grovelling on the ground.*

Clo. I' the name of me!—

Aut. O! help me, help me! pluck but off these rags, and then death, death!   57

Clo. Alack, poor soul! thou hast need of more rags to lay on thee, rather than have these off.   60

Aut. O, sir! the loathsomeness of them offends me more than the stripes I have received, which are mighty ones and millions.

Clo. Alas, poor man! a million of beating may come to a great matter.   65

Aut. I am robbed, sir, and beaten; my money and apparel ta'en from me, and these detestable things put upon me.   68

Clo. What, by a horseman or a footman?

Aut. A footman, sweet sir, a footman.

Clo. Indeed, he should be a footman, by the garments he hath left with thee: if this be a horseman's coat, it hath seen very hot service. Lend me thy hand, I'll help thee: come, lend me thy hand.   [*Helping him up.*

Aut. O! good sir, tenderly, O!   76

Clo. Alas, poor soul!

Aut. O! good sir; softly, good sir! I fear, sir, my shoulder-blade is out.

Clo. How now! canst stand?   80

Aut. Softly, dear sir; [*Picks his pocket.*] good sir, softly. You ha' done me a charitable office.

Clo. Dost lack any money? I have a little money for thee.   84

Aut. No, good sweet sir: no, I beseech you,

sir. I have a kinsman not past three-quarters of
a mile hence, unto whom I was going: I shall
there have money, or anything I want: offer me
no money, I pray you! that kills my heart.   89

Clo. What manner of fellow was he that
robbed you?

Aut. A fellow, sir, that I have known to go
about with trol-my-dames: I knew him once a
servant of the prince. I cannot tell, good sir,
for which of his virtues it was, but he was certainly whipped out of the court.   96

Clo. His vices, you would say: there's no
virtue whipped out of the court: they cherish it,
to make it stay there, and yet it will no more
but abide.   100

Aut. Vices, I would say, sir. I know this man
well: he hath been since an ape-bearer; then a
process-server, a bailiff; then he compassed a
motion of the Prodigal Son, and married a
tinker's wife within a mile where my land and
living lies; and having flown over many knavish
professions, he settled only in rogue: some call
him Autolycus.   108

Clo. Out upon him! Prig, for my life, prig:
he haunts wakes, fairs, and bear-baitings.

Aut. Very true, sir; he, sir, he: that's the
rogue that put me into this apparel.   112

Clo. Not a more cowardly rogue in all
Bohemia: if you had but looked big and spit
at him, he'd have run.

Aut. I must confess to you, sir, I am no
fighter: I am false of heart that way, and that
he knew, I warrant him.   118

Clo. How do you now?

Aut. Sweet sir, much better than I was: I
can stand and walk. I will even take my leave
of you, and pace softly towards my kinsman's.

Clo. Shall I bring thee on the way?

Aut. No, good-faced sir; no, sweet sir.   124

Clo. Then fare thee well: I must go buy
spices for our sheep-shearing.

Aut. Prosper you, sweet sir!—[*Exit* Clown.]
Your purse is not hot enough to purchase your
spice. I'll be with you at your sheep-shearing
too. If I make not this cheat bring out another,
and the shearers prove sheep, let me be unrolled,
and my name put in the book of virtue.   132

> Jog on, jog on, the footpath way,
> And merrily hent the stile-a:
> A merry heart goes all the day,
> Your sad tires in a mile-a.   [*Exit.*

SCENE III.—*The Same. A Lawn before the*
Shepherd's *Cottage.*

Enter FLORIZEL *and* PERDITA.

Flo. These your unusual weeds to each part
of you
Do give a life: no shepherdess, but Flora
Peering in April's front. This your sheep-shear-
ing
Is as a meeting of the petty gods,   4
And you the queen on't.

Per.   Sir, my gracious lord,
To chide at your extremes it not becomes me:

O! pardon, that I name them. Your high self
The gracious mark o' the land, you have obscur'e
With a swain's wearing, and me, poor lowly
maid,
Most goddess-like prank'd up. But that ou
feasts
In every mess have folly, and the feeders
Digest it with a custom, I should blush   12
To see you so attired,—swoon, I think,
To show myself a glass.

Flo.   I bless the time
When my good falcon made her flight across
Thy father's ground.

Per.   Now, Jove afford you cause!   1
To me the difference forges dread; your great-
ness
Hath not been us'd to fear. Even now I tremble
To think, your father, by some accident,
Should pass this way as you did. O, the Fates
How would he look, to see his work, so noble,   2
Vilely bound up? What would he say? Or how
Should I, in these my borrow'd flaunts, behold
The sternness of his presence?

Flo.   Apprehend   2
Nothing but jollity. The gods themselves,
Humbling their deities to love, have taken
The shapes of beasts upon them: Jupiter
Became a bull, and bellow'd; the green Neptune
A ram, and bleated; and the fire-rob'd god, 2
Golden Apollo, a poor humble swain,
As I seem now. Their transformations
Were never for a piece of beauty rarer,   3
Nor in a way so chaste, since my desires
Run not before mine honour, nor my lusts
Burn hotter than my faith.

Per.   O! but, sir,
Your resolution cannot hold, when 'tis   3
Oppos'd, as it must be, by the power of the king
One of these two must be necessities,
Which then will speak, that you must change
this purpose,
Or I my life.

Flo.   Thou dearest Perdita,   4
With these forc'd thoughts, I prithee, darken no
The mirth o' the feast: or I'll be thine, my fair,
Or not my father's; for I cannot be
Mine own, nor anything to any, if   4
I be not thine: to this I am most constant,
Though destiny say no. Be merry, gentle;
Strangle such thoughts as these with any thing
That you behold the while. Your guests are
coming: 4
Lift up your countenance, as it were the day
Of celebration of that nuptial which
We two have sworn shall come.

Per.   O lady Fortune,
Stand you auspicious!

Flo.   See, your guests approach: 5
Address yourself to entertain them sprightly,
And let's be red with mirth.

Enter Shepherd, *with* POLIXENES *and* CAMILLO
disguised; Clown, MOPSA, DORCAS, *and Others.*

Shep. Fie, daughter! when my old wife liv'd,
upon
This day she was both pantler, butler, cook; 5

oth dame and servant; welcom'd all, serv'd
all,
Vould sing her song and dance her turn; now
here,
t upper end o' the table, now i' the middle;
n his shoulder, and his; her face o' fire   60
Vith labour and the thing she took to quench it,
he would to each one sip. You are retir'd,
s if you were a feasted one and not
he hostess of the meeting: pray you, bid   64
hese unknown friends to 's welcome; for it is
. way to make us better friends, more known.
'ome, quench your blushes and present yourself
hat which you are, mistress o' the feast: come
on,   68
.nd bid us welcome to your sheep-shearing,
.s your good flock shall prosper.

   Per.   [*To* POLIXENES.] Sir, welcome:
: is my father's will I should take on me
'he hostess-ship o' the day:—[*To* CAMILLO.]
   You're welcome, sir.   72
iive me those flowers there, Dorcas. Reverend
sirs,
'or you there's rosemary and rue; these keep
eeming and savour all the winter long;
irace and remembrance be to you both,   76
.nd welcome to our shearing!

   Per.   Shepherdess,—
. fair one are you,—well you fit our ages
Vith flowers of winter.

   Per.   Sir, the year growing ancient,
Jot yet on summer's death, nor on the birth 80
)f trembling winter, the fairest flowers o' the
   season
.re our carnations, and streak'd gillyvors,
Vhich some call nature's bastards: of that kind
)ur rustic garden's barren, and I care not   84
'o get slips of them.

   Pol.   Wherefore, gentle maiden,
)o you neglect them?

   Per.   For I have heard it said
'here is an art which in their piedness shares
Vith great creating nature.

   Pol.   Say there be;   88
'et nature is made better by no mean
3ut nature makes that mean: so, over that art,
Vhich you say adds to nature, is an art
'hat nature makes. You see, sweet maid, we
   marry   92
. gentler scion to the wildest stock,
.nd make conceive a bark of baser kind
3y bud of nobler race: this is an art
Vhich does mend nature, change it rather, but
'he art itself is nature.

   Per.   So it is.   97

   Pol. Then make your garden rich in gillyvors,
.nd do not call them bastards.

   Per.   I'll not put
'he dibble in earth to set one slip of them; 100
No more than, were I painted, I would wish
'his youth should say, 'twere well, and only
   therefore
)esire to breed by me. Here's flowers for you;
Jot lavender, mints, savory, marjoram;   104
'he marigold, that goes to bed wi' the sun,
.nd with him rises weeping: these are flowers

Of middle summer, and I think they are given
To men of middle age. You're very welcome. 108

   Cam. I should leave grazing, were I of your
   flock,
And only live by gazing.

   Per.   Out, alas!
You'd be so lean, that blasts of January
Would blow you through and through. Now,
   my fair'st friend,   112
I would I had some flowers o' the spring that
   might
Become your time of day; and yours, and yours,
That wear upon your virgin branches yet
Your maidenheads growing: O Proserpina! 116
For the flowers now that frighted thou let'st fall
From Dis's waggon! daffodils,
That come before the swallow dares, and take
The winds of March with beauty; violets dim,
But sweeter than the lids of Juno's eyes   121
Or Cytherea's breath; pale prime-roses,
That die unmarried, ere they can behold
Bright Phœbus in his strength, a malady   124
Most incident to maids; bold oxlips and
The crown imperial; lilies of all kinds,
The flower-de-luce being one. O! these I lack
To make you garlands of, and my sweet friend,
To strew him o'er and o'er!

   Flo.   What! like a corse? 129

   Per. No, like a bank for love to lie and play
   on;
Not like a corse; or if,—not to be buried,
But quick and in mine arms. Come, take your
   flowers: 132
Methinks I play as I have seen them do
In Whitsun pastorals: sure this robe of mine
Does change my disposition.

   Flo.   What you do
Still betters what is done. When you speak,
   sweet,   136
I'd have you do it ever: when you sing,
I'd have you buy and sell so; so give alms;
Pray so; and, for the ordering your affairs,
To sing them too: when you do dance, I wish
   you   140
A wave o' the sea, that you might ever do
Nothing but that; move still, still so,
And own no other function: each your doing,
So singular in each particular,   144
Crowns what you are doing in the present deed,
That all your acts are queens.

   Per.   O Doricles!
Your praises are too large: but that your youth,
And the true blood which fairly peeps through it,
Do plainly give you out an unstain'd shepherd,
With wisdom I might fear, my Doricles,
You woo'd me the false way.

   Flo.   I think you have
As little skill to fear as I have purpose   152
To put you to 't. But, come; our dance, I pray.
Your hand, my Perdita: so turtles pair
That never mean to part.

   Per.   I'll swear for 'em.

   Pol. This is the prettiest low-born lass that
   ever   156
Ran on the green-sord: nothing she does or
   seems

But smacks of something greater than herself;
Too noble for this place.

Cam.   He tells her something
That makes her blood look out. Good sooth,
  she is   160
The queen of curds and cream.

Clo.   Come on, strike up.

Dor. Mopsa must be your mistress: marry,
  garlic,
To mend her kissing with.

Mop.   Now, in good time!

Clo. Not a word, a word: we stand upon our
  manners.   164
Come, strike up. [*Music. Here a dance of Shep-
                                herds and Shepherdesses.*

Pol. Pray, good shepherd, what fair swain is
  this
Which dances with your daughter?

Shep. They call him Doricles, and boasts
  himself   168
To have a worthy feeding; but I have it
Upon his own report and I believe it:
He looks like sooth. He says he loves my
  daughter:
I think so too; for never gaz'd the moon   172
Upon the water as he'll stand and read
As 'twere my daughter's eyes; and, to be plain,
I think there is not half a kiss to choose
Who loves another best.

Pol.   She dances featly.   176

Shep. So she does any thing, though I report it
That should be silent. If young Doricles
Do light upon her, she shall bring him that
Which he not dreams of.   180

Enter a Servant.

Serv. O master! if you did but hear the pedlar
at the door, you would never dance again after a
tabor and pipe; no, the bagpipe could not move
you. He sings several tunes faster than you'll
tell money; he utters them as he had eaten
ballads and all men's ears grew to his tunes. 186

Clo. He could never come better: he shall
come in: I love a ballad but even too well, if it
be doleful matter merrily set down, or a very
pleasant thing indeed and sung lamentably. 190

Serv. He hath songs for man or woman, of all
sizes; no milliner can so fit his customers with
gloves: he has the prettiest love-songs for maids;
so without bawdry, which is strange; with such
delicate burthens of dildos and fadings, 'jump
her and thump her;' and where some stretch-
mouthed rascal would, as it were, mean mischief
and break a foul gap into the matter, he makes
the maid to answer, 'Whoop, do me no harm,
good man;' puts him off, slights him with
'Whoop, do me no harm, good man.'   201

Pol. This is a brave fellow.

Clo. Believe me, thou talkest of an admirable
conceited fellow. Has he any unbraided wares?

Serv. He hath ribands of all the colours i'
the rainbow; points more than all the lawyers
in Bohemia can learnedly handle, though they
come to him by the gross; inkles, caddisses,
cambrics, lawns: why, he sings 'em over, as they
were gods or goddesses. You would think a

smock were a she-angel, he so chants to th
sleeve-hand and the work about the square on'

Clo. Prithee, bring him in, and let him a
proach singing.   2

Per. Forewarn him that he use no scurrilou
words in 's tunes.   [*Exit* Servan

Clo. You have of these pedlars, that hav
more in them than you'd think, sister.

Per. Ay, good brother, or go about to thin

Enter AUTOLYCUS, *singing.*

Lawn as white as driven snow;   2
Cyprus black as e'er was crow;
Gloves as sweet as damask roses;
Masks for faces and for noses;
Bugle-bracelet, necklace-amber,   2
Perfume for a lady's chamber;
Golden quoifs and stomachers,
For my lads to give their dears;
Pins and poking-sticks of steel;   2
What maids lack from head to heel:
Come buy of me, come; come buy, come buy;
Buy, lads, or else your lasses cry:
Come buy.   2

Clo. If I were not in love with Mopsa, tho
shouldst take no money of me; but being e
thralled as I am, it will also be the bondage
certain ribands and gloves.

Mop. I was promised them against the feas
but they come not too late now.

Dor. He hath promised you more than tha
or there be liars.   2

Mop. He hath paid you all he promised you
may be he has paid you more, which will sham
you to give him again.   2

Clo. Is there no manners left among maid
will they wear their plackets where they shou
bear their faces? Is there not milking-tim
when you are going to bed, or kiln-hole, to whisi
off these secrets, but you must be tittle-tattli
before all our guests? 'Tis well they are whispe
ing: clamour your tongues, and not a word mor

Mop. I have done. Come, you promised r
a tawdry lace and a pair of sweet gloves.   2

Clo. Have I not told thee how I was cozen
by the way, and lost all my money?

Aut. And indeed, sir, there are cozene
abroad; therefore it behoves men to be wary. 2

Clo. Fear not thou, man, thou shalt lo
nothing here.

Aut. I hope so, sir; for I have about r
many parcels of charge.   2

Clo. What hast here? ballads?

Mop. Pray now, buy some: I love a ballad
print, a-life, for then we are sure they are tru

Aut. Here's one to a very doleful tune, ho
a usurer's wife was brought to bed of twen
money-bags at a burden; and how she longed
eat adders' heads and toads carbonadoed.

Mop. Is it true, think you?

Aut. Very true, and but a month old.

Dor. Bless me from marrying a usurer!

Aut. Here's the midwife's name to't, one M
tress Taleporter, and five or six honest wives' th
were present. Why should I carry lies abroa

Mop. Pray you now, buy it.   2

Clo. Come on, lay it by: and let's first see
oe ballads; we'll buy the other things anon.
Aut. Here's another ballad of a fish that
appeared upon the coast on Wednesday the
ourscore of April, forty thousand fathom above
ater, and sung this ballad against the hard
earts of maids: it was thought she was a woman
ad was turned into a cold fish for she would not
xchange flesh with one that loved her. The
allad is very pitiful and as true.   284
Dor. Is it true too, think you?
Aut. Five justices' hands at it, and witnesses
ore than my pack will hold.
Clo. Lay it by too: another.   288
Aut. This is a merry ballad, but a very
retty one.
Mop. Let's have some merry ones.
Aut. Why, this is a passing merry one, and
oes to the tune of 'Two maids wooing a man:'
ere's scarce a maid westward but she sings it:
is in request, I can tell you.   295
Mop. We can both sing it: if thou'lt bear a
art thou shalt hear; 'tis in three parts.
Dor. We had the tune on't a month ago.
Aut. I can bear my part; you must know 'tis
y occupation: have at it with you.   300

Aut.	Get you hence, for I must go,
	Where it fits not you to know.
Dor.	Whither?
Mop.	O! whither? 304
Dor.	Whither?
Mop.	It becomes thy oath full well,
	Thou to me thy secrets tell.
Dor.	Me too: let me go thither. 308
Mop.	Or thou go'st to the grange or mill.
Dor.	If to either, thou dost ill.
Aut.	Neither.
Dor.	What, neither? 312
Aut.	Neither.
Dor.	Thou hast sworn my love to be.
Mop.	Thou hast sworn it more to me:
	Then whither go'st? say whither? 316

Clo. We'll have this song out anon by our-
elves: my father and the gentlemen are in sad
alk, and we'll not trouble them: come, bring
way thy pack after me. Wenches, I'll buy for
ou both. Pedlar, let's have the first choice. Fol-
w me, girls. [*Exit with* DORCAS *and* MOPSA.
Aut. And you shall pay well for 'em.

	Will you buy any tape, 324
	Or lace for your cape,
	My dainty duck, my dear-a?
	Any silk, any thread,
	Any toys for your head, 328
	Of the new'st and fin'st, fin'st wear-a?
	Come to the pedlar;
	Money's a meddler,
	That doth utter all men's ware-a. 332

[*Exit.*

Re-enter Servant.

Serv. Master, there is three carters, three
epherds, three neat-herds, three swine-herds,
aat have made themselves all men of hair;
aey call themselves Saltiers; and they have a

dance which the wenches say is a gallimaufry of
gambols, because they are not in't; but they
themselves are o' the mind,—if it be not too
rough for some that know little but bowling,—
it will please plentifully.   341
Shep. Away! we'll none on't: here has been
too much homely foolery already. I know, sir,
we weary you.   344
Pol. You weary those that refresh us: pray,
let's see these four threes of herdsmen.
Serv. One three of them, by their own report,
sir, hath danced before the king; and not the
worst of the three but jumps twelve foot and a
half by the squier.   350
Shep. Leave your prating: since these good
men are pleased let them come in: but quickly
now.
Serv. Why, they stay at door, sir.   [*Exit.*

Re-enter Servant, *with Twelve Rustics habited
like Satyrs. They dance, and then exeunt.*

Pol. [*To* Shep.] O, father! you'll know more
of that hereafter.
[*To* CAMILLO.] Is it not too far gone? 'Tis time
to part them.   356
He's simple and tells much.   [*To* FLORIZEL.]
How now, fair shepherd!
Your heart is full of something that does take
Your mind from feasting. Sooth, when I was
young,
And handed love as you do, I was wont   360
To load my she with knacks: I would have
ransack'd
The pedlar's silken treasury and have pour'd it
To her acceptance; you have let him go
And nothing marted with him. If your lass   364
Interpretation should abuse and call this
Your lack of love or bounty, you were straited
For a reply, at least if you make a care
Of happy holding her.
Flo.   Old sir, I know   368
She prizes not such trifles as these are.
The gifts she looks from me are pack'd and
lock'd
Up in my heart, which I have given already,
But not deliver'd. O! hear me breathe my life
Before this ancient sir, who, it should seem,   373
Hath sometime lov'd: I take thy hand; this
hand,
As soft as dove's down, and as white as it,
Or Ethiopian's tooth, or the fann'd snow   376
That's bolted by the northern blasts twice o'er.
Pol. What follows this?
How prettily the young swain seems to wash
The hand was fair before! I have put you out:
But to your protestation: let me hear   381
What you profess.
Flo.   Do, and be witness to't.
Pol. And this my neighbour too?
Flo.   And he, and more
Than he, and men, the earth, the heavens, and
all;   384
That, were I crown'd the most imperial monarch,
Thereof most worthy, were I the fairest youth
That ever made eye swerve, had force and know-
ledge

More than was ever man's, I would not prize
    them   388
Without her love: for her employ them all;
Commend them and condemn them to her service
Or to their own perdition.
    Pol.   Fairly offer'd.
    Cam. This shows a sound affection.
    Shep.   But, my daughter, 392
Say you the like to him?
    Per.   I cannot speak
So well, nothing so well; no, nor mean better:
By the pattern of mine own thoughts I cut out
The purity of his.
    Shep.   Take hands; a bargain; 396
And, friends unknown, you shall bear witness
    to't:
I give my daughter to him, and will make
Her portion equal his.
    Flo.   O! that must be   399
I' the virtue of your daughter: one being dead,
I shall have more than you can dream of yet;
Enough then for your wonder. But, come
    on;
Contract us 'fore these witnesses.
    Shep.   Come, your hand;
And, daughter, yours.
    Pol.   Soft, swain, awhile, beseech you.
Have you a father?
    Flo.   I have; but what of him?
    Pol. Knows he of this?
    Flo.   He neither does nor shall.
    Pol. Methinks a father
Is, at the nuptial of his son, a guest   408
That best becomes the table. Pray you, once
    more,
Is not your father grown incapable
Of reasonable affairs? is he not stupid
With age and altering rheums? can he speak?
    hear?   412
Know man from man? dispute his own estate?
Lies he not bed-rid? and again does nothing
But what he did being childish?
    Flo.   No, good sir:
He has his health and ampler strength indeed
Than most have of his age.
    Pol.   By my white beard, 417
You offer him, if this be so, a wrong
Something unfilial. Reason my son
Should choose himself a wife, but as good
    reason   420
The father,—all whose joy is nothing else
But fair posterity,—should hold some counsel
In such a business.
    Flo.   I yield all this;
But for some other reasons, my grave sir, 424
Which 'tis not fit you know, I not acquaint
My father of this business.
    Pol.   Let him know't.
    Flo. He shall not.
    Pol.   Prithee, let him.
    Flo.   No, he must not.
    Shep. Let him, my son: he shall not need to
    grieve   428
At knowing of thy choice.
    Flo.   Come, come, he must not.
Mark our contract.

    Pol.   Mark your divorce, young si[r]
            [*Discovering himse[lf.*
Whom son I dare not call: thou art too base
To be acknowledg'd: thou a sceptre's heir, 4
That thus affect'st a sheep-hook! Thou o[ld]
    traitor,
I am sorry that by hanging thee I can
But shorten thy life one week. And thou, fre[sh]
    piece
Of excellent witchcraft, who of force must kno[w]
The royal fool thou cop'st with,—
    Shep.   O, my heart! 4
    Pol. I'll have thy beauty scratch'd with brie[rs,]
    and made
More homely than thy state. For thee, for
    boy,
If I may ever know thou dost but sigh   4
That thou no more shalt see this knack,—[as]
    never
I mean thou shalt,—we'll bar thee from succe[s-]
    sion;
Not hold thee of our blood, no, not our kin,
Far than Deucalion off: mark thou my word[s.]
Follow us to the court. Thou, churl, for th[is]
    time,   4
Though full of our displeasure, yet we free the[e]
From the dead blow of it. And you, enchan[t-]
    ment,—
Worthy enough a herdsman; yea, him too, 4
That makes himself, but for our honour there[in,]
Unworthy thee,—if ever henceforth thou
These rural latches to his entrance open,
Or hoop his body more with thy embraces, 4
I will devise a death as cruel for thee
As thou art tender to't.   [*Ex[it.*
    Per.   Even here undone!
I was not much afeard; for once or twice
I was about to speak and tell him plainly, 4
The self-same sun that shines upon his cour[t]
Hides not his visage from our cottage, but
Looks on alike. Will't please you, sir, be gon[e?]
I told you what would come of this: beseec[h]
    you,   4
Of your own state take care: this dream [of]
    mine—
Being now awake, I'll queen it no inch furthe[r,]
But milk my ewes and weep.
    Cam.   Why, how now, fathe[r!]
Speak, ere thou diest.
    Shep.   I cannot speak, nor think, 4
Nor dare to know that which I know. O si[r,]
You have undone a man of fourscore three,
That thought to fill his grave in quiet, yea,
To die upon the bed my father died,   4
To lie close by his honest bones: but now
Some hangman must put on my shroud an[d]
    lay me
Where no priest shovels in dust. O curse[d]
    wretch!
That knew'st this was the prince, and would[st]
    adventure   4
To mingle faith with him. Undone! undone[!]
If I might die within this hour, I have liv'[d]
To die when I desire.   [*Ex[it.*
    Flo.   Why look you so upon me[?]
I am but sorry, not afeard; delay'd,   4

But nothing alter'd. What I was, I am:
More straining on for plucking back; not fol-
lowing
My leash unwillingly.
Cam.   Gracious my lord,
You know your father's temper: at this time 480
He will allow no speech, which I do guess
You do not purpose to him; and as hardly
Will he endure your sight as yet, I fear:
Then, till the fury of his highness settle,   484
Come not before him.
Flo.   I not purpose it.
I think, Camillo?
Cam.   Even he, my lord.
Per. How often have I told you 'twould be
thus!
How often said my dignity would last   488
But till 'twere known!
. *Flo.*   It cannot fail but by
The violation of my faith; and then
Let nature crush the sides o' the earth together
And mar the seeds within! Lift up thy looks:
From my succession wipe me, father; I   493
Am heir to my affection.
Cam.   Be advis'd.
Flo. I am; and by my fancy: if my reason
Will thereto be obedient, I have reason;   496
If not, my senses, better pleas'd with madness,
Do bid it welcome.
Cam.   This is desperate, sir.
Flo. So call it; but it does fulfil my vow,
I needs must think it honesty. Camillo,   500
Not for Bohemia, nor the pomp that may
Be thereat glean'd, for all the sun sees or
The close earth wombs or the profound sea
hides
In unknown fathoms, will I break my oath 504
To this my fair belov'd. Therefore, I pray you,
As you have ever been my father's honour'd
friend,
When he shall miss me,—as, in faith, I mean not
To see him any more,—cast your good counsels
Upon his passion: let myself and fortune   509
Tug for the time to come. This you may know
And so deliver, I am put to sea
With her whom here I cannot hold on shore;
And most opportune to our need, I have   513
A vessel rides fast by, but not prepar'd
For this design. What course I mean to hold
Shall nothing benefit your knowledge, nor   516
Concern me the reporting.
Cam.   O my lord!
would your spirit were easier for advice,
Or stronger for your need.
Flo.   Hark, Perdita. [*Takes her aside.*
To CAMILLO.] I'll hear you by and by.
Cam.   He's irremovable,   520
Resolv'd for flight. Now were I happy if
His going I could frame to serve my turn,
Save him from danger, do him love and honour,
Purchase the sight again of dear Sicilia   524
And that unhappy king, my master, whom
so much thirst to see.
Flo.   Now, good Camillo,
am so fraught with curious business that
leave out ceremony.

Cam.   Sir, I think   528
You have heard of my poor services, i' the love
That I have borne your father?
Flo.   Very nobly
Have you deserv'd: it is my father's music
To speak your deeds, not little of his care   532
To have them recompens'd as thought on.
Cam.   Well, my lord,
If you may please to think I love the king
And through him what's nearest to him, which
is
Your gracious self, embrace but my direction,
If your more ponderous and settled project 537
May suffer alteration, on mine honour
I'll point you where you shall have such receiv-
ing
As shall become your highness; where you
may   540
Enjoy your mistress,—from the whom, I see,
There's no disjunction to be made, but by,
As, heavens forfend! your ruin,—marry her;
And with my best endeavours in your absence
Your discontenting father strive to qualify, 545
And bring him up to liking.
Flo.   How, Camillo,
May this, almost a miracle, be done?
That I may call thee something more than man,
And, after that trust to thee.
Cam.   Have you thought on 549
A place whereto you'll go?
Flo.   Not any yet;
But as the unthought-on accident is guilty
To what we wildly do, so we profess   552
Ourselves to be the slaves of chance and flies
Of every wind that blows.
Cam.   Then list to me:
This follows; if you will not change your pur-
pose
But undergo this flight, make for Sicilia,   556
And there present yourself and your fair prin-
cess,—
For so, I see, she must be,—'fore Leontes;
She shall be habited as it becomes
The partner of your bed. Methinks I see   560
Leontes opening his free arms and weeping
His welcomes forth; asks thee, the son, forgive-
ness
As 'twere i' the father's person; kisses the hands
Of your fresh princess; o'er and o'er divides
him   564
'Twixt his unkindness and his kindness: the one
He chides to hell, and bids the other grow
Faster than thought or time.
Flo.   Worthy Camillo,
What colour for my visitation shall I   568
Hold up before him?
Cam.   Sent by the king your father
To greet him and to give him comforts. Sir,
The manner of your bearing towards him, with
What you as from your father shall deliver, 572
Things known betwixt us three, I'll write you
down:
The which shall point you forth at every sitting
What you must say; that he shall not perceive
But that you have your father's bosom there 576
And speak his very heart.

Flo. I am bound to you.
There is some sap in this.

Cam. A course more promising
Than a wild dedication of yourselves
To unpath'd waters, undream'd shores, most
certain 580
To miseries enough: no hope to help you,
But as you shake off one to take another;
Nothing so certain as your anchors, who
Do their best office, if they can but stay you 584
Where you'll be loath to be. Besides, you know
Prosperity's the very bond of love,
Whose fresh complexion and whose heart to-
gether
Affliction alters.

Per. One of these is true: 588
I think affliction may subdue the cheek,
But not take in the mind.

Cam. Yea, say you so?
There shall not at your father's house these
seven years
Be born another such.

Flo. My good Camillo, 592
She is as forward of her breeding as
She is i' the rear o' her birth.

Cam. I cannot say 'tis pity
She lacks instructions, for she seems a mistress
To most that teach.

Per. Your pardon, sir; for this 596
I'll blush you thanks.

Flo. My prettiest Perdita!
But O! the thorns we stand upon. Camillo,
Preserver of my father, now of me,
The med'cine of our house, how shall we do? 600
We are not furnish'd like Bohemia's son,
Nor shall appear in Sicilia.

Cam. My lord,
Fear none of this: I think you know my for-
tunes
Do all lie there: it shall be so my care 604
To have you royally appointed as if
The scene you play were mine. For instance, sir,
That you may know you shall not want, one
word. [*They talk aside.*

Enter AUTOLYCUS.

Aut. Ha, ha! what a fool Honesty is! and
Trust, his sworn brother, a very simple gentleman! I have sold all my trumpery: not a counterfeit stone, not a riband, glass, pomander,
brooch, table-book, ballad, knife, tape, glove,
shoe-tie, bracelet, horn-ring, to keep my pack
from fasting: they throng who should buy first,
as if my trinkets had been hallowed and brought
a benediction to the buyer: by which means
I saw whose purse was best in picture; and
what I saw, to my good use I remembered. My
clown—who wants but something to be a reasonable man,—grew so in love with the wenches'
song that he would not stir his pettitoes till he
had both tune and words; which so drew the
rest of the herd to me that all their other senses
stuck in ears: you might have pinched a placket,
it was senseless; 'twas nothing to geld a codpiece
of a purse; I would have filed keys off that hung
in chains: no hearing, no feeling, but my sir's

song, and admiring the nothing of it; so that, in
this time of lethargy I picked and cut most of
their festival purses; and had not the old man
come in with a whoo-bub against his daughter
and the king's son, and scared my choughs from
the chaff, I had not left a purse alive in the
whole army. 634

[CAMILLO, FLORIZEL, *and* PERDITA
come forward.

Cam. Nay, but my letters, by this means
being there
So soon as you arrive, shall clear that doubt. 636

Flo. And those that you'll procure from King
Leontes—

Cam. Shall satisfy your father.

Per. Happy be you!
All that you speak shows fair.

Cam. [*Seeing* AUTOLYCUS.] Whom have we
here?
We'll make an instrument of this: omit 640
Nothing may give us aid.

Aut. [*Aside.*] If they have overheard me now,
why, hanging.

Cam. How now, good fellow! Why shakest
thou so? Fear not, man; here's no harm intended to thee.

Aut. I am a poor fellow, sir. 647

Cam. Why, be so still; here's nobody will
steal that from thee; yet, for the outside of thy
poverty we must make an exchange; therefore,
discase thee instantly,—thou must think, there's
a necessity in't,—and change garments with this
gentleman: though the pennyworth on his side
be the worst, yet hold thee, there's some boot.

Aut. I am a poor fellow, sir.—[*Aside.*] I
know ye well enough. 656

Cam. Nay, prithee, dispatch: the gentleman
is half flayed already.

Aut. Are you in earnest, sir? [*Aside.*] I
smell the trick on't. 660

Flo. Dispatch, I prithee.

Aut. Indeed, I have had earnest; but I cannot with conscience take it.

Cam. Unbuckle, unbuckle.—
[FLORIZEL *and* AUTOLYCUS *exchange
garments*

Fortunate mistress,—let my prophecy
Come home to ye!—you must retire yourself
Into some covert: take your sweetheart's hat
And pluck it o'er your brows; muffle your face
Dismantle you, and, as you can, disliken 66
The truth of your own seeming; that you may,—
For I do fear eyes over you,—to shipboard
Get undescried.

Per. I see the play so lies 67
That I must bear a part.

Cam. No remedy.
Have you done there?

Flo. Should I now meet my fathe
He would not call me son.

Cam. Nay, you shall have no ha
[*Giving it to* PERDITA
Come, lady, come. Farewell, my friend.

Aut. Adieu, sir. 67

Flo. O Perdita, what have we twain forgot
Pray you, a word. [*They converse apar*

Cam. [Aside.] What I do next shall be to
tell the king
this escape, and whither they are bound; 680
?erein my hope is I shall so prevail
force him after: in whose company
?hall review Sicilia, for whose sight
?ave a woman's longing.
Flo.   Fortune speed us! 684
?us we set on, Camillo, to the sea-side.
Cam. The swifter speed the better.
[Exeunt FLORIZEL, PERDITA, and CAMILLO.
Aut. I understand the business; I hear it.
?have an open ear, a quick eye, and a nimble
?nd, is necessary for a cut-purse: a good nose
?equisite also, to smell out work for the other
?ses. I see this is the time that the unjust
?n doth thrive. What an exchange had this
?en without boot! what a boot is here with this
?hange! Sure, the gods do this year connive
?us, and we may do anything extempore. The
?nce himself is about a piece of iniquity;
?aling away from his father with his clog at
? heels. If I thought it were a piece of
?nesty to acquaint the king withal, I would not
?'t: I hole it the more knavery to conceal it,
?d therein am I constant to my profession.
?ide, aside: here is more matter for a hot
?ain. Every lane's end, every shop, church,
?sion, hanging, yields a careful man work. 704

Re-enter Clown and Shepherd.

Clo. See, see, what a man you are now! There
?no other way but to tell the king she's a
?angeling and none of your flesh and blood.
Shep. Nay, but hear me. 708
Clo. Nay, but hear me.
Shep. Go to, then.
Clo. She being none of your flesh and blood,
?ur flesh and blood has not offended the king;
?d so your flesh and blood is not to be punish-
?by him. Show those things you found about
?r; those secret things, all but what she has
?th her: this being done, let the law go whistle:
?varrant you. 717
?I will tell the king all, every word, yea,
?d his son's pranks too; who, I may say, is no
?nest man neither to his father nor to me,
?go about to make me the king's brother-
?law. 722
Clo. Indeed, brother-in-law was the furthest
?you could have been to him, and then your
?ood had been the dearer by I know not how
?ich an ounce.
Aut. [Aside.] Very wisely, puppies! 727
Shep. Well, let us to the king: there is that
?this fardel will make him scratch his beard.
Aut. [Aside.] I know not what impediment
?is complaint may be to the flight of my
?aster. 732
Clo. Pray heartily he be at palace.
Aut. [Aside.] Though I am not naturally
?nest, I am so sometimes by chance: let me
?cket up my pedlar's excrement. [Takes off
? false beard.] How now, rustics! whither are
?u bound? 738

Shep. To the palace, an it like your worship. 740
Aut. Your affairs there, what, with whom, the
condition of that fardel, the place of your dwelling, your names, your ages, of what having,
breeding, and anything that is fitting to be
known, discover. 745
Clo. We are but plain fellows, sir.
Aut. A lie; you are rough and hairy. Let
me have no lying; it becomes none but tradesmen, and they often give us soldiers the lie; but
we pay them for it with stamped coin, not
stabbing steel; therefore they do not give us the
lie. 752
Clo. Your worship had like to have given us
one, if you had not taken yourself with the
manner. 755
Shep. Are you a courtier, an't like you, sir?
Aut. Whether it like me or no, I am a
courtier. Seest thou not the air of the court in
these enfoldings? hath not my gait in it the
measure of the court? receives not thy nose
court-odour from me? reflect I not on thy baseness court-contempt? Think'st thou, for that I
insinuate, or toaze from thee thy business, I am
therefore no courtier? I am courtier, cap-a-pe,
and one that will either push on or pluck back
thy business there: whereupon I command thee
to open thy affair.
Shep. My business, sir, is to the king. 768
Aut. What advocate hast thou to him?
Shep. I know not, an't like you.
Clo. Advocate's the court-word for a phea-
sant: say you have none. 772
Shep. None, sir; I have no pheasant, cock
nor hen.
Aut. How bless'd are we that are not simple
men!
Yet nature might have made me as these are,
Therefore I'll not disdain. 776
Clo. This cannot be but a great courtier.
Shep. His garments are rich, but he wears
them not handsomely.
Clo. He seems to be the more noble in being
fantastical: a great man, I'll warrant; I know
by the picking on's teeth.
Aut. The fardel there? what's i' the fardel?
Wherefore that box? 784
Shep. Sir, there lies such secrets in this fardel
and box which none must know but the king;
and which he shall know within this hour if I
may come to the speech of him. 788
Aut. Age, thou hast lost thy labour.
Shep. Why, sir?
Aut. The king is not at the palace; he is
gone aboard a new ship to purge melancholy
and air himself: for, if thou be'st capable of
things serious, thou must know the king is full
of grief.
Shep. So 'tis said, sir, about his son, that
should have married a shepherd's daughter. 797
Aut. If that shepherd be not now in hand-
fast, let him fly: the curses he shall have, the
torture he shall feel, will break the back of man,
the heart of monster. 801
Clo. Think you so, sir?

Aut. Not he alone shall suffer what wit can
make heavy and vengeance bitter; but those
that are germane to him, though removed fifty
times, shall all come under the hangman: which
though it be great pity, yet it is necessary. An
old sheep-whistling rogue, a ram-tender, to offer
to have his daughter come into grace! Some
say he shall be stoned; but that death is too
soft for him, say I: draw out throne into a
sheep cote! all deaths are too few, the sharpest
too easy.   813

Clo. Has the old man e'er a son, sir, do you
hear, an't like you, sir?

Aut. He has a son, who shall be flayed alive;
then 'nointed over with honey, set on the head
of a wasp's nest; then stand till he be three
quarters and a dram dead; then recovered again
with aqua-vitæ or some other hot infusion; then,
raw as he is, and in the hottest day prognostication proclaims, shall he be set against a brick-
wall, the sun looking with a southward eye upon
him, where he is to behold him with flies blown
to death. But what talk we of these traitorly
rascals, whose miseries are to be smiled at, their
offences being so capital? Tell me,—for you seem
to be honest plain men,—what you have to the
king: being something gently considered, I'll
bring you where he is aboard, tender your persons to his presence, whisper him in your be-
halfs; and if it be in man besides the king to
effect your suits, here is a man shall do it. 833

Clo. He seems to be of great authority: close
with him, give him gold; and though authority
be a stubborn bear, yet he is oft led by the nose
with gold. Show the inside of your purse to the
outside of his hand, and no more ado. Remember, 'stoned,' and 'flayed alive!'   839

Shep. An't please you, sir, to undertake the
business for us, here is that gold I have: I'll
make it as much more and leave this young
man in pawn till I bring it you.

Aut. After I have done what I promised?   845

Shep. Ay, sir.

Aut. Well, give me the moiety. Are you a
party in this business?   848

Clo. In some sort, sir: but though my case be
a pitiful one, I hope I shall not be flayed out
of it.

Aut. O! that's the case of the shepherd's son:
hang him, he'll be made an example.   853

Clo. Comfort, good comfort! we must to the
king and show our strange sights: he must
know 'tis none of your daughter nor my sister;
we are gone else. Sir, I will give you as much as
this old man does when the business is performed; and remain, as he says, your pawn till
it be brought you.   860

Aut. I will trust you. Walk before toward
the sea-side; go on the right hand; I will but
look upon the hedge and follow you.

Clo. We are blessed in this man, as I may
say, even blessed.   865

Shep. Let's before as he bids us. He was
provided to do us good.

    [*Exeunt* Shepherd *and* Clown.

Aut. If I had a mind to be honest I s
Fortune would not suffer me: she drops boot
in my mouth. I am courted now with a doub
occasion, gold, and a means to do the prir
my master good; which who knows how th
may turn back to my advancement? I w
bring these two moles, these blind ones, aboa
him: if he think it fit to shore them again, a
that the complaint they have to the king co
cerns him nothing, let him call me rogue f
being so far officious; for I am proof again
that title and what shame else belongs to't.
him will I present them: there may be mat
in it.   [*Ex*

ACT V

Scene I.—*Sicilia. A Room in the Palace*
LEONTES.

Enter LEONTES, CLEOMENES, DION, PAULIN/
and Others.

Cleo. Sir, you have done enough, and ha
perform'd
A saint-like sorrow: no fault could you make
Which you have not redeem'd; indeed, pa
down
More penitence than done trespass. At t
last,
Do as the heavens have done, forget your ev
With them forgive yourself.

Leon.   Whilst I rememb
Her and her virtues, I cannot forget
My blemishes in them, and so still think of
The wrong I did myself; which was so muc
That heirless it hath made my kingdom, a
Destroy'd the sweet'st companion that e'er m
Bred his hopes out of.

Paul.   True, too true, my lord;
If one by one you wedded all the world,
Or from the all that are took something goc
To make a perfect woman, she you kill'd
Would be unparallel'd.

Leon.   I think so. Kill'd!
She I kill'd! I did so; but thou strik'st me
Sorely to say I did: it is as bitter
Upon thy tongue as in my thought. Now, go
now
Say so but seldom.

Cleo.   Not at all, good lady:
You might have spoken a thousand things th
would
Have done the time more benefit, and grac'
Your kindness better.

Paul.   You are one of those
Would have him wed again.

Dion.   If you would not so,
You pity not the state, nor the remembrance
Of his most sovereign name; consider little
What dangers, by his highness' fail of issue,
May drop upon his kingdom and devour
Incertain lookers-on. What were more holy
Than to rejoice the former queen is well?
What holier than for royalty's repair,
For present comfort, and for future good,
To bless the bed of majesty again

ith a sweet fellow to't?
Paul.   There is none worthy,
specting her that's gone. Besides, the gods   36
ill have fulfill'd their secret purposes;
r has not the divine Apollo said,
t not the tenour of his oracle,
at King Leontes shall not have an heir
ll his lost child be found? which that it shall,   41
all as monstrous to our human reason
 my Antigonus to break his grave
d come again to me; who, on my life,
d perish with the infant. 'Tis your counsel   44
y lord should to the heavens be contrary,
pose against their wills.—[To LEONTES.]
  Care not for issue;
e crown will find an heir: great Alexander
ft his to the worthiest, so his successor   48
as like to be the best.
Leon.   Good Paulina,
ho hast the memory of Hermione,
 now, in honour; O! that ever I
d squar'd me to thy counsel! then, even now,
night have look'd upon my queen's full eyes,
ve taken treasure from her lips,—
Paul.   And left them
ore rich, for what they yielded.
Leon.   Thou speak'st truth.
 more such wives; therefore, no wife: one   56
 worse,
d better us'd, would make her sainted spirit
gain possess her corpse and on this stage,—
here we're offenders now,—appear soul-vex'd,
d begin, 'Why to me?'
Paul.   Had she such power,   60
e had just cause.
Leon.   She had; and would incense me
 murder her I married.
Paul.   I should so:
ere I the ghost that walk'd, I'd bid you mark   64
er eye, and tell me for what dull part in't
ou chose her; then I'd shriek, that even your
  ears
ould rift to hear me; and the words that
  follow'd
ould be 'Remember mine.'
Leon.   Stars, stars!
d all eyes else dead coals. Fear thou no wife;
 have no wife, Paulina.
Paul.   Will you swear   69
ever to marry but by my free leave?
Leon. Never, Paulina: so be bless'd my spirit!
Paul. Then, good my lords, bear witness to
his oath.   72
Cleo. You tempt him over much.
Paul.   Unless another,
 like Hermione as is her picture,
front his eye.
Cleo.   Good madam,—
Paul.   I have done.
et, if my lord will marry,—if you will, sir,   76
o remedy, but you will,—give me the office
 choose you a queen, she shall not be so young
s was your former; but she shall be such
s, walk'd your first queen's ghost, it should
  take joy
 see her in your arms.

Leon.   My true Paulina,
We shall not marry till thou bidd'st us.
Paul.   That
Shall be when your first queen's again in breath;
Never till then.   84

Enter a Gentleman.

Gent. One that gives out himself Prince
Florizel,
Son of Polixenes, with his princess,—she
The fairest I have yet beheld,—desires access
To your high presence.
Leon.   What with him? he comes not   88
Like to his father's greatness; his approach,
So out of circumstance and sudden, tells us
'Tis not a visitation fram'd, but forc'd
By need and accident. What train?
Gent.   But few,   92
And those but mean.
Leon.   His princess, say you, with him?
Gent. Ay, the most peerless piece of earth, I
think,
That e'er the sun shone bright on.
Paul.   O Hermione!
As every present time doth boast itself   96
Above a better gone, so must thy grave
Give way to what's seen now. Sir, you yourself
Have said and writ so,—but your writing now
Is colder than that theme,—'She had not been,
Nor was not to be equall'd; thus your verse   101
Flow'd with her beauty once: 'tis shrewdly ebb'd
To say you have seen a better.
Gent.   Pardon, madam:
The one I have almost forgot—your pardon—
The other, when she has obtain'd your eye,   105
Will have your tongue too. This is a creature,
Would she begin a sect, might quench the zeal
Of all professors else, make proselytes   108
Of who she but bid follow.
Paul.   How! not women?
Gent. Women will love her, that she is a
woman
More worth than any man; men, that she is
The rarest of all women.
Leon.   Go, Cleomenes;   112
Yourself, assisted with your honour'd friends,
Bring them to our embracement. Still 'tis
strange,
[*Exeunt* CLEOMENES, Lords, *and* Gentleman.
He thus should steal upon us.
Paul.   Had our prince—
Jewel of children—seen this hour, he had pair'd
Well with this lord: there was not full a month
Between their births.
Leon. Prithee, no more: cease! thou know'st
He dies to me again when talk'd of: sure,   120
When I shall see this gentleman, thy speeches
Will bring me to consider that which may
Unfurnish me of reason. They are come.

Re-enter CLEOMENES, *with* FLORIZEL, PERDITA,
and Others.

Your mother was most true to wedlock, prince;
For she did print your royal father off,   125
Conceiving you. Were I but twenty-one,
Your father's image is so hit in you,

His very air, that I should call you brother, 128
As I did him; and speak of something wildly
By us perform'd before. Most dearly welcome!
And you, fair princess,—goddess! O, alas!
I lost a couple, that 'twixt heaven and earth 132
Might thus have stood begetting wonder as
You, gracious couple, do: and then I lost—
All mine own folly—the society,
Amity too, of your brave father, whom, 136
Though bearing misery, I desire my life
Once more to look on him.
 Flo.   By his command
Have I here touch'd Sicilia; and from him
Give you all greetings that a king, at friend, 140
Can send his brother: and, but infirmity,—
Which waits upon worn times,—hath some-
 thing seiz'd
His wish'd ability, he had himself 143
The land and waters 'twixt your throne and his
Measur'd to look upon you, whom he loves—
He bade me say so—more than all the sceptres
And those that bear them living.
 Leon.   O, my brother!—
Good gentleman,—the wrongs I have done thee
 stir 148
Afresh within me, and these thy offices
So rarely kind, are as interpreters
Of my behind-hand slackness! Welcome hither,
As is the spring to the earth. And hath he too
Expos'd this paragon to the fearful usage— 153
At least ungentle—of the dreadful Neptune,
To greet a man not worth her pains, much less
The adventure of her person?
 Flo.   Good my lord, 156
She came from Libya.
 Leon.   Where the war-like Smalus,
That noble honour'd lord, is fear'd and lov'd?
 Flo. Most royal sir, from thence; from him,
 whose daughter
His tears proclaim'd his, parting with her:
 thence— 160
A prosperous south-wind friendly—we have
 cross'd,
To execute the charge my father gave me
For visiting your highness: my best train
I have from your Sicilian shores dismiss'd; 164
Who for Bohemia bend, to signify
Not only my success in Libya, sir,
But my arrival and my wife's, in safety
Here where we are.
 Leon.   The blessed gods 168
Purge all infection from our air whilst you
Do climate here! You have a holy father,
A graceful gentleman; against whose person,
So sacred as it is, I have done sin: 172
For which the heavens, taking angry note,
Have left me issueless; and your father's
 bless'd—
As he from heaven merits it—with you, 175
Worthy his goodness. What might I have been,
Might I a son and daughter now have look'd on,
Such goodly things as you!

Enter a Lord.

 Lord.   Most noble sir,
That which I shall report will bear no credit,

Were not the proof so nigh. Please you, gr
 sir,
Bohemia greets you from himself by me;
Desires you to attach his son, who has—
His dignity and duty both cast off—
Fled from his father, from his hopes, and w
A shepherd's daughter.
 Leon.   Where's Bohemia? speak.
 Lord. Here in your city; I now came fr
 him:
I speak amazedly, and it becomes
My marvel and my message. To your court
Whiles he was hastening,—in the chase it see
Of this fair couple,—meets he on the way
The father of this seeming lady and
Her brother, having both their country quit
With this young prince.
 Flo.   Camillo has betray'd me;
Whose honour and whose honesty till now
Endur'd all weathers.
 Lord.   Lay't so to his char
He's with the king your father.
 Leon.   Who? Camillo?
 Lord. Camillo, sir: I spake with him, w
 now
Has these poor men in question. Never sav
Wretches so quake: they kneel, they kiss t
 earth,
Forswear themselves as often as they speak:
Bohemia stops his ears, and threatens them
With divers deaths in death.
 Per.   O my poor fath
The heaven sets spies upon us, will not have
Our contract celebrated.
 Leon.   You are married?
 Flo. We are not, sir, nor are we like to b
The stars, I see, will kiss the valleys first:
The odds for high and low's alike.
 Leon.   My lord,
Is this the daughter of a king?
 Flo.   She is,
When once she is my wife.
 Leon. That 'once,' I see, by your go
 father's speed,
Will come on very slowly. I am sorry,
Most sorry, you have broken from his liking
Where you were tied in duty; and as sorry
Your choice is not so rich in worth as beauty,
That you might well enjoy her.
 Flo.   Dear, look u
Though Fortune, visible an enemy,
Should chase us with my father, power
 jot
Hath she to change our loves. Beseech yo
 sir,
Remember since you ow'd no more to time
Than I do now; with thought of such aff
 tions,
Step forth mine advocate; at your request
My father will grant precious things as trifl
 Leon. Would he do so, I'd beg your preci
 mistress,
Which he counts but a trifle.
 Paul.   Sir, my liege,
Your eye hath too much youth in 't: not
 month

'ore your queen died, she was more worth
　　such gazes
han what you look on now.

Leon.　　　　　　I thought of her,
ven in these looks I made. [To FLORIZEL.]
　But yet your petition　　　　　　　　228
s yet unanswer'd. I will to your father:
our honour not o'erthrown by your desires,
am friend to them and you; upon which errand
now go toward him. Therefore follow me, 232
nd mark what way I make: come, good my
　lord.　　　　　　　　　　　　[Exeunt.

SCENE II.—*The Same. Before the Palace.*

Enter AUTOLYCUS *and a* Gentleman.

Aut. Beseech you, sir, were you present at
is relation?

Gent. I was by at the opening of the fardel,
eard the old shepherd deliver the manner how
e found it: whereupon, after a little amazed-
ess, we were all commanded out of the cham-
er; only this methought I heard the shepherd
ay, he found the child.　　　　　　　　　8

Aut. I would most gladly know the issue of it.

Gent. I make a broken delivery of the busi-
ess; but the changes I perceived in the king
nd Camillo were very notes of admiration: they
emed almost, with staring on one another, to
ar the cases of their eyes; there was speech in
eir dumbness, language in their very gesture;
ey looked as they had heard of a world ran-
med, or one destroyed: a notable passion of
onder appeared in them; but the wisest be-
older, that knew no more but seeing, could not
y if the importance were joy or sorrow; but in
e extremity of the one it must needs be.　21

Enter another Gentleman.

ere comes a gentleman that haply knows more.
he news, Rogero?

Sec. Gent. Nothing but bonfires: the oracle
fulfilled; the king's daughter is found: such a
eal of wonder is broken out within this hour
at ballad-makers cannot be able to express it.

Enter a third Gentleman.

ere comes the lady Paulina's steward: he can
eliver you more. How goes it now, sir? this
ews which is called true is so like an old tale,
he verity of it is in strong suspicion: has
he king found his heir?　　　　　　　　32

Third Gent. Most true, if ever truth were
regnant by circumstance: that which you hear
ou'll swear you see, there is such unity in the
roofs. The mantle of Queen Hermione, her
ewel about the neck of it, the letters of Anti-
onus found with it, which they know to be his
haracter; the majesty of the creature in re-
emblance of the mother, the affection of noble-
ess which nature shows above her breeding,
nd many other evidences proclaim her with all
ertainty to be the king's daughter. Did you see
he meeting of the two kings?　　　　　　44

Sec. Gent. No.

Third Gent. Then have you lost a sight, which
was to be seen, cannot be spoken of. There
might you have beheld one joy crown another,
so, and in such manner that, it seemed, sorrow
wept to take leave of them, for their joy waded
in tears. There was casting up of eyes, holding
up of hands, with countenances of such distraction that they were to be known by garment,
not by favour. Our king, being ready to leap out
of himself for joy of his found daughter, as if
that joy were now become a loss, cries, 'O, thy
mother, thy mother!' then asks Bohemia forgiveness; then embraces his son-in-law; then
again worries he his daughter with clipping her;
now he thanks the old shepherd, which stands
by like a weather-bitten conduit of many kings'
reigns. I never heard of such another encounter, which lames report to follow it and undoes
description to do it.　　　　　　　　　64

Sec. Gent. What, pray you, became of Antigonus that carried hence the child?

Third Gent. Like an old tale still, which will
have matter to rehearse, though credit be asleep
and not an ear open. He was torn to pieces with
a bear: this avouches the shepherd's son, who
has not only his innocence—which seems much
—to justify him, but a handkerchief and rings
of his that Paulina knows.　　　　　　　73

First Gent. What became of his bark and his
followers?

Third Gent. Wracked, the same instant of
their master's death, and in the view of the shepherd: so that all the instruments which aided to
expose the child were even then lost when it was
found. But, O! the noble combat that 'twixt
joy and sorrow was fought in Paulina. She had
one eye declined for the loss of her husband,
another elevated that the oracle was fulfilled:
she lifted the princess from the earth, and so
locks her in embracing, as if she would pin her
to her heart that she might no more be in
danger of losing.　　　　　　　　　87

First Gent. The dignity of this act was worth
the audience of kings and princes, for by such
was it acted.

Third Gent. One of the prettiest touches of
all, and that which angled for mine eyes,—
caught the water though not the fish,—was when
at the relation of the queen's death, with the
manner how she came to it,—bravely confessed
and lamented by the king,—how attentiveness
wounded his daughter; till, from one sign of
dolour to another, she did, with an 'alas!' I
would fain say, bleed tears, for I am sure my
heart wept blood. Who was most marble there
changed colour; some swounded, all sorrowed:
if all the world could have seen't, the woe had
been universal.　　　　　　　　　103

First Gent. Are they returned to the court?

Third Gent. No; the princess hearing of her
mother's statue, which is in the keeping of
Paulina—a piece many years in doing, and now
newly performed by that rare Italian master,
Julio Romano; who, had he himself eternity
and could put breath into his work, would
beguile Nature of her custom, so perfectly he is

her ape: he so near to Hermione hath done
Hermione that they say one would speak to her
and stand in hope of answer: thither with all
greediness of affection are they gone, and there
they intend to sup.   116

Sec. Gent. I thought she had some great
matter there in hand, for she hath privately,
twice or thrice a day, ever since the death of
Hermione, visited that removed house. Shall
we thither and with our company piece the rejoicing?   122

First Gent. Who would be thence that has
the benefit of access? every wink of an eye some
new grace will be born: our absence makes us
unthrifty to our knowledge. Let's along.   126
             [*Exeunt* Gentlemen.

Aut. Now, had I not the dash of my former
life in me, would preferment drop on my head.
I brought the old man and his son aboard the
prince; told him I heard them talk of a fardel
and I know not what; but he at that time, over-
fond of the shepherd's daughter,—so he then
took her to be,—who began to be much sea-sick,
and himself little better, extremity of weather
continuing, this mystery remained undiscovered.
But 'tis all one to me; for had I been the finder
out of this secret, it would not have relished
among my other discredits. Here come those
I have done good to against my will, and already appearing in the blossoms of their fortune.   141

       Enter Shepherd *and* Clown.

Shep. Come, boy; I am past moe children,
but thy sons and daughters will be all gentlemen born.   144

Clo. You are well met, sir. You denied to
fight with me this other day, because I was no
gentleman born: see you these clothes? say, you
see them not and think me still no gentleman
born: you were best say these robes are not
gentleman born. Give me the lie, do, and try
whether I am not now gentleman born.

Aut. I know you are now, sir, a gentleman
born.   153

Clo. Ay, and have been so any time these
four hours.

Shep. And so have I, boy.   156

Clo. So you have: but I was a gentleman
born before my father; for the king's son took
me by the hand and called me brother; and
then the two kings called my father brother;
and then the prince my brother and the princess
my sister called my father father; and so we
wept: and there was the first gentleman-like
tears that ever we shed.   164

Shep. We may live, son, to shed many more.

Clo. Ay; or else 'twere hard luck, being in so
preposterous estate as we are.

Aut. I humbly beseech you, sir, to pardon
me all the faults I have committed to your worship, and to give me your good report to the
prince my master.

Shep. Prithee, son, do; for we must be gentle,
now we are gentlemen.   173

Clo. Thou wilt amend thy life?

Aut. Ay, an it like your good worship.

Clo. Give me thy hand: I will swear to th
prince thou art as honest a true fellow as any
in Bohemia.   I

Shep. You may say it, but not swear it.

Clo. Not swear it, now I am a gentleman
Let boors and franklins say it, I'll swear it.

Shep. How if it be false, son?   I

Clo. If it be ne'er so false, a true gentlem
may swear it in the behalf of his friend: a
I'll swear to the prince thou art a tall fello
of thy hands and that thou wilt not be drun
but I know thou art no tall fellow of thy han
and that thou wilt be drunk: but I'll swear
and I would thou wouldst be a tall fellow of th
hands.

Aut. I will prove so, sir, to my power.   I

Clo. Ay, by any means prove a tall fellov
if I do not wonder how thou darest venture
be drunk, not being a tall fellow, trust me no
Hark! the kings and the princes, our kindre
are going to see the queen's picture. Com
follow us: we'll be thy good masters.   I
                 [*Exeun*

SCENE III.—*The Same. A Chapel in* PAULINA
             House.

Enter LEONTES, POLIXENES, FLORIZEL, PERDIT
    CAMILLO, PAULINA, Lords, *and* Attendants

Leon. O grave and good Paulina, the gre
    comfort
That I have had of thee!

Paul.   What, sovereign si
I did not well, I meant well. All my services
You have paid home; but that you have vouc
    saf'd,
With your crown'd brother and these your co
    tracted
Heirs of your kingdoms, my poor house
    visit,
It is a surplus of your grace, which never
My life may last to answer.

Leon.   O Paulina!
We honour you with trouble: but we came
To see the statue of our queen: your gallery
Have we pass'd through, not without muc
    content
In many singularities, but we saw not
That which my daughter came to look upon.
The statue of her mother.

Paul.   As she liv'd peerles
So her dead likeness, I do well believe,
Excels whatever yet you look'd upon
Or hand of man hath done; therefore I keep
Lonely, apart. But here it is: prepare
To see the life as lively mock'd as ever
Still sleep mock'd death: behold! and say 't
    well.   2
     [PAULINA *draws back a curtain, and di*
         covers HERMIONE *as a statu*
I like your silence: it the more shows off
Your wonder; but yet speak: first you, m
    liege.
Comes it not something near?

Leon.   Her natural posture!
ide me, dear stone, that I may say, indeed
ou art Hermione; or rather, thou art she
thy not chiding, for she was as tender   26
 infancy and grace. But yet, Paulina,
ermione was not so much wrinkled; nothing
 aged as this seems.
Pol.   O! not by much.   29
Paul. So much the more our carver's excellence;
hich lets go by some sixteen years and makes her
 she liv'd now.
Leon.   As now she might have done, 32
 much to my good comfort, as it is
ow piercing to my soul. O! thus she stood,
ven with such life of majesty,—warm life,
 now it coldly stands,—when first I woo'd her.   36
m asham'd: does not the stone rebuke me
r being more stone than it? O, royal piece!
ere's magic in thy majesty, which has
y evils conjur'd to remembrance, and   40
om thy admiring daughter took the spirits,
anding like stone with thee.
Per.   And give me leave,
nd do not say 'tis superstition, that   43
kneel and then implore her blessing. Lady,
ear queen, that ended when I but began,
ive me that hand of yours to kiss.
Paul.   O, patience!
e statue is but newly fix'd, the colour's
ot dry.   48
Cam. My lord, your sorrow was too sore laid on,
hich sixteen winters cannot blow away,
 many summers dry: scarce any joy
d ever so long live; no sorrow   52
t kill'd itself much sooner.
Pol.   Dear my brother,
t him that was the cause of this have power
 take off so much grief from you as he
ill piece up in himself.
Paul.   Indeed, my lord, 56
I had thought the sight of my poor image
ould thus have wrought you,—for the stone is mine,—
d not have show'd it.
Leon.   Do not draw the curtain.
Paul. No longer shall you gaze on't, lest your fancy   60
ay think anon it moves.
Leon.   Let be, let be!
ould I were dead, but that, methinks, already—
hat was he that did make it? See, my lord,
ould you not deem it breath'd, and that those veins   64
d verily bear blood?
Pol.   Masterly done:
he very life seems warm upon her lip.
Leon. The fixture of her eye has motion in't,
s we are mock'd with art.
Paul.   I'll draw the curtain; 68
y lord's almost so far transported that
e'll think anon it lives.

Leon.   O sweet Paulina!
Make me to think so twenty years together:
Not settled senses of the world can match   72
The pleasure of that madness. Let't alone.
Paul. I am sorry, sir, I have thus far stirr'd you: but
I could afflict you further.
Leon.   Do, Paulina;
For this affliction has a taste as sweet   76
As any cordial comfort. Still, methinks,
There is an air comes from her: what fine chisel
Could ever yet cut breath? Let no man mock me,
For I will kiss her.
Paul.   Good my lord, forbear. 80
The ruddiness upon her lip is wet:
You'll mar it if you kiss it; stain your own
With oily painting. Shall I draw the curtain?
Leon. No, not these twenty years.
Per.   So long could I   84
Stand by, a looker-on.
Paul.   Either forbear,
Quit presently the chapel, or resolve you
For more amazement. If you can behold it,
I'll make the statue move indeed, descend,   88
And take you by the hand; but then you'll think,—
Which I protest against,—I am assisted
By wicked powers.
Leon.   What you can make her do,
I am content to look on: what to speak,   92
I am content to hear; for 'tis as easy
To make her speak as move.
Paul.   It is requir'd
You do awake your faith. Then, all stand still;
Or those that think it is unlawful business   96
I am about, let them depart.
Leon.   Proceed:
No foot shall stir.
Paul.   Music, awake her: strike! [*Music.*
'Tis time; descend; be stone no more: approach;
Strike all that look upon with marvel. Come;
I'll fill your grave up: stir; nay, come away;
Bequeath to death your numbness, for from him
Dear life redeems you. You perceive she stirs:
                    [HERMIONE *comes down.*
Start not; her actions shall be holy as   104
You hear my spell is lawful: do not shun her
Until you see her die again, for then
You kill her double. Nay, present your hand:
When she was young you woo'd her; now in age   108
Is she become the suitor!
Leon. [*Embracing her.*] O! she's warm.
If this be magic, let it be an art
Lawful as eating.
Pol.   She embraces him.
Cam. She hangs about his neck: 112
If she pertain to life let her speak too.
Pol. Ay; and make't manifest where she has liv'd,
Or how stol'n from the dead.
Paul.   That she is living,
Were it but told you, should be hooted at   116
Like an old tale; but it appears she lives,

Though yet she speak not. Mark a little while.
Please you to interpose, fair madam: kneel
And pray your mother's blessing. Turn, good
    lady;   120
Our Perdita is found.

        [*Presenting* PERDITA, *who kneels to*
        HERMIONE.

  Her.   You gods, look down,
And from your sacred vials pour your graces
Upon my daughter's head! Tell me, mine own,
Where hast thou been preserv'd? where liv'd?
    how found   124
Thy father's court? for thou shalt hear that I,
Knowing by Paulina that the oracle
Gave hope thou wast in being, have preserv'd
Myself to see the issue.

  Paul.   There's time enough for that;   128
Lest they desire upon this push to trouble
Your joys with like relation. Go together,
You precious winners all: your exultation
Partake to every one. I, an old turtle,   132
Will wing me to some wither'd bough, and
    there
My mate, that's never to be found again,
Lament till I am lost.

  Leon.   O! peace, Paulina!

Thou shouldst a husband take by my co
    sent,   1
As I by thine a wife: this is a match,
And made between's by vows. Thou hast four
    mine;
But how, is to be question'd; for I saw her,
As I thought dead, and have in vain sa
    many   1
A prayer upon her grave. I'll not seek far,-
For him, I partly know his mind,—to find the
An honourable husband. Come, Camillo,
And take her by the hand; whose worth ar
    honesty   1
Is richly noted, and here justified
By us, a pair of kings. Let's from this place.
What! look upon my brother: both your pa
    dons,
That e'er I put between your holy looks   1
My ill suspicion. This' your son-in-law,
And son unto the king,—whom heavens direc
    ing,
Is troth-plight to your daughter. Good Paulin
Lead us from hence, where we may leisurely 1
Each one demand and answer to his part
Perform'd in this wide gap of time since first
We were dissever'd: hastily lead away. [*Exeun*

THE LIFE AND DEATH OF KING JOHN

DRAMATIS PERSONÆ

KING JOHN.
PRINCE HENRY, Son to the King.
ARTHUR, Duke of Britaine, Nephew to the King.
THE EARL OF PEMBROKE.
THE EARL OF ESSEX.
THE EARL OF SALISBURY.
THE LORD BIGOT.
HUBERT DE BURGH.
ROBERT FAULCONBRIDGE, Son to Sir Robert Faulcon-
  bridge.
PHILIP THE BASTARD, his half-brother.
JAMES GURNEY, Servant to Lady Faulconbridge.
PETER OF POMFRET, a Prophet.
PHILIP, King of France.

LEWIS, the Dauphin.
LYMOGES, Duke of Austria.
CARDINAL PANDULPH, the Pope's Legate.
MELUN, a French Lord.
CHATILLON, Ambassador from France.

QUEEN ELINOR, Mother to King John.
CONSTANCE, Mother to Arthur.
BLANCH OF SPAIN, Niece to King John.
LADY FAULCONBRIDGE.

Lords, Ladies, Citizens of Angiers, Sheriff, Heralds,
  Officers, Soldiers, Messengers, and other Attendants.

SCENE.—*Sometimes in England, and sometimes in France.*

ACT I

SCENE I.—*A Room of State in the Palace.*

Enter KING JOHN, QUEEN ELINOR, PEMBROKE,
ESSEX, SALISBURY, *and Others, with* CHA-
TILLON.

K. John. Now, say, Chatillon, what would
  France with us?
Chat. Thus, after greeting, speaks the King
  of France,
In my behaviour, to the majesty,
The borrow'd majesty of England here.   4
Eli. A strange beginning; 'borrow'd ma-
  jesty!'
K. John. Silence, good mother; hear the
  embassy.
Chat. Philip of France, in right and true
  behalf
Of thy deceased brother Geffrey's son,   8
Arthur Plantagenet, lays most lawful claim
To this fair island and the territories,
To Ireland, Poictiers, Anjou, Touraine, Maine;
Desiring thee to lay aside the sword   12
Which sways usurpingly these several titles,
And put the same into young Arthur's hand,
Thy nephew and right royal sovereign.
K. John. What follows if we disallow of this?
Chat. The proud control of fierce and bloody
  war,   17
To enforce these rights so forcibly withheld.
K. John. Here have we war for war, and
  blood for blood,
Controlment for controlment: so answer France.
Chat. Then take my king's defiance from my
  mouth,   21
The furthest limit of my embassy.
K. John. Bear mine to him, and so depart
  in peace:
Be thou as lightning in the eyes of France;   24
For ere thou canst report I will be there,
The thunder of my cannon shall be heard.
So, hence! Be thou the trumpet of our wrath

And sullen presage of your own decay.   28
An honourable conduct let him have:
Pembroke, look to 't. Farewell, Chatillon.
      [*Exeunt* CHATILLON *and* PEMBROKE.
Eli. What now, my son! have I not ever said
How that ambitious Constance would not cease
Till she had kindled France and all the world   33
Upon the right and party of her son?
This might have been prevented and made whole
With very easy arguments of love,   36
Which now the manage of two kingdoms must
With fearful bloody issue arbitrate.
K. John. Our strong possession and our right
  for us.
Eli. Your strong possession much more than
  your right,   40
Or else it must go wrong with you and me:
So much my conscience whispers in your ear,
Which none but heaven and you and I shall hear.

Enter a Sheriff, *who whispers* ESSEX.

Essex. My liege, here is the strangest con-
  troversy,   44
Come from the country to be judg'd by you,
That e'er I heard: shall I produce the men?
K. John. Let them approach. [*Exit* Sheriff.
Our abbeys and our priories shall pay   48
This expedition's charge.

Re-enter Sheriff, *with* ROBERT FAULCONBRIDGE
    and PHILIP, *his Bastard Brother.*

              What men are you?
Bast. Your faithful subject I, a gentleman
Born in Northamptonshire, and eldest son,
As I suppose, to Robert Faulconbridge,   52
A soldier, by the honour-giving hand
Of Cœur-de-Lion knighted in the field.
K. John. What art thou?
Rob. The son and heir to that same Faul-
  conbridge.   56
K. John. Is that the elder, and art thou the
  heir?
You came not of one mother then, it seems.

Bast. Most certain of one mother, mighty king,
That is well known: and, as I think, one father:
But for the certain knowledge of that truth   61
I put you o'er to heaven and to my mother:
Of that I doubt, as all men's children may.

Eli. Out on thee, rude man! thou dost shame
    thy mother   64
And wound her honour with this diffidence.

Bast. I, madam? no, I have no reason for it;
That is my brother's plea and none of mine;
The which if he can prove, a' pops me out   68
At least from fair five hundred pound a year:
Heaven guard my mother's honour and my
    land!

K. John. A good blunt fellow. Why, being
    younger born,
Doth he lay claim to thine inheritance?   72

Bast. I know not why, except to get the land.
But once he slander'd me with bastardy:
But whe'r I be as true-begot or no,
That still I lay upon my mother's head;   76
But that I am as well-begot, my liege,—
Fair fall the bones that took the pains for me!—
Compare our faces and be judge yourself.
If old Sir Robert did beget us both,   80
And were our father, and this son like him;
O old Sir Robert, father, on my knee
I give heaven thanks I was not like to thee!

K. John. Why, what a madcap hath heaven
    lent us here!

Eli. He hath a trick of Cœur-de-Lion's face;
The accent of his tongue affecteth him.
Do you not read some tokens of my son
In the large composition of this man?   88

K. John. Mine eye hath well examined his
    parts,
And finds them perfect Richard. Sirrah, speak:
What doth move you to claim your brother's
    land?

Bast. Because he hath a half-face, like my
    father.   92
With half that face would he have all my land;
A half-fac'd groat five hundred pound a year!

Rob. My gracious liege, when that my father
    liv'd,
Your brother did employ my father much,— 96

Bast. Well, sir, by this you cannot get my
    land:
Your tale must be how he employ'd my mother.

Rob. And once dispatch'd him in an embassy
To Germany, there with the emperor   100
To treat of high affairs touching that time.
The advantage of his absence took the king,
And in the mean time sojourn'd at my father's;
Where how he did prevail I shame to speak, 104
But truth is truth: large lengths of seas and
    shores
Between my father and my mother lay,—
As I have heard my father speak himself,—
When this same lusty gentleman was got. 108
Upon his death-bed he by will bequeath'd
His lands to me, and took it on his death
That this my mother's son was none of his;
An if he were, he came into the world   112
Full fourteen weeks before the course of time.

Then, good my liege, let me have what is mine
My father's land, as was my father's will.   11

K. John. Sirrah, your brother is legitimate
Your father's wife did after wedlock bear him
And if she did play false, the fault was hers;
Which fault lies on the hazards of all husband
That marry wives. Tell me, how if my brother
Who, as you say, took pains to get this son, 12
Had of your father claim'd this son for his?
In sooth, good friend, your father might have
    kept
This calf bred from his cow from all the world
In sooth he might: then, if he were my brother's
My brother might not claim him; nor you
    father,
Being none of his, refuse him: this concludes
My mother's son did get your father's heir; 12
Your father's heir must have your father's land

Rob. Shall then my father's will be of no
    force
To dispossess that child which is not his?

Bast. Of no more force to dispossess me, sir
Than was his will to get me, as I think.   13

Eli. Whe'r hadst thou rather be a Faulcon
    bridge
And like thy brother, to enjoy thy land,
Or the reputed son of Cœur-de-Lion,   13
Lord of thy presence and no land beside?

Bast. Madam, an if my brother had my shape
And I had his, Sir Robert his, like him;
And if my legs were two such riding-rods,   14
My arms such eel-skins stuff'd, my face so thin
That in mine ear I durst not stick a rose
Lest men should say, 'Look, where three-far
    things goes!'
And, to his shape, were heir to all this land, 14
Would I might never stir from off this place,
I'd give it every foot to have this face:
I would not be Sir Nob in any case.

Eli. I like thee well: wilt thou forsake thy
    fortune,   14
Bequeath thy land to him, and follow me?
I am a soldier and now bound to France.

Bast. Brother, take you my land, I'll take
    my chance.   15
Your face hath got five hundred pounds a year
Yet sell your face for five pence and 'tis dear
Madam, I'll follow you unto the death.

Eli. Nay, I would have you go before me
    thither.

Bast. Our country manners give our better
    way.   15

K. John. What is thy name?

Bast. Philip, my liege, so is my name begun
Philip, good old Sir Robert's wife's eldest son

K. John. From henceforth bear his name
    whose form thou bearest: 16
Kneel thou down Philip, but arise more great
Arise Sir Richard, and Plantagenet.

Bast. Brother by the mother's side, give me
    your hand:
My father gave me honour, yours gave land. 16
Now blessed be the hour, by night or day,
When I was got, Sir Robert was away!

Eli. The very spirit of Plantagenet!
I am thy grandam, Richard: call me so.   168

Bast. Madam, by chance but not by truth;
  what though?
Something about, a little from the right,
In at the window, or else o'er the hatch:
Who dares not stir by day must walk by night,
  And have is have, however men do catch. 173
Near or far off, well won is still well shot,
And I am I, howe'er I was begot.
  K. John. Go, Faulconbridge: now hast thou
  thy desire; 176
A landless knight makes thee a landed squire.
Come, madam, and come, Richard: we must
  speed
For France, for France, for it is more than need.
  Bast. Brother, adieu: good fortune come to
  thee! 180
For thou wast got i' the way of honesty.
    [*Exeunt all but the* BASTARD.
A foot of honour better than I was,
But many a many foot of land the worse.
Well, now can I make any Joan a lady. 184
'Good den, Sir Richard!' 'God-a-mercy, fel-
  low!'
And if his name be George, I'll call him Peter;
For new-made honour doth forget men's names:
Tis too respective and too sociable 188
For your conversion. Now your traveller,
He and his toothpick at my worship's mess,
And when my knightly stomach is suffic'd,
Why then I suck my teeth, and catechize 192
My picked man of countries: 'My dear sir,'—
Thus, leaning on mine elbow, I begin,—
'I shall beseech you,'—that is question now;
And then comes answer like an absey-book:
'O, sir,' says answer, 'at your best command;
At your employment; at your service, sir:'
'No, sir,' says question, 'I, sweet sir, at yours:'
And so, ere answer knows what question would,
Saving in dialogue of compliment, 201
And talking of the Alps and Apennines,
The Pyrenean and the river Po,
It draws toward supper in conclusion so. 204
But this is worshipful society
And fits the mounting spirit like myself;
For he is but a bastard to the time,
That doth not smack of observation; 208
And so am I, whether I smack or no;
And not alone in habit and device,
Exterior form, outward accoutrement,
But from the inward motion to deliver 212
Sweet, sweet, sweet poison for the age's tooth.
Which, though I will not practise to deceive,
Yet, to avoid deceit, I mean to learn;
For it shall strew the footsteps of my rising. 216
But who comes in such haste in riding-robes?
What woman-post is this? hath she no husband
That will take pains to blow a horn before her?

  Enter LADY FAULCONBRIDGE *and* JAMES
    GURNEY.

O me! it is my mother. How now, good lady!
What brings you here to court so hastily? 221
  Lady F. Where is that slave, thy brother?
  where is he,
That holds in chase mine honour up and down?

  Bast. My brother Robert? old Sir Robert's
  son? 224
Colbrand the giant, that same mighty man?
Is it Sir Robert's son that you seek so?
  Lady F. Sir Robert's son! Ay, thou un-
  reverend boy,
Sir Robert's son: why scorn'st thou at Sir
  Robert? 228
He is Sir Robert's son, and so art thou.
  Bast. James Gurney, wilt thou give us leave
  awhile?
  Gur. Good leave, good Philip.
  Bast.   Philip! sparrow! James,
There's toys abroad: anon I'll tell thee more.
    [*Exit* GURNEY.
Madam, I was not old Sir Robert's son: 233
Sir Robert might have eat his part in me
Upon Good-Friday and ne'er broke his fast.
Sir Robert could do well: marry, to confess,
Could he get me? Sir Robert could not do
  it:
We know his handiwork: therefore, good
  mother,
To whom am I beholding for these limbs?
Sir Robert never holp to make this leg. 240
  Lady F. Hast thou conspired with thy bro-
  ther too,
That for thine own gain shouldst defend mine
  honour?
What means this scorn, thou most untoward
  knave?
  Bast. Knight, knight, good mother, Basi-
  lisco-like. 244
What! I am dubb'd; I have it on my shoulder.
But, mother, I am not Sir Robert's son;
I have disclaim'd Sir Robert and my land;
Legitimation, name, and all is gone. 248
Then, good my mother, let me know my father;
Some proper man, I hope; who was it, mother?
  Lady F. Hast thou denied thyself a Faulcon-
  bridge?
  Bast. As faithfully as I deny the devil. 252
  Lady F. King Richard Cœur-de-Lion was
  thy father:
By long and vehement suit I was seduc'd
To make room for him in my husband's bed.
Heaven lay not my transgression to my charge!
Thou art the issue of my dear offence, 257
Which was so strongly urg'd past my defence.
  Bast. Now, by this light, were I to get again,
Madam, I would not wish a better father. 260
Some sins do bear their privilege on earth,
And so doth yours; your fault was not your
  folly:
Needs must you lay your heart at his dispose,
Subjected tribute to commanding love, 264
Against whose fury and unmatched force
The aweless lion could not wage the fight,
Nor keep his princely heart from Richard's
  hand.
He that perforce robs lions of their hearts 268
May easily win a woman's. Ay, my mother,
With all my heart I thank thee for my father!
Who lives and dares but say thou didst not well
When I was got, I'll send his soul to hell. 272
Come, lady, I will show thee to my kin;

And they shall say, when Richard me begot,
If thou hadst said him nay, it had been sin:
Who says it was, he lies: I say, 'twas not. 276
[*Exeunt.*

ACT II

SCENE I.—*France. Before the Walls of
Angiers.*

Enter, on one side, the DUKE OF AUSTRIA, *and
Forces; on the other,* PHILIP, *King of France,
and Forces,* LEWIS, CONSTANCE, ARTHUR, *and
Attendants.*

K. Phi. Before Angiers well met, brave
Austria,
Arthur, that great forerunner of thy blood,
Richard, that robb'd the lion of his heart
And fought the holy wars in Palestine,   4
By this brave duke came early to his grave:
And, for amends to his posterity,
At our importance hither is he come,
To spread his colours, boy, in thy behalf,   8
And to rebuke the usurpation
Of thy unnatural uncle, English John:
Embrace him, love him, give him welcome
hither.
Arth. God shall forgive you Cœur-de-Lion's
death   12
The rather that you give his offspring life,
Shadowing their right under your wings of
war.
I give you welcome with a powerless hand,
But with a heart full of unstained love: 16
Welcome before the gates of Angiers, duke.
K. Phi. A noble boy! Who would not do
thee right?
Aust. Upon thy cheek lay I this zealous kiss,
As seal to this indenture of my love,   20
That to my home I will no more return
Till Angiers, and the right thou hast in France,
Together with that pale, that white-fac'd shore,
Whose foot spurns back the ocean's roaring
tides   24
And coops from other lands her islanders,
Even till that England, hedg'd in with the main,
That water-walled bulwark, still secure
And confident from foreign purposes,   28
Even till that utmost corner of the west
Salute thee for her king: till then, fair boy,
Will I not think of home, but follow arms.
Const. O! take his mother's thanks, a widow's
thanks,   32
Till your strong hand shall help to give him
strength
To make a more requital to your love.
Aust. The peace of heaven is theirs that lift
their swords
In such a just and charitable war.   36
K. Phi. Well then, to work: our cannon shall
be bent
Against the brows of this resisting town.
Call for our chiefest men of discipline,
To cull the plots of best advantages: 40
We'll lay before this town our royal bones,
Wade to the market-place in Frenchmen's
blood,

But we will make it subject to this boy.
Const. Stay for an answer to your embassy,
Lest unadvis'd you stain your swords with
blood.   45
My Lord Chatillon may from England bring
That right in peace which here we urge in
war;
And then we shall repent each drop of blood 48
That hot rash haste so indirectly shed.

Enter CHATILLON.

K. Phi. A wonder, lady! lo, upon thy wish,
Our messenger, Chatillon, is arriv'd!
What England says, say briefly, gentle lord; 51
We coldly pause for thee; Chatillon, speak.
Chat. Then turn your forces from this paltry
siege
And stir them up against a mightier task.
England, impatient of your just demands,   56
Hath put himself in arms: the adverse winds,
Whose leisure I have stay'd, have given him
time
To land his legions all as soon as I;
His marches are expedient to this town,   60
His forces strong, his soldiers confident.
With him along is come the mother-queen,
An Ate, stirring him to blood and strife;
With her her niece, the Lady Blanch of Spain;
With them a bastard of the king's deceas'd; 65
And all the unsettled humours of the land,
Rash, inconsiderate, fiery voluntaries,
With ladies' faces and fierce dragons' spleens, 68
Have sold their fortunes at their native homes,
Bearing their birthrights proudly on their backs,
To make a hazard of new fortunes here.
In brief, a braver choice of dauntless spirits 72
Than now the English bottoms have waft o'er
Did never float upon the swelling tide,
To do offence and scathe in Christendom.
[*Drums heard within.*
The interruption of their churlish drums   76
Cuts off more circumstance: they are at hand,
To parley or to fight; therefore prepare.
K. Phi. How much unlook'd for is this ex-
pedition!
Aust. By how much unexpected, by so much
We must awake endeavour for defence,   81
For courage mounteth with occasion:
Let them be welcome then, we are prepar'd.

Enter KING JOHN, ELINOR, BLANCH, *the* BASTARD,
Lords, and Forces.

K. John. Peace be to France, if France in
peace permit   84
Our just and lineal entrance to our own;
If not, bleed France, and peace ascend to
heaven,
Whiles we, God's wrathful agent, do correct
Their proud contempt that beats his peace to
heaven.   88
K. Phi. Peace be to England, if that war
return
From France to England, there to live in peace.
England we love; and, for that England's sake
With burden of our armour here we sweat: 92
This toil of ours should be a work of thine;

ut thou from loving England art so far
hat thou hast under-wrought his lawful king,
ut off the sequence of posterity,   96
ut-faced infant state, and done a rape
pon the maiden virtue of the crown.
ook here upon thy brother Geffrey's face:
hese eyes, these brows, were moulded out of
  his;   100
his little abstract doth contain that large
Vhich died in Geffrey, and the hand of time
hall draw this brief into as huge a volume.
hat Geffrey was thy elder brother born,   104
nd this his son; England was Geffrey's right
nd this is Geffrey's. In the name of God
ow comes it then that thou art call'd a king,
Vhen living blood doth in these temples beat,
Vhich owe the crown that thou o'ermasterest?
  K. John. From whom hast thou this great
    commission, France,
o draw my answer from thy articles?
  K. Phi. From that supernal judge, that stirs
    good thoughts   112
n any breast of strong authority,
o look into the blots and stains of right:
hat judge hath made me guardian to this
    boy:
Jnder whose warrant I impeach thy wrong, 116
And by whose help I mean to chastise it.
  K. John. Alack! thou dost usurp authority.
  K. Phi. Excuse; it is to beat usurping down.
  Eli. Who is it thou dost call usurper,
    France?   120
  Const. Let me make answer; thy usurping
    son.
  Eli. Out, insolent! thy bastard shall be king,
hat thou mayst be a queen, and check the
    world!
  Const. My bed was ever to thy son as true
s thine was to thy husband, and this boy 125
iker in feature to his father Geffrey
han thou and John in manners; being as like
As rain to water, or devil to his dam.   128
My boy a bastard! By my soul I think
His father never was so true begot;
t cannot be an if thou wert his mother.
  Eli. There's a good mother, boy, that blots
    thy father.   132
  Const. There's a good grandam, boy, that
    would blot thee.
  Aust. Peace!
  Bast.   Hear the crier.
  Aust.   What the devil art thou?
  Bast. One that will play the devil, sir, with
    you,
An a' may catch your hide and you alone. 136
You are the hare of whom the proverb goes,
Vhose valour plucks dead lions by the beard.
'll smoke your skin-coat, an I catch you right.
irrah, look to't; i' faith, I will, i' faith.   140
  Blanch. O! well did he become that lion's
    robe,
That did disrobe the lion of that robe.
  Bast. It lies as sightly on the back of him
As great Alcides' shows upon an ass: 144
ut, ass, I'll take that burden from your back,
Or lay on that shall make your shoulders crack.

  Aust. What cracker is this same that deafs
    our ears
With this abundance of superfluous breath? 148
King,—Lewis, determine what we shall do
    straight.
  K. Phi. Women and fools, break off your
    conference.
King John, this is the very sum of all:
England and Ireland, Anjou, Touraine, Maine,
In right of Arthur do I claim of thee.   153
Wilt thou resign them and lay down thy arms?
  K. John. My life as soon: I do defy thee,
    France.
Arthur of Britaine, yield thee to my hand; 156
And out of my dear love I'll give thee more
Than e'er the coward hand of France can win.
Submit thee, boy.
  Eli.   Come to thy grandam, child.
  Const. Do, child, go to it grandam, child; 160
Give grandam kingdom, and it grandam will
Give it a plum, a cherry, and a fig:
There's a good grandam.
  Arth.   Good my mother, peace!
I would that I were low laid in my grave: 164
I am not worth this coil that's made for me.
  Eli. His mother shames him so, poor boy, he
    weeps.
  Const. Now shame upon you, whe'r she does
    or no!
His grandam's wrongs, and not his mother's
    shames,   168
Draw those heaven-moving pearls from his poor
    eyes,
Which heaven shall take in nature of a fee;
Ay, with these crystal beads heaven shall be
    brib'd
To do him justice and revenge on you.   172
  Eli. Thou monstrous slanderer of heaven
    and earth!
  Const. Thou monstrous injurer of heaven
    and earth!
Call not me slanderer; thou and thine usurp
The dominations, royalties, and rights   176
Of this oppressed boy: this is thy eld'st son's son,
Infortunate in nothing but in thee:
Thy sins are visited in this poor child;
The canon of the law is laid on him,   180
Being but the second generation
Removed from thy sin-conceiving womb.
  K. John. Bedlam, have done.
  Const.   I have but this to say,
That he's not only plagued for her sin,   184
But God hath made her sin and her the plague
On this removed issue, plagu'd for her,
And with her plague, her sin; his injury
Her injury, the beadle to her sin,   188
All punish'd in the person of this child,
And all for her. A plague upon her!
  Eli. Thou unadvised scold, I can produce
A will that bars the title of thy son.   192
  Const. Ay, who doubts that? a will! a wicked
    will;
A woman's will; a canker'd grandam's will!
  K. Phi. Peace, lady! pause, or be more tem-
    perate:
It ill beseems this presence to cry aim   196

To these ill-tuned repetitions.
Some trumpet summon hither to the walls
These men of Angiers: let us hear them speak
Whose title they admit, Arthur's or John's. 200

Trumpet sounds. Enter Citizens *upon the Walls.*

First Cit. Who is it that hath warn'd us to
  the walls?
K. Phi. 'Tis France, for England.
K. John.   England for itself.
You men of Angiers, and my loving subjects,—
K. Phi. You loving men of Angiers, Arthur's
  subjects,   204
Our trumpet call'd you to this gentle parle,—
K. John. For our advantage; therefore hear
  us first.
These flags of France, that are advanced here
Before the eye and prospect of your town,   208
Have hither march'd to your endamagement:
The cannons have their bowels full of wrath,
And ready mounted are they to spit forth
Their iron indignation 'gainst your walls: 212
All preparation for a bloody siege
And merciless proceeding by these French
Confronts your city's eyes, your winking gates;
And but for our approach those sleeping stones,
That as a waist do girdle you about,   217
By the compulsion of their ordinance
By this time from their fixed beds of lime
Had been dishabited, and wide havoc made 220
For bloody power to rush upon your peace.
But on the sight of us your lawful king,—
Who painfully with much expedient march
Have brought a countercheck before your gates,
To save unscratch'd your city's threaten'd
  cheeks,   225
Behold, the French amaz'd vouchsafe a parle;
And now, instead of bullets wrapp'd in fire,
To make a shaking fever in your walls,   228
They shoot but calm words folded up in smoke,
To make a faithless error in your ears:
Which trust accordingly, kind citizens,
And let us in, your king, whose labour'd spirits,
Forwearied in this action of swift speed,   233
Crave harbourage within your city walls.
K. Phi. When I have said, make answer to
  us both.
Lo! in this right hand, whose protection   236
Is most divinely vow'd upon the right
Of him it holds, stands young Plantagenet,
Son to the elder brother of this man,
And king o'er him and all that he enjoys: 240
For this down-trodden equity, we tread
In war-like march these greens before your town,
Being no further enemy to you
Than the constraint of hospitable zeal,   244
In the relief of this oppressed child,
Religiously provokes. Be pleased then
To pay that duty which you truly owe
To him that owes it, namely, this young prince;
And then our arms, like to a muzzled bear, 249
Save in aspect, have all offence seal'd up;
Our cannons' malice vainly shall be spent
Against the invulnerable clouds of heaven; 252
And with a blessed and unvex'd retire,

With unhack'd swords and helmets all un
  bruis'd,
We will bear home that lusty blood again
Which here we came to spout against you
  town,   2
And leave your children, wives, and you, i
  peace.
But if you fondly pass our proffer'd offer,
'Tis not the roundure of your old-fac'd walls
Can hide you from our messengers of war, 2
Though all these English and their discipline
Were harbour'd in their rude circumference
Then tell us, shall your city call us lord,
In that behalf which we have challeng'd it? 2
Or shall we give the signal to our rage
And stalk in blood to our possession?
  First Cit. In brief, we are the King of En
  land's subjects:
For him, and in his right, we hold this town. 2
  K. John. Acknowledge then the king, ar
  let me in.
  First Cit. That can we not; but he that prov
  the king,
To him will we prove loyal: till that time
Have we ramm'd up our gates against the worl
  K. John. Doth not the crown of Englan
  prove the king?   2
And if not that, I bring you witnesses,
Twice fifteen thousand hearts of England
  breed,—
  Bast. Bastards, and else.   27
  K. John. To verify our title with their lives
  K. Phi. As many and as well-born bloods a
  those,—
  Bast. Some bastards too.
  K. Phi. Stand in his face to contradict h
  claim.   28
  First Cit. Till thou compound whose rigl
  is worthiest,
We for the worthiest hold the right from bot
  K. John. Then God forgive the sins of a
  those souls
That to their everlasting residence,   28
Before the dew of evening fall, shall fleet,
In dreadful trial of our kingdom's king!
  K. Phi. Amen, Amen! Mount, chevaliers
  to arms!
  Bast. Saint George, that swing'd the drago
  and e'er since   28
Sits on his horse back at mine hostess' door,
Teach us some fence! [*To* AUSTRIA.] Sirral
  were I at home,
At your den, sirrah, with your lioness,
I would set an ox-head to your lion's hide, 29
And make a monster of you.
  Aust.   Peace! no more.
  Bast. O! tremble, for you hear the lion roa
  K. John. Up higher to the plain; where we'
  set forth
In best appointment all our regiments.   29
  Bast. Speed then, to take advantage of th
  field.
  K. Phi. It shall be so; [*To* LEWIS.] and at th
  other hill
Command the rest to stand. God, and ou
  right!   [*Exeun*

larums and excursions; then a retreat. Enter
a French Herald, *with trumpets, to the gates.*

F. Her. You men of Angiers, open wide your
 gates, 300
And let young Arthur, Duke of Britaine, in,
Who, by the hand of France this day hath made
Much work for tears in many an English mother,
Whose sons lie scatter'd on the bleeding ground;
Many a widow's husband grovelling lies, 305
Coldly embracing the discolour'd earth;
And victory, with little loss, doth play
Upon the dancing banners of the French, 308
Who are at hand, triumphantly display'd,
To enter conquerors and to proclaim
Arthur of Britaine England's king and yours.

Enter English Herald, *with trumpets.*

E. Her. Rejoice, you men of Angiers, ring
 your bells; 312
King John, your king and England's, doth ap-
 proach,
Commander of this hot malicious day.
Their armours, that march'd hence so silver-
 bright,
Hither return all gilt with Frenchmen's blood; 317
There stuck no plume in any English crest
That is removed by a staff of France;
Our colours do return in those same hands
That did display them when we first march'd
 forth; 320
And, like a jolly troop of huntsmen, come
Our lusty English, all with purpled hands
Dy'd in the dying slaughter of their foes.
Open your gates and give the victors way. 324
 First Cit. Heralds, from off our towers we
 might behold,
From first to last, the onset and retire
Of both your armies; whose equality
By our best eyes cannot be censured: 328
Blood hath bought blood, and blows have an-
 swer'd blows;
Strength match'd with strength, and power
 confronted power:
Both are alike; and both alike we like.
One must prove greatest: while they weigh so
 even, 332
We hold our town for neither, yet for both.

Re-enter the two KINGS, *with their powers,
severally.*

 K. John. France, hast thou yet more blood
 to cast away?
Say, shall the current of our right run on?
Whose passage, vex'd with thy impediment, 336
Shall leave his native channel and o'erswell
With course disturb'd even thy confining shores,
Unless thou let his silver water keep
A peaceful progress to the ocean. 340
 K. Phi. England, thou hast not sav'd one
 drop of blood,
In this hot trial, more than we of France;
Rather, lost more: and by this hand I swear,
That sways the earth this climate overlooks, 344
Before we will lay down our just-borne arms,
We'll put thee down, 'gainst whom these arms
 we bear,

Or add a royal number to the dead,
Gracing the scroll that tells of this war's loss 348
With slaughter coupled to the name of kings.
 Bast. Ha, majesty! how high thy glory towers
When the rich blood of kings is set on fire!
O! now doth Death line his dead chaps with
 steel; 352
The swords of soldiers are his teeth, his fangs;
And now he feasts, mousing the flesh of men,
In undetermin'd differences of kings.
Why stand these royal fronts amazed thus?
Cry 'havoc!' kings; back to the stained field,
You equal-potents, fiery-kindled spirits!
Then let confusion of one part confirm
The other's peace; till then, blows, blood, and
 death! 360
 K. John. Whose party do the townsmen yet
 admit?
 K. Phi. Speak, citizens, for England; who's
 your king?
 First Cit. The King of England, when we
 know the king.
 K. Phi. Know him in us, that here hold up
 his right. 364
 K. John. In us, that are our own great deputy,
And bear possession of our person here,
Lord of our presence, Angiers, and of you.
 First Cit. A greater power than we denies all
 this; 368
And, till it be undoubted, we do lock
Our former scruple in our strong-barr'd gates,
Kings of ourselves; until our fears, resolv'd,
Be by some certain king purg'd and depos'd. 372
 Bast. By heaven, these scroyles of Angiers
 flout you, kings,
And stand securely on their battlements
As in a theatre, whence they gape and point
At your industrious scenes and acts of death. 376
Your royal presences be rul'd by me:
Do like the mutines of Jerusalem,
Be friends awhile and both conjointly bend
Your sharpest deeds of malice on this town. 380
By east and west let France and England mount
Their battering cannon charged to the mouths,
Till their soul-fearing clamours have brawl'd
 down
The flinty ribs of this contemptuous city: 384
I'd play incessantly upon these jades,
Even till unfenced desolation
Leave them as naked as the vulgar air.
That done, dissever your united strengths, 388
And part your mingled colours once again;
Turn face to face and bloody point to point;
Then, in a moment, Fortune shall cull forth
Out of one side her happy minion, 392
To whom in favour she shall give the day,
And kiss him with a glorious victory.
How like you this wild counsel, mighty states?
Smacks it not something of the policy? 396
 K. John. Now, by the sky that hangs above
 our heads,
I like it well. France, shall we knit our powers
And lay this Angiers even with the ground;
Then after fight who shall be king of it? 400
 Bast. An if thou hast the mettle of a king,
Being wrong'd as we are by this peevish town,

Turn thou the mouth of thy artillery,
As we will ours, against these saucy walls; 404
And when that we have dash'd them to the ground,
Why then defy each other, and, pell-mell,
Make work upon ourselves, for heaven or hell.
   K. Phi. Let it be so. Say, where will you assault?   408
   K. John. We from the west will send destruction
Into this city's bosom.
   Aust. I from the north.
   K. Phi.   Our thunder from the south
Shall rain their drift of bullets on this town. 412
   Bast. O, prudent discipline! From north to south
Austria and France shoot in each other's mouth:
I'll stir them to it. Come, away, away!
   First Cit. Hear us, great kings: vouchsafe a while to stay,   416
And I shall show you peace and fair-fac'd league;
Win you this city without stroke or wound;
Rescue those breathing lives to die in beds,
That here come sacrifices for the field.   420
Persever not, but hear me, mighty kings.
   K. John. Speak on with favour: we are bent to hear.
   First Cit. That daughter there of Spain, the Lady Blanch,
Is near to England: look upon the years   424
Of Lewis the Dauphin and that lovely maid.
If lusty love should go in quest of beauty,
Where should he find it fairer than in Blanch?
If zealous love should go in search of virtue,
Where should he find it purer than in Blanch?
If love ambitious sought a match of birth,
Whose veins bound richer blood than Lady Blanch?
Such as she is, in beauty, virtue, birth,   432
Is the young Dauphin every way complete:
If not complete of, say he is not she;
And she again wants nothing, to name want,
If want it be not that she is not he: 436
He is the half part of a blessed man,
Left to be finished by such a she;
And she a fair divided excellence,
Whose fulness of perfection lies in him.   440
O! two such silver currents, when they join,
Do glorify the banks that bound them in;
And two such shores to two such streams made one,
Two such controlling bounds shall you be, kings,   444
To these two princes, if you marry them.
This union shall do more than battery can
To our fast-closed gates; for at this match,
With swifter spleen than powder can enforce, 448
The mouth of passage shall we fling wide ope,
And give you entrance; but without this match,
The sea enraged is not half so deaf,
Lions more confident, mountains and rocks 452
More free from motion, no, not death himself
In mortal fury half so peremptory,
As we to keep this city.
   Bast.   Here's a stay,

That shakes the rotten carcase of old Death 456
Out of his rags! Here's a large mouth, indeed,
That spits forth death and mountains, rocks and seas,
Talks as familiarly of roaring lions
As maids of thirteen do of puppy-dogs.   460
What cannoneer begot this lusty blood?
He speaks plain cannon fire, and smoke and bounce;
He gives the bastinado with his tongue;
Our ears are cudgell'd; not a word of his 464
But buffets better than a fist of France.
'Zounds! I was never so bethump'd with words
Since I first call'd my brother's father dad.
   Eli. [*Aside to* KING JOHN.] Son, list to this conjunction, make this match;   468
Give with our niece a dowry large enough;
For by this knot thou shalt so surely tie
Thy now unsur'd assurance to the crown,
That yon green boy shall have no sun to ripe 472
The bloom that promiseth a mighty fruit.
I see a yielding in the looks of France;
Mark how they whisper: urge them while their souls
Are capable of this ambition,   476
Lest zeal, now melted by the windy breath
Of soft petitions, pity and remorse,
Cool and congeal again to what it was.
   First Cit. Why answer not the double majesties   480
This friendly treaty of our threaten'd town?
   K. Phi. Speak England first, that hath been forward first
To speak unto this city: what say you?
   K. John. If that the Dauphin there, thy princely son,   484
Can in this book of beauty read 'I love,'
Her dowry shall weigh equal with a queen:
For Anjou, and fair Touraine, Maine, Poictiers,
And all that we upon this side the sea,—   488
Except this city now by us besieg'd,—
Find liable to our crown and dignity,
Shall gild her bridal bed and make her rich
In titles, honours, and promotions,   492
As she in beauty, education, blood,
Holds hand with any princess of the world.
   K. Phi. What sayst thou, boy? look in the lady's face.
   Lew. I do, my lord; and in her eye I find 496
A wonder, or a wondrous miracle,
The shadow of myself form'd in her eye;
Which, being but the shadow of your son
Becomes a sun, and makes your son a shadow:
I do protest I never lov'd myself   500
Till now infixed I beheld myself,
Drawn in the flattering table of her eye.
            [*Whispers with* BLANCH.
   Bast. Drawn in the flattering table of her eye!
Hang'd in the frowning wrinkle of her brow!
And quarter'd in her heart! he doth espy
Himself love's traitor: this is pity now,
That hang'd and drawn and quarter'd, there should be   508
In such a love so vile a lout as he.
   Blanch. My uncle's will in this respect is mine:

he see aught in you that makes him like,
at anything he sees, which moves his liking,
can with ease translate it to my will;   513
r if you will, to speak more properly,
will enforce it easily to my love.
rther I will not flatter you, my lord,   516
at all I see in you is worthy love,
an this: that nothing do I see in you,
ough churlish thoughts themselves should
  be your judge,
at I can find should merit any hate.   520
K. John. What say these young ones? What
  say you, my niece?
Blanch. That she is bound in honour still
  to do
hat you in wisdom still vouchsafe to say.
K. John. Speak then, Prince Dauphin; can
  you love this lady?   524
Lew. Nay, ask me if I can refrain from love;
r I do love her most unfeignedly.
K. John. Then do I give Volquessen, Touraine, Maine,
ictiers, and Anjou, these five provinces,   528
ith her to thee; and this addition more,
ll thirty thousand marks of English coin.
ilip of France, if thou be pleas'd withal,
ommand thy son and daughter to join hands.
K. Phi. It likes us well. Young princes, close
  your hands.   533
Aust. And your lips too; for I am well assur'd
hat I did so when I was first assur'd.
K. Phi. Now, citizens of Angiers, ope your
  gates,   536
et in that amity which you have made;
r at Saint Mary's chapel presently
he rites of marriage shall be solemniz'd.
not the Lady Constance in this troop?   540
know she is not; for this match made up
er presence would have interrupted much:
here is she and her son? tell me, who knows.
Lew. She is sad and passionate at your highness' tent.   544
K. Phi. And, by my faith, this league that
  we have made
ill give her sadness very little cure.
rother of England, how may we content
his widow lady? In her right we came;   548
hich we, God knows, have turn'd another way,
o our own vantage.
K. John. We will heal up all;
r we'll create young Arthur Duke of Britaine
nd Earl of Richmond; and this rich fair town
Ve make him lord of. Call the Lady Constance:
ome speedy messenger bid her repair
o our solemnity: I trust we shall,
not fill up the measure of her will,   556
et in some measure satisfy her so,
hat we shall stop her exclamation.
o we, as well as haste will suffer us,
o this unlook'd-for unprepared pomp.   560
  [Exeunt all except the BASTARD. *The
  Citizens* retire from the walls.
Bast. Mad world! mad kings! mad composition!
hn, to stop Arthur's title in the whole,
ath willingly departed with a part;

And France, whose armour conscience buckled
  on,   564
Whom zeal and charity brought to the field
As God's own soldier, rounded in the ear
With that same purpose-changer, that sly devil,
That broker, that still breaks the pate of faith,
That daily break-vow, he that wins of all,   569
Of kings, of beggars, old men, young men,
  maids,
Who having no external thing to lose
But the word 'maid,' cheats the poor maid of
  that,   572
That smooth-fac'd gentleman, tickling Com-
  modity,
Commodity, the bias of the world;
The world, who of itself is peized well,
Made to run even upon even ground,   576
Till this advantage, this vile-drawing bias,
This sway of motion, this Commodity,
Makes it take head from all indifferency,
From all direction, purpose, course, intent: 580
And this same bias, this Commodity,
This bawd, this broker, this all-changing word,
Clapp'd on the outward eye of fickle France,
Hath drawn him from his own determin'd aid,
From a resolv'd and honourable war,   585
To a most base and vile-concluded peace.
And why rail I on this Commodity?
But for because he hath not woo'd me yet.   588
Not that I have the power to clutch my hand
When his fair angels would salute my palm;
But for my hand, as unattempted yet,
Like a poor beggar, raileth on the rich.   592
Well, whiles I am a beggar, I will rail,
And say there is no sin but to be rich;
And being rich, my virtue then shall be
To say there is no vice but beggary.   596
Since kings break faith upon Commodity,
Gain, be my lord, for I will worship thee! *[Exit.*

ACT III

SCENE I.—*France. The French King's Tent.*

Enter CONSTANCE, ARTHUR, *and* SALISBURY.

Const. Gone to be married! gone to swear a
  peace!
False blood to false blood join'd! gone to be
  friends!
Shall Lewis have Blanch, and Blanch those
  provinces?
It is not so; thou hast misspoke, misheard;   4
Be well advis'd, tell o'er thy tale again:
It cannot be; thou dost but say 'tis so.
I trust I may not trust thee, for thy word
Is but the vain breath of a common man: 8
Believe me, I do not believe thee, man;
I have a king's oath to the contrary.
Thou shalt be punish'd for thus frighting me,
For I am sick and capable of fears;   12
Oppress'd with wrongs, and therefore full of
  fears;
A widow, husbandless, subject to fears;
A woman, naturally born to fears;
And though thou now confess thou didst but
  jest,   16

With my vex'd spirits I cannot take a truce,
But they will quake and tremble all this day.
What dost thou mean by shaking of thy
  head?
Why dost thou look so sadly on my son? 20
What means that hand upon that breast of
  thine?
Why holds thine eye that lamentable rheum,
Like a proud river peering o'er his bounds?
Be these sad signs confirmers of thy words? 24
Then speak again; not all thy former tale,
But this one word, whether thy tale be true.
  Sal. As true as I believe you think them
  false
That give you cause to prove my saying true. 28
  Const. O! if thou teach me to believe this
  sorrow,
Teach thou this sorrow how to make me die;
And let belief and life encounter so
As doth the fury of two desperate men 32
Which in the very meeting fall and die.
Lewis marry Blanch! O boy! then where art
  thou?
France friend with England what becomes of
  me?
Fellow, be gone! I cannot brook thy sight: 36
This news hath made thee a most ugly man.
  Sal. What other harm have I, good lady,
  done,
But spoke the harm that is by others done?
  Const. Which harm within itself so heinous is
As it makes harmful all that speak of it. 41
  Arth. I do beseech you, madam, be content.
  Const. If thou, that bidd'st me be content,
  wert grim,
Ugly and slanderous to thy mother's womb, 44
Full of unpleasing blots and sightless stains,
Lame, foolish, crooked, swart, prodigious,
Patch'd with foul moles and eye-offending
  marks,
I would not care, I then would be content; 48
For then I should not love thee, no, nor thou
Become thy great birth, nor deserve a crown.
But thou art fair; and at thy birth, dear boy,
Nature and Fortune join'd to make thee great:
Of Nature's gifts thou mayst with lilies boast 53
And with the half-blown rose. But Fortune, O!
She is corrupted, chang'd, and won from
  thee:
She adulterates hourly with thine uncle John, 56
And with her golden hand hath pluck'd on
  France
To tread down fair respect of sovereignty,
And made his majesty the bawd to theirs.
France is a bawd to Fortune and King John, 60
That strumpet Fortune, that usurping John!
Tell me, thou fellow, is not France forsworn?
Envenom him with words, or get thee gone
And leave those woes alone which I alone 64
Am bound to underbear.
  Sal. Pardon me, madam,
I may not go without you to the kings.
  Const. Thou mayst, thou shalt: I will not go
  with thee.
I will instruct my sorrows to be proud; 68
For grief is proud and makes his owner stoop.

To me and to the state of my great grief
Let kings assemble; for my grief 's so great
That no supporter but the huge firm earth
Can hold it up: here I and sorrows sit;
Here is my throne, bid kings come bow to it.
  [*Seats herself on the groun*

Enter KING JOHN, KING PHILIP, LEWIS, BLANC
  ELINOR, *the* BASTARD, DUKE OF AUSTRIA, a
  Attendants.

  K. Phi. 'Tis true, fair daughter; and th
  blessed day
Ever in France shall be kept festival:
To solemnize this day the glorious sun
Stays in his course and plays the alchemist,
Turning with splendour of his precious eye
The meagre cloddy earth to glittering gold:
The yearly course that brings this day about
Shall never see it but a holiday.
  Const. [*Rising.*] A wicked day, and not
  holy day!
What hath this day deserv'd? what hath it do
That it in golden letters should be set
Among the high tides in the calendar?
Nay, rather turn this day out of the week,
This day of shame, oppression, perjury:
Or, if it must stand still, let wives with child
Pray that their burdens may not fall this da
Lest that their hopes prodigiously be cross'
But on this day let seamen fear no wrack;
No bargains break that are not this day mad
This day all things begun come to ill end;
Yea, faith itself to hollow falsehood change
  K. Phi. By heaven, lady, you shall have n
  cause
To curse the fair proceedings of this day:
Have I not pawn'd to you my majesty?
  Const. You have beguil'd me with a counte
  feit
Resembling majesty, which, being touch'd ar
  tried,
Proves valueless: you are forsworn, forswor
You came in arms to spill mine enemies' blood
But now in arms you strengthen it with your
The grappling vigour and rough frown of wa
Is cold in amity and painted peace,
And our oppression hath made up this leagu
Arm, arm, you heavens, against these perjur
  kings!
A widow cries; be husband to me, heavens!
Let not the hours of this ungodly day
Wear out the day in peace; but, ere sunset,
Set armed discord 'twixt these perjur'd king
Hear me! O, hear me!
  Aust. Lady Constance, peace
  Const. War! war! no peace! peace is to m
  a war.
O, Lymoges! O, Austria! thou dost shame
That bloody spoil: thou slave, thou wretc
  thou coward!
Thou little valiant, great in villany!
Thou ever strong upon the stronger side!
Thou Fortune's champion, that dost never fig
But when her humorous ladyship is by
To teach thee safety! thou art perjur'd too, 12
And sooth'st up greatness. What a fool art tho

ramping fool, to brag, and stamp and swear
oon my party! Thou cold-blooded slave,
ast thou not spoke like thunder on my side?
en sworn my soldier? bidding me depend 125
oon thy stars, thy fortune, and thy strength?
id dost thou now fall over to my foes?
iou wear a lion's hide! doff it for shame, 128
id hang a calf's-skin on those recreant limbs.
Aust. O! that a man should speak those
words to me.
Bast. And hang a calf's-skin on those recreant limbs.
Aust. Thou dar'st not say so, villain, for thy
life. 132
Bast. And hang a calf's-skin on those recreant limbs.
K. John. We like not this; thou dost forget
thyself.

Enter PANDULPH.

K. Phi. Here comes the holy legate of the
pope.
Pand. Hail, you anointed deputies of heaven!
o thee, King John, my holy errand is. 137
Pandulph, of fair Milan cardinal,
nd from Pope Innocent the legate here,
o in his name religiously demand 140
'hy thou against the church, our holy mother,
wilfully dost spurn; and, force perforce,
eep Stephen Langton, chosen Archbishop
f Canterbury, from that holy see? 144
iis, in our foresaid holy father's name,
ipe Innocent, I do demand of thee.
K. John. What earthly name to interroga-
tories
an task the free breath of a sacred king? 148
iou canst not, cardinal, devise a name
o slight, unworthy and ridiculous,
o charge me to an answer, as the pope.
ell him this tale; and from the mouth of England 152
idd thus much more: that no Italian priest
iall tithe or toll in our dominions;
it as we under heaven are supreme head,
o under him that great supremacy, 156
'here we do reign, we will alone uphold,
ithout the assistance of a mortal hand:
o tell the pope; all reverence set apart
o him, and his usurp'd authority. 160
K. Phi. Brother of England, you blaspheme
in this.
K. John. Though you and all the kings of
Christendom
re led so grossly by this meddling priest,
reading the curse that money may buy out;
nd, by the merit of vile gold, dross, dust, 165
urchase corrupted pardon of a man,
Tho in that sale sells pardon from himself;
hough you and all the rest so grossly led 168
his juggling witchcraft with revenue cherish;
et I alone, alone do me oppose
gainst the pope, and count his friends my
foes.
Pand. Then, by the lawful power that I have,
hou shalt stand curs'd and excommunicate:
nd blessed shall he be that doth revolt

From his allegiance to a heretic;
And meritorious shall that hand be call'd, 176
Canonized and worshipp'd as a saint,
That takes away by any secret course
Thy hateful life.
Const. O! lawful let it be
That I have room with Rome to curse awhile.
Good father cardinal, cry thou amen 181
To my keen curses; for without my wrong
There is no tongue hath power to curse him
right.
Pand. There's law and warrant, lady, for
my curse. 184
Const. And for mine too: when law can do
no right,
Let it be lawful that law bar no wrong.
Law cannot give my child his kingdom here,
For he that holds his kingdom holds the law:
Therefore, since law itself is perfect wrong, 189
How can the law forbid my tongue to curse?
Pand. Philip of France, on peril of a curse,
Let go the hand of that arch-heretic, 192
And raise the power of France upon his head,
Unless he do submit himself to Rome.
Eli. Look'st thou pale, France? do not let
go thy hand.
Const. Look to that, devil, lest that France
repent, 196
And by disjoining hands, hell lose a soul.
Aust. King Philip, listen to the cardinal.
Bast. And hang a calf's-skin on his recreant
limbs.
Aust. Well, ruffian, I must pocket up these
wrongs, 200
Because—
Bast. Your breeches best may carry them.
K. John. Philip, what sayst thou to the car-
dinal?
Const. What should he say, but as the car-
dinal?
Lew. Bethink you, father; for the difference
Is purchase of a heavy curse from Rome, 205
Or the light loss of England for a friend:
Forego the easier.
Blanch. That's the curse of Rome.
Const. O Lewis, stand fast! the devil tempts
thee here, 208
In likeness of a new untrimmed bride.
Blanch. The Lady Constance speaks not from
her faith,
But from her need.
Const. O! if thou grant my need,
Which only lives but by the death of faith, 212
That need must needs infer this principle,
That faith would live again by death of need:
O! then, tread down my need, and faith mounts
up;
Keep my need up, and faith is trodden down.
K. John. The king is mov'd, and answers
not to this. 217
Const. O! be remov'd from him, and answer
well.
Aust. Do so, King Philip: hang no more in
doubt.
Bast. Hang nothing but a calf's-skin, most
sweet lout. 220

K. Phi. I am perplex'd, and know not what to say.

Pand. What canst thou say but will perplex thee more,
If thou stand excommunicate and curs'd?

K. Phi. Good reverend father, make my person yours, 224
And tell me how you would bestow yourself.
This royal hand and mine are newly knit,
And the conjunction of our inward souls
Married in league, coupled and link'd together
With all religious strength of sacred vows; 229
The latest breath that gave the sound of words
Was deep-sworn faith, peace, amity, true love,
Between our kingdoms and our royal selves; 232
And even before this truce, but new before,
No longer than we well could wash our hands
To clap this royal bargain up of peace,
Heaven knows, they were besmear'd and over-stain'd 236
With slaughter's pencil, where revenge did paint
The fearful difference of incensed kings:
And shall these hands, so lately purg'd of blood,
So newly join'd in love, so strong in both, 240
Unyoke this seizure and this kind regreet?
Play fast and loose with faith? so jest with heaven,
Make such unconstant children of ourselves,
As now again to snatch our palm from palm,
Unswear faith sworn, and on the marriage-bed
Of smiling peace to march a bloody host,
And make a riot on the gentle brow
Of true sincerity? O! holy sir, 248
My reverend father, let it not be so!
Out of your grace, devise, ordain, impose
Some gentle order, and then we shall be bless'd
To do your pleasure and continue friends. 252

Pand. All form is formless, order orderless,
Save what is opposite to England's love.
Therefore to arms! be champion of our church,
Or let the church, our mother, breathe her curse,
A mother's curse, on her revolting son. 257
France, thou mayst hold a serpent by the tongue,
A chafed lion by the mortal paw,
A fasting tiger safer by the tooth, 260
Than keep in peace that hand which thou dost hold.

K. Phi. I may disjoin my hand, but not my faith.

Pand. So mak'st thou faith an enemy to faith:
And like a civil war sett'st oath to oath, 264
Thy tongue against thy tongue. O! let thy vow
First made to heaven, first be to heaven performed;
That is, to be the champion of our church.
What since thou swor'st is sworn against thyself
And may not be performed by thyself; 269
For that which thou hast sworn to do amiss
Is not amiss when it is truly done;
And being not done, where doing tends to ill,
The truth is then most done not doing it. 273
The better act of purposes mistook
Is to mistake again; though indirect,
Yet indirection thereby grows direct, 276
And falsehood falsehood cures, as fire cools fire

Within the scorched veins of one new-burn'
It is religion that doth make vows kept;
But thou hast sworn against religion 2
By what thou swear'st, against the thing tho
swear'st,
And mak'st an oath the surety for thy truth
Against an oath: the truth thou art unsure
To swear, swears only not to be forsworn; 2
Else what a mockery should it be to swear!
But thou dost swear only to be forsworn;
And most forsworn, to keep what thou do
swear.
Therefore thy later vows against thy first 2
Is in thyself rebellion to thyself;
And better conquest never canst thou mak
Than arm thy constant and thy nobler parts
Against these giddy loose suggestions: 2
Upon which better part our prayers come in
If thou vouchsafe them; but, if not, then kno
The peril of our curses light on thee
So heavy as thou shalt not shake them off, 2
But in despair die under their black weight.

Aust. Rebellion, flat rebellion!

Bast. Will't not be
Will not a calf's-skin stop that mouth of thin

Lew. Father, to arms!

Blanch. Upon thy wedding-day? 3
Against the blood that thou hast married?
What! shall our feast be kept with slaughter men?
Shall braying trumpets and loud churlish drum
Clamours of hell, be measures to our pomp? 3
O husband, hear me! ay, alack! how new
Is husband in my mouth; even for that nam
Which till this time my tongue did ne'er pre
nounce,
Upon my knee I beg, go not to arms 3
Against mine uncle.

Const. O! upon my knee,
Made hard with kneeling, I do pray to thee,
Thou virtuous Dauphin, alter not the doom
Forethought by heaven. 3

Blanch. Now shall I see thy love: wh
motive may
Be stronger with thee than the name of wife?

Const. That which upholdeth him that th
upholds,
His honour: O! thine honour, Lewis, thi
honour. 3

Lew. I muse your majesty doth seem so col
When such profound respects do pull you o

Pand. I will denounce a curse upon his hea

K. Phi. Thou shalt not need. England, I
fall from thee. 3

Const. O fair return of banish'd majesty!

Eli. O foul revolt of French inconstancy!

K. John. France, thou shalt rue this ho
within this hour.

Bast. Old Time the clock-setter, that ba
sexton Time, 3
Is it as he will? well then, France shall rue.

Blanch. The sun's o'ercast with blood: fa
day, adieu!
Which is the side that I must go withal?
I am with both: each army hath a hand; 3
And in their rage, I having hold of both,

They whirl asunder and dismember me.
Husband, I cannot pray that thou mayst win;
Uncle, I needs must pray that thou mayst lose;
Father, I may not wish the fortune thine;   333
Grandam, I will not wish thy wishes thrive:
Whoever wins, on that side shall I lose;
Assured loss before the match be play'd.   336

Lew. Lady, with me; with me thy fortune lies.
Blanch. There where my fortune lives, there
my life dies.

K. John. Cousin, go draw our puissance together.   [*Exit* BASTARD.

France, I am burn'd up with inflaming wrath,
A rage whose heat hath this condition,   341
That nothing can allay, nothing but blood,
The blood, and dearest-valu'd blood of France.

K. Phi. Thy rage shall burn thee up, and
thou shalt turn   344
To ashes, ere our blood shall quench that fire:
Look to thyself, thou art in jeopardy.

K. John. No more than he that threats. To
arms let's hie!   [*Exeunt.*

SCENE II.—*The Same. Plains near Angiers.*

Alarums; excursions. Enter the BASTARD, *with
the* DUKE OF AUSTRIA'S *head.*

Bast. Now, by my life, this day grows won-
drous hot;
Some airy devil hovers in the sky
And pours down mischief. Austria's head lie
there,
While Philip breathes.   4

Enter KING JOHN, ARTHUR, *and* HUBERT.

K. John. Hubert, keep this boy. Philip, make
up,
My mother is assailed in our tent,
And ta'en, I fear.

Bast.   My lord, I rescu'd her;
Her highness is in safety, fear you not: 8
But on, my liege; for very little pains
Will bring this labour to a happy end. [*Exeunt.*

SCENE III.—*The Same.*

Alarums; excursions; retreat. Enter KING JOHN,
ELINOR, ARTHUR, *the* BASTARD, HUBERT, *and*
Lords.

K. John. [*To* ELINOR.] So shall it be; your
grace shall stay behind
So strongly guarded. [*To* ARTHUR.] Cousin,
look not sad:
Thy grandam loves thee; and thy uncle will
As dear be to thee as thy father was.   4

Arth. O! this will make my mother die with
grief.

K. John. [*To the* BASTARD.] Cousin, away for
England! haste before;
And, ere our coming, see thou shake the bags
Of hoarding abbots; set at liberty   8
Imprison'd angels: the fat ribs of peace
Must by the hungry now be fed upon:
Use our commission in his utmost force.

Bast. Bell, book, and candle shall not drive
me back   12
When gold and silver becks me to come on.
I leave your highness. Grandam, I will pray,—
If ever I remember to be holy,—
For your fair safety; so I kiss your hand.   16

Eli. Farewell, gentle cousin.

K. John.   Coz, farewell.
[*Exit* BASTARD.

Eli. Come hither, little kinsman; hark, a
word.   [*She takes* ARTHUR *aside.*

K. John. Come hither, Hubert. O my gentle
Hubert,
We owe thee much: within this wall of flesh 20
There is a soul counts thee her creditor,
And with advantage means to pay thy love:
And, my good friend, thy voluntary oath
Lives in this bosom, dearly cherished.   24
Give me thy hand. I had a thing to say,
But I will fit it with some better time.
By heaven, Hubert, I am almost asham'd
To say what good respect I have of thee.   28

Hub. I am much bounden to your majesty.

K. John. Good friend, thou hast no cause
to say so yet;
But thou shalt have; and creep time ne'er so slow,
Yet it shall come for me to do thee good.   32
I had a thing to say, but let it go:
The sun is in the heaven, and the proud day,
Attended with the pleasures of the world,
Is all too wanton and too full of gawds   36
To give me audience: if the midnight bell
Did, with his iron tongue and brazen mouth,
Sound one into the drowsy race of night;
If this same were a churchyard where we stand,
And thou possessed with a thousand wrongs; 41
Or if that surly spirit, melancholy,
Had bak'd thy blood and made it heavy-thick,
Which else runs tickling up and down the veins,
Making that idiot, laughter, keep men's eyes 45
And strain their cheeks to idle merriment,
A passion hateful to my purposes;
Or if that thou couldst see me without eyes, 48
Hear me without thine ears, and make reply
Without a tongue, using conceit alone,
Without eyes, ears, and harmful sound of words;
Then, in despite of brooded watchful day,   52
I would into thy bosom pour my thoughts:
But ah! I will not: yet I love thee well;
And, by my troth, I think thou lov'st me well.

Hub. So well, that what you bid me under-
take,   56
Though that my death were adjunct to my act,
By heaven, I would do it.

K. John.   Do not I know thou wouldst?
Good Hubert! Hubert, Hubert, throw thine eye
On yon young boy: I'll tell thee what, my
friend,   60
He is a very serpent in my way;
And wheresoe'er this foot of mine doth tread
He lies before me: dost thou understand me?
Thou art his keeper.

Hub.   And I'll keep him so   64
That he shall not offend your majesty.

K. John. Death.

Hub.   My lord?

K. John.   **A grave.**
Hub.   He shall not live.
K. John.   Enough.
I could be merry now. Hubert, I love thee;
Well, I'll not say what I intend for thee: 68
Remember. Madam, fare you well:
I'll send those powers o'er to your majesty.
   Eli. My blessing go with thee!
   K. John.   For England, cousin; go:
Hubert shall be your man, attend on you   72
With all true duty. On toward Calais, ho!
                           [*Exeunt.*

SCENE IV.—*The Same. The French King's
Tent.*

Enter KING PHILIP, LEWIS, PANDULPH,
and Attendants.

   K. Phi. So, by a roaring tempest on the flood,
A whole armado of convicted sail
Is scatter'd and disjoin'd from fellowship.
   Pand. Courage and comfort! all shall yet go
   well.   4
   K. Phi. What can go well when we have run
   so ill?
Are we not beaten? Is not Angiers lost?
Arthur ta'en prisoner? divers dear friends slain?
And bloody England into England gone,   8
O'erbearing interruption, spite of France?
   Lew. What he hath won that hath he forti-
   fied:
So hot a speed with such advice dispos'd,
Such temperate order in so fierce a cause,   12
Doth want example: who hath read or heard
Of any kindred action like to this?
   K. Phi. Well could I bear that England had
   this praise,
So we could find some pattern of our shame. 16

Enter CONSTANCE.

Look, who comes here! a grave unto a soul;
Holding the eternal spirit, against her will,
In the vile prison of afflicted breath.
I prithee lady, go away with me.   20
   Const. Lo now! now see the issue of your
   peace.
   K. Phi. Patience, good lady! comfort, gentle
   Constance!
   Const. No, I defy all counsel, all redress,
But that which ends all counsel, true redress, 24
Death, death: O, amiable lovely death!
Thou odoriferous stench! sound rottenness!
Arise forth from the couch of lasting night,
Thou hate and terror to prosperity,   28
And I will kiss thy detestable bones,
And put my eyeballs in thy vaulty brows,
And ring these fingers with thy household worms,
And stop this gap of breath with fulsome dust,
And be a carrion monster like thyself: 33
Come, grin on me; and I will think thou smil'st
And buss thee as thy wife! Misery's love,
O! come to me.
   K. Phi.   O fair affliction, peace!   36
   Const. No, no, I will not, having breath to
   cry:
O! that my tongue were in the thunder's mouth!

Then with a passion would I shake the world
And rouse from sleep that fell anatomy   4
Which cannot hear a lady's feeble voice,
Which scorns a modern invocation.
   Pand. Lady, you utter madness, and no
   sorrow.
   Const. Thou art not holy to belie me so; 4
I am not mad: this hair I tear is mine;
My name is Constance; I was Geffrey's wife;
Young Arthur is my son, and he is lost!
I am not mad: I would to heaven I were!
For then 'tis like I should forget myself:
O! if I could, what grief should I forget.
Preach some philosophy to make me mad,
And thou shalt be canoniz'd, cardinal;   5
For being not mad but sensible of grief,
My reasonable part produces reason
How I may be deliver'd of these woes,
And teaches me to kill or hang myself: 5
If I were mad, I should forget my son,
Or madly think a babe of clouts were he.
I am not mad: too well, too well I feel
The different plague of each calamity.   6
   K. Phi. Bind up those tresses. O! what love
   I note
In the fair multitude of those her hairs:
Where but by chance a silver drop hath fallen
Even to that drop ten thousand wiry friends 6
Do glue themselves in sociable grief,
Like true, inseparable, faithful loves,
Sticking together in calamity.
   Const. To England, if you will.
   K. Phi.   Bind up your hairs. 6
   Const. Yes, that I will; and wherefore will
   do it?
I tore them from their bonds, and cried aloud
'O! that these hands could so redeem my son,
As they have given these hairs their liberty!' 7
But now I envy at their liberty,
And will again commit them to their bonds,
Because my poor child is a prisoner.
And, father cardinal, I have heard you say 7
That we shall see and know our friends in heaven
If that be true, I shall see my boy again;
For since the birth of Cain, the first male child
To him that did but yesterday suspire,   8
There was not such a gracious creature born.
But now will canker-sorrow eat my bud
And chase the native beauty from his cheek,
And he will look as hollow as a ghost,   8
As dim and meagre as an ague's fit,
And so he'll die; and, rising so again,
When I shall meet him in the court of heaven
I shall not know him: therefore never, never 8
Must I behold my pretty Arthur more.
   Pand. You hold too heinous a respect of
   grief.
   Const. He talks to me, that never had a son.
   K. Phi. You are as fond of grief as of your
   child.   92
   Const. Grief fills the room up of my absent
   child,
Lies in his bed, walks up and down with me,
Puts on his pretty looks, repeats his words,
Remembers me of all his gracious parts,   9
Stuffs out his vacant garments with his form;

en have I reason to be fond of grief.
re you well: had you such a loss as I,
ould give better comfort than you do.   100
vill not keep this form upon my head
hen there is such disorder in my wit.
Lord! my boy, my Arthur, my fair son!
y life, my joy, my food, my all the world!   104
y widow-comfort, and my sorrows' cure!
                                        [*Exit.*
K. Phi. I fear some outrage, and I'll follow
  her.   [*Exit.*
Lew. There's nothing in this world can make
  me joy:
fe is as tedious as a twice-told tale,   108
xing the dull ear of a drowsy man;
d bitter shame hath spoil'd the sweet world's
  taste,
at it yields nought but shame and bitterness.
Pand. Before the curing of a strong disease,
en in the instant of repair and health,   113
e fit is strongest: evils that take leave,
their departure most of all show evil.
hat have you lost by losing of this day?   116
Lew. All days of glory, joy, and happiness.
Pand. If you had won it, certainly you had.
, no; when Fortune means to men most
  good,
e looks upon them with a threatening eye.   120
is strange to think how much King John
  hath lost
this which he accounts so clearly won.
e not you griev'd that Arthur is his prisoner?
Lew. As heartily as he is glad he hath him.
Pand. Your mind is all as youthful as your
  blood.   125
ow hear me speak with a prophetic spirit;
r even the breath of what I mean to speak
all blow each dust, each straw, each little rub,
t of the path which shall directly lead   129
y foot to England's throne; and therefore
  mark.
hn hath seiz'd Arthur; and it cannot be,
at whiles warm life plays in that infant's
  veins   132
e misplac'd John should entertain an hour,
e minute, nay, one quiet breath of rest.
sceptre snatch'd with an unruly hand
ust be as boisterously maintain'd as gain'd;
d he that stands upon a slippery place   137
akes nice of no vile hold to stay him up:
at John may stand, then Arthur needs must
  fall;
be it, for it cannot be but so.   140
Lew. But what shall I gain by young Arthur's
  fall?
Pand. You, in the right of Lady Blanch your
  wife,
ay then make all the claim that Arthur did.
Lew. And lose it, life and all, as Arthur did.
Pand. How green you are and fresh in this
  old world!   145
hn lays you plots; the times conspire with you;
r he that steeps his safety in true blood
all find but bloody safety and untrue.   148
is act so evilly borne shall cool the hearts
f all his people and freeze up their zeal,

That none so small advantage shall step forth
To check his reign, but they will cherish it;   152
No natural exhalation in the sky,
No scope of nature, no distemper'd day,
No common wind, no customed event,
But they will pluck away his natural cause   156
And call them meteors, prodigies, and signs,
Abortives, presages, and tongues of heaven,
Plainly denouncing vengeance upon John.
  Lew. May be he will not touch young
    Arthur's life,   160
But hold himself safe in his prisonment.
  Pand. O! sir, when he shall hear of your
    approach,
If that young Arthur be not gone already,
Even at that news he dies; and then the hearts
Of all his people shall revolt from him   165
And kiss the lips of unacquainted change,
And pick strong matter of revolt and wrath
Out of the bloody fingers' ends of John.   168
Methinks I see this hurly all on foot:
And, O! what better matter breeds for you
Than I have nam'd. The bastard Faulconbridge
Is now in England ransacking the church,   172
Offending charity: if but a dozen French
Were there in arms, they would be as a call
To train ten thousand English to their side;
Or as a little snow, tumbled about,   176
Anon becomes a mountain. O noble Dauphin!
Go with me to the king. 'Tis wonderful
What may be wrought out of their discontent
Now that their souls are topful of offence.   180
For England go; I will whet on the king.
  Lew. Strong reasons make strong actions.
    Let us go:
If you say ay, the king will not say no.
                                        [*Exeunt.*

ACT IV

SCENE I.—*Northampton. A Room in the
  Castle.*

Enter HUBERT *and Two* Attendants.

Hub. Heat me these irons hot; and look
    thou stand
Within the arras: when I strike my foot
Upon the bosom of the ground, rush forth,
And bind the boy which you shall find with me
Fast to the chair: be heedful. Hence, and watch.
  First Attend. I hope your warrant will bear
    out the deed.   6
  Hub. Uncleanly scruples! fear not you: look
    to't.   [*Exeunt* Attendants.
Young lad, come forth; I have to say with you.

Enter ARTHUR.

  Arth. Good morrow, Hubert.
  Hub.   Good morrow, little prince.
  Arth. As little prince,—having so great a title
To be more prince,—as may be. You are sad.
  Hub. Indeed, I have been merrier.
  Arth.   Mercy on me!   12
Methinks nobody should be sad but I:
Yet I remember, when I was in France,
Young gentlemen would be as sad as night,

Only for wantonness. By my christendom, 16
So I were out of prison and kept sheep,
I should be as merry as the day is long;
And so I would be here, but that I doubt
My uncle practises more harm to me: 20
He is afraid of me, and I of him.
Is it my fault that I was Geffrey's son?
No, indeed, is 't not; and I would to heaven
I were your son, so you would love me, Hubert.
   Hub. [*Aside.*] If I talk to him with his inno- 25
    cent prate
He will awake my mercy which lies dead:
Therefore I will be sudden and dispatch.
   Arth. Are you sick, Hubert? you look pale 28
    to-day:
In sooth, I would you were a little sick,
That I might sit all night and watch with you:
I warrant I love you more than you do me.
   Hub. [*Aside.*] His words do take possession 32
    of my bosom.
Read here, young Arthur. [*Showing a paper.*]
           [*Aside.*] How now, foolish rheum!
Turning dispiteous torture out of door!
I must be brief, lest resolution drop
Out at mine eyes in tender womanish tears. 36
Can you not read it? is it not fair writ?
   Arth. Too fairly, Hubert, for so foul effect.
Must you with hot irons burn out both mine
    eyes?
   Hub. Young boy, I must.
   Arth.   And will you?
   Hub.   And I will. 40
   Arth. Have you the heart? When your head
    did but ache,
I knit my handkercher about your brows,—
The best I had, a princess wrought it me,—
And I did never ask it you again; 44
And with my hand at midnight held your head,
And like the watchful minutes to the hour,
Still and anon cheer'd up the heavy time,
Saying, 'What lack you?' and, 'Where lies your
    grief?' 48
Or, 'What good love may I perform for you?'
Many a poor man's son would have lain still,
And ne'er have spoke a loving word to you;
But you at your sick-service had a prince. 52
Nay, you may think my love was crafty love,
And call it cunning: do an if you will.
If heaven be pleas'd that you must use me ill,
Why then you must. Will you put out mine
    eyes? 56
These eyes that never did nor never shall
So much as frown on you?
   Hub.   I have sworn to do it;
And with hot irons must I burn them out.
   Arth. Ah! none but in this iron age would
    do it! 60
The iron of itself, though heat red-hot,
Approaching near these eyes, would drink my
    tears
And quench this fiery indignation
Even in the matter of mine innocence; 64
Nay, after that, consume away in rust,
But for containing fire to harm mine eye.
Are you more stubborn-hard than hammer'd
    iron?

An if an angel should have come to me 68
And told me Hubert should put out mine eyes,
I would not have believ'd him; no tongue but
    Hubert's.
   Hub. [*Stamps.*] Come forth.

   Re-enter Attendants, *with cord, irons, &c.*

Do as I bid you do. 72
   Arth. O! save me, Hubert, save me! my eyes
    are out
Even with the fierce looks of these bloody men.
   Hub. Give me the iron, I say, and bind him
    here.
   Arth. Alas! what need you be so boisterous-
    rough? 76
I will not struggle; I will stand stone-still.
For heaven's sake, Hubert, let me not be bound!
Nay, hear me, Hubert: drive these men away,
And I will sit as quiet as a lamb; 80
I will not stir, nor wince, nor speak a word,
Nor look upon the iron angerly.
Thrust but these men away, and I'll forgive you,
Whatever torment you do put me to. 84
   Hub. Go, stand within: let me alone with him.
   First Attend. I am best pleas'd to be from
    such a deed.   [*Exeunt* Attendants.
   Arth. Alas! I then have chid away my friend.
He hath a stern look, but a gentle heart. 88
Let him come back, that his compassion may
Give life to yours.
   Hub.   Come, boy, prepare yourself.
   Arth. Is there no remedy?
   Hub.   None, but to lose your eyes.
   Arth. O heaven! that there were but a mote
    in yours, 92
A grain, a dust, a gnat, a wandering hair,
Any annoyance in that precious sense;
Then feeling what small things are boisterous
    there,
Your vile intent must needs seem horrible. 96
   Hub. Is this your promise? go to, hold your
    tongue.
   Arth. Hubert, the utterance of a brace of
    tongues
Must needs want pleading for a pair of eyes.
Let me not hold my tongue; let me not, Hubert;
Or Hubert, if you will, cut out my tongue, 101
So I may keep mine eyes: O! spare mine eyes,
Though to no use but still to look on you:
Lo! by my troth, the instrument is cold 104
And would not harm me.
   Hub.   I can heat it, boy.
   Arth. No, in good sooth; the fire is dead
    with grief,
Being create for comfort, to be us'd
In undeserv'd extremes: see else yourself; 108
There is no malice in this burning coal;
The breath of heaven hath blown his spirit out,
And strew'd repentant ashes on his head.
   Hub. But with my breath I can revive it,
    boy. 112
   Arth. An if you do you will but make it blush
And glow with shame of your proceedings,
    Hubert:
Nay, it perchance will sparkle in your eyes;
And like a dog that is compell'd to fight, 116

natch at his master that doth tarre him on.
All things that you should use to do me wrong
Deny their office: only you do lack
Creatures of note for mercy-lacking uses. 121
 Hub. Well, see to live; I will not touch thine
  eyes
For all the treasure that thine uncle owes:
Yet am I sworn and I did purpose, boy, 124
With this same very iron to burn them out.
 Arth. O! now you look like Hubert, all this
  while
You were disguised.
 Hub.   Peace! no more. Adieu.
Your uncle must not know but you are dead;
I'll fill these dogged spies with false reports: 129
And, pretty child, sleep doubtless and secure,
That Hubert for the wealth of all the world
Will not offend thee.
 Arth. O heaven! I thank you, Hubert.
 Hub. Silence! no more, go closely in with
  me: 133
Much danger do I undergo for thee. [*Exeunt.*

SCENE II.—*The Same. A Room of State in
the Palace.*

Enter KING JOHN, *crowned*; PEMBROKE, SALIS-
BURY, *and other* Lords. *The* KING *takes his
state.*

 K. John. Here once again we sit, once again
  crown'd,
And look'd upon, I hope, with cheerful eyes.
 Pem. This 'once again,' but that your high-
  ness pleas'd,
Was once superfluous: you were crown'd before,
And that high royalty was ne'er pluck'd off, 5
The faiths of men ne'er stained with revolt;
Fresh expectation troubled not the land
With any long'd-for change or better state. 8
 Sal. Therefore, to be possess'd with double
  pomp,
To guard a title that was rich before,
To gild refined gold, to paint the lily,
To throw a perfume on the violet, 12
To smooth the ice, or add another hue
Into the rainbow, or with taper-light
To seek the beauteous eye of heaven to garnish,
Is wasteful and ridiculous excess. 16
 Pem. But that your royal pleasure must be
  done,
This act is as an ancient tale new told,
And in the last repeating troublesome,
Being urged at a time unseasonable. 20
 Sal. In this the antique and well-noted face
Of plain old form is much disfigured;
And, like a shifted wind unto a sail,
It makes the course of thoughts to fetch about,
Startles and frights consideration, 25
Makes sound opinion sick and truth suspected,
For putting on so new a fashion'd robe.
 Pem. When workmen strive to do better than
  well 28
They do confound their skill in covetousness;
And oftentimes excusing of a fault

Doth make the fault the worse by the excuse:
As patches set upon a little breach 32
Discredit more in hiding of the fault
Than did the fault before it was so patch'd.
 Sal. To this effect, before you were new-
  crown'd,
We breath'd our counsel: but it pleas'd your
  highness 36
To overbear it, and we are all well pleas'd;
Since all and every part of what we would
Doth make a stand at what your highness will.
 K. John. Some reasons of this double coro-
  nation 40
I have possess'd you with and think them strong;
And more, more strong,—when lesser is my
  fear,—
I shall indue you with: meantime but ask
What you would have reform'd that is not well;
And well shall you perceive how willingly 45
I will both hear and grant you your requests.
 Pem. Then I,—as one that am the tongue of
  these
To sound the purposes of all their hearts,— 48
Both for myself and them,—but, chief of all,
Your safety, for the which myself and them
Bend their best studies,—heartily request
The enfranchisement of Arthur; whose restraint
Doth move the murmuring lips of discontent 53
To break into this dangerous argument:
If what in rest you have in right you hold,
Why then your fears,—which, as they say, attend
The steps of wrong,—should move you to mew up
Your tender kinsman, and to choke his days
With barbarous ignorance, and deny his youth
The rich advantage of good exercise? 60
That the time's enemies may not have this
To grace occasions, let it be our suit
That you have bid us ask, his liberty;
Which for our goods we do no further ask 64
Than whereupon our weal, on you depending,
Counts it your weal he have his liberty.

Enter HUBERT.

 K. John. Let it be so: I do commit his youth
To your direction. Hubert, what news with
  you?   [*Taking him apart.*
 Pem. This is the man should do the bloody
  deed; 69
He show'd his warrant to a friend of mine:
The image of a wicked heinous fault
Lives in his eye; that close aspect of his 72
Does show the mood of a much troubled breast;
And I do fearfully believe 'tis done,
What we so fear'd he had a charge to do.
 Sal. The colour of the king doth come and go
Between his purpose and his conscience, 77
Like heralds 'twixt two dreadful battles set:
His passion is so ripe it needs must break.
 Pem. And when it breaks, I fear will issue
  thence 80
The foul corruption of a sweet child's death.
 K. John. We cannot hold mortality's strong
  hand:
Good lords, although my will to give is living,
The suit which you demand is gone and dead:
He tells us Arthur is deceas'd to-night. 85

Sal. Indeed we fear'd his sickness was past
cure.

Pem. Indeed we heard how near his death
he was
Before the child himself felt he was sick: 88
This must be answer'd, either here or hence.

K. John. Why do you bend such solemn
brows on me?
Think you I bear the shears of destiny?
Have I commandment on the pulse of life? 92

Sal. It is apparent foul play; and 'tis shame
That greatness should so grossly offer it:
So thrive it in your game! and so, farewell.

Pem. Stay yet, Lord Salisbury; I'll go with
thee,   96
And find the inheritance of this poor child,
His little kingdom of a forced grave.
That blood which ow'd the breadth of all this
isle,
Three foot of it doth hold: bad world the
while!   100
This must not be thus borne: this will break out
To all our sorrows, and ere long I doubt.
                                        [*Exeunt* Lords.

K. John. They burn in indignation. I repent:
There is no sure foundation set on blood, 104
No certain life achiev'd by others' death.

Enter a Messenger.

A fearful eye thou hast: where is that blood
That I have seen inhabit in those cheeks?
So foul a sky clears not without a storm: 108
Pour down thy weather: how goes all in
France?

Mess. From France to England. Never such
a power
For any foreign preparation
Was levied in the body of a land.   112
The copy of your speed is learn'd by them;
For when you should be told they do prepare,
The tidings come that they are all arriv'd.

K. John. O! where hath our intelligence been
drunk?   116
Where hath it slept? Where is my mother's
care
That such an army could be drawn in France,
And she not hear of it?

Mess.   My liege, her ear
Is stopp'd with dust: the first of April died 120
Your noble mother; and, as I hear, my lord,
The Lady Constance in a frenzy died
Three days before: but this from rumour's
tongue
I idly heard; if true or false I know not.   124

K. John. Withhold thy speed, dreadful occa-
sion!
O! make a league with me, till I have pleas'd
My discontented peers. What! mother dead!
How wildly then walks my estate in France! 128
Under whose conduct came those powers of
France
That thou for truth giv'st out are landed here?

Mess. Under the Dauphin.

K. John.   Thou hast made me giddy
With these ill tidings.

Enter the BASTARD, *and* PETER OF POMFRET.

          Now, what says the world 13
To your proceedings? do not seek to stuff
My head with more ill news, for it is full.

Bast. But if you be afeard to hear the worst
Then let the worst unheard fall on your head

K. John. Bear with me, cousin, for I wa
amaz'd   13
Under the tide; but now I breathe again
Aloft the flood, and can give audience
To any tongue, speak it of what it will.   14

Bast. How I have sped among the clergy
men,
The sums I have collected shall express.
But as I travell'd hither through the land,
I find the people strangely fantasied,
Possess'd with rumours, full of idle dreams,
Not knowing what they fear, but full of fear.
And here's a prophet that I brought with me
From forth the streets of Pomfret, whom
found   14
With many hundreds treading on his heels;
To whom he sung, in rude harsh-sounding rimes
That, ere the next Ascension-day at noon,
Your highness should deliver up your crown. 15

K. John. Thou idle dreamer, wherefore dids
thou so?

Peter. Foreknowing that the truth will fa
out so.

K. John. Hubert, away with him; impriso
him:
And on that day at noon, whereon, he says, 15
I shall yield up my crown, let him be hang'd
Deliver him to safety, and return,
For I must use thee.
            [*Exit* HUBERT, *with* PETER
             O my gentle cousin,
Hear'st thou the news abroad, who are arriv'd

Bast. The French, my lord; men's mouth
are full of it: 16
Besides, I met Lord Bigot and Lord Salisbury
With eyes as red as new-enkindled fire,
And others more, going to seek the grave   16
Of Arthur, whom they say is kill'd to-night
On your suggestion.

K. John.   Gentle kinsman, go,
And thrust thyself into their companies.
I have a way to win their loves again;   16
Bring them before me.

Bast.   I will seek them out.

K. John. Nay, but make haste; the bette
foot before.
O! let me have no subject enemies
When adverse foreigners affright my towns 17
With dreadful pomp of stout invasion.
Be Mercury, set feathers to thy heels,
And fly like thought from them to me again.

Bast. The spirit of the time shall teach m
speed.   17

K. John. Spoke like a sprightful noble gen
tleman.   [*Exit* BASTARD
Go after him; for he perhaps shall need
Some messenger betwixt me and the peers;
And be thou he.

Mess. With all my heart, my liege. [*Exi*

K. John. My mother dead!

Re-enter HUBERT.

Hub. My lord, they say five moons were seen
  to-night:
Four fixed, and the fifth did whirl about
The other four in wondrous motion.   184
K. John. Five moons!
Hub.   Old men and beldams in the streets
Do prophesy upon it dangerously:
Young Arthur's death is common in their
  mouths;
And when they talk of him, they shake their
  heads   188
And whisper one another in the ear;
And he that speaks, doth gripe the hearer's wrist
Whilst he that hears makes fearful action,
With wrinkled brows, with nods, with rolling
  eyes.   192
I saw a smith stand with his hammer, thus,
The whilst his iron did on the anvil cool,
With open mouth swallowing a tailor's news;
Who, with his shears and measure in his hand,
Standing on slippers,—which his nimble haste
Had falsely thrust upon contrary feet,—
Told of a many thousand warlike French,
That were embattailed and rank'd in Kent. 200
Another lean unwash'd artificer
Cuts off his tale and talks of Arthur's death.
K. John. Why seek'st thou to possess me
  with these fears?
Why urgest thou so oft young Arthur's death?
Thy hand hath murder'd him: I had a mighty
  cause   205
To wish him dead, but thou hadst none to kill
  him.
Hub. No had, my lord! why, did you not
  provoke me?
K. John. It is the curse of kings to be at-
  tended   208
By slaves that take their humours for a warrant
To break within the bloody house of life,
And on the winking of authority
To understand a law, to know the meaning 212
Of dangerous majesty, when, perchance, it
  frowns
More upon humour than advis'd respect.
Hub. Here is your hand and seal for what I
  did.
K. John. O! when the last account 'twixt
  heaven and earth   216
Is to be made, then shall this hand and seal
Witness against us to damnation.
How oft the sight of means to do ill deeds
Makes ill deeds done! Hadst not thou been by,
A fellow by the hand of nature mark'd,   221
Quoted and sign'd to do a deed of shame,
This murder had not come into my mind;
But taking note of thy abhorr'd aspect,   224
Finding thee fit for bloody villany,
Apt, liable to be employ'd in danger,
Faintly broke with thee of Arthur's death;
And thou, to be endeared to a king,   228
Made it no conscience to destroy a prince.
Hub. My lord,—
K. John. Hadst thou but shook thy head or
  made a pause
When I spake darkly what I purposed,   232

Or turn'd an eye of doubt upon my face,
As bid me tell my tale in express words,
Deep shame had struck me dumb, made me
  break off,
And those thy fears might have wrought fears
  in me: 236
But thou didst understand me by my signs
And didst in signs again parley with sin;
Yea, without stop, didst let thy heart consent,
And consequently thy rude hand to act   240
The deed which both our tongues held vile to
  name.
Out of my sight, and never see me more!
My nobles leave me; and my state is brav'd,
Even at my gates, with ranks of foreign powers:
Nay, in the body of this fleshly land,   245
This kingdom, this confine of blood and breath,
Hostility and civil tumult reigns
Between my conscience and my cousin's death.
Hub. Arm you against your other enemies,
I'll make a peace between your soul and you.
Young Arthur is alive: this hand of mine
Is yet a maiden and an innocent hand,   252
Not painted with the crimson spots of blood.
Within this bosom never enter'd yet
The dreadful motion of a murderous thought;
And you have slander'd nature in my form, 256
Which, howsoever rude exteriorly,
Is yet the cover of a fairer mind
Than to be butcher of an innocent child.
K. John. Doth Arthur live? O! haste thee
  to the peers,   260
Throw this report on their incensed rage,
And make them tame to their obedience.
Forgive the comment that my passion made
Upon thy feature; for my rage was blind, 264
And foul imaginary eyes of blood
Presented thee more hideous than thou art.
O! answer not; but to my closet bring
The angry lords, with all expedient haste.   268
I conjure thee but slowly; run more fast.
                                               [Exeunt.

SCENE III.—*The Same. Before the Castle.*

Enter ARTHUR, *on the Walls.*

  Arth. The wall is high; and yet will I leap
    down.
Good ground, be pitiful and hurt me not!
There's few or none do know me; if they did,
This ship-boy's semblance hath disguis'd me
  quite.   4
I am afraid; and yet I'll venture it.
If I get down, and do not break my limbs,
I'll find a thousand shifts to get away:
As good to die and go, as die and stay.   8
                                          [Leaps down.
O me! my uncle's spirit is in these stones!
Heaven take my soul, and England keep my
  bones!   *[Dies.*

Enter PEMBROKE, SALISBURY, *and* BIGOT.

  Sal. Lords, I will meet him at Saint Ed-
    mundsbury.
It is our safety, and we must embrace   12
This gentle offer of the perilous time.

Pem. Who brought that letter from the
  cardinal?
Sal. The Count Melun, a noble lord of France;
Whose private with me of the Dauphin's love, 16
Is much more general than these lines import.
  Big. To-morrow morning let us meet him
  then.
Sal. Or rather then set forward; for 'twill be
Two long days' journey, lords, or e'er we meet.

Enter the BASTARD.

  Bast. Once more to-day well met, distem-
  per'd lords! 21
The king by me requests your presence straight.
  Sal. The king hath dispossess'd himself of us:
We will not line his thin bestained cloak 24
With our pure honours, nor attend the foot
That leaves the print of blood where'er it walks.
Return and tell him so: we know the worst.
  Bast. Whate'er you think, good words, I
  think, were best. 28
  Sal. Our griefs, and not our manners,
  reason now.
  Bast. But there is little reason in your grief;
Therefore 'twere reason you had manners now.
  Pem. Sir, sir, impatience hath his privilege.
  Bast. 'Tis true; to hurt his master, no man
  else. 33
  Sal. This is the prison.   [*Seeing* ARTHUR.
                  What is he lies here?
  Pem. O death, made proud with pure and
  princely beauty!
The earth had not a hole to hide this deed. 36
  Sal. Murder, as hating what himself hath
  done,
Doth lay it open to urge on revenge.
  Big. Or when he doom'd this beauty to a
  grave,
Found it too precious-princely for a grave. 40
  Sal. Sir Richard, what think you? Have you
  beheld,
Or have you read, or heard? or could you
think?
Or do you almost think, although you see,
That you do see? could thought, without this
  object, 44
Form such another? This is the very top,
The height, the crest, or crest unto the crest,
Of murder's arms: this is the bloodiest shame,
The wildest savagery, the vilest stroke, 48
That ever wall-eyed wrath or staring rage
Presented to the tears of soft remorse.
  Pem. All murders past do stand excus'd in
  this:
And this, so sole and so unmatchable, 52
Shall give a holiness, a purity,
To the yet unbegotten sin of times;
And prove a deadly bloodshed but a jest,
Exampled by this heinous spectacle. 56
  Bast. It is a damned and a bloody work;
The graceless action of a heavy hand,
If that it be the work of any hand.
  Sal. If that it be the work of any hand! 60
We had a kind of light what would ensue:
It is the shameful work of Hubert's hand;
The practice and the purpose of the king:

From whose obedience I forbid my soul, 6
Kneeling before this ruin of sweet life,
And breathing to his breathless excellence
The incense of a vow, a holy vow,
Never to taste the pleasures of the world, 6
Never to be infected with delight,
Nor conversant with ease and idleness,
Till I have set a glory to this hand,
By giving it the worship of revenge. 7
  Pem. } Our souls religiously confirm th
  Big. } words.

Enter HUBERT.

  Hub. Lords, I am hot with haste in seekin
  you:
Arthur doth live: the king hath sent for you.
  Sal. O! he is bold and blushes not at death
Avaunt, thou hateful villain! get thee gone. 7
  Hub. I am no villain.
  Sal. [*Drawing his sword.*] Must I rob the law
  Bast. Your sword is bright, sir; put it u
  again.
  Sal. Not till I sheathe it in a murderer's ski
  Hub. Stand back, Lord Salisbury, stan
  back, I say: 8
By heaven, I think my sword's as sharp as your
I would not have you, lord, forget yourself,
Nor tempt the danger of my true defence; 8
Lest I, by marking of your rage, forget
Your worth, your greatness, and nobility.
  Big. Out, dunghill! dar'st thou brave a noble
  man?
  Hub. Not for my life; but yet I dare defen
My innocent life against an emperor. 8
  Sal. Thou art a murderer.
  Hub.   Do not prove me so
Yet I am none. Whose tongue soe'er speak
  false,
Not truly speaks; who speaks not truly, lies. 9
  Pem. Cut him to pieces.
  Bast.   Keep the peace, I say
  Sal. Stand by, or I shall gall you, Faulcor
  bridge.
  Bast. Thou wert better gall the devil, Salis
  bury:
If thou but frown on me, or stir thy foot, 9
Or teach thy hasty spleen to do me shame,
I'll strike thee dead. Put up thy sword betime
Or I'll so maul you and your toasting-iron,
That you shall think the devil is come from hel
  Big. What wilt thou do, renowned Faulcor
  bridge? 10
Second a villain and a murderer?
  Hub. Lord Bigot, I am none.
  Big.   Who kill'd this prince
  Hub. 'Tis not an hour since I left him wel
I honour'd him, I lov'd him; and will weep 10
My date of life out for his sweet life's loss.
  Sal. Trust not those cunning waters of hi
  eyes,
For villany is not without such rheum; 10
And he, long traded in it, makes it seem
Like rivers of remorse and innocency.
Away with me, all you whose souls abhor
The uncleanly savours of a slaughter-house;
For I am stifled with this smell of sin. 11

Big. Away toward Bury; to the Dauphin there!

Pem. There tell the king he may inquire us out.   [*Exeunt* Lords.

Bast. Here's a good world! Knew you of this fair work?   116
...yond the infinite and boundless reach
...f mercy, if thou didst this deed of death,
...rt thou damn'd, Hubert.

Hub.   Do but hear me, sir.

Bast. Ha! I'll tell thee what;   120
...ou art damn'd as black—nay, nothing is so black;
...ou art more deep damn'd than Prince Lucifer:
...ere is not yet so ugly a fiend of hell
...s thou shalt be, if thou didst kill this child. 124

Hub. Upon my soul,—

Bast.   If thou didst but consent
...o this most cruel act, do but despair;
...nd if thou want'st a cord, the smallest thread
...aat ever spider twisted from her womb   128
...ill serve to strangle thee; a rush will be a beam
...o hang thee on; or wouldst thou drown thyself,
...t but a little water in a spoon,
...nd it shall be as all the ocean,   132
...ough to stifle such a villain up.
...o suspect thee very grievously.

Hub. If I in act, consent, or sin of thought,
...e guilty of the stealing that sweet breath   136
...hich was embounded in this beauteous clay,
...et hell want pains enough to torture me.
...eft him well.

Bast.   Go, bear him in thine arms.
...m amaz'd, methinks, and lose my way   140
...mong the thorns and dangers of this world.
...ow easy dost thou take all England up!
...om forth this morsel of dead royalty,
...e life, the right and truth of all this realm 144
...fled to heaven; and England now is left
...o tug and scamble and to part by the teeth
...e unow'd interest of proud swelling state.
...ow for the bare-pick'd bone of majesty   148
...oth dogged war bristle his angry crest,
...nd snarleth in the gentle eyes of peace:
...ow powers from home and discontents at
home
...eet in one line; and vast confusion waits,—   152
...s doth a raven on a sick-fallen beast,—
...e imminent decay of wrested pomp.
...ow happy he whose cloak and ceinture can
...old out this tempest. Bear away that child
...nd follow me with speed: I'll to the king: 157
...thousand businesses are brief in hand,
...nd heaven itself doth frown upon the land.
                                    [*Exeunt.*

ACT V

SCENE I.—*The Same. A Room in the Palace.*

Enter KING JOHN, PANDULPH *with the crown, and* Attendants.

K. John. Thus have I yielded up into your hand
...e circle of my glory.

Pand. [*Giving* JOHN *the crown.*] Take again
From this my hand, as holding of the pope,
Your sovereign greatness and authority.   4

K. John. Now keep your holy word: go meet the French,
And from his holiness use all your power
To stop their marches 'fore we are inflam'd.
Our discontented counties do revolt,   8
Our people quarrel with obedience,
Swearing allegiance and the love of soul
To stranger blood, to foreign royalty.
This inundation of mistemper'd humour   12
Rests by you only to be qualified:
Then pause not; for the present time's so sick,
That present medicine must be minister'd,
Or overthrow incurable ensues.   16

Pand. It was my breath that blew this tempest up
Upon your stubborn usage of the pope;
But since you are a gentle convertite,
My tongue shall hush again this storm of war   20
And make fair weather in your blustering land.
On this Ascension-day, remember well,
Upon your oath of service to the pope,
Go I to make the French lay down their arms.
                                    [*Exit.*

K. John. Is this Ascension-day? Did not the prophet   25
Say that before Ascension-day at noon
My crown I should give off? Even so I have:
I did suppose it should be on constraint;   28
But, heaven be thank'd, it is but voluntary.

Enter the BASTARD.

Bast. All Kent hath yielded; nothing there holds out
But Dover Castle: London hath receiv'd,
Like a kind host, the Dauphin and his powers:
Your nobles will not hear you, but are gone   33
To offer service to your enemy;
And wild amazement hurries up and down
The little number of your doubtful friends.   36

K. John. Would not my lords return to me again
After they heard young Arthur was alive?

Bast. They found him dead and cast into the streets,
An empty casket, where the jewel of life   40
By some damn'd hand was robb'd and ta'en away.

K. John. That villain Hubert told me he did live.

Bast. So, on my soul, he did, for aught he knew.
But wherefore do you droop? why look you sad?
Be great in act, as you have been in thought;   45
Let not the world see fear and sad distrust
Govern the motion of a kingly eye:
Be stirring as the time; be fire with fire;   48
Threaten the threatener, and outface the brow
Of bragging horror: so shall inferior eyes,
That borrow their behaviours from the great,
Grow great by your example and put on   52
The dauntless spirit of resolution.
Away! and glister like the god of war
When he intendeth to become the field:
Show boldness and aspiring confidence.   56

What! shall they seek the lion in his den
And fright him there? and make him tremble
there?
O! let it not be said. Forage, and run
To meet displeasure further from the doors, 60
And grapple with him ere he comes so nigh.
   K. John. The legate of the pope hath been
with me,
And I have made a happy peace with him;
And he hath promis'd to dismiss the powers 64
Led by the Dauphin.
   Bast.   O inglorious league!
Shall we, upon the footing of our land,
Send fair-play orders and make compromise,
Insinuation, parley and base truce   68
To arms invasive? shall a beardless boy,
A cocker'd silken wanton, brave our fields,
And flesh his spirit in a war-like soil,
Mocking the air with colours idly spread, 72
And find no check? Let us, my liege, to arms.
Perchance the cardinal cannot make your peace;
Or if he do, let it at least be said
They saw we had a purpose of defence.   76
   K. John. Have thou the ordering of this
present time.
   Bast. Away then, with good courage! yet, I
know,
Our party may well meet a prouder foe.
                              [*Exeunt.*

SCENE II.—*A Plain, near St. Edmundsbury.*
The French Camp.

Enter, in arms, LEWIS, SALISBURY, MELUN, PEM-
BROKE, BIGOT, *and* Soldiers.

   Lew. My Lord Melun, let this be copied out,
And keep it safe for our remembrance.
Return the precedent to these lords again;
That, having our fair order written down,   4
Both they and we, perusing o'er these notes,
May know wherefore we took the sacrament,
And keep our faiths firm and inviolable.
   Sal. Upon our sides it never shall be broken. 8
And, noble Dauphin, albeit we swear
A voluntary zeal, an unurg'd faith
To your proceedings; yet, believe me, prince,
I am not glad that such a sore of time   12
Should seek a plaster by contemn'd revolt,
And heal the inveterate canker of one wound
By making many. O! it grieves my soul
That I must draw this metal from my side 16
To be a widow-maker! O! and there
Where honourable rescue and defence
Cries out upon the name of Salisbury,
But such is the infection of the time,   20
That, for the health and physic of our right,
We cannot deal but with the very hand
Of stern injustice and confused wrong.
And is't not pity, O my grieved friends! 24
That we, the sons and children of this isle,
Were born to see so sad an hour as this?
Wherein we step after a stranger march
Upon her gentle bosom, and fill up   28
Her enemies' ranks,—I must withdraw and weep
Upon the spot of this enforced cause,—

To grace the gentry of a land remote,
And follow unacquainted colours here?
What, here? O nation! that thou couldst
move;
That Neptune's arms, who clippeth thee abo
Would bear thee from the knowledge of thyse
And gripple thee unto a pagan shore;
Where these two Christian armies might co
bine
The blood of malice in a vein of league,
And not to spend it so unneighbourly!
   Lew. A noble temper dost thou show in th
And great affections wrestling in thy bosom
Do make an earthquake of nobility.
O! what a noble combat hast thou fought
Between compulsion and a brave respect.
Let me wipe off this honourable dew,
That silverly doth progress on thy cheeks:
My heart hath melted at a lady's tears,
Being an ordinary inundation;
But this effusion of such manly drops,
This shower, blown up by tempest of the so
Startles mine eyes, and makes me more amaz
Than had I seen the vaulty top of heaven
Figur'd quite o'er with burning meteors.
Lift up thy brow, renowned Salisbury,
And with a great heart heave away this stor
Commend these waters to those baby eyes
That never saw the giant world enrag'd;
Nor met with fortune other than at feasts,
Full warm of blood, of mirth, of gossiping.
Come, come; for thou shalt thrust thy hand
deep
Into the purse of rich prosperity
As Lewis himself: so, nobles, shall you all,
That knit your sinews to the strength of mi

Enter PANDULPH *attended.*

And even there, methinks, an angel spake:
Look, where the holy legate comes apace,
To give us warrant from the hand of heaven,
And on our actions set the name of right
With holy breath.
   Pand.   Hail, noble prince of France!
The next is this: King John hath reconcil'd
Himself to Rome; his spirit is come in
That so stood out against the holy church,
The great metropolis and see of Rome.
Therefore thy threat'ning colours now wind u
And tame the savage spirit of wild war,
That, like a lion foster'd up at hand,
It may lie gently at the foot of peace,
And be no further harmful than in show.
   Lew. Your grace shall pardon me; I will n
back:
I am too high-born to be propertied,
To be a secondary at control,
Or useful serving-man and instrument
To any sovereign state throughout the world
Your breath first kindled the dead coal of wa
Between this chastis'd kingdom and myself,
And brought in matter that should feed th
fire;
And now 'tis far too huge to be blown out
With that same weak wind which enkindled
You taught me how to know the face of right,

quainted me with interest to this land,
a, thrust this enterprise into my heart;
d come you now to tell me John hath made
s peace with Rome? What is that peace to
me? 92
y the honour of my marriage-bed,
ter young Arthur, claim this land for mine;
d, now it is half-conquer'd, must I back
cause that John hath made his peace with
Rome? 96
n I Rome's slave? What penny hath Rome
borne,
nat men provided, what munition sent,
underprop this action? is't not I
at undergo this charge? who else but I, 100
nd such as to my claim are liable,
eat in this business and maintain this war?
ve I not heard these islanders shout out,
ve le roy! as I have bank'd their towns? 104
ve not here the best cards for the game
win this easy match play'd for a crown?
nd shall I now give o'er the yielded set?
o, no, on my soul, it never shall be said. 108
Pand. You look but on the outside of this
work.
Lew. Outside or inside, I will not return
l my attempt so much be glorified
to my ample hope was promised 112
fore I drew this gallant head of war,
nd cull'd these fiery spirits from the world,
outlook conquest and to win renown
en in the jaws of danger and of death. 116
    [*Trumpet sounds.*
hat lusty trumpet thus doth summon us?

Enter the BASTARD, *attended.*

Bast. According to the fair play of the world,
t me have audience; I am sent to speak:
y holy Lord of Milan, from the king 120
ome, to learn how you have dealt for him;
d, as you answer, I do know the scope
d warrant limited unto my tongue.
Pand. The Dauphin is too wilful-opposite,
d will not temporize with my entreaties: 125
flatly says he'll not lay down his arms.
Bast. By all the blood that ever fury breath'd,
e youth says well. Now hear our English
king; 128
r thus his royalty doth speak in me.
is prepar'd; and reason too he should:
is apish and unmannerly approach,
is harness'd masque and unadvised revel, 132
is unhair'd sauciness and boyish troops,
e king doth smile at; and is well prepar'd
whip this dwarfish war, these pigmy arms,
om out the circle of his territories. 136
at hand which had the strength, even at
your door,
cudgel you and make you take the hatch;
dive, like buckets, in concealed wells;
crouch in litter of your stable planks; 140
lie like pawns lock'd up in chests and trunks;
hug with swine; to seek sweet safety out
vaults and prisons; and to thrill and shake,
en at the crying of your nation's crow, 144
inking this voice an armed Englishman:

Shall that victorious hand be feebled here
That in your chambers gave you chastisement?
No! Know, the gallant monarch is in arms, 148
And like an eagle o'er his aiery towers,
To souse annoyance that comes near his nest.
And you degenerate, you ingrate revolts,
You bloody Neroes, ripping up the womb 152
Of your dear mother England, blush for shame:
For your own ladies and pale-visag'd maids
Like Amazons come tripping after drums,
Their thimbles into armed gauntlets change, 156
Their neelds to lances, and their gentle hearts
To fierce and bloody inclination.
 Lew. There end thy brave, and turn thy face
in peace;
We grant thou canst outscold us: fare thee
well; 160
We hold our time too precious to be spent
With such a brabbler.
 Pand.   Give me leave to speak.
 Bast. No, I will speak.
 Lew.   We will attend to neither.
Strike up the drums; and let the tongue of
war 164
Plead for our interest and our being here.
 Bast. Indeed, your drums, being beaten, will
cry out;
And so shall you, being beaten. Do but start
An echo with the clamour of thy drum, 168
And even at hand a drum is ready brac'd
That shall reverberate all as loud as thine;
Sound but another, and another shall
As loud as thine rattle the welkin's ear 172
And mock the deep-mouth'd thunder: for at
hand,—
Not trusting to this halting legate here,
Whom he hath us'd rather for sport than need,—
Is warlike John; and in his forehead sits 176
A bare-ribb'd death, whose office is this day
To feast upon whole thousands of the French.
 Lew. Strike up our drums, to find this danger
out.
 Bast. And thou shalt find it, Dauphin, do
not doubt. [*Exeunt.*

SCENE III.—*The Same. A Field of Battle.*

 Alarums. Enter KING JOHN *and* HUBERT.

 K. John. How goes the day with us? O! tell
me, Hubert.
 Hub. Badly, I fear. How fares your majesty?
 K. John. This fever, that hath troubled me
so long,
Lies heavy on me: O! my heart is sick. 4

 Enter a Messenger.

 Mess. My lord, your valiant kinsman, Faul-
conbridge,
Desires your majesty to leave the field,
And send him word by me which way you go.
 K. John. Tell him, toward Swinstead, to the
abbey there. 8
 Mess. Be of good comfort: for the great
supply
That was expected by the Dauphin here,
Are wrack'd three nights ago on Goodwin sands.

This news was brought to Richard but even now.
The French fight coldly, and retire themselves. 13
K. John. Ay me! this tyrant fever burns me up,
And will not let me welcome this good news.
Set on toward Swinstead: to my litter straight;
Weakness possesseth me, and I am faint.   17
                                    [*Exeunt.*

SCENE IV.—*The Same. Another Part of
the Same.*

Enter SALISBURY, PEMBROKE, BIGOT, *and
Others.*

Sal. I did not think the king so stor'd with
  friends.
Pem. Up once again; put spirit in the French:
If they miscarry we miscarry too.
Sal. That misbegotten devil, Faulconbridge,
In spite of spite, alone upholds the day.   5
Pem. They say King John, sore sick, hath
  left the field.

Enter MELUN *wounded, and led by* Soldiers.

Mel. Lead me to the revolts of England here.
Sal. When we were happy we had other
  names.   8
Pem. It is the Count Melun.
Sal.   Wounded to death.
Mel. Fly, noble English; you are bought and
  sold;
Unthread the rude eye of rebellion,
And welcome home again discarded faith.   12
Seek out King John and fall before his feet;
For if the French be lords of this loud day,
He means to recompense the pains you take
By cutting off your heads. Thus hath he sworn,
And I with him, and many moe with me,   17
Upon the altar at Saint Edmundsbury;
Even on that altar where we swore to you
Dear amity and everlasting love.   20
Sal. May this be possible? may this be true?
Mel. Have I not hideous death within my
  view,
Retaining but a quantity of life,
Which bleeds away, even as a form of wax   24
Resolveth from his figure 'gainst the fire?
What in the world should make me now deceive,
Since I must lose the use of all deceit?
Why should I then be false, since it is true   28
That I must die here and live hence by truth?
I say again, if Lewis do win the day,
He is forsworn, if e'er those eyes of yours
Behold another day break in the east: 32
But even this night, whose black contagious
  breath
Already smokes about the burning crest
Of the old, feeble, and day-wearied sun,
Even this ill night, your breathing shall expire,
Paying the fine of rated treachery   37
Even with a treacherous fine of all your lives,
If Lewis by your assistance win the day.
Commend me to one Hubert with your king;   40
The love of him, and this respect besides,
For that my grandsire was an Englishman,
Awakes my conscience to confess all this.

In lieu whereof, I pray you, bear me hence
From forth the noise and rumour of the fie
Where I may think the remnant of my thoug
In peace, and part this body and my soul
With contemplation and devout desires.
Sal. We do believe thee: and beshrew
  soul
But I do love the favour and the form
Of this most fair occasion, by the which
We will untread the steps of damned flight,
And like a bated and retired flood,
Leaving our rankness and irregular course
Stoop low within those bounds we have o
  look'd,
And calmly run on in obedience,
Even to our ocean, to our great King John
My arm shall give thee help to bear thee her
For I do see the cruel pangs of death
Right in thine eye. Away, my friends! N
  flight;
And happy newness, that intends old right.
                            [*Exeunt, leading off* MEL

SCENE V.—*The Same. The French Camp*
Enter LEWIS *and his Train.*

Lew. The sun of heaven methought w
  loath to set,
But stay'd and made the western welkin blu
When the English measur'd backward th
  own ground
In faint retire. O! bravely came we off,
When with a volley of our needless shot,
After such bloody toil, we bid good night,
And wound our tottering colours clearly up
Last in the field, and almost lords of it!

Enter a Messenger.

Mess. Where is my prince, the Dauphin
Lew.   Here: what new
Mess. The Count Melun is slain; the Engl
  lords,
By his persuasion, are again fall'n off;
And your supply, which you have wish'd so lo
Are cast away and sunk, on Goodwin sands.
Lew. Ah, foul shrewd news! Beshrew
  very heart!
I did not think to be so sad to-night
As this hath made me. Who was he that sai
King John did fly an hour or two before
The stumbling night did part our weary powe
Mess. Whoever spoke it, it is true, my lo
Lew. Well; keep good quarter and good c
  to-night:
The day shall not be up so soon as I,
To try the fair adventure of to-morrow. [*Exet*

SCENE VI.—*An open Place in the neighbourh*
of Swinstead Abbey.

Enter the BASTARD *and* HUBERT, *several*
Hub. Who's there? speak, ho! speak quick
  or I shoot.
Bast. A friend. What art thou?
Hub.   Of the part of Engla

Bast. Whither dost thou go?
Hub. What's that to thee? Why may not I demand   4
thine affairs as well as thou of mine?
Bast. Hubert, I think?
Hub.   Thou hast a perfect thought:
Ill upon all hazards well believe
ou art my friend, that know'st my tongue so well.   8
ho art thou?
Bast.   Who thou wilt: and if thou please,
ou mayst befriend me so much as to think
ome one way of the Plantagenets.
Hub. Unkind remembrance! thou and eyeless night   12
ive done me shame: brave soldier, pardon me,
at any accent breaking from thy tongue
ould 'scape the true acquaintance of mine
ear.
Bast. Come, come; sans compliment, what news abroad?   16
Hub. Why, here walk I in the black brow of night,
find you out.
Bast.   Brief, then; and what's the news?
Hub. O! my sweet sir, news fitting to the night,
ack, fearful, comfortless, and horrible.   20
Bast. Show me the very wound of this ill news:
m no woman; I'll not swound at it.
Hub. The king, I fear, is poison'd by a monk:
eft him almost speechless; and broke out   24
acquaint you with this evil, that you might
e better arm you to the sudden time
an if you had at leisure known of this.
Bast. How did he take it? who did taste to him?   28
Hub. A monk, I tell you; a resolved villain,
hose bowels suddenly burst out: the king
t speaks, and peradventure may recover.
Bast. Whom didst thou leave to tend his majesty?   32
Hub. Why, know you not? the lords are all come back,
d brought Prince Henry in their company;
whose request the king hath pardon'd them,
d they are all about his majesty.   36
Bast. Withhold thine indignation, mighty heaven,
d tempt us not to bear above our power!
tell thee, Hubert, half my power this night,
ssing these flats, are taken by the tide;   40
ese Lincoln Washes have devoured them:
yself, well-mounted, hardly have escap'd.
vay before! conduct me to the king;
oubt he will be dead or ere I come. [*Exeunt.*

SCENE VII.—*The Orchard of Swinstead Abbey.*

Enter PRINCE HENRY, SALISBURY, *and* BIGOT.

P. Hen. It is too late: the life of all his blood
touch'd corruptibly; and his pure brain,—

Which some suppose the soul's frail dwelling-house,—
Doth, by the idle comments that it makes,   4
Foretell the ending of mortality.

Enter PEMBROKE.

Pem. His highness yet doth speak; and holds belief
That, being brought into the open air,
It would allay the burning quality   8
Of that fell poison which assaileth him.
P. Hen. Let him be brought into the orchard here.
Doth he still rage?   [*Exit* BIGOT.
Pem.   He is more patient
Than when you left him: even now he sung. 12
P. Hen. O, vanity of sickness! fierce extremes
In their continuance will not feel themselves.
Death, having prey'd upon the outward parts,
Leaves them invisible; and his siege is now 16
Against the mind, the which he pricks and wounds
With many legions of strange fantasies,
Which, in their throng and press to that last hold,
Confound themselves. 'Tis strange that death should sing.   20
I am the cygnet to this pale faint swan,
Who chants a doleful hymn to his own death,
And from the organ-pipe of frailty sings
His soul and body to their lasting rest.   24
Sal. Be of good comfort, prince; for you are born
To set a form upon that indigest
Which he hath left so shapeless and so rude.

Re-enter BIGOT *and* Attendants *carrying*
KING JOHN *in a chair.*

K. John. Ay, marry, now my soul hath elbow-room;   28
It would not out at windows, nor at doors.
There is so hot a summer in my bosom
That all my bowels crumble up to dust:
I am a scribbled form, drawn with a pen   32
Upon a parchment, and against this fire
Do I shrink up.
P. Hen.   How fares your majesty?
K. John. Poison'd, ill-fare; dead, forsook, cast off;
And none of you will bid the winter come 36
To thrust his icy fingers in my maw;
Nor let my kingdom's rivers take their course
Through my burn'd bosom; nor entreat the north
To make his bleak winds kiss my parched lips 40
And comfort me with cold. I do not ask you much:
I beg cold comfort; and you are so strait
And so ingrateful you deny me that.
P. Hen. O! that there were some virtue in my tears,   44
That might relieve you.
K. John.   The salt in them is hot.
Within me is a hell; and there the poison
Is as a fiend confin'd to tyrannize
On unreprievable condemned blood.   48

Enter the BASTARD.

Bast. O! I am scalded with my violent motion
And spleen of speed to see your majesty.
   K. John. O cousin! thou art come to set mine
      eye:
The tackle of my heart is crack'd and burn'd, 52
And all the shrouds wherewith my life should
      sail
Are turned to one thread, one little hair;
My heart hath one poor string to stay it by,
Which holds but till thy news be uttered;   56
And then all this thou seest is but a clod
And module of confounded royalty.
   Bast. The Dauphin is preparing hitherward,
Where heaven he knows how we shall answer
      him: 60
For in a night the best part of my power,
As I upon advantage did remove,
Were in the Washes all unwarily
Devoured by the unexpected flood.   64
                         [*The* KING *dies.*
   Sal. You breathe these dead news in as dead
      an ear.
My liege! my lord! But now a king, now thus.
   P. Hen. Even so must I run on, and even so
      stop.
What surety of the world, what hope, what stay,
When this was now a king, and now is clay? 69
   Bast. Art thou gone so? I do but stay behind
To do the office for thee of revenge,
And then my soul shall wait on thee to heaven,
As it on earth hath been thy servant still. 73
Now, now, you stars, that move in your right
      spheres,
Where be your powers? Show now your mended
      faiths,
And instantly return with me again,   76
To push destruction and perpetual shame
Out of the weak door of our fainting land.
Straight let us seek, or straight we shall be
      sought:
The Dauphin rages at our very heels.   80

   Sal. It seems you know not then so much
      we.
The Cardinal Pandulph is within at rest,
Who half an hour since came from the Dauph
And brings from him such offers of our peace
As we with honour and respect may take,
With purpose presently to leave this war.
   Bast. He will the rather do it when he sees
Ourselves well sinewed to our defence.
   Sal. Nay, it is in a manner done already;
For many carriages he hath dispatch'd
To the sea-side, and put his cause and quar
To the disposing of the cardinal:
With whom yourself, myself, and other lor
If you think meet, this afternoon will post
To consummate this business happily.
   Bast. Let it be so. And you, my noble prin
With other princes that may best be spar'd,
Shall wait upon your father's funeral.
   P. Hen. At Worcester must his body be
      terr'd;
For so he will'd it.
   Bast.   Thither shall it then.
And happily may your sweet self put on
The lineal state and glory of the land!
To whom, with all submission, on my knee,
I do bequeath my faithful services
And true subjection everlastingly.
   Sal. And the like tender of our love we ma
To rest without a spot for evermore.
   P. Hen. I have a kind soul that would gi
      you thanks,
And knows not how to do it but with tears.
   Bast. O! let us pay the time but needful w
Since it hath been beforehand with our grie
This England never did, nor never shall,
Lie at the proud foot of a conqueror,
But when it first did help to wound itself.
Now these her princes are come home agai
Come the three corners of the world in arms,
And we shall shock them. Nought shall ma
us rue,
If England to itself do rest but true.   [*Exeu*

THE TRAGEDY OF
KING RICHARD THE SECOND

DRAMATIS PERSONÆ

NG RICHARD THE SECOND.
IN OF GAUNT, DUKE ⎫
   of Lancaster, ⎬ Uncles to the King.
MUND OF LANGLEY, ⎪
   Duke of York, ⎭
NRY, surnamed BOLINGBROKE, Duke of Hereford,
   Son to John of Gaunt: afterwards King Henry IV.
KE OF AUMERLE, Son to the Duke of York.
OMAS MOWBRAY, Duke of Norfolk.
KE OF SURREY.
RL OF SALISBURY.
RD BERKELEY.
SHY, ⎫
GOT, ⎬ Servants to King Richard.
EEN, ⎭
RL OF NORTHUMBERLAND.
NRY PERCY, surnamed Hotspur, his Son.

LORD ROSS.
LORD WILLOUGHBY.
LORD FITZWATER.
BISHOP OF CARLISLE.
ABBOT OF WESTMINSTER.
LORD MARSHAL.
SIR PIERCE OF EXTON.
SIR STEPHEN SCROOP.
Captain of a Band of Welshmen.

QUEEN TO KING RICHARD.
DUCHESS OF GLOUCESTER.
DUCHESS OF YORK.
Lady attending on the Queen.

Lords, Heralds, Officers, Soldiers, Gardeners, Keeper,
   Messenger, Groom, and other Attendants.

SCENE.—*Dispersedly in England and Wales.*

ACT I

SCENE I.—*London. A Room in the Palace.*

ter KING RICHARD, *attended;* JOHN OF GAUNT,
   and other Nobles.

K. Rich. Old John of Gaunt, time-honour'd
  Lancaster,
st thou, according to thy oath and band,
ought hither Henry Hereford thy bold son,
re to make good the boisterous late appeal, 4
hich then our leisure would not let us hear,
ainst the Duke of Norfolk, Thomas Mowbray?
Gaunt. I have, my liege.
K. Rich. Tell me, moreover, hast thou
  sounded him,   8
he appeal the duke on ancient malice,
worthily, as a good subject should,
some known ground of treachery in him?
Gaunt. As near as I could sift him on that
  argument,   12
some apparent danger seen in him
m'd at your highness, no inveterate malice.
K. Rich. Then call them to our presence:
  face to face,
d frowning brow to brow, ourselves will hear
e accuser and the accused freely speak: 17
        [Exeunt some Attendants.
gh-stomach'd are they both, and full of ire,
rage deaf as the sea, hasty as fire.

e-enter Attendants, *with* BOLINGBROKE *and*
  MOWBRAY.

Boling. Many years of happy days befall 20
gracious sovereign, my most loving liege!
Mow. Each day still better other's happiness;

Until the heavens, envying earth's good hap,
Add an immortal title to your crown!   24
  K. Rich. We thank you both: yet one but
  flatters us,
As well appeareth by the cause you come;
Namely, to appeal each other of high treason.
Cousin of Hereford, what dost thou object 28
Against the Duke of Norfolk, Thomas Mow-
  bray?
  Boling. First,—heaven be the record to my
  speech!—
In the devotion of a subject's love,
Tendering the precious safety of my prince, 32
And free from other misbegotten hate,
Come I appellant to this princely presence.
Now, Thomas Mowbray, do I turn to thee,
And mark my greeting well; for what I speak 36
My body shall make good upon this earth,
Or my divine soul answer it in heaven.
Thou art a traitor and a miscreant;
Too good to be so and too bad to live,   40
Since the more fair and crystal is the sky,
The uglier seem the clouds that in it fly.
Once more, the more to aggravate the note,
With a foul traitor's name stuff I thy throat; 44
And wish, so please my sovereign, ere I move,
What my tongue speaks, my right drawn sword
  may prove.
  Mow. Let not my cold words here accuse my
  zeal:
'Tis not the trial of a woman's war,   48
The bitter clamour of two eager tongues,
Can arbitrate this cause betwixt us twain;
The blood is hot that must be cool'd for this:
Yet can I not of such tame patience boast 52
As to be hush'd and nought at all to say.

First, the fair reverence of your highness curbs
me
From giving reins and spurs to my free speech; 56
Which else would post until it had return'd
These terms of treason doubled down his throat.
Setting aside his high blood's royalty,
And let him be no kinsman to my liege,
I do defy him, and I spit at him; 60
Call him a slanderous coward and a villain:
Which to maintain I would allow him odds,
And meet him, were I tied to run afoot
Even to the frozen ridges of the Alps, 64
Or any other ground inhabitable,
Wherever Englishman durst set his foot.
Meantime let this defend my loyalty:
By all my hopes, most falsely doth he lie. 68
    Boling. Pale trembling coward, there I throw
my gage,
Disclaiming here the kindred of the king;
And lay aside my high blood's royalty,
Which fear, not reverence, makes thee to ex-
cept: 72
If guilty dread have left thee so much strength
As to take up mine honour's pawn, then stoop:
By that, and all the rites of knighthood else,
Will I make good against thee, arm to arm, 76
What I have spoke, or thou canst worse devise.
    Mow. I take it up; and by that sword I
swear,
Which gently laid my knighthood on my shoul-
der,
I'll answer thee in any fair degree, 80
Or chivalrous design of knightly trial:
And when I mount, alive may I not light,
If I be traitor or unjustly fight!
    K. Rich. What doth our cousin lay to Mow-
bray's charge? 84
It must be great that can inherit us
So much as of a thought of ill in him.
    Boling. Look, what I speak, my life shall
prove it true;
That Mowbray hath receiv'd eight thousand
nobles 88
In name of lendings for your highness' soldiers,
The which he hath detain'd for lewd employ-
ments,
Like a false traitor and injurious villain.
Besides I say and will in battle prove, 92
Or here or elsewhere to the furthest verge
That ever was survey'd by English eye,
That all the treasons for these eighteen years
Complotted and contriv'd in this land, 96
Fetch from false Mowbray their first head and
spring.
Further I say and further will maintain
Upon his bad life to make all this good,
That he did plot the Duke of Gloucester's death,
Suggest his soon-believing adversaries, 101
And consequently, like a traitor coward,
Sluic'd out his innocent soul through streams
of blood:
Which blood, like sacrificing Abel's, cries, 104
Even from the tongueless caverns of the earth,
To me for justice and rough chastisement;
And, by the glorious worth of my descent,
This arm shall do it, or this life be spent. 108

    K. Rich. How high a pitch his resoluti
soars!
Thomas of Norfolk, what sayst thou to this
    Mow. O! let my sovereign turn away h
face
And bid his ears a little while be deaf,
Till I have told this slander of his blood
How God and good men hate so foul a liar.
    K. Rich. Mowbray, impartial are our ey
and ears:
Were he my brother, nay, my kingdom's heir,
As he is but my father's brother's son,—
Now, by my sceptre's awe I make a vow,
Such neighbour nearness to our sacred bloc
Should nothing privilege him, nor partialize
The unstooping firmness of my upright sou
He is our subject, Mowbray; so art thou:
Free speech and fearless I to thee allow.
    Mow. Then, Bolingbroke, as low as to t
heart,
Through the false passage of thy throat, th
liest.
Three parts of that receipt I had for Calais
Disburs'd I duly to his highness' soldiers;
The other part reserv'd I by consent,
For that my sovereign liege was in my debt
Upon remainder of a dear account,
Since last I went to France to fetch his quee
Now swallow down that lie. For Glouceste
death,
I slew him not; but to mine own disgrace
Neglected my sworn duty in that case.
For you, my noble Lord of Lancaster,
The honourable father to my foe,
Once did I lay an ambush for your life,
A trespass that doth vex my grieved soul;
But ere I last receiv'd the sacrament
I did confess it, and exactly begg'd
Your Grace's pardon, and I hope I had it.
This is my fault: as for the rest appeal'd,
It issues from the rancour of a villain,
A recreant and most degenerate traitor;
Which in myself I boldly will defend,
And interchangeably hurl down my gage
Upon this overweening traitor's foot,
To prove myself a loyal gentleman
Even in the best blood chamber'd in his boso
In haste whereof, most heartily I pray
Your highness to assign our trial day.
    K. Rich. Wrath-kindled gentlemen, be ru
by me;
Let's purge this choler without letting bloc
This we prescribe, though no physician;
Deep malice makes too deep incision:
Forget, forgive; conclude and be agreed,
Our doctors say this is no month to bleed.
Good uncle, let this end where it begun;
We'll calm the Duke of Norfolk, you yo
son.
    Gaunt. To be a make-peace shall become
age:
Throw down, my son, the Duke of Norfol
gage.
    K. Rich. And, Norfolk, throw down his.
    Gaunt.   When, Harry, whe
Obedience bids I should not bid again.

K. *Rich.* Norfolk, throw down, we bid; there
   is no boot.   164
Mow. Myself I throw, dread sovereign, at
   thy foot.
 life thou shalt command, but not my shame:
 e one my duty owes; but my fair name,—
spite of death that lives upon my grave,— 168
 dark dishonour's use thou shalt not have.
m disgrac'd, impeach'd, and baffled here,
rc'd to the soul with slander's venom'd spear,
e which no balm can cure but his heart-
   blood   172
ich breath'd this poison.
K. *Rich.*   Rage must be withstood:
ve me his gage: lions make leopards tame.
Mow. Yea, but not change his spots: take
   but my shame,
d I resign my gage. My dear dear lord, 176
 e purest treasure mortal times afford
spotless reputation; that away,
 n are but gilded loam or painted clay.
ewel in a ten-times-barr'd-up chest 180
 a bold spirit in a loyal breast.
ne honour is my life; both grow in one;
ke honour from me, and my life is done:
 en, dear my liege, mine honour let me try;
 that I live and for that will I die. 185
K. *Rich.* Cousin, throw down your gage: do
   you begin.
Boling. O! God defend my soul from such
   deep sin.
all I seem crest-fall'n in my father's sight, 188
 with pale beggar-fear impeach my height
fore this out-dar'd dastard? Ere my tongue
all wound mine honour with such feeble
   wrong,
sound so base a parle, my teeth shall tear 192
 e slavish motive of recanting fear,
 d spit it bleeding in his high disgrace,
here shame doth harbour, even in Mowbray's
   face.   [*Exit* GAUNT.
K. *Rich.* We were not born to sue, but to
   command: 196
hich since we cannot do to make you friends,
 ready, as your lives shall answer it,
 Coventry, upon Saint Lambert's day:
ere shall your swords and lances arbitrate 200
 e swelling difference of your settled hate:
ace we cannot atone you, we shall see
stice design the victor's chivalry.
arshal, command our officers-at-arms 204
 ready to direct these home alarms. [*Exeunt.*

CENE II.—*The Same. A Room in the* DUKE
        OF LANCASTER'S *Palace.*

nter GAUNT *and* DUCHESS OF GLOUCESTER.

Gaunt. Alas! the part I had in Woodstock's
   blood
oth more solicit me than your exclaims,
 stir against the butchers of his life.
 t since correction lieth in those hands 4
hich made the fault that we cannot correct,
 t we our quarrel to the will of heaven;
ho, when they see the hours ripe on earth,

Will rain hot vengeance on offenders' heads. 8
   Duch. Finds brotherhood in thee no sharper
      spur?
Hath love in thy old blood no living fire?
Edward's seven sons, whereof thyself art one,
Were as seven vials of his sacred blood, 12
Or seven fair branches springing from one root:
Some of those seven are dried by nature's course,
Some of those branches by the Destinies cut;
But Thomas, my dear lord, my life, my Gloucester,
One vial full of Edward's sacred blood, 17
One flourishing branch of his most royal root,
Is crack'd, and all the precious liquor spilt;
Is hack'd down, and his summer leaves all vaded,
By envy's hand and murder's bloody axe. 21
Ah, Gaunt! his blood was thine: that bed, that
   womb,
That metal, that self-mould, that fashion'd thee
Made him a man; and though thou liv'st and
   breath'st,   24
Yet art thou slain in him: thou dost consent
In some large measure to thy father's death
In that thou seest thy wretched brother die,
Who was the model of thy father's life. 28
Call it not patience, Gaunt; it is despair:
In suffering thus thy brother to be slaughter'd
Thou show'st the naked pathway to thy life,
Teaching stern murder how to butcher thee: 32
That which in mean men we entitle patience
Is pale cold cowardice in noble breasts.
What shall I say? to safeguard thine own life,
The best way is to venge my Gloucester's death.
   Gaunt. God's is the quarrel; for God's sub-
      stitute,   37
His deputy anointed in his sight,
Hath caus'd his death; the which if wrongfully,
Let heaven revenge, for I may never lift 40
An angry arm against his minister.
   Duch. Where then, alas! may I complain
      myself?
   Gaunt. To God, the widow's champion and
      defence.
   Duch. Why then, I will. Farewell, old Gaunt.
Thou go'st to Coventry, there to behold 45
Our cousin Hereford and fell Mowbray fight:
O! sit my husband's wrongs on Hereford's spear,
That it may enter butcher Mowbray's breast. 48
Or if misfortune miss the first career,
Be Mowbray's sins so heavy in his bosom
That they may break his foaming courser's back,
And throw the rider headlong in the lists, 52
A caitiff recreant to my cousin Hereford!
Farewell, old Gaunt: thy sometimes brother's
   wife
With her companion grief must end her life.
   Gaunt. Sister, farewell; I must to Coventry.
As much good stay with thee as go with me! 57
   Duch. Yet one word more. Grief boundeth
      where it falls,
Not with the empty hollowness, but weight:
I take my leave before I have begun, 60
For sorrow ends not when it seemeth done.
Commend me to my brother, Edmund York.
Lo! this is all: nay, yet depart not so;
Though this be all, do not so quickly go; 64
I shall remember more. Bid him—ah, what?—

With all good speed at Plashy visit me.
Alack! and what shall good old York there see
But empty lodgings and unfurnish'd walls, 68
Unpeopled offices, untrodden stones?
And what hear there for welcome but my groans?
Therefore commend me; let him not come there,
To seek out sorrow that dwells every where. 72
Desolate, desolate will I hence, and die:
The last leave of thee takes my weeping eye.
                                        [*Exeunt.*

SCENE III.—*Open Space, near Coventry. Lists
set out, and a Throne.* Heralds, &c., *attending.*

Enter the Lord Marshal *and* AUMERLE.

Mar. My Lord Aumerle, is Harry Hereford
    arm'd?
Aum. Yea, at all points, and longs to enter in.
Mar. The Duke of Norfolk, sprightfully and
    bold,
Stays but the summons of the appellant's trum-
    pet.   4
Aum. Why then, the champions are pre-
    par'd, and stay
For nothing but his majesty's approach.

Flourish. Enter KING RICHARD, *who takes his
seat on his Throne;* GAUNT, BUSHY, BAGOT,
GREEN, *and Others, who take their places. A
trumpet is sounded, and answered by another
trumpet within. Then enter* MOWBRAY, *in
armour, defendant, preceded by a* Herald.

K. Rich. Marshal, demand of yonder cham-
    pion   8
The cause of his arrival here in arms:
Ask him his name, and orderly proceed
To swear him in the justice of his cause.
    Mar. In God's name, and the king's, say
who thou art,
And why thou com'st thus knightly clad in arms,
Against what man thou com'st, and what thy
    quarrel?   13
Speak truly, on thy knighthood and thine oath;
As so defend thee heaven and thy valour!
    Mow. My name is Thomas Mowbray, Duke
of Norfolk,   16
Who hither come engaged by my oath,—
Which God defend a knight should violate!—
Both to defend my loyalty and truth
To God, my king, and his succeeding issue, 20
Against the Duke of Hereford that appeals me;
And, by the grace of God and this mine arm,
To prove him, in defending of myself,
A traitor to my God, my king, and me: 24
And as I truly fight, defend me heaven!
                                    [*He takes his seat.*

Trumpet sounds. Enter BOLINGBROKE, *appellant, in armour, preceded by a* Herald.

K. Rich. Marshal, ask yonder knight in arms,
Both who he is and why he cometh hither
Thus plated in habiliments of war;   28
And formally, according to our law,
Depose him in the justice of his cause.
    Mar. What is thy name? and wherefore
com'st thou hither,

Before King Richard in his royal lists?
Against whom comest thou? and what's t
    quarrel?
Speak like a true knight, so defend thee heave
    Boling. Harry of Hereford, Lancaster, a
    Derby,
Am I; who ready here do stand in arms,
To prove by God's grace and my body's valo
In lists, on Thomas Mowbray, Duke of Norfo.
That he's a traitor foul and dangerous,
To God of heaven, King Richard, and to me
And as I truly fight, defend me heaven!
    Mar. On pain of death, no person be so bo
Or daring-hardy as to touch the lists,
Except the marshal and such officers
Appointed to direct these fair designs.
    Boling. Lord marshal, let me kiss my so
    reign's hand,
And bow my knee before his majesty:
For Mowbray and myself are like two men
That vow a long and weary pilgrimage;
Then let us take a ceremonious leave
And loving farewell of our several friends.
    Mar. The appellant in all duty greets yo
    highness,
And craves to kiss your hand and take his lea
    K. Rich. [*Descends from his throne.*] We w
    descend and fold him in our arms.
Cousin of Hereford, as thy cause is right,
So be thy fortune in this royal fight!
Farewell, my blood; which if to-day thou she
Lament we may, but not revenge thee dead.
    Boling. O! let no noble eye profane a tear
For me, if I be gor'd with Mowbray's spear.
As confident as is the falcon's flight
Against a bird, do I with Mowbray fight.
My loving lord, I take my leave of you;
Of you, my noble cousin, Lord Aumerle;
Not sick, although I have to do with death,
But lusty, young, and cheerly drawing brea
Lo! as at English feasts, so I regreet
The daintiest last, to make the end most swe
O thou, the earthly author of my blood,
Whose youthful spirit, in me regenerate,
Doth with a two-fold vigour lift me up
To reach at victory above my head,
Add proof unto mine armour with thy praye
And with thy blessings steel my lance's poi
That it may enter Mowbray's waxen coat,
And furbish new the name of John a Gaunt,
Even in the lusty haviour of his son.
    Gaunt. God in thy good cause make th
    prosperous!
Be swift like lightning in the execution;
And let thy blows, doubly redoubled,
Fall like amazing thunder on the casque
Of thy adverse pernicious enemy:
Rouse up thy youthful blood, be valiant and li
    Boling. Mine innocency and Saint Geor
    to thrive!   [*He takes his se*
    Mow. [*Rising.*] However God or fortune ca
    my lot,
There lives or dies, true to King Richard's thron
A loyal, just, and upright gentleman.
Never did captive with a freer heart
Cast off his chains of bondage and embrace

golden uncontroll'd enfranchisement,
re than my dancing soul doth celebrate
s feast of battle with mine adversary. 92
st mighty liege, and my companion peers,
e from my mouth the wish of happy years.
gentle and as jocund as to jest,
I to fight: truth has a quiet breast. 96
. *Rich.* Farewell, my lord: securely I espy
ue with valour couched in thine eye.
ler the trial, marshal, and begin.
[*The* KING *and the* Lords *return
                    to their seats.*
1ar. Harry of Hereford, Lancaster, and
Derby, 100
eive thy lance; and God defend the right!
oling. [*Rising.*] Strong as a tower in hope,
I cry 'amen.'
1ar. [*To an* Officer.] Go bear this lance to
Thomas, Duke of Norfolk.
irst Her. Harry of Hereford, Lancaster,
and Derby, 104
nds here for God, his sovereign, and himself,
pain to be found false and recreant,
prove the Duke of Norfolk, Thomas Mowbray,
raitor to his God, his king, and him; 108
I dares him to set forward to the fight.
ec. Her. Here standeth Thomas Mowbray,
Duke of Norfolk,
pain to be found false and recreant,
h to defend himself and to approve 112
ry of Hereford, Lancaster, and Derby,
God, his sovereign, and to him, disloyal;
rageously and with a free desire,
ending but the signal to begin. 116
1ar. Sound, trumpets; and set forward,
combatants. [*A charge sounded.*
y, stay, the king hath thrown his warder
down.
. *Rich.* Let them lay by their helmets and
their spears,
I both return back to their chairs again: 120
hdraw with us; and let the trumpets sound
ile we return these dukes what we decree.
                        [*A long flourish.*
the Combatants.] Draw near,
I list what with our council we have done.
that our kingdom's earth should not be
soil'd 125
h that dear blood which it hath fostered;
I for our eyes do hate the dire aspect
civil wounds plough'd up with neighbours'
swords; 128
I for we think the eagle-winged pride
sky-aspiring and ambitious thoughts,
h rival-hating envy, set on you
wake our peace, which in our country's
cradle 132
ws the sweet infant breath of gentle sleep;
ich so rous'd up with boist'rous untun'd
drums,
h harsh-resounding trumpets' dreadful bray,
I grating shock of wrathful iron arms, 136
ght from our quiet confines fright fair peace
I make us wade even in our kindred's blood:
refore, we banish you our territories:

You, cousin Hereford, upon pain of life, 140
Till twice five summers have enrich'd our fields,
Shall not regreet our fair dominions,
But tread the stranger paths of banishment.
Boling. Your will be done: this must my
comfort be, 144
That sun that warms you here shall shine on me;
And those his golden beams to you here lent
Shall point on me and gild my banishment.
K. Rich. Norfolk, for thee remains a heavier
doom, 148
Which I with some unwillingness pronounce:
The sly slow hours shall not determinate
The dateless limit of thy dear exile;
The hopeless word of 'never to return' 152
Breathe I against thee, upon pain of life.
Mow. A heavy sentence, my most sovereign
liege,
And all unlook'd for from your highness' mouth:
A dearer merit, not so deep a maim 156
As to be cast forth in the common air,
Have I deserved at your highness' hands.
The language I have learn'd these forty years,
My native English, now I must forego; 160
And now my tongue's use is to me no more
Than an unstringed viol or a harp,
Or like a cunning instrument cas'd up,
Or, being open, put into his hands 164
That knows no touch to tune the harmony:
Within my mouth you have engaol'd my tongue,
Doubly portcullis'd with my teeth and lips;
And dull, unfeeling, barren ignorance 168
Is made my gaoler to attend on me.
I am too old to fawn upon a nurse,
Too far in years to be a pupil now:
What is thy sentence then but speechless death,
Which robs my tongue from breathing native
breath? 173
K. Rich. It boots thee not to be compas-
sionate:
After our sentence plaining comes too late.
Mow. Then, thus I turn me from my coun-
try's light, 176
To dwell in solemn shades of endless night.
                                    [*Retiring.*
K. Rich. Return again, and take an oath with
thee.
Lay on our royal sword your banish'd hands;
Swear by the duty that you owe to God— 180
Our part therein we banish with yourselves—
To keep the oath that we administer:
You never shall,—so help you truth and God!—
Embrace each other's love in banishment; 184
Nor never look upon each other's face;
Nor never write, regreet, nor reconcile
This low'ring tempest of your home-bred hate;
Nor never by advised purpose meet 188
To plot, contrive, or complot any ill
'Gainst us, our state, our subjects, or our land.
Boling. I swear.
Mow. And I, to keep all this. 192
Boling. Norfolk, so far, as to mine enemy:—
By this time, had the king permitted us,
One of our souls had wander'd in the air,
Banish'd this frail sepulchre of our flesh, 196
As now our flesh is banish'd from this land:

Confess thy treasons ere thou fly the realm;
Since thou hast far to go, bear not along
The clogging burden of a guilty soul.   200

Mow. No, Bolingbroke: if ever I were traitor,
My name be blotted from the book of life,
And I from heaven banish'd as from hence!
But what thou art, God, thou, and I do know; 204
And all too soon, I fear, the king shall rue.
Farewell, my liege. Now no way can I stray;
Save back to England, all the world's my way.
                      [*Exit.*

K. Rich. Uncle, even in the glasses of thine
   eyes   208
I see thy grieved heart: thy sad aspect
Hath from the number of his banish'd years
Pluck'd four away.—[*To* BOLINGBROKE.] Six
   frozen winters spent,
Return with welcome home from banishment.

Boling. How long a time lies in one little
   word!   213
Four lagging winters and four wanton springs
End in a word: such is the breath of kings.

Gaunt. I thank my liege, that in regard of me
He shortens four years of my son's exile; 217
But little vantage shall I reap thereby:
For, ere the six years that he hath to spend
Can change their moons and bring their times
   about,   220
My oil-dried lamp and time-bewasted light
Shall be extinct with age and endless night;
My inch of taper will be burnt and done,
And blindfold death not let me see my son. 224

K. Rich. Why, uncle, thou hast many years
   to live.

Gaunt. But not a minute, king, that thou
   canst give:
Shorten my days thou canst with sullen sorrow,
And pluck nights from me, but not lend a mor-
   row;   228
Thou canst help time to furrow me with age,
But stop no wrinkle in his pilgrimage;
Thy word is current with him for my death,
But dead, thy kingdom cannot buy my breath.

K. Rich. Thy son is banish'd upon good
   advice,   233
Whereto thy tongue a party-verdict gave:
Why at our justice seem'st thou then to lower?

Gaunt. Things sweet to taste prove in diges-
   tion sour.   236
You urg'd me as a judge; but I had rather
You would have bid me argue like a father.
O! had it been a stranger, not my child,
To smooth his fault I should have been more
   mild: 240
A partial slander sought I to avoid,
And in the sentence my own life destroy'd.
Alas! I look'd when some of you should say,
I was too strict to make mine own away; 244
But you gave leave to my unwilling tongue
Against my will to do myself this wrong.

K. Rich. Cousin, farewell; and, uncle, bid
   him so:
Six years we banish him, and he shall go. 248
   [*Flourish. Exeunt* KING RICHARD *and Train.*

Aum. Cousin, farewell: what presence must
   not know,

From where you do remain let paper show
   Mar. My lord, no leave take I; for I will ri
As far as land will let me, by your side.

Gaunt. O! to what purpose dost thou ho
   thy words,
That thou return'st no greeting to thy frien

Boling. I have too few to take my leave
   you,
When the tongue's office should be prodigal
To breathe the abundant dolour of the he

Gaunt. Thy grief is but thy absence for a ti

Boling. Joy absent, grief is present for t
   time.

Gaunt. What is six winters? they are quic
   gone.

Boling. To men in joy; but grief makes
   hour ten.

Gaunt. Call it a travel that thou tak'st
   pleasure.

Boling. My heart will sigh when I mis
   it so,
Which finds it an inforced pilgrimage.

Gaunt. The sullen passage of thy weary s
Esteem as foil wherein thou art to set
The precious jewel of thy home return.

Boling. Nay, rather, every tedious stric
   make
Will but remember me what a deal of worl
I wander from the jewels that I love.
Must I not serve a long apprenticehood
To foreign passages, and in the end,
Having my freedom, boast of nothing else
But that I was a journeyman to grief?

Gaunt. All places that the eye of heaven v
Are to a wise man ports and happy havens.
Teach thy necessity to reason thus;
There is no virtue like necessity.
Think not the king did banish thee,
But thou the king. Woe doth the heavier si
Where it perceives it is but faintly borne.
Go, say I sent thee forth to purchase hono
And not the king exil'd thee; or suppose
Devouring pestilence hangs in our air,
And thou art flying to a fresher clime.
Look, what thy soul holds dear, imagine it
To lie that way thou go'st, not whence t
   com'st.
Suppose the singing birds musicians,
The grass whereon thou tread'st the press
   strew'd,
The flowers fair ladies, and thy steps no m
Than a delightful measure or a dance;
For gnarling sorrow hath less power to bite
The man that mocks at it and sets it light.

Boling. O! who can hold a fire in his ha
By thinking on the frosty Caucasus?
Or cloy the hungry edge of appetite
By bare imagination of a feast?
Or wallow naked in December snow
By thinking on fantastic summer's heat?
O, no! the apprehension of the good
Gives but the greater feeling to the worse
Fell sorrow's tooth doth never rankle mo
Than when it bites, but lanceth not the so

Gaunt. Come, come, my son, I'll bring
   on thy way.

d I thy youth and cause, I would not stay.

Boling. Then, England's ground, farewell;
　　sweet soil, adieu:

y mother, and my nurse, that bears me yet!
here'er I wander, boast of this I can,　308
ough banish'd, yet a true-born Englishman.
　　　　　　　　　　　　　　[*Exeunt.*

ENE IV.—*London. A Room in the* KING'S
　　　　　Castle.

ter KING RICHARD, BAGOT, *and* GREEN *at one
　　　door ;* AUMERLE *at another.*

K. Rich. We did observe. Cousin Aumerle,
ow far brought you high Hereford on his way?

Aum. I brought high Hereford, if you call
　　him so,

t to the next highway, and there I left him. 4

K. Rich. And say, what store of parting tears
　　were shed?

Aum. Faith, none for me; except the north-
　　east wind,

hich then blew bitterly against our faces,
vak'd the sleeping rheum, and so by chance 8
d grace our hollow parting with a tear.

K. Rich. What said our cousin when you
　　parted with him?

Aum. 'Farewell:'

d, for my heart disdained that my tongue 12
ould so profane the word, that taught me craft
counterfeit oppression of such grief
at words seem'd buried in my sorrow's grave.
arry, would the word 'farewell' have length-
　　en'd hours　　　　　　　　　　　　16
d added years to his short banishment,
should have had a volume of farewells;
t, since it would not, he had none of me.

K. Rich. He is our cousin, cousin; but 'tis
　　doubt,　　　　　　　　　　　　　20
hen time shall call him home from banish-
　　ment,

hether our kinsman come to see his friends.
irself and Bushy, Bagot here and Green
oserv'd his courtship to the common people,
ow he did seem to dive into their hearts　25
ith humble and familiar courtesy,
hat reverence he did throw away on slaves,
ooing poor craftsmen with the craft of smiles
d patient underbearing of his fortune,　29
'twere to banish their affects with him.
f goes his bonnet to an oyster-wench;
brace of draymen bid God speed him well, 32
d had the tribute of his supple knee,
ith 'Thanks, my countrymen, my loving
　　friends;'
were our England in reversion his,
nd he our subjects' next degree in hope.　36

Green. Well, he is gone; and with him go
　　these thoughts.

ow for the rebels which stand out in Ireland;
xpedient manage must be made, my liege,
e further leisure yield them further means 40
or their advantage and your highness' loss.

K. Rich. We will ourself in person to this war.
nd, for our coffers with too great a court
nd liberal largess are grown somewhat light,

We are enforc'd to farm our royal realm;　45
The revenue whereof shall furnish us
For our affairs in hand. If that come short,
Our substitutes at home shall have blank
　　charters;　　　　　　　　　　　48
Whereto, when they shall know what men are
　　rich,
They shall subscribe them for large sums of gold,
And send them after to supply our wants;
For we will make for Ireland presently.　52

Enter BUSHY.

Bushy, what news?

Bushy. Old John of Gaunt is grievous sick,
　　my lord,
Suddenly taken, and hath sent post-haste
To entreat your majesty to visit him.　　56

K. Rich. Where lies he?

Bushy. At Ely House.

K. Rich. Now, put it, God, in his physician's
　　mind
To help him to his grave immediately!　　60
The lining of his coffers shall make coats
To deck our soldiers for these Irish wars.
Come, gentlemen, let's all go visit him:
Pray God we may make haste, and come too
　　late.　　　　　　　　　　　　　64

All. Amen.　　　　　　　　　　[*Exeunt.*

ACT II

SCENE I.—*London. An Apartment in Ely
　　　　　House.*

GAUNT *on a couch; the* DUKE OF YORK *and
　　　Others standing by him.*

Gaunt. Will the king come, that I may breathe
　　my last
In wholesome counsel to his unstaid youth?

York. Vex not yourself, nor strive not with
　　your breath;
For all in vain comes counsel to his ear.　4

Gaunt. O! but they say the tongues of dying
　　men
Enforce attention like deep harmony:
Where words are scarce, they are seldom spent
　　in vain,
For they breathe truth that breathe their words
　　in pain.　　　　　　　　　　　8
He that no more must say is listen'd more
　　Than they whom youth and ease have taught
　　　to glose:
More are men's ends mark'd than their lives
　　before:
The setting sun, and music at the close,　12
As the last taste of sweets, is sweetest last,
Writ in remembrance more than things long
　　past:
Though Richard my life's counsel would not
　　hear,
My death's sad tale may yet undeaf his ear. 16

York. No; it is stopp'd with other flattering
　　sounds,
As praises of his state: then there are fond
Lascivious metres, to whose venom sound
The open ear of youth doth always listen:　20

Report of fashions in proud Italy,
Whose manners still our tardy apish nation
Limps after in base imitation.
Where doth the world thrust forth a vanity,— 24
So it be new there's no respect how vile,
That is not quickly buzz'd into his ears?
Then all too late comes counsel to be heard,
Where will doth mutiny with wit's regard. 28
Direct not him whose way himself will choose:
'Tis breath thou lack'st, and that breath wilt
    thou lose.
    Gaunt. Methinks I am a prophet new inspir'd,
And thus expiring do foretell of him: 32
His rash fierce blaze of riot cannot last,
For violent fires soon burn out themselves;
Small showers last long, but sudden storms are
    short;
He tires betimes that spurs too fast betimes; 36
With eager feeding food doth choke the feeder:
Light vanity, insatiate cormorant,
Consuming means, soon preys upon itself.
This royal throne of kings, this scepter'd isle, 40
This earth of majesty, this seat of Mars,
This other Eden, demi-paradise,
This fortress built by Nature for herself
Against infection and the hand of war,   44
This happy breed of men, this little world,
This precious stone set in the silver sea,
Which serves it in the office of a wall,
Or as a moat defensive to a house,   48
Against the envy of less happier lands,
This blessed plot, this earth, this realm, this
    England,
This nurse, this teeming womb of royal kings,
Fear'd by their breed and famous by their
    birth,   52
Renowned for their deeds as far from home,—
For Christian service and true chivalry,—
As is the sepulchre in stubborn Jewry
Of the world's ransom, blessed Mary's Son: 56
This land of such dear souls, this dear, dear land,
Dear for her reputation through the world,
Is now leas'd out,—I die pronouncing it,—
Like to a tenement, or pelting farm: 60
England, bound in with the triumphant sea,
Whose rocky shore beats back the envious siege
Of watery Neptune, is now bound in with shame,
With inky blots, and rotten parchment bonds: 64
That England, that was wont to conquer others,
Hath made a shameful conquest of itself.
Ah! would the scandal vanish with my life,
How happy then were my ensuing death.   68

Enter KING RICHARD *and* QUEEN; AUMERLE,
    BUSHY, GREEN, BAGOT, ROSS, *and* WIL-
    LOUGHBY.

    York. The king is come: deal mildly with
        his youth;
For young hot colts, being rag'd, do rage the
    more.
    Queen. How fares our noble uncle, Lan-
        caster?
    K. Rich. What comfort, man? How is't with
        aged Gaunt?   72
    Gaunt. O! how that name befits my com-
        position;

Old Gaunt indeed, and gaunt in being old
Within me grief hath kept a tedious fast;
And who abstains from meat that is not gau
For sleeping England long time have I watch
Watching breeds leanness, leanness is all gau
The pleasure that some fathers feed upon
Is my strict fast, I mean my children's looks;
And therein fasting hast thou made me gau
Gaunt am I for the grave, gaunt as a grave
Whose hollow womb inherits nought but bon
    K. Rich. Can sick men play so nicely w
        their names?
    Gaunt. No; misery makes sport to mock
        self:
Since thou dost seek to kill my name in me
I mock my name, great king, to flatter thee
    K. Rich. Should dying men flatter with th
        that live?
    Gaunt. No, no; men living flatter those t
        die.
    K. Rich. Thou, now a-dying, sayst thou fl
        ter'st me.
    Gaunt. O, no! thou diest, though I the sic
        be.
    K. Rich. I am in health, I breathe, and
        thee ill.
    Gaunt. Now, he that made me knows I
        thee ill;
Ill in myself to see, and in thee seeing ill.
Thy death-bed is no lesser than thy land
Wherein thou liest in reputation sick:
And thou, too careless patient as thou art,
Committ'st thy anointed body to the cure
Of those physicians that first wounded thee
A thousand flatterers sit within thy crown,
Whose compass is no bigger than thy hea
And yet, incaged in so small a verge,
The waste is no whit lesser than thy land.
O! had thy grandsire, with a prophet's eye,
Seen how his son's son should destroy his so
From forth thy reach he would have laid t
    shame,
Deposing thee before thou wert possess'd,
Which art possess'd now to depose thyself.
Why, cousin, wert thou regent of the world,
It were a shame to let this land by lease;
But for thy world enjoying but this land,
Is it not more than shame to shame it so?
Landlord of England art thou now, not ki
Thy state of law is bond-slave to the law,
And—
    K. Rich. And thou a lunatic lean-witted fo
Presuming on an ague's privilege,
Dar'st with thy frozen admonition
Make pale our cheek, chasing the royal blo
With fury from his native residence.
Now, by my seat's right royal majesty,
Wert thou not brother to great Edward's son,
This tongue that runs so roundly in thy head
Should run thy head from thy unrevere
    shoulders.
    Gaunt. O! spare me not, my brother E
        ward's son,
For that I was his father Edward's son.
That blood already, like the pelican,
Hast thou tapp'd out and drunkenly carous

y brother Gloucester, plain well-meaning
soul,— 128
hom fair befall in heaven 'mongst happy
souls!—
ay be a precedent and witness good
at thou respect'st not spilling Edward's
blood:
in with the present sickness that I have; 132
d thy unkindness be like crooked age,
crop at once a too-long wither'd flower.
ve in thy shame, but die not shame with thee!
ese words hereafter thy tormentors be! 136
nvey me to my bed, then to my grave:
ve they to live that love and honour have.
    [*Exit, borne out by his* Attendants.
K. *Rich.* And let them die that age and sullens
have;
r both hast thou, and both become the grave.
York. I do beseech your majesty, impute his
words 141
wayward sickliness and age in him:
loves you, on my life, and holds you dear
Harry, Duke of Hereford, were he here. 144
K. *Rich.* Right, you say true: as Hereford's
love, so his;
theirs, so mine; and all be as it is.

Enter NORTHUMBERLAND.

North. My liege, old Gaunt commends him
to your majesty.
K. *Rich.* What says he? 148
North. Nay, nothing; all is said:
s tongue is now a stringless instrument;
rds, life, and all, old Lancaster hath spent.
York. Be York the next that must be bankrupt so! 152
ough death be poor, it ends a mortal woe.
K. *Rich.* The ripest fruit first falls, and so
doth he:
s time is spent; our pilgrimage must be.
much for that. Now for our Irish wars. 156
must supplant those rough rug-headed kerns,
ich live like venom where no venom else
t only they have privilege to live.
d for these great affairs do ask some charge,
wards our assistance we do seize to us 161
e plate, coin, revenues, and moveables,
ereof our uncle Gaunt did stand possess'd.
York. How long shall I be patient? Ah! how
long 164
all tender duty make me suffer wrong?
t Gloucester's death, nor Hereford's banishment,
t Gaunt's rebukes, nor England's private
wrongs,
r the prevention of poor Bolingbroke 168
out his marriage, nor my own disgrace,
ve ever made me sour my patient cheek,
bend one wrinkle on my sovereign's face.
m the last of noble Edward's sons, 172
whom thy father, Prince of Wales, was first;
war was never lion rag'd more fierce,
peace was never gentle lamb more mild,
an was that young and princely gentleman.
s face thou hast, for even so look'd he, 177
complish'd with the number of thy hours;

But when he frown'd, it was against the French,
And not against his friends; his noble hand 180
Did win what he did spend, and spent not that
Which his triumphant father's hand had won:
His hands were guilty of no kindred's blood,
But bloody with the enemies of his kin. 184
O, Richard! York is too far gone with grief,
Or else he never would compare between.
    K. Rich. Why, uncle, what's the matter?
    York. O! my liege.
Pardon me, if you please; if not, I, pleas'd 188
Not to be pardon'd, am content withal.
Seek you to seize and gripe into your hands
The royalties and rights of banish'd Hereford?
Is not Gaunt dead, and doth not Hereford live?
Was not Gaunt just, and is not Harry true? 193
Did not the one deserve to have an heir?
Is not his heir a well-deserving son?
Take Hereford's rights away, and take from
Time
His charters and his customary rights; 197
Let not to-morrow then ensue to-day;
Be not thyself; for how art thou a king
But by fair sequence and succession? 200
Now, afore God,—God forbid I say true!—
If you do wrongfully seize Hereford's rights,
Call in the letters-patent that he hath
By his attorneys-general to sue 204
His livery, and deny his offer'd homage,
You pluck a thousand dangers on your head,
You lose a thousand well-disposed hearts,
And prick my tender patience to those thoughts
Which honour and allegiance cannot think. 209
    K. Rich. Think what you will: we seize into
our hands
His plate, his goods, his money, and his lands.
    York. I'll not be by the while: my liege, fare-
well: 212
What will ensue hereof, there's none can tell;
But by bad courses may be understood
That their events can never fall out good. [*Exit.*
    K. Rich. Go, Bushy, to the Earl of Wiltshire
straight: 216
Bid him repair to us to Ely House
To see this business. To-morrow next
We will for Ireland; and 'tis time, I trow:
And we create, in absence of ourself, 220
Our uncle York lord governor of England;
For he is just, and always lov'd us well.
Come on, our queen: to-morrow must we part;
Be merry, for our time of stay is short. [*Flourish.*
    [*Exeunt* KING, QUEEN, BUSHY, AUMERLE,
GREEN, *and* BAGOT.
    North. Well, lords, the Duke of Lancaster is
dead. 225
    Ross. And living too; for now his son is duke.
    Willo. Barely in title, not in revenue.
    North. Richly in both, if justice had her right.
    Ross. My heart is great; but it must break
with silence, 229
Ere't be disburden'd with a liberal tongue.
    North. Nay, speak thy mind; and let him
ne'er speak more
That speaks thy words again to do thee harm!
    Willo. Tends that thou'dst speak to the
Duke of Hereford? 233

If it be so, out with it boldly, man;
Quick is mine ear to hear of good towards
  him.
Ross. No good at all that I can do for him, 236
Unless you call it good to pity him,
Bereft and gelded of his patrimony.
North. Now, afore God, 'tis shame such
    wrongs are borne
In him, a royal prince, and many more   240
Of noble blood in this declining land.
The king is not himself, but basely led
By flatterers; and what they will inform,
Merely in hate, 'gainst any of us all,   244
That will the king severely prosecute
'Gainst us, our lives, our children, and our heirs.
Ross. The commons hath he pill'd with
    grievous taxes,
And quite lost their hearts: the nobles hath he
    fin'd   248
For ancient quarrels, and quite lost their hearts.
Willo. And daily new exactions are devis'd;
As blanks, benevolences, and I wot not what:
But what, o' God's name, doth become of this?
North. Wars have not wasted it, for warr'd
    he hath not,   253
But basely yielded upon compromise
That which his ancestors achiev'd with blows.
More hath he spent in peace than they in wars.
Ross. The Earl of Wiltshire hath the realm
    in farm.   257
Willo. The king's grown bankrupt, like a
    broken man.
North. Reproach and dissolution hangeth
    over him.
Ross. He hath not money for these Irish wars,
His burdenous taxations notwithstanding,   261
But by the robbing of the banish'd duke.
North. His noble kinsman: most degenerate
    king!
But, lords, we hear this fearful tempest sing, 264
Yet seek no shelter to avoid the storm;
We see the wind sit sore upon our sails,
And yet we strike not, but securely perish.
Ross. We see the very wrack that we must
    suffer;   268
And unavoided is the danger now,
For suffering so the causes of our wrack.
North. Not so: even through the hollow eyes
    of death
I spy life peering; but I dare not say   272
How near the tidings of our comfort is.
Willo. Nay, let us share thy thoughts, as
    thou dost ours.
Ross. Be confident to speak, Northumber-
    land:
We three are but thyself: and, speaking so, 276
Thy words are but as thoughts; therefore, be
    bold.
North. Then thus: I have from Port le Blanc,
    a bay
In Brittany, receiv'd intelligence
That Harry Duke of Hereford, Rainold Lord
    Cobham,   280
That late broke from the Duke of Exeter,
His brother, Archbishop late of Canterbury,
Sir Thomas Erpingham, Sir John Ramston,

Sir John Norbery, Sir Robert Waterton, a
    Francis Quoint,
All these well furnish'd by the Duke of Britai
With eight tall ships, three thousand men
    war,
Are making hither with all due expedience,
And shortly mean to touch our northern sho
Perhaps they had ere this, but that they stay
The first departing of the king for Ireland.
If then we shall shake off our slavish yoke,
Imp out our drooping country's broken wi
Redeem from broking pawn the blemish
    crown,
Wipe off the dust that hides our sceptre's g
And make high majesty look like itself,
Away with me in post to Ravenspurgh;
But if you faint, as fearing to do so,
Stay and be secret, and myself will go.
Ross. To horse, to horse! urge doubts
    them that fear.
Willo. Hold out my horse, and I will first
    there.   [*Exeu*

SCENE II.—*The Same. A Room in the Pala*

Enter QUEEN, BUSHY, *and* BAGOT.

Bushy. Madam, your majesty is too mu
    sad:
You promis'd, when you parted with the ki
To lay aside life-harming heaviness,
And entertain a cheerful disposition.
Queen. To please the king I did; to ple
    myself
I cannot do it; yet I know no cause
Why I should welcome such a guest as grief,
Save bidding farewell to so sweet a guest
As my sweet Richard: yet, again, methinks,
Some unborn sorrow, ripe in fortune's won
Is coming towards me, and my inward soul
With nothing trembles; at some thing it grie
More than with parting from my lord the ki
Bushy. Each substance of a grief hath twe
    shadows,
Which show like grief itself, but are not so.
For sorrow's eye, glazed with blinding tears,
Divides one thing entire to many objects;
Like perspectives, which rightly gaz'd upon
Show nothing but confusion; ey'd awry
Distinguish form: so your sweet majesty,
Looking awry upon your lord's departure
Finds shapes of grief more than himself to wa
Which, look'd on as it is, is nought but shado
Of what it is not. Then, thrice-gracious que
More than your lord's departure weep n
    more's not seen;
Or if it be, 'tis with false sorrow's eye,
Which for things true weeps things imagina
Queen. It may be so; but yet my inward s
Persuades me it is otherwise: howe'er it be,
I cannot but be sad, so heavy sad,
As, though in thinking on no thought I thi
Makes me with heavy nothing faint and shri
Bushy. 'Tis nothing but conceit, my graci
    lady.
Queen. 'Tis nothing less: conceit is s
    deriv'd

om some forefather grief; mine is not so,
r nothing hath begot my something grief; 36
: something hath the nothing that I grieve:
is in reversion that I do possess;
at what it is, that is not yet known; what
annot name; 'tis nameless woe, I wot. 40

Enter GREEN.

Green. God save your majesty! and well met,
    gentlemen:
ope the king is not yet shipp'd for Ireland.
Queen. Why hop'st thou so? 'tis better hope
    he is, 43
r his designs crave haste, his haste good hope:
en wherefore dost thou hope he is not shipp'd?
Green. That he, our hope, might have retir'd
    his power,
nd driven into despair an enemy's hope,
ho strongly hath set footing in this land: 48
ae banish'd Bolingbroke repeals himself,
nd with uplifted arms is safe arriv'd
t Ravenspurgh.
Queen.   Now God in heaven forbid!
Green. Ah! madam, 'tis too true: and that is
    worse, 52
ae Lord Northumberland, his son young
    Henry Percy,
ae Lords of Ross, Beaumond, and Willoughby,
ith all their powerful friends, are fled to him.
Bushy. Why have you not proclaim'd North-
    umberland 56
nd all the rest of the revolted faction traitors?
Green. We have: whereupon the Earl of
    Worcester
ath broke his staff, resign'd his stewardship,
nd all the household servants fled with him 60
Bolingbroke.
Queen. So, Green, thou art the midwife to
    my woe,
nd Bolingbroke my sorrow's dismal heir:
ow hath my soul brought forth her prodigy, 64
nd I, a gasping new-deliver'd mother,
ave woe to woe, sorrow to sorrow join'd.
Bushy. Despair not, madam.
Queen.   Who shall hinder me?
will despair, and be at enmity 68
ith cozening hope: he is a flatterer,
parasite, a keeper-back of death,
ho gently would dissolve the bands of life,
hich false hope lingers in extremity. 72

Enter YORK.

Green. Here comes the Duke of York.
Queen. With signs of war about his aged
    neck:
! full of careful business are his looks.
ncle, for God's sake, speak comfortable words.
York. Should I do so, I should belie my
    thoughts: 77
omfort's in heaven; and we are on the earth,
here nothing lives but crosses, cares, and grief.
our husband, he is gone to save far off, 80
hilst others come to make him lose at home:
ere am I left to underprop his land,
ho, weak with age, cannot support myself.

Now comes the sick hour that his surfeit made;
Now shall he try his friends that flatter'd him.

Enter a Servant.

Serv. My lord, your son was gone before I
    came.
York. He was? Why, so! go all which way
    it will!
The nobles they are fled, the commons they are
    cold, 88
And will, I fear, revolt on Hereford's side.
Sirrah, get thee to Plashy, to my sister Glouces-
    ter;
Bid her send me presently a thousand pound.
Hold, take my ring. 92
Serv. My lord, I had forgot to tell your lord-
    ship:
To-day, as I came by, I called there;
But I shall grieve you to report the rest.
York. What is't, knave? 96
Serv. An hour before I came the duchess
    died.
York. God for his mercy! what a tide of woes
Comes rushing on this woeful land at once!
I know not what to do: I would to God,— 100
So my untruth had not provok'd him to it,—
The king had cut off my head with my brother's.
What! are there no posts dispatch'd for Ireland?
How shall we do for money for these wars? 104
Come, sister,—cousin, I would say,—pray,
    pardon me.—
Go, fellow, get thee home; provide some carts
And bring away the armour that is there.
                      [*Exit* Servant.
Gentlemen, will you go muster men? If I know
How or which way to order these affairs 109
Thus thrust disorderly into my hands,
Never believe me. Both are my kinsmen:
The one is my sovereign, whom both my oath
And duty bids defend; the other again 113
Is my kinsman, whom the king hath wrong'd,
Whom conscience and my kindred bids to right.
Well, somewhat we must do. Come, cousin, 116
I'll dispose of you. Gentlemen, go muster up
    your men,
And meet me presently at Berkeley Castle.
I should to Plashy too:
But time will not permit. All is uneven, 120
And every thing is left at six and seven.
             [*Exeunt* YORK *and* QUEEN.
Bushy. The wind sits fair for news to go to
    Ireland,
But none returns. For us to levy power
Proportionable to the enemy 124
Is all unpossible.
Green. Besides, our nearness to the king in
    love
Is near the hate of those love not the king.
Bagot. And that's the wavering commons;
    for their love 128
Lies in their purses, and whoso empties them,
By so much fills their hearts with deadly hate.
Bushy. Wherein the king stands generally
    condemn'd.
Bagot. If judgment lie in them, then so do we,
Because we ever have been near the king. 133

Green. Well, I'll for refuge straight to Bristol
  Castle;
The Earl of Wiltshire is already there.
  Bushy. Thither will I with you; for little
  office   136
Will the hateful commons perform for us,
Except like curs to tear us all to pieces.
Will you go along with us?
  Bagot. No; I'll to Ireland to his majesty.
Farewell: if heart's presages be not vain,   141
We three here part that ne'er shall meet again.
  Bushy. That's as York thrives to beat back
  Bolingbroke.
  Green. Alas, poor duke! the task he under-
  takes   144
Is numbering sands and drinking oceans dry:
Where one on his side fights, thousands will fly.
Farewell at once; for once, for all, and ever.
  Bushy. Well, we may meet again.
  Bagot.   I fear me, never. 148
                                        [*Exeunt.*

SCENE III.—*The Wolds in Gloucestershire.*

Enter BOLINGBROKE *and* NORTHUMBERLAND,
                  with Forces.

  Boling. How far is it, my lord, to Berkeley
  now?
  North. Believe me, noble lord,
I am a stranger here in Gloucestershire:
These high wild hills and rough uneven ways 4
Draw out our miles and make them wearisome;
But yet your fair discourse hath been as sugar,
Making the hard way sweet and delectable.
But I bethink me what a weary way   8
From Ravenspurgh to Cotswold will be found
In Ross and Willoughby, wanting your com-
  pany,
Which, I protest, hath very much beguil'd
The tediousness and process of my travel: 12
But theirs is sweeten'd with the hope to have
The present benefit which I possess;
And hope to joy is little less in joy
Than hope enjoy'd: by this the weary lords 16
Shall make their way seem short, as mine hath
  done
By sight of what I have, your noble company.
  Boling. Of much less value is my company
Than your good words. But who comes here?

            Enter HENRY PERCY.

  North. It is my son, young Harry Percy, 21
Sent from my brother Worcester, whenceso-
  ever.
Harry, how fares your uncle?
  H. Percy. I had thought, my lord, to have
  learn'd his health of you.   24
  North. Why, is he not with the queen?
  H. Percy. No, my good lord; he hath forsook
  the court,
Broken his staff of office, and dispers'd
The household of the king.
  North.   What was his reason? 28
He was not so resolv'd when last we spake
  together.

  H. Percy. Because your lordship was pr
  claimed traitor.
But he, my lord, is gone to Ravenspurgh,
To offer service to the Duke of Hereford,
And sent me over by Berkeley to discover
What power the Duke of York had levied ther
Then with direction to repair to Ravenspurg
  North. Have you forgot the Duke of Her
  ford, boy?
  H. Percy. No, my good lord; for that is n
  forgot
Which ne'er I did remember: to my knowled
I never in my life did look on him.
  North. Then learn to know him now: this
  the duke.
  H. Percy. My gracious lord, I tender ye
  my service,
Such as it is, being tender, raw, and young,
Which elder days shall ripen and confirm
To more approved service and desert.
  Boling. I thank thee, gentle Percy; and I
  sure
I count myself in nothing else so happy
As in a soul remembering my good friends;
And as my fortune ripens with thy love,
It shall be still thy true love's recompense:
My heart this covenant makes, my hand th
  seals it.
  North. How far is it to Berkeley? and wh
  stir
Keeps good old York there with his men of wa
  H. Percy. There stands the castle, by yc
  tuft of trees,
Mann'd with three hundred men, as I ha
  heard;
And in it are the Lords of York, Berkeley, ar
  Seymour;
None else of name and noble estimate.

            Enter ROSS *and* WILLOUGHBY.

  North. Here come the Lords of Ross ar
  Willoughby,
Bloody with spurring, fiery-red with haste.
  Boling. Welcome, my lords. I wot your lo
  pursues
A banish'd traitor; all my treasury
Is yet but unfelt thanks, which, more enrich'
Shall be your love and labour's recompense
  Ross. Your presence makes us rich, mo
  noble lord.
  Willo. And far surmounts our labour
  attain it.
  Boling. Evermore thanks, the exchequer
  the poor;
Which, till my infant fortune comes to years
Stands for my bounty. But who comes her

            Enter BERKELEY.

  North. It is my Lord of Berkeley, as I gues
  Berk. My lord of Hereford, my message
  to you.
  Boling. My lord, my answer is—to Lancaste
And I am come to seek that name in Englan
And I must find that title in your tongue
Before I make reply to aught you say.

Berk. Mistake me not, my lord; 'tis not my
    meaning
To raze one title of your honour out:
To you, my lord, I come, what lord you will,   76
From the most gracious regent of this land,
The Duke of York, to know what pricks you on
To take advantage of the absent time
And fright our native peace with self-born arms.

Enter YORK, *attended.*

Boling. I shall not need transport my words
    by you: 81
Here comes his Grace in person.
                    My noble uncle! [*Kneels.*
York. Show me thy humble heart, and not
    thy knee,
Whose duty is deceivable and false.   84
Boling. My gracious uncle—
York. Tut, tut!
Grace me no grace, nor uncle me no uncle:
I am no traitor's uncle; and that word 'grace'
In an ungracious mouth is but profane.   89
Why have those banish'd and forbidden legs
Dar'd once to touch a dust of England's ground?
But then, more 'why?' why have they dar'd to
    march   92
So many miles upon her peaceful bosom,
Frighting her pale-fac'd villages with war
And ostentation of despised arms?
Com'st thou because the anointed king is hence?
Why, foolish boy, the king is left behind,   97
And in my loyal bosom lies his power.
Were I but now the lord of such hot youth
As when brave Gaunt thy father, and myself, 100
Rescu'd the Black Prince, that young Mars of
    men,
From forth the ranks of many thousand French,
O! then, how quickly should this arm of mine,
Now prisoner to the palsy, chastise thee   104
And minister correction to thy fault!
Boling. My gracious uncle, let me know my
    fault:
On what condition stands it and wherein?
York. Even in condition of the worst degree,
In gross rebellion and detested treason: 109
Thou art a banish'd man, and here art come
Before the expiration of thy time,
In braving arms against thy sovereign.   112
Boling. As I was banish'd, I was banish'd
    Hereford;
But as I come, I come for Lancaster.
And, noble uncle, I beseech your Grace
Look on my wrongs with an indifferent eye: 116
You are my father, for methinks in you
I see old Gaunt alive: O! then, my father,
Will you permit that I shall stand condemn'd
A wandering vagabond; my rights and royalties
Pluck'd from my arms perforce and given away
To upstart unthrifts? Wherefore was I born?
If that my cousin king be King of England,
It must be granted I am Duke of Lancaster. 124
You have a son, Aumerle, my noble kinsman;
Had you first died, and he been thus trod down,
He should have found his uncle Gaunt a father,
To rouse his wrongs and chase them to the bay.
I am denied to sue my livery here,   129

And yet my letters-patent give me leave:
My father's goods are all distrain'd and sold,
And these and all are all amiss employ'd. 132
What would you have me do? I am a subject,
And challenge law: attorneys are denied me,
And therefore personally I lay my claim
To my inheritance of free descent.   136
North. The noble duke hath been too much
    abus'd.
Ross. It stands your Grace upon to do him
    right.
Willo. Base men by his endowments are
    made great.
York. My lords of England, let me tell you
    this: 140
I have had feeling of my cousin's wrongs,
And labour'd all I could to do him right;
But in this kind to come, in braving arms,
Be his own carver and cut out his way,   144
To find out right with wrong, it may not be;
And you that do abet him in this kind
Cherish rebellion and are rebels all.
North. The noble duke hath sworn his com-
    ing is   148
But for his own; and for the right of that
We all have strongly sworn to give him aid;
And let him ne'er see joy that breaks that oath!
York. Well, well, I see the issue of these
    arms: 152
I cannot mend it, I must needs confess,
Because my power is weak and all ill left;
But if I could, by him that gave me life,
I would attach you all and make you stoop 156
Unto the sovereign mercy of the king;
But since I cannot, be it known to you
I do remain as neuter. So, fare you well;
Unless you please to enter in the castle   160
And there repose you for this night.
Boling. An offer, uncle, that we will accept:
But we must win your Grace to go with us
To Bristol Castle; which they say is held   164
By Bushy, Bagot, and their complices,
The caterpillars of the commonwealth,
Which I have sworn to weed and pluck away.
York. It may be I will go with you; but yet
    I'll pause: 168
For I am loath to break our country's laws.
Nor friends nor foes, to me welcome you are:
Things past redress are now with me past care.
                                    [*Exeunt.*

SCENE IV.—*A Camp in Wales.*

Enter SALISBURY *and a* Captain.

Cap. My Lord of Salisbury, we have stay'd
    ten days,
And hardly kept our countrymen together,
And yet we hear no tidings from the king;
Therefore we will disperse ourselves: farewell. 4
Sal. Stay yet another day, thou trusty Welsh-
    man:
The king reposeth all his confidence in thee.
Cap. 'Tis thought the king is dead: we will
    not stay.
The bay-trees in our country are all wither'd 8
And meteors fright the fixed stars of heaven,

The pale-fac'd moon looks bloody on the earth
And lean-look'd prophets whisper fearful
    change,
Rich men look sad and ruffians dance and leap,
The one in fear to lose what they enjoy,   13
The other to enjoy by rage and war:
These signs forerun the death or fall of kings.
Farewell: our countrymen are gone and fled, 16
As well assur'd Richard their king is dead.
                                        [*Exit.*
Sal. Ah, Richard! with the eyes of heavy
    mind
I see thy glory like a shooting star
Fall to the base earth from the firmament. 20
Thy sun sets weeping in the lowly west,
Witnessing storms to come, woe, and unrest.
Thy friends are fled to wait upon thy foes,
And crossly to thy good all fortune goes. [*Exit.*

ACT III

SCENE I.—*Bristol.* BOLINGBROKE'S *Camp.*

Enter BOLINGBROKE, YORK, NORTHUMBERLAND,
    HENRY PERCY, WILLOUGHBY, ROSS; Officers
    behind, with BUSHY *and* GREEN *prisoners.*

Boling. Bring forth these men.
Bushy and Green, I will not vex your souls—
Since presently your souls must part your
    bodies—
With too much urging your pernicious lives, 4
For 'twere no charity; yet, to wash your blood
From off my hands, here in the view of men
I will unfold some causes of your deaths.
You have misled a prince, a royal king,   8
A happy gentleman in blood and lineaments,
By you unhappied and disfigur'd clean:
You have in manner with your sinful hours
Made a divorce betwixt his queen and him, 12
Broke the possession of a royal bed,
And stain'd the beauty of a fair queen's cheeks
With tears drawn from her eyes by your foul
    wrongs.
Myself, a prince by fortune of my birth,   16
Near to the king in blood, and near in love
Till you did make him misinterpret me,
Have stoop'd my neck under your injuries,
And sigh'd my English breath in foreign clouds,
Eating the bitter bread of banishment;   21
Whilst you have fed upon my signories,
Dispark'd my parks, and felled my forest woods,
From mine own windows torn my household
    coat,   24
Raz'd out my impress, leaving me no sign,
Save men's opinions and my living blood,
To show the world I am a gentleman.
This and much more, much more than twice
    all this,   28
Condemns you to the death. See them deliver'd
    over
To execution and the hand of death.
    Bushy. More welcome is the stroke of death
    to me
Than Bolingbroke to England. Lords, farewell.

Green. My comfort is, that heaven will take
    our souls   33
And plague injustice with the pains of hell.
    Boling. My Lord Northumberland, see them
    dispatch'd.
        [*Exeunt* NORTHUMBERLAND *and Others,*
                            with BUSHY *and* GREEN.
Uncle, you say the queen is at your house; 36
For God's sake, fairly let her be entreated:
Tell her I send to her my kind commends;
Take special care my greetings be deliver'd.
    York. A gentleman of mine I have dispatch'd
With letters of your love to her at large.   41
    Boling. Thanks, gentle uncle. Come, lords,
    away,
To fight with Glendower and his complices:
Awhile to work, and after holiday.   [*Exeunt.*

SCENE II.—*The Coast of Wales. A Castle
in view.*

Flourish: drums and trumpets. Enter KING
    RICHARD, *the* BISHOP OF CARLISLE, AUMERLE,
    and Soldiers.

    K. Rich. Barkloughly Castle call they this
    at hand?
    Aum. Yea, my lord. How brooks your Grace
    the air,
After your late tossing on the breaking seas?
    K. Rich. Needs must I like it well: I weep
    for joy   4
To stand upon my kingdom once again.
Dear earth, I do salute thee with my hand,
Though rebels wound thee with their horses'
    hoofs:
As a long-parted mother with her child   8
Plays fondly with her tears and smiles in meeting,
So, weeping, smiling, greet I thee, my earth,
And do thee favour with my royal hands.
Feed not my sovereign's foe, my gentle earth, 12
Nor with thy sweets comfort his ravenous sense;
But let thy spiders, that suck up thy venom,
And heavy-gaited toads lie in their way,
Doing annoyance to the treacherous feet   16
Which with usurping steps do trample thee.
Yield stinging nettles to mine enemies;
And when they from thy bosom pluck a flower,
Guard it, I pray thee, with a lurking adder 20
Whose double tongue may with a mortal touch
Throw death upon thy sovereign's enemies.
Mock not my senseless conjuration, lords:
This earth shall have a feeling and these stones
Prove armed soldiers, ere her native king 25
Shall falter under foul rebellion's arms.
    Car. Fear not, my lord: that power that
    made you king
Hath power to keep you king in spite of all. 28
The means that heaven yields must be embrac'd,
And not neglected; else, if heaven would,
And we will not, heaven's offer we refuse,
The proffer'd means of succour and redress. 32
    Aum. He means, my lord, that we are too
    remiss;
Whilst Bolingbroke, through our security,
Grows strong and great in substance and in
    friends.

K. Rich. Discomfortable cousin! know'st
thou not 36
That when the searching eye of heaven is hid
Behind the globe, and lights the lower world,
Then thieves and robbers range abroad un-
seen,
In murders and in outrage bloody here; 40
But when, from under this terrestrial ball
He fires the proud tops of the eastern pines
And darts his light through every guilty hole,
Then murders, treasons, and detested sins, 44
The cloak of night being pluck'd from off their
backs,
Stand bare and naked, trembling at themselves?
So when this thief, this traitor, Bolingbroke,
Who all this while hath revell'd in the night 48
Whilst we were wandering with the antipodes,
Shall see us rising in our throne, the east,
His treasons will sit blushing in his face,
Not able to endure the sight of day, 52
But self-affrighted tremble at his sin.
Not all the water in the rough rude sea
Can wash the balm from an anointed king;
The breath of worldly men cannot depose 56
The deputy elected by the Lord.
For every man that Bolingbroke hath press'd
To lift shrewd steel against our golden crown,
God for his Richard hath in heavenly pay 60
A glorious angel: then, if angels fight,
Weak men must fall, for heaven still guards
the right.

Enter SALISBURY.

Welcome, my lord: how far off lies your power?
Sal. Nor near nor further off, my gracious
lord, 64
Than this weak arm: discomfort guides my
tongue
And bids me speak of nothing but despair.
One day too late, I fear me, noble lord,
Hath clouded all thy happy days on earth. 68
O! call back yesterday, bid time return,
And thou shalt have twelve thousand fighting
men:
To-day, to-day, unhappy day too late,
O'erthrows thy joys, friends, fortune, and thy
state; 72
For all the Welshmen, hearing thou wert dead,
Are gone to Bolingbroke, dispers'd, and fled.
Aum. Comfort, my liege! why looks your
Grace so pale?
K. Rich. But now, the blood of twenty thou-
sand men 76
Did triumph in my face, and they are fled;
And till so much blood thither come again
Have I not reason to look pale and dead?
All souls that will be safe, fly from my side; 80
For time hath set a blot upon my pride.
Aum. Comfort, my liege! remember who you
are.
K. Rich. I had forgot myself. Am I not king?
Awake, thou sluggard majesty! thou sleepest. 84
Is not the king's name twenty thousand names?
Arm, arm, my name! a puny subject strikes
At thy great glory. Look not to the ground,
Ye favourites of a king: are we not high? 88

High be our thoughts: I know my uncle York
Hath power enough to serve our turn. But who
comes here?

Enter SIR STEPHEN SCROOP.

Scroop. More health and happiness betide
my liege
Than can my care-tun'd tongue deliver him! 92
K. Rich. Mine ear is open and my heart pre-
par'd:
The worst is worldly loss thou canst unfold.
Say, is my kingdom lost? why, 'twas my care;
And what loss is it to be rid of care? 96
Strives Bolingbroke to be as great as we?
Greater he shall not be: if he serve God
We'll serve him too, and be his fellow so:
Revolt our subjects? that we cannot mend; 100
They break their faith to God as well as us:
Cry woe, destruction, ruin, loss, decay;
The worst is death, and death will have his day.
Scroop. Glad am I that your highness is so
arm'd 104
To bear the tidings of calamity.
Like an unseasonable stormy day
Which makes the silver rivers drown their shores,
As if the world were all dissolv'd to tears, 108
So high above his limits swells the rage
Of Bolingbroke, covering your fearful land
With hard bright steel and hearts harder than
steel.
White-beards have arm'd their thin and hair-
less scalps 112
Against thy majesty; and boys, with women's
voices,
Strive to speak big, and clap their female joints
In stiff unwieldy arms against thy crown;
Thy very beadsmen learn to bend their bows
Of double-fatal yew against thy state; 117
Yea, distaff-women manage rusty bills
Against thy seat: both young and old rebel,
And all goes worse than I have power to tell. 120
K. Rich. Too well, too well thou tell'st a tale
so ill.
Where is the Earl of Wiltshire? where is Bagot?
What is become of Bushy? where is Green?
That they have let the dangerous enemy 124
Measure our confines with such peaceful steps?
If we prevail, their heads shall pay for it.
I warrant they have made peace with Boling-
broke.
Scroop. Peace have they made with him,
indeed, my lord. 128
K. Rich. O villains, vipers, damn'd without
redemption!
Dogs, easily won to fawn on any man!
Snakes, in my heart-blood warm'd, that sting
my heart!
Three Judases, each one thrice worse than Judas!
Would they make peace? terrible hell make war
Upon their spotted souls for this offence!
Scroop. Sweet love, I see, changing his pro-
perty,
Turns to the sourest and most deadly hate. 136
Again uncurse their souls; their peace is made
With heads and not with hands: those whom
you curse

Have felt the worst of death's destroying wound
And lie full low, grav'd in the hollow ground. 140
   Aum. Is Bushy, Green, and the Earl of Wilt-
shire dead?
   Scroop. Yea, all of them at Bristol lost their
heads.
   Aum. Where is the duke my father with his
power?
   K. Rich. No matter where. Of comfort no
man speak: 144
Let's talk of graves, of worms, and epitaphs;
Make dust our paper, and with rainy eyes
Write sorrow on the bosom of the earth;
Let's choose executors and talk of wills: 148
And yet not so—for what can we bequeath
Save our deposed bodies to the ground?
Our lands, our lives, and all are Bolingbroke's,
And nothing can we call our own but death, 152
And that small model of the barren earth
Which serves as paste and cover to our bones.
For God's sake, let us sit upon the ground
And tell sad stories of the death of kings: 156
How some have been depos'd, some slain in
war,
Some haunted by the ghosts they have depos'd,
Some poison'd by their wives, some sleeping
kill'd;
All murder'd: for within the hollow crown 160
That rounds the mortal temples of a king
Keeps Death his court, and there the antick sits,
Scoffing his state and grinning at his pomp;
Allowing him a breath, a little scene, 164
To monarchize, be fear'd, and kill with looks,
Infusing him with self and vain conceit
As if this flesh which walls about our life
Were brass impregnable; and humour'd thus
Comes at the last, and with a little pin 169
Bores through his castle wall, and farewell king!
Cover your heads, and mock not flesh and blood
With solemn reverence: throw away respect, 172
Tradition, form, and ceremonious duty,
For you have but mistook me all this while:
I live with bread like you, feel want,
Taste grief, need friends: subjected thus, 176
How can you say to me I am a king?
   Car. My lord, wise men ne'er sit and wail
their woes,
But presently prevent the ways to wail.
To fear the foe, since fear oppresseth strength,
Gives in your weakness strength unto your foe,
And so your follies fight against yourself.
Fear and be slain; no worse can come to fight:
And fight and die is death destroying death; 184
Where fearing dying pays death servile breath.
   Aum. My father hath a power; inquire of him
And learn to make a body of a limb.
   K. Rich. Thou chid'st me well. Proud Boling-
broke, I come 188
To change blows with thee for our day of doom.
This ague-fit of fear is over-blown;
An easy task it is, to win our own.—
Say, Scroop, where lies our uncle with his power?
Speak sweetly, man, although thy looks be sour.
   Scroop. Men judge by the complexion of the
sky
The state and inclination of the day;

So may you by my dull and heavy eye, 196
My tongue hath but a heavier tale to say.
I play the torturer, by small and small
To lengthen out the worst that must be spoken.
Your uncle York is join'd with Bolingbroke, 200
And all your northern castles yielded up,
And all your southern gentlemen in arms
Upon his party.
   K. Rich. Thou hast said enough.
[*To* AUMERLE.] Beshrew thee, cousin, which
didst lead me forth 204
Of that sweet way I was in to despair!
What say you now? What comfort have we
now?
By heaven, I'll hate him everlastingly
That bids me be of comfort any more. 208
Go to Flint Castle: there I'll pine away;
A king, woe's slave, shall kingly woe obey.
That power I have, discharge; and let them go
To ear the land that hath some hope to grow,
For I have none: let no man speak again 213
To alter this, for counsel is but vain.
   Aum. My liege, one word.
   K. Rich. He does me double wrong,
That wounds me with the flatteries of his tongue.
Discharge my followers: let them hence away,
From Richard's night to Bolingbroke's fair day.
                  [*Exeunt.*

SCENE III.—*Wales. Before Flint Castle.*

Enter, with drum and colours, BOLINGBROKE *and
Forces;* YORK, NORTHUMBERLAND, *and Others.*

   Boling. So that by this intelligence we learn
The Welshmen are dispers'd and Salisbury
Is gone to meet the king, who lately landed
With some few private friends upon this coast. 4
   North. The news is very fair and good, my
lord:
Richard not far from hence hath hid his head.
   York. It would beseem the Lord Northum-
berland
To say, 'King Richard:' alack the heavy day 8
When such a sacred king should hide his head!
   North. Your Grace mistakes; only to be brief
Left I his title out.
   York. The time hath been,
Would you have been so brief with him, he
would 12
Have been so brief with you, to shorten you,
For taking so the head, your whole head's length.
   Boling. Mistake not, uncle, further than you
should.
   York. Take not, good cousin, further than
you should, 16
Lest you mistake the heavens are o'er our heads.
   Boling. I know it, uncle; and oppose not my-
self
Against their will. But who comes here?

Enter HENRY PERCY.

Welcome, Harry: what, will not this castle
yield? 20
   H. Percy. The castle royally is mann'd, my
lord,
Against thy entrance.

Boling. Royally!
Why, it contains no king?
    H. Percy.   Yes, my good lord, 24
It doth contain a king: King Richard lies
Within the limits of yon lime and stone;
And with him are the Lord Aumerle, Lord
    Salisbury,
Sir Stephen Scroop; besides a clergyman   28
Of holy reverence; who, I cannot learn.
    North. O! belike it is the Bishop of Carlisle.
    Boling. [*To* NORTH.] Noble lord,
Go to the rude ribs of that ancient castle,   32
Through brazen trumpet send the breath of parley
Into his ruin'd ears, and thus deliver:
Henry Bolingbroke
On both his knees doth kiss King Richard's
    hand,   36
And sends allegiance and true faith of heart
To his most royal person; hither come
Even at his feet to lay my arms and power,
Provided that my banishment repeal'd,   40
And lands restor'd again be freely granted.
If not, I'll use the advantage of my power,
And lay the summer's dust with showers of blood
Rain'd from the wounds of slaughter'd Eng-
    lishmen: 44
The which, how far off from the mind of Bol-
    ingbroke
It is, such crimson tempest should bedrench
The fresh green lap of fair King Richard's land,
My stooping duty tenderly shall show.   48
Go, signify as much, while here we march
Upon the grassy carpet of this plain.
Let's march without the noise of threat'ning
    drum,
That from the castle's totter'd battlements   52
Our fair appointments may be well perus'd.
Methinks King Richard and myself should meet
With no less terror than the elements
Of fire and water, when their thundering shock
At meeting tears the cloudy cheeks of heaven.
Be he the fire, I'll be the yielding water:
The rage be his, while on the earth I rain
My waters; on the earth, and not on him.   60
March on, and mark King Richard how he looks.

*A Parley sounded, and answered by a Trumpet
    within. Flourish. Enter on the Walls* KING
    RICHARD, *the* BISHOP OF CARLISLE, AUMERLE,
    SCROOP, *and* SALISBURY.

    H. Percy. See, see, King Richard doth him-
        self appear,
As doth the blushing discontented sun
From out the fiery portal of the east,   64
When he perceives the envious clouds are bent
To dim his glory and to stain the track
Of his bright passage to the occident.
    York. Yet looks he like a king: behold, his
        eye,   68
As bright as is the eagle's, lightens forth
Controlling majesty: alack, alack, for woe,
That any harm should stain so fair a show!
    K. Rich. [*To* NORTHUMBERLAND.] We are
        amaz'd; and thus long have we stood   72
To watch the fearful bending of thy knee,
Because we thought ourself thy lawful king:

And if we be, how dare thy joints forget
To pay their awful duty to our presence?   76
If we be not, show us the hand of God
That hath dismiss'd us from our stewardship;
For well we know, no hand of blood and bone
Can gripe the sacred handle of our sceptre,   80
Unless he do profane, steal, or usurp.
And though you think that all, as you have done,
Have torn their souls by turning them from us,
And we are barren and bereft of friends;   84
Yet know, my master, God omnipotent,
Is mustering in his clouds on our behalf
Armies of pestilence; and they shall strike
Your children yet unborn and unbegot,   88
That lift your vassal hands against my head
And threat the glory of my precious crown.
Tell Bolingbroke,—for yond methinks he is,—
That every stride he makes upon my land   92
Is dangerous treason: he is come to open
The purple testament of bleeding war;
But ere the crown he looks for live in peace,
Ten thousand bloody crowns of mothers'
    sons   96
Shall ill become the flower of England's face,
Change the complexion of her maid-pale peace
To scarlet indignation, and bedew
Her pastures' grass with faithful English blood.
    North. The king of heaven forbid our lord
        the king   101
Should so with civil and uncivil arms
Be rush'd upon! Thy thrice-noble cousin,
Harry Bolingbroke, doth humbly kiss thy hand;
And by the honourable tomb he swears,   105
That stands upon your royal grandsire's bones,
And by the royalties of both your bloods,
Currents that spring from one most gracious
    head,   108
And by the buried hand of war-like Gaunt,
And by the worth and honour of himself,
Comprising all that may be sworn or said,
His coming hither hath no further scope   112
Than for his lineal royalties and to beg
Enfranchisement immediate on his knees:
Which on thy royal party granted once,
His glittering arms he will commend to rust, 116
His barbed steeds to stables, and his heart
To faithful service of your majesty.
This swears he, as he is a prince, is just;
And, as I am a gentleman, I credit him.   120
    K. Rich. Northumberland, say, thus the king
        returns:
His noble cousin is right welcome hither;
And all the number of his fair demands
Shall be accomplish'd without contradiction:
With all the gracious utterance thou hast   125
Speak to his gentle hearing kind commends.
    [NORTHUMBERLAND *retires to* BOLINGBROKE.
[*To* AUMERLE.] We do debase ourself, cousin,
    do we not,
To look so poorly and to speak so fair?   128
Shall we call back Northumberland and send
Defiance to the traitor, and so die?
    Aum. No, good my lord; let's fight with
        gentle words,
Till time lend friends and friends their helpful
    swords.   132

K. Rich. O God! O God! that e'er this tongue
  of mine,
That laid the sentence of dread banishment
On yond proud man, should take it off again
With words of sooth. O! that I were as great
As is my grief, or lesser than my name,   137
Or that I could forget what I have been,
Or not remember what I must be now.
Swell'st thou, proud heart? I'll give thee scope
  to beat,   140
Since foes have scope to beat both thee and me.
Aum. Northumberland comes back from
  Bolingbroke.
K. Rich. What must the king do now? Must
  he submit?
The king shall do it: must he be depos'd?   144
The king shall be contented: must he lose
The name of king? o' God's name, let it go:
I'll give my jewels for a set of beads,
My gorgeous palace for a hermitage,   148
My gay apparel for an almsman's gown,
My figur'd goblets for a dish of wood,
My sceptre for a palmer's walking-staff,
My subjects for a pair of carved saints,   152
And my large kingdom for a little grave,
A little little grave, an obscure grave;
Or I'll be buried in the king's highway,
Some way of common trade, where subjects'
  feet
May hourly trample on their sovereign's head;
For on my heart they tread now whilst I live;
And buried once, why not upon my head?   159
Aumerle, thou weep'st, my tender-hearted
  cousin!
We'll make foul weather with despised tears;
Our sighs and they shall lodge the summer corn,
And make a dearth in this revolting land.
Or shall we play the wantons with our woes,   164
And make some pretty match with shedding
  tears?
As thus; to drop them still upon one place,
Till they have fretted us a pair of graves
Within the earth; and, there inlaid: 'There lies
Two kinsmen digg'd their graves with weeping
  eyes.'   169
Would not this ill do well? Well, well, I see
I talk but idly and you laugh at me.
Most mighty prince, my Lord Northumberland,
What says King Bolingbroke? will his majesty
Give Richard leave to live till Richard die?
You make a leg, and Bolingbroke says ay.
North. My lord, in the base court he doth
  attend   176
To speak with you; may't please you to come
  down?
K. Rich. Down, down, I come; like glister-
  ing Phaethon,
Wanting the manage of unruly jades.
In the base court? Base court, where kings
  grow base,   180
To come at traitors' calls and do them grace.
In the base court? Come down? Down, court!
  down, king!
For night-owls shriek where mounting larks
  should sing.   [*Exeunt from above.*
Boling. What says his majesty?

North.   Sorrow and grief of heart   184
Makes him speak fondly, like a frantic man:
Yet he is come.

Enter KING RICHARD, *and his* Attendants.

Boling. Stand all apart,
And show fair duty to his majesty. [*Kneeling.*
My gracious lord,—   189
K. Rich. Fair cousin, you debase your
  princely knee
To make the base earth proud with kissing it:
Me rather had my heart might feel your love   192
Than my unpleas'd eye see your courtesy.
Up, cousin, up; your heart is up, I know,
Thus high at least, although your knee be low.
Boling. My gracious lord, I come but for
  mine own.   196
K. Rich. Your own is yours, and I am yours,
  and all.
Boling. So far be mine, my most redoubted
  lord,
As my true service shall deserve your love.
K. Rich. Well you deserve: they well deserve
  to have   200
That know the strong'st and surest way to get.
Uncle, give me your hand: nay, dry your eyes;
Tears show their love, but want their remedies.
Cousin, I am too young to be your father,   204
Though you are old enough to be my heir.
What you will have I'll give, and willing too;
For do we must what force will have us do.
Set on towards London. Cousin, is it so?   208
Boling. Yea, my good lord.
K. Rich.   Then I must not say no.
  [*Flourish. Exeunt.*

SCENE IV.—*Langley. The* DUKE OF YORK'S
Garden.

Enter the QUEEN *and two* Ladies.

Queen. What sport shall we devise here in
  this garden,
To drive away the heavy thought of care?
First Lady. Madam, we'll play at bowls.
Queen. 'Twill make me think the world is
  full of rubs,   4
And that my fortune runs against the bias.
First Lady. Madam, we'll dance.
Queen. My legs can keep no measure in de-
  light
When my poor heart no measure keeps in grief:
Therefore, no dancing, girl; some other sport. 9
First Lady. Madam, we'll tell tales.
Queen. Of sorrow or of joy?
First Lady.   Of either, madam.
Queen. Of neither, girl: 12
For if of joy, being altogether wanting,
It doth remember me the more of sorrow;
Or if of grief, being altogether had,
It adds more sorrow to my want of joy: 16
For what I have I need not to repeat,
And what I want it boots not to complain.
First Lady. Madam, I'll sing.
Queen.   'Tis well that thou hast cause;
But thou shouldst please me better wouldst
  thou weep.   20

First Lady. I could weep, madam, would it
  do you good.
  Queen. And I could sing would weeping do
  me good,
And never borrow any tear of thee.
But stay, here come the gardeners: 24
Let's step into the shadow of these trees.
My wretchedness unto a row of pins,
They'll talk of state; for every one doth so
Against a change: woe is forerun with woe. 28

[QUEEN *and* Ladies *retire.*

Enter a Gardener *and two* Servants.

Gard. Go, bind thou up yon dangling apri-
  cocks,
Which, like unruly children, make their sire
Stoop with oppression of their prodigal weight:
Give some supportance to the bending twigs. 32
Go thou, and like an executioner,
Cut off the heads of too fast growing sprays,
That look too lofty in our commonwealth:
All must be even in our government.   36
You thus employ'd, I will go root away
The noisome weeds, that without profit suck
The soil's fertility from wholesome flowers.
  First Serv. Why should we in the compass
  of a pale   40
Keep law and form and due proportion,
Showing, as in a model, our firm estate,
When our sea-walled garden, the whole land,
Is full of weeds, her fairest flowers chok'd up, 44
Her fruit-trees all unprun'd, her hedges ruin'd,
Her knots disorder'd, and her wholesome herbs
Swarming with caterpillars?
  Gard.   Hold thy peace:
He that hath suffer'd this disorder'd spring 48
Hath now himself met with the fall of leaf:
The weeds that his broad-spreading leaves did
  shelter,
That seem'd in eating him to hold him up,
Are pluck'd up root and all by Bolingbroke; 52
I mean the Earl of Wiltshire, Bushy, Green.
  First Serv. What! are they dead?
  Gard.   They are; and Bolingbroke
Hath seiz'd the wasteful king. O! what pity
  is it
That he hath not so trimm'd and dress'd his land
As we this garden. We at time of year   57
Do wound the bark, the skin of our fruit-trees,
Lest, being over-proud with sap and blood,
With too much riches it confound itself: 60
Had he done so to great and growing men,
They might have liv'd to bear and he to taste
Their fruits of duty: superfluous branches
We lop away that bearing boughs may live: 64
Had he done so, himself had borne the crown,
Which waste of idle hours hath quite thrown
  down.
  First Serv. What! think you then the king
shall be depos'd?
  Gard. Depress'd he is already, and depos'd
'Tis doubt he will be: letters came last night 69
To a dear friend of the good Duke of York's,
That tell black tidings.
  Queen. O! I am press'd to death through
  want of speaking.   [*Coming forward.*

Thou, old Adam's likeness, set to dress this
  garden,   73
How dares thy harsh rude tongue sound this
  unpleasing news?
What Eve, what serpent, hath suggested thee
To make a second fall of cursed man?   76
Why dost thou say King Richard is depos'd?
Dar'st thou, thou little better thing than earth,
Divine his downfall? Say, where, when, and
  how
Cam'st thou by these ill tidings? speak, thou
  wretch.   80
  Gard. Pardon me, madam: little joy have I
To breathe these news, yet what I say is true.
King Richard, he is in the mighty hold
Of Bolingbroke; their fortunes both are
  weigh'd:
In your lord's scale is nothing but himself, 85
And some few vanities that make him light;
But in the balance of great Bolingbroke,
Besides himself, are all the English peers, 88
And with that odds he weighs King Richard
  down.
Post you to London and you'll find it so;
I speak no more than every one doth know.
  Queen. Nimble mischance, that art so light
  of foot,   92
Doth not thy embassage belong to me,
And am I last that knows it? O! thou think'st
To serve me last, that I may longest keep
Thy sorrow in my breast. Come, ladies, go, 96
To meet at London London's king in woe.
What! was I born to this, that my sad look
Should grace the triumph of great Boling-
  broke?
Gardener, for telling me these news of woe, 100
Pray God the plants thou graft'st may never
  grow.   [*Exeunt* QUEEN *and* Ladies.
  Gard. Poor queen! so that thy state might
  be no worse,
I would my skill were subject to thy curse.
Here did she fall a tear; here, in this place, 104
I'll set a bank of rue, sour herb of grace:
Rue, even for ruth, here shortly shall be seen,
In the remembrance of a weeping queen.
    [*Exeunt.*

ACT IV

SCENE I.—*London. Westminster Hall.*

*The Lords spiritual on the right side of the throne:
the Lords temporal on the left; the Commons
below. Enter* BOLINGBROKE, AUMERLE, SUR-
REY, NORTHUMBERLAND, HENRY PERCY, FITZ-
WATER, *another* Lord, *the* BISHOP OF CARLISLE,
the ABBOT OF WESTMINSTER, *and* Attendants.
Officers *behind with* BAGOT.

Boling. Call forth Bagot.
Now, Bagot, freely speak thy mind;
What thou dost know of noble Gloucester's
  death,
Who wrought it with the king, and who per-
  form'd   4
The bloody office of his timeless end.

Bagot. Then set before my face the Lord
  Aumerle.
Boling. Cousin, stand forth, and look upon
  that man.
Bagot. My Lord Aumerle, I know your dar-
  ing tongue   8
Scorns to unsay what once it hath deliver'd.
In that dead time when Gloucester's death was
  plotted,
I heard you say, 'Is not my arm of length,
That reacheth from the restful English court 12
As far as Calais, to my uncle's head?'
Amongst much other talk, that very time,
I heard you say that you had rather refuse
The offer of a hundred thousand crowns   16
Than Bolingbroke's return to England;
Adding withal, how blest this land would be
In this your cousin's death.
Aum.   Princes and noble lords,
What answer shall I make to this base man? 20
Shall I so much dishonour my fair stars,
On equal terms to give him chastisement?
Either I must, or have mine honour soil'd
With the attainder of his slanderous lips. 24
There is my gage, the manual seal of death,
That marks thee out for hell: I say thou liest,
And will maintain what thou hast said is
  false
In thy heart-blood, though being all too base 28
To stain the temper of my knightly sword.
Boling. Bagot, forbear; thou shalt not take
  it up.
Aum. Excepting one, I would he were the
  best
In all this presence that hath mov'd me so. 32
Fitz. If that thy valour stand on sympathies,
There is my gage, Aumerle, in gage to thine:
By that fair sun which shows me where thou
  stand'st,
I heard thee say, and vauntingly thou spak'st it,
That thou wert cause of noble Gloucester's
  death.   37
If thou deny'st it twenty times, thou liest;
And I will turn thy falsehood to thy heart,
Where it was forged, with my rapier's point. 40
Aum. Thou dar'st not, coward, live to see
  that day.
Fitz. Now, by my soul, I would it were this
  hour.
Aum. Fitzwater, thou art damn'd to hell for
  this.
H. Percy. Aumerle, thou liest; his honour is
  as true   44
In this appeal as thou art all unjust;
And that thou art so, there I throw my gage,
To prove it on thee to the extremest point
Of mortal breathing: seize it if thou dar'st. 48
Aum. And if I do not may my hands rot off
And never brandish more revengeful steel
Over the glittering helmet of my foe!
Lord. I task the earth to the like, forsworn
  Aumerle;   52
And spur thee on with full as many lies
As may be holla'd in thy treacherous ear
From sun to sun: there is mine honour's pawn;
Engage it to the trial if thou dar'st.   56

Aum. Who sets me else? by heaven, I'll throw
  at all:
I have a thousand spirits in one breast,
To answer twenty thousand such as you.
Surrey. My Lord Fitzwater, I do remember
  well   60
The very time Aumerle and you did talk.
Fitz. 'Tis very true: you were in presence
  then;
And you can witness with me this is true.
Surrey. As false, by heaven, as heaven itself
  is true.   64
Fitz. Surrey, thou liest.
Surrey.   Dishonourable boy!
That lie shall lie so heavy on my sword
That it shall render vengeance and revenge,
Till thou the lie-giver and that lie do lie   68
In earth as quiet as thy father's skull.
In proof whereof, there is my honour's pawn:
Engage it to the trial if thou dar'st.
Fitz. How fondly dost thou spur a forward
  horse!   72
If I dare eat, or drink, or breathe, or live,
I dare meet Surrey in a wilderness,
And spit upon him, whilst I say he lies,
And lies, and lies: there is my bond of faith 76
To tie thee to my strong correction.
As I intend to thrive in this new world,
Aumerle is guilty of my true appeal:
Besides, I heard the banish'd Norfolk say   80
That thou, Aumerle, didst send two of thy men
To execute the noble duke at Calais.
Aum. Some honest Christian trust me with
  a gage.
That Norfolk lies, here do I throw down this, 84
If he may be repeal'd to try his honour.
Boling. These differences shall all rest under
  gage
Till Norfolk be repeal'd: repeal'd he shall be,
And though mine enemy, restor'd again   88
To all his lands and signories; when he's re-
  turn'd,
Against Aumerle we will enforce his trial.
Car. That honourable day shall ne'er be seen.
Many a time hath banish'd Norfolk fought 92
For Jesu Christ in glorious Christian field,
Streaming the ensign of the Christian cross
Against black pagans, Turks, and Saracens;
And toil'd with works of war, retir'd himself 96
To Italy; and there at Venice gave
His body to that pleasant country's earth,
And his pure soul unto his captain Christ,
Under whose colours he had fought so long. 100
Boling. Why, bishop, is Norfolk dead?
Car. As surely as I live, my lord.
Boling. Sweet peace conduct his sweet soul
  to the bosom
Of good old Abraham! Lords appellants, 104
Your differences shall all rest under gage
Till we assign you to your days of trial.

Enter YORK, *attended.*

York. Great Duke of Lancaster, I come to
  thee
From plume-pluck'd Richard; who with willing soul   108

Adopts thee heir, and his high sceptre yields
To the possession of thy royal hand.
Ascend his throne, descending now from him;
And long live Henry, of that name the fourth!
   Boling. In God's name, I'll ascend the regal
    throne.   113
   Car. Marry, God forbid!
Worst in this royal presence may I speak,
Yet best beseeming me to speak the truth. 116
Would God that any in this noble presence
Were enough noble to be upright judge
Of noble Richard! then, true noblesse would
Learn him forbearance from so foul a wrong. 120
What subject can give sentence on his king?
And who sits here that is not Richard's subject?
Thieves are not judg'd but they are by to hear,
Although apparent guilt be seen in them; 124
And shall the figure of God's majesty,
His captain, steward, deputy elect,
Anointed, crowned, planted many years,
Be judg'd by subject and inferior breath, 128
And he himself not present? O! forfend it, God,
That in a Christian climate souls refin'd
Should show so heinous, black, obscene a deed.
I speak to subjects, and a subject speaks, 132
Stirr'd up by God thus boldly for his king.
My Lord of Hereford here, whom you call king,
Is a foul traitor to proud Hereford's king;
And if you crown him, let me prophesy: 136
The blood of English shall manure the ground
And future ages groan for this foul act;
Peace shall go sleep with Turks and infidels,
And in this seat of peace tumultuous wars 140
Shall kin with kin and kind with kind confound;
Disorder, horror, fear and mutiny
Shall here inhabit, and this land be call'd
The field of Golgotha and dead men's skulls. 144
O! if you rear this house against this house,
It will the woefullest division prove
That ever fell upon this cursed earth.
Prevent it, resist it, let it not be so, 148
Lest child, child's children, cry against you
  'woe!'
   North. Well have you argu'd, sir; and, for
    your pains,
Of capital treason we arrest you here.
My Lord of Westminster, be it your charge 152
To keep him safely till his day of trial.
May it please you, lords, to grant the commons'
  suit?
   Boling. Fetch hither Richard, that in com-
    mon view
He may surrender; so we shall proceed   156
Without suspicion.
   York.   I will be his conduct. [*Exit.*
   Boling. Lords, you that here are under our
    arrest,
Procure your sureties for your days of answer.
To CARLISLE.] Little are we beholding to your
  love,   160
And little look'd for at your helping hands.

Re-enter YORK, *with* KING RICHARD, *and* Officers
       bearing the Crown, &c.

   K. Rich. Alack! why am I sent for to a king
Before I have shook off the regal thoughts

Wherewith I reign'd? I hardly yet have learn'd
To insinuate, flatter, bow, and bend my limbs:
Give sorrow leave awhile to tutor me
To this submission. Yet I well remember
The favours of these men: were they not
  mine?   168
Did they not sometime cry, 'All hail!' to me?
So Judas did to Christ: but he, in twelve,
Found truth in all but one; I, in twelve thou-
  sand, none.
God save the king! Will no man say, amen? 172
Am I both priest and clerk? well then, amen.
God save the king! although I be not he;
And yet, amen, if heaven do think him me.
To do what service am I sent for hither? 176
   York. To do that office of thine own good
    will
Which tired majesty did make thee offer,
The resignation of thy state and crown
To Henry Bolingbroke.   180
   K. Rich. Give me the crown. Here, cousin,
    seize the crown;
Here cousin,
On this side my hand and on that side thine.
Now is this golden crown like a deep well 184
That owes two buckets filling one another;
The emptier ever dancing in the air,
The other down, unseen and full of water:
That bucket down and full of tears am I, 188
Drinking my griefs, whilst you mount up on
  high.
   Boling. I thought you had been willing to
    resign.
   K. Rich. My crown, I am; but still my griefs
    are mine.
You may my glories and my state depose, 192
But not my griefs; still am I king of those.
   Boling. Part of your cares you give me with
    your crown.
   K. Rich. Your cares set up do not pluck my
    cares down.
My care is loss of care, by old care done; 196
Your care is gain of care, by new care won.
The cares I give I have, though given away;
They tend the crown, yet still with me they stay.
   Boling. Are you contented to resign the
    crown?   200
   K. Rich. Ay, no; no, ay; for I must nothing
    be;
Therefore no no, for I resign to thee.
Now mark me how I will undo myself:
I give this heavy weight from off my head, 204
And this unwieldy sceptre from my hand,
The pride of kingly sway from out my heart;
With mine own tears I wash away my balm,
With mine own hands I give away my crown, 208
With mine own tongue deny my sacred state,
With mine own breath release all duteous rites:
All pomp and majesty I do forswear;
My manors, rents, revenues, I forego; 212
My acts, decrees, and statutes I deny:
God pardon all oaths that are broke to me!
God keep all vows unbroke are made to thee!
Make me, that nothing have, with nothing
  griev'd,   216
And thou with all pleas'd, that hast all achiev'd!

Long mayst thou live in Richard's seat to sit,
And soon lie Richard in an earthy pit!
God save King Henry, unking'd Richard says,
And send him many years of sunshine days! 221
What more remains?

North. [Offering a paper.] No more, but that
   you read
These accusations and these grievous crimes
Committed by your person and your followers
Against the state and profit of this land; 225
That, by confessing them, the souls of men
May deem that you are worthily depos'd.

K. Rich. Must I do so? and must I ravel out
My weav'd-up follies? Gentle Northumberland,
If thy offences were upon record,
Would it not shame thee in so fair a troop
To read a lecture of them? If thou wouldst, 232
There shouldst thou find one heinous article,
Containing the deposing of a king,
And cracking the strong warrant of an oath,
Mark'd with a blot, damn'd in the book of
   heaven.   236
Nay, all of you that stand and look upon me,
Whilst that my wretchedness doth bait myself,
Though some of you with Pilate wash your
   hands,
Showing an outward pity; yet you Pilates 240
Have here deliver'd me to my sour cross,
And water cannot wash away your sin.

North. My lord, dispatch; read o'er these
   articles.

K. Rich. Mine eyes are full of tears, I cannot
   see: 244
And yet salt water blinds them not so much
But they can see a sort of traitors here.
Nay, if I turn mine eyes upon myself,
I find myself a traitor with the rest; 248
For I have given here my soul's consent
To undeck the pompous body of a king;
Made glory base and sovereignty a slave,
Proud majesty a subject, state a peasant. 252

North. My lord,—

K. Rich. No lord of thine, thou haught in-
   sulting man,
Nor no man's lord; I have no name, no title
No, not that name was given me at the font, 256
But 'tis usurp'd: alack the heavy day!
That I have worn so many winters out,
And know not now what name to call myself.
O! that I were a mockery king of snow, 260
Standing before the sun of Bolingbroke,
To melt myself away in water-drops.
Good king, great king,—and yet not greatly
   good,
An if my word be sterling yet in England, 264
Let it command a mirror hither straight,
That it may show me what a face I have,
Since it is bankrupt of his majesty.

Boling. Go some of you and fetch a looking-
   glass.   *[Exit an* Attendant.

North. Read o'er this paper while the glass
   doth come.   269

K. Rich. Fiend! thou torment'st me ere I
   come to hell.

Boling. Urge it no more, my Lord Northumberland.

North. The commons will not then be satisfied.   272

K. Rich. They shall be satisfied: I'll read
   enough
When I do see the very book indeed
Where all my sins are writ, and that's myself.

Re-enter Attendant, *with a glass.*

Give me the glass, and therein will I read. 276
No deeper wrinkles yet? Hath sorrow struck
So many blows upon this face of mine
And made no deeper wounds? O, flattering
   glass!
Like to my followers in prosperity, 280
Thou dost beguile me. Was this face the face
That every day under his household roof
Did keep ten thousand men? Was this the face
That like the sun did make beholders wink? 284
Was this the face that fac'd so many follies,
And was at last out-fac'd by Bolingbroke?
A brittle glory shineth in this face:
As brittle as the glory is the face; 288
   [Dashes the glass against the ground.
For there it is, crack'd in a hundred shivers.
Mark, silent king, the moral of this sport,
How soon my sorrow hath destroy'd my face.

Boling. The shadow of your sorrow hath
   destroy'd   292
The shadow of your face.

K. Rich.   Say that again.
The shadow of my sorrow! Ha! let's see:
'Tis very true, my grief lies all within;
And these external manners of laments 296
Are merely shadows to the unseen grief
That swells with silence in the tortur'd soul;
There lies the substance: and I thank thee, king,
For thy great bounty, that not only giv'st 300
Me cause to wail, but teachest me the way
How to lament the cause. I'll beg one boon,
And then be gone and trouble you no more.
Shall I obtain it?

Boling.   Name it, fair cousin. 304

K. Rich. 'Fair cousin!' I am greater than
   a king;
For when I was a king, my flatterers
Were then but subjects; being now a subject,
I have a king here to my flatterer. 308
Being so great, I have no need to beg.

Boling. Yet ask.

K. Rich. And shall I have?

Boling. You shall.   312

K. Rich. Then give me leave to go.

Boling. Whither?

K. Rich. Whither you will, so I were from
   your sights.

Boling. Go, some of you convey him to the
   Tower.   316

K. Rich. O, good! convey? conveyers are
   you all,
That rise thus nimbly by a true king's fall.
   [Exeunt KING RICHARD *and* Guard

Boling. On Wednesday next we solemnly set
   down
Our coronation: lords, prepare yourselves. 32
[Exeunt all except the BISHOP OF CARLISLE, *the*
   ABBOT OF WESTMINSTER, *and* AUMERLE

Abbot. A woeful pageant have we here beheld.

Bishop. The woe's to come; the children yet unborn

Shall feel this day as sharp to them as thorn.

Aum. You holy clergymen, is there no plot
To rid the realm of this pernicious blot?　325

Abbot. My lord,
Before I freely speak my mind herein,
You shall not only take the sacrament　328
To bury mine intents, but also to effect
Whatever I shall happen to devise.
I see your brows are full of discontent,
Your hearts of sorrow, and your eyes of tears:
Come home with me to supper; I will lay　333
A plot shall show us all a merry day. [*Exeunt.*

ACT V

Scene I.—*London. A Street leading to the Tower.*

Enter the QUEEN *and* LADIES.

Queen. This way the king will come; this is the way
To Julius Cæsar's ill-erected tower,
To whose flint bosom my condemned lord
Is doom'd a prisoner by proud Bolingbroke. 4
Here let us rest, if this rebellious earth
Have any resting for her true king's queen.

Enter KING RICHARD *and* Guard.

But soft, but see, or rather do not see,
My fair rose wither: yet look up, behold,　8
That you in pity may dissolve to dew,
And wash him fresh again with true-love tears.
Ah! thou, the model where old Troy did stand,
Thou map of honour, thou King Richard's tomb,　12
And not King Richard; thou most beauteous inn,
Why should hard-favour'd grief be lodg'd in thee,
When triumph is become an alehouse guest?

K. Rich. Join not with grief, fair woman, do not so,　16
To make my end too sudden: learn, good soul,
To think our former state a happy dream;
From which awak'd, the truth of what we are
Shows us but this. I am sworn brother, sweet,
To grim Necessity, and he and I　21
Will keep a league till death. Hie thee to France,
And cloister thee in some religious house:
Our holy lives must win a new world's crown, 24
Which our profane hours here have stricken down.

Queen. What! is my Richard both in shape and mind
Transform'd and weaken'd! Hath Bolingbroke depos'd
Thine intellect? hath he been in thy heart? 28
The lion dying thrusteth forth his paw
And wounds the earth, if nothing else, with rage
To be o'erpower'd; and wilt thou, pupil-like,
Take thy correction mildly, kiss the rod,　32

And fawn on rage with base humility,
Which art a lion and a king of beasts?

K. Rich. A king of beasts indeed; if aught but beasts,
I had been still a happy king of men.　36
Good sometime queen, prepare thee hence for France,
Think I am dead, and that even here thou tak'st,
As from my death-bed, my last living leave.
In winter's tedious nights sit by the fire　40
With good old folks, and let them tell thee tales
Of woeful ages, long ago betid;
And ere thou bid good night, to quit their grief,
Tell thou the lamentable tale of me,　44
And send the hearers weeping to their beds:
For why the senseless brands will sympathize
The heavy accent of thy moving tongue,
And in compassion weep the fire out;　48
And some will mourn in ashes, some coal-black,
For the deposing of a rightful king.

Enter NORTHUMBERLAND, *attended.*

North. My lord, the mind of Bolingbroke is chang'd;
You must to Pomfret, not unto the Tower. 52
And, madam, there is order ta'en for you;
With all swift speed you must away to France.

K. Rich. Northumberland, thou ladder wherewithal
The mounting Bolingbroke ascends my throne,
The time shall not be many hours of age　57
More than it is, ere foul sin gathering head
Shall break into corruption. Thou shalt think,
Though he divide the realm and give thee half,
It is too little, helping him to all;　61
And he shall think that thou, which know'st the way
To plant unrightful kings, wilt know again,
Being ne'er so little urg'd, another way　64
To pluck him headlong from the usurped throne.
The love of wicked friends converts to fear;
That fear to hate, and hate turns one or both
To worthy danger and deserved death.　68

North. My guilt be on my head, and there an end.
Take leave and part; for you must part forthwith.

K. Rich. Doubly divorc'd! Bad men, ye violate
A two-fold marriage; 'twixt my crown and me,
And then, betwixt me and my married wife. 73
Let me unkiss the oath 'twixt thee and me;
And yet not so, for with a kiss 'twas made.
Part us, Northumberland: I towards the north,
Where shivering cold and sickness pines the clime;　77
My wife to France: from whence, set forth in pomp,
She came adorned hither like sweet May,
Sent back like Hallowmas or short'st of day. 80

Queen. And must we be divided? must we part?

K. Rich. Ay, hand from hand, my love, and heart from heart.

Queen. Banish us both and send the king with me.

North. That were some love but little po-
licy.   84
Queen. Then whither he goes, thither let me
go.
K. Rich. So two, together weeping, make
one woe.
Weep thou for me in France, I for thee here;
Better far off, than near, be ne'er the near. 88
Go, count thy way with sighs, I mine with
groans.
Queen. So longest way shall have the longest
moans.
K. Rich. Twice for one step I'll groan, the
way being short,
And piece the way out with a heavy heart. 92
Come, come, in wooing sorrow let's be brief,
Since, wedding it, there is such length in grief.
One kiss shall stop our mouths, and dumbly
part;
Thus give I mine, and thus take I thy heart. 96
                                  [*They kiss.*
Queen. Give me mine own again; 'twere no
good part
To take on me to keep and kill thy heart.
                              [*They kiss again.*
So, now I have mine own again, be gone,
That I may strive to kill it with a groan. 100
K. Rich. We make woe wanton with this
fond delay;
Once more, adieu; the rest let sorrow say.
                                    [*Exeunt.*

SCENE II.—*The Same. A Room in the* DUKE OF
                YORK'S *Palace.*

        Enter YORK *and his* DUCHESS.

Duch. My lord, you told me you would tell
the rest,
When weeping made you break the story off,
Of our two cousins coming into London.
York. Where did I leave?
Duch.   At that sad stop, my lord, 4
Where rude misgovern'd hands, from windows'
tops,
Threw dust and rubbish on King Richard's head.
York. Then, as I said, the duke, great Bol-
ingbroke,
Mounted upon a hot and fiery steed,   8
Which his aspiring rider seem'd to know,
With slow but stately pace kept on his course,
While all tongues cried, 'God save thee, Boling-
broke!'
You would have thought the very windows
spake,   12
So many greedy looks of young and old
Through casements darted their desiring eyes
Upon his visage, and that all the walls
With painted imagery had said at once   16
'Jesu preserve thee! welcome, Bolingbroke!'
Whilst he, from one side to the other turning,
Bare-headed, lower than his proud steed's neck,
Bespake them thus, 'I thank you, countrymen:'
And thus still doing, thus he pass'd along. 21
Duch. Alack, poor Richard! where rode he
the whilst?
York. As in a theatre, the eyes of men,

After a well-grac'd actor leaves the stage, 2
Are idly bent on him that enters next,
Thinking his prattle to be tedious;
Even so, or with much more contempt, men'
eyes
Did scowl on Richard: no man cried, 'God sav
him;'   2
No joyful tongue gave him his welcome home
But dust was thrown upon his sacred head,
Which with such gentle sorrow he shook off,
His face still combating with tears and smiles, 3
The badges of his grief and patience,
That had not God, for some strong purpose
steel'd
The hearts of men, they must perforce hav
melted,
And barbarism itself have pitied him.   3
But heaven hath a hand in these events,
To whose high will we bound our calm contents
To Bolingbroke are we sworn subjects now,
Whose state and honour I for aye allow.   4
Duch. Here comes my son Aumerle.
York.   Aumerle that was
But that is lost for being Richard's friend,
And, madam, you must call him Rutland
now.
I am in parliament pledge for his truth   4
And lasting fealty to the new-made king.

            Enter AUMERLE.

Duch. Welcome, my son: who are the violet
now
That strew the green lap of the new come spring
Aum. Madam, I know not, nor I greatl
care not: 4
God knows I had as lief be none as one.
York. Well, bear you well in this new sprin
of time,
Lest you be cropp'd before you come to prime
What news from Oxford? hold those justs an
triumphs?   5
Aum. For aught I know, my lord, they do.
York. You will be there, I know.
Aum. If God prevent it not, I purpose so.
York. What seal is that that hangs withou
thy bosom?   5
Yea, look'st thou pale? let me see the writing
Aum. My lord, 'tis nothing.
York.   No matter then, who sees it
I will be satisfied; let me see the writing.
Aum. I do beseech your Grace to pardor
me: 6
It is a matter of small consequence,
Which for some reasons I would not have seen
York. Which for some reasons, sir, I mear
to see.
I fear, I fear,—
Duch.   What should you fear?   6
'Tis nothing but some bond he's enter'd into
For gay apparel 'gainst the triumph day.
York. Bound to himself! what doth he witl
a bond
That he is bound to? Wife, thou art a fool. 68
Boy, let me see the writing.
Aum. I do beseech you, pardon me; I may
not show it.

York. I will be satisfied; let me see it, I say.
                    [Snatches it, and reads.
Treason! foul treason! villain! traitor! slave! 72
Duch. What is the matter, my lord?
York. Ho! who is within there?

Enter a Servant.

                Saddle my horse.
God for his mercy! what treachery is here!
Duch. Why, what is it, my lord?
York. Give me my boots, I say; saddle my 76
horse.
Now, by mine honour, by my life, my troth,
I will appeach the villain.   *[Exit Servant.*
Duch.   What's the matter?
York. Peace, foolish woman. 80
Duch. I will not peace. What is the matter,
Aumerle?
Aum. Good mother, be content; it is no more
Than my poor life must answer.
Duch.   Thy life answer!
York. Bring me my boots: I will unto the
king. 84

Re-enter Servant with boots.

Duch. Strike him, Aumerle. Poor boy, thou
art amaz'd.
[To Servant.] Hence, villain! never more come
in my sight.   *[Exit Servant.*
York. Give me my boots, I say.
Duch. Why, York, what wilt thou do? 88
Wilt thou not hide the trespass of thine own?
Have we more sons, or are we like to have?
Is not my teeming date drunk up with time?
And wilt thou pluck my fair son from mine age,
And rob me of a happy mother's name? 93
Is he not like thee? is he not thine own?
York. Thou fond, mad woman,
Wilt thou conceal this dark conspiracy? 96
A dozen of them here have ta'en the sacrament,
And interchangeably set down their hands,
To kill the king at Oxford.
Duch.   He shall be none;
We'll keep him here: then, what is that to him?
York. Away, fond woman! were he twenty
times
My son, I would appeach him. 101
Duch.   Hadst thou groan'd for him
As I have done, thou'dst be more pitiful.
But now I know thy mind: thou dost suspect
That I have been disloyal to thy bed, 105
And that he is a bastard, not thy son:
Sweet York, sweet husband, be not of that mind:
He is as like thee as a man may be, 108
Not like to me, nor any of my kin,
And yet I love him.
York.   Make way, unruly woman! *[Exit.*
Duch. After, Aumerle! Mount thee upon his
horse;
Spur post, and get before him to the king, 112
And beg thy pardon ere he do accuse thee.
I'll not be long behind; though I be old,
I doubt not but to ride as fast as York:
And never will I rise up from the ground 116
Till Bolingbroke have pardon'd thee. Away!
be gone.   *[Exeunt.*

SCENE III.—*Windsor. A Room in the Castle.*

Enter BOLINGBROKE *as King;* HENRY PERCY,
and other Lords.

Boling. Can no man tell of my unthrifty son?
'Tis full three months since I did see him last.
If any plague hang over us, 'tis he.
I would to God, my lords, he might be found:
Inquire at London, 'mongst the taverns there,
For there, they say, he daily doth frequent,
With unrestrained loose companions,
Even such, they say, as stand in narrow lanes 8
And beat our watch and rob our passengers;
While he, young wanton and effeminate boy,
Takes on the point of honour to support
So dissolute a crew. 12
H. Percy. My lord, some two days since I
saw the prince,
And told him of these triumphs held at Oxford.
Boling. And what said the gallant?
H. Percy. His answer was: he would unto
the stews, 16
And from the common'st creature pluck a glove,
And wear it as a favour; and with that
He would unhorse the lustiest challenger.
Boling. As dissolute as desperate; yet, through
both, 20
I see some sparkles of a better hope,
Which elder days may happily bring forth.
But who comes here?

Enter AUMERLE.

Aum.   Where is the king?
Boling.   What means
Our cousin, that he stares and looks so wildly?
Aum. God save your Grace! I do beseech
your majesty, 25
To have some conference with your Grace
alone.
Boling. Withdraw yourselves, and leave us
here alone.   *[Exeunt H. PERCY and Lords.*
What is the matter with our cousin now?
Aum. *[Kneels.]* For ever may my knees grow
to the earth, 29
My tongue cleave to my roof within my mouth,
Unless a pardon ere I rise or speak.
Boling. Intended or committed was this fault?
If on the first, how heinous e'er it be, 33
To win thy after-love I pardon thee.
Aum. Then give me leave that I may turn
the key,
That no man enter till my tale be done. 36
Boling. Have thy desire.
               [AUMERLE locks the door.
York. *[Within.]* My liege, beware! look to
thyself;
Thou hast a traitor in thy presence there. 39
Boling. *[Drawing.]* Villain, I'll make thee safe.
Aum. Stay thy revengeful hand; thou hast
no cause to fear.
York. *[Within.]* Open the door, secure, fool-
hardy king:
Shall I for love speak treason to thy face?
Open the door, or I will break it open. 44
            *[BOLINGBROKE unlocks the door; and
                afterwards relocks it.*

Enter YORK.

Boling. What is the matter, uncle? speak;
Recover breath; tell us how near is danger,
That we may arm us to encounter it.
    York. Peruse this writing here, and thou
        shalt know   48
The treason that my haste forbids me show.
    Aum. Remember, as thou read'st, thy pro-
        mise pass'd:
I do repent me; read not my name there;   51
My heart is not confederate with my hand.
    York. 'Twas, villain, ere thy hand did set it
        down.
I tore it from the traitor's bosom, king;
Fear, and not love, begets his penitence.
Forget to pity him, lest thy pity prove   56
A serpent that will sting thee to the heart.
    Boling. O heinous, strong, and bold con-
        spiracy!
O loyal father of a treacherous son!   59
Thou sheer, immaculate, and silver fountain,
From whence this stream through muddy pas-
        sages
Hath held his current and defil'd himself!
Thy overflow of good converts to bad,
And thy abundant goodness shall excuse   64
This deadly blot in thy digressing son.
    York. So shall my virtue be his vice's bawd,
And he shall spend mine honour with his shame,
As thriftless sons their scraping fathers' gold.
Mine honour lives when his dishonour dies,
Or my sham'd life in his dishonour lies: 70
Thou kill'st me in his life; giving him breath,
The traitor lives, the true man's put to death.
    Duch. [*Within.*] What ho, my liege! for God's
        sake let me in.
    Boling. What shrill-voic'd suppliant makes
        this eager cry?
    Duch. [*Within.*] A woman, and thine aunt,
        great king; 'tis I.
Speak with me, pity me, open the door;   76
A beggar begs, that never begg'd before.
    Boling. Our scene is alter'd from a serious
        thing,
And now chang'd to 'The Beggar and the King.'
My dangerous cousin, let your mother in: 80
I know she's come to pray for your foul sin.
                    [AUMERLE *unlocks the door.*
    York. If thou do pardon, whosoever pray,
More sins, for this forgiveness, prosper may.
This fester'd joint cut off, the rest rests sound;
This, let alone, will all the rest confound.   85

Enter DUCHESS.

    Duch. O king! believe not this hard-hearted
        man:
Love, loving not itself, none other can.
    York. Thou frantic woman, what dost thou
        make here?   88
Shall thy old dugs once more a traitor rear?
    Duch. Sweet York, be patient.   [*Kneels.*
                    Hear me, gentle liege.
    Boling. Rise up, good aunt.
    Duch.   Not yet, I thee beseech.
For ever will I walk upon my knees,   92
And never see day that the happy sees,

Till thou give joy; until thou bid me joy,
By pardoning Rutland, my transgressing boy. 95
    Aum. Unto my mother's prayers I bend my
        knee.   [*Kneels.*
    York. Against them both my true joints
        bended be.   [*Kneels.*
Ill mayst thou thrive if thou grant any grace!
    Duch. Pleads he in earnest? look upon his
        face;   99
His eyes do drop no tears, his prayers are in jest;
His words come from his mouth, ours from our
        breast:
He prays but faintly and would be denied;
We pray with heart and soul and all beside:
His weary joints would gladly rise, I know;
Our knees shall kneel till to the ground they
        grow;   105
His prayers are full of false hypocrisy;
Ours of true zeal and deep integrity.
Our prayers do out-pray his; then let them
        have   108
That mercy which true prayer ought to have.
    Boling. Good aunt, stand up.
    Duch.   Nay, do not say 'stand up;'
But 'pardon' first, and afterwards 'stand up.'
An if I were thy nurse, thy tongue to teach, 112
'Pardon' should be the first word of thy speech.
I never long'd to hear a word till now;
Say 'pardon,' king; let pity teach thee how:
The word is short, but not so short as sweet;
No word like 'pardon,' for kings' mouths so
        meet.   117
    York. Speak it in French, king; say, '*par-
        donnez moy.*'
    Duch. Dost thou teach pardon pardon to
        destroy?   119
Ah! my sour husband, my hard-hearted lord,
That sett'st the word itself against the word,
Speak 'pardon' as 'tis current in our land;
The chopping French we do not understand.
Thine eye begins to speak, set thy tongue there;
Or in thy piteous heart plant thou thine ear,
That hearing how our plaints and prayers do
        pierce,   126
Pity may move thee pardon to rehearse.
    Boling. Good aunt, stand up.
    Duch.   I do not sue to stand;
Pardon is all the suit I have in hand.
    Boling. I pardon him, as God shall pardon
        me.   130
    Duch. O happy vantage of a kneeling knee!
Yet am I sick for fear: speak it again;
Twice saying 'pardon' doth not pardon twain,
But makes one pardon strong.
    Boling.   With all my heart
I pardon him.
    Duch.   A god on earth thou art.
    Boling. But for our trusty brother-in-law and
        the abbot,   136
With all the rest of that consorted crew,
Destruction straight shall dog them at the heels.
Good uncle, help to order several powers
To Oxford, or where'er these traitors are:
They shall not live within this world, I swear,
But I will have them, if I once know where.
Uncle, farewell: and cousin too, adieu:

our mother well hath pray'd, and prove you
  true.   144
Duch. Come, my old son: I pray God make
  thee new.   [*Exeunt.*

SCENE IV.—*Another Room in the Castle.*

Enter EXTON *and a* Servant.

Exton. Didst thou not mark the king, what
  words he spake?
Have I no friend will rid me of this living fear?'
  as it not so?
Serv.   Those were his very words.
Exton. 'Have I no friend?' quoth he: he
  spake it twice,   4
nd urg'd it twice together, did he not?
Serv. He did.
Exton. And speaking it, he wistly looked on
  me,
s who should say, 'I would thou wert the man
hat would divorce this terror from my heart;'
Meaning the king at Pomfret. Come, let's go:
am the king's friend, and will rid his foe.
                                          [*Exeunt.*

SCENE V. *Pomfret. The Dungeon of the
  Castle.*

Enter KING RICHARD.

K. Rich. I have been studying how I may
  compare
his prison where I live unto the world:
nd for because the world is populous,
nd here is not a creature but myself,   4
cannot do it; yet I'll hammer it out.
My brain I'll prove the female to my soul;
My soul the father: and these two beget
  generation of still-breeding thoughts,   8
nd these same thoughts people this little world
a humours like the people of this world.
or no thought is contented. The better sort,
s thoughts of things divine, are intermix'd 12
'ith scruples, and do set the word itself
gainst the word:
s thus, 'Come, little ones;' and then again,
t is as hard to come as for a camel   16
o thread the postern of a needle's eye.'
houghts tending to ambition, they do plot
'nlikely wonders; how these vain weak nails
May tear a passage through the flinty ribs   20
of this hard world, my ragged prison walls;
nd, for they cannot, die in their own pride.
houghts tending to content flatter themselves
hat they are not the first of fortune's slaves, 24
or shall not be the last; like silly beggars
Who sitting in the stocks refuge their shame,
hat many have and others must sit there:
nd in this thought they find a kind of ease, 28
earing their own misfortune on the back
of such as have before endur'd the like.
hus play I in one person many people,
nd none contented: sometimes am I king;   32
hen treason makes me wish myself a beggar,
nd so I am: then crushing penury
ersuades me I was better when a king;
hen am I king'd again; and by and by   36

Think that I am unking'd by Bolingbroke,
And straight am nothing: but whate'er I be,
Nor I nor any man that but man is
With nothing shall be pleas'd, till he be eas'd 40
With being nothing. Music do I hear? [*Music.*
Ha, ha! keep time. How sour sweet music is
When time is broke and no proportion kept!
So is it in the music of men's lives.   44
And here have I the daintiness of ear
To check time broke in a disorder'd string;
But for the concord of my state and time
Had not an ear to hear my true time broke.   48
I wasted time, and now doth time waste me;
For now hath time made me his numbering
  clock:
My thoughts are minutes, and with sighs they jar
Their watches on unto mine eyes, the outward
  watch,   52
Whereto my finger, like a dial's point,
Is pointing still, in cleansing them from tears.
Now sir, the sound that tells what hour it is
Are clamorous groans, that strike upon my heart
Which is the bell: so sighs and tears and groans
Show minutes, times, and hours; but my time
Runs posting on in Bolingbroke's proud joy,
While I stand fooling here, his Jack o' the clock.
This music mads me: let it sound no more;   61
For though it have holp madmen to their wits,
In me it seems it will make wise men mad.
Yet blessing on his heart that gives it me!   64
For 'tis a sign of love, and love to Richard
Is a strange brooch in this all-hating world.

Enter Groom of the Stable.

Groom. Hail, royal prince!
K. Rich.   Thanks, noble peer;
The cheapest of us is ten groats too dear.   68
What art thou? and how comest thou hither,
  man,
Where no man never comes but that sad dog
That brings me food to make misfortune live?
Groom. I was a poor groom of thy stable, king,
When thou wert king; who, travelling towards
  York,   73
With much ado at length have gotten leave
To look upon my sometimes royal master's face.
O! how it yearn'd my heart when I beheld   76
In London streets, that coronation day
When Bolingbroke rode on roan Barbary,
That horse that thou so often hast bestrid,
That horse that I so carefully have dress'd.   80
K. Rich. Rode he on Barbary? Tell me,
  gentle friend,
How went he under him?
Groom. So proudly as if he disdain'd the
  ground.
K. Rich. So proud that Bolingbroke was on
  his back!   84
That jade hath eat bread from my royal hand;
This hand hath made him proud with clapping
  him.
Would he not stumble? Would he not fall
  down,—
Since pride must have a fall,—and break the
  neck   88
Of that proud man that did usurp his back?

Forgiveness, horse! why do I rail on thee,
Since thou, created to be aw'd by man,
Wast born to bear? I was not made a horse; 92
And yet I bear a burden like an ass,
Spur-gall'd and tir'd by jauncing Bolingbroke.

Enter Keeper, *with a dish.*

Keep. [*To the* Groom.] Fellow, give place;
here is no longer stay.
K. Rich. If thou love me, 'tis time thou wert
away.   96
Groom. What my tongue dares not, that my
heart shall say.   [*Exit.*
Keep. My lord, will't please you to fall to?
K. Rich. Taste of it first, as thou art wont
to do.
Keep. My lord, I dare not: Sir Pierce of Ex-
ton, who lately came from the king, commands
the contrary.
K. Rich. The devil take Henry of Lancaster,
and thee!
Patience is stale, and I am weary of it.   104
                        [*Strikes the* Keeper.
Keep. Help, help, help!

Enter EXTON *and* Servants, *armed.*

K. Rich. How now! what means death in
this rude assault?
Villain, thine own hand yields thy death's in-
strument.
           [*Snatching a weapon and killing one.*
Go thou and fill another room in hell.   108
           [*He kills another : then* EXTON *strikes
                                   him down.*
That hand shall burn in never-quenching fire
That staggers thus my person. Exton, thy
fierce hand
Hath with the king's blood stain'd the king's
own land.   111
Mount, mount, my soul! thy seat is up on high,
Whilst my gross flesh sinks downward, here to
die.   [*Dies.*
Exton. As full of valour as of royal blood:
Both have I spilt; O! would the deed were good;
For now the devil, that told me I did well, 116
Says that this deed is chronicled in hell.
This dead king to the living king I'll bear.
Take hence the rest and give them burial here.
                                      [*Exeunt.*

SCENE VI.—*Windsor. An Apartment in the
Castle.*

Flourish. Enter BOLINGBROKE *and* YORK, *with*
Lords *and* Attendants.

Boling. Kind uncle York, the latest news we
hear
Is that the rebels have consum'd with fire
Our town of Cicester in Gloucestershire;
But whether they be ta'en or slain we hear not. 4

Enter NORTHUMBERLAND.
Welcome, my lord. What is the news?

North. First, to thy sacred state wish I a
happiness.
The next news is: I have to London sent
The heads of Salisbury, Spencer, Blunt, an
Kent.
The manner of their taking may appear
At large discoursed in this paper here.
Boling. We thank thee, gentle Percy, for th
pains,
And to thy worth will add right worthy gains.

Enter FITZWATER.

Fitz. My lord, I have from Oxford sent
London
The heads of Brocas and Sir Bennet Seely,
Two of the dangerous consorted traitors
That sought at Oxford thy dire overthrow.
Boling. Thy pains, Fitzwater, shall not b
forgot;
Right noble is thy merit, well I wot.

Enter HENRY PERCY, *with the* BISHOP OF
CARLISLE.

H. Percy. The grand conspirator, Abbot
Westminster,
With clog of conscience and sour melancholy,
Hath yielded up his body to the grave;
But here is Carlisle living, to abide
Thy kingly doom and sentence of his pride.
Boling. Carlisle, this is your doom:
Choose out some secret place, some revere
room,
More than thou hast, and with it joy thy lif
So, as thou livest in peace, die free from stri
For though mine enemy thou hast ever been,
High sparks of honour in thee have I seen.

Enter EXTON, *with* Attendants *bearing a coffi*

Exton. Great king, within this coffin I prese
Thy buried fear: herein all breathless lies
The mightiest of thy greatest enemies,
Richard of Bordeaux, by me hither brought.
Boling. Exton, I thank thee not; for the
hast wrought
A deed of slander with thy fatal hand
Upon my head and all this famous land.
Exton. From your own mouth, my lord, d
I this deed.
Boling. They love not poison that do poiso
need,
Nor do I thee: though I did wish him dead,
I hate the murderer, love him murdered.
The guilt of conscience take thou for thy labou
But neither my good word nor princely favou
With Cain go wander through the shade of nig
And never show thy head by day nor light.
Lords, I protest, my soul is full of woe,
That blood should sprinkle me to make me grow
Come, mourn with me for that I do lament,
And put on sullen black incontinent.
I'll make a voyage to the Holy Land,
To wash this blood off from my guilty hand.
March sadly after; grace my mournings her
In weeping after this untimely bier.   [*Exeun*

THE FIRST PART OF
KING HENRY THE FOURTH

DRAMATIS PERSONÆ

ING HENRY THE FOURTH.
ENRY, Prince of Wales,⎫ Sons to the King.
OHN OF LANCASTER,   ⎭
ARL OF WESTMORELAND.
R WALTER BLUNT.
HOMAS PERCY, Earl of Worcester.
ENRY PERCY, Earl of Northumberland.
ENRY PERCY, surnamed Hotspur, his son.
DMUND MORTIMER, Earl of March.
ICHARD SCROOP, Archbishop of York.
RCHIBALD, Earl of Douglas.
WEN GLENDOWER.
R RICHARD VERNON.
R JOHN FALSTAFF.

SIR MICHAEL, a Friend to the Archbishop of York.
POINS.
GADSHILL.
PETO.
BARDOLPH.

LADY PERCY, Wife to Hotspur, and Sister to Mortimer.
LADY MORTIMER, Daughter to Glendower, and Wife to Mortimer.
MISTRESS QUICKLY, Hostess of the Boar's Head Tavern in Eastcheap.

Lords, Officers, Sheriff, Vintner, Chamberlain, Drawers, two Carriers, Travellers, and Attendants.

SCENE.—*England.*

ACT I

SCENE I.—*London. The Palace.*

Enter KING HENRY, WESTMORELAND, *and Others.*

K. Hen. So shaken as we are, so wan with care,
ind we a time for frighted peace to pant,
nd breathe short-winded accents of new broils
o be commenc'd in stronds afar remote.   4
o more the thirsty entrance of this soil
hall daub her lips with her own children's blood;
o more shall trenching war channel her fields,
or bruise her flowerets with the armed hoofs 8
f hostile paces: those opposed eyes,
Vhich, like the meteors of a troubled heaven,
ll of one nature, of one substance bred,
Did lately meet in the intestine shock   12
nd furious close of civil butchery,
hall now, in mutual well-beseeming ranks,
March all one way, and be no more oppos'd
gainst acquaintance, kindred, and allies: 16
he edge of war, like an ill-sheathed knife,
o more shall cut his master. Therefore, friends,
s far as to the sepulchre of Christ,—
Vhose soldier now, under whose blessed cross
Ve are impressed and engag'd to fight,—   21
orthwith a power of English shall we levy,
Vhose arms were moulded in their mother's womb
o chase these pagans in those holy fields 24
Over whose acres walk'd those blessed feet
Vhich fourteen hundred years ago were nail'd
or our advantage on the bitter cross.
ut this our purpose is a twelvemonth old, 28
nd bootless 'tis to tell you we will go:
herefore we meet not now. Then let me hear

Of you, my gentle cousin Westmoreland,
What yesternight our council did decree   32
In forwarding this dear expedience.
  West. My liege, this haste was hot in question,
And many limits of the charge set down
But yesternight; when all athwart there came
A post from Wales loaden with heavy news; 37
Whose worst was, that the noble Mortimer,
Leading the men of Herefordshire to fight
Against the irregular and wild Glendower, 40
Was by the rude hands of that Welshman taken,
And a thousand of his people butchered;
Upon whose dead corpse' there was such misuse,
Such beastly shameless transformation   44
By those Welshwomen done, as may not be
Without much shame re-told or spoken of.
  K. Hen. It seems then that the tidings of this broil
Brake off our business for the Holy Land. 48
  West. This match'd with other like, my gracious lord;
For more uneven and unwelcome news
Came from the north and thus it did import:
On Holy-rood day, the gallant Hotspur there, 52
Young Harry Percy and brave Archibald,
That ever-valiant and approved Scot,
At Holmedon met,
Where they did spend a sad and bloody hour;
As by discharge of their artillery,   57
And shape of likelihood, the news was told;
For he that brought them, in the very heat
And pride of their contention did take horse, 60
Uncertain of the issue any way.
  K. Hen. Here is a dear and true industrious friend,
Sir Walter Blunt, new lighted from his horse,
Stain'd with the variation of each soil   64
Betwixt that Holmedon and this seat of ours;

o

And he hath brought us smooth and welcome
news.
The Earl of Douglas is discomfited;
Ten thousand bold Scots, two and twenty
   knights,   68
Balk'd in their own blood did Sir Walter see
On Holmedon's plains: of prisoners Hotspur
   took
Mordake the Earl of Fife, and eldest son
To beaten Douglas, and the Earls of Athol, 72
Of Murray, Angus, and Menteith.
And is not this an honourable spoil?
A gallant prize? ha, cousin, is it not?
   West. In faith,   76
It is a conquest for a prince to boast of.
   K. Hen. Yea, there thou mak'st me sad and
   mak'st me sin
In envy that my Lord Northumberland
Should be the father to so blest a son,   80
A son who is the theme of honour's tongue;
Amongst a grove the very straightest plant;
Who is sweet Fortune's minion and her pride:
Whilst I, by looking on the praise of him,   84
See riot and dishonour stain the brow
Of my young Harry. O! that it could be prov'd
That some night-tripping fairy had exchang'd
In cradle-clothes our children where they lay, 88
And call'd mine Percy, his Plantagenet.
Then would I have his Harry, and he mine.
But let him from my thoughts. What think
   you, coz,
Of this young Percy's pride? the prisoners, 92
Which he in this adventure hath surpris'd,
To his own use he keeps, and sends me word,
I shall have none but Mordake Earl of Fife.
   West. This is his uncle's teaching, this is
   Worcester,   96
Malevolent to you in all aspects;
Which makes him prune himself, and bristle up
The crest of youth against your dignity.
   K. Hen. But I have sent for him to answer
   this;   100
And for this cause a while we must neglect
Our holy purpose to Jerusalem.
Cousin, on Wednesday next our council we
Will hold at Windsor; so inform the lords: 104
But come yourself with speed to us again;
For more is to be said and to be done
Than out of anger can be uttered.
   West. I will, my liege.   [*Exeunt.*

SCENE II.—*The Same. An Apartment of the*
PRINCE'S.

Enter the PRINCE *and* FALSTAFF.

   Fal. Now, Hal, what time of day is it, lad?
   Prince. Thou art so fat-witted, with drinking
of old sack, and unbuttoning thee after supper,
and sleeping upon benches after noon, that thou
hast forgotten to demand that truly which thou
wouldst truly know. What a devil hast thou to
do with the time of the day? unless hours were
cups of sack, and minutes capons, and clocks
the tongues of bawds, and dials the signs of
leaping-houses, and the blessed sun himself a
fair hot wench in flame-colour'd taffeta, I see no

reason why thou shouldst be so superfluous
demand the time of the day.
   Fal. Indeed, thou comest near me now, H
for we that take purses go by the moon and t
seven stars, and not by Phœbus, he, 'that wa
dering knight so fair.' And, I prithee, sw
wag, when thou art king,—as, God save t
Grace,—majesty, I should say, for grace th
wilt have none,—
   Prince. What! none?
   Fal. No, by my troth; not so much as w
serve to be prologue to an egg and butter.
   Prince. Well, how then? come, round
roundly.
   Fal. Marry, then, sweet wag, when thou a
king, let not us that are squires of the nigh
body be called thieves of the day's beauty:
us be Diana's foresters, gentlemen of the shac
minions of the moon; and let men say, we
men of good government, being governed as t
sea is, by our noble and chaste mistress t
moon, under whose countenance we steal.
   Prince. Thou sayest well, and it holds w
too; for the fortune of us that are the moo
men doth ebb and flow like the sea, being g
verned as the sea is, by the moon. As for pro
now: a purse of gold most resolutely snatch
on Monday night and most dissolutely spent
Tuesday morning; got with swearing 'Lay by
and spent with crying 'Bring in:' now in
low an ebb as the foot of the ladder, and by a
by in as high a flow as the ridge of the gallow
   Fal. By the Lord, thou sayest true, lad. A
is not my hostess of the tavern a most swe
wench?
   Prince. As the honey of Hybla, my old lad
the castle. And is not a buff jerkin a most swe
robe of durance?
   Fal. How now, how now, mad wag! wha
in thy quips and thy quiddities? what a plagu
have I to do with a buff jerkin?
   Prince. Why, what a pox have I to do wi
my hostess of the tavern?
   Fal. Well, thou hast called her to a recko
ing many a time and oft.
   Prince. Did I ever call for thee to pay tl
part?
   Fal. No; I'll give thee thy due, thou ha
paid all there.
   Prince. Yea, and elsewhere, so far as my co
would stretch; and where it would not, I hav
used my credit.
   Fal. Yea, and so used it that, were it not he
apparent that thou art heir apparent—But,
prithee, sweet wag, shall there be gallows stan
ing in England when thou art king, and resol
tion thus fobbed as it is with the rusty curb
old father antick the law? Do not thou, whe
thou art king, hang a thief.
   Prince. No; thou shalt.
   Fal. Shall I? O rare! By the Lord, I'll be
brave judge.
   Prince. Thou judgest false already; I mea
thou shalt have the hanging of the thieves an
so become a rare hangman.
   Fal. Well, Hal, well; and in some sort

mps with my humour as well as waiting in
he court, I can tell you.

Prince. For obtaining of suits? 80

Fal. Yea, for obtaining of suits, whereof the
angman hath no lean wardrobe. 'Sblood, I
m as melancholy as a gib cat, or a lugged bear.

Prince. Or an old lion, or a lover's lute. 84

Fal. Yea, or the drone of a Lincolnshire
agpipe.

Prince. What sayest thou to a hare, or the
melancholy of Moor-ditch? 88

Fal. Thou hast the most unsavory similes,
nd art, indeed, the most comparative, rascal-
est, sweet young prince; but, Hal, I prithee,
rouble me no more with vanity. I would to God
hou and I knew where a commodity of good
ames were to be bought. An old lord of the
ouncil rated me the other day in the street about
ou, sir, but I marked him not; and yet he
alked very wisely, but I regarded him not; and
et he talked wisely, and in the street too. 98

Prince. Thou didst well; for wisdom cries
ut in the streets, and no man regards it. 100

Fal. O! thou hast damnable iteration, and
rt indeed able to corrupt a saint. Thou hast
one much harm upon me, Hal; God forgive
hee for it! Before I knew thee, Hal, I knew
othing; and now am I, if a man should speak
ruly, little better than one of the wicked. I
ust give over this life, and I will give it over;
y the Lord, an I do not, I am a villain: I'll be
amned for never a king's son in Christendom.

Prince. Where shall we take a purse to-
morrow, Jack? 111

Fal. Zounds! where thou wilt, lad, I'll make
ne; an I do not, call me a villain and baffle me.

Prince. I see a good amendment of life in
hee; from praying to purse-taking. 115

Enter POINS, *at a distance.*

Fal. Why, Hal, 'tis my vocation, Hal; 'tis no
in for a man to labour in his vocation. Poins!
Now shall we know if Gadshill have set a match.
O! if men were to be saved by merit, what hole
n hell were hot enough for him? This is the
most omnipotent villain that ever cried 'Stand!'
o a true man. 122

Prince. Good morrow, Ned.

Poins. Good morrow, sweet Hal. What says
Monsieur Remorse? What says Sir John Sack-
nd-Sugar? Jack! how agrees the devil and thee
bout thy soul, that thou soldest him on Good-
Friday last for a cup of Madeira and a cold
apon's leg? 129

Prince. Sir John stands to his word, the devil
hall have his bargain; for he was never yet a
reaker of proverbs: he will give the devil his due.

Poins. Then art thou damned for keeping thy
word with the devil.

Prince. Else he had been damned for cozen-
ng the devil. 136

Poins. But my lads, my lads, to-morrow
morning, by four o'clock, early at Gadshill!
There are pilgrims going to Canterbury with
ich offerings, and traders riding to London with
at purses: I have vizards for you all; you have

horses for yourselves. Gadshill lies to-night in
Rochester; I have bespoke supper to-morrow
night in Eastcheap: we may do it as secure as
sleep. If you will go I will stuff your purses full
of crowns; if you will not, tarry at home and be
hanged. 147

Fal. Hear ye, Yedward: if I tarry at home
and go not, I'll hang you for going.

Poins. You will, chops?

Fal. Hal, wilt thou make one?

Prince. Who, I rob? I a thief? not I, by my
faith. 153

Fal. There's neither honesty, manhood, nor
good fellowship in thee, nor thou camest not of
the blood royal, if thou darest not stand for ten
shillings. 157

Prince. Well, then, once in my days I'll be a
madcap.

Fal. Why, that's well said. 160

Prince. Well, come what will, I'll tarry at
home.

Fal. By the Lord, I'll be a traitor then, when
thou art king. 164

Prince. I care not.

Poins. Sir John, I prithee, leave the prince
and me alone: I will lay him down such reasons
for this adventure that he shall go. 168

Fal. Well, God give thee the spirit of persuasion and him the ears of profiting, that what
thou speakest may move, and what he hears
may be believed, that the true prince may, for
recreation sake, prove a false thief; for the poor
abuses of the time want countenance. Farewell:
you shall find me in Eastcheap. 175

Prince. Farewell, thou latter spring! Farewell, All-hallown summer! [*Exit* FALSTAFF.

Poins. Now, my good sweet honey lord, ride
with us to-morrow: I have a jest to execute that
I cannot manage alone. Falstaff, Bardolph,
Peto, and Gadshill shall rob those men that we
have already waylaid; yourself and I will not be
there; and when they have the booty, if you
and I do not rob them, cut this head from my
shoulders. 185

Prince. But how shall we part with them in
setting forth?

Poins. Why, we will set forth before or after
them, and appoint them a place of meeting,
wherein it is at our pleasure to fail; and then
will they adventure upon the exploit themselves,
which they shall have no sooner achieved but
we'll set upon them. 193

Prince. Yea, but 'tis like that they will know
us by our horses, by our habits, and by every
other appointment, to be ourselves. 196

Poins. Tut! our horses they shall not see,
I'll tie them in the wood; our vizards we will
change after we leave them; and, sirrah, I have
cases of buckram for the nonce, to inmask our
noted outward garments. 201

Prince. Yea, but I doubt they will be too
hard for us.

Poins. Well, for two of them, I know them
to be as true-bred cowards as ever turned back;
and for the third, if he fight longer than he sees
reason, I'll forswear arms. The virtue of this

jest will be, the incomprehensible lies that this
same fat rogue will tell us when we meet at
supper: how thirty, at least, he fought with;
what wards, what blows, what extremities he
endured; and in the reproof of this lies the jest.

  Prince. Well, I'll go with thee: provide us
all things necessary and meet me to-morrow
night in Eastcheap; there I'll sup. Farewell.

  Poins. Farewell, my lord.   [*Exit.*

  Prince. I know you all, and will awhile up-
hold   217
The unyok'd humour of your idleness:
Yet herein will I imitate the sun,
Who doth permit the base contagious clouds
To smother up his beauty from the world, 221
That when he please again to be himself,
Being wanted, he may be more wonder'd at,
By breaking through the foul and ugly mists
Of vapours that did seem to strangle him. 225
If all the year were playing holidays,
To sport would be as tedious as to work;
But when they seldom come, they wish'd for
come,
And nothing pleaseth but rare accidents. 229
So, when this loose behaviour I throw off,
And pay the debt I never promised,
By how much better than my word I am   232
By so much shall I falsify men's hopes;
And like bright metal on a sullen ground,
My reformation, glittering o'er my fault,
Shall show more goodly and attract more eyes
Than that which hath no foil to set it off. 237
I'll so offend to make offence a skill;
Redeeming time when men think least I will.
     [*Exit.*

SCENE III.—*The Same. The Palace.*

Enter KING HENRY, NORTHUMBERLAND, WOR-
CESTER, HOTSPUR, SIR WALTER BLUNT, *and
Others.*

  K. Hen. My blood hath been too cold and
temperate,
Unapt to stir at these indignities,
And you have found me; for accordingly
You tread upon my patience: but, be sure, 4
I will from henceforth rather be myself,
Mighty, and to be fear'd, than my condition,
Which hath been smooth as oil, soft as young
down,
And therefore lost that title of respect   8
Which the proud soul ne'er pays but to the
proud.

  Wor. Our house, my sovereign liege, little
deserves
The scourge of greatness to be us'd on it;
And that same greatness too which our own
hands
Have holp to make so portly.   12

  North. My lord,—

  K. Hen. Worcester, get thee gone; for I do see
Danger and disobedience in thine eye.   16
O, sir, your presence is too bold and peremptory,
And majesty might never yet endure
The moody frontier of a servant brow.

You have good leave to leave us; when we need
Your use and counsel we shall send for you. 21
     [*Exit* WORCESTER.

[*To* NORTHUMBERLAND.] You were about to
speak.

  North. Yea, my good lord,
Those prisoners in your highness' name de-
manded,
Which Harry Percy here at Holmedon took, 24
Were, as he says, not with such strength denied
As is deliver'd to your majesty:
Either envy, therefore, or misprision
Is guilty of this fault and not my son.   28

  Hot. My liege, I did deny no prisoners:
But I remember, when the fight was done,
When I was dry with rage and extreme toil,
Breathless and faint, leaning upon my sword, 32
Came there a certain lord, neat, and trimly
dress'd,
Fresh as a bridegroom; and his chin, new reap'd,
Show'd like a stubble-land at harvest-home:
He was perfumed like a milliner,   36
And 'twixt his finger and his thumb he held
A pouncet-box, which ever and anon
He gave his nose and took't away again;
Who therewith angry, when it next came there,
Took it in snuff: and still he smil'd and talk'd;
And as the soldiers bore dead bodies by,
He call'd them untaught knaves, unmannerly,
To bring a slovenly unhandsome corpse   44
Betwixt the wind and his nobility.
With many holiday and lady terms
He question'd me; among the rest, demanded
My prisoners in your majesty's behalf.   48
I then all smarting with my wounds being cold,
To be so pester'd with a popinjay,
Out of my grief and my impatience
Answer'd neglectingly, I know not what,   52
He should, or he should not; for he made me mad
To see him shine so brisk and smell so sweet
And talk so like a waiting-gentlewoman
Of guns, and drums, and wounds,—God save
the mark!—   56
And telling me the sovereign'st thing on earth
Was parmaceti for an inward bruise;
And that it was great pity, so it was,
This villanous saltpetre should be digg'd   60
Out of the bowels of the harmless earth,
Which many a good tall fellow had destroy'd
So cowardly; and but for these vile guns,
He would himself have been a soldier.   64
This bald unjointed chat of his, my lord,
I answer'd indirectly, as I said;
And I beseech you, let not his report
Come current for an accusation   68
Betwixt my love and your high majesty.

  Blunt. The circumstance consider'd, good
my lord,
Whatever Harry Percy then had said
To such a person and in such a place,   72
At such a time, with all the rest re-told,
May reasonably die and never rise
To do him wrong, or any way impeach
What then he said, so he unsay it now.   76

  K. Hen. Why, yet he doth deny his prisoners,
But with proviso and exception,

That we at our own charge shall ransom straight
His brother-in-law, the foolish Mortimer;   80
Who, on my soul, hath wilfully betray'd
The lives of those that he did lead to fight
Against the great magician, damn'd Glendower,
Whose daughter, as we hear, the Earl of March
Hath lately married. Shall our coffers then   85
Be emptied to redeem a traitor home?
Shall we buy treason, and indent with fears,
When they have lost and forfeited themselves?
No, on the barren mountains let him starve;   89
For I shall never hold that man my friend
Whose tongue shall ask me for one penny cost
To ransom home revolted Mortimer.   92
    Hot. Revolted Mortimer!
He never did fall off, my sovereign liege,
But by the chance of war: to prove that true
Needs no more but one tongue for all those
    wounds,   96
Those mouthed wounds, which valiantly he
    took,
When on the gentle Severn's sedgy bank,
In single opposition, hand to hand,
He did confound the best part of an hour   100
In changing hardiment with great Glendower.
Three times they breath'd and three times did
    they drink,
Upon agreement, of swift Severn's flood,
Who then, affrighted with their bloody looks,   104
Ran fearfully among the trembling reeds,
And hid his crisp head in the hollow bank
Blood-stained with these valiant combatants.
Never did base and rotten policy   108
Colour her working with such deadly wounds;
Nor never could the noble Mortimer
Receive so many, and all willingly:
Then let him not be slander'd with revolt.   112
    K. Hen. Thou dost belie him, Percy, thou
    dost belie him:
He never did encounter with Glendower:
    tell thee,
He durst as well have met the devil alone   116
As Owen Glendower for an enemy.
Art thou not asham'd? But, sirrah, henceforth
Let me not hear you speak of Mortimer:
Send me your prisoners with the speediest
    means,   120
Or you shall hear in such a kind from me
As will displease you. My Lord Northumber-
    land,
We license your departure with your son.
Send us your prisoners, or you'll hear of it.   124
    [Exeunt KING HENRY, BLUNT, and Train.
    Hot. An if the devil come and roar for them,
I will not send them: I will after straight
And tell him so; for I will ease my heart,
Albeit I make a hazard of my head.   128
    North. What! drunk with choler? stay, and
    pause awhile:
Here comes your uncle.

Re-enter WORCESTER.

    Hot.   Speak of Mortimer!
Zounds! I will speak of him; and let my soul
Want mercy if I do not join with him: 132
In his behalf I'll empty all these veins,
And shed my dear blood drop by drop i' the dust,
But I will lift the down-trod Mortimer
As high i' the air as this unthankful king,   136
As this ingrate and canker'd Bolingbroke.
    North. Brother, the king hath made your
    nephew mad.
    Wor. Who struck this heat up after I was
    gone?
    Hot. He will, forsooth, have all my prisoners;
And when I urg'd the ransom once again   141
Of my wife's brother, then his cheek look'd pale,
And on my face he turn'd an eye of death,
Trembling even at the name of Mortimer.   144
    Wor. I cannot blame him: was he not pro-
    claim'd
By Richard that dead is the next of blood?
    North. He was; I heard the proclamation:
And then it was when the unhappy king,—   148
Whose wrongs in us God pardon!—did set forth
Upon his Irish expedition;
From whence he, intercepted, did return
To be depos'd, and shortly murdered.   152
    Wor. And for whose death we in the world's
    wide mouth
Live scandaliz'd and foully spoken of.
    Hot. But, soft! I pray you, did King Richard
    then
Proclaim my brother Edmund Mortimer   156
Heir to the crown?
    North.   He did; myself did hear it.
    Hot. Nay, then I cannot blame his cousin
    king,
That wish'd him on the barren mountains starve.
But shall it be that you, that set the crown   160
Upon the head of this forgetful man,
And for his sake wear the detested blot
Of murd'rous subornation, shall it be,
That you a world of curses undergo,   164
Being the agents, or base second means,
The cords, the ladder, or the hangman rather?
O! pardon me that I descend so low,
To show the line and the predicament   168
Wherein you range under this subtle king.
Shall it for shame be spoken in these days,
Or fill up chronicles in time to come,
That men of your nobility and power,   172
Did gage them both in an unjust behalf,
As both of you—God pardon it!—have done,
To put down Richard, that sweet lovely rose,
And plant this thorn, this canker, Bolingbroke?
And shall it in more shame be further spoken,
That you are fool'd, discarded, and shook off
By him for whom these shames ye underwent?
No; yet time serves wherein you may redeem 180
Your banish'd honours, and restore yourselves
Into the good thoughts of the world again;
Revenge the jeering and disdain'd contempt
Of this proud king, who studies day and night
To answer all the debt he owes to you,   185
Even with the bloody payment of your deaths.
Therefore, I say,—
    Wor.   Peace, cousin! say no more:
And now I will unclasp a secret book,   188
And to your quick-conceiving discontents
I'll read you matter deep and dangerous,
As full of peril and adventurous spirit

As to o'er-walk a current roaring loud,   192
On the unsteadfast footing of a spear.

   Hot. If he fall in, good night! or sink or
     swim:
Send danger from the east unto the west,
So honour cross it from the north to south, 196
And let them grapple: O! the blood more stirs
To rouse a lion than to start a hare.

   North. Imagination of some great exploit
Drives him beyond the bounds of patience. 200

   Hot. By heaven methinks it were an easy
     leap
To pluck bright honour from the pale-fac'd
     moon,
Or dive into the bottom of the deep,
Where fathom-line could never touch the
     ground,   204
And pluck up drowned honour by the locks;
So he that doth redeem her thence might wear
Without corrival all her dignities:
But out upon this half-fac'd fellowship!   208

   Wor. He apprehends a world of figures
     here,
But not the form of what he should attend.
Good cousin, give me audience for a while.

   Hot. I cry you mercy.

   Wor.   Those same noble Scots 212
That are your prisoners,—

   Hot.   I'll keep them all;
By God, he shall not have a Scot of them:
No, if a Scot would save his soul, he shall not:
I'll keep them, by this hand.

   Wor.   You start away, 216
And lend no ear unto my purposes.
Those prisoners you shall keep.

   Hot.   Nay, I will; that's flat:
He said he would not ransom Mortimer;
Forbade my tongue to speak of Mortimer; 220
But I will find him when he lies asleep,
And in his ear I'll holla 'Mortimer!'
Nay,
I'll have a starling shall be taught to speak 224
Nothing but 'Mortimer,' and give it him,
To keep his anger still in motion.

   Wor. Hear you, cousin; a word.

   Hot. All studies here I solemnly defy, 228
Save how to gall and pinch this Bolingbroke:
And that same sword-and-buckler Prince of
     Wales,
But that I think his father loves him not,
And would be glad he met with some mischance,
I would have him poison'd with a pot of ale. 233

   Wor. Farewell, kinsman: I will talk to you
When you are better temper'd to attend.

   North. Why, what a wasp-stung and impa-
     tient fool   236
Art thou to break into this woman's mood,
Tying thine ear to no tongue but thine own!

   Hot. Why, look you, I am whipp'd and
     scourg'd with rods,
Nettled, and stung with pismires, when I hear
Of this vile politician, Bolingbroke.   241
In Richard's time,—what do you call the place?—
A plague upon't—it is in Gloucestershire;—
'Twas where the madcap duke his uncle kept,
His uncle York; where I first bow'd my knee

Unto this king of smiles, this Bolingbroke,
'Sblood!
When you and he came back from Ravens
     purgh.   24

   North. At Berkeley Castle.

   Hot. You say true.
Why, what a candy deal of courtesy
This fawning greyhound then did proffer me
Look,' when his infant fortune came to age,' 25
And 'gentle Harry Percy,' and 'kind cousin.'
O! the devil take such cozeners. God forgive
     me!
Good uncle, tell your tale, for I have done. 25

   Wor. Nay, if you have not, to't again;
We'll stay your leisure.

   Hot.   I have done, i' faith

   Wor. Then once more to your Scottish
     prisoners.
Deliver them up without their ransom straight
And make the Douglas' son your only mean 26
For powers in Scotland; which, for divers
     reasons
Which I shall send you written, be assur'd,
Will easily be granted. [*To* NORTHUMBERLAND.
     You, my lord,   26
Your son in Scotland being thus employ'd,
Shall secretly into the bosom creep
Of that same noble prelate well belov'd,
The Archbishop.   268

   Hot. Of York, is it not?

   Wor. True; who bears hard
His brother's death at Bristol, the Lord Scroop.
I speak not this in estimation,   272
As what I think might be, but what I know
Is ruminated, plotted and set down;
And only stays but to behold the face
Of that occasion that shall bring it on.   276

   Hot. I smell it.
Upon my life it will do wondrous well.

   North. Before the game's afoot thou still
     lett'st slip.

   Hot. Why, it cannot choose but be a noble
     plot: 28
And then the power of Scotland and of York,
To join with Mortimer, ha?

   Wor.   And so they shall.

   Hot. In faith, it is exceedingly well aim'd.

   Wor. And 'tis no little reason bids us speed,
To save our heads by raising of a head;   285
For, bear ourselves as even as we can,
The king will always think him in our debt,
And think we think ourselves unsatisfied,   288
Till he hath found a time to pay us home.
And see already how he doth begin
To make us strangers to his looks of love.

   Hot. He does, he does: we'll be reveng'd on
     him.   292

   Wor. Cousin, farewell: no further go in this,
Than I by letters shall direct your course.
When time is ripe,—which will be suddenly,—
I'll steal to Glendower and Lord Mortimer; 296
Where you and Douglas and our powers at
     once,—
As I will fashion it,—shall happily meet,
To bear our fortunes in our own strong arms,
Which now we hold at much uncertainty. 300

North. Farewell, good brother: we shall
 thrive, I trust.
Hot. Uncle, adieu: O! let the hours be short,
ll fields and blows and groans applaud our
 sport!   [*Exeunt.*

ACT II

Scene I.—*Rochester. An Inn-Yard.*

nter a Carrier, *with a lanthorn in his hand.*

First Car. Heigh-ho! An't be not four by
e day I'll be hanged: Charles' Wain is over
e new chimney, and yet our horse not packed.
hat, ostler!   4
Ost. [*Within.*] Anon, anon.
First Car. I prithee, Tom, beat Cut's saddle,
t a few flocks in the point; the poor jade is
ung in the withers out of all cess.   8

Enter another Carrier.

Sec. Car. Peas and beans are as dank here as
dog, and that is the next way to give poor
les the bots; this house is turned upside down
ce Robin Ostler died.   12
First Car. Poor fellow! never joyed since the
ice of oats rose; it was the death of him.
Sec. Car. I think this be the most villanous
use in all London road for fleas: I am stung
e a tench.   17
First Car. Like a tench! by the mass, there
ne'er a king christen could be better bit than
ave been since the first cock.   20
Sec. Car. Why, they will allow us ne'er a
rdan, and then we leak in the chimney; and
ur chamber-lie breeds fleas like a loach.
First Car. What, ostler! come away and be
nged, come away.   25
Sec. Car. I have a gammon of bacon and
o razes of ginger, to be delivered as far as
aring-cross.   28
First Car. Godsbody! the turkeys in my
nnier are quite starved. What, ostler! A
ague on thee! hast thou never an eye in thy
ad? canst not hear? An 'twere not as good a
ed as drink to break the pate on thee, I am a
ry villain. Come, and be hanged! hast no
ith in thee?

Enter GADSHILL.

Gads. Good morrow, carriers. What's o'clock?
First Car. I think it be two o'clock.   37
Gads. I prithee, lend me thy lanthorn, to see
y gelding in the stable.
First Car. Nay, by God, soft: I know a
ick worth two of that, i' faith.   41
Gads. I prithee, lend me thine.
Sec. Car. Ay, when? canst tell? Lend me
y lanthorn, quoth a'? marry, I'll see thee
nged first.   45
Gads. Sirrah carrier, what time do you mean
come to London?
Sec. Car. Time enough to go to bed with a
ndle, I warrant thee. Come, neighbour Mugs,
e'll call up the gentlemen: they will along
ith company, for they have great charge.
                                  [*Exeunt* Carriers.

Gads. What, ho! chamberlain!   52
Cham. [*Within.*] 'At hand, quoth pick-purse.'
Gads. That's even as fair as, 'at hand, quoth
the chamberlain'; for thou variest no more from
picking of purses than giving direction doth
from labouring; thou layest the plot how.   57

Enter CHAMBERLAIN.

Cham. Good morrow, Master Gadshill. It
holds current that I told you yesternight: there's
a franklin in the wild of Kent hath brought
three hundred marks with him in gold: I heard
him tell it to one of his company last night at
supper; a kind of auditor; one that hath abundance of charge too, God knows what. They are
up already and call for eggs and butter: they
will away presently.
Gads. Sirrah, if they meet not with Saint
Nicholas' clerks, I'll give thee this neck. 68
Cham. No, I'll none of it: I prithee, keep
that for the hangman; for I know thou worship'st Saint Nicholas as truly as a man of
falsehood may.   72
Gads. What talkest thou to me of the
hangman? If I hang I'll make a fat pair of
gallows; for if I hang, old Sir John hangs with
me, and thou knowest he's no starveling. Tut!
there are other Troyans that thou dreamest not
of, the which for sport sake are content to do
the profession some grace; that would, if matters
should be looked into, for their own credit sake
make all whole. I am joined with no foot-land-
rakers, no long-staff sixpenny strikers, none of
these mad mustachio-purple-hued malt worms;
but with nobility and tranquillity, burgomasters
and great oneyers such as can hold in, such as
will strike sooner than speak, and speak sooner
than drink, and drink sooner than pray: and
yet I lie; for they pray continually to their
saint, the commonwealth; or, rather, not pray
to her, but prey on her, for they ride up and
down on her and make her their boots.   91
Cham. What! the commonwealth their
boots? will she hold out water in foul way?
Gads. She will, she will; justice hath liquored
her. We steal as in a castle, cock-sure; we have
the receipt of fern-seed, we walk invisible. 96
Cham. Nay, by my faith, I think you are
more beholding to the night than to fern-seed
for your walking invisible.
Gads. Give me thy hand: thou shalt have a
share in our purchase, as I am a true man. 101
Cham. Nay, rather let me have it, as you are
a false thief.
Gads. Go to; *homo* is a common name to all
men. Bid the ostler bring my gelding out of
the stable. Farewell, you muddy knave.   106
                                          [*Exeunt.*

Scene II.—*The Road by Gadshill.*

Enter the PRINCE *and* POINS.

Poins. Come, shelter, shelter: I have removed Falstaff's horse, and he frets like a
gummed velvet.
Prince. Stand close.   4

Enter FALSTAFF.

Fal. Poins! Poins, and be hanged! Poins!

Prince. Peace, ye fat-kidneyed rascal! What brawling dost thou keep!

Fal. Where's Poins, Hal?   8

Prince. He is walked up to the top of the hill: I'll go seek him.

[*Pretends to seek* POINS, *and retires.*

Fal. I am accursed to rob in that thief's company; the rascal hath removed my horse and tied him I know not where. If I travel but four foot by the squire further afoot I shall break my wind. Well, I doubt not but to die a fair death for all this, if I 'scape hanging for killing that rogue. I have forsworn his company hourly any time this two-and-twenty years, and yet I am bewitched with the rogue's company. If the rascal have not given me medicines to make me love him, I'll be hanged: it could not be else: I have drunk medicines. Poins! Hal! a plague upon you both! Bardolph! Peto! I'll starve ere I'll rob a foot further. An 'twere not as good a deed as drink to turn true man and leave these rogues, I am the veriest varlet that ever chewed with a tooth. Eight yards of uneven ground is threescore and ten miles afoot with me, and the stony-hearted villains know it well enough. A plague upon't when thieves cannot be true one to another! [*They whistle.*] Whew! A plague upon you all! Give me my horse, you rogues; give me my horse and be hanged.   34

Prince. [*Coming forward.*] Peace, ye fat-guts! lie down: lay thine ear close to the ground, and list if thou canst hear the tread of travellers.   38

Fal. Have you any levers to lift me up again, being down? 'Sblood! I'll not bear mine own flesh so far afoot again for all the coin in thy father's exchequer. What a plague mean ye to colt me thus?

Prince. Thou liest: thou art not colted; thou art uncolted.   45

Fal. I prithee, good Prince Hal, help me to my horse, good king's son.

Prince. Out, you rogue! shall I be your ostler?

Fal. Go, hang thyself in thine own heir apparent garters! If I be ta'en I'll peach for this. An I have not ballads made on you all, and sung to filthy tunes, let a cup of sack be my poison: when a jest is so forward, and afoot too! I hate it. 53

Enter GADSHILL.

Gads. Stand.

Fal. So I do, against my will.

Poins. O! 'tis our setter: I know his voice.

Enter BARDOLPH *and* PETO.

Bard. What news?   57

Gads. Case ye, case ye; on with your vizards: there's money of the king's coming down the hill; 'tis going to the king's exchequer.   60

Fal. You lie, you rogue; 'tis going to the king's tavern.

Gads. There's enough to make us all.

Fal. To be hanged.   64

Prince. Sirs, you four shall front them in th narrow lane; Ned Poins and I will walk lowe if they 'scape from your encounter then the light on us.   ·

Peto. How many be there of them?

Gads. Some eight or ten.

Fal. 'Zounds! will they not rob us?

Prince. What! a coward, Sir John Paunch

Fal. Indeed, I am not John of Gaunt, you grandfather; but yet no coward, Hal.

Prince. Well, we leave that to the proof.

Poins. Sirrah Jack, thy horse stands behin the hedge: when thou needst him there tho shalt find him. Farewell, and stand fast.

Fal. Now cannot I strike him if I should t hanged.   ·

Prince. [*Aside to* POINS.] Ned, where are ou disguises?

Poins. Here, hard by; stand close.

[*Exeunt* PRINCE *and* POIN

Fal. Now my masters, happy man be h dole, say I: every man to his business.   ·

Enter Travellers.

First Trav. Come, neighbour; the boy sha lead our horses down the hill; we'll walk afoo awhile, and ease our legs.   ·

Thieves. Stand!

Travellers. Jesu bless us!

Thieves. Strike; down with them; cut the vi lains' throats: ah! whoreson caterpillars! bacor fed knaves! they hate us youth: down wit them; fleece them.

Travellers. O! we are undone, both we an ours for ever.   ·

Fal. Hang ye, gorbellied knaves, are ye ur done? No, ye fat chuffs; I would your sto were here! On, bacons, on! What! ye knave young men must live. You are grand-juror are ye? We'll jure ye, i' faith.   1·

[*Here they rob and bind them. Exeun*

Re-enter the PRINCE *and* POINS.

Prince. The thieves have bound the true mer Now could thou and I rob the thieves and g merrily to London, it would be argument for week, laughter for a month, and a good jest fc ever.   1·

Poins. Stand close; I hear them coming.

Re-enter Thieves.

Fal. Come, my masters; let us share, an then to horse before day. An the Prince an Poins be not two arrant cowards, there's n equity stirring: there's no more valour in tha Poins than in a wild duck.   1·

Prince. Your money!

Poins. Villains!

[*As they are sharing, the* PRINCE *an* POINS *set upon them. They all ru away; and* FALSTAFF, *after a blow c two, runs away too, leaving the boot behind.*

Prince. Got with much ease. Now merril to horse: 1·

The thieves are scatter'd and possess'd with fea

o strongly that they dare not meet each other;
ach takes his fellow for an officer.
way, good Ned. Falstaff sweats to death
nd lards the lean earth as he walks along: 120
Vere 't not for laughing I should pity him.
Poins. How the rogue roar'd!   [*Exeunt.*

CENE III.—*Warkworth. A Room in the Castle.*

Enter HOTSPUR, *reading a letter.*

But for mine own part, my lord, I could be well
contented to be there, in respect of the love I bear
your house.

e could be contented; why is he not then? In
espect of the love he bears our house: he shows
 this he loves his own barn better than he
ves our house. Let me see some more.

The purpose you undertake is dangerous;—   8

Vhy, that's certain: 'tis dangerous to take a
old, to sleep, to drink; but I tell you, my lord
ol, out of this nettle, danger, we pluck this
ower, safety.   12

The purpose you undertake is dangerous; the
friends you have named uncertain; the time itself
unsorted; and your whole plot too light for the
counterpoise of so great an opposition.   16

ay you so, say you so? I say unto you again,
ou are a shallow cowardly hind, and you lie.
Vhat a lack-brain is this! By the Lord, our plot
 a good plot as ever was laid; our friends true
nd constant: a good plot, good friends, and full
f expectation; an excellent plot, very good
iends. What a frosty-spirited rogue is this!
Vhy, my Lord of York commends the plot and
ae general course of the action. 'Zounds! an
 were now by this rascal, I could brain him
ith his lady's fan. Is there not my father, my
ncle, and myself? Lord Edmund Mortimer, my
ord of York, and Owen Glendower? Is there
ot besides the Douglas? Have I not all their
tters to meet me in arms by the ninth of the
ext month, and are they not some of them set
orward already? What a pagan rascal is this!
a infidel! Ha! you shall see now in very sin-
erity of fear and cold heart, will he to the king
nd lay open all our proceedings. O! I could
ivide myself and go to buffets, for moving such
 dish of skim milk with so honourable an
ction. Hang him! let him tell the king; we
re prepared. I will set forward to-night.   40

Enter LADY PERCY.

Iow now, Kate! I must leave you within these
two hours.
Lady P. O, my good lord! why are you thus
alone?
or what offence have I this fortnight been
 banish'd woman from my Harry's bed?   44
ell me, sweet lord, what is 't that takes from
 thee
hy stomach, pleasure, and thy golden sleep?
Vhy dost thou bend thine eyes upon the earth,
nd start so often when thou sitt'st alone? 48
Vhy hast thou lost the fresh blood in thy
 cheeks,
nd given my treasures and my rights of thee

To thick-eyed musing and curst melancholy?
In thy faint slumbers I by thee have watch'd, 52
And heard thee murmur tales of iron wars,
Speak terms of manage to thy bounding steed,
Cry, 'Courage! to the field!' And thou hast
 talk'd
Of sallies and retires, of trenches, tents,   56
Of palisadoes, frontiers, parapets,
Of basilisks, of cannon, culverin,
Of prisoners' ransom, and of soldiers slain,
And all the currents of a heady fight.   60
Thy spirit within thee hath been so at war,
And thus hath so bestirr'd thee in thy sleep,
That beads of sweat have stood upon thy
 brow,
Like bubbles in a late-disturbed stream;   64
And in thy face strange motions have appear'd,
Such as we see when men restrain their breath
On some great sudden hest. O! what portents
 are these?   67
Some heavy business hath my lord in hand,
And I must know it, else he loves me not.
Hot. What, ho!

Enter Servant.

                Is Gilliams with the packet gone?
Serv. He is, my lord, an hour ago.
Hot. Hath Butler brought those horses from
 the sheriff?   72
Serv. One horse, my lord, he brought even
 now.
Hot. What horse? a roan, a crop-ear, is it
 not?
Serv. It is, my lord.
Hot.   That roan shall be my throne.
Well, I will back him straight: O, *Esperance!*
Bid Butler lead him forth into the park.   77
                                [*Exit* Servant.
Lady P. But hear you, my lord.
Hot. What sayst thou, my lady?
Lady P. What is it carries you away?   80
Hot. Why, my horse, my love, my horse.
Lady P. Out, you mad-headed ape!
A weasel hath not such a deal of spleen
As you are toss'd with. In faith,   84
I'll know your business, Harry, that I will.
I fear my brother Mortimer doth stir
About his title, and hath sent for you
To line his enterprise. But if you go—   88
Hot. So far afoot, I shall be weary, love.
Lady P. Come, come, you paraquito, answer
 me
Directly unto this question that I ask.
In faith, I'll break thy little finger, Harry,   92
An if thou wilt not tell me all things true.
Hot. Away,
Away, you trifler! Love! I love thee not,
I care not for thee, Kate: this is no world   96
To play with mammets and to tilt with lips:
We must have bloody noses and crack'd crowns,
And pass them current too. God's me, my
 horse!
What sayst thou, Kate? what wouldst thou
 have with me?   100
Lady P. Do you not love me? do you not,
 indeed?

Well, do not, then; for since you love me not,
I will not love myself. Do you not love me?
Nay, tell me if you speak in jest or no.   104
 Hot. Come, wilt thou see me ride?
And when I am o' horseback, I will swear
I love thee infinitely. But hark you, Kate;
I must not have you henceforth question me   108
Whither I go, nor aught whereabout.
Whither I must, I must; and, to conclude,
This evening must I leave you, gentle Kate.
I know you wise; but yet no further wise   112
Than Harry Percy's wife: constant you are,
But yet a woman: and for secrecy,
No lady closer; for I well believe
Thou wilt not utter what thou dost not know;
And so far will I trust thee, gentle Kate.   117
 Lady P. How! so far?
 Hot. Not an inch further. But, hark you,
Kate;
Whither I go, thither shall you go too;   120
To-day will I set forth, to-morrow you.
Will this content you, Kate?
 Lady P.   It must, of force.
                                [Exeunt.

SCENE IV.—*Eastcheap. A Room in the Boar's
         Head Tavern.*

Enter the PRINCE *and* POINS.

 Prince. Ned, prithee, come out of that fat
room, and lend me thy hand to laugh a little.
 Poins. Where hast been, Hal?   3
 Prince. With three or four loggerheads a-
mongst three or four score hogsheads. I have
sounded the very base string of humility. Sirrah, I am sworn brother to a leash of drawers,
and can call them all by their christen names,
as Tom, Dick, and Francis. They take it already
upon their salvation, that though I be but Prince
of Wales, yet I am the king of courtesy; and tell
me flatly I am no proud Jack, like Falstaff, but
a Corinthian, a lad of mettle, a good boy,—by
the Lord, so they call me,—and when I am king
of England, I shall command all the good lads
in Eastcheap. They call drinking deep, dyeing
scarlet; and when you breathe in your watering,
they cry 'hem!' and bid you play it off. To
conclude, I am so good a proficient in one
quarter of an hour, that I can drink with any
tinker in his own language during my life. I
tell thee, Ned, thou hast lost much honour that
thou wert not with me in this action. But, sweet
Ned,—to sweeten which name of Ned, I give thee
this pennyworth of sugar, clapped even now into
my hand by an underskinker, one that never
spake other English in his life than—'Eight
shillings and sixpence,' and—'You are welcome,'
with this shrill addition,—'Anon, anon, sir!
Score a pint of bastard in the Half-moon,' or
so. But, Ned, to drive away the time till Falstaff
come, I prithee do thou stand in some by-room,
while I question my puny drawer to what end
he gave me the sugar; and do thou never leave
calling 'Francis!' that his tale to me may be
nothing but 'Anon.' Step aside, and I'll show
thee a precedent.   37

 Poins. Francis!
 Prince. Thou art perfect.
 Poins. Francis!   [*Exit* POIN⟨S⟩

Enter FRANCIS.

 Fran. Anon, anon, sir. Look down into th⟨e⟩
Pomgarnet, Ralph.
 Prince. Come hither, Francis.
 Fran. My lord.
 Prince. How long hast thou to serve, Francis⟨?⟩
 Fran. Forsooth, five years, and as much as to—
 Poins. [*Within.*] Francis!
 Fran. Anon, anon, sir.   4⟨
 Prince. Five years! by'r lady a long lease f⟨or⟩
the clinking of pewter. But, Francis, dare⟨st⟩
thou be so valiant as to play the coward wit⟨h⟩
thy indenture and show it a fair pair of hee⟨ls⟩
and run from it?   5⟨
 Fran. O Lord, sir! I'll be sworn upon all th⟨e⟩
books in England, I could find in my heart—
 Poins. [*Within.*] Francis!   5⟨
 Fran. Anon, sir.
 Prince. How old art thou, Francis?
 Fran. Let me see—about Michaelmas next
shall be—   6⟨
 Poins. [*Within.*] Francis!
 Fran. Anon, sir. Pray you, stay a little, m⟨y⟩
lord.
 Prince. Nay, but hark you, Francis. For th⟨e⟩
sugar thou gavest me, 'twas a pennyworth⟨,⟩
was't not?
 Fran. O Lord, sir! I would it had been tw⟨o⟩
 Prince. I will give thee for it a thousan⟨d⟩
pound: ask me when thou wilt and thou sha⟨lt⟩
have it.
 Poins. [*Within.*] Francis!
 Fran. Anon, anon.   7⟨
 Prince. Anon, Francis? No, Francis; b⟨ut⟩
to-morrow, Francis; or, Francis, o' Thurs⟨-⟩
day; or, indeed, Francis, when thou wilt. Bu⟨t⟩
Francis!
 Fran. My lord?
 Prince. Wilt thou rob this leathern-jerki⟨n,⟩
crystal-button, knot-pated, agate-ring, puke⟨-⟩
stocking, caddis-garter, smooth-tongue, Spanish⟨-⟩
pouch,—   8⟨
 Fran. O Lord, sir, who do you mean?
 Prince. Why then, your brown bastard i⟨s⟩
your only drink; for, look you, Francis, you⟨r⟩
white canvas doublet will sully. In Barbary, si⟨r,⟩
it cannot come to so much.
 Fran. What, sir?
 Poins. [*Within.*] Francis!   8⟨
 Prince. Away, you rogue! Dost thou n⟨ot⟩
hear them call?
   [*Here they both call him; the* Drawer *stand⟨s⟩
       amazed, not knowing which way to g⟨o.⟩*

Enter VINTNER.

 Vint. What! standest thou still, and heares⟨t⟩
such a calling? Look to the guests withi⟨n.⟩
[*Exit* FRANCIS.] My lord, old Sir John, wit⟨h⟩
half a dozen more, are at the door: shall I le⟨t⟩
them in?
 Prince. Let them alone awhile, and the⟨n⟩
open the door. [*Exit* VINTNER.] Poins!   9⟨

Re-enter POINS.

Poins. Anon, anon, sir.

Prince. Sirrah, Falstaff and the rest of the ieves are at the door: shall we be merry? 100

Poins. As merry as crickets, my lad. But rk ye; what cunning match have you made th this jest of the drawer? come, what's the ue? 104

Prince. I am now of all humours that have ow'd themselves humours since the old days goodman Adam to the pupil age of this sent twelve o'clock at midnight. [FRANCIS sses the stage, with wine.] What's o'clock, ancis? 110

Fran. Anon, anon, sir. [*Exit.*

Prince. That ever this fellow should have ver words than a parrot, and yet the son of a man! His industry is up-stairs and down-irs; his eloquence the parcel of a reckoning. m not yet of Percy's mind, the Hotspur of the orth; he that kills me some six or seven dozen Scots at a breakfast, washes his hands, and s to his wife, 'Fie upon this quiet life! I nt work.' 'O my sweet Harry,' says she, 'how ny hast thou killed to-day?' 'Give my roan rse a drench,' says he, and answers, 'Some rteen,' an hour after, 'a trifle, a trifle.' I thee call in Falstaff: I'll play Percy, and that mned brawn shall play Dame Mortimer his fe. 'Rivo!' says the drunkard. Call in ribs, l in tallow. 127

ter FALSTAFF, GADSHILL, BARDOLPH, PETO, *and* FRANCIS.

Poins. Welcome, Jack:where hast thou been?

Fal. A plague of all cowards, I say, and a ngeance too! marry, and amen! Give me a p of sack, boy. Ere I lead this life long, I sew nether-stocks and mend them and foot em too. A plague of all cowards! Give me a p of sack, rogue.—Is there no virtue extant? [*He drinks.*

Prince. Didst thou never see Titan kiss a dish butter—pitiful-hearted Titan, that melted at e sweet tale of the sun? if thou didst then hold that compound. 138

Fal. You rogue, here's lime in this sack too: ere is nothing but roguery to be found in llanous man: yet a coward is worse than a cup sack with lime in it, a villanous coward! Go y ways, old Jack; die when thou wilt. If man-od, good manhood, be not forgot upon the ce of the earth, then am I a shotten herring. ere live not three good men unhanged in agland, and one of them is fat and grows old: od help the while! a bad world, I say. I would were a weaver; I could sing psalms or any-ing. A plague of all cowards, I say still.

Prince. How now, wool-sack! what mutter bu? 152

Fal. A king's son! If I do not beat thee out thy kingdom with a dagger of lath, and drive l thy subjects afore thee like a flock of wild ese, I'll never wear hair on my face more. bu Prince of Wales! 157

Prince. Why, you whoreson round man, what's the matter?

Fal. Are you not a coward? answer me to that; and Poins there? 161

Poins. 'Zounds! ye fat paunch, an ye call me coward, I'll stab thee.

Fal. I call thee coward! I'll see thee damned ere I call thee coward; but I would give a thousand pound I could run as fast as thou canst. You are straight enough in the shoulders; you care not who sees your back: call you that backing of your friends? A plague upon such backing! give me them that will face me. Give me a cup of sack: I am a rogue if I drunk to-day. 172

Prince. O villain! thy lips are scarce wiped since thou drunkest last.

Fal. All's one for that. [*He drinks.*] A plague of all cowards, still say I. 176

Prince. What's the matter?

Fal. What's the matter? there be four of us here have ta'en a thousand pound this day morning. 180

Prince. Where is it, Jack? where is it?

Fal. Where is it! taken from us it is: a hundred upon poor four of us.

Prince. What, a hundred, man? 184

Fal. I am a rogue, if I were not at half-sword with a dozen of them two hours together. I have 'scap'd by miracle. I am eight times thrust through the doublet, four through the hose; my buckler cut through and through; my sword hacked like a hand-saw: *ecce signum!* I never dealt better since I was a man: all would not do. A plague of all cowards! Let them speak: if they speak more or less than truth, they are villains and the sons of darkness.

Prince. Speak, sirs; how was it?

Gads. We four set upon some dozen,— 196

Fal. Sixteen, at least, my lord.

Gads. And bound them.

Peto. No, no, they were not bound.

Fal. You rogue, they were bound, every man of them; or I am a Jew else, an Ebrew Jew.

Gads. As we were sharing, some six or seven fresh men set upon us,— 204

Fal. And unbound the rest, and then come in the other.

Prince. What, fought ye with them all?

Fal. All! I know not what ye call all; but if I fought not with fifty of them, I am a bunch of radish: if there were not two or three and fifty upon poor old Jack, then am I no two-legged creature. 212

Prince. Pray God you have not murdered some of them.

Fal. Nay, that's past praying for: I have peppered two of them: two I am sure I have paid, two rogues in buckram suits. I tell thee what, Hal, if I tell thee a lie, spit in my face, call me horse. Thou knowest my old ward; here I lay, and thus I bore my point. Four rogues in buckram let drive at me,— 221

Prince. What, four? thou saidst but two even now.

Fal. Four, Hal; I told thee four.   224

Poins. Ay, ay, he said four.

Fal. These four came all a-front, and mainly thrust at me. I made me no more ado but took all their seven points in my target, thus.   228

Prince. Seven? why, there were but four even now.

Fal. In buckram.

Poins. Ay, four, in buckram suits.   232

Fal. Seven, by these hilts, or I am a villain else.

Prince. Prithee, let him alone; we shall have more anon.   236

Fal. Dost thou hear me, Hal?

Prince. Ay, and mark thee too, Jack.

Fal. Do so, for it is worth the listening to. These nine in buckram that I told thee of,— 240

Prince. So, two more already.

Fal. Their points being broken,—

Poins. Down fell their hose.

Fal. Began to give me ground; but I followed me close, came in foot and hand and with a thought seven of the eleven I paid.

Prince. O monstrous! eleven buckram men grown out of two.   248

Fal. But, as the devil would have it, three misbegotten knaves in Kendal-green came at my back and let drive at me; for it was so dark, Hal, that thou couldst not see thy hand. 252

Prince. These lies are like the father that begets them; gross as a mountain, open, palpable. Why, thou clay-brained guts, thou knotty-pated fool, thou whoreson, obscene, greasy tallowketch,—   257

Fal. What, art thou mad? art thou mad? is not the truth the truth?

Prince. Why, how couldst thou know these men in Kendal-green, when it was so dark thou couldst not see thy hand? come, tell us your reason: what sayest thou to this?   263

Poins. Come, your reason, Jack, your reason.

Fal. What, upon compulsion? 'Zounds! an I were at the strappado, or all the racks in the world, I would not tell you on compulsion. Give you a reason on compulsion! if reasons were as plenty as blackberries I would give no man a reason upon compulsion, I.   270

Prince. I'll be no longer guilty of this sin: this sanguine coward, this bed-presser, this horseback-breaker, this huge hill of flesh;— 273

Fal. 'Sblood, you starveling, you elf-skin, you dried neat's-tongue, you bull's pizzle, you stockfish! O! for breath to utter what is like thee; you tailor's yard, you sheath, you bow-case, you vile standing-tuck;—   278

Prince. Well, breathe awhile, and then to it again; and when thou hast tired thyself in base comparisons, hear me speak but this.   281

Poins. Mark, Jack.

Prince. We two saw you four set on four and you bound them, and were masters of their wealth. Mark now, how a plain tale shall put you down. Then did we two set on you four, and, with a word, out-faced you from your prize, and have it; yea, and can show it you here in the house. And, Falstaff, you carried your guts away

as nimbly, with as quick dexterity, and roar for mercy, and still ran and roared, as ever heard bull-calf. What a slave art thou, to ha thy sword as thou hast done, and then say was in fight! What trick, what device, wh starting-hole canst thou now find out to hi thee from this open and apparent shame?   2

Poins. Come, let's hear, Jack; what tri hast thou now?

Fal. By the Lord, I knew ye as well as that made ye. Why, hear you, my masters: w it for me to kill the heir-apparent? Should I tu upon the true prince? Why, thou knowest I a as valiant as Hercules; but beware instinct; t lion will not touch the true prince. Instinct a great matter, I was a coward on instinct. shall think the better of myself and thee duri my life; I for a valiant lion, and thou for a tr prince. But, by the Lord, lads, I am glad y have the money. Hostess, clap to the door watch to-night, pray to-morrow. Gallants, lac boys, hearts of gold, all the titles of good fello ship come to you! What! shall we be merr shall we have a play extempore?   3

Prince. Content; and the argument shall thy running away.

Fal. Ah! no more of that, Hal, an thou love me!   3

Enter MISTRESS QUICKLY.

Quick. O Jesu! my lord the prince!

Prince. How now, my lady the hostess! wh sayest thou to me?   3

Quick. Marry, my lord, there is a noblema of the court at door would speak with you: says he comes from your father.

Prince. Give him as much as will make him royal man, and send him back again to my moth

Fal. What manner of man is he?   3

Quick. An old man.

Fal. What doth gravity out of his bed midnight? Shall I give him his answer?

Prince. Prithee, do, Jack.

Fal. Faith, and I'll send him packing. [*Ex*

Prince. Now, sirs: by'r lady, you fought fai so did you, Peto; so did you, Bardolph: you a lions too, you ran away upon instinct, you w not touch the true prince; no, fie!

Bard. Faith, I ran when I saw others run. 3

Prince. Faith, tell me now in earnest, ho came Falstaff's sword so hacked?

Peto. Why, he hacked it with his dagger, an said he would swear truth out of England b he would make you believe it was done in figh and persuaded us to do the like.   3

Bard. Yea, and to tickle our noses wi spear-grass to make them bleed, and then to b slubber our garments with it and swear was the blood of true men. I did that I did n this seven year before; I blushed to hear h monstrous devices.   34

Prince. O villain! thou stolest a cup of sac eighteen years ago, and wert taken with th manner, and ever since thou hast blushed e tempore. Thou hadst fire and sword on thy sid and yet thou rannest away. What instinct hadst thou for it?

Bard. [*Pointing to his face.*] My lord, do you see these meteors? do you behold these exhalations?					357

Prince. I do.

Bard. What think you they portend?

Prince. Hot livers and cold purses.					360

Bard. Choler, my lord, if rightly taken.

Prince. No, if rightly taken, halter.—

Re-enter FALSTAFF.

Here comes lean Jack, here comes bare-bone.—How now, my sweet creature of bombast! How long is 't ago, Jack, since thou sawest thine own knee?					366

Fal. My own knee! when I was about thy years, Hal, I was not an eagle's talon in the waist; I could have crept into any alderman's thumb-ring. A plague of sighing and grief! it blows a man up like a bladder. There 's villanous news abroad: here was Sir John Bracy from your father: you must to the court in the morning. That same mad fellow of the north, Percy, and he of Wales, that gave Amaimon the bastinado and made Lucifer cuckold, and swore the devil his true liegeman upon the cross of a Welsh hook—what a plague call you him?					378

Poins. Owen Glendower.

Fal. Owen, Owen, the same; and his son-in-law Mortimer and old Northumberland; and that sprightly Scot of Scots, Douglas, that runs o' horseback up a hill perpendicular.

Prince. He that rides at high speed and with his pistol kills a sparrow flying.					385

Fal. You have hit it.

Prince. So did he never the sparrow.

Fal. Well, that rascal hath good mettle in him; he will not run.					389

Prince. Why, what a rascal art thou then to praise him so for running!

Fal. O' horseback, ye cuckoo! but, afoot he will not budge a foot.					393

Prince. Yes, Jack, upon instinct.

Fal. I grant ye, upon instinct. Well, he is there too, and one Mordake, and a thousand blue-caps more. Worcester is stolen away to-night; thy father's beard is turned white with the news: you may buy land now as cheap as stinking mackerel.					400

Prince. Why then, it is like, if there come a hot June and this civil buffeting hold, we shall buy maidenheads as they buy hob-nails, by the hundreds.					404

Fal. By the mass, lad, thou sayest true; it is like we shall have good trading that way. But tell me, Hal, art thou not horribly afeard? thou being heir apparent, could the world pick thee out three such enemies again as that fiend Douglas, that spirit Percy, and that devil Glendower? Art thou not horribly afraid? doth not thy blood thrill at it?					412

Prince. Not a whit, i' faith; I lack some of thy instinct.

Fal. Well, thou wilt be horribly chid to-morrow when thou comest to thy father: if thou love me, practise an answer.					417

Prince. Do thou stand for my father, and examine me upon the particulars of my life.

Fal. Shall I? content: this chair shall be my state, this dagger my sceptre, and this cushion my crown.					422

Prince. Thy state is taken for a joint-stool, thy golden sceptre for a leaden dagger, and thy precious rich crown for a pitiful bald crown!					425

Fal. Well, an the fire of grace be not quite out of thee, now shalt thou be moved. Give me a cup of sack to make mine eyes look red, that it may be thought I have wept; for I must speak in passion, and I will do it in King Cambyses' vein.					[*Drinks.*

Prince. Well, here is my leg. [*Makes a bow.*

Fal. And here is my speech. Stand aside, nobility.					434

Quick. O Jesu! This is excellent sport, i' faith!

Fal. Weep not, sweet queen, for trickling tears are vain.					436

Quick. O, the father! how he holds his countenance.

Fal. For God's sake, lords, convey my tristful queen,
For tears do stop the flood-gates of her eyes.					440

Quick. O Jesu! he doth it as like one of these harlotry players as ever I see!

Fal. Peace, good pint-pot! peace, good tickle-brain. Harry, I do not only marvel where thou spendest thy time, but also how thou art accompanied: for though the camomile, the more it is trodden on the faster it grows, yet youth, the more it is wasted the sooner it wears. That thou art my son, I have partly thy mother's word, partly my own opinion; but chiefly, a villanous trick of thine eye and a foolish hanging of thy nether lip, that doth warrant me. If then thou be son to me, here lies the point; why, being son to me, art thou so pointed at? Shall the blessed sun of heaven prove a micher and eat blackberries? a question not to be asked. Shall the son of England prove a thief and take purses? a question to be asked. There is a thing, Harry, which thou hast often heard of, and it is known to many in our land by the name of pitch: this pitch, as ancient writers do report, doth defile; so doth the company thou keepest; for, Harry, now I do not speak to thee in drink, but in tears, not in pleasure but in passion, not in words only, but in woes also. And yet there is a virtuous man whom I have often noted in thy company, but I know not his name.					467

Prince. What manner of man, an it like your majesty?

Fal. A goodly portly man, i' faith, and a corpulent; of a cheerful look, a pleasing eye, and a most noble carriage; and, as I think, his age some fifty, or by'r lady, inclining to threescore; and now I remember me, his name is Falstaff: if that man should be lewdly given, he deceiveth me; for, Harry, I see virtue in his looks. If then the tree may be known by the fruit, as the fruit by the tree, then, peremptorily I speak it, there is virtue in that Falstaff: him keep with, the rest

banish. And tell me now, thou naughty varlet,
tell me, where hast thou been this month?

Prince. Dost thou speak like a king? Do
thou stand for me, and I'll play my father. 483

Fal. Depose me? if thou dost it half so
gravely, so majestically, both in word and
matter, hang me up by the heels for a rabbit-
sucker or a poulter's hare.

Prince. Well, here I am set.   488

Fal. And here I stand. Judge, my masters.

Prince. Now, Harry! whence come you?

Fal. My noble lord, from Eastcheap.

Prince. The complaints I hear of thee are
grievous.   493

Fal. 'Sblood, my lord, they are false: nay,
I'll tickle ye for a young prince, i' faith.

Prince. Swearest thou, ungracious boy? henceforth ne'er look on me. Thou art violently carried away from grace: there is a devil haunts
thee in the likeness of a fat old man; a tun of
man is thy companion. Why dost thou converse with that trunk of humours, that bolting-
hutch of beastliness, that swoln parcel of dropsies,
that huge bombard of sack, that stuffed cloak-
bag of guts, that roasted Manningtree ox with
the pudding in his belly, that reverend vice, that
grey iniquity, that father ruffian, that vanity in
years? Wherein is he good but to taste sack and
drink it? wherein neat and cleanly but to carve
a capon and eat it? wherein cunning but in
craft? wherein crafty but in villany? wherein
villanous but in all things? wherein worthy but
in nothing?   512

Fal. I would your Grace would take me with
you: whom means your Grace?

Prince. That villanous abominable misleader
of youth, Falstaff, that old white-bearded Satan.

Fal. My lord, the man I know.   517

Prince. I know thou dost.

Fal. But to say I know more harm in him
than in myself were to say more than I know.
That he is old, the more the pity, his white
hairs do witness it; but that he is, saving your
reverence, a whoremaster, that I utterly deny.
If sack and sugar be a fault, God help the
wicked! If to be old and merry be a sin, then
many an old host that I know is damned: if to
be fat be to be hated, then Pharaoh's lean kine
are to be loved. No, my good lord; banish Peto,
banish Bardolph, banish Poins; but for sweet
Jack Falstaff, kind Jack Falstaff, true Jack Falstaff, valiant Jack Falstaff, and therefore more
valiant, being, as he is, old Jack Falstaff, banish
not him thy Harry's company: banish not him
thy Harry's company: banish plump Jack, and
banish all the world.   535

Prince. I do, I will.   [*A knocking heard.*

[*Exeunt* MISTRESS QUICKLY, FRANCIS, *and*
BARDOLPH.

Re-enter BARDOLPH, *running.*

Bard. O! my lord, my lord, the sheriff with a
most monstrous watch is at the door.

Fal. Out, ye rogue! Play out the play: I
have much to say in the behalf of that Falstaff.

Re-enter MISTRESS QUICKLY.

Quick. O Jesu! my lord, my lord!   541

Prince. Heigh, heigh! the devil rides upon a
fiddle-stick: what's the matter?

Quick. The sheriff and all the watch are at
the door: they are come to search the house.
Shall I let them in?   546

Fal. Dost thou hear, Hal? never call a true
piece of gold a counterfeit: thou art essentially
mad without seeming so.   549

Prince. And thou a natural coward without
instinct.

Fal. I deny your major. If you will deny the
sheriff, so; if not, let him enter: if I become not
a cart as well as another man, a plague on my
bringing up! I hope I shall as soon be strangled
with a halter as another.   556

Prince. Go, hide thee behind the arras: the
rest walk up above. Now, my masters, for a
true face and good conscience.

Fal. Both which I have had; but their date
is out, and therefore I'll hide me.   561

[*Exeunt all but the* PRINCE *and* PETO.

Prince. Call in the sheriff.

Enter Sheriff *and* Carrier.

Now, master sheriff, what's your will with me?

Sher. First, pardon me, my lord. A hue and
cry   564
Hath follow'd certain men unto this house.

Prince. What men?

Sher. One of them is well known, my gracious
lord,
A gross fat man.

Car.   As fat as butter.   568

Prince. The man, I do assure you, is not here
For I myself at this time have employ'd him.
And, sheriff, I will engage my word to thee,
That I will, by to-morrow dinner-time,   572
Send him to answer thee, or any man,
For anything he shall be charg'd withal:
And so let me entreat you leave the house.

Sher. I will, my lord. There are two gentle
men   57
Have in this robbery lost three hundred marks.

Prince. It may be so: if he have robb'd these
men,
He shall be answerable; and so farewell.

Sher. Good night, my noble lord.   58

Prince. I think it is good morrow, is it not

Sher. Indeed, my lord, I think it be two
o'clock.   [*Exeunt* Sheriff *and* Carrier

Prince. This oily rascal is known as well a
Paul's.
Go, call him forth.   58

Peto. Falstaff! fast asleep behind the arras
and snorting like a horse.

Prince. Hark, how hard he fetches breath
Search his pockets. [*He searcheth his pockets
and findeth certain papers.*] What hast thou
found?   59

Peto. Nothing but papers, my lord.

Prince. Let's see what they be: read them

Peto. Item, A capon	. . . . . .	2s. 2d.
Item, Sauce	. . . . .	4d.
Item, Sack, two gallons	. . . .	5s. 8d.
Item, Anchovies and sack after supper		2s. 6d.
Item, Bread		ob.

Prince. O monstrous! but one half-penny-worth of bread to this intolerable deal of sack! What there is else, keep close; we'll read it at more advantage. There let him sleep till day. I'll to the court in the morning. We must all to the wars, and thy place shall be honourable. I'll procure this fat rogue a charge of foot; and, I know, his death will be a march of twelvescore. The money shall be paid back again with advantage. Be with me betimes in the morning; and so good morrow, Peto.   608

Peto. Good morrow, good my lord. [*Exeunt.*

ACT III

SCENE I.—*Bangor. A Room in the Archdeacon's House.*

Enter HOTSPUR, WORCESTER, MORTIMER, *and* GLENDOWER.

Mort. These promises are fair, the parties sure,
And our induction full of prosperous hope.

Hot. Lord Mortimer, and cousin Glendower,
Will you sit down?   4
And uncle Worcester: a plague upon it!
I have forgot the map.

Glend.   No, here it is.
Sit, cousin Percy; sit, good cousin Hotspur;
For by that name as oft as Lancaster   8
Doth speak of you, his cheek looks pale and with
A rising sigh he wishes you in heaven.

Hot. And you in hell, as often as he hears
Owen Glendower spoke of.   12

Glend. I cannot blame him: at my nativity
The front of heaven was full of fiery shapes,
Of burning cressets; and at my birth
The frame and huge foundation of the earth 16
Shak'd like a coward.

Hot. Why, so it would have done at the same
season, if your mother's cat had but kittened,
though yourself had never been born.   20

Glend. I say the earth did shake when I was
born.

Hot. And I say the earth was not of my mind,
If you suppose as fearing you it shook.

Glend. The heavens were all on fire, the earth
did tremble.   24

Hot. O! then the earth shook to see the
heavens on fire,
And not in fear of your nativity.
Diseased nature oftentimes breaks forth
In strange eruptions; oft the teeming earth 28
Is with a kind of colic pinch'd and vex'd
By the imprisoning of unruly wind
Within her womb; which, for enlargement
striving,
Shakes the old beldam earth, and topples down

Steeples and moss-grown towers. At your birth   33
Our grandam earth, having this distemperature,
In passion shook.

Glend.   Cousin, of many men
I do not bear these crossings. Give me leave 36
To tell you once again that at my birth
The front of heaven was full of fiery shapes,
The goats ran from the mountains, and the herds
Were strangely clamorous to the frighted fields.
These signs have mark'd me extraordinary; 41
And all the courses of my life do show
I am not in the roll of common men.
Where is he living, clipp'd in with the sea 44
That chides the banks of England, Scotland, Wales,
Which calls me pupil, or hath read to me?
And bring him out that is but woman's son
Can trace me in the tedious ways of art   48
And hold me pace in deep experiments.

Hot. I think there's no man speaks better Welsh.
I'll to dinner.

Mort. Peace, cousin Percy! you will make
him mad.   52

Glend. I can call spirits from the vasty deep.

Hot. Why, so can I, or so can any man;
But will they come when you do call for them?

Glend. Why, I can teach thee, cousin, to command   56
The devil.

Hot. And I can teach thee, coz, to shame the devil
By telling truth: tell truth and shame the devil.
If thou have power to raise him, bring him hither,   60
And I'll be sworn I have power to shame him hence.
O! while you live, tell truth and shame the devil!

Mort. Come, come;
No more of this unprofitable chat.   64

Glend. Three times hath Henry Bolingbroke made head
Against my power; thrice from the banks of Wye
And sandy-bottom'd Severn have I sent him
Bootless home and weather-beaten back.   68

Hot. Home without boots, and in foul weather too!
How 'scapes he agues, in the devil's name?

Glend. Come, here's the map: shall we divide our right
According to our threefold order ta'en?   72

Mort. The archdeacon hath divided it
Into three limits very equally.
England, from Trent and Severn hitherto,
By south and east, is to my part assign'd: 76
All westward, Wales beyond the Severn shore,
And all the fertile land within that bound,
To Owen Glendower: and, dear coz, to you
The remnant northward, lying off from Trent. 80
And our indentures tripartite are drawn,
Which being sealed interchangeably,
A business that this night may execute,
To-morrow, cousin Percy, you and I   84

And my good Lord of Worcester will set forth
To meet your father and the Scottish power,
As is appointed us, at Shrewsbury.
My father Glendower is not ready yet,   88
Nor shall we need his help these fourteen days.
[*To* GLENDOWER.] Within that space you may
    have drawn togefher
Your tenants, friends, and neighbouring gentle-
    men.
  Glend. A shorter time shall send me to you,
    lords;   92
And in my conduct shall your ladies come,
From whom you now must steal and take no
    leave;
For there will be a world of water shed
Upon the parting of your wives and you.   96
  Hot. Methinks my moiety, north from Bur-
    ton here,
In quantity equals not one of yours:
See how this river comes me cranking in,
And cuts me from the best of all my land   100
A huge half-moon, a monstrous cantle out.
I'll have the current in this place damm'd up,
And here the smug and silver Trent shall run
In a new channel, fair and evenly;   104
It shall not wind with such a deep indent,
To rob me of so rich a bottom here.
  Glend. Not wind! it shall, it must; you see
    it doth.
  Mort. Yea, but   108
Mark how he bears his course, and runs me up
With like advantage on the other side;
Gelding the opposed continent as much,
As on the other side it takes from you.   112
  Wor. Yea, but a little charge will trench him
    here,
And on this north side win this cape of land;
And then he runs straight and even.
  Hot. I'll have it so; a little charge will do it.
  Glend. I will not have it alter'd.
  Hot.   Will not you?   117
  Glend. No, nor you shall not.
  Hot.   Who shall say me nay?
  Glend. Why, that will I.
  Hot.   Let me not understand you then:
Speak it in Welsh.   120
  Glend. I can speak English, lord, as well as
    you,
For I was train'd up in the English court;
Where, being but young, I framed to the harp
Many an English ditty lovely well,   124
And gave the tongue an helpful ornament;
A virtue that was never seen in you.
  Hot. Marry, and I'm glad of it with all my
    heart.
I had rather be a kitten, and cry mew   128
Than one of these same metre ballad-mongers;
I had rather hear a brazen canstick turn'd,
Or a dry wheel grate on the axle-tree;
And that would set my teeth nothing on edge,
Nothing so much as mincing poetry: 133
'Tis like the forc'd gait of a shuffling nag.
  Glend. Come, you shall have Trent turn'd.
  Hot. I do not care: I'll give thrice so much
    land   136
To any well-deserving friend;

But in the way of bargain, mark you me,
I'll cavil on the ninth part of a hair.
Are the indentures drawn? shall we be gone
  Glend. The moon shines fair, you may awa
    by night: 14
I'll haste the writer and withal
Break with your wives of your departure hence
I am afraid my daughter will run mad,   14
So much she doteth on her Mortimer.   [*Exi*
  Mort. Fie, cousin Percy! how you cross m
    father!
  Hot. I cannot choose: sometimes he anger
    me
With telling me of the moldwarp and the an
Of the dreamer Merlin and his prophecies,   14
And of a dragon, and a finless fish,
A clip-wing'd griffin, and a moulten raven,
A couching lion, and a ramping cat,   15
And such a deal of skimble-skamble stuff
As puts me from my faith. I'll tell thee wha
He held me last night at least nine hours
In reckoning up the several devils' names   15
That were his lackeys: I cried 'hum!' and 'wel
    go to.'
But mark'd him not a word. O! he's as tediou
As a tired horse, a railing wife;
Worse than a smoky house. I had rather liv
With cheese and garlick in a windmill, far,   16
Than feed on cates and have him talk to me
In any summer-house in Christendom.
  Mort. In faith, he is a worthy gentleman, 16
Exceedingly well read, and profited
In strange concealments, valiant as a lion
And wondrous affable, and as bountiful
As mines of India. Shall I tell you, cousin? 16
He holds your temper in a high respect,
And curbs himself even of his natural scope
When you do cross his humour; faith, he does
I warrant you, that man is not alive   17
Might so have tempted him as you have done
Without the taste of danger and reproof:
But do not use it oft, let me entreat you.
  Wor. In faith, my lord, you are too wilful
    blame;   17
And since your coming hither have done enoug
To put him quite beside his patience.
You must needs learn, lord, to amend this fault
Though sometimes it show greatness, courage
    blood,—   18
And that's the dearest grace it renders you,—
Yet oftentimes it doth present harsh rage,
Defect of manners, want of government,
Pride, haughtiness, opinion, and disdain: 18
The least of which haunting a nobleman
Loseth men's hearts and leaves behind a stai
Upon the beauty of all parts besides,
Beguiling them of commendation.   18
  Hot. Well, I am school'd; good manners b
    your speed!
Here come our wives, and let us take our leave

Re-enter GLENDOWER, *with the* Ladies.

  Mort. This is the deadly spite that angers me
My wife can speak no English, I no Welsh. 19
  Glend. My daughter weeps; she will not par
    with you:

She'll be a soldier too: she'll to the wars.

Mort. Good father, tell her that she and my
aunt Percy,

Shall follow in your conduct speedily.   196

[GLENDOWER *speaks to* LADY MORTIMER
*in Welsh, and she answers him in the
same.*

Glend. She's desperate here; a peevish self-
will'd harlotry, one that no persuasion can do
good upon. [*She speaks to* MORTIMER *in Welsh.*

Mort. I understand thy looks: that pretty
Welsh   200

Which thou pour'st down from these swelling
heavens

I am too perfect in; and, but for shame,

In such a parley would I answer thee.

[*She speaks again.*

I understand thy kisses and thou mine,   204

And that's a feeling disputation:

But I will never be a truant, love,

Till I have learn'd thy language; for thy tongue

Makes Welsh as sweet as ditties highly penn'd,

Sung by a fair queen in a summer's bower,   209

With ravishing division, to her lute.

Glend. Nay, if you melt, then will she run
mad.   [*She speaks again.*

Mort. O! I am ignorance itself in this.   212

Glend. She bids you

Upon the wanton rushes lay you down

And rest your gentle head upon her lap,

And she will sing the song that pleaseth you,

And on your eye-lids crown the god of sleep,   217

Charming your blood with pleasing heaviness,

Making such difference 'twixt wake and sleep

As is the difference between day and night   220

The hour before the heavenly-harness'd team

Begins his golden progress in the east.

Mort. With all my heart I'll sit and hear her
sing:

By that time will our book, I think, be drawn.

Glend. Do so;   225

And those musicians that shall play to you

Hang in the air a thousand leagues from hence,

And straight they shall be here: sit, and attend.   228

Hot. Come, Kate, thou art perfect in lying
down: come, quick, quick, that I may lay my
head in thy lap.

Lady P. Go, ye giddy goose.   232

[GLENDOWER *speaks some Welsh words,
and music is heard.*

Hot. Now I perceive the devil understands
Welsh;

And 'tis no marvel he is so humorous.

By'r lady, he's a good musician.

Lady P. Then should you be nothing but
musical for you are altogether governed by
humours. Lie still, ye thief, and hear the lady
sing in Welsh.

Hot. I had rather hear Lady, my brach, howl
in Irish.   240

Lady P. Wouldst thou have thy head broken?

Hot. No.

Lady P. Then be still.

Hot. Neither; 'tis a woman's fault.   244

Lady P. Now, God help thee!

Hot. To the Welsh lady's bed.

Lady P. What's that?

Hot. Peace! she sings.   248

[*A Welsh song sung by* LADY MORTIMER.

Hot. Come, Kate, I'll have your song too.

Lady P. Not mine, in good sooth.

Hot. Not yours, 'in good sooth!' Heart!
you swear like a comfit-maker's wife! Not you,
'in good sooth;' and, 'as true as I live;' and,
'as God shall mend me;' and, 'as sure as day:'
And giv'st such sarcenet surety for thy oaths,
As if thou never walk'dst further than Fins-
bury.   256

Swear me, Kate, like a lady as thou art,

A good mouth-filling oath; and leave 'in sooth,'

And such protest of pepper-gingerbread,

To velvet-guards and Sunday-citizens.   260

Come, sing.

Lady P.   I will not sing.

Hot. 'Tis the next way to turn tailor or be
red-breast teacher. An the indentures be drawn,
I'll away within these two hours; and so, come
in when ye will.   [*Exit.*

Glend. Come, come, Lord Mortimer; you are
as slow

As hot Lord Percy is on fire to go.   268

By this our book is drawn; we will but seal,

And then to horse immediately.

Mort. With all my heart.   [*Exeunt.*

SCENE II.—*London. A Room in the Palace.*

Enter KING HENRY, *the* PRINCE, *and* Lords.

K. Hen. Lords, give us leave; the Prince of
Wales and I

Must have some private conference: but be near
at hand,

For we shall presently have need of you.

[*Exeunt* Lords.

I know not whether God will have it so,   4

For some displeasing service I have done,

That, in his secret doom, out of my blood

He'll breed revengement and a scourge for me;

But thou dost in thy passages of life   8

Make me believe that thou art only mark'd

For the hot vengeance and the rod of heaven

To punish my mistreadings. Tell me else,

Could such inordinate and low desires,   12

Such poor, such bare, such lewd, such mean
attempts,

Such barren pleasures, rude society,

As thou art match'd withal and grafted to,

Accompany the greatness of thy blood   16

And hold their level with thy princely heart?

Prince. So please your majesty, I would I
could

Quit all offences with as clear excuse

As well as I am doubtless I can purge   20

Myself of many I am charg'd withal:

Yet such extenuation let me beg,

As, in reproof of many tales devis'd,

Which oft the ear of greatness needs must hear,

By smiling pick-thanks and base newsmongers,

I may, for some things true, wherein my youth

Hath faulty wander'd and irregular,

Find pardon on my true submission.   28

K. Hen. God pardon thee! yet let me wonder,
Harry,
At thy affections, which do hold a wing
Quite from the flight of all thy ancestors.
Thy place in council thou hast rudely lost, 32
Which by thy younger brother is supplied,
And art almost an alien to the hearts
Of all the court and princes of my blood.
The hope and expectation of thy time 36
Is ruin'd, and the soul of every man
Prophetically do forethink thy fall.
Had I so lavish of my presence been,
So common-hackney'd in the eyes of men, 40
So stale and cheap to vulgar company,
Opinion, that did help me to the crown,
Had still kept loyal to possession
And left me in reputeless banishment, 44
A fellow of no mark nor likelihood.
By being seldom seen, I could not stir,
But like a comet I was wonder'd at;
That men would tell their children, 'This is he;'
Others would say, 'Where? which is Boling-
broke?' 49
And then I stole all courtesy from heaven,
And dress'd myself in such humility
That I did pluck allegiance from men's hearts,
Loud shouts and salutations from their mouths,
Even in the presence of the crowned king.
Thus did I keep my person fresh and new;
My presence, like a robe pontifical, 56
Ne'er seen but wonder'd at: and so my state,
Seldom but sumptuous, showed like a feast,
And won by rareness such solemnity.
The skipping king, he ambled up and down 60
With shallow jesters and rash bavin wits,
Soon kindled and soon burnt; carded his state,
Mingled his royalty with capering fools,
Had his great name profaned with their scorns,
And gave his countenance, against his name, 65
To laugh at gibing boys and stand the push
Of every beardless vain comparative;
Grew a companion to the common streets, 68
Enfeoff'd himself to popularity;
That, being daily swallow'd by men's eyes,
They surfeited with honey and began
To loathe the taste of sweetness, whereof a little
More than a little is by much too much. 73
So, when he had occasion to be seen,
He was but as the cuckoo is in June,
Heard, not regarded; seen, but with such eyes
As, sick and blunted with community, 77
Afford no extraordinary gaze,
Such as is bent on sun-like majesty
When it shines seldom in admiring eyes; 80
But rather drows'd and hung their eyelids down,
Slept in his face, and render'd such aspect
As cloudy men use to their adversaries,
Being with his presence glutted, gorg'd, and
full. 84
And in that very line, Harry, stand'st thou;
For thou hast lost thy princely privilege
With vile participation: not an eye
But is aweary of thy common sight, 88
Save mine, which hath desir'd to see thee more;
Which now doth that I would not have it do,
Make blind itself with foolish tenderness.

Prince. I shall hereafter, my thrice graciou
lord,
Be more myself.
   K. Hen.   For all the world,
As thou art to this hour was Richard then
When I from France set foot at Ravenspurg
And even as I was then is Percy now.
Now, by my sceptre and my soul to boot,
He hath more worthy interest to the state
Than thou the shadow of succession;
For of no right, nor colour like to right,
He doth fill fields with harness in the realm,
Turns head against the lion's armed jaws,
And, being no more in debt to years than tho
Leads ancient lords and reverend bishops on
To bloody battles and to bruising arms.
What never-dying honour hath he got
Against renowned Douglas! whose high deed
Whose hot incursions and great name in arm
Holds from all soldiers chief majority,
And military title capital,
Through all the kingdoms that acknowledg
Christ.
Thrice hath this Hotspur, Mars in swathlin
clothes,
This infant warrior, in his enterprises
Discomfited great Douglas; ta'en him once,
Enlarged him and made a friend of him,
To fill the mouth of deep defiance up
And shake the peace and safety of our thror
And what say you to this? Percy, Northumbe
land,
The Archbishop's Grace of York, Dougla
Mortimer,
Capitulate against us and are up.
But wherefore do I tell these news to thee?
Why, Harry, do I tell thee of my foes,
Which art my near'st and dearest enemy?
Thou that art like enough, through vassal fea
Base inclination, and the start of spleen,
To fight against me under Percy's pay,
To dog his heels, and curtsy at his frowns,
To show how much thou art degenerate.
   Prince. Do not think so; you shall not fir
it so:
And God forgive them, that so much ha
sway'd
Your majesty's good thoughts away from m
I will redeem all this on Percy's head,
And in the closing of some glorious day
Be bold to tell you that I am your son;
When I will wear a garment all of blood
And stain my favours in a bloody mask,
Which, wash'd away, shall scour my shame wi
it:
And that shall be the day, whene'er it lights
That this same child of honour and renown
This gallant Hotspur, this all-praised knight,
And your unthought-of Harry chance to mee
For every honour sitting on his helm,—
Would they were multitudes, and on my hea
My shames redoubled!—for the time will con
That I shall make this northern youth exchan
His glorious deeds for my indignities.
Percy is but my factor, good my lord,
To engross up glorious deeds on my behalf;

And I will call him to so strict account
That he shall render every glory up,
Yea, even the slightest worship of his time,
Or I will tear the reckoning from his heart. 152
This, in the name of God, I promise here:
The which, if he be pleas'd I shall perform,
I do beseech your majesty may salve
The long-grown wounds of my intemperance:
If not, the end of life cancels all bands, 157
And I will die a hundred thousand deaths
Ere break the smallest parcel of this vow.
  K. Hen. A hundred thousand rebels die in
this: 160
Thou shalt have charge and sovereign trust
herein.

Enter SIR WALTER BLUNT.

How now, good Blunt! thy looks are full of
speed.
  Blunt. So hath the business that I come to
speak of.
Lord Mortimer of Scotland hath sent word 164
That Douglas and the English rebels met,
The eleventh of this month at Shrewsbury.
A mighty and a fearful head they are,—
If promises be kept on every hand,—   168
As ever offer'd foul play in a state.
  K. Hen. The Earl of Westmoreland set forth
to-day,
With him my son, Lord John of Lancaster;
For this advertisement is five days old.   172
On Wednesday next, Harry, you shall set for-
ward;
On Thursday we ourselves will march: our
meeting
Is Bridgenorth; and Harry, you shall march
Through Gloucestershire; by which account, 176
Our business valued, some twelve days hence
Our general forces at Bridgenorth shall meet.
Our hands are full of business: let's away;
Advantage feeds him fat while men delay. 180
                                        [*Exeunt.*

SCENE III.—*Eastcheap. A Room in the
Boar's Head Tavern.*

Enter FALSTAFF *and* BARDOLPH.

  Fal. Bardolph, am I not fallen away vilely
since this last action? do I not bate? do I not
dwindle? Why, my skin hangs about me like an
old lady's loose gown; I am withered like an old
apple-john. Well, I'll repent, and that suddenly,
while I am in some liking; I shall be out of heart
shortly, and then I shall have no strength to repent. An I have not forgotten what the inside
of a church is made of, I am a peppercorn, a
brewer's horse: the inside of a church! Company, villanous company, hath been the spoil
of me.   12
  Bard. Sir John, you are so fretful, you cannot live long.
  Fal. Why, there is it: come, sing me a bawdy
song; make me merry. I was as virtuously given
as a gentleman need to be; virtuous enough:
swore little; diced not above seven times a week;

went to a bawdy-house not above once in a
quarter—of an hour; paid money that I borrowed three or four times; lived well and in good
compass; and now I live out of all order, out of
all compass.
  Bard. Why, you are so fat, Sir John, that 23
you must needs be out of all compass, out of all
reasonable compass, Sir John.   26
  Fal. Do thou amend thy face, and I'll amend
my life: thou art our admiral, thou bearest the
lanthorn in the poop, but 'tis in the nose of thee:
thou art the Knight of the Burning Lamp.
  Bard. Why, Sir John, my face does you no
harm.   32
  Fal. No, I'll be sworn; I make as good use
of it as many a man doth of a Death's head, or
a *memento mori*: I never see thy face but I think
upon hell-fire and Dives that lived in purple;
for there he is in his robes, burning, burning. If
thou wert any way given to virtue, I would swear
by thy face; my oath should be, 'By this fire,
that's God's angel:' but thou art altogether
given over, and wert indeed, but for the light in
thy face, the son of utter darkness. When thou
rannest up Gadshill in the night to catch my
horse, if I did not think thou hadst been an
ignis fatuus or a ball of wildfire, there's no
purchase in money. O! thou art a perpetual
triumph, an everlasting bonfire-light. Thou hast
saved me a thousand marks in links and torches,
walking with thee in the night betwixt tavern
and tavern: but the sack that thou hast drunk
me would have bought me lights as good cheap
at the dearest chandler's in Europe. I have
maintained that salamander of yours with fire
any time this two-and-thirty years; God reward
me for it!   55
  Bard. 'Sblood, I would my face were in your
belly.
  Fal. God-a-mercy! so should I be sure to be
heart-burned.

Enter MISTRESS QUICKLY.

How now, Dame Partlet the hen! have you
inquired yet who picked my pocket?   61
  Quick. Why, Sir John, what do you think,
Sir John? Do you think I keep thieves in my
house? I have searched, I have inquired, so has
my husband, man by man, boy by boy, servant
by servant: the tithe of a hair was never lost in
my house before.   67
  Fal. You lie, hostess: Bardolph was shaved
and lost many a hair; and I'll be sworn my
pocket was picked. Go to, you are a woman; go.
  Quick. Who, I? No; I defy thee: God's light!
I was never called so in my own house before. 72
  Fal. Go to, I know you well enough.
  Quick. No, Sir John; you do not know me,
Sir John: I know you, Sir John: you owe me
money, Sir John, and now you pick a quarrel to
beguile me of it: I bought you a dozen of shirts
to your back.   78
  Fal. Dowlas, filthy dowlas: I have given
them away to bakers' wives, and they have
made bolters of them.   81
  Quick. Now, as I am true woman, holland of

eight shillings an ell. You owe money here besides, Sir John, for your diet and by-drinkings, and money lent you, four-and-twenty pound. 85

Fal. He had his part of it; let him pay.

Quick. He! alas! he is poor; he hath nothing.

Fal. How! poor? look upon his face; what call you rich? let them coin his nose, let them coin his cheeks. I'll not pay a denier. What! will you make a younker of me? shall I not take mine ease in mine inn but I shall have my pocket picked? I have lost a seal-ring of my grandfather's worth forty mark.

Quick. O Jesu! I have heard the prince tell him, I know not how oft, that that ring was copper.   97

Fal. How! the prince is a Jack, a sneak-cup; 'sblood! an he were here, I would cudgel him like a dog, if he would say so.   100

Enter the PRINCE *and* POINS *marching.* FALSTAFF *meets them, playing on his truncheon like a fife.*

Fal. How now, lad! is the wind in that door, i' faith? must we all march?

Bard. Yea, two and two, Newgate fashion.

Quick. My lord, I pray you, hear me.   104

Prince. What sayest thou, Mistress Quickly? How does thy husband? I love him well, he is an honest man.

Quick. Good my lord, hear me.   108

Fal. Prithee, let her alone, and list to me.

Prince. What sayest thou, Jack?

Fal. The other night I fell asleep here behind the arras and had my pocket picked: this house is turned bawdy-house; they pick pockets. 113

Prince. What didst thou lose, Jack?

Fal. Wilt thou believe me, Hal? three or four bonds of forty pound a-piece, and a seal-ring of my grandfather's.   117

Prince. A trifle; some eight-penny matter.

Quick. So I told him, my lord; and I said I heard your Grace say so: and, my lord, he speaks most vilely of you, like a foul-mouthed man as he is, and said he would cudgel you.   122

Prince. What! he did not?

Quick. There's neither faith, truth, nor womanhood in me else.   125

Fal. There's no more faith in thee than in a stewed prune; nor no more truth in thee than in a drawn fox; and for womanhood, Maid Marian may be the deputy's wife of the ward to thee. Go, you thing, go.

Quick. Say, what thing? what thing?

Fal. What thing! why, a thing to thank God on.   133

Quick. I am no thing to thank God on, I would thou shouldst know it; I am an honest man's wife; and setting thy knighthood aside, thou art a knave to call me so.   137

Fal. Setting thy womanhood aside, thou art a beast to say otherwise.

Quick. Say, what beast, thou knave thou? 140

Fal. What beast! why, an otter.

Prince. An otter, Sir John! why, an otter?

Fal. Why? she's neither fish nor flesh; a man knows not where to have her.   144

Quick. Thou art an unjust man in saying so: thou or any man knows where to have me, thou knave thou!

Prince. Thou sayest true, hostess; and he slanders thee most grossly.   149

Quick. So he doth you, my lord; and said this other day you ought him a thousand pound.

Prince. Sirrah! do I owe you a thousand pound?   153

Fal. A thousand pound, Hal! a million: thy love is worth a million; thou owest me thy love.

Quick. Nay, my lord, he called you Jack, and said he would cudgel you.   157

Fal. Did I, Bardolph?

Bard. Indeed, Sir John, you said so.

Fal. Yea; if he said my ring was copper. 160

Prince. I say 'tis copper: darest thou be as good as thy word now?

Fal. Why, Hal, thou knowest, as thou art but man, I dare; but as thou art prince, I fear thee as I fear the roaring of the lion's whelp. 165

Prince. And why not as the lion?

Fal. The king himself is to be feared as the lion: dost thou think I'll fear thee as I fear thy father? nay, an I do, I pray God my girdle break!   170

Prince. O! if it should, how would thy guts fall about thy knees. But, sirrah, there's no room for faith, truth, or honesty in this bosom of thine; it is all filled up with guts and midriff. Charge an honest woman with picking thy pocket! Why, thou whoreson, impudent, embossed rascal, if there were any thing in thy pocket but tavern reckonings, memorandums of bawdy-houses, and one poor pennyworth of sugar-candy to make thee long-winded; if thy pocket were enriched with any other injuries but these, I am a villain. And yet you will stand to it, you will not pocket up wrong. Art thou not ashamed?   183

Fal. Dost thou hear, Hal? thou knowest in the state of innocency Adam fell; and what should poor Jack Falstaff do in the days of villany? Thou seest I have more flesh than another man, and therefore more frailty. You confess then, you picked my pocket?   189

Prince. It appears so by the story.

Fal. Hostess, I forgive thee. Go make ready breakfast; love thy husband, look to thy servants, cherish thy guests: thou shalt find me tractable to any honest reason: thou seest I am pacified Still! Nay prithee, be gone. [*Exit* MISTRESS QUICKLY.] Now, Hal, to the news at court: for the robbery, lad, how is that answered?   19

Prince. O! my sweet beef, I must still be good angel to thee: the money is paid back again.

Fal. O! I do not like that paying back; 'tis a double labour.

Prince. I am good friends with my father and may do anything.

Fal. Rob me the exchequer the first thing thou dost, and do it with unwashed hands too.

Bard. Do, my lord.

Prince. I have procured thee, Jack, a charge of foot.   20

Fal. I would it had been of horse. Where shall I find one that can steal well? O! for

he thief, of the age of two-and-twenty, or there-
bouts; I am heinously unprovided. Well, God
be thanked for these rebels; they offend none
but the virtuous: I laud them, I praise them.

Prince. Bardolph!

Bard. My lord?   216

Prince. Go bear this letter to Lord John of
  Lancaster,
o my brother John; this to my Lord of Westmoreland.
Go, Poins, to horse, to horse! for thou and I
Have thirty miles to ride ere dinner-time.   220
ack, meet me to-morrow in the Temple-hall
t two o'clock in the afternoon:
here shalt thou know thy charge, and there
  receive
Money and order for their furniture.   224
he land is burning; Percy stands on high;
and either we or they must lower lie.

    [*Exeunt the* PRINCE, POINS, *and* BARDOLPH.

Fal. Rare words! brave world! Hostess, my
  breakfast; come!
O! I could wish this tavern were my drum. 228

                     [*Exit.*

ACT IV

SCENE I.—*The Rebel Camp near Shrewsbury.*

Enter HOTSPUR, WORCESTER, *and* DOUGLAS.

  Hot. Well said, my noble Scot: if speaking
  truth
In this fine age were not thought flattery,
Such attribution should the Douglas have,
As not a soldier of this season's stamp   4
Should go so general current through the world.
By God, I cannot flatter; do defy
The tongues of soothers; but a braver place
In my heart's love hath no man than yourself. 8
Nay, task me to my word; approve me, lord.

  Doug. Thou art the king of honour:
No man so potent breathes upon the ground
But I will beard him.

  Hot.   Do so, and 'tis well.   12

Enter a Messenger, *with letters.*

What letters hast thou there? [*To* DOUGLAS.]
  I can but thank you.

  Mess. These letters come from your father.

  Hot. Letters from him! why comes he not
  himself?

  Mess. He cannot come, my lord: he's grievous sick.   16

  Hot. 'Zounds! how has he the leisure to be
  sick
In such a justling time? Who leads his power?
Under whose government come they along?

  Mess. His letters bear his mind, not I, my
  lord.   20

  Wor. I prithee, tell me, doth he keep his bed?

  Mess. He did, my lord, four days ere I set
  forth;
And at the time of my departure thence
He was much fear'd by his physicians.   24

  Wor. I would the state of time had first been
  whole
Ere he by sickness had been visited:
His health was never better worth than now.

  Hot. Sick now! droop now! this sickness doth
  infect   28
The very life-blood of our enterprise;
'Tis catching hither, even to our camp.
He writes me here, that inward sickness——
And that his friends by deputation could not 32
So soon be drawn; nor did he think it meet
To lay so dangerous and dear a trust
On any soul remov'd but on his own.
Yet doth he give us bold advertisement,   36
That with our small conjunction we should on,
To see how fortune is dispos'd to us;
For, as he writes, there is no quailing now,
Because the king is certainly possess'd   40
Of all our purposes. What say you to it?

  Wor. Your father's sickness is a maim to us.

  Hot. A perilous gash, a very limb lopp'd off:
And yet, in faith, 'tis not; his present want 44
Seems more than we shall find it. Were it good
To set the exact wealth of all our states
All at one cast? to set so rich a main
On the nice hazard of one doubtful hour?   48
It were not good; for therein should we read
The very bottom and the soul of hope,
The very list, the very utmost bound
Of all our fortunes.

  Doug.   Faith, and so we should; 52
Where now remains a sweet reversion:
We may boldly spend upon the hope of what
Is to come in:
A comfort of retirement lives in this.   56

  Hot. A rendezvous, a home to fly unto,
If that the devil and mischance look big
Upon the maidenhead of our affairs.

  Wor. But yet, I would your father had been
  here.   60
The quality and hair of our attempt
Brooks no division. It will be thought
By some, that know not why he is away,
That wisdom, loyalty, and mere dislike   64
Of our proceedings, kept the earl from hence.
And think how such an apprehension
May turn the tide of fearful faction
And breed a kind of question in our cause;   68
For well you know we of the offering side
Must keep aloof from strict arbitrement,
And stop all sight-holes, every loop from
  whence
The eye of reason may pry in upon us: 72
This absence of your father's draws a curtain,
That shows the ignorant a kind of fear
Before not dreamt of.

  Hot.   You strain too far.
I rather of his absence make this use: 76
It lends a lustre and more great opinion,
A larger dare to our great enterprise,
Than if the earl were here; for men must think,
If we without his help, can make a head   80
To push against the kingdom, with his help
We shall o'erturn it topsy-turvy down.
Yet all goes well, yet all our joints are whole.

  Doug. As heart can think: there is not such
  a word   84
Spoke of in Scotland as this term of fear.

Enter SIR RICHARD VERNON.

Hot. My cousin Vernon! welcome, by my soul.

Ver. Pray God my news be worth a welcome, lord.
The Earl of Westmoreland, seven thousand strong,
Is marching hitherwards; with him Prince John.

Hot. No harm: what more?

Ver.   And further, I have learn'd,
The king himself in person is set forth,
Or hitherwards intended speedily,   92
With strong and mighty preparation.

Hot. He shall be welcome too. Where is his son,
The nimble-footed madcap Prince of Wales,
And his comrades, that daff'd the world aside, 96
And bid it pass?

Ver.   All furnish'd, all in arms,
All plum'd like estridges that wing the wind,
Baited like eagles having lately bath'd,
Glittering in golden coats, like images,   100
As full of spirit as the month of May,
And gorgeous as the sun at midsummer,
Wanton as youthful goats, wild as young bulls.
I saw young Harry, with his beaver on,   104
His cushes on his thighs, gallantly arm'd,
Rise from the ground like feather'd Mercury,
And vaulted with such ease into his seat,
As if an angel dropp'd down from the clouds,
To turn and wind a fiery Pegasus   109
And witch the world with noble horsemanship.

Hot. No more, no more: worse than the sun in March
This praise doth nourish agues. Let them come;
They come like sacrifices in their trim,   113
And to the fire-ey'd maid of smoky war
All hot and bleeding will we offer them:
The mailed Mars shall on his altar sit   116
Up to the ears in blood. I am on fire
To hear this rich reprisal is so nigh
And yet not ours. Come, let us me taste my horse,
Who is to bear me like a thunderbolt   120
Against the bosom of the Prince of Wales:
Harry to Harry shall, hot horse to horse,
Meet and ne'er part till one drop down a corse.
O! that Glendower were come.

Ver.   There is more news: 124
I learn'd in Worcester, as I rode along,
He cannot draw his power these fourteen days.

Doug. That's the worst tidings that I hear of yet.

Wor. Ay, by my faith, that bears a frosty sound.   128

Hot. What may the king's whole battle reach unto?

Ver. To thirty thousand.

Hot.   Forty let it be:
My father and Glendower being both away,
The powers of us may serve so great a day. 132
Come, let us take a muster speedily:
Doomsday is near; die all, die merrily.

Doug. Talk not of dying: I am out of fear
Of death or death's hand for this one half year.
                     [*Exeunt.*

SCENE II.—*A public Road near Coventry.*

Enter FALSTAFF *and* BARDOLPH.

Fal. Bardolph, get thee before to Coventry; fill me a bottle of sack: our soldiers shall march through: we'll to Sutton-Co'fil' to-night.

Bard. Will you give me money, captain? 4

Fal. Lay out, lay out.

Bard. This bottle makes an angel.

Fal. An if it do, take it for thy labour; and if it make twenty, take them all, I'll answer the coinage. Bid my Lieutenant Peto meet me at the town's end.   10

Bard. I will, captain: farewell.   [*Exit.*

Fal. If I be not ashamed of my soldiers, I am a soused gurnet. I have misused the king's press damnably. I have got, in exchange of a hundred and fifty soldiers, three hundred and odd pounds. I press me none but good householders, yeomen's sons; inquire me out contracted bachelors, such as had been asked twice on the banns; such a commodity of warm slaves, as had as lief hear the devil as a drum; such as fear the report of a caliver worse than a struck fowl or a hurt wild-duck. I pressed me none but such toasts-and-butter, with hearts in their bellies no bigger than pins' heads, and they have bought out their ser-vices; and now my whole charge consists of ancients, corporals, lieutenants, gentlemen of companies, slaves as ragged as Lazarus in the painted cloth, where the glutton's dogs licked his sores; and such as indeed were never soldiers, but discarded unjust serving-men, younger sons to younger brothers, revolted tapsters and ostlers trade-fallen, the cankers of a calm world and a long peace; ten times more dishonourable ragged than an old faced ancient: and such have I, to fill up the rooms of them that have bought out their services, that you would think that I had a hundred and fifty tattered prodigals, lately come from swine-keeping, from eating draff and husks. A mad fellow met me on the way and told me I had unloaded all the gibbets and pressed the dead bodies. No eye hath seen such scarecrows. I'll not march through Coventry with them, that's flat: nay, and the villains march wide be-twixt the legs, as if they had gyves on; for, in-deed I had the most of them out of prison. There's but a shirt and a half in all my com-pany; and the half shirt is two napkins tacked together and thrown over the shoulders like a herald's coat without sleeves; and the shirt, to say the truth, stolen from my host at Saint Alban's, or the red-nose inn-keeper of Daventry. But that's all one; they'll find linen enough on every hedge.   53

Enter the PRINCE *and* WESTMORELAND.

Prince. How now, blown Jack! how now, quilt!

Fal. What, Hal! How now, mad wag! what a devil dost thou in Warwickshire? My good Lord of Westmoreland, I cry you mercy: I thought your honour had already been at Shrewsbury.

West. Faith, Sir John, 'tis more than time that I were there, and you too; but my powers

are there already. The king, I can tell you, looks
for us all: we must away all night. 63
Fal. Tut, never fear me: I am as vigilant as
a cat to steal cream.
Prince. I think to steal cream indeed, for
thy theft hath already made thee butter. But
tell me, Jack, whose fellows are these that come
after?
Fal. Mine, Hal, mine. 70
Prince. I did never see such pitiful rascals.
Fal. Tut, tut; good enough to toss; food for
powder, food for powder; they'll fill a pit as well
as better: tush, man, mortal men, mortal men.
West. Ay, but, Sir John, methinks they are
exceeding poor and bare; too beggarly. 76
Fal. Faith, for their poverty, I know not
where they had that; and for their bareness, I
am sure they never learned that of me. 79
Prince. No, I'll be sworn; unless you call
three fingers on the ribs bare. But sirrah, make
haste: Percy is already in the field.
Fal. What, is the king encamped?
West. He is, Sir John: I fear we shall stay
too long. 84
Fal. Well,
To the latter end of a fray and the beginning of
a feast
Fits a dull fighter and a keen guest. [*Exeunt.*

SCENE III.—*The Rebel Camp near Shrewsbury.*

Enter HOTSPUR, WORCESTER, DOUGLAS,
and VERNON.

Hot. We'll fight with him to-night.
Wor.   It may not be.
Doug. You give him then advantage.
Ver.   Not a whit.
Hot. Why say you so? looks he not for sup-
ply?
Ver. So do we.
Hot.   His is certain, ours is doubtful. 4
Wor. Good cousin, be advis'd: stir not to-
night.
Ver. Do not, my lord.
Doug.   You do not counsel well:
You speak it out of fear and cold heart.
Ver. Do me no slander, Douglas: by my life,—
And I dare well maintain it with my life,— 9
If well-respected honour bid me on,
I hold as little counsel with weak fear
As you, my lord, or any Scot that this day lives:
Let it be seen to-morrow in the battle 13
Which of us fears.
Doug.   Yea, or to-night.
Ver.   Content.
Hot. To-night, say I.
Ver. Come, come, it may not be. I wonder
much, 16
Being men of such great leading as you are,
That you foresee not what impediments
Drag back our expedition: certain horse
Of my cousin Vernon's are not yet come up: 20
Your uncle Worcester's horse came but to-day;
And now their pride and mettle is asleep,
Their courage with hard labour tame and dull,

That not a horse is half the half of himself. 24
Hot. So are the horses of the enemy
In general, journey-bated and brought low:
The better part of ours are full of rest.
Wor. The number of the king exceedeth ours:
For God's sake, cousin, stay till all come in. 29
[*The trumpet sounds a parley.*

Enter SIR WALTER BLUNT.

Blunt. I come with gracious offers from the
king,
If you vouchsafe me hearing and respect.
Hot. Welcome, Sir Walter Blunt; and would
to God 32
You were of our determination!
Some of us love you well; and even those some
Envy your great deservings and good name,
Because you are not of our quality, 36
But stand against us like an enemy.
Blunt. And God defend but still I should
stand so,
So long as out of limit and true rule
You stand against anointed majesty. 40
But, to my charge. The king hath sent to know
The nature of your griefs, and whereupon
You conjure from the breast of civil peace
Such bold hostility, teaching his duteous land 44
Audacious cruelty. If that the king
Have any way your good deserts forgot,—
Which he confesseth to be manifold,—
He bids you name your griefs; and with all
speed 48
You shall have your desires with interest,
And pardon absolute for yourself and these
Herein misled by your suggestion.
Hot. The king is kind; and well we know the
king 52
Knows at what time to promise, when to pay.
My father and my uncle and myself
Did give him that same royalty he wears;
And when he was not six-and-twenty strong, 56
Sick in the world's regard, wretched and low,
A poor unminded outlaw sneaking home,
My father gave him welcome to the shore;
And when he heard him swear and vow to God
He came but to be Duke of Lancaster, 61
To sue his livery and beg his peace,
With tears of innocency and terms of zeal,
My father, in kind heart and pity mov'd, 64
Swore him assistance and perform'd it too.
Now when the lords and barons of the realm
Perceiv'd Northumberland did lean to him,
The more and less came in with cap and knee;
Met him in boroughs, cities, villages, 69
Attended him on bridges, stood in lanes,
Laid gifts before him, proffer'd him their oaths,
Gave him their heirs, as pages, follow'd him 72
Even at the heels in golden multitudes.
He presently, as greatness knows itself,
Steps me a little higher than his vow
Made to my father, while his blood was poor, 76
Upon the naked shore at Ravenspurgh;
And now, forsooth, takes on him to reform
Some certain edicts and some strait decrees
That lie too heavy on the commonwealth, 80
Cries out upon abuses, seems to weep

Over his country's wrongs; and by this face,
This seeming brow of justice, did he win
The hearts of all that he did angle for;　84
Proceeded further; cut me off the heads
Of all the favourites that the absent king
In deputation left behind him here,
When he was personal in the Irish war.　88
　　Blunt. Tut, I came not to hear this.
　　Hot.　　　　　Then to the point.
In short time after, he depos'd the king;
Soon after that, depriv'd him of his life;
And, in the neck of that, task'd the whole state;
To make that worse, suffer'd his kinsman
　　March—　93
Who is, if every owner were well plac'd,
Indeed his king—to be engag'd in Wales,
There without ransom to lie forfeited;　96
Disgrac'd me in my happy victories;
Sought to entrap me by intelligence;
Rated my uncle from the council-board;
In rage dismiss'd my father from the court; 100
Broke oath on oath, committed wrong on wrong;
And in conclusion drove us to seek out
This head of safety; and withal to pry
Into his title, the which we find　104
Too indirect for long continuance.
　　Blunt. Shall I return this answer to the king?
　　Hot. Not so, Sir Walter: we'll withdraw
　　awhile.
Go to the king; and let there be impawn'd 108
Some surety for a safe return again,
And in the morning early shall my uncle
Bring him our purposes; and so farewell.
　　Blunt. I would you would accept of grace and
　　love.　112
　　Hot. And may be so we shall.
　　Blunt.　　　　　Pray God, you do!
　　　　　　　　　　　　　[*Exeunt.*

SCENE IV.—*York. A Room in the* ARCH-
BISHOP'S *Palace.*

Enter the ARCHBISHOP OF YORK *and*
SIR MICHAEL.

　　Arch. Hie, good Sir Michael; bear this sealed
　　brief
With winged haste to the lord marshal;
This to my cousin Scroop, and all the rest
To whom they are directed. If you knew　4
How much they do import, you would make
　　haste.
　　Sir M. My good lord,
I guess their tenour.
　　Arch.　　　　Like enough you do.
To-morrow, good Sir Michael, is a day　8
Wherein the fortune of ten thousand men
Must bide the touch; for, sir, at Shrewsbury,
As I am truly given to understand,　11
The king with mighty and quick-raised power
Meets with Lord Harry: and, I fear, Sir Michael,
What with the sickness of Northumberland,—
Whose power was in the first proportion,—
And what with Owen Glendower's absence
　　thence,　16
Who with them was a rated sinew too,
And comes not in, o'er-rul'd by prophecies,—

I fear the power of Percy is too weak
To wage an instant trial with the king.　20
　　Sir M. Why, my good lord, you need not
　　fear:
There is the Douglas and Lord Mortimer.
　　Arch. No, Mortimer is not there.
　　Sir M. But there is Mordake, Vernon, Lord
　　Harry Percy,　24
And there's my Lord of Worcester, and a head
Of gallant warriors, noble gentlemen.
　　Arch. And so there is; but yet the king hath
　　drawn
The special head of all the land together:　28
The Prince of Wales, Lord John of Lancaster,
The noble Westmoreland, and war-like Blunt;
And many moe corrivals and dear men
Of estimation and command in arms.　32
　　Sir M. Doubt not, my lord, they shall be well
　　oppos'd.
　　Arch. I hope no less, yet needful 'tis to fear;
And, to prevent the worse, Sir Michael, speed:
For if Lord Percy thrive not, ere the king　36
Dismiss his power, he means to visit us,
For he hath heard of our confederacy,
And 'tis but wisdom to make strong against
　　him:
Therefore make haste. I must go write again 40
To other friends; and so farewell, Sir Michael.
　　　　　　　　　　　　　[*Exeunt.*

ACT V

SCENE I.—*The* KING'S *Camp near Shrewsbury.*

Enter KING HENRY, *the* PRINCE, JOHN OF LAN-
CASTER, SIR WALTER BLUNT, *and* SIR JOHN
FALSTAFF.

　　K. Hen. How bloodily the sun begins to peer
Above yon busky hill! the day looks pale
At his distemperature.
　　Prince.　　　　The southern wind
Doth play the trumpet to his purposes,　4
And by his hollow whistling in the leaves
Foretells a tempest and a blustering day.
　　K. Hen. Then with the losers let it sym-
　　pathize,
For nothing can seem foul to those that win. 8
　　　　　　　　　　　　[*Trumpet sounds*

Enter WORCESTER *and* VERNON.

How now, my Lord of Worcester! 'tis not well
That you and I should meet upon such terms
As now we meet. You have deceiv'd our trust,
And made us doff our easy robes of peace,　12
To crush our old limbs in ungentle steel:
This is not well, my lord; this is not well.
What say you to it? will you again unknit
This churlish knot of all-abhorred war,　16
And move in that obedient orb again
Where you did give a fair and natural light,
And be no more an exhal'd meteor,
A prodigy of fear and a portent　20
Of broached mischief to the unborn times?
　　Wor. Hear me, my liege.
For mine own part, I could be well content

entertain the lag-end of my life　24
ith quiet hours; for I do protest
ave not sought the day of this dislike.
K. Hen. You have not sought it! how comes
it then?
Fal. Rebellion lay in his way, and he found it.
Prince. Peace, chewet, peace!　29
Wor. It pleas'd your majesty to turn your
looks
favour from myself and all our house;
ad yet I must remember you, my lord,　32
e were the first and dearest of your friends.
r you my staff of office did I break
Richard's time; and posted day and night
meet you on the way, and kiss your hand, 36
hen yet you were in place and in account
othing so strong and fortunate as I.
was myself, my brother, and his son,
at brought you home and boldly did outdare
e dangers of the time. You swore to us,　41
nd you did swear that oath at Doncaster,
at you did nothing purpose 'gainst the state,
or claim no further than your new-fall'n right,
e seat of Gaunt, dukedom of Lancaster.　45
this we swore our aid: but, in short space
rain'd down fortune showering on your head,
nd such a flood of greatness fell on you,　48
hat with our help, what with the absent king,
hat with the injuries of a wanton time,
e seeming sufferances that you had borne,
nd the contrarious winds that held the king
long in his unlucky Irish wars,　53
at all in England did repute him dead:
nd from this swarm of fair advantages
ou took occasion to be quickly woo'd　56
gripe the general sway into your hand;
rgot your oath to us at Doncaster;
nd being fed by us you us'd us so
s that ungentle gull, the cuckoo's bird,　60
seth the sparrow: did oppress our nest,
rew by our feeding to so great a bulk
at even our love durst not come near your
sight
r fear of swallowing; but with nimble wing 64
e were enforc'd, for safety's sake, to fly
ut of your sight and raise this present head;
hereby we stand opposed by such means
s you yourself have forg'd against yourself 68
y unkind usage, dangerous countenance,
nd violation of all faith and troth
vorn to us in your younger enterprise.
K. Hen. These things indeed, you have articulate,　72
roclaim'd at market-crosses, read in churches,
o face the garment of rebellion
ith some fine colour that may please the eye
f fickle changelings and poor discontents, 76
hich gape and rub the elbow at the news
f hurlyburly innovation:
nd never yet did insurrection want
ich water-colours to impaint his cause;　80
or moody beggars, starving for a time
f pell-mell havoc and confusion.
Prince. In both our armies there is many a
soul
hall pay full dearly for this encounter,　84

If once they join in trial. Tell your nephew,
The Prince of Wales doth join with all the
world
In praise of Henry Percy: by my hopes,
This present enterprise set off his head,　88
I do not think a braver gentleman,
More active-valiant or more valiant-young,
More daring or more bold, is now alive
To grace this latter age with noble deeds.　92
For my part, I may speak it to my shame,
I have a truant been to chivalry;
And so I hear he doth account me too;
Yet this before my father's majesty—　96
I am content that he shall take the odds
Of his great name and estimation,
And will, to save the blood on either side,
Try fortune with him in a single fight.　100
　K. Hen. And, Prince of Wales, so dare we
venture thee,
Albeit considerations infinite
Do make against it. No, good Worcester, no,
We love our people well; even those we love
That are misled upon your cousin's part;
And, will they take the offer of our grace,
Both he and they and you, yea, every man
Shall be my friend again, and I'll be his.　108
So tell your cousin, and bring me word
What he will do; but if he will not yield,
Rebuke and dread correction wait on us,
And they shall do their office. So, be gone: 112
We will not now be troubled with reply;
We offer fair, take it advisedly.
　　　　　[Exeunt WORCESTER *and* VERNON.
　Prince. It will not be accepted, on my life.
The Douglas and the Hotspur both together
Are confident against the world in arms.　117
　K. Hen. Hence, therefore, every leader to his
charge;
For, on their answer, will we set on them;
And God befriend us, as our cause is just! 120
　　　　[Exeunt KING HENRY, BLUNT, *and* JOHN
　　　　　　　　　　　　OF LANCASTER.
　Fal. Hal, if thou see me down in the battle,
and bestride me, so; 'tis a point of friendship.
　Prince. Nothing but a colossus can do thee
that friendship. Say thy prayers, and farewell.
　Fal. I would it were bed-time, Hal, and all
well.　126
　Prince. Why, thou owest God a death. [*Exit.*
　Fal. 'Tis not due yet: I would be loath to
pay him before his day. What need I be so
forward with him that calls not on me? Well,
'tis no matter; honour pricks me on. Yea, but
how if honour prick me off when I come on?
how then? Can honour set to a leg? No. Or an
arm? No. Or take away the grief of a wound?
No. Honour hath no skill in surgery then? No.
What is honour? a word. What is that word,
honour? Air. A trim reckoning! Who hath it?
he that died o' Wednesday. Doth he feel it?
No. Doth he hear it? No. It is insensible
then? Yea, to the dead. But will it not live
with the living? No. Why? Detraction will not
suffer it. Therefore I'll none of it: honour is a
mere scutcheon; and so ends my catechism. 143
　　　　　　　　　　　　　　　[*Exit.*

SCENE II.—*The Rebel Camp near Shrewsbury.*

Enter WORCESTER *and* VERNON.

Wor. O, no! my nephew must not know,
  Sir Richard,
The liberal kind offer of the king.
  Ver. 'Twere best he did.
  Wor.   Then are we all undone.
It is not possible, it cannot be,   4
The king should keep his word in loving us;
He will suspect us still, and find a time
To punish this offence in other faults:
Suspicion all our lives shall be stuck full of eyes; 8
For treason is but trusted like the fox,
Who, ne'er so tame, so cherish'd, and lock'd up,
Will have a wild trick of his ancestors.
Look how we can, or sad or merrily,   12
Interpretation will misquote our looks,
And we shall feed like oxen at a stall,
The better cherish'd, still the nearer death.
My nephew's trespass may be well forgot, 16
It hath the excuse of youth and heat of blood;
And an adopted name of privilege,
A hare-brain'd Hotspur, govern'd by a spleen.
All his offences live upon my head   20
And on his father's: we did train him on;
And, his corruption being ta'en from us,
We, as the spring of all, shall pay for all.
Therefore, good cousin, let not Harry know 24
In any case the offer of the king.
  Ver. Deliver what you will, I'll say 'tis so.
Here comes your cousin.

Enter HOTSPUR *and* DOUGLAS; Officers *and*
       Soldiers *behind.*

  Hot. My uncle is return'd: deliver up   28
My Lord of Westmoreland. Uncle, what news?
  Wor. The king will bid you battle presently.
  Doug. Defy him by the Lord of Westmoreland.
  Hot. Lord Douglas, go you and tell him so. 32
  Doug. Marry, and shall, and very willingly.
                          [*Exit.*
  Wor. There is no seeming mercy in the king.
  Hot. Did you beg any? God forbid!
  Wor. I told him gently of our grievances, 36
Of his oath-breaking; which he mended thus,
By now forswearing that he is forsworn:
He calls us rebels, traitors; and will scourge
With haughty arms this hateful name in us. 40

Re-enter DOUGLAS.

  Doug. Arm, gentlemen! to arms! for I have
    thrown
A brave defiance in King Henry's teeth,
And Westmoreland, that was engag'd, did bear it;
Which cannot choose but bring him quickly on.
  Wor. The Prince of Wales stepp'd forth be-
    fore the king,   45
And, nephew, challeng'd you to single fight.
  Hot. O! would the quarrel lay upon our heads,
And that no man might draw short breath to-
    day   48
But I and Harry Monmouth. Tell me, tell me,
How show'd his tasking? seem'd it in contempt?
  Ver. No, by my soul; I never in my life
Did hear a challenge urg'd more modestly, 52

Unless a brother should a brother dare
To gentle exercise and proof of arms.
He gave you all the duties of a man,
Trimm'd up your praises with a princely tongu
Spoke your deservings like a chronicle,
Making you ever better than his praise,
By still dispraising praise valu'd with you;
And, which became him like a prince indeed,
He made a blushing cital of himself,
And chid his truant youth with such a grace
As if he master'd there a double spirit
Of teaching and of learning instantly.
There did he pause. But let me tell the worl
If he outlive the envy of this day,
England did never owe so sweet a hope,
So much misconstru'd in his wantonness.
  Hot. Cousin, I think thou art enamoured
On his follies: never did I hear
Of any prince so wild a libertine.
But be he as he will, yet once ere night
I will embrace him with a soldier's arm,
That he shall shrink under my courtesy.
Arm, arm, with speed! And, fellows, soldier
    friends,
Better consider what you have to do,
Than I, that have not well the gift of tongue,
Can lift your blood up with persuasion.

Enter a Messenger.

  Mess. My lord, here are letters for you.
  Hot. I cannot read them now.
O gentlemen! the time of life is short;
To spend that shortness basely were too lon
If life did ride upon a dial's point,
Still ending at the arrival of an hour.
An if we live, we live to tread on kings;
If die, brave death, when princes die with us
Now, for our consciences, the arms are fair,
When the intent of bearing them is just.

Enter another Messenger.

  Mess. My lord, prepare; the king comes o
    apace.
  Hot. I thank him that he cuts me from my tal
For I profess not talking. Only this,—
Let each man do his best: and here draw I
A sword, whose temper I intend to stain
With the best blood that I can meet withal
In the adventure of this perilous day.
Now, *Esperance!* Percy! and set on.
Sound all the lofty instruments of war,
And by that music let us all embrace;
For, heaven to earth, some of us never shall
A second time do such a courtesy.
           [*The trumpets sound. They embrace
                         and exeun

SCENE III.—*Between the Camps.*

*Excursions and Parties fighting. Alarum to th
  Battle. Then enter* DOUGLAS *and* SIR WALTE
  BLUNT, *meeting.*

  Blunt. What is thy name, that in the battl
    thus
Thou crossest me? what honour dost thou see
Upon my head?

Doug.   Know then, my name is Douglas;
And I do haunt thee in the battle thus   4
Because some tell me that thou art a king.

Blunt. They tell thee true.

Doug. The Lord of Stafford dear to-day hath
bought
Thy likeness; for, instead of thee, King Harry, 8
This sword hath ended him: so shall it thee,
Unless thou yield thee as my prisoner.

Blunt. I was not born a yielder, thou proud
Scot;
And thou shalt find a king that will revenge 12
Lord Stafford's death.

[*They fight, and* BLUNT *is slain.*]

Enter HOTSPUR.

Hot. O, Douglas! hadst thou fought at
Holmedon thus,
never had triumph'd upon a Scot.

Doug. All's done, all's won: here breathless
lies the king.   16

Hot. Where?

Doug. Here.

Hot. This, Douglas! no; I know this face full
well;
A gallant knight he was, his name was Blunt;
Semblably furnish'd like the king himself. 21

Doug. A fool go with thy soul, whither it
goes!
A borrow'd title hast thou bought too dear:
Why didst thou tell me that thou wert a
king?   24

Hot. The king hath many marching in his
coats.

Doug. Now, by my sword, I will kill all his
coats;
I'll murder all his wardrobe, piece by piece,
Until I meet the king.

Hot.   Up, and away!   28
Our soldiers stand full fairly for the day.

[*Exeunt.*]

Alarums. Enter FALSTAFF.

Fal. Though I could 'scape shot-free at
London, I fear the shot here; here's no scoring
but upon the pate. Soft! who art thou? Sir
Walter Blunt: there's honour for you! here's
no vanity! I am as hot as molten lead, and as
heavy too: God keep lead out of me! I need
no more weight than mine own bowels. I have
led my ragamuffins where they are peppered:
there's not three of my hundred and fifty left
alive, and they are for the town's end, to beg
during life. But who comes here?   40

Enter the PRINCE.

Prince. What! stand'st thou idle here? lend
me thy sword:
many a nobleman lies stark and stiff
under the hoofs of vaunting enemies,
whose deaths are unreveng'd: prithee, lend
me thy sword.   44

Fal. O Hal! I prithee, give me leave to
breathe awhile. Turk Gregory never did such
deeds in arms as I have done this day. I have
paid Percy, I have made him sure.   48

Prince. He is, indeed; and living to kill thee.
I prithee, lend me thy sword.

Fal. Nay, before God, Hal, if Percy be alive,
thou gett'st not my sword; but take my pistol,
if thou wilt.

Prince. Give it me. What! is it in the case?   53

Fal. Ay, Hal; 'tis hot, 'tis hot: there's that
will sack a city.   56

[*The* PRINCE *draws out a bottle of sack.*]

Prince. What! is't a time to jest and dally
now?   [*Throws it at him, and exit.*]

Fal. Well, if Percy be alive, I'll pierce him.
If he do come in my way, so: if he do not, if I
come in his, willingly, let him make a carbonado
of me. I like not such grinning honour as Sir
Walter hath: give me life; which if I can save,
so; if not, honour comes unlooked for, and
there's an end.   [*Exit.*]

SCENE IV.—*Another Part of the Field.*

Alarums. Excursions. Enter KING HENRY, *the*
PRINCE, JOHN OF LANCASTER, *and* WESTMORE-
LAND.

K. Hen. I prithee,
Harry, withdraw thyself; thou bleed'st too
much.
Lord John of Lancaster, go you with him.

Lanc. Not I, my lord, unless I did bleed too. 4

Prince. I beseech your majesty, make up,
Lest your retirement do amaze your friends.

K. Hen. I will do so.
My Lord of Westmoreland, lead him to his
tent.   8

West. Come, my lord, I'll lead you to your
tent.

Prince. Lead me, my lord? I do not need
your help:
And God forbid a shallow scratch should drive
The Prince of Wales from such a field as this, 12
Where stain'd nobility lies trodden on,
And rebels' arms triumph in massacres!

Lanc. We breathe too long: come, cousin
Westmoreland,
Our duty this way lies: for God's sake, come. 16

[*Exeunt* JOHN OF LANCASTER *and*
WESTMORELAND.

Prince. By God, thou hast deceiv'd me, Lan-
caster;
I did not think thee lord of such a spirit:
Before, I lov'd thee as a brother, John;
But now, I do respect thee as my soul.   20

K. Hen. I saw him hold Lord Percy at the
point
With lustier maintenance than I did look for
Of such an ungrown warrior.

Prince.   O! this boy
Lends mettle to us all.   [*Exit.*]

Alarums. Enter DOUGLAS.

Doug. Another king! they grow like Hydra's
heads: 25
I am the Douglas, fatal to all those
That wear those colours on them: what art
thou,
That counterfeit'st the person of a king?   28

K. Hen. The king himself; who, Douglas, grieves at heart
So many of his shadows thou hast met
And not the very king. I have two boys
Seek Percy and thyself about the field:　32
But, seeing thou fall'st on me so luckily,
I will assay thee; so defend thyself.

Doug. I fear thou art another counterfeit;
And yet, in faith, thou bear'st thee like a king:
But mine I am sure thou art, whoe'er thou be,
And thus I win thee.
　　　　　[*They fight.* KING HENRY *being in
　　　　　danger, re-enter the* PRINCE.

Prince. Hold up thy head, vile Scot, or thou art like
Never to hold it up again! the spirits　40
Of valiant Shirley, Stafford, Blunt, are in my arms:
It is the Prince of Wales that threatens thee,
Who never promiseth but he means to pay.
　　　　　[*They fight:* DOUGLAS *flies.*
Cheerly, my lord: how fares your Grace?　44
Sir Nicholas Gawsey hath for succour sent,
And so hath Clifton: I'll to Clifton straight.

K. Hen. Stay, and breathe awhile.
Thou hast redeem'd thy lost opinion,　48
And show'd thou mak'st some tender of my life,
In this fair rescue thou hast brought to me.

Prince. O God! they did me too much injury
That ever said I hearken'd for your death.　52
If it were so, I might have let alone
The insulting hand of Douglas over you;
Which would have been as speedy in your end
As all the poisonous potions in the world,　56
And sav'd the treacherous labour of your son.

K. Hen. Make up to Clifton: I'll to Sir Nicholas Gawsey.　　　　　[*Exit.*

Enter HOTSPUR.

Hot. If I mistake not, thou art Harry Monmouth.

Prince. Thou speak'st as if I would deny my name.　60

Hot. My name is Harry Percy.

Prince. 　　　　　Why, then, I see
A very valiant rebel of that name.
I am the Prince of Wales; and think not, Percy,
To share with me in glory any more:　64
Two stars keep not their motion in one sphere;
Nor can one England brook a double reign,
Of Harry Percy and the Prince of Wales.

Hot. Nor shall it, Harry; for the hour is come　68
To end the one of us; and would to God
Thy name in arms were now as great as mine!

Prince. I'll make it greater ere I part from thee;
And all the budding honours on thy crest　72
I'll crop, to make a garland for my head.

Hot. I can no longer brook thy vanities.
　　　　　[*They fight.*

Enter FALSTAFF.

Fal. Well said, Hal! to it, Hal! Nay, you shall find no boy's play here, I can tell you.　76

Re-enter DOUGLAS; *he fights with* FALSTAFF, *who falls down as if he were dead, and exit* DOUGLAS. HOTSPUR *is wounded, and falls.*

Hot. O, Harry! thou hast robb'd me of my youth.
I better brook the loss of brittle life
Than those proud titles thou hast won of me:
They wound my thoughts worse than thy sword my flesh:　80
But thought's the slave of life, and life time's fool;
And time, that takes survey of all the world,
Must have a stop. O! I could prophesy,
But that the earthy and cold hand of death 8.
Lies on my tongue. No, Percy, thou art dust,
And food for——　　　　　[*Dies*

Prince. For worms, brave Percy. Fare the well, great heart!
Ill-weav'd ambition, how much art tho' shrunk!
When that this body did contain a spirit,　8
A kingdom for it was too small a bound;
But now, two paces of the vilest earth
Is room enough: this earth, that bears the dead,　9
Bears not alive so stout a gentleman.
If thou wert sensible of courtesy,
I should not make so dear a show of zeal:
But let my favours hide thy mangled face,
And, even in thy behalf, I'll thank myself
For doing these fair rites of tenderness.
Adieu, and take thy praise with thee to heaven
Thy ignomy sleep with thee in the grave,　1
But not remember'd in thy epitaph!
　　　　　[*He spies* FALSTAFF *on the groun*
What! old acquaintance! could not all th flesh
Keep in a little life? Poor Jack, farewell!
I could have better spar'd a better man.　1
O! I should have a heavy miss of thee
If I were much in love with vanity.
Death hath not struck so fat a deer to-day,
Though many dearer, in this bloody fray.　1
Embowell'd will I see thee by and by:
Till then in blood by noble Percy lie.　[*Ex*

Fal. [*Rising.*] Embowelled! if thou embow me to-day, I'll give you leave to powder me ar eat me too, to-morrow. 'Sblood! 'twas time counterfeit, or that hot termagant Scot had pa me scot and lot too. Counterfeit? I lie, I am n counterfeit: to die, is to be a counterfeit; for h is but the counterfeit of a man, who hath n the life of a man; but to counterfeit dying, whe a man thereby liveth, is to be no counterfeit, b the true and perfect image of life indeed. T. better part of valour is discretion; in the whi better part, I have saved my life. 'Zounds! am afraid of this gunpowder Percy though be dead: how, if he should counterfeit too an rise? By my faith I am afraid he would pro the better counterfeit. Therefore I'll make h

sure; yea, and I'll swear I killed him. Why may
not he rise as well as I? Nothing confutes me
but eyes, and nobody sees me: therefore, sirrah
[*stabbing him*], with a new wound in your thigh
come you along with me.

[*He takes* HOSPUR *on his back.*

Re-enter the PRINCE *and* JOHN OF LANCASTER.

Prince. Come, brother John; full bravely
hast thou flesh'd   132
Thy maiden sword.
Lanc.   But, soft! whom have we here?
Did you not tell me this fat man was dead?
Prince. I did; I saw him dead,
Breathless and bleeding on the ground.   136
Art thou alive? or is it fantasy
That plays upon our eyesight? I prithee,
speak;
We will not trust our eyes without our ears:
Thou art not what thou seem'st.   140
Fal. No, that's certain; I am not a double
man: but if I be not Jack Falstaff, then am I a
Jack. There is Percy [*throwing the body down*]:
if your father will do me any honour, so; if not,
let him kill the next Percy himself. I look to
be either earl or duke, I can assure you.
Prince. Why, Percy I killed myself, and saw
thee dead.   147
Fal. Didst thou? Lord, Lord! how this world
is given to lying. I grant you I was down and
out of breath, and so was he; but we rose both
at an instant, and fought a long hour by Shrewsbury clock. If I may be believed, so; if not, let
them that should reward valour bear the sin
upon their own heads. I'll take it upon my
death, I gave him this wound in the thigh: if
the man were alive and would deny it, 'zounds,
would make him eat a piece of my sword.   157
Lanc. This is the strangest tale that e'er I
heard.
Prince. This is the strangest fellow, brother
John.
Come, bring your luggage nobly on your
back: 160
For my part, if a lie may do thee grace,
I'll gild it with the happiest terms I have.
                          [*A retreat is sounded.*
The trumpet sounds retreat; the day is ours.
Come, brother, let us to the highest of the
field,   164
To see what friends are living, who are dead.
               [*Exeunt the* PRINCE *and* JOHN OF
                                       LANCASTER.
Fal. I'll follow, as they say, for reward. He
that rewards me, God reward him! If I do grow
great, I'll grow less; for I'll purge, and leave
sack, and live cleanly, as a nobleman should do.
                                        [*Exit.*

SCENE V.—*Another Part of the Field.*

The trumpets sound. Enter KING HENRY, *the*
PRINCE, JOHN OF LANCASTER, WESTMORELAND,
and Others, with WORCESTER *and* VERNON
prisoners.

K. Hen. Thus ever did rebellion find rebuke.
Ill-spirited Worcester! did we not send grace,
Pardon, and terms of love to all of you?
And wouldst thou turn our offers contrary? 4
Misuse the tenour of thy kinsman's trust?
Three knights upon our party slain to-day,
A noble earl and many a creature else
Had been alive this hour,   8
If like a Christian, thou hadst truly borne
Betwixt our armies true intelligence.
Wor. What I have done my safety urg'd me
to;
And I embrace this fortune patiently,   12
Since not to be avoided it falls on me.
K. Hen. Bear Worcester to the death and
Vernon too:
Other offenders we will pause upon.
          [*Exeunt* WORCESTER *and* VERNON, *guarded.*
How goes the field?   16
Prince. The noble Scot, Lord Douglas, when
he saw
The fortune of the day quite turn'd from him,
The noble Percy slain, and all his men
Upon the foot of fear, fled with the rest;   20
And falling from a hill he was so bruis'd
That the pursuers took him. At my tent
The Douglas is, and I beseech your Grace
I may dispose of him.
K. Hen.   With all my heart.   24
Prince. Then, brother John of Lancaster, to
you
This honourable bounty shall belong.
Go to the Douglas, and deliver him
Up to his pleasure, ransomless, and free: 28
His valour shown upon our crests to-day
Hath taught us how to cherish such high deeds,
Even in the bosom of our adversaries.
Lanc. I thank your Grace for this high cour-
tesy,   32
Which I shall give away immediately.
K. Hen. Then this remains, that we divide
our power.
You, son John, and my cousin Westmoreland
Towards York shall bend you, with your dearest
speed,   36
To meet Northumberland and the prelate Scroop,
Who, as we hear, are busily in arms:
Myself and you, son Harry, will towards Wales,
To fight with Glendower and the Earl of March.
Rebellion in this land shall lose his sway, 41
Meeting the check of such another day:
And since this business so fair is done,
Let us not leave till all our own be won. [*Exeunt.*

THE SECOND PART OF
KING HENRY THE FOURTH

DRAMATIS PERSONÆ

RUMOUR, the Presenter.
KING HENRY THE FOURTH.
HENRY, Prince of Wales; afterwards
    King Henry the Fifth,
THOMAS, Duke of Clarence,   } His Sons.
JOHN OF LANCASTER,
HUMPHREY OF GLOUCESTER,
EARL OF WARWICK,
EARL OF WESTMORELAND,
EARL OF SURREY,   } Of the King's party.
GOWER,
HARCOURT,
BLUNT,
LORD CHIEF JUSTICE of the King's Bench.
A Servant of the Chief Justice.
EARL OF NORTHUMBERLAND,
RICHARD SCROOP, Archbishop
    of York,
LORD MOWBRAY,   } Opposites to the King.
LORD HASTINGS,
LORD BARDOLPH,
SIR JOHN COLEVILE,

TRAVERS and MORTON, Retainers of Northumberland.
SIR JOHN FALSTAFF.
His Page.
BARDOLPH.
PISTOL.
POINS.
PETO.
SHALLOW and SILENCE, Country Justices.
DAVY, Servant to Shallow.
MOULDY, SHADOW, WART, FEEBLE, and BULLCALF
    Recruits.
FANG and SNARE, Sheriff's Officers.
A Porter.
A Dancer, Speaker of the Epilogue.

LADY NORTHUMBERLAND.
LADY PERCY.
MISTRESS QUICKLY, Hostess of a tavern in Eastcheap.
DOLL TEARSHEET.

Lords and Attendants; Officers, Soldiers, Messenger
    Drawers, Beadles, Grooms, &c.

SCENE.—*England.*

INDUCTION

Warkworth. Before NORTHUMBERLAND'S *Castle.*

Enter RUMOUR, *painted full of tongues*

Rum. Open your ears; for which of you will
        stop
The vent of hearing when loud Rumour speaks?
I, from the orient to the drooping west,
Making the wind my post-horse, still unfold   4
The acts commenced on this ball of earth:
Upon my tongues continual slanders ride,
The which in every language I pronounce,
Stuffing the ears of men with false reports.   8
I speak of peace, while covert enmity
Under the smile of safety wounds the world:
And who but Rumour, who but only I,
Make fearful musters and prepar'd defence,   12
Whilst the big year, swoln with some other grief,
Is thought with child by the stern tyrant war,
And no such matter? Rumour is a pipe
Blown by surmises, jealousies, conjectures,   16
And of so easy and so plain a stop
That the blunt monster with uncounted heads,
The still-discordant wavering multitude,
Can play upon it. But what need I thus   20
My well-known body to anatomize
Among my household? Why is Rumour here?
I run before King Harry's victory;
Who in a bloody field by Shrewsbury   24
Hath beaten down young Hotspur and his troops,
Quenching the flame of bold rebellion
Even with the rebels' blood. But what mean I

To speak so true at first? my office is   2
To noise abroad that Harry Monmouth fell
Under the wrath of noble Hotspur's sword,
And that the king before the Douglas' rage
Stoop'd his anointed head as low as death.   3
This have I rumour'd through the peasant tow
Between the royal field of Shrewsbury
And this worm-eaten hold of ragged stone,
Where Hotspur's father, old Northumberland,
Lies crafty-sick. The posts come tiring on,   3
And not a man of them brings other news
Than they have learn'd of me: from Rumour
        tongues
They bring smooth comforts false, worse tha
        true wrongs.   [Exi

ACT I

SCENE I.—*Warkworth. Before* NORTHUMBE
            LAND'S *Castle.*

Enter LORD BARDOLPH.

L. Bard. Who keeps the gate here? ho!
                [*The* Porter *opens the ga*
                            Where is the ear
    Port. What shall I say you are?
L. Bard.   Tell thou the ea
That the Lord Bardolph doth attend him her
    Port. His Lordship is walk'd forth into t
    orchard:
Please it your honour knock but at the gate,
And he himself will answer.

Enter NORTHUMBERLAND.

L. Bard.   Here comes the earl.
               [*Exit* Porter.
North. What news, Lord Bardolph? every
   minute now
ould be the father of some stratagem,   8
e times are wild; contention, like a horse
ll of high feeding, madly hath broke loose
nd bears down all before him.
L. Bard.   Noble earl,
bring you certain news from Shrewsbury. 12
North. Good, an God will!
L. Bard.   As good as heart can wish.
e king is almost wounded to the death;
nd, in the fortune of my lord your son,
ince Harry slain outright; and both the
   Blunts   16
ill'd by the hand of Douglas; young Prince
   John
nd Westmoreland and Stafford fled the field.
nd Harry Monmouth's brawn, the hulk Sir
   John,
prisoner to your son: O! such a day,   20
o fought, so follow'd, and so fairly won,
ame not till now to dignify the times
nce Cæsar's fortunes.
North.   How is this deriv'd?
w you the field? came you from Shrewsbury?
L. Bard. I spake with one, my lord, that
   came from thence;   25
gentleman well bred and of good name,
hat freely render'd me these news for true.
North. Here comes my servant Travers,
   whom I sent   28
n Tuesday last to listen after news.
L. Bard. My lord, I over-rode him on the
   way;
nd he is furnish'd with no certainties
ore than he haply may retail from me.   32

Enter TRAVERS.

North. Now, Travers, what good tidings come
   with you?
Tra. My lord, Sir John Umfrevile turn'd me
   back
ith joyful tidings; and, being better hors'd,
ut-rode me. After him came spurring hard 36
gentleman, almost forspent with speed,
hat stopp'd by me to breathe his bloodied
   horse.
e ask'd the way to Chester; and of him
did demand what news from Shrewsbury. 40
e told me that rebellion had bad luck,
nd that young Harry Percy's spur was cold.
ith that he gave his able horse the head,
nd, bending forward struck his armed heels 44
gainst the panting sides of his poor jade
p to the rowel-head, and, starting so,
e seem'd in running to devour the way,
aying no longer question.
North.   Ha! Again: 48
aid he young Harry Percy's spur was cold?
f Hotspur, Coldspur? that rebellion
ad met ill luck?
L. Bard.   My lord, I'll tell you what:
my young lord your son have not the day, 52

Upon mine honour, for a silken point
I'll give my barony: never talk of it.
   North. Why should the gentleman that rode
   by Travers
Give then such instances of loss?
   L. Bard.   Who, he? 56
He was some hilding fellow that had stolen
The horse he rode on, and, upon my life,
Spoke at a venture. Look, here comes more
   news.

Enter MORTON.

   North. Yea, this man's brow, like to a title-
   leaf,   60
Foretells the nature of a tragic volume:
So looks the strond, whereon the imperious
   flood
Hath left a witness'd usurpation.
Say, Morton, didst thou come from Shrews-
   bury?   64
   Mor. I ran from Shrewsbury, my noble lord;
Where hateful death put on his ugliest mask
To fright our party.
   North.   How doth my son and brother?
Thou tremblest, and the whiteness in thy cheek
Is apter than thy tongue to tell thy errand. 69
Even such a man, so faint, so spiritless,
So dull, so dead in look, so woe-begone,
Drew Priam's curtain in the dead of night, 72
And would have told him half his Troy was
   burn'd;
But Priam found the fire ere he his tongue,
And I my Percy's death ere thou report'st it.
This thou wouldst say, 'Your son did thus and
   thus;   76
Your brother thus; so fought the noble Douglas;'
Stopping my greedy ear with their bold deeds:
But in the end, to stop mine ear indeed,
Thou hast a sigh to blow away this praise,   80
Ending with 'Brother, son, and all are dead.'
   Mor. Douglas is living, and your brother,
   yet;
But, for my lord your son,—
   North.   Why, he is dead.—
See, what a ready tongue suspicion hath!   84
He that but fears the thing he would not know
Hath by instinct knowledge from others' eyes
That what he fear'd is chanced. Yet speak,
   Morton:
Tell thou thy earl his divination lies,   88
And I will take it as a sweet disgrace
And make thee rich for doing me such wrong.
   Mor. You are too great to be by me gainsaid;
Your spirit is too true, your fears too certain.
   North. Yet, for all this, say not that Percy's
   dead.
I see a strange confession in thine eye:
Thou shak'st thy head, and hold'st it fear or sin
To speak a truth. If he be slain, say so;   96
The tongue offends not that reports his death:
And he doth sin that doth belie the dead,
Not he which says the dead is not alive.
Yet the first bringer of unwelcome news   100
Hath but a losing office, and his tongue
Sounds ever after as a sullen bell,
Remember'd knolling a departing friend.

L. Bard. I cannot think, my lord, your son
is dead.   104
Mor. I am sorry I should force you to believe
That which I would to God I had not seen;
But these mine eyes saw him in bloody state,
Rendering faint quittance, wearied and out-
breath'd,   108
To Harry Monmouth; whose swift wrath beat
down
The never-daunted Percy to the earth,
From whence with life he never more sprung up.
In few, his death,—whose spirit lent a fire   112
Even to the dullest peasant in his camp,—
Being bruited once, took fire and heat away
From the best-temper'd courage in his troops;
For from his metal was his party steel'd;   116
Which once in him abated, all the rest
Turn'd on themselves, like dull and heavy lead:
And as the thing that's heavy in itself,
Upon enforcement flies with greatest speed, 120
So did our men, heavy in Hotspur's loss,
Lend to this weight such lightness with their
fear
That arrows fled not swifter toward their aim
Than did our soldiers, aiming at their safety,
Fly from the field. Then was that noble Wor-
cester   125
Too soon ta'en prisoner; and that furious Scot,
The bloody Douglas, whose well-labouring
sword
Had three times slain the appearance of the
king,   128
'Gan vail his stomach, and did grace the shame
Of those that turn'd their backs; and in his
flight,
Stumbling in fear, was took. The sum of all
Is, that the king hath won, and hath sent out
A speedy power to encounter you, my lord,
Under the conduct of young Lancaster
And Westmoreland. This is the news at full.
North. For this I shall have time enough to
mourn.   136
In poison there is physic; and these news,
Having been well, that would have made me sick,
Being sick, have in some measure made me well:
And as the wretch, whose fever-weaken'd joints,
Like strengthless hinges, buckle under life, 141
Impatient of his fit, breaks like a fire
Out of his keeper's arms, even so my limbs,
Weaken'd with grief, being now enrag'd with
grief,   144
Are thrice themselves. Hence, therefore, thou
nice crutch!
A scaly gauntlet now, with joints of steel
Must glove this hand: and hence, thou sickly
quoif!
Thou art a guard too wanton for the head 148
Which princes, flesh'd with conquest, aim to hit.
Now bind my brows with iron; and approach
The ragged'st hour that time and spite dare
bring
To frown upon the enrag'd Northumberland!
Let heaven kiss earth! now let not nature's
hand   153
Keep the wild flood confin'd! let order die!
And let this world no longer be a stage

To feed contention in a lingering act;   1
But let one spirit of the first-born Cain
Reign in all bosoms, that, each heart being s
On bloody courses, the rude scene may end
And darkness be the burier of the dead!   1
Tra. This strained passion doth you wron
my lord.
L. Bard. Sweet earl, divorce not wisdo
from your honour.
Mor. The lives of all your loving complic
Lean on your health; the which, if you give o
To stormy passion must perforce decay.   1
You cast the event of war, my noble lord,
And summ'd the account of chance, before y
said,
'Let us make head.' It was your presurmise 1
That in the dole of blows your son might dro
You knew he walk'd o'er perils, on an edge,
More likely to fall in than to get o'er;
You were advis'd his flesh was capable   1
Of wounds and scars, and that his forward spi
Would lift him where most trade of dang
rang'd:
Yet did you say, 'Go forth;' and none of th
Though strongly apprehended, could   1
strain   1
The stiff-borne action: what hath then befalle
Or what hath this bold enterprise broug
forth,
More than that being which was like to be?
L. Bard. We all that are engaged to this lo
Knew that we ventur'd on such dangerous se
That if we wrought out life 'twas ten to one;
And yet we ventur'd, for the gain propos'd
Chok'd the respect of likely peril fear'd;   1
And since we are o'erset, venture again.
Come, we will all put forth, body and goods.
Mor. 'Tis more than time: and, my mo
noble lord,
I hear for certain, and do speak the truth,   1
The gentle Archbishop of York is up,
With well-appointed powers: he is a man
Who with a double surety binds his followe
My lord your son had only but the corpse', 1
But shadows and the shows of men to fight;
For that same word, rebellion, did divide
The action of their bodies from their souls;
And they did fight with queasiness, constrain
As men drink potions, that their weapo
only
Seem'd on our side: but, for their spirits a
souls,
This word, rebellion, it had froze them up,
As fish are in a pond. But now the bishop 2
Turns insurrection to religion:
Suppos'd sincere and holy in his thoughts,
He's follow'd both with body and with min
And doth enlarge his rising with the blood
Of fair King Richard, scrap'd from Pomfr
stones;
Derives from heaven his quarrel and his caus
Tells them he doth bestride a bleeding land,
Gasping for life under great Bolingbroke; 2
And more and less do flock to follow him.
North. I knew of this before; but, to spe
truth,

his present grief had wip'd it from my mind.
To in with me; and counsel every man   212
the aptest way for safety and revenge:
get posts and letters, and make friends with
    speed:
Never so few, and never yet more need.

                           [Exeunt.

SCENE II.—*London. A Street.*

Enter SIR JOHN FALSTAFF, *with his* Page *bearing his sword and buckler.*

Fal. Sirrah, you giant, what says the doctor
to my water?

Page. He said, sir, the water itself was a good
healthy water; but, for the party that owed it, he
might have more diseases than he knew for. 5

Fal. Men of all sorts take a pride to gird at
me: the brain of this foolish-compounded clay,
man, is not able to invent anything that tends
to laughter, more than I invent or is invented
in me: I am not only witty in myself, but the
cause that wit is in other men. I do here walk
before thee like a sow that hath overwhelmed all
her litter but one. If the prince put thee into
my service for any other reason than to set me
off, why then I have no judgment. Thou whoreson mandrake, thou art fitter to be worn in my
cap than to wait at my heels. I was never
manned with an agate till now; but I will set
you neither in gold nor silver, but in vile apparel,
and send you back again to your master, for a
jewel; the juvenal, the prince your master, whose
chin is not yet fledged. I will sooner have a
beard grow in the palm of my hand than he shall
get one on his cheek; and yet he will not stick
to say, his face is a face-royal: God may finish it
when he will, it is not a hair amiss yet: he may
keep it still as a face-royal, for a barber shall
never earn sixpence out of it; and yet he will
be crowing as if he had writ man ever since his
father was a bachelor. He may keep his own
grace, but he is almost out of mine, I can assure
him. What said Master Dombledon about the
satin for my short cloak and my slops?   33

Page. He said, sir, you should procure him
better assurance than Bardolph; he would not
take his bond and yours: he liked not the
security.   37

Fal. Let him be damned like the glutton!
may his tongue be hotter! A whoreson Achito-
phel! a rascally yea-forsooth knave! to bear a
gentleman in hand, and then stand upon security.
The whoreson smooth-pates do now wear nothing but high shoes, and bunches of keys at their
girdles; and if a man is thorough with them in
honest taking up, then they must stand upon
security. I had as lief they would put ratsbane
in my mouth as offer to stop it with security. I
looked a' should have sent me two and twenty
yards of satin, as I am a true knight, and he
sends me security. Well, he may sleep in security;
for he hath the horn of abundance, and the lightness of his wife shines through it: and yet cannot he see, though he have his own lanthorn to
light him. Where's Bardolph?   54

Page. He's gone into Smithfield to buy your
worship a horse.

Fal. I bought him in Paul's, and he'll buy
me a horse in Smithfield: an I could get me
but a wife in the stews, I were manned, horsed,
and wived.   60

Enter the LORD CHIEF JUSTICE *and*
Servant.

Page. Sir, here comes the nobleman that
committed the prince for striking him about
Bardolph.

Fal. Wait close; I will not see him.   64

Ch. Just. What's he that goes there?

Ser. Falstaff, an't please your lordship.

Ch. Just. He that was in question for the
robbery?   68

Ser. He, my lord; but he hath since done
good service at Shrewsbury, and, as I hear, is
now going with some charge to the Lord John
of Lancaster.   72

Ch. Just. What, to York? Call him back
again.

Ser. Sir John Falstaff!

Fal. Boy, tell him I am deaf.   76

Page. You must speak louder, my master is
deaf.

Ch. Just. I am sure he is, to the hearing of
anything good. Go, pluck him by the elbow; I
must speak with him.

Ser. Sir John!   82

Fal. What! a young knave, and beg! Is there
not wars? is there not employment? doth not
the king lack subjects? do not the rebels want
soldiers? Though it be a shame to be on any
side but one, it is worse shame to beg than to be
on the worst side, were it worse than the name
of rebellion can tell how to make it.

Ser. You mistake me, sir.   90

Fal. Why, sir, did I say you were an honest
man? setting my knighthood and my soldiership aside, I had lied in my throat if I had
said so.   94

Ser. I pray you, sir, then set your knighthood
and your soldiership aside, and give me leave to
tell you you lie in your throat if you say I
am any other than an honest man.   98

Fal. I give thee leave to tell me so! I lay
aside that which grows to me! If thou gett'st
any leave of me, hang me: if thou takest leave,
thou wert better be hanged. You hunt-counter:
hence! avaunt!   103

Ser. Sir, my lord would speak with you.

Ch. Just. Sir John Falstaff, a word with
you.

Fal. My good lord! God give your lordship
good time of day. I am glad to see your lordship abroad; I heard say your lordship was sick:
I hope your lordship goes abroad by advice.
Your lordship, though not clean past your youth,
hath yet some smack of age in you, some relish
of the saltness of time; and I most humbly beseech your lordship to have a reverend care of
your health.   115

Ch. Just. Sir John, I sent for you before your
expedition to Shrewsbury.

Fal. An't please your lordship, I hear his majesty is returned with some discomfort from Wales.   120

Ch. Just. I talk not of his majesty. You would not come when I sent for you.

Fal. And I hear, moreover, his highness is fallen into this same whoreson apoplexy.   124

Ch. Just. Well, heaven mend him! I pray you, let me speak with you.

Fal. This apoplexy is, as I take it, a kind of lethargy, an't please your lordship; a kind of sleeping in the blood, a whoreson tingling.

Ch. Just. What tell you me of it? be it as it is.   131

Fal. It hath its original from much grief, from study and perturbation of the brain. I have read the cause of his effects in Galen: it is a kind of deafness.

Ch. Just. I think you are fallen into the disease, for you hear not what I say to you.   137

Fal. Very well, my lord, very well: rather, an't please you, it is the disease of not listening, the malady of not marking, that I am troubled withal.   141

Ch. Just. To punish you by the heels would amend the attention of your ears; and I care not if I do become your physician.   144

Fal. I am as poor as Job, my lord, but not so patient: your lordship may minister the potion of imprisonment to me in respect of poverty; but how I should be your patient to follow your prescriptions, the wise may make some dram of a scruple, or indeed a scruple itself.   150

Ch. Just. I sent for you, when there were matters against you for your life, to come speak with me.

Fal. As I was then advised by my learned counsel in the laws of this land-service, I did not come.   156

Ch. Just. Well, the truth is, Sir John, you live in great infamy.

Fal. He that buckles him in my belt cannot live in less.   160

Ch. Just. Your means are very slender, and your waste is great.

Fal. I would it were otherwise: I would my means were greater and my waist slenderer.

Ch. Just. You have misled the youthful prince.

Fal. The young prince hath misled me: I am the fellow with the great belly, and he my dog.   168

Ch. Just. Well, I am loath to gall a new-healed wound: your day's service at Shrewsbury hath a little gilded over your night's exploit on Gadshill: you may thank the unquiet time for your quiet o'er-posting that action.   173

Fal. My lord!

Ch. Just. But since all is well, keep it so: wake not a sleeping wolf.   176

Fal. To wake a wolf is as bad as to smell a fox.

Ch. Just. What! you are as a candle, the better part burnt out.   180

Fal. A wassail candle, my lord; all tallow: if I did say of wax, my growth would approve the truth.

Ch. Just. There is not a white hair on you face but should have his effect of gravity. 1

Fal. His effect of gravy, gravy, gravy.

Ch. Just. You follow the young prince u and down, like his ill angel.

Fal. Not so, my lord; your ill angel is ligh but I hope he that looks upon me will take n without weighing: and yet, in some respects, grant, I cannot go, I cannot tell. Virtue is so little regard in these costermonger times th true valour is turned bear-herd: pregnancy made a tapster, and hath his quick wit waste in giving reckonings: all the other gifts apper nent to man, as the malice of this age shap them, are not worth a gooseberry. You that a old consider not the capacities of us that a young; you measure the heat of our livers wi the bitterness of your galls; and we that are the vaward of our youth, I must confess, a wags too.   2

Ch. Just. Do you set down your name in th scroll of youth, that are written down old wi all the characters of age? Have you not a moi eye, a dry hand, a yellow cheek, a white bear a decreasing leg, an increasing belly? Is n your voice broken, your wind short, your ch double, your wit single, and every part abo you blasted with antiquity, and will you yet ca yourself young? Fie, fie, fie, Sir John!   2

Fal. My lord, I was born about three of th clock in the afternoon, with a white head, ar something a round belly. For my voice, I hav lost it with hollaing, and singing of anthem To approve my youth further, I will not: th truth is, I am only old in judgment and unde standing; and he that will caper with me for thousand marks, let him lend me the mone and have at him! For the box o' the ear th the prince gave you, he gave it like a rude princ and you took it like a sensible lord. I hav checked him for it, and the young lion repent marry, not in ashes and sackcloth, but in ne silk and old sack.   2

Ch. Just. Well, God send the prince a bett companion!

Fal. God send the companion a better princ I cannot rid my hands of him.   2

Ch. Just. Well, the king hath severed yc and Prince Harry. I hear you are going wi Lord John of Lancaster against the archbisho and the Earl of Northumberland.   2

Fal. Yea; I thank your pretty sweet wit f it. But look you pray, all you that kiss my lac Peace at home, that our armies join not in a h day; for, by the Lord, I take but two shirts o with me, and I mean not to sweat extraordinar ly: if it be a hot day, and I brandish anything b my bottle, I would I might never spit white agai There is not a dangerous action can peep o his head but I am thrust upon it. Well, I ca not last ever. But it was always yet the trick our English nation, if they have a good thing, make it too common. If you will needs say I a an old man, you should give me rest. I wou to God my name were not so terrible to th enemy as it is: I were better to be eaten to dea

ith rust than to be scoured to nothing with
erpetual motion. 251
Ch. Just. Well, be honest, be honest; and
od bless your expedition.
Fal. Will your lordship lend me a thousand
ound to furnish me forth? 255
Ch. Just. Not a penny; not a penny; you are
oo impatient to bear crosses. Fare you well:
ommend me to my cousin Westmoreland. 258
    [*Exeunt* CHIEF JUSTICE *and* Servant.
Fal. If I do, fillip me with a three-man beetle.
man can no more separate age and covetous-
ess than he can part young limbs and lechery;
ut the gout galls the one, and the pox pinches
he other; and so both the degrees prevent my
urses. Boy! 264
Page. Sir!
Fal. What money is in my purse?
Page. Seven groats and twopence. 267
Fal. I can get no remedy against this con-
umption of the purse: borrowing only lingers
nd lingers it out, but the disease is incurable.
o bear this letter to my Lord of Lancaster;
his to the prince; this to the Earl of Westmore-
nd; and this to old Mistress Ursula, whom I
ave weekly sworn to marry since I perceived
he first white hair on my chin. About it: you
now where to find me. [*Exit* PAGE.] A pox of
his gout! or, a gout of this pox! for the one or
he other plays the rogue with my great toe.
'is no matter if I do halt; I have the wars for
y colour, and my pension shall seem the more
asonable. A good wit will make use of any-
hing; I will turn diseases to commodity. [*Exit.*

SCENE III.—*York. A Room in the* ARCH-
      BISHOP'S *Palace.*

nter the ARCHBISHOP OF YORK, LORD HASTINGS,
   MOWBRAY, *and* BARDOLPH.

Arch. Thus have you heard our cause and
   known our means;
nd, my most noble friends, I pray you all,
peak plainly your opinions of our hopes:
nd first, Lord Marshal, what say you to it? 4
Mowb. I well allow the occasion of our arms;
ut gladly would be better satisfied
ow in our means we should advance ourselves
o look with forehead bold and big enough 8
pon the power and puissance of the king.
Hast. Our present musters grow upon the file
o five-and-twenty thousand men of choice;
nd our supplies live largely in the hope 12
f great Northumberland, whose bosom burns
ith an incensed fire of injuries.
L. Bard. The question, then, Lord Hastings,
   standeth thus:
hether our present five-and-twenty thousand
ay hold up head without Northumberland. 17
Hast. With him, we may.
L. Bard.   Ay, marry, there's the point:
ut if without him we be thought too feeble,
y judgment is, we should not step too far 20
ill we had his assistance by the hand;
or in a theme so bloody-fac'd as this,
onjecture, expectation, and surmise

Of aids incertain should not be admitted. 24
   Arch. 'Tis very true, Lord Bardolph; for,
   indeed
It was young Hotspur's case at Shrewsbury.
   L. Bard. It was, my lord; who lin'd himself
   with hope,
Eating the air on promise of supply, 28
Flattering himself with project of a power
Much smaller than the smallest of his thoughts;
And so, with great imagination
Proper to madmen, led his powers to death, 32
And winking leap'd into destruction.
   Hast. But, by your leave, it never yet did hurt
To lay down likelihoods and forms of hope.
   L. Bard. Yes, if this present quality of war,—
Indeed the instant action,—a cause on foot,
Lives so in hope, as in an early spring
We see the appearing buds; which, to prove fruit,
Hope gives not so much warrant as despair 40
That frosts will bite them. When we mean to
   build,
We first survey the plot, then draw the model;
And when we see the figure of the house,
Then must we rate the cost of the erection; 44
Which if we find outweighs ability,
What do we then but draw anew the model
In fewer offices, or at last desist
To build at all? Much more, in this great work,—
Which is almost to pluck a kingdom down 49
And set another up,—should we survey
The plot of situation and the model,
Consent upon a sure foundation, 52
Question surveyors, know our own estate,
How able such a work to undergo,
To weigh against his opposite; or else,
We fortify in paper, and in figures, 56
Using the names of men instead of men:
Like one that draws the model of a house
Beyond his power to build it; who, half through,
Gives o'er and leaves his part-created cost 60
A naked subject to the weeping clouds,
And waste for churlish winter's tyranny.
   Hast. Grant that our hopes, yet likely of fair
   birth,
Should be still-born, and that we now possess'd
The utmost man of expectation; 65
I think we are a body strong enough,
Even as we are, to equal with the king.
   L. Bard. What! is the king but five-and-
   twenty thousand? 68
   Hast. To us no more; nay, not so much,
   Lord Bardolph.
For his divisions, as the times do brawl,
Are in three heads: one power against the
   French,
And one against Glendower; perforce, a third 72
Must take up us: so is the unfirm king
In three divided, and his coffers sound
With hollow poverty and emptiness.
   Arch. That he should draw his several
   strengths together 76
And come against us in full puissance,
Need not be dreaded.
   Hast.   If he should do so,
He leaves his back unarm'd, the French and
   Welsh

Baying him at the heels: never fear that.   80
   L. Bard. Who is it like should lead his forces
hither?
   Hast. The Duke of Lancaster and West-
moreland;
Against the Welsh, himself and Harry Mon-
mouth:
But who is substituted 'gainst the French   84
I have no certain notice.
   Arch.   Let us on
And publish the occasion of our arms.
The commonwealth is sick of their own choice;
Their over-greedy love hath surfeited.   88
A habitation giddy and unsure
Hath he that buildeth on the vulgar heart.
O thou fond many! with what loud applause
Didst thou beat heaven with blessing Boling-
broke   92
Before he was what thou wouldst have him be:
And being now trimm'd in thine own desires,
Thou, beastly feeder, art so full of him
That thou provok'st thyself to cast him up.   96
So, so, thou common dog, didst thou disgorge
Thy glutton bosom of the royal Richard,
And now thou wouldst eat thy dead vomit up,
And howl'st to find it. What trust is in these
times?   100
They that, when Richard liv'd, would have him
die,
Are now become enamour'd on his grave:
Thou, that threw'st dust upon his goodly head,
When through proud London he came sighing
on   104
After the admired heels of Bolingbroke,
Cry'st now, 'O earth! yield us that king again,
And take thou this!' O, thoughts of men ac-
curst!
Past and to come seem best; things present
worst.   108
   Mowb. Shall we go draw our numbers and
set on?
   Hast. We are time's subjects, and time bids
be gone.   [*Exeunt.*

ACT II

Scene I.—*London. A Street.*

Enter Mistress Quickly: Fang, *and his* Boy,
with her; and Snare *following.*

   Quick. Master Fang, have you entered the
exion?
   Fang. It is entered.
   Quick. Where's your yeoman? Is it a lusty
yeoman? will a' stand to 't?
   Fang. Sirrah, where's Snare?
   Quick. O Lord, ay! good Master Snare.
   Snare. Here, here.
   Fang. Snare, we must arrest Sir John Fal-
staff.   8
   Quick. Yea, good Master Snare; I have en-
tered him and all.   12
   Snare. It may chance cost some of us our
lives, for he will stab.

   Quick. Alas the day! take heed of him: h̵
stabbed me in mine own house, and that mo̵
beastly. In good faith, he cares not wh̵
mischief he doth if his weapon be out: h̵
will foin like any devil; he will spare neith̵
man, woman, nor child.
   Fang. If I can close with him I care not f̵
his thrust.
   Quick. No, nor I neither: I'll be at yo̵
elbow.
   Fang. An I but fist him once; an a' come b̵
within my vice,—
   Quick. I am undone by his going; I warra̵
you, he's an infinitive thing upon my sco̵
Good Master Fang, hold him sure: good Mast̵
Snare, let him not 'scape. A' comes continuant̵
to Pie-corner—saving your manhoods—to b̵
a saddle; and he's indited to dinner to the Lu̵
ber's Head in Lumbert-Street, to Master Smoot̵
the silkman: I pray ye, since my exion is entere̵
and my case so openly known to the world, ̵
him be brought in to his answer. A hundr̵
mark is a long one for a poor lone woman ̵
bear; and I have borne, and borne, and born̵
and have been fubbed off, and fubbed off, a̵
fubbed off, from this day to that day, that it is̵
shame to be thought on. There is no honesty̵
such dealing; unless a woman should be ma̵
an ass, and a beast, to bear every knave's wron̵
Yonder he comes; and that arrant malmse̵
nose knave, Bardolph, with him. Do your office̵
do your offices, Master Fang and Master Snar̵
do me, do me, do me your offices.

Enter Sir John Falstaff, Page, *and* Bardolp̵

   Fal. How now! whose mare's dead? what̵
the matter?
   Fang. Sir John, I arrest you at the suit ̵
Mistress Quickly.
   Fal. Away, varlets! Draw, Bardolph: c̵
me off the villain's head; throw the quea̵
the channel.
   Quick. Throw me in the channel! I'll thro̵
thee in the channel. Wilt thou? wilt thou? th̵
bastardly rogue! Murder, murder! Ah, th̵
honey-suckle villain! wilt thou kill God's offic̵
and the king's? Ah, thou honey-seed rog̵
thou art a honey-seed, a man-queller, and ̵
woman-queller.
   Fal. Keep them off, Bardolph.
   Fang. A rescue! a rescue!
   Quick. Good people, bring a rescue or tw̵
Thou wo't, wo't thou? thou wo't, wo't ta? d̵
do, thou rogue! do, thou hemp-seed!
   Fal. Away, you scullion! you rampallia̵
you fustilarian! I'll tickle your catastrophe.

Enter the Lord Chief Justice, *attended.*

   Ch. Just. What is the matter? keep the pea̵
here, ho!
   Quick. Good my lord, be good to me! I b̵
seech you, stand to me!
   Ch. Just. How now, Sir John! what! are y̵
brawling here?
Doth this become your place, your time ar̵
business?

You should have been well on your way to
  York.
Stand from him, fellow: wherefore hang'st up-
  on him?   76
  Quick. O, my most worshipful lord, an't
please your grace, I am a poor widow of Eastcheap, and he is arrested at my suit.
  Ch. Just. For what sum?   80
  Quick. It is more than for some, my lord; it
is for all, all I have. He hath eaten me out of
house and home; he hath put all my substance
into that fat belly of his: but I will have some of
it out again, or I will ride thee o' nights like the
mare.
  Fal. I think I am as like to ride the mare if
I have any vantage of ground to get up.   88
  Ch. Just. How comes this, Sir John? Fie!
what man of good temper would endure this
tempest of exclamation? Are you not ashamed
to enforce a poor widow to so rough a course to
come by her own?   93
  Fal. What is the gross sum that I owe thee?
  Quick. Marry, if thou wert an honest man,
thyself and the money too. Thou didst swear
to me upon a parcel-gilt goblet, sitting in my
Dolphin-chamber, at the round table, by a seacoal fire, upon Wednesday in Wheeson week,
when the prince broke thy head for liking his
father to a singing-man of Windsor, thou didst
swear to me then, as I was washing thy wound,
to marry me and make me my lady thy wife.
Canst thou deny it? Did not goodwife Keech,
the butcher's wife, come in then and call me
gossip Quickly? coming in to borrow a mess of
vinegar; telling us she had a good dish of
prawns; whereby thou didst desire to eat some,
whereby I told thee they were ill for a green
wound? And didst thou not, when she was gone
down stairs, desire me to be no more so familiarity with such poor people; saying that ere
long they should call me madam? And didst
thou not kiss me and bid me fetch thee thirty
shillings? I put thee now to thy book-oath:
deny it if thou canst.   116
  Fal. My lord, this is a poor mad soul; and
she says up and down the town that her eldest
son is like you. She hath been in good case,
and the truth is, poverty hath distracted her.
But for these foolish officers, I beseech you I
may have redress against them.   122
  Ch. Just. Sir John, Sir John, I am well acquainted with your manner of wrenching the
true cause the false way. It is not a confident
brow, nor the throng of words that come with
such more than impudent sauciness from you,
can thrust me from a level consideration; you
have, as it appears to me, practised upon the
easy-yielding spirit of this woman, and made
her serve your uses both in purse and in person.
  Quick. Yea, in troth, my lord.   132
  Ch. Just. Prithee, peace. Pay her the debt
you owe her, and unpay the villany you have
done her: the one you may do with sterling
money, and the other with current repentance.
  Fal. My lord, I will not undergo this sneap
without reply. You call honourable boldness

impudent sauciness: if a man will make curtsy,
and say nothing, he is virtuous. No, my lord,
my humble duty remembered, I will not be your
suitor: I say to you, I do desire deliverance from
these officers, being upon hasty employment in
the king's affairs.   144
  Ch. Just. You speak as having power to do
wrong: but answer in the effect of your reputation, and satisfy the poor woman.
  Fal. Come hither, hostess. [*Taking her aside.*

Enter GOWER.

  Ch. Just. Now, Master Gower! what news?
  Gow. The king, my lord, and Harry Prince
  of Wales
Are near at hand: the rest the paper tells.
                          [*Gives a letter.*
  Fal. As I am a gentleman.   152
  Quick. Nay, you said so before.
  Fal. As I am a gentleman. Come, no more
words of it.
  Quick. By this heavenly ground I tread on,
I must be fain to pawn both my plate and the
tapestry of my dining-chambers.   158
  Fal. Glasses, glasses, is the only drinking:
and for thy walls, a pretty slight drollery, or the
story of the Prodigal, or the German hunting in
water-work, is worth a thousand of these bed-
hangings and these fly-bitten tapestries. Let it
be ten pound if thou canst. Come, an it were
not for thy humours, there is not a better wench
in England. Go, wash thy face, and draw thy
action. Come, thou must not be in this humour
with me; dost not know me? Come, come, I
know thou wast set on to this.   169
  Quick. Prithee, Sir John, let it be but twenty
nobles: i' faith, I am loath to pawn my plate,
so God save me, la!   172
  Fal. Let it alone; I'll make other shift:
you'll be a fool still.
  Quick. Well, you shall have it, though I pawn
my gown. I hope you'll come to supper. You'll
pay me all together?   177
  Fal. Will I live? [*To* BARDOLPH.] Go, with
her, with her; hook on, hook on.
  Quick. Will you have Doll Tearsheet meet
you at supper?
  Fal. No more words; let's have her.
    [*Exeunt* MISTRESS QUICKLY, BARDOLPH,
                          Officers, *and* Page.
  Ch. Just. I have heard the news better news.
  Fal. What's the news, my good lord?   184
  Ch. Just. Where lay the king last night?
  Gow. At Basingstoke, my lord.
  Fal. I hope, my lord, all's well: what is the
news, my lord?   188
  Ch. Just. Come all his forces back?
  Gow. No; fifteen hundred foot, five hundred
  horse,
Are march'd up to my Lord of Lancaster,
Against Northumberland and the archbishop.
  Fal. Comes the king back from Wales, my
  noble lord?   193
  Ch. Just. You shall have letters of me pre-
sently.
Come, go along with me, good Master Gower.

Fal. My lord!   196
Ch. Just. What's the matter?
Fal. Master Gower, shall I entreat you with me to dinner?
Gow. I must wait upon my good lord here; I thank you, good Sir John.   201
Ch. Just. Sir John, you loiter here too long, being you are to take soldiers up in counties as you go.   204
Fal. Will you sup with me, Master Gower?
Ch. Just. What foolish master taught you these manners, Sir John?
Fal. Master Gower, if they become me not, he was a fool that taught them me. This is the right fencing grace, my lord; tap for tap, and so part fair.   211
Ch. Just. Now the Lord lighten thee! thou art a great fool.   [*Exeunt.*

SCENE II.—*The Same. Another Street.*

Enter the PRINCE *and* POINS.

Prince. Before God, I am exceeding weary.
Poins. Is it come to that? I had thought weariness durst not have attached one of so high blood.   4
Prince. Faith, it does me, though it discolours the complexion of my greatness to acknowledge it. Doth it not show vilely in me to desire small beer?   8
Poins. Why, a prince should not be so loosely studied as to remember so weak a composition.
Prince. Belike then my appetite was not princely got; for, by my troth, I do now remember the poor creature, small beer. But, indeed, these humble considerations make me out of love with my greatness. What a disgrace is it to me to remember thy name, or to know thy face to-morrow! or to take note how many pair of silk stockings thou hast; *viz.* these, and those that were thy peach-coloured ones! or to bear the inventory of thy shirts; as, one for superfluity, and one other for use! But that the tennis-court-keeper knows better than I, for it is a low ebb of linen with thee when thou keepest not racket there; as thou hast not done a great while, because the rest of thy low-countries have made a shift to eat up thy holland: and God knows whether those that bawl out the ruins of thy linen shall inherit his kingdom; but the midwives say the children are not in the fault; whereupon the world increases, and kindreds are mightily strengthened.   31
Poins. How ill it follows, after you have laboured so hard, you should talk so idly! Tell me, how many good young princes would do so, their fathers being so sick as yours at this time is?   36
Prince. Shall I tell thee one thing, Poins?
Poins. Yes, faith, and let it be an excellent good thing.
Prince. It shall serve among wits of no higher breeding than thine.   41
Poins. Go to; I stand the push of your one thing that you will tell.

Prince. Marry, I tell thee, it is not meet that I should be sad, now my father is sick: albeit I could tell to thee,—as to one it pleases me, for fault of a better, to call my friend,—I could be sad, and sad indeed too.   48
Poins. Very hardly upon such a subject.
Prince. By this hand, thou thinkest me as far in the devil's book as thou and Falstaff for obduracy and persistency: let the end try the man. But I tell thee my heart bleeds inwardly that my father is so sick; and keeping such vile company as thou art hath in reason taken from me all ostentation of sorrow.   56
Poins. The reason?
Prince. What wouldst thou think of me if I should weep?
Poins. I would think thee a most princely hypocrite.   61
Prince. It would be every man's thought; and thou art a blessed fellow to think as every man thinks: never a man's thought in the world keeps the road-way better than thine: every man would think me a hypocrite indeed. And what accites your most worshipful thought to think so?
Poins. Why, because you have been so lewd and so much engraffed to Falstaff.   69
Prince. And to thee.
Poins. By this light, I am well spoke on; I can hear it with mine own ears: the worst that they can say of me is that I am a second brother and that I am a proper fellow of my hands; and these two things I confess I cannot help. By the mass, here comes Bardolph.   76

Enter BARDOLPH *and* Page.

Prince. And the boy that I gave Falstaff: a' had him from me Christian; and look, if the fat villain have not transformed him ape.
Bard. God save your Grace!   80
Prince. And yours, most noble Bardolph.
Bard. [*To the* Page.] Come, you virtuous ass, you bashful fool, must you be blushing? wherefore blush you now? What a maidenly man-at-arms are you become! Is it such a matter to get a pottle-pot's maidenhead?   84
Page. A' calls me even now, my lord, through a red lattice, and I could discern no part of his face from the window: at last, I spied his eyes and methought he had made two holes in the ale-wife's new petticoat, and peeped through.
Prince. Hath not the boy profited?   91
Bard. Away, you whoreson upright rabbit, away!
Page. Away, you rascally Althea's dream, away!   95
Prince. Instruct us, boy; what dream, boy?
Page. Marry, my lord, Althea dreamed she was delivered of a firebrand; and therefore I call him her dream.   100
Prince. A crown's worth of good interpretation. There it is, boy.   [*Gives him money.*
Poins. O! that this good blossom could be kept from cankers. Well, there is sixpence to preserve thee.   105
Bard. An you do not make him be hanged among you, the gallows shall have wrong.

Prince. And how doth thy master, Bardolph?

Bard. Well, my lord. He heard of your Grace's coming to town: there's a letter for you.

Poins. Delivered with good respect. And how doth the martlemas, your master? 112

Bard. In bodily health, sir.

Poins. Marry, the immortal part needs a physician; but that moves not him: though that be sick, it dies not. 116

Prince. I do allow this wen to be as familiar with me as my dog; and he holds his place, for look you how he writes. 119

Poins. '*John Falstaff, knight*,'—every man must know that, as oft as he has occasion to name himself: even like those that are akin to the king, for they never prick their finger but they say, 'There is some of the king's blood spilt.' 'How comes that?' says he that takes upon him not to conceive. The answer is as ready as a borrower's cap, 'I am the king's poor cousin, sir.' 128

Prince. Nay, they will be kin to us, or they will fetch it from Japhet. But to the letter:

Poins. *Sir John Falstaff, knight, to the son of the king nearest his father, Harry Prince of Wales, greeting.* Why, this is a certificate.

Prince. Peace! 134

Poins. *I will imitate the honourable Romans in brevity:* sure he means brevity in breath, short-winded.—*I commend me to thee, I commend thee, and I leave thee. Be not too familiar with Poins; for he misuses thy favours so much that he swears thou art to marry his sister Nell. Repent at idle times as thou mayest, and so farewell.* 142

    Thine, by yea and no,—which is as much as to say, as thou usest him, JACK FAL-STAFF, *with my familiars;* JOHN, *with my brothers and sisters, and* SIR JOHN *with all Europe.*

My lord, I'll steep this letter in sack and make him eat it. 149

Prince. That's to make him eat twenty of his words. But do you use me thus, Ned? must I marry your sister? 152

Poins. God send the wench no worse fortune! but I never said so.

Prince. Well, thus we play the fools with the time, and the spirits of the wise sit in the clouds and mock us. Is your master here in London?

Bard. Yes, my lord.

Prince. Where sups he? doth the old boar feed in the old frank? 160

Bard. At the old place, my lord, in East-cheap.

Prince. What company?

Page. Ephesians, my lord, of the old church.

Prince. Sup any women with him? 165

Page. None, my lord, but old Mistress Quickly and Mistress Doll Tearsheet.

Prince. What pagan may that be? 168

Page. A proper gentlewoman, sir, and a kins-woman of my master's.

Prince. Even such kin as the parish heifers are to the town bull. Shall we steal upon them, Ned, at supper? 173

Poins. I am your shadow, my lord; I'll follow you.

Prince. Sirrah, you boy, and Bardolph; no word to your master that I am yet come to town: there's for your silence. [*Gives money.*

Bard. I have no tongue, sir. 179

Page. And for mine, sir, I will govern it.

Prince. Fare ye well; go. [*Exeunt* BARDOLPH *and* Page.] This Doll Tearsheet should be some road.

Poins. I warrant you, as common as the way between Saint Alban's and London. 185

Prince. How might we see Falstaff bestow himself to-night in his true colours, and not ourselves be seen? 188

Poins. Put on two leathern jerkins and aprons, and wait upon him at his table as drawers. 191

Prince. From a god to a bull! a heavy descension! it was Jove's case. From a prince to a prentice! a low transformation! that shall be mine; for in every thing the purpose must weigh with the folly. Follow me, Ned. [*Exeunt.*

SCENE III.—*Warkworth. Before* NORTHUMBER-LAND'S *Castle.*

Enter NORTHUMBERLAND, LADY NORTHUMBER-LAND, *and* LADY PERCY.

North. I pray thee, loving wife, and gentle daughter,

Give even way unto my rough affairs:

Put not you on the visage of the times,

And be like them to Percy troublesome. 4

Lady N. I have given over, I will speak no more:

Do what you will; your wisdom be your guide.

North. Alas! sweet wife, my honour is at pawn;

And, but my going, nothing can redeem it. 8

Lady P. O! yet for God's sake, go not to these wars.

The time was, father, that you broke your word

When you were more endear'd to it than now;

When your own Percy, when my heart's dear Harry, 12

Threw many a northward look to see his father

Bring up his powers; but he did long in vain.

Who then persuaded you to stay at home?

There were two honours lost, yours and your son's: 16

For yours, the God of heaven brighten it!

For his, it stuck upon him as the sun

In the grey vault of heaven; and by his light

Did all the chivalry of England move 20

To do brave acts: he was indeed the glass

Wherein the noble youth did dress themselves:

He had no legs, that practis'd not his gait;

And speaking thick, which nature made his blemish, 24

Became the accents of the valiant;

For those that could speak low and tardily,

Would turn their own perfection to abuse,

To seem like him: so that, in speech, in gait, 28

In diet, in affections of delight,

In military rules, humours of blood,

He was the mark and glass, copy and book,
That fashion'd others. And him, O wondrous
  him!   32
O miracle of men! him did you leave,—
Second to none, unseconded by you,—
To look upon the hideous god of war
In disadvantage; to abide a field   36
Where nothing but the sound of Hotspur's
  name
Did seem defensible: so you left him.
Never, O! never, do his ghost the wrong
To hold your honour more precise and nice 40
With others than with him: let them alone.
The marshal and the archbishop are strong:
Had my sweet Harry had but half their numbers,
To-day might I, hanging on Hotspur's neck, 44
Have talk'd of Monmouth's grave.
      North.   Beshrew your heart,
Fair daughter! you do draw my spirits from me
With new lamenting ancient oversights.
But I must go and meet with danger there, 48
Or it will seek me in another place,
And find me worse provided.
      Lady N.   O! fly to Scotland,
Till that the nobles and the armed commons
Have of their puissance made a little taste. 52
      Lady P. If they get ground and vantage of
  the king,
Then join you with them, like a rib of steel,
To make strength stronger; but, for all our loves,
First let them try themselves. So did your son;
He was so suffer'd: so came I a widow;   57
And never shall have length of life enough
To rain upon remembrance with mine eyes,
That it may grow and sprout as high as heaven,
For recordation to my noble husband.   61
      North. Come, come, go in with me. 'Tis with
  my mind
As with the tide swell'd up unto its height,
That makes a still-stand, running neither way: 64
Fain would I go to meet the archbishop,
But many thousand reasons hold me back.
I will resolve for Scotland: there am I,
Till time and vantage crave my company.   68
                                        [*Exeunt.*

SCENE IV.—*London. A Room in the Boar's
      Head Tavern, in Eastcheap.*

      Enter two Drawers.

  First Draw. What the devil hast thou brought
there? apple-johns? thou knowest Sir John cannot endure an apple-john.   3
  Sec. Draw. Mass, thou sayst true. The prince
once set a dish of apple-johns before him, and
told him there were five more Sir Johns; and,
putting off his hat, said, 'I will now take my
leave of these six dry, round, old withered
knights.' It angered him to the heart; but he
hath forgot that.   10
  First Draw. Why then, cover, and set them
down: and see if thou canst find out Sneak's
noise; Mistress Tearsheet would fain hear some
music. Dispatch: the room where they supped
is too hot; they'll come in straight.   15
  Sec. Draw. Sirrah, here will be the prince

and Master Poins anon; and they will put on
two of our jerkins and aprons; and Sir John
must not know of it: Bardolph hath brought
word.   20
  First Draw. By the mass, here will be old
utis: it will be an excellent stratagem.
  Sec. Draw. I'll see if I can find out Sneak.
                                        [*Exit.*

Enter MISTRESS QUICKLY *and* DOLL TEAR-
      SHEET.

  Quick. I' faith, sweetheart, methinks now you
are in an excellent good temperality: your pul-
sidge beats as extraordinarily as heart would
desire; and your colour, I warrant you, is as
red as any rose; in good truth, la! But, i' faith,
you have drunk too much canaries, and that's
a marvellous searching wine, and it perfumes
the blood ere one can say, What's this? How
do you now?   32
  Dol. Better than I was: hem!
  Quick. Why, that's well said; a good heart's
worth gold. Lo! here comes Sir John.

      Enter FALSTAFF, *singing.*

  Fal. When Arthur first in court—Empty
the jordan.—[*Exit First Drawer.*]—And was a
worthy king. How now, Mistress Doll!   38
  Quick. Sick of a calm: yea, good sooth.
  Fal. So is all her sect; an they be once in a
calm they are sick.   41
  Dol. You muddy rascal, is that all the comfort you give me?
  Fal. You make fat rascals, Mistress Doll. 44
  Dol. I make them! gluttony and diseases
make them; I make them not.
  Fal. If the cook help to make the gluttony, you help to make the diseases, Doll: we
catch of you, Doll, we catch of you; grant that,
my poor virtue, grant that.   50
  Dol. Ay, marry; our chains and our jewels.
  Fal. 'Your brooches, pearls, and owches:'—
for to serve bravely is to come halting off; you
know: to come off the breach with his pike bent
bravely, and to surgery bravely; to venture upon
the charged chambers bravely,—   56
  Dol. Hang yourself, you muddy conger, hang
yourself!
  Quick. By my troth, this is the old fashion:
you two never meet but you fall to some discord:
you are both, in good troth, as rheumatic as two
dry toasts; you cannot one bear with another's
confirmities. What the good-year! one must
bear, and that must be you: you are the weaker
vessel, as they say, the emptier vessel. 64
  Dol. Can a weak empty vessel bear such a
huge full hogshead? there's a whole merchant's
venture of Bourdeaux stuff in him: you have no
seen a hulk better stuffed in the hold. Come
I'll be friends with thee, Jack: thou art going
to the wars; and whether I shall ever see the
again or no, there is nobody cares.   70

      Re-enter First Drawer.

  First Draw. Sir, Ancient Pistol's below, an
would speak with you.

Dol. Hang him, swaggering rascal! let him
t come hither: it is the foul-mouthedest rogue
England.   77
Quick. If he swagger, let him not come here:
, by my faith; I must live amongst my neigh-
urs; I'll no swaggerers: I am in good name
d fame with the very best. Shut the door;
ere comes no swaggerers here: I have not
ed all this while to have swaggering now:
ut the door, I pray you.   84
Fal. Dost thou hear, hostess?
Quick. Pray you, pacify yourself, Sir John:
ere comes no swaggerers here.
Fal. Dost thou hear? it is mine ancient.   88
Quick. Tilly-fally, Sir John, never tell me:
ur ancient swaggerer comes not in my doors.
vas before Master Tisick, the deputy, t'other
y; and, as he said to me,—'twas no longer ago
an Wednesday last,—'Neighbour Quickly,'
ys he;—Master Dumbe, our minister, was by
en;—'Neighbour Quickly,' says he, 'receive
ose that are civil, for,' said he, 'you are in an
name;' now, a' said so, I can tell whereupon;
or,' says he, 'you are an honest woman, and
ell thought on; therefore take heed what guests
u receive: receive,' says he, 'no swaggering
mpanions.' There comes none here:—you
ould bless you to hear what he said. No, I'll
e swaggerers.   103
Fal. He's no swaggerer, hostess; a tame
eater, i' faith; you may stroke him as gently
a puppy greyhound: he will not swagger with
Barbary hen if her feathers turn back in any
ow of resistance. Call him up, drawer.   108
                        [*Exit* First Drawer.
Quick. Cheater, call you him? I will bar no
nest man my house, nor no cheater; but I do
t love swaggering, by my troth; I am the
orse, when one says swagger. Feel, masters,
w I shake; look you, I warrant you.   113
Dol. So you do, hostess.
Quick. Do I? yea, in very truth, do I, an
vere an aspen leaf: I cannot abide swaggerers.

Enter PISTOL, BARDOLPH, *and* Page.

Pist. God save you, Sir John!   117
Fal. Welcome, Ancient Pistol. Here, Pistol,
charge you with a cup of sack: do you dis-
arge upon mine hostess.   120
Pist. I will discharge upon her, Sir John,
th two bullets.
Fal. She is pistol-proof, sir; you shall hardly
fend her.   124
Quick. Come, I'll drink no proofs nor no
ullets: I'll drink no more than will do me
ood, for no man's pleasure, I.
Pist. Then to you, Mistress Dorothy; I will
arge you.   129
Dol. Charge me! I scorn you, scurvy com-
nion. What! you poor, base, rascally, cheat-
g, lack-linen mate! Away, you mouldy rogue,
vay! I am meat for your master.
Pist. I know you, Mistress Dorothy.   134
Dol. Away, you cut-purse rascal! you filthy
ung, away! By this wine, I'll thrust my knife

in your mouldy chaps an you play the saucy
cuttle with me. Away, you bottle-ale rascal!
you basket-hilt stale juggler, you! Since when,
I pray you, sir? God's light! with two points
on your shoulder? much!   141
Pist. God let me not live. I will murder your
ruff for this!
Fal. No more, Pistol: I would not have you
go off here. Discharge yourself of our company,
Pistol.
Quick. No, good captain Pistol; not here,
sweet captain.   148
Dol. Captain! thou abominable damned
cheater, art thou not ashamed to be called
captain? An captains were of my mind, they
would truncheon you out for taking their names
upon you before you have earned them. You
a captain, you slave! for what? for tearing a
poor whore's ruff in a bawdy-house? He a
captain! Hang him, rogue! He lives upon
mouldy stewed prunes and dried cakes. A
captain! God's light, these villains will make
the word captain as odious as the word 'occupy,'
which was an excellent good word before it was
ill sorted: therefore captains had need look to it.
Bard. Pray thee, go down, good ancient. 162
Fal. Hark thee hither, Mistress Doll.
Pist. Not I; I tell thee what, Corporal Bardolph; I could tear her. I'll be revenged of
her.   166
Page. Pray thee, go down.
Pist. I'll see her damned first; to Pluto's
damned lake, by this hand, to the infernal deep,
with Erebus and tortures vile also. Hold hook
and line, say I. Down, down, dogs! down fates!
Have we not Hiren here?   172
Quick. Good Captain Peesel, be quiet; it is
very late, i' faith. I beseek you now, aggravate
your choler.
Pist. These be good humours, indeed! Shall
pack-horses,   176
And hollow pamper'd jades of Asia,
Which cannot go but thirty miles a day,
Compare with Cæsars, and with Cannibals,
And Trojan Greeks? nay, rather damn them
with   180
King Cerberus; and let the welkin roar.
Shall we fall foul for toys?
Quick. By my troth, captain, these are very
bitter words.   184
Bard. Be gone, good ancient: this will grow
to a brawl anon.
Pist. Die men like dogs! give crowns like
pins! Have we not Hiren here?   188
Quick. O' my word, captain, there's none
such here. What the good-year! do you think
I wouid deny her? for God's sake! be quiet.
Pist. Then feed, and be fat, my fair Calipolis.
Come, give's some sack.   193
Si fortuna me tormente, sperato me contento.
Fear we broadsides? no, let the fiend give fire:
Give me some sack; and, sweetheart, lie thou
there.   [*Laying down his sword.*
Come we to full points here, and are *et ceteras*
nothing?   197
Fal. Pistol, I would be quiet.

Pist. Sweet knight, I kiss thy neif. What! we have seen the seven stars.   200

Dol. For God's sake, thrust him down stairs! I cannot endure such a fustian rascal.

Pist. 'Thrust him down stairs!' know we not Galloway nags?   204

Fal. Quoit him down, Bardolph, like a shove-groat shilling: nay, an a' do nothing but speak nothing, a' shall be nothing here.

Bard. Come, get you down stairs.   208

Pist. What! shall we have incision? Shall we imbrue?   [*Snatching up his sword.*
Then death rock me asleep, abridge my doleful days!
Why then, let grievous, ghastly, gaping wounds Untwine the Sisters Three! Come, Atropos, I say!   212

Quick. Here's goodly stuff toward!

Fal. Give me my rapier, boy.

Dol. I pray thee, Jack, I pray thee, do not draw.   216

Fal. Get you down stairs.   [*Drawing.*

Quick. Here's a goodly tumult! I'll forswear keeping house, afore I'll be in these tirrits and frights. So; murder, I warrant now. Alas, alas! put up your naked weapons; put up your naked weapons.   [*Exeunt* BARDOLPH *and* PISTOL.

Dol. I pray thee, Jack, be quiet; the rascal's gone. Ah! you whoreson little valiant villain, you!   225

Quick. Are you not hurt i' the groin? methought a' made a shrewd thrust at your belly.

Re-enter BARDOLPH.

Fal. Have you turned him out o' doors?   228

Bard. Yes, sir: the rascal's drunk. You have hurt him, sir, i' the shoulder.

Fal. A rascal, to brave me!

Dol. Ah, you sweet little rogue, you! Alas, poor ape, how thou sweatest! Come, let me wipe thy face; come on, you whoreson chops. Ah, rogue! i' faith, I love thee. Thou art as valorous as Hector of Troy, worth five of Agamemnon, and ten times better than the Nine Worthies. Ah, villain!

Fal. A rascally slave! I will toss the rogue in a blanket.   240

Dol. Do, an thou darest for thy heart: an thou dost, I'll canvass thee between a pair of sheets.

Enter Music.

Page. The music is come, sir.   244

Fal. Let them play. Play, sirs. Sit on my knee, Doll. A rascal bragging slave! the rogue fled from me like quicksilver.

Dol. I' faith, and thou followedst him like a church. Thou whoreson little tidy Bartholomew boar-pig, when wilt thou leave fighting o' days, and foining o' nights, and begin to patch up thine old body for heaven?   252

Enter behind the PRINCE *and* POINS, *disguised like Drawers.*

Fal. Peace, good Doll! do not speak like a death's head: do not bid me remember mine end.

Dol. Sirrah, what humour is the prince o

Fal. A good shallow young fellow: a' wou have made a good pantler, a' would have chipp bread well.

Dol. They say, Poins has a good wit.

Fal. He a good wit! hang him, baboon! wit is as thick as Tewksbury mustard: there no more conceit in him than is in a mallet.

Dol. Why does the prince love him so, the

Fal. Because their legs are both of a bigne and he plays at quoits well, and eats conger a fennel, and drinks off candles' ends for fla dragons, and rides the wild mare with the boy and jumps upon joint-stools, and swears wit good grace, and wears his boots very smoo like unto the sign of the leg, and breeds no ba with telling of discreet stories; and such oth gambol faculties a' has, that show a weak mi and an able body, for the which the prin admits him: for the prince himself is su another; the weight of a hair will turn t scales between their avoirdupois.

Prince. Would not this nave of a wheel ha his ears cut off?

Poins. Let's beat him before his whore.

Prince. Look, whether the withered eld hath not his poll clawed like a parrot.

Poins. Is it not strange that desire should many years outlive performance?

Fal. Kiss me, Doll.

Prince. Saturn and Venus this year in co junction! what says the almanack to that?

Poins. And, look, whether the fiery Trigo his man, be not lisping to his master's old tabl his note-book, his counsel-keeper.

Fal. Thou dost give me flattering busses.

Dol. By my troth, I kiss thee with a m constant heart.

Fal. I am old, I am old.

Dol. I love thee better than I love e'er scurvy young boy of them all.

Fal. What stuff wilt have a kirtle of? shall receive money o' Thursday; thou sh have a cap to-morrow. A merry song! com it grows late; we'll to bed. Thou'lt forget when I am gone.

Dol. By my troth, thou'lt set me a-weepi an thou sayst so: prove that ever I dress mys handsome till thy return. Well, hearken at t end.

Fal. Some sack, Francis!

Prince. \ [*Coming forward.*] Anon, anc
Poins. / sir.

Fal. Ha! a bastard son of the king's? A art not thou Poins his brother?

Prince. Why, thou globe of sinful continen what a life dost thou lead!

Fal. A better than thou: I am a gentlema thou art a drawer.

Prince. Very true, sir; and I come to dr you out by the ears.

Quick. O! the Lord preserve thy good Gra by my troth, welcome to London. Now, Lord bless that sweet face of thine! O Jes are you come from Wales?

Fal. Thou whoreson mad compound

ajesty, by this light flesh and corrupt blood
ointing to DOLL], thou art welcome.

Dol. How, you fat fool! I scorn you.   324

Poins. My lord, he will drive you out of your
venge and turn all to a merriment, if you take
t the heat.

Prince. You whoreson candle-mine, you, how
ely did you speak of me even now before this
nest, virtuous, civil gentlewoman!

Quick. Blessing on your good heart! and so
e is, by my troth.   332

Fal. Didst thou hear me?

Prince. Yea; and you knew me, as you did
en you ran away by Gadshill: you knew I
is at your back, and spoke it on purpose to try
v patience.   337

Fal. No, no, no; not so; I did not think thou
st within hearing.

Prince. I shall drive you then to confess the
lful abuse; and then I know how to handle
u.

Fal. No abuse, Hal, o' mine honour; no
use.   344

Prince. Not to dispraise me, and call me
ntler and bread-chipper and I know not what?

Fal. No abuse, Hal.

Poins. No abuse!   348

Fal. No abuse, Ned, in the world; honest
ed, none. I dispraised him before the wicked,
at the wicked might not fall in love with him;
which doing I have done the part of a careful
end and a true subject, and thy father is to
ve me thanks for it. No abuse, Hal; none,
ed, none: no, faith, boys, none.   355

Prince. See now, whether pure fear and
tire cowardice doth not make thee wrong this
tuous gentlewoman to close with us? Is she
the wicked? Is thine hostess here of the
cked? Or is thy boy of the wicked? Or honest
rdolph, whose zeal burns in his nose, of the
cked?   362

Poins. Answer, thou dead elm, answer.

Fal. The fiend hath pricked down Bardolph
ecoverable; and his face is Lucifer's privy-
tchen, where he doth nothing but roast malt-
orms. For the boy, there is a good angel about
m; but the devil outbids him too.   368

Prince. For the women?

Fal. For one of them, she is in hell already,
d burns poor souls. For the other, I owe her
oney; and whether she be damned for that, I
ow not.   373

Quick. No, I warrant you.

Fal. No, I think thou art not; I think thou
t quit for that. Marry, there is another in-
tment upon thee, for suffering flesh to be
ten in thy house, contrary to the law; for the
ich I think thou wilt howl.

Quick. All victuallers do so: what's a joint of
utton or two in a whole Lent?   381

Prince. You, gentlewoman,—

Dol. What says your Grace?

Fal. His Grace says that which his flesh
bels against.   [*Knocking within.*

Quick. Who knocks so loud at door? Look
the door there, Francis.

Enter PETO.

Prince. Peto, how now! what news?   388

Peto. The king your father is at Westminster;
And there are twenty weak and wearied posts
Come from the north: and as I came along,
I met and overtook a dozen captains,   392
Bare-headed, sweating, knocking at the taverns,
And asking every one for Sir John Falstaff.

Prince. By heaven, Poins, I feel me much to
blame,
So idly to profane the precious time,   396
When tempest of commotion, like the south,
Borne with black vapour, doth begin to melt
And drop upon our bare unarmed heads.
Give me my sword and cloak. Falstaff, good
night. [*Exeunt the* PRINCE, POINS, PETO, *and*
BARDOLPH.

Fal. Now comes in the sweetest morsel of
the night, and we must hence and leave it un-
picked. [*Knocking within.*] More knocking at
the door!   404

Re-enter BARDOLPH.

How now! what's the matter?

Bard. You must away to court, sir, presently;
A dozen captains stay at door for you.   407

Fal. [*To the* Page]. Pay the musicians, sirrah.
Farewell, hostess; farewell, Doll. You see, my
good wenches, how men of merit are sought
after: the undeserver may sleep when the man
of action is called on. Farewell, good wenches.
If I be not sent away post, I will see you again
ere I go.   414

Dol. I cannot speak; if my heart be not
ready to burst,—well, sweet Jack, have a care
of thyself.   417

Fal. Farewell, farewell.
[*Exeunt* FALSTAFF *and* BARDOLPH.

Quick. Well, fare thee well: I have known
thee these twenty-nine years, come peascod-
time; but an honester, and truer-hearted man,
—well, fare thee well.

Bard. [*Within.*] Mistress Tearsheet!

Quick. What's the matter?   424

Bard. [*Within.*] Bid Mistress Tearsheet come
to my master.

Quick. O! run, Doll, run; run, good Doll.
[*Exeunt.*

ACT III

SCENE I.—*Westminster. A Room in the
Palace.*

Enter KING HENRY *in his night-gown, with a*
Page.

K. Hen. Go, call the Earls of Surrey and of
Warwick;
But, ere they come, bid them o'er-read these
letters,
And well consider of them. Make good speed.
[*Exit* Page.
How many thousand of my poorest subjects 4
Are at this hour asleep! O sleep! O gentle sleep!
Nature's soft nurse, how have I frighted thee,

That thou no more wilt weigh my eyelids down
And steep my senses in forgetfulness? 8
Why rather, sleep, liest thou in smoky cribs,
Upon uneasy pallets stretching thee,
And hush'd with buzzing night-flies to thy
    slumber,
Than in the perfum'd chambers of the great, 12
Under the canopies of costly state,
And lull'd with sound of sweetest melody?
O thou dull god! why liest thou with the vile
In loathsome beds, and leav'st the kingly couch
A watch-case or a common 'larum bell? 17
Wilt thou upon the high and giddy mast
Seal up the ship-boy's eyes, and rock his brains
In cradle of the rude imperious surge, 20
And in the visitation of the winds,
Who take the ruffian billows by the top,
Curling their monstrous heads, and hanging
    them
With deaf'ning clamour in the slippery clouds,
That with the hurly death itself awakes? 25
Canst thou, O partial sleep! give thy repose
To the wet sea-boy in an hour so rude,
And in the calmest and most stillest night, 28
With all appliances and means to boot,
Deny it to a king? Then, happy low, lie down!
Uneasy lies the head that wears a crown.

Enter WARWICK *and* SURREY.

War. Many good morrows to your majesty!
K. Hen. Is it good morrow, lords? 33
War. 'Tis one o'clock, and past.
K. Hen. Why then, good morrow to you all,
    my lords.
Have you read o'er the letters that I sent you?
War. We have, my liege. 37
K. Hen. Then you perceive the body of our
    kingdom,
How foul it is; what rank diseases grow,
And with what danger, near the heart of it. 40
War. It is but as a body, yet, distemper'd,
Which to his former strength may be restor'd
With good advice and little medicine:
My Lord Northumberland will soon be cool'd. 44
  K. Hen. O God! that one might read the
    book of fate,
And see the revolution of the times
Make mountains level, and the continent,—
Weary of solid firmness,—melt itself 48
Into the sea! and, other times, to see
The beachy girdle of the ocean
Too wide for Neptune's hips; how chances
    mock,
And changes fill the cup of alteration 52
With divers liquors! O! if this were seen,
The happiest youth, viewing his progress through,
What perils past, what crosses to ensue,
Would shut the book, and sit him down and die.
'Tis not ten years gone 57
Since Richard and Northumberland, great
    friends,
Did feast together, and in two years after
Were they at wars: it is but eight years since 60
This Percy was the man nearest my soul,
Who like a brother toil'd in my affairs
And laid his love and life under my foot;

Yea, for my sake, even to the eyes of Richard
Gave him defiance. But which of you was by,-
[*To* WARWICK.] You, cousin Nevil, as I ma
    remember,—
When Richard, with his eye brimful of tears
Then check'd and rated by Northumberland,
Did speak these words, now prov'd a prophecy
'Northumberland, thou ladder, by the which
My cousin Bolingbroke ascends my throne;
Though then, God knows, I had no such inten
But that necessity so bow'd the state
That I and greatness were compelled to kiss
'The time shall come,' thus did he follow it,
'The time will come, that foul sin, gatherin
    head,
Shall break into corruption:'—so went on,
Foretelling this same time's condition
And the division of our amity.
  War. There is a history in all men's lives,
Figuring the nature of the times deceas'd;
The which observ'd, a man may prophesy,
With a near aim, of the main chance of thin
As yet not come to life, which in their seeds
And weak beginnings lie intreasured.
Such things become the hatch and brood of tim
And by the necessary form of this
King Richard might create a perfect guess
That great Northumberland, then false to hir
Would of that seed grow to a greater falsenes
Which should not find a ground to root upo
Unless on you.
  K. Hen. Are these things then necessities
Then let us meet them like necessities;
And that same word even now cries out on u
They say the bishop and Northumberland
Are fifty thousand strong.
  War.   It cannot be, my lor
Rumour doth double, like the voice and echo,
The numbers of the fear'd. Please it your Gra
To go to bed: upon my soul, my lord,
The powers that you already have sent forth
Shall bring this prize in very easily.
To comfort you the more, I have receiv'd
A certain instance that Glendower is dead.
Your majesty hath been this fortnight ill,
And these unseason'd hours perforce must ac
Unto your sickness.
  K. Hen.   I will take your counse
And were these inward wars once out of han
We would, dear lords, unto the Holy Land.
                        [*Exeur*

SCENE II.—*Court before* JUSTICE SHALLOW'
    House in Gloucestershire.

Enter SHALLOW *and* SILENCE, *meeting*; MOULD
    SHADOW, WART, FEEBLE, BULLCALF *and* Se
    vants, *behind.*

  Shal. Come on, come on, come on, sir; gi
me your hand, sir, give me your hand, sir:
early stirrer, by the rood! And how doth n
good cousin Silence?
  Sil. Good morrow, good cousin Shallow.
  Shal. And how doth my cousin, your be
fellow? and your fairest daughter and mine, n
god-daughter Ellen?

Sil. Alas! a black ousel, cousin Shallow!

Shal. By yea and nay, sir, I dare say my cousin William is become a good scholar. He is at Oxford still, is he not?   12

Sil. Indeed, sir, to my cost.

Shal. A' must, then, to the inns o' court shortly. I was once of Clement's Inn; where I think they will talk of mad Shallow yet.   16

Sil. You were called 'lusty Shallow' then, cousin.

Shal. By the mass, I was called any thing; and I would have done any thing indeed too, and roundly too. There was I, and Little John Doit of Staffordshire, and black George Barnes, and Francis Pickbone, and Will Squele a Cotsvold man; you had not four such swinge-buckers in all the inns of court again: and, I may say to you, we knew where the *bona-robas* were, and had the best of them all at commandment. Then was Jack Falstaff, now Sir John, a boy, and page to Thomas Mowbray, Duke of Norfolk.

Sil. This Sir John, cousin, that comes hither anon about soldiers?   31

Shal. The same Sir John, the very same. I saw him break Skogan's head at the court gate, when a' was a crack not thus high: and the very same day did I fight with one Sampson Stockfish, a fruiterer, behind Gray's Inn. Jesu! Jesu! the mad days that I have spent; and to see how many of mine old acquaintance are dead!   38

Sil. We shall all follow, cousin.

Shal. Certain, 'tis certain; very sure, very sure: death, as the Psalmist saith, is certain to all; all shall die. How a good yoke of bullocks at Stamford fair?

Sil. Truly, cousin, I was not there.   44

Shal. Death is certain. Is old Double of your own living yet?

Sil. Dead, sir.

Shal. Jesu! Jesu! dead! a' drew a good bow; and dead! a' shot a fine shoot: John a Gaunt loved him well, and betted much money on his head. Dead! a' would have clapped i' the clout at twelve score; and carried you a forehand shaft a fourteen and fourteen and a half, that it would have done a man's heart good to see. How a score of ewes now?   55

Sil. Thereafter as they be: a score of good ewes may be worth ten pounds.

Shal. And is old Double dead?

Sil. Here come two of Sir John Falstaff's men, as I think.   60

Enter BARDOLPH, *and One with him.*

Bard. Good morrow, honest gentlemen: I beseech you, which is Justice Shallow?

Shal. I am Robert Shallow, sir; a poor esquire of this county, and one of the king's justices of the peace: what is your good pleasure with me?   66

Bard. My captain, sir, commends him to you; my captain, Sir John Falstaff: a tall gentleman, by heaven, and a most gallant leader.   69

Shal. He greets me well, sir. I knew him a good backsword man. How doth the good knight? may I ask how my lady his wife doth?

Bard. Sir, pardon; a soldier is better accommodated than with a wife.   74

Shal. It is well said, in faith, sir; and it is well said indeed too. 'Better accommodated!' it is good; yea indeed, is it: good phrases are surely and ever were, very commendable. Accommodated! it comes of *accommodo*: very good; a good phrase.   80

Bard. Pardon me, sir; I have heard the word. 'Phrase,' call you it? By this good day, I know not the phrase; but I will maintain the word with my sword to be a soldier-like word, and a word of exceeding good command, by heaven. Accommodated; that is, when a man is, as they say, accommodated; or, when a man is, being, whereby, a' may be thought to be accommodated, which is an excellent thing.   89

Enter FALSTAFF.

Shal. It is very just. Look, here comes good Sir John. Give me your good hand, give me your worship's good hand. By my troth, you look well and bear your years very well: welcome, good Sir John.   94

Fal. I am glad to see you well, good Master Robert Shallow. Master Surecard, as I think.

Shal. No, Sir John; it is my cousin, Silence, in commission with me.

Fal. Good Master Silence, it well befits you should be of the peace.   100

Sil. Your good worship is welcome.

Fal. Fie! this is hot weather, gentlemen. Have you provided me here half a dozen sufficient men?   104

Shal. Marry, have we, sir. Will you sit?

Fal. Let me see them, I beseech you.

Shal. Where's the roll? where's the roll? where's the roll? Let me see, let me see, let me see. So, so, so, so, so, so, so: yea, marry, sir: Ralph Mouldy! let them appear as I call; let them do so, let them do so. Let me see; where is Mouldy?

Moul. Here, an't please you.   112

Shal. What think you, Sir John? a good-limbed fellow; young, strong, and of good friends.

Fal. Is thy name Mouldy?   116

Moul. Yea, an't please you.

Fal. 'Tis the more time thou wert used.

Shal. Ha, ha, ha! most excellent, i' faith! things that are mouldy lack use: very singular good. In faith, well said, Sir John; very well said.   122

Fal. Prick him.

Moul. I was pricked well enough before, an you could have let me alone: my old dame will be undone now for one to do her husbandry and her drudgery: you need not to have pricked me; there are other men fitter to go out than I.

Fal. Go to: peace, Mouldy! you shall go. Mouldy, it is time you were spent.   130

Moul. Spent!

Shal. Peace, fellow, peace! stand aside: know you where you are? For the other, Sir John: let me see. Simon Shadow!

Fal. Yea, marry, let me have him to sit under: he's like to be a cold soldier.   136

Shal. Where's Shadow?

Shad. Here, sir.

Fal. Shadow, whose son art thou?

Shad. My mother's son, sir.   140

Fal. Thy mother's son! like enough, and thy father's shadow: so the son of the female is the shadow of the male: it is often so, indeed; but not of the father's substance.   144

Shal. Do you like him, Sir John?

Fal. Shadow will serve for summer; prick him, for we have a number of shadows to fill up the muster-book.   148

Shal. Thomas Wart?

Fal. Where's he?

Wart. Here, sir.

Fal. Is thy name Wart?   152

Wart. Yea, sir.

Fal. Thou art a very ragged wart.

Shal. Shall I prick him, Sir John?

Fal. It were superfluous; for his apparel is built upon his back, and the whole frame stands upon pins: prick him no more.   158

Shal. Ha, ha, ha! you can do it, sir; you can do it: I commend you well. Francis Feeble!

Fee. Here, sir.

Fal. What trade art thou, Feeble?

Fee. A woman's tailor, sir.

Shal. Shall I prick him, sir?   164

Fal. You may; but if he had been a man's tailor he'd have pricked you. Wilt thou make as many holes in an enemy's battle as thou hast done in a woman's petticoat?   168

Fee. I will do my good will, sir: you can have no more.

Fal. Well said, good woman's tailor! well said, courageous Feeble! Thou wilt be as valiant as the wrathful dove or most magnanimous mouse. Prick the woman's tailor; well, Master Shallow; deep, Master Shallow.

Fee. I would Wart might have gone, sir. 176

Fal. I would thou wert a man's tailor, that thou mightst mend him, and make him fit to go. I cannot put him to a private soldier that is the leader of so many thousands: let that suffice, most forcible Feeble.   181

Fee. It shall suffice, sir.

Fal. I am bound to thee, reverend Feeble. Who is next?   184

Shal. Peter Bullcalf o' the green!

Fal. Yea, marry, let's see Bullcalf.

Bull. Here, sir.

Fal. 'Fore God, a likely fellow! Come, prick me Bullcalf till he roar again.   189

Bull. O Lord! good my lord captain,—

Fal. What! dost thou roar before thou art pricked?   192

Bull. O Lord, sir! I am a diseased man.

Fal. What disease hast thou?

Bull. A whoreson cold, sir; a cough, sir, which I caught with ringing in the king's affairs upon his coronation day, sir.   197

Fal. Come, thou shalt go to the wars in a gown; we will have away thy cold; and I will take such order that thy friends shall ring for thee. Is here all?   201

Shal. Here is two more called than your number; you must have but four here, sir: an so, I pray you, go in with me to dinner.   20

Fal. Come, I will go drink with you, but cannot tarry dinner. I am glad to see you, b my troth, Master Shallow.

Shal. O, Sir John, do you remember since w lay all night in the windmill in Saint George fields?

Fal. No more of that, good Master Shallow no more of that.   21

Shal. Ha! it was a merry night. And is Jan Nightwork alive?

Fal. She lives, Master Shallow.

Shal. She never could away with me.   21

Fal. Never, never; she would always say sh could not abide Master Shallow.

Shal. By the mass, I could anger her to th heart. She was then a *bona-roba*. Doth sh hold her own well?   22

Fal. Old, old, Master Shallow.

Shal. Nay, she must be old; she cannot choos but be old; certain she's old; and had Robi Nightwork by old Nightwork before I came t Clement's Inn.

Sil. That's fifty-five year ago.   22

Shal. Ha! cousin Silence, that thou hads seen that that this knight and I have seen. Ha Sir John, said I well?

Fal. We have heard the chimes at midnigh Master Shallow.   23

Shal. That we have, that we have, that w have; in faith, Sir John, we have. Our watch word was, 'Hem, boys!' Come, let's to dinner come, let's to dinner. Jesus, the days that w have seen! Come, come.   23

[*Exeunt* FALSTAFF, SHALLOW, an
SILENCE

Bull. Good Master Corporate Bardolph, stan my friend, and here's four Harry ten shillings in French crowns for you. In very truth, sir, I ha as lief be hanged, sir, as go: and yet, for min own part, sir, I do not care; but rather, becaus I am unwilling, and, for mine own part, have desire to stay with my friends: else, sir, I di not care, for mine own part, so much.   24

Bard. Go to; stand aside.

Moul. And, good Master corporal captain, fo my old dame's sake, stand my friend: she ha nobody to do any thing about her, when I am gone; and she is old, and cannot help herself You shall have forty, sir.

Bard. Go to; stand aside.   25

Fee. By my troth, I care not; a man can di but once; we owe God a death. I'll ne'er bear a base mind: an't be my destiny, so; an't be not, so. No man's too good to serve's prince and let it go which way it will, he that dies this year is quit for the next.

Bard. Well said; thou'rt a good fellow.

Fee. Faith, I'll bear no base mind.   26

Re-enter FALSTAFF *and the* Justices.

Fal. Come, sir, which men shall I have?

Shal. Four, of which you please.

Bard. [*To* FALSTAFF.] Sir, a word with you. I have three pound to free Mouldy and Bullcalf

Fal. [*Aside to* BARDOLPH.] Go to; well. 265
Shal. Come, Sir John, which four will you have?
Fal. Do you choose for me. 268
Shal. Marry, then, Mouldy, Bullcalf, Feeble, and Shadow.
Fal. Mouldy, and Bullcalf: for you, Mouldy, stay at home till you are past service: and for your part, Bullcalf, grow till you come unto it: I will none of you. 274
Shal. Sir John, Sir John, do not yourself wrong: they are your likeliest men, and I would have you served with the best. 277
Fal. Will you tell me, Master Shallow, how to choose a man? Care I for the limb, the thewes, the stature, bulk, and big assemblance of a man! Give me the spirit, Master Shallow. Here's Wart; you see what a ragged appearance it is: a' shall charge you and discharge you with the motion of a pewterer's hammer, come off and on swifter than he that gibbets on the brewer's bucket. And this same half-faced fellow, Shadow, give me this man: he presents no mark to the enemy; the foeman may with as great aim level at the edge of a penknife. And, for a retreat; how swiftly will this Feeble the woman's tailor run off! O! give me the spare men, and spare me the great ones. Put me a caliver into Wart's hand, Bardolph. 293
Bard. Hold, Wart, traverse; thus, thus, thus.
Fal. Come, manage me your caliver. So: very well: go to: very good: exceeding good. O, give me always a little, lean, old, chopp'd, bald shot. Well said, i' faith, Wart; thou 'rt a good scab: hold, there's a tester for thee. 299
Shal. He is not his craft's master, he doth not do it right. I remember at Mile-end Green, when I lay at Clement's Inn,—I was then Sir Dagonet in Arthur's show,—there was a little quiver fellow, and a' would manage you his piece thus: and a' would about and about, and come you in, and come you in; 'rah, tah, tah,' would a' say; 'bounce,' would a' say; and away again would a' go, and again would a' come: I shall never see such a fellow. 309
Fal. These fellows will do well, Master Shallow. God keep you, Master Silence: I will not use many words with you. Fare you well, gentlemen both: I thank you: I must a dozen mile to-night. Bardolph, give the soldiers coats.
Shal. Sir John, the Lord bless you! and prosper your affairs! God send us peace! At your return visit our house; let our old acquaintance be renewed: peradventure I will with ye to the court. 319
Fal. 'Fore God I would you would, Master Shallow.
Shal. Go to; I have spoke at a word. God keep you. 323
Fal. Fare you well, gentle gentlemen. [*Exeunt* SHALLOW *and* SILENCE.] On, Bardolph; lead the men away. [*Exeunt* BARDOLPH, *Recruits, &c.*] As I return, I will fetch off these justices: I do see the bottom of Justice Shallow. Lord, Lord! how subject we old men are to this vice of lying. This same starved justice hath done nothing but prate to me of the wildness of his youth and the feats he hath done about Turnbull Street; and every third word a lie, duer paid to the hearer than the Turk's tribute. I do remember him at Clement's Inn like a man made after supper of a cheese-paring: when a' was naked he was for all the world like a forked radish, with a head fantastically carved upon it with a knife: a' was so forlorn that his dimensions to any thick sight were invincible: a' was the very genius of famine; yet lecherous as a monkey, and the whores called him mandrake: a' came ever in the rearward of the fashion and sung those tunes to the over-scutched huswives that he heard the carmen whistle, and sware they were his fancies or his good-nights. And now is this Vice's dagger become a squire, and talks as familiarly of John a Gaunt as if he had been sworn brother to him; and I'll be sworn a' never saw him but once in the Tilt-yard, and then he burst his head for crowding among the marshal's men. I saw it and told John a Gaunt he beat his own name; for you might have thrust him and all his apparel into an eel-skin; the case of a treble hautboy was a mansion for him, a court; and now has he land and beefs. Well, I will be acquainted with him, if I return; and it shall go hard but I will make him a philosopher's two stones to me. If the young dace be a bait for the old pike, I see no reason in the law of nature but I may snap at him. Let time shape, and there an end. [*Exit.*

ACT IV

SCENE I.—*A Forest in Yorkshire.*

Enter the ARCHBISHOP OF YORK, MOWBRAY, HASTINGS, *and Others.*

Arch. What is this forest call'd?
Hast. 'Tis Gaultree Forest, an 't shall please your Grace.
Arch. Here stand, my lords, and send discoverers forth,
To know the numbers of our enemies. 4
Hast. We have sent forth already.
Arch.   'Tis well done.
My friends and brethren in these great affairs,
I must acquaint you that I have receiv'd
New-dated letters from Northumberland; 8
Their cold intent, tenour and substance, thus:
Here doth he wish his person, with such powers
As might hold sortance with his quality;
The which he could not levy; whereupon 12
He is retir'd, to ripe his growing fortunes,
To Scotland; and concludes in hearty prayers
That your attempts may overlive the hazard
And fearful meeting of their opposite. 16
Mowb. Thus do the hopes we have in him touch ground
And dash themselves to pieces.

Enter a Messenger.

Hast.   Now, what news?
Mess. West of this forest, scarcely off a mile,

In goodly form comes on the enemy;   20
And, by the ground they hide, I judge their
    number
Upon or near the rate of thirty thousand.
Mowb. The just proportion that we gave
    them out.
Let us sway on and face them in the field.   24

Enter WESTMORELAND.

Arch. What well-appointed leader fronts us
    here?
Mowb. I think it is my Lord of Westmore-
    land.
West. Health and fair greeting from our
    general,
The Prince, Lord John and Duke of Lancaster.
Arch. Say on, my Lord of Westmoreland, in
    peace,   29
What doth concern your coming.
    West.   Then, my lord,
Unto your Grace do I in chief address
The substance of my speech. If that rebellion
Came like itself, in base and abject routs,   33
Led on by bloody youth, guarded with rags,
And countenanc'd by boys and beggary;
I say, if damn'd commotion so appear'd,   36
In his true, native, and most proper shape,
You, reverend father, and these noble lords
Had not been here, to dress the ugly form
Of base and bloody insurrection   40
With your fair honours. You, lord archbishop,
Whose see is by a civil peace maintain'd,
Whose beard the silver hand of peace hath
    touch'd,
Whose learning and good letters peace hath
    tutor'd,   44
Whose white investments figure innocence,
The dove and very blessed spirit of peace,
Wherefore do you so ill translate yourself
Out of the speech of peace that bears such grace
Into the harsh and boisterous tongue of war;   49
Turning your books to greaves, your ink to
    blood,
Your pens to lances, and your tongue divine
To a loud trumpet and a point of war?   52
    Arch. Wherefore do I this? so the question
    stands.
Briefly to this end: we are all diseas'd;
And, with out surfeiting and wanton hours
Have brought ourselves into a burning fever,   56
And we must bleed for it: of which disease
Our late king, Richard, being infected, died.
But, my most noble Lord of Westmoreland,
I take not on me here as a physician,   60
Nor do I as an enemy to peace
Troop in the throngs of military men;
But rather show a while like fearful war,
To diet rank minds sick of happiness   64
And purge the obstructions which begin to stop
Our very veins of life. Hear me more plainly:
I have in equal balance justly weigh'd
What wrongs our arms may do, what wrongs
    we suffer,   68
And find our griefs heavier than our offences.
We see which way the stream of time doth run
And are enforc'd from our most quiet sphere

By the rough torrent of occasion;   72
And have the summary of all our griefs,
When time shall serve, to show in articles,
Which long ere this we offer'd to the king,
And might by no suit gain our audience.   76
When we are wrong'd and would unfold our
    griefs,
We are denied access unto his person
Even by those men that most have done us
    wrong.
The dangers of the days but newly gone,—   80
Whose memory is written on the earth
With yet appearing blood,—and the examples
Of every minute's instance, present now,
Have put us in these ill-beseeming arms;   84
Not to break peace, or any branch of it,
But to establish here a peace indeed,
Concurring both in name and quality.
    West. When ever yet was your appeal denied?
Wherein have you been galled by the king?
What peer hath been suborn'd to grate on you,
That you should seal this lawless bloody book
Of forg'd rebellion with a seal divine,   92
And consecrate commotion's bitter edge?
    Arch. My brother general, the common-
    wealth,
To brother born an household cruelty,
I make my quarrel in particular.   96
    West. There is no need of any such redress;
Or if there were, it not belongs to you.
    Mowb. Why not to him in part, and to us all
That feel the bruises of the days before,   100
And suffer the condition of these times
To lay a heavy and unequal hand
Upon our honours?
    West.   O! my good Lord Mowbray,
Construe the times to their necessities,   104
And you shall say indeed, it is the time,
And not the king, that doth you injuries.
Yet, for your part, it not appears to me
Either from the king or in the present time
That you should have an inch of any ground
To build a grief on: were you not restor'd   110
To all the Duke of Norfolk's signories,
Your noble and right well-remember'd father's?
    Mowb. What thing, in honour, had my
    father lost,   113
That need to be reviv'd and breath'd in me?
The king that lov'd him as the state stood then,
Was force perforce compell'd to banish him:
And then that Harry Bolingbroke and he, 117
Being mounted and both roused in their seats,
Their neighing coursers daring of the spur,
Their armed staves in charge, their beavers
    down,   120
Their eyes of fire sparkling through sights of
    steel,
And the loud trumpet blowing them together
Then, then, when there was nothing could have
    stay'd
My father from the breast of Bolingbroke, 124
O! when the king did throw his warder down
His own life hung upon the staff he threw;
Then threw he down himself and all their lives
That by indictment and by dint of sword 128
Have since miscarried under Bolingbroke.

West. You speak, Lord Mowbray, now you
  know not what.
he Earl of Hereford was reputed then
  England the most valiant gentleman: 132
Vho knows on whom Fortune would then have
  smil'd?
ut if your father had been victor there,
e ne'er had borne it out of Coventry;
or all the country in a general voice   136
ried hate upon him; and all their prayers and
  love
Vere set on Hereford, whom they doted on
nd bless'd and grac'd indeed, more than the
  king.
ut this is mere digression from my purpose. 140
Iere come I from our princely general
o know your griefs; to tell you from his Grace
hat he will give you audience; and wherein
: shall appear that your demands are just, 144
ou shall enjoy them; every thing set off
hat might so much as think you enemies.
  Mowb. But he hath forc'd us to compel this
  offer,
nd it proceeds from policy, not love.   148
  West. Mowbray, you overween to take it so.
his offer comes from mercy, not from fear:
or, lo! within a ken our army lies
Jpon mine honour, all too confident   152
o give admittance to a thought of fear.
)ur battle is more full of names than yours,
)ur men more perfect in the use of arms,
)ur armour all as strong, our cause the best;
hen reason will our hearts should be as good:
ay you not then our offer is compell'd.
  Mowb. Well, by my will we shall admit no
  parley.
  West. That argues but the shame of your
  offence: 160
\ rotten case abides no handling.
  Hast. Hath the Prince John a full commission,
n very ample virtue of his father,
To hear and absolutely to determine   164
)f what conditions we shall stand upon?
  West. That is intended in the general's name.
muse you make so slight a question.
  Arch. Then take, my Lord of Westmoreland,
  this schedule,   168
'or this contains our general grievances:
:ach several article herein redress'd;
\ll members of our cause, both here and hence,
That are insinew'd to this action,   172
Acquitted by a true substantial form
And present execution of our wills
To us and to our purposes consign'd;
We come within our awful banks again   176
And knit our powers to the arm of peace.
  West. This will I show the general. Please
  you, lords,
n sight of both our battles we may meet;
And either end in peace, which God so frame!
)r to the place of difference call the swords
Which must decide it.
  Arch.   My lord, we will do so.
                  [*Exit* WESTMORELAND.
  Mowb. There is a thing within my bosom
  tells me   183

That no conditions of our peace can stand.
  Hast. Fear you not that: if we can make
  our peace   185
Upon such large terms, and so absolute
As our conditions shall consist upon,
Our peace shall stand as firm as rocky mountains.
  Mowb. Yea, but our valuation shall be such
That every slight and false-derived cause,
Yea, every idle, nice, and wanton reason
Shall to the king taste of this action;   192
That, were our royal faiths martyrs in love,
We shall be winnow'd with so rough a wind
That even our corn shall seem as light as chaff
And good from bad find no partition.   196
  Arch. No, no, my lord. Note this; the king
  is weary
Of dainty and such picking grievances:
For he hath found to end one doubt by death
Revives two greater in the heirs of life;   200
And therefore will he wipe his tables clean,
And keep no tell-tale to his memory
That may repeat and history his loss
To new remembrance; for full well he knows
He cannot so precisely weed this land   205
As his misdoubts present occasion:
His foes are so enrooted with his friends
That, plucking to unfix an enemy,   208
He doth unfasten so and shake a friend.
So that this land, like an offensive wife,
That hath enrag'd him on to offer strokes,
As he is striking, holds his infant up   212
And hangs resolv'd correction in the arm
That was uprear'd to execution.
  Hast. Besides, the king hath wasted all his
  rods
On late offenders, that he now doth lack   216
The very instruments of chastisement;
So that his power, like to a fangless lion,
May offer, but not hold.
  Arch.   'Tis very true:
And therefore be assur'd, my good lord marshal,
If we do now make our atonement well,   221
Our peace will, like a broken limb united,
Grow stronger for the breaking.
  Mowb.   Be it so.
Here is return'd my Lord of Westmoreland. 224

    Re-enter WESTMORELAND.

  West. The prince is here at hand: pleaseth
  your lordship,
To meet his Grace just distance 'tween our
  armies?
  Mowb. Your Grace of York, in God's name
  then, set forward.
  Arch. Before, and greet his Grace: my lord,
  we come.   [*Exeunt.*

  SCENE II.—*Another Part of the Forest.*

Enter, from one side, MOWBRAY, *the* ARCH-
BISHOP, HASTINGS, *and Others: from the other
side,* JOHN OF LANCASTER, WESTMORELAND,
Officers, *and* Attendants.

  Lanc. You are well encounter'd here, my
  cousin Mowbray:
Good day to you, gentle lord archbishop;

And so to you, Lord Hastings, and to all.
My Lord of York, it better show'd with you, 4
When that your flock, assembled by the bell,
Encircled you to hear with reverence
Your exposition on the holy text
Than now to see you here an iron man, 8
Cheering a rout of rebels with your drum,
Turning the word to sword and life to death.
That man that sits within a monarch's heart
And ripens in the sunshine of his favour, 12
Would he abuse the countenance of the king,
Alack! what mischief might he set abroach
In shadow of such greatness. With you, lord
bishop,
It is even so. Who hath not heard it spoken 16
How deep you were within the books of God?
To us, the speaker in his parliament;
To us the imagin'd voice of God himself;
The very opener and intelligencer 20
Between the grace, the sanctities of heaven,
And our dull workings. O! who shall believe
But you misuse the reverence of your place,
Employ the countenance and grace of heaven,
As a false favourite doth his prince's name,
In deeds dishonourable? You have taken up,
Under the counterfeited zeal of God,
The subjects of his substitute, my father; 28
And both against the peace of heaven and him
Have here upswarm'd them.
    Arch.   Good my Lord of Lancaster,
I am not here against your father's peace;
But, as I told my Lord of Westmoreland, 32
The time misorder'd doth, in common sense,
Crowd us and crush us to this monstrous form,
To hold our safety up. I sent your Grace
The parcels and particulars of our grief,— 36
The which hath been with scorn shov'd from
the court,—
Whereon this Hydra son of war is born;
Whose dangerous eyes may well be charm'd
asleep 39
With grant of our most just and right desires,
And true obedience, of this madness cur'd,
Stoop tamely to the foot of majesty.
    Mowb. If not, we ready are to try our fortunes
To the last man.
    Hast.   And though we here fall down, 44
We have supplies to second our attempt:
If they miscarry, theirs shall second them;
And so success of mischief shall be born,
And heir from heir shall hold this quarrel up 48
Whiles England shall have generation.
    Lanc. You are too shallow, Hastings, much
too shallow,
To sound the bottom of the after-times.
    West. Pleaseth your Grace, to answer them
directly 52
How far forth you do like their articles.
    Lanc. I like them all, and do allow them
well;
And swear here, by the honour of my blood,
My father's purposes have been mistook, 56
And some about him have too lavishly
Wrested his meaning and authority.
My lord, these griefs shall be with speed re-
dress'd;

Upon my soul, they shall. If this may plea
you,
Discharge your powers unto their several cou
ties,
As we will ours: and here between the armies
Let's drink together friendly and embrace,
That all their eyes may bear those tokens hon
Of our restored love and amity.
    Arch. I take your princely word for the
redresses.
    Lanc. I give it you, and will maintain n
word:
And thereupon I drink unto your Grace.
    Hast. [*To an* Officer.] Go, captain, and deliv
to the army
This news of peace: let them have pay, a
part:
I know it will well please them: hie thee, captai
                                        [*Exit* Office
    Arch. To you, my noble Lord of Westmor
land.
    West. I pledge your Grace: and, if you kne
what pains
I have bestow'd to breed this present peace
You would drink freely; but my love to yo
Shall show itself more openly hereafter.
    Arch. I do not doubt you.
    West.   I am glad of it.
Health to my lord and gentle cousin, Mowbra
    Mowb. You wish me health in very hap
season;
For I am, on the sudden, something ill.
    Arch. Against ill chances men are ever merr
But heaviness foreruns the good event.
    West. Therefore be merry, coz; since sudd
sorrow
Serves to say thus, Some good thing com
to-morrow.
    Arch. Believe me, I am passing light in spiri
    Mowb. So much the worse if your own ru
be true.   [*Shouts withi*
    Lanc. The word of peace is render'd: har
how they shout!
    Mowb. This had been cheerful, after victor
    Arch. A peace is of the nature of a conques
For then both parties nobly are subdu'd,
And neither party loser.
    Lanc.   Go, my lord,
And let our army be discharged too.
                        [*Exit* WESTMORELAN
And, good my lord, so please you, let o
trains
March by us, that we may peruse the men
We should have cop'd withal.
    Arch. Go, good Lord Hastings,
And, ere they be dismiss'd, let them march b
                            [*Exit* HASTING
    Lanc. I trust, lords, we shall lie to-night t
gether.

Re-enter WESTMORELAND.

Now, cousin, wherefore stands our army stil
    West. The leaders, having charge from yc
to stand,   I
Will not go off until they hear you speak.
    Lanc. They know their duties.

Re-enter HASTINGS.

Hast. My lord, our army is dispers'd already:
like youthful steers unyok'd, they take their
  courses   104
ast, west, north, south; or, like a school broke
  up,
ach hurries toward his home and sporting-
  place.

West. Good tidings, my Lord Hastings; for
  the which
do arrest thee, traitor, of high treason: 108
nd you, lord archbishop, and you, Lord Mowbray,
f capital treason I attach you both.

Mowb. Is this proceeding just and honourable?

West. Is your assembly so?   112

Arch. Will you thus break your faith?

Lanc.   I pawn'd thee none.
promis'd you redress of these same grievances
Vhereof you did complain; which, by mine
  honour,
will perform with a most Christian care. 116
ut for you, rebels, look to taste the due
leet for rebellion and such acts as yours.
Most shallowly did you these arms commence,
ondly brought here and foolishly sent hence.
trike up our drums! pursue the scatter'd
  stray:
od, and not we, hath safely fought to-day.
ome guard these traitors to the block of
  death;   123
reason's true bed, and yielder up of breath.
           [*Exeunt.*

SCENE III.—*Another Part of the Forest.*

Alarums. Excursions. Enter FALSTAFF *and*
COLEVILE, *meeting.*

Fal. What's your name, sir? of what con-
ition are you, and of what place, I pray?

Cole. I am a knight, sir; and my name is
Colevile of the dale.   4

Fal. Well then, Colevile is your name, a
night is your degree, and your place the dale:
olevile shall still be your name, a traitor your
egree, and the dungeon your place, a place
eep enough; so shall you be still Colevile of
1e dale.

Cole. Are not you Sir John Falstaff?   11

Fal. As good a man as he, sir, whoe'er I am.
)o ye yield, sir, or shall I sweat for you? If
do sweat, they are the drops of thy lovers,
nd they weep for thy death: therefore rouse
p fear and trembling, and do observance to
1y mercy.   17

Cole. I think you are Sir John Falstaff, and
a that thought yield me.

Fal. I have a whole school of tongues in this
elly of mine, and not a tongue of them all
peaks any other word but my name. An I had
ut a belly of any indifferency, I were simply the
1ost active fellow in Europe: my womb, my
omb, my womb undoes me. Here comes our
eneral.   26

Enter JOHN OF LANCASTER, WESTMORELAND,
BLUNT, *and Others.*

Lanc. The heat is past, follow no further
  now.
Call in the powers, good cousin Westmoreland.
           [*Exit* WESTMORELAND.
Now, Falstaff, where have you been all this
  while?   29
When everything is ended, then you come:
These tardy tricks of yours will, on my life,
One time or other break some gallows' back. 32

Fal. I would be sorry, my lord, but it should
be thus: I never knew yet but rebuke and check
was the reward of valour. Do you think me a
swallow, an arrow, or a bullet? have I, in my
poor and old motion, the expedition of thought?
I have speeded hither with the very extremest
inch of possibility; I have foundered nine score
and odd posts; and here, travel-tainted as I am,
have, in my pure and immaculate valour, taken
Sir John Colevile of the dale, a most furious
knight and valorous enemy. But what of that?
he saw me, and yielded; that I may justly say
with the hook-nosed fellow of Rome, 'I came,
saw, and overcame.'

Lanc. It was more of his courtesy than your
deserving.   48

Fal. I know not: here he is, and here I yield
him; and I beseech your Grace, let it be booked
with the rest of this day's deeds; or, by the Lord,
I will have it in a particular ballad else, with
mine own picture on the top on't, Colevile
kissing my foot. To the which course if I be
enforced, if you do not all show like gilt two-
pences to me, and I in the clear sky of fame
o'ershine you as much as the full moon doth
the cinders of the element, which show like pins'
heads to her, believe not the word of the noble.
Therefore let me have right, and let desert
mount.   61

Lanc. Thine's too heavy to mount.

Fal. Let it shine then.

Lanc. Thine's too thick to shine.   64

Fal. Let it do something, my good lord, that
may do me good, and call it what you will.

Lanc. Is thy name Colevile?

Cole. It is, my lord.   68

Lanc. A famous rebel art thou, Colevile.

Fal. And a famous true subject took him.

Cole. I am, my lord, but as my betters are
That led me hither: had they been rul'd by
  me   72
You should have won them dearer than you
  have.

Fal. I know not how they sold themselves:
but thou, like a kind fellow, gavest thyself away
gratis, and I thank thee for thee.   76

Re-enter WESTMORELAND.

Lanc. Have you left pursuit?

West. Retreat is made and execution stay'd.

Lanc. Send Colevile with his confederates
To York, to present execution.   80
Blunt, lead him hence, and see you guard him
sure.   [*Exit* BLUNT *and Others with*
           COLEVILE, *guarded.*

And now dispatch we toward the court, my
 lords:
I hear, the king my father is sore sick:
Our news shall go before us to his majesty, 84
Which, cousin [*addressing* WESTMORELAND], you
 shall bear, to comfort him;
And we with sober speed will follow you.

 Fal. My lord, I beseech you, give me leave
  to go,
Through Gloucestershire, and when you come
 to court   88
Stand my good lord, pray, in your good report.

 Lanc. Fare you well, Falstaff: I, in my condition,
Shall better speak of you than you deserve. 91
        [*Exeunt all but* FALSTAFF.

 Fal. I would you had but the wit: 'twere
better than your dukedom. Good faith, this
same young sober-blooded boy doth not love
me; nor a man cannot make him laugh; but
that's no marvel, he drinks no wine. There's
never none of these demure boys come to any
proof; for thin drink doth so over-cool their
blood, and making many fish-meals, that they
fall into a kind of male green-sickness; and then,
when they marry, they get wenches. They
are generally fools and cowards, which some of
us should be too but for inflammation. A good
sherris-sack hath a two-fold operation in it.
It ascends me into the brain; dries me there all
the foolish and dull and crudy vapours which
environ it; makes it apprehensive, quick, forgetive, full of nimble fiery and delectable shapes;
which, deliver'd o'er to the voice, the tongue,
which is the birth, becomes excellent wit. The
second property of your excellent sherris is, the
warming of the blood; which, before cold and
settled, left the liver white and pale, which is
the badge of pusillanimity and cowardice: but
the sherris warms it and makes it course from
the inwards to the parts extreme. It illumineth
the face, which, as a beacon, gives warning to
all the rest of this little kingdom, man, to arm;
and then the vital commoners and inland petty
spirits muster me all to their captain, the heart,
who, great and puffed up with this retinue, doth
any deed of courage; and this valour comes of
sherris. So that skill in the weapon is nothing
without sack, for that sets it a-work; and learning, a mere hoard of gold kept by a devil till
sack commences it and sets it in act and use.
Hereof comes it that Prince Harry is valiant;
for the cold blood he did naturally inherit of
his father, he hath, like lean, sterile, and bare
land, manured, husbanded, and tilled, with excellent endeavour of drinking good and good
store of fertile sherris, that he is become very
hot and valiant. If I had a thousand sons, the
first human principle I would teach them should
be, to forswear thin potations and to addict
themselves to sack.   136

Enter BARDOLPH.

How now, Bardolph?
 Bard. The army is discharged all and gone.
 Fal. Let them go. I'll through Gloucester-

shire; and there will I visit Master Robert
Shallow, esquire: I have him already tempering
between my finger and my thumb, and shortly
will I seal with him. Come away. [*Exeunt.*

SCENE IV.—*Westminster. The Jerusalem
Chamber.*

Enter KING HENRY, CLARENCE, GLOUCESTER,
  WARWICK, *and Others.*

 K. Hen. Now, lords, if God doth give suc-
  cessful end
To this debate that bleedeth at our doors,
We will our youth lead on to higher fields
And draw no swords but what are sanctified.
Our navy is address'd, our power collected,
Our substitutes in absence well invested,
And everything lies level to our wish:
Only, we want a little personal strength;
And pause us, till these rebels, now afoot,
Come underneath the yoke of government.
 War. Both which we doubt not but your
  majesty
Shall soon enjoy.
 K. Hen. Humphrey, my son of Gloucester,
Where is the prince your brother?
 Glo. I think he's gone to hunt, my lord, at
  Windsor.
 K. Hen. And how accompanied?
 Glo.   I do not know, my lord.
 K. Hen. Is not his brother Thomas of Cla-
  rence with him?
 Glo. No, my good lord; he is in presence
  here.
 Cla. What would my lord and father?
 K. Hen. Nothing but well to thee, Thomas
  of Clarence.
How chance thou art not with the prince thy
 brother?
He loves thee, and thou dost neglect him,
 Thomas;
Thou hast a better place in his affection
Than all thy brothers: cherish it, my boy,
And noble offices thou mayst effect
Of mediation, after I am dead,
Between his greatness and thy other brethren:
Therefore omit him not; blunt not his love,
Nor lose the good advantage of his grace
By seeming cold or careless of his will;
For he is gracious, if he be observ'd:
He hath a tear for pity and a hand
Open as day for melting charity;
Yet, notwithstanding, being incens'd, he's flint
As humorous as winter, and as sudden
As flaws congealed in the spring of day.
His temper therefore must be well observ'd:
Chide him for faults, and do it reverently,
When you perceive his blood inclin'd to mirth;
But, being moody, give him line and scope,
Till that his passions, like a whale on ground,
Confound themselves with working. Learn
 this, Thomas,
And thou shalt prove a shelter to thy friends,
A hoop of gold to bind thy brothers in,
That the united vessel of their blood,
Mingled with venom of suggestion—

s, force perforce, the age will pour it in—
hall never leak, though it do work as strong
s aconitum or rash gunpowder.   48
Cla. I shall observe him with all care and
love.
K. Hen. Why art thou not at Windsor with
him, Thomas?
Cla. He is not there to-day; he dines in
London.
K. Hen. And how accompanied? canst thou
tell that?   52
Cla. With Poins and other his continual followers.
K. Hen. Most subject is the fattest soil to
weeds;
nd he, the noble image of my youth,
s overspread with them: therefore my grief 56
tretches itself beyond the hour of death:
he blood weeps from my heart when I do
shape
n forms imaginary the unguided days
nd rotten times that you shall look upon   60
Vhen I am sleeping with my ancestors.
'or when his headstrong riot hath no curb,
Vhen rage and hot blood are his counsellors,
Vhen means and lavish manners meet together,
)! with what wings shall his affections fly 65
owards fronting peril and oppos'd decay.
War. My gracious lord, you look beyond
him quite:
he prince but studies his companions   68
ike a strange tongue, wherein, to gain the
language,
Tis needful that the most immodest word
e look'd upon, and learn'd; which once attain'd,   71
Your highness knows, comes to no further use
ut to be known and hated. So, like gross
terms,
he prince will in the perfectness of time
Cast off his followers; and their memory
hall as a pattern or a measure live,   76
by which his Grace must mete the lives of others,
urning past evils to advantages.
K. Hen. 'Tis seldom when the bee doth leave
her comb
n the dead carrion.

Enter WESTMORELAND.

Who's here? Westmoreland!
West. Health to my sovereign, and new hap-
piness   81
Added to that that I am to deliver!
Prince John your son doth kiss your Grace's
hand:
Mowbray, the Bishop Scroop, Hastings and all
Are brought to the correction of your law.   85
There is not now a rebel's sword unsheath'd,
But Peace puts forth her olive everywhere.
The manner how this action hath been borne,
Here at more leisure may your highness read
With every course in his particular.
K. Hen. O Westmoreland! thou art a sum-
mer bird,   91
Which ever in the haunch of winter sings
The lifting up of day.

Enter HARCOURT.

Look! here's more news.
Har. From enemies heaven keep your ma-
jesty;
And, when they stand against you, may they fall
As those that I am come to tell you of!   96
The Earl Northumberland, and the Lord Bar-
dolph,
With a great power of English and of Scots,
Are by the sheriff of Yorkshire overthrown.
The manner and true order of the fight   100
This packet, please it you, contains at large.
K. Hen. And wherefore should these good
news make me sick?
Will Fortune never come with both hands full
But write her fair words still in foulest letters?
She either gives a stomach and no food;   105
Such are the poor, in health; or else a feast
And takes away the stomach; such are the rich,
That have abundance and enjoy it not.   108
I should rejoice now at this happy news,
And now my sight fails, and my brain is giddy.
O me! come near me, now I am much ill.
Glo. Comfort, your majesty!
Cla.   O my royal father! 112
West. My sovereign lord, cheer up yourself:
look up!
War. Be patient, princes: you do know these
fits
Are with his highness very ordinary:
Stand from him, give him air; he'll straight
be well.   116
Cla. No, no; he cannot long hold out these
pangs:
The incessant care and labour of his mind
Hath wrought the mure that should confine
it in
So thin, that life looks through and will break
out.   120
Glo. The people fear me; for they do observe
Unfather'd heirs and loathly births of nature:
The seasons change their manners, as the year
Had found some months asleep and leap'd
them over.   124
Cla. The river hath thrice flow'd, no ebb
between;
And the old folk, time's doting chronicles,
Say it did so a little time before
That our great-grandsire, Edward, sick'd and
died.   128
War. Speak lower, princes, for the king re-
covers.
Glo. This apoplexy will certain be his end.
K. Hen. I pray you take me up, and bear me
hence
Into some other chamber: softly, pray.   132

SCENE V.—*Another Chamber.*

KING HENRY *lying on a bed:* CLARENCE, GLOU-
CESTER, WARWICK, *and Others in attendance.*

K. Hen. Let there be no noise made, my
gentle friends;
Unless some dull and favourable hand
Will whisper music to my weary spirit.   3
War. Call for the music in the other room.

K. Hen. Set me the crown upon my pillow
     here.
Cla. His eye is hollow, and he changes much.
War. Less noise, less noise!

Enter the PRINCE.

Prince.   Who saw the Duke of Clarence?
Cla. I am here, brother, full of heaviness. 8
Prince. How now! rain within doors, and
     none abroad!
How doth the king?
Glo.   Exceeding ill.
Prince.   Heard he the good news yet?
Tell it him.   11
Glo. He alter'd much upon the hearing it.
Prince. If he be sick with joy, he will recover
without physic.
     War. Not so much noise, my lords. Sweet
prince, speak low;
The king your father is dispos'd to sleep. 16
     Cla. Let us withdraw into the other room.
     War. Will't please your Grace to go along
with us?
     Prince. No; I will sit and watch here by the
king.   [*Exeunt all but the* PRINCE.
Why doth the crown lie there upon his pillow,
Being so troublesome a bedfellow?   21
O polish'd perturbation! golden care!
That keep'st the ports of slumber open wide
To many a watchful night! Sleep with it now!
Yet not so sound, and half so deeply sweet 25
As he whose brow with homely biggin bound
Snores out the watch of night. O majesty!
When thou dost pinch thy bearer, thou dost sit
Like a rich armour worn in heat of day, 29
That scalds with safety. By his gates of breath
There lies a downy feather which stirs not:
Did he suspire, that light and weightless down
Perforce must move. My gracious lord! my
     father!   33
This sleep is sound indeed; this is a sleep
That from this golden rigol hath divorc'd
So many English kings. Thy due from me 36
Is tears and heavy sorrows of the blood,
Which nature, love, and filial tenderness
Shall, O dear father! pay thee plenteously:
My due from thee is this imperial crown, 40
Which, as immediate from thy place and
     blood,
Derives itself to me. Lo! here it sits,
          [*Putting it on his head.*
Which heaven shall guard; and put the world's
     whole strength
Into one giant arm, it shall not force 44
This lineal honour from me. This from thee
Will I to mine leave, as 'tis left to me. [*Exit.*
     K. Hen. [*Waking.*] Warwick! Gloucester!
     Clarence!

Re-enter WARWICK, GLOUCESTER, CLARENCE,
     and the rest.

Cla.   Doth the king call?
War. What would your majesty? How fares
     your Grace?   48
K. Hen. Why did you leave me here alone,
     my lords?

Cla. We left the prince my brother here, my
     liege,
Who undertook to sit and watch by you.
     K. Hen. The Prince of Wales! Where is he?
     let me see him: 52
He is not here.
     War. The door is open; he is gone this way.
     Glo. He came not through the chamber where
     we stay'd.
     K. Hen. Where is the crown? who took it
     from my pillow?   56
     War. When we withdrew, my liege, we left it
     here.
     K. Hen. The prince hath ta'en it hence: go,
     seek him out.
Is he so hasty that he doth suppose
My sleep my death?   60
Find him, my Lord of Warwick; chide him
     hither.   [*Exit* WARWICK.
This part of his conjoins with my disease,
And helps to end me. See, sons, what things
     you are!
How quickly nature falls into revolt 64
When gold becomes her object!
For this the foolish over-careful fathers
Have broke their sleeps with thoughts,
Their brains with care, their bones with in-
     dustry;   68
For this they have engrossed and pil'd up
The canker'd heaps of strange-achieved gold;
For this they have been thoughtful to invest
Their sons with arts and martial exercises: 72
When, like the bee, culling from every flower
The virtuous sweets,
Our thighs packed with wax, our mouths with
     honey,
We bring it to the hive, and like the bees, 76
Are murder'd for our pains. This bitter taste
Yield his engrossments to the ending father.

Re-enter WARWICK.

Now, where is he that will not stay so long
Till his friend sickness hath determin'd me? 80
     War. My lord, I found the prince in the next
     room,
Washing with kindly tears his gentle cheeks,
With such a deep demeanour in great sorrow
That tyranny, which never quaff'd but blood, 84
Would by beholding him, have wash'd his knife
With gentle eye-drops. He is coming hither.
     K. Hen. But wherefore did he take away the
     crown?

Re-enter the PRINCE.

Lo, where he comes. Come hither to me, Harry,
Depart the chamber, leave us here alone. 89
          [*Exeunt* WARWICK, *and the rest.*
     Prince. I never thought to hear you speak
     again.
     K. Hen. Thy wish was father, Harry, to that
     thought:
I stay too long by thee, I weary thee.   92
Dost thou so hunger for my empty chair
That thou wilt needs invest thee with mine
     honours
Before thy hour be ripe? O foolish youth!

hou seek'st the greatness that will overwhelm
　thee.　　　　　　　　　　　　　　　　96
tay but a little; for my cloud of dignity
s held from falling with so weak a wind
hat it will quickly drop: my day is dim.
hou hast stol'n that which after some few
　hours　　　　　　　　　　　　　　　100
Vere thine without offence; and at my death
hou hast seal'd up my expectation:
hy life did manifest thou lov'dst me not,
nd thou wilt have me die assur'd of it.　104
hou hid'st a thousand daggers in thy thoughts,
Vhich thou hast whetted on thy stony heart,
o stab at half an hour of my life.
Vhat! canst thou not forbear me half an hour?
hen get thee gone and dig my grave thyself, 109
And bid the merry bells ring to thine ear
hat thou art crowned, not that I am dead.
et all the tears that should bedew my hearse
e drops of balm to sanctify thy head:　113
nly compound me with forgotten dust;
ive that which gave thee life unto the worms.
luck down my officers, break my decrees;
or now a time is come to mock at form.　117
larry the Fifth is crown'd! Up, vanity!
own, royal state! all you sage counsellors,
　hence!
nd to the English court assemble now,　120
rom every region, apes of idleness!
Now, neighbour confines, purge you of your
　scum:
Have you a ruffian that will swear, drink, dance,
evel the night, rob, murder, and commit　124
he oldest sins the newest kind of ways?
e happy, he will trouble you no more;
ngland shall double gild his treble guilt.
ngland shall give him office, honour, might;
or the fifth Harry from curb'd licence plucks
he muzzle of restraint, and the wild dog
hall flesh his tooth in every innocent.　131
my poor kingdom! sick with civil blows.
When that my care could not withhold thy riots,
What wilt thou do when riot is thy care?
O! thou wilt be a wilderness again,
eopled with wolves, thy old inhabitants.　136
　Prince. O! pardon me, my liege; but for my
　tears,
The moist impediments unto my speech,
had forestall'd this dear and deep rebuke
re you with grief had spoke and I had heard
The course of it so far. There is your crown;
And he that wears the crown immortally
Long guard it yours! If I affect it more
Than as your honour and as your renown, 144
Let me no more from this obedience rise,—
Which my most true and inward duteous spirit
Teacheth,—this prostrate and exterior bending.
God witness with me, when I here came in,
And found no course of breath within your
　majesty,　　　　　　　　　　　　　149
How cold it struck my heart! if I do feign,
O! let me in my present wildness die
And never live to show the incredulous world
The noble change that I have purposed.　153
Coming to look on you, thinking you dead,
And dead almost, my liege, to think you were,

I spake unto the crown as having sense,　156
And thus upbraided it: 'The care on thee de-
　pending
Hath fed upon the body of my father;
Therefore, thou best of gold art worst of gold:
Other, less fine in carat, is more precious,　160
Preserving life in medicine potable:
But thou most fine, most honour'd, most re-
　nown'd,
Hast eat thy bearer up.' Thus, my most royal
　liege,
Accusing it, I put it on my head,　　　164
To try with it, as with an enemy
That had before my face murder'd my father,
The quarrel of a true inheritor.
But if it did infect my blood with joy,　168
Or swell my thoughts to any strain of pride;
If any rebel or vain spirit of mine
Did with the least affection of a welcome
Give entertainment to the might of it,　172
Let God for ever keep it from my head,
And make me as the poorest vassal is
That doth with awe and terror kneel to it!
　K. Hen. O my son!　　　　　　　176
God put it in thy mind to take it hence,
That thou mightst win the more thy father's
　love,
Pleading so wisely in excuse of it.
Come hither, Harry: sit thou by my bed;　180
And hear, I think, the very latest counsel
That ever I shall breathe. God knows, my son,
By what by-paths and indirect crook'd ways
I met this crown; and I myself know well 184
How troublesome it sat upon my head:
To thee it shall descend with better quiet,
Better opinion, better confirmation;
For all the soil of the achievement goes　188
With me into the earth. It seem'd in me
But as an honour snatch'd with boisterous hand,
And I had many living to upbraid
My gain of it by their assistances;　　192
Which daily grew to quarrel and to bloodshed,
Wounding supposed peace. All these bold fears
Thou seest with peril I have answered;
For all my reign hath been but as a scene 196
Acting that argument; and now my death
Changes the mode: for what in me was pur-
　chas'd,
Falls upon thee in a more fairer sort;
So thou the garment wear'st successively.　200
Yet, though thou stand'st more sure than I
　could do,
Thou art not firm enough, since griefs are green;
And all my friends, which thou must make thy
　friends,
Have but their stings and teeth newly ta'en out;
By whose fell working I was first advanc'd, 205
And by whose power I well might lodge a fear
To be again displac'd: which to avoid,
I cut them off; and had a purpose now　208
To lead out many to the Holy Land,
Lest rest and lying still might make them look
Too near unto my state. Therefore, my Harry,
Be it thy course to busy giddy minds　212
With foreign quarrels; that action, hence borne
　out,

May waste the memory of the former days.
More would I, but my lungs are wasted so
That strength of speech is utterly denied me. 216
How I came by the crown, O God, forgive!
And grant it may with thee in true peace live.
   Prince. My gracious liege,
You won it, wore it, kept it, gave it me; 220
Then plain and right must my possession be:
Which I with more than with a common pain
'Gainst all the world will rightfully maintain.

Enter JOHN OF LANCASTER.

  K. Hen. Look, look, here comes my John of
Lancaster. 224
  Lanc. Health, peace, and happiness to my
royal father!
  K. Hen. Thou bring'st me happiness and
peace, son John;
But health, alack, with youthful wings is flown
From this bare wither'd trunk: upon thy sight
My worldly business makes a period. 229
Where is my Lord of Warwick?
  Prince.   My Lord of Warwick!

Re-enter WARWICK *and Others.*

  K. Hen. Doth any name particular belong
Unto the lodging where I first did swound? 232
  War. 'Tis call'd Jerusalem, my noble lord.
  K. Hen. Laud be to God! even there my life
must end.
It hath been prophesied to me many years
I should not die but in Jerusalem, 236
Which vainly I suppos'd the Holy Land.
But bear me to that chamber; there I'll lie:
In that Jerusalem shall Harry die. [*Exeunt.*

ACT V

SCENE I.—*Gloucestershire. A Hall in*
SHALLOW'S *House.*

Enter SHALLOW, FALSTAFF, BARDOLPH, *and*
Page.

  Shal. By cock and pie, sir, you shall not away
to-night. What! Davy, I say.
  Fal. You must excuse me, Master Robert
Shallow. 4
  Shal. I will not excuse you; you shall not be
excused; excuses shall not be admitted; there
is no excuse shall serve; you shall not be excused. Why, Davy! 8

Enter DAVY.

  Davy. Here, sir.
  Shal. Davy, Davy, Davy, Davy, let me see,
Davy; let me see: yea, marry, William cook, bid
him come hither. Sir John, you shall not be
excused. 13
  Davy. Marry, sir, thus; those precepts cannot be served: and again, sir, shall we sow the
headland with wheat? 16
  Shal. With red wheat, Davy. But for William
cook: are there no young pigeons?
  Davy. Yes, sir. Here is now the smith's note
for shoeing and plough-irons. 20

  Shal. Let it be cast and paid. Sir John, yo
shall not be excused.
  Davy. Now, sir, a new link to the bucke
must needs be had: and, sir, do you mean t
stop any of William's wages, about the sack h
lost the other day at Hinckley fair?
  Shal. A' shall answer it. Some pigeon.
Davy, a couple of short-legged hens, a joint o
mutton, and any pretty little tiny kickshaw
tell William cook.
  Davy. Doth the man of war stay all nigh
sir?
  Shal. Yea, Davy. I will use him well.
friend i' the court is better than a penny i
purse. Use his men well, Davy, for they ar
arrant knaves, and will backbite.
  Davy. No worse than they are back-bitten
sir; for they have marvellous foul linen.
  Shal. Well conceited, Davy: about thy bus
ness, Davy.
  Davy. I beseech you, sir, to countenance
William Visor of Wincot against Clemen
Perkes of the hill.
  Shal. There are many complaints, Davy
against that Visor: that Visor is an arran
knave, on my knowledge.
  Davy. I grant your worship that he is
knave, sir; but yet, God forbid, sir, but a knav
should have some countenance at his friend'
request. An honest man, sir, is able to speak fo
himself, when a knave is not. I have serve
your worship truly, sir, this eight years; and
I cannot once or twice in a quarter bear out
knave against an honest man, I have but a ver
little credit with your worship. The knave i
mine honest friend, sir; therefore, I beseec
your worship, let him be countenanced.
  Shal. Go to; I say he shall have no wrong
Look about, Davy. [*Exit* DAVY.] Where are you
Sir John? Come, come, come; off with you
boots. Give me your hand, Master Bardolph.
  Bard. I am glad to see your worship.
  Shal. I thank thee with all my heart, kin
Master Bardolph:—[*To the* Page.] and wel
come, my tall fellow. Come, Sir John.
  Fal. I'll follow you, good Master Rober
Shallow. [*Exit* SHALLOW.] Bardolph, look to
our horses. [*Exeunt* BARDOLPH *and* Page.] If
were sawed into quantities, I should make fou
dozen of such bearded hermit's staves as Maste
Shallow. It is a wonderful thing to see th
semblable coherence of his men's spirits and his
they, by observing him, do bear themselves lik
foolish justices; he, by conversing with them, i
turned into a justice-like serving-man. Thei
spirits are so married in conjunction with th
participation of society that they flock togethe
in consent, like so many wild-geese. If I had
suit to Master Shallow, I would humour his mea
with the imputation of being near their master
if to his men, I would curry with Master Shallow
that no man could better command his servants
It is certain that either wise bearing or ignoran
carriage is caught, as men take diseases, one o
another: therefore let men take heed of thei
company. I will devise matter enough out o

is Shallow to keep Prince Harry in continual
ughter the wearing out of six fashions,—which
four terms, or two actions,—and a' shall laugh
thout intervallums. O! it is much that a lie
th a slight oath and a jest with a sad brow
do with a fellow that never had the ache in
s shoulders. O! you shall see him laugh till
s face be like a wet cloak ill laid up! 94

Shal. [*Within.*] Sir John!

Fal. I come, Master Shallow: I come, Master
aallow. [*Exit.*

ENE II.—*Westminster. An Apartment in the
Palace.*

nter WARWICK *and the* LORD CHIEF JUSTICE.

War. How now, my Lord Chief Justice!
whither away?

Ch. Just. How doth the king?

War. Exceeding well: his cares are now all
ended.

Ch. Just. I hope not dead.

War. He's walk'd the way of nature; 4
nd to our purposes he lives no more.

Ch. Just. I would his majesty had call'd me
with him:

he service that I truly did his life
ath left me open to all injuries. 8

War. Indeed I think the young king loves
you not.

Ch. Just. I know he doth not, and do arm
myself,

o welcome the condition of the time;
hich cannot look more hideously upon me 12
han I have drawn it in my fantasy.

Enter LANCASTER, CLARENCE, GLOUCESTER,
WESTMORELAND *and Others.*

War. Here come the heavy issue of dead
Harry:

! that the living Harry had the temper
f him, the worst of these three gentlemen. 16
ow many nobles then should hold their places,
hat must strike sail to spirits of vile sort!

Ch. Just. O God! I fear all will be overturn'd.

Lanc. Good morrow, cousin Warwick, good
morrow. 20

Glo. } Good morrow, cousin.
Cla. }

Lanc. We meet like men that had forgot to
speak.

War. We do remember; but our argument
all too heavy to admit much talk. 24

Lanc. Well, peace be with him that hath
made us heavy!

Ch. Just. Peace be with us, lest we be heavier!

Glo. O! good my lord, you have lost a friend
indeed; 27
nd I dare swear you borrow not that face
f seeming sorrow; it is sure your own.

Lanc. Though no man be assur'd what grace
to find,
ou stand in coldest expectation.
am the sorrier; would 'twere otherwise. 32

Cla. Well, you must now speak Sir John
Falstaff fair,

Which swims against your stream of quality.

Ch. Just. Sweet princes, what I did, I did in
honour,
Led by the impartial conduct of my soul; 36
And never shall you see that I will beg
A ragged and forestall'd remission.
If truth and upright innocency fail me,
I'll to the king my master that is dead, 40
And tell him who hath sent me after him.

War. Here comes the prince.

Enter KING HENRY THE FIFTH, *attended.*

Ch. Just. Good morrow, and God save your
majesty!

K. Hen. V. This new and gorgeous garment,
majesty, 44
Sits not so easy on me as you think.
Brothers, you mix your sadness with some fear:
This is the English, not the Turkish court;
Not Amurath an Amurath succeeds, 48
But Harry Harry. Yet be sad, good brothers,
For, to speak truth, it very well becomes you:
Sorrow so royally in you appears
That I will deeply put the fashion on 52
And wear it in my heart. Why then, be sad;
But entertain no more of it, good brothers,
Than a joint burden laid upon us all.
For me, by heaven, I bid you be assur'd, 56
I'll be your father and your brother too;
Let me but bear your love, I'll bear your cares:
Yet weep that Harry's dead, and so will I;
But Harry lives that shall convert those tears 60
By number into hours of happiness.

Lanc., &c. We hope no other from your
majesty.

K. Hen. V. You all look strangely on me: [*To
the* CHIEF JUSTICE.] and you most;
You are, I think, assur'd I love you not. 64

Ch. Just. I am assur'd, if I be measur'd rightly,
Your majesty hath no just cause to hate me.

K. Hen. V. No! 67
How might a prince of my great hopes forget
So great indignities you laid upon me?
What! rate, rebuke, and roughly send to prison
The immediate heir of England! Was this easy?
May this be wash'd in Lethe, and forgotten? 72

Ch. Just. I then did use the person of your
father;
The image of his power lay then in me:
And, in the administration of his law,
Whiles I was busy for the commonwealth, 76
Your highness pleased to forget my place,
The majesty and power of law and justice,
The image of the king whom I presented,
And struck me in my very seat of judgment; 80
Whereon, as an offender to your father,
I gave bold way to my authority,
And did commit you. If the deed were ill,
Be you contented, wearing now the garland, 84
To have a son set your decrees at nought,
To pluck down justice from your awful bench,
To trip the course of law, and blunt the sword
That guards the peace and safety of your
person: 88
Nay, more, to spurn at your most royal image
And mock your workings in a second body.

Question your royal thoughts, make the case
  yours;
Be now the father and propose a son,   92
Hear your own dignity so much profan'd,
See your most dreadful laws so loosely slighted,
Behold yourself so by a son disdain'd;
And then imagine me taking your part,   96
And in your power soft silencing your son:
After this cold considerance, sentence me;
And, as you are a king, speak in your state
What I have done that misbecame my place,
My person, or my liege's sov'reignty.   101

K. Hen. V. You are right, justice; and you
  weigh this well;
Therefore still bear the balance and the sword:
And I do wish your honours may increase
Till you do live to see a son of mine   105
Offend you and obey you, as I did.
So shall I live to speak my father's words:
'Happy am I, that have a man so bold   108
That dares do justice on my proper son;
And not less happy, having such a son,
That would deliver up his greatness so
Into the hands of justice.' You did commit me:
For which, I do commit into your hand   113
The unstained sword that you have us'd to bear;
With this remembrance, that you use the same
With the like bold, just, and impartial spirit 116
As you have done 'gainst me. There is my hand:
You shall be as a father to my youth;
My voice shall sound as you do prompt mine ear,
And I will stoop and humble my intents   120
To your well-practis'd wise directions.
And, princes all, believe me, I beseech you;
My father is gone wild into his grave,
For in his tomb lie my affections;   124
And with his spirit sadly I survive,
To mock the expectation of the world,
To frustrate prophecies, and to raze out
Rotten opinion, who hath writ me down   128
After my seeming. The tide of blood in me
Hath proudly flow'd in vanity till now:
Now doth it turn and ebb back to the sea,
Where it shall mingle with the state of floods 132
And flow henceforth in formal majesty.
Now call we our high court of parliament;
And let us choose such limbs of noble counsel,
That the great body of our state may go   136
In equal rank with the best govern'd nation;
That war or peace, or both at once, may be
As things acquainted and familiar to us;
In which you, father, shall have foremost hand.
Our coronation done, we will accite,   141
As I before remember'd, all our state:
And, God consigning to my good intents,
No prince nor peer shall have just cause to say,
God shorten Harry's happy life one day.   145
                    [*Exeunt.*

SCENE III.—*Gloucestershire. The Garden of*
SHALLOW'S *House.*

Enter FALSTAFF, SHALLOW, SILENCE, BARDOLPH,
the Page, *and* DAVY.

Shal. Nay, you shall see mine orchard, where,
in an arbour, we will eat a last year's pippin of
my own graffing, with a dish of caraways, a
so forth; come, cousin Silence; and then to be

Fal. 'Fore God, you have here a good
dwelling, and a rich.

Shal. Barren, barren, barren; beggars a
beggars all, Sir John: marry, good air. Sprea
Davy; spread, Davy: well said, Davy.

Fal. This Davy serves you for good uses;
is your serving-man and your husband.

Shal. A good varlet, a good varlet, a ve
good varlet, Sir John: by the mass, I ha
drunk too much sack at supper: a good varle
Now sit down, now sit down. Come, cousin

Sil. Ah, sirrah! quoth a', we shall

Do nothing but eat, and make good cheer,
  And praise God for the merry year;
When flesh is cheap and females dear,
  And lusty lads roam here and there,
      So merrily,
  And ever among so merrily.

Fal. There's a merry heart! Good Mast
Silence, I'll give you a health for that anon.

Shal. Give Master Bardolph some wine, Dav

Davy. Sweet sir, sit; I'll be with you ano
most sweet sir, sit. Master page, good mast
page, sit. Proface! What you want in me
we'll have in drink: but you must bear: t
heart's all.   [*Ex*

Shal. Be merry, Master Bardolph; and m
little soldier there, be merry.

Sil. Be merry, be merry, my wife has all;
    For women are shrews, both short and tall:
      'Tis merry in hall when beards wag all,
          And welcome merry Shrove-tide.
    Be merry, be merry.

Fal. I did not think Master Silence had bee
a man of this mettle.

Sil. Who, I? I have been merry twice an
once ere now.

Re-enter DAVY.

Davy. There's a dish of leather-coats for yo
                    [*Setting them before* BARDOLP

Shal. Davy!

Davy. Your worship! I'll be with you straigh
A cup of wine, sir?

Sil.   A cup of wine that's brisk and fine
    And drink unto the leman mine;
        And a merry heart lives long-a.

Fal. Well said, Master Silence.

Sil. And we shall be merry, now comes in th
sweet o' the night.

Fal. Health and long life to you, Maste
Silence.

Sil.   Fill the cup, and let it come;
    I'll pledge you a mile to the bottom.

Shal. Honest Bardolph, welcome: if thou wan
est anything and wilt not call, beshrew thy hear
[*To the* Page.] Welcome, my little tiny thie
and welcome indeed too. I'll drink to Maste
Bardolph and to all the cavaleiroes about Londor

Davy. I hope to see London once ere I die.

Bard. An I might see you there, Davy,—

Shal. By the mass, you'll crack a quart to
gether: ha! will you not, Master Bardolph?

Bard. Yea, sir, in a pottle-pot.

Shal. By God's liggens, I thank thee. The
ave will stick by thee, I can assure thee that:
will not out; he is true bred. 68

Bard. And I'll stick by him, sir.

Shal. Why, there spoke a king. Lack nothing:
merry. [*Knocking within.*] Look who's at
or there. Ho! who knocks? [*Exit* DAVY.

Fal. [*To* SILENCE, *who drinks a bumper.*]
hy, now you have done me right. 74

Sil.   Do me right,
     And dub me knight:
          Samingo. 77

't not so?

Fal. 'Tis so.

Sil. Is't so? Why, then, say an old man can
somewhat. 81

Re-enter DAVY.

Davy. An't please your worship, there's one
stol come from the court with news.

Fal. From the court! let him come in. 84

Enter PISTOL.

ow now, Pistol!

Pist. Sir John, God save you, sir!

Fal. What wind blew you hither, Pistol?

Pist. Not the ill wind which blows no man to
good. 88

veet knight, thou art now one of the greatest
en in this realm.

Sil. By'r lady, I think a' be, but goodman
uff of Barson. 92

Pist. Puff!

uff in thy teeth, most recreant coward base!
r John, I am thy Pistol and thy friend,
nd helter-skelter have I rode to thee, 96
nd tidings do I bring and lucky joys
nd golden times and happy news of price.

Fal. I prithee now, deliver them like a man
of this world.

Pist. A foutra for the world and worldlings
base! 100
speak of Africa and golden joys.

Fal. O base Assyrian knight, what is thy
news?
et King Cophetua know the truth thereof.

Sil.   And Robin Hood, Scarlet, and John. 104

Pist. Shall dunghill curs confront the Heli-
cons?
nd shall good news be baffled?
hen, Pistol, lay thy head in Furies' lap.

Shal. Honest gentleman, I know not your
reeding. 109

Pist. Why then, lament therefore.

Shal. Give me pardon, sir: if, sir, you come with
ews from the court, I take it there is but two
ays: either to utter them, or to conceal them.
am, sir, under the king, in some authority.

Pist. Under which king, Bezonian? speak,
or die. 115

Shal. Under King Harry.

Pist.   Harry the Fourth? or Fifth?

Shal. Harry the Fourth.

Pist.   A foutra for thine office!
ir John, thy tender lambkin now is king;

Harry the Fifth's the man. I speak the truth:
When Pistol lies, do this; and fig me, like 120
The bragging Spaniard.

Fal. What! is the old king dead?

Pist. As nail in door: the things I speak are
just. 123

Fal. Away, Bardolph! saddle my horse.
Master Robert Shallow, choose what office thou
wilt in the land, 'tis thine. Pistol, I will double-
charge thee with dignities.

Bard. O joyful day! 128
I would not take a knighthood for my fortune.

Pist. What! I do bring good news.

Fal. Carry Master Silence to bed. Master
Shallow, my Lord Shallow, be what thou wilt, I
am Fortune's steward. Get on thy boots: we'll
ride all night. O sweet Pistol! Away, Bardolph!
[*Exit* BARDOLPH.] Come, Pistol, utter more to
me; and, withal devise something to do thyself
good. Boot, boot, Master Shallow: I know the
young king is sick for me. Let us take any
man's horses; the laws of England are at my
commandment. Happy are they which have
been my friends, and woe unto my lord chief
justice! 142

Pist. Let vultures vile seize on his lungs also!
'Where is the life that late I led?' say they:
Why, here it is: welcome these pleasant days!
                             [*Exeunt.*

SCENE IV.—*London. A Street.*

Enter BEADLES, *dragging in* MISTRESS QUICKLY
and DOLL TEARSHEET.

Quick. No, thou arrant knave: I would to
God I might die that I might have thee hanged;
thou hast drawn my shoulder out of joint.

First Bead. The constables have delivered
her over to me, and she shall have whipping-
cheer enough, I warrant her: there hath been a
man or two lately killed about her. 7

Dol. Nut-hook, nut-hook, you lie. Come on;
I'll tell thee what, thou damned tripe-visaged
rascal, an the child I now go with do miscarry,
thou hadst better thou hadst struck thy mother,
thou paper-faced villain. 12

Quick. O the Lord! that Sir John were come;
he would make this a bloody day to somebody.
But I pray God the fruit of her womb miscarry!

First Bead. If it do, you shall have a dozen
of cushions again; you have but eleven now.
Come, I charge you both go with me; for the
man is dead that you and Pistol beat among you.

Dol. I'll tell thee what, thou thin man in a
censer, I will have you as soundly swinged for
this, you blue-bottle rogue! you filthy famished
correctioner! if you be not swinged, I'll forswear half-kirtles. 24

First Bead. Come, come, you she knight-
errant, come.

Quick. O, that right should thus overcome
might! Well, of sufferance comes ease.

Dol. Come, you rogue, come: bring me to
a justice. 29

Quick. Ay; come, you starved blood-hound.

Dol. Goodman death! goodman bones!

Quick. Thou atomy, thou!   32
Dol. Come, you thin thing; come, you rascal!
First Bead. Very well.   [*Exeunt.*

SCENE V.—*A public Place near Westminster Abbey.*

Enter two Grooms, *strewing rushes.*

First Groom. More rushes, more rushes.
Sec. Groom. The trumpets have sounded
twice.   3
First Groom. It will be two o'clock ere they
come from the coronation. Dispatch, dispatch.
     [*Exeunt.*

Enter FALSTAFF, SHALLOW, PISTOL, BARDOLPH,
and the Page.

Fal. Stand here by me, Master Robert Shal-
low; I will make the king do you grace. I will
leer upon him, as a' comes by: and do but mark
the countenance that he will give me.   9
Pist. God bless thy lungs, good knight.
Fal. Come here, Pistol; stand behind me.
O! if I had had time to have made new liveries,
I would have bestowed the thousand pound I
borrowed of you. But 'tis no matter; this poor
show doth better: this doth infer the zeal I had
to see him.   16
Shal. It doth so.
Fal. It shows my earnestness of affection.
Shal. It doth so.
Fal. My devotion.   20
Shal. It doth, it doth, it doth.
Fal. As it were, to ride day and night; and
not to deliberate, not to remember, not to have
patience to shift me.   24
Shal. It is most certain.
Fal. But to stand stained with travel, and
sweating with desire to see him; thinking of
nothing else; putting all affairs else in oblivion,
as if there were nothing else to be done but to
see him.
Pist. 'Tis *semper idem*, for *absque hoc nihil est:*
'Tis all in every part.   32
Shal. 'Tis so, indeed.
Pist. My knight, I will inflame thy noble
liver,
And make thee rage.
Thy Doll, and Helen of thy noble thoughts,   36
Is in base durance and contagious prison;
Hal'd thither
By most mechanical and dirty hand:
Rouse up revenge from ebon den with fell
Alecto's snake,   40
For Doll is in: Pistol speaks nought but truth.
Fal. I will deliver her.
     [*Shouts within and trumpets sound.*
Pist. There roar'd the sea, and trumpet-
clangor sounds.

Enter KING HENRY THE FIFTH *and his Train, the*
LORD CHIEF JUSTICE *among them.*

Fal. God save thy grace, King Hal! my royal
Hal!   45
Pist. The heavens thee guard and keep, most
royal imp of fame!

Fal. God save thee, my sweet boy!
K. Hen. V. My lord chief justice, speak
that vain man.
Ch. Just. Have you your wits? know ye
what 'tis you speak?
Fal. My king! my Jove! I speak to thee, m
heart!
K. Hen. V. I know thee not, old man: fa
to thy prayers;
How ill white hairs become a fool and jeste
I have long dream'd of such a kind of man,
So surfeit-swell'd, so old, and so profane;
But, being awak'd, I do despise my dream.
Make less thy body hence, and more th
grace;
Leave gormandising; know the grave do
gape
For thee thrice wider than for other men.
Reply not to me with a fool-born jest:
Presume not that I am the thing I was;
For God doth know, so shall the world pe
ceive,
That I have turn'd away my former self;
So will I those that kept me company.
When thou dost hear I am as I have been,
Approach me, and thou shalt be as thou wa
The tutor and the feeder of my riots:
Till then, I banish thee, on pain of death,
As I have done the rest of my misleaders,
Not to come near our person by ten mile.
For competence of life I will allow you,
That lack of means enforce you not to evil;
And, as we hear you do reform yourselves,
We will, according to your strength and qua
ties,
Give you advancement. Be it your charge, m
lord,
To see perform'd the tenour of our word.
Set on. [*Exeunt* KING HENRY V. *and his Tra*
Fal. Master Shallow, I owe you a thousa
pound.
Shal. Ay, marry, Sir John; which I beseec
you to let me have home with me.
Fal. That can hardly be, Master Shallow. I
not you grieve at this: I shall be sent for
private to him. Look you, he must seem th
to the world. Fear not your advancements;
will be the man yet that shall make you great.
Shal. I cannot perceive how, unless y
should give me your doublet and stuff me o
with straw. I beseech you, good Sir John, l
me have five hundred of my thousand.
Fal. Sir, I will be as good as my word: th
that you heard was but a colour.
Shal. A colour that I fear you will die in, S
John.
Fal. Fear no colours: go with me to dinne
Come, Lieutenant Pistol; come, Bardolph:
shall be sent for soon at night.

Re-enter JOHN OF LANCASTER, *the* LORD CHI
JUSTICE; Officers *with them.*

Ch. Just. Go, carry Sir John Falstaff to th
Fleet;
Take all his company along with him.
Fal. My lord, my lord!

Ch. Just. I cannot now speak: I will hear
you soon.　　　　　　　　　　　　　　　100
ake them away.
Pist. *Si fortuna me tormenta, spero contenta.*
　　　　　[Exeunt FALSTAFF, SHALLOW, PISTOL,
　　　　　　BARDOLPH, Page, *and* Officers.
Lanc. I like this fair proceeding of the king's.
e hath intent his wonted followers　　104
hall all be very well provided for;
ut all are banish'd till their conversations
ppear more wise and modest to the world.
Ch. Just. And so they are.　　　　　108
Lanc. The king hath call'd his parliament,
my lord.
Ch. Just. He hath.
Lanc. I will lay odds, that, ere this year expire,
s far as France. I heard a bird so sing,　112
Vhose music, to my thinking, pleas'd the king.
'ome, will you hence?　　　　　　　*[Exeunt.*

EPILOGUE

Spoken by a Dancer.

*First, my fear; then, my curtsy; last my
peech. My fear is, your displeasure, my
urtsy, my duty, and my speech, to beg your
ardon. If you look for a good speech now, you
ndo me; for what I have to say is of mine
wn making; and what indeed I should say
vill, I doubt, prove mine own marring. But to
the purpose, and so to the venture. Be it known
to you,—as it is very well,—I was lately here in
the end of a displeasing play, to pray your
patience for it and to promise you a better. I
did mean indeed to pay you with this; which,
if like an ill venture it come unluckily home, I
break, and you, my gentle creditors, lose. Here,
I promised you I would be, and here I commit
my body to your mercies: bate me some and I
will pay you some; and, as most debtors do,
promise you infinitely.　　　　　　　　18
　　If my tongue cannot entreat you to acquit me,
will you command me to use my legs? and yet
that were but light payment, to dance out of your
debt. But a good conscience will make any
possible satisfaction, and so will I. All the
gentlewomen here have forgiven me: if the
gentlemen will not, then the gentlemen do not
agree with the gentlewomen, which was never
seen before in such an assembly.　　　　27
　　One word more, I beseech you. If you be not
too much cloyed with fat meat, our humble
author will continue the story, with Sir John in
it, and make you merry with fair Katharine of
France: where, for anything I know, Falstaff
shall die of a sweat, unless already a' be killed
with your hard opinions; for Oldcastle died a
martyr, and this is not the man. My tongue is
weary; when my legs are too, I will bid you
good night: and so kneel down before you; but,
indeed, to pray for the queen.　　　　　38*

THE LIFE OF
KING HENRY THE FIFTH

DRAMATIS PERSONÆ

KING HENRY THE FIFTH.
DUKE OF GLOUCESTER,⎫ Brothers to the King.
DUKE OF BEDFORD, ⎭
DUKE OF EXETER, Uncle to the King.
DUKE OF YORK, Cousin to the King.
EARLS OF SALISBURY, WESTMORELAND, and WARWICK.
ARCHBISHOP OF CANTERBURY.
BISHOP OF ELY.
EARL OF CAMBRIDGE.
LORD SCROOP.
SIR THOMAS GREY.
SIR THOMAS ERPINGHAM, GOWER, FLUELLEN, MAC-MORRIS, JAMY, Officers in King Henry's Army.
BATES, COURT, WILLIAMS, Soldiers in the Same.
PISTOL, NYM, BARDOLPH.
Boy.
A Herald.

CHARLES THE SIXTH, King of France.
LEWIS, the Dauphin.
DUKES OF BURGUNDY, ORLEANS, and BOURBON.
The CONSTABLE OF FRANCE.
RAMBURES and GRANDPRÉ, French Lords.
MONTJOY, a French Herald.
Governor of Harfleur.
Ambassadors to the King of England.

ISABEL, Queen of France.
KATHARINE, Daughter to Charles and Isabel.
ALICE, a Lady attending on the Princess Katharine.
Hostess of the Boar's Head Tavern, formerly Mistre Quickly, and now married to Pistol.

Lords, Ladies, Officers, French and English Soldie Citizens, Messengers, and Attendants.

Chorus.

SCENE.—*England; afterwards France.*

Enter Chorus.

Chor. O! for a Muse of fire, that would ascend
The brightest heaven of invention;
A kingdom for a stage, princes to act
And monarchs to behold the swelling scene. 4
Then should the war-like Harry, like himself,
Assume the port of Mars; and at his heels,
Leash'd in like hounds, should famine, sword, and fire
Crouch for employment. But pardon, gentles all,
The flat unraised spirits that hath dar'd 9
On this unworthy scaffold to bring forth
So great an object: can this cockpit hold
The vasty fields of France? or may we cram 12
Within this wooden O the very casques
That did affright the air at Agincourt?
O, pardon! since a crooked figure may
Attest in little place a million; 16
And let us, ciphers to this great accompt,
On your imaginary forces work.
Suppose within the girdle of these walls
Are now confin'd two mighty monarchies, 20
Whose high upreared and abutting fronts
The perilous narrow ocean parts asunder:
Piece out our imperfections with your thoughts:
Into a thousand parts divide one man, 24
And make imaginary puissance;
Think when we talk of horses that you see them
Printing their proud hoofs i' the receiving earth;
For 'tis your thoughts that now must deck our kings, 28
Carry them here and there, jumping o'er times,
Turning the accomplishment of many years
Into an hour-glass: for the which supply,
Admit me Chorus to this history; 3
Who prologue-like your humble patience pray
Gently to hear, kindly to judge, our play. [Exi

ACT I

SCENE I.—*London. An Antechamber in the KING'S Palace.*

Enter the ARCHBISHOP OF CANTERBURY *and th* BISHOP OF ELY.

Cant. My lord, I'll tell you; that self bill urg'd,
Which in th' eleventh year of the last king reign
Was like, and had indeed against us pass'd,
But that the scambling and unquiet time
Did push it out of further question.
Ely. But how, my lord, shall we resist it now
Cant. It must be thought on. If it pas against us,
We lose the better half of our possession;
For all the temporal lands which men devou
By testament have given to the church
Would they strip from us; being valu'd thus:
As much as would maintain, to the king honour,
Full fifteen earls and fifteen hundred knight
Six thousand and two hundred good esquires
And, to relief of lazars and weak age,
Of indigent faint souls past corporal toil, »
A hundred almshouses right well supplied;

nd to the coffers of the king beside,
thousand pounds by the year. Thus runs the
   bill.
Ely. This would drink deep.
Cant.   'Twould drink the cup and all.
Ely. But what prevention?   21
Cant. The king is full of grace and fair regard.
Ely. And a true lover of the holy church.
Cant. The courses of his youth promis'd it
   not.   24
he breath no sooner left his father's body
ut that his wildness, mortified in him,
em'd to die too; yea, at that very moment,
onsideration like an angel came,   28
nd whipp'd the offending Adam out of him,
aving his body as a paradise,
o envelop and contain celestial spirits.
ever was such a sudden scholar made;   32
ever came reformation in a flood,
'ith such a heady currance, scouring faults;
or never Hydra-headed wilfulness
o soon did lose his seat and all at once   36
s in this king.
Ely.   We are blessed in the change.
Cant. Hear him but reason in divinity,
nd, all-admiring, with an inward wish
ou would desire the king were made a prelate: 40
ear him debate of commonwealth affairs,
ou would say it hath been all in all his study:
ist his discourse of war, and you shall hear
   fearful battle render'd you in music: 44
'hich is a wonder how his Grace should glean
   it,
nce his addiction was to courses vain;
is companies unletter'd, rude, and shallow;
is hours fill'd up with riots, banquets,
   sports;   56
nd never noted in him any study,
ny retirement, any sequestration
rom open haunts and popularity.
Ely. The strawberry grows underneath the
   nettle,   60
nd wholesome berries thrive and ripen best
eighbour'd by fruit of baser quality:
nd so the prince obscur'd his contemplation
nder the veil of wildness; which, no doubt, 64
rew like the summer grass, fastest by night,
nseen, yet crescive in his faculty.
Cant. It must be so; for miracles are ceas'd;
nd therefore we must needs admit the means
ow things are perfected.
Ely.   But, my good lord, 69
ow now for mitigation of this bill
rg'd by the commons? Doth his majesty
ncline to it, or no?
Cant.   He seems indifferent, 72
r rather swaying more upon our part

Than cherishing the exhibiters against us;
For I have made an offer to his majesty,
Upon our spiritual convocation,   76
And in regard of causes now in hand,
Which I have open'd to his Grace at large,
As touching France, to give a greater sum
Than ever at one time the clergy yet   80
Did to his predecessors part withal.
   Ely. How did this offer seem receiv'd, my
     lord?
   Cant. With good acceptance of his majesty;
Save that there was not time enough to
   hear,—   84
As I perceiv'd his Grace would fain have done,—
The severals and unhidden passages
Of his true titles to some certain dukedoms,
And generally to the crown and seat of France,
Deriv'd from Edward, his great-grandfather.
   Ely. What was the impediment that broke
     this off?
   Cant. The French ambassador upon that
     instant   91
Crav'd audience; and the hour I think is come
To give him hearing: is it four o'clock?
   Ely. It is.
   Cant. Then go we in to know his embassy;
Which I could with a ready guess declare 96
Before the Frenchman speak a word of it.
   Ely. I'll wait upon you, and I long to hear it.
                              [Exeunt.

SCENE II.—*The Same. The Presence Chamber.*

Enter KING HENRY, GLOUCESTER, BEDFORD,
   EXETER, WARWICK, WESTMORELAND, *and* Attendants.

   K. Hen. Where is my gracious lord of Can-
     terbury?
   Exe. Not here in presence.
   K. Hen.   Send for him, good uncle.
   West. Shall we call in the ambassador, my
     liege?
   K. Hen. Not yet, my cousin: we would be
     resolv'd,   4
Before we hear him, of some things of weight
That task our thoughts, concerning us and
   France.

Enter the ARCHBISHOP OF CANTERBURY *and the*
   BISHOP OF ELY.

   Cant. God and his angels guard your sacred
     throne,
And make you long become it!
   K. Hen.   Sure, we thank you.
My learned lord, we pray you to proceed, 9
And justly and religiously unfold
Why the law Salique that they have in France
Or should, or should not, bar us in our claim. 12
And God forbid, my dear and faithful lord,
That you should fashion, wrest, or bow your
   reading,
Or nicely charge your understanding soul
With opening titles miscreate, whose right 16
Suits not in native colours with the truth;
For God doth know how many now in health
Shall drop their blood in approbation

Of what your reverence shall incite us to. 20
Therefore take heed how you impawn our
  person,
How you awake the sleeping sword of war:
We charge you in the name of God, take heed;
For never two such kingdoms did contend 24
Without much fall of blood; whose guiltless
  drops
Are every one a woe, a sore complaint,
'Gainst him whose wrongs give edge unto the
  swords
That make such waste in brief mortality. 28
Under this conjuration speak, my lord,
And we will hear, note, and believe in heart,
That what you speak is in your conscience wash'd
As pure as sin with baptism. 32
  Cant. Then hear me, gracious sovereign, and
    you peers,
That owe yourselves, your lives, and services
To this imperial throne. There is no bar
To make against your highness' claim to France
But this, which they produce from Pharamond,
In terram Salicam mulieres ne succedant, 38
'No woman shall succeed in Salique land:'
Which Salique land the French unjustly gloze
To be the realm of France, and Pharamond 41
The founder of this law and female bar.
Yet their own authors faithfully affirm
That the land Salique is in Germany, 44
Between the floods of Sala and of Elbe;
Where Charles the Great, having subdu'd the
  Saxons,
There left behind and settled certain French;
Who, holding in disdain the German women
For some dishonest manners of their life,
Establish'd then this law; to wit, no female
Should be inheritrix in Salique land: 51
Which Salique, as I said, 'twixt Elbe and Sala,
Is at this day in Germany call'd Meisen.
Then doth it well appear the Salique law
Was not devised for the realm of France;
Nor did the French possess the Salique land 56
Until four hundred one-and-twenty years
After defunction of King Pharamond,
Idly suppos'd the founder of this law;
Who died within the year of our redemption 60
Four hundred twenty-six; and Charles the Great
Subdu'd the Saxons, and did seat the French
Beyond the river Sala, in the year
Eight hundred five. Besides, their writers say,
King Pepin, which deposed Childeric, 65
Did, as heir general, being descended
Of Blithild, which was daughter to King Clothair,
Make claim and title to the crown of France. 68
Hugh Capet also, who usurp'd the crown
Of Charles the Duke of Loraine, sole heir male
Of the true line and stock of Charles the Great,
To find his title with some shows of truth,— 72
Though in pure truth, it was corrupt and
  naught,—
Convey'd himself as heir to the Lady Lingare,
Daughter to Charlemain, who was the son
To Lewis the emperor, and Lewis the son 76
Of Charles the Great. Also King Lewis the
  Tenth,
Who was sole heir to the usurper Capet,

Could not keep quiet in his conscience,
Wearing the crown of France, till satisfied
That fair Queen Isabel, his grandmother,
Was lineal of the Lady Ermengare,
Daughter to Charles the aforesaid Duke
  Loraine:
By the which marriage the line of Charles th
  Great
Was re-united to the crown of France.
So that, as clear as is the summer's sun,
King Pepin's title, and Hugh Capet's claim,
King Lewis his satisfaction, all appear
To hold in right and title of the female:
So do the kings of France unto this day;
Howbeit they would hold up this Salique la
To bar your highness claiming from the femal
And rather choose to hide them in a net
Than amply to imbar their crooked titles
Usurp'd from you and your progenitors.
  K. Hen. May I with right and conscien
    make this claim?
  Cant. The sin upon my head, dread sov
    reign!
For in the book of Numbers is it writ:
'When the son dies, let the inheritance
Descend unto the daughter.' Gracious lord, i
Stand for your own; unwind your bloody fla
Look back into your mighty ancestors:
Go, my dread lord, to your great-grandsire
  tomb,
From whom you claim; invoke his war-lil
  spirit,   1
And your great-uncle's, Edward the Blac
  Prince,
Who on the French ground play'd a tragedy,
Making defeat on the full power of France
Whiles his most mighty father on a hill 1
Stood smiling to behold his lion's whelp
Forage in blood of French nobility.
O noble English! that could entertain
With half their forces the full pride of Franc
And let another half stand laughing by, 1
All out of work, and cold for action.
  Ely. Awake remembrance of these valia
    dead,
And with your puissant arm renew their feat
You are their heir, you sit upon their throne,
The blood and courage that renowned them
Runs in your veins; and my thrice-puissant lieg
Is in the very May-morn of his youth, 1
Ripe for exploits and mighty enterprises.
  Exe. Your brother kings and monarchs
    the earth
Do all expect that you should rouse yourself,
As did the former lions of your blood. 1
  West. They know your Grace hath cause an
    means and might;
So hath your highness; never King of Englan
Had nobles richer, and more loyal subjects,
Whose hearts have left their bodies here in En
  land   1
And lie pavilion'd in the fields of France.
  Cant. O! let their bodies follow, my de
    liege,
With blood and sword and fire to win yo
  right;

n aid whereof we of the spirituality   132
Vill raise your highness such a mighty sum
s never did the clergy at one time
ring in to any of your ancestors.
  K. Hen. We must not only arm to invade the
    French,   136
ut lay down our proportions to defend
gainst the Scot, who will make road upon us
Vith all advantages.
  Cant. They of those marches, gracious so-
    vereign,   140
hall be a wall sufficient to defend
ur inland from the pilfering borderers.
  K. Hen. We do not mean the coursing
    snatchers only,
ut fear the main intendment of the Scot,   144
Vho hath been still a giddy neighbour to us;
or you shall read that my great-grandfather
lever went with his forces into France
ut that the Scot on his unfurnish'd kingdom
ame pouring, like the tide into a breach,   149
Vith ample and brim fulness of his force,
alling the gleaned land with hot essays,
irding with grievous siege castles and towns;
hat England, being empty of defence,   153
lath shook and trembled at the ill neighbour-
    hood.
  Cant. She hath been then more fear'd than
    harm'd, my liege;
or hear her but exampled by herself: 156
Vhen all her chivalry hath been in France
nd she a mourning widow of her nobles,
he hath herself not only well defended,
ut taken and impounded as a stray   160
he King of Scots; whom she did send to
    France,
o fill King Edward's fame with prisoner kings,
nd make your chronicle as rich with praise
s is the owse and bottom of the sea   164
Vith sunken wrack and sumless treasuries.
  West. But there's a saying very old and true;
    If that you will France win,
      Then with Scotland first begin: 168
or once the eagle England being in prey,
o her unguarded nest the weasel Scot
omes sneaking and so sucks her princely eggs,
laying the mouse in absence of the cat,   172
o tear and havoc more than she can eat.
  Exe. It follows then the cat must stay at
    home:
et that is but a crush'd necessity;
ince we have locks to safeguard necessaries   176
nd pretty traps to catch the petty thieves.
Vhile that the armed hand doth fight abroad
he advised head defends itself at home:
or government, though high and low and
    lower,   180
ut into parts, doth keep in one consent,
ongreeing in a full and natural close,
ike music.
  Cant.   Therefore doth heaven divide
he state of man in divers functions,   184
etting endeavour in continual motion;
o which is fixed, as an aim or butt,
bedience: for so work the honey-bees,
reatures that by a rule in nature teach   188

The act of order to a peopled kingdom.
They have a king and officers of sorts;
Where some, like magistrates, correct at home,
Others, like merchants, venture trade abroad,
Others, like soldiers, armed in their stings,   193
Make boot upon the summer's velvet buds;
Which pillage they with merry march bring
    home
To the tent-royal of their emperor: 196
Who, busied in his majesty, surveys
The singing masons building roofs of gold,
The civil citizens kneading up the honey,
The poor mechanic porters crowding in   200
Their heavy burdens at his narrow gate,
The sad-ey'd justice, with his surly hum,
Delivering o'er to executors pale
The lazy yawning drone. I this infer,   204
That many things, having full reference
To one consent, may work contrariously;
As many arrows, loosed several ways,
Fly to one mark; as many ways meet in one
    town;   208
As many fresh streams meet in one salt sea;
As many lines close in the dial's centre;
So may a thousand actions, once afoot,
End in one purpose, and be all well borne   212
Without defeat. Therefore to France, my liege.
Divide your happy England into four;
Whereof take you one quarter into France,
And you withal shall make all Gallia shake.   216
If we, with thrice such powers left at home,
Cannot defend our own doors from the dog,
Let us be worried and our nation lose
The name of hardiness and policy.   220
  K. Hen. Call in the messengers sent from
    the Dauphin.   [*Exit an* Attendant.
Now are we well resolv'd; and by God's help,
And yours, the noble sinews of our power,
France being ours, we'll bend it to our awe
Or break it all to pieces: or there we'll sit,
Ruling in large and ample empery
O'er France and all her almost kingly dukedoms,
Or lay these bones in an unworthy urn,   228
Tombless, with no remembrance over them:
Either our history shall with full mouth
Speak freely of our acts, or else our grave,
Like Turkish mute, shall have a tongueless
    mouth,   232
Not worshipp'd with a waxen epitaph.

        Enter Ambassadors of France.

Now are we well prepar'd to know the pleasure
Of our fair cousin Dauphin; for we hear
Your greeting is from him, not from the king.
  First Amb. May't please your majesty to
    give us leave   237
Freely to render what we have in charge;
Or shall we sparingly show you far off
The Dauphin's meaning and our embassy?   240
  K. Hen. We are no tyrant, but a Christian
    king;
Unto whose grace our passion is as subject
As are our wretches fetter'd in our prisons:
Therefore with frank and with uncurbed plain-
    ness   244
Tell us the Dauphin's mind.

First Amb.   Thus then, in few.
Your highness, lately sending into France,
Did claim some certain dukedoms, in the right
Of your great predecessor, King Edward the
   Third.   248
In answer of which claim, the prince our master
Says that you savour too much of your youth,
And bids you be advis'd there's nought in
   France
That can be with a nimble galliard won;   252
You cannot revel into dukedoms there.
He therefore sends you, meeter for your spirit,
This tun of treasure; and, in lieu of this,
Desires you let the dukedoms that you claim
Hear no more of you. This the Dauphin speaks.
   K. Hen. What treasure, uncle?
   Exe.   Tennis-balls, my liege.
   K. Hen. We are glad the Dauphin is so
pleasant with us:
His present and your pains we thank you for:
When we have match'd our rackets to these
   balls,   261
We will in France, by God's grace, play a set
Shall strike his father's crown into the hazard.
Tell him he hath made a match with such a
   wrangler   264
That all the courts of France will be disturb'd
With chaces. And we understand him well,
How he comes o'er us with our wilder days,
Not measuring what use we made of them. 268
We never valu'd this poor seat of England;
And therefore, living hence, did give ourself
To barbarous licence; as 'tis ever common
That men are merriest when they are from
   home.   272
But tell the Dauphin I will keep my state,
Be like a king and show my sail of greatness
When I do rouse me in my throne of France:
For that I have laid by my majesty   276
And plodded like a man for working-days,
But I will rise there with so full a glory
That I will dazzle all the eyes of France,
Yea, strike the Dauphin blind to look on us.
And tell the pleasant prince this mock of his
Hath turn'd his balls to gun-stones; and his
   soul
Shall stand sore-charged for the wasteful ven-
   geance
That shall fly with them; for many a thousand
   widows   284
Shall this his mock mock out of their dear hus-
   bands;
Mock mothers from their sons, mock castles
   down;
And some are yet ungotten and unborn
That shall have cause to curse the Dauphin's
   scorn.   288
But this lies all within the will of God,
To whom I do appeal; and in whose name
Tell you the Dauphin I am coming on,
To venge me as I may and to put forth   292
My rightful hand in a well-hallow'd cause.
So get you hence in peace; and tell the Dauphin
His jest will savour but of shallow wit
When thousands weep more than did laugh at
   it.   296

Convey them with safe conduct. Fare you well
            [*Exeunt* Ambassadors
   Exe. This was a merry message.
   K. Hen. We hope to make the sender blush
at it.
Therefore, my lords, omit no happy hour   30
That may give furtherance to our expedition
For we have now no thought in us but France
Save those to God, that run before our business
Therefore let our proportions for these wars
Be soon collected, and all things thought upo
That may with reasonable swiftness add   30
More feathers to our wings; for, God before,
We'll chide this Dauphin at his father's doo
Therefore let every man now task his though
That this fair action may on foot be brough
               [*Exeunt. Flouris*

ACT II

Enter Chorus.

Chor. Now all the youth of England are o
   fire,
And silken dalliance in the wardrobe lies;
Now thrive the armourers, and honour's thoug
Reigns solely in the breast of every man:
They sell the pasture now to buy the horse,
Following the mirror of all Christian kings,
With winged heels, as English Mercuries.
For now sits Expectation in the air
And hides a sword from hilts unto the point
With crowns imperial, crowns and coronets,
Promis'd to Harry and his followers.
The French, advis'd by good intelligence   1
Of this most dreadful preparation,
Shake in their fear, and with pale policy
Seek to divert the English purposes.
O England! model to thy inward greatness,   1
Like little body with a mighty heart,
What mightst thou do, that honour would thee d
Were all thy children kind and natural!
But see thy fault! France hath in thee foun
   out   2
A nest of hollow bosoms, which he fills
With treacherous crowns; and three corrupte
   men,
One, Richard Earl of Cambridge, and the second
Henry Lord Scroop of Masham, and the third
Sir Thomas Grey, knight, of Northumberland,
Have, for the gilt of France,—O guilt, indeed!—
Confirm'd conspiracy with fearful France;
And by their hands this grace of kings mus
   die,—
If hell and treason hold their promises,—
Ere he take ship for France, and in Southampto
Linger your patience on; and well digest
The abuse of distance while we force a play. 3
The sum is paid; the traitors are agreed;
The king is set from London; and the scene
Is now transported, gentles, to Southampton:
There is the playhouse now, there must you sit,
And thence to France shall we convey you safe
And bring you back, charming the narrow sea

give you gentle pass; for, if we may,
'll not offend one stomach with our play. 40
t, till the king come forth and not till then,
to Southampton do we shift our scene.
                                    [*Exit.*

SCENE I.—*London. Eastcheap.*

Enter NYM *and* BARDOLPH.

Bard. Well met, Corporal Nym.
Nym. Good morrow, Lieutenant Bardolph.
Bard. What, are Ancient Pistol and you
ends yet? 4
Nym. For my part, I care not: I say little;
t when time shall serve, there shall be smiles;
t that shall be as it may. I dare not fight;
t I will wink and hold out mine iron. It is a
nple one; but what though? it will toast
eese, and it will endure cold as another man's
ord will: and there's an end. 11
Bard. I will bestow a breakfast to make you
ends, and we'll be all three sworn brothers to
ance: let it be so, good Corporal Nym.
Nym. Faith, I will live so long as I may,
at's the certain of it; and when I cannot live
y longer, I will do as I may: that is my rest,
at is the rendezvous of it. 18
Bard. It is certain, corporal, that he is
rried to Nell Quickly; and, certainly she did
u wrong, for you were troth-plight to her. 21
Nym. I cannot tell; things must be as they
ay: men may sleep, and they may have their
roats about them at that time; and, some say,
ives have edges. It must be as it may: though
tience be a tired mare, yet she will plod.
ere must be conclusions. Well, I cannot tell.

Enter PISTOL *and* Hostess.

Bard. Here comes Ancient Pistol and his
fe. Good corporal, be patient here. How
w, mine host Pistol!
Pist. Base tike, call'st thou me host?
ow, by this hand, I swear, I scorn the term; 32
or shall my Nell keep lodgers.
Host. No, by my troth, not long; for we can-
t lodge and board a dozen or fourteen gentlemen that live honestly by the prick of their
edles, but it will be thought we keep a bawdy-
use straight. [NYM *and* PISTOL *draw.*] O well-
day, Lady! if he be not drawn now: we shall
e wilful adultery and murder committed. 40
Bard. Good lieutenant! good corporal! offer
thing here.
Nym. Pish!
Pist. Pish for thee, Iceland dog! thou prick-
eared cur of Iceland! 44
Host. Good Corporal Nym, show thy valour
d put up your sword.
Nym. Will you shog off? I would have you
lus. [*Sheathing his sword.*
Pist. Solus, egregious dog? O viper vile!
e *solus* in thy most mervailous face;
e *solus* in thy teeth, and in thy throat,
nd in thy hateful lungs, yea, in thy maw,
perdy; 52
nd, which is worse, within thy nasty mouth!

I do retort the *solus* in thy bowels;
For I can take, and Pistol's cock is up,
And flashing fire will follow. 56
Nym. I am not Barbason; you cannot conjure me. I have an humour to knock you in-
differently well. If you grow foul with me, Pistol,
I will scour you with my rapier, as I may, in
fair terms: if you would walk off, I would prick
your guts a little, in good terms, as I may; and
that's the humour of it.
Pist. O braggart vile and damned furious
  wight! 64
The grave doth gape, and doting death is near;
Therefore exhale.
Bard. Hear me, hear me what I say: he that
strikes the first stroke, I'll run him up to the
hilts, as I am a soldier. [*Draws.*
Pist. An oath of mickle might, and fury shall
abate.
Give me thy fist, thy fore-foot to me give;
Thy spirits are most tall. 72
Nym. I will cut thy throat, one time or other,
in fair terms; that is the humour of it.
Pist. Coupe le gorge!
That is the word. I thee defy again. 76
O hound of Crete, think'st thou my spouse to
  get?
No; to the spital go,
And from the powdering-tub of infamy
Fetch forth the lazar kite of Cressid's kind, 80
Doll Tearsheet she by name, and her espouse:
I have, and I will hold, the *quondam* Quickly
For the only she; and—*pauca,* there's enough.
Go to.

Enter the Boy.

Boy. Mine host Pistol, you must come to my
master, and your hostess: he is very sick, and
would to bed. Good Bardolph, put thy face between his sheets and do the office of a warming-
pan. Faith, he's very ill. 89
Bard. Away, you rogue!
Host. By my troth, he'll yield the crow a
pudding one of these days. The king has killed
his heart. Good husband, come home presently.
                     [*Exeunt* Hostess *and* Boy.
Bard. Come, shall I make you two friends?
We must to France together. Why the devil
should we keep knives to cut one another's
throats? 97
Pist. Let floods o'erswell, and fiends for food
howl on!
Nym. You'll pay me the eight shillings I won
of you at betting?
Pist. Base is the slave that pays. 101
Nym. That now I will have; that's the
humour of it.
Pist. As manhood shall compound: push
  home. [*They draw.*
Bard. By this sword, he that makes the first
thrust, I'll kill him; by this sword, I will.
Pist. Sword is an oath, and oaths must have
  their course. 107
Bard. Corporal Nym, an thou wilt be friends,
be friends: an thou wilt not, why then, be enemies with me too. Prithee, put up.

Nym. I shall have my eight shillings I won of you at betting?   112

Pist. A noble shalt thou have, and present pay;
And liquor likewise will I give to thee,
And friendship shall combine, and brotherhood:
I'll live by Nym, and Nym shall live by me.
Is not this just? for I shall sutler be   117
Unto the camp, and profits will accrue.
Give me thy hand.

Nym. I shall have my noble?   120

Pist. In cash most justly paid. [*Paying him.*

Nym. Well then, that's the humour of it.

Re-enter Hostess.

Host. As ever you came of women, come in quickly to Sir John. Ah, poor heart! he is so shaked of a burning quotidian tertian, that it is most lamentable to behold. Sweet men, come to him.

Nym. The king hath run bad humours on the knight; that's the even of it.   129

Pist. Nym, thou hast spoke the right; His heart is fracted and corroborate.

Nym. The king is a good king: but it must be as it may; he passes some humours and careers.   134

Pist. Let us condole the knight; for, lambkins, we will live.   [*Exeunt.*

Scene II.—*Southampton. A Council-chamber.*

Enter EXETER, BEDFORD, *and* WESTMORELAND.

Bed. 'Fore God, his Grace is bold to trust these traitors.

Exe. They shall be apprehended by and by.

West. How smooth and even they do bear themselves!
As if allegiance in their bosoms sat,   4
Crowned with faith and constant loyalty.

Bed. The king hath note of all that they intend,
By interception which they dream not of.

Exe. Nay, but the man that was his bedfellow,
Whom he hath dull'd and cloy'd with gracious favours,   9
That he should, for a foreign purse, so sell
His sovereign's life to death and treachery!

Trumpets sound. Enter KING HENRY, SCROOP, CAMBRIDGE, GREY, Lords, *and* Attendants.

K. Hen. Now sits the wind fair, and we will aboard.   12
My Lord of Cambridge, and my kind Lord of Masham,
And you, my gentle knight, give me your thoughts:
Think you not that the powers we bear with us
Will cut their passage through the force of France,   16
Doing the execution and the act
For which we have in head assembled them?

Scroop. No doubt, my liege, if each man do his best.

K. Hen. I doubt not that; since we are we persuaded
We carry not a heart with us from hence
That grows not in a fair consent with ours;
Nor leave not one behind that doth not wish
Success and conquest to attend on us.

Cam. Never was monarch better fear'd an lov'd
Than is your majesty: there's not, I think, subject
That sits in heart-grief and uneasiness
Under the sweet shade of your government.

Grey. True: those that were your father enemies
Have steep'd their galls in honey, and do ser you
With hearts create of duty and of zeal.

K. Hen. We therefore have great cause thankfulness,
And shall forget the office of our hand,
Sooner than quittance of desert and merit
According to the weight and worthiness.

Scroop. So service shall with steeled sine toil,
And labour shall refresh itself with hope,
To do your Grace incessant services.

K. Hen. We judge no less. Uncle of Exete
Enlarge the man committed yesterday
That rail'd against our person: we consider
It was excess of wine that set him on;
And on his more advice we pardon him.

Scroop. That's mercy, but too much securit
Let him be punish'd, sovereign, lest example
Breed, by his sufferance, more of such a kin

K. Hen. O! let us yet be merciful.

Cam. So may your highness, and yet puni too.

Grey. Sir,
You show great mercy, if you give him life
After the taste of much correction.

K. Hen. Alas! your too much love and ca of me
Are heavy orisons 'gainst this poor wretch.
If little faults, proceeding on distemper,
Shall not be wink'd at, how shall we stret our eye
When capital crimes, chew'd, swallow'd, an digested,
Appear before us? We'll yet enlarge that ma
Though Cambridge, Scroop, and Grey, in the dear care,
And tender preservation of our person,
Would have him punish'd. And now to o French causes:
Who are the late commissioners?

Cam. I one, my lord:
Your highness bade me ask for it to-day.

Scroop. So did you me, my liege.

Grey. And I, my royal sovereign.

K. Hen. Then, Richard, Earl of Cambridg there is yours;
There yours, Lord Scroop of Masham; and, s knight,
Grey of Northumberland, this same is yours:
Read them; and know, I know your worthines
My Lord of Westmoreland, and uncle Exete

e will aboard to-night. Why, how now,
 gentlemen!
hat see you in those papers that you lose   72
 much complexion? Look ye, how they
 change!
heir cheeks are paper. Why, what read you
 there,
hat hath so cowarded and chas'd your blood
it of appearance?

Cam.   I do confess my fault,   76
nd do submit me to your highness' mercy.

Grey. }
Scroop. } To which we all appeal.

K. Hen. The mercy that was quick in us but
 late   79
 your own counsel is suppress'd and kill'd:
ou must not dare, for shame, to talk of mercy;
r your own reasons turn into your bosoms,
 dogs upon their masters, worrying you.
e you, my princes and my noble peers,   84
ese English monsters! My Lord of Cambridge
 here,
ou know how apt our love was to accord
 furnish him with all appertinents
 longing to his honour; and this man   88
th, for a few light crowns, lightly conspir'd,
d sworn unto the practices of France,
 kill us here in Hampton: to the which
is knight, no less for bounty bound to us   92
an Cambridge is, hath likewise sworn. But O!
hat shall I say to thee, Lord Scroop? thou
 cruel,
grateful, savage and inhuman creature!
ou that didst bear the key of all my counsels,
at knew'st the very bottom of my soul,   97
at almost mightst have coin'd me into gold
ouldst thou have practis'd on me for thy use!
ay it be possible that foreign hire   100
uld out of thee extract one spark of evil
at might annoy my finger? 'tis so strange
at, though the truth of it stands off as gross
black from white, my eye will scarcely see it.
eason and murder ever kept together,   105
two yoke-devils sworn to either's purpose,
orking so grossly in a natural cause
at admiration did not whoop at them: 108
t thou, 'gainst all proportion, didst bring in
onder to wait on treason and on murder:
d whatsoever cunning fiend it was
at wrought upon thee so preposterously   112
th got the voice in hell for excellence:
d other devils that suggest by treasons
 botch and bungle up damnation
th patches, colours, and with forms, being
 fetch'd   116
om glistering semblances of piety;
t he that temper'd thee bade thee stand up,
ve thee no instance why thou shouldst do
 treason,
less to dub thee with the name of traitor.
hat same demon that hath gull'd thee thus
ould with his lion gait walk the whole world,
 might return to vasty Tartar back,
d tell the legions, 'I can never win   124
soul so easy as that Englishman's.'
how hast thou with jealousy infected

The sweetness of affiance. Show men dutiful?
Why, so didst thou: seem they grave and
 learned?   128
Why, so didst thou: come they of noble family?
Why, so didst thou: seem they religious?
Why, so didst thou: or are they spare in diet,
Free from gross passion or of mirth or anger,   132
Constant in spirit, not swerving with the blood,
Garnish'd and deck'd in modest complement,
Not working with the eye without the ear,
And but in purged judgment trusting neither?
Such and so finely bolted didst thou seem: 137
And thus thy fall hath left a kind of blot,
To mark the full-fraught man and best indu'd
With some suspicion. I will weep for thee;   140
For this revolt of thine, methinks, is like
Another fall of man. Their faults are open:
Arrest them to the answer of the law;
And God acquit them of their practices!   144

Exe. I arrest thee of high treason, by the
 name of Richard Earl of Cambridge.
I arrest thee of high treason, by the name of
Henry Lord Scroop of Masham.   148
I arrest thee of high treason, by the name of
Thomas Grey, knight, of Northumberland.

Scroop. Our purposes God justly hath dis-
 cover'd,
And I repent my fault more than my death;   152
Which I beseech your highness to forgive,
Although my body pay the price of it.

Cam. For me, the gold of France did not
 seduce,
Although I did admit it as a motive   156
The sooner to effect what I intended:
But God be thanked for prevention;
Which I in sufferance heartily will rejoice,
Beseeching God and you to pardon me.   160

Grey. Never did faithful subject more rejoice
At the discovery of most dangerous treason
Than I do at this hour joy o'er myself,
Prevented from a damned enterprise.   164
My fault, but not my body, pardon, sovereign.

K. Hen. God quit you in his mercy! Hear
 your sentence.
You have conspir'd against our royal person,
Join'd with an enemy proclaim'd, and from his
 coffers   168
Receiv'd the golden earnest of our death;
Wherein you would have sold your king to
 slaughter,
His princes and his peers to servitude,
His subjects to oppression and contempt,   172
And his whole kingdom into desolation.
Touching our person seek we no revenge;
But we our kingdom's safety must so tender,
Whose ruin you have sought, that to her laws
We do deliver you. Get you therefore hence,
Poor miserable wretches, to your death;
The taste whereof, God of his mercy give you
Patience to endure, and true repentance   180
Of all your dear offences! Bear them hence.
            [*Exeunt* CAMBRIDGE, SCROOP, *and*
                      GREY, *guarded.*
Now, lords, for France! the enterprise whereof
Shall be to you, as us, like glorious.
We doubt not of a fair and lucky war,   184

Since God so graciously hath brought to light
This dangerous treason lurking in our way
To hinder our beginnings. We doubt not now
But every rub is smoothed on our way.   188
Then forth, dear countrymen: let us deliver
Our puissance into the hand of God,
Putting it straight in expedition.
Cheerly to sea! the signs of war advance: 192
No king of England, if not king of France.
                                    [*Exeunt.*

SCENE III.—*London. Before a Tavern in
Eastcheap.*

Enter PISTOL, Hostess, NYM, BARDOLPH,
and Boy.

Host. Prithee, honey-sweet husband, let me
bring thee to Staines.
Pist. No; for my manly heart doth yearn.
Bardolph, be blithe; Nym, rouse thy vaunting
veins;   4
Boy, bristle thy courage up; for Falstaff he is
dead,
And we must yearn therefore.
Bard. Would I were with him, wheresome'er
he is, either in heaven or in hell!   8
Host. Nay, sure, he's not in hell: he's in Arthur's bosom, if ever man went to Arthur's bosom. A' made a finer end and went away an it
had been any christom child; a' parted even just
between twelve and one, even at the turning o'
the tide: for after I saw him fumble with the
sheets and play with flowers and smile upon his
fingers' ends, I knew there was but one way; for
his nose was as sharp as a pen, and a' babbled of
green fields. 'How now, Sir John!' quoth I:
'what man! be of good cheer.' So a' cried out
'God, God, God!' three or four times: now I,
to comfort him, bid him a' should not think of
God, I hoped there was no need to trouble himself with any such thoughts yet. So a' bade me
lay more clothes on his feet: I put my hand
into the bed and felt them, and they were as
cold as any stone; then I felt to his knees, and
so upward, and upward, and all was as cold as
any stone.   28
Nym. They say he cried out of sack.
Host. Ay, that a' did.
Bard. And of women.
Host. Nay, that a' did not.   32
Boy. Yes, that a' did; and said they were
devils incarnate.
Host. A' could never abide carnation; 'twas
a colour he never liked.   36
Boy. A' said once, the devil would have him
about women.
Host. A' did in some sort, indeed, handle
women; but then he was rheumatic, and talked
of the whore of Babylon.   41
Boy. Do you not remember a' saw a flea
stick upon Bardolph's nose, and a' said it was
a black soul burning in hell-fire?   44
Bard. Well, the fuel is gone that maintained
that fire: that's all the riches I got in his service.

Nym. Shall we shog? the king will be go
from Southampton.
Pist. Come, let's away. My love, give r
thy lips.
Look to my chattels and my moveables:
Let senses rule, the word is, 'Pitch and pay;'
Trust none;
For oaths are straws, men's faiths are wafe
cakes,
And hold-fast is the only dog, my duck:
Therefore, *caveto* be thy counsellor.
Go, clear thy crystals. Yoke-fellows in arm
Let us to France; like horse-leeches, my bo
To suck, to suck, the very blood to suck!
Boy. And that's but unwholesome foc
they say.
Pist. Touch her soft mouth, and march.
Bard. Farewell, hostess.   [*Kissing h*
Nym. I cannot kiss, that is the humour
it; but, adieu.
Pist. Let housewifery appear: keep close
thee command.
Host. Farewell; adieu.   [*Exeu*

SCENE IV.—*France. An Apartment in the*
FRENCH KING'S *Palace.*

Flourish. Enter the FRENCH KING, *attended; n*
DAUPHIN, *the* DUKES OF BERRI *and* BRITAIN
the CONSTABLE, *and Others.*

Fr. King. Thus come the English with f
power upon us;
And more than carefully it us concerns
To answer royally in our defences.
Therefore the Dukes of Berri and Britaine,
Of Brabant and of Orleans, shall ma
forth,
And you, Prince Dauphin, with all swift d
patch,
To line and new repair our towns of war
With men of courage and with means defer
ant:
For England his approaches makes as fierce
As waters to the sucking of a gulf.
It fits us then to be as provident
As fear may teach us, out of late examples
Left by the fatal and neglected English
Upon our fields.
Dau.   My most redoubted father,
It is most meet we arm us 'gainst the foe;
For peace itself should not so dull a kingdom,
Though war nor no known quarrel were
question,—
But that defences, musters, preparations,
Should be maintain'd, assembled, and collect
As were a war in expectation.
Therefore I say 'tis meet we all go forth
To view the sick and feeble parts of France
And let us do it with no show of fear;
No, with no more than if we heard that Engla
Were busied with a Whitsun morris-dance:
For, my good liege, she is so idly king'd,
Her sceptre so fantastically borne
By a vain, giddy, shallow, humorous youth,
That fear attends her not.

Con. O peace, Prince Dauphin!
You are too much mistaken in this king.
Question your Grace the late ambassadors,
With what great state he heard their embassy,
How well supplied with noble counsellors, 33
How modest in exception, and, withal
How terrible in constant resolution,
And you shall find his vanities forespent 36
Were but the outside of the Roman Brutus,
Covering discretion with a coat of folly;
As gardeners do with ordure hide those roots
That shall first spring and be most delicate. 40
Dau. Well, 'tis not so, my lord high constable;
But though we think it so, it is no matter:
In cases of defence 'tis best to weigh
The enemy more mighty than he seems: 44
To the proportions of defence are fill'd;
Which of a weak and niggardly projection
Doth like a miser spoil his coat with scanting
little cloth.
Fr. King. Think we King Harry strong; 48
And, princes, look you strongly arm to meet
him.
The kindred of him hath been flesh'd upon us,
And he is bred out of that bloody strain
That haunted us in our familiar paths: 52
Witness our too much memorable shame
When Cressy battle fatally was struck
And all our princes captiv'd by the hand
Of that black name, Edward Black Prince of
Wales; 56
Whiles that his mounting sire, on mountain
standing,
Up in the air, crown'd with the golden sun,
Saw his heroical seed, and smil'd to see him
Mangle the work of nature, and deface 60
The patterns that by God and by French fathers
Had twenty years been made. This is a stem
Of that victorious stock; and let us fear
The native mightiness and fate of him. 64

Enter a Messenger.

Mess. Ambassadors from Harry King of
England
To crave admittance to your majesty.
Fr. King. We'll give them present audience.
Go, and bring them.
[*Exeunt* Messenger *and certain* Lords.
You see this chase is hotly follow'd, friends.
Dau. Turn head, and stop pursuit; for
coward dogs 69
Most spend their mouths when what they seem
to threaten
Runs far before them. Good my sovereign,
Take up the English short, and let them know
Of what a monarchy you are the head: 73
Self-love, my liege, is not so vile a sin
As self-neglecting.

Re-enter Lords, *with* EXETER *and Train.*

Fr. King. From our brother England?
Exe. From him; and thus he greets your
majesty. 76
He wills you, in the name of God Almighty,
That you divest yourself, and lay apart

The borrow'd glories that by gift of heaven,
By law of nature and of nations 'long 80
To him and to his heirs; namely, the crown
And all wide-stretched honours that pertain
By custom and the ordinance of times
Unto the crown of France. That you may know
'Tis no sinister nor no awkward claim, 85
Pick'd from the worm-holes of long-vanish'd
days,
Nor from the dust of old oblivion rak'd,
He sends you this most memorable line, 88
[*Gives a pedigree.*
In every branch truly demonstrative;
Willing you overlook this pedigree;
And when you find him evenly deriv'd
From his most fam'd of famous ancestors, 92
Edward the Third, he bids you then resign
Your crown and kingdom, indirectly held
From him the native and true challenger.
Fr. King. Or else what follows? 96
Exe. Bloody constraint; for if you hide the
crown
Even in your hearts, there will he rake for it:
Therefore in fierce tempest is he coming,
In thunder and in earthquake like a Jove, 100
That, if requiring fail, he will compel;
And bids you, in the bowels of the Lord,
Deliver up the crown, and to take mercy
On the poor souls for whom this hungry war 104
Opens his vasty jaws; and on your head
Turning the widows' tears, the orphans' cries,
The dead men's blood, the pining maidens'
groans,
For husbands, fathers, and betrothed lovers, 108
That shall be swallow'd in this controversy.
This is his claim, his threat'ning, and my mes-
sage;
Unless the Dauphin be in presence here,
To whom expressly I bring greeting too. 112
Fr. King. For us, we will consider of this
further:
To-morrow shall you bear our full intent
Back to our brother England.
Dau. For the Dauphin,
I stand here for him: what to him from Eng-
land? 116
Exe. Scorn and defiance, slight regard, con-
tempt,
And anything that may not misbecome
The mighty sender, doth he prize you at.
Thus says my king: an if your father's high-
ness 120
Do not, in grant of all demands at large,
Sweeten the bitter mock you sent his majesty,
He'll call you to so hot an answer of it,
That caves and womby vaultages of France 124
Shall chide your trespass and return your mock
In second accent of his ordinance.
Dau. Say, if my father render fair return,
It is against my will; for I desire 128
Nothing but odds with England: to that end,
As matching to his youth and vanity,
I did present him with the Paris balls.
Exe. He'll make your Paris Louvre shake
for it, 132
Were it the mistress-court of mighty Europe:

And, be assur'd, you'll find a difference—
As we his subjects have in wonder found—
Between the promise of his greener days   136
And these he masters now. Now he weighs time
Even to the utmost grain; that you shall read
In your own losses, if he stay in France.
Fr. King. To-morrow shall you know our
    mind at full.   140
Exe. Dispatch us with all speed, lest that our
    king
Come here himself to question our delay;
For he is footed in this land already.
Fr. King. You shall be soon dispatch'd with
    fair conditions: 144
A night is but small breath and little pause
To answer matters of this consequence.
                    [*Flourish. Exeunt.*

ACT III

Enter Chorus.

Chor. *Thus with imagin'd wing our swift scene
    flies
In motion of no less celerity
Than that of thought. Suppose that you have
    seen*
The well-appointed king at Hampton pier   4
*Embark his royalty; and his brave fleet
With silken streamers the young Phœbus fan-
    ning:
Play with your fancies, and in them behold
Upon the hempen tackle ship-boys climbing;*   8
*Hear the shrill whistle which doth order give
To sounds confus'd; behold the threaden sails,
Borne with the invisible and creeping wind,
Draw the huge bottoms through the furrow'd
    sea,*   12
*Breasting the lofty surge. O! do but think
You stand upon the rivage and behold
A city on the inconstant billows dancing;
For so appears this fleet majestical,*   16
*Holding due course to Harfleur. Follow, follow!
Grapple your minds to sternage of this navy,
And leave your England, as dead midnight still,
Guarded with grandsires, babies, and old women,
Either past or not arriv'd to pith and puissance:
For who is he, whose chin is but enrich'd
With one appearing hair, that will not follow
Those cull'd and choice-drawn cavaliers to
    France?*   24
*Work, work your thoughts, and therein see a
    siege;
Behold the ordenance on their carriages,
With fatal mouths gaping on girded Harfleur.
Suppose the ambassador from the French comes
    back;*   28
*Tells Harry that the king doth offer him
Katharine his daughter; and with her, to dowry,
Some petty and unprofitable dukedoms:
The offer likes not: and the nimble gunner*   32
With linstock now the devilish cannon touches,
            [*Alarum; and chambers go off.*
*And down goes all before them. Still be kind,
And eke out our performance with your mind.*
                                [*Exit.*

SCENE I.—*France. Before Harfleur.*

Alarums. Enter KING HENRY, EXETER, BEDFORI
    GLOUCESTER, *and* Soldiers, *with scalin
    ladders.*

K. Hen. Once more unto the breach, dea
    friends, once more;
Or close the wall up with our English dead!
In peace there's nothing so becomes a man
As modest stillness and humility:
But when the blast of war blows in our ears,
Then imitate the action of the tiger;
Stiffen the sinews, summon up the blood,
Disguise fair nature with hard-favour'd rage;
Then lend the eye a terrible aspect;
Let it pry through the portage of the head
Like the brass cannon; let the brow o'erwhelm
As fearfully as doth a galled rock
O'erhang and jutty his confounded base,
Swill'd with the wild and wasteful ocean.
Now set the teeth and stretch the nostril wid
Hold hard the breath, and bend up every spir
To his full height! On, on, you noblest Englisl
Whose blood is fet from fathers of war-proo
Fathers that, like so many Alexanders,
Have in these parts from morn till even fough
And sheath'd their swords for lack of arg
    ment.
Dishonour not your mothers; now attest
That those whom you call'd fathers did beg
    you.
Be copy now to men of grosser blood,
And teach them how to war. And you, goo
    yeomen,
Whose limbs were made in England, show u
    here
The mettle of your pasture; let us swear
That you are worth your breeding; which
    doubt not;
For there is none of you so mean and base
That hath not noble lustre in your eyes.
I see you stand like greyhounds in the slips,
Straining upon the start. The game's afoot:
Follow your spirit; and, upon this charge
Cry 'God for Harry! England and Saint George
            [*Exeunt. Alarum, and chambers go of*

SCENE II.—*The Same.*

Enter NYM, BARDOLPH, PISTOL, *and* Boy.

Bard. On, on, on, on, on! to the breach,
the breach!
Nym. Pray thee, corporal, stay: the knock
are too hot; and for mine own part, I have n
a case of lives: the humour of it is too hot, th
is the very plain-song of it.
Pist. The plain-song is most just, for h
mours do abound:

    Knocks go and come: God's vassals drop and die
            And sword and shield
            In bloody field
            Doth win immortal fame.

Boy. Would I were in an alehouse in London
I would give all my fame for a pot of ale, an
safety.

Pist. And I: 16

> If wishes would prevail with me,
> My purpose should not fail with me,
> But thither would I hie.

Boy.   As duly,   20

> But not as truly,
> As bird doth sing on bough.

Enter FLUELLEN.

Flu. Up to the breach, you dogs! avaunt, you cullions!   [*Driving them forward.*

Pist. Be merciful, great duke, to men of mould!   24

Abate thy rage, abate thy manly rage!
Abate thy rage, great duke!
Good bawcock, bate thy rage; use lenity, sweet chuck!

Nym. These be good humours! your honour wins bad humours.   29

[*Exeunt* NYM, PISTOL, *and* BARDOLPH, *followed by* FLUELLEN.

Boy. As young as I am, I have observed these three swashers. I am boy to them all three, but all they three, though they would serve me, could not be man to me; for, indeed three such antiques do not amount to a man. For Bardolph, he is white-livered and red-faced; by the means whereof, a' faces it out, but fights not. For Pistol, he hath a killing tongue and a quiet sword; by the means whereof a' breaks words, and keeps whole weapons. For Nym, he hath heard that men of few words are the best men; and therefore he scorns to say his prayers, lest a' should be thought a coward: but his few bad words are matched with as few good deeds; for a' never broke any man's head but his own, and that was against a post when he was drunk. They will steal any thing and call it purchase. Bardolph stole a lute-case, bore it twelve leagues, and sold it for three half-pence. Nym and Bardolph are sworn brothers in filching, and in Calais they stole a fire-shovel;—I knew by that piece of service the men would carry coals,—they would have me as familiar with men's pockets as their gloves or their handkerchers: which makes much against my manhood if I should take from another's pocket to put into mine; for it is plain pocketing up of wrongs. I must leave them and seek some better service: their villany goes against my weak stomach, and therefore I must cast it up.   [*Exit.*

Re-enter FLUELLEN, GOWER *following.*

Gow. Captain Fluellen, you must come presently to the mines: the Duke of Gloucester would speak with you.   62

Flu. To the mines! tell you the duke it is not so good to come to the mines. For look you, the mines is not according to the disciplines of the war; the concavities of it is not sufficient; for, look you, th' athversary—you may discuss into the duke, look you—is digt himself four yards under the countermines; by Cheshu, I think, a' will plow up all if there is not better directions.   71

Gow. The Duke of Gloucester, to whom the order of the siege is given, is altogether directed by an Irishman, a very valiant gentleman, i' faith.

Flu. It is Captain Macmorris, is it not?   76

Gow. I think it be.

Flu. By Cheshu, he is an ass, as in the world: I will verify as much in his peard: he has no more directions in the true disciplines of the wars, look you, of the Roman disciplines, than is a puppy-dog.   82

Enter MACMORRIS *and* JAMY, *at a distance.*

Gow. Here a' comes; and the Scots captain, Captain Jamy, with him.

Flu. Captain Jamy is a marvellous falorous gentleman, that is certain; and of great expedition and knowledge in th' aunchient wars, upon my particular knowledge of his directions: by Cheshu, he will maintain his argument as well as any military man in the world, in the disciplines of the pristine wars of the Romans. 91

Jamy. I say gud day, Captain Fluellen.

Flu. God-den to your worship, good Captain James.

Gow. How now, Captain Macmorris! have you quit the mines? have the pioners given o'er?

Mac. By Chrish, la! tish ill done: the work ish give over, the trumpet sound the retreat. By my hand, I swear, and my father's soul, the work ish ill done; it ish give over: I would have blowed up the town, so Chrish save me, la! in an hour: O! tish ill done, tish ill done; by my hand, tish ill done!   103

Flu. Captain Macmorris, I beseech you now, will you voutsafe me, look you, a few disputations with you, as partly touching or concerning the disciplines of the war, the Roman wars, in the way of argument, look you, and friendly communication; partly to satisfy my opinion, and partly for the satisfaction, look you, of my mind, as touching the direction of the military discipline: that is the point.   112

Jamy. It sall be vary gud, gud feith, gud captains bath: [*Aside.*] and I sall quit you with gud leve, as I may pick occasion; that sall I, marry.

Mac. It is no time to discourse, so Chrish save me: the day is hot, and the weather, and the wars, and the king, and the dukes: it is no time to discourse. The town is beseeched, and the trumpet calls us to the breach; and we talk, and be Chrish, do nothing: 'tis shame for us all; so God sa' me, 'tis shame to stand still; it is shame, by my hand; and there is throats to be cut, and works to be done; and there ish nothing done, so Chrish sa' me, la!   125

Jamy. By the mess, ere theise eyes of mine take themselves to slumber, aile do gud service, or aile lig i' the grund for it; ay, or go to death; and aile pay it as valorously as I may, that sal I suerly do, that is the breff and the long. Marry, I wad full fain heard some question 'tween you tway.   132

Flu. Captain Macmorris, I think, look you, under your correction, there is not many of your nation—   135

Mac. Of my nation! What ish my nation? ish a villain, and a bastard, and a knave, and a rascal? What ish my nation? Who talks of my nation?   139

Flu. Look you, if you take the matter otherwise than is meant, Captain Macmorris, peradventure I shall think you do not use me with that affability as in discretion you ought to use me, look you; being as good a man as yourself, both in the disciplines of wars, and in the derivation of my birth, and in other particularities.   146

Mac. I do not know you so good a man as myself: so Chrish save me, I will cut off your head.   149

Gow. Gentlemen both, you will mistake each other.

Jamy. A! that's a foul fault.

[*A parley sounded.*

Gow. The town sounds a parley.   153

Flu. Captain Macmorris, when there is more better opportunity to be required, look you, I will be so bold as to tell you I know the disciplines of wars; and there is an end. [*Exeunt.*

SCENE III.—*The Same. Before the Gates of Harfleur.*

The Governor *and some* Citizens *on the walls; the* English *forces below. Enter* KING HENRY *and his Train.*

K. Hen. How yet resolves the governor of the town?
This is the latest parle we will admit:
Therefore to our best mercy give yourselves;
Or like to men proud of destruction   4
Defy us to our worst: for, as I am a soldier,—
A name that in my thoughts, becomes me best,—
If I begin the battery once again,
I will not leave the half-achieved Harfleur   8
Till in her ashes she lie buried.
The gates of mercy shall be all shut up,
And the flesh'd soldier, rough and hard of heart,
In liberty of bloody hand shall range   12
With conscience wide as hell, mowing like grass
Your fresh-fair virgins and your flowering infants.
What is it then to me, if impious war,
Array'd in flames like to the prince of fiends, 16
Do, with his smirch'd complexion, all fell feats
Enlink'd to waste and desolation?
What is 't to me, when you yourselves are cause,
If your pure maidens fall into the hand   20
Of hot and forcing violation?
What rein can hold licentious wickedness
When down the hill he holds his fierce career?
We may as bootless spend our vain command   24
Upon the enraged soldiers in their spoil   25
As send precepts to the leviathan
To come ashore. Therefore, you men of Harfleur,
Take pity of your town and of your people,   28
Whiles yet my soldiers are in my command;
Whiles yet the cool and temperate wind of grace
O'erblows the filthy and contagious clouds
Of heady murder, spoil, and villany.   32
If not, why, in a moment, look to see
The blind and bloody soldier with foul hand
Defile the locks of your shrill-shrieking daughters;

Your fathers taken by the silver beards,   36
And their most reverend heads dash'd to the walls;
Your naked infants spitted upon pikes,
Whiles the mad mothers with their howls confus'd
Do break the clouds, as did the wives of Jewry
At Herod's bloody-hunting slaughtermen.   41
What say you? will you yield, and this avoid,
Or, guilty in defence, be thus destroy'd?

Gov. Our expectation hath this day an end:
The Dauphin, whom of succour we entreated,   45
Returns us that his powers are yet not ready
To raise so great a siege. Therefore, great king,
We yield our town and lives to thy soft mercy.
Enter our gates; dispose of us and ours;   49
For we no longer are defensible.

K. Hen. Open your gates! Come, uncle Exeter,
Go you and enter Harfleur; there remain,   52
And fortify it strongly 'gainst the French:
Use mercy to them all. For us, dear uncle,
The winter coming on and sickness growing
Upon our soldiers, we will retire to Calais.   56
To-night in Harfleur will we be your guest;
To-morrow for the march are we addrest.

[*Flourish.* KING HENRY *and his Train enter the town*

SCENE IV.—*Rouen. A Room in the Palace.*

Enter KATHARINE *and* ALICE.

Kath. Alice, tu as esté en Angleterre, et tu parles bien le langage.

Alice. Un peu, madame.

Kath. Je te prie, m'enseignez; il faut que j'apprenne à parler. Comment appellez vous la main en Anglois?

Alice. La main? elle est appellée, de hand.

Kath. De hand. Et les doigts?

Alice. Les doigts? ma foy, je oublie les doigts; mais je me souviendray. Les doigts? je pense qu'ils sont appellés de fingres; ouy, de fingres.   10

Kath. La main, de hand; les doigts, de fingres. Je pense que je suis le bon escolier; j'ai gagné deux mots d'Anglois vistement. Comment appellez vous les ongles?   15

Alice. Les ongles? nous les appellons, de nails.

Kath. De nails. Escoutez; dites moy, si je parle bien: de hands, de fingres, et de nails.

Alice. C'est bien dict, madame; il est fort bon Anglois.   20

Kath. Dites moy l'Anglois pour le bras.

Alice. De arm, madame.

Kath. Et le coude?   23

Alice. De elbow.

Kath. De elbow. Je m'en fais la répétition de tous les mots que vous m'avez appris dès à présent.

Alice. Il est trop difficile, madame, comme je pense.

Kath. Excusez moy, Alice; escoutez: de hand, de fingres, de nails, de arma, de bilbow.   30

Alice. De elbow, madame.

Kath. O *Seigneur Dieu! je m'en oublie; de*
elbow. *Comment appellez vous le col?*
Alice. De nick, *madame.* 36
Kath. De nick. *Et le menton?*
Alice. De chin.
Kath. De sin. *Le col, de nick: le menton, de*
sin.
Alice. Ouy. *Sauf vostre honneur, en vérité*
vous prononcez les mots aussi droict que les
natifs d'Angleterre.
Kath. Je ne doute point d'apprendre par la
grace de Dieu, et en peu de temps. 45
Alice. N'avez vous déjà oublié ce que je vous
ay enseignée?
Kath. Non, je reciteray à vous promptement.
De hand, de fingre, de mails,— 49
Alice. De nails, *madame.*
Kath. De nails, de arme, de ilbow.
Alice. Sauf vostre honneur, d'elbow. 52
Kath. Ainsi dis je; d'elbow, de nick, et de
sin. *Comment appellez vous le pied et la robe?*
Alice. De foot, *madame; et* de coun. 55
Kath. De foot, et de coun? *O Seigneur*
Dieu! ces sont mots de son mauvais, corruptible,
gros, et impudique, et non pour les dames
d'honneur d'user. Je ne voudrois prononcer
ces mots devant les seigneurs de France, pour
tout le monde. Foh! le foot, et le coun. Néant-
moins je reciterai une autre fois ma leçon
ensemble: de hand, de fingre, de nails, d'arm,
d'elbow, de nick, de sin, de foot, de coun. 64
Alice. Excellent, *madame!*
Kath. C'est assez pour une fois: allons nous
à diner. [*Exeunt.*

SCENE V.—*The Same. Another Room in*
the Palace.

Enter the FRENCH KING, *the* DAUPHIN, DUKE
OF BOURBON, *the* CONSTABLE OF FRANCE, *and*
Others.

Fr. King. 'Tis certain, he hath pass'd the
river Somme.
Con. And if he be not fought withal, my lord,
Let us not live in France; let us quit all,
And give our vineyards to a barbarous people. 4
Dau. O *Dieu vivant!* shall a few sprays of us,
The emptying of our fathers' luxury,
Our scions, put in wild and savage stock,
Spirt up so suddenly into the clouds, 8
And overlook their grafters?
Bour. Normans, but bastard Normans, Nor-
man bastards!
Mort de ma vie! if they march along
Unfought withal, but I will sell my dukedom,
To buy a slobbery and a dirty farm 13
In that nook-shotten isle of Albion.
Con. Dieu de battailes! where have they
this mettle? 16
Is not their climate foggy, raw, and dull,
On whom, as in despite, the sun looks pale,
Killing their fruit with frowns? Can sodden
water,
A drench for sur-rein'd jades, their barley-broth,
Decoct their cold blood to such valiant heat? 20
And shall our quick blood, spirited with wine,

Seem frosty? O! for honour of our land,
Let us not hang like roping icicles
Upon our houses' thatch, whiles a more frosty
people 24
Sweat drops of gallant youth in our rich fields;
Poor we may call them in their native lords.
Dau. By faith and honour,
Our madams mock at us, and plainly say 28
Our mettle is bred out; and they will give
Their bodies to the lust of English youth
To new-store France with bastard warriors.
Bour. They bid us to the English dancing-
schools, 32
And teach lavoltas high and swift corantos;
Saying our grace is only in our heels,
And that we are most lofty runaways.
Fr. King. Where is Montjoy the herald?
speed him hence: 36
Let him greet England with our sharp defiance.
Up, princes! and, with spirit of honour edg'd
More sharper than your swords, hie to the field:
Charles Delabreth, High Constable of France; 40
You Dukes of Orleans, Bourbon, and Berri,
Alençon, Brabant, Bar, and Burgundy;
Jaques Chatillon, Rambures, Vaudemont,
Beaumont, Grandpré, Roussi, and Fauconberg,
Foix, Lestrale, Bouciqualt, and Charolois; 45
High dukes, great princes, barons, lords, and
knights,
For your great seats now quit you of great
shames.
Bar Harry England, that sweeps through our
land
With pennons painted in the blood of Harfleur:
Rush on his host, as doth the melted snow
Upon the valleys, whose low vassal seat
The Alps doth spit and void his rheum upon: 52
Go down upon him, you have power enough.
And in a captive chariot into Roan
Bring him our prisoner.
Con. This becomes the great.
Sorry am I his numbers are so few, 56
His soldiers sick and famish'd in their march,
For I am sure when he shall see our army
He'll drop his heart into the sink of fear,
And for achievement offer us his ransom. 60
Fr. King. Therefore, lord constable, haste on
Montjoy,
And let him say to England that we send
To know what willing ransom he will give.
Prince Dauphin, you shall stay with us in Roan.
Dau. Not so, I do beseech your majesty. 65
Fr. King. Be patient, for you shall remain
with us.
Now forth, lord constable and princes all,
And quickly bring us word of England's fall. 68
[*Exeunt.*

SCENE VI.—*The English Camp in Picardy.*

Enter GOWER *and* FLUELLEN.

Gow. How now, Captain Fluellen! come you
from the bridge?
Flu. I assure you, there is very excellent
services committed at the pridge. 4
Gow. Is the Duke of Exeter safe?

Flu. The Duke of Exeter is as magnanimous as Agamemnon; and a man that I love and honour with my soul, and my heart, and my duty, and my life, and my living, and my uttermost power: he is not—God be praised and plessed!—any hurt in the world; but keeps the pridge most valiantly, with excellent discipline. There is an aunchient lieutenant there at the pridge, I think, in my very conscience, he is as valiant a man as Mark Antony; and he is a man of no estimation in the world; but I did see him do as gallant service.   17

Gow. What do you call him?

Flu. He is called Aunchient Pistol.

Gow. I know him not.   20

Enter PISTOL.

Flu. Here is the man.

Pist. Captain, I thee beseech to do me favours:

The Duke of Exeter doth love thee well.

Flu. Ay, I praise God; and I have merited some love at his hands.   25

Pist. Bardolph, a soldier firm and sound of heart,

And of buxom valour, hath, by cruel fate

And giddy Fortune's furious fickle wheel,   28

That goddess blind,

That stands upon the rolling restless stone,—

Flu. By your patience, Aunchient Pistol. Fortune is painted plind, with a muffler afore her eyes, to signify to you that Fortune is plind: and she is painted also with a wheel, to signify to you, which is the moral of it, that she is turning, and inconstant, and mutability, and variation: and her foot, look you, is fixed upon a spherical stone, which rolls, and rolls, and rolls: in good truth, the poet makes a most excellent description of it: Fortune is an excellent moral.   40

Pist. Fortune is Bardolph's foe, and frowns on him;

For he hath stol'n a pax, and hanged must a' be,

A damned death!

Let gallows gape for dog, let man go free   44

And let not hemp his wind-pipe suffocate.

But Exeter hath given the doom of death

For pax of little price.

Therefore, go speak; the duke will hear thy voice;   48

And let not Bardolph's vital thread be cut

With edge of penny cord and vile reproach:

Speak, captain, for his life, and I will thee re-quite.

Flu. Aunchient Pistol, I do partly understand your meaning.   53

Pist. Why then, rejoice therefore.

Flu. Certainly, aunchient, it is not a thing to rejoice at; for, if, look you, he were my brother, I would desire the duke to use his good pleasure and put him to execution; for discipline ought to be used.

Pist. Die and be damn'd; and figo for thy friendship!   60

Flu. It is well.

Pist. The fig of Spain!   [*Exit.*

Flu. Very good.

Gow. Why, this is an arrant counterfeit rascal: I remember him now; a bawd, a cut-purse.   66

Flu. I'll assure you a' uttered as prave words at the pridge as you shall see in a summer's day. But it is very well; what he has spoke to me, that is well, I warrant you, when time is serve.   71

Gow. Why, 'tis a gull, a fool, a rogue, that now and then goes to the wars to grace himself at his return into London under the form of a soldier. And such fellows are perfect in the great commanders' names, and they will learn you by rote where services were done; at such and such a sconce, at such a breach, at such a convoy; who came off bravely, who was shot, who disgraced, what terms the enemy stood on; and this they con perfectly in the phrase of war, which they trick up with new-tuned oaths: and what a beard of the general's cut and a horrid suit of the camp will do among foaming bottles and ale-washed wits, is wonderful to be thought on. But you must learn to know such slanders of the age, or else you may be marvellously mistook.   88

Flu. I tell you what, Captain Gower; I do perceive, he is not the man that he would gladly make show to the world he is: if I find a hole in his coat I will tell him my mind. [*Drum heard.*] Hark you, the king is coming; and I must speak with him from the pridge.

Enter KING HENRY, GLOUCESTER, *and* Soldiers.

Flu. God pless your majesty!

K. Hen. How now, Fluellen! cam'st thou from the bridge?   96

Flu. Ay, so please your majesty. The Duke of Exeter hath very gallantly maintained the pridge: the French is gone off, look you, and there is gallant and most prave passages. Marry, th' athversary was have possession of the pridge, but he is enforced to retire, and the Duke of Exeter is master of the pridge. I can tell your majesty the duke is a prave man.   104

K. Hen. What men have you lost, Fluellen?

Flu. The perdition of th' athversary hath been very great, reasonable great: marry, for my part, I think the duke hath lost never a man but one that is like to be executed for robbing a church; one Bardolph, if your majesty know the man: his face is all bubukles, and whelks, and knobs, and flames o' fire; and his lips blows at his nose, and it is like a coal of fire, sometimes plue and sometimes red; but his nose is executed, and his fire's out.   115

K. Hen. We would have all such offenders so cut off: and we give express charge that in our marches through the country there be nothing compelled from the villages, nothing taken but paid for, none of the French upbraided or abused in disdainful language; for when lenity and cruelty play for a kingdom, the gentler gamester is the soonest winner.

Tucket. Enter MONTJOY.

Mont. You know me by my habit.   124
K. Hen. Well then I know thee: what shall I
  know of thee?
Mont. My master's mind.
K. Hen. Unfold it.   127
Mont. Thus says my king: Say thou to Harry
of England: Though we seemed dead, we did but
sleep: advantage is a better soldier than rashness. Tell him, we could have rebuked him at
Harfleur, but that we thought not good to bruise
an injury till it were full ripe: now we speak
upon our cue, and our voice is imperial: England
shall repent his folly, see his weakness, and admire our sufferance. Bid him therefore consider
of his ransom; which must proportion the losses
we have borne, the subjects we have lost, the
disgrace we have digested; which, in weight to
re-answer, his pettiness would bow under. For
our losses, his exchequer is too poor; for the
effusion of our blood, the muster of his kingdom
too faint a number; and for our disgrace, his
own person, kneeling at our feet, but a weak and
worthless satisfaction. To this add defiance: and
tell him, for conclusion, he hath betrayed his
followers, whose condemnation is pronounced.
So far my king and master, so much my office.
K. Hen. What is thy name? I know thy
  quality.   149
Mont. Montjoy.
K. Hen. Thou dost thy office fairly. Turn
  thee back,
And tell thy king I do not seek him now,   152
But could be willing to march on to Calais
Without impeachment; for, to say the sooth,—
Though 'tis no wisdom to confess so much
Unto an enemy of craft and vantage,—   156
My people are with sickness much enfeebled,
My numbers lessen'd, and those few I have
Almost no better than so many French:
Who, when they were in health, I tell thee,
  herald,   160
I thought upon one pair of English legs
Did march three Frenchmen. Yet, forgive me,
  God,
That I do brag thus! this your air of France
Hath blown that vice in me; I must repent. 164
Go therefore, tell thy master here I am:
My ransom is this frail and worthless trunk,
My army but a weak and sickly guard;
Yet, God before, tell him we will come on,   168
Though France himself and such another neigh-
  bour
Stand in our way. There's for thy labour,
  Montjoy.
Go, bid thy master well advise himself:
If we may pass, we will; if we be hinder'd, 172
We shall your tawny ground with your red
  blood
Discolour: and so, Montjoy, fare you well.
The sum of all our answer is but this:
We would not seek a battle as we are;   176
Nor, as we are, we say we will not shun it:
So tell your master.
Mont. I shall deliver so. Thanks to your
  highness.   [*Exit.*

Glo. I hope they will not come upon us
  now.   180
K. Hen. We are in God's hand, brother, not
  in theirs.
March to the bridge; it now draws toward
  night:
Beyond the river we'll encamp ourselves,
And on to-morrow bid them march away. 184
                                      [*Exeunt.*

SCENE VII.—*The French Camp, near
          Agincourt.*

Enter the CONSTABLE OF FRANCE, *the* LORD RAM-
  BURES, *the* DUKE OF ORLEANS, *the* DAUPHIN,
  and Others.

Con. Tut! I have the best armour of the
world. Would it were day!
Orl. You have an excellent armour; but let
my horse have his due.   4
Con. It is the best horse of Europe.
Orl. Will it never be morning?
Dau. My Lord of Orleans, and my lord high
constable, you talk of horse and armour—   8
Orl. You are as well provided of both as any
prince in the world.
Dau. What a long night is this! I will not
change my horse with any that treads but on
four pasterns. *Ça, ha!* He bounds from the
earth as if his entrails were hairs: *le cheval
volant,* the Pegasus, *qui a les narines de feu!*
When I bestride him, I soar, I am a hawk: he
trots the air; the earth sings when he touches
it; the basest horn of his hoof is more musical
than the pipe of Hermes.
Orl. He's of the colour of the nutmeg.   20
Dau. And of the heat of the ginger. It is a
beast for Perseus: he is pure air and fire; and
the dull elements of earth and water never
appear in him but only in patient stillness while
his rider mounts him: he is indeed a horse; and
all other jades you may call beasts.
Con. Indeed, my lord, it is a most absolute
and excellent horse.   28
Dau. It is the prince of palfreys; his neigh
is like the bidding of a monarch and his countenance enforces homage.
Orl. No more, cousin.   32
Dau. Nay, the man hath no wit that cannot,
from the rising of the lark to the lodging of the
lamb, vary deserved praise on my palfrey: it is
a theme as fluent as the sea; turn the sands into
eloquent tongues, and my horse is argument for
them all. 'Tis a subject for a sovereign to reason on, and for a sovereign's sovereign to ride
on; and for the world—familiar to us, and
unknown—to lay apart their particular functions and wonder at him. I once writ a sonnet in his praise and began thus: 'Wonder of
nature!'—   44
Orl. I have heard a sonnet begin so to one's
mistress.
Dau. Then did they imitate that which I
composed to my courser; for my horse is my
mistress.   49

Orl. Your mistress bears well.

Dau. Me well; which is the prescript praise and perfection of a good and particular mistress.   53

Con. *Ma foi*, methought yesterday your mistress shrewdly shook your back.

Dau. So perhaps did yours.   56

Con. Mine was not bridled.

Dau. O! then belike she was old and gentle; and you rode, like a kern of Ireland, your French hose off and in your straight strossers.   60

Con. You have good judgment in horsemanship.

Dau. Be warned by me, then: they that ride so, and ride not warily, fall into foul bogs. I had rather have my horse to my mistress.   65

Con. I had as lief have my mistress a jade.

Dau. I tell thee, constable, my mistress wears his own hair.   68

Con. I could make as true a boast as that if I had a sow to my mistress.

Dau. *Le chien est retourné à son propre vomissement, et la truie lavée au bourbier:* thou makest use of any thing.   73

Con. Yet do I not use my horse for my mistress: or any such proverb so little kin to the purpose.   76

Ram. My lord constable, the armour that I saw in your tent to-night, are those stars or suns upon it?

Con. Stars, my lord.   80

Dau. Some of them will fall to-morrow, I hope.

Con. And yet my sky shall not want.

Dau. That may be, for you bear a many superfluously, and 'twere more honour some were away.   86

Con. Even as your horse bears your praises; who would trot as well were some of your brags dismounted.   89

Dau. Would I were able to load him with his desert! Will it never be day? I will trot to-morrow a mile, and my way shall be paved with English faces.   93

Con. I will not say so for fear I should be faced out of my way. But I would it were morning, for I would fain be about the ears of the English.   97

Ram. Who will go to hazard with me for twenty prisoners?

Con. You must first go yourself to hazard, ere you have them.   101

Dau. 'Tis midnight: I'll go arm myself.
                                                               [*Exit.*

Orl. The Dauphin longs for morning.

Ram. He longs to eat the English.   104

Con. I think he will eat all he kills.

Orl. By the white hand of my lady, he's a gallant prince.

Con. Swear by her foot, that she may tread out the oath.   109

Orl. He is simply the most active gentleman of France.

Con. Doing is activity, and he will still be doing.   113

Orl. He never did harm, that I heard of.

Con. Nor will do none to-morrow: he will keep that good name still.   116

Orl. I know him to be valiant.

Con. I was told that by one that knows him better than you.

Orl. What's he?   120

Con. Marry, he told me so himself; and he said he cared not who knew it.

Orl. He needs not; it is no hidden virtue in him.   124

Con. By my faith, sir, but it is; never any body saw it but his lackey: 'tis a hooded valour; and when it appears, it will bate.

Orl. 'Ill will never said well.'   128

Con. I will cap that proverb with 'There is flattery in friendship.'

Orl. And I will take up that with 'Give the devil his due.'   132

Con. Well placed: there stands your friend for the devil: have at the very eye of that proverb, with 'A pox of the devil.'

Orl. You are the better at proverbs, by how much 'A fool's bolt is soon shot.'   137

Con. You have shot over.

Orl. 'Tis not the first time you were overshot.

Enter a Messenger.

Mess. My lord high constable, the English lie within fifteen hundred paces of your tents. 141

Con. Who hath measured the ground?

Mess. The Lord Grandpré.

Con. A valiant and most expert gentleman. Would it were day! Alas! poor Harry of England, he longs not for the dawning as we do.

Orl. What a wretched and peevish fellow is this King of England, to mope with his fat-brained followers so far out of his knowledge!

Con. If the English had any apprehension they would run away.   151

Orl. That they lack; for if their heads had any intellectual armour they could never wear such heavy head-pieces.

Ram. That island of England breeds very valiant creatures: their mastiffs are of unmatchable courage.   157

Orl. Foolish curs! that run winking into the mouth of a Russian bear and have their heads crushed like rotten apples. You may as well say that's a valiant flea that dare eat his breakfast on the lip of a lion.   162

Con. Just, just; and the men do sympathize with the mastiffs in robustious and rough coming on, leaving their wits with their wives: and then give them great meals of beef and iron and steel, they will eat like wolves and fight like devils.   168

Orl. Ay, but these English are shrewdly out of beef.

Con. Then shall we find to-morrow they have only stomachs to eat and none to fight. Now is it time to arm; come, shall we about it?   173

Orl. It is now two o'clock: but, let me see, by ten
We shall have each a hundred Englishmen.
                                                             [*Exeunt.*

ACT IV

Enter Chorus.

Now entertain conjecture of a time
When creeping murmur and the poring dark
Fills the wide vessel of the universe.
From camp to camp, through the foul womb of
*   night,*   4
The hum of either army stilly sounds,
That the fix'd sentinels almost receive
The secret whispers of each other's watch:
Fire answers fire, and through their paly flames 8
Each battle sees the other's umber'd face:
Steed threatens steed, in high and boastful neighs
Piercing the night's dull ear; and from the tents
The armourers, accomplishing the knights,   12
With busy hammers closing rivets up,
Give dreadful note of preparation.
The country cocks do crow, the clocks do toll,
And the third hour of drowsy morning name. 16
Proud of their numbers, and secure in soul,
The confident and over-lusty French
Do the low-rated English play at dice;
And chide the cripple tardy-gaited night   20
Who, like a foul and ugly witch, doth limp
So tediously away. The poor condemned English,
Like sacrifices, by their watchful fires
Sit patiently, and inly ruminate   24
The morning's danger, and their gesture sad
Investing lank-lean cheeks and war-worn coats
Presenteth them unto the gazing moon
So many horrid ghosts. O! now, who will be-
*   hold*   28
The royal captain of this ruin'd band
Walking from watch to watch, from tent to tent,
Let him cry 'Praise and glory on his head!'
For forth he goes and visits all his host,   32
Bids them good morrow with a modest smile,
And calls them brothers, friends, and country-
*   men.*
Upon his royal face there is no note
How dread an army hath enrounded him;   36
Nor doth he dedicate one jot of colour
Unto the weary and all-watched night:
But freshly looks and overbears attaint
With cheerful semblance and sweet majesty;   40
That every wretch, pining and pale before,
Beholding him, plucks comfort from his looks.
A largess universal, like the sun
His liberal eye doth give to every one,   44
Thawing cold fear. Then mean and gentle all,
Behold, as may unworthiness define,
A little touch of Harry in the night.
And so our scene must to the battle fly;   48
Where,—O for pity,—we shall much disgrace,
With four or five most vile and ragged foils,
Right ill dispos'd in brawl ridiculous,
The name of Agincourt. Yet sit and see;   52
Minding true things by what their mockeries be.
*   [Exit.*

SCENE I.—*The English Camp at Agincourt.*

Enter KING HENRY, BEDFORD, *and* GLOUCESTER.

K. Hen. Gloucester, 'tis true that we are in
    great danger;
The greater therefore should our courage be.

Goodmorrow, brotherBedford. GodAlmighty!
There is some soul of goodness in things evil, 4
Would men observingly distil it out;
For our bad neighbour makes us early stirrers,
Which is both healthful, and good husbandry:
Besides, they are our outward consciences,   8
And preachers to us all; admonishing
That we should dress us fairly for our end.
Thus may we gather honey from the weed,
And make a moral of the devil himself.   12

Enter ERPINGHAM.

Good morrow, old Sir Thomas Erpingham:
A good soft pillow for that good white head
Were better than a churlish turf of France.
    Erp. Not so, my liege: this lodging likes me
        better,   16
Since I may say, 'Now lie I like a king.'
    K. Hen. 'Tis good for men to love their
        present pains
Upon example; so the spirit is eas'd:
And when the mind is quicken'd, out of doubt,
The organs, though defunct and dead before,
Break up their drowsy grave, and newly move
With casted slough and fresh legerity.
Lend me thy cloak, Sir Thomas. Brothers both,
Commend me to the princes in our camp;   25
Do my good morrow to them; and anon
Desire them all to my pavilion.
    Glo. We shall, my liege.   28
            [*Exeunt* GLOUCESTER *and* BEDFORD.
    Erp. Shall I attend your Grace?
    K. Hen.   No, my good knight:
Go with my brothers to my lords of England:
I and my bosom must debate awhile,
And then I would no other company.   32
    Erp. The Lord in heaven bless thee, noble
        Harry!   [*Exit.*
    K. Hen. God-a-mercy, old heart! thou
        speak'st cheerfully.

Enter PISTOL.

    Pist. Qui va là?
    K. Hen. A friend.   36
    Pist. Discuss unto me; art thou officer?
Or art thou base, common and popular?
    K. Hen. I am a gentleman of a company.
    Pist. Trail'st thou the puissant pike?   40
    K. Hen. Even so. What are you?
    Pist. As good a gentleman as the emperor.
    K. Hen. Then you are a better than the king.
    Pist. The king's a bawcock, and a heart of
        gold,   44
A lad of life, an imp of fame:
Of parents good, of fist most valiant:
I kiss his dirty shoe, and from my heart-string
I love the lovely bully. What's thy name? 48
    K. Hen. Harry *le Roy.*
    Pist. Le Roy! a Cornish name: art thou of
Cornish crew?
    K. Hen. No, I am a Welshman.
    Pist. Know'st thou Fluellen?   52
    K. Hen. Yes.
    Pist. Tell him, I'll knock his leek about his
        pate
Upon Saint Davy's day.

K. Hen. Do not you wear your dagger in your cap that day, lest he knock that about yours. 57

Pist. Art thou his friend?

K. Hen. And his kinsman too.

Pist. The figo for thee then! 60

K. Hen. I thank you. God be with you!

Pist. My name is Pistol called. [*Exit.*

K. Hen. It sorts well with your fierceness.
[*Retires.*

Enter FLUELLEN *and* GOWER, *severally.*

Gow. Captain Fluellen! 64

Flu. So! in the name of Cheshu Christ, speak lower. It is the greatest admiration in the universal world, when the true and auncient prerogatifes and laws of the wars is not kept. If you would take the pains but to examine the wars of Pompey the Great, you shall find, I warrant you, that there is no tiddle-taddle nor pibble-pabble in Pompey's camp; I warrant you, you shall find the ceremonies of the wars, and the cares of it, and the forms of it, and the sobriety of it, and the modesty of it, to be otherwise. 76

Gow. Why, the enemy is loud; you heard him all night.

Flu. If the enemy is an ass and a fool and a prating coxcomb, is it meet, think you, that we should also, look you, be an ass and a fool and a prating coxcomb, in your own conscience now?

Gow. I will speak lower. 83

Flu. I pray you and peseech you that you will. [*Exeunt* GOWER *and* FLUELLEN.

K. Hen. Though it appear a little out of fashion,

There is much care and valour in this Welshman.

Enter JOHN BATES, ALEXANDER COURT, *and* MICHAEL WILLIAMS.

Court. Brother John Bates, is not that the morning which breaks yonder? 89

Bates. I think it be; but we have no great cause to desire the approach of day.

Will. We see yonder the beginning of the day, but I think we shall never see the end of it. Who goes there?

K. Hen. A friend.

Will. Under what captain serve you? 96

K. Hen. Under Sir Thomas Erpingham.

Will. A good old commander and a most kind gentleman: I pray you, what thinks he of our estate? 100

K. Hen. Even as men wracked upon a sand, that look to be washed off the next tide.

Bates. He hath not told his thought to the king? 104

K. Hen. No; nor it is not meet he should. For, though I speak it to you, I think the king is but a man, as I am: the violet smells to him as it doth to me; the element shows to him as it doth to me; all his senses have but human conditions: his ceremonies laid by, in his nakedness he appears but a man; and though his affections are higher mounted than ours, yet when they stoop, they stoop with the like wing. Therefore when he sees reason of fears, as we do,

his fears, out of doubt, be of the same relish a ours are: yet, in reason, no man should posses him with any appearance of fear, lest he, b showing it, should dishearten his army. 11

Bates. He may show what outward courag he will, but I believe, as cold a night as 'tis, h could wish himself in Thames up to the neck and so I would he were, and I by him, at a adventures, so we were quit here. 12

K. Hen. By my troth, I will speak my con science of the king: I think he would not wisl himself any where but where he is.

Bates. Then I would he were here alone; s should he be sure to be ransomed, and a man poor men's lives saved. 12

K. Hen. I dare say you love him not so i to wish him here alone, howsoever you spea this to feel other men's minds. Methinks could not die any where so contented as in th king's company, his cause being just and hi quarrel honourable.

Will. That's more than we know. 13

Bates. Ay, or more than we should seek after for we know enough if we know we are the king' subjects. If his cause be wrong, our obedienc to the king wipes the crime of it out of us. 14

Will. But if the cause be not good, the kin himself hath a heavy reckoning to make; whe all those legs and arms and heads, chopped o in a battle, shall join together at the latter day and cry all, 'We died at such a place;' som swearing, some crying for a surgeon, some upo their wives left poor behind them, some upo the debts they owe, some upon their childre rawly left. I am afeard there are few die we that die in a battle; for how can they charitabl dispose of any thing when blood is their argu ment? Now, if these men do not die well, will be a black matter for the king that led then to it, whom to disobey were against all propor tion of subjection. 15

K. Hen. So, if a son that is by his father sen about merchandise do sinfully miscarry upo the sea, the imputation of his wickedness, by your rule, should be imposed upon his fathe that sent him: or if a servant, under his master' command transporting a sum of money, be as sailed by robbers and die in many irreconcile iniquities, you may call the business of the maste the author of the servant's damnation. But thi is not so: the king is not bound to answer th particular endings of his soldiers, the father o his son, nor the master of his servant; for they purpose not their death when they purpose thei services. Besides, there is no king, be his caus never so spotless, if it come to the arbitremen of swords, can try it out with all unspotted sol diers. Some, peradventure, have on them the guilt of premeditated and contrived murder some, of beguiling virgins with the broken seal of perjury; some, making the wars their bul wark, that have before gored the gentle boson of peace with pillage and robbery. Now, if these men have defeated the law and outrun nativ punishment, though they can outstrip men, the have no wings to fly from God: war is his beadle

ar is his vengeance; so that here men are
unished for before-breach of the king's laws in
ow the king's quarrel: where they feared the
eath they have borne life away, and where they
ould be safe they perish. Then, if they die
nprovided, no more is the king guilty of their
amnation than he was before guilty of those
npieties for the which they are now visited.
very subject's duty is the king's; but every
ubject's soul is his own. Therefore should every
oldier in the wars do as every sick man in his
ed, wash every mote out of his conscience; and
ying so, death is to him advantage; or not
ying, the time was blessedly lost wherein such
reparation was gained: and in him that es-
apes, it were no sin to think, that making God
o free an offer, he let him outlive that day to
e his greatness, and to teach others how they
ould prepare. 199
Will. 'Tis certain, every man that dies ill, the
l upon his own head: the king is not to answer

Bates. I do not desire he should answer for
e; and yet I determine to fight lustily for him.
K. Hen. I myself heard the king say he would
ot be ransomed. 206
Will. Ay, he said so, to make us fight cheer-
lly; but when our throats are cut he may be
nsomed, and we ne'er the wiser.
K. Hen. If I live to see it, I will never trust
is word after. 211
Will. You pay him then. That's a perilous
ot out of an elder-gun, that a poor and a
rivate displeasure can do against a monarch.
ou may as well go about to turn the sun to
e with fanning in his face with a peacock's
ather. You'll never trust his word after!
me, 'tis a foolish saying. 218
K. Hen. Your reproof is something too round;
should be angry with you if the time were conenient. 221
Will. Let it be a quarrel between us, if you
ve.
K. Hen. I embrace it. 224
Will. How shall I know thee again?
K. Hen. Give me any gage of thine, and I
ill wear it in my bonnet: then, if ever thou
arest acknowledge it, I will make it my quarrel.
Will. Here's my glove: give me another of
ine. 230
K. Hen. There.
Will. This will I also wear in my cap: if ever
ou come to me and say after to-morrow, 'This
my glove,' by this hand I will take thee a box
n the ear.
K. Hen. If ever I live to see it, I will challenge
it. 237
Will. Thou darest as well be hanged.
K. Hen. Well, I will do it, though I take thee
n the king's company. 240
W ll. Keep thy word: fare thee well.
Bates. Be friends, you English fools, be
riends: we have French quarrels enow, if you
ould tell how to reckon. 244
K. Hen. Indeed, the French may lay twenty
'rench crowns to one, they will beat us; for

they bear them on their shoulders: but it is no
English treason to cut French crowns, and to-
morrow the king himself will be a clipper. 249
[*Exeunt* Soldiers.
Upon the king! let us our lives, our souls,
Our debts, our careful wives,
Our children, and our sins lay on the king! 252
We must bear all. O hard condition!
Twin-born with greatness, subject to the breath
Of every fool, whose sense no more can feel
But his own wringing. What infinite heart's
ease 256
Must kings neglect that private men enjoy!
And what have kings that privates have not too,
Save ceremony, save general ceremony?
And what art thou, thou idle ceremony? 260
What kind of god art thou, that suffer'st more
Of mortal griefs than do thy worshippers?
What are thy rents? what are thy comings-in?
O ceremony! show me but thy worth: 264
What is thy soul of adoration?
Art thou aught else but place, degree, and form,
Creating awe and fear in other men?
Wherein thou art less happy, being fear'd, 268
Than they in fearing.
What drink'st thou oft, instead of homage
sweet,
But poison'd flattery? O! be sick, great great-
ness,
And bid thy ceremony give thee cure. 272
Think'st thou the fiery fever will go out
With titles blown from adulation?
Will it give place to flexure and low-bending?
Canst thou, when thou command'st the beggar's
knee, 276
Command the health of it? No, thou proud
dream,
That play'st so subtly with a king's repose;
I am a king that find thee; and I know
'Tis not the balm, the sceptre and the ball, 280
The sword, the mace, the crown imperial,
The intertissued robe of gold and pearl,
The farced title running 'fore the king,
The throne he sits on, nor the tide of pomp 284
That beats upon the high shore of this world,
No, not all these, thrice-gorgeous ceremony,
Not all these, laid in bed majestical,
Can sleep so soundly as the wretched slave, 288
Who with a body fill'd and vacant mind
Gets him to rest, cramm'd with distressful bread;
Never sees horrid night, the child of hell,
But, like a lackey, from the rise to set 292
Sweats in the eye of Phœbus, and all night
Sleeps in Elysium; next day after dawn,
Doth rise and help Hyperion to his horse,
And follows so the ever-running year 296
With profitable labour to his grave:
And, but for ceremony, such a wretch,
Winding up days with toil and nights with
sleep,
Had the fore-hand and vantage of a king. 300
The slave, a member of the country's peace,
Enjoys it; but in gross brain little wots
What watch the king keeps to maintain the
peace,
Whose hours the peasant best advantages. 304

Re-enter ERPINGHAM.

Erp. My lord, your nobles, jealous of your absence,
Seek through your camp to find you.
K. Hen. Good old knight,
Collect them all together at my tent:
I'll be before thee.
Erp. I shall do 't, my lord. [*Exit.*
K. Hen. O God of battles! steel my soldiers'
hearts; 309
Possess them not with fear; take from them now
The sense of reckoning, if the opposed numbers
Pluck their hearts from them. Not to-day, O
Lord! 312
O! not to-day, think not upon the fault
My father made in compassing the crown.
I Richard's body have interr'd anew,
And on it have bestow'd more contrite tears
Than from it issu'd forced drops of blood.
Five hundred poor I have in yearly pay,
Who twice a day their wither'd hands hold up
Toward heaven, to pardon blood; and I have
built 320
Two chantries, where the sad and solemn priests
Sing still for Richard's soul. More will I do;
Though all that I can do is nothing worth,
Since that my penitence comes after all, 324
Imploring pardon.

Re-enter GLOUCESTER.

Glo. My liege!
K. Hen. My brother Gloucester's voice! Ay;
I know thy errand, I will go with thee: 328
The day, my friends, and all things stay for me.
[*Exeunt.*

SCENE II.—*The French Camp.*

Enter the DAUPHIN, ORLEANS, RAMBURES, *and Others.*

Orl. The sun doth gild our armour: up, my lords!
Dau. Montez à cheval! My horse! varlet!
lacquais! ha!
Orl. O brave spirit!
Dau. Via! les eaux et la terre! 4
Orl. Rien puis? l'air et le feu.
Dau. Ciel! cousin Orleans.

Enter CONSTABLE.

Now, my lord constable!
Con. Hark how our steeds for present ser-
vice neigh! 8
Dau. Mount them, and make incision in
their hides,
That their hot blood may spin in English eyes,
And dout them with superfluous courage: ha!
Ram. What! will you have them weep our
horses' blood? 12
How shall we then behold their natural tears?

Enter a Messenger.

Mess. The English are embattail'd, you
French peers.
Con. To horse, you gallant princes! straight
to horse!
Do but behold yon poor and starved band, 16

And your fair show shall suck away their soul
Leaving them but the shales and husks of men
There is not work enough for all our hands;
Scarce blood enough in all their sickly veins
To give each naked curtal-axe a stain,
That our French gallants shall to-day draw out
And sheathe for lack of sport: let us but blow on
them,
The vapour of our valour will o'erturn them.
'Tis positive 'gainst all exceptions, lords,
That our superfluous lackeys and our peasant
Who in unnecessary action swarm
About our squares of battle, were enow
To purge this field of such a hilding foe,
Though we upon this mountain's basis by
Took stand for idle speculation:
But that our honours must not. What's to say
A very little little let us do,
And all is done. Then let the trumpets sound
The tucket sonance and the note to mount:
For our approach shall so much dare the field
That England shall couch down in fear and
yield.

Enter GRANDPRÉ.

Grand. Why do you stay so long, my lord
of France?
Yon island carrions desperate of their bones
Ill-favour'dly become the morning field;
Their ragged curtains poorly are let loose,
And our air shakes them passing scornfully:
Big Mars seems bankrupt in their beggar'd host
And faintly through a rusty beaver peeps:
The horsemen sit like fixed candlesticks,
With torch-staves in their hand; and their poor
jades
Lob down their heads, dropping the hides and
hips,
The gum down-roping from their pale-dead
eyes,
And in their pale dull mouths the gimmal bit
Lies foul with chew'd grass, still and motionless
And their executors, the knavish crows,
Fly o'er them, all impatient for their hour.
Description cannot suit itself in words
To demonstrate the life of such a battle
In life so lifeless as it shows itself.
Con. They have said their prayers, and they
stay for death.
Dau. Shall we go send them dinners and
fresh suits,
And give their fasting horses provender,
And after fight with them?
Con. I stay but for my guard: on, to the
field!
I will the banner from a trumpet take,
And use it for my haste. Come, come, away
The sun is high, and we outwear the day.
[*Exeunt.*

SCENE III.—*The English Camp.*

Enter the English host; GLOUCESTER, BEDFORD
EXETER, SALISBURY, *and* WESTMORELAND.

Glo. Where is the king?
Bed. The king himself is rode to view their
battle.

West. Of fighting men they have full threescore thousand.
Exe. There's five to one; besides, they all are
  fresh.   4
Sal. God's arm strike with us! 'tis a fearful
  odds.

od be wi' you, princes all; I'll to my charge:
we no more meet till we meet in heaven,
ren, joyfully, my noble Lord of Bedford,   8
y dear Lord Gloucester, and my good Lord
  Exeter,
nd my kind kinsman, warriors all, adieu!
Bed. Farewell, good Salisbury; and good
  luck go with thee!
Exe. Farewell, kind lord. Fight valiantly to-
  day: 12
nd yet I do thee wrong to mind thee of it,
er thou art fram'd of the firm truth of valour.
                          [*Exit* SALISBURY.
Bed. He is as full of valour as of kindness;
incely in both.

Enter KING HENRY.

West.   O! that we now had here 16
it one ten thousand of those men in England
aat do no work to-day.
K. Hen.   What's he that wishes so?
y cousin Westmoreland? No, my fair cousin:
we are mark'd to die, we are enow   20
o do our country loss; and if to live,
ne fewer men, the greater share of honour.
od's will! I pray thee, wish not one man more.
r Jove, I am not covetous for gold,   24
or care I who doth feed upon my cost;
yearns me not if men my garments wear;
ch outward things dwell not in my desires:
at if it be a sin to covet honour,   28
nm the most offending soul alive.
o, faith, my coz, wish not a man from England:
od's peace! I would not lose so great an
  honour
s one man more, methinks, would share from
  me,   32
er the best hope I have. O! do not wish one
  more:
ather proclaim it, Westmoreland, through
  my host,
aat he which hath no stomach to this fight,
et him depart; his passport shall be made,   36
nd crowns for convoy put into his purse:
e would not die in that man's company
aat fears his fellowship to die with us.
is day is call'd the feast of Crispian: 40
e that outlives this day, and comes safe home,
ill stand a tip-toe when this day is nam'd,
nd rouse him at the name of Crispian.
e that shall live this day, and see old age,   44
ill yearly on the vigil feast his neighbours,
nd say, 'To-morrow is Saint Crispian:'
nen will he strip his sleeve and show his scars,
nd say, 'These wounds I had on Crispin's day.'
d men forget: yet all shall be forgot,   49
it he'll remember with advantages
hat feats he did that day. Then shall our
  names,
miliar in his mouth as household words,   52

Harry the king, Bedford and Exeter,
Warwick and Talbot, Salisbury and Gloucester,
Be in their flowing cups freshly remember'd.
This story shall the good man teach his son; 56
And Crispin Crispian shall ne'er go by,
From this day to the ending of the world,
But we in it shall be remembered;
We few, we happy few, we band of brothers; 60
For he to-day that sheds his blood with me
Shall be my brother; be he ne'er so vile
This day shall gentle his condition:
And gentlemen in England now a-bed   64
Shall think themselves accurs'd they were not
  here,
And hold their manhoods cheap whiles any
  speaks
That fought with us upon Saint Crispin's day.

Re-enter SALISBURY.

  Sal. My sov'reign lord, bestow yourself with
    speed: 68
The French are bravely in their battles set,
And will with all expedience charge on us.
  K. Hen. All things are ready, if our minds
    be so.
  West. Perish the man whose mind is back-
    ward now!   72
  K. Hen. Thou dost not wish more help from
    England, coz?
  West. God's will! my liege, would you and I
    alone,
Without more help, could fight this royal battle!
  K. Hen. Why, now thou hast unwish'd five
    thousand men;   76
Which likes me better than to wish us one.
You know your places: God be with you all!

Tucket. Enter MONTJOY.

  Mont. Once more I come to know of thee,
    King Harry,
If for thy ransom thou wilt now compound, 80
Before thy most assured overthrow:
For certainly thou art so near the gulf
Thou needs must be englutted. Besides, in
  mercy,
The constable desires thee thou wilt mind   84
Thy followers of repentance; that their souls
May make a peaceful and a sweet retire
From off these fields, where, wretches, their
  poor bodies
Must lie and fester.
  K. Hen.   Who hath sent thee now? 88
  Mont. The Constable of France.
  K. Hen. I pray thee, bear my former answer
    back:
Bid them achieve me and then sell my bones.
Good God! why should they mock poor fellows
  thus?   92
The man that once did sell the lion's skin
While the beast liv'd, was kill'd with hunting
  him.
A many of our bodies shall no doubt
Find native graves; upon the which, I trust, 96
Shall witness live in brass of this day's work;
And those that leave their valiant bones in
  France,

Dying like men, though buried in your dung-
hills,
They shall be fam'd; for there the sun shall
greet them,   100
And draw their honours reeking up to heaven,
Leaving their earthly parts to choke your clime,
The smell whereof shall breed a plague in
France.
Mark then abounding valour in our English,
That being dead, like to the bullet's grazing,
Break out into a second course of mischief,
Killing in relapse of mortality.
Let me speak proudly: tell the constable,   108
We are but warriors for the working-day;
Our gayness and our gilt are all besmirch'd
With rainy marching in the painful field;
There's not a piece of feather in our host— 112
Good argument, I hope, we will not fly—
And time hath worn us into slovenry:
But, by the mass, our hearts are in the trim;
And my poor soldiers tell me, yet ere night 116
They'll be in fresher robes, or they will pluck
The gay new coats o'er the French soldiers'
heads,
And turn them out of service. If they do this,—
As, if God please, they shall,—my ransom then
Will soon be levied. Herald, save thou thy
labour;   121
Come thou no more for ransom, gentle herald:
They shall have none, I swear, but these my
joints;
Which if they have as I will leave 'em them,
Shall yield them little, tell the constable.

Mont. I shall, King Harry. And so, fare
thee well:
Thou never shalt hear herald any more. [*Exit.*
K. Hen. I fear thou'lt once more come again
for ransom.   128

Enter YORK.

York. My lord, most humbly on my knee I
beg
The leading of the vaward.
K. Hen. Take it, brave York. Now, soldiers,
march away:
And how thou pleasest, God, dispose the day!
[*Exeunt.*

SCENE IV.—*The Field of Battle.*

Alarums: Excursions. Enter French Soldier,
PISTOL, *and* Boy.

Pist. Yield, cur!
*Fr. Sol. Je pense que vous estes le gentil-
homme de bonne qualité.*
Pist. Quality? Calen O custure me! Art
thou a gentleman?   4
What is thy name? discuss.
Fr. Sol. O Seigneur Dieu!
Pist. O Signieur Dew should be a gentle-
man:—
Perpend my words, O Signieur Dew, and mark:
O Signieur Dew, thou diest on point of fox 9
Except, O signieur, thou do give to me
Egregious ransom.

*Fr. Sol. O, prenez misericorde! ayez pitié
moy!*
Pist. Moy shall not serve; I will have fo
moys;
Or I will fetch thy rim out at thy throat
In drops of crimson blood.
*Fr. Sol. Est-il impossible d'eschapper la fo
de ton bras?*
Pist. Brass, cur!
Thou damned and luxurious mountain goat,
Offer'st me brass?
Fr. Sol. O pardonnez moy!
Pist. Sayst thou me so? is that a ton of moy
Come hither, boy: ask me this slave in Fren
What is his name.
Boy. Escoutez: comment estes vous appel
Fr. Sol. Monsieur le Fer.
Boy. He says his name is Master Fer.
Pist. Master Fer! I'll fer him, and firk hi
and ferret him. Discuss the same in Fren
unto him.
Boy. I do not know the French for fer, a
ferret, and firk.
Pist. Bid him prepare, for I will cut
throat.
Fr. Sol. Que dit-il, monsieur?
*Boy. Il me commande à vous dire que v
faites vous prest; car ce soldat icy est disp
tout à cette heure de couper vostre gorge.*
Pist. Ouy, cuppele gorge, permafoy.
Peasant, unless thou give me crowns, bra
crowns;
Or mangled shalt thou be by this my sword.
*Fr. Sol. O! je vous supplie pour l'amour
Dieu, me pardonner! Je suis le gentilhomme
bonne maison: gardez ma vie, et je vous d
neray deux cents escus.*
Pist. What are his words?
Boy. He prays you to save his life: he i
gentleman of a good house; and, for his rans
he will give you two hundred crowns.
Pist. Tell him, my fury shall abate, and I
The crowns will take.
Fr. Sol. Petit monsieur, que dit-il?
*Boy. Encore qu'il est contre son jurem
de pardonner aucun prisonnier; neant-moi
pour les escus que vous l'avez promis, il
content de vous donner la liberté, le franchi
ment.*
*Fr. Sol. Sur mes genoux, je vous donne m
remerciemens; et je m'estime heureux que
suis tombé entre les mains d'un chevalier,
pense, le plus brave, valiant, et très disting
seigneur d'Angleterre.*
Pist. Expound unto me, boy.
Boy. He gives you, upon his knees, a th
sand thanks; and he esteems himself hap
that he hath fallen into the hands of one—as
thinks—the most brave, valorous, and thri
worthy signieur of England.
Pist. As I suck blood, I will some me
show.—
Follow me!
[*Exeunt* PISTOL *and* French Soldi
Boy. Suivez vous le grand capitaine. I
never know so full a voice issue from so emp

heart: but the saying is true, 'The empty
ssel makes the greatest sound.' Bardolph
d Nym had ten times more valour than this
aring devil i' the old play, that every one
ay pare his nails with a wooden dagger;
d they are both hanged; and so would this
if he durst steal anything adventurously.
nust stay with the lackeys, with the luggage
our camp: the French might have a good
ey of us, if he knew of it; for there is none to
ard it but boys.   [Exit.

SCENE V.—Another Part of the Field.

arums. Enter DAUPHIN, ORLEANS, BOURBON,
CONSTABLE, RAMBURES, and Others.

Con. O diable!
Orl. O seigneur! le jour est perdu! tout est
perdu!
Dau. Mort de ma vie! all is confounded, all!
eproach and everlasting shame
: mocking in our plumes. O meschante
fortune!
o not run away.   [A short alarum.
Con.   Why, all our ranks are broke.
Dau. O perdurable shame! let's stab ourselves.
e these the wretches that we play'd at dice
for?   8
Orl. Is this the king we sent to for his ransom?
Bour. Shame, and eternal shame, nothing
but shame!
et's die in honour! once more back again;
nd he that will not follow Bourbon now, 12
et him go hence, and with his cap in hand,
ke a base pander, hold the chamber-door
hilst by a slave, no gentler than my dog,
is fairest daughter is contaminated.   16
Con. Disorder, that hath spoil'd us, friend
us now!
et us on heaps go offer up our lives.
Orl. We are enough yet living in the field
o smother up the English in our throngs, 20
any order might be thought upon.
Bour. The devil take order now! I'll to the
throng:
et life be short, else shame will be too long.
                                          [Exeunt.

SCENE VI.—Another Part of the Field.

Alarums. Enter KING HENRY and Forces;
EXETER, and Others.

K. Hen. Well have we done, thrice-valiant
countrymen:
ut all's not done; yet keep the French the
field.
Exe. The Duke of York commends him to
your majesty.
K. Hen. Lives he, good uncle? thrice within
this hour   4
saw him down; thrice up again, and fighting;
rom helmet to the spur all blood he was.
Exe. In which array, brave soldier, doth he lie,
arding the plain; and by his bloody side,— 8
oke-fellow to his honour-owing wounds,—

The noble Earl of Suffolk also lies.
Suffolk first died: and York, all haggled over,
Comes to him, where in gore he lay insteep'd, 12
And takes him by the beard, kisses the gashes
That bloodily did yawn upon his face;
And cries aloud, 'Tarry, dear cousin Suffolk!
My soul shall thine keep company to heaven; 16
Tarry, sweet soul, for mine, then fly abreast,
As in this glorious and well-foughten field,
We kept together in our chivalry!'
Upon these words I came and cheer'd him up:
He smil'd me in the face, raught me his hand,
And with a feeble gripe says, 'Dear my lord,
Commend my service to my sovereign.'
So did he turn, and over Suffolk's neck   24
He threw his wounded arm, and kiss'd his lips;
And so espous'd to death, with blood he seal'd
A testament of noble-ending love.
The pretty and sweet manner of it forc'd   28
Those waters from me which I would have
stopp'd;
But I had not so much of man in me,
And all my mother came into mine eyes
And gave me up to tears.
K. Hen.   I blame you not;   32
For, hearing this, I must perforce compound
With mistful eyes, or they will issue too.
                                           [Alarum.
But hark! what new alarum is this same?
The French have reinforc'd their scatter'd men:
Then every soldier kill his prisoners!   37
Give the word through.   [Exeunt.

SCENE VII.—Another Part of the Field.

Alarums. Enter FLUELLEN and GOWER.

Flu. Kill the poys and the luggage! 'tis expressly against the law of arms: 'tis as arrant
a piece of knavery, mark you now, as can be
offer't: in your conscience now, is it not?   4
Gow. 'Tis certain, there's not a boy left alive;
and the cowardly rascals that ran from the
battle have done this slaughter: besides, they
have burned and carried away all that was in
the king's tent; wherefore the king most
worthily hath caused every soldier to cut his
prisoner's throat. O! 'tis a gallant king.   11
Flu. Ay, he was porn at Monmouth, Captain
Gower. What call you the town's name where
Alexander the Pig was born?
Gow. Alexander the Great.   15
Flu. Why, I pray you, is not pig great? The
pig, or the great, or the mighty, or the huge,
or the magnanimous, are all one reckonings,
save the phrase is a little variations.   19
Gow. I think Alexander the Great was born
in Macedon: his father was called Philip of
Macedon, as I take it.
Flu. I think it is in Macedon where Alexander is porn. I tell you, captain, if you look in
the maps of the 'orld, I warrant you sall find,
in the comparisons between Macedon and Monmouth, that the situations, look you, is both
alike. There is a river in Macedon, and there is
also moreover a river at Monmouth: it is called
Wye at Monmouth; but it is out of my prains

what is the name of the other river; but 'tis all one, 'tis alike as my fingers is to my fingers, and there is salmons in both. If you mark Alexander's life well, Harry of Monmouth's life is come after it indifferent well; for there is figures in all things. Alexander,—God knows, and you know,—in his rages, and his furies, and his wraths, and his cholers, and his moods, and his displeasures, and his indignations, and also being a little intoxicates in his prains, did, in his ales and his angers, look you, kill his pest friend, Cleitus.   42

Gow. Our king is not like him in that: he never killed any of his friends.

Flu. It is not well done, mark you now, to take the tales out of my mouth, ere it is made and finished. I speak but in the figures and comparisons of it: as Alexander killed his friend Cleitus, being in his ales and his cups, so also Harry Monmouth, being in his right wits and his good judgments, turned away the fat knight with the great belly-doublet: he was full of jests, and gipes, and knaveries, and mocks; I have forgot his name.   54

Gow. Sir John Falstaff.

Flu. That is he. I'll tell you, there is goot men porn at Monmouth.

Gow. Here comes his majesty.   58

Alarum. Enter KING HENRY, *with a part of the English Forces;* WARWICK, GLOUCESTER, EXETER, *and Others.*

K. Hen. I was not angry since I came to France
Until this instant. Take a trumpet, herald;   60
Ride thou unto the horsemen on yon hill:
If they will fight with us, bid them come down,
Or void the field; they do offend our sight.
If they'll do neither, we will come to them,   64
And make them skirr away, as swift as stones
Enforced from the old Assyrian slings.
Besides, we'll cut the throats of those we have,
And not a man of them that we shall take   68
Shall taste our mercy. Go and tell them so.

Enter MONTJOY.

Exe. Here comes the herald of the French, my liege.

Glo. His eyes are humbler than they us'd to be.

K. Hen. How now! what means this, herald? know'st thou not   72
That I have fin'd these bones of mine for ransom?

Com'st thou again for ransom?

Mont.   No, great king.
I come to thee for charitable licence,
That we may wander o'er this bloody field   76
To book our dead, and then to bury them;
To sort our nobles from our common men;
For many of our princes—woe the while!—
Lie drown'd and soak'd in mercenary blood;   80
So do our vulgar drench their peasant limbs
In blood of princes; and their wounded steeds
Fret fetlock-deep in gore, and with wild rage
Yerk out their armed heels at their dead masters,

Killing them twice. O! give us leave, great kin
To view the field in safety and dispose
Of their dead bodies.

K. Hen.   I tell thee truly, hera
I know not if the day be ours or no;
For yet a many of your horsemen peer
And gallop o'er the field.

Mont.   The day is your
K. Hen. Praised be God, and not o
strength, for it!
What is this castle call'd that stands hard b
Mont. They call it Agincourt.
K. Hen. Then call we this the field of Agi
court,
Fought on the day of Crispin Crispianus.

Flu. Your grandfather of famous memo
an't please your majesty, and your great-un
Edward the Plack Prince of Wales, as I ha
read in the chronicles, fought a most pra
pattle here in France.

K. Hen. They did, Fluellen.

Flu. Your majesty says very true. If yo
majesties is remembered of it, the Welshm
did good service in a garden where leeks d
grow, wearing leeks in their Monmouth cap
which, your majesty know, to this hour is
honourable badge of the service; and I do l
lieve, your majesty takes no scorn to wear t
leek upon Saint Tavy's day.

K. Hen. I wear it for a memorable honou
For I am Welsh, you know, good countryma

Flu. All the water in Wye cannot wash yo
majesty's Welsh plood out of your pody, I c
tell you that: Got pless it and preserve it, as lo
as it pleases his grace, and his majesty too!

K. Hen. Thanks, good my countryman.

Flu. By Jeshu, I am your majesty's countr
man, I care not who know it; I will confess it
all the 'orld: I need not be ashamed of yo
majesty, praised be God, so long as your majes
is an honest man.

K. Hen. God keep me so! Our heralds
with him:
Bring me just notice of the numbers dead
On both our parts. Call yonder fellow hithe
        [*Points to* WILLIAMS. *Exeunt* MONTJ
                                      and Othe

Exe. Soldier, you must come to the king.

K. Hen. Soldier, why wear'st thou that glo
in thy cap?

Will. An't please your majesty, 'tis the ga
of one that I should fight withal, if he be aliv

K. Hen. An Englishman?

Will. An't please your majesty, a rascal th
swaggered with me last night; who, if a' live a
ever dare to challenge this glove, I have sworn
take him a box o' the ear: or, if I can see n
glove in his cap,—which he swore as he was
soldier he would wear if alive,—I will strike
out soundly.

K. Hen. What think you, Captain Fluelle
is it fit this soldier keep his oath?

Flu. He is a craven and a villain else, ar
please your majesty, in my conscience.

K. Hen. It may be his enemy is a gentlema
of great sort, quite from the answer of his degre

Flu. Though he be as good a gentleman as the devil is, as Lucifer and Belzebub himself, it is necessary, look your Grace, that he keep his vow and his oath. If he be perjured, see you now, his reputation is as arrant a villain and a jack-sauce as ever his black shoe trod upon God's ground and his earth, in my conscience, la! 151

K. Hen. Then keep thy vow, sirrah, when thou meetest the fellow.

Will. So I will, my liege, as I live.

K. Hen. Who servest thou under?

Will. Under Captain Gower, my liege. 156

Flu. Gower is a goot captain, and is good knowledge and literatured in the wars.

K. Hen. Call him hither to me, soldier.

Will. I will, my liege.			[*Exit.*

K. Hen. Here, Fluellen; wear thou this favour for me and stick it in thy cap. When Alençon and myself were down together I plucked this glove from his helm: if any man challenge this, he is a friend to Alençon, and an enemy to our person; if thou encounter any such, apprehend him, an thou dost me love. 167

Flu. Your Grace does me as great honours as can be desired in the hearts of his subjects: I would fain see the man that has but two legs that shall find himself aggriefed at this glove, that is all; but I would fain see it once, and please God of his grace that I might see. 173

K. Hen. Knowest thou Gower?

Flu. He is my dear friend, an 't please you.

K. Hen. Pray thee, go seek him, and bring him to my tent. 177

Flu. I will fetch him.			[*Exit.*

K. Hen. My Lord of Warwick, and my brother Gloucester, 180
follow Fluellen closely at the heels.
The glove which I have given him for a favour,
May haply purchase him a box o' the ear;
It is the soldier's; I by bargain should
Wear it myself. Follow, good cousin Warwick:
If that the soldier strike him,—as, I judge 185
by his blunt bearing he will keep his word,—
Some sudden mischief may arise of it;
For I do know Fluellen valiant, 188
And touch'd with choler, hot as gunpowder,
And quickly will return an injury:
Follow and see there be no harm between them.
Go you with me, uncle of Exeter.		[*Exeunt.*

SCENE VIII.—*Before* KING HENRY'S *Pavilion.*

Enter GOWER *and* WILLIAMS.

Will. I warrant it is to knight you, captain.

Enter FLUELLEN.

Flu. God's will and his pleasure, captain, I beseech you now come apace to the king: there is more good toward you peradventure than is in your knowledge to dream of. 5

Will. Sir, know you this glove?

Flu. Know the glove! I know the glove is a glove. 8

Will. I know this; and thus I challenge it.
								[*Strikes him.*

Flu. 'Sblood! an arrant traitor as any 's in the universal 'orld, or in France, or in England.

Gow. How now, sir! you villain! 12

Will. Do you think I'll be forsworn?

Flu. Stand away, Captain Gower; I will give treason his payment into plows, I warrant you.

Will. I am no traitor. 16

Flu. That's a lie in thy throat. I charge you in his majesty's name, apprehend him: he is a friend of the Duke Alençon's.

Enter WARWICK *and* GLOUCESTER.

War. How now, how now! what's the matter?

Flu. My Lord of Warwick, here is,—praised be God for it!—a most contagious treason come to light, look you, as you shall desire in a summer's day. Here is his majesty. 24

Enter KING HENRY *and* EXETER.

K. Hen. How now! what's the matter?

Flu. My liege, here is a villain and a traitor, that, look your Grace, has struck the glove which your majesty is take out of the helmet of Alençon.

Will. My liege, this was my glove; here is the fellow of it; and he that I gave it to in change promised to wear it in his cap: I promised to strike him, if he did: I met this man with my glove in his cap, and I have been as good as my word. 34

Flu. Your majesty hear now,—saving your majesty's manhood,—what an arrant, rascally, beggarly, lousy knave it is. I hope your majesty is pear me testimony and witness, and avouchments, that this is the glove of Alençon that your majesty is give me; in your conscience now.

K. Hen. Give me thy glove, soldier: look, here is the fellow of it. 42
'Twas I, indeed, thou promisedst to strike;
And thou hast given me most bitter terms.

Flu. An't please your majesty, let his neck answer for it, if there is any martial law in the 'orld.

K. Hen. How canst thou make me satisfaction? 49

Will. All offences, my lord, come from the heart: never came any from mine that might offend your majesty. 52

K. Hen. It was ourself thou didst abuse.

Will. Your majesty came not like yourself: you appeared to me but as a common man; witness the night, your garments, your lowliness; and what your highness suffered under that shape, I beseech you, take it for your own fault and not mine: for had you been as I took you for I made no offence; therefore, I beseech your highness, pardon me. 61

K. Hen. Here, uncle Exeter, fill this glove with crowns,
And give it to this fellow. Keep it, fellow;
And wear it for an honour in thy cap 64
Till I do challenge it. Give him the crowns:
And, captain, you must needs be friends with him.

Flu. By this day and this light, the fellow has mettle enough in his belly. Hold, there is twelve pence for you, and I pray you to serve

God, and keep you out of prawls, and prabbles,
and quarrels, and dissensions, and, I warrant
you, it is the better for you. 72
Will. I will none of your money.
Flu. It is with a good will; I can tell you it
will serve you to mend your shoes: come, wherefore should you be so pashful? your shoes is not
so good: 'tis a good shilling, I warrant you, or I
will change it. 78

Enter an English Herald.

K. Hen. Now, herald, are the dead number'd?
Her. Here is the number of the slaughter'd
French. [*Delivers a paper.*
K. Hen. What prisoners of good sort are
taken, uncle? 81
Exe. Charles Duke of Orleans, nephew to the
king;
John Duke of Bourbon, and Lord Bouciqualt:
Of other lords and barons, knights and squires,
Full fifteen hundred, besides common men.
K. Hen. This note doth tell me of ten thou-
sand French
That in the field lie slain: of princes, in this
number, 87
And nobles bearing banners, there lie dead
One hundred twenty-six: added to these,
Of knights, esquires, and gallant gentlemen,
Eight thousand and four hundred; of the which
Five hundred were but yesterday dubb'd knights:
So that, in these ten thousand they have lost,
There are but sixteen hundred mercenaries;
The rest are princes, barons, lords, knights,
squires,
And gentlemen of blood and quality. 96
The names of those their nobles that lie dead:
Charles Delabreth, High Constable of France;
Jaques of Chatillon, Admiral of France;
The master of the cross-bows, Lord Rambures;
Great-master of France, the brave Sir Guischard
Dauphin; 101
John Duke of Alençon; Antony Duke of
Brabant,
The brother to the Duke of Burgundy,
And Edward Duke of Bar: of lusty earls, 104
Grandpré and Roussi, Fauconberg and Foix,
Beaumont and Marle, Vaudemont and Lestrale.
Here was a royal fellowship of death!
Where is the number of our English dead?
[*Herald presents another paper.*
Edward the Duke of York, the Earl of Suffolk,
Sir Richard Ketley, Davy Gam, esquire:
None else of name: and of all other men 111
But five and twenty. O God! thy arm was here;
And not to us, but to thy arm alone,
Ascribe we all. When, without stratagem,
But in plain shock and even play of battle,
Was ever known so great and little loss 116
On one part and on the other? Take it, God,
For it is none but thine!
Exe. 'Tis wonderful!
K. Hen. Come, go we in procession to the
village; 119
And be it death proclaimed through our host
To boast of this or take the praise from God
Which is his only.

Flu. Is it not lawful, an please your majesty
to tell how many is killed? 12
K. Hen. Yes, captain; but with this acknow-
ledgment,
That God fought for us.
Flu. Yes, my conscience, he did us great good
K. Hen. Do we all holy rites: 12
Let there be sung *Non nobis* and *Te Deum*;
The dead with charity enclos'd in clay.
We'll then to Calais; and to England then,
Where ne'er from France arriv'd more happy
men. [*Exeunt*

ACT V

Enter Chorus.

Chor. Vouchsafe to those that have not read
the story,
That I may prompt them: and of such as have
I humbly pray them to admit the excuse
Of time, of numbers, and due course of things,
Which cannot in their huge and proper life
Be here presented. Now we bear the king
Toward Calais: grant him there; there seen,
Heave him away upon your winged thoughts
Athwart the sea. Behold, the English beach
Pales in the flood with men, with wives, and boys,
Whose shouts and claps out-voice the deep
mouth'd sea,
Which, like a mighty whiffler 'fore the king, 1
Seems to prepare his way: so let him land
And solemnly see him set on to London.
So swift a pace hath thought that even now
You may imagine him upon Blackheath; 1
Where that his lords desire him to have borne
His bruised helmet and his bended sword
Before him through the city: he forbids it,
Being free from vainness and self-glorious
pride; 2
Giving full trophy, signal and ostent,
Quite from himself, to God. But now behold,
In the quick forge and working-house of thought,
How London doth pour out her citizens. 2
The mayor and all his brethren in best sort,
Like to the senators of the antique Rome,
With the plebeians swarming at their heels,
Go forth and fetch their conquering Cæsar in:
As, by a lower but loving likelihood, 2
Were now the general of our gracious empress,—
As in good time he may,—from Ireland coming
Bringing rebellion broached on his sword, 3
How many would the peaceful city quit
To welcome him! much more, and much more
cause,
Did they this Harry. Now in London place him
As yet the lamentation of the French 3
Invites the King of England's stay at home,—
The emperor's coming in behalf of France,
To order peace between them;—and omit
All the occurrences, whatever chanc'd, 4
Till Harry's back-return again to France:
There must we bring him; and myself have play'd
The interim, by remembering you 'tis past.
Then brook abridgment, and your eyes advance
After your thoughts, straight back again to
France. [*Exit*

SCENE I.—*France. An English Court of Guard.*

Enter FLUELLEN *and* GOWER.

Gow. Nay, that's right; but why wear you your leek to-day? Saint Davy's day is past.

Flu. There is occasions and causes why and wherefore in all things: I will tell you, asse my friend, Captain Gower. The rascally, scald, beggarly, lousy, pragging knave, Pistol,—which you and yourself and all the 'orld know to be no better than a fellow,—look you now, of no merits, he is come to me and prings me pread and salt yesterday, look you, and pid me eat my leek. It was in a place where I could not preed no contention with him; but I will be so pold as to wear it in my cap till I see him once again, and then I will tell him a little piece of my desires.

Gow. Why, here he comes, swelling like a turkey-cock. 16

Enter PISTOL.

Flu. 'Tis no matter for his swellings nor his turkey-cocks. God pless you, Auncient Pistol! you scurvy, lousy knave, God pless you!

Pist. Ha! art thou bedlam? dost thou thirst, base Troyan, 20 to have me fold up Parca's fatal web? Hence! I am qualmish at the smell of leek.

Flu. I peseech you heartily, scurvy lousy knave, at my desires and my requests and my petitions to eat, look you, this leek; pecause, look you, you do not love it, nor your affections and your appetites and your digestions does not gree with it, I would desire you to eat it. 28

Pist. Not for Cadwallader and all his goats.

Flu. [*Strikes him.*] There is one goat for you. Will you be so good, scald knave, as eat it?

Pist. Base Troyan, thou shalt die. 32

Flu. You say very true, scald knave, when God's will is. I will desire you to live in the mean time and eat your victuals; come, there is sauce for it. [*Strikes him again.*] You called me yesterday mountain-squire, but I will make you to-day a squire of low degree. I pray you, fall to: if you can mock a leek you can eat a leek.

Gow. Enough, captain: you have astonished him. 41

Flu. I say, I will make him eat some part of my leek, or I will peat his pate four days. Bite, I pray you; it is good for your green wound and your ploody coxcomb. 45

Pist. Must I bite?

Flu. Yes, certainly, and out of doubt and out of question too and ambiguities. 48

Pist. By this leek, I will most horribly revenge. I eat and eat, I swear—

Flu. Eat, I pray you: will you have some more sauce to your leek? there is not enough leek to swear by. 53

Pist. Quiet thy cudgel: thou dost see I eat.

Flu. Much good do you, scald knave, heartily. Nay, pray you, throw none away; the skin is good for your broken coxcomb. When you take occasions to see leeks hereafter, I pray you, mock at 'em; that is all.

Pist. Good. 60

Flu. Ay, leeks is good. Hold you, there is a groat to heal your pate.

Pist. Me a groat!

Flu. Yes, verily and in truth, you shall take it; or I have another leek in my pocket, which you shall eat. 66

Pist. I take thy groat in earnest of revenge.

Flu. If I owe you anything I will pay you in cudgels: you shall be a woodmonger, and buy nothing of me but cudgels. God be wi' you, and keep you, and heal your pate. [*Exit.*

Pist. All hell shall stir for this. 72

Gow. Go, go; you are a counterfeit cowardly knave. Will you mock at an ancient tradition, begun upon an honourable respect, and worn as a memorable trophy of predeceased valour, and dare not avouch in your deeds any of your words? I have seen you gleeking and galling at this gentleman twice or thrice. You thought, because he could not speak English in the native garb, he could not therefore handle an English cudgel: you find it otherwise; and henceforth let a Welsh correction teach you a good English condition. Fare ye well. [*Exit.*

Pist. Doth Fortune play the huswife with me now? 85
News have I that my Nell is dead i' the spital
Of malady of France:
And there my rendezvous is quite cut off. 88
Old I do wax, and from my weary limbs
Honour is cudgelled. Well, bawd I'll turn,
And something lean to cutpurse of quick hand.
To England will I steal, and there I'll steal: 92
And patches will I get unto these cudgell'd scars,
And swear I got them in the Gallia wars. [*Exit.*

SCENE II.—*Troyes in Champagne. An Apartment in the* FRENCH KING'S *Palace.*

Enter, from one side, KING HENRY, BEDFORD, GLOUCESTER, EXETER, WARWICK, WESTMORELAND, *and other* Lords; *from the other side, the* FRENCH KING, QUEEN ISABEL, *the* PRINCESS KATHARINE, ALICE *and other* Ladies; *the* DUKE OF BURGUNDY, *and his Train.*

K. Hen. Peace to this meeting, wherefore we are met!
Unto our brother France, and to our sister,
Health and fair time of day; joy and good wishes
To our most fair and princely cousin Katharine;
And, as a branch and member of this royalty, 5
By whom this great assembly is contriv'd,
We do salute you, Duke of Burgundy;
And, princes French, and peers, health to you all! 8

Fr. King. Right joyous are we to behold your face,
Most worthy brother England; fairly met:
So are you, princes English, every one.

Q. Isa. So happy be the issue, brother England, 12
Of this good day and of this gracious meeting,
As we are now glad to behold your eyes;
Your eyes, which hitherto have borne in them

Against the French, that met them in their
bent,   16
The fatal balls of murdering basilisks:
The venom of such looks, we fairly hope,
Have lost their quality, and that this day
Shall change all griefs and quarrels into love. 20
  K. Hen. To cry amen to that, thus we appear.
  Q. Isa. You English princes all, I do salute
you.
  Bur. My duty to you both, on equal love,
Great Kings of France and England! That I
have labour'd   24
With all my wits, my pains, and strong en-
deavours,
To bring your most imperial majesties
Unto this bar and royal interview,
Your mightiness on both parts best can wit-
ness.   28
Since then my office hath so far prevail'd
That face to face, and royal eye to eye,
You have congreeted, let it not disgrace me
If I demand before this royal view,   32
What rub or what impediment there is,
Why that the naked, poor, and mangled Peace,
Dear nurse of arts, plenties, and joyful births,
Should not in this best garden of the world, 36
Our fertile France, put up her lovely visage?
Alas! she hath from France too long been chas'd,
And all her husbandry doth lie on heaps,
Corrupting in its own fertility.   40
Her vine, the merry cheerer of the heart,
Unpruned dies; her hedges even-pleach'd,
Like prisoners wildly overgrown with hair,
Put forth disorder'd twigs; her fallow leas 44
The darnel, hemlock and rank fumitory
Doth root upon, while that the coulter rusts
That should deracinate such savagery;
The even mead, that erst brought sweetly forth
The freckled cowslip, burnet, and green clover,
Wanting the scythe, all uncorrected, rank,
Conceives by idleness, and nothing teems   51
But hateful docks, rough thistles, kecksies, burs,
Losing both beauty and utility;
And as our vineyards, fallows, meads, and
hedges,
Defective in their natures, grow to wildness,
Even so our houses and ourselves and children
Have lost, or do not learn for want of time, 57
The sciences that should become our country,
But grow like savages,—as soldiers will,
That nothing do but meditate on blood,—   60
To swearing and stern looks, diffus'd attire,
And every thing that seems unnatural.
Which to reduce into our former favour
You are assembled; and my speech entreats 64
That I may know the let why gentle Peace
Should not expel these inconveniences,
And bless us with her former qualities.
  K. Hen. If, Duke of Burgundy, you would
the peace,   68
Whose want gives growth to the imperfections
Which you have cited, you must buy that
peace
With full accord to all our just demands;
Whose tenours and particular effects   72
You have, enschedul'd briefly, in your hands.

  Bur. The king hath heard them; to the whi
as yet
There is no answer made.
  K. Hen.   Well then the pea
Which you before so urg'd, lies in his answer.
  Fr. King. I have but with a cursorary eye
O'erglanc'd the articles: pleaseth your Grac
To appoint some of your council presently
To sit with us once more, with better heed
To re-survey them, we will suddenly
Pass our accept and peremptory answer.
  K. Hen. Brother, we shall. Go, uncle Exet
And brother Clarence, and you, brother Glo
cester,
Warwick and Huntingdon, go with the king
And take with you free power to ratify,
Augment, or alter, as your wisdoms best
Shall see advantageable for our dignity,
Anything in or out of our demands,
And we'll consign thereto. Will you, fair siste
Go with the princes, or stay here with us?
  Q. Isa. Our gracious brother, I will go wi
them.
Haply a woman's voice may do some good
When articles too nicely urg'd be stood on.
  K. Hen. Yet leave our cousin Katharine he
with us:
She is our capital demand, compris'd
Within the fore-rank of our articles.
  Q. Isa. She hath good leave.
           [*Exeunt all except* KING HENR
                KATHARINE, *and* ALIC
  K. Hen.   Fair Katharine, and most fai
Will you vouchsafe to teach a soldier terms
Such as will enter at a lady's ear,   1
And plead his love-suit to her gentle heart?
  Kath. Your majesty sall mock at me; I ca
not speak your England.
  K. Hen. O fair Katharine! if you will lo
me soundly with your French heart, I will
glad to hear you confess it brokenly with yo
English tongue. Do you like me, Kate?   1
  Kath. Pardonnez moy, I cannot tell vat
'like me.'
  K. Hen. An angel is like you, Kate; and ye
are like an angel.
  *Kath. Que dit-il? que je suis semblable à l
anges?*   1
  *Alice. Ouy, vrayment, sauf vostre grace, ain
dit-il.*
  K. Hen. I said so, dear Katharine; and
must not blush to affirm it.   1
  *Kath. O bon Dieu! les langues des homm
sont pleines des tromperies.*
  K. Hen. What says she, fair one? that t
tongues of men are full of deceits?   1
  Alice. Ouy, dat de tongues of de mans is
full of deceits: dat is de princess.
  K. Hen. The princess is the better Englis
woman. I' faith, Kate, my wooing is fit for t
understanding: I am glad thou canst speak r
better English; for, if thou couldst, thou would
find me such a plain king that thou would
think I had sold my farm to buy my crown.
know no ways to mince it in love, but direct
to say 'I love you:' then, if you urge me furthe

an to say 'Do you in faith?' I wear out my
uit. Give me your answer; i' faith do: and so
ap hands and a bargain. How say you, lady?

Kath. Sauf vostre honneur, me understand vell.

K. Hen. Marry, if you would put me to verses,
r to dance for your sake, Kate, why you undid
e: for the one, I have neither words nor mea-
ure, and for the other, I have no strength in
easure, yet a reasonable measure in strength.
'I could win a lady at leap-frog, or by vaulting
to my saddle with my armour on my back,
nder the correction of bragging be it spoken,
should quickly leap into a wife. Or if I might
uffet for my love, or bound my horse for her
vours, I could lay on like a butcher and sit
ke a jack-an-apes, never off. But before God,
ate, I cannot look greenly nor gasp out my
oquence, nor I have no cunning in protesta-
on; only downright oaths, which I never use
ll urged, nor never break for urging. If thou
anst love a fellow of this temper, Kate, whose
ice is not worth sun-burning, that never looks
a his glass for love of anything he sees there,
et thine eye be thy cook. I speak to thee plain
oldier: if thou canst love me for this, take me;
' not, to say to thee that I shall die, is true; but
or thy love, by the Lord, no; yet I love thee
oo. And while thou livest, dear Kate, take a
ellow of plain and uncoined constancy, for he
erforce must do thee right, because he hath
ot the gift to woo in other places; for these
ellows of infinite tongue, that can rime them-
elves into ladies' favours, they do always reason
emselves out again. What! a speaker is but a
prater; a rime is but a ballad. A good leg
vill fall, a straight back will stoop, a black beard
vill turn white, a curled pate will grow bald, a
air face will wither, a full eye will wax hollow,
ut a good heart, Kate, is the sun and the
noon; or, rather, the sun, and not the moon;
or it shines bright and never changes, but keeps
is course truly. If thou would have such a one,
ake me; and take me, take a soldier; take a
oldier, take a king. And what sayest thou then to
ny love? speak, my fair, and fairly, I pray thee.

Kath. Is it possible dat I sould love de
nemy of France?   178

K. Hen. No; it is not possible you should
ove the enemy of France, Kate; but, in loving
ne, you should love the friend of France; for
love France so well, that I will not part with
village of it; I will have it all mine: and,
Kate, when France is mine and I am yours,
hen yours is France and you are mine.   185

Kath. I cannot tell vat is dat.

K. Hen. No, Kate? I will tell thee in French,
vhich I am sure will hang upon my tongue like
a new-married wife about her husband's neck,
ardly to be shook off. *Je quand sur le posses-
ion de France, et quand vous avez le possession
le moy,*—let me see, what then? Saint Denis
e my speed!—*donc vostre est France, et vous
istes mienne.* It is as easy for me, Kate, to
onquer the kingdom, as to speak so much
nore French; I shall never move thee in French,
mless it be to laugh at me.   197

Kath. Sauf vostre honneur, le François que
vous parlez est meilleur que l'Anglois lequel je
parle.   200

K. Hen. No, faith, is't not, Kate; but thy
speaking of my tongue, and I thine, most truly
falsely, must needs be granted to be much at
one. But, Kate, dost thou understand thus
much English, Canst thou love me?   205

Kath. I cannot tell.

K. Hen. Can any of your neighbours tell,
Kate? I'll ask them. Come, I know thou lovest
me; and at night when you come into your
closet you'll question this gentlewoman about
me; and I know, Kate, you will to her dispraise
those parts in me that you love with your heart:
but, good Kate, mock me mercifully; the rather,
gentle princess, because I love thee cruelly. If
ever thou be'st mine, Kate,—as I have a saving
faith within me tells me thou shalt,—I get thee
with scambling, and thou must therefore needs
prove a good soldier-breeder. Shall not thou
and I, between Saint Denis and Saint George,
compound a boy, half French, half English,
that shall go to Constantinople and take the
Turk by the beard? shall we not? what sayest
thou, my fair flower-de-luce?

Kath. I do not know dat.   224

K. Hen. No; 'tis hereafter to know, but now
to promise: do but now promise, Kate, you will
endeavour for your French part of such a boy,
and for my English moiety take the word of a
king and a bachelor. How answer you, *la plus
belle Katharine du monde, mon très cher et
divine déesse?*   231

Kath. Your *majesté* ave *fausse* French enough
to deceive de most *sage demoiselle* dat is *en
France.*   234

K. Hen. Now, fie upon my false French! By
mine honour, in true English I love thee, Kate:
by which honour I dare not swear thou lovest
me; yet my blood begins to flatter me that thou
dost, notwithstanding the poor and untempering
effect of my visage. Now beshrew my father's
ambition! he was thinking of civil wars when
he got me: therefore was I created with a stubborn outside, with an aspect of iron, that, when
I come to woo ladies I fright them. But, in
faith, Kate, the elder I wax the better I shall
appear: my comfort is, that old age, that ill
layer-up of beauty, can do no more spoil upon
my face: thou hast me, if thou hast me, at the
worst; and thou shalt wear me, if thou wear me,
better and better. And therefore tell me, most
fair Katharine, will you have me? Put off your
maiden blushes; avouch the thoughts of your
heart with the looks of an empress; take me
by the hand, and say 'Harry of England, I am
thine:' which word thou shalt no sooner bless
mine ear withal, but I will tell thee aloud—
'England is thine, Ireland is thine, France is
thine, and Henry Plantagenet is thine;' who,
though I speak it before his face, if he be not
fellow with the best king, thou shalt find the
best king of good fellows. Come, your answer
in broken music; for thy voice is music, and
thy English broken; therefore, queen of all,

Katharine, break thy mind to me in broken
English: wilt thou have me? 265

Kath. Dat is as it sall please de *roy mon père.*

K. Hen. Nay, it will please him well, Kate;
it shall please him, Kate. 268

Kath. Den it sall also content me.

K. Hen. Upon that I kiss your hand, and I
call you my queen.

Kath. *Laissez, mon seigneur, laissez, laissez!
Ma foy, je ne veux point que vous abaissez vostre
grandeur, en baisant la main d'une vostre in-
digne serviteure: excusez moy, je vous supplie,
mon très puissant seigneur.* 276

K. Hen. Then I will kiss your lips, Kate.

Kath. *Les dames, et demoiselles, pour estre
baisées devant leur noces, il n'est pas la cou-
tume de France.* 280

K. Hen. Madam my interpreter, what says she?

Alice. Dat it is not be de fashion *pour les*
ladies of France,—I cannot tell what is *baiser*
in English. 284

K. Hen. To kiss.

Alice. Your majesty *entendre* bettre *que moy.*

K. Hen. It is not a fashion for the maids in
France to kiss before they are married, would
she say? 289

Alice Ouy, *vrayment.*

K. Hen. O Kate! nice customs curtsy to great
kings. Dear Kate, you and I cannot be confined
within the weak list of a country's fashion: we
are the makers of manners, Kate; and the
liberty that follows our places stops the mouths
of all find-faults, as I will do yours, for uphold-
ing the nice fashion of your country in denying
me a kiss: therefore, patiently, and yielding
[*Kissing her*]. You have witchcraft in your lips,
Kate: there is more eloquence in a sugar touch
of them, than in the tongues of the French
council; and they should sooner persuade
Harry of England than a general petition of
monarchs. Here comes your father. 304

Re-enter the KING *and* QUEEN, BURGUNDY, BED-
FORD, GLOUCESTER, EXETER, WARWICK, WEST-
MORELAND, *and other French and English*
Lords.

Bur. God save your majesty! My royal
cousin, teach you our princess English?

K. Hen. I would have her learn, my fair
cousin, how perfectly I love her; and that is
good English. 309

Bur. Is she not apt?

K. Hen. Our tongue is rough, coz, and my
condition is not smooth; so that, having neither
the voice nor the heart of flattery about me, I
cannot so conjure up the spirit of love in her,
that he will appear in his true likeness. 315

Bur. Pardon the frankness of my mirth if I
answer you for that. If you would conjure in
her, you must make a circle; if conjure up Love
in her in his true likeness, he must appear
naked and blind. Can you blame her then,
being a maid yet rosed over with the virgin
crimson of modesty, if she deny the appearance
of a naked blind boy in her naked seeing self?

It were, my lord, a hard condition for a ma
to consign to. 3

K. Hen. Yet they do wink and yield, as lo
is blind and enforces.

Bur. They are then excused, my lord, wh
they see not what they do. 3

K. Hen. Then, good my lord, teach yo
cousin to consent winking.

Bur. I will wink on her to consent, my lo
if you will teach her to know my meaning: f
maids, well summered and warm kept, are li
flies at Bartholomew-tide, blind, though the
have their eyes; and then they will endure han
ling, which before would not abide looking o

K. Hen. This moral ties me over to tin
and a hot summer; and so I shall catch th
fly, your cousin, in the latter end, and she mu
be blind too. 3

Bur. As love is, my lord, before it loves.

K. Hen. It is so: and you may, some of yo
thank love for my blindness, who cannot se
many a fair French city for one fair Frenc
maid that stands in my way. 3

Fr. King. Yes, my lord, you see them pe
spectively, the cities turned into a maid; fo
they are all girdled with maiden walls that w
hath never entered.

K. Hen. Shall Kate be my wife?

Fr. King. So please you.

K. Hen. I am content; so the maiden citie
you talk of may wait on her: so the maid th
stood in the way for my wish shall show me th
way to my will. 3

Fr. King. We have consented to all terms o
reason.

K. Hen. Is 't so, my lords of England?

West. The king hath granted every article
His daughter first, and then in sequel all, 3
According to their firm proposed natures.

Exe. Only he hath not yet subscribed this
Where your majesty demands, that the King o
France, having any occasion to write for matte
of grant, shall name your highness in this form
and with this addition, in French, *Notre très che
filz Henry roy d'Angleterre, Héretier de France*
and thus in Latin, *Præclarissimus filius noste
Henricus, Rex Angliæ, et Hæres Franciæ.*

Fr. King. Nor this I have not, brother, s
denied,
But your request shall make me let it pass. 37

K. Hen. I pray you then, in love and dea
alliance,
Let that one article rank with the rest;
And thereupon give me your daughter.

Fr. King. Take her, fair son; and from he
blood raise up 37
Issue to me; that the contending kingdoms
Of France and England, whose very shores loo
pale
With envy of each other's happiness,
May cease their hatred, and this dear conjunctio
Plant neighbourhood and Christian-like accor
In their sweet bosoms, that never war advanc
His bleeding sword 'twixt England and fai
France.

All. Amen! 38

K. Hen. Now, welcome, Kate: and bear me
　witness all,
That here I kiss her as my sovereign queen.
　　　　　　　　　　　　　[*Flourish.*

Q. Isa. God, the best maker of all marriages,
Combine your hearts in one, your realms in
　one!
As man and wife, being two, are one in love, 389
So be there 'twixt your kingdoms such a
　spousal
That never may ill office, or fell jealousy,
Which troubles oft the bed of blessed marriage,
Thrust in between the paction of these king-
　doms,
To make divorce of their incorporate league;
That English may as French, French English-
　men,
Receive each other! God speak this Amen! 396
All. Amen!

K. Hen. Prepare we for our marriage: on
　which day,
My Lord of Burgundy, we'll take your oath,
And all the peers', for surety of our leagues. 400

Then shall I swear to Kate, and you to me;
And may our oaths well kept and prosperous
　be!　　　　　　　　[*Sennet. Exeunt.*

Enter Chorus.

Thus far, with rough and all-unable pen,
　Our bending author hath pursu'd the story;
In little room confining mighty men,　　405
　Mangling by starts the full course of their
　　glory.
Small time, but in that small most greatly liv'd
　This star of England: Fortune made his sword,
By which the world's best garden he achiev'd, 409
　And of it left his son imperial lord.
Henry the Sixth, in infant bands crown'd King
　Of France and England, did this king succeed;
Whose state so many had the managing,　413
　That they lost France and made his England
　　bleed:
Which oft our stage hath shown; and, for their
　sake,
In your fair minds let this acceptance take. 416
　　　　　　　　　　　　　　　[*Exit.*

THE FIRST PART OF
KING HENRY THE SIXTH

DRAMATIS PERSONÆ

KING HENRY THE SIXTH.
DUKE OF GLOUCESTER, Uncle to the King, and Protector.
DUKE OF BEDFORD, Uncle to the King, Regent of France.
THOMAS BEAUFORT, Duke of Exeter, Great-uncle to the King.
HENRY BEAUFORT, Great-uncle to the King; Bishop of Winchester, and afterwards Cardinal.
JOHN BEAUFORT, Earl, afterwards Duke, of Somerset.
RICHARD PLANTAGENET, Son of Richard, late Earl of Cambridge; afterwards Duke of York.
EARL OF WARWICK.
EARL OF SALISBURY.
EARL OF SUFFOLK.
LORD TALBOT, afterwards Earl of Shrewsbury.
JOHN TALBOT, his Son.
EDMUND MORTIMER, Earl of March.
SIR JOHN FASTOLFE.
SIR WILLIAM LUCY.
SIR WILLIAM GLANSDALE.
SIR THOMAS GARGRAVE.
WOODVILE, Lieutenant of the Tower. Mayor of London. Mortimer's Keepers. A Lawyer.

VERNON, of the White-Rose, or York Faction.
BASSET, of the Red-Rose, or Lancaster Faction.
CHARLES, Dauphin, and afterwards King of France.
REIGNIER, Duke of Anjou, and titular King of Naples.
DUKE OF BURGUNDY.
DUKE OF ALENÇON.
BASTARD OF ORLEANS.
Governor of Paris.
Master-Gunner of Orleans, and his Son.
General of the French Forces in Bourdeaux.
A French Sergeant.
A Porter.
An old Shepherd, Father to Joan la Pucelle.

MARGARET, Daughter to Reignier; afterwards married to King Henry.
COUNTESS OF AUVERGNE.
JOAN LA PUCELLE, commonly called Joan of Arc.

Lords, Warders of the Tower, Heralds, Officers, Soldiers, Messengers, and Attendants.

Fiends appearing to La Pucelle.

SCENE.—*Partly in England, and partly in France.*

ACT I

SCENE I.—*Westminster Abbey.*

Dead March. Enter the Funeral of KING HENRY THE FIFTH *attended on by the* DUKES OF BEDFORD, GLOUCESTER, *and* EXETER; *the* EARL OF WARWICK, *the* BISHOP OF WINCHESTER, Heralds, &c.

Bed. Hung be the heavens with black, yield day to night!
Comets, importing change of times and states,
Brandish your crystal tresses in the sky,
And with them scourge the bad revolting stars,
That have consented unto Henry's death!   5
King Henry the Fifth, too famous to live long!
England ne'er lost a king of so much worth.
  Glo. England ne'er had a king until his time.   9
Virtue he had, deserving to command:
His brandish'd sword did blind men with his beams;
His arms spread wider than a dragon's wings;
His sparkling eyes, replete with wrathful fire,   12
More dazzled and drove back his enemies
Than mid-day sun fierce bent against their faces.
What should I say? his deeds exceed all speech:
He ne'er lift up his hand but conquered.   16
  Exe. We mourn in black: why mourn we not in blood?
Henry is dead and never shall revive.

Upon a wooden coffin we attend,
And death's dishonourable victory   20
We with our stately presence glorify,
Like captives bound to a triumphant car.
What! shall we curse the planets of mishap
That plotted thus our glory's overthrow?   24
Or shall we think the subtle-witted French
Conjurers and sorcerers, that, afraid of him,
By magic verses have contriv'd his end?
  Win. He was a king bless'd of the King of kings.   28
Unto the French the dreadful judgment-day
So dreadful will not be as was his sight.
The battles of the Lord of hosts he fought:
The church's prayers made him so prosperous.
  Glo. The church! where is it? Had not churchmen pray'd   33
His thread of life had not so soon decay'd:
None do you like but an effeminate prince,
Whom like a school-boy you may over-awe.   36
  Win. Gloucester, whate'er we like thou art protector,
And lookest to command the prince and realm.
Thy wife is proud; she holdeth thee in awe,
More than God or religious churchmen may.   40
  Glo. Name not religion, for thou lov'st the flesh,
And ne'er throughout the year to church thou go'st,
Except it be to pray against thy foes.

Bed. Cease, cease these jars and rest your
  minds in peace! 44
's to the altar: heralds, wait on us:
tead of gold we'll offer up our arms,
ce arms avail not, now that Henry's dead.
sterity, await for wretched years, 48
en at their mothers' moist eyes babes shall
  suck,
r isle be made a marish of salt tears,
d none but women left to wail the dead.
ry the Fifth! thy ghost I invocate: 52
sper this realm, keep it from civil broils!
mbat with adverse planets in the heavens!
ar more glorious star thy soul will make,
an Julius Cæsar, or bright— 56

Enter a Messenger.

Mess. My honourable lords, health to you
  all!
1 tidings bring I to you out of France,
 loss, of slaughter, and discomfiture:
ienne, Champaigne, Rheims, Orleans, 60
is, Guysors, Poictiers, are all quite lost.
Bed. What sayst thou, man, before dead
  Henry's corse?
ak softly; or the loss of those great towns
ll make him burst his lead and rise from
  death. 64
Glo. Is Paris lost? is Roan yielded up?
Henry were recall'd to life again
ese news would cause him once more yield
  the ghost.
Exe. How were they lost? what treachery
  was us'd? 68
Mess. No treachery; but want of men and
  money.
long the soldiers this is muttered,
at here you maintain several factions;
d, whilst a field should be dispatch'd and
  fought, 72
u are disputing of your generals.
e would have lingering wars with little cost;
other would fly swift, but wanteth wings;
hird thinks, without expense at all, 76
guileful fair words peace may be obtain'd.
ake, awake, English nobility!
 not sloth dim your honours new-begot:
pp'd are the flower-de-luces in your arms; 80
England's coat one half is cut away.
Exe. Were our tears wanting to this funeral
ese tidings would call forth their flowing tides.
Bed. Me they concern; Regent I am of
  France. 84
ve me my steeled coat: I'll fight for France.
ay with these disgraceful wailing robes!
unds will I lend the French instead of eyes,
 weep their intermissive miseries. 88

Enter another Messenger.

Sec. Mess. Lords, view these letters, full of
  bad mischance.
nce is revolted from the English quite,
cept some petty towns of no import:
e Dauphin Charles is crowned king in
  Rheims; 92
e Bastard of Orleans with him is join'd;

Reignier, Duke of Anjou, doth take his part;
The Duke of Alençon flieth to his side.
  Exe. The Dauphin crowned king! all fly to
  him! 96
O! whither shall we fly from this reproach?
  Glo. We will not fly, but to our enemies'
  throats.
Bedford, if thou be slack, I'll fight it out.
  Bed. Gloucester, why doubt'st thou of my
  forwardness? 100
An army have I muster'd in my thoughts,
Wherewith already France is overrun.

Enter a third Messenger.

  Third Mess. My gracious lords, to add to
  your laments,
Wherewith you now bedew King Henry's hearse,
I must inform you of a dismal fight 105
Betwixt the stout Lord Talbot and the French.
  Win. What! wherein Talbot overcame? is't
  so?
  Third Mess. O, no! wherein Lord Talbot was
  o'erthrown: 108
The circumstance I'll tell you more at large.
The tenth of August last this dreadful lord,
Retiring from the siege of Orleans,
Having full scarce six thousand in his troop, 112
By three-and-twenty thousand of the French
Was round encompassed and set upon.
No leisure had he to enrank his men;
He wanted pikes to set before his archers; 116
Instead whereof sharp stakes pluck'd out of
  hedges
They pitched in the ground confusedly,
To keep the horsemen off from breaking in.
More than three hours the fight continued; 120
Where valiant Talbot above human thought
Enacted wonders with his sword and lance.
Hundreds he sent to hell, and none durst stand
  him;
Here, there, and every where, enrag'd he flew:
The French exclaim'd the devil was in arms; 125
All the whole army stood agaz'd on him.
His soldiers, spying his undaunted spirit,
A Talbot! a Talbot! cried out amain, 128
And rush'd into the bowels of the battle.
Here had the conquest fully been seal'd up,
If Sir John Fastolfe had not play'd the coward.
He, being in the vaward,—plac'd behind, 132
With purpose to relieve and follow them,—
Cowardly fled, not having struck one stroke.
Hence grew the general wrack and massacre;
Enclosed were they with their enemies. 136
A base Walloon, to win the Dauphin's grace,
Thrust Talbot with a spear into the back,
Whom all France, with their chief assembled
  strength,
Durst not presume to look once in the face. 140
  Bed. Is Talbot slain? then I will slay myself,
For living idly here in pomp and ease
Whilst such a worthy leader, wanting aid,
Unto his dastard foemen is betray'd. 144
  Third Mess. O no! he lives; but is took
  prisoner,
And Lord Scales with him, and Lord Hunger-
  ford:

Most of the rest slaughter'd or took likewise.
  Bed. His ransom there is none but I shall
    pay: 148
I'll hale the Dauphin headlong from his throne;
His crown shall be the ransom of my friend;
Four of their lords I'll change for one of ours.
Farewell, my masters; to my task will I;   152
Bonfires in France forthwith I am to make,
To keep our great Saint George's feast withal:
Ten thousand soldiers with me I will take,
Whose bloody deeds shall make all Europe
    quake.   156
  Third Mess. So you had need; for Orleans is
    besieg'd;
The English army is grown weak and faint;
The Earl of Salisbury craveth supply,
And hardly keeps his men from mutiny,   160
Since they, so few, watch such a multitude.
  Exe. Remember, lords, your oaths to Henry
    sworn,
Either to quell the Dauphin utterly,
Or bring him in obedience to your yoke.   164
  Bed. I do remember it; and here take my
    leave,
To go about my preparation.   [*Exit.*
  Glo. I'll to the Tower with all the haste I
    can,
To view the artillery and munition;   168
And then I will proclaim young Henry king.
                                                  [*Exit.*
  Exe. To Eltham will I, where the young
    king is,
Being ordain'd his special governor;
And for his safety there I'll best devise. [*Exit.*
  Win. Each hath his place and function to
    attend: 173
I am left out; for me nothing remains.
But long I will not be Jack-out-of-office.
The king from Eltham I intend to steal,   176
And sit at chiefest stern of public weal. [*Exit.*

SCENE II.—*France. Before Orleans.*

Flourish. Enter CHARLES, *with his Forces:*
    ALENÇON, REIGNIER, *and Others.*

  Char. Mars his true moving, even as in the
    heavens
So in the earth, to this day is not known.
Late did he shine upon the English side;
Now we are victors; upon us he smiles.   4
What towns of any moment but we have?
At pleasure here we lie near Orleans;
Otherwhiles the famish'd English, like pale
    ghosts,
Faintly besiege us one hour in a month.   8
  Alen. They want their porridge and their fat
    bull-beeves:
Either they must be dieted like mules
And have their provender tied to their mouths,
Or piteous they will look, like drowned mice. 12
  Reig. Let's raise the siege: why live we idly
    here?
Talbot is taken, whom we wont to fear:
Remaineth none but mad-brain'd Salisbury,
And he may well in fretting spend his gall; 16
Nor men nor money hath he to make war.

  Char. Sound, sound alarum! we will rush
    them.
Now for the honour of the forlorn French!
Him I forgive my death that killeth me
When he sees me go back one foot or fly.
                                                  [*Exeu*

Alarums; Excursions; afterwards a retre
  Re-enter CHARLES, ALENÇON, REIGNIER, *a*
    Others.

  Char. Who ever saw the like? what m
    have I!
Dogs! cowards! dastards! I would ne'er ha
    fled
But that they left me 'midst my enemies.
  Reig. Salisbury is a desperate homicide;
He fighteth as one weary of his life:
The other lords, like lions wanting food,
Do rush upon us as their hungry prey.
  Alen. Froissart, a countryman of ours,
    cords,
England all Olivers and Rowlands bred
During the time Edward the Third did reigr
More truly now may this be verified:
For none but Samsons and Goliases,
It sendeth forth to skirmish. One to ten!
Lean-bon'd rascals! who would e'er suppo
They had such courage and audacity?
  Char. Let's leave this town; for they a
    hare-brain'd slaves,
And hunger will enforce them to be more eage
Of old I know them; rather with their teeth
The walls they'll tear down than forsake t
    siege.
  Reig. I think, by some odd gimmals
    device,
Their arms are set like clocks, still to strike o
Else ne'er could they hold out so as they do.
By my consent, we'll e'en let them alone.
  Alen. Be it so.

        Enter the BASTARD OF ORLEANS.

  Bast. Where's the prince Dauphin? I ha
    news for him.
  Char. Bastard of Orleans, thrice welcor
    to us.
  Bast. Methinks your looks are sad, yo
    cheer appall'd:
Hath the late overthrow wrought this offenc
Be not dismay'd, for succour is at hand:
A holy maid hither with me I bring,
Which by a vision sent to her from heaven
Ordained is to raise this tedious siege,
And drive the English forth the bounds
    France.
The spirit of deep prophecy she hath,
Exceeding the nine sibyls of old Rome;
What's past and what's to come she can descr
Speak, shall I call her in? Believe my words,
For they are certain and unfallible.
  Char. Go, call her in. [*Exit* BASTARD.] B
    first, to try her skill,
Reignier, stand thou as Dauphin in my plac
Question her proudly; let thy looks be stern
By this means shall we sound what skill s
    hath.   [*Retire*

Re-enter the BASTARD OF ORLEANS, *with* JOAN LA
PUCELLE *and Others.*

Reig. Fair maid, is 't thou wilt do these won-
　　drous feats?　　　　　　　　　　　64
Joan. Reignier, is 't thou that thinkest to be-
　　guile me?
Where is the Dauphin? Come, come from be-
　　hind;
I know thee well, though never seen before.
Be not amaz'd, there's nothing hid from me: 68
In private will I talk with thee apart.
Stand back, you lords, and give us leave a while.
　　Reig. She takes upon her bravely at first
　　dash.
Joan. Dauphin, I am by birth a shepherd's
　　daughter,　　　　　　　　　　　　72
My wit untrain'd in any kind of art.
Heaven and our Lady gracious hath it pleas'd
To shine on my contemptible estate:
Lo! whilst I waited on my tender lambs, 76
And to sun's parching heat display'd my cheeks,
God's mother deigned to appear to me,
And in a vision full of majesty
Will'd me to leave my base vocation 80
And free my country from calamity:
Her aid she promis'd and assur'd success;
In complete glory she reveal'd herself,
And, whereas I was black and swart before, 84
With those clear rays which she infus'd on me,
That beauty am I bless'd with which you see.
Ask me what question thou canst possible
And I will answer unpremeditated: 88
My courage try by combat, if thou dar'st,
And thou shalt find that I exceed my sex.
Resolve on this, thou shalt be fortunate
If thou receive me for thy war-like mate. 92
　　Char. Thou hast astonish'd me with thy high
　　terms.
Only this proof I'll of thy valour make,
In single combat thou shalt buckle with me,
And if thou vanquishest, thy words are true; 96
Otherwise I renounce all confidence.
Joan. I am prepar'd: here is my keen-edg'd
　　sword,
Deck'd with five flower-de-luces on each side;
The which at Touraine, in Saint Katharine's
　　churchyard,　　　　　　　　　　　100
Out of a great deal of old iron I chose forth.
　　Char. Then come, o' God's name; I fear no
　　woman.
Joan. And, while I live, I'll ne'er fly from a
　　man.
[*They fight, and* JOAN LA PUCELLE *overcomes.*
　　Char. Stay, stay thy hands! thou art an
　　Amazon,　　　　　　　　　　　　104
And fightest with the sword of Deborah.
　　Joan. Christ's mother helps me, else I were
　　too weak.
　　Char. Whoe'er helps thee, 'tis thou that must
　　help me:
Impatiently I burn with thy desire; 108
My heart and hands thou hast at once subdu'd.
Excellent Pucelle, if thy name be so,
Let me be thy servant and not sovereign be;
'Tis the French Dauphin sueth to thee thus. 112
　　Joan. I must not yield to any rites of love,

For my profession's sacred from above:
When I have chased all thy foes from hence,
Then will I think upon a recompense. 116
　　Char. Meantime look gracious on thy pros-
　　trate thrall.
　　Reig. My lord, methinks, is very long in talk.
　　Alen. Doubtless he shrives this woman to
　　her smock;
Else ne'er could he so long protract his speech.
　　Reig. Shall we disturb him, since he keeps
　　no mean?　　　　　　　　　　　　121
　　Alen. He may mean more than we poor men
　　do know:
These women are shrewd tempters with their
　　tongues.
　　Reig. My lord, where are you? what devise
　　you on?　　　　　　　　　　　　124
Shall we give over Orleans, or no?
　　Joan. Why, no, I say, distrustful recreants!
Fight till the last gasp; I will be your guard.
　　Char. What she says, I'll confirm: we'll fight
　　it out.　　　　　　　　　　　　128
　　Joan. Assign'd am I to be the English scourge.
This night the siege assuredly I'll raise:
Expect Saint Martin's summer, halcyon days,
Since I have entered into these wars. 132
Glory is like a circle in the water,
Which never ceaseth to enlarge itself,
Till by broad spreading it disperse to nought.
With Henry's death the English circle ends;
Dispersed are the glories it included. 137
Now am I like that proud insulting ship
Which Cæsar and his fortune bare at once.
　　Char. Was Mahomet inspired with a dove?
Thou with an eagle art inspired then. 141
Helen, the mother of great Constantine,
Nor yet Saint Philip's daughters were like thee.
Bright star of Venus, fall'n down on the earth,
How may I reverently worship thee enough?
　　Alen. Leave off delays and let us raise the
　　siege.　　　　　　　　　　　　146
　　Reig. Woman, do what thou canst to save
　　our honours;
Drive them from Orleans and be immortalis'd.
　　Char. Presently we'll try. Come, let's away
　　about it:
No prophet will I trust if she prove false. 150
　　　　　　　　　　　　　　　　[*Exeunt.*

SCENE III.—*London. Before the Tower.*

Enter at the Gates the DUKE OF GLOUCESTER,
with his Serving-men, *in blue coats.*

Glo. I am come to survey the Tower this day;
Since Henry's death, I fear, there is conveyance.
Where be these warders that they wait not here?
Open the gates! 'Tis Gloucester that calls. 4
　　　　　　　　　　　　　　[*Servants knock.*
First Ward. [*Within.*] Who's there that
　　knocks so imperiously?
First Serv. It is the noble Duke of Glouces-
　　ter.
Sec. Ward. [*Within.*] Whoe'er he be, you may
　　not be let in.
First Serv. Villains, answer you so the Lord
　　Protector?

First Ward. [*Within.*] The Lord protect him!
     so we answer him:
We do not otherwise than we are will'd.
     Glo. Who willed you? or whose will stands
     but mine?
There's none protector of the realm but I.   12
Break up the gates, I'll be your warrantize:
Shall I be flouted thus by dunghill grooms?
[GLOUCESTER's *Men rush at the Tower gates,
     and* WOODVILLE *the Lieutenant speaks within.*
     Wood. What noise is this? what traitors have
     we here?
     Glo. Lieutenant, is it you whose voice I hear?
Open the gates! here's Gloucester that would
     enter.   17
     Wood. [*Within.*] Have patience, noble Duke;
     I may not open;
The Cardinal of Winchester forbids:
From him I have express commandment   20
That thou nor none of thine shall be let in.
     Glo. Faint-hearted Woodvile, prizest him
     'fore me?
Arrogant Winchester, that haughty prelate,
Whom Henry, our late sovereign, ne'er could
     brook?   24
Thou art no friend to God or to the king:
Open the gates, or I'll shut thee out shortly.
     First Serv. Open the gates unto the Lord
     Protector;
Or we'll burst them open, if that you come not
     quickly.   28

Enter WINCHESTER, *attended by* Serving-men *in
     tawny coats.*

     Win. How now, ambitious Humphrey! what
     means this?
     Glo. Peel'd priest, dost thou command me to
     be shut out?
     Win. I do, thou most usurping proditor,
And not protector, of the king or realm.   32
     Glo. Stand back, thou manifest conspirator,
Thou that contriv'dst to murder our dead
     lord;
Thou that giv'st whores indulgences to sin:
I'll canvass thee in thy broad cardinal's hat,   36
If thou proceed in this thy insolence.
     Win. Nay, stand thou back; I will not budge
     a foot:
This be Damascus, be thou cursed Cain,
To slay thy brother Abel, if thou wilt.   40
     Glo. I will not slay thee, but I'll drive thee
     back:
Thy scarlet robes as a child's bearing-cloth
I'll use to carry thee out of this place.
     Win. Do what thou dar'st; I'll beard thee to
     thy face.   44
     Glo. What! am I dar'd and bearded to my
     face?—
Draw, men, for all this privileged place;
Blue coats to tawny-coats. Priest, beware your
     beard; [GLOUCESTER *and his men attack the
                                CARDINAL.
I mean to tug it and to cuff you soundly.   48
Under my feet I stamp thy cardinal's hat,
In spite of pope or dignities of church,
Here by the cheeks I'll drag thee up and down.

     Win. Gloucester, thou'lt answer this before
     the pope.   52
     Glo. Winchester goose! I cry a rope! a rope!
Now beat them hence; why do you let them stay?
Thee I'll chase hence, thou wolf in sheep's array.
Out, tawny coats! out, scarlet hypocrite!   56
Here GLOUCESTER'S *Men beat out the* Cardinal's
     Men, *and enter in the hurly-burly the* Mayor
     of London and his Officers.
     May. Fie, lords! that you, being supreme
     magistrates,
Thus contumeliously should break the peace!
     Glo. Peace, mayor! thou know'st little of my
     wrongs:
Here's Beaufort, that regards nor God nor
     King,
Hath here distrain'd the Tower to his use.   61
     Win. Here's Gloucester, a foe to citizens;
One that still motions war and never peace,
O'ercharging your free purses with large fines,
That seeks to overthrow religion   65
Because he is protector of the realm,
And would have armour here out of the Tower,
To crown himself king and suppress the prince.
     Glo. I will not answer thee with words, but
     blows.   [*Here they skirmish again.*
     May. Nought rests for me, in this tumul-
     tuous strife
But to make open proclamation.
Come, officer: as loud as e'er thou canst;   72
     Cry.
     *Off. All manner of men, assembled here in
arms this day, against God's peace and the
king's, we charge and command you, in his high-
ness' name, to repair to your several dwelling-
places; and not to wear, handle, or use, any
sword, weapon, or dagger, henceforward, upon
pain of death.*   80
     Glo. Cardinal, I'll be no breaker of the law;
But we shall meet and break our minds at large.
     Win. Gloucester, we will meet; to thy cost,
     be sure:
Thy heart-blood I will have for this day's work.
     May. I'll call for clubs if you will not away.
This cardinal's more haughty than the devil.   86
     Glo. Mayor, farewell: thou dost but what
     thou mayst.
     Win. Abominable Gloucester! guard thy head;
For I intend to have it ere long.
     [*Exeunt, severally,* GLOUCESTER *and* WIN-
         CHESTER, *with their* Serving-men.
     May. See the coast clear'd, and then we will
     depart.   90
Good God! these nobles should such stomachs
     bear;
I myself fight not once in forty year. [*Exeunt.*

     SCENE IV.—*France. Before Orleans.*

Enter, on the walls, the Master-Gunner *and
     his* Boy.

     M. Gun. Sirrah, thou know'st how Orleans
     is besieg'd,
And how the English have the suburbs won.
     Son. Father, I know; and oft have shot at them,
Howe'er unfortunate I miss'd my aim.   4

M. Gun. But now thou shalt not. Be thou
rul'd by me:
ief master-gunner am I of this town;
mething I must do to procure me grace.
e prince's espials have informed me   8
ow the English, in the suburbs close entrench'd
ont through a secret gate of iron bars
 yonder tower to overpeer the city,
d thence discover how with most advantage
ey may vex us with shot or with assault. 13
 intercept this inconvenience,
piece of ordnance 'gainst it I have plac'd;
d fully even these three days have I watch'd
 could see them. Now, boy, do thou watch,
r I can stay no longer.   18
 thou spy'st any, run and bring me word;
d thou shalt find me at the Governor's. [*Exit.*
Son. Father, I warrant you; take you no care; 21
 never trouble you if I may spy them. [*Exit.*

ter, on the turrets, the LORDS SALISBURY *and*
TALBOT; SIR WILLIAM GLANSDALE, SIR THOMAS
GARGRAVE, *and Others.*

Sal. Talbot, my life, my joy! again return'd!
ow wert thou handled being prisoner?   24
 by what means got'st thou to be releas'd,
scourse, I prithee, on this turret's top.
Tal. The Duke of Bedford had a prisoner
lled the brave Lord Ponton de Santrailles; 28
r him I was exchang'd and ransomed.
t with a baser man at arms by far
ce in contempt they would have barter'd me:
hich I disdaining scorn'd, and craved death
ther than I would be so vile-esteem'd.   33
fine, redeem'd I was as I desir'd.
t, O! the treacherous Fastolfe wounds my
 heart!
hom with my bare fists I would execute   36
 now had him brought into my power.
Sal. Yet tell'st thou not how thou wert entertain'd.
Tal. With scoffs and scorns and contumelious taunts.
open market-place produc'd they me,   40
 be a public spectacle to all:
re, said they, is the terror of the French,
e scarecrow that affrights our children so.
en broke I from the officers that led me, 44
d with my nails digg'd stones out of the ground
 hurl at the beholders of my shame.
y grisly countenance made others fly.
ne durst come near for fear of sudden death.
iron walls they deem'd me not secure; 49
 great fear of my name 'mongst them was
 spread
at they suppos'd I could rend bars of steel
d spurn in pieces posts of adamant: 52
herefore a guard of chosen shot I had,
at walk'd about me every minute-while;
d if I did but stir out of my bed
ady they were to shoot me to the heart. 56

Enter the Boy *with a linstock.*

Sal. I grieve to hear what torments you endur'd;
t we will be reveng'd sufficiently.

Now it is supper-time in Orleans:
Here, through this grate, I count each one, 60
And view the Frenchmen how they fortify:
Let us look in; the sight will much delight thee.
Sir Thomas Gargrave, and Sir William Glans-
dale,
Let me have your express opinions   64
Where is best place to make our battery next.
Gar. I think at the North gate; for there
stand lords.
Glan. And I, here, at the bulwark of the
bridge.
Tal. For aught I see, this city must be fam-
ish'd,   68
Or with light skirmishes enfeebled.
[*Here they shoot.* SALISBURY *and* SIR
THOMAS GARGRAVE *fall.*
Sal. O Lord! have mercy on us, wretched
sinners.
Gar. O Lord! have mercy on me, woeful
man.
Tal. What chance is this that suddenly hath
cross'd us?   72
Speak, Salisbury; at least, if thou canst speak:
How far'st thou, mirror of all martial men?
One of thy eyes and thy cheek's side struck off!
Accursed tower! accursed fatal hand   76
That hath contriv'd this woeful tragedy!
In thirteen battles Salisbury o'ercame;
Henry the Fifth he first train'd to the wars;
Whilst any trump did sound or drum struck
up,   80
His sword did ne'er leave striking in the field.
Yet liv'st thou, Salisbury? though thy speech
doth fail,
One eye thou hast to look to heaven for grace:
The sun with one eye vieweth all the world. 84
Heaven, be thou gracious to none alive,
If Salisbury wants mercy at thy hands!
Bear hence his body; I will help to bury it.
Sir Thomas Gargrave, hast thou any life? 88
Speak unto Talbot; nay, look up to him.
Salisbury, cheer thy spirit with this comfort;
Thou shalt not die, whiles—
He beckons with his hand and smiles on me, 92
As who should say, 'When I am dead and gone,
Remember to avenge me on the French.'
Plantagenet, I will; and like thee, Nero,
Play on the lute, beholding the towns burn: 96
Wretched shall France be only in my name.
[*It thunders and lightens. An alarum.*
What stir is this? What tumult's in the heavens?
Whence cometh this alarum and the noise?

Enter a Messenger.

Mess. My lord, my lord! the French have
gather'd head: 100
The Dauphin, with one Joan la Pucelle join'd,
A holy prophetess new risen up
Is come with a great power to raise the siege.
[*Here* SALISBURY *lifteth himself
up and groans.*
Tal. Hear, hear how dying Salisbury doth
groan!   104
It irks his heart he cannot be reveng'd.
Frenchmen, I'll be a Salisbury to you:

Pucelle or puzzel, dolphin or dogfish,
Your hearts I'll stamp out with my horse's heels
And make a quagmire of your mingled brains.
Convey me Salisbury into his tent,   110
And then we'll try what these dastard French-
   men dare.
       [*Exeunt, bearing out the bodies.*

SCENE V.—*The Same. Before one of the Gates.*

Alarum. Skirmishings. Enter TALBOT, *pursuing the* DAUPHIN; *drives him in, and exit:
   then enter* JOAN LA PUCELLE, *driving Englishmen before her, and exit after them. Then
   re-enter* TALBOT.

Tal. Where is my strength, my valour, and
   my force?
Our English troops retire, I cannot stay them;
A woman clad in armour chaseth them.

Re-enter JOAN LA PUCELLE.

Here, here she comes. I'll have a bout with thee:
Devil, or devil's dam, I'll conjure thee: 5
Blood will I draw on thee, thou art a witch,
And straightway give thy soul to him thou serv'st.
   Joan. Come, come; 'tis only I that must
   disgrace thee.   [*They fight.*
   Tal. Heavens, can you suffer hell so to pre-
   vail?   9
My breast I'll burst with straining of my courage,
And from my shoulders crack my arms asunder,
But I will chastise this high-minded strumpet. 12
                   [*They fight again.*
   Joan. Talbot, farewell; thy hour is not yet
   come:
I must go victual Orleans forthwith.
      [*A short alarum; then* LA PUCELLE *enters
                the town with* Soldiers.
O'ertake me if thou canst; I scorn thy strength.
Go, go, cheer up thy hunger-starved men;   16
Help Salisbury to make his testament:
This day is ours, as many more shall be. [*Exit.*
   Tal. My thoughts are whirled like a potter's
   wheel;
I know not where I am, nor what I do: 20
A witch, by fear, not force, like Hannibal,
Drives back our troops and conquers as she
   lists:
So bees with smoke, and doves with noisome
   stench,
Are from their hives and houses driven away. 24
They call'd us for our fierceness English dogs;
Now, like to whelps, we crying run away.
                   [*A short alarum.*
Hark, countrymen! either renew the fight,
Or tear the lions out of England's coat;   28
Renounce your soil, give sheep in lions' stead:
Sheep run not half so treacherous from the wolf,
Or horse or oxen from the leopard,
As you fly from your oft-subdued slaves.   32
       [*Alarum. Another skirmish.*
It will not be: retire into your trenches:
You all consented unto Salisbury's death,
For none would strike a stroke in his revenge.
Pucelle is entered into Orleans   36
In spite of us or aught that we could do.

O! would I were to die with Salisbury.
The shame hereof will make me hide my hea
     [*Alarum. Retreat. Exeunt* TALB
                  and his Forces, &

SCENE VI.—*The Same.*

Flourish. Enter, on the walls, JOAN LA PUCELI
   CHARLES, REIGNIER, ALENÇON, *and* Soldiers

   Joan. Advance our waving colours on t
   walls;
Rescu'd is Orleans from the English:
Thus Joan la Pucelle hath perform'd her wor
   Char. Divinest creature, Astræa's daughter
How shall I honour thee for this success?
Thy promises are like Adonis' gardens,
That one day bloom'd and fruitful were tl
   next.
France, triumph in thy glorious prophetess!
Recover'd is the town of Orleans:
More blessed hap did ne'er befall our state.
   Reig. Why ring not out the bells througho
   the town?
Dauphin, command the citizens make bonfi
And feast and banquet in the open streets,
To celebrate the joy that God hath given us.
   Alen. All France will be replete with mir
   and joy,
When they shall hear how we have play'd tl
   men.
   Char. 'Tis Joan, not we, by whom the day
   won;
For which I will divide my crown with her
And all the priests and friars in my realm
Shall in procession sing her endless praise.
A statelier pyramis to her I'll rear
Than Rhodope's or Memphis ever was:
In memory of her when she is dead,
Her ashes, in an urn more precious
Than the rich-jewell'd coffer of Darius,
Transported shall be at high festivals
Before the kings and queens of France.
No longer on Saint Denis will we cry,
But Joan la Pucelle shall be France's saint.
Come in, and let us banquet royally,
After this golden day of victory.
                  [*Flourish. Exeur*

ACT II

SCENE I.—*Before Orleans.*

Enter to the Gates, a French Sergeant, *and
   two* Sentinels.

   Serg. Sirs, take your places and be vigilant
If any noise or soldier you perceive
Near to the walls, by some apparent sign
Let us have knowledge at the court of guard.
   First Sent. Sergeant, you shall.
                       [*Exit* Sergeant
        Thus are poor servitors—
When others sleep upon their quiet beds—
Constrain'd to watch in darkness, rain, and col

Enter TALBOT, BEDFORD, BURGUNDY, *and Forces
with scaling-ladders; their drums beating a
dead march.*

Tal. Lord regent, and redoubted Burgundy,
By whose approach the regions of Artois,   9
Walloon, and Picardy, are friends to us,
This happy night the Frenchmen are secure,
Having all day carous'd and banqueted;   12
Embrace we then this opportunity,
As fitting best to quittance their deceit
Contriv'd by art and baleful sorcery.
    Bed. Coward of France! how much he wrongs
    his fame,   16
Despairing of his own arm's fortitude,
To join with witches and the help of hell!
    Bur. Traitors have never other company.
But what's that Pucelle whom they term so pure?
    Tal. A maid, they say.
    Bed.   A maid, and be so martial! 21
    Bur. Pray God she prove not masculine ere
    long;
If underneath the standard of the French
She carry armour, as she hath begun.   24
    Tal. Well, let them practise and converse
    with spirits.
God is our fortress, in whose conquering name
Let us resolve to scale their flinty bulwarks.
    Bed. Ascend, brave Talbot; we will follow
    thee.   28
    Tal. Not all together: better far, I guess,
That we do make our entrance several ways,
That if it chance the one of us do fail,
The other yet may rise against their force.   32
    Bed. Agreed. I'll to yond corner.
    Bur.   And I to this.
    Tal. And here will Talbot mount, or make
    his grave.
Now, Salisbury, for thee, and for the right
Of English Henry, shall this night appear   36
How much in duty I am bound to both.
    [*The English scale the walls, crying, 'Saint
    George!' 'A Talbot!' and all enter the town.*
    First Sent. Arm, arm! the enemy doth make
    assault!

*The French leap over the Walls in their shirts.
Enter, several ways,* BASTARD OF ORLEANS,
ALENÇON, *and* REIGNIER, *half ready, and half
unready.*

    Alen. How now, my lords! what! all un-
    ready so?
    Bast. Unready! ay, and glad we 'scap'd so
    well.   40
    Reig. 'Twas time, I trow, to wake and leave
    our beds,
Hearing alarums at our chamber-doors.
    Alen. Of all exploits since first I follow'd
    arms,
Ne'er heard I of a war-like enterprise   44
More venturous or desperate than this.
    Bast. I think this Talbot be a fiend of hell.
    Reig. If not of hell, the heavens, sure, favour
    him.
    Alen. Here cometh Charles: I marvel how
    he sped.   48
    Bast. Tut! holy Joan was his defensive guard.

Enter CHARLES *and* JOAN LA PUCELLE.
    Char. Is this thy cunning, thou deceitful
    dame?
Didst thou at first, to flatter us withal,
Make us partakers of a little gain,   52
That now our loss might be ten times so much?
    Joan. Wherefore is Charles impatient with
    his friend?
At all times will you have my power alike?
Sleeping or waking must I still prevail,   56
Or will you blame and lay the fault on me?
Improvident soldiers! had your watch been good,
This sudden mischief never could have fall'n.
    Char. Duke of Alençon, this was your de-
    fault,
That, being captain of the watch to-night,   61
Did look no better to that weighty charge.
    Alen. Had all your quarters been so safely
    kept
As that whereof I had the government,   64
We had not been thus shamefully surpris'd.
    Bast. Mine was secure.
    Reig.   And so was mine, my lord.
    Char. And for myself, most part of all this
    night,
Within her quarter and mine own precinct 68
I was employ'd in passing to and fro,
About relieving of the sentinels:
Then how or which way should they first break
    in?
    Joan. Question, my lords, no further of the
    case,
How or which way: 'tis sure they found some   72
    place
But weakly guarded, where the breach was
    made.
And now there rests no other shift but this;
To gather our soldiers, scatter'd and dispers'd,
And lay new platforms to endamage them.   77

Alarum. Enter an English Soldier, *crying, 'A
Talbot! a Talbot!' They fly, leaving their
clothes behind.*

    Sold. I'll be so bold to take what they have
    left.
The cry of Talbot serves me for a sword;
For I have loaden me with many spoils,   80
Using no other weapon but his name.   [*Exit.*

SCENE II.—*Orleans. Within the Town.*

Enter TALBOT, BEDFORD, BURGUNDY, *a* Captain,
and Others.

    Bed. The day begins to break, and night is
    fled,
Whose pitchy mantle over-veil'd the earth.
Here sound retreat, and cease our hot pursuit.
                                    [*Retreat sounded.*
    Tal. Bring forth the body of old Salisbury, 4
And here advance it in the market-place,
The middle centre of this cursed town.
Now have I paid my vow unto his soul;
For every drop of blood was drawn from him 8
There hath at least five Frenchmen died to-
    night.

And that hereafter ages may behold
What ruin happen'd in revenge of him,
Within their chiefest temple I'll erect   12
A tomb wherein his corse shall be interr'd:
Upon the which, that every one may read,
Shall be engrav'd the sack of Orleans,
The treacherous manner of his mournful death,
And what a terror he had been to France.   17
But, lords, in all our bloody massacre,
I muse we met not with the Dauphin's grace,
His new-come champion, virtuous Joan of Arc,
Nor any of his false confederates.   21
 Bed. 'Tis thought, Lord Talbot, when the
  fight began,
Rous'd on the sudden from their drowsy beds,
They did amongst the troops of armed men   24
Leap o'er the walls for refuge in the field.
 Bur. Myself—as far as I could well discern
For smoke and dusky vapours of the night—
Am sure I scar'd the Dauphin and his trull,   28
When arm in arm they both came swiftly run-
  ning,
Like to a pair of loving turtle-doves
That could not live asunder day or night.
After that things are set in order here,   32
We'll follow them with all the power we have.

   Enter a Messenger.

 Mess. All hail, my lords! Which of this
  princely train
Call ye the war-like Talbot, for his acts
So much applauded through the realm of
  France?   36
 Tal. Here is the Talbot: who would speak
  with him?
 Mess. The virtuous lady, Countess of Au-
  vergne,
With modesty admiring thy renown,
By me entreats, great lord, thou wouldst vouch-
  safe   40
To visit her poor castle where she lies,
That she may boast she hath beheld the man
Whose glory fills the world with loud report.
 Bur. Is it even so? Nay, then, I see our wars
Will turn into a peaceful comic sport,   45
When ladies crave to be encounter'd with.
You may not, my lord, despise her gentle suit.
 Tal. Ne'er trust me then; for when a world
  of men   48
Could not prevail with all their oratory,
Yet hath a woman's kindness over-rul'd:
And therefore tell her I return great thanks,
And in submission will attend on her.   52
Will not your honours bear me company?
 Bed. No, truly; it is more than manners
  will;
And I have heard it said, unbidden guests
Are often welcomest when they are gone.   56
 Tal. Well then, alone,—since there's no re-
  medy,—
I mean to prove this lady's courtesy.
Come hither, captain. [*Whispers.*] You perceive
  my mind.
 Capt. I do, my lord, and mean accordingly.
      [*Exeunt.*

SCENE III.—*Auvergne. Court of the Castle.*
  Enter the COUNTESS *and her* Porter.

 Count. Porter, remember what I gave
  charge;
And when you have done so, bring the keys
  me.
 Port. Madam, I will. [*Ex*
 Count. The plot is laid: if all things fall o
  right,
I shall as famous be by this exploit
As Scythian Tomyris by Cyrus' death.
Great is the rumour of this dreadful knight,
And his achievements of no less account:
Fain would mine eyes be witness with mi
  ears,
To give their censure of these rare reports.

   Enter Messenger *and* TALBOT.

 Mess. Madam,
According as your ladyship desir'd,
By message crav'd, so is Lord Talbot come.
 Count. And he is welcome. What! is this t
  man?
 Mess. Madam, it is.
 Count. Is this the scourge of France
Is this the Talbot, so much fear'd abroad,
That with his name the mothers still their babe
I see report is fabulous and false:
I thought I should have seen some Hercules
A second Hector, for his grim aspect,
And large proportion of his strong-knit limb
Alas! this is a child, a silly dwarf:
It cannot be this weak and writhled shrimp
Should strike such terror to his enemies.
 Tal. Madam, I have been bold to troub
  you;
But since your ladyship is not at leisure,
I'll sort some other time to visit you.
 Count. What means he now? Go ask hi
  whither he goes.
 Mess. Stay, my Lord Talbot; for my la
  craves
To know the cause of your abrupt departure.
 Tal. Marry, for that she's in a wrong beli
I go to certify her Talbot's here.

   Re-enter Porter, *with keys.*

 Count. If thou be he, then art thou prisone
 Tal. Prisoner! to whom?
 Count. To me, blood-thirsty lord
And for that cause I train'd thee to my hous
Long time thy shadow hath been thrall
  me,
For in my gallery thy picture hangs:
But now the substance shall endure the like,
And I will chain these legs and arms of thin
That hast by tyranny, these many years
Wasted our country, slain our citizens,
And sent our sons and husbands captive.
 Tal. Ha, ha, ha!
 Count. Laughest thou, wretch? thy mir
  shall turn to moan.
 Tal. I laugh to see your ladyship so fond
To think that you have aught but Talbot
  shadow,

Whereon to practise your severity.

Count. Why, art not thou the man?

Tal.　　　　　　　　　　I am, indeed.　　48

Count. Then have I substance too.

Tal. No, no, I am but shadow of myself:
You are deceiv'd, my substance is not here;
For what you see is but the smallest part　52
And least proportion of humanity.
I tell you, madam, were the whole frame here,
It is of such a spacious lofty pitch,
Your roof were not sufficient to contain it.　56

Count. This is a riddling merchant for the nonce;
He will be here, and yet he is not here:
How can these contrarieties agree?

Tal. That will I show you presently.　60

He winds a horn. Drums strike up; a peal of ordnance. The Gates being forced, enter Soldiers.

How say you, madam? are you now persuaded
That Talbot is but shadow of himself?
These are his substance, sinews, arms, and strength,
With which he yoketh your rebellious necks,　64
Razeth your cities, and subverts your towns,
And in a moment makes them desolate.

Count. Victorious Talbot! pardon my abuse:
I find thou art no less than fame hath bruited,
And more than may be gather'd by thy shape.
Let my presumption not provoke thy wrath;
For I am sorry that with reverence
I did not entertain thee as thou art.　72

Tal. Be not dismay'd, fair lady; nor misconster
The mind of Talbot as you did mistake
The outward composition of his body.
What you have done hath not offended me;　76
Nor other satisfaction do I crave,
But only, with your patience, that we may
Taste of your wine and see what cates you have;
For soldiers' stomachs always serve them well.

Count. With all my heart, and think me honoured　81
To feast so great a warrior in my house.

[*Exeunt.*

SCENE IV.—*London. The Temple Garden.*

Enter the EARLS OF SOMERSET, SUFFOLK, *and* WARWICK; RICHARD PLANTAGENET, VERNON, *and a* Lawyer.

Plan. Great lords, and gentlemen, what means this silence?
Dare no man answer in a case of truth?

Suf. Within the Temple hall we were too loud;
The garden here is more convenient.　4

Plan. Then say at once if I maintain'd the truth,
Or else was wrangling Somerset in the error?

Suf. Faith, I have been a truant in the law,
And never yet could frame my will to it;　8
And therefore frame the law unto my will.

Som. Judge you, my Lord of Warwick, then, between us.

War. Between two hawks, which flies the higher pitch;
Between two dogs, which hath the deeper mouth;　12
Between two blades, which bears the better temper;
Between two horses, which doth bear him best;
Between two girls, which hath the merriest eye;
I have perhaps, some shallow spirit of judgment;　16
But in these nice sharp quillets of the law,
Good faith, I am no wiser than a daw.

Plan. Tut, tut! here is a mannerly forbearance:
The truth appears so naked on my side,　20
That any purblind eye may find it out.

Som. And on my side it is so well apparell'd,
So clear, so shining, and so evident,
That it will glimmer through a blind man's eye.

Plan. Since you are tongue-tied, and so loath to speak,　25
In dumb significants proclaim your thoughts:
Let him that is a true-born gentleman,
And stands upon the honour of his birth,　28
If he suppose that I have pleaded truth,
From off this brier pluck a white rose with me.

Som. Let him that is no coward nor no flatterer,
But dare maintain the party of the truth,　32
Pluck a red rose from off this thorn with me.

War. I love no colours, and, without all colour
Of base insinuating flattery
I pluck this white rose with Plantagenet.　36

Suf. I pluck this red rose with young Somerset:
And say withal I think he held the right.

Ver. Stay, lords and gentlemen, and pluck no more,
Till you conclude that he, upon whose side　40
The fewest roses are cropp'd from the tree,
Shall yield the other in the right opinion.

Som. Good Master Vernon, it is well objected:
If I have fewest I subscribe in silence.　44

Plan. And I.

Ver. Then for the truth and plainness of the case,
I pluck this pale and maiden blossom here,
Giving my verdict on the white rose side.　48

Som. Prick not your finger as you pluck it off,
Lest bleeding you do paint the white rose red,
And fall on my side so, against your will.

Ver. If I, my lord, for my opinion bleed,　52
Opinion shall be surgeon to my hurt,
And keep me on the side where still I am.

Som. Well, well, come on: who else?

Law. [*To* SOMERSET.] Unless my study and my books be false,　56
The argument you held was wrong in you,
In sign whereof I pluck a white rose too.

Plan. Now, Somerset, where is your argument?

Som. Here, in my scabbard; meditating that　60
Shall dye your white rose in a bloody red.

Plan. Meantime, your cheeks do counterfeit
   our roses;
For pale they look with fear, as witnessing
The truth on our side.
   Som.   No, Plantagenet, 64
'Tis nor for fear but anger that thy cheeks
Blush for pure shame to counterfeit our roses,
And yet thy tongue will not confess thy error.
   Plan. Hath not thy rose a canker, Somerset?
   Som. Hath not thy rose a thorn, Planta-
   genet? 69
   Plan. Ay, sharp and piercing, to maintain
   his truth;
Whiles thy consuming canker eats his falsehood.
   Som. Well, I'll find friends to wear my bleed-
   ing roses, 72
That shall maintain what I have said is true,
Where false Plantagenet dare not be seen.
   Plan. Now, by this maiden blossom in my
   hand,
I scorn thee and thy faction, peevish boy. 76
   Suf. Turn not thy scorns this way, Planta-
   genet.
   Plan. Proud Pole, I will, and scorn both him
   and thee.
   Suf. I'll turn my part thereof into thy throat.
   Som. Away, away! good William de la Pole:
We grace the yeoman by conversing with him.
   War. Now, by God's will thou wrong'st him,
   Somerset: 82
His grandfather was Lionel, Duke of Clarence,
Third son to the third Edward, King of England.
Spring crestless yeomen from so deep a root?
   Plan. He bears him on the place's privilege,
Or durst not, for his craven heart, say thus.
   Som. By Him that made me, I'll maintain
   my words 88
On any plot of ground in Christendom.
Was not thy father, Richard Earl of Cambridge,
For treason executed in our late king's days?
And, by his treason stand'st not thou attainted,
Corrupted, and exempt from ancient gentry?
His trespass yet lives guilty in thy blood; 94
And, till thou be restor'd, thou art a yeoman.
   Plan. My father was attached, not attainted
Condemn'd to die for treason, but no traitor;
And that I'll prove on better men than Somerset,
Were growing time once ripen'd to my will.
For your partaker Pole and you yourself, 100
I'll note you in my book of memory,
To scourge you for this apprehension:
Look to it well and say you are well warn'd.
   Som. Ah, thou shalt find us ready for thee
   still, 104
And know us by these colours for thy foes;
For these my friends in spite of thee shall wear.
   Plan. And, by my soul, this pale and angry rose,
As cognizance of my blood-drinking hate, 108
Will I for ever and my faction wear,
Until it wither with me to my grave
Or flourish to the height of my degree.
   Suf. Go forward, and be chok'd with thy
   ambition: 112
And so farewell until I meet thee next.   [*Exit.*
   Som. Have with thee, Pole. Farewell, am-
   bitious Richard.   [*Exit.*

   Plan. How I am brav'd and must perforc
   endure it!
   War. This blot that they object against you
   house 11
Shall be wip'd our in the next parliament,
Call'd for the truce of Winchester and Glouces
   ter;
And if thou be not then created York,
I will not live to be accounted Warwick. 12
Meantime in signal of my love to thee,
Against proud Somerset and William Pole,
Will I upon thy party wear this rose.
And here I prophesy: this brawl to-day,
Grown to this faction in the Temple garden,
Shall send between the red rose and the whit
A thousand souls to death and deadly night.
   Plan. Good Master Vernon, I am bound t
   you, 12
That you on my behalf would pluck a flower.
   Ver. In your behalf still would I wear th
   same.
   Law. And so will I.
   Plan. Thanks, gentle sir. 13
Come, let us four to dinner: I dare say
This quarrel will drink blood another day.
                                     [*Exeunt*

SCENE V.—*London. A Room in the Tower.*

Enter MORTIMER, *brought in a chair by
   two Gaolers.*

   Mor. Kind keepers of my weak decaying age
Let dying Mortimer here rest himself.
Even like a man new haled from the rack,
So fare my limbs with long imprisonment;
And these gray locks, the pursuivants of death
Nestor-like aged, in an age of care,
Argue the end of Edmund Mortimer.
These eyes, like lamps whose wasting oil i
   spent,
Wax dim, as drawing to their exigent;
Weak shoulders, overborne with burdening grief
And pithless arms, like to a wither'd vine
That droops his sapless branches to the ground
Yet are these feet, whose strengthless stay i
   numb, 1
Unable to support this lump of clay,
Swift-winged with desire to get a grave,
As witting I no other comfort have. 1
But tell me, keeper, will my nephew come?
   First Keep. Richard Plantagenet, my lord
   will come:
We sent unto the Temple, unto his chamber;
And answer was return'd that he will come. 2
   Mor. Enough: my soul shall then be satisfied
Poor gentleman! his wrong doth equal mine.
Since Henry Monmouth first began to reign,
Before whose glory I was great in arms, 2
This loathsome sequestration have I had;
And even since then hath Richard been obscur'd
Depriv'd of honour and inheritance.
But now the arbitrator of despairs, 2
Just death, kind umpire of men's miseries,
With sweet enlargement doth dismiss me hence
I would his troubles likewise were expir'd,
That so he might recover what was lost. 3

Enter RICHARD PLANTAGENET.

First Keep. My lord, your loving nephew
now is come.

Mor. Richard Plantagenet, my friend, is he
come?

Plan. Ay, noble uncle, thus ignobly us'd,
our nephew, late despised Richard, comes. 36

Mor. Direct mine arms I may embrace his
neck,
And in his bosom spend my latter gasp:
O! tell me when my lips do touch his cheeks,
That I may kindly give one fainting kiss. 40
And now declare, sweet stem from York's great
stock,
Why didst thou say of late thou wert despis'd?

Plan. First, lean thine aged back against
mine arm;
And in that ease, I'll tell thee my disease. 44
This day, in argument upon a case,
Some words there grew 'twixt Somerset and me;
Among which terms he us'd a lavish tongue
And did upbraid me with my father's death: 48
Which obloquy set bars before his tongue,
Else with the like I had requited him.
Therefore, good uncle, for my father's sake,
In honour of a true Plantagenet,   52
And for alliance sake, declare the cause
My father, Earl of Cambridge, lost his head.

Mor. That cause, fair nephew, that im-
prison'd me,
And hath detain'd me all my flow'ring youth 56
Within a loathsome dungeon, there to pine,
Was cursed instrument of his decease.

Plan. Discover more at large what cause that
was,
For I am ignorant and cannot guess.   60

Mor. I will, if that my fading breath permit,
And death approach not ere my tale be done.
Henry the Fourth, grandfather to this king,
Depos'd his nephew Richard, Edward's son, 64
The first-begotten, and the lawful heir
Of Edward king, the third of that descent:
During whose reign the Percies of the North,
Finding his usurpation most unjust,   68
Endeavour'd my advancement to the throne.
The reason mov'd these warlike lords to this
Was, for that—young King Richard thus re-
mov'd,
Leaving no heir begotten of his body—   72
Was the next by birth and parentage;
For by my mother I derived am
From Lionel Duke of Clarence, the third son
To King Edward the Third; whereas he   76
From John of Gaunt doth bring his pedigree,
Being but fourth of that heroic line.
But mark: as, in this haughty great attempt
They laboured to plant the rightful heir, 80
I lost my liberty, and they their lives.
Long after this, when Henry the Fifth
Succeeding his father Bolingbroke, did reign,
Thy father, Earl of Cambridge, then deriv'd 84
From famous Edmund Langley, Duke of York,
Marrying my sister that thy mother was,
Again in pity of my hard distress
Levied an army, weening to redeem   88
And have install'd me in the diadem;

But, as the rest, so fell that noble earl,
And was beheaded. Thus the Mortimers,
In whom the title rested, were suppress'd. 92

Plan. Of which, my lord, your honour is the
last.

Mor. True; and thou seest that I no issue
have,
And that my fainting words do warrant death:
Thou art my heir; the rest I wish thee gather: 96
But yet be wary in thy studious care.

Plan. Thy grave admonishments prevail with
me.
But yet methinks my father's execution
Was nothing less than bloody tyranny.   100

Mor. With silence, nephew, be thou politic:
Strong-fixed is the house of Lancaster,
And like a mountain, not to be remov'd.
But now thy uncle is removing hence,   104
As princes do their courts, when they are cloy'd
With long continuance in a settled place.

Plan. O uncle! would some part of my young
years
Might but redeem the passage of your age. 108

Mor. Thou dost then wrong me,—as the
slaughterer doth,
Which giveth many wounds when one will kill.—
Mourn not, except thou sorrow for my good;
Only give order for my funeral: 112
And so farewell; and fair be all thy hopes,
And prosperous be thy life in peace and war!
                                         [*Dies.*

Plan. And peace, no war, befall thy parting
soul!
In prison hast thou spent a pilgrimage,   116
And like a hermit overpass'd thy days.
Well, I will lock his counsel in my breast;
And what I do imagine let that rest.
Keepers, convey him hence; and I myself   120
Will see his burial better than his life.
      [*Exeunt* Keepers, *bearing out the body
                              of* MORTIMER.
Here dies the dusky torch of Mortimer,
Chok'd with ambition of the meaner sort:
And, for those wrongs, those bitter injuries, 124
Which Somerset hath offer'd to my house,
I doubt not but with honour to redress;
And therefore haste I to the parliament,
Either to be restored to my blood,   128
Or make my ill the advantage of my good.
                                         [*Exit.*

ACT III

SCENE I.—*London. The Parliament House.*

Flourish. Enter KING HENRY, EXETER, GLOU-
CESTER, WARWICK, SOMERSET, *and* SUFFOLK;
the BISHOP OF WINCHESTER, RICHARD PLANTA-
GENET, *and Others.* GLOUCESTER *offers to put
up a bill;* WINCHESTER *snatches it, and tears it.*

Win. Com'st thou with deep premeditated
lines,
With written pamphlets studiously devis'd,
Humphrey of Gloucester? If thou canst accuse,
Or aught intend'st to lay unto my charge, 4
Do it without invention, suddenly;

As I, with sudden and extemporal speech
Purpose to answer what thou canst object.
  Glo. Presumptuous priest! this place com-
    mands my patience   8
Or thou shouldst find thou hast dishonour'd me.
Think not, although in writing I preferr'd
The manner of thy vile outrageous crimes,
That therefore I have forg'd, or am not able 12
Verbatim to rehearse the method of my pen:
No, prelate; such is thy audacious wickedness,
Thy lewd, pestiferous, and dissentious pranks,
As very infants prattle of thy pride. 16
Thou art a most pernicious usurer,
Froward by nature, enemy to peace;
Lascivious, wanton, more than well beseems
A man of thy profession and degree; 20
And for thy treachery, what's more manifest?
In that thou laid'st a trap to take my life
As well at London Bridge as at the Tower.
Beside, I fear me, if thy thoughts were sifted, 24
The king, thy sov'reign, is not quite exempt
From envious malice of thy swelling heart.
  Win. Gloucester, I do defy thee. Lords,
    vouchsafe
To give me hearing what I shall reply. 28
If I were covetous, ambitious, or perverse,
As he will have me, how am I so poor?
Or how haps it I seek not to advance
Or raise myself, but keep my wonted calling? 32
And for dissension, who preferreth peace
More than I do, except I be provok'd?
No, my good lords, it is not that offends;
It is not that that hath incens'd the duke: 36
It is, because no one should sway but he;
No one but he should be about the king;
And that engenders thunder in his breast,
And makes him roar these accusations forth. 40
  Glo.   As good!
Thou bastard of my grandfather!
  Win. Ay, lordly sir; for what are you, I pray,
But one imperious in another's throne? 44
  Glo. Am I not protector, saucy priest?
  Win. And am not I a prelate of the church?
  Glo. Yes, as an outlaw in a castle keeps,
And useth it to patronage his theft. 48
  Win. Unreverent Gloucester!
  Glo.   Thou art reverent.
Touching thy spiritual function, not thy life.
  Win. Rome shall remedy this.
  War.   Roam thither then.
  Som. My lord, it were your duty to forbear.
  War. Ay, see the bishop be not overborne.
  Som. Methinks my lord should be religious,
And know the office that belongs to such.
  War. Methinks his lordship should be
    humbler; 56
It fitteth not a prelate so to plead.
  Som. Yes, when his holy state is touch'd so
    near.
  War. State holy, or unhallow'd, what of
    that?
Is not his Grace protector to the king? 60
  Plan. [*Aside.*] Plantagenet, I see, must hold
    his tongue,
Lest it be said, 'Speak, sirrah, when you should;'

Must your bold verdict enter talk with lords
Else would I have a fling at Winchester.
  K. Hen. Uncles of Gloucester and of Win
    chester,
The special watchmen of our English weal,
I would prevail, if prayers might prevail,
To join your hearts in love and amity.
O! what a scandal is it to our crown,
That two such noble peers as ye should jar.
Believe me, lords, my tender years can tell
Civil dissension is a viperous worm,
That gnaws the bowels of the commonwealth
  [*A noise within;* 'Down with the tawny coats!
What tumult's this?
  War.   An uproar, I dare warran
Begun through malice of the bishop's men.
  [*A noise again within;* 'Stones! Stones!

Enter the Mayor of London, *attended.*

  May. O, my good lords, and virtuous Henry
Pity the city of London, pity us!
The bishop and the Duke of Gloucester's men
Forbidden late to carry any weapon,
Have fill'd their pockets full of pebble stones,
And banding themselves in contrary parts
Do pelt so fast at one another's pate,
That many have their giddy brains knock'
    out:
Our windows are broke down in every street,
And we for fear compell'd to shut our shops

Enter, skirmishing, the Serving-men of GLOU
CESTER *and* WINCHESTER, *with bloody pates.*

  K. Hen. We charge you, on allegiance t
    ourself,
To hold your slaught'ring hands, and keep th
    peace.—
Pray, uncle Gloucester, mitigate this strife.
  First Serv. Nay, if we be forbidden stones
we'll fall to it with our teeth.
  Sec. Serv. Do what ye dare, we are a
    resolute.   [*Skirmish again*
  Glo. You of my household, leave this peevis
    broil,
And set this unaccustom'd fight aside.
  Third Serv. My lord, we know your Grace t
    be a man
Just and upright, and, for your royal birth,
Inferior to none but to his majesty;
And ere that we will suffer such a prince,
So kind a father of the commonweal,
To be disgraced by an inkhorn mate,
We and our wives and children all will fight,
And have our bodies slaught'red by thy foes.
  First Serv. Ay, and the very parings of ou
    nails
Shall pitch a field when we are dead.
                    [*Skirmish again*
  Glo.   Stay, stay, I say
And, if you love me, as you say you do,
Let me persuade you to forbear a while.
  K. Hen. O! how this discord doth afflict m
    soul!
Can you, my Lord of Winchester, behold
My sighs and tears and will not once relent?
Who should be pitiful if you be not?

Or who should study to prefer a peace
If holy churchmen take delight in broils?
  War. Yield, my Lord Protector; yield, Win-
    chester;   112
Except you mean with obstinate repulse
To slay your sov'reign and destroy the realm.
You see what mischief and what murder too
Hath been enacted through your enmity;   116
Then be at peace, except ye thirst for blood.
  Win. He shall submit or I will never yield.
  Glo. Compassion on the king commands me
    stoop;   120
Or I would see his heart out ere the priest
Should ever get that privilege of me.
  War. Behold, my Lord of Winchester, the
    duke
Hath banish'd moody discontented fury,
As by his smoothed brows it doth appear: 124
Why look you still so stern and tragical?
  Glo. Here, Winchester, I offer thee my hand.
  K. Hen. Fie, uncle Beaufort! I have heard
    you preach,
That malice was a great and grievous sin;   128
And will not you maintain the thing you teach,
But prove a chief offender in the same?
  War. Sweet king! the bishop hath a kindly
    gird.
For shame, my Lord of Winchester, relent! 132
What! shall a child instruct you what to do?
  Win. Well, Duke of Gloucester, I will yield
    to thee;
Love for thy love and hand for hand I give.
  Glo. [*Aside.*] Ay; but I fear me, with a hollow
    heart.   136
See here, my friends and loving countrymen,
This token serveth for a flag of truce,
Betwixt ourselves and all our followers.
So help me God, as I dissemble not!   140
  Win. [*Aside.*] So help me God, as I intend it
    not!
  K. Hen. O loving uncle, kind Duke of Glou-
    cester,
How joyful am I made by this contract!
Away, my masters! trouble us no more;   144
But join in friendship, as your lords have done.
  First Serv. Content: I'll to the surgeon's.
  Sec. Serv.   And so will I.
  Third Serv. And I will see what physic the
    tavern affords.
            [*Exeunt* Mayor, Serving-men, *&c.*
  War. Accept this scroll, most gracious sove-
    reign,   148
Which in the right of Richard Plantagenet
We do exhibit to your majesty.
  Glo. Well urg'd, my Lord of Warwick: for,
    sweet prince,
An if your Grace mark every circumstance, 152
You have great reason to do Richard right;
Especially for those occasions
At Eltham-place I told your majesty.
  K. Hen. And those occasions, uncle, were of
    force;   156
Therefore, my loving lords, our pleasure is
That Richard be restored to his blood.
  War. Let Richard be restored to his blood;
So shall his father's wrongs be recompens'd. 160

  Win. As will the rest, so willeth Winchester.
  K. Hen. If Richard will be true, not that
    alone,
But all the whole inheritance I give
That doth belong unto the house of York, 164
From whence you spring by lineal descent.
  Plan. Thy humble servant vows obedience,
And humble service till the point of death.
  K. Hen. Stoop then and set your knee against
    my foot;   168
And, in reguerdon of that duty done,
I girt thee with the valiant sword of York:
Rise, Richard, like a true Plantagenet,
And rise created princely Duke of York. 172
  Plan. And so thrive Richard as thy foes may
    fall!
And as my duty springs, so perish they
That grudge one thought against your majesty!
  All. Welcome, high prince, the mighty Duke
    of York!   176
  Som. [*Aside.*] Perish, base prince, ignoble
    Duke of York!
  Glo. Now, will it best avail your majesty
To cross the seas and to be crown'd in France.
The presence of a king engenders love   180
Amongst his subjects and his loyal friends,
As it disanimates his enemies.
  K. Hen. When Gloucester says the word,
    King Henry goes;
For friendly counsel cuts off many foes.   184
  Glo. Your ships already are in readiness.
        [*Flourish. Exeunt all except* EXETER.
  Exe. Ay, we may march in England or in
    France,
Not seeing what is likely to ensue.
This late dissension grown betwixt the peers
Burns under feigned ashes of forg'd love
And will at last break out into a flame:
As fester'd members rot but by degree,
Till bones and flesh and sinews fall away, 192
So will this base and envious discord breed.
And now I fear that fatal prophecy
Which in the time of Henry, nam'd the Fifth,
Was in the mouth of every sucking babe; 196
That Henry born at Monmouth should win all;
And Henry born at Windsor should lose all:
Which is so plain that Exeter doth wish
His days may finish ere that hapless time. 200
                                      [*Exit.*

SCENE II.—*France. Before Roan.*

Enter JOAN LA PUCELLE, *disguised, and* Soldiers
  *dressed like countrymen, with sacks upon their
  backs.*

  Joan. These are the city gates, the gates of
    Roan,
Through which our policy must make a breach:
Take heed, be wary how you place your words;
Talk like the vulgar sort of market-men   4
That come to gather money for their corn.
If we have entrance,—as I hope we shall,—
And that we find the slothful watch but weak,
I'll by a sign give notice to our friends,   8
That Charles the Dauphin may encounter them.
  First Sold. Our sacks shall be a mean to sack
    the city,

And we be lords and rulers over Roan;
Therefore we'll knock. [*Knocks.*
   Guard. [*Within.*] *Qui est là?* 13
   Joan. Paisans, pauvres gens de France:
Poor market-folks that come to sell their corn.
   Guard. [*Opening the gates.*] Enter, go in; the
     market-bell is rung. 16
   Joan. Now, Roan, I'll shake thy bulwarks
     to the ground.
       [JOAN LA PUCELLE, &c., *enter the city.*

Enter CHARLES, *the* BASTARD OF ORLEANS,
     ALENÇON, *and Forces.*

   Char. Saint Denis bless this happy strata-
     gem!
And once again we'll sleep secure in Roan.
   Bast. Here enter'd Pucelle and her prac-
     tisants; 20
Now she is there how will she specify
Where is the best and safest passage in?
   Alen. By thrusting out a torch from yonder
     tower;
Which, once discern'd, shows that her mean-
     ing is, 24
No way to that, for weakness, which she enter'd.

Enter JOAN LA PUCELLE *on a battlement, holding
    out a torch burning.*

   Joan. Behold! this is the happy wedding
     torch
That joineth Roan unto her countrymen, 27
But burning fatal to the Talbotites! [*Exit.*
   Bast. See, noble Charles, the beacon of our
     friend,
The burning torch in yonder turret stands.
   Char. Now shine it like a comet of revenge,
A prophet to the fall of all our foes! 32
   Alen. Defer no time, delays have dangerous
     ends;
Enter, and cry 'The Dauphin!' presently,
And then do execution on the watch.
       [*They enter the town.*

Alarum. Enter TALBOT *in an Excursion.*

   Tal. France, thou shalt rue this treason with
     thy tears, 36
If Talbot but survive thy treachery.
Pucelle, that witch, that damned sorceress,
Hath wrought this hellish mischief unawares,
That hardly we escap'd the pride of France. 40
       [*Exit.*

Alarum: Excursions. Enter from the town, BED-
   FORD, *brought in sick in a chair. Enter* TALBOT
   and BURGUNDY, *and the English Forces. Then,
   enter on the walls,* JOAN LA PUCELLE, CHARLES,
   the BASTARD OF ORLEANS, ALENÇON, *and
   Others.*

   Joan. Good morrow, gallants! Want ye
     corn for bread?
I think the Duke of Burgundy will fast
Before he'll buy again at such a rate.
'Twas full of darnel; do you like the taste? 44
   Bur. Scoff on, vile fiend and shameless
     courtezan!
I trust ere long to choke thee with thine own,

And make thee curse the harvest of that corn.
   Char. Your Grace may starve perhaps, be-
     fore that time. 48
   Bed. O! let no words, but deeds, revenge this
     treason!
   Joan. What will you do, good grey-beard?
     break a lance,
And run a tilt at death within a chair?
   Tal. Foul fiend of France, and hag of all
     despite, 52
Encompass'd with thy lustful paramours!
Becomes it thee to taunt his valiant age
And twit with cowardice a man half dead?
Damsel, I'll have a bout with you again, 56
Or else let Talbot perish with this shame.
   Joan. Are you so hot, sir? Yet, Pucelle, hold
     thy peace;
If Talbot do but thunder, rain will follow.
      [TALBOT *and the rest consult together.*
God speed the parliament! who shall be the
     speaker? 60
   Tal. Dare ye come forth and meet us in the
     field?
   Joan. Belike your lordship takes us then for
     fools,
To try if that our own be ours or no.
   Tal. I speak not to that railing Hecate, 64
But unto thee, Alençon, and the rest;
Will ye, like soldiers, come and fight it out?
   Alen. Signior, no.
   Tal. Signior, hang! base muleters of
     France! 68
Like peasant foot-boys do they keep the walls,
And dare not take up arms like gentlemen.
   Joan. Away, captains! let's get us from the
     walls;
For Talbot means no goodness, by his looks. 72
God be wi' you, my lord! we came but to tell
     you
That we are here.
      [*Exeunt* JOAN LA PUCELLE, &c.,
       from the Walls.
   Tal. And there will we be too, ere it be long,
Or else reproach be Talbot's greatest fame! 76
Vow, Burgundy, by honour of thy house,—
Prick'd on by public wrongs sustain'd in
     France,—
Either to get the town again, or die;
And I, as sure as English Henry lives, 80
And as his father here was conqueror,
As sure as in this late-betrayed town
Great Cœur-de-lion's heart was buried,
So sure I swear to get the town or die. 84
   Bur. My vows are equal partners with thy
     vows.
   Tal. But, ere we go, regard this dying prince,
The valiant Duke of Bedford. Come, my lord,
We will bestow you in some better place, 88
Fitter for sickness and for crazy age.
   Bed. Lord Talbot, do not so dishonour me:
Here will I sit before the walls of Roan,
And will be partner of your weal or woe. 92
   Bur. Courageous Bedford, let us now per-
     suade you.
   Bed. Not to be gone from hence; for once I
     read,

That stout Pendragon in his litter, sick,
Came to the field and vanquished his foes: 96
Methinks I should revive the soldiers' hearts,
Because I ever found them as myself.

Tal. Undaunted spirit in a dying breast!
Then be it so: heavens keep old Bedford
safe! 100
And now no more ado, brave Burgundy,
But gather we our forces out of hand,
And set upon our boasting enemy.

[*Exeunt all but* BEDFORD *and* Attendants.

Alarum: Excursions; in one of which, enter SIR
JOHN FASTOLFE *and a* Captain.

Cap. Whither away, Sir John Fastolfe, in
such haste? 104
Fast. Whither away! to save myself by flight:
We are like to have the overthrow again.
Cap. What! will you fly, and leave Lord
Talbot?
Fast. Ay,
All the Talbots in the world, to save my life.
[*Exit.*
Cap. Cowardly knight! ill fortune follow
thee! [*Exit.*

Retreat: Excursions. Re-enter, from the town,
JOAN LA PUCELLE, ALENÇON, CHARLES, *&c.,*
and exeunt, flying.

Bed. Now, quiet soul, depart when Heaven
please, 110
For I have seen our enemies' overthrow.
What is the trust or strength of foolish man?
They, that of late were daring with their scoffs
Are glad and fain by flight to save themselves.
[*Dies, and is carried off in his chair.*

Alarum. Re-enter TALBOT, BURGUNDY,
and Others.

Tal. Lost, and recover'd in a day again!
This is a double honour, Burgundy: 116
Yet heavens have glory for this victory!
Bur. Warlike and martial Talbot, Burgundy
Enshrines thee in his heart, and there erects
Thy noble deeds as valour's monument. 120
Tal. Thanks, gentle duke. But where is
Pucelle now?
I think her old familiar is asleep.
Now where's the Bastard's braves, and Charles
his gleeks?
What! all amort? Roan hangs her head for
grief, 124
That such a valiant company are fled.
Now will we take some order in the town,
Placing therein some expert officers,
And then depart to Paris to the king; 128
For there young Henry with his nobles lie.
Bur. What wills Lord Talbot pleaseth Bur-
gundy.
Tal. But yet, before we go, let's not forget
The noble Duke of Bedford late deceas'd, 132
But see his exequies fulfill'd in Roan:
A braver soldier never couched lance,
A gentler heart did never sway in court;
But kings and mightiest potentates must die, 136
For that's the end of human misery. [*Exeunt.*

SCENE III.—*The Plains near Roan.*

Enter CHARLES, *the* BASTARD OF ORLEANS, ALEN-
ÇON, JOAN LA PUCELLE, *and Forces.*

Joan. Dismay not, princes, at this accident,
Nor grieve that Roan is so recovered:
Care is no cure, but rather corrosive,
For things that are not to be remedied. 4
Let frantic Talbot triumph for a while,
And like a peacock sweep along his tail;
We'll pull his plumes and take away his train,
If Dauphin and the rest will be but rul'd. 8
Char. We have been guided by thee hitherto,
And of thy cunning had no diffidence:
One sudden foil shall never breed distrust.
Bast. Search out thy wit for secret policies,
And we will make thee famous through the
world. 13
Alen. We'll set thy statue in some holy place
And have thee reverenc'd like a blessed saint:
Employ thee, then, sweet virgin, for our
good. 16
Joan. Then thus it must be; this doth Joan
devise:
By fair persuasions, mix'd with sugar'd words,
We will entice the Duke of Burgundy
To leave the Talbot and to follow us. 20
Char. Ay, marry, sweeting, if we could do
that,
France were no place for Henry's warriors;
Nor should that nation boast it so with us,
But be extirped from our provinces. 24
Alen. For ever should they be expuls'd from
France,
And not have title of an earldom here.
Joan. Your honours shall perceive how I
will work
To bring this matter to the wished end. 28
[*Drums heard afar off.*
Hark! by the sound of drum you may perceive
Their powers are marching unto Paris-ward.

Here sound an English march. Enter, and pass
over, TALBOT *and his Forces.*

There goes the Talbot, with his colours spread,
And all the troops of English after him. 32

A French march. Enter the DUKE OF BURGUNDY
and his Forces.

Now in the rearward comes the duke and his:
Fortune in favour makes him lag behind.
Summon a parley; we will talk with him.
[*A parley.*
Char. A parley with the Duke of Burgundy!
Bur. Who craves a parley with the Bur-
gundy? 37
Joan. The princely Charles of France, thy
countryman.
Bur. What sayst thou, Charles? for I am
marching hence.
Char. Speak, Pucelle, and enchant him with
thy words. 40
Joan. Brave Burgundy, undoubted hope of
France!
Stay, let thy humble handmaid speak to thee.

Bur. Speak on; but be not over-tedious.

Joan. Look on thy country, look on fertile
France, 44
And see the cities and the towns defac'd
By wasting ruin of the cruel foe.
As looks the mother on her lowly babe
When death doth close his tender dying eyes, 48
See, see the pining malady of France;
Behold the wounds, the most unnatural wounds,
Which thou thyself hast giv'n her woeful
breast.
O! turn thy edged sword another way; 52
Strike those that hurt, and hurt not those that
help.
One drop of blood drawn from thy country's
bosom,
Should grieve thee more than streams of foreign
gore: 55
Return thee therefore, with a flood of tears,
And wash away thy country's stained spots.

Bur. Either she hath bewitch'd me with her
words,
Or nature makes me suddenly relent.

Joan. Besides, all French and France ex-
claims on thee, 60
Doubting thy birth and lawful progeny.
Who join'st thou with but with a lordly nation
That will not trust thee but for profit's sake?
When Talbot hath set footing once in France,
And fashion'd thee that instrument of ill, 65
Who then but English Henry will be lord,
And thou be thrust out like a fugitive?
Call we to mind, and mark but this for proof,
Was not the Duke of Orleans thy foe,
And was he not in England prisoner?
But when they heard he was thine enemy,
They set him free, without his ransom paid, 72
In spite of Burgundy and all his friends.
See then, thou fight'st against thy countrymen!
And join'st with them will be thy slaughter-
men.
Come, come, return; return, thou wand'ring
lord; 76
Charles and the rest will take thee in their
arms.

Bur. I am vanquished; these haughty words
of hers
Have batter'd me like roaring cannon-shot,
And made me almost yield upon my knees. 80
Forgive me, country, and sweet countrymen!
And, lords, accept this hearty kind embrace:
My forces and my power of men are yours.
So, farewell, Talbot; I'll no longer trust thee.

Joan. Done like a Frenchman: turn, and
turn again! 85

Char. Welcome, brave duke! thy friendship
makes us fresh.

Bast. And doth beget new courage in our
breasts.

Alen. Pucelle hath bravely play'd her part
in this, 88
And doth deserve a coronet of gold.

Char. Now let us on, my lords, and join our
powers:
And seek how we may prejudice the foe.
           [Exeunt.

SCENE IV.—*Paris. A Room in the Palace.*

Enter KING HENRY, GLOUCESTER, BISHOP OF
WINCHESTER, YORK, SUFFOLK, SOMERSET,
WARWICK, EXETER; VERNON, BASSET, *and
Others. To them with his* Soldiers, TALBOT.

Tal. My gracious prince, and honourable
peers,
Hearing of your arrival in this realm,
I have a while giv'n truce unto my wars,
To do my duty to my sovereign: 4
In sign whereof, this arm,—that hath reclaim'd
To your obedience fifty fortresses,
Twelve cities, and seven walled towns of strength,
Beside five hundred prisoners of esteem,— 8
Lets fall his sword before your highness' feet,
           [Kneels.
And with submissive loyalty of heart,
Ascribes the glory of his conquest got,
First to my God, and next unto your Grace. 12

K. Hen. Is this the Lord Talbot, uncle
Gloucester,
That hath so long been resident in France?

Glo. Yes, if it please your majesty, my
liege.

K. Hen. Welcome, brave captain and vic-
torious lord! 16
When I was young,—as yet I am not old,—
I do remember how my father said,
A stouter champion never handled sword.
Long since we were resolved of your truth, 20
Your faithful service and your toil in war;
Yet never have you tasted our reward,
Or been reguerdon'd with so much as thanks,
Because till now we never saw your face: 24
Therefore, stand up; and for these good deserts,
We here create you Earl of Shrewsbury;
And in our coronation take your place.
   [Flourish. Exeunt all but VERNON
          and BASSET.

Ver. Now, sir, to you, that were so hot at
sea, 28
Disgracing of these colours that I wear
In honour of my noble Lord of York,
Dar'st thou maintain the former words thou
spak'st? 31

Bas. Yes, sir: as well as you dare patronage
The envious barking of your saucy tongue
Against my lord the Duke of Somerset.

Ver. Sirrah, thy lord I honour as he is.

Bas. Why, what is he? as good a man as
York. 36

Ver. Hark ye; not so: in witness, take ye
that.   *[Strikes him.*

Bas. Villain, thou know'st the law of arms
is such
That, whoso draws a sword, 'tis present death,
Or else this blow should broach thy dearest
blood. 40
But I'll unto his majesty, and crave
I may have liberty to venge this wrong;
When thou shalt see I'll meet thee to thy cost.

Ver. Well, miscreant, I'll be there as soon
as you; 44
And, after, meet you sooner than you would.
           [Exeunt.

ACT IV

SCENE I.—*Paris. A Room of State.*

Enter KING HENRY, GLOUCESTER, EXETER, YORK,
SUFFOLK, SOMERSET, *the* BISHOP OF WIN-
CHESTER, WARWICK, TALBOT, *the* Governor
of Paris, *and Others.*

Glo. Lord bishop, set the crown upon his
head.

Win. God save King Henry, of that name
the sixth.

Glo. Now, Governor of Paris, take your
oath,—   [*Governor kneels.*
That you elect no other king but him,   4
Esteem none friends but such as are his friends,
And none your foes but such as shall pretend
Malicious practices against his state:
This shall ye do, so help you righteous God! 8
[*Exeunt* Governor *and his Train.*

Enter SIR JOHN FASTOLFE.

Fast. My gracious sovereign, as I rode from
Calais,
To haste unto your coronation,
A letter was deliver'd to my hands,
Writ to your Grace from the Duke of Burgundy.
Tal. Shame to the Duke of Burgundy and
thee!   13
I vow'd, base knight, when I did meet thee next,
To tear the garter from thy craven's leg;
[*Plucking it off.*
Which I have done, because unworthily   16
Thou wast installed in that high degree.
Pardon me, princely Henry, and the rest:
This dastard, at the battle of Patay,
When but in all I was six thousand strong, 20
And that the French were almost ten to one,
Before we met or that a stroke was given,
Like to a trusty squire did run away:
In which assault we lost twelve hundred men;
Myself, and divers gentlemen beside,   25
Were there surpris'd and taken prisoners.
Then judge, great lords, if I have done amiss;
Or whether that such cowards ought to wear 28
This ornament of knighthood, yea, or no?
Glo. To say the truth, this fact was infamous
And ill beseeming any common man,
Much more a knight, a captain and a leader. 32
Tal. When first this order was ordain'd, my
lords,
Knights of the garter were of noble birth,
Valiant and virtuous, full of haughty courage,
Such as were grown to credit by the wars; 36
Not fearing death, nor shrinking for distress,
But always resolute in most extremes.
He then that is not furnish'd in this sort
Doth but usurp the sacred name of knight, 40
Profaning this most honourable order;
And should—if I were worthy to be judge—
Be quite degraded, like a hedge-born swain
That doth presume to boast of gentle blood. 44
K. Hen. Stain to thy countrymen! thou
hear'st thy doom.
Be packing therefore, thou that wast a knight;
Henceforth we banish thee on pain of death.
[*Exit* FASTOLFE.

And now, my Lord Protector, view the letter 48
Sent from our uncle Duke of Burgundy.
Glo. [*Viewing superscription.*] What means
his Grace, that he hath chang'd his style?
No more, but plain and bluntly, *To the King!*
Hath he forgot he is his sovereign?   52
Or doth this churlish superscription
Pretend some alteration in good will?
What's here? *I have, upon especial cause,*
Mov'd with compassion of my country's wrack,
Together with the pitiful complaints   57
Of such as your oppression feeds upon,
Forsaken your pernicious faction,
And join'd with Charles, the rightful King of
France.   60
O, monstrous treachery! Can this be so,
That in alliance, amity, and oaths,
There should be found such false dissembling
guile?
K. Hen. What! doth my uncle Burgundy
revolt?   64
Glo. He doth, my lord, and is become your
foe.
K. Hen. Is that the worst this letter doth
contain?
Glo. It is the worst, and all, my lord, he
writes.
K. Hen. Why then, Lord Talbot there shall
talk with him,   68
And give him chastisement for this abuse.
How say you, my lord? are you not content?
Tal. Content, my liege! Yes: but that I am
prevented,
I should have begg'd I might have been em-
ploy'd.   72
K. Hen. Then gather strength, and march
unto him straight:
Let him perceive how ill we brook his treason,
And what offence it is to flout his friends.
Tal. I go, my lord; in heart desiring still 76
You may behold confusion of your foes. [*Exit.*

Enter VERNON *and* BASSET.

Ver. Grant me the combat, gracious sove-
reign!
Bas. And me, my lord; grant me the combat
too!
York. This is my servant: hear him, noble
prince!   80
Som. And this is mine: sweet Henry, favour
him!
K. Hen. Be patient, lords; and give them
leave to speak.
Say, gentlemen, what makes you thus exclaim?
And wherefore crave you combat? or with
whom?   84
Ver. With him, my lord; for he hath done
me wrong.
Bas. And I with him; for he hath done me
wrong.
K. Hen. What is that wrong whereof you
both complain?
First let me know, and then I'll answer you. 88
Bas. Crossing the sea from England into
France,
This fellow here, with envious carping tongue,

Upbraided me about the rose I wear;
Saying, the sanguine colour of the leaves   92
Did represent my master's blushing cheeks,
When stubbornly he did repugn the truth
About a certain question in the law
Argu'd betwixt the Duke of York and him; 96
With other vile and ignominious terms:
In confutation of which rude reproach,
And in defence of my lord's worthiness,
I crave the benefit of law of arms.   100
  Ver. And that is my petition, noble lord:
For though he seem with forged quaint conceit,
To set a gloss upon his bold intent,
Yet know, my lord, I was provok'd by him; 104
And he first took exceptions at this badge,
Pronouncing, that the paleness of this flower
Bewray'd the faintness of my master's heart.
  York. Will not this malice, Somerset, be
left?   108
  Som. Your private grudge, my Lord of York,
will out,
Though ne'er so cunningly you smother it.
  K. Hen. Good Lord! what madness rules in
brain-sick men,
When, for so slight and frivolous a cause, 112
Such factious emulations shall arise!
Good cousins both, of York and Somerset,
Quiet yourselves, I pray, and be at peace.
  York. Let this dissension first be tried by
fight,   116
And then your highness shall command a peace.
  Som. The quarrel toucheth none but us alone;
Betwixt ourselves let us decide it, then.
  York. There is my pledge; accept it, Somer-
set.   120
  Ver. Nay, let it rest where it began at first.
  Bas. Confirm it so, mine honourable lord.
  Glo. Confirm it so! Confounded be your
strife!
And perish ye, with your audacious prate! 124
Presumptuous vassals! are you not asham'd,
With this immodest clamorous outrage
To trouble and disturb the king and us?—
And you, my lords, methinks you do not well 128
To bear with their perverse objections;
Much less to take occasion from their mouths
To raise a mutiny betwixt yourselves:
Let me persuade you take a better course. 132
  Exe. It grieves his highness: good my lords,
be friends.
  K. Hen. Come hither, you that would be
combatants.
Henceforth I charge you, as you love our favour,
Quite to forget this quarrel and the cause. 136
And you, my lords, remember where we are;
In France, amongst a fickle wav'ring nation.
If they perceive dissension in our looks,
And that within ourselves we disagree,   140
How will their grudging stomachs be provok'd
To wilful disobedience, and rebel!
Beside, what infamy will there arise,
When foreign princes shall be certified   144
That for a toy, a thing of no regard,
King Henry's peers and chief nobility
Destroy'd themselves, and lost the realm of
France!

O! think upon the conquest of my father, 14
My tender years, and let us not forego
That for a trifle that was bought with blood!
Let me be umpire in this doubtful strife.
I see no reason, if I wear this rose,   15
                    [*Putting on a red rose*
That any one should therefore be suspicious
I more incline to Somerset than York:
Both are my kinsmen, and I love them both.
As well they may upbraid me with my crown,
Because, forsooth, the King of Scots is crown'd
But your discretions better can persuade
Than I am able to instruct or teach:
And therefore, as we hither came in peace, 16
So let us still continue peace and love.
Cousin of York, we institute your Grace
To be our regent in these parts of France:
And, good my Lord of Somerset, unite   16
Your troops of horsemen with his bands of foot
And like true subjects, sons of your progenitors
Go cheerfully together and digest
Your angry choler on your enemies.   16
Ourself, my Lord Protector, and the rest,
After some respite will return to Calais;
From thence to England; where I hope er
long
To be presented by your victories,   17
With Charles, Alençon, and that traitorou
rout.
      [*Flourish. Exeunt all but* YORK, WARWICK
                            EXETER, *and* VERNON
  War. My Lord of York, I promise you, th
king
Prettily, methought, did play the orator.
  York. And so he did; but yet I like it not,
In that he wears the badge of Somerset.   17
  War. Tush! that was but his fancy, blam
him not;
I dare presume, sweet prince, he thought n
harm.
  York. An if I wist he did,—But let it rest;
Other affairs must now be managed.   18
      [*Exeunt* YORK, WARWICK, *and* VERNON
  Exe. Well didst thou, Richard, to suppress
thy voice;
For had the passions of thy heart burst out,
I fear we should have seen decipher'd there
More rancorous spite, more furious raging
broils,
Than yet can be imagin'd or suppos'd.
But howsoe'er, no simple man that sees
This jarring discord of nobility,   188
This shouldering of each other in the court,
This factious bandying of their favourites,
But that it doth presage some ill event.
'Tis much when sceptres are in children's hands
But more, when envy breeds unkind division:
There comes the ruin, there begins confusion.
                                         [*Exit*

SCENE II.—*Before Bourdeaux.*

Enter TALBOT, *with his Forces.*

  Tal. Go to the gates of Bourdeaux, trumpeter;
Summon their general unto the wall.

*Trumpet sounds a parley. Enter, on the Walls,
the* General *of the French Forces, and Others.*

English John Talbot, captains, calls you forth,
Servant in arms to Harry King of England; 4
And thus he would: Open your city gates,
Be humble to us, call my sov'reign yours,
And do him homage as obedient subjects,
And I'll withdraw me and my bloody power; 8
But, if you frown upon this proffer'd peace,
You tempt the fury of my three attendants,
Lean famine, quartering steel, and climbing
   fire;
Who in a moment even with the earth 12
Shall lay your stately and air-braving towers,
If you forsake the offer of their love.

Gen. Thou ominous and fearful owl of
   death,
Our nation's terror and their bloody scourge! 16
The period of thy tyranny approacheth.
On us thou canst not enter but by death;
For, I protest, we are well fortified,
And strong enough to issue out and fight: 20
If thou retire, the Dauphin, well appointed,
Stands with the snares of war to tangle thee:
On either hand thee there are squadrons
   pitch'd,
To wall thee from the liberty of flight; 24
And no way canst thou turn thee for redress
But death doth front thee with apparent spoil,
And pale destruction meets thee in the face.
Ten thousand French have ta'en the sacrament,
To rive their dangerous artillery 29
Upon no Christian soul but English Talbot.
Lo! there thou stand'st, a breathing valiant
   man,
Of an invincible unconquer'd spirit: 32
This is the latest glory of thy praise,
That I, thy enemy, 'due thee withal;
For ere the glass, that now begins to run,
Finish the process of his sandy hour, 36
These eyes, that see thee now well coloured,
Shall see thee wither'd, bloody, pale, and dead.
             [Drum afar off.
Hark! hark! the Dauphin's drum, a warning
   bell,
Sings heavy music to thy timorous soul; 40
And mine shall ring thy dire departure out.
    [Exeunt General, *&c., from the Walls.*

Tal. He fables not; I hear the enemy:
Out, some light horsemen, and peruse their
   wings.
O! negligent and heedless discipline; 44
How are we park'd and bounded in a pale,
A little herd of England's timorous deer,
Maz'd with a yelping kennel of French curs!
If we be English deer, be then, in blood; 48
Not rascal-like, to fall down with a pinch,
But rather moody-mad and desperate stags,
Turn on the bloody hounds with heads of steel,
And make the cowards stand aloof at bay: 52
Sell every man his life as dear as mine,
And they shall find dear deer of us, my friends.
God and Saint George, Talbot and England's
   right,
Prosper our colours in this dangerous fight! 56
                  [Exeunt.

SCENE III.—*Plains in Gascony.*

Enter YORK, *with Forces; to him a
Messenger.*

York. Are not the speedy scouts return'd
   again,
That dogg'd the mighty army of the Dauphin?

Mess. They are return'd, my lord; and give
   it out,
That he is march'd to Bourdeaux with his power,
To fight with Talbot. As he march'd along, 5
By your espials were discovered
Two mightier troops than that the Dauphin led,
Which join'd with him and made their march
   for Bourdeaux. 8

York. A plague upon that villain Somerset,
That thus delays my promised supply
Of horsemen that were levied for this siege!
Renowned Talbot doth expect my aid, 12
And I am louted by a traitor villain,
And cannot help the noble chevalier.
God comfort him in this necessity!
If he miscarry, farewell wars in France. 16

Enter SIR WILLIAM LUCY.

Lucy. Thou princely leader of our English
   strength,
Never so needful on the earth of France,
Spur to the rescue of the noble Talbot,
Who now is girdled with a waist of iron 20
And hemm'd about with grim destruction.
To Bourdeaux, war-like duke! To Bourdeaux,
   York!
Else, farewell Talbot, France, and England's
   honour.

York. O God! that Somerset, who in proud
   heart 24
Doth stop my cornets, were in Talbot's place!
So should we save a valiant gentleman
By forfeiting a traitor and a coward.
Mad ire and wrathful fury, make me weep 28
That thus we die, while remiss traitors sleep.

Lucy. O! send some succour to the distress'd lord.

York. He dies, we lose; I break my war-like
   word;
We mourn, France smiles; we lose, they daily
   get; 32
All 'long of this vile traitor Somerset.

Lucy. Then God take mercy on brave Tal-
   bot's soul;
And on his son young John, whom two hours
   since
I met in travel toward his war-like father. 36
This seven years did not Talbot see his son;
And now they meet where both their lives are
   done.

York. Alas! what joy shall noble Talbot
   have,
To bid his young son welcome to his grave? 40
Away! vexation almost stops my breath
That sunder'd friends greet in the hour of death.
Lucy, farewell: no more my fortune can,
But curse the cause I cannot aid the man. 44
Maine, Blois, Poictiers, and Tours, are won
   away,

'Long all of Somerset and his delay.
[*Exit, with his* Soldiers.
Lucy. Thus, while the vulture of sedition
Feeds in the bosom of such great commanders,
Sleeping neglection doth betray to loss   49
The conquest of our scarce cold conqueror,
That ever living man of memory,
Henry the Fifth: whiles they each other cross,
Lives, honours, lands, and all hurry to loss. 53
[*Exit.*

SCENE IV.—*Other Plains in Gascony.*

Enter SOMERSET, *with his Army; a Captain of*
TALBOT'S *with him.*

Som. It is too late; I cannot send them now:
This expedition was by York and Talbot
Too rashly plotted: all our general force
Might with a sally of the very town   4
Be buckled with: the over-daring Talbot
Hath sullied all his gloss of former honour
By this unheedful, desperate, wild adventure:
York set him on to fight and die in shame,   8
That, Talbot dead, great York might bear the
name.
Cap. Here is Sir William Lucy, who with me
Set from our o'ermatch'd forces forth for aid.

Enter SIR WILLIAM LUCY.

Som. How now, Sir William! whither were
you sent?   12
Lucy. Whither, my lord? from bought and
sold Lord Talbot;
Who, ring'd about with bold adversity,
Cries out for noble York and Somerset,
To beat assailing death from his weak legions:
And whiles the honourable captain there   17
Drops bloody sweat from his war-wearied limbs,
And, in advantage lingering, looks for rescue,
You, his false hopes, the trust of England's
honour,   20
Keep off aloof with worthless emulation.
Let not your private discord keep away
The levied succours that should lend him aid,
While he, renowned noble gentleman,   24
Yields up his life unto a world of odds:
Orleans the Bastard, Charles, Burgundy,
Alençon, Reignier, compass him about,
And Talbot perisheth by your default.   28
Som. York set him on; York should have
sent him aid.
Lucy. And York as fast upon your Grace
exclaims;
Swearing that you withhold his levied host
Collected for this expedition.   32
Som. York lies; he might have sent and had
the horse:
I owe him little duty, and less love;
And take foul scorn to fawn on him by sending.
Lucy. The fraud of England, not the force
of France,   36
Hath now entrapp'd the noble-minded Talbot.
Never to England shall he bear his life,
But dies, betray'd to fortune by your strife.
Som. Come, go; I will dispatch the horse-
men straight: 40
Within six hours they will be at his aid.

Lucy. Too late comes rescue: he is ta'en or
slain,
For fly he could not if he would have fled;
And fly would Talbot never, though he might. 44
Som. If he be dead, brave Talbot, then adieu!
Lucy. His fame lives in the world, his shame
in you.   [*Exeunt.*

SCENE V.—*The English Camp near
Bourdeaux.*

Enter TALBOT *and* JOHN *his Son.*

Tal. O young John Talbot! I did send for
thee
To tutor thee in stratagems of war,
That Talbot's name might be in thee reviv'd
When sapless age, and weak unable limbs
Should bring thy father to his drooping chair
But,—O malignant and ill-boding stars!
Now thou art come unto a feast of death,
A terrible and unavoided danger:
Therefore, dear boy, mount on my swiftes
horse,
And I'll direct thee how thou shalt escape
By sudden flight: come, dally not, be gone.
John. Is my name Talbot? and am I you
son?   1
And shall I fly? O! if you love your mother,
Dishonour not her honourable name,
To make a bastard and a slave of me:
The world will say he is not Talbot's blood 1
That basely fled when noble Talbot stood.
Tal. Fly, to revenge my death, if I be slain
John. He that flies so will ne'er return again
Tal. If we both stay, we both are sure to die
John. Then let me stay; and, father, do you
fly?   2
Your loss is great, so your regard should be
My worth unknown, no loss is known in me.
Upon my death the French can little boast; 2
In yours they will, in you all hopes are lost.
Flight cannot stain the honour you have won
But mine it will that no exploit have done:
You fled for vantage everyone will swear; 2
But if I bow, they'll say it was for fear.
There is no hope that ever I will stay
If the first hour I shrink and run away.
Here, on my knee, I beg mortality,   3
Rather than life preserv'd with infamy.
Tal. Shall all thy mother's hopes lie in on
tomb?
John. Ay, rather than I'll shame my mother
womb.
Tal. Upon my blessing I command thee g
John. To fight I will, but not to fly the foe.
Tal. Part of thy father may be sav'd in thee
John. No part of him but will be shame in me
Tal. Thou never hadst renown, nor cans
not lose it.   4
John. Yes, your renowned name: shall fligl
abuse it?
Tal. Thy father's charge shall clear thee from
that stain.
John. You cannot witness for me, bein
slain.
If death be so apparent, then both fly.   4

Tal. And leave my followers here to fight
and die?
y age was never tainted with such shame.
John. And shall my youth be guilty of such
blame?
[C]an more can I be sever'd from your side 48
[C]an can yourself yourself in twain divide.
[Na]y, go, do what you will, the like do I;
[O]r live I will not if my father die.
Tal. Then here I take my leave of thee, fair
son, 52
[Tu]rn to eclipse thy life this afternoon.
[Co]me, side by side together live and die,
[An]d soul with soul from France to heaven fly.

SCENE VI.—A Field of Battle.

[Al]arum: Excursions, wherein TALBOT'S Son is
hemmed about, and TALBOT rescues him.

Tal. Saint George and victory! fight, sol-
diers, fight!
[Th]e regent hath with Talbot broke his word,
[An]d left us to the rage of France his sword.
[W]here is John Talbot? Pause, and take thy
breath: 4
[I g]ave thee life and rescu'd thee from death.
John. O! twice my father, twice am I thy
son:
[Th]e life thou gav'st me first was lost and done,
[Til]l with thy war-like sword, despite of fate, 8
[I] my determin'd time thou gav'st new date.
Tal. When from the Dauphin's crest thy
sword struck fire,
[It] warm'd thy father's heart with proud desire
[Of] bold-fac'd victory. Then leaden age, 12
[Qui]cken'd with youthful spleen and war-like
rage,
[be]at down Alençon, Orleans, Burgundy,
[an]d from the pride of Gallia rescu'd thee.
[Th]e ireful bastard Orleans,—that drew blood 16
[fr]om thee, my boy, and had the maidenhood
[of] thy first fight,—I soon encountered
[an]d, interchanging blows, I quickly shed
[so]me of his bastard blood; and, in disgrace, 20
[I] spoke him thus, 'Contaminated, base,
[an]d misbegotten blood I spill of thine,
[m]ean and right poor, for that pure blood of
mine
[wh]ich thou didst force from Talbot, my brave
boy:' 24
[He]re, purposing the Bastard to destroy,
[ca]me in strong rescue. Speak, thy father's care,
[ar]t thou not weary, John? How dost thou fare?
[Wi]lt thou yet leave the battle, boy, and fly, 28
[No]w thou art seal'd the son of chivalry?
[Fl]y, to revenge my death when I am dead;
[Th]e help of one stands me in little stead.
[O!] too much folly is it, well I wot, 32
[To] hazard all our lives in one small boat.
[If] I to-day die not with Frenchmen's rage,
[To]-morrow I shall die with mickle age:
[By] me they nothing gain an if I stay; 36
[']Tis but the short'ning of my life one day.
[In] thee thy mother dies, our household's name,
[M]y death's revenge, thy youth, and England's
fame.

All these and more we hazard by thy stay; 40
All these are sav'd if thou wilt fly away.
John. The sword of Orleans hath not made
me smart;
These words of yours draw life-blood from my
heart.
On that advantage, bought with such a shame, 45
To save a paltry life and slay bright fame,
Before young Talbot from old Talbot fly,
The coward horse that bears me fall and die!
And like me to the peasant boys of France, 48
To be shame's scorn and subject of mischance!
Surely, by all the glory you have won,
An if I fly, I am not Talbot's son:
Then talk no more of flight, it is no boot; 52
If son to Talbot, die at Talbot's foot.
Tal. Then follow thou thy desperate sire of
Crete,
Thou Icarus. Thy life to me is sweet:
If thou wilt fight, fight by thy father's side, 56
And, commendable prov'd, let's die in pride.
[Exeunt.

SCENE VII.—Another Part of the Field.

Alarum: Excursions. Enter Old TALBOT,
wounded, led by a Servant.

Tal. Where is my other life?—mine own is
gone;—
O! where's young Talbot? where is valiant
John?
Triumphant death, smear'd with captivity,
Young Talbot's valour makes me smile at thee.
When he perceiv'd me shrink and on my knee,
His bloody sword he brandish'd over me,
And like a hungry lion did commence
Rough deeds of rage and stern impatience; 8
But when my angry guardant stood alone,
Tendering my ruin and assail'd of none,
Dizzy-ey'd fury and great rage of heart
Suddenly made him from my side to start 12
Into the clust'ring battle of the French;
And in that sea of blood my boy did drench
His overmounting spirit; and there died
My Icarus, my blossom, in his pride. 16

Enter Soldiers, bearing the body of
Young TALBOT.

Serv. O, my dear lord! lo, where your son is
borne!
Tal. Thou antick, death, which laugh'st us
here to scorn,
Anon, from thy insulting tyranny,
Coupled in bonds of perpetuity, 20
Two Talbots, winged through the lither sky,
In thy despite shall 'scape mortality.
O! thou, whose wounds become hard-favour'd
death,
Speak to thy father ere thou yield thy breath; 24
Brave death by speaking whe'r he will or no;
Imagine him a Frenchman and thy foe.
Poor boy! he smiles, methinks, as who should
say,
Had death been French, then death had died
to-day. 28
Come, come, and lay him in his father's arms:

My spirit can no longer bear these harms.
Soldiers, adieu! I have what I would have,
Now my old arms are young John Talbot's
  grave.   [Dies.

Alarums. Exeunt Soldiers and Servant, leaving
  the two bodies. Enter CHARLES, ALENÇON,
  BURGUNDY, the BASTARD OF ORLEANS, JOAN
  LA PUCELLE, and Forces.

  Char. Had York and Somerset brought res-
cue in
We should have found a bloody day of this.
  Bast. How the young whelp of Talbot's,
  raging-wood,   35
Did flesh his puny sword in Frenchmen's blood!
  Joan. Once I encounter'd him, and thus I
said:
'Thou maiden youth, be vanquish'd by a maid:'
But with a proud majestical high scorn,
He answer'd thus: 'Young Talbot was not born
To be the pillage of a giglot wench.'   41
So, rushing in the bowels of the French,
He left me proudly, as unworthy fight.
  Bur. Doubtless he would have made a noble
  knight;   44
See, where he lies inhearsed in the arms
Of the most bloody nurser of his harms.
  Bast. Hew them to pieces, hack their bones
asunder,
Whose life was England's glory, Gallia's won-
der.   48
  Char. O, no! forbear; for that which we
have fled
During the life, let us not wrong it dead.

  Enter SIR WILLIAM LUCY, attended: a French
    Herald preceding.

  Lucy. Herald, conduct me to the Dauphin's
tent,
To know who hath obtain'd the glory of the day.
  Char. On what submissive message art thou
sent?   53
  Lucy. Submission, Dauphin! 'tis a mere
French word;
We English warriors wot not what it means.
I come to know what prisoners thou hast
ta'en,   56
And to survey the bodies of the dead.
  Char. For prisoners ask'st thou? hell our
prison is.
But tell me whom thou seek'st.
  Lucy. Where is the great Alcides of the field,
Valiant Lord Talbot, Earl of Shrewsbury? 61
Created, for his rare success in arms,
Great Earl of Washford, Waterford, and
  Valence;
Lord Talbot of Goodrig and Urchinfield,   64
Lord Strange of Blackmere, Lord Verdun of
  Alton,
Lord Cromwell of Wingfield, Lord Furnival of
  Sheffield,
The thrice-victorious Lord of Falconbridge;
Knight of the noble order of Saint George, 68
Worthy Saint Michael and the Golden Fleece;
Great mareschal to Henry the Sixth
Of all his wars within the realm of France?

  Joan. Here is a silly stately style indeed!
The Turk, that two-and-fifty kingdoms hath
Writes not so tedious a style as this.
Him that thou magnifiest with all these tit[l
Stinking and fly-blown lies here at our feet.
  Lucy. Is Talbot slain, the Frenchmen's o[
Your kingdom's terror and black Nemesis[
O! were mine eye-balls into bullets turn'd,
That I in rage might shoot them at your fac[
O! that I could but call these dead to life!
It were enough to fright the realm of Franc[
Were but his picture left among you here
It would amaze the proudest of you all.
Give me their bodies, that I may bear th[
  hence,
And give them burial as beseems their wor[
  Joan. I think this upstart is old Talb[
  ghost,
He speaks with such a proud commanding spi[
For God's sake, let him have 'em; to keep th[
  here
They would but stink and putrefy the air.
  Char. Go, take their bodies hence.
  Lucy.   I'll bear them hen[
But from their ashes shall be rear'd
A phoenix that shall make all France afeard[
  Char. So we be rid of them, do with 'em w[
  thou wilt.
And now to Paris, in this conquering vein[
All will be ours now bloody Talbot's slain.
                           [Exeu[

ACT V

SCENE I.—London. A Room in the Palace[

Enter KING HENRY, GLOUCESTER, and EXETE[

  K. Hen. Have you perus'd the letters fr[
  the pope,
The emperor, and the Earl of Armagnac?
  Glo. I have, my lord; and their intent is th[
They humbly sue unto your excellence
To have a godly peace concluded of
Between the realms of England and of Fran[
  K. Hen. How doth your Grace affect th[
  motion?
  Glo. Well, my good lord; and as the o[
  means
To stop effusion of our Christian blood,
And stablish quietness on every side.
  K. Hen. Ay, marry, uncle; for I alw[
  thought
It was both impious and unnatural
That such immanity and bloody strife
Should reign among professors of one fait[
  Glo. Beside, my lord, the sooner to effe[
And surer bind this knot of amity,
The Earl of Armagnac, near knit to Charles[
A man of great authority in France,
Proffers his only daughter to your Grace
In marriage, with a large and sumptuous dow[
  K. Hen. Marriage, uncle! alas! my years[
  young,
And fitter is my study and my books

...an wanton dalliance with a paramour.
...t call the ambassadors; and, as you please, 24
... let them have their answers every one:
...hall be well content with any choice
...nds to God's glory and my country's weal.

...ter a Legate, *and two* Ambassadors, *with*
WINCHESTER, *now* CARDINAL BEAUFORT, *and*
habited accordingly.

Exe. [*Aside.*] What! is my Lord of Winchester
install'd, 28
...d call'd unto a cardinal's degree?
...en, I perceive that will be verified
...nry the Fifth did sometime prophesy,—
'...once he come to be a cardinal, 32
...'ll make his cap co-equal with the crown.'
K. Hen. My lords ambassadors, your several
suits
...ve been consider'd, and debated on.
...ur purpose is both good and reasonable; 36
...d therefore are we certainly resolv'd
... draw conditions of a friendly peace;
...hich by my Lord of Winchester we mean
...all be transported presently to France. 40
Glo. And for the proffer of my lord your
master,
...ave inform'd his highness so at large,
...—liking of the lady's virtuous gifts,
...r beauty, and the value of her dower,— 44
... doth intend she shall be England's queen.
K. Hen. [*To the Ambassador.*] In argument
and proof of which contract,
...ar her this jewel, pledge of my affection.
...d so, my lord protector, see them guarded, 48
...d safely brought to Dover; where inshipp'd
...mmit them to the fortune of the sea.
    [*Exeunt* KING HENRY *and Train;* GLOU-
      CESTER, EXETER, *and Ambassadors.*
Win. Stay, my lord legate: you shall first
receive
...e sum of money which I promised 52
...ould be deliver'd to his holiness
...r clothing me in these grave ornaments.
Leg. I will attend upon your lordship's
leisure.
Win. [*Aside.*] Now Winchester will not submit, I trow, 56
...be inferior to the proudest peer.
...mphrey of Gloucester, thou shalt well perceive
...at neither in birth or for authority
...e bishop will be overborne by thee: 60
...either make thee stoop and bend thy knee,
...sack this country with a mutiny. [*Exeunt.*

SCENE II.—*France. Plains in Anjou.*

...ter CHARLES, BURGUNDY, ALENÇON, JOAN LA
  PUCELLE, *and Forces, marching.*

Char. These news, my lord, may cheer our
drooping spirits;
...s said the stout Parisians do revolt,
...d turn again unto the war-like French.
Alen. Then, march to Paris, royal Charles of
France, 4
...d keep not back your powers in dalliance.

Joan. Peace be amongst them if they turn
  to us;
Else, ruin combat with their palaces!

    Enter a Scout.

Scout. Success unto our valiant general, 8
And happiness to his accomplices!
Char. What tidings send our scouts? I
prithee speak.
Scout. The English army, that divided was
Into two parties, is now conjoin'd in one, 12
And means to give you battle presently.
Char. Somewhat too sudden, sirs, the warn-
ing is:
But we will presently provide for them.
Bur. I trust the ghost of Talbot is not there:
Now he is gone, my lord, you need not fear.
Joan. Of all base passions, fear is most
accurs'd.
Command the conquest, Charles, it shall be
thine;
Let Henry fret and all the world repine. 20
Char. Then on, my lords; and France be
fortunate! [*Exeunt.*

SCENE III.—*France. Before Angiers.*

Alarum: Excursions. Enter JOAN LA PUCELLE.

Joan. The regent conquers and the French-
men fly.
Now help, ye charming spells and periapts;
And ye choice spirits that admonish me
And give me signs of future accidents: 4
    [*Thunder.*
You speedy helpers, that are substitutes
Under the lordly monarch of the north,
Appear, and aid me in this enterprise!

    Enter Fiends.

This speedy and quick appearance argues proof
Of your accustom'd diligence to me. 9
Now, ye familiar spirits, that are cull'd
Out of the powerful regions under earth,
Help me this once, that France may get the field.
    [*They walk, and speak not.*
O! hold me not with silence over-long. 13
Where I was wont to feed you with my blood,
I'll lop a member off and give it you,
In earnest of a further benefit, 16
So you do condescend to help me now.
    [*They hang their heads.*
No hope to have redress? My body shall
Pay recompense, if you will grant my suit.
    [*They shake their heads.*
Cannot my body nor blood-sacrifice 20
Entreat you to your wonted furtherance?
Then take my soul; my body, soul, and all,
Before that England give the French the foil.
    [*They depart.*
See! they forsake me. Now the time is come, 24
That France must vail her lofty-plumed crest,
And let her head fall into England's lap.
My ancient incantations are too weak,
And hell too strong for me to buckle with: 28
Now, France, thy glory droopeth to the dust.
    [*Exit.*

Alarum. Enter French and English fighting:
JOAN LA PUCELLE *and* YORK *fight hand to hand:*
JOAN LA PUCELLE *is taken. The French fly.*

York. Damsel of France, I think I have you
fast:
Unchain your spirits now with spelling charms,
And try if they can gain your liberty.   32
A goodly prize, fit for the devil's grace!
See how the ugly witch doth bend her brows,
As if with Circe she would change my shape.
  Joan. Chang'd to a worser shape thou canst
not be.   36
  York. O! Charles the Dauphin is a proper
man;
No shape but his can please your dainty eye.
  Joan. A plaguing mischief light on Charles
and thee!
And may ye both be suddenly surpris'd   40
By bloody hands, in sleeping on your beds!
  York. Fell banning hag, enchantress, hold
thy tongue!
  Joan. I prithee, give me leave to curse a while.
  York. Curse, miscreant, when thou comest
to the stake.   [*Exeunt.*

Alarum. Enter SUFFOLK, *with* MARGARET *in his
hand.*

  Suf. Be what thou wilt, thou art my prisoner.
    [*Gazes on her.*
O fairest beauty! do not fear nor fly,
For I will touch thee but with reverent hands,
I kiss these fingers for eternal peace,   48
And lay them gently on thy tender side.
What art thou? say, that I may honour thee.
  Mar. Margaret my name, and daughter to a
king,
The King of Naples, whosoe'er thou art.   52
  Suf. An earl I am, and Suffolk am I call'd.
Be not offended, nature's miracle.
Thou art allotted to be ta'en by me:
So doth the swan her downy cygnets save,   56
Keeping them prisoners underneath her wings.
Yet if this servile usage once offend,
Go and be free again, as Suffolk's friend.
    [*She turns away as going.*
O stay! I have no power to let her pass;   60
My hand would free her, but my heart says no.
As plays the sun upon the glassy streams,
Twinkling another counterfeited beam,
So seems this gorgeous beauty to mine eyes.   64
Fain would I woo her, yet I dare not speak:
I'll call for pen and ink and write my mind.
Fie, De la Pole! disable not thyself;
Hast not a tongue? is she not here thy pri-
soner?   68
Wilt thou be daunted at a woman's sight?
Ay; beauty's princely majesty is such
Confounds the tongue and makes the senses
rough.
  Mar. Say, Earl of Suffolk,—if thy name be
so,—   72
What ransom must I pay before I pass?
For I perceive, I am thy prisoner.
  Suf. [*Aside.*] How canst thou tell she will
deny thy suit,

Before thou make a trial of her love?
  Mar. Why speak'st thou not? what rans[
must I pay?
  Suf. [*Aside.*] She's beautiful and therefore
be woo'd,
She is a woman, therefore to be won.
  Mar. Wilt thou accept of ransom, yea or r
  Suf. [*Aside.*] Fond man! remember that th
hast a wife;
Then how can Margaret be thy paramour?
  Mar. I were best to leave him, for he
not hear.
  Suf. [*Aside.*] There all is marr'd; there lie
cooling card.
  Mar. He talks at random; sure, the ma
mad.
  Suf. [*Aside.*] And yet a dispensation may
had.
  Mar. And yet I would that you would
swer me.
  Suf. [*Aside.*] I'll win this Lady Margaret.]
whom?
Why, for my king: tush! that's a wooden th
  Mar. [*Overhearing him.*] He talks of wo
it is some carpenter.
  Suf. [*Aside.*] Yet so my fancy may be satisfi
And peace established between these realms.
But there remains a scruple in that too;
For though her father be the King of Nap
Duke of Anjou and Maine, yet is he poor,
And our nobility will scorn the match.
  Mar. Hear ye, captain? Are you not
leisure?
  Suf. [*Aside.*] It shall be so, disdain they n
so much:
Henry is youthful and will quickly yield.
Madam, I have a secret to reveal.
  Mar. [*Aside.*] What though I be enthrall
he seems a knight,
And will not any way dishonour me.
  Suf. Lady, vouchsafe to listen what I sa
  Mar. [*Aside.*] Perhaps I shall be rescu'd
the French;
And then I need not crave his courtesy.
  Suf. Sweet madam, give me hearing i
cause—
  Mar. Tush, women have been captivate
now.
  Suf. Lady, wherefore talk you so?
  Mar. I cry you mercy, 'tis but *quid* for q
  Suf. Say, gentle princess, would you not s
pose
Your bondage happy to be made a queen?
  Mar. To be a queen in bondage is more
Than is a slave in base servility;
For princes should be free.
  Suf.   And so shall y
If happy England's royal king be free.
  Mar. Why, what concerns his freedom u
me?
  Suf. I'll undertake to make thee Hen
queen,
To put a golden sceptre in thy hand
And set a precious crown upon thy head,
If thou wilt condescend to be my—
  Mar.   What?

Suf.   His love. 120

Mar. I am unworthy to be Henry's wife.

Suf. No, gentle madam; I unworthy am
To woo so fair a dame to be his wife
And have no portion in the choice myself. 124
Now say you, madam, are you so content?

Mar. An if my father please, I am content.

Suf. Then call our captains and our colours
forth!
And, madam, at your father's castle walls 128
We'll crave a parley, to confer with him.
[*Troops come forward.*

Parley sounded. Enter REIGNIER *on the Walls.*

Suf. See, Reignier, see thy daughter prisoner!

Reig. To whom?

Suf.   To me.

Reig.   Suffolk, what remedy?
I am a soldier, and unapt to weep, 132
Or to exclaim on Fortune's fickleness.

Suf. Yes, there is remedy enough, my lord:
Consent, and for thy honour, give consent,
Thy daughter shall be wedded to my king, 136
Whom I with pain have woo'd and won thereto;
And this her easy-held imprisonment
Hath gain'd thy daughter princely liberty.

Reig. Speaks Suffolk as he thinks?

Suf.   Fair Margaret knows 140
That Suffolk doth not flatter, face, or feign.

Reig. Upon thy princely warrant, I descend
To give thee answer of thy just demand.
[*Exit from the walls.*

Suf. And here I will expect thy coming. 144

Trumpets sound. Enter REIGNIER, *below.*

Reig. Welcome, brave earl, into our territories:
Command in Anjou what your honour pleases.

Suf. Thanks, Reignier, happy for so sweet a
child,
Fit to be made companion with a king. 148
What answer makes your Grace unto my suit?

Reig. Since thou dost deign to woo her little
worth
To be the princely bride of such a lord,
Upon condition I may quietly 152
Enjoy mine own, the county Maine and Anjou,
Free from oppression or the stroke of war,
My daughter shall be Henry's if he please.

Suf. That is her ransom; I deliver her; 156
And those two counties I will undertake
Your Grace shall well and quietly enjoy.

Reig. And I again, in Henry's royal name,
As deputy unto that gracious king, 160
Give thee her hand for sign of plighted faith.

Suf. Reignier of France, I give thee kingly
thanks,
Because this is in traffic of a king:
[*Aside.*] And yet, methinks, I could be well con-
tent 164
To be mine own attorney in this case.
I'll over then, to England with this news,
And make this marriage to be solemniz'd.
So farewell, Reignier: set this diamond safe,
In golden palaces, as it becomes. 169

Reig. I do embrace thee, as I would embrace
The Christian prince, King Henry, were he here.

Mar. Farewell, my lord. Good wishes,
praise, and prayers 172
Shall Suffolk ever have of Margaret. [*Going.*

Suf. Farewell, sweet madam! but hark you,
Margaret;
No princely commendations to my king?

Mar. Such commendations as become a
maid, 176
A virgin, and his servant, say to him.

Suf. Words sweetly plac'd and modestly
directed.
But madam, I must trouble you again,
No loving token to his majesty? 180

Mar. Yes, my good lord; a pure unspotted
heart,
Never yet taint with love, I send the king.

Suf. And this withal.   [*Kisses her.*

Mar. That for thyself: I will not so presume,
To send such peevish tokens to a king. 185
[*Exeunt* REIGNIER *and* MARGARET.

Suf. O! wert thou for myself! But Suffolk,
stay;
Thou mayst not wander in that labyrinth;
There Minotaurs and ugly treasons lurk. 188
Solicit Henry with her wondrous praise:
Bethink thee on her virtues that surmount
And natural graces that extinguish art;
Repeat their semblance often on the seas, 192
That, when thou com'st to kneel at Henry's feet,
Thou mayst bereave him of his wits with wonder.
[*Exit.*

SCENE IV.—*Camp of the* DUKE OF YORK,
in Anjou.

Enter YORK, WARWICK, *and Others.*

York. Bring forth that sorceress, condemn'd
to burn.

Enter JOAN LA PUCELLE, *guarded; and a*
Shepherd.

Shep. Ah, Joan! this kills thy father's heart
outright.
Have I sought every country far and near,
And, now it is my chance to find thee out, 4
Must I behold thy timeless cruel death?
Ah, Joan! sweet daughter Joan, I'll die with
thee.

Joan. Decrepit miser! base ignoble wretch!
I am descended of a gentler blood: 8
Thou art no father nor no friend of mine.

Shep. Out, out! My lords, an please you, 'tis
not so;
I did beget her, all the parish knows:
Her mother liveth yet, can testify 12
She was the first fruit of my bachelorship.

War. Graceless! wilt thou deny thy parentage?

York. This argues what her kind of life hath
been:
Wicked and vile; and so her death concludes. 16

Shep. Fie, Joan, that thou wilt be so obstacle!
God knows, thou art a collop of my flesh;
And for thy sake have I shed many a tear:
Deny me not, I prithee, gentle Joan. 20

Joan. Peasant, avaunt! You have suborn'd
this man,

Of purpose to obscure my noble birth.

Shep. 'Tis true, I gave a noble to the priest,
The morn that I was wedded to her mother. 24
Kneel down and take my blessing, good my girl.
Wilt thou not stoop? Now cursed be the time
Of thy nativity! I would the milk
Thy mother gave thee, when thou suck'dst her breast,   28
Had been a little ratsbane for thy sake!
Or else, when thou didst keep my lambs a-field
I wish some ravenous wolf had eaten thee!
Dost thou deny thy father, cursed drab?   32
O! burn her, burn her! hanging is too good.
                                        [*Exit.*

York. Take her away; for she hath liv'd too long,
To fill the world with vicious qualities.

Joan. First, let me tell you whom you have condemn'd: 36
Not me begotten of a shepherd swain,
But issu'd from the progeny of kings;
Virtuous and holy; chosen from above,
By inspiration of celestial grace,   40
To work exceeding miracles on earth.
I never had to do with wicked spirits:
But you,—that are polluted with your lusts,
Stain'd with the guiltless blood of innocents, 44
Corrupt and tainted with a thousand vices,—
Because you want the grace that others have,
You judge it straight a thing impossible
To compass wonders but by help of devils. 48
No misconceived! Joan of Arc hath been
A virgin from her tender infancy,
Chaste and immaculate in very thought;
Whose maiden blood, thus rigorously effus'd, 52
Will cry for vengeance at the gates of heaven.

York. Ay, ay: away with her to execution!

War. And hark ye, sirs; because she is a maid,
Spare for no fagots, let there be enow: 56
Place barrels of pitch upon the fatal stake,
That so her torture may be shortened.

Joan. Will nothing turn your unrelenting hearts?
Then, Joan, discover thine infirmity;   60
That warranteth by law to be thy privilege.
I am with child, ye bloody homicides:
Murder not then the fruit within my womb,
Although ye hale me to a violent death.   64

York. Now, heaven forefend! the holy maid with child!

War. The greatest miracle that e'er ye wrought!
Is all your strict preciseness come to this?

York. She and the Dauphin have been juggling: 68
I did imagine what would be her refuge.

War. Well, go to; we will have no bastards live;
Especially since Charles must father it.

Joan. You are deceiv'd; my child is none of his: 72
It was Alençon that enjoy'd my love.

York. Alençon! that notorious Machiavel!
It dies an if it had a thousand lives.

Joan. O! give me leave, I have deluded you:

'Twas neither Charles, nor yet the duke I nam'd
But Reignier, King of Naples, that prevail'd.

War. A married man: that's most intoler able.

York. Why, here's a girl! I think she know not well,   8
There were so many, whom she may accuse.

War. It 's sign she hath been liberal and free

York. And yet, forsooth, she is a virgin pure
Strumpet, thy words condemn thy brat and thee
Use no entreaty, for it is in vain.   8

Joan. Then lead me hence; with whom leave my curse:
May never glorious sun reflex his beams
Upon the country where you make abode; 8
But darkness and the gloomy shade of death
Environ you, till mischief and despair
Drive you to break your necks or hang your selves!   [*Exit, guarded*

York. Break thou in pieces and consume t ashes,   9
Thou foul accursed minister of hell!

Enter CARDINAL BEAUFORT, *attended.*

Car. Lord regent, I do greet your excellenc
With letters of commission from the king.
For know, my lords, the states of Christendom
Mov'd with remorse of these outrageous broils
Have earnestly implor'd a general peace   9
Betwixt our nation and the aspiring French;
And here at hand the Dauphin, and his train,
Approacheth to confer about some matter. 10

York. Is all our travail turn'd to this effect
After the slaughter of so many peers,
So many captains, gentlemen, and soldiers, 10.
That in this quarrel have been overthrown,
And sold their bodies for their country's benefit
Shall we at last conclude effeminate peace?
Have we not lost most part of all the towns, 10
By treason, falsehood, and by treachery,
Our great progenitors had conquered?
O! Warwick, Warwick! I foresee with grief
The utter loss of all the realm of France.   11

War. Be patient, York: if we conclude peace,
It shall be with such strict and severe covenant
As little shall the Frenchmen gain thereby.

Enter CHARLES, *attended;* ALENÇON, *the* BASTAR
OF ORLEANS, REIGNIER, *and Others.*

Char. Since, lords of England, it is thu agreed,   11
That peaceful truce shall be proclaim'd i France,
We come to be informed by yourselves
What the conditions of that league must be.

York. Speak, Winchester; for boiling choler chokes   12
The hollow passage of my poison'd voice,
By sight of these our baleful enemies.

Car. Charles, and the rest, it is enacted thus
That, in regard King Henry gives consent,   12.
Of mere compassion and of lenity,
To ease your country of distressful war,
And suffer you to breathe in fruitful peace,
You shall become true liegemen to his crown

And, Charles, upon condition thou wilt swear
To pay him tribute, and submit thyself,
Thou shalt be plac'd as viceroy under him,
And still enjoy thy regal dignity.   132
    Alen. Must he be then, as shadow of himself?
Adorn his temples with a coronet,
And yet, in substance and authority,
Retain but privilege of a private man?   136
This proffer is absurd and reasonless.
    Char. 'Tis known already that I am possess'd
With more than half the Gallian territories,
And therein reverenc'd for their lawful king: 140
Shall I, for lucre of the rest unvanquish'd,
Detract so much from that prerogative
As to be call'd but viceroy of the whole?
No, lord ambassador; I'll rather keep   144
That which I have than, coveting for more,
Be cast from possibility of all.
    York. Insulting Charles! hast thou by secret
        means
Us'd intercession to obtain a league,   148
And now the matter grows to compromise,
Stand'st thou aloof upon comparison?
Either accept the title thou usurp'st,
Of benefit proceeding from our king   152
And not of any challenge of desert,
Or we will plague thee with incessant wars.
    Reig. My lord, you do not well in obstinacy
To cavil in the course of this contract: 156
If once it be neglected, ten to one,
We shall not find like opportunity.
    Alen. [*Aside to* CHARLES.] To say the truth,
    it is your policy
To save your subjects from such massacre 160
And ruthless slaughters as are daily seen
By our proceeding in hostility;
And therefore take this compact of a truce,
Although you break it when your pleasure
    serves.   164
    War. How sayst thou, Charles? shall our
        condition stand?
    Char. It shall;
Only reserv'd, you claim no interest
In any of our towns of garrison.   168
    York. Then swear allegiance to his majesty;
As thou art knight, never to disobey
Nor be rebellious to the crown of England,
Thou, nor thy nobles, to the crown of England.
        [CHARLES, &c., *give tokens of fealty.*
So, now dismiss your army when ye please;
Hang up your ensigns, let your drums be still,
For here we entertain a solemn peace. [*Exeunt.*

SCENE V.—*London. A Room in the Palace.*

Enter KING HENRY, *in conference with* SUFFOLK;
    GLOUCESTER *and* EXETER *following.*

    K. Hen. Your wondrous rare description,
        noble earl,
Of beauteous Margaret hath astonish'd me:
Her virtues, graced with external gifts,
Do breed love's settled passions in my heart: 4
And like as rigour of tempestuous gusts
Provokes the mightiest hulk against the tide,
So am I driven by breath of her renown
Either to suffer shipwreck, or arrive   8

Where I may have fruition of her love.
    Suf. Tush! my good lord, this superficial tale
Is but a preface of her worthy praise:
The chief perfections of that lovely dame— 12
Had I sufficient skill to utter them—
Would make a volume of enticing lines,
Able to ravish any dull conceit:
And, which is more, she is not so divine,   16
So full replete with choice of all delights,
But with as humble lowliness of mind
She is content to be at your command;
Command, I mean, of virtuous chaste intents,
To love and honour Henry as her lord.   21
    K. Hen. And otherwise will Henry ne'er pre-
        sume.
Therefore, my Lord Protector, give consent
That Margaret may be England's royal queen.
    Glo. So should I give consent to flatter sin.
You know, my lord, your highness is betroth'd
Unto another lady of esteem;
How shall we then dispense with that contract,
And not deface your honour with reproach? 29
    Suf. As doth a ruler with unlawful oaths;
Or one that, at a triumph having vow'd
To try his strength, forsaketh yet the lists   32
By reason of his adversary's odds.
A poor earl's daughter is unequal odds,
And therefore may be broke without offence.
    Glo. Why, what, I pray, is Margaret more
        than that?   36
Her father is no better than an earl,
Although in glorious titles he excel.
    Suf. Yes, my good lord, her father is a king,
The King of Naples and Jerusalem;   40
And of such great authority in France
As his alliance will confirm our peace,
And keep the Frenchmen in allegiance.   43
    Glo. And so the Earl of Armagnac may do,
Because he is near kinsman unto Charles.
    Exe. Beside, his wealth doth warrant liberal
        dower,
Where Reignier sooner will receive than give.
    Suf. A dower, my lords! disgrace not so your
        king,   48
That he should be so abject, base, and poor,
To choose for wealth and not for perfect love.
Henry is able to enrich his queen,
And not to seek a queen to make him rich: 52
So worthless peasants bargain for their wives,
As market-men for oxen, sheep, or horse.
Marriage is a matter of more worth
Than to be dealt in by attorneyship: 56
Not whom we will, but whom his Grace affects,
Must be companion of his nuptial bed;
And therefore, lords, since he affects her most,
It most of all these reasons bindeth us,   60
In our opinions she should be preferr'd.
For what is wedlock forced, but a hell,
An age of discord and continual strife?
Whereas the contrary bringeth bliss,   64
And is a pattern of celestial peace.
Whom should we match with Henry, being a
        king,
But Margaret, that is daughter to a king?
Her peerless feature, joined with her birth, 68
Approves her fit for none but for a king:

Her valiant courage and undaunted spirit—
More than in women commonly is seen—
Will answer our hope in issue of a king;   72
For Henry, son unto a conqueror,
Is likely to beget more conquerors,
If with a lady of so high resolve
As is fair Margaret he be link'd in love.   76
Then yield, my lords; and here conclude with
  me
That Margaret shall be queen, and none but she.
   K. Hen. Whether it be through force of your
  report,
My noble lord of Suffolk, or for that   80
My tender youth was never yet attaint
With any passion of inflaming love,
I cannot tell; but this I am assur'd,
I feel such sharp dissension in my breast,   84
Such fierce alarums both of hope and fear,
As I am sick with working of my thoughts.
Take, therefore, shipping; post, my lord, to
  France;
Agree to any covenants, and procure   88
That Lady Margaret do vouchsafe to come

To cross the seas to England and be crown'd
King Henry's faithful and anointed queen:
For your expenses and sufficient charge,   92
Among the people gather up a tenth.
Be gone, I say; for till you do return
I rest perplexed with a thousand cares.
And you, good uncle, banish all offence: 96
If you do censure me by what you were,
Not what you are, I know it will excuse
This sudden execution of my will.
And so, conduct me, where, from company
I may revolve and ruminate my grief.   *[Exit.*
   Glo. Ay, grief, I fear me, both at first and
  last.   *[Exeunt* GLOUCESTER *and* EXETER.
   Suf. Thus Suffolk hath prevail'd; and thus
  he goes,   103
As did the youthful Paris once to Greece;
With hope to find the like event in love,
But prosper better than the Trojan did.
Margaret shall now be queen, and rule the
  king;   107
But I will rule both her, the king, and realm.
                            [Exit.

THE SECOND PART OF
KING HENRY THE SIXTH

DRAMATIS PERSONÆ

KING HENRY THE SIXTH.
HUMPHREY, Duke of Gloucester, his Uncle.
CARDINAL BEAUFORT, Bishop of Winchester, Great-Uncle to the King.
RICHARD PLANTAGENET, Duke of York.
EDWARD and RICHARD, his Sons.
DUKE OF SOMERSET,
DUKE OF SUFFOLK,
DUKE OF BUCKINGHAM, } of the King's Party.
LORD CLIFFORD,
YOUNG CLIFFORD, his Son,
EARL OF SALISBURY, } of the York Faction.
EARL OF WARWICK,
LORD SCALES, Governor of the Tower.
SIR HUMPHREY STAFFORD, and WILLIAM STAFFORD, his Brother.
LORD SAY.
A Sea-captain, Master, and Master's Mate.
WALTER WHITMORE.
SIR JOHN STANLEY.
Two Gentlemen, prisoners with Suffolk.
VAUX.
MATTHEW GOFFE.
JOHN HUME and JOHN SOUTHWELL, Priests.

BOLINGBROKE, a Conjurer.
A Spirit raised by him.
THOMAS HORNER, an Armourer.
PETER, his Man.
Clerk of Chatham.
Mayor of St. Alban's.
SIMPCOX, an Impostor.
Two Murderers.
JACK CADE, a Rebel.
GEORGE BEVIS, JOHN HOLLAND, DICK the Butcher, SMITH the Weaver, MICHAEL, &c., Followers of Cade.
ALEXANDER IDEN, a Kentish Gentleman.

MARGARET, Queen to King Henry.
ELEANOR, Duchess of Gloucester.
MARGERY JOURDAIN, a Witch.
Wife to Simpcox.

Lords, Ladies, and Attendants; Herald, Petitioners, Aldermen, a Beadle, Sheriff, and Officers; Citizens, Prentices, Falconers, Guards, Soldiers, Messengers, &c.

SCENE.—*In various parts of England.*

ACT I

SCENE I.—*London. A room of State in the Palace.*

Flourish of Trumpets: then hautboys. Enter, on one side, KING HENRY, DUKE OF GLOUCESTER, SALISBURY, WARWICK, *and* CARDINAL BEAUFORT; *on the other*, QUEEN MARGARET, *led in by* SUFFOLK; YORK, SOMERSET, BUCKINGHAM, *and Others, following.*

Suf. As by your high imperial majesty
I had in charge at my depart for France,
As procurator to your excellence,
To marry Princess Margaret for your Grace; 4
So, in the famous ancient city, Tours,
In presence of the Kings of France and Sicil,
The Dukes of Orleans, Calaber, Britaine, and Alençon,
Seven earls, twelve barons, and twenty reverend bishops, 8
I have perform'd my task, and was espous'd:
And humbly now upon my bended knee,
In sight of England and her lordly peers,
Deliver up my title in the queen 12
To your most gracious hands, that are the substance
Of that great shadow I did represent;
The happiest gift that ever marquess gave,
The fairest queen that ever king receiv'd. 16

K. Hen. Suffolk, arise. Welcome, Queen Margaret:
I can express no kinder sign of love
Than this kind kiss. O Lord! that lends me life,
Lend me a heart replete with thankfulness! 20
For thou hast given me in this beauteous face
A world of earthly blessings to my soul,
If sympathy of love unite our thoughts.
Q. Mar. Great King of England and my gracious lord, 24
The mutual conference that my mind hath had
By day, by night, waking, and in my dreams,
In courtly company, or at my beads,
With you, mine alderliefest sovereign, 28
Makes me the bolder to salute my king
With ruder terms, such as my wit affords,
And over-joy of heart doth minister.
K. Hen. Her sight did ravish, but her grace in speech, 32
Her words y-clad with wisdom's majesty,
Makes me from wondering fall to weeping joys;
Such is the fulness of my heart's content.
Lords, with one cheerful voice welcome my love. 36
All. Long live Queen Margaret, England's happiness!
Q. Mar. We thank you all. [*Flourish.*
Suf. My Lord Protector, so it please your Grace,

Here are the articles of contracted peace 40
Between our sovereign and the French King
Charles,
For eighteen months concluded by consent.

Glo. Imprimis, *It is agreed between the
French king, Charles, and William De la Pole,
Marquess of Suffolk, ambassador for Henry
King of England, that the said Henry shall
espouse the Lady Margaret, daughter unto
Reignier King of Naples, Sicilia, and Jerusalem, and crown her Queen of England ere the
thirtieth of May next ensuing.* Item, *That
the duchy of Anjou and the county of Maine
shall be released and delivered and delivered to the king her
father.—* [*Lets the paper fall.*

K. Hen. Uncle, how now!

Glo. Pardon me, gracious lord;
Some sudden qualm hath struck me at the heart
And dimm'd mine eyes, that I can read no
further. 56

K. Hen. Uncle of Winchester, I pray, read on.

Car. Item, *It is further agreed between
them, that the duchies of Anjou and Maine
shall be released and delivered over to the king
her father; and she sent over of the King of
England's own proper cost and charges, without having any dowry.*

K. Hen. They please us well. Lord mar-
quess, kneel down: 64
We here create thee the first Duke of Suffolk,
And girt thee with the sword. Cousin of York,
We here discharge your Grace from being
regent
I' the parts of France, till term of eighteen
months 68
Be full expir'd. Thanks, uncle Winchester,
Gloucester, York, Buckingham, Somerset,
Salisbury, and Warwick;
We thank you all for this great favour done, 72
In entertainment to my princely queen.
Come, let us in, and with all speed provide
To see her coronation be perform'd.

[*Exeunt* KING, QUEEN, *and* SUFFOLK.

Glo. Brave peers of England, pillars of the
state, 76
To you Duke Humphrey must unload his grief,
Your grief, the common grief of all the land.
What! did my brother Henry spend his youth,
His valour, coin, and people, in the wars? 80
Did he so often lodge in open field,
In winter's cold, and summer's parching heat,
To conquer France, his true inheritance?
And did my brother Bedford toil his wits, 84
To keep by policy what Henry got?
Have you yourselves, Somerset, Buckingham,
Brave York, Salisbury, and victorious Warwick,
Receiv'd deep scars in France and Normandy?
Or hath mine uncle Beaufort and myself, 89
With all the learned council of the realm,
Studied so long, sat in the council-house
Early and late, debating to and fro 92
How France and Frenchmen might be kept in
awe?
And hath his highness in his infancy
Been crown'd in Paris, in despite of foes?
And shall these labours and these honours die?

Shall Henry's conquest, Bedford's vigilance,
Your deeds of war and all our counsel die?
O peers of England! shameful is this league,
Fatal this marriage, cancelling your fame, 100
Blotting your names from books of memory,
Razing the characters of your renown,
Defacing monuments of conquer'd France,
Undoing all, as all had never been. 104

Car. Nephew, what means this passionat
discourse,
This peroration with such circumstance?
For France, 'tis ours; and we will keep it stil

Glo. Ay, uncle; we will keep it, if we can;
But now it is impossible we should. 108
Suffolk, the new-made duke that rules the roas
Hath given the duchies of Anjou and Maine
Unto the poor King Reignier, whose large styl
Agrees not with the leanness of his purse. 112

Sal. Now, by the death of him who died fo
all,
These counties were the keys of Normandy.
But wherefore weeps Warwick, my valiant son

War. For grief that they are past recovery
For, were there hope to conquer them again,
My sword should shed hot blood, mine eye
no tears. 118
Anjou and Maine! myself did win them both
Those provinces these arms of mine did conquer
And are the cities, that I got with wounds,
Deliver'd up again with peaceful words?
Mort Dieu! 122

York. For Suffolk's duke, may he be suffo
cate,
That dims the honour of this war-like isle!
France should have torn and rent my very hear
Before I would have yielded to this league. 126
I never read but England's kings have had
Large sums of gold and dowries with their wives
And our King Henry gives away his own,
To match with her that brings no vantages. 130

Glo. A proper jest, and never heard before
That Suffolk should demand a whole fifteent
For costs and charges in transporting her!
She should have stay'd in France, and starv'
in France, 134
Before—

Car. My Lord of Gloucester, now you gro
too hot:
It was the pleasure of my lord the king.

Glo. My Lord of Winchester, I know you
mind: 140
'Tis not my speeches that you do mislike,
But 'tis my presence that doth trouble ye.
Rancour will out: proud prelate, in thy face
I see thy fury. If I longer stay 144
We shall begin our ancient bickerings.
Lordings, farewell; and say, when I am gone
I prophesied France will be lost ere long. [*Exi.*

Car. So, there goes our protector in a rage
'Tis known to you he is mine enemy, 14
Nay, more, an enemy unto you all,
And no great friend, I fear me, to the king.
Consider lords, he is the next of blood, 15
And heir apparent to the English crown:
Had Henry got an empire by his marriage,
And all the wealthy kingdoms of the west,

here's reason he should be displeas'd at it.
.ook to it, lords; let not his smoothing words
ewitch your hearts; be wise and circumspect.
Vhat though the common people favour him,
Calling him, 'Humphrey, the good Duke of
  Gloucester;'   160
Clapping their hands, and crying with loud voice,
Jesu maintain your royal excellence!'
Vith 'God preserve the good Duke Humphrey!'
fear me, lords, for all this flattering gloss, 164
Ie will be found a dangerous protector.
  Buck. Why should he then protect our
  sovereign,
Ie being of age to govern of himself?
Cousin of Somerset, join you with me, 168
And all together, with the Duke of Suffolk,
Ve'll quickly hoise Duke Humphrey from his
  seat.
  Car. This weighty business will not brook
  delay;
'll to the Duke of Suffolk presently. [*Exit.*
  Som. Cousin of Buckingham, though Hum-
  phrey's pride 173
And greatness of his place be grief to us,
Yet let us watch the haughty cardinal:
His insolence is more intolerable 176
Than all the princes in the land beside:
f Gloucester be displac'd, he'll be protector.
  Buck. Or thou, or I, Somerset, will be pro-
  tector,
Despite Duke Humphrey or the cardinal. 180
      [*Exeunt* BUCKINGHAM *and* SOMERSET.
  Sal. Pride went before, ambition follows
  him.
While these do labour for their own preferment,
Behoves it us to labour for the realm.
never saw but Humphrey, Duke of Gloucester,
Did bear him like a noble gentleman. 185
Oft have I seen the haughty cardinal
More like a soldier than a man o' the church,
As stout and proud as he were lord of all, 188
Swear like a ruffian and demean himself
Unlike the ruler of a commonweal.
Varwick, my son, the comfort of my age,
Thy deeds, thy plainness, and thy house-
  keeping, 192
Have won the greatest favour of the commons,
Excepting none but good Duke Humphrey:
And, brother York, thy acts in Ireland,
n bringing them to civil discipline, 196
Thy late exploits done in the heart of France,
When thou wert regent for our sovereign,
Have made thee fear'd and honour'd of the
  people.
Join we together for the public good, 200
n what we can to bridle and suppress
The pride of Suffolk and the cardinal,
With Somerset's and Buckingham's ambition;
And, as we may, cherish Duke Humphrey's
  deeds, 204
While they do tend the profit of the land.
  War. So God help Warwick, as he loves the
  land,
And common profit of his country!
  York. [*Aside.*] And so says York, for he hath
  greatest cause. 208

  Sal. Then let's make haste away, and look
  unto the main.
  War. Unto the main! O father, Maine is lost!
That Maine which by main force Warwick did
  win,
And would have kept so long as breath did last:
Main chance, father, you meant; but I meant
  Maine, 213
Which I will win from France, or else be slain.
      [*Exeunt* WARWICK *and* SALISBURY.
  York. Anjou and Maine are given to the
  French;
Paris is lost; the state of Normandy 216
Stands on a tickle point now they are gone.
Suffolk concluded on the articles,
The peers agreed, and Henry was well pleas'd
To change two dukedoms for a duke's fair
  daughter. 220
I cannot blame them all: what is't to them?
'Tis thine they give away, and not their own.
Pirates may make cheap pennyworths of their
  pillage,
And purchase friends, and give to courtezans,
Still revelling like lords till all be gone; 225
While as the silly owner of the goods
Weeps over them, and wrings his hapless hands,
And shakes his head, and trembling stands
  aloof,
While all is shar'd and all is borne away, 229
Ready to starve and dare not touch his own:
So York must sit and fret and bite his tongue
While his own lands are bargain'd for and sold.
Methinks the realms of England, France, and
  Ireland 233
Bear that proportion to my flesh and blood
As did the fatal brand Althæa burn'd
Unto the prince's heart of Calydon. 236
Anjou and Maine both given unto the French!
Cold news for me, for I had hope of France,
Even as I have of fertile England's soil.
A day will come when York shall claim his own;
And therefore I will take the Nevils' parts 241
And make a show of love to proud Duke Hum-
  phrey,
And, when I spy advantage, claim the crown,
For that's the golden mark I seek to hit. 244
Nor shall proud Lancaster usurp my right,
Nor hold the sceptre in his childish fist,
Nor wear the diadem upon his head,
Whose church-like humours fit not for a crown.
Then, York, be still awhile, till time do serve:
Watch thou and wake when others be asleep,
To pry into the secrets of the state;
Till Henry, surfeiting in joys of love, 252
With his new bride and England's dear-bought
  queen,
And Humphrey with the peers be fall'n at jars:
Then will I raise aloft the milk-white rose,
With whose sweet smell the air shall be per-
  fum'd, 256
And in my standard bear the arms of York,
To grapple with the house of Lancaster;
And, force perforce, I'll make him yield the
  crown,
Whose bookish rule hath pull'd fair England
  down. [*Exit.*

SCENE II.—*The Same. A Room in the* DUKE
    OF GLOUCESTER'S *House.*

Enter GLOUCESTER *and his* DUCHESS.

Duch. Why droops my lord, like over-ripen'd
    corn
Hanging the head at Ceres' plenteous load?
Why doth the great Duke Humphrey knit his
    brows,
As frowning at the favours of the world?   4
Why are thine eyes fix'd to the sullen earth,
Gazing on that which seems to dim thy sight?
What seest thou there? King Henry's diadem
Enchas'd with all the honours of the world? 8
If so, gaze on, and grovel on thy face,
Until thy head be circled with the same.
Put forth thy hand, reach at the glorious gold:
What! is 't too short? I'll lengthen it with
    mine;   12
And having both together heav'd it up,
We'll both together lift our heads to heaven,
And never more abase our sight so low
As to vouchsafe one glance unto the ground.
    Glo. O Nell, sweet Nell, if thou dost love thy
    lord,   17
Banish the canker of ambitious thoughts:
And may that thought, when I imagine ill
Against my king and nephew, virtuous Henry,
Be my last breathing in this mortal world! 21
My troublous dream this night doth make me
    sad.
    Duch. What dream'd my lord? tell me, and
    I'll requite it
With sweet rehearsal of my morning's dream.
    Glo. Methought this staff, mine office-badge
    in court,
Was broke in twain; by whom I have forgot,
But, as I think, it was by the cardinal;
And on the pieces of the broken wand   28
Were plac'd the heads of Edmund Duke of
    Somerset,
And William De la Pole, first Duke of Suffolk.
This was my dream: what it doth bode, God
    knows.
    Duch. Tut! this was nothing but an argu-
    ment   32
That he that breaks a stick of Gloucester's grove
Shall lose his head for his presumption.
But list to me, my Humphrey, my sweet duke:
Methought I sat in seat of majesty   36
In the cathedral church of Westminster,
And in that chair where kings and queens are
    crown'd;
Where Henry and Dame Margaret kneel'd to
    me,
And on my head did set the diadem.   40
    Glo. Nay, Eleanor, then must I chide out-
    right:
Presumptuous dame! ill-nurtur'd Eleanor!
Art thou not second woman in the realm,
And the protector's wife, belov'd of him?   44
Hast thou not worldly pleasure at command,
Above the reach or compass of thy thought?
And wilt thou still be hammering treachery,
To tumble down thy husband and thyself   48
From top of honour to disgrace's feet?

Away from me, and let me hear no more.
    Duch. What, what, my lord! are you so
    choleric
With Eleanor, for telling but her dream?   52
Next time I'll keep my dreams unto myself,
And not be check'd.
    Glo. Nay, be not angry; I am pleas'd again.

Enter a Messenger.

    Mess. My Lord Protector, 'tis his highness'
    pleasure   56
You do prepare to ride unto Saint Alban's,
Whereas the king and queen do mean to hawk.
    Glo. I go. Come, Nell, thou wilt ride with us?
    Duch. Yes, my good lord, I'll follow pre-
    sently.   60
           [*Exeunt* GLOUCESTER *and* Messenger.
Follow I must; I cannot go before,
While Gloucester bears this base and humble
    mind.
Were I a man, a duke, and next of blood,
I would remove these tedious stumbling-blocks
And smooth my way upon their headless necks
And, being a woman, I will not be slack
To play my part in Fortune's pageant.
Where are you there? Sir John! nay, fear not,
    man,   68
We are alone; here's none but thee and I.

Enter HUME.

    Hume. Jesus preserve your royal majesty!
    Duch. What sayst thou? majesty! I am but
    Grace.
    Hume. But, by the grace of God, and Hume's
    advice,   72
Your Grace's title shall be multiplied.
    Duch. What sayst thou, man? hast thou as
    yet conferr'd
With Margery Jourdain, the cunning witch,
With Roger Bolingbroke, the conjurer?   76
And will they undertake to do me good?
    Hume. This they have promised, to show
    your highness
A spirit rais'd from depth of under ground,
That shall make answer to such questions   80
As by your Grace shall be propounded him.
    Duch. It is enough: I'll think upon the
    questions.
When from Saint Alban's we do make return
We'll see these things effected to the full.   84
Here, Hume, take this reward; make merry,
    man,
With thy confed'rates in this weighty cause.
                      [*Exit.*
    Hume. Hume must make merry with the
    duchess' gold;
Marry and shall. But how now, Sir John
    Hume!
Seal up your lips, and give no words but mum:
The business asketh silent secrecy.
Dame Eleanor gives gold to bring the witch:
Gold cannot come amiss, were she a devil.   92
Yet have I gold flies from another coast:
I dare not say from the rich cardinal
And from the great and new-made Duke of
    Suffolk;

I do find it so: for, to be plain,   96
ey, knowing Dame Eleanor's aspiring humour,
ve hired me to undermine the duchess
d buzz these conjurations in her brain.
ey say, 'A crafty knave does need no broker;'
am I Suffolk and the cardinal's broker.
me, if you take not heed, you shall go near
call them both a pair of crafty knaves.
ll, so it stands; and thus, I fear, at last   104
me's knavery will be the duchess' wrack,
d her attainture will be Humphrey's fall.
t how it will I shall have gold for all. [Exit.

SCENE III.—*The Same. A Room in the
Palace.*

er three or four Petitioners, PETER, *the Armourer's man, being one.*

irst Pet. My masters, let's stand close: my
d Protector will come this way by and by,
then we may deliver our supplications in
quill.   4
ec. Pet. Marry, the Lord protect him, for
s a good man! Jesu bless him!

Enter SUFFOLK *and* QUEEN MARGARET.

irst Pet. Here a' comes, methinks, and the
en with him. I'll be the first, sure.   8
ec. Pet. Come back, fool! this is the Duke
Suffolk and not my Lord Protector.
uf. How now, fellow! wouldst anything
ith me?   12
irst Pet. I pray, my lord, pardon me: I took
or my Lord Protector.
. Mar. [*Glancing at the Superscriptions.*]
my Lord Protector! are your supplications
is lordship? Let me see them: what is thine?
irst Pet. Mine is, an't please your Grace,
inst John Goodman, my Lord Cardinal's
n, for keeping my house, and lands, my wife
all, from me.   21
uf. Thy wife too! that is some wrong indeed.
at's yours? What's here? *Against the
e of Suffolk, for enclosing the commons of
ford!* How now, sir knave!   25
ec. Pet. Alas! sir, I am but a poor peti-
er of our whole township.
eter. [*Presenting his petition.*] Against my
ster, Thomas Horner, for saying that the
e of York was rightful heir to the crown.
. Mar. What sayst thou? Did the Duke of
k say he was rightful heir to the crown? 32
eter. That my master was? No, forsooth:
master said that he was; and that the king
an usurper.
uf. Who is there?   36

Enter Servants.

e this fellow in, and send for his master
a pursuivant presently. We'll hear more
our matter before the king.
[*Exeunt* Servants *with* PETER.
. Mar. And as for you, that love to be pro-
ected   40
er the wings of our protector's grace,

Begin your suits anew and sue to him.
                    [*Tears the petitions.*
Away, base cullions! Suffolk, let them go.
   All. Come, let's be gone.   44
                    [*Exeunt* Petitioners.
   Q. Mar. My Lord of Suffolk, say, is this the
      guise,
Is this the fashion of the court of England?
Is this the government of Britain's isle,
And this the royalty of Albion's king?   48
What! shall King Henry be a pupil still
Under the surly Gloucester's governance?
Am I a queen in title and in style,
And must be made a subject to a duke?   52
I tell thee, Pole, when in the city Tours
Thou ran'st a tilt in honour of my love,
And stol'st away the ladies' hearts of France,
I thought King Henry had resembled thee 56
In courage, courtship, and proportion:
But all his mind is bent to holiness,
To number Ave-Maries on his beads;
His champions are the prophets and apostles;
His weapons holy saws of sacred writ;   61
His study is his tilt-yard, and his loves
Are brazen images of canoniz'd saints.
I would the college of the cardinals   64
Would choose him pope, and carry him to
   Rome,
And set the triple crown upon his head:
That were a state fit for his holiness.
   Suf. Madam, be patient; as I was cause 68
Your highness came to England, so will I
In England work your Grace's full content.
   Q. Mar. Beside the haught protector, have
      we Beaufort
The imperious churchman, Somerset, Bucking-
      ham,   72
And grumbling York; and not the least of these
But can do more in England than the king.
   Suf. And he of these that can do most of all
Cannot do more in England than the Nevils: 76
Salisbury and Warwick are no simple peers.
   Q. Mar. Not all these lords do vex me half
      so much
As that proud dame, the Lord Protector's wife:
She sweeps it through the court with troops of
      ladies,   80
More like an empress than Duke Humphrey's
      wife.
Strangers in court do take her for the queen:
She bears a duke's revenues on her back,
And in her heart she scorns our poverty.   84
Shall I not live to be aveng'd on her?
Contemptuous base-born callot as she is,
She vaunted 'mongst her minions t'other day
The very train of her worst wearing gown 88
Was better worth than all my father's lands,
Till Suffolk gave two dukedoms for his daughter.
   Suf. Madam, myself have lim'd a bush for
      her,
And plac'd a quire of such enticing birds 92
That she will light to listen to the lays,
And never mount to trouble you again.
So, let her rest: and, madam, list to me;
For I am bold to counsel you in this.   96
Although we fancy not the cardinal,

Yet must we join with him and with the lords
Till we have brought Duke Humphrey in dis-
grace.   99
As for the Duke of York, this late complaint
Will make but little for his benefit:
So, one by one, we'll weed them all at last,
And you yourself shall steer the happy helm.

Sound a sennet. Enter KING HENRY, YORK, *and*
SOMERSET; DUKE *and* DUCHESS OF GLOUCESTER,
CARDINAL BEAUFORT, BUCKINGHAM, SALIS-
BURY, *and* WARWICK.

K. Hen. For my part, noble lords, I care not
which;   104
Or Somerset or York, all's one to me.
York. If York have ill demean'd himself in
France,
Then let him be denay'd the regentship.
Som. If Somerset be unworthy of the place,
Let York be regent; I will yield to him.   109
War. Whether your Grace be worthy, yea or
no,
Dispute not that: York is the worthier.
Car. Ambitious Warwick, let thy betters
speak.   112
War. The cardinal's not my better in the
field.
Buck. All in this presence are thy betters,
Warwick.
War. Warwick may live to be the best of
all.
Sal. Peace, son! and show some reason,
Buckingham,   116
Why Somerset should be preferr'd in this.
Q. Mar. Because the king, forsooth, will
have it so.
Glo. Madam, the king is old enough himself
To give his censure: these are no women's
matters.   120
Q. Mar. If he be old enough, what needs
your Grace
To be protector of his excellence?
Glo. Madam, I am protector of the realm;
And at his pleasure will resign my place.   124
Suf. Resign it then and leave thine insolence.
Since thou wert king,—as who is king but
thou?—
The commonwealth hath daily run to wrack;
The Dauphin hath prevail'd beyond the seas;
And all the peers and nobles of the realm .129
Have been as bondmen to thy sovereignty.
Car. The commons hast thou rack'd; the
clergy's bags
Are lank and lean with thy extortions.   132
Som. Thy sumptuous buildings and thy
wife's attire
Have cost a mass of public treasury.
Buck. Thy cruelty in execution
Upon offenders hath exceeded law,   136
And left thee to the mercy of the law.
Q. Mar. Thy sale of offices and towns in
France,
If they were known, as the suspect is great,
Would make thee quickly hop without thy head.
[Exit GLOUCESTER. *The* QUEEN *drops
her fan.*

Give me my fan: what, minion! can ye not?
[*Giving the* DUCHESS *a box on the ear*
I cry you mercy, madam, was it you?
Duch. Was't I? yea, I it was, proud French
woman:
Could I come near your beauty with my nail
I'd set my ten commandments in your face. 14
K. Hen. Sweet aunt, be quiet; 'twas against
her will.
Duch. Against her will! Good king, look
to't in time;
She'll hamper thee and dandle thee like a
baby:
Though in this place most master wear no
breeches,   14
She shall not strike Dame Eleanor unreveng'd
[*Exit*
Buck. Lord Cardinal, I will follow Eleanor
And listen after Humphrey, how he proceeds
She's tickled now; her fume can need no spur
She'll gallop far enough to her destruction.
[*Exit* BUCKINGHAM

Re-enter GLOUCESTER.

Glo. Now, lords, my choler being over-blown
With walking once about the quadrangle,   15
I come to talk of commonwealth affairs.
As for your spiteful false objections,
Prove them, and I lie open to the law:
But God in mercy so deal with my soul   16
As I in duty love my king and country!
But to the matter that we have in hand.
I say, my sov'reign, York is meetest man
To be your regent in the realm of France.   16
Suf. Before we make election, give me leave
To show some reason, of no little force,
That York is most unmeet of any man.
York. I'll tell thee, Suffolk, why I am un-
meet: 16
First, for I cannot flatter thee in pride;
Next, if I be appointed for the place,
My Lord of Somerset will keep me here,
Without discharge, money, or furniture,   1
Till France be won into the Dauphin's hand
Last time I danc'd attendance on his will
Till Paris was besieg'd, famish'd, and lost.
War. That can I witness; and a fouler fact
Did never traitor in the land commit.   1
Suf. Peace, headstrong Warwick!
War. Image of pride, why should I hold my
peace?

Enter Servants *of* SUFFOLK, *bringing in*
HORNER *and* PETER.

Suf. Because here is a man accus'd of trea-
son:
Pray God the Duke of York excuse himself!
York. Doth any one accuse York for a traitor
K. Hen. What mean'st thou, Suffolk? tell
me, what are these?
Suf. Please it your majesty, this is the man
That doth accuse his master of high treason.
His words were these: that Richard, Duke of
York,
Was rightful heir unto the English crown,
And that your majesty was an usurper.

K. Hen. Say, man, were these thy words?

Hor. An't shall please your majesty, I never id nor thought any such matter: God is my itness, I am falsely accused by the villain. 192

Pet. By these ten bones, my lords, he did eak them to me in the garret one night, as e were scouring my Lord of York's armour.

York. Base dunghill villain, and mechanical, ll have thy head for this thy traitor's speech. do beseech your royal majesty 198 et him have all the rigour of the law.

Hor. Alas! my lord, hang me if ever I spake e words. My accuser is my prentice; and hen I did correct him for his fault the other ay, he did vow upon his knees he would be even ith me: I have good witness of this: therefore beseech your majesty, do not cast away an onest man for a villain's accusation.

K. Hen. Uncle, what shall we say to this in law? 207

Glo. This doom, my lord, if I may judge. et Somerset be regent o'er the French, ecause in York this breeds suspicion; nd let these have a day appointed them or single combat in convenient place; 212 or he hath witness of his servant's malice. his is the law, and this Duke Humphrey's doom.

K. Hen. Then be it so. My Lord of Somerset, Ve make your Grace lord regent o'er the French. 216

Som. I humbly thank your royal majesty.

Hor. And I accept the combat willingly.

Pet. Alas! my lord, I cannot fight: for God's ake, pity my case! the spite of man prevaileth gainst me. O Lord, have mercy upon me! I nall never be able to fight a blow. O Lord, my eart!

Glo. Sirrah, or you must fight, or else be hang'd. 224

K. Hen. Away with them to prison; and the day f combat shall be the last of the next month. ome, Somerset, we'll see thee sent away.
[*Exeunt.*

SCENE IV.—*The Same. The* DUKE OF GLOUCESTER'S *Garden.*

nter MARGERY JOURDAIN, HUME, SOUTHWELL, *and* BOLINGBROKE.

Hume. Come, my masters; the duchess, I ll you, expects performance of your promises.

Boling. Master Hume, we are therefore proided. Will her ladyship behold and hear our xorcisms? 5

Hume. Ay; what else? fear you not her ourage.

Boling. I have heard her reported to be a oman of invincible spirit: but it shall be conenient, Master Hume, that you be by her aloft vhile we be busy below; and so, I pray you, o in God's name, and leave us. [*Exit* HUME.] 1other Jourdain, be you prostrate, and grovel n the earth; John Southwell, read you; and t us to our work.

Enter DUCHESS *aloft,* HUME *following.*

Duch. Well said, my masters, and welcome all. 16
To this gear the sooner the better.

Boling. Patience, good lady; wizards know their times:
Deep night, dark night, the silent of the night,
The time of night when Troy was set on fire; 20
The time when screech-owls cry, and ban-dogs howl,
And spirits walk, and ghosts break up their graves,
That time best fits the work we have in hand.
Madam, sit you, and fear not: whom we raise
We will make fast within a hallow'd verge. 25
[*Here they perform the ceremonies belonging, and make the circle;* BOLINGBROKE, *or* SOUTHWELL *reads,* Conjuro te, *&c. It thunders and lightens terribly; then the Spirit* riseth.

Spir. Adsum.

M. Jourd. Asmath!
By the eternal God, whose name and power 28
Thou tremblest at, answer that I shall ask;
For till thou speak, thou shalt not pass from hence.

Spir. Ask what thou wilt. That I had said and done!

Boling. First, of the king: what shall of him become? 32

Spir. The Duke yet lives that Henry shall depose;
But him outlive, and die a violent death.
[*As the* Spirit *speaks,* SOUTHWELL *writes the answers.*

Boling. What fate awaits the Duke of Suffolk?

Spir. By water shall he die and take his end.

Boling. What shall befall the Duke of Somerset? 37

Spir. Let him shun castles:
Safer shall he be upon the sandy plains
Than where castles mounted stand. 40
Have done, for more I hardly can endure.

Boling. Descend to darkness and the burning lake!
False fiend, avoid!
[*Thunder and lightning.* Spirit *descends.*

Enter YORK *and* BUCKINGHAM, *hastily, with their Guards, and Others.*

York. Lay hands upon these traitors and their trash. 44
Beldam, I think we watch'd you at an inch.
What! madam, are you there? the king and commonweal
Are deeply indebted for this piece of pains:
My Lord Protector will, I doubt it not, 48
See you well guerdon'd for these good deserts.

Duch. Not half so bad as thine to England's king,
Injurious duke, that threat'st where is no cause.

Buck. True, madam, none at all. What call you this? [*Showing her the papers.*
Away with them! let them be clapp'd up close

And kept asunder. You, madam, shall with us:
Stafford, take her to thee.—   55

    [*Exeunt above*, DUCHESS *and* HUME
                 guarded.

We'll see your trinkets here all forthcoming.
All, away!

    [*Exeunt* SOUTHWELL, BOLINGBROKE, &c.,
                 guarded.

    York. Lord Buckingham, methinks you
     watch'd her well:
A pretty plot, well chosen to build upon!
Now, pray, my lord, let's see the devil's writ.
What have we here?   61
The duke yet lives that Henry shall depose;
But him outlive, and die a violent death.
Why, this is just,   64
Aio te, Æacida, Romanos vincere posse.
Well, to the rest:
Tell me what fate awaits the Duke of Suffolk?
By water shall he die and take his end.   68
What shall betide the Duke of Somerset?
Let him shun castles;
Safer shall he be upon the sandy plains
Than where castles mounted stand.   72
Come, come, my lords; these oracles
Are hardly attain'd, and hardly understood.
The king is now in progress towards Saint
    Alban's;
With him, the husband of this lovely lady: 76
Thither go these news as fast as horse can carry
    them,
A sorry breakfast for my Lord Protector.
    Buck. Your Grace shall give me leave, my
     Lord of York,
To be the post, in hope of his reward.   80
    York. At your pleasure, my good lord.
Who's within there, ho!

        Enter a Serving-man.

Invite my Lords of Salisbury and Warwick
To sup with me to-morrow night. Away!

        [*Flourish. Exeunt.*

ACT II

SCENE I.—*St. Alban's.*

Enter KING HENRY, QUEEN MARGARET, GLOUCES-
TER, CARDINAL BEAUFORT, *and* SUFFOLK, *with*
Falconers, *hollaing.*

    Q. Mar. Believe me, lords, for flying at the
     brook,
I saw not better sport these seven years' day:
Yet, by your leave, the wind was very high,
And, ten to one, old Joan had not gone out.   4
    K. Hen. But what a point, my lord, your
     falcon made,
And what a pitch she flew above the rest!
To see how God in all his creatures works!
Yea, man and birds are fain of climbing high. 8
    Suf. No marvel, an it like your majesty,
My Lord Protector's hawks do tower so well;
They know their master loves to be aloft,
And bears his thoughts above his falcon's pitch.
    Glo. My lord, 'tis but a base ignoble mind

That mounts no higher than a bird can soar.
    Car. I thought as much; he'd be above
     clouds.
    Glo. Ay, my Lord Cardinal; how think y
     by that?
Were it not good your Grace could fly to h
     ven?
    K. Hen. The treasury of everlasting joy.
    Car. Thy heaven is on earth; thine eyes a
     thoughts
Beat on a crown, the treasure of thy heart;
Pernicious protector, dangerous peer,
That smooth'st it so with king and comm
     weal!
    Glo. What! cardinal, is your priestho
     grown peremptory?
Tantæne animis cælestibus iræ?
Churchmen so hot? good uncle, hide su
     malice;
With such holiness can you do it?
    Suf. No malice, sir; no more than well b
     comes
So good a quarrel and so bad a peer.
    Glo. As who, my lord?
    Suf.   Why, as you, my lo
An't like your lordly lord-protectorship.
    Glo. Why, Suffolk, England knows thi
     insolence.
    Q. Mar. And thy ambition, Gloucester.
    K. Hen.   I prithee, peace,
Good queen, and whet not on these furio
     peers;
For blessed are the peacemakers on earth.
    Car. Let me be blessed for the peace I ma
Against this proud protector with my sword!
    Glo. [*Aside to the* CARDINAL.] Faith, ho
     uncle, would 'twere come to that!
    Car. [*Aside to* GLOUCESTER.] Marry, wh
     thou dar'st.
    Glo. [*Aside to the* CARDINAL.] Make up
     factious numbers for the matter;
In thine own person answer thy abuse.
    Car. [*Aside to* GLOUCESTER.] Ay, where th
     dar'st not peep: an if thou dar'st,
This evening on the east side of the grove.
    K. Hen. How now, my lords!
    Car.   Believe me, cousin Glouceste
Had not your man put up the fowl so sudden
We had had more sport. [*Aside to* GLOUCE
     TER.] Come with thy two-hand sword.
    Glo. True, uncle.
    Car. Are you advis'd? [*Aside to* GLOUCE
     TER] the east side of the grove.
    Glo. [*Aside to the* CARDINAL.] Cardinal,
     am with you.
    K. Hen. Why, how now, uncle Gloucester
    Glo. Talking of hawking; nothing else, m
     lord.—
[*Aside to the* CARDINAL.] Now, by God's mothe
     priest, I'll shave your crown
For this, or all my fence shall fail.
    Car. [*Aside to* GLOUCESTER.] *Medice teipsu*
Protector, see to't well, protect yourself.
    K. Hen. The winds grow high; so do you
     stomachs, lords.
How irksome is this music to my heart!   5

n such strings jar, what hope of harmony?
y, my lords, let me compound this strife.

Enter One, crying, 'A Miracle.'

). What means this noise?
w, what miracle dost thou proclaim?   60
ie. A miracle! a miracle!
f. Come to the king, and tell him what
iracle.
ie. Forsooth, a blind man at Saint Alban's
rine,
in this half hour hath receiv'd his sight;
an that ne'er saw in his life before.   65
Hen. Now, God be prais'd, that to be-
eving souls
s light in darkness, comfort in despair!

r the Mayor of Saint Alban's, *and his*
ethren, and SIMPCOX, *borne between two*
rsons in a chair; his Wife and a great multi-
de following.

ir. Here comes the townsmen on procession,
resent your highness with the man.   69
Hen. Great is his comfort in this earthly
ale,
ough by his sight his sin be multiplied.
o. Stand by, my masters; bring him near
he king: 72
highness' pleasure is to talk with him.
Hen. Good fellow, tell us here the circumstance,
t we for thee may glorify the Lord.
it! hast thou been long blind, and now
estor'd?   76
imp. Born blind, an't please your Grace.
ife. Ay, indeed, was he.
if. What woman is this?
ife. His wife, an't like your worship.   80
o. Hadst thou been his mother, thou
ouldst have better told.
Hen. Where wert thou born?
imp. At Berwick in the north, an't like
our Grace.
Hen. Poor soul! God's goodness hath
een great to thee: 84
never day nor night unhallow'd pass,
still remember what the Lord hath done.
Mar. Tell me, good fellow, cam'st thou
here by chance,
of devotion, to this holy shrine?   88
imp. God knows, of pure devotion; being
call'd
undred times and oft'ner in my sleep,
ood Saint Alban; who said, 'Simpcox, come;
ie, offer at my shrine, and I will help thee.'
ife. Most true, forsooth; and many time
and oft   93
self have heard a voice to call him so.
ar. What! art thou lame?
imp.   Ay, God Almighty help me!
uf. How cam'st thou so?
imp.   A fall off of a tree.   96
ife. A plum-tree, master.
lo.   How long hast thou been blind?
imp. O! born so, master.
lo.   What! and wouldst climb a tree?

Simp. But that in all my life, when I was a
youth.
Wife. Too true; and bought his climbing very
dear.   100
Glo. Mass, thou lov'dst plums well, that
wouldst venture so.
Simp. Alas! master, my wife desir'd some
damsons,
And made me climb with danger of my life.
Glo. A subtle knave! but yet it shall not
serve.   104
Let me see thine eyes: wink now: now open
them:
In my opinion yet thou seest not well.
Simp. Yes, master, clear as day; I thank
God and Saint Alban.
Glo. Sayst thou me so? What colour is this
cloak of?   108
Simp. Red, master; red as blood.
Glo. Why, that's well said. What colour is
my gown of?
Simp. Black, forsooth; coal-black, as jet.
K. Hen. Why then, thou know'st what colour
jet is of?   112
Suf. And yet, I think, jet did he never see.
Glo. But cloaks and gowns before this day a
many.
Wife. Never, before this day, in all his life.
Glo. Tell me, sirrah, what's my name?   116
Simp. Alas! master, I know not.
Glo. What's his name?
Simp. I know not.
Glo. Nor his?   120
Simp. No, indeed, master.
Glo. What's thine own name?
Simp. Saunder Simpcox, an if it please you,
master.
Glo. Then, Saunder, sit there, the lyingest
knave in Christendom. If thou hadst been born
blind, thou mightst as well have known all our
names as thus to name the several colours we do
wear. Sight may distinguish of colours, but
suddenly to nominate them all, it is impossible.
My lords, Saint Alban here hath done a miracle;
and would ye not think that cunning to be great,
that could restore this cripple to his legs again?
Simp. O, master, that you could!   133
Glo. My masters of Saint Alban's, have you
not beadles in your town, and things called
whips?   136
May. Yes, my lord, if it please your Grace.
Glo. Then send for one presently.
May. Sirrah, go fetch the beadle hither
straight.   [*Exit an* Attendant.
Glo. Now fetch me a stool hither by and by.
[*A stool brought out.*] Now, sirrah, if you mean
to save yourself from whipping, leap me over
this stool and run away.   144
Simp. Alas! master, I am not able to stand
alone:
You go about to torture me in vain.

Re-enter Attendant, *and a* Beadle *with a whip.*

Glo. Well, sir, we must have you find your
legs. Sirrah beadle, whip him till he leap over
that same stool.   149

Bead. I will, my lord. Come on, sirrah; off with your doublet quickly.

Simp. Alas! master, what shall I do? I am not able to stand.   153

[*After the* Beadle *hath hit him once, he leaps over the stool, and runs away: and the people follow and cry,* 'A miracle!']

K. Hen. O God! seest thou this, and bear'st so long?

Q. Mar. It made me laugh to see the villain run.

Glo. Follow the knave; and take this drab away.   156

Wife. Alas! sir, we did it for pure need.

Glo. Let them be whipp'd through every market town

Till they come to Berwick, from whence they came.   [*Exeunt* Mayor, Beadle, Wife, &c.

Car. Duke Humphrey has done a miracle to-day.   160

Suf. True; made the lame to leap and fly away.

Glo. But you have done more miracles than I; You made in a day, my lord, whole towns to fly.

Enter BUCKINGHAM.

K. Hen. What tidings with our cousin Buckingham?   164

Buck. Such as my heart doth tremble to unfold.

A sort of naughty persons, lewdly bent,
Under the countenance and confederacy
Of Lady Eleanor, the protector's wife,   168
The ringleader and head of all this rout,
Have practis'd dangerously against your state,
Dealing with witches and with conjurers:
Whom we have apprehended in the fact;   172
Raising up wicked spirits from under-ground,
Demanding of King Henry's life and death,
And other of your highness' privy council,
As more at large your Grace shall understand.

Car. And so, my Lord Protector, by this means   177

Your lady is forthcoming yet at London.
This news, I think, hath turn'd your weapon's edge;

'Tis like, my lord, you will not keep your hour.

Glo. Ambitious churchman, leave to afflict my heart: 181

Sorrow and grief have vanquish'd all my powers;
And, vanquish'd as I am, I yield to thee,
Or to the meanest groom.   184

K. Hen. O God! what mischiefs work the wicked ones,

Heaping confusion on their own heads thereby.

Q. Mar. Gloucester, see here the tainture of thy nest;

And look thyself be faultless, thou wert best.

Glo. Madam, for myself, to heaven I do appeal,
How I have lov'd my king and commonweal;
And, for my wife, I know not how it stands.
Sorry I am to hear what I have heard: 192
Noble she is, but if she have forgot
Honour and virtue, and convers'd with such
As, like to pitch, defile nobility,

I banish her my bed and company,   1
And give her, as a prey, to law and shame,
That hath dishonour'd Gloucester's hone name.

K. Hen. Well, for this night we will repo us here:

To-morrow toward London back again,   2
To look into this business thoroughly,
And call these foul offenders to their answer
And poise the cause in justice' equal scales,
Whose beam stands sure, whose rightful cau prevails.   [*Flourish. Exeu*

SCENE II.—*London. The* DUKE OF YORK'S *Garden.*

Enter YORK, SALISBURY, *and* WARWICK.

York. Now, my good Lords of Salisbury a Warwick,

Our simple supper ended, give me leave,
In this close walk to satisfy myself,
In craving your opinion of my title,
Which is infallible to England's crown.

Sal. My lord, I long to hear it at full.

War. Sweet York, begin; and if thy claim good,

The Nevils are thy subjects to command.

York. Then thus:

Edward the Third, my lords, had seven son
The first, Edward the Black Prince, Prince Wales;

The second, William of Hatfield; and the thi
Lionel, Duke of Clarence; next to whom
Was John of Gaunt, the Duke of Lancaster
The fifth was Edmund Langley, Duke of Yo
The sixth was Thomas of Woodstock, Duke Gloucester;

William of Windsor was the seventh and la
Edward the Black Prince died before his fath
And left behind him Richard, his only son
Who after Edward the Third's death, reig as king;

Till Henry Bolingbroke, Duke of Lancaster
The eldest son and heir of John of Gaunt,
Crown'd by the name of Henry the Fourth
Seiz'd on the realm, depos'd the rightful king
Sent his poor queen to France, from whence came,

And him to Pomfret; where as all you kno
Harmless Richard was murder'd traitorous

War. Father, the duke hath told the tru

Thus got the house of Lancaster the crown

York. Which now they hold by force and by right;

For Richard, the first son's heir, being dea
The issue of the next son should have reign'd

Sal. But William of Hatfield died with an heir.

York. The third son, Duke of Clarence, f whose line

I claim the crown, had issue, Philippe a daugh
Who married Edmund Mortimer, Earl March:

Edmund had issue Roger, Earl of March:
Roger had issue Edmund, Anne, and Elea

l. This Edmund, in the reign of Boling-
-roke,
have read, laid claim unto the crown;   40
but for Owen Glendower, had been king,
, kept him in captivity till he died.
to the rest.
rk.   His eldest sister, Anne,
mother, being heir unto the crown,   44
ried Richard, Earl of Cambridge, who was
on
Edmund Langley, Edward the Third's fifth
on.
er I claim the kingdom: she was heir
Roger, Earl of March; who was the son 48
Edmund Mortimer; who married Philippe,
daughter unto Lionel, Duke of Clarence;
if the issue of the eldest son
eed before the younger, I am king.   52
ar. What plain proceeding is more plain
han this?
ry doth claim the crown from John of
Gaunt,
fourth son; York claims it from the third.
Lionel's issue fails, his should not reign: 56
ils not yet, but flourishes in thee,
, in thy sons, fair slips of such a stock.
n, father Salisbury, kneel we together,
, in this private plot be we the first   60
t shall salute our rightful sovereign
h honour of his birthright to the crown.
oth. Long live our sovereign Richard, England's king!
ork. We thank you, lords! But I am not
your king   64
I be crown'd, and that my sword be stain'd
h heart-blood of the house of Lancaster;
t that's not suddenly to be perform'd,
with advice and silent secrecy.   68
you as I do in these dangerous days,
k at the Duke of Suffolk's insolence,
Beaufort's pride, at Somerset's ambition,
Buckingham and all the crew of them,   72
they have snar'd the shepherd of the flock,
t virtuous prince, the good Duke Humphrey:
that they seek; and they, in seeking that
ll find their deaths, if York can prophesy. 76
al. My lord, break we off; we know your
mind at full.
Var. My heart assures me that the Earl of
Warwick
ll one day make the Duke of York a king.
ork. And, Nevil, this I do assure myself,
hard shall live to make the Earl of Warwick
e greatest man in England but the king.
                                        [*Exeunt*.

SCENE III.—*The Same. A Hall of Justice*.

mpets sounded. Enter KING HENRY, QUEEN
MARGARET, GLOUCESTER, YORK, SUFFOLK, *and*
ALISBURY; *the* DUCHESS OF GLOUCESTER,
ARGERY JOURDAIN, SOUTHWELL, HUME, *and*
OLINGBROKE, *under guard.*

. Hen. Stand forth, Dame Eleanor Cobham, Gloucester's wife.
ight of God and us, your guilt is great:

Receive the sentence of the law for sins
Such as by God's book are adjudg'd to death.
You four, from hence to prison back again;
From thence, unto the place of execution:
The witch in Smithfield shall be burn'd to
ashes,   7
And you three shall be strangled on the gallows.
You, madam, for you are more nobly born,
Despoiled of your honour in your life,
Shall, after three days' open penance done,
Live in your country here, in banishment,   12
With Sir John Stanley, in the Isle of Man.
  Duch. Welcome is banishment; welcome
were my death.
  Glo. Eleanor, the law, thou seest, hath
judged thee: 15
I cannot justify whom the law condemns.—
          [*Exeunt the* DUCHESS, *and the other*
                              Prisoners, guarded.
Mine eyes are full of tears, my heart of grief.
Ah, Humphrey! this dishonour in thine age
Will bring thy head with sorrow to the ground.
I beseech your majesty, give me leave to go;
Sorrow would solace and mine age would ease.
  K. Hen. Stay, Humphrey, Duke of Glouces-
ter: ere thou go,
Give up thy staff: Henry will to himself
Protector be; and God shall be my hope,   24
My stay, my guide, and lantern to my feet.
And go in peace, Humphrey; no less belov'd
Than when thou wert protector to thy king.
  Q. Mar. I see no reason why a king of
years   28
Should be to be protected like a child.
God and King Henry govern England's helm!
Give up your staff, sir, and the king his realm.
  Glo. My staff! here, noble Henry, is my
staff: 32
As willingly do I the same resign
As e'er thy father Henry made it mine;
And even as willingly at thy feet I leave it
As others would ambitiously receive it.   36
Farewell, good king! when I am dead and gone,
May honourable peace attend thy throne.
                                        [*Exit*.
  Q. Mar. Why, now is Henry king, and Mar-
garet queen;
And Humphrey, Duke of Gloucester, scarce
himself,   40
That bears so shrewd a maim: two pulls at
once;
His lady banish'd, and a limb lopp'd off;
This staff of honour raught: there let it stand,
Where it best fits to be, in Henry's hand.   44
  Suf. Thus droops this lofty pine and hangs
his sprays;
Thus Eleanor's pride dies in her youngest days.
  York. Lords, let him go. Please it your
majesty
This is the day appointed for the combat;   48
And ready are the appellant and defendant,
The armourer and his man, to enter the lists,
So please your highness to behold the fight.
  Q. Mar. Ay, good my lord; for purposely
therefore   52
Left I the court, to see this quarrel tried.

K. Hen. O' God's name, see the lists and all
things fit:
Here let them end it; and God defend the right!
York. I never saw a fellow worse bested, 56
Or more afraid to fight, than is the appellant,
The servant of this armourer, my lords.

Enter, on one side, HORNER, *and his* Neighbours
*drinking to him so much that he is drunk; and
he enters bearing his staff with a sand-bag
fastened to it; a drum before him: on the other
side,* PETER, *with a drum and a sand-bag; and*
Prentices *drinking to him.*

First Neigh. Here, neighbour Horner, I drink
to you in a cup of sack: and fear not, neighbour, you shall do well enough.   61
Sec. Neigh. And here, neighbour, here's a
cup of charneco.
Third Neigh. And here's a pot of good
double beer, neighbour: drink, and fear not
your man.
Hor. Let it come, i' faith, and I'll pledge you
all; and a fig for Peter!   68
First Pren. Here, Peter, I drink to thee; and
be not afraid.
Sec. Pren. Be merry, Peter, and fear not thy
master: fight for credit of the prentices.   72
Peter. I thank you all: drink, and pray for
me, I pray you; for, I think, I have taken my
last draught in this world. Here, Robin, an if I
die, I give thee my apron: and, Will, thou shalt
have my hammer: and here, Tom, take all the
money that I have. O Lord bless me! I pray
God, for I am never able to deal with my master,
he hath learnt so much fence already.   80
Sal. Come, leave your drinking and fall to
blows. Sirrah, what's thy name?
Peter. Peter, forsooth.
Sal. Peter! what more?   84
Peter. Thump.
Sal. Thump! then see thou thump thy master well.
Hor. Masters, I am come hither, as it were,
upon my man's instigation, to prove him a
knave, and myself an honest man: and touch-
ing the Duke of York, I will take my death I
never meant him any ill, nor the king, nor the
queen; and therefore, Peter, have at thee with
a downright blow!   94
York. Dispatch: this knave's tongue begins
to double.
Sound, trumpets, alarum to the combatants.
[*Alarum. They fight, and* PETER *strikes
down his Master.*
Hor. Hold, Peter, hold! I confess, I confess
treason.   [*Dies.*
York. Take away his weapon. Fellow, thank
God, and the good wine in thy master's way.
Peter. O God! have I overcome mine enemies
in this presence? O Peter! thou hast prevailed
in right!
K. Hen. Go, take hence that traitor from
our sight;   104
For by his death we do perceive his guilt:
And God in justice hath reveal'd to us
The truth and innocence of this poor fellow,

Which he had thought to have murder'd wr
fully.
Come, fellow, follow us for thy reward.
[*Sound a flourish. Ex*

SCENE IV.—*The Same. A Street.*

Enter GLOUCESTER *and* Serving-men, *i
mourning cloaks.*

Glo. Thus sometimes hath the brightes
a cloud;
And after summer evermore succeeds
Barren winter, with his wrathful nipping c
So cares and joys abound, as seasons flee
Sirs, what's o'clock?
Serv.   Ten, my lord.
Glo. Ten is the hour that was appointe
To watch the coming of my punish'd duch
Uneath may she endure the flinty streets,
To tread them with her tender-feeling fee
Sweet Nell, ill can thy noble mind abrook
The abject people, gazing on thy face
With envious looks still laughing at thy sh
That erst did follow thy proud chariot whee
When thou didst ride in triumph through
streets.
But, soft! I think she comes; and I'll prep
My tear-stain'd eyes to see her miseries.

Enter the DUCHESS OF GLOUCESTER, *with pa
pinned upon her back, in a white sheet, her
bare, and a taper burning in her hand;* SIR J
STANLEY, *a* Sheriff, *and* Officers.

Serv. So please your Grace, we'll take
from the sheriff.
Glo. No, stir not, for your lives; let her
by.
Duch. Come you, my lord, to see my c
shame?
Now thou dost penance too. Look! how
gaze.
See! how the giddy multitude do point,
And nod their heads, and throw their eye
thee.
Ah, Gloucester, hide thee from their ha
looks,
And, in thy closet pent up, rue my shame,
And ban thine enemies, both mine and th
Glo. Be patient, gentle Nell; forget this g
Duch. Ay, Gloucester, teach me to fo
myself;
For whilst I think I am thy wedded wife,
And thou a prince, protector of this land,
Methinks I should not thus be led along,
Mail'd up in shame, with papers on my b
And follow'd with a rabble that rejoice
To see my tears and hear my deep-fet gro
The ruthless flint doth cut my tender feet,
And when I start, the envious people laug
And bid me be advised how I tread.
Ah, Humphrey! can I bear this shameful yo
Trow'st thou that e'er I'll look upon the wo
Or count them happy that enjoy the sun?
No; dark shall be my light, and night my d
To think upon my pomp shall be my hell.
Sometime I'll say, I am Duke Humphrey's w

d he a prince and ruler of the land:
t so he rul'd and such a prince he was　44
he stood by whilst I, his forlorn duchess,
as made a wonder and a pointing-stock
every idle rascal follower.
t be thou mild and blush not at my shame;
or stir at nothing till the axe of death
ing over thee, as, sure, it shortly will;
r Suffolk, he that can do all in all　51
ith her that hateth thee, and hates us all,
d York, and impious Beaufort, that false
priest,
ve all lim'd bushes to betray thy wings;
d, fly thou how thou canst, they'll tangle
thee;
t fear not thou, until thy foot be snar'd,　56
r never seek prevention of thy foes.
Glo. Ah, Nell! forbear: thou aimest all awry;
ust offend before I be attainted;
d I twenty times so many foes,　60
d each of them had twenty times their power,
I these could not procure me any scath,
long as I am loyal, true, and crimeless.
ouldst have me rescue thee from this reproach?　64
hy, yet thy scandal were not wip'd away,
t I in danger for the breach of law.
iy greatest help is quiet, gentle Nell:
ray thee, sort thy heart to patience;　68
iese few days' wonder will be quickly worn.

Enter a Herald.

Her. I summon your Grace to his majesty's
rliament, holden at Bury the first of this
xt month.　72
Glo. And my consent ne'er ask'd herein
before!
iis is close dealing. Well, I will be there.
　　　　　　　　　　　　[_Exit_ Herald.
y Nell, I take my leave: and, master sheriff,
t not her penance exceed the king's commission.　76
Sher. An't please your Grace, here my commission stays;
d Sir John Stanley is appointed now
) take her with him to the Isle of Man.
Glo. Must you, Sir John, protect my lady
here?　80
Stan. So am I given in charge, may't please
your Grace.
Glo. Entreat her not the worse in that I pray
ɔu use her well. The world may laugh again;
d I may live to do you kindness if　84
ou do it her: and so, Sir John, farewell.
Duch. What! gone, my lord, and bid me not
farewell!
Glo. Witness my tears, I cannot stay to speak.
　　　[_Exeunt_ GLOUCESTER _and_ Serving-men.
Duch. Art thou gone too? All comfort go
with thee!　88
r none abides with me: my joy is death;
ath, at whose name I oft have been afear'd,
cause I wish'd this world's eternity.
nley, I prithee, go, and take me hence;　92
are not whither, for I beg no favour,
ly convey me where thou art commanded.

Stan. Why, madam, that is to the Isle of
Man;
There to be us'd according to your state.　96
Duch. That's bad enough, for I am but re-
proach:
And shall I then be us'd reproachfully?
Stan. Like to a duchess, and Duke Hum-
phrey's lady:
According to that state you shall be us'd.　100
Duch. Sheriff, farewell, and better than I fare,
Although thou hast been conduct of my shame.
Sher. It is my office; and, madam, pardon
me.
Duch. Ay, ay, farewell; thy office is dis-
charg'd.　104
Come, Stanley, shall we go?
Stan. Madam, your penance done, throw off
this sheet,
And go we to attire you for our journey.
Duch. My shame will not be shifted with my
sheet:　108
No; it will hang upon my richest robes,
And show itself, attire me how I can.
Go, lead the way; I long to see my prison.
　　　　　　　　　　　　　　　[_Exeunt._

ACT III

SCENE I.—_The Abbey at Bury St. Edmund's._

Sound a sennet. Enter to the Parliament, KING
HENRY, QUEEN MARGARET, CARDINAL BEAU-
FORT, SUFFOLK, YORK, BUCKINGHAM, _and
Others._

K. Hen. I muse my Lord of Gloucester is
not come:
'Tis not his wont to be the hindmost man,
Whate'er occasion keeps him from us now.
Q. Mar. Can you not see? or will ye not
observe　4
The strangeness of his alter'd countenance?
With what a majesty he bears himself,
How insolent of late he is become,
How proud, how peremptory, and unlike him-
self?　8
We know the time since he was mild and affable,
An if we did but glance a far-off look,
Immediately he was upon his knee,
That all the court admir'd him for submission:
But meet him now, and, be it in the morn,　13
When everyone will give the time of day,
He knits his brow and shows an angry eye,
And passeth by with stiff unbowed knee,　16
Disdaining duty that to us belongs.
Small curs are not regarded when they grin,
But great men tremble when the lion roars;
And Humphrey is no little man in England.　20
First note that he is near you in descent,
And should you fall, he is the next will mount.
Me seemeth then it is no policy,
Respecting what a rancorous mind he bears,　24
And his advantage following your decease,
That he should come about your royal person
Or be admitted to your highness' council.
By flattery hath he won the commons' hearts,　28

And when he please to make commotion,
'Tis to be fear'd they all will follow him.
Now 'tis the spring, and weeds are shallow-
  rooted;
Suffer them now and they'll o'ergrow the gar-
  den,   32
And choke the herbs for want of husbandry.
The reverent care I bear unto my lord
Made me collect these dangers in the duke.
If it be fond, call it a woman's fear;   36
Which fear if better reasons can supplant,
I will subscribe and say I wrong'd the duke.
My Lord of Suffolk, Buckingham, and York,
Reprove my allegation if you can   40
Or else conclude my words effectual.

  Suf. Well hath your highness seen into this
    duke;
And had I first been put to speak my mind,
I think I should have told your Grace's tale. 44
The duchess, by his subornation,
Upon my life, began her devilish practices:
Or if he were not privy to those faults,
Yet, by reputing of his high descent,   48
As, next the king he was successive heir,
And such high vaunts of his nobility,
Did instigate the bedlam brain-sick duchess,
By wicked means to frame our sovereign's fall.
Smooth runs the water where the brook is deep,
And in his simple show he harbours treason.
The fox barks not when he would steal the lamb:
No, no, my sov'reign; Gloucester is a man 56
Unsounded yet, and full of deep deceit.

  Car. Did he not, contrary to form of law,
Devise strange deaths for small offences done?

  York. And did he not, in his protectorship,
Levy great sums of money through the realm
For soldiers' pay in France, and never sent it?
By means whereof the towns each day revolted.

  Buck. Tut! these are petty faults to faults
    unknown,   64
Which time will bring to light in smooth Duke
  Humphrey.

  K. Hen. My lords, at once: the care you
    have of us,
To mow down thorns that would annoy our foot,
Is worthy down praise; but shall I speak my con-
  science,   68
Our kinsman Gloucester is as innocent
From meaning treason to our royal person,
As is the sucking lamb or harmless dove.
The duke is virtuous, mild, and too well given
To dream on evil, or to work my downfall.

  Q. Mar. Ah! what's more dangerous than
    this fond affiance!
Seems he a dove? his feathers are but borrow'd,
For he's disposed as the hateful raven: 76
Is he a lamb? his skin is surely lent him,
For he's inclin'd as is the ravenous wolf.
Who cannot steal a shape that means deceit?
Take heed, my lord; the welfare of us all 80
Hangs on the cutting short that fraudful man.

Enter SOMERSET.

  Som. All health unto my gracious sovereign!

  K. Hen. Welcome, Lord Somerset. What
    news from France?

  Som. That all your interest in those territori
Is utterly bereft you; all is lost.

  K. Hen. Cold news, Lord Somerset: b
    God's will be done!

  York. [*Aside.*] Cold news for me; for I ha
    hope of France,
As firmly as I hope for fertile England.
Thus are my blossoms blasted in the bud,
And caterpillars eat my leaves away;
But I will remedy this gear ere long,
Or sell my title for a glorious grave.

Enter GLOUCESTER.

  Glo. All happiness unto my lord the king
Pardon, my liege, that I have stay'd so long

  Suf. Nay, Gloucester, know that thou a
    come too soon,
Unless thou wert more loyal than thou art:
I do arrest thee of high treason here.

  Glo. Well, Suffolk's duke, thou shalt not s
    me blush,
Nor change my countenance for this arrest:
A heart unspotted is not easily daunted.
The purest spring is not so free from mud
As I am clear from treason to my sovereign.
Who can accuse me? wherein am I guilty?

  York. 'Tis thought, my lord, that you to
    bribes of France,   i
And, being protector, stay'd the soldiers' pa
By means whereof his highness hath lost Franc

  Glo. Is it but thought so? What are th
    that think it?
I never robb'd the soldiers of their pay,   i
Nor ever had one penny bribe from France.
So help me God, as I have watch'd the nigh
Ay, night by night, in studying good for Englan
That doit that e'er I wrested from the king,
Or any groat I hoarded to my use,
Be brought against me at my trial-day!
No; many a pound of mine own proper sto
Because I would not tax the needy commo
Have I disbursed to the garrisons,   i
And never ask'd for restitution.

  Car. It serves you well, my lord, to say
    much.

  Glo. I say no more than truth, so help
    God!

  York. In your protectorship you did dev
Strange tortures for offenders, never heard
That England was defam'd by tyranny.

  Glo. Why, 'tis well known that, whiles I w
    protector,   i
Pity was all the fault that was in me;
For I should melt at an offender's tears,
And lowly words were ransom for their fau
Unless it were a bloody murderer,   i
Or foul felonious thief that fleec'd poor pa
  sengers,
I never gave them condign punishment:
Murder, indeed, that bloody sin, I tortur'd
Above the felon or what trespass else.

  Suf. My lord, these faults are easy, quick
    answer'd:
But mightier crimes are laid unto your char
Whereof you cannot easily purge yourself.
I do arrest you in his highness' name;   i

d here commit you to my Lord Cardinal
keep until your further time of trial.

. Hen. My Lord of Gloucester, 'tis my
special hope   139
at you will clear yourself from all suspect:
conscience tells me you are innocent.

lo. Ah! gracious lord, these days are
dangerous.

tue is chok'd with foul ambition,
d charity chas'd hence by rancour's hand;
il subornation is predominant,   145
d equity exil'd your highness' land.
iow their complot is to have my life;
d if my death might make this island happy,
d prove the period of their tyranny,   149
ould expend it with all willingness;
: mine is made the prologue to their play;
r thousands more, that yet suspect no peril,
ll not conclude their plotted tragedy.   153
ufort's red sparkling eyes blab his heart's
malice,
d Suffolk's cloudy brow his stormy hate;
irp Buckingham unburdens with his tongue
e envious load that lies upon his heart;   157
d dogged York, that reaches at the moon,
iose overweening arm I have pluck'd back,
false accuse doth level at my life: 160
d you, my sov'reign lady, with the rest,
useless have laid disgraces on my head,
d with your best endeavour have stirr'd up
liefest liege to be mine enemy.   164
, all of you have laid your heads together;
yself had notice of your conventicles;
d all to make away my guiltless life.
hall not want false witness to condemn me,
r store of treasons to augment my guilt; 169
e ancient proverb will be well effected:
staff is quickly found to beat a dog.'

Car. My liege, his railing is intolerable. 172
those that care to keep your royal person
om treason's secret knife and traitor's rage
thus upbraided, chid, and rated at,
d the offender granted scope of speech, 176
will make them cool in zeal unto your Grace.

Suf. Hath he not twit our sovereign lady here
ith ignominious words, though clerkly
couch'd,
if she had suborned some to swear   180
lse allegations to o'erthrow his state?

Q. Mar. But I can give the loser leave to
chide.

Glo. Far truer spoke than meant: I lose,
indeed;
shrew the winners, for they play'd me false!
id well such losers may have leave to speak.

Buck. He'll wrest the sense and hold us here
all day.

rd Cardinal, he is your prisoner.

Car. Sirs, take away the duke, and guard
him sure.   188

Glo. Ah! thus King Henry throws away his
crutch
fore his legs be firm to bear his body:
ius the shepherd beaten from thy side,
id wolves are gnarling who shall gnaw thee
first.   192

Ah! that my fear were false, ah! that it were;
For, good King Henry, thy decay I fear.
  [*Exeunt* Attendants *with* GLOUCESTER.

K. Hen. My lords, what to your wisdoms
seemeth best
Do or undo, as if ourself were here.   196

Q. Mar. What! will your highness leave the
parliament?

K. Hen. Ay, Margaret; my heart is drown'd
with grief,
Whose flood begins to flow within mine eyes,
My body round engirt with misery,   200
For what's more miserable than discontent?
Ah! uncle Humphrey, in thy face I see
The map of honour, truth, and loyalty;
And yet, good Humphrey, is the hour to come
That e'er I prov'd thee false, or fear'd thy faith.
What low'ring star now envies thy estate,
That these great lords, and Margaret our queen,
Do seek subversion of thy harmless life? 208
Thou never didst them wrong, nor no man
wrong;
And as the butcher takes away the calf,
And binds the wretch, and beats it when it strays,
Bearing it to the bloody slaughter-house,   212
Even so, remorseless, have they borne him hence;
And as the dam runs lowing up and down,
Looking the way her harmless young one went,
And can do nought but wail her darling's loss;
Even so myself bewails good Gloucester's case,
With sad unhelpful tears, and with dimm'd eyes
Look after him, and cannot do him good;
So mighty are his vowed enemies.   220
His fortunes I will weep; and, 'twixt each groan,
Say 'Who's a traitor, Gloucester he is none.'
  [*Exit.*

Q. Mar. Fair lords, cold snow melts with
the sun's hot beams.
Henry my lord is cold in great affairs,   224
Too full of foolish pity; and Gloucester's show
Beguiles him as the mournful crocodile
With sorrow snares relenting passengers;
Or as the snake, roll'd in a flow'ring bank, 228
With shining checker'd slough, doth sting a
child
That for the beauty thinks it excellent.
Believe me, lords, were none more wise than I,—
And yet herein I judge mine own wit good,—
This Gloucester should be quickly rid the world,
To rid us from the fear we have of him.

Car. That he should die is worthy policy;
And yet we want a colour for his death.   236
'Tis meet he be condemn'd by course of law.

Suf. But in my mind that were no policy:
The king will labour still to save his life;
The commons haply rise to save his life;   240
And yet we have but trivial argument,
More than mistrust, that shows him worthy
death.

York. So that, by this, you would not have
him die.

Suf. Ah! York, no man alive so fain as I.

York. 'Tis York that hath more reason for
his death.   245
But my Lord Cardinal, and you, my Lord of
Suffolk,

Say as you think, and speak it from your souls,
Were't not all one an empty eagle were set
To guard the chicken from a hungry kite,   249
As place Duke Humphrey for the king's pro-
    tector?
    Q. Mar. So the poor chicken should be sure
of death.
    Suf. Madam, 'tis true: and were't not mad-
ness, then,   252
To make the fox surveyor of the fold?
Who, being accus'd a crafty murderer,
His guilt should be but idly posted over
Because his purpose is not executed.   256
No; let him die, in that he is a fox,
By nature prov'd an enemy to the flock,
Before his chaps be stain'd with crimson blood,
As Humphrey, prov'd by reasons, to my liege.
And do not stand on quillets how to slay him:
Be it by gins, by snares, by subtilty,
Sleeping or waking, 'tis no matter how,
So he be dead; for that is good deceit   264
Which mates him first that first intends deceit.
    Q. Mar. Thrice noble Suffolk, 'tis resolutely
spoke.
    Suf. Not resolute, except so much were done,
For things are often spoke and seldom meant;
But, that my heart accordeth with my tongue,
Seeing the deed is meritorious,
And to preserve my sovereign from his foe,
Say but the word and I will be his priest.   272
    Car. But I would have him dead, my Lord
of Suffolk,
Ere you can take due orders for a priest:
Say you consent and censure well the deed,
And I'll provide his executioner;   276
I tender to the safety of my liege.
    Suf. Here is my hand, the deed is worthy
doing.
    Q. Mar. And so say I.
    York. And I: and now we three have spoke
it,   280
It skills not greatly who impugns our doom.

Enter a Messenger.

    Mess. Great lords, from Ireland am I come
amain,
To signify that rebels there are up,
And put the Englishmen unto the sword.   284
Send succours, lords, and stop the rage betime,
Before the wound do grow uncurable;
For, being green, there is great hope of help.
    Car. A breach that craves a quick expedient
stop!   288
What counsel give you in this weighty cause?
    York. That Somerset be sent as regent
thither.
'Tis meet that lucky ruler be employ'd;   291
Witness the fortune he hath had in France.
    Som. If York, with all his far-fet policy,
Had been the regent there instead of me,
He never would have stay'd in France so long.
    York. No, not to lose it all, as thou hast
done: 296
I rather would have lost my life betimes
Than bring a burden of dishonour home,
By staying there so long till all were lost.

Show me one scar character'd on thy skin:
Men's flesh preserv'd so whole do seldom w
    Q. Mar. Nay then, this spark will pro
raging fire,
If wind and fuel be brought to feed it witl
No more, good York; sweet Somerset, be s
Thy fortune, York, hadst thou been regent th
Might happily have prov'd far worse than
    York. What! worse than nought? nay, t
a shame take all.
    Som. And in the number thee, that wish
shame.
    Car. My Lord of York, try what your fort
is.
The uncivil kerns of Ireland are in arms
And temper clay with blood of Englishme
To Ireland will you lead a band of men,
Collected choicely, from each county some
And try your hap against the Irishmen?
    York. I will, my lord, so please his maje
    Suf. Why, our authority is his consent,
And what we do establish he confirms:
Then, noble York, take thou this task in ha
    York. I am content: provide me soldi
lords,
Whiles I take order for mine own affairs.
    Suf. A charge, Lord York, that I will
perform'd.
But now return we to the false Duke Humphi
    Car. No more of him; for I will deal with
That henceforth he shall trouble us no more.
And so break off; the day is almost spent.
Lord Suffolk, you and I must talk of that eve
    York. My Lord of Suffolk, within fourt
days
At Bristol I expect my soldiers;
For there I'll ship them all for Ireland.
    Suf. I'll see it truly done, my Lord of Yc
    [*Exeunt all except* YO
    York. Now, York, or never, steel thy fear
thoughts,
And change misdoubt to resolution:
Be that thou hop'st to be, or what thou art
Resign to death; it is not worth the enjoyi
Let pale-fac'd fear keep with the mean-b
man,
And find no harbour in a royal heart.
Faster than spring-time showers comes thou
on thought,
And not a thought but thinks on dignity.
My brain, more busy than the labouring spid
Weaves tedious snares to trap mine enemi
Well, nobles, well; 'tis politicly done,
To send me packing with a host of men:
I fear me you but warm the starved snake,
Who, cherish'd in your breasts, will sting y
hearts.
'Twas men I lack'd, and you will give them n
I take it kindly; yet be well assur'd
You put sharp weapons in a madman's han
Whiles I in Ireland nourish a mighty band,
I will stir up in England some black storm
Shall blow ten thousand souls to heaven or he
And this fell tempest shall not cease to rage
Until the golden circuit on my head,
Like to the glorious sun's transparent bea

o calm the fury of this mad-bred flaw.
nd, for a minister of my intent,
have seduc'd a headstrong Kentishman,
ohn Cade of Ashford,   357
o make commotion, as full well he can,
nder the title of John Mortimer.
 Ireland have I seen this stubborn Cade   360
ppose himself against a troop of kerns,
nd fought so long, till that his thighs with
    darts
Vere almost like a sharp-quill'd porpentine:
nd, in the end being rescu'd, I have seen   364
im caper upright like a wild Morisco,
haking the bloody darts as he his bells.
ull often, like a shag-hair'd crafty kern,
lath he conversed with the enemy,   368
nd undiscover'd come to me again,
nd given me notice of their villanies.
his devil here shall be my substitute;   371
or that John Mortimer, which now is dead,
n face, in gait, in speech, he doth resemble;
y this I shall perceive the commons' mind,
low they affect the house and claim of York.
ay he be taken, rack'd, and tortured,   376
know no pain they can inflict upon him
Vill make him say I mov'd him to those arms.
ay that he thrive,—as 'tis great like he will,—
Vhy, then from Ireland come I with my
    strength,   380
nd reap the harvest which that rascal sow'd;
or, Humphrey being dead, as he shall be,
nd Henry put apart, the next for me. [*Exit.*

CENE II.—*Bury St. Edmund's. A Room in the
    Palace.*

Enter certain Murderers, *hastily.*

First Mur. Run to my Lord of Suffolk; let
    him know
Ve have dispatch'd the duke, as he com-
    manded.
Sec. Mur. O! that it were to do. What have
    we done?
)idst ever hear a man so penitent?   4

Enter SUFFOLK.

First Mur. Here comes my lord.
Suf. Now, sirs, have you dispatch'd this
    thing?
First Mur. Ay, my good lord, he's dead.
Suf. Why, that's well said. Go, get you to
    my house;   8
will reward you for this venturous deed.
he king and all the peers are here at hand.
Iave you laid fair the bed? is all things well,
According as I gave directions?   12
First Mur. 'Tis, my good lord.
Suf. Away! be gone.   [*Exeunt* Murderers.

ound trumpets. Enter KING HENRY, QUEEN
MARGARET, CARDINAL BEAUFORT, SOMERSET,
Lords, *and Others.*

K. Hen. Go, call our uncle to our presence
    straight;
ay, we intend to try his Grace to-day,   16
f he be guilty, as 'tis published.

Suf. I'll call him presently, my noble lord.
    [*Exit.*
K. Hen. Lords, take your places; and, I pray
    you all,
Proceed no straiter 'gainst our uncle Gloucester
Than from true evidence, of good esteem,   21
He be approv'd in practice culpable.
Q. Mar. God forbid any malice should pre-
    vail
That faultless may condemn a nobleman!   24
Pray God, he may acquit him of suspicion!
K. Hen. I thank thee, Meg; these words con-
    tent me much.

Re-enter SUFFOLK.

How now! why look'st thou pale? why trem-
    blest thou?
Where is our uncle? what's the matter, Suf-
    folk?   28
Suf. Dead in his bed, my lord; Gloucester
    is dead.
Q. Mar. Marry, God forfend!
Car. God's secret judgment: I did dream to-
    night
The duke was dumb, and could not speak a
    word.   [*The* KING *swoons.*
Q. Mar. How fares my lord? Help, lords!
    the king is dead.   33
Som. Rear up his body; wring him by the
    nose.
Q. Mar. Run, go, help, help! O Henry, ope
    thine eyes!
Suf. He doth revive again. Madam, be
    patient.   36
K. Hen. O heavenly God!
Q. Mar.   How fares my gracious lord?
Suf. Comfort, my sovereign! gracious Henry,
    comfort!
K. Hen. What! doth my Lord of Suffolk
    comfort me?
Came he right now to sing a raven's note,   40
Whose dismal tune bereft my vital powers,
And thinks he that the chirping of a wren,
By crying comfort from a hollow breast,
Can chase away the first-conceived sound?   44
Hide not thy poison with such sugar'd words:
Lay not thy hands on me; forbear, I say:
Their touch affrights me as a serpent's sting.
Thou baleful messenger, out of my sight!   48
Upon thy eyeballs murderous tyranny
Sits in grim majesty to fright the world.
Look not upon me, for thine eyes are wounding:
Yet do not go away; come, basilisk,   52
And kill the innocent gazer with thy sight;
For in the shade of death I shall find joy,
In life but double death, now Gloucester's dead.
Q. Mar. Why do you rate my Lord of Suf-
    folk thus?   56
Although the duke was enemy to him,
Yet he, most Christian-like, laments his death:
And for myself, foe as he was to me,
Might liquid tears or heart-offending groans
Or blood-consuming sighs recall his life,   61
I would be blind with weeping, sick with groans,
Look pale as primrose with blood-drinking
    sighs,

And all to have the noble duke alive.   64
What know I how the world may deem of me?
For it is known we were but hollow friends:
It may be judg'd I made the duke away:
So shall my name with slander's tongue be
    wounded,   68
And princes' courts be fill'd with my reproach.
This get I by his death. Ay me, unhappy!
To be a queen, and crown'd with infamy!
  K. Hen. Ah! woe is me for Gloucester,
    wretched man.   72
  Q. Mar. Be woe for me, more wretched than
    he is.
What! dost thou turn away and hide thy face?
I am no loathsome leper; look on me.   75
What! art thou, like the adder, waxen deaf?
Be poisonous too and kill thy forlorn queen.
Is all thy comfort shut in Gloucester's tomb?
Why, then, Dame Margaret was ne'er thy joy:
Erect his statua and worship it,   80
And make my image but an alehouse sign.
Was I for this nigh wrack'd upon the sea,
And twice by awkward wind from England's
    bank
Drove back again unto my native clime?   84
What boded this, but well forewarning wind
Did seem to say, 'Seek not a scorpion's nest,
Nor set no footing on this unkind shore?'
What did I then, but curs'd the gentle gusts   88
And he that loos'd them forth their brazen
    caves;
And bid them blow towards England's blessed
    shore,
Or turn our stern upon a dreadful rock?
Yet Æolus would not be a murderer,   92
But left that hateful office unto thee:
The pretty vaulting sea refus'd to drown me,
Knowing that thou wouldst have me drown'd
    on shore
With tears as salt as sea through thy unkind-
    ness: 96
The splitting rocks cower'd in the sinking sands,
And would not dash me with their ragged sides,
Because thy flinty heart, more hard than they,
Might in thy palace perish Margaret.   100
As far as I could ken thy chalky cliffs,
When from thy shore the tempest beat us back,
I stood upon the hatches in the storm,
And when the dusky sky began to rob   104
My earnest-gaping sight of thy land's view,
I took a costly jewel from my neck,
A heart it was, bound in with diamonds,
And threw it towards thy land: the sea receiv'd
    it,   108
And so I wish'd thy body might my heart:
And even with this I lost fair England's view,
And bid mine eyes be packing with my heart,
And call'd them blind and dusky spectacles
For losing ken of Albion's wished coast.   113
How often have I tempted Suffolk's tongue—
The agent of thy foul inconstancy—
To sit and witch me, as Ascanius did   116
When he to madding Dido would unfold
His father's acts, commenc'd in burning Troy!
Am I not witch'd like her? or thou not false like
    him?

Ay me! I can no more. Die, Margaret!   12₍
For Henry weeps that thou dost live so long

Noise within. Enter WARWICK *and* SALISBURY
  The Commons *press to the door.*

  War. It is reported, mighty sovereign,
That good Duke Humphrey trait'rously is mu₍
    der'd
By Suffolk and the Cardinal Beaufort's mean₍
The commons, like an angry hive of bees   12
That want their leader, scatter up and down
And care not who they sting in his revenge.
Myself have calm'd their spleenful mutiny,   12₍
Until they hear the order of his death.
  K. Hen. That he is dead, good Warwick, 'ti
    too true;
But how he died God knows, not Henry.
Enter his chamber, view his breathless corpse
And comment then upon his sudden death.   13₍
  War. That shall I do, my liege. Stay, Sali₍
    bury,
With the rude multitude till I return.

    [WARWICK *goes into an inner chamber*
                  SALISBURY *retire₍*
  K. Hen. O! Thou that judgest all things
    stay my thoughts,   13₍
My thoughts that labour to persuade my sou₍
Some violent hands were laid on Humphrey'
    life.
If my suspect be false, forgive me, God,
For judgment only doth belong to thee.   14
Fain would I go to chafe his paly lips
With twenty thousand kisses, and to drain
Upon his face an ocean of salt tears,
To tell my love unto his deaf dumb trunk,   14
And with my fingers feel his hand unfeeling:
But all in vain are these mean obsequies,
And to survey his dead and earthly image
What were it but to make my sorrow greater

Re-enter WARWICK *and Others bearing*
    GLOUCESTER'S *body on a bed.*

  War. Come hither, gracious sovereign, view
    this body.   14₍
  K. Hen. That is to see how deep my grave i₍
    made;
For with his soul fled all my worldly solace,
For seeing him I see my life in death.   15₍
  War. As surely as my soul intends to live
With that dread King that took our state upo₍
    him
To free us from his Father's wrathful curse,
I do believe that violent hands were laid   15₍
Upon the life of this thrice-famed duke.
  Suf. A dreadful oath, sworn with a solemn
    tongue!
What instance gives Lord Warwick for his vow ₍
  War. See how the blood is settled in his face.
Oft have I seen a timely-parted ghost,   16₍
Of ashy semblance, meagre, pale, and bloodless,
Being all descended to the labouring heart;
Who, in the conflict that it holds with death,
Attracts the same for aidance 'gainst the enemy;
Which with the heart there cools, and ne'er
    returneth   166
To blush and beautify the cheek again.

But see, his face is black and full of blood,
His eyeballs further out than when he liv'd,
Staring full ghastly like a strangled man;
His hair uprear'd, his nostrils stretch'd with
   struggling: 171
His hands abroad display'd, as one that grasp'd
And tugg'd for life, and was by strength subdu'd.
Look on the sheets, his hair, you see, is sticking;
His well-proportion'd beard made rough and
   rugged,
Like to the summer's corn by tempest lodg'd.
It cannot be but he was murder'd here;   177
The least of all these signs were probable.
  Suf. Why, Warwick, who should do the duke
   to death?
Myself and Beaufort had him in protection;
And we, I hope, sir, are no murderers.   181
  War. But both of you were vow'd Duke
  Humphrey's foes,
And you, forsooth, had the good duke to keep:
'Tis like you would not feast him like a friend,
And 'tis well seen he found an enemy.   185
  Q. Mar. Then you, belike, suspect these
  noblemen
As guilty of Duke Humphrey's timeless death.
  War. Who finds the heifer dead, and bleed-
  ing fresh,   188
And sees fast by a butcher with an axe,
But will suspect 'twas he that made the
  slaughter?
Who finds the partridge in the puttock's nest,
But may imagine how the bird was dead,   192
Although the kite soar with unbloodied beak?
Even so suspicious is this tragedy.
  Q. Mar. Are you the butcher, Suffolk?
  where's your knife?
Is Beaufort term'd a kite? where are his talons?
  Suf. I wear no knife to slaughter sleeping
  men;   197
But here's a vengeful sword, rusted with ease,
That shall be scoured in his rancorous heart
That slanders me with murder's crimson badge.
Say, if thou dar'st, proud Lord of Warwickshire,
That I am faulty in Duke Humphrey's death.
  [*Exeunt* CARDINAL BEAUFORT, SOMERSET,
          and *Others.*
  War. What dares not Warwick, if false Suf-
  folk dare him?
  Q. Mar. He dares not calm his contumelious
  spirit,   204
Nor cease to be an arrogant controller,
Though Suffolk dare him twenty thousand times.
  War. Madam, be still, with reverence may I
  say;
For every word you speak in his behalf   208
Is slander to your royal dignity.
  Suf. Blunt-witted lord, ignoble in de-
  meanour!
If ever lady wrong'd her lord so much,
Thy mother took into her blameful bed   212
Some stern untutor'd churl, and noble stock
Was graft with crab-tree slip; whose fruit thou
  art,
And never of the Nevils' noble race.
  War. But that the guilt of murder bucklers
  thee,   216

And I should rob the deathsman of his fee,
Quitting thee thereby of ten thousand shames,
And that my sov'reign's presence makes me
  mild,   219
I would, false murd'rous coward, on thy knee
Make thee beg pardon for thy passed speech,
And say it was thy mother that thou meant'st;
That thou thyself wast born in bastardy:
And after all this fearful homage done,   224
Give thee thy hire, and send thy soul to hell,
Pernicious blood-sucker of sleeping men.
  Suf. Thou shalt be waking while I shed thy
  blood,
If from this presence thou dar'st go with me.
  War. Away even now, or I will drag thee
  hence: 229
Unworthy though thou art, I'll cope with thee,
And do some service to Duke Humphrey's
  ghost.   [*Exeunt* SUFFOLK *and* WARWICK.
  K. Hen. What stronger breastplate than a
  heart untainted!   232
Thrice is he arm'd that hath his quarrel just,
And he but naked, though lock'd up in steel,
Whose conscience with injustice is corrupted.
  Q. Mar. What noise is this? [*A noise within.*

Re-enter SUFFOLK *and* WARWICK, *with their
      weapons drawn.*

  K. Hen. Why, how now, lords! your wrath-
  ful weapons drawn   237
Here in our presence! dare you be so bold?
Why, what tumultuous clamour have we here?
  Suf. The traitorous Warwick, with the men
  of Bury,   240
Set all upon me, mighty sovereign.

Noise of a crowd within. Re-enter SALISBURY.

  Sal. [*Speaking to those within.*] Sirs, stand
  apart; the king shall know your mind.
Dread lord, the commons send you word by me,
Unless false Suffolk straight be done to death,
Or banished fair England's territories,   245
They will by violence tear him from your palace
And torture him with grievous lingering death.
They say, by him the good Duke Humphrey
  died;   248
They say, in him they fear your highness' death;
And mere instinct of love and loyalty,
Free from a stubborn opposite intent,   251
As being thought to contradict your liking,
Makes them thus forward in his banishment.
They say, in care of your most royal person,
That if your highness should intend to sleep,
And charge that no man should disturb your
  rest   256
In pain of your dislike or pain of death,
Yet, notwithstanding such a strait edict,
Were there a serpent seen, with forked tongue,
That slily glided towards your majesty,   260
It were but necessary you were wak'd,
Lest, being suffer'd in that harmful slumber,
The mortal worm might make the sleep eternal:
And therefore do they cry, though you forbid,
That they will guard you, whe'r you will or no,
From such fell serpents as false Suffolk is;
With whose envenomed and fatal sting,   267

Your loving uncle, twenty times his worth,
They say, is shamefully bereft of life.
　　Commons. [*Within.*] An answer from the
king, my Lord of Salisbury!
　　Suf. 'Tis like the commons, rude unpolish'd
hinds,　　　　　　　　　　　　　　　271
Could send such message to their sovereign;
But you, my lord, were glad to be employ'd,
To show how quaint an orator you are:
But all the honour Salisbury hath won
Is that he was the lord ambassador,　　276
Sent from a sort of tinkers to the king.
　　Commons. [*Within.*] An answer from the
king, or we will all break in!
　　K. Hen. Go, Salisbury, and tell them all
from me,　　　　　　　　　　　　　279
I thank them for their tender loving care;
And had I not been cited so by them,
Yet did I purpose as they do entreat;
For, sure, my thoughts do hourly prophesy
Mischance unto my state by Suffolk's means:
And therefore, by his majesty I swear,　285
Whose far unworthy deputy I am,
He shall not breathe infection in this air
But three days longer, on the pain of death.
　　　　　　　　　　　　[*Exit* SALISBURY.
　　Q. Mar. O Henry! let me plead for gentle
Suffolk.
　　K. Hen. Ungentle queen, to call him gentle
Suffolk!　　　　　　　　　　　　290
No more, I say; if thou dost plead for him
Thou wilt but add increase unto my wrath.
Had I but said, I would have kept my word,
But when I swear, it is irrevocable.
[*To* SUFFOLK.] If after three days' space thou
here be'st found
On any ground that I am ruler of,　　296
The world shall not be ransom for thy life.
Come, Warwick, come, good Warwick, go with
me;
I have great matters to impart to thee.
　　[*Exeunt* KING HENRY, WARWICK, Lords, &c.
　　Q. Mar. Mischance and sorrow go along
with you!　　　　　　　　　　　300
Heart's discontent and sour affliction
Be playfellows to keep you company!
There's two of you; the devil make a third,
And threefold vengeance tend upon your steps!
　　Suf. Cease, gentle queen, these execrations,
And let thy Suffolk take his heavy leave.
　　Q. Mar. Fie, coward woman and soft-
hearted wretch!　　　　　　　　307
Hast thou not spirit to curse thine enemy?
　　Suf. A plague upon them! Wherefore should
I curse them?
Would curses kill, as doth the mandrake's groan,
I would invent as bitter-searching terms,
As curst, as harsh and horrible to hear,　312
Deliver'd strongly through my fixed teeth,
With full as many signs of deadly hate,
As lean-fac'd Envy in her loathsome cave.
My tongue should stumble in mine earnest
words,　　　　　　　　　　　　316
Mine eyes should sparkle like the beaten flint;
My hair be fix'd on end, as one distract;
Ay, every joint should seem to curse and ban:

And even now my burden'd heart would brea
Should I not curse them. Poison be their drink
Gall, worse than gall, the daintiest that the
taste!　　　　　　　　　　　　　32
Their sweetest shade a grove of cypress tree
Their chiefest prospect murdering basilisks!
Their softest touch as smart as lizard's stings!
Their music frightful as the serpent's hiss,
And boding screech-owls make the concert ful
All the foul terrors in dark-seated hell—　32
　　Q. Mar. Enough, sweet Suffolk; thou tor
ment'st thyself;
And these dread curses, like the sun 'gainst glas
Or like an over-charged gun, recoil,
And turn the force of them upon thyself.　33
　　Suf. You bade me ban, and will you bid m
leave?
Now, by the ground that I am banish'd from
Well could I curse away a winter's night,
Though standing naked on a mountain top,
Where biting cold would never let grass grow
And think it but a minute spent in sport.
　　Q. Mar. O! let me entreat thee, cease! Giv
me thy hand,　　　　　　　　　33
That I may dew it with my mournful tears;
Nor let the rain of heaven wet this place,
To wash away my woeful monuments.
O! could this kiss be printed in thy hand,
　　　　　　　　　　　[*Kisses his hand*
That thou mightst think upon these by the seal
Through whom a thousand sighs are breath'c
for thee.　　　　　　　　　　　34
So, get thee gone, that I may know my grief
'Tis but surmis'd whiles thou art standing by,
As one that surfeits thinking on a want.　34
I will repeal thee, or, be well assur'd,
Adventure to be banished myself;
And banished I am, if but from thee.
Go; speak not to me; even now be gone.　35
O! go not yet. Even thus two friends condemn'c
Embrace and kiss, and take ten thousand leaves
Loather a hundred times to part than die.
Yet now farewell; and farewell life with thee
　　Suf. Thus is poor Suffolk ten times banished
Once by the king, and three times thrice by thee
'Tis not the land I care for, wert thou thence;
A wilderness is populous enough,　　　36
So Suffolk had thy heavenly company:
For where thou art, there is the world itself,
With every several pleasure in the world,
And where thou art not, desolation.　　364
I can no more: live thou to joy thy life;
Myself to joy in nought but that thou liv'st.

Enter VAUX.

　　Q. Mar. Whither goes Vaux so fast? what
news, I prithee?
　　Vaux. To signify unto his majesty　　368
That Cardinal Beaufort is at point of death;
For suddenly a grievous sickness took him,
That makes him gasp and stare, and catch the
air,
Blaspheming God, and cursing men on earth
Sometime he talks as if Duke Humphrey's ghost
Were by his side; sometime he calls the king,
And whispers to his pillow, as to him,

secrets of his overcharged soul: 376
I am sent to tell his majesty
even now he cries aloud for him.
. *Mar.* Go tell this heavy message to the
king.　　　　　　　　　　[*Exit* VAUX.
me! what is this world! what news are these!
wherefore grieve I at an hour's poor loss,
itting Suffolk's exile, my soul's treasure?
y only, Suffolk, mourn I not for thee,
with the southern clouds contend in tears,
irs for the earth's increase, mine for my
sorrows? 385
w get thee hence: the king, thou know'st, is
coming;
hou be found by me thou art but dead.
uf. If I depart from thee I cannot live; 388
I in thy sight to die, what were it else
like a pleasant slumber in thy lap?
re could I breathe my soul into the air, 392
mild and gentle as the cradle babe,
ng with mother's dug between its lips;
ere, from thy sight, I should be raging mad,
d cry out for thee to close up mine eyes,
have thee with thy lips to stop my mouth:
shouldst thou either turn my flying soul,
I should breathe it so into thy body,
d then it liv'd in sweet Elysium.
die by thee, were but to die in jest; 400
m thee to die were torture more than death.
let me stay, befall what may befall!
. Mar. Away! though parting be a fretful
corsive,
applied to a deathful wound. 404
France, sweet Suffolk: let me hear from
thee;
wheresoe'er thou art in this world's globe,
have an Iris that shall find thee out.
uf. I go.
Mar. And take my heart with thee. 408
uf. A jewel, lock'd into the woefull'st cask
at ever did contain a thing of worth.
n as a splitted bark, so sunder we:
s way fall I to death.
. Mar.　　　　　This way for me. 412
　　　　　　　　　[*Exeunt severally.*

SCENE III.—*London.* CARDINAL BEAUFORT'S
Bedchamber.

er KING HENRY, SALISBURY, WARWICK, *and
Others. The* CARDINAL *in bed;* Attendants
ith him.

K. Hen. How fares my lord? speak, Beaufort, to thy sovereign.
Car. If thou be'st death, I'll give thee England's treasure,
ough to purchase such another island,
thou wilt let me live, and feel no pain. 4
K. Hen. Ah! what a sign it is of evil life
ere death's approach is seen so terrible.
War. Beaufort, it is thy sov'reign speaks to
thee. 7
Car. Bring me unto my trial when you will.
ed he not in his bed? where should he die?
n I make men live whe'r they will or no?
torture me no more, I will confess.

Alive again? then show me where he is: 12
I'll give a thousand pound to look upon him.
He hath no eyes, the dust hath blinded them.
Comb down his hair; look! look! it stands up-
right, 15
Like lime-twigs set to catch my winged soul.
Give me some drink; and bid the apothecary
Bring the strong poison that I bought of him.
K. Hen. O thou eternal Mover of the
heavens!
Look with a gentle eye upon this wretch; 20
O! beat away the busy meddling fiend
That lays strong siege unto this wretch's soul,
And from his bosom purge this black despair.
War. See how the pangs of death do make
him grin! 24
Sal. Disturb him not! let him pass peace-
ably.
K. Hen. Peace to his soul, if God's good
pleasure be!
Lord Cardinal, if thou think'st on heaven's
bliss, 27
Hold up thy hand, make signal of thy hope.
He dies, and makes no sign. O God, forgive
him!
War. So bad a death argues a monstrous life.
K. Hen. Forbear to judge, for we are sinners
all. 31
Close up his eyes, and draw the curtain close;
And let us all to meditation. [*Exeunt.*

ACT IV

SCENE I.—*Kent. The Seashore near Dover.*

Firing heard at Sea. Then enter from a boat, a
Captain, *a* Master, *a* Master's-Mate, WALTER
WHITMORE, *and Others; with them* SUFFOLK
disguised, and other Gentlemen, *prisoners.*

Cap. The gaudy, blabbing, and remorseful
day
Is crept into the bosom of the sea,
And now loud-howling wolves arouse the jades
That drag the tragic melancholy night; 4
Who with their drowsy, slow, and flagging wings
Clip dead men's graves, and from their misty
jaws
Breathe foul contagious darkness in the air.
Therefore bring forth the soldiers of our prize, 8
For, whilst our pinnace anchors in the Downs
Here shall they make their ransom on the sand,
Or with their blood stain this discolour'd shore.
Master, this prisoner freely give I thee: 12
And thou that art his mate make boot of this;
The other [*Pointing to* SUFFOLK], Walter Whit-
more, is thy share.
First Gent. What is my ransom, master? let
me know.
Mast. A thousand crowns, or else lay down
your head. 16
Mate. And so much shall you give, or off
goes yours.
Cap. What! think you much to pay two
thousand crowns,

And bear the name and port of gentlemen?
Cut both the villains' throats! for die you shall:
The lives of those which we have lost in fight
Cannot be counterpois'd with such a petty sum!

    First Gent. I'll give it, sir; and therefore
spare my life.
    Sec. Gent. And so will I, and write home for
it straight.   24
    Whit. I lost mine eye in laying the prize
aboard,
[*To* SUFFOLK.] And therefore to revenge it shalt
thou die;
And so should these if I might have my will.
    Cap. Be not so rash: take ransom; let him
live.   28
    Suf. Look on my George; I am a gentleman:
Rate me at what thou wilt, thou shalt be paid.
    Whit. And so am I; my name is Walter
Whitmore.
How now! why start'st thou? what! doth
death affright?   32
    Suf. Thy name affrights me, in whose sound
is death.
A cunning man did calculate my birth,
And told me that by *Water* I should die: 35
Yet let not this make thee be bloody-minded;
Thy name is—*Gaultier*, being rightly sounded.
    Whit. *Gaultier*, or *Walter*, which it is I care
not;
Never yet did base dishonour blur our name
But with our sword we wip'd away the blot: 40
Therefore, when merchant-like I sell revenge,
Broke be my sword, my arms torn and defac'd,
And I proclaim'd a coward through the world!
                   [*Lays hold on* SUFFOLK.
    Suf. Stay, Whitmore; for thy prisoner is a
prince,   44
The Duke of Suffolk, William de la Pole.
    Whit. The Duke of Suffolk muffled up in
rags!
    Suf. Ay, but these rags are no part of the
duke:
Jove sometimes went disguis'd, and why not I?
    Cap. But Jove was never slain, as thou shalt
be.   49
    Suf. Obscure and lowly swain, King Henry's
blood,
The honourable blood of Lancaster,
Must not be shed by such a jaded groom.   52
Hast thou not kiss'd thy hand and held my
stirrup?
Bare-headed plodded by my foot-cloth mule,
And thought thee happy when I shook my head?
How often hast thou waited at my cup,   56
Fed from my trencher, kneel'd down at the board,
When I have feasted with Queen Margaret?
Remember it and let it make thee crest-fall'n;
Ay, and allay this thy abortive pride.   60
How in our voiding lobby hast thou stood
And duly waited for my coming forth?
This hand of mine hath writ in thy behalf,
And therefore shall it charm thy riotous tongue.
    Whit. Speak, captain, shall I stab the for-
lorn swain?   65
    Cap. First let my words stab him, as he hath
me.

    Suf. Base slave, thy words are blunt, an[d so]
art thou.
    Cap. Convey him hence, and on our l[ong]
boat's side
Strike off his head.
    Suf.   Thou dar'st not for thy o[wn.]
    Cap. Yes, Pole.
    Suf.   Pole!
    Cap.   Pool! Sir Pool! l[ord!]
Ay, kennel, puddle, sink; whose filth and [mud]
Troubles the silver spring where England dri[nks.]
Now will I dam up this thy yawning mout[h]
For swallowing the treasure of the realm[:]
Thy lips, that kiss'd the queen, shall swee[p the]
ground;
And thou, that smil'dst at good Duke H[um-]
phrey's death,
Against the senseless winds shall grin in va[in,]
Who in contempt shall hiss at thee again:
And wedded be thou to the hags of hell,
For daring to affy a mighty lord
Unto the daughter of a worthless king,
Having neither subject, wealth, nor diade[m.]
By devilish policy art thou grown great,
And, like ambitious Sylla, overgorg'd
With gobbets of thy mother's bleeding hea[rt.]
By thee Anjou and Maine were sold to Fra[nce;]
The false revolting Normans thorough th[ee]
Disdain to call us lord, and Picardy
Hath slain their governors, surpris'd our for[ts,]
And sent the ragged soldiers wounded ho[me.]
The princely Warwick, and the Nevils all,
Whose dreadful swords were never draw[n in]
vain,
As hating thee, are rising up in arms:
And now the house of York, thrust from [the]
crown
By shameful murder of a guiltless king,
And lofty proud encroaching tyranny,
Burns with revenging fire; whose hop[eful]
colours
Advance our half-fac'd sun, striving to sh[ine,]
Under the which is writ *Invitis nubibus.*
The commons here in Kent are up in arms;
And to conclude, reproach and beggary
Is crept into the palace of our king,
And all by thee. Away! convey him henc[e.]
    Suf. O! that I were a god, to shoot f[orth]
thunder
Upon these paltry, servile, abject drudges.
Small things make base men proud: this vil[lain]
here,
Being captain of a pinnace, threatens mo[re]
Than Bargulus the strong Illyrian pirate.
Drones suck not eagles' blood, but rob '[bee-]
hives.
It is impossible that I should die
By such a lowly vassal as thyself.
Thy words move rage, and not remorse in [me:]
I go of message from the queen to France[:]
I charge thee, waft me safely cross the Chan[nel.]
    Cap. Walter!
    Whit. Come, Suffolk, I must waft thee to [thy]
death.
    Suf. Gelidus timor occupat artus: 'tis th[y]
fear.

Whit. Thou shalt have cause to fear before I
leave thee.

What! are ye daunted now? now will ye stoop?

First Gent. My gracious lord, entreat him,
speak him fair. 120

Suf. Suffolk's imperial tongue is stern and
rough,

Us'd to command, untaught to plead for favour.

Far be it we should honour such as these

With humble suit: no, rather let my head 124

Stoop to the block than these knees bow to any

Save to the God of heaven, and to my king;

And sooner dance upon a bloody pole

Than stand uncover'd to the vulgar groom.

True nobility is exempt from fear: 129

More can I bear than you dare execute.

Cap. Hale him away, and let him talk no
more.

Suf. Come, soldiers, show what cruelty ye
can, 132

That this my death may never be forgot.

Great men oft die by vile bezonians.

A Roman sworder and banditto slave

Murder'd sweet Tully; Brutus' bastard hand

Stabb'd Julius Cæsar; savage islanders 137

Pompey the Great; and Suffolk dies by pirates.

     [*Exit with* SUFFOLK, WHITMORE *and Others.*

Cap. And as for these whose ransom we have
set,

It is our pleasure one of them depart: 140

Therefore come you with us and let him go.

     [*Exeunt all but first* Gentleman.

Re-enter WHITMORE, *with* SUFFOLK'S *body.*

Whit. There let his head and lifeless body lie,

Until the queen his mistress bury it.   [*Exit.*

First Gent. O barbarous and bloody spectacle! 144

His body will I bear unto the king:

If he revenge it not, yet will his friends;

So will the queen, that living held him dear.

     [*Exit with the body.*

SCENE II.—*Blackheath.*

Enter GEORGE BEVIS *and* JOHN HOLLAND.

Geo. Come, and get thee a sword, though
made of a lath: they have been up these two
days.

John. They have the more need to sleep now
then. 5

Geo. I tell thee, Jack Cade the clothier means
to dress the commonwealth, and turn it, and set
a new nap upon it.

John. So he had need, for 'tis threadbare.
Well, I say it was never merry world in England
since gentlemen came up.

Geo. O miserable age! Virtue is not regarded
in handicrafts-men. 13

John. The nobility think scorn to go in
leather aprons.

Geo. Nay, more; the king's council are no
good workmen.

John. True; and yet it is said, 'Labour in thy
vocation:' which is as much to say as, let the

magistrates be labouring men; and therefore
should we be magistrates. 21

Geo. Thou hast hit it; for there's no better
sign of a brave mind than a hard hand.

John. I see them! I see them! There's
Best's son, the tanner of Wingham,— 25

Geo. He shall have the skins of our enemies
to make dog's-leather of.

John. And Dick the butcher,— 28

Geo. Then is sin struck down like an ox, and
iniquity's throat cut like a calf.

John. And Smith the weaver,—

Geo. Argo, their thread of life is spun. 32

John. Come, come, let's fall in with them.

Drum. Enter CADE, DICK *the Butcher,* SMITH *the
Weaver, and a Sawyer, with infinite numbers.*

Cade. We John Cade, so termed of our supposed father,—

Dick. [*Aside.*] Or rather, of stealing a cade
of herrings. 37

Cade. For our enemies shall fall before us,
inspired with the spirit of putting down kings
and princes,—Command silence. 40

Dick. Silence!

Cade. My father was a Mortimer.—

Dick. [*Aside.*] He was an honest man, and a
good bricklayer. 44

Cade. My mother a Plantagenet,—

Dick. [*Aside.*] I knew her well; she was a
midwife.

Cade. My wife descended of the Lacies,— 48

Dick. [*Aside.*] She was, indeed, a pedlar's
daughter, and sold many laces.

Smith. [*Aside.*] But now of late, not able to
travel with her furred pack, she washes bucks
here at home. 53

Cade. Therefore am I of an honourable
house.

Dick. [*Aside.*] Ay, by my faith, the field is
honourable; and there was he born, under a
hedge; for his father had never a house but the
cage.

Cade. Valiant I am. 60

Smith. [*Aside.*] A' must needs, for beggary
is valiant.

Cade. I am able to endure much.

Dick. [*Aside.*] No question of that, for I have
seen him whipped three market-days together.

Cade. I fear neither sword nor fire.

Smith. [*Aside.*] He need not fear the sword,
for his coat is of proof. 68

Dick. [*Aside.*] But methinks he should stand
in fear of fire, being burnt i' the hand for stealing of sheep.

Cade. Be brave, then; for your captain is
brave, and vows reformation. There shall be
in England seven halfpenny loaves sold for a
penny; the three-hooped pot shall have ten
hoops; and I will make it felony to drink small
beer. All the realm shall be in common, and in
Cheapside shall my palfrey go to grass. And
when I am king,—as king I will be,—

All. God save your majesty! 80

Cade. I thank you, good people: there shall
be no money; all shall eat and drink on my

score; and I will apparel them all in one livery,
that they may agree like brothers, and worship
me their lord.   85

Dick. The first thing we do, let's kill all the
lawyers.

Cade. Nay, that I mean to do. Is not this
a lamentable thing, that of the skin of an innocent lamb should be made parchment! that
parchment, being scribbled o'er, should undo a
man? Some say the bee stings; but I say, 'tis
the bee's wax, for I did but seal once to a thing,
and I was never mine own man since. How
now! who's there?   95

Enter some, bringing in the Clerk of Chatham.

Smith. The clerk of Chatham: he can write
and read and cast accompt.

Cade. O monstrous!

Smith. We took him setting of boys' copies.

Cade. Here's a villain!   100

Smith. Has a book in his pocket with red
letters in 't.

Cade. Nay, then he is a conjurer.

Dick. Nay, he can make obligations, and
write court-hand.   105

Cade. I am sorry for 't: the man is a proper
man, of mine honour; unless I find him guilty,
he shall not die. Come hither, sirrah, I must
examine thee. What is thy name?   109

Clerk. Emmanuel.

Dick. They use to write it on the top of
letters. 'Twill go hard with you.   112

Cade. Let me alone. Dost thou use to write
thy name, or hast thou a mark to thyself, like
an honest plain-dealing man?

Clerk. Sir, I thank God, I have been so well
brought up, that I can write my name.   117

All. He hath confessed: away with him! he's
a villain and a traitor.

Cade. Away with him! I say: hang him with
his pen and ink-horn about his neck.   121

[*Exeunt some with the* Clerk.

Enter MICHAEL.

Mich. Where's our general?

Cade. Here I am, thou particular fellow.

Mich. Fly, fly, fly! Sir Humphrey Stafford
and his brother are hard by, with the king's
forces.   126

Cade. Stand, villain, stand, or I'll fell thee
down. He shall be encountered with a man as
good as himself: he is but a knight, is a'?

Mich. No.

Cade. To equal him, I will make myself a
knight presently. [*Kneels.*] Rise up Sir John
Mortimer. [*Rises.*] Now have at him.   133

Enter SIR HUMPHREY STAFFORD *and* WILLIAM
  his Brother, with drum and Forces.

Staf. Rebellious hinds, the filth and scum of
Kent,
Mark'd for the gallows, lay your weapons down;
Home to your cottages, forsake this groom:
The king is merciful, if you revolt.   137

W. Staf. But angry, wrathful, and inclin'd
to blood,

If you go forward: therefore yield, or die.

Cade. As for these silken-coated slaves, I
pass not: 140
It is to you, good people, that I speak,
O'er whom, in time to come I hope to reign;
For I am rightful heir unto the crown.

Staf. Villain! thy father was a plasterer;
And thou thyself a shearman, art thou not? 145

Cade. And Adam was a gardener.

W. Staf. And what of that?

Cade. Marry, this: Edmund Mortimer, Earl
of March,   148
Married the Duke of Clarence' daughter, did
he not?

Staf. Ay, sir.

Cade. By her he had two children at one
birth.

W. Staf. That's false.   152

Cade. Ay, there's the question; but I say,
'tis true:
The elder of them, being put to nurse,
Was by a beggar-woman stol'n away;
And, ignorant of his birth and parentage, 156
Became a bricklayer when he came to age:
His son am I; deny it if you can.

Dick. Nay, 'tis too true; therefore he shall be
king.

Smith. Sir, he made a chimney in my father's
house, and the bricks are alive at this day to
testify it; and therefore deny it not.

Staf. And will you credit this base drudge's
words,
That speaks he knows not what?   164

All. Ay, marry, will we; therefore get ye
gone.

W. Staf. Jack Cade, the Duke of York hath
taught you this.

Cade. [*Aside.*] He lies, for I invented it myself. Go to, sirrah; tell the king from me, that,
for his father's sake, Henry the Fifth, in whose
time boys went to span-counter for French
crowns, I am content he shall reign; but I'll be
protector over him.   172

Dick. And furthermore, we'll have the Lord
Say's head for selling the dukedom of Maine.

Cade. And good reason; for thereby is England mained, and fain to go with a staff, but
that my puissance holds it up. Fellow kings, I
tell you that that Lord Say hath gelded the
commonwealth, and made it a eunuch; and
more than that, he can speak French; and
therefore he is a traitor.   181

Staf. O gross and miserable ignorance!

Cade. Nay, answer, if you can: the Frenchmen are our enemies; go to then, I ask but
this, can he that speaks with the tongue of an
enemy be a good counsellor, or no?

All. No, no; and therefore we'll have his head.

W. Staf. Well, seeing gentle words will not
prevail,   188
Assail them with the army of the king.

Staf. Herald, away; and throughout every
town
Proclaim them traitors that are up with Cade;
That those which fly before the battle ends 192
May, even in their wives' and children's sight,

Be hang'd up for example at their doors:
And you, that be the king's friends, follow
　me.
　　[*Exeunt the two* STAFFORDS *and Forces.*
Cade. And you, that love the commons,
　follow me.　　　　　　　　196
Now show yourselves men; 'tis for liberty.
We will not leave one lord, one gentleman:
Spare none but such as go in clouted shoon,
For they are thrifty honest men, and such　200
As would, but that they dare not take our
　parts.
Dick. They are all in order, and march to-
　ward us.
Cade. But then are we in order when we are
most out of order. Come, march! forward!　204
　　　　　　　　　　　　　　[*Exeunt.*

SCENE III.—*Another Part of Blackheath.*

*Alarums. The two parties enter and fight, and
both the* STAFFORDS *are slain.*

Cade. Where's Dick, the butcher of Ashford?
Dick. Here, sir.
Cade. They fell before thee like sheep and
oxen, and thou behavedst thyself as if thou
hadst been in thine own slaughter-house: therefore thus will I reward thee, the Lent shall be
as long again as it is; and thou shalt have a
licence to kill for a hundred lacking one.　8
Dick. I desire no more.
Cade. And, to speak truth, thou deservest no
less. This monument of the victory will I bear:
[*Puts on* SIR HUMPHREY STAFFORD'S *armour.*]
and the bodies shall be dragged at my horse'
heels, till I do come to London, where we will
have the Mayor's sword borne before us.　14
Dick. If we mean to thrive and do good,
break open the gaols and let out the prisoners.
Cade. Fear not that, I warrant thee. Come;
let's march towards London.　　[*Exeunt.*

SCENE IV.—*London. A Room in the Palace.*

Enter KING HENRY, *reading a Supplication; the*
DUKE OF BUCKINGHAM *and* LORD SAY *with
him: at a distance,* QUEEN MARGARET, *mourning over* SUFFOLK'S *head.*

Q. Mar. Oft have I heard that grief softens
　the mind,
And makes it fearful and degenerate;
Think therefore on revenge, and cease to
　weep.
But who can cease to weep and look on this?　4
Here may his head lie on my throbbing breast;
But where's the body that I should embrace?
Buck. What answer makes your Grace to the
rebels' supplication?　　　　　8
K. Hen. I'll send some holy bishop to entreat;
For God forbid so many simple souls
Should perish by the sword! And I myself,
Rather than bloody war shall cut them short,　12
Will parley with Jack Cade their general.
But stay, I'll read it over once again.
Q. Mar. Ah, barbarous villains! hath this
lovely face

Rul'd like a wandering planet over me,　16
And could it not enforce them to relent,
That were unworthy to behold the same?
K. Hen. Lord Say, Jack Cade hath sworn to
　have thy head.
Say. Ay, but I hope your highness shall have
　his.　　　　　　　　　　20
K. Hen. How now, madam!
Still lamenting and mourning for Suffolk's
　death?
I fear me, love, if that I had been dead,
Thou wouldest not have mourn'd so much for
　me.　　　　　　　　　　24
Q. Mar. No, my love; I should not mourn,
　but die for thee.

Enter a Messenger.

K. Hen. How now! what news? why com'st
　thou in such haste?
Mess. The rebels are in Southwark; fly, my
　lord!　　　　　　　　　　27
Jack Cade proclaims himself Lord Mortimer,
Descended from the Duke of Clarence' house,
And calls your Grace usurper openly,
And vows to crown himself in Westminster.
His army is a ragged multitude　　　32
Of hinds and peasants, rude and merciless:
Sir Humphrey Stafford and his brother's death
Hath given them heart and courage to proceed.
All scholars, lawyers, courtiers, gentlemen,　36
They call false caterpillars, and intend their
　death.
K. Hen. O graceless men! they know not
　what they do.
Buck. My gracious lord, retire to Killing-
　worth,
Until a power be rais'd to put them down.　40
Q. Mar. Ah! were the Duke of Suffolk now
　alive,
These Kentish rebels would be soon appeas'd.
K. Hen. Lord Say, the traitors hate thee,
Therefore away with us to Killingworth.　44
Say. So might your Grace's person be in
　danger.
The sight of me is odious in their eyes;
And therefore in this city will I stay,
And live alone as secret as I may.　　48

Enter a second Messenger.

Sec. Mess. Jack Cade hath gotten London
　bridge;
The citizens fly and forsake their houses;
The rascal people, thirsting after prey,
Join with the traitor; and they jointly swear　52
To spoil the city and your royal court.
Buck. Then linger not, my lord; away! take
　horse.
K. Hen. Come, Margaret; God, our hope,
　will succour us.
Q. Mar. My hope is gone, now Suffolk is
　deceas'd.　　　　　　　56
K. Hen. [*To* LORD SAY.] Farewell, my lord:
　trust not the Kentish rebels.
Buck. Trust nobody, for fear you be betray'd.
Say. The trust I have is in mine innocence,
And therefore am I bold and resolute. [*Exeunt.*

SCENE V.—*The Same. The Tower.*

Enter LORD SCALES *and Others, on the Walls.
Then enter certain* Citizens, *below.*

Scales. How now! is Jack Cade slain?

First Cit. No, my lord, nor likely to be slain;
for they have won the bridge, killing all those
that withstand them. The Lord Mayor craves
aid of your honour from the Tower, to defend
the city from the rebels.

Scales. Such aid as I can spare you shall
command;
But I am troubled here with them myself;   8
The rebels have assay'd to win the Tower.
But get you to Smithfield and gather head,
And thither I will send you Matthew Goffe:
Fight for your king, your country, and your
lives;   12
And so, farewell, for I must hence again.
                                    [*Exeunt.*

SCENE VI.—*London. Cannon Street.*

Enter JACK CADE, *and his Followers. He strikes
his staff on London-stone.*

Cade. Now is Mortimer lord of this city. And
here, sitting upon London-stone, I charge and
command that, of the city's cost, the pissing-
conduit run nothing but claret wine this first
year of our reign. And now, henceforward, it
shall be treason for any that calls me other than
Lord Mortimer.

Enter a Soldier, *running.*

Sold. Jack Cade! Jack Cade!

Cade. Knock him down there.
                                [*They kill him.*

Smith. If this fellow be wise, he'll never call
you Jack Cade more: I think he hath a very
fair warning.   12

Dick. My lord, there's an army gathered together in Smithfield.

Cade. Come then, let's go fight with them.
But first, go and set London-bridge on fire, and,
if you can, burn down the Tower too. Come,
let's away.   [*Exeunt.*

SCENE VII.—*The Same. Smithfield.*

Alarums. Enter, on one side, CADE *and his company; on the other,* Citizens, *and the* KING'S
Forces, *headed by* MATTHEW GOFFE. *They
fight; the* Citizens *are routed, and* MATTHEW
GOFFE *is slain.*

Cade. So, sirs:—Now go some and pull down
the Savoy; others to the inns of court: down
with them all.

Dick. I have a suit unto your lordship.   4

Cade. Be it a lordship, thou shalt have it for
that word.

Dick. Only that the laws of England may
come out of your mouth.   8

John. [*Aside.*] Mass, 'twill be sore law then;
for he was thrust in the mouth with a spear,
and 'tis not whole yet.

Smith. [*Aside.*] Nay, John, it will be stink-

ing law; for his breath stinks with eating
toasted cheese.   14

Cade. I have thought upon it; it shall be so.
Away! burn all the records of the realm: my
mouth shall be the parliament of England.

John. [*Aside.*] Then we are like to have
biting statutes, unless his teeth be pulled out.

Cade. And henceforward all things shall be
in common.   21

Enter a Messenger.

Mess. My lord, a prize, a prize! here's the
Lord Say, which sold the towns in France; he
that made us pay one-and-twenty fifteens, and
one shilling to the pound, the last subsidy. 25

Enter GEORGE BEVIS, *with the* LORD SAY.

Cade. Well, he shall be beheaded for it ten
times. Ah! thou say, thou serge, nay, thou
buckram lord; now art thou within point-
blank of our jurisdiction regal. What canst
thou answer to my majesty for giving up of
Normandy unto Monsieur Basimecu, the Dauphin of France? Be it known unto thee by
these presence, even the presence of Lord Mortimer, that I am the besom that must sweep
the court clean of such filth as thou art. Thou
hast most traitorously corrupted the youth of
the realm in erecting a grammar-school; and
whereas, before, our fore-fathers had no other
books but the score and the tally, thou hast
caused printing to be used; and, contrary to
the king, his crown, and dignity, thou hast built
a paper-mill. It will be proved to thy face that
thou hast men about thee that usually talk of
a noun and a verb, and such abominable words
as no Christian ear can endure to hear. Thou
hast appointed justices of peace, to call poor
men before them about matters they were not
able to answer. Moreover, thou hast put them
in prison; and because they could not read
thou hast hanged them; when indeed only for
that cause they have been most worthy to live.
Thou dost ride on a foot-cloth, dost thou not?

Say. What of that?   5

Cade. Marry, thou oughtest not to let thy
horse wear a cloak, when honester men than
thou go in their hose and doublets.   5

Dick. And work in their shirt too; as myself
for example, that am a butcher.

Say. You men of Kent,—

Dick. What say you of Kent?   6

Say. Nothing but this: 'tis *bona terra, ma-
gens.*

Cade. Away with him! away with him! he
speaks Latin.

Say. Hear me but speak, and bear me where
you will.

Kent, in the Commentaries Cæsar writ,
Is term'd the civil'st place of all this isle:
Sweet is the country, because full of riches;
The people liberal, valiant, active, wealthy;
Which makes me hope you are not void of pity.
I sold not Maine, I lost not Normandy;
Yet, to recover them, would lose my life.
Justice with favour have I always done;

rayers and tears have mov'd me, gifts could
    never.
When have I aught exacted at your hands,
ut to maintain the king, the realm, and you?
arge gifts have I bestow'd on learned clerks, 76
ecause my book preferr'd me to the king,
nd seeing ignorance is the curse of God,
nowledge the wing wherewith we fly to heaven,
nless you be possess'd with devilish spirits, 80
ou cannot but forbear to murder me:
his tongue hath parley'd unto foreign kings
or your behoof,—
  Cade. Tut! when struck'st thou one blow in
e field?   85
  Say. Great men have reaching hands: oft
  have I struck
hose that I never saw, and struck them dead.
  Geo. O monstrous coward! what, to come
hind folks!   89
  Say. These cheeks are pale for watching for
  your good.
  Cade. Give him a box o' the ear, and that
ill make 'em red again.   92
  Say. Long sitting, to determine poor men's
  causes,
ath made me full of sickness and diseases.
  Cade. Ye shall have a hempen caudle then,
d the help of hatchet.   96
  Dick. Why dost thou quiver, man?
  Say. The palsy, and not fear, provokes me.
  Cade. Nay, he nods at us; as who should say,
l be even with you: I'll see if his head will
and steadier on a pole, or no. Take him away
d behead him.   102
  Say. Tell me wherein have I offended most?
ave I affected wealth, or honour? speak.
re my chests fill'd up with extorted gold?
my apparel sumptuous to behold?
hom have I injur'd, that ye seek my death?
nese hands are free from guiltless blood-
  shedding,   108
his breast from harbouring foul deceitful
  thoughts.
! let me live.
  Cade. [*Aside.*] I feel remorse in myself with
s words; but I'll bridle it: he shall die, an it
e but for pleading so well for his life. Away
ith him! he has a familiar under his tongue;
e speaks not o' God's name. Go, take him
vay, I say, and strike off his head presently;
d then break into his son-in-law's house, Sir
mes Cromer, and strike off his head, and
ring them both upon two poles hither.   119
  All. It shall be done.
  Say. Ah, countrymen! if when you make
  your prayers,
od should be so obdurate as yourselves,
ow would it fare with your departed souls?
nd therefore yet relent, and save my life. 124
  Cade. Away with him! and do as I com-
and ye. [*Exeunt some, with* LORD SAY.] The
roudest peer in the realm shall not wear a
ead on his shoulders, unless he pay me tribute;
ere shall not a maid be married, but she shall
ay to me her maidenhead, ere they have it;
en shall hold of me *in capite;* and we charge

and command that their wives be as free as
heart can wish or tongue can tell.   133
  Dick. My lord, when shall we go to Cheap-
side and take up commodities upon our bills?
  Cade. Marry, presently.   136
  All. O! brave!

Re-enter Rebels, with the heads of LORD SAY
and his Son-in-law.

  Cade. But is not this braver? Let them kiss
one another, for they loved well when they were
alive. Now part them again, lest they consult
about the giving up of some more towns in
France. Soldiers, defer the spoil of the city
until night: for with these borne before us, instead of maces, will we ride through the streets;
and at every corner have them kiss. Away! 145
                              [*Exeunt.*

SCENE VIII.—*The Same. Southwark.*

Alarum. Enter CADE *and all his Rabblement.*

  Cade. Up Fish Street! down St. Magnus'
corner! kill and knock down! throw them into
Thames! [*A parley sounded, then a retreat.*]
What noise is this I hear? Dare any be so bold
to sound retreat or parley, when I command
them kill?

Enter BUCKINGHAM, *and Old* CLIFFORD, *with
Forces.*

  Buck. Ay, here they be that dare and will
disturb thee.
Know, Cade, we come ambassadors from the
  king   8
Unto the commons whom thou hast misled;
And here pronounce free pardon to them all
That will forsake thee and go home in peace.
  Clif. What say ye, countrymen? will ye
  relent,   12
And yield to mercy, whilst 'tis offer'd you,
Or let a rebel lead you to your deaths?
Who loves the king, and will embrace his pardon,
Fling up his cap, and say 'God save his
  majesty!'   16
Who hateth him, and honours not his father,
Henry the Fifth, that made all France to quake,
Shake he his weapon at us, and pass by.
  All. God save the king! God save the king!
  Cade. What! Buckingham and Clifford, are
ye so brave? And you, base peasants, do ye
believe him? will you needs be hanged with your
pardons about your necks? Hath my sword
therefore broke through London Gates, that you
should leave me at the White Hart in Southwark? I thought ye would never have given out
these arms till you had recovered your ancient
freedom; but you are all recreants and dastards,
and delight to live in slavery to the nobility.
Let them break your backs with burdens, take
your houses over your heads, ravish your wives
and daughters before your faces: for me, I will
make shift for one, and so, God's curse light
upon you all!   35
  All. We'll follow Cade, we'll follow Cade!
  Clif. Is Cade the son of Henry the Fifth,

That thus you do exclaim you'll go with him?
Will he conduct you through the heart of France,
And make the meanest of you earls and dukes?
Alas! he hath no home, no place to fly to;   41
Nor knows he how to live but by the spoil,
Unless by robbing of your friends and us.
Were 't not a shame, that whilst you live at jar,
The fearful French, whom you late vanquished,
Should make a start o'er seas and vanquish you?
Methinks already in this civil broil
I see them lording it in London streets,   48
Crying *Villiago!* unto all they meet.
Better ten thousand base-born Cades miscarry,
Than you should stoop unto a Frenchman's
     mercy.
To France, to France! and get what you have
     lost;   52
Spare England, for it is your native coast.
Henry hath money, you are strong and manly;
God on our side, doubt not of victory.
     All. A Clifford! a Clifford! we'll follow the
king and Clifford.   57
     Cade. [*Aside.*] Was ever feather so lightly
blown to and fro as this multitude? The name of
Henry the Fifth hales them to a hundred mischiefs, and makes them leave me desolate. I see
them lay their heads together to surprise me.
My sword make way for me, for here is no staying. In despite of the devils and hell, have
through the very middest of you! and heavens
and honour be witness, that no want of resolution
in me, but only my followers' base and ignominious treasons, makes me betake me to my heels.
     [*Exit.*
     Buck. What, is he fled? go some, and follow
him;
And he that brings his head unto the king
Shall have a thousand crowns for his reward.
     [*Exeunt some of them.*
Follow me, soldiers: we'll devise a mean   72
To reconcile you all unto the king. [*Exeunt.*

SCENE IX.—*Kenilworth Castle.*

Trumpets sounded. Enter KING HENRY, QUEEN
     MARGARET, *and* SOMERSET, *on the terrace.*

     K. Hen. Was ever king that joy'd an earthly
throne,
And could command no more content than I?
No sooner was I crept out of my cradle
But I was made a king at nine months old: 4
Was never subject long'd to be a king
As I do long and wish to be a subject.

Enter BUCKINGHAM *and Old* CLIFFORD.

     Buck. Health, and glad tidings, to your
majesty!
     K. Hen. Why, Buckingham, is the traitor
Cade surpris'd?   8
Or is he but retir'd to make him strong?

Enter, below, a number of CADE'S *followers,
     with halters about their necks.*

     Clif. He's fled, my lord, and all his powers
do yield;
And humbly thus, with halters on their necks,

Expect your highness' doom, of life, or death.
     K. Hen. Then, heaven, set ope thy everlast-
     ing gates,
To entertain my vows of thanks and praise!
Soldiers, this day have you redeem'd your lives
And show'd how well you love your prince and
     country:
Continue still in this so good a mind,
And Henry, though he be infortunate,
Assure yourselves, will never be unkind:
And so, with thanks and pardon to you all,
I do dismiss you to your several countries.
     All. God save the king! God save the king!

Enter a Messenger.

     Mess. Please it your Grace to be advertised
The Duke of York is newly come from Ireland,
And with a puissant and a mighty power
Of Gallowglasses, and stout kerns,
Is marching hitherward in proud array;
And still proclaimeth, as he comes along,
His arms are only to remove from thee
The Duke of Somerset, whom he terms a traitor.
     K. Hen. Thus stands my state, 'twixt Cade
     and York distress'd;
Like to a ship, that, having scap'd a tempest,
Is straightway calm'd, and boarded with a pirate:
But now is Cade driven back, his men dispers'd;
And now is York in arms to second him.
I pray thee, Buckingham, go and meet him,
And ask him what's the reason of these arms.
Tell him I'll send Duke Edmund to the Tower;
And, Somerset, we will commit thee thither
Until his army be dismiss'd from him.
     Som. My lord,
I'll yield myself to prison willingly,
Or unto death, to do my country good.
     K. Hen. In any case, be not too rough in
     terms;
For he is fierce and cannot brook hard language.
     Buck. I will, my lord; and doubt not so to
     deal
As all things shall redound unto your good.
     K. Hen. Come, wife, let's in, and learn to
     govern better;
For yet may England curse my wretched reign.
     [*Exeunt*

SCENE X.—*Kent. Iden's Garden.*

Enter CADE.

     Cade. Fie on ambition! fie on myself, that
have a sword, and yet am ready to famish!
These five days have I hid me in these woods and
durst not peep out, for all the country is laid
for me; but now I am so hungry, that if I might
have a lease of my life for a thousand years I
could stay no longer. Wherefore, on a brick
wall have I climbed into this garden, to see if I
can eat grass, or pick a sallet another while,
which is not amiss to cool a man's stomach this
hot weather. And I think this word 'sallet'
was born to do me good: for many a time, but
for a sallet, my brain-pan had been cleft with a
brown bill; and many a time, when I have been
dry, and bravely marching, it hath served me

instead of a quart-pot to drink in; and now the word 'sallet' must serve me to feed on. 17

Enter IDEN *with* Servants *behind.*

Iden. Lord! who would live turmoiled in the court,
And may enjoy such quiet walks as these?
This small inheritance my father left me 20
Contenteth me, and worth a monarchy.
I seek not to wax great by others' waning,
Or gather wealth I care not with what envy:
Sufficeth that I have maintains my state, 24
And sends the poor well pleased from my gate.
Cade. [*Aside.*] Here's the lord of the soil
come to seize me for a stray, for entering his
fee-simple without leave. Ah, villain! thou wilt
betray me, and get a thousand crowns of the
king by carrying my head to him; but I'll make
thee eat iron like an ostrich, and swallow my
sword like a great pin, ere thou and I part. 32
Iden. Why, rude companion, whatsoe'er
thou be,
I know thee not; why then should I betray thee?
Is't not enough to break into my garden,
And like a thief to come to rob my grounds, 36
Climbing my walls in spite of me the owner,
But thou wilt brave me with these saucy terms?
Cade. Brave thee! ay, by the best blood that
ever was broached, and beard thee too. Look on
me well: I have eat no meat these five days;
yet, come thou and thy five men, and if I do
not leave you all as dead as a door-nail, I pray
God I may never eat grass more. 44
Iden. Nay, it shall ne'er be said, while Eng-
land stands,
That Alexander Iden, an esquire of Kent,
Took odds to combat a poor famish'd man.
Oppose thy steadfast-gazing eyes to mine, 48
See if thou canst out-face me with thy looks:
Set limb to limb, and thou art far the lesser;
Thy hand is but a finger to my fist;
Thy leg a stick compared with this truncheon;
My foot shall fight with all the strength thou
hast; 53
And if mine arm be heaved in the air
Thy grave is digg'd already in the earth.
As for more words, whose greatness answers
words, 56
Let this my sword report what speech forbears.
Cade. By my valour, the most complete
champion that ever I heard! Steel, if thou turn
the edge, or cut not out the burly-boned clown
in chines of beef ere thou sleep in thy sheath, I
beseech Jove on my knees, thou mayst be turned
to hobnails. [*They fight;* CADE *falls.*] O, I am
slain! Famine and no other hath slain me: let
ten thousand devils come against me, and give
me but the ten meals I have lost, and I'll defy
them all. Wither, garden; and be henceforth a
burying-place to all that do dwell in this house,
because the unconquered soul of Cade is fled.
Iden. Is't Cade that I have slain, that monstrous traitor? 70
Sword, I will hallow thee for this thy deed,
And hang thee o'er my tomb when I am dead:
Ne'er shall this blood be wiped from thy point,

But thou shalt wear it as a herald's coat, 74
To emblaze the honour that thy master got.
Cade. Iden, farewell; and be proud of thy
victory. Tell Kent from me, she hath lost her
best man, and exhort all the world to be
cowards; for I, that never feared any, am van-
quished by famine, not by valour. [*Dies.*
Iden. How much thou wrong'st me, heaven
be my judge. 81
Die, damned wretch, the curse of her that bare
thee!
And as I thrust thy body in with my sword,
So wish I I might thrust thy soul to hell. 84
Hence will I drag thee headlong by the heels
Unto a dunghill which shall be thy grave,
And there cut off thy most ungracious head;
Which I will bear in triumph to the king, 88
Leaving thy trunk for crows to feed upon.
[*Exit, with* Servants, *dragging out
the body.*

ACT V

SCENE I.—*Kent. Fields between Dartford and
Blackheath.*

The KING'S *camp on one side. On the other, enter*
YORK, *and his army of Irish, with drum and
colours.*

York. From Ireland thus comes York to
claim his right,
And pluck the crown from feeble Henry's head:
Ring, bells, aloud; burn, bonfires, clear and
bright,
To entertain great England's lawful king. 4
Ah *sancta majestas,* who would not buy thee
dear?
Let them obey that know not how to rule;
This hand was made to handle nought but gold:
I cannot give due action to my words, 8
Except a sword, or sceptre balance it.
A sceptre shall it have, have I a soul,
On which I'll toss the flower-de-luce of France.

Enter BUCKINGHAM.

Whom have we here? Buckingham, to disturb
me? 12
The king hath sent him, sure: I must dissemble.
Buck. York, if thou meanest well, I greet
thee well.
York. Humphrey of Buckingham, I accept
thy greeting. 15
Art thou a messenger, or come of pleasure?
Buck. A messenger from Henry, our dread
liege,
To know the reason of these arms in peace;
Or why thou,—being a subject as I am,—
Against thy oath and true allegiance sworn,
Shouldst raise so great a power without his leave,
Or dare to bring thy force so near the court.
York. [*Aside.*] Scarce can I speak, my choler
is so great: 23
O! I could hew up rocks and fight with flint,
I am so angry at these abject terms;
And now, like Ajax Telamonius,

On sheep or oxen could I spend my fury.
I am far better born than is the king,   28
More like a king, more kingly in my thoughts;
But I must make fair weather yet awhile,
Till Henry be more weak, and I more strong.
[*Aloud.*] Buckingham, I prithee, pardon me,
That I have given no answer all this while;   33
My mind was troubled with deep melancholy.
The cause why I have brought this army hither
Is to remove proud Somerset from the king,
Seditious to his Grace and to the state.
     Buck. That is too much presumption on thy
          part:
But if thy arms be to no other end,
The king hath yielded unto thy demand: 40
The Duke of Somerset is in the Tower.
     York. Upon thine honour, is he a prisoner?
     Buck. Upon mine honour, he is a prisoner.
     York. Then, Buckingham, I do dismiss my
          powers.   44
Soldiers, I thank you all; disperse yourselves;
Meet me to-morrow in Saint George's field,
You shall have pay, and everything you wish,
And let my sov'reign, virtuous Henry,   48
Command my eldest son, nay, all my sons,
As pledges of my fealty and love;
I'll send them all as willing as I live:
Lands, goods, horse, armour, anything I have
Is his to use, so Somerset may die.   53
     Buck. York, I commend this kind submission:
We twain will go into his highness' tent.

          Enter KING HENRY, *attended.*

     K. Hen. Buckingham, doth York intend no
          harm to us,   56
That thus he marcheth with thee arm in arm?
     York. In all submission and humility
York doth present himself unto your highness.
     K. Hen. Then what intend these forces thou
          dost bring?   60
     York. To heave the traitor Somerset from hence,
And fight against that monstrous rebel, Cade,
Who since I heard to be discomfited.

          Enter IDEN, *with* CADE'S *head.*

     Iden. If one so rude and of so mean condi-
          tion   64
May pass into the presence of a king,
Lo! I present your Grace a traitor's head,
The head of Cade, whom I in combat slew.
     K. Hen. The head of Cade! Great God, how
          just art thou!   68
O! let me view his visage, being dead,
That living wrought me such exceeding trouble.
Tell me, my friend, art thou the man that slew
          him?
     Iden. I was, an't like your majesty.   72
     K. Hen. How art thou call'd, and what is
          thy degree?
     Iden. Alexander Iden, that's my name;
A poor esquire of Kent, that loves this king.
     Buck. So please it you, my lord, 'twere not
          amiss   76
He were created knight for his good service.
     K. Hen. Iden, kneel down. [*He kneels.*] Rise
          up a knight.

We give thee for reward a thousand marks;
And will, that thou henceforth attend on us. 80
     Iden. May Iden live to merit such a bounty,
And never live but true unto his liege!
     K. Hen. See! Buckingham! Somerset comes
          with the queen:
Go, bid her hide him quickly from the duke. 84

          Enter QUEEN MARGARET *and* SOMERSET.

     Q. Mar. For thousand Yorks he shall not
          hide his head,
But boldly stand and front him to his face.
     York. How now! is Somerset at liberty?
Then, York, unloose thy long-imprison'd
          thoughts   88
And let thy tongue be equal with thy heart.
Shall I endure the sight of Somerset?
False king! why hast thou broken faith with me,
Knowing how hardly I can brook abuse?   92
King did I call thee? no, thou art not king;
Not fit to govern and rule multitudes,
Which dar'st not, no, nor canst not rule a traitor.
That head of thine doth not become a crown;
Thy hand is made to grasp a palmer's staff, 97
And not to grace an awful princely sceptre.
That gold must round engirt these brows of
          mine,
Whose smile and frown, like to Achilles' spear,
Is able with the change to kill and cure.   101
Here is a hand to hold a sceptre up,
And with the same to act controlling laws.
Give place: by heaven, thou shalt rule no
          more   104
O'er him whom heaven created for thy ruler.
     Som. O monstrous traitor:—I arrest thee,
          York,
Of capital treason 'gainst the king and crown.
Obey, audacious traitor; kneel for grace. 108
     York. Wouldst have me kneel? first let me
          ask of these
If they can brook I bow a knee to man.
Sirrah, call in my sons to be my bail:
          [*Exit an Attendant.*
I know ere they will have me go to ward,   112
They'll pawn their swords for my enfranchise-
          ment.
     Q. Mar. Call hither Clifford; bid him come
          amain,
To say if that the bastard boys of York
Shall be the surety for their traitor father. 116
          [*Exit* BUCKINGHAM.
     York. O blood-bespotted Neapolitan,
Outcast of Naples, England's bloody scourge!
The sons of York, thy betters in their birth,
Shall be their father's bail; and bane to those
That for my surety will refuse the boys!   121

Enter EDWARD *and* RICHARD PLANTAGENET,
     *with Forces at one side; at the other, with
     Forces also,* Old CLIFFORD *and his Son.*

See where they come: I'll warrant they'll make
     it good.
     Q. Mar. And here comes Clifford, to deny
          their bail.
     Clif. [*Kneeling.*] Health and all happiness to
          my lord the king!   124

York. I thank thee, Clifford: say, what news
with thee?
ay, do not fright us with an angry look:
e are thy sov'reign, Clifford, kneel again;
or thy mistaking so, we pardon thee. 128
Clif. This is my king, York, I do not mistake;
ıt thou mistak'st me much to think I do.
› Bedlam with him! is the man grown mad?
K. Hen. Ay, Clifford; a bedlam and ambitious humour 132
Takes him oppose himself against his king.
Clif. He is a traitor; let him to the Tower,
nd chop away that factious pate of his.
Q. Mar. He is arrested, but will not obey:
is sons, he says, shall give their words for
him. 137
York. Will you not, sons?
Edw. Ay, noble father, if our words will serve.
Rich. And if words will not, then our weapons shall. 140
Clif. Why, what a brood of traitors have we
here!
York. Look in a glass, and call thy image so:
am thy king, and thou a false-heart traitor.
all hither to the stake my two brave bears, 144
hat with the very shaking of their chains
hey may astonish these fell-lurking curs:
id Salisbury and Warwick come to me.

rums. Enter WARWICK *and* SALISBURY, *with
Forces.*

Clif. Are these thy bears? we'll bait thy
bears to death, 148
nd manacle the bear-ward in their chains
thou dar'st bring them to the baiting-place.
Rich. Oft have I seen a hot o'erweening cur
un back and bite, because he was withheld;
'ho, being suffer'd with the bear's fell paw,
ath clapp'd his tail between his legs, and
cried:
nd such a piece of service will you do,
you oppose yourselves to match Lord Warwick. 156
Clif. Hence, heap of wrath, foul indigested
lump,
s crooked in thy manners as thy shape!
York. Nay, we shall heat you thoroughly
anon.
Clif. Take heed, lest by your heat you burn
yourselves. 160
K. Hen. Why, Warwick, hath thy knee forgot to bow?
ld Salisbury, shame to thy silver hair,
hou mad misleader of thy brain-sick son!
What! wilt thou on thy death-bed play the
ruffian, 164
nd seek for sorrow with thy spectacles?
! where is faith? O, where is loyalty?
it be banish'd from the frosty head,
Where shall it find a harbour in the earth? 167
Wilt thou go dig a grave to find out war,
nd shame thine honourable age with blood?
Why art thou old, and want'st experience?
r wherefore dost abuse it, if thou hast it?
or shame! in duty bend thy knee to me, 173
hat bows unto the grave with mickle age.

Sal. My lord, I have consider'd with myself
The title of this most renowned duke; 176
And in my conscience do repute his Grace
The rightful heir to England's royal seat.
K. Hen. Hast thou not sworn allegiance
unto me?
Sal. I have. 180
K. Hen. Canst thou dispense with heaven
for such an oath?
Sal. It is a great sin to swear unto a sin,
But greater sin to keep a sinful oath.
Who can be bound by any solemn vow 184
To do a murderous deed, to rob a man,
To force a spotless virgin's chastity,
To reave the orphan of his patrimony,
To wring the widow from her custom'd right,
And have no other reason for this wrong 189
But that he was bound by a solemn oath?
Q. Mar. A subtle traitor needs no sophister.
K. Hen. Call Buckingham, and bid him arm
himself. 192
York. Call Buckingham, and all the friends
thou hast,
I am resolv'd for death, or dignity.
Clif. The first I warrant thee, if dreams prove
true.
War. You were best to go to bed and dream
again, 196
To keep thee from the tempest of the field.
Clif. I am resolv'd to bear a greater storm
Than any thou canst conjure up to-day;
And that I'll write upon thy burgonet, 200
Might I but know thee by thy household badge.
War. Now, by my father's badge, old Nevil's
crest,
The rampant bear chain'd to the ragged staff,
This day I'll wear aloft my burgonet,— 204
As on a mountain-top the cedar shows,
That keeps his leaves in spite of any storm,—
Even to affright thee with the view thereof.
Clif. And from thy burgonet I'll rend thy
bear, 208
And tread it underfoot with all contempt,
Despite the bear-ward that protects the bear.
Y. Clif. And so to arms, victorious father,
To quell the rebels and their complices. 212
Rich. Fie! charity! for shame! speak not in
spite,
For you shall sup with Jesu Christ to-night.
Y. Clif. Foul stigmatic, that's more than
thou canst tell.
Rich. If not in heaven, you'll surely sup in
hell. [*Exeunt severally.*

SCENE II.—*Saint Alban's.*

Alarums: Excursions. Enter WARWICK.

War. Clifford of Cumberland, 'tis Warwick
calls:
And if thou dost not hide thee from the bear,
Now, when the angry trumpet sounds alarm,
And dead men's cries do fill the empty air, 4
Clifford, I say, come forth, and fight with
me!
Proud northern lord, Clifford of Cumberland,
Warwick is hoarse with calling thee to arms.

Enter YORK.

How now, my noble lord! what! all afoot?   8
York. The deadly-handed Clifford slew my
    steed;
But match to match I have encounter'd him,
And made a prey for carrion kites and crows
Even of the bonny beast he lov'd so well.   12

Enter Old CLIFFORD.

War. Of one or both of us the time is come.
York. Hold, Warwick! seek thee out some
    other chase,
For I myself must hunt this deer to death.
War. Then, nobly, York; 'tis for a crown
    thou fight'st.   16
As I intend, Clifford, to thrive to-day,
It grieves my soul to leave thee unassail'd.
                                    [*Exit.*
Clif. What seest thou in me, York? why
    dost thou pause?
York. With thy brave bearing should I be in
    love,   20
But that thou art so fast mine enemy.
Clif. Nor should thy prowess want praise
    and esteem,
But that 'tis shown ignobly and in treason.
York. So let it help me now against thy sword
As I in justice and true right express it.   25
Clif. My soul and body on the action both!
York. A dreadful lay! address thee instantly.
Clif. La fin couronne les œuvres.   28
        [*They fight, and* CLIFFORD *falls and dies.*
York. Thus war hath given thee peace, for
    thou art still.
Peace with his soul, heaven, if it be thy will!
                                    [*Exit.*

Enter Young CLIFFORD.

Y. Clif. Shame and confusion! all is on the
    rout: 31
Fear frames disorder, and disorder wounds
Where it should guard. O war! thou son of hell,
Whom angry heavens do make their minister,
Throw in the frozen bosoms of our part
Hot coals of vengeance! Let no soldier fly:
He that is truly dedicate to war   37
Hath no self-love; nor he that loves himself
Hath not essentially, but by circumstance,
The name of valour. [*Seeing his father's body.*
        O! let the vile world end,   40
And the premised flames of the last day
Knit heaven and earth together;
Now let the general trumpet blow his blast,
Particularities and petty sounds   44
To cease!—Wast thou ordain'd, dear father,
To lose thy youth in peace, and to achieve
The silver livery of advised age,   47
And, in thy reverence and thy chair-days thus
To die in ruffian battle? Even at this sight
My heart is turn'd to stone: and while 'tis mine
It shall be stony. York not our old men spares;
No more will I their babes: tears virginal   52
Shall be to me even as the dew to fire;
And beauty, that the tyrant oft reclaims,
Shall to my flaming wrath be oil and flax.
Henceforth I will not have to do with pity: 56

Meet I an infant of the house of York,
Into as many gobbets will I cut it
As wild Medea young Absyrtus did:
In cruelty will I seek out my fame.   6
Come, thou new ruin of old Clifford's house
                        [*Taking up the body*
As did Æneas old Anchises bear,
So bear I then upon my manly shoulders;
But then Æneas bare a living load,   6
Nothing so heavy as these woes of mine. [*Exi*

Enter RICHARD *and* SOMERSET, *fighting;*
    SOMERSET *is killed.*

Rich. So, lie thou there;
For underneath an alehouse' paltry sign,
The Castle in Saint Alban's, Somerset   6
Hath made the wizard famous in his death.
Sword, hold thy temper; heart, be wrathful still
Priests pray for enemies, but princes kill. [*Exi*

Alarums: Excursions. Enter KING HENRY, QUEE
    MARGARET, *and Others, retreating.*

Q. Mar. Away, my lord! you are slow: fo
    shame, away!
K. Hen. Can we outrun the heavens? goo
    Margaret, stay.
Q. Mar. What are you made of? you'll no
    fight nor fly:
Now is it manhood, wisdom, and defence,
To give the enemy way, and to secure us   7
By what we can, which can no more but fly.
                        [*Alarum afar o*
If you be ta'en, we then should see the botto
Of all our fortunes: but if we haply scape,
As well we may, if not through your neglec
We shall to London get, where you are lov'e
And where this breach now in our fortune
    made
May readily be stopp'd.

Re-enter Young CLIFFORD.

Y. Clif. But that my heart's on future mi
    chief set,   8
I would speak blasphemy ere bid you fly;
But fly you must: uncurable discomfit
Reigns in the hearts of all our present parts.
Away, for your relief! and we will live   8
To see their day and them our fortune give.
Away, my lord, away!   [*Exeun*

SCENE III.—*Field near Saint Alban's.*

Alarum. Retreat. Flourish; then enter YOR
    RICHARD, WARWICK, *and* Soldiers, *with dru*
    and colours.

York. Of Salisbury, who can report of hin
That winter lion, who in rage forgets
Aged contusions and all brush of time,
And, like a gallant in the brow of youth,
Repairs him with occasion? this happy day
Is not itself, nor have we won one foot,
If Salisbury be lost.
Rich.   My noble father,
Three times to-day I holp him to his horse,
Three times bestrid him; thrice I led him off,

Persuaded him from any further act:
But still, where danger was, still there I met him;
And like rich hangings in a homely house, 12
So was his will in his old feeble body.
But, noble as he is, look where he comes.

Enter SALISBURY.

Sal. Now, by my sword, well hast thou fought
By the mass, so did we all. I thank you,
  Richard: 16
God knows how long it is I have to live;
And it hath pleas'd him that three times to-
  day
You have defended me from imminent death.
Well, lords, we have not got that which we
  have: 20

'Tis not enough our foes are this time fled,
Being opposites of such repairing nature.
  York. I know our safety is to follow them;
For, as I hear, the king is fled to London, 24
To call a present court of parliament:
Let us pursue him ere the writs go forth:—
What says Lord Warwick? shall we after them?
  War. After them! nay, before them, if we
  can. 28
Now, by my hand, lords, 'twas a glorious
  day:
Saint Alban's battle, won by famous York,
Shall be eterniz'd in all age to come.
Sound, drums and trumpets, and to London
  all: 32
And more such days as these to us befall!
[*Exeunt.*

THE THIRD PART OF
KING HENRY THE SIXTH

DRAMATIS PERSONÆ

KING HENRY THE SIXTH.
EDWARD, Prince of Wales, his Son.
LEWIS THE ELEVENTH, King of France.
DUKE OF SOMERSET,
DUKE OF EXETER,
EARL OF OXFORD,
EARL OF NORTHUMBERLAND,
EARL OF WESTMORELAND,
LORD CLIFFORD, } on King Henry's side.
RICHARD PLANTAGENET, Duke of York.
EDWARD, Earl of March, afterwards King
   Edward the Fourth,
EDMUND, Earl of Rutland,
GEORGE, afterwards Duke of Clarence, } his Sons.
RICHARD, afterwards Duke of Gloucester,
DUKE OF NORFOLK,
MARQUESS OF MONTAGUE,
EARL OF WARWICK,
EARL OF PEMBROKE,
LORD HASTINGS,
LORD STAFFORD, } of the Duke of York's Party.

SIR JOHN MORTIMER, }
SIR HUGH MORTIMER, } Uncles to the Duke of York.
HENRY, EARL OF RICHMOND, a Youth.
LORD RIVERS, Brother to Lady Grey.
SIR WILLIAM STANLEY.
SIR JOHN MONTGOMERY.
SIR JOHN SOMERVILLE.
Tutor to Rutland.
Mayor of York.
Lieutenant of the Tower.
A Nobleman.
Two Keepers. A Huntsman.
A Son that has killed his Father.
A Father that has killed his Son.

QUEEN MARGARET.
LADY GREY, afterwards Queen to Edward the Fourth.
BONA, Sister to the French Queen.

Soldiers, and other Attendants on King Henry and King Edward, Messengers, Watchmen, &c.

SCENE.—*During part of the Third Act, in France; during the rest of the Play, in England.*

ACT I

SCENE I.—*London. The Parliament-House.*

Drums. Some Soldiers *of* YORK'S *party break in. Then, enter the* DUKE OF YORK, EDWARD, RICHARD, NORFOLK, MONTAGUE, WARWICK, *and Others, with white roses in their hats.*

War. I wonder how the king escap'd our hands.

York. While we pursu'd the horsemen of the north,
He slily stole away and left his men:
Whereat the great Lord of Northumberland, 4
Whose warlike ears could never brook retreat,
Cheer'd up the drooping army; and himself,
Lord Clifford, and Lord Stafford, all abreast,
Charg'd our main battle's front, and breaking in 8
Were by the swords of common soldiers slain.

Edw. Lord Stafford's father, Duke of Buckingham,
Is either slain or wounded dangerously;
I cleft his beaver with a downright blow: 12
That this is true, father, behold his blood.

[Showing his bloody sword.

Mont. And, brother, here's the Earl of Wiltshire's blood, *[To* YORK, *showing his.*
Whom I encounter'd as the battles join'd.

Rich. Speak thou for me, and tell them what I did. *[Throwing down the* DUKE OF SOMERSET'S *head.*

York. Richard hath best deserv'd of all my sons. 17

But, is your Grace dead, my Lord of Somerset?

Norf. Such hope have all the line of John of Gaunt!

Rich. Thus do I hope to shake King Henry's head. 20

War. And so do I. Victorious Prince of York,
Before I see thee seated in that throne
Which now the house of Lancaster usurps,
I vow by heaven these eyes shall never close. 24
This is the palace of the fearful king,
And this the regal seat: possess it, York;
For this is thine, and not King Henry's heirs'.

York. Assist me, then, sweet Warwick, and I will; 28
For hither we have broken in by force.

Norf. We'll all assist you; he that flies shall die.

York. Thanks, gentle Norfolk. Stay by me, my lords;
And, soldiers, stay and lodge by me this night. 32

War. And when the king comes, offer him no violence,
Unless he seek to thrust you out perforce.

[The Soldiers *retire.*

York. The queen this day here holds her parliament,
But little thinks we shall be of her council: 36
By words or blows here let us win our right.

Rich. Arm'd as we are, let's stay within this house.

War. The bloody parliament shall this be call'd,
Unless Plantagenet, Duke of York, be king, 40

And bashful Henry depos'd, whose cowardice
Hath made us by-words to our enemies.

  York. Then leave me not, my lords; be
resolute;
I mean to take possession of my right.   44

  War. Neither the king, nor he that loves
him best,
The proudest he that holds up Lancaster,
Dares stir a wing if Warwick shake his bells.
I'll plant Plantagenet, root him up who dares.
Resolve thee, Richard; claim the English crown.

  [WARWICK *leads* YORK *to the throne,*
who seats himself.

Flourish. Enter KING HENRY, CLIFFORD, NORTH-
UMBERLAND, WESTMORELAND, EXETER, *and*
Others, with red roses in their hats.

  K. Hen. My lords, look where the sturdy
rebel sits,
Even in the chair of state! belike he means—
Back'd by the power of Warwick, that false
peer—   52
To aspire unto the crown and reign as king.
Earl of Northumberland, he slew thy father,
And thine, Lord Clifford; and you both have
vow'd revenge
On him, his sons, his favourites, and his friends.

  North. If I be not, heavens be reveng'd on
me!   57

  Clif. The hope thereof makes Clifford mourn
in steel.

  West. What! shall we suffer this? let's pluck
him down:
My heart for anger burns; I cannot brook it. 60

  K. Hen. Be patient, gentle Earl of Westmoreland.

  Clif. Patience is for poltroons, such as he:
He durst not sit there had your father liv'd.
My gracious lord, here in the parliament   64
Let us assail the family of York.

  North. Well hast thou spoken, cousin: be
it so.

  K. Hen. Ah! know you not the city favours
them,
And they have troops of soldiers at their beck?

  Exe. But when the duke is slain they'll
quickly fly.   69

  K. Hen. Far be the thought of this from
Henry's heart,
To make a shambles of the parliament-house!
Cousin of Exeter, frowns, words, and threats, 72
Shall be the war that Henry means to use.

  [*They advance to the* DUKE.
Thou factious Duke of York, descend my throne,
And kneel for grace and mercy at my feet;
I am thy sovereign.

  York.   I am thine.   76

  Exe. For shame! come down: he made thee
Duke of York.

  York. 'Twas my inheritance, as the earldom
was.

  Exe. Thy father was a traitor to the crown.

  War. Exeter, thou art a traitor to the crown
In following this usurping Henry.   81

  Clif. Whom should he follow but his natural
king?

  War. True, Clifford; and that's Richard,
Duke of York.

  K. Hen. And shall I stand, and thou sit in
my throne?   84

  York. It must and shall be so: content thyself.

  War. Be Duke of Lancaster: let him be king.

  West. He is both king and Duke of Lancaster;
And that the Lord of Westmoreland shall maintain.   88

  War. And Warwick shall disprove it. You
forget
That we are those which chas'd you from the
field
And slew your fathers, and with colours spread
March'd through the city to the palace gates. 92

  North. Yes, Warwick, I remember it to my
grief;
And, by his soul, thou and thy house shall rue it.

  West. Plantagenet, of thee, and these thy
sons,
Thy kinsmen and thy friends, I'll have more
lives   96
Than drops of blood were in my father's veins.

  Clif. Urge it no more; lest that instead of
words,
I send thee, Warwick, such a messenger
As shall revenge his death before I stir.   100

  War. Poor Clifford! how I scorn his worthless threats.

  York. Will you we show our title to the
crown?
If not, our swords shall plead it in the field.

  K. Hen. What title hast thou, traitor, to the
crown?   104
Thy father was, as thou art, Duke of York;
Thy grandfather, Roger Mortimer, Earl of
March;
I am the son of Henry the Fifth,
Who made the Dauphin and the French to stoop,
And seiz'd upon their towns and provinces.

  War. Talk not of France, sith thou hast lost
it all.

  K. Hen. The Lord Protector lost it, and not I:
When I was crown'd I was but nine months old.

  Rich. You are old enough now, and yet,
methinks, you lose.   113
Father, tear the crown from the usurper's head.

  Edw. Sweet father, do so; set it on your head.

  Mont. [*To* YORK.] Good brother, as thou
lov'st and honour'st arms,   116
Let's fight it out and not stand cavilling thus.

  Rich. Sound drums and trumpets, and the
king will fly.

  York. Sons, peace!

  K. Hen. Peace thou! and give King Henry
leave to speak.   120

  War. Plantagenet shall speak first: hear him,
lords;
And be you silent and attentive too,
For he that interrupts him shall not live.

  K. Hen. Think'st thou that I will leave my
kingly throne,   124
Wherein my grandsire and my father sat?
No: first shall war unpeople this my realm;
Ay, and their colours, often borne in France,

And now in England to our heart's great sorrow,
Shall be my winding-sheet. Why faint you,
  lords?   129
My title's good, and better far than his.
  War. Prove it, Henry, and thou shalt be
  king.
  K. Hen. Henry the Fourth by conquest got
  the crown.   132
  York. 'Twas by rebellion against his king.
  K. Hen. [*Aside.*] I know not what to say:
  my title's weak.
[*Aloud.*] Tell me, may not a king adopt an heir?
  York. What then?   136
  K. Hen. An if he may, then am I lawful
  king;
For Richard, in the view of many lords,
Resign'd the crown to Henry the Fourth,
Whose heir my father was, and I am his.   140
  York. He rose against him, being his sove-
  reign,
And made him to resign his crown perforce.
  War. Suppose, my lords, he did it uncon-
  strain'd,
Think you 'twere prejudicial to his crown? 144
  Exe. No; for he could not so resign his
  crown
But that the next heir should succeed and reign.
  K. Hen. Art thou against us, Duke of Exeter?
  Exe. His is the right, and therefore pardon
  me.   148
  York. Why whisper you, my lords, and an-
  swer not?
  Exe. My conscience tells me he is lawful king.
  K. Hen. [*Aside.*] All will revolt from me, and
  turn to him.
  North. Plantagenet, for all the claim thou
  lay'st,   152
Think not that Henry shall be so depos'd.
  War. Depos'd he shall be in despite of all.
  North. Thou art deceiv'd: 'tis not thy south-
  ern power,
Of Essex, Norfolk, Suffolk, nor of Kent, 156
Which makes thee thus presumptuous and
  proud,
Can set the duke up in despite of me.
  Clif. King Henry, be thy title right or wrong,
Lord Clifford vows to fight in thy defence: 160
May that ground gape and swallow me alive,
Where I shall kneel to him that slew my father!
  K. Hen. O Clifford, how thy words revive
  my heart!
  York. Henry of Lancaster, resign thy crown.
What mutter you, or what conspire you, lords?
  War. Do right unto this princely Duke of
  York,   166
Or I will fill the house with armed men,
And o'er the chair of state, where now he sits,
Write up his title with usurping blood.
        [*He stamps with his foot, and the
                Soldiers show themselves.*
  K. Hen. My Lord of Warwick, hear me but
  one word:—
Let me for this my life-time reign as king.
  York. Confirm the crown to me and to mine
  heirs,   172
And thou shalt reign in quiet while thou liv'st.

  K. Hen. I am content: Richard Plantagenet,
Enjoy the kingdom after my decease.
  Clif. What wrong is this unto the prince
  your son!   176
  War. What good is this to England and
  himself!
  West. Base, fearful, and despairing Henry!
  Clif. How hast thou injur'd both thyself
  and us!
  West. I cannot stay to hear these articles.
  North. Nor I.   181
  Clif. Come, cousin, let us tell the queen these
  news.
  West. Farewell, faint-hearted and degene-
  rate king,
In whose cold blood no spark of honour bides.
  North. Be thou a prey unto the house of
  York,   185
And die in bands for this unmanly deed!
  Clif. In dreadful war mayst thou be over-
  come,
Or live in peace abandon'd and despis'd! 188
        [*Exeunt* NORTHUMBERLAND, CLIFFORD,
              and WESTMORELAND.
  War. Turn this way, Henry, and regard them
  not.
  Exe. They seek revenge and therefore will
  not yield.
  K. Hen. Ah! Exeter.
  War.   Why should you sigh, my lord?
  K. Hen. Not for myself, Lord Warwick, but
  my son,   192
Whom I unnaturally shall disinherit.
But be it as it may; I here entail
The crown to thee and to thine heirs for ever;
Conditionally, that here thou take an oath 196
To cease this civil war, and, whilst I live,
To honour me as thy king and sovereign;
And neither by treason nor hostility
To seek to put me down and reign thyself. 200
  York. This oath I willingly take and will
  perform.   [*Coming from the throne.*
  War. Long live King Henry! Plantagenet,
  embrace him.
  K. Hen. And long live thou and these thy
  forward sons!
  York. Now York and Lancaster are recon-
  cil'd.   204
  Exe. Accurs'd be he that seeks to make them
  foes!   [*Sennet. The* Lords *come forward.*
  York. Farewell, my gracious lord; I'll to my
  castle.
  War. And I'll keep London with my sol-
  diers.   207
  Norf. And I to Norfolk with my followers.
  Mont. And I unto the sea from whence I
  came. [*Exeunt* YORK *and his Sons*, WAR-
  WICK, NORFOLK, MONTAGUE, Soldiers, *and*
  Attendants.
  K. Hen. And I, with grief and sorrow, to the
  court.

Enter QUEEN MARGARET *and the* PRINCE OF
WALES.

  Exe. Here comes the queen, whose looks bewray her anger:

l steal away.   [*Going.*
K. Hen.   Exeter, so will I.   [*Going.*
Q. Mar. Nay, go not from me; I will follow
  thee.   213
K. Hen. Be patient, gentle queen, and I will
  stay.
Q. Mar. Who can be patient in such extremes?
h! wretched man; would I had died a maid,
nd never seen thee, never borne thee son,
eing thou hast prov'd so unnatural a father.
ath he deserv'd to lose his birthright thus?
adst thou but lov'd him half so well as I, 220
r felt that pain which I did for him once,
r nourish'd him as I did with my blood,
ou wouldst have left thy dearest heart-blood
  there,
ather than have made that savage duke thine
  heir,   224
nd disinherited thine only son.
Prince. Father, you cannot disinherit me:
  you be king, why should not I succeed?
K. Hen. Pardon me, Margaret; pardon me,
  sweet son;   228
e Earl of Warwick, and the duke, enforc'd
  me.
Q. Mar. Enforc'd thee! art thou king, and
  wilt be forc'd?
shame to hear thee speak. Ah! timorous
  wretch;   231
ou hast undone thyself, thy son, and me;
nd given unto the house of York such head
 thou shalt reign but by their sufferance.
 entail him and his heirs unto the crown,
hat is it but to make thy sepulchre,   236
nd creep into it far before thy time?
arwick is chancellor and the Lord of Calais;
ern Faulconbridge commands the narrow seas;
e duke is made protector of the realm; 240
nd shalt thou be safe? such safety finds
e trembling lamb environed with wolves.
ad I been there, which am a silly woman,
e soldiers should have toss'd me on their
  pikes   244
fore I would have granted to that act;
t thou preferr'st thy life before thine honour:
nd seeing thou dost, I here divorce myself,
th from thy table, Henry, and thy bed, 248
atil that act of parliament be repeal'd
hereby my son is disinherited.
e northern lords that have forsworn thy
  colours
ill follow mine, if once they see them spread;
nd spread they shall be, to thy foul disgrace,
nd utter ruin of the house of York.
us do I leave thee. Come, son, let's away;
r army is ready; come, we'll after them. 256
K. Hen. Stay, gentle Margaret, and hear me
  speak.
Q. Mar. Thou hast spoke too much already:
  get thee gone.
K. Hen. Gentle son Edward, thou wilt stay
  with me?
Q. Mar. Ay, to be murder'd by his enemies.
Prince. When I return with victory from the
  field   261

I'll see your Grace: till then, I'll follow her.
Q. Mar. Come, son, away; we may not linger
  thus.   [*Exeunt* QUEEN MARGARET *and the*
                          PRINCE OF WALES.
K. Hen. Poor queen! how love to me and to
  her son   264
Hath made her break out into terms of rage.
Reveng'd may she be on that hateful duke,
Whose haughty spirit, winged with desire,
Will cost my crown, and like an empty eagle
Tire on the flesh of me and of my son! 269
The loss of those three lords torments my heart:
I'll write unto them, and entreat them fair.
Come, cousin; you shall be the messenger. 272
  Exe. And I, I hope, shall reconcile them all.
                                    [*Exeunt.*

SCENE II.—*A Room in Sandal Castle, near
         Wakefield, in Yorkshire.*

Enter EDWARD, RICHARD, *and* MONTAGUE.

Rich. Brother, though I be youngest, give
  me leave.
Edw. No, I can better play the orator.
Mont. But I have reasons strong and forcible.

            Enter YORK.

York. Why, how now, sons and brother! at
  a strife?   4
What is your quarrel? how began it first?
Edw. No quarrel, but a slight contention.
York. About what?
Rich. About that which concerns your Grace
  and us;   8
The crown of England, father, which is yours.
York. Mine, boy? not till King Henry be
  dead.
Rich. Your right depends not on his life or
  death.
Edw. Now you are heir, therefore enjoy it
  now: 12
By giving the house of Lancaster leave to
  breathe,
It will outrun you, father, in the end.
York. I took an oath that he should quietly
  reign.
Edw. But for a kingdom any oath may be
  broken: 16
I would break a thousand oaths to reign one
  year.
Rich. No; God forbid your Grace should be
  forsworn.
York. I shall be, if I claim by open war.
Rich. I'll prove the contrary, if you'll hear
  me speak.   20
York. Thou canst not, son; it is impossible.
Rich. An oath is of no moment, being not
  took
Before a true and lawful magistrate
That hath authority over him that swears: 24
Henry had none, but did usurp the place;
Then, seeing 'twas he that made you to depose,
Your oath, my lord, is vain and frivolous.
Therefore, to arms! And, father, do but think
How sweet a thing it is to wear a crown, 29
Within whose circuit is Elysium,

And all that poets feign of bliss and joy.
Why do we linger thus? I cannot rest   32
Until the white rose that I wear be dy'd
Even in the lukewarm blood of Henry's heart.
  York. Richard, enough, I will be king, or
  die.
Brother, thou shalt to London presently,   36
And whet on Warwick to this enterprise.
Thou, Richard, shalt unto the Duke of Norfolk,
And tell him privily of our intent.
You, Edward, shall unto my Lord Cobham,   40
With whom the Kentishmen will willingly
  rise:
In them I trust; for they are soldiers,
Witty, courteous, liberal, full of spirit.
While you are thus employ'd, what resteth
  more,   44
But that I seek occasion how to rise,
And yet the king not privy to my drift,
Nor any of the house of Lancaster?

Enter a Messenger.

But, stay: what news? why com'st thou in such
  post?   48
  Mess. The queen with all the northern earls
  and lords
Intend here to besiege you in your castle.
She is hard by with twenty thousand men,
And therefore fortify your hold, my lord.   52
  York. Ay, with my sword. What! think'st
  thou that we fear them?
Edward and Richard, you shall stay with
  me;
My brother Montague shall post to London:
Let noble Warwick, Cobham, and the rest,   56
Whom we have left protectors of the king,
With powerful policy strengthen themselves,
And trust not simple Henry nor his oaths.
  Mont. Brother, I go; I'll win them, fear it
  not: 60
And thus most humbly I do take my leave.
      [*Exit.*

Enter SIR JOHN *and* SIR HUGH MORTIMER.

  York. Sir John, and Sir Hugh Mortimer,
  mine uncles!
You are come to Sandal in a happy hour;
The army of the queen mean to besiege us.   64
  Sir John. She shall not need, we'll meet her
  in the field.
  York. What! with five thousand men?
  Rich. Ay, with five hundred, father, for a
  need:
A woman's general; what should we fear?   68
      [*A march afar off.*
  Edw. I hear their drums; let's set our men
  in order,
And issue forth and bid them battle straight.
  York. Five men to twenty! though the odds
  be great,
I doubt not, uncle, of our victory.   72
Many a battle have I won in France,
When as the enemy hath been ten to one:
Why should I not now have the like success?
      [*Alarum. Exeunt.*

SCENE III.—*Field of Battle between Sand*
      Castle and Wakefield.

Alarums: Excursions. Enter RUTLAND *and* I
      Tutor.

  Rut. Ah, whither shall I fly to 'scape the
  hands?
Ah! tutor, look, where bloody Clifford come

Enter CLIFFORD *and* Soldiers.

  Clif. Chaplain, away! thy priesthood sav
  thy life.
As for the brat of this accursed duke,
Whose father slew my father, he shall die.
  Tut. And I, my lord, will bear him compar
  Clif. Soldiers, away with him.
  Tut. Ah! Clifford, murder not this innoce
  child,
Lest thou be hated both of God and man!
      [*Exit, forced off by Soldie*
  Clif. How now! is he dead already? Or
  it fear
That makes him close his eyes? I'll open the
  Rut. So looks the pent-up lion o'er
  wretch
That trembles under his devouring paws;
And so he walks, insulting o'er his prey,
And so he comes to rend his limbs asunde
Ah! gentle Clifford, kill me with thy sword,
And not with such a cruel threatening lool
Sweet Clifford! hear me speak before I die:
I am too mean a subject for thy wrath;
Be thou reveng'd on men, and let me live.
  Clif. In vain thou speak'st, poor boy; i
  father's blood
Hath stopp'd the passage where thy wor
  should enter.
  Rut. Then let my father's blood open it aga
He is a man, and, Clifford, cope with him.
  Clif. Had I thy brethren here, their lives a
  thine
Were not revenge sufficient for me;
No, if I digg'd up thy forefathers' graves,
And hung their rotten coffins up in chains,
It could not slake mine ire, nor ease my hea
The sight of any of the house of York
Is as a fury to torment my soul;
And till I root out their accursed line,
And leave not one alive, I live in hell.
Therefore—   [*Lifting his han*
  Rut. O! let me pray before I take my dea
To thee I pray; sweet Clifford, pity me!
  Clif. Such pity as my rapier's point affor
  Rut. I never did thee harm: why wilt th
  slay me?
  Clif. Thy father hath.
  Rut.   But 'twas ere I was bo
Thou hast one son; for his sake pity me,
Lest in revenge thereof, sith God is just,
He be as miserably slain as I.
Ah! let me live in prison all my days;
And when I give occasion of offence,
Then let me die, for now thou hast no cause
  Clif. No cause!
Thy father slew my father; therefore, die.
      [*Stabs h*

Rut. Dii faciant laudis summa sit ista tuæ!
[*Dies.*

Clif. Plantagenet! I come, Plantagenet! 49
And this thy son's blood cleaving to my blade
Shall rust upon my weapon, till thy blood,
Congeal'd with this, do make me wipe off both.
[*Exit.*

SCENE IV.—*Another Part of the Plains.*

Alarum. Enter YORK.

York. The army of the queen hath got the
field:
My uncles both are slain in rescuing me;
And all my followers to the eager foe   3
Turn back and fly, like ships before the wind,
Or lambs pursu'd by hunger-starved wolves.
My sons, God knows what hath bechanced
them:
But this I know, they have demean'd themselves
Like men born to renown by life or death. 8
Three times did Richard make a lane to me,
And thrice cried, 'Courage, father! fight it out!'
And full as oft came Edward to my side,   12
With purple falchion, painted to the hilt
In blood of those that had encounter'd him:
And when the hardiest warriors did retire,
Richard cried, 'Charge! and give no foot of
ground!'   15
And cried, 'A crown, or else a glorious tomb!
A sceptre, or an earthly sepulchre!'
With this, we charg'd again; but, out, alas!
We bodg'd again: as I have seen a swan   19
With bootless labour swim against the tide,
And spend her strength with over-matching
waves.   [*A short alarum within.*
Ah, hark! the fatal followers do pursue;
And I am faint and cannot fly their fury;
And were I strong I would not shun their
fury: 24
The sands are number'd that make up my life;
Here must I stay, and here my life must end.

Enter QUEEN MARGARET, CLIFFORD, NORTH-
UMBERLAND, *the young* PRINCE, *and* Soldiers.
Come, bloody Clifford, rough Northumberland,
I dare your quenchless fury to more rage: 28
I am your butt, and I abide your shot.
North. Yield to our mercy, proud Planta-
genet.
Clif. Ay, to such mercy as his ruthless arm
With downright payment show'd unto my
father.   32
Now Phæthon hath tumbled from his car,
And made an evening at the noontide prick.
York. My ashes, as the phœnix, may bring
forth
A bird that will revenge upon you all;   36
And in that hope I throw mine eyes to heaven,
Scorning whate'er you can afflict me with.
Why come you not? what! multitudes, and fear?
Clif. So cowards fight when they can fly no
further;   40
So doves do peck the falcon's piercing talons;
So desperate thieves, all hopeless of their lives,
Breathe out invectives 'gainst the officers.

York. O Clifford! but bethink thee once
again,   44
And in thy thought o'er-run my former time;
And, if thou canst for blushing, view this face,
And bite thy tongue, that slanders him with
cowardice
Whose frown hath made thee faint and fly ere
this.   48
Clif. I will not bandy with thee word for
word,
But buckle with thee blows, twice two for one.
[*Draws.*
Q. Mar. Hold, valiant Clifford! for a thou-
sand causes
I would prolong awhile the traitor's life. 52
Wrath makes him deaf: speak thou, Northum-
berland.
North. Hold, Clifford! do not honour him
so much
To prick thy finger, though to wound his heart.
What valour were it, when a cur doth grin, 56
For one to thrust his hand between his teeth,
When he might spurn him with his foot away?
It is war's prize to take all vantages,
And ten to one is no impeach of valour.   60
[*They lay hands on* YORK, *who struggles.*
Clif. Ay, ay; so strives the woodcock with
the gin.
North. So doth the cony struggle in the net.
[YORK *is taken prisoner.*
York. So triumph thieves upon their con-
quer'd booty;
So true men yield, with robbers so o'er-matched.
North. What would your Grace have done
unto him now?   65
Q. Mar. Brave warriors, Clifford and North-
umberland,
Come, make him stand upon this molehill here,
That raught at mountains with outstretched
arms,   68
Yet parted but the shadow with his hand.
What! was it you that would be England's
king?
Was't you that revell'd in our parliament,
And made a preachment of your high descent?
Where are your mess of sons to back you
now?   73
The wanton Edward, and the lusty George?
And where's that valiant crook-back prodigy,
Dicky your boy, that with his grumbling voice
Was wont to cheer his dad in mutinies?
Or, with the rest, where is your darling Rutland?
Look, York: I stain'd this napkin with the
blood   79
That valiant Clifford with his rapier's point
Made issue from the bosom of the boy;
And if thine eyes can water for his death,
I give thee this to dry thy cheeks withal. 83
Alas, poor York! but that I hate thee deadly,
I should lament thy miserable state.
I prithee grieve, to make me merry, York.
What! hath thy fiery heart so parch'd thine
entrails
That not a tear can fall for Rutland's death?
Why art thou patient, man? thou shouldst be
mad;   89

And I, to make thee mad, do mock thee thus.
Stamp, rave, and fret, that I may sing and dance.
Thou wouldst be fee'd, I see, to make me sport:
York cannot speak unless he wear a crown. 93
A crown for York! and, lords, bow low to him:
Hold you his hands whilst I do set it on.
          [*Putting a paper crown on his head.*
Ay, marry, sir, now looks he like a king! 96
Ay, this is he that took King Henry's chair;
And this is he was his adopted heir.
But how is it that great Plantagenet
Is crown'd so soon, and broke his solemn oath?
As I bethink me, you should not be king 101
Till our King Henry had shook hands with
          death.
And will you pale your head in Henry's glory,
And rob his temples of the diadem, 104
Now in his life, against your holy oath?
O! 'tis a fault too-too unpardonable.
Off with the crown; and, with the crown, his
          head;
And, whilst we breathe, take time to do him
          dead. 108
     Clif. That is my office, for my father's sake.
     Q. Mar. Nay, stay; let's hear the orisons he
          makes.
     York. She-wolf of France, but worse than
          wolves of France,
Whose tongue more poisons than the adder's
          tooth! 112
How ill-beseeming is it in thy sex
To triumph, like an Amazonian trull,
Upon their woes whom fortune captivates!
But that thy face is, visor-like, unchanging, 116
Made impudent with use of evil deeds,
I would assay, proud queen, to make thee
          blush:
To tell thee whence thou cam'st, of whom
          deriv'd,
Were shame enough to shame thee, wert thou
          not shameless. 120
Thy father bears the type of King of Naples,
Of both the Sicils and Jerusalem;
Yet not so wealthy as an English yeoman.
Hath that poor monarch taught thee to insult?
It needs not, nor it boots thee not, proud queen,
Unless the adage must be verified, 126
That beggars mounted run their horse to death.
'Tis beauty that doth oft make women proud;
But, God he knows, thy share thereof is small:
'Tis virtue that doth make them most admir'd;
The contrary doth make thee wonder'd at:
'Tis government that makes them seem divine;
The want thereof makes thee abominable. 133
Thou art as opposite to every good
As the Antipodes are unto us,
Or as the south to the septentrion. 136
O tiger's heart wrapp'd in a woman's hide!
How couldst thou drain the life-blood of the
          child,
To bid the father wipe his eyes withal,
And yet be seen to bear a woman's face? 140
Women are soft, mild, pitiful, and flexible;
Thou stern, obdurate, flinty, rough, remorseless.
Bidd'st thou me rage? why, now thou hast thy
          wish:

Wouldst have me weep? why, now thou hast
          thy will; 144
For raging wind blows up incessant showers,
And when the rage allays, the rain begins.
These tears are my sweet Rutland's obsequies,
And every drop cries vengeance for his death,
'Gainst thee, fell Clifford, and thee, false French-
          woman. 149
     North. Beshrew me, but his passion moves
          me so
That hardly can I check my eyes from tears.
     York. That face of his the hungry cannibals
Would not have touch'd, would not have
          stain'd with blood; 153
But you are more inhuman, more inexorable,—
O! ten times more, than tigers of Hyrcania.
See, ruthless queen, a hapless father's tears:
This cloth thou dipp'dst in blood of my sweet
          boy, 157
And I with tears do wash the blood away.
Keep thou the napkin, and go boast of this;
          [*Giving back the handkerchief.*
And if thou tell'st the heavy story right, 160
Upon my soul, the hearers will shed tears;
Yea, even my foes will shed fast-falling tears,
And say, 'Alas! it was a piteous deed!'
There, take the crown, and, with the crown, my
          curse, 164
And in thy need such comfort come to thee
As now I reap at thy too cruel hand!
Hard-hearted Clifford, take me from the world!
My soul to heaven, my blood upon your heads!
     North. Had he been slaughter-man to all
          my kin, 169
I should not for my life but weep with him,
To see how inly sorrow gripes his soul.
     Q. Mar. What! weeping-ripe, my Lord
          Northumberland? 172
Think but upon the wrong he did us all,
And that will quickly dry thy melting tears.
     Clif. Here's for my oath; here's for my
          father's death. [*Stabbing him.*
     Q. Mar. And here's to right our gentle-
          hearted king. [*Stabbing him.*
     York. Open thy gate of mercy, gracious
          God! 177
My soul flies through these wounds to seek out
          thee. [*Dies.*
     Q. Mar. Off with his head, and set it on
          York gates;
So York may overlook the town of York. 180
          [*Flourish. Exeunt*

ACT II

SCENE I.—*A Plain near Mortimer's Cross in
          Herefordshire.*

Drums. Enter EDWARD *and* RICHARD, *with their
          Forces, marching.*

     Edw. I wonder how our princely father
          'scap'd,
Or whether he be 'scap'd away or no
From Clifford's and Northumberland's pursuit:
Had he been ta'en we should have heard the
          news;

Iad he been slain we should have heard the
 news;
 r had he 'scap'd, methinks we should have
 heard
 he happy tidings of his good escape.
 Iow fares my brother? why is he so sad? 8
    Rich. I cannot joy until I be resolv'd
 Where our right valiant father is become.
 saw him in the battle range about,   11
 nd watch'd him how he singled Clifford forth.
 Iethought he bore him in the thickest troop
 s doth a lion in a herd of neat;
 r as a bear, encompass'd round with dogs,
 Vho having pinch'd a few and made them cry,
 he rest stand all aloof and bark at him.   17
 o far'd our father with his enemies;
 o fled his enemies my war-like father:
 Iethinks, 'tis prize enough to be his son. 20
 ee how the morning opes her golden gates,
 nd takes her farewell of the glorious sun;
 Iow well resembles it the prime of youth,
 rimm'd like a younker prancing to his love. 24
    Edw. Dazzle mine eyes, or do I see three suns?
    Rich. Three glorious suns, each one a per-
 fect sun;
 Iot separated with the racking clouds,
 ut sever'd in a pale clear-shining sky.   28
 ee, see! they join, embrace, and seem to kiss,
 s if they vow'd some league inviolable:
 Iow are they but one lamp, one light, one sun.
 a this the heaven figures some event.   32
    Edw. 'Tis wondrous strange, the like yet
 never heard of.
 think it cites us, brother, to the field;
 hat we, the sons of brave Plantagenet,
 ach one already blazing by our meeds,   36
 hould notwithstanding join our lights together,
 nd over-shine the earth, as this the world.
 Vhate'er it bodes, henceforward will I bear
 pon my target three fair-shining suns.   40
    Rich. Nay, bear three daughters: by your
 leave I speak it,
 ou love the breeder better than the male.

Enter a Messenger.

ut what art thou, whose heavy looks foretell
 ome dreadful story hanging on thy tongue?
    Mess. Ah! one that was a woeful looker-on,
 Then as the noble Duke of York was slain,
 our princely father, and my loving lord.
    Edw. O! speak no more, for I have heard
 too much.   48
    Rich. Say how he died, for I will hear it all.
    Mess. Environed he was with many foes,
 nd stood against them, as the hope of Troy
 gainst the Greeks that would have enter'd
 Troy.   52
 ut Hercules himself must yield to odds;
 nd many strokes, though with a little axe,
 ew down and fell the hardest-timber'd oak.
 y many hands your father was subdu'd;   56
 ut only slaughter'd by the ireful arm
 f unrelenting Clifford and the queen,
 Tho crown'd the gracious duke in high despite;

Laugh'd in his face; and when with grief he
 wept,   60
The ruthless queen gave him to dry his cheeks,
A napkin steeped in the harmless blood
Of sweet young Rutland, by rough Clifford
 slain:
And after many scorns, many foul taunts,   64
They took his head, and on the gates of York
They set the same; and there it doth remain,
The saddest spectacle that e'er I view'd.
    Edw. Sweet Duke of York! our prop to lean
 upon,   68
Now thou art gone, we have no staff, no
 stay!
O Clifford! boist'rous Clifford! thou hast slain
The flower of Europe for his chivalry;
And treacherously hast thou vanquish'd him,
For hand to hand he would have vanquish'd
 thee.   73
Now my soul's palace is become a prison:
Ah! would she break from hence, that this my
 body
Might in the ground be closed up in rest,   76
For never henceforth shall I joy again,
Never, O! never, shall I see more joy.
    Rich. I cannot weep, for all my body's mois-
 ture
Scarce serves to quench my furnace-burning
 heart: 80
Nor can my tongue unload my heart's great
 burden;
For self-same wind, that I should speak withal
Is kindling coals that fire all my breast,
And burn me up with flames, that tears would
 quench.   84
To weep is to make less the depth of grief:
Tears then, for babes; blows and revenge for
 me!
Richard, I bear thy name; I'll venge thy death,
Or die renowned by attempting it.   88
    Edw. His name that valiant duke hath left
 with thee;
His dukedom and his chair with me is left.
    Rich. Nay, if thou be that princely eagle's
 bird,   91
Show thy descent by gazing 'gainst the sun:
For chair and dukedom, throne and kingdom
 say;
Either that is thine, or else thou wert not his.

March. Enter WARWICK *and the* MARQUESS OF
 MONTAGUE, *with Forces.*

    War. How now, fair lords! What fare?
 what news abroad?
    Rich. Great Lord of Warwick, if we should
 recount   96
Our baleful news, and at each word's deliv'rance
Stab poniards in our flesh till all were told,
The words would add more anguish than the
 wounds.
O valiant lord! the Duke of York is slain. 100
    Edw. O Warwick! Warwick! that Planta-
 genet
Which held thee dearly as his soul's redemp-
 tion,
Is by the stern Lord Clifford done to death.

War. Ten days ago I drown'd these news in
  tears, 104
And now, to add more measure to your woes,
I come to tell you things sith then befallen.
After the bloody fray at Wakefield fought,
Where your brave father breath'd his latest
  gasp, 108
Tidings, as swiftly as the posts could run,
Were brought me of your loss and his de-
  part.
I, then in London, keeper of the king,
Muster'd my soldiers, gather'd flocks of friends,
And very well appointed, as I thought, 113
March'd towards Saint Alban's to intercept the
  queen,
Bearing the king in my behalf along;
For by my scouts I was advertised 116
That she was coming with a full intent
To dash our late decree in parliament,
Touching King Henry's oath and your suc-
  cession. 119
Short tale to make, we at Saint Alban's met,
Our battles join'd, and both sides fiercely fought:
But whether 'twas the coldness of the king,
Who look'd full gently on his war-like queen,
That robb'd my soldiers of their heated spleen;
Or whether 'twas report of her success; 125
Or more than common fear of Clifford's rigour,
Who thunders to his captives blood and death,
I cannot judge: but, to conclude with truth,
Their weapons like to lightning came and went;
Our soldiers'—like the night-owl's lazy flight,
Or like a lazy thresher with a flail— 131
Fell gently down, as if they struck their friends.
I cheer'd them up with justice of our cause,
With promise of high pay, and great rewards:
But all in vain; they had no heart to fight,
And we in them no hope to win the day; 136
So that we fled: the king unto the queen;
Lord George your brother, Norfolk, and my-
  self,
In haste, post-haste, are come to join with
  you; 139
For in the marches here we heard you were,
Making another head to fight again.
Edw. Where is the Duke of Norfolk, gentle
  Warwick?
And when came George from Burgundy to
  England?
War. Some six miles off the duke is with the
  soldiers; 144
And for your brother, he was lately sent
From your kind aunt, Duchess of Burgundy,
With aid of soldiers to this needful war.
Rich. 'Twas odds, belike, when valiant War-
  wick fled: 148
Oft have I heard his praises in pursuit,
But ne'er till now his scandal of retire.
War. Nor now my scandal, Richard, dost
  thou hear;
For thou shalt know, this strong right hand of
  mine 152
Can pluck the diadem from faint Henry's head,
And wring the awful sceptre from his fist,
Were he as famous, and as bold in war
As he is fam'd for mildness, peace, and prayer.

Rich. I know it well, Lord Warwick; blame
  me not: 1
'Tis love I bear thy glories makes me speak.
But, in this troublous time what 's to be done
Shall we go throw away our coats of steel, 1
And wrap our bodies in black mourning gowns
Numb'ring our Ave-Maries with our beads?
Or shall we on the helmets of our foes
Tell our devotion with revengeful arms? 1
If for the last, say 'Ay,' and to it, lords.
War. Why, therefore Warwick came to seek
  you out;
And therefore comes my brother Montague.
Attend me, lords. The proud insulting queen
With Clifford and the haught Northumberland
And of their feather many more proud birds
Have wrought the easy-melting king like wax
He swore consent to your succession, 1
His oath enrolled in the parliament;
And now to London all the crew are gone,
To frustrate both his oath and what beside
May make against the house of Lancaster. 1
Their power, I think, is thirty thousand strong
Now, if the help of Norfolk and myself,
With all the friends that thou, brave Earl
  March,
Amongst the loving Welshmen canst procure
Will but amount to five and twenty thousand,
Why, *Via!* to London will we march amain,
And once again bestride our foaming steeds
And once again cry, 'Charge upon our foes!
But never once again turn back and fly. 1
Rich. Ay, now methinks I hear great War-
  wick speak:
Ne'er may he live to see a sunshine day,
That cries 'Retire,' if Warwick bid him stay
Edw. Lord Warwick, on thy shoulder will
  lean; 1
And when thou fail'st—as God forbid the
  hour!—
Must Edward fall, which peril heaven forfend
War. No longer Earl of March, but Duke
  York: 1
The next degree is England's royal throne;
For King of England shalt thou be proclaim'
In every borough as we pass along;
And he that throws not up his cap for joy 1
Shall for the fault make forfeit of his head.
King Edward, valiant Richard, Montague,
Stay we no longer dreaming of renown,
But sound the trumpets, and about our task.
Rich. Then, Clifford, were thy heart as hard
  as steel,— 2
As thou hast shown it flinty by thy deeds,—
I come to pierce it, or to give thee mine.
Edw. Then strike up, drums! God, and
  Saint George for us! 2

Enter a Messenger.

War. How now! what news?
Mess. The Duke of Norfolk sends you word
  by me,
The queen is coming with a puissant host;
And craves your company for speedy counsel
War. Why then it sorts; brave warriors
  let's away.   [*Exeunt*

SCENE II.—*Before York.*

ourish. Enter KING HENRY, QUEEN MARGARET, *the* PRINCE OF WALES, CLIFFORD *and* NORTHUMBERLAND, *with drums and trumpets.*

Q. Mar. Welcome, my lord, to this brave town of York.
onder's the head of that arch-enemy,
    hat sought to be encompass'd with your crown: 3
    oth not the object cheer your heart, my lord?
K. Hen. Ay, as the rocks cheer them that fear their wrack:
    o see this sight, it irks my very soul.
    ithhold revenge, dear God! 'tis not my fault,
    or wittingly have I infring'd my vow.   8
Clif. My gracious liege, this too much lenity
    nd harmful pity must be laid aside.
    o whom do lions cast their gentle looks?
    ot to the beast that would usurp their den.
    hose hand is that the forest bear doth lick?
    ot his that spoils her young before her face.
    ho 'scapes the lurking serpent's mortal sting?
    ot he that sets his foot upon her back.   16
    he smallest worm will turn being trodden on,
    nd doves will peck in safeguard of their brood.
    mbitious York did level at thy crown;
    hou smiling while he knit his angry brows: 20
    e, but a duke, would have his son a king,
    nd raise his issue like a loving sire;
    hou, being a king, bless'd with a goodly son,
    idst yield consent to disinherit him,   24
    hich argu'd thee a most unloving father.
    nreasonable creatures feed their young;
    nd though man's face be fearful to their eyes,
    et, in protection of their tender ones,   28
    ho hath not seen them, even with those wings
    hich sometime they have us'd with fearful flight,
    ake war with him that climb'd unto their nest,
    ffering their own lives in their young's defence?
    or shame, my liege! make them your precedent.
    ere it not pity that this goodly boy
    ould lose his birthright by his father's fault,
    nd long hereafter say unto his child,   36
    What my great grandfather and grandsire got,
    y careless father fondly gave away'?
    h! what a shame were this. Look on the boy;
    nd let his manly face, which promiseth   40
    iccessful fortune, steel thy melting heart
    o hold thine own and leave thine own with him.
K. Hen. Full well hath Clifford play'd the orator,
    ferring arguments of mighty force.   44
    ut, Clifford, tell me, didst thou never hear
    hat things ill got had ever bad success?
    nd happy always was it for that son
    hose father for his hoarding went to hell?
    ll leave my son my virtuous deeds behind;
    nd would my father had left me no more!
    or all the rest is held at such a rate   51
    s brings a thousand-fold more care to keep
    han in possession any jot of pleasure.
    h! cousin York, would thy best friends did know

How it doth grieve me that thy head is here!
Q. Mar. My lord, cheer up your spirits: our foes are nigh,   56
And this soft courage makes your followers faint.
You promis'd knighthood to our forward son:
Unsheathe your sword, and dub him presently.
Edward, kneel down.   60
K. Hen. Edward Plantagenet, arise a knight;
And learn this lesson, draw thy sword in right.
Prince. My gracious father, by your kingly leave,
I'll draw it as apparent to the crown,   64
And in that quarrel use it to the death.
Clif. Why, that is spoken like a toward prince.

Enter a Messenger.

Mess. Royal commanders, be in readiness:
For with a band of thirty thousand men   68
Comes Warwick, backing of the Duke of York;
And in the towns, as they do march along,
Proclaims him king, and many fly to him:
Darraign your battle, for they are at hand.   72
Clif. I would your highness would depart the field:
The queen hath best success when you are absent.
Q. Mar. Ay, good my lord, and leave us to our fortune.
K. Hen. Why, that's my fortune too; therefore I'll stay.   76
North. Be it with resolution then to fight.
Prince. My royal father, cheer these noble lords,
And hearten those that fight in your defence:
Unsheathe your sword, good father: cry, 'Saint George!'   80

March. Enter EDWARD, GEORGE, RICHARD, WARWICK, NORFOLK, MONTAGUE, *and* Soldiers.

Edw. Now, perjur'd Henry, wilt thou kneel for grace,
And set thy diadem upon my head;
Or bide the mortal fortune of the field?
Q. Mar. Go, rate thy minions, proud insulting boy!   84
Becomes it thee to be thus bold in terms
Before thy sovereign and thy lawful king?
Edw. I am his king, and he should bow his knee;
I was adopted heir by his consent: 88
Since when, his oath is broke; for, as I hear,
You, that are king, though he do wear the crown,
Have caus'd him, by new act of parliament,
To blot out me, and put his own son in.   92
Clif. And reason too:
Who should succeed the father but the son?
Rich. Are you there, butcher? O! I cannot speak.
Clif. Ay, crook-back; here I stand to answer thee,   96
Or any he the proudest of thy sort.
Rich. 'Twas you that kill'd young Rutland, was it not?
Clif. Ay, and old York, and yet not satisfied.

Rich. For God's sake, lords, give signal to
  the fight.   100
War. What sayst thou, Henry, wilt thou yield
  the crown?
Q. Mar. Why, how now, long-tongu'd War-
  wick! dare you speak?
When you and I met at Saint Alban's last,
Your legs did better service than your hands.
War. Then 'twas my turn to fly, and now
  'tis thine.   105
Clif. You said so much before, and yet you
  fled.
War. 'Twas not your valour, Clifford, drove
  me thence.
North. No, nor your manhood that durst
  make you stay.   108
Rich. Northumberland, I hold thee rever-
  ently.
Break off the parley; for scarce I can refrain
The execution of my big-swoln heart
Upon that Clifford, that cruel child-killer. 112
Clif. I slew thy father: call'st thou him a
  child?
Rich. Ay, like a dastard and a treacherous
  coward,
As thou didst kill our tender brother Rutland;
But ere sun-set I'll make him curse the deed.
K. Hen. Have done with words, my lords,
  and hear me speak.   117
Q. Mar. Defy them, then, or else hold close
  thy lips.
K. Hen. I prithee, give no limits to my
  tongue:
I am a king, and privileg'd to speak.   120
Clif. My liege, the wound that bred this
  meeting here
Cannot be cur'd by words; therefore be still.
Rich. Then, executioner, unsheathe thy
  sword.
By him that made us all, I am resolv'd   124
That Clifford's manhood lies upon his tongue.
Edw. Say, Henry, shall I have my right or
  no?
A thousand men have broke their fasts to-day,
That ne'er shall dine unless thou yield the
  crown.   128
War. If thou deny, their blood upon thy
  head;
For York in justice puts his armour on.
Prince. If that be right which Warwick says
  is right,   131
There is no wrong, but everything is right.
Rich. Whoever got thee, there thy mother
  stands;
For well I wot thou hast thy mother's tongue.
Q. Mar. But thou art neither like thy sire
  nor dam,
But like a foul misshapen stigmatic,   136
Mark'd by the destinies to be avoided,
As venom toads, or lizards' dreadful stings.
Rich. Iron of Naples hid with English gilt,
Whose father bears the title of a king,—   140
As if a channel should be call'd the sea,—
Sham'st thou not, knowing whence thou art
  extraught,
To let thy tongue detect thy base-born heart?

Edw. A wisp of straw were worth a thousan
  crowns,   1
To make this shameless callet know herself.
Helen of Greece was fairer far than thou,
Although thy husband may be Menelaus;
And ne'er was Agamemnon's brother wrong
By that false woman as this king by thee.
His father revell'd in the heart of France,
And tam'd the king, and made the Dauph
  stoop;   1
And had he match'd according to his state,
He might have kept that glory to this day;
But when he took a beggar to his bed,
And grac'd thy poor sire with his bridal day,
Even then that sunshine brew'd a shower f
  him,   1
That wash'd his father's fortunes forth
  France,
And heap'd sedition on his crown at home.
For what hath broach'd this tumult but th
  pride?
Hadst thou been meek our title still had slep
And we, in pity of the gentle king,   1
Had slipp'd our claim until another age.
Geo. But when we saw our sunshine ma
  thy spring,
And that thy summer bred us no increase, 1
We set the axe to thy usurping root;
And though the edge hath something hit ou
  selves,
Yet know thou, since we have begun to strik
We'll never leave, till we have hewn thee dow
Or bath'd thy growing with our heated blood
Edw. And in this resolution I defy thee;
Not willing any longer conference,   1
Since thou deny'st the gentle king to speak.
Sound trumpets!—let our bloody colours wav
And either victory, or else a grave.
Q. Mar. Stay, Edward.
Edw. No, wrangling woman, we'll no long
  stay: 1
These words will cost ten thousand lives th
  day.   [*Exeun*

SCENE III.—*A Field of Battle between Towt*
  and Saxton, in Yorkshire.

Alarums: Excursions. Enter WARWICK.

War. Forspent with toil, as runners with
  race,
I lay me down a little while to breathe;
For strokes receiv'd, and many blows repai
Have robb'd my strong-knit sinews of the
  strength,
And spite of spite needs must I rest a while.

Enter EDWARD, *running.*

Edw. Smile, gentle heaven! or strike, u
  gentle death!
For this world frowns, and Edward's sun
  clouded.
War. How now, my lord! what hap? wh
  hope of good?

Enter GEORGE.

Geo. Our hap is loss, our hope but sad despa

r ranks are broke, and ruin follows us.
at counsel give you? whither shall we fly?
Edw. Bootless is flight, they follow us with
wings; 12
d weak we are and cannot shun pursuit.

Enter RICHARD.

Rich. Ah! Warwick, why hast thou withdrawn thyself?
y brother's blood the thirsty earth hath
drunk,
ach'd with the steely point of Clifford's lance;
d in the very pangs of death he cried, 17
e to a dismal clangor heard from far,
arwick, revenge! brother, revenge my death!'
underneath the belly of their steeds, 20
at stain'd their fetlocks in his smoking blood,
e noble gentleman gave up the ghost.
War. Then let the earth be drunken with our
blood:
kill my horse because I will not fly. 24
y stand we like soft-hearted women here,
iling our losses, whiles the foe doth rage;
d look upon, as if the tragedy 27
re play'd in jest by counterfeiting actors?
re on my knee I vow to God above,
never pause again, never stand still
either death hath clos'd these eyes of mine,
fortune given me measure of revenge. 32
Edw. O Warwick! I do bend my knee with
thine:
d in this vow do chain my soul to thine.
d, ere my knee rise from the earth's cold
face,
row my hands, mine eyes, my heart to thee,
ou setter up and plucker down of kings, 37
eeching thee, if with thy will it stands
at to my foes this body must be prey,
t that thy brazen gates of heaven may ope,
d give sweet passage to my sinful soul!
w, lords, take leave until we meet again,
ere'er it be, in heaven or in earth.
Rich. Brother, give me thy hand; and, gentle
Warwick, 44
me embrace thee in my weary arms:
hat did never weep, now melt with woe
at winter should cut off our spring-time so.
War. Away, away! Once more, sweet lords,
farewell. 48
Geo. Yet let us all together to our troops,
d give them leave to fly that will not stay,
d call them pillars that will stand to us;
d if we thrive, promise them such rewards
victors wear at the Olympian games.
is may plant courage in their quailing breasts;
r yet is hope of life and victory.
rslow no longer; make we hence amain. 56
[*Exeunt.*

SCENE IV.—*Another Part of the Field.*

Excursions. Enter RICHARD *and* CLIFFORD.

Rich. Now, Clifford, I have singled thee
alone.
ppose this arm is for the Duke of York,
d this for Rutland; both bound to revenge,

Wert thou environ'd with a brazen wall. 4
Clif. Now, Richard, I am with thee here
alone.
This is the hand that stabb'd thy father York,
And this the hand that slew thy brother Rut-
land;
And here's the heart that triumphs in their
death 8
And cheers these hands that slew thy sire and
brother,
To execute the like upon thyself;
And so, have at thee!
[*They fight.* WARWICK *enters;* CLIFFORD *flies.*
Rich. Nay, Warwick, single out some other
chase; 12
For I myself will hunt this wolf to death.
[*Exeunt.*

SCENE V.—*Another Part of the Field.*

Alarum. Enter KING HENRY.

K. Hen. This battle fares like to the morn-
ing's war,
When dying clouds contend with growing light,
What time the shepherd, blowing of his nails,
Can neither call it perfect day nor night. 4
Now sways it this way, like a mighty sea
Forc'd by the tide to combat with the wind;
Now sways it that way, like the self-same sea
Forc'd to retire by fury of the wind: 8
Sometime the flood prevails, and then the wind;
Now one the better, then another best;
Both tugging to be victors, breast to breast,
Yet neither conqueror nor conquered: 12
So is the equal poise of this fell war.
Here on this molehill will I sit me down.
To whom God will, there be the victory!
For Margaret my queen, and Clifford too, 16
Have chid me from the battle; swearing both
They prosper best of all when I am thence.
Would I were dead! if God's good will were so;
For what is in this world but grief and woe? 20
O God! methinks it were a happy life,
To be no better than a homely swain;
To sit upon a hill, as I do now,
To carve out dials quaintly, point to point, 24
Thereby to see the minutes how they run,
How many make the hour full complete;
How many hours bring about the day;
How many days will finish up the year; 28
How many years a mortal man may live.
When this is known, then to divide the times:
So many hours must I tend my flock;
So many hours must I take my rest; 32
So many hours must I contemplate;
So many hours must I sport myself;
So many days my ewes have been with young;
So many weeks ere the poor fools will ean; 36
So many years ere I shall shear the fleece:
So minutes, hours, days, months, and years,
Pass'd over to the end they were created,
Would bring white hairs unto a quiet grave. 40
Ah! what a life were this! how sweet! how lovely!
Gives not the hawthorn bush a sweeter shade
To shepherds, looking on their silly sheep,
Than doth a rich embroider'd canopy 44

To kings, that fear their subjects' treachery?
O, yes! it doth; a thousand-fold it doth.
And to conclude, the shepherd's homely curds,
His cold thin drink out of his leather bottle, 48
His wonted sleep under a fresh tree's shade,
All which secure and sweetly he enjoys,
Is far beyond a prince's delicates,
His viands sparkling in a golden cup, 52
His body couched in a curious bed,
When care, mistrust, and treason wait on him.

Alarum. Enter a Son *that hath killed his Father,
with the dead body.*

Son. Ill blows the wind that profits nobody.
This man whom hand to hand I slew in fight, 56
May be possessed with some store of crowns;
And I, that haply take them from him now,
May yet ere night yield both my life and them
To some man else, as this dead man doth me. 60
Who's this? O God! it is my father's face,
Whom in this conflict I unwares have kill'd.
O heavy times, begetting such events!
From London by the king was I press'd forth; 64
My father, being the Earl of Warwick's man,
Came on the part of York, press'd by his master;
And I, who at his hands receiv'd my life,
Have by my hands of life bereaved him. 68
Pardon me, God, I knew not what I did!
And pardon, father, for I knew not thee!
My tears shall wipe away these bloody marks;
And no more words till they have flow'd their fill.
K. Hen. O piteous spectacle! O bloody times!
Whiles lions war and battle for their dens,
Poor harmless lambs abide their enmity. 75
Weep, wretched man, I'll aid thee tear for tear;
And let our hearts and eyes, like civil war,
Be blind with tears, and break o'ercharg'd with
grief.

Enter a Father *that hath killed his Son, with the
body in his arms.*

Fath. Thou that so stoutly hast resisted me,
Give me thy gold, if thou hast any gold, 80
For I have bought it with a hundred blows.
But let me see: is this our foeman's face?
Ah! no, no, no, it is mine only son.
Ah! boy, if any life be left in thee, 84
Throw up thine eye: see, see! what showers arise,
Blown with the windy tempest of my heart,
Upon thy wounds, that kill mine eye and heart.
O! pity, God, this miserable age. 88
What stratagems, how fell, how butcherly,
Erroneous, mutinous, and unnatural,
This deadly quarrel daily doth beget!
O boy! thy father gave thee life too soon, 92
And hath bereft thee of thy life too late.
K. Hen. Woe above woe! grief more than
common grief!
O! that my death would stay these ruthful deeds.
O! pity, pity; gentle heaven, pity. 96
The red rose and the white are on his face,
The fatal colours of our striving houses:
The one his purple blood right well resembles;
The other his pale cheeks, methinks, presenteth:
Wither one rose, and let the other flourish! 101
If you contend, a thousand lives must wither.

Son. How will my mother for a father's dea[th]
Take on with me and ne'er be satisfied!
Fath. How will my wife for slaughter of [my]
son
Shed seas of tears and ne'er be satisfied!
K. Hen. How will the country for these wo[e]
ful chances
Misthink the king and not be satisfied!
Son. Was ever son so ru'd a father's deat[h]
Fath. Was ever father so bemoan'd a so[n]
K. Hen. Was ever king so griev'd for su[b]
jects' woe?
Much is your sorrow; mine, ten times so mu[ch]
Son. I'll bear thee hence, where I may we[ep]
my fill. [*Exit with the bo*[dy]
Fath. These arms of mine shall be thy win[d]
ing-sheet;
My heart, sweet boy, shall be thy sepulchr[e]
For from my heart thine image ne'er shall g[o]
My sighing breast shall be thy funeral bell;
And so obsequious will thy father be,
E'en for the loss of thee, having no more,
As Priam was for all his valiant sons.
I'll bear thee hence; and let them fight that w[ill]
For I have murder'd where I should not kill.
[*Exit with the bo*[dy]
K. Hen. Sad-hearted men, much overgo[ne]
with care,
Here sits a king more woeful than you are.

Alarum. Excursions. Enter QUEEN MARGARE[T],
PRINCE OF WALES, *and* EXETER.

Prince. Fly, father, fly! for all your frien[ds]
are fled,
And Warwick rages like a chafed bull.
Away! for death doth hold us in pursuit.
Q. Mar. Mount you, my lord; towards B[er]
wick post amain.
Edward and Richard, like a brace of greyhoun[ds]
Having the fearful flying hare in sight,
With fiery eyes sparkling for very wrath,
And bloody steel grasp'd in their ireful han[ds]
Are at our backs; and therefore hence ama[in]
Exe. Away! for vengeance comes along w[ith]
them.
Nay, stay not to expostulate; make speed,
Or else come after: I'll away before.
K. Hen. Nay, take me with thee, good sw[eet]
Exeter:
Not that I fear to stay, but love to go
Whither the queen intends. Forward! awa[y]
[*Exeu*[nt]

SCENE VI.—*The Same.*

A loud alarum. Enter CLIFFORD, *wounded.*

Clif. Here burns my candle out; ay, here [he]
dies,
Which, while it lasted, gave King Henry lig[ht]
O Lancaster! I fear thy overthrow
More than my body's parting with my soul[.]
My love and fear glu'd many friends to the[e]
And, now I fall, thy tough commixtures m[elt]
Impairing Henry, strengthening misproud Y[ork]
The common people swarm like summer flies[;]
And whither fly the gnats but to the sun?
And who shines now but Henry's enemies?

Phœbus! hadst thou never given consent
at Phæthon should check thy fiery steeds, 12
y burning car never had scorch'd the earth;
nd, Henry, hadst thou sway'd as kings should do,
r as thy father and his father did,
iving no ground unto the house of York, 16
ey never then had sprung like summer flies;
and ten thousand in this luckless realm
ad left no mourning widows for our death,
nd thou this day hadst kept thy chair in peace.
r what doth cherish weeds but gentle air? 21
nd what makes robbers bold but too much
   lenity?
otless are plaints, and cureless are my wounds;
o way to fly, nor strength to hold out flight: 24
he foe is merciless, and will not pity;
or at their hands I have deserv'd no pity.
he air hath got into my deadly wounds,
nd much effuse of blood doth make me faint.
ome, York and Richard, Warwick and the rest;
stabb'd your fathers' bosoms, split my breast.
                            [He faints.

larum and Retreat. Enter EDWARD, GEORGE,
  RICHARD, MONTAGUE, WARWICK, *and* Soldiers.

Edw. Now breathe we, lords: good fortune
   bids us pause,
nd smooth the frowns of war with peaceful
   looks. 32
ome troops pursue the bloody-minded queen,
hat led calm Henry, though he were a king,
s doth a sail, fill'd with a fretting gust,
ommand an argosy to stem the waves. 36
ut think you, lords, that Clifford fled with
   them?
War. No, 'tis impossible he should escape;
or, though before his face I speak the words,
our brother Richard mark'd him for the grave;
nd wheresoe'er he is, he's surely dead. 41
             [CLIFFORD *groans and dies.*
Edw. Whose soul is that which takes her
   heavy leave?
Rich. A deadly groan, like life and death's
   departing.
Edw. See who it is: and now the battle's
   ended, 44
friend or foe let him be gently us'd.
Rich. Revoke that doom of mercy, for 'tis
   Clifford;
/ho not contented that he lopp'd the branch
 hewing Rutland when his leaves put forth, 48
ut set his murd'ring knife unto the root
rom whence that tender spray did sweetly
   spring,
mean our princely father, Duke of York.
War. From off the gates of York fetch down
   the head, 52
our father's head, which Clifford placed there;
stead whereof let this supply the room:
Teasure for measure must be answered.
   Edw. Bring forth that fatal screech-owl to
   our house, 56
hat nothing sung but death to us and ours:
Tow death shall stop his dismal threatening
   sound,

And his ill-boding tongue no more shall speak.
      [Attendants *bring the body forward.*
War. I think his understanding is bereft. 60
Speak, Clifford; dost thou know who speaks to
   thee?
Dark cloudy death o'ershades his beams of life,
And he nor sees, nor hears us what we say.
   Rich. O! would he did; and so perhaps he
   doth: 64
'Tis but his policy to counterfeit,
Because he would avoid such bitter taunts
Which in the time of death he gave our father.
   Geo. If so thou think'st, vex him with eager
   words. 68
Rich. Clifford! ask mercy and obtain no grace.
Edw. Clifford, repent in bootless penitence.
War. Clifford! devise excuses for thy faults.
Geo. While we devise fell tortures for thy
   faults. 72
Rich. Thou didst love York, and I am son to
   York.
Edw. Thou pitiedst Rutland, I will pity thee.
Geo. Where's Captain Margaret, to fence
   you now?
War. They mock thee, Clifford: swear as
   thou wast wont. 76
Rich. What! not an oath? nay, then the
   world goes hard
When Clifford cannot spare his friends an oath.
I know by that he's dead; and, by my soul,
If this right hand would buy two hours' life,
That I in all despite might rail at him, 81
This hand should chop it off, and with the issuing
   blood
Stifle the villain whose unstaunched thirst
York and young Rutland could not satisfy.
   War. Ay, but he's dead: off with the traitor's
   head, 85
And rear it in the place your father's stands.
And now to London with triumphant march,
There to be crowned England's royal king:
From whence shall Warwick cut the sea to
   France, 89
And ask the Lady Bona for thy queen.
So shalt thou sinew both these lands together;
And, having France thy friend, thou shalt not
   dread 92
The scatter'd foe that hopes to rise again;
For though they cannot greatly sting to hurt,
Yet look to have them buzz to offend thine
   ears.
First will I see the coronation, 96
And then to Brittany I'll cross the sea,
To effect this marriage, so it please my lord.
   Edw. Even as thou wilt, sweet Warwick, let
   it be;
For on thy shoulder do I build my seat, 100
And never will I undertake the thing
Wherein thy counsel and consent is wanting.
Richard, I will create thee Duke of Gloucester;
And George, of Clarence; Warwick, as ourself,
Shall do and undo as him pleaseth best. 105
   Rich. Let me be Duke of Clarence, George of
   Gloucester,
For Gloucester's dukedom is too ominous.
   War. Tut! that's a foolish observation: 108

Richard, be Duke of Gloucester. Now to London,
To see these honours in possession.   [*Exeunt.*

ACT III

Scene I.—*A Chase in the North of England.*

Enter two Keepers, *with cross-bows in their hands.*

First Keep. Under this thick-grown brake
    we'll shroud ourselves;
For through this laund anon the deer will come;
And in this covert will we make our stand,
Culling the principal of all the deer.   4
    Sec. Keep. I'll stay above the hill, so both
    may shoot.
    First Keep. That cannot be; the noise of thy
    cross-bow
Will scare the herd, and so my shoot is lost.
Here stand we both, and aim we at the best: 8
And, for the time shall not seem tedious,
I'll tell thee what befell me on a day
In this self place where now we mean to stand.
    Sec. Keep. Here comes a man; let's stay till
    he be past.   12

Enter KING HENRY, *disguised, with a prayerbook.*

    K. Hen. From Scotland am I stol'n, even of
    pure love,
To greet mine own land with my wishful sight.
No, Harry, Harry, 'tis no land of thine;
Thy place is fill'd, thy sceptre wrung from thee
Thy balm wash'd off wherewith thou wast
    anointed: 17
No bending knee will call thee Cæsar now,
No humble suitors press to speak for right,
No, not a man comes for redress of thee;   20
For how can I help them, and not myself?
    First Keep. Ay, here's a deer whose skin's a
    keeper's fee:
This is the quondam king; let's seize upon him.
    K. Hen. Let me embrace thee, sour adversity,
For wise men say it is the wisest course.   25
    Sec. Keep. Why linger we? let us lay hands
    upon him.
    First Keep. Forbear awhile; we'll hear a
    little more.
    K. Hen. My queen and son are gone to
    France for aid;   28
And, as I hear, the great commanding Warwick
Is thither gone, to crave the French king's sister
To wife for Edward. If this news be true,
Poor queen and son, your labour is but lost;
For Warwick is a subtle orator,   33
And Lewis a prince soon won with moving
    words.
By this account then Margaret may win him,
For she's a woman to be pitied much: 36
Her sighs will make a battery in his breast;
Her tears will pierce into a marble heart;
The tiger will be mild while she doth mourn;
And Nero will be tainted with remorse,   40
To hear and see her plaints, her brinish tears.
Ay, but she's come to beg; Warwick, to give:
She on his left side craving aid for Henry;

He on his right asking a wife for Edward.
She weeps, and says her Henry is depos'd;
He smiles, and says his Edward is install'd;
That she, poor wretch, for grief can speak
    more:
Whiles Warwick tells his title, smooths t
    wrong,
Inferreth arguments of mighty strength,
And in conclusion wins the king from her,
With promise of his sister, and what else,
To strengthen and support King Edward's pla
O Margaret! thus 'twill be; and thou, poor so
Art then forsaken, as thou went'st forlorn.
    Sec. Keep. Say, what art thou, that talk
    of kings and queens?
    K. Hen. More than I seem, and less th
    I was born to:
A man at least, for less I should not be;
And men may talk of kings, and why not I
    Sec. Keep. Ay, but thou talk'st as if th
    wert a king.
    K. Hen. Why, so I am, in mind; and tha
    enough.
    Sec. Keep. But, if thou be a king, where
    thy crown?
    K. Hen. My crown is in my heart, not
    my head;
Not deck'd with diamonds and Indian ston
Nor to be seen: my crown is call'd content;
A crown it is that seldom kings enjoy.
    Sec. Keep. Well, if you be a king crown
    with content,
Your crown content and you must be content
To go along with us; for, as we think,
You are the king King Edward hath depos'
And we his subjects, sworn in all allegiance
Will apprehend you as his enemy.
    K. Hen. But did you never swear, and bre
    an oath?
    Sec. Keep. No, never such an oath; nor w
    not now.
    K. Hen. Where did you dwell when I w
    King of England?
    Sec. Keep. Here in this country, where
    now remain.
    K. Hen. I was anointed king at nine mont
    old;
My father and my grandfather were kings,
And you were sworn true subjects unto me
And tell me, then, have you not broke yo
    oaths?
    First Keep. No;
For we were subjects but while you were kin
    K. Hen. Why, am I dead? do I not breatl
    a man?
Ah! simple men, you know not what you swea
Look, as I blow this feather from my face,
And as the air blows it to me again,
Obeying with my wind when I do blow,
And yielding to another when it blows,
Commanded always by the greater gust;
Such is the lightness of you common men.
But do not break your oaths; for of that sin
My mild entreaty shall not make you guilty
Go where you will, the king shall be con
    manded;

d be you kings: command, and I'll obey.

First Keep. We are true subjects to the king,
King Edward.

K. Hen. So would you be again to Henry,
he were seated as King Edward is. 96

First Keep. We charge you, in God's name,
and in the king's,
go with us unto the officers.

K. Hen. In God's name, lead; your king's
name be obey'd:
d what God will, that let your king perform;
d what he will, I humbly yield unto. [*Exeunt.*

CENE II.—*London. A Room in the Palace.*

ter KING EDWARD, GLOUCESTER, CLARENCE,
and LADY GREY.

K. Edw. Brother of Gloucester, at Saint
Alban's field
is lady's husband, Sir John Grey, was slain,
s lands then seiz'd on by the conqueror:
r suit is now, to repossess those lands; 4
hich we in justice cannot well deny,
cause in quarrel of the house of York
e worthy gentleman did lose his life.

Glo. Your highness shall do well to grant her
suit; 8
were dishonour to deny it her.

K. Edw. It were no less: but yet I'll make a
pause.

Glo. [*Aside to* CLARENCE.] Yea; is it so? 12
ee the lady hath a thing to grant
fore the king will grant her humble suit.

Clar. [*Aside to* GLOUCESTER.] He knows the
game: how true he keeps the wind!

Glo. [*Aside to* CLARENCE.] Silence!

K. Edw. Widow, we will consider of your
suit, 16
d come some other time to know our mind.

L. Grey. Right gracious lord, I cannot brook
delay:
ay it please your highness to resolve me now,
d what your pleasure is shall satisfy me. 20

Glo. [*Aside to* CLARENCE.] Ay, widow? then
I'll warrant you all your lands,
a if what pleases him shall pleasure you,
ght closer, or, good faith, you'll catch a blow.

Clar. [*Aside to* GLOUCESTER.] I fear her not,
unless she chance to fall. 24

Glo. [*Aside to* CLARENCE.] God forbid that!
for he'll take vantages.

K. Edw. How many children hast thou,
widow? tell me.

Clar. [*Aside to* GLOUCESTER.] I think he means
to beg a child of her.

Glo. [*Aside to* CLARENCE.] Nay, whip me,
then; he'll rather give her two. 28

L. Grey. Three, my most gracious lord.

Glo. [*Aside to* CLARENCE.] You shall have
four, if you'll be rul'd by him.

K. Edw. 'Twere pity they should lose their
father's lands.

L. Grey. Be pitiful, dread lord, and grant it
then. 32

K. Edw. Lords, give us leave: I'll try this
widow's wit.

Glo. [*Aside to* CLARENCE.] Ay, good leave
have you; for you will have leave,
Till youth take leave and leave you to the
crutch. [*Retiring with* CLARENCE.

K. Edw. Now, tell me, madam, do you love
your children? 36

L. Grey. Ay, full as dearly as I love myself.

K. Edw. And would you not do much to do
them good?

L. Grey. To do them good I would sustain
some harm.

K. Edw. Then get your husband's lands, to
do them good. 40

L. Grey. Therefore I came unto your majesty.

K. Edw. I'll tell you how these lands are to
be got.

L. Grey. So shall you bind me to your highness' service.

K. Edw. What service wilt thou do me, if I
give them? 44

L. Grey. What you command, that rests in
me to do.

K. Edw. But you will take exceptions to my
boon.

L. Grey. No, gracious lord, except I cannot
do it.

K. Edw. Ay, but thou canst do what I mean
to ask. 48

L. Grey. Why, then I will do what your
Grace commands.

Glo. [*Aside to* CLARENCE.] He plies her hard;
and much rain wears the marble.

Clar. [*Aside to* GLOUCESTER.] As red as fire!
nay, then her wax must melt.

L. Grey. Why stops my lord? shall I not
hear my task? 52

K. Edw. An easy task: 'tis but to love a king.

L. Grey. That's soon perform'd, because I
am a subject.

K. Edw. Why then, thy husband's lands I
freely give thee.

L. Grey. I take my leave with many thousand thanks. 56

Glo. [*Aside to* CLARENCE.] The match is made;
she seals it with a curtsy.

K. Edw. But stay thee; 'tis the fruits of love
I mean.

L. Grey. The fruits of love I mean, my loving
liege. 59

K. Edw. Ay, but, I fear me, in another sense.
What love think'st thou I sue so much to get?

L. Grey. My love till death, my humble
thanks, my prayers:
That love which virtue begs and virtue grants.

K. Edw. No, by my troth, I did not mean
such love. 64

L. Grey. Why, then you mean not as I
thought you did.

K. Edw. But now you partly may perceive
my mind.

L. Grey. My mind will never grant what I
perceive
Your highness aims at, if I aim aright. 68

K. Edw. To tell thee plain, I aim to lie with thee.

L. Grey. To tell you plain, I had rather lie
in prison.

K. Edw. Why, then thou shalt not have thy
husband's lands.

L. Grey. Why, then mine honesty shall be
my dower;   72
For by that loss I will not purchase them.

K. Edw. Therein thou wrong'st thy children
mightily.

L. Grey. Herein your highness wrongs both
them and me.

But, mighty lord, this merry inclination   76
Accords not with the sadness of my suit:
Please you dismiss me, either with 'ay,' or 'no.'

K. Edw. Ay, if thou wilt say 'ay' to my request;

No, if thou dost say 'no' to my demand.   80

L. Grey. Then, no, my lord. My suit is at
an end.

Glo. [*Aside to* CLARENCE.] The widow likes
him not, she knits her brows.

Clar. [*Aside to* GLOUCESTER.] He is the blunt-
est wooer in Christendom.

K. Edw. [*Aside.*] Her looks do argue her re-
plete with modesty;   84
Her words do show her wit incomparable;
All her perfections challenge sovereignty:
One way or other, she is for a king;
And she shall be my love, or else my queen. 88
Say that King Edward take thee for his queen?

L. Grey. 'Tis better said than done, my
gracious lord:
I am a subject fit to jest withal,
But far unfit to be a sovereign.   92

K. Edw. Sweet widow, by my state I swear
to thee,
I speak no more than what my soul intends;
And that is, to enjoy thee for my love.

L. Grey. And that is more than I will yield
unto.   96
I know I am too mean to be your queen,
And yet too good to be your concubine.

K. Edw. You cavil, widow: I did mean, my
queen.

L. Grey. 'Twill grieve your Grace my sons
should call you father.   100

K. Edw. No more than when my daughters
call thee mother.
Thou art a widow, and thou hast some chil-
dren;
And, by God's mother, I, being but a bachelor,
Have other some: why, 'tis a happy thing 104
To be the father unto many sons.
Answer no more, for thou shalt be my queen.

Glo. [*Aside to* CLARENCE.] The ghostly father
now hath done his shrift.

Clar. [*Aside to* GLOUCESTER.] When he was
made a shriver, 'twas for shift.   108

K. Edw. Brothers, you muse what chat we
two have had.

Glo. The widow likes it not, for she looks
very sad.

K. Edw. You'd think it strange if I should
marry her.

Clar. To whom, my lord?

K. Edw.   Why, Clarence, to myself.

Glo. That would be ten days' wonder at the
least.   113

Clar. That's a day longer than a wonder las▮

Glo. By so much is the wonder in extreme▮

K. Edw. Well, jest on, brothers: I can t▮
you both   ▮
Her suit is granted for her husband's lands.

Enter a Nobleman.

Nob. My gracious lord, Henry your foe ▮
taken,
And brought as prisoner to your palace gate▮

K. Edw. See that he be convey'd unto t▮
Tower: ▮
And go we, brothers, to the man that took hi▮
To question of his apprehension.
Widow, go you along. Lords, use her honou▮
ably.   [*Exeunt all but* GLOUCESTE▮

Glo. Ay, Edward will use women honou▮
ably.   ▮
Would he were wasted, marrow, bones, and a▮
That from his loins no hopeful branch m▮
spring,
To cross me from the golden time I look fo▮
And yet, between my soul's desire and me— ▮
The lustful Edward's title buried,—
Is Clarence, Henry, and his son young Edwar▮
And all the unlook'd for issue of their bodie▮
To take their rooms, ere I can place myself: ▮
A cold premeditation for my purpose!
Why then, I do but dream on sovereignty;
Like one that stands upon a promontory,
And spies a far-off shore where he would trea▮
Wishing his foot were equal with his eye; ▮
And chides the sea that sunders him from thenc▮
Saying, he'll lade it dry to have his way:
So do I wish the crown, being so far off,   ▮
And so I chide the means that keep me from ▮
And so I say I'll cut the causes off,
Flattering me with impossibilities.
My eye's too quick, my heart o'erweens t▮
much,   ▮
Unless my hand and strength could equ▮
them.
Well, say there is no kingdom then for Richar▮
What other pleasure can the world afford?
I'll make my heaven in a lady's lap,   ▮
And deck my body in gay ornaments,
And witch sweet ladies with my words and look▮
O miserable thought! and more unlikely
Than to accomplish twenty golden crowns. ▮
Why, love forswore me in my mother's wom▮
And, for I should not deal in her soft laws,
She did corrupt frail nature with some bribe▮
To shrink mine arm up like a wither'd shru▮
To make an envious mountain on my back,
Where sits deformity to mock my body;
To shape my legs of an unequal size;
To disproportion me in every part,   1▮
Like to a chaos, or an unlick'd bear-whelp
That carries no impression like the dam.
And am I then a man to be belov'd?
O monstrous fault! to harbour such a thoug▮
Then, since this earth affords no joy to me 1▮
But to command, to check, to o'erbear such
As are of better person than myself,
I'll make my heaven to dream upon the crow▮
And, whiles I live, to account this world but he▮

ntil my mis-shap'd trunk that bears this head
e round impaled with a glorious crown.
nd yet I know not how to get the crown, 172
or many lives stand between me and home:
nd I, like one lost in a thorny wood,
nat rents the thorns and is rent with the thorns,
eking a way and straying from the way; 176
ot knowing how to find the open air,
ut toiling desperately to find it out,
orment myself to catch the English crown:
nd from that torment I will free myself, 180
r hew my way out with a bloody axe.
hy, I can smile, and murder while I smile,
nd cry, 'Content,' to that which grieves my
  heart,
nd wet my cheeks with artificial tears, 184
nd frame my face to all occasions.
l drown more sailors than the mermaid shall;
l slay more gazers than the basilisk;
l play the orator as well as Nestor, 188
eceive more slily than Ulysses could,
nd, like a Sinon, take another Troy.
an add colours to the chameleon, 191
nange shapes with Proteus for advantages,
nd set the murd'rous Machiavel to school.
an I do this, and cannot get a crown?
ut! were it further off, I'll pluck it down. [*Exit.*

SCENE III.—*France. A Room in the Palace.*

ourish. Enter LEWIS *the French King, his
sister* LADY BONA, *attended: his Admiral
called* BOURBON; *the King takes his state.
Then enter* QUEEN MARGARET, PRINCE ED-
WARD, *and the* EARL OF OXFORD. LEWIS *sits,
and riseth up again.*

K. Lew. Fair Queen of England, worthy
  Margaret,
t down with us: it ill befits thy state
nd birth, that thou shouldst stand while Lewis
  doth sit.
Q. Mar. No, mighty King of France: now
  Margaret 4
ust strike her sail, and learn a while to serve
here kings command. I was, I must confess,
reat Albion's queen in former golden days;
it now mischance hath trod my title down, 8
nd with dishonour laid me on the ground,
here I must take like seat unto my fortune,
nd to my humble seat conform myself.
K. Lew. Why, say, fair queen, whence springs
  this deep despair? 12
Q. Mar. From such a cause as fills mine
  eyes with tears
nd stops my tongue, while heart is drown'd in
  cares.
K. Lew. Whate'er it be, be thou still like
  thyself,
nd sit thee by our side. [*Seats her by him.*]
  Yield not thy neck 16
 fortune's yoke, but let thy dauntless mind
ill ride in triumph over all mischance.
 plain, Queen Margaret, and tell thy grief;
shall be eas'd, if France can yield relief. 20
Q. Mar. Those gracious words revive my
  drooping thoughts,

And give my tongue-tied sorrows leave to speak.
Now, therefore, be it known to noble Lewis,
That Henry, sole possessor of my love, 24
Is of a king become a banish'd man,
And forc'd to live in Scotland a forlorn;
While proud ambitious Edward Duke of York
Usurps the regal title and the seat 28
Of England's true-anointed lawful king.
This is the cause that I, poor Margaret,
With this my son, Prince Edward, Henry's heir,
Am come to crave thy just and lawful aid; 32
And if thou fail us, all our hope is done.
Scotland hath will to help, but cannot help;
Our people and our peers are both misled,
Our treasure seiz'd, our soldiers put to flight, 36
And, as thou seest, ourselves in heavy plight.
K. Lew. Renowned queen, with patience
  calm the storm,
While we bethink a means to break it off.
Q. Mar. The more we stay, the stronger
  grows our foe. 40
K. Lew. The more I stay, the more I'll suc-
  cour thee.
Q. Mar. O! but impatience waiteth on true
  sorrow:
And see where comes the breeder of my sorrow.

Enter WARWICK, *attended.*

K. Lew. What's he, approacheth boldly to
  our presence? 44
Q. Mar. Our Earl of Warwick, Edward's
  greatest friend.
K. Lew. Welcome, brave Warwick! What
  brings thee to France?
  [*Descending from his state.* QUEEN
    MARGARET *rises.*
Q. Mar. Ay, now begins a second storm to
  rise;
For this is he that moves both wind and tide. 48
War. From worthy Edward, King of Albion,
My lord and sovereign, and thy vowed friend,
I come, in kindness and unfeigned love,
First, to do greetings to thy royal person; 52
And then to crave a league of amity;
And lastly to confirm that amity
With nuptial knot, if thou vouchsafe to grant
That virtuous Lady Bona, thy fair sister, 56
To England's king in lawful marriage.
Q. Mar. If that go forward, Henry's hope is
  done.
War. [*To* BONA.] And, gracious madam, in
  our king's behalf,
I am commanded, with your leave and favour, 60
Humbly to kiss your hand, and with my tongue
To tell the passion of my sov'reign's heart;
Where fame, late entering at his heedful ears,
Hath plac'd thy beauty's image and thy virtue.
Q. Mar. King Lewis and Lady Bona, hear
  me speak, 65
Before you answer Warwick. His demand
Springs not from Edward's well-meant honest
  love,
But from deceit bred by necessity; 68
For how can tyrants safely govern home,
Unless abroad they purchase great alliance?
To prove him tyrant this reason may suffice,

That Henry liveth still; but were he dead,   72
Yet here Prince Edward stands, King Henry's
    son.
Look, therefore, Lewis, that by this league and
    marriage
Thou draw not on thy danger and dishonour;
For though usurpers sway the rule awhile,   76
Yet heavens are just, and time suppresseth
    wrongs.
War. Injurious Margaret!
Prince.   And why not queen?
War. Because thy father Henry did usurp,
And thou no more art prince than she is queen.
Oxf. Then Warwick disannuls great John of
    Gaunt,   81
Which did subdue the greatest part of Spain;
And, after John of Gaunt, Henry the Fourth,
Whose wisdom was a mirror to the wisest;   84
And, after that wise prince, Henry the Fifth,
Who by his prowess conquered all France:
From these our Henry lineally descends.
War. Oxford, how haps it, in this smooth
    discourse,   88
You told me not how Henry the Sixth hath lost
All that which Henry the Fifth had gotten?
Methinks these peers of France should smile at
    that.
But for the rest, you tell a pedigree   92
Of threescore and two years; a silly time
To make prescription for a kingdom's worth.
Oxf. Why, Warwick, canst thou speak against
    thy liege,
Whom thou obeyedst thirty and six years,   96
And not bewray thy treason with a blush?
War. Can Oxford, that did ever fence the
    right,
Now buckler falsehood with a pedigree?
For shame! leave Henry, and call Edward king.
Oxf. Call him my king, by whose injurious
    doom   101
My elder brother, the Lord Aubrey Vere,
Was done to death? and more than so, my
    father,
Even in the downfall of his mellow'd years,
When nature brought him to the door of death?
No, Warwick, no; while life upholds this arm,
This arm upholds the house of Lancaster.
War. And I the house of York.   108
K. Lew. Queen Margaret, Prince Edward,
    and Oxford,
Vouchsafe at our request to stand aside,
While I use further conference with Warwick.
                    [*They stand aloof.*
Q. Mar. Heaven grant that Warwick's words
    bewitch him not!   112
K. Lew. Now, Warwick, tell me, even upon
    thy conscience,
Is Edward your true king? for I were loath
To link with him that were not lawful chosen.
War. Thereon I pawn my credit and mine
    honour.   116
K. Lew. But is he gracious in the people's
    eye?
War. The more that Henry was unfortunate.
K. Lew. Then further, all dissembling set
    aside,

Tell me for truth the measure of his love
Unto our sister Bona.
War.   Such it seems
As may beseem a monarch like himself.
Myself have often heard him say and swear
That this his love was an eternal plant,
Whereof the root was fix'd in virtue's grou
The leaves and fruit maintain'd with beaut
    sun,
Exempt from envy, but not from disdain,
Unless the Lady Bona quit his pain.
K. Lew. Now, sister, let us hear your fi
    resolve.
Bona. Your grant, or your denial, shall
    mine:
[*To* WARWICK.] Yet I confess that often ere t
    day,
When I have heard your king's desert recount
Mine ear hath tempted judgment to desire.
K. Lew. Then, Warwick, thus: our sis
    shall be Edward's;
And now forthwith shall articles be drawn
Touching the jointure that your king m
    make,
Which with her dowry shall be counterpois
Draw near, Queen Margaret, and be a witn
That Bona shall be wife to the English kin
Prince. To Edward, but not to the Engl
    king.
Q. Mar. Deceitful Warwick! it was thy dev
By this alliance to make void my suit:
Before thy coming Lewis was Henry's frien
K. Lew. And still is friend to him and M
    garet:
But if your title to the crown be weak,
As may appear by Edward's good success,
Then 'tis but reason that I be releas'd
From giving aid which late I promised.
Yet shall you have all kindness at my hand
That your estate requires and mine can yie
War. Henry now lives in Scotland at his ea
Where having nothing, nothing can he lose.
And as for you yourself, our quondam quee
You have a father able to maintain you,
And better 'twere you troubled him than Franc
Q. Mar. Peace! impudent and shamele
    Warwick, peace;
Proud setter up and puller down of kings;
I will not hence, till, with my talk and tear
Both full of truth, I make King Lewis beho
Thy sly conveyance and thy lord's false love;
For both of you are birds of self-same feathe
                    [*A horn winded with*
K. Lew. Warwick, this is some post to us
    thee.

Enter a Post.

Mess. My lord ambassador, these letters a
    for you,
Sent from your brother, Marquess Montagu
These from our king unto your majesty;
[*To* MARGARET.] And, madam, these for yo
    from whom I know not.
                    [*They all read their letter*
Oxf. I like it well that our fair queen ar
    mistress

miles at her news, while Warwick frowns at
  his.   168
Prince. Nay, mark how Lewis stamps as he
  were nettled:
.ope all's for the best.
K. Lew. Warwick, what are thy news? and
  yours, fair queen?
Q. Mar. Mine, such as fill my heart with
  unhop'd joys.   172
War. Mine, full of sorrow and heart's discontent.
K. Lew. What! has your king married the
  Lady Grey?
.id now, to soothe your forgery and his,
.nds me a paper to persuade me patience? 176
.this the alliance that he seeks with France?
.are he presume to scorn us in this manner?
Q. Mar. I told your majesty as much before:
.is proveth Edward's love and Warwick's
  honesty.   180
War. King Lewis, I here protest, in sight of
  heaven,
.id by the hope I have of heavenly bliss,
.at I am clear from this misdeed of Edward's;
.o more my king, for he dishonours me;   184
.it most himself, if he could see his shame.
.id I forget that by the house of York
.y father came untimely to his death?
.id I let pass the abuse done to my niece?   188
.id I impale him with the regal crown?
.id I put Henry from his native right?
.id am I guerdon'd at the last with shame?
.iame on himself! for my desert is honour: 192
.id, to repair my honour, lost for him,
.iere renounce him and return to Henry.
.y noble queen, let former grudges pass,
.id henceforth I am thy true servitor.   196
.vill revenge his wrong to Lady Bona,
.id replant Henry in his former state.
Q. Mar. Warwick, these words have turn'd
  my hate to love;
.id I forgive and quite forget old faults,   200
.idjoy that thou becom'st King Henry's friend.
War. So much his friend, ay, his unfeigned
  friend,
.iat, if King Lewis vouchsafe to furnish us
.ith some few bands of chosen soldiers,   204
.I undertake to land them on our coast,
.id force the tyrant from his seat by war.
.is not his new-made bride shall succour him:
.id as for Clarence, as my letters tell me, 208
.e's very likely now to fall from him,
.irmatching more for wanton lust than honour,
.r than for strength and safety of our country.
Bona. Dear brother, how shall Bona be reveng'd,   212
.it by thy help to this distressed queen?
Q. Mar. Renowned prince, how shall poor
  Henry live,
.nless thou rescue him from foul despair?
Bona. My quarrel and this English queen's
  are one.   216
War. And mine, fair Lady Bona, joins with
  yours.
K. Lew. And mine with hers, and thine and
  Margaret's.

Therefore, at last, I firmly am resolv'd
You shall have aid.   220
  Q. Mar. Let me give humble thanks for all
    at once.
  K. Lew. Then, England's messenger, return
    in post,
And tell false Edward, thy supposed king,
That Lewis of France is sending over masquers,
To revel it with him and his new bride.   225
Thou seest what's past; go fear thy king withal.
  Bona. Tell him, in hope he'll prove a widower
    shortly,
I'll wear the willow garland for his sake.   228
  Q. Mar. Tell him, my mourning weeds are
    laid aside,
And I am ready to put armour on.
  War. Tell him from me, that he hath done
    me wrong,
And therefore I'll uncrown him ere't be long.
There's thy reward: be gone. [*Exit* Messenger.
  K. Lew. But, Warwick, thou   233
Thou and Oxford, with five thousand men,
Shall cross the seas, and bid false Edward battle;
And, as occasion serves, this noble queen   236
And prince shall follow with a fresh supply.
Yet ere thou go, but answer me one doubt:
What pledge have we of thy firm loyalty?
  War. This shall assure my constant loyalty:
That if our queen and this young prince agree,
I'll join mine eldest daughter and my joy
To him forthwith in holy wedlock bands.
  Q. Mar. Yes, I agree, and thank you for your
    motion.   244
Son Edward, she is fair and virtuous,
Therefore delay not, give thy hand to Warwick;
And, with thy hand, thy faith irrevocable,
That only Warwick's daughter shall be thine.
  Prince. Yes, I accept her, for she well de-
    serves it;   249
And here, to pledge my vow, I give my hand.
        [*He gives his hand to* WARWICK.
  K. Lew. Why stay we now? These soldiers
    shall be levied,
And thou, Lord Bourbon, our high admiral, 252
Shall waft them over with our royal fleet.
I long till Edward fall by war's mischance,
For mocking marriage with a dame of France.
        [*Exeunt all except* WARWICK.
  War. I came from Edward as ambassador,
But I return his sworn and mortal foe: 257
Matter of marriage was the charge he gave me,
But dreadful war shall answer his demand.
Had he none else to make a stale but me?   260
Then none but I shall turn his jest to sorrow.
I was the chief that rais'd him to the crown,
And I'll be chief to bring him down again:
Not that I pity Henry's misery,   264
But seek revenge on Edward's mockery. [*Exit.*

ACT IV

SCENE I.—*London. A Room in the Palace.*

Enter GLOUCESTER, CLARENCE, SOMERSET,
  MONTAGUE, *and Others.*

  Glo. Now tell me, brother Clarence, what
    think you

Of this new marriage with the Lady Grey?
Hath not our brother made a worthy choice?
   Clar. Alas! you know, 'tis far from hence to
   France;   4
How could he stay till Warwick made return?
   Som. My lords, forbear this talk; here comes
   the king.
   Glo. And his well-chosen bride.
   Clar. I mind to tell him plainly what I think. 7

Flourish. Enter KING EDWARD, *attended;* LADY
GREY, *as Queen;* PEMBROKE, STAFFORD, HAST-
INGS, *and Others.*

   K. Edw. Now, brother Clarence, how like
you our choice,
That you stand pensive, as half malcontent?
   Clar. As well as Lewis of France, or the Earl
of Warwick;
Which are so weak of courage and in judgment
That they'll take no offence at our abuse.   13
   K. Edw. Suppose they take offence without
a cause,
They are but Lewis and Warwick: I am Ed-
ward,
Your king and Warwick's, and must have my
will.   16
   Glo. And you shall have your will, because
our king:
Yet hasty marriage seldom proveth well.
   K. Edw. Yea, brother Richard, are you of-
fended too?
   Glo. Not I: 20
No, God forbid, that I should wish them sever'd
Whom God hath join'd together; ay, and 'twere
pity
To sunder them that yoke so well together.
   K. Edw. Setting your scorns and your mis-
like aside,   24
Tell me some reason why the Lady Grey
Should not become my wife and England's
queen:
And you too, Somerset and Montague,
Speak freely what you think.   28
   Clar. Then this is mine opinion: that King
Lewis
Becomes your enemy for mocking him
About the marriage of the Lady Bona.
   Glo. And Warwick, doing what you gave in
charge,   32
Is now dishonoured by this new marriage.
   K. Edw. What if both Lewis and Warwick
be appeas'd
By such invention as I can devise?
   Mont. Yet to have join'd with France in
such alliance   36
Would more have strengthen'd this our com-
monwealth
'Gainst foreign storms, than any home-bred
marriage.
   Hast. Why, knows not Montague, that of
itself
England is safe, if true within itself?   40
   Mont. Yes; but the safer when 'tis back'd
with France.
   Hast. 'Tis better using France than trusting
France:

Let us be back'd with God and with the seas
Which he hath given for fence impregnable,
And with their helps only defend ourselve
In them and in ourselves our safety lies.
   Clar. For this one speech Lord Hastings w
deserves
To have the heir of the Lord Hungerford.
   K. Edw. Ay, what of that? it was my v
and grant;
And for this once my will shall stand for la
   Glo. And yet methinks your Grace hath n
done well,
To give the heir and daughter of Lord Sca
Unto the brother of your loving bride:
She better would have fitted me or Clarenc
But in your bride you bury brotherhood.
   Clar. Or else you would not have besto
the heir
Of the Lord Bonville on your new wife's s
And leave your brothers to go speed elsewhe
   K. Edw. Alas, poor Clarence, is it for a w
That thou art malcontent? I will provide th
   Clar. In choosing for yourself you shov
your judgment,
Which being shallow, you shall give me le
To play the broker on mine own behalf;
And to that end I shortly mind to leave you.
   K. Edw. Leave me, or tarry, Edward will
king,
And not be tied unto his brother's will.
   Q. Eliz. My lords, before it pleas'd
majesty
To raise my state to title of a queen,
Do me but right, and you must all confess
That I was not ignoble of descent;
And meaner than myself have had like fortu
But as this title honours me and mine,
So your dislikes, to whom I would be pleasi
Do cloud my joys with danger and with sorr
   K. Edw. My love, forbear to fawn upon th
frowns:
What danger or what sorrow can befall th
So long as Edward is thy constant friend,
And their true sovereign, whom they must obe
Nay, whom they shall obey, and love t
too,
Unless they seek for hatred at my hands;
Which if they do, yet will I keep thee safe,
And they shall feel the vengeance of my wra
   Glo. [*Aside.*] I hear, yet say not much, l
think the more.

Enter a Messenger.

   K. Edw. Now, messenger, what letters
what news
From France?
   Mess. My sovereign liege, no letters; a
few words;
But such as I, without your special pard
Dare not relate.
   K. Edw. Go to, we pardon thee: therefo
in brief,
Tell me their words as near as thou canst gu
them.
What answer makes King Lewis unto c
letters?

Mess. At my depart these were his very
    words: 92
'Go tell false Edward, thy supposed king,
That Lewis of France is sending over masquers,
To revel it with him and his new bride.'
K. Edw. Is Lewis so brave? belike he thinks
    me Henry. 96
But what said Lady Bona to my marriage?
Mess. These were her words, utter'd with
    mild disdain:
'Tell him, in hope he'll prove a widower shortly,
I'll wear the willow garland for his sake.' 100
K. Edw. I blame not her, she could say little
    less;
She had the wrong. But what said Henry's
    queen?
For I have heard that she was there in place.
Mess. 'Tell him,' quoth she, 'my mourning
    weeds are done, 104
And I am ready to put armour on.'
K. Edw. Belike she minds to play the Ama-
    zon.
But what said Warwick to these injuries?
Mess. He, more incens'd against your majesty
Than all the rest, discharg'd me with these
    words: 109
'Tell him from me that he hath done me wrong,
And therefore I'll uncrown him ere 't be long.'
K. Edw. Ha! durst the traitor breathe out
    so proud words? 112
Well, I will arm me, being thus forewarn'd:
They shall have wars, and pay for their pre-
    sumption.
But say, is Warwick friends with Margaret?
Mess. Ay, gracious sovereign; they are so
    link'd in friendship, 116
That young Prince Edward marries Warwick's
    daughter.
Clar. Belike the elder; Clarence will have
    the younger.
Now, brother king, farewell, and sit you fast,
For I will hence to Warwick's other daughter;
That, though I want a kingdom, yet in marriage
I may not prove inferior to yourself.
You, that love me and Warwick, follow me.
    [*Exit* CLARENCE, *and* SOMERSET *follows.*
Glo. [*Aside.*] Not I. 124
My thoughts aim at a further matter; I
Stay not for love of Edward, but the crown.
K. Edw. Clarence and Somerset both gone
    to Warwick!
Yet am I arm'd against the worst can happen,
And haste is needful in this desperate case.
Pembroke and Stafford, you in our behalf
Go levy men, and make prepare for war:
They are already, or quickly will be landed: 132
Myself in person will straight follow you,
    [*Exeunt* PEMBROKE *and* STAFFORD.
But ere I go, Hastings and Montague,
Resolve my doubt. You twain, of all the rest,
Are near to Warwick by blood, and by alliance:
Tell me if you love Warwick more than me?
If it be so, then both depart to him; 138
I rather wish you foes than hollow friends:
But if you mind to hold your true obedience,
Give me assurance with some friendly vow

That I may never have you in suspect.
Mont. So God help Montague as he proves
    true!
Hast. And Hastings as he favours Edward's
    cause! 144
K. Edw. Now, brother Richard, will you
    stand by us?
Glo. Ay, in despite of all that shall withstand
    you.
K. Edw. Why, so! then am I sure of victory.
Now therefore let us hence; and lose no hour
Till we meet Warwick with his foreign power.
    [*Exeunt.*

SCENE II.—*A Plain in Warwickshire.*

Enter WARWICK *and* OXFORD, *with French and
other Forces.*

War. Trust me, my lord, all hitherto goes
    well;
The common people by numbers swarm to us.

Enter CLARENCE *and* SOMERSET.

But see where Somerset and Clarence come!
Speak suddenly, my lords, are we all friends?
Clar. Fear not that, my lord. 5
War. Then, gentle Clarence, welcome unto
    Warwick;
And welcome, Somerset: I hold it cowardice,
To rest mistrustful where a noble heart 8
Hath pawn'd an open hand in sign of love;
Else might I think that Clarence, Edward's
    brother,
Were but a feigned friend to our proceedings:
But welcome, sweet Clarence; my daughter
    shall be thine. 12
And now what rests, but in night's coverture,
Thy brother being carelessly encamp'd,
His soldiers lurking in the towns about,
And but attended by a simple guard, 16
We may surprise and take him at our pleasure?
Our scouts have found the adventure very easy:
That as Ulysses, and stout Diomede,
With sleight and manhood stole to Rhesus'
    tents, 20
And brought from thence the Thracian fatal
    steeds;
So we, well cover'd with the night's black
    mantle,
At unawares may beat down Edward's guard,
And seize himself; I say not, slaughter him,
For I intend but only to surprise him. 25
You, that will follow me to this attempt,
Applaud the name of Henry with your leader.
    [*They all cry* 'Henry!'
Why, then, let's on our way in silent sort. 28
For Warwick and his friends, God and Saint
    George! [*Exeunt.*

SCENE III.—EDWARD'S *Camp near Warwick.*

Enter certain Watchmen *to guard the
KING'S tent.*

First Watch. Come on, my masters, each
    man take his stand;
The king, by this, is set him down to sleep.

Sec. Watch. What, will he not to bed?
First Watch. Why, no: for he hath made a   4
solemn vow
Never to lie and take his natural rest
Till Warwick or himself be quite suppress'd.
Sec. Watch. To-morrow then belike shall be
the day,
If Warwick be so near as men report.   8
Third Watch. But say, I pray, what noble-
man is that
That with the king here resteth in his tent?
First Watch. 'Tis the Lord Hastings, the
king's chiefest friend.
Third Watch. O! is it so? But why com-
mands the king   12
That his chief followers lodge in towns about
him,
While he himself keeps in the cold field?
Sec. Watch. 'Tis the more honour, because
the more dangerous.
Third Watch. Ay, but give me worship and
quietness;   16
I like it better than a dangerous honour.
If Warwick knew in what estate he stands,
'Tis to be doubted he would waken him.
First Watch. Unless our halberds did shut
up his passage.   20
Sec. Watch. Ay; wherefore else guard we his
royal tent,
But to defend his person from night-foes?

Enter WARWICK, CLARENCE, OXFORD, SOMERSET,
and Forces.

War. This is his tent; and see where stand
his guard.   23
Courage, my masters! honour now or never!
But follow me, and Edward shall be ours.
First Watch. Who goes there?
Sec. Watch. Stay, or thou diest.
     [WARWICK *and the rest cry all,* 'War-
wick! Warwick!' *and set upon the*
Guard; *who fly, crying,* 'Arm! Arm!'
WARWICK *and the rest following them.*

*Drums beating, and Trumpets sounding, re-
enter* WARWICK *and the rest, bringing the*
KING *out in his gown, sitting in a chair.*
GLOUCESTER *and* HASTINGS *fly over the stage.*

Som.   What are they that fly there?
War. Richard and Hastings: let them go;
here's the duke.   28
K. Edw. The duke! Why, Warwick, when
we parted last,
Thou call'dst me king!
War.   Ay, but the case is alter'd:
When you disgrac'd me in my embassade,
Then I degraded you from being king,   32
And come now to create you Duke of York.
Alas! how should you govern any kingdom,
That know not how to use ambassadors,
Nor how to be contented with one wife,   36
Nor how to use your brothers brotherly,
Nor how to study for the people's welfare,
Nor how to shroud yourself from enemies?
K. Edw. Yea, brother of Clarence, art thou
here too?   40
Nay, then, I see that Edward needs must down.

Yet, Warwick, in despite of all mischance,
Of thee thyself, and all thy complices,
Edward will always bear himself as king: 44
Though Fortune's malice overthrow my state,
My mind exceeds the compass of her wheel.
War. Then, for his mind, be Edward Eng-
land's king: [*Takes off his crown.*
But Henry now shall wear the English crown, 48
And be true king indeed, thou but the shadow.
My Lord of Somerset, at my request,
See that forthwith Duke Edward be convey'd
Unto my brother, Archbishop of York.   52
When I have fought with Pembroke and his
fellows,
I'll follow you, and tell what answer
Lewis and the Lady Bona send to him:
Now, for a while farewell, good Duke of
York.   56
K. Edw. What fates impose, that men must
needs abide;
It boots not to resist both wind and tide.
          [*Exit, led out;* SOMERSET *with him.*
Oxf. What now remains, my lords, for us to
do,
But march to London with our soldiers?   60
War. Ay, that's the first thing that we have
to do;
To free King Henry from imprisonment,
And see him seated in the regal throne.
          [*Exeunt.*

SCENE IV.—*London. A Room in the Palace.*

Enter QUEEN ELIZABETH *and* RIVERS.

Riv. Madam, what makes you in this sudden
change?
Q. Eliz. Why, brother Rivers, are you yet to
learn
What late misfortune is befall'n King Edward?
Riv. What! loss of some pitch'd battle
against Warwick?   4
Q. Eliz. No, but the loss of his own royal
person.
Riv. Then is my sovereign slain?
Q. Eliz. Ay, almost slain, for he is taken
prisoner;
Either betray'd by falsehood of his guard   8
Or by his foe surpris'd at unawares:
And, as I further have to understand,
Is now committed to the Bishop of York,
Fell Warwick's brother, and by that our foe.
Riv. These news, I must confess, are full of
grief;   13
Yet, gracious madam, bear it as you may:
Warwick may lose, that now hath won the day.
Q. Eliz. Till then fair hope must hinder life's
decay.   16
And I the rather wean me from despair
For love of Edward's offspring in my womb:
This is it that makes me bridle passion,
And bear with mildness my misfortune's cross;
Ay, ay, for this I draw in many a tear,   21
And stop the rising of blood-sucking sighs,
Lest with my sighs or tears I blast or drown
King Edward's fruit, true heir to the English
crown.   24

Riv. But, madam, where is Warwick then become?

Q. Eliz. I am inform'd that he comes towards London,
To set the crown once more on Henry's head:
Guess thou the rest; King Edward's friends must down.   28
But, to prevent the tyrant's violence,—
For trust not him that hath once broken faith,—
I'll hence forthwith unto the sanctuary,
To save at least the heir of Edward's right: 32
There shall I rest secure from force and fraud.
Come, therefore; let us fly while we may fly:
If Warwick take us we are sure to die. [*Exeunt.*

SCENE V.—*A Park near Middleham Castle in Yorkshire.*

Enter GLOUCESTER, HASTINGS, SIR WILLIAM STANLEY, *and Others.*

Glo. Now, my Lord Hastings and Sir William Stanley,
Leave off to wonder why I drew you hither,
Into this chiefest thicket of the park.
Thus stands the case. You know, our king, my brother,   4
Is prisoner to the bishop here, at whose hands
He hath good usage and great liberty,
And often but attended with weak guard,
Comes hunting this way to disport himself. 8
I have advertis'd him by secret means,
That if about this hour he make this way,
Under the colour of his usual game,
He shall here find his friends, with horse and men   12
To set him free from his captivity.

Enter KING EDWARD *and a* Huntsman.

Hunt. This way, my lord, for this way lies the game.
K. Edw. Nay, this way, man: see where the huntsmen stand.
Now, brother of Gloucester, Lord Hastings, and the rest,   16
Stand you thus close, to steal the bishop's deer?
Glo. Brother, the time and case requireth haste.
Your horse stands ready at the park corner.
K. Edw. But whither shall we then?   20
Hast. To Lynn, my lord; and ship from thence to Flanders.
Glo. Well guess'd, believe me; for that was my meaning.
K. Edw. Stanley, I will requite thy forwardness.
Glo. But wherefore stay we? 'tis no time to talk.   24
K. Edw. Huntsman, what sayst thou? wilt thou go along?
Hunt. Better do so than tarry and be hang'd.
Glo. Come then, away; let's ha' no more ado.
K. Edw. Bishop, farewell: shield thee from Warwick's frown,   28
And pray that I may repossess the crown.
[*Exeunt.*

SCENE VI.—*A Room in the Tower.*

Enter KING HENRY, CLARENCE, WARWICK, SOMERSET, *young* RICHMOND, OXFORD, MONTAGUE, Lieutenant of the Tower, *and* Attendants.

K. Hen. Master lieutenant, now that God and friends
Have shaken Edward from the regal seat,
And turn'd my captive state to liberty,
My fear to hope, my sorrows unto joys,   4
At our enlargement what are thy due fees?
Lieu. Subjects may challenge nothing of their sovereigns;
But if a humble prayer may prevail,
I then crave pardon of your majesty.   8
K. Hen. For what, lieutenant? for well using me?
Nay, be thou sure, I'll well requite thy kindness,
For that it made my imprisonment a pleasure;
Ay, such a pleasure as encaged birds   12
Conceive, when, after many moody thoughts
At last by notes of household harmony
They quite forget their loss of liberty.
But, Warwick, after God, thou set'st me free,
And chiefly therefore I thank God and thee;
He was the author, thou the instrument.   18
Therefore, that I may conquer Fortune's spite
By living low, where Fortune cannot hurt me,
And that the people of this blessed land
May not be punish'd with my thwarting stars,
Warwick, although my head still wear the crown,
I here resign my government to thee,   24
For thou art fortunate in all thy deeds.
War. Your Grace hath still been fam'd for virtuous;
And now may seem as wise as virtuous,
By spying and avoiding Fortune's malice;   28
For few men rightly temper with the stars:
Yet in this one thing let me blame your Grace,
For choosing me when Clarence is in place.
Clar. No, Warwick, thou art worthy of the sway,   32
To whom the heavens, in thy nativity,
Adjudg'd an olive branch and laurel crown,
As likely to be blest in peace, and war;
And therefore I yield thee my free consent. 36
War. And I choose Clarence only for protector.
K. Hen. Warwick and Clarence, give me both your hands:
Now join your hands, and with your hands your hearts,
That no dissension hinder government: 40
I make you both protectors of this land,
While I myself will lead a private life,
And in devotion spend my latter days,
To sin's rebuke and my Creator's praise. 44
War. What answers Clarence to his sovereign's will?
Clar. That he consents, if Warwick yield consent;
For on thy fortune I repose myself.
War. Why then, though loath, yet must I be content: 48

We'll yoke together, like a double shadow
To Henry's body, and supply his place;
I mean, in bearing weight of government,
While he enjoys the honour and his ease.   52
And, Clarence, now then it is more than needful
Forthwith that Edward be pronounc'd a traitor,
And all his lands and goods confiscate.

   Clar. What else? and that succession be
  determin'd.   56

   War. Ay, therein Clarence shall not want
his part.

   K. Hen. But, with the first of all your chief
affairs,
Let me entreat, for I command no more,
That Margaret your queen, and my son Edward,
Be sent for, to return from France with speed:
For, till I see them here, by doubtful fear
My joy of liberty is half eclips'd.

   Clar. It shall be done, my sov'reign, with all
  speed.   64

   K. Hen. My Lord of Somerset, what youth
is that
Of whom you seem to have so tender care?

   Som. My liege, it is young Henry, Earl of
Richmond.

   K. Hen. Come hither, England's hope: [*Lays
his hand on his head.*] If secret powers   68
Suggest but truth to my divining thoughts,
This pretty lad will prove our country's bliss.
His looks are full of peaceful majesty,
His head by nature fram'd to wear a crown,
His hand to wield a sceptre, and himself   73
Likely in time to bless a regal throne.
Make much of him, my lords; for this is he
Must help you more than you are hurt by me.

Enter a Post.

   War. What news, my friend?   77

   Mess. That Edward is escaped from your
brother,
And fled, as he hears since, to Burgundy.

   War. Unsavoury news! but how made he
escape?   80

   Mess. He was convey'd by Richard Duke of
Gloucester,
And the Lord Hastings, who attended him
In secret ambush on the forest side,
And from the bishop's huntsmen rescu'd him:
For hunting was his daily exercise.   85

   War. My brother was too careless of his
charge.
But let us hence, my sovereign, to provide
A salve for any sore that may betide.   88

   [*Exeunt* KING HENRY, WARWICK, CLARENCE,
    Lieutenant, *and* Attendants.

   Som. My lord, I like not of this flight of
Edward's;
For doubtless Burgundy will yield him help,
And we shall have more wars before 't be long.
As Henry's late presaging prophecy   92
Did glad my heart with hope of this young
Richmond,
So doth my heart misgive me, in these conflicts
What may befall him to his harm and ours:
Therefore, Lord Oxford, to prevent the worst,
Forthwith we'll send him hence to Brittany,

Till storms be past of civil enmity.

   Oxf. Ay, for if Edward repossess the crown
'Tis like that Richmond with the rest shall
down.   100

   Som. It shall be so; he shall to Brittany.
Come, therefore, let's about it speedily. [*Exeunt*

SCENE VII.—*Before York.*

Enter KING EDWARD, GLOUCESTER, HASTINGS
and Forces.

   K. Edw. Now, brother Richard, Lord Hast-
ings, and the rest,
Yet thus far Fortune maketh us amends,
And says, that once more I shall interchange
My waned state for Henry's regal crown.   4
Well have we pass'd, and now repass'd the seas,
And brought desired help from Burgundy:
What then remains, we being thus arriv'd
From Ravenspurgh haven before the gates of
York,   8
But that we enter, as into our dukedom?

   Glo. The gates made fast! Brother, I like not
this;
For many men that stumble at the threshold
Are well foretold that danger lurks within.   12

   K. Edw. Tush, man! abodements must not
now affright us.
By fair or foul means we must enter in,
For hither will our friends repair to us.

   Hast. My liege, I'll knock once more to
summon them.   16

Enter, on the Walls, the Mayor of York *and
his Brethren.*

   May. My lords, we were forewarned of your
coming,
And shut the gates for safety of ourselves;
For now we owe allegiance unto Henry.

   K. Edw. But, Master Mayor, if Henry be
your king,   20
Yet Edward, at the least, is Duke of York.

   May. True, my good lord, I know you for
no less.

   K. Edw. Why, and I challenge nothing but
my dukedom,
As being well content with that alone.   24

   Glo. [*Aside.*] But when the fox hath once got
in his nose,
He'll soon find means to make the body follow.

   Hast. Why, Master Mayor, why stand you
in a doubt?   27
Open the gates; we are King Henry's friends.

   May. Ay, say you so? the gates shall then be
open'd.   [*Exit, with* Aldermen, *above.*

   Glo. A wise stout captain, and soon persuaded.

   Hast. The good old man would fain that all
were well,   31
So 'twere not 'long of him; but being enter'd,
I doubt not, I, but we shall soon persuade
Both him and all his brothers unto reason.

Re-enter the Mayor *and two* Aldermen.

   K. Edw. So, Master Mayor: these gates must
not be shut
But in the night, or in the time of war.   36

What! fear not, man, but yield me up the keys;
							[*Takes his keys.*
For Edward will defend the town and thee,
And all those friends that deign to follow me.

Enter MONTGOMERY *and Forces.*

Glo. Brother, this is Sir John Montgomery,
Our trusty friend, unless I be deceiv'd.		41
K. Edw. Welcome, Sir John! but why come
	you in arms?
Mont. To help King Edward in his time of
	storm,
As every loyal subject ought to do.		44
K. Edw. Thanks, good Montgomery; but we
	now forget
Our title to the crown, and only claim
Our dukedom till God please to send the rest.
Mont. Then fare you well, for I will hence
	again:							48
I came to serve a king and not a duke.
Drummer, strike up, and let us march away.
							[*A march begun.*
K. Edw. Nay, stay, Sir John, awhile; and
	we'll debate
By what safe means the crown may be re-
	cover'd.							52
Mont. What talk you of debating? in few
	words,
If you'll not here proclaim yourself our king,
I'll leave you to your fortune, and be gone
To keep them back that come to succour you.
Why shall we fight, if you pretend no title?		57
Glo. Why, brother, wherefore stand you on
	nice points?
K. Edw. When we grow stronger then we'll
	make our claim;
Till then, 'tis wisdom to conceal our mean-
	ing.							60
Hast. Away with scrupulous wit! now arms
	must rule.
Glo. And fearless minds climb soonest unto
	crowns.
Brother, we will proclaim you out of hand;
The bruit thereof will bring you many friends.
K. Edw. Then be it as you will; for 'tis my
	right,							65
And Henry but usurps the diadem.
Mont. Ay, now my sov'reign speaketh like
	himself;
And now will I be Edward's champion.		68
Hast. Sound, trumpet! Edward shall be
	here proclaim'd;
Come, fellow soldier, make thou proclamation.
							[*Gives him a paper. Flourish.*
Sold. Edward the Fourth, *by the grace of
God, King of England and France, and Lord
of Ireland, &c.*						73
Mont. And whosoe'er gainsays King Ed-
	ward's right,
By this I challenge him to single fight.
							[*Throws down his gauntlet.*
All. Long live Edward the Fourth!		76
K. Edw. Thanks, brave Montgomery;—and
	thanks unto you all:
If Fortune serve me, I'll requite this kindness.
Now, for this night, let's harbour here in York

And when the morning sun shall raise his car
Above the border of this horizon,		81
We'll forward towards Warwick, and his mates;
For well I wot that Henry is no soldier.
Ah, froward Clarence, how evil it beseems thee
To flatter Henry, and forsake thy brother!	85
Yet, as we may, we'll meet both thee and
	Warwick.
Come on, brave soldiers: doubt not of the day;
And, that once gotten, doubt not of large pay.
							[*Exeunt.*

SCENE VIII.—*London. A Room in the
							Palace.*

Flourish.   Enter KING HENRY, WARWICK,
	CLARENCE, MONTAGUE, EXETER, *and* OXFORD.

War. What counsel, lords? Edward from
	Belgia,
With hasty Germans and blunt Hollanders,
Hath pass'd in safety through the narrow seas,
And with his troops doth march amain to
	London;						4
And many giddy people flock to him.
Oxf. Let's levy men, and beat him back again.
Clar. A little fire is quickly trodden out,
Which, being suffer'd, rivers cannot quench.	8
War. In Warwickshire I have true-hearted
	friends,
Not mutinous in peace, yet bold in war;
Those will I muster up; and thou, son Clarence,
Shalt stir up in Suffolk, Norfolk, and in Kent,
The knights and gentlemen to come with thee:
Thou, brother Montague, in Buckingham,
Northampton, and in Leicestershire, shalt find
Men well inclin'd to hear what thou com-
	mand'st:						16
And thou, brave Oxford, wondrous well be-
	lov'd
In Oxfordshire, shalt muster up thy friends.
My sov'reign, with the loving citizens,
Like to his island girt in with the ocean,	20
Or modest Dian circled with her nymphs,
Shall rest in London till we come to him.
Fair lords, take leave, and stand not to reply.
Farewell, my sovereign.				24
K. Hen. Farewell, my Hector, and my Troy's
	true hope.
Clar. In sign of truth, I kiss your highness'
	hand.
K. Hen. Well-minded Clarence, be thou for-
	tunate!
Mont. Comfort, my lord; and so, I take my
	leave.						28
Oxf. [*Kissing* HENRY'S *hand.*] And thus I seal
	my truth, and bid adieu.
K. Hen. Sweet Oxford, and my loving Mon-
	tague,
And all at once, once more a happy farewell.
War. Farewell, sweet lords: let's meet at
	Coventry.						32
							[*Exeunt all but* KING HENRY *and* EXETER.
K. Hen. Here at the palace will I rest awhile.
Cousin of Exeter, what thinks your lordship?
Methinks the power that Edward hath in field
Should not be able to encounter mine.		36

Exe. The doubt is that he will seduce the
  rest.
K. Hen. That's not my fear; my meed hath
  got me fame:
I have not stopp'd mine ears to their demands,
Nor posted off their suits with slow delays; 40
My pity hath been balm to heal their wounds,
My mildness hath allay'd their swelling griefs,
My mercy dried their water-flowing tears;
I have not been desirous of their wealth; 44
Nor much oppress'd them with great subsidies,
Nor forward of revenge, though they much
  err'd.
Then why should they love Edward more than
  me?
No, Exeter, these graces challenge grace: 48
And, when the lion fawns upon the lamb,
The lamb will never cease to follow him.
    [*Shout within,* 'A Lancaster! A Lancaster!'
Exe. Hark, hark, my lord! what shouts are
  these?

Enter KING EDWARD, GLOUCESTER, *and* Soldiers.

K. Edw. Seize on the shame-fac'd Henry!
  bear him hence; 52
And once again proclaim us King of England.
You are the fount that makes small brooks to
  flow:
Now stops thy spring; my sea shall suck them
  dry,
And swell so much the higher by their ebb. 56
Hence with him to the Tower! let him not speak.
    [*Exeunt some with* KING HENRY.
And, lords, towards Coventry bend we our
  course,
Where peremptory Warwick now remains:
The sun shines hot; and, if we use delay, 60
Cold biting winter mars our hop'd-for hay.
Glo. Away betimes, before his forces join,
And take the great-grown traitor unawares:
Brave warriors, march amain towards Coventry.
    [*Exeunt.*

ACT V

SCENE I.—*Coventry.*

Enter, upon the Walls, WARWICK, *the* Mayor of
Coventry, *two* Messengers, *and Others.*

War. Where is the post that came from
  valiant Oxford?
How far hence is thy lord, mine honest fellow?
  First Mess. By this at Dunsmore, marching
  hitherward. 3
War. How far off is our brother Montague?
Where is the post that came from Montague?
  Sec. Mess. By this at Daintry, with a puis-
  sant troop.

Enter SIR JOHN SOMERVILLE.

War. Say, Somerville, what says my loving
  son? 7
And, by thy guess, how nigh is Clarence now?
  Som. At Southam I did leave him with his
  forces,
And do expect him here some two hours hence.
    [*Drum heard.*

War. Then Clarence is at hand, I hear his
  drum.
Som. It is not his, my lord; here Southam lies:
The drum your honour hears marcheth from
  Warwick. 13
War. Who should that be? belike, unlook'd
  for friends.
Som. They are at hand, and you shall quickly
  know.

Enter KING EDWARD, GLOUCESTER, *and Forces.*

K. Edw. Go, trumpet, to the walls, and
  sound a parle. 16
Glo. See how the surly Warwick mans the
  wall.
War. O, unbid spite! is sportful Edward
  come?
Where slept our scouts, or how are they seduc'd,
That we could hear no news of his repair? 20
K. Edw. Now, Warwick, wilt thou ope the
  city gates,
Speak gentle words, and humbly bend thy
  knee?—
Call Edward king, and at his hands beg mercy?
And he shall pardon thee these outrages. 24
  War. Nay, rather, wilt thou draw thy forces
  hence,—
Confess who set thee up and pluck'd thee
  down?—
Call Warwick patron, and be penitent;
And thou shalt still remain the Duke of York.
  Glo. I thought, at least, he would have said
  the king; 29
Or did he make the jest against his will?
  War. Is not a dukedom, sir, a goodly gift?
  Glo. Ay, by my faith, for a poor earl to give
I'll do thee service for so good a gift. 33
  War. 'Twas I that gave the kingdom to thy
  brother.
  K. Edw. Why then 'tis mine, if but by War-
  wick's gift.
  War. Thou art no Atlas for so great a weight
And, weakling, Warwick takes his gift again
And Henry is my king, Warwick his subject.
  K. Edw. But Warwick's king is Edward's
  prisoner;
And, gallant Warwick, do but answer this, 40
What is the body, when the head is off?
  Glo. Alas! that Warwick had no more fore-
  cast,
But, whiles he thought to steal the single ten,
The king was slily finger'd from the deck. 44
You left poor Henry at the bishop's palace,
And, ten to one, you'll meet him in the Tower.
  K. Edw. 'Tis even so; yet you are Warwick
  still.
  Glo. Come, Warwick, take the time; kneel
  down, kneel down: 48
Nay, when? strike now, or else the iron cools.
  War. I had rather chop this hand off at a blow
And with the other fling it at thy face,
Than bear so low a sail to strike to thee. 52
  K. Edw. Sail how thou canst, have wind and
  tide thy friend;
This hand, fast wound about thy coal-black hair
Shall, whiles thy head is warm and new cut off

Write in the dust this sentence with thy blood:
'Wind-changing Warwick now can change no
more.'   57

Enter OXFORD, *with Soldiers, drum, and colours.*

War. O cheerful colours! see where Oxford
  comes!
Oxf. Oxford, Oxford, for Lancaster!
            [*He and his Forces enter the city.*
Glo. The gates are open, let us enter too.   60
K. Edw. So other foes may set upon our
  backs.
Stand we in good array; for they no doubt
Will issue out again and bid us battle:
If not, the city being but of small defence,   64
We'll quickly rouse the traitors in the same.
War. O! welcome, Oxford! for we want thy
  help.

Enter MONTAGUE, *with Soldiers, drum, and
                    colours.*

Mont. Montague, Montague, for Lancaster!
            [*He and his Forces enter the city.*
Glo. Thou and thy brother both shall buy
  this treason   68
Even with the dearest blood your bodies bear.
K. Edw. The harder match'd, the greater
  victory:
My mind presageth happy gain, and conquest.

Enter SOMERSET, *with Soldiers, drum, and
                    colours.*

Som. Somerset, Somerset, for Lancaster! 72
            [*He and his Forces enter the city.*
Glo. Two of thy name, both Dukes of Somer-
  set,
Have sold their lives unto the house of York;
And thou shalt be the third, if this sword hold.

Enter CLARENCE, *with Forces, drum, and
                    colours.*

War. And lo! where George of Clarence
  sweeps along,   76
Of force enough to bid his brother battle;
With whom an upright zeal to right prevails
More than the nature of a brother's love.
Come, Clarence, come; thou wilt, if Warwick
  call.   80
Clar. Father of Warwick, know you what
  this means?
            [*Taking the red rose out of his hat.*
Look here, I throw my infamy at thee:
I will not ruinate my father's house,
Who gave his blood to lime the stones together,
And set up Lancaster. Why, trow'st thou,
  Warwick,   85
That Clarence is so harsh, so blunt, unnatural,
To bend the fatal instruments of war
Against his brother and his lawful king?   88
Perhaps thou wilt object my holy oath:
To keep that oath were more impiety
Than Jephthah's, when he sacrific'd his daughter.
I am so sorry for my trespass made   92
That, to deserve well at my brother's hands,
I here proclaim myself thy mortal foe;

With resolution, wheresoe'er I meet thee—
As I will meet thee if thou stir abroad—   96
To plague thee for thy foul misleading me.
And so, proud-hearted Warwick, I defy thee,
And to my brother turn my blushing cheeks.
Pardon me, Edward, I will make amends;   100
And, Richard, do not frown upon my faults,
For I will henceforth be no more unconstant.
K. Edw. Now welcome more, and ten times
  more belov'd,
Than if thou never hadst deserv'd our hate.   104
Glo. Welcome, good Clarence; this is
  brother-like.
War. O passing traitor, perjur'd, and unjust?
K. Edw. What, Warwick, wilt thou leave the
  town, and fight?   107
Or shall we beat the stones about thine ears?
War. Alas! I am not coop'd here for defence:
I will away towards Barnet presently,
And bid thee battle, Edward, if thou dar'st.
K. Edw. Yes, Warwick, Edward dares, and
  leads the way.   112
Lords, to the field; Saint George and victory!
                                    [*March. Exeunt.*

SCENE II.—*A Field of Battle near Barnet.*

Alarums and Excursions. Enter KING EDWARD,
    bringing in WARWICK, *wounded.*

K. Edw. So, lie thou there: die thou, and
  die our fear;
For Warwick was a bug that fear'd us all.
Now Montague, sit fast; I seek for thee,
That Warwick's bones may keep thine company.
                                            [*Exit.*
War. Ah! who is nigh? come to me, friend
  or foe,   5
And tell me who is victor, York or Warwick?
Why ask I that? my mangled body shows,
My blood, my want of strength, my sick heart
  shows,   8
That I must yield my body to the earth,
And, by my fall, the conquest to my foe.
Thus yields the cedar to the axe's edge,   11
Whose arms gave shelter to the princely eagle,
Under whose shade the ramping lion slept,
Whose top branch overpeer'd Jove's spreading
  tree,
And kept low shrubs from winter's powerful
  wind.
These eyes, that now are dimm'd with death's
  black veil,   16
Have been as piercing as the mid-day sun,
To search the secret treasons of the world:
The wrinkles in my brows, now fill'd with blood,
Were liken'd oft to kingly sepulchres;   20
For who liv'd king, but I could dig his grave?
And who durst smile when Warwick bent his
  brow?
Lo! now my glory smear'd in dust and blood;
My parks, my walks, my manors that I had,   24
Even now forsake me; and, of all my lands
Is nothing left me but my body's length.
Why, what is pomp, rule, reign, but earth and
  dust?
And, live we how we can, yet die we must.   28

Enter OXFORD *and* SOMERSET.

Som. Ah! Warwick, Warwick, wert thou as
we are,
We might recover all our loss again.
The queen from France hath brought a puis-
sant power;
Even now we heard the news. Ah! couldst
thou fly.　　　　　　　　　　　　32
War. Why, then, I would not fly. Ah!
Montague,
If thou be there, sweet brother, take my hand,
And with thy lips keep in my soul awhile.
Thou lov'st me not; for, brother, if thou didst,
Thy tears would wash this cold congealed blood
That glues my lips and will not let me speak.
Come quickly, Montague, or I am dead.
　　Som. Ah! Warwick, Montague hath breath'd
his last;　　　　　　　　　　　　40
And to the latest gasp, cried out for Warwick,
And said, 'Commend me to my valiant brother.'
And more he would have said; and more he
spoke,
Which sounded like a clamour in a vault,　44
That mought not be distinguish'd: but at last
I well might hear, deliver'd with a groan,
'O! farewell, Warwick!'
　　War. Sweet rest his soul! Fly, lords, and
save yourselves;　　　　　　　　48
For Warwick bids you all farewell, to meet in
heaven.　　　　　　　　　　　[*Dies.*
　　Oxf. Away, away, to meet the queen's great
power.
　　　[*Exeunt, bearing off* WARWICK'S *body.*

SCENE III.—*Another Part of the Field.*

Flourish. Enter KING EDWARD, *in triumph: with*
CLARENCE, GLOUCESTER, *and the rest.*

K. Edw. Thus far our fortune keeps an up-
ward course,
And we are grac'd with wreaths of victory.
But in the midst of this bright-shining day,
I spy a black, suspicious, threat'ning cloud,　4
That will encounter with our glorious sun,
Ere he attain his easeful western bed:
I mean, my lords, those powers that the queen
Hath rais'd in Gallia, have arriv'd our coast,　8
And, as we hear, march on to fight with us.
　　Clar. A little gale will soon disperse that
cloud,
And blow it to the source from whence it came:
Thy very beams will dry those vapours up,　12
For every cloud engenders not a storm.
　　Glo. The queen is valu'd thirty thousand
strong,
And Somerset, with Oxford, fled to her:
If she have time to breathe, be well assur'd　16
Her faction will be full as strong as ours.
　　K. Edw. We are advertis'd by our loving
friends
That they do hold their course toward Tewks-
bury.
We, having now the best at Barnet field,　20
Will thither straight, for willingness rids way;
And, as we march our strength will be augmented

In every county as we go along.
Strike up the drum! cry 'Courage!' and away
　　　　　　　　　　[*Flourish. Exeunt*

SCENE IV.—*Plains near Tewksbury.*

March. Enter QUEEN MARGARET, PRINCE ED-
WARD, SOMERSET, OXFORD, *and* Soldiers.

　　Q. Mar. Great lords, wise men ne'er sit and
wail their loss,
But cheerly seek how to redress their harms.
What though the mast be now blown over-board,
The cable broke, the holding anchor lost,
And half our sailors swallow'd in the flood?
Yet lives our pilot still: is't meet that he
Should leave the helm and like a fearful lad
With tearful eyes add water to the sea,
And give more strength to that which hath too
much;
Whiles in his moan the ship splits on the rock
Which industry and courage might have sav'd?
Ah! what a shame! ah, what a fault were this
Say, Warwick was our anchor; what of that?
And Montague our top-mast; what of him?
Our slaughter'd friends the tackles; what of
these?
Why, is not Oxford here another anchor?　　1
And Somerset, another goodly mast?
The friends of France our shrouds and tacklings
And, though unskilful, why not Ned and I
For once allow'd the skilful pilot's charge?
We will not from the helm, to sit and weep,
But keep our course, though the rough wind
say no,
From shelves and rocks that threaten us with
wrack.
As good to chide the waves as speak them fair
And what is Edward but a ruthless sea?　　2
What Clarence but a quicksand of deceit?
And Richard but a ragged fatal rock?
All those the enemies to our poor bark.　　2
Say you can swim; alas! 'tis but a while:
Tread on the sand; why, there you quickly sink
Bestride the rock; the tide will wash you off,
Or else you famish; that's a threefold death.　3
This speak I, lords, to let you understand,
In case some one of you would fly from us,
That there's no hop'd-for mercy with th
brothers
More than with ruthless waves, with sands an
rocks.　　　　　　　　　　　　3
Why, courage, then! what cannot be avoided
'Twere childish weakness to lament or fear.
　　Prince. Methinks a woman of this valian
spirit
Should, if a coward heard her speak thes
words,　　　　　　　　　　　　4
Infuse his breast with magnanimity,
And make him, naked, foil a man at arms.
I speak not this, as doubting any here;
For did I but suspect a fearful man,　　　4
He should have leave to go away betimes,
Lest in our need he might infect another,
And make him of like spirit to himself.
If any such be here, as God forbid!　　　4
Let him depart before we need his help.

Oxf. Women and children of so high a
courage,
And warriors faint! why, 'twere perpetual
shame.
O brave young prince! thy famous grandfather
Doth live again in thee: long mayst thou live
To bear his image and renew his glories!
  Som. And he, that will not fight for such a
hope,
Go home to bed, and, like the owl by day, 56
If he arise, be mock'd and wonder'd at.
  Q. Mar. Thanks, gentle Somerset: sweet
Oxford, thanks.
  Prince. And take his thanks that yet hath
nothing else.

Enter a Messenger.

  Mess. Prepare you, lords, for Edward is at
hand, 60
Ready to fight; therefore be resolute.
  Oxf. I thought no less: it is his policy
To haste thus fast, to find us unprovided.
  Som. But he's deceiv'd; we are in readiness.
  Q. Mar. This cheers my heart to see your
forwardness. 65
  Oxf. Here pitch our battle; hence we will
not budge.

March. Enter, at a distance, KING EDWARD,
CLARENCE, GLOUCESTER, *and Forces.*

  K. Edw. Brave followers, yonder stands the
thorny wood,
Which, by the heavens' assistance, and your
strength, 68
Must by the roots be hewn up yet ere night.
I need not add more fuel to your fire,
For well I wot ye blaze to burn them out:
Give signal to the fight, and to it, lords. 72
  Q. Mar. Lords, knights, and gentlemen,
what I should say
My tears gainsay; for every word I speak,
Ye see, I drink the water of mine eyes.
Therefore, no more but this: Henry, your
sovereign, 76
Is prisoner to the foe; his state usurp'd,
His realm a slaughter house, his subjects slain,
His statutes cancell'd, and his treasure spent;
And yonder is the wolf that makes this spoil. 80
You fight in justice: then, in God's name, lords,
Be valiant, and give signal to the fight.
[Exeunt both armies.

SCENE V.—*Another Part of the Same.*

*Alarums: Excursions: and afterwards a retreat.
Then enter* KING EDWARD, CLARENCE, GLOU-
CESTER, *and Forces; with* QUEEN MARGARET,
OXFORD, *and* SOMERSET *prisoners.*

  K. Edw. Now, here a period of tumultuous
broils.
Away with Oxford to Hames Castle straight:
For Somerset, off with his guilty head.
Go, bear them hence; I will not hear them
speak. 4
  Oxf. For my part, I'll not trouble thee with
words.

  Som. Nor I, but stoop with patience to my
fortune.
[Exeunt OXFORD *and* SOMERSET, *guarded.*
  Q. Mar. So part we sadly in this troublous
world,
To meet with joy in sweet Jerusalem. 8
  K. Edw. Is proclamation made, that who
finds Edward
Shall have a high reward, and he his life?
  Glo. It is: and lo, where youthful Edward
comes.

Enter Soldiers, *with* PRINCE EDWARD.

  K. Edw. Bring forth the gallant: let us hear
him speak. 12
What! can so young a thorn begin to prick?
Edward, what satisfaction canst thou make,
For bearing arms, for stirring up my subjects,
And all the trouble thou hast turn'd me to? 16
  Prince. Speak like a subject, proud ambi-
tious York!
Suppose that I am now my father's mouth:
Resign thy chair, and where I stand kneel thou,
Whilst I propose the self-same words to thee,
Which, traitor, thou wouldst have me answer
to. 21
  Q. Mar. Ah! that thy father had been so
resolv'd.
  Glo. That you might still have worn the
petticoat,
And ne'er have stol'n the breech from Lan-
caster. 24
  Prince. Let Æsop fable in a winter's night;
His currish riddles sort not with this place.
  Glo. By heaven, brat, I'll plague you for
that word.
  Q. Mar. Ay, thou wast born to be a plague
to men. 28
  Glo. For God's sake, take away this captive
scold.
  Prince. Nay, take away this scolding crook-
back rather.
  K. Edw. Peace, wilful boy, or I will charm
your tongue.
  Clar. Untutor'd lad, thou art too malapert.
  Prince. I know my duty; you are all un-
dutiful: 33
Lascivious Edward, and thou perjur'd George,
And thou mis-shapen Dick, I tell ye all,
I am your better, traitors as ye are; 36
And thou usurp'st my father's right and mine.
  K. Edw. Take that, the likeness of this railer
here. *[Stabs him.*
  Glo. Sprawl'st thou? take that, to end thy
agony. *[Stabs him.*
  Clar. And there's for twitting me with per-
jury. *[Stabs him.*
  Q. Mar. O, kill me too! 41
  Glo. Marry, and shall. *[Offers to kill her.*
  K. Edw. Hold, Richard, hold! for we have
done too much.
  Glo. Why should she live, to fill the world
with words? 44
  K. Edw. What! doth she swoon? use means
for her recovery.

Glo. Clarence, excuse me to the king, my
     brother;
I'll hence to London on a serious matter:
Ere ye come there, be sure to hear some news.
     Clar. What? what?   49
     Glo. The Tower! the Tower!   [*Exit.*
     Q. Mar. O Ned, sweet Ned! speak to thy
     mother, boy!
Canst thou not speak? O traitors! murderers!
They that stabb'd Cæsar shed no blood at all,
Did not offend, nor were not worthy blame,
If this foul deed were by, to equal it:
He was a man; this, in respect, a child;   56
And men ne'er spend their fury on a child.
What's worse than murderer, that I may name
     it?
No, no, my heart will burst, an if I speak:
And I will speak, that so my heart may burst.
Butchers and villains! bloody cannibals!   61
How sweet a plant have you untimely cropp'd!
You have no children, butchers! if you had,
The thought of them would have stirr'd up
     remorse: 64
But if you ever chance to have a child,
Look in his youth to have him so cut off
As, deathsmen, you have rid this sweet young
     prince!
     K. Edw. Away with her! go, bear her hence
     perforce.   68
     Q. Mar. Nay, never bear me hence, dispatch
     me here:
Here sheathe thy sword, I'll pardon thee my
     death.
What! wilt thou not? then, Clarence, do it
     thou.
     Clar. By heaven, I will not do thee so much
     ease.   72
     Q. Mar. Good Clarence, do; sweet Clarence,
     do thou do it.
     Clar. Didst thou not hear me swear I would
     not do it?
     Q. Mar. Ay, but thou usest to forswear thy-
     self:
'Twas sin before, but now 'tis charity.   76
What! wilt thou not? Where is that devil's
     butcher,
Hard-favour'd Richard? Richard, where art
     thou?
Thou art not here: murder is thy alms-deed;
Petitioners for blood thou ne'er put'st back. 80
     K. Edw. Away, I say! I charge ye, bear her
     hence.
     Q. Mar. So come to you and yours, as to
     this prince!   [*Exit, led out forcibly.*
     K. Edw. Where's Richard gone?
     Clar. To London, all in post; and, as I
     guess,   84
To make a bloody supper in the Tower.
     K. Edw. He's sudden if a thing comes in
     his head.
Now march we hence: discharge the common
     sort   87
With pay and thanks, and let's away to London
And see our gentle queen how well she fares;
By this, I hope, she hath a son for me.
     [*Exeunt.*

SCENE VI.—*London. A Room in the Tower.*

KING HENRY *is discovered sitting with a book
in his hand, the* Lieutenant *attending. Ente*
GLOUCESTER.

     Glo. Good day, my lord. What! at your book
     so hard?
     K. Hen. Ay, my good lord:—my lord,
     should say rather;
'Tis sin to flatter, 'good' was little better:
'Good Gloucester' and 'good devil' were alike
And both preposterous; therefore, not 'goo
     lord.'
     Glo. Sirrah, leave us to ourselves: we mus
     confer.   [*Exit Lieutenant*
     K. Hen. So flies the reckless shepherd from
     the wolf;
So first the harmless sheep doth yield his fleece
And next his throat unto the butcher's knife.
What scene of death hath Roscius now to act
     Glo. Suspicion always haunts the guilty
     mind;
The thief doth fear each bush an officer.   1
     K. Hen. The bird that hath been limed in a
     bush,
With trembling wings misdoubteth every bush
And I, the hapless male to one sweet bird,
Have now the fatal object in my eye   1
Where my poor young was lim'd, was caught
     and kill'd.
     Glo. Why, what a peevish fool was that o
     Crete,
That taught his son the office of a fowl!
And yet, for all his wings, the fool was drown'd
     K. Hen. I, Dædalus; my poor boy, Icarus;
Thy father, Minos, that denied our course;
The sun, that sear'd the wings of my sweet boy
Thy brother Edward, and thyself the sea,   2
Whose envious gulf did swallow up his life.
Ah! kill me with thy weapon, not with words.
My breast can better brook thy dagger's poin
Than can my ears that tragic history.   28
But wherefore dost thou come? is't for my
     life?
     Glo. Think'st thou I am an executioner?
     K. Hen. A persecutor, I am sure, thou art:
If murd'ring innocents be executing,   3
Why, then thou art an executioner.
     Glo. Thy son I kill'd for his presumption.
     K. Hen. Hadst thou been kill'd, when firs
     thou didst presume,
Thou hadst not liv'd to kill a son of mine.   3
And thus I prophesy: that many a thousand,
Which now mistrust no parcel of my fear,
And many an old man's sigh, and many a
     widow's,   3
And many an orphan's water-standing eye,
Men for their sons', wives for their husbands'
And orphans for their parents' timeless death
Shall rue the hour that ever thou wast born.
The owl shriek'd at thy birth, an evil sign;   4
The night-crow cried, aboding luckless time;
Dogs howl'd, and hideous tempest shook dow
     trees!
The raven rook'd her on the chimney's top,
And chattering pies in dismal discords sung.   4

hy mother felt more than a mother's pain,
nd yet brought forth less than a mother's
 hope;
o wit an indigest deformed lump,
ot like the fruit of such a goodly tree. 52
eeth hadst thou in thy head when thou wast
 born,
o signify thou cam'st to bite the world:
nd, if the rest be true which I have heard,
hou cam'st— 56
 Glo. I'll hear no more: die, prophet, in thy
 speech: [*Stabs him.*
or this, amongst the rest, was I ordain'd.
 K. Hen. Ay, and for much more slaughter
 after this.
, God forgive my sins, and pardon thee! [*Dies.*
 Glo. What! will the aspiring blood of Lancaster 61
ink in the ground? I thought it would have
 mounted.
ee how my sword weeps for the poor king's
 death!
! may such purple tears be always shed 64
rom those that wish the downfall of our house.
any spark of life be yet remaining,
own, down to hell; and say I sent thee thither,
 [*Stabs him again.*
that have neither pity, love, nor fear. 68
deed, 'tis true, that Henry told me of;
or I have often heard my mother say
came into the world with my legs forward.
ad I not reason, think ye, to make haste, 72
nd seek their ruin that usurp'd our right?
he midwife wonder'd, and the women cried
! Jesus bless us, he is born with teeth.'
nd so I was; which plainly signified 76
hat I should snarl and bite and play the dog.
hen, since the heavens have shap'd my body so,
et hell make crook'd my mind to answer it.
have no brother, I am like no brother; 80
nd this word 'love,' which greybeards call
 divine,
e resident in men like one another
nd not in me: I am myself alone.
larence, beware; thou keep'st me from the
 light: 84
ut I will sort a pitchy day for thee;
or I will buzz abroad such prophecies
hat Edward shall be fearful of his life;
nd then, to purge his fear, I'll be thy death. 88
ing Henry and the prince his son are gone:
larence, thy turn is next, and then the rest,
ounting myself but bad till I be best.
'll throw thy body in another room, 92
nd triumph, Henry, in thy day of doom.
 [*Exit with the body.*

SCENE VII.—*The same. A Room in the Palace.*

ING EDWARD is discovered sitting on his throne: QUEEN ELIZABETH *with the infant Prince,* CLARENCE, GLOUCESTER, HASTINGS, *and Others, near him.*

 K. Edw. Once more we sit in England's
 royal throne,

Re-purchas'd with the blood of enemies.
What valiant foemen like to autumn's corn,
Have we mow'd down, in tops of all their
 pride! 4
Three Dukes of Somerset, threefold renown'd
For hardy and undoubted champions;
Two Cliffords, as the father and the son;
And two Northumberlands: two braver men
Ne'er spurr'd their coursers at the trumpet's
 sound;
With them, the two brave bears, Warwick and
 Montague,
That in their chains fetter'd the kingly lion,
And made the forest tremble when they
 roar'd. 12
Thus have we swept suspicion from our seat,
And made our footstool of security.
Come hither, Bess, and let me kiss my boy.
Young Ned, for thee thine uncles and my-
 self 16
Have in our armours watch'd the winter's
 night;
Went all a-foot in summer's scalding heat,
That thou might'st repossess the crown in
 peace;
And of our labours thou shalt reap the gain.
 Glo. [*Aside.*] I'll blast his harvest, if your
 head were laid; 21
For yet I am not look'd on in the world.
This shoulder was ordain'd so thick to heave;
And heave it shall some weight, or break my
 back: 24
Work thou the way, and thou shalt execute.
 K. Edw. Clarence and Gloucester, love my
 lovely queen;
And kiss your princely nephew, brothers both.
 Clar. The duty, that I owe unto your
 majesty 28
I seal upon the lips of this sweet babe.
 K. Edw. Thanks, noble Clarence; worthy
 brother, thanks.
 Glo. And, that I love the tree from whence
 thou sprang'st,
Witness the loving kiss I give the fruit. 32
[*Aside.*] To say the truth, so Judas kiss'd his
 master,
And cried 'all hail!' when as he meant all
 harm.
 K. Edw. Now am I seated as my soul de-
 lights,
Having my country's peace and brothers' loves.
 Clar. What will your Grace have done with
 Margaret?
Reignier, her father, to the King of France
Hath pawn'd the Sicils and Jerusalem,
And hither have they sent it for her ransom.
 K. Edw. Away with her, and waft her hence
 to France. 41
And now what rests but that we spend the time
With stately triumphs, mirthful comic shows,
Such as befit the pleasure of the court? 44
Sound, drums and trumpets! farewell, sour
 annoy!
For here, I hope, begins our lasting joy.
 [*Exeunt.*

THE TRAGEDY OF
KING RICHARD THE THIRD

DRAMATIS PERSONÆ

KING EDWARD THE FOURTH.
EDWARD, Prince of Wales; afterwards King Edward the Fifth,
RICHARD, Duke of York, } Sons to the King.
GEORGE, Duke of Clarence,
RICHARD, Duke of Gloucester, afterwards King Richard the Third, } Brothers to the King.
A young Son of Clarence.
HENRY, Earl of Richmond; afterwards King Henry the Seventh.
CARDINAL BOURCHIER, Archbishop of Canterbury.
THOMAS ROTHERHAM, Archbishop of York.
JOHN MORTON, Bishop of Ely.
DUKE OF BUCKINGHAM.
DUKE OF NORFOLK.
EARL OF SURREY, his Son.
EARL RIVERS, Brother to King Edward's Queen.
MARQUESS OF DORSET, and LORD GREY, her Sons.
EARL OF OXFORD.
LORD HASTINGS.
LORD STANLEY, called also EARL OF DERBY.
LORD LOVEL.
SIR THOMAS VAUGHAN.
SIR RICHARD RATCLIFF.
SIR WILLIAM CATESBY.

SIR JAMES TYRRELL.
SIR JAMES BLOUNT.
SIR WALTER HERBERT.
SIR ROBERT BRAKENBURY, Lieutenant of the Tower.
SIR WILLIAM BRANDON.
CHRISTOPHER URSWICK, a Priest.
Another Priest.
Lord Mayor of London. Sheriff of Wiltshire.
TRESSEL and BERKELEY, Gentlemen attending on Lady Anne.

ELIZABETH, Queen of King Edward the Fourth.
MARGARET, Widow of King Henry the Sixth.
DUCHESS OF YORK, Mother to King Edward the Fourth, Clarence, and Gloucester.
LADY ANNE, Widow of Edward, Prince of Wales, Son to King Henry the Sixth; afterwards married to the Duke of Gloucester.
LADY MARGARET PLANTAGENET, a young Daughter of Clarence.

Lords, and other Attendants; two Gentlemen, a Pursuivant, Scrivener, Citizens, Murderers, Messengers, Ghosts of those murdered by Richard the Third, Soldiers, &c.

SCENE.—England.

ACT I

SCENE I.—London. A Street.

Enter GLOUCESTER.

Glo. Now is the winter of our discontent
Made glorious summer by this sun of York;
And all the clouds that lour'd upon our house
In the deep bosom of the ocean buried.   4
Now are our brows bound with victorious wreaths;
Our bruised arms hung up for monuments;
Our stern alarums changed to merry meetings;
Our dreadful marches to delightful measures.
Grim-visag'd war hath smooth'd his wrinkled front;
And now,—instead of mounting barbed steeds,
To fright the souls of fearful adversaries,—
He capers nimbly in a lady's chamber   12
To the lascivious pleasing of a lute.
But I, that am not shap'd for sportive tricks,
Nor made to court an amorous looking-glass;
I, that am rudely stamp'd, and want love's majesty   16
To strut before a wanton ambling nymph;
I, that am curtail'd of this fair proportion,
Cheated of feature by dissembling nature,
Deform'd, unfinish'd, sent before my time   20
Into this breathing world, scarce half made up,

And that so lamely and unfashionable
That dogs bark at me, as I halt by them;
Why, I, in this weak piping time of peace,   24
Have no delight to pass away the time,
Unless to see my shadow in the sun
And descant on mine own deformity:
And therefore, since I cannot prove a lover,   28
To entertain these fair well-spoken days,
I am determined to prove a villain,
And hate the idle pleasures of these days.
Plots have I laid, inductions dangerous,   32
By drunken prophecies, libels, and dreams,
To set my brother Clarence and the king
In deadly hate the one against the other:
And if King Edward be as true and just   36
As I am subtle, false, and treacherous,
This day should Clarence closely be mew'd up
About a prophecy, which says, that G
Of Edward's heirs the murderer shall be.   40
Dive, thoughts, down to my soul: here Clarence comes.

Enter CLARENCE, guarded, and BRAKENBURY.

Brother, good day: what means this armed guard
That waits upon your Grace?
Clar.   His majesty,
Tendering my person's safety, hath appointed
This conduct to convey me to the Tower.

Glo. Upon what cause?
Clar.   Because my name is George.
Glo. Alack! my lord, that fault is none of
yours;   47
e should, for that, commit your godfathers.
! belike his majesty hath some intent
nat you should be new-christen'd in the Tower,
ut what's the matter, Clarence? may I know?
Clar. Yea, Richard, when I know; for
I protest   52
s yet I do not: but, as I can learn,
e hearkens after prophecies and dreams;
nd from the cross-row plucks the letter G,
nd says a wizard told him that by G   56
is issue disinherited should be;
nd, for my name of George begins with G,
follows in his thought that I am he.   59
hese, as I learn, and such like toys as these,
ave mov'd his highness to commit me now.
Glo. Why, this it is, when men are rul'd by
women;
is not the king that sends you to the Tower;
ly Lady Grey, his wife, Clarence, 'tis she   64
hat tempers him to this extremity.
as it not she and that good man of worship,
ntony Woodville, her brother there,
hat made him send Lord Hastings to the
Tower,   68
rom whence this present day he is deliver'd?
'e are not safe, Clarence; we are not safe.
Clar. By heaven, I think there is no man
secure
ut the queen's kindred and night-walking
heralds   72
hat trudge betwixt the king and Mistress
Shore.
eard you not what a humble suppliant
ord Hastings was to her for his delivery?
Glo. Humbly complaining to her deity   76
ot my lord chamberlain his liberty.
l tell you what; I think it is our way,
' we will keep in favour with the king,
o be her men and wear her livery: 80
he jealous o'er-worn widow and herself,
nce that our brother dubb'd them gentlewomen,
re mighty gossips in our monarchy.
Brak. I beseech your Graces both to pardon
me;   84
is majesty hath straitly given in charge
hat no man shall have private conference,
f what degree soever, with your brother.
Glo. Even so; an please your worship,
Brakenbury,   88
ou may partake of anything we say:
'e speak no treason, man: we say the king
' wise and virtuous, and his noble queen
ell struck in years, fair, and not jealous;   92
'e say that Shore's wife hath a pretty foot,
. cherry lip, a bonny eye, a passing pleasing
tongue;
nd that the queen's kindred are made gentle-
folks.
low say you, sir? can you deny all this?   96
Brak. With this, my lord, myself have
nought to do.

Glo. Naught to do with Mistress Shore! I
tell thee, fellow,
He that doth naught with her, excepting one,
Were best to do it secretly, alone.   100
Brak. What one, my lord?
Glo. Her husband, knave. Wouldst thou
betray me?
Brak. I beseech your Grace to pardon me;
and withal
Forbear your conference with the noble duke.
Clar. We know thy charge, Brakenbury, and
will obey.   105
Glo. We are the queen's abjects, and must
obey.
Brother, farewell: I will unto the king;
And whatsoe'er you will employ me in,   108
Were it to call King Edward's widow sister,
I will perform it to enfranchise you.
Meantime, this deep disgrace in brotherhood
Touches me deeper than you can imagine. 112
Clar. I know it pleaseth neither of us well.
Glo. Well, your imprisonment shall not be
long;
I will deliver you, or else lie for you:
Meantime, have patience.
Clar.   I must perforce: farewell.
[*Exeunt* CLARENCE, BRAKENBURY, *and*
Guard.
Glo. Go, tread the path that thou shalt ne'er
return,   117
Simple, plain Clarence! I do love thee so
That I will shortly send thy soul to heaven,
If heaven will take the present at our hands.
But who comes here? the new-deliver'd Hast-
ings!   121

Enter HASTINGS.

Hast. Good time of day unto my gracious
lord!
Glo. As much unto my good lord chamber-
lain!
Well are you welcome to this open air.   124
How hath your lordship brook'd imprison-
ment?
Hast. With patience, noble lord, as prisoners
must:
But I shall live, my lord, to give them thanks
That were the cause of my imprisonment.
Glo. No doubt, no doubt; and so shall Cla-
rence too;   129
For they that were your enemies are his,
And have prevail'd as much on him as you.
Hast. More pity that the eagles should be
mew'd,   132
While kites and buzzards prey at liberty.
Glo. What news abroad?
Hast. No news so bad abroad as this at home;
The king is sickly, weak, and melancholy, 136
And his physicians fear him mightily.
Glo. Now by Saint Paul, this news is bad
indeed.
O! he hath kept an evil diet long,
And over-much consum'd his royal person:
'Tis very grievous to be thought upon.   141
What, is he in his bed?
Hast.   He is.

Glo. Go you before, and I will follow you.
[*Exit* HASTINGS.
He cannot live, I hope; and must not die   144
Till George be pack'd with post-horse up to
heaven.
I'll in, to urge his hatred more to Clarence,
With lies well steel'd with weighty arguments;
And, if I fail not in my deep intent,   148
Clarence hath not another day to live:
Which done, God take King Edward to his
mercy,
And leave the world for me to bustle in!
For then I'll marry Warwick's youngest
daughter.   152
What though I kill'd her husband and her
father,
The readiest way to make the wench amends
Is to become her husband and her father:
The which will I; not all so much for love   156
As for another secret close intent,
By marrying her, which I must reach unto.
But yet I run before my horse to market:
Clarence still breathes; Edward still lives and
reigns: 160
When they are gone, then must I count my
gains.   [*Exit.*

SCENE II.—*London. Another Street.*

Enter the corpse of KING HENRY THE SIXTH,
borne in an open coffin; Gentlemen *bearing
halberds to guard it; and* LADY ANNE, *as
mourner.*

Anne. Set down, set down your honourable
load,
If honour may be shrouded in a hearse,
Whilst I a while obsequiously lament
The untimely fall of virtuous Lancaster.   4
Poor key-cold figure of a holy king!
Pale ashes of the house of Lancaster!
Thou bloodless remnant of that royal blood!
Be it lawful that I invocate thy ghost,   8
To hear the lamentations of poor Anne,
Wife to thy Edward, to thy slaughter'd son,
Stabb'd by the self-same hand that made these
wounds!
Lo, in these windows that let forth thy life,   12
I pour the helpless balm of my poor eyes.
O! cursed be the hand that made these holes;
Cursed the heart that had the heart to do it!
Cursed the blood that let this blood from
hence!   16
More direful hap betide that hated wretch,
That makes us wretched by the death of thee,
Than I can wish to adders, spiders, toads,
Or any creeping venom'd thing that lives!   20
If ever he have child, abortive be it,
Prodigious, and untimely brought to light,
Whose ugly and unnatural aspect
May fright the hopeful mother at the view;   24
And that be heir to his unhappiness!
If ever he have wife, let her be made
More miserable by the death of him
Than I am made by my young lord and thee!
Come, now toward Chertsey with your holy
load,   29

Taken from Paul's to be interred there;
And still, as you are weary of the weight,
Rest you, whiles I lament King Henry's corse.
[*The Bearers take up the corpse and advan*

Enter GLOUCESTER.

Glo. Stay, you that bear the corse, and se
down.
Anne. What black magician conjures up th
fiend,
To stop devoted charitable deeds?
Glo. Villains! set down the corse; or,
Saint Paul,
I'll make a corse of him that disobeys.
First Gent. My lord, stand back, and let t
coffin pass.
Glo. Unmanner'd dog! stand thou wher
command:
Advance thy halberd higher than my brea
Or, by Saint Paul, I'll strike thee to my foot,
And spurn upon thee, beggar, for thy boldne
[*The Bearers set down the cof*
Anne. What! do you tremble? are you
afraid?
Alas! I blame you not; for you are mortal,
And mortal eyes cannot endure the devil.
Avaunt! thou dreadful minister of hell,
Thou hadst but power over his mortal body
His soul thou canst not have: therefore, be go
Glo. Sweet saint, for charity, be not so cur
Anne. Foul devil, for God's sake hence, a
trouble us not;
For thou hast made the happy earth thy he
Fill'd it with cursing cries and deep exclaims.
If thou delight to view thy heinous deeds,
Behold this pattern of thy butcheries.
O! gentlemen; see, see! dead Henry's woun
Open their congeal'd mouths and bleed afres
Blush, blush, thou lump of foul deformity,
For 'tis thy presence that exhales this blood
From cold and empty veins, where no blo
dwells:
Thy deed, inhuman and unnatural,
Provokes this deluge most unnatural.
O God! which this blood mad'st, revenge
death;
O earth! which this blood drink'st, revenge
death;
Either heaven with lightning strike the m
derer dead,
Or earth, gape open wide, and eat him quic
As thou dost swallow up this good king's bloc
Which his hell-govern'd arm hath butchere
Glo. Lady, you know no rules of charity,
Which renders good for bad, blessings for curs
Anne. Villain, thou know'st no law of G
nor man:
No beast so fierce but knows some touch
pity.
Glo. But I know none, and therefore am
beast.
Anne. O! wonderful, when devils tell t
truth.
Glo. More wonderful when angels are
angry.
Vouchsafe, divine perfection of a woman,

these supposed evils, to give me leave,   76
  circumstance, but to acquit myself.

Anne. Vouchsafe, diffus'd infection of a man,
  r these known evils, but to give me leave,
  circumstance, to curse thy cursed self.   80

Glo. Fairer than tongue can name thee, let
  me have
me patient leisure to excuse myself.

Anne. Fouler than heart can think thee, thou
  canst make
 excuse current, but to hang thyself.   84

Glo. By such despair I should accuse myself.

Anne. And by despairing shouldst thou stand
  excus'd
 r doing worthy vengeance on thyself,
 hich didst unworthy slaughter upon others.

Glo. Say that I slew them not.

Anne.   Then say they were not slain:
 t dead they are, and, devilish slave, by thee.

Glo. I did not kill your husband.

Anne.   Why, then he is alive.

Glo. Nay, he is dead; and slain by Edward's
  hand.   92

Anne. In thy foul throat thou liest: Queen
  Margaret saw
 y murderous falchion smoking in his blood;
 e which thou once didst bend against her
  breast,
 t that thy brothers beat aside the point.   96

Glo. I was provoked by her sland'rous tongue,
  at laid their guilt upon my guiltless shoulders.

Anne. Thou wast provoked by thy bloody
  mind,   99
 at never dreamt on aught but butcheries.
 dst thou not kill this king?

Glo. I grant ye.

Anne. Dost grant me, hedge-hog? Then,
  God grant me too
 ou mayst be damned for that wicked deed!
  he was gentle, mild, and virtuous.   105

Glo. The fitter for the King of heaven, that
  hath him.

Anne. He is in heaven, where thou shalt
  never come.

Glo. Let him thank me, that help'd to send
  him thither;   108
 r he was fitter for that place than earth.

Anne. And thou unfit for any place but hell.

Glo. Yes, one place else, if you will hear me
  name it.

Anne. Some dungeon.

Glo.   Your bed-chamber.

Anne. Ill rest betide the chamber where thou
  liest!   113

Glo. So will it, madam, till I lie with you.

Anne. I hope so.

Glo.   I know so. But, gentle Lady Anne,
  leave this keen encounter of our wits,   116
 d fall somewhat into a slower method,
 not the causer of the timeless deaths
 these Plantagenets, Henry and Edward,
  blameful as the executioner?   120

Anne. Thou wast the cause, and most accurs'd effect;

Glo. Your beauty was the cause of that effect;
  ur beauty, that did haunt me in my sleep

To undertake the death of all the world,   124
So might I live one hour in your sweet bosom.

Anne. If I thought that, I tell thee, homicide,
These nails should rend that beauty from my
  cheeks.

Glo. These eyes could not endure that
  beauty's wrack;   128
You should not blemish it if I stood by:
As all the world is cheered by the sun,
So I by that; it is my day, my life.

Anne. Black night o'ershade thy day, and
  death thy life!   132

Glo. Curse not thyself, fair creature; thou
  art both.

Anne. I would I were, to be reveng'd on thee.

Glo. It is a quarrel most unnatural,
To be reveng'd on him that loveth thee.   136

Anne. It is a quarrel just and reasonable,
To be reveng'd on him that kill'd my husband.

Glo. He that bereft thee, lady, of thy husband,
Did it to help thee to a better husband.   140

Anne. His better doth not breathe upon the
  earth.

Glo. He lives that loves thee better than he
  could.

Anne. Name him.

Glo.   Plantagenet.

Anne.   Why, that was he.

Glo. The self-same name, but one of better
  nature.   144

Anne. Where is he?

Glo.   Here. [*She spitteth at
  him.*] Why dost thou spit at me?

Anne. Would it were mortal poison, for thy
  sake!

Glo. Never came poison from so sweet a
  place.   147

Anne. Never hung poison on a fouler toad.
Out of my sight! thou dost infect mine eyes.

Glo. Thine eyes, sweet lady, have infected
  mine.

Anne. Would they were basilisks, to strike
  thee dead!

Glo. I would they were, that I might die at
  once;   152
For now they kill me with a living death.
Those eyes of thine from mine have drawn salt
  tears,
Sham'd their aspects with store of childish
  drops;   155
These eyes, which never shed remorseful tear;
No, when my father York and Edward wept
To hear the piteous moan that Rutland made
When black-fac'd Clifford shook his sword at
  him;
Nor when thy war-like father like a child,   160
Told the sad story of my father's death,
And twenty times made pause to sob and weep,
That all the standers-by had wet their cheeks,
Like trees bedash'd with rain: in that sad time,
My manly eyes did scorn an humble tear;   165
And what these sorrows could not thence ex-
  hale,
Thy beauty hath, and made them blind with
  weeping.
I never su'd to friend, nor enemy;   168

My tongue could never learn sweet smoothing
    words;
But, now thy beauty is propos'd my fee,
My proud heart sues, and prompts my tongue
    to speak. [*She looks scornfully at him.*
Teach not thy lip such scorn, for it was made 172
For kissing, lady, not for such contempt.
If thy revengeful heart cannot forgive,
Lo! here I lend thee this sharp-pointed sword;
Which if thou please to hide in this true breast,
And let the soul forth that adoreth thee, 177
I lay it open to the deadly stroke,
And humbly beg the death upon my knee.
    [*He lays his breast open: she offers at
            it with his sword.*
Nay, do not pause; for I did kill King Henry;
But 'twas thy beauty that provoked me. 181
Nay, now dispatch; 'twas I that stabb'd young
    Edward; [*She again offers at his breast.*
But 'twas thy heavenly face that set me on.
              [*She lets fall the sword.*
Take up the sword again, or take up me. 184
    Anne. Arise, dissembler: though I wish thy
    death,
I will not be thy executioner.
    Glo. Then bid me kill myself, and I will do it.
    Anne. I have already.
    Glo.   That was in thy rage:
Speak it again, and, even with the word, 189
This hand, which for thy love did kill thy love,
Shall, for thy love, kill a far truer love:
To both their deaths shalt thou be accessary. 192
    Anne. I would I knew thy heart.
    Glo. 'Tis figur'd in my tongue.
    Anne. I fear me both are false.
    Glo. Then never man was true. 196
    Anne. Well, well, put up your sword.
    Glo. Say, then, my peace is made.
    Anne. That shalt thou know hereafter.
    Glo. But shall I live in hope? 200
    Anne. All men, I hope, live so.
    Glo. Vouchsafe to wear this ring.
    Anne. To take is not to give.
              [*She puts on the ring.*
    Glo. Look, how my ring encompasseth thy
    finger, 204
Even so thy breast encloseth my poor heart;
Wear both of them, for both of them are thine.
And if thy poor devoted servant may
But beg one favour at thy gracious hand, 208
Thou dost confirm his happiness for ever.
    Anne. What is it?
    Glo. That it may please you leave these sad
    designs
To him that hath most cause to be a mourner,
And presently repair to Crosby-place; 213
Where, after I have solemnly interr'd
At Chertsey monastery this noble king,
And wet his grave with my repentant tears,
I will with all expedient duty see you: 217
For divers unknown reasons, I beseech you,
Grant me this boon.
    Anne. With all my heart; and much it joys
    me too 220
To see you are become so penitent.
Tressel and Berkeley, go along with me.

    Glo. Bid me farewell.
    Anne.   'Tis more than you deser
But since you teach me how to flatter you,
Imagine I have said farewell already.
           [*Exeunt* LADY ANNE, TRESSEL,
                         BERKEL
    Glo. Sirs, take up the corse.
    Gent. Toward Chertsey, noble lord?
    Glo. No, to White-Friars; there attend
    coming. [*Exeunt all but* GLOUCEST
Was ever woman in this humour woo'd?
Was ever woman in this humour won?
I'll have her; but I will not keep her long.
What! I, that kill'd her husband, and his fat
To take her in her heart's extremest hate;
With curses in her mouth, tears in her ey
The bleeding witness of her hatred by;
Having God, her conscience, and these t
    against me,
And nothing I to back my suit withal
But the plain devil and dissembling looks
And yet to win her, all the world to nothing
Ha!
Hath she forgot already that brave prince,
Edward, her lord, whom I, some three mon
    since,
Stabb'd in my angry mood at Tewksbury?
A sweeter and a lovelier gentleman,
Fram'd in the prodigality of nature,
Young, valiant, wise, and, no doubt, right ro
The spacious world cannot again afford:
And will she yet abase her eyes on me,
That cropp'd the golden prime of this sv
    prince,
And made her widow to a woeful bed?
On me, whose all not equals Edward's moie
On me, that halt and am misshapen thus?
My dukedom to a beggarly denier
I do mistake my person all this while:
Upon my life, she finds, although I canno
Myself to be a marvellous proper man.
I'll be at charges for a looking-glass,
And entertain a score or two of tailors,
To study fashions to adorn my body:
Since I am crept in favour with myself,
I will maintain it with some little cost.
But first I'll turn yon fellow in his grave,
And then return lamenting to my love.
Shine out, fair sun, till I have bought a glass
That I may see my shadow as I pass. [*E

SCENE III.—*London. A Room in the Pal*

    Enter QUEEN ELIZABETH, LORD RIVERS, a
             LORD GREY.

    Riv. Have patience, madam: there's
    doubt his majesty
Will soon recover his accustom'd health.
    Grey. In that you brook it ill, it makes
    worse:
Therefore, for God's sake, entertain good c
    fort,
And cheer his Grace with quick and m
    words.
    Q. Eliz. If he were dead, what would be
    on me?

Grey. No other harm but loss of such a lord.

Q. Eliz. The loss of such a lord includes all
harms.   8

Grey. The heavens have bless'd you with a
goodly son,

be your comforter when he is gone.

Q. Eliz. Ah! he is young; and his minority
put into the trust of Richard Gloucester,   12
man that loves not me, nor none of you.

Riv. Is it concluded he shall be protector?

Q. Eliz. It is determin'd, not concluded yet:
ut so it must be if the king miscarry.   16

Enter BUCKINGHAM *and* STANLEY.

Grey. Here come the Lords of Buckingham
and Stanley.

Buck. Good time of day unto your royal
Grace!

Stan. God make your majesty joyful as you
have been!

Q. Eliz. The Countess Richmond, good my
Lord of Stanley,   20
o your good prayer will scarcely say amen.

et, Stanley, notwithstanding she's your wife,
nd loves not me, be you, good lord, assur'd
hate not you for her proud arrogance.   24

Stan. I do beseech you, either not believe
he envious slanders of her false accusers;
r, if she be accus'd on true report,
ear with her weakness, which, I think, proceeds
rom wayward sickness, and no grounded
malice.   29

Q. Eliz. Saw you the king to-day, my Lord
of Stanley?

Stan. But now the Duke of Buckingham
and I,
re come from visiting his majesty.   32

Q. Eliz. What likelihood of his amendment,
lords?

Buck. Madam, good hope; his Grace speaks
cheerfully.

Q. Eliz. God grant him health! did you confer with him?

Buck. Ay, madam: he desires to make atonement   36
etween the Duke of Gloucester and your
brothers,
nd between them and my lord chamberlain;
nd sent to warn them to his royal presence.

Q. Eliz. Would all were well! But that will
never be.   40
fear our happiness is at the highest.

Enter GLOUCESTER, HASTINGS, *and* DORSET.

Glo. They do me wrong, and I will not endure it:
Vho are they that complain unto the king,
hat I, forsooth, am stern and love them not?
y holy Paul, they love his Grace but lightly
hat fill his ears with such dissentious rumours.
ecause I cannot flatter and speak fair,
mile in men's faces, smooth, deceive, and cog,
uck with French nods and apish courtesy,   49
must be held a rancorous enemy.
annot a plain man live and think no harm,
ut this his simple truth must be abus'd   52
y silken, sly, insinuating Jacks?

Grey. To whom in all this presence speaks
your Grace?

Glo. To thee, that hast nor honesty nor grace.
When have I injur'd thee? when done thee
wrong?   56
Or thee? or thee? or any of your faction?
A plague upon you all! His royal person,—
Whom God preserve better than you would
wish!—
Cannot be quiet scarce a breathing-while,   60
But you must trouble him with lewd complaints.

Q. Eliz. Brother of Gloucester, you mistake
the matter.
The king, on his own royal disposition,
And not provok'd by any suitor else,   64
Aiming, belike, at your interior hatred,
That in your outward action shows itself
Against my children, brothers, and myself,
Makes him to send; that thereby he may
gather   68
The ground of your ill-will, and so remove it.

Glo. I cannot tell; the world is grown so bad
That wrens make prey where eagles dare not
perch:
Since every Jack became a gentleman   72
There's many a gentle person made a Jack.

Q. Eliz. Come, come, we know your mean-
ing, brother Gloucester;
You envy my advancement and my friends'.
God grant we never may have need of you!   76

Glo. Meantime, God grants that we have
need of you:
Our brother is imprison'd by your means,
Myself disgrac'd, and the nobility
Held in contempt; while great promotions
Are daily given to ennoble those   81
That scarce, some two days since, were worth
a noble.

Q. Eliz. By him that rais'd me to this care-
ful height
From that contented hap which I enjoy'd,   84
I never did incense his majesty
Against the Duke of Clarence, but have been
An earnest advocate to plead for him.
My lord, you do me shameful injury,   88
Falsely to draw me in these vile suspects.

Glo. You may deny that you were not the
mean
Of my Lord Hastings' late imprisonment.

Riv. She may, my lord; for—   92

Glo. She may, Lord Rivers! why, who knows
not so?
She may do more, sir, than denying that:
She may help you to many fair preferments,
And then deny her aiding hand therein,   96
And lay those honours on your high deserts.
What may she not? She may,—ay, marry,
may she,—

Riv. What, marry, may she?

Glo. What, marry, may she! marry with a
king,   100
A bachelor, a handsome stripling too.
I wis your grandam had a worser match.

Q. Eliz. My Lord of Gloucester, I have too
long borne
Your blunt upbraidings and your bitter scoffs;

By heaven, I will acquaint his majesty   105
Of those gross taunts that oft I have endur'd.
I had rather be a country servantmaid
Than a great queen, with this condition,   108
To be so baited, scorn'd, and stormed at:
Small joy have I in being England's queen.

Enter QUEEN MARGARET, *behind.*

  Q. Mar. [*Apart.*] And lessen'd be that small,
    God, I beseech him!
Thy honour, state, and seat is due to me.   112
  Glo. What! threat you me with telling of the
    king?
Tell him, and spare not: look, what I have said
I will avouch in presence of the king:
I dare adventure to be sent to the Tower.   116
'Tis time to speak; my pains are quite forgot.
  Q. Mar. [*Apart.*] Out, devil! I remember
    them too well:
Thou kill'dst my husband Henry in the Tower,
And Edward, my poor son, at Tewksbury.   120
  Glo. Ere you were queen, ay, or your hus-
    band king,
I was a pack-horse in his great affairs,
A weeder-out of his proud adversaries,
A liberal rewarder of his friends;   124
To royalize his blood I spilt mine own.
  Q. Mar. Ay, and much better blood than his,
    or thine.
  Glo. In all which time you and your husband
    Grey
Were factious for the house of Lancaster;
And, Rivers, so were you. Was not your hus-
    band   129
In Margaret's battle at Saint Alban's slain?
Let me put in your minds, if you forget,
What you have been ere now, and what you are;
Withal, what I have been, and what I am.   133
  Q. Mar. A murderous villain, and so still
    thou art.
  Glo. Poor Clarence did forsake his father,
    Warwick,
Ay, and forswore himself,—which Jesu par-
    don!—   136
  Q. Mar. Which God revenge!
  Glo. To fight on Edward's party for the
    crown;
And for his meed, poor lord, he is mew'd up.
I would to God my heart were flint, like Ed-
    ward's;   140
Or Edward's soft and pitiful, like mine:
I am too childish-foolish for this world.
  Q. Mar. Hie thee to hell for shame, and
    leave this world,
Thou cacodemon! there thy kingdom is.   144
  Riv. My Lord of Gloucester, in those busy
    days
Which here you urge to prove us enemies,
We follow'd then our lord, our lawful king;
So should we you, if you should be our king.
  Glo. If I should be! I had rather be a pedlar.
Far be it from my heart the thought thereof!
  Q. Eliz. As little joy, my lord, as you suppose
You should enjoy, were you this country's king,
As little joy you may suppose in me   153
That I enjoy, being the queen thereof.

  Q. Mar. As little joy enjoys the queen thereof;
For I am she, and altogether joyless.   156
I can no longer hold me patient.   [*Advancing.*
Hear me, you wrangling pirates, that fall out
In sharing that which you have pill'd from me!
Which of you trembles not that looks on me?
If not, that, I being queen, you bow like sub-
    jects,   161
Yet that, by you depos'd, you quake like rebels?
Ah! gentle villain, do not turn away.
  Glo. Foul wrinkled witch, what mak'st thou
    in my sight?   164
  Q. Mar. But repetition of what thou hast
    marr'd;
That will I make before I let thee go.
  Glo. Wert thou not banished on pain of
    death?
  Q. Mar. I was; but I do find more pain in
    banishment   168
Than death can yield me here by my abode.
A husband and a son thou ow'st to me;
And thou, a kingdom; all of you, allegiance:
This sorrow that I have by right is yours,   172
And all the pleasures you usurp are mine.
  Glo. The curse my noble father laid on thee,
When thou didst crown his war-like brows with
    paper,
And with thy scorns drew'st rivers from his
    eyes;   176
And then, to dry them, gav'st the duke a clout
Steep'd in the faultless blood of pretty Rutland;
His curses, then from bitterness of soul
Denounc'd against thee, are all fall'n upon
    thee;   180
And God, not we, hath plagu'd thy bloody deed.
  Q. Eliz. So just is God, to right the innocent.
  Hast. O! 'twas the foulest deed to slay that
    babe,
And the most merciless, that e'er was heard of.
  Riv. Tyrants themselves wept when it was
    reported.   185
  Dors. No man but prophesied revenge for it.
  Buck. Northumberland, then present, wept
    to see it.
  Q. Mar. What! were you snarling all before
    I came,   188
Ready to catch each other by the throat,
And turn you all your hatred now on me?
Did York's dread curse prevail so much with
    heaven
That Henry's death, my lovely Edward's death,
Their kingdom's loss, my woeful banishment,
Should all but answer for that peevish brat?
Can curses pierce the clouds and enter heaven?
Why then, give way, dull clouds, to my quick
    curses!   197
Though not by war, by surfeit die your king,
As ours by murder, to make him a king!
Edward, thy son, that now is Prince of Wales,
For Edward, my son, which was Prince of Wales,
Die in his youth by like untimely violence!
Thyself a queen, for me that was a queen,
Outlive thy glory, like my wretched self!
Long mayst thou live to wail thy children's
    loss,   205
And see another, as I see thee now,

eck'd in thy rights, as thou art stall'd in mine!
ong die thy happy days before thy death;
nd, after many lengthen'd hours of grief, 208
ie neither mother, wife, nor England's queen!
ivers, and Dorset, you were standers by,—
nd so wast thou, Lord Hastings,—when my
　　son
as stabb'd with bloody daggers: God, I pray
　　him, 212
aat none of you may live your natural age,
it by some unlook'd accident cut off.
Glo. Have done thy charm, thou hateful
　　wither'd hag!
Q. Mar. And leave out thee? stay, dog, for
　　thou shalt hear me. 216
heaven have any grievous plague in store
xceeding those that I can wish upon thee,
! let them keep it till thy sins be ripe,
nd then hurl down their indignation 220
n thee, the troubler of the poor world's peace.
he worm of conscience still begnaw thy soul!
hy friends suspect for traitors while thou liv'st
nd take deep traitors for thy dearest friends!
o sleep close up that deadly eye of thine, 225
nless it be while some tormenting dream
ffrights thee with a hell of ugly devils!
hou elvish-mark'd, abortive, rooting hog! 228
hou that wast seal'd in thy nativity
he slave of nature and the son of hell!
hou slander of thy mother's heavy womb!
hou loathed issue of thy father's loins! 232
hou rag of honour! thou detested—
　　Glo. Margaret!
　　Q. Mar.　　　Richard!
　　Glo.　　　　　　　Ha!
　　Q. Mar.　　　　I call thee not.
　　Glo. I cry thee mercy then, for I did think
hat thou hadst call'd me all these bitter names.
　　Q. Mar. Why, so I did; but look'd for no
　　reply. 237
! let me make the period to my curse.
　　Glo. 'Tis done by me, and ends in 'Mar-
　　garet.'
　　Q. Eliz. Thus have you breath'd your curse
　　against yourself. 240
　　Q. Mar. Poor painted queen, vain flourish
　　of my fortune!
Vhy strew'st thou sugar on that bottled spider,
Vhose deadly web ensnareth thee about?
ool, fool! thou whet'st a knife to kill thyself.
he day will come that thou shalt wish for me
o help thee curse this pois'nous bunch-back'd
　　toad.
　　Hast. False-boding woman, end thy frantic
　　curse,
est to thy harm thou move our patience. 248
　　Q. Mar. Foul shame upon you! you have all
　　mov'd mine.
　　Riv. Were you well serv'd, you would be
　　taught your duty.
　　Q. Mar. To serve me well, you all should do
　　me duty,
each me to be your queen, and you my sub-
　　jects: 252
! serve me well, and teach yourselves that duty.
　　Dor. Dispute not with her, she is lunatic.

　　Q. Mar. Peace! Master marquess, you are
　　malapert:
Your fire-new stamp of honour is scarce cur-
　　rent. 256
O! that your young nobility could judge
What 'twere to lose it, and be miserable!
They that stand high have many blasts to shake
　　them,
And if they fall, they dash themselves to pieces.
　　Glo. Good counsel, marry: learn it, learn it,
　　marquess. 261
　　Dor. It touches you, my lord, as much as me.
　　Glo. Ay, and much more; but I was born so
　　high,
Our aery buildeth in the cedar's top, 264
And dallies with the wind, and scorns the sun.
　　Q. Mar. And turns the sun to shade; alas!
　　alas!
Witness my son, now in the shade of death;
Whose bright out-shining beams thy cloudy
　　wrath 268
Hath in eternal darkness folded up.
Your aery buildeth in our aery's nest:
O God! that seest it, do not suffer it;
As it was won with blood, lost be it so! 272
　　Buck. Peace, peace! for shame, if not for
　　charity.
　　Q. Mar. Urge neither charity nor shame to
　　me:
Uncharitably with me have you dealt,
And shamefully my hopes by you are butcher'd.
My charity is outrage, life my shame; 277
And in that shame still live my sorrow's rage!
　　Buck. Have done, have done.
　　Q. Mar. O princely Buckingham! I'll kiss
　　thy hand, 280
In sign of league and amity with thee:
Now fair befall thee and thy noble house!
Thy garments are not spotted with our blood,
Nor thou within the compass of my curse. 284
　　Buck. Nor no one here; for curses never
　　pass
The lips of those that breathe them in the air.
　　Q. Mar. I will not think but they ascend the
　　sky,
And there awake God's gentle-sleeping peace.
O Buckingham! take heed of yonder dog: 289
Look, when he fawns, he bites; and when he
　　bites
His venom tooth will rankle to the death:
Have not to do with him, beware of him; 292
Sin, death and hell have set their marks on him,
And all their ministers attend on him.
　　Glo. What doth she say, my Lord of Buck-
　　ingham?
　　Buck. Nothing that I respect, my gracious
　　lord. 296
　　Q. Mar. What! dost thou scorn me for my
　　gentle counsel,
And soothe the devil that I warn thee from?
O! but remember this another day,
When he shall split thy very heart with sor-
　　row, 300
And say poor Margaret was a prophetess.
Live each of you the subject to his hate,
And he to yours, and all of you to God's! [*Exit.*

Hast. My hair doth stand on end to hear her
curses.   304
Riv. And so doth mine. I muse why she's
at liberty.
Glo. I cannot blame her: by God's holy
mother,
She hath had too much wrong, and I repent
My part thereof that I have done to her.   308
    Q. Eliz. I never did her any, to my know-
ledge.
    Glo. Yet you have all the vantage of her
wrong.
I was too hot to do somebody good,
That is too cold in thinking of it now.   312
Marry, as for Clarence, he is well repaid;
He is frank'd up to fatting for his pains:
God pardon them that are the cause thereof!
    Riv. A virtuous and a Christian-like con-
clusion,   316
To pray for them that have done scath to us.
    Glo. So do I ever [*Aside*], being well-advis'd;
For had I curs'd now, I had curs'd myself.

Enter CATESBY.

Cates. Madam, his majesty doth call for you;
And for your Grace; and you, my noble lords.
    Q. Eliz. Catesby, I come. Lords, will you go
with me?
    Riv. We wait upon your Grace.
              [*Exeunt all but* GLOUCESTER.
    Glo. I do the wrong, and first begin to brawl.
The secret mischiefs that I set abroach   325
I lay unto the grievous charge of others.
Clarence, whom I, indeed, have cast in dark-
ness,
I do beweep to many simple gulls;   328
Namely, to Stanley, Hastings, Buckingham;
And tell them 'tis the queen and her allies
That stir the king against the duke my brother.
Now they believe it; and withal whet me   332
To be reveng'd on Rivers, Vaughan, Grey;
But then I sigh, and, with a piece of scripture,
Tell them that God bids us do good for evil:
And thus I clothe my naked villany   336
With old odd ends stol'n forth of holy writ,
And seem a saint when most I play the devil.

Enter two Murderers.

But soft! here come my executioners.
How now, my hardy, stout resolved mates!   340
Are you now going to dispatch this thing?
    First Murd. We are, my lord; and come to
have the warrant,
That we may be admitted where he is.   343
    Glo. Well thought upon; I have it here about
me: [*Gives the warrant.*
When you have done, repair to Crosby-place.
But, sirs, be sudden in the execution,
Withal obdurate, do not hear him plead;
For Clarence is well-spoken, and perhaps   348
May move your hearts to pity, if you mark
him.
    First Murd. Tut, tut, my lord, we will not
stand to prate;
Talkers are no good doers: be assur'd
We go to use our hands and not our tongues.   352

    Glo. Your eyes drop millstones, when fools'
eyes fall tears:
I like you, lads; about your business straight;
Go, go, dispatch.
    First Murd.   We will, my noble lord.
              [*Exeunt.*

SCENE IV.—*The Same. The Tower.*

Enter CLARENCE *and* BRAKENBURY.

Brak. Why looks your Grace so heavily to-
day?
    Clar. O, I have pass'd a miserable night,
So full of ugly sights, of ghastly dreams,
That, as I am a Christian faithful man,   4
I would not spend another such a night,
Though 'twere to buy a world of happy days,
So full of dismal terror was the time.
    Brak. What was your dream, my lord? I
pray you, tell me.   8
    Clar. Methought that I had broken from the
Tower,
And was embark'd to cross to Burgundy;
And in my company my brother Gloucester,
Who from my cabin tempted me to walk   12
Upon the hatches: hence we look'd toward
England,
And cited up a thousand heavy times,
During the wars of York and Lancaster,
That had befall'n us. As we pac'd along   16
Upon the giddy footing of the hatches,
Methought that Gloucester stumbled; and, in
falling,
Struck me, that thought to stay him, overboard,
Into the tumbling billows of the main.   20
Lord, Lord! methought what pain it was to
drown:
What dreadful noise of water in mine ears!
What sights of ugly death within mine eyes!
Methought I saw a thousand fearful wracks;   24
A thousand men that fishes gnaw'd upon;
Wedges of gold, great anchors, heaps of pearl,
Inestimable stones, unvalu'd jewels,
All scatter'd in the bottom of the sea.   28
Some lay in dead men's skulls; and in those holes
Where eyes did once inhabit, there were crept
As 'twere in scorn of eyes, reflecting gems,
That woo'd the slimy bottom of the deep,   32
And mock'd the dead bones that lay scatter'd by
    Brak. Had you such leisure in the time of
death
To gaze upon those secrets of the deep?
    Clar. Methought I had; and often did I
strive   36
To yield the ghost; but still the envious flood
Stopt in my soul, and would not let it forth
To find the empty, vast, and wandering air;
But smother'd it within my panting bulk,   40
Which almost burst to belch it in the sea.
    Brak. Awak'd you not with this sore agony?
    Clar. No, no, my dream was lengthen'd after
life;
O! then began the tempest to my soul.   44
I pass'd, methought, the melancholy flood,
With that grim ferryman which poets write of,
Unto the kingdom of perpetual night.

e first that there did greet my stranger soul,
as my great father-in-law, renowned Warwick;   49
ho cried aloud, 'What scourge for perjury
n this dark monarchy afford false Clarence?'
d so he vanish'd: then came wandering by 52
shadow like an angel, with bright hair
abbled in blood; and he shriek'd out aloud,
'larence is come,—false, fleeting, perjur'd
   Clarence,
at stabb'd me in the field by Tewksbury;— 56
ize on him! Furies, take him unto torment.'
ith that, methought, a legion of foul fiends
aviron'd me, and howled in mine ears
ch hideous cries, that, with the very noise
rembling wak'd, and, for a season after   61
uld not believe but that I was in hell,
ch terrible impression made my dream.
Brak. No marvel, lord, though it affrighted
   you;   64
am afraid, methinks, to hear you tell it.
Clar. O Brakenbury! I have done these
   things
hat now give evidence against my soul,
or Edward's sake; and see how he requites
   me.   68
God! if my deep prayers cannot appease thee,
ut thou wilt be aveng'd on my misdeeds,
et execute thy wrath on me alone:
! spare my guiltless wife and my poor children,   72
pray thee, gentle keeper, stay by me;
y soul is heavy, and I fain would sleep.
Brak. I will, my lord. God give your Grace
   good rest!   [CLARENCE *sleeps.*
orrow breaks seasons and reposing hours, 76
fakes the night morning, and the noon-tide
   night.
rinces have but their titles for their glories,
n outward honour for an inward toil;
nd, for unfelt imaginations,   80
hey often feel a world of restless cares:
o that, between their titles and low names,
here's nothing differs but the outward fame.

Enter the two Murderers.

First Murd. Ho! who's here?   84
Brak. What wouldst thou, fellow? and how
   cam'st thou thither?
First Murd. I would speak with Clarence, and
   came hither on my legs.
Brak. What! so brief?   88
Sec. Murd. 'Tis better, sir, than to be
   tedious.—
et him see our commission, and talk no more.
   [*A paper is delivered to* BRAKENBURY,
      who reads it.
Brak. I am, in this, commanded to deliver
he noble Duke of Clarence to your hands:
will not reason what is meant hereby,   93
ecause I will be guiltless of the meaning.
here lies the duke asleep, and there the keys.
'll to the king; and signify to him   96
hat thus I have resign'd to you my charge.
First Murd. You may, sir; 'tis a point of
isdom: fare you well.   [*Exit* BRAKENBURY.

Sec. Murd. What! shall we stab him as he
sleeps?   101
First Murd. No; he'll say 'twas done cowardly, when he wakes.
Sec. Murd. When he wakes! why, fool, he
shall never wake till the judgment-day.   105
First Murd. Why, then he'll say we stabbed
him sleeping.
Sec. Murd. The urging of that word
'judgment' hath bred a kind of remorse in
me.   110
First Murd. What! art thou afraid?
Sec. Murd. Not to kill him, having a warrant
for it; but to be damn'd for killing him, from
the which no warrant can defend me.
First Murd. I thought thou hadst been resolute.   116
Sec. Murd. So I am, to let him live.
First Murd. I'll back to the Duke of Glou-
cester, and tell him so.
Sec. Murd. Nay, I prithee, stay a little: I
hope my holy humour will change; it was wont
to hold me but while one tells twenty.
First Murd. How dost thou feel thyself
now?   124
Sec. Murd. Some certain dregs of conscience
are yet within me.
First Murd. Remember our reward when
the deed's done.   128
Sec. Murd. 'Zounds! he dies: I had forgot
the reward.
First Murd. Where's thy conscience now?
Sec. Murd. In the Duke of Gloucester's purse.
First Murd. So when he opens his purse to
give us our reward, thy conscience flies out.
Sec. Murd. 'Tis no matter; let it go: there's
few or none will entertain it.   136
First Murd. What if it come to thee again?
Sec. Murd. I'll not meddle with it; it makes
a man a coward; a man cannot steal, but it
accuseth him; a man cannot swear, but it checks
him; a man cannot lie with his neighbour's wife,
but it detects him: 'tis a blushing shamefast
spirit, that mutinies in a man's bosom; it fills
one full of obstacles; it made me once restore
a purse of gold that I found; it beggars any
man that keeps it; it is turned out of all towns
and cities for a dangerous thing; and every
man that means to live well, endeavours to
trust to himself and live without it.   149
First Murd. 'Zounds! it is even now at my
elbow, persuading me not to kill the duke.
Sec. Murd. Take the devil in thy mind, and
believe him not: he would insinuate with thee
but to make thee sigh.
First Murd. Tut, I am strong-framed; he
cannot prevail with me.   156
Sec. Murd. Spoke like a tall fellow that respects his reputation. Come, shall we to this
gear?
First Murd. Take him over the costard with
the hilts of thy sword, and then throw him into
the malmsey-butt in the next room.
Sec. Murd. O, excellent device! make a sop
of him.   164
First Murd. Soft! he wakes.

Sec. Murd. Strike!

First Murd. No, we'll reason with him.

Clar. Where art thou, keeper? give me a cup of wine.   169

First Murd. You shall have wine enough, my lord, anon.

Clar. In God's name, what art thou?   172

First Murd. A man, as you are.

Clar. But not, as I am, royal.

First Murd. Nor you, as we are, loyal.

Clar. Thy voice is thunder, but thy looks are humble.   176

First Murd. My voice is now the king's, my looks mine own.

Clar. How darkly, and how deadly dost thou speak!

Your eyes do menace me: why look you pale?
Who sent you hither? Wherefore do you come?

Both Murd. To, to, to—   181

Clar. To murder me?

Both Murd. Ay, ay.

Clar. You scarcely have the hearts to tell me so,   184
And therefore cannot have the hearts to do it.
Wherein, my friends, have I offended you?

First Murd. Offended us you have not, but the king.

Clar. I shall be reconcil'd to him again.   188

Sec. Murd. Never, my lord; therefore prepare to die.

Clar. Are you call'd forth from out a world of men
To slay the innocent? What is my offence?
Where is the evidence that doth accuse me?
What lawful quest have given their verdict up
Unto the frowning judge? or who pronounc'd
The bitter sentence of poor Clarence' death?
Before I be convict by course of law,   196
To threaten me with death is most unlawful.
I charge you, as you hope to have redemption
By Christ's dear blood shed for our grievous sins,
That you depart and lay no hands on me;   200
The deed you undertake is damnable.

First Murd. What we will do, we do upon command.

Sec. Murd. And he that hath commanded is our king.

Clar. Erroneous vassal! the great King of kings   204
Hath in the table of his law commanded
That thou shalt do no murder: will you, then,
Spurn at his edict and fulfil a man's?   207
Take heed; for he holds vengeance in his hand,
To hurl upon their heads that break his law.

Sec. Murd. And that same vengeance doth he hurl on thee,
For false forswearing and for murder too:
Thou didst receive the sacrament to fight   212
In quarrel of the house of Lancaster.

First Murd. And, like a traitor to the name of God,
Didst break that vow, and, with thy treacherous blade
Unripp'dst the bowels of thy sovereign's son.   216

Sec. Murd. Whom thou wast sworn to cherish and defend.

First Murd. How canst thou urge God's dreadful law to us,
When thou hast broke it in such dear degree?

Clar. Alas! for whose sake did I that ill deed?   220
For Edward, for my brother, for his sake:
He sends you not to murder me for this;
For in that sin he is as deep as I.
If God will be avenged for the deed,   224
O! know you yet, he doth it publicly:
Take not the quarrel from his powerful arm;
He needs no indirect or lawless course
To cut off those that have offended him.   228

First Murd. Who made thee then a bloody minister,
When gallant-springing, brave Plantagenet,
That princely novice, was struck dead by thee?

Clar. My brother's love, the devil, and my rage.   232

First Murd. Thy brother's love, our duty, and thy fault,
Provoke us hither now to slaughter thee.

Clar. If you do love my brother, hate not me;
I am his brother, and I love him well.   236
If you are hir'd for meed, go back again,
And I will send you to my brother Gloucester,
Who shall reward you better for my life
Than Edward will for tidings of my death.   240

Sec. Murd. You are deceiv'd, your brother Gloucester hates you.

Clar. O, no! he loves me, and he holds me dear:
Go you to him from me.

Both Murd.   Ay, so we will.

Clar. Tell him, when that our princely father York   244
Bless'd his three sons with his victorious arm,
And charg'd us from his soul to love each other,
He little thought of this divided friendship:
Bid Gloucester think on this, and he will weep.

First Murd. Ay, millstones; as he lesson'd us to weep.   249

Clar. O! do not slander him, for he is kind.

First Murd. Right;
As snow in harvest. Thou deceiv'st thyself:
'Tis he that sends us to destroy you here.

Clar. It cannot be; for he bewept my fortune,
And hugg'd me in his arms, and swore, with sobs,
That he would labour my delivery.   253

First Murd. Why, so he doth, when he delivers you
From this earth's thraldom to the joys of heaven.

Sec. Murd. Make peace with God, for you must die, my lord.

Clar. Hast thou that holy feeling in thy soul,   260
To counsel me to make my peace with God,
And art thou yet to thy own soul so blind,
That thou wilt war with God by murdering me?
O! sirs, consider, he that set you on   264
To do this deed, will hate you for the deed.

Sec. Murd. What shall we do?

Clar.   Relent and save your souls.
First Murd. Relent! 'tis cowardly, and wo-
    manish.
Clar. Not to relent, is beastly, savage,
    devilish.   268
'hich of you, if you were a prince's son,
eing pent from liberty, as I am now,
   two such murd'rers as yourselves came to
    you,
'ould not entreat for life?   272
Iy friend, I spy some pity in thy looks;
I if thine eye be not a flatterer,
.ome thou on my side, and entreat for me,
.s you would beg, were you in my distress: 276
  begging prince what beggar pities not?
Sec. Murd. Look behind you, my lord.
First Murd. [*Stabs him.*] Take that, and that:
    if all this will not do,
.ll drown you in the malmsey-butt within. 280
                      [*Exit with the body.*
Sec. Murd. A bloody deed, and desperately
    dispatch'd!
.ow fain, like Pilate, would I wash my hands
.f this most grievous murder.

Re-enter first Murderer.

First Murd. How now! what mean'st thou,
    that thou help'st me not?   284
.y heaven, the duke shall know how slack you
    have been.
Sec. Murd. I would he knew that I had sav'd
    his brother!
.ake thou the fee, and tell him what I say;
.or I repent me that the duke is slain.   [*Exit.*
First Murd. So do not I: go, coward as
    thou art.   289
.ell, I'll go hide the body in some hole,
.ill that the duke give order for his burial:
.nd when I have my meed, I will away;   292
.or this will out, and here I must not stay.
                           [*Exit.*

ACT II

SCENE I.—*London. A Room in the Palace.*

'nter KING EDWARD *sick,* QUEEN ELIZABETH,
DORSET, RIVERS, HASTINGS, BUCKINGHAM,
GREY, *and Others.*

K. Edw. Why, so: now have I done a good
    day's work.
'ou peers, continue this united league:
.every day expect an embassage
'rom my Redeemer to redeem me hence;   4
.nd more in peace my soul shall part to heaven,
.ince I have made my friends at peace on earth.
.ivers and Hastings, take each other's hand;
.issemble not your hatred, swear your love. 8
Riv. By heaven, my soul is purg'd from
    grudging hate;
.nd with my hand I seal my true heart's love.
Hast. So thrive I, as I truly swear the like!
K. Edw. Take heed you dally not before
    your king;   12
.est he that is the supreme King of kings
.onfound your hidden falsehood, and award
.ither of you to be the other's end.

Hast. So prosper I, as I swear perfect love!
Riv. And I, as I love Hastings with my heart!
K. Edw. Madam, yourself are not exempt in
    this,
Nor you, son Dorset, Buckingham, nor you;
You have been factious one against the other. 20
Wife, love Lord Hastings, let him kiss your hand;
And what you do, do it unfeignedly.
Q. Eliz. There, Hastings; I will never more
    remember
Our former hatred, so thrive I and mine!   24
    K. Edw. Dorset, embrace him; Hastings,
    love lord marquess.
Dor. This interchange of love, I here protest,
Upon my part shall be inviolable.
    Hast. And so swear I.   [*They embrace.*
    K. Edw. Now, princely Buckingham, seal
    thou this league   29
With thy embracements to my wife's allies,
And make me happy in your unity.
    Buck. [*To the* QUEEN.] Whenever Bucking-
    ham doth turn his hate   32
Upon your Grace, but with all duteous love
Doth cherish you and yours, God punish me
With hate in those where I expect most love!
When I have most need to employ a friend, 36
And most assured that he is a friend,
Deep, hollow, treacherous, and full of guile,
Be he unto me! This do I beg of God,
When I am cold in love to you or yours.   40
                           [*They embrace.*
    K. Edw. A pleasing cordial, princely Buck-
    ingham,
Is this thy vow unto my sickly heart.
There wanteth now our brother Gloucester here
To make the blessed period of this peace.   44
    Buck. And in good time, here comes the
    noble duke.

Enter GLOUCESTER.

    Glo. Good morrow to my sovereign king
    and queen;
And princely peers, a happy time of day!
    K. Edw. Happy, indeed, as we have spent
    the day.   48
Gloucester, we have done deeds of charity;
Made peace of enmity, fair love of hate,
Between these swelling wrong-incensed peers.
    Glo. A blessed labour, my most sovereign
    lord.   52
Among this princely heap, if any here,
By false intelligence, or wrong surmise,
Hold me a foe;
If I unwittingly, or in my rage,   56
Have aught committed that is hardly borne
By any in this presence, I desire
To reconcile me to his friendly peace:
'Tis death to me to be at enmity;   60
I hate it, and desire all good men's love.
First, madam, I entreat true peace of you,
Which I will purchase with my duteous service;
Of you, my noble cousin Buckingham,   64
If ever any grudge were lodg'd between us;
Of you, Lord Rivers, and Lord Grey, of you,
That all without desert have frown'd on me;
Of you, Lord Woodvile, and Lord Scales, of you

Dukes, earls, lords, gentlemen; indeed, of all.
I do not know that Englishman alive
With whom my soul is any jot at odds
More than the infant that is born to-night: 72
I thank my God for my humility.
Q. Eliz. A holy day shall this be kept here-
after:
I would to God all strifes were well compounded.
My sov'reign lord, I do beseech your highness 76
To take our brother Clarence to your grace.
Glo. Why, madam, have I offer'd love for this,
To be so flouted in this royal presence?
Who knows not that the gentle duke is dead? 80
                              [*They all start.*
You do him injury to scorn his corse.
  K. Edw. Who knows not he is dead! who
knows he is?
  Q. Eliz. All-seeing heaven, what a world is
this!
  Buck. Look I so pale, Lord Dorset, as the
rest? 84
  Dor. Ay, my good lord; and no man in the
presence
But his red colour hath forsook his cheeks.
  K. Edw. Is Clarence dead? the order was
revers'd.
  Glo. But he, poor man, by your first order
died, 88
And that a winged Mercury did bear;
Some tardy cripple bore the countermand,
That came too lag to see him buried. 91
God grant that some, less noble and less loyal,
Nearer in bloody thoughts, and not in blood,
Deserve not worse than wretched Clarence did,
And yet go current from suspicion.

Enter STANLEY.

  Stan. A boon, my sov'reign, for my service
done! 96
  K. Edw. I prithee, peace: my soul is full of
sorrow.
  Stan. I will not rise, unless your highness
hear me.
  K. Edw. Then say at once, what is it thou
request'st.
  Stan. The forfeit, sovereign, of my servant's
life; 100
Who slew to-day a riotous gentleman
Lately attendant on the Duke of Norfolk.
  K. Edw. Have I a tongue to doom my
brother's death, 103
And shall that tongue give pardon to a slave?
My brother kill'd no man, his fault was thought;
And yet his punishment was bitter death.
Who su'd to me for him? who, in my wrath,
Kneel'd at my feet, and bade me be advis'd?
Who spoke of brotherhood? who spoke of love?
Who told me how the poor soul did forsake
The mighty Warwick, and did fight for me?
Who told me, in the field at Tewksbury, 112
When Oxford had me down, he rescu'd me,
And said, 'Dear brother, live, and be a king?'
Who told me, when we both lay in the field
Frozen almost to death, how he did lap me
Even in his garments; and did give himself,
All thin and naked, to the numb cold night?

All this from my remembrance brutish wrat
Sinfully pluck'd, and not a man of you   1
Had so much grace to put it in my mind.
But when your carters or your waiting-vassa
Have done a drunken slaughter, and defac'd
The precious image of our dear Redeemer,
You straight are on your knees for pardo
pardon;   1
And I, unjustly too, must grant it you;
But for my brother not a man would speak,
Nor I, ungracious, speak unto myself
For him, poor soul. The proudest of you all
Have been beholding to him in his life,
Yet none of you would once beg for his life.
O God! I fear, thy justice will take hold   1
On me and you and mine and yours for this.
Come, Hastings, help me to my closet. O! po
Clarence!
        [*Exeunt* KING EDWARD, QUEEN, HASTING
                    RIVERS, DORSET, *and* GRE
  Glo. This is the fruit of rashness. Mark
you not
How that the guilty kindred of the queen   1
Look'd pale when they did hear of Clarenc
death?
O! they did urge it still unto the king:
God will revenge it. Come, lords; will you g
To comfort Edward with our company?   1
  Buck. We wait upon your Grace. [*Exeun*

SCENE II.—*The Same. A Room in the Palac*

Enter the DUCHESS OF YORK, *with a Son an*
            Daughter *of* CLARENCE.

  Boy. Good grandam, tell us, is our fath
dead?
  Duch. No, boy.
  Daugh. Why do you wring your hands, an
beat your breast,
And cry—'O Clarence, my unhappy son?'
  Boy. Why do you look on us, and shak
your head,
And call us orphans, wretches, castaways,
If that our noble father be alive?
  Duch. My pretty cousins, you mistake m
much;
I do lament the sickness of the king,
As loath to lose him, not your father's death
It were lost sorrow to wail one that's lost.
  Boy. Then, grandam, you conclude that h
is dead.   1
The king mine uncle is to blame for it:
God will revenge it; whom I will importune
With earnest prayers all to that effect.
  Daugh. And so will I.   1
  Duch. Peace, children, peace! the king dot
love you well:
Incapable and shallow innocents,
You cannot guess who caus'd your father'
death.
  Boy. Grandam, we can; for my good uncl
Gloucester   2
Told me, the king, provok'd to 't by the queen
Devis'd impeachments to imprison him:
And when my uncle told me so, he wept,
And pitied me, and kindly kiss'd my cheek; 2

Bade me rely on him, as on my father,
And he would love me dearly as his child.

  Duch. Ah! that deceit should steal such
    gentle shape,
And with a virtuous vizard hide deep vice.   28
He is my son, ay, and therein my shame,
Yet from my dugs he drew not this deceit.

  Boy. Think you my uncle did dissemble,
    grandam?

  Duch. Ay, boy.

  Boy. I cannot think it. Hark! what noise is   32
    this?

Enter QUEEN ELIZABETH, *distractedly;* RIVERS
    and DORSET *following her.*

  Q. Eliz. Oh! who shall hinder me to wail and
    weep,
To chide my fortune, and torment myself?
I'll join with black despair against my soul,   36
And to myself become an enemy.

  Duch. What means this scene of rude im-
    patience?

  Q. Eliz. To make an act of tragic violence:
Edward, my lord, thy son, our king, is dead!   40
Why grow the branches now the root is wither'd?
Why wither not the leaves that want their sap?
If you will live, lament: if die, be brief,
That our swift-winged souls may catch the king's;   44
Or, like obedient subjects, follow him
To his new kingdom of perpetual rest.

  Duch. Ah! so much interest have I in thy
    sorrow
As I had title in thy noble husband.   48
I have bewept a worthy husband's death,
And liv'd with looking on his images;
But now two mirrors of his princely semblance
Are crack'd in pieces by malignant death,   52
And I for comfort have but one false glass,
That grieves me when I see my shame in him.
Thou art a widow; yet thou art a mother,
And hast the comfort of thy children left thee:
But death hath snatch'd my husband from mine
    arms,   57
And pluck'd two crutches from my feeble limbs,
Clarence and Edward. O! what cause have I—
Thine being but a moiety of my grief—   60
To overgo thy plaints, and drown thy cries!

  Boy. Ah, aunt, you wept not for our father's
    death;
How can we aid you with our kindred tears?

  Daugh. Our fatherless distress was left un-
    moan'd;   64
Your widow-dolour likewise be unwept.

  Q. Eliz. Give me no help in lamentation;
I am not barren to bring forth complaints:
All springs reduce their currents to mine eyes,
That I, being govern'd by the wat'ry moon,   69
May send forth plenteous tears to drown the
    world!
Ah! for my husband, for my dear Lord Edward!

  Chil. Ah! for our father, for our dear Lord
    Clarence!

  Duch. Alas! for both, both mine, Edward   72
    and Clarence.

  Q. Eliz. What stay had I but Edward? and
    he's gone.

  Chil. What stay had ٧
    he's gone.

  Duch. What stays had I bu
    are gone.

  Q. Eliz. Was never widow had so ؟

  Chil. Were never orphans had so de؟

  Duch. Was never mother had so dear a
Alas! I am the mother of these griefs:
Their woes are parcell'd, mine are general.
She for an Edward weeps, and so do I;
I for a Clarence weep, so doth not she:
These babes for Clarence weep, and so do I;   84
I for an Edward weep, so do not they:
Alas! you three, on me, threefold distress'd,
Pour all your tears; I am your sorrow's nurse,
And I will pamper it with lamentation.   88

  Dor. Comfort, dear mother: God is much
    displeas'd
That you take with unthankfulness his doing.
In common worldly things 'tis call'd ungrateful
With dull unwillingness to repay a debt   92
Which with a bounteous hand was kindly lent;
Much more to be thus opposite with heaven,
For it requires the royal debt it lent you.

  Riv. Madam, bethink you, like a careful
    mother,   96
Of the young prince your son: send straight for
    him;
Let him be crown'd; in him your comfort lives.
Drown desperate sorrow in dead Edward's
    grave,   99
And plant your joys in living Edward's throne.

Enter GLOUCESTER, BUCKINGHAM, STANLEY,
    HASTINGS, RATCLIFF, *and Others.*

  Glo. Sister, have comfort: all of us have cause
To wail the dimming of our shining star;
But none can cure their harms by wailing them.
Madam, my mother, I do cry you mercy;   104
I did not see your Grace: humbly on my knee
I crave your blessing.

  Duch. God bless thee! and put meekness in
    thy mind,
Love, charity, obedience, and true duty.   108

  Glo. Amen; [*Aside.*] and make me die a
    good old man!
That is the butt-end of a mother's blessing;
I marvel that her Grace did leave it out.

  Buck. You cloudy princes and heart-sorrow-
    ing peers,   112
That bear this heavy mutual load of moan,
Now cheer each other in each other's love:
Though we have spent our harvest of this king,
We are to reap the harvest of his son.   116
The broken rancour of your high-swoln hearts,
But lately splinter'd, knit, and join'd together,
Must gently be preserv'd, cherish'd, and kept:
Me seemeth good, that, with some little train,
Forthwith from Ludlow the young prince be
    fetch'd   121
Hither to London, to be crown'd our king.

  Riv. Why with some little train, my Lord of
    Buckingham?

  Buck. Marry, my lord, lest, by a multitude,
The new-heal'd wound of malice should break
    out;   125

more dangerous,
green and yet un-

commanding rein,
please himself, 129
harm apparent,
be prevented.
made peace with all of
132

and true in me.
nd so, I think, in all:
en, it should be put
To no a... hood of breach, 136
Which haply by... company might be urg'd:
Therefore I say with noble Buckingham,
That it is meet so few should fetch the prince.
Hast. And so say I. 140
Glo. Then be it so: and go we to determine
Who they shall be that straight shall post to
Ludlow.
Madam, and you my mother, will you go
To give your censures in this business? 144
    [*Exeunt all except* BUCKINGHAM *and*
        GLOUCESTER.

Buck. My lord, whoever journeys to the
prince,
For God's sake, let not us two stay at home:
For by the way I'll sort occasion,
As index to the story we late talk'd of, 148
To part the queen's proud kindred from the
prince.
Glo. My other self, my counsel's consistory,
My oracle, my prophet! My dear cousin,
I, as a child, will go by thy direction, 152
Towards Ludlow then, for we'll not stay be-
hind.   [*Exeunt.*

SCENE III.—*The Same. A Street.*

Enter two Citizens, *meeting.*

First Cit. Good morrow, neighbour: whither
away so fast?
Sec. Cit. I promise you, I scarcely know
myself:
Hear you the news abroad?
    First Cit. Ay; that the king is dead.
Sec. Cit. Ill news, by'r lady; seldom comes
the better: 4
I fear, I fear, 'twill prove a giddy world.

Enter a third Citizen.

Third Cit. Neighbours, God speed!
First Cit. Give you good morrow, sir.
Third Cit. Doth the news hold of good King
Edward's death?
Sec. Cit. Ay, sir, it is too true; God help the
while! 8
Third Cit. Then, masters, look to see a
troublous world.
First Cit. No, no; by God's good grace, his
son shall reign.
Third Cit. Woe to that land that's govern'd
by a child!
Sec. Cit. In him there is a hope of govern-
ment, 12
That in his nonage council under him,

And in his full and ripen'd years himself,
No doubt, shall then and till then govern well.
    First Cit. So stood the state when Henry the
Sixth 16
Was crown'd at Paris but at nine months old.
    Third Cit. Stood the state so? no, no, good
friends, God wot;
For then this land was famously enrich'd
With politic grave counsel; then the king 20
Had virtuous uncles to protect his Grace.
    First Cit. Why, so hath this, both by his
father and mother.
    Third Cit. Better it were they all came by
his father,
Or by his father there were none at all; 24
For emulation, who shall now be nearest,
Will touch us all too near, if God prevent not.
O! full of danger is the Duke of Gloucester!
And the queen's sons and brothers haught and
proud; 28
And were they to be rul'd, and not to rule,
This sickly land might solace as before.
    First Cit. Come, come, we fear the worst;
all will be well.
    Third Cit. When clouds are seen, wise men
put on their cloaks; 32
When great leaves fall, then winter is at hand;
When the sun sets, who doth not look for night?
Untimely storms make men expect a dearth.
All may be well; but, if God sort it so, 36
'Tis more than we deserve, and I expect.
    Sec. Cit. Truly, the hearts of men are full of
fear:
You cannot reason almost with a man
That looks not heavily and full of dread. 40
    Third Cit. Before the days of change, still is
it so:
By a divine instinct men's minds mistrust
Ensuing danger; as, by proof, we see
The waters swell before a boisterous storm. 44
But leave it all to God. Whither away?
    Sec. Cit. Marry, we were sent for to the
justices.
    Third Cit. And so was I: I'll bear you
company.   [*Exeunt.*

SCENE IV.—*The Same. A Room in the
Palace.*

Enter the ARCHBISHOP OF YORK, *the young* DUKE
OF YORK, QUEEN ELIZABETH, *and the* DUCHESS
OF YORK.

Arch. Last night, I hear, they lay at North-
ampton;
At Stony-Stratford they do rest to-night:
To-morrow, or next day, they will be here.
    Duch. I long with all my heart to see the
prince. 4
I hope he is much grown since last I saw him.
    Q. Eliz. But I hear, no; they say my son of
York
Hath almost overta'en him in his growth.
    York. Ay, mother, but I would not have it so.
    Duch. Why, my young cousin, it is good to
grow. 9

York. Grandam, one night, as we did sit at
    supper,
My uncle Rivers talk'd how I did grow
More than my brother: 'Ay,' quoth my uncle
    Gloucester,   12
Small herbs have grace, great weeds do grow
    apace:'
And since, methinks, I would not grow so fast,
Because sweet flowers are slow and weeds make
    haste.
Duch. Good faith, good faith, the saying did
    not hold   16
In him that did object the same to thee:
He was the wretched'st thing when he was young,
So long a-growing, and so leisurely,
That, if his rule were true, he should be gracious.
Arch. And so, no doubt, he is, my gracious
    madam.   21
Duch. I hope he is; but yet let mothers doubt.
York. Now, by my troth, if I had been re-
    member'd,
I could have given my uncle's grace a flout,   24
To touch his growth nearer than he touch'd
    mine.
Duch. How, my young York? I prithee, let
    me hear it.
York. Marry, they say my uncle grew so fast,
That he could gnaw a crust at two hours old: 28
'Twas full two years ere I could get a tooth.
Grandam, this would have been a biting jest.
Duch. I prithee, pretty York, who told thee
    this?
York. Grandam, his nurse.   32
Duch. His nurse! why, she was dead ere thou
    wast born.
York. If 'twere not she, I cannot tell who
    told me.
Q. Eliz. A parlous boy: go to, you are too
    shrewd.
Arch. Good madam, be not angry with the
    child.   36
Q. Eliz. Pitchers have ears.

Enter a Messenger.

Arch. Here comes a messenger. What news?
Mess. Such news, my lord, as grieves me to
    report.
Q. Eliz. How doth the prince?
Mess.   Well, madam, and in health.
Duch. What is thy news?   41
Mess. Lord Rivers and Lord Grey are sent
    to Pomfret,
With them Sir Thomas Vaughan, prisoners.
Duch. Who hath committed them?
Mess.   The mighty dukes,   44
Gloucester and Buckingham.
Arch.   For what offence?
Mess. The sum of all I can I have disclos'd:
Why or for what the nobles were committed
Is all unknown to me, my gracious lord.   48
Q. Eliz. Ah me! I see the ruin of my house!
The tiger now hath seiz'd the gentle hind;
Insulting tyranny begins to jet
Upon the innocent and aweless throne: 52
Welcome, destruction, death, and massacre!
I see, as in a map, the end of all.

Duch. Accursed and unquiet wrangling days,
How many of you have mine eyes beheld! 56
My husband lost his life to get the crown,
And often up and down my sons were toss'd,
For me to joy and weep their gain and loss:
And being seated, and domestic broils   60
Clean over-blown, themselves, the conquerors
Make war upon themselves; brother to brother,
Blood to blood, self against self: O! preposter-
    ous
And frantic outrage, end thy damned spleen; 64
Or let me die, to look on death no more.
Q. Eliz. Come, come, my boy; we will to
    sanctuary.
Madam, farewell.
Duch.   Stay, I will go with you.
Q. Eliz. You have no cause.
Arch. [*To the* QUEEN.] My gracious lady, go;
And thither bear your treasure and your goods
For my part, I'll resign unto your Grace
The seal I keep: and so betide to me
As well I tender you and all of yours!   72
Come; I'll conduct you to the sanctuary.
                                      [*Exeunt.*

ACT III

SCENE I.—*The Same. A Street.*

The Trumpets sound. Enter the PRINCE OF WALES,
    GLOUCESTER, BUCKINGHAM, CATESBY, CARDI-
    NAL BOURCHIER, *and Others.*

Buck. Welcome, sweet prince, to London, to
    your chamber.
Glo. Welcome, dear cousin, my thoughts'
    sovereign;
The weary way hath made you melancholy.
Prince. No, uncle; but our crosses on the
    way   4
Have made it tedious, wearisome, and heavy:
I want more uncles here to welcome me.
Glo. Sweet prince, the untainted virtue of
    your years
Hath not yet div'd into the world's deceit: 8
No more can you distinguish of a man
Than of his outward show; which, God he
    knows,
Seldom or never jumpeth with the heart.
Those uncles which you want were dangerous;
Your Grace attended to their sugar'd words, 13
But look'd not on the poison of their hearts:
God keep you from them, and from such false
    friends!
Prince. God keep me from false friends! but
    they were none.   16
Glo. My lord, the Mayor of London comes to
    greet you.

Enter the Lord Mayor *and his Train.*

May. God bless your Grace with health and
    happy days!
Prince. I thank you, good my lord; and
    thank you all.
I thought my mother and my brother York 20
Would long ere this have met us on the way:
Fie! what a slug is Hastings, that he comes not
To tell us whether they will come or no.

Enter HASTINGS.

Buck. And in good time here comes the
   sweating lord.   24
Prince. Welcome, my lord. What, will our
   mother come?
Hast. On what occasion, God he knows,
   not I,
The queen your mother, and your brother York,
Have taken sanctuary: the tender prince   28
Would fain have come with me to meet your
   Grace,
But by his mother was perforce withheld.
Buck. Fie! what an indirect and peevish
   course   31
Is this of hers! Lord Cardinal, will your Grace
Persuade the queen to send the Duke of York
Unto his princely brother presently?
If she deny, Lord Hastings, go with him,
And from her jealous arms pluck him perforce.
Card. My Lord of Buckingham, if my weak
   oratory   37
Can from his mother win the Duke of York,
Anon expect him here; but if she be obdurate
To mild entreaties, God in heaven forbid   40
We should infringe the holy privilege
Of blessed sanctuary! not for all this land
Would I be guilty of so great a sin.
Buck. You are too senseless-obstinate, my
   lord,   44
Too ceremonious and traditional:
Weigh it but with the grossness of this age,
You break not sanctuary in seizing him.
The benefit thereof is always granted   48
To those whose dealings have deserv'd the place
And those who have the wit to claim the place:
This prince hath neither claim'd it, nor deserv'd
   it;   51
And therefore, in mine opinion, cannot have it:
Then, taking him from thence that is not there,
You break no privilege nor charter there.
Oft have I heard of sanctuary men,
But sanctuary children ne'er till now.   56
Card. My lord, you shall o'er-rule my mind
   for once.
Come on, Lord Hastings, will you go with me?
Hast. I go, my lord.
Prince. Good lords, make all the speedy
   haste you may.   60
            [*Exeunt* CARDINAL BOURCHIER *and*
                                          HASTINGS.
Say, uncle Gloucester, if our brother come,
Where shall we sojourn till our coronation?
Glo. Where it seems best unto your royal
   self.
If I may counsel you, some day or two   64
Your highness shall repose you at the Tower:
Then where you please, and shall be thought
   most fit
For your best health and recreation.
Prince. I do not like the Tower, of any place:
Did Julius Cæsar build that place, my lord? 69
Buck. He did, my gracious lord, begin that
   place,
Which, since, succeeding ages have re-edified.
Prince. Is it upon record, or else reported 72

Successively from age to age, he built it?
Buck. Upon record, my gracious lord.
Prince. But say, my lord, it were not regis-
   ter'd,
Methinks the truth should live from age to age
As 'twere retail'd to all posterity,   7
Even to the general all-ending day.
   Glo. [*Aside.*] So wise so young, they say, d
   never live long.
Prince. What say you, uncle?   8
   Glo. I say, without characters, fame live
   long.
[*Aside.*] Thus, like the formal Vice, Iniquity,
I moralize two meanings in one word.
Prince. That Julius Cæsar was a famou
   man;   8
With what his valour did enrich his wit,
His wit set down to make his valour live:
Death makes no conquest of this conqueror,
For now he lives in fame, though not in life. 8
I'll tell you what, my cousin Buckingham,—
Buck. What, my gracious lord?
Prince. An if I live until I be a man,
I'll win our ancient right in France again, 9
Or die a soldier, as I liv'd a king.
Glo. [*Aside.*] Short summers lightly have
   forward spring.

Enter YORK, HASTINGS, *and* CARDINAL
                       BOURCHIER.

Buck. Now, in good time, here comes th
   Duke of York.
Prince. Richard of York! how fares ou
   loving brother?   9
York. Well, my dread lord; so must I ca
   you now.
Prince. Ay, brother, to our grief, as it i
   yours:
Too late he died that might have kept that title
Which by his death hath lost much majesty. 10
Glo. How fares our cousin, noble Lord c
   York?
York. I thank you, gentle uncle. O, my lord
You said that idle weeds are fast in growth:
The prince my brother hath outgrown me fa
Glo. He hath, my lord.
York.   And therefore is he idle? 10
Glo. O, my fair cousin, I must not say so.
York. Then he is more beholding to yo
   than I.
Glo. He may command me as my sovereign
But you have power in me as in a kinsman. 1c
York. I pray you, uncle, give me this dagge
Glo. My dagger, little cousin? with all m
   heart.
Prince. A beggar, brother?   11
York. Of my kind uncle, that I know wi
   give;
And, being but a toy, which is no grief to give
Glo. A greater gift than that I'll give m
   cousin.
York. A greater gift! O, that's the swor
   to it.
Glo. Ay, gentle cousin, were it light enough
York. O, then, I see, you'll part but wit
   light gifts;

In weightier things you'll say a beggar nay.
　Glo. It is too weighty for your Grace to wear.
　York. I weigh it lightly, were it heavier. 121
　Glo. What! would you have my weapon,
　　little lord?
　York. I would, that I might thank you, as
　　you call me.
　Glo. How?　　　　　　　　　　　　124
　York. Little.
　Prince. My Lord of York will still be cross
　　in talk.
Uncle, your Grace knows how to bear with
　him.
　York. You mean, to bear me, not to bear
　　with me:　　　　　　　　　　　128
Uncle, my brother mocks both you and me.
Because that I am little, like an ape,
He thinks that you should bear me on your
　shoulders.
　Buck. With what a sharp provided wit he
　　reasons!　　　　　　　　　　　132
To mitigate the scorn he gives his uncle,
He prettily and aptly taunts himself:
So cunning and so young is wonderful.
　Glo. My lord, will't please you pass along? 137
Myself and my good cousin Buckingham
Will to your mother, to entreat of her
To meet you at the Tower and welcome you.
　York. What! will you go unto the Tower,
　　my lord?　　　　　　　　　　140
　Prince. My Lord Protector needs will have
　　it so.
　York. I shall not sleep in quiet at the Tower.
　Glo. Why, what would you fear?
　York. Marry, my uncle Clarence' angry
　　ghost:　　　　　　　　　　　144
My grandam told me he was murder'd there.
　Prince. I fear no uncles dead.
　Glo. Nor none that live, I hope.
　Prince. An if they live, I hope, I need not
　　fear.　　　　　　　　　　　148
But come, my lord; and, with a heavy heart,
Thinking on them, go I unto the Tower.
　　　　　[*Sennet. Exeunt all but* GLOUCESTER,
　　　　　BUCKINGHAM, *and* CATESBY.
　Buck. Think you, my lord, this little prating
　　York
Was not incensed by his subtle mother　152
To taunt and scorn you thus opprobriously?
　Glo. No doubt, no doubt: O! 'tis a parlous
　　boy;
Bold, quick, ingenious, forward, capable:
He's all the mother's, from the top to toe. 156
　Buck. Well, let them rest. Come hither,
　　Catesby; thou art sworn
As deeply to effect what we intend
As closely to conceal what we impart.
Thou know'st our reasons urg'd upon the
　way:　　　　　　　　　　　160
What think'st thou? is it not an easy matter
To make William Lord Hastings of our mind,
For the instalment of this noble duke
In the seat royal of this famous isle?　164
　Cate. He for his father's sake so loves the
　　prince
That he will not be won to aught against him.

　Buck. What think'st thou then of Stanley?
　　what will he?
　Cate. He will do all in all as Hastings doth.
　Buck. Well then, no more but this: go,
　　gentle Catesby,　　　　　　　169
And, as it were far off, sound thou Lord Hast-
　ings,
How he doth stand affected to our purpose;
And summon him to-morrow to the Tower, 172
To sit about the coronation.
If thou dost find him tractable to us,
Encourage him, and tell him all our reasons:
If he be leaden, icy-cold, unwilling,　176
Be thou so too, and so break off the talk,
And give us notice of his inclination;
For we to-morrow hold divided councils,
Wherein thyself shalt highly be employ'd. 180
　Glo. Commend me to Lord William: tell him,
　　Catesby,
His ancient knot of dangerous adversaries
To-morrow are let blood at Pomfret Castle;
And bid my lord, for joy of this good news, 184
Give Mistress Shore one gentle kiss the more.
　Buck. Good Catesby, go, effect this business
　　soundly.
　Cate. My good lords both, with all the heed
　　I can.
　Glo. Shall we hear from you, Catesby, ere
　　we sleep?　　　　　　　　　188
　Cate. You shall, my lord.
　Glo. At Crosby-place, there shall you find us
　　both.　　　　　　　　　[*Exit* CATESBY.
　Buck. Now, my lord, what shall we do if we
　　perceive
Lord Hastings will not yield to our complots?
　Glo. Chop off his head; something we will
　　determine:　　　　　　　　193
And, look, when I am king, claim thou of me
The earldom of Hereford, and all the moveables
Whereof the king my brother stood possess'd.
　Buck. I'll claim that promise at your Grace's
　　hand.　　　　　　　　　197
　Glo. And look to have it yielded with all
　　kindness.
Come, let us sup betimes, that afterwards
We may digest our complots in some form. 200
　　　　　　　　　　　　　[*Exeunt.*

SCENE II.—*The Same. Before* LORD HASTINGS'
　　　　　　　　House.

Enter a Messenger.

　Mess. [*Knocking.*] My lord! my lord!
　Hast. [*Within.*] Who knocks?
　Mess. One from the Lord Stanley.
　Hast. [*Within.*] What is't o'clock?　　4
　Mess. Upon the stroke of four.

Enter HASTINGS.

　Hast. Cannot my Lord Stanley sleep these
　　tedious nights?
　Mess. So it appears by that I have to say.
First, he commends him to your noble self.
　Hast. What then?
　Mess. Then certifies your lordship, that this
　　night

He dreamt the boar had razed off his helm:
Besides, he says there are two councils held; 12
And that may be determin'd at the one
Which may make you and him to rue at the other.
Therefore he sends to know your lordship's pleasure,
If you will presently take horse with him, 16
And with all speed post with him towards the north,
To shun the danger that his soul divines.
  Hast. Go, fellow, go, return unto thy lord;
Bid him not fear the separated councils: 20
His honour and myself are at the one,
And at the other is my good friend Catesby;
Where nothing can proceed that toucheth us
Whereof I shall not have intelligence. 24
Tell him his fears are shallow, wanting instance:
And for his dreams, I wonder he's so fond
To trust the mockery of unquiet slumbers.
To fly the boar before the boar pursues, 28
Were to incense the boar to follow us
And make pursuit where he did mean no chase.
Go, bid thy master rise and come to me;
And we will both together to the Tower, 32
Where, he shall see, the boar will use us kindly.
  Mess. I'll go, my lord, and tell him what
you say.   [*Exit.*

Enter CATESBY.

  Cate. Many good morrows to my noble lord!
  Hast. Good morrow, Catesby; you are early
stirring. 36
What news, what news, in this our tottering state?
  Cate. It is a reeling world, indeed, my lord;
And I believe will never stand upright
Till Richard wear the garland of the realm. 40
  Hast. How! wear the garland! dost thou
mean the crown?
  Cate. Ay, my good lord.
  Hast. I'll have this crown of mine cut from
my shoulders
Before I'll see the crown so foul misplac'd. 44
But canst thou guess that he doth aim at it?
  Cate. Ay, on my life; and hopes to find you
forward
Upon his party for the gain thereof:
And thereupon he sends you this good news, 48
That this same very day your enemies,
The kindred of the queen, must die at Pomfret.
  Hast. Indeed, I am no mourner for that
news,
Because they have been still my adversaries; 52
But that I'll give my voice on Richard's side,
To bar my master's heirs in true descent,
God knows I will not do it, to the death.
  Cate. God keep your lordship in that gra-
cious mind! 56
  Hast. But I shall laugh at this a twelve-
month hence,
That they which brought me in my master's
hate,
I live to look upon their tragedy. 59
Well, Catesby, ere a fortnight make me older,
I'll send some packing that yet think not on't.

  Cate. 'Tis a vile thing to die, my gracious
lord,
When men are unprepar'd and look not for it.
  Hast. O monstrous, monstrous! and so falls
it out 64
With Rivers, Vaughan, Grey; and so 'twill do
With some men else, who think themselves as
safe
As thou and I; who, as thou know'st, are dear
To princely Richard and to Buckingham. 68
  Cate. The princes both make high account
of you;
[*Aside.*] For they account his head upon the
bridge.
  Hast. I know they do, and I have well de-
serv'd it.

Enter STANLEY.

Come on, come on; where is your boar-spear,
man? 72
Fear you the boar, and go so unprovided?
  Stan. My lord, good morrow; good morrow
Catesby:
You may jest on, but by the holy rood,
I do not like these several councils, I. 76
  Hast. My lord, I hold my life as dear as you
do yours;
And never, in my days, I do protest,
Was it so precious to me as 'tis now.
Think you, but that I know our state secure, 80
I would be so triumphant as I am?
  Stan. The lords at Pomfret, when they rode
from London,
Were jocund and suppos'd their state was sure,
And they indeed had no cause to mistrust; 84
But yet you see how soon the day o'ercast.
This sudden stab of rancour I misdoubt;
Pray God, I say, I prove a needless coward!
What, shall we toward the Tower? the day is
spent. 88
  Hast. Come, come, have with you. Wot
you what, my lord?
To-day the lords you talk of are beheaded.
  Stan. They, for their truth, might better
wear their heads,
Than some that have accus'd them wear their
hats. 92
But come, my lord, let's away.

Enter a Pursuivant.

  Hast. Go on before; I'll talk with this good
fellow.   [*Exeunt* STANLEY *and* CATESBY.
How now, sirrah! how goes the world with
thee?
  Purs. The better that your lordship please
to ask. 96
  Hast. I tell thee, man, 'tis better with me
now
Than when I met thee last where now we meet:
Then was I going prisoner to the Tower,
By the suggestion of the queen's allies; 100
But now, I tell thee,—keep it to thyself,—
This day those enemies are put to death,
And I in better state than e'er I was.
  Purs. God hold it to your honour's good
content! 104

Hast. Gramercy, fellow: there, drink that
  for me.   [*Throws him his purse.*
Purs. God save your lordship.   [*Exit.*

        Enter a Priest.

Pr. Well met, my lord; I am glad to see your
  honour.
Hast. I thank thee, good Sir John, with all
  my heart.   108
I am in your debt for your last exercise;
Come the next Sabbath, and I will content you.

     Enter BUCKINGHAM.

Buck. What, talking with a priest, lord
  chamberlain?
Your friends at Pomfret, they do need the priest:
Your honour hath no shriving work in hand. 113
  Hast. Good faith, and when I met this holy
  man,
The men you talk of came into my mind.
What, go you toward the Tower?   116
  Buck. I do, my lord; but long I shall not
  stay:
I shall return before your lordship thence.
  Hast. Nay, like enough, for I stay dinner
  there.
  Buck. [*Aside.*] And supper too, although
  thou know'st it not.   120
Come, will you go?
  Hast.   I'll wait upon your lordship.
                         [*Exeunt.*

  SCENE III.—*Pomfret. Before the Castle.*

Enter RATCLIFF, *with halberds, carrying* RIVERS,
  GREY, *and* VAUGHAN *to death.*

Riv. Sir Richard Ratcliff, let me tell thee
  this:
To-day shalt thou behold a subject die
For truth, for duty, and for loyalty.
  Grey. God bless the prince from all the pack
  of you!   4
A knot you are of damned blood-suckers.
  Vaugh. You live that shall cry woe for this
  hereafter.
  Rat. Dispatch; the limit of your lives is out.
  Riv. O Pomfret, Pomfret! O thou bloody
  prison!   8
Fatal and ominous to noble peers!
Within the guilty closure of thy walls
Richard the Second here was hack'd to death;
And, for more slander to thy dismal seat,   12
We give thee up our guiltless blood to drink.
  Grey. Now Margaret's curse is fall'n upon
  our heads,
When she exclaim'd on Hastings, you, and I,
For standing by when Richard stabb'd her
  son.   16
  Riv. Then curs'd she Richard, then curs'd
  she Buckingham,
Then curs'd she Hastings: O! remember, God,
To hear her prayer for them, as now for us;
And for my sister and her princely sons,   20
Be satisfied, dear God, with our true blood,
Which, as thou know'st, unjustly must be spilt.
  Rat. Make haste; the hour of death is expiate.

Riv. Come, Grey, come, Vaughan; let us
  here embrace: 24
And take our leave until we meet in heaven.
                        [*Exeunt.*

   SCENE IV.—*London. The Tower.*

BUCKINGHAM, STANLEY, HASTINGS, *the* BISHOP
  OF ELY, RATCLIFF, LOVEL, *and Others, sitting
  at a table. Officers of the Council attending.*

Hast. My lords, at once: the cause why we
  are met
Is to determine of the coronation:
In God's name, speak, when is the royal day?
  Buck. Are all things ready for that royal
  time?   4
  Stan. It is; and wants but nomination.
  Ely. To-morrow then I judge a happy day.
  Buck. Who knows the Lord Protector's mind
  herein?
Who is most inward with the noble duke?   8
  Ely. Your Grace, we think, should soonest
  know his mind.
  Buck. We know each other's faces; for our
  hearts,
He knows no more of mine than I of yours;
Nor I of his, my lord, than you of mine.   12
Lord Hastings, you and he are near in love.
  Hast. I thank his Grace, I know he loves me
  well;
But, for his purpose in the coronation,
I have not sounded him, nor he deliver'd   16
His gracious pleasure any way therein:
But you, my noble lords, may name the time;
And in the duke's behalf I'll give my voice,
Which, I presume, he'll take in gentle part. 20

     Enter GLOUCESTER.

Ely. In happy time, here comes the duke
  himself.
  Glo. My noble lords and cousins all, good
  morrow.
I have been long a sleeper; but, I trust,
My absence doth neglect no great design,   24
Which by my presence might have been con-
  cluded.
  Buck. Had you not come upon your cue, my
  lord,
William Lord Hastings had pronounc'd your
  part,
I mean, your voice, for crowning of the king. 28
  Glo. Than my Lord Hastings no man might
  be bolder:
His lordship knows me well, and loves me well.
My Lord of Ely, when I was last in Holborn,
I saw good strawberries in your garden there; 32
I do beseech you send for some of them.
  Ely. Marry, and will, my lord, with all my
  heart.   [*Exit.*
  Glo. Cousin of Buckingham, a word with
  you.   [*Takes him aside.*
Catesby hath sounded Hastings in our busi-
  ness,   36
And finds the testy gentleman so hot,
That he will lose his head ere give consent
His master's child, as worshipfully he terms it,

Shall lose the royalty of England's throne. 40
Buck. Withdraw yourself a while; I'll go
with you.
    [*Exeunt* GLOUCESTER *and* BUCKINGHAM.
Stan. We have not yet set down this day of
triumph.
To-morrow, in my judgment, is too sudden;
For I myself am not so well provided 44
As else I would be, were the day prolong'd.

Re-enter BISHOP OF ELY.

Ely. Where is my lord, the Duke of Glou-
cester?
I have sent for these strawberries.
Hast. His Grace looks cheerfully and smooth
this morning: 48
There's some conceit or other likes him well,
When that he bids good morrow with such
spirit.
I think there's never a man in Christendom
Can lesser hide his hate or love than he; 52
For by his face straight shall you know his heart.
Stan. What of his heart perceiv'd you in his
face
By any livelihood he show'd to-day?
Hast. Marry, that with no man here he is
offended; 56
For, were he, he had shown it in his looks.

Re-enter GLOUCESTER *and* BUCKINGHAM.

Glo. I pray you all, tell me what they deserve
That do conspire my death with devilish plots
Of damned witchcraft, and that have prevail'd 60
Upon my body with their hellish charms?
Hast. The tender love I bear your Grace, my
lord,
Makes me most forward in this princely presence
To doom th' offenders, whosoe'er they be: 64
I say, my lord, they have deserved death.
Glo. Then be your eyes the witness of their evil.
Look how I am bewitch'd; behold mine arm
Is like a blasted sapling, wither'd up: 68
And this is Edward's wife, that monstrous witch
Consorted with that harlot strumpet Shore,
That by their witchcraft thus have marked me.
Hast. If they have done this thing, my noble
lord,— 72
Glo. If! thou protector of this damned
strumpet,
Talk'st thou to me of ifs? Thou art a traitor:
Off with his head! now, by Saint Paul, I swear,
I will not dine until I see the same. 76
Lovel and Ratcliff, look that it be done:
The rest, that love me, rise, and follow me.
    [*Exeunt all but* HASTINGS, RATCLIFF,
        and LOVEL.
Hast. Woe, woe, for England! not a whit for
me;
For I, too fond, might have prevented this. 80
Stanley did dream the boar did raze his helm;
And I did scorn it, and disdain'd to fly.
Three times to-day my foot-cloth horse did
stumble,
And startled when he looked upon the Tower, 84
As loath to bear me to the slaughter-house.
O! now I need the priest that spake to me:

I now repent I told the pursuivant,
As too triumphing, how mine enemies 88
To-day at Pomfret bloodily were butcher'd
And I myself secure in grace and favour.
O Margaret, Margaret! now thy heavy curse
Is lighted on poor Hastings' wretched head. 92
Rat. Come, come, dispatch; the duke would
be at dinner:
Make a short shrift, he longs to see your head.
Hast. O momentary grace of mortal man,
Which we more hunt for than the grace of
God! 96
Who builds his hope in air of your good looks,
Lives like a drunken sailor on a mast;
Ready with every nod to tumble down
Into the fatal bowels of the deep. 100
Lov. Come, come, dispatch; 'tis bootless to
exclaim.
Hast. O bloody Richard! miserable Eng-
land!
I prophesy the fearfull'st time to thee
That ever wretched age hath look'd upon. 104
Come, lead me to the block; bear him my head:
They smile at me who shortly shall be dead.
    Exeunt.

SCENE V.—*London. The Tower Walls.*

Enter GLOUCESTER *and* BUCKINGHAM, *in rotten
armour, marvellous ill-favoured.*

Glo. Come, cousin, canst thou quake, and
change thy colour,
Murder thy breath in middle of a word,
And then again begin, and stop again,
As if thou wert distraught and mad with terror?
Buck. Tut! I can counterfeit the deep
tragedian, 5
Speak and look back, and pry on every side,
Tremble and start at wagging of a straw,
Intending deep suspicion: ghastly looks 8
Are at my service, like enforced smiles;
And both are ready in their offices,
At any time, to grace my stratagems.
But what! is Catesby gone? 12
Glo. He is; and, see, he brings the mayor
along.

Enter the Lord Mayor *and* CATESBY.

Buck. Lord Mayor,—
Glo. Look to the drawbridge there!
Buck. Hark! a drum.
Glo. Catesby, o'erlook the walls. 16
Buck. Lord Mayor, the reason we have
sent,—
Glo. Look back, defend thee; here are ene-
mies.
Buck. God and our innocency defend and
guard us!

Enter LOVEL *and* RATCLIFF, *with* HASTINGS' *head.*

Glo. Be patient, they are friends, Ratcliff and
Lovel. 20
Lov. Here is the head of that ignoble traitor,
The dangerous and unsuspected Hastings.
Glo. So dear I lov'd the man, that I must weep.
I took him for the plainest harmless creature 24

at breath'd upon the earth a Christian;
ade him my book, wherein my soul recorded
he history of all her secret thoughts:
smooth he daub'd his vice with show of
    virtue,   28
at, his apparent open guilt omitted,
mean his conversation with Shore's wife,
e liv'd from all attainder of suspect.
  Buck. Well, well, he was the covert'st shel-
    ter'd traitor   32
at ever liv'd.
ould you imagine, or almost believe,—
ere't not that by great preservation
e live to tell it, that the subtle traitor   36
his day had plotted, in the council-house,
murder me and my good Lord of Glou-
    cester?
  May. Had he done so?
  Glo. What! think you we are Turks or in-
    fidels?   40
r that we would, against the form of law,
roceed thus rashly in the villain's death,
ut that the extreme peril of the case,
he peace of England and our person's safety,   44
nforc'd us to this execution?
  May. Now, fair befall you! he deserv'd his
    death;
nd your good Graces both have well pro-
    ceeded,
o warn false traitors from the like attempts.   48
never look'd for better at his hands,
fter he once fell in with Mistress Shore.
  Buck. Yet had we not determin'd he should die,
ntil your lordship came to see his end: 52
hich now the loving haste of these our friends,
omething against our meaning, hath pre-
    vented:
ecause, my lord, we would have had you heard
he traitor speak, and timorously confess   56
he manner and the purpose of his treason;
hat you might well have signified the same
nto the citizens, who haply may
isconster us in him, and wail his death.   60
  May. But, my good lord, your Grace's word
    shall serve,
s well as I had seen and heard him speak:
nd do not doubt, right noble princes both,
ut I'll acquaint our duteous citizens   64
ith all your just proceedings in this cause.
  Glo. And to that end we wish'd your lordship
    here,
o avoid the censures of the carping world.
  Buck. But since you come too late of our
    intent,   68
et witness what you hear we did intend:
nd so, my good Lord Mayor, we bid farewell.
    [Exit Lord Mayor.
  Glo. Go, after, after, cousin Buckingham,
he mayor towards Guildhall hies him in all
    post: 72
here, at your meetest vantage of the time,
fer the bastardy of Edward's children:
ell them how Edward put to death a citizen,
nly for saying he would make his son   76
eir to the crown; meaning indeed his house,
hich by the sign thereof was termed so.

Moreover, urge his hateful luxury
And bestial appetite in change of lust;   80
Which stretch'd unto their servants, daughters,
    wives,
Even where his raging eye or savage heart
Without control lusted to make a prey.
Nay, for a need, thus far come near my
    person: 84
Tell them, when that my mother went with child
Of that insatiate Edward, noble York
My princely father then had wars in France;
And, by true computation of the time,   88
Found that the issue was not his begot;
Which well appeared in his lineaments,
Being nothing like the noble duke my father.
Yet touch this sparingly, as 'twere far off;   92
Because, my lord, you know my mother lives.
  Buck. Doubt not, my lord, I'll play the
    orator
As if the golden fee for which I plead
Were for myself: and so, my lord, adieu.   96
  Glo. If you thrive well, bring them to Bay-
    nard's Castle;
Where you shall find me well accompanied
With reverend fathers and well-learned bishops.
  Buck. I go; and towards three or four
    o'clock   100
Look for the news that the Guildhall affords.
    [Exit.
  Glo. Go, Lovel, with all speed to Doctor
    Shaw;
[To CATESBY.] Go thou to Friar Penker; bid
    them both
Meet me within this hour at Baynard's Castle.
    [Exeunt LOVEL *and* CATESBY.
Now will I in, to take some privy order,   105
To draw the brats of Clarence out of sight;
And to give notice that no manner person
Have any time recourse unto the princes. *[Exit.*

SCENE VI.—*The Same. A Street.*

Enter a Scrivener.

  Scriv. Here is the indictment of the good
    Lord Hastings;
Which in a set hand fairly is engross'd,
That it may be to-day read o'er in Paul's:
And mark how well the sequel hangs together.   4
Eleven hours I have spent to write it over,
For yesternight by Catesby was it sent me.
The precedent was full as long a-doing;
And yet within these five hours Hastings liv'd,   8
Untainted, unexamin'd, free, at liberty.
Here's a good world the while! Who is so gross
That cannot see this palpable device?
Yet who so bold but says he sees it not?   12
Bad is the world; and all will come to naught,
When such ill dealing must be seen in thought.
    [Exit.

SCENE VII.—*The Same. The Court of Baynard's Castle.*

Enter GLOUCESTER *and* BUCKINGHAM, *meeting.*

  Glo. How now, how now! what say the
    citizens?
  Buck. Now, by the holy mother of our Lord,

The citizens are mum, say not a word.
 Glo. Touch'd you the bastardy of Edward's
  children? 4
 Buck. I did; with his contract with Lady
  Lucy,
And his contract by deputy in France;
The insatiate greediness of his desires,
And his enforcement of the city wives; 8
His tyranny for trifles; his own bastardy,
As being got, your father then in France,
And his resemblance, being not like the duke:
Withal I did infer your lineaments, 12
Being the right idea of your father,
Both in your form and nobleness of mind;
Laid open all your victories in Scotland,
Your discipline in war, wisdom in peace, 16
Your bounty, virtue, fair humility;
Indeed, left nothing fitting for your purpose
Untouch'd or slightly handled in discourse;
And when my oratory drew toward end, 20
I bade them that did love their country's good
Cry 'God save Richard, England's royal king!'
 Glo. And did they so?
 Buck. No, so God help me, they spake not a
  word; 24
But, like dumb statuas or breathing stones,
Star'd each on other, and look'd deadly pale.
Which when I saw, I reprehended them;
And ask'd the mayor what meant this wilful
 silence: 28
His answer was, the people were not wont
To be spoke to but by the recorder.
Then he was urg'd to tell my tale again:
'Thus saith the duke, thus hath the duke
 infer'd;' 32
But nothing spoke in warrant from himself.
When he had done, some followers of mine own,
At lower end of the hall, hurl'd up their caps,
And some ten voices cried, 'God save King
 Richard!' 36
And thus I took the vantage of those few,
'Thanks, gentle citizens and friends,' quoth I;
'This general applause and cheerful shout
Argues your wisdom and your love to Richard:'
And even here brake off, and came away. 41
 Glo. What tongueless blocks were they!
  would they not speak?
Will not the mayor then and his brethren come?
 Buck. The mayor is here at hand. Intend
  some fear; 44
Be not you spoke with but by mighty suit:
And look you get a prayer-book in your hand,
And stand between two churchmen, good my
 lord:
For on that ground I'll make a holy descant: 48
And be not easily won to our requests;
Play the maid's part, still answer nay, and take it.
 Glo. I go; and if you plead as well for them
As I can say nay to thee for myself, 52
No doubt we bring it to a happy issue.
 Buck. Go, go, up to the leads! the Lord
  Mayor knocks. [*Exit* GLOUCESTER.

Enter the Lord Mayor, Aldermen, *and* Citizens.
Welcome, my lord: I dance attendance here;
I think the duke will not be spoke withal. 56

Enter, from the Castle, CATESBY.

Now, Catesby! what says your lord to my re-
 quest?
 Cate. He doth entreat your Grace, my noble
  lord,
To visit him to-morrow or next day.
He is within, with two right reverend fathers,
Divinely bent to meditation;
And in no worldly suit would he be mov'd,
To draw him from his holy exercise.
 Buck. Return, good Catesby, to the gracious
  duke:
Tell him, myself, the mayor and aldermen,
In deep designs in matter of great moment,
No less importing than our general good,
Are come to have some conference with his
 Grace.
 Cate. I'll signify so much unto him straight.
              [*Exit.*
 Buck. Ah, ha, my lord, this prince is not an
  Edward!
He is not lolling on a lewd day-bed,
But on his knees at meditation;
Not dallying with a brace of courtezans,
But meditating with two deep divines;
Not sleeping, to engross his idle body,
But praying, to enrich his watchful soul.
Happy were England, would this virtuous prince
Take on his Grace the sovereignty thereof:
But sore, I fear, we shall not win him to it.
 May. Marry, God defend his Grace should
  say us nay!
 Buck. I fear he will. Here Catesby comes
  again.

Re-enter CATESBY.

Now, Catesby, what says his Grace?
 Cate. He wonders to what end you have
  assembled
Such troops of citizens to come to him,
His Grace not being warn'd thereof before:
My lord, he fears you mean no good to him.
 Buck. Sorry I am my noble cousin should
Suspect me that I mean no good to him.
By heaven, we come to him in perfect love;
And so once more return, and tell his Grace.
           [*Exit* CATESBY.
When holy and devout religious men
Are at their beads, 'tis much to draw them
 thence;
So sweet is zealous contemplation.

Enter GLOUCESTER, *in a gallery above, between*
 two Bishops. CATESBY *returns.*

 May. See, where his Grace stands 'tween two
  clergymen!
 Buck. Two props of virtue for a Christian
  prince,
To stay him from the fall of vanity;
And, see, a book of prayer in his hand;
True ornament to know a holy man.
Famous Plantagenet, most gracious prince,
Lend favourable ear to our requests, 10
And pardon us the interruption
Of thy devotion, and right Christian zeal.

Glo. My lord, there needs no such apology;
to beseech your Grace to pardon me,   104
who, earnest in the service of my God,
deferr'd the visitation of my friends.
But, leaving this, what is your Grace's pleasure?
Buck. Even that, I hope, which pleaseth God
above,   108
and all good men of this ungovern'd isle.
Glo. I do suspect I have done some offence
that seems disgracious in the city's eye;
and that you come to reprehend my ignorance.
Buck. You have, my lord: would it might
please your Grace,   113
to our entreaties to amend your fault!
Glo. Else wherefore breathe I in a Christian
land?
Buck. Know then, it is your fault that you
resign   116
the supreme seat, the throne majestical,
the sceptred office of your ancestors,
your state of fortune and your due of birth,
the lineal glory of your royal house;   120
to the corruption of a blemish'd stock;
whiles, in the mildness of your sleepy thoughts,—
which here we waken to our country's good,—
this noble isle doth want her proper limbs;   124
her face defac'd with scars of infamy,
her royal stock graft with ignoble plants,
and almost shoulder'd in the swallowing gulf
of dark forgetfulness and deep oblivion.   128
which to recure we heartily solicit
your gracious self to take on you the charge
and kingly government of this your land;
not as protector, steward, substitute,   132
or lowly factor for another's gain;
but as successively from blood to blood,
your right of birth, your empery, your own.
for this, consorted with the citizens,   136
your very worshipful and loving friends,
and by their vehement instigation,
in this just cause come I to move your Grace.
Glo. I cannot tell, if to depart in silence 140
or bitterly to speak in your reproof,
best fitteth my degree or your condition:
if not to answer, you might haply think
tongue-tied ambition, not replying, yielded   144
to bear the golden yoke of sov'reignty,
which fondly you would here impose on me;
or to reprove you for this suit of yours,
if season'd with your faithful love to me,   148
then, on the other side, I check'd my friends.
therefore, to speak, and to avoid the first,
and then, in speaking, not to incur the last,
definitively thus I answer you.   152
Your love deserves my thanks; but my desert
unmeritable shuns your high request.
First, if all obstacles were cut away,
and that my path were even to the crown,   156
as the ripe revenue and due of birth,
yet so much is my poverty of spirit,
so mighty and so many my defects,
that I would rather hide me from my greatness,
being a bark to brook no mighty sea,   161
than in my greatness covet to be hid,
and in the vapour of my glory smother'd.
But, God be thank'd, there is no need of me;   164

And much I need to help you, were there need;
The royal tree hath left us royal fruit,
Which, mellow'd by the stealing hours of time,
Will well become the seat of majesty,   168
And make, no doubt, us happy by his reign.
On him I lay that you would lay on me,
The right and fortune of his happy stars;
Which God defend that I should wring from
him!   172
Buck. My lord, this argues conscience in
your Grace;
But the respects thereof are nice and trivial,
All circumstances well considered.
You say that Edward is your brother's son: 176
So say we too, but not by Edward's wife;
For first was he contract to Lady Lucy,
Your mother lives a witness to his vow,
And afterward by substitute betroth'd   180
To Bona, sister to the King of France.
These both put by, a poor petitioner,
A care-craz'd mother to a many sons,
A beauty-waning and distressed widow,   184
Even in the afternoon of her best days,
Made prize and purchase of his wanton eye,
Seduc'd the pitch and height of his degree
To base declension and loath'd bigamy: 188
By her, in his unlawful bed, he got
This Edward, whom our manners call the prince.
More bitterly could I expostulate,
Save that, for reverence to some alive,   192
I give a sparing limit to my tongue.
Then, good my lord, take to your royal self
This proffer'd benefit of dignity;
If not to bless us and the land withal,   196
Yet to draw forth your noble ancestry
From the corruption of abusing times,
Unto a lineal true-derived course.
May. Do, good my lord; your citizens
entreat you.   200
Buck. Refuse not, mighty lord, this proffer'd
love.
Cate. O! make them joyful: grant their law-
ful suit!
Glo. Alas! why would you heap those cares
on me?
I am unfit for state and majesty: 204
I do beseech you, take it not amiss,
I cannot nor I will not yield to you.
Buck. If you refuse it, as, in love and zeal,
Loath to depose the child, your brother's son;
As well we know your tenderness of heart   209
And gentle, kind, effeminate remorse,
Which we have noted in you to your kindred,
And egally, indeed, to all estates,   212
Yet whether you accept our suit or no,
Your brother's son shall never reign our king;
But we will plant some other in the throne,
To the disgrace and downfall of your house: 216
And in this resolution here we leave you.
Come, citizens, we will entreat no more.
                              [*Exit* BUCKINGHAM *and*
                                        Citizens.
Cate. Call them again, sweet prince; accept
their suit:
If you deny them, all the land will rue it.   220
Glo. Will you enforce me to a world of cares?

Call them again: I am not made of stone,
But penetrable to your kind entreats,
[*Exit* CATESBY.
Albeit against my conscience and my soul. 224

Re-enter BUCKINGHAM *and the rest.*

Cousin of Buckingham, and sage, grave men,
Since you will buckle fortune on my back,
To bear her burden, whe'r I will or no,
I must have patience to endure the load: 228
But if black scandal or foul-fac'd reproach
Attend the sequel of your imposition,
Your mere enforcement shall acquittance me
From all the impure blots and stains thereof;
For God doth know, and you may partly see, 233
How far I am from the desire of this.
  May. God bless your Grace! we see it, and
    will say it.
  Glo. In saying so, you shall but say the truth.
  Buck. Then I salute you with this royal title:
Long live King Richard, England's worthy king!
  All. Amen.
  Buck. To-morrow may it please you to be
    crown'd?   240
  Glo. Even when you please, for you will have
    it so.
  Buck. To-morrow then we will attend your
    Grace:
And so most joyfully we take our leave.
  Glo. [*To the* Bishops.] Come, let us to our
    holy work again.   244
Farewell, my cousin;—farewell, gentle friends.
[*Exeunt.*

ACT IV

SCENE I.—*London. Before the Tower.*

Enter on one side, QUEEN ELIZABETH, DUCHESS
OF YORK, *and* MARQUESS OF DORSET; *on the
other,* ANNE, DUCHESS OF GLOUCESTER, *leading*
LADY MARGARET PLANTAGENET, CLARENCE'S
young daughter.

  Duch. Who meets us here? my niece Plan-
    tagenet,
Led in the hand of her kind aunt of Gloucester?
Now, for my life, she's wand'ring to the Tower,
On pure heart's love, to greet the tender princes.
Daughter, well met.
  Anne.   God give your Graces both 5
A happy and a joyful time of day!
  Q. Eliz. As much to you, good sister!
    whither away?
  Anne. No further than the Tower; and, as
    I guess,   8
Upon the like devotion as yourselves,
To gratulate the gentle princes there.
  Q. Eliz. Kind sister, thanks: we'll enter all
    together:—

Enter BRAKENBURY.

And, in good time, here the lieutenant comes. 12
Master lieutenant, pray you, by your leave,
How doth the prince, and my young son of York?
  Brak. Right well, dear madam. By your
    patience,

I may not suffer you to visit them:
The king hath strictly charg'd the contrary.
  Q. Eliz. The king! who's that?
  Brak.   I mean the Lord Protecto
  Q. Eliz. The Lord protect him from th
    kingly title!
Hath he set bounds between their love and m
I am their mother; who shall bar me from then
  Duch. I am their father's mother; I will s
    them.
  Anne. Their aunt I am in law, in love the
    mother:
Then bring me to their sights; I'll bear t'
    blame,
And take thy office from thee, on my peril.
  Brak. No, madam, no, I may not leave it s
I am bound by oath, and therefore pardon m
[*Ex*

Enter STANLEY.

  Stan. Let me but meet you, ladies, one ho
    hence,
And I'll salute your Grace of York as moth
And reverend looker-on, of two fair queens
[*To the* DUCHESS OF GLOUCESTER.] Come, m
    dam, you must straight to Westminster,
There to be crowned Richard's royal queen.
  Q. Eliz. Ah! cut my lace asunder,
That my pent heart may have some scope to be
Or else I swoon with this dead-killing news.
  Anne. Despiteful tidings! O! unpleasi
    news!
  Dor. Be of good cheer: mother, how fai
    your Grace?
  Q. Eliz. O, Dorset! speak not to me, get th
    gone;
Death and destruction dog thee at the heels:
Thy mother's name is ominous to children.
If thou wilt outstrip death, go cross the seas,
And live with Richmond, from the reach of he
Go, hie thee, hie thee, from this slaughter-hou
Lest thou increase the number of the dead,
And make me die the thrall of Margaret's cur
Nor mother, wife, nor England's counted quee
  Stan. Full of wise care is this your couns
    madam.
[*To* DORSET.] Take all the swift advantage of t
    hours;
You shall have letters from me to my son
In your behalf, to meet you on the way:
Be not ta'en tardy by unwise delay.
  Duch. O ill-dispersing wind of misery!
O! my accursed womb, the bed of death,
A cockatrice hast thou hatch'd to the world,
Whose unavoided eye is murderous!
  Stan. Come, madam, come; I in all ha
    was sent.
  Anne. And I with all unwillingness will g
O! would to God that the inclusive verge
Of golden metal that must round my brow
Were red-hot steel to sear me to the brain.
Anointed let me be with deadly venom;
And die, ere men can say 'God save the quee
  Q. Eliz. Go, go, poor soul, I envy not t
    glory;
To feed my humour, wish thyself no harm.

Anne. No! why? When he, that is my husband now

ame to me, as I follow'd Henry's corse;

hen scarce the blood was well wash'd from his hands,

hich issu'd from my other angel husband, 68

nd that dead saint which then I weeping follow'd;

! when I say, I look'd on Richard's face,

his was my wish, 'Be thou,' quoth I, 'accurs'd,

or making me so young, so old a widow! 72

nd, when thou wedd'st, let sorrow haunt thy bed;

nd be thy wife—if any be so mad—

Iore miserable by the life of thee

han thou hast made me by my dear lord's death!' 76

o! ere I can repeat this curse again,

ithin so small a time, my woman's heart

rossly grew captive to his honey words, 79

nd prov'd the subject of mine own soul's curse;

hich hitherto hath held mine eyes from rest;

or never yet one hour in his bed

id I enjoy the golden dew of sleep,

ut with his timorous dreams was still awak'd.

esides, he hates me for my father Warwick, 85

nd will, no doubt, shortly be rid of me.

Q. Eliz. Poor heart, adieu! I pity thy complaining.

Anne. No more than with my soul I mourn for yours. 88

Q. Eliz. Farewell! thou woeful welcomer of glory!

Anne. Adieu, poor soul, that tak'st thy leave of it!

Duch. [*To* DORSET.] Go thou to Richmond, and good fortune guide thee!

To ANNE.] Go thou to Richard, and good angels tend thee! 92

To Q. ELIZABETH.] Go thou to sanctuary, and good thoughts possess thee!

to my grave, where peace and rest lie with me!

ighty odd years of sorrow have I seen,

nd each hour's joy wrack'd with a week of teen.

Q. Eliz. Stay yet, look back with me unto the Tower. 97

ity, you ancient stones, those tender babes

hom envy hath immur'd within your walls,

ough cradle for such little pretty ones! 100

tude ragged nurse, old sullen playfellow

or tender princes, use my babies well.

o foolish sorrow bids your stones farewell.

[*Exeunt.*]

SCENE II.—*The Same. A Room of State in the Palace.*

ennet. RICHARD, *in pomp, crowned:* BUCKINGHAM, CATESBY, *a* Page, *and Others.*

K. Rich. Stand all apart. Cousin of Buckingham.

Buck. My gracious sovereign!

K. Rich. Give me thy hand. [*He ascends the throne.*] Thus high, by thy advice,

nd thy assistance, is King Richard seated: 4

ut shall we wear these glories for a day?

Or shall they last, and we rejoice in them?

Buck. Still live they, and for ever let them last!

K. Rich. Ah! Buckingham, now do I play the touch, 8

To try if thou be current gold indeed:

Young Edward lives: think now what I would speak.

Buck. Say on, my loving lord.

K. Rich. Why, Buckingham, I say, I would be king. 12

Buck. Why, so you are, my thrice-renowned liege.

K. Rich. Ha! am I king? 'Tis so: but Edward lives.

Buck. True, noble prince.

K. Rich. O bitter consequence,

That Edward still should live! 'True, noble prince!' 16

Cousin, thou wast not wont to be so dull:

Shall I be plain? I wish the bastards dead;

And I would have it suddenly perform'd.

What sayst thou now? speak suddenly, be brief. 20

Buck. Your Grace may do your pleasure.

K. Rich. Tut, tut! thou art all ice, thy kindness freezes:

Say, have I thy consent that they shall die?

Buck. Give me some little breath, some pause, dear lord, 24

Before I positively speak in this:

I will resolve you herein presently. [*Exit.*]

Cate. [*Aside to another.*] The king is angry: see, he gnaws his lip.

K. Rich. [*Descends from his throne.*] I will converse with iron-witted fools 28

And unrespective boys: none are for me

That look into me with considerate eyes.

High-reaching Buckingham grows circumspect. Boy! 32

Page. My lord!

K. Rich. Know'st thou not any whom corrupting gold

Will tempt unto a close exploit of death?

Page. I know a discontented gentleman, 36

Whose humble means match not his haughty spirit:

Gold were as good as twenty orators,

And will, no doubt, tempt him to anything.

K. Rich. What is his name?

Page. His name, my lord, is Tyrrell.

K. Rich. I partly know the man: go, call him hither. [*Exit* Page.

The deep-revolving witty Buckingham

No more shall be the neighbour to my counsel.

Hath he so long held out with me untir'd, 44

And stops he now for breath? well, be it so.

Enter STANLEY.

How now, Lord Stanley! what's the news?

Stan. Know, my loving lord,

The Marquess Dorset, as I hear, is fled 48

To Richmond, in the parts where he abides.

K. Rich. Come hither, Catesby: rumour it abroad,

That Anne my wife is very grievous sick;

I will take order for her keeping close.   52
Inquire me out some mean poor gentleman,
Whom I will marry straight to Clarence'
    daughter:
The boy is foolish, and I fear not him.
Look, how thou dream'st! I say again, give out 56
That Anne my queen is sick, and like to die:
About it; for it stands me much upon,
To stop all hopes whose growth may damage
    me.   [Exit CATESBY.
I must be married to my brother's daughter, 60
Or else my kingdom stands on brittle glass.
Murder her brothers, and then marry her!
Uncertain way of gain! But I am in
So far in blood, that sin will pluck on sin: 64
Tear-falling pity dwells not in this eye.

Re-enter Page, *with* TYRRELL.

Is thy name Tyrrell?
    Tyr. James Tyrrell, and your most obedient
        subject.
    K. Rich. Art thou, indeed?
    Tyr.   Prove me, my gracious lord. 68
    K. Rich. Dar'st thou resolve to kill a friend
        of mine?
    Tyr. Please you; but I had rather kill two
        enemies,
    K. Rich. Why, then thou hast it: two deep
        enemies,
Foes to my rest, and my sweet sleep's disturbers,
Are they that I would have thee deal upon. 73
Tyrrell, I mean those bastards in the Tower.
    Tyr. Let me have open means to come to
        them,
And soon I'll rid you from the fear of them. 76
    K. Rich. Thou sing'st sweet music. Hark,
        come hither, Tyrrell:
Go, by this token: rise, and lend thine ear.
                            [*Whispers.*
There is no more but so: say it is done,
And I will love thee, and prefer thee for it.   80
    Tyr. I will dispatch it straight.   [*Exit.*

Re-enter BUCKINGHAM.

    Buck. My lord, I have consider'd in my mind
The late demand that you did sound me in.
    K. Rich. Well, let that rest. Dorset is fled
        to Richmond.   84
    Buck. I hear the news, my lord.
    K. Rich. Stanley, he is your wife's son: well,
        look to it.
    Buck. My lord, I claim the gift, my due by
        promise,
For which your honour and your faith is
        pawn'd;   88
The earldom of Hereford and the moveables
Which you have promised I shall possess.
    K. Rich. Stanley, look to your wife: if she
        convey
Letters to Richmond, you shall answer it. 92
    Buck. What says your highness to my just
        request?
    K. Rich. I do remember me, Henry the
        Sixth
Did prophesy that Richmond should be king,
When Richmond was a little peevish boy. 96

A king! perhaps—
    Buck. My lord!
    K. Rich. How chance the prophet could n
        at that time
Have told me, I being by, that I should k
        him?   1
    Buck. My lord, your promise for the ea
        dom,—
    K. Rich. Richmond! When last I was
        Exeter,
The mayor in courtesy show'd me the castle
And call'd it Rougemont: at which name
        started,   1
Because a bard of Ireland told me once
I should not live long after I saw Richmond.
    Buck. My lord!
    K. Rich. Ay, what's o'clock?   1
    Buck. I am thus bold to put your Grace
        mind
Of what you promis'd me.
    K. Rich. Well, but what is't o'clock?
    Buck.   Upon the stroke of te
    K. Rich. Well, let it strike.
    Buck.   Why let it strike?
    K. Rich. Because that, like a Jack, th
        keep'st the stroke
Betwixt thy begging and my meditation.
I am not in the giving vein to-day.
    Buck. Why, then resolve me whe'r you wi
        or no.
    K. Rich. Thou troublest me: I am not in t
        vein.   [*Exeunt* KING RICHARD *and Tra*
    Buck. And is it thus? repays he my de
        service
With such contempt? made I him king for thi
O, let me think on Hastings, and be gone 1
To Brecknock, while my fearful head is on.
                                    [*Ex.*

SCENE III.—*The Same.*

Enter TYRRELL.

    Tyr. The tyrannous and bloody act is don
The most arch deed of piteous massacre
That ever yet this land was guilty of.
Dighton and Forrest, whom I did suborn
To do this piece of ruthless butchery,
Albeit they were flesh'd villains, bloody dog
Melting with tenderness and mild compassio
Wept like to children in their death's sad stor
'Oh! thus,' quoth Dighton, 'lay the gent
    babes:'
'Thus, thus,' quoth Forrest, 'girdling o
    another
Within their alabaster innocent arms:
Their lips were four red roses on a stalk,
Which in their summer beauty kiss'd each othe
A book of prayers on their pillow lay;
Which once,' quoth Forrest, 'almost chang
    my mind;
But, O, the devil'—there the villain stopp'd;
When Dighton thus told on: 'We smothered
The most replenished sweet work of nature,
That from the prime creation e'er she fram'd
Hence both are gone with conscience and r
    morse;   2

they could not speak; and so I left them both,
to bear this tidings to the bloody king:
and here he comes.

Enter KING RICHARD.

                    All health, my sovereign lord!
K. Rich. Kind Tyrrell, am I happy in thy
     news?
Tyr. If to have done the thing you gave in
     charge
Beget your happiness, be happy then,
For it is done.
K. Rich.   But didst thou see them dead?
Tyr. I did, my lord.
K. Rich.   And buried, gentle Tyrrell?
Tyr. The chaplain of the Tower hath buried
     them;   29
But how or in what place I do not know.
K. Rich. Come to me, Tyrrell, soon at after-
     supper,
When thou shalt tell the process of their
     death.   32
Meantime, but think how I may do thee good,
And be inheritor of thy desire.
Farewell till then.
Tyr.   I humbly take my leave. [*Exit.*
K. Rich. The son of Clarence have I pent up
     close;   36
His daughter meanly have I match'd in mar-
     riage;
The sons of Edward sleep in Abraham's bosom,
And Anne my wife hath bid the world good
     night.
Now, for I know the Breton Richmond aims 40
At young Elizabeth, my brother's daughter,
And, by that knot, looks proudly on the crown,
To her go I, a jolly thriving wooer.

Enter CATESBY.

Cate. My lord!   44
K. Rich. Good or bad news, that thou com'st
     in so bluntly?
Cate. Bad news, my lord: Morton is fled to
     Richmond;
And Buckingham, back'd with the hardy Welsh-
     men,
Is in the field, and still his power increaseth. 48
K. Rich. Ely with Richmond troubles me
     more near
Than Buckingham and his rash-levied strength.
Come; I have learn'd that fearful commenting
Is leaden servitor to dull delay: 52
Delay leads impotent and snail-pac'd beggary:
Then fiery expedition be my wing,
Jove's Mercury, and herald for a king!
Go, muster men: my counsel is my shield; 56
We must be brief when traitors brave the field.
                              [*Exeunt.*

SCENE IV.—*The Same. Before the Palace.*

Enter QUEEN MARGARET.

Q. Mar. So, now prosperity begins to mellow
And drop into the rotten mouth of death.
Here in these confines slily have I lurk'd
To watch the waning of mine enemies.   4

A dire induction am I witness to,
And will to France, hoping the consequence
Will prove as bitter, black, and tragical.
Withdraw thee, wretched Margaret: who comes
     here?   8

Enter QUEEN ELIZABETH *and the* DUCHESS OF
     YORK.

Q. Eliz. Ah! my poor princes! ah, my tender
     babes,
My unblown flowers, new-appearing sweets,
If yet your gentle souls fly in the air
And be not fix'd in doom perpetual,   12
Hover about me with your airy wings,
And hear your mother's lamentation.
Q. Mar. Hover about her; say, that right
     for right
Hath dimm'd your infant morn to aged night. 16
Duch. So many miseries have craz'd my
     voice,
That my woe-wearied tongue is still and mute.
Edward Plantagenet, why art thou dead?
Q. Mar. Plantagenet doth quit Plantagenet;
Edward for Edward pays a dying debt.   21
Q. Eliz. Wilt thou, O God! fly from such
     gentle lambs,
And throw them in the entrails of the wolf?
When didst thou sleep when such a deed was
     done?   24
Q. Mar. When holy Harry died, and my
     sweet son.
Duch. Dead life, blind sight, poor mortal
     living ghost,
Woe's scene, world's shame, grave's due by life
     usurp'd,
Brief abstract and record of tedious days, 28
Rest thy unrest on England's lawful earth,
                              [*Sitting down.*
Unlawfully made drunk with innocent blood!
Q. Eliz. Ah! that thou wouldst as soon
     afford a grave
As thou canst yield a melancholy seat;   32
Then would I hide my bones, not rest them here.
Ah! who hath any cause to mourn but I?
                         [*Sitting down by her.*
Q. Mar. If ancient sorrow be most reverend,
Give mine the benefit of seniory,   36
And let my griefs frown on the upper hand,
If sorrow can admit society.
                         [*Sitting down with them.*
Tell o'er your woes again by viewing mine:
I had an Edward, till a Richard kill'd him; 40
I had a Harry, till a Richard kill'd him:
Thou hadst an Edward, till a Richard kill'd him;
Thou hadst a Richard, till a Richard kill'd him.
Duch. I had a Richard too, and thou didst
     kill him;   44
I had a Rutland too, thou holp'st to kill him.
Q. Mar. Thou hadst a Clarence too, and
     Richard kill'd him.
From forth the kennel of thy womb hath crept
A hell-hound that doth hunt us all to death: 48
That dog, that had his teeth before his eyes,
To worry lambs, and lap their gentle blood,
That foul defacer of God's handiwork,
That excellent grand-tyrant of the earth,   52

That reigns in galled eyes of weeping souls,
Thy womb let loose, to chase us to our graves.
O! upright, just, and true-disposing God,
How do I thank thee that this carnal cur   56
Preys on the issue of his mother's body,
And makes her pew-fellow with others' moan.
    Duch. O! Harry's wife, triumph not in my
    woes:
God witness with me, I have wept for thine. 60
    Q. Mar. Bear with me; I am hungry for
    revenge,
And now I cloy me with beholding it.
Thy Edward he is dead, that kill'd my Edward;
Thy other Edward dead, to quit my Edward; 64
Young York he is but boot, because both they
Match not the high perfection of my loss:
Thy Clarence he is dead that stabb'd my Ed-
    ward;
And the beholders of this tragic play,   68
The adulterate Hastings, Rivers, Vaughan,
    Grey,
Untimely smother'd in their dusky graves.
Richard yet lives, hell's black intelligencer,
Only reserv'd their factor, to buy souls   72
And send them thither; but at hand, at hand,
Ensues his piteous and unpitied end:
Earth gapes, hell burns, fiends roar, saints pray,
To have him suddenly convey'd from hence. 76
Cancel his bond of life, dear God! I pray,
That I may live to say, The dog is dead.
    Q. Eliz. O! thou didst prophesy the time
    would come
That I should wish for thee to help me curse 80
That bottled spider, that foul bunchback'd
    toad.
    Q. Mar. I call'd thee then vain flourish of
    my fortune;
I call'd thee then poor shadow, painted queen;
The presentation of but what I was;   84
The flattering index of a direful pageant;
One heav'd a-high to be hurl'd down below;
A mother only mock'd with two fair babes;
A dream of what thou wert, a breath, a bubble,
A sign of dignity, a garish flag,   89
To be the aim of every dangerous shot;
A queen in jest, only to fill the scene.
Where is thy husband now? where be thy
    brothers?   92
Where are thy children? wherein dost thou
    joy?
Who sues and kneels and cries God save the
    queen?
Where be the bending peers that flatter'd thee?
Where be the thronging troops that follow'd
    thee?   96
Decline all this, and see what now thou art:
For happy wife, a most distressed widow;
For joyful mother, one that wails the name;
For one being su'd to, one that humbly sues; 100
For queen, a very caitiff crown'd with care;
For one that scorn'd at me, now scorn'd of me;
For one being fear'd of all, now fearing one;
For one commanding all, obey'd of none. 104
Thus hath the course of justice whirl'd about,
And left thee but a very prey to time;
Having no more but thought of what thou wert,

To torture thee the more, being what thou a
Thou didst usurp my place, and dost thou n
Usurp the just proportion of my sorrow?   1
Now thy proud neck bears half my burden
    yoke;
From which even here, I slip my wearied hea
And leave the burden of it all on thee.   1
Farewell, York's wife, and queen of sad mi
    chance;
These English woes shall make me smile
    France.
    Q. Eliz. O thou, well skill'd in curses, sta
    awhile,   1
And teach me how to curse mine enemies.
    Q. Mar. Forbear to sleep the night, and fa
    the day;
Compare dead happiness with living woe;
Think that thy babes were fairer than they we
And he that slew them fouler than he is: 1
Bettering thy loss makes the bad causer wors
Revolving this will teach thee how to curse.
    Q. Eliz. My words are dull; O! quicken the
    with thine!   1
    Q. Mar. Thy woes will make them shar
    and pierce like mine.   [*Ex*
    Duch. Why should calamity be full of word
    Q. Eliz. Windy attorneys to their client woe
Airy succeeders of intestate joys,   1
Poor breathing orators of miseries!
Let them have scope: though what they
    impart
Help nothing else, yet do they ease the hea
    Duch. If so, then be not tongue tied: go wi
    me,   1
And in the breath of bitter words let's smoth
My damned son, that thy two sweet so
    smother'd.   [*A trumpet hear*
The trumpet sounds: be copious in exclaims

    Enter KING RICHARD, *and his Train,
    marching.*

    K. Rich. Who intercepts me in my exped
    tion?   1
    Duch. O! she that might have intercepte
    thee,
By strangling thee in her accursed womb,
From all the slaughters, wretch, that thou ha
    done!
    Q. Eliz. Hid'st thou that forehead with
    golden crown,   1
Where should be branded, if that right we
    right,
The slaughter of the prince that ow'd that crow
And the dire death of my poor sons an
    brothers?
Tell me, thou villain slave, where are my chi
    dren?   1
    Duch. Thou toad, thou toad, where is th
    brother Clarence
And little Ned Plantagenet, his son?
    Q. Eliz. Where is the gentle Rivers, Vaugha
    Grey?
    Duch. Where is kind Hastings?   1
    K. Rich. A flourish, trumpets! strike alaru
    drums!
Let not the heavens hear these tell-tale wome

Rail on the Lord's anointed. Strike, I say!
                              [*Flourish. Alarums.*
  Either be patient, and entreat me fair,   152
Or with the clamorous report of war
Thus will I drown your exclamations.
  Duch. Art thou my son?
  K. Rich. Ay; I thank God, my father, and
    yourself.   156
  Duch. Then patiently hear my impatience.
  K. Rich. Madam, I have a touch of your
    condition,
That cannot brook the accent of reproof.
  Duch. O, let me speak!
  K. Rich.   Do, then; but I'll not hear. 160
  Duch. I will be mild and gentle in my words.
  K. Rich. And brief, good mother; for I am
    in haste.
  Duch. Art thou so hasty? I have stay'd for
    thee,
God knows, in torment and in agony.   164
  K. Rich. And came I not at last to comfort
    you?
  Duch. No, by the holy rood, thou know'st it
    well,
Thou cam'st on earth to make the earth my hell.
A grievous burden was thy birth to me;   168
Tetchy and wayward was thy infancy;
Thy school-days frightful, desperate, wild and
    furious;
Thy prime of manhood daring, bold, and ven-
    turous;
Thy age confirm'd, proud, subtle, sly, and
    bloody,   172
More mild, but yet more harmful, kind in
    hatred:
What comfortable hour canst thou name
That ever grac'd me in thy company?
  K. Rich. Faith, none, but Humphrey Hour,
    that call'd your Grace   176
To breakfast once forth of my company.
If I be so disgracious in your eye,
Let me march on, and not offend you, madam.
Strike up the drum!
  Duch.   I prithee, hear me speak.   180
  K. Rich. You speak too bitterly.
  Duch.   Hear me a word;
For I shall never speak to thee again.
  K. Rich. So!
  Duch. Either thou wilt die by God's just
    ordinance,   184
Ere from this war thou turn a conqueror;
Or I with grief and extreme age shall perish
And never look upon thy face again.
Therefore take with thee my most grievous
    curse,   188
Which, in the day of battle, tire thee more
Than all the complete armour that thou wear'st!
My prayers on the adverse party fight;
And there the little souls of Edward's children
Whisper the spirits of thine enemies   193
And promise them success and victory.
Bloody thou art, bloody will be thy end;
Shame serves thy life and doth thy death attend.
                                        [*Exit.*
  Q. Eliz. Though far more cause, yet much
    less spirit to curse   197

Abides in me: I say amen to her.   [*Going.*
  K. Rich. Stay, madam; I must talk a word
    with you.
  Q. Eliz. I have no moe sons of the royal
    blood   200
For thee to slaughter: for my daughters,
    Richard,
They shall be praying nuns, not weeping queens;
And therefore level not to hit their lives.
  K. Rich. You have a daughter call'd Eliza-
    beth,   204
Virtuous and fair, royal and gracious.
  Q. Eliz. And must she die for this? O! let
    her live,
And I'll corrupt her manners, stain her beauty;
Slander myself as false to Edward's bed;   208
Throw over her the veil of infamy:
So she may live unscarr'd of bleeding slaughter,
I will confess she was not Edward's daughter.
  K. Rich. Wrong not her birth; she is of royal
    blood.   212
  Q. Eliz. To save her life, I'll say she is not so.
  K. Rich. Her life is safest only in her birth.
  Q. Eliz. And only in that safety died her
    brothers.
  K. Rich. Lo! at their births good stars were
    opposite!   216
  Q. Eliz. No, to their lives ill friends were
    contrary.
  K. Rich. All unavoided is the doom of des-
    tiny.
  Q. Eliz. True, when avoided grace makes
    destiny.
My babes were destin'd to a fairer death,   220
If grace had bless'd thee with a fairer life.
  K. Rich. You speak as if that I had slain my
    cousins.
  Q. Eliz. Cousins, indeed; and by their uncle
    cozen'd
Of comfort, kingdom, kindred, freedom, life. 224
Whose hands soever lanc'd their tender hearts
Thy head, all indirectly, gave direction:
No doubt the murderous knife was dull and
    blunt
Till it was whetted on thy stone-hard heart, 228
To revel in the entrails of my lambs.
But that still use of grief makes wild grief tame,
My tongue should to thy ears not name my boys
Till that my nails were anchor'd in thine eyes;
And I, in such a desperate bay of death,   233
Like a poor bark, of sails and tackling reft,
Rush all to pieces on thy rocky bosom.
  K. Rich. Madam, so thrive I in my enter-
    prise   236
And dangerous success of bloody wars,
As I intend more good to you and yours
Than ever you or yours by me were harm'd.
  Q. Eliz. What good is cover'd with the face
    of heaven,   240
To be discover'd, that can do me good?
  K. Rich. The advancement of your children,
    gentle lady.
  Q. Eliz. Up to some scaffold, there to lose
    their heads?
  K. Rich. No, to the dignity and height of
    fortune,   244

The high imperial type of this earth's glory.
  Q. Eliz. Flatter my sorrow with report of it:
Tell me what state, what dignity, what honour,
Canst thou demise to any child of mine? 248
  K. Rich. Even all I have; ay, and myself and
    all,
Will I withal endow a child of thine;
So in the Lethe of thy angry soul
Thou drown the sad remembrance of those
    wrongs 252
Which thou supposest I have done to thee.
  Q. Eliz. Be brief, lest that the process of thy
    kindness
Last longer telling than thy kindness' date.
  K. Rich. Then know, that from my soul I
    love thy daughter. 256
  Q. Eliz. My daughter's mother thinks it with
    her soul.
  K. Rich. What do you think?
  Q. Eliz. That thou dost love my daughter
    from thy soul:
So from thy soul's love didst thou love her
    brothers; 260
And from my heart's love I do thank thee for
    it.
  K. Rich. Be not too hasty to confound my
    meaning:
I mean, that with my soul I love thy daughter,
And do intend to make her Queen of England.
  Q. Eliz. Well then, who dost thou mean
    shall be her king? 265
  K. Rich. Even he that makes her queen:
    who else should be?
  Q. Eliz. What! thou?
  K. Rich. Even so: what think you of it? 268
  Q. Eliz. How canst thou woo her?
  K. Rich.   That I would learn of you,
As one being best acquainted with her humour.
  Q. Eliz. And wilt thou learn of me?
  K. Rich.   Madam, with all my heart.
  Q. Eliz. Send to her, by the man that slew
    her brothers, 272
A pair of bleeding hearts; thereon engrave
Edward and York; then haply will she weep:
Therefore present to her, as sometime Margaret
Did to thy father, steep'd in Rutland's blood, 276
A handkerchief, which, say to her, did drain
The purple sap from her sweet brother's body,
And bid her wipe her weeping eyes withal.
If this inducement move her not to love, 280
Send her a letter of thy noble deeds;
Tell her thou mad'st away her uncle Clarence,
Her uncle Rivers; ay, and for her sake,
Mad'st quick conveyance with her good aunt
    Anne. 284
  K. Rich. You mock me, madam; this is not
    the way
To win your daughter.
  Q. Eliz.   There is no other way
Unless thou couldst put on some other shape,
And not be Richard that hath done all this. 288
  K. Rich. Say, that I did all this for love of
    her?
  Q. Eliz. Nay, then indeed, she cannot choose
    but hate thee,
Having bought love with such a bloody spoil.

  K. Rich. Look, what is done cannot be no
    amended: 29
Men shall deal unadvisedly sometimes,
Which after-hours give leisure to repent.
If I did take the kingdom from your sons,
To make amends I'll give it to your daughte
If I have kill'd the issue of your womb, 2
To quicken your increase, I will beget
Mine issue of your blood upon your daughte
A grandam's name is little less in love 30
Than is the doting title of a mother;
They are as children but one step below,
Even of your mettle, of your very blood;
Of all one pain, save for a night of groans 30
Endur'd of her for whom you bid like sorrow
Your children were vexation to your youth
But mine shall be a comfort to your age.
The loss you have is but a son being king, 30
And by that loss your daughter is made quee
I cannot make you what amends I would,
Therefore accept such kindness as I can.
Dorset your son, that with a fearful soul 3
Leads discontented steps in foreign soil,
This fair alliance quickly shall call home
To high promotions and great dignity:
The king that calls your beauteous daughte
    wife, 3
Familiarly shall call thy Dorset brother;
Again shall you be mother to a king,
And all the ruins of distressful times
Repair'd with double riches of content. 3
What! we have many goodly days to see:
The liquid drops of tears that you have shed
Shall come again, transform'd to orient pear
Advantaging their loan with interest 3
Of ten times double gain of happiness.
Go then, my mother; to thy daughter go:
Make bold her bashful years with your e
    perience;
Prepare her ears to hear a wooer's tale; 3
Put in her tender heart the aspiring flame
Of golden sovereignty; acquaint the princess
With the sweet silent hours of marriage joys
And when this arm of mine hath chastised 3
The petty rebel, dull-brain'd Buckingham,
Bound with triumphant garlands will I come
And lead thy daughter to a conqueror's be
To whom I will retail my conquest won, 3
And she shall be sole victress, Cæsar's Cæsa
  Q. Eliz. What were I best to say? her father
    brother
Would be her lord? Or shall I say, her uncle
Or, he that slew her brothers and her uncles
Under what title shall I woo for thee, 3
That God, the law, my honour, and her love
Can make seem pleasing to her tender years
  K. Rich. Infer fair England's peace by th
    alliance. 3
  Q. Eliz. Which she shall purchase with st
    lasting war.
  K. Rich. Tell her, the king, that may com
    mand, entreats.
  Q. Eliz. That at her hands which the king
    King forbids.
  K. Rich. Say, she shall be a high and might
    queen. 3

Q. Eliz. To wail the title, as her mother doth.

K. Rich. Say, I will love her everlastingly.

Q. Eliz. But how long shall that title 'ever' last?

K. Rich. Sweetly in force unto her fair life's end.   352

Q. Eliz. But how long fairly shall her sweet life last?

K. Rich. As long as heaven and nature lengthens it.

Q. Eliz. As long as hell and Richard likes of it.

K. Rich. Say, I, her sovereign, am her subject low.   356

Q. Eliz. But she, your subject, loathes such sovereignty.

K. Rich. Be eloquent in my behalf to her.

Q. Eliz. An honest tale speeds best being plainly told.

K. Rich. Then plainly to her tell my loving tale.   360

Q. Eliz. Plain and not honest is too harsh a style.

K. Rich. Your reasons are too shallow and too quick.

Q. Eliz. O, no! my reasons are too deep and dead;

.oo deep and dead, poor infants, in their graves.

K. Rich. Harp not on that string, madam; that is past.   365

Q. Eliz. Harp on it still shall I till heart-strings break.

K. Rich. Now, by my George, my garter, and my crown,—

Q. Eliz. Profan'd, dishonour'd, and the third usurp'd.   368

K. Rich. I swear,—

Q. Eliz.   By nothing; for this is no oath.

hy George, profan'd, hath lost his holy honour;

hy garter, blemish'd, pawn'd his knightly virtue;   371

hy crown, usurp'd, disgrac'd his kingly glory.

something thou wouldst swear to be believ'd,

wear, then, by something that thou hast not wrong'd.   374

K. Rich. Now, by the world,—

Q. Eliz.   'Tis full of thy foul wrongs.

K. Rich. My father's death,—

Q. Eliz. Thy life hath that dishonour'd.

K. Rich. Then, by myself,—

Q. Eliz.   Thyself is self-misus'd.

K. Rich. Why, then, by God,—

Q. Eliz.   God's wrong is most of all.

' thou hadst fear'd to break an oath by him,

he unity the king my husband made   380

fad not been broken, nor my brothers died:

' thou hadst fear'd to break an oath by him,

' he imperial metal, circling now thy head,

fad grac'd the tender temples of my child, 384

.nd both the princes had been breathing here,

Vhich now, too tender bed-fellows for dust,

hy broken faith hath made a prey for worms.

Vhat canst thou swear by now?

K. Rich.   The time to come.   388

Q. Eliz. That thou hast wronged in the time o'erpast;

For I myself have many tears to wash

Hereafter time for time past wrong'd by thee.

The children live, whose parents thou hast slaughter'd,   392

Ungovern'd youth, to wail it in their age:

The parents live, whose children thou hast butcher'd,

Old barren plants, to wail it with their age.

Swear not by time to come; for that thou hast

Misus'd ere us'd, by times ill-us'd o'erpast. 397

K. Rich. As I intend to prosper, and repent,

So thrive I in my dangerous affairs

Of hostile arms! myself myself confound! 400

Heaven and fortune bar me happy hours!

Day, yield me not thy light; nor, night, thy rest!

Be opposite all planets of good luck

To my proceeding, if, with pure heart's love, 404

Immaculate devotion, holy thoughts,

I tender not thy beauteous princely daughter!

In her consists my happiness and thine;

Without her, follows to myself, and thee, 408

Herself, the land, and many a Christian soul,

Death, desolation, ruin, and decay:

It cannot be avoided but by this;

It will not be avoided but by this.   412

Therefore, dear mother,—I must call you so,—

Be the attorney of my love to her:

Plead what I will be, not what I have been;

Not my deserts, but what I will deserve: 416

Urge the necessity and state of times,

And be not peevish-fond in great designs.

Q. Eliz. Shall I be tempted of the devil thus?

K. Rich. Ay, if the devil tempt thee to do good.   420

Q. Eliz. Shall I forget myself to be myself?

K. Rich. Ay, if your self's remembrance wrong yourself.

Q. Eliz. Yet thou didst kill my children.

K. Rich. But in your daughter's womb I bury them: 424

Where, in that nest of spicery, they shall breed

Selves of themselves, to your recomfiture.

Q. Eliz. Shall I go win my daughter to thy will?

K. Rich. And be a happy mother by the deed.

Q. Eliz. I go. Write to me very shortly, 429

And you shall understand from me her mind.

K. Rich. Bear her my true love's kiss; and so farewell.

                [*Kissing her. Exit* QUEEN ELIZABETH.

Relenting fool, and shallow changing woman!

Enter RATCLIFF; CATESBY *following.*

How now! what news?   433

Rat. Most mighty sovereign, on the western coast

Rideth a puissant navy; to the shores

Throng many doubtful hollow-hearted friends,

Unarm'd, and unresolv'd to beat them back. 437

'Tis thought that Richmond is their admiral;

And there they hull, expecting but the aid

Of Buckingham to welcome them ashore.   440

K. Rich. Some light-foot friend post to the Duke of Norfolk:

Ratcliff, thyself, or Catesby; where is he?

Cate. Here, my good lord.

K. Rich.   Catesby, fly to the duke.

Cate. I will, my lord, with all convenient
haste.   444

K. Rich. Ratcliff, come hither. Post to Salisbury:

When thou com'st thither,—[*To* CATESBY.]
Dull, unmindful villain,

Why stay'st thou here, and go'st not to the
duke?

Cate. First, mighty liege, tell me your high-
ness' pleasure,   448

What from your Grace I shall deliver to him.

K. Rich. O! true, good Catesby: bid him
levy straight

The greatest strength and power he can make,

And meet me suddenly at Salisbury.   452

Cate. I go.   [*Exit.*

Rat. What, may it please you, shall I do at
Salisbury?

K. Rich. Why, what wouldst thou do there
before I go?

Rat. Your highness told me I should post
before.   456

Enter STANLEY.

K. Rich. My mind is chang'd. Stanley, what
news with you?

Stan. None good, my liege, to please you
with the hearing;

Nor none so bad but well may be reported.

K. Rich. Hoyday, a riddle! neither good nor
bad!   460

What need'st thou run so many miles about,

When thou mayst tell thy tale the nearest way?

Once more, what news?

Stan.   Richmond is on the seas.

K. Rich. There let him sink, and be the seas
on him!   464

White-liver'd runagate! what doth he there?

Stan. I know not, mighty sovereign, but by
guess.

K. Rich. Well, as you guess?

Stan. Stirr'd up by Dorset, Buckingham,
and Morton,   468

He makes for England, here to claim the crown.

K. Rich. Is the chair empty? is the sword
unsway'd?

Is the king dead? the empire unpossess'd?

What heir of York is there alive but we?   472

And who is England's king but great York's
heir?

Then, tell me, what makes he upon the seas?

Stan. Unless for that, my liege, I cannot
guess.

K. Rich. Unless for that he comes to be your
liege,   476

You cannot guess wherefore the Welshman
comes.

Thou wilt revolt and fly to him I fear.

Stan. No, my good lord; therefore mistrust
me not.

K. Rich. Where is thy power then to beat
him back?   480

Where be thy tenants and thy followers?

Are they not now upon the western shore,

Safe-conducting the rebels from their ships?

Stan. No, my good lord, my friends are
the north.   4

K. Rich. Cold friends to me: what do th
in the north

When they should serve their sovereign in t
west?

Stan. They have not been commande
mighty king:

Pleaseth your majesty to give me leave,   4

I'll muster up my friends, and meet your Grac

Where and what time your majesty shall pleas

K. Rich. Ay, ay, thou wouldst be gone
join with Richmond:

But I'll not trust thee.

Stan.   Most mighty sovereign, 4

You have no cause to hold my friendship doub
ful.

I never was nor never will be false.

K. Rich. Go then and muster men: but lea
behind

Your son, George Stanley: look your heart
firm,   4

Or else his head's assurance is but frail.

Stan. So deal with him as I prove true
you.   [*Ex*

Enter a Messenger.

Mess. My gracious sovereign, now in Devo
shire,

As I by friends am well advertised,   5

Sir Edward Courtney, and the haughty prelat

Bishop of Exeter, his brother there,

With many moe confederates are in arms.

Enter a second Messenger.

Sec. Mess. In Kent, my liege, the Guildfor
are in arms;   5

And every hour more competitors

Flock to the rebels, and their power grov
strong.

Enter a third Messenger.

Third Mess. My lord, the army of gre
Buckingham—

K. Rich. Out on ye, owls! nothing but son
of death?   [*He strikes hi*

There, take thou that, till thou bring bett
news.   5

Third Mess. The news I have to tell yo
majesty

Is, that by sudden floods and fall of waters,

Buckingham's army is dispers'd and scatter'

And he himself wander'd away alone,   5

No man knows whither.

K. Rich.   I cry thee mercy:

There is my purse, to cure that blow of thin

Hath any well-advised friend proclaim'd   5

Reward to him that brings the traitor in?

Third Mess. Such proclamation hath be
made, my liege.

Enter a fourth Messenger.

Fourth Mess. Sir Thomas Lovel, and Lo
Marquess Dorset,

'Tis said, my liege, in Yorkshire are in arms: 5

But this good comfort bring I to your highnes

he Breton navy is dispers'd by tempest.
ichmond, in Dorsetshire, sent out a boat
nto the shore to ask those on the banks   524
' they were his assistants, yea or no;
'ho answer'd him, they came from Buckingham
'pon his party: he, mistrusting them,
[ois'd sail, and made away for Brittany.   528
  K. Rich. March on, march on, since we are
  up in arms;
' not to fight with foreign enemies,
et to beat down these rebels here at home.

Re-enter CATESBY.

  Cate. My liege, the Duke of Buckingham is
  taken,   532
hat is the best news: that the Earl of Richmond
s with a mighty power landed at Milford
s colder news, but yet they must be told.
  K. Rich. Away towards Salisbury! while we
  reason here,   536
. royal battle might be won and lost.
ome one take order Buckingham be brought
o Salisbury; the rest march on with me.
                                    [*Exeunt.*

SCENE V.—*The Same. A Room in* LORD
STANLEY'S *House.*

nter STANLEY *and* SIR CHRISTOPHER URSWICK.

  Stan. Sir Christopher, tell Richmond this
  from me:
hat in the sty of this most bloody boar
ly son George Stanley is frank'd up in hold:
' I revolt, off goes young George's head;   4
he fear of that holds off my present aid.
o, get thee gone: commend me to thy lord.
'ithal, say that the queen hath heartily consented
le should espouse Elizabeth her daughter. 8
ut, tell me, where is princely Richmond now?
  Chris. At Pembroke, or at Ha'rford-west, in
  Wales.
  Stan. What men of name resort to him?
  Chris. Sir Walter Herbert, a renowned
  soldier,   12
ir Gilbert Talbot, Sir William Stanley,
'xford, redoubted Pembroke, Sir James Blunt,
nd Rice ap Thomas, with a valiant crew;
nd many other of great name and worth: 16
nd towards London do they bend their power,
' by the way they be not fought withal.
  Stan. Well, hie thee to thy lord; I kiss his
  hand:
ly letter will resolve him of my mind.   20
arewell.   [*Exeunt.*

ACT V

SCENE I.—*Salisbury. An open Place.*

nter the Sheriff *and* Guard, *with* BUCKINGHAM,
led to execution.

  Buck. Will not King Richard let me speak
  with him?

  Sher. No, my good lord; therefore be patient.
  Buck. Hastings, and Edward's children, Grey
  and Rivers,
Holy King Henry, and thy fair son Edward,   4
Vaughan, and all that have miscarried
By underhand corrupted foul injustice,
If that your moody discontented souls
Do through the clouds behold this present hour,
Even for revenge mock my destruction!   9
This is All-Souls' day, fellows, is it not?
  Sher. It is, my lord.
  Buck. Why, then All-Souls' day is my body's
  doomsday.   12
This is the day that, in King Edward's time,
I wish'd might fall on me, when I was found
False to his children or his wife's allies;
This is the day wherein I wish'd to fall   16
By the false faith of him whom most I trusted;
This, this All-Souls' day to my fearful soul
Is the determin'd respite of my wrongs.
That high All-Seer which I dallied with   20
Hath turn'd my feigned prayer on my head,
And given in earnest what I begg'd in jest.
Thus doth he force the swords of wicked men
To turn their own points on their masters'
  bosoms: 24
Thus Margaret's curse falls heavy on my neck:
'When he,' quoth she, 'shall split thy heart
  with sorrow,
Remember Margaret was a prophetess.'   27
Come, lead me, officers, to the block of shame:
Wrong hath but wrong, and blame the due of
  blame.   [*Exeunt.*

SCENE II.—*A Plain near Tamworth.*

Enter with drum and colours, RICHMOND, OX-
FORD, SIR JAMES BLUNT, SIR WALTER HERBERT,
and Others, with Forces, marching.

  Richm. Fellows in arms, and my most loving
  friends,
Bruis'd underneath the yoke of tyranny,
Thus far into the bowels of the land
Have we march'd on without impediment: 4
And here receive we from our father Stanley
Lines of fair comfort and encouragement.
The wretched, bloody, and usurping boar,
That spoil'd your summer fields and fruitful
  vines,   8
Swills your warm blood like wash, and makes
  his trough
In your embowell'd bosoms, this foul swine
Is now even in the centre of this isle,
Near to the town of Leicester, as we learn: 12
From Tamworth thither is but one day's march.
In God's name, cheerly on, courageous friends,
To reap the harvest of perpetual peace
By this one bloody trial of sharp war.   16
  Oxf. Every man's conscience is a thousand
  men,
To fight against this guilty homicide.
  Herb. I doubt not but his friends will turn
  to us.
  Blunt. He hath no friends but what are
  friends for fear,   20
Which in his dearest need will fly from him.

Richm. All for our vantage: then, in God's
name, march:
True hope is swift, and flies with swallow's
wings;
Kings it makes gods, and meaner creatures
kings.   [*Exeunt.*

SCENE III.—*Bosworth Field.*

Enter KING RICHARD *and Forces; the* DUKE OF
NORFOLK, EARL OF SURREY, *and Others.*

K. Rich. Here pitch our tent, even here in
Bosworth field.
My Lord of Surrey, why look you so sad?
Sur. My heart is ten times lighter than my
looks.
K. Rich. My Lord of Norfolk,—
Nor.   Here, most gracious liege. 4
K. Rich. Norfolk, we must have knocks; ha!
must we not?
Nor. We must both give and take, my loving
lord.
K. Rich. Up with my tent! here will I lie to-
night;
[*Soldiers begin to set up the* KING'S *tent.*
But where to-morrow? Well, all's one for that. 8
Who hath descried the number of the traitors?
Nor. Six or seven thousand is their utmost
power.
K. Rich. Why, our battalia trebles that ac-
count;
Besides, the king's name is a tower of strength,
Which they upon the adverse faction want. 13
Up with the tent! Come, noble gentlemen,
Let us survey the vantage of the ground;
Call for some men of sound direction: 16
Let's lack no discipline, make no delay;
For, lords, to-morrow is a busy day. [*Exeunt.*

Enter on the other side of the field, RICHMOND,
SIR WILLIAM BRANDON, OXFORD, *and other*
Officers. *Some of the* Soldiers *pitch* RICH-
MOND'S *tent.*

Richm. The weary sun hath made a golden set,
And, by the bright track of his fiery car,   20
Gives token of a goodly day to-morrow.
Sir William Brandon, you shall bear my stan-
dard.
Give me some ink and paper in my tent:
I'll draw the form and model of our battle, 24
Limit each leader to his several charge,
And part in just proportion our small power.
My Lord of Oxford, you, Sir William Brandon,
And you, Sir Walter Herbert, stay with me. 28
The Earl of Pembroke keeps his regiment:
Good Captain Blunt, bear my good-night to him,
And by the second hour in the morning
Desire the earl to see me in my tent.   32
Yet one thing more, good captain, do for me;
Where is Lord Stanley quarter'd, do you know?
Blunt. Unless I have mista'en his colours
much,—
Which, well I am assur'd, I have not done,— 36
His regiment lies half a mile at least
South from the mighty power of the king.
Richm. If without peril it be possible,

Good Captain Blunt, bear my good-night t
him,
And give him from me this most needful not
Blunt. Upon my life, my lord, I'll undertake
And so, God give you quiet rest to-night!
Richm. Good-night, good Captain Blun
Come, gentlemen,
Let us consult upon to-morrow's business;
In to my tent, the air is raw and cold.
[*They withdraw into the ten*

Enter, to his tent, KING RICHARD, NORFOLK,
RATCLIFF, *and* CATESBY.

K. Rich. What is't o'clock?
Cate.   It's supper-time, my lor
It's nine o'clock.
K. Rich.   I will not sup to-night.
Give me some ink and paper.
What, is my beaver easier than it was,
And all my armour laid into my tent?
Cate. It is, my liege; and all things are
readiness.
K. Rich. Good Norfolk, hie thee to th
charge;
Use careful watch; choose trusty sentinels.
Nor. I go, my lord.
K. Rich. Stir with the lark to-morrow, gen
Norfolk.
Nor. I warrant you, my lord.   [*Ex*
K. Rich. Ratcliff!
Rat. My lord?
K. Rich.   Send out a pursuivant at arr
To Stanley's regiment; bid him bring his pow
Before sun-rising, lest his son George fall
Into the blind cave of eternal night.
Fill me a bowl of wine. Give me a watch.
Saddle white Surrey for the field to-morrow.
Look that my staves be sound, and not t
heavy.
Ratcliff!
Rat. My lord!
K. Rich. Saw'st thou the melancholy Lo
Northumberland?
Rat. Thomas the Earl of Surrey, and himse
Much about cock-shut time, from troop to troo
Went through the army, cheering up the so
diers.
K. Rich. So, I am satisfied. Give me a bo
of wine:
I have not that alacrity of spirit,
Nor cheer of mind, that I was wont to have.
Set it down. Is ink and paper ready?
Rat. It is, my lord.
K. Rich. Bid my guard watch; leave me.
Ratcliff, about the mid of night come to my te
And help to arm me. Leave me, I say.
[KING RICHARD *retires into his ten*
Exeunt RATCLIFF *and* CATESB

RICHMOND'S *tent opens, and discovers him a*
his Officers, &c.

Enter STANLEY.

Stan. Fortune and victory sit on thy helm
Richm. All comfort that the dark night c
afford

e to thy person, noble father-in-law!
ell me, how fares our loving mother?
Stan. I, by attorney, bless thee from thy
  mother, 84
ho prays continually for Richmond's good:
o much for that. The silent hours steal on,
nd flaky darkness breaks within the east.
n brief, for so the season bids us be, 88
repare thy battle early in the morning,
nd put thy fortune to the arbitrement
f bloody strokes and mortal-staring war.
as I may,—that which I would I cannot,— 92
ith best advantage will deceive the time,
nd aid thee in this doubtful shock of arms:
ut on my side I may not be too forward,
est, being seen, my brother, tender George, 96
e executed in his father's sight.
arewell: the leisure and the fearful time
uts off the ceremonious vows of love
nd ample interchange of sweet discourse, 100
hich so long sunder'd friends should dwell
  upon:
od give us leisure for these rites of love!
nce more, adieu: be valiant, and speed well!
  Richm. Good lords, conduct him to his regiment. 104
l strive, with troubled thoughts, to take a nap,
est leaden slumber peise me down to-morrow,
hen I should mount with wings of victory.
nce more, good-night, kind lords and gentlemen. *[Exeunt all but* RICHMOND.
thou, whose captain I account myself, 109
ook on my forces with a gracious eye;
t in their hands thy bruising irons of wrath,
at they may crush down with a heavy fall 112
e usurping helmets of our adversaries!
ake us thy ministers of chastisement,
at we may praise thee in thy victory!
thee I do commend my watchful soul, 116
re I let fall the windows of mine eyes:
eeping and waking, O! defend me still!
      [Sleeps.

he Ghost of PRINCE EDWARD, *Son to Henry
the Sixth, rises between the two tents.*
Ghost. [*To* KING RICHARD.] Let me sit heavy
  on thy soul to-morrow!
hink how thou stab'dst me in my prime of
  youth 120
t Tewksbury: despair, therefore, and die!
Be cheerful, Richmond; for the wronged souls
f butcher'd princes fight in thy behalf:
ing Henry's issue, Richmond, comforts thee.

The Ghost of KING HENRY THE SIXTH *rises.*
Ghost. [*To* KING RICHARD.] When I was
  mortal, my anointed body 125
y thee was punched full of deadly holes:
hink on the Tower and me; despair and die!
enry the Sixth bids thee despair and die. 128
[*To* RICHARD.] Virtuous and holy, be thou
  conqueror!
arry, that prophesied thou shouldst be the
  king,
oth comfort thee in thy sleep: live thou and
  flourish!

The Ghost of CLARENCE *rises.*
Ghost. [*To* KING RICHARD.] Let me sit heavy
  on thy soul to-morrow! 132
I, that was wash'd to death with fulsome wine,
Poor Clarence, by thy guile betray'd to death!
To-morrow in the battle think on me,
And fall thy edgeless sword: despair, and die!
[*To* RICHMOND.] Thou offspring of the house
  of Lancaster, 137
The wronged heirs of York do pray for thee:
Good angels guard thy battle! live, and flourish!

The Ghosts of RIVERS, GREY, *and* VAUGHAN *rise.*
Ghost of RIVERS. [*To* KING RICHARD.] Let me
  sit heavy on thy soul to-morrow! 140
Rivers, that died at Pomfret! despair, and die!
Ghost of GREY. [*To* KING RICHARD.] Think
  upon Grey, and let thy soul despair.
Ghost of VAUGHAN. [*To* KING RICHARD.]
  Think upon Vaughan, and with guilty fear
Let fall thy pointless lance: despair, and die!—
All Three. [*To* RICHMOND.] Awake! and think
  our wrongs in Richard's bosom 145
Will conquer him: awake, and win the day!

The Ghost of HASTINGS *rises.*
Ghost. [*To* KING RICHARD.] Bloody and guilty,
  guiltily awake;
And in a bloody battle end thy days! 148
Think on Lord Hastings, so despair, and die!—
[*To* RICHMOND.] Quiet, untroubled soul,
  awake, awake!
Arm, fight, and conquer, for fair England's
  sake!

The Ghosts of the two young PRINCES *rise.*
Ghosts. [*To* KING RICHARD.] Dream on thy
  cousins smother'd in the Tower; 152
Let us be lead within thy bosom, Richard,
And weigh thee down to ruin, shame, and death!
Thy nephews' souls bid thee despair, and die!
[*To* RICHMOND.] Sleep, Richmond, sleep in
  peace, and wake in joy; 156
Good angels guard thee from the boar's annoy!
Live, and beget a happy race of kings!
Edward's unhappy sons do bid thee flourish.

The Ghost of LADY ANNE *rises.*
Ghost. [*To* KING RICHARD.] Richard, thy wife,
  that wretched Anne thy wife, 160
That never slept a quiet hour with thee,
Now fills thy sleep with perturbations:
To-morrow in the battle think on me,
And fall thy edgeless sword: despair, and die!
[*To* RICHMOND.] Thou quiet soul, sleep thou
  a quiet sleep; 165
Dream of success and happy victory!
Thy adversary's wife doth pray for thee.

The Ghost of BUCKINGHAM *rises.*
Ghost. [*To* KING RICHARD.] The first was I that
  help'd thee to the crown; 168
The last was I that felt thy tyranny.
O! in the battle think on Buckingham,
And die in terror of thy guiltiness!

Dream on, dream on, of bloody deeds and death:
Fainting, despair; despairing, yield thy breath!
[*To* RICHMOND.] I died for hope ere I could
  lend thee aid: 174
But cheer thy heart, and be thou not dismay'd;
God and good angels fight on Richmond's side;
And Richard falls in height of all his pride.

[*The Ghosts vanish.* KING RICHARD
starts out of his dream.

K. Rich. Give me another horse! bind up
  my wounds!   178
Have mercy, Jesu! Soft! I did but dream.
O coward conscience, how dost thou afflict me!
The lights burn blue. It is now dead midnight.
Cold fearful drops stand on my trembling flesh.
What! do I fear myself? there's none else by:
Richard loves Richard; that is, I am I.   184
Is there a murderer here? No. Yes, I am:
Then fly: what! from myself? Great reason why:
Lest I revenge. What! myself upon myself?
Alack! I love myself. Wherefore? for any good
That I myself have done unto myself?   189
O! no: alas! I rather hate myself
For hateful deeds committed by myself.
I am a villain. Yet I lie; I am not.   192
Fool, of thyself speak well: fool, do not flatter.
My conscience hath a thousand several tongues,
And every tongue brings in a several tale,
And every tale condemns me for a villain.   196
Perjury, perjury, in the high'st degree;
Murder, stern murder, in the dir'st degree;
All several sins, all us'd in each degree,   199
Throng to the bar, crying all, 'Guilty! guilty!'
I shall despair. There is no creature loves me;
And if I die, no soul will pity me:
Nay, wherefore should they, since that I myself
Find in myself no pity to myself?   204
Methought the souls of all that I had murder'd
Came to my tent; and every one did threat
To-morrow's vengeance on the head of Richard.

Enter RATCLIFF.

Rat. My lord!   208
K. Rich. 'Zounds! who's there?
Rat. Ratcliff, my lord; 'tis I. The early vil-
  lage cock
Hath twice done salutation to the morn;
Your friends are up, and buckle on their
  armour.   212
K. Rich. O Ratcliff! I have dream'd a fear-
  ful dream.
What thinkest thou, will our friends prove all
  true?
Rat. No doubt, my lord.
K. Rich.   O Ratcliff! I fear, I fear,—
Rat. Nay, good my lord, be not afraid of
  shadows.   216
K. Rich. By the apostle Paul, shadows to-night
Have struck more terror to the soul of Richard
Than can the substance of ten thousand sol-
  diers
Armed in proof, and led by shallow Richmond.
It is not yet near day. Come, go with me;   221
Under our tents I'll play the eaves-dropper,
To hear if any mean to shrink from me.

[*Exeunt.*

RICHMOND *wakes. Enter* OXFORD *and Other*

Lords. Good morrow, Richmond!   22
Richm. Cry mercy, lords, and watchf
  gentlemen,
That you have ta'en a tardy sluggard here.
Lords. How have you slept, my lord?
Richm. The sweetest sleep, the fairest-bodi
  dreams
That ever enter'd in a drowsy head,
Have I since your departure had, my lords.
Methought their souls, whose bodies Richa
  murder'd,
Came to my tent and cried on victory: 2
I promise you, my heart is very jocund
In the remembrance of so fair a dream.
How far into the morning is it, lords?
Lords. Upon the stroke of four.   2
Richm. Why, then 'tis time to arm and gi
  direction.

His oration to his Soldiers.

More than I have said, loving countrymen,
The leisure and enforcement of the time
Forbids to dwell on: yet remember this,   2
God and our good cause fight upon our sid
The prayers of holy saints and wronged sou
Like high-rear'd bulwarks, stand before our face
Richard except, those whom we fight against 2
Had rather have us win than him they follo
For what is he they follow? truly, gentlemen
A bloody tyrant and a homicide;
One rais'd in blood, and one in blood establish'
One that made means to come by what he hat
And slaughter'd those that were the means
  help him;
A base foul stone, made precious by the foil
Of England's chair, where he is falsely set; 2
One that hath ever been God's enemy.
Then, if you fight against God's enemy,
God will in justice, ward you as his soldiers
If you do sweat to put a tyrant down,
You sleep in peace, the tyrant being slain;
If you do fight against your country's foes,
Your country's fat shall pay your pains t
  hire;
If you do fight in safeguard of your wives, 2
Your wives shall welcome home the conqueror
If you do free your children from the sword
Your children's children quit it in your age.
Then, in the name of God and all these righ
Advance your standards, draw your willi
  swords.   2
For me, the ransom of my bold attempt
Shall be this cold corse on the earth's cold fac
But if I thrive, the gain of my attempt   2
The least of you shall share his part thereof.
Sound drums and trumpets, boldly and che
  fully;
God and Saint George! Richmond and victor
[*Exeu*

Re-enter KING RICHARD, RATCLIFF, Attendan
and Forces.

K. Rich. What said Northumberland
  touching Richmond?   2

Rat. That he was never trained up in arms.

K. Rich. He said the truth: and what said Surrey then?

Rat. He smil'd, and said, 'The better for our purpose.'

K. Rich. He was i' the right; and so, indeed, it is. [*Clock strikes.*
ll the clock there. Give me a calendar. 277
ho saw the sun to-day?

Rat. Not I, my lord.

K. Rich. Then he disdains to shine; for by the book
e should have brav'd the east an hour ago: 280
black day will it be to somebody.
atcliff!

Rat. My lord?

K. Rich. The sun will not be seen to-day;
he sky doth frown and lower upon our army.
would these dewy tears were from the ground.
ot shine to-day! Why, what is that to me
fore than to Richmond? for the self-same heaven
hat frowns on me looks sadly upon him. 288

Enter NORFOLK.

Nor. Arm, arm, my lord! the foe vaunts in the field.

K. Rich. Come, bustle, bustle; caparison my horse.
all up Lord Stanley, bid him bring his power:
will lead forth my soldiers to the plain, 292
nd thus my battle shall be ordered:
y foreward shall be drawn out all in length
onsisting equally of horse and foot;
ur archers shall be placed in the midst: 296
ohn Duke of Norfolk, Thomas Earl of Surrey,
hall have the leading of this foot and horse.
hey thus directed, we will follow
the main battle, whose puissance on either side 300
hall be well winged with our chiefest horse.
his, and Saint George to boot! What think'st thou, Norfolk?

Nor. A good direction, war-like sovereign.
his found I on my tent this morning. 304
[*Giving a scroll.*

K. Rich. Jockey of Norfolk, be not too bold,
or Dickon thy master is bought and sold.
thing devised by the enemy.
o, gentlemen; every man to his charge: 308
et not our babbling dreams affright our souls;
onscience is but a word that cowards use,
)evis'd at first to keep the strong in awe:
)ur strong arms be our conscience, swords our law. 312
1arch on, join bravely, let us to't pell-mell;
f not to heaven, then hand in hand to hell.

His oration to his Army.

Vhat shall I say more than I have inferr'd?
Remember whom you are to cope withal: 316
A sort of vagabonds, rascals, and run-aways,
A scum of Bretons and base lackey peasants,
Vhom their o'er-cloyed country vomits forth
'o desperate adventures and assur'd destruction. 320

You sleeping safe, they bring you to unrest;
You having lands, and bless'd with beauteous wives,
They would restrain the one, distain the other.
And who doth lead them but a paltry fellow, 324
Long kept in Britaine at our mother's cost?
A milksop, one that never in his life
Felt so much cold as over shoes in snow? 327
Let's whip these stragglers o'er the sea again;
Lash hence these overweening rags of France,
These famish'd beggars, weary of their lives;
Who, but for dreaming on this fond exploit,
For want of means, poor rats, had hang'd themselves: 332
If we be conquer'd, let men conquer us,
And not these bastard Bretons; whom our fathers
Have in their own land beaten, bobb'd, and thump'd,
And, on record, left them the heirs of shame. 336
Shall these enjoy our lands? lie with our wives?
Ravish our daughters? [*Drum afar off.*
Hark! I hear their drum.
Fight, gentlemen of England! fight, bold yeomen! 339
Draw, archers, draw your arrows to the head!
Spur your proud horses hard, and ride in blood;
Amaze the welkin with your broken staves!

Enter a Messenger.

What says Lord Stanley? will he bring his power?

Mess. My lord, he doth deny to come. 344

K. Rich. Off with his son George's head!

Nor. My lord, the enemy is pass'd the marsh:
After the battle let George Stanley die.

K. Rich. A thousand hearts are great within my bosom: 348
Advance our standards! set upon our foes!
Our ancient word of courage, fair Saint George,
Inspire us with the spleen of fiery dragons!
Upon them! Victory sits upon our helms. 352
[*Exeunt.*

SCENE IV.—*Another Part of the Field.*

Alarum: Excursions. Enter NORFOLK *and Forces; to him* CATESBY.

Cate. Rescue, my Lord of Norfolk! rescue, rescue!
The king enacts more wonders than a man,
Daring an opposite to every danger:
His horse is slain, and all on foot he fights, 4
Seeking for Richmond in the throat of death.
Rescue, fair lord, or else the day is lost!

Alarum. Enter KING RICHARD.

K. Rich. A horse! a horse! my kingdom for a horse!

Cate. Withdraw, my lord; I'll help you to a horse. 8

K. Rich. Slave! I have set my life upon a cast,
And I will stand the hazard of the die.
I think there be six Richmonds in the field;
Five have I slain to-day, instead of him.— 12
A horse! a horse! my kingdom for a horse!
[*Exeunt.*

X

Alarums. Enter from opposite sides KING
RICHARD *and* RICHMOND, *and exeunt fighting.
Retreat and flourish. Then re-enter* RICH-
MOND, STANLEY, *bearing the crown, with
divers other* Lords, *and Forces.*

  Richm. God and your arms be prais'd, vic-
    torious friends;
The day is ours, the bloody dog is dead.
  Stan. Courageous Richmond, well hast thou
    acquit thee!   16
Lo! here, this long-usurped royalty
From the dead temples of this bloody wretch
Have I pluck'd off, to grace thy brows withal:
Wear it, enjoy it, and make much of it.   20
  Richm. Great God of heaven, say amen to
    all!
But, tell me, is young George Stanley living?
  Stan. He is, my lord, and safe in Leicester
    town;
Whither, if you please, we may withdraw us. 24
  Richm. What men of name are slain on
    either side?
  Stan. John Duke of Norfolk, Walter Lord
    Ferrers,
Sir Robert Brakenbury, and Sir William Bran-
    don.
  Richm. Inter their bodies as becomes their
    births: 28
Proclaim a pardon to the soldiers fled

That in submission will return to us;
And then, as we have ta'en the sacrament,
We will unite the white rose and the red:
Smile, heaven, upon this fair conjunction,
That long hath frown'd upon their enmity!
What traitor hears me, and says not amen?
England hath long been mad, and scarr'd he
  self;
The brother blindly shed the brother's bloo
The father rashly slaughter'd his own son,
The son, compell'd, been butcher to the sir
All this divided York and Lancaster,
Divided in their dire division,
O! now, let Richmond and Elizabeth,
The true succeeders of each royal house,
By God's fair ordinance conjoin together;
And let their heirs—God, if thy will be so,—
Enrich the time to come with smooth-fac
  peace,
With smiling plenty, and fair prosperous day
Abate the edge of traitors, gracious Lord,
That would reduce these bloody days again,
And make poor England weep in streams
  blood!
Let them not live to taste this land's increas
That would with treason wound this fair land
  peace!
Now civil wounds are stopp'd, peace lives agai
That she may long live here, God say amen!
                         [Exeun

THE FAMOUS HISTORY OF THE LIFE OF
KING HENRY THE EIGHTH

DRAMATIS PERSONÆ

KING HENRY THE EIGHTH.
CARDINAL WOLSEY.
CARDINAL CAMPEIUS.
CAPUCIUS, Ambassador from the Emperor Charles the Fifth.
CRANMER, Archbishop of Canterbury.
DUKE OF NORFOLK.
DUKE OF SUFFOLK.
DUKE OF BUCKINGHAM.
EARL OF SURREY.
Lord Chancellor.
Lord Chamberlain.
GARDINER, Bishop of Winchester.
BISHOP OF LINCOLN.
LORD ABERGAVENNY.
LORD SANDS.
SIR THOMAS LOVELL.
SIR HENRY GUILDFORD.
SIR ANTHONY DENNY.
SIR NICHOLAS VAUX.
Secretaries to Wolsey.

CROMWELL, Servant to Wolsey.
GRIFFITH, Gentleman-Usher to Queen Katharine.
Three Gentlemen.
Garter King-at-Arms.
DOCTOR BUTTS, Physician to the King.
Surveyor to the Duke of Buckingham.
BRANDON, and a Sergeant-at-Arms.
Door-keeper of the Council Chamber.
Porter, and his Man.
Page to Gardiner.
A Crier.

QUEEN KATHARINE, Wife to King Henry; afterwards divorced.
ANNE BULLEN, her Maid of Honour; afterwards Queen.
An Old Lady, Friend to Anne Bullen.
PATIENCE, Woman to Queen Katharine.

Several Lords and Ladies in the Dumb Shows; Women attending upon the Queen; Spirits which appear to her; Scribes, Officers, Guards, and other Attendants.

SCENE.—*Chiefly in London and Westminster; once, at Kimbolton.*

PROLOGUE

I come no more to make you laugh: things now,
That bear a weighty and a serious brow,
Sad, high, and working, full of state and woe,
Such noble scenes as draw the eye to flow,   4
We now present. Those that can pity, here
May, if they think it well, let fall a tear;
The subject will deserve it. Such as give
Their money out of hope they may believe,   8
May here find truth too. Those that come to see
Only a show or two, and so agree
The play may pass, if they be still and willing,
I'll undertake may see away their shilling   12
Richly in two short hours. Only they
That come to hear a merry, bawdy play,
A noise of targets, or to see a fellow
In a long motley coat guarded with yellow,   16
Will be deceiv'd; for, gentle hearers, know,
To rank our chosen truth with such a show
As fool and fight is, besides forfeiting
Our own brains, and the opinion that we bring,   21
Will leave us never an understanding friend.
Therefore, for goodness' sake, and as you are
known
The first and happiest hearers of the town,   24
Be sad, as we would make ye: think ye see
The very persons of our noble story
As they were living; think you see them great,
And follow'd with the general throng and sweat   28
Of thousand friends; then, in a moment see
How soon this mightiness meets misery:

And if you can be merry then, I'll say
A man may weep upon his wedding day.   32

ACT I

SCENE I.—*London. An Antechamber in the Palace.*

Enter at one door the DUKE OF NORFOLK; *at the other, the* DUKE OF BUCKINGHAM *and the* LORD ABERGAVENNY.

Buck. Good morrow, and well met. How have you done,
Since last we saw in France?
Nor.   I thank your Grace,
Healthful; and ever since a fresh admirer
Of what I saw there.
Buck.   An untimely ague   4
Stay'd me a prisoner in my chamber, when
Those suns of glory, those two lights of men,
Met in the vale of Andren.
Nor.   'Twixt Guynes and Arde:
I was then present, saw them salute on horse-
back;   8
Beheld them, when they lighted, how they clung
In their embracement, as they grew together;
Which had they, what four thron'd ones could
have weigh'd
Such a compounded one?
Buck.   All the whole time   12
I was my chamber's prisoner.
Nor.   Then you lost
The view of earthly glory: men might say,
Till this time, pomp was single, but now married

To one above itself. Each following day   16
Became the next day's master, till the last
Made former wonders its. To-day the French
All clinquant, all in gold, like heathen gods,
Shone down the English; and to-morrow they
Made Britain India: every man that stood   21
Show'd like a mine. Their dwarfish pages were
As cherubins, all gilt: the madams, too,
Not us'd to toil, did almost sweat to bear   24
The pride upon them, that their very labour
Was to them as a painting. Now this masque
Was cried incomparable; and the ensuing night
Made it a fool, and beggar. The two kings, 28
Equal in lustre, were now best, now worst,
As presence did present them; him in eye,
Still him in praise; and, being present both,
'Twas said they saw but one; and no discerner
Durst wag his tongue in censure. When these
     suns—   33
For so they phrase 'em—by their heralds chal-
     leng'd
The noble spirits to arms, they did perform
Beyond thought's compass; that former fabu-
     lous story,   36
Being now seen possible enough, got credit
That Bevis was believ'd.
   Buck.   O! you go far.
   Nor. As I belong to worship, and affect
In honour honesty, the tract of every thing   40
Would by a good discourser lose some life,
Which action's self was tongue to. All was
     royal;
To the disposing of it nought rebell'd,
Order gave each thing view; the office did   44
Distinctly his full function.
   Buck.   Who did guide,
I mean, who set the body and the limbs
Of this great sport together, as you guess?
   Nor. One, certes, that promises no element 48
In such a business.
   Buck.   I pray you, who, my lord?
   Nor. All this was order'd by the good dis-
     cretion
Of the right reverend Cardinal of York.
   Buck. The devil speed him! no man's pie is
     freed   52
From his ambitious finger. What had he
To do in these fierce vanities? I wonder
That such a keech can with his very bulk
Take up the rays o' the beneficial sun,   56
And keep it from the earth.
   Nor.   Surely, sir,
There's in him stuff that puts him to these ends;
For, being not propp'd by ancestry, whose grace
Chalks successors their way, nor call'd upon 60
For high feats done to the crown; neither allied
To eminent assistants: but, spider-like,
Out of his self-drawing web, he gives us note,
The force of his own merit makes his way;   64
A gift that heaven gives for him, which buys
A place next to the king.
   Aber.   I cannot tell
What heaven hath given him: let some graver eye
Pierce into that; but I can see his pride   68
Peep through each part of him: whence has he
     that?

If not from hell, the devil is a niggard,
Or has given all before, and he begins
A new hell in himself.
   Buck.   Why the devil,
Upon this French going-out, took he upon him
Without the privity o' the king, to appoint
Who should attend on him? He makes up th
     file
Of all the gentry; for the most part such
To whom as great a charge as little honour
He meant to lay upon: and his own letter,—
The honourable board of council out,—
Must fetch him in he papers.
   Aber.   I do know
Kinsmen of mine, three at the least, that ha
By this so sicken'd their estates, that never
They shall abound as formerly.
   Buck.   O! many
Have broke their backs with laying mano
     on 'em   8
For this great journey. What did this vanity
But minister communication of
A most poor issue?
   Nor.   Grievingly I think,
The peace between the French and us no
     values   8
The cost that did conclude it.
   Buck.   Every man,
After the hideous storm that follow'd, was
A thing inspir'd; and, not consulting, broke
Into a general prophecy: That this tempest,
Dashing the garment of this peace, aboded
The sudden breach on 't.
   Nor.   Which is budded ou
For France hath flaw'd the league, and ha
     attach'd
Our merchants' goods at Bourdeaux.
   Aber.   Is it therefore
The ambassador is silenc'd?
   Nor.   Marry, is 't.
   Aber. A proper title of a peace; and pu
     chas'd
At a superfluous rate!
   Buck.   Why, all this business
Our reverend cardinal carried.
   Nor.   Like it your Grace, 1
The state takes notice of the private differenc
Betwixt you and the cardinal. I advise you,-
And take it from a heart that wishes toward
     you
Honour and plenteous safety,—that you rea
The cardinal's malice and his potency   1
Together; to consider further that
What his high hatred would effect wants no
A minister in his power. You know his natur
That he's revengeful; and I know his sword r
Hath a sharp edge: it's long, and 't may be sai
It reaches far; and where 'twill not extend,
Thither he darts it. Bosom up my counsel, 1
You'll find it wholesome. Lo where comes th
     rock
That I advise your shunning.

Enter CARDINAL WOLSEY,—*the Purse born*
     before him,—certain of the Guard, *and tw*
     Secretaries *with papers. The* CARDINAL *in h*

passage fixeth his eye on BUCKINGHAM, *and*
BUCKINGHAM *on him, both full of disdain.*

Wol. The Duke of Buckingham's surveyor,
  ha?
Vhere's his examination?
First Secr.   Here, so please you. 116
Wol. Is he in person ready?
First Secr.   Ay, please your Grace.
Wol. Well, we shall then know more; and
  Buckingham
hall lessen this big look.
              [Exeunt WOLSEY, *and Train.*
Buck. This butcher's cur is venom-mouth'd,
  and I   120
Iave not the power to muzzle him; therefore
  best
Not wake him in his slumber. A beggar's book
Dutworths a noble's blood.
Nor.   What! are you chaf'd?
Ask God for temperance; that's the appliance
  only   124
Vhich your disease requires.
Buck.   I read in's looks
Matter against me; and his eye revil'd
Me, as his abject object: at this instant
Ie bores me with some trick: he's gone to the
  king;   128
'll follow, and out-stare him.
Nor.   Stay, my lord,
And let your reason with your choler question
Vhat 'tis you go about. To climb steep hills
Requires slow pace at first: anger is like   132
A full-hot horse, who being allow'd his way,
Self-mettle tires him. Not a man in England
Can advise me like you: be to yourself
As you would to your friend.
Buck.   I'll to the king; 136
And from a mouth of honour quite cry down
This Ipswich fellow's insolence, or proclaim
There's difference in no persons.
Nor.   Be advis'd;
Ieat not a furnace for your foe so hot   140
That it do singe yourself. We may outrun
By violent swiftness that which we run at,
And lose by overrunning. Know you not, 143
The fire that mounts the liquor till it run o'er,
n seeming to augment it wastes it? Be advis'd:
say again, there is no English soul
More stronger to direct you than yourself,
f with the sap of reason you would quench, 148
Or but allay, the fire of passion.
Buck.   Sir,
am thankful to you, and I'll go along
By your prescription: but this top-proud fellow
Whom from the flow of gall I name not, but 152
from sincere motions,—by intelligence,
And proofs as clear as founts in July, when
We see each grain of gravel,—I do know
To be corrupt and treasonous.
Nor.   Say not, 'treasonous.' 156
Buck. To the king I'll say't; and make my
  vouch as strong
As shore of rock. Attend. This holy fox,
Or wolf, or both,—for he is equal ravenous
As he is subtle, and as prone to mischief   160

As able to perform't, his mind and place
Infecting one another, yea, reciprocally,
Only to show his pomp as well in France
As here at home, suggests the king our master
To this last costly treaty, the interview,   165
That swallow'd so much treasure, and like a
  glass
Did break i' the rinsing.
Nor.   Faith, and so it did.
Buck. Pray give me favour, sir. This cunning
  cardinal   168
The articles o' the combination drew
As himself pleas'd; and they were ratified
As he cried, 'Thus let be,' to as much end
As give a crutch to the dead. But our count-
  cardinal   172
Has done this, and 'tis well; for worthy Wolsey,
Who cannot err, he did it. Now this follows,—
Which, as I take it, is a kind of puppy
To the old dam, treason, Charles the emperor,
Under pretence to see the queen his aunt,— 177
For 'twas indeed his colour, but he came
To whisper Wolsey,—here makes visitation:
His fears were, that the interview betwixt 180
England and France might, through their amity,
Breed him some prejudice; for from this league
Peep'd harms that menac'd him. He privily
Deals with our cardinal, and, as I trow,   184
Which I do well; for, I am sure the emperor
Paid ere he promis'd; whereby his suit was
  granted
Ere it was ask'd; but when the way was made,
And pav'd with gold, the emperor thus desir'd:
That he would please to alter the king's course,
And break the foresaid peace. Let the king
  know—
As soon he shall by me—that thus the cardinal
Does buy and sell his honour as he pleases, 192
And for his own advantage.
Nor.   I am sorry
To hear this of him; and could wish he were
Something mistaken in't.
Buck.   No, not a syllable:
I do pronounce him in that very shape   196
He shall appear in proof.

Enter BRANDON; *a* Sergeant-at-Arms *before
  him.*

Bran. Your office, sergeant; execute it.
Serg.   Sir,
My Lord the Duke of Buckingham, and Earl
Of Hereford, Stafford, and Northampton, I 200
Arrest thee of high treason, in the name
Of our most sovereign king.
Buck.   Lo you, my lord,
The net has fall'n upon me! I shall perish
Under device and practice.
Bran.   I am sorry 204
To see you ta'en from liberty, to look on
The business present. 'Tis his highness' plea-
  sure
You shall to the Tower.
Buck.   It will help me nothing
To plead mine innocence, for that dye is on me
Which makes my whit'st part black. The will
  of heaven   209

Be done in this and all things! I obey.
O! my Lord Abergavenny, fare you well!
Bran. Nay, he must bear you company. [*To
ABERGAVENNY.*] The king 212
Is pleas'd you shall to the Tower, till you know
How he determines further.
Aber. As the duke said,
The will of heaven be done, and the king's
pleasure
By me obey'd!
Bran. Here is a warrant from 216
The king to attach Lord Montacute; and the
bodies
Of the duke's confessor, John de la Car,
One Gilbert Peck, his chancellor,—
Buck. So, so; 219
These are the limbs o' the plot: no more, I hope.
Bran. A monk o' the Chartreux.
Buck. O! Nicholas Hopkins?
Bran. He.
Buck. My surveyor is false; the o'er-great
cardinal
Hath show'd him gold. My life is spann'd
already:
I am the shadow of poor Buckingham, 224
Whose figure even this instant cloud puts on,
By dark'ning my clear sun. My lord, farewell.
[*Exeunt.*

SCENE II.—*The Council Chamber.*

Enter the KING, *leaning on the* CARDINAL'S
shoulder, the Lords of the Council, SIR
THOMAS LOVELL, *Officers, and* Attendants.
The CARDINAL *places himself under the* KING'S
feet on the right side.

K. Hen. My life itself, and the best heart of it,
Thanks you for this great care: I stood i' the level
Of a full-charg'd confederacy, and give thanks
To you that chok'd it. Let be call'd before us 4
That gentleman of Buckingham's; in person
I'll hear him his confessions justify;
And point by point the treasons of his master
He shall again relate. 8

A noise within, crying, 'Room for the Queen!'
Enter QUEEN KATHARINE, *ushered by the* DUKES
OF NORFOLK *and* SUFFOLK: *she kneels. The*
KING *riseth from his state, takes her up, kisses,
and placeth her by him.*

Q. Kath. Nay, we must longer kneel: I am
a suitor.
K. Hen. Arise, and take place by us: half
your suit
Never name to us; you have half our power:
The other moiety, ere you ask, is given; 12
Repeat your will, and take it.
Q. Kath. Thank your majesty.
That you would love yourself, and in that love
Not unconsider'd leave your honour, nor
The dignity of your office, is the point 16
Of my petition.
K. Hen. Lady mine, proceed.
Q. Kath. I am solicited, not by a few,
And those of true condition, that your subjects
Are in great grievance: there have been com-
missions 20

Sent down among 'em, which hath flaw'd th
heart
Of all their loyalties: wherein, although,
My good Lord Cardinal, they vent reproache
Most bitterly on you, as putter-on
Of these exactions, yet the king our master,—
Whose honour heaven shield from soil!—eve
he escapes not
Language unmannerly; yea, such which break
The sides of loyalty, and almost appears
In loud rebellion.
Nor. Not almost appears,
It doth appear; for, upon these taxations,
The clothiers all, not able to maintain
The many to them 'longing, have put off
The spinsters, carders, fullers, weavers, who,
Unfit for other life, compell'd by hunger
And lack of other means, in desperate manne
Daring the event to the teeth, are all in ur
roar,
And danger serves among them.
K. Hen. Taxation!
Wherein? and what taxation? My Lord Car
dinal,
You that are blam'd for it alike with us,
Know you of this taxation?
Wol. Please you, sir,
I know but of a single part in aught
Pertains to the state; and front but in that fil
Where others tell steps with me.
Q. Kath. No, my lord
You know no more than others; but you fram
Things that are known alike; which are no
wholesome
To those which would not know them, and ye
must
Perforce be their acquaintance. These exac
tions,
Whereof my sov'reign would have note, the
are
Most pestilent to the hearing; and to bear 'em
The back is sacrifice to the load. They say
They are devis'd by you, or else you suffer
Too hard an exclamation.
K. Hen. Still exaction!
The nature of it? In what kind, let's know,
Is this exaction?
Q. Kath. I am much too venturous
In tempting of your patience; but am bolden'c
Under your promis'd pardon. The subjects
grief
Comes through commissions, which compe
from each
The sixth part of his substance, to be levied
Without delay; and the pretence for this
Is nam'd, your wars in France. This make
bold mouths:
Tongues spit their duties out, and cold heart
freeze
Allegiance in them; their curses now
Live where their prayers did; and it's come to
pass,
This tractable obedience is a slave
To each incensed will. I would your highness
Would give it quick consideration, for
There is no primer business.

K. Hen. By my life,
his is against our pleasure.

Wol. And for me, 68
have no further gone in this than by
a single voice, and that not pass'd me but
By learned approbation of the judges. If I am
'raduc'd by ignorant tongues, which neither
know 72
My faculties nor person, yet will be
The chronicles of my doing, let me say
'Tis but the fate of place, and the rough brake
That virtue must go through. We must not
stint 76
Our necessary actions, in the fear
To cope malicious censurers; which ever,
As rav'nous fishes, do a vessel follow
That is new-trimm'd, but benefit no further 80
Than vainly longing. What we oft do best,
By sick interpreters, once weak ones, is
Not ours, or not allow'd; what worst, as oft,
Hitting a grosser quality, is cried up 84
For our best act. If we shall stand still,
In fear our motion will be mock'd or carp'd at,
We should take root here where we sit, or sit
Tate-statues only.

K. Hen. Things done well, 88
And with a care, exempt themselves from fear;
Things done without example, in their issue
Are to be fear'd. Have you a precedent
Of this commission? I believe, not any. 92
We must not rend our subjects from our laws,
And stick them in our will. Sixth part of each?
A trembling contribution! Why, we take
From every tree, lop, bark, and part o' the
timber; 96
And, though we leave it with a root, thus
hack'd,
The air will drink the sap. To every county
Where this is question'd, send our letters, with
Free pardon to each man that has denied 100
The force of this commission. Pray, look to't;
put it to your care.

Wol. [*To the* Secretary.] A word with you.
Let there be letters writ to every shire,
Of the king's grace and pardon. The griev'd
commons 104
Hardly conceive of me; let it be nois'd
That through our intercession this revokement
And pardon comes: I shall anon advise you
Further in the proceeding. [*Exit* Secretary.

Enter Surveyor.

Q. Kath. I am sorry that the Duke of Buckingham 109
Is run in your displeasure.

K. Hen. It grieves many:
The gentleman is learn'd, and a most rare
speaker,
To nature none more bound; his training such
That he may furnish and instruct great teachers,
And never seek for aid out of himself. Yet see,
When these so noble benefits shall prove
Not well dispos'd, the mind growing once cor-
rupt, 116
They turn to vicious forms, ten times more ugly
Than ever they were fair. This man so complete,

Who was enroll'd 'mongst wonders, and when
we,
Almost with ravish'd listening, could not find
His hour of speech a minute; he, my lady, 121
Hath into monstrous habits put the graces
That once were his, and is become as black
As if besmear'd in hell. Sit by us; you shall
hear— 124
This was his gentleman in trust—of him
Things to strike honour sad. Bid him recount
The fore-recited practices; whereof
We cannot feel too little, hear too much. 128

Wol. Stand forth; and with bold spirit relate
what you,
Most like a careful subject, have collected
Out of the Duke of Buckingham.

K. Hen. Speak freely.
Surv. First, it was usual with him, every day
It would infect his speech, that if the king 133
Should without issue die, he'd carry it so
To make the sceptre his. These very words
I've heard him utter to his son-in-law, 136
Lord Abergavenny, to whom by oath he
menac'd
Revenge upon the cardinal.

Wol. Please your highness, note
This dangerous conception in this point.
Not friended by his wish, to your high person
His will is most malignant; and it stretches 141
Beyond you, to your friends.

Q. Kath. My learn'd Lord Cardinal,
Deliver all with charity.

K. Hen. Speak on:
How grounded he his title to the crown 144
Upon our fail? to this point hast thou heard him
At any time speak aught?

Surv. He was brought to this
By a vain prophecy of Nicholas Hopkins.

K. Hen. What was that Hopkins?
Surv. Sir, a Chartreux friar,
His confessor, who fed him every minute 149
With words of sovereignty.

K. Hen. How know'st thou this?
Surv. Not long before your highness sped to
France,
The duke being at the Rose, within the parish
Saint Lawrence Poultney, did of me demand 153
What was the speech among the Londoners
Concerning the French journey: I replied,
Men fear'd the French would prove perfidious,
To the king's danger. Presently the duke 157
Said, 'twas the fear, indeed; and that he
doubted
'Twould prove the verity of certain words
Spoke by a holy monk; 'that oft,' says he, 160
'Hath sent to me, wishing me to permit
John de la Car, my chaplain, a choice hour
To hear from him a matter of some moment:
Whom after under the confession's seal 164
He solemnly had sworn, that what he spoke,
My chaplain to no creature living but
To me should utter, with demure confidence
This pausingly ensu'd: neither the king nor's
heirs, 168
Tell you the duke—shall prosper: bid him
strive

To gain the love o' the commonalty: the duke
Shall govern England.'
  Q. Kath.   If I know you well,
You were the duke's surveyor, and lost your
    office   172
On the complaint o' the tenants: take good
    heed
You charge not in your spleen a noble person,
And spoil your nobler soul. I say, take heed;
Yes, heartily beseech you.
  K. Hen.   Let him on.   176
Go forward.
  Surv.   On my soul, I'll speak but truth.
I told my lord the duke, by the devil's illusions
The monk might be deceiv'd; and that 'twas
    dangerous for him
To ruminate on this so far, until   180
It forg'd him some design, which, being believ'd,
It was much like to do. He answer'd, 'Tush!
It can do me no damage;' adding further,
That had the king in his last sickness fail'd, 184
The cardinal's and Sir Thomas Lovell's heads
Should have gone off.
  K. Hen.   Ha! what, so rank? Ah, ha!
There's mischief in this man. Canst thou say
    further?
  Surv. I can, my liege.
  K. Hen.   Proceed.
  Surv.   Being at Greenwich,
After your highness had reprov'd the duke 189
About Sir William Blomer,—
  K. Hen.   I remember
Of such a time: being my sworn servant,
The duke retain'd him his. But on; what
    hence?   192
  Surv. 'If,' quoth he, 'I for this had been com-
    mitted,
As, to the Tower, I thought, I would have play'd
The part my father meant to act upon
The usurper Richard; who, being at Salisbury,
Made suit to come in's presence; which if
    granted,   197
As he made semblance of his duty, would
Have put his knife into him.'
  K. Hen.   A giant traitor!
  Wol. Now, madam, may his highness live
    in freedom,   200
And this man out of prison?
  Q. Kath.   God mend all!
  K. Hen. There's something more would out
of thee? what sayst?
  Surv. After 'the duke his father,' with 'the
    knife,'
He stretch'd him, and, with one hand on his
    dagger,   204
Another spread on's breast, mounting his eyes,
He did discharge a horrible oath; whose tenour
Was, were he evil us'd, he would outgo
His father by as much as a performance 208
Does an irresolute purpose.
  K. Hen.   There's his period;
To sheathe his knife in us. He is attach'd;
Call him to present trial: if he may
Find mercy in the law, 'tis his; if none, 212
Let him not seek 't of us: by day and night!
He's traitor to the height.   [*Exeunt.*

SCENE III.—*A Room in the Palace.*

Enter the Lord Chamberlain *and* LORD SAND

  Cham. Is 't possible the spells of Franc
should juggle
Men into such strange mysteries?
  Sands.   New custom
Though they be never so ridiculous,
Nay, let 'em be unmanly, yet are follow'd.
  Cham. As far as I see, all the good our Eng
lish
Have got by the late voyage is but merely
A fit or two o' the face; but they are shrew
ones;
For when they hold 'em, you would swea
directly
Their very noses had been counsellors
To Pepin or Clotharius, they keep state so.
  Sands. They have all new legs, and lam
ones: one would take it,
That never saw 'em pace before, the spavin
Or springhalt reign'd among 'em.
  Cham.   Death! my lor
Their clothes are after such a pagan cut too,
That, sure, they've worn out Christendom.

Enter SIR THOMAS LOVELL.

                      How now
What news, Sir Thomas Lovell?
  Lov.   Faith, my lor
I hear of none, but the new proclamation
That's clapp'd upon the court-gate.
  Cham.   What is 't for
  Lov. The reformation of our travell'd ga
lants,
That fill the court with quarrels, talk, an
tailors.   2
  Cham. I am glad 'tis there: now I woul
pray our monsieurs
To think an English courtier may be wise,
And never see the Louvre.
  Lov.   They must either—
For so run the conditions—leave those rem
nants   2
Of fool and feather that they got in France,
With all their honourable points of ignoranc
Pertaining thereunto,—as fights and fireworks
Abusing better men than they can be,   2
Out of a foreign wisdom;—renouncing clean
The faith they have in tennis and tall stockings
Short blister'd breeches, and those types o
travel,
And understand again like honest men;   3
Or pack to their old playfellows: there, I take i
They may, *cum privilegio*, wear away
The lag end of their lewdness, and be laugh'd at
  Sands. 'Tis time to give 'em physic, thei
diseases   3
Are grown so catching.
  Cham.   What a loss our ladie
Will have of these trim vanities!
  Lov.   Ay, marry
There will be woe indeed, lords: the sly whore
sons
Have got a speeding trick to lay down ladies; 4

French song and a fiddle has no fellow.

Sands. The devil fiddle 'em! I am glad they're going:
For, sure, there's no converting of 'em: now
An honest country lord, as I am, beaten   44
A long time out of play, may bring his plain-song
And have an hour of hearing; and, by 'r lady,
Held current music too.

Cham.   Well said, Lord Sands;
Your colt's tooth is not cast yet.

Sands.   No, my lord;   48
Nor shall not, while I have a stump.

Cham.   Sir Thomas,
Whither were you a-going?

Lov.   To the cardinal's:
Your lordship is a guest too.

Cham.   O! 'tis true:
This night he makes a supper, and a great one,
To many lords and ladies; there will be   53
The beauty of this kingdom, I'll assure you.

Lov. That churchman bears a bounteous mind indeed,
A hand as fruitful as the land that feeds us;   56
His dews fall everywhere.

Cham.   No doubt he's noble;
He had a black mouth that said other of him.

Sands. He may, my lord; he has where-withal: in him
Sparing would show a worse sin than ill doctrine: 60
Men of his way should be most liberal;
They are set here for examples.

Cham.   True, they are so;
But few now give so great ones. My barge stays;
Your lordship shall along. Come, good Sir Thomas,   64
We shall be late else; which I would not be,
For I was spoke to, with Sir Henry Guildford,
This night to be comptrollers.

Sands.   I am your lordship's.
[*Exeunt.*

SCENE IV.—*The Presence-chamber in York-Place.*

Hautboys. A small table under a state for CARDINAL WOLSEY, *a longer table for the guests. Enter, at one door,* ANNE BULLEN, *and divers Lords, Ladies, and Gentlewomen, as guests; at another door, enter* SIR HENRY GUILDFORD.

Guild. Ladies, a general welcome from his Grace
Salutes ye all; this night he dedicates
To fair content and you. None here, he hopes,
In all this noble bevy, has brought with her   4
One care abroad; he would have all as merry
As, first, good company, good wine, good welcome
Can make good people.

Enter Lord Chamberlain, LORD SANDS, *and* SIR THOMAS LOVELL.

                  O, my lord! you're tardy:
The very thought of this fair company   8

Clapp'd wings to me.

Cham. You are young, Sir Harry Guildford.

Sands. Sir Thomas Lovell, had the cardinal
But half my lay-thoughts in him, some of these
Should find a running banquet ere they rested,
I think would better please 'em: by my life,   13
They are a sweet society of fair ones.

Lov. O! that your lordship were but now confessor
To one or two of these!

Sands.   I would I were;   16
They should find easy penance.

Lov.   Faith, how easy?

Sands. As easy as a down-bed would afford it.

Cham. Sweet ladies, will it please you sit? Sir Harry,
Place you that side, I'll take the charge of this;
His Grace is ent'ring. Nay you must not freeze;
Two women plac'd together makes cold weather:
My Lord Sands, you are one will keep 'em waking;
Pray, sit between these ladies.

Sands.   By my faith,   24
And thank your lordship. By your leave, sweet ladies: [*Seats himself between* ANNE BULLEN *and another* Lady.
If I chance to talk a little wild, forgive me;
I had it from my father.

Anne.   Was he mad, sir?

Sands. O! very mad, exceeding mad; in love too: 28
But he would bite none; just as I do now,
He would kiss you twenty with a breath.
[*Kisses her.*

Cham.   Well said, my lord.
So, now you're fairly seated. Gentlemen,
The penance lies on you, if these fair ladies   32
Pass away frowning.

Sands.   For my little cure,
Let me alone.

Hautboys. Enter CARDINAL WOLSEY, *attended, and takes his state.*

Wol. You're welcome, my fair guests: that noble lady,
Or gentleman, that is not freely merry,   36
Is not my friend: this, to confirm my welcome;
And to you all, good health. [*Drinks.*

Sands.   Your Grace is noble:
Let me have such a bowl may hold my thanks,
And save me so much talking.

Wol.   My Lord Sands,   40
I am beholding to you: cheer your neighbours.
Ladies, you are not merry: gentlemen,
Whose fault is this?

Sands.   The red wine first must rise
In their fair cheeks, my lord; then, we shall have 'em   44
Talk us to silence.

Anne.   You are a merry gamester,
My Lord Sands.

Sands.   Yes, if I make my play.
Here's to your ladyship; and pledge it, madam,
For 'tis to such a thing,—

Anne.   You cannot show me.   48

Sands. I told your Grace they would talk

anon.   [*Drum and trumpets within;
                          chambers discharged.*
Wol.   What's that?
Cham. Look out there, some of ye.
                              [*Exit a* Servant.
Wol.   What war-like voice,
And to what end, is this? Nay, ladies, fear
    not;
By all the laws of war you 're privileg'd.   52

                   Re-enter Servant.

Cham. How now, what is't?
    Serv.   A noble troop of strangers;
For so they seem: they've left their barge and
    landed;
And hither make, as great ambassadors
From foreign princes.
    Wol.   Good Lord Chamberlain,   56
Go, give 'em welcome; you can speak the
    French tongue;
And, pray, receive 'em nobly, and conduct 'em
Into our presence, where this heaven of beauty
Shall shine at full upon them. Some attend
    him.
    [*Exit the* Lord Chamberlain, *attended. All
              arise, and tables removed.*
You have now a broken banquet; but we'll
    mend it.   61
A good digestion to you all; and once more
I shower a welcome on ye; welcome all.

Hautboys. Enter the KING, *and Others, as
    masquers, habited like shepherds, ushered by
    the* Lord Chamberlain. *They pass directly
    before the* CARDINAL, *and gracefully salute
    him.*

A noble company! what are their pleasures?
    Cham. Because they speak no English, thus
        they pray'd   65
To tell your Grace: that, having heard by fame
Of this so noble and so fair assembly
This night to meet here, they could do no less,
Out of the great respect they bear to beauty, 69
But leave their flocks; and, under your fair
    conduct,
Crave leave to view these ladies, and entreat
An hour of revels with 'em.
    Wol.   Say, Lord Chamberlain,
They have done my poor house grace; for which
    I pay 'em   73
A thousand thanks, and pray 'em take their
    pleasures.
    [*They choose* Ladies *for the dance. The* KING
              chooses ANNE BULLEN.
    K. Hen. The fairest hand I ever touch'd! O
        beauty,
Till now I never knew thee! [*Music. Dance.*
Wol. My lord.
    Cham.   Your Grace?
Wol.   Pray tell them thus much from me:
There should be one amongst 'em, by his person,
More worthy this place than myself; to whom,
If I but knew him, with my love and duty   80
I would surrender it.
    Cham.   I will, my lord.
                    [*Whispers the Masquers.*

Wol. What say they?
Cham.   Such a one, they all confes
There is, indeed; which they would have you
    Grace
Find out, and he will take it.
    Wol.   Let me see then.   8
                      [*Comes from his stat*
By all your good leaves, gentlemen, here I'
    make
My royal choice.
    K. Hen. [*Unmasking.*] You have found hin
        cardinal.
You hold a fair assembly; you do well, lord:
You are a churchman, or, I'll tell you, cardina
I should judge now unhappily.
    Wol.   I am glad   8
Your Grace is grown so pleasant.
    K. Hen.   My Lord Chamberlai
Prithee, come hither. What fair lady 's that'
    Cham. An't please your Grace, Sir Thoma
        Bullen's daughter,
The Viscount Rochford, one of her highnes
    women.
    K. Hen. By heaven, she is a dainty on
        Sweetheart,
I were unmannerly to take you out,
And not to kiss you. A health, gentlemen! 9
Let it go round.
    Wol. Sir Thomas Lovell, is the banquet read
I' the privy chamber?
    Lov.   Yes, my lord.
    Wol.   Your Grac
I fear, with dancing is a little heated.   1
    K. Hen. I fear, too much.
    Wol.   There's fresher air, my lor
In the next chamber.
    K. Hen. Lead in your ladies, every on
        Sweet partner,
I must not yet forsake you. Let's be merry: 1
Good my Lord Cardinal, I have half a doze
    healths
To drink to these fair ladies, and a measure
To lead 'em once again; and then let's drea
Who's best in favour. Let the music knock i
                       [*Exeunt with trumpet*

ACT II

SCENE I.—*Westminster. A Street.*

Enter two Gentlemen, *meeting.*

First Gent. Whither away so fast?
Sec. Gent.   O! God save y
E'en to the hall, to hear what shall become
Of the great Duke of Buckingham.
    First Gent.   I'll save yo
That labour, sir. All's now done but the cer
    mony
Of bringing back the prisoner.
    Sec. Gent.   Were you there
First Gent. Yes, indeed, was I.
Sec. Gent. Pray speak what has happen'
First Gent. You may guess quickly what.
Sec. Gent.   Is he found guilty
First Gent. Yes, truly is he, and condemn
    upon't.
Sec. Gent. I am sorry for 't.

First Gent.   So are a number more.
Sec. Gent. But, pray, how pass'd it?
First Gent. I'll tell you in a little. The great duke
Came to the bar; where, to his accusations 12
He pleaded still not guilty, and alleg'd
Many sharp reasons to defeat the law.
The king's attorney on the contrary
Urg'd on the examinations, proofs, confessions
Of divers witnesses, which the duke desir'd 17
To have brought, *vivâ voce*, to his face:
At which appear'd against him his surveyor;
Sir Gilbert Peck his chancellor; and John Car
Confessor to him; with that devil-monk, 21
Hopkins, that made this mischief.
       Sec. Gent.   That was he
That fed him with his prophecies?
       First Gent.   The same.
All these accus'd him strongly; which he fain
Would have flung from him, but, indeed, he
       could not: 25
And so his peers, upon this evidence,
Have found him guilty of high treason. Much
He spoke, and learnedly, for life; but all 28
Was either pitied in him or forgotten.
Sec. Gent. After all this how did he bear
       himself?
First Gent. When he was brought again to
       the bar, to hear
His knell rung out, his judgment, he was stirr'd
With such an agony, he sweat extremely, 33
And something spoke in choler, ill, and hasty:
But he fell to himself again, and sweetly
In all the rest show'd a most noble patience. 36
Sec. Gent. I do not think he fears death.
       First Gent.   Sure, he does not;
He never was so womanish; the cause
He may a little grieve at.
       Sec. Gent.   Certainly
The cardinal is the end of this.
       First Gent.   'Tis likely 40
By all conjectures: first, Kildare's attainder,
Then deputy of Ireland; who, remov'd,
Earl Surrey was sent thither, and in haste too,
Lest he should help his father.
       Sec. Gent.   That trick of state 44
Was a deep envious one.
       First Gent.   At his return,
No doubt he will requite it. This is noted,
And generally, whoever the king favours,
The cardinal instantly will find employment, 48
And far enough from court too.
Sec. Gent.   All the commons
Hate him perniciously, and o' my conscience,
Wish him ten fathom deep: this duke as much
They love and dote on; call him bounteous
       Buckingham, 52
The mirror of all courtesy;—
       First Gent.   Stay there, sir,
And see the noble ruin'd man you speak of.

Enter BUCKINGHAM *from his arraignment; Tip-
staves before him; the axe with the edge towards him; halberds on each side: with him*
SIR THOMAS LOVELL, SIR NICHOLAS VAUX, SIR
WILLIAM SANDS, *and common people.*

Sec. Gent. Let's stand close, and behold him.

Buck.   All good people,
You that thus far have come to pity me, 56
Hear what I say, and then go home and lose me.
I have this day receiv'd a traitor's judgment,
And by that name must die: yet, heaven bear
       witness,
And if I have a conscience, let it sink me, 60
Even as the axe falls, if I be not faithful!
The law I bear no malice for my death,
'T has done upon the premises but justice;
But those that sought it I could wish more
       Christians: 64
Be what they will, I heartily forgive 'em.
Yet let 'em look they glory not in mischief,
Nor build their evils on the graves of great men;
For then my guiltless blood must cry against
       'em. 68
For further life in this world I ne'er hope,
Nor will I sue, although the king have mercies
More than I dare make faults. You few that
       lov'd me,
And dare be bold to weep for Buckingham, 72
His noble friends and fellows, whom to leave
Is only bitter to him, only dying,
Go with me, like good angels, to my end;
And, as the long divorce of steel falls on me, 76
Make of your prayers one sweet sacrifice,
And lift my soul to heaven. Lead on, o' God's
       name.
Lov. I do beseech your Grace, for charity,
If ever any malice in your heart 80
Were hid against me, now to forgive me frankly.
Buck. Sir Thomas Lovell, I as free forgive
       you
As I would be forgiven: I forgive all.
There cannot be those numberless offences 84
'Gainst me that I cannot take peace with: no
       black envy
Shall mark my grave. Commend me to his
       Grace;
And, if he speak of Buckingham, pray, tell him
You met him half in heaven. My vows and
       prayers 88
Yet are the king's; and, till my soul forsake,
Shall cry for blessings on him: may he live
Longer than I have time to tell his years!
Ever belov'd and loving may his rule be! 92
And when old time shall lead him to his end,
Goodness and he fill up one monument!
Lov. To the water side I must conduct your
       Grace;
Then give my charge up to Sir Nicholas Vaux,
Who undertakes you to your end.
Vaux.   Prepare there! 97
The duke is coming: see the barge be ready;
And fit it with such furniture as suits
The greatness of his person.
Buck.   Nay, Sir Nicholas, 100
Let it alone; my state now will but mock me.
When I came hither, I was Lord High
       Constable,
And Duke of Buckingham; now, poor Edward
       Bohun:
Yet I am richer than my base accusers, 104
That never knew what truth meant: I now
       seal it;

And with that blood will make them one day
  groan for't.
My noble father, Henry of Buckingham,
Who first rais'd head against usurping Richard,
Flying for succour to his servant Banister, 109
Being distress'd, was by that wretch betray'd,
And without trial fell: God's peace be with him!
Henry the Seventh succeeding, truly pitying
My father's loss, like a most royal prince, 113
Restor'd me to my honours, and, out of ruins,
Made my name once more noble. Now his son,
Henry the Eighth, life, honour, name, and all 116
That made me happy, at one stroke has taken
For ever from the world. I had my trial,
And, must needs say, a noble one; which makes
  me
A little happier than my wretched father: 120
Yet thus far we are one in fortunes; both
Fell by our servants, by those men we lov'd
  most:
A most unnatural and faithless service!
Heaven has an end in all; yet, you that hear me,
This from a dying man receive as certain: 125
Where you are liberal of your loves and counsels
Be sure you be not loose; for those you make
  friends
And give your hearts to, when they once per-
  ceive 128
The least rub in your fortunes, fall away
Like water from ye, never found again
But where they mean to sink ye. All good
  people,
Pray for me! I must now forsake ye: the last
  hour 132
Of my long weary life is come upon me.
Farewell:
And when you would say something that is sad,
Speak how I fell. I have done; and God forgive
  me! [Exeunt BUCKINGHAM and Train.
First Gent. O! this is full of pity! Sir, it calls,
I fear, too many curses on their heads
That were the authors.
  Sec. Gent. If the duke be guiltless,
'Tis full of woe; yet I can give you inkling 140
Of an ensuing evil, if it fall,
Greater than this.
  First Gent. Good angels keep it from us!
What may it be? You do not doubt my faith,
  sir?
  Sec. Gent. This secret is so weighty, 'twill re-
  quire 144
A strong faith to conceal it.
  First Gent. Let me have it;
I do not talk much.
  Sec. Gent. I am confident:
You shall, sir. Did you not of late days hear
A buzzing of a separation 148
Between the king and Katharine?
  First Gent. Yes, but it held not;
For when the king once heard it, out of anger
He sent command to the lord mayor straight
To stop the rumour, and allay those tongues
That durst disperse it.
  Sec. Gent. But that slander, sir,
Is found a truth now; for it grows again 154
Fresher than e'er it was; and held for certain

The king will venture at it. Either the cardina
Or some about him near, have, out of malice
To the good queen, possess'd him with a scrup
That will undo her: to confirm this too,
Cardinal Campeius is arriv'd, and lately; 1
As all think, for this business.
  First Gent. 'Tis the cardina
And merely to revenge him on the emperor
For not bestowing on him, at his asking,
The archbishopric of Toledo, this is purpos'
  Sec. Gent. I think you have hit the mar
  but is't not cruel 1
That she should feel the smart of this? T
  cardinal
Will have his will, and she must fall.
  First Gent. 'Tis woeful.
We are too open here to argue this; 1
Let's think in private more. [Exeun

SCENE II.—An Antechamber in the Palace

Enter the Lord Chamberlain, reading a letter

  Cham. My lord, The horses your lordsh
sent for, with all the care I had, I saw we
chosen, ridden, and furnished. They we
young and handsome, and of the best breed
the north. When they were ready to set out f
London, a man of my Lord Cardinal's, by con
mission and main power, took them from m
with this reason: His master would be serve
before a subject, if not before the king; whic
stopped our mouths, sir.
I fear he will indeed. Well, let him have then
He will have all, I think.

  Enter the DUKES OF NORFOLK and SUFFOLK.

  Nor. Well met, my Lord Chamberlain.
  Cham. Good day to both your Graces.
  Suf. How is the king employ'd?
  Cham. I left him privat
Full of sad thoughts and troubles.
  Nor. What's the cause
  Cham. It seems the marriage with his brother
  wife
Has crept too near his conscience.
  Suf. No; his conscienc
Has crept too near another lady.
  Nor. 'Tis so:
This is the cardinal's doing, the king-cardinal
That blind priest, like the eldest son of Fortune
Turns what he list. The king will know him on
  day.
  Suf. Pray God he do! he'll never know him
  self else.
  Nor. How holily he works in all his business
And with what zeal! for, now he has crack'd th
  league 2
Between us and the emperor, the queen's grea
  nephew,
He dives into the king's soul, and there scatter
Dangers, doubts, wringing of the conscience,
Fears, and despairs; and all these for his mar
  riage: 2
And out of all these, to restore the king,
He counsels a divorce; a loss of her,
That like a jewel has hung twenty years 3

About his neck, yet never lost her lustre;
Of her, that loves him with that excellence
That angels love good men with; even of her,
That, when the greatest stroke of fortune falls,
Will bless the king: and is not this course pious?
    Cham. Heaven keep me from such counsel!
'Tis most true   38
These news are every where; every tongue
    speaks 'em,
And every true heart weeps for't. All that dare
Look into these affairs, see this main end,   41
The French king's sister. Heaven will one day
    open
The king's eyes, that so long have slept upon
This bold bad man.
    Suf.   And free us from his slavery.
    Nor. We had need pray,   45
And heartily, for our deliverance;
Or this imperious man will work us all
From princes into pages. All men's honours 48
Lie like one lump before him, to be fashion'd
Into what pitch he please.
    Suf.   For me, my lords,
I love him not, nor fear him; there's my creed.
As I am made without him, so I'll stand,   52
If the king please; his curses and his blessings
Touch me alike, they're breath I not believe in.
I knew him, and I know him; so I leave him
To him that made him proud, the pope.
    Nor.   Let's in;
And with some other business put the king 57
From these sad thoughts, that work too much
    upon him.
My lord, you'll bear us company?
    Cham.   Excuse me;
The king hath sent me otherwhere: besides, 60
You'll find a most unfit time to disturb him:
Health to your lordships.
    Nor. Thanks, my good Lord Chamberlain.
                    [*Exit* Lord Chamberlain.

NORFOLK *opens a folding-door. The* KING *is
discovered sitting and reading pensively.*

    Suf. How sad he looks! sure, he is much
afflicted.
    K. Hen. Who is there, ha?
    Nor.   Pray God he be not angry.
    K. Hen. Who's there I say? How dare you
thrust yourselves   65
Into my private meditations?
Who am I, ha?
    Nor. A gracious king that pardons all of-
fences   68
Malice ne'er meant: our breach of duty this way
Is business of estate; in which we come
To know your royal pleasure.
    K. Hen.   Ye are too bold.
Go to; I'll make ye know your times of business:
Is this an hour for temporal affairs, ha?   73

    Enter WOLSEY *and* CAMPEIUS.

Who's there? my good Lord Cardinal? O! my
    Wolsey,
The quiet of my wounded conscience;
Thou art a cure fit for a king. [*To* CAMPEIUS.]
You're welcome,   76

Most learned reverend sir, into our kingdom:
Use us, and it. [*To* WOLSEY.] My good lord,
    have great care
I be not found a talker.
    Wol.   Sir, you cannot.
I would your Grace would give us but an hour
Of private conference.
    K. Hen. [*To* NORFOLK *and* SUFFOLK.] We are
busy: go.   81
    Nor. [*Aside to* SUFFOLK.] This priest has no
pride in him!
    Suf. [*Aside to* NORFOLK.] Not to speak of;
I would not be so sick though for his place:
But this cannot continue.
    Nor. [*Aside to* SUFFOLK.] If it do,   84
I'll venture one have-at-him.
    Suf. [*Aside to* NORFOLK.] I another.
              [*Exeunt* NORFOLK *and* SUFFOLK.
    Wol. Your Grace has given a precedent of
wisdom
Above all princes, in committing freely
Your scruple to the voice of Christendom. 88
Who can be angry now? what envy reach you?
The Spaniard, tied by blood and favour to her,
Must now confess, if they have any goodness,
The trial just and noble. All the clerks,   92
I mean the learned ones, in Christian kingdoms
Have their free voices: Rome, the nurse of judg-
ment,
Invited by your noble self, hath sent
One general tongue unto us, this good man, 96
This just and learned priest, Cardinal Cam-
peius;
Whom once more I present unto your highness.
    K. Hen. And once more in my arms I bid him
welcome,
And thank the holy conclave for their loves:
They have sent me such a man I would have
wish'd for.   101
    Cam. Your Grace must needs deserve all
strangers' loves,
You are so noble. To your highness' hand
I tender my commission, by whose virtue,—
The court of Rome commanding,—you, my Lord
Cardinal of York, are join'd with me, their servant,
In the impartial judging of this business.
    K. Hen. Two equal men. The queen shall be
acquainted   108
Forthwith for what you come. Where's Gar-
diner?
    Wol. I know your majesty has always lov'd
her
So dear in heart, not to deny her that
A woman of less place might ask by law,   112
Scholars, allow'd freely to argue for her.
    K. Hen. Ay, and the best, she shall have; and
my favour
To him that does best: God forbid else. Car-
dinal,   115
Prithee, call Gardiner to me, my new secretary:
I find him a fit fellow.   [*Exit* WOLSEY.

    Re-enter WOLSEY, *with* GARDINER.

    Wol. [*Aside to* GARDINER.] Give me your
hand; much joy and favour to you;
You are the king's now.

Gard. [Aside to WOLSEY.] But to be commanded
For ever by your Grace, whose hand has rais'd me.   120
K. Hen. Come hither, Gardiner.
    [They converse apart.
Cam. My Lord of York, was not one Doctor Pace
In this man's place before him?
Wol.   Yes, he was.
Cam. Was he not held a learned man?
Wol.   Yes, surely. 124
Cam. Believe me, there's an ill opinion spread then
Even of yourself, Lord Cardinal.
Wol.   How! of me?
Cam. They will not stick to say, you envied him,
And fearing he would rise, he was so virtuous,
Kept him a foreign man still; which so griev'd him   129
That he ran mad and died.
Wol.   Heaven's peace be with him!
That's Christian care enough: for living murmurers
There's places of rebuke. He was a fool,   132
For he would needs be virtuous: that good fellow,
If I command him, follows my appointment:
I will have none so near else. Learn this, brother,   135
We live not to be grip'd by meaner persons.
K. Hen. Deliver this with modesty to the queen.
    [Exit GARDINER.
The most convenient place that I can think of
For such receipt of learning, is Black-Friars;
There ye shall meet about this weighty business.
My Wolsey, see it furnish'd. O my lord!   141
Would it not grieve an able man to leave
So sweet a bedfellow? But, conscience, conscience!
O! 'tis a tender place, and I must leave her.   144
    [Exeunt.

SCENE III.—An Antechamber in the QUEEN'S Apartments.

Enter ANNE BULLEN and an Old Lady.

Anne. Not for that neither: here's the pang that pinches!
His highness having liv'd so long with her, and she
So good a lady that no tongue could ever
Pronounce dishonour of her; by my life,   4
She never knew harm-doing; O! now, after
So many courses of the sun enthron'd,
Still growing in a majesty and pomp, the which
To leave a thousand-fold more bitter than   8
'Tis sweet at first to acquire, after this process
To give her the avaunt! it is a pity
Would move a monster.
Old Lady.   Hearts of most hard temper
Melt and lament for her.
Anne.   O! God's will; much better   12
She ne'er had known pomp: though 't be temporal,

Yet, if that quarrel, Fortune, do divorce
It from the bearer, 'tis a sufferance panging
As soul and body's severing.
Old Lady.   Alas! poor lady, 16
She's a stranger now again.
Anne.   So much the more
Must pity drop upon her. Verily,
I swear, 'tis better to be lowly born,
And range with humble livers in content,   20
Than to be perk'd up in a glist'ring grief
And wear a golden sorrow.
Old Lady.   Our content
Is our best having.
Anne.   By my troth and maidenhead
I would not be a queen.
Old Lady.   Beshrew me, I would, 24
And venture maidenhead for 't; and so would you,
For all this spice of your hypocrisy.
You, that have so fair parts of woman on you,
Have too a woman's heart; which ever yet   28
Affected eminence, wealth, sovereignty:
Which, to say sooth, are blessings; and which gifts—
Saving your mincing—the capacity
Of your soft cheveril conscience would receive,
If you might please to stretch it.
Anne.   Nay, good troth. 33
Old Lady. Yes, troth, and troth; you would not be a queen?
Anne. No, not for all the riches under heaven.
Old Lady. 'Tis strange: a three-pence bow'd would hire me,   36
Old as I am, to queen it. But, I pray you,
What think you of a duchess? have you limbs
To bear that load of title?
Anne.   No, in truth.
Old Lady. Then you are weakly made. Pluck off a little: 40
I would not be a young count in your way,
For more than blushing comes to: if your back
Cannot vouchsafe this burden, 'tis too weak
Ever to get a boy.
Anne.   How you do talk!   44
I swear again, I would not be a queen
For all the world.
Old Lady.   In faith, for little England
You'd venture an emballing: I myself
Would for Carnarvonshire, although there 'long'd
No more to the crown but that. Lo! who comes here?   49

Enter the Lord Chamberlain.

Cham. Good morrow, ladies. What were 't worth to know
The secret of your conference?
Anne.   My good lord,
Not your demand; it values not your asking: 52
Our mistress' sorrows we were pitying.
Cham. It was a gentle business, and becoming
The action of good women: there is hope
All will be well.
Anne.   Now, I pray God, amen! 56
Cham. You bear a gentle mind, and heavenly blessings

Follow such creatures. That you may, fair lady,
Perceive I speak sincerely, and high note's
Ta'en of your many virtues, the king's majesty
Commends his good opinion of you, and 61
Does purpose honour to you no less flowing
Than Marchioness of Pembroke; to which title
A thousand pound a year, annual support, 64
Out of his grace he adds.

Anne.   I do not know
What kind of my obedience I should tender;
More than my all is nothing, nor my prayers
Are not words duly hallow'd, nor my wishes 68
More worth than empty vanities; yet prayers
    and wishes
Are all I can return. Beseech your lordship,
Vouchsafe to speak my thanks and my obe-
    dience,
As from a blushing handmaid, to his highness,
Whose health and royalty I pray for.

Cham.   Lady, 73
I shall not fail to approve the fair conceit
The king hath of you. [*Aside.*] I have perus'd
    her well;
Beauty and honour in her are so mingled 76
That they have caught the king; and who knows
    yet
But from this lady may proceed a gem
To lighten all this isle? [*To her.*] I'll to the king,
And say, I spoke with you.

Anne.   My honour'd lord. 80
    [*Exit* LORD CHAMBERLAIN.

Old Lady. Why, this it is; see, see!
I have been begging sixteen years in court,
Am yet a courtier beggarly, nor could
Come pat betwixt too early and too late; 84
For any suit of pounds; and you, O fate!
A very fresh-fish here,—fie, fie, upon
This compell'd fortune!—have your mouth fill'd
    up
Before you open it.

Anne.   This is strange to me. 88
Old Lady. How tastes it? is it bitter? forty
    pence, no.
There was a lady once,—'tis an old story,—
That would not be a queen, that would she not,
For all the mud in Egypt: have you heard it?
Anne. Come, you are pleasant.
Old Lady.   With your theme I could
O'ermount the lark. The Marchioness of Pem-
    broke!
A thousand pounds a year, for pure respect!
No other obligation! By my life 96
That promises more thousands: honour's train
Is longer than his foreskirt. By this time
I know your back will bear a duchess: say,
Are you not stronger than you were?
Anne.   Good lady, 100
Make yourself mirth with your particular fancy,
And leave me out on 't. Would I had no being,
If this salute my blood a jot: it faints me,
To think what follows. 104
The queen is comfortless, and we forgetful
In our long absence. Pray, do not deliver
What here you've heard to her.
Old Lady.   What do you think me?
    [*Exeunt.*

SCENE IV.—*A Hall in Black-Friars.*

*Trumpets, sennet, and cornets. Enter two Ver-
gers, with short silver wands; next them, two
Scribes, in the habit of doctors; after them,
the* ARCHBISHOP OF CANTERBURY, *alone; after
him, the* BISHOPS OF LINCOLN, ELY, ROCHES-
TER, *and* SAINT ASAPH; *next them, at some
small distance, follows a* Gentleman *bearing
the purse, with the great seal, and a cardinal's
hat; then two* Priests, *bearing each a silver
cross; then a* Gentleman-Usher *bare-headed,
accompanied with a* Sergeant-at-Arms, *bearing a silver mace; then two* Gentlemen, *bearing two great silver pillars; after them, side
by side, the two* CARDINALS; *two* Noblemen
with the sword and mace. Then enter the
KING *and* QUEEN, *and their Trains. The* KING
takes place under the cloth of state; the two
CARDINALS *sit under him as judges. The*
QUEEN *takes place at some distance from the*
KING. *The* BISHOPS *place themselves on each
side the court, in manner of a consistory;
below them, the* Scribes. *The* Lords *sit next
the* BISHOPS. *The* Crier *and the rest of the*
Attendants *stand in convenient order about
the Stage.*

Wol. Whilst our commission from Rome is
    read,
Let silence be commanded.
K. Hen.   What's the need?
It hath already publicly been read,
And on all sides the authority allow'd; 4
You may then spare that time.
Wol.   Be 't so. Proceed.
Scribe. Say, Henry King of England, come
    into the court.
Crier. Henry King of England, come into the
    court.
K. Hen. Here.
Scribe. Say, Katharine Queen of England,
    come into the court.
Crier. Katharine Queen of England, come
    into the court.
    [*The* QUEEN *makes no answer, rises out of
    her chair, goes about the court, comes to
    the* KING, *and kneels at his feet; then
    speaks.*
Q. Kath. Sir, I desire you do me right and
    justice;
And to bestow your pity on me; for 12
I am a most poor woman, and a stranger,
Born out of your dominions; having here
No judge indifferent, nor no more assurance
Of equal friendship and proceeding. Alas! sir,
In what have I offended you? what cause 17
Hath my behaviour given to your displeasure,
That thus you should proceed to put me off
And take your good grace from me? Heaven
    witness, 20
I have been to you a true and humble wife,
At all times to your will conformable;
Ever in fear to kindle your dislike,
Yea, subject to your countenance, glad or sorry
As I saw it inclin'd. When was the hour 25
I ever contradicted your desire,

Or made it not mine too? Or which of your
friends 27
Have I not strove to love, although I knew
He were mine enemy? what friend of mine
That had to him deriv'd your anger, did I
Continue in my liking? nay, gave notice
He was from thence discharg'd. Sir, call to
mind 32
That I have been your wife, in this obedience
Upward of twenty years, and have been blest
With many children by you: if, in the course
And process of this time, you can report, 36
And prove it too, against mine honour aught,
My bond to wedlock, or my love and duty,
Against your sacred person, in God's name
Turn me away; and let the foul'st contempt
Shut door upon me, and so give me up 41
To the sharp'st kind of justice. Please you, sir,
The king, your father, was reputed for
A prince most prudent, of an excellent 44
And unmatch'd wit and judgment: Ferdinand,
My father, King of Spain, was reckon'd one
The wisest prince that there had reign'd by
many
A year before: it is not to be question'd 48
That they had gather'd a wise council to them
Of every realm, that did debate this business,
Who deem'd our marriage lawful. Wherefore I
humbly
Beseech you, sir, to spare me, till I may 52
Be by my friends in Spain advis'd, whose coun-
sel
I will implore: if not, i' the name of God,
Your pleasure be fulfill'd!
  Wol.   You have here, lady,—
And of your choice,—these reverend fathers;
men 56
Of singular integrity and learning,
Yea, the elect o' the land, who are assembled
To plead your cause. It shall be therefore boot-
less
That longer you desire the court, as well 60
For your own quiet, as to rectify
What is unsettled in the king.
  Cam.   His Grace
Hath spoken well and justly: therefore, madam,
It's fit this royal session do proceed, 64
And that, without delay, their arguments
Be now produc'd and heard.
  Q. Kath.   Lord Cardinal,
To you I speak.
  Wol.   Your pleasure, madam?
  Q. Kath.   Sir,
I am about to weep; but, thinking that 68
We are a queen,—or long have dream'd so,—
certain
The daughter of a king, my drops of tears
I'll turn to sparks of fire.
  Wol.   Be patient yet.
  Q. Kath. I will, when you are humble; nay,
before. 72
Or God will punish me. I do believe,
Induc'd by potent circumstances, that
You are mine enemy; and make my challenge
You shall not be my judge; for it is you 76
Have blown this coal betwixt my lord and me,

Which God's dew quench! Therefore I say
again,
I utterly abhor, yea, from my soul 79
Refuse you for my judge, whom, yet once more,
I hold my most malicious foe, and think not
At all a friend to truth.
  Wol.   I do profess
You speak not like yourself; who ever yet
Have stood to charity, and display'd the effects
Of disposition gentle, and of wisdom 85
O'ertopping woman's power. Madam, you do
me wrong:
I have no spleen against you; nor injustice
For you or any: how far I have proceeded, 88
Or how far further shall, is warranted
By a commission from the consistory,
Yea, the whole consistory of Rome. You charge
me
That I have blown this coal: I do deny it. 92
The king is present: if it be known to him
That I gainsay my deed, how may he wound,
And worthily, my falsehood; yea, as much
As you have done my truth. If he know 96
That I am free of your report, he knows
I am not of your wrong. Therefore in him
It lies to cure me; and the cure is, to
Remove these thoughts from you: the which
before 100
His highness shall speak in, I do beseech
You, gracious madam, to unthink your speaking,
And to say so no more.
  Q. Kath.   My lord, my lord,
I am a simple woman, much too weak 104
To oppose your cunning. You're meek and
humble-mouth'd;
You sign your place and calling, in full seeming,
With meekness and humility; but your heart
Is cramm'd with arrogancy, spleen, and pride.
You have, by fortune and his highness' favours,
Gone slightly o'er low steps, and now are
mounted 109
Where powers are your retainers, and your
words,
Domestics to you, serve your will as 't please
Yourself pronounce their office. I must tell
you, 113
You tender more your person's honour than
Your high profession spiritual; that again
I do refuse you for my judge; and here, 116
Before you all, appeal unto the pope,
To bring my whole cause 'fore his holiness
And to be judg'd by him.
  [*She curtsies to the* KING, *and offers to
depart.*
  Cam.   The queen is obstinate,
Stubborn to justice, apt to accuse it, and 120
Disdainful to be tried by 't: 'tis not well.
She's going away.
  K. Hen. Call her again.
  Crier. Katharine Queen of England, come
into the court. 124
  Grif. Madam, you are call'd back.
  Q. Kath. What need you note it? pray you,
keep your way:
When you are call'd, return. Now, the Lord
help!

hey vex me past my patience. Pray you, pass
on: 128
will not tarry; no, nor ever more
pon this business my appearance make
1 any of their courts.
    [*Exeunt* QUEEN, *and her* Attendants.
K. Hen.   Go thy ways, Kate:
hat man i' the world who shall report he has
  better wife, let him in nought be trusted, 133
or speaking false in that: thou art, alone,—
' thy rare qualities, sweet gentleness,
hy meekness saint-like, wife-like government,
beying in commanding, and thy parts 137
overeign and pious else, could speak thee out,—
he queen of earthly queens. She's noble born;
.nd, like her true nobility, she has 140
.arried herself towards me.
Wol.   Most gracious sir,
1 humblest manner I require your highness,
hat it shall please you to declare, in hearing
f all these ears,—for where I am robb'd and
  bound 144
here must I be unloos'd, although not there
t once, and fully satisfied,—whether ever I
id broach this business to your highness, or
aid any scruple in your way, which might
iduce you to the question on't? or ever 149
iave to you, but with thanks to God for such
. royal lady, spake one the least word that
  might
e to the prejudice of her present state, 152
r touch of her good person?
K. Hen.   My Lord Cardinal,
do excuse you; yea, upon mine honour,
free you from't. You are not to be taught
hat you have many enemies, that know not
/hy they are so, but, like to village curs, 157
ark when their fellows do: by some of these
he queen is put in anger. You're excus'd:
ut will you be more justified? you ever 160
iave wish'd the sleeping of this business; never
)esir'd it to be stirr'd; but oft have hinder'd,
  oft,
he passages made toward it. On my honour,
speak my good Lord Cardinal to this point,
.nd thus far clear him. Now, what mov'd me
  to't, 165
will be bold with time and your attention:
hen mark the inducement. Thus it came; give
  heed to't:
Iy conscience first receiv'd a tenderness, 168
cruple, and prick, on certain speeches utter'd
y the Bishop of Bayonne, then French ambassador,
/ho had been hither sent on the debating
. marriage 'twixt the Duke of Orleans and
ur daughter Mary. I' the progress of this
  business, 173
.re a determinate resolution, he—
mean, the bishop—did require a respite;
/herein he might the king his lord advertise 176
/hether our daughter were legitimate,
.especting this our marriage with the dowager,
ometimes our brother's wife. This respite
  shook
he bosom of my conscience, enter'd me, 180

Yea, with a splitting power, and made to tremble
The region of my breast; which forc'd such way,
That many maz'd considerings did throng,
And press'd in with this caution. First, me-
  thought 184
I stood not in the smile of heaven, who had
Commanded nature, that my lady's womb,
If it conceiv'd a male child by me, should
Do no more offices of life to't than 188
The grave does to the dead; for her male issue
Or died where they were made, or shortly after
This world had air'd them. Hence I took a
  thought
This was a judgment on me; that my kingdom,
Well worthy the best heir o' the world, should
  not 193
Be gladded in't by me. Then follows that
I weigh'd the danger which my realms stood in
By this my issue's fail; and that gave to me
Many a groaning throe. Thus hulling in 197
The wild sea of my conscience, I did steer
Toward this remedy, whereupon we are
Now present here together; that's to say, 200
I meant to rectify my conscience, which
I then did feel full sick, and yet not well,
By all the rev'rend fathers of the land
And doctors learn'd. First, I began in private
With you, my Lord of Lincoln; you remember
How under my oppression I did reek, 206
When I first mov'd you.
Lin.   Very well, my liege.
K. Hen. I have spoke long: be pleas'd your-
  self to say 208
How far you satisfied me.
Lin.   So please your highness,
The question did at first so stagger me,
Bearing a state of mighty moment in't,
And consequence of dread, that I committed 212
The daring'st counsel that I had to doubt;
And did entreat your highness to this course
Which you are running here.
K. Hen.   Then I mov'd you,
My Lord of Canterbury, and got your leave
To make this present summons. Unsolicited
I left no reverend person in this court;
But by particular consent proceeded 219
Under your hands and seals: therefore, go on;
For no dislike i' the world against the person
Of the good queen, but the sharp thorny
  points
Of my alleged reasons drive this forward.
Prove but our marriage lawful, by my life
And kingly dignity, we are contented 225
To wear our mortal state to come with her,
Katharine our queen, before the primest creature
That's paragon'd o' the world.
Cam.   So please your highness, 228
The queen being absent, 'tis a needful fitness
That we adjourn this court till further day:
Meanwhile must be an earnest motion 231
Made to the queen, to call back her appeal
She intends unto his holiness.
             [*They rise to depart.*
K. Hen.   [*Aside.*]   I may perceive
These cardinals trifle with me: I abhor
This dilatory sloth and tricks of Rome. 235

My learn'd and well-beloved servant Cranmer,
Prithee, return: with thy approach, I know,
My comfort comes along. Break up the court:
I say, set on.

[*Exeunt, in manner as they entered.*]

ACT III

SCENE I.—*The Palace at Bridewell. A Room in the* QUEEN'S *Apartment.*

The QUEEN *and her Women at work.*

Q. Kath. Take thy lute, wench: my soul grows
  sad with troubles;
Sing and disperse 'em, if thou canst. Leave
  working.

SONG

Orpheus with his lute made trees,
  And the mountain tops that freeze,   4
    Bow themselves, when he did sing:
To his music plants and flowers
Ever sprung; as sun and showers
  There had made a lasting spring.   8

Every thing that heard him play,
  Even the billows of the sea,
    Hung their heads, and then lay by.
In sweet music is such art,   12
Killing care and grief of heart
Fall asleep, or hearing, die.

Enter a GENTLEMAN.

Q. Kath. How now!
Gent. An't please your Grace, the two great
  cardinals   16
Wait in the presence.
Q. Kath.   Would they speak with me?
Gent. They will'd me say so, madam.
Q. Kath.   Pray their Graces
To come near. [*Exit* Gentleman.] What can be
  their business
With me, a poor weak woman, fall'n from favour?
I do not like their coming, now I think on 't.
They should be good men, their affairs as right-
  eous;   22
But all hoods make not monks.

Enter WOLSEY *and* CAMPEIUS.

Wol.   Peace to your highness!
Q. Kath. Your Graces find me here part of
  a housewife;   24
I would be all, against the worst may happen.
What are your pleasures with me, reverend lords?
Wol. May it please you, noble madam, to
  withdraw   27
Into your private chamber, we shall give you
The full cause of our coming.
Q. Kath.   Speak it here;
There's nothing I have done yet, o' my con-
  science,
Deserves a corner: would all other women
Could speak this with as free a soul as I do! 32
My lords, I care not—so much I am happy
Above a number—if my actions
Were tried by every tongue, every eye saw 'em,
Envy and base opinion set against 'em,   36
I know my life so even. If your business
Seek me out, and that way I am wife in,
Out with it boldly: truth loves open dealing.

Wol. Tanta est erga te mentis integrita
  regina serenissima,—
Q. Kath. O, good my lord, no Latin;
I am not such a truant since my coming
As not to know the language I have liv'd in:
A strange tongue makes my cause more strange,
  suspicious;
Pray, speak in English: here are some will thank
  you,
If you speak truth, for their poor mistress' sake;
Believe me, she has had much wrong. Lord
  Cardinal,
The willing'st sin I ever yet committed
May be absolv'd in English.
Wol.   Noble lady,
I am sorry my integrity should breed,—
And service to his majesty and you,—
So deep suspicion, where all faith was meant.
We come not by the way of accusation,
To taint that honour every good tongue blesses,
Nor to betray you any way to sorrow,
You have too much, good lady; but to know
How you stand minded in the weighty difference
Between the king and you; and to deliver,
Like free and honest men, our just opinions
And comforts to your cause.
Cam.   Most honour'd madam,
My Lord of York, out of his noble nature,
Zeal and obedience he still bore your Grace,
Forgetting, like a good man, your late censure
Both of his truth and him,—which was too far,—
Offers, as I do, in sign of peace,
His service and his counsel.
Q. Kath.   [*Aside.*] To betray me.—
My lords, I thank you both for your good will;
Ye speak like honest men,—pray God, ye prove
  so!—
But how to make ye suddenly an answer,
In such a point of weight, so near mine honour,—
More near my life, I fear,—with my weak wit,
And to such men of gravity and learning,
In truth, I know not. I was set at work
Among my maids; full little, God knows, look-
  ing
Either for such men or such business.
For her sake that I have been,—for I feel
The last fit of my greatness,—good your Grace,
Let me have time and counsel for my cause.
Alas! I am a woman, friendless, hopeless.
Wol. Madam, you wrong the king's love with
  these fears;
Your hopes and friends are infinite.
Q. Kath.   In England
But little for my profit. Can you think, lords,
That any Englishman dare give me counsel?
Or be a known friend, 'gainst his highness' plea-
  sure,—
Though he be grown so desperate to be honest,—
And live a subject? Nay, forsooth, my friends,
They that must weigh out my afflictions,
They that my trust must grow to, live not here:
They are, as all my other comforts, far hence
In mine own country, lords.
Cam.   I would your Grace
Would leave your griefs, and take my counsel.
Q. Kath.   How, sir?

Cam. Put your main cause into the king's
protection;   92
e's loving and most gracious: 'twill be much
oth for your honour better and your cause;
or if the trial of the law o'ertake ye,
ou'll part away disgrac'd.
Wol.   He tells you rightly. 96
Q. Kath. Ye tell me what ye wish for both;
my ruin.
this your Christian counsel? out upon ye!
eaven is above all yet; there sits a judge
at no king can corrupt.
Cam.   Your rage mistakes us. 100
Q. Kath. The more shame for ye! holy men I
thought ye,
pon my soul, two reverend cardinal virtues;
t cardinal sins and hollow hearts I fear ye.
end 'em, for shame, my lords. Is this your
comfort?   104
e cordial that ye bring a wretched lady,
woman lost among ye, laugh'd at, scorn'd?
will not wish ye half my miseries,   107
have more charity; but say, I warn'd ye:
ke heed, for heaven's sake, take heed, lest at
once
he burden of my sorrows fall upon ye.
Wol. Madam, this is a mere distraction;
ou turn the good we offer into envy.   112
Q. Kath. Ye turn me into nothing: woe upon
ye,
nd all such false professors! Would ye have
me,—
ye have any justice, any pity;   115
ye be anything but churchmen's habits,—
t my sick cause into his hands that hates me?
las! he has banish'd me his bed already,
is love, too long ago! I am old, my lords,
nd all the fellowship I hold now with him
only my obedience. What can happen   121
o me above this wretchedness? all your studies
ake me a curse like this.
Cam.   Your fears are worse.
Q. Kath. Have I liv'd thus long—let me speak
myself,   124
nce virtue finds no friends—a wife, a true one?
woman, I dare say without vain-glory,
ever yet branded with suspicion?
ave I with all my full affections   128
ill met the king? lov'd him next heaven?
obey'd him?
een, out of fondness, superstitious to him?
lmost forgot my prayers to content him?
nd am I thus rewarded? 'tis not well, lords. 132
ring me a constant woman to her husband,
ne that ne'er dream'd a joy beyond his pleasure,
nd to that woman, when she has done most,
et will I add an honour, a great patience. 136
Wol. Madam, you wander from the good we
aim at.
Q. Kath. My lord, I dare not make myself so
guilty,
o give up willingly that noble title   139
our master wed me to: nothing but death
hall e'er divorce my dignities.
Wol.   Pray hear me.

Q. Kath. Would I had never trod this English
earth,
Or felt the flatteries that grow upon it!
Ye have angels' faces, but heaven knows your
hearts.   144
What will become of me now, wretched lady?
I am the most unhappy woman living.
[*To her women.*] Alas! poor wenches, where are
now your fortunes?   147
Shipwrack'd upon a kingdom, where no pity,
No friends, no hope; no kindred weep for me;
Almost no grave allow'd me. Like the lily,
That once was mistress of the field and flourish'd,
I'll hang my head and perish.
Wol.   If your Grace
Could but be brought to know our ends are
honest,   153
You'd feel more comfort. Why should we, good
lady,
Upon what cause, wrong you? alas! our places,
The way of our profession is against it: 156
We are to cure such sorrows, not to sow them.
For goodness' sake, consider what you do;
How you may hurt yourself, ay, utterly
Grow from the king's acquaintance, by this
carriage.   160
The hearts of princes kiss obedience,
So much they love it; but to stubborn spirits
They swell, and grow as terrible as storms.
I know you have a gentle, noble temper,   164
A soul as even as a calm: pray think us
Those we profess, peace-makers, friends, and
servants.
Cam. Madam, you'll find it so. You wrong
your virtues
With these weak women's fears: a noble spirit,
As yours was put into you, ever casts   169
Such doubts, as false coin, from it. The king
loves you;
Beware you lose it not: for us, if you please
To trust us in your business, we are ready
To use our utmost studies in your service.
Q. Kath. Do what ye will, my lords: and,
pray, forgive me
If I have us'd myself unmannerly.
You know I am a woman, lacking wit   176
To make a seemly answer to such persons.
Pray do my service to his majesty;
He has my heart yet; and shall have my prayers
While I shall have my life. Come, reverend
fathers,   180
Bestow your counsels on me: she now begs
That little thought, when she set footing here,
She should have bought her dignities so dear.
[*Exeunt.*

SCENE II.—*Antechamber to the* KING'S
Apartment.

Enter the DUKE OF NORFOLK, *the* DUKE OF
SUFFOLK, *the* EARL OF SURREY, *and the* Lord
Chamberlain.
Nor. If you will now unite in your com-
plaints,
And force them with a constancy, the cardinal
Cannot stand under them: if you omit

The offer of this time, I cannot promise 4
But that you shall sustain moe new disgraces
With these you bear already.
 Sur.   I am joyful
To meet the least occasion that may give me
Remembrance of my father-in-law, the duke, 8
To be reveng'd on him.
 Suf.   Which of the peers
Have uncontemn'd gone by him, or at least
Strangely neglected? when did he regard
The stamp of nobleness in any person, 12
Out of himself?
 Cham. My lords, you speak your pleasures:
What he deserves of you and me, I know;
What we can do to him,—though now the time
Gives way to us,—I much fear. If you cannot
Bar his access to the king, never attempt 17
Any thing on him, for he hath a witchcraft
Over the king in's tongue.
 Nor.   O! fear him not;
His spell in that is out: the king hath found
Matter against him that for ever mars 21
The honey of his language. No, he's settled,
Not to come off, in his displeasure.
 Sur.   Sir,
I should be glad to hear such news as this 24
Once every hour.
 Nor.   Believe it, this is true:
In the divorce his contrary proceedings
Are all unfolded; wherein he appears
As I would wish mine enemy.
 Sur.   How came 28
His practices to light?
 Suf.   Most strangely.
 Sur.   O! how? how?
 Suf. The cardinal's letter to the pope mis-
 carried,
And came to the eye o' the king; wherein was
 read,
That the cardinal did entreat his holiness 32
To stay the judgment o' the divorce; for if
It did take place, 'I do,' quoth he, 'perceive
My king is tangled in affection to 35
A creature of the queen's, Lady Anne Bullen.'
 Sur. Has the king this?
 Suf.   Believe it.
 Sur.   Will this work?
 Cham. The king in this perceives him, how
 he coasts
And hedges his own way. But in this point
All his tricks founder, and he brings his physic
After his patient's death: the king already 41
Hath married the fair lady.
 Sur.   Would he had!
 Suf. May you be happy in your wish, my
 lord!
For I profess, you have it.
 Sur.   Now all my joy 44
Trace the conjunction!
 Suf.   My amen to't!
 Nor.   All men's.
 Suf. There's order given for her coronation:
Marry, this is yet but young, and may be left
To some ears unrecounted. But, my lords,
She is a gallant creature, and complete 49
In mind and feature: I persuade me, from her

Will fall some blessing to this land, which shall
In it be memoriz'd.
 Sur.   But will the king 52
Digest this letter of the cardinal's?
The Lord forbid!
 Nor.   Marry, amen!
 Suf.   No, no;
There be moe wasps that buzz about his nose
Will make this sting the sooner. Cardinal Cam-
 peius 56
Is stol'n away to Rome; hath ta'en no leave;
Has left the cause o' the king unhandled; and
Is posted, as the agent of our cardinal,
To second all his plot. I do assure you 60
The king cried Ha! at this.
 Cham.   Now, God incense him,
And let him cry Ha! louder.
 Nor.   But, my lord,
When returns Cranmer?
 Suf. He is return'd in his opinions, which
Have satisfied the king for his divorce, 65
Together with all famous colleges
Almost in Christendom. Shortly, I believe,
His second marriage shall be publish'd, and
Her coronation. Katherine no more 69
Shall be call'd queen, but princess dowager,
And widow to Prince Arthur.
 Nor.   This same Cranmer's
A worthy fellow, and hath ta'en much pain
In the king's business.
 Suf.   He has; and we shall see him
For it an archbishop.
 Nor.   So I hear.
 Suf.   'Tis so. The cardinal!

Enter WOLSEY *and* CROMWELL.

 Nor.   Observe, observe; he's moody
 Wol. The packet, Cromwell, 70
Gave't you the king?
 Crom. To his own hand, in his bedchamber
 Wol. Look'd he o' the inside of the paper?
 Crom.   Presently
He did unseal them; and the first he view'd,
He did it with a serious mind; a heed 8
Was in his countenance. You he bade
Attend him here this morning.
 Wol.   Is he ready
To come abroad?
 Crom.   I think, by this he is. 8
 Wol. Leave me awhile. [*Exit* CROMWELL
[*Aside.*] It shall be to the Duchess of Alençon,
The French King's sister; he shall marry her.
Anne Bullen! No; I'll no Anne Bullens for him
There's more in't than fair visage. Bullen! 8
No, we'll no Bullens. Speedily I wish
To hear from Rome. The Marchioness of Pem
 broke!
 Nor. He's discontented.
 Suf.   May be he hears the kin
Does whet his anger to him.
 Sur.   Sharp enough, 9
Lord, for thy justice!
 Wol. The late queen's gentlewoman,
 knight's daughter,
To be her mistress' mistress! the queen's queen

This candle burns not clear: 'tis I must snuff it;
Then, out it goes. What though I know her
    virtuous
And well deserving? yet I know her for   99
A spleeny Lutheran; and not wholesome to
Our cause, that she should lie i' the bosom of
Our hard-rul'd king. Again, there is sprung up
A heretic, an arch one, Cranmer; one
Hath crawl'd into the favour of the king,   104
And is his oracle.

Nor.   He is vex'd at something.

Sur. I would 'twere something that would
    fret the string,
The master-cord on's heart!

Enter the KING, *reading a schedule; and*
    LOVELL.

Suf.   The king, the king!

K. Hen. What piles of wealth hath he ac-
    cumulated   108
To his own portion! and what expense by the
    hour
Seems to flow from him! How, i' the name of
    thrift,
Does he rake this together? Now, my lords,
Saw you the cardinal?

Nor.   My lord, we have   112
Stood here observing him; some strange com-
    motion
Is in his brain: he bites his lip, and starts;
Stops on a sudden, looks upon the ground,
Then lays his finger on his temple; straight 116
Springs out into fast gait; then stops again,
Strikes his breast hard; and anon he casts
His eye against the moon: in most strange
    postures
We have seen him set himself.

K. Hen.   It may well be: 120
There is a mutiny in's mind. This morning
Papers of state he sent me to peruse,
As I requir'd; and wot you what I found
There, on my conscience, put unwittingly? 124
Forsooth, an inventory, thus importing;
The several parcels of his plate, his treasure,
Rich stuffs and ornaments of household, which
    find at such a proud rate that it out-speaks
Possession of a subject.

Nor.   It's heaven's will: 129
Some spirit put this paper in the packet
To bless your eye withal.

K. Hen.   If we did think
His contemplation were above the earth, 132
And fix'd on spiritual object, he should still
Dwell in his musings: but I am afraid
His thinkings are below the moon, not worth
His serious considering.

    [*He takes his seat, and whispers*
        LOVELL, *who goes to* WOLSEY.

Wol.   Heaven forgive me! 136
Ever God bless your highness!

K. Hen.   Good my lord,
You are full of heavenly stuff, and bear the in-
    ventory
Of your best graces in your mind, the which
You were now running o'er: you have scarce
    time   140

To steal from spiritual leisure a brief span
To keep your earthly audit: sure, in that
I deem you an ill husband, and am glad
To have you therein my companion.

Wol.   Sir, 144
For holy offices I have a time; a time
To think upon the part of business which
I bear i' the state; and nature does require
Her times of preservation, which perforce 148
I, her frail son, amongst my brethren mortal,
Must give my tendance to.

K. Hen.   You have said well.

Wol. And ever may your highness yoke to-
    gether,
As I will lend you cause, my doing well   152
With my well saying!

K. Hen.   'Tis well said again;
And 'tis a kind of good deed to say well:
And yet words are no deeds. My father lov'd
    you: 155
He said he did; and with his deed did crown
His word upon you. Since I had my office,
I have kept you next my heart; have not alone
Employ'd you where high profits might come
    home,
But par'd my present havings, to bestow   160
My bounties upon you.

Wol. [*Aside.*] What should this mean?

Sur. [*Aside.*] The Lord increase this business!

K. Hen.   Have I not made you
The prime man of the state? I pray you, tell
    me
If what I now pronounce you have found true;
And if you may confess it, say withal,   165
If you are bound to us or no. What say you?

Wol. My sovereign, I confess your royal graces,
Shower'd on me daily, have been more than
    could   168
My studied purposes requite; which went
Beyond all man's endeavours: my endeavours
Have ever come too short of my desires,   171
Yet fil'd with my abilities. Mine own ends
Have been mine so, that evermore they pointed
To the good of your most sacred person and
The profit of the state. For your great graces
Heap'd upon me, poor undeserver, I   176
Can nothing render but allegiant thanks,
My prayers to heaven for you, my loyalty,
Which ever has and ever shall be growing,
Till death, that winter, kill it.

K. Hen.   Fairly answer'd; 180
A loyal and obedient subject is
Therein illustrated; the honour of it
Does pay the act of it, as, i' the contrary,
The foulness is the punishment. I presume
That as my hand has open'd bounty to you,
My heart dropp'd love, my power rain'd honour,
    more   187
On you than any; so your hand and heart,
Your brain, and every function of your power,
Should, notwithstanding that your bond of duty,
As 'twere in love's particular, be more
To me, your friend, than any.

Wol.   I do profess, 191
That for your highness' good I ever labour'd
More than mine own; that am, have, and will be.

Though all the world should crack their duty to
    you,
And throw it from their soul; though perils did
Abound as thick as thought could make 'em, and
Appear in forms more horrid, yet my duty, 197
As doth a rock against the chiding flood,
Should the approach of this wild river break,
And stand unshaken yours.
    K. Hen.   'Tis nobly spoken. 200
Take notice, lords, he has a loyal breast,
For you have seen him open't. Read o'er this;
                [*Giving him papers.*
And after, this: and then to breakfast with
What appetite you have.
    [*Exit* KING, *frowning upon* CARDINAL
    WOLSEY; *the* Nobles *throng after*
    him, smiling, and whispering.
    Wol.   What should this mean? 204
What sudden anger's this? how have I reap'd it?
He parted frowning from me, as if ruin
Leap'd from his eyes: so looks the chafed lion
Upon the daring huntsman that has gall'd him;
Then makes him nothing. I must read this
    paper,   209
I fear, the story of his anger. 'Tis so;
This paper has undone me! 'Tis the account
Of all that world of wealth I have drawn together
For mine own ends; indeed, to gain the popedom,
And fee my friends in Rome. O negligence!
Fit for a fool to fall by: what cross devil 215
Made me put this main secret in the packet
I sent the king? Is there no way to cure this?
No new device to beat this from his brains?
I know 'twill stir him strongly; yet I know
A way, if it take right, in spite of fortune 220
Will bring me off again. What's this?—'To the
    Pope!'
The letter, as I live, with all the business
I writ to's holiness. Nay then, farewell!
I have touch'd the highest point of all my great-
    ness;   224
And from that full meridian of my glory,
I haste now to my setting: I shall fall
Like a bright exhalation in the evening,
And no man see me more.   228

Re-enter the DUKES OF NORFOLK *and* SUFFOLK,
the EARL OF SURREY, *and the* Lord Chamberlain.

    Nor. Hear the king's pleasure, cardinal: who
    commands you
To render up the great seal presently
Into our hands; and to confine yourself
To Asher-house, my Lord of Winchester's, 232
Till you hear further from his highness.
    Wol.   Stay,
Where's your commission, lord? words cannot
carry
Authority so weighty.
    Suf.   Who dare cross 'em,
Bearing the king's will from his mouth expressly?
    Wol. Till I find more than will or words to
do it,   237
I mean your malice, know, officious lords,
I dare and must deny it. Now I feel
Of what coarse metal ye are moulded, envy:

How eagerly ye follow my disgraces, 24
As if it fed ye! and how sleek and wanton
Ye appear in every thing may bring my ruin
Follow your envious courses, men of malice;
You have Christian warrant for 'em, and, n
    doubt,   24
In time will find their fit rewards. That seal
You ask with such a violence, the king—
Mine and your master—with his own hand gav
    me;   24
Bade me enjoy it with the place and honours
During my life; and to confirm his goodnes
Tied it by letters-patents: now who'll take it
    Sur. The king, that gave it.
    Wol.   It must be himself then. 25
    Sur. Thou art a proud traitor, priest.
    Wol.   Proud lord, thou liest
Within these forty hours Surrey durst better
Have burnt that tongue than said so.
    Sur.   Thy ambition
Thou scarlet sin, robb'd this bewailing land
Of noble Buckingham, my father-in-law: 25
The heads of all thy brother cardinals—
With thee and all thy best parts bound to
    gether—
Weigh'd not a hair of his. Plague of you
    policy!   26
You sent me deputy for Ireland,
Far from his succour, from the king, from al
That might have mercy on the fault thou gav'
    him;   26
Whilst your great goodness, out of holy pity
Absolv'd him with an axe.
    Wol.   This and all else
This talking lord can lay upon my credit,
I answer is most false. The duke by law
Found his deserts: how innocent I was   26
From any private malice in his end,
His noble jury and foul cause can witness.
If I lov'd many words, lord, I should tell you
You have as little honesty as honour,   27
That in the way of loyalty and truth
Toward the king, my ever royal master,
Dare mate a sounder man than Surrey can be
And all that love his follies.
    Sur.   By my soul, 27
Your long coat, priest, protects you; thou
    shouldst feel
My sword i' the life-blood of thee else. My lords
Can ye endure to hear this arrogance?
And from this fellow? If we live thus tamely
To be thus jaded by a piece of scarlet, 28
Farewell nobility; let his Grace go forward,
And dare us with his cap like larks.
    Wol.   All goodnes
Is poison to thy stomach.
    Sur.   Yes, that goodness 28
Of gleaning all the land's wealth into one,
Into your own hands, cardinal, by extortion;
The goodness of your intercepted packets,
You writ to the pope against the king; you
    goodness,   28
Since you provoke me, shall be most notorious
My Lord of Norfolk, as you are truly noble,
As you respect the common good, the state
Of our despis'd nobility, our issues,   29

Who, if he live, will scarce be gentlemen,
Produce the grand sum of his sins, the articles
Collected from his life; I'll startle you
Worse than the sacring bell, when the brown
    wench   296
Lay kissing in your arms, Lord Cardinal.
    Wol. How much, methinks, I could despise
    this man,
But that I am bound in charity against it!
    Nor. Those articles, my lord, are in the king's
    hand;   300
But, thus much, they are foul ones.
    Wol.   So much fairer
And spotless shall mine innocence arise
When the king knows my truth.
    Sur.   This cannot save you:
I thank my memory, I yet remember   304
Some of these articles; and out they shall.
Now, if you can blush, and cry 'guilty,' cardinal,
You'll show a little honesty.
    Wol.   Speak on, sir;
I dare your worst objections; if I blush,   308
It is to see a nobleman want manners.
    Sur. I had rather want those than my head.
Have at you!
First, that, without the king's assent or know-
    ledge,   311
You wrought to be a legate; by which power
You maim'd the jurisdiction of all bishops.
    Nor. Then, that in all you writ to Rome, or else
To foreign princes, *Ego et Rex meus*   314
Was still inscrib'd; in which you brought the
    king
To be your servant.
    Suf. Then, that without the knowledge
Either of king or council, when you went
Ambassador to the emperor, you made bold
To carry into Flanders the great seal.   320
    Sur. Item, you sent a large commission
To Gregory de Cassado, to conclude,
Without the king's will or the state's allowance,
A league between his highness and Ferrara.
    Suf. That, out of mere ambition, you have
    caus'd   325
Your holy hat to be stamp'd on the king's coin.
    Sur. Then, that you have sent innumerable
    substance,—
By what means got I leave to your own con-
    science,—   328
To furnish Rome, and to prepare the ways
You have for dignities; to the mere undoing
Of all the kingdom. Many more there are;
Which, since they are of you, and odious,   332
will not taint my mouth with.
    Cham.   O my lord!
Press not a falling man too far; 'tis virtue:
His faults lie open to the laws; let them,
Not you, correct him. My heart weeps to see
    him   336
So little of his great self.
    Sur.   I forgive him.
    Suf. Lord Cardinal, the king's further plea-
    sure is,
Because all those things you have done of late,
By your power legatine, within this kingdom,
Fall into the compass of a *præmunire*,   341

That therefore such a writ be su'd against you;
To forfeit all your goods, lands, tenements,
Chattels, and whatsoever, and to be   344
Out of the king's protection. This is my charge.
    Nor. And so we'll leave you to your medita-
    tions
How to live better. For your stubborn answer
About the giving back the great seal to us,
The king shall know it, and, no doubt, shall
    thank you.
So fare you well, my little good Lord Cardinal.   349
        [Exeunt all except WOLSEY.
    Wol. So farewell to the little good you bear
    me.   351
Farewell! a long farewell, to all my greatness!
This is the state of man: to-day he puts forth
The tender leaves of hopes; to-morrow blossoms,
And bears his blushing honours thick upon him;
The third day comes a frost, a killing frost;
And, when he thinks, good easy man, full surely
His greatness is a-ripening, nips his root,   358
And then he falls, as I do. I have ventur'd,
Like little wanton boys that swim on bladders,
This many summers in a sea of glory,   361
But far beyond my depth: my high-blown pride
At length broke under me, and now has left me,
Weary and old with service, to the mercy   364
Of a rude stream, that must for ever hide me.
Vain pomp and glory of this world, I hate ye:
I feel my heart new open'd. O! how wretched
Is that poor man that hangs on princes' favours!
There is, betwixt that smile we would aspire to,
That sweet aspect of princes, and their ruin,
More pangs and fears than wars or women have;
And when he falls, he falls like Lucifer,   372
Never to hope again.

Enter CROMWELL, *and stands amazed.*
        Why, how now, Cromwell!
    Crom. I have no power to speak, sir.
    Wol.   What! amaz'd
At my misfortunes? can thy spirit wonder
A great man should decline? Nay, an you weep,
I am fall'n indeed.
    Crom.   How does your Grace?
    Wol.   Why, well;   377
Never so truly happy, my good Cromwell.
I know myself now; and I feel within me
A peace above all earthly dignities,   380
A still and quiet conscience. The king has cur'd
    me,
I humbly thank his Grace; and from these
    shoulders,
These ruin'd pillars, out of pity taken   383
A load would sink a navy, too much honour:
O! 'tis a burden, Cromwell, 'tis a burden
Too heavy for a man that hopes for heaven.
    Crom. I am glad your Grace has made that
    right use of it.
    Wol. I hope I have: I am able now, methinks,—
Out of a fortitude of soul I feel,—   389
To endure more miseries and greater far
Than my weak-hearted enemies dare offer.
What news abroad?
    Crom.   The heaviest and the worst,
Is your displeasure with the king.

Wol.   God bless him! 393
Crom. The next is, that Sir Thomas More is chosen
Lord Chancellor in your place.
Wol.   That's somewhat sudden:
But he's a learned man. May he continue 396
Long in his highness' favour, and do justice
For truth's sake and his conscience; that his bones,
When he has run his course and sleeps in blessings,
May have a tomb of orphans' tears wept on 'em!
What more? 401
Crom. That Cranmer is return'd with welcome,
Install'd Lord Archbishop of Canterbury.
Wol. That's news indeed.
Crom.   Last, that the Lady Anne,
Whom the king hath in secrecy long married,
This day was view'd in open, as his queen, 405
Going to chapel; and the voice is now
Only about her coronation.
Wol. There was the weight that pull'd me down. O Cromwell! 408
The king has gone beyond me: all my glories
In that one woman I have lost for ever.
No sun shall ever usher forth mine honours,
Or gild again the noble troops that waited 412
Upon my smiles. Go, get thee from me, Cromwell;
I am a poor fall'n man, unworthy now
To be thy lord and master: seek the king;—
That sun, I pray, may never set!—I have told him 416
What, and how true thou art: he will advance thee;
Some little memory of me will stir him—
I know his noble nature—not to let 419
Thy hopeful service perish too. Good Cromwell,
Neglect him not; make use now, and provide
For thine own future safety.
Crom.   O my lord!
Must I then, leave you? must I needs forego
So good, so noble, and so true a master? 424
Bear witness all that have not hearts of iron,
With what a sorrow Cromwell leaves his lord.
The king shall have my service; but my prayers
For ever and for ever, shall be yours. 428
Wol. Cromwell, I did not think to shed a tear
In all my miseries; but thou hast forc'd me,
Out of thy honest truth, to play the woman.
Let's dry our eyes: and thus far hear me, Cromwell; 432
And, when I am forgotten, as I shall be,
And sleep in dull cold marble, where no mention
Of me more must be heard of, say, I taught thee,
Say, Wolsey, that once trod the ways of glory,
And sounded all the depths and shoals of honour, 437
Found thee a way, out of his wrack, to rise in;
A sure and safe one, though thy master miss'd it.
Mark but my fall, and that that ruin'd me. 440

Cromwell, I charge thee, fling away ambition:
By that sin fell the angels; how can man then,
The image of his Maker, hope to win by't?
Love thyself last: cherish those hearts that hate thee; 444
Corruption wins not more than honesty.
Still in thy right hand carry gentle peace,
To silence envious tongues: be just, and fear not.
Let all the ends thou aim'st at be thy country's,
Thy God's, and truth's; then if thou fall'st, O Cromwell! 449
Thou fall'st a blessed martyr. Serve the king;
And,—prithee, lead me in:
There take an inventory of all I have, 452
To the last penny; 'tis the king's: my robe,
And my integrity to heaven is all
I dare now call mine own. O Cromwell, Cromwell! 455
Had I but serv'd my God with half the zeal
I serv'd my king, he would not in mine age
Have left me naked to mine enemies.
Crom. Good sir, have patience.
Wol.   So I have. Farewell
The hopes of court! my hopes in heaven do dwell.   [*Exeunt.*

ACT IV

SCENE I.—*A Street in Westminster.*

Enter two Gentlemen, *meeting.*

First Gen. You're well met once again.
Sec. Gen.   So are you.
First Gen. You come to take your stand here, and behold
The Lady Anne pass from her coronation?
Sec. Gen. 'Tis all my business. At our last encounter
The Duke of Buckingham came from his trial.
First Gen. 'Tis very true: but that time offer'd sorrow;
This, general joy.
Sec. Gen.   'Tis well: the citizens,
I am sure, have shown at full their royal minds
As, let 'em have their rights, they are ever forward,
In celebration of this day with shows,
Pageants, and sights of honour.
First Gen.   Never greater,
Nor, I'll assure you, better taken, sir. 1
Sec. Gen. May I be bold to ask what that contains,
That paper in your hand?
First Gen.   Yes; 'tis the list
Of those that claim their offices this day
By custom of the coronation.
The Duke of Suffolk is the first, and claims
To be high-steward; next, the Duke of Norfolk,
He to be earl marshal: you may read the rest.
Sec. Gen. I thank you, sir: had I not known those customs,
I should have been beholding to your paper.
But, I beseech you, what's become of Katharine,
The princess dowager? how goes her business?
First Gen. That I can tell you too. The Archbishop
Of Canterbury, accompanied with other

earned and reverend fathers of his order,
eld a late court at Dunstable, six miles off
rom Ampthill, where the princess lay; to
   which   28
ae was often cited by them, but appear'd not:
nd, to be short, for not appearance and
he king's late scruple, by the main assent
f all these learned men she was divorc'd, 32
nd the late marriage made of none effect:
nce which she was remov'd to Kimbolton,
'here she remains now sick.

Sec. Gen.   Alas! good lady!
                   [*Trumpets.*
he trumpets sound: stand close, the queen is
   coming.   [*Hautboys.*

THE ORDER OF THE CORONATION.

A lively flourish of trumpets.

Two Judges.
Lord Chancellor, *with the purse and mace*
  before him.
Choristers, *singing.*   [*Music.*
Mayor of London, *bearing the mace. Then*
  Garter, *in his coat of arms, and on his head*
  a gilt copper crown.
MARQUESS DORSET, *bearing a sceptre of gold,*
  on his head a demi-coronal of gold. With
  him, the EARL OF SURREY, *bearing the rod of*
  silver with the dove, crowned with an earl's
  coronet. Collars of SS.
DUKE OF SUFFOLK, *in his robe of estate, his*
  coronet on his head, bearing a long white
  wand, as high-steward. With him, the DUKE
  OF NORFOLK, *with the rod of marshalship,*
  a coronet on his head. Collars of SS.
A canopy borne by four of the Cinque-ports;
  under it, the QUEEN *in her robe; in her hair*
  richly adorned with pearl, crowned. On
  each side of her, the BISHOPS OF LONDON *and*
  WINCHESTER.
The old DUCHESS OF NORFOLK, *in a coronal*
  of gold, wrought with flowers, bearing the
  QUEEN'S *train.*
Certain Ladies *or* Countesses, *with plain*
  circlets of gold without flowers.

They pass over the stage in order and state.

Sec. Gen. A royal train, believe me. These I
  know;   37
ho's that that bears the sceptre?
First Gen.   Marquess Dorset:
nd that the Earl of Surrey with the rod.
Sec. Gen. A bold brave gentleman. That
  should be   40
ae Duke of Suffolk?
First Gen.   'Tis the same; high-steward.
Sec. Gen. And that my Lord of Norfolk?
First Gen.   Yes.
Sec. Gen. [*Looking on the* QUEEN.] Heaven
  bless thee!
aou hast the sweetest face I ever look'd on.
r, as I have a soul, she is an angel;   44
ar king has all the Indies in his arms,
nd more and richer, when he strains that lady:
:annot blame his conscience.
First Gen.   They that bear

The cloth of honour over her, are four barons
Of the Cinque-ports.
  Sec. Gen. Those men are happy; and so are
    all are near her.
I take it, she that carries up the train
Is that old noble lady, Duchess of Norfolk. 52
  First Gen. It is; and all the rest are count-
    esses.
  Sec. Gen. Their coronets say so. These are
    stars indeed;
And sometimes falling ones.
  First Gen.   No more of that.
           [*Exit Procession, with a great*
           flourish of trumpets.

Enter a third Gentleman.

God save you, sir: Where have you been broil-
  ing?   56
  Third Gen. Among the crowd i' the Abbey;
    where a finger
Could not be wedg'd in more: I am stifled
With the mere rankness of their joy.
  Sec. Gen.   You saw
The ceremony?
  Third Gen.   That I did.
  First Gen.   How was it? 60
  Third Gen. Well worth the seeing.
  Sec. Gen.   Good sir, speak it to us.
  Third Gen. As well as I am able. The rich
    stream
Of lords and ladies, having brought the queen
To a prepar'd place in the choir, fell off   64
A distance from her; while her Grace sat down
To rest awhile, some half an hour or so,
In a rich chair of state, opposing freely
The beauty of her person to the people. 68
Believe me, sir, she is the goodliest woman
That ever lay by man: which when the people
Had the full view of, such a noise arose
As the shrouds make at sea in a stiff tempest, 72
As loud, and to as many tunes: hats, cloaks,—
Doublets, I think,—flew up; and had their
  faces
Been loose, this day they had been lost. Such
  joy
I never saw before. Great-bellied women, 76
That had not half a week to go, like rams
In the old time of war, would shake the press,
And make 'em reel before them. No man living
Could say, 'This is my wife,' there; all were
  woven 80
So strangely in one piece.
  Sec. Gen.   But, what follow'd?
  Third Gen. At length her Grace rose, and
    with modest paces
Came to the altar; where she kneel'd, and,
  saint-like,
Cast her fair eyes to heaven and pray'd de-
  voutly. 84
Then rose again and bow'd her to the people:
When by the Archbishop of Canterbury
She had all the royal makings of a queen;
As holy oil, Edward Confessor's crown, 88
The rod, and bird of peace, and all such em-
  blems
Laid nobly on her: which perform'd, the choir,

With all the choicest music of the kingdom,
Together sung *Te Deum*. So she parted,   92
And with the same full state pac'd back again
To York-place, where the feast is held.
   First Gen.   Sir,
You must no more call it York-place, that's
   past;
For, since the cardinal fell, that title's lost: 96
'Tis now the king's, and call'd Whitehall.
   Third Gen.   I know it;
But 'tis so lately alter'd that the old name
Is fresh about me.
   Sec. Gen.   What two reverend bishops
Were those that went on each side of the
   queen?   100
   Third Gen. Stokesly and Gardiner; the one
   of Winchester,—
Newly preferr'd from the king's secretary,—
The other, London.
   Sec. Gen.   He of Winchester
Is held no great good lover of the archbishop's,
The virtuous Cranmer.
   Third Gen.   All the land knows that:
However, yet there's no great breach; when it
   comes,   106
Cranmer will find a friend will not shrink from
   him.
   Sec. Gen. Who may that be, I pray you?
   Third Gen.   Thomas Cromwell:
A man in much esteem with the king, and truly
A worthy friend. The king
Has made him master o' the jewel house,
And one, already, of the privy-council.   112
   Sec. Gen. He will deserve more.
   Third Gen.   Yes, without all doubt.
Come, gentlemen, ye shall go my way, which
Is to the court, and there ye shall be my guests;
Something I can command. As I walk thither,
I'll tell ye more.
   Both.   You may command us, sir.   117
                         [*Exeunt.*

   SCENE II.—*Kimbolton.*

Enter KATHARINE, *Dowager, sick: led between*
        GRIFFITH *and* PATIENCE.

   Grif. How does your Grace?
   Kath.   O Griffith: sick to death!
My legs, like loaden branches, bow to the earth,
Willing to leave their burden. Reach a chair:
So; now, methinks, I feel a little ease.   4
Didst thou not tell me, Griffith, as thou ledd'st
   me,
That the great child of honour, Cardinal
   Wolsey,
Was dead?
   Grif. Yes, madam; but I think your Grace,
Out of the pain you suffer'd, gave no ear to 't. 8
   Kath. Prithee, good Griffith, tell me how he
   died:
If well, he stepp'd before me, happily,
For my example.
   Grif.   Well, the voice goes, madam:
For after the stout Earl Northumberland   12
Arrested him at York, and brought him for-
   ward,

As a man sorely tainted, to his answer,
He fell sick suddenly, and grew so ill
He could not sit his mule.
   Kath.   Alas! poor man.
   Grif. At last, with easy roads, he came
   Leicester;
Lodg'd in the abbey, where the reverend abbo
With all his covent, honourably receiv'd hir
To whom he gave these words: 'O! fath
   abbot,
An old man, broken with the storms of stat
Is come to lay his weary bones among ye;
Give him a little earth for charity.'
So went to bed, where eagerly his sickness
Pursu'd him still; and three nights after thi
About the hour of eight,—which he himself
Foretold should be his last,—full of repentanc
Continual meditations, tears, and sorrows,
He gave his honours to the world again,
His blessed part to heaven, and slept in peac
   Kath. So may he rest; his faults lie gently o
   him!
Yet thus far, Griffith, give me leave to spea
   him,
And yet with charity. He was a man
Of an unbounded stomach, ever ranking
Himself with princes; one, that by suggestio
Tied all the kingdom; simony was fair-play;
His own opinion was his law; i' the presenc
He would say untruths, and be ever double
Both in his words and meaning. He was neve
But where he meant to ruin, pitiful;
His promises were, as he then was, mighty;
But his performance, as he is now, nothing:
Of his own body he was ill, and gave
The clergy ill example.
   Grif.   Noble madam,
Men's evil manners live in brass; their virtu
We write in water. May it please your highne
To hear me speak his good now?
   Kath.   Yes, good Griffit
I were malicious else.
   Grif.   This cardinal,
Though from a humble stock, undoubtedly
Was fashion'd to much honour from his cradl
He was a scholar, and a ripe and good one;
Exceeding wise, fair-spoken, and persuading;
Lofty and sour to them that lov'd him not;
But, to those men that sought him sweet a
   summer.
And though he were unsatisfied in getting,—
Which was a sin,—yet in bestowing, madam,
He was most princely. Ever witness for him
Those twins of learning that he rais'd in you
Ipswich, and Oxford! one of which fell with hir
Unwilling to outlive the good that did it;
The other, though unfinish'd, yet so famous
So excellent in art, and still so rising,
That Christendom shall ever speak his virtu
His overthrow heap'd happiness upon him;
For then, and not till then, he felt himself,
And found the blessedness of being little:
And, to add greater honours to his age
Than man could give him, he died fearing Go
   Kath. After my death I wish no other heral
No other speaker of my living actions,

keep mine honour from corruption,
t such an honest chronicler as Griffith. 72
hom I most hated living, thou hast made me,
ith thy religious truth and modesty,
ow in his ashes honour. Peace be with him!
tience, be near me still; and set me lower: 76
ave not long to trouble thee. Good Griffith,
use the musicians play me that sad note
am'd my knell, whilst I sit meditating
that celestial harmony I go to. 80
      [Sad and solemn music.

Grif. She is asleep: good wench, let's sit
down quiet,
r fear we wake her: softly, gentle Patience.

*e Vision. Enter, solemnly tripping one after
another, six Personages, clad in white robes,
wearing on their heads garlands of bays, and
golden vizards on their faces; branches of
bays or palm in their hands. They first
congee unto her, then dance; and, at certain
changes, the first two hold a spare garland
over her head; at which, the other four make
reverend curtsies: then, the two that held the
garland deliver the same to the other next
two, who observe the same order in their
changes, and holding the garland over her
head: which done, they deliver the same garland to the last two, who likewise observe
the same order, at which,—as it were by
inspiration,—she makes in her sleep signs
of rejoicing, and holdeth up her hands to
heaven: and so in their dancing they vanish,
carrying the garland with them. The music
continues.*

Kath. Spirits of peace, where are ye? Are ye
all gone,
nd leave me here in wretchedness behind ye?
Grif. Madam, we are here.
Kath.   It is not you I call for: 85
aw ye none enter since I slept?
Grif.   None, madam.
Kath. No? Saw you not, even now, a blessed
troop
vite me to a banquet; whose bright faces
ast thousand beams upon me, like the sun?
hey promis'd me eternal happiness, 90
nd brought me garlands, Griffith, which I
feel
am not worthy yet to wear: I shall assuredly.
Grif. I am most joyful, madam, such good
dreams 93
ossess your fancy.
Kath.   Bid the music leave,
hey are harsh and heavy to me. *[Music ceases.*
Pat.   Do you note
ow much her Grace is alter'd on the sudden?
ow long her face is drawn? How pale she
looks, 97
nd of an earthy cold? Mark her eyes!
Grif. She is going, wench. Pray, pray.
Pat. Heaven comfort her! 100

Enter a Messenger.

Mess. An't like your Grace,—
Kath.   You are a saucy fellow:

Deserve we no more reverence?
Grif.   You are to blame,
Knowing she will not lose her wonted great-
ness,
To use so rude behaviour; go to, kneel. 104
Mess. I humbly do entreat your highness'
pardon;
My haste made me unmannerly. There is
staying
A gentleman, sent from the king, to see you.
Kath. Admit him entrance, Griffith: but this
fellow 108
Let me ne'er see again.
      [Exeunt GRIFFITH *and* Messenger.

Re-enter GRIFFITH, *with* CAPUCIUS.
       If my sight fail not,
You should be lord ambassador from the
emperor,
My royal nephew, and your name Capucius.
Cap. Madam, the same; your servant.
Kath.   O my lord! 112
The times and titles now are alter'd strangely
With me since first you knew me. But, I pray
you,
What is your pleasure with me?
Cap.   Noble lady,
First, mine own service to your Grace; the
next, 116
The king's request that I would visit you;
Who grieves much for your weakness, and by me
Sends you his princely commendations, 119
And heartily entreats you take good comfort.
Kath. O! my good lord, that comfort comes
too late;
'Tis like a pardon after execution:
That gentle physic, given in time, had cur'd
me;
But now I am past all comforts here but prayers.
How does his highness?
Cap.   Madam, in good health. 125
Kath. So may he ever do! and ever flourish,
When I shall dwell with worms, and my poor
name
Banish'd the kingdom. Patience, is that letter
I caus'd you write, yet sent away?
Pat.   No, madam. 129
      [Giving it to KATHARINE.
Kath. Sir, I most humbly pray you to deliver
This to my lord the king.
Cap.   Most willing, madam.
Kath. In which I have commended to his
goodness 132
The model of our chaste loves, his young
daughter:
The dews of heaven fall thick in blessings on
her!
Beseeching him to give her virtuous breeding,—
She is young, and of a noble modest nature, 136
I hope she will deserve well,—and a little
To love her for her mother's sake, that lov'd
him,
Heaven knows how dearly. My next poor peti-
tion
Is, that his noble Grace would have some pity
Upon my wretched women, that so long 141

Have follow'd both my fortunes faithfully:
Of which there is not one, I dare avow,—
And now I should not lie,—but will deserve, 144
For virtue, and true beauty of the soul,
For honesty and decent carriage,
A right good husband, let him be a noble;
And, sure, those men are happy that shall have
'em.   148
The last is, for my men: they are the poorest,
But poverty could never draw 'em from me;
That they may have their wages duly paid 'em,
And something over to remember me by: 152
If heaven had pleas'd to have given me longer
    life
And able means, we had not parted thus.
These are the whole contents: and, good my
    lord,
By that you love the dearest in this world, 156
As you wish Christian peace to souls departed,
Stand these poor people's friend, and urge the
    king
To do me this last right.
    Cap.   By heaven, I will,
Or let me lose the fashion of a man! 160
    Kath. I thank you, honest lord. Remember me
In all humility unto his highness:
Say his long trouble now is passing
Out of this world; tell him, in death I bless'd
    him,   164
For so I will. Mine eyes grow dim. Farewell,
My lord. Griffith, farewell. Nay, Patience,
You must not leave me yet: I must to bed;
Call in more women. When I am dead, good
    wench,   168
Let me be us'd with honour: strew me over
With maiden flowers, that all the world may
    know
I was a chaste wife to my grave: embalm me,
Then lay me forth: although unqueen'd, yet
    like   172
A queen, and daughter to a king, inter me.
I can no more. [Exeunt, leading KATHARINE.

ACT V

SCENE I.—London. A Gallery in the Palace.

Enter GARDINER, Bishop of Winchester, a Page
with a torch before him, met by SIR THOMAS
LOVELL.

    Gar. It's one o'clock, boy, is 't not?
    Boy.   It has struck.
    Gar. These should be hours for necessities,
Not for delights; times to repair our nature
With comforting repose, and not for us   4
To waste these times. Good hour of night, Sir
    Thomas!
Whither so late?
    Lov.   Came you from the king, my lord?
    Gar. I did, Sir Thomas; and left him at
    primero
With the Duke of Suffolk.
    Lov.   I must to him too, 8
Before he go to bed. I'll take my leave.
    Gar. Not yet, Sir Thomas Lovell. What's
the matter?
It seems you are in haste: an if there be

No great offence belongs to 't, give your frie
Some touch of your late business: affairs, t
    walk—
As they say spirits do—at midnight, have
In them a wilder nature than the business
That seeks dispatch by day.
    Lov.   My lord, I love you,
And durst commend a secret to your ear
Much weightier than this work. The queen's
    labour,
They say, in great extremity; and fear'd
She'll with the labour end.
    Gar.   The fruit she goes with
I pray for heartily, that it may find
Good time, and live: but for the stock,
    Thomas,
I wish it grubb'd up now.
    Lov.   Methinks I coul
Cry the amen; and yet my conscience says
She's a good creature, and, sweet lady, do
Deserve our better wishes.
    Gar.   But, sir, sir,
Hear me, Sir Thomas: you're a gentleman
Of mine own way; I know you wise, religio
And, let me tell you, it will ne'er be well,
'Twill not, Sir Thomas Lovell, take 't of m
Till Cranmer, Cromwell, her two hands, and s
Sleep in their graves.
    Lov.   Now, sir, you speak of two
The most remark'd i' the kingdom. As
    Cromwell,
Beside that of the jewel-house, is made mas
O' the rolls, and the king's secretary; further,
Stands in the gap and trade of moe preferme
With which the time will load him. The ar
    bishop
Is the king's hand and tongue; and who d
    speak
One syllable against him?
    Gar.   Yes, yes, Sir Thom
There are that dare; and I myself have ventu
To speak my mind of him: and indeed this d
Sir,—I may tell it you,—I think I have
Incens'd the lords o' the council that he is-
For so I know he is, they know he is—
A most arch heretic, a pestilence
That does infect the land: with which th
    mov'd
Have broken with the king; who hath so f
Given ear to our complaint,—of his great gr
And princely care, foreseeing those fell misch
Our reasons laid before him,—hath comman
To-morrow morning to the council-board
He be convented. He's a rank weed, Sir Thom
And we must root him out. From your affa
I hinder you too long: good-night, Sir Thom
    Lov. Many good-nights, my lord. I rest y
    servant.   [Exeunt GARDINER and Pa

Enter the KING and SUFFOLK.

    K. Hen. Charles, I will play no more
    night;
My mind's not on 't; you are too hard for n
    Suf. Sir, I did never win of you before.
    K. Hen. But little, Charles;
Nor shall not when my fancy's on my play.

ow, Lovell, from the queen what is the news?
Lov. I could not personally deliver to her
hat you commanded me, but by her woman
ent your message; who return'd her thanks
the great'st humbleness, and desir'd your
highness 65
ost heartily to pray for her.
K. Hen. What sayst thou, ha?
pray for her? what! is she crying out?
Lov. So said her woman; and that her sufferance made 68
most each pang a death.
K. Hen. Alas! good lady.
Suf. God safely quit her of her burden, and
ith gentle travail, to the gladding of
our highness with an heir!
K. Hen. 'Tis midnight, Charles; 72
ithee, to bed; and in thy prayers remember
ie estate of my poor queen. Leave me alone;
or I must think of that which company
ould not be friendly to.
Suf. I wish your highness 76
quiet night; and my good mistress will
emember in my prayers.
K. Hen. Charles, good-night.
[*Exit* SUFFOLK.

Enter SIR ANTHONY DENNY.

ell, Sir, what follows?
Den. Sir, I have brought my lord the arch-
bishop, 80
s you commanded me.
K. Hen. Ha! Canterbury?
Den. Ay, my good lord.
K. Hen. 'Tis true: where is he, Denny?
Den. He attends your highness' pleasure.
K. Hen. Bring him to us.
[*Exit* DENNY.
Lov. [*Aside.*] This is about that which the
bishop spake: 84
am happily come hither.

Re-enter DENNY, *with* CRANMER.

K. Hen. Avoid the gallery.
[LOVELL *seems to stay.*
a! I have said. Begone.
hat!— [*Exeunt* LOVELL *and* DENNY.
Cran. I am fearful. Wherefore frowns he
thus? 88
is his aspect of terror: all 's not well.
K. Hen. How now, my lord! You do desire to
know
herefore I sent for you.
Cran. [*Kneeling.*] It is my duty
o attend your highness' pleasure.
K. Hen. Pray you, arise,
y good and gracious Lord of Canterbury. 93
ome, you and I must walk a turn together;
have news to tell you: come, come, give me
your hand.
h! my good lord, I grieve at what I speak, 96
nd am right sorry to repeat what follows.
have, and most unwillingly, of late
eard many grievous, I do say, my lord,
rievous complaints of you; which, being consider'd, 100

Have mov'd us and our council, that you shall
This morning come before us; where, I know,
You cannot with such freedom purge yourself,
But that, till further trial in those charges 104
Which will require your answer, you must take
Your patience to you, and be well contented
To make your house our Tower: you a brother
of us,
It fits we thus proceed, or else no witness 108
Would come against you.
Cran. [*Kneeling.*] I humbly thank your high-
ness;
And am right glad to catch this good occasion
Most throughly to be winnow'd, where my chaff
And corn shall fly asunder; for I know 112
There's none stands under more calumnious
tongues
Than I myself, poor man.
K. Hen. Stand up, good Canterbury:
Thy truth and thy integrity is rooted 115
In us, thy friend: give me thy hand, stand up:
Prithee, let's walk. Now, by my holidame,
What manner of man are you? My lord, I look'd
You would have given me your petition, that
I should have ta'en some pains to bring to-
gether 120
Yourself and your accusers; and to have heard
you,
Without indurance, further.
Cran. Most dread liege,
The good I stand on is my truth and honesty:
If they shall fail, I, with mine enemies, 124
Will triumph o'er my person; which I weigh
not,
Being of those virtues vacant. I fear nothing
What can be said against me.
K. Hen. Know you not
How your state stands i' the world, with the
whole world? 128
Your enemies are many, and not small; their
practices
Must bear the same proportion; and not ever
The justice and the truth o' the question carries
The due o' the verdict with it. At what ease
Might corrupt minds procure knaves as corrupt
To swear against you? such things have been
done.
You are potently oppos'd, and with a malice
Of as great size. Ween you of better luck, 136
I mean in perjur'd witness, than your master,
Whose minister you are, whiles here he liv'd
Upon this naughty earth? Go to, go to;
You take a precipice for no leap of danger, 140
And woo your own destruction.
Cran. God and your majesty
Protect mine innocence! or I fall into
The trap is laid for me!
K. Hen. Be of good cheer;
They shall no more prevail than we give way
to. 144
Keep comfort to you; and this morning see
You do appear before them. If they shall
chance,
In charging you with matters, to commit you,
The best persuasions to the contrary 148
Fail not to use, and with what vehemency

The occasion shall instruct you: if entreaties
Will render you no remedy, this ring
Deliver them, and your appeal to us   152
There make before them. Look! the good man
weeps;
He's honest, on mine honour. God's blest
mother!
I swear he is true-hearted; and a soul   155
None better in my kingdom. Get you gone,
And do as I have bid you. [*Exit* CRANMER.] He
has strangled
His language in his tears.

Enter an Old Lady.

Gent. [*Within.*] Come back: what mean you?
Old L. I'll not come back; the tidings that I
bring   160
Will make my boldness manners. Now, good
angels
Fly o'er thy royal head, and shade thy person
Under their blessed wings!
K. Hen.   Now, by thy looks
I guess thy message. Is the queen deliver'd?
Say, ay; and of a boy.
Old L.   Ay, ay, my liege;   165
And of a lovely boy: the God of heaven
Both now and ever bless her! 'tis a girl,
Promises boys hereafter. Sir, your queen   168
Desires your visitation, and to be
Acquainted with this stranger: 'tis as like you
As cherry is to cherry.
K. Hen.   Lovell!

Re-enter LOVELL.

Lov.   Sir!
K. Hen. Give her a hundred marks. I'll to
the queen.   [*Exit.*
Old L. A hundred marks! By this light, I'll
ha' more.   173
An ordinary groom is for such payment:
I will have more, or scold it out of him.
Said I for this the girl was like to him?   176
I will have more, or else unsay 't; and now,
While it is hot, I'll put it to the issue. [*Exeunt.*

SCENE II.—*The Lobby before the Council-
Chamber.*

Enter CRANMER; Pursuivants, Pages, &c.,
attending.

Cran. I hope I am not too late; and yet the
gentleman,
That was sent to me from the council, pray'd
me
To make great haste. All fast? what means this?
Ho!
Who waits there?

Enter KEEPER.

Sure, you know me?
Keep.   Yes, my lord;   4
But yet I cannot help you.
Cran.   Why?
Keep. Your Grace must wait till you be
call'd for.

Enter DOCTOR BUTTS.

Cran.   S
Butts. [*Aside.*] This is a piece of malice.
am glad
I came this way so happily: the king
Shall understand it presently.
Cran.   [*Aside.*] 'Tis Butts,
The king's physician. As he past along,
How earnestly he cast his eyes upon me.
Pray heaven he sound not my disgrace! F
certain,
This is of purpose laid by some that hate me,
God turn their hearts! I never sought th
malice,—
To quench mine honour: they would shame
make me
Wait else at door, a fellow-counsellor,
'Mong boys, grooms, and lackeys. But th
pleasures
Must be fulfill'd, and I attend with patience

Enter, at a window above, the KING *and* BUT

Butts. I'll show your Grace the strange
sight,—
K. Hen.   What's that, Butt
Butts. I think your highness saw this ma
a day.
K. Hen. Body o' me, where is it?
Butts.   There, my lor
The high promotion of his Grace of Cante
bury;
Who holds his state at door, 'mongst pursui
ants,
Pages, and footboys.
K. Hen.   Ha! 'Tis he, indeed:
Is this the honour they do one another?
'Tis well there's one above 'em yet. I h
thought
They had parted so much honesty among 'em,
At least, good manners,—as not thus to suffer
A man of his place, and so near our favour,
To dance attendance on their lordships' ple
sures,
And at the door too, like a post with packe
By holy Mary, Butts, there's knavery:
Let 'em alone, and draw the curtain close;
We shall hear more anon.   [*Exeunt abo*

SCENE III.—*The Council-Chamber.*

Enter the Lord Chancellor, *the* DUKE OF SUFFOL
the DUKE OF NORFOLK, EARL OF SURREY, Lo
Chamberlain, GARDINER, *and* CROMWEL
The Chancellor *places himself at the upp
end of the table on the left hand; a seat bei
left void above him, as for the* ARCHBISHOP *
CANTERBURY. *The rest seat themselves
order on each side.* CROMWELL *at the low
end as secretary.* Keeper *at the door.*

Chan. Speak to the business, Master secr
tary:
Why are we met in council?
Crom.   Please your honou
The chief cause concerns his Grace of Canterbu
Gar. Has he had knowledge of it?
Crom.   Yes.

Nor.   Who waits there? 4
Keep. Without, my noble lords?
Gar.   Yes.
Keep.   My lord archbishop:
d has done half-an-hour, to know your
  pleasures.
Chan. Let him come in.
Keep.   Your Grace may enter now.
      [CRANMER enters and approaches the
                           council-table.
Chan. My good lord archbishop, I'm very
  sorry   8
 sit here at this present and behold
at chair stand empty: but we all are men,
  our own natures frail, and capable
 our flesh; few are angels: out of which frailty
d want of wisdom, you, that best should
  teach us,   13
ve misdemean'd yourself, and not a little,
ward the king first, then his laws, in filling
e whole realm, by your teaching and your
  chaplains,—   16
r so we are inform'd,—with new opinions,
vers and dangerous; which are heresies,
d, not reform'd, may prove pernicious   19
Gar. Which reformation must be sudden too,
y noble lords; for those that tame wild horses
ce 'em not in their hands to make 'em gentle,
t stop their mouths with stubborn bits, and
  spur 'em,
l they obey the manage. If we suffer—   24
t of our easiness and childish pity
 one man's honour—this contagious sickness,
rewell all physic: and what follows then?
mmotions, uproars, with a general taint 28
 the whole state: as, of late days, our neigh-
      bours,
e upper Germany, can dearly witness,
t freshly pitied in our memories.
Cran. My good lords, hitherto in all the
  progress   32
th of my life and office, I have labour'd,
d with no little study, that my teaching
d the strong course of my authority
ight go one way, and safely; and the end 36
as ever, to do well: nor is there living,—
speak it with a single heart, my lords,—
man that more detests, more stirs against,
th in his private conscience and his place,
efacers of a public peace, than I do.   41
ay heaven the king may never find a heart
ith less allegiance in it! Men, that make
vy and crooked malice nourishment   44
re bite the best. I do beseech your lordships
at, in this case of justice, my accusers,
 what they will, may stand forth face to face,
d freely urge against me.
Suf.   Nay, my lord, 48
at cannot be: you are a counsellor,
d by that virtue no man dare accuse you.
Gar. My lord, because we have business of
  more moment,
e will be short with you. 'Tis his highness'
  pleasure,   52
d our consent, for better trial of you,
om hence you be committed to the Tower;

Where, being but a private man again,
You shall know many dare accuse you boldly,
More than, I fear, you are provided for.   57
   Cran. Ah! my good Lord of Winchester, I
  thank you;
You are always my good friend: if your will pass,
I shall both find your lordship judge and juror,
You are so merciful. I see your end;   61
'Tis my undoing: love and meekness, lord,
Become a churchman better than ambition:
Win straying souls with modesty again,   64
Cast none away. That I shall clear myself,
Lay all the weight ye can upon my patience,
I make as little doubt, as you do conscience,
In doing daily wrongs. I could say more,   68
But reverence to your calling makes me modest.
   Gar. My lord, my lord, you are a sectary;
That's the plain truth: your painted gloss dis-
      covers,
To men that understand you, words and weak-
      ness.   72
   Crom. My Lord of Winchester, you are a little,
By your good favour, too sharp; men so noble,
However faulty, yet should find respect
For what they have been: 'tis a cruelty   76
To load a falling man.
   Gar.   Good Master secretary,
I cry your honour mercy; you may, worst
Of all this table, say so.
   Crom.   Why, my lord?
   Gar. Do not I know you for a favourer 80
Of this new sect? ye are not sound.
   Crom.   Not sound?
   Gar. Not sound, I say.
   Crom.   Would you were half so honest!
Men's prayers then would seek you, not their
      fears.
   Gar. I shall remember this bold language.
   Crom.   Do. 84
Remember your bold life too.
   Chan.   This is too much;
Forbear, for shame, my lords.
   Gar.   I have done.
   Crom.   And I.
   Chan. Then thus for you, my lord: it stands
      agreed,
I take it, by all voices, that forthwith   88
You be convey'd to the Tower a prisoner;
There to remain till the king's further pleasure
Be known unto us. Are you all agreed, lords?
   All. We are.
   Cran.   Is there no other way of mercy,
But I must needs to the Tower, my lords?
   Gar.   What other 93
Would you expect? You are strangely trouble-
      some.
Let some o' the guard be ready there.

Enter Guard.

   Cran.   For me?
Must I go like a traitor thither?
   Gar.   Receive him, 96
And see him safe i' the Tower.
   Cran.   Stay, good my lords;
I have a little yet to say. Look there, my lords;
By virtue of that ring I take my cause   99

Out of the gripes of cruel men, and give it
To a most noble judge, the king my master.
 Chan. This is the king's ring,
 Sur.   'Tis no counterfeit.
 Suf. 'Tis the right ring, by heaven! I told ye all,
When we first put this dangerous stone a-rolling,
'Twould fall upon ourselves.
 Nor.   Do you think, my lords, 105
The king will suffer but the little finger
Of this man to be vex'd?
 Cham.   'Tis now too certain:
How much more is his life in value with him?
Would I were fairly out on't.
 Crom.   My mind gave me,
In seeking tales and informations
Against this man—whose honesty the devil
And his disciples only envy at—   112
Ye blew the fire that burns ye: now have at ye!

Enter the KING, *frowning on them: he takes*
his seat.

 Gar. Dread sovereign, how much are we
  bound to heaven
In daily thanks, that gave us such a prince;
Not only good and wise, but most religious: 116
One that in all obedience makes the Church
The chief aim of his honour; and, to strengthen
That holy duty, out of dear respect,
His royal self in judgment comes to hear 120
The cause betwixt her and this great offender.
 K. Hen. You were ever good at sudden com-
  mendations,
Bishop of Winchester; but know, I come not
To hear such flattery now, and in my presence;
They are too thin and bare to hide offences 125
To me you cannot reach; you play the spaniel,
And think with wagging of your tongue to win
 me;
But, whatsoe'er thou tak'st me for, I'm sure
Thou hast a cruel nature and a bloody. 129
[*To* CRANMER.] Good man, sit down. Now let
 me see the proudest
He, that dares most, but wag his finger at thee:
By all that's holy, he had better starve 132
Than but once think this place becomes thee not.
 Sur. May it please your Grace,—
 K. Hen.   No, sir, it does not please me.
I had thought I had had men of some under-
 standing
And wisdom of my council; but I find none.
Was it discretion, lords, to let this man, 137
This good man,—few of you deserve that title,—
This honest man, wait like a lousy footboy
At chamber-door? and one as great as you are?
Why, what a shame was this! Did my com-
 mission   141
Bid ye so far forget yourselves? I gave ye
Power as he was a counsellor to try him,
Not as a groom. There's some of ye, I see,
More out of malice than integrity,   145
Would try him to the utmost, had ye mean;
Which ye shall never have while I live.
 Chan.   Thus far,
My most dread sov'reign, may it like your
 Grace   148

To let my tongue excuse all. What was pu
 pos'd
Concerning his imprisonment, was rather—
If there be faith in men—meant for his trial
And fair purgation to the world, than malice, i
I'm sure, in me.
 K. Hen. Well, well, my lords, respect hi
Take him, and use him well; he's worthy of
I will say thus much for him, if a prince
May be beholding to a subject, I   1
Am, for his love and service, so to him.
Make me no more ado, but all embrace hir
Be friends, for shame, my lords! My Lord
 Canterbury,
I have a suit which you must not deny me;
That is, a fair young maid that yet war
 baptism,
You must be godfather, and answer for her
 Cran. The greatest monarch now alive m
  glory
In such an honour: how may I deserve it, 1
That am a poor and humble subject to you
 K. Hen. Come, come, my lord, you'd spa
your spoons: you shall have two noble partne
with you; the old Duchess of Norfolk, and La
Marquess Dorset: will these please you?   1
Once more, my Lord of Winchester, I char
 you,
Embrace and love this man.
 Gar.   With a true hea
And brother-love I do it.
 Cran.   And let heaven
Witness, how dear I hold this confirmation.
 K. Hen. Good man! those joyful tears sho
 thy true heart:
The common voice, I see, is verified
Of thee, which says thus, 'Do my Lord
 Canterbury   1
A shrewd turn, and he is your friend for eve
Come, lords, we trifle time away; I long
To have this young one made a Christian.
As I have made ye one, lords, one remain; r
So I grow stronger, you more honour gain.
            [*Exeunt.*

SCENE IV.—*The Palace-Yard.*

Noise and tumult within. Enter Porter *and*
his Man.

 Port. You'll leave your noise anon, ye rasca
Do you take the court for Paris-garden? ye ru
slaves, leave your gaping.
 [*Within.*] Good Master porter, I belong
the larder.
 Port. Belong to the gallows, and be hange
you rogue! Is this a place to roar in? Fet
me a dozen crab-tree staves, and strong one
these are but switches to 'em. I'll scratch yo
heads: you must be seeing christenings! I
you look for ale and cakes here, you ru
rascals?
 Man. Pray, sir, be patient: 'tis as mu
 impossible—
Unless we sweep 'em from the door wi
 cannons—
To scatter 'em, as 'tis to make 'em sleep

On May-day morning; which will never be. 16
We may as well push against Paul's as stir 'em.
Port. How got they in, and be hang'd?
Man. Alas, I know not; how gets the tide in?
As much as one sound cudgel of four foot— 20
you see the poor remainder—could distribute,
made no spare, sir.
Port.   You did nothing, sir.
Man. I am not Samson, nor Sir Guy, nor
   Colbrand,
To mow 'em down before me; but if I spar'd any
That had a head to hit, either young or old,
He or she, cuckold or cuckold-maker,   26
Let me ne'er hope to see a chine again;
And that I would not for a cow, God save her!
[*Within.*] Do you hear, Master porter?   29
Port. I shall be with you presently, good
Master puppy. Keep the door close, sirrah.
Man. What would you have me do?   32
Port. What should you do, but knock 'em
down by the dozens? Is this Moorfields to
muster in? or have we some strange Indian
with the great tool come to court, the women so
besiege us? Bless me, what a fry of fornication
is at door! On my Christian conscience, this
one christening will beget a thousand: here will
be father, godfather, and all together.   40
Man. The spoons will be the bigger, sir. There
is a fellow somewhat near the door, he should be
a brazier by his face, for, o' my conscience,
twenty of the dog days now reign in 's nose: all
that stand about him are under the line, they
need no other penance. That fire-drake did I
hit three times on the head, and three times was
his nose discharged against me: he stands there,
like a mortar-piece, to blow us. There was a
haberdasher's wife of small wit near him, that
railed upon me till her pinked porringer fell off
her head, for kindling such a combustion in the
state. I missed the meteor once, and hit that
woman, who cried out, 'Clubs!' when I might
see from far some forty truncheoners draw to
her succour, which were the hope o' the Strand,
where she was quartered. They fell on; I made
good my place; at length they came to the
broomstaff to me; I defied 'em still; when
suddenly a file of boys behind 'em, loose shot,
delivered such a shower of pebbles, that I was
fain to draw mine honour in, and let 'em win the
work. The devil was amongst 'em, I think, surely. 64
Port. These are the youths that thunder at a
playhouse, and fight for bitten apples; that no
audience, but the Tribulation of Tower-hill, or
the Limbs of Limehouse, their dear brothers, are
able to endure. I have some of 'em in *Limbo
Patrum*, and there they are like to dance these
three days; besides the running banquet of two
beadles, that is to come.   72

Enter the Lord Chamberlain.

Cham. Mercy o' me, what a multitude are
here!
They grow still too, from all parts they are
   coming,
As if we kept a fair here! Where are these
   porters,

These lazy knaves? Ye have made a fine hand,
   fellows: 76
There's a trim rabble let in. Are all these
Your faithful friends o' the suburbs? We shall
   have
Great store of room, no doubt, left for the ladies,
When they pass back from the christening.
Port.   An't please your honour,   80
We are but men; and what so many may do,
Not being torn a-pieces, we have done:
An army cannot rule 'em.
Cham.   As I live,
If the king blame me for't, I'll lay ye all   84
By the heels, and suddenly; and on your heads
Clap round fines for neglect: ye're lazy knaves;
And here ye lie baiting of bombards, when
Ye should do service. Hark! the trumpets
   sound;   88
They're come already from the christening.
Go, break among the press, and find a way out
To let the troop pass fairly, or I'll find
A Marshalsea shall hold ye play these two
   months.   92
Port. Make way there for the princess.
Man.   You great fellow,
Stand close up, or I'll make your head ache.
Port. You i' the camlet, get up o' the rail:
I'll pick you o'er the pales else.   [*Exeunt.*

SCENE V.—*The Palace.*

Enter trumpets, sounding; then two Aldermen,
   Lord Mayor, Garter, CRANMER, DUKE OF
   NORFOLK, *with his marshal's staff,* DUKE OF
   SUFFOLK, *two* Noblemen *bearing great stand-
   ing-bowls for the christening gifts; then, four*
   Noblemen *bearing a canopy, under which the*
   DUCHESS OF NORFOLK, *godmother, bearing
   the child, richly habited in a mantle, &c.,
   train borne by a* Lady; *then follows the* MAR-
   CHIONESS OF DORSET, *the other godmother,
   and* Ladies. *The troop pass once about the
   stage, and* Garter *speaks.*

Gart. Heaven, from thy endless goodness,
send prosperous life, long, and ever happy, to
the high and mighty Princess of England, Elizabeth!   4

Flourish. Enter KING *and Train.*

Cran. [*Kneeling.*] And to your royal Grace,
   and the good queen,
My noble partners, and myself, thus pray:
All comfort, joy, in this most gracious lady,
Heaven ever laid up to make parents happy, 8
May hourly fall upon ye!
K. Hen. Thank you, good lord archbishop:
What is her name?
Cran.   Elizabeth.
K. Hen.   Stand up, lord.
   [*The* KING *kisses the Child.*
With this kiss take my blessing; God protect
   thee!
Into whose hand I give thy life.
Cran.   Amen.   12
K. Hen. My noble gossips, ye have been too
   prodigal:

Y

I thank ye heartily: so shall this lady
When she has so much English.
　　　Cran.　　　　　Let me speak, sir,
For heaven now bids me; and the words I utter
Let none think flattery, for they'll find 'em
　　truth.
This royal infant,—heaven still move about
　　her!—
Though in her cradle, yet now promises　19
Upon this land a thousand thousand blessings,
Which time shall bring to ripeness: she shall
　　be—
But few now living can behold that goodness—
A pattern to all princes living with her,
And all that shall succeed: Saba was never 24
More covetous of wisdom and fair virtue
Than this pure soul shall be: all princely graces,
That mould up such a mighty piece as this is,
With all the virtues that attend the good,　28
Shall still be doubled on her; truth shall nurse
　　her;
Holy and heavenly thoughts still counsel her;
She shall be lov'd and fear'd; her own shall
　　bless her;
Her foes shake like a field of beaten corn,　32
And hang their heads with sorrow; good grows
　　with her.
In her days every man shall eat in safety
Under his own vine what he plants; and sing
The merry songs of peace to all his neighbours.
God shall be truly known; and those about her
From her shall read the perfect ways of honour,
And by those claim their greatness, not by
　　blood.　　　　　　　　　　39
Nor shall this peace sleep with her; but as when
The bird of wonder dies, the maiden phœnix,
Her ashes new-create another heir
As great in admiration as herself,
So shall she leave her blessedness to one,—　44
When heaven shall call her from this cloud of
　　darkness,—
Who, from the sacred ashes of her honour,
Shall star-like rise, as great in fame as she was,
And so stand fix'd. Peace, plenty, love, truth,
　　terror,　　　　　　　　　　48
That were the servants to this chosen infant,
Shall then be his, and like a vine grow to him:
Wherever the bright sun of heaven shall shine,
His honour and the greatness of his name　52

Shall be, and make new nations; he shall flou
　　rish,
And, like a mountain cedar, reach his branche
To all the plains about him; our children's chil
　　dren
Shall see this, and bless heaven.
　　K. Hen.　　　　　Thou speakest wonders
　　Cran. She shall be, to the happiness of Eng
　　land,　　　　　　　　　　　　5
An aged princess; many days shall see her,
And yet no day without a deed to crown it.
Would I had known no more! but she must die
She must, the saints must have her, yet a virgin
A most unspotted lily shall she pass
To the ground, and all the world shall mourn
　　her.
　　K. Hen. O lord archbishop!　　　　　6
Thou hast made me now a man: never, befor
This happy child, did I get any thing.
This oracle of comfort has so pleas'd me,
That when I am in heaven, I shall desire　6
To see what this child does, and praise my
　　Maker.
I thank ye all. To you, my good Lord Mayor
And your good brethren, I am much beholding
I have receiv'd much honour by your presence
And ye shall find me thankful. Lead the way
　　lords;　　　　　　　　　　　　7
Ye must all see the queen, and she must thank
　　ye;
She will be sick else. This day, no man think
He has business at his house; for all shall stay
This little one shall make it holiday. [*Exeunt*

EPILOGUE

'Tis ten to one, this play can never please
All that are here: some come to take their ease
And sleep an act or two; but those, we fear,
We've frighted with our trumpets; so, 'tis clear
They'll say 'tis naught: others, to hear the city
Abus'd extremely, and to cry, 'That's witty!'
Which we have not done neither: that, I fear,
All the expected good we're like to hear
For this play at this time, is only in
The merciful construction of good women;
For such a one we show'd 'em: if they smile,
And say 'twill do, I know, within a while　　1
All the best men are ours; for 'tis ill hap
If they hold when their ladies bid 'em clap.

TROILUS AND CRESSIDA

DRAMATIS PERSONÆ

PRIAM, King of Troy.

HECTOR,
TROILUS,
PARIS, } his Sons.
DEIPHOBUS,
HELENUS,

MARGARELON, a Bastard Son of Priam.

ENEAS, } Trojan Commanders.
ANTENOR,

CALCHAS, a Trojan Priest, taking part with the Greeks.

PANDARUS, Uncle to Cressida.

AGAMEMNON, the Grecian General.

MENELAUS, his Brother.

ACHILLES,
AJAX, } Grecian Commanders.
ULYSSES,

NESTOR,
DIOMEDES, } Grecian Commanders.
PATROCLUS,

THERSITES, a deformed and scurrilous Grecian.

ALEXANDER, Servant to Cressida.

Servant to Troilus.

Servant to Paris.

Servant to Diomedes.

HELEN, Wife to Menelaus.

ANDROMACHE, Wife to Hector.

CASSANDRA, Daughter to Priam; a prophetess.

CRESSIDA, Daughter to Calchas.

Trojan and Greek Soldiers, and Attendants.

SCENE.—*Troy, and the Grecian Camp before it.*

PROLOGUE

In Troy there lies the scene. From isles of Greece
The princes orgulous, their high blood chaf'd,
Have to the port of Athens sent their ships,
Fraught with the ministers and instruments 4
Of cruel war: sixty and nine, that wore
Their crownets regal, from the Athenian bay
Put forth toward Phrygia; and their vow is made
To ransack Troy, within whose strong immures 8
The ravish'd Helen, Menelaus' queen,
With wanton Paris sleeps; and that's the quarrel.
To Tenedos they come,
And the deep-drawing barks do there disgorge
Their war-like fraughtage: now on Dardan
*   plains* 13
The fresh and yet unbruised Greeks do pitch
Their brave pavilions: Priam's six-gated city,
Dardan, and Tymbria, Ilias, Chetas, Trojan,
And Antenorides, with massy staples 17
And corresponsive and fulfilling bolts,
Sperr up the sons of Troy.
Now expectation, tickling skittish spirits, 20
On one and other side, Trojan and Greek,
Sets all on hazard. And hither am I come
A prologue arm'd, but not in confidence
Of author's pen or actor's voice, but suited 24
In like conditions as our argument,
To tell you, fair beholders, that our play
Leaps o'er the vaunt and firstlings of those broils,
Beginning in the middle; starting thence away
To what may be digested in a play. 29
Like or find fault; do as your pleasures are:
Now good or bad, 'tis but the chance of war.

ACT I

SCENE I.—*Troy. Before* PRIAM'S *Palace.*

Enter TROILUS *armed, and* PANDARUS.

Tro. Call here my varlet, I'll unarm again:
Why should I war without the walls of Troy,
That find such cruel battle here within?
Each Trojan that is master of his heart, 4
Let him to field; Troilus, alas! has none.

Pan. Will this gear ne'er be mended?

Tro. The Greeks are strong, and skilful to
their strength,
Fierce to their skill, and to their fierceness
valiant; 8
But I am weaker than a woman's tear,
Tamer than sleep, fonder than ignorance,
Less valiant than the virgin in the night,
And skilless as unpractis'd infancy. 12

Pan. Well, I have told you enough of this:
for my part, I'll not meddle nor make no further.
He that will have a cake out of the wheat must
tarry the grinding. 16

Tro. Have I not tarried?

Pan. Ay, the grinding; but you must tarry
the bolting.

Tro. Have I not tarried? 20

Pan. Ay, the bolting; but you must tarry
the leavening.

Tro. Still have I tarried.

Pan. Ay, to the leavening; but here's yet in
the word 'hereafter' the kneading, the making
of the cake, the heating of the oven, and the
baking; nay, you must stay the cooling too, or
you may chance to burn your lips. 28

Tro. Patience herself, what goddess e'er she
be,
Doth lesser blench at sufferance than I do.
At Priam's royal table do I sit;
And when fair Cressid comes into my thoughts,—
So, traitor! 'when she comes'!—When is she
thence? 33

Pan. Well, she looked yesternight fairer than
ever I saw her look, or any woman else.

Tro. I was about to tell thee: when my heart,
As wedged with a sigh, would rive in twain, 37
Lest Hector or my father should perceive me,
I have—as when the sun doth light a storm—

Buried this sigh in wrinkle of a smile;   40
But sorrow, that is couch'd in seeming gladness,
Is like that mirth fate turns to sudden sadness.
  Pan. An her hair were not somewhat darker
than Helen's,—well, go to,—there were no more
comparison between the women: but, for my
part, she is my kinswoman; I would not, as they
term it, praise her, but I would somebody had
heard her talk yesterday, as I did: I will not
dispraise your sister Cassandra's wit, but—   49
  Tro. O Pandarus! I tell thee, Pandarus,—
When I do tell thee, there my hopes lie drown'd,
Reply not in how many fathoms deep   52
They lie indrench'd. I tell thee I am mad
In Cressid's love: thou answer'st, she is fair;
Pour'st in the open ulcer of my heart
Her eyes, her hair, her cheek, her gait, her voice;
Handlest in thy discourse, O! that her hand, 57
In whose comparison all whites are ink,
Writing their own reproach; to whose soft
seizure
The cygnet's down is harsh, and spirit of sense
Hard as the palm of ploughman: this thou
tell'st me,   61
As true thou tell'st me, when I say I love her;
But, saying thus, instead of oil and balm,
Thou lay'st in every gash that love hath given
me   64
The knife that made it.
  Pan. I speak no more than truth.
  Tro. Thou dost not speak so much.
  Pan. Faith, I'll not meddle in't. Let her be
as she is: if she be fair, 'tis the better for her;
an she be not, she has the mends in her own
hands.   71
  Tro. Good Pandarus, how now, Pandarus!
  Pan. I have had my labour for my travail;
ill-thought on of her, and ill-thought of you:
gone between, and between, but small thanks
for my labour.   76
  Tro. What! art thou angry, Pandarus? what!
with me?
  Pan. Because she's kin to me, therefore she's
not so fair as Helen: an she were not kin to me,
she would be as fair on Friday as Helen is on
Sunday. But what care I? I care not an she
were a black-a-moor; 'tis all one to me.
  Tro. Say I she is not fair?   83
  Pan. I do not care whether you do or no.
She's a fool to stay behind her father: let her
to the Greeks; and so I'll tell her the next time
I see her. For my part, I'll meddle nor make
no more i' the matter.   88
  Tro. Pandarus,—
  Pan. Not I.
  Tro. Sweet Pandarus,—
  Pan. Pray you, speak no more to me! I will
leave all as I found it, and there an end.   93
        [*Exit* PANDARUS. *An alarum.*
  Tro. Peace, you ungracious clamours! peace,
rude sounds!
Fools on both sides! Helen must needs be fair,
When with your blood you daily paint her thus.
I cannot fight upon this argument;   97
It is too starv'd a subject for my sword.

But Pandarus,—O gods! how do you plague me
I cannot come to Cressid but by Pandar; 100
And he's as tetchy to be woo'd to woo
As she is stubborn-chaste against all suit.
Tell me, Apollo, for thy Daphne's love,
What Cressid is, what Pandar, and what we? 10
Her bed is India; there she lies, a pearl:
Between our Ilium and where she resides
Let it be call'd the wild and wandering flood
Ourself the merchant, and this sailing Panda
Our doubtful hope, our convoy and our bark. 10

Alarum. Enter ÆNEAS.

  Æne. How now, Prince Troilus! wherefore
not afield?
  Tro. Because not there: this woman's an
swer sorts,
For womanish it is to be from thence.   11
What news, Æneas, from the field to-day?
  Æne. That Paris is returned home, and hurt
  Tro. By whom, Æneas?
  Æne.   Troilus, by Menelaus
  Tro. Let Paris bleed: 'tis but a scar to scorn
Paris is gor'd with Menelaus' horn. [*Alarum*
  Æne. Hark, what good sport is out of town
to-day!   11
  Tro. Better at home, if 'would I might' wer
'may.'
But to the sport abroad: are you bound thither
  Æne. In all swift haste.
  Tro.   Come, go we then together
                                  [*Exeunt*

SCENE II.—*The Same. A Street.*

Enter CRESSIDA *and* ALEXANDER.

  Cres. Who were those went by?
  Alex.   Queen Hecuba and Helen
  Cres. And whither go they?
  Alex.   Up to the eastern tower
Whose height commands as subject all the vale
To see the battle. Hector, whose patience
Is as a virtue fix'd, to-day was mov'd:
He chid Andromache, and struck his armourer
And, like as there were husbandry in war,
Before the sun rose he was harness'd light,
And to the field goes he; where every flower
Did, as a prophet, weep what it foresaw
In Hector's wrath.
  Cres.   What was his cause of anger
  Alex. The noise goes, this: there is amon
the Greeks   1
A lord of Trojan blood, nephew to Hector;
They call him Ajax.
  Cres.   Good; and what of him
  Alex. They say he is a very man *per se*
And stands alone.   1
  Cres. So do all men, unless they are drunk
sick, or have no legs.
  Alex. This man, lady, hath robbed man
beasts of their particular additions: he is a
valiant as the lion, churlish as the bear, slow a
the elephant: a man into whom nature hath s
crowded humours that his valour is crushed int
folly, his folly sauced with discretion: there i

o man hath a virtue that he hath not a glimpse
f, nor any man an attaint but he carries some
tain of it. He is melancholy without cause, and
merry against the hair; he hath the joints of
very thing, but every thing so out of joint that
ne is a gouty Briareus, many hands and no use;
or purblind Argus, all eyes and no sight.   31
  Cres. But how should this man, that makes
ne smile, make Hector angry?
  Alex. They say he yesterday coped Hector in
he battle and struck him down; the disdain
nd shame whereof hath ever since kept Hector
asting and waking.   37
  Cres. Who comes here?

Enter PANDARUS.

  Alex. Madam, your uncle Pandarus.
  Cres. Hector's a gallant man.   40
  Alex. As may be in the world, lady.
  Pan. What's that? what's that?
  Cres. Good morrow, uncle Pandarus.
  Pan. Good morrow, cousin Cressid. What
lo you talk of? Good morrow, Alexander.
How do you, cousin? When were you at Ilium?
  Cres. This morning, uncle.   47
  Pan. What were you talking of when I
ame? Was Hector armed and gone ere ye
ame to Ilium? Helen was not up, was she?
  Cres. Hector was gone, but Helen was not up.
  Pan. E'en so: Hector was stirring early. 52
  Cres. That were we talking of, and of his anger.
  Pan. Was he angry?
  Cres. So he says here.
  Pan. True, he was so; I know the cause too:
ne'll lay about him to-day, I can tell them that:
nd there's Troilus will not come far behind
nim; let them take heed of Troilus, I can tell
hem that too.   60
  Cres. What! is he angry too?
  Pan. Who, Troilus? Troilus is the better
nan of the two.
  Cres. O Jupiter! there's no comparison. 64
  Pan. What! not between Troilus and Hector?
Do you know a man if you see him?
  Cres. Ay, if I ever saw him before and knew
him.   68
  Pan. Well, I say Troilus is Troilus.
  Cres. Then you say as I say; for I am sure
ne is not Hector.
  Pan. No, nor Hector is not Troilus in some
degrees.   73
  Cres. 'Tis just to each of them; he is himself.
  Pan. Himself! Alas, poor Troilus, I would
ne were.   76
  Cres. So he is.
  Pan. Condition, I had gone bare-foot to India.
  Cres. He is not Hector.
  Pan. Himself! no, he's not himself. Would
' were himself: well, the gods are above;
ime must friend or end: well, Troilus, well, I
vould my heart were in her body. No, Hector
s not a better man than Troilus.   84
  Cres. Excuse me.
  Pan. He is elder.
  Cres. Pardon me, pardon me.

  Pan. Th' other's not come to't; you shall tell
me another tale when the other's come to't.
Hector shall not have his wit this year.
  Cres. He shall not need it if he have his own.
  Pan. Nor his qualities.   92
  Cres. No matter.
  Pan. Nor his beauty.
  Cres. 'Twould not become him; his own's
better.   96
  Pan. You have no judgment, niece: Helen
herself swore th' other day, that Troilus, for a
brown favour,—for so 'tis I must confess,—not
brown neither,—   100
  Cres. No, but brown.
  Pan. Faith, to say truth, brown and not
brown.
  Cres. To say the truth, true and not true. 104
  Pan. She prais'd his complexion above Paris.
  Cres. Why, Paris hath colour enough.
  Pan. So he has.
  Cres. Then Troilus should have too much: if
she praised him above, his complexion is higher
than his: he having colour enough, and the
other higher, is too flaming a praise for a good
complexion. I had as lief Helen's golden tongue
had commended Troilus for a copper nose. 113
  Pan. I swear to you, I think Helen loves him
better than Paris.
  Cres. Then she's a merry Greek indeed. 116
  Pan. Nay, I am sure she does. She came to
him th' other day into the compassed window,
and, you know, he has not past three or four
hairs on his chin,—   120
  Cres. Indeed, a tapster's arithmetic may soon
bring his particulars therein to a total.
  Pan. Why, he is very young; and yet will he,
within three pound, lift as much as his brother
Hector.   125
  Cres. Is he so young a man, and so old a
lifter?
  Pan. But to prove to you that Helen loves
him: she came and puts me her white hand to
his cloven chin,—   130
  Cres. Juno have mercy! how came it cloven?
  Pan. Why, you know, 'tis dimpled. I think
his smiling becomes him better than any man
in all Phrygia.
  Cres. O! he smiles valiantly.
  Pan. Does he not?   136
  Cres. O! yes, an 'twere a cloud in autumn.
  Pan. Why, go to, then. But to prove to you
that Helen loves Troilus,—
  Cres. Troilus will stand to the proof, if
you'll prove it so.   141
  Pan. Troilus! why he esteems her no more
than I esteem an addle egg.
  Cres. If you love an addle egg as well as you
love an idle head, you would eat chickens i' the
shell.   146
  Pan. I cannot choose but laugh, to think
how she tickled his chin: indeed, she has a
marvell's white hand, I must needs confess,—
  Cres. Without the rack.   150
  Pan. And she takes upon her to spy a white
hair on his chin.
  Cres. Alas! poor chin! many a wart is richer.

Pan. But there was such laughing: Queen Hecuba laughed that her eyes ran o'er.

Cres. With millstones.   156

Pan. And Cassandra laughed.

Cres. But there was more temperate fire under the pot of her eyes: did her eyes run o'er too?

Pan. And Hector laughed.   160

Cres. At what was all this laughing?

Pan. Marry, at the white hair that Helen spied on Troilus' chin.

Cres. An't had been a green hair, I should have laughed too.   165

Pan. They laughed not so much at the hair as at his pretty answer.

Cres. What was his answer?   168

Pan. Quoth she, 'Here's but one-and-fifty hairs on your chin, and one of them is white.'

Cres. This is her question.

Pan. That's true; make no question of that. 'One-and-fifty hairs,' quoth he, 'and one white: that white hair is my father, and all the rest are his sons.' 'Jupiter!' quoth she, 'which of these hairs is Paris, my husband?' 'The forked one,' quoth he; 'pluck't out, and give it him.' But there was such laughing, and Helen so blushed, and Paris so chafed, and all the rest so laughed, that it passed.   180

Cres. So let it now, for it has been a great while going by.

Pan. Well, cousin, I told you a thing yesterday; think on't.   184

Cres. So I do.

Pan. I'll be sworn 'tis true: he will weep you, an 'twere a man born in April.

Cres. And I'll spring up in his tears, an 'twere a nettle against May. [*A retreat sounded.*

Pan. Hark! they are coming from the field. Shall we stand up here, and see them as they pass toward Ilium? good niece, do; sweet niece, Cressida.

Cres. At your pleasure.   193

Pan. Here, here; here's an excellent place: here we may see most bravely. I'll tell you them all by their names as they pass by, but mark Troilus above the rest.   197

Cres. Speak not so loud.

ÆNEAS passes over the stage.

Pan. That's Æneas: is not that a brave man? he's one of the flowers of Troy, I can tell you: but mark Troilus; you shall see anon. 201

ANTENOR passes over.

Cres. Who's that?

Pan. That's Antenor: he has a shrewd wit, I can tell you; and he's a man good enough: he's one o' the soundest judgments in Troy, whosoever, and a proper man of person. When comes Troilus? I'll show you Troilus anon: if he see me, you shall see him nod at me. 208

Cres. Will he give you the nod?

Pan. You shall see.

Cres. If he do, the rich shall have more.

HECTOR passes over.

Pan. That's Hector, that, that, look you, that; there's a fellow! Go thy way, Hector! There's

a brave man, niece. O brave Hector! Look how he looks! there's a countenance! Is't not a brave man?   216

Cres. O! a brave man.

Pan. Is a' not? It does a man's heart good. Look you what hacks are on his helmet! look you yonder, do you see? look you there: there's no jesting; there's laying on, take't off who will, as they say: there be hacks!   222

Cres. Be those with swords?

Pan. Swords? any thing, he cares not; an the devil come to him, it's all one: by God's lid, it does one's heart good. Yonder comes Paris, yonder comes Paris.   227

PARIS crosses over.

Look ye yonder, niece: is't not a gallant man too, is't not? Why, this is brave now. Who said he came hurt home to-day? he's not hurt: why, this will do Helen's heart good now, ha! Would I could see Troilus now! You shall see Troilus anon.   233

Cres. Who's that?

HELENUS passes over.

Pan. That's Helenus. I marvel where Troilus is. That's Helenus. I think he went not forth to-day. That's Helenus.   237

Cres. Can Helenus fight, uncle?

Pan. Helenus? no, yes, he'll fight indifferent well. I marvel where Troilus is. Hark! do you not hear the people cry, 'Troilus?' Helenus is a priest.   242

Cres. What sneaking fellow comes yonder?

TROILUS passes over.

Pan. Where? yonder? that's Deiphobus. 'Tis Troilus! there's a man, niece! Hem! Brave Troilus! the prince of chivalry!   246

Cres. Peace! for shame, peace!

Pan. Mark him; note him: O brave Troilus! look well upon him, niece: look you how his sword is bloodied, and his helmet more hacked than Hector's; and how he looks, and how he goes! O admirable youth! he ne'er saw three-and-twenty. Go thy way, Troilus, go thy way! Had I a sister were a grace, or a daughter a goddess, he should take his choice. O admirable man! Paris? Paris is dirt to him; and, I warrant, Helen, to change, would give an eye to boot.

Cres. Here come more.   259

Soldiers pass over.

Pan. Asses, fools, dolts! chaff and bran, chaff and bran! porridge after meat! I could live and die i' the eyes of Troilus. Ne'er look, ne'er look; the eagles are gone: crows and daws, crows and daws! I had rather be such a man as Troilus than Agamemnon and all Greece. 265

Cres. There is among the Greeks Achilles, a better man than Troilus.

Pan. Achilles! a drayman, a porter, a very camel.   269

Cres. Well, well.

Pan. 'Well, well!' Why, have you any dis-cretion? have you any eyes? Do you know what a man is? Is not birth, beauty, good shape, discourse, manhood, learning, gentleness, virtue, youth, liberality, and so forth, the spice and salt that season a man?   276

Cres. Ay, a minced man: and then to be baked with no date in the pie, for then the man's date's out.

Pan. You are such a woman! one knows not at what ward you lie.   281

Cres. Upon my back, to defend my belly; upon my wit, to defend my wiles; upon my secrecy, to defend mine honesty; my mask, to defend my beauty; and you, to defend all these: and at all these wards I lie, at a thousand watches.

Pan. Say one of your watches.   288

Cres. Nay, I'll watch you for that; and that's one of the chiefest of them too: if I cannot ward what I would not have hit, I can watch you for telling how I took the blow; unless it swell past hiding, and then it's past watching.   293

Pan. You are such another!

Enter TROILUS' Boy.

Boy. Sir, my lord would instantly speak with you.   296

Pan. Where?

Boy. At your own house; there he unarms him.

Pan. Good boy, tell him I come. [*Exit* Boy.] I doubt he be hurt. Fare ye well, good niece.

Cres. Adieu, uncle.

Pan. I'll be with you, niece, by and by.

Cres. To bring, uncle?

Pan. Ay, a token from Troilus.   304

Cres. By the same token, you are a bawd.

[*Exit* PANDARUS.

Words, vows, gifts, tears, and love's full sacrifice
He offers in another's enterprise;
But more in Troilus thousand-fold I see   308
Than in the glass of Pandar's praise may be.
Yet hold I off. Women are angels, wooing;
Things won are done; joy's soul lies in the doing;
That she belov'd knows nought that knows not this: 312
Men prize the thing ungain'd more than it is:
That she was never yet, that ever knew
Love got so sweet as when desire did sue.
Therefore this maxim out of love I teach: 316
Achievement is command; ungain'd, beseech:
Then though my heart's content firm love doth bear,
Nothing of that shall from mine eyes appear.

[*Exeunt.*

SCENE III.—*The Grecian Camp. Before*
AGAMEMNON'S *Tent.*

Sennet. Enter AGAMEMNON, NESTOR, ULYSSES,
MENELAUS, *and Others.*

Agam. Princes,
What grief hath set the jaundice on your cheeks?
The ample proposition that hope makes
In all designs begun on earth below   4
Fails in the promis'd largeness: checks and disasters
Grow in the veins of actions highest rear'd;
As knots, by the conflux of meeting sap,
Infect the sound pine and divert his grain   8
Tortive and errant from his course of growth.
Nor, princes, is it matter new to us
That we come short of our suppose so far
That after seven years' siege yet Troy walls stand;   10
Sith every action that hath gone before,
Whereof we have record, trial did draw
Bias and thwart, not answering the aim,
And that unbodied figure of the thought   16
That gave't surmised shape. Why then, you princes,
Do you with cheeks abash'd behold our works,
And call them shames? which are indeed nought else
But the protractive trials of great Jove,   20
To find persistive constancy in men:
The fineness of which metal is not found
In Fortune's love; for then, the bold and coward,
The wise and fool, the artist and unread,   24
The hard and soft, seem all affin'd and kin:
But, in the wind and tempest of her frown,
Distinction, with a broad and powerful fan,
Puffing at all, winnows the light away;   28
And what hath mass or matter, by itself
Lies rich in virtue and unmingled.

Nest. With due observance of thy god-like seat,
Great Agamemnon, Nestor shall apply   32
Thy latest words. In the reproof of chance
Lies the true proof of men: the sea being smooth,
How many shallow bauble boats dare sail
Upon her patient breast, making their way   36
With those of nobler bulk!
But let the ruffian Boreas once enrage
The gentle Thetis, and anon behold
The strong-ribb'd bark through liquid mountains cut,   40
Bounding between the two moist elements,
Like Perseus' horse: where's then the saucy boat
Whose weak untimber'd sides but even now
Co-rivall'd greatness? either to harbour fled,   44
Or made a toast for Neptune. Even so
Doth valour's show and valour's worth divide
In storms of fortune; for in her ray and brightness
The herd hath more annoyance by the breese   48
Than by the tiger; but when the splitting wind
Makes flexible the knees of knotted oaks,
And flies fled under shade, why then the thing of courage,
As rous'd with rage, with rage doth sympathize,
And with an accent tun'd in self-same key,   53
Retorts to chiding fortune.

Ulyss.   Agamemnon,
Thou great commander, nerve and bone of Greece,
Heart of our numbers, soul and only spirit,   56
In whom the tempers and the minds of all
Should be shut up, hear what Ulysses speaks.
Besides the applause and approbation

The which, [*To* AGAMEMNON] most mighty for
thy place and sway,   60
[*To* NESTOR.] And thou most reverend for thy
stretch'd-out life,
I give to both your speeches, which were such
As Agamemnon and the hand of Greece
Should hoid up high in brass; and such again
As venerable Nestor, hatch'd in silver,   65
Should with a bond of air, strong as the axle-
tree
On which heaven rides, knit all the Greekish
ears
To his experienc'd tongue, yet let it please
both,   68
Thou great, and wise, to hear Ulysses speak.
   Agam. Speak, Prince of Ithaca; and be't of
less expect
That matter needless, of importless burden,
Divide thy lips, than we are confident,   72
When rank Thersites opes his mastick jaws,
We shall hear music, wit, and oracle.
   Ulyss. Troy, yet upon his basis, had been
down,
And the great Hector's sword had lack'd a
master,   76
But for these instances.
The specialty of rule hath been neglected:
And look, how many Grecian tents do stand
Hollow upon this plain, so many hollow fac-
tions.   80
When that the general is not like the hive
To whom the foragers shall all repair,
What honey is expected? Degree being vizarded,
The unworthiest shows as fairly in the mask.
The heavens themselves, the planets, and this
centre   85
Observe degree, priority, and place,
Insisture, course, proportion, season, form,
Office, and custom, in all line of order: 88
And therefore is the glorious planet Sol
In noble eminence enthron'd and spher'd
Amidst the other; whose med'cinable eye
Corrects the ill aspects of planets evil,   92
And posts, like the commandment of a king,
Sans check, to good and bad: but when the
planets
In evil mixture to disorder wander,
What plagues, and what portents, what mutiny,
What raging of the sea, shaking of earth,   97
Commotion in the winds, frights, changes,
horrors,
Divert and crack, rend and deracinate
The unity and married calm of states   100
Quite from their fixure! O! when degree is
shak'd,
Which is the ladder to all high designs,
The enterprise is sick. How could communities,
Degrees in schools, and brotherhoods in cities,
Peaceful commerce from dividable shores, 105
The primogenitive and due of birth,
Prerogative of age, crowns, sceptres, laurels,
But by degree, stand in authentic place? 108
Take but degree away, untune that string,
And, hark! what discord follows; each thing
meets
In mere oppugnancy: the bounded waters

Should lift their bosoms higher than the shores
And make a sop of all this solid globe: 11
Strength should be lord of imbecility,
And the rude son should strike his father dead
Force should be right; or rather, right and
wrong—   11
Between whose endless jar justice resides—
Should lose their names, and so should justice
too.
Then every thing includes itself in power,
Power into will, will into appetite;   12
And appetite, a universal wolf,
So doubly seconded with will and power,
Must make perforce a universal prey,
And last eat up himself. Great Agamemnon,
This chaos, when degree is suffocate,   12
Follows the choking.
And this neglection of degree it is
That by a pace goes backward, with a purpose
It hath to climb. The general's disdain'd 12
By him one step below, he by the next,
That next by him beneath; so every step,
Exampled by the first pace that is sick   13
Of his superior, grows to an envious fever
Of pale and bloodless emulation:
And 'tis this fever that keeps Troy on foot,
Not her own sinews. To end a tale of length,
Troy in our weakness lives, not in her strength
   Nest. Most wisely hath Ulysses here dis
cover'd
The fever whereof all our power is sick.
   Agam. The nature of the sickness found
Ulysses,   14
What is the remedy?
   Ulyss. The great Achilles, whom opinion
crowns
The sinew and the forehand of our host,
Having his ear full of his airy fame,   14
Grows dainty of his worth, and in his tent
Lies mocking our designs. With him Patroclu
Upon a lazy bed the livelong day
Breaks scurril jests,   14
And with ridiculous and awkward action—
Which, slanderer, he imitation calls—
He pageants us. Sometime, great Agamemnon
Thy topless deputation he puts on   15
And, like a strutting player, whose conceit
Lies in his hamstring, and doth think it rich
To hear the wooden dialogue and sound
'Twixt his stretch'd footing and the scaffold
age,—   15
Such to-be-pitied and o'er-wrested seeming
He acts thy greatness in:—and when he speaks
'Tis like a chime a mending; with terms un
squar'd,
Which, from the tongue of roaring Typho
dropp'd,   16
Would seem hyperboles. At this fusty stuff
The large Achilles, on his press'd bed lolling,
From his deep chest laughs out a loud applause
Cries, 'Excellent! 'tis Agamemnon just.   16
Now play me Nestor; hem, and stroke thy beard
As he being drest to some oration.'
That's done;—as near as the extremest ends
Of parallels, like as Vulcan and his wife:—
Yet good Achilles still cries, 'Excellent!   16

is Nestor right. Now play him me, Patroclus,
ming to answer in a night alarm.'
d then, forsooth, the faint defects of age 172
ust be the scene of mirth; to cough and spit,
d with a palsy-fumbling on his gorget,
ake in and out the rivet: and at this sport
　Valour dies; cries, 'O! enough, Patroclus;
　give me ribs of steel; I shall split all　177
pleasure of my spleen.' And in this fashion,
I our abilities, gifts, natures, shapes,
verals and generals of grace exact,　180
hievements, plots, orders, preventions,
citements to the field, or speech for truce,
ccess or loss, what is or is not, serves
　stuff for these two to make paradoxes. 184
Nest. And in the imitation of these twain—
hom, as Ulysses says, opinion crowns
th an imperial voice—many are infect.
ax is grown self-will'd, and bears his head 188
such a rein, in full as proud a place
　broad Achilles; keeps his tent like him;
akes factious feasts; rails on our state of war,
ld as an oracle, and sets Thersites—　192
slave whose gall coins slanders like a mint—
match us in comparison with dirt;
weaken and discredit our exposure,
w rank soever rounded in with danger. 196
Ulyss. They tax our policy, and call it
　cowardice;
unt wisdom as no member of the war;
restall prescience, and esteem no act
t that of hand: the still and mental parts, 200
at do contrive how many hands shall strike,
hen fitness calls them on, and know by measure
' their observant toil the enemies' weight,—
hy, this hath not a finger's dignity:　204
ey call this bed-work, mappery, closet-war;
that the ram that batters down the wall,
r the great swing and rudeness of his poise,
ey place before his hand that made the engine,
those that with the fineness of their souls
' reason guide his execution.　210
Nest. Let this be granted, and Achilles' horse
akes many Thetis' sons.　[A tucket.
Agam. What trumpet? look, Menelaus.
Men. From Troy.

Enter ÆNEAS.

Agam. What would you 'fore our tent?
Æne. Is this great Agamemnon's tent, I
　pray you?　216
Agam. Even this.
Æne. May one, that is a herald and a prince,
o a fair message to his kingly ears?
Agam. With surety stronger than Achilles'
　arm　220
ore all the Greekish heads, which with one
　voice
ll Agamemnon head and general.
Æne. Fair leave and large security. How
　may
stranger to those most imperial looks　224
now them from eyes of other mortals?
Agam.　　　　　　　　　　How!
Æne. Ay;
sk, that I might waken reverence,

And bid the cheek be ready with a blush 228
Modest as morning when she coldly eyes
The youthful Phœbus:
Which is that god in office, guiding men?
Which is the high and mighty Agamemnon? 232
　Agam. This Trojan scorns us; or the men of
　　Troy
Are ceremonious courtiers.
　Æne. Courtiers as free, as debonair, unarm'd,
As bending angels; that's their fame in peace:
But when they would seem soldiers, they have
　galls,　237
Good arms, strong joints, true swords; and,
　Jove's accord,
Nothing so full of heart. But peace, Æneas!
Peace, Trojan! lay thy finger on thy lips! 240
The worthiness of praise distains his worth,
If that the prais'd himself bring the praise forth;
But what the repining enemy commends,
That breath fame blows; that praise, sole pure,
　transcends.　244
　Agam. Sir, you of Troy, call you yourself
　　Æneas?
　Æne. Ay, Greek, that is my name.
　Agam. What's your affair, I pray you?
　Æne. Sir, pardon; 'tis for Agamemnon's ears.
　Agam. He hears nought privately that comes
　　from Troy.　249
　Æne. Nor I from Troy come not to whisper
　　him:
I bring a trumpet to awake his ear,
To set his sense on the attentive bent,　252
And then to speak.
　Agam.　　　　Speak frankly as the wind:
It is not Agamemnon's sleeping hour;
That thou shalt know, Trojan, he is awake,
He tells thee so himself.
　Æne.　　　　Trumpet, blow aloud, 256
Send thy brass voice through all these lazy tents;
And every Greek of mettle, let him know,
What Troy means fairly shall be spoke aloud.
　　　　　　　　　　　　[Trumpet sounds.
We have, great Agamemnon, here in Troy, 260
A prince called Hector,—Priam is his father,—
Who in this dull and long-continu'd truce
Is rusty grown: he bade me take a trumpet,
And to this purpose speak: king's, princes, lords!
If there be one among the fair'st of Greece 265
That holds his honour higher than his ease,
That seeks his praise more than he fears his
　peril,
That knows his valour, and knows not his fear,
That loves his mistress more than in confes-
　sion,　269
With truant vows to her own lips he loves,
And dare avow her beauty and her worth
In other arms than hers,—to him this challenge.
Hector, in view of Trojans and of Greeks, 273
Shall make it good, or do his best to do it,
He hath a lady wiser, fairer, truer,
Than ever Greek did compass in his arms; 276
And will to-morrow with his trumpet call,
Mid-way between your tents and walls of Troy,
To rouse a Grecian that is true in love:
If any come, Hector shall honour him;　280
If none, he'll say in Troy when he retires,

The Grecian dames are sunburnt, and not worth
The splinter of a lance. Even so much.
  Agam. This shall be told our lovers, Lord
    Æneas; 284
If none of them have soul in such a kind,
We left them all at home: but we are soldiers;
And may that soldier a mere recreant prove,
That means not, hath not, or is not in love! 288
If then one is, or hath, or means to be,
That one meets Hector; if none else, I am he.
  Nest. Tell him of Nestor, one that was a
    man
When Hector's grandsire suck'd: he is old now;
But if there be not in our Grecian host 293
One noble man that hath one spark of fire
To answer for his love, tell him from me,
I'll hide my silver beard in a gold beaver, 296
And in my vantbrace put this wither'd brawn;
And, meeting him, will tell him that my lady
Was fairer than his grandam, and as chaste
As may be in the world: his youth in flood, 300
I'll prove this truth with my three drops of
    blood.
  Æne. Now heavens forbid such scarcity of
    youth!
  Ulyss. Amen.
  Agam. Fair Lord Æneas, let me touch your
    hand; 304
To our pavilion shall I lead you first.
Achilles shall have word of this intent;
So shall each lord of Greece, from tent to tent:
Yourself shall feast with us before you go, 308
And find the welcome of a noble foe.
        [*Exeunt all but* ULYSSES *and* NESTOR.
  Ulyss. Nestor!
  Nest. What says Ulysses?
  Ulyss. I have a young conception in my
    brain; 312
Be you my time to bring it to some shape.
  Nest. What is't?
  Ulyss. This 'tis:
Blunt wedges rive hard knots: the seeded pride
That hath to this maturity blown up 317
In rank Achilles, must or now be cropp'd,
Or, shedding, breed a nursery of like evil,
To overbulk us all.
  Nest. Well, and how? 320
  Ulyss. This challenge that the gallant Hector
    sends,
However it is spread in general name,
Relates in purpose only to Achilles.
  Nest. The purpose is perspicuous even as
    substance 324
Whose grossness little characters sum up:
And, in the publication, make no strain, ,
But that Achilles, were his brain as barren
As banks of Libya,—though, Apollo knows, 328
'Tis dry enough,—will with great speed of judg-
    ment,
Ay, with celerity, find Hector's purpose
Pointing on him.
  Ulyss. And wake him to the answer, think
    you? 332
  Nest. Yes, 'tis most meet: whom may you
    else oppose,
That can from Hector bring those honours off,

If not Achilles? Though't be a sportful comba
Yet in the trial much opinion dwells; 3
For here the Trojans taste our dear'st reput
With their fin'st palate: and trust to me, Ulyss
Our imputation shall be oddly pois'd
In this wild action; for the success,
Although particular, shall give a scantling
Of good or bad unto the general;
And in such indexes, although small pricks
To their subsequent volumes, there is seen 3
The baby figure of the giant mass
Of things to come at large. It is suppos'd
He that meets Hector issues from our choi
And choice, being mutual act of all our souls, 3
Makes merit her election, and doth boil,
As 'twere from forth us all, a man distill'd
Out of our virtues; who miscarrying,
What heart receives from hence the conqueri
    part,
To steel a strong opinion to themselves?
Which entertain'd, limbs are his instrument
In no less working than are swords and bo
Directive by the limbs.
  Ulyss. Give pardon to my speech:
Therefore 'tis meet Achilles meet not Hecto
Let us like merchants show our foulest war
And think perchance they'll sell; if not, 3
The lustre of the better yet to show
Shall show the better. Do not consent
That ever Hector and Achilles meet;
For both our honour and our shame in this
Are dogg'd with two strange followers.
  Nest. I see them not with my old eyes: wh
    are they?
  Ulyss. What glory our Achilles shares fr
    Hector,
Were he not proud, we all should share wi
    him: 3
But he already is too insolent;
And we were better parch in Afric sun
Than in the pride and salt scorn of his eyes
Should he 'scape Hector fair: if he were foil'd,
Why then we did our main opinion crush
In taint of our best man. No; make a lotte
And by device let blockish Ajax draw
The sort to fight with Hector: among o
    selves 3
Give him allowance as the worthier man,
For that will physic the great Myrmidon
Who broils in loud applause; and make h
    fall
His crest that prouder than blue Iris bends. 3
If the dull brainless Ajax come safe off,
We'll dress him up in voices: if he fail,
Yet go we under our opinion still
That we have better men. But, hit or miss, 3
Our project's life this shape of sense assum
Ajax employ'd plucks down Achilles' plum
  Nest. Ulysses,
Now I begin to relish thy advice; 3
And I will give a taste of it forthwith
To Agamemnon: go we to him straight.
Two curs shall tame each other: pride alon
Must tarre the 'mastiffs on, as 'twere the
    bone. [*Exeu*

ACT II

SCENE I.—*A Part of the Grecian Camp.*

Enter AJAX *and* THERSITES.

Ajax. Thersites!

Ther. Agamemnon, how if he had boils? full, over, generally?

Ajax. Thersites!   4

Ther. And those boils did run? Say so, did not the general run then? were not that a botchy core?

Ajax. Dog!   8

Ther. Then would come some matter from him: I see none now.

Ajax. Thou bitch-wolf's son, canst thou not hear? feel, then.   [*Strikes him.*

Ther. The plague of Greece upon thee, thou mongrel beef-witted lord!

Ajax. Speak then, thou vinewedst leaven, speak: I will beat thee into handsomeness. 16

Ther. I shall sooner rail thee into wit and holiness: but I think thy horse will sooner con an oration than thou learn a prayer without book. Thou canst strike, canst thou? a red murrain o' thy jade's tricks!   21

Ajax. Toadstool, learn me the proclamation.

Ther. Dost thou think I have no sense, thou strikest me thus?   24

Ajax. The proclamation!

Ther. Thou art proclaimed a fool, I think.

Ajax. Do not, porpentine, do not: my fingers itch.   28

Ther. I would thou didst itch from head to foot, and I had the scratching of thee; I would make thee the loathsomest scab of Greece. When thou art forth in the incursions, thou strikest as slow as another.   33

Ajax. I say, the proclamation!

Ther. Thou grumblest and railest every hour on Achilles, and thou art as full of envy at his greatness as Cerberus is at Proserpina's beauty, ay, that thou barkest at him.

Ajax. Mistress Thersites!

Ther. Thou shouldst strike him.   40

Ajax. Cobloaf!

Ther. He would pun thee into shivers with his fist, as a sailor breaks a biscuit.

Ajax. You whoreson cur.   [*Beating him.*

Ther. Do, do.   45

Ajax. Thou stool for a witch!

Ther. Ay, do, do; thou sodden-witted lord! thou hast no more brain than I have in mine elbows; an assinego may tutor thee: thou scurvy-valiant ass! thou art here but to thrash Trojans; and thou art bought and sold among those of any wit, like a barbarian slave. If thou use to beat me, I will begin at thy heel, and tell what thou art by inches, thou thing of no bowels, thou!

Ajax. You dog!

Ther. You scurvy lord!   56

Ajax. You cur!   [*Beating him.*

Ther. Mars his idiot! do, rudeness; do, camel; do, do.

Enter ACHILLES *and* PATROCLUS.

Achil. Why, how now, Ajax! wherefore do you this?   60
How now, Thersites! what's the matter, man?

Ther. You see him there, do you?

Achil. Ay; what's the matter?

Ther. Nay, look upon him.   64

Achil. So I do: what's the matter?

Ther. Nay, but regard him well.

Achil. 'Well!' why, so I do.

Ther. But yet you look not well upon him; for, whosoever you take him to be, he is Ajax. 69

Achil. I know that, fool.

Ther. Ay, but that fool knows not himself.

Ajax. Therefore I beat thee.   72

Ther. Lo, lo, lo, lo, what modicums of wit he utters! his evasions have ears thus long. I have bobbed his brain more than he has beat my bones: I will buy nine sparrows for a penny, and his *pia mater* is not worth the ninth part of a sparrow. This lord, Achilles, Ajax, who wears his wit in his belly, and his guts in his head, I'll tell you what I say of him.   80

Achil. What?

Ther. I say, this Ajax,—
   [AJAX *offers to strike him.*

Achil. Nay, good Ajax.

Ther. Has not so much wit—   84

Achil. Nay, I must hold you.

Ther. As will stop the eye of Helen's needle, for whom he comes to fight.

Achil. Peace, fool!   88

Ther. I would have peace and quietness, but the fool will not: he there; that he; look you there.

Ajax. O thou damned cur! I shall—   92

Achil. Will you set your wit to a fool's?

Ther. No, I warrant you; for a fool's will shame it.

Patr. Good words, Thersites.   96

Achil. What's the quarrel?

Ajax. I bade the vile owl go learn me the tenour of the proclamation, and he rails upon me.   100

Ther. I serve thee not.

Ajax. Well, go to, go to.

Ther. I serve here voluntary.

Achil. Your last service was sufferance, 'twas not voluntary; no man is beaten voluntary: Ajax was here the voluntary, and you as under an impress.   107

Ther. Even so; a great deal of your wit too lies in your sinews, or else there be liars. Hector shall have a great catch if he knock out either of your brains: a' were as good crack a fusty nut with no kernel.   112

Achil. What, with me too, Thersites?

Ther. There's Ulysses and old Nestor, whose wit was mouldy ere your grandsires had nails on their toes, yoke you like draught-oxen, and make you plough up the wars.   117

Achil. What, what?

Ther. Yes, good sooth: to, Achilles! to, Ajax! to!   120

Ajax. I shall cut out your tongue.

Ther. 'Tis no matter; I shall speak as much as thou afterwards.

Patr. No more words, Thersites; peace! 124

Ther. I will hold my peace when Achilles' brach bids me, shall I?

Achil. There's for you, Patroclus.

Ther. I will see you hanged, like clotpoles, ere I come any more to your tents: I will keep where there is wit stirring and leave the faction of fools.   [*Exit.*

Patr. A good riddance.   132

Achil. Marry, this, sir, is proclaim'd through all our host:

That Hector, by the fifth hour of the sun,
Will, with a trumpet, 'twixt our tents and Troy
To-morrow morning call some knight to arms
That hath a stomach; and such a one that dare 137
Maintain—I know not what: 'tis trash. Farewell.

Ajax. Farewell. Who shall answer him?

Achil. I know not: it is put to lottery; otherwise,   140
He knew his man.

Ajax. O, meaning you. I will go learn more of it.   [*Exeunt.*

SCENE II.—*Troy. A Room in* PRIAM'S *Palace.*

Enter PRIAM, HECTOR, TROILUS, PARIS, *and*
HELENUS.

Pri. After so many hours, lives, speeches spent,
Thus once again says Nestor from the Greeks:
'Deliver Helen, and all damage else,
As honour, loss of time, travail, expense,   4
Wounds, friends, and what else dear that is consum'd
In hot digestion of this cormorant war,
Shall be struck off.' Hector, what say you to 't?

Hect. Though no man lesser fears the Greeks than I,   8
As far as toucheth my particular,
Yet, dread Priam,
There is no lady of more softer bowels,
More spongy to suck in the sense of fear,   12
More ready to cry out 'Who knows what follows?'
Than Hector is. The wound of peace is surety,
Surety secure; but modest doubt is call'd
The beacon of the wise, the tent that searches 16
To the bottom of the worst. Let Helen go:
Since the first sword was drawn about this question,
Every tithe soul, 'mongst many thousand dismes,
Hath been as dear as Helen; I mean, of ours:
If we have lost so many tenths of ours,   21
To guard a thing not ours nor worth to us,
Had it our name, the value of one ten,
What merit's in that reason which denies   24
The yielding of her up?

Tro.   Fie, fie! my brother,
Weigh you the worth and honour of a king
So great as our dread father in a scale
Of common ounces? will you with counters sum
The past proportion of his infinite?   29
And buckle in a waist most fathomless

With spans and inches so diminutive
As fears and reasons? fie, for godly shame!

Hel. No marvel, though you bite so sharp reasons,
You are so empty of them. Should not o father
Bear the great sway of his affairs with reaso
Because your speech hath none that tells h so?

Tro. You are for dreams and slumbers, br ther priest;
You fur your gloves with reason. Here a your reasons:
You know an enemy intends you harm;
You know a sword employ'd is perilous,
And reason flies the object of all harm:
Who marvels then, when Helenus beholds
A Grecian and his sword, if he do set
The very wings of reason to his heels,
And fly like chidden Mercury from Jove,
Or like a star disorb'd? Nay, if we talk of reaso
Let's shut our gates and sleep: manhood a honour
Should have hare-hearts, would they but f their thoughts
With this cramm'd reason: reason and respe
Make livers pale, and lustihood deject.

Hect. Brother, she is not worth what s doth cost
The holding.

Tro.   What is aught but as 'tis valu'

Hect. But value dwells not in particular wi
It holds his estimate and dignity
As well wherein 'tis precious of itself
As in the prizer. 'Tis mad idolatry
To make the service greater than the god;
And the will dotes that is inclinable
To what infectiously itself affects,
Without some image of the affected merit.

Tro. I take to-day a wife, and my electio
Is led on in the conduct of my will;
My will enkindled by mine eyes and ears,
Two traded pilots 'twixt the dangerous shores
Of will and judgment. How may I avoid,
Although my will distaste what it elected,
The wife I chose? there can be no evasion
To blench from this and to stand firm honour.
We turn not back the silks upon the mercha
When we have soil'd them, nor the remaind viands
We do not throw in unrespective sink
Because we now are full. It was thought me
Paris should do some vengeance on the Greek
Your breath of full consent bellied his sails;
The seas and winds—old wranglers—took truce
And did him service: he touch'd the por desir'd,
And for an old aunt whom the Greeks he captive
He brought a Grecian queen, whose youth ar freshness
Wrinkles Apollo's, and makes stale the morr ing.
Why keep we her? the Grecians keep our aun

she worth keeping? why, she is a pearl, 81
hose price hath launch'd above a thousand
 ships,
d turn'd crown'd kings to merchants.
you'll avouch 'twas wisdom Paris went,— 84
 you must needs, for you all cried 'Go, go,'—
you'll confess he brought home noble prize,—
 you must needs, for you all clapp'd your
 hands,
d cry'd 'Inestimable!'—why do you now 88
e issue of your proper wisdoms rate,
d do a deed that Fortune never did,
ggar the estimation which you priz'd
cher than sea and land? O! theft most base,
at we have stol'n what we do fear to keep? 93
t thieves unworthy of a thing so stol'n,
at in their country did them that disgrace
e fear to warrant in our native place. 96
Cas. [*Within.*] Cry, Trojans, cry!
Pri.   What noise? what shriek?
Tro. 'Tis our mad sister, I do know her voice.
Cas. [*Within.*] Cry, Trojans!
Hect. It is Cassandra. 100

   Enter CASSANDRA, *raving.*

Cas. Cry, Trojans, cry! lend me ten thousand
 eyes,
d I will fill them with prophetic tears.
Hect. Peace, sister, peace!
Cas. Virgins and boys, mid-age and wrinkled
 eld, 104
ft infancy, that nothing canst but cry,
dd to my clamours! let us pay betimes
moiety of that mass of moan to come.
y, Trojans, cry! practise your eyes with tears!
roy must not be, nor goodly Ilion stand; 109
ur firebrand brother, Paris, burns us all.
ry, Trojans, cry! a Helen and a woe!
ry, cry! Troy burns, or else let Helen go. [*Exit.*
Hect. Now, youthful Troilus, do not these
 high strains 113
f divination in our sister work
me touches of remorse? or is your blood
madly hot that no discourse of reason, 116
or fear of bad success in a bad cause,
an qualify the same?
 Tro.   Why, brother Hector,
e may not think the justness of each act
ich and no other than event doth form it, 120
or once deject the courage of our minds,
ecause Cassandra's mad: her brain-sick rap-
 tures
annot distaste the goodness of a quarrel
hich hath our several honours all engag'd 124
o make it gracious. For my private part,
am no more touch'd than all Priam's sons;
nd Jove forbid there should be done amongst
 us
uch things as might offend the weakest spleen
o fight for and maintain. 129
 Par. Else might the world convince of levity
s well my undertakings as your counsels;
ut I attest the gods, your full consent 132
ave wings to my propension and cut off
ll fears attending on so dire a project:
or what, alas! can these my single arms?

What propugnation is in one man's valour, 136
To stand the push and enmity of those
This quarrel would excite? Yet, I protest,
Were I alone to pass the difficulties,
And had as ample power as I have will, 140
Paris should ne'er retract what he hath done,
Nor faint in the pursuit.
 Pri.   Paris, you speak
Like one besotted on your sweet delights:
You have the honey still, but these the gall; 144
So to be valiant is no praise at all.
 Par. Sir, I propose not merely to myself
The pleasure such a beauty brings with it;
But I would have the soil of her fair rape 148
Wip'd off, in honourable keeping her.
What treason were it to the ransack'd queen,
Disgrace to your great worths, and shame to me,
Now to deliver her possession up, 152
On terms of base compulsion! Can it be
That so degenerate a strain as this
Should once set footing in your generous
 bosoms?
There's not the meanest spirit on our party 156
Without a heart to dare or sword to draw
When Helen is defended, nor none so noble
Whose life were ill bestow'd or death unfam'd
Where Helen is the subject: then, I say, 160
Well may we fight for her, whom, we know well,
The world's large spaces cannot parallel.
 Hect. Paris and Troilus, you have both said
 well;
And on the cause and question now in hand 164
Have gloz'd, but superficially; not much
Unlike young men, whom Aristotle thought
Unfit to hear moral philosophy.
The reasons you allege do more conduce 168
To the hot passion of distemper'd blood
Than to make up a free determination
'Twixt right and wrong; for pleasure and re-
 venge
Have ears more deaf than adders to the voice
Of any true decision. Nature craves 173
All dues be render'd to their owners: now,
What nearer debt in all humanity
Than wife is to the husband? if this law 176
Of nature be corrupted through affection,
And that great minds, of partial indulgence
To their benumbed wills, resist the same;
There is a law in each well-order'd nation 180
To curb those raging appetites that are
Most disobedient and refractory.
If Helen then be wife to Sparta's king,
As it is known she is, these moral laws 184
Of nature, and of nations, speak aloud
To have her back return'd: thus to persist
In doing wrong extenuates not wrong,
But makes it much more heavy. Hector's
 opinion 188
Is this, in way of truth; yet, ne'ertheless,
My spritely brethren, I propend to you
In resolution to keep Helen still;
For 'tis a cause that hath no mean dependance
Upon our joint and several dignities. 193
 Tro. Why, there you touch'd the life of our
 design:
Were it not glory that we more affected

Than the performance of our heaving spleens,
I would not wish a drop of Trojan blood 197
Spent more in her defence. But, worthy Hector,
She is a theme of honour and renown,
A spur to valiant and magnanimous deeds, 200
Whose present courage may beat down our foes,
And fame in time to come canonize us;
For, I presume, brave Hector would not lose
So rich advantage of a promis'd glory   204
As smiles upon the forehead of this action
For the wide world's revenue.

   Hect.   I am yours,
You valiant offspring of great Priamus.
I have a roisting challenge sent amongst 208
The dull and factious nobles of the Greeks
Will strike amazement to their drowsy spirits.
I was advertis'd their great general slept
Whilst emulation in the army crept: 212
This, I presume, will wake him.   [*Exeunt.*

SCENE III.—*The Grecian Camp. Before*
ACHILLES' *Tent.*

Enter THERSITES.

   Ther. How now, Thersites! what, lost in the labyrinth of thy fury! Shall the elephant Ajax carry it thus? he beats me, and I rail at him: O worthy satisfaction! Would it were otherwise; that I could beat him, whilst he railed at me. 'Sfoot, I'll learn to conjure and raise devils, but I'll see some issue of my spiteful execrations. Then there's Achilles, a rare enginer. If Troy be not taken till these two undermine it, the walls will stand till they fall of themselves. O! thou great thunder-darter of Olympus, forget that thou art Jove the king of gods, and, Mercury, lose all the serpentine craft of thy caduceus, if ye take not that little little less than little wit from them that they have; which short-armed ignorance itself knows is so abundant scarce it will not in circumvention deliver a fly from a spider, without drawing their massy irons and cutting the web. After this, the vengeance on the whole camp! or, rather, the Neapolitan bone-ache! for that, methinks, is the curse dependant on those that war for a placket. I have said my prayers, and devil Envy say Amen. What, ho! my Lord Achilles!   24

Enter PATROCLUS.

   Patr. Who's there? Thersites! Good Thersites, come in and rail.
   Ther. If I could have remembered a gilt counterfeit, thou wouldst not have slipped out of my contemplation: but it is no matter; thyself upon thyself! The common curse of mankind, folly and ignorance, be thine in great revenue! heaven bless thee from a tutor, and discipline come not near thee! Let thy blood be thy direction till thy death! then, if she that lays thee out says thou art a fair corpse, I'll be sworn and sworn upon't she never shrouded any but lazars. Amen. Where's Achilles? 37
   Patr. What! art thou devout? wast thou in prayer?

   Ther. Ay; the heavens hear me!

Enter ACHILLES.

   Achil. Who's there?
   Patr. Thersites, my lord.
   Achil. Where, where? Art thou come? W
my cheese, my digestion, why hast thou
served thyself in to my table so many mea
Come, what's Agamemnon?
   Ther. Thy commander, Achilles. Then
me, Patroclus, what's Achilles?
   Patr. Thy lord, Thersites. Then tell me
pray thee, what's thyself?
   Ther. Thy knower, Patroclus. Then tell r
Patroclus, what art thou?
   Patr. Thou mayst tell that knowest.
   Achil. O! tell, tell.
   Ther. I'll decline the whole question. A
memnon commands Achilles; Achilles is
lord; I am Patroclus' knower; and Patroclu
a fool.
   Patr. You rascal!
   Ther. Peace, fool! I have not done.
   Achil. He is a privileged man. Procee
Thersites.
   Ther. Agamemnon is a fool; Achilles is
fool; Thersites is a fool; and, as aforesa
Patroclus is a fool.
   Achil. Derive this; come.
   Ther. Agamemnon is a fool to offer to co
mand Achilles; Achilles is a fool to be co
manded of Agamemnon; Thersites is a fool
serve such a fool; and Patroclus is a fo
positive.
   Patr. Why am I a fool?
   Ther. Make that demand to the Creator.
suffices me thou art. Look you, who con
here?
   Achil. Patroclus, I'll speak with nobod
Come in with me, Thersites.   [*Ex*
   Ther. Here is such patchery, such jugglir
and such knavery! all the argument is
cuckold and a whore; a good quarrel to dra
emulous factions and bleed to death upon. No
the dry serpigo on the subject! and war a
lechery confound all!   [*Ex*

Enter AGAMEMNON, ULYSSES, NESTOR, DIO-
MEDES, *and* AJAX.

   Agam. Where is Achilles?
   Patr. Within his tent; but ill-dispos'd, n
lord.
   Agam. Let it be known to him that we a
here.
He shent our messengers; and we lay by
Our appertainments, visiting of him:
Let him be told so; lest perchance he think
We dare not move the question of our place
Or know not what we are.
   Patr.   I shall say so to hir
                         [*Exi*
   Ulyss. We saw him at the opening of h
tent:
He is not sick.
   Ajax. Yes, lion-sick, sick of proud heart: yo
may call it melancholy if you will favour th

an; but, by my head, 'tis pride: but why,
ay? let him show us a cause. A word, my
d. [*Takes* AGAMEMNON *aside.*
Nest. What moves Ajax thus to bay at him?
Ulyss. Achilles hath inveigled his fool from
n. 101
Nest. Who, Thersites?
Ulyss. He.
Nest. Then will Ajax lack matter, if he have
st his argument. 105
Ulyss. No; you see, he is his argument that
s his argument, Achilles.
Nest. All the better; their fraction is more
r wish than their faction: but it was a strong
mposure a fool could disunite.
Ulyss. The amity that wisdom knits not folly
ay easily untie. Here comes Patroclus. 112

Re-enter PATROCLUS.

Nest. No Achilles with him.
Ulyss. The elephant hath joints, but none for
urtesy: his legs are legs for necessity, not for
xure. 116
Patr. Achilles bids me say, he is much sorry
any thing more than your sport and pleasure
id move your greatness and this noble state
o call upon him; he hopes it is no other 120
it, for your health and your digestion sake,
n after-dinner's breath.
Agam. Hear you, Patroclus:
'e are too well acquainted with these answers:
it his evasion, wing'd thus swift with scorn,
annot outfly our apprehensions. 125
uch attribute he hath, and much the reason
hy we ascribe it to him; yet all his virtues,
ot virtuously on his own part beheld, 128
o in our eyes begin to lose their gloss,
ea, like fair fruit in an unwholesome dish,
re like to rot untasted. Go and tell him,
'e come to speak with him; and you shall not
sin 132
you do say we think him over-proud
nd under-honest, in self-assumption greater
han in the note of judgment; and worthier
than himself
ere tend the savage strangeness he puts
on, 136
isguise the holy strength of their command,
nd underwrite in an observing kind
is humorous predominance; yea, watch
is pettish lunes, his ebbs, his flows, as if 140
he passage and whole carriage of this action
ode on his tide. Go tell him this, and add,
hat if he overhold his price so much,
'e'll none of him; but let him, like an engine
ot portable, lie under this report: 145
3ring action hither, this cannot go to war:'
stirring dwarf we do allowance give
efore a sleeping giant: tell him so. 148
Patr. I shall; and bring his answer presently. [*Exit.*
Agam. In second voice we'll not be satisfied;
Ve come to speak with him. Ulysses, enter
you. [*Exit* ULYSSES.
Ajax. What is he more than another? 152
Agam. No more than what he thinks he is.

Ajax. Is he so much? Do you not think he
thinks himself a better man than I am?
Agam. No question. 156
Ajax. Will you subscribe his thought, and
say he is?
Agam. No, noble Ajax; you are as strong,
as valiant, as wise, no less noble, much more
gentle, and altogether more tractable. 161
Ajax. Why should a man be proud? How
doth pride grow? I know not what pride is.
Agam. Your mind is the clearer, Ajax, and
your virtues the fairer. He that is proud eats
up himself: pride is his own glass, his own
trumpet, his own chronicle; and whatever
praises itself but in the deed, devours the deed
in the praise. 169
Ajax. I do hate a proud man, as I hate the
engendering of toads.
Nest. [*Aside.*] Yet he loves himself: is't not
strange? 173

Re-enter ULYSSES.

Ulyss. Achilles will not to the field to-
morrow.
Agam. What's his excuse?
Ulyss. He doth rely on none,
But carries on the stream of his dispose 176
Without observance or respect of any,
In will peculiar and in self-admission.
Agam. Why will he not upon our fair re-
quest
Untent his person and share the air with us?
Ulyss. Things small as nothing, for request's
sake only, 181
He makes important: possess'd he is with great-
ness,
And speaks not to himself but with a pride
That quarrels at self-breath: imagin'd worth
Holds in his blood such swoln and hot dis-
course, 185
That 'twixt his mental and his active parts
Kingdom'd Achilles in commotion rages
And batters down himself: what should I say?
He is so plaguy proud, that the death-tokens
of it 189
Cry 'No recovery.'
Agam. Let Ajax go to him.
Dear lord, go you and meet him in his tent:
'Tis said he holds you well, and will be led 192
At your request a little from himself.
Ulyss. O Agamemnon! let it not be so.
We'll consecrate the steps that Ajax makes
When they go from Achilles: shall the proud
lord 196
That bastes his arrogance with his own seam,
And never suffers matter of the world
Enter his thoughts, save such as do revolve
And ruminate himself, shall he be worshipp'd
Of that we hold an idol more than he? 201
No, this thrice-worthy and right valiant lord
Must not so stale his palm, nobly acquir'd;
Nor, by my will, assubjugate his merit, 204
As amply titled as Achilles is,
By going to Achilles:
That were to enlard his fat-already pride,
And add more coals to Cancer when he burns

With entertaining great Hyperion. 209
This lord go to him! Jupiter forbid,
And say in thunder, 'Achilles go to him.'
Nest. [*Aside.*] O! this is well; he rubs the
vein of him. 213
Dio. [*Aside.*] And how his silence drinks up
this applause!
Ajax. If I go to him, with my armed fist 216
I'll pash him o'er the face.
Agam. O, no! you shall not go.
Ajax. An a' be proud with me, I'll pheeze
his pride.
Let me go to him. 220
Ulyss. Not for the worth that hangs upon
our quarrel.
Ajax. A paltry, insolent fellow!
Nest. [*Aside.*] How he describes himself!
Ajax. Can he not be sociable? 224
Ulyss. [*Aside.*] The raven chides blackness.
Ajax. I'll let his humours blood.
Agam. [*Aside.*] He will be the physician
that should be the patient. 228
Ajax. An all men were o' my mind,—
Ulyss. [*Aside.*] Wit would be out of fashion.
Ajax. A' should not bear it so, a' should eat
swords first: shall pride carry it? 232
Nest. [*Aside.*] An't would, you'd carry half.
Ulyss. [*Aside.*] A' would have ten shares.
Ajax. I will knead him; I will make him
supple.
Nest. [*Aside.*] He's not yet through warm:
force him with praises: pour in, pour in; his
ambition is dry. 238
Ulyss. [*To* AGAMEMNON.] My lord, you feed
too much on this dislike.
Nest. Our noble general, do not do so. 240
Dio. You must prepare to fight without
Achilles.
Ulyss. Why, 'tis this naming of him does
him harm.
Here is a man—but 'tis before his face;
I will be silent.
Nest. Wherefore should you so? 244
He is not emulous, as Achilles is.
Ulyss. Know the whole world, he is as
valiant.
Ajax. A whoreson dog, that shall palter thus
with us! Would he were a Trojan! 248
Nest. What a vice were it in Ajax now,—
Ulyss. If he were proud,—
Dio. Or covetous of praise,—
Ulyss. Ay, or surly borne,— 252
Dio. Or strange, or self-affected!
Ulyss. Thank the heavens, lord, thou art of
sweet composure;
Praise him that got thee, her that gave thee
suck:
Fam'd be thy tutor, and thy parts of nature 256
Thrice-fam'd, beyond all erudition:
But he that disciplin'd thy arms to fight,
Let Mars divide eternity in twain,
And give him half: and, for thy vigour, 260
Bull-bearing Milo his addition yield
To sinewy Ajax. I will not praise thy wisdom,
Which, like a bourn, a pale, a shore, confines
Thy spacious and dilated parts: here's Nestor

Instructed by the antiquary times,
He must, he is, he cannot but be wise;
But pardon, father Nestor, were your days
As green as Ajax, and your brain so temper
You should not have the eminence of him,
But be as Ajax.
Ajax. Shall I call you father?
Ulyss. Ay, my good son.
Dio. Be rul'd by him, Lord Aj
Ulyss. There is no tarrying here; the h
Achilles
Keeps thicket. Please it our great general
To call together all his state of war;
Fresh kings are come to Troy: to-morrow,
We must with all our main of power stand fa
And here's a lord,—come knights from east
west,
And cull their flower, Ajax shall cope the be
Agam. Go we to council. Let Achilles slee
Light boats sail swift, though greater hu
draw deep. [*Exeu*

ACT III

SCENE I.—*Troy*. PRIAM'S *Palace*.

Enter PANDARUS *and a* Servant.

Pan. Friend! you! pray you, a word: do n
you follow the young Lord Paris?
Serv. Ay, sir, when he goes before me.
Pan. You depend upon him, I mean?
Serv. Sir, I do depend upon the Lord.
Pan. You depend upon a noble gentlema
I must needs praise him.
Serv. The Lord be praised!
Pan. You know me, do you not?
Serv. Faith, sir, superficially.
Pan. Friend, know me better. I am t
Lord Pandarus.
Serv. I hope I shall know your hono
better.
Pan. I do desire it.
Serv. You are in the state of grace.
Pan. Grace! not so, friend; honour a
lordship are my titles. [*Music within.*] Wh
music is this?
Serv. I do but partly know, sir: it is mus
in parts.
Pan. Know you the musicians?
Serv. Wholly, sir.
Pan. Who play they to?
Serv. To the hearers, sir.
Pan. At whose pleasure, friend?
Serv. At mine, sir, and theirs that love musi
Pan. Command, I mean, friend.
Serv. Who shall I command, sir?
Pan. Friend, we understand not one anothe
I am too courtly, and thou art too cunning.
whose request do these men play?
Serv. That's to't, indeed, sir. Marry, sir,
the request of Paris my lord, who is there
person; with him the mortal Venus, the hear
blood of beauty, love's invisible soul.
Pan. Who, my cousin Cressida?
Serv. No, sir, Helen: could you not find o
that by her attributes?
Pan. It should seem, fellow, that thou ha

...not seen the Lady Cressida. I come to speak
with Paris from the Prince Troilus: I will make
a complimental assault upon him, for my business seethes. 44

Serv. Sodden business: there's a stewed
phrase, indeed.

Enter PARIS *and* HELEN, *attended.*

Pan. Fair be to you, my lord, and to all this
fair company! fair desires, in all fair measures,
fairly guide them! especially to you, fair queen!
fair thoughts be your fair pillow! 50

Helen. Dear lord, you are full of fair words.

Pan. You speak your fair pleasure, sweet
queen. Fair prince, here is good broken music.

Par. You have broke it, cousin; and, by my
life, you shall make it whole again: you shall
piece it out with a piece of your performance.
Nell, he is full of harmony. 57

Pan. Truly, lady, no.

Helen. O, sir!

Pan. Rude, in sooth; in good sooth, very
rude. 61

Par. Well said, my lord! Well, you say so
in fits.

Pan. I have business to my lord, dear queen.
My lord, will you vouchsafe me a word? 65

Helen. Nay, this shall not hedge us out:
we'll hear you sing, certainly.

Pan. Well, sweet queen, you are pleasant
with me. But, marry, thus, my lord. My dear
lord and most esteemed friend, your brother
Troilus—

Helen. My Lord Pandarus; honey-sweet
lord,— 73

Pan. Go to, sweet queen, go to: commends
himself most affectionately to you.

Helen. You shall not bob us out of our
melody: if you do, our melancholy upon your
head!

Pan. Sweet queen, sweet queen! that's a
sweet queen, i' faith. 80

Helen. And to make a sweet lady sad is a
sour offence.

Pan. Nay, that shall not serve your turn;
that shall it not, in truth, la! Nay, I care not
for such words: no, no. And, my lord, he
desires you, that if the king call for him at
supper, you will make his excuse.

Helen. My Lord Pandarus,— 88

Pan. What says my sweet queen, my very
sweet queen?

Par. What exploit's in hand? where sups he
to-night? 92

Helen. Nay, but my lord,—

Pan. What says my sweet queen! My
cousin will fall out with you. You must know
where he sups. 96

Par. I'll lay my life, with my disposer
Cressida.

Pan. No, no, no such matter; you are wide.
Come, your disposer is sick. 100

Par. Well, I'll make excuse.

Pan. Ay, good my lord. Why should you
say Cressida? no, your poor disposer's sick.

Par. I spy. 104

Pan. You spy! what do you spy? Come,
give me an instrument. Now, sweet queen.

Helen. Why, this is kindly done.

Pan. My niece is horribly in love with a
thing you have, sweet queen. 109

Helen. She shall have it, my lord, if it be not
my Lord Paris.

Pan. He! no, she'll none of him; they two
are twain. 113

Helen. Falling in, after falling out, may
make them three.

Pan. Come, come, I'll hear no more of this.
I'll sing you a song now. 117

Helen. Ay, ay, prithee now. By my troth,
sweet lord, thou hast a fine forehead.

Pan. Ay, you may, you may. 120

Helen. Let thy song be love: this love will
undo us all. O Cupid, Cupid, Cupid!

Pan. Love! ay, that it shall, i' faith.

Par. Ay, good now, love, love, nothing but
love. 125

Pan. In good troth, it begins so:
[*Sings.*]

> Love, love, nothing but love, still more!
>   For, oh! love's bow 128
>   Shoots buck and doe:
>   The shaft confounds,
>   Not that it wounds,
> But tickles still the sore. 132
> These lovers cry O! O! they die!
>   Yet that which seems the wound to kill,
>   Doth turn O! O! to ha! ha! he!
>   So dying love lives still: 136
> O! O! a while, but ha! ha! ha!
> O! O! groans out for ha! ha! ha!

Heigh-ho!

Helen. In love, i' faith, to the very tip of the
nose. 141

Par. He eats nothing but doves, love; and
that breeds hot blood, and hot blood begets hot
thoughts, and hot thoughts beget hot deeds, and
hot deeds is love. 145

Pan. Is this the generation of love? hot
blood? hot thoughts, and hot deeds? Why,
they are vipers: is love a generation of vipers?
Sweet lord, who's a-field to-day? 149

Par. Hector, Deiphobus, Helenus, Antenor,
and all the gallantry of Troy: I would fain have
armed to-day, but my Nell would not have it so.
How chance my brother Troilus went not? 153

Helen. He hangs the lip at something: you
know all, Lord Pandarus.

Pan. Not I, honey-sweet queen. I long to
hear how they sped to-day. You'll remember
your brother's excuse?

Par. To a hair.

Pan. Farewell, sweet queen. 160

Helen. Commend me to your niece.

Pan. I will, sweet queen.
                    [*Exit. A retreat sounded.*

Par. They're come from field: let us to
Priam's hall
To greet the warriors. Sweet Helen, I must
    woo you 164
To help unarm our Hector: his stubborn buckles,
With these your white enchanting fingers
    touch'd,

Shall more obey than to the edge of steel
Or force of Greekish sinews; you shall do
more   168
Than all the island kings,—disarm great Hec-
tor.
   Helen. 'Twill make us proud to be his ser-
vant, Paris;
Yea, what he shall receive of us in duty
Gives us more palm in beauty than we have, 172
Yea, overshines ourself.
   Par. Sweet, above thought I love thee.
                          [*Exeunt.*

SCENE II.—*The Same.* PANDARUS' *Orchard.*

Enter PANDARUS *and* TROILUS' *Boy, meeting.*

   Pan. How now! where's thy master? at my
cousin Cressida's?
   Boy. No, sir; he stays for you to conduct him
thither.   4

Enter TROILUS.

   Pan. O! here he comes. How now, how now!
   Tro. Sirrah, walk off.   [*Exit Boy.*
   Pan. Have you seen my cousin?
   Tro. No, Pandarus: I stalk about her door,
Like a strange soul upon the Stygian banks 9
Staying for waftage. O! be thou my Charon,
And give me swift transportation to those fields
Where I may wallow in the lily-beds   12
Propos'd for the deserver! O gentle Pandarus!
From Cupid's shoulder pluck his painted
wings,
And fly with me to Cressid.
   Pan. Walk here i' the orchard. I'll bring
her straight.   [*Exit.*
   Tro. I am giddy, expectation whirls me round.
The imaginary relish is so sweet
That it enchants my sense. What will it be
When that the watery palate tastes indeed 20
Love's thrice-repured nectar? death, I fear me,
Swounding destruction, or some joy too fine,
Too subtle-potent, tun'd too sharp in sweet-
ness
For the capacity of my ruder powers: 24
I fear it much; and I do fear besides
That I shall lose distinction in my joys;
As doth a battle, when they charge on heaps
The enemy flying.   28

Re-enter PANDARUS.

   Pan. She's making her ready: she'll come
straight: you must be witty now. She does so
blush, and fetches her wind so short, as if she
were frayed with a sprite: I'll fetch her. It is
the prettiest villain: she fetches her breath as
short as a new-ta'en sparrow.   [*Exit.*
   Tro. Even such a passion doth embrace my
bosom;
My heart beats thicker than a fev'rous pulse; 36
And all my powers do their bestowing lose,
Like vassalage at unawares encountering
The eye of majesty.

Re-enter PANDARUS *with* CRESSIDA.

   Pan. Come, come, what need you blush?

shame's a baby. Here he is now: swear the
oaths now to her that you have sworn to me.
What! are you gone again? you must be watched
ere you be made tame, must you? Come your
ways, come your ways; an you draw backward
we'll put you i' the fills. Why do you not speak
to her? Come, draw this curtain, and let's see
your picture. Alas the day, how loath you are
to offend day-light! an 'twere dark, you'd close
sooner. So, so; rub on, and kiss the mistress.
How now! a kiss in fee-farm! build there, carpenter; the air is sweet. Nay, you shall fight
your hearts out ere I part you. The falcon as the
tercel, for all the ducks i' the river: go to, go to.
   Tro. You have bereft me of all words, lady.
   Pan. Words pay no debts, give her deeds:
but she'll bereave you of the deeds too if she
call your activity in question. What! billing
again? Here's 'In witness whereof the parties
interchangeably'—Come in, come in: I'll go
get a fire.   [*Exit.*
   Cres. Will you walk in, my lord?
   Tro. O Cressida! how often have I wished
me thus!   64
   Cres. Wished, my lord! The gods grant,—O
my lord!
   Tro. What should they grant? what makes
this pretty abruption? What too curious dreg
espies my sweet lady in the fountain of our love?
   Cres. More dregs than water, if my fears
have eyes.
   Tro. Fears make devils of cherubins; they
never see truly.   72
   Cres. Blind fear, that seeing reason leads,
finds safer footing than blind reason stumbling
without fear: to fear the worst oft cures the
worse.   77
   Tro. O! let my lady apprehend no fear: in all
Cupid's pageant there is presented no monster.
   Cres. Nor nothing monstrous neither?   80
   Tro. Nothing but our undertakings; when
we vow to weep seas, live in fire, eat rocks, tame
tigers; thinking it harder for our mistress to
devise imposition enough than for us to undergo
any difficulty imposed. This is the monstruosity
in love, lady, that the will is infinite, and the
execution confined; that the desire is boundless,
and the act a slave to limit.   88
   Cres. They say all lovers swear more performance than they are able, and yet reserve
an ability that they never perform; vowing
more than the perfection of ten and discharging
less than the tenth part of one. They that have
the voice of lions and the act of hares, are they
not monsters?   95
   Tro. Are there such? such are not we.
Praise us as we are tasted, allow us as we prove;
our head shall go bare, till merit crown it. No
perfection in reversion shall have a praise in
present: we will not name desert before his
birth, and, being born, his addition shall be
humble. Few words to fair faith: Troilus shall
be such to Cressid, as what envy can say worst
shall be a mock for his truth; and what truth
can speak truest not truer than Troilus.   105
   Cres. Will you walk in, my lord?

Re-enter PANDARUS.

Pan. What! blushing still? have you not
done talking yet?   108

Cres. Well, uncle, what folly I commit, I
dedicate to you.

Pan. I thank you for that: if my lord get
a boy of you, you'll give him me. Be true to
my lord; if he flinch, chide me for it.   113

Tro. You know now your hostages; your
uncle's word, and my firm faith.

Pan. Nay, I'll give my word for her too.
Our kindred, though they be long ere they are
wooed, they are constant being won: they are
burrs, I can tell you; they'll stick where they
are thrown.   120

Cres. Boldness comes to me now, and brings
me heart:
Prince Troilus, I have lov'd you night and day
For many weary months.

Tro.   Why was my Cressid then so hard to
win?   124

Cres. Hard to seem won; but I was won, my
lord,
With the first glance that ever—pardon me—
If I confess much you will play the tyrant.
I love you now; but, till now, not so much   128
But I might master it: in faith, I lie;
My thoughts were like unbridled children, grown
Too headstrong for their mother. See, we fools!
Why have I blabb'd? who shall be true to us   132
When we are so unsecret to ourselves?
But, though I lov'd you well, I woo'd you not;
And yet, good faith, I wish'd myself a man,
Or that we women had men's privilege   136
Of speaking first. Sweet, bid me hold my tongue;
For in this rapture I shall surely speak
The thing I shall repent. See, see! your silence,
Cunning in dumbness, from my weakness draws
My very soul of counsel. Stop my mouth.   141

Tro. And shall, albeit sweet music issues
thence.

Pan. Pretty, i' faith.

Cres. My lord, I do beseech you, pardon me;
'Twas not my purpose thus to beg a kiss: 145
I am asham'd: O heavens! what have I done?
For this time will I take my leave, my lord.

Tro. Your leave, sweet Cressid?   148

Pan. Leave! an you take leave till to-morrow
morning,—

Cres. Pray you, content you.

Tro.   What offends you, lady?

Cres. Sir, mine own company.   152

Tro. You cannot shun yourself.

Cres. Let me go and try:
I have a kind of self resides with you;
But an unkind self, that itself will leave,   156
To be another's fool. I would be gone:
Where is my wit? I speak I know not what.

Tro. Well know they what they speak that
speak so wisely.

Cres. Perchance, my lord, I show more craft
than love;   160
And fell so roundly to a large confession,
To angle for your thoughts: but you are wise,
Or else you love not, for to be wise, and love,

Exceeds man's might; that dwells with gods
above.   164

Tro. O! that I thought it could be in a
woman—
As if it can I will presume in you—
To feed for aye her lamp and flames of love;
To keep her constancy in plight and youth,   168
Outliving beauty's outward, with a mind
That doth renew swifter than blood decays:
Or that persuasion could but thus convince me,
That my integrity and truth to you   172
Might be affronted with the match and weight
Of such a winnow'd purity in love;
How were I then uplifted! but, alas!
I am as true as truth's simplicity,   176
And simpler than the infancy of truth.

Cres. In that I'll war with you.

Tro.   O virtuous fight!
When right with right wars who shall be most
right.
True swains in love shall in the world to come
Approve their truths by Troilus: when their
rimes,   181
Full of protest, of oath, and big compare,
Want similes, truth tir'd with iteration,
As true as steel, as plantage to the moon,   184
As sun to day, as turtle to her mate,
As iron to adamant, as earth to the centre,
Yet, after all comparisons of truth,
As truth's authentic author to be cited,   188
'As true as Troilus' shall crown up the verse
And sanctify the numbers.

Cres.   Prophet may you be!
If I be false, or swerve a hair from truth,
When time is old and hath forgot itself,   192
When waterdrops have worn the stones of Troy,
And blind oblivion swallow'd cities up,
And mighty states characterless are grated
To dusty nothing, yet let memory,   196
From false to false, among false maids in love
Upbraid my falsehood! when they have said 'as
false
As air, as water, wind, or sandy earth,
As fox to lamb, as wolf to heifer's calf,   200
Pard to the hind, or stepdame to her son;'
Yea, let them say, to stick the heart of false-
hood,
'As false as Cressid.'

Pan. Go to, a bargain made; seal it, seal it:
I'll be the witness. Here I hold your hand, here
my cousin's. If ever you prove false one to another, since I have taken such pains to bring you
together, let all pitiful goers-between be called to
the world's end after my name; call them all
Pandars; let all constant men be Troiluses, all
false women Cressids, and all brokers-between
Pandars! say, Amen.   212

Tro. Amen.

Cres. Amen.

Pan. Amen. Whereupon I will show you a
chamber and a bed; which bed, because it shall
not speak of your pretty encounters, press it to
death: away!
And Cupid grant all tongue-tied maidens here
Bed, chamber, Pandar to provide this gear! 220
                                          [*Exeunt.*

SCENE III.—*The Grecian Camp.*

Enter AGAMEMNON, ULYSSES, DIOMEDES, NESTOR, AJAX, MENELAUS, *and* CALCHAS.

Cal. Now, princes, for the service I have done you,
The advantage of the time prompts me aloud
To call for recompense. Appear it to your mind
That through the sight I bear in things to come,
I have abandon'd Troy, left my possession, 5
Incurr'd a traitor's name; expos'd myself,
From certain and possess'd conveniences,
To doubtful fortunes; sequestering from me all
That time, acquaintance, custom, and condition
Made tame and most familiar to my nature;
And here, to do you service, have become
As new into the world, strange, unacquainted:
I do beseech you, as in way of taste, 13
To give me now a little benefit,
Out of those many register'd in promise,
Which, you say, live to come in my behalf. 16
     Agam. What wouldst thou of us, Trojan? make demand.
     Cal. You have a Trojan prisoner, call'd Antenor,
Yesterday took: Troy holds him very dear.
Oft have you—often have you thanks therefore— 20
Desir'd my Cressid in right great exchange,
Whom Troy hath still denied; but this Antenor
I know is such a wrest in their affairs
That their negociations all must slack, 24
Wanting his manage; and they will almost
Give us a prince of blood, a son of Priam,
In change of him: let him be sent, great princes,
And he shall buy my daughter; and her presence 28
Shall quite strike off all service I have done,
In most accepted pain.
     Agam.   Let Diomedes bear him,
And bring us Cressid hither: Calchas shall have
What he requests of us. Good Diomed, 32
Furnish you fairly for this interchange:
Withal bring word if Hector will to-morrow
Be answer'd in his challenge: Ajax is ready.
     Dio. This shall I undertake; and 'tis a burden 36
Which I am proud to bear.
     [*Exeunt* DIOMEDES *and* CALCHAS.

Enter ACHILLES *and* PATROCLUS, *before their tent.*

Ulyss. Achilles stands in the entrance of his tent:
Please it our general to pass strangely by him,
As if he were forgot; and, princes all, 40
Lay negligent and loose regard upon him:
I will come last. 'Tis like he'll question me
Why such unplausive eyes are bent on him:
If so, I have derision med'cinable 44
To use between your strangeness and his pride,
Which his own will shall have desire to drink.
It may do good: pride hath no other glass
To show itself but pride, for supple knees 48
Feed arrogance and are the poor man's fees.
     Agam. We'll execute your purpose, and put on

A form of strangeness as we pass along:
So do each lord, and either greet him not, 5
Or else disdainfully, which shall shake him more
Than if not look'd on. I will lead the way.
     Achil. What! comes the general to speak with me?
You know my mind; I'll fight no more 'gainst Troy.
     Agam. What says Achilles? would he aught with us? 5
     Nest. Would you, my lord, aught with the general?
     Achil. No.
     Nest. Nothing, my lord. 6
     Agam. The better.
          [*Exeunt* AGAMEMNON *and* NESTOR.
     Achil. Good day, good day.
     Men. How do you? how do you? [*Exit*
     Achil. What! does the cuckold scorn me? 6
     Ajax. How now, Patroclus?
     Achil. Good morrow, Ajax.
     Ajax. Ha?
     Achil. Good morrow. 6
     Ajax. Ay, and good next day too. [*Exit*
     Achil. What mean these fellows? Know they not Achilles?
     Patr. They pass by strangely: they were us'd to bend,
To send their smiles before them to Achilles; 7
To come as humbly as they us'd to creep
To holy altars.
     Achil.   What! am I poor of late?
'Tis certain, greatness, once fall'n out with fortune,
Must fall out with men too: what the declin'd is
He shall as soon read in the eyes of others 7
As feel in his own fall; for men, like butterflies
Show not their mealy wings but to the summer,
And not a man, for being simply man, 8
Hath any honour, but honour for those honours
That are without him, as places, riches, and favour,
Prizes of accident as oft as merit:
Which when they fall, as being slippery standers, 8
The love that lean'd on them as slippery too,
Do one pluck down another, and together
Die in the fall. But 'tis not so with me:
Fortune and I are friends: I do enjoy 8
At ample point all that I did possess,
Save these men's looks; who do, methinks, find out
Something not worth in me such rich beholding
As they have often given. Here is Ulysses; 9
I'll interrupt his reading.
How now, Ulysses!
     Ulyss.   Now, great Thetis' son!
     Achil. What are you reading?
     Ulyss.   A strange fellow here
Writes me,
          That man, how dearly ever parted,
How much in having, or without or in, 9
Cannot make boast to have that which he hath
Nor feels not what he owes but by reflection;
As when his virtues shining upon others 10
Heat them, and they retort that heat again
To the first giver.

Achil. This is not strange, Ulysses!
The beauty that is borne here in the face
The bearer knows not, but commends itself 104
To others' eyes: nor doth the eye itself—
That most pure spirit of sense—behold itself,
Not going from itself; but eye to eye oppos'd
Salutes each other with each other's form; 108
For speculation turns not to itself
Till it hath travell'd and is mirror'd there
Where it may see itself. This is not strange at all.
    Ulyss. I do not strain at the position, 112
It is familiar, but at the author's drift;
Who in his circumstance expressly proves
That no man is the lord of any thing—
Though in and of him there be much consist-
    ing— 116
Till he communicate his parts to others:
Nor doth he of himself know them for aught
Till he behold them form'd in the applause
Where they're extended; who, like an arch,
    reverberates 120
The voice again, or, like a gate of steel
Fronting the sun, receives and renders back
His figure and his heat. I was much rapt in
    this;
And apprehended here immediately 124
The unknown Ajax.
Heavens, what a man is there! a very horse,
That has he knows not what. Nature, what
    things there are,
Most abject in regard, and dear in use! 128
What things again most dear in the esteem
And poor in worth! Now shall we see to-
    morrow,
An act that very chance doth throw upon him,
Ajax renown'd. O heavens! what some men
    do; 132
While some men leave to do.
How some men creep in skittish Fortune's hall,
Whiles others play the idiots in her eyes!
How one man eats into another's pride, 136
While pride is fasting in his wantonness!
To see these Grecian lords! why, even already
They clap the lubber Ajax on the shoulder,
As if his foot were on brave Hector's breast, 140
And great Troy shrinking.
    Achil. I do believe it; for they pass'd by me
As misers do by beggars, neither gave to me
Good word or look: what! are my deeds forgot?
    Ulyss. Time hath, my lord, a wallet at his
        back, 145
Wherein he puts alms for oblivion,
A great-siz'd monster of ingratitudes:
Those scraps are good deeds past; which are
    devour'd 148
As fast as they are made, forgot as soon
As done: perseverance, dear my lord,
Keeps honour bright: to have done, is to hang
Quite out of fashion, like a rusty mail 152
In monumental mockery. Take the instant
    way;
For honour travels in a strait so narrow
Where one but goes abreast: keep, then, the
    path;
For emulation hath a thousand sons 156
That one by one pursue: if you give way,

Or hedge aside from the direct forthright,
Like to an enter'd tide they all rush by
And leave you hindmost; 160
Or, like a gallant horse fall'n in first rank,
Lie there for pavement to the abject rear,
O'errun and trampled on: then what they do in
    present,
Though less than yours in past, must o'ertop
    yours; 164
For time is like a fashionable host,
That slightly shakes his parting guest by the
    hand,
And with his arms outstretch'd, as he would fly,
Grasps in the comer: welcome ever smiles, 168
And farewell goes out sighing. O! let not virtue
    seek
Remuneration for the thing it was;
For beauty, wit,
High birth, vigour of bone, desert in service, 172
Love, friendship, charity, are subjects all
To envious and calumniating time.
One touch of nature makes the whole world kin,
That all with one consent praise new-born
    gawds, 176
Though they are made and moulded of things
    past,
And give to dust that is a little gilt
More laud than gilt o'er-dusted.
The present eye praises the present object: 180
Then marvel not, thou great and complete man,
That all the Greeks begin to worship Ajax;
Since things in motion sooner catch the eye
Than what not stirs. The cry went once on
    thee, 184
And still it might, and yet it may again,
If thou wouldst not entomb thyself alive,
And case thy reputation in thy tent;
Whose glorious deeds, but in these fields of late,
Made emulous missions 'mongst the gods
    themselves, 189
And drave great Mars to faction.
    Achil. Of this my privacy
I have strong reasons.
    Ulyss. But 'gainst your privacy
The reasons are more potent and heroical. 192
'Tis known, Achilles, that you are in love
With one of Priam's daughters.
    Achil. Ha! known!
    Ulyss. Is that a wonder? 196
The providence that's in a watchful state
Knows almost every grain of Plutus' gold,
Finds bottom in the uncomprehensive deeps,
Keeps place with thought, and almost, like the
    gods, 200
Does thoughts unveil in their dumb cradles.
There is a mystery—with whom relation
Durst never meddle—in the soul of state,
Which hath an operation more divine 204
Than breath or pen can give expressure to.
All the commerce that you have had with Troy
As perfectly is ours as yours, my lord;
And better would it fit Achilles much 208
To throw down Hector than Polyxena;
But it must grieve young Pyrrhus now at home,
When fame shall in our islands sound her
    trump,

And all the Greekish girls shall tripping sing,
'Great Hector's sister did Achilles win,   213
But our great Ajax bravely beat down him.'
Farewell, my lord: I as your lover speak;
The fool slides o'er the ice that you should
  break.   [*Exit.*

Patr. To this effect, Achilles, have I mov'd
you.   217
A woman impudent and mannish grown
Is not more loath'd than an effeminate man
In time of action. I stand condemn'd for this:
They think my little stomach to the war   221
And your great love to me restrains you thus.
Sweet, rouse yourself; and the weak wanton
  Cupid
Shall from your neck unloose his amorous
  fold,   224
And, like a dew-drop from the lion's mane,
Be shook to air.

Achil.   Shall Ajax fight with Hector?
Patr. Ay; and perhaps receive much honour
  by him.
Achil. I see my reputation is at stake;   228
My fame is shrewdly gor'd.

Patr.   O! then, beware;
Those wounds heal ill that men do give them-
  selves:
Omission to do what is necessary
Seals a commission to a blank of danger;   232
And danger, like an ague, subtly taints
Even then when we sit idly in the sun.

Achil. Go call Thersites hither, sweet Patro-
  clus:
I'll send the fool to Ajax and desire him   236
T' invite the Trojan lords after the combat
To see us here unarmed. I have a woman's
  longing,
An appetite that I am sick withal,
To see great Hector in his weeds of peace; 240
To talk with him and to behold his visage,
Even to my full of view. A labour sav'd!

Enter THERSITES.

Ther. A wonder!
Achil. What?   244
Ther. Ajax goes up and down the field, asking for himself.
Achil. How so?
Ther. He must fight singly to-morrow with
Hector, and is so prophetically proud of an
heroical cudgelling that he raves in saying
nothing.
Achil. How can that be?   252
Ther. Why, he stalks up and down like a
peacock, a stride and a stand; ruminates like a
hostess that hath no arithmetic but her brain to
set down her reckoning; bites his lip with a
politic regard, as who should say 'There were wit
in this head, an 'twould out;' and so there is,
but it lies as coldly in him as fire in a flint, which
will not show without knocking. The man's
undone for ever; for if Hector break not his
neck i' the combat, he'll break 't himself in vain-
glory. He knows not me; I said, 'Good morrow,
Ajax;' and he replies, 'Thanks, Agamemnon.'
What think you of this man that takes me for

the general? He's grown a very land-fish, lan-
guageless, a monster. A plague of opinion! a
man may wear it on both sides, like a leather
jerkin.   269
Achil. Thou must be my ambassador to him,
Thersites.
Ther. Who, I? why, he'll answer nobody; he
professes not answering; speaking is for beggars;
he wears his tongue in his arms. I will put on
his presence: let Patroclus make demands to me,
you shall see the pageant of Ajax.   276
Achil. To him, Patroclus: tell him, I humbly
desire the valiant Ajax to invite the most valorous Hector to come unarmed to my tent; and to
procure safe-conduct for his person of the mag-
nanimous and most illustrious, six-or-seven-
times-honoured captain-general of the Grecian
army, Agamemnon, et cætera. Do this.
Patr. Jove bless great Ajax!   284
Ther. Hum!
Patr. I come from the worthy Achilles,—
Ther. Ha!
Patr. Who most humbly desires you to in-
vite Hector to his tent,—   289
Ther. Hum!
Patr. And to procure safe-conduct from
Agamemnon.   292
Ther. Agamemnon!
Patr. Ay, my lord.
Ther. Ha!
Patr. What say you to 't?   296
Ther. God be wi' you, with all my heart.
Patr. Your answer, sir.
Ther. If to-morrow be a fair day, by eleven
o'clock it will go one way or other; howsoever,
he shall pay for me ere he has me.   301
Patr. Your answer, sir.
Ther. Fare you well, with all my heart.
Achil. Why, but he is not in this tune, is he?
Ther. No, but he's out o' tune thus. What
music will be in him when Hector has knocked
out his brains, I know not; but, I am sure,
none, unless the fiddler Apollo get his sinews to
make catlings on.   309
Achil. Come, thou shalt bear a letter to him
straight.
Ther. Let me bear another to his horse, for
that's the more capable creature.   313
Achil. My mind is troubled, like a fountain
  stirr'd;
And I myself see not the bottom of it.

  [*Exeunt* ACHILLES *and* PATROCLUS.

Ther. Would the fountain of your mind were
clear again, that I might water an ass at it!
I had rather be a tick in a sheep than such a
valiant ignorance.   [*Exit.*

ACT IV

SCENE I.—*Troy. A Street.*

Enter, on one side, ÆNEAS, *and* Servant *with a
torch; on the other,* PARIS, DEIPHOBUS, ANTE-
NOR, DIOMEDES, *and Others, with torches.*

Par. See, ho! who is that there?
Dei.   It is the Lord Æneas.

Æne. Is the prince there in person?
Had I so good occasion to lie long
As you, Prince Paris, nothing but heavenly
   business   4
Should rob my bed-mate of my company.
  Dio. That's my mind too. Good morrow,
   Lord Æneas.
  Par. A valiant Greek, Æneas; take his hand:
Witness the process of your speech, wherein 8
You told how Diomed, a whole week by days,
Did haunt you in the field.
  Æne.   Health to you, valiant sir,
During all question of the gentle truce;
But when I meet you arm'd, as black defiance 12
As heart can think or courage execute.
  Dio. The one and other Diomed embraces.
Our bloods are now in calm, and, so long,
  health!
But when contention and occasion meet, 16
By Jove, I'll play the hunter for thy life
With all my force, pursuit, and policy.
  Æne. And thou shalt hunt a lion, that will fly
With his face backward. In humane gentleness,
Welcome to Troy! now, by Anchises' life, 21
Welcome, indeed! By Venus' hand I swear,
No man alive can love in such a sort
The thing he means to kill more excellently. 24
  Dio. We sympathize. Jove, let Æneas live,
If to my sword his fate be not the glory,
A thousand complete courses of the sun!
But, in mine emulous honour, let him die, 28
With every joint a wound, and that to-morrow!
  Æne. We know each other well.
  Dio. We do; and long to know each other
  worse.
  Par. This is the most despiteful gentle greet-
  ing,   32
The noblest hateful love, that e'er I heard of.
What business, lord, so early?
  Æne. I was sent for to the king; but why,
  I know not.
  Par. His purpose meets you: 'twas to bring
  this Greek   36
To Calchas' house, and there to render him,
For the enfreed Antenor, the fair Cressid.
Let's have your company; or, if you please,
Haste there before us. I constantly do think— 40
Or rather, call my thought a certain know-
  ledge—
My brother Troilus lodges there to-night:
Rouse him and give him note of our approach,
With the whole quality wherefore: I fear 44
We shall be much unwelcome.
  Æne.   That I assure you:
Troilus had rather Troy were borne to Greece
Than Cressid borne from Troy.
  Par.   There is no help;
The bitter disposition of the time   48
Will have it so. On, lord; we'll follow you.
  Æne. Good morrow, all.   [*Exit.*
  Par. And tell me, noble Diomed; faith, tell
  me true,
Even in the soul of sound good-fellowship, 52
Who, in your thoughts, merits fair Helen best—
Myself or Menelaus?
  Dio.   Both alike:

He merits well to have her that doth seek her—
Not making any scruple of her soilure— 56
With such a hell of pain and world of charge,
And you as well to keep her that defend her—
Not palating the taste of her dishonour—
With such a costly loss of wealth and friends: 60
He, like a puling cuckold, would drink up
The lees and dregs of a flat tamed piece;
You, like a lecher, out of whorish loins
Are pleas'd to breed out your inheritors: 64
Both merits pois'd, each weighs nor less nor
  more;
But he as he, the heavier for a whore.
  Par. You are too bitter to your country-
  woman.
  Dio. She's bitter to her country. Hear me,
  Paris: 68
For every false drop in her bawdy veins
A Grecian's life hath sunk; for every scruple
Of her contaminated carrion weight
A Trojan hath been slain. Since she could
  speak,   72
She hath not given so many good words breath
As for her Greeks and Trojans suffer'd death.
  Par. Fair Diomed, you do as chapmen do,
Dispraise the thing that you desire to buy; 76
But we in silence hold this virtue well,
We'll not commend what we intend to sell.
Here lies our way.   [*Exeunt.*

SCENE II.—*The Same. A Court before*
    PANDARUS' *House.*

    Enter TROILUS *and* CRESSIDA.

  Tro. Dear, trouble not yourself: the morn is
  cold.
  Cres. Then, sweet my lord, I'll call mine
  uncle down:
He shall unbolt the gates.
  Tro.   Trouble him not;
To bed, to bed: sleep kill those pretty eyes, 4
And give as soft attachment to thy senses
As infants' empty of all thought!
  Cres.   Good morrow then.
  Tro. I prithee now, to bed.
  Cres.   Are you aweary of me?
  Tro. O Cressida! but that the busy day, 8
Wak'd by the lark, hath rous'd the ribald
  crows,
And dreaming night will hide our joys no
  longer,
I would not from thee.
  Cres.   Night hath been too brief.
  Tro. Beshrew the witch! with venomous
  wights she stays   12
As tediously as hell, but flies the grasps of love
With wings more momentary-swift than
  thought.
You will catch cold, and curse me.
  Cres.   Prithee, tarry:
You men will never tarry.   16
O foolish Cressid! I might have still held off,
And then you would have tarried. Hark!
  there's one up.
  Pan. [*Within.*] What! are all the doors open
  here?

Tro. It is your uncle.   20
Cres. A pestilence on him! now will he be mocking: I shall have such a life!

Enter PANDARUS.

Pan. How now, how now! how go maidenheads?
Here, you maid! where's my cousin Cressid? 24
Cres. Go hang yourself, you naughty mocking uncle!
You bring me to do—and then you flout me too.
Pan. To do what? to do what? let her say what: what have I brought you to do?   28
Cres. Come, come; beshrew your heart! you'll ne'er be good,
Nor suffer others.
Pan. Ha, ha! Alas, poor wretch! a poor capocchia! hast not slept to-night? would he not, a naughty man, let it sleep? a bugbear take him!
Cres. Did not I tell you? 'would he were knock'd o' the head!   [*Knocking within.*
Who's that at door? good uncle, go and see. 36
My lord, come you again into my chamber:
You smile, and mock me, as if I meant naughtily.
Tro. Ha, ha!
Cres. Come, you are deceiv'd, I think of no such thing.   [*Knocking within.*
How earnestly they knock! Pray you, come in:
I would not for half Troy have you seen here.
      [*Exeunt* TROILUS *and* CRESSIDA.
Pan. [*Going to the door.*] Who's there? what's the matter? will you beat down the door? How now! what's the matter?   45

Enter ÆNEAS.

Æne. Good morrow, lord, good morrow.
Pan. Who's there? my Lord Æneas! By my troth,
I knew you not: what news with you so early?
Æne. Is not Prince Troilus here?   49
Pan. Here! what should he do here?
Æne. Come, he is here, my lord: do not deny him: it doth import him much to speak with me.
Pan. Is he here, say you? 'tis more than I know, I'll be sworn: for my own part, I came in late. What should he do here?   56
Æne. Who! nay, then: come, come, you'll do him wrong ere you're 'ware. You'll be so true to him, to be false to him. Do not you know of him, but yet go fetch him hither; go. 60

Re-enter TROILUS.

Tro. How now! what's the matter?
Æne. My lord, I scarce have leisure to salute you,
My matter is so rash: there is at hand
Paris your brother, and Deiphobus,   64
The Grecian Diomed, and our Antenor
Deliver'd to us; and for him forthwith,
Ere the first sacrifice, within this hour,
We must give up to Diomedes' hand   68
The Lady Cressida.
Tro.   Is it so concluded?

Æne. By Priam, and the general state of Troy:
They are at hand and ready to effect it.
Tro. How my achievements mock me!   72
I will go meet them: and, my Lord Æneas,
We met by chance; you did not find me here.
Æne. Good, good, my lord; the secrets of nature
Have not more gift in taciturnity.   76
      [*Exeunt* TROILUS *and* ÆNEAS.
Pan. Is't possible? no sooner got but lost?
The devil take Antenor! the young prince will go mad: a plague upon Antenor! I would they had broke 's neck!   80

Enter CRESSIDA.

Cres. How now! What is the matter? Who was here?
Pan. Ah! ah!
Cres. Why sigh you so profoundly? where's my lord? gone! Tell me, sweet uncle, what's the matter?
Pan. Would I were as deep under the earth as I am above!   88
Cres. O the gods! what's the matter?
Pan. Prithee, get thee in. Would thou hadst ne'er been born! I knew thou wouldst be his death. O poor gentleman! A plague upon Antenor!   93
Cres. Good uncle, I beseech you, on my knees I beseech you, what's the matter?
Pan. Thou must be gone, wench, thou must be gone; thou art changed for Antenor. Thou must to thy father, and be gone from Troilus: 'twill be his death; 'twill be his bane; he cannot bear it.   100
Cres. O you immortal gods! I will not go.
Pan. Thou must.
Cres. I will not, uncle: I have forgot my father;
I know no touch of consanguinity;   104
No kin, no love, no blood, no soul so near me
As the sweet Troilus. O you gods divine!
Make Cressid's name the very crown of falsehood
If ever she leave Troilus! Time, force, and death,
Do to this body what extremes you can;   109
But the strong base and building of my love
Is as the very centre of the earth,
Drawing all things to it. I'll go in and weep,—
Pan. Do, do.   113
Cres. Tear my bright hair, and scratch my praised cheeks,
Crack my clear voice with sobs, and break my heart
With sounding Troilus. I will not go from Troy.   [*Exeunt.*

SCENE III.—*The Same. Before* PANDARUS' *House.*

Enter PARIS, TROILUS, ÆNEAS, DEIPHOBUS, ANTENOR, *and* DIOMEDES.

Par. It is great morning, and the hour prefix'd
Of her delivery to this valiant Greek

nes fast upon. Good my brother Troilus,
 you the lady what she is to do,   4
 haste her to the purpose.
ro.   Walk into her house;
bring her to the Grecian presently:
 to his hand when I deliver her,
nk it an altar, and thy brother Troilus   8
riest, there offering to it his own heart. [*Exit.*
ar. I know what 'tis to love;
 would, as I shall pity, I could help!
ase you walk in, my lords.   [*Exeunt.*

SCENE IV.—*The Same. A Room in
PANDARUS' House.*

Enter PANDARUS *and* CRESSIDA.

'an. Be moderate, be moderate.
'res. Why tell you me of moderation?
 grief is fine, full, perfect, that I taste,
 violenteth in a sense as strong   4
'hat which causeth it: how can I moderate it?
 could temporize with my affection,
brew it to a weak and colder palate,
 like allayment could I give my grief: 8
 love admits no qualifying dross;
 more my grief, in such a precious loss.

Enter TROILUS.

'an. Here, here, here he comes. Ah! sweet
ducks.
'res. [*Embracing him.*] O Troilus! Troilus!
'an. What a pair of spectacles is here! Let
embrace too. 'O heart,' as the goodly say-
is,—

   O heart, heavy heart,   16
   Why sigh'st thou without breaking?

n he answers again,

   Because thou canst not ease thy smart
   By friendship nor by speaking.   20

re was never a truer rime. Let us cast away
hing, for we may live to have need of such a
se: we see it, we see it. How now, lambs!
ro. Cressid, I love thee in so strain'd a
purity,   24
t the bless'd gods, as angry with my fancy,
re bright in zeal than the devotion which
d lips blow to their deities, take thee from
me.
res. Have the gods envy?   28
an. Ay, ay, ay, ay; 'tis too plain a case.
res. And is it true that I must go from Troy?
ro. A hateful truth.
res.   What! and from Troilus too?
ro. From Troy and Troilus.
res.   Is it possible? 32
ro. And suddenly; where injury of chance
s back leave-taking, justles roughly by
 time of pause, rudely beguiles our lips
 all rejoindure, forcibly prevents   36
 lock'd embrasures, strangles our dear vows
n in the birth of our own labouring breath.
 two, that with so many thousand sighs
 buy each other, must poorly sell ourselves
th the rude brevity and discharge of one. 41
urious time now with a robber's haste

Crams his rich thievery up, he knows not how:
As many farewells as be stars in heaven,   44
With distinct breath and consign'd kisses to
   them,
He fumbles up into a loose adieu,
And scants us with a single famish'd kiss,
Distasted with the salt of broken tears.   48
   Æne. [*Within.*] My lord, is the lady ready?
   Tro. Hark! you are call'd: some say the
     Genius so
Cries 'Come!' to him that instantly must die.
Bid them have patience; she shall come anon.
   Pan. Where are my tears? rain, to lay this
wind, or my heart will be blown up by root!
                 [*Exit.*
   Cres. I must then to the Grecians?
   Tro.   No remedy.
   Cres. A woeful Cressid 'mongst the merry
     Greeks!   56
When shall we see again?
   Tro. Hear me, my love. Be thou but true of
     heart,—
   Cres. I true! how now! what wicked deem
     is this?
   Tro. Nay, we must use expostulation kindly,
For it is parting from us: 61
I speak not 'be thou true,' as fearing thee,
For I will throw my glove to Death himself,
That there's no maculation in thy heart;   64
But, 'be thou true,' say I, to fashion in
My sequent protestation; be thou true,
And I will see thee.
   Cres. O! you shall be expos'd, my lord, to
     dangers   68
As infinite as imminent; but I'll be true.
   Tro. And I'll grow friend with danger. Wear
     this sleeve.
   Cres. And you this glove. When shall I see
     you?
   Tro. I will corrupt the Grecian sentinels, 72
To give thee nightly visitation.
But yet, be true.
   Cres.   O heavens! 'be true' again!
   Tro. Hear why I speak it, love:
The Grecian youths are full of quality;   76
They're loving, well compos'd, with gifts of
   nature,
Flowing and swelling o'er with arts and exer-
   cise:
How novelty may move, and parts with person,
Alas! a kind of godly jealousy,—   80
Which, I beseech you, call a virtuous sin,—
Makes me afear'd.
   Cres.   O heavens! you love me not.
   Tro. Die I a villain, then!
In this I do not call your faith in question 84
So mainly as my merit: I cannot sing,
Nor heel the high lavolt, nor sweeten talk,
Nor play at subtle games; fair virtues all,
To which the Grecians are most prompt and
   pregnant: 88
But I can tell that in each grace of these
There lurks a still and dumb-discoursive devil
That tempts most cunningly. But be not
   tempted.
   Cres. Do you think I will?   92

Tro. No.
But something may be done that we will not:
And sometimes we are devils to ourselves
When we will tempt the frailty of our powers,
Presuming on their changeful potency.   97
    Æne. [*Within.*] Nay, good my lord,—
    Tro.   Come, kiss; and let us part.
    Par. [*Within.*] Brother Troilus!
    Tro.   Good brother, come you hither;
And bring Æneas and the Grecian with you. 100
    Cres. My lord, will you be true?
    Tro. Who, I? alas, it is my vice, my fault:
While others fish with craft for great opinion,
I with great truth catch mere simplicity;   104
Whilst some with cunning gild their copper
    crowns,
With truth and plainness I do wear mine bare.
Fear not my truth; the moral of my wit
Is plain, and true; there's all the reach of it.

Enter ÆNEAS, PARIS, ANTENOR, DEIPHOBUS,
    and DIOMEDES.

Welcome, Sir Diomed! Here is the lady   109
Which for Antenor we deliver you:
At the port, lord, I'll give her to thy hand,
And by the way possess thee what she is.   112
Entreat her fair; and, by my soul, fair Greek,
If e'er thou stand at mercy of my sword,
Name Cressid, and thy life shall be as safe
As Priam is in Ilion.
    Dio.   Fair Lady Cressid,   116
So please you, save the thanks this prince ex-
    pects:
The lustre in your eye, heaven in your cheek,
Pleads your fair usage; and to Diomed
You shall be mistress, and command him wholly.
    Tro. Grecian, thou dost not use me cour-
    teously,   121
To shame the zeal of my petition to thee
In praising her: I tell thee, lord of Greece,
She is as far high-soaring o'er thy praises 124
As thou unworthy to be call'd her servant.
I charge thee use her well, even for my charge;
For, by the dreadful Pluto, if thou dost not,
Though the great bulk Achilles be thy guard,
I'll cut thy throat.
    Dio.   O! be not mov'd, Prince Troilus:
Let me be privileg'd by my place and message
To be a speaker free; when I am hence,
I'll answer to my lust; and know you, lord, 132
I'll nothing do on charge: to her own worth
She shall be priz'd; but that you say 'be't so,'
I'll speak it in my spirit and honour, 'no.'
    Tro. Come, to the port. I'll tell thee, Diomed,
This brave shall oft make thee to hide thy
    head.   137
Lady, give me your hand, and, as you walk,
To our own selves bend we our needful talk.
        [*Exeunt* TROILUS, CRESSIDA, *and*
            DIOMEDES. *Trumpet sounded.*
    Par. Hark! Hector's trumpet.
    Æne.   How have we spent this morning!
The prince must think me tardy and remiss, 141
That swore to ride before him to the field.
    Par. 'Tis Troilus' fault. Come, come, to field
with him.

Dei. Let us make ready straight.   144
    Æne. Yea, with a bridegroom's fresh alac-
    rity,
Let us address to tend on Hector's heels:
The glory of our Troy doth this day lie
On his fair worth and single chivalry. [*Exeunt*

SCENE V.—*The Grecian Camp. Lists set out.*

Enter AJAX, *armed;* AGAMEMNON, ACHILLES
    PATROCLUS, MENELAUS, ULYSSES, NESTOR, *and*
    Others.

Agam. Here art thou in appointment fresh
    and fair,
Anticipating time with starting courage.
Give with thy trumpet a loud note to Troy,
Thou dreadful Ajax; that the appalled air
May pierce the head of the great combatant
And hale him hither.
    Ajax.   Thou, trumpet, there's my purse
Now crack thy lungs, and split thy brazen pipe
Blow, villain, till thy sphered bias cheek
Outswell the colic of puff'd Aquilon.
Come, stretch thy chest, and let thy eyes spout
    blood;
Thou blow'st for Hector.   [*Trumpet sound.*
    Ulyss. No trumpet answers.
    Achil.   'Tis but early days.
    Agam. Is not yond Diomed with Calchas
    daughter?
    Ulyss. 'Tis he, I ken the manner of his gait
He rises on the toe: that spirit of his
In aspiration lifts him from the earth.

Enter DIOMEDES, *with* CRESSIDA.

    Agam. Is this the Lady Cressid?
    Dio.   Even she
    Agam. Most dearly welcome to the Greeks
    sweet lady.
    Nest. Our general doth salute you with
    kiss.
    Ulyss. Yet is the kindness but particular;
'Twere better she were kiss'd in general.
    Nest. And very courtly counsel: I'll begin.
So much for Nestor.
    Achil. I'll take that winter from your lips
    fair lady:
Achilles bids you welcome.
    Men. I had good argument for kissing once
    Patr. But that's no argument for kissing
    now;
For thus popp'd Paris in his hardiment,
And parted thus you and your argument.
    Ulyss. O, deadly gall, and theme of all our
    scorns!
For which we lose our heads to gild his horn
    Patr. The first was Menelaus' kiss; this
    mine:
Patroclus kisses you.
    Men.   O! this is trim.
    Patr. Paris and I, kiss evermore for him.
    Men. I'll have my kiss, sir. Lady, by your
    leave.
    Cres. In kissing, do you render or receive?
    Patr. Both take and give.
    Cres.   I'll make my match to live

e kiss you take is better than you give;
refore no kiss.

Men. I'll give you boot; I'll give you three for one. 40

Cres. You're an odd man; give even, or give none.

Men. An odd man, lady! every man is odd.

Cres. No, Paris is not; for, you know 'tis true,
at you are odd, and he is even with you. 44

Men. You fillip me o' the head.

Cres. No, I'll be sworn.

Ulyss. It were no match, your nail against his horn.

y I, sweet lady, beg a kiss of you?

Cres. You may.

Ulyss. I do desire it.

Cres. Why, beg, then. 48

Ulyss. Why, then, for Venus' sake, give me a kiss,
en Helen is a maid again, and his.

Cres. I am your debtor; claim it when 'tis due.

Ulyss. Never's my day, and then a kiss of you. 52

Dio. Lady, a word: I'll bring you to your father. [DIOMEDES *leads out* CRESSIDA.

Nest. A woman of quick sense.

Ulyss. Fie, fie upon her!
ere's language in her eye, her cheek, her lip,
y, her foot speaks; her wanton spirits look out 56
every joint and motive of her body.
these encounterers, so glib of tongue,
at give a coasting welcome ere it comes,
d wide unclasp the tables of their thoughts
every tickling reader, set them down 61
r sluttish spoils of opportunity
d daughters of the game. [Trumpet within.

All. The Trojans' trumpet.

Agam. Yonder comes the troop. 64

nter HECTOR, *armed;* ÆNEAS, TROILUS, *and other Trojans, with Attendants.*

Æne. Hail, all you state of Greece! what shall be done
him that victory commands? or do you purpose
victor shall be known? will you the knights
all to the edge of all extremity 68
rsue each other, or shall be divided
any voice or order of the field?
ctor bade ask.

Agam. Which way would Hector have it?

Æne. He cares not; he'll obey conditions. 72

Achil. 'Tis done like Hector; but securely done,
little proudly, and great deal misprising
e knight oppos'd.

Æne. If not Achilles, sir, hat is your name?

Achil. If not Achilles, nothing. 76

Æne. Therefore Achilles; but, whate'er, know this:
the extremity of great and little,
lour and pride excel themselves in Hector;
The one almost as infinite as all, 80
The other blank as nothing. Weigh him well,
And that which looks like pride is courtesy.
This Ajax is half made of Hector's blood:
In love whereof half Hector stays at home; 84
Half heart, half hand, half Hector comes to seek
This blended knight, half Trojan, and half Greek.

Achil. A maiden battle, then? O! I perceive you.

Re-enter DIOMEDES.

Agam. Here is Sir Diomed. Go, gentle knight, 88
Stand by our Ajax: as you and Lord Æneas
Consent upon the order of their fight,
So be it; either to the uttermost,
Or else a breath: the combatants being kin 92
Half stints their strife before their strokes begin.
[AJAX *and* HECTOR *enter the lists.*

Ulyss. They are oppos'd already.

Agam. What Trojan is that same that looks so heavy?

Ulyss. The youngest son of Priam, a true knight: 96
Not yet mature, yet matchless; firm of word,
Speaking in deeds and deedless in his tongue;
Not soon provok'd, nor being provok'd soon calm'd:
His heart and hand both open and both free; 100
For what he has he gives, what thinks he shows;
Yet gives he not till judgment guide his bounty,
Nor dignifies an impure thought with breath.
Manly as Hector, but more dangerous; 104
For Hector, in his blaze of wrath, subscribes
To tender objects; but he in heat of action
Is more vindicative than jealous love.
They call him Troilus, and on him erect 108
A second hope, as fairly built as Hector.
Thus says Æneas; one that knows the youth
Even to his inches, and with private soul
Did in great Ilion thus translate him to me. 112
[Alarum. HECTOR *and* AJAX *fight.*

Agam. They are in action.

Nest. Now, Ajax, hold thine own!

Tro. Hector, thou sleep'st; awake thee!

Agam. His blows are well dispos'd: there, Ajax!

Dio. You must no more. [Trumpets cease.

Æne. Princes, enough, so please you. 116

Ajax. I am not warm yet; let us fight again.

Dio. As Hector pleases.

Hect. Why, then will I no more:
Thou art, great lord, my father's sister's son,
A cousin-german to great Priam's seed; 120
The obligation of our blood forbids
A gory emulation 'twixt us twain.
Were thy commixtion Greek and Trojan so
That thou couldst say, 'This hand is Grecian all,
And this is Trojan; the sinews of this leg 125
All Greek, and this all Troy; my mother's blood
Runs on the dexter cheek, and this sinister
Bounds in my father's,' by Jove multipotent, 128
Thou shouldst not bear from me a Greekish member
Wherein my sword had not impressure made

Of our rank feud. But the just gods gainsay
That any drop thou borrow'dst from thy mother,
My sacred aunt, should by my mortal sword 133
Be drain'd! Let me embrace thee, Ajax;
By him that thunders, thou hast lusty arms;
Hector would have them fall upon him thus:
Cousin, all honour to thee!
    Ajax.   I thank thee, Hector:
Thou art too gentle and too free a man:
I came to kill thee, cousin, and bear hence
A great addition earned in thy death.   140
    Hect. Not Neoptolemus so mirable,
On whose bright crest Fame with her loud'st oyes
Cries, 'This is he!' could promise to himself
A thought of added honour torn from Hector.
    Æne. There is expectance here from both
the sides,   145
What further you will do.
    Hect.   We'll answer it;
The issue is embracement: Ajax, farewell.
    Ajax. If I might in entreaties find success,—
As seld I have the chance,—I would desire 149
My famous cousin to our Grecian tents.
    Dio. 'Tis Agamemnon's wish, and great
Achilles
Doth long to see unarm'd the valiant Hector.
    Hect. Æneas, call my brother Troilus to me,
And signify this loving interview
To the expecters of our Trojan part;
Desire them home. Give me thy hand, my
cousin;   156
I will go eat with thee and see your knights.
    Ajax. Great Agamemnon comes to meet us
here.
    Hect. The worthiest of them tell me name
by name;
But for Achilles, mine own searching eyes 160
Shall find him by his large and portly size.
    Agam. Worthy of arms! as welcome as to
one
That would be rid of such an enemy;
But that's no welcome; understand more clear,
What's past and what's to come is strew'd with
husks   165
And formless ruin of oblivion;
But in this extant moment, faith and troth,
Strain'd purely from all hollow bias-drawing,168
Bids thee, with most divine integrity,
From heart of very heart, great Hector, wel-
come.
    Hect. I thank thee, most imperious Aga-
memnon.
    Agam. [*To* TROILUS.] My well-fam'd Lord of
Troy, no less to you.   172
    Men. Let me confirm my princely brother's
greeting:
You brace of war-like brothers, welcome hither.
    Hect. Whom must we answer?
    Æne.   The noble Menelaus.
    Hect. O! you, my lord? by Mars his gaunt-
let, thanks!   176
Mock not that I affect the untraded oath:
Your *quondam* wife swears still by Venus' glove:
She's well, but bade me not commend her to
you.

    Men. Name her not now, sir; she's a dea[d]
theme.
    Hect. O! pardon; I offend.
    Nest. I have, thou gallant Trojan, seen th[ee]
oft,
Labouring for destiny, make cruel way
Through ranks of Greekish youth: and I ha[ve]
seen thee,
As hot as Perseus, spur thy Phrygian steed,
Despising many forfeits and subduements,
When thou hast hung thy advanc'd sword i'
air,
Not letting it decline on the declin'd;
That I have said to some my standers-by,
'Lo! Jupiter is yonder, dealing life!'
And I have seen thee pause and take thy brea[th]
When that a ring of Greeks have hemm'd th[ee]
in,
Like an Olympian wrestling: this have I see[n];
But this thy countenance, still lock'd in ste[el],
I never saw till now. I knew thy grandsire,
And once fought with him: he was a sold[ier]
good;
But, by great Mars, the captain of us all,
Never like thee. Let an old man embrace the[e],
And, worthy warrior, welcome to our tents[.]
    Æne. 'Tis the old Nestor.
    Hect. Let me embrace thee, good old chro[n]-
icle,
That hast so long walk'd hand in hand wi[th]
time:
Most reverend Nestor, I am glad to clasp the[e].
    Nest. I would my arms could match thee in
contention,
As they contend with thee in courtesy.
    Hect. I would they could.
    Nest. Ha!
By this white beard, I'd fight with thee [to-]
morrow.
Well, welcome, welcome! I have seen t[he]
time.—
    Ulyss. I wonder now how yonder city stan[ds]
When we have here her base and pillar by [us].
    Hect. I know your favour, Lord Ulysses, we[ll].
Ah! sir, there's many a Greek and Trojan dea[d],
Since first I saw yourself and Diomed
In Ilion, on your Greekish embassy.
    Ulyss. Sir, I foretold you then what wou[ld]
ensue:
My prophecy is but half his journey yet;
For yonder walls, that pertly front your tow[n],
Yond towers, whose wanton tops do buss t[he]
clouds,
Must kiss their own feet.
    Hect.   I must not believe you:
There they stand yet, and modestly I think,
The fall of every Phrygian stone will cost
A drop of Grecian blood: the end crowns a[ll],
And that old common arbitrator, Time,
Will one day end it.
    Ulyss.   So to him we leave it.
Most gentle and most valiant Hector, welcom[e].
After the general, I beseech you next
To feast with me and see me at my tent.
    Achil. I shall forestall thee, Lord Ulysse[s],
thou!

w, Hector, I have fed mine eyes on thee;
ave with exact view perus'd thee, Hector,
d quoted joint by joint.   Is this Achilles? 232
1chil. I am Achilles.
1ect. Stand fair, I pray thee: let me look on thee.
1chil. Behold thy fill.
1ect.   Nay, I have done already.
1chil. Thou art too brief: I will the second time,   236
I would buy thee, view thee limb by limb.
1ect. O! like a book of sport thou 'lt read me o'er;
t there's more in me than thou understand'st.
1y dost thou so oppress me with thine eye?
1chil. Tell me, you heavens, in which part of his body   241
all I destroy him? whether there, or there, or there?
at I may give the local wound a name,
d make distinct the very breach whereout 244
ctor's great spirit flew. Answer me, heavens!
1ect. It would discredit the bless'd gods, proud man,
answer such a question. Stand again:
ink'st thou to catch my life so pleasantly 248
to prenominate in nice conjecture
1ere thou wilt hit me dead?
1chil.   I tell thee, yea.
1ect. Wert thou an oracle to tell me so,
not believe thee. Henceforth guard thee well,
r I'll not kill thee there, nor there, nor there;
t, by the furge that stithied Mars his helm,
kill thee every where, yea, o'er and o'er.
1u wisest Grecians, pardon me this brag; 256
s insolence draws folly from my lips;
t I'll endeavour deeds to match these words,
may I never—
1jax.   Do not chafe thee, cousin:
d you, Achilles, let these threats alone, 260
1 accident or purpose bring you to 't:
1u may have every day enough of Hector,
1ou have stomach. The general state, I fear,
n scarce entreat you to be odd with him. 264
1ect. I pray you, let us see you in the field;
1 have had pelting wars since you refus'd
1e Grecians' cause.
1chil.   Dost thou entreat me, Hector?
-morrow do I meet thee, fell as death; 268
-night all friends.
1ect.   Thy hand upon that match.
1gam. First, all you peers of Greece, go to my tent;
1ere in the full convive we afterwards,
Hector's leisure and your bounties shall 272
1ncur together, severally entreat him.
1at loud the tabourines, let the trumpets blow,
1at this great soldier may his welcome know.
     [Exeunt all except TROILUS *and* ULYSSES.
Tro. My Lord Ulysses, tell me, I beseech you,
what place of the field doth Calchas keep?
Ulyss. At Menelaus' tent, most princely Troilus:
1ere Diomed doth feast with him to-night;
1ho neither looks upon the heaven nor earth,

But gives all gaze and bent of amorous view 281
On the fair Cressid.
Tro. Shall I, sweet lord, be bound to thee so much,
After we part from Agamemnon's tent, 284
To bring me thither?
Ulyss.   You shall command me, sir.
As gentle tell me, of what honour was
This Cressida in Troy? Had she no lover there
That wails her absence?   288
Tro. O, sir! to such as boasting show their scars
A mock is due. Will you walk on, my lord?
She was belov'd, she lov'd; she is, and doth:
But still sweet love is food for fortune's tooth.
     [Exeunt.

ACT V

SCENE I.—*The Grecian Camp. Before*
ACHILLES' *Tent.*

Enter ACHILLES *and* PATROCLUS.

Achil. I'll heat his blood with Greekish wine to-night,
Which with my scimitar I'll cool to-morrow.
Patroclus, let us feast him to the height.
Patr. Here comes Thersites.

Enter THERSITES.

Achil. How now, thou core of envy! 4
Thou crusty batch of nature, what's the news?
Ther. Why, thou picture of what thou seemest, and idol of idiot-worshippers, here's a letter for thee. 8
Achil. From whence, fragment?
Ther. Why, thou full dish of fool, from Troy.
Patr. Who keeps the tent now?
Ther. The surgeon's box, or the patient's wound. 13
Patr. Well said, adversity! and what need these tricks?
Ther. Prithee, be silent, boy: I profit not by thy talk: thou art thought to be Achilles' male varlet. 18
Patr. Male varlet, you rogue! what's that?
Ther. Why, his masculine whore. Now, the rotten diseases of the south, the guts-griping, ruptures, catarrhs, loads o' gravel i' the back, lethargies, cold palsies, raw eyes, dirt-rotten livers, wheezing lungs, bladders full of imposthume, sciaticas, lime-kilns i' the palm, incurable bone-ache, and the rivelled fee-simple of the tetter, take and take again such preposterous discoveries! 28
Patr. Why, thou damnable box of envy, thou, what meanest thou to curse thus?
Ther. Do I curse thee?
Patr. Why, no, you ruinous butt, you whoreson indistinguishable cur, no. 33
Ther. No! why art thou then exasperate, thou idle immaterial skein of sleave silk, thou green sarcenet flap for a sore eye, thou tassel of a prodigal's purse, thou? Ah! how the poor world is pestered with such water-flies, diminutives of nature.
Patr. Out, gall! 40

Ther. Finch egg!

Achil. My sweet Patroclus, I am thwarted quite
From my great purpose in to-morrow's battle.
Here is a letter from Queen Hecuba, 44
A token from her daughter, my fair love,
Both taxing me and gaging me to keep
An oath that I have sworn. I will not break it:
Fall Greeks; fail fame; honour or go or stay;
My major vow lies here, this I'll obey. 49
Come, come, Thersites, help to trim my tent;
This night in banqueting must all be spent.
Away, Patroclus! 52
[*Exeunt* ACHILLES *and* PATROCLUS.

Ther. With too much blood and too little brain, these two may run mad; but if with too much brain, and too little blood they do, I'll be a curer of madmen. Here's Agamemnon, an honest fellow enough, and one that loves quails, but he has not so much brain as ear-wax: and the goodly transformation of Jupiter there, his brother, the bull, the primitive statue, and oblique memorial of cuckolds; a thrifty shoeing-horn in a chain, hanging at his brother's leg, to what form but that he is should wit larded with malice and malice forced with wit turn him to? To an ass, were nothing: he is both ass and ox; to an ox, were nothing: he is both ox and ass. To be a dog, a mule, a cat, a fitchew, a toad, a lizard, an owl, a puttock, or a herring without a roe, I would not care; but to be Menelaus! I would conspire against destiny. Ask me not what I would be, if I were not Thersites, for I care not to be the louse of a lazar, so I were not Menelaus. Hey-day! spirits and fires! 74

Enter HECTOR, TROILUS, AJAX, AGAMEMNON, ULYSSES, NESTOR, MENELAUS, *and* DIOMEDES, *with lights.*

Agam. We go wrong, we go wrong.

Ajax. No, yonder 'tis;
There, where we see the lights.

Hect. I trouble you. 76

Ajax. No, not a whit.

Ulyss. Here comes himself to guide you.

Re-enter ACHILLES.

Achil. Welcome, brave Hector; welcome, princes all.

Agam. So now, fair prince of Troy, I bid good-night.
Ajax commands the guard to tend on you. 80

Hect. Thanks and good-night to the Greeks' general.

Men. Good-night, my lord.

Hect. Good-night, sweet Lord Menelaus.

Ther. Sweet draught: 'sweet,' quoth a'! sweet sink, sweet sewer. 85

Achil. Good-night and welcome both at once, to those
That go or tarry.

Agam. Good-night. 88
[*Exeunt* AGAMEMNON *and* MENELAUS.

Achil. Old Nestor tarries; and you too, Diomed,

Keep Hector company an hour or two.

Dio. I cannot, lord; I have important busin
The tide whereof is now. Good-night, gr
Hector.

Hect. Give me your hand.

Ulyss. [*Aside to* TROILUS.] Follow his to
he goes to Calchas' tent.
I'll keep you company.

Tro. Sweet sir, you honour me.

Hect. And so, good-night
[*Exit* DIOMEDES; ULYSSES
TROILUS *follow.*

Achil. Come, come, enter my tent.
[*Exeunt* ACHILLES, HECTOR, A
and NEST

Ther. That same Diomed's a false-hear rogue, a most unjust knave; I will no more tr him when he leers than I will a serpent wh he hisses. He will spend his mouth, and p mise, like Brabbler the hound; but when performs, astronomers foretell it: it is p digious, there will come some change: the s borrows of the moon when Diomed keeps word. I will rather leave to see Hector, t not to dog him: they say he keeps a Tro drab, and uses the traitor Calchas' tent. after. Nothing but lechery! all incontin varlets. [*E*

SCENE II.—*The Same. Before* CALCHAS' *T*

Enter DIOMEDES.

Dio. What, are you up here, ho! speak.

Cal. [*Within.*] Who calls?

Dio. Diomed. Calchas, I think. Wher
your daughter?

Cal. [*Within.*] She comes to you.

Enter TROILUS *and* ULYSSES, *at a distance
after them* THERSITES.

Ulyss. Stand where the torch may not c
cover us.

Enter CRESSIDA.

Tro. Cressid comes forth to him.

Dio. How now, my char

Cres. Now, my sweet guardian! Hark
word with you. [*Whispe*

Tro. Yea, so familiar!

Ulyss. She will sing any man at first sigh

Ther. And any man may sing her, if he c
take her cliff; she's noted.

Dio. Will you remember?

Cres. Remember! yes.

Dio. Nay, but do, then;
And let your mind be coupled with your wor

Tro. What should she remember?

Ulyss. List!

Cres. Sweet honey Greek, tempt me no mo
to folly.

Ther. Roguery!

Dio. Nay, then,—

Cres. I'll tell you what,—

Dio. Foh, foh! come, tell a pin: you a
forsworn.

Cres. In faith, I cannot. What would you
have me do?

Ther. A juggling trick,—to be secretly open.

Dio. What did you swear you would bestow
on me? 24

Cres. I prithee, do not hold me to mine
oath;

I me do anything but that, sweet Greek.

Dio. Good-night.

Tro. Hold, patience! 28

Ulyss. How now, Trojan?

Cres. Diomed,—

Dio. No, no, good-night; I'll be your fool no
more.

Tro. Thy better must.

Cres. Hark! one word in your ear. 32

Tro. O plague and madness!

Ulyss. You are mov'd, prince; let us depart,
I pray you,

st your displeasure should enlarge itself

wrathful terms. This place is dangerous; 36

e time right deadly. I beseech you, go.

Tro. Behold, I pray you!

Ulyss. Nay, good my lord, go off:
u flow to great distraction; come, my lord.

Tro. I pray thee, stay.

Ulyss. You have not patience; come. 40

Tro. I pray you, stay. By hell, and all hell's
torments,

ill not speak a word!

Dio. And so, good-night.

Cres. Nay, but you part in anger.

Tro. Doth that grieve thee?
wither'd truth!

Ulyss. Why, how now, lord!

Tro. By Jove, 44
ill be patient.

Cres. Guardian!—why, Greek!

Dio. Foh, foh! adieu; you palter.

Cres. In faith, I do not: come hither once
again.

Ulyss. You shake, my lord, at something:
will you go? 48
u will break out.

Tro. She strokes his cheek!

Ulyss. Come, come.

Tro. Nay, stay; by Jove, I will not speak
a word:

ere is between my will and all offences

guard of patience: stay a little while. 52

Ther. How the devil Luxury, with his fat
mp and potato finger, tickles these together!
y, lechery, fry!

Dio. But will you, then? 56

Cres. In faith, I will, la; never trust me else.

Dio. Give me some token for the surety of it.

Cres. I'll fetch you one. [*Exit.*

Ulyss. You have sworn patience.

Tro. Fear me not, sweet lord; 60
ill not be myself, nor have cognition
what I feel: I am all patience.

Re-enter CRESSIDA.

Ther. Now the pledge! now, now, now!

Cres. Here, Diomed, keep this sleeve. 64

Tro. O beauty! where is thy faith?

Ulyss. My lord,—

Tro. I will be patient; outwardly I will.

Cres. You look upon that sleeve; behold it
well.

He lov'd me—O false wench!—Give't to me
again. 68

Dio. Whose was't?

Cres. It is no matter, now I have't again.

I will not meet with you to-morrow night.

I prithee, Diomed, visit me no more.

Ther. Now she sharpens: well said, whetstone! 72

Dio. I shall have it.

Cres. What, this?

Dio. Ay, that.

Cres. O! all you gods. O pretty, pretty
pledge!

Thy master now lies thinking in his bed

Of thee and me; and sighs, and takes my glove,

And gives memorial dainty kisses to it, 77

As I kiss thee. Nay, do not snatch it from me;

He that takes that doth take my heart withal.

Dio. I had your heart before; this follows it.

Tro. I did swear patience. 81

Cres. You shall not have it, Diomed; faith
you shall not;

I'll give you something else.

Dio. I will have this. Whose was it?

Cres. 'Tis no matter.

Dio. Come, tell me whose it was. 85

Cres. 'Twas one's that loved me better than
you will.

But, now you have it, take it.

Dio. Whose was it?

Cres. By all Diana's waiting-women yond, 88

And by herself, I will not tell you whose.

Dio. To-morrow will I wear it on my helm,

And grieve his spirit that dares not challenge it.

Tro. Wert thou the devil, and wor'st it on
thy horn, 92

It should be challeng'd.

Cres. Well, well, 'tis done, 'tis past: and yet
it is not:

I will not keep my word.

Dio. Why then, farewell;

Thou never shalt mock Diomed again. 96

Cres. You shall not go: one cannot speak a
word,

But it straight starts you.

Dio. I do not like this fooling.

Ther. Nor I, by Pluto: but that that likes
not me

Pleases me best. 100

Dio. What, shall I come? the hour?

Cres. Ay, come:—O Jove!—

Do come:—I shall be plagu'd.

Dio. Farewell till then.

Cres. Good-night: I prithee, come.—

[*Exit* DIOMEDES.

Troilus, farewell! one eye yet looks on thee, 104

But with my heart the other eye doth see.

Ah! poor our sex; this fault in us I find,

The error of our eye directs our mind.

What error leads must err. O! then conclude

Minds sway'd by eyes are full of turpitude. 109

[*Exit.*

Ther. A proof of strength she could not pub-
lish more,
Unless she said, 'My mind is now turn'd whore.'
Ulyss. All 's done, my lord.
Tro. It is.
Ulyss. Why stay we, then?
Tro. To make a recordation to my soul 113
Of every syllable that here was spoke.
But if I tell how these two did co-act,
Shall I not lie in publishing a truth? 116
Sith yet there is a credence in my heart,
An esperance so obstinately strong,
That doth invert the attest of eyes and ears,
As if those organs had deceptious functions,
Created only to calumniate. 121
Was Cressid here?
Ulyss. I cannot conjure, Trojan.
Tro. She was not, sure.
Ulyss. Most sure she was.
Tro. Why, my negation hath no taste of
madness. 124
Ulyss. Nor mine, my lord: Cressid was here
but now.
Tro. Let it not be believ'd for womanhood!
Think we had mothers; do not give advantage
To stubborn critics, apt, without a theme, 128
For depravation, to square the general sex
By Cressid's rule: rather think this not Cressid.
Ulyss. What hath she done, prince, that can
soil our mothers?
Tro. Nothing at all, unless that this were she.
Ther. Will he swagger himself out on's own
eyes? 133
Tro. This she? no, this is Diomed's Cressida.
If beauty have a soul, this is not she;
If souls guide vows, if vows be sanctimony, 136
If sanctimony be the gods' delight,
If there be rule in unity itself,
This is not she. O madness of discourse,
That cause sets up with and against itself; 140
Bi-fold authority! where reason can revolt
Without perdition, and loss assume all reason
Without revolt: this is, and is not, Cressid.
Within my soul there doth conduce a fight 144
Of this strange nature that a thing inseparate
Divides more wider than the sky and earth;
And yet the spacious breadth of this division
Admits no orifice for a point as subtle 148
As Ariachne's broken woof to enter.
Instance, O instance! strong as Pluto's gates:
Cressid is mine, tied with the bonds of heaven:
Instance, O instance! strong as heaven itself;
The bonds of heaven are slipp'd, dissolv'd, and
loos'd; 153
And with another knot, five-finger-tied,
The fractions of her faith, orts of her love,
The fragments, scraps, the bits, and greasy
reliques 156
Of her o'er-eaten faith, are bound to Diomed.
Ulyss. May worthy Troilus be half attach'd
With that which here his passion doth express?
Tro. Ay, Greek; and that shall be divulged
well 160
In characters as red as Mars his heart
Inflam'd with Venus: never did young man
fancy

With so eternal and so fix'd a soul.
Hark, Greek: as much as I do Cressid love,
So much by weight hate I her Diomed;
That sleeve is mine that he'll bear on his hel[
Were it a casque compos'd by Vulcan's ski[
My sword should bite it. Not the dreadful sp[
Which shipmen do the hurricano call,
Constring'd in mass by the almighty sun,
Shall dizzy with more clamour Neptune's e[
In his descent than shall my prompted swo[
Falling on Diomed.
Ther. He'll tickle it for his concupy.
Tro. O Cressid! O false Cressid! false, fa[
false!
Let all untruths stand by thy stained name,
And they'll seem glorious.
Ulyss. O! contain yours[
Your passion draws ears hither.

Enter ÆNEAS.

Æne. I have been seeking you this hour,
lord.
Hector, by this, is arming him in Troy:
Ajax, your guard, stays to conduct you ho[
Tro. Have with you, prince. My courte[
lord, adieu.
Farewell, revolted fair! and Diomed,
Stand fast, and wear a castle on thy head!
Ulyss. I'll bring you to the gates.
Tro. Accept distracted thanks.
[*Exeunt* TROILUS, ÆNEAS, *and* ULYS[
Ther. Would I could meet that rogue D[
med! I would croak like a raven; I would bo[
I would bode. Patroclus would give me a[
thing for the intelligence of this whore:
parrot will not do more for an almond t[
he for a commodious drab. Lechery, leche[
still, wars and lechery: nothing else ho[
fashion. A burning devil take them! [E

SCENE III.—*Troy. Before* PRIAM'S *Palace.*
Enter HECTOR and ANDROMACHE.

And. When was my lord so much ungen[
temper'd,
To stop his ears against admonishment?
Unarm, unarm, and do not fight to-day.
Hect. You train me to offend you; get
you in:
By all the everlasting gods, I'll go.
And. My dreams will, sure, prove omin[
to the day.
Hect. No more, I say.

Enter CASSANDRA.

Cas. Where is my brother Hecto[
And. Here, sister; arm'd, and bloody in
intent.
Consort with me in loud and dear petition
Pursue we him on knees; for I have dream[
Of bloody turbulence, and this whole nigh[
Hath nothing been but shapes and forms [
slaughter.
Cas. O! 'tis true.
Hect. Ho! bid my trumpet sou[
Cas. No notes of sally, for the heavens, sw[
brother.

Hect. Be gone, I say: the gods have heard me swear.

Cas. The gods are deaf to hot and peevish vows: 16
hey are polluted offerings, more abhorr'd
han spotted livers in the sacrifice.

And. O! be persuaded: do not count it holy
o hurt by being just: it is as lawful,   20
or we would give much, to use violent thefts,
nd rob in the behalf of charity.

Cas. It is the purpose that makes strong the vow;
ut vows to every purpose must not hold.   24
narm, sweet Hector.

Hect.   Hold you still, I say;
ine honour keeps the weather of my fate:
ife every man holds dear; but the dear man
olds honour far more precious-dear than life.

Enter TROILUS.

ow now, young man! mean'st thou to fight to-day?   29

And. Cassandra, call my father to persuade.
                        [*Exit* CASSANDRA.

Hect. No, faith, young Troilus; doff thy harness, youth;   32
am to-day i' the vein of chivalry:
et grow thy sinews till their knots be strong,
nd tempt not yet the brushes of the war.
narm thee, go, and doubt thou not, brave boy,
l stand to-day for thee and me and Troy.   36

Tro. Brother, you have a vice of mercy in you,
hich better fits a lion than a man.

Hect. What vice is that, good Troilus? chide me for it.

Tro. When many times the captive Grecian falls,   40
ven in the fan and wind of your fair sword,
ou bid them rise, and live.

Hect. O! 'tis fair play.

Tro.   Fool's play, by heaven, Hector.

Hect. How now! how now!

Tro.   For the love of all the gods,   44
et's leave the hermit pity with our mothers,
nd when we have our armours buckled on,
he venom'd vengeance ride upon our swords,
ur them to ruthful work, rein them from ruth.   48

Hect. Fie, savage, fie!

Tro.   Hector, then 'tis wars.

Hect. Troilus, I would not have you fight to-day.

Tro. Who should withhold me?
ot fate, obedience, nor the hand of Mars   52
eckoning with fiery truncheon my retire;
ot Priamus and Hecuba on knees,
heir eyes o'ergalled with recourse of tears;
or you, my brother, with your true sword drawn,   56
ppos'd to hinder me, should stop my way,
ut by my ruin.

Re-enter CASSANDRA, *with* PRIAM.

Cas. Lay hold upon him, Priam, hold him fast:

He is thy crutch; now if thou lose thy stay,   60
Thou on him leaning, and all Troy on thee,
Fall all together.

Pri.   Come, Hector, come; go back:
The wife hath dream'd; thy mother hath had visions;
Cassandra doth foresee; and I myself   64
Am like a prophet suddenly enrapt,
To tell thee that this day is ominous:
Therefore, come back.

Hect.   Æneas is a-field;
And I do stand engag'd to many Greeks,   68
Even in the faith of valour, to appear
This morning to them.

Pri.   Ay, but thou shalt not go.

Hect. I must not break my faith.
You know me dutiful; therefore, dear sir,   72
Let me not shame respect, but give me leave
To take that course by your consent and voice,
Which you do here forbid me, royal Priam.

Cas. O Priam! yield not to him.

And.   Do not, dear father.   76

Hect. Andromache, I am offended with you:
Upon the love you bear me, get you in.
                        [*Exit* ANDROMACHE.

Tro. This foolish, dreaming, superstitious girl
Makes all these bodements.

Cas.   O farewell! dear Hector.   80
Look! how thou diest; look! how thy eye turns pale;
Look! how thy wounds do bleed at many vents!
Hark! how Troy roars: how Hecuba cries out!
How poor Andromache shrills her dolours forth!   84
Behold, distraction, frenzy, and amazement,
Like witless anticks, one another meet,
And all cry Hector! Hector's dead! O Hector!

Tro. Away! Away!   88

Cas. Farewell. Yet, soft! Hector, I take my leave:
Thou dost thyself and all our Troy deceive.
                        [*Exit.*

Hect. You are amaz'd, my liege, at her exclaim.
Go in and cheer the town: we'll forth and fight;
Do deeds worth praise and tell you them at night.   93

Pri. Farewell: the gods with safety stand about thee!
                [*Exeunt severally* PRIAM *and* HECTOR.
                        Alarums.

Tro. They are at it, hark! Proud Diomed, believe,
I come to lose my arm, or win my sleeve.   96

As TROILUS *is going out, enter, from the other side*, PANDARUS.

Pan. Do you hear, my lord? do you hear?

Tro. What now?

Pan. Here's a letter come from yond poor girl.

Tro. Let me read.   100

Pan. A whoreson tisick, a whoreson rascally tisick so troubles me, and the foolish fortune of

Z

this girl; and what one thing, what another, that I shall leave you one o' these days: and I have a rheum in mine eyes too, and such an ache in my bones that, unless a man were cursed, I cannot tell what to think on't. What says she there? 108

Tro. Words, words, mere words, no matter from the heart;
The effect doth operate another way.

[*Tearing the letter.*

Go, wind to wind, there turn and change together.
My love with words and errors still she feeds,
But edifies another with her deeds. 113

[*Exeunt severally.*

SCENE IV.—*Between Troy and the Grecian Camp.*

Alarums. Excursions. Enter THERSITES.

Ther. Now they are clapper-clawing one another; I'll go look on. That dissembling abominable varlet, Diomed, has got that same scurvy doting foolish young knave's sleeve of Troy there in his helm: I would fain see them meet; that that same young Trojan ass, that loves the whore there, might send that Greekish whoremasterly villain, with the sleeve, back to the dissembling luxurious drab, on a sleeveless errand. O' the other side, the policy of those crafty swearing rascals,—that stale old mouse-eaten dry cheese, Nestor, and that same dog-fox, Ulysses, is not proved worth a blackberry: they set me up, in policy, that mongrel cur, Ajax, against that dog of as bad a kind, Achilles; and now is the cur Ajax prouder than the cur Achilles, and will not arm to-day; whereupon the Grecians begin to proclaim barbarism, and policy grows into an ill opinion. Soft! here comes sleeve, and t' other. 20

Enter DIOMEDES, TROILUS *following.*

Tro. Fly not; for shouldst thou take the river Styx,
I would swim after.
Dio. Thou dost miscall retire:
I do not fly; but advantageous care
Withdrew me from the odds of multitude. 24
Have at thee!
Ther. Hold thy whore, Grecian! now for thy whore, Trojan! now the sleeve, now the sleeve!

[*Exeunt* TROILUS *and* DIOMEDES, *fighting.*

Enter HECTOR.

Hect. What art thou, Greek? art thou for Hector's match? 28
Art thou of blood and honour?
Ther. No, no, I am a rascal; a scurvy railing knave; a very filthy rogue.
Hect. I do believe thee: live. [*Exit.*
Ther. God-a-mercy, that thou wilt believe me; but a plague break thy neck for frighting me! What's become of the wenching rogues? I think they have swallowed one another: I would laugh at that miracle; yet, in a sort, lechery eats itself. I'll seek them. [*Exit.*

SCENE V.—*Another Part of the Plains.*

Enter DIOMEDES *and a* Servant.

Dio. Go, go, my servant, take thou Troilu horse;
Present the fair steed to my Lady Cressid:
Fellow, commend my service to her beauty:
Tell her I have chastis'd the amorous Trojan,
And am her knight by proof.
Serv. I go, my lord. [*Exe*

Enter AGAMEMNON.

Agam. Renew, renew! The fierce Polydam
Hath beat down Menon; bastard Margarelo
Hath Doreus prisoner,
And stands colossus-wise, waving his beam,
Upon the pashed corses of the kings
Epistrophus and Cedius; Polixenes is slain;
Amphimachus, and Thoas, deadly hurt;
Patroclus ta'en, or slain; and Palamedes
Sore hurt and bruis'd; the dreadful Sagittar
Appals our numbers: haste we, Diomed,
To reinforcement, or we perish all.

Enter NESTOR.

Nest. Go, bear Patroclus' body to Achille
And bid the snail-pac'd Ajax arm for shame
There is a thousand Hectors in the field:
Now here he fights on Galathe his horse,
And there lacks work; anon he's there afoo
And there they fly or die, like scaled sculls
Before the belching whale; then is he yonde
And there the strawy Greeks, ripe for his edg
Fall down before him, like the mower's swath
Here, there, and everywhere, he leaves an
takes,
Dexterity so obeying appetite
That what he will he does; and does so muc
That proof is called impossibility.

Enter ULYSSES.

Ulyss. O! courage, courage, princes; gre
Achilles
Is arming, weeping, cursing, vowing vengeanc
Patroclus' wounds have rous'd his drowsy bloo
Together with his mangled Myrmidons,
That noseless, handless, hack'd and chipp'
come to him,
Crying on Hector. Ajax hath lost a friend,
And foams at mouth, and he is arm'd and
it,
Roaring for Troilus, who hath done to-day
Mad and fantastic execution,
Engaging and redeeming of himself
With such a careless force and forceless care
As if that luck, in very spite of cunning,
Bade him win all.

Enter AJAX.

Ajax. Troilus! thou coward Troilus! [*Exi*
Dio. Ay, there, there
Nest. So, so, we draw together.

Enter ACHILLES.

Achil. Where is this Hector
Come, come, thou boy-queller, show thy face;

Know what it is to meet Achilles angry:
Hector! where's Hector? I will none but
Hector.   [*Exeunt.*

SCENE VI.—*Another Part of the Plains.*
Enter AJAX.

Ajax. Troilus, thou coward Troilus, show
thy head!

Enter DIOMEDES.

Dio. Troilus, I say! where's Troilus?
Ajax.   What wouldst thou?
Dio. I would correct him.
Ajax. Were I the general, thou shouldst have
my office   4
Ere that correction. Troilus, I say! what,
Troilus!

Enter TROILUS.

Tro. O traitor Diomed! Turn thy false face,
thou traitor!
And pay thy life thou ow'st me for my horse!
Dio. Ha! art thou there?   8
Ajax. I'll fight with him alone: stand,
Diomed.
Dio. He is my prize; I will not look upon.
Tro. Come, both you cogging Greeks; have
at you both!   [*Exeunt, fighting.*

Enter HECTOR.

Hect. Yea, Troilus? O, well fought, my
youngest brother!   12

Enter ACHILLES.

Achil. Now I do see thee. Ha! have at thee,
Hector!
Hect. Pause, if thou wilt.
Achil. I do disdain thy courtesy, proud
Trojan.
Be happy that my arms are out of use: 16
My rest and negligence befriend thee now,
But thou anon shalt hear of me again;
Till when, go seek thy fortune.   [*Exit.*
Hect.   Fare thee well:—
I would have been much more a fresher man, 20
Had I expected thee. How now, my brother!

Re-enter TROILUS.

Tro. Ajax hath ta'en Æneas: shall it be?
No, by the flame of yonder glorious heaven,
He shall not carry him: I'll be ta'en too,   24
Or bring him off. Fate, hear me what I say!
I reck not though I end my life to-day. [*Exit.*

Enter One in sumptuous armour.

Hect. Stand, stand, thou Greek; thou art a
goodly mark.
No? wilt thou not? I like thy armour well; 28
I'll frush it, and unlock the rivets all,
But I'll be master of it. Wilt thou not, beast,
abide?
Why then, fly on, I'll hunt thee for thy hide.
                                            [*Exeunt.*

SCENE VII.—*Another Part of the Plains.*
Enter ACHILLES, *with Myrmidons.*

Achil. Come here about me, you my Myrmidons;

Mark what I say. Attend me where I wheel:
Strike not a stroke, but keep yourselves in
breath:
And when I have the bloody Hector found, 4
Empale him with your weapons round about;
In fellest manner execute your aims.
Follow me, sirs, and my proceedings eye:
It is decreed, Hector the great must die.   8
                                            [*Exeunt.*

Enter MENELAUS *and* PARIS, *fighting; then*
THERSITES.

Ther. The cuckold and the cuckold-maker
are at it. Now, bull! now, dog! 'Loo, Paris,
'loo! now, my double-henned sparrow! 'loo,
Paris, 'loo! The bull has the game: 'ware
horns, ho!   [*Exeunt* PARIS *and* MENELAUS.

Enter MARGARELON.

Mar. Turn, slave, and fight.
Ther. What art thou?
Mar. A bastard son of Priam's.   16
Ther. I am a bastard too; I love bastards: I
am a bastard begot, bastard instructed, bastard
in mind, bastard in valour, in every thing illegitimate. One bear will not bite another, and
wherefore should one bastard? Take heed, the
quarrel's most ominous to us: if the son of a
whore fight for a whore, he tempts judgment.
Farewell, bastard.   [*Exit.*
Mar. The devil take thee, coward!   [*Exit.*

SCENE VIII.—*Another Part of the Plains.*
Enter HECTOR.

Hect. Most putrefied core, so fair without,
Thy goodly armour thus hath cost thy life.
Now is my day's work done; I'll take good
breath:
Rest, sword; thou hast thy fill of blood and
death.   [*Puts off his helmet, and hangs
                        his shield behind him.*

Enter ACHILLES *and* Myrmidons.

Achil. Look, Hector, how the sun begins to
set;   5
How ugly night comes breathing at his heels:
Even with the vail and darking of the sun,
To close the day up, Hector's life is done.   8
Hect. I am unarm'd; forego this vantage,
Greek.
Achil. Strike, fellows, strike! this is the man
I seek.   [HECTOR *falls.*
So, Ilion, fall thou next! now, Troy, sink down!
Here lies thy heart, thy sinews, and thy bone. 12
On! Myrmidons, and cry you all amain,
'Achilles hath the mighty Hector slain.'—
                            [*A retreat sounded.*
Hark! a retreat upon our Grecian part.
Myr. The Trojan trumpets sound the like,
my lord.   16
Achil. The dragon wing of night o'erspreads
the earth,
And, stickler-like, the armies separates.
My half-supp'd sword, that frankly would have
fed,

Pleas'd with this dainty bait, thus goes to bed.—
                                        [*Sheathes his sword.*
Come, tie his body to my horse's tail;   21
Along the field I will the Trojan trail. [*Exeunt.*

SCENE IX.—*Another Part of the Plains.*

Enter AGAMEMNON, AJAX, MENELAUS, NESTOR,
   DIOMEDES, *and Others marching. Shouts within.*

Agam. Hark! hark! what shout is that?
Nest.   Peace, drums!
                              [*Within.*] Achilles!
Achilles! Hector's slain! Achilles!
   Dio. The bruit is, Hector's slain, and by
Achilles.
   Ajax. If it be so, yet bragless let it be;   4
Great Hector was a man as good as he.
   Agam. March patiently along. Let one be
sent
To pray Achilles see us at our tent.
If in his death the gods have us befriended,   8
Great Troy is ours, and our sharp wars are
ended.   [*Exeunt marching.*

SCENE X.—*Another Part of the Plains.*

Enter ÆNEAS *and* Trojans.

Æne. Stand, ho! yet are we masters of the
field.
Never go home; here starve we out the night.

Enter TROILUS.

Tro. Hector is slain.
All.   Hector! the gods forbid!
Tro. He's dead; and at the murderer's horse's
tail,   4
In beastly sort, dragg'd through the shameful
field.
Frown on, you heavens, effect your rage with
speed!
Sit, gods, upon your thrones, and smile at Troy!
I say, at once let your brief plagues be mercy, 8
And linger not our sure destructions on!
   Æne. My lord, you do discomfort all the
host.
   Tro. You understand me not that tell me so.
I do not speak of flight, of fear, of death;   12
But dare all imminence that gods and men
Address their dangers in. Hector is gone:

Who shall tell Priam so, or Hecuba?
Let him that will a screech-owl aye be call'd 16
Go in to Troy, and say there Hector's dead:
There is a word will Priam turn to stone,
Make wells and Niobes of the maids and wives,
Cold statues of the youth: and, in a word,   20
Scare Troy out of itself. But march away:
Hector is dead; there is no more to say.
Stay yet. You vile abominable tents,
Thus proudly pight upon our Phrygian plains,
Let Titan rise as early as he dare,   25
I'll through and through you! And, thou great-
      siz'd coward,
No space of earth shall sunder our two hates:
I'll haunt thee like a wicked conscience still, 28
That mouldeth goblins swift as frenzy's thoughts.
Strike a free march to Troy! with comfort go:
Hope of revenge shall hide our inward woe.
                [*Exeunt* ÆNEAS *and* Trojan Forces.

As TROILUS *is going out, enter, from the other
      side,* PANDARUS.

Pan. But hear you, hear you!   32
Tro. Hence, broker lackey! ignomy and
      shame
Pursue thy life, and live aye with thy name!
                                          [*Exit.*
Pan. A goodly medicine for my aching bones!
O world! world! world! thus is the poor agent
despised. O traitors and bawds, how earnestly
are you set a-work, and how ill requited! why
should our endeavour be so loved, and the performance so loathed? what verse for it? what
instance for it?—Let me see!—   41

   Full merrily the humble-bee doth sing,
   Till he hath lost his honey and his sting;
   And being once subdu'd in armed tail,   44
   Sweet honey and sweet notes together fail.

Good traders in the flesh, set this in your
painted cloths.
   As many as be here of pander's hall,   48
   Your eyes, half out, weep out at Pandar's fall;
   Or if you cannot weep, yet give some groans,
      Though not for me, yet for your aching bones.
   Brethren and sisters of the hold-door trade,   52
   Some two months hence my will shall here be made;
   It should be now, but that my fear is this,
   Some galled goose of Winchester would hiss.
   Till then I'll sweat, and seek about for eases; 56
   And at that time bequeath you my diseases.
                                          [*Exit.*

CORIOLANUS

DRAMATIS PERSONÆ

CAIUS MARCIUS, afterwards Caius Marcius Coriolanus.
TITUS LARTIUS, } Generals against the Volscians.
COMINIUS,
MENENIUS AGRIPPA, Friend to Coriolanus.
SICINIUS VELUTUS, } Tribunes of the People.
JUNIUS BRUTUS,
YOUNG MARCIUS, Son to Coriolanus.
Roman Herald.
TULLUS AUFIDIUS, General of the Volscians.
Lieutenant to Aufidius.
Conspirators with Aufidius.
NICANOR, a Roman.

A Citizen of Antium.
ADRIAN, a Volsce.
Two Volscian Guards.

VOLUMNIA, Mother to Coriolanus.
VIRGILIA, Wife to Coriolanus.
VALERIA, Friend to Virgilia.
Gentlewoman, attending on Virgilia.

Roman and Volscian Senators, Patricians, Ædiles,
Lictors, Soldiers, Citizens, Messengers, Servants
to Aufidius, and other Attendants.

SCENE.—*Rome and the Neighbourhood; Corioli and the Neighbourhood; Antium.*

ACT I

SCENE I.—*Rome. A Street.*

Enter a Company of mutinous Citizens, *with staves, clubs, and other weapons.*

First Cit. Before we proceed any further, hear me speak.

All. Speak, speak.

First Cit. You are all resolved rather to die than to famish?   5

All. Resolved, resolved.

First Cit. First, you know Caius Marcius is chief enemy to the people.   8

All. We know't, we know't.

First Cit. Let us kill him, and we'll have corn at our own price. Is't a verdict?

All. No more talking on't; let it be done. Away, away!   13

Sec. Cit. One word, good citizens.

First Cit. We are accounted poor citizens, the patricians good. What authority surfeits on would relieve us. If they would yield us but the superfluity, while it were wholesome, we might guess they relieved us humanely; but they think we are too dear: the leanness that afflicts us, the object of our misery, is as an inventory to particularise their abundance; our sufferance is a gain to them. Let us revenge this with our pikes, ere we become rakes: for the gods know I speak this in hunger for bread, not in thirst for revenge.   26

Sec. Cit. Would you proceed especially against Caius Marcius?

First Cit. Against him first: he's a very dog to the commonalty.

Sec. Cit. Consider you what services he has done for his country?   32

First Cit. Very well; and could be content to give him good report for't, but that he pays himself with being proud.

Sec. Cit. Nay, but speak not maliciously.   36

First Cit. I say unto you, what he hath done famously, he did it to that end: though soft-conscienced men can be content to say it was for his country, he did it to please his mother,

and to be partly proud; which he is, even to the altitude of his virtue.   42

Sec. Cit. What he cannot help in his nature, you account a vice in him. You must in no way say he is covetous.   45

First Cit. If I must not, I need not be barren of accusations: he hath faults, with surplus, to tire in repetition. [*Shouts within.*] What shouts are these? The other side o' the city is risen: why stay we prating here? to the Capitol!

All. Come, come.

First Cit. Soft! who comes here?   52

Enter MENENIUS AGRIPPA.

Sec. Cit. Worthy Menenius Agrippa; one that hath always loved the people.

First Cit. He's one honest enough: would all the rest were so!   56

Men. What work 's, my countrymen, in hand? Where go you
With bats and clubs? The matter? Speak, I pray you.

First Cit. Our business is not unknown to the senate; they have had inkling this fortnight what we intend to do, which now we'll show 'em in deeds. They say poor suitors have strong breaths: they shall know we have strong arms too.   64

Men. Why, masters, my good friends, mine honest neighbours,
Will you undo yourselves?

First Cit. We cannot, sir; we are undone already.   68

Men. I tell you, friends, most charitable care
Have the patricians of you. For your wants,
Your suffering in this dearth, you may as well
Strike at the heaven with your staves as lift them   72
Against the Roman state, whose course will on
The way it takes, cracking ten thousand curbs
Of more strong link asunder than can ever
Appear in your impediment. For the dearth,
The gods, not the patricians, make it, and   77
Your knees to them, not arms, must help.
Alack!

You are transported by calamity
Thither where more attends you; and you slander 80
The helms o' the state, who care for you like fathers,
When you curse them as enemies.
First Cit. Care for us! True, indeed! They ne'er cared for us yet: suffer us to famish, and their storehouses crammed with grain; make edicts for usury, to support usurers; repeal daily any wholesome act established against the rich, and provide more piercing statutes daily to chain up and restrain the poor. If the wars eat us not up, they will; and there's all the love they bear us.
Men. Either you must 92
Confess yourselves wondrous malicious,
Or be accus'd of folly. I shall tell you
A pretty tale: it may be you have heard it;
But, since it serves my purpose, I will venture
To scale't a little more. 97
First Cit. Well, I'll hear it, sir; yet you must not think to fob off our disgrace with a tale; but, an't please you, deliver. 100
Men. There was a time when all the body's members
Rebell'd against the belly; thus accus'd it:
That only like a gulf it did remain
I' the midst o' the body, idle and unactive, 104
Still cupboarding the viand, never bearing
Like labour with the rest, where the other instruments
Did see and hear, devise, instruct, walk, feel,
And, mutually participate, did minister 108
Unto the appetite and affection common
Of the whole body. The belly answer'd,—
First Cit. Well, sir, what answer made the belly? 112
Men. Sir, I shall tell you.—With a kind of smile,
Which ne'er came from the lungs, but even thus—
For, look you, I may make the belly smile
As well as speak—it tauntingly replied 116
To the discontented members, the mutinous parts
That envied his receipt; even so most fitly
As you malign our senators for that
They are not such as you.
First Cit. Your belly's answer? What! 121
The kingly crowned head, the vigilant eye,
The counsellor heart, the arm our soldier,
Our steed the leg, the tongue our trumpeter,
With other muniments and petty helps 124
In this our fabric, if that they—
Men. What then?—
'Fore me, this fellow speaks! what then? what then?
First Cit. Should by the cormorant belly be restrain'd,
Who is the sink o' the body,—
Men. Well, what then? 128
First Cit. The former agents, if they did complain,
What could the belly answer?
Men. I will tell you;

If you'll bestow a small, of what you have little
Patience a while, you'll hear the belly's answer.
First Cit. You're long about it.
Men. Note me this, good friend; 13
Your most grave belly was deliberate,
Not rash like his accusers, and thus answer'd
'True is it, my incorporate friends,' quoth he
'That I receive the general food at first, 13
Which you do live upon; and fit it is;
Because I am the store-house and the shop
Of the whole body: but, if you do remember
I send it through the rivers of your blood, 14
Even to the court, the heart, to the seat o' th' brain;
And, through the cranks and offices of man,
The strongest nerves and small inferior veins
From me receive that natural competency 14
Whereby they live. And though that all at once
You, my good friends,'—this says the belly mark me,—
First Cit. Ay, sir; well, well.
Men. 'Though all at once canno
See what I do deliver out to each, 14
Yet I can make my audit up, that all
From me do back receive the flour of all,
And leave me but the bran.' What say you to't
First Cit. It was an answer: how apply yo this? 15
Men. The senators of Rome are this goo belly,
And you the mutinous members; for, examin
Their counsels and their cares, digest thing rightly
Touching the weal o' the common, you sha find 15
No public benefit which you receive
But it proceeds or comes from them to you,
And no way from yourselves. What do yo think, 16
You, the great toe of this assembly?
First Cit. I the great toe? Why the great toe
Men. For that, being one o' the lowest, basest poorest,
Of this most wise rebellion, thou go'st fore most: 16
Thou rascal, that art worst in blood to run,
Lead'st first to win some vantage.
But make you ready your stiff bats and clubs
Rome and her rats are at the point of battle
The one side must have bale.

Enter CAIUS MARCIUS.

Hail, noble Marcius
Mar. Thanks.—What's the matter, you dis sentious rogues,
That, rubbing the poor itch of your opinion,
Make yourselves scabs?
First Cit. We have ever your good word
Mar. He that will give good words to the will flatter 17
Beneath abhorring. What would you have, yo curs,
That like nor peace nor war? the one affrigh you,
The other makes you proud. He that trusts t you, 17

Where he should find you lions, finds you hares;
Where foxes, geese: you are no surer, no,
han is the coal of fire upon the ice,
Or hailstone in the sun. Your virtue is,   180
To make him worthy whose offence subdues
     him,
And curse that justice did it. Who deserves
     greatness
Deserves your hate; and your affections are
A sick man's appetite, who desires most that 184
Which would increase his evil. He that depends
Upon your favours swims with fins of lead
And hews down oaks with rushes. Hang ye!
     Trust ye?
With every minute you do change a mind, 188
And call him noble that was now your hate,
Him vile that was your garland. What's the
     matter,
That in these several places of the city
You cry against the noble senate, who,   192
Under the gods, keep you in awe, which else
Would feed on one another? What's their seek-
     ing?
     Men. For corn at their own rates; whereof
     they say
The city is well stor'd.
     Mar.   Hang 'em! They say! 196
They'll sit by the fire, and presume to know
What's done i' the Capitol; who's like to rise,
Who thrives, and who declines; side factions,
     and give out
Conjectural marriages; making parties strong,
And feebling such as stand not in their liking,
Below their cobbled shoes. They say there's
     grain enough!   202
Would the nobility lay aside their ruth,
And let me use my sword, I'd make a quarry
With thousands of these quarter'd slaves, as
     high   205
As I could pick my lance.
     Men. Nay, these are almost thoroughly per-
     suaded;
For though abundantly they lack discretion, 208
Yet are they passing cowardly. But, I beseech
     you,
What says the other troop?
     Mar.   They are dissolv'd: hang 'em!
They said they were an-hungry; sigh'd forth
     proverbs:
That hunger broke stone walls; that dogs must
     eat;   212
That meat was made for mouths; that the gods
     sent not
Corn for the rich men only. With these shreds
They vented their complainings; which being
     answer'd,
And a petition granted them, a strange one,—
To break the heart of generosity,   217
And make bold power look pale,—they threw
     their caps
As they would hang them on the horns o' the
     moon,
Shouting their emulation.
     Men.   What is granted them?
     Mar. Five tribunes to defend their vulgar
     wisdoms,   221

Of their own choice: one's Junius Brutus,
Sicinius Velutus, and I know not—'Sdeath!
The rabble should have first unroof'd the city,
Ere so prevail'd with me; it will in time   225
Win upon power, and throw forth greater
     themes
For insurrection's arguing.
     Men.   This is strange.
     Mar. Go; get you home, you fragments! 228

     Enter a Messenger, *hastily.*

     Mess. Where's Caius Marcius?
     Mar.   Here: what's the matter?
     Mess. The news is, sir, the Volsces are in
     arms.
     Mar. I am glad on't; then we shall ha' means
     to vent
Our musty superfluity. See, our best elders. 232

Enter COMINIUS, TITUS LARTIUS, *and other* Sena-
     tors; JUNIUS BRUTUS *and* SICINIUS VELUTUS.

     First Sen. Marcius, 'tis true that you have
     lately told us;
The Volsces are in arms.
     Mar.   They have a leader,
Tullus Aufidius, that will put you to 't.
I sin in envying his nobility,   236
And were I anything but what I am,
I would wish me only he.
     Com.   You have fought together.
     Mar. Were half to half the world by the ears,
     and he
Upon my party, I'd revolt, to make   240
Only my wars with him: he is a lion
That I am proud to hunt.
     First Sen.   Then, worthy Marcius,
Attend upon Cominius to these wars.
     Com. It is your former promise.
     Mar.   Sir, it is;   244
And I am constant. Titus Lartius, thou
Shalt see me once more strike at Tullus' face.
What! art thou stiff? stand'st out?
     Tit.   No, Caius Marcius;
I'll lean upon one crutch and fight with
     t'other,   248
Ere stay behind this business.
     Men.   O! true-bred.
     First Sen. Your company to the Capitol;
     where I know
Our greatest friends attend us.
     Tit.   [*To* COMINIUS.] Lead you on:
[*To* MARCIUS.] Follow Cominius; we must fol-
     low you;   252
Right worthy you priority.
     Com.   Noble Marcius!
     First Sen. [*To the* Citizens.] Hence! to your
     homes! be gone.
     Mar.   Nay, let them follow:
The Volsces have much corn; take these rats
     thither
To gnaw their garners. Worshipful mutiners,
Your valour puts well forth; pray, follow. 257
[*Exeunt* Senators, COMINIUS, MARCIUS, TITUS,
     and MENENIUS. Citizens *steal away.*
     Sic. Was ever man so proud as is this Mar-
     cius?

Bru. He has no equal.

Sic. When we were chosen tribunes for the
people,—   260

Bru. Mark'd you his lip and eyes?

Sic.   Nay, but his taunts.

Bru. Being mov'd, he will not spare to gird
the gods.

Sic. Bemock the modest moon.

Bru. The present wars devour him; he is
grown   264
Too proud to be so valiant.

Sic.   Such a nature,
Tickled with good success, disdains the shadow
Which he treads on at noon. But I do wonder
His insolence can brook to be commanded 268
Under Cominius.

Bru.   Fame, at the which he aims,
In whom already he is well grac'd, cannot
Better be held nor more attain'd than by
A place below the first; for what miscarries 272
Shall be the general's fault, though he perform
To the utmost of a man; and giddy censure
Will then cry out of Marcius 'O! if he
Had borne the business.'

Sic.   Besides, if things go well, 276
Opinion, that so sticks on Marcius, shall
Of his demerits rob Cominius.

Bru.   Come:
Half all Cominius' honours are to Marcius,
Though Marcius earn'd them not; and all his
faults   280
To Marcius shall be honours, though indeed
In aught he merit not.

Sic.   Let's hence and hear
How the dispatch is made; and in what fashion,
More than his singularity, he goes   284
Upon this present action.

Bru.   Let's along. [*Exeunt.*

SCENE II.—*Corioli. The Senate-house.*

Enter TULLUS AUFIDIUS *and Senators.*

First Sen. So, your opinion is, Aufidius,
That they of Rome are enter'd in our counsels,
And know how we proceed.

Auf.   Is it not yours?
What ever have been thought on in this state, 4
That could be brought to bodily act ere Rome
Had circumvention? 'Tis not four days gone
Since I heard thence; these are the words: I
think
I have the letter here; yes, here it is.   8
*They have press'd a power, but it is not known
Whether for east, or west: the dearth is great;
The people mutinous; and it is rumour'd,
Cominius, Marcius, your old enemy,—*   12
*Who is of Rome worse hated than of you,—
And Titus Lartius, a most valiant Roman,
These three lead on this preparation
Whither 'tis bent: most likely 'tis for you:*   16
Consider of it.

First Sen. Our army's in the field:
We never yet made doubt but Rome was ready
To answer us.

Auf.   Nor did you think it folly
To keep your great pretences veil'd till when 20
They needs must show themselves; which in
the hatching,
It seem'd, appear'd to Rome. By the discovery
We shall be shorten'd in our aim, which was
To take in many towns ere almost Rome   24
Should know we were afoot.

Sec. Sen.   Noble Aufidius,
Take your commission; hie you to your bands;
Let us alone to guard Corioli:
If they set down before's, for the remove   28
Bring up your army; but, I think you'll find
They've not prepared for us.

Auf.   O! doubt not that;
I speak from certainties. Nay, more;
Some parcels of their power are forth already, 32
And only hitherward. I leave your honours.
If we and Caius Marcius chance to meet,
'Tis sworn between us we shall ever strike
Till one can do no more.

All.   The gods assist you! 36

Auf. And keep your honours safe!

First Sen.   Farewell.

Sec. Sen.   Farewell.

All. Farewell.   [*Exeunt.*

SCENE III.—*Rome. A Room in* MARCIUS'S
House.

Enter VOLUMNIA *and* VIRGILIA: *they set them
down on two low stools and sew.*

Vol. I pray you, daughter, sing; or express
yourself in a more comfortable sort. If my son
were my husband, I would freelier rejoice in that
absence wherein he won honour than in the
embracements of his bed where he would show
most love. When yet he was but tender-bodied
and the only son of my womb, when youth with
comeliness plucked all gaze his way, when for a
day of kings' entreaties a mother should not sell
him an hour from her beholding, I, considering
how honour would become such a person, that
it was no better than picture-like to hang by the
wall, if renown made it not stir, was pleased to
let him seek danger where he was like to find
fame. To a cruel war I sent him; from whence
he returned, his brows bound with oak. I tell
thee, daughter, I sprang not more in joy at first
hearing he was a man-child than now in first
seeing he had proved himself a man.   19

Vir. But had he died in the business, madam;
how then?

Vol. Then, his good report should have been
my son; I therein would have found issue. Hear
me profess sincerely: had I a dozen sons, each
in my love alike, and none less dear than thine
and my good Marcius, I had rather had eleven
die nobly for their country than one voluptu-
ously surfeit out of action.   28

Enter a Gentlewoman.

Gen. Madam, the Lady Valeria is come to
visit you.

Vir. Beseech you, give me leave to retire
myself.

Vol. Indeed, you shall not.   32
Methinks I hear hither your husband's drum

ee him pluck Aufidius down by the hair,
s children from a bear, the Volsces shunning
    him:
Methinks I see him stamp thus, and call thus:
Come on, you cowards! you were got in fear,
hough you were born in Rome.' His bloody
    brow
'ith his mail'd hand then wiping, forth he goes,
ike to a harvestman that's task'd to mow 40
r all or lose his hire.
    Vir. His bloody brow! O Jupiter! no blood.
    Vol. Away, you fool! it more becomes a man
han gilt his trophy: the breasts of Hecuba, 44
'hen she did suckle Hector, look'd not lovelier
han Hector's forehead when it spit forth blood
t Grecian swords, contemning. Tell Valeria
'e are fit to bid her welcome.   48
                              [*Exit* Gentlewoman.
    Vir. Heavens bless my lord from fell Aufidius!
    Vol. He'll beat Aufidius' head below his knee,
nd tread upon his neck.

Re-enter Gentlewoman, *with* VALERIA *and
            an* Usher.

    Val. My ladies both, good day to you. 52
    Vol. Sweet madam.
    Vir. I am glad to see your ladyship.
    Val. How do you both? you are manifest
ousekeepers. What are you sewing here? A
ie spot, in good faith. How does your little
n?   58
    Vir. I thank your ladyship; well, good
adam.
    Vol. He had rather see the swords and hear
drum, than look upon his schoolmaster. 61
    Val. O' my word, the father's son; I'll swear
is a very pretty boy. O' my troth, I looked
oon him o' Wednesday half an hour together:
 has such a confirmed countenance. I saw
m run after a gilded butterfly; and when he
ught it, he let it go again; and after it again;
id over and over he comes, and up again;
tched it again: or whether his fall enraged
m, or how 'twas, he did so set his teeth and
ar it; O! I warrant, how he mammocked it!
    Vol. One on 's father's moods.   72
    Val. Indeed, la, 'tis a noble child.
    Vir. A crack, madam.
    Val. Come, lay aside your stitchery; I must
ave you play the idle huswife with me this
ternoon.   77
    Vir. No, good madam; I will not out of
oors.
    Val. Not out of doors!
    Vol. She shall, she shall.   80
    Vir. Indeed, no, by your patience; I'll not
ver the threshold till my lord return from the
ars.
    Vol. Fie! you confine yourself most un-
asonably. Come; you must go visit the good
dy that lies in.   86
    Vir. I will wish her speedy strength, and visit
er with my prayers; but I cannot go thither.
    Vol. Why, I pray you?
    Vir. 'Tis not to save labour, nor that I want
ve.   91

    Val. You would be another Penelope; yet,
they say, all the yarn she spun in Ulysses'
absence did but fill Ithaca full of moths. Come;
I would your cambric were sensible as your
finger, that you might leave pricking it for pity.
Come, you shall go with us.   97
    Vir. No, good madam, pardon me; indeed, I
will not forth.
    Val. In truth, la, go with me; and I'll tell
you excellent news of your husband.   101
    Vir. O, good madam, there can be none yet.
    Val. Verily, I do not jest with you; there
came news from him last night.   104
    Vir. Indeed, madam?
    Val. In earnest, it's true; I heard a senator
speak it. Thus it is: The Volsces have an army
forth; against whom Cominius the general is
gone, with one part of our Roman power: your
lord and Titus Lartius are set down before their
city Corioli; they nothing doubt prevailing and
to make it brief wars. This is true, on mine
honour; and so, I pray, go with us.   113
    Vir. Give me excuse, good madam; I will
obey you in every thing hereafter.
    Vol. Let her alone, lady: as she is now she
will but disease our better mirth.   117
    Val. In troth, I think she would. Fare you
well then. Come, good sweet lady. Prithee,
Virgilia, turn thy solemness out o' door, and go
along with us.   121
    Vir. No, at a word, madam; indeed I must
not. I wish you much mirth.
    Val. Well then, farewell.   [*Exeunt.*

SCENE IV.—*Before Corioli.*

Enter, with drum and colours, MARCIUS, TITUS
LARTIUS, Officers, *and* Soldiers. *To them a*
Messenger.

    Mar. Yonder comes news: a wager they have
    met.
    Lart. My horse to yours, no.
    Mar.   'Tis done.
    Lart.   Agreed.
    Mar. Say, has our general met the enemy?
    Mess. They lie in view, but have not spoke
    as yet.   4
    Lart. So the good horse is mine.
    Mar.   I'll buy him of you.
    Lart. No, I'll nor sell nor give him; lend you
    him I will
For half a hundred years. Summon the town.
    Mar. How far off lie these armies?
    Mess.   Within this mile and half. 8
    Mar. Then shall we hear their 'larum, and
    they ours.
Now, Mars, I prithee, make us quick in work,
That we with smoking swords may march from
    hence,
To help our fielded friends! Come, blow thy
    blast.   12

A Parley sounded. Enter, on the Walls, two
        Senators, *and Others.*

Tullus Aufidius, is he within your walls?
    First Sen. No, nor a man that fears you less
    than he,

That's lesser than a little. Hark, our drums
                         [*Drums afar off.*
Are bringing forth our youth: we'll break our
    walls,   16
Rather than they shall pound us up: our gates,
Which yet seem shut, we have but pinn'd with
    rushes;
They'll open of themselves. Hark you, far off!
                         [*Alarum afar off.*
There is Aufidius: list, what work he makes 20
Amongst your cloven army.
    Mar.   O! they are at it!
    Lart. Their noise be our instruction. Lad-
    ders, ho!

    The Volsces *enter, and pass over the stage.*

    Mar. They fear us not, but issue forth their
    city.
Now put your shields before your hearts, and
    fight   24
With hearts more proof than shields. Advance,
    brave Titus:
They do disdain us much beyond our thoughts,
Which makes me sweat with wrath. Come on,
    my fellows:
He that retires, I'll take him for a Volsce,   28
And he shall feel mine edge.

    Alarum. The Romans are beaten back to their
       trenches. Re-enter MARCIUS.

    Mar. All the contagion of the south light on
    you,
You shames of Rome! you herd of—Boils and
    plagues
Plaster you o'er, that you may be abhorr'd 32
Further than seen, and one infect another
Against the wind a mile! You souls of geese,
That bear the shapes of men, how have you run
From slaves that apes would beat! Pluto and
    hell!   36
All hurt behind; backs red, and faces pale
With flight and agu'd fear! Mend and charge
    home,
Or, by the fires of heaven, I'll leave the foe
And make my wars on you; look to 't: come on;
If you'll stand fast, we'll beat them to their
    wives,   41
As they us to our trenches follow'd.

    Another alarum. The Volsces *and* Romans *re-*
       enter, and the fight is renewed. The Volsces
       retire into Corioli, and MARCIUS *follows them*
       to the gates.

So, now the gates are ope: now prove good
    seconds:
'Tis for the followers Fortune widens them, 44
Not for the fliers: mark me, and do the like.
                         [*He enters the gates.*
    First Sol. Foolhardiness! not I.
    Sec. Sol.   Nor I.
                      [MARCIUS *is shut in.*
    Third Sol. See, they have shut him in.
    All.   To the pot, I warrant him.
                      [*Alarum continues.*

    Re-enter TITUS LARTIUS.

    Lart. What is become of Marcius?

    All.   Slain, sir, doubtless.
    First Sol. Following the fliers at the ve
    heels,
With them he enters; who, upon the sudde
Clapp'd-to their gates; he is himself alone,
To answer all the city.
    Lart.   O noble fellow!
Who, sensibly, outdares his senseless sword
And, when it bows, stands up. Thou art le
    Marcius:
A carbuncle entire, as big as thou art,
Were not so rich a jewel. Thou wast a sold
Even to Cato's wish, not fierce and terrible
Only in strokes; but, with thy grim looks a
The thunder-like percussion of thy sounds,
Thou mad'st thine enemies shake, as if t
    world
Were feverous and did tremble.

    Re-enter MARCIUS, *bleeding, assaulted by*
            the enemy.

    First Sol.   Look, sir!
    Lart.   O! 'tis Marciu
Let's fetch him off, or make remain alike.
                  [*They fight, and all enter the ci*

    SCENE V.—*Corioli. A Street.*

    Enter certain Romans, *with spoils.*

    First Rom. This will I carry to Rome.
    Sec. Rom. And I this.
    Third Rom. A murrain on't! I took this t
    silver.   [*Alarum continues still afar o*

    Enter MARCIUS *and* TITUS LARTIUS, *with a*
                trumpet.

    Mar. See here these movers that do pri
    their hours
At a crack'd drachme! Cushions, leaden spoo
Irons of a doit, doublets that hangmen wou
Bury with those that wore them, these ba
    slaves,
Ere yet the fight be done, pack up. Down wi
    them!
And hark, what noise the general makes! 7
    him!
There is the man of my soul's hate, Aufidiu
Piercing our Romans: then, valiant Titus, ta
Convenient numbers to make good the city,
Whilst I, with those that have the spirit, w
    haste
To help Cominius.
    Lart.   Worthy sir, thou bleed's
Thy exercise hath been too violent
For a second course of fight.
    Mar.   Sir, praise me not;
My work hath yet not warm'd me: fare ye
    well:
The blood I drop is rather physical
Than dangerous to me: to Aufidius thus
I will appear, and fight.
    Lart.   Now the fair goddess, Fortune,
Fall deep in love with thee; and her great charr
Misguide thy opposers' swords! Bold gentl
    man,
Prosperity be thy page!

Mar.   Thy friend no less
..an those she places highest! So, farewell. 24
Lart. Thou worthiest Marcius!—
                              [*Exit* MARCIUS.
.., sound thy trumpet in the market-place;
..ll thither all the officers of the town.
..here they shall know our mind. Away! 28
                              [*Exeunt.*

SCENE VI.—*Near the Camp of* COMINIUS.

Enter COMINIUS *and Forces, retreating.*

.Com. Breathe you, my friends: well fought;
    we are come off
..ke Romans, neither foolish in our stands,
..r cowardly in retire: believe me, sirs,
..e shall be charg'd again. Whiles we have
    struck,   4
..interims and conveying gusts we have heard
..e charges of our friends. Ye Roman gods!
..ad their successes as we wish our own,
..at both our powers, with smiling fronts en-
    countering,   8
..ay give you thankful sacrifice.

Enter a Messenger.

                              Thy news?
Mess. The citizens of Corioli have issu'd,
..d given to Lartius and to Marcius battle:
..aw our party to their trenches driven, 12
..d then I came away.
Com.   Though thou speak'st truth,
..ethinks thou speak'st not well. How long is't
    since?
Mess. Above an hour, my lord.
Com. 'Tis not a mile; briefly we heard their
    drums: 16
..ow couldst thou in a mile confound an hour,
..d bring thy news so late?
Mess.   Spies of the Volsces
..eld me in chase, that I was forc'd to wheel
..ree or four miles about; else had I, sir, 20
..alf an hour since brought my report.
Com.   Who's yonder,
..at does appear as he were flay'd? O gods!
..e has the stamp of Marcius; and I have
..efore-time seen him thus.
Mar. [*Within.*] Come I too late? 24
Com. The shepherd knows not thunder from
    a tabor,
..ore than I know the sound of Marcius' tongue
..om every meaner man.

Enter MARCIUS.

Mar.   Come I too late?
Com. Ay, if you come not in the blood of
    others,   28
..ut mantled in your own.
Mar.   O! let me clip ye
..arms as sound as when I woo'd, in heart
..s merry as when our nuptial day was done,
..nd tapers burn'd to bedward.
Com.   Flower of warriors. 32
..ow is't with Titus Lartius?
Mar. As with a man busied about decrees:
..ondemning some to death, and some to exile;

Ransoming him, or pitying, threat'ning the
    other;   36
Holding Corioli in the name of Rome,
Even like a fawning greyhound in the leash,
To let him slip at will.
Com.   Where is that slave
Which told me they had beat you to your
    trenches?   40
Where is he? Call him hither.
Mar.   Let him alone;
He did inform the truth: but for our gentlemen,
The common file—a plague! tribunes for
    them!—
The mouse ne'er shunn'd the cat as they did
    budge   44
From rascals worse than they.
Com.   But how prevail'd you?
Mar. Will the time serve to tell? I do not
    think.
Where is the enemy? Are you lords o' the field?
If not, why cease you till you are so?   48
Com. Marcius, we have at disadvantage
    fought,
And did retire to win our purpose.
Mar. How lies their battle? Know you on
    which side
They have plac'd their men of trust?
Com.   As I guess, Marcius, 52
Their bands i' the vaward are the Antiates,
Of their best trust; o'er them Aufidius,
Their very heart of hope.
Mar.   I do beseech you,
By all the battles wherein we have fought, 56
By the blood we have shed together, by the vows
We have made to endure friends, that you
    directly
Set me against Aufidius and his Antiates;
And that you not delay the present, but, 60
Filling the air with swords advanc'd and darts,
We prove this very hour.
Com.   Though I could wish
You were conducted to a gentle bath,
And balms applied to you, yet dare I never 64
Deny your asking: take your choice of those
That best can aid your action.
Mar.   Those are they
That most are willing. If any such be here—
As it were sin to doubt—that love this painting
Wherein you see me smear'd; if any fear 69
Lesser his person than an ill report;
If any think brave death outweighs bad life,
And that his country's dearer than himself; 72
Let him, alone, or so many so minded,
Wave thus, to express his disposition,
And follow Marcius.
        [*They all shout, and wave their swords;
            take him up in their arms, and cast up
            their caps.*
O! me alone? Make you a sword of me? 76
If these shows be not outward, which of you
But is four Volsces? None of you but is
Able to bear against the great Aufidius
A shield as hard as his. A certain number, 80
Though thanks to all, must I select from all:
    the rest
Shall bear the business in some other fight,

As cause will be obey'd. Please you to march;
And four shall quickly draw out my command,
Which men are best inclin'd.
Com. March on, my fellows: 85
Make good this ostentation, and you shall
Divide in all with us. [*Exeunt.*

SCENE VII.—*The Gates of Corioli.*

TITUS LARTIUS, *having set a guard upon* CORIOLI,
going with drum and trumpet towards COMINIUS
and CAIUS MARCIUS, *enters with a* Lieutenant,
a party of Soldiers, *and a* Scout.

Lart. So; let the ports be guarded: keep your
duties,
As I have set them down. If I do send, dispatch
Those centuries to our aid; the rest will serve
For a short holding: if we lose the field, 4
We cannot keep the town.
Lieu. Fear not our care, sir.
Lart. Hence, and shut your gates upon us.
Our guider, come; to the Roman camp conduct
us. [*Exeunt.*

SCENE VIII.—*A Field of Battle between the
Roman and the Volscian Camps.*

Alarum. Enter from opposite sides MARCIUS
and AUFIDIUS.

Mar. I'll fight with none but thee; for I do
hate thee
Worse than a promise-breaker.
Auf. We hate alike:
Not Afric owns a serpent I abhor
More than thy fame and envy. Fix thy foot. 4
Mar. Let the first budger die the other's
slave,
And the gods doom him after!
Auf. If I fly, Marcius,
Halloo me like a hare.
Mar. Within these three hours, Tullus, 8
Alone I fought in your Corioli walls,
And made what work I pleas'd; 'tis not my
blood
Wherein thou seest me mask'd; for thy revenge
Wrench up thy power to the highest.
Auf. Wert thou the Hector 12
That was the whip of your bragg'd progeny,
Thou shouldst not 'scape me here.—
[*They fight, and certain* Volsces *come to the
aid of* AUFIDIUS.
Officious, and not valiant, you have sham'd me
In your condemned seconds. 16
[*Exeunt fighting, all driven in by* MARCIUS.

SCENE IX.—*The Roman Camp.*

*Alarum. A retreat sounded. Flourish. Enter
from one side,* COMINIUS *and* Romans; *from
the other side,* MARCIUS, *with his arm in a scarf,
and other* Romans.

Com. If I should tell thee o'er this thy day's
work,
Thou'lt not believe thy deeds: but I'll report it
Where senators shall mingle tears with smiles,
Where great patricians shall attend and shrug,
I' the end, admire; where ladies shall be frighted,

And, gladly quak'd, hear more; where the du[ll]
Tribunes,
That, with the fusty plebeians, hate thin[e]
honours,
Shall say, against their hearts,
'We thank the gods our Rome hath such
soldier!'
Yet cam'st thou to a morsel of this feast,
Having fully din'd before.

Enter TITUS LARTIUS, *with his power, from
the pursuit.*

Lart. O general,
Here is the steed, we the caparison:
Hadst thou beheld—
Mar. Pray now, no more: my mothe[r]
Who has a charter to extol her blood,
When she does praise me grieves me. I hav[e]
done
As you have done; that's what I can; induc'[d]
As you have been; that's for my country:
He that has but effected his good will
Hath overta'en mine act.
Com. You shall not be
The grave of your deserving; Rome must kno[w]
The value of her own: 'twere a concealment [2?]
Worse than a theft, no less than a traducemen[t]
To hide your doings; and to silence that,
Which, to the spire and top of praises vouch'[d]
Would seem but modest. Therefore, I beseec[h]
you,—
In sign of what you are, not to reward
What you have done,—before our army hea[r]
me.
Mar. I have some wounds upon me, and the[y]
smart 2
To hear themselves remember'd.
Com. Should they no[t]
Well might they fester 'gainst ingratitude,
And tent themselves with death. Of all th[e]
horses,
Whereof we have ta'en good, and good store, o[f]
all 3
The treasure, in this field achiev'd and city,
We render thee the tenth; to be ta'en forth,
Before the common distribution,
At your only choice.
Mar. I thank you, general; 3[?]
But cannot make my heart consent to take
A bribe to pay my sword: I do refuse it;
And stand upon my common part with thos[e]
That have beheld the doing. 4
[*A long flourish. They all cry '*Marcius!
Marcius!*' cast up their caps and lances*
COMINIUS *and* LARTIUS *stand bare.*
Mar. May these same instruments, which
you profane,
Never sound more! When drums and trumpet[s]
shall
I' the field prove flatterers, let courts and citie[s]
be
Made all of false-fac'd soothing! 4
When steel grows soft as is the parasite's silk
Let him be made a coverture for the wars!
No more, I say! For that I have not wash'd
My nose that bled, or foil'd some debile wretch

Which, without note, here's many else have
       done,   49
You shout me forth
In acclamations hyperbolical;
As if I lov'd my little should be dieted   52
In praises sauc'd with lies.
    Com.   Too modest are you;
More cruel to your good report than grateful
To us that give you truly. By your patience,
If 'gainst yourself you be incens'd, we'll put you,
Like one that means his proper harm, in
       manacles,   57
Then reason safely with you. Therefore, be it
       known,
As to us, to all the world, that Caius Marcius
Wears this war's garland; in token of the which,
My noble steed, known to the camp, I give him,
With all his trim belonging; and from this time,
For what he did before Corioli, call him,
With all the applause and clamour of the host,
CAIUS MARCIUS CORIOLANUS! Bear   65
The addition nobly ever!
    All. Caius Marcius Coriolanus!
       [*Flourish. Trumpets sound, and drums.*
    Cor. I will go wash;   68
And when my face is fair, you shall perceive
Whether I blush, or no: howbeit, I thank you.
I mean to stride your steed, and at all times
To undercrest your good addition   72
To the fairness of my power.
    Com.   So, to our tent;
Where, ere we do repose us, we will write
To Rome of our success. You, Titus Lartius,
Must to Corioli back: send us to Rome   76
The best, with whom we may articulate,
For their own good and ours.
    Lart.   I shall, my lord.
    Cor. The gods begin to mock me. I, that now
Refus'd most princely gifts, am bound to beg 80
Of my lord general.
    Com.   Take it; 'tis yours. What is't?
    Cor. I sometime lay here in Corioli
At a poor man's house; he us'd me kindly:
He cried to me; I saw him prisoner;   84
But then Aufidius was within my view,
And wrath o'erwhelm'd my pity: I request you
To give my poor host freedom.
    Com.   O! well begg'd!
Were he the butcher of my son, he should   88
Be free as is the wind. Deliver him, Titus.
    Lart. Marcius, his name?
    Cor.   By Jupiter! forgot.
I am weary; yea, my memory is tir'd.
Have we no wine here?
    Com.   Go we to our tent: 92
The blood upon your visage dries; 'tis time
It should be look'd to: come.   [*Exeunt.*

SCENE X.—*The Camp of the* Volsces.

Flourish. Cornets. Enter TULLUS AUFIDIUS,
    bloody, with two or three Soldiers.

    Auf. The town is ta'en!
    First Sol. 'Twill be deliver'd back on good
condition.
    Auf. Condition!

I would I were a Roman; for I cannot,   4
Being a Volsce, be that I am. Condition!
What good condition can a treaty find
I' the part that is at mercy? Five times, Marcius,
I have fought with thee; so often hast thou beat
       me,   8
And wouldst do so, I think, should we encounter
As often as we eat. By the elements,
If e'er again I meet him beard to beard,
He is mine, or I am his: mine emulation   12
Hath not that honour in't it had; for where
I thought to crush him in an equal force—
True sword to sword—I'll potch at him some
       way
Or wrath or craft may get him.
    First Sol.   He's the devil. 16
    Auf. Bolder, though not so subtle. My
       valour's poison'd
With only suffering stain by him; for him
Shall fly out of itself. Nor sleep nor sanctuary,
Being naked, sick, nor fane nor Capitol,   20
The prayers of priests, nor times of sacrifice,
Embarquements all of fury, shall lift up
Their rotten privilege and custom 'gainst
My hate to Marcius. Where I find him, were it
At home, upon my brother's guard, even there
Against the hospitable canon, would I
Wash my fierce hand in's heart. Go you to the
       city;
Learn how 'tis held, and what they are that
       must   28
Be hostages for Rome.
    First Sol.   Will not you go?
    Auf. I am attended at the cypress grove: I
       pray you—
'Tis south the city mills—bring me word thither
How the world goes, that to the pace of it 32
I may spur on my journey.
    First Sol.   I shall, sir. [*Exeunt.*

ACT II

SCENE I.—*Rome. A Public Place.*

Enter MENENIUS, SICINIUS, *and* BRUTUS.

    Men. The augurer tells me we shall have
news to-night.
    Bru. Good or bad?
    Men. Not according to the prayer of the
people, for they love not Marcius.   5
    Sic. Nature teaches beasts to know their
friends.
    Men. Pray you, who does the wolf love? 8
    Sic. The lamb.
    Men. Ay, to devour him; as the hungry
plebeians would the noble Marcius.
    Bru. He's a lamb indeed, that baes like a
bear.   13
    Men. He's a bear indeed, that lives like a
lamb. You two are old men; tell me one thing
that I shall ask you.   16
    Sic. }
    Bru. } Well, sir.
    Men. In what enormity is Marcius poor in,
that you two have not in abundance?
    Bru. He's poor in no one fault, but stored
with all.   21

Sic. Especially in pride.

Bru. And topping all others in boasting.

Men. This is strange now: do you two know how you are censured here in the city, I mean of us o' the right-hand file? Do you? 26

Both. Why, how are we censured?

Men. Because you talk of pride now,—Will you not be angry?

Both. Well, well, sir; well. 30

Men. Why, 'tis no great matter; for a very little thief of occasion will rob you of a great deal of patience: give your dispositions the reins, and be angry at your pleasures; at the least, if you take it as a pleasure to you in being so. You blame Marcius for being proud?

Bru. We do it not alone, sir. 37

Men. I know you can do very little alone; for your helps are many, or else your actions would grow wondrous: your abilities are too infant-like, for doing much alone. You talk of pride: O! that you could turn your eyes towards the napes of your necks, and make but an interior survey of your good selves. O! that you could. 45

Bru. What then, sir?

Men. Why, then you should discover a brace of unmeriting, proud, violent, testy magistrates—alias fools—as any in Rome. 49

Sic. Menenius, you are known well enough too.

Men. I am known to be a humorous patrician, and one that loves a cup of hot wine with not a drop of allaying Tiber in't; said to be something imperfect in favouring the first complaint; hasty and tinder-like upon too trivial motion; one that converses more with the buttock of the night than with the forehead of the morning. What I think I utter, and spend my malice in my breath. Meeting two such wealsmen as you are,—I cannot call you Lycurguses, —if the drink you give me touch my palate adversely, I make a crooked face at it. I cannot say your worships have delivered the matter well when I find the ass in compound with the major part of your syllables; and though I must be content to bear with those that say you are reverend grave men, yet they lie deadly that tell you have good faces. If you see this in the map of my microcosm, follows it that I am known well enough too? What harm can your bisson conspectuities glean out of this character, if I be known well enough too? 73

Bru. Come, sir, come, we know you well enough.

Men. You know neither me, yourselves, nor anything. You are ambitious for poor knaves' caps and legs: you wear out a good wholesome forenoon in hearing a cause between an orange-wife and a fosset-seller, and then rejourn the controversy of three-pence to a second day of audience. When you are hearing a matter between party and party, if you chance to be pinched with the colic, you make faces like mummers, set up the bloody flag against all patience, and, in roaring for a chamber-pot, dismiss the controversy bleeding, the more entangled by your hearing: all the peace you make in their cause is, calling both the parties knaves. You are a pair of strange ones. 9

Bru. Come, come, you are well understood to be a perfecter giber for the table than a necessary bencher in the Capitol. 9

Men. Our very priests must become mockers if they shall encounter such ridiculous subjects as you are. When you speak best unto the purpose it is not worth the wagging of your beards; and your beards deserve not so honourable a grave as to stuff a botcher's cushion, or to be entombed in an ass's pack-saddle. Yet you must be saying Marcius is proud; who, in cheap estimation, is worth all your predecessors since Deucalion, though peradventure some of the best of 'em were hereditary hangmen. Good den to your worships: more of your conversation would infect my brain, being the herdsmen of the beastly plebeians: I will be bold to take my leave of you. [BRUTUS *and* SICINIUS *go aside.*

Enter VOLUMNIA, VIRGILIA, *and* VALERIA.

How now, my as fair as noble ladies,—and the moon, were she earthly, no nobler,—whither do you follow your eyes so fast? 11

Vol. Honourable Menenius, my boy Marcius approaches; for the love of Juno, let's go.

Men. Ha! Marcius coming home?

Vol. Ay, worthy Menenius; and with most prosperous approbation. 11

Men. Take my cap, Jupiter, and I thank thee. Hoo! Marcius coming home!

Vol. } Nay, 'tis true.
Vir. }

Vol. Look, here's a letter from him: the state hath another, his wife another; and, I think, there's one at home for you.

Men. I will make my very house reel to-night. A letter for me! 12

Vir. Yes, certain, there's a letter for you; I saw it.

Men. A letter for me! It gives me an estate of seven years' health; in which time I will make a lip at the physician: the most sovereign prescription in Galen is but empiricutic, and, to this preservative, of no better report than a horse-drench. Is he not wounded? he was wont to come home wounded. 13

Vir. O! no, no, no.

Vol. O! he is wounded, I thank the gods for't.

Men. So do I too, if it be not too much. Brings a' victory in his pocket? The wounds become him.

Vol. On 's brows, Menenius; he comes the third time home with the oaken garland. 14

Men. Has he disciplined Aufidius soundly?

Vol. Titus Lartius writes they fought together, but Aufidius got off.

Men. And 'twas time for him too, I'll warrant him that: an he had stayed by him I would not have been so fidiused for all the chests in Corioli, and the gold that's in them. Is the senate possessed of this? 14

Vol. Good ladies, let's go. Yes, yes, yes; the senate has letters from the general, wherein he

ives my son the whole name of the war. He
ath in this action outdone his former deeds
oubly.   153
  Val. In troth there's wondrous things spoke
f him.
  Men. Wondrous! ay, I warrant you, and not
vithout his true purchasing.   157
  Vir. The gods grant them true!
  Vol. True! pow, wow.
  Men. True! I'll be sworn they are true.
Vhere is he wounded? [*To the* Tribunes.] God
ave your good worships! Marcius is coming
1ome: he has more cause to be proud. [*To*
/OLUMNIA.] Where is he wounded?   164
  Vol. I' the shoulder, and i' the left arm: there
vill be large cicatrices to show the people when
1e shall stand for his place. He received in the
epulse of Tarquin seven hurts i' the body. 168
  Men. One i' the neck, and two i' the thigh,
1here's nine that I know.
  Vol. He had, before this last expedition,
wenty-five wounds upon him.   172
  Men. Now, it's twenty-seven: every gash was
1n enemy's grave. [*A shout and flourish.*]
1ark! the trumpets.
  Vol. These are the ushers of Marcius: before
1im he carries noise, and behind him he leaves
ears: 178
Death, that dark spirit, in's nervy arm doth lie;
Vhich, being advanc'd, declines, and then men
  die.

A Sennet. Trumpets sound. Enter COMINIUS *and*
  TITUS LARTIUS; *between them,* CORIOLANUS,
  crowned with an oaken garland; with Captains,
  Soldiers, *and a* Herald.

  Her. Know, Rome, that all alone Marcius
    did fight
Within Corioli gates: where he hath won,
With fame, a name to Caius Marcius; these
1n honour follows Coriolanus.   184
Welcome to Rome, renowned **Coriolanus**!
                  [*Flourish.*
  All. Welcome to Rome, renowned Coriolanus!
  Cor. No more of this; it does offend my heart:
Pray now, no more.
  Com.   Look, sir, your mother!
  Cor.   O!
You have, I know, petition'd all the gods 189
For my prosperity.   [*Kneels.*
  Vol.   Nay, my good soldier, up;
My gentle Marcius, worthy Caius, and
By deed-achieving honour newly nam'd,— 192
What is it?—Coriolanus must I call thee?
But O! thy wife!—
  Cor.   My gracious silence, hail!
Wouldst thou have laugh'd had I come coffin'd
  home,
That weep'st to see me triumph? Ah! my dear,
Such eyes the widows in Corioli wear,   197
And mothers that lack sons.
  Men.   Now, the gods crown thee!
  Cor. And live you yet? [*To* VALERIA.] O my
  sweet lady, pardon.
  Vol. I know not where to turn: O! welcome
  home;   200

And welcome, general; and ye're welcome all.
  Men. A hundred thousand welcomes: I could
  weep,
And I could laugh; I am light, and heavy. Wel-
  come.
A curse begnaw at very root on's heart   204
That is not glad to see thee! You are three
That Rome should dote on; yet, by the faith of
  men,
We have some old crab-trees here at home that
  will not
Be grafted to your relish. Yet, welcome, war-
  riors!   208
We call a nettle but a nettle, and
The faults of fools but folly.
  Com.   Ever right.
  Cor. Menenius, ever, ever.
  Her. Give way there, and go on!
  Cor. [*To* VOLUMNIA *and* VALERIA.] Your
  hand, and yours: 212
Ere in our own house I do shade my head,
The good patricians must be visited;
From whom I have receiv'd not only greetings,
But with them change of honours.
  Vol.   I have liv'd 216
To see inherited my very wishes,
And the buildings of my fancy: only
There's one thing wanting, which I doubt not
  but
Our Rome will cast upon thee.
  Cor.   Know, good mother, 220
I had rather be their servant in my way
Than sway with them in theirs.
  Com. On, to the Capitol!
        [*Flourish. Cornets. Exeunt in state, as*
          before. The Tribunes *remain.*
  Bru. All tongues speak of him, and the
  bleared sights   224
Are spectacled to see him: your prattling nurse
Into a rapture lets her baby cry
While she chats him: the kitchen malkin pins
Her richest lockram 'bout her reechy neck, 228
Clambering the walls to eye him: stalls, bulks,
  windows,
Are smother'd up, leads fill'd, and ridges hors'd
With variable complexions, all agreeing   231
In earnestness to see him: seld-shown flamens
Do press among the popular throngs, and puff
To win a vulgar station: our veil'd dames
Commit the war of white and damask in
Their nicely-gawded cheeks to the wanton spoil
Of Phœbus' burning kisses: such a pother 237
As if that whatsoever god who leads him
Were slily crept into his human powers,
And gave him graceful posture.
  Sic.   On the sudden 240
I warrant him consul.
  Bru.   Then our office may,
During his power, go sleep.
  Sic. He cannot temperately transport his
  honours
From where he should begin and end, but will
Lose those he hath won.
  Bru.   In that there's comfort. 245
  Sic. Doubt not, the commoners, for whom
  we stand,

But they upon their ancient malice will
Forget with the least cause these his new
    honours,   248
Which that he'll give them, make I as little
    question
As he is proud to do't.
  Bru.   I heard him swear,
Were he to stand for consul, never would he
Appear i' the market-place, nor on him put 252
The napless vesture of humility;
Nor, showing, as the manner is, his wounds
To the people, beg their stinking breaths.
  Sic.   'Tis right.
  Bru. It was his word. O! he would miss it
    rather   256
Than carry it but by the suit o' the gentry to him
And the desire of the nobles.
  Sic.   I wish no better
Than have him hold that purpose and to put it
In execution.
  Bru. 'Tis most like he will.   260
  Sic. It shall be to him then, as our good wills,
A sure destruction.
  Bru.   So it must fall out
To him or our authorities. For an end,
We must suggest the people in what hatred 264
He still hath held them; that to his power he
    would
Have made them mules, silenc'd their pleaders,
    and
Dispropertied their freedoms; holding them,
In human action and capacity, 268
Of no more soul nor fitness for the world
Than camels in the war; who have their provand
Only for bearing burdens, and sore blows
For sinking under them.
  Sic.   This, as you say, suggested 272
At some time when his soaring insolence
Shall teach the people—which time shall not want,
If he be put upon 't; and that's as easy
As to set dogs on sheep—will be his fire 276
To kindle their dry stubble; and their blaze
Shall darken him for ever.

          Enter a Messenger.

  Bru.   What's the matter?
  Mess. You are sent for to the Capitol. 'Tis
    thought
That Marcius shall be consul.   280
I have seen the dumb men throng to see him, and
The blind to hear him speak: matrons flung
    gloves,
Ladies and maids their scarfs and handkerchers
Upon him as he pass'd; the nobles bended, 284
As to Jove's statue, and the commons made
A shower and thunder with their caps and shouts:
I never saw the like.
  Bru.   Let's to the Capitol;
And carry with us ears and eyes for the time, 288
But hearts for the event.
  Sic.   Have with you. [*Exeunt.*

    SCENE II.—*The Same. The Capitol.*
    Enter two Officers to lay cushions.

  First Off. Come, come, they are almost here.
How many stand for consulships?

  Sec. Off. Three, they say; but 'tis thought o
every one Coriolanus will carry it.
  First Off. That's a brave fellow; but he'
vengeance proud, and loves not the commo
people.
  Sec. Off. Faith, there have been many grea
men that have flattered the people, who ne'e
loved them; and there be many that they hav
loved, they know not wherefore: so that if the
love they know not why, they hate upon n
better a ground. Therefore, for Coriolanu
neither to care whether they love or hate hin
manifests the true knowledge he has in thei
disposition; and out of his noble carelessnes
lets them plainly see't.   1
  First Off. If he did not care whether he ha
their love or no, he waved indifferently 'twix
doing them neither good nor harm; but he seek
their hate with greater devotion than they ca
render it him; and leaves nothing undone tha
may fully discover him their opposite. Now, t
seem to affect the malice and displeasure of th
people is as bad as that which he dislikes, t
flatter them for their love.   2
  Sec. Off. He hath deserved worthily of hi
country; and his ascent is not by such eas
degrees as those who, having been supple an
courteous to the people, bonneted, without an
further deed to have them at all into thei
estimation and report; but he hath so plante
his honours in their eyes, and his actions i
their hearts, that for their tongues to be silen
and not confess so much, were a kind of in
grateful injury; to report otherwise, were
malice, that, giving itself the lie, would pluc
reproof and rebuke from every ear that hear
it.
  First Off. No more of him; he is a worth
man: make way, they are coming.   4

A Sennet. Enter, with Lictors *before them,* COMI
    NIUS *the Consul,* MENENIUS, CORIOLANUS, *man*
    other Senators, SICINIUS *and* BRUTUS. *The*
    Senators *take their places; the* Tribunes *tak*
    theirs also by themselves.

  Men. Having determin'd of the Volsces, anc
To send for Titus Lartius, it remains,
As the main point of this our after-meeting, 4
To gratify his noble service that
Hath thus stood for his country: therefore
    please you,
Most reverend and grave elders, to desire
The present consul, and last general   4
In our well-found successes, to report
A little of that worthy work perform'd
By Caius Marcius Coriolanus, whom
We meet here both to thank and to remembe
With honours like himself.
  First Sen.   Speak, good Cominius: 5
Leave nothing out for length, and make us thin
Rather our state's defective for requital,
Than we to stretch it out. [*To the Tribunes.*
    Masters o' the people,   5
We do request your kindest ears, and, after,
Your loving motion toward the common body
To yield what passes here.

Sic.   We are convented
Upon a pleasing treaty, and have hearts   60
Inclinable to honour and advance
The theme of our assembly.

Bru.   Which the rather
We shall be bless'd to do, if he remember
A kinder value of the people than   64
He hath hereto priz'd them at.

Men.   That's off, that's off;
I would you rather had been silent. Please you
To hear Cominius speak?

Bru.   Most willingly;
But yet my caution was more pertinent   68
Than the rebuke you give it.

Men.   He loves your people;
But tie him not to be their bedfellow.
Worthy Cominius, speak.

[CORIOLANUS *rises, and offers to go away.*
               Nay, keep your place.

First Sen. Sit, Coriolanus; never shame to
hear   72
What you have nobly done.

Cor.   Your honours' pardon:
I had rather have my wounds to heal again
Than hear say how I got them.

Bru.   Sir, I hope
My words disbench'd you not.

Cor.   No, sir: yet oft, 76
When blows have made me stay, I fled from
words.
You sooth'd not, therefore hurt not. But your
people,
I love them as they weigh.

Men.   Pray now, sit down.

Cor. I had rather have one scratch my head
i' the sun   80
When the alarum were struck than idly sit
To hear my nothings monster'd.   [*Exit.*

Men.   Masters of the people,
Your multiplying spawn how can he flatter,—
That's thousand to one good one,—when you
now see   84
He had rather venture all his limbs for honour
Than one on 's ears to hear it. Proceed, Comi-
nius.

Com. I shall lack voice: the deeds of Corio-
lanus
Should not be utter'd feebly. It is held   88
That valour is the chiefest virtue, and
Most dignifies the haver: if it be,
The man I speak of cannot in the world
Be singly counterpois'd. At sixteen years, 92
When Tarquin made a head for Rome, he fought
Beyond the mark of others; our then dictator,
Whom with all praise I point at, saw him fight,
When with his Amazonian chin he drove 96
The bristled lips before him. He bestrid
An o'er-press'd Roman, and i' the consul's view
Slew three opposers: Tarquin's self he met,
And struck him on his knee: in that day's
feats,   100
When he might act the woman in the scene,
He prov'd best man i' the field, and for his meed
Was brow-bound with the oak. His pupil age
Man-enter'd thus, he waxed like a sea, 104
And in the brunt of seventeen battles since

He lurch'd all swords of the garland. For this
last,
Before and in Corioli, let me say,
I cannot speak him home: he stopp'd the fliers,
And by his rare example made the coward 109
Turn terror into sport: as weeds before
A vessel under sail, so men obey'd,
And fell below his stem: his sword, death's
stamp, 112
Where it did mark, it took; from face to foot
He was a thing of blood, whose every motion
Was tim'd with dying cries: alone he enter'd
The mortal gate of the city, which he painted
With shunless destiny; aidless came off, 117
And with a sudden re-enforcement struck
Corioli like a planet. Now all's his:
When by and by the din of war 'gan pierce 120
His ready sense; then straight his doubled spirit
Re-quicken'd what in flesh was fatigate,
And to the battle came he; where he did
Run reeking o'er the lives of men, as if 124
'Twere a perpetual spoil; and till we call'd
Both field and city ours, he never stood
To ease his breast with panting.

Men.   Worthy man!

First Sen. He cannot but with measure fit
the honours   128
Which we devise him.

Com.   Our spoils he kick'd at,
And look'd upon things precious as they were
The common muck o' the world: he covets less
Than misery itself would give; rewards 132
His deeds with doing them, and is content
To spend the time to end it.

Men.   He's right noble:
Let him be call'd for.

First Sen.   Call Coriolanus.

Off. He doth appear.   136

Re-enter CORIOLANUS.

Men. The senate, Coriolanus, are well pleas'd
To make thee consul.

Cor.   I do owe them still
My life and services.

Men.   It then remains
That you do speak to the people.

Cor.   I do beseech you,
Let me o'erleap that custom, for I cannot 141
Put on the gown, stand naked, and entreat them,
For my wounds' sake, to give their suffrage:
please you,
That I may pass this doing.

Sic.   Sir, the people 144
Must have their voices; neither will they bate
One jot of ceremony.

Men.   Put them not to 't:
Pray you, go fit you to the custom, and
Take to you, as your predecessors have, 148
Your honour with your form.

Cor.   It is a part
That I shall blush in acting, and might well
Be taken from the people.

Bru. [*Aside to* SICINIUS.] Mark you that?

Cor. To brag unto them, thus I did, and thus;
Show them the unaching scars which I should
hide,   153

As if I had receiv'd them for the hire
Of their breath only!
Men. Do not stand upon 't.
We recommend to you, tribunes of the people,
Our purpose to them; and to our noble consul
Wish we all joy and honour.
Sen. To Coriolanus come all joy and honour!
    [*Flourish. Exeunt all but* SICINIUS
    and BRUTUS.
Bru. You see how he intends to use the
    people. 160
Sic. May they perceive 's intent! He will re-
    quire them,
As if he did contemn what he requested
Should be in them to give.
Bru. Come; we'll inform them
Of our proceedings here: on the market-place
I know they do attend us. [*Exeunt.*

SCENE III.—*The Same. The Forum.*

Enter several Citizens.

First Cit. Once, if he do require our voices,
we ought not to deny him.
Sec. Cit. We may, sir, if we will. 3
Third Cit. We have power in ourselves to do
it, but it is a power that we have no power to
do; for if he show us his wounds, and tell us his
deeds, we are to put our tongues into those
wounds and speak for them; so, if he tell us his
noble deeds, we must also tell him our noble
acceptance of them. Ingratitude is monstrous,
and for the multitude to be ingrateful were to
make a monster of the multitude; of the which,
we being members, should bring ourselves to be
monstrous members. 14
First Cit. And to make us no better thought
of, a little help will serve; for once we stood up
about the corn, he himself stuck not to call us
the many-headed multitude. 18
Third Cit. We have been called so of many;
not that our heads are some brown, some black,
some abram, some bald, but that our wits are
so diversely coloured: and truly I think, if all
our wits were to issue out of one skull, they
would fly east, west, north, south; and their
consent of one direct way should be at once to
all the points o' the compass.
Sec. Cit. Think you so? Which way do you
judge my wit would fly? 28
Third Cit. Nay, your wit will not so soon out
as another man's will; 'tis strongly wedged up
in a block-head; but if it were at liberty, 'twould,
sure, southward. 32
Sec. Cit. Why that way?
Third Cit. To lose itself in a fog; where
being three parts melted away with rotten dews,
the fourth would return for conscience' sake, to
help to get thee a wife. 37
Sec. Cit. You are never without your tricks:
you may, you may.
Third Cit. Are you all resolved to give your
voices? But that's no matter, the greater part
carries it. I say, if he would incline to the
people, there was never a worthier man. 43

Re-enter CORIOLANUS, *in a gown of humility,*
and MENENIUS.

Here he comes, and in a gown of humility:
mark his behaviour. We are not to stay all
together, but to come by him where he stands,
by ones, by twos, and by threes. He's to make
his requests by particulars; wherein every one
of us has a single honour, in giving him our own
voices with our own tongues: therefore follow
me, and I'll direct you how you shall go by him.
All. Content, content. [*Exeunt* Citizens.
Men. O, sir, you are not right: have you not
    known 53
The worthiest men have done 't?
Cor. What must I say?
'I pray, sir,'—Plague upon 't! I cannot bring
My tongue to such a pace. 'Look, sir, my
    wounds! 56
I got them in my country's service, when
Some certain of your brethren roar'd and ran
From the noise of our own drums.'
Men. O me! the gods!
You must not speak of that: you must desire
    them 60
To think upon you.
Cor. Think upon me! Hang 'em!
I would they would forget me, like the virtues
Which our divines lose by 'em.
Men. You'll mar all:
I'll leave you. Pray you, speak to 'em, I pray
    you, 64
In wholesome manner.
Cor. Bid them wash their faces,
And keep their teeth clean. [*Exit* MENENIUS.
    So, here comes a brace.

Re-enter two Citizens.

You know the cause, sir, of my standing here?
First Cit. We do, sir; tell us what hath
brought you to 't. 69
Cor. Mine own desert.
Sec. Cit. Your own desert!
Cor. Ay, not mine own desire. 72
First Cit. How! not your own desire?
Cor. No, sir, 'twas never my desire yet to
trouble the poor with begging.
First Cit. You must think, if we give you
any thing, we hope to gain by you. 7
Cor. Well, then, I pray, your price o' the
consulship?
First Cit. The price is, to ask it kindly. 8
Cor. Kindly! sir, I pray, let me ha' t: I have
wounds to show you, which shall be yours i'
private. Your good voice, sir; what say you
Sec. Cit. You shall ha' t, worthy sir. 8
Cor. A match, sir. There is in all two worth
voices begged. I have your alms: adieu.
First Cit. But this is something odd.
Sec. Cit. An 'twere to give again,—but 't
no matter. [*Exeunt the two* Citizen

Re-enter two other Citizens.

Cor. Pray you now, if it may stand with th
tune of your voices that I may be consul,
have here the customary gown.

Third Cit. You have deserved nobly of your country, and you have not deserved nobly.

Cor. Your enigma?   95

Third Cit. You have been a scourge to her enemies, you have been a rod to her friends; you have not indeed loved the common people.

Cor. You should account me the more virtuous that I have not been common in my love. I will, sir, flatter my sworn brother the people, to earn a dearer estimation of them; 'tis a condition they account gentle: and since the wisdom of their choice is rather to have my hat than my heart, I will practise the insinuating nod, and be off to them most counterfeitly; that is, sir, I will counterfeit the bewitchment of some popular man, and give it bountifully to the desirers. Therefore, beseech you, I may be consul.   110

Fourth Cit. We hope to find you our friend, and therefore give you our voices heartily.

Third Cit. You have received many wounds for your country.   114

Cor. I will not seal your knowledge with showing them. I will make much of your voices, and so trouble you no further.   117

Both Cit. The gods give you joy, sir, heartily!
[*Exeunt.*

Cor. Most sweet voices!
Better it is to die, better to starve,   120
Than crave the hire which first we do deserve.
Why in this woolvish toge should I stand here,
To beg of Hob and Dick, that do appear,
Their needless vouches? Custom calls me to 't:
What custom wills, in all things should we do 't,
The dust on antique time would lie unswept,
And mountainous error be too highly heap'd
For truth to o'er-peer. Rather than fool it so,
Let the high office and the honour go   129
To one that would do thus. I am half through;
The one part suffer'd, the other will I do.
Here come more voices.   132

Re-enter three other Citizens.

Your voices: for your voices I have fought;
Watch'd for your voices; for your voices bear
Of wounds two dozen odd; battles thrice six
I have seen and heard of; for your voices have
Done many things, some less, some more; your voices: 137
Indeed, I would be consul.

Fifth Cit. He has done nobly, and cannot go without any honest man's voice.   140

Sixth Cit. Therefore let him be consul. The gods give him joy, and make him good friend to the people!

All. Amen, amen.   144
God save thee, noble consul! [*Exeunt* Citizens.

Cor.   Worthy voices!

Re-enter MENENIUS, *with* BRUTUS *and* SICINIUS.

Men. You have stood your limitation; and the tribunes
Endue you with the people's voice: remains
That, in the official marks invested, you   148
Anon do meet the senate.

Cor.   Is this done?

Sic. The custom of request you have discharg'd:
The people do admit you, and are summon'd
To meet anon, upon your approbation.   152

Cor. Where? at the senate-house?

Sic.   There, Coriolanus.

Cor. May I change these garments?

Sic. You may, sir.

Cor. That I'll straight do; and, knowing myself again,   156
Repair to the senate-house.

Men. I'll keep you company. Will you along?

Bru. We stay here for the people.

Sic.   Fare you well.
[*Exeunt* CORIOLANUS *and* MENENIUS.
He has it now; and by his looks, methinks,   160
'Tis warm at 's heart.

Bru.   With a proud heart he wore
His humble weeds. Will you dismiss the people?

Re-enter Citizens.

Sic. How now, my masters! have you chose this man?

First Cit. He has our voices, sir.   164

Bru. We pray the gods he may deserve your love.

Sec. Cit. Amen, sir. To my poor unworthy notice,
He mock'd us when he begg'd our voices.

Third Cit.   Certainly,
He flouted us downright.   168

First Cit. No, 'tis his kind of speech; he did not mock us.

Sec. Cit. Not one amongst us, save yourself, but says
He used us scornfully. he should have show'd us
His marks of merit, wounds receiv'd for 's country.   172

Sic. Why, so he did, I am sure.

All.   No, no; no man saw 'em.

Third Cit. He said he had wounds, which he could show in private;
And with his hat, thus waving it in scorn,
'I would be consul,' says he: 'aged custom,   176
But by your voices, will not so permit me;
Your voices therefore:' when we granted that,
Here was, 'I thank you for your voices, thank you,
Your most sweet voices: now you have left your voices   180
I have no further with you.' Was not this mockery?

Sic. Why, either were you ignorant to see 't,
Or, seeing it, of such childish friendliness
To yield your voices?

Bru.   Could you not have told him
As you were lesson'd, when he had no power,   185
But was a petty servant to the state,
He was your enemy, ever spake against
Your liberties and the charters that you bear
I' the body of the weal; and now, arriving   189
A place of potency and sway o' the state,
If he should still malignantly remain
Fast foe to the plebeii, your voices might   192
Be curses to yourselves? You should have said

That as his worthy deeds did claim no less
Than what he stood for, so his gracious nature
Would think upon you for your voices and 196
Translate his malice towards you into love,
Standing your friendly lord.

Sic.   Thus to have said,
As you were fore-advis'd, had touch'd his spirit
And tried his inclination; from him pluck'd 200
Either his gracious promise, which you might,
As cause had call'd you up, have held him to;
Or else it would have gall'd his surly nature,
Which easily endures not article   204
Tying him to aught; so, putting him to rage,
You should have ta'en the advantage of his
    choler,
And pass'd him unelected.

Bru.   Did you perceive
He did solicit you in free contempt   208
When he did need your loves, and do you think
That his contempt shall not be bruising to you
When he hath power to crush? Why, had your
    bodies
No heart among you? or had you tongues to cry
Against the rectorship of judgment?

Sic.   Have you 213
Ere now denied the asker? and now again
Of him that did not ask, but mock, bestow
Your su'd-for tongues?   216

Third Cit. He's not confirm'd; we may deny
    him yet.

Sec. Cit. And will deny him:

I'll have five hundred voices of that sound.

First Cit. Ay, twice five hundred and their
    friends to piece 'em.   220

Bru. Get you hence instantly, and tell those
    friends,
They have chose a consul that will from them
    take
Their liberties; make them of no more voice
Than dogs that are as often beat for barking 224
As therefore kept to do so.

Sic.   Let them assemble;
And, on a safer judgment, all revoke
Your ignorant election. Enforce his pride,
And his old hate unto you; besides, forget
    not   228
With what contempt he wore the humble weed;
How in his suit he scorn'd you; but your loves,
Thinking upon his services, took from you
The apprehension of his present portance, 232
Which most gibingly, ungravely, he did fashion
After the inveterate hate he bears you.

Bru.   Lay
A fault on us, your tribunes; that we labour'd,—
No impediment between,—but that you must
Cast your election on him.

Sic.   Say, you chose him 237
More after our commandment than as guided
By your own true affections; and that, your
    minds,
Pre-occupied with what you rather must do 240
That what you should, made you against the
    grain
To voice him consul: lay the fault on us.

Bru. Ay, spare us not. Say we read lectures
    to you,

How youngly he began to serve his country, 244
How long continu'd, and what stock he springs of,
The noble house o' the Marcians, from whence
    came
That Ancus Marcius, Numa's daughter's son,
Who, after great Hostilius, here was king; 248
Of the same house Publius and Quintus were,
That our best water brought by conduits hither;
And Censorinus, that was so surnam'd,—
And nobly nam'd so, twice being censor,— 252
Was his great ancestor.

Sic.   One thus descended,
That hath, beside, well in his person wrought
To be set high in place, we did commend
To your remembrances: but you have found,
Scaling his present bearing with his past, 257
That he's your fixed enemy, and revoke
Your sudden approbation.

Bru.   Say you ne'er had done 't—
Harp on that still—but by our putting on; 260
And presently, when you have drawn your
    number,
Repair to the Capitol.

All.   We will so; almost all
Repent in their election.   [*Exeunt* Citizens.

Bru.   Let them go on;
This mutiny were better put in hazard   264
Than stay, past doubt, for greater.
If, as his nature is, he fall in rage
With their refusal, both observe and answer
The vantage of his anger.

Sic.   To the Capitol, come: 268
We will be there before the stream o' the people;
And this shall seem, as partly 'tis, their own,
Which we have goaded onward.   [*Exeunt.*

ACT III

SCENE I.—*Rome. A Street.*

Cornets. Enter CORIOLANUS, MENENIUS, COMI-
NIUS, TITUS LARTIUS, Senators, *and* Patricians.

Cor. Tullus Aufidius then had made new
    head?

Lart. He had, my lord; and that it was which
    caus'd
Our swifter composition.

Cor. So then the Volsces stand but as at first,
Ready, when time shall prompt them, to make
    road   5
Upon 's again.

Com.   They are worn, lord consul, so
That we shall hardly in our ages see
Their banners wave again.

Cor.   Saw you Aufidius? 8

Lart. On safe-guard he came to me; and did
    curse
Against the Volsces, for they had so vilely
Yielded the town: he is retir'd to Antium.

Cor. Spoke he of me?

Lart.   He did, my lord.

Cor.   How? what? 12

Lart. How often he had met you, sword to
    sword:
That of all things upon the earth he hated

our person most, that he would pawn his
fortunes
o hopeless restitution, so he might 16
e call'd your vanquisher.
  Cor.   At Antium lives he?
  Lart. At Antium.
  Cor. I wish I had a cause to seek him there,
o oppose his hatred fully. Welcome home. 20

Enter SICINIUS *and* BRUTUS.

ehold! these are the tribunes of the people,
he tongues o' the common mouth: I do despise
  them;
or they do prank them in authority
gainst all noble sufferance.
  Sic.   Pass no further. 24
  Cor. Ha! what is that?
  Bru. It will be dangerous to go on: no further.
  Cor. What makes this change?
  Men.   The matter?
  Com. Hath he not pass'd the noble and the
  common? 28
  Bru. Cominius, no.
  Cor.   Have I had children's voices?
  First Sen. Tribunes, give way; he shall to
  the market-place.
  Bru. The people are incens'd against him.
  Sic.   Stop,
r all will fall in broil.
  Cor.   Are these your herd? 32
/ust these have voices, that can yield them now,
nd straight disclaim their tongues? What are
  your offices?
ou being their mouths, why rule you not their
  teeth?
ave you not set them on?
  Men.   Be calm, be calm. 36
  Cor. It is a purpos'd thing, and grows by plot,
o curb the will of the nobility:
uffer 't, and live with such as cannot rule
Nor ever will be rul'd.
  Bru.   Call 't not a plot: 40
he people cry you mock'd them, and of late,
When corn was given them gratis, you repin'd;
candall'd the suppliants for the people, call'd
  them
ime-pleasers, flatterers, foes to nobleness. 44
  Cor. Why, this was known before.
  Bru.   Not to them all.
  Cor. Have you inform'd them sithence?
  Bru.   How! I inform them!
  Cor. You are like to do such business.
  Bru.   Not unlike,
ach way, to better yours. 48
  Cor. Why then should I be consul? By yond
  clouds,
et me deserve so ill as you, and make me
our fellow tribune.
  Sic.   You show too much of that
or which the people stir; if you will pass 52
o where you are bound, you must inquire your
  way,
Vhich you are out of, with a gentler spirit;
r never be so noble as a consul,
Nor yoke with him for tribune.
  Men.   Let's be calm. 56

  Com. The people are abus'd; set on. This
  paltering
Becomes not Rome, nor has Coriolanus
Deserv'd this so dishonour'd rub, laid falsely
I' the plain way of his merit.
  Cor.   Tell me of corn! 60
This was my speech, and I will speak 't again,—
  Men. Not now, not now.
  First Sen.   Not in this heat, sir, now.
  Cor. Now, as I live, I will. My nobler friends,
I crave their pardons: 64
For the mutable, rank-scented many, let them
Regard me as I do not flatter, and
Therein behold themselves: I say again,
In soothing them we nourish 'gainst our senate
The cockle of rebellion, insolence, sedition, 69
Which we ourselves have plough'd for, sow'd
  and scatter'd,
By mingling them with us, the honour'd num-
  ber;
Who lack'd not virtue, no, nor power, but that
Which they have given to beggars.
  Men.   Well, no more. 73
  First Sen. No more words, we beseech you.
  Cor.   How! no more!
As for my country I have shed my blood,
Not fearing outward force, so shall my lungs 76
Coin words till they decay against those measles,
Which we disdain should tetter us, yet sought
The very way to catch them.
  Bru.   You speak o' the people,
As if you were a god to punish, not 80
A man of their infirmity.
  Sic.   'Twere well
We let the people know 't.
  Men.   What, what? his choler?
  Cor. Choler!
Were I as patient as the midnight sleep, 84
By Jove, 'twould be my mind!
  Sic.   It is a mind
That shall remain a poison where it is,
Not poison any further.
  Cor.   Shall remain!
Hear you this Triton of the minnows? mark
  you 88
His absolute 'shall?'
  Com.   'Twas from the canon.
  Cor.   'Shall!'
O good but most unwise patricians! why,
You grave but reckless senators, have you thus
Given Hydra here to choose an officer, 92
That with his peremptory 'shall,' being but
The horn and noise o' the monster's, wants not
  spirit
To say he'll turn your current in a ditch,
And make your channel his? If he have power,
Then vail your ignorance; if none, awake 97
Your dangerous lenity. If you are learned,
Be not as common fools; if you are not,
Let them have cushions by you. You are ple-
  beians 100
If they be senators; and they are no less,
When, both your voices blended, the great'st
  taste
Most palates theirs. They choose their magis-
  trate,

And such a one as he, who puts his 'shall,' 104
His popular 'shall,' against a graver bench
Than ever frown'd in Greece. By Jove himself!
It makes the consuls base; and my soul aches
To know, when two authorities are up, 108
Neither supreme, how soon confusion
May enter 'twixt the gap of both and take
The one by the other.
    Com.   Well, on to the market-place.
    Cor. Whoever gave that counsel, to give forth
The corn o' the store-house gratis, as 'twas us'd
Sometime in Greece,—
    Men.   Well, well; no more of that.
    Cor. Though there the people had more
absolute power,
I say, they nourish'd disobedience, fed 116
The ruin of the state.
    Bru.   Why, shall the people give
One that speaks thus their voice?
    Cor.   I'll give my reasons,
More worthier than their voices. They know
the corn 119
Was not our recompense, resting well assur'd
They ne'er did service for 't. Being press'd to
the war,
Even when the navel of the state was touch'd,
They would not thread the gates: this kind of
service 123
Did not deserve corn gratis. Being i' the war,
Their mutinies and revolts, wherein they show'd
Most valour, spoke not for them. The accusa-
tion
Which they have often made against the senate,
All cause unborn, could never be the motive 128
Of our so frank donation. Well, what then?
How shall this bisson multitude digest
The senate's courtesy? Let deeds express
What's like to be their words: 'We did request
it; 132
We are the greater poll, and in true fear
They gave us our demands.' Thus we debase
The nature of our seats, and make the rabble
Call our cares, fears; which will in time break
ope 136
The locks o' the senate, and bring in the crows
To peck the eagles.
    Men.   Come, enough.
    Bru. Enough, with over-measure.
    Cor.   No, take more:
What may be sworn by, both divine and human,
Seal what I end withal! This double worship,141
Where one part does disdain with cause, the
other
Insult without all reason; where gentry, title,
wisdom,
Cannot conclude, but by the yea and no 144
Of general ignorance,—it must omit
Real necessities, and give way the while
To unstable slightness: purpose so barr'd, it
follows
Nothing is done to purpose. Therefore, beseech
you,— 148
You that will be less fearful than discreet,
That love the fundamental part of state
More than you doubt the change on 't, that
prefer

A noble life before a long, and wish 152
To jump a body with a dangerous physic
That's sure of death without it, at once pluck out
The multitudinous tongue; let them not lick
The sweet which is their poison. Your dis-
honour 156
Mangles true judgment, and bereaves the state
Of that integrity which should become it,
Not having the power to do the good it would,
For the ill which doth control 't.
    Bru.   He has said enough. 160
    Sic. He has spoken like a traitor, and shall
answer
As traitors do.
    Cor. Thou wretch! despite o'erwhelm thee!
What should the people do with these bald
tribunes? 164
On whom depending, their obedience fails
To the greater bench. In a rebellion,
When what's not meet, but what must be, was
law,
Then were they chosen: in a better hour, 168
Let what is meet be said it must be meet,
And throw their power i' the dust.
    Bru. Manifest treason!
    Sic.   This a consul? no.
    Bru. The ædiles, ho! Let him be appre-
hended. 172

Enter an Ædile.

    Sic. Go, call the people; [*Exit Ædile*] in
whose name, myself
Attach thee as a traitorous innovator,
A foe to the public weal: obey, I charge thee,
And follow to thine answer.
    Cor.   Hence, old goat! 176
    Sen. We'll surety him.
    Com.   Aged sir, hands off.
    Cor. Hence, rotten thing! or I shall shake
thy bones
Out of thy garments.
    Sic.   Help, ye citizens!

*Re-enter Ædiles, with Others, and a rabble of
Citizens.*

    Men. On both sides more respect. 180
    Sic. Here's he that would take from you all
your power.
    Bru. Seize him, ædiles!
    Citizens. Down with him!—down with him!—
    Sen. Weapons!—weapons!—weapons!—184
    [*They all bustle about* CORIOLANUS, *crying*
Tribunes!—patricians!—citizens!—What ho!—
Sicinius!—Brutus!—Coriolanus!—Citizens!
Peace!—Peace!—Peace!—Stay!—Hold!—Peace!
    Men. What is about to be?—I am out of
breath; 188
Confusion's near; I cannot speak. You, tri-
bunes
To the people! Coriolanus, patience!
Speak, good Sicinius.
    Sic.   Hear me, people; peace!
    Citizens. Let's hear our tribune:—Peace!—
Speak, speak, speak. 192
    Sic. You are at point to lose your liberties:

Marcius would have all from you; Marcius,
Whom late you have nam'd for consul.
Men.   Fie, fie, fie!
This is the way to kindle, not to quench. 196
First Sen. To unbuild the city and to lay all
flat.
Sic. What is the city but the people?
Citizens.   True,
The people are the city.
Bru. By the consent of all, we were establish'd
The people's magistrates.
Citizens.   You so remain. 201
Men. And so are like to do.
Com. That is the way to lay the city flat;
To bring the roof to the foundation,   204
And bury all, which yet distinctly ranges,
In heaps and piles of ruin.
Sic.   This deserves death.
Bru. Or let us stand to our authority,
Or let us lose it. We do here pronounce, 208
Upon the part o' the people, in whose power
We were elected theirs, Marcius is worthy
Of present death.
Sic.   Therefore lay hold of him;
Bear him to the rock Tarpeian, and from thence
Into destruction cast him.
Bru.   Ædiles, seize him! 213
Citizens. Yield, Marcius, yield!
Men.   Hear me one word;
Beseech you, tribunes, hear me but a word.
Æd. Peace, peace!   216
Men. Be that you seem, truly your country's
friends,
And temperately proceed to what you would
Thus violently redress.
Bru.   Sir, those cold ways,
That seem like prudent helps, are very poisonous
Where the disease is violent. Lay hands upon
him,   221
And bear him to the rock.
Cor.   No, I'll die here.
                        [*Drawing his sword.*
There's some among you have beheld me fight-
ing:
Come, try upon yourselves what you have seen
me.   224
Men. Down with that word! Tribunes, with-
draw awhile.
Bru. Lay hands upon him.
Men.   Help Marcius, help,
You that be noble; help him, young and old!
Citizens. Down with him!—down with him!
    [*In this mutiny the Tribunes, the Ædiles,
                and the People are beat in.*
Men. Go, get you to your house; be gone,
away!   229
All will be naught else.
Sec. Sen.   Get you gone.
Cor.   Stand fast;
We have as many friends as enemies.
Men. Shall it be put to that?
First Sen.   The gods forbid!
I prithee, noble friend, home to thy house; 233
Leave us to cure this cause.
Men.   For 'tis a sore upon us,
You cannot tent yourself: be gone, beseech you.

Com. Come, sir, along with us.   236
Cor. I would they were barbarians,—as they
are,
Though in Rome litter'd,—not Romans,—as
they are not,
Though calv'd i' the porch o' the Capitol,—
Men.   Be gone;
Put not your worthy rage into your tongue; 240
One time will owe another.
Cor.   On fair ground
I could beat forty of them.
Men.   I could myself
Take up a brace o' the best of them; yea, the
two tribunes.
Com. But now 'tis odds beyond arithmetic;
And manhood is call'd foolery when it stands 245
Against a falling fabric. Will you hence,
Before the tag return? whose rage doth rend
Like interrupted waters and o'erbear   248
What they are us'd to bear.
Men.   Pray you, be gone.
I'll try whether my old wit be in request
With those that have but little: this must be
patch'd
With cloth of any colour.
Com.   Nay, come away. 252
[*Exeunt* CORIOLANUS, COMINIUS, *and Others.*
First Pat. This man has marr'd his fortune.
Men. His nature is too noble for the world:
He would not flatter Neptune for his trident,
Or Jove for's power to thunder. His heart's his
mouth: 256
What his breast forges, that his tongue must
vent;
And, being angry, does forget that ever
He heard the name of death. [*A noise within.*
Here's goodly work!
Sec. Pat.   I would they were a-bed!
Men. I would they were in Tiber! What the
vengeance!   261
Could he not speak 'em fair?

Re-enter BRUTUS *and* SICINIUS, *with the rabble.*

Sic.   Where is this viper
That would depopulate the city and
Be every man himself?
Men.   You worthy tribunes,—
Sic. He shall be thrown down the Tarpeian
rock   265
With rigorous hands: he hath resisted law,
And therefore law shall scorn him further trial
Than the severity of the public power, 268
Which he so sets at nought.
First Cit.   He shall well know
The noble tribunes are the people's mouths,
And we their hands.
Citizens.   He shall, sure on't.
Men.   Sir, sir,—
Sic. Peace!   272
Men. Do not cry havoc, where you should
but hunt
With modest warrant.
Sic.   Sir, how comes 't that you
Have holp to make this rescue?
Men.   Hear me speak:
As I do know the consul's worthiness,   275

So can I name his faults.

Sic.   Consul! what consul?

Men. The Consul Coriolanus.

Bru.   He consul!

Citizens. No, no, no, no, no.

Men. If, by the tribunes' leave, and yours,
  good people,   280
I may be heard, I would crave a word or two,
The which shall turn you to no further harm
Than so much loss of time.

Sic.   Speak briefly then;
For we are peremptory to dispatch   284
This viperous traitor. To eject him hence
Were but one danger, and to keep him here
Our certain death; therefore it is decreed
He dies to-night.

Men.   Now the good gods forbid   288
That our renowned Rome, whose gratitude
Towards her deserved children is enroll'd
In Jove's own book, like an unnatural dam
Should now eat up her own!   292

Sic. He's a disease that must be cut away.

Men. O! he's a limb that has but a disease;
Mortal to cut it off; to cure it easy.
What has he done to Rome that's worthy
  death?   296
Killing our enemies, the blood he hath lost,—
Which, I dare vouch, is more than that he hath
By many an ounce,—he dropp'd it for his coun-
  try;
And what is left, to lose it by his country, 300
Were to us all, that do't and suffer it,
A brand to th' end o' the world.

Sic.   This is clean kam.

Bru. Merely awry: when he did love his
  country
It honour'd him.

Men.   The service of the foot   304
Being once gangren'd, is not then respected
For what before it was.

Bru.   We'll hear no more.
Pursue him to his house, and pluck him thence,
Lest his infection, being of catching nature, 308
Spread further.

Men.   One word more, one word.
This tiger-footed rage, when it shall find
The harm of unscann'd swiftness, will, too late,
Tie leaden pounds to's heels. Proceed by pro-
  cess;   312
Lest parties—as he is belov'd—break out,
And sack great Rome with Romans.

Bru.   If 'twere so,—

Sic. What do ye talk?
Have we not had a taste of his obedience? 316
Our aediles smote? ourselves resisted? Come!

Men. Consider this: he has been bred i' the
  wars
Since he could draw a sword, and is ill school'd
In bolted language; meal and bran together 320
He throws without distinction. Give me leave,
I'll go to him, and undertake to bring him
Where he shall answer by a lawful form,—
In peace,—to his utmost peril.

First Sen.   Noble tribunes, 324
It is the humane way: the other course
Will prove too bloody, and the end of it

Unknown to the beginning.

Sic.   Noble Menenius
Be you then as the people's officer.   32
Masters, lay down your weapons.

Bru.   Go not home

Sic. Meet on the market-place. We'll atten
  you there:
Where, if you bring not Marcius, we'll procee
In our first way.   33

Men. I'll bring him to you.
[*To the* Senators.] Let me desire your company
  He must come,
Or what is worst will follow.

First Sen.   Pray you, let's to him
                                          [*Exeun*

SCENE II.—*The Same. A Room in* CORIO-
          LANUS'S *House.*

Enter CORIOLANUS *and* Patricians.

Cor. Let them pull all about mine ears; pre
  sent me
Death on the wheel, or at wild horses' heels;
Or pile ten hills on the Tarpeian rock,
That the precipitation might down stretch
Below the beam of sight; yet will I still
Be thus to them.

First Pat.   You do the nobler.

Cor. I muse my mother
Does not approve me further, who was wont
To call them woollen vassals, things created
To buy and sell with groats, to show bare head
In congregations, to yawn, be still, and wonder
When one but of my ordinance stood up   1
To speak of peace or war.

Enter VOLUMNIA.

                    I talk of you:
Why did you wish me milder? Would you have
  me
False to my nature? Rather say I play
The man I am.

Vol.   O! sir, sir, sir,   1
I would have had you put your power well on
Before you had worn it out.

Cor.   Let go.

Vol. You might have been enough the man
  you are
With striving less to be so: lesser had been 2
The thwarting of your dispositions if
You had not show'd them how you were dis-
  pos'd,
Ere they lack'd power to cross you.

Cor.   Let them hang.

Vol. Ay, and burn too.   24

Enter MENENIUS *and* Senators.

Men. Come, come; you have been too rough,
  something too rough;
You must return and mend it.

First Sen.   There's no remedy;
Unless, by not so doing, our good city
Cleave in the midst, and perish.

Vol.   Pray be counsell'd. 28
I have a heart of mettle apt as yours,
But yet a brain that leads my use of anger

o better vantage.
Men.   Well said, noble woman!
efore he should thus stoop to the herd, but
    that   32
he violent fit o' the time craves it as physic
or the whole state, I would put mine armour on,
'hich I can scarcely bear.
Cor.   What must I do?
Men. Return to the tribunes.
Cor.   Well, what then? what then? 36
Men. Repent what you have spoke.
Cor. For them! I cannot do it to the gods;
'ust I then do 't to them?
Vol.   You are too absolute;
hough therein you can never be too noble, 40
ut when extremities speak. I have heard you
    say,
onour and policy, like unsever'd friends,
the war do grow together: grant that, and
    tell me,
a peace what each of them by th' other lose, 44
hat they combine not there.
Cor.   Tush, tush!
Men.   A good demand.
Vol. If it be honour in your wars to seem
he same you are not,—which, for your best
    ends,
ou adopt your policy,—how is it less or worse,
hat it shall hold companionship in peace 49
/ith honour, as in war, since that to both
    stands in like request?
Cor.   Why force you this?
Vol. Because that now it lies you on to
    speak   52
o the people; not by your own instruction,
or by the matter which your heart prompts
    you,
ut with such words that are but rooted in
our tongue, though but bastards and syllables
f no allowance to your bosom's truth.   57
ow, this no more dishonours you at all
han to take in a town with gentle words,
/hich else would put you to your fortune and
he hazard of much blood.   61
would dissemble with my nature where
'ly fortunes and my friends at stake requir'd
should do so in honour: I am in this,   64
our wife, your son, these senators, the nobles;
nd you will rather show our general louts
ow you can frown than spend a fawn upon
    'em,
or the inheritance of their loves and safe-
    guard   68
f what that want might ruin.
Men.   Noble lady!
'ome, go with us; speak fair; you may salve so,
'ot what is dangerous present, but the loss
f what is past.
Vol.   I prithee now, my son,   72
'io to them, with this bonnet in thy hand;
nd thus far having stretch'd it,—here be with
    them,
hy knee bussing the stones,—for in such busi-
    ness
ction is eloquence, and the eyes of the igno-
    rant   76

More learned than the ears,—waving thy head,
Which often, thus, correcting thy stout heart,
Now humble as the ripest mulberry
That will not hold the handling: or say to them,
Thou art their soldier, and being bred in broils
Hast not the soft way which, thou dost confess
Were fit for thee to use as they to claim,
In asking their good loves; but thou wilt frame
Thyself, forsooth, hereafter theirs, so far   85
As thou hast power and person.
Men.   This but done,
Even as she speaks, why, their hearts were
    yours;
For they have pardons, being ask'd, as free 88
As words to little purpose.
Vol.   Prithee now,
Go, and be rul'd; although I know thou hadst
    rather
Follow thine enemy in a fiery gulf
Than flatter him in a bower. Here is Cominius.

Enter COMINIUS.

Com. I have been i' the market-place; and,
    sir, 'tis fit   93
You make strong party, or defend yourself
By calmness or by absence: all's in anger.
Men. Only fair speech.
Com.   I think 'twill serve if he 96
Can thereto frame his spirit.
Vol.   He must, and will.
Prithee now, say you will, and go about it.
Cor. Must I go show them my unbarbed
    sconce?
Must I with my base tongue give to my noble
    heart   100
A lie that it must bear? Well, I will do 't:
Yet, were there but this single plot to lose,
This mould of Marcius, they to dust should
    grind it,
And throw 't against the wind. To the market-
    place!   104
You have put me now to such a part which
    never
I shall discharge to the life.
Com.   Come, come, we'll prompt you.
Vol. I prithee now, sweet son, as thou hast
    said
My praises made thee first a soldier, so,   108
To have my praise for this, perform a part
Thou hast not done before.
Cor.   Well, I must do 't:
Away, my disposition, and possess me
Some harlot's spirit! My throat of war be
    turn'd,
Which quired with my drum, into a pipe   113
Small as a eunuch, or the virgin voice
That babies lulls asleep! The smiles of knaves
Tent in my cheeks, and school-boys' tears take
    up   116
The glasses of my sight! A beggar's tongue
Make motion through my lips, and my arm'd
    knees,
Who bow'd but in my stirrup, bend like his
That hath receiv'd an alms! I will not do 't, 120
Lest I surcease to honour mine own truth,
And by my body's action teach my mind

A most inherent baseness.

Vol.   At thy choice then:
To beg of thee it is my more dishonour   124
Than thou of them. Come all to ruin; let
Thy mother rather feel thy pride than fear
Thy dangerous stoutness, for I mock at death
With as big heart as thou. Do as thou list, 128
Thy valiantness was mine, thou suck'dst it
   from me,
But owe thy pride thyself.

Cor.   Pray, be content:
Mother, I am going to the market-place;
Chide me no more. I'll mountebank their
  loves,   132
Cog their hearts from them, and come home
  belov'd
Of all the trades in Rome. Look, I am going:
Commend me to my wife. I'll return consul,
Or never trust to what my tongue can do 136
I' the way of flattery further.

Vol.   Do your will. [*Exit.*

Com. Away! the tribunes do attend you:
  arm yourself
To answer mildly; for they are prepar'd
With accusations, as I hear, more strong 140
Than are upon you yet.

Men. The word is 'mildly.'

Cor.   Pray you, let us go:
Let them accuse me by invention, I
Will answer in mine honour.

Men.   Ay, but mildly. 144

Cor. Well, mildly be it then. Mildly!
                    [*Exeunt.*

SCENE III.—*The Same. The Forum.*

Enter SICINIUS *and* BRUTUS.

Bru. In this point charge him home, that he
  affects
Tyrannical power: if he evade us there,
Enforce him with his envy to the people,
And that the spoil got on the Antiates   4
Was ne'er distributed.—

Enter an ÆDILE.

What, will he come?

Æd.   He's coming.

Bru.   How accompanied?

Æd. With old Menenius, and those senators
That always favour'd him.

Sic.   Have you a catalogue 8
Of all the voices that we have procur'd,
Set down by the poll?

Æd.   I have; 'tis ready.

Sic. Have you collected them by tribes?

Æd.   I have.

Sic. Assemble presently the people hither; 12
And when they hear me say, 'It shall be so,
I' the right and strength o' the commons,' be it
  either
For death, for fine, or banishment, then let
  them,
If I say, fine, cry 'fine,'—if death, cry 'death,' 16
Insisting on the old prerogative
And power i' the truth o' the cause.

Æd.   I shall inform them.

Bru. And when such time they have beg
  to cry,
Let them not cease, but with a din confus'd
Enforce the present execution
Of what we chance to sentence.

Æd.   Very well.

Sic. Make them be strong and ready for th
  hint,
When we shall hap to give't them.

Bru.   Go about it.
                [*Exit Ædi*
Put him to choler straight. He hath been us
Ever to conquer, and to have his worth
Of contradiction: being once chaf'd, he cann
Be rein'd again to temperance; then he spea
What's in his heart; and that is there whi
  looks
With us to break his neck.

Sic.   Well, here he com

Enter CORIOLANUS, MENENIUS, COMINIUS,
  Senators, *and* Patricians.

Men. Calmly, I do beseech you.

Cor. Ay, as an ostler, that for the poor
  piece
Will bear the knave by the volume. T
  honour'd gods
Keep Rome in safety, and the chairs of justi
Supplied with worthy men! plant love among u
Throng our large temples with the shows
  peace,
And not our streets with war!

First Sen.   Amen, amen

Men. A noble wish.

Re-enter ÆDILE, *with* Citizens.

Sic.   Draw near, ye peopl

Æd. List to your tribunes; audience; peac
  I say.

Cor. First, hear me speak.

Both Tri.   Well, say. Peace, ho!

Cor. Shall I be charg'd no further than th
  present?
Must all determine here?

Sic.   I do demand,
If you submit you to the people's voices,
Allow their officers, and are content
To suffer lawful censure for such faults
As shall be prov'd upon you?

Cor.   I am content.

Men. Lo! citizens, he says he is content:
The war-like service he has done, conside
  think
Upon the wounds his body bears, which sho
Like graves i' the holy churchyard.

Cor.   Scratches with brie
Scars to move laughter only.

Men.   Consider furthe
That when he speaks not like a citizen,
You find him like a soldier: do not take
His rougher accents for malicious sounds,
But, as I say, such as become a soldier,
Rather than envy you.

Com.   Well, well; no more.

Cor. What is the matter,
That being pass'd for consul with full voice

m so dishonour'd that the very hour
ou take it off again?
Sic.　　　　　　　　Answer to us.　60
Cor. Say, then: 'tis true, I ought so.
Sic. We charge you, that you have contriv'd
　to take
om Rome all season'd office, and to wind
ourself into a power tyrannical;　64
or which you are a traitor to the people.
Cor. How! Traitor!
Men.　　Nay, temperately; your promise.
Cor. The fires i' the lowest hell fold-in the
　people!
all me their traitor! Thou injurious tribune!
ithin thine eyes sat twenty thousand deaths,
thy hands clutch'd as many millions, in
ay lying tongue both numbers, I would say
hou liest' unto thee with a voice as free　72
s I do pray the gods.
Sic.　　　　　　Mark you this, people?
Citizens. To the rock!—to the rock with him!
Sic.　　　　　　　　Peace!
e need not put new matter to his charge:
hat you have seen him do, and heard him
　speak,　76
eating your officers, cursing yourselves,
pposing laws with strokes, and here defying
hose whose great power must try him; even
　this,
o criminal and in such capital kind,　80
eserves the extremest death.
Bru.　　　　　　But since he hath
rv'd well for Rome,—
Cor.　　　　What do you prate of service?
Bru. I talk of that, that know it.
Cor.　　　　　　　　You!
Men. Is this the promise that you made your
　mother?　84
Com. Know, I pray you,—
Cor.　　　　　　I'll know no further:
et them pronounce the steep Tarpeian death,
agabond exile, flaying, pent to linger
ut with a grain a day, I would not buy　88
heir mercy at the price of one fair word,
or check my courage for what they can give,
o have 't with saying 'Good morrow.'
Sic.　　　　　　For that he has,—
s much as in him lies,—from time to time　92
nvied against the people, seeking means
o pluck away their power, as now at last
iven hostile strokes, and that not in the pre-
　sence
f dreaded justice, but on the ministers　96
hat do distribute it; in the name o' the people,
nd in the power of us the tribunes, we,
ven from this instant, banish him our city,
a peril of precipitation　100
rom off the rock Tarpeian, never more
o enter our Rome gates: i' the people's name,
say, it shall be so.
Citizens. It shall be so,—It shall be so,—Let
　him away.—　104
e's banish'd, and it shall be so.
Com. Hear me, my masters, and my com-
　mon friends,—
Sic. He's sentenc'd; no more hearing.

Com.　　　　　　Let me speak:
I have been consul, and can show for Rome 108
Her enemies' marks upon me. I do love
My country's good with a respect more tender,
More holy, and profound, than mine own life,
My dear wife's estimate, her womb's increase,
And treasure of my loins; then if I would 113
Speak that—
Sic.　　We know your drift: speak what?
Bru. There's no more to be said, but he is
　banish'd,
As enemy to the people and his country: 116
It shall be so.
Citizens.　　It shall be so,—it shall be so.
Cor. You common cry of curs! whose breath
　I hate
As reek o' the rotten fens, whose loves I prize
As the dead carcases of unburied men　120
That do corrupt my air, I banish you;
And here remain with your uncertainty!
Let every feeble rumour shake your hearts!
Your enemies, with nodding of their plumes, 124
Fan you into despair! Have the power still
To banish your defenders; till at length
Your ignorance,—which finds not, till it feels,—
Making but reservation of yourselves,—　128
Still your own foes,—deliver you as most
Abated captives to some nation
That won you without blows! Despising,
For you, the city, thus I turn my back:　132
There is a world elsewhere.
　[Exeunt CORIOLANUS, COMINIUS, MENENIUS,
　　　　　　Senators, and Patricians.
Æd. The people's enemy is gone, is gone!
Citizens. Our enemy is banish'd!—he is
　gone!—Hoo! hoo!
　　[They all shout and throw up their caps.
Sic. Go, see him out at gates, and follow him,
As he hath follow'd you, with all despite; 137
Give him deserv'd vexation. Let a guard
Attend us through the city.
Citizens. Come, come,—let us see him out at
　gates! come!　140
The gods preserve our noble tribunes! Come!
　　　　　　　　　　[Exeunt.

ACT IV

SCENE I.—*Rome. Before a Gate of the City.*

Enter CORIOLANUS, VOLUMNIA, VIRGILIA, MENE-
　NIUS, COMINIUS, *and several young* Patricians.

Cor. Come, leave your tears: a brief farewell:
　the beast
With many heads butts me away. Nay, mother,
Where is your ancient courage? you were us'd,
To say extremity was the trier of spirits;　4
That common chances common men could bear;
That when the sea was calm all boats alike
Show'd mastership in floating; fortune's blows,
When most struck home, being gentle wounded,
　craves　8
A noble cunning: you were us'd to load me
With precepts that would make invincible
The heart that conn'd them.
Vir. O heavens! O heavens!
Cor.　　　　　　Nay, I prithee, woman,—

Vol. Now the red pestilence strike all trades
in Rome,　　　　13
And occupations perish!
　Cor.　　　　What, what, what!
I shall be lov'd when I am lack'd. Nay, mother,
Resume that spirit, when you were wont to say,
If you had been the wife of Hercules,　　17
Six of his labours you'd have done, and sav'd
Your husband so much sweat. Cominius,
Droop not; adieu. Farewell, my wife! my
mother!　　　　20
I'll do well yet. Thou old and true Menenius,
Thy tears are salter than a younger man's.
And venomous to thine eyes. My sometime
general,
I have seen thee stern, and thou hast oft beheld
Heart-hardening spectacles; tell these sad
women　　25
'Tis fond to wail inevitable strokes
As 'tis to laugh at them. My mother, you wot
well
My hazards still have been your solace; and 28
Believe 't not lightly,—though I go alone
Like to a lonely dragon, that his fen
Makes fear'd and talk'd of more than seen,—
your son
Will or exceed the common or be caught　　32
With cautelous baits and practice.
　Vol.　　　　My first son,
Whither wilt thou go? Take good Cominius
With thee awhile: determine on some course,
More than a wild exposture to each chance 36
That starts i' the way before thee.
　Cor.　　　　O the gods!
　Com. I'll follow thee a month, devise with
thee
Where thou shalt rest, that thou mayst hear of us,
And we of thee: so, if the time thrust forth 40
A cause for thy repeal, we shall not send
O'er the vast world to seek a single man,
And lose advantage, which doth ever cool
I' the absence of the needer.
　Cor.　　　　Fare ye well:　　44
Thou hast years upon thee; and thou art too full
Of the wars' surfeits, to go rove with one
That's yet unbruis'd: bring me but out at gate.
Come, my sweet wife, my dearest mother, and 48
My friends of noble touch, when I am forth,
Bid me farewell, and smile. I pray you, come.
While I remain above the ground you shall
Hear from me still; and never of me aught 52
But what is like me formerly.
　Men.　　　　That's worthily
As any ear can hear. Come, let's not weep.
If I could shake off but one seven years
From these old arms and legs, by the good gods,
I'd with thee every foot.
　Cor.　　　　Give me thy hand:　57
Come.　　　　[Exeunt.

SCENE II.—The Same. A Street near
the Gate.

Enter SICINIUS, BRUTUS, and an Ædile.

　Sic. Bid them all home; he's gone, and we'll
no further.

The nobility are vex'd, whom we see have side
In his behalf.
　Bru.　　　　Now we have shown our powe
Let us seem humbler after it is done
Than when it was a-doing.
　Sic.　　　　Bid them home;
Say their great enemy is gone, and they
Stand in their ancient strength.
　Bru.　　　　Dismiss them hom
　　　　[Exit Ædil

Enter VOLUMNIA, VIRGILIA, and MENENIUS.
Here comes his mother.
　Sic.　　　　Let's not meet her.
　Bru.　　　　Wh
　Sic. They say she's mad.
　Bru. They have ta'en note of us: keep c
your way.
　Vol. O! you're well met. The hoarded plagu
o' the gods
Requite your love!
　Men.　　　　Peace, peace! be not so lou
　Vol. If that I could for weeping, you shou
hear,—
Nay, and you shall hear some. [To BRUTUS
Will you be gone?
　Vir. [To SICINIUS.] You shall stay too.
would I had the power
To say so to my husband.
　Sic.　　　　Are you mankind?
　Vol. Ay, fool; is that a shame? Note b
this fool.
Was not a man my father? Hadst thou foxsh
To banish him that struck more blows for Rom
Than thou hast spoken words?
　Sic.　　　　O blessed heavens
　Vol. More noble blows than ever thou wi
words;
And for Rome's good. I'll tell thee what; y
go:
Nay, but thou shalt stay too: I would my so
Were in Arabia, and thy tribe before him,
His good sword in his hand.
　Sic.　　　　What then?
　Vir.　　　　What then
He'd make an end of thy posterity.
　Vol. Bastards and all.
Good man, the wounds that he does bear fo
Rome!
　Men. Come, come: peace!
　Sic. I would he had continu'd to his countr
As he began, and not unknit himself
The noble knot he made.
　Bru.　　　　I would he had.
　Vol. 'I would he had!' 'Twas you incens
the rabble:
Cats, that can judge as fitly of his worth
As I can of those mysteries which heaven
Will not have earth to know.
　Bru.　　　　Pray, let us go.
　Vol. Now, pray, sir, get you gone:
You have done a brave deed. Ere you go, hea
this:
As far as doth the Capitol exceed
The meanest house in Rome, so far my son,—
This lady's husband here, this, do you see,—

...om you have banish'd, does exceed you all.
Bru. Well, well, we'll leave you.
Sic.   Why stay we to be baited
th one that wants her wits?
Vol.   Take my prayers with you.
                                    [*Exeunt* Tribunes.
...ould the gods had nothing else to do   45
... to confirm my curses! Could I meet 'em
... once a day, it would unclog my heart
... what lies heavy to 't.
Men.   You have told them home,
...d, by my troth, you have cause. You'll sup
... with me?   49
Vol. Anger's my meat; I sup upon myself,
...d so shall starve with feeding. Come, let's
... go.
...ave this faint puling and lament as I do, 52
... anger, Juno-like. Come, come, come.
Men. Fie, fie, fie!   [*Exeunt.*

SCENE III.—*A Highway between Rome and Antium.*

Enter a Roman *and a* Volsce, *meeting.*

Rom. I know you well, sir, and you know
...: your name I think is Adrian.
Vols. It is so, sir: truly, I have forgot you.
Rom. I am a Roman; and my services are,
you are, against 'em: know you me yet? 5
Vols. Nicanor? No.
Rom. The same, sir.
Vols. You had more beard, when I last saw
...u; but your favour is well approved by your
...ngue. What's the news in Rome? I have a
...te from the Volscian state to find you out
...re: you have well saved me a day's journey.
Rom. There hath been in Rome strange in-
...rrections: the people against the senators,
...tricians: and nobles.   15
Vols. Hath been! Is it ended then? Our
...te thinks not so; they are in a most war-like
...eparation, and hope to come upon them in
... heat of their division.   19
Rom. The main blaze of it is past, but a small
...ing would make it flame again. For the nobles
...ceive so to heart the banishment of that
...rthy Coriolanus, that they are in a ripe apt-
...ss to take all power from the people and to
...uck from them their tribunes for ever. This
...s glowing, I can tell you, and is almost
...ature for the violent breaking out.
Vols. Coriolanus banished!   28
Rom. Banished, sir.
Vols. You will be welcome with this intelli-
...nce, Nicanor.   31
Rom. The day serves well for them now. I
...ve heard it said, the fittest time to corrupt a
...an's wife is when she's fallen out with her
...usband. Your noble Tullus Aufidius will
...ppear well in these wars, his great opposer,
...oriolanus, being now in no request of his
...untry.   38
Vols. He cannot choose. I am most for-
...unate, thus accidentally to encounter you: you
...ave ended my business, and I will merrily
...ccompany you home.   42

Rom. I shall, between this and supper, tell
you most strange things from Rome; all tending
to the good of their adversaries. Have you an
army ready, say you?   46
Vols. A most royal one: the centurions and
their charges distinctly billeted, already in the
entertainment, and to be on foot at an hour's
warning.   50
Rom. I am joyful to hear of their readiness,
and am the man, I think, that shall set them in
present action. So, sir, heartily well met, and
most glad of your company.
Vols. You take my part from me, sir; I have
the most cause to be glad of yours.   56
Rom. Well, let us go together.   [*Exeunt.*

SCENE IV.—*Antium. Before* AUFIDIUS' *House.*

Enter CORIOLANUS, *in mean apparel, disguised and muffled.*

Cor. A goodly city is this Antium. City,
'Tis I that made thy widows: many an heir
Of these fair edifices 'fore my wars
Have I heard groan and drop: then, know me
not,   4
Lest that thy wives with spits and boys with
stones
In puny battle slay me.

Enter a Citizen.

                              Save you, sir.
Cit. And you.
Cor.   Direct me, if it be your will,
Where great Aufidius lies. Is he in Antium? 8
Cit. He is, and feasts the nobles of the state
At his house this night.
Cor.   Which is his house, beseech you?
Cit. This, here before you.
Cor.   Thank you, sir. Farewell.
                                    [*Exit* Citizen.
O world! thy slippery turns. Friends now fast
sworn,   12
Whose double bosoms seem to wear one heart,
Whose hours, whose bed, whose meal, and
exercise,
Are still together, who twin, as 'twere, in love
Unseparable, shall within this hour,   16
On a dissension of a doit, break out
To bitterest enmity: so, fellest foes,
Whose passions and whose plots have broke
their sleep
To take the one the other, by some chance, 20
Some trick not worth an egg, shall grow dear
friends
And interjoin their issues. So with me:
My birth-place hate I, and my love's upon
This enemy town. I'll enter: if he slay me, 24
He does fair justice; if he give me way,
I'll do his country service.   [*Exit.*

SCENE V.—*The Same. A Hall in* AUFIDIUS' *House.*

Music within. Enter a Servingman.

First Serv. Wine, wine, wine! What service
is here! I think our fellows are asleep. [*Exit.*

Enter a Second Servingman.

Sec. Serv. Where's Cotus? my master calls
for him. Cotus! [*Exit.*

Enter CORIOLANUS.

Cor. A goodly house: the feast smells well;
but I 5
Appear not like a guest.

Re-enter the First Servingman.

First Serv. What would you have, friend?
Whence are you? Here's no place for you:
pray, go to the door. [*Exit.*
Cor. I have deserv'd no better entertain-
ment,
In being Coriolanus. 11

Re-enter Second Servingman.

Sec. Serv. Whence are you, sir? Has the
porter his eyes in his head, that he gives en-
trance to such companions? Pray, get you out.
Cor. Away!
Sec. Serv. 'Away!' Get you away. 16
Cor. Now, thou art troublesome.
Sec. Serv. Are you so brave? I'll have you
talked with anon.

Enter a Third Servingman. *Re-enter the First.*

Third Serv. What fellow's this? 20
First Serv. A strange one as ever I looked on:
I cannot get him out o' the house: prithee, call
my master to him.
Third Serv. What have you to do here,
fellow? Pray you, avoid the house. 25
Cor. Let me but stand; I will not hurt your
hearth.
Third Serv. What are you? 28
Cor. A gentleman.
Third Serv. A marvellous poor one.
Cor. True, so I am.
Third Serv. Pray you, poor gentleman, take
up some other station; here's no place for you;
pray you, avoid: come. 34
Cor. Follow your function; go, and batten
on cold bits. [*Pushes him away.*
Third Serv. What, you will not? Prithee,
tell my master what a strange guest he has here.
Sec. Serv. And I shall. [*Exit.*
Third Serv. Where dwell'st thou? 40
Cor. Under the canopy.
Third Serv. 'Under the canopy!'
Cor. Ay.
Third Serv. Where's that? 44
Cor. I' the city of kites and crows.
Third Serv. 'I' the city of kites and crows!'
What an ass it is! Then thou dwell'st with
daws too? 48
Cor. No; I serve not thy master.
Third Serv. How sir! Do you meddle with
my master?
Cor. Ay; 'tis an honester service than to
meddle with thy mistress. 53
Thou prat'st, and prat'st: serve with thy
trencher. Hence. [*Beats him away.*

Enter AUFIDIUS *and First* Servingman.

Auf. Where is this fellow?
Sec. Serv. Here, sir: I'd have beaten him l
a dog, but for disturbing the lords within.
Auf. Whence com'st thou? what woul
thou? Thy name?
Why speak'st not? Speak, man: what's
name?
Cor. [*Unmuffling.*] If, Tullus,
Not yet thou know'st me, and, seeing me, d
not
Think me for the man I am, necessity
Commands me name myself.
Auf. What is thy nan
[*Servants ret*
Cor. A name unmusical to the Volscians' ea
And harsh in sound to thine.
Auf. Say, what's thy name?
Thou hast a grim appearance, and thy face
Bears a command in't; though thy tackl
torn,
Thou show'st a noble vessel. What's thy nan
Cor. Prepare thy brow to frown. Know
thou me yet?
Auf. I know thee not. Thy name?
Cor. My name is Caius Marcius, who h
done
To thee particularly, and to all the Volsces,
Great hurt and mischief; thereto witness n
My surname, Coriolanus: the painful servi
The extreme dangers, and the drops of blo
Shed for my thankless country, are requited
But with that surname; a good memory,
And witness of the malice and displeasure
Which thou shouldst bear me: only that na
remains;
The cruelty and envy of the people,
Permitted by our dastard nobles, who
Have all forsook me, hath devour'd the res
And suffer'd me by the voice of slaves to b
Whoop'd out of Rome. Now this extremity
Hath brought me to thy hearth; not out of ho]
Mistake me not, to save my life; for if
I had fear'd death, of all the men i' the wo
I would have 'voided thee; but in mere spi
To be full quit of those my banishers,
Stand I before thee here. Then if thou hast
A heart of wreak in thee, that will revenge
Thine own particular wrongs and stop tho
maims
Of shame seen through thy country, speed tl
straight,
And make my misery serve thy turn: so use
That my revengeful services may prove
As benefits to thee, for I will fight
Against my canker'd country with the splee
Of all the under fiends. But if so be
Thou dar'st not this, and that to prove mc
fortunes
Thou art tir'd, then, in a word, I also am l
Longer to live most weary, and present
My throat to thee and to thy ancient malic
Which not to cut would show thee but a fo
Since I have ever follow'd thee with hate, l
Drawn tuns of blood out of thy country's brea

nd cannot live but to thy shame, unless
be to do thee service.
Auf. O Marcius, Marcius!
ch word thou hast spoke hath weeded from
  my heart 108
root of ancient envy. If Jupiter
ould from yond cloud speak divine things,
nd say, ''Tis true,' I'd not believe them more
an thee, all noble Marcius. Let me twine
ine arms about that body, where against 113
y grained ash a hundred times hath broke,
nd scarr'd the moon with splinters: here I clip
ue anvil of my sword, and do contest 116
s hotly and as nobly with thy love
s ever in ambitious strength I did
ntend against thy valour. Know thou first,
ov'd the maid I married; never man 120
gh'd truer breath; but that I see thee here,
nou noble thing! more dances my rapt heart
nan when I first my wedded mistress saw
stride my threshold. Why, thou Mars! I tell
  thee, 124
e have a power on foot; and I had purpose
nce more to hew thy target from thy brawn,
close mine arm for 't. Thou hast beat me out 127
welve several times, and I have nightly since
reamt of encounters 'twixt thyself and me;
e have been down together in my sleep,
nbuckling helms, fisting each other's throat,
nd wak'd half dead with nothing. Worthy
  Marcius, 132
ad we no quarrel else to Rome, but that
nou art thence banish'd, we would muster all
rom twelve to seventy, and, pouring war
to the bowels of ungrateful Rome, 136
ke a bold flood o'er-bear. O! come; go in,
nd take our friendly senators by the hands,
ho now are here, taking their leaves of me,
ho am prepar'd against your territories, 140
hough not for Rome itself.
Cor. You bless me, gods!
Auf. Therefore, most absolute sir, if thou
  wilt have
he leading of thine own revenges, take
he one half of my commission, and set down,
s best thou art experienc'd, since thou know'st
hy country's strength and weakness, thine own
  ways;
hether to knock against the gates of Rome,
r rudely visit them in parts remote, 148
o fright them, ere destroy. But come in:
et me commend thee first to those that shall
ay yea to thy desires. A thousand welcomes!
nd more a friend than e'er an enemy; 152
et, Marcius, that was much. Your hand:
  most welcome!
  [*Exeunt* CORIOLANUS *and* AUFIDIUS.
First Serv. [*Advancing.*] Here's a strange
  teration!
Sec. Serv. By my hand, I had thought to
ave strucken him with a cudgel; and yet my
ind gave me his clothes made a false report of
im. 159
First Serv. What an arm he has! He turned
ne about with his finger and his thumb, as one
ould set up a top.

Sec. Serv. Nay, I knew by his face that there
was something in him: he had, sir, a kind of face,
methought,—I cannot tell how to term it. 165
First Serv. He had so; looking as it were,—
would I were hanged but I thought there was
more in him than I could think. 168
Sec. Serv. So did I, I'll be sworn: he is simply
the rarest man i' the world.
First Serv. I think he is; but a greater
soldier than he you wot on. 172
Sec. Serv. Who? my master?
First Serv. Nay, it's no matter for that.
Sec. Serv. Worth six on him.
First Serv. Nay, not so neither; but I take
him to be the greater soldier. 177
Sec. Serv. Faith, look you, one cannot tell
how to say that: for the defence of a town our
general is excellent. 180
First Serv. Ay, and for an assault too.

Re-enter Third Servingman.

Third Serv. O slaves! I can tell you news;
news, you rascals.
First Serv. } What, what, what? let's partake.
Sec. Serv. }
Third Serv. I would not be a Roman, of all
nations; I had as lief be a condemned man. 186
First Serv. } Wherefore? wherefore?
Sec. Serv. }
Third Serv. Why, here's he that was wont to
thwack our general, Caius Marcius.
First Serv. Why do you say 'thwack our
general?' 191
Third Serv. I do not say, 'thwack our gene-
ral;' but he was always good enough for him.
Sec. Serv. Come, we are fellows and friends:
he was ever too hard for him; I have heard him
say so himself. 196
First Serv. He was too hard for him,—directly
to say the truth on't: before Corioli he scotched
him and notched him like a carbonado.
Sec. Serv. An he had been cannibally given,
he might have broiled and eaten him too. 201
First Serv. But, more of thy news.
Third Serv. Why, he is so made on here
within, as if he were son and heir to Mars; set
at upper end o' the table; no question asked
him by any of the senators, but they stand bald
before him. Our general himself makes a mistress
of him; sanctifies himself with 's hand, and turns
up the white o' the eye to his discourse. But the
bottom of the news is, our general is cut i' the
middle, and but one half of what he was yesterday, for the other has half, by the entreaty and
grant of the whole table. He'll go, he says, and
sowle the porter of Rome gates by the ears: he
will mow down all before him, and leave his
passage polled. 216
Sec. Serv. And he's as like to do't as any
man I can imagine.
Third Serv. Do't! he will do't; for—look
you, sir—he has as many friends as enemies;
which friends, sir—as it were—durst not—look
you, sir—show themselves—as we term it—his
friends, whilst he's in directitude.
First Serv. Directitude! what's that? 224

Sec. Serv. But when they shall see, sir, his crest up again, and the man in blood, they will out of their burrows, like conies after rain, and revel all with him.   228

First Serv. But when goes this forward?

Third Serv. To-morrow; to-day; presently. You shall have the drum struck up this afternoon; 'tis, as it were, a parcel of their feast, and to be executed ere they wipe their lips.   233

Sec. Serv. Why, then we shall have a stirring world again. This peace is nothing but to rust iron, increase tailors, and breed ballad-makers.

First Serv. Let me have war, say I; it exceeds peace as far as day does night; it's spritely, waking, audible, and full of vent. Peace is a very apoplexy, lethargy; mulled, deaf, sleepy, insensible; a getter of more bastard children than war's a destroyer of men.   242

Sec. Serv. 'Tis so: and as war, in some sort, may be said to be a ravisher, so it cannot be denied but peace is a great maker of cuckolds.

First Serv. Ay, and it makes men hate one another.   247

Third Serv. Reason: because they then less need one another. The wars for my money. I hope to see Romans as cheap as Volscians. They are rising, they are rising.   251

All. In, in, in, in!   [*Exeunt.*

SCENE VI.—*Rome. A Public Place.*

Enter SICINIUS *and* BRUTUS.

Sic. We hear not of him, neither need we fear him;
His remedies are tame i' the present peace
And quietness o' the people, which before
Were in wild hurry. Here do we make his friends   4
Blush that the world goes well, who rather had,
Though they themselves did suffer by 't, behold
Dissentious numbers pestering streets, than see
Our tradesmen singing in their shops and going
About their functions friendly.   9

Enter MENENIUS.

Bru. We stood to 't in good time. Is this Menenius?

Sic. 'Tis he, 'tis he. O! he is grown most kind Of late. Hail, sir!

Men.   Hail to you both!   12

Sic. Your Coriolanus is not much miss'd But with his friends: the commonwealth doth stand,
And so would do, were he more angry at it.

Men. All's well; and might have been much better, if   16
He could have temporiz'd.

Sic.   Where is he, hear you?

Men. Nay, I hear nothing: his mother and his wife
Hear nothing from him.

Enter three or four Citizens.

Citizens. The gods preserve you both!

Sic.   Good den, our neighbours.   20

Bru. Good den to you all, good den to you all.

First Cit. Ourselves, our wives, and children
on our knees,
Are bound to pray for you both.

Sic.   Live, and thriv

Bru. Farewell, kind neighbours: we wish Coriolanus
Had lov'd you as we did.

Citizens.   Now the gods keep yo

Sic. } Farewell, farewell. [*Exeunt Citizens*
Bru. }

Sic. This is a happier and more comely tir
Than when these fellows ran about the stree
Crying confusion.

Bru.   Caius Marcius was
A worthy officer i' the war; but insolent,
O'ercome with pride, ambitious past all thin
ing,
Self-loving,—

Sic.   And affecting one sole throne,
Without assistance.

Men.   I think not so.

Sic. We should by this, to all our lamentatio
If he had gone forth consul, found it so.

Bru. The gods have well prevented it, a
Rome
Sits safe and still without him.

Enter an ÆDILE.

Æd.   Worthy tribune
There is a slave, whom we have put in priso
Reports, the Volsces with two several powe
Are enter'd in the Roman territories,
And with the deepest malice of the war
Destroy what lies before them.

Men.   'Tis Aufidiu
Who, hearing of our Marcius' banishment,
Thrusts forth his horns again into the world;
Which were inshell'd when Marcius stood f
Rome,
And durst not once peep out.

Sic. Come, what talk you of Marcius?

Bru. Go see this rumourer whipp'd. It ca
not be
The Volsces dare break with us.

Men.   Cannot be!
We have record that very well it can,
And three examples of the like have been
Within my age. But reason with the fellow,
Before you punish him, where he heard this
Lest you shall chance to whip your informatio
And beat the messenger who bids beware
Of what is to be dreaded.

Sic.   Tell not me:
I know this cannot be.

Bru.   Not possible.

Enter a Messenger.

Mess. The nobles in great earnestness a
going
All to the senate-house: some news is come,
That turns their countenances.

Sic.   'Tis this slave.—
Go whip him 'fore the people's eyes: his raisin
Nothing but his report.

Mess.   Yes, worthy sir,
The slave's report is seconded; and more,

[M]ore fearful, is deliver'd.
Sic. What more fearful? 64
Mess. It is spoke freely out of many mouths—
[N]ow probable I do not know—that Marcius,
[J]oin'd with Aufidius, leads a power 'gainst
Rome,
[A]nd vows revenge as spacious as between 68
[t]he young'st and oldest thing.
Sic. This is most likely.
Bru. Rais'd only, that the weaker sort may
wish
[G]ood Marcius home again.
Sic. The very trick on 't.
Men. This is unlikely: 72
[H]e and Aufidius can no more atone,
[t]han violentest contrariety.

Enter another Messenger.

Sec. Mess. You are sent for to the senate:
[a] fearful army, led by Caius Marcius, 76
[a]ssociated with Aufidius, rages
[u]pon our territories; and have already
[o]'erborne their way, consum'd with fire, and
took
[w]hat lay before them. 80

Enter COMINIUS.

Com. O! you have made good work!
Men. What news? what news?
Com. You have holp to ravish your own
daughters, and
[t]o melt the city leads upon your pates,
[t]o see your wives dishonour'd to your noses,—
Men. What's the news? what's the news? 85
Com. Your temples burned in their cement,
and
[y]our franchises, whereon you stood, confin'd
[i]nto an auger's bore.
Men. Pray now, your news?—88
[y]ou have made fair work, I fear me. Pray, your
news?
[I]f Marcius should be join'd with Volscians,—
Com. If!
[H]e is their god: he leads them like a thing
[M]ade by some other deity than Nature, 92
[t]hat shapes man better; and they follow him,
[a]gainst us brats, with no less confidence
[t]han boys pursuing summer butterflies,
[o]r butchers killing flies.
Men. You have made good work, 96
[y]ou, and your apron-men; you that stood so
much
[U]pon the voice of occupation and
[t]he breath of garlic-eaters!
Com. He will shake
[y]our Rome about your ears.
Men. As Hercules 100
[D]id shake down mellow fruit. You have made
fair work!
Bru. But is this true, sir?
Com. Ay; and you'll look pale
[b]efore you find it other. All the regions
[D]o smilingly revolt; and who resist 104
[a]re mock'd for valiant ignorance,
[a]nd perish constant fools. Who is 't can blame
him?

Your enemies, and his, find something in him.
Men. We are all undone unless 108
The noble man have mercy.
Com. Who shall ask it?
The tribunes cannot do 't for shame; the people
Deserve such pity of him as the wolf
Does of the shepherds: for his best friends, if
they 112
Should say, 'Be good to Rome,' they charg'd
him even
As those should do that had deserv'd his hate,
And therein show'd like enemies.
Men. 'Tis true:
If he were putting to my house the brand 116
That should consume it, I have not the face
To say, 'Beseech you, cease.'—You have made
fair hands,
You and your crafts! you have crafted fair!
Com. You have brought
A trembling upon Rome, such as was never 120
So incapable of help.
Sic. } Say not we brought it.
Bru. }
Men. How! Was it we? We lov'd him; but,
like beasts
And cowardly nobles, gave way unto your
clusters,
Who did hoot him out o' the city.
Com. But I fear 124
They'll roar him in again. Tullus Aufidius,
The second name of men, obeys his points
As if he were his officer: desperation
Is all the policy, strength, and defence, 128
That Rome can make against them.

Enter a troop of Citizens.

Men. Here come the clusters.
And is Aufidius with him? You are they
That made the air unwholesome, when you
cast
Your stinking greasy caps in hooting at 132
Coriolanus' exile. Now he's coming;
And not a hair upon a soldier's head
Which will not prove a whip: as many cox-
combs
As you threw caps up will he tumble down, 136
And pay you for your voices. 'Tis no matter;
If he could burn us all into one coal,
We have deserv'd it.
Citizens. Faith, we hear fearful news.
First Cit. For mine own part,
When I said banish him, I said 'twas pity. 141
Sec. Cit. And so did I.
Third Cit. And so did I; and, to say the
truth, so did very many of us. That we did we
did for the best; and though we willingly con-
sented to his banishment, yet it was against our
will.
Com. You're goodly things, you voices!
Men. You have made
Good work, you and your cry! Shall's to the
Capitol? 149
Com. O! ay; what else?
[*Exeunt* COMINIUS *and* MENENIUS.
Sic. Go, masters, get you home; be not dis-
may'd:

These are a side that would be glad to have 152
This true which they so seem to fear. Go home,
And show no sign of fear.

First Cit. The gods be good to us! Come,
masters, let's home. I ever said we were i' the
wrong when we banished him.   157

Sec. Cit. So did we all. But come, let's home.
                              [*Exeunt* Citizens.

Bru. I do not like this news.
Sic. Nor I.   160
Bru. Let's to the Capitol. Would half my
    wealth
Would buy this for a lie!
Sic.   Pray let us go. [*Exeunt.*

SCENE VII.—*A Camp at a small distance
              from Rome.*

Enter AUFIDIUS *and his* Lieutenant.

Auf. Do they still fly to the Roman?
Lieu. I do not know what witchcraft's in
    him, but
Your soldiers use him as the grace 'fore meat,
Their talk at table, and their thanks at end; 4
And you are darken'd in this action, sir,
Even by your own.
Auf.   I cannot help it now,
Unless, by using means, I lame the foot
Of our design. He bears himself more proudlier,
Even to my person, than I thought he would 9
When first I did embrace him; yet his nature
In that's no changeling, and I must excuse
What cannot be amended.
Lieu.   Yet, I wish, sir,— 12
I mean for your particular,—you had not
Join'd in commission with him; but either
Had borne the action of yourself, or else
To him had left it solely.   16
Auf. I understand thee well; and be thou
    sure,
When he shall come to his account, he knows
    not
What I can urge against him. Although it
    seems,
And so he thinks, and is no less apparent 20
To the vulgar eye, that he bears all things fairly,
And shows good husbandry for the Volscian
    state,
Fights dragon-like, and does achieve as soon
As draw his sword; yet he hath left undone 24
That which shall break his neck or hazard mine,
Whene'er we come to our account.
Lieu. Sir, I beseech you, think you he'll carry
    Rome?
Auf. All places yield to him ere he sits down;
And the nobility of Rome are his: 29
The senators and patricians love him too:
The tribunes are no soldiers; and their people
Will be as rash in the repeal as hasty   32
To expel him thence. I think he'll be to Rome
As is the osprey to the fish, who takes it
By sovereignty of nature. First he was
A noble servant to them, but he could not 36
Carry his honours even; whether 'twas pride,
Which out of daily fortune ever taints
The happy man; whether defect of judgment,

To fail in the disposing of those chances 40
Which he was lord of; or whether nature,
Not to be other than one thing, not moving
From the casque to the cushion, but command-
    ing peace
Even with the same austerity and garb 44
As he controll'd the war; but one of these,
As he hath spices of them all, not all,
For I dare so far free him, made him fear'd,
So hated, and so banish'd: but he has a merit 48
To choke it in the utterance. So our virtues
Lie in the interpretation of the time;
And power, unto itself most commendable,
Hath not a tomb so evident as a chair 52
To extol what it hath done.
One fire drives out one fire; one nail, one nail;
Rights by rights falter, strengths by strengths
    do fail.
Come, let's away. When, Caius, Rome is thine,
Thou art poor'st of all; then shortly art thou
    mine.   [*Exeunt.*

ACT V

SCENE I.—*Rome. A Public Place.*

Enter MENENIUS, COMINIUS, SICINIUS, BRUTUS,
                and Others.

Men. No, I'll not go: you hear what he hath
    said
Which was sometime his general; who lov'd
    him
In a most dear particular. He call'd me father:
But what o' that? Go, you that banish'd him; 4
A mile before his tent fall down, and kneel
The way into his mercy. Nay, if he coy'd
To hear Cominius speak, I'll keep at home.
Com. He would not seem to know me.
Men.   Do you hear? 8
Com. Yet one time he did call me by my
    name.
I urg'd our old acquaintance, and the drops
That we have bled together. Coriolanus
He would not answer to; forbad all names; 12
He was a kind of nothing, titleless,
Till he had forg'd himself a name o' the fire
Of burning Rome.
Men. Why, so: you have made good work!
A pair of tribunes that have rack'd for Rome, 16
To make coals cheap: a noble memory!
Com. I minded him how royal 'twas to
    pardon
When it was less expected: he replied,
It was a bare petition of a state 20
To one whom they had punish'd.
Men.   Very well.
Could he say less?
Com. I offer'd to awaken his regard
For's private friends: his answer to me was, 24
He could not stay to pick them in a pile
Of noisome musty chaff: he said 'twas folly,
For one poor grain or two, to leave unburnt
And still to nose the offence.
Men.   For one poor grain or two! 28
I am one of those: his mother, wife, his child,
And this brave fellow too, we are the grains:
You are the musty chaff, and you are smelt

Above the moon. We must be burnt for you. 32
Sic. Nay, pray, be patient: if you refuse your
aid
in this so-never-needed help, yet do not
Upbraid 's with our distress. But, sure, if you
Would be your country's pleader, your good
tongue,   36
More than the instant army we can make,
Might stop our countryman.
Men.   No; I'll not meddle.
Sic. Pray you, go to him.
Men. What should I do?   40
Bru. Only make trial what your love can do
For Rome, towards Marcius.
Men.   Well; and say that Marcius
Return me, as Cominius is return'd,
Unheard; what then?   44
But as a discontented friend, grief-shot
With his unkindness? say 't be so?
Sic.   Yet your good will
Must have that thanks from Rome, after the
measure
As you intended well.
Men.   I'll undertake it: 48
I think he'll hear me. Yet, to bite his lip,
And hum at good Cominius, much unhearts me.
He was not taken well; he had not din'd:
The veins unfill'd, our blood is cold, and then 52
We pout upon the morning, are unapt
To give or to forgive; but when we have stuff'd
These pipes and these conveyances of our blood
With wine and feeding, we have supper souls 56
Than in our priest-like fasts: therefore, I'll
watch him
Till he be dieted to my request,
And then I'll set upon him.
Bru. You know the very road into his kind-
ness,   60
And cannot lose your way.
Men.   Good faith, I'll prove him,
Speed how it will. I shall ere long have know-
ledge
Of my success.   [*Exit.*
Com.   He'll never hear him.
Sic.   Not?
Com. I tell you he does sit in gold, his eye 64
Red as 'twould burn Rome, and his injury
The gaoler to his pity. I kneel'd before him;
'Twas very faintly he said 'Rise;' dismiss'd me
Thus, with his speechless hand: what he would
do   68
He sent in writing after me; what he would not,
Bound with an oath to yield to his conditions:
So that all hope is vain
Unless his noble mother and his wife,   72
Who, as I hear, mean to solicit him
For mercy to his country. Therefore let 's hence,
And with our fair entreaties haste them on.
                                    [*Exeunt.*

SCENE II.—*The Volscian Camp before Rome.
The Guards at their stations.*

            Enter to them, MENENIUS.

First Guard. Stay! whence are you?
Sec. Guard.   Stand! and go back.

Men. You guard like men; 'tis well; but, by
your leave,
I am an officer of state, and come
To speak with Coriolanus.
First Guard.   From whence?
Men.   From Rome.
First Guard. You may not pass; you must
return: our general   5
Will no more hear from thence.
Sec. Guard. You'll see your Rome embrac'd
with fire before
You'll speak with Coriolanus.
Men.   Good my friends,
If you have heard your general talk of Rome, 9
And of his friends there, it is lots to blanks
My name hath touch'd your ears: it is Mene-
nius.
First Guard. Be it so; go back: the virtue of
your name   12
Is not here passable.
Men.   I tell thee, fellow,
Thy general is my lover: I have been
The book of his good acts, whence men have
read
His fame unparallel'd, haply amplified;   16
For I have ever glorified my friends—
Of whom he 's chief—with all the size that verity
Would without lapsing suffer: nay, sometimes,
Like to a bowl upon a subtle ground,   20
I have tumbled past the throw, and in his praise
Have almost stamp'd the leasing. Therefore,
fellow,
I must have leave to pass.
First Guard. Faith, sir, if you had told as
many lies in his behalf as you have uttered words
in your own, you should not pass here; no,
though it were as virtuous to lie as to live
chastely. Therefore go back.   28
Men. Prithee, fellow, remember my name is
Menenius, always factionary on the party of
your general.
Sec. Guard. Howsoever you have been his
liar—as you say you have—I am one that,
telling true under him, must say you cannot
pass. Therefore go back.   35
Men. Has he dined, canst thou tell? for I
would not speak with him till after dinner.
First Guard. You are a Roman, are you?
Men. I am as thy general is.   39
First Guard. Then you should hate Rome, as
he does. Can you, when you have pushed out
your gates the very defender of them, and, in a
violent popular ignorance, given your enemy
your shield, think to front his revenges with the
easy groans of old women, the virginal palms of
your daughters, or with the palsied intercession
of such a decayed dotant as you seem to be?
Can you think to blow out the intended fire your
city is ready to flame in with such weak breath
as this? No, you are deceived; therefore, back
to Rome, and prepare for your execution: you
are condemned, our general has sworn you out
of reprieve and pardon.   53
Men. Sirrah, if thy captain knew I were here,
he would use me with estimation.
Sec. Guard. Come, my captain knows you not.

Men. I mean, thy general.   57

First Guard. My general cares not for you. Back, I say: go, lest I let forth your half-pint of blood; back, that's the utmost of your having: back.   61

Men. Nay, but, fellow, fellow,—

Enter CORIOLANUS *and* AUFIDIUS.

Cor. What's the matter?

Men. Now, you companion, I'll say an errand for you: you shall know now that I am in estimation; you shall perceive that a Jack guardant cannot office me from my son Coriolanus: guess, but by my entertainment with him, if thou standest not i' the state of hanging, or of some death more long in spectatorship, and crueller in suffering; behold now presently, and swound for what's to come upon thee. [*To* CORIOLANUS.] The glorious gods sit in hourly synod about thy particular prosperity, and love thee no worse than thy old father Menenius does! O my son! my son! thou art preparing fire for us; look thee, here's water to quench it. I was hardly moved to come to thee; but being assured none but myself could move thee, I have been blown out of your gates with sighs; and conjure thee to pardon Rome, and thy petitionary countrymen. The good gods assuage thy wrath, and turn the dregs of it upon this varlet here; this, who, like a block, hath denied my access to thee.   85

Cor. Away!

Men. How! away!

Cor. Wife, mother, child, I know not. My affairs   88
Are servanted to others: though I owe
My revenge properly, my remission lies
In Volscian breasts. That we have been familiar,
Ingrate forgetfulness shall poison, rather   92
Than pity note how much. Therefore, be gone:
Mine ears against your suits are stronger than
Your gates against my force. Yet, for I lov'd thee,
Take this along; I writ it for thy sake,   96
                 [*Gives a paper.*
And would have sent it. Another word, Menenius,
I will not hear thee speak. This man, Aufidius,
Was my belov'd in Rome: yet thou behold'st!   100

Auf. You keep a constant temper.
            [*Exeunt* CORIOLANUS *and* AUFIDIUS.

First Guard. Now, sir, is your name Menenius?

Sec. Guard. 'Tis a spell, you see, of much power. You know the way home again.

First Guard. Do you hear how we are shent for keeping your greatness back?   105

Sec. Guard. What cause, do you think, I have to swound?

Men. I neither care for the world, nor your general: for such things as you, I can scarce think there's any, ye're so slight. He that hath a will to die by himself fears it not from another. Let your general do his worst. For you, be that you are, long; and your misery increase with your age! I say to you, as I was said to, Away!
                           [*Exit.*

First Guard. A noble fellow, I warrant him.

Sec. Guard. The worthy fellow is our general: he is the rock, the oak not to be wind-shaken.
                       [*Exeunt.*

SCENE III.—*The Tent of* CORIOLANUS.

Enter CORIOLANUS, AUFIDIUS, *and Others.*

Cor. We will before the walls of Rome tomorrow
Set down our host. My partner in this action,
You must report to the Volscian lords, how plainly
I have borne this business.

Auf.   Only their ends   4
You have respected; stopp'd your ears against
The general suit of Rome; never admitted
A private whisper; no, not with such friends
That thought them sure of you.

Cor.   This last old man,   8
Whom with a crack'd heart I have sent to Rome,
Lov'd me above the measure of a father;
Nay, godded me indeed. Their latest refuge
Was to send him; for whose old love I have,   12
Though I show'd sourly to him, once more offer'd
The first conditions, which they did refuse,
And cannot now accept, to grace him only
That thought he could do more. A very little 16
I have yielded to; fresh embassies and suits,
Nor from the state, nor private friends, hereafter
Will I lend ear to. [*Shout within.*] Ha! what shout is this?
Shall I be tempted to infringe my vow   20
In the same time 'tis made? I will not.

Enter, in mourning habits, VIRGILIA, VOLUMNIA, *leading young* MARCIUS, VALERIA, *and Attendants.*

My wife comes foremost; then the honour'd mould
Wherein this trunk was fram'd, and in her hand
The grandchild to her blood. But out, affection!   24
All bond and privilege of nature, break!
Let it be virtuous to be obstinate.
What is that curtsy worth? or those doves' eyes,
Which can make gods forsworn? I melt, and am not   28
Of stronger earth than others. My mother bows,
As if Olympus to a molehill should
In supplication nod; and my young boy
Hath an aspect of intercession, which   32
Great nature cries, 'Deny not.' Let the Volsces
Plough Rome, and harrow Italy; I'll never
Be such a gosling to obey instinct, but stand
As if a man were author of himself   36
And knew no other kin.

Vir.   My lord and husband!

Cor. These eyes are not the same I wore in Rome.

Vir. The sorrow that delivers us thus chang'd Makes you think so.

Cor.   Like a dull actor now, 40
have forgot my part, and I am out,
'ven to a full disgrace. Best of my flesh,
'orgive my tyranny; but do not say
'or that, 'Forgive our Romans.' O! a kiss 44
.ong as my exile, sweet as my revenge!
Jow, by the jealous queen of heaven, that kiss
carried from thee, dear, and my true lip
Iath virgin'd it e'er since. You gods! I prate,
.nd the most noble mother of the world 49
.eave unsaluted. Sink, my knee, i' the earth;
                              [*Kneels.*
)f thy deep duty more impression show
han that of common sons.
Vol.   O! stand up bless'd; 52
Vhilst, with no softer cushion than the flint,
I kneel before thee, and unproperly
how duty, as mistaken all this while
ietween the child and parent.   [*Kneels.*
Cor.   What is this? 56
'our knees to me! to your corrected son!
'hen let the pebbles on the hungry beach
'illip the stars; then let the mutinous winds
itrike the proud cedars 'gainst the fiery sun, 60
Iurd'ring impossibility, to make
Vhat cannot be, slight work.
Vol.   Thou art my warrior;
holp to frame thee. Do you know this lady?
Cor. The noble sister of Publicola, 64
'he moon of Rome; chaste as the icicle
'hat's curdied by the frost from purest snow,
.nd hangs on Dian's temple: dear Valeria!
Vol. This is a poor epitome of yours, 68
                    [*Pointing to the* Child.
Vhich by the interpretation of full time
Iay show like all yourself.
Cor.   The god of soldiers,
Vith the consent of supreme Jove, inform
'hy thoughts with nobleness; that thou mayst
    prove   72
'o shame unvulnerable, and stick i' the wars
.ike a great sea-mark, standing every flaw,
.nd saving those that eye thee!
Vol.   Your knee, sirrah.
Cor. That's my brave boy! 76
Vol. Even he, your wife, this lady, and my-
    self,
.re suitors to you.
Cor.   I beseech you, peace:
)r, if you'd ask, remember this before:
'he things I have forsworn to grant may never
ie held by you denials. Do not bid me 81
)ismiss my soldiers, or capitulate
.gain with Rome's mechanics: tell me not
Vherein I seem unnatural: desire not 84
'o allay my rages and revenges with
'our colder reasons.
Vol.   O! no more, no more;
'ou have said you will not grant us any thing;
'or we have nothing else to ask but that 88
Vhich you deny already: yet we will ask;
'hat, if you fail in our request, the blame
Iay hang upon your hardness. Therefore,
    hear us.
Cor. Aufidius, and you Volsces, mark; for
    we'll   92

Hear nought from Rome in private. Your re-
    quest?
Vol. Should we be silent and not speak, our
    raiment
And state of bodies would bewray what life
We have led since thy exile. Think with thyself
How more unfortunate than all living women
Are we come hither: since that thy sight, which
    should   98
Make our eyes flow with joy, hearts dance with
    comforts,
Constrains them weep, and shake with fear and
    sorrow;   100
Making the mother, wife, and child to see
The son, the husband, and the father tearing
His country's bowels out. And to poor we
Thine enmity's most capital: thou barr'st us 104
Our prayers to the gods, which is a comfort
That all but we enjoy; for how can we,
Alas! how can we for our country pray,
Whereto we are bound, together with thy vic-
    tory,   108
Whereto we are bound? Alack! or we must lose
The country, our dear nurse, or else thy person,
Our comfort in the country. We must find
An evident calamity, though we had 112
Our wish, which side should win; for either thou
Must, as a foreign recreant, be led
With manacles through our streets, or else
Triumphantly tread on thy country's ruin, 116
And bear the palm for having bravely shed
Thy wife and children's blood. For myself, son,
I purpose not to wait on Fortune till
These wars determine: if I cannot persuade
    thee   120
Rather to show a noble grace to both parts
Than seek the end of one, thou shalt no sooner
March to assault thy country than to tread—
Trust to't, thou shalt not—on thy mother's
    womb,   124
That brought thee to this world.
Vir.   Ay, and mine,
That brought you forth this boy, to keep your
    name
Living to time.
Boy.   A' shall not tread on me:
I'll run away till I am bigger, but then I'll fight. 128
Cor. Not of a woman's tenderness to be,
Requires nor child nor woman's face to see.
I have sat too long.   [*Rising.*
Vol. Nay, go not from us thus.
If it were so, that our request did tend 132
To save the Romans, thereby to destroy
The Volsces whom you serve, you might con-
    demn us,
As poisonous of your honour: no; our suit
Is, that you reconcile them: while the Volsces
May say, 'This mercy we have show'd;' the
    Romans,   137
'This we receiv'd;' and each in either side
Give the all-hail to thee, and cry, 'Be bless'd
For making up this peace!' Thou know'st,
    great son,   140
The end of war's uncertain; but this certain,
That, if thou conquer Rome, the benefit
Which thou shalt thereby reap is such a name

Whose repetition will be dogg'd with curses; 144
Whose chronicle thus writ: 'The man was noble,
But with his last attempt he wip'd it out,
Destroy'd his country, and his name remains
To the ensuing age abhorr'd.' Speak to me,
   son!   148
Thou hast affected the fine strains of honour,
To imitate the graces of the gods;
To tear with thunder the wide cheeks o' the air,
And yet to charge the sulphur with a bolt 152
That should but rive an oak. Why dost not
   speak?
Think'st thou it honourable for a noble man
Still to remember wrongs? Daughter, speak
   you:
He cares not for your weeping. Speak thou,
   boy: 156
Perhaps thy childishness will move him more
Than can our reasons. There is no man in the
   world
More bound to's mother; yet here he lets me
   prate
Like one i' the stocks. Thou hast never in thy
   life   160
Show'd thy dear mother any courtesy;
When she—poor hen! fond of no second
   brood—
Has cluck'd thee to the wars, and safely home,
Loaden with honour. Say my request's unjust,
And spurn me back; but if it be not so, 165
Thou art not honest, and the gods will plague
   thee,
That thou restrain'st from me the duty which
To a mother's part belongs. He turns away:
Down, ladies; let us shame him with our knees.
To his surname Coriolanus 'longs more pride
Than pity to our prayers. Down: an end;
This is the last: so we will home to Rome, 172
And die among our neighbours. Nay, behold us.
This boy, that cannot tell what he would have,
But kneels and holds up hands for fellowship,
Does reason our petition with more strength 176
Than thou hast to deny 't. Come, let us go:
This fellow had a Volscian to his mother;
His wife is in Corioli, and his child
Like him by chance. Yet give us our dispatch:
I am hush'd until our city be a-fire, 181
And then I'll speak a little.

   Cor. [*Holding* VOLUMNIA *by the hand, silent.*]
                  O, mother, mother,
What have you done? Behold! the heavens do
   ope,
The gods look down, and this unnatural scene
They laugh at. O my mother! mother! O! 185
You have won a happy victory to Rome;
But, for your son, believe it, O! believe it,
Most dangerously you have with him pre-
   vail'd, 188
If not most mortal to him. But let it come.
Aufidius, though I cannot make true wars,
I'll frame convenient peace. Now, good Aufi-
   dius,
Were you in my stead, would you have heard
A mother less, or granted less, Aufidius? 193
   Auf. I was mov'd withal.
   Cor.   I dare be sworn you were:

And, sir, it is no little thing to make
Mine eyes to sweat compassion. But, good sir
What peace you'll make, advise me: for my
   part, 19
I'll not to Rome, I'll back with you; and pray
   you,
Stand to me in this cause. O mother! wife!
   Auf. [*Aside.*] I am glad thou hast set thy
   mercy and thy honour 20
At difference in thee: out of that I'll work
Myself a former fortune.
         [*The ladies make signs to* CORIOLANUS
   Cor.   Ay, by and by;
But we will drink together; and you shall bea
A better witness back than words, which we, 20.
On like conditions, would have counter-seal'd
Come, enter with us. Ladies, you deserve
To have a temple built you: all the swords
In Italy, and her confederate arms, 20
Could not have made this peace. [*Exeunt

SCENE IV.—*Rome. A Public Place.*

Enter MENENIUS *and* SICINIUS.

   Men. See you yond coign o' the Capitol, yone
corner-stone?
   Sic. Why, what of that?
   Men. If it be possible for you to displace
with your little finger, there is some hope the
ladies of Rome, especially his mother, may
prevail with him. But I say, there is no hope
in't. Our throats are sentenced and stay upon
execution.
   Sic. Is't possible that so short a time can
alter the condition of a man?
   Men. There is difference between a grub and
a butterfly; yet your butterfly was a grub.
Marcius is grown from man to dragon: he ha
wings; he's more than a creeping thing.
   Sic. He loved his mother dearly.
   Men. So did he me; and he no more remem
bers his mother now than an eight-year-old
horse. The tartness of his face sours ripe
grapes: when he walks, he moves like an engine
and the ground shrinks before his treading: he
is able to pierce a corslet with his eye; talks like
a knell, and his hum is a battery. He sits in his
state, as a thing made for Alexander. Wha
he bids be done is finished with his bidding. He
wants nothing of a god but eternity and a
heaven to throne in.
   Sic. Yes, mercy, if you report him truly. 2
   Men. I paint him in the character. Mark
what mercy his mother shall bring from him
there is no more mercy in him than there is
milk in a male tiger; that shall our poor city
find: and all this is 'long of you. 3
   Sic. The gods be good unto us!
   Men. No, in such a case the gods will not be
good unto us. When we banished him, we
respected not them; and, he returning to break
our necks, they respect not us.

Enter a Messenger.

   Mess. Sir, if you'd save your life, fly to your
   house:

The plebeians have got your fellow-tribune, 40
And hale him up and down; all swearing, if
The Roman ladies bring not comfort home,
They'll give him death by inches.

Enter a second Messenger.

Sic. What's the news?
Sec. Mess. Good news, good news! the ladies
have prevail'd, 44
The Volscians are dislodg'd, and Marcius gone.
A merrier day did never yet greet Rome,
No, not the expulsion of the Tarquins.
Sic. Friend,
Art thou certain this is true? is it most certain? 48
Sec. Mess. As certain as I know the sun is
fire:
Where have you lurk'd that you make doubt
of it?
Ne'er through an arch so hurried the blown
tide,
As the recomforted through the gates. Why,
hark you! 52
[*Trumpets and hautboys sounded, and drums
beaten, all together. Shouting also within.*
The trumpets, sackbuts, psalteries, and fifes,
Tabors, and cymbals, and the shouting Romans,
Make the sun dance. Hark you! [*A shout within.*
Men. This is good news:
We'll go meet the ladies. This Volumnia 56
Is worth of consuls, senators, patricians,
A city full; of tribunes, such as you,
A sea and land full. You have pray'd well to-
day: 59
This morning for ten thousand of your throats
I'd not have given a doit. Hark, how they joy!
[*Music still and shouts.*
Sic. First, the gods bless you for your tidings;
next,
Accept my thankfulness.
Sec. Mess. Sir, we have all
Great cause to give great thanks.
Sic. They are near the city? 64
Sec. Mess. Almost at point to enter.
Sic. We will meet them,
And help the joy. [*Going.*

*Enter the Ladies, accompanied by Senators,
Patricians, and People. They pass over the
stage.*

First Sen. Behold our patroness, the life of
Rome!
Call all your tribes together, praise the gods, 68
And make triumphant fires; strew flowers before
them:
Unshout the noise that banish'd Marcius;
Repeal him with the welcome of his mother;
Cry, 'Welcome, ladies, welcome!'
All. Welcome, ladies, 72
Welcome! [*A flourish with drums and
trumpets. Exeunt.*

SCENE V.—*Corioli. A Public Place.*

Enter TULLUS AUFIDIUS, *with Attendants.*

Auf. Go tell the lords o' the city I am here:
Deliver them this paper: having read it,
Bid them repair to the market-place; where I,
Even in theirs and in the commons' ears, 4
Will vouch the truth of it. Him I accuse
The city ports by this hath enter'd, and
Intends to appear before the people, hoping
To purge himself with words: dispatch. 8
[*Exeunt* Attendants.

Enter three or four Conspirators *of* AUFIDIUS'
faction.

Most welcome!
First Con. How is it with our general?
Auf. Even so
As with a man by his own alms empoison'd,
And with his charity slain.
Sec. Con. Most noble sir, 12
If you do hold the same intent wherein
You wish'd us parties, we'll deliver you
Of your great danger.
Auf. Sir, I cannot tell:
We must proceed as we do find the people. 16
Third Con. The people will remain uncertain
whilst
'Twixt you there's difference; but the fall of
either
Makes the survivor heir of all.
Auf. I know it;
And my pretext to strike at him admits 20
A good construction. I rais'd him, and I pawn'd
Mine honour for his truth: who being so
heighten'd,
He water'd his new plants with dews of flattery,
Seducing so my friends; and, to this end, 24
He bow'd his nature, never known before
But to be rough, unswayable, and free.
Third Con. Sir, his stoutness
When he did stand for consul, which he lost 28
By lack of stooping,—
Auf. That I would have spoke of:
Being banish'd for't, he came unto my hearth;
Presented to my knife his throat: I took him;
Made him joint-servant with me; gave him way
In all his own desires; nay, let him choose 33
Out of my files, his projects to accomplish,
My best and freshest men; serv'd his design-
ments
In mine own person; holp to reap the fame 36
Which he did end all his; and took some pride
To do myself this wrong: till, at the last,
I seem'd his follower, not partner; and
He wag'd me with his countenance, as if 40
I had been mercenary.
First Con. So he did, my lord:
The army marvell'd at it; and, in the last,
When we had carried Rome, and that we look'd
For no less spoil than glory,—
Auf. There was it; 44
For which my sinews shall be stretch'd upon him.
At a few drops of women's rheum, which are
As cheap as lies, he sold the blood and labour
Of our great action: therefore shall he die, 48
And I'll renew me in his fall. But, hark!
[*Drums and trumpets sound, with
great shouts of the People.*
First Con. Your native town you enter'd
like a post,

And had no welcomes home; but he returns,
Splitting the air with noise.
   Sec. Con.   And patient fools, 52
Whose children he hath slain, their base throats tear
With giving him glory.
   Third Con.   Therefore, at your vantage,
Ere he express himself, or move the people
With what he would say, let him feel your sword,   56
Which we will second. When he lies along,
After your way his tale pronounc'd shall bury
His reasons with his body.
   Auf.   Say no more:
Here come the lords.   60

     Enter the Lords *of the city.*

   Lords. You are most welcome home.
   Auf.   I have not deserv'd it.
But, worthy lords, have you with heed perus'd
What I have written to you?
   Lords.   We have.
   First Lord.   And grieve to hear 't.
What faults he made before the last, I think 64
Might have found easy fines; but there to end
Where he was to begin, and give away
The benefit of our own levies, answering us
With our own charge, making a treaty where 68
There was a yielding, this admits no excuse.
   Auf. He approaches: you shall hear him.

   Enter CORIOLANUS, *with drums and colours; a*
     crowd of Citizens *with him.*

   Cor. Hail, lords! I am return'd your soldier;
No more infected with my country's love 72
Than when I parted hence, but still subsisting
Under your great command. You are to know,
That prosperously I have attempted and
With bloody passage led your wars even to 76
The gates of Rome. Our spoils we have brought home
Do more than counterpoise a full third part
The charges of the action. We have made peace
With no less honour to the Antiates 80
Than shame to the Romans; and we here deliver,
Subscrib'd by the consuls and patricians,
Together with the seal o' the senate, what
We have compounded on.
   Auf.   Read it not, noble lords; 84
But tell the traitor in the highest degree
He hath abus'd your powers.
   Cor. Traitor! How now?
   Auf.   Ay, traitor, Marcius.
   Cor.   Marcius!
   Auf. Ay, Marcius, Caius Marcius. Dost thou think   88
I'll grace thee with that robbery, thy stol'n name
Coriolanus in Corioli?
You lords and heads of the state, perfidiously
He has betray'd your business, and given up, 92
For certain drops of salt, your city Rome,
I say 'your city,' to his wife and mother;
Breaking his oath and resolution like
A twist of rotten silk, never admitting   96

Counsel o' the war, but at his nurse's tears
He whin'd and roar'd away your victory,
That pages blush'd at him, and men of heart
Look'd wondering each at other.
   Cor.   Hear'st thou, Mars? 100
   Auf. Name not the god, thou boy of tears.
   Cor.   Ha!
   Auf. No more.
   Cor. Measureless liar, thou hast made my heart
Too great for what contains it. Boy! O slave!
Pardon me, lords, 'tis the first time that ever 105
I was forc'd to scold. Your judgments, my grave lords,
Must give this cur the lie: and his own notion—
Who wears my stripes impress'd upon him, that   108
Must bear my beating to his grave—shall join
To thrust the lie unto him.
   First Lord. Peace, both, and hear me speak.
   Cor. Cut me to pieces, Volsces; men and lads,   112
Stain all your edges on me. Boy! False hound!
If you have writ your annals true, 'tis there,
That, like an eagle in a dove-cote, I
Flutter'd your Volscians in Corioli: 116
Alone I did it. Boy!
   Auf.   Why, noble lords,
Will you be put in mind of his blind fortune,
Which was your shame, by this unholy braggart,
'Fore your own eyes and ears?
   Conspirators.   Let him die for't. 120
   All the People. Tear him to pieces.—Do it presently.—He killed my son.—My daughter.
—He killed my cousin Marcus.—He killed my father.   124
   Sec. Lord. Peace, ho! no outrage: peace!
The man is noble and his fame folds in
This orb o' the earth. His last offences to us
Shall have judicious hearing. Stand, Aufidius,
And trouble not the peace.
   Cor.   O! that I had him, 129
With six Aufidiuses, or more, his tribe,
To use my lawful sword!
   Auf.   Insolent villain!
   Conspirators. Kill, kill, kill, kill, kill him!
   [AUFIDIUS *and the* Conspirators *draw*
     and kill CORIOLANUS, *who falls:* AU-
     FIDIUS *stands on his body.*
   Lords.   Hold, hold, hold, hold! 132
   Auf. My noble masters, hear me speak.
   First Lord.   O Tullus
   Sec. Lord. Thou hast done a deed whereat valour will weep.
   Third Lord. Tread not upon him. Master all, be quiet.
Put up your swords.   136
   Auf. My lords, when you shall know,—as in this rage,
Provok'd by him, you cannot,—the great danger
Which this man's life did owe you, you'll rejoice
That he is thus cut off. Please it your honour
To call me to your senate, I'll deliver   141
Myself your loyal servant, or endure
Your heaviest censure.

First Lord. Bear from hence his body;
And mourn you for him! Let him be regarded
As the most noble corse that ever herald 145
Did follow to his urn.

Sec. Lord. His own impatience
Takes from Aufidius a great part of blame.
Let's make the best of it.

Auf. My rage is gone, 148
And I am struck with sorrow. Take him up:
Help, three o' the chiefest soldiers; I'll be one,
Beat thou the drum, that it speak mournfully;
Trail your steel pikes. Though in this city he
Hath widow'd and unchilded many a one, 153
Which to this hour bewail the injury,
Yet he shall have a noble memory.
Assist.

[*Exeunt, bearing the body of* CORIOLANUS.
A dead march sounded.

TITUS ANDRONICUS

DRAMATIS PERSONÆ

SATURNINUS, Son to the late Emperor of Rome, and afterwards declared Emperor.
BASSIANUS, Brother to Saturninus, in love with Lavinia.
TITUS ANDRONICUS, a Roman, General against the Goths.
MARCUS ANDRONICUS, Tribune of the People, and brother to Titus.

LUCIUS,
QUINTUS,
MARTIUS,
MUTIUS,
} Sons to Titus Andronicus.

YOUNG LUCIUS, a Boy, Son to Lucius.
PUBLIUS, Son to Marcus Andronicus.

SEMPRONIUS,
CAIUS,
VALENTINE,
} Kinsmen to Titus.

ÆMILIUS, a noble Roman.
ALARBUS,
DEMETRIUS,
CHIRON,
} Sons to Tamora.
AARON, a Moor, beloved by Tamora.
A Captain, Tribune, Messenger, and Clown; Romans.
Goths and Romans.

TAMORA, Queen of the Goths.
LAVINIA, Daughter to Titus Andronicus.
A Nurse, and a black Child.

Senators, Tribunes, Officers, Soldiers, and Attendants.

SCENE.—*Rome, and the Country near it.*

ACT I

SCENE I.—*Rome.*

The Tomb of the Andronici appearing. The Tribunes and Senators aloft; and then enter SATURNINUS *and his Followers at one door, and* BASSIANUS *and his Followers at the other, with drum and colours.*

Sat. Noble patricians, patrons of my right,
Defend the justice of my cause with arms;
And, countrymen, my loving followers,
Plead my successive title with your swords: 4
I am his first-born son that was the last
That wore the imperial diadem of Rome;
Then let my father's honours live in me,
Nor wrong mine age with this indignity. 8

Bas. Romans, friends, followers, favourers of my right,
If ever Bassianus, Cæsar's son,
Were gracious in the eyes of royal Rome,
Keep then this passage to the Capitol, 12
And suffer not dishonour to approach
The imperial seat, to virtue consecrate,
To justice, continence, and nobility;
But let desert in pure election shine, 16
And, Romans, fight for freedom in your choice.

Enter MARCUS ANDRONICUS, *aloft, with the crown.*

Mar. Princes, that strive by factions and by friends
Ambitiously for rule and empery,
Know that the people of Rome, for whom we stand 20
A special party, have, by common voice,
In election for the Roman empery,
Chosen Andronicus, surnamed Pius,
For many good and great deserts to Rome: 24
A nobler man, a braver warrior,
Lives not this day within the city walls:
He by the senate is accited home

From weary wars against the barbarous Goths;
That, with his sons, a terror to our foes, 29
Hath yok'd a nation, strong, train'd up in arms.
Ten years are spent since first he undertook
This cause of Rome, and chastised with arms 32
Our enemies' pride: five times he hath return'd
Bleeding to Rome, bearing his valiant sons
In coffins from the field;
And now at last, laden with honour's spoils, 36
Returns the good Andronicus to Rome,
Renowned Titus, flourishing in arms.
Let us entreat, by honour of his name,
Whom worthily you would have now succeed, 40
And in the Capitol and senate's right,
Whom you pretend to honour and adore,
That you withdraw you and abate your strength;
Dismiss your followers, and, as suitors should,
Plead your deserts in peace and humbleness. 45

Sat. How fair the tribune speaks to calm my thoughts!

Bas. Marcus Andronicus, so I do affy
In thy uprightness and integrity, 48
And so I love and honour thee and thine,
Thy noble brother Titus and his sons,
And her to whom my thoughts are humbled all,
Gracious Lavinia, Rome's rich ornament, 52
That I will here dismiss my loving friends,
And to my fortunes and the people's favour
Commit my cause in balance to be weigh'd.
[*Exeunt the Followers of* BASSIANUS.

Sat. Friends, that have been thus forward in my right, 56
I thank you all and here dismiss you all;
And to the love and favour of my country
Commit myself, my person, and the cause.
[*Exeunt the Followers of* SATURNINUS.
Rome, be as just and gracious unto me 60
As I am confident and kind to thee.
Open the gates, and let me in.

Bas. Tribunes, and me, a poor competitor.
[*Flourish. They go up into the
Senate-house*

Enter a Captain.

Cap. Romans, make way! the good Andro-
nicus,   64
Patron of virtue, Rome's best champion,
Successful in the battles that he fights,
With honour and with fortune is return'd
From where he circumscribed with his sword, 68
And brought to yoke, the enemies of Rome.

Drums and trumpets sounded, and then enter
MARTIUS *and* MUTIUS; *after them two Men*
bearing a coffin covered with black; then LUCIUS
and QUINTUS. *After them* TITUS ANDRONICUS;
and then TAMORA, *with* ALARBUS, CHIRON,
DEMETRIUS, AARON, *and other* Goths, *prisoners;*
Soldiers *and people following. The bearers set*
down the coffin, and TITUS *speaks.*

Tit. Hail, Rome, victorious in thy mourning
weeds!
Lo! as the bark, that hath discharg'd her fraught,
Returns with precious lading to the bay   72
From whence at first she weigh'd her anchorage,
Cometh Andronicus, bound with laurel boughs,
To re-salute his country with his tears,
Tears of true joy for his return to Rome.   76
Thou great defender of this Capitol,
Stand gracious to the rites that we intend!
Romans, of five-and-twenty valiant sons,
Half of the number that King Priam had,   80
Behold the poor remains, alive, and dead!
These that survive let Rome reward with love;
These that I bring unto their latest home,
With burial among their ancestors: 84
Here Goths have given me leave to sheathe my
sword,
Titus, unkind and careless of thine own,
Why suffer'st thou thy sons, unburied yet
To hover on the dreadful shore of Styx?   88
Make way to lay them by their brethren.
                              [*The tomb is opened.*
There greet in silence, as the dead are wont,
And sleep in peace, slain in your country's wars!
O sacred receptacle of my joys,   92
Sweet cell of virtue and nobility,
How many sons of mine hast thou in store,
That thou wilt never render to me more!
Luc. Give us the proudest prisoner of the
Goths,   96
That we may hew his limbs, and on a pile
Ad manes fratrum sacrifice his flesh,
Before this earthy prison of their bones;
That so the shadows be not unappeas'd,   100
Nor we disturb'd with prodigies on earth.
Tit. I give him you, the noblest that survives,
The eldest son of this distressed queen.
Tam. Stay, Roman brethren! Gracious con-
queror,   104
Victorious Titus, rue the tears I shed,
A mother's tears in passion for her son:
And if thy sons were ever dear to thee,
O! think my son to be as dear to me.   108
Sufficeth not that we are brought to Rome,
To beautify thy triumphs and return,
Captive to thee and to thy Roman yoke;
But must my sons be slaughter'd in the streets 112

For valiant doings in their country's cause?
O! if to fight for king and commonweal
Were piety in thine, it is in these.
Andronicus, stain not thy tomb with blood: 116
Wilt thou draw near the nature of the gods?
Draw near them then in being merciful;
Sweet mercy is nobility's true badge:
Thrice-noble Titus, spare my first-born son. 120
Tit. Patient yourself, madam, and pardon
me.
These are their brethren, whom your Goths
beheld
Alive and dead, and for their brethren slain
Religiously they ask a sacrifice: 124
To this your son is mark'd, and die he must,
To appease their groaning shadows that are
gone.
Luc. Away with him! and make a fire straight;
And with our swords, upon a pile of wood, 128
Let's hew his limbs till they be clean consum'd.
        [*Exeunt* LUCIUS, QUINTUS, MARTIUS, *and*
                            MUTIUS, *with* ALARBUS.
Tam. O cruel, irreligious piety!
Chi. Was ever Scythia half so barbarous?
Dem. Oppose not Scythia to ambitious Rome.
Alarbus goes to rest, and we survive   133
To tremble under Titus' threatening look.
Then, madam, stand resolv'd; but hope withal
The self-same gods, that arm'd the Queen of
Troy   136
With opportunity of sharp revenge
Upon the Thracian tyrant in his tent,
May favour Tamora, the Queen of Goths—
When Goths were Goths, and Tamora was
queen—   140
To quit the bloody wrongs upon her foes.

Re-enter LUCIUS, QUINTUS, MARTIUS, *and*
MUTIUS, *with their swords bloody.*

Luc. See, lord and father, how we have per-
form'd
Our Roman rites. Alarbus' limbs are lopp'd,
And entrails feed the sacrificing fire,   144
Whose smoke, like incense, doth perfume the
sky.
Remaineth nought but to inter our brethren,
And with loud 'larums welcome them to Rome.
Tit. Let it be so; and let Andronicus   148
Make this his latest farewell to their souls.
        [*Trumpets sounded, and the coffin laid*
                              in the tomb.
In peace and honour rest you here, my sons;
Rome's readiest champions, repose you here in
rest,
Secure from worldly chances and mishaps! 152
Here lurks no treason, here no envy swells,
Here grow no damned drugs, here are no storms,
No noise, but silence and eternal sleep:
In peace and honour rest you here, my sons! 156

Enter LAVINIA.

Lav. In peace and honour live Lord Titus
long;
My noble lord and father, live in fame!
Lo! at this tomb my tributary tears
I render for my brethren's obsequies;   160

And at thy feet I kneel, with tears of joy
Shed on the earth for thy return to Rome.
O! bless me here with thy victorious hand,
Whose fortunes Rome's best citizens applaud.

Tit. Kind Rome, that hast thus lovingly
reserv'd 165
The cordial of mine age to glad my heart!
Lavinia, live; outlive thy father's days,
And fame's eternal date, for virtue's praise! 168

Enter MARCUS ANDRONICUS *and* Tribunes; *re-enter* SATURNINUS, BASSIANUS, *and Others.*

Mar. Long live Lord Titus, my beloved
brother,
Gracious triumpher in the eyes of Rome,

Tit. Thanks, gentle Tribune, noble brother
Marcus.

Mar. And welcome, nephews, from success-
ful wars, 172
You that survive, and you that sleep in fame!
Fair lords, your fortunes are alike in all,
That in your country's service drew your
swords;
But safer triumph is this funeral pomp, 176
That hath aspir'd to Solon's happiness,
And triumphs over chance in honour's bed.
Titus Andronicus, the people of Rome,
Whose friend in justice thou hast ever been, 180
Send thee by me, their tribune and their trust,
This palliament of white and spotless hue;
And name thee in election for the empire,
With these our late-deceased emperor's sons:184
Be *candidatus* then, and put it on,
And help to set a head on headless Rome.

Tit. A better head her glorious body fits
Than his that shakes for age and feebleness. 188
What should I don this robe, and trouble you?
Be chosen with proclamations to-day,
To-morrow yield up rule, resign my life,
And set abroad new business for you all? 192
Rome, I have been thy soldier forty years,
And led my country's strength successfully,
And buried one-and-twenty valiant sons,
Knighted in field, slain manfully in arms, 196
In right and service of their noble country.
Give me a staff of honour for mine age,
But not a sceptre to control the world:
Upright he held it, lords, that held it last. 200

Mar. Titus, thou shalt obtain and ask the
empery.

Sat. Proud and ambitious tribune, canst thou
tell?

Tit. Patience, Prince Saturninus.

Sat. Romans, do me right!
Patricians, draw your swords, and sheathe
them not 204
Till Saturninus be Rome's emperor.
Andronicus, would thou wert shipp'd to hell,
Rather than rob me of the people's hearts!

Luc. Proud Saturnine, interrupter of the
good 208
That noble-minded Titus means to thee!

Tit. Content thee, prince; I will restore to
thee
The people's hearts, and wean them from themselves.

Bas. Andronicus, I do not flatter thee, 212
But honour thee, and will do till I die:
My faction if thou strengthen with thy friends,
I will most thankful be; and thanks to men
Of noble minds is honourable meed. 216

Tit. People of Rome, and people's tribunes
here,
I ask your voices and your suffrages:
Will you bestow them friendly on Andronicus?

Tribunes. To gratify the good Andronicus,
And gratulate his safe return to Rome, 221
The people will accept whom he admits.

Tit. Tribunes, I thank you; and this suit I
make,
That you create your emperor's eldest son, 224
Lord Saturnine; whose virtues will, I hope,
Reflect on Rome as Titan's rays on earth,
And ripen justice in this commonweal;
Then, if you will elect by my advice, 228
Crown him, and say, 'Long live our emperor!'

Mar. With voices and applause of every sort,
Patricians and plebeians, we create
Lord Saturninus Rome's great emperor, 232
And say, 'Long live our Emperor Saturnine!'
[*A long flourish.*

Sat. Titus Andronicus, for thy favours done
To us in our election this day,
I give thee thanks in part of thy deserts, 236
And will with deeds requite thy gentleness:
And, for an onset, Titus, to advance
Thy name and honourable family,
Lavinia will I make my empress, 240
Rome's royal mistress, mistress of my heart,
And in the sacred Pantheon her espouse.
Tell me, Andronicus, doth this motion please
thee?

Tit. It doth, my worthy lord; and in this
match 244
I hold me highly honour'd of your Grace:
And here in sight of Rome to Saturnine,
King and commander of our commonweal,
The wide world's emperor, do I consecrate 248
My sword, my chariot, and my prisoners;
Presents well worthy Rome's imperious lord:
Receive them then, the tribute that I owe,
Mine honour's ensigns humbled at thy feet. 252

Sat. Thanks, noble Titus, father of my life!
How proud I am of thee and of thy gifts
Rome shall record, and, when I do forget
The least of these unspeakable deserts, 256
Romans, forget your fealty to me.

Tit. [*To* TAMORA.] Now, madam, are you
prisoner to an emperor;
To him that, for your honour and your state,
Will use you nobly and your followers. 260

Sat. A goodly lady, trust me; of the hue
That I would choose, were I to choose anew.
Clear up, fair queen, that cloudy countenance:
Though chance of war hath wrought this change
of cheer, 264
Thou com'st not to be made a scorn in Rome:
Princely shall be thy usage every way.
Rest on my word, and let not discontent 267
Daunt all your hopes: madam, he comforts you
Can make you greater than the Queen of Goths.
Lavinia, you are not displeas'd with this?

Lav. Not I, my lord; sith true nobility
Warrants these words in princely courtesy. 272
Sat. Thanks, sweet Lavinia. Romans, let us
go;
Ransomless here we set our prisoners free:
Proclaim our honours, lords, with trump and
drum.   [*Flourish.* SATURNINUS *courts*
TAMORA *in dumb show.*
Bas. Lord Titus, by your leave, this maid is
mine.   [*Seizing* LAVINIA.
Tit. How, sir! Are you in earnest then, my
lord?   277
Bas. Ay, noble Titus; and resolv'd withal
To do myself this reason and this right.
Mar. Suum cuique is our Roman justice: 280
This prince in justice seizeth but his own.
Luc. And that he will, and shall, if Lucius
live.
Tit. Traitors, avaunt! Where is the em-
peror's guard?
Treason, my lord! Lavinia is surpris'd.   284
Sat. Surpris'd! By whom?
Bas.   By him that justly may
Bear his betroth'd from all the world away.
[*Exeunt* MARCUS *and* BASSIANUS
with LAVINIA.
Mut. Brothers, help to convey her hence
away,
And with my sword I'll keep this door safe. 288
[*Exeunt* LUCIUS, QUINTUS, *and* MARTIUS.
Tit. Follow, my lord, and I'll soon bring her
back.
Mut. My lord, you pass not here.
Tit.   What! villain boy;
Barr'st me my way in Rome? [*Stabs* MUTIUS.
Mut.   Help, Lucius, help! [*Dies.*

Re-enter LUCIUS.

Luc. My lord, you are unjust; and, more
than so,   292
In wrongful quarrel you have slain your son.
Tit. Nor thou, nor he, are any sons of mine;
My sons would never so dishonour me.
Traitor, restore Lavinia to the emperor.   296
Luc. Dead, if you will; but not to be his wife
That is another's lawful promis'd love. [*Exit.*
Sat. No, Titus, no; the emperor needs her not,
Nor her, nor thee, nor any of thy stock: 300
I'll trust, by leisure, him that mocks me once;
Thee never, nor thy traitorous haughty sons,
Confederates all thus to dishonour me.
Was none in Rome to make a stale   304
But Saturnine? Full well, Andronicus,
Agreed these deeds with that proud brag of
thine,
That saidst I begg'd the empire at thy hands.
Tit. O monstrous! what reproachful words
are these?   308
Sat. But go thy ways; go, give that changing
piece
To him that flourish'd for her with his sword.
A valiant son-in-law thou shalt enjoy;
One fit to bandy with thy lawless sons,   312
To ruffle in the commonwealth of Rome.
Tit. These words are razors to my wounded
heart.

Sat. And therefore, lovely Tamora, Queen of
Goths,
That like the stately Phœbe 'mongst her nymphs, 316
Dost overshine the gallant'st dames of Rome,
If thou be pleas'd with this my sudden choice,
Behold, I choose thee, Tamora, for my bride,
And will create thee Empress of Rome.   320
Speak, Queen of Goths, dost thou applaud my
choice?
And here I swear by all the Roman gods,
Sith priest and holy water are so near,
And tapers burn so bright, and every thing 324
In readiness for Hymenæus stand,
I will not re-salute the streets of Rome,
Or climb my palace, till from forth this place
I lead espous'd my bride along with me.   328
Tam. And here, in sight of heaven, to Rome
I swear,
If Saturnine advance the Queen of Goths,
She will a handmaid be to his desires,
A loving nurse, a mother to his youth.   332
Sat. Ascend, fair queen, Pantheon. Lords,
accompany
Your noble emperor, and his lovely bride,
Sent by the heavens for Prince Saturnine,
Whose wisdom hath her fortune conquered: 336
There shall we consummate our spousal rights.
[*Exeunt all but* TITUS.
Tit. I am not bid to wait upon this bride.
Titus, when wert thou wont to walk alone, 339
Dishonour'd thus, and challenged of wrongs?

Re-enter MARCUS, LUCIUS, QUINTUS, *and*
MARTIUS.

Mar. O! Titus, see, O! see what thou hast
done;
In a bad quarrel slain a virtuous son.
Tit. No, foolish tribune, no; no son of mine,
Nor thou, nor these, confederates in the deed 344
That hath dishonour'd all our family:
Unworthy brother, and unworthy sons!
Luc. But let us give him burial, as becomes;
Give Mutius burial with our brethren.   348
Tit. Traitors, away! he rests not in this tomb.
This monument five hundred years hath stood,
Which I have sumptuously re-edified:
Here none but soldiers and Rome's servitors 352
Repose in fame; none basely slain in brawls.
Bury him where you can; he comes not here.
Mar. My lord, this is impiety in you.
My nephew Mutius' deeds do plead for him; 356
He must be buried with his brethren.
Quin.}
Mart.} And shall, or him we will accompany.
Tit. And shall! What villain was it spake
that word?
Quin. He that would vouch it in any place
but here.   360
Tit. What! would you bury him in my de-
spite?
Mar. No, noble Titus; but entreat of thee
To pardon Mutius, and to bury him.
Tit. Marcus, even thou hast struck upon my
crest,   364
And, with these boys, mine honour thou hast
wounded:

My foes I do repute you every one;
So, trouble me no more, but get you gone.
Mart. He is not with himself; let us with-
    draw.   368
Quin. Not I, till Mutius' bones be buried.
        [MARCUS *and the sons of* TITUS *kneel.*
Mar. Brother, for in that name doth nature
    plead,—
Quin. Father, and in that name doth nature
    speak,—
Tit. Speak thou no more, if all the rest will
    speed.   372
Mar. Renowned Titus, more than half my
    soul,—
Luc. Dear father, soul and substance of us
    all,—
Mar. Suffer thy brother Marcus to inter
His noble nephew here in virtue's nest,   376
That died in honour and Lavinia's cause.
Thou art a Roman; be not barbarous:
The Greeks upon advice did bury Ajax
That slew himself; and wise Laertes' son   380
Did graciously plead for his funerals.
Let not young Mutius then, that was thy joy,
Be barr'd his entrance here.
Tit.   Rise, Marcus, rise.
The dismall'st day is this that e'er I saw,   384
To be dishonour'd by my sons in Rome!
Well, bury him, and bury me the next.
            [MUTIUS *is put into the tomb.*
Luc. There lie thy bones, sweet Mutius, with
    thy friends,
Till we with trophies do adorn thy tomb.   388
All. [*Kneeling.*] No man shed tears for noble
    Mutius;
He lives in fame that died in virtue's cause.
Mar. My lord,—to step out of these dreary
    dumps,—
How comes it that the subtle Queen of Goths 392
Is of a sudden thus advanc'd in Rome?
Tit. I know not, Marcus; but I know it is,
Whether by device or no, the heavens can tell.
Is she not, then, beholding to the man   396
That brought her for this high good turn so far?
Mar. Yes, and will nobly him remunerate.

Flourish. Re-enter, on one side, SATURNINUS,
    attended, TAMORA, DEMETRIUS, CHIRON, *and*
    AARON: *on the other side,* BASSIANUS, LAVINIA,
    and Others.

Sat. So, Bassianus, you have play'd your
    prize:
God give you joy, sir, of your gallant bride. 400
Bas. And you of yours, my lord! I say no
    more,
Nor wish no less; and so I take my leave.
Sat. Traitor, if Rome have law or we have
    power,
Thou and thy faction shall repent this rape. 404
Bas. Rape call you it, my lord, to seize my
    own,
My true-betrothed love and now my wife?
But let the laws of Rome determine all;
Meanwhile, I am possess'd of that is mine. 408
Sat. 'Tis good, sir: you are very short with
    us;

But, if we live, we'll be as sharp with you.
Bas. My lord, what I have done, as best I
    may,
Answer I must and shall do with my life.   412
Only thus much I give your Grace to know:
By all the duties that I owe to Rome,
This noble gentleman, Lord Titus here,
Is in opinion and in honour wrong'd;   416
That, in the rescue of Lavinia,
With his own hand did slay his youngest son,
In zeal to you and highly mov'd to wrath
To be controll'd in that he frankly gave: 420
Receive him then to favour, Saturnine,
That hath express'd himself in all his deeds
A father and a friend to thee and Rome.
Tit. Prince Bassianus, leave to plead my
    deeds: 424
'Tis thou and those that have dishonour'd me.
Rome and the righteous heavens be my judge,
How I have lov'd and honour'd Saturnine!
Tam. My worthy lord, if ever Tamora   428
Were gracious in those princely eyes of thine,
Then hear me speak indifferently for all;
And at my suit, sweet, pardon what is past.
Sat. What, madam! be dishonour'd openly,
And basely put it up without revenge?   433
Tam. Not so, my lord; the gods of Rome
    forfend
I should be author to dishonour you!
But on mine honour dare I undertake   436
For good Lord Titus' innocence in all,
Whose fury not dissembled speaks his griefs.
Then, at my suit, look graciously on him;
Lose not so noble a friend on vain suppose, 440
Nor with sour looks afflict his gentle heart.
[*Aside to* SATURNINUS.] My lord, be rul'd by
    me, be won at last;
Dissemble all your griefs and discontents:
You are but newly planted in your throne; 444
Lest then, the people, and patricians too,
Upon a just survey, take Titus' part,
And so supplant you for ingratitude,
Which Rome reputes to be a heinous sin, 448
Yield at entreats, and then let me alone.
I'll find a day to massacre them all,
And raze their faction and their family,
The cruel father, and his traitorous sons, 452
To whom I sued for my dear son's life;
And make them know what 'tis to let a queen
Kneel in the streets and beg for grace in vain.
[*Aloud.*] Come, come, sweet emperor; come,
    Andronicus;   456
Take up this good old man, and cheer the heart
That dies in tempest of thy angry frown.
Sat. Rise, Titus, rise; my empress hath pre-
    vail'd.   459
Tit. I thank your majesty, and her, my lord.
These words, these looks, infuse new life in me.
Tam. Titus, I am incorporate in Rome,
A Roman now adopted happily,
And must advise the emperor for his good. 463
This day all quarrels die, Andronicus;
And let it be mine honour, good my lord,
That I have reconcil'd your friends and you.
For you, Prince Bassianus, I have pass'd 467
My word and promise to the emperor,

That you will be more mild and tractable.
And fear not, lords, and you, Lavinia,
By my advice, all humbled on your knees, 472
You shall ask pardon of his majesty.
Luc. We do; and vow to heaven and to his
highness,
That what we did was mildly, as we might,
Tendering our sister's honour and our own. 476
Mar. That on mine honour here I do protest.
Sat. Away, and talk not; trouble us no more.
Tam. Nay, nay, sweet emperor, we must all
be friends:
The tribune and his nephews kneel for grace; 480
I will not be denied: sweet heart, look back.
Sat. Marcus, for thy sake, and thy brother's
here,
And at my lovely Tamora's entreats,
I do remit these young men's heinous faults: 484
Stand up.
Lavinia, though you left me like a churl,
I found a friend, and sure as death I swore
I would not part a bachelor from the priest. 488
Come; if the emperor's court can feast two brides,
You are my guest, Lavinia, and your friends.
This day shall be a love-day, Tamora.
Tit. To-morrow, an it please your majesty 492
To hunt the panther and the hart with me,
With horn and hound we'll give your Grace
bon jour.
Sat. Be it so, Titus, and gramercy too.
                        [*Trumpets. Exeunt.*

ACT II

SCENE I.—*Rome. Before the Palace.*

Enter AARON.

Aar. Now climbeth Tamora Olympus' top,
Safe out of Fortune's shot; and sits aloft,
Secure of thunder's crack or lightning flash,
Advanc'd above pale envy's threat'ning reach. 4
As when the golden sun salutes the morn,
And, having gilt the ocean with his beams,
Gallops the zodiac in his glistering coach,
And overlooks the highest-peering hills;   8
So Tamora.
Upon her wit doth earthly honour wait
And virtue stoops and trembles at her frown.
Then, Aaron, arm thy heart, and fit thy thoughts
To mount aloft with thy imperial mistress, 13
And mount her pitch, whom thou in triumph
long
Hast prisoner held, fetter'd in amorous chains,
And faster bound to Aaron's charming eyes 16
Than is Prometheus tied to Caucasus.
Away with slavish weeds and servile thoughts!
I will be bright, and shine in pearl and gold,
To wait upon this new-made empress.   20
To wait, said I? to wanton with this queen,
This goddess, this Semiramis, this nymph,
This siren, that will charm Rome's Saturnine,
And see his ship wrack and his commonweal's. 24
Holla! what storm is this?

Enter DEMETRIUS *and* CHIRON, *braving.*

Dem. Chiron, thy years want wit, thy wit
wants edge

And manners, to intrude where I am grac'd,
And may, for aught thou know'st, affected be. 28
Chi. Demetrius, thou dost over-ween in all
And so in this, to bear me down with braves.
'Tis not the difference of a year or two
Makes me less gracious or thee more fortunate:
I am as able and as fit as thou   33
To serve, and to deserve my mistress' grace;
And that my sword upon thee shall approve,
And plead my passions for Lavinia's love. 36
Aar. Clubs, clubs! these lovers will not keep
the peace.
Dem. Why, boy, although our mother, un-
advis'd,
Gave you a dancing-rapier by your side,
Are you so desperate grown, to threat your
friends?   40
Go to; have your lath glu'd within your sheath
Till you know better how to handle it.
Chi. Meanwhile, sir, with the little skill I
have,
Full well shalt thou perceive how much I dare.
Dem. Ay, boy, grow ye so brave? [*They draw.*
Aar.   Why, how now, lords! 45
So near the emperor's palace dare you draw,
And maintain such a quarrel openly?
Full well I wot the ground of all this grudge: 48
I would not for a million of gold
The cause were known to them it most con-
cerns;
Nor would your noble mother for much more
Be so dishonour'd in the court of Rome.   52
For shame, put up.
Dem.   Not I, till I have sheath'd
My rapier in his bosom, and withal
Thrust those reproachful speeches down his
throat   55
That he hath breath'd in my dishonour here.
Chi. For that I am prepar'd and full resolv'd,
Foul-spoken coward, that thunder'st with thy
tongue,
And with thy weapon nothing dar'st perform!
Aar. Away, I say!   60
Now, by the gods that war-like Goths adore,
This petty brabble will undo us all.
Why, lords, and think you not how dangerous
It is to jet upon a prince's right?   64
What! is Lavinia then become so loose,
Or Bassianus so degenerate,
That for her love such quarrels may be broach'd
Without controlment, justice, or revenge? 68
Young lords, beware! an should the empress
know
This discord's ground, the music would not
please.
Chi. I care not, I, knew she and all the world:
I love Lavinia more than all the world.   72
Dem. Youngling, learn thou to make some
meaner choice:
Lavinia is thine elder brother's hope.
Aar. Why, are ye mad? or know ye not in
Rome
How furious and impatient they be,   76
And cannot brook competitors in love?
I tell you, lords, you do but plot your deaths
By this device.

Chi.   Aaron, a thousand deaths
Would I propose, to achieve her whom I love. 80
Aar. To achieve her! how?
Dem.   Why mak'st thou it so strange?
She is a woman, therefore may be woo'd;
She is a woman, therefore may be won;
She is Lavinia, therefore must be lov'd.   84
What, man! more water glideth by the mill
Than wots the miller of; and easy it is
Of a cut loaf to steal a shive, we know:
Though Bassianus be the emperor's brother, 88
Better than he have worn Vulcan's badge.
Aar. [*Aside.*] Ay, and as good as Saturninus
may.
Dem. Then why should he despair that knows
to court it
With words, fair looks, and liberality?   92
What! hast thou not full often struck a doe,
And borne her cleanly by the keeper's nose?
Aar. Why, then, it seems, some certain snatch
or so
Would serve your turns.
Chi.   Ay, so the turn were serv'd. 96
Dem. Aaron, thou hast hit it.
Aar.   Would you had hit it too!
Then should not we be tir'd with this ado.
Why, hark ye, hark ye! and are you such fools
To square for this? Would it offend you then 100
That both should speed?
Chi.   Faith, not me.
Dem. Nor me, so I were one.
Aar. For shame, be friends, and join for that
you jar:
'Tis policy and stratagem must do   104
That you affect; and so must you resolve,
That what you cannot as you would achieve,
You must perforce accomplish as you may.
Take this of me: Lucrece was not more chaste
Than this Lavinia, Bassianus' love.   109
A speedier course than lingering languishment
Must we pursue, and I have found the path.
My lords, a solemn hunting is in hand;   112
There will the lovely Roman ladies troop:
The forest walks are wide and spacious,
And many unfrequented plots there are
Fitted by kind for rape and villany: 116
Single you thither then this dainty doe,
And strike her home by force, if not by words:
This way, or not at all, stand you in hope.
Come, come, our empress, with her sacred wit
To villany and vengeance consecrate,   121
Will we acquaint with all that we intend;
And she shall file our engines with advice,
That will not suffer you to square yourselves, 124
But to your wishes' height advance you both.
The emperor's court is like the house of Fame,
The palace full of tongues, of eyes, and ears:
The woods are ruthless, dreadful, deaf, and dull;
There speak, and strike, brave boys, and take
your turns;   129
There serve your lusts, shadow'd from heaven's
eye,
And revel in Lavinia's treasury.
Chi. Thy counsel, lad, smells of no cowardice.
Dem. Sit fas aut nefas, till I find the stream
To cool this heat, a charm to calm these fits,

Per Styga, per manes vehor.   [*Exeunt*

SCENE II.—*A Forest.*

Horns and cry of hounds heard. Enter TITUS
ANDRONICUS, *with* Hunters, &c.; MARCUS,
LUCIUS, QUINTUS, *and* MARTIUS.

Tit. The hunt is up, the morn is bright and
grey,
The fields are fragrant and the woods are green.
Uncouple here and let us make a bay,
And wake the emperor and his lovely bride,
And rouse the prince and ring a hunter's peal,
That all the court may echo with the noise.
Sons, let it be your charge, as it is ours,
To attend the emperor's person carefully: 8
I have been troubled in my sleep this night,
But dawning day new comfort hath inspir'd.
[*A cry of hounds, and horns winded
in a peal.*

Enter SATURNINUS, TAMORA, BASSIANUS, LA-
VINIA, DEMETRIUS, CHIRON, *and* Attendants.

Many good morrows to your majesty;
Madam, to you as many and as good;   12
I promised your Grace a hunter's peal.
Sat. And you have rung it lustily, my lord;
Somewhat too early for new-married ladies.
Bas. Lavinia, how say you?
Lav.   I say, no; 16
I have been broad awake two hours and more.
Sat. Come on, then; horse and chariots let
us have,
And to our sport.—[*To* TAMORA.] Madam, now
shall ye see
Our Roman hunting.
Mar.   I have dogs, my lord, 20
Will rouse the proudest panther in the chase,
And climb the highest promontory top.
Tit. And I have horse will follow where the
game
Makes way, and run like swallows o'er the plain.
Dem. [*Aside.*] Chiron, we hunt not, we, with
horse nor hound,   25
But hope to pluck a dainty doe to ground.
[*Exeunt.*

SCENE III.—*A lonely Part of the Forest.*

Enter AARON, *with a bag of gold.*

Aar. He that had wit would think that I had
none,
To bury so much gold under a tree,
And never after to inherit it.
Let him that thinks of me so abjectly   4
Know that this gold must coin a stratagem,
Which, cunningly effected, will beget
A very excellent piece of villany:
And so repose, sweet gold, for their unrest
That have their alms out of the empress' chest.
[*Hides the gold.*

Enter TAMORA.

Tam. My lovely Aaron, wherefore look'st
thou sad,
When every thing doth make a gleeful boast?

he birds chant melody on every bush,   12
he snake lies rolled in the cheerful sun,
he green leaves quiver with the cooling wind,
nd make a chequer'd shadow on the ground.
Jnder their sweet shade, Aaron, let us sit,   16
nd, whilst the babbling echo mocks the
    hounds,
eplying shrilly to the well-tun'd horns,
s if a double hunt were heard at once,
et us sit down and mark their yelping noise; 20
nd after conflict, such as was suppos'd
he wandering prince and Dido once enjoy'd,
Vhen with a happy storm they were surpris'd,
nd curtain'd with a counsel-keeping cave, 24
Ve may, each wreathed in the other's arms,
Jur pastimes done, possess a golden slumber;
Vhiles hounds and horns and sweet melodious
    birds
3e unto us as is a nurse's song   28
Jf lullaby to bring her babe asleep.

    Aar. Madam, though Venus govern your
    desires,
aturn is dominator over mine:
Vhat signifies my deadly-standing eye,   32
Иy silence and my cloudy melancholy,
Иy fleece of woolly hair that now uncurls
ven as an adder when she doth unroll
'o do some fatal execution?   36
Jo, madam, these are no venereal signs:
'engeance is in my heart, death in my hand,
3lood and revenge are hammering in my head.
Iark, Tamora, the empress of my soul,   40
Vhich never hopes more heaven than rests in
    thee,
'his is the day of doom for Bassianus;
Iis Philomel must lose her tongue to-day,
'hy sons make pillage of her chastity,   44
\nd wash their hands in Bassianus' blood.
.eest thou this letter? take it up, I pray thee,
\nd give the king this fatal-plotted scroll.
Jow question me no more; we are espied; 48
Iere comes a parcel of our hopeful booty,
Vhich dreads not yet their lives' destruction.

    Tam. Ah! my sweet Moor, sweeter to me
    than life.

    Aar. No more, great empress; Bassianus
    comes: 52
3e cross with him; and I'll go fetch thy sons
'o back thy quarrels, whatsoe'er they be. [*Exit.*

    Enter BASSIANUS *and* LAVINIA.

    Bas. Who have we here? Rome's royal em-
    press,
Jnfurnish'd of her well-beseeming troop? 56
Jr is it Dian, habited like her,
Vho hath abandoned her holy groves,
'o see the general hunting in this forest?

    Tam. Saucy controller of our private steps!
Iad I the power that some say Dian had,   61
'hy temples should be planted presently
Vith horns, as was Actæon's; and the hounds
Should drive upon thy new-transformed limbs,
Jnmannerly intruder as thou art!   65

    Lav. Under your patience, gentle empress,
Tis thought you have a goodly gift in horning;
\nd to be doubted that your Moor and you 68

Are singled forth to try experiments.
Jove shield your husband from his hounds
    to-day!
'Tis pity they should take him for a stag.

    Bas. Believe me, queen, your swarth Cim-
    merian   72
Doth make your honour of his body's hue,
Spotted, detested, and abominable.
Why are you sequester'd from all your train,
Dismounted from your snow-white goodly
    steed,
And wander'd hither to an obscure plot,   77
Accompanied but with a barbarous Moor,
If foul desire had not conducted you?

    Lav. And, being intercepted in your sport, 80
Great reason that my noble lord be rated
For sauciness. I pray you, let us hence,
And let her joy her raven-colour'd love;
This valley fits the purpose passing well.   84

    Bas. The king my brother shall have note of
    this.

    Lav. Ay, for these slips have made him noted
    long:
Good king, to be so mightily abus'd!

    Tam. Why have I patience to endure all
    this?   88

    Enter DEMETRIUS *and* CHIRON.

    Dem. How now, dear sovereign, and our
    gracious mother!
Why doth your highness look so pale and wan?

    Tam. Have I not reason, think you, to look
    pale?
These two have 'tic'd me hither to this place: 92
A barren detested vale, you see, it is;
The trees, though summer, yet forlorn and lean,
O'ercome with moss and baleful mistletoe:
Here never shines the sun; here nothing breeds,
Unless the nightly owl or fatal raven: 97
And when they show'd me this abhorred pit,
They told me, here, at dead time of the night,
A thousand fiends, a thousand hissing snakes,
Ten thousand swelling toads, as many urchins,
Would make such fearful and confused cries,
As any mortal body hearing it
Should straight fall mad, or else die suddenly.
No sooner had they told this hellish tale,   105
But straight they told me they would bind me
    here
Unto the body of a dismal yew,
And leave me to this miserable death: 108
And then they called me foul adulteress,
Lascivious Goth, and all the bitterest terms
That ever ear did hear to such effect;
And, had you not by wondrous fortune come, 112
This vengeance on me had they executed.
Revenge it, as you love your mother's life,
Or be ye not henceforth call'd my children.

    Dem. This is a witness that I am thy son. 116
                    [*Stabs* BASSIANUS.

    Chi. And this for me, struck home to show
    my strength.
         [*Also stabs* BASSIANUS, *who dies.*

    Lav. Ay, come, Semiramis, nay, barbarous
    Tamora;
For no name fits thy nature but thy own.

Tam. Give me thy poniard; you shall know,
my boys,   120
Your mother's hand shall right your mother's
wrong.
Dem. Stay, madam; here is more belongs
to her:
First thrash the corn, then after burn the straw.
This minion stood upon her chastity,   124
Upon her nuptial vow, her loyalty,
And with that painted hope she braves your
mightiness:
And shall she carry this unto her grave?
Chi. An if she do, I would I were an eunuch.
Drag hence her husband to some secret hole, 129
And make his dead trunk pillow to our lust.
Tam. But when ye have the honey ye desire,
Let not this wasp outlive, us both to sting. 132
Chi. I warrant you, madam, we will make
that sure.
Come, mistress, now perforce we will enjoy
That nice-preserved honesty of yours.
Lav. O Tamora! thou bear'st a woman's
face,—   136
Tam. I will not hear her speak; away with
her!
Lav. Sweet lords, entreat her hear me but a
word.
Dem. Listen, fair madam: let it be your glory
To see her tears; but be your heart to them 140
As unrelenting flint to drops of rain.
Lav. When did the tiger's young ones teach
the dam?
O! do not learn her wrath; she taught it thee;
The milk thou suck'dst from her did turn to
marble;   144
Even at thy teat thou hadst thy tyranny.
Yet every mother breeds not sons alike:
[*To* CHIRON.] Do thou entreat her show a
woman pity.
Chi. What! wouldst thou have me prove
myself a bastard?   148
Lav. 'Tis true! the raven doth not hatch a
lark:
Yet have I heard, O! could I find it now,
The lion mov'd with pity did endure
To have his princely paws par'd all away. 152
Some say that ravens foster forlorn children,
The whilst their own birds famish in their nests:
O! be to me, though thy hard heart say no,
Nothing so kind, but something pitiful.   156
Tam. I know not what it means; away with
her!
Lav. O, let me teach thee! for my father's
sake,
That gave thee life when well he might have
slain thee,
Be not obdurate, open thy deaf ears.   160
Tam. Hadst thou in person ne'er offended
me,
Even for his sake am I pitiless.
Remember, boys, I pour'd forth tears in vain
To save your brother from the sacrifice;   164
But fierce Andronicus would not relent:
Therefore, away with her, and use her as you
will;
The worse to her, the better lov'd of me.

Lav. O Tamora! be call'd a gentle queen, 16
And with thine own hands kill me in this place
For 'tis not life that I have begg'd so long;
Poor I was slain when Bassianus died.
Tam. What begg'st thou then? fond woman
let me go.   17
Lav. 'Tis present death I beg: and one thin
more
That womanhood denies my tongue to tell.
O! keep me from their worse than killing lus
And tumble me into some loathsome pit,   17
Where never man's eye may behold my body
Do this, and be a charitable murderer.
Tam. So should I rob my sweet sons of the
fee:
No, let them satisfy their lust on thee.   18
Dem. Away! for thou hast stay'd us here too
long.
Lav. No grace! no womanhood! Ah, beast
creature,
The blot and enemy to our general name.
Confusion fall—   18
Chi. Nay, then I'll stop your mouth. Brin
thou her husband:
This is the hole where Aaron bid us hide hin
        [DEMETRIUS *throws the body of* BASSIANU
            into the pit; then exeunt DEMETRIU
            and CHIRON, *dragging off* LAVINIA.
Tam. Farewell, my sons: see that you mak
her sure.
Ne'er let my heart know merry cheer indeed 18
Till all the Andronici be made away.
Now will I hence to seek my lovely Moor,
And let my spleenful sons this trull deflower.
                                            [*Exi*

Enter AARON, *with* QUINTUS *and* MARTIUS.

Aar. Come on, my lords, the better foot be
fore: 19
Straight will I bring you to the loathsome pit
Where I espied the panther fast asleep.
Quin. My sight is very dull, whate'er it bodes
Mart. And mine, I promise you: were't no
for shame,   19
Well could I leave our sport to sleep awhile.
                              [*Falls into the pit*
Quin. What! art thou fall'n? What subtl
hole is this,
Whose mouth is cover'd with rude-growing
briers,   19
Upon whose leaves are drops of new-shed bloo
As fresh as morning's dew distill'd on flowers
A very fatal place it seems to me.
Speak, brother, hast thou hurt thee with the
fall?
Mart. O brother! with the dismall'st objec
hurt   20
That ever eye with sight made heart lament.
Aar. [*Aside.*] Now will I fetch the king t
find them here,
That he thereby may give a likely guess
How these were they that made away his brother
                                            [*Exit*
Mart. Why dost not comfort me, and help
me out   20
From this unhallow'd and blood-stained hole

Quin. I am surprised with an uncouth fear;
A chilling sweat o'erruns my trembling joints:
My heart suspects more than mine eye can
    see.   213
Mart. To prove thou hast a true-divining
    heart,
Aaron and thou look down into this den,
And see a fearful sight of blood and death. 216
Quin. Aaron is gone; and my compassionate
    heart
Will not permit mine eyes once to behold
The thing whereat it trembles by surmise.
O! tell me how it is; for ne'er till now   220
Was I a child, to fear I know not what.
Mart. Lord Bassianus lies embrewed here,
All on a heap, like to a slaughter'd lamb,
In this detested, dark, blood-drinking pit. 224
Quin. If it be dark, how dost thou know 'tis he?
Mart. Upon his bloody finger he doth wear
A precious ring, that lightens all the hole,
Which, like a taper in some monument, 228
Doth shine upon the dead man's earthy cheeks,
And shows the ragged entrails of the pit:
So pale did shine the moon on Pyramus
When he by night lay bath'd in maiden blood.
O brother! help me with thy fainting hand, 233
If fear hath made thee faint, as me it hath,
Out of this fell devouring receptacle,
As hateful as Cocytus' misty mouth. 236
Quin. Reach me thy hand, that I may help
    thee out;
Or, wanting strength to do thee so much good
I may be pluck'd into the swallowing womb
Of this deep pit, poor Bassianus' grave. 240
I have no strength to pluck thee to the brink.
Mart. Nor I no strength to climb without
    thy help.
Quin. Thy hand once more; I will not loose
    again,
Till thou art here aloft, or I below. 244
Thou canst not come to me: I come to thee.
                 [Falls in.

Re-enter AARON *with* SATURNINUS.

Sat. Along with me: I'll see what hole is
    here,
And what he is that now is leap'd into it.
Say, who art thou that lately didst descend 248
Into this gaping hollow of the earth?
Mart. The unhappy son of old Andronicus;
Brought hither in a most unlucky hour,
To find thy brother Bassianus dead. 252
Sat. My brother dead! I know thou dost but
    jest:
He and his lady both are at the lodge,
Upon the north side of this pleasant chase;
'Tis not an hour since I left him there. 256
Mart. We know not where you left him all
    alive;
But, out alas! here have we found him dead.

Enter TAMORA, *with* Attendants; TITUS ANDRO-
    NICUS, *and* LUCIUS.

Tam. Where is my lord, the king?
Sat. Here, Tamora; though griev'd with kill-
    ing grief. 260

Tam. Where is thy brother Bassianus?
Sat. Now to the bottom dost thou search my
    wound:
Poor Bassianus here lies murdered.
Tam. Then all too late I bring this fatal writ,
                 [Giving a letter.
The complot of this timeless tragedy; 265
And wonder greatly that man's face can fold
In pleasing smiles such murderous tyranny.
    Sat. And if we miss to meet him hand-
      somely, 268
Sweet huntsman, Bassianus 'tis we mean,
Do thou so much as dig the grave for him:
Thou know'st our meaning. Look for thy reward
Among the nettles of the elder-tree 272
Which overshades the mouth of that same pit
Where we decreed to bury Bassianus:
Do this, and purchase us thy lasting friends.
O Tamora! was ever heard the like? 276
This is the pit, and this the elder-tree.
Look, sirs, if you can find the huntsman out
That should have murder'd Bassianus here.
Aar. My gracious lord, here is the bag of
    gold. 280
Sat. [*To* TITUS.] Two of thy whelps, fell curs
    of bloody kind,
Have here bereft my brother of his life.
Sirs, drag them from the pit unto the prison:
There let them bide until we have devis'd 284
Some never-heard-of torturing pain for them.
Tam. What! are they in this pit? O won-
    drous thing!
How easily murder is discovered!
Tit. High emperor, upon my feeble knee 288
I beg this boon with tears not lightly shed;
That this fell fault of my accursed sons,
Accursed, if the fault be prov'd in them,—
Sat. If it be prov'd! you see it is apparent. 292
Who found this letter? Tamora, was it you?
Tam. Andronicus himself did take it up.
Tit. I did, my lord: yet let me be their bail;
For, by my father's reverend tomb, I vow 296
They shall be ready at your highness' will
To answer their suspicion with their lives.
Sat. Thou shalt not bail them: see thou fol-
    low me.
Some bring the murder'd body, some the mur-
    derers: 300
Let them not speak a word; the guilt is plain;
For, by my soul, were there worse end than
    death,
That end upon them should be executed.
Tam. Andronicus, I will entreat the king: 304
Fear not thy sons, they shall do well enough.
Tit. Come, Lucius, come; stay not to talk
    with them.   *[Exeunt severally.*

SCENE IV.—*Another Part of the Forest.*

Enter DEMETRIUS *and* CHIRON, *with* LAVINIA,
    ravished; her hands cut off, and her tongue
    cut out.

Dem. So, now go tell, an if thy tongue can
    speak,
Who 'twas that cut thy tongue and ravish'd
    thee.

Chi. Write down thy mind, bewray thy meaning so;
An if thy stumps will let thee play the scribe. 4
Dem. See, how with signs and tokens she can scrowl.
Chi. Go home, call for sweet water, wash thy hands.
Dem. She hath no tongue to call, nor hands to wash;
And so let's leave her to her silent walks. 8
Chi. An 'twere my case, I should go hang myself.
Dem. If thou hadst hands to help thee knit the cord.

[*Exeunt* DEMETRIUS *and* CHIRON.

Enter MARCUS.

Mar. Who's this? my niece, that flies away so fast?
Cousin, a word; where is your husband? 12
If I do dream, would all my wealth would wake me!
If I do wake, some planet strike me down,
That I may slumber in eternal sleep!
Speak, gentle niece, what stern ungentle hands 16
Have lopp'd and hew'd and made thy body bare
Of her two branches, those sweet ornaments,
Whose circling shadows kings have sought to sleep in,
And might not gain so great a happiness 20
As have thy love? Why dost not speak to me?
Alas! a crimson river of warm blood,
Like to a bubbling fountain stirr'd with wind,
Doth rise and fall between thy rosed lips, 24
Coming and going with thy honey breath.
But, sure, some Tereus hath deflower'd thee,
And, lest thou shouldst detect him, cut thy tongue.
Ah! now thou turn'st away thy face for shame; 28
And, notwithstanding all this loss of blood, 29
As from a conduit with three issuing spouts,
Yet do thy cheeks look red as Titan's face
Blushing to be encounter'd with a cloud. 32
Shall I speak for thee? shall I say 'tis so?
O! that I knew thy heart; and knew the beast,
That I might rail at him to ease my mind.
Sorrow concealed, like to an oven stopp'd, 36
Doth burn the heart to cinders where it is.
Fair Philomela, she but lost her tongue,
And in a tedious sampler sew'd her mind:
But, lovely niece, that mean is cut from thee; 40
A craftier Tereus hast thou met withal,
And he hath cut those pretty fingers off,
That could have better sew'd than Philomel.
O! had the monster seen those lily hands 44
Tremble, like aspen-leaves, upon a lute,
And make the silken strings delight to kiss them,
He would not, then, have touch'd them for his life;
Or had he heard the heavenly harmony 48
Which that sweet tongue hath made,
He would have dropp'd his knife, and fell asleep,
As Cerberus at the Thracian poet's feet.
Come, let us go, and make thy father blind; 52

For such a sight will blind a father's eye:
One hour's storm will drown the fragrant meads;
What will whole months of tears thy father's eyes?
Do not draw back, for we will mourn with thee: 56
O! could our mourning ease thy misery.

[*Exeunt.*

ACT III

SCENE I.—*Rome. A Street.*

Enter Senators, Tribunes, *and* Officers of Justice, *with* MARTIUS *and* QUINTUS, *bound, passing on to the place of execution;* TITUS *going before, pleading.*

Tit. Hear me, grave fathers! noble tribunes, stay!
For pity of mine age, whose youth was spent
In dangerous wars, whilst you securely slept;
For all my blood in Rome's great quarrel shed;
For all the frosty nights that I have watch'd; 5
And for these bitter tears, which now you see
Filling the aged wrinkles in my cheeks;
Be pitiful to my condemned sons, 8
Whose souls are not corrupted as 'tis thought.
For two and twenty sons I never wept,
Because they died in honour's lofty bed.
For these, these, tribunes, in the dust I write 12

[*He throws himself on the ground.*

My heart's deep languor and my soul's sad tears.
Let my tears stanch the earth's dry appetite;
My sons' sweet blood will make it shame and blush.   [*Exeunt* Senators, Tribunes, &c.,
with the Prisoners.
O earth! I will befriend thee more with rain, 16
That shall distil from these two ancient urns,
Than youthful April shall with all his showers:
In summer's drought I'll drop upon thee still;
In winter with warm tears I'll melt the snow, 20
And keep eternal spring-time on thy face,
So thou refuse to drink my dear sons' blood.

Enter LUCIUS, *with his sword drawn.*

O reverend tribunes! O gentle, aged men!
Unbind my sons, reverse the doom of death: 24
And let me say, that never wept before,
My tears are now prevailing orators.
Luc. O noble father, you lament in vain:
The tribunes hear you not, no man is by; 28
And you recount your sorrows to a stone.
Tit. Ah! Lucius, for thy brothers let me plead.
Grave tribunes, once more I entreat of you,—
Luc. My gracious lord, no tribune hears you speak. 32
Tit. Why, 'tis no matter, man: if they did hear,
They would not mark me, or if they did mark,
They would not pity me, yet plead I must,
All bootless unto them. 36
Therefore I tell my sorrows to the stones,
Who, though they cannot answer my distress,
Yet in some sort they are better than the tribunes,
For that they will not intercept my tale. 40

When I do weep, they humbly at my feet
Receive my tears, and seem to weep with me;
And, were they but attired in grave weeds,
Rome could afford no tribune like to these. 44
A stone is soft as wax, tribunes more hard than
  stones;
A stone is silent, and offendeth not,
And tribunes with their tongues doom men to
  death.   [*Rises.*
But wherefore stand'st thou with thy weapon
  drawn?   48
   Luc. To rescue my two brothers from their
  death;
For which attempt the judges have pronounc'd
My everlasting doom of banishment.
   Tit. O happy man! they have befriended
  thee.   52
Why, foolish Lucius, dost thou not perceive
That Rome is but a wilderness of tigers?
Tigers must prey; and Rome affords no prey
But me and mine: how happy art thou then, 56
From these devourers to be banished!
But who comes with our brother Marcus here?

     Enter MARCUS *and* LAVINIA.

   Mar. Titus, prepare thy aged eyes to weep;
Or, if not so, thy noble heart to break: 60
  bring consuming sorrow to thine age.
   Tit. Will it consume me? let me see it then.
   Mar. This was thy daughter.
   Tit. Why, Marcus, so she is. 64
   Luc. Ay me! this object kills me.
   Tit. Faint-hearted boy, arise, and look upon
  her.
Speak, Lavinia, what accursed hand
Hath made thee handless in thy father's sight?
What fool hath added water to the sea, 69
Or brought a faggot to bright-burning Troy?
My grief was at the height before thou cam'st;
And now, like Nilus, it disdaineth bounds. 72
Give me a sword, I'll chop off my hands too;
For they have fought for Rome, and all in vain;
And they have nurs'd this woe, in feeding life;
In bootless prayer have they been held up, 76
And they have serv'd me to effectless use:
Now all the service I require of them
Is that the one will help to cut the other.
'Tis well, Lavinia, that thou hast no hands, 80
For hands, to do Rome service, are but vain.
   Luc. Speak, gentle sister, who hath martyr'd
  thee?
   Mar. O! that delightful engine of her
  thoughts,
That blabb'd them with such pleasing elo-
  quence, 84
Is torn from forth that pretty hollow cage,
Where, like a sweet melodious bird, it sung
Sweet varied notes, enchanting every ear.
   Luc. O! say thou for her, who hath done
  this deed? 88
   Mar. O! thus I found her straying in the park,
Seeking to hide herself, as doth the deer,
That hath receiv'd some unrecuring wound.
   Tit. It was my dear; and he that wounded
  her 92
Hath hurt me more than had he kill'd me dead:

For now I stand as one upon a rock
Environ'd with a wilderness of sea,
Who marks the waxing tide grow wave by wave,
Expecting ever when some envious surge 97
Will in his brinish bowels swallow him.
This way to death my wretched sons are gone;
Here stands my other son, a banish'd man, 100
And here my brother, weeping at my woes:
But that which gives my soul the greatest spurn,
Is dear Lavinia, dearer than my soul.
Had I but seen thy picture in this plight 104
It would have madded me: what shall I do
Now I behold thy lively body so?
Thou hast no hands to wipe away thy tears,
Nor tongue to tell me who hath martyr'd thee:
Thy husband he is dead, and for his death 109
Thy brothers are condemn'd, and dead by this.
Look! Marcus; ah! son Lucius, look on her:
When I did name her brothers, then fresh tears
Stood on her cheeks, as doth the honey-dew 113
Upon a gather'd lily almost wither'd.
   Mar. Perchance she weeps because they
  kill'd her husband;
Perchance because she knows them innocent.
   Tit. If they did kill thy husband, then be
  joyful, 117
Because the law hath ta'en revenge on them.
No, no, they would not do so foul a deed;
Witness the sorrow that their sister makes. 120
Gentle Lavinia, let me kiss thy lips;
Or make some sign how I may do thee ease.
Shall thy good uncle, and thy brother Lucius,
And thou, and I, sit round about some foun-
  tain, 124
Looking all downwards, to behold our cheeks
How they are stain'd, like meadows yet not dry,
With miry slime left on them by a flood?
And in the fountain shall we gaze so long 128
Till the fresh taste be taken from that clearness,
And made a brine-pit with our bitter tears?
Or shall we cut away our hands, like thine?
Or shall we bite our tongues, and in dumb
  shows 132
Pass the remainder of our hateful days?
What shall we do? let us, that have our tongues,
Plot some device of further misery,
To make us wonder'd at in time to come. 136
   Luc. Sweet father, cease your tears; for at
  your grief
See how my wretched sister sobs and weeps.
   Mar. Patience, dear niece. Good Titus, dry
  thine eyes.
   Tit. Ah! Marcus, Marcus, brother; well I
  wot 140
Thy napkin cannot drink a tear of mine,
For thou, poor man, hast drown'd it with thine
  own.
   Luc. Ah! my Lavinia, I will wipe thy cheeks.
   Tit. Mark, Marcus, mark! I understand her
  signs: 144
Had she a tongue to speak, now would she say
That to her brother which I said to thee:
His napkin, with his true tears all bewet,
Can do no service on her sorrowful cheeks. 148
O! what a sympathy of woe is this;
As far from help as limbo is from bliss.

Enter AARON.

Aar. Titus Andronicus, my lord the emperor
Sends thee this word: that, if thou love thy
    sons,   152
Let Marcus, Lucius, or thyself, old Titus,
Or any one of you, chop off your hand,
And send it to the king: he for the same
Will send thee hither both thy sons alive;   156
And that shall be the ransom for their fault.
Tit. O gracious emperor! O gentle Aaron!
Did ever raven sing so like a lark,
That gives sweet tidings of the sun's uprise? 160
With all my heart, I'll send the emperor my
    hand:
Good Aaron, wilt thou help to chop it off?
Luc. Stay, father! for that noble hand of
    thine,
That hath thrown down so many enemies, 164
Shall not be sent; my hand will serve the turn:
My youth can better spare my blood than you;
And therefore mine shall save my brothers'
    lives.
Mar. Which of your hands hath not de-
    fended Rome,   168
And rear'd aloft the bloody battle-axe,
Writing destruction on the enemy's castle?
O! none of both but are of high desert:
My hand hath been but idle; let it serve   172
To ransom my two nephews from their death;
Then have I kept it to a worthy end.
Aar. Nay, come, agree whose hand shall go
    along,
For fear they die before their pardon come. 176
Mar. My hand shall go.
Luc.   By heaven, it shall not go!
Tit. Sirs, strive no more: such wither'd herbs
    as these
Are meet for plucking up, and therefore mine.
Luc. Sweet father, if I shall be thought thy
    son,   180
Let me redeem my brothers both from death.
Mar. And for our father's sake, and mother's
    care,
Now let me show a brother's love to thee.
Tit. Agree between you; I will spare my
    hand.   184
Luc. Then I'll go fetch an axe.
Mar.   But I will use the axe.
    [*Exeunt* LUCIUS *and* MARCUS.
Tit. Come hither, Aaron; I'll deceive them
    both:
Lend me thy hand, and I will give thee mine.
Aar. [*Aside.*] If that be call'd deceit, I will
    be honest,   188
And never, whilst I live, deceive men so:
But I'll deceive you in another sort,
And that you'll say, ere half an hour pass.
    [*Cuts off* TITUS' *hand.*

Re-enter LUCIUS *and* MARCUS.

Tit. Now stay your strife: what shall be is
    dispatch'd.   192
Good Aaron, give his majesty my hand:

Tell him it was a hand that warded him
From thousand dangers; bid him bury it;
More hath it merited; that let it have.   196
As for my sons, say I account of them
As jewels purchas'd at an easy price;
And yet dear too, because I bought mine own.
Aar. I go, Andronicus; and for thy hand,
Look by and by to have thy sons with thee. 201
[*Aside.*] Their heads, I mean. O! how this
    villany
Doth fat me with the very thoughts of it.
Let fools do good, and fair men call for grace,
Aaron will have his soul black like his face. 205
    [*Exit.*
Tit. O! here I lift this one hand up to heaven,
And bow this feeble ruin to the earth:
If any power pities wretched tears,   208
To that I call! [*To* LAVINIA.] What! wilt thou
    kneel with me?
Do, then, dear heart; for heaven shall hear our
    prayers,
Or with our sighs we'll breathe the welkin
    dim,   211
And stain the sun with fog, as sometime clouds
When they do hug him in their melting bosoms.
Mar. O! brother, speak with possibilities,
And do not break into these deep extremes.
Tit. Is not my sorrow deep, having no
    bottom?   216
Then be my passions bottomless with them.
Mar. But yet let reason govern thy lament.
Tit. If there were reason for these miseries,
Then into limits could I bind my woes.   220
When heaven doth weep, doth not the earth
    o'erflow?
If the winds rage, doth not the sea wax mad,
Threat'ning the welkin with his big-swoln face?
And wilt thou have a reason for this coil? 224
I am the sea; hark! how her sighs do blow;
She is the weeping welkin, I the earth:
Then must my sea be moved with her sighs;
Then must my earth with her continual tears
Become a deluge, overflow'd and drown'd; 229
For why my bowels cannot hide her woes,
But like a drunkard must I vomit them.
Then give me leave, for losers will have leave 232
To ease their stomachs with their bitter tongues.

Enter a Messenger, *with two heads and
a hand.*

Mess. Worthy Andronicus, ill art thou re-
    paid
For that good hand thou sent'st the emperor.
Here are the heads of thy two noble sons, 236
And here's thy hand, in scorn to thee sent back:
Thy griefs their sports, thy resolution mock'd;
That woe is me to think upon thy woes,
More than remembrance of my father's death.
    [*Exit.*
Mar. Now let hot Ætna cool in Sicily,   241
And be my heart an ever burning hell!
These miseries are more than may be borne.
To weep with them that weep doth ease some
    deal,   244
But sorrow flouted at is double death.

Luc. Ah! that this sight should make so deep
  a wound,
nd yet detested life not shrink thereat,   247
hat ever death should let life bear his name,
Where life hath no more interest but to breathe.
  [LAVINIA *kisses* TITUS.
Mar. Alas! poor heart; that kiss is comfortless
s frozen water to a starved snake.
Tit. When will this fearful slumber have an
  end?   252
Mar. Now, farewell, flattery: die, Andronicus;
hou dost not slumber: see, thy two sons' heads,
hy war-like hand, thy mangled daughter here;
hy other banish'd son, with this dear sight 256
ruck pale and bloodless; and thy brother, I,
ven like a stony image, cold and numb.
h! now no more will I control my griefs.
ent off thy silver hair, thy other hand   260
nawing with thy teeth; and be this dismal
  sight
he closing up of our most wretched eyes!
ow is a time to storm; why art thou still?
Tit. Ha, ha, ha!   264
Mar. Why dost thou laugh? it fits not with
  this hour.
Tit. Why, I have not another tear to shed:
esides, this sorrow is an enemy,
nd would usurp upon my watery eyes,   268
nd make them blind with tributary tears:
hen which way shall I find Revenge's cave?
or these two heads do seem to speak to me,
nd threat me I shall never come to bliss   272
ill all these mischiefs be return'd again
ven in their throats that have committed
  them.
ome, let me see what task I have to do.
ou heavy people, circle me about,   276
hat I may turn me to each one of you,
nd swear unto my soul to right your wrongs.
he vow is made. Come, brother, take a head;
nd in this hand the other will I bear.   280
avinia, thou shalt be employ'd in these things:
ear thou my hand, sweet wench, between thy
  teeth.
s for thee, boy, go get thee from my sight;
hou art an exile, and thou must not stay: 284
ie to the Goths, and raise an army there:
nd if you love me, as I think you do,
et's kiss and part, for we have much to do.
  [*Exeunt* TITUS, MARCUS, *and* LAVINIA.
Luc. Farewell, Andronicus, my noble father;
he woefull'st man that ever liv'd in Rome: 289
arewell, proud Rome; till Lucius come again,
He leaves his pledges dearer than his life.
arewell, Lavinia, my noble sister;   292
O! would thou wert as thou tofore hast been;
ut now nor Lucius nor Lavinia lives
ut in oblivion and hateful griefs.
f Lucius live, he will requite your wrongs, 296
And make proud Saturnine and his empress
eg at the gates like Tarquin and his queen.
ow will I to the Goths, and raise a power,
o be reveng'd on Rome and Saturnine.   300
  [*Exit.*

SCENE II.—*The Same. A Room in* TITUS'
  House. A Banquet set out.

Enter TITUS, MARCUS, LAVINIA, *and young*
  LUCIUS, *a Boy.*

Tit. So, so; now sit; and look you eat no
  more
Than will preserve just so much strength in us
As will revenge these bitter woes of ours.
Marcus, unknit that sorrow-wreathen knot: 4
Thy niece and I, poor creatures, want our hands,
And cannot passionate our ten-fold grief
With folded arms. This poor right hand of
  mine
Is left to tyrannize upon my breast;   8
And when my heart, all mad with misery,
Beats in this hollow prison of my flesh,
Then thus I thump it down.
  [*To* LAVINIA.] Thou map of woe, that thus dost
    talk in signs!   12
When thy poor heart beats with outrageous
  beating
Thou canst not strike it thus to make it still.
Wound it with sighing, girl, kill it with groans;
Or get some little knife between thy teeth, 16
And just against thy heart make thou a hole;
That all the tears that thy poor eyes let fall
May run into that sink, and, soaking in,
Drown the lamenting fool in sea-salt tears. 20
Mar. Fie, brother, fie! teach her not thus to
  lay
Such violent hands upon her tender life.
Tit. How now! has sorrow made thee dote
  already?
Why, Marcus, no man should be mad but I.   24
What violent hands can she lay on her life?
Ah! wherefore dost thou urge the name of
  hands;
To bid Æneas tell the tale twice o'er,
How Troy was burnt and he made miserable?   28
O! handle not the theme, to talk of hands,
Lest we remember still that we have none.
Fie, fie! how franticly I square my talk,
As if we should forget we had no hands,   32
If Marcus did not name the word of hands.
Come, let's fall to; and, gentle girl, eat this:
Here is no drink. Hark, Marcus, what she says;
I can interpret all her martyr'd signs;   36
She says she drinks no other drink but tears,
Brew'd with her sorrow, mash'd upon her
  cheeks.
Speechless complainer, I will learn thy thought;
In thy dumb action will I be as perfect   40
As begging hermits in their holy prayers:
Thou shalt not sigh, nor hold thy stumps to
  heaven,
Nor wink, nor nod, nor kneel, nor make a sign,
But I of these will wrest an alphabet,   44
And by still practice learn to know thy meaning.
Boy. Good grandsire, leave these bitter deep
  laments:
Make my aunt merry with some pleasing tale.
Mar. Alas! the tender boy, in passion mov'd,
Doth weep to see his grandsire's heaviness. 49
Tit. Peace, tender sapling; thou art made of
  tears,

And tears will quickly melt thy life away.
[MARCUS *strikes the dish with a knife.*
What dost thou strike at, Marcus, with thy
knife? 52
Mar. At that that I have kill'd, my lord; a
fly.
Tit. Out on thee, murderer! thou kill'st my
heart;
Mine eyes are cloy'd with view of tyranny:
A deed of death, done on the innocent, 56
Becomes not Titus' brother. Get thee gone;
I see, thou art not for my company.
Mar. Alas! my lord, I have but kill'd a fly.
Tit. But how if that fly had a father and a
mother? 60
How would he hang his slender gilded wings
And buzz lamenting doings in the air!
Poor harmless fly,
That, with his pretty buzzing melody, 64
Came here to make us merry! and thou hast
kill'd him.
Mar. Pardon me, sir; it was a black ill-
favour'd fly,
Like to the empress' Moor; therefore I kill'd
him.
Tit. O, O, O! 68
Then pardon me for reprehending thee,
For thou hast done a charitable deed.
Give me thy knife, I will insult on him;
Flattering myself, as if it were the Moor 72
Come hither purposely to poison me.
There's for thyself, and that's for Tamora.
Ah! sirrah,
Yet I think we are not brought so low, 76
But that between us we can kill a fly
That comes in likeness of a coal-black Moor.
Mar. Alas! poor man; grief has so wrought
on him,
He takes false shadows for true substances. 80
Tit. Come, take away. Lavinia, go with me:
I'll to thy closet; and go read with thee
Sad stories chanced in the times of old.
Come, boy, and go with me: thy sight is young,
And thou shalt read when mine begins to dazzle.
[*Exeunt.*

ACT IV

SCENE I.—*Rome.* TITUS' *Garden.*

Enter TITUS *and* MARCUS. *Then enter young*
LUCIUS, LAVINIA *running after him.*

Boy. Help, grandsire, help! my aunt Lavinia
Follows me everywhere, I know not why:
Good uncle Marcus, see how swift she comes:
Alas! sweet aunt, I know not what you mean. 4
Mar. Stand by me, Lucius; do not fear thine
aunt.
Tit. She loves thee, boy, too well to do thee
harm.
Boy. Ay, when my father was in Rome, she
did.
Mar. What means my niece Lavinia by these
signs? 8
Tit. Fear her not, Lucius: somewhat doth
she mean.
See, Lucius, see how much she makes of thee;

Somewhither would she have thee go with her
Ah! boy; Cornelia never with more care
Read to her sons, than she hath read to thee
Sweet poetry and Tully's Orator.
Mar. Canst thou not guess wherefore she
plies thee thus?
Boy. My lord, I know not, I, nor can I guess
Unless some fit or frenzy do possess her;
For I have heard my grandsire say full oft,
Extremity of griefs would make men mad;
And I have read that Hecuba of Troy
Ran mad through sorrow; that made me to fear
Although, my lord, I know my noble aunt
Loves me as dear as e'er my mother did,
And would not, but in fury, fright my youth;
Which made me down to throw my books an
fly,
Causeless, perhaps. But pardon me, sweet aunt
And, madam, if my uncle Marcus go,
I will most willingly attend your ladyship.
Mar. Lucius, I will.
[LAVINIA *turns over the books which*
LUCIUS *had let fall*
Tit. How now, Lavinia! Marcus, what mean
this?
Some book there is that she desires to see.
Which is it, girl, of these? Open them, boy.
But thou art deeper read, and better skill'd;
Come, and take choice of all my library,
And so beguile thy sorrow, till the heavens
Reveal the damn'd contriver of this deed.
Why lifts she up her arms in sequence thus?
Mar. I think she means that there was more
than one
Confederate in the fact: ay, more there was;
Or else to heaven she heaves them for revenge
Tit. Lucius, what book is that she tosseth so
Boy. Grandsire, 'tis Ovid's Metamorphoses
My mother gave it me.
Mar. For love of her that's gone
Perhaps, she cull'd it from among the rest.
Tit. Soft! see how busily she turns the leaves
[*Helping her*
What would she find? Lavinia, shall I read?
This is the tragic tale of Philomel,
And treats of Tereus' treason and his rape;
And rape, I fear, was root of thine annoy.
Mar. See, brother, see! note how she quote
the leaves.
Tit. Lavinia, wert thou thus surpris'd, sweet
girl,
Ravish'd and wrong'd, as Philomela was,
Forc'd in the ruthless, vast, and gloomy woods
See, see!
Ay, such a place there is, where we did hunt,
O! had we never, never hunted there,—
Pattern'd by that the poet here describes,
By nature made for murders and for rapes.
Mar. O! why should nature build so foul a
den,
Unless the gods delight in tragedies?
Tit. Give signs, sweet girl, for here are none
but friends,
What Roman lord it was durst do the deed:
Or slunk not Saturnine, as Tarquin erst,
That left the camp to sin in Lucrece' bed?

Mar. Sit down, sweet niece: brother, sit
   down by me.
pollo, Pallas, Jove, or Mercury,
spire me, that I may this treason find!
y lord, look here; look here, Lavinia: 68
his sandy plot is plain; guide, if thou canst,
his after me.
   [*He writes his name with his staff, and
     guides it with his feet and mouth.*
   I have writ my name
'ithout the help of any hand at all.
urs'd be that heart that forc'd us to this shift!
'rite thou, good niece, and here display at last
'hat God will have discover'd for revenge. 74
eaven guide thy pen to print thy sorrows plain,
hat we may know the traitors and the truth!
   [*She takes the staff in her mouth, and guides
     it with her stumps, and writes.*
   Tit. O! do you read, my lord, what she hath
   writ?   77
tuprum, *Chiron, Demetrius.*
   Mar. What, what! the lustful sons of Tamora
erformers of this heinous, bloody deed?   80
   Tit. Magni dominator poli,
am lentus audis scelera? tam lentus vides?
   Mar. O! calm thee, gentle lord; although I
   know
here is enough written upon this earth   84
o stir a mutiny in the mildest thoughts
nd arm the minds of infants to exclaims.
Iy lord, kneel down with me; Lavinia, kneel;
nd kneel, sweet boy, the Roman Hector's hope;
nd swear with me, as, with the woeful fere 89
nd father of that chaste dishonour'd dame,
ord Junius Brutus sware for Lucrece' rape,
hat we will prosecute by good advice   92
Iortal revenge upon these traitorous Goths,
nd see their blood, or die with this reproach.
   Tit. 'Tis sure enough, an you knew how;
ut if you hunt these bear-whelps, then beware:
he dam will wake, an if she wind you once: 97
he 's after the lion deeply still in league,
nd lulls him whilst she playeth on her back,
nd when he sleeps will she do what she list. 100
'ou're a young huntsman, Marcus; let it alone;
nd, come, I 'll go get a leaf of brass,
nd with a gad of steel will write these words,
nd lay it by: the angry northern wind   104
Vill blow these sands like Sibyl's leaves abroad,
nd where 's your lesson then? Boy, what say
   you?
   Boy. I say, my lord, that if I were a man,
'heir mother's bed-chamber should not be safe
'or these bad bondmen to the yoke of Rome. 109
   Mar. Ay, that 's my boy! thy father hath full
   oft
'or his ungrateful country done the like.
   Boy. And, uncle, so will I, an if I live.   112
   Tit. Come, go with me into mine armoury:
ucius, I'll fit thee; and withal my boy
hall carry from me to the empress' sons
resents that I intend to send them both: 116
'ome, come; thou 'lt do thy message, wilt thou
   not?
   Boy. Ay, with my dagger in their bosoms,
   grandsire.

Tit. No, boy, not so; I'll teach thee another
   course.
Lavinia, come. Marcus, look to my house; 120
Lucius and I'll go brave it at the court:
Ay, marry, will we, sir; and we'll go waited on.
   [*Exeunt* TITUS, LAVINIA, *and* Boy.
   Mar. O heavens! can you hear a good man
   groan,
And not relent or not compassion him?   124
Marcus, attend him in his ecstasy,
That hath more scars of sorrow in his heart
Than foemen's marks upon his batter'd shield;
But yet so just that he will not revenge.   128
Revenge, ye heavens, for old Andronicus! [*Exit.*

SCENE II.—*The Same. A Room in the Palace.*

Enter, from one side, AARON, DEMETRIUS, *and*
CHIRON; *from the other young* LUCIUS, *and
an* Attendant, *with a bundle of weapons, and
verses writ upon them.*

   Chi. Demetrius, here 's the son of Lucius;
He hath some message to deliver us.
   Aar. Ay, some mad message from his mad
   grandfather.
   Boy. My lords, with all the humbleness I
   may,   4
I greet your honours from Andronicus;
[*Aside.*] And pray the Roman gods, confound
   you both!
   Dem. Gramercy, lovely Lucius: what's the
   news?
   Boy. [*Aside.*] That you are both decipher'd,
   that 's the news,   8
For villains mark'd with rape. [*Aloud.*] May it
   please you,
My grandsire, well advis'd, hath sent by me
The goodliest weapons of his armoury,
To gratify your honourable youth,   12
The hope of Rome, for so he bade me say;
And so I do, and with his gifts present
Your lordships, that whenever you have need,
You may be armed and appointed well.   16
And so I leave you both: [*Aside.*] like bloody
   villains.   [*Exeunt* Boy *and* Attendant.
   Dem. What's here? A scroll; and written
   round about?
Let 's see:—
[*Reads.*] '*Integer vitæ, scelerisque purus,*   20
     Non eget Mauri jaculis, nec arcu.
   Chi. O! 'tis a verse in Horace; I know it well:
I read it in the grammar long ago.
   Aar. Ay just, a verse in Horace; right, you
   have it.   24
[*Aside.*] Now, what a thing it is to be an ass!
Here 's no sound jest! the old man hath found
   their guilt
And sends them weapons wrapp'd about with
   lines,
That wound, beyond their feeling, to the quick;
But were our witty empress well afoot,   29
She would applaud Andronicus' conceit:
But let her rest in her unrest awhile.
[*To them.*] And now, young lords, was 't not a
   happy star   32
Led us to Rome, strangers, and more than so,

Captives, to be advanced to this height?
It did me good before the palace gate
To brave the tribune in his brother's hearing. 36
  Dem. But me more good, to see so great a lord
Basely insinuate and send us gifts.
  Aar. Had he not reason, Lord Demetrius?
Did you not use his daughter very friendly? 40
  Dem. I would we had a thousand Roman dames
At such a bay, by turn to serve our lust.
  Chi. A charitable wish and full of love.
  Aar. Here lacks but your mother for to say amen. 44
  Chi. And that would she for twenty thousand more.
  Dem. Come, let us go and pray to all the gods
For our beloved mother in her pains.
  Aar. [*Aside.*] Pray to the devils; the gods have given us over. [*Trumpets sound.*
  Dem. Why do the emperor's trumpets flourish thus? 49
  Chi. Belike, for joy the emperor hath a son.
  Dem. Soft! who comes here?

Enter a Nurse, *with a blackamoor Child.*

  Nur. Good morrow, lords. O! tell me, did you see 52
Aaron the Moor?
  Aar. Well, more or less, or ne'er a whit at all,
Here Aaron is; and what with Aaron now?
  Nur. O gentle Aaron! we are all undone. 56
Now help, or woe betide thee evermore!
  Aar. Why, what a caterwauling dost thou keep!
What dost thou wrap and fumble in thine arms?
  Nur. O! that which I would hide from heaven's eye, 60
Our empress' shame, and stately Rome's disgrace!
She is deliver'd, lords, she is deliver'd.
  Aar. To whom?
  Nur. I mean, she's brought a-bed.
  Aar. Well, God give her good rest! What hath he sent her? 64
  Nur. A devil.
  Aar. Why, then she's the devil's dam: a joyful issue.
  Nur. A joyless, dismal, black, and sorrowful issue.
Here is the babe, as loathsome as a toad 68
Amongst the fairest breeders of our clime.
The empress sends it thee, thy stamp, thy seal,
And bids thee christen it with thy dagger's point.
  Aar. 'Zounds, ye whore! is black so base a hue? 72
Sweet blowse, you are a beauteous blossom, sure.
  Dem. Villain, what hast thou done?
  Aar. That which thou canst not undo.
  Chi. Thou hast undone our mother. 76
  Aar. Villain, I have done thy mother.
  Dem. And therein, hellish dog, thou hast undone.
Woe to her chance, and damn'd her loathed choice!

Accurs'd the offspring of so foul a fiend!
  Chi. It shall not live.
  Aar. It shall not die.
  Nur. Aaron, it must; the mother wills it s[o]
  Aar. What! must it, nurse? then let no ma[n] but I
Do execution on my flesh and blood.
  Dem. I'll broach the tadpole on my rapier['s] point:
Nurse, give it me; my sword shall soon dispatc[h] it.
  Aar. Sooner this sword shall plough th[y] bowels up.
      [*Takes the Child from the* Nurs[e]
                and draw[s]
Stay, murderous villains! will you kill yo[ur] brother?
Now, by the burning tapers of the sky,
That shone so brightly when this boy was go[t]
He dies upon my scimitar's sharp point
That touches this my first-born son and heir[.]
I tell you, younglings, not Enceladus,
With all his threatening band of Typhon['s] brood,
Nor great Alcides, nor the god of war,
Shall seize this prey out of his father's hand[s]
What, what, ye sanguine, shallow-hearted boy[s]
Ye white-lim'd walls! ye alehouse painted sign[s]
Coal-black is better than another hue, 10[0]
In that it scorns to bear another hue;
For all the water in the ocean
Can never turn the swan's black legs to whit[e]
Although she lave them hourly in the flood. 10[
Tell the empress from me, I am of age
To keep mine own, excuse it how she can.
  Dem. Wilt thou betray thy noble mistre[ss] thus?
  Aar. My mistress is my mistress; this m[y] self; 10[
The vigour, and the picture of my youth:
This before all the world do I prefer;
This maugre all the world will I keep safe,
Or some of you shall smoke for it in Rome.
  Dem. By this our mother is for ever sham['d]
  Chi. Rome will despise her for this fo[ul] escape.
  Nur. The emperor in his rage will doom he[r] death.
  Chi. I blush to think upon this ignomy. 11[
  Aar. Why, there's the privilege your beaut[y] bears.
Fie, treacherous hue! that will betray wit[h] blushing
The close enacts and counsels of the heart:
Here's a young lad fram'd of another leer: 12[
Look how the black slave smiles upon the fathe[r]
As who should say, 'Old lad, I am thine own[']
He is your brother, lords, sensibly fed
Of that self blood that first gave life to you; 12[
And from that womb where you imprison'[d]
were
He is enfranchised and come to light:
Nay, he is your brother by the surer side,
Although my seal be stamped in his face. 1[
  Nur. Aaron, what shall I say unto the em[press?]

Dem. Advise thee, Aaron, what is to be done,
nd we will all subscribe to thy advice:
ve thou the child, so we may all be safe. 132
Aar. Then sit we down, and let us all consult,
[y son and I will have the wind of you:
eep there; now talk at pleasure of your safety.
[*They sit.*
Dem. How many women saw this child of
his? 136
Aar. Why, so, brave lords! when we join in
league,
am a lamb; but if you brave the Moor,
he chafed boar, the mountain lioness,
he ocean swells not so as Aaron storms. 140
ut say, again, how many saw the child?
Nur. Cornelia the midwife, and myself,
nd no one else but the deliver'd empress.
Aar. The empress, the midwife, and yourself: 144
wo may keep counsel when the third's away:
o to the empress; tell her this I said:
[*Stabbing her.*
Weke, weke!'
o cries a pig prepared to the spit. 148
Dem. What mean'st thou, Aaron? Wherefore didst thou this?
Aar. O lord, sir, 'tis a deed of policy:
hall she live to betray this guilt of ours,
long-tongu'd babbling gossip? no, lords, no.
nd now be it known to you my full intent. 153
[ot far, one Muli lives, my countryman;
[is wife but yesternight was brought to bed.
[is child is like to her, fair as you are: 156
o pack with him, and give the mother gold,
nd tell them both the circumstance of all,
nd how by this their child shall be advanc'd,
nd be received for the emperor's heir, 160
nd substituted in the place of mine,
o calm this tempest whirling in the court;
nd let the emperor dandle him for his own.
Mark ye, lords; you see, I have given her physic.
[*Pointing to the* Nurse.
nd you must needs bestow her funeral; 165
he fields are near, and you are gallant grooms.
his done, see that you take no longer days,
ut send the midwife presently to me. 168
he midwife and the nurse well made away,
hen let the ladies tattle what they please.
Chi. Aaron, I see thou wilt not trust the air
with secrets.
Dem. For this care of Tamora, 172
Ierself and hers are highly bound to thee.
[*Exeunt* DEMETRIUS *and* CHIRON,
bearing off the Nurse's *body.*
Aar. Now to the Goths, as swift as swallow
flies;
here to dispose this treasure in mine arms,
nd secretly to greet the empress' friends. 176
Come on, you thick-lipp'd slave, I'll bear you
hence;
or it is you that puts us to our shifts:
'll make you feed on berries and on roots,
nd feed on curds and whey, and suck the goat,
nd cabin in a cave, and bring you up 181
o be a warrior, and command a camp.
[*Exit with the* Child.

SCENE III.—*The Same. A Public Place.*

Enter TITUS, *bearing arrows, with letters on the ends of them; with him* MARCUS, *young* LUCIUS, PUBLIUS, SEMPRONIUS, CAIUS, *and other* Gentlemen, *with bows.*

Tit. Come, Marcus, come; kinsmen, this is
the way.
Sir boy, now let me see your archery:
Look ye draw home enough, and 'tis there
straight.
Terras Astræa reliquit: 4
Be you remember'd, Marcus, she's gone, she's
fled.
Sirs, take you to your tools. You, cousins, shall
Go sound the ocean, and cast your nets;
Happily you may find her in the sea; 8
Yet there's as little justice as at land.
No; Publius and Sempronius, you must do it;
'Tis you must dig with mattock and with spade,
And pierce the inmost centre of the earth: 12
Then, when you come to Pluto's region,
I pray you, deliver him this petition;
Tell him, it is for justice and for aid,
And that it comes from old Andronicus, 16
Shaken with sorrows in ungrateful Rome.
Ah! Rome. Well, well; I made thee miserable
What time I threw the people's suffrages
On him that thus doth tyrannize o'er me. 20
Go, get you gone; and pray be careful all,
And leave you not a man-of-war unsearch'd:
This wicked emperor may have shipp'd her
hence;
And, kinsmen, then we may go pipe for justice.
Mar. O Publius! is not this a heavy case, 25
To see thy noble uncle thus distract?
Pub. Therefore, my lord, it highly us concerns
By day and night to attend him carefully, 28
And feed his humour kindly as we may,
Till time beget some careful remedy.
Mar. Kinsmen, his sorrows are past remedy.
Join with the Goths, and with revengeful war 32
Take wreak on Rome for this ingratitude,
And vengeance on the traitor Saturnine.
Tit. Publius, how now! how now, my masters!
What! have you met with her? 36
Pub. No, my good lord; but Pluto sends you
word,
If you will have Revenge from hell, you shall:
Marry, for Justice, she is so employ'd,
He thinks, with Jove in heaven, or somewhere
else, 40
So that perforce you must needs stay a time.
Tit. He doth me wrong to feed me with delays.
I'll dive into the burning lake below,
And pull her out of Acheron by the heels. 44
Marcus, we are but shrubs, no cedars we;
No big-bon'd men fram'd of the Cyclops' size;
But metal, Marcus, steel to the very back,
Yet wrung with wrongs more than our backs
can bear: 48
And sith there's no justice in earth nor hell,
We will solicit heaven and move the gods
To send down Justice for to wreak our wrongs.
Come, to this gear. You are a good archer,

Marcus.   [*He gives them the arrows.*
Ad Jovem, that's for you: here, *ad Apollinem:*
Ad Martem, that's for myself:
Here, boy, to Pallas: here, to Mercury:
To Saturn, Caius, not to Saturnine;   56
You were as good to shoot against the wind.
To it, boy! Marcus, loose when I bid.
Of my word, I have written to effect;
There's not a god left unsolicited.   60
     Mar. Kinsmen, shoot all your shafts into
          the court:
We will afflict the emperor in his pride.
     Tit. Now, masters, draw. [*They shoot.*] O!
          well said, Lucius!
Good boy, in Virgo's lap: give it Pallas.   64
     Mar. My lord, I aim a mile beyond the moon;
Your letter is with Jupiter by this.
     Tit. Ha! Publius, Publius, what hast thou
          done?
See, see! thou hast shot off one of Taurus' horns.
     Mar. This was the sport, my lord: when
          Publius shot,   69
The Bull, being gall'd, gave Aries such a knock
That down fell both the Ram's horns in the court;
And who should find them but the empress'
          villain?   72
She laugh'd, and told the Moor, he should not
          choose
But give them to his master for a present.
     Tit. Why, there it goes: God give his lord-
          ship joy!

Enter a Clown, *with a basket, and two pigeons
          in it.*

News! news from heaven! Marcus, the post is
          come.   76
Sirrah, what tidings? have you any letters?
Shall I have justice? what says Jupiter?
     Clo. O! the gibbet-maker? He says that he
hath taken them down again, for the man must
not be hanged till the next week.   81
     Tit. But what says Jupiter, I ask thee?
     Clo. Alas! sir, I know not Jupiter; I never
drank with him in all my life.   84
     Tit. Why, villain, art not thou the carrier?
     Clo. Ay, of my pigeons, sir; nothing else.
     Tit. Why, didst thou not come from heaven?
     Clo. From heaven! alas! sir, I never came
there. God forbid I should be so bold to press
to heaven in my young days. Why, I am going
with my pigeons to the tribunal plebs, to take
up a matter of brawl betwixt my uncle and one
of the emperial's men.   93
     Mar. Why, sir, that is as fit as can be to
serve for your oration; and let him deliver the
pigeons to the emperor from you.   96
     Tit. Tell me, can you deliver an oration to
the emperor with a grace?
     Clo. Nay, truly, sir, I could never say grace
in all my life.   100
     Tit. Sirrah, come hither: make no more ado,
But give your pigeons to the emperor:
By me thou shalt have justice at his hands.
Hold, hold; meanwhile, here's money for thy
          charges.   104
Give me pen and ink.

Sirrah, can you with a grace deliver a supplic
tion?
     Clo. Ay, sir.
     Tit. Then here is a supplication for yo
And when you come to him, at the first a
proach you must kneel; then kiss his foot; the
deliver up your pigeons; and then look for yo
reward. I'll be at hand, sir; see you do it bravel
     Clo. I warrant you, sir; let me alone.   1
     Tit. Sirrah, hast thou a knife? Come, l
me see it.
Here, Marcus, fold it in the oration;
For thou hast made it like a humble supplian
And when thou hast given it to the emperor, 1
Knock at my door, and tell me what he say
     Clo. God be with you, sir; I will.
     Tit. Come, Marcus, let us go. Publius, follo
me.   [*Exeur*

SCENE IV.—*The Same. Before the Palace.*

Enter SATURNINUS, TAMORA, DEMETRIUS, CHIRO:
Lords, *and Others:* SATURNINUS *with the arro*
in his hand that TITUS *shot.*

     Sat. Why, lords, what wrongs are thes
          Was ever seen
An emperor of Rome thus overborne,
Troubled, confronted thus; and, for the exter
Of egal justice, us'd in such contempt?
My lords, you know, as do the mightful gods,—
However these disturbers of our peace
Buzz in the people's ears,—there nought ha
          pass'd,
But even with law, against the wilful sons
Of old Andronicus. And what an if
His sorrows have so overwhelm'd his wits,
Shall we be thus afflicted in his wreaks,
His fits, his frenzy, and his bitterness?
And now he writes to heaven for his redress
See, here's to Jove, and this to Mercury;
This to Apollo; this to the god of war;
Sweet scrolls to fly about the streets of Rome!
What's this but libelling against the senate,
And blazoning our injustice every where?
A goodly humour, is it not, my lords?
As who would say, in Rome no justice were.
But if I live, his feigned ecstasies
Shall be no shelter to these outrages;
But he and his shall know that justice lives
In Saturninus' health; whom, if she sleep,
He'll so awake, as she in fury shall
Cut off the proud'st conspirator that lives.
     Tam. My gracious lord, my lovely Saturnin
Lord of my life, commander of my thoughts, a
Calm thee, and bear the faults of Titus' age,
The effects of sorrow for his valiant sons,
Whose loss hath pierc'd him deep and scarr'
          his heart;
And rather comfort his distressed plight
Than prosecute the meanest or the best
For these contempts.—[*Aside.*] Why, thus
          shall become
High-witted Tamora to gloze with all:
But, Titus, I have touch'd thee to the quick, a
Thy life-blood out: if Aaron now be wise,
Then is all safe, the anchor's in the port.

Enter Clown.

ow now, good fellow! wouldst thou speak with
 us?

Clo. Yea, forsooth, an your mistership be
 emperial. 40

Tam. Empress I am, but yonder sits the
 emperor.

Clo. 'Tis he. God and Saint Stephen give you
 good den.

have brought you a letter and a couple of
 pigeons here.

   [SATURNINUS *reads the letter.*

Sat. Go, take him away, and hang him presently. 44

Clo. How much money must I have?

Tam. Come, sirrah, you must be hanged.

Clo. Hanged! By'r lady, then I have brought
 a neck to a fair end. [*Exit, guarded.*

Sat. Despiteful and intolerable wrongs! 49

all I endure this monstrous villany?

now from whence this same device proceeds:

ay this be borne? As if his traitorous sons, 52

nat died by law for murder of our brother,

ave by my means been butcher'd wrongfully!

o, drag the villain hither by the hair;

or age nor honour shall shape privilege. 56

or this proud mock I'll be thy slaughterman;

y frantic wretch, that holp'st to make me great,

hope thyself should govern Rome and me.

Enter ÆMILIUS.

hat news with thee, Æmilius? 60

Æmil. Arm, arm, my lord! Rome never had
 more cause.

he Goths have gather'd head, and with a power

f high-resolved men, bent to the spoil,

hey hither march amain, under conduct 64

f Lucius, son to old Andronicus;

ho threats, in course of this revenge, to do

s much as ever Coriolanus did.

Sat. Is war-like Lucius general of the Goths?

hese tidings nip me, and I hang the head 69

s flowers with frost or grass beat down with
 storms.

y, now begin our sorrows to approach:

is he the common people love so much; 72

Iyself hath often heard them say,

hen I have walked like a private man,

hat Lucius' banishment was wrongfully,

nd they have wish'd that Lucius were their
 emperor, 76

Tam. Why should you fear? is not your city
 strong?

Sat. Ay, but the citizens favour Lucius,

nd will revolt from me to succour him.

Tam. King, be thy thoughts imperious, like
 thy name. 80

s the sun dimm'd, that gnats do fly in it?

he eagle suffers little birds to sing,

nd is not careful what they mean thereby,

nowing that with the shadow of his wings 84

Ie can at pleasure stint their melody;

ven so mayst thou the giddy men of Rome,

hen cheer thy spirit; for know, thou emperor,

will enchant the old Andronicus 88

With words more sweet, and yet more dangerous,

Than baits to fish, or honey-stalks to sheep,

Whenas the one is wounded with the bait,

The other rotted with delicious feed. 92

Sat. But he will not entreat his son for us.

Tam. If Tamora entreat him, then he will:

For I can smooth and fill his aged ear

With golden promises, that, were his heart 96

Almost impregnable, his old ears deaf,

Yet should both ear and heart obey my tongue.

[*To* ÆMILIUS.] Go thou before, be our ambassador:

Say that the emperor requests a parley 100

Of war-like Lucius, and appoint the meeting,

Even at his father's house, the old Andronicus.

Sat. Æmilius, do this message honourably:

And if he stand on hostage for his safety, 104

Bid him demand what pledge will please him
 best.

Æmil. Your bidding shall I do effectually.

          [*Exit.*

Tam. Now will I to that old Andronicus,

And temper him with all the art I have, 108

To pluck proud Lucius from the war-like Goths,

And now, sweet emperor, be blithe again,

And bury all thy fear in my devices.

Sat. Then go successfully, and plead to him.

          [*Exeunt.*

ACT V

SCENE I.—*Plains near Rome.*

Flourish. Enter LUCIUS, *and an army of* Goths,
 with drums and colours.

Luc. Approved warriors, and my faithful
 friends,

I have received letters from great Rome,

Which signify what hate they bear their emperor,

And how desirous of our sight they are. 4

Therefore, great lords, be, as your titles witness,

Imperious and impatient of your wrongs;

And wherein Rome hath done you any scath,

Let him make treble satisfaction. 8

First Goth. Brave slip, sprung from the great
 Andronicus,

Whose name was once our terror, now our
 comfort;

Whose high exploits and honourable deeds

Ingrateful Rome requites with foul contempt, 12

Be bold in us: we'll follow where thou lead'st,

Like stinging bees in hottest summer's day

Led by their master to the flower'd fields,

And be aveng'd on cursed Tamora. 16

Goths. And, as he saith, so say we all with
 him.

Luc. I humbly thank him, and I thank you
 all.

But who comes here, led by a lusty Goth?

Enter a Goth, *leading* AARON, *with his* Child
 in his arms.

Sec. Goth. Renowned Lucius, from our
 troops I stray'd, 20

To gaze upon a ruinous monastery;

And as I earnestly did fix mine eye

Upon the wasted building, suddenly
I heard a child cry underneath a wall.   24
I made unto the noise; when soon I heard
The crying babe controll'd with this discourse:
'Peace, tawny slave, half me and half thy dam!
Did not thy hue bewray whose brat thou art,   28
Had nature lent thee but thy mother's look,
Villain, thou mightst have been an emperor:
But where the bull and cow are both milk-white,
They never do beget a coal-black calf.   32
Peace, villain, peace!'—even thus he rates the
    babe,—
'For I must bear thee to a trusty Goth;
Who, when he knows thou art the empress'
    babe,
Will hold thee dearly for thy mother's sake.' 36
With this, my weapon drawn, I rush'd upon
    him,
Surpris'd him suddenly, and brought him hither,
To use as you think needful of the man.
    Luc. O worthy Goth, this is the incarnate
    devil   40
That robb'd Andronicus of his good hand:
This is the pearl that pleas'd your empress' eye,
And here's the base fruit of his burning lust.
Say, wall-ey'd slave, whither wouldst thou con-
    vey   44
This growing image of thy fiend-like face?
Why dost not speak? What! deaf? not a word?
A halter, soldiers! hang him on this tree,
And by his side his fruit of bastardy.   48
    Aar. Touch not the boy; he is of royal blood.
    Luc. Too like the sire for ever being good.
First hang the child, that he may see it sprawl;
A sight to vex the father's soul withal.   52
Get me a ladder.   [*A ladder brought,
        which* AARON *is made to ascend.*
    Aar.   Lucius, save the child;
And bear it from me to the empress.
If thou do this, I'll show thee wondrous things,
That highly may advantage thee to hear: 56
If thou wilt not, befall what may befall,
I'll speak no more but 'Vengeance rot you all!'
    Luc. Say on; and if it please me which thou
    speak'st,
Thy child shall live, and I will see it nourish'd.
    Aar. An if it please thee! why, assure thee,
    Lucius,   61
'Twill vex thy soul to hear what I shall speak;
For I must talk of murders, rapes, and mas-
    sacres,
Acts of black night, abominable deeds,   64
Complots of mischief, treason, villanies
Ruthful to hear, yet piteously perform'd:
And this shall all be buried by my death,
Unless thou swear to me my child shall live.   68
    Luc. Tell on thy mind: I say, thy child shall
    live.
    Aar. Swear that he shall, and then I will
    begin.
    Luc. Who should I swear by? thou believ'st
    no god:
That granted, how canst thou believe an oath?
    Aar. What if I do not? as, indeed, I do not;
Yet, for I know thou art religious,
And hast a thing within thee called conscience,

With twenty popish tricks and ceremonies,
Which I have seen thee careful to observe,
Therefore I urge thy oath; for that I know
An idiot holds his bauble for a god,
And keeps the oath which by that god he swear
To that I'll urge him: therefore thou shalt vo
By that same god, what god soe'er it be,
That thou ador'st and hast in reverence,
To save my boy, to nourish and bring him u
Or else I will discover nought to thee.
    Luc. Even by my god I swear to thee I wi
    Aar. First, know thou, I begot him on t
    empress.
    Luc. O most insatiate and luxurious woma
    Aar. Tut! Lucius, this was but a deed
    charity
To that which thou shalt hear of me anon.
'Twas her two sons that murder'd Bassianus
They cut thy sister's tongue and ravish'd her,
And cut her hands and trimm'd her as tho
    saw'st.
    Luc. O detestable villain! call'st thou th
    trimming?
    Aar. Why, she was wash'd, and cut, ar
    trimm'd, and 'twas
Trim sport for them that had the doing of it.
    Luc. O barbarous, beastly villains, like th
    self!
    Aar. Indeed, I was their tutor to instru
    them.
That codding spirit had they from their moth
As sure a card as ever won the set;
That bloody mind, I think, they learn'd of m
As true a dog as ever fought at head.
Well, let my deeds be witness of my worth.
I train'd thy brethren to that guileful hole
Where the dead corpse of Bassianus lay;
I wrote the letter that thy father found,
And hid the gold within the letter mention'd
Confederate with the queen and her two son
And what not done, that thou hast cause to ru
Wherein I had no stroke of mischief in it?
I play'd the cheater for thy father's hand,
And, when I had it, drew myself apart,
And almost broke my heart with extrem
    laughter.
I pry'd me through the crevice of a wall
When, for his hand, he had his two sons' head
Beheld his tears, and laugh'd so heartily,
That both mine eyes were rainy like to his:
And when I told the empress of this sport,
She swounded almost at my pleasing tale,
And for my tidings gave me twenty kisses.
    First Goth. What! canst thou say all th
    and never blush?
    Aar. Ay, like a black dog, as the saying is
    Luc. Art thou not sorry for these heinou
    deeds?
    Aar. Ay, that I had not done a thousan
    more.
Even now I curse the day, and yet, I think,
Few come within the compass of my curse,
Wherein I did not some notorious ill:
As kill a man, or else devise his death;
Ravish a maid, or plot the way to do it;
Accuse some innocent, and forswear myself,

t deadly enmity between two friends;
ake poor men's cattle break their necks; 132
t fire on barns and hay-stacks in the night,
nd bid the owners quench them with their
    tears,
t have I digg'd up dead men from their graves,
nd set them upright at their dear friends'
    doors,   136
ven when their sorrows almost were forgot;
nd on their skins, as on the bark of trees,
ave with my knife carved in Roman letters,
.et not your sorrow die, though I am dead.' 140
ut! I have done a thousand dreadful things
s willingly as one would kill a fly,
nd nothing grieves me heartily indeed
ut that I cannot do ten thousand more. 144

Luc. Bring down the devil, for he must not
    die
) sweet a death as hanging presently.

Aar. If there be devils, would I were a devil,
o live and burn in everlasting fire,   148
) I might have your company in hell,
ut to torment you with my bitter tongue!

Luc. Sirs, stop his mouth, and let him speak
    no more.

Enter a Goth.

Goth. My lord, there is a messenger from
    Rome   152
esires to be admitted to your presence.

Luc. Let him come near.

Enter ÆMILIUS.

Velcome, Æmilius! what's the news from
    Rome?

Æmil. Lord Lucius, and you princes of the
    Goths,   156
he Roman emperor greets you all by me;
nd, for he understands you are in arms,
e craves a parley at your father's house,
'illing you to demand your hostages,   160
nd they shall be immediately deliver'd.

First Goth. What says our general?

Luc. Æmilius, let the emperor give his
    pledges
nto my father and my uncle Marcus,   164
nd we will come. March away.   [*Exeunt.*

SCENE II.—*Rome. Before* TITUS' *House.*

Enter TAMORA, DEMETRIUS, *and* CHIRON,
    disguised.

Tam. Thus, in this strange and sad habili-
    ment,
will encounter with Andronicus,
nd say I am Revenge, sent from below
o join with him and right his heinous wrongs.
nock at his study, where, they say, he keeps, 5
o ruminate strange plots of dire revenge;
ell him, Revenge is come to join with him,
nd work confusion on his enemies.   8
    [*They knock.*

Enter TITUS, *above.*

Tit. Who doth molest my contemplation?
it your trick to make me ope the door,
hat so my sad decrees may fly away,

And all my study be to no effect?   12
You are deceiv'd; for what I mean to do,
See here, in bloody lines I have set down;
And what is written shall be executed.

Tam. Titus, I am come to talk with thee. 16

Tit. No, not a word; how can I grace my talk,
Wanting a hand to give it action?
Thou hast the odds of me; therefore no more.

Tam. If thou didst know me, thou wouldst
    talk with me.   20

Tit. I am not mad; I know thee well enough:
Witness this wretched stump, witness these
    crimson lines;
Witness these trenches made by grief and care;
Witness the tiring day and heavy night;   24
Witness all sorrow, that I know thee well
For our proud empress, mighty Tamora.
Is not thy coming for my other hand?

Tam. Know, thou sad man, I am not
    Tamora;   28
She is thy enemy, and I thy friend:
I am Revenge, sent from the infernal kingdom,
To ease the gnawing vulture of thy mind,
By working wreakful vengeance on thy foes. 32
Come down, and welcome me to this world's
    light;
Confer with me of murder and of death.
There's not a hollow cave or lurking-place,
No vast obscurity or misty vale,   36
Where bloody murder or detested rape
Can couch for fear, but I will find them out;
And in their ears tell them my dreadful name,
Revenge, which makes the foul offender quake.

Tit. Art thou Revenge? and art thou sent to
    me,   41
To be a torment to mine enemies?

Tam. I am; therefore come down, and wel-
    come me.

Tit. Do me some service ere I come to thee.
Lo, by thy side where Rape and Murder stands;
Now give some surance that thou art Revenge:
Stab them, or tear them on thy chariot-wheels,
And then I'll come and be thy waggoner,   48
And whirl along with thee about the globe.
Provide two proper palfreys, black as jet,
To hale thy vengeful waggon swift away,
And find out murderers in their guilty caves: 52
And when thy car is loaden with their heads,
I will dismount, and by the waggon-wheel
Trot like a servile footman all day long,
Even from Hyperion's rising in the east   56
Until his very downfall in the sea:
And day by day I'll do this heavy task,
So thou destroy Rapine and Murder there.

Tam. These are my ministers, and come with
    me.   60

Tit. Are these thy ministers? what are they
    call'd?

Tam. Rapine and Murder; therefore called
    so,
'Cause they take vengeance of such kind of men.

Tit. Good Lord, how like the empress' sons
    they are,   64
And you the empress! but we worldly men
Have miserable, mad, mistaking eyes.
O sweet Revenge! now do I come to thee;

And, if one arm's embracement will content
thee,   68
I will embrace thee in it by and by. [*Exit above.*
  Tam. This closing with him fits his lunacy.
Whate'er I forge to feed his brain-sick fits,
Do you uphold and maintain in your speeches, 72
For now he firmly takes me for Revenge;
And, being credulous in this mad thought,
I'll make him send for Lucius his son;
And, whilst I at a banquet hold him sure,   76
I'll find some cunning practice out of hand
To scatter and disperse the giddy Goths,
Or, at the least, make them his enemies.
See, here he comes, and I must ply my theme. 80

Enter TITUS.

  Tit. Long have I been forlorn, and all for
thee:
Welcome, dread Fury, to my woeful house:
Rapine and Murder, you are welcome too.
How like the empress and her sons you are! 84
Well are you fitted had you but a Moor:
Could not all hell afford you such a devil?
For well I wot the empress never wags
But in her company there is a Moor;   88
And would you represent our queen aright,
It were convenient you had such a devil.
But welcome as you are. What shall we do?
  Tam. What wouldst thou have us do, An-
dronicus?   92
  Dem. Show me a murderer, I'll deal with
him.
  Chi. Show me a villain that hath done a rape,
And I am sent to be reveng'd on him.
  Tam. Show me a thousand that have done
thee wrong,   96
And I will be revenged on them all.
  Tit. Look round about the wicked streets of
Rome,
And when thou find'st a man that's like thyself,
Good Murder, stab him; he's a murderer.   100
Go thou with him; and when it is thy hap
To find another that is like to thee,
Good Rapine, stab him; he's a ravisher.
Go thou with them; and in the emperor's
court   104
There is a queen attended by a Moor;
Well mayst thou know her by thy own pro-
portion,
For up and down she doth resemble thee:
I pray thee, do on them some violent death; 108
They have been violent to me and mine.
  Tam. Well hast thou lesson'd us; this shall
we do.
But would it please thee, good Andronicus,
To send for Lucius, thy thrice-valiant son, 112
Who leads towards Rome a band of war-like
Goths,
And bid him come and banquet at thy house:
When he is here, even at thy solemn feast,
I will bring in the empress and her sons,   116
The emperor himself, and all thy foes,
And at thy mercy shall they stoop and kneel,
And on them shalt thou ease thy angry heart.
What says Andronicus to this device?   120
  Tit. Marcus, my brother! 'tis sad Titus calls.

Enter MARCUS.

Go, gentle Marcus, to thy nephew Lucius;
Thou shalt inquire him out among the Goth
Bid him repair to me, and bring with him 1.
Some of the chiefest princes of the Goths;
Bid him encamp his soldiers where they are
Tell him, the emperor and the empress too
Feast at my house, and he shall feast with ther
This do thou for my love; and so let him, 1
As he regards his aged father's life.
  Mar. This will I do, and soon return agai
                                       [*Ex*
  Tam. Now will I hence about thy business, 1
And take my ministers along with me.
  Tit. Nay, nay, let Rape and Murder sta
with me;
Or else I'll call my brother back again,
And cleave to no revenge but Lucius.   1
  Tam. [*Aside to her sons.*] What say yo
boys? will you abide with him,
Whiles I go tell my lord the emperor
How I have govern'd our determin'd jest?
Yield to his humour, smooth and speak hi
fair,   1
And tarry with him till I turn again.
  Tit. [*Aside.*] I know them all, though the
suppose me mad;
And will o'er-reach them in their own device
A pair of cursed hell-hounds and their dam. 1
  Dem. [*Aside to* TAMORA.] Madam, depart
pleasure; leave us here.
  Tam. Farewell, Andronicus: Revenge no
goes
To lay a complot to betray thy foes.
                                   [*Exit* TAMOR
  Tit. I know thou dost; and, sweet Reveng
farewell.   1
  Chi. Tell us, old man, how shall we be er
ploy'd?
  Tit. Tut! I have work enough for you to d
Publius, come hither, Caius, and Valentine!

Enter PUBLIUS *and Others.*

  Pub. What is your will?   1
  Tit. Know you these two?
  Pub. The empress' sons,
I take them, Chiron and Demetrius.
  Tit. Fie, Publius, fie! thou art too mu
deceiv'd;   1
The one is Murder, Rape is the other's nam
And therefore bind them, gentle Publius;
Caius and Valentine, lay hands on them;
Oft have you heard me wish for such an hou
And now I find it: therefore bind them sure, n
And stop their mouths, if they begin to cry.
             [*Exit.* PUBLIUS, &c., *seize* CHIR(
                               and DEMETRIL
  Chi. Villains, forbear! we are the empres
sons.
  Pub. And therefore do we what we are cor
manded.   1
Stop close their mouths, let them not speak
word.
Is he sure bound? look that you bind them fa

Re-enter TITUS, *with* LAVINIA; *she bearing a basin, and he a knife.*

Tit. Come, come, Lavinia; look, thy foes are bound.

rs, stop their mouths, let them not speak to me,   168
let them hear what fearful words I utter.
villains, Chiron and Demetrius!
ere stands the spring whom you have stain'd with mud,
his goodly summer with your winter mix'd. 172
ou kill'd her husband, and for that vile fault
wo of her brothers were condemn'd to death,
ly hand cut off and made a merry jest:
oth her sweet hands, her tongue, and that more dear   176
han hands or tongue, her spotless chastity,
nhuman traitors, you constrain'd and forc'd.
Vhat would you say if I should let you speak?
illains! for shame you could not beg for grace.
Mark, wretches! how I mean to martyr you. 181
his one hand yet is left to cut your throats,
Vhilst that Lavinia 'tween her stumps doth hold
he basin that receives your guilty blood.   184
ou know your mother means to feast with me,
nd calls herself Revenge, and thinks me mad.
Mark! villains, I will grind your bones to dust,
nd with your blood and it I'll make a paste;
nd of the paste a coffin I will rear,   189
nd make two pasties of your shameful heads;
nd bid that strumpet, your unhallow'd dam,
ike to the earth swallow her own increase. 192
his is the feast that I have bid her to,
nd this the banquet she shall surfeit on;
or worse than Philomel you us'd my daughter,
nd worse than Procne I will be reveng'd. 196
nd now prepare your throats. Lavinia, come.
                              [*He cuts their throats.*
Receive the blood: and when that they are dead,
et me go grind their bones to powder small,
nd with this hateful liquor temper it;   200
nd in that paste let their vile heads be bak'd.
Come, come, be every one officious
o make this banquet, which I wish may prove
More stern and bloody than the Centaurs' feast.
o, now bring them in, for I will play the cook,
nd see them ready 'gainst their mother comes.
                        [*Exeunt, bearing the dead bodies.*

SCENE III.—*The Same. Court of Titus' House. A banquet set out.*

Enter LUCIUS, MARCUS *and* Goths, *with* AARON *prisoner.*

Luc. Uncle Marcus, since it is my father's mind
hat I repair to Rome, I am content.
First Goth. And ours with thine, befall what fortune will.
Luc. Good uncle, take you in this barbarous Moor,   4
his ravenous tiger, this accursed devil;
et him receive no sustenance, fetter him,
ill he be brought unto the empress' face,

For testimony of her foul proceedings: 8
And see the ambush of our friends be strong;
I fear the emperor means no good to us.
Aar. Some devil whisper curses in mine ear,
And prompt me, that my tongue may utter forth   12
The venomous malice of my swelling heart!
Luc. Away, inhuman dog! unhallow'd slave!
Sirs, help our uncle to convey him in.
                [*Exeunt* Goths, *with* AARON. *Trumpets sound.*
The trumpets show the emperor is at hand. 16

Enter SATURNINUS *and* TAMORA, *with* ÆMILIUS, Senators, Tribunes, *and* Others.

Sat. What! hath the firmament more suns than one?
Luc. What boots it thee, to call thyself a sun?
Mar. Rome's emperor, and nephew, break the parle;
These quarrels must be quietly debated.   20
The feast is ready which the careful Titus
Hath ordain'd to an honourable end,
For peace, for love, for league, and good to Rome:
Please you, therefore, draw nigh, and take your places.   24
Sat. Marcus, we will.   [*Hautboys sound.*

Enter TITUS, *dressed like a cook,* LAVINIA, *veiled, young* LUCIUS, *and Others.* TITUS *places the dishes on the table.*

Tit. Welcome, my gracious lord; welcome, dread queen;
Welcome, ye war-like Goths; welcome, Lucius;
And welcome, all. Although the cheer be poor,
'Twill fill your stomachs; please you eat of it. 29
Sat. Why art thou thus attir'd, Andronicus?
Tit. Because I would be sure to have all well
To entertain your highness, and your empress.
Tam. We are beholding to you, good Andronicus.   33
Tit. An if your highness knew my heart, you were.
My lord the emperor, resolve me this:
Was it well done of rash Virginius   36
To slay his daughter with his own right hand,
Because she was enforced, stain'd, and deflower'd?
Sat. It was, Andronicus.
Tit. Your reason, mighty lord?   40
Sat. Because the girl should not survive her shame,
And by her presence still renew his sorrows.
Tit. A reason mighty, strong, and effectual;
A pattern, precedent, and lively warrant,   44
For me most wretched, to perform the like.
Die, die, Lavinia, and thy shame with thee;
And with thy shame thy father's sorrow die!
                              [*Kills* LAVINIA.
Sat. What hast thou done, unnatural and unkind?   48
Tit. Kill'd her, for whom my tears have made me blind.
I am as woeful as Virginius was,

And have a thousand times more cause than he
To do this outrage: and it is now done.   52

   Sat. What! was she ravish'd? tell who did
the deed.

   Tit. Will't please you eat? will't please your
highness feed?

   Tam. Why hast thou slain thine only daughter
thus?

   Tit. Not I; 'twas Chiron and Demetrius: 56
They ravish'd her, and cut away her tongue:
And they, 'twas they, that did her all this wrong.

   Sat. Go fetch them hither to us presently.

   Tit. Why, there they are both, baked in that
pie;   60
Whereof their mother daintily hath fed,
Eating the flesh that she herself hath bred.
'Tis true, 'tis true; witness my knife's sharp
point.   [*Kills* TAMORA.

   Sat. Die, frantic wretch, for this accursed
deed!   [*Kills* TITUS.

   Luc. Can the son's eye behold his father
bleed?   65
There's meed for meed, death for a deadly deed!
   [*Kills* SATURNINUS. *A great tumult. The
   people in confusion disperse.* MARCUS,
   LUCIUS, *and their partisans, go up into
   the balcony.*

   Mar. You sad-fac'd men, people and sons of
Rome,
By uproar sever'd, like a flight of fowl   68
Scatter'd by winds and high tempestuous gusts,
O! let me teach you how to knit again
This scatter'd corn into one mutual sheaf,
These broken limbs again into one body;   72
Lest Rome herself be bane unto herself,
And she whom mighty kingdoms curtsy to,
Like a forlorn and desperate castaway,
Do shameful execution on herself.   76
But if my frosty signs and chaps of age,
Grave witnesses of true experience,
Cannot induce you to attend my words,
[*To* LUCIUS.] Speak, Rome's dear friend, as erst
our ancestor,   80
When with his solemn tongue he did discourse
To love-sick Dido's sad attending ear
The story of that baleful burning night
When subtle Greeks surpris'd King Priam's
Troy;   84
Tell us what Sinon hath bewitch'd our ears,
Or who hath brought the fatal engine in
That gives our Troy, our Rome, the civil wound.
My heart is not compact of flint nor steel,   88
Nor can I utter all our bitter grief,
But floods of tears will drown my oratory,
And break my very utterance, even in the time
When it should move you to attend me most, 92
Lending your kind commiseration.
Here is a captain, let him tell the tale;
Your hearts will throb and weep to hear him
speak.

   Luc. Then, noble auditory, be it known to
you,   96
That cursed Chiron and Demetrius
Were they that murdered our emperor's
brother;
And they it was that ravished our sister.   99

For their fell faults our brothers were beheade
Our father's tears despis'd, and basely cozen
Of that true hand that fought Rome's quarr
out,
And sent her enemies unto the grave:
Lastly, myself unkindly banished,   10
The gates shut on me, and turn'd weeping ou
To beg relief among Rome's enemies;
Who drown'd their enmity in my true tears,
And op'd their arms to embrace me as
friend: 10
And I am the turn'd forth, be it known to yo
That have preserv'd her welfare in my blood
And from her bosom took the enemy's poin
Sheathing the steel in my adventurous body. 11
Alas! you know I am no vaunter, I;
My scars can witness, dumb although they ar
That my report is just and full of truth.
But, soft! methinks I do digress too much, 11
Citing my worthless praise: O! pardon me;
For when no friends are by, men praise them
selves.

   Mar. Now is my turn to speak. Behold th
child;
Of this was Tamora delivered,   12
The issue of an irreligious Moor,
Chief architect and plotter of these woes.
The villain is alive in Titus' house,
Damn'd as he is, to witness this is true.   12
Now judge what cause had Titus to revenge
These wrongs, unspeakable, past patience,
Or more than any living man could bear.
Now you have heard the truth, what say yo
Romans?   12
Have we done aught amiss, show us wherein
And, from the place where you behold us now
The poor remainder of Andronici
Will, hand in hand, all headlong cast us dowr
And on the ragged stones beat forth our brains
And make a mutual closure of our house.
Speak, Romans, speak! and if you say we shal
Lo! hand in hand, Lucius and I will fall.   13

   Æmil. Come, come, thou reverend man c
Rome,
And bring our emperor gently in thy hand,
Lucius, our emperor; for well I know
The common voice do cry it shall be so.   14

   Romans. Lucius, all hail! Rome's royal em
peror!

   Mar. [*To* Attendants.] Go, go into old Titus
sorrowful house,
And hither hale that misbelieving Moor,
To be adjudg'd some direful slaughtering death
As punishment for his most wicked life.   14
             [*Exeunt* Attendants

LUCIUS, MARCUS, *and the Others descend.*

   Romans. Lucius, all hail! Rome's graciou
governor!

   Luc. Thanks, gentle Romans: may I gover
so,
To heal Rome's harms, and wipe away her woe
But, gentle people, give me aim awhile,   14
For nature puts me to a heavy task.
Stand all aloof; but, uncle, draw you near,
To shed obsequious tears upon this trunk. 15

I take this warm kiss on thy pale cold lips,
         [Kisses TITUS.
These sorrowful drops upon thy blood-stain'd face,
The last true duties of thy noble son!
 Mar. Tear for tear, and loving kiss for kiss,
Thy brother Marcus tenders on thy lips: 157
O! were the sum of these that I should pay
Countless and infinite, yet would I pay them.
 Luc. Come hither, boy; come, come, and
  learn of us   160
To melt in showers: thy grandsire lov'd thee
  well:
Many a time he danc'd thee on his knee,
Sung thee asleep, his loving breast thy pillow;
Many a matter hath he told to thee, 164
Meet and agreeing with thine infancy;
In that respect, then, like a loving child,
Shed yet some small drops from thy tender
  spring,
Because kind nature doth require it so: 168
Friends should associate friends in grief and
  woe.
Bid him farewell; commit him to the grave;
Do him that kindness, and take leave of him.
 Boy. O grandsire, grandsire! even with all
  my heart   172
Would I were dead, so you did live again.
O Lord! I cannot speak to him for weeping;
My tears will choke me if I ope my mouth.

  Re-enter Attendants, *with* AARON.

 First Rom. You sad Andronici, have done
  with woes: 176

Give sentence on this execrable wretch,
That hath been breeder of these dire events.
 Luc. Set him breast-deep in earth, and famish
  him;
There let him stand, and rave, and cry for
  food: 180
If any one relieves or pities him,
For the offence he dies. This is our doom:
Some stay to see him fasten'd in the earth.
 Aar. O! why should wrath be mute, and fury
  dumb?   184
I am no baby, I, that with base prayers
I should repent the evils I have done.
Ten thousand worse than ever yet I did
Would I perform, if I might have my will: 188
If one good deed in all my life I did,
I do repent it from my very soul.
 Luc. Some loving friends convey the em-
  peror hence,
And give him burial in his father's grave. 192
My father and Lavinia shall forthwith
Be closed in our household's monument.
As for that heinous tiger, Tamora,
No funeral rite, nor man in mournful weeds, 196
No mournful bell shall ring her burial;
But throw her forth to beasts and birds of
  prey.
Her life was beast-like, and devoid of pity;
And, being so, shall have like want of pity.
See justice done on Aaron, that damn'd Moor,
By whom our heavy haps had their beginning:
Then, afterwards, to order well the state,
That like events may ne'er it ruinate. 204
          [Exeunt.

ROMEO AND JULIET

DRAMATIS PERSONÆ

ESCALUS, Prince of Verona.
PARIS, a young Nobleman, Kinsman to the Prince.
MONTAGUE, ⎱ Heads of two Houses at variance with
CAPULET, ⎰ each other.
Uncle to Capulet.
ROMEO, son to Montague.
MERCUTIO, Kinsman to the Prince, ⎱
BENVOLIO, Nephew to Montague, ⎰ Friends to Romeo.
TYBALT, Nephew to Lady Capulet.
FRIAR LAURENCE, a Franciscan.
FRIAR JOHN, of the same Order.
BALTHASAR, Servant to Romeo.
SAMPSON, ⎱ Servants to Capulet.
GREGORY, ⎰

PETER, Servant to Juliet's Nurse.
ABRAHAM, Servant to Montague.
An Apothecary.
Three Musicians.
Page to Mercutio; Page to Paris; another Page; an Officer.

LADY MONTAGUE, Wife to Montague.
LADY CAPULET, Wife to Capulet.
JULIET, Daughter to Capulet.
Nurse to Juliet.

Citizens of Verona; male and female Kinsfolk to both Houses; Masquers, Guards, Watchmen and Attendants.

Chorus.

SCENE.—*Verona: Once (in the Fifth Act), at Mantua.*

PROLOGUE

Enter Chorus.

Chor. Two households, both alike in dignity,
  In fair Verona, where we lay our scene,
From ancient grudge break to new mutiny,
  Where civil blood makes civil hands unclean.
From forth the fatal loins of these two foes   5
  A pair of star-cross'd lovers take their life;
Whose misadventur'd piteous overthrows
  Do with their death bury their parents' strife.
The fearful passage of their death-mark'd love,
  And the continuance of their parents' rage,
Which, but their children's end, nought could remove,
Is now the two hours' traffick of our stage;   12
The which if you with patient ears attend,
What here shall miss, our toil shall strive to mend.
                     [Exit.

ACT I

SCENE I.—*Verona. A Public Place.*

Enter SAMPSON *and* GREGORY, *armed with swords and bucklers.*

Sam. Gregory, o' my word, we'll not carry coals.

Gre. No, for then we should be colliers.

Sam. I mean, an we be in choler, we'll draw.

Gre. Ay, while you live, draw your neck out o' the collar.   6

Sam. I strike quickly, being moved.

Gre. But thou art not quickly moved to strike.

Sam. A dog of the house of Montague moves me.   10

Gre. To move is to stir, and to be valiant is to stand; therefore, if thou art moved, thou runnest away.

Sam. A dog of that house shall move me to stand: I will take the wall of any man or maid of Montague's.   16

Gre. That shows thee a weak slave; for the weakest goes to the wall.

Sam. 'Tis true; and therefore women, being the weaker vessels, are ever thrust to the wall: therefore I will push Montague's men from the wall, and thrust his maids to the wall.

Gre. The quarrel is between our masters and us their men.

Sam. 'Tis all one, I will show myself a tyrant: 24 when I have fought with the men, I will be cruel with the maids; I will cut off their heads.

Gre. The heads of the maids?   28

Sam. Ay, the heads of the maids, or their maidenheads; take it in what sense thou wilt.

Gre. They must take it in sense that feel it.

Sam. Me they shall feel while I am able to stand; and 'tis known I am a pretty piece of flesh.   34

Gre. 'Tis well thou art not fish; if thou hadst, thou hadst been poor John. Draw thy tool; here comes two of the house of the Montagues. 37

Enter ABRAHAM *and* BALTHASAR.

Sam. My naked weapon is out; quarrel, I will back thee.

Gre. How! turn thy back and run?   40

Sam. Fear me not.

Gre. No, marry; I fear thee!

Sam. Let us take the law of our sides; let them begin.   44

Gre. I will frown as I pass by, and let them take it as they list.

Sam. Nay, as they dare. I will bite my thumb at them; which is a disgrace to them, if they bear it.   49

Abr. Do you bite your thumb at us, sir?

Sam. I do bite my thumb, sir.

Abr. Do you bite your thumb at us, sir? 52

Sam. [*Aside to* GREGORY.] Is the law of our side if I say ay?

Gre. [*Aside to* SAMPSON.] No.

Sam. No, sir, I do not bite my thumb at you, sir; but I bite my thumb, sir.   57

Gre. Do you quarrel, sir?

Abr. Quarrel, sir! no, sir.

Sam. If you do, sir, I am for you: I serve as good a man as you.   61

Abr. No better.

Sam. Well, sir.

Gre. [*Aside to* SAMPSON.] Say, 'better;' here comes one of my master's kinsmen.   65

Sam. Yes, better, sir.

Abr. You lie.

Sam. Draw, if you be men. Gregory, remember thy swashing blow.   [*They fight.*

Enter BENVOLIO.

Ben. Part, fools!
Put up your swords; you know not what you
   do.   [*Beats down their swords.*

Enter TYBALT.

Tyb. What! art thou drawn among these
   heartless hinds?   72
Turn thee, Benvolio, look upon thy death.

Ben. I do but keep the peace: put up thy
   sword,
Or manage it to part these men with me.

Tyb. What! drawn, and talk of peace? I hate
   the word,   76
As I hate hell, all Montagues, and thee.
Have at thee, coward!   [*They fight.*

*Enter several persons of both houses, who join
the fray; then enter* Citizens, *with clubs and
partisans.*

Citizens. Clubs, bills, and partisans! strike!
   beat them down!
Down with the Capulets! down with the Montagues!   80

Enter CAPULET *in his gown, and* LADY
   CAPULET.

Cap. What noise is this? Give me my long
   sword, ho!

Lady Cap. A crutch, a crutch! Why call you
   for a sword?

Cap. My sword, I say! Old Montague is come,
And flourishes his blade in spite of me.   84

Enter MONTAGUE *and* LADY MONTAGUE.

Mon. Thou villain Capulet! Hold me not;
   let me go.

Lady Mon. Thou shalt not stir one foot to
   seek a foe.

Enter PRINCE *with his Train.*

Prin. Rebellious subjects, enemies to peace,
Profaners of this neighbour-stained steel,— 88
Will they not hear? What ho! you men, you
   beasts,
That quench the fire of your pernicious rage
With purple fountains issuing from your veins,
On pain of torture, from those bloody hands 92
Throw your mis-temper'd weapons to the
   ground,
And hear the sentence of your moved prince.

Three civil brawls, bred of an airy word,
By thee, old Capulet, and Montague,   96
Have thrice disturb'd the quiet of our streets,
And made Verona's ancient citizens
Cast by their grave beseeming ornaments,
To wield old partisans, in hands as old,   100
Canker'd with peace, to part your canker'd hate.
If ever you disturb our streets again
Your lives shall pay the forfeit of the peace.
For this time, all the rest depart away: 104
You, Capulet, shall go along with me;
And, Montague, come you this afternoon
To know our further pleasure in this case,
To old Free-town, our common judgment-place.
Once more, on pain of death, all men depart. 109
   [*Exeunt all but* MONTAGUE, LADY MON-
      TAGUE, *and* BENVOLIO.

Mon. Who set this ancient quarrel new a-
   broach?
Speak, nephew, were you by when it began?

Ben. Here were the servants of your adver-
   sary   112
And yours close fighting ere I did approach:
I drew to part them; in the instant came
The fiery Tybalt, with his sword prepar'd,
Which, as he breath'd defiance to my ears, 116
He swung about his head, and cut the winds,
Who, nothing hurt withal hiss'd him in scorn.
While we were interchanging thrusts and blows,
Came more and more, and fought on part and
   part,   120
Till the prince came, who parted either part.

Lady Mon. O! where is Romeo? saw you
   him to-day?
Right glad I am he was not at this fray.

Ben. Madam, an hour before the worshipp'd
   sun   124
Peer'd forth the golden window of the east,
A troubled mind drave me to walk abroad;
Where, underneath the grove of sycamore
That westward rooteth from the city's side, 128
So early walking did I see your son:
Towards him I made; but he was ware of me,
And stole into the covert of the wood:
I, measuring his affections by my own,   132
That most are busied when they're most alone,
Pursu'd my humour not pursuing his,
And gladly shunn'd who gladly fled from me.

Mon. Many a morning hath he there been
   seen,   136
With tears augmenting the fresh morning's dew,
Adding to clouds more clouds with his deep
   sighs:
But all so soon as the all-cheering sun
Should in the furthest east begin to draw   140
The shady curtains from Aurora's bed,
Away from light steals home my heavy son,
And private in his chamber pens himself,
Shuts up his windows, locks fair daylight out,
And makes himself an artificial night.   145
Black and portentous must this humour prove
Unless good counsel may the cause remove.

Ben. My noble uncle, do you know the cause?

Mon. I neither know it nor can learn of him.

Ben. Have you importun'd him by any
   means?

Mon. Both by myself and many other friends:
But he, his own affections' counsellor,   152
Is to himself, I will not say how true,
But to himself so secret and so close,
So far from sounding and discovery,
As is the bud bit with an envious worm,   156
Ere he can spread his sweet leaves to the air,
Or dedicate his beauty to the sun.
Could we but learn from whence his sorrows
  grow,
We would as willingly give cure as know.   160
  Ben. See where he comes: so please you, step
  aside;
I'll know his grievance, or be much denied.
  Mon. I would thou wert so happy by thy
  stay,
To hear true shrift. Come, madam, let's away.
          [*Exeunt* MONTAGUE *and* LADY.

Enter ROMEO.

  Ben. Good morrow, cousin.
  Rom.   Is the day so young?   165
  Ben. But new struck nine.
  Rom. Ay me! sad hours seem long.
Was that my father that went hence so fast?
  Ben. It was. What sadness lengthens
  Romeo's hours?   168
  Rom. Not having that, which having, makes
  them short.
  Ben. In love?
  Rom. Out—
  Ben. Of love?   172
  Rom. Out of her favour, where I am in love.
  Ben. Alas! that love, so gentle in his view,
Should be so tyrannous and rough in proof.
  Rom. Alas! that love, whose view is muffled
  still,   176
Should, without eyes, see pathways to his will.
Where shall we dine? O me! What fray was
  here?
Yet tell me not, for I have heard it all.
Here's much to do with hate, but more with
  love: 180
Why then, O brawling love! O loving hate!
O any thing! of nothing first create.
O heavy lightness! serious vanity!
Mis-shapen chaos of well-seeming forms!   184
Feather of lead, bright smoke, cold fire, sick
  health!
Still-waking sleep, that is not what it is!
This love feel I, that feel no love in this.
Dost thou not laugh?
  Ben.   No, coz, I rather weep.   188
  Rom. Good heart, at what?
  Ben. At thy good heart's oppression.
  Rom. Why, such is love's transgression.
Griefs of mine own lie heavy in my breast,   192
Which thou wilt propagate to have it press'd
With more of thine: this love that thou hast
  shown
Doth add more grief to too much of mine own.
Love is a smoke rais'd with the fume of sighs;
Being purg'd, a fire sparkling in lovers' eyes; 197
Being vex'd, a sea nourish'd with lovers' tears:
What is it else? a madness most discreet,
A choking gall, and a preserving sweet.   200

Farewell, my coz.   [*Going*
  Ben.   Soft, I will go along;
An if you leave me so, you do me wrong.
  Rom. Tut! I have lost myself; I am not here
This is not Romeo, he's some other where. 20.
  Ben. Tell me in sadness, who is that you love
  Rom. What! shall I groan and tell thee?
  Ben.   Groan! why, no
But sadly tell me who.
  Rom. Bid a sick man in sadness make his
  will;   20?
Ah! word ill urg'd to one that is so ill.
In sadness, cousin, I do love a woman.
  Ben. I aim'd so near when I suppos'd you
  lov'd.
  Rom. A right good mark-man! And she's
  fair I love.   21.
  Ben. A right fair mark, fair coz, is soonest
  hit.
  Rom. Well, in that hit you miss: she'll not
  be hit
With Cupid's arrow; she hath Dian's wit;
And, in strong proof of chastity well arm'd, 21(
From love's weak childish bow she lives un
  harm'd.
She will not stay the siege of loving terms,
Nor bide the encounter of assailing eyes,
Nor ope her lap to saint-seducing gold: 22(
O! she is rich in beauty; only poor
That, when she dies, with beauty dies her store
  Ben. Then she hath sworn that she will still
  live chaste?
  Rom. She hath, and in that sparing makes
  huge waste;   22(
For beauty, starv'd with her severity,
Cuts beauty off from all posterity.
She is too fair, too wise, wisely too fair,
To merit bliss by making me despair: 22?
She hath forsworn to love, and in that vow
Do I live dead that live to tell it now.
  Ben. Be rul'd by me; forget to think of her.
  Rom. O! teach me how I should forget to
  think.   23?
  Ben. By giving liberty unto thine eyes:
Examine other beauties.
  Rom.   'Tis the way
To call hers exquisite, in question more.
These happy masks that kiss fair ladies' brows
Being black put us in mind they hide the fair; 23?
He, that is strucken blind cannot forget
The precious treasure of his eyesight lost:
Show me a mistress that is passing fair,   24(
What doth her beauty serve but as a note
Where I may read who pass'd that passing fair?
Farewell: thou canst not teach me to forget.
  Ben. I'll pay that doctrine, or else die in debt.
          [*Exeunt.*

SCENE II.—*The Same. A Street.*

Enter CAPULET, PARIS, *and* Servant.

  Cap. But Montague is bound as well as I,
In penalty alike; and 'tis not hard, I think,
For men so old as we to keep the peace.
  Par. Of honourable reckoning are you both;
And pity 'tis you liv'd at odds so long.   5

But now, my lord, what say you to my suit?

Cap. But saying o'er what I have said before:
My child is yet a stranger in the world,   8
She hath not seen the change of fourteen years;
Let two more summers wither in their pride
Ere we may think her ripe to be a bride.

Par. Younger than she are happy mothers
made.   12

Cap. And too soon marr'd are those so early
made.
Earth hath swallow'd all my hopes but she,
She is the hopeful lady of my earth:
But woo her, gentle Paris, get her heart,   16
My will to her consent is but a part;
An she agree, within her scope of choice
Lies my consent and fair according voice.
This night I hold an old accustom'd feast,   20
Whereto I have invited many a guest
Such as I love; and you, among the store,
One more, most welcome, makes my number
more.
At my poor house look to behold this night   24
Earth-treading stars that make dark heaven
light:
Such comfort as do lusty young men feel
When well-apparel'd April on the heel
Of limping winter treads, even such delight   28
Among fresh female buds shall you this night
Inherit at my house; hear all, all see,
And like her most whose merit most shall be:
Which on more view, of many mine being one   32
May stand in number, though in reckoning
none.
Come, go with me. [*To Servant, giving him a
paper.*] Go, sirrah, trudge about
Through fair Verona; find those persons out
Whose names are written there, and to them
say,   36
My house and welcome on their pleasure stay.
                    [*Exeunt* CAPULET *and* PARIS.

Serv. Find them out whose names are written
here! It is written that the shoemaker should
meddle with his yard, and the tailor with his
last, the fisher with his pencil, and the painter
with his nets; but I am sent to find those
persons, whose names are here writ, and can
never find what names the writing person hath
here writ. I must to the learned. In good
time.

Enter BENVOLIO *and* ROMEO.

Ben. Tut! man, one fire burns out another's
burning,
One pain is lessen'd by another's anguish;   48
Turn giddy, and be holp by backward turning;
One desperate grief cures with another's lan-
guish:
Take thou some new infection to thy eye,
And the rank poison of the old will die.   52

Rom. Your plantain leaf is excellent for that.

Ben. For what, I pray thee?

Rom.   For your broken shin.

Ben. Why, Romeo, art thou mad?

Rom. Not mad, but bound more than a madman is;   56
Shut up in prison, kept without my food,

Whipp'd and tormented, and—Good den, good
fellow.

Serv. God gi' good den. I pray, sir, can you
read?

Rom. Ay, mine own fortune in my misery.   60

Serv. Perhaps you have learn'd it without
book: but, I pray, can you read any thing you
see?

Rom. Ay, if I know the letters and the language.   64

Serv. Ye say honestly; rest you merry!
                    [*Offering to go.*

Rom. Stay, fellow; I can read.
*Signior Martino and his wife and daugh-
ters; County Anselme and his beauteous sis-
ters; the lady widow of Vitruvio; Signior
Placentio, and his lovely nieces; Mercutio and
his brother Valentine; mine uncle Capulet, his
wife and daughters; my fair niece Rosaline;
Livia; Signior Valentio and his cousin Tybalt;
Lucio and the lively Helena.*
A fair assembly: whither should they come?

Serv. Up.   76

Rom. Whither?

Serv. To supper; to our house.

Rom. Whose house?

Serv. My master's.   80

Rom. Indeed, I should have asked you that
before.

Serv. Now I'll tell you without asking. My
master is the great rich Capulet; and if you be
not of the house of Montagues, I pray, come
and crush a cup of wine. Rest you merry!
                    [*Exit.*

Ben. At this same ancient feast of Capulet's,
Sups the fair Rosaline, whom thou so lov'st,   88
With all the admired beauties of Verona:
Go thither; and, with unattainted eye
Compare her face with some that I shall show,
And I will make thee think thy swan a crow.   92

Rom. When the devout religion of mine eye
Maintains such falsehood, then turn tears to
fires!
And these, who often drown'd could never die,
Transparent heretics, be burnt for liars!   96
One fairer than my love! the all-seeing sun
Ne'er saw her match since first the world begun.

Ben. Tut! you saw her fair, none else being by,
Herself pois'd with herself in either eye;   100
But in that crystal scales let there be weigh'd
Your lady's love against some other maid
That I will show you shining at this feast,
And she shall scant show well that now shows
best.   104

Rom. I'll go along, no such sight to be shown,
But to rejoice in splendour of mine own.
                    [*Exeunt.*

SCENE III.—*The Same. A Room in* CAPULET'S
House.

Enter LADY CAPULET *and* Nurse.

Lady Cap. Nurse, where's my daughter? call
her forth to me.

Nurse. Now, by my maidenhead, at twelve
year old,—

I bade her come. What, lamb! what, lady-bird!
God forbid! where's this girl? what, Juliet! 4

Enter JULIET.

Jul. How now! who calls?
Nurse. Your mother.
Jul.   Madam, I am here.
What is your will?
Lady Cap. This is the matter. Nurse, give
leave awhile.
We must talk in secret: nurse, come back again; 8
I have remember'd me, thou's hear our counsel.
Thou know'st my daughter's of a pretty age.
Nurse. Faith, I can tell her age unto an hour.
Lady Cap. She's not fourteen.
Nurse.   I'll lay fourteen of my teeth— 12
And yet to my teen be it spoken I have but four—
She is not fourteen. How long is it now
To Lammas-tide?
Lady Cap.   A fortnight and odd days.
Nurse. Even or odd, of all days in the year,
Come Lammas-eve at night shall she be four-
teen.   17
Susan and she—God rest all Christian souls!—
Were of an age. Well, Susan is with God;
She was too good for me. But, as I said, 20
On Lammas-eve at night shall she be fourteen;
That shall she, marry; I remember it well.
'Tis since the earthquake now eleven years;
And she was wean'd, I never shall forget it, 24
Of all the days of the year, upon that day;
For I had then laid wormwood to my dug,
Sitting in the sun under the dove-house wall;
My lord and you were then at Mantua. 28
Nay, I do bear a brain:—but, as I said,
When it did taste the wormwood on the nipple
Of my dug and felt it bitter, pretty fool!
To see it tetchy and fall out with the dug. 32
'Shake,' quoth the dove-house: 'twas no need,
I trow,
To bid me trudge:
And since that time it is eleven years;
For then she could stand high lone; nay, by the
rood,   36
She could have run and waddled all about;
For even the day before she broke her brow:
And then my husband—God be with his soul!
A' was a merry man—took up the child: 40
'Yea,' quoth he, 'dost thou fall upon thy face?
Thou wilt fall backward when thou hast more
wit;
Wilt thou not, Jule?' and, by my halidom,
The pretty wretch left crying, and said 'Ay.' 44
To see now how a jest shall come about!
I warrant, an I should live a thousand years,
I never should forget it: 'Wilt thou not, Jule?'
quoth he;
And, pretty fool, it stinted and said 'Ay.' 48
Lady Cap. Enough of this; I pray thee, hold
thy peace.
Nurse. Yes, madam. Yet I cannot choose
but laugh,
To think it should leave crying, and say 'Ay.'
And yet, I warrant, it had upon its brow 52
A bump as big as a young cockerel's stone;
A parlous knock; and it cried bitterly:

'Yea,' quoth my husband, 'fall'st upon thy face?
Thou wilt fall backward when thou com'st to
age;   56
Wilt thou not, Jule?' it stinted and said 'Ay.'
Jul. And stint thou too, I pray thee, nurse,
say I.
Nurse. Peace, I have done. God mark thee
to his grace!
Thou wast the prettiest babe that e'er I nursed:
An I might live to see thee married once, 61
I have my wish.
Lady Cap. Marry, that 'marry' is the very
theme
I came to talk of. Tell me, daughter Juliet, 64
How stands your disposition to be married?
Jul. It is an honour that I dream not of.
Nurse. An honour! were not I thine only
nurse,
I would say thou hadst suck'd wisdom from
thy teat.   68
Lady Cap. Well, think of marriage now:
younger than you,
Here in Verona, ladies of esteem,
Are made already mothers: by my count,
I was your mother much upon these years 72
That you are now a maid. Thus then in brief,
The valiant Paris seeks you for his love.
Nurse. A man, young lady! lady, such a man
As all the world—why, he's a man of wax. 76
Lady Cap. Verona's summer hath not such
a flower.
Nurse. Nay, he's a flower; in faith, a very
flower.
Lady Cap. What say you? can you love the
gentleman?
This night you shall behold him at our feast; 80
Read o'er the volume of young Paris' face
And find delight writ there with beauty's pen;
Examine every married lineament,
And see how one another lends content; 84
And what obscur'd in this fair volume lies
Find written in the margent of his eyes.
This precious book of love, this unbound lover,
To beautify him, only lacks a cover: 88
The fish lives in the sea, and 'tis much pride
For fair without the fair within to hide:
That book in many eyes doth share the glory,
That in gold clasps locks in the golden story: 92
So shall you share all that he doth possess,
By having him making yourself no less.
Nurse. No less! nay, bigger; women grow by
men.
Lady Cap. Speak briefly, can you like of
Paris' love?   96
Jul. I'll look to like, if looking liking move:
But no more deep will I endart mine eye
Than your consent gives strength to make it fly

Enter a Servant.

Serv. Madam, the guests are come, supper
served up, you called, my young lady asked for
the nurse cursed in the pantry, and everything
in extremity. I must hence to wait; I beseech
you, follow straight.   10
Lady Cap. We follow thee. Juliet, the county
stays.

Nurse. Go, girl, seek happy nights to happy
days. [*Exeunt.*

ꜱCENE IV.—*The Same. A Street*

Enter ROMEO, MERCUTIO, BENVOLIO, *with five or
six Maskers, Torch-Bearers, and Others.*

Rom. What! shall this speech be spoke for
our excuse,
Or shall we on without apology?
Ben. The date is out of such prolixity:
We'll have no Cupid hood-wink'd with a scarf, 4
Bearing a Tartar's painted bow of lath,
Scaring the ladies like a crow-keeper;
Nor no without-book prologue, faintly spoke
After the prompter, for our entrance: 8
But, let them measure us by what they will,
We'll measure them a measure, and be gone.
Rom. Give me a torch: I am not for this
ambling;
Being but heavy, I will bear the light. 12
Mer. Nay, gentle Romeo, we must have you
dance.
Rom. Not I, believe me: you have dancing
shoes
With nimble soles; I have a soul of lead
So stakes me to the ground I cannot move. 16
Mer. You are a lover; borrow Cupid's wings,
And soar with them above a common bound.
Rom. I am too sore enpierced with his shaft
To soar with his light feathers; and so bound 20
I cannot bound a pitch above dull woe:
Under love's heavy burden do I sink.
Mer. And, to sink in it, should you burden
love;
Too great oppression for a tender thing. 24
Rom. Is love a tender thing? it is too rough,
Too rude, too boisterous; and it pricks like
thorn.
Mer. If love be rough with you, be rough
with love;
Prick love for pricking, and you beat love
down. 28
Give me a case to put my visage in:
[*Putting on a mask.*
A visor for a visor! what care I,
What curious eye doth quote deformities?
Here are the beetle brows shall blush for me. 32
Ben. Come, knock and enter; and no sooner
in,
But every man betake him to his legs.
Rom. A torch for me; let wantons, light of
heart,
Tickle the senseless rushes with their heels, 36
For I am proverb'd with a grandsire phrase;
I'll be a candle-holder, and look on.
The game was ne'er so fair, and I am done.
Mer. Tut! dun's the mouse, the constable's
own word: 40
If thou art Dun, we'll draw thee from the mire,
Of—save your reverence—love, wherein thou
stick'st
Up to the ears. Come, we burn daylight, ho!
Rom. Nay, that's not so.
Mer. I mean, sir, in delay 44
We waste our lights in vain, like lamps by day.

Take our good meaning, for our judgment sits
Five times in that ere once in our five wits.
Rom. And we mean well in going to this
masque; 48
But 'tis no wit to go.
Mer. Why, may one ask?
Rom. I dream'd a dream to-night.
Mer. And so did I.
Rom. Well, what was yours?
Mer. That dreamers often lie.
Rom. In bed asleep, while they do dream
things true. 52
Mer. O! then, I see, Queen Mab hath been
with you.
Ben. Queen Mab! What's she?
Mer. She is the fairies' midwife, and she
comes
In shape no bigger than an agate-stone 56
On the fore-finger of an alderman,
Drawn with a team of little atomies
Athwart men's noses as they lie asleep:
Her waggon-spokes made of long spinners' legs;
The cover, of the wings of grasshoppers; 61
The traces, of the smallest spider's web;
The collars, of the moonshine's watery beams;
Her whip, of cricket's bone; the lash, of film; 64
Her waggoner, a small grey-coated gnat,
Not half so big as a round little worm
Prick'd from the lazy finger of a maid;
Her chariot is an empty hazel-nut, 68
Made by the joiner squirrel or old grub,
Time out o' mind the fairies' coach-makers.
And in this state she gallops night by night
Through lovers' brains, and then they dream of
love; 72
O'er courtiers' knees, that dream on curtsies
straight;
O'er lawyers' fingers, who straight dream on
fees;
O'er ladies' lips, who straight on kisses dream;
Which oft the angry Mab with blisters plagues,
Because their breaths with sweetmeats tainted
are. 77
Sometimes she gallops o'er a courtier's nose,
And then dreams he of smelling out a suit;
And sometimes comes she with a tithe-pig's tail,
Tickling a parson's nose as a' lies asleep, 81
Then dreams he of another benefice;
Sometime she driveth o'er a soldier's neck,
And then dreams he of cutting foreign throats,
Of breaches, ambuscadoes, Spanish blades, 85
Of healths five fathom deep; and then anon
Drums in his ear, at which he starts and wakes;
And, being thus frighted, swears a prayer or
two, 88
And sleeps again. This is that very Mab
That plats the manes of horses in the night;
And bakes the elf-locks in foul sluttish hairs,
Which once untangled much misfortune bodes;
This is the hag, when maids lie on their backs,
That presses them and learns them first to bear,
Making them women of good carriage:
This is she—
Rom. Peace, peace! Mercutio, peace! 96
Thou talk'st of nothing.
Mer. True, I talk of dreams,

Which are the children of an idle brain,
Begot of nothing but vain fantasy;
Which is as thin of substance as the air, 100
And more inconstant than the wind, who woos
Even now the frozen bosom of the north,
And, being anger'd, puffs away from thence,
Turning his face to the dew-dropping south. 104

Ben. This wind you talk of blows us from
ourselves;
Supper is done, and we shall come too late.

Rom. I fear too early; for my mind misgives
Some consequence yet hanging in the stars 108
Shall bitterly begin his fearful date
With this night's revels, and expire the term
Of a despised life clos'd in my breast
By some vile forfeit of untimely death. 112
But he, that hath the steerage of my course,
Direct my sail! On, lusty gentlemen!

Ben. Strike, drum. [*Exeunt.*

SCENE V.—*The Same. A Hall in* CAPULET'S
House.

Musicians *waiting. Enter* Servingmen.

First Serv. Where's Potpan, that he helps
not to take away? he shift a trencher! he scrape
a trencher!

Sec. Serv. When good manners shall lie all
in one or two men's hands, and they unwashed
too, 'tis a foul thing. 6

First Serv. Away with the joint-stools, remove the court-cupboard, look to the plate.
Good thou, save me a piece of marchpane; and,
as thou lovest me, let the porter let in Susan
Grindstone and Nell. Antony! and Potpan!

Sec. Serv. Ay, boy; ready. 12

First Serv. You are looked for and called
for, asked for and sought for in the great
chamber.

Third Serv. We cannot be here and there
too. 17

Sec. Serv. Cheerly, boys; be brisk awhile, and
the longer liver take all. [*They retire behind.*

Enter CAPULET *and* JULIET *and Others of his
house, meeting the Guests and Maskers.*

Cap. Welcome, gentlemen! ladies that have
their toes 20
Unplagu'd with corns will walk about with you.
Ah ha! my mistresses, which of you all
Will now deny to dance? she that makes dainty,
she,
I'll swear, hath corns; am I come near ye
now? 24
Welcome, gentlemen! I have seen the day
That I have worn a visor, and could tell
A whispering tale in a fair lady's ear
Such as would please; 'tis gone, 'tis gone, 'tis
gone. 28
You are welcome, gentlemen! Come, musi-
cians, play.
A hall! a hall! give room, and foot it, girls.
[*Music plays, and they dance.*
More light, ye knaves! and turn the tables up,
And quench the fire, the room has grown too
hot. 32

Ah! sirrah, this unlook'd-for sport comes well
Nay, sit, nay, sit, good cousin Capulet,
For you and I are past our dancing days;
How long is 't now since last yourself and I 3
Were in a mask?

Sec. Cap. By'r Lady, thirty years.

Cap. What, man! 'tis not so much, 'tis no
so much:
'Tis since the nuptial of Lucentio,
Come Pentecost as quickly as it will, 4
Some five and twenty years; and then we mask'c

Sec. Cap. 'Tis more, 'tis more; his son i
elder, sir.
His son is thirty.

Cap. Will you tell me that?
His son was but a ward two years ago. 4

Rom. What lady is that which doth enric
the hand
Of yonder knight?

Serv. I know not, sir.

Rom. O! she doth teach the torches to bur
bright. 4
It seems she hangs upon the cheek of night
Like a rich jewel in an Ethiop's ear;
Beauty too rich for use, for earth too dear!
So shows a snowy dove trooping with crows, 5
As yonder lady o'er her fellows shows.
The measure done, I'll watch her place of stand
And, touching hers, make blessed my rude hanc
Did my heart love till now? forswear it, sight
For I ne'er saw true beauty till this night.

Tyb. This, by his voice, should be a Montague
Fetch me my rapier, boy. What! dares the slav
Come hither, cover'd with an antick face, 6
To fleer and scorn at our solemnity?
Now, by the stock and honour of my kin,
To strike him dead I hold it not a sin.

Cap. Why, how now, kinsman! wherefor
storm you so? 6

Tyb. Uncle, this is a Montague, our foe;
A villain that is hither come in spite,
To scorn at our solemnity this night.

Cap. Young Romeo, is it?

Tyb. 'Tis he, that villain Romeo. 6

Cap. Content thee, gentle coz, let him alone
He bears him like a portly gentleman;
And, to say truth, Verona brags of him
To be a virtuous and well-govern'd youth. 7
I would not for the wealth of all this town
Here in my house do him disparagement;
Therefore be patient, take no note of him:
It is my will; the which if thou respect, 7
Show a fair presence and put off these frowns
An ill-beseeming semblance for a feast.

Tyb. It fits, when such a villain is a guest:
I'll not endure him.

Cap. He shall be endur'd: 8
What! goodman boy; I say, he shall, go to;
Am I the master here, or you? go to.
You'll not endure him! God shall mend m
soul!
You'll make a mutiny among my guests! 8
You'll set cock-a-hoop! you'll be the man

Tyb. Why, uncle, 'tis a shame.

Cap. Go to, go to
You are a saucy boy—is 't so indeed?—

his trick may chance to scathe you.—I know
what: 88
ou must contrary me! marry, 'tis time.
ell said, my hearts! You are a princox; go:
e quiet, or—More light, more light!—For
shame!
ll make you quiet. What! cheerly, my hearts!

Tyb. Patience perforce with wilful choler
meeting 93
Makes my flesh tremble in their different greeting.
will withdraw; but this intrusion shall
Now seeming sweet convert to bitter gall. [*Exit.*

om. [*To* JULIET.] If I profane with my un-
worthiest hand 97
This holy shrine, the gentle sin is this;
My lips, two blushing pilgrims, ready stand
To smooth that rough touch with a tender kiss.

ul. Good pilgrim, you do wrong your hand
too much, 101
Which mannerly devotion shows in this;
or saints have hands that pilgrims' hands do
touch,
And palm to palm is holy palmers' kiss. 104

om. Have not saints lips, and holy palmers
too?

Jul. Ay, pilgrim, lips that they must use in
prayer.

om. O! then, dear saint, let lips do what hands
do;
They pray, grant thou, lest faith turn to despair. 108

Jul. Saints do not move, though grant for
prayers' sake.

Rom. Then move not, while my prayers'
effect I take.
Thus from my lips, by thine, my sin is purg'd.
[*Kissing her.*

Jul. Then have my lips the sin that they have
took. 112

om. Sin from my lips? O trespass sweetly
urg'd!
Give me my sin again.

Jul. You kiss by the book.

Nurse. Madam, your mother craves a word
with you.

Rom. What is her mother?

Nurse. Marry, bachelor,
Her mother is the lady of the house, 117
And a good lady, and a wise, and virtuous:
nurs'd her daughter, that you talk'd withal;
tell you he that can lay hold of her 120
Shall have the chinks.

Rom. Is she a Capulet?
O dear account! my life is my foe's debt.

Ben. Away, be gone; the sport is at the best.

Rom. Ay, so I fear; the more is my unrest.

Cap. Nay, gentlemen, prepare not to be
gone; 125
We have a trifling foolish banquet towards.
Is it e'en so? Why then, I thank you all;
I thank you, honest gentlemen; good-night. 128
More torches here! Come on then, let's to bed.
Ah! sirrah, by my fay, it waxes late;
I'll to my rest. [*Exeunt all except* JULIET
and Nurse.

Jul. Come hither, nurse. What is yond
gentleman? 132

Nurse. The son and heir of old Tiberio.

Jul. What's he that now is going out of door?

Nurse. Marry, that, I think, be young Petruchio.

Jul. What's he, that follows there, that
would not dance? 136

Nurse. I know not.

Jul. Go, ask his name.—If he be married,
My grave is like to be my wedding bed.

Nurse. His name is Romeo, and a Montague;
The only son of your great enemy. 141

Jul. My only love sprung from my only hate!
Too early seen unknown, and known too late!
Prodigious birth of love it is to me, 144
That I must love a loathed enemy.

Nurse. What's this, what's this?

Jul. A rime I learn'd even now
Of one I danc'd withal.
[*One calls within,* 'JULIET!']

Nurse. Anon, anon!—
Come, let's away; the strangers are all gone. 148
[*Exeunt.*

PROLOGUE

Enter Chorus.

Chor. Now old desire doth in his death-bed lie,
And young affection gapes to be his heir;
That fair for which love groan'd for and would
die,
With tender Juliet match'd, is now not fair.
Now Romeo is belov'd and loves again, 5
Alike bewitched by the charm of looks,
But to his foe suppos'd he must complain,
And she steal love's sweet bait from fearful
hooks: 8
Being held a foe, he may not have access
To breathe such vows as lovers us'd to swear;
And she as much in love, her means much less
To meet her new-beloved any where: 12
But passion lends them power, time means, to
meet,
Tempering extremity with extreme sweet.
[Exit.

ACT II

SCENE I.—*Verona. A Lane by the wall of*
CAPULET'S *Orchard.*

Enter ROMEO

Rom. Can I go forward when my heart is
here?
Turn back, dull earth, and find thy centre out.
[*He climbs the wall, and leaps down
within it.*

Enter BENVOLIO *and* MERCUTIO.

Ben. Romeo! my cousin Romeo!

Mer. He is wise;
And, on my life, hath stol'n him home to bed. 4

Ben. He ran this way, and leap'd this orchard
wall:
Call, good Mercutio.

Mer. Nay, I'll conjure too.

Romeo! humours! madman! passion! lover!
Appear thou in the likeness of a sigh; 8
Speak but one rime and I am satisfied;
Cry but 'Ay me!' couple but 'love' and 'dove;'
Speak to my gossip Venus one fair word.
One nickname for her purblind son and heir, 12
Young Adam Cupid, he that shot so trim
When King Cophetua lov'd the beggar-maid.
He heareth not, he stirreth not, he moveth not;
The ape is dead, and I must conjure him. 16
I conjure thee by Rosaline's bright eyes,
By her high forehead, and her scarlet lip,
By her fine foot, straight leg, and quivering
    thigh,
And the demesnes that there adjacent lie, 20
That in thy likeness thou appear to us.
    Ben. An if he hear thee, thou wilt anger him.
    Mer. This cannot anger him: 'twould anger
    him
To raise a spirit in his mistress' circle 24
Of some strange nature, letting it there stand
Till she had laid it, and conjur'd it down;
That were some spite: my invocation
Is fair and honest, and in his mistress' name 28
I conjure only but to raise up him.
    Ben. Come, he hath hid himself among these
    trees,
To be consorted with the humorous night:
Blind is his love and best befits the dark. 32
    Mer. If love be blind, love cannot hit the
    mark.
Now will he sit under a medlar tree,
And wish his mistress were that kind of fruit
As maids call medlars, when they laugh alone.
O Romeo! that she were, O! that she were 37
An open *et cætera*, thou a poperin pear.
Romeo, good night: I'll to my truckle-bed;
This field-bed is too cold for me to sleep: 40
Come, shall we go?
    Ben.   Go, then; for 'tis in vain
To seek him here that means not to be found.
                                    [*Exeunt.*

SCENE II.—*The Same.* CAPULET'S *Orchard.*

Enter ROMEO.

    Rom. He jests at scars, that never felt a
    wound.
          [JULIET *appears above at a window.*
But, soft! what light through yonder window
    breaks?
It is the east, and Juliet is the sun!
Arise, fair sun, and kill the envious moon, 4
Who is already sick and pale with grief,
That thou her maid art far more fair than she:
Be not her maid, since she is envious;
Her vestal livery is but sick and green, 8
And none but fools do wear it; cast it off.
It is my lady; O! it is my love:
O! that she knew she were.
She speaks, yet she says nothing: what of that?
Her eye discourses; I will answer it. 13
I am too bold, 'tis not to me she speaks:
Two of the fairest stars in all the heaven,
Having some business, do entreat her eyes 16
To twinkle in their spheres till they return.

What if her eyes were there, they in her head
The brightness of her cheek would shame those
    stars
As daylight doth a lamp; her eyes in heaven
Would through the airy region stream so bright
That birds would sing and think it were not
    night.
See! how she leans her cheek upon her hand,
O! that I were a glove upon that hand,
That I might touch that cheek.
    Jul.   Ay me!
    Rom.   She speaks.
O! speak again, bright angel; for thou art
As glorious to this night, being o'er my head
As is a winged messenger of heaven
Unto the white-upturned wond'ring eyes
Of mortals, that fall back to gaze on him
When he bestrides the lazy-pacing clouds,
And sails upon the bosom of the air.
    Jul. O Romeo, Romeo! wherefore art thou
    Romeo?
Deny thy father, and refuse thy name;
Or, if thou wilt not, be but sworn my love,
And I'll no longer be a Capulet.
    Rom. [*Aside.*] Shall I hear more, or shall I
    speak at this?
    Jul. 'Tis but thy name that is my enemy;
Thou art thyself though, not a Montague.
What's Montague? it is nor hand, nor foot,
Nor arm, nor face, nor any other part
Belonging to a man. O! be some other name
What's in a name? that which we call a rose
By any other name would smell as sweet;
So Romeo would, were he not Romeo call'd,
Retain that dear perfection which he owes
Without that title. Romeo, doff thy name;
And for that name, which is no part of thee,
Take all myself.
    Rom.   I take thee at thy word.
Call me but love, and I'll be new baptiz'd;
Henceforth I never will be Romeo.
    Jul. What man art thou, that, thus bescreen'd
    in night,
So stumblest on my counsel?
    Rom.   By a name
I know not how to tell thee who I am:
My name, dear saint, is hateful to myself,
Because it is an enemy to thee:
Had I it written, I would tear the word.
    Jul. My ears have not yet drunk a hundred
    words
Of that tongue's uttering, yet I know the sound
Art thou not Romeo, and a Montague?
    Rom. Neither, fair maid, if either thee dis-
    like.
    Jul. How cam'st thou hither, tell me, and
    wherefore?
The orchard walls are high and hard to climb
And the place death, considering who thou art
If any of my kinsmen find thee here.
    Rom. With love's light wings did I o'er
    perch these walls;
For stony limits cannot hold love out,
And what love can do that dares love attempt
Therefore thy kinsmen are no stop to me.
    Jul. If they do see thee they will murder thee

Rom. Alack! there lies more peril in thine eye
han twenty of their swords: look thou but
   sweet,   72
nd I am proof against their enmity.
Jul. I would not for the world they saw thee
   here.
Rom. I have night's cloak to hide me from
   their eyes;
nd but thou love me, let them find me here;
ly life were better ended by their hate,   77
han death prorogued, wanting of thy love.
Jul. By whose direction found'st thou out
   this place?
Rom. By Love, that first did prompt me to
   inquire;   80
e lent me counsel, and I lent him eyes.
am no pilot; yet, wert thou as far
s that vast shore wash'd with the furthest sea,
would adventure for such merchandise.   84
Jul. Thou know'st the mask of night is on
   my face,
lse would a maiden blush bepaint my cheek
or that which thou hast heard me speak to-
   night.
ain would I dwell on form, fain, fain deny 88
Vhat I have spoke: but farewell compliment!
Oost thou love me? I know thou wilt say 'Ay;'
nd I will take thy word; yet, if thou swear'st,
'hou mayst prove false; at lovers' perjuries, 92
hey say, Jove laughs. O gentle Romeo!
f thou dost love, pronounce it faithfully:
Or if thou think'st I am too quickly won,
'll frown and be perverse and say thee nay, 96
o thou wilt woo; but else, not for the world.
n truth, fair Montague, I am too fond,
nd therefore thou mayst think my haviour
   light:
Sut trust me, gentleman, I'll prove more true 100
'han those that have more cunning to be
   strange.
should have been more strange, I must confess,
Sut that thou over-heard'st, ere I was 'ware,
My true love's passion: therefore pardon me,
And not impute this yielding to light love, 105
Vhich the dark night hath so discovered.
Rom. Lady, by yonder blessed moon I swear
'hat tips with silver all these fruit-tree tops,—
Jul. O! swear not by the moon, the incon-
   stant moon,   109
'hat monthly changes in her circled orb,
est that thy love prove likewise variable.
Rom. What shall I swear by?
Jul.   Do not swear at all;
Or, if thou wilt, swear by thy gracious self, 113
Vhich is the god of my idolatry.
And I'll believe thee.
  Rom.   If my heart's dear love—
Jul. Well, do not swear. Although I joy in
   thee,   116
have no joy of this contract to-night:
t is too rash, too unadvis'd, too sudden;
'oo like the lightning, which doth cease to be
Ere one can say it lightens. Sweet, good-night!
'his bud of love, by summer's ripening breath,
May prove a beauteous flower when next we
   meet.

Good-night, good-night! as sweet repose and
   rest
Come to thy heart as that within my breast! 124
  Rom. O! wilt thou leave me so unsatisfied?
  Jul. What satisfaction canst thou have to-
   night?
  Rom. The exchange of thy love's faithful vow
   for mine.
  Jul. I gave thee mine before thou didst re-
   quest it;   128
And yet I would it were to give again.
  Rom. Wouldst thou withdraw it? for what
   purpose, love?
  Jul. But to be frank, and give it thee again.
And yet I wish but for the thing I have: 132
My bounty is as boundless as the sea,
My love as deep; the more I give to thee,
The more I have, for both are infinite.
                  [*Nurse calls within.*
I hear some noise within; dear love, adieu! 136
Anon, good nurse! Sweet Montague, be true.
Stay but a little, I will come again. [*Exit above.*
  Rom. O blessed, blessed night! I am afeard,
Being in night, all this is but a dream,   140
Too flattering-sweet to be substantial.

Re-enter JULIET, *above.*

  Jul. Three words, dear Romeo, and good-
   night indeed.
If that thy bent of love be honourable,
Thy purpose marriage, send me word to-
   morrow,   144
By one that I'll procure to come to thee,
Where, and what time, thou wilt perform the rite;
And all my fortunes at thy foot I'll lay,
And follow thee my lord throughout the world.
  Nurse. [*Within.*] Madam!   149
  Jul. I come, anon.—But if thou mean'st not
   well,
I do beseech thee,—
  Nurse. [*Within.*] Madam!
  Jul.   By and by; I come:—
To cease thy suit, and leave me to my grief: 152
To-morrow will I send.
  Rom.   So thrive my soul,—
  Jul. A thousand times good-night!
                   [*Exit above.*
  Rom. A thousand times the worse, to want
   thy light.
Love goes toward love, as schoolboys from
   their books;   156
But love from love, toward school with heavy
   looks.   [*Retiring.*

Re-enter JULIET, *above.*

  Jul. Hist! Romeo, hist! O! for a falconer's
   voice,
To lure this tassel-gentle back again.
Bondage is hoarse, and may not speak aloud, 160
Else would I tear the cave where Echo lies,
And make her airy tongue more hoarse than
   mine,
With repetition of my Romeo's name.
  Rom. It is my soul that calls upon my name:
How silver-sweet sound lovers' tongues by
   night,   165

Like softest music to attending ears!

Jul. Romeo!

Rom.   My dear!

Jul.   At what o'clock to-morrow
Shall I send to thee?

Rom.   At the hour of nine. 168

Jul. I will not fail; 'tis twenty years till then.
I have forgot why I did call thee back.

Rom. Let me stand here till thou remember it

Jul. I shall forget, to have thee still stand
   there,   172
Remembering how I love thy company.

Rom. And I'll still stay, to have thee still
   forget,
Forgetting any other home but this.

Jul. 'Tis almost morning; I would have thee
   gone;   176
And yet no further than a wanton's bird,
Who lets it hop a little from her hand,
Like a poor prisoner in his twisted gyves,
And with a silk thread plucks it back again, 180
So loving-jealous of his liberty.

Rom. I would I were thy bird.

Jul.   Sweet, so would I:
Yet I should kill thee with much cherishing.
Good-night, good-night! parting is such sweet
   sorrow   184
That I shall say good-night till it be morrow.
       [*Exit.*

Rom. Sleep dwell upon thine eyes, peace in
   thy breast!
Would I were sleep and peace, so sweet to rest!
Hence will I to my ghostly father's cell,   188
His help to crave, and my dear hap to tell.
       [*Exit.*

SCENE III.—*The Same.* FRIAR LAURENCE'S
Cell.

Enter FRIAR LAURENCE, *with a basket.*

Fri. L. The grey-ey'd morn smiles on the
   frowning night,
Chequering the eastern clouds with streaks of
   light,
And flecked darkness like a drunkard reels
From forth day's path and Titan's fiery wheels:
Now, ere the sun advance his burning eye   5
The day to cheer and night's dank dew to dry,
I must up-fill this osier cage of ours
With baleful weeds and precious-juiced flowers.
The earth that's nature's mother is her tomb; 9
What is her burying grave that is her womb,
And from her womb children of divers kind
We sucking on her natural bosom find,   12
Many for many virtues excellent,
None but for some, and yet all different.
O! mickle is the powerful grace that lies
In herbs, plants, stones, and their true quali-
   ties: 16
For nought so vile that on the earth doth live
But to the earth some special good doth give,
Nor aught so good but strain'd from that fair use
Revolts from true birth, stumbling on abuse: 20
Virtue itself turns vice, being misapplied,
And vice sometime's by action dignified,
Within the infant rind of this weak flower

Poison hath residence and medicine power: 24
For this, being smelt, with that part cheers each
   part;
Being tasted, slays all senses with the heart.
Two such opposed foes encamp them still
In man as well as herbs, grace and rude will; 28
And where the worser is predominant,
Full soon the canker death eats up that plant.

Enter ROMEO.

Rom. Good morrow, father!

Fri. L.   Benedicite!
What early tongue so sweet saluteth me?   32
Young son, it argues a distemper'd head
So soon to bid good morrow to thy bed:
Care keeps his watch in every old man's eye,
And where care lodges, sleep will never lie; 36
But where unbruised youth with unstuff'd brain
Doth couch his limbs, there golden sleep doth
   reign:
Therefore thy earliness doth me assure
Thou art up-rous'd by some distemperature; 40
Or if not so, then here I hit it right,
Our Romeo hath not been in bed to-night.

Rom. That last is true; the sweeter rest was
   mine.

Fri. L. God pardon sin! wast thou with
   Rosaline?   44

Rom. With Rosaline, my ghostly father?
   no;
I have forgot that name, and that name's woe.

Fri. L. That's my good son: but where hast
   thou been, then?

Rom. I'll tell thee, ere thou ask it me again.
I have been feasting with mine enemy,   49
Where on a sudden one hath wounded me,
That's by me wounded: both our remedies
Within thy help and holy physic lies: 52
I bear no hatred, blessed man; for, lo!
My intercession likewise steads my foe.

Fri. L. Be plain, good son, and homely in
   thy drift;
Riddling confession finds but riddling shrift. 56

Rom. Then plainly know my heart's dear
   love is set
On the fair daughter of rich Capulet:
As mine on hers, so hers is set on mine;
And all combin'd, save what thou must com-
   bine   60
By holy marriage: when and where and how
We met we woo'd and made exchange of vow,
I'll tell thee as we pass; but this I pray,
That thou consent to marry us to-day.   64

Fri. L. Holy Saint Francis! what a change is
   here!
Is Rosaline, whom thou didst love so dear,
So soon forsaken? young men's love then lies
Not truly in their hearts, but in their eyes. 68
Jesu Maria! what a deal of brine
Hath wash'd thy sallow cheeks for Rosaline!
How much salt water thrown away in waste,
To season love, that of it doth not taste!   72
The sun not yet thy sighs from heaven clears
Thy old groans ring yet in my ancient ears;
Lo! here upon thy cheek the stain doth sit
Of an old tear that is not wash'd off yet.   76

If e'er thou wast thyself and these woes thine,
Thou and these woes were all for Rosaline:
And art thou chang'd? pronounce this sentence
   then:
Women may fall, when there's no strength in
   men.   80
   Rom. Thou chidd'st me oft for loving Rosa-
line.
   Fri. L. For doting, not for loving, pupil
mine.
   Rom. And bad'st me bury love.
   Fri. L.   Not in a grave,
To lay one in, another out to have.   84
   Rom. I pray thee, chide not; she, whom I
love now
Doth grace for grace and love for love allow;
The other did not so.
   Fri. L.   O! she knew well
Thy love did read by rote and could not spell. 88
But come, young waverer, come, go with me,
In one respect I'll thy assistant be;
For this alliance may so happy prove,
To turn your households' rancour to pure love.
   Rom. O! let us hence; I stand on sudden
haste.   93
   Fri. L. Wisely and slow; they stumble that
run fast.   [*Exeunt.*

SCENE IV.—*The Same. A Street.*

Enter BENVOLIO *and* MERCUTIO.

   Mer. Where the devil should this Romeo be?
Came he not home to-night?
   Ben. Not to his father's; I spoke with his
man.
   Mer. Why that same pale hard-hearted
      wench, that Rosaline,   4
Torments him so, that he will sure run mad.
   Ben. Tybalt, the kinsman of old Capulet,
Hath sent a letter to his father's house.
   Mer. A challenge, on my life.   8
   Ben. Romeo will answer it.
   Mer. Any man that can write may answer a
letter.
   Ben. Nay, he will answer the letter's master,
how he dares, being dared.   12
   Mer. Alas! poor Romeo, he is already dead;
stabbed with a white wench's black eye; shot
through the ear with a love-song; the very pin
of his heart cleft with the blind bow-boy's
butt-shaft; and is he a man to encounter
Tybalt?
   Ben. Why, what is Tybalt?   19
   Mer. More than prince of cats, I can tell you.
O! he is the courageous captain of compliments.
He fights as you sing prick-song, keeps time,
distance, and proportion; rests me his minim
rest, one, two, and the third in your bosom; the
very butcher of a silk button, a duellist, a duellist; a gentleman of the very first house, of
the first and second cause. Ah! the immortal
passado! the punto reverso! the hay!   28
   Ben. The what?
   Mer. The pox of such antick, lisping, affecting
fantasticoes, these new tuners of accents!—'By
Jesu, a very good blade!—a very tall man! a very

good whore.'—Why, is not this a lamentable
thing, grandsire, that we should be thus afflicted
with these strange flies, these fashion-mongers,
these *pardonnez-mois*, who stand so much on
the new form that they cannot sit at ease on
the old bench? O, their *bons*, their *bons*!   38

Enter ROMEO.

   Ben. Here comes Romeo, here comes Romeo.
   Mer. Without his roe, like a dried herring.
O flesh, flesh, how art thou fishified! Now is he
for the numbers that Petrarch flowed in: Laura
to his lady was but a kitchen-wench; marry,
she had a better love to be-rime her; Dido a
dowdy; Cleopatra a gipsy; Helen and Hero
hildings and harlots; Thisbe, a grey eye or so,
but not to the purpose. Signior Romeo, *bon
jour!* there's a French salutation to your French
slop. You gave us the counterfeit fairly last
night.
   Rom. Good morrow to you both. What
counterfeit did I give you?   52
   Mer. The slip, sir, the slip; can you not conceive?
   Rom. Pardon, good Mercutio, my business
was great; and in such a case as mine a man
may strain courtesy.   57
   Mer. That's as much as to say, such a case
as yours constrains a man to bow in the hams.
   Rom. Meaning—to curtsy.   60
   Mer. Thou hast most kindly hit it.
   Rom. A most courteous exposition.
   Mer. Nay, I am the very pink of courtesy.
   Rom. Pink for flower.   64
   Mer. Right.
   Rom. Why, then, is my pump well flowered.
   Mer. Well said; follow me this jest now till
thou hast worn out the pump, that, when the
single sole of it is worn, the jest may remain
after the wearing sole singular.
   Rom. O single-soled jest! solely singular for
the singleness.   72
   Mer. Come between us, good Benvolio; my
wit faints.
   Rom. Switch and spurs, switch and spurs;
or I'll cry a match.   71
   Mer. Nay, if thy wits run the wild-goose
chase, I have done, for thou hast more of the
wild-goose in one of thy wits than, I am sure,
I have in my whole five. Was I with you there
for the goose?   81
   Rom. Thou wast never with me for anything
when thou wast not here for the goose.
   Mer. I will bite thee by the ear for that jest.
   Rom. Nay, good goose, bite not.   85
   Mer. Thy wit is a very bitter sweeting; it is
a most sharp sauce.
   Rom. And is it not then well served in to a
sweet goose?   89
   Mer. O! here's a wit of cheveril, that stretches
from an inch narrow to an ell broad.
   Rom. I stretch it out for that word 'broad;'
which added to the goose, proves thee far and
wide a broad goose.   94
   Mer. Why, is not this better now than groaning for love? now art thou sociable, now art thou

Romeo; now art thou what thou art, by art as
well as by nature: for this drivelling love is like
a great natural, that runs lolling up and down
to hide his bauble in hole.   100

Ben. Stop there, stop there.

Mer. Thou desirest me to stop in my tale
against the hair.

Ben. Thou wouldst else have made thy tale
large.   105

Mer. O! thou art deceived; I would have
made it short; for I was come to the whole
depth of my tale, and meant indeed to occupy
the argument no longer.   109

Rom. Here's goodly gear!

Enter Nurse *and* PETER.

Mer. A sail, a sail!

Ben. Two, two; a shirt and a smock.   112

Nurse. Peter!

Peter. Anon!

Nurse. My fan, Peter.

Mer. Good Peter, to hide her face; for her
fan's the fairer face.   117

Nurse. God ye good morrow, gentlemen.

Mer. God ye good den, fair gentlewoman.

Nurse. Is it good den?   120

Mer. 'Tis no less, I tell you; for the bawdy
hand of the dial is now upon the prick of noon.

Nurse. Out upon you! what a man are you?

Rom. One, gentlewoman, that God hath
made for himself to mar.   125

Nurse. By my troth, it is well said; 'for himself to mar,' quoth a'?—Gentlemen, can any of
you tell me where I may find the young Romeo?

Rom. I can tell you; but young Romeo will
be older when you have found him than he was
when you sought him: I am the youngest of
that name, for fault of a worse.   132

Nurse. You say well.

Mer. Yea! is the worst well? very well took,
i' faith; wisely, wisely.

Nurse. If you be he, sir, I desire some confidence with you.   137

Ben. She will indite him to some supper.

Mer. A bawd, a bawd, a bawd! So ho!

Rom. What hast thou found?   140

Mer. No hare, sir; unless a hare, sir, in a
lenten pie, that is something stale and hoar ere
it be spent.   [*Sings.*

An old hare hoar, and an old hare hoar,   144
  Is very good meat in Lent:
But a hare that is hoar, is too much for a score,
  When it hoars ere it be spent.

Romeo, will you come to your father's? we'll to
dinner thither.   149

Rom. I will follow you.

Mer. Farewell, ancient lady; farewell,

Lady, lady, lady.   152

[*Exeunt* MERCUTIO *and* BENVOLIO.

Nurse. Marry, farewell! I pray you, sir,
what saucy merchant was this, that was so full
of his ropery?

Rom. A gentleman, nurse, that loves to hear
himself talk, and will speak more in a minute
than he will stand to in a month.   158

Nurse. An a' speak anything against me, I'll
take him down, an a' were lustier than he is,
and twenty such Jacks; and if I cannot, I'll find
those that shall. Scurvy knave! I am none of
his flirt-gills; I am none of his skeins-mates.
[*To* PETER.] And thou must stand by too, and
suffer every knave to use me at his pleasure! 165

Peter. I saw no man use you at his pleasure;
if I had, my weapon should quickly have been
out, I warrant you. I dare draw as soon as
another man, if I see occasion in a good quarrel,
and the law on my side.   170

Nurse. Now, afore God, I am so vexed, that
every part about me quivers. Scurvy knave!
Pray you, sir, a word; and as I told you, my
young lady bade me inquire you out; what she
bid me say I will keep to myself; but first let
me tell ye, if ye should lead her into a fool's
paradise, as they say, it were a very gross kind
of behaviour, as they say: for the gentlewoman
is young; and, therefore, if you should deal
double with her, truly it were an ill thing to be
offered to any gentlewoman, and very weak
dealing.   182

Rom. Nurse, commend me to thy lady and
mistress. I protest unto thee,—

Nurse. Good heart! and, i' faith, I will tell
her as much. Lord, Lord! she will be a joyful
woman.   187

Rom. What wilt thou tell her, nurse? thou
dost not mark me.

Nurse. I will tell her, sir, that you do protest; which, as I take it, is a gentlemanlike
offer.   192

Rom. Bid her devise
Some means to come to shrift this afternoon;
And there she shall at Friar Laurence' cell,
Be shriv'd and married. Here is for thy pains.

Nurse. No, truly, sir; not a penny.   197

Rom. Go to; I say, you shall.

Nurse. This afternoon, sir? well, she shall be
there.   200

Rom. And stay, good nurse; behind the
  abbey wall:
Within this hour my man shall be with thee,
And bring thee cords made like a tackled stair;
Which to the high top-gallant of my joy   204
Must be my convoy in the secret night.
Farewell! Be trusty, and I'll quit thy pains.
Farewell! Commend me to thy mistress.

Nurse. Now God in heaven bless thee! Hark
  you, sir.   208

Rom. What sayst thou, my dear nurse?

Nurse. Is your man secret? Did you ne'er
  hear say,
Two may keep counsel, putting one away?

Rom. I warrant thee my man's as true as
  steel.   212

Nurse. Well, sir; my mistress is the sweetest
lady—Lord, Lord!—when 'twas a little prating
thing,—O! there's a nobleman in town, one
Paris, that would fain lay knife aboard; but
she, good soul, had as lief see a toad, a very
toad, as see him. I anger her sometimes and
tell her that Paris is the properer man; but, I'll
warrant you, when I say so, she looks as pale as

any clout in the versal world. Doth not rosemary and Romeo begin both with a letter?

Rom. Ay, nurse: what of that? both with
an R.   224

Nurse. Ah! mocker; that's the dog's name.
R is for the—No; I know it begins with some
other letter: and she had the prettiest sententious of it, of you and rosemary, that it would
do you good to hear it.   229

Rom. Commend me to thy lady.

Nurse. Ay, a thousand times. [*Exit* ROMEO.]
Peter!   232

Peter. Anon!

Nurse. Before, and apace.   [*Exeunt.*

SCENE V.—*The Same.* CAPULET'S *Garden.*

Enter JULIET.

Jul. The clock struck nine when I did send
the nurse;
In half an hour she promis'd to return.
Perchance she cannot meet him: that's not so.
O! she is lame: love's heralds should be
thoughts,   4
Which ten times faster glide than the sun's
beams,
Driving back shadows over lowering hills:
Therefore do nimble-pinion'd doves draw Love,
And therefore hath the wind-swift Cupid wings.
Now is the sun upon the highmost hill   9
Of this day's journey, and from nine till twelve
Is three long hours, yet she is not come.
Had she affections, and warm youthful blood, 12
She'd be as swift in motion as a ball;
My words would bandy her to my sweet love,
And his to me:
But old folks, many feign as they were dead; 16
Unwieldy, slow, heavy and pale as lead.

Enter Nurse *and* PETER.

O God! she comes. O honey nurse! what news?
Hast thou met with him? Send thy man away.

Nurse. Peter, stay at the gate. [*Exit* PETER.

Jul. Now, good sweet nurse: O Lord! why
look'st thou sad?   21
Though news be sad, yet tell them merrily;
If good, thou sham'st the music of sweet news
By playing it to me with so sour a face.   24

Nurse. I am aweary, give me leave awhile:
Fie, how my bones ache! What a jaunce have
I had!

Jul. I would thou hadst my bones, and I thy
news.
Nay, come, I pray thee, speak; good, good
nurse, speak.   28

Nurse. Jesu! what haste? can you not stay
awhile?
Do you not see that I am out of breath?

Jul. How art thou out of breath when thou
hast breath
To say to me that thou art out of breath?   32
The excuse that thou dost make in this delay
Is longer than the tale thou dost excuse.
Is thy news good, or bad? answer to that;
Say either, and I'll stay the circumstance: 36
Let me be satisfied, is't good or bad?

Nurse. Well, you have made a simple choice;
you know not how to choose a man: Romeo!
no, not he; though his face be better than any
man's, yet his leg excels all men's; and for a
hand, and a foot, and a body, though they be
not to be talked on, yet they are past compare.
He is not the flower of courtesy, but I'll warrant
him, as gentle as a lamb. Go thy ways, wench;
serve God. What! have you dined at home?

Jul. No, no: but all this did I know before.
What says he of our marriage? what of that?

Nurse. Lord! how my head aches; what a
head have I!   49
It beats as it would fall in twenty pieces.
My back o' t'other side; O! my back, my back!
Beshrew your heart for sending me about,
To catch my death with jauncing up and down.

Jul. I' faith, I am sorry that thou art not well.
Sweet, sweet, sweet nurse, tell me, what says
my love?   55

Nurse. Your love says, like an honest gentleman, and a courteous, and a kind, and a handsome, and, I warrant, a virtuous,—Where is
your mother?

Jul. Where is my mother! why, she is with-
in;   60
Where should she be? How oddly thou repliest:
'Your love says, like an honest gentleman,
Where is your mother?'

Nurse.   O! God's lady dear,
Are you so hot? Marry, come up, I trow;   64
Is this the poultice for my aching bones?
Henceforward do your messages yourself.

Jul. Here's such a coil! come, what says
Romeo?

Nurse. Have you got leave to go to shrift
to-day?   68

Jul. I have.

Nurse. Then hie you hence to Friar Laurence'
cell,
There stays a husband to make you a wife:
Now comes the wanton blood up in your cheeks,
They'll be in scarlet straight at any news. 73
Hie you to church; I must another way,
To fetch a ladder, by the which your love
Must climb a bird's nest soon when it is dark;
I am the drudge and toil in your delight,   77
But you shall bear the burden soon at night.
Go; I'll to dinner: hie you to the cell.

Jul. Hie to high fortune! Honest nurse, farewell.   [*Exeunt.*

SCENE VI.—*The Same.* FRIAR LAURENCE'S
Cell.

Enter FRIAR LAURENCE *and* ROMEO.

Fri. L. So smile the heaven upon this holy
act,
That after hours with sorrow chide us not!

Rom. Amen, amen! but come what sorrow
can,
It cannot countervail the exchange of joy   4
That one short minute gives me in her sight:
Do thou but close our hands with holy words,
Then love-devouring death do what he dare;
It is enough I may but call her mine.

Fri. L. These violent delights have violent ends,
And in their triumph die, like fire and powder,
Which, as they kiss consume: the sweetest honey
Is loathsome in his own deliciousness   12
And in the taste confounds the appetite:
Therefore love moderately; long love doth so;
Too swift arrives as tardy as too slow.

Enter JULIET.

Here comes the lady: O! so light a foot   16
Will ne'er wear out the everlasting flint;
A lover may bestride the gossamer
That idles in the wanton summer air,
And yet not fall; so light is vanity.   20
Jul. Good even to my ghostly confessor.
Fri. L. Romeo shall thank thee, daughter,
    for us both.
Jul. As much to him, else are his thanks too
    much.
Rom. Ah! Juliet, if the measure of thy joy
Be heap'd like mine, and that thy skill be more   25
To blazon it, then sweeten with thy breath
This neighbour air, and let rich music's tongue
Unfold the imagin'd happiness that both   28
Receive in either by this dear encounter.
Jul. Conceit, more rich in matter than in
    words,
Brags of his substance, not of ornament:
They are but beggars that can count their
    worth;   32
But my true love is grown to such excess
I cannot sum up half my sum of wealth.
Fri. L. Come, come with me, and we will
    make short work;
For, by your leaves, you shall not stay alone   36
Till holy church incorporate two in one.
                                        [*Exeunt.*

ACT III

SCENE I.—*Verona. A Public Place.*

Enter MERCUTIO, BENVOLIO, Page, *and* Servants.

Ben. I pray thee, good Mercutio, let's retire:
The day is hot, the Capulets abroad,
And, if we meet, we shall not 'scape a brawl;
For now, these hot days, is the mad blood stir-
    ring.   4
Mer. Thou art like one of those fellows that
when he enters the confines of a tavern claps
me his sword upon the table and says, 'God
send me no need of thee!' and by the operation
of the second cup draws him on the drawer,
when, indeed, there is no need.
Ben. Am I like such a fellow?   11
Mer. Come, come, thou art as hot a Jack in
thy mood as any in Italy; and as soon moved to
be moody, and as soon moody to be moved.
Ben. And what to?   15
Mer. Nay, an there were two such, we should
have none shortly, for one would kill the other.
Thou! why, thou wilt quarrel with a man that
hath a hair more or a hair less in his beard than
thou hast. Thou wilt quarrel with a man for
cracking nuts, having no other reason but because thou hast hazel eyes. What eye, but such

an eye, would spy out such a quarrel? Thy
head is as full of quarrels as an egg is full of
meat, and yet thy head hath been beaten as
addle as an egg for quarrelling. Thou hast
quarrelled with a man for coughing in the
street, because he hath wakened thy dog that
hath lain asleep in the sun. Didst thou not fall
out with a tailor for wearing his new doublet
before Easter? with another, for tying his new
shoes with old riband? and yet thou wilt tutor
me from quarrelling!   33
Ben. An I were so apt to quarrel as thou art,
any man should buy the fee-simple of my life
for an hour and a quarter.   36
Mer. The fee-simple! O simple!
Ben. By my head, here come the Capulets.
Mer. By my heel, I care not.

Enter TYBALT, *and Others.*

Tyb. Follow me close, for I will speak to them.
Gentlemen, good den! a word with one of you.
Mer. And but one word with one of us?
Couple it with something; make it a word and
a blow.   44
Tyb. You shall find me apt enough to that,
sir, an you will give me occasion.
Mer. Could you not take some occasion with-
out giving?   48
Tyb. Mercutio, thou consort'st with Romeo,—
Mer. Consort! What! dost thou make us
minstrels? an thou make minstrels of us, look
to hear nothing but discords: here's my fiddle-
stick; here's that shall make you dance.
'Zounds! consort!
Ben. We talk here in the public haunt of
men:
Either withdraw unto some private place,   56
Or reason coldly of your grievances,
Or else depart; here all eyes gaze on us.
Mer. Men's eyes were made to look, and let
them gaze;
I will not budge for no man's pleasure, I.   60

Enter ROMEO.

Tyb. Well, peace be with you, sir. Here
comes my man.
Mer. But I'll be hang'd, sir, if he wear your
livery:
Marry, go before to field, he'll be your follower;
Your worship in that sense may call him 'man.'
Tyb. Romeo, the hate I bear thee can afford
No better term than this,—thou art a villain.
Rom. Tybalt, the reason that I have to love
    thee *dramatic irony*
Doth much excuse the appertaining rage   68
To such a greeting; villain am I none,
Therefore farewell; I see thou know'st me not.
Tyb. Boy, this shall not excuse the injuries
That thou hast done me; therefore turn and
    draw.   72
Rom. I do protest I never injur'd thee,
But love thee better than thou canst devise,
Till thou shalt know the reason of my love:
And so, good Capulet, which name I tender   76
As dearly as my own, be satisfied.
Mer. O calm, dishonourable, vile submission!

Alla stoccata carries it away.   [*Draws.*

Tybalt, you rat-catcher, will you walk?   80

  Tyb. What wouldst thou have with me?

  Mer. Good king of cats, nothing but one of
your nine lives, that I mean to make bold withal,
and, as you shall use me hereafter, dry-beat the
rest of the eight. Will you pluck your sword
out of his pilcher by the ears? make haste, lest
mine be about your ears ere it be out.

  Tyb. [*Drawing.*] I am for you.   88

  Rom. Gentle Mercutio, put thy rapier up.

  Mer. Come, sir, your passado. [*They fight.*

  Rom. Draw, Benvolio; beat down their weapons.

Gentlemen, for shame, forbear this outrage! 92

Tybalt, Mercutio, the prince expressly hath

Forbidden bandying in Verona streets.

Hold, Tybalt! good Mercutio!

      [*Exeunt* TYBALT *and his Partisans.*

  Mer.   I am hurt.

A plague o' both your houses! I am sped. 96

Is he gone, and hath nothing?

  Ben.   What! art thou hurt?

  Mer. Ay, ay, a scratch, a scratch; marry, 'tis
    enough.

Where is my page? Go, villain, fetch a surgeon.

      [*Exit* Page.

  Rom. Courage, man; the hurt cannot be
much.   100

  Mer. No, 'tis not so deep as a well, nor so wide
as a church door; but 'tis enough, 'twill serve:
ask for me to-morrow, and you shall find me a
grave man. I am peppered, I warrant, for this
world. A plague o' both your houses! 'Zounds,
a dog, a rat, a mouse, a cat, to scratch a man to
death! a braggart, a rogue, a villain, that fights
by the book of arithmetic! Why the devil came
you between us? I was hurt under your arm. 109

  Rom. I thought all for the best.

  Mer. Help me into some house, Benvolio,
Or I shall faint. A plague o' both your houses!
They have made worms' meat of me: I have
it,   113

And soundly too:—your houses!

      [*Exeunt* MERCUTIO *and* BENVOLIO.

  Rom. This gentleman, the prince's near ally,
My very friend, hath got his mortal hurt 116
In my behalf; my reputation stain'd
With Tybalt's slander, Tybalt, that an hour
Hath been my kinsman. O sweet Juliet!
Thy beauty hath made me effeminate, 120
And in my temper soften'd valour's steel!

Re-enter BENVOLIO.

  Ben. O Romeo, Romeo! brave Mercutio's
dead;

That gallant spirit hath aspir'd the clouds,

Which too untimely here did scorn the earth.

  Rom. This day's black fate on more days
doth depend;   125

This but begins the woe others must end.

Re-enter TYBALT.

  Ben. Here comes the furious Tybalt back
again.

  Rom. Alive! in triumph! and Mercutio slain!

Away to heaven, respective lenity,   129

And fire-ey'd fury be my conduct now!

Now, Tybalt, take the villain back again

That late thou gav'st me; for Mercutio's soul

Is but a little way above our heads,   133

Staying for thine to keep him company:

Either thou, or I, or both, must go with him.

  Tyb. Thou wretched boy, that didst consort
    him here,   136

Shalt with him hence.

  Rom.   This shall determine that.

      [*They fight*: TYBALT *falls.*

  Ben. Romeo, away! be gone!

The citizens are up, and Tybalt slain.

Stand not amaz'd: the prince will doom thee

    death   140

If thou art taken: hence! be gone! away!

  Rom. O! I am Fortune's fool.

  Ben.   Why dost thou stay?

      [*Exit* ROMEO.

Enter Citizens, &c.

  First Cit. Which way ran he that kill'd Mer-
    cutio?

Tybalt, that murderer, which way ran he? 144

  Ben. There lies that Tybalt.

  First Cit.   Up, sir, go with me.

I charge thee in the prince's name, obey.

Enter PRINCE, *attended*: MONTAGUE, CAPULET, *their Wives, and Others.*

  Prin. Where are the vile beginners of this
    fray?

  Ben. O noble prince! I can discover all   148

The unlucky manage of this fatal brawl:

There lies the man, slain by young Romeo,

That slew thy kinsman, brave Mercutio.

  Lady Cap. Tybalt, my cousin! O my bro-
    ther's child!   152

O prince! O cousin! husband! O! the blood is
    spill'd

Of my dear kinsman. Prince, as thou art true,

For blood of ours shed blood of Montague.

O cousin, cousin!   156

  Prin. Benvolio, who began this bloody fray?

  Ben. Tybalt, here slain, whom Romeo's hand
    did slay;

Romeo, that spoke him fair, bade him bethink

How nice the quarrel was, and urg'd withal 160

Your high displeasure: all this, uttered

With gentle breath, calm look, knees humbly
    bow'd,

Could not take truce with the unruly spleen

Of Tybalt deaf to peace, but that he tilts   164

With piercing steel at bold Mercutio's breast,

Who, all as hot, turns deadly point to point,

And, with a martial scorn, with one hand beats

Cold death aside, and with the other sends 168

It back to Tybalt, whose dexterity

Retorts it: Romeo he cries aloud,

'Hold, friends! friends, part!' and, swifter than
    his tongue

His agile arm beats down their fatal points, 172

And 'twixt them rushes; underneath whose arm

An envious thrust from Tybalt hit the life

Of stout Mercutio, and then Tybalt fled;

But by and by comes back to Romeo,   176
Who had but newly entertain'd revenge,
And to't they go like lightning, for, ere I
Could draw to part them, was stout Tybalt
slain,
And, as he fell, did Romeo turn and fly.   180
This is the truth, or let Benvolio die.

Lady Cap. He is a kinsman to the Montague;
Affection makes him false, he speaks not true:
Some twenty of them fought in this black strife
And all those twenty could but kill one life. 185
I beg for justice, which thou, prince, must give;
Romeo slew Tybalt, Romeo must not live.

Prin. Romeo slew him, he slew Mercutio;
Who now the price of his dear blood doth owe?

Mon. Not Romeo, prince, he was Mercutio's
friend,
His fault concludes but what the law should end,
The life of Tybalt.

Prin.   And for that offence   192
Immediately we do exile him hence:
I have an interest in your hate's proceeding,
My blood for your rude brawls doth lie a-bleed-
ing;
But I'll amerce you with so strong a fine   196
That you shall all repent the loss of mine.
I will be deaf to pleading and excuses;
Nor tears nor prayers shall purchase out abuses;
Therefore use none; let Romeo hence in haste,
Else, when he's found, that hour is his last.   201
Bear hence this body and attend our will:
Mercy but murders, pardoning those that kill.
                              [*Exeunt.*

SCENE II.—*The Same.* CAPULET'S *Orchard.*

Enter JULIET.

Jul. Gallop apace, you fiery-footed steeds,
Towards Phœbus' lodging; such a waggoner
As Phæthon would whip you to the west,
And bring in cloudy night immediately.   4
Spread thy close curtain, love-performing night!
That runaway's eyes may wink, and Romeo
Leap to these arms, untalk'd of and unseen!
Lovers can see to do their amorous rites   8
By their own beauties; or, if love be blind,
It best agrees with night. Come, civil night,
Thou sober-suited matron, all in black,
And learn me how to lose a winning match,   12
Play'd for a pair of stainless maidenhoods:
Hood my unmann'd blood, bating in my cheeks,
With thy black mantle; till strange love, grown
bold,
Think true love acted simple modesty.   16
Come, night! come, Romeo! come, thou day in
night!
For thou wilt lie upon the wings of night,
Whiter than new snow on a raven's back.
Come, gentle night; come, loving, black-brow'd
night,   20
Give me my Romeo: and, when he shall die,
Take him and cut him out in little stars,
And he will make the face of heaven so fine
That all the world will be in love with night, 24
And pay no worship to the garish sun.
O! I have bought the mansion of a love,

But not possess'd it, and, though I am sold,
Not yet enjoy'd. So tedious is this day   28
As is the night before some festival
To an impatient child that hath new robes
And may not wear them. O! here comes my
nurse,

Enter Nurse *with cords.*

And she brings news; and every tongue that
speaks   32
But Romeo's name speaks heavenly eloquence.
Now nurse, what news? What hast thou there?
the cords
That Romeo bade thee fetch?

Nurse.   Ay, ay, the cords.
                        [*Throws them down.*

Jul. Ah me! what news? why dost thou wring
thy hands?   36

Nurse. Ah well-a-day! he's dead, he's dead,
he's dead!
We are undone, lady, we are undone!
Alack the day! he's gone, he's killed, he's dead!

Jul. Can heaven be so envious?

Nurse.   Romeo can,   40
Though heaven cannot. O! Romeo, Romeo;
Who ever would have thought it? Romeo!

Jul. What devil art thou that dost torment
me thus?
This torture should be roar'd in dismal hell.
Hath Romeo slain himself? say thou but 'I,'
And that bare vowel, 'I,' shall poison more
Than the death-darting eye of cockatrice:
I am not I, if there be such an 'I;'   48
Or those eyes shut that make thee answer 'I.
If he be slain, say 'I;' or if not 'no:'
Brief sounds determine of my weal or woe.

Nurse. I saw the wound, I saw it with mine
eyes,   52
God save the mark! here on his manly breast
A piteous corse, a bloody piteous corse;
Pale, pale as ashes, all bedaub'd in blood,
All in gore blood; I swounded at the sight.   56

Jul. O break, my heart!—poor bankrupt
break at once!
To prison, eyes, ne'er look on liberty!
Vile earth, to earth resign; end motion here;
And thou and Romeo press one heavy bier! 60

Nurse. O Tybalt, Tybalt! the best friend I had!
O courteous Tybalt! honest gentleman!
That ever I should live to see thee dead!

Jul. What storm is this that blows so con-
trary?   64
Is Romeo slaughter'd, and is Tybalt dead?
My dearest cousin, and my dearer lord?
Then, dreadful trumpet, sound the general
doom!
For who is living if those two are gone?   68

Nurse. Tybalt is gone, and Romeo banished;
Romeo, that kill'd him, he is banished.

Jul. O God! did Romeo's hand shed Tybalt's
blood?

Nurse. It did, it did; alas the day! it did. 72

Jul. O serpent heart, hid with a flowering face!
Did ever dragon keep so fair a cave?
Beautiful tyrant! fiend angelical!
Dove-feather'd raven! wolvish-ravening lamb!

Despised substance of divinest show!   77
Just opposite to what thou justly seem'st;
A damned saint, an honourable villain!
O, nature! what hadst thou to do in hell   80
When thou didst bower the spirit of a fiend
In mortal paradise of such sweet flesh?
Was ever book containing such vile matter
So fairly bound? O! that deceit should dwell
In such a gorgeous palace.
    Nurse.   There's no trust, 85
No faith, no honesty in men; all naught,
All perjur'd, all dissemblers, all forsworn.
Ah! where's my man? give me some *aqua*
    vitæ: 88
These griefs, these woes, these sorrows make
    me old.
Shame come to Romeo!
    Jul.   Blister'd be thy tongue
For such a wish! he was not born to shame:
Upon his brow shame is asham'd to sit;   92
For 'tis a throne where honour may be crown'd
Sole monarch of the universal earth.
O! what a beast was I to chide at him.
    Nurse. Will you speak well of him that kill'd
    your cousin?   96
    Jul. Shall I speak ill of him that is my hus-
    band?
Ah! poor my lord, what tongue shall smooth
    thy name,
When I, thy three-hours wife, have mangled it?
But, wherefore, villain, didst thou kill my
    cousin?   100
That villain cousin would have kill'd my hus-
    band:
Back, foolish tears, back to your native spring;
Your tributary drops belong to woe,
Which you, mistaking, offer up to joy.   104
My husband lives, that Tybalt would have slain;
And Tybalt's dead, that would have slain my
    husband:
All this is comfort; wherefore weep I then?
Some word there was, worser than Tybalt's
    death,   108
That murder'd me: I would forget it fain;
But O! it presses to my memory,
Like damned guilty deeds to sinners' minds.
'Tybalt is dead, and Romeo banished!'   112
That 'banished,' that one word 'banished,'
Hath slain ten thousand Tybalts. Tybalt's death
Was woe enough, if it had ended there:
Or, if sour woe delights in fellowship,   116
And needly will be rank'd with other griefs,
Why follow'd not, when she said 'Tybalt's dead,'
Thy father, or thy mother, nay, or both,   119
Which modern lamentation might have mov'd?
But with a rearward following Tybalt's death,
'Romeo is banished!' to speak that word
Is father, mother, Tybalt, Romeo, Juliet,
All slain, all dead: 'Romeo is banished!'   124
There is no end, no limit, measure, bound
In that word's death; no words can that woe
    sound.—
Where is my father and my mother, nurse?
    Nurse. Weeping and wailing over Tybalt's
    corse: 128
Will you go to them? I will bring you thither.

    Jul. Wash they his wounds with tears: mine
    shall be spent,
When theirs are dry, for Romeo's banishment.
Take up those cords. Poor ropes, you are be-
    guil'd,   132
Both you and I, for Romeo is exil'd:
He made you for a highway to my bed,
But I, a maid, die maiden-widowed.
Come, cords; come, nurse; I'll to my wedding
    bed;   136
And death, not Romeo, take my maidenhead!
    Nurse. Hie to your chamber; I'll find Romeo
To comfort you: I wot well where he is.
Hark ye, your Romeo will be here to-night: 140
I'll to him; he is hid at Laurence' cell.
    Jul. O! find him; give this ring to my true
    knight,
And bid him come to take his last farewell.
                         [*Exeunt.*

[handwritten: Juliet is the stronger in adversity]

SCENE III.—*The Same.* FRIAR LAURENCE'S
                 Cell.

          Enter FRIAR LAURENCE.

    Fri. L. Romeo, come forth; come forth, thou
    fearful man:
Affliction is enamour'd of thy parts,
And thou art wedded to calamity.

            Enter ROMEO.

    Rom. Father, what news? what is the prince's
    doom?   4
What sorrow craves acquaintance at my hand,
That I yet know not?
    Fri. L.   Too familiar
Is my dear son with such sour company:
I bring thee tidings of the prince's doom.   8
    Rom. What less than doomsday is the prince's
    doom?
    Fri. L. A gentler judgment vanish'd from his
    lips,
Not body's death, but body's banishment.
    Rom. Ha! banishment! be merciful, say
    'death;'   12
For exile hath more terror in his look,
Much more than death: do not say 'banish-
    ment.'
    Fri. L. Hence from Verona art thou banished.
Be patient, for the world is broad and wide. 16
    Rom. There is no world without Verona walls,
But purgatory, torture, hell itself.
Hence banished is banish'd from the world,
And world's exile is death; then 'banished,' 20
Is death mis-term'd. Calling death 'banished,'
Thou cutt'st my head off with a golden axe,
And smil'st upon the stroke that murders me.
    Fri. L. O deadly sin! O rude unthankfulness!
Thy fault our law calls death; but the kind
    prince,   25
Taking thy part, hath rush'd aside the law,
And turn'd that black word death to banish-
    ment:
This is dear mercy, and thou seest it not.   28
    Rom. 'Tis torture, and not mercy: heaven is
    here,
Where Juliet lives; and every cat and dog

And little mouse, every unworthy thing,
Live here in heaven and may look on her; 32
But Romeo may not: more validity,
More honourable state, more courtship lives
In carrion flies than Romeo: they may seize
On the white wonder of dear Juliet's hand, 36
And steal immortal blessing from her lips,
Who, even in pure and vestal modesty,
Still blush, as thinking their own kisses sin;
Flies may do this, but I from this must fly: 40
They are free men, but I am banished.
And sayst thou yet that exile is not death?
Hadst thou no poison mix'd, no sharp-ground
    knife,
No sudden mean of death, though ne'er so
    mean,   44
But 'banished' to kill me? 'Banished!'
O friar! the damned use that word in hell;
Howlings attend it: how hast thou the heart,
Being a divine, a ghostly confessor,   48
A sin-absolver, and my friend profess'd,
To mangle me with that word 'banished?'
    Fri. L. Thou fond mad man, hear me but
    speak a word.
    Rom. O! thou wilt speak again of banish-
    ment.   52
    Fri. L. I'll give thee armour to keep off that
    word;
Adversity's sweet milk, philosophy,
To comfort thee, though thou art banished.
    Rom. Yet 'banished!' Hang up philosophy!
Unless philosophy can make a Juliet,   57
Displant a town, reverse a prince's doom,
It helps not, it prevails not: talk no more.
    Fri. L. O! then I see that madmen have no
    ears.   60
    Rom. How should they, when that wise men
    have no eyes?
    Fri. L. Let me dispute with thee of thy estate.
    Rom. Thou canst not speak of that thou dost
    not feel:
Wert thou as young as I, Juliet thy love,   64
An hour but married, Tybalt murdered,
Doting like me, and like me banished,
Then mightst thou speak, then mightst thou
    tear thy hair,
And fall upon the ground, as I do now,   68
Taking the measure of an unmade grave.
                          [*Knocking within.*
    Fri. L. Arise; one knocks: good Romeo,
    hide thyself.
    Rom. Not I; unless the breath of heart-sick
    groans,
Mist-like, infold me from the search of eyes. 72
                               [*Knocking.*
    Fri. L. Hark! how they knock. Who's
    there? Romeo arise;
Thou wilt be taken. Stay awhile! Stand up;
                               [*Knocking.*
Run to my study. By and by! God's will!
What wilfulness is this! I come, I come!   76
                               [*Knocking.*
Who knocks so hard? whence come you? what's
    your will?
    Nurse. [*Within.*] Let me come in, and you
    shall know my errand:

I come from Lady Juliet.
    Fri. L.   Welcome, then.

                 Enter Nurse.

    Nurse. O holy friar! O! tell me, holy friar
Where is my lady's lord? where's Romeo?   8
    Fri. L. There on the ground, with his own
    tears made drunk.
    Nurse. O! he is even in my mistress' case,
Just in her case!
    Fri. L.   O woeful sympathy!   8
Piteous predicament! Even so lies she,
Blubbering and weeping, weeping and blubber-
    ing.
Stand up, stand up; stand, an you be a man:
For Juliet's sake, for her sake, rise and stand
Why should you fall into so deep an O?   8
    Rom. Nurse!
    Nurse. Ah, sir! ah, sir! Well, death's the end
    of all.
    Rom. Spak'st thou of Juliet? how is it with
    her?   92
Doth she not think me an old murderer,
Now I have stain'd the childhood of our joy
With blood remov'd but little from her own?
Where is she? and how doth she? and what
    says   96
My conceal'd lady to our cancell'd love?
    Nurse. O! she says nothing, sir, but weeps
    and weeps;
And now falls on her bed; and then starts up,
And Tybalt calls, and then on Romeo cries, 100
And then down falls again.
    Rom.   As if that name,
Shot from the deadly level of a gun,
Did murder her; as that name's cursed hand
Murder'd her kinsman. O! tell me, friar, tell
    me,   104
In what vile part of this anatomy
Doth my name lodge? tell me, that I may sack
The hateful mansion.   [*Drawing his sword.*
    Fri. L.   Hold thy desperate hand:
Art thou a man? thy form cries out thou art:
Thy tears are womanish; thy wild acts denote
The unreasonable fury of a beast:
Unseemly woman in a seeming man;
Or ill-beseeming beast in seeming both!   112
Thou hast amaz'd me: by my holy order,
I thought thy disposition better temper'd.
Hast thou slain Tybalt? wilt thou slay thyself?
And slay thy lady that in thy life lives,   116
By doing damned hate upon thyself?
Why rail'st thou on thy birth, the heaven, and
    earth?
Since birth, and heaven, and earth, all three do
    meet
In thee at once, which thou at once wouldst
    lose.   120
Fie, fie! thou sham'st thy shape, thy love, thy
    wit,
Which, like a usurer, abound'st in all,
And usest none in that true use indeed
Which should bedeck thy shape, thy love, thy
    wit.   124
Thy noble shape is but a form of wax,
Digressing from the valour of a man

Thy dear love, sworn, but hollow perjury,
Killing that love which thou hast vow'd to
  cherish;   128
Thy wit, that ornament to shape and love,
Misshapen in the conduct of them both,
Like powder in a skilless soldier's flask,
To set a-fire by thine own ignorance,   132
And thou dismember'd with thine own defence.
What! rouse thee, man; thy Juliet is alive,
For whose dear sake thou wast but lately dead;
There art thou happy: Tybalt would kill thee,
But thou slew'st Tybalt; there art thou happy
  too: 137
The law that threaten'd death becomes thy
  friend,
And turns it to exile; there art thou happy:
A pack of blessings light upon thy back;   140
Happiness courts thee in her best array;
But, like a misbehav'd and sullen wench,
Thou pout'st upon thy fortune and thy love.
Take heed, take heed, for such die miserable. 144
Go, get thee to thy love, as was decreed,
Ascend her chamber, hence and comfort her;
But look thou stay not till the watch be set,
For then thou canst not pass to Mantua;   148
Where thou shalt live, till we can find a time
To blaze your marriage, reconcile your friends,
Beg pardon of the prince, and call thee back
With twenty hundred thousand times more joy
Than thou went'st forth in lamentation.   153
Go before, nurse: commend me to thy lady;
And bid her hasten all the house to bed,
Which heavy sorrow makes them apt unto: 156
Romeo is coming.

Nurse. O Lord! I could have stay'd here all
  the night
To hear good counsel: O! what learning is.
My lord, I'll tell my lady you will come. 160

Rom. Do so, and bid my sweet prepare to
  chide.

Nurse. Here, sir, a ring she bid me give you,
  sir.
Hie you, make haste, for it grows very late.
                                        [*Exit.*

Rom. How well my comfort is reviv'd by
  this!   164

Fri. L. Go hence; good-night; and here
  stands all your state:
Either be gone before the watch be set,
Or by the break of day disguis'd from hence:
Sojourn in Mantua; I'll find out your man, 168
And he shall signify from time to time
Every good hap to you that chances here.
Give me thy hand; 'tis late: farewell; good-
  night.

Rom. But that a joy past joy calls out on me,
It were a grief so brief to part with thee: 173
Farewell.   [*Exeunt.*

SCENE IV.—*The Same. A Room in* CAPULET'S
  House.

Enter CAPULET, LADY CAPULET, *and* PARIS.

Cap. Things have fall'n out, sir, so unluckily,
That we have had no time to move our daughter:
Look you, she lov'd her kinsman Tybalt dearly,

And so did I: well, we were born to die.   4
'Tis very late, she'll not come down to-night:
I promise you, but for your company,
I would have been a-bed an hour ago.

Par. These times of woe afford no time to
  woo.   8

Madam, good-night: commend me to your
  daughter.

Lady Cap. I will, and know her mind early
  to-morrow;
To-night she's mew'd up to her heaviness.

Cap. Sir Paris, I will make a desperate ten-
  der   12
Of my child's love: I think she will be rul'd
In all respects by me; nay, more, I doubt it not.
Wife, go you to her ere you go to bed;
Acquaint her here of my son Paris' love;   16
And bid her, mark you me, on Wednesday
  next—
But, soft! what day is this?

Par.   Monday, my lord.

Cap. Monday! ha, ha! Well, Wednesday is
  too soon;
O' Thursday let it be: o' Thursday, tell her, 20
She shall be married to this noble earl.
Will you be ready? do you like this haste?
We'll keep no great ado; a friend or two;
For, hark you, Tybalt being slain so late, 24
It may be thought we held him carelessly,
Being our kinsman, if we revel much.
Therefore we'll have some half a dozen friends,
And there an end. But what say you to Thurs-
  day?   28

Par. My lord, I would that Thursday were
  to-morrow.

Cap. Well, get you gone: o' Thursday be it
  then.
Go you to Juliet ere you go to bed,
Prepare her, wife, against this wedding-day. 32
Farewell, my lord. Light to my chamber, ho!
Afore me! it is so very very late,
That we may call it early by and by.
Good-night.   [*Exeunt.*

SCENE V.—*The Same.* JULIET'S *Chamber.*

Enter ROMEO *and* JULIET.

Jul. Wilt thou be gone? it is not yet near day:
It was the nightingale, and not the lark,
That pierc'd the fearful hollow of thine ear;
Nightly she sings on yon pomegranate tree: 4
Believe me, love, it was the nightingale.

Rom. It was the lark, the herald of the morn,
No nightingale: look, love, what envious streaks
Do lace the severing clouds in yonder east: 8
Night's candles are burnt out, and jocund day
Stands tiptoe on the misty mountain tops:
I must be gone and live, or stay and die.

Jul. Yon light is not daylight, I know it, I: 13
It is some meteor that the sun exhales,
To be to thee this night a torch-bearer,
And light thee on thy way to Mantua:
Therefore stay yet; thou need'st not to be gone.

Rom. Let me be ta'en, let me be put to
  death;   17
I am content, so thou wilt have it so.

I'll say yon grey is not the morning's eye,
'Tis but the pale reflex of Cynthia's brow; 20
Nor that is not the lark, whose notes do beat
The vaulty heaven so high above our heads:
I have more care to stay than will to go:
Come, death, and welcome! Juliet wills it so. 24
How is 't, my soul? let's talk; it is not day.

Jul. It is, it is; hie hence, be gone, away!
It is the lark that sings so out of tune,
Straining harsh discords and unpleasing sharps.
Some say the lark makes sweet division; 29
This doth not so, for she divideth us:
Some say the lark and loathed toad change
  eyes;
O! now I would they had chang'd voices too, 32
Since arm from arm that voice doth us affray,
Hunting thee hence with hunts-up to the day.
O! now be gone; more light and light it grows.

Rom. More light and light; more dark and
  dark our woes.   36

Enter Nurse.

Nurse. Madam!
Jul. Nurse!
Nurse. Your lady mother is coming to your
  chamber: 39
The day is broke; be wary, look about. [*Exit.*
Jul. Then, window, let day in, and let life out.
Rom. Farewell, farewell! one kiss, and I'll
  descend.   [*Descends.*
Jul. Art thou gone so? my lord, my love, my
  friend!
I must hear from thee every day in the hour, 44
For in a minute there are many days:
O! by this count I shall be much in years
Ere I again behold my Romeo.
Rom. Farewell!   48
I will omit no opportunity
That may convey my greetings, love, to thee.
Jul. O! think'st thou we shall ever meet
  again?
Rom. I doubt it not; and all these woes shall
  serve   52
For sweet discourses in our time to come.
Jul. O God! I have an ill-divining soul:
Methinks I see thee, now thou art so low,
As one dead in the bottom of a tomb: 56
Either my eyesight fails, or thou look'st pale.
Rom. And trust me, love, in my eye so do you:
Dry sorrow drinks our blood. Adieu! adieu!
                                       [*Exit.*
Jul. O fortune, fortune! all men call thee
  fickle: 60
If thou art fickle, what dost thou with him
That is renown'd for faith? Be fickle, fortune;
For then, I hope, thou wilt not keep him long,
But send him back.   64
Lady Cap. [*Within.*] Ho, daughter! are you
  up?
Jul. Who is 't that calls? is it my lady mother?
Is she not down so late, or up so early?
What unaccustom'd cause procures her hither?

Enter LADY CAPULET.

Lady Cap. Why, how now, Juliet!
Jul.   Madam, I am not well. 69

Lady Cap. Evermore weeping for your cou
  sin's death?
What! wilt thou wash him from his grave wit
  tears?
And if thou couldst, thou couldst not make hir
  live;   7
Therefore, have done: some grief shows much
  of love;
But much of grief shows still some want of wi
Jul. Yet let me weep for such a feeling loss
Lady Cap. So shall you feel the loss, but no
  the friend   7
Which you weep for.
Jul.   Feeling so the loss,
I cannot choose but ever weep the friend.
Lady Cap. Well, girl, thou weep'st not so
  much for his death,
As that the villain lives which slaughter'd him
Jul. What villain, madam?
Lady Cap.   That same villain, Romeo
Jul. [*Aside.*] Villain and he be many mile
  asunder.   8
God pardon him! I do, with all my heart;
And yet no man like he doth grieve my heart
Lady Cap. That is because the traitor mur
  derer lives.   8
Jul. Ay, madam, from the reach of these m
  hands.
Would none but I might venge my cousin'
  death!
Lady Cap. We will have vengeance for it
  fear thou not: 8
Then weep no more. I'll send to one in Mantua
Where that same banish'd runagate doth live
Shall give him such an unaccustom'd dram
That he shall soon keep Tybalt company: 9
And then, I hope, thou wilt be satisfied.
Jul. Indeed, I never shall be satisfied
With Romeo, till I behold him—dead—
Is my poor heart so for a kinsman vex'd: 9
Madam, if you could find out but a man
To bear a poison, I would temper it,
That Romeo should, upon receipt thereof,
Soon sleep in quiet. O! how my heart abhor
To hear him nam'd, and cannot come to him
To wreak the love I bore my cousin Tybalt
Upon his body that hath slaughter'd him.
Lady Cap. Find thou the means, and I'll find
  such a man.   10
But now I'll tell thee joyful tidings, girl.
Jul. And joy comes well in such a needy
  time:
What are they, I beseech your ladyship?
Lady Cap. Well, well, thou hast a careful
  father, child;   10
One who, to put thee from thy heaviness,
Hath sorted out a sudden day of joy
That thou expect'st not, nor I look'd not for.
Jul. Madam, in happy time, what day is that?
Lady Cap. Marry, my child, early next
  Thursday morn   11
The gallant, young, and noble gentleman,
The County Paris, at Saint Peter's church,
Shall happily make thee there a joyful bride. 116
Jul. Now, by Saint Peter's church, and Peter
  too,

nearly gives herself away (handwritten annotation)

le shall not make me there a joyful bride.
wonder at this haste; that I must wed
re he that should be husband comes to woo.
pray you, tell my lord and father, madam, 121
will not marry yet; and, when I do, I swear,
t shall be Romeo, whom you know I hate,
Rather than Paris. These are news indeed! 124

Lady Cap. Here comes your father; tell him
   so yourself,
And see how he will take it at your hands.

Enter CAPULET *and* Nurse.

Cap. When the sun sets, the air doth drizzle
   dew;
But for the sunset of my brother's son   128
It rains downright.
How now! a conduit, girl? what! still in tears?
Evermore showering? In one little body
Thou counterfeit'st a bark, a sea, a wind; 132
For still thy eyes, which I may call the sea,
Do ebb and flow with tears; the bark thy body is,
Sailing in this salt flood; the winds, thy sighs;
Who, raging with thy tears, and they with
   them,   136
Without a sudden calm, will overset
Thy tempest-tossed body. How now, wife!
Have you deliver'd to her our decree?
Lady Cap. Ay, sir; but she will none, she
   gives you thanks.   140
would the fool were married to her grave!
Cap. Soft! take me with you, take me with
   you, wife.
How! will she none? doth she not give us thanks?
Is she not proud? doth she not count her bless'd,
Unworthy as she is, that we have wrought 145
So worthy a gentleman to be her bridegroom?
Jul. Not proud, you have; but thankful, that
   you have:
Proud can I never be of what I hate,   148
But thankful even for hate, that is meant love.
Cap. How now! how now, chop-logic! What
   is this?
Proud,' and 'I thank you,' and 'I thank you
   not;'
And yet 'not proud;' mistress minion, you, 152
Thank me no thankings, nor proud me no
   prouds,
But fettle your fine joints 'gainst Thursday next,
To go with Paris to Saint Peter's church,
Or I will drag thee on a hurdle thither.   156
Out, you green-sickness carrion! out, you bag-
   gage! *very bad breathed away* (handwritten)
You tallow face! *angry* (handwritten)
Lady Cap. Fie, fie! what, are you mad?
Jul. Good father, I beseech you on my knees, 160
Hear me with patience but to speak a word.
Cap. Hang thee, young baggage! disobedient
   wretch!
I tell thee what, get thee to church o' Thursday,
Or never after look me in the face.
Speak not, reply not, do not answer me;   164
My fingers itch.—Wife, we scarce thought us
   bless'd
That God had lent us but this only child;
But now I see this one is one too much,
And that we have a curse in having her.   168

Out on her, hilding!
   Nurse.   God in heaven bless her!
You are to blame, my lord, to rate her so.
Cap. And why, my lady wisdom? hold your
   tongue,   171
Good prudence; smatter with your gossips, go.
Nurse. I speak no treason.
Cap.   O! God ye good den.
Nurse. May not one speak?
Cap.   Peace, you mumbling fool;
Utter your gravity o'er a gossip's bowl;
For here we need it not.
Lady Cap.   You are too hot. 176
Cap. God's bread! it makes me mad.
Day, night, hour, tide, time, work, play,
Alone, in company, still my care hath been
To have her match'd; and having now provided
A gentleman of noble parentage,   181
Of fair demesnes, youthful, and nobly train'd,
Stuff'd, as they say, with honourable parts,
Proportion'd as one's thought would wish a
   man;   184
And then to have a wretched puling fool,
A whining mammet, in her fortune's tender,
To answer 'I'll not wed,' 'I cannot love,'
'I am too young,' 'I pray you, pardon me;' 188
But, an you will not wed, I'll pardon you:
Graze where you will, you shall not house with
   me:
Look to 't, think on 't, I do not use to jest.
Thursday is near; lay hand on heart, advise. 192
An you be mine, I'll give you to my friend;
An you be not, hang, beg, starve, die in the
   streets,
For, by my soul, I'll ne'er acknowledge thee,
Nor what is mine shall never do thee good. 196
Trust to 't, bethink you; I'll not be forsworn.
           [*Exit.*
Jul. Is there no pity sitting in the clouds,
That sees into the bottom of my grief?
O! sweet my mother, cast me not away: 200
Delay this marriage for a month, a week;
Or, if you do not, make the bridal bed
In that dim monument where Tybalt lies.
Lady Cap. Talk not to me, for I'll not speak
   a word.   204
Do as thou wilt, for I have done with thee. [*Exit.*
Jul. O God! O nurse! how shall this be pre-
   vented?
My husband is on earth, my faith in heaven;
How shall that faith return again to earth, 208
Unless that husband send it me from heaven
By leaving earth? comfort me, counsel me.
Alack, alack! that heaven should practise strata-
   gems
Upon so soft a subject as myself!   212
What sayst thou? hast thou not a word of joy?
Some comfort, nurse?
   Nurse.   Faith, here it is. Romeo
Is banished; and all the world to nothing
That he dares ne'er come back to challenge you;
Or, if he do, it needs must be by stealth.   217
Then, since the case so stands as now it doth,
I think it best you married with the county.
O! he's a lovely gentleman;   220
Romeo's a dishclout to him: an eagle, madam,

Hath not so green, so quick, so fair an eye
As Paris hath. Beshrew my very heart,
I think you are happy in this second match, 224
For it excels your first: or if it did not,
Your first is dead; or 'twere as good he were,
As living here and you no use of him.
  Jul. Speakest thou from thy heart?
  Nurse.   And from my soul too; 228
Or else beshrew them both.
  Jul.   Amen!
  Nurse.   What!
  Jul. Well, thou hast comforted me marvellous much.
Go in; and tell my lady I am gone,
Having displeas'd my father, to Laurence' cell,
To make confession and to be absolv'd.   233
  Nurse. Marry, I will; and this is wisely done.
                            [*Exit.*
  Jul. Ancient damnation! O most wicked
    fiend!   236
Is it more sin to wish me thus forsworn,
Or to dispraise my lord with that same tongue
Which she hath prais'd him with above compare
So many thousand times? Go, counsellor;
Thou and my bosom henceforth shall be twain.
I'll to the friar, to know his remedy: 241
If all else fail, myself have power to die. [*Exit.*

ACT IV

SCENE I.—*Verona.* FRIAR LAURENCE'S *Cell.*

Enter FRIAR LAURENCE *and* PARIS.

  Fri. L. On Thursday, sir? the time is very
    short.
  Par. My father Capulet will have it so;
And I am nothing slow to slack his haste.
  Fri. L. You say you do not know the lady's
    mind: 4
Uneven is the course, I like it not.
  Par. Immoderately she weeps for Tybalt's
    death,
And therefore have I little talk'd of love;
For Venus smiles not in a house of tears.   8
Now, sir, her father counts it dangerous
That she doth give her sorrow so much sway,
And in his wisdom hastes our marriage
To stop the inundation of her tears;   12
Which, too much minded by herself alone,
May be put from her by society.
Now do you know the reason of this haste.
  Fri. L. [*Aside.*] I would I knew not why it
    should be slow'd.   16
Look, sir, here comes the lady towards my cell.

Enter JULIET.

  Par. Happily met, my lady and my wife!
  Jul. That may be, sir, when I may be a wife.
  Par. That may be must be, love, on Thursday next.   20
  Jul. What must be shall be.
  Fri. L.   That's a certain text.
  Par. Come you to make confession to this
    father?
  Jul. To answer that, I should confess to you.
  Par. Do not deny to him that you love me.
  Jul. I will confess to you that I love him. 25

  Par. So will ye, I am sure, that you love me
  Jul. If I do so, it will be of more price,
Being spoke behind your back, than to you
    face.
  Par. Poor soul, thy face is much abus'd wit
    tears.
  Jul. The tears have got small victory by that
For it was bad enough before their spite.
  Par. Thou wrong'st it, more than tears, wit
    that report.
  Jul. That is no slander, sir, which is a truth
And what I spake, I spake it to my face.
  Par. Thy face is mine, and thou hast slander'
    it.
  Jul. It may be so, for it is not mine own.
Are you at leisure, holy father, now;
Or shall I come to you at evening mass?
  Fri. L. My leisure serves me, pensive daugh
    ter, now:
My lord, we must entreat the time alone.   4
  Par. God shield, I should disturb devotion
Juliet, on Thursday early will I rouse you:
Till then, adieu; and keep this holy kiss. [*Exi*
  Jul. O! shut the door! and when thou has
    done so,
Come weep with me; past hope, past cure, pas
    help!
  Fri. L. Ah! Juliet, I already know thy grief
It strains me past the compass of my wits:
I hear thou must, and nothing may prorogue i
On Thursday next be married to this county.
  Jul. Tell me not, friar, that thou hear'st o
    this,
Unless thou tell me how I may prevent it:
If, in thy wisdom, thou canst give no help, 5
Do thou but call my resolution wise,
And with this knife I'll help it presently.
God join'd my heart and Romeo's, thou ou
    hands;
And ere this hand, by thee to Romeo seal'd, 5
Shall be the label to another deed,
Or my true heart with treacherous revolt
Turn to another, this shall slay them both.
Therefore, out of thy long-experienc'd time, 6
Give me some present counsel; or behold,
'Twixt my extremes and me this bloody knif
Shall play the umpire, arbitrating that
Which the commission of thy years and art 6
Could to no issue of true honour bring.
Be not so long to speak; I long to die,
If what thou speak'st speak not of remedy.
  Fri. L. Hold, daughter; I do spy a kind o
    hope,   6
Which craves as desperate an execution
As that is desperate which we would prevent
If, rather than to marry County Paris,
Thou hast the strength of will to slay thyself, 7
Then is it likely thou wilt undertake
A thing like death to chide away this shame,
That cop'st with death himself to 'scape from it
And, if thou dar'st, I'll give thee remedy.   7
  Jul. O! bid me leap, rather than marry Paris
From off the battlements of yonder tower;
Or walk in thievish ways; or bid me lurk
Where serpents are; chain me with roaring
    bears;   8

)r shut me nightly in a charnel-house,
)'er-cover'd quite with dead men's rattling
　　bones,
Vith reeky shanks, and yellow chapless skulls;
)r bid me go into a new-made grave　　84
And hide me with a dead man in his shroud;
'hings that, to hear them told, have made me
　　tremble;
And I will do it without fear or doubt,
'o live an unstain'd wife to my sweet love.　88
　Fri. L. Hold, then; go home, be merry, give
　　consent
'o marry Paris: Wednesday is to-morrow:
'o-morrow night look that thou lie alone,
.et not thy nurse lie with thee in thy chamber:
'ake thou this vial, being then in bed,　　93
And this distilled liquor drink thou off;
Vhen presently through all thy veins shall run
A cold and drowsy humour, for no pulse　　96
hall keep his native progress, but surcease;
'o warmth, no breath, shall testify thou liv'st;
'he roses in thy lips and cheeks shall fade
'o paly ashes; thy eyes' windows fall,　　100
.ike death, when he shuts up the day of life;
:ach part, depriv'd of supple government,
hall, stiff and stark and cold, appear like death;
And in this borrow'd likeness of shrunk death
'hou shalt continue two-and-forty hours,　105
And then awake as from a pleasant sleep.
Jow, when the bridegroom in the morning
　　comes
'o rouse thee from thy bed, there art thou dead:
'hen—as the manner of our country is—　109
n thy best robes uncover'd on the bier,
'hou shalt be borne to that same ancient vault
Vhere all the kindred of the Capulets lie.　112
n the mean time, against thou shalt awake,
hall Romeo by my letters know our drift,
And hither shall he come; and he and I
Vill watch thy waking, and that very night　116
hall Romeo bear thee hence to Mantua.
And this shall free thee from this present shame;
f no unconstant toy, nor womanish fear,
Abate thy valour in the acting it.　　120
　Jul. Give me, give me! O! tell me not of fear!
　Fri. L. Hold; get you gone, be strong and
　　prosperous
n this resolve. I'll send a friar with speed
'o Mantua, with my letters to thy lord.　124
　Jul. Love, give me strength! and strength
　　shall help afford.
'arewell, dear father!　　　　　[*Exeunt.*

SCENE II.—*The Same. Hall in* CAPULET'S
House.

Enter CAPULET, LADY CAPULET, Nurse, *and*
Servingmen.

　Cap. So many guests invite as here are writ.
　　　　　　　　　　　[*Exit Servant.*
irrah, go hire me twenty cunning cooks.
　Sec. Serv. You shall have none ill, sir; for
'll try if they can lick their fingers.　4
　Cap. How canst thou try them so?
　Sec. Serv. Marry, sir, 'tis an ill cook that
annot lick his own fingers: therefore he that

cannot lick his fingers goes not with me.　　8
　Cap. Go, be gone.　[*Exit Second Servant.*
We shall be much unfurnish'd for this time.
What! is my daughter gone to Friar Laurence?
　Nurse. Ay, forsooth.　　　　12
　Cap. Well, she may chance to do some good
　　on her: ⸢Coming round.⸣
A peevish self-will'd harlotry it is.
　Nurse. See where she comes from shrift with
　merry look.　　　　　　　16

Enter JULIET.

　Cap. How now, my headstrong! where have
　　you been gadding?
　Jul. Where I have learn'd me to repent the
　　sin
Of disobedient opposition
To you and your behests; and am enjoin'd 20
By holy Laurence to fall prostrate here,
And beg your pardon. Pardon, I beseech you!
Henceforward I am ever rul'd by you.
　Cap. Send for the county; go tell him of
　　this:　　　　　　　　24
I'll have this knot knit up to-morrow morning.
　Jul. I met the youthful lord at Laurence'
　　cell;
And gave him what becomed love I might,
Not stepping o'er the bounds of modesty.　28
　Cap. Why, I'm glad on't; this is well: stand
　　up:
This is as't should be. Let me see the county;
Ay, marry, go, I say, and fetch him hither.
Now, afore God! this reverend holy friar,　32
All our whole city is much bound to him.
　Jul. Nurse, will you go with me into my
　　closet,
To help me sort such needful ornaments
As you think fit to furnish me to-morrow? 36
　Lady Cap. No, not till Thursday; there is
　　time enough.
　Cap. Go, nurse, go with her. We'll to church
　to-morrow.　　[*Exeunt* JULIET *and* Nurse.
　Lady Cap. We shall be short in our pro-
　　vision:
'Tis now near night.
　Cap.　　　　Tush! I will stir about, 40
And all things shall be well, I warrant thee,
　wife:
Go thou to Juliet, help to deck up her;
I'll not to bed to-night; let me alone;
I'll play the housewife for this once. What, ho!
They are all forth: well, I will walk myself 45
To County Paris, to prepare him up
Against to-morrow. My heart is wondrous
　light,
Since this same wayward girl is so reclaim'd. 48
　　　　　　　　　　　　[*Exeunt.*

SCENE III.—*The Same.* JULIET'S *Chamber.*

Enter JULIET *and* Nurse.

　Jul. Ay, those attires are best; but, gentle
　nurse,
I pray thee, leave me to myself to-night;
For I have need of many orisons
To move the heavens to smile upon my state, 4

Which, well thou know'st, is cross and full of
   sin.

Enter LADY CAPULET.

Lady Cap. What! are you busy, ho? need
   you my help?
Jul. No, madam; we have cull'd such neces-
   saries
As are behoveful for our state to-morrow: 8
So please you, let me now be left alone,
And let the nurse this night sit up with you;
For I am sure, you have your hands full all
In this so sudden business.
   Lady Cap.   Good-night: 12
Get thee to bed, and rest; for thou hast need.
      [*Exeunt* LADY CAPULET *and* Nurse.
Jul. Farewell! God knows when we shall
   meet again.
I have a faint cold fear thrills through my veins,
That almost freezes up the heat of life: 16
I'll call them back again to comfort me:
Nurse! What should she do here?
My dismal scene I needs must act alone.
Come, vial.   20
What if this mixture do not work at all?
Shall I be married then to-morrow morning?
No, no; this shall forbid it: lie thou there.
      [*Laying down a dagger.*
What if it be a poison, which the friar   24
Subtly hath minister'd to have me dead,
Lest in this marriage he should be dishonour'd
Because he married me before to Romeo?
I fear it is: and yet, methinks, it should not, 28
For he hath still been tried a holy man.
I will not entertain so bad a thought.
How if, when I am laid into the tomb,
I wake before the time that Romeo   32
Come to redeem me? there's a fearful point!
Shall I not then be stifled in the vault,
To whose foul mouth no healthsome air breathes
   in,
And there die strangled ere my Romeo comes?
Or, if I live, is it not very like,   37
The horrible conceit of death and night,
Together with the terror of the place,
As in a vault, an ancient receptacle,   40
Where, for these many hundred years, the bones
Of all my buried ancestors are pack'd;
Where bloody Tybalt, yet but green in earth,
Lies festering in his shroud; where, as they say, 44
At some hours in the night spirits resort:
Alack, alack! is it not like that I,
So early waking, what with loathsome smells,
And shrieks like mandrakes' torn out of the
   earth,   48
That living mortals, hearing them, run mad:
O! if I wake, shall I not be distraught,
Environed with all these hideous fears,
And madly play with my forefathers' joints, 52
And pluck the mangled Tybalt from his shroud?
And, in this rage, with some great kinsman's
   bone,
As with a club, dash out my desperate brains?
O, look! methinks I see my cousin's ghost 56
Seeking out Romeo, that did spit his body
Upon a rapier's point. Stay, Tybalt, stay!

Romeo, I come! this do I drink to thee.
   [*She falls upon her bed within the curtains.*

SCENE IV.—*The Same.* Hall *in* CAPULET'S
      House.

Enter LADY CAPULET *and* Nurse.

Lady Cap. Hold, take these keys, and fetch
   more spices, nurse.
Nurse. They call for dates and quinces in the
   pastry.

Enter CAPULET.

Cap. Come, stir, stir, stir! the second cock
   hath crow'd,
The curfew bell hath rung, 'tis three o'clock: 4
Look to the bak'd meats, good Angelica:
Spare not for cost.
Nurse.   Go, go, you cot-quean, go;
Get you to bed; faith, you'll be sick to-morrow
For this night's watching.   8
   Cap. No, not a whit; what! I have watch'd
   ere now
All night for lesser cause, and ne'er been sick.
   Lady Cap. Ay, you have been a mouse-hunt
   in your time;
But I will watch you from such watching now.
      [*Exeunt* LADY CAPULET *and* Nurse.
   Cap. A jealous-hood, a jealous-hood!

Enter three or four Servingmen, *with spits,
      logs, and baskets*

               Now, fellow, 13
What's there?
First Serv. Things for the cook, sir; but I
   know not what.
Cap. Make haste, make haste. [*Exit firs
   Serving-man.*] Sirrah, fetch drier logs: 16
Call Peter, he will show thee where they are.
Sec. Serv. I have a head, sir, that will fin
   out logs,
And never trouble Peter for the matter. [*Exit
Cap. Mass, and well said; a merry whore
   son, ha!   20
Thou shalt be logger-head. Good faith! 'tis day
The county will be here with music straight
For so he said he would. [*Music within.*] I hea
   him near.
Nurse! Wife! what, ho! What, nurse, I say!

Re-enter Nurse.

Go waken Juliet, go and trim her up;   2
I'll go and chat with Paris. Hie, make haste,
Make haste; the bridegroom he is come already
Make haste, I say.   [*Exeunt

SCENE V.—*The Same.* JULIET'S *Chamber.*

Enter Nurse.

Nurse. Mistress! what, mistress! Juliet! fast
   I warrant her, she:
Why, lamb! why, lady! fie, you slug-a-bed!
Why, love, I say! madam! sweet-heart! why
   bride!
What! not a word? you take your pennyworth
   now;
Sleep for a week; for the next night, I warran

he County Paris hath set up his rest,
hat you shall rest but little. God forgive me,
arry, and amen, how sound is she asleep! 8
needs must wake her. Madam, madam,
madam!
y, let the county take you in your bed;
e'll fright you up, i' faith. Will it not be?
hat, dress'd! and in your clothes! and down
again! 12
must needs wake you. Lady! lady! lady!
las! alas! Help! help! my lady's dead!
! well-a-day, that ever I was born.
me *aqua-vitæ*, ho! My lord! my lady! 16

Enter LADY CAPULET.

Lady Cap. What noise is here?
Nurse. O lamentable day!
Lady Cap. What is the matter?
Nurse. Look, look! O heavy day!
Lady Cap. O me, O me! my child, my only
life,
evive, look up, or I will die with thee! 20
elp, help! Call help.

Enter CAPULET.

Cap. For shame! bring Juliet forth; her lord
is come.
Nurse. She's dead, deceas'd, she's dead;
alack the day!
Lady Cap. Alack the day! she's dead, she's
dead! she's dead! 24
Cap. Ha! let me see her. Out, alas! she's
cold;
er blood is settled, and her joints are stiff;
fe and these lips have long been separated:
eath lies on her like an untimely frost 28
pon the sweetest flower of all the field.
Nurse. O lamentable day!
Lady Cap. O woeful time!
Cap. Death, that hath ta'en her hence to
make me wail,
ies up my tongue, and will not let me speak. 32

Enter FRIAR LAURENCE, *and* PARIS, *with*
Musicians.

Fri. L. Come, is the bride ready to go to
church?
Cap. Ready to go, but never to return.
son! the night before thy wedding-day
ath Death lain with thy wife. There she lies, 36
lower as she was, deflowered by him.
eath is my son-in-law, Death is my heir;
y daughter he hath wedded: I will die,
nd leave him all; life, living, all is Death's! 40
Par. Have I thought long to see this morning's face,
nd doth it give me such a sight as this?
Lady Cap. Accurs'd, unhappy, wretched,
hateful day!
ost miserable hour, that e'er time saw 44
a lasting labour of his pilgrimage!
ut one, poor one, one poor and loving child,
ut one thing to rejoice and solace in,
nd cruel death hath catch'd it from my sight! 48
Nurse. O woe! O woeful, woeful, woeful
day!

Most lamentable day, most woeful day,
That ever, ever, I did yet behold!
O day! O day! O day! O hateful day! 52
Never was seen so black a day as this:
O woeful day, O woeful day!
Par. Beguil'd, divorced, wronged, spited,
slain!
Most detestable death, by thee beguil'd, 56
By cruel cruel thee quite overthrown!
O love! O life! not life, but love in death!
Cap. Despis'd, distressed, hated, martyr'd,
kill'd!
Uncomfortable time, why cam'st thou now 60
To murder, murder our solemnity?
O child! O child! my soul, and not my child!
Dead art thou! dead! alack, my child is dead;
And with my child my joys are buried! 64
Fri. L. Peace, ho! for shame! confusion's
cure lives not
In these confusions. Heaven and yourself
Had part in this fair maid; now heaven hath all,
And all the better is it for the maid: 68
Your part in her you could not keep from death,
But heaven keeps his part in eternal life.
The most you sought was her promotion,
For 'twas your heaven she should be advanc'd,
And weep ye now, seeing she is advanc'd 73
Above the clouds, as high as heaven itself?
O! in this love, you love your child so ill,
That you run mad, seeing that she is well: 76
She's not well married that lives married long;
But she's best married that dies married young.
Dry up your tears, and stick your rosemary
On this fair corse; and, as the custom is, 80
In all her best array bear her to church;
For though fond nature bids us all lament,
Yet nature's tears are reason's merriment.
Cap. All things that we ordained festival, 84
Turn from their office to black funeral;
Our instruments to melancholy bells,
Our wedding cheer to a sad burial feast,
Our solemn hymns to sullen dirges change, 88
Our bridal flowers serve for a buried corse,
And all things change them to the contrary.
Fri. L. Sir, go you in; and, madam, go with
him;
And go, Sir Paris; every one prepare 92
To follow this fair corse unto her grave.
The heavens do lower upon you for some ill;
Move them no more by crossing their high will.
[*Exeunt* CAPULET, LADY CAPULET, PARIS,
and Friar.
First Mus. Faith, we may put up our pipes,
and be gone. 97
Nurse. Honest good fellows, ah! put up, put
up, for, well you know, this is a pitiful case.
[*Exit.*
First Mus. Ay, by my troth, the case may be
amended. 101

Enter PETER.

Pet. Musicians! O! musicians, 'Heart's ease,
Heart's ease:' O! an ye will have me live, play
'Heart's ease.' 104
First Mus. Why 'Heart's ease?'
Pet. O! musicians, because my heart itself

plays 'My heart is full of woe;' O! play me
some merry dump, to comfort me.   108

Sec. Mus. Not a dump we; 'tis no time to
play now.

Pet. You will not then?

Musicians. No.   112

Pet. I will then give it you soundly.

First Mus. What will you give us?

Pet. No money, on my faith! but the gleek;
I will give you the minstrel.   116

First Mus. Then will I give you the serving-
creature.

Pet. Then will I lay the serving-creature's
dagger on your pate, I will carry no crotchets:
I'll re you, I'll fa you. Do you note me?   121

First Mus. An you re us, and fa us, you
note us.

Sec. Mus. Pray you, put up your dagger,
and put out your wit.   125

Pet. Then have at you with my wit! I will
dry-beat you with an iron wit, and put up my
iron dagger. Answer me like men: 128

When griping grief the heart doth wound,
    And doleful dumps the mind oppress,
Then music with her silver sound—

Why 'silver sound?' why 'music with her silver
sound?' What say you, Simon Catling?   133

First Mus. Marry, sir, because silver hath a
sweet sound.

Pet. Pretty! What say you, Hugh Rebeck?

Sec. Mus. I say 'silver sound,' because musicians sound for silver.

Pet. Pretty too! What say you, James
Soundpost?   140

Third Mus. Faith, I know not what to say.

Pet. O! I cry you mercy; you are the singer:
I will say for you. It is, 'music with her silver
sound,' because musicians have no gold for
sounding: 145

Then music with her silver sound
    With speedy help doth lend redress.

[*Exit.*

First Mus. What a pestilent knave is this
same!   149

Sec. Mus. Hang him, Jack! Come, we'll in
here; tarry for the mourners, and stay dinner.

[*Exeunt.*

ACT V

Scene I.—*Mantua. A Street.*

Enter ROMEO.

Rom. If I may trust the flattering truth of
sleep,
My dreams presage some joyful news at hand:
My bosom's lord sits lightly in his throne;
And all this day an unaccustom'd spirit   4
Lifts me above the ground with cheerful
thoughts.
I dreamt my lady came and found me dead;—
Strange dream, that gives a dead man leave to
think,—
And breath'd such life with kisses in my lips, 8
That I reviv'd, and was an emperor.

Ah me! how sweet is love itself possess'd,
When but love's shadows are so rich in joy!

Enter BALTHASAR, *booted.*

News from Verona! How now, Balthasar? 12
Dost thou not bring me letters from the friar?
How doth my lady? Is my father well?
How fares my Juliet? That I ask again;
For nothing can be ill if she be well.   16

Bal. Then she is well, and nothing can be ill:
Her body sleeps in Capel's monument,
And her immortal part with angels lives.
I saw her laid low in her kindred's vault,   20
And presently took post to tell it you.
O! pardon me for bringing these ill news,
Since you did leave it for my office, sir.

Rom. Is it even so? then I defy you, stars!
Thou know'st my lodging: get me ink and
paper,   25
And hire post-horses; I will hence to-night.

Bal. I do beseech you, sir, have patience:
Your looks are pale and wild, and do import
Some misadventure.

Rom.   Tush, thou art deceiv'd:
Leave me, and do the thing I bid thee do.
Hast thou no letters to me from the friar?

Bal. No, my good lord.

Rom.   No matter; get thee gone, 3
And hire those horses: I'll be with thee straight.

[*Exit BALTHASAR*

Well, Juliet, I will lie with thee to-night.
Let's see for means: O mischief! thou art swift
To enter in the thoughts of desperate men.
I do remember an apothecary,
And hereabouts he dwells, which late I note
In tatter'd weeds, with overwhelming brows,
Culling of simples; meagre were his looks,
Sharp misery had worn him to the bones:
And in his needy shop a tortoise hung,
An alligator stuff'd, and other skins
Of ill-shap'd fishes; and about his shelves
A beggarly account of empty boxes,
Green earthen pots, bladders, and musty seeds,
Remnants of packthread, and old cakes of roses
Were thinly scatter'd, to make up a show.
Noting this penury, to myself I said
And if a man did need a poison now,
Whose sale is present death in Mantua,
Here lives a caitiff wretch would sell it him.
O! this same thought did but fore-run my need
And this same needy man must sell it me.
As I remember, this should be the house:
Being holiday, the beggar's shop is shut.
What, ho! apothecary!

Enter Apothecary.

Ap.   Who calls so loud?

Rom. Come hither, man. I see that thou art
poor;
Hold, there is forty ducats; let me have
A dram of poison, such soon-speeding gear
As will disperse itself through all the veins
That the life-weary taker may fall dead,
And that the trunk may be discharg'd of breath
As violently as hasty powder fir'd
Doth hurry from the fatal cannon's womb.

Ap. Such mortal drugs I have; but Mantua's law
death to any he that utters them.

Rom. Art thou so bare, and full of wretchedness,   63
nd fear'st to die? famine is in thy cheeks,
eed and oppression starveth in thine eyes,
ontempt and beggary hang upon thy back;
he world is not thy friend nor the world's law:
he world affords no law to make thee rich; 73
hen be not poor, but break it, and take this.

Ap. My poverty, but not my will, consents.

Rom. I pay thy poverty, and not thy will. 76

Ap. Put this in any liquid thing you will,
nd drink it off; and, if you had the strength
f twenty men, it would dispatch you straight.

Rom. There is thy gold, worse poison to
men's souls,   80
oing more murders in this loathsome world
han these poor compounds that thou mayst
not sell:
sell thee poison, thou hast sold me none.
arewell; buy food, and get thyself in flesh. 84
ome, cordial and not poison, go with me
o Juliet's grave, for there must I use thee.
                                          [*Exeunt.*

SCENE II.—*Verona.* FRIAR LAURENCE'S *Cell.*

Enter FRIAR JOHN.

Fri. J. Holy Franciscan friar! brother, ho!

Enter FRIAR LAURENCE.

Fri. L. This same should be the voice of
Friar John.
Welcome from Mantua: what says Romeo?
r, if his mind be writ, give me his letter.   4

Fri. J. Going to find a bare-foot brother out,
ne of our order, to associate me,
ere in this city visiting the sick,
nd finding him, the searchers of the town, 8
uspecting that we both were in a house
Where the infectious pestilence did reign,
eal'd up the doors, and would not let us forth;
o that my speed to Mantua there was stay'd. 12

Fri. L. Who bare my letter then to Romeo?

Fri. J. I could not send it, here it is again,
'or get a messenger to bring it thee,
o fearful were they of infection.   16

Fri. L. Unhappy fortune! by my brotherhood,
he letter was not nice, but full of charge
f dear import; and the neglecting it
lay do much danger. Friar John, go hence;
et me an iron crow, and bring it straight 21
nto my cell.

Fri. J.   Brother, I'll go and bring it thee.
                                          [*Exit.*

Fri. L. Now must I to the monument alone;
Within these three hours will fair Juliet wake: 24
he will beshrew me much that Romeo
ath had no notice of these accidents;
ut I will write again to Mantua,
nd keep her at my cell till Romeo come: 28
oor living corse, clos'd in a dead man's tomb!
                                          [*Exit.*

SCENE III.—*The Same. A Churchyard; in it
a Monument belonging to the* CAPULETS.

Enter PARIS, *and his Page, bearing flowers and
a torch.*

Par. Give me thy torch, boy: hence, and
stand aloof;
Yet put it out, for I would not be seen.
Under yond yew-trees lay thee all along,
Holding thine ear close to the hollow ground: 4
So shall no foot upon the churchyard tread,
Being loose, unfirm with digging up of graves,
But thou shalt hear it: whistle then to me,
As signal that thou hear'st something approach.
Give me those flowers. Do as I bid thee; go. 9

Page. [*Aside.*] I am almost afraid to stand
alone
Here in the churchyard; yet I will adventure.
                                          [*Retires.*

Par. Sweet flower, with flowers thy bridal
bed I strew,   12
O woe! thy canopy is dust and stones;
Which with sweet water nightly I will dew,
Or, wanting that, with tears distill'd by moans:
The obsequies that I for thee will keep   16
Nightly shall be to strew thy grave and weep.
                              [*The* Page *whistles.*
The boy gives warning something doth ap-
proach.
What cursed foot wanders this way to-night,
To cross my obsequies and true love's rite? 20
What! with a torch?—muffle me, night, awhile.
                                          [*Retires.*

Enter ROMEO *and* BALTHASAR, *with a torch,
mattock, &c.*

Rom. Give me that mattock, and the wrenching
iron.
Hold, take this letter; early in the morning
See thou deliver it to my lord and father. 24
Give me the light: upon thy life I charge thee,
Whate'er thou hear'st or seest, stand all aloof,
And do not interrupt me in my course.
Why I descend into this bed of death,   28
Is partly, to behold my lady's face;
But chiefly to take thence from her dead finger
A precious ring, a ring that I must use
In dear employment: therefore hence, be gone:
But, if thou, jealous, dost return to pry 33
In what I further shall intend to do,
By heaven, I will tear thee joint by joint,
And strew this hungry churchyard with thy
limbs.   36
The time and my intents are savage-wild,
More fierce and more inexorable far
Than empty tigers or the roaring sea.

Bal. I will be gone, sir, and not trouble you. 40

Rom. So shalt thou show me friendship.
Take thou this:
Live, and be prosperous; and farewell, good
fellow.

Bal. [*Aside.*] For all this same, I'll hide me
here about:
His looks I fear, and his intents I doubt. 44
                                          [*Retires.*

Rom. Thou detestable maw, thou womb of
death,
Gorg'd with the dearest morsel of the earth,
Thus I enforce thy rotten jaws to open,
                    [*Opens the tomb.*
And, in despite, I'll cram thee with more food!
   Par. This is that banish'd haughty Mon-
tague,   49
That murder'd my love's cousin, with which grief
It is supposed the fair creature died;
And here is come to do some villanous shame 52
To the dead bodies: I will apprehend him.—
                   [*Comes forward.*
Stop thy unhallow'd toil, vile Montague,
Can vengeance be pursu'd further than death?
Condemned villain, I do apprehend thee: 56
Obey, and go with me; for thou must die.
   Rom. I must, indeed; and therefore came I
hither.
Good gentle youth, tempt not a desperate man;
Fly hence and leave me: think upon these gone;
Let them affright thee. I beseech thee, youth,
Put not another sin upon my head
By urging me to fury: O! be gone:
By heaven, I love thee better than myself. 64
For I come hither arm'd against myself:
Stay not, be gone; live, and hereafter say
A madman's mercy bade thee run away.
   Par. I do defy thy conjurations,   68
And apprehend thee for a felon here.
   Rom. Wilt thou provoke me? then have at
thee, boy!   [*They fight.*
   Page. O Lord! they fight: I will go call the
watch.   [*Exit.*
   Par. [*Falls.*] O, I am slain!—If thou be
merciful,   72
Open the tomb, lay me with Juliet.   [*Dies.*
   Rom. In faith, I will. Let me peruse this face:
Mercutio's kinsman, noble County Paris!
What said my man when my betossed soul 76
Did not attend him as we rode? I think
He told me Paris should have married Juliet:
Said he not so? or did I dream it so?
Or am I mad, hearing him talk of Juliet, 80
To think it was so? O! give me thy hand,
One writ with me in sour misfortune's book:
I'll bury thee in a triumphant grave;
A grave? O, no! a lanthorn, slaughter'd youth,
For here lies Juliet, and her beauty makes 85
This vault a feasting presence full of light.
Death, lie thou there, by a dead man interr'd,
         [*Laying* PARIS *in the tomb.*
How oft when men are at the point of death 88
Have they been merry! which their keepers call
A lightning before death: O! how may I
Call this a lightning? O my love! my wife!
Death, that hath suck'd the honey of thy breath,
Hath had no power yet upon thy beauty: 93
Thou art not conquer'd; beauty's ensign yet
Is crimson in thy lips and in thy cheeks,
And death's pale flag is not advanced there. 96
Tybalt, liest thou there in thy bloody sheet?
O! what more favour can I do to thee,
Than with that hand that cut thy youth in twain
To sunder his that was thine enemy?   100
Forgive me, cousin! Ah! dear Juliet,

Why art thou yet so fair? Shall I believe
That unsubstantial Death is amorous,
And that the lean abhorred monster keeps 104
Thee here in dark to be his paramour?
For fear of that I still will stay with thee,
And never from this palace of dim night
Depart again: here, here will I remain   108
With worms that are thy chambermaids; O!
here
Will I set up my everlasting rest,
And shake the yoke of inauspicious stars
From this world-wearied flesh. Eyes, look your
last!   112
Arms, take your last embrace! and, lips, O you
The doors of breath, seal with a righteous kiss
A dateless bargain to engrossing death!
Come, bitter conduct, come, unsavoury guide!
Thou desperate pilot, now at once run on 117
The dashing rocks thy sea-sick weary bark!
Here's to my love! [*Drinks.*] O true apothecary!
Thy drugs are quick. Thus with a kiss I die. 120
                           [*Dies.*

Enter, at the other end of the Churchyard, FRIAR
LAURENCE, *with a lanthorn, crow, and spade.*

   Fri. L. Saint Francis be my speed! how oft
to-night
Have my old feet stumbled at graves! Who's
there?
   Bal. Here's one, a friend, and one that knows
you well.
   Fri. L. Bliss be upon you! Tell me, good my
friend,   124
What torch is yond, that vainly lends his light
To grubs and eyeless skulls? as I discern,
It burneth in the Capel's monument.
   Bal. It doth so, holy sir; and there's my
master,   128
One that you love.
   Fri. L.   Who is it?
   Bal.   Romeo.
   Fri. L. How long hath he been there?
   Bal.   Full half an hour.
   Fri. L. Go with me to the vault.
   Bal.   I dare not, sir.
My master knows not but I am gone hence; 133
And fearfully did menace me with death
If I did stay to look on his intents.
   Fri. L. Stay then, I'll go alone. Fear comes
upon me;
O! much I fear some ill unlucky thing.   137
   Bal. As I did sleep under this yew-tree here
I dreamt my master and another fought,
And that my master slew him.
   Fri. L.   [*Advances.*] Romeo!
Alack, alack! what blood is this which stains 141
The stony entrance of this sepulchre?
What mean these masterless and gory swords
To lie discolour'd by this place of peace?
                  [*Enters the tomb.*
Romeo! O, pale! Who else? what! Paris too?
And steep'd in blood? Ah! what an unkind
hour   147
Is guilty of this lamentable chance.
The lady stirs.   [JULIET *wakes.*
   Jul. O, comfortable friar! where is my lord?

do remember well where I should be, 149
And there I am. Where is my Romeo?
[*Noise within.*
Fri. L. I hear some noise. Lady, come from
that nest
Of death, contagion, and unnatural sleep: 152
A greater power than we can contradict
Hath thwarted our intents: come, come away.
Thy husband in thy bosom there lies dead;
And Paris too: come, I'll dispose of thee 156
Among a sisterhood of holy nuns.
Stay not to question, for the watch is coming;
Come, go, good Juliet.—[*Noise again.*] I dare
no longer stay.
Jul. Go, get thee hence, for I will not away.
[*Exit* FRIAR LAURENCE.
What's here? a cup, clos'd in my true love's
hand? 161
Poison, I see, hath been his timeless end.
O churl! drunk all, and left no friendly drop
To help me after! I will kiss thy lips; 164
Haply, some poison yet doth hang on them,
To make me die with a restorative. [*Kisses him.*
Thy lips are warm!
First Watch. [*Within.*] Lead, boy: which way?
Jul. Yea, noise? then I'll be brief. O happy
dagger! [*Snatching* ROMEO's *dagger.*
This is thy sheath; [*Stabs herself.*] there rest,
and let me die. 170
[*Falls on* ROMEO's *body and dies.*

Enter Watch, *with the* Page *of* PARIS.

Page. This is the place; there where the torch
doth burn.
First Watch. The ground is bloody; search
about the churchyard. 172
Go, some of you, whoe'er you find, attach.
[*Exeunt some of the* Watch.
Pitiful sight! here lies the county slain,
And Juliet bleeding, warm, and newly dead,
Who here hath lain these two days buried. 176
Go, tell the prince, run to the Capulets,
Raise up the Montagues, some others search:
[*Exeunt others of the* Watch.
We see the ground whereon these woes do lie;
But the true ground of all these piteous woes
We cannot without circumstance descry. 181

Re-enter some of the Watch, *with* BALTHASAR.

Sec. Watch. Here's Romeo's man; we found
him in the churchyard.
First Watch. Hold him in safety, till the
prince come hither.

Re-enter other of the Watch, *with* FRIAR
LAURENCE.

Third Watch. Here is a friar, that trembles,
sighs, and weeps; 184
We took this mattock and this spade from him,
As he was coming from this churchyard side.
First Watch. A great suspicion: stay the friar
too. 187

Enter the PRINCE *and* Attendants.

Prince. What misadventure is so early up,
That calls our person from our morning's rest?

Enter CAPULET, LADY CAPULET, *and Others.*

Cap. What should it be, that they so shriek
abroad?
Lady Cap. The people in the street cry
Romeo,
Some Juliet, and some Paris; and all run 192
With open outcry toward our monument.
Prince. What fear is this which startles in
our ears?
First Watch. Sovereign, here lies the County
Paris slain;
And Romeo dead; and Juliet, dead before, 196
Warm and new kill'd.
Prince. Search, seek, and know how this foul
murder comes.
First Watch. Here is a friar, and slaughter'd
Romeo's man;
With instruments upon them, fit to open 200
These dead men's tombs.
Cap. O, heaven!—O wife! look how our
daughter bleeds!
This dagger hath mista'en!—for, lo, his house
Is empty on the back of Montague— 204
And is mis-sheathed in my daughter's bosom.
Lady Cap. O me! this sight of death is as a
bell,
That warns my old age to a sepulchre.

Enter MONTAGUE *and Others.*

Prince. Come, Montague: for thou art early
up, 208
To see thy son and heir more early down.
Mon. Alas! my liege, my wife is dead to-
night;
Grief of my son's exile hath stopp'd her breath.
What further woe conspires against mine
age? 212
Prince. Look, and thou shalt see.
Mon. O thou untaught! what manners is in
this,
To press before thy father to a grave?
Prince. Seal up the mouth of outrage for a
while, 216
Till we can clear these ambiguities,
And know their spring, their head, their true
descent;
And then will I be general of your woes,
And lead you even to death: meantime for-
bear, 220
And let mischance be slave to patience.
Bring forth the parties of suspicion.
Fri. L. I am the greatest, able to do least,
Yet most suspected, as the time and place 224
Doth make against me, of this direful murder;
And here I stand, both to impeach and purge
Myself condemned and myself excus'd.
Prince. Then say at once what thou dost
know in this. 228
Fri. L. I will be brief, for my short date of
breath
Is not so long as is a tedious tale.
Romeo, there dead, was husband to that Juliet;
And she, there dead, that Romeo's faithful wife:
I married them; and their stolen marriage-day
Was Tybalt's doomsday, whose untimely death

Banish'd the new-made bridegroom from this
city;
For whom, and not for Tybalt, Juliet pin'd. 236
You, to remove that siege of grief from her,
Betroth'd, and would have married her perforce,
To County Paris: then comes she to me,
And, with wild looks bid me devise some mean
To rid her from this second marriage, 241
Or in my cell there would she kill herself.
Then gave I her,—so tutor'd by my art,—
A sleeping potion; which so took effect 244
As I intended, for it wrought on her
The form of death: meantime I writ to Romeo
That he should hither come as this dire night,
To help to take her from her borrow'd grave, 248
Being the time the potion's force should cease.
But he which bore my letter, Friar John,
Was stay'd by accident, and yesternight
Return'd my letter back. Then, all alone, 252
At the prefixed hour of her waking,
Came I to take her from her kindred's vault,
Meaning to keep her closely at my cell,
Till I conveniently could send to Romeo: 256
But, when I came,—some minute ere the time
Of her awakening,—here untimely lay
The noble Paris and true Romeo dead.
She wakes; and I entreated her come forth, 260
And bear this work of heaven with patience;
But then a noise did scare me from the tomb,
And she, too desperate, would not go with me,
But, as it seems, did violence on herself. 264
All this I know; and to the marriage
Her nurse is privy: and, if aught in this
Miscarried by my fault, let my old life
Be sacrific'd, some hour before his time, 268
Unto the rigour of severest law.
   Prince. We still have known thee for a holy
      man.
Where's Romeo's man? what can he say in this?
   Bal. I brought my master news of Juliet's
      death; 272
And then in post he came from Mantua
To this same place, to this same monument.

This letter he early bid me give his father,
And threaten'd me with death, going in th
   vault, 27
If I departed not and left him there.
   Prince. Give me the letter; I will look on it
Where is the county's page that rais'd the watch
Sirrah, what made your master in this place ?
   Page. He came with flowers to strew hi
      lady's grave, 28
And bid me stand aloof, and so I did;
Anon, comes one with light to ope the tomb
And by and by my master drew on him; 28
And then I ran away to call the watch.
   Prince. This letter doth make good the friar'
      words,
Their course of love, the tidings of her death
And here he writes that he did buy a poison 28
Of a poor 'pothecary, and therewithal
Came to this vault to die, and lie with Juliet.
Where be these enemies ?—Capulet ! Montague
See what a scourge is laid upon your hate, 29
That heaven finds means to kill your joys with
   love;
And I, for winking at your discords too,
Have lost a brace of kinsmen: all are punish'd
   Cap. O brother Montague! give me thy
      hand: 29
This is my daughter's jointure, for no more
Can I demand.
   Mon.   But I can give thee more;
For I will raise her statue in pure gold;
That while Verona by that name is known, 30
There shall no figure at such rate be set
As that of true and faithful Juliet.
   Cap. As rich shall Romeo by his lady lie;
Poor sacrifices of our enmity!   30
   Prince. A glooming peace this morning with
      it brings;
The sun, for sorrow, will not show his head
Go hence, to have more talk of these sad things
   Some shall be pardon'd, and some punished
For never was a story of more woe
Than this of Juliet and her Romeo.   [*Exeunt*

TIMON OF ATHENS

DRAMATIS PERSONÆ

TIMON, a noble Athenian.

LUCIUS,
LUCULLUS, } flattering Lords.
SEMPRONIUS,

VENTIDIUS, one of Timon's false Friends.

APEMANTUS, a churlish Philosopher.

ALCIBIADES, an Athenian Captain.

FLAVIUS, Steward to Timon.

FLAMINIUS,
LUCILIUS, } Servants to Timon.
SERVILIUS,

CAPHIS,
PHILOTUS,
TITUS, } Servants to Timon's Creditors.
LUCIUS,
HORTENSIUS,

Servants of Ventidius, and of Varro and Isidore (two of Timon's Creditors).

Three Strangers.

An Old Athenian.

A Page.

A Fool.

Poet, Painter, Jeweller, and Merchant.

PHRYNIA,
TIMANDRA, } Mistresses to Alcibiades.

Lords, Senators, Officers, Soldiers, Thieves, and Attendants.

CUPID and Amazons in the Masque.

SCENE.—*Athens, and the neighbouring Woods.*

ACT I

SCENE I.—*Athens. A Hall in* TIMON'S *House.*

Enter Poet, Painter, Jeweller, Merchant, *and Others, at several doors.*

Poet. Good day, sir.
Pain.   I am glad you're well.
Poet. I have not seen you long. How goes the world?
Pain. It wears, sir, as it grows.
Poet.   Ay, that's well known;
But what particular rarity? what strange,   4
Which manifold record not matches? See,
Magic of bounty! all these spirits thy power
Hath conjur'd to attend. I know the merchant.
Pain. I know them both; th' other's a jeweller.   8
Mer. O! 'tis a worthy lord.
Jew.   Nay, that's most fix'd.
Mer. A most incomparable man, breath'd, as it were,
To an untirable and continuate goodness:
He passes.
Jew.   I have a jewel here—   12
Mer. O! pray, let's see't: for the Lord Timon, sir?
Jew. If he will touch the estimate: but, for that—
Poet. When we for recompense have prais'd the vile,
It stains the glory in that happy verse   16
Which aptly sings the good.
Mer. [*Looking at the jewel.*] 'Tis a good form.
Jew. And rich: here is a water, look ye.
Pain. You are rapt, sir, in some work, some dedication
To the great lord.
Poet.   A thing slipp'd idly from me.
Our poesy is as a gum, which oozes   21
From whence 'tis nourish'd: the fire i' the flint
Shows not till it be struck; our gentle flame
Provokes itself, and, like the current flies   24
Each bound it chafes. What have you there?
Pain. A picture, sir. When comes your book forth?
Poet. Upon the heels of my presentment, sir.
Let's see your piece.   28
Pain. 'Tis a good piece.
Poet. So 'tis: this comes off well and excellent.
Pain. Indifferent.
Poet.   Admirable! How this grace
Speaks his own standing! what a mental power
This eye shoots forth! how big imagination   33
Moves in this lip! to the dumbness of the gesture
One might interpret.
Pain. It is a pretty mocking of the life.   36
Here is a touch; is't good?
Poet.   I'll say of it,
It tutors nature: artificial strife
Lives in these touches, livelier than life.

Enter certain Senators, *who pass over the stage.*

Pain. How this lord is follow'd!   40
Poet. The senators of Athens: happy man!
Pain. Look, more!
Poet. You see this confluence, this great flood of visitors.
I have, in this rough work, shap'd out a man,   44
Whom this beneath world doth embrace and hug
With amplest entertainment: my free drift
Halts not particularly, but moves itself
In a wide sea of wax: no levell'd malice   48
Infects one comma in the course I hold;
But flies an eagle flight, bold and forth on,
Leaving no tract behind.
Pain. How shall I understand you?
Poet.   I will unbolt to you.   52
You see how all conditions, how all minds—

As well of glib and slippery creatures as
Of grave and austere quality—tender down
Their services to Lord Timon: his large fortune,
Upon his good and gracious nature hanging, 57
Subdues and properties to his love and tendance
All sorts of hearts; yea, from the glass-fac'd
flatterer
To Apemantus, that few things loves better 60
Than to abhor himself: even he drops down
The knee before him and returns in peace
Most rich in Timon's nod.
  Pain.   I saw them speak together.
  Poet. Sir, I have upon a high and pleasant
hill   64
Feign'd Fortune to be thron'd: the base o' the
mount
Is rank'd with all deserts, all kind of natures,
That labour on the bosom of this sphere
To propagate their states: amongst them all, 68
Whose eyes are on this sovereign lady fix'd,
One do I personate of Lord Timon's frame,
Whom Fortune with her ivory hand wafts to
her;
Whose present grace to present slaves and ser-
vants   72
Translates his rivals.
  Pain.   'Tis conceiv'd to scope.
This throne, this Fortune, and this hill, me-
thinks,
With one man beckon'd from the rest below,
Bowing his head against the steepy mount 76
To climb his happiness, would be well express'd
In our condition.
  Poet.   Nay, sir, but hear me on.
All those which were his fellows but of late,
Some better than his value, on the moment 80
Follow his strides, his lobbies fill with tendance,
Rain sacrificial whisperings in his ear,
Make sacred even his stirrup, and through him
Drink the free air.
  Pain.   Ay, marry, what of these? 84
  Poet. When Fortune in her shift and change
of mood
Spurns down her late belov'd, all his dependants
Which labour'd after him to the mountain's
top
Even on their knees and hands, let him slip
down,   88
Not one accompanying his declining foot.
  Pain. 'Tis common:
A thousand moral paintings I can show
That shall demonstrate these quick blows of
Fortune's   92
More pregnantly than words. Yet you do well
To show Lord Timon that mean eyes have seen
The foot above the head.

Trumpets sound. Enter LORD TIMON, *address-
ing himself courteously to every suitor; a*
Messenger *from* VENTIDIUS *talking with him;*
LUCILIUS *and other servants following.*

  Tim.   Imprison'd is he, say you?
  Mess. Ay, my good lord: five talents is his
debt,   96
His means most short, his creditors most strait:
Your honourable letter he desires

To those have shut him up; which, failing,
Periods his comfort.
  Tim.   Noble Ventidius! Well; 100
I am not of that feather to shake off
My friend when he must need me. I do know
him
A gentleman that well deserves a help,
Which he shall have: I'll pay the debt and free
him.   104
  Mess. Your lordship ever binds him.
  Tim. Commend me to him. I will send his
ransom;
And being enfranchis'd, bid him come to me.
'Tis not enough to help the feeble up, 108
But to support him after. Fare you well.
  Mess. All happiness to your honour. [*Exit*

Enter an Old Athenian.

  Old Ath. Lord Timon, hear me speak.
  Tim.   Freely, good father.
  Old Ath. Thou hast a servant nam'd Lucilius.
  Tim. I have so: what of him? 112
  Old Ath. Most noble Timon, call the man
before thee.
  Tim. Attends he here or no? Lucilius!
  Luc. Here, at your lordship's service. 116
  Old Ath. This fellow here, Lord Timon, this
thy creature,
By night frequents my house. I am a man
That from my first have been inclin'd to thrift
And my estate deserves an heir more rais'd 120
Than one which holds a trencher.
  Tim.   Well; what further?
  Old Ath. One only daughter have I, no kin
else,
On whom I may confer what I have got:
The maid is fair, o' the youngest for a bride, 124
And I have bred her at my dearest cost
In qualities of the best. This man of thine
Attempts her love: I prithee, noble lord,
Join with me to forbid him her resort; 128
Myself have spoke in vain.
  Tim.   The man is honest.
  Old Ath. Therefore he will be, Timon:
His honesty rewards him in itself;
It must not bear my daughter.
  Tim.   Does she love him? 132
  Old Ath. She is young and apt:
Our own precedent passions do instruct us
What levity 's in youth.
  Tim. [*To* LUCILIUS.] Love you the maid?
  Luc. Ay, my good lord, and she accepts of it.
  Old Ath. If in her marriage my consent be
missing,   136
I call the gods to witness, I will choose
Mine heir from forth the beggars of the world
And dispossess her all.
  Tim.   How shall she be endow'd
If she be mated with an equal husband? 140
  Old Ath. Three talents on the present; in
future, all.
  Tim. This gentleman of mine hath serv'd me
long:
To build his fortune I will strain a little, 144
For 'tis a bond in men. Give him thy daughter

What you bestow, in him I'll counterpoise,
And make him weigh with her.

Old Ath.   Most noble lord,
Pawn me to this your honour, she is his.   148
Tim. My hand to thee; mine honour on my
    promise.
Luc. Humbly I thank your lordship: never
    may
That state or fortune fall into my keeping
Which is not ow'd to you!   152

            [*Exeunt* LUCILIUS *and* Old Athenian.

Poet. Vouchsafe my labour, and long live
    your lordship!
Tim. I thank you; you shall hear from me
    anon:
Go not away. What have you there, my friend?
Pain. A piece of painting, which I do be-
    seech   156
Your lordship to accept.
Tim.   Painting is welcome.
The painting is almost the natural man;
For since dishonour traffics with man's nature,
He is but outside: these pencil'd figures are 160
Even such as they give out. I like your work;
And you shall find I like it: wait attendance
Till you hear further from me.
Pain.   The gods preserve you!
Tim. Well fare you, gentleman: give me your
    hand;   164
We must needs dine together. Sir, your jewel
Hath suffer'd under praise.
Jew.   What, my lord! dispraise?
Tim. A mere satiety of commendations.
If I should pay you for't as 'tis extoll'd,   168
It would unclew me quite.
Jew.   My lord, 'tis rated
As those which sell would give: but you well
    know,
Things of like value, differing in the owners,
Are prized by their masters. Believe 't, dear
    lord,   172
You mend the jewel by the wearing it.
Tim. Well mock'd.
Mer. No, my good lord; he speaks the com-
    mon tongue,
Which all men speak with him.   176
Tim. Look, who comes here. Will you be
    chid?

            Enter APEMANTUS.

Jew. We'll bear, with your lordship.
Mer.   He'll spare none.
Tim. Good morrow to thee, gentle Apeman-
    tus!
Apem. Till I be gentle, stay thou for thy good
    morrow;   180
When thou art Timon's dog, and these knaves
    honest.
Tim. Why dost thou call them knaves? thou
    know'st them not.
Apem. Are they not Athenians?
Tim. Yes.   184
Apem. Then I repent not.
Jew. You know me, Apemantus?
Apem. Thou know'st I do; I call'd thee by
thy name.   188

Tim. Thou art proud, Apemantus.
Apem. Of nothing so much as that I am not
like Timon.
Tim. Whither art going?   192
Apem. To knock out an honest Athenian's
brains.
Tim. That's a deed thou'lt die for.
Apem. Right, if doing nothing be death by
the law.   197
Tim. How likest thou this picture, Apeman-
tus?
Apem. The best, for the innocence.   200
Tim. Wrought he not well that painted it?
Apem. He wrought better that made the
painter; and yet he's but a filthy piece of work.
Pain. You're a dog.   204
Apem. Thy mother's of my generation:
what's she, if I be a dog?
Tim. Wilt dine with me, Apemantus?
Apem. No; I eat not lords.   208
Tim. An thou shouldst, thou'dst anger ladies.
Apem. O! they eat lords; so they come by
great bellies.
Tim. That's a lascivious apprehension. 212
Apem. So thou apprehendest it, take it for
thy labour.
Tim. How dost thou like this jewel, Ape-
mantus?   216
Apem. Not so well as plain-dealing, which
will not cost a man a doit.
Tim. What dost thou think 'tis worth?
Apem. Not worth my thinking. How now,
poet!   221
Poet. How now, philosopher!
Apem. Thou liest.
Poet. Art not one?   224
Apem. Yes.
Poet. Then I lie not.
Apem. Art not a poet?
Poet. Yes.   228
Apem. Then thou liest: look in thy last work,
where thou hast feigned him a worthy fellow.
Poet. That's not feigned; he is so.   231
Apem. Yes, he is worthy of thee, and to pay
thee for thy labour: he that loves to be flattered
is worthy o' the flatterer. Heavens, that I were
a lord!   235
Tim. What wouldst do then, Apemantus?
Apem. Even as Apemantus does now; hate
a lord with my heart.   238
Tim. What, thyself?
Apem. Ay.
Tim. Wherefore?   241
Apem. That I had no angry wit to be a lord.
Art not thou a merchant?
Mer. Ay, Apemantus.   244
Apem. Traffic confound thee, if the gods will
not!
Mer. If traffic do it, the gods do it.
Apem. Traffic's thy god, and thy god con-
found thee!   249

            Trumpet sounds. Enter a Servant.

Tim. What trumpet's that?
Serv. 'Tis Alcibiades, and some twenty horse,
All of companionship.   252

Tim. Pray, entertain them; give them guide
to us.   [*Exeunt some* Attendants.
You must needs dine with me. Go not you hence
Till I have thanked you; when dinner's done,
Show me this piece. I am joyful of your sights.

Enter ALCIBIADES, *with his Company.*

Most welcome, sir!
Apem.   So, so, there!   257
Aches contract and starve your supple joints!
That there should be small love 'mongst these
sweet knaves,
And all this courtesy! The strain of man's
bred out   260
Into baboon and monkey.
Alcib. Sir, you have sav'd my longing, and
I feed
Most hungerly on your sight.
Tim.   Right welcome, sir!
Ere we depart, we'll share a bounteous time 264
In different pleasures. Pray you, let us in.
          [*Exeunt all except* APEMANTUS.

Enter two Lords.

First Lord. What time o' day is 't, Apemantus?
Apem. Time to be honest.
First Lord. That time serves still.   268
Apem. The more accursed thou, that still
omitt'st it.
Sec. Lord. Thou art going to Lord Timon's
feast?
Apem. Ay; to see meat fill knaves and wine
heat fools.   272
Sec. Lord. Fare thee well, fare thee well.
Apem. Thou art a fool to bid me farewell
twice.
Sec. Lord. Why, Apemantus?
Apem. Shouldst have kept one to thyself, for
I mean to give thee none.   277
First Lord. Hang thyself!
Apem. No, I will do nothing at thy bidding:
make thy requests to thy friend.   280
Sec. Lord. Away, unpeaceable dog! or I'll
spurn thee hence.
Apem. I will fly, like a dog, the heels of an
ass.   [*Exit.*
First Lord. He's opposite to humanity.
Come, shall we in,   285
And taste Lord Timon's bounty? he outgoes
The very heart of kindness.
Sec. Lord. He pours it out; Plutus, the god
of gold,   288
Is but his steward: no meed but he repays
Sevenfold above itself; no gift to him
But breeds the giver a return exceeding   291
All use of quittance.
First Lord.   The noblest mind he carries
That ever govern'd man.
Sec. Lord. Long may he live in fortunes!
Shall we in?   295
First Lord. I'll keep you company. [*Exeunt.*

SCENE II.—*The Same. A Room of State in*
TIMON'S *House.*

*Hautboys playing loud music. A great banquet
served in;* FLAVIUS *and Others attending: then*

enter LORD TIMON, ALCIBIADES, Lords, *an*
Senators, VENTIDIUS *and* Attendants. *The*
comes, dropping after all, APEMANTUS *discon*
tentedly, like himself.

Ven. Most honour'd Timon,
It hath pleas'd the gods to remember my father'*s*
age,
And call him to long peace.
He is gone happy, and has left me rich:
Then, as in grateful virtue I am bound
To your free heart, I do return those talents,
Doubled with thanks and service, from whos*e*
help
I deriv'd liberty.
Tim.   O! by no means,   *8*
Honest Ventidius; you mistake my love;
I gave it freely ever; and there's none
Can truly say he gives, if he receives:
If our betters play at that game, we must no
dare   *12*
To imitate them; faults that are rich are fair.
Ven. A noble spirit.
          [*They all stand ceremoniously looking*
on TIMON
Tim. Nay, my lords, ceremony was but devis'*d*
at first
To set a gloss on faint deeds, hollow welcomes,
Recanting goodness, sorry ere 'tis shown;   *1*
But where there is true friendship, there need*s*
none.
Pray, sit; more welcome are ye to my fortune*s*
Than my fortunes to me.   [*They sit*
First Lord. My lord, we always have con-
fess'd it.   *2*
Apem. Ho, ho! confess'd it; hang'd it, have
you not?
Tim. O! Apemantus, you are welcome.
Apem.   No,
You shall not make me welcome: *24*
I come to have thee thrust me out of doors.
Tim. Fie! thou 'rt a churl; ye've got a humou*r*
there
Does not become a man; 'tis much to blame.
They say, my lords, *Ira furor brevis est;*   *28*
But yond man is ever angry.
Go, let him have a table by himself,
For he does neither affect company,
Nor is he fit for it, indeed.   *32*
Apem. Let me stay at thine apperil, Timon*:*
I come to observe; I give thee warning on't.
Tim. I take no heed of thee; thou'rt a*n*
Athenian, therefore, welcome. I myself would
have no power; prithee, let my meat make thee
silent.   *36*
Apem. I scorn thy meat; 'twould choke me,
for I should
Ne'er flatter thee. O you gods! what a number
Of men eat Timon, and he sees them not.   *40*
It grieves me to see so many dip their meat
In one man's blood; and all the madness is,
He cheers them up too.   *44*
I wonder men dare trust themselves with men*:*
Methinks they should invite them without
knives;
Good for their meat, and safer for their lives.

There's much example for't; the fellow that 48
sits next him now, parts bread with him, and
pledges
The breath of him in a divided draught,
Is the readiest man to kill him: 't has been prov'd.
If I were a huge man, I should fear to drink at
meals;   52
Lest they should spy my wind-pipe's dangerous
notes:
Great men should drink with harness on their
throats.
  Tim. My lord, in heart; and let the health
go round.
  Sec. Lord. Let it flow this way, my good lord.
  Apem. Flow this way! A brave fellow! he
keeps his tides well. Those healths will make
thee and thy state look ill, Timon.
Here's that which is too weak to be a sinner, 60
Honest water, which ne'er left man i' the mire:
This and my food are equals, there's no odds:
Feasts are too proud to give thanks to the gods.

Immortal gods, I crave no pelf;   64
I pray for no man but myself:
Grant I may never prove so fond,
To trust man on his oath or bond;
Or a harlot for her weeping;   68
Or a dog that seems a-sleeping;
Or a keeper with my freedom;
Or my friends, if I should need 'em.
Amen. So fall to't: 72
Rich men sin, and I eat root.

[*Eats and drinks.*

Much good dich thy good heart, Apemantus!
  Tim. Captain Alcibiades, your heart's in the
field now.   76
  Alcib. My heart is ever at your service, my
lord.
  Tim. You had rather be at a breakfast of
enemies than a dinner of friends.   80
  Alcib. So they were bleeding-new, my lord,
there's no meat like 'em: I could wish my best
friend at such a feast.
  Apem. 'Would all those flatterers were thine
enemies then, that then thou mightst kill 'em
and bid me to 'em.   86
  First Lord. Might we but have that happiness, my lord, that you would once use our
hearts, whereby we might express some part
of our zeals, we should think ourselves for ever
perfect.   91
  Tim. O! no doubt, my good friends, but the
gods themselves have provided that I shall have
much help from you: how had you been my
friends else? why have you that charitable title
from thousands, did not you chiefly belong to
my heart? I have told more of you to myself
than you can with modesty speak in your own
behalf; and thus far I confirm you. O you
gods! think I, what need we have any friends, if
we should ne'er have need of 'em? they were the
most needless creatures living should we ne'er
have use for 'em, and would most resemble
sweet instruments hung up in cases, that keep
their sounds to themselves. Why, I have often
wished myself poorer that I might come nearer
to you. We are born to do benefits; and what

better or properer can we call our own than the
riches of our friends? O! what a precious comfort 'tis, to have so many, like brothers, com-
manding one another's fortunes. O joy! e'en
made away ere it can be born. Mine eyes cannot
hold out water, methinks: to forget their faults,
I drink to you.
  Apem. Thou weepest to make them drink,
Timon.   116
  Sec. Lord. Joy had the like conception in our
eyes,
And, at that instant, like a babe, sprung up.
  Apem. Ho, ho! I laugh to think that babe a
bastard.
  Third Lord. I promise you, my lord, you
mov'd me much.   120
  Apem. Much!   [*Tucket sounded.*
  Tim. What means that trump?

Enter a Servant.

How now!
  Serv. Please you, my lord, there are certain
ladies most desirous of admittance.   124
  Tim. Ladies? What are their wills?
  Serv. There comes with them a forerunner,
my lord, which bears that office, to signify their
pleasures.   128
  Tim. I pray, let them be admitted.

Enter CUPID.

  Cup. Hail to thee, worthy Timon; and to all
That of his bounties taste! The five best senses
Acknowledge thee their patron; and come
freely   132
To gratulate thy plenteous bosom. Th' ear,
Taste, touch, smell, pleas'd from thy table rise;
They only now come but to feast thine eyes.
  Tim. They are welcome all; let 'em have
kind admittance: 136
Music, make their welcome!   [*Exit* CUPID.
  First Lord. You see, my lord, how ample
you're belov'd.

Music. Re-enter CUPID, *with a masque of* Ladies
as Amazons, *with lutes in their hands, dancing
and playing.*

  Apem. Hoy-day! what a sweep of vanity
comes this way:
They dance! they are mad women.   140
Like madness is the glory of this life,
As this pomp shows to a little oil and root.
We make ourselves fools to disport ourselves;
And spend our flatteries to drink those men 144
Upon whose age we void it up again,
With poisonous spite and envy.
Who lives that's not depraved or depraves?
Who dies that bears not one spurn to their
graves   148
Of their friend's gift?
I should fear those that dance before me now
Would one day stamp upon me: it has been
done;
Men shut their doors against a setting sun. 152

The Lords *rise from table, with much adoring
of* TIMON; *and to show their loves each singles*

out an Amazon, *and all dance, men with women,*
a lofty strain or two to the hautboys, and cease.

Tim. You have done our pleasures much
grace, fair ladies,
Set a fair fashion on our entertainment,
Which was not half so beautiful and kind;
You have added worth unto 't and lustre, 156
And entertain'd me with mine own device;
I am to thank you for 't.
First Lady. My lord, you take us even at the
best.
Apem. Faith, for the worst is filthy; and
would not hold taking, I doubt me. 161
Tim. Ladies, there is an idle banquet
Attends you: please you to dispose yourselves.
All Lad. Most thankfully, my lord. 164
[*Exeunt* CUPID *and* Ladies.

Tim. Flavius!
Flav. My lord!
Tim. The little casket bring me hither.
Flav. Yes, my lord. [*Aside.*] More jewels yet!
There is no crossing him in 's humour; 168
Else I should tell him well, i' faith, I should,
When all 's spent, he'd be cross'd then, an he
could.
'Tis pity bounty had not eyes behind,
That man might ne'er be wretched for his mind.
[*Exit.*

First Lord. Where be our men? 173
Serv. Here, my lord, in readiness.
Sec. Lord. Our horses!

Re-enter FLAVIUS *with the Casket.*

Tim. O, my friends! I have one word to say
to you; 176
Look you, my good lord,
I must entreat you, honour me so much
As to advance this jewel; accept it and wear it,
Kind my lord. 180
First Lord. I am so far already in your gifts—
All. So are we all.

Enter a Servant.

Serv. My lord, there are certain nobles of the
senate
Newly alighted, and come to visit you. 184
Tim. They are fairly welcome.
Flav. I beseech your honour,
Vouchsafe me a word; it does concern you near.
Tim. Near! why then another time I'll hear
thee.
I prithee, let 's be provided to show them enter-
tainment. 188
Flav. [*Aside.*] I scarce know how.

Enter another Servant.

Sec. Serv. May it please your honour, Lord
Lucius,
Out of his free love, hath presented to you
Four milk-white horses, trapp'd in silver. 192
Tim. I shall accept them fairly; let the presents
Be worthily entertain'd.

Enter a third Servant.

How now! what news?
Third Serv. Please you, my lord, that honourable gentleman, Lord Lucullus, entreats your

company to-morrow to hunt with him, and has
sent your honour two brace of greyhounds. 198
Tim. I'll hunt with him; and let them be
receiv'd,
Not without fair reward.
Flav. [*Aside.*] What will this come to?
He commands us to provide, and give great
gifts, 201
And all out of an empty coffer:
Nor will he know his purse, or yield me this,
To show him what a beggar his heart is, 204
Being of no power to make his wishes good.
His promises fly so beyond his state
That what he speaks is all in debt; he owes
For every word: he is so kind that he now 208
Pays interest for 't; his land's put to their books.
Well, would I were gently put out of office
Before I were forc'd out!
Happier he that has no friend to feed 212
Than such as do e'en enemies exceed.
I bleed inwardly for my lord. [*Exit.*
Tim. You do yourselves
Much wrong, you bate too much of your own
merits:
Here, my lord, a trifle of our love. 216
Sec. Lord. With more than common thanks
I will receive it.
Third Lord. O! he's the very soul of bounty.
Tim. And now I remember, my lord, you
gave
Good words the other day of a bay courser 220
I rode on: it is yours, because you lik'd it.
Third Lord. O! I beseech you, pardon me,
my lord, in that.
Tim. You may take my word, my lord; I
know no man
Can justly praise but what he does affect: 224
I weigh my friend's affection with mine own;
I'll tell you true. I'll call to you.
All Lords. O! none so welcome.
Tim. I take all and your several visitations
So kind to heart, 'tis not enough to give; 228
Methinks, I could deal kingdoms to my friends,
And ne'er be weary. Alcibiades,
Thou art a soldier, therefore seldom rich;
It comes in charity to thee; for all thy living
Is 'mongst the dead, and all the lands thou hast
Lie in a pitch'd field.
Alcib. Ay, defil'd land, my lord.
First Lord. We are so virtuously bound,—
Tim. And so
Am I to you.
Sec. Lord. So infinitely endear'd,— 236
Tim. All to you. Lights, more lights!
First Lord. The best of happiness,
Honour, and fortunes, keep with you, Lord
Timon!
Tim. Ready for his friends.
[*Exeunt* ALCIBIADES, Lords, &c.
Apem. What a coil 's here!
Serving of becks and jutting out of bums! 240
I doubt whether their legs be worth the sums
That are given for 'em. Friendship 's full of
dregs:
Methinks, false hearts should never have sound
legs.

Thus honest fools lay out their wealth on curt-
    sies.   244
Tim. Now, Apemantus, if thou wert not
    sullen,
I would be good to thee.
    Apem. No, I'll nothing; for if I should be
bribed too, there would be none left to rail upon
thee, and then thou wouldst sin the faster. Thou
givest so long, Timon, I fear me thou wilt give
away thyself in paper shortly: what need these
feasts, pomps, and vain-glories?   252
    Tim. Nay, an you begin to rail on society
once, I am sworn not to give regard to you.
Farewell; and come with better music. [*Exit.*
    Apem. So: 256
Thou wilt not hear me now; thou shalt not then;
I'll lock thy heaven from thee.
O! that men's ears should be
To counsel deaf, but not to flattery.   [*Exit.*

ACT II

SCENE I.—*Athens. A Room in a* Senator's
House.

Enter a Senator, *with papers in his hand.*

    Sen. And late, five thousand: to Varro and
    to Isidore
He owes nine thousand; besides my former sum,
Which makes it five-and-twenty. Still in motion
Of raging waste! It cannot hold; it will not. 4
If I want gold, steal but a beggar's dog
And give it Timon, why, the dog coins gold;
If I would sell my horse, and buy twenty more
Better than he, why, give my horse to Timon, 8
Ask nothing, give it him, it foals me, straight,
And able horses. No porter at his gate,
But rather one that smiles and still invites
All that pass by. It cannot hold; no reason 12
Can found his state in safety. Caphis, ho!
Caphis, I say!

Enter CAPHIS.

    Caph.   Here, sir; what is your pleasure?
    Sen. Get on your cloak, and haste you to
    Lord Timon;
Importune him for my moneys; be not ceas'd 16
With slight denial, nor then silenc'd when—
'Commend me to your master'—and the cap
Plays in the right hand, thus;—but tell him,
My uses cry to me; I must serve my turn 20
Out of mine own; his days and times are past,
And my reliances on his fracted dates
Have smit my credit: I love and honour him,
But must not break my back to heal his finger;
Immediate are my needs, and my relief 25
Must not be toss'd and turn'd to me in words,
But find supply immediate. Get you gone:
Put on a most importunate aspect, 28
A visage of demand; for, I do fear,
When every feather sticks in his own wing,
Lord Timon will be left a naked gull,
Which flashes now a phœnix. Get you gone. 32
    Caph. I go, sir.
    Sen. 'I go, sir!' Take the bonds along with
    you,
And have the dates in compt.

    Caph.   I will, sir.
    Sen.   Go. [*Exeunt.*

SCENE II.—*The Same. A Hall in* TIMON'S
House.

Enter FLAVIUS, *with many bills in his hand.*

    Flav. No care, no stop! so senseless of ex-
    pense,
That he will neither know how to maintain it,
Nor cease his flow of riot: takes no account
How things go from him, nor resumes no care 4
Of what is to continue: never mind
Was to be so unwise, to be so kind.
What shall be done? He will not hear, till feel:
I must be round with him, now he comes from
    hunting.   8
Fie, fie, fie, fie!

Enter CAPHIS, *and the* Servants *of* ISIDORE
and VARRO.

    Caph.   Good even, Varro. What!
You come for money?
    Var. Serv.   Is 't not your business too?
    Caph. It is: and yours too, Isidore?
    Isid. Serv.   It is so.
    Caph. Would we were all discharg'd!
    Var. Serv.   I fear it. 12
    Caph. Here comes the lord!

Enter TIMON, ALCIBIADES, *and* Lords, *&c.*

    Tim. So soon as dinner 's done, we'll forth
    again,
My Alcibiades. With me? what is your will?
    Caph. My lord, here is a note of certain dues.
    Tim. Dues! Whence are you?
    Caph.   Of Athens here, my lord. 17
    Tim. Go to my steward.
    Caph. Please it your lordship, he hath put
    me off
To the succession of new days this month: 20
My master is awak'd by great occasion
To call upon his own; and humbly prays
That with your other noble parts you'll suit
In giving him his right.
    Tim.   Mine honest friend, 24
I prithee, but repair to me next morning.
    Caph. Nay, good my lord,—
    Tim.   Contain thyself, good friend.
    Var. Serv. One Varro's servant, my good
    lord,—
    Isid. Serv.   From Isidore;
He humbly prays your speedy payment. 28
    Caph. If you did know, my lord, my master's
    wants,—
    Var. Serv. 'Twas due on forfeiture, my lord,
    six weeks
And past.
    Isid. Serv. Your steward puts me off, my
    lord; 32
And I am sent expressly to your lordship.
    Tim. Give me breath.
I do beseech you, good my lords, keep on;
I'll wait upon you instantly.
              [*Exeunt* ALCIBIADES *and* Lords.
    [*To* FLAVIUS.] Come hither: pray you, 36
How goes the world, that I am thus encounter'd

With clamorous demands of date-broke bonds,
And the detention of long-since-due debts,
Against my honour?
Flav. Please you, gentlemen, 40
The time is unagreeable to this business:
Your importunacy cease till after dinner,
That I may make his lordship understand
Wherefore you are not paid.
Tim. Do so, my friends. 44
See them well entertained. [*Exit.*
Flav. Pray, draw near. [*Exit.*

Enter APEMANTUS *and* Fool.

Caph. Stay, stay; here comes the fool with
Apemantus: let's ha' some sport with 'em.
Var. Serv. Hang him, he'll abuse us. 48
Isid. Serv. A plague upon him, dog!
Var. Serv. How dost, fool?
Apem. Dost dialogue with thy shadow?
Var. Serv. I speak not to thee. 52
Apem. No; 'tis to thyself. [*To the* Fool.]
Come away.
Isid. Serv. [*To* VAR. Serv.] There's the fool
hangs on your back already. 56
Apem. No, thou stand'st single; thou'rt not
on him yet.
Caph. Where's the fool now?
Apem. He last asked the question. Poor
rogues, and usurers' men! bawds between gold
and want! 61
All Serv. What are we, Apemantus?
Apem. Asses.
All Serv. Why? 64
Apem. That you ask me what you are, and do
not know yourselves. Speak to 'em, fool.
Fool. How do you, gentlemen?
All Serv. Gramercies, good fool. How does
your mistress? 69
Fool. She's e'en setting on water to scald
such chickens as you are. Would we could see
you at Corinth! 72
Apem. Good! gramercy.

Enter Page.

Fool. Look you, here comes my mistress'
page.
Page. [*To the* Fool.] Why, how now, captain!
what do you in this wise company? How dost
thou, Apemantus?
Apem. Would I had a rod in my mouth, that
I might answer thee profitably. 80
Page. Prithee, Apemantus, read me the
superscription of these letters: I know not
which is which.
Apem. Canst not read? 84
Page. No.
Apem. There will little learning die then
that day thou art hanged. This is to Lord
Timon; this to Alcibiades. Go; thou wast born
a bastard, and thou'lt die a bawd. 89
Page. Thou wast whelped a dog, and thou
shalt famish a dog's death. Answer not; I am
gone. [*Exit* Page.
Apem. E'en so thou outrunn'st grace.—
Fool, I will go with you to Lord Timon's.
Fool. Will you leave me there?

Apem. If Timon stay at home. You three
serve three usurers? 97
All Serv. Ay; would they served us!
Apem. So would I, as good a trick as ever
hangman served thief. 100
Fool. Are you three usurers' men?
All Serv. Ay, fool.
Fool. I think no usurer but has a fool to his
servant: my mistress is one, and I am her fool.
When men come to borrow of your masters,
they approach sadly, and go away merry; but
they enter my mistress' house merrily, and go
away sadly: the reason of this? 108
Var. Serv. I could render one.
Apem. Do it, then, that we may account thee
a whoremaster and a knave; which, notwithstanding, thou shalt be no less esteemed. 112
Var. Serv. What is a whoremaster, fool?
Fool. A fool in good clothes, and something
like thee. 'Tis a spirit: sometime 't appears
like a lord; sometime like a lawyer; sometime
like a philosopher, with two stones more than 's
artificial one. He is very often like a knight;
and generally in all shapes that man goes up
and down in from fourscore to thirteen, this
spirit walks in. 121
Var. Serv. Thou art not altogether a fool.
Fool. Nor thou altogether a wise man: as
much foolery as I have, so much wit thou
lackest. 125
Apem. That answer might have become Apemantus.
All Serv. Aside, aside; here comes Lord
Timon. 129

Re-enter TIMON *and* FLAVIUS.

Apem. Come with me, fool, come.
Fool. I do not always follow lover, elder
brother and woman; sometime the philosopher.
[*Exeunt* APEMANTUS *and* Fool.
Flav. Pray you, walk near: I'll speak with
you anon. [*Exeunt* Servants.
Tim. You make me marvel: wherefore, ere
this time,
Had you not fully laid my state before me,
That I might so have rated my expense 136
As I had leave of means?
Flav. You would not hear me,
At many leisures I propos'd.
Tim. Go to:
Perchance some single vantages you took,
When my indisposition put you back; 140
And that unaptness made your minister,
Thus to excuse yourself.
Flav. O my good lord!
At many times I brought in my accounts,
Laid them before you; you would throw them
off, 144
And say you found them in mine honesty.
When for some trifling present you have bid me
Return so much, I have shook my head, and
wept;
Yea, 'gainst the authority of manners, pray'd
you 148
To hold your hand more close: I did endure
Not seldom, nor no slight checks, when I have

rompted you in the ebb of your estate
And your great flow of debts. My loved lord, 152
'hough you hear now, too late, yet now 's a time,
he greatest of your having lacks a half
'o pay your present debts.
   Tim.   Let all my land be sold.
   Flav. 'Tis all engag'd, some forfeited and
    gone;   156
And what remains will hardly stop the mouth
Of present dues; the future comes apace:
What shall defend the interim? and at length
How goes our reckoning?   160
   Tim. To Lacedæmon did my land extend.
   Flav. O my good lord! the world is but a word;
Were it all yours to give it in a breath,
How quickly were it gone!
   Tim.   You tell me true. 164
   Flav. If you suspect my husbandry or false-
    hood,
Call me before the exactest auditors,
And set me on the proof. So the gods bless me
When all our offices have been oppress'd 168
With riotous feeders, when our vaults have wept
With drunken spilth of wine, when every room
Hath blaz'd with lights and bray'd with min-
    strelsy,
I have retir'd me to a wasteful cock,   172
And set mine eyes at flow.
   Tim.   Prithee, no more.
   Flav. Heavens! have I said, the bounty of
    this lord!
How many prodigal bits have slaves and peasants
This night englutted! Who is not Timon's? 176
What heart, head, sword, force, means, but is
    Lord Timon's?
Great Timon, noble, worthy, royal Timon!
Ah! when the means are gone that buy this
    praise,   179
The breath is gone whereof this praise is made:
Feast-won, fast-lost; one cloud of winter
    showers,
These flies are couch'd.
   Tim.   Come, sermon me no further;
No villanous bounty yet hath pass'd my heart;
Unwisely, not ignobly, have I given.   184
Why dost thou weep? Canst thou the conscience
    lack,
To think I shall lack friends? Secure thy heart;
If I would broach the vessels of my love,
And try the argument of hearts by borrowing,
Men and men's fortunes could I frankly use 189
As I can bid thee speak.
   Flav.   Assurance bless your thoughts!
   Tim. And, in some sort, these wants of mine
    are crown'd,
That I account them blessings; for by these 192
Shall I try friends. You shall perceive how you
Mistake my fortunes; I am wealthy in my friends.
Within there! Flaminius! Servilius!

   Enter FLAMINIUS, SERVILIUS, *and other*
                Servants.

   Serv. My lord! my lord!   196
   Tim. I will dispatch you severally: you, to
Lord Lucius; to Lord Lucullus you: I hunted
with his honour to-day; you, to Sempronius.

Commend me to their loves; and I am proud,
say, that my occasions have found time to use
them toward a supply of money: let the request
be fifty talents.
   Flam. As you have said, my lord.   204
   Flav. [*Aside.*] Lord Lucius, and Lucullus?
    hum!
   Tim. [*To another* Servant.] Go you, sir, to
    the senators,—
Of whom, even to the state's best health, I have
Deserv'd this hearing,—bid 'em send o' the in-
    stant   208
A thousand talents to me.
   Flav.   I have been bold,—
For that I knew it the most general way,—
To them to use your signet and your name;
But they do shake their heads, and I am here
No richer in return.
   Tim.   Is't true? can't be?   213
   Flav. They answer, in a joint and corporate
    voice,
That now they are at fall, want treasure, cannot
Do what they would; are sorry; you are honour-
    able;   216
But yet they could have wish'd; they know not;
Something hath been amiss; a noble nature
May catch a wrench; would all were well; 'tis pity;
And so, intending other serious matters,   220
After distasteful looks and these hard fractions,
With certain half-caps and cold-moving nods
They froze me into silence.
   Tim.   You gods, reward them!
Prithee, man, look cheerly. These old fellows
Have their ingratitude in them hereditary; 225
Their blood is cak'd, 'tis cold, it seldom flows;
'Tis lack of kindly warmth they are not kind;
And nature, as it grows again toward earth, 228
Is fashion'd for the journey, dull and heavy.
[*To a* Servant.] Go to Ventidius.—[*To* FLA-
    VIUS.] Prithee, be not sad,
Thou art true and honest; ingenuously I speak,
No blame belongs to thee.—[*To* Servant.] Ven-
    tidius lately   232
Buried his father; by whose death he's stepp'd
Into a great estate; when he was poor,
Imprison'd and in scarcity of friends,
I clear'd him with five talents; greet him from
    me;   236
Bid him suppose some good necessity
Touches his friend, which craves to be remem-
    ber'd
With those five talents. [*Exit* Servant.] [*To*
    FLAVIUS.] That had, give't these fellows
To whom 'tis instant due. Ne'er speak, or think
That Timon's fortunes 'mong his friends can sink.
   Flav. I would I could not think it: that
    thought is bounty's foe;   242
Being free itself, it thinks all others so. [*Exeunt.*

ACT III

SCENE I.—*Athens. A Room in* LUCULLUS'
               House.

FLAMINIUS *waiting. Enter a* Servant *to him.*

   Serv. I have told my lord of you; he is coming down to you.

Flam. I thank you, sir.

Enter LUCULLUS.

Serv. Here's my lord. 4
Lucul. [*Aside.*] One of Lord Timon's men! a gift, I warrant. Why, this hits right; I dreamt of a silver bason and ewer to-night. Flaminius, honest Flaminius, you are very respectively welcome, sir. Fill me some wine. [*Exit* Servant.] And how does that honourable, complete, free-hearted gentleman of Athens, thy very bountiful good lord and master? 12
Flam. His health is well, sir.
Lucul. I am right glad that his health is well, sir. And what hast thou there under thy cloak, pretty Flaminius? 16
Flam. Faith, nothing but an empty box, sir; which, in my lord's behalf, I come to entreat your honour to supply; who, having great and instant occasion to use fifty talents, hath sent to your lordship to furnish him, nothing doubting your present assistance therein. 22
Lucul. La, la, la, la! 'nothing doubting,' says he? Alas! good lord; a noble gentleman 'tis, if he would not keep so good a house. Many a time and often I ha' dined with him, and told him on't; and come again to supper to him, of purpose to have him spend less; and yet he would embrace no counsel, take no warning by my coming. Every man has his fault, and honesty is his; I ha' told him on't, but I could ne'er get him from it. 32

Re-enter Servant with wine.

Serv. Please your lordship, here is the wine.
Lucul. Flaminius, I have noted thee always wise. Here's to thee.
Flam. Your lordship speaks your pleasure. 36
Lucul. I have observed thee always for a towardly prompt spirit, give thee thy due, and one that knows what belongs to reason; and canst use the time well, if the time use thee well: good parts in thee. [*To the* Servant.]—Get you gone, sirrah.—[*Exit* Servant.] Draw nearer, honest Flaminius. Thy lord's a bountiful gentleman; but thou art wise, and thou knowest well enough, although thou comest to me, that this is no time to lend money, especially upon bare friendship, without security. Here's three solidares for thee: good boy, wink at me, and say thou sawest me not. Fare thee well. 49
Flam. Is't possible the world should so much differ,
And we alive that liv'd? Fly, damned baseness,
To him that worships thee. 52
[*Throwing the money away.*]
Lucul. Ha! now I see thou art a fool, and fit for thy master. [*Exit.*]
Flam. May these add to the number that may scald thee!
Let molten coin be thy damnation, 56
Thou disease of a friend, and not himself!
Has friendship such a faint and milky heart
It turns in less than two nights? O you gods!
I feel my master's passion. This slave unto his honour 60

Has my lord's meat in him:
Why should it thrive and turn to nutriment
When he is turn'd to poison?
O! may diseases only work upon't, 64
And, when he's sick to death, let not that part of nature
Which my lord paid for, be of any power
To expel sickness, but prolong his hour. [*Exit.*

SCENE II.—*The Same. A Public Place.*

Enter LUCIUS, *with three* Strangers.

Luc. Who, the Lord Timon? he is my very good friend, and an honourable gentleman.
First Stran. We know him for no less, though we are but strangers to him. But I can tell you one thing, my lord, and which I hear from common rumours: now Lord Timon's happy hours are done and past, and his estate shrinks from him. 8
Luc. Fie, no, do not believe it; he cannot want for money.
Sec. Stran. But believe you this, my lord, that, not long ago, one of his men was with the Lord Lucullus, to borrow so many talents, nay, urged extremely for't, and showed what necessity belonged to't, and yet was denied. 16
Luc. How!
Sec. Stran. I tell you, denied, my lord.
Luc. What a strange case was that! now, before the gods, I am ashamed on't. Denied that honourable man! there was very little honour showed in't. For my own part, I must needs confess, I have received some small kindnesses from him, as money, plate, jewels, and such like trifles, nothing comparing to his; yet, had he mistook him, and sent to me, I should ne'er have denied his occasion so many talents. 26

Enter SERVILIUS.

Servil. See, by good hap, yonder's my lord; I have sweat to see his honour. [*To* LUCIUS.] My honoured lord!
Luc. Servilius! you are kindly met, sir. Fare thee well: commend me to thy honourable virtuous lord, my very exquisite friend. 32
Servil. May it please your honour, my lord hath sent—
Luc. Ha! what has he sent? I am so much endeared to that lord; he's ever sending: how shall I thank him, thinkest thou? And what has he sent now? 38
Servil. He has only sent his present occasion now, my lord; requesting your lordship to supply his instant use with so many talents. 41
Luc. I know his lordship is but merry with me;
He cannot want fifty-five hundred talents.
Servil. But in the mean time he wants less, my lord. 44
If his occasion were not virtuous,
I should not urge it half so faithfully.
Luc. Dost thou speak seriously, Servilius?
Servil. Upon my soul, 'tis true, sir. 48
Luc. What a wicked beast was I to disfurnish myself against such a good time, when I might

ha' shown myself honourable! how unluckily it happened, that I should purchase the day before for a little part, and undo a great deal of honour! Servilius, now, before the gods, I am not able to do; the more beast, I say; I was sending to use Lord Timon myself, these gentlemen can witness; but I would not, for the wealth of Athens, I had done it now. Commend me bountifully to his good lordship; and I hope his honour will conceive the fairest of me, because I have no power to be kind: and tell him this from me, I count it one of my greatest afflictions say, that I cannot pleasure such an honourable gentleman. Good Servilius, will you befriend me so far as to use mine own words to him?   66

Servil. Yes, sir, I shall.

Luc. I'll look you out a good turn, Servilius.
                              [*Exit* SERVILIUS.
True, as you said, Timon is shrunk indeed;
And he that's once denied will hardly speed.
                                          [*Exit.*

First Stran. Do you observe this, Hostilius?

Sec. Stran. Ay, too well.

First Stran. Why this is the world's soul;
  and just of the same piece   72
Is every flatterer's spirit. Who can call him
His friend that dips in the same dish? for, in
My knowing, Timon has been this lord's father,
And kept his credit with his purse,   76
Supported his estate; nay, Timon's money
Has paid his men their wages: he ne'er drinks
But Timon's silver treads upon his lip;
And yet, O! see the monstrousness of man, 80
When he looks out in an ungrateful shape,
He does deny him, in respect of his,
What charitable men afford to beggars.

Third Stran. Religion groans at it.

First Stran.   For mine own part, 84
I never tasted Timon in my life,
Nor came any of his bounties over me,
To mark me for his friend; yet, I protest,
For his right noble mind, illustrious virtue, 88
And honourable carriage,
Had his necessity made use of me,
I would have put my wealth into donation,
And the best half should have return'd to him, 92
So much I love his heart. But, I perceive,
Men must learn now with pity to dispense;
For policy sits above conscience.   [*Exeunt.*

SCENE III.—*The Same. A Room in* SEMPRONIUS'S *House.*

Enter SEMPRONIUS *and a* Servant *of* TIMON'S.

Sem. Must he needs trouble me in't. Hum!
'bove all others?
He might have tried Lord Lucius, or Lucullus;
And now Ventidius is wealthy too,
Whom he redeem'd from prison: all these 4
Owe their estates unto him.

Serv.   My lord,
They have all been touch'd and found base
  metal, for
They have all denied him.

Sem.   How! have they denied him?

Have Ventidius and Lucullus denied him? 8
And does he send to me? Three? hum!
It shows but little love or judgment in him:
Must I be his last refuge? His friends, like physicians,
Thrice give him over; must I take the cure upon
  me?   12
He has much disgrac'd me in't; I'm angry at
  him,
That might have known my place. I see no sense
  for't,
But his occasions might have woo'd me first;
For, in my conscience, I was the first man 16
That e'er received gift from him:
And does he think so backwardly of me now,
That I'll requite it last? No:
So it may prove an argument of laughter   20
To the rest, and I 'mongst lords be thought a
  fool.
I had rather than the worth of thrice the sum,
He had sent to me first, but for my mind's sake
I'd such a courage to do him good. But now
  return,   24
And with their faint reply this answer join;
Who bates mine honour shall not know my
  coin.   [*Exit.*

Serv. Excellent! Your lordship's a goodly
villain. The devil knew not what he did when
he made man politic; he crossed himself by't:
and I cannot think but in the end the villanies
of man will set him clear. How fairly this lord
strives to appear foul! takes virtuous copies to
be wicked, like those that under hot ardent zeal
would set whole realms on fire:
Of such a nature is his politic love.
This was my lord's best hope; now all are fled 36
Save only the gods. Now his friends are dead,
Doors, that were ne'er acquainted with their
  wards
Many a bounteous year, must be employ'd
Now to guard sure their master: 40
And this is all a liberal course allows;
Who cannot keep his wealth must keep his
  house.   [*Exit.*

SCENE IV.—*The Same. A Hall in* TIMON'S *House.*

Enter two Servants *of* VARRO, *and the* Servant *of* LUCIUS, *meeting* TITUS, HORTENSIUS, *and other* Servants *to* TIMON'S *Creditors, waiting his coming out.*

First Var. Serv. Well met; good morrow,
Titus and Hortensius.

Tit. The like to you, kind Varro.

Hor.   Lucius!
What! do we meet together!

Luc. Ser.   Ay, and I think
One business does command us all; for mine 4
Is money.

Tit. So is theirs and ours.

Enter PHILOTUS.

Luc. Serv.   And Sir Philotus too!

Phi. Good day at once.

Luc. Serv.   Welcome, good brother.

What do you think the hour?

Phi. Labouring for nine. 8

Luc. Serv. So much?

Phi. Is not my lord seen yet?

Luc. Serv. Not yet.

Phi. I wonder on't; he was wont to shine at seven.

Luc. Serv. Ay, but the days are waxed shorter

You must consider that a prodigal course 12
Is like the sun's; but not, like his, recoverable.
I fear,
'Tis deepest winter in Lord Timon's purse;
That is, one may reach deep enough, and yet 16
Find little.

Phi. I am of your fear for that.

Tit. I'll show you how to observe a strange event.
Your lord sends now for money.

Hor. Most true, he does.

Tit. And he wears jewels now of Timon's gift,
For which I wait for money. 21

Hor. It is against my heart.

Luc. Serv. Mark, how strange it shows,
Timon in this should pay more than he owes:
And e'en as if your lord should wear rich jewels,
And send for money for 'em. 25

Hor. I'm weary of this charge, the gods can witness:
I know my lord hath spent of Timon's wealth,
And now ingratitude makes it worse than stealth. 28

First Var. Serv. Yes, mine's three thousand crowns; what's yours?

Luc. Serv. Five thousand mine.

First Var. Serv. 'Tis much deep : and it should seem by the sum,
Your master's confidence was above mine; 32
Else, surely, his had equall'd.

Enter FLAMINIUS.

Tit. One of Lord Timon's men.

Luc. Serv. Flaminius! Sir, a word. Pray, is my lord ready to come forth? 36

Flam. No, indeed, he is not.

Tit. We attend his lordship; pray, signify so much.

Flam. I need not tell him that; he knows you are too diligent. [*Exit* FLAMINIUS.

Enter FLAVIUS *in a cloak, muffled.*

Luc. Serv. Ha! is not that his steward muffled so?
He goes away in a cloud: call him, call him.

Tit. Do you hear, sir? 44

Sec. Var. Serv. By your leave, sir.

Flav. What do you ask of me, my friend?

Tit. We wait for certain money here, sir.

Flav. Ay,
If money were as certain as your waiting, 48
'Twere sure enough.
Why then preferr'd you not your sums and bills,
When your false masters eat of my lord's meat?
Then they could smile and fawn upon his debts,
And take down the interest into their gluttonous maws. 53

You do yourselves but wrong to stir me up;
Let me pass quietly:
Believe't, my lord and I have made an end; 56
I have no more to reckon, he to spend.

Luc. Serv. Ay, but this answer will not serve.

Flav. If 'twill not serve, 'tis not so base as you;
For you serve knaves. [*Exit.*

First Var. Serv. How! what does his cashiered worship mutter? 62

Sec. Var. Serv. No matter what; he's poor, and that's revenge enough. Who can speak broader than he that has no house to put his head in? such may rail against great buildings.

Enter SERVILIUS.

Tit. O! here's Servilius; now we shall know some answer. 68

Servil. If I might beseech you, gentlemen, to repair some other hour, I should derive much from't; for, take't of my soul, my lord leans wondrously to discontent. His comfortable temper has forsook him; he's much out of health, and keeps his chamber.

Luc. Serv. Many do keep their chambers are not sick:
And, if it be so far beyond his health, 76
Methinks he should the sooner pay his debts,
And make a clear way to the gods.

Servil. Good gods!

Tit. We cannot take this for answer, sir.

Flam. [*Within.*] Servilius, help! my lord! my lord! 80

Enter TIMON *in a rage;* FLAMINIUS *following.*

Tim. What! are my doors oppos'd against my passage?
Have I been ever free, and must my house
Be my retentive enemy, my gaol?
The place which I have feasted, does it now, 84
Like all mankind, show me an iron heart?

Luc. Serv. Put in now, Titus.

Tit. My lord, here is my bill.

Luc. Serv. Here's mine. 88

Hor. And mine, my lord.

Both Var. Serv. And ours, my lord.

Phi. All our bills.

Tim. Knock me down with 'em: cleave me to the girdle. 92

Luc. Serv. Alas! my lord,—

Tim. Cut my heart in sums.

Tit. Mine, fifty talents.

Tim. Tell out my blood. 96

Luc. Serv. Five thousand crowns, my lord.

Tim. Five thousand drops pays that. What yours? and yours?

First Var. Serv. My lord,—

Sec. Var. Serv. My lord,— 100

Tim. Tear me, take me; and the gods fall upon you! [*Exit.*

Hor. Faith, I perceive our masters may throw their caps at their money: these debts may well be called desperate ones, for a madman owes 'em. [*Exeunt.*

Re-enter TIMON *and* FLAVIUS.

Tim. They have e'en put my breath from me, the slaves!
Creditors? devils!
Flav. My dear lord,—   108
Tim. What if it should be so?
Flav. My lord,—
Tim. I'll have it so. My steward!
Flav. Here, my lord.   112
Tim. So fitly! Go, bid all my friends again,
Lucius, Lucullus, and Sempronius; all:
I'll once more feast the rascals.
Flav.   O my lord!
You only speak from your distracted soul; 116
There is not so much left to furnish out
A moderate table.
Tim.   Be't not in thy care: go.
I charge thee, invite them all: let in the tide
Of knaves once more; my cook and I'll provide.
                                   [*Exeunt.*

SCENE V.—*The Same. The Senate House.*

The Senate sitting.

First Sen. My lord, you have my voice to it;
   the fault's
Bloody; 'tis necessary he should die;
Nothing emboldens sin so much as mercy.
Sec. Sen. Most true; the law shall bruise him.

Enter ALCIBIADES, *attended.*

Alcib. Honour, health, and compassion to
   the senate!   5
First Sen. Now, captain.
Alcib. I am a humble suitor to your virtues;
For pity is the virtue of the law,   8
And none but tyrants use it cruelly.
It pleases time and fortune to lie heavy
Upon a friend of mine, who, in hot blood,
Hath stepp'd into the law, which is past depth
To those that without heed do plunge into't. 13
He is a man, setting his fate aside,
Of comely virtues;
Nor did he soil the fact with cowardice,— 16
An honour in him which buys out his fault,—
But, with a noble fury and fair spirit,
Seeing his reputation touch'd to death,
He did oppose his foe;   20
And with such sober and unnoted passion
He did behave his anger, ere 'twas spent,
As if he had but prov'd an argument.
First Sen. You undergo too strict a paradox,
Striving to make an ugly deed look fair: 25
Your words have took such pains as if they
   labour'd
To bring manslaughter into form, and set
   quarrelling
Upon the head of valour; which indeed   28
Is valour misbegot, and came into the world
When sects and factions were newly born.
He's truly valiant that can wisely suffer
The worst that man can breathe, and make his
   wrongs   32
His outsides, to wear them like his raiment,
   carelessly,

And ne'er prefer his injuries to his heart,
To bring it into danger.
If wrongs be evils and enforce us kill,   36
What folly 'tis to hazard life for ill!
Alcib. My lord,—
First Sen. You cannot make gross sins look
   clear;
To revenge is no valour, but to bear.   40
Alcib. My lords, then, under favour, pardon
   me,
If I speak like a captain.
Why do fond men expose themselves to battle,
And not endure all threats? sleep upon't, 44
And let the foes quietly cut their throats
Without repugnancy? If there be
Such valour in the bearing, what make we
Abroad? why then, women are more valiant 48
That stay at home, if bearing carry it,
And the ass more captain than the lion, the
   felon
Loaden with irons wiser than the judge,
If wisdom be in suffering. O my lords!   52
As you are great, be pitifully good:
Who cannot condemn rashness in cold blood?
To kill, I grant, is sin's extremest gust;
But, in defence, by mercy, 'tis most just. 56
To be in anger is impiety;
But who is man that is not angry?
Weigh but the crime with this.
Sec. Sen. You breathe in vain.
Alcib.   In vain! his service done 60
At Lacedæmon and Byzantium
Were a sufficient briber for his life.
First Sen. What's that?
Alcib. I say, my lords, he has done fair ser-
   vice,   64
And slain in fight many of your enemies.
How full of valour did he bear himself
In the last conflict, and made plenteous wounds!
Sec. Sen. He has made too much plenty with
   'em;   68
He's a sworn rioter; he has a sin that often
Drowns him and takes his valour prisoner;
If there were no foes, that were enough
To overcome him; in that beastly fury   72
He has been known to commit outrages
And cherish factions; 'tis inferr'd to us,
His days are foul and his drink dangerous.
First Sen. He dies.   76
Alcib. Hard fate! he might have died in war.
My lords, if not for any parts in him,—
Though his right arm might purchase his own
   time,
And be in debt to none,—yet, more to move you
Take my deserts to his, and join 'em both; 81
And, for I know your reverend ages love
Security, I'll pawn my victories, all
My honour to you, upon his good returns. 84
If by this crime he owes the law his life,
Why, let the war receive't in valiant gore;
For law is strict, and war is nothing more.
First Sen. We are for law; he dies: urge it
   no more,   88
On height of our displeasure. Friend, or bro-
   ther,
He forfeits his own blood that spills another.

Alcib. Must it be so? it must not be. My lords,
I do beseech you, know me. 92
Sec. Sen. How!
Alcib. Call me to your remembrances.
Third Sen. What!
Alcib. I cannot think but your age has forgot me;
It could not else be I should prove so base, 96
To sue, and be denied such common grace.
My wounds ache at you.
First Sen. Do you dare our anger?
'Tis in few words, but spacious in effect;
We banish thee for ever.
Alcib. Banish me! 100
Banish your dotage; banish usury,
That makes the senate ugly.
First Sen. If, after two days' shine, Athens contain thee,
Attend our weightier judgment. And, not to swell our spirit, 104
He shall be executed presently.
[*Exeunt* Senators.
Alcib. Now the gods keep you old enough; that you may live
Only in bone, that none may look on you!
I am worse than mad: I have kept back their foes, 108
While they have told their money and let out
Their coin upon large interest; I myself
Rich only in large hurts: all those for this?
Is this the balsam that the usuring senate 112
Pours into captains' wounds? Banishment!
It comes not ill; I hate not to be banish'd;
It is a cause worthy my spleen and fury,
That I may strike at Athens. I'll cheer up 116
My discontented troops, and lay for hearts.
'Tis honour with most lands to be at odds;
Soldiers should brook as little wrongs as gods.
[*Exit.*

SCENE VI.—*The Same. A Room of State in*
TIMON's *House.*

Music. Tables set out: Servants attending.
Enter divers Lords, Senators, *and Others, at several doors.*

First Lord. The good time of day to you, sir.
Sec. Lord. I also wish it you. I think this honourable lord did but try us this other day. 3
First Lord. Upon that were my thoughts tiring when we encountered: I hope it is not so low with him as he made it seem in the trial of his several friends.
Sec. Lord. It should not be, by the persuasion of his new feasting. 9
First Lord. I should think so: he hath sent me an earnest inviting, which many my near occasions did urge me to put off; but he hath conjured me beyond them, and I must needs appear. 14
Sec. Lord. In like manner was I in debt to my importunate business, but he would not hear my excuse. I am sorry, when he sent to borrow of me, that my provision was out.
First Lord. I am sick of that grief too, as I understand how all things go. 20

Sec. Lord. Every man here's so. What would he have borrowed you?
First Lord. A thousand pieces.
Sec. Lord. A thousand pieces! 24
First Lord. What of you?
Third Lord. He sent to me, sir,—Here he comes.

Enter TIMON *and* Attendants.

Tim. With all my heart, gentlemen both;
and how fare you? 29
First Lord. Ever at the best, hearing well of your lordship.
Sec. Lord. The swallow follows not summer more willing than we your lordship. 33
Tim. [*Aside.*] Nor more willingly leaves winter; such summer-birds are men. Gentlemen, our dinner will not recompense this long stay: feast your ears with the music awhile, if they will fare so harshly o' the trumpet's sound; we shall to't presently. 39
First Lord. I hope it remains not unkindly with your lordship that I returned you an empty messenger.
Tim. O! sir, let it not trouble you.
Sec. Lord. My noble lord,— 44
Tim. Ah! my good friend, what cheer?
Sec. Lord. My most honourable lord, I am e'en sick of shame, that when your lordship this other day sent to me I was so unfortunate a beggar.
Tim. Think not on't, sir. 49
Sec. Lord. If you had sent but two hours before,—
Tim. Let it not cumber your better remembrance. [*The banquet brought in.*] Come, bring in all together.
Sec. Lord. All covered dishes!
First Lord. Royal cheer, I warrant you. 56
Third Lord. Doubt not that, if money and the season can yield it.
First Lord. How do you? What's the news?
Third Lord. Alcibiades is banished: hear you of it? 61
First Lord. } Alcibiades banished!
Sec. Lord. }
Third Lord. 'Tis so, be sure of it.
First Lord. How? how? 64
Sec. Lord. I pray you, upon what?
Tim. My worthy friends, will you draw near?
Third Lord. I'll tell you more anon. Here's a noble feast toward. 68
Sec. Lord. This is the old man still.
Third Lord. Will't hold? will't hold?
Sec. Lord. It does; but time will—and so—
Third Lord. I do conceive. 72
Tim. Each man to his stool, with that spur as he would to the lip of his mistress: your diet shall be in all places alike. Make not a city feast of it, to let the meat cool ere we can agree upon the first place: sit, sit. The gods require our thanks.— 78
You great benefactors sprinkle our society with thankfulness. For your own gifts, make yourselves praised: but reserve still to give, lest your deities be despised. Lend to each man enough, that one need not lend to another; for,

ere your godheads to borrow of men, men
ould forsake the gods. Make the meat be
loved more than the man that gives it. Let
 assembly of twenty be without a score of
lains: if there sit twelve women at the table,
t a dozen of them be as they are. The rest of
ur fees, O gods! the senators of Athens, to-
ther with the common lag of people, what is
niss in them, you gods, make suitable for
struction. For these my present friends, as
ey are to me nothing, so in nothing bless
em, and to nothing are they welcome.
ncover, dogs, and lap.   96
        [The dishes uncovered are full
                of warm water.
Some speak. What does his lordship mean?
Some other. I know not.
Tim. May you a better feast never behold,
ou knot of mouth-friends! smoke and luke-
    warm water   100
your perfection. This is Timon's last;
'ho, stuck and spangled with your flatteries,
 ashes it off, and sprinkles in your faces
        [Throwing the water in their faces.
our reeking villany. Live loath'd, and long,104
lost smiling, smooth, detested parasites,
ourteous destroyers, affable wolves, meek
    bears,
ou fools of fortune, trencher-friends, time's flies,
ap and knee slaves, vapours, and minute-jacks!
f man and beast the infinite malady   109
rust you quite o'er! What! dost thou go?
oft! take thy physic first,—thou too,—and
    thou;—
ay, I will lend thee money, borrow none. 112
        [Throws the dishes at them.
'hat! all in motion? Henceforth be no feast,
'hereat a villain's not a welcome guest.
urn, house! sink, Athens! henceforth hated be
f Timon man and all humanity!   *[Exit.*

Re-enter the Lords, Senators, &c.

First Lord. How now, my lords!   117
Sec. Lord. Know you the quality of Lord
imon's fury?
Third Lord. Push! did you see my cap? 120
Fourth Lord. I have lost my gown.
First Lord. He's but a mad lord, and nought
ut humour sways him. He gave me a jewel th'
ther day, and now he has beat it out of my hat:
id you see my jewel?   125
Third Lord. Did you see my cap?
Sec. Lord. Here 'tis.
Fourth Lord. Here lies my gown.   128
First Lord. Let's make no stay.
Sec. Lord. Lord Timon's mad.
Third Lord.   I feel 't upon my bones.
Fourth Lord. One day he gives us diamonds,
    next day stones.   *[Exeunt.*

ACT IV

SCENE I.—*Without the Walls of Athens.*
Enter TIMON.

Tim. Let me look back upon thee. O thou
    wall,

That girdlest in those wolves, dive in the earth,
And fence not Athens! Matrons, turn incon-
    tinent!
Obedience fail in children! slaves and fools, 4
Pluck the grave wrinkled senate from the bench,
And minister in their steads! To general filths
Convert, o' the instant, green virginity!
Do 't in your parents' eyes! Bankrupts, hold
    fast;   8
Rather than render back, out with your knives,
And cut your trusters' throats! Bound ser-
    vants, steal!—
Large-handed robbers your grave masters are,—
And pill by law. Maid, to thy master's bed; 12
Thy mistress is o' the brothel! Son of sixteen,
Pluck the lin'd crutch from thy old limping sire,
With it beat out his brains! Piety, and fear,
Religion to the gods, peace, justice, truth, 16
Domestic awe, night-rest and neighbourhood,
Instruction, manners, mysteries and trades,
Degrees, observances, customs and laws,
Decline to your confounding contraries, 20
And let confusion live! Plagues incident to men,
Your potent and infectious fevers heap
On Athens, ripe for stroke! Thou cold sciatica,
Cripple our senators, that their limbs may halt
As lamely as their manners! Lust and liberty
Creep in the minds and marrows of our youth,
That 'gainst the stream of virtue they may strive,
And drown themselves in riot! Itches, blains, 28
Sow all the Athenian bosoms, and their crop
Be general leprosy! Breath infect breath,
That their society, as their friendship, may
Be merely poison! Nothing I'll bear from thee
But nakedness, thou detestable town!   33
Take thou that too, with multiplying bans!
Timon will to the woods; where he shall find
The unkindest beast more kinder than mankind.
The gods confound—hear me, you good gods
    all—   37
The Athenians both within and out that wall!
And grant, as Timon grows, his hate may grow
To the whole race of mankind, high and low!
                  Amen. *[Exit.*

SCENE II.—*Athens. A Room in* TIMON'S
House.

Enter FLAVIUS, *with two or three* Servants.

First Serv. Hear you, Master steward!
    where's our master?
Are we undone? cast off? nothing remaining?
    Flav. Alack! my fellows, what should I say
to you?
Let me be recorded by the righteous gods,   4
I am as poor as you.
    First Serv.   Such a house broke!
So noble a master fall'n! All gone! and not
One friend to take his fortune by the arm,
And go along with him!
    Sec. Serv.   As we do turn our backs 8
From our companion thrown into his grave,
So his familiars to his buried fortunes
Slink all away, leave their false vows with him,
Like empty purses pick'd; and his poor self, 12
A dedicated beggar to the air,

With his disease of all-shunn'd poverty,
Walks, like contempt, alone. More of our fellows.

Enter other Servants.

Flav. All broken implements of a ruin'd
house.   16
Third Serv. Yet do our hearts wear Timon's
livery,
That see I by our faces; we are fellows still,
Serving alike in sorrow. Leak'd is our bark,
And we, poor mates, stand on the dying deck, 20
Hearing the surges threat: we must all part
Into this sea of air.
Flav.   Good fellows all,
The latest of my wealth I'll share amongst you.
Wherever we shall meet, for Timon's sake 24
Let's yet be fellows; let's shake our heads, and
say,
As 'twere a knell unto our master's fortunes,
'We have seen better days.' Let each take some;
                          [*Giving them money.*
Nay, put out all your hands. Not one word
more: 28
Thus part we rich in sorrow, parting poor.
             [*They embrace, and part several ways.*
O! the fierce wretchedness that glory brings us.
Who would not wish to be from wealth exempt,
Since riches point to misery and contempt? 32
Who would be so mock'd with glory? or so live,
But in a dream of friendship?
To have his pomp and all what state compounds
But only painted, like his varnish'd friends? 36
Poor honest lord! brought low by his own heart,
Undone by goodness. Strange, unusual blood,
When man's worst sin is he does too much good!
Who then dares to be half so kind agen?   40
For bounty, that makes gods, does still mar men.
My dearest lord, bless'd, to be most accurs'd,
Rich, only to be wretched, thy great fortunes
Are made thy chief afflictions. Alas! kind lord,
He's flung in rage from this ingrateful seat 45
Of monstrous friends;
Nor has he with him to supply his life,
Or that which can command it.   48
I'll follow and inquire him out:
I'll ever serve his mind with my best will;
Whilst I have gold I'll be his steward still. [*Exit.*

Scene III.—*Woods and Cave near the
Sea-shore.*

Enter TIMON *from the Cave.*

Tim. O blessed breeding sun! draw from the
earth
Rotten humidity; below thy sister's orb
Infect the air! Twinn'd brothers of one womb,
Whose procreation, residence and birth,   4
Scarce is dividant, touch them with several for-
tunes;
The greater scorns the lesser: not nature,
To whom all sores lay siege, can bear great for-
tune,
But by contempt of nature.   8
Raise me this beggar, and deny't that lord;
The senator shall bear contempt hereditary,

The beggar native honour.
It is the pasture lards the rother's sides,
The want that makes him lean. Who dare
who dares,
In purity of manhood stand upright,
And say, 'This man's a flatterer?' if one be,
So are they all; for every grize of fortune
Is smooth'd by that below: the learned pate
Ducks to the golden fool: all is oblique;
There's nothing level in our cursed natures
But direct villany. Therefore, be abhorr'd 2
All feasts, societies, and throngs of men!
His semblable, yea, himself, Timon disdains
Destruction fang mankind! Earth, yield m
roots!   [*Diggin*
Who seeks for better of thee, sauce his palate 2
With thy most operant poison! What is here
Gold! yellow, glittering, precious gold! N
gods,
I am no idle votarist. Roots, you clear heavens
Thus much of this will make black white, fo
fair,   2
Wrong right, base noble, old young, cowar
valiant.
Ha! you gods, why this? What this, you gods
Why, this
Will lug your priests and servants from you
sides,
Pluck stout men's pillows from below the
head: 3
This yellow slave
Will knit and break religions; bless the accurs'd
Make the hoar leprosy ador'd; place thieves,
And give them title, knee, and approbation, 3
With senators on the bench; this is it
That makes the wappen'd widow wed again;
She, whom the spital-house and ulcerous sore
Would cast the gorge at, this embalms an
spices   4
To the April day again. Come, damned earth
Thou common whore of mankind, that putt's
odds
Amond the rout of nations, I will make thee
Do thy right nature.—[*March afar off.*] Ha!
drum? thou'rt quick,   4
But yet I'll bury thee: thou'lt go, strong thie
When gouty keepers of thee cannot stand:
Nay, stay thou out for earnest.
                                     [*Keeping some gold*

Enter ALCIBIADES, *with drum and fife, in war
like manner;* PHRYNIA *and* TIMANDRA.

Alcib. What art thou there? speak.   4
Tim. A beast, as thou art. The canker gnaw
thy heart,
For showing me again the eyes of man!
Alcib. What is thy name? Is man so hate
ful to thee,
That art thyself a man?
Tim. I am *Misanthropos*, and hate mankind 5.
For thy part, I do wish thou wert a dog,
That I might love thee something.
Alcib.   I know thee well
But in thy fortunes am unlearn'd and strange
Tim. I know thee too; and more than tha
I know thee   5

I not desire to know. Follow thy drum;
With man's blood paint the ground, gules,
gules;
Religious canons, civil laws are cruel;	60
Then what should war be? This fell whore of
thine
Hath in her more destruction than thy sword
For all her cherubin look.

Phry.	Thy lips rot off!

Tim. I will not kiss thee; then the rot re-
turns	64
To thine own lips again.

Alcib. How came the noble Timon to this
change?

Tim. As the moon does, by wanting light to
give:
But then renew I could not like the moon;	68
There were no suns to borrow of.

Alcib. Noble Timon, what friendship may I
do thee?

Tim. None, but to maintain my opinion.

Alcib. What is it, Timon?	72

Tim. Promise me friendship, but perform
none: if thou wilt not promise, the gods plague
thee, for thou art a man! if thou dost perform,
confound thee, for thou art a man!	76

Alcib. I have heard in some sort of thy
miseries.

Tim. Thou saw'st them, when I had prosperity.

Alcib. I see them now; then was a blessed
time.

Tim. As thine is now, held with a brace of
harlots.	80

Timan. Is this the Athenian minion, whom
the world
Voic'd so regardfully?

Tim.	Art thou Timandra?

Timan.	Yes.

Tim. Be a whore still; they love thee not that
use thee:
Give them diseases, leaving with thee their lust.
Make use of thy salt hours; season the slaves	85
for tubs and baths; bring down rose-cheeked
youth
To the tub-fast and the diet.

Timan.	Hang thee, monster!

Alcib. Pardon him, sweet Timandra, for his
wits	88
Are drown'd and lost in his calamities.
I have but little gold of late, brave Timon,
The want whereof doth daily make revolt
In my penurious band: I have heard and griev'd
How cursed Athens, mindless of thy worth,	93
Forgetting thy great deeds, when neighbour
states,
But for thy sword and fortune, trod upon
them,—

Tim. I prithee, beat thy drum, and get thee
gone.	96

Alcib. I am thy friend, and pity thee, dear
Timon.

Tim. How dost thou pity him whom thou
dost trouble?
I had rather be alone.

Alcib.	Why, fare thee well:

Here is some gold for thee.

Tim.	Keep it, I cannot eat it.	100

Alcib. When I have laid proud Athens on a
heap,—

Tim. Warr'st thou 'gainst Athens?

Alcib. Ay, Timon, and have cause.

Tim. The gods confound them all in thy con-
quest; and	104
Thee after, when thou hast conquer'd!

Alcib.	Why me, Timon?

Tim. That, by killing of villians. thou wast
born to conquer
My country.
Put up thy gold: go on,—here's gold,—go on;
Be as a planetary plague, when Jove	109
Will o'er some high-vic'd city hang his poison
In the sick air: let not thy sword skip one.
Pity not honour'd age for his white beard;	112
He is a usurer. Strike me the counterfeit matron;
It is her habit only that is honest,
Herself 's a bawd. Let not the virgin's cheek
Make soft thy trenchant sword; for those milk-
paps,	116
That through the window-bars bore at men's
eyes,
Are not within the leaf of pity writ,
But set them down horrible traitors. Spare not
the babe,
Whose dimpled smiles from fools exhaust their
mercy,	120
Think it a bastard, whom the oracle
Hath doubtfully pronounc'd thy throat shall cut,
And mince it sans remorse. Swear against
objects;
Put armour on thine ears and on thine eyes,	124
Whose proof nor yells of mothers, maids, nor
babes,
Nor sight of priests in holy vestments bleeding,
Shall pierce a jot. There's gold to pay thy
soldiers:
Make large confusion; and, thy fury spent,	128
Confounded be thyself! Speak not, be gone.

Alcib. Hast thou gold yet? I'll take the gold
thou giv'st me,
Not all thy counsel.

Tim. Dost thou, or dost thou not, heaven's
curse upon thee!	132

Phry. } Give us some gold, good Timon:
Timan. } hast thou more?

Tim. Enough to make a whore forswear her
trade,
And to make whores a bawd. Hold up, you
sluts,
Your aprons mountant: you are not oathable,
Although, I know, you'll swear, terribly swear
Into strong shudders and to heavenly agues	138
The immortal gods that hear you, spare your
oaths,
I'll trust to your conditions: be whores still;
And he whose pious breath seeks to convert you,
Be strong in whore, allure him, burn him up;
Let your close fire predominate his smoke,
And be no turncoats: yet may your pains, six
months,	144
Be quite contrary: and thatch your poor thin
roofs

With burdens of the dead; some that were
  hang'd,
No matter; wear them, betray with them:
  whore still;
Paint till a horse may mire upon your face: 148
A pox of wrinkles!
  Phry. }
  Timan. } Well, more gold. What then?
Believe 't, that we'll do anything for gold.
  Tim. Consumptions sow   152
In hollow bones of man; strike their sharp shins,
And mar men's spurring. Crack the lawyer's
  voice,
That he may never more false title plead,
Nor sound his quillets shrilly: hoar the flamen,
That scolds against the quality of flesh,   157
And not believes himself: down with the nose,
Down with it flat; take the bridge quite away
Of him that, his particular to foresee,   160
Smells from the general weal: make curl'd-pate
  ruffians bald,
And let the unscarr'd braggarts of the war
Derive some pain from you: plague all,
That your activity may defeat and quell   164
The source of all erection. There's more gold;
Do you damn others, and let this damn you,
And ditches grave you all!
  Phry. } More counsel with more money,
  Timan. } bounteous Timon.   168
  Tim. More whore, more mischief first; I have
  given you earnest.
  Alcib. Strike up the drum towards Athens!
  Farewell, Timon:
If I thrive well, I'll visit thee again.
  Tim. If I hope well, I'll never see thee more.
  Alcib. I never did thee harm.   173
  Tim. Yes, thou spok'st well of me.
  Alcib.   Call'st thou that harm?
  Tim. Men daily find it. Get thee away, and
  take
Thy beagles with thee.
  Alcib.   We but offend him. Strike!
    [*Drum beats. Exeunt* ALCIBIADES,
        PHRYNIA, *and* TIMANDRA.
  Tim. That nature, being sick of man's un-
  kindness,   177
Should yet be hungry! Common mother, thou,
    [*Digging.*
Whose womb unmeasurable, and infinite breast,
Teems, and feeds all; whose self-same mettle,
Whereof thy proud child, arrogant man, is
  puff'd,   181
Engenders the black toad and adder blue,
The gilded newt and eyeless venom'd worm,
With all the abhorred births below crisp heaven
Whereon Hyperion's quickening fire doth shine;
Yield him, who all thy human sons doth hate,
From forth thy plenteous bosom, one poor root!
Ensear thy fertile and conceptious womb, 188
Let it no more bring out ingrateful man!
Go great with tigers, dragons, wolves, and
  bears;
Teem with new monsters, whom thy upward
  face
Hath to the marbled mansion all above   192
Never presented! O! a root; dear thanks:

Dry up thy marrows, vines and plough-torn
  leas;
Whereof ingrateful man, with liquorish draughts
And morsels unctuous, greases his pure mind,
That from it all consideration slips!   197

    Enter APEMANTUS.
More man! Plague! plague!
  Apem. I was directed hither: men report
Thou dost affect my manners, and dost use
  them.   200
  Tim. 'Tis, then, because thou dost not keep
  a dog
Whom I would imitate: consumption catch
  thee!
  Apem. This is in thee a nature but infected;
A poor unmanly melancholy sprung   204
From change of fortune. Why this spade? this
  place?
This slave-like habit? and these looks of care?
Thy flatterers yet wear silk, drink wine, lie soft,
Hug their diseas'd perfumes, and have forgot
That ever Timon was. Shame not these woods
By putting on the cunning of a carper.   210
Be thou a flatterer now, and seek to thrive
By that which has undone thee: hinge thy knee,
And let his very breath, whom thou'lt observe,
Blow off thy cap; praise his most vicious strain,
And call it excellent. Thou wast told thus;
Thou gav'st thine ears, like tapsters that bid
  welcome,   216
To knaves and all approachers: 'tis most just
That thou turn rascal; hadst thou wealth again,
Rascals should have 't. Do not assume my like-
  ness.
  Tim. Were I like thee I'd throw away myself.
  Apem. Thou hast cast away thyself, being
  like thyself;   221
A madman so long, now a fool. What! think'st
That the bleak air, thy boisterous chamberlain,
Will put thy shirt on warm? will these moss'd
  trees,   224
That have outliv'd the eagle, page thy heels
And skip when thou point'st out? will the cold
  brook,
Candied with ice, caudle thy morning taste
To cure the o'er-night's surfeit? Call the crea-
  tures   228
Whose naked natures live in all the spite
Of wreakful heaven, whose bare unhoused
  trunks
To the conflicting elements expos'd,
Answer mere nature; bid them flatter thee; 23
O! thou shalt find—
  Tim.   A fool of thee. Depart.
  Apem. I love thee better now than e'er I did
  Tim. I hate thee worse.
  Apem.   Why?
  Tim.   Thou flatter'st misery
  Apem. I flatter not, but say thou art a caitif
  Tim. Why dost thou seek me out?
  Apem.   To vex thee. 23
  Tim. Always a villain's office, or a fool's.
Dost please thyself in 't?
  Apem.   Ay.
  Tim.   What! a knave too

Apem. If thou didst put this sour-cold habit
on   240
To castigate thy pride, 'twere well; but thou
Dost it enforcedly; thou'dst courtier be again
Wert thou not beggar. Willing misery
Outlives incertain pomp, is crown'd before; 244
The one is filling still, never complete;
The other, at high wish: best state, contentless,
Hath a distracted and most wretched being,
Worse than the worst, content.   248
Thou hadst desire to die, being miserable.
  Tim. Not by his breath that is more miserable.
Thou art a slave, whom Fortune's tender arm
With favour never clasp'd, but bred a dog. 252
Hadst thou, like us from our first swath, proceeded
The sweet degrees that this brief world affords
To such as may the passive drudges of it
Freely command, thou wouldst have plung'd
thyself   256
In general riot; melted down thy youth
In different beds of lust; and never learn'd
The icy precepts of respect, but follow'd
The sugar'd game before thee. But myself, 260
Who had the world as my confectionary,
The mouths, the tongues, the eyes, and hearts of
men
At duty, more than I could frame employment,
That numberless upon me stuck as leaves 264
Do on the oak, have with one winter's brush
Fell from their boughs and left me open, bare
For every storm that blows; I, to bear this,
That never knew but better, is some burden: 268
Thy nature did commence in sufferance, time
Hath made thee hard in't. Why shouldst thou
hate men?
They never flatter'd thee: what hast thou given?
If thou wilt curse, thy father, that poor rag, 272
Must be thy subject, who in spite put stuff
To some she beggar and compounded thee
Poor rogue hereditary. Hence! be gone!
If thou hadst not been born the worst of men,
Thou hadst been a knave and flatterer.
  Apem.   Art thou proud yet? 277
  Tim. Ay, that I am not thee.
  Apem.   I, that I was
No prodigal.
  Tim.   I, that I am one now:
Were all the wealth I have shut up in thee, 280
I'd give thee leave to hang it. Get thee gone.
That the whole life of Athens were in this!
Thus would I eat it.   [*Eating a root.*
  Apem.   Here; I will mend thy feast.
  Tim. First mend my company, take away
thyself.   284
  Apem. So I shall mend mine own, by the lack
of thine.
  Tim. 'Tis not well mended so, it is but
botch'd;
If not, I would it were.
  Apem. What wouldst thou have to Athens?
  Tim. Thee thither in a whirlwind. If thou wilt,
Tell them there I have gold; look, so I have.
  Apem. Here is no use for gold.
  Tim.   The best and truest;

For here it sleeps, and does no hired harm. 292
  Apem. Where liest o' nights, Timon?
  Tim.   Under that 's above me.
Where feed'st thou o' days, Apemantus?
  Apem. Where my stomach finds meat; or,
rather, where I eat it.   296
  Tim. Would poison were obedient and knew
my mind!
  Apem. Where wouldst thou send it?
  Tim. To sauce thy dishes.
  Apem. The middle of humanity thou never
knewest, but the extremity of both ends. When
thou wast in thy gilt and thy perfume, they
mocked thee for too much curiosity; in thy
rags thou knowest none, but art despised for
the contrary. There's a medlar for thee; eat it.
  Tim. On what I hate I feed not.   306
  Apem. Dost hate a medlar?
  Tim. Ay, though it look like thee.
  Apem. An thou hadst hated meddlers sooner,
thou shouldst have loved thyself better now.
What man didst thou ever know unthrift that
was beloved after his means?   312
  Tim. Who, without those means thou talkest
of, didst thou ever know beloved?
  Apem. Myself.
  Tim. I understand thee; thou hadst some
means to keep a dog.   317
  Apem. What things in the world canst thou
nearest compare to thy flatterers?
  Tim. Women nearest; but men, men are the
things themselves. What wouldst thou do with
the world, Apemantus, if it lay in thy power?
  Apem. Give it the beasts, to be rid of the
men.   324
  Tim. Wouldst thou have thyself fall in the
confusion of men, and remain a beast with the
beasts?
  Apem. Ay, Timon.   328
  Tim. A beastly ambition, which the gods
grant thee to attain to. If thou wert the lion,
the fox would beguile thee; if thou wert the
lamb, the fox would eat thee; if thou wert the
fox, the lion would suspect thee, when peradventure thou wert accused by the ass; if thou
wert the ass, thy dulness would torment thee,
and still thou livedst but as a breakfast to the
wolf; if thou wert the wolf, thy greediness
would afflict thee, and oft thou shouldst hazard
thy life for thy dinner; wert thou the unicorn,
pride and wrath would confound thee and make
thine own self the conquest of thy fury; wert
thou a bear, thou wouldst be killed by the
horse; wert thou a horse, thou wouldst be
seized by the leopard; wert thou a leopard,
thou wert german to the lion, and the spots of
thy kindred were jurors on thy life; all thy
safety were remotion, and thy defence absence.
What beast couldst thou be, that were not
subject to a beast? and what a beast art thou
already, that seest not thy loss in transformation!   350
  Apem. If thou couldst please me with speaking to me, thou mightst have hit upon it here;
the commonwealth of Athens is become a forest
of beasts.

Tim. How has the ass broke the wall, that
thou art out of the city? 357

Apem. Yonder comes a poet and a painter:
the plague of company light upon thee! I will
fear to catch it, and give way. When I know
not what else to do, I'll see thee again. 361

Tim. When there is nothing living but thee,
thou shalt be welcome. I had rather be a beggar's dog than Apemantus. 364

Apem. Thou art the cap of all the fools alive.

Tim. Would thou wert clean enough to spit
upon!

Apem. A plague on thee! thou art too bad
to curse!

Tim. All villains that do stand by thee are
pure. 368

Apem. There is no leprosy but what thou
speak'st.

Tim. If I name thee.
I'll beat thee, but I should infect my hands.

Apem. I would my tongue could rot them off!

Tim. Away, thou issue of a mangy dog! 373
Choler does kill me that thou art alive;
I swound to see thee.

Apem. Would thou wouldst burst!

Tim. Away,
Thou tedious rogue! I am sorry I shall lose 376
A stone by thee. [*Throws a stone at him.*

Apem. Beast!

Tim. Slave!

Apem. Toad!

Tim. Rogue, rogue, rogue!
I am sick of this false world, and will love nought
But even the mere necessities upon't.
Then, Timon, presently prepare thy grave; 380
Lie where the light foam of the sea may beat
Thy grave-stone daily: make thine epitaph,
That death in me at others' lives may laugh.
[*Looking on the gold.*
O thou sweet king-killer, and dear divorce 384
'Twixt natural son and sire! thou bright defiler
Of Hymen's purest bed! thou valiant Mars!
Thou ever young, fresh, lov'd, and delicate
wooer,
Whose blush doth thaw the consecrated snow
That lies on Dian's lap! thou visible god, 389
That solder'st close impossibilities,
And mak'st them kiss! that speak'st with every
tongue,
To every purpose! O thou touch of hearts! 392
Think, thy slave man rebels, and by thy virtue
Set them into confounding odds, that beasts
May have the world in empire.

Apem. Would 'twere so:
But not till I am dead; I'll say thou'st gold:
Thou wilt be throng'd to shortly.

Tim. Throng'd to?

Apem. Ay.

Tim. Thy back, I prithee.

Apem. Love, and love thy misery!

Tim. Long live so, and so die!
[*Exit* APEMANTUS.
I am quit.
More things like men! Eat, Timon, and abhor
them. 400

Enter Thieves.

First Thief. Where should he have this gold?
It is some poor fragment, some slender ort o
his remainder. The mere want of gold, and th
falling-from of his friends, drove him into thi
melancholy. 40

Sec. Thief. It is noised he hath a mass o
treasure.

Third Thief. Let us make the assay upo
him: if he care not for't, he will supply u
easily; if he covetously reserve it, how shall
get it?

Sec. Thief. True; for he bears it not abou
him, 'tis hid. 41

First Thief. Is not this he?

Thieves. Where?

Sec. Thief. 'Tis his description.

Third Thief. He; I know him. 41

All. Save thee, Timon.

Tim. Now, thieves?

All. Soldiers, not thieves.

Tim. Both too; and women's sons. 42

Thieves. We are not thieves, but men tha
much do want.

Tim. Your greatest want is, you want muc
of meat.
Why should you want? Behold, the earth hatl
roots;
Within this mile break forth a hundred springs
The oaks bear mast, the briers scarlet hips; 42
The bounteous housewife, nature, on each bus
Lays her full mess before you. Want! wh
want?

First Thief. We cannot live on grass, o
berries, water, 42
As beasts, and birds, and fishes.

Tim. Nor on the beasts themselves, the birds
and fishes;
You must eat men. Yet thanks I must you co
That you are thieves profess'd, that you worl
not 43
In holier shapes; for there is boundless theft
In limited professions. Rascal thieves,
Here's gold. Go, suck the subtle blood o' the
grape, 43
Till the high fever seethe your blood to froth
And so 'scape hanging: trust not the physician
His antidotes are poison, and he slays
More than you rob: take wealth and lives to
gether;
Do villany, do, since you protest to do't, 44
Like workmen. I'll example you with thievery
The sun 's a thief, and with his great attractio
Robs the vast sea; the moon 's an arrant thie
And her pale fire she snatches from the sun; 44
The sea's a thief, whose liquid surge resolves
The moon into salt tears; the earth's a thief,
That feeds and breeds by a composture stolen
From general excrement, each thing 's a thief
The laws, your curb and whip, in their roug
power 44
Have uncheck'd theft. Love not yourselves
away!
Rob one another. There's more gold; cu
throats;

ll that you meet are thieves. To Athens go,
reak open shops; nothing can you steal 453
ut thieves do lose it: steal no less for this
give you; and gold confound you howsoe'er!
men. 456
Third Thief. He has almost charmed me
om my profession, by persuading me to it.
First Thief. 'Tis in the malice of mankind
hat he thus advises us; not to have us thrive in
ur mystery. 461
Sec. Thief. I'll believe him as an enemy, and
ive over my trade.
First Thief. Let us first see peace in Athens;
here is no time so miserable but a man may be
rue. [*Exeunt* Thieves.

Enter FLAVIUS.

Flav. O you gods!
s yond despised and ruinous man my lord? 468
ull of decay and failing? O monument
And wonder of good deeds evilly bestow'd!
What an alteration of honour
Has desperate want made! 472
What viler thing upon the earth than friends
Who can bring noblest minds to basest ends!
How rarely does it meet with this time's guise,
When man was wish'd to love his enemies! 476
Grant I may ever love, and rather woo
Those that would mischief me than those that
do!
He hath caught me in his eye: I will present
My honest grief unto him; and, as my lord, 480
Still serve him with my life. My dearest master!

TIMON *comes forward.*

Tim. Away! what art thou?
Flav. Have you forgot me, sir?
Tim. Why dost ask that? I have forgot all
men;
Then, if thou grant'st thou'rt a man, I have
forgot thee. 484
Flav. An honest poor servant of yours.
Tim. Then I know thee not:
I never had an honest man about me; ay all
I kept were knaves, to serve in meat to villains.
Flav. The gods are witness, 488
Ne'er did poor steward wear a truer grief
For his undone lord than mine eyes for you.
Tim. What! dost thou weep? Come nearer.
Then I love thee,
Because thou art a woman, and disclaim'st 492
Flinty mankind; whose eyes do never give,
But thorough lust and laughter. Pity's sleeping:
Strange times, that weep with laughing, not
with weeping!
Flav. I beg of you to know me, good my lord,
To accept my grief and whilst this poor wealth
lasts 497
To entertain me as your steward still.
Tim. Had I a steward
So true, so just, and now so comfortable? 500
It almost turns my dangerous nature mild.
Let me behold thy face. Surely, this man
Was born of woman.
Forgive my general and exceptless rashness, 504
You perpetual sober gods! I do proclaim

One honest man, mistake me not, but one;
No more, I pray, and he's a steward.
How fain would I have hated all mankind! 508
And thou redeem'st thyself: but all, save thee,
I fell with curses.
Methinks thou art more honest now than wise;
For, by oppressing and betraying me, 512
Thou mightst have sooner got another service:
For many so arrive at second masters
Upon their first lord's neck. But tell me true,—
For I must ever doubt, though ne'er so sure,—
Is not thy kindness subtle, covetous, 517
If not a usuring kindness and as rich men deal
gifts,
Expecting in return twenty for one?
Flav. No, my most worthy master; in whose
breast 520
Doubt and suspect, alas! are plac'd too late.
You should have fear'd false times when you
did feast;
Suspect still comes when an estate is least.
That which I show, heaven knows, is merely love,
Duty and zeal to your unmatched mind, 525
Care of your food and living; and, believe it,
My most honour'd lord,
For any benefit that points to me, 528
Either in hope, or present, I'd exchange
For this one wish, that you had power and wealth
To requite me by making rich yourself.
Tim. Look thee, 'tis so. Thou singly honest
man, 532
Here, take: the gods out of my misery,
Have sent thee treasure. Go, live rich and
happy;
But this condition'd: thou shalt build from men;
Hate all, curse all, show charity to none, 536
But let the famish'd flesh slide from the bone,
Ere thou relieve the beggar; give to dogs
What thou deny'st to men; let prisons swallow
'em,
Debts wither 'em to nothing; be men like blasted
woods, 540
And may diseases lick up their false bloods!
And so, farewell and thrive.
Flav. O! let me stay
And comfort you, my master.
Tim. If thou hatest
Curses, stay not; fly, whilst thou'rt bless'd and
free: 544
Ne'er see thou man, and let me ne'er see thee.
[*Exeunt severally.*

ACT V

SCENE I.—*The Woods. Before* TIMON'S *Cave.*

Enter Poet *and* Painter.

Pain. As I took note of the place, it cannot
be far where he abides.
Poet. What's to be thought of him? Does
the rumour hold for true that he is so full of
gold? 5
Pain. Certain: Alcibiades reports it; Phrynia
and Timandra had gold of him: he likewise
enriched poor straggling soldiers with great
quantity. 'Tis said he gave unto his steward a
mighty sum. 10

Poet. Then this breaking of his has been but a try for his friends.

Pain. Nothing else; you shall see him a palm in Athens again, and flourish with the highest. Therefore 'tis not amiss we tender our loves to him, in this supposed distress of his: it will show honestly in us, and is very likely to load our purposes with what they travel for, if it be a just and true report that goes of his having.

Poet. What have you now to present unto him?

Pain. Nothing at this time but my visitation; only, I will promise him an excellent piece.

Poet. I must serve him so too; tell him of an intent that's coming towards him.

Pain. Good as the best. Promising is the very air o' the time; it opens the eyes of expectation; performance is ever the duller for his act; and, but in the plainer and simpler kind of people, the deed of saying is quite out of use. To promise is most courtly and fashionable; performance is a kind of will or testament which argues a great sickness in his judgment that makes it.   33

Enter TIMON *from his cave.*

Tim. [*Aside.*] Excellent workman! Thou canst not paint a man so bad as is thyself.

Poet. I am thinking what I shall say I have provided for him: it must be a personating of himself; a satire against the softness of prosperity, with a discovery of the infinite flatteries that follow youth and opulency.   40

Tim. [*Aside.*] Must thou needs stand for a villain in thine own work? Wilt thou whip thine own faults in other men? Do so, I have gold for thee.   44

Poet. Nay, let's seek him:
Then do we sin against our own estate,
When we may profit meet, and come too late.

Pain. True;   48
When the day serves, before black-corner'd night,
Find what thou want'st by free and offer'd light. Come.

Tim. [*Aside.*] I'll meet you at the turn. What a god's gold,   52
That he is worshipp'd in a baser temple
Than where swine feed!
'Tis thou that rigg'st the bark and plough'st the foam,
Settlest admired reverence in a slave: 56
To thee be worship; and thy saints for aye
Be crown'd with plagues that thee alone obey.
Fit I meet them.   [*Advancing.*

Poet. Hail, worthy Timon!

Pain.   Our late noble master!   60

Tim. Have I once liv'd to see two honest men?

Poet. Sir,
Having often of your open bounty tasted,   63
Hearing you were retir'd, your friends fall'n off,
Whose thankless natures—O abhorred spirits!
Not all the whips of heaven are large enough—
What! to you,
Whose star-like nobleness gave life and influence
To their whole being! I am rapt, and cannot cover   69

The monstrous bulk of this ingratitude
With any size of words.

Tim. Let it go naked, men may see't the better:
You, that are honest, by being what you are
Make them best seen and known.

Pain.   He and myself
Have travell'd in the great shower of your gifts,
And sweetly felt it.

Tim.   Ay, you are honest men.

Pain. We are hither come to offer you our service.

Tim. Most honest men! Why, how shall I requite you?
Can you eat roots and drink cold water? no.

Both. What we can do, we'll do, to do you service.

Tim. Ye're honest men. Ye've heard that I have gold;
I am sure you have: speak truth; ye're honest men.

Pain. So it is said, my noble lord; but therefore
Came not my friend nor I.

Tim. Good honest men! Thou draw'st counterfeit
Best in all Athens: thou'rt, indeed, the best;
Thou counterfeit'st most lively.

Pain.   So, so, my lord.

Tim. E'en so, sir, as I say. And, for thy fiction,
Why, thy verse swells with stuff so fine and smooth
That thou art even natural in thine art.
But for all this, my honest-natur'd friends,
I must needs say you have a little fault:
Marry, 'tis not monstrous in you, neither wish I
You take much pains to mend.

Both.   Beseech your honour—
To make it known to us.

Tim.   You'll take it ill.

Both. Most thankfully, my lord.

Tim.   Will you indeed?

Both. Doubt it not, worthy lord.

Tim. There's never a one of you but trusts a knave,
That mightily deceives you.

Both.   Do we, my lord?

Tim. Ay, and you hear him cog, see him dissemble,
Know his gross patchery, love him, feed him,
Keep in your bosom; yet remain assur'd
That he's a made-up villain.

Pain. I know none such, my lord.

Poet.   Nor I.

Tim. Look you, I love you well; I'll give you gold,
Rid me these villains from your companies:
Hang them or stab them, drown them in a draught,
Confound them by some course, and come to me,
I'll give you gold enough.

Both. Name them, my lord; let's know them.

Tim. You that way and you this, but two in company;

ch man apart, all single and alone,   112
et an arch-villain keeps him company.
, where thou art two villains shall not be,
me not near him. [*To the* Poet.] If thou
  would not reside
ence! pack! there's gold; ye came for gold,
  ye slaves: 117
ou have done work for me, there's payment:
  hence!
ou are an alchemist, make gold of that.
ut, rascal dogs!   120
[*Beats them out and then returns to his cave.*

    Enter FLAVIUS *and two* Senators.

Flav. It is in vain that you would speak with
  Timon;
or he is set so only to himself
hat nothing but himself, which looks like man,
  friendly with him.
First Sen.   Bring us to his cave: 124
is our part and promise to the Athenians
o speak with Timon.
Sec. Sen.   At all times alike
len are not still the same: 'twas time and griefs
hat fram'd him thus: time, with his fairer
  hand,   128
ffering the fortunes of his former days,
he former man may make him. Bring us to
  him,
nd chance it as it may.
Flav.   Here is his cave.   131
eace and content be here! Lord Timon!
  Timon!
ook out, and speak to friends. The Athenians,
y two of their most reverend senate, greet thee:
peak to them, noble Timon.

    Enter TIMON, *from his cave.*

Tim. Thou sun, that comfort'st, burn! Speak,
  and be hang'd: 136
or each true word, a blister! and each false
e as a cauterizing to the root o' the tongue,
onsuming it with speaking!
First Sen.   Worthy Timon,—
Tim. Of none but such as you, and you of
  Timon.   140
Sec. Sen. The senators of Athens greet thee,
  Timon.
Tim. I thank them; and would send them
  back the plague,
ould I but catch it for them.
First Sen.   O! forget
/hat we are sorry for ourselves in thee.   144
he senators with one consent of love
ntreat thee back to Athens; who have thought
n special dignities, which vacant lie
or thy best use and wearing.
Sec. Sen.   They confess   148
oward thee forgetfulness too general, gross;
/hich now the public body, which doth seldom
lay the recanter, feeling in itself
lack of Timon's aid, hath sense withal   152
f its own fail, restraining aid to Timon;
nd send forth us, to make their sorrow'd
  render,
ogether with a recompense more fruitful

Than their offence can weigh down by the dram;
Ay, even such heaps and sums of love and wealth
As shall to thee block out what wrongs were
  theirs,
And write in thee the figures of their love,
Ever to read them thine.
Tim.   You witch me in it;   160
Surprise me to the very brink of tears:
Lend me a fool's heart and a woman's eyes,
And I'll beweep these comforts, worthy sena-
  tors.
First Sen. Therefore so please thee to return
  with us,   164
And of our Athens—thine and ours—to take
The captainship, thou shalt be met with thanks,
Allow'd with absolute power, and thy good
  name
Live with authority: so soon we shall drive back
Of Alcibiades the approaches wild;   169
Who, like a boar too savage, doth root up
His country's peace.
Sec. Sen. And shakes his threat'ning sword
Against the walls of Athens.
First Sen.   Therefore, Timon,—   172
Tim. Well, sir, I will; therefore, I will, sir;
  thus:—
If Alcibiades kill my countrymen,
Let Alcibiades know this of Timon,
That Timon cares not. But if he sack fair
  Athens,   176
And take our goodly aged men by the beards,
Giving our holy virgins to the stain
Of contumelious, beastly, mad-brain'd war;
Then let him know, and tell him Timon speaks
  it,   180
In pity of our aged and our youth
I cannot choose but tell him, that I care not,
And let him take't at worst; for their knives
  care not
While you have throats to answer: for myself,
There's not a whittle in the unruly camp   185
But I do prize it at my love before
The reverend'st throat in Athens. So I leave
  you
To the protection of the prosperous gods,   188
As thieves to keepers.
Flav.   Stay not; all's in vain.
Tim. Why, I was writing of my epitaph;
It will be seen to-morrow. My long sickness
Of health and living now begins to mend,   192
And nothing brings me all things. Go; live
  still:
Be Alcibiades your plague, you his,
And last so long enough!
First Sen.   We speak in vain.
Tim. But yet I love my country, and am
  not   196
One that rejoices in the common wrack,
As common bruit doth put it.
First Sen.   That's well spoke.
Tim. Commend me to my loving country-
  men,—
First Sen. These words become your lips as
  they pass through them.   200
Sec. Sen. And enter in our ears like great
  triumphers

In their applauding gates.

Tim. Commend me to them;
And tell them, that, to ease them of their griefs,
Their fears of hostile strokes, their aches, losses,
Their pangs of love, with other incident throes
That nature's fragile vessel doth sustain
In life's uncertain voyage, I will some kindness
do them:
I'll teach them to prevent wild Alcibiades'
wrath. 208

Sec. Sen. I like this well; he will return again.

Tim. I have a tree which grows here in my
close,
That mine own use invites me to cut down,
And shortly must I fell it; tell my friends, 212
Tell Athens, in the sequence of degree,
From high to low throughout, that whoso
please
To stop affliction, let him take his haste,
Come hither, ere my tree hath felt the axe, 216
And hang himself. I pray you, do my greeting.

Flav. Trouble him no further; thus you still
shall find him.

Tim. Come not to me again; but say to
Athens,
Timon hath made his everlasting mansion 220
Upon the beached verge of the salt flood;
Who once a day with his embossed froth
The turbulent surge shall cover: thither come,
And let my grave-stone be your oracle. 224
Lips, let sour words go by and language end:
What is amiss plague and infection mend!
Graves only be men's works and death their
gain!
Sun, hide thy beams! Timon hath done his
reign. [*Exit.*

First Sen. His discontents are unremovably
Coupled to nature.

Sec. Sen. Our hope in him is dead: let us
return,
And strain what other means is left unto us 232
In our dear peril.

First Sen. It requires swift foot. [*Exeunt.*

SCENE II.—*Before the Walls of Athens.*

Enter two Senators *and a* Messenger.

First Sen. Thou hast painfully discover'd:
are his files
As full as thy report?

Mess. I have spoke the least;
Besides, his expedition promises
Present approach. 4

Sec. Sen. We stand much hazard if they
bring not Timon.

Mess. I met a courier, one mine ancient
friend,
Whom, though in general part we were oppos'd,
Yet our old love made a particular force, 8
And made us speak like friends: this man was
riding
From Alcibiades to Timon's cave,
With letters of entreaty, which imported
His fellowship i' the cause against your city, 12
In part for his sake mov'd.

First Sen. Here come our brothers.

Enter Senators *from* TIMON.

Third Sen. No talk of Timon, nothing
him expect.
The enemies' drum is heard, and fearful scour
Doth choke the air with dust. In, and prepa
Ours is the fall, I fear; our foes the snare.
[*Exeu*

SCENE III.—*The Woods.* TIMON'S *Cave, an*
rude Tomb seen.

Enter a Soldier, *seeking* TIMON.

Sold. By all description this should be t
place.
Who's here? speak, ho! No answer! What
this?
Timon is dead, who hath outstretch'd his spa
Some beast rear'd this; here does not live
man.
Dead, sure; and this his grave. What's on t
tomb
I cannot read; the character I'll take with wa
Our captain hath in every figure skill;
An ag'd interpreter, though young in days.
Before proud Athens he's set down by this,
Whose fall the mark of his ambition is. [*Ex*

SCENE IV.—*Before the Walls of Athens.*

Trumpets sound. Enter ALCIBIADES *with hi*
Powers.

Alcib. Sound to this coward and lascivio
town
Our terrible approach. [*A parley sounde*

Enter Senators, *on the Walls.*

Till now you have gone on, and fill'd the tin
With all licentious measure, making your wills
The scope of justice; till now myself and su
As slept within the shadow of your power
Have wander'd with our travers'd arms, a
breath'd
Our sufferance vainly. Now the time is flush,
When crouching marrow, in the bearer stron
Cries of itself, 'No more:' now breathless wro
Shall sit and pant in your great chairs of eas
And pursy insolence shall break his wind
With fear and horrid flight.

First Sen. Noble and youn
When thy first griefs were but a mere conce
Ere thou hadst power or we had cause of fea
We sent to thee, to give thy rages balm,
To wipe out our ingratitude with loves
Above their quantity.

Sec. Sen. So did we woo
Transformed Timon to our city's love
By humble message and by promis'd means: :
We were not all unkind, nor all deserve
The common stroke of war.

First Sen. These walls of ou
Were not erected by their hands from whom
You have receiv'd your grief; nor are they suc
That these great towers, trophies, and schoo
should fall
For private faults in them.

Sec. Sen.   Nor are they living
ho were the motives that you first went out;
ame that they wanted cunning in excess   28
ath broke their hearts. March, noble lord,
to our city with thy banners spread:
' decimation, and a tithed death,—
thy revenges hunger for that food   32
hich nature loathes,—take thou the destin'd
  tenth,
nd by the hazard of the spotted die
t die the spotted.
  First Sen.   All have not offended;
or those that were, it is not square to take   36
n those that are, revenges: crimes, like lands,
re not inherited. Then, dear countryman,
'ing in thy ranks, but leave without thy rage:
»are thy Athenian cradle, and those kin   40
hich in the bluster of thy wrath must fall
ith those that have offended. like a shepherd,
pproach the fold and cull th' infected forth,
it kill not all together.
  Sec. Sen.   What thou wilt,   44
hou rather shalt enforce it with thy smile
han hew to 't with thy sword.
  First Sen.   Set but thy foot
gainst our rampir'd gates, and they shall ope,
» thou wilt send thy gentle heart before,   48
o say thou 'lt enter friendly.
  Sec. Sen.   Throw thy glove,
r any token of thine honour else,
hat thou wilt use the wars as thy redress
nd not as our confusion, all thy powers   52
hall make their harbour in our town, till we
ave seal'd thy full desire.
  Alcib.   Then there 's my glove;
escend, and open thy uncharged ports:
hose enemies of Timon's and mine own   56
'hom you yourselves shall set out for reproof,

Fall, and no more; and, to atone your fears
With my more noble meaning, not a man
Shall pass his quarter, or offend the stream   60
Of regular justice in your city's bounds,
But shall be render'd to your public laws
At heaviest answer.
  Both.   'Tis most nobly spoken.
  Alcib. Descend, and keep your words.   64
  [*The* Senators *descend, and open the gates.*

Enter a Soldier.

  Sold. My noble general, Timon is dead;
Entomb'd upon the very hem o' the sea:
And on his grave-stone this insculpture, which
With wax I brought away, whose soft impression
Interprets for my poor ignorance.   69
  *Alcib. Here lies a wretched corse, of wretched
    soul bereft:*
*Seek not my name: a plague consume you wicked
    caitiffs left!*
*Here lie I, Timon; who, alive, all living men did
    hate:*   72
*Pass by, and curse thy fill; but pass and stay not
    here thy gait.*
These well express in thee thy latter spirits:
Though thou abhorr'dst in us our human griefs,
Scorn'dst our brain's flow and those our drop-
    lets which   76
From niggard nature fall, yet rich conceit
Taught thee to make vast Neptune weep for aye
On thy low grave, on faults forgiven. Dead
Is noble Timon; of whose memory   80
Hereafter more. Bring me into your city,
And I will use the olive with my sword;
Make war breed peace; make peace stint war;
    make each
Prescribe to other as each other's leech.   84
Let our drums strike.   [*Exeunt.*

JULIUS CÆSAR

DRAMATIS PERSONÆ

JULIUS CÆSAR.
OCTAVIUS CÆSAR,
MARCUS ANTONIUS,
M. ÆMILIUS LEPIDUS,
} Triumvirs after the Death of Julius Cæsar.

CICERO,
PUBLIUS,
POPILIUS LENA,
} Senators.

MARCUS BRUTUS,
CASSIUS,
CASCA,
TREBONIUS,
LIGARIUS,
DECIUS BRUTUS,
METELLUS CIMBER,
CINNA,
} Conspirators against Julius Cæsar.

FLAVIUS and MARULLUS, Tribunes.
ARTEMIDORUS, a Sophist of Cnidos.
A Soothsayer.
CINNA, a Poet.
Another Poet.
LUCILIUS, TITINIUS, MESSALA, Young CATO, and VOLUM-
NIUS; Friends to Brutus and Cassius.
VARRO, CLITUS, CLAUDIUS, STRATO, LUCIUS, DARDA-
NIUS; Servants to Brutus.
PINDARUS, Servant to Cassius.

CALPHURNIA, Wife to Cæsar.
PORTIA, Wife to Brutus.

Senators, Citizens, Guards, Attendants, &c.

SCENE.—*During a great part of the Play, at* Rome; *afterwards, Sardis and near Philippi.*

ACT I

SCENE I.—*Rome. A Street.*

Enter FLAVIUS, MARULLUS, *and certain*
Commoners.

Flav. Hence! home, you idle creatures, get
you home:
Is this a holiday? What! know you not,
Being mechanical, you ought not walk
Upon a labouring day without the sign   4
Of your profession? Speak, what trade art thou?
First Com. Why, sir, a carpenter.
Mar. Where is thy leather apron, and thy
rule?
What dost thou with thy best apparel on?   8
You, sir, what trade are you?
Second Com. Truly, sir, in respect of a fine
workman, I am but, as you would say, a cobbler.
Mar. But what trade art thou? Answer me
directly.   12
Sec. Com. A trade, sir, that, I hope, I may
use with a safe conscience; which is, indeed, sir,
a mender of bad soles.
Mar. What trade, thou knave? thou naughty
knave, what trade?   16
Sec. Com. Nay, I beseech you, sir, be not out
with me: yet, if you be out, sir, I can mend you.
Mar. What meanest thou by that? Mend
me, thou saucy fellow!   20
Sec. Com. Why, sir, cobble you.
Flav. Thou art a cobbler, art thou?
Sec. Com. Truly, sir, all that I live by is with
the awl: I meddle with no tradesman's matters,
nor women's matters, but with awl. I am, indeed, sir, a surgeon to old shoes; when they are
in great danger, I recover them. As proper men
as ever trod upon neat's leather have gone upon
my handiwork.   29
Flav. But wherefore art not in thy shop to-
day?
Why dost thou lead these men about the streets?

Sec. Com. Truly, sir, to wear out their shoes,
to get myself into more work. But, indeed, sir,
we make holiday to see Cæsar and to rejoice in
his triumph.
Mar. Wherefore rejoice? What conquest
brings he home?   36
What tributaries follow him to Rome
To grace in captive bonds his chariot wheels?
You blocks, you stones, you worse than sense-
less things!
O you hard hearts, you cruel men of Rome,   40
Knew you not Pompey? Many a time and oft
Have you climb'd up to walls and battlements,
To towers and windows, yea, to chimney-tops,
Your infants in your arms, and there have sat
The livelong day, with patient expectation,   4
To see great Pompey pass the streets of Rome
And when you saw his chariot but appear,
Have you not made a universal shout,   4
That Tiber trembled underneath her banks,
To hear the replication of your sounds
Made in her concave shores?
And do you now put on your best attire?   5
And do you now cull out a holiday?
And do you now strew flowers in his way,
That comes in triumph over Pompey's blood?
Be gone!   5
Run to your houses, fall upon your knees,
Pray to the gods to intermit the plague
That needs must light on this ingratitude.
Flav. Go, go, good countrymen, and, for this
fault   6
Assemble all the poor men of your sort;
Draw them to Tiber banks, and weep your
tears
Into the channel, till the lowest stream
Do kiss the most exalted shores of all.   6
               [*Exeunt all the* Commoners.
See whe'r their basest metal be not mov'd;
They vanish tongue-tied in their guiltiness.
Go you down that way towards the Capitol;

his way will I. Disrobe the images   68
you do find them deck'd with ceremonies.
Mar. May we do so?
ou know it is the feast of Lupercal.
Flav. It is no matter; let no images   72
e hung with Cæsar's trophies. I'll about
nd drive away the vulgar from the streets:
o do you too where you perceive them thick.
hese growing feathers pluck'd from Cæsar's
        wing   76
Vill make him fly an ordinary pitch,
Tho else would soar above the view of men
nd keep us all in servile fearfulness. [*Exeunt.*

SCENE II.—*The Same. A Public Place.*

nter, in procession, with music, CÆSAR; AN-
TONY, *for the course;* CALPHURNIA, PORTIA,
DECIUS, CICERO, BRUTUS, CASSIUS, *and* CASCA;
*a great crowd following, among them a Sooth-
sayer.*

Cæs. Calphurnia!
Casca.   Peace, ho! Cæsar speaks.
                                [*Music ceases.*
Cæs.   Calphurnia!
Cal. Here, my lord.
Cæs. Stand you directly in Antonius' way
Vhen he doth run his course. Antonius!   4
Ant. Cæsar, my lord.
Cæs. Forget not, in your speed, Antonius,
o touch Calphurnia; for our elders say,
he barren, touched in this holy chase,   8
hake off their sterile curse.
Ant.   I shall remember:
Vhen Cæsar says 'Do this,' it is perform'd.
Cæs. Set on; and leave no ceremony out.
                                    [*Music.*
Sooth. Cæsar!   12
Cæs. Ha! Who calls?
Casca. Bid every noise be still: peace yet
    again!   [*Music ceases.*
Cæs. Who is it in the press that calls on me?
hear a tongue, shriller than all the music, 16
ry 'Cæsar.' Speak; Cæsar is turn'd to hear.
Sooth. Beware the ides of March.
Cæs.   What man is that?
Bru. A soothsayer bids you beware the ides
    of March.
Cæs. Set him before me; let me see his face.
Cas. Fellow, come from the throng; look
    upon Cæsar.   21
Cæs. What sayst thou to me now? Speak
    once again.
Sooth. Beware the ides of March.
Cæs. He is a dreamer; let us leave him: pass.
        [*Sennet. Exeunt all but* BRUTUS *and*
                        CASSIUS.
Cas. Will you go see the order of the course?
Bru. Not I.
Cas. I pray you, do.
Bru. I am not gamesome: I do lack some
    part   28
f that quick spirit that is in Antony.
et me not hinder, Cassius, your desires;
ll leave you.
Cas. Brutus, I do observe you now of late: 32

I have not from your eyes that gentleness
And show of love as I was wont to have:
You bear too stubborn and too strange a hand
Over your friend that loves you.
Bru.   Cassius,   36
Be not deceiv'd: if I have veil'd my look,
I turn the trouble of my countenance
Merely upon myself. Vexed I am
Of late with passions of some difference,   40
Conceptions only proper to myself,
Which give some soil perhaps to my behaviours;
But let not therefore my good friends be
            griev'd,—
Among which number, Cassius, be you one,—44
Nor construe any further my neglect,
Than that poor Brutus, with himself at war,
Forgets the shows of love to other men.
Cas. Then, Brutus, I have much mistook
    your passion;   48
By means whereof this breast of mine hath
    buried
Thoughts of great value, worthy cogitations.
Tell me, good Brutus, can you see your face?
Bru. No, Cassius; for the eye sees not itself,
But by reflection, by some other things.   53
Cas. 'Tis just:
And it is very much lamented, Brutus,
That you have no such mirrors as will turn   56
Your hidden worthiness into your eye,
That you might see your shadow. I have heard,
Where many of the best respect in Rome,—
Except immortal Cæsar,—speaking of Brutus.   61
And groaning underneath this age's yoke,
Have wish'd that noble Brutus had his eyes.
Bru. Into what dangers would you lead me,
    Cassius,
That you would have me seek into myself   64
For that which is not in me?
Cas. Therefore, good Brutus, be prepar'd to
    hear;
And, since you know you cannot see yourself
So well as by reflection, I, your glass,   68
Will modestly discover to yourself
That of yourself which you yet know not of.
And be not jealous on me, gentle Brutus:
Were I a common laugher, or did use   72
To stale with ordinary oaths my love
To every new protester; if you know
That I do fawn on men and hug them hard,
And after scandal them; or if you know   76
That I profess myself in banqueting
To all the rout, then hold me dangerous.
                            [*Flourish and shout.*
Bru. What means this shouting? I do fear
    the people
Choose Cæsar for their king.
Cas.   Ay, do you fear it? 80
Then must I think you would not have it so.
Bru. I would not, Cassius; yet I love him
    well.
But wherefore do you hold me here so long?
What is it that you would impart to me?   84
If it be aught toward the general good,
Set honour in one eye and death i' the other,
And I will look on both indifferently;
For let the gods so speed me as I love   88

The name of honour more than I fear death.

Cas. I know that virtue to be in you, Brutus,
As well as I do know your outward favour.
Well, honour is the subject of my story.   92
I cannot tell what you and other men
Think of this life; but, for my single self,
I had as lief not be as live to be
In awe of such a thing as I myself.   96
I was born free as Cæsar; so were you:
We both have fed as well, and we can both
Endure the winter's cold as well as he:
For once, upon a raw and gusty day,   100
The troubled Tiber chafing with her shores,
Cæsar said to me, 'Dar'st thou, Cassius, now
Leap in with me into this angry flood,
And swim to yonder point?' Upon the word,
Accoutred as I was, I plunged in   105
And bade him follow; so, indeed he did.
The torrent roar'd, and we did buffet it
With lusty sinews, throwing it aside   108
And stemming it with hearts of controversy;
But ere we could arrive the point propos'd,
Cæsar cried, 'Help me, Cassius, or I sink!'
I, as Æneas, our great ancestor,   112
Did from the flames of Troy upon his shoulder
The old Anchises bear, so from the waves of
    Tiber
Did I the tired Cæsar. And this man
Is now become a god, and Cassius is   116
A wretched creature and must bend his body
If Cæsar carelessly but nod on him.
He had a fever when he was in Spain,
And when the fit was on him, I did mark   120
How he did shake; 'tis true, this god did shake
His coward lips did from their colour fly,
And that same eye whose bend doth awe the
    world
Did lose his lustre; I did hear him groan;   124
Ay, and that tongue of his that bade the Romans
Mark him and write his speeches in their books,
Alas! it cried, 'Give me some drink, Titinius,'
As a sick girl. Ye gods, it doth amaze me,   128
A man of such a feeble temper should
So get the start of the majestic world,
And bear the palm alone. [*Flourish. Shout.*
Bru.   Another general shout!
I do believe that these applauses are   132
For some new honours that are heaped on
    Cæsar.

Cas. Why, man, he doth bestride the narrow
    world
Like a Colossus; and we petty men
Walk under his huge legs, and peep about   136
To find ourselves dishonourable graves.
Men at some time are masters of their fates:
The fault, dear Brutus, is not in our stars,
But in ourselves, that we are underlings.   140
Brutus and Cæsar: what should be in that
    'Cæsar'?
Why should that name be sounded more than
    yours?
Write them together, yours is as fair a name;
Sound them, it doth become the mouth as
    well;   144
Weigh them, it is as heavy; conjure with 'em,
'Brutus' will start a spirit as soon as 'Cæsar.'

Now, in the names of all the gods at once,
Upon what meat doth this our Cæsar feed,   148
That he is grown so great? Age, thou art sham'd!
Rome, thou hast lost the breed of noble bloods!
When went there by an age, since the great flood,
But it was fam'd with more than with one man?
When could they say, till now, that talk'd of
    Rome,   153
That her wide walls encompass'd but one man?
Now is it Rome indeed and room enough,
When there is in it but one only man.   156
O! you and I have heard our fathers say,
There was a Brutus once that would have
    brook'd
Th' eternal devil to keep his state in Rome
As easily as a king.   160
Bru. That you do love me, I am nothing
    jealous;
What you would work me to, I have some aim:
How I have thought of this and of these times,
I shall recount hereafter; for this present,   164
I would not, so with love I might entreat you,
Be any further mov'd. What you have said
I will consider; what you have to say
I will with patience hear, and find a time   168
Both meet to hear and answer such high things
Till then, my noble friend, chew upon this:
Brutus had rather be a villager
Than to repute himself a son of Rome   172
Under these hard conditions as this time
Is like to lay upon us.
Cas.   I am glad
That my weak words have struck but thus much
    show
Of fire from Brutus.   176
Bru. The games are done and Cæsar is re
    turning.
Cas. As they pass by, pluck Casca by th
    sleeve,
And he will, after his sour fashion, tell you
What hath proceeded worthy note to-day.   180

Re-enter CÆSAR *and his Train.*

Bru. I will do so. But, look you, Cassius,
The angry spot doth glow on Cæsar's brow,
And all the rest look like a chidden train:
Calphurnia's cheek is pale, and Cicero   184
Looks with such ferret and such fiery eyes
As we have seen him in the Capitol,
Being cross'd in conference by some senator
Cas. Casca will tell us what the matter is.   188
Cæs. Antonius!
Ant. Cæsar.
Cæs. Let me have men about me that are fa
Sleek-headed men and such as sleep o' night
Yond Cassius has a lean and hungry look;   19
He thinks too much: such men are dangerou
Ant. Fear him not, Cæsar, he's not dange
    ous;
He is a noble Roman, and well given.   19
Cæs. Would he were fatter! but I fear hi
    not:
Yet if my name were liable to fear,
I do not know the man I should avoid
So soon as that spare Cassius. He reads much
He is a great observer, and he looks   2

uite through the deeds of men; he loves no
  plays,
s thou dost, Antony; he hears no music;
ldom he smiles, and smiles in such a sort 204
s if he mock'd himself, and scorn'd his spirit
hat could be mov'd to smile at any thing.
ch men as he be never at heart's ease
hiles they behold a greater than themselves,
nd therefore are they very dangerous.   209
rather tell thee what is to be fear'd
han what I fear, for always I am Cæsar.
ome on my right hand, for this ear is deaf, 212
nd tell me truly what thou think'st of him.

    [*Sennet. Exeunt* CÆSAR *and his Train.*
           CASCA *stays behind.*
Casca. You pull'd me by the cloak; would
  you speak with me?
Bru. Ay, Casca; tell us what hath chanc'd
  to-day,
hat Cæsar looks so sad.   216
Casca. Why, you were with him, were you
  not?
Bru. I should not then ask Casca what had
  chanc'd.
Casca. Why, there was a crown offered him;
d, being offered him, he put it by with the
ck of his hand, thus; and then the people fell
  shouting.
Bru. What was the second noise for?
Casca. Why, for that too.   224
Cas. They shouted thrice: what was the last
  cry for?
Casca. Why, for that too.
Bru. Was the crown offered him thrice?
Casca. Ay, marry, was't, and he put it by
rice, every time gentler than other; and at every
tting-by mine honest neighbours shouted.
Cas. Who offered him the crown?
Casca. Why, Antony.   232
Bru. Tell us the manner of it, gentle Casca.
Casca. I can as well be hanged as tell the
anner of it: it was mere foolery; I did not
ark it. I saw Mark Antony offer him a crown;
t 'twas not a crown neither, 'twas one of these
ronets; and, as I told you, he put it by once;
ut, for all that, to my thinking, he would fain
ve had it. Then he offered it to him again;
en he put it by again; but, to my thinking, he
as very loath to lay his fingers off it. And then
e offered it the third time; he put it the third
me by; and still as he refused it the rabblement
outed and clapped their chopped hands, and
rew up their sweaty night-caps, and uttered
ch a deal of stinking breath because Cæsar
efused the crown, that it had almost choked
æsar; for he swounded and fell down at it: and
r mine own part, I durst not laugh, for fear of
pening my lips and receiving the bad air.
Cas. But soft, I pray you: what! did Cæsar
  swound?   252
Casca. He fell down in the market-place, and
amed at mouth, and was speechless.
Bru. 'Tis very like: he hath the falling-sickness.
Cas. No, Cæsar hath it not; but you, and I,
nd honest Casca, we have the falling-sickness.

Casca. I know not what you mean by that;
but I am sure Cæsar fell down. If the tag-rag
people did not clap him and hiss him, according
as he pleased and displeased them, as they use
to do the players in the theatre, I am no true
man.   263
Bru. What said he, when he came unto himself?
Casca. Marry, before he fell down, when he
perceiv'd the common herd was glad he refused
the crown, he plucked me ope his doublet and
offered them his throat to cut. An I had been a
man of any occupation, if I would not have taken
him at a word, I would I might go to hell among
the rogues. And so he fell. When he came to
himself again, he said, if he had done or said
any thing amiss, he desired their worships to
think it was his infirmity. Three or four
wenches, where I stood, cried, 'Alas! good soul,'
and forgave him with all their hearts: but
there's no heed to be taken of them; if Cæsar
had stabbed their mothers, they would have
done no less.   279
Bru. And after that he came, thus sad, away?
Casca. Ay.
Cas. Did Cicero say any thing?
Casca. Ay, he spoke Greek.
Cas. To what effect?   284
Casca. Nay, an I tell you that, I'll ne'er look
you i' the face again; but those that understood
him smiled at one another and shook their
heads; but, for mine own part, it was Greek to
me. I could tell you more news too; Marullus
and Flavius, for pulling scarfs off Cæsar's images,
are put to silence. Fare you well. There was
more foolery yet, if I could remember it.   292
Cas. Will you sup with me to-night, Casca?
Casca. No, I am promised forth.
Cas. Will you dine with me to-morrow?
Casca. Ay, if I be alive, and your mind hold,
and your dinner worth the eating.   297
Cas. Good; I will expect you.
Casca. Do so. Farewell, both.   [*Exit.*
Bru. What a blunt fellow is this grown to
  be!   300
He was quick mettle when he went to school.
Cas. So is he now in execution
Of any bold or noble enterprise,
However he puts on this tardy form.   304
This rudeness is a sauce to his good wit,
Which gives men stomach to digest his words
With better appetite.
Bru. And so it is. For this time I will leave
  you: 308
To-morrow, if you please to speak with me,
I will come home to you; or, if you will,
Come home to me, and I will wait for you.
Cas. I will do so: till then, think of the world.
                  [*Exit* BRUTUS.
Well, Brutus, thou art noble; yet, I see,   313
Thy honourable metal may be wrought
From that it is dispos'd: therefore 'tis meet
That noble minds keep ever with their likes; 316
For who so firm that cannot be seduced?
Cæsar doth bear me hard; but he loves Brutus:
If I were Brutus now and he were Cassius

He should not humour me. I will this night,
In several hands, in at his windows throw, 321
As if they came from several citizens,
Writings all tending to the great opinion
That Rome holds of his name; wherein ob-
scurely   324
Cæsar's ambition shall be glanced at:
And after this let Cæsar seat him sure;
For we will shake him, or worse days endure.
                                     [*Exit.*

SCENE III.—*The Same. A Street.*

*Thunder and lightning. Enter, from opposite
sides,* CASCA, *with his sword drawn, and*
CICERO.

Cic. Good even, Casca: brought you Cæsar
home?
Why are you breathless? and why stare you so?
  Casca. Are not you mov'd, when all the sway
    of earth
Shakes like a thing unfirm? O Cicero!   4
I have seen tempests, when the scolding winds
Have riv'd the knotty oaks; and I have seen
The ambitious ocean swell and rage and foam,
To be exalted with the threat'ning clouds: 8
But never till to-night, never till now,
Did I go through a tempest dropping fire.
Either there is a civil strife in heaven,
Or else the world, too saucy with the gods, 12
Incenses them to send destruction.
  Cic. Why, saw you any thing more wonder-
ful?
  Casca. A common slave—you know him well
    by sight—
Held up his left hand, which did flame and burn
Like twenty torches join'd; and yet his hand, 17
Not sensible of fire, remain'd unscorch'd.
Besides,—I have not since put up my sword,—
Against the Capitol I met a lion,   20
Who glar'd upon me, and went surly by,
Without annoying me; and there were drawn
Upon a heap a hundred ghastly women,
Transformed with their fear, who swore they
    saw   24
Men all in fire walk up and down the streets.
And yesterday the bird of night did sit,
Even at noon-day, upon the market-place,
Hooting and shrieking. When these prodigies
Do so conjointly meet, let not men say   29
'These are their reasons, they are natural;'
For, I believe, they are portentous things
Unto the climate that they point upon.   32
  Cic. Indeed, it is a strange-disposed time:
But men may construe things after their fashion,
Clean from the purpose of the things them-
selves.
Comes Cæsar to the Capitol to-morrow?   36
  Casca. He doth; for he did bid Antonius
Send word to you he would be there to-morrow.
  Cic. Good-night then, Casca: this disturbed
    sky
Is not to walk in.
  Casca.   Farewell, Cicero. [*Exit* CICERO.

Enter CASSIUS.

Cas. Who's there?

Casca.   A Roman.
Cas.   Casca, by your voice.
Casca. Your ear is good. Cassius, what night
    is this!
Cas. A very pleasing night to honest men.
Casca. Who ever knew the heavens menace
    so?
Cas. Those that have known the earth so full
    of faults.
For my part, I have walk'd about the streets,
Submitting me unto the perilous night,
And, thus unbraced, Casca, as you see,   48
Have bar'd my bosom to the thunder-stone;
And, when the cross blue lightning seem'd to
    open
The breast of heaven, I did present myself
Even in the aim and very flash of it.   52
  Casca. But wherefore did you so much tempt
    the heavens?
It is the part of men to fear and tremble
When the most mighty gods by tokens send
Such dreadful heralds to astonish us.   56
  Cas. You are dull, Casca, and those sparks of
    life
That should be in a Roman you do want,
Or else you use not. You look pale, and gaze,
And put on fear, and cast yourself in wonder, 60
To see the strange impatience of the heavens;
But if you would consider the true cause
Why all these fires, why all these gliding ghosts,
Why birds and beasts, from quality and kind,
Why old men, fools, and children calculate; 65
Why all these things change from their ordi-
nance,
Their natures, and pre-formed faculties,
To monstrous quality, why, you shall find 68
That heaven hath infus'd them with these spirits
To make them instruments of fear and warning
Unto some monstrous state.
Now could I, Casca, name to thee a man   72
Most like this dreadful night,
That thunders, lightens, opens graves, and
    roars
As doth the lion in the Capitol,
A man no mightier than thyself or me   76
In personal action, yet prodigious grown
And fearful as these strange eruptions are.
  Casca. 'Tis Cæsar that you mean; is it not,
    Cassius?
  Cas. Let it be who it is: for Romans now 80
Have thews and limbs like to their ancestors;
But, woe the while! our fathers' minds are dead,
And we are govern'd with our mothers' spirits;
Our yoke and sufferance show us womanish. 84
  Casca. Indeed, they say the senators to-mor-
row
Mean to establish Cæsar as a king;
And he shall wear his crown by sea and land,
In every place, save here in Italy.   88
  Cas. I know where I will wear this dagger
    then;
Cassius from bondage will deliver Cassius:
Therein, ye gods, you make the weak most
    strong;
Therein, ye gods, you tyrants do defeat: 92
Nor stony tower, nor walls of beaten brass,

or airless dungeon, nor strong links of iron,
an be retentive to the strength of spirit;
ut life, being weary of those worldly bars, 96
ever lacks power to dismiss itself.
  I know this, know all the world besides,
hat part of tyranny that I do bear
can shake off at pleasure.   [*Thunder still.*
  Casca.   So can I: 100
o every bondman in his own hand bears
he power to cancel his captivity.
  Cas. And why should Cæsar be a tyrant then?
oor man! I know he would not be a wolf 104
ut that he sees the Romans are but sheep;
te were no lion were not Romans hinds.
hose that with haste will make a mighty fire
egin it with weak straws; what trash is Rome,
Vhat rubbish, and what offal, when it serves 109
or the base matter to illuminate
o vile a thing as Cæsar! But, O grief!
Vhere hast thou led me? I, perhaps, speak this
efore a willing bondman; then I know   113
Iy answer must be made: but I am arm'd,
.nd dangers are to me indifferent.
  Casca. You speak to Casca, and to such a
      man   116
hat is no fleering tell-tale. Hold, my hand:
e factious for redress of all these griefs,
.nd I will set this foot of mine as far
.s who goes furthest.
  Cas.   There's a bargain made. 120
Now know you, Casca, I have mov'd already
ome certain of the noblest-minded Romans
'o undergo with me an enterprise
Of honourable-dangerous consequence;   124
.nd I do know by this they stay for me
n Pompey's porch: for now, this fearful night,
'here is no stir, or walking in the streets;
.nd the complexion of the element   128
n favour's like the work we have in hand,
Most bloody, fiery, and most terrible.
  Casca. Stand close awhile, for here comes
      one in haste.
  Cas. 'Tis Cinna; I do know him by his gait:
Ie is a friend.

          Enter CINNA.

          Cinna, where haste you so? 133
  Cin. To find out you. Who's that? Metellus
      Cimber?
  Cas. No, it is Casca; one incorporate
'o our attempts. Am I not stay'd for, Cinna?
  Cin. I am glad on't. What a fearful night is
      this!   137
'here's two or three of us have seen strange
      sights.
  Cas. Am I not stay'd for? Tell me.
  Cin.   Yes, you are.
O Cassius! if you could   140
But win the noble Brutus to our party—
  Cas. Be you content. Good Cinna, take this
      paper,
.nd look you lay it in the prætor's chair,
Vhere Brutus may but find it; and throw this
n at his window; set this up with wax   145
Jpon old Brutus' statue: all this done,
Repair to Pompey's porch, where you shall find us.

Is Decius Brutus and Trebonius there?   148
  Cin. All but Metellus Cimber; and he's gone
To seek you at your house. Well, I will hie,
And so bestow these papers as you bade me.
  Cas. That done, repair to Pompey's theatre.
                              [*Exit* CINNA.
Come, Casca, you and I will yet ere day 153
See Brutus at his house: three parts of him
Is ours already, and the man entire
Upon the next encounter yields him ours. 156
  Casca. O! he sits high in all the people's
      hearts:
And that which would appear offence in us,
His countenance, like richest alchemy,
Will change to virtue and to worthiness. 160
  Cas. Him and his worth and our great need
      of him
You have right well conceited. Let us go,
For it is after midnight; and ere day
We will awake him and be sure of him.   164
                              [*Exeunt.*

            ACT II

  SCENE I.—*Rome.* BRUTUS' *Orchard.*

          Enter BRUTUS.

  Bru. What, Lucius! ho!
I cannot, by the progress of the stars,
Give guess how near to day. Lucius, I say!
I would it were my fault to sleep so soundly. 4
When, Lucius, when! Awake, I say! what,
      Lucius!

          Enter LUCIUS.

  Luc. Call'd you, my lord?
  Bru. Get me a taper in my study, Lucius:
When it is lighted, come and call me here. 8
  Luc. I will, my lord.   [*Exit.*
  Bru. It must be by his death: and, for my
      part,
I know no personal cause to spurn at him,
But for the general. He would be crown'd: 12
How that might change his nature, there's the
      question:
It is the bright day that brings forth the adder;
And that craves wary walking. Crown him?—
      that!
And then, I grant, we put a sting in him, 16
That at his will he may do danger with.
The abuse of greatness is when it disjoins
Remorse from power; and, to speak truth of
      Cæsar,
I have not known when his affections sway'd 20
More than his reason. But 'tis a common proof,
That lowliness is young ambition's ladder,
Whereto the climber-upward turns his face;
But when he once attains the upmost round, 24
He then unto the ladder turns his back,
Looks in the clouds, scorning the base degrees
By which he did ascend. So Cæsar may:
Then, lest he may, prevent. And, since the
      quarrel   28
Will bear no colour for the thing he is,
Fashion it thus; that what he is, augmented,
Would run to these and these extremities;
And therefore think him as a serpent's egg 32

Which, hatch'd, would, as his kind, grow mis-
    chievous,
And kill him in the shell.

Re-enter LUCIUS.

Luc. The taper burneth in your closet, sir.
Searching the window for a flint, I found   36
This paper, thus seal'd up; and I am sure
It did not lie there when I went to bed.
Bru. Get you to bed again; it is not day.
Is not to-morrow, boy, the ides of March?   40
Luc. I know not, sir.
Bru. Look in the calendar, and bring me
    word.
Luc. I will, sir.   [*Exit.*
Bru. The exhalations whizzing in the air 44
Give so much light that I may read by them.
                           [*Opens the letter.*
Brutus, thou sleep'st: awake and see thyself.
Shall Rome, &c., speak, strike, redress!
Brutus, thou sleep'st: awake!   48
Such instigations have been often dropp'd
Where I have took them up.
'Shall Rome, &c.' Thus must I piece it out:
Shall Rome stand under one man's awe? What,
    Rome?   52
My ancestors did from the streets of Rome
The Tarquin drive, when he was call'd a king.
'Speak, strike, redress!' Am I entreated
To speak, and strike? O Rome! I make thee
    promise;   56
If the redress will follow, thou receiv'st
Thy full petition at the hand of Brutus!

Re-enter LUCIUS.

Luc. Sir, March is wasted fourteen days.
                           [*Knocking within.*
Bru. 'Tis good. Go to the gate: somebody
    knocks.   [*Exit* LUCIUS.
Since Cassius first did whet me against Cæsar,
I have not slept.
Between the acting of a dreadful thing
And the first motion, all the interim is   64
Like a phantasma, or a hideous dream:
The genius and the mortal instruments
Are then in council; and the state of man,
Like to a little kingdom, suffers then   68
The nature of an insurrection.

Re-enter LUCIUS.

Luc. Sir, 'tis your brother Cassius at the
    door,
Who doth desire to see you.
Bru.   Is he alone?
Luc. No, sir, there are more with him.
Bru.   Do you know them? 72
Luc. No, sir; their hats are pluck'd about
    their ears,
And half their faces buried in their cloaks,
That by no means I may discover them
By any mark of favour.
Bru.   Let 'em enter.   76
                           [*Exit* LUCIUS.
They are the faction. O conspiracy!
Sham'st thou to show thy dangerous brow by
    night,

When evils are most free? O! then by day   78
Where wilt thou find a cavern dark enough   80
To mask thy monstrous visage? Seek none,
    conspiracy;
Hide it in smiles and affability:
For if thou path, thy native semblance on,
Not Erebus itself were dim enough   84
To hide thee from prevention.

Enter the Conspirators, CASSIUS, CASCA, DECIUS,
    CINNA, METELLUS CIMBER, *and* TREBONIUS.

Cas. I think we are too bold upon your rest:
Good morrow, Brutus; do we trouble you?
Bru. I have been up this hour, awake all
    night.   88
Know I these men that come along with you?
Cas. Yes, every man of them; and no man
    here
But honours you; and every one doth wish
You had but that opinion of yourself   92
Which every noble Roman bears of you.
This is Trebonius.
Bru.   He is welcome hither.
Cas. This, Decius Brutus.
Bru.   He is welcome too.
Cas. This, Casca; this, Cinna;   96
And this, Metellus Cimber.
Bru.   They are all welcome.
What watchful cares do interpose themselves
Betwixt your eyes and night?
Cas. Shall I entreat a word?   100
          [BRUTUS *and* CASSIUS *whisper.*
Dec. Here lies the east: doth not the day
    break here?
Casca. No.
Cin. O! pardon, sir, it doth; and yon grey
    lines
That fret the clouds are messengers of day. 104
Casca. You shall confess that you are both
    deceiv'd.
Here, as I point my sword, the sun arises;
Which is a great way growing on the south,
Weighing the youthful season of the year. 108
Some two months hence up higher toward the
    north
He first presents his fire; and the high east
Stands, as the Capitol, directly here.
Bru. Give me your hands all over, one by
    one.   112
Cas. And let us swear our resolution.
Bru. No, not an oath: if not the face of men,
The sufferance of our souls, the time's abuse,
If these be motives weak, break off betimes, 116
And every man hence to his idle bed;
So let high-sighted tyranny range on,
Till each man drop by lottery. But if these,
As I am sure they do, bear fire enough   120
To kindle cowards and to steel with valour
The melting spirits of women, then, country-
    men,
What need we any spur but our own cause
To prick us to redress? what other bond   124
Than secret Romans, that have spoke the word
And will not palter? and what other oath
Than honesty to honesty engag'd,
That this shall be, or we will fall for it? 128

Swear priests and cowards and men cautelous,
Old feeble carrions and such suffering souls
That welcome wrongs; unto bad causes swear
Such creatures as men doubt; but do not stain
The even virtue of our enterprise, 133
Nor th' insuppressive mettle of our spirits,
To think that or our cause or our performance
Did need an oath; when every drop of blood 136
That every Roman bears, and nobly bears,
Is guilty of a several bastardy,
If he do break the smallest particle
Of any promise that hath pass'd from him. 140
  Cas. But what of Cicero? Shall we sound
him?
I think he will stand very strong with us.
  Casca. Let us not leave him out.
  Cin.   No, by no means.
  Met. O! let us have him; for his silver hairs
Will purchase us a good opinion 145
And buy men's voices to commend our deeds:
It shall be said his judgment rul'd our hands;
Our youths and wildness shall no whit appear,
But all be buried in his gravity. 149
  Bru. O! name him not: let us not break with
him;
For he will never follow any thing
That other men begin.
  Cas.   Then leave him out. 152
  Casca. Indeed he is not fit.
  Dec. Shall no man else be touch'd but only
Cæsar?
  Cas. Decius, well urg'd. I think it is not meet,
Mark Antony, so well belov'd of Cæsar, 156
Should outlive Cæsar: we shall find of him
A shrewd contriver; and, you know, his means,
If he improve them, may well stretch so far
As to annoy us all; which to prevent, 160
Let Antony and Cæsar fall together.
  Bru. Our course will seem too bloody, Caius
Cassius,
To cut the head off and then hack the limbs,
Like wrath in death and envy afterwards; 164
For Antony is but a limb of Cæsar.
Let us be sacrificers, but not butchers, Caius.
We all stand up against the spirit of Cæsar;
And in the spirit of men there is no blood: 168
O! then that we could come by Cæsar's spirit,
And not dismember Cæsar. But, alas!
Cæsar must bleed for it. And, gentle friends,
Let's kill him boldly, but not wrathfully; 172
Let's carve him as a dish fit for the gods,
Not hew him as a carcass fit for hounds:
And let our hearts, as subtle masters do,
Stir up their servants to an act of rage, 176
And after seem to chide 'em. This shall make
Our purpose necessary and not envious;
Which so appearing to the common eyes,
We shall be call'd purgers, not murderers. 180
And, for Mark Antony, think not of him;
For he can do no more than Cæsar's arm
When Cæsar's head is off.
  Cas.   Yet I fear him;
For in the engrafted love he bears to Cæsar— 184
  Bru. Alas! good Cassius, do not think of
him:
If he love Cæsar, all that he can do

Is to himself, take thought and die for Cæsar:
And that were much he should; for he is given
To sports, to wildness, and much company. 189
  Treb. There is no fear in him; let him not
die:
For he will live, and laugh at this hereafter.
                        [*Clock strikes.*
  Bru. Peace! count the clock.
  Cas.   The clock hath stricken three. 192
  Treb. 'Tis time to part.
  Cas.   But it is doubtful yet
Whether Cæsar will come forth to-day or no;
For he is superstitious grown of late,
Quite from the main opinion he held once 196
Of fantasy, of dreams, and ceremonies.
It may be, these apparent prodigies,
The unaccustom'd terror of this night,
And the persuasion of his augurers, 200
May hold him from the Capitol to-day.
  Dec. Never fear that: if he be so resolv'd,
I can o'ersway him; for he loves to hear
That unicorns may be betray'd with trees, 204
And bears with glasses, elephants with holes,
Lions with toils, and men with flatterers;
But when I tell him he hates flatterers,
He says he does, being then most flattered. 208
Let me work;
For I can give his humour the true bent,
And I will bring him to the Capitol.
  Cas. Nay, we will all of us be there to fetch
him. 212
  Bru. By the eighth hour: is that the utter-
most?
  Cin. Be that the uttermost, and fail not then.
  Met. Caius Ligarius doth bear Cæsar hard,
Who rated him for speaking well of Pompey:
I wonder none of you have thought of him. 217
  Bru. Now, good Metellus, go along by him:
He loves me well, and I have given him reasons;
Send him but hither, and I'll fashion him. 220
  Cas. The morning comes upon's: we'll leave
you, Brutus.
And, friends, disperse yourselves; but all re-
member
What you have said, and show yourselves true
Romans.
  Bru. Good gentlemen, look fresh and merrily;
Let not our looks put on our purposes, 225
But bear it as our Roman actors do,
With untir'd spirits and formal constancy:
And so good morrow to you every one. 228
              [*Exeunt all except* BRUTUS.
Boy! Lucius! Fast asleep? It is no matter;
Enjoy the honey-heavy dew of slumber:
Thou hast no figures nor no fantasies
Which busy care draws in the brains of men;
Therefore thou sleep'st so sound. 233

           Enter PORTIA.

  Por.   Brutus, my lord!
  Bru. Portia, what mean you? Wherefore rise
you now?
It is not for your health thus to commit
Your weak condition to the raw cold morning.
  Por. Nor for yours neither. You've un-
gently, Brutus, 237

Stole from my bed; and yesternight at supper
You suddenly arose, and walk'd about,
Musing and sighing, with your arms across, 240
And when I ask'd you what the matter was,
You star'd upon me with ungentle looks.
I urg'd you further; then you scratch'd your
  head,
And too impatiently stamp'd with your foot; 244
Yet I insisted, yet you answer'd not,
But, with an angry wafture of your hand,
Gave sign for me to leave you. So I did,
Fearing to strengthen that impatience   248
Which seem'd too much enkindled, and withal
Hoping it was but an effect of humour,
Which sometime hath his hour with every man.
It will not let you eat, nor talk, nor sleep, 252
And could it work so much upon your shape
As it hath much prevail'd on your condition,
I should not know you, Brutus. Dear my lord,
Make me acquainted with your cause of grief.
  Bru. I am not well in health, and that is all. 257
  Por. Brutus is wise, and were he not in health,
He would embrace the means to come by it.
  Bru. Why, so I do. Good Portia, go to
bed.   260
  Por. Is Brutus sick, and is it physical
To walk unbraced and suck up the humours
Of the dank morning? What! is Brutus sick,
And will he steal out of his wholesome bed 264
To dare the vile contagion of the night,
And tempt the rheumy and unpurged air
To add unto his sickness? No, my Brutus;
You have some sick offence within your mind,
Which, by the right and virtue of my place, 269
I ought to know of; and, upon my knees,
I charm you, by my once-commended beauty,
By all your vows of love, and that great vow 272
Which did incorporate and make us one,
That you unfold to me, your self, your half,
Why are you heavy, and what men to-night
Have had resort to you; for here have been 276
Some six or seven, who did hide their faces
Even from darkness.
  Bru.   Kneel not, gentle Portia.
  Por. I should not need, if you were gentle
    Brutus.
Within the bond of marriage, tell me, Brutus,
Is it excepted, I should know no secrets   281
That appertain to you? Am I yourself
But, as it were, in sort of limitation,
To keep with you at meals, comfort your bed,
And talk to you sometimes? Dwell I but in the
  suburbs   285
Of your good pleasure? If it be no more,
Portia is Brutus' harlot, not his wife.
  Bru. You are my true and honourable
    wife,   288
As dear to me as are the ruddy drops
That visit my sad heart.
  Por. If this were true then should I know
    this secret.
I grant I am a woman, but, withal,   292
A woman that Lord Brutus took to wife;
I grant I am a woman, but, withal,
A woman well-reputed, Cato's daughter.
Think you I am no stronger than my sex,   296

Being so father'd and so husbanded?
Tell me your counsels, I will not disclose 'em
I have made strong proof of my constancy,
Giving myself a voluntary wound   300
Here, in the thigh: can I bear that with patience
And not my husband's secrets?
  Bru.   O ye gods!
Render me worthy of this noble wife.
                         [*Knocking within*
Hark, hark! one knocks. Portia, go in awhile
And by and by thy bosom shall partake   305
The secrets of my heart.
All my engagements I will construe to thee,
All the charactery of my sad brows.   308
Leave me with haste.   [*Exit* PORTIA
                    Lucius, who's that knocks?

    Re-enter LUCIUS *with* LIGARIUS.

  Luc. Here is a sick man that would speak
with you.
  Bru. Caius Ligarius, that Metellus spoke of.
Boy, stand aside. Caius Ligarius! how?   312
  Lig. Vouchsafe good morrow from a feeble
tongue.
  Bru. O! what a time have you chose out,
brave Caius,
To wear a kerchief. Would you were not sick.
  Lig. I am not sick if Brutus have in hand
Any exploit worthy the name of honour.   317
  Bru. Such an exploit have I in hand, Ligarius,
Had you a healthful ear to hear of it.
  Lig. By all the gods that Romans bow before
I here discard my sickness. Soul of Rome! 321
Brave son, deriv'd from honourable loins!
Thou, like an exorcist, hast conjur'd up
My mortified spirit. Now bid me run,   324
And I will strive with things impossible;
Yea, get the better of them. What's to do?
  Bru. A piece of work that will make sick men
whole.
  Lig. But are not some whole that we must
make sick?   328
  Bru. That must we also. What it is, my Caius,
I shall unfold to thee as we are going
To whom it must be done.
  Lig.   Set on your foot,
And with a heart new-fir'd I follow you, 332
To do I know not what; but it sufficeth
That Brutus leads me on.
  Bru.   Follow me then.
                              [*Exeunt.*

SCENE II.—*The Same.* CÆSAR'S *House.*

    Thunder and lightning. Enter CÆSAR
        in his night-gown.

  Cæs. Nor heaven nor earth have been at
peace to-night:
Thrice hath Calphurnia in her sleep cried out,
'Help, ho! They murder Cæsar!' Who's within?

        Enter a Servant.
  Serv. My lord!   4
  Cæs. Go bid the priests do present sacrifice,
And bring me their opinions of success.
  Serv. I will, my lord.   [*Exit.*

Enter CALPHURNIA.

Cal. What mean you, Cæsar? Think you to
walk forth? 8
You shall not stir out of your house to-day.
Cæs. Cæsar shall forth: the things that
threaten'd me
Ne'er look'd but on my back; when they shall
see
The face of Cæsar, they are vanished. 12
Cal. Cæsar, I never stood on ceremonies,
Yet now they fright me. There is one within,
Besides the things that we have heard and seen,
Recounts most horrid sights seen by the watch.
A lioness hath whelped in the streets; 17
And graves have yawn'd and yielded up their
dead;
Fierce fiery warriors fought upon the clouds,
In ranks and squadrons and right form of war,
Which drizzled blood upon the Capitol; 21
The noise of battle hurtled in the air,
Horses did neigh, and dying men did groan,
And ghosts did shriek and squeal about the
streets. 24
O Cæsar! these things are beyond all use,
And I do fear them.
Cæs. What can be avoided
Whose end is purpos'd by the mighty gods?
Yet Cæsar shall go forth; for these predictions
Are to the world in general as to Cæsar. 29
Cal. When beggars die there are no comets
seen;
The heavens themselves blaze forth the death of
princes.
Cæs. Cowards die many times before their
deaths; 32
The valiant never taste of death but once.
Of all the wonders that I yet have heard,
It seems to me most strange that men should
fear;
Seeing that death, a necessary end, 36
Will come when it will come.

Re-enter Servant. (priests)
What say the augurers?
Serv. They would not have you to stir forth
to-day.
Plucking the entrails of an offering forth,
They could not find a heart within the beast. 40
Cæs. The gods do this in shame of cowardice:
Cæsar should be a beast without a heart
If he should stay at home to-day for fear.
No, Cæsar shall not; danger knows full well 44
That Cæsar is more dangerous than he:
We are two lions litter'd in one day,
And I the elder and more terrible:
And Cæsar shall go forth.
Cal. Alas! my lord, 48
Your wisdom is consum'd in confidence.
Do not go forth to-day: call it my fear
That keeps you in the house, and not your own.
We'll send Mark Antony to the senate-house, 52
And he shall say you are not well to-day:
Let me, upon my knee, prevail in this.
Cæs. Mark Antony shall say I am not well;
And, for thy humour, I will stay at home. 56

Enter DECIUS.

Here's Decius Brutus, he shall tell them so.
Dec. Cæsar, all hail! Good morrow, worthy
Cæsar:
I come to fetch you to the senate-house.
Cæs. And you are come in very happy time
To bear my greeting to the senators, 61
And tell them that I will not come to-day:
Cannot, is false, and that I dare not, falser;
I will not come to-day: tell them so, Decius. 64
Cal. Say he is sick.
Cæs. Shall Cæsar send a lie?
Have I in conquest stretch'd mine arm so far
To be afeard to tell greybeards the truth?
Decius, go tell them Cæsar will not come. 68
Dec. Most mighty Cæsar, let me know some
cause,
Lest I be laugh'd at when I tell them so.
Cæs. The cause is in my will: I will not come;
That is enough to satisfy the senate: 72
But for your private satisfaction,
Because I love you, I will let you know:
Calphurnia here, my wife, stays me at home:
She dreamt to-night she saw my statua, 76
Which, like a fountain with a hundred spouts,
Did run pure blood; and many lusty Romans
Came smiling, and did bathe their hands in it:
And these does she apply for warnings and por-
tents, 80
And evils imminent; and on her knee
Hath begg'd that I will stay at home to-day.
Dec. This dream is all amiss interpreted;
It was a vision fair and fortunate: 84
Your statue spouting blood in many pipes,
In which so many smiling Romans bath'd,
Signifies that from you great Rome shall suck
Reviving blood, and that great men shall press
For tinctures, stains, relics, and cognizance. 89
This by Calphurnia's dream is signified.
Cæs. And this way have you well expounded
it.
Dec. I have, when you have heard what I
can say: 92
And know it now: the senate have concluded
To give this day a crown to mighty Cæsar.
If you shall send them word you will not come,
Their minds may change. Besides, it were a
mock 96
Apt to be render'd, for some one to say
'Break up the senate till another time,
When Cæsar's wife shall meet with better
dreams.'
If Cæsar hide himself, shall they not whisper 100
'Lo! Cæsar is afraid?'
Pardon me, Cæsar; for my dear dear love
To your proceeding bids me tell you this,
And reason to my love is liable. 104
Cæs. How foolish do your fears seem now,
Calphurnia!
I am ashamed I did yield to them.
Give me my robe, for I will go:

Enter PUBLIUS, BRUTUS, LIGARIUS, METELLUS,
CASCA, TREBONIUS, *and* CINNA.

And look where Publius is come to fetch me. 108

(marginalia: Cæsar prophesying / his own death)

Pub. Good morrow, Cæsar.
Cæs.   Welcome, Publius.
What! Brutus, are you stirr'd so early too?
Good morrow, Casca. Caius Ligarius,
Cæsar was ne'er so much your enemy   112
As that same ague which hath made you lean.
What is't o'clock?
Bru.   Cæsar, 'tis strucken eight.
Cæs. I thank you for your pains and courtesy.

[handwritten: passage of time is very marked.]

     Enter ANTONY.

See! Antony, that revels long o' nights,   116
Is notwithstanding up. Good morrow, Antony.
Ant. So to most noble Cæsar.
Cæs.   Bid them prepare within:
I am to blame to be thus waited for.
Now, Cinna; now, Metellus; what, Trebonius!
I have an hour's talk in store for you;   121
Remember that you call on me to-day:
Be near me, that I may remember you.
Treb. Cæsar, I will:—[*Aside.*] and so near
will I be,   124
That your best friends shall wish I had been
further.
Cæs. Good friends, go in, and taste some
wine with me;
And we, like friends, will straightway go to-
gether.
Bru. [*Aside.*] That every like is not the same,
O Cæsar!   128
The heart of Brutus yearns to think upon.

[handwritten: Brutus is very fond of Cæsar even though he has joined in the conspiracy.]

    [Exeunt.

    SCENE III.—*The Same. A Street near
the Capitol.*

    Enter ARTEMIDORUS, *reading a paper.*

Art. Cæsar, beware of Brutus; take heed of
Cassius; come not near Casca: have an eye to
Cinna; trust not Trebonius; mark well Metellus Cimber; Decius Brutus loves thee not; thou
hast wronged Caius Ligarius. There is but one
mind in all these men, and it is bent against
Cæsar. If thou be'st not immortal, look about
you: security gives way to conspiracy. The
mighty gods defend thee! Thy lover,   9
          ARTEMIDORUS.

Here will I stand till Cæsar pass along,
And as a suitor will I give him this.   12
My heart laments that virtue cannot live
Out of the teeth of emulation.
If thou read this, O Cæsar! thou mayst live;
If not, the Fates with traitors do contrive. [*Exit.*

    SCENE IV.—*The Same. Another Part of the
same Street, before the House of* BRUTUS.

    Enter PORTIA *and* LUCIUS.

Por. I prithee, boy, run to the senate-house;
Stay not to answer me, but get thee gone.
Why dost thou stay?
Luc.   To know my errand, madam.
Por. I would have had thee there, and here
again,   4
Ere I can tell thee what thou shouldst do there.
O constancy! be strong upon my side;

Set a huge mountain 'tween my heart and
tongue;
I have a man's mind, but a woman's might. 8
How hard it is for women to keep counsel!
Art thou here yet?
Luc.   Madam, what shall I do?
Run to the Capitol, and nothing else?
And so return to you, and nothing else?   12
Por. Yes, bring me word, boy, if thy lord
look well,
For he went sickly forth; and take good note
What Cæsar doth, what suitors press to him.
Hark, boy! what noise is that?   16
Luc. I hear none, madam.
Por.   Prithee, listen well:
I heard a bustling rumour, like a fray,
And the wind brings it from the Capitol.
Luc. Sooth, madam, I hear nothing.   20

    Enter the Soothsayer.

Por. Come hither, fellow: which way hast
thou been?
Sooth. At mine own house, good lady.
Por. What is't o'clock? *[handwritten: Time again]*
Sooth.   About the ninth hour, lady.
Por. Is Cæsar yet gone to the Capitol?   24
Sooth. Madam, not yet: I go to take my
stand,
To see him pass on to the Capitol.
Por. Thou hast some suit to Cæsar, hast
thou not?
Sooth. That I have, lady: if it will please
Cæsar   28
To be so good to Cæsar as to hear me,
I shall beseech him to befriend himself.
Por. Why, know'st thou any harm 's in-
tended towards him?
Sooth. None that I know will be, much that
I fear may chance.   32
Good morrow to you. Here the street is narrow:
The throng that follows Cæsar at the heels,
Of senators, of prætors, common suitors,
Will crowd a feeble man almost to death: 36
I'll get me to a place more void, and there
Speak to great Cæsar as he comes along. [*Exit.*
Por. I must go in. Ay me! how weak a thing
The heart of woman is. O Brutus!   40
The heavens speed thee in thine enterprise.
Sure, the boy heard me: Brutus hath a suit
That Cæsar will not grant. O! I grow faint.
Run, Lucius, and commend me to my lord;   44
Say I am merry: come to me again,
And bring me word what he doth say to thee.
          [*Exeunt, severally.*

          ACT III

    SCENE I.—*Rome. Before the Capitol; the
Senate sitting above.*

    A crowd of People; among them ARTEMIDORUS
and the Soothsayer. *Flourish. Enter* CÆSAR,
BRUTUS, CASSIUS, CASCA, DECIUS, METELLUS,
TREBONIUS, CINNA, ANTONY, LEPIDUS, POPI-
LIUS, PUBLIUS, *and Others.*

    Cæs. [*To the* Soothsayer.] The ides of March
are come.

Sooth. Ay, Cæsar; but not gone.
Art. Hail, Cæsar! Read this schedule.
Dec. Trebonius doth desire you to o'er-read, 4
t your best leisure, this his humble suit.
Art. O Cæsar! read mine first; for mine 's a suit
hat touches Cæsar nearer. Read it, great
Cæs. What touches us ourself shall be last serv'd.   8
Art. Delay not, Cæsar; read it instantly.
Cæs. What! is the fellow mad?
Pub.   Sirrah, give place.
Cæs. What! urge you your petitions in the street?
ome to the Capitol.   12

CÆSAR goes up to the Senate-House, the rest following. All the Senators rise.

Pop. I wish your enterprise to-day may thrive.
Cas. What enterprise, Popilius?
Pop.   Fare you well.
          [*Advances to* CÆSAR.
Bru. What said Popilius Lena?
Cas. He wish'd to-day our enterprise might thrive.   16
fear our purpose is discovered.
Bru. Look, how he makes to Cæsar: mark him.
Cas. Casca, be sudden, for we fear prevention.
rutus, what shall be done? If this be known, 20
assius or Cæsar never shall turn back,
or I will slay myself.
Bru.   Cassius, be constant:
opilius Lena speaks not of our purposes;
or, look, he smiles, and Cæsar doth not change.   24
Cas. Trebonius knows his time; for, look you, Brutus,
[h]e draws Mark Antony out of the way.
          [*Exeunt* ANTONY *and* TREBONIUS. CÆSAR *and the Senators take their seats.*
Dec. Where is Metellus Cimber? Let him go,
nd presently prefer his suit to Cæsar.   28
Bru. He is address'd; press near and second him.
Cin. Casca, you are the first that rears your hand.
Casca. Are we all ready? What is now amiss,
hat Cæsar and his senate must redress?   32
Met. Most high, most mighty, and most puissant Cæsar,
Tetellus Cimber throws before thy seat
[a] humble heart,—   [*Kneeling.*
Cæs.   I must prevent thee, Cimber.
hese couchings and these lowly courtesies, 36
Tight fire the blood of ordinary men,
nd turn pre-ordinance and first decree
nto the law of children. Be not fond,
o think that Cæsar bears such rebel blood 40
hat will be thaw'd from the true quality
Vith that which melteth fools; I mean sweet words,
.ow-crooked curtsies, and base spaniel fawning.

Thy brother by decree is banished: 44
If thou dost bend and pray and fawn for him,
I spurn thee like a cur out of my way.
Know, Cæsar doth not wrong, nor without cause
Will he be satisfied.   48
Met. Is there no voice more worthy than my own,
To sound more sweetly in great Cæsar's ear
For the repealing of my banish'd brother?
Bru. I kiss thy hand, but not in flattery, Cæsar;   52
Desiring thee, that Publius Cimber may
Have an immediate freedom of repeal.
Cæs. What, Brutus!
Cas.   Pardon, Cæsar; Cæsar, pardon:
As low as to thy foot doth Cassius fall,   56
To beg enfranchisement for Publius Cimber.
Cæs. I could be well mov'd if I were as you;
If I could pray to move, prayers would move me;
But I am constant as the northern star,   60
Of whose true-fix'd and resting quality
There is no fellow in the firmament.
The skies are painted with unnumber'd sparks,
They are all fire and every one doth shine,   64
But there's but one in all doth hold his place:
So, in the world; 'tis furnish'd well with men,
And men are flesh and blood, and apprehensive;
Yet in the number I do know but one   68
That unassailable holds on his rank,
Unshak'd of motion: and that I am he,
Let me a little show it, even in this,
That I was constant Cimber should be banish'd,
And constant do remain to keep him so.   73
Cin. O Cæsar,—
Cæs.   Hence! Wilt thou lift up Olympus!
Dec. Great Cæsar,—
Cæs.   Doth not Brutus bootless kneel?
Casca. Speak, hands, for me!   76
          [*They stab Cæsar.*
Cæs. Et tu, Brute? Then fall, Cæsar! [*Dies.*
Cin. Liberty! Freedom! Tyranny is dead!
Run hence, proclaim, cry it about the streets.
Cas. Some to the common pulpits, and cry out,   80
'Liberty, freedom, and enfranchisement!'
Bru. People and senators be not affrighted;
Fly not; stand still; ambition's debt is paid.
Casca. Go to the pulpit, Brutus.
Dec.   And Cassius too.   84
Bru. Where's Publius?
Cin. Here, quite confounded with this mutiny.
Met. Stand fast together, lest some friend of Cæsar's
Should chance—   88
Bru. Talk not of standing. Publius, good cheer;
There is no harm intended to your person,
Nor to no Roman else; so tell them, Publius.
Cas. And leave us, Publius; lest that the people,   92
Rushing on us, should do your age some mischief.
Bru. Do so; and let no man abide this deed
But we the doers.

Re-enter TREBONIUS.

Cas. Where's Antony?

Tre. Fled to his house amaz'd. 96
Men, wives and children stare, cry out and run
As it were doomsday.

Bru. Fates, we will know your pleasures.
That we shall die, we know; 'tis but the time
And drawing days out, that men stand upon. 100

Casca. Why, he that cuts off twenty years
of life
Cuts off so many years of fearing death.

Bru. Grant that, and then is death a benefit:
So are we Cæsar's friends, that have abrid'd 104
His time of fearing death. Stoop, Romans,
stoop,
And let us bathe our hands in Cæsar's blood
Up to the elbows, and besmear our swords:
Then walk we forth, even to the market-place;
And waving our red weapons o'er our heads, 109
Let's all cry, 'Peace, freedom, and liberty!'

Cas. Stoop, then, and wash. How many ages
hence
Shall this our lofty scene be acted o'er, 112
In states unborn and accents yet unknown!

Bru. How many times shall Cæsar bleed in
sport,
That now on Pompey's basis lies along
No worthier than the dust!

Cas. So oft as that shall be, 116
So often shall the knot of us be call'd
The men that gave their country liberty.

Dec. What! shall we forth?

Cas. Ay, every man away:
Brutus shall lead; and we will grace his heels
With the most boldest and best hearts of
Rome. 121

Enter a Servant.

Bru. Soft! who comes here? A friend of
Antony's.

Serv. Thus, Brutus, did my master bid me
kneel;
Thus did Mark Antony bid me fall down; 124
And, being prostrate, thus he bade me say:
Brutus is noble, wise, valiant, and honest;
Cæsar was mighty, bold, royal, and loving:
Say I love Brutus, and I honour him; 128
Say I fear'd Cæsar, honour'd him, and lov'd
him.
If Brutus will vouchsafe that Antony
May safely come to him, and be resolv'd
How Cæsar hath deserv'd to lie in death, 132
Mark Antony shall not love Cæsar dead
So well as Brutus living; but will follow
The fortunes and affairs of noble Brutus
Thorough the hazards of this untrod state 136
With all true faith. So says my master Antony.

Bru. Thy master is a wise and valiant Roman;
I never thought him worse.
Tell him, so please him come unto this place,
He shall be satisfied; and, by my honour, 141
Depart untouch'd.

Serv. I'll fetch him presently. [*Exit.*

Bru. I know that we shall have him well to
friend.

Cas. I wish we may: but yet have I a mind

That fears him much; and my misgiving still
Falls shrewdly to the purpose. 146

Re-enter ANTONY.

Bru. But here comes Antony. Welcome,
Mark Antony.

Ant. O mighty Cæsar! dost thou lie so low?
Are all thy conquests, glories, triumphs, spoils,
Shrunk to this little measure? Fare thee well.
I know not, gentlemen, what you intend, 151
Who else must be let blood, who else is rank:
If I myself, there is no hour so fit
As Cæsar's death's hour, nor no instrument
Of half that worth as those your swords, made
rich
With the most noble blood of all this world. 156
I do beseech ye, if ye bear me hard,
Now, whilst your purpled hands do reek and
smoke,
Fulfil your pleasure. Live a thousand years,
I shall not find myself so apt to die: 160
No place will please me so, no mean of death,
As here by Cæsar, and by you cut off,
The choice and master spirits of this age.

Bru. O Antony! beg not your death of us.
Though now we must appear bloody and
cruel, 165
As, by our hands and this our present act,
You see we do, yet see you but our hands
And this the bleeding business they have done:
Our hearts you see not; they are pitiful; 169
And pity to the general wrong of Rome—
As fire drives out fire, so pity pity—
Hath done this deed on Cæsar. For your part,
To you our swords have leaden points, Mark
Antony; 173
Our arms, in strength of malice, and our hearts
Of brothers' temper, do receive you in
With all kind love, good thoughts, and reve-
rence. 176

Cas. Your voice shall be as strong as any
man's
In the disposing of new dignities.

Bru. Only be patient till we have appeas'd
The multitude, beside themselves with fear, 180
And then we will deliver you the cause
Why I, that did love Cæsar when I struck him,
Have thus proceeded.

Ant. I doubt not of your wisdom.
Let each man render me his bloody hand: 184
First, Marcus Brutus, will I shake with you;
Next, Caius Cassius, do I take your hand;
Now, Decius Brutus, yours; now yours, Metel-
lus;
Yours, Cinna; and, my valiant Casca, yours; 188
Though last, not least in love, yours, good Tre-
bonius.
Gentlemen all,—alas! what shall I say?
My credit now stands on such slippery ground,
That one of two bad ways you must conceit me,
Either a coward or a flatterer. 192
That I did love thee, Cæsar, O! 'tis true:
If then thy spirit look upon us now,
Shall it not grieve thee dearer than thy death
To see thy Antony making his peace, 196
Shaking the bloody fingers of thy foes,

Most noble! in the presence of thy corse?
Had I as many eyes as thou hast wounds, 200
Weeping as fast as they stream forth thy blood,
It would become me better than to close
In terms of friendship with thine enemies.
Pardon me, Julius! Here wast thou bay'd,
    brave hart; 204
Here didst thou fall; and here thy hunters stand,
Sign'd in thy spoil, and crimson'd in thy leth.
O world! thou wast the forest to this hart;
And this, indeed, O world! the heart of thee. 208
How like a deer, strucken by many princes,
Dost thou here lie!
    Cas. Mark Antony,—
    Ant.   Pardon me, Caius Cassius:
The enemies of Cæsar shall say this; 212
Then, in a friend, it is cold modesty.
    Cas. I blame you not for praising Cæsar so;
But what compact mean you to have with us?
Will you be prick'd in number of our friends, 216
Or shall we on, and not depend on you?
    Ant. Therefore I took your hands, but was
indeed
Sway'd from the point by looking down on
    Cæsar.
Friends am I with you all, and love you all, 220
Upon this hope, that you shall give me reasons
Why and wherein Cæsar was dangerous.
    Bru. Or else were this a savage spectacle.
Our reasons are so full of good regard 224
That were you, Antony, the son of Cæsar,
You should be satisfied.
    Ant.   That's all I seek:
And am moreover suitor that I may
Produce his body to the market place; 228
And in the pulpit, as becomes a friend,
Speak in the order of his funeral.
    Bru. You shall, Mark Antony.
    Cas.   Brutus, a word with you.
[*Aside to* BRUTUS.] You know not what you do;
    do not consent 232
That Antony speak in his funeral:
Know you how much the people may be mov'd
By that which he will utter?
    Bru.   By your pardon;
I will myself into the pulpit first, 236
And show the reason of our Cæsar's death:
What Antony shall speak, I will protest
He speaks by leave and by permission,
And that we are contented Cæsar shall 240
Have all true rites and lawful ceremonies.
It shall advantage more than do us wrong.
    Cas. I know not what may fall; I like it not.
    Bru. Mark Antony, here, take you Cæsar's
    body. 244
You shall not in your funeral speech blame us,
But speak all good you can devise of Cæsar,
And say you do 't by our permission;
Else shall you not have any hand at all 248
About his funeral; and you shall speak
In the same pulpit whereto I am going,
After my speech is ended.
    Ant.   Be it so;
I do desire no more. 252
    Bru. Prepare the body then, and follow us.
        [*Exeunt all but* ANTONY.

    Ant. O! pardon me, thou bleeding piece of
    earth,
That I am meek and gentle with these butchers;
Thou art the ruins of the noblest man 256
That ever lived in the tide of times.
Woe to the hand that shed this costly blood!
Over thy wounds now do I prophesy,
Which like dumb mouths do ope their ruby
    lips, 260
To beg the voice and utterance of my tongue,
A curse shall light upon the limbs of men;
Domestic fury and fierce civil strife
Shall cumber all the parts of Italy; 264
Blood and destruction shall be so in use,
And dreadful objects so familiar,
That mothers shall but smile when they behold
Their infants quarter'd with the hands of war;
All pity chok'd with custom of fell deeds: 269
And Cæsar's spirit, ranging for revenge,
With Ate by his side come hot from hell,
Shall in these confines with a monarch's voice
Cry 'Havoc!' and let slip the dogs of war; 273
That this foul deed shall smell above the earth
With carrion men, groaning for burial.

        Enter a Servant.

You serve Octavius Cæsar, do you not? 276
    Serv. I do, Mark Antony.
    Ant. Cæsar did write for him to come to
Rome.
    Serv. He did receive his letters, and is coming;
And bid me say to you by word of mouth— 280
        [*Seeing the body.*
O Cæsar!—
    Ant. Thy heart is big, get thee apart and
weep.
Passion, I see, is catching; for mine eyes,
Seeing those beads of sorrow stand in thine, 284
Began to water. Is thy master coming?
    Serv. He lies to-night within seven leagues of
Rome.
    Ant. Post back with speed, and tell him what
hath chanc'd:
Here is a mourning Rome, a dangerous Rome,
No Rome of safety for Octavius yet; 289
Hie hence and tell him so. Yet, stay awhile;
Thou shalt not back till I have borne this corpse
Into the market-place; there shall I try, 292
In my oration, how the people take
The cruel issue of these bloody men;
According to the which thou shalt discourse
To young Octavius of the state of things. 296
Lend me your hand.
        [*Exeunt, with* CÆSAR'S *body.*

    SCENE II.—*The Same. The Forum.*

    Enter BRUTUS *and* CASSIUS, *and a throng of*
        Citizens.

    Citizens. We will be satisfied: let us be satis-
fied.
    Bru. Then follow me, and give me audience,
friends.
Cassius, go you into the other street,
And part the numbers.   4
Those that will hear me speak, let 'em stay here;

Those that will follow Cassius, go with him;
And public reasons shall be rendered
Of Cæsar's death.

First Cit. I will hear Brutus speak. 8
Sec. Cit. I will hear Cassius; and compare
their reasons,
When severally we hear them rendered.

[*Exit* CASSIUS, *with some of the* Citizens;
BRUTUS *goes into the pulpit.*

Third Cit. The noble Brutus is ascended:
silence!

Bru. Be patient till the last. 12
Romans, countrymen, and lovers! hear me for
my cause; and be silent, that you may hear:
believe me for mine honour, and have respect to
mine honour, that you may believe: censure me
in your wisdom, and awake your senses, that
you may the better judge. If there be any in this
assembly, any dear friend of Cæsar's, to him I
say, that Brutus' love to Cæsar was no less than
his. If then that friend demand why Brutus
rose against Cæsar, this is my answer: Not that
I loved Cæsar less, but that I loved Rome more.
Had you rather Cæsar were living, and die all
slaves, than that Cæsar were dead, to live all free
men? As Cæsar loved me, I weep for him; as
he was fortunate, I rejoice at it; as he was
valiant, I honour him; but, as he was ambitious,
I slew him. There is tears for his love; joy for
his fortune; honour for his valour; and death
for his ambition. Who is here so base that
would be a bondman? If any, speak; for him
have I offended. Who is here so rude that
would not be a Roman? If any, speak; for him
have I offended. Who is here so vile that will
not love his country? If any, speak; for him
have I offended. I pause for a reply. 37

Citizens. None, Brutus, none.

Bru. Then none have I offended. I have
done no more to Cæsar, than you shall do to
Brutus. The question of his death is enrolled
in the Capitol; his glory not extenuated, wherein he was worthy, nor his offences enforced, for
which he suffered death. 44

Enter ANTONY *and Others, with* CÆSAR'S *body.*

Here comes his body, mourned by Mark Antony:
who, though he had no hand in his death, shall
receive the benefit of his dying, a place in the
commonwealth; as which of you shall not?
With this I depart: that, as I slew my best lover
for the good of Rome, I have the same dagger
for myself, when it shall please my country to
need my death. 52

Citizens. Live, Brutus! live! live!
First Cit. Bring him with triumph home
unto his house.
Sec. Cit. Give him a statue with his ancestors.
Third Cit. Let him be Cæsar.
Fourth Cit. Cæsar's better parts
Shall be crown'd in Brutus. 57
First Cit. We'll bring him to his house with
shouts and clamours.
Bru. My countrymen,—
Sec. Cit. Peace! silence! Brutus speaks.
First Cit. Peace, ho! 60

Bru. Good countrymen, let me depart alone,
And, for my sake, stay here with Antony.
Do grace to Cæsar's corpse, and grace his speech
Tending to Cæsar's glories, which Mark Antony,
By our permission, is allow'd to make. 65
I do entreat you, not a man depart,
Save I alone, till Antony have spoke. [*Exit.*
First Cit. Stay, ho! and let us hear Mark
Antony. 68
Third Cit. Let him go up into the public
chair;
We'll hear him. Noble Antony, go up.
Ant. For Brutus' sake, I am beholding to
you. [*Goes up.*
Fourth Cit. What does he say of Brutus?
Third Cit. He says, for Brutus' sake,
He finds himself beholding to us all. 73
Fourth Cit. 'Twere best he speak no harm of
Brutus here.
First Cit. This Cæsar was a tyrant.
Third Cit. Nay, that's certain:
We are bless'd that Rome is rid of him. 76
Sec. Cit. Peace! let us hear what Antony can
say.
Ant. You gentle Romans,—
Citizens. Peace, ho! let us hear him.
Ant. Friends, Romans, countrymen, lend me
your ears;
I come to bury Cæsar, not to praise him. 80
The evil that men do lives after them,
The good is oft interred with their bones;
So let it be with Cæsar. The noble Brutus
Hath told you Cæsar was ambitious; 84
If it were so, it was a grievous fault,
And grievously hath Cæsar answer'd it.
Here, under leave of Brutus and the rest,—
For Brutus is an honourable man; 88
So are they all, all honourable men,—
Come I to speak in Cæsar's funeral.
He was my friend, faithful and just to me:
But Brutus says he was ambitious; 92
And Brutus is an honourable man.
He hath brought many captives home to Rome,
Whose ransoms did the general coffers fill:
Did this in Cæsar seem ambitious? 96
When that the poor have cried, Cæsar hath
wept;
Ambition should be made of sterner stuff:
Yet Brutus says he was ambitious;
And Brutus is an honourable man. 100
You all did see that on the Lupercal
I thrice presented him a kingly crown,
Which he did thrice refuse: was this ambition?
Yet Brutus says he was ambitious; 104
And, sure, he is an honourable man.
I speak not to disprove what Brutus spoke,
But here I am to speak what I do know.
You all did love him once, not without cause:
What cause withholds you then to mourn for
him? 109
O judgment! thou art fled to brutish beasts,
And men have lost their reason. Bear with me;
My heart is in the coffin there with Cæsar, 112
And I must pause till it come back to me.
First Cit. Methinks there is much reason in
his sayings.

Sec. Cit. If thou consider rightly of the matter,
æsar has had great wrong.
Third Cit.   Has he, masters? 116
fear there will a worse come in his place.
Fourth Cit. Mark'd ye his words? He would not take the crown;
herefore 'tis certain he was not ambitious.
First Cit. If it be found so, some will dear abide it.   120
Sec. Cit. Poor soul! his eyes are red as fire with weeping.
Third Cit. There's not a nobler man in Rome than Antony.
Fourth Cit. Now mark him; he begins again to speak.
Ant. But yesterday the word of Cæsar might
lave stood against the world; now lies he there,
And none so poor to do him reverence.
) masters! if I were dispos'd to stir
Your hearts and minds to mutiny and rage, 128
should do Brutus wrong, and Cassius wrong,
Who, you all know, are honourable men.
will not do them wrong; I rather choose
To wrong the dead, to wrong myself, and you,
Than I will wrong such honourable men. 133
But here's a parchment with the seal of Cæsar;
found it in his closet, 'tis his will.
et but the commons hear this testament— 136
Which, pardon me, I do not mean to read—
And they would go and kiss dead Cæsar's wounds,
And dip their napkins in his sacred blood,
Yea, beg a hair of him for memory,   140
And, dying, mention it within their wills,
Bequeathing it as a rich legacy
Unto their issue.
Fourth Cit. We'll hear the will: read it, Mark Antony.   144
Citizens. The will, the will! we will hear Cæsar's will.
Ant. Have patience, gentle friends; I must not read it:
t is not meet you know how Cæsar lov'd you.
You are not wood, you are not stones, but men;
And, being men, hearing the will of Cæsar, 149
t will inflame you, it will make you mad.
Tis good you know not that you are his heirs;
For if you should, O! what would come of it.
Fourth Cit. Read the will! we'll hear it, Antony;   153
You shall read us the will, Cæsar's will.
Ant. Will you be patient? Will you stay awhile?
I have o'ershot myself to tell you of it.   156
I fear I wrong the honourable men
Whose daggers have stabb'd Cæsar; I do fear it.
Fourth Cit. They were traitors: honourable men!
Citizens. The will! the testament!   160
Sec. Cit. They were villains, murderers. The will! read the will.
Ant. You will compel me then to read the will?
Then make a ring about the corpse of Cæsar,
And let me show you him that made the will. 164

Shall I descend? and will you give me leave?
Citizens. Come down.
Sec. Cit. Descend.   [ANTONY *comes down.*
Third Cit. You shall have leave.   168
Fourth Cit. A ring; stand round.
First Cit. Stand from the hearse; stand from the body.
Sec. Cit. Room for Antony; most noble Antony.
Ant. Nay, press not so upon me; stand far off.   172
Citizens. Stand back! room! bear back!
Ant. If you have tears, prepare to shed them now.
You all do know this mantle: I remember
The first time ever Cæsar put it on;   176
'Twas on a summer's evening, in his tent,
That day he overcame the Nervii.
Look! in this place ran Cassius' dagger through:
See what a rent the envious Casca made: 180
Through this the well-beloved Brutus stabb'd;
And, as he pluck'd his cursed steel away,
Mark how the blood of Cæsar follow'd it,
As rushing out of doors, to be resolv'd   184
If Brutus so unkindly knock'd or no;
For Brutus, as you know, was Cæsar's angel:
Judge, O you gods! how dearly Cæsar lov'd him.
This was the most unkindest cut of all;   188
For when the noble Cæsar saw him stab,
Ingratitude, more strong than traitors' arms,
Quite vanquish'd him: then burst his mighty heart;
And, in his mantle muffling up his face,   192
Even at the base of Pompey's statua,
Which all the while ran blood, great Cæsar fell.
O! what a fall was there, my countrymen;
Then I, and you, and all of us fell down, 196
Whilst bloody treason flourish'd o'er us.
O! now you weep, and I perceive you feel
The dint of pity; these are gracious drops.
Kind souls, what! weep you when you but behold   200
Our Cæsar's vesture wounded? Look you here,
Here is himself, marr'd, as you see, with traitors.
First Cit. O piteous spectacle!
Sec. Cit. O noble Cæsar!   204
Third Cit. O woeful day!
Fourth Cit. O traitors! villains!
First Cit. O most bloody sight!
Sec. Cit. We will be revenged.   208
Citizens. Revenge!—About!—Seek!—Burn!
Fire!—Kill!—Slay! Let not a traitor live.
Ant. Stay, countrymen!
First Citizen. Peace there! Hear the noble Antony.   212
Sec. Cit. We'll hear him, we'll follow him, we'll die with him.
Ant. Good friends, sweet friends, let me not stir you up
To such a sudden flood of mutiny.
They that have done this deed are honourable:
What private griefs they have, alas! I know not,   217
That made them do it; they are wise and honourable,

And will, no doubt, with reasons answer you.
I come not, friends, to steal away your hearts:
I am no orator, as Brutus is;   221
But, as you know me all, a plain blunt man,
That love my friend; and that they know full
    well
That gave me public leave to speak of him. 224
For I have neither wit, nor words, nor worth,
Action, nor utterance, nor the power of speech,
To stir men's blood: I only speak right on;
I tell you that which you yourselves do know,
Show you sweet Cæsar's wounds, poor poor
    dumb mouths,   229
And bid them speak for me: but were I Brutus,
And Brutus Antony, there were an Antony
Would ruffle up your spirits, and put a tongue
In every wound of Cæsar, that should move 233
The stones of Rome to rise and mutiny.

Citizens. We'll mutiny.
First Cit. We'll burn the house of Brutus.
Third Cit. Away, then! come, seek the con-
    spirators.   237
Ant. Yet hear me, countrymen; yet hear me
    speak.
Citizens. Peace, ho!—Hear Antony,—most
    noble Antony.
Ant. Why, friends, you go to do you know
    not what.   240
Wherein hath Cæsar thus deserv'd your loves?
Alas! you know not: I must tell you then.
You have forgot the will I told you of.
Citizens. Most true. The will! let's stay and
    hear the will.   244
Ant. Here is the will, and under Cæsar's seal.
To every Roman citizen he gives,
To every several man, seventy-five drachmas.
Sec. Cit. Most noble Cæsar! we'll revenge
    his death.   248
Third Cit. O royal Cæsar!
Ant. Hear me with patience.
Citizens. Peace, ho!
Ant. Moreover, he hath left you all his walks,
His private arbours, and new-planted orchards,
On this side Tiber; he hath left them you,
And to your heirs for ever; common pleasures,
To walk abroad, and recreate yourselves. 256
Here was a Cæsar! when comes such another?
First Cit. Never, never! Come, away, away!
We'll burn his body in the holy place,
And with the brands fire the traitors' houses.
Take up the body.   261
Sec. Cit. Go fetch fire.
Third Cit. Pluck down benches.
Fourth Cit. Pluck down forms, windows, any
    thing.   [*Exeunt* Citizens, *with the body.*
Ant. Now let it work: mischief, thou art
    afoot,   265
Take thou what course thou wilt!

Enter a Servant.

                        How now, fellow!
Serv. Sir, Octavius is already come to Rome.
Ant. Where is he?   268
Serv. He and Lepidus are at Cæsar's house.
Ant. And thither will I straight to visit him.
He comes upon a wish. Fortune is merry,

And in this mood will give us any thing. 272
Serv. I heard him say Brutus and Cassius
Are rid like madmen through the gates of Rome.
Ant. Belike they had some notice of the
    people,   275
How I had mov'd them. Bring me to Octavius.
                                          [*Exeunt.*

SCENE III.—*The Same. A Street.*

Enter CINNA, *the Poet.*

Cin. I dreamt to-night that I did feast with
    Cæsar,
And things unlucky charge my fantasy:
I have no will to wander forth of doors,
Yet something leads me forth.   4

Enter Citizens.

First Cit. What is your name?
Sec. Cit. Whither are you going?
Third Cit. Where do you dwell?
Fourth Cit. Are you a married man, or a
bachelor?   9
Sec. Cit. Answer every man directly.
First Cit. Ay, and briefly.
Fourth Cit. Ay, and wisely.   12
Third Cit. Ay, and truly, you were best.
Cin. What is my name? Whither am I
going? Where do I dwell? Am I a married
man, or a bachelor? Then, to answer every
man directly and briefly, wisely and truly:
wisely I say, I am a bachelor.   18
Sec. Cit. That's as much as to say, they are
fools that marry; you'll bear me a bang for
that, I fear. Proceed; directly.   21
Cin. Directly, I am going to Cæsar's funeral.
First Cit. As a friend or an enemy?
Cin. As a friend.   24
Sec. Cit. That matter is answered directly.
Fourth Cit. For your dwelling, briefly.
Cin. Briefly, I dwell by the Capitol.
Third Cit. Your name, sir, truly.   28
Cin. Truly, my name is Cinna.
Sec. Cit. Tear him to pieces; he's a con-
spirator.
Cin. I am Cinna the poet, I am Cinna the
poet.   33
Fourth Cit. Tear him for his bad verses, tear
him for his bad verses.
Cin. I am not Cinna the conspirator.
Sec. Cit. It is no matter, his name's Cinna;
pluck but his name out of his heart, and turn
him going.   39
Third Cit. Tear him, tear him! Come,
brands, ho! firebrands! To Brutus', to Cassius';
burn all. Some to Decius' house, and some to
Casca's; some to Ligarius'. Away! go! 43
                                          [*Exeunt.*

ACT IV

SCENE I.—*Rome. A Room in* ANTONY'S
    House.

ANTONY, OCTAVIUS, *and* LEPIDUS, *seated at a
    table.*

Ant. These many then shall die; their names
    are prick'd.

Oct. Your brother too must die; consent you,
  Lepidus?
Lep. I do consent.
Oct.   Prick him down, Antony.
Lep. Upon condition Publius shall not live, 4
Who is your sister's son, Mark Antony.
Ant. He shall not live; look, with a spot I
  damn him.
But, Lepidus, go you to Cæsar's house;
Fetch the will hither, and we shall determine 8
How to cut off some charge in legacies.
Lep. What! shall I find you here?
Oct. Or here or at the Capitol.
                              [*Exit* LEPIDUS.
Ant. This is a slight unmeritable man,   12
Meet to be sent on errands: is it fit,
The three-fold world divided, he should stand
One of the three to share it?
Oct.   So you thought him;
And took his voice who should be prick'd to die,
In our black sentence and proscription.   17
Ant. Octavius, I have seen more days than
  you:
And though we lay these honours on this man,
To ease ourselves of divers slanderous loads, 20
He shall but bear them as the ass bears gold,
To groan and sweat under the business,
Either led or driven, as we point the way; 23
And having brought our treasure where we will,
Then take we down his load, and turn him off,
Like to the empty ass, to shake his ears,
And graze in commons.
Oct.   You may do your will;
But he's a tried and valiant soldier.   28
Ant. So is my horse, Octavius; and for that
I do appoint him store of provender.
It is a creature that I teach to fight,
To wind, to stop, to run directly on,   32
His corporal motion govern'd by my spirit.
And, in some taste, is Lepidus but so;
He must be taught, and train'd, and bid go forth;
A barren-spirited fellow; one that feeds   36
On abject orts, and imitations,
Which, out of use and stal'd by other men,
Begin his fashion: do not talk of him
But as a property. And now, Octavius,   40
Listen great things: Brutus and Cassius
Are levying powers; we must straight make
  head;
Therefore let our alliance be combin'd,
Our best friends made, and our best means
  stretch'd out;   44
And let us presently go sit in council,
How covert matters may be best disclos'd,
And open perils surest answered.
Oct. Let us do so: for we are at the stake, 48
And bay'd about with many enemies;
And some that smile have in their hearts, I fear,
Millions of mischiefs.   [*Exeunt.*

hornibly an look out for usurpers.

SCENE II.—*Camp near Sardis. Before*
            BRUTUS' *Tent.*

Drum. Enter BRUTUS, LUCILIUS, LUCIUS, *and*
  Soldiers: TITINIUS *and* PINDARUS *meet them.*

Bru. Stand, ho!

Lucil. Give the word, ho! and stand.
Bru. What now, Lucilius! is Cassius near?
Lucil. He is at hand; and Pindarus is come 4
To do you salutation from his master.
        [PINDARUS *gives a letter to* BRUTUS.
Bru. He greets me well. Your master, Pin-
  darus,
In his own change, or by ill officers,
Hath given me some worthy cause to wish 8
Things done, undone; but, if he be at hand,
I shall be satisfied.
Pin.   I do not doubt
But that my noble master will appear
Such as he is, full of regard and honour.   12
Bru. He is not doubted. A word, Lucilius;
How he receiv'd you, let me be resolv'd.
Lucil. With courtesy and with respect
  enough;
But not with such familiar instances,   16
Nor with such free and friendly conference,
As he hath us'd of old.
Bru.   Thou hast describ'd
A hot friend cooling. Ever note, Lucilius,
When love begins to sicken and decay,   20
It useth an enforced ceremony.
There are no tricks in plain and simple faith;
But hollow men, like horses hot at hand,
Make gallant show and promise of their
  mettle;   24
But when they should endure the bloody spur,
They fall their crests, and, like deceitful jades,
Sink in the trial. Comes his army on?
Lucil. They mean this night in Sardis to be
  quarter'd;   28
The greater part, the horse in general,
Are come with Cassius.
Bru.   Hark! he is arriv'd.
              [*Low march within.*
March gently on to meet him.

        Enter CASSIUS *and* Soldiers.

Cas. Stand, ho!   32
Bru. Stand, ho! Speak the word along.
First Sold. Stand!
Sec. Sold. Stand!
Third Sold. Stand!   36
Cas. Most noble brother, you have done me
  wrong.
Bru. Judge me, you gods! Wrong I mine
  enemies?
And, if not so, how should I wrong a brother?
Cas. Brutus, this sober form of yours hides
  wrongs;   40
And when you do them—
Bru.   Cassius, be content;
Speak your griefs softly: I do know you well.
Before the eyes of both our armies here,
Which should perceive nothing but love from
  us,   44
Let us not wrangle: bid them move away;
Then in my tent, Cassius, enlarge your griefs,
And I will give you audience.
Cas.   Pindarus,
Bid our commanders lead their charges off 48
A little from this ground.
Bru. Lucilius, do you the like; and let no man

Come to our tent till we have done our con-
ference.
Let Lucius and Tintinius guard our door. 52
[Exeunt.

SCENE III.—Within the Tent of BRUTUS.

Enter BRUTUS and CASSIUS.

Cas. That you have wrong'd me doth appear
in this:
You have condemn'd and noted Lucius Pella
For taking bribes here of the Sardians;
Wherein my letters, praying on his side, 4
Because I knew the man, were slighted off.
Bru. You wrong'd yourself to write in such
a case.
Cas. In such a time as this it is not meet
That every nice offence should bear his com-
ment. 8
Bru. Let me tell you, Cassius, you yourself
Are much condemn'd to have an itching palm;
To sell and mart your offices for gold
To undeservers.
Cas. I an itching palm! 12
You know that you are Brutus that speak this,
Or, by the gods, this speech were else your last.
Bru. The name of Cassius honours this cor-
ruption,
And chastisement doth therefore hide his head.
Cas. Chastisement! 17
Bru. Remember March, the ides of March
remember:
Did not great Julius bleed for justice' sake?
What villain touch'd his body, that did stab, 20
And not for justice? What! shall one of us,
That struck the foremost man of all this world
But for supporting robbers, shall we now
Contaminate our fingers with base bribes, 24
And sell the mighty space of our large honours
For so much trash as may be grasped thus?
I had rather be a dog, and bay the moon,
Than such a Roman.
Cas. Brutus, bay not me; 28
I'll not endure it: you forget yourself,
To hedge me in. I am a soldier, I,
Older in practice, abler than yourself
To make conditions.
Bru. Go to; you are not, Cassius. 32
Cas. I am.
Bru. I say you are not.
Cas. Urge me no more, I shall forget myself;
Have mind upon your health; tempt me no
further. 36
Bru. Away, slight man!
Cas. Is't possible?
Bru. Hear me, for I will speak.
Must I give way and room to your rash choler?
Shall I be frighted when a madman stares? 40
Cas. O ye gods! ye gods! Must I endure all
this?
Bru. All this! ay, more: fret till your proud
heart break;
Go show your slaves how choleric you are,
And make your bondmen tremble. Must I
budge? 44
Must I observe you? Must I stand and crouch

Under your testy humour? By the gods,
You shall digest the venom of your spleen,
Though it do split you; for, from this day forth,
I'll use you for my mirth, yea, for my laughter,
When you are waspish.
Cas. Is it come to this?
Bru. You say you are a better soldier:
Let it appear so; make your vaunting true, 52
And it shall please me well. For mine own part,
I shall be glad to learn of noble men.
Cas. You wrong me every way; you wrong
me, Brutus;
I said an elder soldier, not a better: 56
Did I say, 'better?'
Bru. If you did, I care not.
Cas. When Cæsar liv'd, he durst not thus
have mov'd me.
Bru. Peace, peace! you durst not so have
tempted him.
Cas. I durst not! 60
Bru. No.
Cas. What! durst not tempt him!
Bru. For your life you durst not.
Cas. Do not presume too much upon my
love;
I may do that I shall be sorry for. 64
Bru. You have done that you should be
sorry for.
There is no terror, Cassius, in your threats;
For I am arm'd so strong in honesty
That they pass by me as the idle wind, 68
Which I respect not. I did send to you
For certain sums of gold, which you denied me;
For I can raise no money by vile means:
By heaven, I had rather coin my heart, 72
And drop my blood for drachmas, than to wring
From the hard hands of peasants their vile trash
By any indirection. I did send
To you for gold to pay my legions, 76
Which you denied me: was that done like
Cassius?
Should I have answer'd Caius Cassius so?
When Marcus Brutus grows so covetous,
To lock such rascal counters from his friends, 80
Be ready, gods, with all your thunderbolts;
Dash him to pieces!
Cas. I denied you not.
Bru. You did.
Cas. I did not: he was but a fool
That brought my answer back. Brutus hath
riv'd my heart. 84
A friend should bear his friend's infirmities,
But Brutus makes mine greater than they are.
Bru. I do not, till you practise them on me.
Cas. You love me not.
Bru. I do not like your faults. 88
Cas. A friendly eye could never see such
faults.
Bru. A flatterer's would not, though they do
appear
As huge as high Olympus.
Cas. Come, Antony, and young Octavius,
come, 92
Revenge yourselves alone on Cassius,
For Cassius is aweary of the world;
Hated by one he loves; brav'd by his brother;

Check'd like a bondman; all his faults observ'd,
Set in a note-book, learn'd, and conn'd by rote,
To cast into my teeth. O! I could weep
My spirit from mine eyes. There is my dagger,
And here my naked breast; within, a heart 100
Dearer than Plutus' mine, richer than gold:
If that thou be'st a Roman, take it forth;
I, that denied thee gold, will give my heart:
Strike, as thou didst at Cæsar; for, I know, 104
When thou didst hate him worst, thou lov'dst
        him better
Than ever thou lov'dst Cassius.
    Bru.   Sheathe your dagger:
Be angry when you will, it shall have scope;
Do what you will, dishonour shall be humour.
O Cassius! you are yoked with a lamb 109
That carries anger as the flint bears fire,
Who, much enforced, shows a hasty spark,
And straight is cold again.
    Cas.   Hath Cassius liv'd 112
To be but mirth and laughter to his Brutus,
When grief and blood ill-temper'd vexeth him?
    Bru. When I spoke that I was ill-temper'd
too.
    Cas. Do you confess so much? Give me your
hand.   116
    Bru. And my heart too.
    Cas.   O Brutus!
    Bru.   What's the matter?
    Cas. Have not you love enough to bear with
me,
When that rash humour which my mother gave
me
Makes me forgetful?
    Bru.   Yes, Cassius; and from henceforth
When you are over-earnest with your Brutus, 121
He'll think your mother chides, and leave you
so.   [*Noise within.*
    Poet. [*Within.*] Let me go in to see the
generals;
There is some grudge between 'em, 'tis not meet
They be alone.   125
    Lucil. [*Within.*] You shall not come to them.
    Poet. [*Within.*] Nothing but death shall stay
me.

Enter Poet, followed by LUCILIUS, TITINIUS,
        and LUCIUS.

    Cas. How now! What's the matter? 128
    Poet. For shame, you generals! What do
you mean?
Love, and be friends, as two such men should be;
For I have seen more years, I'm sure, than ye.
    Cas. Ha, ha! how vilely doth this cynic rime!
    Bru. Get you hence, sirrah; saucy fellow,
hence!   133
    Cas. Bear with him, Brutus; 'tis his fashion.
    Bru. I'll know his humour, when he knows
his time:
What should the wars do with these jigging
fools?   136
Companion, hence!
    Cas.   Away, away! be gone.
                              [*Exit Poet.*
    Bru. Lucilius and Titinius, bid the com-
manders

Prepare to lodge their companies to-night.
    Cas. And come yourselves, and bring Mes-
sala with you,   140
Immediately to us.
                [*Exeunt* LUCILIUS *and* TITINIUS.
    Bru. Lucius, a bowl of wine! [*Exit* LUCIUS.
    Cas. I did not think you could have been so
angry.
    Bru. O Cassius! I am sick of many griefs.
    Cas. Of your philosophy you make no use 144
If you give place to accidental evils.
    Bru. No man bears sorrow better: Portia is
dead.
    Cas. Ha! Portia!
    Bru. She is dead.   148
    Cas. How 'scap'd I killing when I cross'd
you so?
O insupportable and touching loss!
Upon what sickness?
    Bru.   Impatient of my absence,
And grief that young Octavius with Mark
Antony   152
Have made themselves so strong;—for with
her death
That tidings came:—with this she fell distract,
And, her attendants absent, swallow'd fire.
    Cas. And died so?
    Bru.   Even so.
    Cas.   O ye immortal gods! 156

Enter LUCIUS, *with wine and tapers.*

    Bru. Speak no more of her. Give me a bowl
of wine.
In this I bury all unkindness, Cassius. [*Drinks.*
    Cas. My heart is thirsty for that noble pledge.
Fill, Lucius, till the wine o'erswell the cup; 160
I cannot drink too much of Brutus' love.
                                        [*Drinks.*
    Bru. Come in, Titinius.   [*Exit* LUCIUS.

Re-enter TITINIUS, *with* MESSALA.

                        Welcome, good Messala.
Now sit we close about this taper here,
And call in question our necessities.   164
    Cas. Portia, art thou gone?
    Bru.   No more, I pray you.
Messala, I have here received letters,
That young Octavius and Mark Antony
Come down upon us with a mighty power, 168
Bending their expedition towards Philippi.
    Mes. Myself have letters of the self-same
tenour.
    Bru. With what addition?
    Mes. That by proscription and bills of out-
lawry,   172
Octavius, Antony, and Lepidus,
Have put to death an hundred senators.
    Bru. Therein our letters do not well agree;
Mine speak of seventy senators that died 176
By their proscriptions, Cicero being one.
    Cas. Cicero one!
    Mes.   Cicero is dead,
And by that order of proscription.
Had you your letters from your wife, my lord?
    Bru. No, Messala.   181
    Mes. Nor nothing in your letters writ of her?

Bru. Nothing, Messala.

Mes. That, methinks, is strange.

Bru. Why ask you? Hear you aught of her in yours? 184

Mes. No, my lord.

Bru. Now, as you are a Roman, tell me true.

Mes. Then like a Roman bear the truth I tell:
For certain she is dead, and by strange manner.

Bru. Why, farewell, Portia. We must die,
Messala: 189
With meditating that she must die once,
I have the patience to endure it now.

Mes. Even so great men great losses should endure. 192

Cas. I have as much of this in art as you,
But yet my nature could not bear it so.

Bru. Well, to our work alive. What do you think
Of marching to Philippi presently? 196

Cas. I do not think it good.

Bru. Your reason?

Cas. This is it:
'Tis better that the enemy seek us:
So shall he waste his means, weary his soldiers,
Doing himself offence; whilst we, lying still, 200
Are full of rest, defence, and nimbleness.

Bru. Good reasons must, of force, give place to better,
The people 'twixt Philippi and this ground
Do stand but in a forc'd affection; 204
For they have grudg'd us contribution:
The enemy, marching along by them,
By them shall make a fuller number up,
Come on refresh'd, new-added, and encourag'd;
From which advantage shall we cut him off, 209
If at Philippi we do face him there,
These people at our back.

Cas. Hear me, good brother.

Bru. Under your pardon. You must note beside, 212
That we have tried the utmost of our friends,
Our legions are brim-full, our cause is ripe:
The enemy increaseth every day;
We, at the height, are ready to decline. 216
There is a tide in the affairs of men,
Which, taken at the flood, leads on to fortune;
Omitted, all the voyage of their life
Is bound in shallows and in miseries. 220
On such a full sea are we now afloat;
And we must take the current when it serves,
Or lose our ventures.

Cas. Then, with your will, go on;
We'll along ourselves, and meet them at Philippi. 224

Bru. The deep of night is crept upon our talk,
And nature must obey necessity,
Which we will niggard with a little rest.
There is no more to say?

Cas. No more. Good-night: 228
Early to-morrow will we rise, and hence.

Bru. Lucius!

Re-enter LUCIUS.

My gown. [*Exit* LUCIUS.
Farewell, good Messala:

Good-night, Titinius. Noble, noble Cassius,
Good-night, and good repose.

Cas. O my dear brother! 232
This was an ill beginning of the night:
Never come such division 'tween our souls!
Let it not, Brutus.

Bru. Every thing is well.

Cas. Good-night, my lord.

Bru. Good-night, good brother. 236

Tit. } Good-night, Lord Brutus.
Mes. }

Bru. Farewell, every one.
[*Exeunt* CASSIUS, TITINIUS, *and* MESSALA.

Re-enter LUCIUS, *with the gown.*

Give me the gown. Where is thy instrument?

Luc. Here in the tent.

Bru. What! thou speak'st drowsily?
Poor knave, I blame thee not; thou art o'er-watch'd. 240
Call Claudius and some other of my men;
I'll have them sleep on cushions in my tent.

Luc. Varro! and Claudius!

Enter VARRO *and* CLAUDIUS.

Var. Calls my lord? 244

Bru. I pray you, sirs, lie in my tent and sleep:
It may be I shall raise you by and by
On business to my brother Cassius.

Var. So please you, we will stand and watch your pleasure. 248

Bru. I will not have it so; lie down, good sirs;
It may be I shall otherwise bethink me.
Look, Lucius, here's the book I sought for so;
I put it in the pocket of my gown. 252
[VARRO *and* CLAUDIUS *lie down.*

Luc. I was sure your lordship did not give it me.

Bru. Bear with me, good boy, I am much forgetful.
Canst thou hold up thy heavy eyes awhile,
And touch thy instrument a strain or two? 256

Luc. Ay, my lord, an't please you.

Bru. It does, my boy:
I trouble thee too much, but thou art willing.

Luc. It is my duty, sir.

Bru. I should not urge thy duty past thy might; 260
I know young bloods look for a time of rest.

Luc. I have slept, my lord, already.

Bru. It was well done, and thou shalt sleep again;
I will not hold thee long: if I do live, 264
I will be good to thee. [*Music, and a Song.*
This is a sleepy tune: O murderous slumber!
Lay'st thou thy leaden mace upon my boy,
That plays thee music? Gentle knave, good-night; 268
I will not do thee so much wrong to wake thee.
If thou dost nod, thou break'st thy instrument;
I'll take it from thee; and, good boy, good-night.
Let me see, let me see; is not the leaf turn'd down 272
Where I left reading? Here it is, I think.

Enter the Ghost of CÆSAR.

ow ill this taper burns! Ha! who comes here?
think it is the weakness of mine eyes
hat shapes this monstrous apparition.   276
comes upon me. Art thou any thing?
rt thou some god, some angel, or some devil,
hat mak'st my blood cold and my hair to
  stare?
>eak to me what thou art.   280
Ghost. Thy evil spirit, Brutus.
Bru.   Why com'st thou?
Ghost. To tell thee thou shalt see me at
  Philippi.
Bru. Well; then I shall see thee again?
Ghost.   Ay, at Philippi.
Bru. Why, I will see thee at Philippi then.
                     [*Ghost vanishes.*
ow I have taken heart thou vanishest: 285
spirit, I would hold more talk with thee.
>y, Lucius! Varro! Claudius! Sirs, awake!
laudius!   288
Luc. The strings, my lord, are false.
Bru. He thinks he still is at his instrument.
ucius, awake!
Luc. My lord!   292
Bru. Didst thou dream, Lucius, that thou so
  criedst out?
Luc. My lord, I do not know that I did cry.
Bru. Yes, that thou didst. Didst thou see
  any thing?
Luc. Nothing, my lord.   296
Bru. Sleep again, Lucius. Sirrah, Claudius!
ellow thou! awake!
Var. My lord!
Clau. My lord!   300
Bru. Why did you so cry out, sirs, in your
  sleep?
Var. } Did we, my lord?
Clau. }
Bru.   Ay: saw you any thing?
Var. No, my lord, I saw nothing.
Clau.   Nor I, my lord.
Bru. Go, and commend me to my brother
  Cassius.   304
id him set on his powers betimes before,
nd we will follow.
Var. } It shall be done, my lord.
Clau. }
                      [*Exeunt.*

ACT V

SCENE I.—*The Plains of Philippi.*

Enter OCTAVIUS, ANTONY, *and their Army.*

Oct. Now, Antony, our hopes are answered:
ou said the enemy would not come down,
ut keep the hills and upper regions;
proves not so; their battles are at hand;   4
ney mean to warn us at Philippi here,
nswering before we do demand of them.
Ant. Tut! I am in their bosoms, and I know
herefore they do it: they could be content 8
> visit other places; and come down
ith fearful bravery, thinking by this face

To fasten in our thoughts that they have courage;
But 'tis not so.

Enter a Messenger.

Mess.   Prepare you, generals: 12
The enemy comes on in gallant show;
Their bloody sign of battle is hung out,
And something to be done immediately.
Ant. Octavius, lead your battle softly on, 16
Upon the left hand of the even field.
Oct. Upon the right hand I; keep thou the
  left.
Ant. Why do you cross me in this exigent?
Oct. I do not cross you; but I will do so. 20
                     [*March.*

Drum. Enter BRUTUS, CASSIUS, *and their Army;*
  LUCILIUS, TITINIUS, MESSALA, *and Others.*

Bru. They stand, and would have parley.
Cas. Stand fast, Titinius: we must out and
  talk.
Oct. Mark Antony, shall we give sign of
  battle?
Ant. No, Cæsar, we will answer on their
  charge.   24
Make forth; the generals would have some
  words.
Oct. Stir not until the signal.
Bru. Words before blows: is it so, country-
  men?
Oct. Not that we love words better, as you do.
Bru. Good words are better than bad strokes,
  Octavius.   29
Ant. In your bad strokes, Brutus, you give
  good words:
Witness the hole you made in Cæsar's heart,
Crying, 'Long live! hail, Cæsar!'
Cas.   Antony,   32
The posture of your blows are yet unknown;
But for your words, they rob the Hybla bees,
And leave them honeyless.
Ant.   Not stingless too.
Bru. O! yes, and soundless too;   36
For you have stol'n their buzzing, Antony,
And very wisely threat before you sting.
Ant. Villains! you did not so when your vile
  daggers
Hack'd one another in the sides of Cæsar: 40
You show'd your teeth like apes, and fawn'd
  like hounds,
And bow'd like bondmen, kissing Cæsar's feet;
Whilst damned Casca, like a cur, behind
Struck Cæsar on the neck. O you flatterers! 44
Cas. Flatterers! Now, Brutus, thank your-
  self:
This tongue had not offended so to-day,
If Cassius might have rul'd.
Oct. Come, come, the cause: if arguing make
  us sweat,   48
The proof of it will turn to redder drops.
Look;
I draw a sword against conspirators;
When think you that the sword goes up again?
Never, till Cæsar's three-and-thirty wounds 53
Be well aveng'd; or till another Cæsar

Have added slaughter to the sword of traitors.

Bru. Cæsar, thou canst not die by traitors' hands,   56
Unless thou bring'st them with thee.

Oct.   So I hope;
I was not born to die on Brutus' sword.

Bru. O! if thou wert the noblest of thy strain,
Young man, thou couldst not die more honour-
able.   60

Cas. A peevish schoolboy, worthless of such honour,
Join'd with a masquer and a reveller.

Ant. Old Cassius still!

Oct.   Come, Antony; away!
Defiance, traitors, hurl we in your teeth.   64
If you dare fight to-day, come to the field;
If not, when you have stomachs.

[*Exeunt* OCTAVIUS, ANTONY, *and their Army.*

Cas. Why now, blow wind, swell billow, and swim bark!
The storm is up, and all is on the hazard.   68

Bru. Ho!
Lucilius! hark, a word with you.

Lucil.   My lord?

[BRUTUS *and* LUCILIUS *talk apart.*

Cas. Messala!

Mes.   What says my general?

Cas.   Messala,
This is my birth-day; as this very day   72
Was Cassius born. Give me thy hand, Messala:
Be thou my witness that against my will,
As Pompey was, am I compell'd to set
Upon one battle all our liberties.   76
You know that I held Epicurus strong,
And his opinion; now I change my mind,
And partly credit things that do presage.
Coming from Sardis, on our former ensign 80
Two mighty eagles fell, and there they perch'd,
Gorging and feeding from our soldiers' hands;
Who to Philippi here consorted us:
This morning are they fled away and gone 84
And in their stead do ravens, crows, and kites
Fly o'er our heads, and downward look on us,
As we were sickly prey: their shadows seem
A canopy most fatal, under which   88
Our army lies, ready to give up the ghost.

Mes. Believe not so.

Cas.   I but believe it partly,
For I am fresh of spirit and resolv'd
To meet all perils very constantly.   92

Bru. Even so, Lucilius.

Cas.   Now, most noble Brutus,
The gods to-day stand friendly, that we may,
Lovers in peace, lead on our days to age!
But since the affairs of men rest still uncertain,
Let's reason with the worst that may befall. 97
If we do lose this battle, then is this
The very last time we shall speak together:
What are you then, determined to do?   100

Bru. Even by the rule of that philosophy
By which I did blame Cato for the death
Which he did give himself; I know not how,
But I do find it cowardly and vile,   104
For fear of what might fall, so to prevent
The time of life: arming myself with patience,
To stay the providence of some high powers

That govern us below.

Cas.   Then, if we lose this battle,
You are contented to be led in triumph
Thorough the streets of Rome?

Bru. No, Cassius, no: think not, thou no
Roman,
That ever Brutus will go bound to Rome;
He bears too great a mind: but this same c
Must end that work the ides of March begu
And whether we shall meet again I know n
Therefore our everlasting farewell take:
For ever, and for ever, farewell, Cassius!
If we do meet again, why, we shall smile;
If not, why then, this parting was well mad

Cas. For ever, and for ever, farewell, Brut
If we do meet again, we'll smile indeed;
If not, 'tis true this parting was well made.

Bru. Why, then, lead on. O! that a m
might know
The end of this day's business, ere it come;
But it sufficeth that the day will end,
And then the end is known. Come, ho! awa
[*Exeu*

SCENE II.—*The Same. The Field of Battle*

Alarum. Enter BRUTUS *and* MESSALA.

Bru. Ride, ride, Messala, ride, and give th
bills
Unto the legions on the other side.
[*Loud alaru*
Let them set on at once, for I perceive
But cold demeanour in Octavius' wing,
And sudden push gives them the overthrow
Ride, ride, Messala: let them all come dow
[*Exeu*

SCENE III.—*Another Part of the Field.*

Alarum. Enter CASSIUS *and* TITINIUS.

Cas. O! look, Titinius, look, the villains
Myself have to mine own turn'd enemy;
This ensign here of mine was turning back;
I slew the coward, and did take it from him

Tit. O Cassius! Brutus gave the word
early;
Who, having some advantage on Octavius,
Took it too eagerly: his soldiers fell to spoi
Whilst we by Antony are all enclos'd.

Enter PINDARUS.

Pin. Fly further off, my lord, fly further o
Mark Antony is in your tents, my lord:
Fly, therefore, noble Cassius, fly far off.

Cas. This hill is far enough. Look, loo
Titinius;
Are those my tents where I perceive the fire

Tit. They are, my lord.

Cas.   Titinius, if thou lov'st r
Mount thou my horse, and hide thy spurs
him,
Till he have brought thee up to yonder troo
And here again; that I may rest assur'd
Whether yond troops are friend or enemy.

Tit. I will be here again, even with a thoug
[*E.*

Cas. Go, Pindarus, get higher on that hill;
My sight was ever thick; regard Titinius,   21
And tell me what thou not'st about the field.
                    [PINDARUS *ascends the hill.*
This day I breathed first; time is come round,
And where I did begin, there shall I end;   24
My life is run his compass. Sirrah, what news?
Pin. [*Above.*] O my lord!
Cas. What news?
Pin. Titinius is enclosed round about   28
With horsemen, that make to him on the spur;
Yet he spurs on: now they are almost on him;
Low, Titinius! now some light; O! he lights
too;
He's ta'en; [*Shout.*] and, hark! they shout for
joy.   32
Cas. Come down; behold no more.
O, coward that I am, to live so long,
To see my best friend ta'en before my face!

PINDARUS *descends.*

Come hither, sirrah: 36
In Parthia did I take thee prisoner;
And then I swore thee, saving of thy life,
That whatsoever I did bid thee do,
Thou shouldst attempt it. Come now, keep
thine oath;   40
Now be a freeman; and with this good sword,
That ran through Cæsar's bowels, search this
bosom.
Stand not to answer; here, take thou the hilts;
And, when my face is cover'd, as 'tis now,   44
Guide thou the sword. Cæsar, thou art reveng'd,
Even with the sword that kill'd thee.   [*Dies.*
Pin. So, I am free; yet would not so have
been;   48
Durst I have done my will. O Cassius,
Far from this country Pindarus shall run,
Where never Roman shall take note of him.
                              [*Exit.*

Re-enter TITINIUS *with* MESSALA.

Mes. It is but change, Titinius; for Octavius
Is overthrown by noble Brutus' power,   52
As Cassius' legions are by Antony.
Tit. These tidings will well comfort Cassius.
Mes. Where did you leave him?
Tit.   All disconsolate,
With Pindarus his bondman, on this hill.   56
Mes. Is not that he that lies upon the
ground?
Tit. He lies not like the living. O my heart!
Mes. Is not that he?
Tit.   No, this was he, Messala,
But Cassius is no more. O setting sun!   60
As in thy red rays thou dost sink to-night,
So in his red blood Cassius' day is set;
The sun of Rome is set. Our day is gone;
Clouds, dews, and dangers come; our deeds are
done.   64
Mistrust of my success hath done this deed.
Mes. Mistrust of good success hath done this
deed.
O hateful error, melancholy's child!

Why dost thou show to the apt thoughts of
men   68
The things that are not? O error! soon con-
ceiv'd,
Thou never com'st unto a happy birth,
But kill'st the mother that engender'd thee.
Tit. What, Pindarus! Where art thou, Pin-
darus?   72
Mes. Seek him, Titinius, whilst I go to meet
The noble Brutus, thrusting this report
Into his ears; I may say, thrusting it;
For piercing steel and darts envenomed   76
Shall be as welcome to the ears of Brutus
As tidings of this sight.
Tit.   Hie you, Messala,
And I will seek for Pindarus the while.
                    [*Exit* MESSALA.
Why didst thou send me forth, brave Cassius?
Did I not meet thy friends? and did not they 81
Put on my brows this wreath of victory,
And bid me give it thee? Didst thou not hear
their shouts?
Alas! thou hast misconstru'd every thing.   84
But, hold thee, take this garland on thy brow;
Thy Brutus bid me give it thee, and I
Will do his bidding. Brutus, come apace,
And see how I regarded Caius Cassius.   88
By your leave, gods: this is a Roman's part:
Come, Cassius' sword, and find Titinius' heart.
                    [*Kills himself.*

Alarum. Re-enter MESSALA, *with* BRUTUS, *Young*
CATO, STRATO, VOLUMNIUS, *and* LUCILIUS.

Bru. Where, where, Messala, doth his body
lie?   91
Mes. Lo, yonder: and Titinius mourning it.
Bru. Titinius' face is upward.
Cato.   He is slain.
Bru. O Julius Cæsar! thou art mighty yet!
Thy spirit walks abroad, and turns our swords
In our own proper entrails.   [*Low alarums.*
Cato.   Brave Titinius!   96
Look whe'r he have not crown'd dead Cassius!
Bru. Are yet two Romans living such as
these?
The last of all the Romans, fare thee well!
It is impossible that ever Rome   100
Should breed thy fellow. Friends, I owe more
tears
To this dead man than you shall see me pay.—
I shall find time, Cassius, I shall find time.—
Come therefore, and to Thassos send his
body: 104
His funerals shall not be in our camp,
Lest it discomfort us. Lucilius, come;
And come, young Cato;—let us to the field.
Labeo and Flavius, set our battles on: 108
'Tis three o'clock; and, Romans, yet ere night
We shall try fortune in a second fight. [*Exeunt.*

SCENE IV.—*Another Part of the Field.*

Alarum. Enter fighting, Soldiers *of both armies;
then* BRUTUS, *Young* CATO, LUCILIUS, *and*
Others.

Bru. Yet, countrymen, O! yet hold up your
heads!

Cato. What bastard doth not? Who will go with me?
I will proclaim my name about the field:
I am the son of Marcus Cato, ho!
A foe to tyrants, and my country's friend;
I am the son of Marcus Cato, ho!
   Bru. And I am Brutus, Marcus Brutus, I;
Brutus, my country's friend; know me for
   Brutus!   [*Exit, charging the enemy.*
      CATO *is overpowered, and falls.*
   Lucil. O young and noble Cato, art thou down?   9
Why, now thou diest as bravely as Titinius,
And mayst be honour'd being Cato's son.
   First Sold. Yield, or thou diest.
   Lucil.   Only I yield to die: 12
There is so much that thou wilt kill me straight.
                          [*Offering money.*
Kill Brutus, and be honour'd in his death.
   First Sold. We must not. A noble prisoner!
   Sec. Sold. Room, ho! Tell Antony, Brutus
is ta'en.   16
   First Sold. I'll tell the news: here comes the general.

Enter ANTONY.

Brutus is ta'en, my lord.
   Ant. Where is he?
   Lucil. Safe, Antony; Brutus is safe enough:
I dare assure thee that no enemy   21
Shall ever take alive the noble Brutus:
The gods defend him from so great a shame!
When you do find him, or alive or dead,   24
He will be found like Brutus, like himself.
   Ant. This is not Brutus, friend; but, I assure you,
A prize no less in worth. Keep this man safe,
Give him all kindness: I had rather have   28
Such men my friends than enemies. Go on,
And see whe'r Brutus be alive or dead,
And bring us word unto Octavius' tent,
How every thing is chanc'd.   [*Exeunt.*

SCENE V.—*Another Part of the Field.*

Enter BRUTUS, DARDANIUS, CLITUS, STRATO, *and* VOLUMNIUS.

   Bru. Come, poor remains of friends, rest on this rock.
   Cli. Statilius show'd the torch-light; but, my lord,
He came not back: he is or ta'en or slain.
   Bru. Sit thee down, Clitus: slaying is the word;   4
It is a deed in fashion. Hark thee, Clitus.
                          [*Whispers.*
   Cli. What, I, my lord? No, not for all the world.
   Bru. Peace, then! no words.
   Cli.   I'll rather kill myself.
   Bru. Hark thee, Dardanius.   [*Whispers.*
   Dar.   Shall I do such a deed? 8
   Cli. O, Dardanius!
   Dar. O, Clitus!
   Cli. What ill request did Brutus make to thee?
   Dar. To kill him, Clitus. Look, he meditates.

   Cli. Now is that noble vessel full of grief, 13
That it runs over even at his eyes.
   Bru. Come hither, good Volumnius: list a word.
   Vol. What says my lord?
   Bru.   Why this, Volumnius: 16
The ghost of Cæsar hath appear'd to me
Two several times by night; at Sardis once,
And this last night here in Philippi fields.
I know my hour is come.
   Vol.   Not so, my lord. 20
   Bru. Nay, I am sure it is, Volumnius.
Thou seest the world, Volumnius, how it goes;
Our enemies have beat us to the pit:
It is more worthy to leap in ourselves,   24
Than tarry till they push us. Good Volumnius,
Thou know'st that we two went to school together:
Even for that our love of old, I prithee,
Hold thou my sword-hilts, whilst I run on it. 28
   Vol. That's not an office for a friend, my lord.
                          [*Alarum still.*
   Cli. Fly, fly, my lord! there is no tarrying here.
   Bru. Farewell to you; and you; and you, Volumnius.
Strato, thou hast been all this while asleep; 32
Farewell to thee too, Strato. Countrymen,
My heart doth joy that yet, in all my life,
I found no man but he was true to me.
I shall have glory by this losing day,   36
More than Octavius and Mark Antony
By this vile conquest shall attain unto.
So fare you well at once; for Brutus' tongue
Hath almost ended his life's history: 40
Night hangs upon mine eyes; my bones would rest,
That have but labour'd to attain this hour.
         [*Alarum. Cry within,* 'Fly, fly, fly!'
   Cli. Fly, my lord, fly.
   Bru.   Hence! I will follow.
         [*Exeunt* CLITUS, DARDANIUS, *and*
                          VOLUMNIUS.
I prithee, Strato, stay thou by thy lord: 44
Thou art a fellow of a good respect;
Thy life hath had some smatch of honour in it:
Hold then my sword, and turn away thy face,
While I do run upon it. Wilt thou, Strato? 48
   Stra. Give me your hand first: fare you well, my lord.
   Bru. Farewell, good Strato.—[*He runs on his sword.*] Cæsar, now be still;
I kill'd not thee with half so good a will. [*Dies.*

Alarum. Retreat. Enter OCTAVIUS, ANTONY, MESSALA, LUCILIUS, *and Army.*

   Oct. What man is that?
   Mes. My master's man. Strato, where is thy master?
   Stra. Free from the bondage you are in, Messala;
The conquerors can but make a fire of him:
For Brutus only overcame himself,
And no man else hath honour by his death.
   Lucil. So Brutus should be found. I thank thee, Brutus,

hat thou hast prov'd Lucilius' saying true.
  Oct. All that serv'd Brutus, I will entertain
   them.   60
ellow, wilt thou bestow thy time with me?
  Stra. Ay, if Messala will prefer me to you.
  Oct. Do so, good Messala.
  Mes. How died my master, Strato?   64
  Stra. I held the sword, and he did run on it.
  Mes. Octavius, then take him to follow thee,
hat did the latest service to my master.
  Ant. This was the noblest Roman of them all; 68
ll the conspirators save only he
Did that they did in envy of great Cæsar;
He only, in a general honest thought
And common good to all, made one of them. 72
His life was gentle, and the elements
So mix'd in him that Nature might stand up
And say to all the world, 'This was a man!'
  Oct. According to his virtue let us use him,
With all respect and rites of burial.   77
Within my tent his bones to-night shall lie,
Most like a soldier, order'd honourably.
So, call the field to rest; and let's away,   80
To part the glories of this happy day. [*Exeunt.*

MACBETH

DRAMATIS PERSONÆ

DUNCAN, King of Scotland.
MALCOLM, } his Sons.
DONALBAIN, }
MACBETH, } Generals of the King's Army.
BANQUO, }
MACDUFF, }
LENNOX, }
ROSS, } Noblemen of Scotland.
MENTEITH, }
ANGUS, }
CAITHNESS, }
FLEANCE, Son to Banquo.
SIWARD, Earl of Northumberland, General of the English Forces.
YOUNG SIWARD, his Son.
SEYTON, an Officer attending Macbeth.

Boy, Son to Macduff.
An English Doctor.
A Scotch Doctor.
A Sergeant.
A Porter.
An Old Man.

LADY MACBETH.
LADY MACDUFF.
Gentlewoman attending on Lady Macbeth.

HECATE and Three Witches.
Lords, Gentlemen, Officers, Soldiers, Murderers, Attendants, and Messengers. The Ghost of Banquo, and other Apparitions.

SCENE.—*Scotland; England.*

ACT I

SCENE I.—*A desert Heath.*

Thunder and lightning. Enter three Witches.

First Witch. When shall we three meet again
In thunder, lightning, or in rain?
Sec. Witch. When the hurlyburly 's done,
When the battle 's lost and won. 4
Third Witch. That will be ere the set of sun.
First Witch. Where the place?
Sec. Witch. Upon the heath.
Third Witch. There to meet with Macbeth.
First Witch. I come, Graymalkin! 8
Sec. Witch. Paddock calls.
Third Witch. Anon.
All. Fair is foul, and foul is fair:
Hover through the fog and filthy air. [*Exeunt.*

SCENE II.—*A Camp near Forres.*

Alarum within. Enter KING DUNCAN, MALCOLM, DONALBAIN, LENNOX, *with* Attendants, *meeting a bleeding* Sergeant.

Dun. What bloody man is that? He can report,
As seemeth by his plight, of the revolt
The newest state.
Mal. This is the sergeant
Who, like a good and hardy soldier fought 4
'Gainst my captivity. Hail, brave friend!
Say to the king the knowledge of the broil
As thou didst leave it.
Serg. Doubtful it stood;
As two spent swimmers, that do cling together 8
And choke their art. The merciless Macdonwald—
Worthy to be a rebel, for to that
The multiplying villanies of nature
Do swarm upon him—from the western isles 12
Of kerns and gallowglasses is supplied;

And fortune, on his damned quarrel smiling,
Show'd like a rebel's whore: but all 's too weak;
For brave Macbeth,—well he deserves that name,— 16
Disdaining fortune, with his brandish'd steel,
Which smok'd with bloody execution,
Like valour's minion carv'd out his passage
Till he fac'd the slave; 20
Which ne'er shook hands, nor bade farewell to him,
Till he unseam'd him from the nave to the chaps,
And fix'd his head upon our battlements. 23
Dun. O valiant cousin! worthy gentleman!
Serg. As whence the sun 'gins his reflection
Shipwracking storms and direful thunders break,
So from that spring whence comfort seem'd to come
Discomfort swells. Mark, King of Scotland, mark: 28
No sooner justice had with valour arm'd
Compell'd these skipping kerns to trust their heels,
But the Norweyan lord surveying vantage,
With furbish'd arms and new supplies of men 32
Began a fresh assault.
Dun. Dismay'd not this
Our captains, Macbeth and Banquo?
Serg. Yes;
As sparrows eagles, or the hare the lion.
If I say sooth, I must report they were 36
As cannons overcharg'd with double cracks;
So they
Doubly redoubled strokes upon the foe:
Except they meant to bathe in reeking wounds
Or memorize another Golgotha, 4
I cannot tell—
But I am faint, my gashes cry for help.
Dun. So well thy words become thee as thy wounds; 4

hey smack of honour both. Go, get him surgeons. [*Exit* Sergeant, *attended.*

Enter ROSS.

Vho comes here?
  Mal. The worthy Thane of Ross.
  Len. What a haste looks through his eyes!
    So should he look
'hat seems to speak things strange.
  Ross. God save the king! 48
  Dun. Whence cam'st thou, worthy thane?
  Ross. From Fife, great king;
Vhere the Norweyan banners flout the sky
nd fan our people cold. Norway himself,
Vith terrible numbers, 52
ssisted by that most disloyal traitor,
'he Thane of Cawdor, began a dismal conflict;
ill that Bellona's bridegroom, lapp'd in proof,
Confronted him with self-comparisons, 56
'oint against point, rebellious arm 'gainst arm,
'urbing his lavish spirit: and, to conclude,
'he victory fell on us.—
  Dun. Great happiness!
  Ross. That now 60
weno, the Norways' king, craves composition;
'or would we deign him burial of his men
'ill he disbursed, at Saint Colme's Inch,
'en thousand dollars to our general use. 64
  Dun. No more that Thane of Cawdor shall
    deceive
)ur bosom interest. Go pronounce his present
    death,
\nd with his former title greet Macbeth.
  Ross. I'll see it done. 68
  Dun. What he hath lost noble Macbeth hath
    won. [*Exeunt.*

SCENE III.—*A Heath.*

Thunder. Enter the three Witches.

First Witch. Where hast thou been, sister?
Sec. Witch. Killing swine.
Third Witch. Sister, where thou?
First Witch. A sailor's wife had chestnuts in
    her lap, 4
\nd munch'd, and munch'd, and munch'd:
'Give me,' quoth I:
Aroint thee, witch!' the rump-fed ronyon cries.
Ier husband's to Aleppo gone, master o' the
    Tiger:
3ut in a sieve I'll thither sail, 8
\nd, like a rat without a tail,
'll do, I'll do, and I'll do.
Sec. Witch. I'll give thee a wind.
First Witch. Thou'rt kind. 12
Third Witch. And I another.
First Witch. I myself have all the other;
\nd the very ports they blow,
\ll the quarters that they know 16
' the shipman's card.
'll drain him dry as hay:
3leep shall neither night nor day
Iang upon his pent-house lid; 20
Ie shall live a man forbid.
Veary se'nnights nine times nine
3hall he dwindle, peak and pine:

Though his bark cannot be lost, 24
Yet it shall be tempest-tost.
Look what I have.
  Sec. Witch. Show me, show me.
  First Witch. Here I have a pilot's thumb, 28
Wrack'd as homeward he did come.
    [*Drum within.*
  Third Witch. A drum! a drum!
Macbeth doth come.
  All. The weird sisters, hand in hand, 32
Posters of the sea and land,
Thus do go about, about:
Thrice to thine, and thrice to mine,
And thrice again, to make up nine. 36
Peace! the charm 's wound up.

Enter MACBETH *and* BANQUO.

  Macb. So foul and fair a day I have not seen.
  Ban. How far is't call'd to Forres? What
    are these,
So wither'd and so wild in their attire, 40
That look not like th' inhabitants o' the earth,
And yet are on't? Live you? or are you aught
That man may question? You seem to under-
    stand me,
By each at once her choppy finger laying 44
Upon her skinny lips: you should be women,
And yet your beards forbid me to interpret
That you are so.
  Macb. Speak, if you can: what are you?
  First Witch. All hail, Macbeth! hail to thee,
    Thane of Glamis! 48
  Sec. Witch. All hail, Macbeth! hail to thee,
    Thane of Cawdor!
  Third Witch. All hail, Macbeth! that shalt
    be king hereafter.
  Ban. Good sir, why do you start, and seem
    to fear
Things that do sound so fair? I' the name of
    truth, 52
Are ye fantastical, or that indeed
Which outwardly ye show? My noble partner
You greet with present grace and great pre-
    diction
Of noble having and of royal hope, 56
That he seems rapt withal: to me you speak
    not.
If you can look into the seeds of time,
And say which grain will grow and which will
    not,
Speak then to me, who neither beg nor fear 60
Your favours nor your hate.
  First Witch. Hail!
  Sec. Witch. Hail!
  Third Witch. Hail! 64
  First Witch. Lesser than Macbeth, and
    greater.
  Sec. Witch. Not so happy, yet much happier.
  Third Witch. Thou shalt get kings, though
    thou be none:
So, all hail, Macbeth and Banquo! 68
  First Witch. Banquo and Macbeth, all hail!
  Macb. Stay, you imperfect speakers, tell me
    more:
By Sinel's death I know I am Thane of Glamis;
But how of Cawdor? the Thane of Cawdor lives,

A prosperous gentleman; and to be king 73
Stands not within the prospect of belief
No more than to be Cawdor. Say, from whence
You owe this strange intelligence? or why 76
Upon this blasted heath you stop our way
With such prophetic greeting? Speak, I charge
  you.   [Witches *vanish*.
  Ban. The earth hath bubbles, as the water
    has,
And these are of them. Whither are they
    vanish'd?   80
  Macb. Into the air, and what seem'd corporal
    melted
As breath into the wind. Would they had stay'd!
  Ban. Were such things here as we do speak
    about?
Or have we eaten on the insane root   84
That takes the reason prisoner?
  Macb. Your children shall be kings.
  Ban.   You shall be king.
  Macb. And Thane of Cawdor too; went it
    not so?
  Ban. To the self-same tune and words.
    Who's here?   88

Enter ROSS *and* ANGUS.

  Ross. The king hath happily receiv'd, Mac-
    beth,
The news of thy success; and when he reads
Thy personal venture in the rebels' fight,
His wonders and his praises do contend   92
Which should be thine or his. Silenc'd with
    that,
In viewing o'er the rest o' the self-same day,
He finds thee in the stout Norweyan ranks,
Nothing afeard of what thyself didst make, 96
Strange images of death. As thick as hail
Came post with post, and every one did bear
Thy praises in his kingdom's great defence,
And pour'd them down before him.
  Ang.   We are sent 100
To give thee from our royal master thanks;
Only to herald thee into his sight,
Not pay thee.
  Ross. And, for an earnest of a greater honour,
He bade me, from him, call thee Thane of Caw-
    dor: 105
In which addition, hail, most worthy thane!
For it is thine.
  Ban.   What! can the devil speak true?
  Macb. The Thane of Cawdor lives: why do
    you dress me   108
In borrow'd robes?
  Ang.   Who was the thane lives yet;
But under heavy judgment bears that life
Which he deserves to lose. Whether he was
    combin'd
With those of Norway, or did line the rebel 112
With hidden help or vantage, or that with both
He labour'd in his country's wrack, I know not;
But treasons capital, confess'd and prov'd,
Have overthrown him.
  Macb. [*Aside.*] Glamis, and Thane of Caw-
    dor:
The greatest is behind. [*To* ROSS *and* ANGUS.]
  Thanks for your pains.   117

[*To* BANQUO.] Do you not hope your children
    shall be kings,
When those that gave the Thane of Cawdor to
    me
Promis'd no less to them?
  Ban.   That, trusted home, 120
Might yet enkindle you unto the crown,
Besides the Thane of Cawdor. But 'tis strange:
And oftentimes, to win us to our harm,
The instruments of darkness tell us truths, 124
Win us with honest trifles, to betray's
In deepest consequence.
Cousins, a word, I pray you.
  Macb. [*Aside.*]   Two truths are told,
As happy prologues to the swelling act   128
Of the imperial theme. I thank you, gentlemen.
[*Aside.*] This supernatural soliciting
Cannot be ill, cannot be good; if ill,
Why hath it given me earnest of success, 132
Commencing in a truth? I am Thane of Caw-
    dor:
If good, why do I yield to that suggestion
Whose horrid image doth unfix my hair
And make my seated heart knock at my ribs,
Against the use of nature? Present fears 137
Are less than horrible imaginings;
My thought, whose murder yet is but fantastical,
Shakes so my single state of man that function
Is smother'd in surmise, and nothing is   141
But what is not.
  Ban.   Look, how our partner's rapt
  Macb. [*Aside.*] If chance will have me king
    why, chance may crown me,
Without my stir.
  Ban.   New honours come upon him, 14
Like our strange garments, cleave not to their
    mould
But with the aid of use.
  Macb.   [*Aside.*] Come what come may
Time and the hour runs through the roughest
    day.
  Ban. Worthy Macbeth, we stay upon your
    leisure.   14
  Macb. Give me your favour: my dull brain
    was wrought
With things forgotten. Kind gentlemen, your
    pains
Are register'd where every day I turn
The leaf to read them. Let us toward the king
Think upon what hath chanc'd; and, at more
    time,   15
The interim having weigh'd it, let us speak
Our free hearts each to other.
  Ban.   Very gladly.
  Macb. Till then, enough. Come, friends. 15
                                       [*Exeunt*

SCENE IV.—*Forres. A Room in the Palace.*

Flourish. Enter DUNCAN, MALCOLM, DONAL-
    BAIN, LENNOX, *and* Attendants.

  Dun. Is execution done on Cawdor? Are not
Those in commission yet return'd?
  Mal.   My liege
They are not yet come back; but I have spoke
With one that saw him die; who did report

That very frankly he confess'd his treasons,
Implor'd your highness' pardon and set forth
A deep repentance. Nothing in his life
Became him like the leaving it; he died   8
As one that had been studied in his death
To throw away the dearest thing he ow'd,
As 'twere a careless trifle.
  Dun.   There's no art
To find the mind's construction in the face: 12
He was a gentleman on whom I built
An absolute trust.

Enter MACBETH, BANQUO, ROSS *and* ANGUS.
                O worthiest cousin!
The sin of my ingratitude even now
Was heavy on me. Thou art so far before   16
That swiftest wing of recompense is slow
To overtake thee; would thou hadst less deserv'd,
That the proportion both of thanks and payment
Might have been mine! only I have left to say, 20
More is thy due than more than all can pay.
  Macb. The service and the loyalty I owe,
In doing it, pays itself. Your highness' part
Is to receive our duties: and our duties   24
Are to your throne and state, children and servants;
Which do but what they should, by doing everything
Safe toward your love and honour.
  Dun.   Welcome hither:
I have begun to plant thee, and will labour 28
To make thee full of growing. Noble Banquo,
That hast no less deserv'd, nor must be known
No less to have done so, let me infold thee
And hold thee to my heart.
  Ban.   There if I grow, 32
The harvest is your own.
  Dun.   My plenteous joys
Wanton in fulness, seek to hide themselves
In drops of sorrow. Sons, kinsmen, thanes,
And you whose places are the nearest, know 36
We will establish our estate upon
Our eldest, Malcolm, whom we name hereafter
The Prince of Cumberland; which honour must
Not unaccompanied invest him only,   40
But signs of nobleness, like stars, shall shine
On all deservers. From hence to Inverness,
And bind us further to you.
  Macb. The rest is labour, which is not us'd
    for you: 44
I'll be myself the harbinger, and make joyful
The hearing of my wife with your approach;
So, humbly take my leave.
  Dun.   My worthy Cawdor!
  Macb. [*Aside.*] The Prince of Cumberland!
    that is a step 48
On which I must fall down, or else o'er-leap,
For in my way it lies. Stars, hide your fires!
Let not light see my black and deep desires;
The eye wink at the hand; yet let that be   52
Which the eye fears, when it is done, to see.
                  [*Exit.*
  Dun. True, worthy Banquo; he is full so
  valiant,

And in his commendations I am fed;
It is a banquet to me. Let's after him,   56
Whose care is gone before to bid us welcome:
It is a peerless kinsman.   [*Flourish. Exeunt.*

SCENE V.—*Inverness.* MACBETH'S *Castle.*

Enter LADY MACBETH, *reading a letter.*

They met me in the day of success; and I have learned by the perfectest report, they have more in them than mortal knowledge. When I burned in desire to question them further, they made themselves air, into which they vanished. Whiles I stood rapt in the wonder of it, came missives from the king, who all-hailed me, 'Thane of Cawdor;' by which title, before, these weird sisters saluted me, and referred me to the coming on of time, with, 'Hail, king that shalt be!' This have I thought good to deliver thee, my dearest partner of greatness, that thou mightest not lose the dues of rejoicing, by being ignorant of what greatness is promised thee. Lay it to thy heart, and farewell.

Glamis thou art, and Cawdor; and shalt be 16
What thou art promis'd. Yet do I fear thy nature:
It is too full o' the milk of human kindness
To catch the nearest way; thou wouldst be great,
Art not without ambition, but without   20
The illness should attend it; what thou wouldst highly,
That thou wouldst holily; wouldst not play false,
And yet wouldst wrongly win; thou'dst have, great Glamis,
That which cries, 'Thus thou must do, if thou have it';   24
And that which rather thou dost fear to do
Than wishest should be undone. Hie thee hither,
That I may pour my spirits in thine ear,
And chastise with the valour of my tongue 28
All that impedes thee from the golden round,
Which fate and metaphysical aid doth seem
To have thee crown'd withal.

Enter a Messenger.

                What is your tidings?
  Mess. The king comes here to-night.
  Lady M.   Thou'rt mad to say it. 32
Is not thy master with him? who, were't so,
Would have inform'd for preparation.
  Mess. So please you, it is true: our thane is coming;
One of my fellows had the speed of him,   36
Who, almost dead for breath, had scarcely more
Than would make up his message.
  Lady M.   Give him tending;
He brings great news.—[*Exit* Messenger.] The raven himself is hoarse
That croaks the fatal entrance of Duncan   40
Under my battlements. Come, you spirits
That tend on mortal thoughts! unsex me here,
And fill me from the crown to the toe top full
Of direst cruelty; make thick my blood,   44

Stop up the access and passage to remorse,
That no compunctious visitings of nature
Shake my fell purpose, nor keep peace between
The effect and it! Come to my woman's breasts,
And take my milk for gall, you murdering minis-
ters,   49
Wherever in your sightless substances
You wait on nature's mischief! Come, thick
night,
And pall thee in the dunnest smoke of hell, 52
That my keen knife see not the wound it makes,
Nor heaven peep through the blanket of the
dark,
To cry, 'Hold, hold!'

Enter MACBETH.

Great Glamis! worthy Cawdor!
Greater than both, by the all-hail hereafter! 56
Thy letters have transported me beyond
This ignorant present, and I feel now
The future in the instant.
      Macb.   My dearest love,
Duncan comes here to-night.
      Lady M.   And when goes hence? 60
      Macb. To-morrow, as he purposes.
      Lady M.   O! never
Shall sun that morrow see.
Your face, my thane, is as a book where men
May read strange matters. To beguile the time,
Look like the time; bear welcome in your eye,
Your hand, your tongue: look like the innocent
flower,
But be the serpent under 't. He that's coming
Must be provided for; and you shall put   68
This night's great business into my dispatch;
Which shall to all our nights and days to come
Give solely sovereign sway and masterdom.
      Macb. We will speak further.
      Lady M.   Only look up clear; 72
To alter favour ever is to fear.
Leave all the rest to me.   [*Exeunt.*

SCENE VI.—*The Same. Before the Castle.*

Hautboys and torches. Enter DUNCAN, MAL-
COLM, DONALBAIN, BANQUO, LENNOX, MAC-
DUFF, ROSS, ANGUS, *and* Attendants.

      Dun. This castle hath a pleasant seat; the air
Nimbly and sweetly recommends itself
Unto our gentle senses.
      Ban.   This guest of summer,
The temple-haunting martlet, does approve 4
By his lov'd mansionry that the heaven's breath
Smells wooingly here: no jutty, frieze,
Buttress, nor coign of vantage, but this bird
Hath made his pendent bed and procreant
cradle: 8
Where they most breed and haunt, I have ob-
serv'd
The air is delicate.

Enter LADY MACBETH.

      Dun.   See, see, our honour'd hostess!
The love that follows us sometime is our trouble,
Which still we thank as love. Herein I teach
you   12

How you shall bid God 'eyld us for your pains,
And thank us for your trouble.
      Lady M.   All our service,
In every point twice done, and then done double,
Were poor and single business, to contend 16
Against those honours deep and broad where-
with
Your majesty loads our house: for those of old,
And the late dignities heap'd up to them,
We rest your hermits.
      Dun. Where's the Thane of Cawdor? 20
We cours'd him at the heels, and had a purpose
To be his purveyor; but he rides well,
And his great love, sharp as his spur, hath holp
him
To his home before us. Fair and noble hostess,
We are your guest to-night.
      Lady M.   Your servants ever 25
Have theirs, themselves, and what is theirs, in
compt,
To make their audit at your highness' pleasure,
Still to return your own.
      Dun.   Give me your hand; 28
Conduct me to mine host: we love him highly,
And shall continue our graces towards him.
By your leave, hostess.   [*Exeunt.*

SCENE VII.—*The Same. A Room in the
Castle.*

*Hautboys and torches. Enter, and pass over
the stage, a* Sewer, *and divers* Servants *with
dishes and service. Then, enter* MACBETH.

      Macb. If it were done when 'tis done, then
'twere well
It were done quickly; if the assassination
Could trammel up the consequence, and catch
With his surcease success; that but this blow 4
Might be the be-all and the end-all here,
But here, upon this bank and shoal of time,
We'd jump the life to come. But in these cases
We still have judgment here; that we but teach
Bloody instructions, which, being taught, re-
turn   9
To plague the inventor; this even-handed justice
Commends the ingredients of our poison'd
chalice
To our own lips. He's here in double trust: 12
First, as I am his kinsman and his subject,
Strong both against the deed; then, as his host
Who should against his murderer shut the door,
Not bear the knife myself. Besides, this Duncan
Hath borne his faculties so meek, hath been 17
So clear in his great office, that his virtues
Will plead like angels trumpet-tongu'd against
The deep damnation of his taking-off;   20
And pity, like a naked new-born babe,
Striding the blast, or heaven's cherubin, hors'd
Upon the sightless couriers of the air,
Shall blow the horrid deed in every eye,   24
That tears shall drown the wind. I have no spur
To prick the sides of my intent, but only
Vaulting ambition, which o'er-leaps itself
And falls on the other. —

Enter LADY MACBETH.
                  How now! what news? 28

Lady M. He has almost supp'd: why have you left the chamber?
Macb. Hath he ask'd for me?
Lady M. Know you not he has?
Macb. We will proceed no further in this business:
He hath honour'd me of late; and I have bought 32
Golden opinions from all sorts of people,
Which would be worn now in their newest gloss,
Not cast aside so soon.
Lady M. Was the hope drunk,
Wherein you dress'd yourself? hath it slept since, 36
And wakes it now, to look so green and pale
At what it did so freely? From this time
Such I account thy love. Art thou afeard
To be the same in thine own act and valour 40
As thou art in desire? Wouldst thou have that
Which thou esteem'st the ornament of life,
And live a coward in thine own esteem,
Letting 'I dare not' wait upon 'I would,' 44
Like the poor cat i' the adage?
Macb. Prithee, peace.
I dare do all that may become a man;
Who dares do more is none.
Lady M. What beast was't, then,
That made you break this enterprise to me? 48
When you durst do it then you were a man;
And, to be more than what you were, you would
Be so much more the man. Nor time nor place
Did then adhere, and yet you would make both: 52
They have made themselves, and that their fitness now
Does unmake you. I have given suck, and know
How tender 'tis to love the babe that milks me:
I would, while it was smiling in my face, 56
Have pluck'd my nipple from his boneless gums,
And dash'd the brains out, had I so sworn as you
Have done to this.
Macb. If we should fail,—
Lady M. We fail!
But screw your courage to the sticking-place, 60
And we'll not fail. When Duncan is asleep,
Whereto the rather shall his day's hard journey
Soundly invite him, his two chamberlains
Will I with wine and wassail so convince 64
That memory, the warder of the brain,
Shall be a fume, and the receipt of reason
A limbeck only; when in swinish sleep
Their drenched natures lie, as in a death, 68
What cannot you and I perform upon
The unguarded Duncan? what not put upon
His spongy officers, who shall bear the guilt
Of our great quell?
Macb. Bring forth men-children only; 72
For thy undaunted mettle should compose
Nothing but males. Will it not be receiv'd,
When we have mark'd with blood those sleepy two 75
Of his own chamber and us'd their very daggers,
That they have done't?
Lady M. Who dares receive it other,
As we shall make our griefs and clamour roar

Upon his death?
Macb. I am settled, and bend up
Each corporal agent to this terrible feat. 80
Away, and mock the time with fairest show:
False face must hide what the false heart doth know. *[Exeunt.*

ACT II

SCENE I.—*Inverness. Court within the Castle.*

Enter BANQUO *and* FLEANCE, *with a* Servant *bearing a torch before him.*

Ban. How goes the night, boy?
Fle. The moon is down; I have not heard the clock.
Ban. And she goes down at twelve.
Fle. I take't, 'tis later, sir.
Ban. Hold, take my sword. There's husbandry in heaven; 4
Their candles are all out. Take thee that too.
A heavy summons lies like lead upon me,
And yet I would not sleep: merciful powers!
Restrain in me the cursed thoughts that nature
Gives way to in repose.

Enter MACBETH, *and a* Servant *with a torch.*
Give me my sword.— 9
Who's there?
Macb. A friend.
Ban. What, sir! not yet at rest? The king's a-bed: 12
He hath been in unusual pleasure, and
Sent forth great largess to your offices.
This diamond he greets your wife withal,
By the name of most kind hostess; and shut up
In measureless content.
Macb. Being unprepar'd, 17
Our will became the servant to defect,
Which else should free have wrought.
Ban. All's well.
I dreamt last night of the three weird sisters: 20
To you they have show'd some truth.
Macb. I think not of them:
Yet, when we can entreat an hour to serve,
We would spend it in some words upon that business,
If you would grant the time.
Ban. At your kind'st leisure. 24
Macb. If you shall cleave to my consent, when 'tis,
It shall make honour for you.
Ban. So I lose none
In seeking to augment it, but still keep
My bosom franchis'd and allegiance clear, 28
I shall be counsell'd.
Macb. Good repose the while!
Ban. Thanks, sir: the like to you.
[Exeunt BANQUO *and* FLEANCE.
Macb. Go bid thy mistress, when my drink is ready
She strike upon the bell. Get thee to bed. 32
[Exit Servant.
Is this a dagger which I see before me,
The handle toward my hand? Come, let me clutch thee:

I have thee not, and yet I see thee still.
Art thou not, fatal vision, sensible   36
To feeling as to sight? or art thou but
A dagger of the mind, a false creation,
Proceeding from the heat-oppressed brain?
I see thee yet, in form as palpable   40
As this which now I draw.
Thou marshall'st me the way that I was going;
And such an instrument I was to use.
Mine eyes are made the fools o' the other
senses,   44
Or else worth all the rest: I see thee still;
And on thy blade and dudgeon gouts of blood,
Which was not so before. There's no such
thing:
It is the bloody business which informs   48
Thus to mine eyes. Now o'er the one half-
world
Nature seems dead, and wicked dreams abuse
The curtain'd sleep; witchcraft celebrates
Pale Hecate's offerings; and wither'd murder, 52
Alarum'd by his sentinel, the wolf,
Whose howl's his watch, thus with his stealthy
pace,
With Tarquin's ravishing strides, toward his
design
Moves like a ghost. Thou sure and firm-set
earth,   56
Hear not my steps, which way they walk, for fear
The very stones prate of my whereabout,
And take the present horror from the time,
Which now suits with it. Whiles I threat he
lives: 60
Words to the heat of deeds too cold breath
gives.   [A bell rings.
I go, and it is done; the bell invites me.
Hear it not, Duncan; for it is a knell
That summons thee to heaven or to hell.   64
[Exit.

SCENE II.—*The Same.*

Enter LADY MACBETH.

Lady M. That which hath made them drunk
hath made me bold,
What hath quench'd them hath given me fire.
Hark!
Peace!
It was the owl that shriek'd, the fatal bellman, 4
Which gives the stern'st good-night. He is
about it:
The doors are open, and the surfeited grooms
Do mock their charge with snores: I have
drugg'd their possets,
That death and nature do contend about them,
Whether they live or die.   9
Macb. [*Within.*] Who's there? what, ho!
Lady M. Alack! I am afraid they have awak'd,
And 'tis not done; the attempt and not the deed
Confounds us. Hark! I laid their daggers
ready;   13
He could not miss them. Had he not resembled
My father as he slept I had done't. My husband!

Enter MACBETH.

Macb. I have done the deed. Didst thou not
hear a noise?   16

Lady M. I heard the owl scream and the
crickets cry.
Did not you speak?
Macb.   When?
Lady M.   Now.
Macb.   As I descended?
Lady M. Ay.
Macb. Hark!   20
Who lies i' the second chamber?
Lady M.   Donalbain.
Macb. [*Looking on his hands.*] This is a sorry
sight.
Lady M. A foolish thought to say a sorry
sight.
Macb. There's one did laugh in's sleep, and
one cried 'Murder!'   24
That they did wake each other: I stood and
heard them;
But they did say their prayers, and address'd
them
Again to sleep.
Lady M.   There are two lodg'd together.
Macb. One cried 'God bless us!' and 'Amen'
the other;   28
As they had seen me with these hangman's
hands.
Listening their fear, I could not say 'Amen',
When they did say 'God bless us!'
Lady M.   Consider it not so deeply
Macb. But wherefore could not I pronounce
'Amen'?   32
I had most need of blessing, and 'Amen'
Stuck in my throat.
Lady M. These deeds must not be thought
After these ways; so, it will make us mad.
Macb. Methought I heard a voice cry 'Sleep
no more!   36
Macbeth does murder sleep', the innocent sleep
Sleep that knits up the ravell'd sleave of care
The death of each day's life, sore labour's bath
Balm of hurt minds, great nature's second
course,   40
Chief nourisher in life's feast,—
Lady M.   What do you mean
Macb. Still it cried, 'Sleep no more!' to all
the house:
'Glamis hath murder'd sleep, and therefore
Cawdor
Shall sleep no more, Macbeth shall sleep no
more!'   44
Lady M. Who was it that thus cried? Why,
worthy thane,
You do unbend your noble strength to think
So brainsickly of things. Go get some water
And wash this filthy witness from your hand.
Why did you bring these daggers from the
place?
They must lie there: go carry them, and smear
The sleepy grooms with blood.
Macb.   I'll go no more
I am afraid to think what I have done;
Look on't again I dare not.
Lady M.   Infirm of purpose
Give me the daggers. The sleeping and the dead
Are but as pictures; 'tis the eye of childhood
That fears a painted devil. If he do bleed,

ll gild the faces of the grooms withal;
or it must seem their guilt.
       [Exit. Knocking within.
 Macb.   Whence is that knocking?
How is 't with me, when every noise appals me?
What hands are here! Ha! they pluck out mine
 eyes.   60
Will all great Neptune's ocean wash this blood
 clean from my hand? No, this my hand will
 rather
The multitudinous seas incarnadine,
Making the green one red.   64

   Re-enter LADY MACBETH.

 Lady M. My hands are of your colour, but I
 shame
To wear a heart so white.—[*Knocking within.*]
 I hear a knocking
At the south entry; retire we to our chamber;
A little water clears us of this deed; 68
How easy is it, then! Your constancy
Hath left you unattended. [*Knocking within.*]
 Hark! more knocking.
Get on your night-gown, lest occasion call us,
And show us to be watchers. Be not lost 72
So poorly in your thoughts.
 Macb. To know my deed 'twere best not
 know myself.   [*Knocking within.*
Wake Duncan with thy knocking! I would thou
 couldst!   [*Exeunt.*

  SCENE III.—*The Same.*

 Knocking within. Enter a Porter.

 Porter. Here's a knocking, indeed! If a man
were porter of hell-gate he should have old
turning the key. [*Knocking within.*] Knock,
knock, knock! Who's there, i' the name of
Beelzebub? Here's a farmer that hanged himself on the expectation of plenty: come in time;
have napkins enough about you; here you'll
sweat for 't. [*Knocking within.*] Knock, knock!
Who's there i' the other devil's name! Faith,
here's an equivocator, that could swear in both
the scales against either scale; who committed
treason enough for God's sake, yet could not
equivocate to heaven: O! come in, equivocator.
[*Knocking within.*] Knock, knock, knock! Who's
here? Faith, here's an English tailor come
hither for stealing out of a French hose: come
in, tailor; here you may roast your goose.
[*Knocking within.*] Knock, knock; never at
quiet! What are you? But this place is too
cold for hell. I'll devil-porter it no further:
I had thought to have let in some of all professions, that go the primrose way to the everlasting bonfire. [*Knocking within.*] Anon, anon!
pray you, remember the porter. 24
        [Opens the gate.

 Enter MACDUFF *and* LENNOX.

 Macd. Was it so late, friend, ere you went
 to bed,
That you do lie so late?
 Port. Faith, sir, we were carousing till the
second cock; and drink, sir, is a great provoker
of three things.   29

 Macd. What three things does drink especially provoke?
 Port. Marry, sir, nose-painting, sleep, and
urine. Lechery, sir, it provokes, and unpro-
vokes; it provokes the desire, but it takes away
the performance. Therefore much drink may
be said to be an equivocator with lechery; it
makes him, and it mars him; it sets him on,
and it takes him off; it persuades him, and dis-
heartens him; makes him stand to, and not
stand to; in conclusion, equivocates him in a
sleep, and, giving him the lie, leaves him. 41
 Macd. I believe drink gave thee the lie last
night.
 Port. That it did, sir, i' the very throat o' me:
but I requited him for his lie; and, I think, being
too strong for him, though he took up my legs
sometime, yet I made a shift to cast him.
 Macd. Is thy master stirring? 48

   Enter MACBETH.

Our knocking has awak'd him; here he comes.
 Len. Good morrow, noble sir.
 Macb.   Good morrow, both.
 Macd. Is the king stirring, worthy thane?
 Macb.   Not yet.
 Macd. He did command me to call timely
 on him: 52
I have almost slipp'd the hour.
 Macb.   I'll bring you to him.
 Macd. I know this is a joyful trouble to you;
But yet 'tis one.
 Macb. The labour we delight in physics pain.
This is the door.
 Macd.   I'll make so bold to call, 57
For 'tis my limited service.   [*Exit.*
 Len. Goes the king hence to-day?
 Macb.   He does: he did appoint so.
 Len. The night has been unruly: where we
 lay,   60
Our chimneys were blown down; and, as they
 say,
Lamentings heard i' the air; strange screams of
 death,
And prophesying with accents terrible
Of dire combustion and confus'd events 64
New hatch'd to the woeful time. The obscure
 bird
Clamour'd the livelong night: some say the
 earth
Was feverous and did shake.
 Macb.   'Twas a rough night.
 Len. My young remembrance cannot parallel
A fellow to it.   69

   Re-enter MACDUFF.

 Macd. O horror! horror! horror! Tongue
 nor heart
Cannot conceive nor name thee!
 Macb. }
 Len. }   What's the matter?
 Macd. Confusion now hath made his master-
 piece!   72
Most sacrilegious murder hath broke ope
The Lord's anointed temple, and stole thence
The life o' the building!

Macb. What is 't you say? the life?   76
Len. Mean you his majesty?
Macd. Approach the chamber, and destroy
   your sight
With a new Gorgon: do not bid me speak;
See, and then speak yourselves.
          [*Exeunt* MACBETH *and* LENNOX.
          Awake! awake! 80
Ring the alarum-bell. Murder and treason!
Banquo and Donalbain! Malcolm! awake!
Shake off this downy sleep, death's counterfeit,
And look on death itself! up, up, and see   84
The great doom's image! Malcolm! Banquo!
As from your graves rise up, and walk like
   sprites,
To countenance this horror! Ring the bell.
          [*Bell rings.*

      Enter LADY MACBETH.

Lady M. What's the business,   88
That such a hideous trumpet calls to parley
The sleepers of the house? speak, speak!
Macd.   O gentle lady!
'Tis not for you to hear what I can speak;
The repetition in a woman's ear   92
Would murder as it fell.

      Enter BANQUO.

          O Banquo! Banquo!
Our royal master 's murder'd!
Lady M.   Woe, alas!
What! in our house?
Ban.   Too cruel any where.
Dear Duff, I prithee, contradict thyself,   96
And say it is not so.

    Re-enter MACBETH *and* LENNOX.

Macb. Had I but died an hour before this
   chance
I had liv'd a blessed time; for, from this instant,
There's nothing serious in mortality,   100
All is but toys; renown and grace is dead,
The wine of life is drawn, and the mere lees
Is left this vault to brag of.

     Enter MALCOLM *and* DONALBAIN.

Don. What is amiss?
Macb.   You are, and do not know 't:
The spring, the head, the fountain of your blood
Is stopp'd; the very source of it is stopp'd.
Macd. Your royal father 's murder'd.
Mal.   O! by whom?
Len. Those of his chamber, as it seem'd, had
   done 't: 108
Their hands and faces were all badg'd with
   blood;
So were their daggers, which unwip'd we found
Upon their pillows: they star'd, and were dis-
   tracted; no man's life
Was to be trusted with them.   112
Macb. O! yet I do repent me of my fury,
That I did kill them.
Macd.   Wherefore did you so?
Macb. Who can be wise, amaz'd, temperate
   and furious,
Loyal and neutral, in a moment? No man: 116

The expedition of my violent love
Outran the pauser, reason. Here lay Duncan,
His silver skin lac'd with his golden blood;
And his gash'd stabs look'd like a breach in
   nature   120
For ruin's wasteful entrance: there, the mur-
   derers,
Steep'd in the colours of their trade, their dag-
   gers
Unmannerly breech'd with gore: who could
   refrain,
That had a heart to love, and in that heart 124
Courage to make 's love known?
Lady M.   Help me hence, ho!
Macd. Look to the lady.
Mal. [*Aside to* DONALBAIN.] Why do we hold
   our tongues,
That most may claim this argument for ours?
Don. [*Aside to* MALCOLM.] What should be
   spoken   128
Here where our fate, hid in an auger-hole,
May rush and seize us? Let's away: our tears
Are not yet brew'd.
Mal. [*Aside to* DONALBAIN.] Nor our strong
   sorrow
Upon the foot of motion.
Ban.   Look to the lady: 13
       [LADY MACBETH *is carried out*
And when we have our naked frailties hid,
That suffer in exposure, let us meet,
And question this most bloody piece of work
To know it further. Fears and scruples shake us
In the great hand of God I stand, and thence 13
Against the undivulg'd pretence I fight
Of treasonous malice.
Macd.   And so do I.
All.   So all.
Macb. Let's briefly put on manly readiness
And meet i' the hall together.
All.   Well contented. 14
     [*Exeunt all but* MALCOLM *and* DONALBAIN
Mal. What will you do? Let's not consort
   with them.
To show an unfelt sorrow is an office
Which the false man does easy. I'll to England
Don. To Ireland, I; our separated fortune
Shall keep us both the safer: where we are,
There's daggers in men's smiles: the near in
   blood,
The nearer bloody.
Mal.   This murderous shaft that's shot
Hath not yet lighted, and our safest way   1
Is to avoid the aim: therefore, to horse;
And let us not be dainty of leave-taking,
But shift away: there's warrant in that theft
Which steals itself when there's no mercy left
          [*Exeur*

    SCENE IV.—*The Same. Without the Castle*

     Enter ROSS *and an* Old Man.

Old Man. Threescore and ten I can remember well;
Within the volume of which time I have seen
Hours dreadful and things strange, but this sore
   night

Hath trifled former knowings.
  Ross.   Ah! good father, 4
Thou seest, the heavens, as troubled with man's
     act,
Threaten his bloody stage: by the clock 'tis day,
And yet dark night strangles the travelling lamp.
Is't night's predominance, or the day's shame,
That darkness does the face of earth entomb, 9
When living light should kiss it?
  Old Man.   'Tis unnatural,
Even like the deed that's done. On Tuesday last,
A falcon, towering in her pride of place,   12
Was by a mousing owl hawk'd at and kill'd.
  Ross. And Duncan's horses,—a thing most
     strange and certain,—
Beauteous and swift, the minions of their race,
Turn'd wild in nature, broke their stalls, flung
     out,   16
Contending 'gainst obedience, as they would
Make war with mankind.
  Old Man.   'Tis said they eat each other.
  Ross. They did so; to the amazement of mine
     eyes,
That look'd upon't. Here comes the good
     Macduff.   20

Enter MACDUFF.

How goes the world, sir, now?
  Macd.   Why, see you not?
  Ross. Is't known who did this more than
     bloody deed?
  Macd. Those that Macbeth hath slain.
  Ross.   Alas, the day!
What good could they pretend?
  Macd.   They were suborn'd. 24
Malcolm and Donalbain, the king's two sons,
Are stol'n away and fled, which puts upon them
Suspicion of the deed.
  Ross.   'Gainst nature still!
Thriftless ambition, that wilt ravin up   28
Thine own life's means! Then 'tis most like
The sovereignty will fall upon Macbeth.
  Macd. He is already nam'd, and gone to Scone
To be invested.
  Ross.   Where is Duncan's body?   32
  Macd. Carried to Colmekill;
The sacred storehouse of his predecessors
And guardian of their bones.
  Ross.   Will you to Scone?
  Macd. No, cousin, I'll to Fife.
  Ross.   Well, I will thither. 36
  Macd. Well, may you see things well done
     there: adieu!
Lest our old robes sit easier than our new!
  Ross. Farewell, father.
  Old Man. God's benison go with you; and
     with those   40
That would make good of bad, and friends of
     foes!   [*Exeunt.*

ACT III

SCENE I.—*Forres. A Room in the Palace.*
Enter BANQUO.

  Ban. Thou hast it now: King, Cawdor,
     Glamis, all,
As the weird women promis'd; and, I fear,
Thou play'dst most foully for't; yet it was said
It should not stand in thy posterity,   4
But that myself should be the root and father
Of many kings. If there come truth from
     them,—
As upon thee, Macbeth, their speeches shine,—
Why, by the verities on thee made good,   8
May they not be my oracles as well,
And set me up in hope? But, hush! no more.

Sennet sounded. Enter MACBETH, *as king;* LADY
     MACBETH, *as queen;* LENNOX, ROSS, Lords,
     Ladies, *and* Attendants.

  Macb. Here's our chief guest.
  Lady M.   If he had been forgotten
It had been as a gap in our great feast,   12
And all-thing unbecoming.
  Macb. To-night we hold a solemn supper, sir,
And I'll request your presence.
  Ban.   Let your highness
Command upon me; to the which my duties 16
Are with a most indissoluble tie
For ever knit.
  Macb. Ride you this afternoon?
  Ban. Ay, my good lord.   20
  Macb. We should have else desir'd your
     good advice—
Which still hath been both grave and pros-
     perous—
In this day's council; but we'll take to-morrow.
Is't far you ride?   24
  Ban. As far, my lord, as will fill up the time
'Twixt this and supper; go not my horse the
     better,
I must become a borrower of the night
For a dark hour or twain.
  Macb.   Fail not our feast. 28
  Ban. My lord, I will not.
  Macb. We hear our bloody cousins are be-
     stow'd
In England and in Ireland, not confessing
Their cruel parricide, filling their hearers 32
With strange invention; but of that to-morrow,
When therewithal we shall have cause of state
Craving us jointly. Hie you to horse; adieu
Till you return at night. Goes Fleance with you?
  Ban. Ay, my good lord: our time does call
     upon's.   37
  Macb. I wish your horses swift and sure of
     foot;
And so I do commend you to their backs.
Farewell.   [*Exit* BANQUO.
Let every man be master of his time   41
Till seven at night; to make society
The sweeter welcome, we will keep ourself
Till supper-time alone; while then, God be with
     you!   [*Exeunt all but* MACBETH
                            and an Attendant.
Sirrah, a word with you. Attend those men 45
Our pleasure?
  Atten. They are, my lord, without the palace
     gate.
  Macb. Bring them before us. [*Exit* Attend-
     ant.] To be thus is nothing;   48

But to be safely thus. Our fears in Banquo
Stick deep, and in his royalty of nature
Reigns that which would be fear'd: 'tis much
  he dares,
And, to that dauntless temper of his mind, 52
He hath a wisdom that doth guide his valour
To act in safety. There is none but he
Whose being I do fear; and under him
My genius is rebuk'd, as it is said 56
Mark Antony's was by Cæsar. He chid the
  sisters
When first they put the name of king upon me,
And bade them speak to him; then, prophet-like,
They hail'd him father to a line of kings. 60
Upon my head they plac'd a fruitless crown,
And put a barren sceptre in my gripe,
Thence to be wrench'd with an unlineal hand,
No son of mine succeeding. If't be so, 64
For Banquo's issue have I fil'd my mind;
For them the gracious Duncan have I murder'd;
Put rancours in the vessel of my peace
Only for them; and mine eternal jewel 68
Given to the common enemy of man,
To make them kings, the seed of Banquo kings!
Rather than so, come fate into the list,
And champion me to the utterance! Who's
  there? 72

Re-enter Attendant, *with two* Murderers.

Now go to the door, and stay there till we call.
  [*Exit* Attendant.
Was it not yesterday we spoke together?
  First Mur. It was, so please your highness.
  Macb. Well then, now
Have you consider'd of my speeches? Know 76
That it was he in the times past which held you
So under fortune, which you thought had been
Our innocent self. This I made good to you
In our last conference, pass'd in probation with
  you, 80
How you were borne in hand, how cross'd, the
  instruments,
Who wrought with them, and all things else
  that might
To half a soul and to a notion craz'd
Say, 'Thus did Banquo.'
  First Mur. You made it known to us. 84
  Macb. I did so; and went further, which is now
Our point of second meeting. Do you find
Your patience so predominant in your nature
That you can let this go? Are you so gospell'd
To pray for this good man and for his issue, 89
Whose heavy hand hath bow'd you to the grave
And beggar'd yours for ever?
  First Mur. We are men, my liege.
  Macb. Ay, in the catalogue ye go for men; 92
As hounds and greyhounds, mongrels, spaniels,
  curs,
Shoughs, water-rugs, and demi-wolves, are clept
All by the name of dogs: the valu'd file
Distinguishes the swift, the slow, the subtle, 96
The housekeeper, the hunter, every one
According to the gift which bounteous nature
Hath in him clos'd; whereby he does receive
Particular addition, from the bill 100
That writes them all alike: and so of men.

Now, if you have a station in the file,
Not i' the worst rank of manhood, say it;
And I will put that business in your bosoms, 104
Whose execution takes your enemy off,
Grapples you to the heart and love of us,
Who wear our health but sickly in his life,
Which in his death were perfect.
  Sec. Mur. I am one, my liege, 108
Whom the vile blows and buffets of the world
Have so incens'd that I am reckless what
I do to spite the world.
  First Mur. And I another,
So weary with disasters, tugg'd with fortune, 112
That I would set my life on any chance,
To mend it or be rid on't.
  Macb. Both of you
Know Banquo was your enemy.
  Sec. Mur. True, my lord.
  Macb. So is he mine; and in such bloody
  distance 116
That every minute of his being thrusts
Against my near'st of life: and though I could
With bare-fac'd power sweep him from my sight
And bid my will avouch it, yet I must not, 120
For certain friends that are both his and mine,
Whose loves I may not drop, but wail his fall
Whom I myself struck down; and thence it is
That I to your assistance do make love, 124
Masking the business from the common eye
For sundry weighty reasons.
  Sec. Mur. We shall, my lord,
Perform what you command us.
  First Mur. Though our lives—
  Macb. Your spirits shine through you. With-
  in this hour at most 128
I will advise you where to plant yourselves,
Acquaint you with the perfect spy o' the time,
The moment on't; for't must be done to-night,
And something from the palace; always thought
That I require a clearness: and with him— 133
To leave no rubs nor botches in the work—
Fleance his son, that keeps him company,
Whose absence is no less material to me 136
Than is his father's, must embrace the fate
Of that dark hour. Resolve yourselves apart
I'll come to you anon.
  Sec. Mur. We are resolv'd, my lord.
  Macb. I'll call upon you straight: abide with-
  in. [*Exeunt* Murderers.
It is concluded: Banquo, thy soul's flight, 141
If it find heaven, must find it out to-night. [*Exit*

SCENE II.—*The Same. Another Room in
  the Palace.*

Enter LADY MACBETH *and a* Servant.

  Lady M. Is Banquo gone from court?
  Serv. Ay, madam, but returns again to-night.
  Lady M. Say to the king, I would attend his
  leisure
For a few words.
  Serv. Madam, I will. [*Exit*
  Lady M. Nought's had, all's spent,
Where our desire is got without content:
'Tis safer to be that which we destroy
Than by destruction dwell in doubtful joy.

Enter MACBETH.

low now, my lord! why do you keep alone, 8
)f sorriest fancies your companions making,
Jsing those thoughts which should indeed have
          died
Vith them they think on? Things without all
          remedy
hould be without regard: what's done is done.

Macb. We have scotch'd the snake, not kill'd
          it: 13
he'll close and be herself, whilst our poor
          malice
Remains in danger of her former tooth.
But let the frame of things disjoint, both the
          worlds suffer,   16
Ere we will eat our meal in fear, and sleep
n the affliction of these terrible dreams
That shake us nightly. Better be with the dead,
Vhom we, to gain our peace, have sent to peace,
Than on the torture of the mind to lie   21
n restless ecstasy. Duncan is in his grave;
After life's fitful fever he sleeps well;
Treason has done his worst: nor steel, nor
          poison,   24
Malice domestic, foreign levy, nothing
Can touch him further.

Lady M.   Come on;
Gentle my lord, sleek o'er your rugged looks;
Be bright and jovial among your guests to-night.

Macb. So shall I, love; and so, I pray, be you.
Let your remembrance apply to Banquo;
Present him eminence, both with eye and
          tongue:
Unsafe the while, that we   32
Must lave our honours in these flattering
          streams,
And make our faces vizards to our hearts,
Disguising what they are.

Lady M.   You must leave this.

Macb. O! full of scorpions is my mind, dear
          wife;   36
Thou know'st that Banquo and his Fleance
          lives.

Lady M. But in them nature's copy's not
          eterne.

Macb. There's comfort yet; they are assail-
          able;
Then be thou jocund. Ere the bat hath flown 40
His cloister'd flight, ere, to black Hecate's sum-
          mons
The shard-borne beetle with his drowsy hums
Hath rung night's yawning peal, there shall be
          done
A deed of dreadful note.

Lady M.   What's to be done? 44

Macb. Be innocent of the knowledge, dearest
          chuck,
Till thou applaud the deed. Come, seeling night,
Scarf up to the tender eye of pitiful day,
And with thy bloody and invisible hand   48
Cancel and tear to pieces that great bond
Which keeps me pale! Light thickens, and the
          crow
Makes wing to the rooky wood;
Good things of day begin to droop and drowse,

Whiles night's black agents to their preys do
          rouse.   53
Thou marvell'st at my words: but hold thee
          still;
Things bad begun make strong themselves by
          ill:
So, prithee, go with me.   [*Exeunt.*

SCENE III.—*The Same. A Park, with a Road
          leading to the Palace.*

Enter three Murderers.

First Mur. But who did bid thee join with us?

Third Mur.   Macbeth.

Sec. Mur. He needs not our mistrust, since
          he delivers
Our offices and what we have to do
To the direction just.

First Mur.   Then stand with us.   4
The west yet glimmers with some streaks of day:
Now spurs the lated traveller apace
To gain the timely inn; and near approaches
The subject of our watch.

Third Mur.   Hark! I hear horses.   8

Ban. [*Within.*] Give us a light there, ho!

Sec. Mur.   Then 'tis he: the rest
That are within the note of expectation
Already are i' the court.

First Mur.   His horses go about.

Third Mur. Almost a mile; but he does
          usually,   12
So all men do, from hence to the palace gate
Make it their walk.

Sec. Mur.   A light, a light!

Third Mur.   'Tis he.

First Mur. Stand to't.

Enter BANQUO *and* FLEANCE, *with a torch.*

Ban. It will be rain to-night.

First Mur.   Let it come down. 16
                    [*They set upon* BANQUO.

Ban. O, treachery! Fly, good Fleance, fly,
          fly, fly!
Thou mayst revenge. O slave!
                    [*Dies.* FLEANCE *escapes.*

Third Mur. Who did strike out the light?

First Mur.   Was't not the way?

Third Mur. There's but one down; the son
          is fled.

Sec. Mur.   We have lost 20
Best half of our affair.

First Mur. Well, let's away, and say how
          much is done.   [*Exeunt.*

SCENE IV.—*The Same. A Room of State in
          the Palace.*

A Banquet prepared. Enter MACBETH, LADY MAC-
BETH, ROSS, LENNOX, Lords, *and* Attendants.

Macb. You know your own degrees; sit
          down: at first and last,
The hearty welcome.

Lords.   Thanks to your majesty.

Macb. Ourself will mingle with society
And play the humble host.   4
Our hostess keeps her state, but in best time
We will require her welcome.

Lady M. Pronounce it for me, sir, to all our
friends;
For my heart speaks they are welcome.   8

Enter First Murderer, *to the door.*

Macb. See, they encounter thee with their
hearts' thanks;
Both sides are even: here I'll sit i' the midst:
Be large in mirth; anon, we'll drink a measure
The table round. [*Approaching the door.*]
There's blood upon thy face.   12
Mur. 'Tis Banquo's, then.
Macb. 'Tis better thee without than he within.
Is he dispatch'd?
Mur. My lord, his throat is cut; that I did
for him.   16
Macb. Thou art the best o' the cut-throats;
yet he 's good
That did the like for Fleance: if thou didst it,
Thou art the nonpareil.
Mur.   Most royal sir,
Fleance is 'scap'd.   20
Macb. Then comes my fit again: I had else
been perfect;
Whole as the marble, founded as the rock,
As broad and general as the casing air:
But now I am cabin'd, cribb'd, confin'd, bound
in   24
To saucy doubts and fears. But Banquo 's safe?
Mur. Ay, my good lord; safe in a ditch he
bides,
With twenty trenched gashes on his head,
The least a death to nature.
Macb.   Thanks for that. 28
There the grown serpent lies: the worm that 's fled
Hath nature that in time will venom breed,
No teeth for the present. Get thee gone; to-
morrow
We'll hear ourselves again.   [*Exit* Murderer.
Lady M.   My royal lord,   32
You do not give the cheer: the feast is sold
That is not often vouch'd, while 'tis a-making,
'Tis given with welcome: to feed were best at
home;
From thence, the sauce to meat is ceremony; 36
Meeting were bare without it.
Macb.   Sweet remembrancer!
Now good digestion wait on appetite,
And health on both!
Len.   May it please your highness sit?
[*The Ghost of* BANQUO *enters, and
sits in* MACBETH'S *place.*
Macb. Here had we now our country's
honour roof'd,   40
Were the grac'd person of our Banquo present;
Who may I rather challenge for unkindness
Than pity for mischance!
Ross.   His absence, sir,
Lays blame upon his promise. Please 't your
highness   44
To grace us with your royal company.
Macb. The table 's full.
Len.   Here is a place reserv'd, sir.
Macb. Where?
Len. Here, my good lord. What is 't that
moves your highness?   48

Macb. Which of you have done this?
Lords.   What, my good lord?
Macb. Thou canst not say I did it: never
shake
Thy gory locks at me.
Ross. Gentlemen, rise; his highness is not
well.   52
Lady M. Sit, worthy friends: my lord is
often thus,
And hath been from his youth: pray you, keep
seat;
The fit is momentary; upon a thought
He will again be well. If much you note him 56
You shall offend him and extend his passion:
Feed and regard him not. Are you a man?
Macb. Ay, and a bold one, that dare look on
that
Which might appal the devil.
Lady M.   O proper stuff! 60
This is the very painting of your fear;
This is the air-drawn dagger which, you said
Led you to Duncan. O! these flaws and starts—
Impostors to true fear—would well become 64
A woman's story at a winter's fire,
Authoriz'd by her grandam. Shame itself!
Why do you make such faces? When all 's done
You look but on a stool.   68
Macb. Prithee, see there! behold! look! lo!
how say you?
Why, what care I? If thou canst nod, speak too.
If charnel-houses and our graves must send
Those that we bury back, our monuments 72
Shall be the maws of kites. [*Ghost disappears.*
Lady M. What! quite unmann'd in folly?
Macb. If I stand here, I saw him.
Lady M.   Fie, for shame!
Macb. Blood hath been shed ere now, i' the
olden time,
Ere human statute purg'd the gentle weal; 76
Ay, and since too, murders have been perform'd
Too terrible for the ear: the times have been,
That, when the brains were out, the man would
die,
And there an end; but now they rise again, 80
With twenty mortal murders on their crowns,
And push us from our stools: this is more strange
Than such a murder is.
Lady M.   My worthy lord,
Your noble friends do lack you.
Macb.   I do forget. 84
Do not muse at me, my most worthy friends;
I have a strange infirmity, which is nothing
To those that know me. Come, love and health
to all;
Then, I'll sit down. Give me some wine; fill full.
I drink to the general joy of the whole table, 89
And to our dear friend Banquo, whom we miss;
Would he were here! to all, and him, we thirst,
And all to all.
Lords.   Our duties, and the pledge. 92

Re-enter Ghost.

Macb. Avaunt! and quit my sight! Let the
earth hide thee!
Thy bones are marrowless, thy blood is cold;

hou hast no speculation in those eyes
hich thou dost glare with.
Lady M.   Think of this, good peers,
ut as a thing of custom: 'tis no other;   97
nly it spoils the pleasure of the time.
Macb. What man dare, I dare:
pproach thou like the rugged Russian bear,
he arm'd rhinoceros, or the Hyrcan tiger;   101
ake any shape but that, and my firm nerves
hall never tremble: or be alive again,
nd dare me to the desert with thy sword;   104
trembling I inhabit then, protest me
he baby of a girl. Hence, horrible shadow!
nreal mockery, hence!   [*Ghost vanishes.*
                                 Why, so; being gone,
am a man again. Pray you, sit still.   108
Lady M. You have displac'd the mirth,
  broke the good meeting,
ith most admir'd disorder.
Macb.   Can such things be
nd overcome us like a summer's cloud,
ithout our special wonder? You make me
  strange   112
ven to the disposition that I owe,
hen now I think you can behold such sights,
nd keep the natural ruby of your cheeks,
hen mine are blanch'd with fear.
Ross.   What sights, my lord? 116
Lady M. I pray you, speak not; he grows
  worse and worse:
uestion enrages him. At once, good-night:
tand not upon the order of your going,
ut go at once.
Len.   Good-night; and better health 120
ttend his majesty!
Lady M.   A kind good-night to all!
                 [*Exeunt* Lords *and* Attendants.
Macb. It will have blood, they say; blood
  will have blood:
tones have been known to move and trees to
  speak;
ugurs and understood relations have   124
y maggot-pies and choughs and rooks brought
  forth
he secret'st man of blood. What is the night?
Lady M. Almost at odds with morning,
  which is which.
Macb. How sayst thou, that Macduff denies
  his person   128
t our great bidding?
Lady M.   Did you send to him, sir?
Macb. I hear it by the way; but I will send.
here's not a one of them but in his house
keep a servant fee'd. I will to-morrow—   132
nd betimes I will—to the weird sisters:
ore shall they speak; for now I am bent to
  know,
y the worst means, the worst. For mine own
  good
ll causes shall give way: I am in blood   136
tepp'd in so far, that, should I wade no more,
eturning were as tedious as go o'er.
trange things I have in head that will to hand,
hich must be acted ere they may be scann'd.
Lady M. You lack the season of all natures,
  sleep.   141

Macb. Come, we'll to sleep. My strange and
  self-abuse
Is the initiate fear that wants hard use:
We are yet but young in deed.   [*Exeunt.*

SCENE V.—*A Heath.*

Thunder. Enter the three Witches, *meeting*
HECATE.

First Witch. Why, how now, Hecate! you
  look angrily.
Hec. Have I not reason, beldams as you are,
Saucy and overbold? How did you dare
To trade and traffic with Macbeth   4
In riddles and affairs of death;
And I, the mistress of your charms,
The close contriver of all harms,
Was never call'd to bear my part,   8
Or show the glory of our art?
And, which is worse, all you have done
Hath been but for a wayward son,
Spiteful and wrathful; who, as others do,   12
Loves for his own ends, not for you.
But make amends now: get you gone,
And at the pit of Acheron
Meet me i' the morning: thither he   16
Will come to know his destiny:
Your vessels and your spells provide,
Your charms and every thing beside.
I am for the air; this night I'll spend   20
Unto a dismal and a fatal end:
Great business must be wrought ere noon:
Upon the corner of the moon
There hangs a vaporous drop profound;   24
I'll catch it ere it come to ground:
And that distill'd by magic sleights
Shall raise such artificial sprites
As by the strength of their illusion   28
Shall draw him on to his confusion:
He shall spurn fate, scorn death, and bear
His hopes 'bove wisdom, grace, and fear;
And you all know security   32
Is mortals' chiefest enemy.
 [*Song within,* 'Come away, come away,' &c.
Hark! I am call'd; my little spirit, see,
Sits in a foggy cloud, and stays for me. [*Exit.*
First Witch. Come, let's make haste; she'll
  soon be back again.   [*Exeunt.*

SCENE VI.—*Forres. A Room in the Palace.*

Enter LENNOX *and another* Lord.

Len. My former speeches have but hit your
  thoughts,
Which can interpret further: only, I say,
Things have been strangely borne. The gracious
  Duncan
Was pitied of Macbeth: marry, he was dead: 4
And the right-valiant Banquo walk'd too late;
Whom, you may say, if 't please you, Fleance
  kill'd,
For Fleance fled: men must not walk too late.
Who cannot want the thought how monstrous 8
It was for Malcolm and for Donalbain
To kill their gracious father? damned fact!
How it did grieve Macbeth! did he not straight

In pious rage the two delinquents tear,   12
That were the slaves of drink and thralls of
    sleep?
Was not that nobly done? Ay, and wisely too;
For 'twould have anger'd any heart alive
To hear the men deny't. So that, I say,   16
He has borne all things well; and I do think
That, had he Duncan's sons under his key,—
As, an't please heaven, he shall not,—they
    should find
What 'twere to kill a father; so should Fleance.
But, peace! for from broad words, and 'cause
    he fail'd   21
His presence at the tyrant's feast, I hear,
Macduff lives in disgrace. Sir, can you tell
Where he bestows himself?
  Lord.   The son of Duncan, 24
From whom this tyrant holds the due of birth,
Lives in the English court, and is receiv'd
Of the most pious Edward with such grace
That the malevolence of fortune nothing   28
Takes from his high respect. Thither Macduff
Is gone to pray the holy king, upon his aid
To wake Northumberland and war-like Siward:
That, by the help of these—with him above 32
To ratify the work—we may again
Give to our tables meat, sleep to our nights,
Free from our feasts and banquets bloody
    knives,
Do faithful homage and receive free honours;
All which we pine for now. And this report 37
Hath so exasperate the king that he
Prepares for some attempt at war.
  Len.   Sent he to Macduff?
  Lord. He did: and with an absolute, 'Sir,
    not I',   40
The cloudy messenger turns me his back,
And hums, as who should say, 'You'll rue the
    time
That clogs me with this answer'.
  Len.   And that well might
Advise him to a caution to hold what distance
His wisdom can provide. Some holy angel 45
Fly to the court of England and unfold
His message ere he come, that a swift blessing
May soon return to this our suffering country 48
Under a hand accurs'd!
  Lord.   I'll send my prayers with him!
                                    [*Exeunt.*

ACT IV

Scene I.—*A Cavern. In the middle, a boiling
        Cauldron.*

  Thunder. Enter the three Witches.

First Witch. Thrice the brinded cat hath
    mew'd.
Sec. Witch. Thrice and once the hedge-pig
    whin'd.
Third Witch. Harper cries: 'Tis time, 'tis
    time.
First Witch. Round about the cauldron go; 4
    In the poison'd entrails throw.
  Toad, that under cold stone
  Days and nights hast thirty-one
  Swelter'd venom sleeping got,   8

Boil thou first i' the charmed pot.
All. Double, double toil and trouble;
  Fire burn and cauldron bubble.
Sec. Witch. Fillet of a fenny snake,   12
  In the cauldron boil and bake;
  Eye of newt, and toe of frog,
  Wool of bat, and tongue of dog,
  Adder's fork, and blind-worm's sting,   16
  Lizard's leg, and howlet's wing,
  For a charm of powerful trouble,
  Like a hell-broth boil and bubble.
All. Double, double toil and trouble;   20
  Fire burn and cauldron bubble.
Third Witch. Scale of dragon, tooth of wolf,
  Witches' mummy, maw and gulf
  Of the ravin'd salt-sea shark,   24
  Root of hemlock digg'd i' the dark,
  Liver of blaspheming Jew,
  Gall of goat, and slips of yew
  Sliver'd in the moon's eclipse,   28
  Nose of Turk, and Tartar's lips,
  Finger of birth-strangled babe
  Ditch-deliver'd by a drab,
  Make the gruel thick and slab: 32
  Add thereto a tiger's chaudron,
  For the ingredients of our cauldron.
All. Double, double toil and trouble;
  Fire burn and cauldron bubble.   36
Sec. Witch. Cool it with a baboon's blood,
  Then the charm is firm and good.

Enter HECATE.

Hec. O! well done! I commend your pains,
  And every one shall share i' the gains.   40
  And now about the cauldron sing,
  Like elves and fairies in a ring,
  Enchanting all that you put in.
    [*Music and a song,* 'Black Spirits,' &c.
Sec. Witch. By the pricking of my thumbs, 44
  Something wicked this way comes.
      Open, locks,
      Whoever knocks.

Enter MACBETH.

Macb. How now, you secret, black, and mid-
    night hags!   48
What is't you do?
  All.   A deed without a name.
  Macb. I conjure you, by that which you
    profess,—
Howe'er you come to know it,—answer me:
Though you untie the winds and let them fight 52
Against the churches; though the yesty waves
Confound and swallow navigation up;
Though bladed corn be lodg'd and trees blown
    down;
Though castles topple on their warders' heads
Though palaces and pyramids do slope   5
Their heads to their foundations; though the
    treasure
Of Nature's germens tumble all together,
Even till destruction sicken; answer me   6
To what I ask you.
  First Witch.   Speak.
  Sec. Witch.   Demand.
  Third Witch.   We'll answer

First Witch. Say if thou'dst rather hear it
  from our mouths,
Or from our masters'?
Macb.   Call 'em: let me see 'em.
First Witch. Pour in sow's blood, that hath
  eaten   64
  Her nine farrow; grease, that's sweaten
  From the murderer's gibbet throw
  Into the flame.
All.   Come, high or low;
  Thyself and office deftly show.   68

Thunder. First Apparition *of an armed Head.*

Macb. Tell me, thou unknown power,—
First Witch.   He knows thy thought:
  Hear his speech, but say thou nought.
First App. Macbeth! Macbeth! Macbeth!
  beware Macduff;
  Beware the Thane of Fife. Dismiss me. Enough.
                                      [*Descends.*
Macb. Whate'er thou art, for thy good cau-
  tion thanks;   73
  Thou hast harp'd my fear aright. But one word
  more,—
First Witch. He will not be commanded:
  here's another,
  More potent than the first.   76

   Thunder. Second Apparition, *a bloody
                Child.*

Sec. App. Macbeth! Macbeth! Macbeth!—
Macb. Had I three ears, I'd hear thee.
Sec. App. Be bloody, bold, and resolute;
  laugh to scorn
  The power of man, for none of woman born 80
  Shall harm Macbeth.   [*Descends.*
Macb. Then live, Macduff: what need I fear
  of thee?
  But yet I'll make assurance double sure,
  And take a bond of fate: thou shalt not live; 84
  That I may tell pale-hearted fear it lies,
  And sleep in spite of thunder.

Thunder. Third Apparition, *a Child crowned,
  with a tree in his hand.*

                      What is this,
  That rises like the issue of a king,
  And wears upon his baby brow the round   88
  And top of sovereignty?
All.   Listen, but speak not to't.
Third App. Be lion-mettled, proud, and take
  no care
  Who chafes, who frets, or where conspirers are:
  Macbeth shall never vanquish'd be until   92
  Great Birnam wood to high Dunsinane hill
  Shall come against him.   [*Descends.*
Macb.   That will never be:
  Who can impress the forest, bid the tree
  Unfix his earth-bound root? Sweet bodements!
  good!   96
  Rebellion's head, rise never till the wood
  Of Birnam rise, and our high-plac'd Macbeth
  Shall live the lease of nature, pay his breath
  To time and mortal custom. Yet my heart 100
  Throbs to know one thing: tell me—if your art
  Can tell so much,—shall Banquo's issue ever

Reign in this kingdom?
All.   Seek to know no more.
Macb. I will be satisfied: deny me this, 104
And an eternal curse fall on you! Let me know.
Why sinks that cauldron? and what noise is
  this?   [*Hautboys.*
First Witch. Show!
Sec. Witch. Show!   108
Third Witch. Show!
All. Show his eyes, and grieve his heart;
Come like shadows, so depart.

*A show of Eight Kings; the last with a glass in
  his hand;* BANQUO'S Ghost *following.*

Macb. Thou art too like the spirit of Banquo;
  down!   112
Thy crown does sear mine eyeballs: and thy hair,
Thou other gold-bound brow, is like the first:
A third is like the former. Filthy hags!
Why do you show me this? A fourth! Start,
  eyes!   116
What! will the line stretch out to the crack of
  doom?
Another yet? A seventh! I'll see no more:
And yet the eighth appears, who bears a glass
Which shows me many more; and some I see
That two-fold balls and treble sceptres carry. 121
Horrible sight! Now, I see, 'tis true;
For the blood-bolter'd Banquo smiles upon me,
And points at them for his. [*Apparitions vanish.*
                    What! is this so? 124
First Witch. Ay, sir, all this is so: but why
Stands Macbeth thus amazedly?
Come, sisters, cheer we up his sprites,
And show the best of our delights.   128
I'll charm the air to give a sound,
While you perform your antick round,
That this great king may kindly say,
Our duties did his welcome pay.   132
      [*Music. The* Witches *dance, and then
              vanish with* HECATE.
Macb. Where are they? Gone? Let this
  pernicious hour
Stand aye accursed in the calendar!
Come in, without there!

              Enter LENNOX.

Len.   What's your Grace's will?
Macb. Saw you the weird sisters?
Len.   No, my lord. 136
Macb. Came they not by you?
Len.   No indeed, my lord.
Macb. Infected be the air whereon they ride,
And damn'd all those that trust them! I did
  hear
The galloping of horse: who was't came by? 140
Len. 'Tis two or three, my lord, that bring
  you word
Macduff is fled to England.
Macb.   Fled to England!
Len. Ay, my good lord.
Macb. Time, thou anticipat'st my dread ex-
  ploits;   144
The flighty purpose never is o'ertook
Unless the deed go with it; from this moment
The very firstlings of my heart shall be

The firstlings of my hand. And even now, 148
To crown my thoughts with acts, be it thought
and done:
The castle of Macduff I will surprise;
Seize upon Fife; give to the edge of the sword 152
His wife, his babes, and all unfortunate souls
That trace him in his line. No boasting like a
fool;
This deed I'll do, before this purpose cool:
But no more sights! Where are these gentle-
men?
Come, bring me where they are.   [*Exeunt.*

SCENE II.—*Fife.* MACDUFF'S *Castle.*

Enter LADY MACDUFF, *her Son, and* ROSS.

L. Macd. What had he done to make him
fly the land?
Ross. You must have patience, madam.
L. Macd.   He had none:
His flight was madness: when our actions do
not,
Our fears do make us traitors.
Ross.   You know not 4
Whether it was his wisdom or his fear.
L. Macd. Wisdom! to leave his wife, to leave
his babes,
His mansion and his titles in a place
From whence himself does fly? He loves us
not; 8
He wants the natural touch; for the poor wren,
The most diminutive of birds, will fight—
Her young ones in her nest—against the owl.
All is the fear and nothing is the love; 12
As little is the wisdom, where the flight
So runs against all reason.
Ross.   My dearest coz,
I pray you, school yourself: but, for your hus-
band,
He is noble, wise, judicious, and best knows 16
The fits o' the season. I dare not speak much
further:
But cruel are the times, when we are traitors
And do not know ourselves, when we hold
rumour
From what we fear, yet know not what we fear,
But float upon a wild and violent sea 21
Each way and move. I take my leave of you:
Shall not be long but I'll be here again.
Things at the worst will cease, or else climb up-
ward 24
To what they were before. My pretty cousin,
Blessing upon you!
L. Macd. Father'd he is, and yet he's father-
less.
Ross. I am so much a fool, should I stay
longer, 28
It would be my disgrace, and your discomfort:
I take my leave at once.   [*Exit.*
L. Macd.   Sirrah, your father's dead:
And what will you do now? How will you live?
Son. As birds do, mother.
L. Macd. What! with worms and flies? 32
Son. With what I get, I mean; and so do they.
L. Macd. Poor bird! thou'dst never fear the
net nor lime,

The pit-fall nor the gin.
Son. Why should I, mother? Poor birds
they are not set for. 36
My father is not dead, for all your saying.
L. Macd. Yes, he is dead: how wilt thou do
for a father?
Son. Nay, how will you do for a husband?
L. Macd. Why, I can buy me twenty at any
market. 40
Son. Then you'll buy 'em to sell again.
L. Macd. Thou speak'st with all thy wit;
and yet, i' faith,
With wit enough for thee.
Son. Was my father a traitor, mother? 44
L. Macd. Ay, that he was.
Son. What is a traitor?
L. Macd. Why, one that swears and lies.
Son. And be all traitors that do so? 48
L. Macd. Every one that does so is a traitor,
and must be hanged.
Son. And must they all be hanged that swear
and lie?
L. Macd. Every one.
Son. Who must hang them? 52
L. Macd. Why, the honest men.
Son. Then the liars and swearers are fools,
for there are liars and swearers enow to beat the
honest men, and hang up them. 56
L. Macd. Now God help thee, poor monkey!
But how wilt thou do for a father?
Son. If he were dead, you'd weep for him: if
you would not, it were a good sign that I should
quickly have a new father. 61
L. Macd. Poor prattler, how thou talk'st!

Enter a Messenger.

Mess. Bless you, fair dame! I am not to you
known,
Though in your state of honour I am perfect. 64
I doubt some danger does approach you nearly:
If you will take a homely man's advice,
Be not found here; hence, with your little ones.
To fright you thus, methinks, I am too savage;
To do worse to you were fell cruelty, 69
Which is too nigh your person. Heaven pre-
serve you!
I dare abide no longer.   [*Exit.*
L. Macd.   Whither should I fly?
I have done no harm. But I remember now 72
I am in this earthly world, where, to do harm
Is often laudable, to do good sometime
Accounted dangerous folly; why then, alas!
Do I put up that womanly defence, 76
To say I have done no harm?

Enter Murderers.

                          What are these faces?
Mur. Where is your husband?
L. Macd. I hope in no place so unsanctified
Where such as thou mayst find him.
Mur.   He's a traitor. 80
Son. Thou liest, thou shag-hair'd villain.
Mur.   What! you egg
Young fry of treachery!   [*Stabbing him.*
Son.   He has killed me, mother

Run away, I pray you!   [*Dies.*
   [*Exit* LADY MACDUFF, *crying* 'Murder',
      and pursued by the Murderers.

SCENE III.—*England. Before the* KING'S
Palace.

Enter MALCOLM *and* MACDUFF.

Mal. Let us seek out some desolate shade,
   and there
Weep our sad bosoms empty.
Macd.   Let us rather
Hold fast the mortal sword, and like good men
Bestride our down-fall'n birthdom; each new
   morn   4
New widows howl, new orphans cry, new sor-
   rows
Strike heaven on the face, that it resounds
As if it felt with Scotland and yell'd out
Like syllable of dolour.
Mal.   What I believe I'll wail, 8
What know believe, and what I can redress,
As I shall find the time to friend, I will.
What you have spoke, it may be so perchance.
This tyrant, whose sole name blisters our tongues,
Was once thought honest: you have lov'd him
   well;   13
He hath not touch'd you yet. I am young; but
   something
You may deserve of him through me, and wis-
   dom
To offer up a weak, poor, innocent lamb 16
To appease an angry god.
Macd. I am not treacherous.
Mal.   But Macbeth is.
A good and virtuous nature may recoil
In an imperial charge. But I shall crave your
   pardon;   20
That which you are my thoughts cannot trans-
   pose;
Angels are bright still, though the brightest fell;
Though all things foul would wear the brows of
   grace,
Yet grace must still look so.
Macd.   I have lost my hopes. 24
Mal. Perchance even there where I did find
   my doubts.
Why in that rawness left you wife and child—
Those precious motives, those strong knots of
   love—
Without leave-taking? I pray you,   28
Let not my jealousies be your dishonours,
But mine own safeties: you may be rightly just,
Whatever I shall think.
Macd.   Bleed, bleed, poor country!
Great tyranny, lay thou thy basis sure, 32
For goodness dares not check thee! wear thou
   thy wrongs;
The title is affeer'd! Fare thee well, lord:
I would not be the villain that thou think'st
For the whole space that's in the tyrant's grasp,
And the rich East to boot.
Mal.   Be not offended: 37
I speak not as in absolute fear of you.
I think our country sinks beneath the yoke;
It weeps, it bleeds, and each new day a gash 40

Is added to her wounds: I think withal,
There would be hands uplifted in my right;
And here from gracious England have I offer
Of goodly thousands: but, for all this, 44
When I shall tread upon the tyrant's head,
Or wear it on my sword, yet my poor country
Shall have more vices than it had before,
More suffer, and more sundry ways than ever, 48
By him that shall succeed.
Macd.   What should he be?
Mal. It is myself I mean; in whom I know
All the particulars of vice so grafted,
That, when they shall be open'd, black Macbeth
Will seem as pure as snow, and the poor state 53
Esteem him as a lamb, being compar'd
With my confineless harms.
Macd.   Not in the legions
Of horrid hell can come a devil more damn'd 56
In evils to top Macbeth.
Mal.   I grant him bloody,
Luxurious, avaricious, false, deceitful,
Sudden, malicious, smacking of every sin
That has a name; but there's no bottom, none,
In my voluptuousness: your wives, your daugh-
   ters,   61
Your matrons, and your maids, could not fill up
The cistern of my lust; and my desire
All continent impediments would o'erbear 64
That did oppose my will; better Macbeth
Than such an one to reign.
Macd.   Boundless intemperance
In nature is a tyranny; it hath been
Th' untimely emptying of the happy throne, 68
And fall of many kings. But fear not yet
To take upon you what is yours; you may
Convey your pleasures in a spacious plenty,
And yet seem cold, the time you may so hood-
   wink.   72
We have willing dames enough; there cannot
   be
That vulture in you, to devour so many
As will to greatness dedicate themselves,
Finding it so inclin'd.
Mal.   With this there grows 76
In my most ill-compos'd affection such
A stanchless avarice that, were I king,
I should cut off the nobles for their lands,
Desire his jewels and this other's house; 80
And my more-having would be as a sauce
To make me hunger more, that I should forge
Quarrels unjust against the good and loyal,
Destroying them for wealth.
Macd.   This avarice 84
Sticks deeper, grows with more pernicious root
Than summer-seeming lust, and it hath been
The sword of our slain kings: yet do not fear;
Scotland hath foisons to fill up your will, 88
Of your mere own; all these are portable,
With other graces weigh'd.
Mal. But I have none: the king-becoming
   graces,
As justice, verity, temperance, stableness, 92
Bounty, perseverance, mercy, lowliness,
Devotion, patience, courage, fortitude,
I have no relish of them, but abound
In the division of each several crime, 96

Acting it many ways. Nay, had I power, I should
Pour the sweet milk of concord into hell,
Uproar the universal peace, confound
All unity on earth.

Macd.   O Scotland, Scotland! 100

Mal. If such a one be fit to govern, speak:
I am as I have spoken.

Macd.   Fit to govern!
No, not to live. O nation miserable,
With an untitled tyrant bloody-scepter'd, 104
When shalt thou see thy wholesome days again,
Since that the truest issue of thy throne
By his own interdiction stands accurs'd,
And does blaspheme his breed? Thy royal
     father 108
Was a most sainted king; the queen that bore
     thee,
Oft'ner upon her knees than on her feet,
Died every day she liv'd. Fare thee well!
These evils thou repeat'st upon thyself 112
Have banish'd me from Scotland. O my breast,
Thy hope ends here!

Mal.   Macduff, this noble passion,
Child of integrity, hath from my soul
Wip'd the black scruples, reconcil'd my thoughts
To thy good truth and honour. Devilish Mac-
     beth 117
By many of these trains hath sought to win me
Into his power, and modest wisdom plucks me
From over-credulous haste; but God above 120
Deal between thee and me! for even now
I put myself to thy direction, and
Unspeak mine own detraction, here abjure
The taints and blames I laid upon myself, 124
For strangers to my nature. I am yet
Unknown to woman, never was forsworn,
Scarcely have coveted what was mine own;
At no time broke my faith, would not betray 128
The devil to his fellow, and delight
No less in truth than life; my first false speaking
Was this upon myself. What I am truly,
Is thine and my poor country's to command; 132
Whither indeed, before thy here-approach,
Old Siward, with ten thousand war-like men,
Already at a point, was setting forth.
Now we'll together, and the chance of goodness
Be like our warranted quarrel. Why are you
     silent? 137

Macd. Such welcome and unwelcome things
     at once
'Tis hard to reconcile.

Enter a Doctor.

Mal. Well; more anon. Comes the king
     forth, I pray you? 140

Doct. Ay, sir; there are a crew of wretched
     souls
That stay his cure; their malady convinces
The great assay of art; but, at his touch,
Such sanctity hath heaven given his hand, 144
They presently amend.

Mal.   I thank you, doctor.
         [*Exit* Doctor.

Macd. What's the disease he means?

Mal.   'Tis call'd the evil:
A most miraculous work in this good king,

Which often, since my here-remain in Englan
I have seen him do. How he solicits heaven, 1.
Himself best knows; but strangely-visite
     people,
All swoln and ulcerous, pitiful to the eye,
The mere despair of surgery, he cures; 1
Hanging a golden stamp about their necks,
Put on with holy prayers; and 'tis spoken
To the succeeding royalty he leaves
The healing benediction. With this strang
     virtue, 1!
He hath a heavenly gift of prophecy,
And sundry blessings hang about his throne
That speak him full of grace.

Macd.   See, who comes here

Mal. My countryman; but yet I know hi
     not. 16

Enter ROSS.

Macd. My ever-gentle cousin, welcom
     hither.

Mal. I know him now. Good God, betime
     remove
The means that make us strangers!

Ross.   Sir, amen

Macd. Stands Scotland where it did?

Ross.   Alas! poor country; 16
Almost afraid to know itself. It cannot
Be call'd our mother, but our grave; wher
     nothing,
But who knows nothing, is once seen to smile
Where sighs and groans and shrieks that ren
     the air 16
Are made, not mark'd; where violent sorrov
     seems
A modern ecstasy; the dead man's knell
Is there scarce ask'd for who; and good men's live
Expire before the flowers in their caps, 17
Dying or ere they sicken.

Macd.   O! relation
Too nice, and yet too true!

Mal.   What's the newest grief

Ross. That of an hour's age doth hiss th
     speaker;
Each minute teems a new one.

Macd.   How does my wife? 17

Ross. Why, well.

Macd.   And all my children?

Ross.   Well too

Macd. The tyrant has not batter'd at thei
     peace?

Ross. No; they were well at peace when I di
     leave 'em.

Macd. Be not a niggard of your speech: hov
     goes't? 18

Ross. When I came hither to transport th
     tidings,
Which I have heavily borne, there ran a rumou
Of many worthy fellows that were out;
Which was to my belief witness'd the rather 18.
For that I saw the tyrant's power a-foot.
Now is the time of help; your eye in Scotlan
Would create soldiers, make our women fight
To doff their dire distresses.

Mal.   Be't their comfort, 18
We are coming thither. Gracious England hath

[s]ent us good Siward and ten thousand men;
[a]n older and a better soldier none
[t]hat Christendom gives out.

Ross.   Would I could answer 192
[t]his comfort with the like! But I have words
[t]hat would be howl'd out in the desert air,
[W]here hearing should not latch them.

Macd.   What concern they?
[t]he general cause? or is it a fee-grief   196
[d]ue to some single breast?

Ross.   No mind that's honest
[b]ut in it shares some woe, though the main part
[p]ertains to you alone.

Macd.   If it be mine
[k]eep it not from me; quickly let me have it. 200

Ross. Let not your ears despise my tongue
   for ever,
[W]hich shall possess them with the heaviest
   sound
[t]hat ever yet they heard.

Macd.   Hum! I guess at it.

Ross. Your castle is surpris'd; your wife and
   babes   204
[s]avagely slaughter'd; to relate the manner,
[W]ere, on the quarry of these murder'd deer,
[T]o add the death of you.

Mal.   Merciful heaven!
[W]hat! man; ne'er pull your hat upon your
   brows;   208
[G]ive sorrow words; the grief that does not speak
[W]hispers the o'er-fraught heart and bids it
   break.

Macd. My children too?

Ross.   Wife, children, servants, all
[t]hat could be found.

Macd.   And I must be from thence! 212
[M]y wife kill'd too?

Ross.   I have said.

Mal.   Be comforted:
[L]et's make us medicine of our great revenge,
[T]o cure this deadly grief.

Macd. He has no children. All my pretty
   ones?   216
[D]id you say all? O hell-kite! All?
[W]hat! all my pretty chickens and their dam
[A]t one fell swoop?

Mal.   Dispute it like a man.

Macd.   I shall do so;
[B]ut I must also feel it as a man: 220
[I] cannot but remember such things were,
[T]hat were most precious to me. Did heaven
   look on,
[A]nd would not take their part? Sinful Macduff!
[T]hey were all struck for thee. Naught that I
   am,   224
[N]ot for their own demerits, but for mine,
[F]ell slaughter on their souls. Heaven rest them
   now!

Mal. Be this the whetstone of your sword:
   let grief
[C]onvert to anger; blunt not the heart, enrage
   it.   228

Macd. O! I could play the woman with mine
   eyes,
[A]nd braggart with my tongue. But, gentle
   heavens,

Cut short all intermission; front to front   231
Bring thou this fiend of Scotland and myself;
Within my sword's length set him; if he 'scape,
Heaven forgive him too!

Mal.   This tune goes manly.
Come, go we to the king; our power is ready;
Our lack is nothing but our leave. Macbeth 236
Is ripe for shaking, and the powers above
Put on their instruments. Receive what cheer
   you may;
The night is long that never finds the day.

                              [*Exeunt.*

ACT V

SCENE I.—*Dunsinane. A Room in the Castle.*

Enter a Doctor of Physic *and a* Waiting-Gentle-
woman.

Doct. I have two nights watched with you,
but can perceive no truth in your report. When
was it she last walked?   3

Gen. Since his majesty went into the field,
I have seen her rise from her bed, throw her
night-gown upon her, unlock her closet, take
forth paper, fold it, write upon't, read it, afterwards seal it, and again return to bed; yet all
this while in a most fast sleep.   9

Doct. A great perturbation in nature, to
receive at once the benefit of sleep and do the
effects of watching! In this slumbery agitation,
besides her walking and other actual performances, what, at any time, have you heard her say?

Gen. That, sir, which I will not report after
her.   16

Doct. You may to me, and 'tis most meet you
should.

Gen. Neither to you nor any one, having no
witness to confirm my speech.   20

Enter LADY MACBETH, *with a taper.*

Lo you! here she comes. This is her very guise;
and, upon my life, fast asleep. Observe her;
stand close.

Doct. How came she by that light?   24

Gen. Why, it stood by her: she has light by
her continually; 'tis her command.

Doct. You see, her eyes are open.

Gen. Ay, but their sense is shut.   28

Doct. What is it she does now? Look, how
she rubs her hands.

Gen. It is an accustomed action with her, to
seem thus washing her hands. I have known
her to continue in this a quarter of an hour. 33

Lady M. Yet here's a spot.

Doct. Hark! she speaks. I will set down
what comes from her, to satisfy my remembrance the more strongly.   37

Lady M. Out, damned spot! out, I say! One;
two: why, then, 'tis time to do 't. Hell is murky!
Fie, my lord, fie! a soldier, and afeard? What
need we fear who knows it, when none can call
our power to account? Yet who would have
thought the old man to have had so much
blood in him?   44

Doct. Do you mark that?

Lady M. The Thane of Fife had a wife:

where is she now? What! will these hands ne'er be clean? No more o' that, my lord, no more o' that: you mar all with this starting.   49

Doct. Go to, go to; you have known what you should not.

Gen. She has spoke what she should not, I am sure of that: Heaven knows what she has known.   54

Lady M. Here's the smell of the blood still: all the perfumes of Arabia will not sweeten this little hand. Oh! oh! oh!   57

Doct. What a sigh is there! The heart is sorely charged.

Gen. I would not have such a heart in my bosom for the dignity of the whole body.   61

Doct. Well, well, well.

Gen. Pray God it be, sir.

Doct. This disease is beyond my practice: yet I have known those which have walked in their sleep who have died holily in their beds.   66

Lady M. Wash your hands, put on your night-gown; look not so pale. I tell you yet again, Banquo's buried; he cannot come out on's grave.

Doct. Even so?   71

Lady M. To bed, to bed: there's knocking at the gate. Come, come, come, come, give me your hand. What's done cannot be undone. To bed, to bed, to bed.   [*Exit.*

Doct. Will she go now to bed?   76

Doct. Foul whisperings are abroad. Unnatural deeds Do breed unnatural troubles; infected minds To their deaf pillows will discharge their secrets; More needs she the divine than the physician.   81 God, God forgive us all! Look after her; Remove from her the means of all annoyance, And still keep eyes upon her. So, good-night: My mind she has mated, and amaz'd my sight. I think, but dare not speak.

Gen.   Good-night, good doctor. [*Exeunt.*

SCENE II.—*The Country near Dunsinane.*

Enter, with drum and colours, MENTEITH, CAITH-NESS, ANGUS, LENNOX, *and* Soldiers.

Ment. The English power is near, led on by Malcolm, His uncle Siward, and the good Macduff. Revenges burn in them; for their dear causes Would to the bleeding and the grim alarm   4 Excite the mortified man.

Ang.   Near Birnam wood Shall we well meet them; that way are they coming.

Caith. Who knows if Donalbain be with his brother?

Len. For certain, sir, he is not: I have a file Of all the gentry: there is Siward's son,   9 And many unrough youths that even now Protest their first of manhood.

Ment.   What does the tyrant?

Caith. Great Dunsinane he strongly fortifies. Some say he's mad; others that lesser hate him Do call it valiant fury; but, for certain,

He cannot buckle his distemper'd cause Within the belt of rule.

Ang.   Now does he feel His secret murders sticking on his hands; Now minutely revolts upbraid his faith-breac Those he commands move only in comman Nothing in love; now does he feel his title Hang loose about him, like a giant's robe Upon a dwarfish thief.

Ment.   Who then shall blam His pester'd senses to recoil and start, When all that is within him does condemn Itself for being there?

Caith.   Well, march we on, To give obedience where 'tis truly ow'd; Meet we the medicine of the sickly weal, And with him pour we in our country's purge Each drop of us.

Len.   Or so much as it needs To dew the sovereign flower and drown th weeds. Make we our march towards Birnam.

[*Exeunt, marchin*

SCENE III.—*Dunsinane. A Room in the Castle.*

Enter MACBETH, Doctor, *and* Attendants.

Macb. Bring me no more reports; let the fly all: Till Birnam wood remove to Dunsinane I cannot taint with fear. What's the boy Ma colm? Was he not born of woman? The spirits th know All mortal consequences have pronounc'd n thus: 'Fear not, Macbeth; no man that's born woman Shall e'er have power upon thee.' Then fl false thanes, And mingle with the English epicures: The mind I sway by and the heart I bear Shall never sag with doubt nor shake with fea

Enter a Servant.

The devil damn thee black, thou cream-fac' loon! Where gott'st thou that goose look?

Serv. There is ten thousand—

Macb.   Geese, villain?

Serv.   Soldiers, si

Macb. Go, prick thy face, and over-red th fear, Thou lily-liver'd boy. What soldiers, patch? Death of thy soul! those linen cheeks of thir Are counsellors to fear. What soldiers, whey face?

Serv. The English force, so please you.

Macb. Take thy face hence. [*Exit Servant* Seyton!—I am sick at heart When I behold—Seyton, I say!—This push a Will cheer me ever or disseat me now. I have liv'd long enough: my way of life Is fall'n into the sear, the yellow leaf: And that which should accompany old age, a

...s honour, love, obedience, troops of friends,
must not look to have; but, in their stead,
curses, not loud but deep, mouth-honour,
        breath,
Which the poor heart would fain deny, and
        dare not.   28
Seyton!

Enter SEYTON.

Sey. What is your gracious pleasure?
Macb.   What news more?
Sey. All is confirm'd, my lord, which was
        reported.
Macb. I'll fight till from my bones my flesh
        be hack'd.   32
Give me my armour.
Sey.   'Tis not needed yet.
Macb. I'll put it on.
Send out more horses, skirr the country round;
Hang those that talk of fear. Give me mine
        armour.   36
How does your patient, doctor?
Doct.   Not so sick, my lord,
As she is troubled with thick-coming fancies,
That keep her from her rest.
Macb.   Cure her of that:
Canst thou not minister to a mind diseas'd, 40
Pluck from the memory a rooted sorrow,
Raze out the written troubles of the brain,
And with some sweet oblivious antidote
Cleanse the stuff'd bosom of that perilous stuff
Which weighs upon the heart?
Doct.   Therein the patient 45
Must minister to himself.
Macb. Throw physic to the dogs; I'll none
        of it.
Come, put mine armour on; give me my staff.
Seyton, send out.—Doctor, the thanes fly from
        me.—   49
Come, sir, dispatch.—If thou couldst, doctor,
        cast
The water of my land, find her disease,
And purge it to a sound and pristine health, 52
I would applaud thee to the very echo,
That should applaud again.—Pull't off, I say.—
What rhubarb, senna, or what purgative drug
Would scour these English hence? Hear'st thou
        of them?   56
Doct. Ay, my good lord; your royal prepara-
        tion
Makes us hear something.
Macb.   Bring it after me.
I will not be afraid of death and bane
Till Birnam forest come to Dunsinane.   60
Doct. [*Aside.*] Were I from Dunsinane away
        and clear,
Profit again should hardly draw me here.
                                    [*Exeunt.*

SCENE IV.—*Country near Birnam Wood.*

Enter, with drum and colours, MALCOLM, Old
SIWARD *and his* Son, MACDUFF, MENTEITH,
CAITHNESS, ANGUS, LENNOX, ROSS, *and* Soldiers
marching.

Mal. Cousins, I hope the days are near at
        hand

That chambers will be safe.
Men.   We doubt it nothing.
Siw. What wood is this before us?
Men. The wood of Birnam.   4
Mal. Let every soldier hew him down a bough
And bear't before him: thereby shall we shadow
The numbers of our host, and make discovery
Err in report of us.
Sold.   It shall be done. 8
Siw. We learn no other but the confident
        tyrant
Keeps still in Dunsinane, and will endure
Our setting down before 't.
Mal.   'Tis his main hope;
For where there is advantage to be given, 12
Both more and less have given him the revolt,
And none serve with him but constrained things
Whose hearts are absent too.
Macd.   Let our just censures
Attend the true event, and put we on   16
Industrious soldiership.
Siw.   The time approaches
That will with due decision make us know
What we shall say we have and what we owe.
Thoughts speculative their unsure hopes relate,
But certain issue strokes must arbitrate,   21
Towards which advance the war.
                                    [*Exeunt, marching.*

SCENE V.—*Dunsinane. Within the Castle.*

Enter, with drum and colours, MACBETH, SEYTON,
and Soldiers.

Macb. Hang out our banners on the out-
        ward walls;
The cry is still, 'They come'; our castle's strength
Will laugh a siege to scorn; here let them lie
Till famine and the ague eat them up;   4
Were they not forc'd with those that should be
        ours,
We might have met them dareful, beard to
        beard,
And beat them backward home.
                                    [*A cry of women within.*
                     What is that noise?
Sey. It is the cry of women, my good lord. 8
                                    [*Exit.*
Macb. I have almost forgot the taste of fears.
The time has been my senses would have cool'd
To hear a night-shriek, and my fell of hair
Would at a dismal treatise rouse and stir   12
As life were in 't. I have supp'd full with horrors;
Direness, familiar to my slaughterous thoughts,
Cannot once start me.

Re-enter SEYTON.

                     Wherefore was that cry?
Sey. The queen, my lord, is dead.   16
Macb. She should have died hereafter;
There would have been a time for such a word.
To-morrow, and to-morrow, and to-morrow,
Creeps in this petty pace from day to day, 20
To the last syllable of recorded time;
And all our yesterdays have lighted fools
The way to dusty death. Out, out, brief candle!
Life's but a walking shadow, a poor player 24

That struts and frets his hour upon the stage,
And then is heard no more; it is a tale
Told by an idiot, full of sound and fury,
Signifying nothing.   28

Enter a Messenger.

Thou com'st to use thy tongue; thy story quickly.
  Mess. Gracious my lord,
I should report that which I say I saw,
But know not how to do it.
  Macb.   Well, say, sir.   32
  Mess. As I did stand my watch upon the hill,
I look'd towards Birnam, and anon, methought,
The wood began to move.
  Macb.   Liar and slave!
  Mess. Let me endure your wrath if 't be not
   so:
Within this three mile may you see it coming;
I say, a moving grove.
  Macb.   If thou speak'st false,
Upon the next tree shalt thou hang alive,
Till famine cling thee; if thy speech be sooth,
I care not if thou dost for me as much.   41
I pull in resolution and begin
To doubt the equivocation of the fiend
That lies like truth; 'Fear not, till Birnam wood
Do come to Dunsinane'; and now a wood   45
Comes toward Dunsinane. Arm, arm, and out!
If this which he avouches does appear,
There is nor flying hence, nor tarrying here.   48
I 'gin to be aweary of the sun,
And wish the estate o' the world were now un-
  done.
Ring the alarum-bell! Blow, wind! come,
  wrack!
At least we'll die with harness on our back.   52
                           [*Exeunt.*

SCENE VI.—*The Same. A Plain before the
Castle.*

Enter, with drum and colours, MALCOLM, *Old*
SIWARD, MACDUFF, &c., *and their Army, with
boughs.*

  Mal. Now near enough; your leavy screens
   throw down,
And show like those you are. You, worthy
  uncle,
Shall, with my cousin, your right-noble son,
Lead our first battle; worthy Macduff and we   4
Shall take upon 's what else remains to do,
According to our order.
  Siw.   Fare you well.
Do we but find the tyrant's power to-night,
Let us be beaten, if we cannot fight.   8
  Macd. Make all our trumpets speak; give
  them all breath,
Those clamorous harbingers of blood and death.
                           [*Exeunt.*

SCENE VII.—*The Same. Another Part
of the Plain.*

Alarums. Enter MACBETH.

  Macb. They have tied me to a stake; I cannot fly,

But bear-like I must fight the course. What's
  he
That was not born of woman? Such a one
Am I to fear, or none.   4

Enter Young SIWARD.

  Young Siw. What is thy name?
  Macb.   Thou'lt be afraid to hear it.
  Young Siw. No; though thou call'st thyself
  a hotter name
Than any is in hell.
  Macb.   My name's Macbeth.
  Young Siw. The devil himself could not pro-
  nounce a title   8
More hateful to mine ear.
  Macb.   No, nor more fearful.
  Young Siw. Thou liest, abhorred tyrant;
  with my sword
I'll prove the lie thou speak'st.
        [*They fight and Young* SIWARD *is slain.*
  Macb.   Thou wast born of woman:
But swords I smile at, weapons laugh to scorn,
Brandish'd by man that's of a woman born.   13
                              [*Exit.*

Alarums. Enter MACDUFF.

  Macd. That way the noise is. Tyrant, show
  thy face:
If thou be'st slain and with no stroke of mine,
My wife and children's ghosts will haunt me
  still.   16
I cannot strike at wretched kerns, whose arms
Are hir'd to bear their staves: either thou,
  Macbeth,
Or else my sword with an unbatter'd edge
I sheathe again undeeded. There thou shouldst
  be;   20
By this great clatter, one of greatest note
Seems bruited. Let me find him, fortune!
And more I beg not.   [*Exit. Alarums.*

Enter MALCOLM *and Old* SIWARD.

  Siw. This way, my lord; the castle's gently
  render'd: 24
The tyrant's people on both sides do fight;
The noble thanes do bravely in the war;
The day almost itself professes yours,
And little is to do.
  Mal.   We have met with foes   28
That strike beside us.
  Siw.   Enter, sir, the castle.
                          [*Exeunt. Alarums.*

Re-enter MACBETH.

  Macb. Why should I play the Roman fool
  and die
On mine own sword? whiles I see lives, the gashes
Do better upon them.

Re-enter MACDUFF.

  Macd.   Turn, hell-hound, turn!   32
  Macb. Of all men else I have avoided thee:
But get thee back; my soul is too much charg'd
With blood of thine already.
  Macd.   I have no words.
My voice is in my sword, thou bloodier villain   36

han terms can give thee out!   [They fight.
Macb.   Thou losest labour:
s easy mayst thou the intrenchant air
'ith thy keen sword impress as make me bleed:
et fall thy blade on vulnerable crests;   40
bear a charmed life, which must not yield
o one of woman born.
Macd.   Despair thy charm;
nd let the angel whom thou still hast serv'd
ell thee, Macduff was from his mother's womb
ntimely ripp'd.   45
Macb. Accursed be that tongue that tells me so,
or it hath cow'd my better part of man:
nd be these juggling fiends no more believ'd, 48
hat palter with us in a double sense;
hat keep the word of promise to our ear,
nd break it to our hope. I'll not fight with thee.
Macd. Then yield thee, coward,   52
nd live to be the show and gaze o' the time:
Ve'll have thee, as our rarer monsters are,
ainted upon a pole, and underwrit,
Here may you see the tyrant.'
Macb.   I will not yield, 56
'o kiss the ground before young Malcolm's feet,
nd to be baited with the rabble's curse.
'hough Birnam wood be come to Dunsinane,
And thou oppos'd, being of no woman born, 60
'et I will try the last: before my body
throw my war-like shield. Lay on, Macduff,
And damn'd be him that first cries, 'Hold,
    enough!'   [*Exeunt, fighting.*

*Retreat. Flourish. Re-enter, with drum and
colours,* MALCOLM, *Old* SIWARD, ROSS, Thanes,
and Soldiers.

Mal. I would the friends we miss were safe
    arriv'd.   64
Siw. Some must go off; and yet, by these I
    see,
o great a day as this is cheaply bought.
Mal. Macduff is missing, and your noble son.
Ross. Your son, my lord, has paid a soldier's
    debt: 68
He only liv'd but till he was a man;
The which no sooner had his prowess confirm'd
n the unshrinking station where he fought,
But like a man he died.

Siw.   Then he is dead? 72
Ross. Ay, and brought off the field. Your
    cause of sorrow
Must not be measur'd by his worth, for then
It hath no end.
Siw.   Had he his hurts before?
Ross. Ay, on the front.
Siw. Why then, God's soldier be he! 76
Had I as many sons as I have hairs,
I would not wish them to a fairer death:
And so, his knell is knoll'd.
Mal.   He's worth more sorrow,
And that I'll spend for him.
Siw.   He's worth no more; 80
They say, he parted well, and paid his score:
And so, God be with him! Here comes newer
    comfort.

Re-enter MACDUFF, *with* MACBETH'S *head.*

Macd. Hail, king! for so thou art. Behold,
    where stands
The usurper's cursed head: the time is free: 84
I see thee compass'd with thy kingdom's pearl,
That speak my salutation in their minds;
Whose voices I desire aloud with mine;
Hail, King of Scotland!
All.   Hail, King of Scotland! 88
                                [*Flourish.*

Mal. We shall not spend a large expense of
    time
Before we reckon with your several loves,
And make us even with you. My thanes and
    kinsmen,
Henceforth be earls, the first that ever Scotland
In such an honour nam'd. What's more to
    do,   93
Which would be planted newly with the time,
As calling home our exil'd friends abroad
That fled the snares of watchful tyranny; 96
Producing forth the cruel ministers
Of this dead butcher and his fiend-like queen,
Who, as 'tis thought, by self and violent hands
Took off her life; this, and what needful else 100
That calls upon us, by the grace of Grace
We will perform in measure, time, and place:
So, thanks to all at once and to each one,
Whom we invite to see us crown'd at Scone. 104
                            [*Flourish. Exeunt.*

HAMLET
PRINCE OF DENMARK

DRAMATIS PERSONÆ

CLAUDIUS, King of Denmark.
HAMLET, Son to the late, and Nephew to the present King.
FORTINBRAS, Prince of Norway.
HORATIO, Friend to Hamlet.
POLONIUS, Lord Chamberlain.
LAERTES, his Son.
VOLTIMAND,
CORNELIUS,
ROSENCRANTZ, } Courtiers.
GUILDENSTERN,
OSRIC,
A Gentleman,
A Priest.

MARCELLUS, } Officers.
BERNARDO,
FRANCISCO, a Soldier.
REYNALDO, Servant to Polonius.
A Captain.
English Ambassadors.
Players. Two Clowns, Grave-diggers.

GERTRUDE, Queen of Denmark and Mother to Hamlet.
OPHELIA, Daughter to Polonius.

Lords, Ladies, Officers, Soldiers, Sailors, Messengers, and Attendants.

Ghost of Hamlet's Father.

SCENE.—*Elsinore.*

ACT I

SCENE I.—*Elsinore. A Platform before the Castle.*

FRANCISCO *at his post. Enter to him* BERNARDO.

Ber. Who's there?
Fran. Nay, answer me; stand, and unfold yourself.
Ber. Long live the king!
Fran. Bernardo? 4
Ber. He.
Fran. You come most carefully upon your hour.
Ber. 'Tis now struck twelve; get thee to bed, Francisco.
Fran. For this relief much thanks; 'tis bitter cold, 8
And I am sick at heart.
Ber. Have you had quiet guard?
Fran. Not a mouse stirring.
Ber. Well, good-night.
If you do meet Horatio and Marcellus, 12
The rivals of my watch, bid them make haste.
Fran. I think I hear them. Stand, ho! Who's there?

Enter HORATIO *and* MARCELLUS.

Hor. Friends to this ground.
Mar. And liegemen to the Dane.
Fran. Give you good-night.
Mar. O! farewell, honest soldier: 16
Who hath reliev'd you?
Fran. Bernardo has my place.
Give you good-night. [*Exit.*
Mar. Holla! Bernardo!
Ber. Say,

What! is Horatio there?
Hor. A piece of him.
Ber. Welcome, Horatio; welcome, good Marcellus. 20
Mar. What! has this thing appear'd again to-night?
Ber. I have seen nothing.
Mar. Horatio says 'tis but our fantasy,
And will not let belief take hold of him 24
Touching this dreaded sight twice seen of us:
Therefore I have entreated him along
With us to watch the minutes of this night;
That if again this apparition come, 28
He may approve our eyes and speak to it.
Hor. Tush, tush! 'twill not appear.
Ber. Sit down awhile,
And let us once again assail your ears,
That are so fortified against our story, 32
What we two nights have seen.
Hor. Well, sit we down,
And let us hear Bernardo speak of this.
Ber. Last night of all,
When yond same star that's westward from the pole 36
Had made his course to illume that part of heaven
Where now it burns, Marcellus and myself,
The bell then beating one,—
Mar. Peace! break thee off; look, where it comes again! 40

Enter Ghost.

Ber. In the same figure, like the king that's dead.
Mar. Thou art a scholar; speak to it, Horatio.
Ber. Looks it not like the king? mark it, Horatio.

Hor. Most like: it harrows me with fear and
wonder.   44
Ber. It would be spoke to.
Mar.   Question it, Horatio.
Hor. What art thou that usurp'st this time
of night,
ogether with that fair and war-like form
ι which the majesty of buried Denmark   48
id sometimes march? by heaven I charge thee,
speak!
Mar. It is offended.
Ber.   See! it stalks away.
Hor. Stay! speak, speak! I charge thee,
speak!   [*Exit* Ghost.
Mar. 'Tis gone, and will not answer.   52
Ber. How now, Horatio! you tremble and
look pale:
ι not this something more than fantasy?
Vhat think you on't?
Hor. Before my God, I might not this believe
Vithout the sensible and true avouch
·f mine own eyes.
Mar.   Is it not like the king?
Hor. As thou art to thyself:
uch was the very armour he had on   60
Vhen he the ambitious Norway combated;
o frown'd he once, when, in an angry parle,
ιe smote the sledded Polacks on the ice.
'is strange.   64
Mar. Thus twice before, and jump at this
dead hour,
Vith martial stalk hath he gone by our watch.
Hor. In what particular thought to work I
know not;
ut in the gross and scope of my opinion,   68
his bodes some strange eruption to our state.
Mar. Good now, sit down, and tell me, he
that knows,
Vhy this same strict and most observant watch
o nightly toils the subject of the land;   72
ιnd why such daily cast of brazen cannon,
ιnd foreign mart for implements of war;
Vhy such impress of shipwrights, whose sore
task
)oes not divide the Sunday from the week;   76
Vhat might be toward, that this sweaty haste
)oth make the night joint-labourer with the
day:
Vho is't that can inform me?
Hor.   That can I;
ιt least, the whisper goes so. Our last king,   80
Vhose image even but now appear'd to us,
Vas, as you know, by Fortinbras of Norway,
'hereto prick'd on by a most emulate pride,
)ar'd to the combat; in which our valiant
Hamlet—   84
'or so this side of our known world esteem'd
him—
)id slay this Fortinbras; who, by a seal'd compact,
Vell ratified by law and heraldry,
)id forfeit with his life all those his lands   88
Vhich he stood seiz'd of, to the conqueror;
ιgainst the which, a moiety competent
Vas gaged by our king; which had return'd

To the inheritance of Fortinbras,   92
Had he been vanquisher; as, by the same
covenant,
And carriage of the article design'd,
His fell to Hamlet. Now, sir, young Fortinbras,
Of unimproved mettle hot and full,   96
Hath in the skirts of Norway here and there
Shark'd up a list of lawless resolutes,
For food and diet, to some enterprise
That hath a stomach in't; which is no other—
As it doth well appear unto our state—   101
But to recover of us, by strong hand
And terms compulsative, those foresaid lands
So by his father lost. And this, I take it,   104
Is the main motive of our preparations,
The source of this our watch and the chief head
Of this post-haste and romage in the land.
Ber. I think it be no other but e'en so;   108
Well may it sort that this portentous figure
Comes armed through our watch, so like the
king
That was and is the question of these wars.
Hor. A mote it is to trouble the mind's eye. 112
In the most high and palmy state of Rome,
A little ere the mightiest Julius fell,
The graves stood tenantless and the sheeted
dead
Did squeak and gibber in the Roman streets; 116
As stars with trains of fire and dews of blood,
Disasters in the sun; and the moist star
Upon whose influence Neptune's empire stands
Was sick almost to doomsday with eclipse; 120
And even the like precurse of fierce events,
As harbingers preceding still the fates
And prologue to the omen coming on,
Have heaven and earth together demonstrated
Unto our climatures and countrymen.   125
But, soft! behold! lo! where it comes again.

Re-enter Ghost.

I'll cross it, though it blast me. Stay, illusion!
If thou hast any sound, or use of voice,   128
Speak to me:
If there be any good thing to be done,
That may to thee do ease and grace to me,
Speak to me: 132
If thou art privy to thy country's fate,
Which happily foreknowing may avoid,
O! speak;
Or if thou hast uphoarded in thy life   136
Extorted treasure in the womb of earth,
For which, they say, you spirits oft walk in
death,   [*Cock crows.*
Speak of it: stay, and speak! Stop it, Mar-
cellus.   139
Mar. Shall I strike at it with my partisan?
Hor. Do, if it will not stand.
Ber.   'Tis here!
Hor.   'Tis here! [*Exit* Ghost.
Mar. 'Tis gone!
We do it wrong, being so majestical,
To offer it the show of violence;   144
For it is, as the air, invulnerable,
And our vain blows malicious mockery.
Ber. It was about to speak when the cock
crew.

Hor. And then it started like a guilty thing
Upon a fearful summons. I have heard, 149
The cock, that is the trumpet to the morn,
Doth with his lofty and shrill-sounding throat
Awake the god of day; and at his warning, 152
Whether in sea or fire, in earth or air,
The extravagant and erring spirit hies
To his confine; and of the truth herein
This present object made probation. 156
Mar. It faded on the crowing of the cock.
Some say that ever 'gainst that season comes
Wherein our Saviour's birth is celebrated,
The bird of dawning singeth all night long; 160
And then, they say, no spirit can walk abroad;
The nights are wholesome; then no planets
    strike,
No fairy takes, nor witch hath power to charm,
So hallow'd and so gracious is the time. 164
Hor. So have I heard and do in part believe it.
But, look, the morn in russet mantle clad,
Walks o'er the dew of yon high eastern hill;
Break we our watch up; and by my advice 168
Let us impart what we have seen to-night
Unto young Hamlet; for, upon my life,
This spirit, dumb to us, will speak to him.
Do you consent we shall acquaint him with it,
As needful in our loves, fitting our duty? 173
Mar. Let's do't, I pray; and I this morning
    know
Where we shall find him most conveniently.
                                    [*Exeunt.*

SCENE II.—*A Room of State in the Castle.*

Enter the KING, QUEEN, HAMLET, POLONIUS,
LAERTES, VOLTIMAND, CORNELIUS, Lords, *and*
Attendants.

King. Though yet of Hamlet our dear bro-
    ther's death
The memory be green, and that it us befitted
To bear our hearts in grief and our whole king-
    dom
To be contracted in one brow of woe, 4
Yet so far hath discretion fought with nature
That we with wisest sorrow think on him,
Together with remembrance of ourselves,
Therefore, our sometime sister, now our queen,
The imperial jointress of this war-like state, 9
Have we, as 'twere with a defeated joy,
With one auspicious and one dropping eye,
With mirth in funeral and with dirge in mar-
    riage, 12
In equal scale weighing delight and dole,
Taken to wife: nor have we herein barr'd
Your better wisdoms, which have freely gone
With this affair along: for all, our thanks. 16
Now follows, that you know, young Fortinbras,
Holding a weak supposal of our worth,
Or thinking by our late dear brother's death
Our state to be disjoint and out of frame, 20
Colleagued with the dream of his advantage,
He hath not fail'd to pester us with message,
Importing the surrender of those lands
Lost by his father, with all bands of law, 24
To our most valiant brother. So much for him.
Now for ourself and for this time of meeting.

Thus much the business is: we have here wr
To Norway, uncle of young Fortinbras, 2
Who, impotent and bed-rid, scarcely hears
Of this his nephew's purpose, to suppress
His further gait herein; in that the levies,
The lists and full proportions, are all made 3
Out of his subject; and we here dispatch
You, good Cornelius, and you, Voltimand,
For bearers of this greeting to old Norway,
Giving to you no further personal power 3
To business with the king more than the scop
Of these dilated articles allow.
Farewell and let your haste commend your duty
    Cor.) In that and all things will we show ou
    Vol.) duty. 4
    King. We doubt it nothing: heartily fare
        well.
                    [*Exeunt* VOLTIMAND *and* CORNELIUS
And now, Laertes, what's the news with you
You told us of some suit; what is 't, Laertes?
You cannot speak of reason to the Dane, 4
And lose your voice; what wouldst thou beg
    Laertes,
That shall not be my offer, not thy asking?
The head is not more native to the heart,
The hand more instrumental to the mouth, 4
Than is the throne of Denmark to thy father
What wouldst thou have, Laertes?
    Laer.   Dread my lord
Your leave and favour to return to France;
From whence though willingly I came to Den
    mark, 5
To show my duty in your coronation,
Yet now, I must confess, that duty done,
My thoughts and wishes bend again toward
    France
And bow them to your gracious leave and
    pardon. 5
    King. Have you your father's leave? Wha
        says Polonius?
    Pol. He hath, my lord, wrung from me my
        slow leave
By laboursome petition, and at last
Upon his will I seal'd my hard consent: 6
I do beseech you, give him leave to go.
    King. Take thy fair hour, Laertes; time be
        thine,
And thy best graces spend it at thy will.
But now, my cousin Hamlet, and my son,— 6
    Ham. [*Aside.*] A little more than kin, and
        less than kind.
    King. How is it that the clouds still hang on
        you?
    Ham. Not so, my lord; I am too much i' the
        sun.
    Queen. Good Hamlet, cast thy nighted colour
        off, 6
And let thine eye look like a friend on Denmark.
Do not for ever with thy vailed lids
Seek for thy noble father in the dust:
Thou know'st 'tis common; all that live must
    die, 7
Passing through nature to eternity.
    Ham. Ay, madam, it is common.
    Queen.   If it be,
Why seems it so particular with thee?

Ham. Seems, madam! Nay, it is; I know not
  'seems.'   76
'Tis not alone my inky cloak, good mother,
Nor customary suits of solemn black,
Nor windy suspiration of forc'd breath,
No, nor the fruitful river in the eye,   80
Nor the dejected haviour of the visage,
Together with all forms, modes, shows of grief,
That can denote me truly; these indeed seem,
For they are actions that a man might play: 84
But I have that within which passeth show;
These but the trappings and the suits of woe.
  King. 'Tis sweet and commendable in your
    nature, Hamlet,
To give these mourning duties to your father: 88
But, you must know, your father lost a father;
That father lost, lost his; and the survivor bound
In filial obligation for some term
To do obsequious sorrow; but to persever 92
In obstinate condolement is a course
Of impious stubbornness; 'tis unmanly grief:
It shows a will most incorrect to heaven,
A heart unfortified, a mind impatient,   96
An understanding simple and unschool'd:
For what we know must be and is as common
As any the most vulgar thing to sense,
Why should we in our peevish opposition 100
Take it to heart? Fie! 'tis a fault to heaven,
A fault against the dead, a fault to nature,
To reason most absurd, whose common theme
Is death of fathers, and who still hath cried, 104
From the first corse till he that died to-day,
'This must be so'. We pray you, throw to earth
This unprevailing woe, and think of us
As of a father; for let the world take note, 108
You are the most immediate to our throne;
And with no less nobility of love
Than that which dearest father bears his son
Do I impart toward you. For your intent 112
In going back to school in Wittenberg,
It is most retrograde to our desire;
And we beseech you, bend you to remain
Here, in the cheer and comfort of our eye, 116
Our chiefest courtier, cousin, and our son.
  Queen. Let not thy mother lose her prayers,
    Hamlet:
I pray thee, stay with us; go not to Wittenberg.
  Ham. I shall in all my best obey you, madam.
  King. Why, 'tis a loving and a fair reply:
Be as ourself in Denmark. Madam, come;
This gentle and unforc'd accord of Hamlet
Sits smiling to my heart; in grace whereof, 124
No jocund health that Denmark drinks to-day,
But the great cannon to the clouds shall tell,
And the king's rouse the heavens shall bruit
  again,
Re-speaking earthly thunder. Come away. 128
          [*Exeunt all except* HAMLET.
  Ham. O! that this too too solid flesh would
    melt,
Thaw and resolve itself into a dew;
Or that the Everlasting had not fix'd
His canon 'gainst self-slaughter! O God! O
  God!   132
How weary, stale, flat, and unprofitable
Seem to me all the uses of this world.

Fie on't! O fie! 'tis an unweeded garden,
That grows to seed; things rank and gross in
  nature   136
Possess it merely. That it should come to this!
But two months dead: nay, not so much, not
  two:
So excellent a king; that was, to this,
Hyperion to a satyr; so loving to my mother 140
That he might not beteem the winds of heaven
Visit her face too roughly. Heaven and earth!
Must I remember? why, she would hang on him,
As if increase of appetite had grown   144
By what it fed on; and yet, within a month,
Let me not think on't: Frailty, thy name is
  woman!
A little month; or ere those shoes were old
With which she follow'd my poor father's body,
Like Niobe, all tears; why she, even she,— 149
O God! a beast, that wants discourse of reason,
Would have mourn'd longer,—married with
  mine uncle,
My father's brother, but no more like my father
Than I to Hercules: within a month,   153
Ere yet the salt of most unrighteous tears
Had left the flushing in her galled eyes,
She married. O! most wicked speed, to post
With such dexterity to incestuous sheets. 157
It is not nor it cannot come to good;
But break, my heart, for I must hold my tongue!

Enter HORATIO, MARCELLUS, *and* BERNARDO.

  Hor. Hail to your lordship!
  Ham.   I am glad to see you well: 160
Horatio, or I do forget myself.
  Hor. The same, my lord, and your poor ser-
    vant ever.
  Ham. Sir, my good friend; I'll change that
    name with you.
And what make you from Wittenberg, Horatio?
Marcellus?   165
  Mar. My good lord,—
  Ham. I am very glad to see you. [*To* BER-
    NARDO.] Good even, sir.
But what, in faith, make you from Wittenberg?
  Hor. A truant disposition, good my lord. 169
  Ham. I would not hear your enemy say so,
Nor shall you do mine ear that violence,
To make it truster of your own report   172
Against yourself; I know you are no truant.
But what is your affair in Elsinore?
We'll teach you to drink deep ere you depart.
  Hor. My lord, I came to see your father's
    funeral.   176
  Ham. I pray thee, do not mock me, fellow-
    student;
I think it was to see my mother's wedding.
  Hor. Indeed, my lord, it follow'd hard upon.
  Ham. Thrift, thrift, Horatio! the funeral
    bak'd meats   180
Did coldly furnish forth the marriage tables.
Would I had met my dearest foe in heaven
Ere I had ever seen that day, Horatio!
My father, methinks I see my father.   184
  Hor. O! where, my lord?
  Ham.   In my mind's eye, Horatio.
  Hor. I saw him once; he was a goodly king.

Ham. He was a man, take him for all in all,
I shall not look upon his like again.   188
Hor. My lord, I think I saw him yesternight.
Ham. Saw who?
Hor. My lord, the king your father.
Ham.   The king, my father!
Hor. Season your admiration for a while   192
With an attent ear, till I may deliver,
Upon the witness of these gentlemen,
This marvel to you.
Ham.   For God's love, let me hear.
Hor. Two nights together had these gentle-
    men,   196
Marcellus and Bernardo, on their watch,
In the dead vast and middle of the night,
Been thus encounter'd: a figure like your father,
Armed at points exactly, cap-a-pe,   200
Appears before them, and with solemn march
Goes slow and stately by them: thrice he walk'd
By their oppress'd and fear-surprised eyes,
Within his truncheon's length; whilst they, dis-
    till'd   204
Almost to jelly with the act of fear,
Stand dumb and speak not to him. This to me
In dreadful secrecy impart they did,
And I with them the third night kept the watch;
Where, as they had deliver'd, both in time,   209
Form of the thing, each word made true and good
The apparition comes. I knew your father;
These hands are not more like.
Ham.   But where was this?
Mar. My lord, upon the platform where we
    watch'd.   213
Ham. Did you not speak to it?
Hor.   My lord, I did;
But answer made it none: yet once methought
It lifted up its head and did address   216
Itself to motion, like as it would speak;
But even then the morning cock crew loud,
And at the sound it shrunk in haste away
And vanish'd from our sight.
Ham.   'Tis very strange.   220
Hor. As I do live, my honour'd lord, 'tis true;
And we did think it writ down in our duty
To let you know of it.
Ham. Indeed, indeed, sirs, but this troubles
    me.   224
Hold you the watch to-night?
Mar. }
Ber. }   We do, my lord.
Ham. Arm'd, say you?
Mar. }
Ber. }   Arm'd, my lord.
Ham.   From top to toe?
Mar. } My lord, from head to foot.
Ber. }
Ham. Then saw you not his face?   228
Hor. O yes! my lord; he wore his beaver up.
Ham. What! look'd he frowningly?
Hor. A countenance more in sorrow than in
    anger.
Ham. Pale or red?   232
Hor. Nay, very pale.
Ham.   And fix'd his eyes upon you?
Hor. Most constantly.
Ham.   I would I had been there.

Hor. It would have much amaz'd you.
Ham. Very like, very like. Stay'd it long? 236
Hor. While one with moderate haste might
    tell a hundred.
Mar. } Longer, longer.
Ber. }
Hor. Not when I saw it.
Ham.   His beard was grizzled, no?
Hor. It was, as I have seen it in his life,   240
A sable silver'd.
Ham.   I will watch to-night;
Perchance 'twill walk again.
Hor.   I warrant it will.
Ham. If it assume my noble father's person,
I'll speak to it, though hell itself should gape 244
And bid me hold my peace. I pray you all,
If you have hitherto conceal'd this sight,
Let it be tenable in your silence still;
And whatsoever else shall hap to-night,   248
Give it an understanding, but no tongue:
I will requite your loves. So, fare you well.
Upon the platform, 'twixt eleven and twelve,
I'll visit you.
All.   Our duty to your honour.   252
Ham. Your loves, as mine to you. Farewell.
    [*Exeunt* HORATIO, MARCELLUS, *and*
        BERNARDO.
My father's spirit in arms! all is not well;
I doubt some foul play: would the night were
    come!
Till then sit still, my soul: foul deeds will rise, 256
Though all the earth o'erwhelm them, to men's
    eyes.   [*Exit.*

SCENE III.—*A Room in* POLONIUS' *House.*

Enter LAERTES *and* OPHELIA.

Laer. My necessaries are embark'd; farewell:
And, sister, as the winds give benefit
And convoy is assistant, do not sleep,
But let me hear from you.
Oph.   Do you doubt that? 4
Laer. For Hamlet, and the trifling of his
    favour,
Hold it a fashion and a toy in blood,
A violet in the youth of primy nature,
Forward, not permanent, sweet, not lasting, 8
The perfume and suppliance of a minute;
No more.
Oph.   No more but so?
Laer.   Think it no more:
For nature, crescent, does not grow alone
In thews and bulk; but, as this temple waxes, 12
The inward service of the mind and soul
Grows wide withal. Perhaps he loves you now,
And now no soil nor cautel doth besmirch
The virtue of his will; but you must fear,   16
His greatness weigh'd, his will is not his own,
For he himself is subject to his birth;
He may not, as unvalu'd persons do,
Carve for himself, for on his choice depends 20
The safety and the health of the whole state;
And therefore must his choice be circumscrib'd
Unto the voice and yielding of that body
Whereof he is the head. Then if he says he loves
    you,   24

t fits your wisdom so far to believe it
As he in his particular act and place
May give his saying deed; which is no further
Than the main voice of Denmark goes withal. 28
Then weigh what loss your honour may sustain,
If with too credent ear you list his songs,
Or lose your heart, or your chaste treasure open
To his unmaster'd importunity.　　　　　　32
Fear it, Ophelia, fear it, my dear sister;
And keep you in the rear of your affection,
Out of the shot and danger of desire.
The chariest maid is prodigal enough　　36
If she unmask her beauty to the moon;
Virtue herself 'scapes not calumnious strokes;
The canker galls the infants of the spring
Too oft before their buttons be disclos'd, 40
And in the morn and liquid dew of youth
Contagious blastments are most imminent.
Be wary then; best safety lies in fear:
Youth to itself rebels, though none else near. 44
　　Oph. I shall th' effect of this good lesson keep,
As watchman to my heart. But, good my
　　brother,
Do not, as some ungracious pastors do,
Show me the steep and thorny way to heaven,
Whiles, like a puff'd and reckless libertine, 49
Himself the primrose path of dalliance treads,
And recks not his own rede.
　　Laer.　　　　　　　　　　O! fear me not.
I stay too long; but here my father comes. 52

Enter POLONIUS.

A double blessing is a double grace;
Occasion smiles upon a second leave.
　　Pol. Yet here, Laertes! aboard, aboard, for
　　shame!
The wind sits in the shoulder of your sail, 56
And you are stay'd for. There, my blessing with
　　thee!
And these few precepts in thy memory
Look thou character. Give thy thoughts no
　　tongue,
Nor any unproportion'd thought his act.　60
Be thou familiar, but by no means vulgar;
The friends thou hast, and their adoption tried,
Grapple them to thy soul with hoops of steel;
But do not dull thy palm with entertainment 64
Of each new-hatch'd, unfledg'd comrade. Be-
　　ware
Of entrance to a quarrel, but, being in,
Bear't that th' opposed may beware of thee.
Give every man thine ear, but few thy voice; 68
Take each man's censure, but reserve thy judg-
　　ment.
Costly thy habit as thy purse can buy,
But not express'd in fancy; rich, not gaudy;
For the apparel oft proclaims the man,　72
And they in France of the best rank and station
Are most select and generous, chief in that.
Neither a borrower, nor a lender be;
For loan oft loses both itself and friend,　76
And borrowing dulls the edge of husbandry.
This above all: to thine own self be true,
And it must follow, as the night the day,
Thou canst not then be false to any man.　80
Farewell; my blessing season this in thee!

　　Laer. Most humbly do I take my leave, my
　　lord.
　　Pol. The time invites you; go, your servants
　　tend.
　　Laer. Farewell, Ophelia; and remember well
What I have said to you.
　　Oph.　　　　　　'Tis in my memory lock'd,
And you yourself shall keep the key of it.　84
　　Laer. Farewell.　　　　　　　　[*Exit.*
　　Pol. What is't, Ophelia, he hath said to you?
　　Oph. So please you, something touching the
　　Lord Hamlet.
　　Pol. Marry, well bethought:
'Tis told me, he hath very oft of late
Given private time to you; and you yourself 92
Have of your audience been most free and
　　bounteous.
If it be so,—as so 'tis put on me,
And that in way of caution,—I must tell you,
You do not understand yourself so clearly 96
As it behoves my daughter and your honour.
What is between you? give me up the truth.
　　Oph. He hath, my lord, of late made many
　　tenders
Of his affection to me.　　　　　　　100
　　Pol. Affection! pooh! you speak like a green
　　girl,
Unsifted in such perilous circumstance.
Do you believe his tenders, as you call them?
　　Oph. I do not know, my lord, what I should
　　think.　　　　　　　　　　　　104
　　Pol. Marry, I'll teach you: think yourself a
　　baby,
That you have ta'en these tenders for true pay,
Which are not sterling. Tender yourself more
　　dearly;
Or,—not to crack the wind of the poor phrase,
Running it thus,—you'll tender me a fool. 109
　　Oph. My lord, he hath importun'd me with
　　love
In honourable fashion.
　　Pol. Ay, fashion you may call it: go to, go to.
　　Oph. And hath given countenance to his
　　speech, my lord,　　　　　　　　113
With almost all the holy vows of heaven.
　　Pol. Ay, springes to catch woodcocks. I do
　　know,
When the blood burns, how prodigal the soul 116
Lends the tongue vows: these blazes, daughter,
Giving more light than heat, extinct in both,
Even in their promise, as it is a-making,
You must not take for fire. From this time 120
Be somewhat scanter of your maiden presence;
Set your entreatments at a higher rate
Than a command to parley. For Lord Hamlet,
Believe so much in him, that he is young, 124
And with a larger tether may he walk
Than may be given you: in few, Ophelia,
Do not believe his vows, for they are brokers,
Not of that dye which their investments show,
But mere implorators of unholy suits,　129
Breathing like sanctified and pious bawds,
The better to beguile. This is for all:
I would not, in plain terms, from this time forth,
Have you so slander any moment's leisure, 133
As to give words or talk with the Lord Hamlet.

Look to't, I charge you; come your ways.

Oph. I shall obey, my lord.   [*Exeunt.*

SCENE IV.—*The Platform.*

Enter HAMLET, HORATIO, *and* MARCELLUS.

Ham. The air bites shrewdly; it is very cold.

Hor. It is a nipping and an eager air.

Ham. What hour now?

Hor.   I think it lacks of twelve.

Mar. No, it is struck.   4

Hor. Indeed? I heard it not: then it draws
    near the season

Wherein the spirit held his wont to walk.
    [*A flourish of trumpets, and ordnance
                    shot off, within.*

What does this mean, my lord?

Ham. The king doth wake to-night and takes
    his rouse,   8

Keeps wassail, and the swaggering up-spring
    reels;

And, as he drains his draughts of Rhenish down,

The kettle-drum and trumpet thus bray out

The triumph of his pledge.

Hor.   Is it a custom?   12

Ham. Ay, marry, is't:

But to my mind,—though I am native here

And to the manner born,—it is a custom

More honour'd in the breach than the obser-
    vance.   16

This heavy-headed revel east and west

Makes us traduc'd and tax'd of other nations;

They clepe us drunkards, and with swinish
    phrase

Soil our addition; and indeed it takes   20

From our achievements, though perform'd at
    height,

The pith and marrow of our attribute.

So, oft it chances in particular men,

That for some vicious mole of nature in them, 24

As, in their birth,—wherein they are not guilty,

Since nature cannot choose his origin,—

By the o'ergrowth of some complexion,

Oft breaking down the pales and forts of reason,

Or by some habit that too much o'er-leavens 29

The form of plausive manners; that these men,

Carrying, I say, the stamp of one defect,

Being nature's livery, or fortune's star,   32

Their virtues else, be they as pure as grace,

As infinite as man may undergo,

Shall in the general censure take corruption

From that particular fault: the dram of eale 36

Doth all the noble substance of a doubt,

To his own scandal.

Enter GHOST.

Hor.   Look, my lord, it comes.

Ham. Angels and ministers of grace defend
    us!

Be thou a spirit of health or goblin damn'd, 40

Bring with thee airs from heaven or blasts from
    hell,

Be thy intents wicked or charitable,

Thou com'st in such a questionable shape

That I will speak to thee: I'll call thee Hamlet,

King, father; royal Dane, O! answer me: 45

Let me not burst in ignorance; but tell

Why thy canoniz'd bones, hearsed in death,

Have burst their cerements; why the sepulchre,

Wherein we saw thee quietly inurn'd,   49

Hath op'd his ponderous and marble jaws,

To cast thee up again. What may this mean,

That thou, dead corse, again in complete steel 52

Revisit'st thus the glimpses of the moon,

Making night hideous; and we fools of nature

So horridly to shake our disposition

With thoughts beyond the reaches of our
    souls?   56

Say, why is this? wherefore? what should we do?
    [*The Ghost beckons* HAMLET.

Hor. It beckons you to go away with it,

As if it some impartment did desire

To you alone.

Mar. Look, with what courteous action   60

It waves you to a more removed ground:

But do not go with it.

Hor.   No, by no means.

Ham. It will not speak; then, will I follow it.

Hor. Do not, my lord.

Ham. Why, what should be the fear?   64

I do not set my life at a pin's fee;

And for my soul, what can it do to that,

Being a thing immortal as itself?

It waves me forth again; I'll follow it.   68

Hor. What if it tempt you toward the flood,
    my lord,

Or to the dreadful summit of the cliff

That beetles o'er his base into the sea,

And there assume some other horrible form, 72

Which might deprive your sovereignty of reason

And draw you into madness? think of it;

The very place puts toys of desperation,

Without more motive, into every brain   76

That looks so many fathoms to the sea

And hears it roar beneath.

Ham. It waves me still. Go on, I'll follow
    thee.

Mar. You shall not go, my lord.

Ham.   Hold off your hands! 80

Hor. Be rul'd; you shall not go.

Ham.   My fate cries out,

And makes each petty artery in this body

As hardy as the Nemean lion's nerve.

    [*Ghost beckons*

Still am I call'd. Unhand me, gentlemen,   84
    [*Breaking from them*

By heaven! I'll make a ghost of him that lets
    me:

I say, away! Go on, I'll follow thee.

    [*Exeunt Ghost and* HAMLET.

Hor. He waxes desperate with imagination

Mar. Let's follow; 'tis not fit thus to obey
    him.   8

Hor. Have after. To what issue will this
    come?

Mar. Something is rotten in the state of
    Denmark.

Hor. Heaven will direct it.

Mar.   Nay, let's follow him
    [*Exeunt.*

SCENE V.—*Another Part of the Platform.*

Enter Ghost *and* HAMLET.

Ham. Whither wilt thou lead me? speak;
  I'll go no further.
Ghost. Mark me.
Ham.   I will.
Ghost.   My hour is almost come,
When I to sulphurous and tormenting flames
Must render up myself.
Ham.   Alas! poor ghost.   4
Ghost. Pity me not, but lend thy serious hearing
To what I shall unfold.
Ham.   Speak; I am bound to hear.
Ghost. So art thou to revenge, when thou
  shalt hear.
Ham. What?   8
Ghost. I am thy father's spirit;
Doom'd for a certain term to walk the night,
And for the day confin'd to fast in fires,
Till the foul crimes done in my days of nature
Are burnt and purg'd away. But that I am
  forbid   13
To tell the secrets of my prison-house,
I could a tale unfold whose lightest word
Would harrow up thy soul, freeze thy young
  blood,   16
Make thy two eyes, like stars, start from their
  spheres,
Thy knotted and combined locks to part,
And each particular hair to stand an end,
Like quills upon the fretful porpentine: 20
But this eternal blazon must not be
To ears of flesh and blood. List, list, O list!
If thou didst ever thy dear father love—
Ham. O God!   24
Ghost. Revenge his foul and most unnatural
  murder.
Ham. Murder!
Ghost. Murder most foul, as in the best it is;
But this most foul, strange, and unnatural. 28
Ham. Haste me to know't, that I, with
  wings as swift
As meditation or the thoughts of love,
May sweep to my revenge.
Ghost.   I find thee apt;
And duller shouldst thou be than the fat weed
That rots itself in ease on Lethe wharf, 33
Wouldst thou not stir in this. Now, Hamlet,
  hear:
'Tis given out that, sleeping in mine orchard,
A serpent stung me; so the whole ear of Den-
  mark   36
Is by a forged process of my death
Rankly abus'd; but know, thou noble youth,
The serpent that did sting thy father's life
Now wears his crown.
Ham.   O my prophetic soul! 40
My uncle!
Ghost. Ay, that incestuous, that adulterate
  beast,
With witchcraft of his wit, with traitrous gifts,—
O wicked wit and gifts, that have the power 44
So to seduce!—won to his shameful lust
The will of my most seeming-virtuous queen.

O Hamlet! what a falling-off was there;
From me, whose love was of that dignity   48
That it went hand in hand even with the vow
I made to her in marriage; and to decline
Upon a wretch whose natural gifts were poor
To those of mine!   52
But virtue, as it never will be mov'd,
Though lewdness court it in a shape of heaven,
So lust, though to a radiant angel link'd,
Will sate itself in a celestial bed,   56
And prey on garbage.
But, soft! methinks I scent the morning air;
Brief let me be. Sleeping within mine orchard,
My custom always in the afternoon,   60
Upon my secure hour thy uncle stole,
With juice of cursed hebona in a vial,
And in the porches of mine ears did pour
The leperous distilment; whose effect 64
Holds such an enmity with blood of man
That swift as quicksilver it courses through
The natural gates and alleys of the body,
And with a sudden vigour it doth posset 68
And curd, like eager droppings into milk,
The thin and wholesome blood: so did it mine,
And a most instant tetter bark'd about,
Most lazar-like, with vile and loathsome crust,
All my smooth body.   73
Thus was I, sleeping, by a brother's hand,
Of life, of crown, of queen, at once dispatch'd;
Cut off even in the blossoms of my sin, 76
Unhousel'd, disappointed, unanel'd,
No reckoning made, but sent to my account
With all my imperfections on my head:
O, horrible! O, horrible! most horrible! 80
If thou hast nature in thee, bear it not;
Let not the royal bed of Denmark be
A couch for luxury and damned incest.
But, howsoever thou pursu'st this act,   84
Taint not thy mind, nor let thy soul contrive
Against thy mother aught; leave her to heaven,
And to those thorns that in her bosom lodge,
To prick and sting her. Fare thee well at once!
The glow-worm shows the matin to be near, 89
And 'gins to pale his uneffectual fire;
Adieu, adieu! Hamlet, remember me. [*Exit.*
Ham. O all you host of heaven! O earth!
  What else?   92
And shall I couple hell? O fie! Hold, hold,
  my heart!
And you, my sinews, grow not instant old,
But bear me stiffly up! Remember thee!
Ay, thou poor ghost, while memory holds a seat
In this distracted globe. Remember thee! 97
Yea, from the table of my memory
I'll wipe away all trivial fond records,
All saws of books, all forms, all pressures past,
That youth and observation copied there; 101
And thy commandment all alone shall live
Within the book and volume of my brain,
Unmix'd with baser matter: yes, by heaven! 104
O most pernicious woman!
O villain, villain, smiling, damned villain!
My tables,—meet it is I set it down,
That one may smile, and smile, and be a villain;
At least I'm sure it may be so in Denmark: 109
                                  [*Writing.*

So, uncle, there you are. Now to my word;
It is, 'Adieu, adieu! remember me'.
I have sworn 't.   112
  Hor. [*Within.*] My lord! my lord!
  Mar. [*Within.*]   Lord Hamlet!
  Hor. [*Within.*]   Heaven secure him!
  Mar. [*Within.*] So be it!
  Hor. [*Within.*] Hillo, ho, ho, my lord!
  Ham. Hillo, ho, ho, boy! come, bird, come.

     Enter HORATIO *and* MARCELLUS.

  Mar. How is 't, my noble lord?
  Hor.   What news, my lord? 117
  Ham. O! wonderful.
  Hor.   Good my lord, tell it.
  Ham. No; you will reveal it.
  Hor. Not I, my lord, by heaven!
  Mar.   Nor I, my lord. 120
  Ham. How say you, then; would heart of
    man once think it?
But you'll be secret?
  Mar. }
  Hor. }   Ay, by heaven, my lord.
  Ham. There's ne'er a villain dwelling in all
    Denmark,
But he's an arrant knave.   124
  Hor. There needs no ghost, my lord, come
    from the grave,
To tell us this.
  Ham.   Why, right; you are i' the right;
And so, without more circumstance at all,
I hold it fit that we shake hands and part; 128
You, as your business and desire shall point
    you,—
For every man hath business and desire,
Such as it is,—and, for mine own poor part,
Look you, I'll go pray.   132
  Hor. These are but wild and whirling words,
    my lord.
  Ham. I am sorry they offend you, heartily;
Yes, faith, heartily.
  Hor.   There's no offence, my lord.
  Ham. Yes, by Saint Patrick, but there is,
    Horatio,   136
And much offence, too. Touching this vision
    here,
It is an honest ghost, that let me tell you;
For your desire to know what is between us,
O'ermaster 't as you may. And now, good
    friends,   140
As you are friends, scholars, and soldiers,
Give me one poor request.
  Hor. What is 't, my lord? we will.
  Ham. Never make known what you have
    seen to-night.   144
  Hor. }
  Mar. } My lord, we will not.
  Ham.   Nay, but swear 't.
  Hor.   In faith,
My lord, not I.
  Mar.   Nor I, my lord, in faith.
  Ham. Upon my sword.
  Mar.   We have sworn, my lord, already.
  Ham. Indeed, upon my sword, indeed. 148
  Ghost. [*Beneath.*] Swear.

  Ham. Ah, ha, boy! sayst thou so? art thou
    there, true-penny?
Come on,—you hear this fellow in the cellar-
    age,—
Consent to swear.
  Hor.   Propose the oath, my lord. 152
  Ham. Never to speak of this that you have
    seen,
Swear by my sword.
  Ghost. [*Beneath.*] Swear.
  Ham. Hic et ubique? then we'll shift our
    ground.   156
Come hither, gentlemen,
And lay your hands again upon my sword:
Never to speak of this that you have heard,
Swear by my sword.   160
  Ghost. [*Beneath.*] Swear.
  Ham. Well said, old mole! canst work i' the
    earth so fast?
A worthy pioner! once more remove, good
    friends.
  Hor. O day and night, but this is wondrous
    strange!   164
  Ham. And therefore as a stranger give it
    welcome.
There are more things in heaven and earth,
    Horatio,
Than are dreamt of in your philosophy.
But come;   168
Here, as before, never, so help you mercy,
How strange or odd soe'er I bear myself,
As I perchance hereafter shall think meet
To put an antic disposition on,   172
That you, at such times seeing me, never shall,
With arms encumber'd thus, or this head-shake,
Or by pronouncing of some doubtful phrase,
As, 'Well, well, we know', or, 'We could, an if
    we would';   176
Or, 'If we list to speak', or, 'There be, an if they
    might';
Or such ambiguous giving out, to note
That you know aught of me: this not to do,
So grace and mercy at your most need help you,
Swear.   180
  Ghost. [*Beneath.*] Swear.   [*They swear.*
  Ham. Rest, rest, perturbed spirit! So, gentle-
    men,
With all my love I do commend me to you:
And what so poor a man as Hamlet is   184
May do, to express his love and friending to you,
God willing, shall not lack. Let us go in to-
    gether;
And still your fingers on your lips, I pray.
The time is out of joint; O cursed spite,   188
That ever I was born to set it right!
Nay, come, let 's go together.   [*Exeunt.*

ACT II

SCENE I.—*A Room in* POLONIUS' *House.*

    Enter POLONIUS *and* REYNALDO.

  Pol. Give him this money and these notes,
    Reynaldo.
  Rey. I will, my lord.
  Pol. You shall do marvellous wisely, good
    Reynaldo,

Before you visit him, to make inquiry 4
Of his behaviour.
  Rey.   My lord, I did intend it.
  Pol. Marry, well said, very well said. Look
    you, sir,
Inquire me first what Danskers are in Paris;
And how, and who, what means, and where they
    keep, 8
What company, at what expense; and finding
By this encompassment and drift of question
That they do know my son, come you more
    nearer
Than your particular demands will touch it: 12
Take you, as 'twere, some distant knowledge of
    him;
As thus, 'I know his father, and his friends,
And, in part, him'; do you mark this, Reynaldo?
  Rey. Ay, very well, my lord. 16
  Pol. 'And, in part, him; but', you may say,
    'not well:
But if't be he I mean, he's very wild,
Addicted so and so'; and there put on him
What forgeries you please; marry, none so rank
As may dishonour him; take heed of that; 21
But, sir, such wanton, wild, and usual slips
As are companions noted and most known
To youth and liberty.
  Rey.   As gaming, my lord? 24
  Pol. Ay, or drinking, fencing, swearing, quar-
    relling,
Drabbing; you may go so far.
  Rey. My lord, that would dishonour him.
  Pol. Faith, no; as you may season it in the
    charge. 28
You must not put another scandal on him,
That he is open to incontinency;
That's not my meaning; but breathe his faults
    so quaintly
That they may seem the taints of liberty, 32
The flash and outbreak of a fiery mind,
A savageness in unreclaimed blood,
Of general assault.
  Rey.   But, my good lord,—
  Pol. Wherefore should you do this?
  Rey.   Ay, my lord, 36
I would know that.
  Pol.   Marry, sir, here's my drift;
And, I believe, it is a fetch of warrant:
You laying these slight sullies on my son,
As 'twere a thing a little soil'd i' the working, 40
Mark you,
Your party in converse, him you would sound,
Having ever seen in the prenominate crimes
The youth you breathe of guilty, be assur'd, 44
He closes with you in this consequence;
'Good sir', or so; or 'friend', or 'gentleman',
According to the phrase or the addition
Of man and country.
  Rey.   Very good, my lord. 48
  Pol. And then, sir, does he this,—he does,—
what was I about to say? By the mass I was
about to say something: where did I leave?
  Rey. At 'closes in the consequence.' 52
At 'friend or so', and 'gentleman'.
  Pol. At 'closes in the consequence', ay, marry;
He closes with you thus: 'I know the gentleman;

I saw him yesterday, or t' other day, 56
Or then, or then; with such, or such and, as
    you say,
There was a' gaming; there o'ertook in 's rouse;
There falling out at tennis'; or perchance,
'I saw him enter such a house of sale', 60
Videlicet, a brothel, or so forth.
See you now;
Your bait of falsehood takes this carp of truth;
And thus do we of wisdom and of reach, 64
With windlasses, and with assays of bias,
By indirections find directions out:
So by my former lecture and advice
Shall you my son. You have me, have you not?
  Rey. My lord, I have.
  Pol.   God be wi' you; fare you well. 69
  Rey. Good my lord!
  Pol. Observe his inclination in yourself.
  Rey. I shall, my lord. 72
  Pol. And let him ply his music.
  Rey.   Well, my lord.
  Pol. Farewell!   [*Exit* REYNALDO.

      Enter OPHELIA.
    How now, Ophelia! what's the matter?
  Oph. Alas! my lord, I have been so affrighted.
  Pol. With what, in the name of God? 76
  Oph. My lord, as I was sewing in my closet,
Lord Hamlet, with his doublet all unbrac'd;
No hat upon his head; his stockings foul'd,
Ungarter'd, and down-gyved to his ancle; 80
Pale as his shirt; his knees knocking each other;
And with a look so piteous in purport
As if he had been loosed out of hell
To speak of horrors, he comes before me. 84
  Pol. Mad for thy love?
  Oph.   My lord, I do not know;
But truly I do fear it.
  Pol.   What said he?
  Oph. He took me by the wrist and held me
    hard,
Then goes he to the length of all his arm, 88
And, with his other hand thus o'er his brow,
He falls to such perusal of my face
As he would draw it. Long stay'd he so;
At last, a little shaking of mine arm, 92
And thrice his head thus waving up and down,
He rais'd a sigh so piteous and profound
That it did seem to shatter all his bulk
And end his being. That done, he lets me go, 96
And, with his head over his shoulder turn'd,
He seem'd to find his way without his eyes;
For out o' doors he went without their help,
And to the last bended their light on me. 100
  Pol. Come, go with me; I will go seek the
    king.
This is the very ecstasy of love,
Whose violent property fordoes itself
And leads the will to desperate undertakings
As oft as any passion under heaven 105
That does afflict our natures. I am sorry.
What! have you given him any hard words of
    late?
  Oph. No, my good lord: but, as you did com-
    mand, 108
I did repel his letters and denied

His access to me.
Pol. That hath made him mad.
I am sorry that with better heed and judgment
I had not quoted him; I fear'd he did but trifle,
And meant to wrack thee; but, beshrew my
jealousy! 113
By heaven, it is as proper to our age
To cast beyond ourselves in our opinions
As it is common for the younger sort 116
To lack discretion. Come, go we to the king:
This must be known; which, being kept close,
might move
More grief to hide than hate to utter love.
Come. [*Exeunt.*

SCENE II.—*A Room in the Castle.*

Enter KING, QUEEN, ROSENCRANTZ, GUILDEN-
STERN, *and* Attendants.

King. Welcome, dear Rosencrantz and Guil-
denstern!
Moreover that we much did long to see you,
The need we have to use you did provoke
Our hasty sending. Something have you heard
Of Hamlet's transformation; so I call it, 5
Since nor the exterior nor the inward man
Resembles that it was. What it should be
More than his father's death, that thus hath put
him 8
So much from the understanding of himself,
I cannot dream of: I entreat you both,
That, being of so young days brought up with him,
And since so neighbour'd to his youth and
humour, 12
That you vouchsafe your rest here in our court
Some little time; so by your companies
To draw him on to pleasures, and to gather,
So much as from occasion you may glean, 16
Whe'r aught to us unknown afflicts him thus,
That, open'd, lies within our remedy.
Queen. Good gentlemen, he hath much talk'd
of you;
And sure I am two men there are not living 20
To whom he more adheres. If it will please you
To show us so much gentry and good will
As to expend your time with us awhile,
For the supply and profit of our hope, 24
Your visitation shall receive such thanks
As fits a king's remembrance.
Ros. Both your majesties
Might, by the sovereign power you have of us,
Put your dread pleasures more into command
Than to entreaty.
Guil. But we both obey, 29
And here give up ourselves, in the full bent,
To lay our service freely at your feet,
To be commanded. 32
King. Thanks, Rosencrantz and gentle Guil-
denstern.
Queen. Thanks, Guildenstern and gentle
Rosencrantz;
And I beseech you instantly to visit
My too much changed son. Go, some of you, 36
And bring these gentlemen where Hamlet is.
Guil. Heavens make our presence, and our
practices

Pleasant and helpful to him!
Queen. Ay, amen!
[*Exeunt* ROSENCRANTZ, GUILDENSTERN, *and
some* Attendants.

Enter POLONIUS.

Pol. The ambassadors from Norway, my
good lord, 40
Are joyfully return'd.
King. Thou still hast been the father of good
news.
Pol. Have I, my lord? Assure you, my good
liege,
I hold my duty, as I hold my soul, 44
Both to my God and to my gracious king;
And I do think—or else this brain of mine
Hunts not the trail of policy so sure
As it hath us'd to do—that I have found 48
The very cause of Hamlet's lunacy.
King. O! speak of that; that do I long to hear.
Pol. Give first admittance to the ambassa-
dors;
My news shall be the fruit to that great feast. 52
King. Thyself do grace to them, and bring
them in. [*Exit* POLONIUS.
He tells me, my sweet queen, that he hath found
The head and source of all your son's distemper.
Queen. I doubt it is no other but the main;
His father's death, and our o'erhasty marriage.
King. Well, we shall sift him.

Re-enter POLONIUS, *with* VOLTIMAND *and*
CORNELIUS.

Welcome, my good friends!
Say, Voltimand, what from our brother Nor-
way?
Volt. Most fair return of greetings, and de-
sires. 60
Upon our first, he sent out to suppress
His nephew's levies, which to him appear'd
To be a preparation 'gainst the Polack;
But, better look'd into, he truly found 64
It was against your highness: whereat griev'd,
That so his sickness, age, and impotence
Was falsely borne in hand, sends out arrests
On Fortinbras; which he, in brief, obeys, 68
Receives rebuke from Norway, and, in fine,
Makes vow before his uncle never more
To give the assay of arms against your majesty.
Whereon old Norway, overcome with joy, 72
Gives him three thousand crowns in annual fee,
And his commission to employ those soldiers,
So levied as before, against the Polack;
With an entreaty, herein further shown, 76
[*Giving a paper.*
That it might please you to give quiet pass
Through your dominions for this enterprise,
On such regards of safety and allowance
As therein are set down.
King. It likes us well; 80
And at our more consider'd time we'll read,
Answer, and think upon this business:
Meantime we thank you for your well-took
labour.
Go to your rest; at night we'll feast together:

[M]ost welcome home.

[*Exeunt* VOLTIMAND *and* CORNELIUS.

Pol.   This business is well ended.   85
[M]y liege, and madam, to expostulate
[W]hat majesty should be, what duty is,
[W]hy day is day, night night, and time is time,
[W]ere nothing but to waste night, day, and time.
[T]herefore, since brevity is the soul of wit,
[A]nd tediousness the limbs and outward
    flourishes,
[I] will be brief. Your noble son is mad: 92
[M]ad call I it; for, to define true madness,
[W]hat is 't but to be nothing else but mad?
[B]ut let that go.

Queen.   More matter, with less art.

Pol. Madam, I swear I use no art at all. 96
[T]hat he is mad, 'tis true; 'tis true 'tis pity;
[A]nd pity 'tis 'tis true: a foolish figure;
[B]ut farewell it, for I will use no art.
[M]ad let us grant him, then; and now remains
[T]hat we find out the cause of this effect,   101
[O]r rather say, the cause of this defect,
[F]or this effect defective comes by cause;
[T]hus it remains, and the remainder thus.
[P]erpend.   105
[I] have a daughter, have while she is mine;
[W]ho, in her duty and obedience, mark,
[H]ath given me this: now, gather, and surmise.
[T]o the celestial, and my soul's idol, the most
    beautified Ophelia;   109
[T]hat's an ill phrase, a vile phrase; 'beautified'
[i]s a vile phrase; but you shall hear. Thus:
[I]n her excellent white bosom, these, &c.— 112

Queen. Came this from Hamlet to her?

Pol. Good madam, stay awhile; I will be
    faithful.

    Doubt thou the stars are fire;
      Doubt that the sun doth move;   116
    Doubt truth to be a liar;
      But never doubt I love.
O dear Ophelia! I am ill at these numbers: I
[h]ave not art to reckon my groans; but that I love
[t]hee best, O most best! believe it. Adieu.
    Thine evermore, most dear lady, whilst
      this machine is to him,
          H*AMLET.*
[T]his in obedience hath my daughter shown me;
[A]nd more above, hath his solicitings,
[A]s they fell out by time, by means, and place,
[A]ll given to mine ear.

King.   But how hath she   128
[R]eceiv'd his love?

Pol.   What do you think of me?

King. As of a man faithful and honourable.

Pol. I would fain prove so. But what might
    you think,   131
[W]hen I had seen this hot love on the wing,—
[A]s I perceiv'd it, I must tell you that,
[B]efore my daughter told me,—what might you,
[O]r my dear majesty, your queen here, think,
[I]f I had play'd the desk or table-book,   136
[O]r given my heart a winking, mute and dumb,
[O]r look'd upon this love with idle sight;
[W]hat might you think? No, I went round to
    work,
[A]nd my young mistress thus I did bespeak: 140

'Lord Hamlet is a prince, out of thy star;
This must not be': and then I precepts gave her,
That she should lock herself from his resort,
Admit no messengers, receive no tokens.   144
Which done, she took the fruits of my advice;
And he, repulsed,—a short tale to make,—
Fell into a sadness, then into a fast,
Thence to a watch, thence into a weakness, 148
Thence to a lightness; and by this declension
Into the madness wherein now he raves,
And all we wail for.

King.   Do you think 'tis this?

Queen. It may be, very likely.   152

Pol. Hath there been such a time,—I'd fain
    know that,—
That I have positively said, ''Tis so',
When it prov'd otherwise?

King.   Not that I know.

Pol. Take this from this, if this be otherwise:

      [*Pointing to his head and shoulder.*
If circumstances lead me, I will find
Where truth is hid, though it were hid indeed
Within the centre.

King.   How may we try it further?

Pol. You know sometimes he walks four
    hours together   160
Here in the lobby.

Queen.   So he does indeed.

Pol. At such a time I'll loose my daughter
    to him;
Be you and I behind an arras then;
Mark the encounter; if he love her not,   164
And be not from his reason fallen thereon,
Let me be no assistant for a state,
But keep a farm, and carters.

King.   We will try it.

Queen. But look, where sadly the poor wretch
    comes reading.   168

Pol. Away! I do beseech you, both away.
I'll board him presently.

    [*Exeunt* KING, QUEEN, *and* Attendants.

Enter HAMLET, *reading.*

          O! give me leave.
How does my good Lord Hamlet?

Ham. Well, God a-mercy.   172

Pol. Do you know me, my lord?

Ham. Excellent well; you are a fishmonger.

Pol. Not I, my lord.

Ham. Then I would you were so honest a
man.   177

Pol. Honest, my lord!

Ham. Ay, sir; to be honest, as this world
goes, is to be one man picked out of ten thousand.   181

Pol. That's very true, my lord.

Ham. For if the sun breed maggots in a dead
dog, being a good kissing carrion,—Have you a
daughter?   185

Pol. I have, my lord.

Ham. Let her not walk i' the sun; conception
is a blessing; but not as your daughter may conceive. Friend, look to 't.   189

Pol. [*Aside.*] How say you by that? Still
harping on my daughter: yet he knew me not
at first; he said I was a fishmonger: he is far

gone, far gone: and truly in my youth I suffered
much extremity for love; very near this. I'll
speak to him again. What do you read, my lord?

Ham. Words, words, words.   196

Pol. What is the matter, my lord?

Ham. Between who?

Pol. I mean the matter that you read, my
lord.   200

Ham. Slanders, sir: for the satirical rogue
says here that old men have grey beards, that
their faces are wrinkled, their eyes purging thick
amber and plum-tree gum, and that they have a
plentiful lack of wit, together with most weak
hams: all which, sir, though I most powerfully
and potently believe, yet I hold it not honesty to
have it thus set down; for you yourself, sir,
should be old as I am, if, like a crab, you could
go backward.   210

Pol. [*Aside.*] Though this be madness, yet
there is method in't. Will you walk out of the
air, my lord?

Ham. Into my grave?   214

Pol. Indeed, that is out o' the air. [*Aside.*]
How pregnant sometimes his replies are! a
happiness that often madness hits on, which
reason and sanity could not so prosperously be
delivered of. I will leave him, and suddenly
contrive the means of meeting between him and
my daughter. My honourable lord, I will most
humbly take my leave of you.   222

Ham. You cannot, sir, take from me any
thing that I will more willingly part withal;
except my life, except my life, except my life.

Pol. Fare you well, my lord.   [*Going.*

Ham. These tedious old fools!

Enter ROSENCRANTZ *and* GUILDENSTERN.

Pol. You go to seek the Lord Hamlet; there
he is.   228

Ros. [*To* POLONIUS.] God save you, sir!
          [*Exit* POLONIUS.

Guil. Mine honoured lord!

Ros. My most dear lord!

Ham. My excellent good friends! How dost
thou, Guildenstern? Ah, Rosencrantz! Good
lads, how do ye both?   234

Ros. As the indifferent children of the earth.

Guil. Happy in that we are not over happy;
On Fortune's cap we are not the very button.

Ham. Nor the soles of her shoe?   238

Ros. Neither, my lord.

Ham. Then you live about her waist, or in
the middle of her favours?   241

Guil. Faith, her privates we.

Ham. In the secret parts of Fortune? O!
most true; she is a strumpet. What news?   244

Ros. None, my lord, but that the world's
grown honest.

Ham. Then is doomsday near; but your news
is not true. Let me question more in particular:
what have you, my good friends, deserved at the
hands of Fortune, that she sends you to prison
hither?

Guil. Prison, my lord!   252

Ham. Denmark's a prison.

Ros. Then is the world one.

Ham. A goodly one: in which there a
many confines, wards, and dungeons, Denmar
being one o' the worst.   2

Ros. We think not so, my lord.

Ham. Why, then, 'tis none to you; for there
nothing either good or bad, but thinking mak
it so: to me it is a prison.   2

Ros. Why, then your ambition makes it on
'tis too narrow for your mind.

Ham. O God! I could be bounded in a nu
shell, and count myself a king of infinite spac
were it not that I have bad dreams.

Guil. Which dreams, indeed, are ambitio
for the very substance of the ambitious is mere
the shadow of a dream.   2

Ham. A dream itself is but a shadow.

Ros. Truly, and I hold ambition of so ai
and light a quality that it is but a shadow
shadow.   2

Ham. Then are our beggars bodies, and o
monarchs and outstretched heroes the beggar
shadows. Shall we to the court? for, by my fa
I cannot reason.   2

Ros. }
Guil. } We'll wait upon you.

Ham. No such matter; I will not sort yo
with the rest of my servants, for, to speak to yo
like an honest man, I am most dreadfully a
tended. But, in the beaten way of friendshi
what make you at Elsinore?

Ros. To visit you, my lord; no other occ
sion.   28

Ham. Beggar that I am, I am even poor i
thanks; but I thank you: and sure, dear friend
my thanks are too dear a halfpenny. Were yo
not sent for? Is it your own inclining? Is
a free visitation? Come, come, deal justly wit
me: come, come; nay, speak.

Guil. What should we say, my lord?   29

Ham. Why anything, but to the purpos
You were sent for; and there is a kind of cor
fession in your looks which your modesties hav
not craft enough to colour: I know the goo
king and queen have sent for you.   29

Ros. To what end, my lord?

Ham. That you must teach me. But let m
conjure you, by the rights of our fellowshi
by the consonancy of our youth, by the obl
gation of our ever-preserved love, and by wha
more dear a better proposer could charge yo
withal, be even and direct with me, whethe
you were sent for or no!   30

Ros. [*Aside to* GUILDENSTERN.] What sa
you?

Ham. [*Aside.*] Nay, then, I have an eye o
you. If you love me, hold not off.   30

Guil. My lord, we were sent for.

Ham. I will tell you why; so shall my antic
pation prevent your discovery, and your secrec
to the king and queen moult no feather. I hav
of late,—but wherefore I know not,—lost all m
mirth, forgone all custom of exercises; an
indeed it goes so heavily with my dispositio
that this goodly frame, the earth, seems to me
sterile promontory; this most excellent canopy
the air, look you, this brave o'erhanging firma

nent, this majestical roof fretted with golden
ire, why, it appears no other thing to me but
a foul and pestilent congregation of vapours.
What a piece of work is a man! How noble in
eason! how infinite in faculty! in form, in
noving, how express and admirable! in action
now like an angel! in apprehension how like a
god! the beauty of the world! the paragon of
animals! And yet, to me, what is this quintes-
sence of dust? man delights not me; no, nor
woman neither, though, by your smiling, you
seem to say so. 331

Ros. My lord, there was no such stuff in my
thoughts.

Ham. Why did you laugh then, when I said,
man delights not me'? 335

Ros. To think, my lord, if you delight not
in man, what lenten entertainment the players
shall receive from you: we coted them on the
way; and hither are they coming, to offer you
service. 340

Ham. He that plays the king shall be welcome; his majesty shall have tribute of me; the
adventurous knight shall use his foil and target;
the lover shall not sigh gratis; the humorous
man shall end his part in peace; the clown shall
make those laugh whose lungs are tickle o' the
sere; and the lady shall say her mind freely,
or the blank verse shall halt for't. What players
are they? 349

Ros. Even those you were wont to take delight
in, the tragedians of the city.

Ham. How chances it they travel? their
residence, both in reputation and profit, was
better both ways. 354

Ros. I think their inhibition comes by the
means of the late innovation.

Ham. Do they hold the same estimation they
did when I was in the city? Are they so followed?

Ros. No, indeed they are not. 359

Ham. How comes it? Do they grow rusty?

Ros. Nay, their endeavour keeps in the wonted
pace: but there is, sir, an aery of children, little
eyases, that cry out on the top of question, and
are most tyrannically clapped for't: these are
now the fashion, and so berattle the common
stages,—so they call them,—that many wearing
rapiers are afraid of goose-quills, and dare scarce
come thither. 368

Ham. What! are they children? who maintains 'em? how are they escoted? Will they
pursue the quality no longer than they can
sing? will they not say afterwards, if they should
grow themselves to common players,—as it is
most like, if their means are no better,—their
writers do them wrong, to make them exclaim
against their own succession? 376

Ros. Faith, there has been much to-do on
both sides: and the nation holds it no sin to
tarre them to controversy: there was, for a while,
no money bid for argument, unless the poet and
the player went to cuffs in the question. 381

Ham. Is it possible?

Guil. O! there has been much throwing about
of brains. 384

Ham. Do the boys carry it away?

Ros. Ay, that they do, my lord; Hercules and
his load too. 387

Ham. It is not very strange; for my uncle is
King of Denmark, and those that would make
mows at him while my father lived, give twenty,
forty, fifty, a hundred ducats a-piece for his
picture in little. 'Sblood, there is something in
this more than natural, if philosophy could find
it out. [*Flourish of trumpets within.*

Guil. There are the players. 395

Ham. Gentlemen, you are welcome to Elsinore. Your hands, come then; the appurtenance
of welcome is fashion and ceremony: let me
comply with you in this garb, lest my extent to
the players—which, I tell you, must show fairly
outward—should more appear like entertainment than yours. You are welcome; but my
uncle-father and aunt-mother are deceived.

Guil. In what, my dear lord? 404

Ham. I am but mad north-north-west: when
the wind is southerly I know a hawk from a
handsaw.

Enter POLONIUS.

Pol. Well be with you, gentlemen! 408

Ham. Hark you, Guildenstern; and you too;
at each ear a hearer: that great baby you see
there is not yet out of his swaddling-clouts. 411

Ros. Happily he's the second time come to
them; for they say an old man is twice a child.

Ham. I will prophesy he comes to tell me
of the players; mark it. You say right, sir; o'
Monday morning; 'twas so indeed. 416

Pol. My lord, I have news to tell you.

Ham. My lord, I have news to tell you. When
Roscius was an actor in Rome,—

Pol. The actors are come hither, my lord.

Ham. Buzz, buzz! 421

Pol. Upon my honour,—

Ham. Then came each actor on his ass,—

Pol. The best actors in the world, either for
tragedy, comedy, history, pastoral, pastoral-
comical, historical-pastoral, tragical-historical,
tragical-comical-historical-pastoral, scene indi-
vidable, or poem unlimited: Seneca cannot be
too heavy, nor Plautus too light. For the law
of writ and the liberty, these are the only men.

Ham. O Jephthah, judge of Israel, what a
treasure hadst thou! 432

Pol. What a treasure had he, my lord?

Ham. Why

> *One fair daughter and no more,*
> *The which he loved passing well.* 436

Pol. [*Aside.*] Still on my daughter.

Ham. Am I not i' the right, old Jephthah?

Pol. If you call me Jephthah, my lord, I have
a daughter that I love passing well. 440

Ham. Nay, that follows not.

Pol. What follows, then, my lord?

Ham. Why,

> *As by lot, God wot.* 444

And then, you know,

> *It came to pass, as most like it was.—*

The first row of the pious chanson will show you
more; for look where my abridgment comes.

Enter four or five Players.

You are welcome, masters; welcome, all. I am glad to see thee well: welcome, good friends. O, my old friend! Thy face is valanced since I saw thee last: comest thou to beard me in Denmark? What! my young lady and mistress! By'r lady, your ladyship is nearer heaven than when I saw you last, by the altitude of a chopine. Pray God, your voice, like a piece of uncurrent gold, be not cracked within the ring. Masters, you are all welcome. We'll e'en to't like French falconers, fly at anything we see: we'll have a speech straight. Come, give us a taste of your quality; come, a passionate speech. 461

First Play. What speech, my good lord?

Ham. I heard thee speak me a speech once, but it was never acted; or, if it was, not above once; for the play, I remember, pleased not the million; 'twas caviare to the general: but it was—as I received it, and others, whose judgments in such matters cried in the top of mine—an excellent play, well digested in the scenes, set down with as much modesty as cunning. I remember one said there were no sallets in the lines to make the matter savoury, nor no matter in the phrase that might indict the author of affectation; but called it an honest method, as wholesome as sweet, and by very much more handsome than fine. One speech in it I chiefly loved; 'twas Æneas' tale to Dido; and thereabout of it especially, where he speaks of Priam's slaughter. If it live in your memory, begin at this line: let me see, let me see:— 480
The rugged Pyrrhus, like the Hyrcanian beast,—
'tis not so, it begins with Pyrrhus:—
The rugged Pyrrhus, he, whose sable arm,
Black as his purpose, did the night resemble
When he lay couched in the ominous horse, 485
Hath now this dread and black complexion smear'd
With heraldry more dismal; head to foot
Now is he total gules; horridly trick'd 488
With blood of fathers, mothers, daughters, sons,
Bak'd and impasted with the parching streets,
That lend a tyrannous and damned light
To their vile murders: roasted in wrath and fire,
And thus o'er-sized with coagulate gore,
With eyes like carbuncles, the hellish Pyrrhus
Old grandsire Priam seeks.
So proceed you. 496

Pol. 'Fore God, my lord, well spoken; with good accent and good discretion.

First Play. *Anon, he finds him*
Striking too short at Greeks; his antique sword,
Rebellious to his arm, lies where it falls, 500
Repugnant to command. Unequal match'd,
Pyrrhus at Priam drives; in rage strikes wide;
But with the whiff and wind of his fell sword
The unnerved father falls. Then senseless Ilium,
Seeming to feel this blow, with flaming top
Stoops to his base, and with a hideous crash
Takes prisoner Pyrrhus' ear: for lo! his sword,
Which was declining on the milky head 508
Of reverend Priam, seem'd i' the air to stick:
So, as a painted tyrant, Pyrrhus stood,

And like a neutral to his will and matter,
Did nothing. 512
But, as we often see, against some storm,
A silence in the heavens, the rack stand still,
The bold winds speechless and the orb below
As hush as death, anon the dreadful thunder 516
Doth rend the region; so, after Pyrrhus' pause,
Aroused vengeance sets him new a-work;
And never did the Cyclops' hammers fall
On Mars's armour, forg'd for proof eterne, 520
With less remorse than Pyrrhus' bleeding sword
Now falls on Priam.
Out, out, thou strumpet, Fortune! All you gods,
In general synod, take away her power; 524
Break all the spokes and fellies from her wheel,
And bowl the round nave down the hill of heaven,
As low as to the fiends!

Pol. This is too long. 528

Ham. It shall to the barber's, with your beard. Prithee, say on: he's for a jig or a tale of bawdry, or he sleeps. Say on; come to Hecuba. 532

First Play. *But who, O! who had seen the mobled queen—*

Ham. 'The mobled queen'?—

Pol. That's good; 'mobled queen' is good.

First Play. *Run barefoot up and down,*
threat'ning the flames 536
With bisson rheum; a clout upon that head
Where late the diadem stood; and, for a robe,
About her lank and all o'er-teemed loins,
A blanket, in the alarm of fear caught up; 540
Who this had seen, with tongue in venom steep'd,
'Gainst Fortune's state would treason have pronounc'd:
But if the gods themselves did see her then,
When she saw Pyrrhus make malicious sport
In mincing with his sword her husband's limbs, 545
The instant burst of clamour that she made—
Unless things mortal move them not at all—
Would have made milch the burning eyes of heaven, 548
And passion in the gods.

Pol. Look! wh'er he has not turned his colour and has tears in's eyes. Prithee, no more. 551

Ham. 'Tis well; I'll have thee speak out the rest soon. Good my lord, will you see the players well bestowed? Do you hear, let them be well used; for they are the abstracts and brief chronicles of the time: after your death you were better have a bad epitaph than their ill report while you live.

Pol. My lord, I will use them according to their desert. 560

Ham. God's bodikins, man, much better; use every man after his desert, and who should 'scape whipping? Use them after your own honour and dignity: the less they deserve, the more merit is in your bounty. Take them in. 565

Pol. Come, sirs.

Ham. Follow him, friends: we'll hear a play to-morrow. [*Exit* POLONIUS, *with all the* Players *but the First.*] Dost thou hear me, old friend; can you play the Murder of Gonzago? 570

First Play. Ay, my lord.

Ham. We'll ha't to-morrow night. You could

or a need, study a speech of some dozen or six-
een lines, which I would set down and insert
1't, could you not?

First Play. Ay, my lord.   576

Ham. Very well. Follow that lord; and look
ou mock him not. [*Exit* First Player.] [*To* RO-
ENCRANTZ *and* GUILDENSTERN.] My good
riends, I'll leave you till night; you are wel-
ome to Elsinore.   581

Ros. Good my lord!

[*Exeunt* ROSENCRANTZ *and* GUILDENSTERN.
Ham. Ay, so, God be wi' ye! Now I am alone.
)! what a rogue and peasant slave am I: 584
s it not monstrous that this player here,
But in a fiction, in a dream of passion,
Could force his soul so to his own conceit 587
hat from her working all his visage wann'd,
'ears in his eyes, distraction in's aspect,
A broken voice, and his whole function suiting
Vith forms to his conceit? and all for nothing!
'or Hecuba!   592
Vhat's Hecuba to him or he to Hecuba
hat he should weep for her? What would he do
Iad he the motive and the cue for passion
hat I have? He would drown the stage with
     tears,   596
And cleave the general ear with horrid speech,
Make mad the guilty and appal the free,
Confound the ignorant, and amaze indeed
he very faculties of eyes and ears.   600
Yet I,
A dull and muddy-mettled rascal, peak,
Like John-a-dreams, unpregnant of my cause,
And can say nothing; no, not for a king,   604
Jpon whose property and most dear life
A damn'd defeat was made. Am I a coward?
Vho calls me villain? breaks my pate across?
Plucks off my beard and blows it in my face? 608
'weaks me by the nose? gives me the lie i' the
     throat,
As deep as to the lungs? Who does me this?
Ia!
Swounds, I should take it, for it cannot be 612
But I am pigeon-liver'd, and lack gall
To make oppression bitter, or ere this
should have fatted all the region kites
Vith this slave's offal. Bloody, bawdy villain!
Remorseless, treacherous, lecherous, kindless
     villain!   617
)! vengeance!
Vhy, what an ass am I! This is most brave
That I, the son of a dear father murder'd, 620
Prompted to my revenge by heaven and hell,
Must, like a whore, unpack my heart with words,
And fall a-cursing, like a very drab,
A scullion!   624
'ie upon't! foh! About, my brain! I have
     heard,
That guilty creatures sitting at a play
Iave by the very cunning of the scene
Been struck so to the soul that presently   628
They have proclaim'd their malefactions;
'or murder, though it have no tongue, will
     speak
Vith most miraculous organ. I'll have these
     players

Play something like the murder of my father 632
Before mine uncle; I'll observe his looks;
I'll tent him to the quick: if he but blench
I know my course. The spirit that I have seen
May be the devil: and the devil hath power 636
To assume a pleasing shape; yea, and perhaps
Out of my weakness and my melancholy—
As he is very potent with such spirits—
Abuses me to damn me. I'll have grounds 640
More relative than this: the play's the thing
Wherein I'll catch the conscience of the king.
                                             [*Exit.*

ACT III

SCENE I.—*A Room in the Castle.*

Enter KING, QUEEN, POLONIUS, OPHELIA,
     ROSENCRANTZ, *and* GUILDENSTERN.

King. And can you, by no drift of circum-
     stance,
Get from him why he puts on this confusion,
Grating so harshly all his days of quiet
With turbulent and dangerous lunacy?   4

Ros. He does confess he feels himself dis-
     tracted;
But from what cause he will by no means speak.

Guil. Nor do we find him forward to be
     sounded,
But, with a crafty madness, keeps aloof,   8
When we would bring him on to some confes-
     sion
Of his true state.

Queen.   Did he receive you well?

Ros. Most like a gentleman.

Guil. But with much forcing of his disposi-
     tion.   12

Ros. Niggard of question, but of our de-
     mands
Most free in his reply.

Queen.   Did you assay him
To any pastime?

Ros. Madam, it so fell out that certain
     players   16
We o'er-raught on the way; of these we told
     him,
And there did seem in him a kind of joy
To hear of it: they are about the court,
And, as I think, they have already order   20
This night to play before him.

Pol.   'Tis most true;
And he beseech'd me to entreat your majesties
To hear and see the matter.

King. With all my heart; and it doth much
     content me   24
To hear him so inclin'd.
Good gentlemen, give him a further edge,
And drive his purpose on to these delights.

Ros. We shall, my lord.

[*Exeunt* ROSENCRANTZ *and* GUILDENSTERN.
King.   Sweet Gertrude, leave us too;
For we have closely sent for Hamlet hither, 29
That he, as 'twere by accident, may here
Affront Ophelia.
Her father and myself, lawful espials,   32
Will so bestow ourselves, that, seeing, unseen,

We may of their encounter frankly judge,
And gather by him, as he is behav'd,
If 't be the affliction of his love or no   36
That thus he suffers for.
  Queen.   I shall obey you.
And for your part, Ophelia, I do wish
That your good beauties be the happy cause
Of Hamlet's wildness; so shall I hope your
    virtues   40
Will bring him to his wonted way again,
To both your honours.
  Oph.   Madam, I wish it may.
                           [*Exit* QUEEN.
  Pol. Ophelia, walk you here. Gracious, so
    please you,
We will bestow ourselves. [*To* OPHELIA.] Read
    on this book;   44
That show of such an exercise may colour
Your loneliness. We are oft to blame in this,
'Tis too much prov'd, that with devotion's visage
And pious action we do sugar o'er   48
The devil himself.
  King. [*Aside.*] O! 'tis too true;
How smart a lash that speech doth give my
    conscience!
The harlot's cheek, beautied with plastering art,
Is not more ugly to the thing that helps it 52
Than is my deed to my most painted word:
O heavy burden!
  Pol. I hear him coming; let's withdraw, my
    lord.   [*Exeunt* KING *and* POLONIUS.

Enter HAMLET.

  Ham. To be, or not to be: that is the ques-
    tion: 56
Whether 'tis nobler in the mind to suffer
The slings and arrows of outrageous fortune,
Or to take arms against a sea of troubles,
And by opposing end them? To die: to sleep;
No more; and, by a sleep to say we end   61
The heart-ache and the thousand natural shocks
That flesh is heir to, 'tis a consummation
Devoutly to be wish'd. To die, to sleep;   64
To sleep: perchance to dream: ay, there's the
    rub;
For in that sleep of death what dreams may
    come
When we have shuffled off this mortal coil,
Must give us pause. There's the respect   68
That makes calamity of so long life;
For who would bear the whips and scorns of
    time,
The oppressor's wrong, the proud man's con-
    tumely,
The pangs of dispriz'd love, the law's delay, 72
The insolence of office, and the spurns
That patient merit of the unworthy takes,
When he himself might his quietus make
With a bare bodkin? who would fardels bear, 76
To grunt and sweat under a weary life,
But that the dread of something after death,
The undiscover'd country from whose bourn
No traveller returns, puzzles the will,   80
And makes us rather bear those ills we have
Than fly to others that we know not of?

Thus conscience does make cowards of us all;
And thus the native hue of resolution   84
Is sicklied o'er with the pale cast of thought,
And enterprises of great pith and moment
With this regard their currents turn awry,
And lose the name of action. Soft you now! 88
The fair Ophelia! Nymph, in thy orisons
Be all my sins remember'd.
  Oph.   Good my lord,
How does your honour for this many a day?
  Ham. I humbly thank you; well, well, well.
  Oph. My lord, I have remembrances of yours,
That I have longed long to re-deliver;
I pray you, now receive them.
  Ham.   No, not I;
I never gave you aught.   96
  Oph. My honour'd lord, you know right well
    you did;
And, with them, words of so sweet breath
    compos'd
As made the things more rich: their perfume
    lost,
Take these again; for to the noble mind   100
Rich gifts wax poor when givers prove unkind.
There, my lord.
  Ham. Ha, ha! are you honest?
  Oph. My lord!   104
  Ham. Are you fair?
  Oph. What means your lordship?
  Ham. That if you be honest and fair, your
honesty should admit no discourse to your
beauty.   109
  Oph. Could beauty, my lord, have better com-
merce than with honesty?
  Ham. Ay, truly; for the power of beauty will
sooner transform honesty from what it is to a
bawd than the force of honesty can translate
beauty into his likeness: this was sometime a
paradox, but now the time gives it proof. I did
love thee once.   117
  Oph. Indeed, my lord, you made me believe
so.
  Ham. You should not have believed me; for
virtue cannot so inoculate our old stock but we
shall relish of it: I loved you not.   123
  Oph. I was the more deceived.
  Ham. Get thee to a nunnery: why wouldst
thou be a breeder of sinners? I am myself
indifferent honest; but yet I could accuse me of
such things that it were better my mother had
not borne me. I am very proud, revengeful,
ambitious; with more offences at my beck than
I have thoughts to put them in, imagination
to give them shape, or time to act them in.
What should such fellows as I do crawling
between heaven and earth? We are arrant
knaves, all; believe none of us. Go thy ways to
a nunnery. Where's your father?   13
  Oph. At home, my lord.
  Ham. Let the doors be shut upon him, that
he may play the fool nowhere but in 's own
house. Farewell.
  Oph. O! help him, you sweet heavens!   14
  Ham. If thou dost marry, I'll give thee this
plague for thy dowry: be thou as chaste as ice,
as pure as snow, thou shalt not escape calumny.

Get thee to a nunnery, go; farewell. Or, if thou
wilt needs marry, marry a fool; for wise men
know well enough what monsters you make of
them. To a nunnery, go; and quickly too.
Farewell.   148

Oph. O heavenly powers, restore him!

Ham. I have heard of your paintings too,
well enough; God hath given you one face, and
you make yourselves another: you jig, you
amble, and you lisp, and nickname God's creatures, and make your wantonness your ignorance.
Go to, I'll no more on't; it hath made me mad.
I say, we will have no more marriages; those
that are married already, all but one, shall live;
the rest shall keep as they are. To a nunnery, go.
                                          [*Exit.*

Oph. O! what a noble mind is here o'er-
thrown:
The courtier's, soldier's, scholar's, eye, tongue,
sword;   160
The expectancy and rose of the fair state,
The glass of fashion and the mould of form,
The observ'd of all observers, quite, quite down!
And I, of ladies most deject and wretched, 164
That suck'd the honey of his music vows,
Now see that noble and most sovereign reason,
Like sweet bells jangled, out of tune and harsh;
That unmatch'd form and feature of blown
youth   168
Blasted with ecstasy: O! woe is me,
To have seen what I have seen, see what I see!

Re-enter KING *and* POLONIUS.

King. Love! his affections do not that way
tend;
Nor what he spake, though it lack'd form a
little,   172
Was not like madness. There's something in
his soul
O'er which his melancholy sits on brood;
And, I do doubt, the hatch and the disclose
Will be some danger; which for to prevent, 176
have in quick determination
Thus set it down: he shall with speed to England,
For the demand of our neglected tribute:
Haply the seas and countries different   180
With variable objects shall expel
This something-settled matter in his heart,
Whereon his brains still beating puts him thus
From fashion of himself. What think you on't?

Pol. It shall do well: but yet do I believe 185
The origin and commencement of his grief
Sprung from neglected love. How now, Ophelia!
You need not tell us what Lord Hamlet said;
We heard it all. My lord, do as you please; 189
But, if you hold it fit, after the play,
Let his queen mother all alone entreat him
To show his griefs: let her be round with him; 192
And I'll be plac'd, so please you, in the ear
Of all their conference. If she find him not,
To England send him, or confine him where
Our wisdom best shall think.

King.   It shall be so: 196
Madness in great ones must not unwatch'd go.
                                        [*Exeunt.*

SCENE II.—*A Hall in the Castle.*

Enter HAMLET *and certain* Players.

Ham. Speak the speech, I pray you, as I pronounced it to you, trippingly on the tongue; but
if you mouth it, as many of your players do, I
had as lief the town-crier spoke my lines. Nor
do not saw the air too much with your hand,
thus; but use all gently: for in the very torrent,
tempest, and—as I may say—whirlwind of
passion, you must acquire and beget a temperance, that may give it smoothness. O! it offends
me to the soul to hear a robustious periwig-
pated fellow tear a passion to tatters, to very
rags, to split the ears of the groundlings, who
for the most part are capable of nothing but
inexplicable dumb-shows and noise: I would
have such a fellow whipped for o'er-doing
Termagant; it out-herods Herod: pray you,
avoid it.   17

First Play. I warrant your honour.

Ham. Be not too tame neither, but let your
own discretion be your tutor: suit the action to
the word, the word to the action; with this
special observance, that you o'erstep not the
modesty of nature; for anything so overdone is
from the purpose of playing, whose end, both at
the first and now, was and is, to hold, as 'twere,
the mirror up to nature; to show virtue her own
feature, scorn her own image, and the very age
and body of the time his form and pressure.
Now, this overdone, or come tardy off, though it
make the unskilful laugh, cannot but make the
judicious grieve; the censure of which one must
in your allowance o'erweigh a whole theatre of
others. O! there be players that I have seen
play, and heard others praise, and that highly,
not to speak it profanely, that, neither having
the accent of Christians nor the gait of Christian,
pagan, nor man, have so strutted and bellowed
that I have thought some of nature's journey-
men had made men and not made them well,
they imitated humanity so abominably.   40

First Play. I hope we have reformed that
indifferently with us.

Ham. O! reform it altogether. And let those
that play your clowns speak no more than is
set down for them; for there be of them that
will themselves laugh, to set on some quantity of
barren spectators to laugh too, though in the
mean time some necessary question of the play
be then to be considered; that's villanous, and
shows a most pitiful ambition in the fool that
uses it. Go, make you ready. [*Exeunt* Players.

Enter POLONIUS, ROSENCRANTZ, *and*
GUILDENSTERN.

How now, my lord! will the king hear this piece
of work?   52

Pol. And the queen too, and that presently.

Ham. Bid the players make haste.
                                 [*Exit* POLONIUS.
Will you two help to hasten them?

Ros. } We will, my lord.   56
Guil. }
                [*Exeunt* ROSENCRANTZ *and* GUILDENSTERN.

Ham. What, ho! Horatio!

Enter HORATIO.

Hor. Here, sweet lord, at your service.

Ham. Horatio, thou art e'en as just a man
As e'er my conversation cop'd withal.   60

Hor. O! my dear lord,—

Ham.   Nay, do not think I flatter;
For what advancement may I hope from thee,
That no revenue hast but thy good spirits
To feed and clothe thee? Why should the poor
   be flatter'd?   64
No; let the candied tongue lick absurd pomp,
And crook the pregnant hinges of the knee
Where thrift may follow fawning. Dost thou
   hear?
Since my dear soul was mistress of her choice
And could of men distinguish, her election   69
Hath seal'd thee for herself; for thou hast been
As one, in suffering all, that suffers nothing,
A man that fortune's buffets and rewards   72
Hast ta'en with equal thanks; and bless'd are
   those
Whose blood and judgment are so well co-
   mingled
That they are not a pipe for fortune's finger
To sound what stop she please. Give me that
   man   76
That is not passion's slave, and I will wear him
In my heart's core, ay, in my heart of heart,
As I do thee. Something too much of this.
There is a play to-night before the king;   80
One scene of it comes near the circumstance
Which I have told thee of my father's death:
I prithee, when thou seest that act afoot,
Even with the very comment of thy soul   84
Observe mine uncle; if his occulted guilt
Do not itself unkennel in one speech,
It is a damned ghost that we have seen,
And my imaginations are as foul   88
As Vulcan's stithy. Give him heedful note;
For I mine eyes will rivet to his face,
And after we will both our judgments join
In censure of his seeming.

Hor.   Well, my lord: 92
If he steal aught the whilst this play is playing,
And 'scape detecting, I will pay the theft.

Ham. They are coming to the play; I must
   be idle:
Get you a place.   96

Danish march. A Flourish. Enter KING, QUEEN,
POLONIUS, OPHELIA, ROSENCRANTZ, GUILDEN-
STERN, *and Others.*

King. How fares our cousin Hamlet?

Ham. Excellent, i' faith; of the chameleon's
dish: I eat the air, promise-crammed; you cannot feed capons so.   100

King. I have nothing with this answer, Hamlet; these words are not mine.

Ham. No, nor mine now. [*To* POLONIUS.]
My lord, you played once i' the university, you
say?   105

Pol. That did I, my lord, and was accounted
a good actor.

Ham. And what did you enact?   108

Pol. I did enact Julius Cæsar: I was killed
i' the Capitol; Brutus killed me.

Ham. It was a brute part of him to kill so
capital a calf there. Be the players ready? 112

Ros. Ay, my lord; they stay upon your
patience.

Queen. Come hither, my good Hamlet, sit by
me.   116

Ham. No, good mother, here's metal more
attractive.

Pol. [*To the* KING.] O ho! do you mark that?

Ham. Lady, shall I lie in your lap?   120
       [*Lying down at* OPHELIA'S *feet.*

Oph. No, my lord.

Ham. I mean, my head upon your lap?

Oph. Ay, my lord.

Ham. Do you think I meant country matters?

Oph. I think nothing, my lord.   125

Ham. That's a fair thought to lie between
maids' legs.

Oph. What is, my lord?   128

Ham. Nothing.

Oph. You are merry, my lord.

Ham. Who, I?

Oph. Ay, my lord.   132

Ham. O God, your only jig-maker. What
should a man do but be merry? for, look you,
how cheerfully my mother looks, and my father
died within's two hours.   136

Oph. Nay, 'tis twice two months, my lord.

Ham. So long? Nay, then, let the devil wear
black, for I'll have a suit of sables. O heavens!
die two months ago, and not forgotten yet?
Then there's hope a great man's memory may
outlive his life half a year; but, by'r lady, he
must build churches then, or else shall he suffer
not thinking on, with the hobby-horse, whose
epitaph is, 'For, O! for, O! the hobby-horse is
forgot'.   146

Hautboys play. The dumb-show enters.

Enter a King *and a* Queen, *very lovingly; the*
Queen *embracing him, and he her. She kneels
and makes show of protestation unto him.
He takes her up, and declines his head upon
her neck; lays him down upon a bank of
flowers: she, seeing him asleep, leaves him.
Anon comes in a fellow, takes off his crown,
kisses it, and pours poison in the* King's *ears,
and exit. The* Queen *returns, finds the* King
dead, and makes passionate action. The
Poisoner, *with some two or three* Mutes, *comes
in again, seeming to lament with her. The
dead body is carried away. The* Poisoner
wooes the Queen *with gifts; she seems loath
and unwilling awhile, but in the end accepts
his love.*   [*Exeunt.*

Oph. What means this, my lord?

Ham. Marry, this is miching mallecho; it
means mischief.   148

Oph. Belike this show imports the argument
of the play.

Enter Prologue.

Ham. We shall know by this fellow: the
players cannot keep counsel; they'll tell all. 152

Oph. Will he tell us what this show meant?
Ham. Ay, or any show that you'll show
im; be not you ashamed to show, he'll not
name to tell you what it means.   157
Oph. You are naught, you are naught. I'll
mark the play.
Pro. For us and for our tragedy,   160
  Here stooping to your clemency,
  We beg your hearing patiently.
Ham. Is this a prologue, or the posy of a
ing?   164
Oph. 'Tis brief, my lord.
Ham. As woman's love.

Enter two Players, King and Queen.

P. King. Full thirty times hath Phœbus' cart
  gone round   167
Neptune's salt wash and Tellus' orbed ground,
And thirty dozen moons with borrow'd sheen
About the world have times twelve thirties been,
Since love our hearts and Hymen did our hands
Unite commutual in most sacred bands.   172
P. Queen. So many journeys may the sun and
  moon
Make us again count o'er ere love be done!
But, woe is me! you are so sick of late,   175
So far from cheer and from your former state,
That I distrust you. Yet, though I distrust,
Discomfort you, my lord, it nothing must;
For women's fear and love holds quantity,
In neither aught, or in extremity.   180
Now, what my love is, proof hath made you know;
And as my love is siz'd, my fear is so.
Where love is great, the littlest doubts are fear;
Where little fears grow great, great love grows
  there.   184
P. King. Faith, I must leave thee, love, and
  shortly too;
My operant powers their functions leave to do:
And thou shalt live in this fair world behind,
Honour'd, belov'd; and haply one as kind   188
For husband shalt thou—
P. Queen.   O! confound the rest:
Such love must needs be treason in my breast:
In second husband let me be accurst;
None wed the second but who kill'd the first.   192
Ham. [*Aside.*] Wormwood, wormwood.
P. Queen. The instances that second marriage
  move,
Are base respects of thrift, but none of love;
A second time I kill my husband dead,   196
When second husband kisses me in bed.
P. King. I do believe you think what now you
  speak;
But what we do determine oft we break.
Purpose is but the slave to memory,   200
Of violent birth, but poor validity;
Which now, like fruit unripe, sticks on the tree,
But fall unshaken when they mellow be.
Most necessary 'tis that we forget   204
To pay ourselves what to ourselves is debt;
What to ourselves in passion we propose,
The passion ending, doth the purpose lose.
The violence of either grief or joy   208
Their own enactures with themselves destroy;

Where joy most revels grief doth most lament,
Grief joys, joy grieves, on slender accident.
This world is not for aye, nor 'tis not strange,
That even our love should with our fortunes
  change;   213
For 'tis a question left us yet to prove
Whe'r love lead fortune or else fortune love.
The great man down, you mark his favourite
  flies;   216
The poor advanc'd makes friends of enemies.
And hitherto doth love on fortune tend,
For who not needs shall never lack a friend;
And who in want a hollow friend doth try   220
Directly seasons him his enemy.
But, orderly to end where I begun,
Our wills and fates do so contrary run
That our devices still are overthrown,   224
Our thoughts are ours, their ends none of our own:
So think thou wilt no second husband wed;
But die thy thoughts when thy first lord is dead.
P. Queen. Nor earth to me give food, nor
  heaven light!   228
Sport and repose lock from me day and night!
To desperation turn my trust and hope!
An anchor's cheer in prison be my scope!
Each opposite that blanks the face of joy   232
Meet what I would have well, and it destroy!
Both here and hence pursue me lasting strife,
If, once a widow, ever I be wife!
Ham. If she should break it now!   236
P. King. 'Tis deeply sworn. Sweet, leave me
  here awhile;
My spirits grow dull, and fain I would beguile
The tedious day with sleep.   [*Sleeps.*
P. Queen.   Sleep rock thy brain;
And never come mischance between us twain!
    [*Exit.*
Ham. Madam, how like you this play?   241
Queen. The lady doth protest too much, me-
thinks.
Ham. O! but she'll keep her word.   244
King. Have you heard the argument? Is
there no offence in't?
Ham. No, no, they do but jest, poison in jest;
no offence i' the world.   248
King. What do you call the play?
Ham. The Mouse-trap. Marry, how? Tropically. This play is the image of a murder
done in Vienna: Gonzago is the duke's name;
his wife, Baptista. You shall see anon; 'tis a
knavish piece of work: but what of that? your
majesty and we that have free souls, it touches
us not: let the galled jade wince, our withers are
unwrung.   257

Enter Player as Lucianus.

This is one Lucianus, nephew to the king.
Oph. You are a good chorus, my lord.
Ham. I could interpret between you and
your love, if I could see the puppets dallying. 261
Oph. You are keen, my lord, you are keen.
Ham. It would cost you a groaning to take
off my edge.   264
Oph. Still better, and worse.
Ham. So you must take your husbands.
Begin, murderer; pox, leave thy damnable

faces, and begin. Come; the croaking raven
doth bellow for revenge. 269

Luc. *Thoughts black, hands apt, drugs fit,
        and time agreeing;*
Confederate season, else no creature seeing;
Thou mixture rank, of midnight weeds collected,
With Hecate's ban thrice blasted, thrice infected,
Thy natural magic and dire property, 274
On wholesome life usurp immediately.

[*Pours the poison into the Sleeper's ears.*
Ham. He poisons him i' the garden for's
estate. His name's Gonzago; the story is extant,
and writ in very choice Italian. You shall see
anon how the murderer gets the love of Gonzago's wife. 280

Oph. The king rises.

Ham. What! frighted with false fire?

Queen. How fares my lord?

Pol. Give o'er the play. 284

King. Give me some light: away!

All. Lights, lights, lights!

[*Exeunt all except* HAMLET *and* HORATIO.
Ham. Why, let the stricken deer go weep,
        The hart ungalled play; 288
        For some must watch, while some must
            sleep:
        So runs the world away.
Would not this, sir, and a forest of feathers, if
the rest of my fortunes turn Turk with me, with
two Provincial roses on my razed shoes, get me
a fellowship in a cry of players, sir?

Hor. Half a share.

Ham. A whole one, I. 296
        For thou dost know, O Damon dear,
        This realm dismantled was
        Of Jove himself; and now reigns here
        A very, very—pajock. 300

Hor. You might have rimed.

Ham. O good Horatio! I'll take the ghost's
word for a thousand pound. Didst perceive?

Hor. Very well, my lord. 304

Ham. Upon the talk of the poisoning?

Hor. I did very well note him.

Ham. Ah, ha! Come, some music! come,
the recorders! 308
        For if the king like not the comedy,
        Why then, belike he likes it not, perdy.
Come, some music!

Re-enter ROSENCRANTZ *and* GUILDENSTERN.

Guil. Good my lord, vouchsafe me a word
with you. 313

Ham. Sir, a whole history.

Guil. The king, sir,—

Ham. Ay, sir, what of him? 316

Guil. Is in his retirement marvellous distempered.

Ham. With drink, sir?

Guil. No, my lord, rather with choler. 320

Ham. Your wisdom should show itself more
richer to signify this to his doctor; for, for me
to put him to his purgation would perhaps
plunge him into far more choler. 324

Guil. Good my lord, put your discourse into
some frame, and start not so wildly from my
affair.

Ham. I am tame, sir; pronounce. 328

Guil. The queen, your mother, in most great
affliction of spirit, hath sent me to you.

Ham. You are welcome. 331

Guil. Nay, good my lord, this courtesy is
not of the right breed. If it shall please you
to make me a wholesome answer, I will do
your mother's commandment; if not, your
pardon and my return shall be the end of my
business. 337

Ham. Sir, I cannot.

Guil. What, my lord?

Ham. Make you a wholesome answer; my
wit's diseased; but, sir, such answer as I can
make, you shall command; or, rather, as you
say, my mother: therefore no more, but to the
matter: my mother, you say,— 344

Ros. Then, thus she says: your behaviour hath
struck her into amazement and admiration.

Ham. O wonderful son, that can so astonish
a mother! But is there no sequel at the heels
of this mother's admiration? Impart. 349

Ros. She desires to speak with you in her
closet ere you go to bed.

Ham. We shall obey, were she ten times our
mother. Have you any further trade with us?

Ros. My lord, you once did love me.

Ham. So I do still, by these pickers and
stealers. 356

Ros. Good my lord, what is your cause of
distemper? you do surely bar the door upon
your own liberty, if you deny your griefs to your
friend. 360

Ham. Sir, I lack advancement.

Ros. How can that be when you have the
voice of the king himself for your succession in
Denmark? 364

Ham. Ay, sir, but 'While the grass grows',—
the proverb is something musty.

Enter Players, *with recorders.*

O! the recorders: let me see one. To withdraw
with you: why do you go about to recover the
wind of me, as if you would drive me into a toil?

Guil. O! my lord, if my duty be too bold, my
love is too unmannerly.

Ham. I do not well understand that. Will
you play upon this pipe? 373

Guil. My lord, I cannot.

Ham. I pray you.

Guil. Believe me, I cannot. 376

Ham. I do beseech you.

Guil. I know no touch of it, my lord.

Ham. 'Tis as easy as lying; govern these
ventages with your finger and thumb, give it
breath with your mouth, and it will discourse
most eloquent music. Look you, these are the
stops.

Guil. But these cannot I command to any
utterance of harmony; I have not the skill. 385

Ham. Why, look you now, how unworthy a
thing you make of me. You would play upon
me; you would seem to know my stops; you
would pluck out the heart of my mystery; you
would sound me from my lowest note to the top
of my compass; and there is much music, ex-

cellent voice, in this little organ, yet cannot you make it speak. 'Sblood, do you think I am easier to be played on than a pipe? Call me what instrument you will, though you can fret me, you cannot play upon me. 396

Enter POLONIUS.

God bless you, sir!

Pol. My lord, the queen would speak with you, and presently.

Ham. Do you see yonder cloud that's almost in shape of a camel?

Pol. By the mass, and 'tis like a camel, indeed.

Ham. Methinks it is like a weasel.

Pol. It is backed like a weasel. 404

Ham. Or like a whale?

Pol. Very like a whale.

Ham. Then I will come to my mother by and by. [*Aside.*] They fool me to the top of my bent. [*Aloud.*] I will come by and by. 409

Pol. I will say so. [*Exit.*

Ham. By and by is easily said. Leave me, friends. [*Exeunt all but HAMLET.*
'Tis now the very witching time of night, 413
When churchyards yawn and hell itself breathes out
Contagion to this world: now could I drink hot blood,
And do such bitter business as the day 416
Would quake to look on. Soft! now to my mother.
O heart! lose not thy nature; let not ever
The soul of Nero enter this firm bosom;
Let me be cruel, not unnatural; 420
I will speak daggers to her, but use none;
My tongue and soul in this be hypocrites;
How in my words soever she be shent,
To give them seals never, my soul, consent! 424
[*Exit.*

SCENE III.—*A Room in the Castle.*

Enter KING, ROSENCRANTZ, and GUILDENSTERN.

King. I like him not, nor stands it safe with us
To let his madness range. Therefore prepare you;
I your commission will forthwith dispatch,
And he to England shall along with you. 4
The terms of our estate may not endure
Hazard so dangerous as doth hourly grow
Out of his lunacies.

Guil. We will ourselves provide.
Most holy and religious fear it is 8
To keep those many many bodies safe
That live and feed upon your majesty.

Ros. The single and peculiar life is bound
With all the strength and armour of the mind
To keep itself from noyance; but much more 13
That spirit upon whose weal depend and rest
The lives of many. The cease of majesty
Dies not alone, but, like a gulf doth draw 16
What's near it with it; it is a massy wheel,
Fix'd on the summit of the highest mount,
To whose huge spokes ten thousand lesser things
Are mortis'd and adjoin'd; which, when it falls, 20
Each small annexment, petty consequence,

Attends the boisterous ruin. Never alone
Did the king sigh, but with a general groan.

King. Arm you, I pray you, to this speedy voyage; 24
For we will fetters put upon this fear,
Which now goes too free-footed.

Ros. }
Guil. } We will haste us.

Exeunt ROSENCRANTZ and GUILDENSTERN.

Enter POLONIUS.

Pol. My lord, he's going to his mother's closet:
Behind the arras I'll convey myself 28
To hear the process; I'll warrant she'll tax him home;
And, as you said, and wisely was it said,
'Tis meet that some more audience than a mother,
Since nature makes them partial, should o'erhear 32
The speech, of vantage. Fare you well, my liege:
I'll call upon you ere you go to bed
And tell you what I know.

King. Thanks, dear my lord.
[*Exit POLONIUS.*
O! my offence is rank, it smells to heaven; 36
It hath the primal eldest curse upon't;
A brother's murder! Pray can I not,
Though inclination be as sharp as will:
My stronger guilt defeats my strong intent; 40
And, like a man to double business bound,
I stand in pause where I shall first begin,
And both neglect. What if this cursed hand
Were thicker than itself with brother's blood, 44
Is there not rain enough in the sweet heavens
To wash it white as snow? Whereto serves mercy
But to confront the visage of offence?
And what's in prayer but this two-fold force, 48
To be forestalled, ere we come to fall,
Or pardon'd, being down? Then, I'll look up;
My fault is past. But, O! what form of prayer
Can serve my turn? 'Forgive me my foul murder'? 52
That cannot be; since I am still possess'd
Of those effects for which I did the murder,
My crown, mine own ambition, and my queen.
May one be pardon'd and retain the offence? 56
In the corrupted currents of this world
Offence's gilded hand may shove by justice,
And oft 'tis seen the wicked prize itself
Buys out the law; but 'tis not so above; 60
There is no shuffling, there the action lies
In his true nature, and we ourselves compell'd
Even to the teeth and forehead of our faults
To give in evidence. What then? what rests? 65
Try what repentance can: what can it not?
Yet what can it, when one can not repent?
O wretched state! O bosom black as death!
O limed soul, that struggling to be free 68
Art more engaged! Help, angels! make assay;
Bow, stubborn knees; and heart with strings of steel
Be soft as sinews of the new-born babe.
All may be well. [*Retires and kneels.*

Enter HAMLET.

Ham. Now might I do it pat, now he is pray-
ing;   73
And now I'll do't: and so he goes to heaven;
And so am I reveng'd. That would be scann'd:
A villain kills my father; and for that,   76
I, his sole son, do this same villain send
To heaven.
Why, this is hire and salary, not revenge.
He took my father grossly, full of bread,   80
With all his crimes broad blown, as flush as May;
And how his audit stands who knows save
heaven?
But in our circumstance and course of thought
'Tis heavy with him. And am I then reveng'd,
To take him in the purging of his soul,   85
When he is fit and season'd for his passage?
No.
Up, sword, and know thou a more horrid
hent;   88
When he is drunk asleep, or in his rage,
Or in the incestuous pleasure of his bed,
At gaming, swearing, or about some act
That has no relish of salvation in't;   92
Then trip him, that his heels may kick at heaven,
And that his soul may be as damn'd and black
As hell, whereto it goes. My mother stays:
This physic but prolongs thy sickly days. [*Exit.*

The KING *rises and advances.*

King. My words fly up, my thoughts remain
below: 97
Words without thoughts never to heaven go.
                                                        [*Exit.*

SCENE IV.—*The* QUEEN'S *Apartment.*

Enter QUEEN *and* POLONIUS.

Pol. He will come straight. Look you lay
home to him;
Tell him his pranks have been too broad to bear
with,
And that your Grace hath screen'd and stood
between
Much heat and him. I'll silence me e'en here. 4
Pray you, be round with him.
Ham. [*Within.*] Mother, mother, mother!
Queen.   I'll warrant you;
Fear me not. Withdraw, I hear him coming.
POLONIUS *hides behind the arras.*

Enter HAMLET.

Ham. Now, mother, what's the matter?   8
Queen. Hamlet, thou hast thy father much
offended.
Ham. Mother, you have my father much
offended.
Queen. Come, come, you answer with an idle
tongue.
Ham. Go, go, you question with a wicked
tongue.   12
Queen. Why, how now, Hamlet!
Ham.   What's the matter now?
Queen. Have you forgot me?
Ham.   No, by the rood, not so:
You are the queen, your husband's brother's
wife;

And,—would it were not so!—you are m
mother.   1
Queen. Nay then, I'll set those to you tha
can speak.
Ham. Come, come, and sit you down; yo
shall not budge;
You go not, till I set you up a glass
Where you may see the inmost part of you. 2
Queen. What wilt thou do? thou wilt no
murder me?
Help, help, ho!
Pol. [*Behind.*] What, ho! help! help! help
Ham. [*Draws.*] How now! a rat? Dead, fo
a ducat, dead!
                        [*Makes a pass through the arras
Pol. [*Behind.*] O! I am slain.   2
Queen. O me! what hast thou done?
Ham. Nay, I know not: is it the king?
Queen. O! what a rash and bloody deed i
this!
Ham. A bloody deed! almost as bad, goo
mother,   2
As kill a king, and marry with his brother.
Queen. As kill a king!
Ham.   Ay, lady, 'twas my word
[*Lifts up the arras and discovers* POLONIUS
[*To* POLONIUS.] Thou wretched, rash, intrudin
fool, farewell!
I took thee for thy better; take thy fortune; 3
Thou find'st to be too busy is some danger.
Leave wringing of your hands: peace! sit yo
down,
And let me wring your heart; for so I shall
If it be made of penetrable stuff,   3
If damned custom have not brass'd it so
That it is proof and bulwark against sense.
Queen. What have I done that thou dar's
wag thy tongue
In noise so rude against me?
Ham.   Such an act   4
That blurs the grace and blush of modesty,
Calls virtue hypocrite, takes off the rose
From the fair forehead of an innocent love
And sets a blister there, makes marriage vows
As false as dicers' oaths; O! such a deed   4
As from the body of contraction plucks
The very soul, and sweet religion makes
A rhapsody of words; heaven's face doth glow
Yea, this solidity and compound mass,   4
With tristful visage, as against the doom,
Is thought-sick at the act.
Queen.   Ay me! what act,
That roars so loud and thunders in the index
Ham. Look here, upon this picture, and on
this;   5
The counterfeit presentment of two brothers.
See, what a grace was seated on this brow;
Hyperion's curls, the front of Jove himself, 5
An eye like Mars, to threaten and command,
A station like the herald Mercury
New-lighted on a heaven-kissing hill,
A combination and a form indeed,   6
Where every god did seem to set his seal,
To give the world assurance of a man.
This was your husband: look you now, what
follows.

Iere is your husband; like a mildew'd ear, 64
Blasting his wholesome brother. Have you
   eyes?
Could you on this fair mountain leave to feed,
And batten on this moor? Ha! have you eyes?
You cannot call it love, for at your age   68
The hey-day in the blood is tame, it's humble,
And waits upon the judgment; and what judg-
   ment
Would step from this to this? Sense, sure, you
   have,
Else could you not have motion; but sure, that
   sense   72
Is apoplex'd; for madness would not err,
Nor sense to ecstasy was ne'er so thrall'd
But it reserv'd some quantity of choice,   75
To serve in such a difference. What devil was't
That thus hath cozen'd you at hoodman-blind?
Eyes without feeling, feeling without sight,
Ears without hands or eyes, smelling sans all,
Or but a sickly part of one true sense   80
Could not so mope.
O shame! where is thy blush? Rebellious hell,
If thou canst mutine in a matron's bones,
To flaming youth let virtue be as wax,   84
And melt in her own fire: proclaim no shame
When the compulsive ardour gives the charge,
Since frost itself as actively doth burn,
And reason panders will.
   Queen.   O Hamlet! speak no more;
Thou turn'st mine eyes into my very soul;   89
And there I see much black and grained spots
As will not leave their tinct.
   Ham.   Nay, but to live
In the rank sweat of an enseamed bed,   92
Stew'd in corruption, honeying and making love
Over the nasty sty,—
   Queen.   O! speak to me no more;
These words like daggers enter in mine ears;
No more, sweet Hamlet!
   Ham.   A murderer, and a villain;
A slave that is not twentieth part the tithe 97
Of your precedent lord; a vice of kings;
A cut-purse of the empire and the rule,
That from a shelf the precious diadem stole, 100
And put it in his pocket!
   Queen.   No more!
   Ham. A king of shreds and patches,—

         Enter Ghost.

Save me, and hover o'er me with your wings,
You heavenly guards! What would your gra-
   cious figure?   104
   Queen. Alas! he's mad!
   Ham. Do you not come your tardy son to
   chide,
That, laps'd in time and passion, lets go by
The important acting of your dread command?
O! say.
   Ghost. Do not forget: this visitation   109
Is but to whet thy almost blunted purpose.
But, look! amazement on thy mother sits;
O! step between her and her fighting soul; 112
Conceit in weakest bodies strongest works:
Speak to her, Hamlet.
   Ham.   How is it with you, lady?

   Queen. Alas! how is't with you,
That you do bend your eye on vacancy   116
And with the incorporal air do hold discourse?
Forth at your eyes your spirits wildly peep;
And, as the sleeping soldiers in the alarm,
Your bedded hair, like life in excrements, 120
Starts up and stands an end. O gentle son!
Upon the heat and flame of thy distemper
Sprinkle cool patience. Whereon do you look?
   Ham. On him, on him! Look you, how pale
   he glares!   124
His form and cause conjoin'd, preaching to
   stones,
Would make them capable. Do not look upon
   me;
Lest with this piteous action you convert
My stern effects: then what I have to do   128
Will want true colour; tears perchance for
   blood.
   Queen. To whom do you speak this?
   Ham.   Do you see nothing there?
   Queen. Nothing at all; yet all that is I see.
   Ham. Nor did you nothing hear?
   Queen.   No, nothing but ourselves.
   Ham. Why, look you there! look, how it
   steals away;   133
My father, in his habit as he liv'd;
Look! where he goes, even now, out at the
   portal.   [*Exit* Ghost.
   Queen. This is the very coinage of your
   brain: 136
This bodiless creation ecstasy
Is very cunning in.
   Ham. Ecstasy!
My pulse, as yours, doth temperately keep time,
And makes as healthful music. It is not mad-
   ness   141
That I have utter'd: bring me to the test,
And I the matter will re-word, which madness
Would gambol from. Mother, for love of grace,
Lay not that flattering unction to your soul, 145
That not your trespass but my madness speaks;
It will but skin and film the ulcerous place,
Whiles rank corruption, mining all within, 148
Infects unseen. Confess yourself to heaven;
Repent what's past; avoid what is to come;
And do not spread the compost on the weeds
To make them ranker. Forgive me this my
   virtue;   152
For in the fatness of these pursy times
Virtue itself of vice must pardon beg,
Yea, curb and woo for leave to do him good.
   Queen. O Hamlet! thou hast cleft my heart
   in twain.   156
   Ham. O! throw away the worser part of it,
And live the purer with the other half.
Good night; but go not to mine uncle's bed;
Assume a virtue, if you have it not.   160
That monster, custom, who all sense doth eat,
Of habits devil, is angel yet in this,
That to the use of actions fair and good
He likewise gives a frock or livery,   164
That aptly is put on. Refrain to-night;
And that shall lend a kind of easiness
To the next abstinence: the next more easy;
For use almost can change the stamp of nature,

And master ev'n the devil or throw him out 169
With wondrous potency. Once more, good-
night:
And when you are desirous to be bless'd,
I'll blessing beg of you. For this same lord, 172
            [*Pointing to* POLONIUS.
I do repent: but heaven hath pleas'd it so,
To punish me with this, and this with me,
That I must be their scourge and minister.
I will bestow him, and will answer well 176
The death I gave him. So, again, good-night.
I must be cruel only to be kind:
Thus bad begins and worse remains behind.
One word more, good lady.
  Queen.   What shall I do? 180
  Ham. Not this, by no means, that I bid you do:
Let the bloat king tempt you again to bed;
Pinch wanton on your cheek; call you his mouse;
And let him, for a pair of reechy kisses, 184
Or paddling in your neck with his damn'd fingers,
Make you to ravel all this matter out,
That I essentially am not in madness,
But mad in craft. 'Twere good you let him
know; 188
For who that's but a queen, fair, sober, wise,
Would from a paddock, from a bat, a gib,
Such dear concernings hide? who would do so?
No, in despite of sense and secrecy, 192
Unpeg the basket on the house's top,
Let the birds fly, and, like the famous ape,
To try conclusions, in the basket creep,
And break your own neck down. 196
  Queen. Be thou assur'd, if words be made of
breath,
And breath of life, I have no life to breathe
What thou hast said to me.
  Ham. I must to England; you know that?
  Queen.   Alack!
I had forgot: 'tis so concluded on. 201
  Ham. There's letters seal'd; and my two
schoolfellows,
Whom I will trust as I will adders fang'd,
They bear the mandate; they must sweep my way,
And marshal me to knavery. Let it work; 205
For 'tis the sport to have the engineer
Hoist with his own petar: and it shall go hard
But I will delve one yard below their mines, 208
And blow them at the moon. O! 'tis most sweet,
When in one line two crafts directly meet.
This man shall set me packing;
I'll lug the guts into the neighbour room. 212
Mother, good-night. Indeed this counsellor
Is now most still, most secret, and most grave,
Who was in life a foolish prating knave.
Come, sir, to draw toward an end with you. 216
Good-night, mother.
    [*Exeunt severally;* HAMLET *dragging in
the body of* POLONIUS.

ACT IV

Scene I.—*A Room in the Castle.*

Enter KING, QUEEN, ROSENCRANTZ, *and*
GUILDENSTERN.

  King. There's matter in these sighs, these
profound heaves:

You must translate; 'tis fit we understand them.
Where is your son?
  Queen. [*To* ROSENCRANTZ *and* GUILDEN-
STERN.] Bestow this place on us a little
while. 4
    [*Exeunt* ROSENCRANTZ *and* GUILDENSTERN.
Ah! my good lord, what have I seen to-night.
  King. What, Gertrude? How does Hamlet?
  Queen. Mad as the sea and wind, when both
contend
Which is the mightier. In his lawless fit, 8
Behind the arras hearing something stir,
Whips out his rapier, cries, 'A rat! a rat!'
And, in his brainish apprehension, kills
The unseen good old man.
  King.   O heavy deed! 12
It had been so with us had we been there.
His liberty is full of threats to all;
To you yourself, to us, to every one.
Alas! how shall this bloody deed be answer'd?
It will be laid to us, whose providence 17
Should have kept short, restrain'd, and out of
haunt,
This mad young man: but so much was our love,
We would not understand what was most fit, 20
But, like the owner of a foul disease,
To keep it from divulging, let it feed
Even on the pith of life. Where is he gone?
  Queen. To draw apart the body he hath
kill'd; 24
O'er whom his very madness, like some ore
Among a mineral of metals base,
Shows itself pure: he weeps for what is done.
  King. O Gertrude! come away. 28
The sun no sooner shall the mountains touch
But we will ship him hence; and this vile deed
We must, with all our majesty and skill,
Both countenance and excuse. Ho! Guilden-
stern! 32

Re-enter ROSENCRANTZ *and* GUILDENSTERN.

Friends both, go join you with some further aid:
Hamlet in madness hath Polonius slain,
And from his mother's closet hath he dragg'd
him:
Go seek him out; speak fair, and bring the body
Into the chapel. I pray you, haste in this. 37
    [*Exeunt* ROSENCRANTZ *and* GUILDENSTERN.
Come, Gertrude, we'll call up our wisest friends;
And let them know both what we mean to do,
And what's untimely done: so, haply, slander,
Whose whisper o'er the world's diameter, 41
As level as the cannon to his blank
Transports his poison'd shot, may miss our
name,
And hit the woundless air. O! come away; 44
My soul is full of discord and dismay. [*Exeunt.*

Scene II.—*Another Room in the Same.*

Enter HAMLET.

  Ham. Safely stowed.
  Ros. ⎱ [*Within.*] Hamlet! Lord Hamlet!
  Guil.⎰
  Ham. What noise? who calls on Hamlet?
O! here they come.

Enter ROSENCRANTZ *and* GUILDENSTERN.

Ros. What have you done, my lord, with the dead body?

Ham. Compounded it with dust, whereto 'tis kin.

Ros. Tell us where 'tis, that we may take it thence
And bear it to the chapel.   8

Ham. Do not believe it.

Ros. Believe what?

Ham. That I can keep your counsel and not mine own. Besides, to be demanded of a sponge! what replication should be made by the son of a king?   14

Ros. Take you me for a sponge, my lord?

Ham. Ay, sir, that soaks up the king's countenance, his rewards, his authorities. But such officers do the king best service in the end: he keeps them, like an ape, in the corner of his jaw; first mouthed, to be last swallowed: when he needs what you have gleaned, it is but squeezing you, and, sponge, you shall be dry again.   23

Ros. I understand you not, my lord.

Ham. I am glad of it: a knavish speech sleeps in a foolish ear.

Ros. My lord, you must tell us where the body is, and go with us to the king.   28

Ham. The body is with the king, but the king is not with the body. The king is a thing—

Guil. A thing, my lord!

Ham. Of nothing: bring me to him. Hide fox, and all after.   [*Exeunt.*

SCENE III.—*Another Room in the Same.*

Enter KING, *attended.*

King. I have sent to seek him, and to find the body.
How dangerous is it that this man goes loose!
Yet must not we put the strong law on him:
He's lov'd of the distracted multitude,   4
Who like not in their judgment, but their eyes;
And where 'tis so, the offender's scourge is weigh'd,
But never the offence. To bear all smooth and even,
This sudden sending him away must seem   8
Deliberate pause: diseases desperate grown
By desperate appliance are reliev'd,
Or not at all.

Enter ROSENCRANTZ.
                    How now! what hath befall'n?

Ros. Where the dead body is bestow'd, my lord,   12
We cannot get from him.

King.   But where is he?

Ros. Without, my lord; guarded, to know your pleasure.

King. Bring him before us.

Ros. Ho, Guildenstern! bring in my lord. 16

Enter HAMLET *and* GUILDENSTERN.

King. Now, Hamlet, where's Polonius?

Ham. At supper.

King. At supper! Where?

Ham. Not where he eats, but where he is eaten: a certain convocation of politic worms are e'en at him. Your worm is your only emperor for diet: we fat all creatures else to fat us, and we fat ourselves for maggots: your fat king and your lean beggar is but variable service; two dishes, but to one table: that's the end.

King. Alas, alas!   28

Ham. A man may fish with the worm that hath eat of a king, and eat of the fish that hath fed of that worm.

King. What dost thou mean by this?   32

Ham. Nothing, but to show you how a king may go a progress through the guts of a beggar.

King. Where is Polonius?   35

Ham. In heaven; send thither to see: if your messenger find him not there, seek him i' the other place yourself. But, indeed, if you find him not within this month, you shall nose him as you go up the stairs into the lobby. 40

King. [*To some* Attendants.] Go seek him there.

Ham. He will stay till you come.
                    [*Exeunt* Attendants.

King. Hamlet, this deed, for thine especial safety,
Which we do tender, as we dearly grieve   44
For that which thou hast done, must send thee hence
With fiery quickness: therefore prepare thyself;
The bark is ready, and the wind at help,
The associates tend, and every thing is bent 48
For England!

Ham.   For England!

King.   Ay, Hamlet.

Ham.   Good.

King. So is it, if thou knew'st our purposes.

Ham. I see a cherub that sees them. But, come; for England! Farewell, dear mother. 52

King. Thy loving father, Hamlet.

Ham. My mother: father and mother is man and wife, man and wife is one flesh, and so, my mother. Come, for England!   [*Exit.*

King. Follow him at foot; tempt him with speed aboard: 57
Delay it not, I'll have him hence to-night.
Away! for every thing is seal'd and done
That else leans on the affair: pray you, make haste.   60
                    [*Exeunt* ROSENCRANTZ *and* GUILDENSTERN.
And England if my love thou hold'st at aught,—
As my great power thereof may give thee sense,
Since yet thy cicatrice looks raw and red
After the Danish sword, and thy free awe   64
Pays homage to us,—thou mayst not coldly set
Our sovereign process, which imports at full,
By letters conjuring to that effect,
The present death of Hamlet. Do it, England;
For like the hectic in my blood he rages,   69
And thou must cure me. Till I know 'tis done,
Howe'er my haps, my joys were ne'er begun.
                                        [*Exit.*

SCENE IV.—*A Plain in Denmark.*

Enter FORTINBRAS, *a* Captain, *and* Soldiers, *marching.*

For. Go, captain, from me greet the Danish king;
Tell him that, by his licence, Fortinbras
Claims the conveyance of a promis'd march
Over his kingdom. You know the rendezvous.
If that his majesty would aught with us,
We shall express our duty in his eye,
And let him know so.
  Cap.   I will do't, my lord.
  For. Go softly on.   8
           [*Exeunt* FORTINBRAS *and* Soldiers.

Enter HAMLET, ROSENCRANTZ, GUILDENSTERN, *&c.*

  Ham. Good sir, whose powers are these?
  Cap. They are of Norway, sir.
  Ham. How purpos'd, sir, I pray you?
  Cap. Against some part of Poland.   12
  Ham. Who commands them, sir?
  Cap. The nephew to old Norway, Fortinbras.
  Ham. Goes it against the main of Poland, sir,
Or for some frontier?   16
  Cap. Truly to speak, and with no addition,
We go to gain a little patch of ground
That hath in it no profit but the name.
To pay five ducats, five, I would not farm it; 20
Nor will it yield to Norway or the Pole
A ranker rate, should it be sold in fee.
  Ham. Why, then the Polack never will defend it.
  Cap. Yes, 'tis already garrison'd.   24
  Ham. Two thousand souls and twenty thousand ducats
Will not debate the question of this straw:
This is the imposthume of much wealth and peace,
That inward breaks, and shows no cause without   28
Why the man dies. I humbly thank you, sir.
  Cap. God be wi' you, sir.   [*Exit.*
  Ros.   Will't please you go, my lord?
  Ham. I'll be with you straight. Go a little before.   [*Exeunt all except* HAMLET.
How all occasions do inform against me,   32
And spur my dull revenge! What is a man,
If his chief good and market of his time
Be but to sleep and feed? a beast, no more.
Sure he that made us with such large discourse,
Looking before and after, gave us not
That capability and god-like reason
To fust in us unus'd. Now, whe'r it be
Bestial oblivion, or some craven scruple   40
Of thinking too precisely on the event,
A thought, which, quarter'd, hath but one part wisdom,
And ever three parts coward, I do not know
Why yet I live to say 'This thing 's to do'; 44
Sith I have cause and will and strength and means
To do't. Examples gross as earth exhort me:
Witness this army of such mass and charge

Led by a delicate and tender prince,   4
Whose spirit with divine ambition puff'd
Makes mouths at the invisible event,
Exposing what is mortal and unsure
To all that fortune, death and danger dare, 5
Even for an egg-shell. Rightly to be great
Is not to stir without great argument,
But greatly to find quarrel in a straw
When honour 's at the stake. How stand I then
That have a father kill'd, a mother stain'd, 5
Excitements of my reason and my blood,
And let all sleep, while, to my shame, I see
The imminent death of twenty thousand men
That, for a fantasy and trick of fame,   6
Go to their graves like beds, fight for a plot
Whereon the numbers cannot try the cause,
Which is not tomb enough and continent   6
To hide the slain? O! from this time forth,
My thoughts be bloody, or be nothing worth
                   [*Exit*

SCENE V.—*Elsinore. A Room in the Castle*

Enter QUEEN, HORATIO, *and a* Gentleman.

  Queen. I will not speak with her.
  Gent. She is importunate, indeed distract:
Her mood will needs be pitied.
  Queen.   What would she have?
  Gent. She speaks much of her father; says she hears
There 's tricks i' the world; and hems, and beats her heart;
Spurns enviously at straws; speaks things in doubt,
That carry but half sense: her speech is nothing
Yet the unshaped use of it doth move
The hearers to collection; they aim at it,
And botch the words up fit to their own thoughts
Which, as her winks, and nods, and gestures yield them,
Indeed would make one think there might be thought,   12
Though nothing sure, yet much unhappily.
  Hor. 'Twere good she were spoken with, for she may strew
Dangerous conjectures in ill-breeding minds.
  Queen. Let her come in. [*Exit Gentleman*
To my sick soul, as sin's true nature is,   1
Each toy seems prologue to some great amiss:
So full of artless jealousy is guilt,
It spills itself in fearing to be spilt.   2

Re-enter Gentleman, *with* OPHELIA.

  Oph. Where is the beauteous majesty of Denmark?
  Queen. How now, Ophelia!
  Oph. How should I your true love know
          From another one?   24
    By his cockle hat and staff,
        And his sandal shoon.
  Queen. Alas! sweet lady, what imports this song?
  Oph. Say you? nay, pray you, mark.   28
    He is dead and gone, lady,
        He is dead and gone;
    At his head a grass-green turf,
        At his heels a stone.   32

O, ho!
Queen. Nay, but Ophelia,—
Oph. Pray you, mark.

White his shroud as the mountain snow,—   36

Enter KING.

Queen. Alas! look here, my lord.
Oph.   Larded with sweet flowers;
        Which bewept to the grave did go
        With true-love showers.   40

King. How do you, pretty lady?
Oph. Well, God 'ild you! They say the owl
was a baker's daughter. Lord! we know what
we are, but know not what we may be. God be
at your table!   45
King. Conceit upon her father.
Oph. Pray you, let's have no words of this; but
when they ask you what it means, say you this:

        To-morrow is Saint Valentine's day,   49
        All in the morning betime,
        And I a maid at your window,
        To be your Valentine:
        Then up he rose, and donn'd his clothes,   52
        And dupp'd the chamber door;
        Let in the maid, that out a maid
        Never departed more.   56

King. Pretty Ophelia!
Oph. Indeed, la! without an oath, I'll make
an end on 't:

        By Gis and by Saint Charity,
        Alack, and fie for shame!   60
        Young men will do 't, if they come to 't;
        By Cock they are to blame.
        Quoth she, before you tumbled me,
        You promis'd me to wed: 64
        So would I ha' done, by yonder sun,
        An thou hadst not come to my bed.

King. How long hath she been thus?   67
Oph. I hope all will be well. We must be
patient: but I cannot choose but weep, to think
they should lay him i' the cold ground. My
brother shall know of it: and so I thank you
for your good counsel. Come, my coach! Good-
night, ladies; good-night, sweet ladies; good-
night, good-night.   [*Exit.*
King. Follow her close; give her good watch,
I pray you.   [*Exit* HORATIO.
O! this is the poison of deep grief; it springs   76
All from her father's death. O Gertrude, Ger-
trude!
When sorrows come, they come not single spies,
But in battalions. First, her father slain;
Next, your son gone; but he most violent
author   80
Of his own just remove: the people muddied,
Thick and unwholesome in their thoughts and
whispers,
For good Polonius' death; and we have done
but greenly,
In hugger-mugger to inter him: poor Ophelia
Divided from herself and her fair judgment,   85
Without the which we are pictures, or mere
beasts:
Last, and as much containing as all these,
Her brother is in secret come from France,   88
Feeds on his wonder, keeps himself in clouds,

And wants not buzzers to infect his ear
With pestilent speeches of his father's death;
Wherein necessity, of matter beggar'd,   92
Will nothing stick our person to arraign
In ear and ear. O my dear Gertrude! this,
Like to a murdering-piece, in many places
Gives me superfluous death.   [*A noise within.*
Queen.   Alack! what noise is this?

Enter a Gentleman.

King. Where are my Switzers? Let them
guard the door.   97
What is the matter?
Gen.   Save yourself, my lord;
The ocean, overpeering of his list,
Eats not the flats with more impetuous haste
Than young Laertes, in a riotous head,   101
O'erbears your officers. The rabble call him
lord;
And, as the world were now but to begin,
Antiquity forgot, custom not known,   104
The ratifiers and props of every word,
They cry, 'Choose we; Laertes shall be king!'
Caps, hands, and tongues, applaud it to the
clouds,
'Laertes shall be king, Laertes king!'   108
Queen. How cheerfully on the false trail they
cry!
O! this is counter, you false Danish dogs!
King. The doors are broke.   [*Noise within.*

Enter LAERTES, *armed;* Danes *following.*

Laer. Where is the king? Sirs, stand you all
without.   112
Danes. No, let's come in.
Laer.   I pray you, give me leave.
Danes. We will, we will.
                [*They retire without the door.*
Laer. I thank you: keep the door. O thou
vile king!
Give me my father.
Queen.   Calmly, good Laertes.   116
Laer. That drop of blood that's calm pro-
claims me bastard,
Cries cuckold to my father, brands the harlot
Even here, between the chaste unsmirched brow
Of my true mother.
King.   What is the cause, Laertes,
That thy rebellion looks so giant-like?   121
Let him go, Gertrude; do not fear our person:
There's such divinity doth hedge a king,
That treason can but peep to what it would,
Acts little of his will. Tell me, Laertes,   125
Why thou art thus incens'd. Let him go, Ger-
trude.
Speak, man.
Laer. Where is my father?
King.   Dead.
Queen.   But not by him.
King. Let him demand his fill.   128
Laer. How came he dead? I'll not be juggled
with.
To hell, allegiance! vows, to the blackest devil!
Conscience and grace, to the profoundest pit!
I dare damnation. To this point I stand,   132
That both the worlds I give to negligence,

Let come what comes; only I'll be reveng'd
Most throughly for my father.

King.   Who shall stay you?

Laer. My will, not all the world: 136
And, for my means, I'll husband them so well,
They shall go far with little.

King.   Good Laertes,
If you desire to know the certainty
Of your dear father's death, is't writ in your
revenge,   140
That, swoopstake, you will draw both friend and
foe,
Winner and loser?

Laer. None but his enemies.

King.   Will you know them then?

Laer. To his good friends thus wide I'll ope
my arms;   144
And like the kind life-rendering pelican,
Repast them with my blood.

King.   Why, now you speak
Like a good child and a true gentleman.
That I am guiltless of your father's death, 148
And am most sensibly in grief for it,
It shall as level to your judgment pierce
As day does to your eye.

Danes.   [*Within.*] Let her come in.

Laer. How now! what noise is that?   152

Re-enter OPHELIA.

O heat, dry up my brains! tears seven times salt,
Burn out the sense and virtue of mine eye!
By heaven, thy madness shall be paid by weight,
Till our scale turn the beam. O rose of May!
Dear maid, kind sister, sweet Ophelia!   157
O heavens! is't possible a young maid's wits
Should be as mortal as an old man's life?
Nature is fine in love, and where 'tis fine   160
It sends some precious instance of itself
After the thing it loves.

Oph.   They bore him barefac'd on the bier;
    Hey non nonny, nonny, hey nonny;   164
    And in his grave rain'd many a tear;—

Fare you well, my dove!

Laer. Hadst thou thy wits, and didst persuade revenge,
It could not move thus.   168

Oph.   You must sing, a-down a-down,
    And you call him a-down-a.

O how the wheel becomes it! It is the false
steward that stole his master's daughter.   172

Laer. This nothing's more than matter.

Oph. There's rosemary, that's for remembrance; pray, love, remember: and there is
pansies, that's for thoughts.   176

Laer. A document in madness, thoughts and
remembrance fitted.

Oph. There's fennel for you, and columbines;
there's rue for you; and here's some for me;
we may call it herb of grace o' Sundays. O! you
must wear your rue with a difference. There's a
daisy; I would give you some violets, but they
withered all when my father died. They say he
made a good end,—   185

For bonny sweet Robin is all my joy.

Laer. Thought and affliction, passion, hell
itself,
She turns to favour and to prettiness.   188

Oph.   And will he not come again?
    And will he not come again?
      No, no, he is dead;
      Go to thy death-bed,   192
    He never will come again.
    His beard was as white as snow
    All flaxen was his poll,
      He is gone, he is gone,   196
      And we cast away moan:
    God ha' mercy on his soul!

And of all Christian souls! I pray God. God be
wi' ye!   [*Exit.*

Laer. Do you see this, O God?   201

King. Laertes, I must common with your
grief,
Or you deny me right. Go but apart,
Make choice of whom your wisest friends you
will,   204
And they shall hear and judge 'twixt you and
me.
If by direct or by collateral hand
They find us touch'd, we will our kingdom give,
Our crown, our life, and all that we call ours, 208
To you in satisfaction; but if not,
Be you content to lend your patience to us,
And we shall jointly labour with your soul
To give it due content.

Laer.   Let this be so: 212
His means of death, his obscure burial,
No trophy, sword, nor hatchment o'er his bones,
No noble rite nor formal ostentation,
Cry to be heard, as 'twere from heaven to earth,
That I must call't in question.

King.   So you shall;   217
And where the offence is let the great axe fall.
I pray you go with me.   [*Exeunt.*

SCENE VI.—*Another Room in the Same.*

Enter HORATIO *and a* Servant.

Hor. What are they that would speak with
me?

Serv. Sailors, sir: they say, they have letters
for you.

Hor. Let them come in.   [*Exit* Servant.
I do not know from what part of the world 4
I should be greeted, if not from Lord Hamlet.

Enter Sailors.

First Sail. God bless you, sir.

Hor. Let him bless thee too.

Sec. Sail. He shall, sir, an't please him.
There's a letter for you, sir;—it comes from
the ambassador that was bound for England;—
if your name be Horatio, as I am let to know
it is.   12

*Hor. Horatio, when thou shalt have over-
looked this, give these fellows some means to the
king: they have letters for him. Ere we were
two days old at sea, a pirate of very war-like
appointment gave us chase. Finding ourselves
too slow of sail, we put on a compelled valour;
in the grapple I boarded them: on the instant
they got clear of our ship, so I alone became*

*heir prisoner. They have dealt with me like
'hieves of mercy, but they knew what they did;
' am to do a good turn for them. Let the king
¡ave the letters I have sent; and repair thou to
ne with as much haste as thou wouldst fly
¡eath. I have words to speak in thine ear will
¡nake thee dumb; yet are they much too light
'or the bore of the matter. These good fellows
¡will bring thee where I am. Rosencrantz and
Guildenstern hold their course for England: of
them I have much to tell thee. Farewell.*

He that thou knowest thine,   32
HAMLET.

Come, I will give you way for these your letters;
And do't the speedier, that you may direct me
To him from whom you brought them. [Exeunt.

SCENE VII.—*Another Room in the Same.*

Enter KING and LAERTES.

King. Now must your conscience my acquit-
     tance seal,
And you must put me in your heart for friend,
Sith you have heard, and with a knowing ear,
That he which hath your noble father slain   4
Pursu'd my life.

Laer.   It well appears: but tell me
Why you proceeded not against these feats,
So crimeful and so capital in nature,
As by your safety, wisdom, all things else,   8
You mainly were stirr'd up.

King.   O! for two special reasons;
Which may to you, perhaps, seem much un-
     sinew'd,
But yet to me they are strong. The queen his
     mother
Lives almost by his looks, and for myself,— 12
My virtue or my plague, be it either which,—
She's so conjunctive to my life and soul,
That, as the star moves not but in his sphere,
I could not but by her. The other motive,   16
Why to a public count I might not go,
Is the great love the general gender bear him;
Who, dipping all his faults in their affection,
Would, like the spring that turneth wood to
     stone,   20
Convert his gyves to graces; so that my arrows,
Too slightly timber'd for so loud a wind,
Would have reverted to my bow again,
And not where I had aim'd them.   24

Laer. And so have I a noble father lost;
A sister driven into desperate terms,
Whose worth, if praises may go back again,
Stood challenger on mount of all the age   28
For her perfections. But my revenge will come.

King. Break not your sleeps for that; you
     must not think
That we are made of stuff so flat and dull
That we can let our beard be shook with danger
And think it pastime. You shortly shall hear
     more;   33
I lov'd your father, and we love ourself,
And that, I hope, will teach you to imagine,—

Enter a Messenger.

How now! what news?

Mess.   Letters, my lord, from Hamlet:
This to your majesty; this to the queen.   37
King. From Hamlet! who brought them?
Mess. Sailors, my lord, they say; I saw them
     not:
They were given me by Claudio, he receiv'd   40
Of him that brought them.
King.   Laertes, you shall hear them.
Leave us.   [*Exit* Messenger.

*High and mighty, you shall know I am set
naked on your kingdom. To-morrow shall I
beg leave to see your kingly eyes; when I shall,
first asking your pardon thereunto, recount the
occasions of my sudden and more strange return.*
                              HAMLET.

What should this mean? Are all the rest come
     back?   49
Or is it some abuse and no such thing?
Laer. Know you the hand?
King.   'Tis Hamlet's character. 'Naked',
And in a postscript here, he says, 'alone'.   52
Can you advise me?
Laer. I'm lost in it, my lord. But let him
     come:
It warms the very sickness in my heart,
That I shall live and tell him to his teeth,   56
'Thus diddest thou'.
King.   If it be so, Laertes,
As how should it be so? how otherwise?
Will you be rul'd by me?
Laer.   Ay, my lord;
So you will not o'er-rule me to a peace.   60
King. To thine own peace. If he be now re-
     turn'd,
As checking at his voyage, and that he means
No more to undertake it, I will work him
To an exploit, now ripe in my device,   64
Under the which he shall not choose but fall;
And for his death no wind of blame shall breathe,
But even his mother shall uncharge the practice
And call it accident.
Laer.   My lord, I will be rul'd;   68
The rather, if you could devise it so
That I might be the organ.
King.   It falls right.
You have been talk'd of since your travel much,
And that in Hamlet's hearing, for a quality   72
Wherein, they say, you shine; your sum of parts
Did not together pluck such envy from him
As did that one, and that, in my regard,
Of the unworthiest siege.
Laer.   What part is that, my lord?   76
King. A very riband in the cap of youth,
Yet needful too; for youth no less becomes
The light and careless livery that it wears
Than settled age his sables and his weeds,   80
Importing health and graveness. Two months
     since
Here was a gentleman of Normandy:
I've seen myself, and serv'd against, the French,
And they can well on horseback; but this gal-
lant   84
Had witchcraft in't, he grew into his seat,
And to such wondrous doing brought his horse,
As he had been incorps'd and demi-natur'd

With the brave beast; so far he topp'd my
  thought, 88
That I, in forgery of shapes and tricks,
Come short of what he did.
  Laer. A Norman was 't?
  King. A Norman.
  Laer. Upon my life, Lamord.
  King. The very same. 92
  Laer. I know him well; he is the brooch
    indeed
And gem of all the nation.
  King. He made confession of you,
And gave you such a masterly report 96
For art and exercise in your defence,
And for your rapier most especially,
That he cried out, 'twould be a sight indeed
If one could match you; the scrimers of their
  nation, 100
He swore, had neither motion, guard, nor eye,
If you oppos'd them. Sir, this report of his
Did Hamlet so envenom with his envy
That he could nothing do but wish and beg 104
Your sudden coming o'er, to play with him.
Now, out of this,—
  Laer. What out of this, my lord?
  King. Laertes, was your father dear to you?
Or are you like the painting of a sorrow, 108
A face without a heart?
  Laer. Why ask you this?
  King. Not that I think you did not love your
    father,
But that I know love is begun by time,
And that I see, in passages of proof, 112
Time qualifies the spark and fire of it.
There lives within the very flame of love
A kind of wick or snuff that will abate it,
And nothing is at a like goodness still, 116
For goodness, growing to a plurisy,
Dies in his own too-much. That we would do,
We should do when we would, for this 'would'
  changes,
And hath abatements and delays as many 120
As there are tongues, are hands, are accidents;
And then this 'should' is like a spendthrift sigh,
That hurts by easing. But, to the quick o' the
  ulcer;
Hamlet comes back; what would you undertake
To show yourself your father's son in deed 125
More than in words?
  Laer. To cut his throat i' the church.
  King. No place, indeed, should murder sanc-
    tuarize;
Revenge should have no bounds. But, good
  Laertes, 128
Will you do this, keep close within your chamber.
Hamlet return'd shall know you are come home;
We'll put on those shall praise your excellence,
And set a double varnish on the fame 132
The Frenchman gave you, bring you, in fine,
  together,
And wager on your heads: he, being remiss,
Most generous and free from all contriving,
Will not peruse the foils; so that, with ease 136
Or with a little shuffling, you may choose
A sword unbated, and, in a pass of practice
Requite him for your father.

  Laer. I will do 't;
And, for that purpose, I'll anoint my sword. 140
I bought an unction of a mountebank,
So mortal that, but dip a knife in it,
Where it draws blood no cataplasm so rare,
Collected from all simples that have virtue 144
Under the moon, can save the thing from death
That is but scratch'd withal; I'll touch my point
With this contagion, that, if I gall him slightly,
It may be death.
  King. Let's further think of this; 148
Weigh what convenience both of time and
  means
May fit us to our shape. If this should fail,
And that our drift look through our bad per-
  formance 152
'Twere better not assay'd; therefore this project
Should have a back or second, that might hold,
If this should blast in proof. Soft! let me see:
We'll make a solemn wager on your cunnings:
I ha 't: 156
When in your motion you are hot and dry,—
As make your bouts more violent to that end,—
And that he calls for drink, I'll have prepar'd
  him
A chalice for the nonce, whereon but sipping,
If he by chance escape your venom'd stuck, 161
Our purpose may hold there. But stay! what
  noise?

Enter QUEEN.

How now, sweet queen!
  Queen. One woe doth tread upon another's
    heel, 164
So fast they follow: your sister's drown'd,
  Laertes.
  Laer. Drown'd! O, where?
  Queen. There is a willow grows aslant a
    brook,
That shows his hoar leaves in the glassy stream;
There with fantastic garlands did she come, 169
Of crow-flowers, nettles, daisies, and long
  purples,
That liberal shepherds give a grosser name,
But our cold maids do dead men's fingers call
  them: 172
There, on the pendent boughs her coronet weeds
Clambering to hang, an envious sliver broke,
When down her weedy trophies and herself
Fell in the weeping brook. Her clothes spread
  wide, 176
And, mermaid-like, awhile they bore her up;
Which time she chanted snatches of old tunes,
As one incapable of her own distress,
Or like a creature native and indu'd 180
Unto that element; but long it could not be
Till that her garments, heavy with their drink,
Pull'd the poor wretch from her melodious lay
To muddy death.
  Laer. Alas! then, she is drown'd? 184
  Queen. Drown'd, drown'd.
  Laer. Too much of water hast thou, poor
    Ophelia,
And therefore I forbid my tears; but yet
It is our trick, nature her custom holds, 188
Let shame say what it will; when these are gone

The woman will be out. Adieu, my lord!
I have a speech of fire, that fain would blaze,
But that this folly douts it.　　　　[*Exit.*
　King.　　　　　Let's follow, Gertrude.
How much I had to do to calm his rage! 193
Now fear I this will give it start again;
Therefore let's follow.　　　　　[*Exeunt.*

ACT V

SCENE I.—*A Churchyard.*

Enter two Clowns, *with spades and mattock.*

First Clo. Is she to be buried in Christian
burial that wilfully seeks her own salvation?
　Sec. Clo. I tell thee she is; and therefore
make her grave straight: the crowner hath sat
on her, and finds it Christian burial.　　5
　First Clo. How can that be, unless she
drowned herself in her own defence?
　Sec. Clo. Why, 'tis found so.
　First Clo. It must be *se offendendo*; it cannot be else. For here lies the point: if I drown
myself wittingly it argues an act; and an act
hath three branches; it is, to act, to do, and to
perform: argal, she drowned herself wittingly.
　Sec. Clo. Nay, but hear you, goodman delver—
　First Clo. Give me leave. Here lies the
water; good: here stands the man; good: if the
man go to this water, and drown himself, it is,
will he, nill he, he goes; mark you that? but if
the water come to him, and drown him, he
drowns not himself: argal, he that is not guilty
of his own death shortens not his own life. 21
　Sec. Clo. But is this law?
　First Clo. Ay, marry, is 't; crowner's quest
law.　　　　24
　Sec. Clo. Will you ha' the truth on 't? If this
had not been a gentlewoman she should have
been buried out o' Christian burial.　　27
　First Clo. Why, there thou sayest; and the
more pity that great folk should have countenance in this world to drown or hang themselves more than their even Christian. Come,
my spade. There is no ancient gentlemen but
gardeners, ditchers, and grave-makers; they
hold up Adam's profession.　　34
　Sec. Clo. Was he a gentleman?
　First Clo. A' was the first that ever bore arms.
　Sec. Clo. Why, he had none.　　37
　First Clo. What! art a heathen? How dost
thou understand the Scripture? The Scripture
says, Adam digged; could he dig without arms?
I'll put another question to thee; if thou an-
swerest me not to the purpose, confess thyself—
　Sec. Clo. Go to.　　43
　First Clo. What is he that builds stronger
than either the mason, the shipwright, or the
carpenter?
　Sec. Clo. The gallows-maker; for that frame
outlives a thousand tenants.　　48
　First Clo. I like thy wit well, in good faith;
the gallows does well, but how does it well? it
does well to those that do ill; now thou dost ill
to say the gallows is built stronger than the
church: argal, the gallows may do well to thee.
To 't again; come.

　Sec. Clo. Who builds stronger than a mason,
a shipwright, or a carpenter?　　56
　First Clo. Ay, tell me that, and unyoke.
　Sec. Clo. Marry, now I can tell.
　First Clo. To 't.
　Sec. Clo. Mass, I cannot tell.　　60

Enter HAMLET *and* HORATIO *at a distance.*

　First Clo. Cudgel thy brains no more about
it, for your dull ass will not mend his pace with
beating; and, when you are asked this question
next, say, 'a grave-maker': the houses that he
makes last till doomsday. Go, get thee to
Yaughan; fetch me a stoup of liquor.
　　　　　[*Exit Second* Clown.
First Clown digs, and sings.

In youth, when I did love, did love,
　Methought it was very sweet,
To contract, O! the time, for-a my behove,
　O! methought there was nothing meet.　　68

　Ham. Has this fellow no feeling of his business, that he sings at grave-making?　　72
　Hor. Custom hath made it in him a property
of easiness.
　Ham. 'Tis e'en so; the hand of little employment hath the daintier sense.　　76
　First Clo.

But age, with his stealing steps,
　Hath claw'd me in his clutch,
And hath shipped me intil the land,
　As if I had never been such.　　80
　　　　　[*Throws up a skull.*

　Ham. That skull had a tongue in it, and
could sing once; how the knave jowls it to the
ground, as if it were Cain's jaw-bone, that did
the first murder! This might be the pate of a
politician, which this ass now o'er-offices, one
that would circumvent God, might it not? 86
　Hor. It might, my lord.
　Ham. Or of a courtier, which could say,
'Good morrow, sweet lord! How dost thou,
good lord?' This might be my Lord Such-a-
one, that praised my Lord Such-a-one's horse,
when he meant to beg it, might it not?　　92
　Hor. Ay, my lord.
　Ham. Why, e'en so, and now my Lady
Worm's; chapless, and knocked about the mazzard with a sexton's spade. Here's fine revolution, an we had the trick to see 't. Did these
bones cost no more the breeding but to play at
loggats with 'em? mine ache to think on 't.
　First Clo.

A pick-axe, and a spade, a spade,　　100
　For and a shrouding sheet;
O! a pit of clay for to be made
　For such a guest is meet.
　　　　　[*Throws up another skull.*

　Ham. There's another; why may not that be
the skull of a lawyer? Where be his quiddities
now, his quillets, his cases, his tenures, and his
tricks? why does he suffer this rude knave now
to knock him about the sconce with a dirty
shovel, and will not tell him of his action of
battery? Hum! This fellow might be in 's time
a great buyer of land, with his statutes, his re-

cognizances, his fines, his double vouchers, his recoveries; is this the fine of his fines, and the recovery of his recoveries, to have his fine pate full of fine dirt? will his vouchers vouch him no more of his purchases, and double ones too, than the length and breadth of a pair of indentures? The very conveyance of his lands will hardly lie in this box, and must the inheritor himself have no more, ha?   120

Hor. Not a jot more, my lord.

Ham. Is not parchment made of sheep-skins?

Hor. Ay, my lord, and of calf-skins too. 123

Ham. They are sheep and calves which seek out assurance in that. I will speak to this fellow. Whose grave's this, sir?

First Clo. Mine, sir,

> O! a pit of clay for to be made   128
> For such a guest is meet.

Ham. I think it be thine, indeed; for thou liest in't.

First Clo. You lie out on't, sir, and therefore it is not yours; for my part, I do not lie in't, and yet it is mine.   134

Ham. Thou dost lie in't, to be in't and say it is thine: 'tis for the dead, not for the quick; therefore thou liest.

First Clo. 'Tis a quick lie, sir; 'twill away again, from me to you.

Ham. What man dost thou dig it for?   140

First Clo. For no man, sir.

Ham. What woman, then?

First Clo. For none, neither.

Ham. Who is to be buried in't?   144

First Clo. One that was a woman, sir; but, rest her soul, she's dead.

Ham. How absolute the knave is! we must speak by the card, or equivocation will undo us. By the Lord, Horatio, these three years I have taken note of it; the age is grown so picked that the toe of the peasant comes so near the heel of the courtier, he galls his kibe. How long hast thou been a grave-maker?   153

First Clo. Of all the days i' the year, I came to't that day that our last King Hamlet overcame Fortinbras.   156

Ham. How long is that since?

First Clo. Cannot you tell that? every fool can tell that; it was the very day that young Hamlet was born; he that is mad, and sent into England.   161

Ham. Ay, marry; why was he sent into England?

First Clo. Why, because he was mad: he shall recover his wits there; or, if he do not, 'tis no great matter there.   166

Ham. Why?

First Clo. 'Twill not be seen in him there; there the men are as mad as he.   169

Ham. How came he mad?

First Clo. Very strangely, they say.

Ham. How strangely?   172

First Clo. Faith, e'en with losing his wits.

Ham. Upon what ground?

First Clo. Why, here in Denmark; I have been sexton here, man and boy, thirty years. 176

Ham. How long will a man lie i' the earth ere he rot?

First Clo. Faith, if he be not rotten before he die,—as we have many pocky corses now-adays, that will scarce hold the laying in,—he will last you some eight year or nine year; a tanner will last you nine year.

Ham. Why he more than another?   182

First Clo. Why, sir, his hide is so tanned with his trade that he will keep out water a great while, and your water is a sore decayer of your whoreson dead body. Here's a skull now; this skull hath lain you i' the earth three-and-twenty years.   190

Ham. Whose was it?

First Clo. A whoreson mad fellow's it was: whose do you think it was?

Ham. Nay, I know not.   194

First Clo. A pestilence on him for a mad rogue! a' poured a flagon of Rhenish on my head once. This same skull, sir, was Yorick's skull, the king's jester.

Ham. This!

First Clo. E'en that.   200

Ham. Let me see.—[*Takes the skull.*]—Alas! poor Yorick. I knew him, Horatio; a fellow of infinite jest, of most excellent fancy; he hath borne me on his back a thousand times; and now, how abhorred in my imagination it is! my gorge rises at it. Here hung those lips that I have kissed I know not how oft. Where be your gibes now? your gambols? your songs? your flashes of merriment, that were wont to set the table on a roar? Not one now, to mock your own grinning? quite chapfallen? Now get you to my lady's chamber, and tell her, let her paint an inch thick, to this favour she must come; make her laugh at that. Prithee, Horatio, tell me one thing.

Hor. What's that, my lord?   216

Ham. Dost thou think Alexander looked o' this fashion i' the earth?

Hor. E'en so.

Ham. And smelt so? pah!   220

> [*Puts down the skull.*

Hor. E'en so, my lord.

Ham. To what base uses we may return, Horatio! Why may not imagination trace the noble dust of Alexander, till he find it stopping a bung-hole?   225

Hor. 'Twere to consider too curiously, to consider so.

Ham. No, faith, not a jot; but to follow him thither with modesty enough, and likelihood to lead it; as thus: Alexander died, Alexander was buried, Alexander returneth into dust; the dust is earth; of earth we make loam, and why of that loam, whereto he was converted, might they not stop a beer-barrel?

> Imperious Cæsar, dead and turn'd to clay,
> Might stop a hole to keep the wind away: 236
> O! that that earth, which kept the world in awe,
> Should patch a wall to expel the winter's flaw.

But soft! but soft! aside: here comes the king.

Enter Priests, &c., *in procession: the Corpse of*
OPHELIA, LAERTES *and Mourners following;*
KING, QUEEN, *their Trains, &c.*

The queen, the courtiers: who is that they fol-
  low?   240
And with such maimed rites? This doth betoken
The corse they follow did with desperate hand
Fordo its own life; 'twas of some estate.
Couch we awhile, and mark.   244
                    [*Retiring with* HORATIO.

Laer. What ceremony else?
Ham.   That is Laertes,
A very noble youth: mark.
Laer. What ceremony else?
First Priest. Her obsequies have been as far
  enlarg'd   248
As we have warrantise: her death was doubt-
  ful,
And, but that great command o'ersways the
  order,
She should in ground unsanctified have lodg'd
Till the last trumpet; for charitable prayers, 252
Shards, flints, and pebbles should be thrown on
  her;
Yet here she is allow'd her virgin crants,
Her maiden strewments, and the bringing home
Of bell and burial.   256
Laer. Must there no more be done?
First Priest.   No more be done:
We should profane the service of the dead,
To sing a requiem, and such rest to her
As to peace-parted souls.
Laer.   Lay her i' the earth;   260
And from her fair and unpolluted flesh
May violets spring! I tell thee, churlish priest,
A ministering angel shall my sister be,
When thou liest howling.
Ham.   What! the fair Ophelia?   264
Queen. Sweets to the sweet: farewell!
                    [*Scattering flowers.*
I hop'd thou shouldst have been my Hamlet's
  wife;
I thought thy bride-bed to have deck'd, sweet
  maid,
And not have strew'd thy grave.
Laer.   O! treble woe   268
Fall ten times treble on that cursed head
Whose wicked deed thy most ingenious sense
Depriv'd thee of. Hold off the earth awhile,
Till I have caught her once more in mine arms.
                    [*Leaps into the grave.*
Now pile your dust upon the quick and dead,
Till of this flat a mountain you have made, 274
To o'er-top old Pelion or the skyish head
Of blue Olympus.
Ham. [*Advancing.*] What is he whose grief
Bears such an emphasis? whose phrase of sor-
  row   277
Conjures the wandering stars, and makes them
  stand
Like wonder-wounded hearers? this is I,
Hamlet the Dane.   [*Leaps into the grave.*
Laer.   The devil take thy soul!   280
                    [*Grapples with him.*
Ham. Thou pray'st not well.

I prithee, take thy fingers from my throat;
For though I am not splenetive and rash
Yet have I in me something dangerous,   284
Which let thy wisdom fear. Away thy hand!
King. Pluck them asunder.
Queen.   Hamlet! Hamlet!
All. Gentlemen,—
Hor.   Good my lord, be quiet.
       [*The* Attendants *part them, and they
                come out of the grave.*
Ham. Why, I will fight with him upon this
  theme   288
Until my eyelids will no longer wag.
Queen. O my son! what theme?
Ham. I lov'd Ophelia: forty thousand bro-
  thers
Could not, with all their quantity of love, 292
Make up my sum. What wilt thou do for her?
King. O! he is mad, Laertes.
Queen. For love of God, forbear him.
Ham. 'Swounds, show me what thou'lt do:
Woo't weep? woo't fight? woo't fast? woo't
  tear thyself?   297
Woo't drink up eisel? eat a crocodile?
I'll do't. Dost thou come here to whine?
To outface me with leaping in her grave?   300
Be buried quick with her, and so will I:
And, if thou prate of mountains, let them throw
Millions of acres on us, till our ground,
Singeing his pate against the burning zone, 304
Make Ossa like a wart! Nay, an thou'lt mouth,
I'll rant as well as thou.
Queen.   This is mere madness:
And thus a while the fit will work on him;
Anon, as patient as the female dove,   308
When that her golden couplets are disclos'd,
His silence will sit drooping.
Ham.   Hear you, sir;
What is the reason that you use me thus?
I lov'd you ever: but it is no matter;   312
Let Hercules himself do what he may,
The cat will mew and dog will have his day.
                                    [*Exit.*
King. I pray you, good Horatio, wait upon
  him.   [*Exit* HORATIO.
[*To* LAERTES.] Strengthen your patience in our
  last night's speech;   316
We'll put the matter to the present push.
Good Gertrude, set some watch over your son.
This grave shall have a living monument:
An hour of quiet shortly shall we see;   320
Till then, in patience our proceeding be.
                                  [*Exeunt.*

SCENE II.—*A Hall in the Castle.*

Enter HAMLET *and* HORATIO.

Ham. So much for this, sir: now shall you
  see the other;
You do remember all the circumstance?
Hor. Remember it, my lord?
Ham. Sir, in my heart there was a kind of
  fighting   4
That would not let me sleep; methought I lay
Worse than the mutines in the bilboes. Rashly,—
And prais'd be rashness for it, let us know,

Our indiscretion sometimes serves us well 8
When our deep plots do pall; and that should teach us
There's a divinity that shapes our ends,
Rough-hew them how we will.
 Hor.   That is most certain.
 Ham. Up from my cabin, 12
My sea-gown scarf'd about me, in the dark
Grop'd I to find out them, had my desire,
Finger'd their packet, and in fine withdrew
To mine own room again; making so bold— 16
My fears forgetting manners—to unseal
Their grand commission; where I found, Horatio,
O royal knavery! an exact command,
Larded with many several sorts of reasons 20
Importing Denmark's health, and England's too,
With, ho! such bugs and goblins in my life,
That, on the supervise, no leisure bated,
No, not to stay the grinding of the axe, 24
My head should be struck off.
 Hor.   Is't possible?
 Ham. Here's the commission: read it at more leisure.
But wilt thou hear me how I did proceed?
 Hor. I beseech you. 28
 Ham. Being thus be-netted round with villanies,—
Ere I could make a prologue to my brains
They had begun the play,—I sat me down,
Devis'd a new commission, wrote it fair; 32
I once did hold it, as our statists do,
A baseness to write fair, and labour'd much
How to forget that learning; but, sir, now
It did me yeoman's service. Wilt thou know 36
The effect of what I wrote?
 Hor.   Ay, good my lord.
 Ham. An earnest conjuration from the king,
As England was his faithful tributary,
As love between them like the palm should flourish, 40
As peace should still her wheaten garland wear,
And stand a comma 'tween their amities,
And many such-like 'As'es of great charge,
That, on the view and knowing of these contents, 44
Without debatement further, more or less,
He should the bearers put to sudden death,
Not shriving-time allow'd.
 Hor.   How was this seal'd?
 Ham. Why, even in that was heaven ordinant. 48
I had my father's signet in my purse,
Which was the model of that Danish seal;
Folded the writ up in form of the other,
Subscrib'd it, gave't th' impression, plac'd it safely, 52
The changeling never known. Now, the next day
Was our sea-fight, and what to this was sequent
Thou know'st already.
 Hor. So Guildenstern and Rosencrantz go to't. 56
 Ham. Why, man, they did make love to this employment;

They are not near my conscience; their defeat
Does by their own insinuation grow.
'Tis dangerous when the baser nature comes 60
Between the pass and fell-incensed points
Of mighty opposites.
 Hor.   Why, what a king is this!
 Ham. Does it not, thinks't thee, stand me now upon—
He that hath kill'd my king and whor'd my mother, 64
Popp'd in between the election and my hopes,
Thrown out his angle for my proper life,
And with such cozenage—is't not perfect conscience
To quit him with this arm? and is't not to be damn'd 68
To let this canker of our nature come
In further evil?
 Hor. It must be shortly known to him from England
What is the issue of the business there. 72
 Ham. It will be short: the interim is mine;
And a man's life's no more than to say 'One.'
But I am very sorry, good Horatio,
That to Laertes I forgot myself; 76
For, by the image of my cause, I see
The portraiture of his: I'll count his favours:
But, sure, the bravery of his grief did put me
Into a towering passion.
 Hor.   Peace! who comes here? 80

    Enter OSRIC.

 Osr. Your lordship is right welcome back to Denmark.
 Ham. I humbly thank you, sir. [*Aside to* HORATIO.] Dost know this water-fly? 84
 Hor. [*Aside to* HAMLET.] No, my good lord.
 Ham. [*Aside to* HORATIO.] Thy state is the more gracious; for 'tis a vice to know him. He hath much land, and fertile: let a beast be lord of beasts, and his crib shall stand at the king's mess: 'tis a chough; but, as I say, spacious in the possession of dirt. 91
 Osr. Sweet lord, if your lordship were at leisure, I should impart a thing to you from his majesty.
 Ham. I will receive it, sir, with all diligence of spirit. Your bonnet to his right use; 'tis for the head. 97
 Osr. I thank your lordship, 'tis very hot.
 Ham. No, believe me, 'tis very cold; the wind is northerly. 100
 Osr. It is indifferent cold, my lord, indeed.
 Ham. But yet methinks it is very sultry and hot for my complexion. 103
 Osr. Exceedingly, my lord; it is very sultry, as 'twere, I cannot tell how. But, my lord, his majesty bade me signify to you that he has laid a great wager on your head. Sir, this is the matter,— 108
 Ham. I beseech you, remember—
   [HAMLET *moves him to put on his hat.*
 Osr. Nay, good my lord; for mine ease, in good faith. Sir, here is newly come to court Laertes; believe me, an absolute gentleman, full of most excellent differences, of very soft society

nd great showing; indeed, to speak feelingly of
im, he is the card or calendar of gentry, for you
hall find in him the continent of what part a
entleman would see. 117

Ham. Sir, his definement suffers no perdition
n you; though, I know, to divide him invento-
ially would dizzy the arithmetic of memory, and
et but yaw neither, in respect of his quick sail.
3ut, in the verity of extolment, I take him to be
a soul of great article; and his infusion of such
dearth and rareness, as, to make true diction of
im, his semblable is his mirror; and who else
vould trace him, his umbrage, nothing more.

Osr. Your lordship speaks most infallibly of
im. 128

Ham. The concernancy, sir? why do we wrap
he gentleman in our more rawer breath?

Osr. Sir?

Hor. Is't not possible to understand in another tongue? You will do't, sir, really. 133

Ham. What imports the nomination of this
entleman?

Osr. Of Laertes? 136

Hor. His purse is empty already; all's
golden words are spent.

Ham. Of him, sir.

Osr. I know you are not ignorant— 140

Ham. I would you did, sir; in faith, if you
did, it would not much approve me. Well, sir.

Osr. You are not ignorant of what excellence
Laertes is— 144

Ham. I dare not confess that, lest I should
compare with him in excellence; but, to know a
nan well, were to know himself. 147

Osr. I mean, sir, for his weapon; but in the
imputation laid on him by them, in his meed
ie's unfellowed.

Ham. What's his weapon?

Osr. Rapier and dagger. 152

Ham. That's two of his weapons; but, well.

Osr. The king, sir, hath wagered with him six
3arbary horses; against the which he has imponed, as I take it, six French rapiers and
poniards, with their assigns, as girdle, hangers,
nd so: three of the carriages, in faith, are very
dear to fancy, very responsive to the hilts, most
delicate carriages, and of very liberal conceit. 160

Ham. What call you the carriages?

Hor. I knew you must be edified by the margent, ere you had done.

Osr. The carriages, sir, are the hangers. 164

Ham. The phrase would be more german to
he matter, if we could carry cannon by our
ides; I would it might be hangers till then.
3ut, on; six Barbary horses against six French
words, their assigns, and three liberal-conceited
carriages; that's the French bet against the
Danish. Why is this 'imponed,' as you call it?

Osr. The king, sir, hath laid, that in a dozen
passes between yourself and him, he shall not
exceed you three hits; he hath laid on twelve
or nine, and it would come to immediate trial,
f your lordship would vouchsafe the answer. 176

Ham. How if I answer no?

Osr. I mean, my lord, the opposition of your
person in trial.

Ham. Sir, I will walk here in the hall; if it
please his majesty, 'tis the breathing time of day
with me; let the foils be brought, the gentleman
willing, and the king hold his purpose, I will win
for him an I can; if not, I will gain nothing but
my shame and the odd hits. 185

Osr. Shall I re-deliver you so?

Ham. To this effect, sir; after what flourish
your nature will. 188

Osr. I commend my duty to your lordship.

Ham. Yours, yours. [*Exit* OSRIC.] He does
well to commend it himself; there are no
tongues else for's turn. 192

Hor. This lapwing runs away with the shell
on his head.

Ham. He did comply with his dug before he
sucked it. Thus has he—and many more of the
same bevy, that I know the drossy age dotes
on—only got the tune of the time and outward
habit of encounter, a kind of yesty collection
which carries them through and through the
most fond and winnowed opinions; and do but
blow them to their trial, the bubbles are out. 202

Enter a Lord.

Lord. My lord, his majesty commended him
to you by young Osric, who brings back to him,
that you attend him in the hall; he sends to
know if your pleasure hold to play with Laertes,
or that you will take longer time. 207

Ham. I am constant to my purposes; they
follow the king's pleasure: if his fitness speaks,
mine is ready; now, or whensoever, provided I
be so able as now.

Lord. The king, and queen, and all are coming down. 213

Ham. In happy time.

Lord. The queen desires you to use some
gentle entertainment to Laertes before you fall
to play. 217

Ham. She well instructs me. [*Exit* Lord.

Hor. You will lose this wager, my lord.

Ham. I do not think so; since he went into
France, I have been in continual practice; I
shall win at the odds. But thou wouldst not
think how ill all's here about my heart; but it
is no matter. 224

Hor. Nay, good my lord,—

Ham. It is but foolery; but it is such a kind
of gain-giving as would perhaps trouble a
woman. 228

Hor. If your mind dislike any thing, obey it;
I will forestal their repair hither, and say you
are not fit. 231

Ham. Not a whit, we defy augury; there's a
special providence in the fall of a sparrow. If it
be now, 'tis not to come; if it be not to come, it
will be now; if it be not now, yet it will come:
the readiness is all. Since no man has aught
of what he leaves, what is't to leave betimes?
Let be. 238

Enter KING, QUEEN, LAERTES, Lords, OSRIC, *and*
Attendants *with foils, &c.*

King. Come, Hamlet, come, and take this
hand from me.

[*The* KING *puts the hand of* LAERTES
into that of HAMLET.

Ham. Give me your pardon, sir; I've done
you wrong;
But pardon't, as you are a gentleman.
This presence knows,
And you must needs have heard, how I am
punish'd
With sore distraction. What I have done, 244
That might your nature, honour and exception
Roughly awake, I here proclaim was madness.
Was't Hamlet wrong'd Laertes? Never Ham-
let:
If Hamlet from himself be ta'en away,   248
And when he's not himself does wrong Laertes,
Then Hamlet does it not; Hamlet denies it.
Who does it then? His madness. If 't be so,
Hamlet is of the faction that is wrong'd; 252
His madness is poor Hamlet's enemy.
Sir, in this audience,
Let my disclaiming from a purpos'd evil
Free me so far in your most generous thoughts,
That I have shot mine arrow o'er the house, 257
And hurt my brother.
    Laer.   I am satisfied in nature,
Whose motive, in this case, should stir me most
To my revenge; but in my terms of honour 260
I stand aloof, and will no reconcilement,
Till by some elder masters, of known honour,
I have a voice and precedent of peace,
To keep my name ungor'd. But till that time,
I do receive your offer'd love like love,   265
And will not wrong it.
    Ham.   I embrace it freely;
And will this brother's wager frankly play.
Give us the foils. Come on.
    Laer.   Come, one for me. 268
    Ham. I'll be your foil, Laertes; in mine
ignorance
Your skill shall, like a star i' the darkest night,
Stick fiery off indeed.
    Laer.   You mock me, sir.
    Ham. No, by this hand.   272
    King. Give them the foils, young Osric.
Cousin Hamlet,
You know the wager?
    Ham.   Very well, my lord.
Your Grace hath laid the odds o' the weaker
side.
    King. I do not fear it; I have seen you both;
But since he is better'd, we have therefore odds.
    Laer. This is too heavy; let me see another.
    Ham. This likes me well. These foils have
all a length?
    Osr. Ay, my good lord.   280
                        [*They prepare to play.*
    King. Set me the stoups of wine upon that
table.
If Hamlet give the first or second hit,
Or quit in answer of the third exchange,
Let all the battlements their ordnance fire; 284
The king shall drink to Hamlet's better breath;
And in the cup an union shall he throw,
Richer than that which four successive kings
In Denmark's crown have worn. Give me the
cups;   288

And let the kettle to the trumpet speak,
The trumpet to the cannoneer without,
The cannons to the heavens, the heavens t
earth,
'Now the king drinks to Hamlet!' Come, begin
And you, the judges, bear a wary eye.   29
    Ham. Come on, sir.
    Laer.   Come, my lord. [*They play*
    Ham.   One.
    Laer.   No.
    Ham.   Judgment
    Osr. A hit, a very palpable hit.
    Laer.   Well; again
    King. Stay; give me drink. Hamlet, thi
pearl is thine;   29
Here's to thy health. Give him the cup.
    [*Trumpets sound; and cannon shot off within*
    Ham. I'll play this bout first; set it by awhile
Come.—[*They play.*] Another hit; what sa
you?
    Laer. A touch, a touch, I do confess.   3c
    King. Our son shall win.
    Queen.   He's fat, and scant of breath
Here, Hamlet, take my napkin, rub thy brows
The queen carouses to thy fortune, Hamlet.
    Ham. Good madam!
    King.   Gertrude, do not drink. 30
    Queen. I will, my lord; I pray you, pardo
me.
    King. [*Aside.*] It is the poison'd cup! it i
too late.
    Ham. I dare not drink yet, madam; by an
by.
    Queen. Come, let me wipe thy face.   30
    Laer. My lord, I'll hit him now.
    King.   I do not think't
    Laer. [*Aside.*] And yet 'tis almost 'gainst m
conscience.
    Ham. Come, for the third, Laertes. You bu
dally;
I pray you pass with your best violence.   31
I am afeard you make a wanton of me.
    Laer. Say you so? come on.   [*They play*
    Osr. Nothing, neither way.
    Laer. Have at you now.
            [LAERTES *wounds* HAMLET; *then, i*
            scuffling, they change rapiers, an
            HAMLET *wounds* LAERTES.
    King.   Part them! they are incens'd
    Ham. Nay, come, again. [*The* QUEEN *falls*
    Osr.   Look to the queen there, ho
    Hor. They bleed on both sides. How is it
my lord?
    Osr. How is it, Laertes?
    Laer. Why, as a woodcock to mine ow
springe, Osric;   32
I am justly kill'd with mine own treachery.
    Ham. How does the queen?
    King.   She swounds to see them bleed
    Queen. No, no, the drink, the drink,—O m
dear Hamlet!   32
The drink, the drink; I am poison'd.   [*Dies*
    Ham. O villany! Ho! let the door be lock'd
Treachery! seek it out.   [LAERTES *falls*
    Laer. It is here, Hamlet. Hamlet, thou ar
slain;

No medicine in the world can do thee good; 328
In thee there is not half an hour of life;
The treacherous instrument is in thy hand,
Unbated and envenom'd. The foul practice
Hath turn'd itself on me; lo! here I lie, 332
Never to rise again. Thy mother's poison'd.
I can no more. The king, the king's to blame.

   Ham. The point envenom'd too!—

Then, venom, to thy work.   [*Stabs the* KING.

   All. Treason! treason! 337

   King. O! yet defend me, friends; I am but
hurt.

   Ham. Here, thou incestuous, murderous,
damned Dane,
Drink off this potion;—is thy union here? 340
Follow my mother.   [KING *dies.*

   Laer.   He is justly serv'd:
It is a poison temper'd by himself.
Exchange forgiveness with me, noble Hamlet:
Mine and my father's death come not upon thee,
Nor thine on me!   [*Dies.*

   Ham. Heaven make thee free of it! I follow
thee. 346
I am dead, Horatio. Wretched queen, adieu!
You that look pale and tremble at this chance,
That are but mutes or audience to this act, 349
Had I but time,—as this fell sergeant, death,
Is strict in his arrest,—O! I could tell you—
But let it be. Horatio, I am dead; 352
Thou liv'st; report me and my cause aright
To the unsatisfied.

   Hor.   Never believe it;
I am more an antique Roman than a Dane:
Here's yet some liquor left.

   Ham.   As thou'rt a man, 356
Give me the cup: let go; by heaven, I'll have't.
O God! Horatio, what a wounded name,
Things standing thus unknown, shall live be-
hind me.
If thou didst ever hold me in thy heart, 360
Absent thee from felicity awhile,
And in this harsh world draw thy breath in pain,
To tell my story.

   [*March afar off, and shot within.*
What war-like noise is this?

   Osr. Young Fortinbras, with conquest come
from Poland, 364
To the ambassadors of England gives
This war-like volley.

   Ham.   O! I die, Horatio;
The potent poison quite o'er-crows my spirit:
I cannot live to hear the news from England, 368
But I do prophesy the election lights
On Fortinbras: he has my dying voice;
So tell him, with the occurrents, more and less,
Which have solicited—The rest is silence. [*Dies.*

   Hor. Now cracks a noble heart. Good-night,
sweet prince, 373
And flights of angels sing thee to thy rest!
Why does the drum come hither?
   [*March within.*

Enter FORTINBRAS, *the English* Ambassadors,
and Others.

   Fort. Where is this sight?

   Hor.   What is it ye would see? 376
If aught of woe or wonder, cease your search.

   Fort. This quarry cries on havoc. O proud
death!
What feast is toward in thine eternal cell,
That thou so many princes at a shot 380
So bloodily hast struck?

   First Amb.   The sight is dismal;
And our affairs from England come too late:
The ears are senseless that should give us hear-
ing,
To tell him his commandment is fulfill'd, 384
That Rosencrantz and Guildenstern are dead.
Where should we have our thanks?

   Hor.   Not from his mouth,
Had it the ability of life to thank you: 387
He never gave commandment for their death.
But since, so jump upon this bloody question,
You from the Polack wars, and you from
England,
Are here arriv'd, give order that these bodies
High on a stage be placed to the view; 392
And let me speak to the yet unknowing world
How these things came about: so shall you
hear
Of carnal, bloody, and unnatural acts,
Of accidental judgments, casual slaughters; 396
Of deaths put on by cunning and forc'd cause,
And, in this upshot, purposes mistook
Fall'n on the inventors' heads; all this can I
Truly deliver.

   Fort.   Let us haste to hear it, 400
And call the noblest to the audience.
For me, with sorrow I embrace my fortune;
I have some rights of memory in this kingdom,
Which now to claim my vantage doth invite
me. 404

   Hor. Of that I shall have also cause to speak,
And from his mouth whose voice will draw on
more:
But let this same be presently perform'd,
Even while men's minds are wild, lest more mis-
chance 408
On plots and errors happen.

   Fort.   Let four captains
Bear Hamlet, like a soldier, to the stage;
For he was likely, had he been put on,
To have prov'd most royally: and, for his pas-
sage, 412
The soldiers' music and the rites of war
Speak loudly for him.
Take up the bodies: such a sight as this
Becomes the field, but here shows much amiss.
Go, bid the soldiers shoot. 417

   [*A dead march. Exeunt, bearing off the
bodies; after which a peal of ordnance
is shot off.*

KING LEAR

DRAMATIS PERSONÆ

LEAR, King of Britain.
KING OF FRANCE.
DUKE OF BURGUNDY.
DUKE OF CORNWALL.
DUKE OF ALBANY.
EARL OF KENT.
EARL OF GLOUCESTER.
EDGAR, Son to Gloucester.
EDMUND, Bastard Son to Gloucester.
CURAN, a Courtier.
OSWALD, Steward to Goneril.
Old Man, Tenant to Gloucester.
Doctor.

Fool.
An Officer, employed by Edmund.
A Gentleman, Attendant on Cordelia.
A Herald.
Servants to Cornwall.

GONERIL,
REGAN, } Daughters to Lear.
CORDELIA,

Knights of Lear's Train, Officers, Messengers, Soldiers, and Attendants.

SCENE.—*Britain.*

ACT I

SCENE I.—*A Room of State in* KING LEAR'S *Palace.*

Enter KENT, GLOUCESTER, *and* EDMUND.

Kent. I thought the king had more affected the Duke of Albany than Cornwall.

Glo. It did always seem so to us; but now, in the division of the kingdom, it appears not which of the dukes he values most; for equalities are so weighed that curiosity in neither can make choice of either's moiety.

Kent. Is not this your son, my lord? 8

Glo. His breeding, sir, hath been at my charge: I have so often blushed to acknowledge him, that now I am brazed to it.

Kent. I cannot conceive you. 12

Glo. Sir, this young fellow's mother could; whereupon she grew round-wombed, and had, indeed, sir, a son for her cradle ere she had a husband for her bed. Do you smell a fault? 16

Kent. I cannot wish the fault undone, the issue of it being so proper.

Glo. But I have a son, sir, by order of law, some year elder than this, who yet is no dearer in my account: though this knave came somewhat saucily into the world before he was sent for, yet was his mother fair; there was good sport at his making, and the whoreson must be acknowledged. Do you know this noble gentleman, Edmund? 26

Edm. No, my lord.

Glo. My Lord of Kent: remember him hereafter as my honourable friend.

Edm. My services to your lordship.

Kent. I must love you, and sue to know you better. 32

Edm. Sir, I shall study deserving.

Glo. He hath been out nine years, and away he shall again. The king is coming.

Sennet. Enter LEAR, CORNWALL, ALBANY, GONERIL, REGAN, CORDELIA, *and* Attendants.

Lear. Attend the Lords of France and Burgundy, Gloucester. 36

Glo. I shall, my liege.

[*Exeunt* GLOUCESTER *and* EDMUND.

Lear. Meantime we shall express our darker purpose.

Give me the map there. Know that we have divided

In three our kingdom; and 'tis our fast intent

To shake all cares and business from our age, 41

Conferring them on younger strengths, while we

Unburden'd crawl toward death. Our son of Cornwall,

And you, our no less loving son of Albany, 44

We have this hour a constant will to publish

Our daughters' several dowers, that future strife

May be prevented now. The princes, France and Burgundy,

Great rivals in our youngest daughter's love, 48

Long in our court have made their amorous sojourn,

And here are to be answer'd. Tell me, my daughters,—

Since now we will divest us both of rule,

Interest of territory, cares of state,— 52

Which of you shall we say doth love us most?

That we our largest bounty may extend

Where nature doth with merit challenge. Goneril,

Our eldest-born, speak first. 56

Gon. Sir, I love you more than words can wield the matter;

Dearer than eye-sight, space, and liberty;

Beyond what can be valu'd, rich or rare;

No less than life, with grace, health, beauty, honour; 60

As much as child e'er lov'd, or father found;

A love that makes breath poor and speech unable;

Beyond all manner of so much I love you.

Cor. [*Aside.*] What shall Cordelia do? Love, and be silent. 64

Lear. Of all these bounds, even from this line to this,

With shadowy forests and with champains rich'd,

With plenteous rivers and wide-skirted meads,

We make thee lady: to thine and Albany's issue

e this perpetual. What says our second
daughter, 69
'ur dearest Regan, wife to Cornwall? Speak.
  Reg. I am made of that self metal as my
sister,
nd prize me at her worth. In my true heart
find she names my very deed of love; 73
'nly she comes too short: that I profess
Iyself an enemy to all other joys
Vhich the most precious square of sense possesses 76
nd find I am alone felicitate
1 your dear highness' love.
  Cor. [*Aside.*] Then, poor Cordelia!
nd yet not so; since, I am sure, my love's
lore richer than my tongue. 80
  Lear. To thee and thine, hereditary ever,
emain this ample third of our fair kingdom,
Io less in space, validity, and pleasure,
han that conferr'd on Goneril. Now, our
joy, 84
lthough our last, not least; to whose young
love
he vines of France and milk of Burgundy
trive to be interess'd; what can you say to
draw
. third more opulent than your sisters? Speak.
  Cor. Nothing, my lord. 89
  Lear. Nothing?
  Cor. Nothing.
  Lear. Nothing will come of nothing: speak
again. 92
  Cor. Unhappy that I am, I cannot heave
Iy heart into my mouth: I love your majesty
ccording to my bond; nor more nor less.
  Lear. How, how, Cordelia! mend your speech
a little, 96
est you may mar your fortunes.
  Cor. Good my lord,
'ou have begot me, bred me, lov'd me: I
eturn those duties back as are right fit,
bey you, love you, and most honour you. 100
Vhy have my sisters husbands, if they say
'hey love you all? Haply, when I shall wed,
hat lord whose hand must take my plight shall
carry
Ialf my love with him, half my care and duty:
ure I shall never marry like my sisters, 105
o love my father all.
  Lear. But goes thy heart with this?
  Cor. Ay, good my lord.
  Lear. So young, and so untender? 108
  Cor. So young, my lord, and true.
  Lear. Let it be so; thy truth then be thy dower:
'or, by the sacred radiance of the sun,
'he mysteries of Hecate and the night, 112
y all the operation of the orbs
'rom whom we do exist and cease to be,
Iere I disclaim all my paternal care,
'ropinquity and property of blood, 116
nd as a stranger to my heart and me
Iold thee from this for ever. The barbarous
Scythian,
Jr he that makes his generation messes
'o gorge his appetite, shall to my bosom 120
te as well neighbour'd, pitied, and reliev'd,

As thou my sometime daughter.
  Kent. Good my liege,—
  Lear. Peace, Kent!
Come not between the dragon and his wrath. 124
I lov'd her most, and thought to set my rest
On her kind nursery. Hence, and avoid my
sight!
So be my grave my peace, as here I give
Her father's heart from her! Call France. Who
stirs? 128
Call Burgundy. Cornwall and Albany,
With my two daughters' dowers digest the third;
Let pride, which she calls plainness, marry her.
I do invest you jointly with my power, 132
Pre-eminence, and all the large effects
That troop with majesty. Ourself by monthly
course,
With reservation of a hundred knights,
By you to be sustain'd, shall our abode 136
Make with you by due turn. Only we shall retain
The name and all th' addition to a king;
The sway, revenue, execution of the rest,
Beloved sons, be yours: which to confirm, 140
This coronet part between you.
  Kent. Royal Lear,
Whom I have ever honour'd as my king,
Lov'd as my father, as my master follow'd,
As my great patron thought on in my prayers,—
  Lear. The bow is bent and drawn; make
from the shaft. 145
  Kent. Let it fall rather, though the fork invade
The region of my heart: be Kent unmannerly
When Lear is mad. What wouldst thou do, old
man? 148
Think'st thou that duty shall have dread to
speak
When power to flattery bows? To plainness
honour's bound
When majesty falls to folly. Reserve thy state;
And, in thy best consideration, check 152
This hideous rashness: answer my life my
judgment,
Thy youngest daughter does not love thee least;
Nor are those empty-hearted whose low sound
Reverbs no hollowness.
  Lear. Kent, on thy life, no more.
  Kent. My life I never held but as a pawn 157
To wage against thine enemies; nor fear to
lose it,
Thy safety being the motive.
  Lear. Out of my sight!
  Kent. See better, Lear; and let me still re-
main 160
The true blank of thine eye.
  Lear. Now, by Apollo,—
  Kent. Now, by Apollo, king,
Thou swear'st thy gods in vain.
  Lear. O vassal! miscreant!
      [*Laying his hand on his sword.*
  Alb. } Dear sir, forbear. 164
  Corn. }
  Kent. Do;
Kill thy physician, and the fee bestow
Upon the foul disease. Revoke thy gift;
Or, whilst I can vent clamour from my throat,
I'll tell thee thou dost evil.

Lear.   Hear me, recreant! 169
On thine allegiance, hear me!
Since thou hast sought to make us break our
    vow,—
Which we durst never yet,—and, with strain'd
    pride   172
To come betwixt our sentence and our power,—
Which nor our nature nor our place can bear,—
Our potency made good, take thy reward.
Five days we do allot thee for provision   176
To shield thee from diseases of the world;
And, on the sixth, to turn thy hated back
Upon our kingdom: if, on the tenth day follow-
    ing
Thy banish'd trunk be found in our dominions,
The moment is thy death. Away! By Jupiter,
This shall not be revok'd.   182
    Kent. Fare thee well, king; sith thus thou
        wilt appear,
Freedom lives hence, and banishment is here.
[*To* CORDELIA.] The gods to their dear shelter
    take thee, maid,   185
That justly think'st, and hast most rightly said!
[*To* REGAN *and* GONERIL.] And your large
    speeches may your deeds approve,
That good effects may spring from words of
    love.   188
Thus Kent, O princes! bids you all adieu;
He'll shape his old course in a country new.
                                          [*Exit.*

Flourish. Re-enter GLOUCESTER, *with* FRANCE,
    BURGUNDY, *and* Attendants.

    Glo. Here's France and Burgundy, my noble
        lord.
    Lear. My Lord of Burgundy,   192
We first address toward you, who with this king
Hath rivall'd for our daughter. What, in the
    least,
Will you require in present dower with her,
Or cease your quest of love?
    Bur.   Most royal majesty, 196
I crave no more than hath your highness offer'd,
Nor will you tender less.
    Lear.   Right noble Burgundy,
When she was dear to us we did hold her so.
But now her price is fall'n. Sir, there she
    stands: 200
If aught within that little-seeming substance,
Or all of it, with our displeasure piec'd,
And nothing more, may fitly like your Grace,
She's there, and she is yours.
    Bur.   I know no answer. 204
    Lear. Will you, with those infirmities she
        owes,
Unfriended, new-adopted to our hate,
Dower'd with our curse, and stranger'd with
    our oath,
Take her, or leave her?
    Bur.   Pardon me, royal sir; 208
Election makes not up on such conditions.
    Lear. Then leave her, sir; for, by the power
        that made me,
I tell you all her wealth.—[*To* FRANCE.] For
    you, great king,
I would not from your love make such a stray

To match you where I hate; therefore, beseech
    you   212
To avert your liking a more worthier way
Than on a wretch whom nature is asham'd
Almost to acknowledge hers.
    France.   This is most strange, 216
That she, who even but now was your best object,
The argument of your praise, balm of your age,
The best, the dearest, should in this trice of time
Commit a thing so monstrous, to dismantle 220
So many folds of favour. Sure, her offence
Must be of such unnatural degree
That monsters it, or your fore-vouch'd affection
Fall into taint; which to believe of her,   224
Must be a faith that reason without miracle
Could never plant in me.
    Cor.   I yet beseech your majesty—
If for I want that glib and oily art
To speak and purpose not; since what I well
    intend,   228
I'll do't before I speak—that you make known
It is no vicious blot nor other foulness,
No unchaste action, or dishonour'd step,
That hath depriv'd me of your grace and favour;
But even for want of that for which I am richer,
A still-soliciting eye, and such a tongue
That I am glad I have not, though not to have it
Hath lost me in your liking.
    Lear.   Better thou   236
Hadst not been born than not to have pleas'd
    me better.
    France. Is it but this? a tardiness in nature
Which often leaves the history unspoke
That it intends to do? My Lord of Burgundy,
What say you to the lady? Love is not love 241
When it is mingled with regards that stand
Aloof from the entire point. Will you have her?
She is herself a dowry.
    Bur.   Royal Lear,   244
Give but that portion which yourself propos'd,
And here I take Cordelia by the hand,
Duchess of Burgundy.
    Lear. Nothing: I have sworn; I am firm. 248
    Bur. I am sorry, then, you have so lost a
        father
That you must lose a husband.
    Cor.   Peace be with Burgundy!
Since that respects of fortune are his love,
I shall not be his wife.
    France. Fairest Cordelia, that art most rich
        being poor;   252
Most choice, forsaken; and most lov'd, despis'd!
Thee and thy virtues here I seize upon:
Be it lawful I take up what's cast away.   256
Gods, gods! 'tis strange that from their cold'st
    neglect
My love should kindle to inflam'd respect.
Thy dowerless daughter, king, thrown to my
    chance,
Is queen of us, of ours, and our fair France: 260
Not all the dukes of waterish Burgundy
Shall buy this unpriz'd precious maid of me.
Bid them farewell, Cordelia, though unkind:
Thou losest here, a better where to find.   264
    Lear. Thou hast her, France; let her be thine
        for we

Have no such daughter, nor shall ever see
That face of hers again, therefore be gone
Without our grace, our love, our benison. 268
Come, noble Burgundy.

[*Flourish. Exeunt* LEAR, BURGUNDY, CORN-
WALL, ALBANY, GLOUCESTER, *and*
Attendants.

France. Bid farewell to your sisters.
Cor. The jewels of our father, with wash'd
eyes
Cordelia leaves you: I know you what you
are; 272
And like a sister am most loath to call
Your faults as they are nam'd. Use well our
father:
To your professed bosoms I commit him:
But yet, alas! stood I within his grace, 276
I would prefer him to a better place.
So farewell to you both.
Reg. Prescribe not us our duties.
Gon. Let your study
Be to content your lord, who hath receiv'd you
At fortune's alms; you have obedience scanted,
And well are worth the want that you have
wanted. 282
Cor. Time shall unfold what plighted cun-
ning hides;
Who covers faults, at last shame them derides.
Well may you prosper!
France. Come, my fair Cordelia.
[*Exit* FRANCE *and* CORDELIA.
Gon. Sister, it is not little I have to say of
what most nearly appertains to us both. I think
our father will hence to-night. 288
Reg. That's most certain, and with you;
next month with us.
Gon. You see how full of changes his age is;
the observation we have made of it hath not
been little: he always loved our sister most; and
with what poor judgment he hath now cast her
off appears too grossly.
Reg. 'Tis the infirmity of his age; yet he
hath ever but slenderly known himself. 297
Gon. The best and soundest of his time hath
been but rash; then, must we look to receive
from his age, not alone the imperfections of
long-engraffed condition, but, therewithal the
unruly waywardness that infirm and choleric
years bring with them. 303
Reg. Such unconstant starts are we like to
have from him as this of Kent's banishment.
Gon. There is further compliment of leave-
taking between France and him. Pray you, let
us hit together: if our father carry authority
with such dispositions as he bears, this last
surrender of his will but offend us. 310
Reg. We shall further think on't.
Gon. We must do something, and i' the heat.
[*Exeunt.*

SCENE II.—*A Hall in the* EARL OF
GLOUCESTER'S *Castle.*

Enter EDMUND, *with a letter.*

Edm. Thou, Nature, art my goddess; to thy
law

My services are bound. Wherefore should I
Stand in the plague of custom, and permit
The curiosity of nations to deprive me, 4
For that I am some twelve or fourteen moon-
shines
Lag of a brother? Why bastard? wherefore
base?
When my dimensions are as well compact,
My mind as generous, and my shape as true, 8
As honest madam's issue? Why brand they us
With base? with baseness? bastardy? base,
base?
Who in the lusty stealth of nature take
More composition and fierce quality 12
Than doth, within a dull, stale, tired bed,
Go to the creating a whole tribe of fops,
Got 'tween asleep and wake? Well then,
Legitimate Edgar, I must have your land: 16
Our father's love is to the bastard Edmund
As to the legitimate. Fine word, 'legitimate!'
Well, my legitimate, if this letter speed,
And my invention thrive, Edmund the base 20
Shall top the legitimate:—I grow, I prosper;
Now, gods, stand up for bastards!

Enter GLOUCESTER.

Glo. Kent banished thus! And France in
choler parted!
And the king gone to-night! subscrib'd his
power! 24
Confin'd to exhibition! All this done
Upon the gad! Edmund, how now! what news?
Edm. So please your lordship, none.
[*Putting up the letter.*
Glo. Why so earnestly seek you to put up
that letter? 29
Edm. I know no news, my lord.
Glo. What paper were you reading?
Edm. Nothing, my lord. 32
Glo. No? What needed then that terrible
dispatch of it into your pocket? the quality of
nothing hath not such need to hide itself. Let's
see; come; if it be nothing, I shall not need
spectacles. 37
Edm. I beseech you, sir, pardon me; it is a
letter from my brother that I have not all o'er-
read, and for so much as I have perused, I find
it not fit for your o'er-looking. 41
Glo. Give me the letter, sir.
Edm. I shall offend, either to detain or give
it. The contents, as in part I understand them,
are to blame. 45
Glo. Let's see, let's see.
Edm. I hope, for my brother's justification,
he wrote this but as an essay or taste of my
virtue. 49
*Glo. This policy and reverence of age makes
the world bitter to the best of our times; keeps
our fortunes from us till our oldness cannot
relish them. I begin to find an idle and fond
bondage in the oppression of aged tyranny, who
sways, not as it hath power, but as it is suffered.
Come to me, that of this I may speak more. If
our father would sleep till I waked him, you
should enjoy half his revenue for ever, and live
the beloved of your brother,* EDGAR.—*Hum!*

Conspiracy! 'Sleep till I waked him, you should enjoy half his revenue.'—My son Edgar! Had he a hand to write this? a heart and brain to breed it in? When came this to you? Who brought it?   64

Edm. It was not brought me, my lord; there's the cunning of it; I found it thrown in at the casement of my closet.

Glo. You know the character to be your brother's?   69

Edm. If the matter were good, my lord, I durst swear it were his; but, in respect of that, I would fain think it were not.   72

Glo. It is his.

Edm. It is his hand, my lord; but I hope his heart is not in the contents.

Glo. Hath he never heretofore sounded you in this business?   77

Edm. Never, my lord: but I have often heard him maintain it to be fit that, sons at perfect age, and fathers declined, the father should be as ward to the son, and the son manage his revenue.   82

Glo. O villain, villain! His very opinion in the letter! Abhorred villain! Unnatural, detested, brutish villain! worse than brutish! Go, sirrah, seek him; I'll apprehend him. Abominable villain! Where is he?   87

Edm. I do not well know, my lord. If it shall please you to suspend your indignation against my brother till you can derive from him better testimony of his intent, you shall run a certain course; where, if you violently proceed against him, mistaking his purpose, it would make a great gap in your own honour, and shake in pieces the heart of his obedience. I dare pawn down my life for him, that he hath writ this to feel my affection to your honour, and to no other pretence of danger.   98

Glo. Think you so?

Edm. If your honour judge it meet, I will place you where you shall hear us confer of this, and by an auricular assurance have your satisfaction; and that without any further delay than this very evening.   104

Glo. He cannot be such a monster—

Edm. Nor is not, sure.

Glo.—to his father, that so tenderly and entirely loves him. Heaven and earth! Edmund, seek him out; wind me into him, I pray you: frame the business after your own wisdom. I would unstate myself to be in a due resolution.

Edm. I will seek him, sir, presently; convey the business as I shall find means, and acquaint you withal.   114

Glo. These late eclipses in the sun and moon portend no good to us: though the wisdom of nature can reason it thus and thus, yet nature finds itself scourged by the sequent effects. Love cools, friendship falls off, brothers divide: in cities, mutinies; in countries, discord; in palaces, treason; and the bond cracked between son and father. This villain of mine comes under the prediction; there's son against father: the king falls from bias of nature; there's father against child. We have seen the best of our time:

machinations, hollowness, treachery, and all ruinous disorders, follow us disquietly to our graves. Find out this villain, Edmund; it shall lose thee nothing: do it carefully. And the noble and true-hearted Kent banished! his offence, honesty! 'Tis strange!   [*Exit.*

Edm. This is the excellent foppery of the world, that, when we are sick in fortune,—often the surfeit of our own behaviour,—we make guilty of our disasters the sun, the moon, and the stars; as if we were villains by necessity, fools by heavenly compulsion, knaves, thieves, and treachers by spherical predominance, drunkards, liars, and adulterers by an enforced obedience of planetary influence; and all that we are evil in, by a divine thrusting on: an admirable evasion of whoremaster man, to lay his goatish disposition to the charge of a star! My father compounded with my mother under the dragon's tail, and my nativity was under *ursa major;* so that it follows I am rough and lecherous. 'Sfoot! I should have been that I am had the maidenliest star in the firmament twinkled on my bastardizing. Edgar—   149

Enter EDGAR.

and pat he comes, like the catastrophe of the old comedy: my cue is villanous melancholy, with a sigh like Tom o' Bedlam. O, these eclipses do portend these divisions! *Fa, sol, la, mi.*

Edg. How now, brother Edmund! What serious contemplation are you in?   156

Edm. I am thinking, brother, of a prediction I read this other day, what should follow these eclipses.

Edg. Do you busy yourself with that?   160

Edm. I promise you the effects he writes of succeed unhappily; as of unnaturalness between the child and the parent; death, dearth, dissolutions of ancient amities; divisions in state; menaces and maledictions against king and nobles; needless diffidences, banishment of friends, dissipation of cohorts, nuptial breaches, and I know not what.   168

Edg. How long have you been a sectary astronomical?

Edm. Come, come; when saw you my father last?   172

Edg. The night gone by.

Edm. Spake you with him?

Edg. Ay, two hours together.

Edm. Parted you in good terms? Found you no displeasure in him by word or countenance?

Edg. None at all.   179

Edm. Bethink yourself wherein you may have offended him; and at my entreaty forbear his presence till some little time hath qualified the heat of his displeasure, which at this instant so rageth in him that with the mischief of your person it would scarcely allay.   185

Edg. Some villain hath done me wrong.

Edm. That's my fear. I pray you have a continent forbearance till the speed of his rage goes slower, and, as I say, retire with me to my

odging, from whence I will fitly bring you to
hear my lord speak. Pray you, go; there's my
key. If you do stir abroad, go armed.   192
  Edg. Armed, brother!
  Edm. Brother, I advise you to the best; go
armed; I am no honest man if there be any good
meaning toward you; I have told you what I
have seen and heard; but faintly, nothing like
he image and horror of it; pray you, away.
  Edg. Shall I hear from you anon?
  Edm. I do serve you in this business.   200
                              [*Exit* EDGAR.
A credulous father, and a brother noble,
Whose nature is so far from doing harms
That he suspects none; on whose foolish
    honesty
My practices ride easy! I see the business.   204
Let me, if not by birth, have lands by wit:
All with me's meet that I can fashion fit. [*Exit.*

SCENE III.—*A Room in the* DUKE OF ALBANY'S *Palace.*

Enter GONERIL *and* OSWALD *her Steward.*

  Gon. Did my father strike my gentleman for
chiding of his fool?
  Osw. Ay, madam.
  Gon. By day and night he wrongs me; every
    hour   4
He flashes into one gross crime or other,
That sets us all at odds: I'll not endure it:
His knights grow riotous, and himself upbraids
    us
On every trifle. When he returns from hunting
will not speak with him; say I am sick: 9
If you come slack of former services,
You shall do well; the fault of it I'll answer.
  Osw. He's coming, madam; I hear him.   12
                              [*Horns within.*
  Gon. Put on what weary negligence you
    please,
You and your fellows; I'd have it come to ques-
    tion:
If he distaste it, let him to my sister,
Whose mind and mine, I know, in that are one,16
Not to be over-rul'd. Idle old man,
That still would manage those authorities
That he hath given away! Now, by my life,
Old fools are babes again, and must be us'd 20
With checks as flatteries, when they are seen
    abus'd.
Remember what I have said.
  Osw.   Well, madam.
  Gon. And let his knights have colder looks
    among you;
What grows of it, no matter; advise your fellows
    so: 24
would breed from hence occasions, and I shall,
That I may speak: I'll write straight to my sister
To hold my very course. Prepare for dinner.
                              [*Exeunt.*

SCENE IV.—*A Hall in the Same.*

Enter KENT, *disguised.*

  Kent. If but as well I other accents borrow,
That can my speech diffuse, my good intent

May carry through itself to that full issue
For which I raz'd my likeness. Now, banish'd
    Kent,   4
If thou canst serve where thou dost stand con-
    demn'd,
So may it come, thy master, whom thou lov'st,
Shall find thee full of labours.

Horns within. *Enter* LEAR, Knights, *and*
Attendants.

  Lear. Let me not stay a jot for dinner: go,
get it ready. [*Exit an* Attendant.] How now!
what art thou?   10
  Kent. A man, sir.
  Lear. What dost thou profess? What wouldst
thou with us?
  Kent. I do profess to be no less than I seem;
to serve him truly that will put me in trust; to
love him that is honest; to converse with him
that is wise, and says little; to fear judgment; to
fight when I cannot choose; and to eat no fish.
  Lear. What art thou?   19
  Kent. A very honest-hearted fellow, and as
poor as the king.
  Lear. If thou be as poor for a subject as he
is for a king, thou art poor enough. What
wouldst thou?   24
  Kent. Service.
  Lear. Whom wouldst thou serve?
  Kent. You.
  Lear. Dost thou know me, fellow?   28
  Kent. No, sir; but you have that in your
countenance which I would fain call master.
  Lear. What's that?
  Kent. Authority.   32
  Lear. What services canst thou do?
  Kent. I can keep honest counsel, ride, run,
mar a curious tale in telling it, and deliver a
plain message bluntly; that which ordinary men
are fit for, I am qualified in, and the best of me
is diligence.   38
  Lear. How old art thou?
  Kent. Not so young, sir, to love a woman for
singing, nor so old to dote on her for any thing;
I have years on my back forty-eight.   42
  Lear. Follow me; thou shalt serve me: if I
like thee no worse after dinner I will not part
from thee yet. Dinner, ho! dinner! Where's
my knave? my fool? Go you and call my fool
hither.   [*Exit an* Attendant.

Enter OSWALD.

You, you, sirrah, where's my daughter?   48
  Osw. So please you,—   [*Exit.*
  Lear. What says the fellow there? Call the
clotpoll back. [*Exit a* Knight.] Where's my
fool, ho? I think the world's asleep. How now!
where's that mongrel?   53

Re-enter Knight.

  Knight. He says, my lord, your daughter is
not well.
  Lear. Why came not the slave back to me
when I called him?   57
  Knight. Sir, he answered me in the roundest
manner, he would not.

Lear. He would not! 60

Knight. My lord, I know not what the matter is; but, to my judgment, your highness is not entertained with that ceremonious affection as you were wont; there's a great abatement of kindness appears as well in the general dependants as in the duke himself also and your daughter.

Lear. Ha! sayest thou so? 68

Knight. I beseech you, pardon me, my lord, if I be mistaken; for my duty cannot be silent when I think your highness wronged. 71

Lear. Thou but rememberest me of mine own conception: I have perceived a most faint neglect of late; which I have rather blamed as mine own jealous curiosity than as a very pretence and purpose of unkindness: I will look further into't. But where's my fool? I have not seen him this two days. 78

Knight. Since my young lady's going into France, sir, the fool hath much pined him away.

Lear. No more of that; I have noted it well. Go you and tell my daughter I would speak with her. [*Exit an* Attendant. Go you, call hither my fool. [*Exit an* Attendant.

Re-enter OSWALD.

O! you sir, you, come you hither, sir. Who am I, sir? 86

Osw. My lady's father.

Lear. 'My lady's father!' my lord's knave: you whoreson dog! you slave! you cur! 89

Osw. I am none of these, my lord; I beseech your pardon.

Lear. Do you bandy looks with me, you rascal? [*Striking him.*

Osw. I'll not be struck, my lord. 94

Kent. Nor tripped neither, you base football player. [*Tripping up his heels.*

Lear. I thank thee, fellow; thou servest me, and I'll love thee. 98

Kent. Come, sir, arise, away! I'll teach you differences: away, away! If you will measure your lubber's length again, tarry; but away! Go to; have you wisdom? so.
[*Pushes* OSWALD *out.*

Lear. Now, my friendly knave, I thank thee: there's earnest of thy service. 104
[*Gives* KENT *money.*

Enter Fool.

Fool. Let me hire him too: here's my coxcomb. [*Offers* KENT *his cap.*

Lear. How now, my pretty knave! how dost thou? 108

Fool. Sirrah, you were best take my coxcomb.

Kent. Why, fool?

Fool. Why? for taking one's part that's out of favour. Nay, an thou canst not smile as the wind sits, thou'lt catch cold shortly: there, take my coxcomb. Why, this fellow has banished two on's daughters, and did the third a blessing against his will: if thou follow him thou must needs wear my coxcomb. How now, nuncle! Would I had two coxcombs and two daughters!

Lear. Why, my boy? 119

Fool. If I gave them all my living, I'd kee my coxcombs myself. There's mine; beg an other of thy daughters.

Lear. Take heed, sirrah; the whip. 12

Fool. Truth's a dog must to kennel; he mu be whipped out when Lady the brach may stan by the fire and stink.

Lear. A pestilent gall to me!

Fool. [*To* KENT.] Sirrah, I'll teach thee speech. 12

Lear. Do.

Fool. Mark it, nuncle:—
  Have more than thou showest, 13
  Speak less than thou knowest,
  Lend less than thou owest,
  Ride more than thou goest,
  Learn more than thou trowest, 13
  Set less than thou throwest;
  Leave thy drink and thy whore,
  And keep in-a-door,
  And thou shalt have more 14
  Than two tens to a score.

Kent. This is nothing, fool.

Fool. Then 'tis like the breath of an unfee' lawyer, you gave me nothing for't. Can yo make no use of nothing, nuncle? 14

Lear. Why, no, boy; nothing can be mad out of nothing.

Fool. [*To* KENT.] Prithee, tell him, so muc the rent of his land comes to: he will not be lieve a fool. 15

Lear. A bitter fool!

Fool. Dost thou know the difference, my boy between a bitter fool and a sweet fool? 15

Lear. No, lad; teach me.

Fool. That lord that counsell'd thee
  To give away thy land, 15
  Come place him here by me,
  Do thou for him stand:
  The sweet and bitter fool
  Will presently appear; 16
  The one in motley here,
  The other found out there.

Lear. Dost thou call me fool, boy?

Fool. All thy other titles thou hast give away; that thou wast born with. 16

Kent. This is not altogether fool, my lord.

Fool. No, faith, lords and great men will no let me; if I had a monopoly out, they woul have part on't, and ladies too: they will not le me have all fool to myself; they'll be snatching Nuncle, give me an egg, and I'll give thee tw crowns. 17

Lear. What two crowns shall they be?

Fool. Why, after I have cut the egg i' the middle and eat up the meat, the two crowns o the egg. When you clovest thy crown i' the middle, and gavest away both parts, thou bores thine ass on thy back o'er the dirt: thou hads little wit in thy bald crown when thou gavest thy golden one away. If I speak like myself i this, let him be whipped that first finds it so. 18

  Fools had ne'er less grace in a year;
    For wise men are grown foppish,
  And know not how their wits to wear, 18
    Their manners are so apish.

Lear. When were you wont to be so full of songs, sirrah? 187

Fool. I have used it, nuncle, ever since thou madest thy daughters thy mothers; for when thou gavest them the rod and puttest down thine own breeches.

> Then they for sudden joy did weep, 192
> And I for sorrow sung,
> That such a king should play bo-peep,
> And go the fools among. 195

Prithee, nuncle, keep a schoolmaster that can teach thy fool to lie: I would fain learn to lie.

Lear. An you lie, sirrah, we'll have you whipped. 199

Fool. I marvel what kin thou and thy daughters are: they'll have me whipped for speaking true, thou'lt have me whipped for lying; and sometimes I am whipped for holding my peace. I had rather be any kind o' thing than a fool; and yet I would not be thee, nuncle; thou hast pared thy wit o' both sides, and left nothing i' the middle: here comes one o' the parings. 208

Enter GONERIL.

Lear. How now, daughter! what makes that frontlet on? Methinks you are too much of late i' the frown. 211

Fool. Thou wast a pretty fellow when thou hadst no need to care for her frowning; now thou art an O without a figure. I am better than thou art now; I am a fool, thou art nothing. [*To* GONERIL.] Yes, forsooth, I will hold my tongue; so your face bids me, though you say nothing.

> Mum, mum;
> He that keeps nor crust nor crumb, 220
> Weary of all, shall want some.

That's a shealed peascod. [*Pointing to* LEAR.

Gon. Not only, sir, this your all-licens'd fool, But other of your insolent retinue 224 Do hourly carp and quarrel, breaking forth In rank and not-to-be-endured riots. Sir, I had thought, by making this well known unto you, To have found a safe redress; but now grow fearful, 228 By what yourself too late have spoke and done, That you protect this course, and put it on By your allowance; which if you should, the fault Would not 'scape censure, nor the redresses sleep, 232 Which, in the tender of a wholesome weal, Might in their working do you that offence, Which else were shame, that then necessity Will call discreet proceeding. 236

Fool. For you trow, nuncle,

> The hedge-sparrow fed the cuckoo so long,
> That it had it head bit off by it young.

So out went the candle, and we were left darkling. 240

Lear. Are you our daughter?

Gon. I would you would make use of your good wisdom,

Whereof I know you are fraught; and put away These dispositions which of late transform you From what you rightly are. 245

Fool. May not an ass know when the cart draws the horse? Whoop, Jug! I love thee.

Lear. Does any here know me? This is not Lear: 248 Does Lear walk thus? speak thus? Where are his eyes? Either his notion weakens, his discernings Are lethargied. Ha! waking? 'tis not so. Who is it that can tell me who I am? 252

Fool. Lear's shadow.

Lear. I would learn that; for, by the marks of sovereignty, knowledge and reason, I should be false persuaded I had daughters. 256

Fool. Which they will make an obedient father.

Lear. Your name, fair gentlewoman?

Gon. This admiration, sir, is much o' the favour 260 Of other your new pranks. I do beseech you To understand my purposes aright: As you are old and reverend, should be wise. Here do you keep a hundred knights and squires; 264 Men so disorder'd, so debosh'd, and bold, That this our court, infected with their manners, Shows like a riotous inn: epicurism and lust Make it more like a tavern or a brothel 268 Than a grac'd palace. The shame itself doth speak For instant remedy; be then desir'd By her that else will take the thing she begs, A little to disquantity your train; 272 And the remainder, that shall still depend, To be such men as may besort your age, Which know themselves and you.

Lear. 　　　　　　　Darkness and devils! Saddle my horses; call my train together. 276 Degenerate bastard! I'll not trouble thee: Yet have I left a daughter.

Gon. You strike my people, and your disorder'd rabble Make servants of their betters. 280

Enter ALBANY.

Lear. Woe, that too late repents;

　　[*To* ALBANY.] O! sir, are you come? Is it your will? Speak, sir. Prepare my horses. Ingratitude, thou marble-hearted fiend, More hideous, when thou show'st thee in a child, 284 Than the sea-monster.

Alb. 　　　　　　Pray, sir, be patient.

Lear. [*To* GONERIL.] Detested kite! thou liest: My train are men of choice and rarest parts, That all particulars of duty know, 288 And in the most exact regard support The worships of their name. O most small fault, How ugly didst thou in Cordelia show! Which, like an engine, wrench'd my frame of nature 292 From the fix'd place, drew from my heart all love,

And added to the gall. O Lear, Lear, Lear!
Beat at this gate, that let thy folly in,   295
                    [*Striking his head.*
And thy dear judgment out: Go, go, my people.
  Alb. My lord, I am guiltless, as I am ignorant
Of what hath mov'd you.
  Lear.   It may be so, my lord.
Hear, Nature, hear! dear goddess, hear!
Suspend thy purpose, if thou didst intend 300
To make this creature fruitful!
Into her womb convey sterility!
Dry up in her the organs of increase,
And from her derogate body never spring 304
A babe to honour her! If she must teem,
Create her child of spleen, that it may live
And be a thwart disnatur'd torment to her!
Let it stamp wrinkles in her brow of youth, 308
With cadent tears fret channels in her cheeks,
Turn all her mother's pains and benefits
To laughter and contempt, that she may feel
How sharper than a serpent's tooth it is   312
To have a thankless child! Away, away! [*Exit.*
  Alb. Now, gods that we adore, whereof
comes this?
  Gon. Never afflict yourself to know the cause;
But let his disposition have that scope   316
That dotage gives it.

Re-enter LEAR.

  Lear. What! fifty of my followers at a clap,
Within a fortnight?
  Alb.   What's the matter, sir?
  Lear. I'll tell thee. [*To* GONERIL.] Life and
death! I am asham'd   320
That thou hast power to shake my manhood
thus,
That these hot tears, which break from me per-
force,
Should make thee worth them. Blasts and fogs
upon thee!
Th' untented woundings of a father's curse 324
Pierce every sense about thee! Old fond eyes,
Beweep this cause again, I'll pluck ye out,
And cast you, with the waters that you lose,
To temper clay. Yea, is it come to this?   328
Let it be so: I have another daughter,
Who, I am sure, is kind and comfortable:
When she shall hear this of thee, with her nails
She'll flay thy wolvish visage. Thou shalt find
That I'll resume the shape which thou dost
think   333
I have cast off for ever; thou shalt, I warrant
thee. [*Exeunt* LEAR, KENT, *and* Attendants.
  Gon. Do you mark that?
  Alb. I cannot be so partial, Goneril,   336
To the great love I bear you.—
  Gon. Pray you, content. What, Oswald, ho!
[*To the Fool.*] You, sir, more knave than fool,
after your master.
  Fool. Nuncle Lear, nuncle Lear! tarry, and
take the fool with thee.   341
        A fox, when one has caught her,
        And such a daughter,
        Should sure to the slaughter,   344
        If my cap would buy a halter;
        So the fool follows after.   [*Exit.*

  Gon. This man hath had good counsel. A
hundred knights!
'Tis politic and safe to let him keep   34
At point a hundred knights; yes, that on every
dream,
Each buzz, each fancy, each complaint, dislike,
He may enguard his dotage with their powers,
And hold our lives in mercy. Oswald, I say! 35
  Alb. Well, you may fear too far.
  Gon.   Safer than trust too far
Let me still take away the harms I fear,
Not fear still to be taken: I know his heart.
What he hath utter'd I have writ my sister; 35
If she sustain him and his hundred knights,
When I have show'd the unfitness,—

Re-enter OSWALD.

                    How now, Oswald
What! have you writ that letter to my sister?
  Osw. Ay, madam.   36
  Gon. Take you some company, and away to
horse:
Inform her full of my particular fear;
And thereto add such reasons of your own
As may compact it more. Get you gone,   36
And hasten your return. [*Exit* OSWALD.] No
no, my lord,
This milky gentleness and course of yours
Though I condemn not, yet, under pardon,
You are much more attask'd for want of wis-
dom   36
Than prais'd for harmful mildness.
  Alb. How far your eyes may pierce I cannot
tell:
Striving to better, oft we mar what's well.
  Gon. Nay, then—   37
  Alb. Well, well; the event.   [*Exeunt.*

SCENE V.—*Court before the Same.*

Enter LEAR, KENT, *and* Fool.

  Lear. Go you before to Gloucester with these
letters. Acquaint my daughter no further with
any thing you know than comes from her
demand out of the letter. If your diligence be
not speedy I shall be there before you.   5
  Kent. I will not sleep, my lord, till I have
delivered your letter.   [*Exit.*
  Fool. If a man's brains were in 's heels, were 't
not in danger of kibes?   9
  Lear. Ay, boy.
  Fool. Then, I prithee, be merry; thy wit shall
not go slip-shod.   12
  Lear. Ha, ha, ha!
  Fool. Shalt see thy other daughter will use
thee kindly; for though she's as like this as a
crab is like an apple, yet I can tell what I can
tell.   17
  Lear. What canst tell, boy?
  Fool. She will taste as like this as a crab does
to a crab. Thou canst tell why one's nose
stands i' the middle on's face?   21
  Lear. No.
  Fool. Why, to keep one's eyes of either side's
nose, that what a man cannot smell out, he
may spy into.   25

Lear. I did her wrong,—

Fool. Canst tell how an oyster makes his
shell?   28

Lear. No.

Fool. Nor I neither; but I can tell why a
snail has a house.

Lear. Why?   32

Fool. Why, to put his head in; not to give
away to his daughters, and leave his horns
without a case.

Lear. I will forget my nature. So kind a
father! Be my horses ready?   37

Fool. Thy asses are gone about 'em. The
reason why the seven stars are no more than
even is a pretty reason.   40

Lear. Because they are not eight?

Fool. Yes, indeed: thou wouldst make a good
fool.

Lear. To take it again perforce! Monster ingratitude!   45

Fool. If thou wert my fool, nuncle, I'd have
thee beaten for being old before thy time.

Lear. How's that?   48

Fool. Thou shouldst not have been old before
thou hadst been wise.

Lear. O! let me not be mad, not mad, sweet
heaven;

Keep me in temper; I would not be mad!   52

Enter Gentleman.

How now! Are the horses ready?

Gent. Ready, my lord.

Lear. Come, boy.

Fool. She that's a maid now, and laughs at
my departure,   56
Shall not be a maid long, unless things be cut
shorter.   [*Exeunt.*

ACT II

SCENE I.—*A Court within the Castle of the*
EARL OF GLOUCESTER.

Enter EDMUND *and* CURAN, *meeting.*

Edm. Save thee, Curan.

Cur. And you, sir. I have been with your
father, and given him notice that the Duke of
Cornwall and Regan his duchess will be here
with him to-night.   5

Edm. How comes that?

Cur. Nay, I know not. You have heard of
the news abroad? I mean the whispered ones,
for they are yet but ear-kissing arguments?   9

Edm. Not I: pray you, what are they?

Cur. Have you heard of no likely wars toward,
'twixt the Dukes of Cornwall and Albany?   12

Edm. Not a word.

Cur. You may do then, in time. Fare you
well, sir.   [*Exit.*

Edm. The duke be here to-night! The better!
best!   16
This weaves itself perforce into my business.
My father hath set guard to take my brother;
And I have one thing, of a queasy question,
Which I must act. Briefness and fortune, work!
Brother, a word; descend: brother, I say!   21

Enter EDGAR.

My father watches: O sir! fly this place;
Intelligence is given where you are hid;
You have now the good advantage of the
night.   24
Have you not spoken 'gainst the Duke of Corn-
wall?
He's coming hither, now, i' the night, i' the
haste,
And Regan with him; have you nothing said
Upon his party 'gainst the Duke of Albany?   28
Advise yourself.

Edg.   I am sure on't, not a word.

Edm. I hear my father coming; pardon me;
In cunning I must draw my sword upon you;
Draw; seem to defend yourself; now 'quit you
well.   32
Yield;—come before my father. Light, ho!
here!
Fly, brother. Torches! torches! So, farewell.
                                    [*Exit* EDGAR.
Some blood drawn on me would beget opinion
                              [*Wounds his arm.*
Of my more fierce endeavour: I have seen
drunkards   36
Do more than this in sport. Father! father!
Stop, stop! No help?

Enter GLOUCESTER, *and* Servants *with torches.*

Glo. Now, Edmund, where's the villain?

Edm. Here stood he in the dark, his sharp
sword out,   40
Mumbling of wicked charms, conjuring the
moon
To stand auspicious mistress.

Glo.   But where is he?

Edm. Look, sir, I bleed.

Glo.   Where is the villain, Edmund?

Edm. Fled this way, sir. When by no means
he could—   44

Glo. Pursue him, ho! Go after. [*Exeunt
some* Servants.] 'By no means' what?

Edm. Persuade me to the murder of your
lordship;
But that I told him, the revenging gods
'Gainst parricides did all their thunders bend;
Spoke with how manifold and strong a bond   49
The child was bound to the father; sir, in fine,
Seeing how loathly opposite I stood
To his unnatural purpose, in fell motion,   52
With his prepared sword he charges home
My unprovided body, lanc'd mine arm:
But when he saw my best alarum'd spirits
Bold in the quarrel's right, rous'd to the en-
counter,   56
Or whether gasted by the noise I made,
Full suddenly he fled.

Glo.   Let him fly far:
Not in this land shall he remain uncaught;
And found——dispatch. The noble duke my
master,   60
My worthy arch and patron, comes to-night:
By his authority I will proclaim it,
That he which finds him shall deserve our
thanks,

Bringing the murderous coward to the stake; 64
He that conceals him, death.

Edm. When I dissuaded him from his intent,
And found him pight to do it, with curst speech
I threaten'd to discover him: he replied, 68
'Thou unpossessing bastard! dost thou think,
If I would stand against thee, would the reposal
Of any trust, virtue, or worth, in thee
Make thy words faith'd? No: what I should
deny,— 72
As this I would; ay, though thou didst produce
My very character,—I'd turn it all
To thy suggestion, plot, and damned practice:
And thou must make a dullard of the world, 76
If they not thought the profits of my death
Were very pregnant and potential spurs
To make thee seek it.'

Glo. Strong and fasten'd villain!
Would he deny his letter? I never got him. 80
[*Tucket within.*
Hark! the duke's trumpets. I know not why he
comes.
All ports I'll bar; the villain shall not 'scape;
The duke must grant me that: besides, his pic-
ture
I will send far and near, that all the kingdom 84
May have due note of him; and of my land,
Loyal and natural boy, I'll work the means
To make thee capable.

Enter CORNWALL, REGAN, *and* Attendants.

Corn. How now, my noble friend! since I
came hither,— 88
Which I can call but now,—I have heard strange
news.

Reg. If it be true, all vengeance comes too
short
Which can pursue the offender. How dost, my
lord?

Glo. O! madam, my old heart is crack'd, it's
crack'd. 92

Reg. What! did my father's godson seek your
life?
He whom my father nam'd? your Edgar?

Glo. O! lady, lady, shame would have it hid.

Reg. Was he not companion with the riotous
knights 96
That tend upon my father?

Glo. I know not, madam; 'tis too bad, too
bad.

Edm. Yes, madam, he was of that consort.

Reg. No marvel then though he were ill
affected; 100
'Tis they have put him on the old man's death,
To have the expense and waste of his revenues.
I have this present evening from my sister
Been well-inform'd of them, and with such
cautions 104
That if they come to sojourn at my house,
I'll not be there.

Corn. Nor I, assure thee, Regan.
Edmund, I hear that you have shown your
father
A child-like office.

Edm. 'Twas my duty, sir. 108

Glo. He did bewray his practice; and receiv'd

This hurt you see, striving to apprehend him

Corn. Is he pursu'd?

Glo. Ay, my good lor

Corn. If he be taken he shall never more i
Be fear'd of doing harm; make your own pu
pose,
How in my strength you please. For yo
Edmund,
Whose virtue and obedience doth this insta
So much commend itself, you shall be ours: i
Natures of such deep trust we shall much nee
You we first seize on.

Edm. I shall serve you, sir,
Truly, however else.

Glo. For him I thank your Grac

Corn. You know not why we came to vis
you,— 1:

Reg. Thus out of season, threading dark-ey
night:
Occasions, noble Gloucester, of some prize,
Wherein we must have use of your advice.
Our father he hath writ, so hath our sister, 1:
Of differences, which I best thought it fit
To answer from our home; the several me
sengers
From hence attend dispatch. Our good ol
friend,
Lay comforts to your bosom, and bestow 1:
Your needful counsel to our businesses,
Which craves the instant use.

Glo. I serve you, madan
Your Graces are right welcome. [*Exeun*

SCENE II.—*Before* GLOUCESTER'S *Castle.*

Enter KENT *and* OSWALD, *severally.*

Osw. Good dawning to thee, friend: art (
this house?

Kent. Ay.

Osw. Where may we set our horses?

Kent. I' the mire.

Osw. Prithee, if thou lovest me, tell me.

Kent. I love thee not.

Osw. Why, then I care not for thee.

Kent. If I had thee in Lipsbury pinfold,
would make thee care for me.

Osw. Why dost thou use me thus? I kno
thee not.

Kent. Fellow, I know thee.

Osw. What dost thou know me for?

Kent. A knave, a rascal, an eater of broke
meats; a base, proud, shallow, beggarly, thre
suited, hundred-pound, filthy, worsted-stockin
knave; a lily-liver'd, action-taking knave;
whoreson, glass-gazing, superserviceable, finic
rogue; one-trunk-inheriting slave; one tha
wouldst be a bawd, in way of good servic
and art nothing but the composition of
knave, beggar, coward, pandar, and the so
and heir of a mongrel bitch: one whom I wi
beat into clamorous whining if thou denie
the least syllable of thy addition. 2

Osw. Why, what a monstrous fellow a
thou, thus to rail on one that is neither know
of thee nor knows thee!

Kent. What a brazen-faced varlet art tho

deny thou knowest me! Is it two days since
tripped up thy heels and beat thee before
the king? Draw, you rogue; for, though it be
ight, yet the moon shines: I'll make a sop o'
the moonshine of you.   [*Drawing his sword.*]
Draw, you whoreson, cullionly, barber-monger,
raw.   37

  Osw. Away! I have nothing to do with thee.

  Kent. Draw, you rascal; you come with let-
ers against the king, and ake vanity the pup-
et's part against the royalty of her father.
Draw, you rogue, or I'll so carbonado your
hanks: draw, you rascal; come your ways.

  Osw. Help, ho! murder! help! 44

  Kent. Strike, you slave; stand, rogue, stand;
ou neat slave, strike.   [*Beating him.*

  Osw. Help, oh! murder! murder!

     Enter EDMUND *with his rapier drawn.*

  Edm. How now! What's the matter? 48
                           [*Parting them.*

  Kent. With you, goodman boy, if you please:
come,
ll flesh ye; come on, young master.

  Enter CORNWALL, REGAN, GLOUCESTER, *and*
               Servants.

  Glo. Weapons! arms! What's the matter
here?

  Corn. Keep peace, upon your lives: 52
He dies that strikes again. What is the matter?

  Reg. The messengers from our sister and the
king.

  Corn. What is your difference? speak.

  Osw. I am scarce in breath, my lord. 56

  Kent. No marvel, you have so bestirred your
alour. You cowardly rascal, nature disclaims
a thee: a tailor made thee.

  Corn. Thou art a strange fellow; a tailor
make a man? 61

  Kent. Ay, a tailor, sir: a stone-cutter or a
ainter could not have made him so ill, though
hey had been but two hours o' the trade. 64

  Corn. Speak yet, how grew your quarrel?

  Osw. This ancient ruffian, sir, whose life I
ave spar'd at suit of his grey beard,— 67

  Kent. Thou whoreson zed! thou unnecessary
etter! My lord, if you will give me leave, I will
read this unbolted villain into mortar, and
aub the wall of a jakes with him. Spare my
rey beard, you wagtail!

  Corn. Peace, sirrah!
ou beastly knave, know you no reverence?

  Kent. Yes, sir; but anger hath a privilege.

  Corn. Why art thou angry? 76

  Kent. That such a slave as this should wear
    a sword,
Who wears no honesty. Such smiling rogues as
    these,
Like rats, oft bite the holy cords a-twain
Which are too intrinse t' unloose; smooth every
    passion 80
That in the natures of their lords rebel;
Bring oil to fire, snow to their colder moods;
Renege, affirm, and turn their halcyon beaks

With every gale and vary of their masters, 84
Knowing nought, like dogs, but following.
A plague upon your epileptic visage!
Smile you my speeches, as I were a fool?
Goose, if I had you upon Sarum plain, 88
I'd drive ye cackling home to Camelot.

  Corn. What! art thou mad, old fellow?

  Glo. How fell you out? say that.

  Kent. No contraries hold more antipathy 92
Than I and such a knave.

  Corn. Why dost thou call him knave? What
    is his fault?

  Kent. His countenance likes me not.

  Corn. No more, perchance, does mine, nor
his, nor hers. 97

  Kent. Sir, 'tis my occupation to be plain:
I have seen better faces in my time
Than stands on any shoulder that I see 100
Before me at this instant.

  Corn.   This is some fellow,
Who, having been prais'd for bluntness, doth
    affect
A saucy roughness, and constrains the garb
Quite from his nature: he cannot flatter, he, 104
An honest mind and plain, he must speak truth:
An they will take it, so; if not, he's plain.
These kind of knaves I know, which in this
    plainness
Harbour more craft and more corrupter ends
Than twenty silly-ducking observants, 109
That stretch their duties nicely.

  Kent. Sir, in good sooth, in sincere verity,
Under the allowance of your grand aspect, 112
Whose influence, like the wreath of radiant fire
On flickering Phœbus' front,—

  Corn.   What mean'st by this?

  Kent. To go out of my dialect, which you
discommend so much. I know, sir, I am no
flatterer: he that beguiled you in a plain accent
was a plain knave; which for my part I will not
be, though I should win your displeasure to entreat me to 't. 120

  Corn. What was the offence you gave him?

  Osw. I never gave him any:
It pleas'd the king his master very late
To strike at me, upon his misconstruction; 124
When he, conjunct, and flattering his dis-
    pleasure,
Tripp'd me behind; being down, insulted, rail'd,
And put upon him such a deal of man,
That worthied him, got praises of the king 128
For him attempting who was self-subdu'd;
And, in the fleshment of this dread exploit,
Drew on me here again.

  Kent.   None of these rogues and cowards
But Ajax is their fool.

  Corn.   Fetch forth the stocks! 132
You stubborn ancient knave, you reverend brag-
    gart,
We'll teach you.

  Kent.   Sir, I am too old to learn,
Call not your stocks for me; I serve the king,
On whose employment I was sent to you; 136
You shall do small respect, show too bold malice
Against the grace and person of my master,
Stocking his messenger.

Corn. Fetch forth the stocks! As I have life and honour, 140
There shall he sit till noon.

Reg. Till noon! Till night, my lord; and all night too.

Kent. Why, madam, if I were your father's dog,
You should not use me so.

Reg. Sir, being his knave, I will. 144

Corn. This is a fellow of the self-same colour
Our sister speaks of. Come, bring away the stocks. [*Stocks brought out.*

Glo. Let me beseech your Grace not to do so.
His fault is much, and the good king his master 148
Will check him for 't: your purpos'd low correction
Is such as basest and contemned'st wretches
For pilferings and most common trespasses
Are punish'd with: the king must take it ill, 152
That he, so slightly valu'd in his messenger,
Should have him thus restrain'd.

Corn. I'll answer that.

Reg. My sister may receive it much more worse
To have her gentleman abus'd, assaulted, 156
For following her affairs. Put in his legs.

[*KENT is put in the stocks.*
Come, my good lord, away.

[*Exeunt all but* GLOUCESTER *and* KENT.

Glo. I am sorry for thee, friend; 'tis the duke's pleasure,
Whose disposition, all the world well knows, 160
Will not be rubb'd nor stopp'd: I'll entreat for thee.

Kent. Pray, do not, sir. I have watch'd and travell'd hard;
Some time I shall sleep out, the rest I'll whistle.
A good man's fortune may grow out at heels: 164
Give you good morrow!

Glo. The duke's to blame in this; 'twill be ill taken. [*Exit.*

Kent. Good king, that must approve the common saw,
Thou out of heaven's benediction com'st 168
To the warm sun.
Approach, thou beacon to this under globe,
That by thy comfortable beams I may
Peruse this letter. Nothing almost sees miracles
But misery: I know 'tis from Cordelia, 173
Who hath most fortunately been inform'd
Of my obscured course; and shall find time
From this enormous state, seeking to give 176
Losses their remedies. All weary and o'er-watch'd,
Take vantage, heavy eyes, not to behold
This shameful lodging.
Fortune, good night, smile once more; turn thy wheel! [*He sleeps.*

SCENE III.—*A Part of the Heath.*

Enter EDGAR.

Edg. I heard myself proclaim'd;
And by the happy hollow of a tree
Escap'd the hunt. No port is free; no place,
That guard, and most unusual vigilance, 4
Does not attend my taking. While I may 'scape
I will preserve myself; and am bethought
To take the basest and most poorest shape
That ever penury, in contempt of man, 8
Brought near to beast; my face I'll grime with filth,
Blanket my loins, elf all my hair in knots,
And with presented nakedness outface
The winds and persecutions of the sky. 12
The country gives me proof and precedent
Of Bedlam beggars, who with roaring voices,
Strike in their numb'd and mortified bare arms
Pins, wooden pricks, nails, sprigs of rosemary;
And with this horrible object, from low farms,
Poor pelting villages, sheep-cotes, and mills,
Sometime with lunatic bans, sometime with prayers,
Enforce their charity. Poor Turlygood! poor Tom! 20
That's something yet: Edgar I nothing am.
[*Exit.*

SCENE IV.—*Before* GLOUCESTER'S *Castle.*
KENT *in the stocks.*

Enter LEAR, Fool, *and* Gentleman.

Lear. 'Tis strange that they should so depart from home,
And not send back my messenger.

Gent. As I learn'd,
The night before there was no purpose in them
Of this remove.

Kent. Hail to thee, noble master! 4

Lear. Ha!
Mak'st thou this shame thy pastime?

Kent. No, my lord.

Fool. Ha, ha! he wears cruel garters. Horses are tied by the head, dogs and bears by the neck, monkeys by the loins, and men by the legs: when a man is over-lusty at legs, then he wears wooden nether-stocks.

Lear. What's he that hath so much thy place mistook 12
To set thee here?

Kent. It is both he and she,
Your son and daughter.

Lear. No.

Kent. Yes. 16

Lear. No, I say.

Kent. I say, yea.

Lear. No, no; they would not.

Kent. Yes, they have. 20

Lear. By Jupiter, I swear, no.

Kent. By Juno, I swear, ay.

Lear. They durst not do 't;
They could not, would not do 't; 'tis worse than murder,
To do upon respect such violent outrage. 24
Resolve me, with all modest haste, which way
Thou mightst deserve, or they impose, this usage,
Coming from us.

Kent. My lord, when at their home
I did commend your highness' letters to them,

Ere I was risen from the place that show'd 29
My duty kneeling, there came a reeking post,
Stew'd in his haste, half breathless, panting
    forth
From Goneril his mistress salutations; 32
Deliver'd letters, spite of intermission,
Which presently they read: on whose contents
They summon'd up their meiny, straight took
    horse;
Commanded me to follow, and attend 36
The leisure of their answer; gave me cold looks:
And meeting here the other messenger,
Whose welcome, I perceiv'd, had poison'd
    mine,—
Being the very fellow which of late 40
Display'd so saucily against your highness,—
Having more man than wit about me,—drew:
He rais'd the house with loud and coward cries.
Your son and daughter found this trespass
    worth 44
The shame which here it suffers.
    Fool. Winter's not gone yet, if the wild geese
fly that way.

> Fathers that wear rags 48
>   Do make their children blind,
> But fathers that bear bags
>   Shall see their children kind.
> Fortune, that arrant whore, 52
>   Ne'er turns the key to the poor.

But for all this thou shalt have as many dolours
for thy daughters as thou canst tell in a year.
    Lear. O! how this mother swells up toward
my heart; 56
Hysterica passio! down, thou climbing sorrow!
Thy element's below. Where is this daughter?
    Kent. With the earl, sir: here within.
    Lear. Follow me not; stay here.   [*Exit.*
    Gent. Made you no more offence than what
you speak of?
    Kent. None.
How chance the king comes with so small a
number? 64
    Fool. An thou hadst been set i' the stocks for
that question, thou hadst well deserved it.
    Kent. Why, fool? 67
    Fool. We'll set thee to school to an ant, to
teach thee there's no labouring i' the winter. All
that follow their noses are led by their eyes but
blind men; and there's not a nose among twenty
but can smell him that's stinking. Let go thy
hold when a great wheel runs down a hill, lest it
break thy neck with following it; but the great
one that goes up the hill, let him draw thee after.
When a wise man gives thee better counsel, give
me mine again: I would have none but knaves
follow it, since a fool gives it.

> That sir which serves and seeks for gain,
>   And follows but for form, 80
> Will pack when it begins to rain,
>   And leave thee in the storm.
> But I will tarry; the fool will stay,
>   And let the wise man fly: 84
> The knave turns fool that runs away;
>   The fool no knave, perdy.

    Kent. Where learn'd you this, fool?
    Fool. Not i' the stocks, fool. 88

Re-enter LEAR, *with* GLOUCESTER.

    Lear. Deny to speak with me! They are sick!
they are weary,
They have travell'd hard to-night! Mere fetches,
The images of revolt and flying off.
Fetch me a better answer.
    Glo.   My dear lord, 92
You know the fiery quality of the duke;
How unremovable and fix'd he is
In his own course.
    Lear. Vengeance! plague! death! confusion!
Fiery! what quality? Why, Gloucester, Glou-
cester, 97
I'd speak with the Duke of Cornwall and his
wife.
    Glo. Well, my good lord, I have inform'd
them so.
    Lear. Inform'd them! Dost thou understand
me, man? 100
    Glo. Ay, my good lord.
    Lear. The king would speak with Cornwall;
the dear father
Would with his daughter speak, commands her
service: 103
Are they inform'd of this? My breath and blood!
Fiery! the fiery duke! Tell the hot duke that—
No, but not yet; may be he is not well:
Infirmity doth still neglect all office
Whereto our health is bound; we are not our-
selves 108
When nature, being oppress'd, commands the
mind
To suffer with the body. I'll forbear;
And am fall'n out with my more headier will,
To take the indispos'd and sickly fit 112
For the sound man. Death on my state! [*Look-
ing on* KENT.] Wherefore
Should he sit here? This act persuades me
That this remotion of the duke and her
Is practice only. Give me my servant forth. 116
Go, tell the duke and's wife I'd speak with them
Now, presently: bid them come forth and hear
me,
Or at their chamber-door I'll beat the drum
Till it cry sleep to death. 120
    Glo. I would have all well betwixt you.
                                    [*Exit.*
    Lear. O, me! my heart, my rising heart! but,
down!
    Fool. Cry to it, nuncle, as the cockney did to
the eels when she put 'em i' the paste alive; she
knapped 'em o' the coxcombs with a stick, and
cried, 'Down, wantons, down!' 'Twas her
brother that, in pure kindness to his horse,
buttered his hay. 128

Enter CORNWALL, REGAN, GLOUCESTER,
    and Servants.

    Lear. Good morrow to you both.
    Corn.   Hail to your Grace!
                    [KENT *is set at liberty.*
    Reg. I am glad to see your highness.
    Lear. Regan, I think you are; I know what
reason
I have to think so: if thou shouldst not be glad,

I would divorce me from thy mother's tomb, 133
Sepulchring an adult'ress.—[*To* KENT.] O! are
you free?
Some other time for that. Beloved Regan,
Thy sister's naught: O Regan! she hath tied 136
Sharp-tooth'd unkindness, like a vulture, here:
[*Points to his heart.*
I can scarce speak to thee; thou'lt not believe
With how deprav'd a quality—O Regan!
  Reg. I pray you, sir, take patience. I have
hope 140
You less know how to value her desert
Than she to scant her duty.
  Lear.   Say, how is that?
  Reg. I cannot think my sister in the least
Would fail her obligation: if, sir, perchance 144
She have restrain'd the riots of your followers,
'Tis on such ground, and to such wholesome end,
As clears her from all blame.
  Lear. My curses on her!
  Reg.   O, sir! you are old; 148
Nature in you stands on the very verge
Of her confine: you should be rul'd and led
By some discretion that discerns your state
Better than you yourself. Therefore I pray you
That to our sister you do make return; 153
Say, you have wrong'd her, sir.
  Lear.   Ask her forgiveness?
Do you but mark how this becomes the house:
'Dear daughter, I confess that I am old; 156
Age is unnecessary: on my knees I beg
                  [*Kneeling.*
That you'll vouchsafe me raiment, bed, and
food.'
  Reg. Good sir, no more; these are unsightly
tricks:
Return you to my sister.
  Lear.   [*Rising.*] Never, Regan. 160
She hath abated me of half my train;
Look'd black upon me; struck me with her
tongue,
Most serpent-like, upon the very heart.
All the stor'd vengeances of heaven fall 164
On her ingrateful top! Strike her young bones,
You taking airs, with lameness!
  Corn.   Fie, sir, fie!
  Lear. You nimble lightnings, dart your blind-
ing flames
Into her scornful eyes! Infect her beauty, 168
You fen-suck'd fogs, drawn by the powerful sun,
To fall and blast her pride!
  Reg. O the blest gods! So will you wish
on me,
When the rash mood is on. 172
  Lear. No, Regan, thou shalt never have my
curse:
Thy tender-hefted nature shall not give
Thee o'er to harshness: her eyes are fierce, but
thine
Do comfort and not burn. 'Tis not in thee 176
To grudge my pleasures, to cut off my train,
To bandy hasty words, to scant my sizes,
And, in conclusion, to oppose the bolt
Against my coming in: thou better know'st 180
The offices of nature, bond of childhood,
Effects of courtesy, dues of gratitude;

Thy half o' the kingdom hast thou not forgot,
Wherein I thee endow'd.
  Reg.   Good sir, to the purpose. 184
  Lear. Who put my man i' the stocks?
                  [*Tucket within.*
  Corn.   What trumpet's that?
  Reg. I know't, my sister's; this approves her
letter,
That she would soon be here. Is your lady come?

                Enter OSWALD.

  Lear. This is a slave, whose easy-borrow'd
pride 188
Dwells in the fickle grace of her he follows.
Out, varlet, from my sight!
  Corn.   What means your Grace?
  Lear. Who stock'd my servant? Regan, I
have good hope
Thou didst not know on't. Who comes here?
O heavens, 192

                Enter GONERIL.

If you do love old men, if your sweet sway
Allow obedience, if yourselves are old,
Make it your cause; send down and take my
part!
[*To* GONERIL.] Art not asham'd to look upon
this beard? 196
O Regan, wilt thou take her by the hand?
  Gon. Why not by the hand, sir? How have
I offended?
All's not offence that indiscretion finds
And dotage terms so.
  Lear.   O sides! you are too tough;
Will you yet hold? How came my man i' the
stocks? 200
  Corn. I set him there, sir: but his own dis-
orders
Deserv'd much less advancement.
  Lear.   You! did you?
  Reg. I pray you, father, being weak, seem so.
If, till the expiration of your month, 205
You will return and sojourn with my sister,
Dismissing half your train, come then to me:
I am now from home, and out of that provision
Which shall be needful for your entertainment
  Lear. Return to her? and fifty men dismiss'd?
No, rather I abjure all roofs, and choose
To wage against the enmity o' the air; 212
To be a comrade with the wolf and owl,
Necessity's sharp pinch! Return with her!
Why, the hot-blooded France, that dowerless
took
Our youngest born, I could as well be brought
To knee his throne, and squire-like, pension beg
To keep base life afoot. Return with her!
Persuade me rather to be slave and sumpter
To this detested groom. [*Pointing at* OSWALD
  Gon.   At your choice, sir. 220
  Lear. I prithee, daughter, do not make me
mad:
I will not trouble thee, my child; farewell.
We'll no more meet, no more see one another;
But yet thou art my flesh, my blood, my
daughter; 22?
Or rather a disease that's in my flesh,

Which I must needs call mine: thou art a boil,
A plague-sore, an embossed carbuncle,
In my corrupted blood. But I'll not chide
thee; 228
Let shame come when it will, I do not call it:
I do not bid the thunder-bearer shoot,
Nor tell tales of thee to high-judging Jove.
Mend when thou canst; be better at thy
leisure: 232
I can be patient; I can stay with Regan,
I and my hundred knights.
   Reg.   Not altogether so:
I look'd not for you yet, nor am provided
For your fit welcome. Give ear, sir, to my
sister; 236
For those that mingle reason with your passion
Must be content to think you old, and so—
But she knows what she does.
   Lear.   Is this well spoken?
   Reg. I dare avouch it, sir: what! fifty fol-
lowers? 240
Is it not well? What should you need of more?
Yea, or so many, sith that both charge and
danger
Speak 'gainst so great a number? How, in one
house,
Should many people, under two commands, 244
Hold amity? 'Tis hard; almost impossible.
   Gon. Why might not you, my lord, receive
attendance
From those that she calls servants, or from
mine?
   Reg. Why not, my lord? If then they chanc'd
to slack you 248
We could control them. If you will come to
me,—
For now I spy a danger,—I entreat you
To bring but five-and-twenty; to no more
Will I give place or notice. 252
   Lear. I gave you all—
   Reg.   And in good time you gave it.
   Lear. Made you my guardians, my deposi-
taries,
But kept a reservation to be follow'd
With such a number. What! must I come to
you 256
With five-and-twenty? Regan, said you so?
   Reg. And speak't again, my lord; no more
with me.
   Lear. Those wicked creatures yet do look
well-favour'd,
When others are more wicked; not being the
worst 260
Stands in some rank of praise. [*To* GONERIL.]
I'll go with thee:
Thy fifty yet doth double five-and-twenty,
And thou art twice her love.
   Gon.   Hear me, my lord.
What need you five-and-twenty, ten, or five, 264
To follow in a house, where twice so many
Have a command to tend you?
   Reg.   What need one?
   Lear. O! reason not the need; our basest
beggars
Are in the poorest thing superfluous: 268
Allow not nature more than nature needs,

Man's life is cheap as beast's. Thou art a lady;
If only to go warm were gorgeous,
Why, nature needs not what thou gorgeous
wear'st, 272
Which scarcely keeps thee warm. But, for true
need,—
You heavens, give me that patience, patience I
need!
You see me here, you gods, a poor old man,
As full of grief as age; wretched in both! 276
If it be you that stir these daughters' hearts
Against their father, fool me not so much
To bear it tamely; touch me with noble anger,
And let not women's weapons, water-drops, 280
Stain my man's cheeks! No, you unnatural
hags,
I will have such revenges on you both
That all the world shall—I will do such things,—
What they are yet I know not,—but they shall
be 284
The terrors of the earth. You think I'll weep;
No, I'll not weep:
I have full cause of weeping, but this heart
Shall break into a hundred thousand flaws 288
Or ere I'll weep. O fool! I shall go mad.
       [*Exeunt* LEAR, GLOUCESTER, KENT, *and* Fool.
   Corn. Let us withdraw; 'twill be a storm.
              [*Storm heard at a distance.*
   Reg. This house is little: the old man and
his people
Cannot be well bestow'd. 292
   Gon. 'Tis his own blame; hath put himself
from rest,
And must needs taste his folly.
   Reg. For his particular, I'll receive him
gladly,
But not one follower.
   Gon.   So am I purpos'd. 296
Where is my Lord of Gloucester?
   Corn. Follow'd the old man forth. He is
return'd.

Re-enter GLOUCESTER.

   Glo. The king is in high rage.
   Corn.   Whither is he going?
   Glo. He calls to horse; but will I know not
whither. 300
   Corn. 'Tis best to give him way; he leads
himself.
   Gon. My lord, entreat him by no means to
stay.
   Glo. Alack! the night comes on, and the
bleak winds
Do sorely ruffle; for many miles about 304
There's scarce a bush.
   Reg.   O! sir, to wilful men,
The injuries that they themselves procure
Must be their schoolmasters. Shut up your
doors;
He is attended with a desperate train, 308
And what they may incense him to, being apt
To have his ear abus'd, wisdom bids fear.
   Corn. Shut up your doors, my lord; 'tis a
wild night:
My Regan counsels well: come out o' the storm.
                  [*Exeunt.*

ACT III

SCENE I.—*A Heath.*

A storm, with thunder and lightning. Enter
KENT *and a Gentleman, meeting.*

Kent. Who's here, beside foul weather?

Gent. One minded like the weather, most
unquietly.

Kent. I know you. Where's the king?

Gent. Contending with the fretful elements;
Bids the wind blow the earth into the sea,   5
Or swell the curled waters 'bove the main,
That things might change or cease; tears his
white hair,
Which the impetuous blasts, with eyeless rage,   8
Catch in their fury, and make nothing of;
Strives in his little world of man to out-scorn
The to-and-fro-conflicting wind and rain.
This night, wherein the cub-drawn bear would
couch,   12
The lion and the belly-pinched wolf
Keep their fur dry, unbonneted he runs,
And bids what will take all.

Kent.   But who is with him?

Gent. None but the fool, who labours to out-
jest   16
His heart-struck injuries.

Kent.   Sir, I do know you;
And dare, upon the warrant of my note,
Commend a dear thing to you. There is divi-
sion,
Although as yet the face of it be cover'd   20
With mutual cunning, 'twixt Albany and Corn-
wall;
Who have—as who have not, that their great
stars
Thron'd and set high—servants, who seem no
less,
Which are to France the spies and speculations
Intelligent of our state; what hath been seen,   25
Either in snuffs and packings of the dukes,
Or the hard rein which both of them have borne
Against the old kind king; or something deeper,
Whereof perchance these are but furnishings;   29
But, true it is, from France there comes a power
Into this scatter'd kingdom; who already,
Wise in our negligence, have secret feet   32
In some of our best ports, and are at point
To show their open banner. Now to you:
If on my credit you dare build so far
To make your speed to Dover, you shall find   36
Some that will thank you, making just report
Of how unnatural and bemadding sorrow
The king hath cause to plain.
I am a gentleman of blood and breeding,   40
And from some knowledge and assurance offer
This office to you.

Gent. I will talk further with you.

Kent.   No, do not.
For confirmation that I am much more   44
Than my out-wall, open this purse, and take
What it contains. If you shall see Cordelia,—
As doubt not but you shall,—show her this
ring,
And she will tell you who your fellow is   48
That yet you do not know. Fie on this storm!

I will go seek the king.

Gent. Give me your hand. Have you no
more to say?

Kent. Few words, but, to effect, more than
all yet;   52
That, when we have found the king,—in which
your pain
That way, I'll this,—he that first lights on him
Holla the other.   [*Exeunt severally.*

SCENE II.—*Another Part of the Heath.*
Storm still.

Enter LEAR *and* Fool.

Lear. Blow, winds, and crack your cheeks!
rage! blow!
You cataracts and hurricanoes, spout
Till you have drench'd our steeples, drown'd
the cocks!
You sulphurous and thought-executing fires,   4
Vaunt-couriers to oak-cleaving thunderbolts,
Singe my white head! And thou, all-shaking
thunder,
Strike flat the thick rotundity o' the world!
Crack nature's moulds, all germens spill at once
That ingrateful man!   9

Fool. O nuncle, court holy-water in a dry
house is better than this rain-water out o' door.
Good nuncle, in, and ask thy daughters' blessing;
here's a night pities neither wise man nor fool.

Lear. Rumble thy bellyful! Spit, fire! spout,
rain!   14
Nor rain, wind, thunder, fire, are my daughters:
I tax not you, you elements, with unkindness;
I never gave you kingdom, call'd you children,
You owe me no subscription: then, let fall
Your horrible pleasure; here I stand, your slave,
A poor, infirm, weak, and despis'd old man.   20
But yet I call you servile ministers,
That have with two pernicious daughters join'd
Your high-engender'd battles 'gainst a head
So old and white as this. O! O! 'tis foul.   24

Fool. He that has a house to put his head in
has a good head-piece.

The cod-piece that will house
  Before the head has any,   28
The head and he shall louse;
  So beggars marry many.
The man that makes his toe
  What he his heart should make,   32
Shall of a corn cry woe,
  And turn his sleep to wake.

For there was never yet fair woman but she
made mouths in a glass.   36

Enter KENT.

Lear. No, I will be the pattern of all patience;
I will say nothing.

Kent. Who's there?

Fool. Marry, here's grace and a cod-piece;
that's a wise man and a fool.   41

Kent. Alas! sir, are you here? things that
love night
Love not such nights as these; the wrathful
skies
Gallow the very wanderers of the dark,   44

And make them keep their caves. Since I was
man
Such sheets of fire, such bursts of horrid thunder,
Such groans of roaring wind and rain, I never
Remember to have heard; man's nature cannot
carry 48
The affliction nor the fear.
Lear. Let the great gods,
That keep this dreadful pother o'er our heads,
Find out their enemies now. Tremble, thou
wretch,
That hast within thee undivulged crimes, 52
Unwhipp'd of justice; hide thee, thou bloody
hand;
Thou perjur'd, and thou simular of virtue
That art incestuous; caitiff, to pieces shake,
That under covert and convenient seeming 56
Hast practis'd on man's life; close pent-up
guilts,
Rive your concealing continents, and cry
These dreadful summoners grace. I am a man
More sinn'd against than sinning.
Kent. Alack! bare-headed!
Gracious my lord, hard by here is a hovel; 61
Some friendship will it lend you 'gainst the
tempest;
Repose you there while I to this hard house,—
More harder than the stone whereof 'tis rais'd,—
Which even but now, demanding after you, 65
Denied me to come in, return and force
Their scanted courtesy.
Lear. My wits begin to turn.
Come on, my boy. How dost, my boy? Art
cold? 68
I am cold myself. Where is this straw, my fellow?
The art of our necessities is strange,
That can make vile things precious. Come, your
hovel.
Poor fool and knave, I have one part in my
heart 72
That's sorry yet for thee.
Fool.

He that has a little tiny wit,
  With hey, ho, the wind and the rain,
Must make content with his fortunes fit, 76
  Though the rain it raineth every day.

Lear. True, my good boy. Come, bring us to
this hovel. [*Exeunt* LEAR *and* KENT.
Fool. This is a brave night to cool a courtezan.
I'll speak a prophecy ere I go: 80
When priests are more in word than matter;
When brewers mar their malt with water;
When nobles are their tailors' tutors;
No heretics burn'd, but wenches' suitors; 84
When every case in law is right;
No squire in debt, nor no poor knight;
When slanders do not live in tongues;
Nor cutpurses come not to throngs; 88
When usurers tell their gold i' the field;
And bawds and whores do churches build;
Then shall the realm of Albion
Come to great confusion: 92
Then comes the time, who lives to see't,
That going shall be us'd with feet.
This prophecy Merlin shall make; for I live
before his time. [*Exit.*

SCENE III.—*A Room in* GLOUCESTER'S
Castle.

Enter GLOUCESTER *and* EDMUND.

Glo. Alack, alack! Edmund, I like not this
unnatural dealing. When I desired their leave
that I might pity him, they took from me the
use of mine own house; charged me, on pain of
their perpetual displeasure, neither to speak of
him, entreat for him, nor any way sustain him.
Edm. Most savage, and unnatural! 7
Glo. Go to; say you nothing. There is
division between the dukes, and a worse matter
than that. I have received a letter this night;
'tis dangerous to be spoken; I have locked the
letter in my closet. These injuries the king now
bears will be revenged home; there's part of
a power already footed; we must incline to the
king. I will seek him and privily relieve him;
go you and maintain talk with the duke, that
my charity be not of him perceived. If he ask
for me, I am ill and gone to bed. If I die for it,
as no less is threatened me, the king, my old
master, must be relieved. There is some strange
thing toward, Edmund; pray you, be careful. 21
[*Exit.*
Edm. This courtesy, forbid thee, shall the
duke
Instantly know; and of that letter too:
This seems a fair deserving, and must draw me
That which my father loses; no less than all: 25
The younger rises when the old doth fall. [*Exit.*

SCENE IV.—*The Heath. Before a Hovel.*

Enter LEAR, KENT, *and* Fool.

Kent. Here is the place, my lord; good my
lord, enter:
The tyranny of the open night's too rough
For nature to endure. [*Storm still.*
Lear. Let me alone.
Kent. Good my lord, enter here.
Lear. Wilt break my heart? 4
Kent. I'd rather break mine own. Good my
lord, enter.
Lear. Thou think'st 'tis much that this con-
tentious storm
Invades us to the skin: so 'tis to thee;
But where the greater malady is fix'd, 8
The lesser is scarce felt. Thou'dst shun a bear;
But if thy flight lay toward the roaring sea,
Thou'dst meet the bear i' the mouth. When
the mind's free
The body's delicate; the tempest in my mind 12
Doth from my senses take all feeling else
Save what beats there. Filial ingratitude!
Is it not as this mouth should tear this hand
For lifting food to't? But I will punish home: 16
No, I will weep no more. In such a night
To shut me out! Pour on; I will endure.
In such a night as this! O Regan, Goneril!
Your old kind father, whose frank heart gave
all,— 20
O! that way madness lies; let me shun that;
No more of that.
Kent. Good my lord, enter here.

Lear. Prithee, go in thyself; seek thine own ease:
This tempest will not give me leave to ponder 24
On things would hurt me more. But I'll go in.
[*To the* Fool.] In, boy; go first. You houseless poverty,—
Nay, get thee in. I'll pray, and then I'll sleep.
[Fool *goes in.*
Poor naked wretches, wheresoe'er you are, 28
That bide the pelting of this pitiless storm,
How shall your houseless heads and unfed sides,
Your loop'd and window'd raggedness, defend you
From seasons such as these? O! I have ta'en 32
Too little care of this. Take physic, pomp;
Expose thyself to feel what wretches feel,
That thou mayst shake the superflux to them,
And show the heavens more just. 36
Edg. [*Within.*] Fathom and half, fathom and half! Poor Tom!
[*The* Fool *runs out from the hovel.*
Fool. Come not in here, nuncle; here's a spirit.
Help me! help me!
Kent. Give me thy hand.. Who's there? 40
Fool. A spirit, a spirit: he says his name's poor Tom.
Kent. What art thou that dost grumble there i' the straw?
Come forth.

Enter EDGAR *disguised as a madman.*

Edg. Away! the foul fiend follows me! 44
Through the sharp hawthorn blow the winds.
Hum! go to thy cold bed and warm thee.
Lear. Didst thou give all to thy two daughters?
And art thou come to this? 48
Edg. Who gives anything to poor Tom? whom the foul fiend hath led through fire and through flame, through ford and whirlpool, o'er bog and quagmire; that hath laid knives under his pillow, and halters in his pew; set ratsbane by his porridge; made him proud of heart, to ride on a bay trotting-horse over four-inched bridges, to course his own shadow for a traitor. Bless thy five wits! Tom's a-cold. O! do de, do de, do de. Bless thee from whirlwinds, star-blasting, and taking! Do poor Tom some charity, whom the foul fiend vexes. There could I have him now, and there, and there again, and there.
[*Storm still.*
Lear. What! have his daughters brought him to this pass?
Couldst thou save nothing? Didst thou give them all?
Fool. Nay, he reserved a blanket, else we had been all shamed. 65
Lear. Now all the plagues that in the pendulous air
Hang fated o'er men's faults light on thy daughters!
Kent. He hath no daughters, sir. 68
Lear. Death, traitor! nothing could have subdu'd nature
To such a lowness, but his unkind daughters.

Is it the fashion that discarded fathers
Should have thus little mercy on their flesh? 72
Judicious punishment! 'twas this flesh begot
Those pelican daughters.
Edg. Pillicock sat on Pillicock-hill:
Halloo, halloo, loo, loo! 76
Fool. This cold night will turn us all to fools and madmen.
Edg. Take heed o' the foul fiend. Obey thy parents; keep thy word justly; swear not; commit not with man's sworn spouse; set not thy sweet heart on proud array. Tom's a-cold. 82
Lear. What hast thou been?
Edg. A servingman, proud in heart and mind; that curled my hair, wore gloves in my cap, served the lust of my mistress's heart, did the act of darkness with her; swore as many oaths as I spake words, and broke them in the sweet face of heaven; one that slept in the contriving of lust, and waked to do it. Wine loved I deeply, dice dearly, and in woman out-paramoured the Turk: false of heart, light of ear, bloody of hand; hog in sloth, fox in stealth, wolf in greediness, dog in madness, lion in prey. Let not the creaking of shoes nor the rustling of silks betray thy poor heart to woman: keep thy foot out of brothels, thy hand out of plackets, thy pen from lenders' books, and defy the foul fiend. Still through the hawthorn blows the cold wind; says suum, mun ha no nonny. Dolphin my boy, my boy; sessa! let him trot by. [*Storm still.*
Lear. Why, thou wert better in thy grave than to answer with thy uncovered body this extremity of the skies. Is man no more than this? Consider him well. Thou owest the worm no silk, the beast no hide, the sheep no wool, the cat no perfume. Ha! here's three on's are sophisticated; thou art the thing itself; unaccommodated man is no more but such a poor, bare, forked animal as thou art. Off, off, you lendings! Come; unbutton here. 112
[*Tearing off his clothes.*
Fool. Prithee, nuncle, be contented; 'tis a naughty night to swim in. Now a little fire in a wide field were like an old lecher's heart; a small spark, all the rest on's body cold. Look! here comes a walking fire. 117

Enter GLOUCESTER *with a torch.*

Edg. This is the foul fiend Flibbertigibbet: he begins at curfew, and walks till the first cock; he gives the web and the pin, squints the eye, and makes the harelip; mildews the white wheat, and hurts the poor creature of earth. 122

Swithold footed thrice the old;
He met the night-mare, and her nine-fold;
Bid her alight,
And her troth plight,
And aroint thee, witch, aroint thee!

Kent. How fares your Grace? 128
Lear. What's he?
Kent. Who's there? What is't you seek?
Glo. What are you there? Your names?
Edg. Poor Tom; that eats the swimming frog, the toad, the tadpole, the wall-newt, and the

water; that in the fury of his heart, when
the foul fiend rages, eats cow-dung for sallets;
swallows the old rat and the ditch-dog; drinks
the green mantle of the standing pool; who is
whipped from tithing to tithing, and stock-
punished, and imprisoned; who hath had three
suits to his back, six shirts to his body, horse to
ride, and weapon to wear;   141

But mice and rats and such small deer
Have been Tom's food for seven long year.

Beware my follower. Peace, Smulkin! peace,
thou fiend.   145
　Glo. What! hath your Grace no better com-
pany?
　Edg. The prince of darkness is a gentleman;
Modo he's call'd, and Mahu.
　Glo. Our flesh and blood, my lord, is grown
so vile,
That it doth hate what gets it.   150
　Edg. Poor Tom's a-cold.
　Glo. Go in with me. My duty cannot suffer
To obey in all your daughters' hard commands:
Though their injunction be to bar my doors, 154
And let this tyrannous night take hold upon
you,
Yet have I ventur'd to come seek you out 156
And bring you where both fire and food is ready.
　Lear. First let me talk with this philosopher.
What is the cause of thunder?
　Kent. Good my lord, take his offer; go into
the house.   160
　Lear. I'll talk a word with this same learned
Theban.
What is your study?
　Edg. How to prevent the fiend, and to kill
vermin.
　Lear. Let me ask you one word in private.
　Kent. Importune him once more to go, my
lord;   165
His wits begin to unsettle.
　Glo.　　Canst thou blame him? [*Storm still.*
His daughters seek his death. Ah! that good
Kent;
He said it would be thus, poor banish'd man!
Thou sayst the king grows mad; I'll tell thee,
friend,   169
I am almost mad myself. I had a son,
Now outlaw'd from my blood; he sought my life,
But lately, very late; I lov'd him, friend, 172
No father his son dearer; true to tell thee,
　　　　　　　　　　　　[*Storm continues.*
The grief hath craz'd my wits. What a night's
this!
I do beseech your Grace,—
　Lear.　　　　O! cry you mercy, sir.
Noble philosopher, your company.   176
　Edg. Tom's a-cold.
　Glo. In, fellow, there, into the hovel: keep
thee warm.
　Lear. Come, let's in all.
　Kent.　　　　This way, my lord.
　Lear.　　　　　　　　With him;
I will keep still with my philosopher.   180
　Kent. Good my lord, soothe him; let him
take the fellow.

　Glo. Take him you on.
　Kent. Sirrah, come on; go along with us.
　Lear. Come, good Athenian.
　Glo. No words, no words: hush.
　Edg. Child Rowland to the dark tower came,
His word was still, Fie, foh, and fum,
I smell the blood of a British man. 187
　　　　　　　　　　　　　　　[*Exeunt.*

SCENE V.—*A Room in* GLOUCESTER'S *Castle.*

Enter CORNWALL *and* EDMUND.

　Corn. I will have my revenge ere I depart
his house.
　Edm. How, my lord, I may be censured, that
nature thus gives way to loyalty, something
fears me to think of.   5
　Corn. I now perceive it was not altogether
your brother's evil disposition made him seek
his death; but a provoking merit, set a-work by
a reproveable badness in himself.   9
　Edm. How malicious is my fortune, that I
must repent to be just! This is the letter he
spoke of, which approves him an intelligent
party to the advantages of France. O heavens!
that this treason were not, or not I the detector!
　Corn. Go with me to the duchess.
　Edm. If the matter of this paper be certain,
you have mighty business in hand.   17
　Corn. True, or false, it hath made thee Earl
of Gloucester. Seek out where thy father is,
that he may be ready for our apprehension. 20
　Edm. [*Aside.*] If I find him comforting the
king, it will stuff his suspicion more fully. I
will persever in my course of loyalty, though
the conflict be sore between that and my blood.
　Corn. I will lay trust upon thee; and thou
shalt find a dearer father in my love. [*Exeunt.*

SCENE VI.—*A Chamber in a Farmhouse adjoining the Castle.*

Enter GLOUCESTER, LEAR, KENT, Fool, *and*
EDGAR.

　Glo. Here is better than the open air; take
it thankfully. I will piece out the comfort with
what addition I can: I will not be long from
you.   4
　Kent. All the power of his wits has given way
to his impatience. The gods reward your kindness!   [*Exit* GLOUCESTER.
　Edg. Fraterretto calls me, and tells me Nero
is an angler in the lake of darkness. Pray,
innocent, and beware the foul fiend.
　Fool. Prithee, nuncle, tell me whether a
madman be a gentleman or a yeoman!   12
　Lear. A king, a king!
　Fool. No; he's a yeoman that has a gentleman to his son; for he's a mad yeoman that
sees his son a gentleman before him.   16
　Lear. To have a thousand with red burning
spits
Come hizzing in upon 'em,—
　Edg. The foul fiend bites my back.
　Fool. He's mad that trusts in the tameness

of a wolf, a horse's health, a boy's love, or a whore's oath.

Lear. It shall be done; I will arraign them straight.

[*To* EDGAR.] Come, sit thou here, most learned justicer;   24

[*To the* Fool.] Thou, sapient sir, sit here. Now, you she foxes!

Edg. Look, where he stands and glares! wantest thou eyes at trial, madam?

Come o'er the bourn, Bessy, to me,—   28

Fool. Her boat hath a leak,
     And she must not speak
Why she dares not come over to thee.

Edg. The foul fiend haunts poor Tom in the voice of a nightingale. Hopdance cries in Tom's belly for two white herring. Croak not, black angel; I have no food for thee.

Kent. How do you, sir? Stand you not so amaz'd: 36
Will you lie down and rest upon the cushions?

Lear. I'll see their trial first. Bring in their evidence.

[*To* EDGAR.] Thou robed man of justice, take thy place;

[*To the* Fool.] And thou, his yoke-fellow of equity,   40
Bench by his side. [*To* KENT.] You are o' the commission,
Sit you too.

Edg. Let us deal justly.

     Sleepest or wakest thou, jolly shepherd?   44
          Thy sheep be in the corn;
     And for one blast of thy minikin mouth,
          Thy sheep shall take no harm.

Purr! the cat is grey.   48

Lear. Arraign her first; 'tis Goneril. I here take my oath before this honourable assembly, she kicked the poor king her father.

Fool. Come hither, mistress. Is your name Goneril?   53

Lear. She cannot deny it.

Fool. Cry you mercy, I took you for a joint-stool.

Lear. And here's another, whose warp'd looks proclaim   56
What store her heart is made on. Stop her there!

Arms, arms, sword, fire! Corruption in the place!

False justicer, why hast thou let her 'scape?

Edg. Bless thy five wits!   60

Kent. O pity! Sir, where is the patience now That you so oft have boasted to retain?

Edg. [*Aside.*] My tears begin to take his part so much,
They'll mar my counterfeiting.   64

Lear. The little dogs and all,
Tray, Blanch, and Sweet-heart, see, they bark at me.

Edg. Tom will throw his head at them.

Avaunt, you curs!   68
     Be thy mouth or black or white,
     Tooth that poisons if it bite;
     Mastiff, greyhound, mongrel grim,
     Hound or spaniel, brach or lym;   72

Or bobtail tike or trundle-tail;
Tom will make them weep and wail:
For, with throwing thus my head,
Dogs leap the hatch, and all are fled.   76
Do de, de, de. Sessa! Come, march to wakes and fairs and market-towns. Poor Tom, thy horn is dry.   79

Lear. Then let them anatomize Regan, see what breeds about her heart. Is there any cause in nature that makes these hard hearts? [*To* EDGAR.] You, sir, I entertain you for one of my hundred; only I do not like the fashion of your garments: you will say, they are Persian attire; but let them be changed.

Kent. Now, good my lord, lie here and rest awhile.   88

Lear. Make no noise, make no noise; draw the curtains: so, so, so. We'll go to supper i' the morning: so, so, so.

Fool. And I'll go to bed at noon.   92

Re-enter GLOUCESTER.

Glo. Come hither, friend: where is the king my master?

Kent. Here, sir; but trouble him not, his wits are gone.   96

Glo. Good friend, I prithee, take him in thy arms;
I have o'erheard a plot of death upon him.
There is a litter ready; lay him in 't,
And drive toward Dover, friend, where thou shalt meet   100
Both welcome and protection. Take up thy master:
If thou shouldst dally half an hour, his life,
With thine, and all that offer to defend him,
Stand in assured loss. Take up, take up;   104
And follow me, that will to some provision Give thee quick conduct.

Kent.   Oppress'd nature sleeps:
This rest might yet have balm'd thy broken sinews,
Which, if convenience will not allow,   108
Stand in hard cure.—[*To the* Fool.] Come, help to bear thy master;
Thou must not stay behind.

Glo.   Come, come, away.
          [*Exeunt* KENT, GLOUCESTER, *and the*
               Fool, *bearing away* LEAR.

Edg. When we our betters see bearing our woes,
We scarcely think our miseries our foes.   112
Who alone suffers suffers most i' the mind,
Leaving free things and happy shows behind;
But then the mind much sufferance doth o'erskip,
When grief hath mates, and bearing fellowship.   116
How light and portable my pain seems now,
When that which makes me bend makes the king bow;
He childed as I father'd! Tom, away!
Mark the high noises, and thyself bewray   120
When false opinion, whose wrong thought defiles thee,
In thy just proof repeals and reconciles thee.

What will hap more to-night, safe 'scape the king!
Lurk, lurk. [Exit.

SCENE VII.—A Room in GLOUCESTER'S Castle.

Enter CORNWALL, REGAN, GONERIL, EDMUND,
and Servants.

Corn. Post speedily to my lord your husband;
show him this letter: the army of France is
landed. Seek out the traitor Gloucester.
[Exeunt some of the Servants.
Reg. Hang him instantly. 4
Gon. Pluck out his eyes.
Corn. Leave him to my displeasure. Edmund,
keep you our sister company: the revenges we
are bound to take upon your traitorous father
are not fit for your beholding. Advise the duke,
where you are going, to a most festinate preparation: we are bound to the like. Our posts shall
be swift and intelligent betwixt us. Farewell,
dear sister: farewell, my Lord of Gloucester. 13

Enter OSWALD.

How now? Where's the king?
Osw. My Lord of Gloucester hath convey'd
him hence:
Some five or six and thirty of his knights, 16
Hot questrists after him, met him at gate;
Who, with some other of the lord's dependants,
Are gone with him toward Dover, where they
boast
To have well-armed friends.
Corn. Get horses for your mistress. 20
Gon. Farewell, sweet lord, and sister.
Corn. Edmund, farewell.
[Exeunt GONERIL, EDMUND, and
OSWALD.
Go seek the traitor Gloucester,
Pinion him like a thief, bring him before us.
[Exeunt other Servants.
Though well we may not pass upon his life 24
Without the form of justice, yet our power
Shall do a courtesy to our wrath, which men
May blame but not control. Who's there?
The traitor?

Re-enter Servants, with GLOUCESTER.

Reg. Ingrateful fox! 'tis he. 28
Corn. Bind fast his corky arms.
Glo. What mean your Graces? Good my
friends, consider
You are my guests: do me no foul play, friends.
Corn. Bind him, I say. [Servants bind him.
Reg. Hard, hard. O filthy traitor!
Glo. Unmerciful lady as you are, I'm none. 33
Corn. To this chair bind him. Villain, thou
shalt find— [REGAN plucks his beard.
Glo. By the kind gods, 'tis most ignobly done
To pluck me by the beard. 36
Reg. So white, and such a traitor!
Glo. Naughty lady,
These hairs, which thou dost ravish from my
chin,
Will quicken, and accuse thee: I am your host:
With robbers' hands my hospitable favours 40
You should not ruffle thus. What will you do?

Corn. Come, sir, what letters had you late
from France?
Reg. Be simple-answer'd, for we know the
truth.
Corn. And what confederacy have you with
the traitors 44
Late footed in the kingdom?
Reg. To whose hands have you sent the
lunatic king?
Speak.
Glo. I have a letter guessingly set down, 48
Which came from one that's of a neutral heart,
And not from one oppos'd.
Corn. Cunning.
Reg. And false.
Corn. Where hast thou sent the king?
Glo. To Dover.
Reg. Wherefore to Dover? Wast thou not
charg'd at peril— 52
Corn. Wherefore to Dover? Let him answer
that.
Glo. I am tied to the stake, and I must stand
the course.
Reg. Wherefore to Dover? 55
Glo. Because I would not see thy cruel nails
Pluck out his poor old eyes; nor thy fierce sister
In his anointed flesh stick boarish fangs.
The sea, with such a storm as his bare head
In hell-black night endur'd, would have buoy'd
up, 60
And quench'd the stelled fires;
Yet, poor old heart, he holp the heavens to rain.
If wolves had at thy gate howl'd that dern time,
Thou shouldst have said, 'Good porter, turn
the key,' 64
All cruels else subscrib'd: but I shall see
The winged vengeance overtake such children.
Corn. See't shalt thou never. Fellows, hold
the chair.
Upon these eyes of thine I'll set my foot. 68
Glo. He that will think to live till he be old,
Give me some help! O cruel! O ye gods!
[GLOUCESTER'S eye put out.
Reg. One side will mock another; the other
too.
Corn. If you see vengeance—
First Serv. Hold your hand, my lord:
I have serv'd you ever since I was a child, 73
But better service have I never done you
Than now to bid you hold.
Reg. How now, you dog!
First Serv. If you did wear a beard upon
your chin, 76
I'd shake it on this quarrel. What do you mean?
Corn. My villain! [Draws.
First Serv. Nay then, come on, and take the
chance of anger. [Draws. They fight.
CORNWALL is wounded.
Reg. Give me thy sword. A peasant stand up
thus! [Takes a sword and runs
at him behind.
First Serv. O! I am slain. My lord, you have
one eye left 81
To see some mischief on him. O! [Dies.
Corn. Lest it see more, prevent it. Out, vile
jelly!

Where is thy lustre now?   84
  Glo. All dark and comfortless. Where's my
   son Edmund?
Edmund, enkindle all the sparks of nature
To quit this horrid act.
  Reg.   Out, treacherous villain!
Thou call'st on him that hates thee; it was he
That made the overture of thy treasons to us, 89
Who is too good to pity thee.
  Glo. O my follies! Then Edgar was abus'd.
Kind gods, forgive me that, and prosper him! 92
  Reg. Go thrust him out at gates, and let him
   smell
His way to Dover. [*Exit one with* GLOUCESTER.]
        How is't, my lord? How look you?
  Corn. I have receiv'd a hurt. Follow me,
   lady.
Turn out that eyeless villain; throw this slave
Upon the dunghill. Regan, I bleed apace: 97
Untimely comes this hurt. Give me your arm.
        [*Exit* CORNWALL *led by* REGAN.
  Sec. Serv. I'll never care what wickedness I do
If this man come to good.
  Third Serv.   If she live long, 100
And, in the end, meet the old course of death,
Women will all turn monsters.
  Sec. Serv. Let's follow the old earl, and get
   the Bedlam
To lead him where he would: his roguish mad-
   ness   104
Allows itself to any thing.
  Third Serv. Go thou; I'll fetch some flax,
   and whites of eggs,
To apply to his bleeding face. Now, heaven
   help him!   [*Exeunt severally.*

ACT IV

Scene I.—*The Heath.*

Enter EDGAR.

  Edg. Yet better thus, and known to be con-
   temn'd,
Than still contemn'd and flatter'd. To be worst,
The lowest and most dejected thing of fortune,
Stands still in esperance, lives not in fear: 4
The lamentable change is from the best;
The worst returns to laughter. Welcome, then,
Thou unsubstantial air that I embrace:
The wretch that thou hast blown unto the worst
Owes nothing to thy blasts. But who comes
   here?   9

Enter GLOUCESTER, *led by an old* Man.

My father, poorly led? World, world, O world!
But that thy strange mutations make us hate thee,
Life would not yield to age.
  Old Man.   O my good lord! 12
I have been your tenant, and your father's
   tenant,
These fourscore years.
  Glo. Away, get thee away; good friend, be
   gone;
Thy comforts can do me no good at all;   16
Thee they may hurt.
  Old Man.   You cannot see your way.

  Glo. I have no way, and therefore want no
   eyes;
I stumbled when I saw. Full oft 'tis seen,
Our means secure us, and our mere defects 2
Prove our commodities. Ah! dear son Edgar
The food of thy abused father's wrath;
Might I but live to see thee in my touch,
I'd say I had eyes again.
  Old Man.   How now! Who's there? 2
  Edg. [*Aside.*] O gods! Who is't can say, '
   am at the worst?'
I am worse than e'er I was.
  Old Man.   'Tis poor mad Tom
  Edg. [*Aside.*] And worse I may be yet; th
   worst is not,
So long as we can say, 'This is the worst.' 2
  Old Man. Fellow, where goest?
  Glo.   Is it a beggar-man
  Old Man. Madman and beggar too.
  Glo. He has some reason, else he could no
   beg.
I' the last night's storm I such a fellow saw, 3
Which made me think a man a worm: my so
Came then into my mind; and yet my mind
Was then scarce friends with him: I have hear
   more since.
As flies to wanton boys, are we to the gods; 3
They kill us for their sport.
  Edg.   [*Aside.*] How should this be
Bad is the trade that must play fool to sorrow
Angering itself and others.—[*To* GLOUCESTER.
   Bless thee, master!
  Glo. Is that the naked fellow?
  Old Man.   Ay, my lord
  Glo. Then, prithee, get thee gone. If, for m
   sake,   4
Thou wilt o'ertake us, hence a mile or twain,
I' the way toward Dover, do it for ancient love
And bring some covering for this naked soul 4
Who I'll entreat to lead me.
  Old Man.   Alack, sir! he is mad
  Glo. 'Tis the times' plague, when madme
   lead the blind.
Do as I bid thee, or rather do thy pleasure;
Above the rest, be gone.   4
  Old Man. I'll bring him the best 'parel tha
   I have,
Come on't what will.   [*Exit
  Glo. Sirrah, naked fellow,—
  Edg. Poor Tom's a-cold. [*Aside.*] I canno
   daub it further.   5
  Glo. Come hither, fellow.
  Edg. [*Aside.*] And yet I must. Bless thy swee
   eyes, they bleed.
  Glo. Know'st thou the way to Dover?   5
  Edg. Both stile and gate, horse-way and foot-
path. Poor Tom hath been scared out of hi
good wits: bless thee, good man's son, from the
foul fiend! Five fiends have been in poor Tom
at once; of lust, as Obidicut; Hobbididance
prince of dumbness; Mahu, of stealing; Modo
of murder; and Flibbertigibbet, of mopping and
mowing; who since possesses chambermaids
and waiting-women. So, bless thee, master! 6
  Glo. Here, take this purse, thou whom the
   heavens' plagues

Have humbled to all strokes: that I am wretched
Makes thee the happier: heavens, deal so still!
Let the superfluous and lust-dieted man,   68
That slaves your ordinance, that will not see
Because he doth not feel, feel your power
    quickly;
So distribution should undo excess,
And each man have enough. Dost thou know
    Dover?   72
    Edg. Ay, master.
    Glo. There is a cliff, whose high and bending
    head
Looks fearfully in the confined deep;
Bring me but to the very brim of it,   76
And I'll repair the misery thou dost bear
With something rich about me; from that place
I shall no leading need.
    Edg.   Give me thy arm:
Poor Tom shall lead thee.   [*Exeunt.*

SCENE II.—*Before the* DUKE OF ALBANY'S
    Palace.

Enter GONERIL *and* EDMUND.

    Gon. Welcome, my lord; I marvel our mild
    husband
Not met us on the way. [*Enter* OSWALD.] Now,
    where's your master?
    Osw. Madam, within; but never man so
    chang'd.
I told him of the army that was landed;   4
He smil'd at it: I told him you were coming;
His answer was, 'The worse:' of Gloucester's
    treachery,
And of the loyal service of his son,
When I inform'd him, then he call'd me sot, 8
And told me I had turn'd the wrong side out:
What most he should dislike seems pleasant to
    him;
What like, offensive.
    Gon. [*To* EDMUND.] Then, shall you go no
    further.
It is the cowish terror of his spirit   12
That dares not undertake; he'll not feel wrongs
Which tie him to an answer. Our wishes on the
    way
May prove effects. Back, Edmund, to my
    brother;
Hasten his musters and conduct his powers: 16
I must change arms at home, and give the dis-
    taff
Into my husband's hands. This trusty servant
Shall pass between us; ere long you are like to
    hear,
If you dare venture in your own behalf,   20
A mistress's command. Wear this; spare
    speech;   [*Giving a favour.*
Decline your head: this kiss, if it durst speak,
Would stretch thy spirits up into the air.
Conceive, and fare thee well.   24
    Edm. Yours in the ranks of death.
    Gon.   My most dear Gloucester!
    [*Exit* EDMUND.
O! the difference of man and man!
To thee a woman's services are due:
My fool usurps my bed.

    Osw. Madam, here comes my lord. [*Exit.*

Enter ALBANY.

    Gon. I have been worth the whistle.
    Alb.   O Goneril! 29
You are not worth the dust which the rude
    wind
Blows in your face. I fear your disposition:
That nature, which contemns its origin,   32
Cannot be border'd certain in itself;
She that herself will sliver and disbranch
From her material sap, perforce must wither
And come to deadly use.   36
    Gon. No more; the text is foolish.
    Alb. Wisdom and goodness to the vile seem
    vile;
Filths savour but themselves. What have you
done?
Tigers, not daughters, what have you perform'd?
A father, and a gracious aged man,   41
Whose reverence the head-lugg'd bear would lick,
Most barbarous, most degenerate! have you
    madded.
Could my good brother suffer you to do it? 44
A man, a prince, by him so benefited!
If that the heavens do not their visible spirits
Send quickly down to tame these vile offences,
It will come,   48
Humanity must perforce prey on itself,
Like monsters of the deep.
    Gon.   Milk-liver'd man!
That bear'st a cheek for blows, a head for
    wrongs;
Who hast not in thy brows an eye discerning 52
Thine honour from thy suffering; that not
    know'st
Fools do those villains pity who are punish'd
Ere they have done their mischief. Where's thy
    drum?
France spreads his banners in our noiseless
    land,   56
With plumed helm thy slayer begins threats,
Whilst thou, a moral fool, sitt'st still, and criest
'Alack! why does he so?'
    Alb.   See thyself, devil!
Proper deformity seems not in the fiend   60
So horrid as in woman.
    Gon.   O vain fool!
    Alb. Thou changed and self-cover'd thing,
    for shame,
Be-monster not thy feature. Were't my fitness
To let these hands obey my blood,   64
They are apt enough to dislocate and tear
Thy flesh and bones; howe'er thou art a fiend,
A woman's shape doth shield thee.
    Gon. Marry, your manhood.—Mew!   68

Enter a Messenger.

    Alb. What news?
    Mess. O! my good lord, the Duke of Corn-
    wall's dead;
Slain by his servant, going to put out
The other eye of Gloucester.
    Alb.   Gloucester's eyes! 72
    Mess. A servant that he bred, thrill'd with
    remorse,

Oppos'd against the act, bending his sword
To his great master; who, thereat enrag'd,
Flew on him, and amongst them fell'd him
  dead; 76
But not without that harmful stroke, which
  since
Hath pluck'd him after.
   Alb.   This shows you are above,
You justicers, that these our nether crimes
So speedily can venge! But, O poor Gloucester!
Lost he his other eye?
   Mess.   Both, both, my lord. 81
This letter, madam, craves a speedy answer;
'Tis from your sister.
   Gon.   [*Aside.*] One way I like this well;
But being widow, and my Gloucester with her,
May all the building in my fancy pluck 85
Upon my hateful life: another way,
This news is not so tart. [*To* Messenger.] I'll
  read and answer.   [*Exit.*
   Alb. Where was his son when they did take
  his eyes? 88
   Mess. Come with my lady hither.
   Alb.   He is not here.
   Mess. No, my good lord; I met him back
  again.
   Alb. Knows he the wickedness?
   Mess. Ay, my good lord; 'twas he inform'd
  against him, 92
And quit the house on purpose that their punishment
Might have the freer course.
   Alb.   Gloucester, I live
To thank thee for the love thou show'dst the
  king,
And to revenge thine eyes. Come hither, friend:
Tell me what more thou knowest.   [*Exeunt.*

SCENE III.—*The French Camp, near Dover.*

Enter KENT *and a* Gentleman.

   Kent. Why the King of France is so suddenly
gone back know you the reason?
   Gent. Something he left imperfect in the
state, which since his coming forth is thought
of; which imports to the kingdom so much fear
and danger, that his personal return was most
required and necessary. 7
   Kent. Who hath he left behind him general?
   Gent. The Marshal of France, Monsieur la
Far.
   Kent. Did your letters pierce the queen to
any demonstration of grief? 12
   Gent. Ay, sir; she took them, read them in
my presence;
And now and then an ample tear trill'd down
Her delicate cheek; it seem'd she was a queen
Over her passion; who, most rebel-like, 16
Sought to be king o'er her.
   Kent.   O! then it mov'd her.
   Gent. Not to a rage; patience and sorrow
strove
Who should express her goodliest. You have
  seen
Sunshine and rain at once; her smiles and tears
Were like a better way; those happy smilets 21

That play'd on her ripe lip seem'd not to know
What guests were in her eyes; which parted
  thence,
As pearls from diamonds dropp'd. In brief, 24
Sorrow would be a rarity most belov'd,
If all could so become it.
   Kent.   Made she no verbal question?
   Gent. Faith, once or twice she heav'd the
  name of 'father'
Pantingly forth, as if it press'd her heart; 28
Cried, 'Sisters! sisters! Shame of ladies! sisters!
Kent! father! sisters! What, i' the storm? i' the
  night?
Let pity not be believed!' There she shook
The holy water from her heavenly eyes, 32
And clamour-moisten'd, then away she started
To deal with grief alone.
   Kent.   It is the stars,
The stars above us, govern our conditions;
Else one self mate and make could not beget 36
Such different issues. You spoke not with her
since?
   Gent. No.
   Kent. Was this before the king return'd?
   Gent.   No, since.
   Kent. Well, sir, the poor distress'd Lear's
  i' the town, 40
Who sometime, in his better tune, remembers
What we are come about, and by no means
Will yield to see his daughter.
   Gent.   Why, good sir?
   Kent. A sovereign shame so elbows him: his
  own unkindness, 44
That stripp'd her from his benediction, turn'd
  her
To foreign casualties, gave her dear rights
To his dog-hearted daughters,—these things
  sting
His mind so venomously that burning shame
Detains him from Cordelia.
   Gent.   Alack! poor gentleman. 49
   Kent. Of Albany's and Cornwall's powers
  you heard not?
   Gent. 'Tis so, they are afoot.
   Kent. Well, sir, I'll bring you to our master
  Lear, 52
And leave you to attend him. Some dear cause
Will in concealment wrap me up awhile;
When I am known aright, you shall not grieve
Lending me this acquaintance. I pray you, go
Along with me.   [*Exeunt.*

SCENE IV.—*The Same. A Tent.*

Enter with drum and colours, CORDELIA, Doctor,
and Soldiers.

   Cor. Alack! 'tis he: why, he was met even now
As mad as the vex'd sea; singing aloud;
Crown'd with rank fumiter and furrow weeds,
With burdocks, hemlock, nettles, cuckoo-
  flowers, 4
Darnel, and all the idle weeds that grow
In our sustaining corn. A century send forth;
Search every acre in the high-grown field,
And bring him to our eye. [*Exit an* Officer.
                  What can man's wisdom 8

In the restoring his bereaved sense?
He that helps him take all my outward worth.
  Doc. There is means, madam;
Our foster-nurse of nature is repose,   12
The which he lacks; that to provoke in him,
Are many simples operative, whose power
Will close the eye of anguish.
  Cor.   All bless'd secrets,
All you unpublish'd virtues of the earth,   16
Spring with my tears! be aidant and remediate
In the good man's distress! Seek, seek for him,
Lest his ungovern'd rage dissolve the life
That wants the means to lead it.

Enter a Messenger.

  Mess.   News, madam; 20
The British powers are marching hitherward.
  Cor. 'Tis known before; our preparation stands
In expectation of them. O dear father!
It is thy business that I go about;   24
Therefore great France
My mourning and important tears hath pitied,
No blown ambition doth our arms incite,
But love, dear love, and our ag'd father's right,
Soon may I hear and see him!   [*Exeunt.*

SCENE V.—*A Room in* GLOUCESTER'S *Castle.*

Enter REGAN *and* OSWALD.

  Reg. But are my brother's powers set forth?
  Osw.   Ay, madam.
  Reg. Himself in person there?
  Osw.   Madam, with much ado:
Your sister is the better soldier.
  Reg. Lord Edmund spake not with your lord
    at home?   4
  Osw. No, madam.
  Reg. What might import my sister's letter
    to him?
  Osw. I know not, lady.
  Reg. Faith, he is posted hence on serious
    matter.   8
It was great ignorance, Gloucester's eyes being
    out,
To let him live; where he arrives he moves
All hearts against us. Edmund, I think, is gone,
In pity of his misery, to dispatch   12
His nighted life; moreover, to descry
The strength o' the enemy.
  Osw. I must needs after him, madam, with
    my letter.
  Reg. Our troops set forth to-morrow; stay
    with us,   16
The ways are dangerous.
  Osw.   I may not, madam;
My lady charg'd my duty in this business.
  Reg. Why should she write to Edmund?
    Might not you
Transport her purposes by word? Belike,   20
Something—I know not what. I'll love thee
    much,
Let me unseal the letter.
  Osw.   Madam, I had rather—
  Reg. I know your lady does not love her
    husband;

I am sure of that: and at her late being here 24
She gave strange œilliades and most speaking
    looks
To noble Edmund. I know you are of her bosom.
  Osw. I, madam!
  Reg. I speak in understanding; you are, I
    know't: 28
Therefore I do advise you, take this note:
My lord is dead; Edmund and I have talk'd,
And more convenient is he for my hand
Than for your lady's. You may gather more. 32
If you do find him, pray you, give him this,
And when your mistress hears thus much from
    you,
I pray desire her call her wisdom to her:
So, fare you well.   36
If you do chance to hear of that blind traitor,
Preferment falls on him that cuts him off.
  Osw. Would I could meet him, madam: I
    would show
What party I do follow.
  Reg.   Fare thee well. [*Exeunt.*

SCENE VI.—*The Country near Dover.*

Enter GLOUCESTER, *and* EDGAR *dressed like a
peasant.*

  Glo. When shall I come to the top of that
    same hill?
  Edg. You do climb up it now; look how we
    labour.
  Glo. Methinks the ground is even.
  Edg.   Horrible steep:
Hark! do you hear the sea?
  Glo.   No, truly.   4
  Edg. Why, then your other senses grow im-
    perfect
By your eyes' anguish.
  Glo.   So may it be, indeed.
Methinks thy voice is alter'd, and thou speak'st
In better phrase and matter than thou didst. 8
  Edg. Y'are much deceiv'd; in nothing am I
    chang'd
But in my garments.
  Glo.   Methinks you're better spoken.
  Edg. Come on, sir; here's the place: stand
    still.
How fearful   12
And dizzy 'tis to cast one's eyes so low!
The crows and choughs that wing the midway air
Show scarce so gross as beetles; half way down
Hangs one that gathers samphire, dreadful
    trade!   16
Methinks he seems no bigger than his head.
The fishermen that walk upon the beach
Appear like mice, and yond tall anchoring bark
Diminish'd to her cock, her cock a buoy   20
Almost too small for sight. The murmuring
    surge,
That on the unnumber'd idle pebbles chafes,
Cannot be heard so high. I'll look no more,
Lest my brain turn, and the deficient sight 24
Topple down headlong.
  Glo.   Set me where you stand.
  Edg. Give me your hand; you are now within
    a foot

Of the extreme verge: for all beneath the moon
Would I not leap upright.
Glo. Let go my hand. 28
Here, friend, 's another purse; in it a jewel
Well worth a poor man's taking: fairies and
gods
Prosper it with thee! Go thou further off;
Bid me farewell, and let me hear thee going. 32
Edg. Now fare you well, good sir.
Glo. With all my heart.
Edg. Why I do trifle thus with his despair
Is done to cure it.
Glo. O you mighty gods!
This world I do renounce, and, in your sights, 36
Shake patiently my great affliction off;
If I could bear it longer, and not fall
To quarrel with your great opposeless wills,
My snuff and loathed part of nature should 40
Burn itself out. If Edgar live, O, bless him!
Now fellow, fare thee well. [*He falls forward.*
Edg. Gone, sir: farewell.
[*Aside.*] And yet I know not how conceit may
rob
The treasury of life when life itself 44
Yields to the theft; had he been where he thought
By this had thought been past. Alive or dead?
[*To* GLOUCESTER.] Ho, you sir! friend! Hear
you, sir? speak!
Thus might he pass indeed; yet he revives. 48
What are you, sir?
Glo. Away and let me die.
Edg. Hadst thou been aught but gossamer,
feathers, air,
So many fathom down precipitating,
Thou'dst shiver'd like an egg; but thou dost
breathe, 52
Hast heavy substance, bleed'st not, speak'st, art
sound.
Ten masts at each make not the altitude
Which thou hast perpendicularly fell:
Thy life's a miracle. Speak yet again. 56
Glo. But have I fallen or no?
Edg. From the dread summit of this chalky
bourn.
Look up a-height; the shrill-gorg'd lark so far
Cannot be seen or heard: do but look up. 60
Glo. Alack! I have no eyes.
Is wretchedness depriv'd that benefit
To end itself by death? 'Twas yet some comfort,
When misery could beguile the tyrant's rage, 64
And frustrate his proud will.
Edg. Give me your arm:
Up: so. How is't? Feel you your legs? You
stand.
Glo. Too well, too well.
Edg. This is above all strangeness.
Upon the crown o' the cliff, what thing was that
Which parted from you?
Glo. A poor unfortunate beggar. 69
Edg. As I stood here below methought his
eyes
Were two full moons; he had a thousand noses,
Horns whelk'd and wav'd like the enridged sea:
It was some fiend; therefore, thou happy father,
Think that the clearest gods, who make them
honours 74

Of men's impossibilities, have preserv'd thee.
Glo. I do remember now; henceforth I'll bear
Affliction till it do cry out itself 77
'Enough, enough,' and die. That thing you
speak of
I took it for a man; often 'twould say
'The fiend, the fiend:' he led me to that place.
Edg. Bear free and patient thoughts. But
who comes here? 81

Enter LEAR, *fantastically dressed with
flowers.*
The safer sense will ne'er accommodate
His master thus.
Lear. No, they cannot touch me for coining;
I am the king himself. 85
Edg. O thou side-piercing sight!
Lear. Nature's above art in that respect.
There's your press-money. That fellow handles
his bow like a crow-keeper: draw me a clothier's
yard. Look, look! a mouse. Peace, peace!
this piece of toasted cheese will do't. There's
my gauntlet; I'll prove it on a giant. Bring
up the brown bills. O! well flown, bird; i' the
clout, i' the clout: hewgh! Give the word.
Edg. Sweet marjoram.
Lear. Pass. 96
Glo. I know that voice.
Lear. Ha! Goneril, with a white beard!
They flatter'd me like a dog, and told me I had
white hairs in my beard ere the black ones were
there. To say 'ay' and 'no' to everything
I said! 'Ay' and 'no' too was no good divinity. When the rain came to wet me once and
the wind to make me chatter, when the thunder
would not peace at my bidding, there I found
'em, there I smelt 'em out. Go to, they are not
men o' their words: they told me I was every
thing; 'tis a lie, I am not ague-proof. 108
Glo. The trick of that voice I do well re-
member:
Is't not the king?
Lear. Ay, every inch a king:
When I do stare, see how the subject quakes.
I pardon that man's life. What was thy cause? 112
Adultery?
Thou shalt not die: die for adultery! No:
The wren goes to't, and the small gilded fly
Does lecher in my sight. 116
Let copulation thrive; for Gloucester's bastard
son
Was kinder to his father than my daughters
Got 'tween the lawful sheets.
To't luxury, pell-mell! for I lack soldiers. 120
Behold yond simpering dame,
Whose face between her forks presageth snow;
That minces virtue, and does shake the head
To hear of pleasure's name; 124
The fitchew nor the soiled horse goes to't
With a more riotous appetite.
Down from the waist they are Centaurs,
Though women all above: 128
But to the girdle do the gods inherit,
Beneath is all the fiends':
There's hell, there's darkness, there is the sul-
phurous pit, 131

Burning, scalding, stench, consumption; fie, fie,
fie! pah, pah! Give me an ounce of civet, good
apothecary, to sweeten my imagination: there's
money for thee.
　Glo. O! let me kiss that hand!　　　　　136
　Lear. Let me wipe it first; it smells of mortality.
　Glo. O ruin'd piece of nature! This great
world
Shall so wear out to nought. Dost thou know
me?　　　　　139
　Lear. I remember thine eyes well enough.
Dost thou squiny at me? No, do thy worst,
blind Cupid; I'll not love. Read thou this
challenge; mark but the penning of it.
　Glo. Were all the letters suns, I could not see.
　Edg. [*Aside.*] I would not take this from report; it is,　　　　　145
And my heart breaks at it.
　Lear. Read.
　Glo. What! with the case of eyes?　　　　　148
　Lear. O, ho! are you there with me? No
eyes in your head, nor no money in your purse?
Your eyes are in a heavy case, your purse in a
light: yet you see how this world goes.　　　　　152
　Glo. I see it feelingly.
　Lear. What! art mad? A man may see how
this world goes with no eyes. Look with thine
ears: see how yond justice rails upon yon simple
thief. Hark, in thine ear: change places; and,
handy-dandy, which is the justice, which is the
thief? Thou hast seen a farmer's dog bark at a
beggar?　　　　　160
　Glo. Ay, sir.
　Lear. And the creature run from the cur?
There thou mightst behold the great image of
authority; a dog's obey'd in office.　　　　　164
Thou rascal beadle, hold thy bloody hand!
Why dost thou lash that whore? Strip thine
own back;
Thou hotly lust'st to use her in that kind
For which thou whipp'st her. The usurer hangs
the cozener.　　　　　168
Through tatter'd clothes small vices do appear;
Robes and furr'd gowns hide all. Plate sin with
gold,
And the strong lance of justice hurtless breaks;
Arm it in rags, a pigmy's straw doth pierce it.
None does offend, none, I say none; I'll able
'em:　　　　　173
Take that of me, my friend, who have the power
To seal the accuser's lips. Get thee glass eyes;
And, like a scurvy politician, seem　　　　　176
To see the things thou dost not. Now, now,
now, now;
Pull off my boots; harder, harder; so.
　Edg. [*Aside.*] O! matter and impertinency
mix'd;
Reason in madness!　　　　　180
　Lear. If thou wilt weep my fortunes, take
my eyes;
I know thee well enough; thy name is Gloucester:
Thou must be patient; we came crying hither:
Thou know'st the first time that we smell the air 184
We waul and cry. I will preach to thee: mark.

　Glo. Alack! alack the day!
　Lear. When we are born, we cry that we are
come
To this great stage of fools. This' a good block!
It were a delicate stratagem to shoe　　　　　189
A troop of horse with felt; I'll put it in proof,
And when I have stol'n upon these sons-in-law,
Then, kill, kill, kill, kill, kill, kill!　　　　　192

Enter Gentleman, *with* Attendants.

　Gent. O! here he is; lay hand upon him. Sir,
Your most dear daughter—
　Lear. No rescue? What! a prisoner? I am
even
The natural fool of fortune. Use me well; 196
You shall have ransom. Let me have surgeons;
I am cut to the brains.
　Gent.　　　　　You shall have any thing.
　Lear. No seconds? All myself?
Why this would make a man a man of salt, 200
To use his eyes for garden water-pots,
Ay, and laying autumn's dust.
　Gent.　　　　　Good sir,—
　Lear. I will die bravely as a bridegroom.
What!
I will be jovial: come, come; I am a king, 204
My masters, know you that?
　Gent. You are a royal one, and we obey you.
　Lear. Then there's life in it. Nay, an you
get it, you shall get it by running. Sa, sa, sa, sa.
　　　　　[*Exit.* Attendants *follow.*
　Gent. A sight most pitiful in the meanest
wretch,　　　　　209
Past speaking of in a king! Thou hast one
daughter,
Who redeems nature from the general curse
Which twain have brought her to.　　　　　212
　Edg. Hail, gentle sir!
　Gent.　　　　　Sir, speed you: what's your will?
　Edg. Do you hear aught, sir, of a battle
toward?
　Gent. Most sure and vulgar; every one hears
that,
Which can distinguish sound.
　Edg.　　　　　But, by your favour, 216
How near's the other army?
　Gent. Near, and on speedy foot; the main
descry
Stands on the hourly thought.
　Edg.　　　　　I thank you, sir: that's all.
　Gent. Though that the queen on special cause
is here,　　　　　220
Her army is mov'd on.
　Edg.　　　　　I thank you, sir.
　　　　　[*Exit* Gentleman.
　Glo. You ever-gentle gods, take my breath
from me:
Let not my worser spirit tempt me again
To die before you please!
　Edg.　　　　　Well pray you, father. 224
　Glo. Now, good sir, what are you?
　Edg. A most poor man, made tame to fortune's blows;
Who, by the art of known and feeling sorrows,
Am pregnant to good pity. Give me your hand
I'll lead you to some biding.

Glo. Hearty thanks: 229
The bounty and the benison of heaven
To boot, and boot!

Enter OSWALD.

Osw. A proclaim'd prize! Most happy!
That eyeless head of thine was first fram'd flesh
To raise my fortunes. Thou old unhappy
traitor, 233
Briefly thyself remember: the sword is out
That must destroy thee.
Glo. Now let thy friendly hand
Put strength enough to 't. [EDGAR *interposes.*
Osw. Wherefore, bold peasant, 236
Dar'st thou support a publish'd traitor? Hence;
Lest that infection of his fortune take
Like hold on thee. Let go his arm.
Edg. Chill not let go, zur, without vurther
'casion. 241
Osw. Let go, slave, or thou diest.
Edg. Good gentleman, go your gait, and let
poor volk pass. An chud ha' bin zwaggered
out of my life, 'twould not ha' bin zo long as
'tis by a vortnight. Nay, come not near th' old
man; keep out, che vor ye, or ise try whether
your costard or my ballow be the harder. Chill
be plain with you. 249
Osw. Out, dunghill!
Edg. Chill pick your teeth, zur. Come; no
matter vor your foins. 252
[*They fight and* EDGAR *knocks him down.*
Osw. Slave, thou hast slain me. Villain, take
my purse.
If ever thou wilt thrive, bury my body;
And give the letters which thou find'st about me
To Edmund Earl of Gloucester; seek him out
Upon the English party: O! untimely death. 257
[*Dies.*
Edg. I know thee well: a serviceable villain;
As duteous to the vices of thy mistress
As badness would desire.
Glo. What! is he dead? 260
Edg. Sit you down, father; rest you.
Let's see his pockets: these letters that he speaks
of
May be my friends. He's dead; I am only sorry
He had no other deaths-man. Let us see: 264
Leave, gentle wax; and, manners, blame us not:
To know our enemies' minds, we'd rip their
hearts;
Their papers, is more lawful.

*Let our reciprocal vows be remembered. You
have many opportunities to cut him off; if
your will want not, time and place will be
fruitfully offered. There is nothing done if he
return the conqueror; then am I the prisoner,
and his bed my goal; from the loathed warmth
whereof deliver me, and supply the place for
your labour.*

Your—wife, so I would say— 276
Affectionate servant,
GONERIL.

O undistinguish'd space of woman's will!
A plot upon her virtuous husband's life, 280
And the exchange my brother! Here, in the
sands,

Thee I'll rake up, the post unsanctified
Of murderous lechers; and in the mature time
With this ungracious paper strike the sight 284
Of the death-practis'd duke. For him 'tis well
That of thy death and business I can tell.
Glo. The king is mad: how stiff is my vile
sense,
That I stand up, and have ingenious feeling 288
Of my huge sorrows! Better I were distract:
So should my thoughts be sever'd from my
griefs,
And woes by wrong imaginations lose
The knowledge of themselves. [*Drums afar off.*
Edg. Give me your hand: 292
Far off, methinks, I hear the beaten drum.
Come, father, I'll bestow you with a friend.
[*Exeunt.*

SCENE VII.—*A Tent in the French Camp.*

Enter CORDELIA, KENT, Doctor, *and* Gentleman.

Cor. O thou good Kent! how shall I live and
work
To match thy goodness? My life will be too
short,
And every measure fail me.
Kent. To be acknowledg'd, madam, is o'er-
paid. 4
All my reports go with the modest truth,
Nor more nor clipp'd, but so.
Cor. Be better suited:
These weeds are memories of those worser
hours:
I prithee, put them off.
Kent. Pardon me, dear madam; 8
Yet to be known shortens my made intent:
My boon I make it that you know me not
Till time and I think meet.
Cor. Then be 't so, my good lord.—[*To the
Doctor.*] How does the king? 12
Doc. Madam, sleeps still.
Cor. O you kind gods,
Cure this great breach in his abused nature!
The untun'd and jarring senses, O! wind up 16
Of this child-changed father!
Doc. So please your majesty
That we may wake the king? he hath slept long.
Cor. Be govern'd by your knowledge, and
proceed
I' the sway of your own will. Is he array'd? 20

Enter LEAR *in his chair, carried by*
Servants.

Gent. Ay, madam; in the heaviness of sleep,
We put fresh garments on him.
Doc. Be by, good madam, when we do awake
him;
I doubt not of his temperance.
Cor. Very well. [*Music.*
Doc. Please you, draw near. Louder the
music there. 25
Cor. O my dear father! Restoration, hang
Thy medicine on my lips, and let this kiss
Repair those violent harms that my two sisters
Have in thy reverence made!
Kent. Kind and dear princess! 29

Cor. Had you not been their father, these
     white flakes
Had challeng'd pity of them. Was this a face
To be expos'd against the warring winds?   32
To stand against the deep dread-bolted thunder?
In the most terrible and nimble stroke
Of quick cross lightning? to watch—poor
     perdu!—
With this thin helm? Mine enemy's dog,   36
Though he had bit me, should have stood that
     night
Against my fire. And wast thou fain, poor
     father,
To hovel thee with swine and rogues forlorn,
In short and musty straw? Alack, alack!   40
'Tis wonder that thy life and wits at once
Had not concluded all. He wakes; speak to
     him.
Doc. Madam, do you; 'tis fittest.
Cor. How does my royal lord? How fares
     your majesty?   44
Lear. You do me wrong to take me out o'
     the grave:
Thou art a soul in bliss; but I am bound
Upon a wheel of fire, that mine own tears
Do scald like molten lead.
Cor.   Sir, do you know me?   48
Lear. You are a spirit, I know; when did
     you die?
Cor. Still, still, far wide.
Doc. He's scarce awake; let him alone awhile.
Lear. Where have I been? Where am I? Fair
     day-light?   52
I am mightily abus'd. I should even die with
     pity
To see another thus. I know not what to say.
I will not swear these are my hands: let's see;
I feel this pin prick. Would I were assur'd   56
Of my condition!
Cor.   O! look upon me, sir,
And hold your hands in benediction o'er me.
No, sir, you must not kneel.
Lear.   Pray, do not mock me:
I am a very foolish fond old man,   60
Fourscore and upward, not an hour more or
     less;
And, to deal plainly,
I fear I am not in my perfect mind.
Methinks I should know you and know this
     man;   64
Yet I am doubtful: for I am mainly ignorant
What place this is, and all the skill I have
Remembers not these garments; nor I know not
Where I did lodge last night. Do not laugh at
     me;   68
For, as I am a man, I think this lady
To be my child Cordelia.
Cor.   And so I am, I am.
Lear. Be your tears wet? Yes, faith. I pray,
     weep not:
If you have poison for me, I will drink it.   72
I know you do not love me; for your sisters
Have, as I do remember, done me wrong:
You have some cause, they have not.
Cor.   No cause, no cause.
Lear. Am I in France?

Kent.   In your own kingdom, sir.
Lear. Do not abuse me.   77
Doc. Be comforted, good madam; the great
     rage,
You see, is kill'd in him; and yet it is danger
To make him even o'er the time he has lost.   80
Desire him to go in; trouble him no more
Till further settling.
Cor. Will't please your highness walk?
Lear.   You must bear with me.
Pray you now, forget and forgive: I am old and
     foolish.   [*Exeunt* LEAR, CORDELIA, DOC-
           TOR, *and* Attendants.
Gent. Holds it true, sir, that the Duke of
Cornwall was so slain?
Kent. Most certain, sir.
Gent. Who is conductor of his people?   88
Kent. As 'tis said, the bastard son of Glouces-
ter.
Gent. They say Edgar, his banished son, is
with the Earl of Kent in Germany.
Kent. Report is changeable. 'Tis time to
look about; the powers of the kingdom
approach apace.   94
Gent. The arbitrement is like to be bloody.
Fare you well, sir.   [*Exit.*
Kent. My point and period will be throughly
wrought,   97
Or well or ill, as this day's battle's fought.
                                   [*Exit.*

ACT V

SCENE I.—*The British Camp near Dover.*

Enter, with drum and colours, EDMUND, REGAN,
     Officers, Soldiers, *and Others.*

Edm. Know of the duke if his last purpose
     hold,
Or whether since he is advis'd by aught
To change the course; he's full of alteration
And self-reproving; bring his constant pleasure.
                 [*To an* Officer, *who goes out.*
Reg. Our sister's man is certainly miscarried.
Edm. 'Tis to be doubted, madam.
Reg.   Now, sweet lord,
You know the goodness I intend upon you:
Tell me, but truly, but then speak the truth,   8
Do you not love my sister?
Edm.   In honour'd love.
Reg. But have you never found my brother's
     way
To the forefended place?
Edm.   That thought abuses you.
Reg. I am doubtful that you have been con-
junct   12
And bosom'd with her, as far as we call hers.
Edm. No, by mine honour, madam.
Reg. I never shall endure her: dear my lord,
Be not familiar with her.
Edm.   Fear me not.   16
She and the duke her husband!

Enter with drums and colours, ALBANY,
     GONERIL, *and* Soldiers.

Gon. [*Aside.*] I had rather lose the battle
than that sister

Should loosen him and me.

Alb. Our very loving sister, well be-met. 20
Sir, this I heard, the king is come to his daughter,
With others; whom the rigour of our state
Forc'd to cry out. Where I could not be honest
I never yet was valiant: for this business, 24
It toucheth us, as France invades our land,
Not bolds the king, with others, whom, I fear,
Most just and heavy causes make oppose.

Edm. Sir, you speak nobly.

Reg.   Why is this reason'd? 28

Gon. Combine together 'gainst the enemy;
For these domestic and particular broils
Are not the question here.

Alb.   Let's then determine
With the ancient of war on our proceeding. 32

Edm. I shall attend you presently at your tent.

Reg. Sister, you'll go with us?

Gon. No.

Reg. 'Tis most convenient; pray you, go
with us.   36

Gon. [*Aside.*] O, ho! I know the riddle.
[*Aloud.*] I will go.

Enter EDGAR, *disguised.*

Edg. If e'er your Grace had speech with man
so poor,
Hear me one word.

Alb.   I'll overtake you. Speak.
[*Exeunt* EDMUND, REGAN, GONERIL, Officers,
           Soldiers, *and* Attendants.

Edg. Before you fight the battle, ope this
letter.   40
If you have victory, let the trumpet sound
For him that brought it: wretched though I
seem,
I can produce a champion that will prove
What is avouched there. If you miscarry, 44
Your business of the world hath so an end,
And machination ceases. Fortune love you!

Alb. Stay till I have read the letter.

Edg.   I was forbid it.
When time shall serve, let but the herald cry, 48
And I'll appear again.

Alb. Why, fare thee well: I will o'erlook thy
paper.   [*Exit* EDGAR.

Re-enter EDMUND.

Edm. The enemy's in view; draw up your
powers.
Here is the guess of their true strength and
forces   52
By diligent discovery; but your haste
Is now urg'd on you.

Alb.   We will greet the time. [*Exit.*

Edm. To both these sisters have I sworn my
love;
Each jealous of the other, as the stung 56
Are of the adder. Which of them shall I take?
Both? one? or neither? Neither can be enjoy'd
If both remain alive: to take the widow
Exasperates, makes mad her sister Goneril; 60
And hardly shall I carry out my side,
Her husband being alive. Now then, we'll use
His countenance for the battle; which being done
Let her who would be rid of him devise 64

His speedy taking off. As for the mercy
Which he intends to Lear, and to Cordelia,
The battle done, and they within our power,
Shall never see his pardon; for my state 68
Stands on me to defend, not to debate. [*Exit.*

SCENE II.—*A Field between the two Camps.*

Alarum within. Enter, with drum and colours,
   LEAR, CORDELIA, *and their Forces; and exeunt.*
Enter EDGAR *and* GLOUCESTER.

Edg. Here, father, take the shadow of this
tree
For your good host; pray that the right may thrive.
If ever I return to you again,
I'll bring you comfort.

Glo.   Grace go with you, sir!
                          [*Exit* EDGAR.

Alarum; afterwards a retreat. Re-enter
           EDGAR.

Edg. Away, old man! give me thy hand;
away!
King Lear hath lost, he and his daughter ta'en:
Give me thy hand; come on.

Glo. No further, sir; a man may rot even
here.

Edg. What! in ill thoughts again? Men must
endure
Their going hence, even as their coming hither:
Ripeness is all. Come on.

Glo.   And that's true too.
                          [*Exeunt.*

SCENE III.—*The British Camp, near Dover.*

Enter, in conquest, with drum and colours,
   EDMUND; LEAR *and* CORDELIA, *prisoners;*
   Officers, Soldiers, &c.

Edm. Some officers take them away: good
guard,
Until their greater pleasures first be known
That are to censure them.

Cor.   We are not the first
Who, with best meaning, have incurr'd the
worst.
For thee, oppressed king, am I cast down;
Myself could else out-frown false Fortune's
frown.
Shall we not see these daughters and these
sisters?

Lear. No, no, no, no! Come, let's away to
prison;
We two alone will sing like birds i' the cage:
When thou dost ask me blessing, I'll kneel down
And ask of thee forgiveness: so we'll live,
And pray, and sing, and tell old tales, and
laugh   12
At gilded butterflies, and hear poor rogues
Talk of court news; and we'll talk with them
too,
Who loses and who wins; who's in, who's out;
And take upon's the mystery of things, 16
As if we were God's spies: and we'll wear out,
In a wall'd prison, packs and sets of great ones
That ebb and flow by the moon.

Edm.   Take them away.

Lear. Upon such sacrifices, my Cordelia, 20
The gods themselves throw incense. Have I
    caught thee?
He that parts us shall bring a brand from heaven,
And fire us hence like foxes. Wipe thine eyes;
The goujeers shall devour them, flesh and fell, 24
Ere they shall make us weep: we'll see 'em starve
    first.
Come.   [*Exeunt* LEAR *and* CORDELIA, *guarded.*

Edm. Come hither, captain; hark,
Take thou this note; [*Giving a paper.*] go follow
    them to prison: 28
One step I have advanc'd thee; if thou dost
As this instructs thee, thou dost make thy way
To noble fortunes; know thou this, that men
Are as the time is; to be tender-minded   32
Does not become a sword; thy great employ-
    ment
Will not bear question; either say thou'lt do't,
Or thrive by other means.
Offi.   I'll do't, my lord.
Edm. About it; and write happy when thou
    hast done.   36
Mark,—I say, instantly, and carry it so
As I have set it down.
Offi. I cannot draw a cart nor eat dried oats;
If it be man's work I will do it.   [*Exit.*

Flourish. Enter ALBANY, GONERIL, REGAN,
    Officers, *and* Attendants.

Alb. Sir, you have show'd to-day your valiant
    strain,   41
And fortune led you well; you have the captives
Who were the opposites of this day's strife;
We do require them of you, so to use them 44
As we shall find their merits and our safety
May equally determine.
Edm.   Sir, I thought it fit
To send the old and miserable king
To some retention, and appointed guard; 48
Whose age has charms in it, whose title more,
To pluck the common bosom on his side,
And turn our impress'd lances in our eyes
Which do command them. With him I sent the
    queen;   52
My reason all the same; and they are ready
To-morrow, or at further space, to appear
Where you shall hold your session. At this time
We sweat and bleed; the friend hath lost his
    friend,   56
And the best quarrels, in the heat, are curs'd
By those that feel their sharpness;
The question of Cordelia and her father
Requires a fitter place.
Alb.   Sir, by your patience, 60
I hold you but a subject of this war,
Not as a brother.
Reg.   That's as we list to grace him:
Methinks our pleasure might have been de-
    manded,
Ere you had spoke so far. He led our powers, 64
Bore the commission of my place and person;
The which immediacy may well stand up,
And call itself your brother.
Gon.   Not so hot;

In his own grace he doth exalt himself   68
More than in your addition.
Reg.   In my rights,
By me invested, he compeers the best.
Gon. That were the most, if he should hus-
    band you.
Reg. Jesters do oft prove prophets.
Gon.   Holla, holla! 72
That eye that told you so look'd but a-squint.
Reg. Lady, I am not well; else I should
    answer
From a full-flowing stomach. General,
Take thou my soldiers, prisoners, patrimony; 76
Dispose of them, of me; the walls are thine;
Witness the world, that I create thee here
My lord and master.
Gon.   Mean you to enjoy him?
Alb. The let-alone lies not in your good
    will.   80
Edm. Nor in thine, lord.
Alb.   Half-blooded fellow, yes.
Reg. [*To* EDMUND.] Let the drum strike, and
    prove my title thine.
Alb. Stay yet; hear reason. Edmund, I arrest
    thee
On capital treason; and, in thy arrest,   84
This gilded serpent. [*Pointing to* GONERIL.] For
    your claim, fair sister,
I bar it in the interest of my wife;
'Tis she is sub-contracted to this lord,
And I, her husband, contradict your bans. 88
If you will marry, make your love to me,
My lady is bespoke.
Gon.   An interlude!
Alb. Thou art arm'd, Gloucester; let the
    trumpet sound:
If none appear to prove upon thy person 92
Thy heinous, manifest, and many treasons,
There is my pledge; [*Throws down a glove.*] I'll
    prove it on thy heart,
Ere I taste bread, thou art in nothing less
Than I have here proclaim'd thee.
Reg.   Sick! O sick! 96
Gon. [*Aside.*] If not, I'll ne'er trust medicine.
Edm. There's my exchange: [*Throws down
    a glove.*] what in the world he is
That names me traitor, villain-like he lies.
Call by thy trumpet: he that dares approach,
On him, on you, who not? I will maintain 101
My truth and honour firmly.
Alb. A herald, ho!
Edm.   A herald, ho! a herald!
Alb. Trust to thy single virtue; for thy sol-
    diers,   104
All levied in my name, have in my name
Took their discharge.
Reg.   My sickness grows upon me.
Alb. She is not well; convey her to my tent.
                [*Exit* REGAN, *led.*
Come hither, herald,

Enter a Herald.

         Let the trumpet sound,— 108
And read out this.
Offi. Sound, trumpet! [*A trumpet sounds.*

Her. If any man of quality or degree within
the lists of the army will maintain upon
Edmund, supposed Earl of Gloucester, that he
is a manifold traitor, let him appear at the
third sound of the trumpet. He is bold in his
defence.   116
Edm. Sound!   [*First Trumpet.*
Her. Again!   [*Second Trumpet.*
Her. Again!   [*Third Trumpet.*
                        [*Trumpet answers within.*

Enter EDGAR, *armed, with a Trumpet before
        him.*

Alb. Ask him his purposes, why he appears
Upon this call o' the trumpet.
Her.   What are you? 121
Your name? your quality? and why you answer
This present summons?
Edg.   Know, my name is lost;
By treason's tooth bare-gnawn and canker-bit;
Yet am I noble as the adversary   125
I come to cope.
Alb.   Which is that adversary?
Edg. What's he that speaks for Edmund
Earl of Gloucester?
Edm. Himself: what sayst thou to him?
Edg.   Draw thy sword, 128
That, if my speech offend a noble heart,
Thy arm may do thee justice; here is mine:
Behold, it is the privilege of mine honours,
My oath, and my profession: I protest,   132
Maugre thy strength, youth, place, and emi-
        nence,
Despite thy victor sword and fire-new fortune,
Thy valour and thy heart, thou art a traitor,
False to thy gods, thy brother, and thy father,
Conspirant 'gainst this high illustrious prince,
And, from the extremest upward of thy head
To the descent and dust below thy foot,
A most toad-spotted traitor. Say thou 'No,' 140
This sword, this arm, and my best spirits are
        bent
To prove upon thy heart, whereto I speak,
Thou liest.
Edm.   In wisdom I should ask thy name;
But since thy outside looks so fair and war-like,
And that thy tongue some say of breeding
        breathes,   145
What safe and nicely I might well delay
By rule of knighthood, I disdain and spurn;
Back do I toss these treasons to thy head, 148
With the hell-hated lie o'erwhelm thy heart,
Which, for they yet glance by and scarcely
        bruise,
This sword of mine shall give them instant way,
Where they shall rest for ever. Trumpets,
        speak!   152
        [*Alarums. They fight.* EDMUND *falls.*
Alb. Save him, save him!
Gon.   This is practice, Gloucester:
By the law of arms thou wast not bound to
        answer
An unknown opposite; thou art not vanquish'd,
But cozen'd and beguil'd.
Alb.   Shut your mouth, dame, 156
Or with this paper shall I stop it. Hold, sir;

Thou worse than any name, read thine own evil:
No tearing, lady; I perceive you know it.
                [*Gives the letter to* EDMUND.
Gon. Say, if I do, the laws are mine, not
        thine: 160
Who can arraign me for 't?   [*Exit.*
Alb.   Most monstrous!
Know'st thou this paper?
Edm.   Ask me not what I know.
Alb. Go after her: she's desperate; govern
        her.   [*Exit an Officer.*
Edm. What you have charg'd me with, that
        have I done,   164
And more, much more; the time will bring it
        out:
'Tis past, and so am I. But what art thou
That hast this fortune on me? If thou 'rt noble,
I do forgive thee.
Edg.   Let's exchange charity. 168
I am no less in blood than thou art, Edmund;
If more, the more thou hast wrong'd me.
My name is Edgar, and thy father's son.
The gods are just, and of our pleasant vices 172
Make instruments to plague us:
The dark and vicious place where thee he got
Cost him his eyes.
Edm.   Thou hast spoken right, 'tis true;
The wheel is come full circle; I am here.   176
Alb. Methought thy very gait did prophesy
A royal nobleness: I must embrace thee:
Let sorrow split my heart, if ever I
Did hate thee or thy father.
Edg.   Worthy prince, I know't. 180
Alb. Where have you hid yourself?
How have you known the miseries of your
        father?
Edg. By nursing them, my lord. List a brief
        tale:
And, when 'tis told, O! that my heart would
        burst,   184
The bloody proclamation to escape
That follow'd me so near,—O! our lives' sweet-
        ness,
That we the pain of death would hourly die
Rather than die at once!—taught me to shift 188
Into a madman's rags, to assume a semblance
That very dogs disdain'd: and in this habit
Met I my father with his bleeding rings,
Their precious stones new lost; became his
        guide,   192
Led him, begg'd for him, sav'd him from de-
        spair;
Never,—O fault!—reveal'd myself unto him,
Until some half hour past, when I was arm'd;
Not sure, though hoping, of this good success,
I ask'd his blessing, and from first to last 197
Told him my pilgrimage: but his flaw'd heart,—
Alack! too weak the conflict to support;
'Twixt two extremes of passion, joy and grief,
Burst smilingly.
Edm. This speech of yours hath mov'd me
And shall perchance do good; but speak you
        on;   202
You look as you had something more to say
Alb. If there be more, more woeful, hold i
        in;   20

For I am almost ready to dissolve,
Hearing of this.
   Edg.   This would have seem'd a period
To such as love not sorrow; but another,
To amplify too much, would make much more,
And top extremity.   209
Whilst I was big in clamour came there a man,
Who, having seen me in my worst estate,
Shunn'd my abhorr'd society; but then, finding
Who 'twas that so endur'd, with his strong arms
He fasten'd on my neck, and bellow'd out
As he'd burst heaven; threw him on my father;
Told the most piteous tale of Lear and him 216
That ever ear receiv'd; which in recounting
His grief grew puissant, and the strings of life
Began to crack: twice then the trumpet sounded,
And there I left him tranc'd.
   Alb.   But who was this? 220
   Edg. Kent, sir, the banish'd Kent; who in
disguise
Follow'd his enemy king, and did him service
Improper for a slave.

Enter a Gentleman, *with a bloody knife.*

   Gent. Help, help! O help!
   Edg.   What kind of help?
   Alb.   Speak, man. 224
   Edg. What means that bloody knife?
   Kent.   'Tis hot, it smokes;
It came even from the heart of—O! she's dead.
   Alb. Who dead? speak, man.
   Gent. Your lady, sir, your lady: and her
sister   228
By her is poison'd; she confesses it.
   Edm. I was contracted to them both: all
three
Now marry in an instant.
   Edg.   Here comes Kent.
   Alb. Produce the bodies, be they alive or
dead: 232
This judgment of the heavens, that makes us
tremble,
Touches us not with pity.   [*Exit* Gentleman.

Enter KENT.

               O! is this he?
The time will not allow the compliment
Which very manners urges.
   Kent.   I am come   236
To bid my king and master aye good-night;
Is he not here?
   Alb.   Great thing of us forgot!
Speak, Edmund, where's the king? and where's
Cordelia?
Seest thou this object, Kent?   240
   [*The bodies of* GONERIL *and* REGAN
                  are brought in.
   Kent. Alack! why thus?
   Edm.   Yet Edmund was belov'd:
The one the other poison'd for my sake,
And after slew herself.
   Alb. Even so. Cover their faces.   244
   Edm. I pant for life: some good I mean to do
Despite of mine own nature. Quickly send,
Be brief in it, to the castle; for my writ
Is on the life of Lear and on Cordelia.   248

Nay, send in time.
   Alb.   Run, run! O run!
   Edg. To whom, my lord? Who has the office?
send
Thy token of reprieve.
   Edm. Well thought on: take my sword, 252
Give it the captain.
   Alb.   Haste thee, for thy life.
                     [*Exit* EDGAR.
   Edm. He hath commission from thy wife and
me
To hang Cordelia in the prison, and
To lay the blame upon her own despair,   256
That she fordid herself.
   Alb. The gods defend her! Bear him hence
awhile.   [EDMUND *is borne off.*

Enter LEAR, *with* CORDELIA *dead in his arms;*
   EDGAR, Officer, *and Others.*

   Lear. Howl, howl, howl, howl! O! you are
men of stones:
Had I your tongues and eyes, I'd use them so
That heaven's vaults should crack. She's gone
for ever.   261
I know when one is dead, and when one lives;
She's dead as earth. Lend me a looking-glass;
If that her breath will mist or stain the stone,
Why, then she lives.
   Kent.   Is this the promis'd end? 265
   Edg. Or image of that horror?
   Alb.   Fall and cease?
   Lear. This feather stirs; she lives! if it be so,
It is a chance which does redeem all sorrows 268
That ever I have felt.
   Kent. [*Kneeling.*] O, my good master!
   Lear. Prithee, away.
   Edg.   'Tis noble Kent, your friend.
   Lear. A plague upon you, murderers, traitors
all!
I might have sav'd her; now, she's gone for ever!
Cordelia, Cordelia! stay a little. Ha!   273
What is 't thou sayst? Her voice was ever soft,
Gentle and low, an excellent thing in woman.
I kill'd the slave that was a hanging thee.   276
   Off. 'Tis true, my lord, he did.
   Lear.   Did I not, fellow?
I have seen the day, with my good biting falchion
I would have made them skip: I am old now,
And these same crosses spoil me. Who are you?
Mine eyes are not o' the best: I'll tell you
straight.   281
   Kent. If fortune brag of two she lov'd and
hated,
One of them we behold.
   Lear. This is a dull sight. Are you not Kent?
   Kent.   The same, 284
Your servant Kent. Where is your servant
Caius?
   Lear. He's a good fellow, I can tell you that;
He'll strike, and quickly too. He's dead and
rotten.
   Kent. No, my good lord; I am the very
man—   289
   Lear. I'll see that straight.
   Kent. That, from your first of difference and
decay,

Have follow'd your sad steps.

Lear.   You are welcome hither.

Kent. Nor no man else; all 's cheerless, dark,
and deadly;   292
Your eldest daughters have fordone themselves,
And desperately are dead.

Lear.   Ay, so I think.

Alb. He knows not what he says, and vain
it is
That we present us to him.

Edg   Very bootless. 296

Enter an Officer.

Off. Edmund is dead, my lord.

Alb.   That's but a trifle here.
You lords and noble friends, know our in-
tent;
What comfort to this great decay may come
Shall be applied: for us, we will resign,   300
During the life of this old majesty,
To him our absolute power:—[*To* EDGAR *and*
KENT.] You, to your rights;
With boot and such addition as your honours
Have more than merited. All friends shall taste
The wages of their virtue, and all foes   305
The cup of their deservings. O! see, see!

Lear. And my poor fool is hang'd! No, no,
no life!
Why should a dog, a horse, a rat, have life, 308

And thou no breath at all? Thou'lt come no
more,
Never, never, never, never, never!
Pray you, undo this button: thank you, sir.
Do you see this? Look on her, look, her lips, 312
Look there, look there!   [*Dies.*

Edg.   He faints!—my lord, my lord!

Kent. Break, heart; I prithee, break.

Edg.   Look up, my lord.

Kent. Vex not his ghost: O! let him pass;
he hates him
That would upon the rack of this tough world
Stretch him out longer.

Edg.   He is gone, indeed. 317

Kent. The wonder is he hath endur'd so long:
He but usurp'd his life.

Alb. Bear them from hence. Our present
business   320
Is general woe. [*To* KENT *and* EDGAR.] Friends
of my soul, you twain
Rule in this realm, and the gor'd state sustain.

Kent. I have a journey, sir, shortly to go;
My master calls me, I must not say no.   324

Alb. The weight of this sad time we must
obey;
Speak what we feel, not what we ought to say.
The oldest hath borne most: we that are young,
Shall never see so much, nor live so long. 328

[*Exeunt, with a dead march.*

OTHELLO

THE MOOR OF VENICE

DRAMATIS PERSONÆ

DUKE OF VENICE.
BRABANTIO, a Senator. Other Senators.
GRATIANO, Brother to Brabantio.
LODOVICO, Kinsman to Brabantio.
OTHELLO, a noble Moor; in the service of the Venetian State.
CASSIO, his Lieutenant.
IAGO, his Ancient.
RODERIGO, a Venetian Gentleman.
MONTANO, Othello's predecessor in the Government of Cyprus.

Clown, Servant to Othello.

DESDEMONA, Daughter to Brabantio, and Wife to Othello.
EMILIA, Wife to Iago.
BIANCA, Mistress to Cassio.

Sailor, Officers, Gentlemen, Messengers, Musicians, Heralds, Attendants.

SCENE.—*For the first Act, in Venice; during the rest of the Play, at a Sea-Port in Cyprus.*

ACT I

SCENE I.—*Venice. A Street.*

Enter RODERIGO *and* IAGO.

Rod. Tush! Never tell me; I take it much unkindly
That thou, Iago, who hast had my purse
As if the strings were thine, shouldst know of this.
Iago. 'Sblood, but you will not hear me: 4
If ever I did dream of such a matter,
Abhor me.
Rod. Thou told'st me thou didst hold him in thy hate.
Iago. Despise me if I do not. Three great ones of the city, 8
In personal suit to make me his lieutenant,
Off-capp'd to him; and, by the faith of man,
I know my price, I am worth no worse a place;
But he, as loving his own pride and purposes, 12
Evades them, with a bombast circumstance
Horribly stuff'd with epithets of war;
And, in conclusion,
Nonsuits my mediators; for, 'Certes,' says he, 16
'I have already chose my officer.'
And what was he?
Forsooth, a great arithmetician,
One Michael Cassio, a Florentine, 20
A fellow almost damn'd in a fair wife;
That never set a squadron in the field,
Nor the division of a battle knows
More than a spinster; unless the bookish theoric, 24
Wherein the toged consuls can propose 25
As masterly as he: mere prattle, without practice,
Is all his soldiership. But he, sir, had the election;
And I—of whom his eyes had seen the proof 28
At Rhodes, at Cyprus,—and on other grounds
Christian and heathen—must be be-lee'd and calm'd

By debitor and creditor; this counter-caster,
He, in good time, must his lieutenant be, 32
And I—God bless the mark!—his Moorship's ancient.
Rod. By heaven, I rather would have been his hangman.
Iago. Why, there's no remedy: 'tis the curse of the service,
Preferment goes by letter and affection, 36
Not by the old gradation, where each second
Stood heir to the first. Now, sir, be judge yourself,
Whe'r I in any just term am affin'd
To love the Moor.
Rod.   I would not follow him then. 40
Iago. O! sir, content you;
I follow him to serve my turn upon him;
We cannot all be masters, nor all masters
Cannot be truly follow'd. You shall mark 44
Many a duteous and knee-crooking knave,
That, doting on his own obsequious bondage,
Wears out his time, much like his master's ass,
For nought but provender, and when he's old, cashier'd; 48
Whip me such honest knaves. Others there are
Who, trimm'd in forms and visages of duty,
Keep yet their hearts attending on themselves,
And, throwing but shows of service on their lords, 52
Do well thrive by them, and when they have lin'd their coats
Do themselves homage: these fellows have some soul;
And such a one do I profess myself. For, sir, 56
It is as sure as you are Roderigo,
Were I the Moor, I would not be Iago:
In following him, I follow but myself;
Heaven is my judge, not I for love and duty, 60
But seeming so, for my peculiar end:
For when my outward action doth demonstrate
The native act and figure of my heart

In compliment extern, 'tis not long after
But I will wear my heart upon my sleeve 64
For daws to peck at: I am not what I am.

Rod. What a full fortune does the thick-lips
owe,
If he can carry 't thus!

Iago. Call up her father; 67
Rouse him, make after him, poison his delight,
Proclaim him in the streets, incense her kins-
men,
And, though he in a fertile climate dwell,
Plague him with flies; though that his joy be joy,
Yet throw such changes of vexation on 't 72
As it may lose some colour.

Rod. Here is her father's house; I'll call aloud.

Iago. Do; with like timorous accent and dire
yell
As when, by night and negligence, the fire 76
Is spied in populous cities.

Rod. What, ho! Brabantio! Signior Brabantio, ho!

Iago. Awake! what, ho! Brabantio! thieves!
thieves! thieves!
Look to your house, your daughter, and your
bags! 80
Thieves! thieves!

Enter BRABANTIO, *above, at a window.*

Bra. What is the reason of this terrible summons?
What is the matter there?

Rod. Signior, is all your family within? 84

Iago. Are your doors lock'd?

Bra. Why? wherefore ask you this?

Iago. 'Zounds! sir, you're robb'd; for shame,
put on your gown;
Your heart is burst, you have lost half your soul;
Even now, now, very now, an old black ram 88
Is tupping your white ewe. Arise, arise!
Awake the snorting citizens with the bell,
Or else the devil will make a grandsire of you.
Arise, I say.

Bra. What! have you lost your wits? 92

Rod. Most reverend signior, do you know
my voice?

Bra. Not I, what are you?

Rod. My name is Roderigo.

Bra. The worser welcome:
I have charg'd thee not to haunt about my
doors: 96
In honest plainness thou hast heard me say
My daughter is not for thee; and now, in mad-
ness,
Being full of supper and distempering draughts,
Upon malicious knavery dost thou come 100
To start my quiet.

Rod. Sir, sir, sir!

Bra. But thou must needs be sure
My spirit and my place have in them power
To make this bitter to thee.

Rod. Patience, good sir. 104

Bra. What tell'st thou me of robbing? this is
Venice;
My house is not a grange.

Rod. Most grave Brabantio,
In simple and pure soul I come to you. 107

Iago. 'Zounds! sir, you are one of those that
will not serve God if the devil bid you. Because
we come to do you service and you think we are
ruffians, you'll have your daughter covered with
a Barbary horse; you'll have your nephews neigh
to you; you'll have coursers for cousins and
gennets for germans. 114

Bra. What profane wretch art thou?

Iago. I am one, sir, that comes to tell you,
your daughter and the Moor are now making
the beast with two backs.

Bra. Thou art a villain.

Iago. You are—a senator.

Bra. This thou shalt answer; I know thee,
Roderigo. 120

Rod. Sir, I will answer any thing. But, I be-
seech you,
If 't be your pleasure and most wise consent,—
As partly, I find, it is,—that your fair daughter,
At this odd-even and dull-watch o' the night, 124
Transported with no worse nor better guard
But with a knave of common hire, a gondolier,
To the gross clasps of a lascivious Moor,— 127
If this be known to you, and your allowance,
We then have done you bold and saucy wrongs;
But if you know not this, my manners tell me
We have your wrong rebuke. Do not believe
That, from the sense of all civility, 132
I thus would play and trifle with your reverence:
Your daughter, if you have not given her leave,
I say again, hath made a gross revolt;
Tying her duty, beauty, wit and fortunes 136
In an extravagant and wheeling stranger
Of here and every where. Straight satisfy your-
self:
If she be in her chamber or your house,
Let loose on me the justice of the state 140
For thus deluding you.

Bra. Strike on the tinder, ho!
Give me a taper! call up all my people!
This accident is not unlike my dream;
Belief of it oppresses me already. 144
Light, I say! light! [*Exit, from above.*

Iago. Farewell, for I must leave you:
It seems not meet nor wholesome to my place
To be produc'd, as, if I stay, I shall,
Against the Moor; for, I do know the state, 148
However this may gall him with some check,
Cannot with safety cast him; for he's embark'd
With such loud reason to the Cyprus wars,—
Which even now stand in act,—that, for their
souls, 152
Another of his fathom they have none,
To lead their business; in which regard,
Though I do hate him as I do hell-pains,
Yet, for necessity of present life, 156
I must show out a flag and sign of love,
Which is indeed but sign. That you shall surely
find him,
Lead to the Sagittary the raised search;
And there will I be with him. So, farewell. 160
[*Exit.*

Enter below, BRABANTIO, *and* Servants *with
torches.*

Bra. It is too true an evil: gone she is,

nd what's to come of my despised time
s nought but bitterness. Now, Roderigo,
Vhere didst thou see her? O, unhappy girl!
Vith the Moor, sayst thou? Who would be a
  father! 165
low didst thou know 'twas she? O, she deceives me
ast thought. What said she to you? Get more
  tapers!
aise all my kindred! Are they married, think
  you? 168
  Rod. Truly, I think they are.
  Bra. O heaven! How got she out? O, treason
  of the blood:
athers, from hence trust not your daughters'
  minds
y what you see them act. Are there not charms
y which the property of youth and maidhood
lay be abus'd? Have you not read, Roderigo,
f some such thing?
  Rod. Yes, sir, I have indeed.
  Bra. Call up my brother. O! that you had
  had her. 176
ome one way, some another! Do you know
Vhere we may apprehend her and the Moor?
  Rod. I think I can discover him, if you please
o get good guard and go along with me. 180
  Bra. Pray you, lead on. At every house I'll
  call;
may command at most. Get weapons, ho!
nd raise some special officers of night.
m, good Roderigo; I'll deserve your pains. 184
                  [Exeunt.

SCENE II.—*Another Street.*

Enter OTHELLO, IAGO, *and* Attendants, *with torches.*

  Iago. Though in the trade of war I have slain
  men,
et do I hold it very stuff o' the conscience
o do no contriv'd murder: I lack iniquity
ometimes to do me service. Nine or ten times 4
  had thought to have yerk'd him here under
  the ribs.
  Oth. 'Tis better as it is.
  Iago. Nay, but he prated,
nd spoke such scurvy and provoking terms
gainst your honour 8
hat, with the little godliness I have,
did full hard forbear him. But, I pray, sir,
re you fast married? Be assur'd of this,
hat the magnifico is much belov'd, 12
nd hath in his effect a voice potential
s double as the duke's; he will divorce you,
)r put upon you what restraint and grievance
he law—with all his might to enforce it on— 16
Vill give him cable.
  Oth. Let him do his spite:
ly services which I have done the signiory
hall out-tongue his complaints. 'Tis yet to
  know, 19
Vhich when I know that boasting is an honour
shall promulgate, I fetch my life and being
rom men of royal siege, and my demerits
lay speak unbonneted to as proud a fortune

As this that I have reach'd; for know, Iago, 24
But that I love the gentle Desdemona,
I would not my unhoused free condition
Put into circumscription and confine
For the sea's worth. But, look! what lights come
  yond? 28
  Iago. Those are the raised father and his
  friends:
You were best go in.
  Oth. Not I; I must be found:
My parts, my title, and my perfect soul
Shall manifest me rightly. Is it they? 32
  Iago. By Janus, I think no.

Enter CASSIO *and certain* Officers, *with torches.*

  Oth. The servants of the duke, and my lieu-
  tenant.
The goodness of the night upon you, friends!
What is the news?
  Cas. The duke does greet you, general, 36
And he requires your haste-post-haste appear-
  ance,
Even on the instant.
  Oth. What is the matter, think you?
  Cas. Something from Cyprus, as I may
  divine.
It is a business of some heat; the galleys 40
Have sent a dozen sequent messengers
This very night at one another's heels,
And many of the consuls, rais'd and met,
Are at the duke's already. You have been hotly
  call'd for; 44
When, being not at your lodging to be found,
The senate hath sent about three several quests
To search you out.
  Oth. 'Tis well I am found by you.
I will but spend a word here in the house, 48
And go with you. *[Exit.*
  Cas. Ancient, what makes he here?
  Iago. Faith, he to-night hath boarded a land
  carrack;
If it prove lawful prize, he's made for ever.
  Cas. I do not understand.
  Iago. He's married.
  Cas. To who? 52

Re-enter OTHELLO.

  Iago. Marry, to—Come, captain, will you go?
  Oth. Have with you.
  Cas. Here comes another troop to seek for
  you.
  Iago. It is Brabantio. General, be advis'd;
He comes to bad intent.

Enter BRABANTIO, RODERIGO, *and* Officers, *with torches and weapons.*

  Oth. Holla! stand there! 56
  Rod. Signior, it is the Moor.
  Bra. Down with him, thief!
             [They draw on both sides.
  Iago. You, Roderigo! come sir, I am for you.
  Oth. Keep up your bright swords, for the
  dew will rust them.
Good signior, you shall more command with
  years 60

Than with your weapons.

Bra. O thou foul thief! where hast thou
    stow'd my daughter?
Damn'd as thou art, thou hast enchanted her;
For I'll refer me to all things of sense,   64
If she in chains of magic were not bound,
Whether a maid so tender, fair, and happy,
So opposite to marriage that she shunn'd
The wealthy curled darlings of our nation, 68
Would ever have, to incur a general mock,
Run from her guardage to the sooty bosom
Of such a thing as thou; to fear, not to delight.
Judge me the world, if 'tis not gross in sense 72
That thou hast practis'd on her with foul charms,
Abus'd her delicate youth with drugs or minerals
That weaken motion: I'll have't disputed on;
'Tis probable, and palpable to thinking.   76
I therefore apprehend and do attach thee
For an abuser of the world, a practiser
Of arts inhibited and out of warrant.
Lay hold upon him: if he do resist,   80
Subdue him at his peril.

Oth.   Hold your hands,
Both you of my inclining, and the rest:
Were it my cue to fight, I should have known it
Without a prompter. Where will you that I go
To answer this your charge?

Bra.   To prison; till fit time 85
Of law and course of direct session
Call thee to answer.

Oth.   What if I do obey?
How may the duke be therewith satisfied,   88
Whose messengers are here about my side,
Upon some present business of the state
To bring me to him?

Off.   'Tis true, most worthy signior;
The duke's in council, and your noble self,   92
I am sure, is sent for.

Bra.   How! the duke in council!
In this time of the night! Bring him away.
Mine's not an idle cause: the duke himself,
Or any of my brothers of the state,   96
Cannot but feel this wrong as 'twere their own;
For if such actions may have passage free,
Bond-slaves and pagans shall our statesmen be.
                          [*Exeunt.*

SCENE III.—*A Council Chamber. The* DUKE *and*
Senators *sitting at a table.* Officers *attending.*

Duke. There is no composition in these news
That gives them credit.

First Sen. Indeed, they are disproportion'd;
My letters say a hundred and seven galleys.

Duke. And mine, a hundred and forty.

Sec. Sen.   And mine, two hundred: 4
But though they jump not on a just account,—
As in these cases, where the aim reports,
'Tis oft with difference,—yet do they all con-
    firm
A Turkish fleet, and bearing up to Cyprus. 8

Duke. Nay, it is possible enough to judg-
    ment:
I do not so secure me in the error,
But the main article I do approve
In fearful sense.

Sailor. [*Within.*] What, ho! what, ho! what,
    ho!   12

Off. A messenger from the galleys.

Enter a Sailor.

Duke.   Now, what's the business?

Sail. The Turkish preparation makes for
    Rhodes;
So was I bid report here to the state
By Signior Angelo.   16

Duke. How say you by this change?

First Sen.   This cannot be,
By no assay of reason; 'tis a pageant
To keep us in false gaze. When we consider
The importance of Cyprus to the Turk,   20
And let ourselves again but understand,
That as it more concerns the Turk than Rhodes,
So may he with more facile question bear it,
For that it stands not in such war-like brace, 24
But altogether lacks the abilities
That Rhodes is dress'd in: if we make thought
    of this,
We must not think the Turk is so unskilful
To leave that latest which concerns him first, 28
Neglecting an attempt of ease and gain,
To wake and wage a danger profitless.

Duke. Nay, in all confidence, he's not for
    Rhodes.

Off. Here is more news.   32

Enter a Messenger.

Mess. The Ottomites, reverend and gracious,
Steering with due course toward the isle of
    Rhodes,
Have there injointed them with an after fleet.

First Sen. Ay, so I thought. How many, as
    you guess?   36

Mess. Of thirty sail; and now they do re-stem
Their backward course, bearing with frank
    appearance
Their purposes toward Cyprus. Signior Mon-
    tano,
Your trusty and most valiant servitor,   40
With his free duty recommends you thus,
And prays you to believe him.

Duke. 'Tis certain then, for Cyprus.
Marcus Luccicos, is not he in town?   44

First Sen. He's now in Florence.

Duke. Write from us to him; post-post-haste
    dispatch.

First Sen. Here comes Brabantio and the
    valiant Moor.

Enter BRABANTIO, OTHELLO, IAGO, RODERIGO,
and Officers.

Duke. Valiant Othello, we must straight em-
    ploy you   48
Against the general enemy Ottoman.
[*To* BRABANTIO.] I did not see you; welcome,
    gentle signior;
We lack'd your counsel and your help to-night.

Bra. So did I yours. Good your grace, par-
    don me;   52
Neither my place nor aught I heard of business
Hath rais'd me from my bed, nor doth the
    general care

ake hold of me, for my particular grief
of so flood-gate and o'erbearing nature   56
hat it engluts and swallows other sorrows
nd it is still itself.

Duke.   Why, what's the matter?

Bra. My daughter! O! my daughter.

Duke. ⎫
Sen. ⎬   Dead?

Bra.   Ay, to me;
he is abus'd, stol'n from me, and corrupted 60
y spells and medicines bought of mounte-
    banks;
or nature so preposterously to err,
eing not deficient, blind, or lame of sense,
ans witchcraft could not.   64

Duke. Whoe'er he be that in this foul pro-
    ceeding
lath thus beguil'd your daughter of herself
nd you of her, the bloody book of law
ou shall yourself read in the bitter letter 68
fter your own sense; yea, though our proper
    son
tood in your action.

Bra.   Humbly I thank your Grace.
lere is the man, this Moor; whom now, it
    seems,
our special mandate for the state affairs,   72
lath hither brought.

Duke. ⎫
Sen. ⎬   We are very sorry for it.

Duke. [*To* OTHELLO.] What, in your own
    part, can you say to this?

Bra. Nothing, but this is so.

Oth. Most potent, grave, and reverend sig-
    niors,   76
ly very noble and approv'd good masters,
'hat I have ta'en away this old man's daughter,
t is most true; true, I have married her:
'he very head and front of my offending   80
lath this extent, no more. Rude am I in my
    speech,
nd little bless'd with the soft phrase of peace;
'or since these arms of mine had seven years'
    pith,
ill now some nine moons wasted, they have us'd
heir dearest action in the tented field;   85
And little of this great world can I speak,
,lore than pertains to feats of broil and battle;
\nd therefore little shall I grace my cause 88
n speaking for myself. Yet, by your gracious
    patience,
will a round unvarnish'd tale deliver
)f my whole course of love; what drugs, what
    charms,
Vhat conjuration, and what mighty magic, 92
'or such proceeding I am charg'd withal,
won his daughter.

Bra.   A maiden never bold;
)f spirit so still and quiet, that her motion
3lush'd at herself; and she, in spite of nature,
)f years, of country, credit, every thing, 97
'o fall in love with what she fear'd to look on!
t is a judgment maim'd and most imperfect
'hat will confess perfection so could err   100
\gainst all rules of nature, and must be driven
'o find out practices of cunning hell,

Why this should be. I therefore vouch again
That with some mixtures powerful o'er the
    blood,   104
Or with some dram conjur'd to this effect,
He wrought upon her.

Duke.   To vouch this, is no proof,
Without more certain and more overt test
Than these thin habits and poor likelihoods 108
Of modern seeming do prefer against him.

First Sen. But, Othello, speak:
Did you by indirect and forced courses
Subdue and poison this young maid's affec-
    tions;   112
Or came it by request and such fair question
As soul to soul affordeth?

Oth.   I do beseech you,
Send for the lady to the Sagittary,
And let her speak of me before her father: 116
If you do find me foul in her report,
The trust, the office I do hold of you,
Not only take away, but let your sentence
Even fall upon my life.

Duke.   Fetch Desdemona hither.

Oth. Ancient, conduct them; you best know
    the place.   121
                    [*Exeunt* IAGO *and* Attendants.
And, till she come, as truly as to heaven
I do confess the vices of my blood,
So justly to your grave ears I'll present   124
How I did thrive in this fair lady's love,
And she in mine.

Duke. Say it, Othello.

Oth. Her father lov'd me; oft invited me;
Still question'd me the story of my life   129
From year to year, the battles, sieges, fortunes
That I have pass'd.
I ran it through, even from my boyish days 132
To the very moment that he bade me tell it;
Wherein I spake of most disastrous chances,
Of moving accidents by flood and field,
Of hair-breadth 'scapes i' the imminent deadly
    breach,   136
Of being taken by the insolent foe
And sold to slavery, of my redemption thence
And portance in my travel's history;
Wherein of antres vast and desarts idle,   140
Rough quarries, rocks and hills whose heads
    touch heaven,
It was my hint to speak, such was the process;
And of the Cannibals that each other eat,
The Anthropophagi, and men whose heads 144
Do grow beneath their shoulders. This to hear
Would Desdemona seriously incline;
But still the house-affairs would draw her
    thence;
Which ever as she could with haste dispatch,
She'd come again, and with a greedy ear 149
Devour up my discourse. Which I observing,
Took once a pliant hour, and found good means
To draw from her a prayer of earnest heart 152
That I would all my pilgrimage dilate,
Whereof by parcels she had something heard,
But not intentively: I did consent;
And often did beguile her of her tears,   156
When I did speak of some distressful stroke
That my youth suffer'd. My story being done,

She gave me for my pains a world of sighs:
She swore, in faith, 'twas strange, 'twas passing
   strange;   160
'Twas pitiful, 'twas wondrous pitiful:
She wish'd she had not heard it, yet she wish'd
That heaven had made her such a man; she
   thank'd me,
And bade me, if I had a friend that lov'd her,
I should but teach him how to tell my story, 165
And that would woo her. Upon this hint I
   spake:
She lov'd me for the dangers I had pass'd,
And I lov'd her that she did pity them.   168
This only is the witchcraft I have us'd:
Here comes the lady; let her witness it.

   Enter DESDEMONA, IAGO, *and* Attendants.

   Duke. I think this tale would win my daugh-
   ter too.
Good Brabantio,   172
Take up this mangled matter at the best;
Men do their broken weapons rather use
Than their bare hands.
   Bra.   I pray you, hear her speak:
If she confess that she was half the wooer, 176
Destruction on my head, if my bad blame
Light on the man! Come hither, gentle mis-
   tress:
Do you perceive in all this noble company
Where most you owe obedience?
   Des.   My noble father,
I do perceive here a divided duty: 181
To you I am bound for life and education;
My life and education both do learn me
How to respect you; you are the lord of duty,
I am hitherto your daughter: but here's my
   husband;   185
And so much duty as my mother show'd
To you, preferring you before her father,
So much I challenge that I may profess 188
Due to the Moor my lord.
   Bra. God be with you! I have done.
Please it your Grace, on to the state affairs:
I had rather to adopt a child than get it.
Come hither, Moor: 192
I here do give thee that with all my heart
Which, but thou hast already, with all my heart
I would keep from thee. For your sake, jewel,
I am glad at soul I have no other child; 196
For thy escape would teach me tyranny,
To hang clogs on them. I have done, my lord.
   Duke. Let me speak like yourself and lay a
   sentence,
Which as a grize or step, may help these lovers
Into your favour.   201
When remedies are past, the griefs are ended
By seeing the worst, which late on hopes de-
   pended.
To mourn a mischief that is past and gone 204
Is the next way to draw new mischief on.
What cannot be preserv'd when Fortune takes,
Patience her injury a mockery makes.
The robb'd that smiles steals something from
   the thief;   208
He robs himself that spends a bootless grief.
   Bra. So let the Turk of Cyprus us beguile;

We lose it not so long as we can smile.
He bears the sentence well that nothing bear
But the free comfort which from thence h
   hears;
But he bears both the sentence and the sorrow
That, to pay grief, must of poor patience bo
   row.
These sentences, to sugar, or to gall,   2
Being strong on both sides, are equivocal:
But words are words; I never yet did hear
That the bruis'd heart was pierced through th
   ear.
I humbly beseech you, proceed to the affairs
   state.   22
   Duke. The Turk with a most mighty prepar
tion makes for Cyprus. Othello, the fortitude
the place is best known to you; and thoug
we have there a substitute of most allowe
sufficiency, yet opinion, a sovereign mistress
effects, throws a more safer voice on you: yo
must therefore be content to slubber the gloss
your new fortunes with this more stubborn an
boisterous expedition.   2
   Oth. The tyrant custom, most grave senator
Hath made the flinty and steel couch of war
My thrice-driven bed of down: I do agnize 2
A natural and prompt alacrity
I find in hardness, and do undertake
These present wars against the Ottomites.
Most humbly therefore bending to your stat
I crave fit disposition for my wife,   2
Due reference of place and exhibition,
With such accommodation and besort
As levels with her breeding.
   Duke.   If you please, 2
Be't at her father's.
   Bra.   I'll not have it so.
   Oth. Nor I.
   Des. Nor I; I would not there reside,
To put my father in impatient thoughts   2
By being in his eye. Most gracious duke,
To my unfolding lend your gracious ear;
And let me find a charter in your voice
To assist my simpleness.   2
   Duke. What would you, Desdemona?
   Des. That I did love the Moor to live wi
   him,
My downright violence and storm of fortun
May trumpet to the world; my heart's subdu
Even to the very quality of my lord;   2
I saw Othello's visage in his mind,
And to his honours and his valiant parts
Did I my soul and fortunes consecrate.   2
So that, dear lords, if I be left behind,
A moth of peace, and he go to the war,
The rites for which I love him are bereft m
And I a heavy interim shall support
By his dear absence. Let me go with him.
   Oth. Let her have your voices.
Vouch with me, heaven, I therefore beg it n
To please the palate of my appetite,   2
Nor to comply with heat,—the young affect
In me defunct,—and proper satisfaction,
But to be free and bounteous to her mind;
And heaven defend your good souls that y
   think   2

will your serious and great business scant
'or she is with me. No, when light-wing'd toys
)f feather'd Cupid seel with wanton dulness
My speculative and offic'd instruments,	272
hat my disports corrupt and taint my business,
Let housewives make a skillet of my helm,
And all indign and base adversities
Make head against my estimation!	276

Duke. Be it as you shall privately determine,
Either for her stay or going. The affair cries haste,
And speed must answer it.

First Sen. You must away to-night.

Oth.	With all my heart. 280

Duke. At nine i' the morning here we'll meet
again.
)thello, leave some officer behind,
And he shall our commission bring to you;
With such things else of quality and respect 284
As doth import you.

Oth.	So please your Grace, my ancient;
A man he is of honesty and trust:
To his conveyance I assign my wife,
With what else needful your good grace shall
think	288
To be sent after me.

Duke.	Let it be so.
Good night to every one. [*To* BRABANTIO.]
And, noble signior,
If virtue no delighted beauty lack,
Your son-in-law is far more fair than black. 292

First Sen. Adieu, brave Moor! use Desdemona well.

Bra. Look to her, Moor, if thou hast eyes to
see:
She has deceiv'd her father, and may thee.

[*Exeunt* DUKE, Senators, Officers, &c.

Oth. My life upon her faith! Honest Iago,
My Desdemona must I leave to thee:	297
prithee, let thy wife attend on her;
And bring them after in the best advantage.
Come, Desdemona; I have but an hour	300
Of love, of worldly matters and direction,
To spend with thee: we must obey the time.

[*Exeunt* OTHELLO *and* DESDEMONA.

Rod. Iago!

Iago. What sayst thou, noble heart?	304

Rod. What will I do, think'st thou?

Iago. Why, go to bed, and sleep.

Rod. I will incontinently drown myself.

Iago. Well, if thou dost, I shall never love
thee after. Why, thou silly gentleman!	309

Rod. It is silliness to live when to live is
torment; and then have we a prescription to die
when death is our physician.	312

Iago. O! villanous; I have looked upon the
world for four times seven years, and since I
could distinguish betwixt a benefit and an
injury, I never found man that knew how to
love himself. Ere I would say, I would drown
myself for the love of a guinea-hen, I would
change my humanity with a baboon.	319

Rod. What should I do? I confess it is my
shame to be so fond; but it is not in my virtue
to amend it.	322

Iago. Virtue! a fig! 'tis in ourselves that we
are thus, or thus. Our bodies are our gardens,
to the which our wills are gardeners; so that if we
will plant nettles or sow lettuce, set hyssop and
weed up thyme, supply it with one gender of herbs
or distract it with many, either to have it sterile
with idleness or manured with industry, why,
the power and corrigible authority of this lies in
our wills. If the balance of our lives had not
one scale of reason to poise another of sensuality, the blood and baseness of our natures would
conduct us to most preposterous conclusions;
but we have reason to cool our raging motions,
our carnal stings, our unbitted lusts, whereof I
take this that you call love to be a sect or scion.

Rod. It cannot be.	338

Iago. It is merely a lust of the blood and a
permission of the will. Come, be a man. Drown
thyself! drown cats and blind puppies. I have
professed me thy friend, and I confess me knit
to thy deserving with cables of perdurable tough-
ness; I could never better stead thee than now.
Put money in thy purse; follow these wars;
defeat thy favour with a usurped beard; I say,
put money in thy purse. It cannot be that
Desdemona should long continue her love to the
Moor,—put money in thy purse,—nor he his to
her. It was a violent commencement in her,
and thou shalt see an answerable sequestration;
put but money in thy purse. These Moors are
changeable in their wills;—fill thy purse with
money:—the food that to him now is as luscious
as locusts, shall be to him shortly as bitter as
coloquintida. She must change for youth: when
she is sated with his body, she will find the error
of her choice. She must have change, she must:
therefore put money in thy purse. If thou wilt
needs damn thyself, do it a more delicate way
than drowning. Make all the money thou canst.
If sanctimony and a frail vow betwixt an erring
barbarian and a supersubtle Venetian be not too
hard for my wits and all the tribe of hell, thou
shalt enjoy her; therefore make money. A pox
of drowning thyself! it is clean out of the way:
seek thou rather to be hanged in compassing
thy joy than to be drowned and go without her.

Rod. Wilt thou be fast to my hopes, if I
depend on the issue?	370

Iago. Thou art sure of me: go, make money.
I have told thee often, and I re-tell thee again
and again, I hate the Moor: my cause is hearted:
thine hath no less reason. Let us be conjunctive in our revenge against him; if thou canst
cuckold him, thou dost thyself a pleasure, me a
sport. There are many events in the womb of
time which will be delivered. Traverse; go:
provide thy money. We will have more of this
to-morrow. Adieu.	380

Rod. Where shall we meet i' the morning?

Iago. At my lodging.

Rod. I'll be with thee betimes.

Iago. Go to; farewell. Do you hear, Rode-
rigo?	384

Rod. What say you?

Iago. No more of drowning, do you hear?

Rod. I am changed. I'll sell all my land.

Iago. Go to; farewell! put money enough in
your purse.	[*Exit* RODERIGO.

Thus do I ever make my fool my purse;   389
For I mine own gain'd knowledge should pro-
  fane,
If I would time expend with such a snipe
But for my sport and profit. I hate the Moor,
And it is thought abroad that 'twixt my sheets
He has done my office: I know not if 't be true,
But I, for mere suspicion in that kind,
Will do as if for surety. He holds me well; 396
The better shall my purpose work on him.
Cassio's a proper man; let me see now:
To get his place; and to plume up my will
In double knavery; how, how? Let's see: 400
After some time to abuse Othello's ear
That he is too familiar with his wife:
He hath a person and a smooth dispose
To be suspected; framed to make women false.
The Moor is of a free and open nature,   405
That thinks men honest that but seem to be so,
And will as tenderly be led by the nose
As asses are.   408
I have 't; it is engender'd: hell and night
Must bring this monstrous birth to the world's
  light.   [*Exit.*

ACT II

SCENE I.—*A Sea-port Town in Cyprus.*
  An open place near the Quay.

Enter MONTANO *and two Gentlemen.*

Mon. What from the cape can you discern at
  sea?
First Gent. Nothing at all: it is a high-
  wrought flood;
I cannot 'twixt the heaven and the main
Descry a sail.   4
Mon. Methinks the wind hath spoke aloud at
  land;
A fuller blast ne'er shook our battlements;
If it hath ruffian'd so upon the sea,
What ribs of oak, when mountains melt on them,
Can hold the mortise? what shall we hear of
  this?   9
Sec. Gent. A segregation of the Turkish fleet;
For do but stand upon the foaming shore,
The chidden billow seems to pelt the clouds; 12
The wind-shak'd surge, with high and mon-
  strous mane,
Seems to cast water on the burning bear
And quench the guards of the ever-fixed pole:
I never did like molestation view   16
On the enchafed flood.
Mon.   If that the Turkish fleet
Be not enshelter'd and embay'd, they are
  drown'd;
It is impossible they bear it out.

Enter a third Gentleman.

Third Gent. News, lads! our wars are done.
The desperate tempest hath so bang'd the Turks
That their designment halts; a noble ship of
  Venice
Hath seen a grievous wrack and sufferance
On most part of their fleet.   24
Mon. How! is this true?
Third Gent.   The ship is here put in,

A Veronesa; Michael Cassio,
Lieutenant to the war-like Moor Othello,
Is come on shore: the Moor himself 's at sea, 28
And is in full commission here for Cyprus.
Mon. I am glad on 't; 'tis a worthy governor.
Third Gent. But this same Cassio, though he
  speak of comfort
Touching the Turkish loss, yet he looks sadly 32
And prays the Moor be safe; for they were
  parted
With foul and violent tempest.
Mon.   Pray heaven he be;
For I have serv'd him, and the man commands
Like a full soldier. Let's to the sea-side, ho! 36
As well to see the vessel that's come in
As to throw out our eyes for brave Othello,
Even till we make the main and the aerial blue
An indistinct regard.
Third Gent.   Come, let's do so;   40
For every minute is expectancy
Of more arrivance.

Enter CASSIO.

Cas. Thanks, you the valiant of this war-like
  isle,
That so approve the Moor. O! let the heavens
Give him defence against the elements,   45
For I have lost him on a dangerous sea.
Mon. Is he well shipp'd?
Cas. His bark is stoutly timber'd, and his
  pilot   48
Of very expert and approv'd allowance;
Therefore my hopes, not surfeited to death,
Stand in bold cure.
    [*Within*, 'A sail!—a sail!—a sail!'

Enter a Messenger.

Cas. What noise?   52
Mess. The town is empty; on the brow o' the
  sea
Stand ranks of people, and they cry, 'A sail!
Cas. My hopes do shape him for the go-
  vernor.   [*Guns heard*
Sec. Gent. They do discharge their shot of
  courtesy;   56
Our friends at least.
Cas.   I pray you, sir, go forth,
And give us truth who 'tis that is arriv'd.
Sec. Gent. I shall.   [*Exit*
Mon. But, good lieutenant, is your general
  wiv'd?   60
Cas. Most fortunately: he hath achiev'd a
  maid
That paragons description and wild fame;
One that excels the quirks of blazoning pens,
And in th' essential vesture of creation   64
Does tire the ingener.

Re-enter second Gentleman.

    How now! who has put in?
Sec. Gent. 'Tis one Iago, ancient to the
  general.
Cas. He has had most favourable and happy
  speed:
Tempests themselves, high seas, and howling
  winds,   68

The gutter'd rocks, and congregated sands,
Traitors ensteep'd to clog the guiltless keel,
As having sense of beauty, do omit
Their mortal natures, letting go safely by   72
The divine Desdemona.

Mon.   What is she?

Cas. She that I spake of, our great captain's
captain,
Left in the conduct of the bold Iago,
Whose footing here anticipates our thoughts 76
A se'nnight's speed. Great Jove, Othello guard,
And swell his sail with thine own powerful
breath,
That he may bless this bay with his tall ship,
Make love's quick pants in Desdemona's arms,
Give renew'd fire to our extincted spirits,   81
And bring all Cyprus comfort!

Enter DESDEMONA, EMILIA, IAGO, RODERIGO,
and Attendants.

                          O! behold,
The riches of the ship is come on shore.
Ye men of Cyprus, let her have your knees.   84
Hail to thee, lady! and the grace of heaven,
Before, behind thee, and on every hand,
Enwheel thee round!

Des.   I thank you, valiant Cassio.
What tidings can you tell me of my lord?   88

Cas. He is not yet arriv'd; nor know I aught
But that he's well, and will be shortly here.

Des. O! but I fear—How lost you company?

Cas. The great contention of the sea and
skies   92
Parted our fellowship. But hark! a sail.
  [*Cry within,* 'A sail!—a sail!' *Guns heard.*

Sec. Gent. They give their greeting to the
citadel:
This likewise is a friend.

Cas.   See for the news!
                        [*Exit* Gentleman.
Good ancient, you are welcome:—[*To* EMILIA.]
welcome, mistress.   96
Let it not gall your patience, good Iago,
That I extend my manners; 'tis my breeding
That gives me this bold show of courtesy.
                            [*Kissing her.*

Iago. Sir, would she give you so much of her
lips   100
As of her tongue she oft bestows on me,
You'd have enough.

Des.   Alas! she has no speech.

Iago. In faith, too much;
I find it still when I have list to sleep: 104
Marry, before your ladyship, I grant,
She puts her tongue a little in her heart,
And chides with thinking.

Emil. You have little cause to say so.   108

Iago. Come on, come on; you are pictures
out of doors,
Bells in your parlours, wild cats in your kitchens,
Saints in your injuries, devils being offended,
Players in your housewifery, and housewives in
your beds.   112

Des. O! fie upon thee, slanderer.

Iago. Nay, it is true, or else I am a Turk:
You rise to play and go to bed to work.

Emil. You shall not write my praise.

Iago.   No, let me not. 116

Des. What wouldst thou write of me, if thou
shouldst praise me?

Iago. O gentle lady, do not put me to 't,
For I am nothing if not critical.

Des. Come on; assay. There's one gone to
the harbour?   120

Iago. Ay, madam.

Des. I am not merry, but I do beguile
The thing I am by seeming otherwise.
Come, how wouldst thou praise me?   124

Iago. I am about it; but indeed my inven-
tion
Comes from my pate as birdlime does from
frize;
It plucks out brains and all: but my muse
labours,
And thus she is deliver'd.   128
If she be fair and wise, fairness and wit,
The one's for use, the other useth it.

Des. Well prais'd! How if she be black and
witty?

Iago. If she be black, and thereto have a
wit,   132
She'll find a white that shall her blackness fit.

Des. Worse and worse.

Emil. How if fair and foolish?

Iago. She never yet was foolish that was fair,
For even her folly help'd her to an heir.   137

Des. These are old fond paradoxes to make
fools laugh i' the alehouse. What miserable
praise hast thou for her that's foul and foolish?

Iago. There's none so foul and foolish thereunto   141
But does foul pranks which fair and wise ones do.

Des. O heavy ignorance! thou praisest the
worst best. But what praise couldst thou bestow on a deserving woman indeed, one that
in the authority of her merit, did justly put on
the vouch of very malice itself?

Iago. She that was ever fair and never proud,
Had tongue at will and yet was never loud, 149
Never lack'd gold and yet went never gay,
Fled from her wish and yet said 'Now I may,'
She that being anger'd, her revenge being nigh,
Bade her wrong stay and her displeasure fly, 153
She that in wisdom never was so frail
To change the cod's head for the salmon's tail,
She that could think and ne'er disclose her mind,
See suitors following and not look behind, 157
She was a wight, if ever such wight were,—

Des. To do what?

Iago. To suckle fools and chronicle small beer.

Des. O most lame and impotent conclusion!
Do not learn of him, Emilia, though he be thy
husband. How say you, Cassio? is he not a
most profane and liberal counsellor?   164

Cas. He speaks home, madam; you may
relish him more in the soldier than in the
scholar.   167

Iago. [*Aside.*] He takes her by the palm; ay,
well said, whisper; with as little a web as this
will I ensnare as great a fly as Cassio. Ay, smile
upon her, do; I will gyve thee in thine own
courtship. You say true, 'tis so, indeed. If

such tricks as these strip you out of your
lieutenantry, it had been better you had not
kissed your three fingers so oft, which now
again you are most apt to play the sir in.
Very good; well kissed! an excellent courtesy!
'tis so, indeed. Yet again your fingers to your
lips? would they were clyster-pipes for your
sake! [*A trumpet heard.*] The Moor! I know
his trumpet.   181

  Cas. 'Tis truly so.
  Des. Let's meet him and receive him.
  Cas. Lo! where he comes.   184

    Enter OTHELLO *and* Attendants.

  Oth. O my fair warrior!
  Des.   My dear Othello!
  Oth. It gives me wonder great as my content
To see you here before me. O my soul's joy!
If after every tempest come such calms,   188
May the winds blow till they have waken'd
    death!
And let the labouring bark climb hills of seas
Olympus-high, and duck again as low
As hell's from heaven! If it were now to die,   192
'Twere now to be most happy, for I fear
My soul hath her content so absolute
That not another comfort like to this
Succeeds in unknown fate.
  Des.   The heavens forbid   196
But that our loves and comforts should increase
Even as our days do grow!
  Oth.   Amen to that, sweet powers!
I cannot speak enough of this content;
It stops me here; it is too much of joy: 200
And this, and this, the greatest discords be,
                          [*Kissing her.*
That e'er our hearts shall make!
  Iago.   [*Aside.*] O! you are well tun'd now,
But I'll set down the pegs that make this music,
As honest as I am.
  Oth.   Come, let us to the castle.   204
News, friends; our wars are done, the Turks are
    drown'd.
How does my old acquaintance of this isle?
Honey, you shall be well desir'd in Cyprus;
I have found great love amongst them. O my
    sweet,   208
I prattle out of fashion, and I dote
In mine own comforts. I prithee, good Iago,
Go to the bay and disembark my coffers.
Bring thou the master to the citadel;   212
He is a good one, and his worthiness
Does challenge much respect. Come, Desde-
    mona,
Once more well met at Cyprus.
        [*Exeunt all except* IAGO *and* RODERIGO.
  Iago. Do thou meet me presently at the
harbour. Come hither. If thou be'st valiant,
as they say base men being in love have then
a nobility in their natures more than is native to
them, list me. The lieutenant to-night watches
on the court of guard: first, I must tell thee this,
Desdemona is directly in love with him.
  Rod. With him! why, 'tis not possible.   223
  Iago. Lay thy finger thus, and let thy soul
be instructed. Mark me with what violence she

first loved the Moor but for bragging and tellin
her fantastical lies; and will she love him sti
for prating? let not thy discreet heart think i
Her eye must be fed; and what delight sha
she have to look on the devil? When the bloo
is made dull with the act of sport, there shoul
be, again to inflame it, and to give satiety
fresh appetite, loveliness in favour, sympath
in years, manners, and beauties; all which th
Moor is defective in. Now, for want of the
required conveniences, her delicate tenderne
will find itself abused, begin to heave the gorg
disrelish and abhor the Moor; very nature wi
instruct her in it, and compel her to son
second choice. Now, sir, this granted, as it is
most pregnant and unforced position, who stand
so eminently in the degree of this fortune a
Cassio does? a knave very voluble, no furth
conscionable than in putting on the mere for
of civil and humane seeming, for the bett
compassing of his salt and most hidden loo
affection? why, none; why, none: a slipper an
subtle knave, a finder-out of occasions, that ha
an eye can stamp and counterfeit advantage
though true advantage never present itself;
devilish knave! Besides, the knave is handsom
young, and hath all those requisites in him tha
folly and green minds look after; a pestilen
complete knave! and the woman hath four
him already.   2

  Rod. I cannot believe that in her; she is fu
of most blessed condition.
  Iago. Blessed fig's end! the wine she drink
is made of grapes; if she had been blessed sh
would never have loved the Moor; blessed pu
ding! Didst thou not see her paddle with th
palm of his hand? didst not mark that?
  Rod. Yes, that I did; but that was but cou
tesy.   2

  Iago. Lechery, by this hand! an index an
obscure prologue to the history of lust and fo
thoughts. They met so near with their lips, th
their breaths embraced together. Villano
thoughts, Roderigo! when these mutualities s
marshal the way, hard at hand comes the mast
and main exercise, the incorporate conclusio
Pish! But, sir, be you ruled by me: I ha
brought you from Venice. Watch you to-nigh
for the command, I'll lay't upon you: Cass
knows you not. I'll not be far from you: do yc
find some occasion to anger Cassio, either
speaking too loud, or tainting his disciplin
or from what other course you please, whic
the time shall more favourably minister.
  Rod. Well.   2

  Iago. Sir, he is rash and very sudden i
choler, and haply may strike at you: provol
him, that he may; for even out of that will
cause these of Cyprus to mutiny, whose qua
fication shall come into no true taste again b
by the displanting of Cassio. So shall you hav
a shorter journey to your desires by the mea
I shall then have to prefer them; and the in
pediment most profitably removed, without th
which there were no expectation of our pro
perity.   2

Rod. I will do this, if I can bring it to any
opportunity.

Iago. I warrant thee. Meet me by and by at
the citadel: I must fetch his necessaries ashore.
Farewell.   296

Rod. Adieu.   [*Exit.*

Iago. That Cassio loves her, I do well believe it;

that she loves him, 'tis apt, and of great credit:
The Moor, howbeit that I endure him not, 300
Is of a constant, loving, noble nature;
And I dare think he'll prove to Desdemona
A most dear husband. Now, I do love her too;
Not out of absolute lust,—though peradventure
I stand accountant for as great a sin,—   305
But partly led to diet my revenge,
For that I do suspect the lusty Moor
Hath leap'd into my seat; the thought whereof
Doth like a poisonous mineral gnaw my in-
wards;   309
And nothing can or shall content my soul
Till I am even'd with him, wife for wife;
Or failing so, yet that I put the Moor   312
At least into a jealousy so strong
That judgment cannot cure. Which thing to do,
If this poor trash of Venice, whom I trash
For his quick hunting, stand the putting-on,
I'll have our Michael Cassio on the hip;   317
Abuse him to the Moor in the rank garb,
For I fear Cassio with my night-cap too,
Make the Moor thank me, love me, and re-
ward me   320
For making him egregiously an ass
And practising upon his peace and quiet
Even to madness. 'Tis here, but yet confus'd:
Knavery's plain face is never seen till us'd. 324
[*Exit.*

Scene II.—*A Street.*

Enter a Herald *with a proclamation; People following.*

Her. It is Othello's pleasure, our noble and
valiant general, that, upon certain tidings now
arrived, importing the mere perdition of the
Turkish fleet, every man put himself into triumph; some to dance, some to make bonfires,
each man to what sport and revels his addiction
leads him; for, besides these beneficial news,
is the celebration of his nuptial. So much was
his pleasure should be proclaimed. All offices
are open, and there is full liberty of feasting
from this present hour of five till the bell have
told eleven. Heaven bless the isle of Cyprus
and our noble general Othello!   [*Exeunt.*

Scene III.—*A Hall in the Castle.*

Enter OTHELLO, DESDEMONA, CASSIO, *and* Attendants.

Oth. Good Michael, look you to the guard
to-night:
Let's teach ourselves that honourable stop,
Not to outsport discretion.

Cas. Iago hath direction what to do;   4
But, notwithstanding, with my personal eye

Will I look to 't.

Oth.   Iago is most honest.
Michael, good night; to-morrow with your
earliest
Let me have speech with you. [*To* DESDEMONA.]
Come, my dear love,   8
The purchase made, the fruits are to ensue;
That profit 's yet to come 'twixt me and you.
Good night.
[*Exeunt* OTHELLO, DESDEMONA, *and*
Attendants.

Enter IAGO.

Cas. Welcome, Iago; we must to the watch.

Iago. Not this hour, lieutenant; 'tis not yet
ten o' the clock. Our general cast us thus early
for the love of his Desdemona, who let us not
therefore blame; he hath not yet made wanton
the night with her, and she is sport for Jove. 17

Cas. She's a most exquisite lady.

Iago. And, I'll warrant her, full of game.

Cas. Indeed, she is a most fresh and delicate
creature.   21

Iago. What an eye she has! methinks it
sounds a parley of provocation.

Cas. An inviting eye; and yet methinks right
modest.   25

Iago. And when she speaks, is it not an
alarum to love?

Cas. She is indeed perfection.   28

Iago. Well, happiness to their sheets! Come,
lieutenant, I have a stoup of wine, and here
without are a brace of Cyprus gallants that
would fain have a measure to the health of black
Othello.   33

Cas. Not to-night, good Iago: I have very
poor and unhappy brains for drinking: I could
well wish courtesy would invent some other
custom of entertainment.   37

Iago. O! they are our friends; but one cup:
I'll drink for you.

Cas. I have drunk but one cup to-night, and
that was craftily qualified too, and, behold,
what innovation it makes here: I am unfortunate in the infirmity, and dare not task my
weakness with any more.   44

Iago. What, man! 'tis a night of revels; the
gallants desire it.

Cas. Where are they?

Iago. Here at the door; I pray you, call
them in.   49

Cas. I'll do 't; but it dislikes me.   [*Exit.*

Iago. If I can fasten but one cup upon him,
With that which he hath drunk to-night already,
He'll be as full of quarrel and offence   53
As my young mistress' dog. Now, my sick fool
Roderigo,
Whom love hath turn'd almost the wrong side out,
To Desdemona hath to-night carous'd   56
Potations pottle deep; and he's to watch.
Three lads of Cyprus, noble swelling spirits,
That hold their honours in a wary distance,
The very elements of this war-like isle,   60
Have I to-night fluster'd with flowing cups,
And they watch too. Now, 'mongst this flock of
drunkards,

Am I to put our Cassio in some action
That may offend the isle. But here they come.
If consequence do but approve my dream, 65
My boat sails freely, both with wind and stream.

Re-enter CASSIO, *with him* MONTANO, *and* Gentlemen. Servant *following with wine.*

Cas. 'Fore God, they have given me a rouse
already. 68
Mon. Good faith, a little one; not past a
pint, as I am a soldier.
Iago. Some wine, ho!

    And let me the canakin clink, clink; 72
    And let me the canakin clink:
      A soldier's a man;
      A life's but a span;
    Why then let a soldier drink. 76

Some wine, boys!
Cas. 'Fore God, an excellent song.
Iago. I learned it in England, where indeed
they are most potent in potting; your Dane,
your German, and your swag-bellied Hollander,
—drink, ho!—are nothing to your English.
Cas. Is your Englishman so expert in his
drinking? 84
Iago. Why, he drinks you with facility your
Dane dead drunk; he sweats not to overthrow
your Almain; he gives your Hollander a vomit
ere the next pottle can be filled. 88
Cas. To the health of our general!
Mon. I am for it, lieutenant; and I'll do you
justice.
Iago. O sweet England! 92

    King Stephen was a worthy peer,
      His breeches cost him but a crown;
    He held them sixpence all too dear,
      With that he call'd the tailor lown. 96
    He was a wight of high renown,
      And thou art but of low degree:
    'Tis pride that pulls the country down,
      Then take thine auld cloak about thee. 100

Some wine, ho!
Cas. Why, this is a more exquisite song than
the other.
Iago. Will you hear 't again? 104
Cas. No; for I hold him to be unworthy of
his place that does those things. Well, God's
above all; and there be souls must be saved, and
there be souls must not be saved. 108
Iago. It's true, good lieutenant.
Cas. For mine own part,—no offence to the
general, nor any man of quality,—I hope to be
saved. 112
Iago. And so do I too, lieutenant.
Cas. Ay; but, by your leave, not before me;
the lieutenant is to be saved before the ancient.
Let's have no more of this; let's to our affairs.
God forgive us our sins! Gentlemen, let's look
to our business. Do not think, gentlemen, I am
drunk: this is my ancient; this is my right
hand, and this is my left hand. I am not drunk
now; I can stand well enough, and speak well
enough. 122
All. Excellent well.
Cas. Why, very well, then; you must not
think then that I am drunk.   [*Exit.*

Mon. To the platform, masters; come, let
  set the watch.
Iago. You see this fellow that is gone before
He is a soldier fit to stand by Cæsar 12
And give direction; and do but see his vice;
'Tis to his virtue a just equinox,
The one as long as the other; 'tis pity of him
I fear the trust Othello puts him in, 1
On some odd time of his infirmity,
Will shake this island.
Mon.   But is he often thus?
Iago. 'Tis evermore the prologue to his sleep
He'll watch the horologe a double set, 1
If drink rock not his cradle.
Mon.   It were well
The general were put in mind of it.
Perhaps he sees it not; or his good nature
Prizes the virtue that appears in Cassio, 14
And looks not on his evils. Is not this true?

Enter RODERIGO.

Iago. [*Aside to him.*] How now, Roderigo
I pray you, after the lieutenant; go.
                [*Exit* RODERIGO
Mon. And 'tis great pity that the noble Moor
Should hazard such a place as his own second
With one of an ingraft infirmity;
It were an honest action to say
So to the Moor.
Iago.   Not I, for this fair island:
I do love Cassio well, and would do much
To cure him of this evil. But hark! what noise
          [*Cry within,* 'Help! Help

Re-enter CASSIO, *driving in* RODERIGO.

Cas. You rogue! you rascal!
Mon.   What's the matter, lieutenant
Cas. A knave teach me my duty! 1
I'll beat the knave into a twiggen bottle.
Rod. Beat me!
Cas.   Dost thou prate, rogue?
                [*Striking* RODERIGO
Mon. [*Staying him.*] Nay, good lieutenant
I pray you, sir, hold your hand.
Cas.   Let me go, sir, 1
Or I'll knock you o'er the mazzard.
Mon.   Come, come; you're drunk
Cas. Drunk!   [*They fight*
Iago. [*Aside to* RODERIGO.] Away, I say! g
out, and cry a mutiny.   [*Exit* RODERIGO
Nay, good lieutenant! God's will, gentlemen
Help, ho! Lieutenant! sir! Montano! sir!
Help, masters! Here's a goodly watch indeed
                [*Bell ring*
Who's that that rings the bell? *Diablo,* ho!
The town will rise: God's will! lieutenant, hold
You will be sham'd for ever.

Re-enter OTHELLO *and* Attendants.

Oth.   What is the matter here? 1
Mon. 'Zounds! I bleed still; I am hurt to
  the death.
Oth. Hold, for your lives!
Iago. Hold, ho, lieutenant! Sir! Montano
  gentlemen! 1
Have you forgot all sense of place and duty?

Hold! the general speaks to you; hold for shame!

Oth. Why, how now, ho! from whence ariseth this?

Are we turn'd Turks, and to ourselves do that
Which heaven hath forbid the Ottomites? 173
For Christian shame put by this barbarous brawl;
He that stirs next to carve for his own rage
Holds his soul light; he dies upon his motion.
Silence that dreadful bell! it frights the isle 177
From her propriety. What is the matter, masters?
Honest Iago, that look'st dead with grieving,
Speak, who began this? on thy love, I charge
thee.   180

Iago. I do not know; friends all but now, even now,
In quarter and in terms like bride and groom
Devesting them for bed; and then, but now,—
As if some planet had unwitted men,—   184
Swords out, and tilting one at other's breast,
In opposition bloody. I cannot speak
Any beginning to this peevish odds,
And would in action glorious I had lost   188
Those legs that brought me to a part of it!

Oth. How comes it, Michael, you are thus forgot?

Cas. I pray you, pardon me; I cannot speak.

Oth. Worthy Montano, you were wont be
civil;   192
The gravity and stillness of your youth
The world hath noted, and your name is great
In mouths of wisest censure: what's the matter,
That you unlace your reputation thus   196
And spend your rich opinion for the name
Of a night-brawler? give me answer to it.

Mon. Worthy Othello, I am hurt to danger;
Your officer, Iago, can inform you,   200
While I spare speech, which something now
offends me,
Of all that I do know; nor know I aught
By me that's said or done amiss this night,
Unless self-charity be sometimes a vice, 204
And to defend ourselves it be a sin
When violence assails us.

Oth.   Now, by heaven,
My blood begins my safer guides to rule,
And passion, having my best judgment collied,
Assays to lead the way. If I once stir,   209
Or do but lift this arm, the best of you
Shall sink in my rebuke. Give me to know
How this foul rout began, who set it on;   212
And he that is approv'd in this offence,
Though he had twinn'd with me—both at a birth—
Shall lose me. What! in a town of war,
Yet wild, the people's hearts brimful of fear, 216
To manage private and domestic quarrel,
In night, and on the court and guard of safety!
'Tis monstrous. Iago, who began't?

Mon. If partially affin'd, or leagu'd in office,
Thou dost deliver more or less than truth, 221
Thou art no soldier.

Iago.   Touch me not so near;
I had rather have this tongue cut from my mouth
Than it should do offence to Michael Cassio; 224

Yet, I persuade myself, to speak the truth
Shall nothing wrong him. Thus it is, general.
Montano and myself being in speech,
There comes a fellow crying out for help, 228
And Cassio following with determin'd sword
To execute upon him. Sir, this gentleman
Steps in to Cassio, and entreats his pause;
Myself the crying fellow did pursue,   232
Lest by his clamour, as it so fell out,
The town might fall in fright; he, swift of foot,
Outran my purpose, and I return'd the rather
For that I heard the clink and fall of swords,
And Cassio high in oath, which till to-night 237
I ne'er might say before. When I came back,—
For this was brief,—I found them close together,
At blow and thrust, even as again they were 240
When you yourself did part them.
More of this matter can I not report:
But men are men; the best sometimes forget:
Though Cassio did some little wrong to him, 244
As men in rage strike those that wish them best,
Yet, surely Cassio, I believe, receiv'd
From him that fled some strange indignity,
Which patience could not pass.

Oth.   I know, Iago, 248
Thy honesty and love doth mince this matter,
Making it light to Cassio. Cassio, I love thee;
But never more be officer of mine.

Enter DESDEMONA, *attended.*

Look! if my gentle love be not rais'd up; 252
[*To* CASSIO.] I'll make thee an example.

Des.   What's the matter?

Oth. All's well now, sweeting; come away to
bed.
Sir, for your hurts, myself will be your surgeon.
Lead him off.   [MONTANO *is led off.*
Iago, look with care about the town,   257
And silence those whom this vile brawl dis-
tracted.
Come, Desdemona; 'tis the soldiers' life,
To have their balmy slumbers wak'd with strife.
                [*Exeunt all but* IAGO *and* CASSIO.

Iago. What! are you hurt, lieutenant? 261

Cas. Ay; past all surgery.

Iago. Marry, heaven forbid!

Cas. Reputation, reputation, reputation! O!
I have lost my reputation. I have lost the immortal part of myself, and what remains is
bestial. My reputation, Iago, my reputation!

Iago. As I am an honest man, I thought you
had received some bodily wound; there is more
offence in that than in reputation. Reputation
is an idle and most false imposition; oft got
without merit, and lost without deserving: you
have lost no reputation at all, unless you repute
yourself such a loser. What! man; there are
ways to recover the general again; you are but
now cast in his mood, a punishment more in
policy than in malice; even so as one would beat
his offenceless dog to affright an imperious lion.
Sue to him again, and he is yours.   279

Cas. I will rather sue to be despised than to
deceive so good a commander with so slight, so
drunken, and so indiscreet an officer. Drunk!
and speak parrot! and squabble, swagger, swear,

and discourse fustian with one's own shadow!
O thou invisible spirit of wine! if thou hast no
name to be known by, let us call thee devil!

Iago. What was he that you followed with
your sword? What had he done to you? 288

Cas. I know not.

Iago. Is't possible?

Cas. I remember a mass of things, but nothing distinctly; a quarrel, but nothing wherefore. O God! that men should put an enemy in
their mouths to steal away their brains; that
we should, with joy, pleasance, revel, and applause, transform ourselves into beasts. 296

Iago. Why, but you are now well enough;
how came you thus recovered?

Cas. It hath pleased the devil drunkenness to
give place to the devil wrath; one unperfectness
shows me another, to make me frankly despise
myself. 302

Iago. Come, you are too severe a moraler.
As the time, the place, and the condition of this
country stands, I could heartily wish this had
not befallen, but since it is as it is, mend it for
your own good. 307

Cas. I will ask him for my place again; he
shall tell me I am a drunkard! Had I as many
mouths as Hydra, such an answer would stop
them all. To be now a sensible man, by and by
a fool, and presently a beast! O strange! Every
inordinate cup is unblessed and the ingredient is
a devil. 314

Iago. Come, come; good wine is a good
familiar creature if it be well used; exclaim no
more against it. And, good lieutenant, I think
you think I love you. 318

Cas. I have well approved it, sir. I drunk!

Iago. You or any man living may be drunk
at some time, man. I'll tell you what you shall
do. Our general's wife is now the general: I
may say so in this respect, for that he hath devoted and given up himself to the contemplation,
mark, and denotement of her parts and graces;
confess yourself freely to her; importune her;
she'll help to put you in your place again. She
is of so free, so kind, so apt, so blessed a disposition, that she holds it a vice in her goodness not
to do more than she is requested. This broken
joint between you and her husband entreat her
to splinter; and my fortunes against any lay
worth naming, this crack of your love shall
grow stronger than it was before. 334

Cas. You advise me well.

Iago. I protest, in the sincerity of love and
honest kindness. 337

Cas. I think it freely; and betimes in the
morning I will beseech the virtuous Desdemona
to undertake for me. I am desperate of my
fortunes if they check me here. 341

Iago. You are in the right. Good night,
lieutenant; I must to the watch.

Cas. Good night, honest Iago!   [*Exit.*

Iago. And what's he then that says I play
the villain? 345
When this advice is free I give and honest,
Probal to thinking and indeed the course
To win the Moor again? For 'tis most easy 348

The inclining Desdemona to subdue
In any honest suit; she's fram'd as fruitful
As the free elements. And then for her
To win the Moor, were't to renounce his bap-
tism, 35
All seals and symbols of redeemed sin,
His soul is so enfetter'd to her love,
That she may make, unmake, do what she list
Even as her appetite shall play the god 35
With his weak function. How am I then a villain
To counsel Cassio to this parallel course,
Directly to his good? Divinity of hell!
When devils will the blackest sins put on, 36
They do suggest at first with heavenly shows,
As I do now; for while this honest fool
Plies Desdemona to repair his fortunes,
And she for him pleads strongly to the Moor, 36
I'll pour this pestilence into his ear
That she repeals him for her body's lust;
And, by how much she strives to do him good
She shall undo her credit with the Moor. 36
So will I turn her virtue into pitch,
And out of her own goodness make the net
That shall enmesh them all.

Re-enter RODERIGO.

              How now, Roderigo

Rod. I do follow here in the chase, not like a
hound that hunts, but one that fills up the cry
My money is almost spent; I have been to-night
exceedingly well cudgelled; and I think the issue
will be, I shall have so much experience for my
pains; and so, with no money at all and a little
more wit, return again to Venice.

Iago. How poor are they that have not pa-
tience!
What wound did ever heal but by degrees? 38
Thou know'st we work by wit and not by witch-
craft,
And wit depends on dilatory time.
Does't not go well? Cassio hath beaten thee,
And thou by that small hurt hast cashiered
Cassio. 38
Though other things grow fair against the sun
Yet fruits that blossom first will first be ripe:
Content thyself awhile. By the mass, 'tis morning
Pleasure and action make the hours seem short
Retire thee; go where thou art billeted: 38
Away, I say; thou shalt know more hereafter
Nay, get thee gone. [*Exit* RODERIGO.] Two
things are to be done,
My wife must move for Cassio to her mistress;
I'll set her on; 39
Myself the while to draw the Moor apart,
And bring him jump when he may Cassio find
Soliciting his wife: ay, that's the way: 39
Dull not device by coldness and delay. [*Exit.*

ACT III

SCENE I.—*Cyprus. Before the Castle.*

Enter CASSIO, *and some* Musicians.

Cas. Masters, play here, I will content your
pains;
Something that's brief; and bid 'Good morrow,
general.'   [*Music.*

Enter Clown.

Clo. Why, masters, have your instruments been in Naples, that they speak i' the nose thus?
First Mus. How, sir, how?   5
Clo. Are these, I pray you, wind-instruments?
First Mus. Ay, marry, are they, sir.
Clo. O! thereby hangs a tail.   8
First Mus. Whereby hangs a tale, sir?
Clo. Marry, sir, by many a wind-instrument that I know. But, masters, here's money for you; and the general so likes your music, that he desires you, for love's sake, to make no more noise with it.   14
First Mus. Well, sir, we will not.
Clo. If you have any music that may not be heard, to't again; but, as they say, to hear music the general does not greatly care.   18
First Mus. We have none such, sir.
Clo. Then put up your pipes in your bag, for I'll away. Go; vanish into air; away!   21
                               [*Exeunt* Musicians.
Cas. Dost thou hear, mine honest friend?
Clo. No, I hear not your honest friend; I hear you.   24
Cas. Prithee, keep up thy quillets. There's a poor piece of gold for thee. If the gentlewoman that attends the general's wife be stirring, tell her there's one Cassio entreats her a little favour of speech: wilt thou do this?   29
Clo. She is stirring, sir: if she will stir hither, I shall seem to notify unto her.
Cas. Do, good my friend.   [*Exit* Clown.

Enter IAGO.

                            In happy time, Iago. 32
Iago. You have not been a-bed, then?
Cas. Why, no; the day had broke
Before we parted. I have made bold, Iago,
To send in to your wife; my suit to her   36
Is, that she will to virtuous Desdemona
Procure me some access.
Iago.   I'll send her to you presently;
And I'll devise a mean to draw the Moor
Out of the way, that your converse and business
May be more free.   41
Cas. I humbly thank you for't.   [*Exit* IAGO.
                               I never knew
A Florentine more kind and honest.

Enter EMILIA.

Emil. Good morrow, good lieutenant: I am sorry   44
For your displeasure; but all will soon be well.
The general and his wife are talking of it,
And she speaks for you stoutly: the Moor replies
That he you hurt is of great fame in Cyprus 48
And great affinity, and that in wholesome wisdom
He might not but refuse you; but he protests he loves you,
And needs no other suitor but his likings
To take the saf'st occasion by the front   52
To bring you in again.
Cas.   Yet, I beseech you,
If you think fit, or that it may be done,

Give me advantage of some brief discourse
With Desdemona alone.
Emil.   Pray you, come in: 56
I will bestow you where you shall have time
To speak your bosom freely.
Cas.   I am much bound to you.
                                        [*Exeunt.*

SCENE II.—*A Room in the Castle.*

Enter OTHELLO, IAGO, *and* Gentlemen.

Oth. These letters give, Iago, to the pilot,
And by him do my duties to the senate;
That done, I will be walking on the works;
Repair there to me.
Iago.   Well, my good lord, I'll do't. 4
Oth. This fortification, gentlemen, shall we see't?
Gent. We'll wait upon your lordship.
                                        [*Exeunt.*

SCENE III.—*Before the Castle.*

Enter DESDEMONA, CASSIO, *and* EMILIA.

Des. Be thou assur'd, good Cassio, I will do
All my abilities in thy behalf.
Emil. Good madam, do: I warrant it grieves my husband,
As if the case were his.   4
Des. O! that's an honest fellow. Do not doubt, Cassio,
But I will have my lord and you again
As friendly as you were.
Cas.   Bounteous madam,
Whatever shall become of Michael Cassio,   8
He's never anything but your true servant.
Des. I know't; I thank you. You do love my lord;
You have known him long; and be you well assur'd
He shall in strangeness stand no further off 12
Than in a politic distance.
Cas.   Ay, but, lady,
That policy may either last so long,
Or feed upon such nice and waterish diet,
Or breed itself so out of circumstance,   16
That, I being absent and my place supplied,
My general will forget my love and service.
Des. Do not doubt that; before Emilia here
I give thee warrant of thy place. Assure thee, 20
If I do vow a friendship, I'll perform it
To the last article; my lord shall never rest;
I'll watch him tame, and talk him out of patience;
His bed shall seem a school, his board a shrift; 24
I'll intermingle every thing he does
With Cassio's suit. Therefore be merry, Cassio;
For thy solicitor shall rather die
Than give thy cause away.   28

Enter OTHELLO, *and* IAGO *at a distance.*

Emil. Madam, here comes my lord.
Cas. Madam, I'll take my leave.
Des. Why, stay, and hear me speak.
Cas. Madam, not now; I am very ill at ease,
Unfit for mine own purposes.   33
Des. Well, do your discretion. [*Exit* CASSIO.

Iago. Ha! I like not that.
Oth. What dost thou say?
Iago. Nothing, my lord: or if—I know not
what. 36
Oth. Was not that Cassio parted from my
wife?
Iago. Cassio, my lord? No, sure, I cannot
think it
That he would steal away so guilty-like,
Seeing you coming.
Oth. I do believe 'twas he. 40
Des. How now, my lord!
I have been talking with a suitor here,
A man that languishes in your displeasure.
Oth. Who is't you mean? 44
Des. Why, your lieutenant, Cassio. Good
my lord,
If I have any grace or power to move you,
His present reconciliation take;
For if he be not one that truly loves you, 48
That errs in ignorance and not in cunning,
I have no judgment in an honest face.
I prithee call him back.
Oth. Went he hence now?
Des. Ay, sooth; so humbled, 52
That he hath left part of his grief with me,
To suffer with him. Good love, call him back.
Oth. Not now, sweet Desdemona; some other
time.
Des. But shall't be shortly?
Oth. The sooner, sweet, for you. 56
Des. Shall't be to-night at supper?
Oth. No, not to-night.
Des. To-morrow dinner then?
Oth. I shall not dine at home;
I meet the captains at the citadel.
Des. Why then, to-morrow night; or Tues-
day morn; 60
On Tuesday noon, or night; on Wednesday
morn:
I prithee name the time, but let it not
Exceed three days: in faith, he's penitent;
And yet his trespass, in our common reason,—
Save that they say, the wars must make ex-
amples 65
Out of their best,—is not almost a fault
To incur a private check. When shall he come?
Tell me, Othello: I wonder in my soul, 68
What you could ask me that I should deny,
Or stand so mammering on. What! Michael
Cassio,
That came a wooing with you, and so many a time,
When I have spoke of you dispraisingly, 72
Hath ta'en your part; to have so much to do
To bring him in! Trust me, I could do much.—
Oth. Prithee, no more; let him come when
he will;
I will deny thee nothing.
Des. Why, this is not a boon; 76
'Tis as I should entreat you wear your gloves,
Or feed on nourishing dishes, or keep you warm,
Or sue to you to do a peculiar profit
To your own person; nay, when I have a suit 80
Wherein I mean to touch your love indeed,
It shall be full of poise and difficult weight,
And fearful to be granted.

Oth. I will deny thee nothing:
Whereon, I do beseech thee, grant me this, 84
To leave me but a little to myself.
Des. Shall I deny you? no . farewell, my lord.
Oth. Farewell, my Desdemona: I'll come to
thee straight.
Des. Emilia, come. Be as your fancies teach
you; 88
Whate'er you be, I am obedient.
[*Exit, with* EMILIA.
Oth. Excellent wretch! Perdition catch my
soul
But I do love thee! and when I love thee not,
Chaos is come again. 92
Iago. My noble lord,—
Oth. What dost thou say, Iago?
Iago. Did Michael Cassio, when you woo'd
my lady,
Know of your love?
Oth. He did, from first to last: why dost thou
ask? 96
Iago. But for a satisfaction of my thought;
No further harm.
Oth. Why of thy thought, Iago?
Iago. I did not think he had been acquainted
with her.
Oth. O! yes; and went between us very oft.
Iago. Indeed! 101
Oth. Indeed! ay, indeed; discern'st thou
aught in that?
Is he not honest?
Iago. Honest, my lord?
Oth. Honest! ay, honest.
Iago. My lord, for aught I know. 104
Oth. What dost thou think?
Iago. Think, my lord!
Oth. Think, my lord!
By heaven, he echoes me,
As if there were some monster in his thought
Too hideous to be shown. Thou dost mean
something: 108
I heard thee say but now, thou lik'dst not that,
When Cassio left my wife; what didst not like?
And when I told thee he was of my counsel
In my whole course of wooing, thou criedst,
'Indeed!' 112
And didst contract and purse thy brow together,
As if thou then hadst shut up in thy brain
Some horrible conceit. If thou dost love me,
Show me thy thought. 116
Iago. My lord, you know I love you.
Oth. I think thou dost;
And, for I know thou art full of love and honesty,
And weigh'st thy words before thou giv'st them
breath,
Therefore these stops of thine fright me the
more; 120
For such things in a false disloyal knave
Are tricks of custom, but in a man that's just
They are close delations, working from the
heart
That passion cannot rule.
Iago. For Michael Cassio, 124
I dare be sworn I think that he is honest.
Oth. I think so too.
Iago. Men should be what they seem;

Or those that be not, would they might seem
  none!
Oth. Certain, men should be what they seem.
Iago. Why then, I think Cassio's an honest
  man.   129
Oth. Nay, yet there's more in this.
I pray thee, speak to me as to thy thinkings,
As thou dost ruminate, and give thy worst of
  thoughts   132
The worst of words.
  Iago.   Good my lord, pardon me;
Though I am bound to every act of duty,
I am not bound to that all slaves are free to.
Utter my thoughts? Why, say they are vile and
  false;   136
As where's that palace whereinto foul things
Sometimes intrude not? who has a breast so
  pure
But some uncleanly apprehensions
Keep leets and law days, and in session sit 140
With meditations lawful?
  Oth. Thou dost conspire against thy friend,
  Iago,
If thou but think'st him wrong'd, and mak'st
  his ear
A stranger to thy thoughts.
  Iago.   I do beseech you, 144
Though I perchance am vicious in my guess,—
As, I confess, it is my nature's plague
To spy into abuses, and oft my jealousy
Shapes faults that are not,—that your wisdom
  yet,   148
From one that so imperfectly conceits,
Would take no notice, nor build yourself a
  trouble
Out of his scattering and unsure observance.
It were not for your quiet nor your good, 152
Nor for my manhood, honesty, or wisdom,
To let you know my thoughts.
  Oth.   What dost thou mean?
  Iago. Good name in man and woman, dear
  my lord,
Is the immediate jewel of their souls: 156
Who steals my purse steals trash; 'tis some-
  thing, nothing;
'Twas mine, 'tis his, and has been slave to thou-
  sands;
But he that filches from me my good name
Robs me of that which not enriches him, 160
And makes me poor indeed.
  Oth. By heaven, I'll know thy thoughts.
  Iago. You cannot, if my heart were in your
  hand;
Nor shall not, whilst 'tis in my custody. 164
  Oth. Ha!
  Iago.   O! beware, my lord, of jealousy;
It is the green-ey'd monster which doth mock
The meat it feeds on; that cuckold lives in bliss
Who, certain of his fate, loves not his wronger;
But, O! what damned minutes tells he o'er 169
Who dotes, yet doubts; suspects, yet soundly
  loves!
  Oth. O misery!
  Iago. Poor and content is rich, and rich
  enough,   172
But riches fineless is as poor as winter

To him that ever fears he shall be poor.
Good heaven, the souls of all my tribe defend
From jealousy!
  Oth.   Why, why is this?   176
Think'st thou I'd make a life of jealousy,
To follow still the changes of the moon
With fresh suspicions? No; to be once in doubt
Is once to be resolved. Exchange me for a goat
When I shall turn the business of my soul 181
To such exsufflicate and blown surmises,
Matching thy inference. 'Tis not to make me
  jealous
To say my wife is fair, feeds well, loves com-
  pany,   184
Is free of speech, sings, plays, and dances well;
Where virtue is, these are more virtuous:
Nor from mine own weak merits will I draw
The smallest fear, or doubt of her revolt; 188
For she had eyes, and chose me. No, Iago;
I'll see before I doubt; when I doubt, prove;
And, on the proof, there is no more but this,
Away at once with love or jealousy!   192
  Iago. I am glad of it; for now I shall have
  reason
To show the love and duty that I bear you
With franker spirit; therefore, as I am bound,
Receive it from me; I speak not yet of proof. 196
Look to your wife; observe her well with Cassio;
Wear your eye thus, not jealous nor secure:
I would not have your free and noble nature
Out of self-bounty be abus'd; look to't: 200
I know our country disposition well;
In Venice they do let heaven see the pranks
They dare not show their husbands; their best
  conscience
Is not to leave't undone, but keep't unknown.
  Oth. Dost thou say so?   205
  Iago. She did deceive her father, marrying
  you;
And when she seem'd to shake and fear your
  looks,
She lov'd them most.
  Oth.   And so she did.
  Iago.   Why, go to, then; 208
She that so young could give out such a seeming,
To seel her father's eyes up close as oak,
He thought 'twas witchcraft; but I am much to
  blame;
I humbly do beseech you of your pardon   212
For too much loving you.
  Oth.   I am bound to thee for ever.
  Iago. I see, this hath a little dash'd your
  spirits.
  Oth. Not a jot, not a jot.
  Iago.   I' faith, I fear it has.
I hope you will consider what is spoke   216
Comes from my love. But, I do see you're
  mov'd;
I am to pray you not to strain my speech
To grosser issues nor to larger reach
Than to suspicion.   220
  Oth. I will not.
  Iago.   Should you do so, my lord,
My speech should fall into such vile success
As my thoughts aim not at. Cassio 's my worthy
  friend—

My lord, I see you're mov'd.
    Oth.   No, not much mov'd: 224
I do not think but Desdemona's honest.
    Iago. Long live she so! and long live you to
    think so!
    Oth. And, yet, how nature erring from it-
    self,—
    Iago. Ay, there's the point: as, to be bold
    with you,   228
Not to affect many proposed matches
Of her own clime, complexion, and degree,
Whereto, we see, in all things nature tends;
Foh! one may smell in such, a will most rank,
Foul disproportion, thoughts unnatural.   233
But pardon me; I do not in position
Distinctly speak of her, though I may fear
Her will, recoiling to her better judgment, 236
May fall to match you with her country forms
And happily repent.
    Oth.   Farewell, farewell:
If more thou dost perceive, let me know more;
Set on thy wife to observe. Leave me, Iago. 240
    Iago. My lord, I take my leave.   [*Going.*
    Oth. Why did I marry? This honest creature,
    doubtless,
Sees and knows more, much more, than he un-
    folds.
    Iago. [*Returning.*] My lord, I would I might
    entreat your honour   244
To scan this thing no further; leave it to time.
Although 'tis fit that Cassio have his place,
For, sure he fills it up with great ability,
Yet, if you please to hold him off awhile, 248
You shall by that perceive him and his means:
Note if your lady strain his entertainment
With any strong or vehement importunity;
Much will be seen in that. In the mean time, 252
Let me be thought too busy in my fears,
As worthy cause I have to fear I am,
And hold her free, I do beseech your honour.
    Oth. Fear not my government.   256
    Iago. I once more take my leave.   [*Exit.*
    Oth. This fellow's of exceeding honesty,
And knows all qualities, with a learned spirit,
Of human dealings; if I do prove her haggard,
Though that her jesses were my dear heart-
    strings,   261
I'd whistle her off and let her down the wind,
To prey at fortune. Haply, for I am black,
And have not those soft parts of conversation
That chamberers have, or, for I am declin'd 265
Into the vale of years—yet that's not much—
She's gone, I am abus'd; and my relief
Must be to loathe her. O curse of marriage! 268
That we can call these delicate creatures ours,
And not their appetites. I had rather be a toad,
And live upon the vapour of a dungeon,
Than keep a corner in the thing I love   272
For others' uses. Yet, 'tis the plague of great
    ones;
Prerogativ'd are they less than the base;
'Tis destiny unshunnable, like death:
Even then this forked plague is fated to us 276
When we do quicken.
              Look! where she comes.
If she be false, O! then heaven mocks itself.

I'll not believe it.

    Re-enter DESDEMONA *and* EMILIA.

    Des.   How now, my dear Othello!
Your dinner and the generous islanders   280
By you invited, do attend your presence.
    Oth. I am to blame.
    Des.   Why do you speak so faintly?
Are you not well?
    Oth. I have a pain upon my forehead here. 284
    Des. Faith, that's with watching; 'twill away
    again:
Let me but bind it hard, within this hour
It will be well.
    Oth.   Your napkin is too little:
              [*She drops her handkerchief.*
Let it alone. Come, I'll go in with you.   288
    Des. I am very sorry that you are not well.
          [*Exeunt* OTHELLO *and* DESDEMONA.
    Emil. I am glad I have found this napkin;
This was her first remembrance from the Moor;
My wayward husband hath a hundred times 292
Woo'd me to steal it, but she so loves the token,
For he conjur'd her she should ever keep it,
That she reserves it evermore about her
To kiss and talk to. I'll have the work ta'en out,
And give't Iago: 297
What he will do with it heaven knows, not I;
I nothing but to please his fantasy.

    Enter IAGO.

    Iago. How now! what do you here alone? 300
    Emil. Do not you chide; I have a thing for
    you.
    Iago. A thing for me? It is a common thing—
    Emil. Ha!
    Iago. To have a foolish wife.   304
    Emil. O! is that all? What will you give me
    now
For that same handkerchief?
    Iago.   What handkerchief?
    Emil. What handkerchief!
Why, that the Moor first gave to Desdemona:
That which so often you did bid me steal. 309
    Iago. Hast stol'n it from her?
    Emil. No, faith; she let it drop by negligence,
And, to the advantage, I, being there, took't up.
Look, here it is.
    Iago.   A good wench; give it me. 313
    Emil. What will you do with't, that you have
    been so earnest
To have me filch it?
    Iago. Why, what's that to you? [*Snatches it.*
    Emil. If it be not for some purpose of im-
    port   317
Give't me again; poor lady! she'll run mad
When she shall lack it.
    Iago. Be not acknown on't; I have use for
    it.   320
Go, leave me.   [*Exit* EMILIA.
I will in Cassio's lodging lose this napkin,
And let him find it; trifles light as air
Are to the jealous confirmations strong   324
As proofs of holy writ; this may do something.
The Moor already changes with my poison:
Dangerous conceits are in their natures poisons,

Vhich at the first are scarce found to distaste,
3ut with a little act upon the blood,   329
3urn like the mines of sulphur. I did say so:
Look! where he comes!

Enter OTHELLO.

Not poppy, nor mandragora,
Nor all the drowsy syrups of the world,   332
shall ever medicine thee to that sweet sleep
Vhich thou ow'dst yesterday.

Oth.   Ha! ha! false to me?

Iago. Why, how now, general! no more of
that.

Oth. Avaunt! be gone! thou hast set me on
the rack;   336
swear 'tis better to be much abus'd
han but to know't a little.

Iago.   How now, my lord!

Oth. What sense had I of her stol'n hours of
lust?   339
saw't not, thought it not, it harm'd not me;
slept the next night well, was free and merry;
found not Cassio's kisses on her lips;
He that is robb'd, not wanting what is stol'n,
Let him not know't and he's not robb'd at all.

Iago. I am sorry to hear this.   345

Oth. I had been happy, if the general camp,
Pioners and all, had tasted her sweet body,
So I had nothing known. O! now, for ever 348
Farewell the tranquil mind; farewell content!
Farewell the plumed troop and the big wars
That make ambition virtue! O, farewell!
Farewell the neighing steed, and the shrill
trump,   352
The spirit-stirring drum, the ear-piercing fife,
The royal banner, and all quality,
Pride, pomp, and circumstance of glorious war!
And, O you mortal engines, whose rude throats
The immortal Jove's dread clamours counter-
feit,   357
Farewell! Othello's occupation's gone!

Iago. Is it possible, my lord?

Oth. Villain, be sure thou prove my love a
whore,   360
Be sure of it; give me the ocular proof;
Or, by the worth of mine eternal soul,
Thou hadst been better have been born a dog
Than answer my wak'd wrath.

Iago.   Is't come to this?

Oth. Make me to see't; or, at the least, so
prove it,   365
That the probation bear no hinge nor loop
To hang a doubt on; or woe upon thy life!

Iago. My noble lord,—   368

Oth. If thou dost slander her and torture me,
Never pray more; abandon all remorse;
On horror's head horrors accumulate;
Do deeds to make heaven weep, all earth
amaz'd;   372
For nothing canst thou to damnation add
Greater than that.

Iago.   O grace! O heaven forgive me!
Are you a man! have you a soul or sense?
God be wi' you; take mine office. O wretched
fool!   376
That liv'st to make thine honesty a vice.

O monstrous world! Take note, take note, O
world!
To be direct and honest is not safe.
I thank you for this profit, and, from hence 380
I'll love no friend, sith love breeds such offence.

Iago. I should be wise; for honesty's a fool,
And loses that it works for.

Oth.   By the world, 384
I think my wife be honest and think she is not;
I think that thou art just and think thou art
not.
I'll have some proof. Her name, that was as
fresh
As Dian's visage, is now begrim'd and black 388
As mine own face. If there be cords or knives,
Poison or fire or suffocating streams,
I'll not endure it. Would I were satisfied!

Iago. I see, sir, you are eaten up with pas-
sion.   392
I do repent me that I put it to you.
You would be satisfied?

Oth.   Would! nay, I will.

Iago. And may; but how? how satisfied, my
lord?
Would you, the supervisor, grossly gape on; 396
Behold her tupp'd?

Oth.   Death and damnation! O!

Iago. It were a tedious difficulty, I think,
To bring them to that prospect; damn them
then,
If ever mortal eyes do see them bolster   400
More than their own! What then? how then?
What shall I say? Where's satisfaction?
It is impossible you should see this,
Were they as prime as goats, as hot as monkeys,
As salt as wolves in pride, and fools as gross 405
As ignorance made drunk; but yet, I say,
If imputation, and strong circumstances,
Which lead directly to the door of truth, 408
Will give you satisfaction, you may have it.

Oth. Give me a living reason she's disloyal.

Iago. I do not like the office;
But, sith I am enter'd in this cause so far, 412
Prick'd to't by foolish honesty and love,
I will go on. I lay with Cassio lately;
And, being troubled with a raging tooth,
I could not sleep.   416
There are a kind of men so loose of soul
That in their sleeps will mutter their affairs;
One of this kind is Cassio.
In sleep I heard him say, 'Sweet Desdemona, 420
Let us be wary, let us hide our loves!'
And then, sir, would he gripe and wring my
hand,
Cry, 'O, sweet creature!' and then kiss me hard,
As if he pluck'd up kisses by the roots, 424
That grew upon my lips; then laid his leg
Over my thigh, and sigh'd, and kiss'd; and then
Cried, 'Cursed fate, that gave thee to the Moor!'

Oth. O monstrous! monstrous!

Iago.   Nay, this was but his dream.

Oth. But this denoted a foregone conclusion:
'Tis a shrewd doubt, though it be but a dream.

Iago. And this may help to thicken other
proofs

That do demonstrate thinly.

Oth.   I'll tear her all to pieces. 432

Iago. Nay, but be wise; yet we see nothing done;

She may be honest yet. Tell me but this:
Have you not sometimes seen a handkerchief
Spotted with strawberries in your wife's hand?

   Oth. I gave her such a one; 'twas my first gift.   437

   Iago. I know not that; but such a handkerchief—

I am sure it was your wife's—did I to-day
See Cassio wipe his beard with.

Oth.   If it be that,— 440

Iago. If it be that, or any that was hers,
It speaks against her with the other proofs.

   Oth. O! that the slave had forty thousand lives;

One is too poor, too weak for my revenge. 444
Now do I see 'tis true. Look here, Iago;
All my fond love thus do I blow to heaven:
'Tis gone.   447
Arise, black vengeance, from the hollow hell!
Yield up, O love! thy crown and hearted throne
To tyrannous hate. Swell, bosom, with thy fraught,
For 'tis of aspics' tongues!

Iago.   Yet be content.

Oth. O! blood, blood, blood!   452

Iago. Patience, I say; your mind, perhaps, may change.

Oth. Never, Iago. Like to the Pontick sea,
Whose icy current and compulsive course
Ne'er feels retiring ebb, but keeps due on 456
To the Propontic and the Hellespont,
Even so my bloody thoughts, with violent pace,
Shall ne'er look back, ne'er ebb to humble love,
Till that a capable and wide revenge   460
Swallow them up.   [*Kneels.*
     Now, by yond marble heaven,
In the due reverence of a sacred vow
I here engage my words.

Iago.   Do not rise yet. [*Kneels.*
Witness, you ever-burning lights above!   464
You elements that clip us round about!
Witness, that here Iago doth give up
The execution of his wit, hands, heart,
To wrong'd Othello's service! Let him command,   468
And to obey shall be in me remorse,
What bloody business ever.

Oth.   I greet thy love,
Not with vain thanks, but with acceptance bounteous,
And will upon the instant put thee to't: 472
Within these three days let me hear thee say
That Cassio's not alive.

Iago. My friend is dead; 'tis done at your request:
But let her live.

Oth. Damn her, lewd minx! O, damn her!
Come, go with me apart; I will withdraw 477
To furnish me with some swift means of death
For the fair devil. Now art thou my lieutenant.

   Iago. I am your own for ever.   [*Exeunt.*

SCENE IV.—*Before the Castle.*

Enter DESDEMONA, EMILIA, *and* Clown.

Des. Do you know, sirrah, where Lieutenant Cassio lies?

Clo. I dare not say he lies any where.

Des. Why, man?

Clo. He is a soldier; and for one to say a soldier lies, is stabbing.

Des. Go to; where lodges he?

Clo. To tell you where he lodges is to tell you where I lie.

Des. Can anything be made of this?

Clo. I know not where he lodges, and for me to devise a lodging, and say he lies here or he lies there, were to lie in mine own throat.

Des. Can you inquire him out, and be edified by report?

Clo. I will catechize the world for him; that is, make questions, and by them answer.

Des. Seek him, bid him come hither; tell him I have moved my lord in his behalf, and hope all will be well.

Clo. To do this is within the compass of man's wit, and therefore I will attempt the doing it.   [*Exit.*

Des. Where should I lose that handkerchief, Emilia?

Emil. I know not, madam.

Des. Believe me, I had rather have lost my purse
Full of cruzadoes; and, but my noble Moor
Is true of mind, and made of no such baseness
As jealous creatures are, it were enough
To put him to ill thinking.

Emil.   Is he not jealous?

Des. Who! he? I think the sun where he was born
Drew all such humours from him.

Emil.   Look! where he comes.

Des. I will not leave him now till Cassio
Be call'd to him.

Enter OTHELLO.

     How is't with you, my lord?

Oth. Well, my good lady. [*Aside.*] O! hardness to dissemble.
How do you, Desdemona?

Des.   Well, my good lord.

Oth. Give me your hand. This hand is moist, my lady.   3

Des. It yet has felt no age nor known no sorrow.

Oth. This argues fruitfulness and liberal heart;
Hot, hot, and moist; this hand of yours requires 4
A sequester from liberty, fasting and prayer,
Much castigation, exercise devout;
For here's a young and sweating devil here,
That commonly rebels. 'Tis a good hand, 4
A frank one.

Des.   You may, indeed, say so;
For 'twas that hand that gave away my heart.

Oth. A liberal hand; the hearts of old gave hands,

But our new heraldry is hands not hearts. 48
  Des. I cannot speak of this. Come now, your
    promise.
  Oth. What promise, chuck?
  Des. I have sent to bid Cassio come speak
    with you.
  Oth. I have a salt and sorry rheum offends
    me.								52
Lend me thy handkerchief.
  Des.				Here, my lord.
  Oth. That which I gave you.
  Des.			I have it not about me.
  Oth. Not?
  Des.		No, indeed, my lord.
  Oth.				That is a fault.
That handkerchief						56
Did an Egyptian to my mother give;
She was a charmer, and could almost read
The thoughts of people; she told her, while she
    kept it,
'Twould make her amiable and subdue my
    father							60
Entirely to her love, but if she lost it
Or made a gift of it, my father's eye
Should hold her loathed, and his spirits should
    hunt
After new fancies. She dying gave it me;	64
And bid me, when my fate would have me wive,
To give it her. I did so: and take heed on 't;
Make it a darling like your precious eye;
To lose 't or give 't away, were such perdition 68
As nothing else could match.
  Des.			Is 't possible?
  Oth. 'Tis true; there 's magic in the web of
    it;
A sibyl, that had number'd in the world
The sun to course two hundred compasses, 72
In her prophetic fury sew'd the work;
The worms were hallow'd that did breed the
    silk,
And it was dy'd in mummy which the skilful
Conserv'd of maidens' hearts.
  Des.		Indeed! is 't true? 76
  Oth. Most veritable; therefore look to 't well.
  Des. Then would to heaven that I had never
    seen it!
  Oth. Ha! wherefore?
  Des. Why do you speak so startingly and
    rash?							80
  Oth. Is 't lost? is 't gone? speak, is it out o'
    the way?
  Des. Heaven bless us!
  Oth.				Say you?
  Des. It is not lost; but what an if it were?
  Oth. How!							84
  Des. I say, it is not lost.
  Oth.			Fetch 't, let me see 't.
  Des. Why, so I can, sir, but I will not now.
This is a trick to put me from my suit:
Pray you let Cassio be receiv'd again.		88
  Oth. Fetch me the handkerchief; my mind
    misgives.
  Des. Come, come;
You'll never meet a more sufficient man.
  Oth. The handkerchief!
  Des.			I pray, talk me of Cassio. 92

  Oth. The handkerchief!
  Des.			A man that all his time
Hath founded his good fortunes on your love,
Shar'd dangers with you,—
  Oth. The handkerchief!
  Des.		In sooth you are to blame. 96
  Oth. Away!						[*Exit.*
  Emil. Is not this man jealous?
  Des. I ne'er saw this before.
Sure, there 's some wonder in this handker-
    chief;							100
I am most unhappy in the loss of it.
  Emil. 'Tis not a year or two shows us a man;
They are all but stomachs, and we all but food;
They eat us hungerly, and when they are full
They belch us. Look you! Cassio and my hus-
    band.							105

Enter IAGO *and* CASSIO.

  Iago. There is no other way; 'tis she must
    do 't:
And, lo! the happiness: go and importune her.
  Des. How now, good Cassio! what 's the news
    with you?						108
  Cas. Madam, my former suit: I do beseech
    you
That by your virtuous means I may again
Exist, and be a member of his love
Whom I with all the office of my heart	112
Entirely honour; I would not be delay'd.
If my offence be of such mortal kind
That nor my service past, nor present sorrows,
Nor purpos'd merit in futurity,			116
Can ransom me into his love again,
But to know so must be my benefit;
So shall I clothe me in a forc'd content,
And shut myself up in some other course 120
To fortune's alms.
  Des.		Alas! thrice-gentle Cassio!
My advocation is not now in tune;
My lord is not my lord; nor should I know him,
Were I in favour as in humour alter'd.	124
So help me every spirit sanctified,
As I have spoken for you all my best
And stood within the blank of his displeasure
For my free speech. You must awhile be
    patient;						128
What I can do I will, and more I will
Than for myself I dare: let that suffice you.
  Iago. Is my lord angry?
  Emil.			He went hence but now,
And, certainly in strange unquietness.	132
  Iago. Can he be angry? I have seen the
    cannon,
When it hath blown his ranks into the air,
And, like the devil, from his very arm	135
Puff'd his own brother; and can he be angry?
Something of moment then; I will go meet him;
There 's matter in 't indeed, if he be angry.
  Des. I prithee, do so. [*Exit* IAGO.] Some-
    thing, sure, of state,
Either from Venice, or some unhatch'd practice
Made demonstrable here in Cyprus to him, 141
Hath puddled his clear spirit; and, in such
    cases
Men's natures wrangle with inferior things,

Though great ones are their object. 'Tis even so;
For let our finger ache, and it indues   145
Our other healthful members ev'n to that sense
Of pain. Nay, we must think men are not gods,
Nor of them look for such observancy   148
As fits the bridal. Beshrew me much, Emilia,
I was—unhandsome warrior as I am—
Arraigning his unkindness with my soul;
But now I find I had suborn'd the witness,   152
And he's indicted falsely.

Emil. Pray heaven it be state-matters, as you
      think,
And no conception, nor no jealous toy
Concerning you.   156

Des. Alas the day! I never gave him cause.

Emil. But jealous souls will not be answer'd
      so;
They are not ever jealous for the cause,
But jealous for they are jealous; 'tis a monster
Begot upon itself, born on itself.   161

Des. Heaven keep that monster from
      Othello's mind!

Emil. Lady, amen.

Des. I will go seek him. Cassio, walk here-
      about;   164
If I do find him fit, I'll move your suit
And seek to effect it to my uttermost.

Cas. I humbly thank your ladyship.

            [*Exeunt* DESDEMONA *and* EMILIA.

            Enter BIANCA.

Bian. Save you, friend Cassio!

Cas.   What make you from home?
How is it with you, my most fair Bianca? 169
I' faith, sweet love, I was coming to your house.

Bian. And I was going to your lodging,
      Cassio.
What! keep a week away? seven days and
      nights?   172
Eight score eight hours? and lovers' absent
      hours,
More tedious than the dial eight score times?
O weary reckoning!

Cas.   Pardon me, Bianca,
I have this while with leaden thoughts been
      press'd,   176
But I shall, in a more continuate time,
Strike off this score of absence. Sweet Bianca.

      [*Giving her* DESDEMONA'S *handkerchief.*
Take me this work out.

Bian.   O Cassio! whence came this?
This is some token from a newer friend;   180
To the felt absence now I feel a cause;
Is't come to this? Well, well.

Cas.   Go to, woman!
Throw your vile guesses in the devil's teeth,
From whence you have them. You are jealous
      now   184
That this is from some mistress, some remem-
      brance:
No, in good troth, Bianca.

Bian.   Why, whose is it?

Cas. I know not, sweet; I found it in my
      chamber.
I like the work well; ere it be demanded,— 188
As like enough it will,—I'd have it copied;

Take it and do't; and leave me for this time.

Bian. Leave you! wherefore?

Cas. I do attend here on the general,   192
And think it no addition nor my wish
To have him see me woman'd.

Bian.   Why, I pray you?

Cas. Not that I love you not.

Bian.   But that you do not love me.
I pray you, bring me on the way a little   196
And say if I shall see you soon at night.

Cas. 'Tis but a little way that I can bring
      you,
For I attend here; but I'll see you soon.

Bian. 'Tis very good; I must be circum-
      stanc'd.   [*Exeunt.*

            ACT IV

SCENE I.—*Cyprus. Before the Castle.*

      Enter OTHELLO *and* IAGO.

Iago. Will you think so?

Oth.   Think so, Iago!

Iago.   What!
To kiss in private?

Oth.   An unauthoriz'd kiss.

Iago. Or to be naked with her friend a-bed
An hour or more, not meaning any harm? 4

Oth. Naked a-bed, Iago, and not mean harm?
It is hypocrisy against the devil:
They that mean virtuously, and yet do so,
The devil their virtue tempts, and they tempt
      heaven.   8

Iago. If they do nothing, 'tis a venial slip;
But if I give my wife a handkerchief,—

Oth. What then?

Iago. Why, then, 'tis hers, my lord; and,
      being hers,   12
She may, I think, bestow't on any man.

Oth. She is protectress of her honour too;
May she give that?

Iago. Her honour is an essence that's not
      seen;   16
They have it very oft that have it not:
But for the handkerchief,—

Oth. By heaven, I would most gladly have
      forgot it:—
Thou said'st,—O! it comes o'er my memory, 20
As doth the raven o'er the infected house,
Boding to all,—he had my handkerchief.

Iago. Ay, what of that?

Oth.   That's not so good now.

Iago.   What,
If I had said I had seen him do you wrong? 24
Or heard him say, as knaves be such abroad,
Who having, by their own importunate suit,
Or voluntary dotage of some mistress,
Convinced or supplied them, cannot choose 28
But they must blab.

Oth.   Hath he said any thing?

Iago. He hath, my lord; but be you well
      assur'd,
No more than he'll unswear.

Oth.   What hath he said?

Iago. Faith, that he did—I know not what
      he did.   32

Oth. What? what?

Iago. Lie—
Oth.   With her?
Iago.   With her, on her; what you will.
Oth. Lie with her! lie on her! We say, lie on
her, when they belie her. Lie with her! that's
fulsome. Handkerchief,—confessions,—hand-
kerchief! To confess, and be hanged for his
labour. First, to be hanged, and then to confess:
I tremble at it. Nature would not invest herself
in such shadowing passion without some instruc-
tion. It is not words that shake me thus. Pish!
Noses, ears, and lips. Is it possible?—Confess!
—Handkerchief!—O devil! [*Falls in a trance.*
Iago. Work on,   45
My medicine, work! Thus credulous fools are
    caught;
And many worthy and chaste dames even thus,
All guiltless, meet reproach. What, ho! my
    lord!   48
My lord, I say! Othello!

Enter CASSIO.

                            How now, Cassio!
Cas. What's the matter?
Iago. My lord is fallen into an epilepsy;
This is his second fit; he had one yesterday. 52
Cas. Rub him about the temples.
Iago.   No, forbear;
The lethargy must have his quiet course,
If not he foams at mouth, and by and by
Breaks out to savage madness. Look! he stirs;
Do you withdraw yourself a little while,   57
He will recover straight; when he is gone,
I would on great occasion speak with you.
                                  [*Exit* CASSIO.
How is it, general? have you not hurt your
    head?   60
Oth. Dost thou mock me?
Iago.   I mock you! no, by heaven.
Would you would bear your fortune like a man!
Oth. A horned man's a monster and a beast.
Iago. There's many a beast then, in a popu-
    lous city,   64
And many a civil monster.
Oth. Did he confess it?
Iago.   Good sir, be a man;
Think every bearded fellow that's but yok'd
May draw with you; there's millions now
    alive   68
That nightly lie in those unproper beds
Which they dare swear peculiar; your case is
    better.
O! 'tis the spite of hell, the fiend's arch-mock,
To lip a wanton in a secure couch,   72
And to suppose her chaste. No, let me know;
And knowing what I am I know what she shall
    be.
Oth. O! thou art wise; 'tis certain.
Iago.   Stand you awhile apart;
Confine yourself but in a patient list.   76
Whilst you were here o'erwhelmed with your
    grief,—
A passion most unsuiting such a man,—
Cassio came hither; I shifted him away,
And laid good 'scuse upon your ecstasy;   80
Bade him anon return and here speak with me;

The which he promis'd. Do but encave your-
    self,
And mark the fleers, the gibes, and notable
    scorns,
That dwell in every region of his face;   84
For I will make him tell the tale anew,
Where, how, how oft, how long ago, and when
He hath, and is again to cope your wife:
I say, but mark his gesture. Marry, patience;
Or I shall say you are all in all in spleen,   89
And nothing of a man.
Oth.   Dost thou hear, Iago?
I will be found most cunning in my patience;
But—dost thou hear?—most bloody.
Iago.   That's not amiss; 92
But yet keep time in all. Will you withdraw?
                          [OTHELLO *goes apart.*
Now will I question Cassio of Bianca,
A housewife that by selling her desires
Buys herself bread and clothes; it is a creature
That dotes on Cassio; as 'tis the strumpet's
    plague   97
To beguile many and be beguil'd by one.
He, when he hears of her, cannot refrain
From the excess of laughter. Here he comes:

Re-enter CASSIO.

As he shall smile, Othello shall go mad;   101
And his unbookish jealousy must construe
Poor Cassio's smiles, gestures, and light be-
    haviour
Quite in the wrong. How do you now, lieu-
    tenant?   104
Cas. The worser that you give me the addi-
    tion
Whose want even kills me.
Iago. Ply Desdemona well, and you are sure
    on't.
[*Speaking lower.*] Now, if this suit lay in
    Bianca's power,   108
How quickly should you speed!
Cas.   Alas! poor caitiff!
Oth. Look! how he laughs already!
Iago. I never knew woman love man so.
Cas. Alas! poor rogue, I think, i' faith, she
    loves me.   112
Oth. Now he denies it faintly, and laughs it
    out.
Iago. Do you hear, Cassio?
Oth.   Now he importunes him
To tell it o'er: go to; well said, well said.
Iago. She gives it out that you shall marry
    her;   116
Do you intend it?
Cas. Ha, ha, ha!
Oth. Do you triumph, Roman? do you
    triumph?   119
Cas. I marry her! what? a customer? I
prithee, bear some charity to my wit; do not
think it so unwholesome. Ha, ha, ha!
Oth. So, so, so, so. They laugh that win.
Iago. Faith, the cry goes that you shall
marry her.   125
Cas. Prithee, say true.
Iago. I am a very villain else.
Oth. Have you scored me? Well.   128

Cas. This is the monkey's own giving out: she is persuaded I will marry her, out of her own love and flattery, not out of my promise.

Oth. Iago beckons me; now he begins the story. 133

Cas. She was here even now; she haunts me in every place. I was the other day talking on the sea bank with certain Venetians, and thither come this bauble, and, by this hand, she falls me thus about my neck;—

Oth. Crying, 'O dear Cassio!' as it were; his gesture imports it. 140

Cas. So hangs and lolls and weeps upon me; so hales and pulls me; ha, ha, ha!

Oth. Now he tells how she plucked him to my chamber. O! I see that nose of yours, but not the dog I shall throw it to. 145

Cas. Well, I must leave her company.

Iago. Before me! look, where she comes.

Cas. 'Tis such another fitchew! marry, a perfumed one. 149

Enter BIANCA.

What do you mean by this haunting of me?

Bian. Let the devil and his dam haunt you! What did you mean by that same handkerchief you gave me even now? I was a fine fool to take it. I must take out the work! A likely piece of work, that you should find it in your chamber, and not know who left it there! This is some minx's token, and I must take out the work! There, give it your hobby-horse; wheresoever you had it I'll take out no work on't.

Cas. How now, my sweet Bianca! how now, how now! 161

Oth. By heaven, that should be my handkerchief!

Bian. An you'll come to supper to-night, you may; an you will not, come when you are next prepared for. [*Exit.*

Iago. After her, after her.

Cas. Faith, I must; she'll rail in the street else. 169

Iago. Will you sup there?

Cas. Faith, I intend so.

Iago. Well, I may chance to see you, for I would very fain speak with you. 173

Cas. Prithee, come; will you?

Iago. Go to; say no more. [*Exit* CASSIO.

Oth. [*Advancing.*] How shall I murder him, Iago? 177

Iago. Did you perceive how he laughed at his vice?

Oth. O! Iago! 180

Iago. And did you see the handkerchief?

Oth. Was that mine?

Iago. Yours, by this hand; and to see how he prizes the foolish woman your wife! she gave it him, and he hath given it his whore. 185

Oth. I would have him nine years a-killing. A fine woman! a fair woman! a sweet woman!

Iago. Nay, you must forget that. 188

Oth. Ay, let her rot, and perish, and be damned to-night; for she shall not live. No, my heart is turned to stone; I strike it, and it hurts my hand. O! the world hath not a sweeter creature; she might lie by an emperor's side and command him tasks.

Iago. Nay, that's not your way. 195

Oth. Hang her! I do but say what she is. So delicate with her needle! An admirable musician! O, she will sing the savageness out of a bear. Of so high and plenteous wit and invention! 200

Iago. She's the worse for all this.

Oth. O! a thousand, a thousand times. And then, of so gentle a condition!

Iago. Ay, too gentle. 204

Oth. Nay, that's certain;—but yet the pity of it, Iago! O! Iago, the pity of it, Iago!

Iago. If you are so fond over her iniquity, give her patent to offend; for, if it touch not you, it comes near nobody. 209

Oth. I will chop her into messes. Cuckold me!

Iago. O! 'tis foul in her. 212

Oth. With mine officer!

Iago. That's fouler.

Oth. Get me some poison, Iago; this night: I'll not expostulate with her, lest her body and beauty unprovide my mind again. This night, Iago. 218

Iago. Do it not with poison, strangle her in her bed, even the bed she hath contaminated.

Oth. Good, good; the justice of it pleases; very good.

Iago. And for Cassio, let me be his undertaker; you shall hear more by midnight. 224

Oth. Excellent good. [*A trumpet within.*] What trumpet is that same?

Iago. Something from Venice, sure. 'Tis Lodovico,
Come from the duke; and see, your wife is with him. 228

Enter LODOVICO, DESDEMONA, *and* Attendants.

Lod. God save you, worthy general!

Oth. With all my heart, sir.

Lod. The duke and senators of Venice greet you. [*Gives him a packet.*

Oth. I kiss the instrument of their pleasures.
[*Opens the packet, and reads.*

Des. And what's the news, good cousin Lodovico? 232

Iago. I am very glad to see you, signior; Welcome to Cyprus.

Lod. I thank you. How does Lieutenant Cassio?

Iago. Lives, sir. 236

Des. Cousin, there's fall'n between him and my lord
An unkind breach; but you shall make all well.

Oth. Are you sure of that?

Des. My lord? 240

Oth. *This fail you not to do, as you will—*

Lod. He did not call; he's busy in the paper. Is there division 'twixt my lord and Cassio?

Des. A most unhappy one; I would do much To atone them, for the love I bear to Cassio. 245

Oth. Fire and brimstone!

Des. My lord?

Oth. Are you wise?

Des. What! is he angry?

Lod.   May be the letter mov'd him;
For, as I think, they do command him home,
Deputing Cassio in his government.   249
Des. Trust me, I am glad on 't.
Oth.   Indeed!
Des.   My lord?
Oth. I am glad to see you mad.
Des.   Why, sweet Othello?
Oth. Devil!   [*Strikes her.*
Des.   I have not deserved this.   252
Lod. My lord, this would not be believ'd in
    Venice,
Though I should swear I saw 't: 'tis very much;
Make her amends, she weeps.
Oth.   O devil, devil!
If that the earth could teem with woman's tears,
Each drop she falls would prove a crocodile. 257
Out of my sight!
Des.   I will not stay to offend you.
                                 [*Going.*
Lod. Truly, an obedient lady;
I do beseech your lordship, call her back. 260
Oth. Mistress!
Des.   My lord?
Oth.   What would you with her, sir?
Lod. Who, I, my lord?
Oth. Ay; you did wish that I would make
    her turn:
Sir, she can turn, and turn, and yet go on, 264
And turn again; and she can weep, sir, weep;
And she's obedient, as you say, obedient,
Very obedient. Proceed you in your tears.
Concerning this, sir, O—well-painted passion!—
I am commanded home. Get you away;   269
I'll send for you anon. Sir, I obey the mandate,
And will return to Venice. Hence! avaunt!
                        [*Exit* DESDEMONA.
Cassio shall have my place. And, sir, to-night,
I do entreat that we may sup together;   273
You are welcome, sir, to Cyprus. Goats and
    monkeys!   [*Exit.*
Lod. Is this the noble Moor whom our full
    senate
Call all-in-all sufficient? is this the noble nature
Whom passion could not shake? whose solid
    virtue   277
The shot of accident nor dart of chance
Could neither graze nor pierce?
Iago.   He is much chang'd.
Lod. Are his wits safe? is he not light of
    brain?   280
Iago. He's that he is; I may not breathe my
    censure.
What he might be, if, what he might, he is not,
I would to heaven he were!
Lod.   What! strike his wife!
Iago. Faith, that was not so well; yet would
    I knew   284
That stroke would prove the worst!
Lod.   Is it his use?
Or did the letters work upon his blood,
And new-create this fault?
Iago.   Alas, alas!   288
It is not honesty in me to speak. You shall ob-
    serve him,

And his own courses will denote him so
That I may save my speech. Do but go after
And mark how he continues.   292
Lod. I am sorry that I am deceiv'd in him.
                                 [*Exeunt.*

SCENE II.—*A Room in the Castle.*

Enter OTHELLO *and* EMILIA.

Oth. You have seen nothing, then?
Emil. Nor ever heard, nor ever did suspect.
Oth. Yes, you have seen Cassio and her to-
    gether.
Emil. But then I saw no harm, and then I
    heard   4
Each syllable that breath made up between
    them.
Oth. What! did they never whisper?
Emil.   Never, my lord.
Oth. Nor send you out o' the way?
Emil.   Never.
Oth. To fetch her fan, her gloves, her mask,
    nor nothing?   8
Emil. Never, my lord.
Oth. That's strange.
Emil. I durst, my lord, to wager she is
    honest,   11
Lay down my soul at stake: if you think other,
Remove your thought; it doth abuse your
    bosom.
If any wretch have put this in your head,
Let heaven requite it with the serpent's curse!
For, if she be not honest, chaste, and true, 16
There's no man happy; the purest of their wives
Is foul as slander.
Oth.   Bid her come hither; go.
                             [*Exit* EMILIA.
She says enough; yet she's a simple bawd
That cannot say as much. This is a subtle
    whore,   20
A closet lock and key of villanous secrets;
And yet she'll kneel and pray; I have seen her
    do 't.

Re-enter EMILIA *with* DESDEMONA.

Des. My lord, what is your will?
Oth.   Pray, chuck, come hither.
Des. What is your pleasure?
Oth.   Let me see your eyes; 24
Look in my face.
Des.   What horrible fancy's this?
Oth. [*To* EMILIA.] Some of your function,
    mistress;
Leave procreants alone and shut the door;
Cough or cry 'hem' if any body come;   28
Your mystery, your mystery; nay, dispatch.
                             [*Exit* EMILIA.
Des. Upon my knees, what doth your speech
    import?
I understand a fury in your words,
But not the words.   32
Oth. Why, what art thou?
Des.   Your wife, my lord; your true
And loyal wife.
Oth.   Come, swear it, damn thyself;
Lest, being like one of heaven, the devils them-
    selves

Should fear to seize thee; therefore be double-
    damn'd; 36
Swear thou art honest.
  Des. Heaven doth truly know it.
  Oth. Heaven truly knows that thou art false
as hell.
  Des. To whom, my lord? with whom? how
am I false?
  Oth. Ah! Desdemona; away, away, away! 40
  Des. Alas, the heavy day!—Why do you
weep?
Am I the motive of these tears, my lord?
If haply you my father do suspect
An instrument of this your calling back, 44
Lay not your blame on me; if you have lost him,
Why, I have lost him too.
  Oth. Had it pleas'd heaven
To try me with affliction, had he rain'd
All kinds of sores, and shames, on my bare
    head, 48
Steep'd me in poverty to the very lips,
Given to captivity me and my utmost hopes,
I should have found in some part of my soul
A drop of patience; but, alas! to make me 52
The fixed figure for the time of scorn
To point his slow and moving finger at;
Yet could I bear that too; well, very well.
But there, where I have garner'd up my heart,
Where either I must live or bear no life, 57
The fountain from the which my current runs
Or else dries up; to be discarded thence!
Or keep it as a cistern for foul toads 60
To knot and gender in! Turn thy complexion
    there,
Patience, thou young and rose-lipp'd cherubin;
Ay, there, look grim as hell!
  Des. I hope my noble lord esteems me
    honest. 64
  Oth. O! ay; as summer flies are in the
    shambles,
That quicken even with blowing. O thou weed!
Who art so lovely fair and smell'st so sweet
That the sense aches at thee, would thou hadst
ne'er been born. 68
  Des. Alas! what ignorant sin have I com-
    mitted?
  Oth. Was this fair paper, this most goodly
    book,
Made to write 'whore' upon? What com-
    mitted!
Committed! O thou public commoner! 72
I should make very forges of my cheeks,
That would to cinders burn up modesty,
Did I but speak thy deeds. What committed!
Heaven stops the nose at it and the moon winks,
The bawdy wind that kisses all it meets 77
Is hush'd within the hollow mine of earth,
And will not hear it. What committed!
Impudent strumpet!
  Des. By heaven, you do me wrong. 80
  Oth. Are not you a strumpet?
  Des. No, as I am a Christian.
If to preserve this vessel for my lord
From any other foul unlawful touch
Be not to be a strumpet, I am none. 84
  Oth. What! not a whore?

  Des. No, as I shall be sav'd.
  Oth. Is it possible?
  Des. O! heaven forgive us.
  Oth. I cry you mercy, then;
I took you for that cunning whore of Venice 88
That married with Othello. You, mistress,
That have the office opposite to Saint Peter,
And keep the gate of hell!

Re-enter EMILIA.

                    You, you, ay, you!
We have done our course; there's money for
    your pains. 92
I pray you, turn the key and keep our counsel.
                                    [*Exit.*
  Emil. Alas! what does this gentleman con-
    ceive?
How do you, madam? how do you, my good
    lady?
  Des. Faith, half asleep. 96
  Emil. Good madam, what's the matter with
my lord?
  Des. With who?
  Emil. Why, with my lord, madam.
  Des. Who is thy lord?
  Emil. He that is yours, sweet lady. 100
  Des. I have none; do not talk to me, Emilia;
I cannot weep, nor answer have I none,
But what should go by water. Prithee, to-night
Lay on my bed my wedding sheets: remember;
And call thy husband hither.
  Emil. Here is a change indeed! 105
                                    [*Exit.*
  Des. 'Tis meet I should be us'd so, very meet.
How have I been behav'd, that he might stick
The small'st opinion on my least misuse? 108

Re-enter EMILIA, *with* IAGO.

  Iago. What is your pleasure, madam? How
is it with you?
  Des. I cannot tell. Those that do teach
    young babes
Do it with gentle means and easy tasks; 112
He might have chid me so; for, in good faith,
I am a child to chiding.
  Iago. What's the matter, lady?
  Emil. Alas! Iago, my lord hath so bewhor'd
    her,
Thrown such despite and heavy terms upon her,
As true hearts cannot bear. 117
  Des. Am I that name, Iago?
  Iago. What name, fair lady?
  Des. Such as she says my lord did say I was.
  Emil. He call'd her whore; a beggar in his
    drink 120
Could not have laid such terms upon his callat.
  Iago. Why did he so?
  Des. I do not know; I am sure I am none
    such.
  Iago. Do not weep, do not weep. Alas the
    day! 124
  Emil. Has she forsook so many noble
    matches,
Her father and her country and her friends,
To be call'd whore? would it not make one
weep?

Des. It is my wretched fortune.

Iago.　　　　　　Beshrew him for it! 128
How comes this trick upon him?

Des.　　　　　　Nay, heaven doth know.

Emil. I will be hang'd, if some eternal villain,
Some busy and insinuating rogue,
Some cogging cozening slave, to get some
　　office,　　　　　　　　　　　　132
Have not devis'd this slander; I'll be hang'd
　　else.

Iago. Fie! there is no such man; it is im-
　　possible.

Des. If any such there be, heaven pardon him!

Emil. A halter pardon him, and hell gnaw
　　his bones!　　　　　　　　　　136
Why should he call her whore? who keeps her
　　company?
What place? what time? what form? what likeli-
　　hood?
The Moor's abus'd by some most villanous
　　knave,
Some base notorious knave, some scurvy fellow.
O heaven! that such companions thou'dst un-
　　fold,　　　　　　　　　　　　141
And put in every honest hand a whip
To lash the rascals naked through the world,
Even from the east to the west!

Iago.　　　　　　Speak within door. 144

Emil. O! fie upon them. Some such squire
　　he was
That turn'd your wit the seamy side without,
And made you to suspect me with the Moor.

Iago. You are a fool; go to.

Des.　　　　　　O good Iago, 148
What shall I do to win my lord again?
Good friend, go to him; for, by this light of
　　heaven,
I know not how I lost him. Here I kneel:
If e'er my will did trespass 'gainst his love, 152
Either in discourse of thought or actual deed,
Or that mine eyes, mine ears, or any sense,
Delighted them in any other form;
Or that I do not yet, and ever did,　　156
And ever will, though he do shake me off
To beggarly divorcement, love him dearly,
Comfort forswear me! Unkindness may do
　　much;
And his unkindness may defeat my life, 160
But never taint my love. I cannot say 'whore:'
It does abhor me now I speak the word;
To do the act that might the addition earn
Not the world's mass of vanity could make me.

Iago. I pray you be content, 'tis but his
　　humour;　　　　　　　　　　165
The business of the state does him offence,
And he does chide with you.

Des.　　　　　　If 'twere no other,—

Iago. 'Tis but so, I warrant. [*Trumpets.*
Hark! how these instruments summon to sup-
　　per;　　　　　　　　　　　　169
The messengers of Venice stay the meat:
Go in, and weep not; all things shall be well.

　　　　　[*Exeunt* DESDEMONA *and* EMILIA.

Enter RODERIGO.

How now, Roderigo!　　　　　　172

Rod. I do not find that thou dealest justly
with me.

Iago. What in the contrary?

Rod. Every day thou daffest me with some
device, Iago; and rather, as it seems to me now,
keepest from me all conveniency, than suppliest
me with the least advantage of hope. I will indeed no longer endure it, nor am I yet persuaded
to put up in peace what already I have foolishly
suffered.　　　　　　　　　　182

Iago. Will you hear me, Roderigo?

Rod. Faith, I have heard too much, for your
words and performances are no kin together.

Iago. You charge me most unjustly.　186

Rod. With nought but truth. I have wasted
myself out of my means. The jewels you have
had from me to deliver to Desdemona would
half have corrupted a votarist; you have told
me she has received them, and returned me
expectations and comforts of sudden respect
and acquaintance, but I find none.　　193

Iago. Well; go to; very well.

Rod. Very well! go to! I cannot go to, man;
nor 'tis not very well: by this hand, I say, it is
very scurvy, and begin to find myself fobbed in it.

Iago. Very well.　　　　　　198

Rod. I tell you 'tis not very well. I will make
myself known to Desdemona; if she will return
me my jewels, I will give over my suit and repent my unlawful solicitation; if not, assure
yourself I will seek satisfaction of you.

Iago. You have said now.　　　204

Rod. Ay, and said nothing, but what I protest intendment of doing.

Iago. Why, now I see there's mettle in thee,
and even from this instant do build on thee a
better opinion than ever before. Give me thy
hand, Roderigo; thou hast taken against me a
most just exception; but yet, I protest, I have
dealt most directly in thy affair.　・212

Rod. It hath not appeared.

Iago. I grant indeed it hath not appeared,
and your suspicion is not without with judgment. But, Roderigo, if thou hast that in thee
indeed, which I have greater reason to believe
now than ever, I mean purpose, courage, and
valour, this night show it: if thou the next
night following enjoy not Desdemona, take
me from this world with treachery and devise
engines for my life.

Rod. Well, what is it? is it within reason and
compass?　　　　　　　　　　224

Iago. Sir, there is especial commission come
from Venice to depute Cassio in Othello's place.

Rod. Is that true? why, then Othello and
Desdemona return again to Venice.　228

Iago. O, no! he goes into Mauritania, and
takes away with him the fair Desdemona, unless his abode be lingered here by some accident;
wherein none can be so determinate as the removing of Cassio.　　　　　　233

Rod. How do you mean, removing of him?

Iago. Why, by making him uncapable of
Othello's place; knocking out his brains.

Rod. And that you would have me do? 237

Iago. Ay; if you dare do yourself a profit

and a right. He sups to-night with a harlotry, and thither will I go to him; he knows not yet of his honourable fortune. If you will watch his going thence,—which I will fashion to fall out between twelve and one,—you may take him at your pleasure; I will be near to second your attempt, and he shall fall between us. Come, stand not amazed at it, but go along with me; I will show you such a necessity in his death that you shall think yourself bound to put it on him. It is now high supper-time, and the night grows to waste; about it. 250

Rod. I will hear further reason for this.

Iago. And you shall be satisfied. [*Exeunt.*

SCENE III.—*Another Room in the Castle.*

Enter OTHELLO, LODOVICO, DESDEMONA, EMILIA, *and* Attendants.

Lod. I do beseech you, sir, trouble yourself no further.

Oth. O! pardon me; 'twill do me good to walk.

Lod. Madam, good night; I humbly thank your ladyship.

Des. Your honour is most welcome.

Oth. Will you walk, sir? O! Desdemona,— 5

Des. My lord?

Oth. Get you to bed on the instant; I will be returned forthwith; dismiss your attendant there; look it be done. 9

Des. I will, my lord.

[*Exeunt* OTHELLO, LODOVICO, *and* Attendants.

Emil. How goes it now? he looks gentler than he did.

Des. He says he will return incontinent; 12 He hath commanded me to go to bed, And bade me to dismiss you.

Emil. Dismiss me!

Des. It was his bidding; therefore, good Emilia, Give me my nightly wearing, and adieu: 16 We must not now displease him.

Emil. I would you had never seen him.

Des. So would not I; my love doth so approve him, That even his stubbornness, his checks and frowns,— 20 Prithee, unpin me,—have grace and favour in them.

Emil. I have laid those sheets you bade me on the bed.

Des. All 's one. Good faith! how foolish are our minds! If I do die before thee, prithee, shroud me 24 In one of those same sheets.

Emil. Come, come, you talk.

Des. My mother had a maid call'd Barbara; She was in love, and he she lov'd prov'd mad And did forsake her; she had a song of 'willow;' 28 An old thing 'twas, but it express'd her fortune, And she died singing it; that song to-night Will not go from my mind; I have much to do

But to go hang my head all at one side, 3 And sing it like poor Barbara. Prithee, dispatch

Emil. Shall I go fetch your night-gown?

Des. No, unpin me here This Lodovico is a proper man.

Emil. A very handsome man. 3

Des. He speaks well.

Emil. I know a lady in Venice would hav walked barefoot to Palestine for a touch of hi nether lip. 4

Des. The poor soul sat sighing by a sycamore tree, Sing all a green willow; Her hand on her bosom, her head on her knee, Sing willow, willow, willow: 4 The fresh streams ran by her, and murmur' her moans; Sing willow, willow, willow: Her salt tears fell from her, and soften'd th stones;—

Lay by these:— 4

Sing willow, willow, willow:

Prithee, hie thee; he'll come anon.—

Sing all a green willow must be my garland. Let nobody blame him, his scorn I approve,—

Nay, that's not next. Hark! who is it tha knocks?

Emil. It is the wind.

Des. I call'd my love false love; but what said h then? 5 Sing willow, willow, willow: If I court moe women, you'll couch with mo men.

So, get thee gone; good night. Mine eyes de itch; Doth that bode weeping?

Emil. 'Tis neither here nor there

Des. I have heard it said so. O! these mer these men! 6 Dost thou in conscience think, tell me, Emilia That there be women do abuse their husband In such gross kind?

Emil. There be some such, no question

Des. Wouldst thou do such a deed for all th world? 6

Emil. Why, would not you?

Des. No, by this heavenly light

Emil. Nor I neither by this heavenly light I might do't as well i' the dark. 6

Des. Wouldst thou do such a deed for all th world?

Emil. The world is a huge thing; 'tis a grea price For a small vice.

Des. In troth, I think thou wouldst no

Emil. In troth, I think I should, and undo when I had done. Marry, I would not do suc a thing for a joint-ring, nor measures of lawn nor for gowns, petticoats, nor caps, nor any pett exhibition; but for the whole world, who woul not make her husband a cuckold to make hir a monarch? I should venture purgatory for'

Des. Beshrew me, if I would do such a wron For the whole world. 8

Emil. Why, the wrong is but a wrong i' th

world; and having the world for your labour,
'tis a wrong in your own world, and you might
quickly make it right.   84

Des. I do not think there is any such woman.

Emil. Yes, a dozen; and as many to the
vantage, as would store the world they played
for.   88
But I do think it is their husbands' faults
If wives do fall. Say that they slack their duties,
And pour our treasures into foreign laps,
Or else break out in peevish jealousies,   92
Throwing restraint upon us; or, say they strike us,
Or scant our former having in despite;
Why, we have galls, and though we have some
    grace,
Yet have we some revenge. Let husbands know
Their wives have sense like them; they see and
    smell,
And have their palates both for sweet and sour, 97
As husbands have. What is it that they do
When they change us for others? Is it sport?
I think it is; and doth affection breed it?   101
I think it doth; is't frailty that thus errs?
It is so too; and have not we affections,
Desires for sport, and frailty, as men have? 104
Then, let them use us well; else let them know,
The ills we do, their ills instruct us so.

Des. Good night, good night; heaven me such
    usage send,
Not to pick bad from bad, but by bad mend! 108
                                   [*Exeunt.*

ACT V

SCENE I.—*Cyprus. A Street.*

Enter IAGO *and* RODERIGO.

Iago. Here, stand behind this bulk; straight
    will he come:
Wear thy good rapier bare, and put it home.
Quick, quick; fear nothing; I'll be at thy elbow.
It makes us, or it mars us; think on that,   4
And fix most firm thy resolution.

Rod. Be near at hand; I may miscarry in't.

Iago. Here, at thy hand: be bold, and take
    thy stand.   [*Retires.*

Rod. I have no great devotion to the deed; 8
And yet he has given me satisfying reasons:
'Tis but a man gone: forth, my sword; he dies.

Iago. I have rubb'd this young quat almost
    to the sense,
And he grows angry. Now, whether he kill
    Cassio,   12
Or Cassio him, or each do kill the other,
Every way makes my gain: live Roderigo,
He calls me to a restitution large
Of gold and jewels that I bobb'd from him, 16
As gifts to Desdemona;
It must not be: if Cassio do remain,
He hath a daily beauty in his life
That makes me ugly; and, besides, the Moor 20
May unfold me to him; there stand I in much
    peril.
No, he must die. But so; I hear him coming.

Enter CASSIO.

Rod. I know his gait; 'tis he. Villain, thou
    diest!   [*Makes a pass at* CASSIO.

Cas. That thrust had been mine enemy in-
    deed   24
But that my coat is better than thou know'st;
I will make proof of thine.
                [*Draws, and wounds* RODERIGO.

Rod.   O! I am slain.
                [IAGO *from behind wounds* CASSIO *in
                    the leg, and exit.*

Cas. I am maim'd for ever. Help, ho! mur-
    der! murder!   [*Falls.*

Enter OTHELLO, *at a distance.*

Oth. The voice of Cassio: Iago keeps his
    word.

Rod. O! villain that I am!

Oth.   It is e'en so.   29

Cas. O, help, ho! light! a surgeon!

Oth. 'Tis he: O brave Iago, honest and just!
That hast such noble sense of thy friend's
    wrong;   32
Thou teachest me. Minion, your dear lies dead,
And your unblest fate hies; strumpet, I come!
Forth of my heart those charms, thine eyes, are
    blotted;
Thy bed lust-stain'd shall with lust's blood be
    spotted.   [*Exit.*

Enter LODOVICO *and* GRATIANO, *at a distance.*

Cas. What ho! no watch? no passage? mur-
    der! murder!

Gra. 'Tis some mischance; the cry is very   37
    direful.

Cas. O, help!

Lod. Hark!

Rod. O wretched villain!   40

Lod. Two or three groan.: it is a heavy night;
These may be counterfeits; let's think't unsafe
To come in to the cry without more help.   44

Rod. Nobody come? then shall I bleed to
    death.

Lod. Hark!

Re-enter IAGO, *with a light.*

Gra. Here's one comes in his shirt, with light
    and weapons.

Iago. Who's there? whose noise is this that
    cries on murder?   48

Lod. We do not know.

Iago.   Did not you hear a cry?

Cas. Here, here! for heaven's sake, help me.

Iago.   What's the matter?

Gra. This is Othello's ancient, as I take it.

Lod. The same indeed; a very valiant fellow.

Iago. What are you here that cry so griev-
    ously?   53

Cas. Iago? O! I am spoil'd, undone by vil-
    lains!
Give me some help.

Iago. O me, lieutenant! what villains have
    done this?   56

Cas. I think that one of them is hereabout,
And cannot make away.

Iago.   O treacherous villains!
[*To* LODOVICO *and* GRATIANO.] What are you
    there? come in, and give some help.

Rod. O! help me here.   60

Cas. That's one of them.

Iago.   O murderous slave! O villain!

[*Stabs* RODERIGO.

Rod. O damn'd Iago! O inhuman dog!

Iago. Kill men i' the dark! Where be these bloody thieves?

How silent is this town! Ho! murder! murder!

What may you be? are you of good or evil? 65

Lod. As you shall prove us, praise us.

Iago. Signior Lodovico?

Lod. He, sir.   68

Iago. I cry you mercy. Here's Cassio hurt by villains.

Gra. Cassio!

Iago. How is it, brother?

Cas. My leg is cut in two.

Iago.   Marry, heaven forbid, 72

Light, gentlemen; I'll bind it with my shirt.

Enter BIANCA.

Bian. What is the matter, ho? who is't that cried?

Iago. Who is't that cried!

Bian. O my dear Cassio! my sweet Cassio! 76

O Cassio, Cassio, Cassio!

Iago. O notable strumpet! Cassio, may you suspect

Who they should be that have thus mangled you?

Cas. No.   80

Gra. I am sorry to find you thus; I have been to seek you.

Iago. Lend me a garter. So. O! for a chair, To bear him easily hence!

Bian. Alas! he faints! O Cassio, Cassio, Cassio!   84

Iago. Gentlemen all, I do suspect this trash To be a party in this injury.

Patience awhile, good Cassio. Come, come.

Lend me a light. Know we this face, or no? 88

Alas! my friend and my dear countryman,

Roderigo? no: yes, sure, O heaven! Roderigo.

Gra. What! of Venice?

Iago. Even he, sir: did you know him?

Gra.   Know him! ay. 92

Iago. Signior Gratiano? I cry you gentle pardon;

These bloody accidents must excuse my manners,

That so neglected you.

Gra.   I am glad to see you.

Iago. How do you, Cassio? O! a chair, a chair!   96

Gra. Roderigo!   [*A chair brought in.*

Iago. He, he, 'tis he.—O! that's well said; the chair:

Some good men bear him carefully from hence;

I'll fetch the general's surgeon. [*To* BIANCA.]

For you, mistress,   100

Save you your labour. He that lies slain here, Cassio,

Was my dear friend. What malice was between you?

Cas. None in the world; nor do I know the man.

Iago. [*To* BIANCA.] What! look you pale? O! bear him out o' the air—   104

[CASSIO *and* RODERIGO *are borne off.*

Stay you, good gentlemen. Look you pale, mistress?—

Do you perceive the gastness of her eye?

Nay, if you stare, we shall hear more anon.

Behold her well; I pray you, look upon her: 108

Do you see, gentlemen? nay, guiltiness will speak

Though tongues were out of use.

Enter EMILIA.

Emil. 'Las! what's the matter? what's the matter, husband?

Iago. Cassio hath here been set on in the dark   112

By Roderigo and fellows that are 'scap'd:

He's almost slain, and Roderigo dead.

Emil. Alas! good gentleman; alas! good Cassio!

Iago. This is the fruit of whoring. Prithee, Emilia,   116

Go know of Cassio where he supp'd to-night.

What! do you shake at that?

Bian. He supp'd at my house; but I therefore shake not.

Iago. O! did he so? I charge you, go with me.

Emil. Fie, fie upon thee, strumpet!   121

Bian. I am no strumpet, but of life as honest

As you that thus abuse me.

Emil.   As I! foh! fie upon thee!

Iago. Kind gentlemen, let's go see poor Cassio dress'd.   124

Come, mistress, you must tell's another tale.

Emilia, run you to the citadel,

And tell my lord and lady what hath happ'd.

Will you go on afore? [*Aside.*] This is the night

That either makes me or fordoes me quite. 129

[*Exeunt.*

SCENE II.—*A Bedchamber in the Castle.* DESDEMONA *in bed asleep. A light burning.*

Enter OTHELLO.

Oth. It is the cause, it is the cause, my soul

Let me not name it to you, you chaste stars!

It is the cause. Yet I'll not shed her blood,

Nor scar that whiter skin of hers than snow,

And smooth as monumental alabaster.

Yet she must die, else she'll betray more men

Put out the light, and then put out the light:

If I quench thee, thou flaming minister,

I can again thy former light restore,

Should I repent me; but once put out thy light

Thou cunning'st pattern of excelling nature,

I know not where is that Promethean heat 1

That can thy light relume. When I have pluck'd the rose,

I cannot give it vital growth again,

It needs must wither: I'll smell it on the tree.

[*Kisses her*

O balmy breath, that dost almost persuade 1

Justice to break her sword! One more, one more.

Be thus when thou art dead, and I will kill thee

And love thee after. One more, and this the last:

So sweet was ne'er so fatal. I must weep,   2

But they are cruel tears; this sorrow's heavenly,
It strikes where it doth love. She wakes.
Des. Who's there? Othello?
Oth.   Ay, Desdemona.
Des. Will you come to bed, my lord?   24
Oth. Have you pray'd to-night, Desdemona?
Des.   Ay, my lord.
Oth. If you bethink yourself of any crime
Unreconcil'd as yet to heaven and grace,
Solicit for it straight.   28
  Des. Alas! my lord, what may you mean by
that?
Oth. Well, do it, and be brief; I will walk by:
I would not kill thy unprepared spirit;
No; heaven forfend! I would not kill thy soul.
Des. Talk you of killing?
Oth.   Ay, I do.
Des.   Then heaven 33
Have mercy on me!
Oth.   Amen! with all my heart.
Des. If you say so, I hope you will not kill
me.
Oth. Hum!   36
Des. And yet I fear you; for you are fatal
then
When your eyes roll so. Why I should fear I
know not,
Since guiltiness I know not; but yet I feel I fear.
Oth. Think on thy sins.
Des.   They are loves I bear to you. 40
Oth. Ay, and for that thou diest.
Des. That death's unnatural that kills for
loving.
Alas! why gnaw you so your nether lip?
Some bloody passion shakes your very frame; 44
These are portents, but yet, I hope, I hope
They do not point on me.
Oth.   Peace, and be still!
Des. I will so. What's the matter?
Oth. That handkerchief which I so lov'd and
gave thee   48
Thou gav'st to Cassio.
Des.   No, by my life and soul!
Send for the man and ask him.
Oth.   Sweet soul, take heed,
Take heed of perjury; thou 'rt on thy death-bed.
Des. Ay, but not yet to die.
Oth.   Yes, presently; 52
Therefore confess thee freely of thy sin;
For to deny each article with oath
Cannot remove nor choke the strong conception
That I do groan withal. Thou art to die.   56
Des. Then Lord have mercy on me!
Oth.   I say, amen.
Des. And have you mercy too! I never did
Offend you in my life; never lov'd Cassio
But with such general warranty of heaven 60
As I might love; I never gave him token.
Oth. By heaven, I saw my handkerchief in 's
hand.
O perjur'd woman! thou dost stone my heart,
And mak'st me call what I intend to do   64
A murder, which I thought a sacrifice:
I saw the handkerchief.
Des.   He found it then;
I never gave it him. Send for him hither;

Let him confess a truth.
Oth.   He hath confess'd. 68
Des. What, my lord?
Oth. That he hath us'd thee.
Des.   How? unlawfully?
Oth. Ay.
Des.   He will not say so.
Oth.   No; his mouth is stopp'd:
Honest Iago hath ta'en order for 't.   72
Des. O! my fear interprets. What! is he
dead?
Oth. Had all his hairs been lives, my great
revenge
Had stomach for them all.
Des. Alas! he is betray'd and I undone.   76
Oth. Out, strumpet! Weep'st thou for him
to my face?
Des. O! banish me, my lord, but kill me not!
Oth. Down, strumpet!
Des. Kill me to-morrow; let me live to-night!
Oth. Nay, if you strive,—   80
Des. But half an hour!
Oth.   Being done, there is no pause.
Des. But while I say one prayer!
Oth.   It is too late. [*He smothers her.*
Emil. [*Within.*] My lord, my lord! what, ho!
my lord, my lord!   84
Oth. What noise is this? Not dead? not yet
quite dead?
I that am cruel am yet merciful;
I would not have thee linger in thy pain.
So, so.
Emil. [*Within.*] What, ho! my lord, my lord!
Oth.   Who's there? 88
Emil. [*Within.*] O! good my lord, I would
speak a word with you!
Oth. Yes; 'tis Emilia: by and by. She's dead.
'Tis like she comes to speak of Cassio's death;
The noise was high. Ha! no more moving? 92
Still as the grave. Shall she come in? Were 't
good?
I think she stirs again: no. What's best to do?
If she come in she'll sure speak to my wife:
My wife! my wife! what wife? I have no wife:
O, insupportable! O heavy hour!   97
Methinks it should be now a huge eclipse
Of sun and moon, and that the affrighted globe
Should yawn at alteration.
Emil.   [*Within.*] I do beseech you 100
That I may speak with you, O! good my lord.
Oth. I had forgot thee: O! come in, Emilia:
Soft, by and by: let me the curtains draw.
Where art thou?   [*Unlocks the door.*

Enter EMILIA.

      What's the matter with thee now? 104
Emil. O! my good lord, yonder 's foul mur-
der done.
Oth. What! now?
Emil.   But now, my lord.
Oth. It is the very error of the moon;
She comes more near the earth than she was
wont,   108
And makes men mad.
Emil. Cassio, my lord, has kill'd a young
Venetian

Call'd Roderigo.

Oth.   Roderigo kill'd!
And Cassio kill'd?

Emil.   No, Cassio is not kill'd.   112

Oth. Not Cassio kill'd! then murder's out of tune,
And sweet revenge grows harsh.

Des. O! falsely, falsely murder'd.

Emil.   Alas! what cry is that?

Oth. That! what?   116

Emil. Out, and alas! that was my lady's voice:
Help! Help, ho! help! O lady, speak again!
Sweet Desdemona! O! sweet mistress, speak.

Des. A guiltless death I die.   120

Emil. O! who hath done this deed?

Des. Nobody; I myself; farewell:
Commend me to my kind lord. O! farewell!
                    [*Dies.*

Oth. Why, how should she be murder'd?

Emil.   Alas! who knows? 124

Oth. You heard her say herself it was not I.

Emil. She said so; I must needs report the truth.

Oth. She's like a liar gone to burning hell;
'Twas I that kill'd her.

Emil.   O! the more angel she,
And you the blacker devil.   129

Oth. She turn'd to folly, and she was a whore.

Emil. Thou dost belie her, and thou art a devil.

Oth. She was false as water.

Emil.   Thou art rash as fire to say
That she was false: O! she was heavenly true.

Oth. Cassio did tup her; ask thy husband else.
O! I were damn'd beneath all depth in hell
But that I did proceed upon just grounds   136
To this extremity. Thy husband knew it all.

Emil. My husband!

Oth. Thy husband.

Emil. That she was false to wedlock?   140

Oth. Ay, with Cassio. Nay, had she been true,
If heaven would make me such another world
Of one entire and perfect chrysolite,
I'd not have sold her for it.   144

Emil. My husband!

Oth.   Ay, 'twas he that told me first:
An honest man he is, and hates the slime
That sticks on filthy deeds.

Emil.   My husband!

Oth. What needs this iterance, woman? I say thy husband.   148

Emil. O mistress! villany hath made mocks with love.
My husband say that she was false!

Oth.   He, woman;
I say, thy husband: dost understand the word?
My friend, thy husband, honest, honest Iago. 152

Emil. If he say so, may his pernicious soul
Rot half a grain a day! he lies to the heart:
She was too fond of her most filthy bargain.

Oth. Ha!   156

Emil. Do thy worst:
This deed of thine is no more worthy heaven
Than thou wast worthy her.

Oth.   Peace! you were best.

Emil. Thou hast not half the power to do me harm   160
As I have to be hurt. O gull! O dolt!
As ignorant as dirt! thou hast done a deed,—
I care not for thy sword; I'll make thee known,
Though I lost twenty lives. Help! help, ho! help!   164
The Moor has kill'd my mistress! Murder! murder!

Enter MONTANO, GRATIANO, IAGO, *and Others.*

Mon. What is the matter? How now, general!

Emil. O! are you come, Iago? you have done well,
That men must lay their murders on your neck.

Gra. What is the matter?   169

Emil. Disprove this villain if thou be'st a man:
He says thou told'st him that his wife was false.
I know thou didst not, thou 'rt not such a villain.
Speak, for my heart is full.   173

Iago. I told him what I thought, and told no more
Than what he found himself was apt and true.

Emil. But did you ever tell him she was false?   176

Iago. I did.

Emil. You told a lie, an odious damned lie;
Upon my soul, a lie, a wicked lie.
She false with Cassio! Did you say with Cassio?

Iago. With Cassio, mistress. Go to, charm your tongue.   181

Emil. I will not charm my tongue; I am bound to speak.
My mistress here lies murder'd in her bed.

All. O heavens forfend!   184

Emil. And your reports have set the murder on.

Oth. Nay, stare not, masters; it is true, indeed.

Gra. 'Tis a strange truth.

Mon. O monstrous act!

Emil.   Villany! villany! villany!
I think upon 't, I think, I smell 't; O villany! 189
I thought so then; I'll kill myself for grief.
O! villany, villany!

Iago. What! are you mad? I charge you, get you home.   192

Emil. Good gentlemen, let me have leave to speak:
'Tis proper I obey him, but not now.
Perchance, Iago, I will ne'er go home.

Oth. O! O! O!   [*Falls on the bed.*

Emil.   Nay, lay thee down and roar,
For thou hast kill'd the sweetest innocent   197
That e'er did lift up eye.

Oth.   O! she was foul.
I scarce did know you, uncle. There lies your niece,
Whose breath, indeed, these hands have newly stopp'd: 200
I know this act shows terrible and grim.

Gra. Poor Desdemona! I am glad thy father's dead.

Thy match was mortal to him, and pure grief
Shore his old thread in twain: did he live now,
This sight would make him do a desperate turn,
Yea, curse his better angel from his side,
And fall to reprobation.

Oth. 'Tis pitiful; but yet Iago knows   208
That she with Cassio hath the act of shame
A thousand times committed; Cassio confess'd it:
And she did gratify his amorous works
With that recognizance and pledge of love 212
Which I first gave her. I saw it in his hand:
It was a handkerchief, an antique token
My father gave my mother.

Emil.   O heaven! O heavenly powers!
Iago.   Come, hold your peace.
Emil. 'Twill out, 'twill out; I hold my peace,
sir? no;   217
No, I will speak as liberal as the north;
Let heaven and men and devils, let them all,
All, all, cry shame against me, yet I'll speak. 220
Iago. Be wise, and get you home.
Emil.   I will not.

[IAGO *offers to stab* EMILIA.
Gra.   Fie!
Your sword upon a woman?

Emil. O thou dull Moor! that handkerchief
thou speak'st of
I found by fortune and did give my husband;
For often, with a solemn earnestness,   225
More than, indeed, belong'd to such a trifle,
He begg'd of me to steal it.
Iago.   Villanous whore!
Emil. She give it Cassio! no, alas! I found
it,   228
And I did give 't my husband.
Iago.   Filth, thou liest!
Emil. By heaven, I do not, I do not, gentle-
men.
O murderous coxcomb! what should such a fool
Do with so good a wife?
Oth.   Are there no stones in heaven
But what serve for the thunder? Precious vil-
lain!   [*He runs at* IAGO. IAGO *stabs*
                              EMILIA, *and exit.*
Gra. The woman falls: sure, he has kill'd his
wife.
Emil. Ay, ay; O! lay me by my mistress' side.
Gra. He's gone; but his wife's kill'd.   236
Mon. 'Tis a notorious villain. Take you this
weapon,
Which I have here recover'd from the Moor.
Come, guard the door without; let him not pass,
But kill him rather. I'll after that same villain,
For 'tis a damned slave.

[*Exeunt* MONTANO *and* GRATIANO.
Oth.   I am not valiant neither, 241
But every puny whipster gets my sword.
But why should honour outlive honesty?
Let it go all.
Emil.   What did thy song bode, lady? 244
Hark, canst thou hear me? I will play the swan,
And die in music:—

        Willow, willow, willow.

Moor, she was chaste; she lov'd thee, cruel
Moor;

So come my soul to bliss as I speak true; 249
So speaking as I think, I die, I die.   [*Dies.*
Oth. I have another weapon in this chamber;
It is a sword of Spain, the ice brook's temper.
O! here it is. Uncle, I must come forth.   253
Gra. [*Within.*] If thou attempt it, it will cost
thee dear:
Thou hast no weapon, and perforce must suffer.
Oth. Look in upon me then, and speak with
me,   256
Or, naked as I am, I will assault thee.

                Re-enter GRATIANO.

Gra. What is the matter?
Oth.   Behold! I have a weapon;
A better never did itself sustain
Upon a soldier's thigh: I have seen the day, 260
That with this little arm, and this good sword,
I have made my way through more impediments
Than twenty times your stop: but, O vain boast!
Who can control his fate? 'tis not so now. 264
Be not afraid, though you do see me weapon'd;
Here is my journey's end, here is my butt,
And very sea-mark of my utmost sail.
Do you go back dismay'd? 'tis a lost fear; 268
Man but a rush against Othello's breast,
And he retires. Where should Othello go?
Now how dost thou look now? O ill-starr'd
wench!
Pale as thy smock! when we shall meet at
compt,   272
This look of thine will hurl my soul from heaven,
And fiends will snatch at it. Cold, cold, my girl!
Even like thy chastity.
O! cursed, cursed slave. Whip me, ye devils, 276
From the possession of this heavenly sight!
Blow me about in winds! roast me in sulphur!
Wash me in steep-down gulfs of liquid fire!
O Desdemona! Desdemona! dead!   280
Oh! Oh! Oh!

Enter LODOVICO, MONTANO, CASSIO *carried in a
chair, and* Officers *with* IAGO, *prisoner.*

Lod. Where is this rash and most unfortu-
nate man?
Oth. That's he that was Othello; here I am.
Lod. Where is that viper? bring the villain
forth.   284
Oth. I look down towards his feet; but that's
a fable.
If that thou be'st a devil, I cannot kill thee.
                              [*Wounds* IAGO.
Lod. Wrench his sword from him.
Iago.   I bleed, sir; but not kill'd.
Oth. I am not sorry neither; I'd have thee
live;   288
For, in my sense, 'tis happiness to die.
Lod. O thou Othello! that wert once so good,
Fall'n in the practice of a damned slave,
What shall be said of thee?
Oth.   Why, any thing: 292
An honourable murderer, if you will;
For nought did I in hate, but all in honour.
Lod. This wretch hath part confess'd his
villany:
Did you and he consent in Cassio's death? 296

Oth. Ay.

Cas Dear general, I never gave you cause.

Oth. I do believe it, and I ask your pardon.
Will you, I pray, demand that demi-devil 300
Why he hath thus ensnar'd my soul and body?

Iago. Demand me nothing: what you know,
you know:
From this time forth I never will speak word.

Lod. What! not to pray?

Gra. Torments will ope your lips.

Oth. Well, thou dost best. 305

Lod. Sir, you shall understand what hath
befall'n,
Which, as I think, you know not. Here is a letter
Found in the pocket of the slain Roderigo, 308
And here another; the one of them imports
The death of Cassio to be undertook
By Roderigo.

Oth. O villain!

Cas. Most heathenish and most gross!

Lod. Now here's another discontented paper,
Found in his pocket too; and this, it seems,
Roderigo meant to have sent this damned vil-
lain,
But that, belike, Iago in the interim 316
Came in and satisfied him.

Oth. O the pernicious caitiff!
How came you, Cassio, by that handkerchief
That was my wife's?

Cas. I found it in my chamber;
And he himself confess'd but even now 320
That there he dropp'd it for a special purpose
Which wrought to his desire.

Oth. O fool! fool! fool!

Cas. There is besides in Roderigo's letter
How he upbraids Iago that he made him 324
Brave me upon the watch; whereon it came
That I was cast: and even but now he spake,
After long seeming dead, Iago hurt him,
Iago set him on. 328

Lod. You must forsake this room and go
with us;
Your power and your command is taken off,
And Cassio rules in Cyprus. For this slave,
If there be any cunning cruelty 332
That can torment him much and hold him long,

It shall be his. You shall close prisoner rest.
Till that the nature of your fault be known
To the Venetian state. Come, bring him away.

Oth. Soft you; a word or two before you
go. 337
I have done the state some service, and they
know't;
No more of that. I pray you, in your letters,
When you shall these unlucky deeds relate, 340
Speak of me as I am; nothing extenuate,
Nor set down aught in malice: then, must you
speak
Of one that lov'd not wisely but too well; 343
Of one not easily jealous, but, being wrought,
Perplex'd in the extreme; of one whose hand,
Like the base Indian, threw a pearl away
Richer than all his tribe; of one whose subdu'd
eyes
Albeit unused to the melting mood, 348
Drop tears as fast as the Arabian trees
Their med'cinable gum. Set you down this;
And say besides, that in Aleppo once,
Where a malignant and a turban'd Turk 352
Beat a Venetian and traduc'd the state,
I took by the throat the circumcised dog,
And smote him thus. [*Stabs himself.*

Lod. O bloody period!

Gra. All that's spoke is marr'd.

Oth. I kiss'd thee ere I kill'd thee; no way
but this, [*Falling upon* DESDEMONA.
Killing myself to die upon a kiss. [*Dies.*

Cas. This did I fear, but thought he had no
weapon;
For he was great of heart.

Lod. [*To* IAGO.] O Spartan dog! 360
More fell than anguish, hunger, or the sea.
Look on the tragic loading of this bed;
This is thy work; the object poisons sight;
Let it be hid. Gratiano, keep the house, 364
And seize upon the fortunes of the Moor,
For they succeed on you. To you, lord governor,
Remains the censure of this hellish villain,
The time, the place, the torture; O! enforce it.
Myself will straight aboard, and to the state 369
This heavy act with heavy heart relate.

[*Exeunt.*

ANTONY AND CLEOPATRA

DRAMATIS PERSONÆ

MARK ANTONY,
OCTAVIUS CÆSAR, } Triumvirs.
M. ÆMILIUS LEPIDUS,
SEXTUS POMPEIUS.

DOMITIUS ENOBARBUS,
VENTIDIUS,
EROS,
SCARUS,   } Friends to Antony.
DERCETAS,
DEMETRIUS,
PHILO,

MECÆNAS,
AGRIPPA,
DOLABELLA,   } Friends to Cæsar.
PROCULEIUS,
THYREUS,
GALLUS,

MENAS,
MENECRATES, } Friends to Pompey.
VARRIUS,

TAURUS, Lieutenant-General to Cæsar.
CANIDIUS, Lieutenant-General to Antony.
SILIUS, an Officer under Ventidius.
EUPHRONIUS, Ambassador from Antony to Cæsar.
ALEXAS,
MARDIAN,
SELEUCUS, } Attendants on Cleopatra.
DIOMEDES,
A Soothsayer.
A Clown.

CLEOPATRA, Queen of Egypt.
OCTAVIA, sister to Cæsar, and wife to Antony.
CHARMIAN, } Attendants on Cleopatra.
IRAS,

Officers, Soldiers, Messengers, and other Attendants.

SCENE.—*In several parts of the Roman Empire.*

ACT I

SCENE I.—*Alexandria. A Room in* CLEOPATRA'S *Palace.*

Enter DEMETRIUS *and* PHILO.

Phi. Nay, but this dotage of our general's
O'erflows the measure; those his goodly eyes,
That o'er the files and musters of the war
Have glow'd like plated Mars, now bend, now turn   4
The office and devotion of their view
Upon a tawny front; his captain's heart,
Which in the scuffles of great fights hath burst
The buckles on his breast, reneges all temper,   8
And is become the bellows and the fan
To cool a gipsy's lust. Look! where they come.

Flourish. Enter ANTONY *and* CLEOPATRA, *with their Trains; Eunuchs fanning her.*

Take but good note, and you shall see in him   12
The triple pillar of the world transform'd
Into a strumpet's fool; behold and see.
Cleo. If it be love indeed, tell me how much.
Ant. There's beggary in the love that can be reckon'd.
Cleo. I'll set a bourn how far to be belov'd.   16
Ant. Then must thou needs find out new heaven, new earth.

Enter an Attendant.

Att. News, my good lord, from Rome.
Ant.   Grates me; the sum.
Cleo. Nay, hear them, Antony:
Fulvia, perchance, is angry; or, who knows   20
If the scarce-bearded Cæsar have not sent
His powerful mandate to you, 'Do this, or this;

Take in that kingdom, and enfranchise that;
Perform't, or else we damn thee.'
Ant.   How, my love!   24
Cleo. Perchance! nay, and most like;
You must not stay here longer; your dismission
Is come from Cæsar; therefore hear it, Antony.
Where's Fulvia's process? Cæsar's I would say? both?   28
Call in the messengers. As I am Egypt's queen,
Thou blushest, Antony, and that blood of thine
Is Cæsar's homager; else so thy cheek pays shame
When shrill-tongu'd Fulvia scolds. The messengers.   32
Ant. Let Rome in Tiber melt, and the wide arch
Of the rang'd empire fall! Here is my space.
Kingdoms are clay; our dungy earth alike
Feeds beast as man; the nobleness of life   36
Is to do thus; when such a mutual pair
                      [*Embracing.*
And such a twain can do't, in which I bind.
On pain of punishment, the world to weet
We stand up peerless.
Cleo.   Excellent falsehood!   40
Why did he marry Fulvia and not love her?
I'll seem the fool I am not; Antony
Will be himself.
Ant.   But stirr'd by Cleopatra.
Now, for the love of Love and her soft hours,   44
Let's not confound the time with conference harsh:
There's not a minute of our lives should stretch
Without some pleasure now. What sport to-night?
Cleo. Hear the ambassadors.
Ant.   Fie, wrangling queen!   48

Whom every thing becomes, to chide, to laugh,
To weep; whose every passion fully strives
To make itself, in thee, fair and admir'd.
No messenger, but thine; and all alone,   52
To-night we'll wander through the streets and
          note
The qualities of people. Come, my queen;
Last night you did desire it: speak not to us.
          [*Exeunt* ANTONY *and* CLEOPATRA, *with*
                              their Train.
Dem. Is Cæsar with Antonius priz'd so slight?
Phi. Sir, sometimes, when he is not Antony,
He comes too short of that great property
Which still should go with Antony.
Dem.   I am full sorry
That he approves the common liar, who   60
Thus speaks of him at Rome; but I will hope
Of better deeds to-morrow. Rest you happy!
                              [*Exeunt.*

SCENE II.—*The Same. Another Room.*

Enter CHARMIAN, IRAS, ALEXAS, *and*
          a Soothsayer.

Char. Lord Alexas, sweet Alexas, most any
thing Alexas, almost most absolute Alexas,
where's the soothsayer that you praised so to
the queen? O! that I knew this husband,
which, you say, must charge his horns with
garlands.   6
Alex. Soothsayer!
Sooth. Your will?   8
Char. Is this the man? Is't you, sir, that
know things?
Sooth. In nature's infinite book of secrecy
A little I can read.
Alex.   Show him your hand.   12

Enter ENOBARBUS.

Eno. Bring in the banquet quickly; wine
          enough
Cleopatra's health to drink.
Char. Good sir, give me good fortune.
Sooth. I make not, but foresee.   16
Char. Pray then, foresee me one.
Sooth. You shall be yet far fairer than you
          are.
Char. He means in flesh.
Iras. No, you shall paint when you are old.
Char. Wrinkles forbid!   21
Alex. Vex not his prescience; be attentive.
Char. Hush!
Sooth. You shall be more beloving than
belov'd.   24
Char. I had rather heat my liver with drinking.
Alex. Nay, hear him.
Char. Good now, some excellent fortune!
Let me be married to three kings in a forenoon,
and widow them all; let me have a child at fifty,
to whom Herod of Jewry may do homage; find
me to marry me with Octavius Cæsar, and com-
panion me with my mistress.   32
Sooth. You shall outlive the lady whom you
serve.
Char. O excellent! I love long life better than
figs.

Sooth. You have seen and prov'd a faire
          former fortune
Than that which is to approach.   3
Char. Then, belike, my children shall hav
no names; prithee, how many boys and wenche
must I have?
Sooth. If every of your wishes had a womb
And fertile every wish, a million.   4
Char. Out, fool! I forgive thee for a witch
Alex. You think none but your sheets ar
privy to your wishes.   4
Char. Nay, come, tell Iras hers.
Alex. We'll know all our fortunes.
Eno. Mine, and most of our fortunes, to
night, shall be,—drunk to bed.   4
Iras. There's a palm presages chastity, i
nothing else.
Char. E'en as the overflowing Nilus presageth
famine.   5
Iras. Go, you wild bedfellow, you canno
soothsay.
Char. Nay, if an oily palm be not a fruitfu
prognostication, I cannot scratch mine ea
Prithee, tell her but a worky-day fortune.   5
Sooth. Your fortunes are alike.
Iras. But how? but how? give me particulars
Sooth. I have said.   6
Iras. Am I not an inch of fortune bette
than she?
Char. Well, if you were but an inch of for
tune better than I, where would you choose it
Iras. Not in my husband's nose.   6
Char. Our worser thoughts heaven mend
Alexas,—come, his fortune, his fortune. O
let him marry a woman that cannot go, swee
Isis, I beseech thee; and let her die too, and giv
him a worse; and let worse follow worse, till th
worst of all follow him laughing to his grave
fifty-fold a cuckold! Good Isis, hear me thi
prayer, though thou deny me a matter of mor
weight; good Isis, I beseech thee!   7
Iras. Amen. Dear goddess, hear that praye
of the people! for, as it is a heart-breaking to se
a handsome man loose-wived, so it is deadl
sorrow to behold a foul knave uncuckolded
therefore, dear Isis, keep decorum, and fortun
him accordingly!   8
Char. Amen.
Alex. Lo, now! if it lay in their hands t
make me a cuckold, they would make themselve
whores, but they'd do't!   8
Eno. Hush! here comes Antony.
Char.   Not he; the queen

Enter CLEOPATRA.

Cleo. Saw you my lord?
Eno. No, lady.
Cleo. Was he not here?   8
Char. No, madam.
Cleo. He was dispos'd to mirth; but on th
          sudden
A Roman thought hath struck him. Enobarbus
·*Eno.* Madam!   9
Cleo. Seek him, and bring him hither
          Where's Alexas?

Alex. Here, at your service. My lord approaches.

Enter ANTONY, *with a* Messenger *and* Attendants.

Cleo. We will not look upon him; go with us.
    [*Exeunt* CLEOPATRA, ENOBARBUS, ALEXAS, IRAS, CHARMIAN, Soothsayer, *and* Attendants.
Mess. Fulvia thy wife first came into the field.
Ant. Against my brother Lucius? 97
Mess. Ay:
But soon that war had end, and the time's state
Made friends of them, jointing their force 100
'gainst Cæsar,
Whose better issue in the war, from Italy
Upon the first encounter drave them.
Ant.   Well, what worst?
Mess. The nature of bad news infects the teller.
Ant. When it concerns the fool, or coward. On; 104
Things that are past are done with me. 'Tis thus:
Who tells me true, though in his tale lay death,
I hear him as he flatter'd.
Mess.   Labienus—
This is stiff news—hath, with his Parthian force
Extended Asia; from Euphrates 109
His conquering banner shook from Syria
To Lydia and to Ionia: whilst—
Ant. Antony, thou wouldst say,— 112
Mess. O! my lord.
Ant. Speak to me home, mince not the general tongue;
Name Cleopatra as she is call'd in Rome;
Rail thou in Fulvia's phrase; and taunt my faults 116
With such full licence as both truth and malice
Have power to utter. O! then we bring forth weeds
When our quick winds lie still; and our ills told us
Is as our earing. Fare thee well awhile. 120
Mess. At your noble pleasure.   [*Exit.*
Ant. From Sicyon, ho, the news! Speak there!
First Att. The man from Sicyon, is there such an one?
Sec. Att. He stays upon your will.
Ant.   Let him appear. 124
These strong Egyptian fetters I must break,
Or lose myself in dotage.

Enter another Messenger.
                    What are you?
Sec. Mess. Fulvia thy wife is dead.
Ant.   Where died she?
Sec. Mess. In Sicyon: 128
Her length of sickness, with what else more serious
Importeth thee to know, this bears.
                    [*Giving a letter.*
Ant.   Forbear me.
                    [*Exit Second* Messenger.
There's a great spirit gone! Thus did I desire it:

What our contempts do often hurl from us 132
We wish it ours again; the present pleasure,
By revolution lowering, does become
The opposite of itself: she's good, being gone;
The hand could pluck her back that shov'd her on. 136
I must from this enchanting queen break off;
Ten thousand harms, more than the ills I know,
My idleness doth hatch. How now! Enobarbus!

Re-enter ENOBARBUS.

Eno. What's your pleasure, sir? 140
Ant. I must with haste from hence.
Eno. Why, then, we kill all our women. We see how mortal an unkindness is to them; if they suffer our departure, death's the word. 144
Ant. I must be gone.
Eno. Under a compelling occasion let women die; it were pity to cast them away for nothing; though between them and a great cause they should be esteemed nothing. Cleopatra, catching but the least noise of this, dies instantly; I have seen her die twenty times upon far poorer moment. I do think there is mettle in death which commits some loving act upon her, she hath such a celerity in dying. 154
Ant. She is cunning past man's thought.
Eno. Alack! sir, no; her passions are made of nothing but the finest part of pure love. We cannot call her winds and waters sighs and tears; they are greater storms and tempests than almanacs can report: this cannot be cunning in her; if it be, she makes a shower of rain as well as Jove. 162
Ant. Would I had never seen her!
Eno. O, sir! you had then left unseen a wonderful piece of work which not to have been blessed withal would have discredited your travel.
Ant. Fulvia is dead.
Eno. Sir? 168
Ant. Fulvia is dead.
Eno. Fulvia!
Ant. Dead.
Eno. Why, sir, give the gods a thankful sacrifice. When it pleaseth their deities to take the wife of a man from him, it shows to man the tailors of the earth; comforting therein, that when old robes are worn out, there are members to make new. If there were no more women but Fulvia, then had you indeed a cut, and the case to be lamented: this grief is crowned with consolation; your old smock brings forth a new petticoat; and indeed the tears live in an onion that should water this sorrow.
Ant. The business she hath broached in the state
Cannot endure my absence. 184
Eno. And the business you have broached here cannot be without you; especially that of Cleopatra's, which wholly depends on your abode. 188
Ant. No more light answers. Let our officers
Have notice what we purpose. I shall break
The cause of our expedience to the queen,
And get her leave to part. For not alone 192
The death of Fulvia, with more urgent touches,

Do strongly speak to us, but the letters too
Of many our contriving friends in Rome
Petition us at home. Sextus Pompeius 196
Hath given the dare to Cæsar, and commands
The empire of the sea; our slippery people—
Whose love is never link'd to the deserver
Till his deserts are past—begin to throw 200
Pompey the Great and all his dignities
Upon his son; who, high in name and power,
Higher than both in blood and life, stands up
For the main soldier, whose quality, going on,
The sides o' the world may danger. Much is
breeding, 205
Which, like the courser's hair, hath yet but life,
And not a serpent's poison. Say, our pleasure,
To such whose place is under us, requires 208
Our quick remove from hence.
Eno. I shall do it.   [Exeunt.

SCENE III.—The Same. Another Room.

Enter CLEOPATRA, CHARMIAN, IRAS, and
ALEXAS.

Cleo. Where is he?
Char.   I did not see him since.
Cleo. See where he is, who's with him, what
he does;
I did not send you: if you find him sad,
Say I am dancing; if in mirth, report 4
That I am sudden sick: quick, and return.
          [Exit ALEXAS.
Char. Madam, methinks, if you did love him
dearly,
You do not hold the method to enforce
The like from him.
Cleo.   What should I do I do not? 8
Char. In each thing give him way, cross him
in nothing.
Cleo. Thou teachest like a fool; the way to
lose him.
Char. Tempt him not so too far; I wish, for-
bear:
In time we hate that which we often fear. 12
But here comes Antony.

Enter ANTONY.

Cleo.   I am sick and sullen.
Ant. I am sorry to give breathing to my pur-
pose,—
Cleo. Help me away, dear Charmian, I shall
fall:
It cannot be thus long, the sides of nature 16
Will not sustain it.
Ant.   Now, my dearest queen,—
Cleo. Pray you, stand further from me.
Ant.   What's the matter?
Cleo. I know, by that same eye, there's some
good news.
What says the married woman? You may go:
Would she had never given you leave to come!
Let her not say 'tis I that keep you here;
I have no power upon you; hers you are.
Ant. The gods best know,—
Cleo.   O! never was there queen 24
So mightily betray'd; yet at the first
I saw the treasons planted.

Ant.   Cleopatra,—
Cleo. Why should I think you can be mine
and true,
Though you in swearing shake the throned
gods, 28
Who have been false to Fulvia? Riotous mad-
ness,
To be entangled with those mouth-made vows,
Which break themselves in swearing!
Ant.   Most sweet queen,—
Cleo. Nay, pray you, seek no colour for your
going, 32
But bid farewell, and go: when you su'd stay-
ing
Then was the time for words; no going then:
Eternity was in our lips and eyes,
Bliss in our brows bent; none our parts so
poor 36
But was a race of heaven; they are so still,
Or thou, the greatest soldier of the world,
Art turn'd the greatest liar.
Ant.   How now, lady!
Cleo. I would I had thy inches; thou shouldst
know 40
There were a heart in Egypt.
Ant.   Hear me, queen:
The strong necessity of time commands
Our services awhile, but my full heart
Remains in use with you. Our Italy 44
Shines o'er with civil swords; Sextus Pompeius
Makes his approaches to the port of Rome;
Equality of two domestic powers
Breeds scrupulous faction. The hated, grown
to strength, 48
Are newly grown to love; the condemn'd
Pompey,
Rich in his father's honour, creeps apace
Into the hearts of such as have not thriv'd 51
Upon the present state, whose numbers threaten;
And quietness, grown sick of rest, would purge
By any desperate change. My more particular,
And that which most with you should safe my
going, 56
Is Fulvia's death.
Cleo. Though age from folly could not give
me freedom,
It does from childishness: can Fulvia die?
Ant. She's dead, my queen:
Look here, and at thy sovereign leisure read 60
The garboils she awak'd; at the last, best,
See when and where she died.
Cleo.   O most false love!
Where be the sacred vials thou shouldst fill
With sorrowful water? Now I see, I see, 64
In Fulvia's death, how mine receiv'd shall be.
Ant. Quarrel no more, but be prepar'd to
know
The purposes I bear, which are or cease
As you shall give the advice. By the fire 68
That quickens Nilus' slime, I go from hence
Thy soldier, servant, making peace or war
As thou affect'st.
Cleo.   Cut my lace, Charmian, come
But let it be: I am quickly ill, and well; 7
So Antony loves.
Ant.   My precious queen, forbear

And give true evidence to his love which stands
An honourable trial.
 Cleo.   So Fulvia told me.
I prithee, turn aside and weep for her; 76
Then bid adieu to me, and say the tears
Belong to Egypt: good now, play one scene
Of excellent dissembling, and let it look
Like perfect honour.
 Ant. You'll heat my blood; no more.
 Cleo. You can do better yet, but this is
  meetly. 81
 Ant. Now, by my sword,—
 Cleo.   And target, Still he mends;
But this is not the best. Look, prithee, Char-
 mian,
How this Herculean Roman does become 84
The carriage of his chafe.
 Ant. I'll leave you, lady.
 Cleo.   Courteous lord, one word.
Sir, you and I must part, but that's not it:
Sir, you and I have lov'd, but there's not it; 88
That you know well: something it is I would,—
O! my oblivion is a very Antony,
And I am all forgotten.
 Ant.   But that your royalty
Holds idleness your subject, I should take you
For idleness itself.
 Cleo. 'Tis sweating labour 93
To bear such idleness so near the heart
As Cleopatra this. But, sir, forgive me;
Since my becomings kill me when they do not 96
Eye well to you: your honour calls you hence;
Therefore be deaf to my unpitied folly,
And all the gods go with you! Upon your sword
Sit laurel victory! and smooth success 100
Be strew'd before your feet!
 Ant.   Let us go. Come;
Our separation so abides and flies,
That thou, residing here, go'st yet with me,
And I, hence fleeting, here remain with thee. 104
Away!   *[Exeunt.*

SCENE IV.—*Rome. A Room in* CÆSAR'S
House.

Enter OCTAVIUS CÆSAR, LEPIDUS, *and
Attendants.*

 Cæs. You may see, Lepidus, and henceforth
  know,
It is not Cæsar's natural vice to hate
Our great competitor. From Alexandria
This is the news: he fishes, drinks, and wastes 4
The lamps of night in revel; is not more man-
 like
Than Cleopatra, nor the queen of Ptolemy
More womanly than he; hardly gave audience,
 or
Vouchsaf'd to think he had partners: you shall
 find there 8
A man who is the abstract of all faults
That all men follow.
 Lep. I must not think there are
Evils enow to darken all his goodness;
His faults in him seem as the spots of heaven, 12
More fiery by night's blackness; hereditary
Rather than purchas'd; what he cannot change

Than what he chooses.
 Cæs. You are too indulgent. Let us grant
  it is not 16
Amiss to tumble on the bed of Ptolemy,
To give a kingdom for a mirth, to sit
And keep the turn of tippling with a slave,
To reel the streets at noon, and stand the
  buffet 20
With knaves that smell of sweat; say this be-
  comes him,—
As his composure must be rare indeed
Whom these things cannot blemish,—yet must
  Antony
No way excuse his soils, when we do bear 24
So great weight in his lightness. If he fill'd
His vacancy with his voluptuousness,
Full surfeits and the dryness of his bones
Call on him for't; but to confound such
  time 28
That drums him from his sport, and speaks as
  loud
As his own state and ours, 'tis to be chid
As we rate boys, who, being mature in know-
  ledge,
Pawn their experience to their present pleasure,
And so rebel to judgment.

Enter a Messenger.

 Lep.   Here's more news. 33
 Mess. Thy biddings have been done, and
  every hour,
Most noble Cæsar, shalt thou have report
How 'tis abroad. Pompey is strong at sea, 36
And it appears he is belov'd of those
That only have fear'd Cæsar; to the ports
The discontents repair, and men's reports
Give him much wrong'd.
 Cæs. I should have known no less.
It hath been taught us from the primal state, 41
That he which is was wish'd until he were;
And the ebb'd man, ne'er lov'd till ne'er worth
  love,
Comes dear'd by being lack'd. This common
  body, 44
Like to a vagabond flag upon the stream,
Goes to and back, lackeying the varying tide,
To rot itself with motion.
 Mess. Cæsar, I bring thee word,
Menecrates and Menas, famous pirates, 48
Make the sea serve them, which they ear and
  wound
With keels of every kind: many hot inroads
They make in Italy; the borders maritime
Lack blood to think on't, and flush youth re-
  volt; 52
No vessel can peep forth, but 'tis as soon
Taken as seen; for Pompey's name strikes more
Than could his war resisted.
 Cæs.   Antony,
Leave thy lascivious wassails. When thou once
Wast beaten from Modena, where thou slew'st
Hirtius and Pansa, consuls, at thy heel
Did famine follow, whom thou fought'st against,
Though daintily brought up, with patience
  more 60
Than savages could suffer; thou didst drink

The stale of horses and the gilded puddle
Which beasts would cough at; thy palate then
    did deign
The roughest berry on the rudest hedge;   64
Yea, like the stag, when snow the pasture sheets,
The barks of trees thou browsed'st; on the Alps
It is reported thou didst eat strange flesh,
Which some did die to look on; and all this—   68
It wounds thy honour that I speak it now—
Was borne so like a soldier, that thy cheek
So much as lank'd not.
    Lep.   'Tis pity of him.
    Cæs. Let his shames quickly   72
Drive him to Rome. 'Tis time we twain
Did show ourselves i' the field; and to that end
Assemble me immediate council; Pompey
Thrives in our idleness.
    Lep.   To-morrow, Cæsar, 76
I shall be furnish'd to inform you rightly
Both what by sea and land I can be able
To front this present time.
    Cæs.   Till which encounter,
It is my business too. Farewell.   80
    Lep. Farewell, my lord. What you shall
    know meantime
Of stirs abroad, I shall beseech you, sir,
To let me be partaker.
    Cæs.   Doubt not, sir;
I knew it for my bond.   [*Exeunt.*

SCENE V.—*Alexandria. A Room in the Palace.*

Enter CLEOPATRA, CHARMIAN, IRAS, *and* MARDIAN.

    Cleo. Charmian!
    Char. Madam!
    Cleo. Ha, ha!
Give me to drink mandragora.
    Char.   Why, madam? 4
    Cleo. That I might sleep out this great gap of time
My Antony is away.
    Char.   You think of him too much.
    Cleo. O! 'tis treason.
    Char.   Madam, I trust, not so.
    Cleo. Thou, eunuch Mardian!
    Mar.   What's your highness' pleasure? 8
    Cleo. Not now to hear thee sing; I take no pleasure
In aught a eunuch has. 'Tis well for thee,
That, being unseminar'd, thy freer thoughts
May not fly forth of Egypt. Hast thou affec-
    tions?   12
    Mar. Yes, gracious madam.
    Cleo. Indeed!
    Mar. Not in deed, madam; for I can do nothing
But what in deed is honest to be done;   16
Yet have I fierce affections, and think
What Venus did with Mars.
    Cleo.   O Charmian!
Where think'st thou he is now? Stands he, or sits he?
Or does he walk? or is he on his horse?   20
O happy horse, to bear the weight of Antony!

Do bravely, horse, for wot'st thou whom thou
    mov'st?
The demi-Atlas of this earth, the arm
And burgonet of men. He's speaking now, 2
Or murmuring 'Where's my serpent of old
    Nile?'
For so he calls me. Now I feed myself
With most delicious poison. Think on me,
That am with Phœbus' amorous pinches black
And wrinkled deep in time? Broad-fronted
    Cæsar,   2
When thou wast here above the ground I was
A morsel for a monarch, and great Pompey
Would stand and make his eyes grow in my
    brow;   3
There would he anchor his aspect and die
With looking on his life.

Enter ALEXAS.

    Alex.   Sovereign of Egypt, hail!
    Cleo. How much unlike art thou Mark
    Antony!
Yet, coming from him, that great medicine
    hath   3
With his tinct gilded thee.
How goes it with my brave Mark Antony?
    Alex. Last thing he did, dear queen,
He kiss'd, the last of many doubled kisses, 4
This orient pearl. His speech sticks in my heart.
    Cleo. Mine ear must pluck it thence.
    Alex.   'Good friend,' quoth he,
'Say, the firm Roman to great Egypt sends
This treasure of an oyster; at whose foot, 4
To mend the petty present, I will piece
Her opulent throne with kingdoms; all the east
Say thou, shall call her mistress.' So he nodded
And soberly did mount an arm-gaunt steed, 4
Who neigh'd so high that what I would have
    spoke
Was beastly dumb'd by him.
    Cleo.   What! was he sad or merry?
    Alex. Like to the time o' the year between the extremes
Of hot and cold; he was nor sad nor merry. 5
    Cleo. O well-divided disposition! Note him,
Note him, good Charmian, 'tis the man; but
    note him:
He was not sad, for he would shine on those
That make their looks by his; he was not
    merry,   5
Which seem'd to tell them his remembrance lay
In Egypt with his joy; but between both:
O heavenly mingle! Be'st thou sad or merry,
The violence of either thee becomes, 6
So does it no man else. Mett'st thou my posts?
    Alex. Ay, madam, twenty several messengers
Why do you send so thick?
    Cleo.   Who's born that day
When I forget to send to Antony, 6
Shall die a beggar. Ink and paper, Charmian.
Welcome, my good Alexas. Did I, Charmian,
Ever love Cæsar so?
    Char.   O! that brave Cæsar!
    Cleo. Be chok'd with such another emphasis!
Say the brave Antony.
    Char.   The valiant Cæsar! 6

Cleo. By Isis, I will give thee bloody teeth,
If thou with Cæsar paragon again
My man of men.
Char.				By your most gracious pardon, 72
I sing but after you.
Cleo.					My salad days,
When I was green in judgment, cold in blood,
To say as I said then! But come, away;
Get me ink and paper: 76
He shall have every day a several greeting,
Or I'll unpeople Egypt.				[*Exeunt.*

ACT II

SCENE I.—*Messina. A Room in* POMPEY'S
House.

Enter POMPEY, MENECRATES, *and* MENAS.

Pom. If the great gods be just, they shall
assist
The deeds of justest men.
Mene.				Know, worthy Pompey,
That what they do delay, they not deny.
Pom. Whiles we are suitors to their throne,
decays					4
The thing we sue for.
Mene.			We, ignorant of ourselves,
Beg often our own harms, which the wise powers
Deny us for our good; so find we profit
By losing of our prayers.
Pom.				I shall do well:	8
The people love me, and the sea is mine;
My powers are crescent, and my auguring hope
Says it will come to the full. Mark Antony
In Egypt sits at dinner, and will make	12
No wars without doors; Cæsar gets money
where
He loses hearts; Lepidus flatters both,
Of both is flatter'd; but he neither loves,
Nor either cares for him.
Men.				Cæsar and Lepidus 16
Are in the field; a mighty strength they carry.
Pom. Where have you this? 'tis false.
Men.					From Silvius, sir.
Pom. He dreams; I know they are in Rome
together,
Looking for Antony. But all the charms of love,
Salt Cleopatra, soften thy wan'd lip!	21
Let witchcraft join with beauty, lust with both!
Tie up the libertine in a field of feasts,
Keep his brain fuming; Epicurean cooks	24
Sharpen with cloyless sauce his appetite,
That sleep and feeding may prorogue his honour
Even till a Lethe'd dulness!

Enter VARRIUS.

						How now, Varrius!
Var. This is most certain that I shall de-
liver:						28
Mark Antony is every hour in Rome
Expected; since he went from Egypt 'tis
A space for further travel.
Pom.				I could have given less matter
A better ear. Menas, I did not think	32
This amorous surfeiter would have donn'd his
helm
For such a petty war; his soldiership

Is twice the other twain. But let us rear
The higher our opinion, that our stirring	36
Can from the lap of Egypt's widow pluck
The ne'er-lust-wearied Antony.
Men.					I cannot hope
Cæsar and Antony shall well greet together;
His wife that's dead did trespasses to Cæsar, 40
His brother warr'd upon him, although I think
Not mov'd by Antony.
Pom.				I know not, Menas,
How lesser enmities may give way to greater.
Were't not that we stand up against them all 44
'Twere pregnant they should square between
themselves,
For they have entertained cause enough
To draw their swords; but how the fear of us
May cement their divisions and bind up	48
The petty difference, we yet not know.
Be it as our gods will have't! It only stands
Our lives upon, to use our strongest hands.
Come, Menas.					[*Exeunt.*

SCENE II.—*Rome. A Room in* LEPIDUS'
House.

Enter ENOBARBUS *and* LEPIDUS.

Lep. Good Enobarbus, 'tis a worthy deed,
And shall become you well, to entreat your
captain
To soft and gentle speech.
Eno.				I shall entreat him
To answer like himself: if Cæsar move him,	4
Let Antony look over Cæsar's head,
And speak as loud as Mars. By Jupiter,
Were I the wearer of Antonius' beard,
I would not shave't to-day.
Lep.					'Tis not a time	8
For private stomaching.
Eno.				Every time
Serves for the matter that is then born in't.
Lep. But small to greater matters must give
way.
Eno. Not if the small come first.
Lep.				Your speech is passion; 12
But, pray you, stir no embers up. Here comes
The noble Antony.

Enter ANTONY *and* VENTIDIUS.

Eno.				And yonder, Cæsar.

Enter CÆSAR, MECÆNAS, *and* AGRIPPA.

Ant. If we compose well then, to Parthia:
Hark ye, Ventidius.
Cæs.				I do not know,	16
Mecænas; ask Agrippa.
Lep.				Noble friends,
That which combin'd us was most great, and
let not
A leaner action rend us. What's amiss,
May it be gently heard; when we debate	20
Our trivial difference loud, we do commit
Murder in healing wounds; then, noble part-
ners,—
The rather for I earnestly beseech,—
Touch you the sourest points with sweetest
terms,					24
Nor curstness grow to the matter.

Ant. 'Tis spoken well.
Were we before our armies, and to fight,
I should do thus.
  Cæs. Welcome to Rome. 28
  Ant. Thank you.
  Cæs. Sit.
  Ant. Sit, sir.
  Cæs. Nay, then. 32
  Ant. I learn, you take things ill which are
    not so,
Or being, concern you not.
  Cæs. I must be laugh'd at
If, or for nothing or a little, I
Should say myself offended, and with you 36
Chiefly i' the world; more laugh'd at that I
  should
Once name you derogately, when to sound your
  name
It not concern'd me.
  Ant. My being in Egypt, Cæsar,
What was't to you? 40
  Cæs. No more than my residing here at
  Rome
Might be to you in Egypt; yet, if you there
Did practise on my state, your being in Egypt
Might be my question.
  Ant. How intend you, practis'd? 44
  Cæs. You may be pleas'd to catch at mine
  intent
By what did here befall me. Your wife and
  brother
Made wars upon me, and their contestation
Was theme for you, you were the word of war.
  Ant. You do mistake your business; my
  brother never 49
Did urge me in his act: I did inquire it;
And have my learning from some true reports,
That drew their swords with you. Did he not
  rather 52
Discredit my authority with yours,
And make the wars alike against my stomach,
Having alike your cause? Of this my letters
Before did satisfy you. If you'll patch a
  quarrel, 56
As matter whole you n' have to make it with,
It must not be with this.
  Cæs. You praise yourself
By laying defects of judgment to me, but
You patch'd up your excuses.
  Ant. Not so, not so; 60
I know you could not lack, I am certain on't,
Very necessity of this thought, that I,
Your partner in the cause 'gainst which he
  fought,
Could not with graceful eyes attend those wars
Which fronted mine own peace. As for my
  wife, 65
I would you had her spirit in such another:
The third o' the world is yours, which with a
  snaffle
You may pace easy, but not such a wife. 68
  Eno. Would we had all such wives, that the
men might go to wars with the women!
  Ant. So much uncurbable, her garboils,
  Cæsar,
Made out of her impatience,—which not wanted

Shrewdness of policy too,—I grieving grant 73
Did you too much disquiet; for that you must
But say I could not help it.
  Cæs. I wrote to you
When rioting in Alexandria; you 76
Did pocket up my letters, and with taunts
Did gibe my missive out of audience.
  Ant. Sir,
He fell upon me, ere admitted: then
Three kings I had newly feasted, and did want 80
Of what I was i' the morning; but next day
I told him of myself, which was as much
As to have ask'd him pardon. Let this fellow
Be nothing of our strife; if we contend, 84
Out of our question wipe him.
  Cæs. You have broken
The article of your oath, which you shall never
Have tongue to charge me with.
  Lep. Soft, Cæsar!
  Ant. No,
Lepidus, let him speak: 88
The honour's sacred which he talks on now,
Supposing that I lack'd it. But on, Cæsar;
The article of my oath.
  Cæs. To lend me arms and aid when I re-
  quir'd them, 92
The which you both denied.
  Ant. Neglected, rather;
And then, when poison'd hours had bound me
  up
From mine own knowledge. As nearly as I may,
I'll play the penitent to you; but mine honesty
Shall not make poor my greatness, nor my
  power 97
Work without it. Truth is, that Fulvia,
To have me out of Egypt, made wars here;
For which myself, the ignorant motive, do 100
So far ask pardon as befits mine honour
To stoop in such a case.
  Lep. 'Tis noble spoken.
  Mec. If it might please you, to enforce no
  further
The griefs between ye: to forget them quite 104
Were to remember that the present need
Speaks to atone you.
  Lep. Worthily spoken, Mecænas.
  Eno. Or, if you borrow one another's love
for the instant, you may, when you hear no
more words of Pompey, return it again: you
shall have time to wrangle in when you have
nothing else to do. 111
  Ant. Thou art a soldier only; speak no more.
  Eno. That truth should be silent I had almost
forgot.
  Ant. You wrong this presence; therefore
  speak no more.
  Eno. Go to, then; your considerate stone. 116
  Cæs. I do not much dislike the matter, but
The manner of his speech; for it cannot be
We shall remain in friendship, our conditions
So differing in their acts. Yet, if I knew 120
What hoop should hold us stanch, from edge to
  edge
O' the world I would pursue it.
  Agr. Give me leave, Cæsar.
  Cæs. Speak, Agrippa.

Agr. Thou hast a sister by the mother's side,
Admir'd Octavia; great Mark Antony   125
s now a widower.

Cæs.   Say not so, Agrippa:
f Cleopatra heard you, your reproof
Were well deserv'd of rashness.   128

Ant. I am not married, Cæsar; let me hear
Agrippa further speak.

Agr. To hold you in perpetual amity,
To make you brothers, and to knit your
    hearts   132
With an unslipping knot, take Antony
Octavia to his wife; whose beauty claims
No worse a husband than the best of men,
Whose virtue and whose general graces speak
That which none else can utter. By this mar-
    riage,   137
All little jealousies which now seem great,
And all great fears which now import their
    dangers,
Would then be nothing; truths would be but
    tales   140
Where now half tales be truths; her love to both
Would each to other and all loves to both
Draw after her. Pardon what I have spoke,
For 'tis a studied, not a present thought, 144
By duty ruminated.

Ant.   Will Cæsar speak?

Cæs. Not till he hears how Antony is touch'd
With what is spoke already.

Ant.   What power is in Agrippa,
f I would say, 'Agrippa, be it so,'   148
To make this good?

Cæs.   The power of Cæsar, and
His power unto Octavia.

Ant.   May I never
To this good purpose, that so fairly shows,
Dream of impediment! Let me have thy hand;
Further this act of grace, and from this hour 153
The heart of brothers govern in our loves
And sway our great designs!

Cæs.   There is my hand.
A sister I bequeath you, whom no brother
Did ever love so dearly; let her live   157
To join our kingdoms and our hearts, and never
Fly off our loves again!

Lep.   Happily, amen!

Ant. I did not think to draw my sword 'gainst
Pompey,   160
For he hath laid strange courtesies and great
Of late upon me; I must thank him only,
Lest my remembrance suffer ill report;
At heel of that, defy him.

Lep.   Time calls upon 's: 164
Of us must Pompey presently be sought,
Or else he seeks out us.

Ant.   Where lies he?

Cæs. About the Mount Misenum.

Ant.   What's his strength
By land?

Cæs.   Great and increasing; but by sea 168
He is an absolute master.

Ant.   So is the fame.
Would we had spoke together! Haste we for it;
Yet, ere we put ourselves in arms, dispatch we
The business we have talk'd of.

Cæs.   With most gladness; 172
And do invite you to my sister's view,
Whither straight I'll lead you.

Ant.   Let us, Lepidus,
Not lack your company.

Lep.   Noble Antony,
Not sickness should detain me.   176
    [*Flourish. Exeunt* CÆSAR, ANTONY,
                      and LEPIDUS.

Mec. Welcome from Egypt, sir.

Eno. Half the heart of Cæsar, worthy Mecænas! My honourable friend, Agrippa!

Agr. Good Enobarbus!   180

Mec. We have cause to be glad that matters
are so well digested. You stayed well by't in
Egypt.

Eno. Ay, sir; we did sleep day out of countenance, and made the night light with drinking.

Mec. Eight wild boars roasted whole at a
breakfast, and but twelve persons there; is this
true?   188

Eno. This was but as a fly by an eagle; we
had much more monstrous matter of feast,
which worthily deserved noting.

Mec. She's a most triumphant lady, if report
be square to her.   193

Eno. When she first met Mark Antony she
pursed up his heart, upon the river of Cydnus.

Agr. There she appeared indeed, or my re-
porter devised well for her.   197

Eno. I will tell you.
The barge she sat in, like a burnish'd throne,
Burn'd on the water; the poop was beaten gold,
Purple the sails, and so perfumed, that   201
The winds were love-sick with them, the oars
    were silver,
Which to the tune of flutes kept stroke, and
    made
The water which they beat to follow faster, 204
As amorous of their strokes. For her own per-
    son,
It beggar'd all description; she did lie
In her pavilion,—cloth-of-gold of tissue,—
O'er-picturing that Venus where we see   208
The fancy outwork nature; on each side her
Stood pretty-dimpled boys, like smiling Cupids,
With divers-colour'd fans, whose wind did seem
To glow the delicate cheeks which they did cool,
And what they undid did.

Agr.   O! rare for Antony. 213

Eno. Her gentlewomen, like the Nereides,
So many mermaids, tended her i' the eyes,
And made their bends adornings; at the helm
A seeming mermaid steers; the silken tackle 217
Swell with the touches of those flower-soft
    hands,
That yarely frame the office. From the barge
A strange invisible perfume hits the sense 220
Of the adjacent wharfs. The city cast
Her people out upon her, and Antony,
Enthron'd i' the market-place, did sit alone,
Whistling to the air; which, but for vacancy,
Had gone to gaze on Cleopatra too   225
And made a gap in nature.

Agr.   Rare Egyptian!

Eno. Upon her landing, Antony sent to her,

Invited her to supper; she replied   228
It should be better he became her guest,
Which she entreated. Our courteous Antony,
Whom ne'er the word of 'No' woman heard
    speak,
Being barber'd ten times o'er, goes to the feast,
And, for his ordinary pays his heart   233
For what his eyes eat only.

Agr.   Royal wench!
She made great Cæsar lay his sword to bed;
He plough'd her, and she cropp'd.

Eno.   I saw her once
Hop forty paces through the public street; 237
And having lost her breath, she spoke, and
    panted
That she did make defect perfection,
And, breathless, power breathe forth.   240

Mec. Now Antony must leave her utterly.

Eno. Never; he will not:
Age cannot wither her, nor custom stale
Her infinite variety; other women cloy   244
The appetites they feed, but she makes hungry
Where most she satisfies; for vilest things
Become themselves in her, that the holy priests
Bless her when she is riggish.   248

Mec. If beauty, wisdom, modesty, can settle
The heart of Antony, Octavia is
A blessed lottery to him.

Agr.   Let us go.
Good Enobarbus, make yourself my guest 252
Whilst you abide here.

Eno.   Humbly, sir, I thank you.
                        [*Exeunt.*

SCENE III.—*The Same. A Room in* CÆSAR'S
    House.

Enter CÆSAR, ANTONY, OCTAVIA *between them;*
    Attendants.

Ant. The world and my great office will some-
    times
Divide me from your bosom.

Oct.   All which time
Before the gods my knee shall bow my prayers
To them for you.

Ant.   Good night, sir. My Octavia, 4
Read not my blemishes in the world's report;
I have not kept my square, but that to come
Shall all be done by the rule. Good night, dear
    lady.

Oct. Good night, sir.   8

Cæs. Good night.
                [*Exeunt* CÆSAR *and* OCTAVIA.

Enter Soothsayer.

Ant. Now, sirrah; you do wish yourself in
Egypt?

Sooth. Would I had never come from thence,
    nor you
Thither!   12

Ant. If you can, your reason?

Sooth.   I see it in
My motion, have it not in my tongue: but yet
Hie you to Egypt again.

Ant.   Say to me,

Whose fortunes shall rise higher, Cæsar's or
mine?   16

Sooth. Cæsar's.
Therefore, O Antony! stay not by his side;
Thy demon—that's thy spirit which keeps thee,
    —is
Noble, courageous, high, unmatchable,   20
Where Cæsar's is not; but near him thy angel
Becomes a fear, as being o'erpower'd; therefore
Make space enough between you.

Ant.   Speak this no more.

Sooth. To none but thee; no more but when
    to thee.   24
If thou dost play with him at any game
Thou art sure to lose, and, of that natural luck,
He beats thee 'gainst the odds; thy lustre thickens
When he shines by. I say again, thy spirit 28
Is all afraid to govern thee near him,
But he away, 'tis noble.

Ant.   Get thee gone:
Say to Ventidius I would speak with him.
                    [*Exit* Soothsayer.
He shall to Parthia. Be it art or hap   32
He hath spoken true; the very dice obey him,
And in our sports my better cunning faints
Under his chance; if we draw lots he speeds,
His cocks do win the battle still of mine   36
When it is all to nought, and his quails ever
Beat mine, inhoop'd, at odds. I will to Egypt;
And though I make this marriage for my peace,
I' the east my pleasure lies.

Enter VENTIDIUS.

                O! come, Ventidius, 40
You must to Parthia; your commission's ready;
Follow me, and receive't.   [*Exeunt.*

SCENE IV.—*The Same. A Street.*

Enter LEPIDUS, MECÆNAS, *and* AGRIPPA.

Lep. Trouble yourselves no further; pray you
    hasten
Your generals after.

Agr.   Sir, Mark Antony
Will e'en but kiss Octavia, and we'll follow.

Lep. Till I shall see you in your soldier's
    dress,
Which will become you both, farewell.

Mec.   We shall,
As I conceive the journey, be at the Mount
Before you, Lepidus.

Lep.   Your way is shorter;
My purposes do draw me much about: 8
You'll win two days upon me.

Mec. } Sir, good success!
Agr. }

Lep. Farewell.   [*Exeunt*

SCENE V.—*Alexandria. A Room in the Palace.*

Enter CLEOPATRA, CHARMIAN, IRAS, ALEXAS,
    and Attendant.

Cleo. Give me some music; music, moody
    food
Of us that trade in love.

Attend.   The music, ho!

Enter MARDIAN.

Cleo. Let it alone; let's to billiards: come,
	Charmian.
Char. My arm is sore; best play with Mar-
	dian.	4
Cleo. As well a woman with a eunuch play'd
As with a woman. Come, you'll play with me,
	sir?
Mar. As well as I can, madam.
Cleo. And when good will is show'd, though't
	come too short,	8
The actor may plead pardon. I'll none now.
Give me mine angle; we'll to the river: there—
My music playing far off—I will betray
Tawny-finn'd fishes; my bended hook shall
	pierce	12
Their slimy jaws; and, as I draw them up,
I'll think them every one an Antony,
And say, 'Ah, ha!' you're caught.
Char.			'Twas merry when
You wager'd on your angling; when your diver
Did hang a salt-fish on his hook, which he	17
With fervency drew up.
Cleo.			That time—O times!—
I laugh'd him out of patience; and that night
I laugh'd him into patience: and next morn,	20
Ere the ninth hour, I drunk him to his bed;
Then put my tires and mantles on him, whilst
I wore his sword Philippan.

Enter a Messenger.

			O! from Italy;
Ram thou thy fruitful tidings in mine ears,	24
That long time have been barren.
Mess.			Madam, madam,—
Cleo. Antony's dead! if thou say so, villain,
Thou kill'st thy mistress; but well and free,
If thou so yield him, there is gold, and here	28
My bluest veins to kiss; a hand that kings
Have lipp'd, and trembled kissing.
Mess. First, madam, he is well.
Cleo.			Why, there's more gold.
But, sirrah, mark, we use	32
To say the dead are well: bring it to that,
The gold I give thee will I melt, and pour
Down thy ill-uttering throat.
Mess. Good madam, hear me.
Cleo.			Well, go to, I will;	36
But there's no goodness in thy face; if Antony
Be free and healthful, so tart a favour
To trumpet such good tidings! if not well,
Thou shouldst come like a Fury crown'd with
	snakes,	40
Not like a formal man.
Mess.			Will't please you hear me?
Cleo. I have a mind to strike thee ere thou
	speak'st:
Yet, if thou say Antony lives, is well,
Or friends with Cæsar, or not captive to him,
I'll set thee in a shower of gold, and hail	45
Rich pearls upon thee.
Mess.			Madam, he's well.
Cleo.			Well said.
Mess. And friends with Cæsar.
Cleo.			Thou 'rt an honest man.

Mess. Cæsar and he are greater friends than
	ever.	48
Cleo. Make thee a fortune from me.
Mess.			But yet, madam,—
Cleo. I do not like 'but yet,' it does allay
The good precedence; fie upon 'but yet!'
'But yet' is as a gaoler to bring forth	52
Some monstrous malefactor. Prithee, friend,
Pour out the pack of matter to mine ear,
The good and bad together. He's friends with
	Cæsar;
In state of health, thou sayst; and thou sayst,
	free.	56
Mess. Free, madam! no; I made no such
	report:
He's bound unto Octavia.
Cleo.			For what good turn?
Mess. For the best turn i' the bed.
Cleo.			I am pale, Charmian!
Mess. Madam, he's married to Octavia.	60
Cleo. The most infectious pestilence upon
	thee!		[*Strikes him down.*
Mess. Good madam, patience.
Cleo.			What say you? Hence,
			[*Strikes him again.*
Horrible villain! or I'll spurn thine eyes
Like balls before me; I'll unhair thy head:	64
			[*She hales him up and down.*
Thou shalt be whipp'd with wire, and stew'd in
	brine,
Smarting in lingering pickle.
Mess.			Gracious madam,
I, that do bring the news made not the match.
Cleo. Say 'tis not so, a province I will give
	thee,	68
And make thy fortunes proud; the blow thou
	hadst
Shall make thy peace for moving me to rage,
And I will boot thee with what gift beside
Thy modesty can beg.
Mess.			He's married, madam.	72
Cleo. Rogue! thou hast liv'd too long.
			[*Draws a knife.*
Mess.			Nay, then I'll run.
What mean you, madam? I have made no
	fault.			[*Exit.*
Char. Good madam, keep yourself within
	yourself;
The man is innocent.	76
Cleo. Some innocents 'scape not the thunder-
	bolt.
Melt Egypt into Nile! and kindly creatures
Turn all to serpents! Call the slave again:
Though I am mad, I will not bite him. Call.	80
Char. He is afeard to come.
Cleo.			I will not hurt him.
			[*Exit* CHARMIAN.
These hands do lack nobility, that they strike
A meaner than myself; since I myself
Have given myself the cause.

Re-enter CHARMIAN, *and* Messenger.

			Come hither, sir.	84
Though it be honest, it is never good
To bring bad news; give to a gracious message
A host of tongues, but let ill tidings tell

Themselves when they be felt.

Mess.   I have done my duty.

Cleo. Is he married?   89
I cannot hate thee worser than I do
If thou again say 'Yes.'

Mess.   He's married, madam.

Cleo. The gods confound thee! dost thou
hold there still?   92

Mess. Should I lie, madam?

Cleo.   O! I would thou didst,
So half my Egypt were submerg'd and made
A cistern for scal'd snakes. Go, get thee hence;
Hadst thou Narcissus in thy face, to me   96
Thou wouldst appear most ugly. He is married?

Mess. I crave your highness' pardon.

Cleo.   He is married?

Mess. Take no offence that I would not offend
you;
To punish me for what you make me do   100
Seems much unequal; he's married to Octavia.

Cleo. O! that his fault should make a knave
of thee,
That art not what thou'rt sure of. Get thee
hence;
The merchandise which thou hast brought from
Rome   104
Are all too dear for me; lie they upon thy hand
And be undone by 'em!   [*Exit* Messenger.

Char.   Good your highness, patience.

Cleo. In praising Antony I have disprais'd
Cæsar.

Char. Many times, madam.

Cleo.   I am paid for 't now.   108
Lead me from hence;
I faint. O Iras! Charmian! 'Tis no matter.
Go to the fellow, good Alexas; bid him
Report the feature of Octavia, her years,   112
Her inclination, let him not leave out
The colour of her hair: bring me word quickly.
          [*Exit* ALEXAS.
Let him for ever go:—let him not—Charmian!—
Though he be painted one way like a Gorgon,
The other way's a Mars. [*To* MARDIAN.] Bid
you Alexas   117
Bring me word how tall she is. Pity me, Char-
mian,
But do not speak to me. Lead me to my chamber.
          [*Exeunt.*

SCENE VI.—*Near Misenum.*

Flourish. Enter POMPEY *and* MENAS, *at one side,
with drum and trumpet; at the other,* CÆSAR,
ANTONY, LEPIDUS, ENOBARBUS, MECÆNAS, *with
Soldiers marching.*

Pom. Your hostages I have, so have you
mine;
And we shall talk before we fight.

Cæs.   Most meet
That first we come to words, and therefore have
we
Our written purposes before us sent;   4
Which if thou hast consider'd, let us know
If 'twill tie up thy discontented sword,
And carry back to Sicily much tall youth
That else must perish here.

Pom.   To you all three,   8
The senators alone of this great world,
Chief factors for the gods, I do not know
Wherefore my father should revengers want,
Having a son and friends; since Julius Cæsar,
Who at Philippi the good Brutus ghosted,   13
There saw you labouring for him. What was 't
That mov'd pale Cassius to conspire? and what
Made the all-honour'd, honest Roman, Brutus,
With the arm'd rest, courtiers of beauteous free-
dom,   17
To drench the Capitol, but that they would
Have one man but a man? And that is it
Hath made me rig my navy, at whose burden   20
The anger'd ocean foams, with which I meant
To scourge the ingratitude that despiteful Rome
Cast on my noble father.

Cæs.   Take your time.

Ant. Thou canst not fear us, Pompey, with
thy sails;   24
We'll speak with thee at sea: at land, thou
know'st
How much we do o'er-count thee.

Pom.   At land, indeed,
Thou dost o'er-count me of my father's house;
But, since the cuckoo builds not for himself,   28
Remain in 't as thou mayst.

Lep.   Be pleas'd to tell us—
For this is from the present—how you take
The offers we have sent you.

Cæs.   There's the point.

Ant. Which do not be entreated to, but
weigh   32
What it is worth embrac'd.

Cæs.   And what may follow,
To try a larger fortune.

Pom.   You have made me offer
Of Sicily, Sardinia; and I must
Rid all the sea of pirates; then, to send   36
Measures of wheat to Rome; this 'greed upon,
To part with unhack'd edges, and bear back
Our targets undinted.

Cæs. \
Ant. } That's our offer.
Lep. /

Pom.   Know, then,
I came before you here a man prepar'd   40
To take this offer; but Mark Antony
Put me to some impatience. Though I lose
The praise of it by telling, you must know,
When Cæsar and your brother were at blows,   44
Your mother came to Sicily and did find
Her welcome friendly.

Ant.   I have heard it, Pompey;
And am well studied for a liberal thanks
Which I do owe you.

Pom.   Let me have your hand: 48
I did not think, sir, to have met you here.

Ant. The beds i' the east are soft; and thanks
to you,
That call'd me timelier than my purpose hither,
For I have gain'd by 't.

Cæs.   Since I saw you last,   52
There is a change upon you.

Pom.   Well, I know not
What counts harsh Fortune casts upon my face,

CENE VI]   989   ANTONY AND CLEOPATRA

But in my bosom shall she never come
To make my heart her vassal.
  Lep.   Well met here. 56
  Pom. I hope so, Lepidus. Thus we are agreed.
crave our composition may be written
And seal'd between us.
                 That's the next to do.
  Pom. We'll feast each other ere we part; and
let's 60
Draw lots who shall begin.
  Ant.   That will I, Pompey.
  Pom. No, Antony, take the lot:
But, first or last, your fine Egyptian cookery
Shall have the fame. I have heard that Julius
Cæsar 64
Grew fat with feasting there.
  Ant.   You have heard much.
  Pom. I have fair meanings, sir.
  Ant.   And fair words to them.
  Pom. Then, so much have I heard;
And I have heard Apollodorus carried— 68
  Eno. No more of that: he did so.
  Pom.   What, I pray you?
  Eno. A certain queen to Cæsar in a mattress.
  Pom. I know thee now; how far'st thou,
    soldier?
  Eno.   Well;
And well am I like to do; for I perceive 72
Four feasts are toward.
  Eno.   Let me shake thy hand;
I never hated thee. I have seen thee fight,
When I have envied thy behaviour.
  Eno.   Sir,
I never lov'd you much, but I ha' prais'd ye 76
When you have well deserv'd ten times as much
As I have said you did.
  Pom.   Enjoy thy plainness,
It nothing ill becomes thee.
Aboard my galley I invite you all: 80
Will you lead, lords?
  Cæs. ⎫
  Ant.   ⎬   Show us the way, sir.
  Lep. ⎭
  Pom.   Come.
  [*Exeunt all except* MENAS *and* ENOBARBUS.
  Men. Thy father, Pompey, would ne'er have
made this treaty. You and I have known, sir.
  Eno. At sea, I think. 84
  Men. We have, sir.
  Eno. You have done well by water.
  Men. And you by land.
  Eno. I will praise any man that will praise
me; though it cannot be denied what I have
done by land. 90
  Men. Nor what I have done by water.
  Eno. Yes, something you can deny for your
own safety; you have been a great thief by sea.
  Men. And you by land. 94
  Eno. There I deny my land service. But
give me your hand, Menas; if our eyes had
authority, here they might take two thieves
kissing.
  Men. All men's faces are true, whatsoe'er
their hands are. 100
  Eno. But there is never a fair woman has a
true face.

  Men. No slander; they steal hearts.
  Eno. We came hither to fight with you. 104
  Men. For my part, I am sorry it is turned to
a drinking. Pompey doth this day laugh away
his fortune.
  Eno. If he do, sure, he cannot weep it back
again. 109
  Men. You have said, sir. We looked not for
Mark Antony here: pray you, is he married to
Cleopatra? 112
  Eno. Cæsar's sister is called Octavia.
  Men. True, sir; she was the wife of Caius
Marcellus.
  Eno. But she is now the wife of Marcus
Antonius. 117
  Men. Pray ye, sir?
  Eno. 'Tis true.
  Men. Then is Cæsar and he for ever knit
together. 121
  Eno. If I were bound to divine of this unity,
I would not prophesy so.
  Men. I think the policy of that purpose
made more in the marriage than the love of the
parties. 126
  Eno. I think so too; but you shall find the
band that seems to tie their friendship together
will be the very strangler of their amity. Octavia
is of a holy, cold, and still conversation. 130
  Men. Who would not have his wife so?
  Eno. Not he that himself is not so; which is
Mark Antony. He will to his Egyptian dish
again; then, shall the sighs of Octavia blow the
fire up in Cæsar, and, as I said before, that
which is the strength of their amity shall prove
the immediate author of their variance. Antony
will use his affection where it is; he married but
his occasion here.
  Men. And thus it may be. Come, sir, will
you aboard? I have a health for you. 141
  Eno. I shall take it, sir: we have used our
throats in Egypt.
  Men. Come; let's away.   [*Exeunt.*

SCENE VII.—*On board* POMPEY'S *Galley off
Misenum.*

Music. Enter two or three Servants, *with a
banquet.*

  First Serv. Here they'll be, man. Some o'
their plants are ill-rooted already; the least
wind i' the world will blow them down.
  Sec. Serv. Lepidus is high-coloured. 4
  First Serv. They have made him drink alms-
drink.
  Sec. Serv. As they pinch one another by the
disposition, he cries out, 'No more;' reconciles
them to his entreaty, and himself to the drink.
  First Serv. But it raises the greater war between him and his discretion. 11
  Sec. Serv. Why, this it is to have a name in
great men's fellowship; I had as lief have a reed
that will do me no service as a partisan I could
not heave. 15
  First Serv. To be called into a huge sphere,
and not to be seen to move in't, are the holes
where eyes should be, which pitifully disaster
the cheeks.

A sennet sounded. Enter CÆSAR, ANTONY, LEPI-
DUS, POMPEY, AGRIPPA, MECÆNAS, ENOBARBUS,
MENAS, *with other* Captains.

Ant. Thus do they, sir. They take the flow
    o' the Nile   20
By certain scales i' the pyramid; they know
By the height, the lowness, or the mean, if dearth
Or foison follow. The higher Nilus swells
The more it promises; as it ebbs, the seedsman
Upon the slime and ooze scatters his grain, 25
And shortly comes to harvest.

Lep. You've strange serpents there.

Ant. Ay, Lepidus.   28

Lep. Your serpent of Egypt is bred now of
your mud by the operation of your sun; so is
your crocodile.

Ant. They are so.   32

Pom. Sit,—and some wine! A health to
Lepidus!

Lep. I am not so well as I should be, but I'll
ne'er out.

Eno. Not till you have slept; I fear me you'll
be in till then.

Lep. Nay, certainly, I have heard the Ptolemies' pyramises are very goodly things; without
contradiction, I have heard that.   41

Men. Pompey, a word.

Pom. Say in mine ear; what is 't?

Men. Forsake thy seat, I do beseech thee,
captain,   44
And hear me speak a word.

Pom.   Forbear me till anon.
This wine for Lepidus!

Lep. What manner o' thing is your crocodile?

Ant. It is shaped, sir, like itself, and it is as
broad as it hath breadth; it is just so high as it
is, and moves with it own organs; it lives by
that which nourisheth it; and the elements
once out of it, it transmigrates.   52

Lep. What colour is it of?

Ant. Of it own colour too.

Lep. 'Tis a strange serpent.

Ant. 'Tis so; and the tears of it are wet. 56

Cæs. Will this description satisfy him?

Ant. With the health that Pompey gives him,
else he is a very epicure.

Pom. Go hang, sir, hang! Tell me of that?
away!   60
Do as I bid you. Where's this cup I call'd for?

Men. If for the sake of merit thou wilt hear
me,
Rise from thy stool.

Pom.   I think thou'rt mad. The matter?
                     [*Walks aside.*

Men. I have ever held my cap off to thy fortunes.   64

Pom. Thou hast serv'd me with much faith.
What's else to say?
Be jolly, lords.

Ant.   These quick-sands, Lepidus,
Keep off them, for you sink.

Men. Wilt thou be lord of all the world?

Pom.   What sayst thou? 68

Men. Wilt thou be lord of the whole world?
That's twice.

Pom. How should that be?

Men.   But entertain it,
And though thou think me poor, I am the man
Will give thee all the world.

Pom.   Hast thou drunk well? 72

Men. No, Pompey, I have kept me from the
cup.
Thou art, if thou dar'st be, the earthly Jove:
Whate'er the ocean pales, or sky inclips,
Is thine, if thou wilt ha't.

Pom.   Show me which way. 76

Men. These three world-sharers, these com-
petitors,
Are in thy vessel: let me cut the cable;
And, when we are put off, fall to their throats:
All there is thine.

Pom.   Ah! this thou shouldst have done,
And not have spoke on 't. In me 'tis villany; 81
In thee 't had been good service. Thou must
    know
'Tis not my profit that does lead mine honour;
Mine honour it. Repent that e'er thy tongue
Hath so betray'd thine act; being done un-
    known,   85
I should have found it afterwards well done,
But must condemn it now. Desist, and drink.

Men. [*Aside.*] For this,   88
I'll never follow thy pall'd fortunes more.
Who seeks, and will not take when once 'tis
    offer'd,
Shall never find it more.

Pom.   This health to Lepidus!

Ant. Bear him ashore. I'll pledge it for him,
Pompey.   92

Eno. Here's to thee, Menas!

Men.   Enobarbus, welcome!

Pom. Fill till the cup be hid.

Eno. There's a strong fellow, Menas.
      [*Pointing to the* Attendant *who carries
      off* LEPIDUS.

Men. Why?   96

Eno. A' bears the third part of the world,
man; see't not?

Men. The third part then is drunk; would
it were all,
That it might go on wheels!   100

Eno. Drink thou; increase the reels.

Men. Come.

Pom. This is not yet an Alexandrian feast.

Ant. It ripens towards it. Strike the vessels,
ho!   104
Here is to Cæsar!

Cæs.   I could well forbear 't.
It's monstrous labour, when I wash my brain,
And it grows fouler.

Ant.   Be a child o' the time.

Cæs. Possess it, I'll make answer;   108
But I had rather fast from all four days
Than drink so much in one.

Eno. [*To* ANTONY.] Ha! my brave emperor;
Shall we dance now the Egyptian Bacchanals,
And celebrate our drink?

Pom.   Let's ha't, good soldier. 112

Ant. Come, let's all take hands,
Till that the conquering wine hath steep'd our
    sense

In soft and delicate Lethe.

Eno.   All take hands.
Make battery to our ears with the loud music; 116
The while I'll place you; then the boy shall sing,
The holding every man shall bear as loud
As his strong sides can volley.

[*Music plays.* ENOBARBUS *places them
hand in hand.*

SONG

Come, thou monarch of the vine,   120
Plumpy Bacchus, with pink eyne!
In thy fats our cares be drown'd,
With thy grapes our hairs be crown'd:
Cup us, till the world go round,   124
Cup us, till the world go round!

Cæs. What would you more? Pompey, good
night. Good brother,
Let me request you off; our graver business
Frowns at this levity. Gentle lords, let's part;
You see we have burnt our cheeks; strong Eno-
barb   129
Is weaker than the wine, and mine own tongue
Splits what it speaks; the wild disguise hath
almost
Antick'd us all. What needs more words? Good
night.   132
Good Antony, your hand.
Pom.   I'll try you on the shore.
Ant. And shall, sir. Give 's your hand.
Pom.   O, Antony!
You have my father's house,—But, what? we
are friends.
Come down into the boat.
Eno.   Take heed you fall not. 136
[*Exeunt* POMPEY, CÆSAR, ANTONY,
and Attendants.

Menas, I'll not on shore.
Men.   No, to my cabin.
These drums! these trumpets, flutes! what!
Let Neptune hear we bid a loud farewell
To these great fellows: sound and be hang'd!
sound out!   140
[*A flourish of trumpets with drums.*
Eno. Hoo! says a'. There's my cap.
Men. Hoo! noble captain! come. [*Exeunt.*

ACT III

SCENE I.—*A Plain in Syria.*

Enter VENTIDIUS, *in triumph, with* SILIUS *and
other* Romans, Officers, *and* Soldiers; *the dead
body of* PACORUS *borne before him.*

Ven. Now, darting Parthia, art thou struck;
and now
Pleas'd fortune does of Marcus Crassus' death
Make me revenger. Bear the king's son's body
Before our army. Thy Pacorus, Orodes,   4
Pays this for Marcus Crassus.
Sil.   Noble Ventidius,
Whilst yet with Parthian blood thy sword is
warm,
The fugitive Parthians follow; spur through
Media,
Mesopotamia, and the shelters whither   8
The routed fly; so thy grand captain Antony
Shall set thee on triumphant chariots and

Put garlands on thy head.
Ven.   O Silius, Silius!
I have done enough; a lower place, note well, 12
May make too great an act; for learn this, Silius,
Better to leave undone than by our deed
Acquire too high a fame when him we serve's
away.
Cæsar and Antony have ever won   16
More in their officer than person; Sossius,
One of my place in Syria, his lieutenant,
For quick accumulation of renown,
Which he achiev'd by the minute, lost his
favour.   20
Who does i' the wars more than his captain can
Becomes his captain's captain; and ambition,
The soldier's virtue, rather makes choice of loss
Than gain which darkens him.   24
I could do more to do Antonius good,
But 'twould offend him; and in his offence
Should my performance perish.
Sil.   Thou hast, Ventidius, that
Without the which a soldier, and his sword, 28
Grants scarce distinction. Thou wilt write to
Antony?
Ven. I'll humbly signify what in his name,
That magical word of war, we have effected;
How, with his banners and his well-paid ranks,
The ne'er-yet-beaten horse of Parthia   33
We have jaded out o' the field.
Sil.   Where is he now?
Ven. He purposeth to Athens; whither, with
what haste
The weight we must convey with's will permit,
We shall appear before him. On, there; pass
along.   [*Exeunt.*

SCENE II.—*Rome. A Room in* CÆSAR'S *House.*

Enter AGRIPPA *and* ENOBARBUS, *meeting.*

Agr. What! are the brothers parted?
Eno. They have dispatch'd with Pompey; he
is gone;
The other three are sealing. Octavia weeps
To part from Rome; Cæsar is sad; and Lepidus,
Since Pompey's feast, as Menas says, is troubled
With the green sickness.
Agr.   'Tis a noble Lepidus.
Eno. A very fine one. O! how he loves Cæsar.
Agr. Nay, but how dearly he adores Mark
Antony!   8
Eno. Cæsar? Why, he's the Jupiter of men.
Agr. What's Antony? The god of Jupiter.
Eno. Spake you of Cæsar? How! the non-
pareil!
Agr. O, Antony! O thou Arabian bird!   12
Eno. Would you praise Cæsar, say, 'Cæsar,'
go no further.
Agr. Indeed, he plied them both with excel-
lent praises.
Eno. But he loves Cæsar best; yet he loves
Antony.
Hoo! hearts, tongues, figures, scribes, bards,
poets, cannot   16
Think, speak, cast, write, sing, number; hoo!
His love to Antony. But as for Cæsar,
Kneel down, kneel down, and wonder.

Agr.   Both he loves.
Eno. They are his shards, and they their beetle.
[*Trumpets within.*] So;
This is to horse. Adieu, noble Agrippa.   21
Agr. Good fortune, worthy soldier, and fare-
well.

Enter CÆSAR, ANTONY, LEPIDUS, *and* OCTAVIA.

Ant. No further, sir.
Cæs. You take from me a great part of my-
self;   24
Use me well in 't. Sister, prove such a wife
As my thoughts make thee, and as my furthest
band
Shall pass on thy approof. Most noble Antony,
Let not the piece of virtue, which is set   28
Betwixt us as the cement of our love
To keep it builded, be the ram to batter
The fortress of it; for better might we
Have lov'd without this mean, if on both parts
This be not cherish'd.
Ant.   Make me not offended 33
In your distrust.
Cæs.   I have said.
Ant.   You shall not find,
Though you be therein curious, the least cause
For what you seem to fear. So, the gods keep
you,   36
And make the hearts of Romans serve your
ends!
We will here part.
Cæs. Farewell, my dearest sister, fare thee well:
The elements be kind to thee, and make   40
Thy spirits all of comfort! fare thee well.
Oct. My noble brother!
Ant. The April 's in her eyes; it is love's spring,
And these the showers to bring it on. Be cheer-
ful.   44
Oct. Sir, look well to my husband's house;
and—
Cæs.   What,
Octavia?
Oct. I'll tell you in your ear.
Ant. Her tongue will not obey her heart, nor
can
Her heart obey her tongue; the swan's down-
feather,   48
That stands upon the swell at full of tide,
And neither way inclines.
Eno. [*Aside to* AGRIPPA.] Will Cæsar weep?
Agr.   He has a cloud in 's face.
Eno. He were the worse for that were he a
horse;   52
So is he, being a man.
Agr.   Why, Enobarbus,
When Antony found Julius Cæsar dead
He cried almost to roaring; and he wept
When at Philippi he found Brutus slain.   56
Eno. That year, indeed, he was troubled with
a rheum;
What willingly he did confound he wail'd,
Believe 't, till I wept too.
Cæs.   No, sweet Octavia,
You shall hear from me still; the time shall not
Out-go my thinking on you.
Ant.   Come, sir, come; 61

I'll wrestle with you in my strength of love:
Look, here I have you; thus I let you go,
And give you to the gods.
Cæs.   Adieu; be happy! 64
Lep. Let all the number of the stars give light
To thy fair way!
Cæs.   Farewell, farewell!
                                  [*Kisses* OCTAVIA.
Ant.   Farewell!
                          [*Trumpets sound. Exeunt.*

SCENE III.—*Alexandria. A Room in the*
            Palace.

Enter CLEOPATRA, CHARMIAN, IRAS, *and*
            ALEXAS.

Cleo. Where is the fellow?
Alex.   Half afeard to come.
Cleo. Go to, go to.
            Enter a Messenger.
                    Come hither, sir.
Alex.   Good majesty,
Herod of Jewry dare not look upon you
But when you are well pleas'd.
Cleo.   That Herod's head 4
I'll have; but how, when Antony is gone
Through whom I might command it? Come
thou near.
Mess. Most gracious majesty!
Cleo.   Didst thou behold
Octavia?
Mess. Ay, dread queen.
Cleo.   Where?
Mess.   Madam, in Rome; 8
I look'd her in the face, and saw her led
Between her brother and Mark Antony.
Cleo. Is she as tall as me?
Mess.   She is not, madam.
Cleo. Didst hear her speak? is she shrill-
tongu'd, or low?   12
Mess. Madam, I heard her speak; she is low-
voic'd.
Cleo. That 's not so good. He cannot like her
long.
Char. Like her! O Isis! 'tis impossible.
Cleo. I think so, Charmian: dull of tongue,
and dwarfish!   16
What majesty is in her gait? Remember,
If e'er thou look'dst on majesty.
Mess.   She creeps;
Her motion and her station are as one;
She shows a body rather than a life,   20
A statue than a breather.
Cleo.   Is this certain?
Mess. Or I have no observance.
Char.   Three in Egypt
Cannot make better note.
Cleo.   He 's very knowing,
I do perceive 't. There 's nothing in her yet. 24
The fellow has good judgment.
Char.   Excellent.
Cleo. Guess at her years, I prithee.
Mess.   Madam,
She was a widow,—
Cleo.   Widow! Charmian, hark.
Mess. And I do think she 's thirty.   28

Cleo. Bear'st thou her face in mind? is't long
or round?
Mess. Round even to faultiness.
Cleo. For the most part, too, they are foolish
that are so.
Her hair, what colour?   32
Mess. Brown, madam; and her forehead
As low as she would wish it.
Cleo.   There's gold for thee:
Thou must not take my former sharpness ill.
I will employ thee back again; I find thee 36
Most fit for business. Go, make thee ready;
Our letters are prepar'd.   [*Exit* Messenger.
Char.   A proper man.
Cleo. Indeed, he is so; I repent me much
That so I harried him. Why, methinks, by him,
This creature's no such thing.
Char.   Nothing, madam. 41
Cleo. The man hath seen some majesty, and
should know.
Char. Hath he seen majesty? Isis else de-
fend,
And serving you so long!   44
Cleo. I have one thing more to ask him yet,
good Charmian:
But 'tis no matter; thou shalt bring him to me
Where I will write. All may be well enough. 47
Char. I warrant you, madam.   [*Exeunt.*

SCENE IV.—*Athens. A Room in* ANTONY'S
House.

Enter ANTONY *and* OCTAVIA.

Ant. Nay, nay, Octavia, not only that,
That were excusable, that, and thousands more
Of semblable import, but he hath wag'd
New wars 'gainst Pompey; made his will, and
read it   4
To public ear:
Spoke scantly of me; when perforce he could
not
But pay me terms of honour, cold and sickly
He vented them; most narrow measure lent
me;   8
When the best hint was given him, he not took't,
Or did it from his teeth.
Oct.   O my good lord!
Believe not all; or, if you must believe,
Stomach not all. A more unhappy lady,   12
If this division chance, ne'er stood between,
Praying for both parts:
The good gods will mock me presently,
When I shall pray, 'O! bless my lord and hus-
band';   16
Undo that prayer, by crying out as loud,
'O! bless my brother!' Husband win, win
brother,
Prays, and destroys the prayer; no midway
'Twixt these extremes at all.
Ant.   Gentle Octavia, 20
Let your best love draw to that point which
seeks
Best to preserve it. If I lose mine honour
I lose myself; better I were not yours
Than yours so branchless. But, as you re-
quested,   24

Yourself shall go between's; the mean time,
lady,
I'll raise the preparation of a war
Shall stain your brother; make your soonest
haste,
So your desires are yours.
Oct.   Thanks to my lord. 28
The Jove of power make me most weak, most
weak,
Your reconciler! Wars 'twixt you twain would
be
As if the world should cleave, and that slain men
Should solder up the rift.   32
Ant. When it appears to you where this be-
gins,
Turn your displeasure that way; for our faults
Can never be so equal that your love
Can equally move with them. Provide your
going;   36
Choose your own company, and command what
cost
Your heart has mind to.   [*Exeunt.*

SCENE V.—*The Same. Another Room.*

Enter ENOBARBUS *and* EROS, *meeting.*

Eno. How now, friend Eros!
Eros. There's strange news come, sir.
Eno. What, man?
Eros. Cæsar and Lepidus have made wars
upon Pompey.   5
Eno. This is old: what is the success?
Eros. Cæsar, having made use of him in the
wars 'gainst Pompey, presently denied him
rivality, would not let him partake in the glory
of the action; and not resting here, accuses him
of letters he had formerly wrote to Pompey;
upon his own appeal, seizes him: so the poor
third is up, till death enlarge his confine. 13
Eno. Then, world, thou hast a pair of chaps,
no more;
And throw between them all the food thou hast,
They'll grind the one the other. Where's An-
tony?   16
Eros. He's walking in the garden—thus: and
spurns
The rush that lies before him; cries, 'Fool,
Lepidus!'
And threats the throat of that his officer
That murder'd Pompey.
Eno.   Our great navy's rigg'd. 20
Eros. For Italy and Cæsar. More, Domitius;
My lord desires you presently: my news
I might have told hereafter.
Eno.   'Twill be naught;
But let it be. Bring me to Antony.   24
Eros. Come, sir.   [*Exeunt.*

SCENE VI.—*Rome. A Room in* CÆSAR'S
House.

Enter CÆSAR, AGRIPPA, *and* MECÆNAS.

Cæs. Contemning Rome, he has done all this
and more
In Alexandria; here's the manner of 't;
I' the market-place, on a tribunal silver'd,
Cleopatra and himself in chairs of gold

Were publicly enthron'd; at the feet sat
Cæsarion, whom they call my father's son,
And all the unlawful issue that their lust
Since then hath made between them. Unto her
He gave the 'stablishment of Egypt; made her 9
Of Lower Syria, Cyprus, Lydia,
Absolute queen.

Mec.   This in the public eye?

Cæs. I' the common show-place, where they
     exercise.   12
His sons he there proclaim'd the kings of kings;
Great Media, Parthia, and Armenia
He gave to Alexander; to Ptolemy he assign'd
Syria, Cilicia, and Phœnicia. She   16
In the habiliments of the goddess Isis
That day appear'd; and oft before gave audi-
     ence,
As 'tis reported, so.

Mec.   Let Rome be thus
Informed.

Agr.   Who, queasy with his insolence 20
Already, will their good thoughts call from him.

Cæs. The people know it; and have now
     receiv'd
His accusations.

Agr.   Whom does he accuse?

Cæs. Cæsar; and that, having in Sicily 24
Sextus Pompeius spoil'd, we had not rated him
His part o' the isle; then does he say, he lent me
Some shipping unrestor'd; lastly, he frets
That Lepidus of the triumvirate   28
Should be depos'd; and, being, that we detain
All his revenue.

Agr.   Sir, this should be answer'd.

Cæs. 'Tis done already, and the messenger
     gone.
I have told him, Lepidus was grown too cruel; 32
That he his high authority abus'd,
And did deserve his change: for what I have
     conquer'd,
I grant him part; but then, in his Armenia,
And other of his conquer'd kingdoms, I   36
Demand the like.

Mec.   He'll never yield to that.

Cæs. Nor must not then be yielded to in this.

Enter OCTAVIA, *with her Train.*

Oct. Hail, Cæsar, and my lord! hail, most
     dear Cæsar!

Cæs. That ever I should call thee cast-
     away!   40

Oct. You have not call'd me so, nor have you
     cause.

Cæs. Why have you stol'n upon us thus?
     You come not
Like Cæsar's sister; the wife of Antony
Should have an army for an usher, and   44
The neighs of horse to tell of her approach
Long ere she did appear; the trees by the way
Should have borne men; and expectation
     fainted,
Longing for what it had not; nay, the dust 48
Should have ascended to the roof of heaven,
Rais'd by your populous troops. But you are
     come
A market-maid to Rome, and have prevented

The ostentation of our love, which, left un-
     shown,   52
Is often left unlov'd: we should have met you
By sea and land, supplying every stage
With an augmented greeting.

Oct.   Good my lord,
To come thus was I not constrain'd, but did it 56
On my free-will. My lord, Mark Antony,
Hearing that you prepar'd for war, acquainted
My grieved ear withal; whereon, I begg'd
His pardon for return.

Cæs.   Which soon he granted, 60
Being an obstruct 'tween his lust and him.

Oct. Do not say so, my lord.

Cæs.   I have eyes upon him,
And his affairs come to me on the wind.
Where is he now?

Oct.   My lord, in Athens.   64

Cæs. No, my most wrong'd sister; Cleopatra
Hath nodded him to her. He hath given his
     empire
Up to a whore; who now are levying
The kings o' the earth for war. He hath assem-
     bled   68
Bocchus, the King of Libya; Archelaus,
Of Cappadocia; Philadelphos, King
Of Paphlagonia; the Thracian king, Adallas;
King Malchus of Arabia; King of Pont;   72
Herod of Jewry; Mithridates, King
Of Comagene; Polemon and Amintas,
The Kings of Mede and Lycaonia,
With a more larger list of sceptres.

Oct.   Ay me, most wretched, 76
That have my heart parted betwixt two friends
That do afflict each other!

Cæs.   Welcome hither:
Your letters did withhold our breaking forth,
Till we perceiv'd both how you were wrong led 80
And we in negligent danger. Cheer your heart;
Be you not troubled with the time, which drives
O'er your content these strong necessities,
But let determin'd things to destiny   84
Hold unbewail'd their way. Welcome to Rome;
Nothing more dear to me. You are abus'd
Beyond the mark of thought, and the high gods,
To do you justice, make their ministers   88
Of us and those that love you. Best of comfort,
And ever welcome to us.

Agr.   Welcome, lady.

Mec. Welcome, dear madam.
Each heart in Rome does love and pity you; 92
Only the adulterous Antony, most large
In his abominations, turns you off,
And gives his potent regiment to a trull,
That noises it against us.

Oct.   Is it so, sir?   96

Cæs. Most certain. Sister, welcome; pray
     you,
Be ever known to patience; my dearest sister!
          [*Exeunt.*

SCENE VII.—ANTONY's *Camp, near to the
          Promontory of* ACTIUM.

Enter CLEOPATRA *and* ENOBARBUS.

Cleo. I will be even with thee, doubt it not.

Eno. But why, why, why?

Cleo. Thou hast forspoke my being in these wars,
And sayst it is not fit.

Eno.   Well, is it, is it?   4

Cleo. If not denounc'd against us, why should not we
Be there in person?

Eno.   [*Aside.*] Well, I could reply:
If we should serve with horse and mares together,
The horse were merely lost; the mares would bear   8
A soldier and his horse.

Cleo.   What is 't you say?

Eno. Your presence needs must puzzle Antony;
Take from his heart, take from his brain, from 's time,
What should not then be spar'd. He is already
Traduc'd for levity, and 'tis said in Rome   13
That Photinus a eunuch and your maids
Manage this war.

Cleo.   Sink Rome, and their tongues rot
That speak against us! A charge we bear i' the war,   16
And, as the president of my kingdom, will
Appear there for a man. Speak not against it;
I will not stay behind.

Eno.   Nay, I have done.
Here comes the emperor.

Enter ANTONY *and* CANIDIUS.

Ant. Is it not strange, Canidius,   20
That from Tarentum and Brundusium
He could so quickly cut the Ionian sea,
And take in Toryne? You have heard on't, sweet?

Cleo. Celerity is never more admir'd   24
Than by the negligent.

Ant.   A good rebuke,
Which might have well becom'd the best of men,
To taunt at slackness. Canidius, we
Will fight with him by sea.

Cleo.   By sea! What else?   28

Can. Why will my lord do so?

Ant. For that he dares us to 't.

Eno. So hath my lord dar'd him to single fight.

Can. Ay, and to wage his battle at Pharsalia,
Where Cæsar fought with Pompey; but these offers,   32
Which serve not for his vantage, he shakes off;
And so should you.

Eno. Your ships are not well mann'd;
Your mariners are muleters, reapers, people
Ingross'd by swift impress; in Cæsar's fleet   36
Are those that often have 'gainst Pompey fought:
Their ships are yare; yours, heavy. No disgrace
Shall fall you for refusing him at sea,
Being prepar'd for land.

Ant.   By sea, by sea.   40

Eno. Most worthy sir, you therein throw away
The absolute soldiership you have by land;
Distract your army, which doth most consist
Of war-mark'd footmen; leave unexecuted   44
Your own renowned knowledge; quite forego
The way which promises assurance; and
Give up yourself merely to chance and hazard
From firm security.

Ant.   I'll fight at sea.   48

Cleo. I have sixty sails, Cæsar none better.

Ant. Our overplus of shipping will be burn;
And with the rest, full-mann'd, from the head of Actium
Beat the approaching Cæsar. But if we fail,   52
We then can do 't at land.

Enter a Messenger.

                    Thy business?

Mess. The news is true, my lord; he is descried;
Cæsar has taken Toryne.

Ant. Can he be there in person? 'tis impossible;   56
Strange that his power should be. Canidius,
Our nineteen legions thou shalt hold by land,
And our twelve thousand horse. We'll to our ship:
Away, my Thetis!

Enter a Soldier.

                    How now, worthy soldier!   60

Sold. O noble emperor! do not fight by sea;
Trust not to rotten planks: do you misdoubt
This sword and these my wounds? Let the Egyptians
And the Phœnicians go a-ducking; we   64
Have used to conquer, standing on the earth,
And fighting foot to foot.

Ant.   Well, well: away!
[*Exeunt* ANTONY, CLEOPATRA, *and* ENOBARBUS.

Sold. By Hercules, I think I am i' the right.

Can. Soldier, thou art; but his whole action grows   68
Not in the power on 't: so our leader 's led,
And we are women's men.

Sold.   You keep by land
The legions and the horse whole, do you not?

Can. Marcus Octavius, Marcus Justeius,   72
Publicola, and Cælius, are for sea;
But we keep whole by land. This speed of Cæsar's
Carries beyond belief.

Sold.   While he was yet in Rome
His power went out in such distractions as   76
Beguil'd all spies.

Can.   Who's his lieutenant, hear you?

Sold. They say, one Taurus.

Can.   Well I know the man.

Enter a Messenger.

Mess. The emperor calls Canidius.

Can. With news the time 's with labour, and throes forth   80
Each minute some.   [*Exeunt.*

SCENE VIII.—*A Plain near* ACTIUM.

Enter CÆSAR, TAURUS, Officers, *and Others.*

Cæs. Taurus!

Taur. My lord?

Cæs. Strike not by land; keep whole: pro-
voke not battle,
Till we have done at sea. Do not exceed 4
The prescript of this scroll: our fortune lies
Upon this jump. [*Exeunt.*

Enter ANTONY *and* ENOBARBUS.

Ant. Set we our squadrons on yond side o'
the hill,
In eye of Cæsar's battle; from which place 8
We may the number of the ships behold,
And so proceed accordingly. [*Exeunt.*

Enter CANIDIUS, *marching with his land army one
way over the stage; and* TAURUS, *the lieutenant
of* CÆSAR, *the other way. After their going in
is heard the noise of a sea-fight.*

Alarum. Re-enter ENOBARBUS.

Eno. Naught, naught, all naught! I can be-
hold no longer.
The Antoniad, the Egyptian admiral, 12
With all their sixty, fly, and turn the rudder;
To see't mine eyes are blasted.

Enter SCARUS.

Scar. Gods and goddesses,
All the whole synod of them!
Eno. What's thy passion?
Scar. The greater cantle of the world is lost
With very ignorance; we have kiss'd away 17
Kingdoms and provinces.
Eno. How appears the fight?
Scar. On our side like the token'd pestilence,
Where death is sure. Yon ribaudred nag of
Egypt, 20
Whom leprosy o'ertake! i' the midst o' the fight,
When vantage like a pair of twins appear'd,
Both as the same, or rather ours the elder,
The breese upon her, like a cow in June, 24
Hoists sails and flies.
Eno. That I beheld:
Mine eyes did sicken at the sight, and could not
Endure a further view.
Scar. She once being loof'd,
The noble ruin of her magic, Antony, 28
Claps on his sea-wing, and like a doting mallard,
Leaving the fight in height, flies after her.
I never saw an action of such shame.
Experience, manhood, honour, ne'er before 32
Did violate so itself.
Eno. Alack, alack!

Enter CANIDIUS.

Can. Our fortune on the sea is out of breath,
And sinks most lamentably. Had our general
Been what he knew himself, it had gone well: 36
O! he has given example for our flight
Most grossly by his own.
Eno. Ay, are you thereabouts?
Why, then, good night, indeed.
Can. Towards Peloponnesus are they fled. 40
Scar. 'Tis easy to't; and there I will attend
What further comes.
Can. To Cæsar will I render
My legions and my horse; six kings already

Show me the way of yielding.
Eno. I'll yet follow 44
The wounded chance of Antony, though my
reason
Sits in the wind against me. [*Exeunt.*

SCENE IX.—*Alexandria. A Room in the
Palace.*

Enter ANTONY *and* Attendants.

Ant. Hark! the land bids me tread no more
upon't;
It is asham'd to bear me. Friends, come hither:
I am so lated in the world that I
Have lost my way for ever. I have a ship 4
Laden with gold; take that, divide it; fly,
And make your peace with Cæsar.
Att. Fly! not we.
Ant. I have fled myself, and have instructed
cowards
To run and show their shoulders. Friends, be
gone; 8
I have myself resolv'd upon a course
Which has no need of you; be gone:
My treasure's in the harbour, take it. O!
I follow'd that I blush to look upon: 12
My very hairs do mutiny, for the white
Reprove the brown for rashness, and they them
For fear and doting. Friends, be gone; you
shall 15
Have letters from me to some friends that will
Sweep your way for you. Pray you, look not
sad,
Nor make replies of loathness; take the hint
Which my despair proclaims; let that be left
Which leaves itself; to the sea-side straightway:
I will possess you of that ship and treasure. 21
Leave me, I pray, a little; pray you now:
Nay, do so; for, indeed, I have lost command,
Therefore I pray you. I'll see you by and by. 24
[*Sits down.*

Enter EROS *following* CLEOPATRA, *led by*
CHARMIAN *and* IRAS.

Eros. Nay, gentle madam, to him, comfort
him.
Iras. Do, most dear queen.
Char. Do! Why, what else?
Cleo. Let me sit down. O Juno! 28
Ant. No, no, no, no, no.
Eros. See you here, sir?
Ant. O fie, fie, fie!
Char. Madam! 32
Iras. Madam; O good empress!
Eros. Sir, sir!
Ant. Yes, my lord, yes. He, at Philippi kept
His sword e'en like a dancer, while I struck 36
The lean and wrinkled Cassius; and 'twas I
That the mad Brutus ended: he alone
Dealt on lieutenantry, and no practice had
In the brave squares of war: yet now—No
matter. 40
Cleo. Ah! stand by.
Eros. The queen, my lord, the queen.
Iras. Go to him, madam, speak to him;
He is unqualited with very shame. 44

Cleo. Well then, sustain me: O!
Eros. Most noble sir, arise; the queen ap-
proaches;
Her head's declin'd, and death will seize her, but
Your comfort makes the rescue.   48
Ant. I have offended reputation,
A most unnoble swerving.
Eros.   Sir, the queen.
Ant. O! whither hast thou led me, Egypt?
See,
How I convey my shame out of thine eyes   52
By looking back what I have left behind
'Stroy'd in dishonour.
Cleo.   O my lord, my lord!
Forgive my fearful sails: I little thought
You would have follow'd.
Ant.   Egypt, thou knew'st too well   56
My heart was to thy rudder tied by the strings,
And thou shouldst tow me after; o'er my spirit
Thy full supremacy thou knew'st, and that
Thy beck might from the bidding of the gods   60
Command me.
Cleo.   O! my pardon.
Ant.   Now I must
To the young man send humble treaties, dodge
And palter in the shifts of lowness, who
With half the bulk o' the world play'd as I
pleas'd,   64
Making and marring fortunes. You did know
How much you were my conqueror, and that
My sword, made weak by my affection, would
Obey it on all cause.
Cleo.   Pardon, pardon!   68
Ant. Fall not a tear, I say; one of them rates
All that is won and lost. Give me a kiss;
Even this repays me. We sent our schoolmaster;
Is he come back? Love, I am full of lead.   72
Some wine, within there, and our viands! For-
tune knows,
We scorn her most when most she offers blows.
                                    [*Exeunt.*

SCENE X.—*Egypt.* CÆSAR'S *Camp.*

Enter CÆSAR, DOLABELLA, THYREUS, *and
Others.*

Cæs. Let him appear that's come from An-
tony.
Know you him?
Dol.   Cæsar, 'tis his schoolmaster:
An argument that he is pluck'd, when hither
He sends so poor a pinion of his wing,   4
Which had superfluous kings for messengers
Not many moons gone by.

Enter EUPHRONIUS.

Cæs.   Approach, and speak.
Euph. Such as I am, I come from Antony:
I was of late as petty to his ends   8
As is the morn-dew on the myrtle-leaf
To his grand sea.
Cæs.   Be't so. Declare thine office.
Euph. Lord of his fortunes he salutes thee,
and
Requires to live in Egypt; which not granted,   12
He lessens his requests, and to thee sues

To let him breathe between the heavens and
earth,
A private man in Athens; this for him.
Next, Cleopatra does confess thy greatness,   16
Submits her to thy might, and of thee craves
The circle of the Ptolemies for her heirs,
Now hazarded to thy grace.
Cæs.   For Antony,
I have no ears to his request. The queen   20
Of audience nor desire shall fail, so she
From Egypt drive her all-disgraced friend,
Or take his life there; this if she perform,
She shall not sue unheard. So to them both.   24
Euph. Fortune pursue thee!
Cæs.   Bring him through the bands.
                            [*Exit* EUPHRONIUS.
[*To* THYREUS.] To try thy eloquence, now 'tis
time; dispatch.
From Antony win Cleopatra; promise,
And in our name, what she requires; add
more,   28
From thine invention, offers. Women are not
In their best fortunes strong, but want will
perjure
The ne'er-touch'd vestal. Try thy cunning,
Thyreus;
Make thine own edict for thy pains, which we   32
Will answer as a law.
Thyr.   Cæsar, I go.
Cæs. Observe how Antony becomes his flaw,
And what thou think'st his very action speaks
In every power that moves.
Thyr.   Cæsar, I shall. [*Exeunt.*

SCENE XI.—*Alexandria. A Room in the
Palace.*

Enter CLEOPATRA, ENOBARBUS, CHARMIAN,
and IRAS.

Cleo. What shall we do, Enobarbus?
Eno.   Think, and die.
Cleo. Is Antony or we, in fault for this?
Eno. Antony only, that would make his will
Lord of his reason. What though you fled
From that great face of war, whose several
ranges
Frighted each other, why should he follow?
The itch of his affection should not then
Have nick'd his captainship; at such a point,   8
When half to half the world oppos'd, he being
The mered question. 'Twas a shame no less
Than was his loss, to course your flying flags,
And leave his navy gazing.
Cleo.   Prithee, peace.   12

Enter ANTONY, *with* EUPHRONIUS.

Ant. Is that his answer?
Euph. Ay, my lord.
Ant. The queen shall then have courtesy,
so she
Will yield us up?
Euph.   He says so.
Ant.   Let her know't, 16
To the boy Cæsar send this grizzled head,
And he will fill thy wishes to the brim
With principalities,

Cleo.   That head, my lord?
Ant. To him again. Tell him he wears the
rose   20
Of youth upon him, from which the world
          should note
Something particular; his coin, ships, legions,
May be a coward's, whose ministers would pre-
          vail
Under the service of a child as soon   24
As i' the command of Cæsar: I dare him there-
          fore
To lay his gay comparisons apart,
And answer me declin'd, sword against sword,
Ourselves alone. I'll write it: follow me.   28
          [*Exeunt* ANTONY *and* EUPHRONIUS.
Eno. [*Aside.*] Yes, like enough, high-battled
          Cæsar will
Unstate his happiness, and be stag'd to the show
Against a sworder! I see men's judgments are
A parcel of their fortunes, and things outward
Do draw the inward quality after them,   33
To suffer all alike. That he should dream,
Knowing all measures, the full Cæsar will
Answer his emptiness! Cæsar, thou hast sub-
          du'd   36
His judgment too.

Enter an Attendant.

Att.   A messenger from Cæsar.
Cleo. What! no more ceremony? See! my
          women;
Against the blown rose may they stop their nose,
That kneel'd unto the buds. Admit him, sir. 40
          [*Exit* Attendant.
Eno. [*Aside.*] Mine honesty and I begin to
          square.
The loyalty well held to fools does make
Our faith mere folly; yet he that can endure
To follow with allegiance a fall'n lord,   44
Does conquer him that did his master conquer,
And earns a place i' the story.

Enter THYREUS.

Cleo.   Cæsar's will?
Thyr. Hear it apart.
Cleo.   None but friends; say boldly.
Thyr. So, haply, are they friends to An-
          tony.   48
Eno. He needs as many, sir, as Cæsar has,
Or needs not us. If Cæsar please, our master
Will leap to be his friend; for us, you know
Whose he is we are, and that is Cæsar's.
Thyr.   So. 52
Thus then, thou most renown'd: Cæsar en-
          treats,
Not to consider in what case thou stand'st,
Further than he is Cæsar.
Cleo.   Go on; right royal.
Thyr. He knows that you embrace not An-
          tony   56
As you did love, but as you fear'd him.
Cleo.   O!
Thyr. The scars upon your honour there-
          fore he
Does pity, as constrained blemishes,

Not as deserv'd.
Cleo.   He is a god, and knows   60
What is most right. Mine honour was not
          yielded,
But conquer'd merely.
Eno. [*Aside.*] To be sure of that,
I will ask Antony. Sir, sir, thou'rt so leaky,
That we must leave thee to thy sinking, for 64
Thy dearest quit thee.   [*Exit.*
Thyr.   Shall I say to Cæsar
What you require of him? for he partly begs
To be desir'd to give. It much would please
          him,
That of his fortunes you should make a staff 68
To lean upon; but it would warm his spirits
To hear from me you had left Antony,
And put yourself under his shroud,
The universal landlord.
Cleo.   What's your name?   72
Thyr. My name is Thyreus.
Cleo.   Most kind messenger,
Say to great Cæsar this: in deputation
I kiss his conqu'ring hand; tell him, I am prompt
To lay my crown at 's feet, and there to kneel; 76
Tell him, from his all-obeying breath I hear
The doom of Egypt.
Thyr.   'Tis your noblest course.
Wisdom and fortune combating together,
If that the former dare but what it can,   80
No chance may shake it. Give me grace to lay
My duty on your hand.
Cleo.   Your Cæsar's father oft,
When he hath mus'd of taking kingdoms in,
Bestow'd his lips on that unworthy place,   84
As it rain'd kisses.

Re-enter ANTONY *and* ENOBARBUS.

Ant.   Favours, by Jove that thunders!
What art thou, fellow?
Thyr.   One that but performs
The bidding of the fullest man, and worthiest
To have command obey'd.
Eno. [*Aside.*] You will be whipp'd. 88
Ant. Approach there! Ah, you kite! Now,
          gods and devils!
Authority melts from me: of late, when I cried
          'Ho!'
Like boys unto a muss, kings would start forth,
And cry, 'Your will?' Have you no ears? I am
Antony yet.

Enter Attendants.

          Take hence this Jack and whip him. 93
Eno. [*Aside.*] 'Tis better playing with a lion's
          whelp
Than with an old one dying.
Ant.   Moon and stars!
Whip him. Were 't twenty of the greatest tribu-
          taries   96
That do acknowledge Cæsar, should I find them
So saucy with the hand of—she here, what's
          her name,
Since she was Cleopatra? Whip him, fellows,
Till, like a boy, you see him cringe his face 100
And whine aloud for mercy; take him hence.

Thyr. Mark Antony,—

  Ant.   Tug him away; being whipp'd,
Bring him again; this Jack of Cæsar's shall
Bear us an errand to him.   104
     · [*Exeunt* Attendants *with* THYREUS.
You were half blasted ere I knew you: ha!
Have I my pillow left unpress'd in Rome,
Forborne the getting of a lawful race,
And by a gem of women, to be abus'd   108
By one that looks on feeders?

  Cleo.   Good my lord,—

  Ant. You have been a boggler ever:
But when we in our viciousness grow hard,—
O misery on 't!—the wise gods seel our eyes; 112
In our own filth drop our clear judgments; make
     us
Adore our errors; laugh at 's while we strut
To our confusion.

  Cleo.   O! is 't come to this?

  Ant. I found you as a morsel, cold upon 116
Dead Cæsar's trencher; nay, you were a frag-
     ment
Of Cneius Pompey's; besides what hotter hours,
Unregister'd in vulgar fame, you have
Luxuriously pick'd out; for, I am sure,   120
Though you can guess what temperance should
     be,
You know not what it is.

  Cleo.   Wherefore is this?

  Ant. To let a fellow that will take rewards
And say 'God quit you!' be familiar with 124
My playfellow, your hand; this kingly seal
And plighter of high hearts. O! that I were
Upon the hill of Basan, to outroar
The horned herd; for I have savage cause; 128
And to proclaim it civilly were like
A halter'd neck, which does the hangman thank
For being yare about him.

      Re-enter Attendants, *with* THYREUS.
               Is he whipp'd?

  First Att. Soundly, my lord.

  Ant.   Cried he? and begg'd a' pardon?

  First Att. He did ask favour.   133

  Ant. If that thy father live, let him repent
Thou wast not made his daughter; and be thou
     sorry
To follow Cæsar in his triumph, since   136
Thou hast been whipp'd for following him:
     henceforth,
The white hand of a lady fever thee,
Shake thou to look on 't. Get thee back to
     Cæsar,
Tell him thy entertainment; look, thou say 140
He makes me angry with him; for he seems
Proud and disdainful, harping on what I am.
Not what he knew I was: he makes me angry;
And at this time most easy 'tis to do 't,   144
When my good stars, that were my former
     guides,
Have empty left their orbs, and shot their fires
Into the abysm of hell. If he mislike
My speech and what is done, tell him he has 148
Hipparchus, my enfranchèd bondman, whom
He may at pleasure whip, or hang, or torture,
As he shall like, to quit me: urge it thou:

Hence with thy stripes; be gone!   152
                   [*Exit* THYREUS.

  Cleo. Have you done yet?

  Ant.   Alack! our terrene moon
Is now eclips'd; and it portends alone
The fall of Antony.

  Cleo.   I must stay his time.

  Ant. To flatter Cæsar, would you mingle
     eyes   156
With one that ties his points?

  Cleo.   Not know me yet?

  Ant. Cold-hearted toward me?

  Cleo.   Ah! dear, if I be so,
From my cold heart let heaven engender hail,
And poison it in the source; and the first stone
Drop in my neck: as it determines, so   161
Dissolve my life. The next Cæsarion smite,
Till by degrees the memory of my womb,
Together with my brave Egyptians all,   164
By the discandying of this pelleted storm,
Lie graveless, till the flies and gnats of Nile
Have buried them for prey!

  Ant.   I am satisfied.
Cæsar sits down in Alexandria, where   168
I will oppose his fate. Our force by land
Hath nobly held; our sever'd navy too
Have knit again, and fleet, threat'ning most
     sea-like.
Where hast thou been, my heart? Dost thou
     hear, lady?   172
If from the field I shall return once more
To kiss these lips, I will appear in blood;
I and my sword will earn our chronicle:
There's hope in 't yet.

  Cleo.   That's my brave lord! 176

  Ant. I will be treble-sinew'd, hearted, breath'd,
And fight maliciously; for when mine hours
Were nice and lucky, men did ransom lives
Of me for jests; but now I'll set my teeth, 180
And send to darkness all that stop me. Come,
Let's have one other gaudy night: call to me
All my sad captains; fill our bowls once more;
Let's mock the midnight bell.

  Cleo.   It is my birth-day: 184
I had thought to have held it poor; but, since
     my lord
Is Antony again, I will be Cleopatra.

  Ant. We will yet do well.

  Cleo. Call all his noble captains to my lord.

  Ant. Do so, we'll speak to them; and to-night
I'll force   189
The wine peep through their scars. Come on,
     my queen;
There's sap in 't yet. The next time I do fight
I'll make death love me, for I will contend 192
Even with his pestilent scythe.
                [*Exeunt all but* ENOBARBUS.

  Eno. Now he'll outstare the lightning. To be
     furious
Is to be frighted out of fear, and in that mood
The dove will peck the estridge; and I see still, 196
A diminution in our captain's brain
Restores his heart. When valour preys on
     reason
It eats the sword it fights with. I will seek
Some way to leave him.   [*Exit.*

ACT IV

SCENE I.—*Before Alexandria.* CÆSAR'S *Camp.*

Enter CÆSAR, *reading a letter;* AGRIPPA, MECÆNAS, *and Others.*

Cæs. He calls me boy, and chides as he had power
To beat me out of Egypt; my messenger
He hath whipp'd with rods; dares me to personal combat,
Cæsar to Antony. Let the old ruffian know   4
I have many other ways to die; meantime
Laugh at his challenge.

Mec.   Cæsar must think,
When one so great begins to rage, he's hunted
Even to falling. Give him no breath, but now   8
Make boot of his distraction: never anger
Made good guard for itself.

Cæs.   Let our best heads
Know that to-morrow the last of many battles
We mean to fight. Within our files there are,   12
Of those that serv'd Mark Antony but late,
Enough to fetch him in. See it done;
And feast the army; we have store to do't,
And they have earn'd the waste. Poor Antony!
                        [*Exeunt.*

SCENE II.—*Alexandria. A Room in the Palace.*

Enter ANTONY, CLEOPATRA, ENOBARBUS, CHARMIAN, IRAS, ALEXAS, *and Others.*

Ant. He will not fight with me, Domitius.
Eno.   No.
Ant. Why should he not?
Eno. He thinks, being twenty times of better fortune,
He is twenty men to one.
Ant.   To-morrow, soldier,   4
By sea and land I'll fight: or I will live,
Or bathe my dying honour in the blood
Shall make it live again. Woo't thou fight well?
Eno. I'll strike, and cry, 'Take all.'
Ant.   Well said; come on.   8
Call forth my household servants; let's to-night
Be bounteous at our meal.

Enter three or four Servitors.

                Give me thy hand,
Thou hast been rightly honest; so hast thou;
Thou; and thou, and thou: you have serv'd me well,   12
And kings have been your fellows.
Cleo.   What means this?
Eno. [*Aside to* CLEOPATRA.] 'Tis one of those odd tricks which sorrow shoots
Out of the mind.
Ant.   And thou art honest too.
I wish I could be made so many men,   16
And all of you clapp'd up together in
An Antony, that I might do you service
So good as you have done.
Servants.   The gods forbid!
Ant. Well, my good fellows, wait on me to-night,   20

Scant not my cups, and make as much of me
As when mine empire was your fellow too,
And suffer'd my command.
Cleo. [*Aside to* ENOBARBUS.] What does he mean?
Eno. [*Aside to* CLEOPATRA.] To make his followers weep.
Ant.   Tend me to-night;   24
May be it is the period of your duty:
Haply, you shall not see me more; or if,
A mangled shadow: perchance to-morrow
You'll serve another master. I look on you   28
As one that takes his leave. Mine honest friends,
I turn you not away; but, like a master
Married to your good service, stay till death.
Tend me to-night two hours, I ask no more,   32
And the gods yield you for't!
Eno.   What mean you, sir,
To give them this discomfort? Look, they weep;
And I, an ass, am onion-ey'd: for shame,
Transform us not to women.
Ant.   Ho, ho, ho!   36
Now, the witch take me, if I meant it thus!
Grace grow where those drops fall! My hearty friends,
You take me in too dolorous a sense,
For I spake to you for your comfort; did desire you   40
To burn this night with torches. Know, my hearts,
I hope well of to-morrow; and will lead you
Where rather I'll expect victorious life
Than death and honour. Let's to supper, come,   44
And drown consideration.   [*Exeunt.*

SCENE III.—*The Same. Before the Palace.*

Enter two Soldiers *to their guard.*

First Sold. Brother, good night; to-morrow is the day.
Sec. Sold. It will determine one way; fare you well.
Heard you of nothing strange about the streets?
First Sold. Nothing. What news?   4
Sec. Sold. Belike, 'tis but a rumour. Good night to you.
First Sold. Well, sir, good night.

Enter two other Soldiers.

Sec. Sold. Soldiers, have careful watch.
Third Sold. And you. Good night, good night.
[*The first two place themselves at their posts.*
Fourth Sold. Here we:
            [*They take their posts.*
            And if to-morrow   9
Our navy thrive, I have an absolute hope
Our landmen will stand up.
Third Sold.   'Tis a brave army,
And full of purpose.
        [*Music of hautboys under the stage.*
Fourth Sold. Peace! what noise?
First Sold.   List, list!   12
Sec. Sold. Hark!
First Sold.   Music i' the air.

Third Sold.　　　　　Under the earth.
Fourth Sold. It signs well, does it not?
Third Sold.　　　　　　　　No.
First Sold.　　　　　Peace, I say!
What should this mean?
Sec. Sold. 'Tis the god Hercules, whom An-
　tony lov'd,　　　　　　　　　　　16
Now leaves him.
First Sold. Walk; let's see if other watch-
　men
Do hear what we do.
　　　　　　[*They advance to another post.*
Sec. Sold.　　　　How now, masters!
Soldiers.　　　　　　　　How now!—
How now!—do you hear this?
First Sold.　　　　Ay; is't not strange?
Third Sold. Do you hear, masters? do you
　hear?　　　　　　　　　　　　20
First Sold. Follow the noise so far as we
　have quarter;
Let's see how't will give off.
Soldiers. [*Speaking together.*] Content.—'Tis
　strange.　　　　　　　　　[*Exeunt.*

SCENE IV.—*The Same. A Room in the
Palace.*

Enter ANTONY *and* CLEOPATRA; CHARMIAN,
and Others, attending.

Ant. Eros! mine armour, Eros!
Cleo.　　　　　　　　Sleep a little.
Ant. No, my chuck. Eros, come; mine
　armour, Eros!

Enter EROS, *with armour.*

Come, good fellow, put mine iron on:
If Fortune be not ours to-day, it is　　　4
Because we brave her. Come.
Cleo.　　　　　Nay, I'll help too.
What's this for?
Ant.　　　Ah! let be, let be; thou art
The armourer of my heart: false, false; this,
　this.
Cleo. Sooth, la! I'll help: thus it must be.
Ant.　　　　　　　　Well, well; 8
We shall thrive now. Seest thou, my good
　fellow?
Go put on thy defences.
Eros.　　　　　Briefly, sir.
Cleo. Is not this buckled well?
Ant.　　　　Rarely, rarely:
He that unbuckles this, till we do please　12
To daff't for our repose, shall hear a storm.
Thou fumblest, Eros; and my queen's a squire
More tight at this than thou: dispatch. O love!
That thou couldst see my wars to-day, and
　knew'st　　　　　　　　　　16
The royal occupation, thou shouldst see
A workman in't.

Enter an armed Soldier.

　　　　Good morrow to thee; welcome;
Thou look'st like him that knows a war-like
　charge:
To business that we love we rise betime,　20
And go to't with delight.

Sold.　　　　　A thousand, sir,
Early though't be, have on their riveted trim,
And at the port expect you.
　　　　　　[*Shout. Trumpets flourish.*

Enter Captains *and* Soldiers.

Capt. The morn is fair. Good morrow,
　general.　　　　　　　　　　24
All. Good morrow, general.
Ant.　　　　　'Tis well blown, lads.
This morning, like the spirit of a youth
That means to be of note, begins betimes.
So, so; come, give me that: this way; well said. 28
Fare thee well, dame, whate'er becomes of me;
This is a soldier's kiss. [*Kisses her.*] Rebukeable
And worthy shameful check it were, to stand
On more mechanic compliment; I'll leave thee
Now, like a man of steel. You that will fight, 33
Follow me close; I'll bring you to't. Adieu.
　　　　　　[*Exeunt* ANTONY, EROS, Captains,
　　　　　　　　　　　　　　and Soldiers.
Char. Please you, retire to your chamber.
Cleo.　　　　　　　　Lead me.
He goes forth gallantly. That he and Cæsar
　might　　　　　　　　　　　　36
Determine this great war in single fight!
Then, Antony,—but now.—Well, on. [*Exeunt.*

SCENE V.—*Alexandria.* ANTONY'S *Camp.*

Trumpets sound. Enter ANTONY *and* EROS; *a
Soldier meeting them.*

Sold. The gods make this a happy day to
　Antony!
Ant. Would thou and those thy scars had
　once prevail'd
To make me fight at land!
Sold.　　　　Hadst thou done so,
The kings that have revolted, and the soldier 4
That has this morning left thee, would have still
Follow'd thy heels.
Ant.　　　Who's gone this morning?
Sold.　　　　　　　　Who!
One ever near thee: call for Enobarbus,
He shall not hear thee; or from Cæsar's camp 8
Say, 'I am none of thine'.
Ant.　　　　　What sayst thou?
Sold.　　　　　　　　Sir,
He is with Cæsar.
Eros.　　　Sir, his chests and treasure
He has not with him.
Ant.　　　　Is he gone?
Sold.　　　　　Most certain.
Ant. Go, Eros, send his treasure after; do it;
Detain no jot, I charge thee. Write to him— 13
I will subscribe—gentle adieus and greetings;
Say that I wish he never find more cause
To change a master. O! my fortunes have 16
Corrupted honest men. Dispatch. Enobarbus!
　　　　　　　　　　　　　[*Exeunt.*

SCENE VI.—*Before Alexandria.* CÆSAR'S
Camp.

Flourish. Enter CÆSAR, *with* AGRIPPA, ENO-
BARBUS, *and Others.*

Cæs. Go forth, Agrippa, and begin the fight:

Our will is Antony be took alive;
Make it so known.
  Agr. Cæsar, I shall.   [*Exit.*
  Cæs. The time of universal peace is near: 5
Prove this a prosperous day, the three-nook'd
    world
Shall bear the olive freely.

Enter a Messenger.

  Mess.   Antony
Is come into the field.
  Cæs.   Go charge Agrippa 8
Plant those that have revolted in the van,
That Antony may seem to spend his fury
Upon himself.   [*Exeunt* CÆSAR *and his Train.*
  Eno. Alexas did revolt, and went to Jewry on
Affairs of Antony; there did persuade   13
Great Herod to incline himself to Cæsar,
And leave his master Antony: for this pains
Cæsar hath hang'd him. Canidius and the rest
That fell away have entertainment, but   17
No honourable trust. I have done ill,
Of which I do accuse myself so sorely
That I will joy no more.

Enter a Soldier *of* CÆSAR'S.

  Sold.   Enobarbus, Antony 20
Hath after thee sent all thy treasure, with
His bounty overplus: the messenger
Came on my guard; and at thy tent is now
Unloading of his mules.
  Eno.   I give it you.   24
  Sold. Mock not, Enobarbus.
I tell you true: best you saf'd the bringer
Out of the host; I must attend mine office
Or would have done't myself. Your emperor 28
Continues still a Jove.   [*Exit.*
  Eno. I am alone the villain of the earth,
And feel I am so most. O Antony!
Thou mine of bounty, how wouldst thou have
    paid   32
My better service, when my turpitude
Thou dost so crown with gold! This blows my
    heart:
If swift thought break it not, a swifter mean
Shall outstrike thought; but thought will do't,
    I feel.   36
I fight against thee! No: I will go seek
Some ditch, wherein to die; the foul'st best fits
My latter part of life.   [*Exit.*

SCENE VII.—*Field of Battle between the Camps.*

Alarum. Drums and trumpets. Enter AGRIPPA
    and Others.

  Agr. Retire, we have engag'd ourselves too
far.
Cæsar himself has work, and our oppression
Exceeds what we expected.   [*Exeunt.*

Alarum. Enter ANTONY, *and* SCARUS *wounded.*

  Scar. O my brave emperor, this is fought
    indeed!   4
Had we done so at first, we had droven them
home

With clouts about their heads.
  Ant.   Thou bleed'st apace.
  Scar. I had a wound here that was like a T,
But now 'tis made an H.
  Ant.   They do retire.   8
  Scar. We'll beat 'em into bench-holes: I have
    yet
Room for six scotches more.

Enter EROS.

  Eros. They are beaten, sir; and our advan-
    tage serves
For a fair victory.
  Scar.   Let us score their backs, 12
And snatch 'em up, as we take hares, behind:
'Tis sport to maul a runner.
  Ant.   I will reward thee
Once for thy sprightly comfort, and ten-fold
For thy good valour. Come thee on.
  Scar.   I'll halt after. [*Exeunt.*

SCENE VIII.—*Under the Walls of Alexandria.*

Alarum. Enter ANTONY, *marching;* SCARUS,
    and Forces.

  Ant. We have beat him to his camp; run
    one before
And let the queen know of our gests. To-
    morrow,
Before the sun shall see 's, we'll spill the blood
That has to-day escap'd. I thank you all;   4
For doughty-handed are you, and have fought
Not as you serv'd the cause, but as't had been
Each man's like mine; you have shown all
    Hectors.
Enter the city, clip your wives, your friends, 8
Tell them your feats; whilst they with joyful
    tears
Wash the congealment from your wounds, and
    kiss
The honour'd gashes whole. [*To* SCARUS.] Give
me thy hand:

Enter CLEOPATRA, *attended.*

To this great fairy I'll commend thy acts,   12
Make her thanks bless thee. O thou day o'
    world!
Chain mine arm'd neck; leap thou, attire and
    all,
Through proof of harness to my heart, and there
Ride on the pants triumphing.
  Cleo.   Lord of lords! 16
O infinite virtue! com'st thou smiling from
The world's great snare uncaught?
  Ant.   My nightingale,
We have beat them to their beds. What, girl!
    though grey
Do something mingle with our younger brown,
    yet ha' we   20
A brain that nourishes our nerves, and can
Get goal for goal of youth. Behold this man;
Commend unto his lips thy favouring hand:
Kiss it, my warrior: he hath fought to-day 24
As if a god, in hate of mankind, had
Destroy'd in such a shape.
  Cleo.   I'll give thee, friend,

An armour all of gold; it was a king's.

Ant. He has deserv'd it, were it carbuncled
Like holy Phœbus' car. Give me thy hand: 29
Through Alexandria make a jolly march;
Bear our hack'd targets like the men that owe
  them:
Had our great palace the capacity   32
To camp this host, we all would sup together
And drink carouses to the next day's fate,
Which promises royal peril. Trumpeters,
With brazen din blast you the city's ear,   36
Make mingle with our rattling tabourines,
That heaven and earth may strike their sounds
  together,
Applauding our approach.   [*Exeunt.*

SCENE IX.—CÆSAR'S *Camp.*

Sentinels *on their post.*

First Sold. If we be not reliev'd within this
  hour,
We must return to the court of guard: the night
Is shiny, and they say we shall embattle
By the second hour i' the morn.

Sec. Sold.   This last day was 4
A shrewd one to 's.

Enter ENOBARBUS.

Eno.   O! bear me witness, night,—
Third Sold. What man is this?
Sec. Sold.   Stand close and list him.
Eno. Be witness to me, O thou blessed moon,
When men revolted shall upon record   8
Bear hateful memory, poor Enobarbus did
Before thy face repent!
First Sold.   Enobarbus!
Third Sold.   Peace!
Hark further.
Eno. O sovereign mistress of true melancholy,
The poisonous damp of night disponge upon
  me,   13
That life, a very rebel to my will,
May hang no longer on me; throw my heart
Against the flint and hardness of my fault, 16
Which, being dried with grief, will break to
  powder,
And finish all foul thoughts. O Antony!
Nobler than my revolt is infamous,
Forgive me in thine own particular;   20
But let the world rank me in register
A master-leaver and a fugitive.
O Antony! O Antony!   [*Dies.*
Sec. Sold. Let's speak to him.   24
First Sold. Let's hear him, for the things he
  speaks
May concern Cæsar.
Third Sold.   Let's do so. But he sleeps.
First Sold. Swounds rather; for so bad a
  prayer as his
Was never yet for sleep.
Sec. Sold.   Go we to him.   28
Third Sold. Awake, sir, awake! speak to us.
Sec. Sold.   Hear you, sir?
First Sold. The hand of death hath raught
  him.   [*Drums afar off.*
      Hark! the drums

Demurely wake the sleepers. Let us bear him
To the court of guard; he is of note: our hour
Is fully out.
Third Sold. Come on, then;   33
He may recover yet.   [*Exeunt with the body.*

SCENE X.—*Between the two Camps.*

Enter ANTONY *and* SCARUS, *with Forces,
marching.*

Ant. Their preparation is to-day by sea;
We please them not by land.
Scar.   For both, my lord.
Ant. I would they'd fight i' the fire or i' the
  air;
We'd fight there too. But this it is; our foot 4
Upon the hills adjoining to the city
Shall stay with us; order for sea is given,
They have put forth the haven,   7
Where their appointment we may best discover
And look on their endeavour.   [*Exeunt.*

Enter CÆSAR, *and his Forces, marching.*

Cæs. But being charg'd, we will be still by
  land,
Which, as I take't, we shall; for his best force
Is forth to man his galleys. To the vales,   12
And hold our best advantage!   [*Exeunt.*

Re-enter ANTONY *and* SCARUS.

Ant. Yet they are not join'd. Where yond
  pine does stand
I shall discover all; I'll bring thee word
Straight how 'tis like to go.   [*Exit.*
Scar.   Swallows have built 16
In Cleopatra's sails their nests; the augurers
Say they know not, they cannot tell; look grimly,
And dare not speak their knowledge. Antony
Is valiant, and dejected; and, by starts,   20
His fretted fortunes give him hope and fear
Of what he has and has not.
      [*Alarum afar off, as at a sea-fight.*

Re-enter ANTONY.

Ant.   All is lost!
This foul Egyptian hath betrayed me;
My fleet hath yielded to the foe, and yonder 24
They cast their caps up and carouse together
Like friends long lost. Triple-turn'd whore!
  'tis thou
Hast sold me to this novice, and my heart
Makes only wars on thee. Bid them all fly; 28
For when I am reveng'd upon my charm,
I have done all. Bid them all fly; be gone.
      [*Exit* SCARUS.
O sun! thy uprise shall I see no more;
Fortune and Antony part here; even here   32
Do we shake hands. All come to this? The
  hearts
That spaniel'd me at heels, to whom I gave
Their wishes, do discandy, melt their sweets
On blossoming Cæsar; and this pine is bark'd,
That overtopp'd them all. Betray'd I am. 37
O this false soul of Egypt! this grave charm,
Whose eyes beck'd forth my wars, and call'd
  them home,

Whose bosom was my crownet, my chief end, 40
Like a right gipsy, hath, at fast and loose,
Beguil'd me to the very heart of loss.
What, Eros! Eros!

Enter CLEOPATRA.

Ah! thou spell. Avaunt!
Cleo. Why is my lord enrag'd against his
love? 44
Ant. Vanish, or I shall give thee thy de-
serving,
And blemish Cæsar's triumph. Let him take
thee,
And hoist thee up to the shouting plebeians;
Follow his chariot, like the greatest spot 48
Of all thy sex; most monster-like, be shown
For poor'st diminutives, for doits; and let
Patient Octavia plough thy visage up
With her prepared nails. [*Exit* CLEOPATRA.
'Tis well thou'rt gone, 52
If it be well to live; but better 'twere
Thou fell'st into my fury, for one death
Might have prevented many. Eros, ho!
The shirt of Nessus is upon me; teach me, 56
Alcides, thou mine ancestor, thy rage;
Let me lodge Lichas on the horns o' the moon;
And with those hands, that grasp'd the heaviest
club,
Subdue my worthiest self. The witch shall die:
To the young Roman boy she hath sold me, and
I fall 61
Under this plot; she dies for 't. Eros, ho!
[*Exit.*

SCENE XI.—*Alexandria. A Room in the
Palace.*

Enter CLEOPATRA, CHARMIAN, IRAS, *and*
MARDIAN.

Cleo. Help me, my women! O! he is more
mad
Than Telamon for his shield; the boar of
Thessaly
Was never so emboss'd.
Char. To the monument!
There lock yourself, and send him word you are
dead. 4
The soul and body rive not more in parting
Than greatness going off.
Cleo. To the monument!
Mardian, go tell him I have slain myself:
Say that the last I spoke was 'Antony', 8
And word it, prithee, piteously. Hence,
Mardian, and bring me how he takes my death.
To the monument! [*Exeunt.*

SCENE XII.—*The Same. Another Room.*

Enter ANTONY *and* EROS.

Ant. Eros, thou yet behold'st me?
Eros. Ay, noble lord.
Ant. Sometimes we see a cloud that's dra-
gonish;
A vapour sometime like a bear or lion,
A tower'd citadel, a pendant rock, 4
A forked mountain, or blue promontory
With trees upon 't, that nod unto the world

And mock our eyes with air: thou hast seen
these signs;
They are black vesper's pageants.
Eros. Ay, my lord. 8
Ant. That which is now a horse, even with
a thought
The rack dislimns, and makes it indistinct,
As water is in water.
Eros. It does, my lord.
Ant. My good knave, Eros, now thy captain
is 12
Even such a body: here I am Antony;
Yet cannot hold this visible shape, my knave.
I made these wars for Egypt; and the queen, 15
Whose heart I thought I had, for she had mine,
Which whilst it was mine had annex'd unto 't
A million more, now lost; she, Eros, has
Pack'd cards with Cæsar, and false-play'd my
glory
Unto an enemy's triumph. 20
Nay, weep not, gentle Eros; there is left us
Ourselves to end ourselves.

Enter MARDIAN.

O! thy vile lady;
She has robb'd me of my sword.
Mar. No, Antony;
My mistress lov'd thee, and her fortunes min-
gled 24
With thine entirely.
Ant. Hence, saucy eunuch; peace!
She hath betray'd me and shall die the death.
Mar. Death of one person can be paid but
once,
And that she has discharg'd. What thou wouldst
do 28
Is done unto thy hand; the last she spake
Was, 'Antony! most noble Antony!'
Then in the midst a tearing groan did break
The name of Antony; it was divided 32
Between her heart and lips. She render'd life,
Thy name so buried in her.
Ant. Dead, then?
Mar. Dead.
Ant. Unarm, Eros; the long day's task is
done,
And we must sleep. [*To* MARDIAN.] That thou
depart'st hence safe, 36
Does pay thy labour richly; go. [*Exit* MARDIAN.
Off, pluck off:
The seven-fold shield of Ajax cannot keep
The battery from my heart. O! cleave, my
sides;
Heart, once be stronger than thy continent, 40
Crack thy frail case! Apace, Eros, apace.
No more a soldier; bruised pieces, go;
You have been nobly borne. From me awhile.
[*Exit* EROS.
I will o'ertake thee, Cleopatra, and 44
Weep for my pardon. So it must be, for now
All length is torture; since the torch is out,
Lie down, and stray no further. Now all labour
Mars what it does; yea, very force entangles 48
Itself with strength; seal then, and all is done.
Eros!—I come, my queen.—Eros!—Stay for
me:

Where souls do couch on flowers, we'll hand in
hand,
And with our sprightly port make the ghosts
gaze; 52
Dido and her Æneas shall want troops,
And all the haunt be ours. Come, Eros! Eros!

Re-enter EROS.

Eros. What would my lord?
Ant. Since Cleopatra died,
I have liv'd in such dishonour, that the gods 56
Detest my baseness. I, that with my sword
Quarter'd the world, and o'er green Neptune's
back
With ships made cities, condemn myself to lack
The courage of a woman; less noble mind 60
Than she, which by her death our Cæsar tells
'I am conqueror of myself'. Thou art sworn,
Eros,
Than, when the exigent should come,—which
now
Is come indeed,—when I should see behind me
The inevitable prosecution of 65
Disgrace and horror, that, on my command,
Thou then wouldst kill me: do't; the time is
come.
Thou strik'st not me, 'tis Cæsar thou defeat'st.
Put colour in thy cheek.
Eros. The gods withhold me!
Shall I do that which all the Parthian darts,
Though enemy, lost aim and could not?
Ant. Eros,
Wouldst thou be window'd in great Rome, and
see 72
Thy master thus with pleach'd arms, bending
down
His corrigible neck, his face subdu'd
To penetrative shame, whilst the wheel'd seat
Of fortunate Cæsar, drawn before him, branded
His baseness that ensu'd?
Eros. I would not see't.
Ant. Come, then; for with a wound I must
be cur'd.
Draw that thy honest sword, which thou hast
worn
Most useful for thy country.
Eros. O, sir! pardon me. 80
Ant. When I did make thee free, swor'st thou
not then
To do this when I bade thee? Do it at once,
Or thy precedent services are all
But accidents unpurpos'd. Draw, and come. 84
Eros. Turn from me then that noble coun-
tenance,
Wherein the worship of the whole world lies.
Ant. Lo thee! [*Turning from him.*
Eros. My sword is drawn.
Ant. Then let it do at once 88
The thing why thou hast drawn it.
Eros. My dear master,
My captain, and my emperor, let me say,
Before I strike this bloody stroke, farewell.
Ant. 'Tis said, man; and farewell. 92
Eros. Farewell, great chief. Shall I strike
now?
Ant. Now, Eros.

Eros. Why, there then; thus do I escape the
sorrow [*Kills himself.*
Of Antony's death.
Ant. Thrice-nobler than myself!
Thou teachest me, O valiant Eros, what 96
I should, and thou couldst not. My queen and
Eros
Have by their brave instruction got upon me
A nobleness in record; but I will be
A bridegroom in my death, and run into't 100
As to a lover's bed. Come, then; and, Eros,
Thy master dies thy scholar: to do thus
[*Falls on his sword.*
I learn'd of thee. How! not dead? not dead?
The guard, ho! O! dispatch me.

Enter DERCETAS *and* Guard.

First Guard. What's the noise? 104
Ant. I have done my work ill, friends: O I
make an end
Of what I have begun.
Sec. Guard. The star is fallen.
First Guard. And time is at his period.
All. Alas, and woe!
Ant. Let him that loves me strike me dead.
First Guard. Not I. 108
Sec. Guard. Nor I.
Third Guard. Nor any one. [*Exeunt* Guard.
Der. Thy death and fortunes bid thy followers
fly.
This sword but shown to Cæsar, with this
tidings, 112
Shall enter me with him.

Enter DIOMEDES.

Dio. Where's Antony?
Der. There, Diomed, there.
Dio. Lives he?
Wilt thou not answer, man? [*Exit* DERCETAS.
Ant. Art thou there, Diomed? Draw thy
sword, and give me 116
Sufficing strokes for death.
Dio. Most absolute lord,
My mistress Cleopatra sent me to thee.
Ant. When did she send thee?
Dio. Now, my lord.
Ant. Where is she?
Dio. Lock'd in her monument. She had a
prophesying fear 120
Of what hath come to pass; for when she saw—
Which never shall be found—you did suspect
She had dispos'd with Cæsar, and that your rage
Would not be purg'd, she sent you word she
was dead; 124
But, fearing since how it might work, hath sent
Me to proclaim the truth; and I am come,
I dread, too late.
Ant. Too late, good Diomed. Call my guard,
I prithee. 128
Dio. What, ho! the emperor's guard! The
guard, what, ho!
Come, your lord calls!

Enter four or five of the Guard *of* ANTONY.

Ant. Bear me, good friends, where Cleopatra
bides;
'Tis the last service that I shall command you.

First Guard. Woe, woe are we, sir, you may not live to wear   133
All your true followers out.
All.   Most heavy day!
Ant. Nay, good my fellows, do not please sharp fate
To grace it with your sorrows; bid that welcome
Which comes to punish us, and we punish it 137
Seeming to bear it lightly. Take me up;
I have led you oft; carry me now, good friends,
And have my thanks for all.   140

[*Exeunt, bearing* ANTONY.

SCENE XIII.—*The Same. A Monument.*

Enter CLEOPATRA *and her maids aloft, with*
CHARMIAN *and* IRAS.

Cleo. O Charmian! I will never go from hence.
Char. Be comforted, dear madam.
Cleo.   No, I will not.
All strange and terrible events are welcome,
But comforts we despise; our size of sorrow, 4
Proportion'd to our cause, must be as great
As that which makes it.

Enter, below, DIOMEDES.

    How now! is he dead?
Dio. His death's upon him, but not dead.
Look out o' the other side your monument; 8
His guard have brought him thither.

Enter, below, ANTONY, *borne by the* Guard.

Cleo.   O sun!
Burn the great sphere thou mov'st in; darkling stand
The varying star o' the world. O Antony,
Antony, Antony! Help, Charmian, help, Iras, help;   12
Help, friends below! let's draw him hither.
Ant.   Peace!
Not Cæsar's valour hath o'erthrown Antony,
But Antony's hath triumph'd on itself.
Cleo. So it should be, that none but Antony 16
Should conquer Antony; but woe 'tis so!
Ant. I am dying, Egypt, dying; only
I here importune death awhile, until
Of many thousand kisses the poor last 20
I lay upon thy lips.
Cleo.   I dare not, dear,—
Dear my lord, pardon,—I dare not,
Lest I be taken: not the imperious show
Of the full-fortun'd Cæsar ever shall 24
Be brooch'd with me; if knife, drugs, serpents, have
Edge, sting, or operation, I am safe:
Your wife Octavia, with her modest eyes
And still conclusion, shall acquire no honour 28
Demuring upon me. But come, come, Antony,—
Help me, my women,—we must draw thee up.
Assist, good friends.
Ant.   O! quick, or I am gone.
Cleo. Here's sport indeed! How heavy weighs my lord!   32
Our strength is all gone into heaviness,
That makes the weight. Had I great Juno's power,

The strong-wing'd Mercury should fetch thee up,
And set thee by Jove's side. Yet come a little, 36
Wishers were ever fools. O! come, come, come;

[*They heave* ANTONY *aloft to* CLEOPATRA.

And welcome, welcome! die where thou hast liv'd;
Quicken with kissing; had my lips that power,
Thus would I wear them out.
All.   A heavy sight! 40
Ant. I am dying, Egypt, dying:
Give me some wine, and let me speak a little.
Cleo. No, let me speak; and let me rail so high,
That the false housewife Fortune break her wheel.   44
Provok'd by my offence.
Ant.   One word, sweet queen.
Of Cæsar seek your honour with your safety. O!
Cleo. They do not go together.
Ant.   Gentle, hear me:
None about Cæsar trust, but Proculeius. 48
Cleo. My resolution and my hands I'll trust;
None about Cæsar.
Ant. The miserable change now at my end
Lament nor sorrow at; but please your thoughts
In feeding them with those my former fortunes
Wherein I liv'd, the greatest prince o' the world,
The noblest; and do now not basely die,
Not cowardly put off my helmet to 56
My countryman; a Roman by a Roman
Valiantly vanquish'd. Now my spirit is going;
I can no more.
Cleo.   Noblest of men, woo't die?
Hast thou no care of me? shall I abide 60
In this dull world, which in thy absence is
No better than a sty? O! see my women,

[ANTONY *dies.*

The crown o' the earth doth melt. My lord!
O! wither'd is the garland of the war, 64
The soldier's pole is fall'n; young boys and girls
Are level now with men; the odds is gone,
And there is nothing left remarkable
Beneath the visiting moon.   [*Swoons.*
Char.   O, quietness, lady! 68
Iras. She is dead too, our sovereign.
Char.   Lady!
Iras.   Madam!
Char. O madam, madam, madam!
Iras.   Royal Egypt!
Empress!
Char. Peace, peace, Iras!   72
Cleo. No more, but e'en a woman, and commanded
By such poor passion as the maid that milks
And does the meanest chares. It were for me
To throw my sceptre at the injurious gods; 76
To tell them that this world did equal theirs
Till they had stol'n our jewel. All 's but naught;
Patience is sottish, and impatience does
Become a dog that's mad; then is it sin 80
To rush into the secret house of death,
Ere death dare come to us? How do you, women?
What, what! good cheer! Why, how now, Charmian!

My noble girls! Ah, women, women, look! 84
Our lamp is spent, it's out. Good sirs, take
  heart;—
We'll bury him; and then, what's brave, what's
  noble,
Let s do it after the high Roman fashion,
And make death proud to take us. Come,
  away; 88
This case of that huge spirit now is cold;
Ah! women, women. Come; we have no friend
But resolution, and the briefest end.
      [Exeunt; those above bearing
        off ANTONY's body.

ACT V

SCENE I.—*Alexandria.* CÆSAR'S *Camp.*

Enter CÆSAR, AGRIPPA, DOLABELLA, MECÆNAS,
    GALLUS, PROCULEIUS, *and Others.*

Cæs. Go to him, Dolabella, bid him yield;
Being so frustrate, tell him he mocks
The pauses that he makes.
Dol.   Caesar, I shall. [*Exit.*

Enter DERCETAS, *with the sword of* ANTONY.

Cæs. Wherefore is that? and what art thou
  that dar'st 4
Appear thus to us?
Der.   I am call'd Dercetas;
Mark Antony I serv'd, who best was worthy
Best to be serv'd; whilst he stood up and spoke
He was my master, and I wore my life 8
To spend upon his haters. If thou please
To take me to thee, as I was to him
I'll be to Caesar; if thou pleasest not,
I yield thee up my life.
Cæs.   What is't thou sayst? 12
Der. I say, O Caesar, Antony is dead.
Cæs. The breaking of so great a thing should
  make
A greater crack; the round world
Should have shook lions into civil streets, 16
And citizens to their dens. The death of Antony
Is not a single doom; in the name lay
A moiety of the world.
Der.   He is dead, Caesar;
Not by a public minister of justice, 20
Nor by a hired knife; but that self hand,
Which writ his honour in the acts it did,
Hath, with the courage which the heart did
  lend it,
Splitted the heart. This is his sword; 24
I robb'd his wound of it; behold it stain'd
With his most noble blood.
Cæs.   Look you sad, friends?
The gods rebuke me, but it is tidings
To wash the eyes of kings.
Agr.   And strange it is, 28
That nature must compel us to lament
Our most persisted deeds.
Mec.   His taints and honours
Wag'd equal with him.
Agr.   A rarer spirit never
Did steer humanity; but you, gods, will give us
Some faults to make us men. Caesar is touch'd.
Mec. When such a spacious mirror's set be-
  fore him,

He needs must see himself.
Cæs.   O Antony!
I have follow'd thee to this; but we do lance 36
Diseases in our bodies: I must perforce
Have shown to thee such a declining day,
Or look on thine; we could not stall together
In the whole world. But yet let me lament, 40
With tears as sovereign as the blood of hearts,
That thou, my brother, my competitor
In top of all design, my mate in empire,
Friend and companion in the front of war, 44
The arm of mine own body, and the heart
Where mine his thoughts did kindle, that our
  stars,
Unreconciliable, should divide
Our equalness to this. Hear me, good friends,—

Enter an Egyptian.

But I will tell you at some meeter season: 49
The business of this man looks out of him;
We'll hear him what he says. Whence are you?
Egyp. A poor Egyptian yet. The queen my
  mistress, 52
Confin'd in all she has, her monument,
Of thy intents desires instruction,
That she preparedly may frame herself
To the way she's forc'd to.
Cæs.   Bid her have good heart; 56
She soon shall know of us, by some of ours,
How honourable and how kindly we
Determine for her; for Caesar cannot live
To be ungentle.
Egyp.   So the gods preserve thee! 60
                          [*Exit.*
Cæs. Come hither, Proculeius. Go and say,
We purpose her no shame; give her what com-
  forts
The quality of her passion shall require,
Lest, in her greatness, by some mortal stroke 64
She do defeat us; for her life in Rome
Would be eternal in our triumph. Go,
And with your speediest bring us what she says,
And how you find of her.
Pro.   Caesar, I shall. [*Exit.*
Cæs. Gallus, go you along. [*Exit* GALLUS.
                  Where's Dolabella,
To second Proculeius?
Agr. | Dolabella!
Mec. |
Cæs. Let him alone, for I remember now
How he's employ'd; he shall in time be ready.
Go with me to my tent; where you shall see 73
How hardly I was drawn into this war;
How calm and gentle I proceeded still
In all my writings. Go with me, and see 76
What I can show in this.   [*Exeunt.*

SCENE II.—*The Same. The Monument.*

Enter aloft, CLEOPATRA, CHARMIAN, *and* IRAS.

Cleo. My desolation does begin to make
A better life. 'Tis paltry to be Caesar;
Not being Fortune, he's but Fortune's knave,
A minister of her will; and it is great 4
To do that thing that ends all other deeds,
Which shackles accidents, and bolts up change,

Which sleeps, and never palates more the dug,
The beggar's nurse and Cæsar's.   8

Enter, below, PROCULEIUS, GALLUS, *and* Soldiers.

Pro. Cæsar sends greeting to the Queen of
  Egypt;
And bids thee study on what fair demands
Thou mean'st to have him grant thee.
    Cleo.   What's thy name?
Pro. My name is Proculeius.
    Cleo.   Antony   12
Did tell me of you, bade me trust you; but
I do not greatly care to be deceiv'd,
That have no use for trusting. If your master
Would have a queen his beggar, you must tell
  him,   16
That majesty, to keep decorum, must
No less beg than a kingdom: if he please
To give me conquer'd Egypt for my son,
He gives me so much of mine own as I   20
Will kneel to him with thanks.
    Pro.   Be of good cheer;
You're fall'n into a princely hand, fear no-
  thing.
Make your full reference freely to my lord,
Who is so full of grace, that it flows over   24
On all that need; let me report to him
Your sweet dependancy, and you shall find
A conqueror that will pray in aid for kindness
Where he for grace is kneel'd to.
    Cleo.   Pray you, tell him   28
I am his fortune's vassal, and I send him
The greatness he has got. I hourly learn
A doctrine of obedience, and would gladly
Look him i' the face.
    Pro.   This I'll report, dear lady: 32
Have comfort, for I know your plight is pitied
Of him that caus'd it.
    Gal. You see how easily she may be surpris'd.
    [PROCULEIUS *and two of the* Guard *ascend
    the monument by a ladder, and come be-
    hind* CLEOPATRA. *Some of the* Guard
    *unbar and open the gates, discovering
    the lower room of the monument.*
[*To* PROCULEIUS *and the* Guard.] Guard her till
  Cæsar come.   [*Exit.*
Iras. Royal queen!   37
Char. O Cleopatra! thou art taken, queen.
Cleo. Quick, quick, good hands.
                        [*Drawing a dagger.*
Pro.   Hold, worthy lady, hold!
                [*Seizes and disarms her.*
Do not yourself such wrong, who are in this   40
Reliev'd, but not betray'd.
    Cleo.   What, of death too,
That rids our dogs of languish?
    Pro.   Cleopatra,
Do not abuse my master's bounty by
The undoing of yourself; let the world see   44
His nobleness well acted, which your death
Will never let come forth.
    Cleo.   Where art thou, death?
Come hither, come! come, come, and take a
  queen
Worth many babes and beggars!
    Pro.   O! temperance, lady.

Cleo. Sir, I will eat no meat, I'll not drink,
  sir;   49
If idle talk will once be necessary,
I'll not sleep neither. This mortal house I'll ruin,
Do Cæsar what he can. Know, sir, that I   52
Will not wait pinion'd at your master's court,
Nor once be chastis'd with the sober eye
Of dull Octavia. Shall they hoist me up
And show me to the shouting varletry   56
Of censuring Rome? Rather a ditch in Egypt
Be gentle grave unto me! rather on Nilus' mud
Lay me stark nak'd, and let the water-flies
Blow me into abhorring! rather make   60
My country's high pyramides my gibbet,
And hang me up in chains!
    Pro.   You do extend
These thoughts of horror further than you shall
Find cause in Cæsar.

        Enter DOLABELLA.

    Dol.   Proculeius,   64
What thou hast done thy master Cæsar knows,
And he hath sent for thee; as for the queen,
I'll take her to my guard.
    Pro.   So, Dolabella,
It shall content me best; be gentle to her.   68
[*To* CLEOPATRA.] To Cæsar I will speak what
  you shall please,
If you'll employ me to him.
    Cleo.   Say, I would die.
        [*Exeunt* PROCULEIUS *and* Soldiers.
Dol. Most noble empress, you have heard of
  me?
Cleo. I cannot tell.
    Dol.   Assuredly you know me.   72
Cleo. No matter, sir, what I have heard or
  known.
You laugh when boys or women tell their
  dreams;
Is't not your trick?
    Dol.   I understand not, madam.
Cleo. I dream'd there was an Emperor An-
  tony: 76
O! such another sleep, that I might see
But such another man.
    Dol.   If it might please ye,—
Cleo. His face was as the heavens, and therein
  stuck
A sun and moon, which kept their course, and
  lighted   80
The little O, the earth.
    Dol.   Most sovereign creature,—
Cleo. His legs bestrid the ocean; his rear'd
  arm
Crested the world; his voice was propertied
As all the tuned spheres, and that to friends;   84
But when he meant to quail and shake the orb,
He was as rattling thunder. For his bounty,
There was no winter in't, an autumn 'twas
That grew the more by reaping; his delights   88
Were dolphin-like, they show'd his back above
The element they liv'd in; in his livery
Walk'd crowns and crownets, realms and islands
  were
As plates dropp'd from his pocket.
    Dol.   Cleopatra,—   92

Cleo. Think you there was, or might be, such
a man
As this I dream'd of?
Dol. Gentle madam, no.
Cleo. You lie, up to the hearing of the gods.
But, if there be, or ever were, one such, 96
It's past the size of dreaming; nature wants
stuff
To vie strange forms with fancy; yet to imagine
An Antony were nature's piece 'gainst fancy,
Condemning shadows quite.
Dol. Hear me, good madam. 100
Your loss is as yourself, great; and you bear it
As answering to the weight: would I might
never
O'ertake pursu'd success, but I do feel,
By the rebound of yours, a grief that smites 104
My very heart at root.
Cleo. I thank you, sir.
Know you what Cæsar means to do with me?
Dol. I am loath to tell you what I would you
knew.
Cleo. Nay, pray you, sir,—
Dol. Though he be honourable,— 108
Cleo. He'll lead me then in triumph?
Dol. Madam, he will; I know't.
[*Within,* 'Make way there!—Cæsar!

Enter CÆSAR, GALLUS, PROCULEIUS, MECÆNAS,
SELEUCUS, *and* Attendants.

Cæs. Which is the Queen of Egypt?
Dol. It is the emperor, madam. 112
[CLEOPATRA *kneels.*
Cæs. Arise, you shall not kneel.
I pray you, rise; rise, Egypt.
Cleo. Sir, the gods
Will have it thus; my master and my lord
I must obey.
Cæs. Take to you no hard thoughts; 116
The record of what injuries you did us,
Though written in our flesh, we shall remember
As things but done by chance.
Cleo. Sole sir o' the world,
I cannot project mine own cause so well 120
To make it clear; but do confess I have
Been laden with like frailties which before
Have often sham'd our sex.
Cæs. Cleopatra, know,
We will extenuate rather than enforce: 124
If you apply yourself to our intents,—
Which towards you are most gentle,—you shall
find
A benefit in this change; but if you seek
To lay on me a cruelty, by taking 128
Antony's course, you shall bereave yourself
Of my good purposes, and put your children
To that destruction which I'll guard them from,
If thereon you rely. I'll take my leave. 132
Cleo. And may through all the world: 'tis
yours; and we,
Your scutcheons, and your signs of conquest,
shall
Hang in what place you please. Here, my good
lord.
Cæs. You shall advise me in all for Cleopatra.

Cleo. [*Giving a Scroll.*] This is the brief of
money, plate, and jewels, 137
I am possess'd of: 'tis exactly valued;
Not petty things admitted. Where's Seleucus?
Sel. Here, madam. 140
Cleo. This is my treasurer; let him speak, my
lord,
Upon his peril, that I have reserv'd
To myself nothing. Speak the truth, Seleucus.
Sel. Madam, 144
I had rather seal my lips, than, to my peril,
Speak that which is not.
Cleo. What have I kept back?
Sel. Enough to purchase what you have made
known.
Cæs. Nay, blush not, Cleopatra; I approve
Your wisdom in the deed.
Cleo. See! Cæsar! O, behold, 149
How pomp is follow'd; mine will now be yours;
And, should we shift estates, yours would be
mine.
The ingratitude of this Seleucus does 152
Even make me wild. O slave! of no more trust
Than love that's hir'd. What! goest thou back?
thou shalt
Go back, I warrant thee; but I'll catch thine eyes,
Though they had wings: slave, soulless villain,
dog! 156
O rarely base!
Cæs. Good queen, let us entreat you.
Cleo. O Cæsar! what a wounding shame is
this,
That thou, vouchsafing here to visit me,
Doing the honour of thy lordliness 160
To one so meek, that mine own servant should
Parcel the sum of my disgraces by
Addition of his envy. Say, good Cæsar,
That I some lady trifles have reserv'd, 164
Immoment toys, things of such dignity
As we greet modern friends withal; and say,
Some nobler token I have kept apart
For Livia and Octavia, to induce 168
Their mediation; must I be unfolded
With one that I have bred? The gods! it smites
me
Beneath the fall I have. [*To* SELEUCUS.] Prithee,
go hence;
Or I shall show the cinders of my spirits 172
Through the ashes of my chance. Wert thou a
man,
Thou wouldst have mercy on me.
Cæs. Forbear, Seleucus.
[*Exit* SELEUCUS.
Cleo. Be it known that we, the greatest, are
misthought
For things that others do; and, when we fall, 176
We answer others' merits in our name,
Are therefore to be pitied.
Cæs. Cleopatra,
Not what you have reserv'd, nor what acknow-
ledg'd,
Put we i' the roll of conquest: still be't yours,
Bestow it at your pleasure; and believe, 181
Cæsar's no merchant, to make prize with you
Of things that merchants sold. Therefore be
cheer'd;

Make not your thoughts your prisons: no, dear
   queen;   184
For we intend so to dispose you as
Yourself shall give us counsel. Feed, and sleep:
Our care and pity is so much upon you,
That we remain your friend; and so, adieu. 188
  Cleo. My master, and my lord!
  Cæs.   Not so. Adieu.
    [*Flourish. Exeunt* CÆSAR *and his Train.*
  Cleo. He words me, girls, he words me, that
    I should not
Be noble to myself: but, hark thee, Charmian.
    [*Whispers* CHARMIAN.
  Iras. Finish, good lady; the bright day is
    done,   192
And we are for the dark.
  Cleo.   Hie thee again:
I have spoke already, and it is provided;
Go, put it to the haste.
  Char.   Madam, I will.

      Re-enter DOLABELLA.

  Dol. Where is the queen?
  Char.   Behold, sir. [*Exit.*
  Cleo.   Dolabella! 196
  Dol. Madam, as thereto sworn by your com-
    mand,
Which my love makes religion to obey,
I tell you this: Cæsar through Syria
Intends his journey; and within three days 200
You with your children will he send before.
Make your best use of this; I have perform'd
Your pleasure and my promise.
  Cleo.   Dolabella,
I shall remain your debtor.
  Dol.   I your servant. 204
Adieu, good queen; I must attend on Cæsar.
  Cleo. Farewell, and thanks.
    [*Exit* DOLABELLA.
    Now, Iras, what think'st thou?
Thou, an Egyptian puppet, shall be shown
In Rome, as well as I; mechanic slaves   208
With greasy aprons, rules and hammers, shall
Uplift us to the view; in their thick breaths,
Rank of gross diet, shall we be enclouded,
And forc'd to drink their vapour.
  Iras.   The gods forbid! 212
  Cleo. Nay, 'tis most certain, Iras. Saucy
    lictors
Will catch at us, like strumpets, and scald rimers
Ballad us out o' tune; the quick comedians
Extemporally will stage us, and present   216
Our Alexandrian revels. Antony
Shall be brought drunken forth, and I shall see
Some squeaking Cleopatra boy my greatness
I' the posture of a whore.
  Iras.   O, the good gods! 220
  Cleo. Nay, that's certain.
  Iras. I'll never see it; for, I am sure my nails
Are stronger than mine eyes.
  Cleo.   Why, that's the way
To fool their preparation, and to conquer 224
Their most absurd intents.

      Re-enter CHARMIAN.
      Now, Charmian,

Show me, my women, like a queen; go fetch
My best attires; I am again for Cydnus,
To meet Mark Antony. Sirrah Iras, go.   228
Now, noble Charmian, we'll dispatch indeed;
And, when thou hast done this chare, I'll give
    thee leave
To play till doomsday. Bring our crown and
    all.   [*Exit* IRAS. *A noise heard.*
Wherefore's this noise?

      Enter one of the Guard.

  Guard.   Here is a rural fellow 232
That will not be denied your highness' presence:
He brings you figs.
  Cleo. Let him come in. [*Exit* Guard.] What
    poor an instrument
May do a noble deed! he brings me liberty. 236
My resolution 's plac'd, and I have nothing
Of woman in me; now from head to foot
I am marble-constant, now the fleeting moon
No planet is of mine.

  Re-enter Guard, *with a* Clown *bringing in a*
    basket.

  Guard.   This is the man.   240
  Cleo. Avoid, and leave him. [*Exit* Guard.
Hast thou the pretty worm of Nilus there,
That kills and pains not?
  Clo. Truly, I have him; but I would not
be the party that should desire you to touch
him, for his biting is immortal; those that do
die of it do seldom or never recover.
  Cleo. Remember'st thou any that have died
on't?   248
  Clo. Very many, men and women too. I
heard of one of them no longer than yesterday;
a very honest woman, but something given to
lie, as a woman should not do but in the way of
honesty, how she died of the biting of it, what
pain she felt. Truly, she makes a very good
report o' the worm; but he that will believe all
that they say shall never be saved by half that
they do. But this is most fallible, the worm's
an odd worm.   258
  Cleo. Get thee hence; farewell.
  Clo. I wish you all joy of the worm.   260
    [*Sets down the basket.*
  Cleo. Farewell.
  Clo. You must think this, look you, that the
worm will do his kind.
  Cleo. Ay, ay; farewell.   264
  Clo. Look you, the worm is not to be
trusted but in the keeping of wise people; for
indeed there is no goodness in the worm.
  Cleo. Take thou no care; it shall be heeded.
  Clo. Very good. Give it nothing, I pray you,
for it is not worth the feeding.   270
  Cleo. Will it eat me?
  Clo. You must not think I am so simple
but I know the devil himself will not eat a
woman; I know that a woman is a dish for the
gods, if the devil dress her not. But, truly,
these same whoreson devils do the gods great
harm in their women, for in every ten that
they make, the devils mar five.   278
  Cleo. Well, get thee gone; farewell.

Clo. Yes, forsooth; I wish you joy of the worm.
                                               [*Exit.*

Re-enter IRAS, *with a robe, crown, &c.*

Cleo. Give me my robe, put on my crown; I
      have   282
Immortal longings in me; now no more
The juice of Egypt's grape shall moist this lip.
Yare, yare, good Iras; quick. Methinks I hear
Antony call; I see him rouse himself
To praise my noble act; I hear him mock
The luck of Cæsar, which the gods give men 288
To excuse their after wrath: husband, I come:
Now to that name my courage prove my title!
I am fire, and air; my other elements
I give to baser life. So; have you done?   292
Come then, and take the last warmth of my lips.
Farewell, kind Charmian; Iras, long farewell.
            [*Kisses them.* IRAS *falls and dies.*
Have I the aspic in my lips? Dost fall?
If thou and nature can so gently part,   296
The stroke of death is as a lover's pinch,
Which hurts, and is desir'd. Dost thou lie still?
If thus thou vanishest, thou tell'st the world
It is not worth leave-taking.   300
     Char. Dissolve, thick cloud, and rain; that I
may say,
The gods themselves do weep.
     Cleo.   This proves me base:
If she first meet the curled Antony,
He'll make demand of her, and spend that kiss
Which is my heaven to have. Come, thou mortal
wretch,   305
     [*To the asp, which she applies to her breast.*
With thy sharp teeth this knot intrinsicate
Of life at once untie; poor venomous fool,
Be angry, and dispatch. O! couldst thou
speak,   308
That I might hear thee call great Cæsar ass
Unpolicied.
     Char.   O eastern star!
     Cleo.   Peace, peace!
Dost thou not see my baby at my breast,
That sucks the nurse asleep?
     Char.   O, break! O, break! 312
     Cleo. As sweet as balm, as soft as air, as
gentle,—
O Antony!—Nay, I will take thee too.
          [*Applying another asp to her arm.*
What should I stay—   [*Dies.*
     Char. In this vile world? So, fare thee
well.   316
Now boast thee, death, in thy possession lies
A lass unparallel'd. Downy windows, close;
And golden Phœbus never be beheld
Of eyes again so royal! Your crown's awry; 320
I'll mend it, and then play.

Enter the Guard, *rushing in.*

First Guard. Where is the queen?
     Char.   Speak softly, wake her not.
First Guard. Cæsar hath sent—
     Char.   Too slow a messenger.
                              [*Applies an asp.*

O! come apace, dispatch; I partly feel thee. 324
     First Guard. Approach, ho! All 's not well;
Cæsar 's beguil'd.
     Sec. Guard. There's Dolabella sent from
Cæsar; call him.
     First Guard. What work is here! Charmian,
is this well done?
     Char. It is well done, and fitting for a prin-
cess   328
Descended of so many royal kings.
Ah! soldier.   [*Dies.*

Re-enter DOLABELLA.

Dol. How goes it here?
     Sec. Guard.   All dead.
     Dol.   Cæsar, thy thoughts
Touch their effects in this; thyself art coming
To see perform'd the dreaded act which thou 333
So sought'st to hinder.
     [*Within,* 'A way there!—a way for Cæsar!'

Re-enter CÆSAR *and all his Train.*

Dol. O! sir, you are too sure an augurer;
That you did fear is done.
     Cæs.   Bravest at the last, 336
She levell'd at our purposes, and, being royal,
Took her own way. The manner of their deaths?
I do not see them bleed.
     Dol.   Who was last with them?
First Guard. A simple countryman that
brought her figs: 340
This was his basket.
     Cæs.   Poison'd then.
     First Guard.   O Cæsar!
This Charmian liv'd but now; she stood, and
spake:
I found her trimming up the diadem
On her dead mistress; tremblingly she stood, 344
And on the sudden dropp'd.
     Cæs.   O noble weakness!
If they had swallow'd poison 'twould appear
By external swelling; but she looks like sleep,
As she would catch another Antony   348
In her strong toil of grace.
     Dol.   Here, on her breast,
There is a vent of blood, and something blown;
The like is on her arm.
     First Guard. This is an aspic's trail; and these
fig-leaves   352
Have slime upon them, such as the aspic leaves
Upon the caves of Nile.
     Cæs.   Most probable
That so she died; for her physician tells me
She hath pursu'd conclusions infinite   356
Of easy ways to die. Take up her bed;
And bear her women from the monument.
She shall be buried by her Antony:
No grave upon the earth shall clip in it   360
A pair so famous. High events as these
Strike those that make them; and their story is
No less in pity than his glory which
Brought them to be lamented. Our army shall,
In solemn show, attend this funeral,   365
And then to Rome. Come, Dolabella, see
High order in this great solemnity. [*Exeunt.*

CYMBELINE

DRAMATIS PERSONÆ

CYMBELINE, King of Britain.
CLOTEN, Son to the Queen by a former Husband.
POSTHUMUS LEONATUS, a Gentleman, Husband to Imogen.
BELARIUS, a banished Lord, disguised under the name of Morgan.
GUIDERIUS, } Sons to Cymbeline, disguised under the names of Polydore and Cadwal, supposed
ARVIRAGUS, } Sons to Morgan.
PHILARIO, Friend to Posthumus, } Italians.
IACHIMO, Friend to Philario, }
A French Gentleman, Friend to Philario.
CAIUS LUCIUS, General of the Roman Forces.
A Roman Captain.
Two British Captains.

PISANIO, Servant to Posthumus.
CORNELIUS, a Physician.
Two Lords of Cymbeline's Court.
Two Gentlemen of the same.
Two Gaolers.

QUEEN, Wife to Cymbeline.
IMOGEN, Daughter to Cymbeline by a former Queen.
HELEN, a Lady attending on Imogen.

Lords, Ladies, Roman Senators, Tribunes, a Dutch Gentleman, a Spanish Gentleman, a Soothsayer, Musicians, Officers, Captains, Soldiers, Messengers, and other Attendants.

Apparitions.

SCENE.—*Sometimes in Britain, sometimes in Italy.*

ACT I

SCENE I.—*Britain. The Garden of* CYMBELINE'S *Palace.*

Enter two Gentlemen.

First Gent. You do not meet a man but frowns; our bloods
No more obey the heavens than our courtiers
Still seem as does the king.
    Sec. Gent.   But what's the matter?
First Gent. His daughter, and the heir of 's kingdom, whom   4
He purpos'd to his wife's sole son,—a widow
That late he married,—hath referr'd herself
Unto a poor but worthy gentleman. She 's wedded;
Her husband banish'd, she imprison'd: all   8
Is outward sorrow, though I think the king
Be touch'd at very heart.
    Sec. Gent.   None but the king?
First Gent. He hath lost her too; so is the queen,
That most desir'd the match; but not a courtier,
Although they wear their faces to the bent   13
Of the king's looks, hath a heart that is not
Glad at the thing they scowl at.
    Sec. Gent.   And why so?
First Gent. He that hath miss'd the princess is a thing   16
Too bad for bad report; and he that hath her,—
I mean that married her, alack! good man!
And therefore banish'd—is a creature such
As, to seek through the regions of the earth   20
For one his like, there would be something failing
In him that should compare. I do not think
So fair an outward and such stuff within
Endows a man but he.
    Sec. Gent.   You speak him far.   24
First Gent. I do extend him, sir, within himself,

Crush him together rather than unfold
His measure duly.
    Sec. Gent.   What's his name and birth?
First Gent. I cannot delve him to the root: his father   28
Was called Sicilius, who did join his honour
Against the Romans with Cassibelan,
But had his titles by Tenantius whom
He serv'd with glory and admir'd success,   32
So gain'd the sur-addition Leonatus;
And had, besides this gentleman in question,
Two other sons, who in the wars o' the time
Died with their swords in hand; for which their father—   36
Then old and fond of issue—took such sorrow
That he quit being, and his gentle lady,
Big of this gentleman, our theme, deceas'd
As he was born. The king, he takes the babe   40
To his protection; calls him Posthumus Leonatus;
Breeds him and makes him of his bedchamber,
Puts to him all the learnings that his time
Could make him the receiver of; which he took,   45
As we do air, fast as 'twas minister'd,
And in's spring became a harvest; liv'd in court,
Which rare it is to do—most prais'd, most lov'd;
A sample to the youngest, to the more mature   49
A glass that feated them, and to the graver
A child that guided dotards; to his mistress,
For whom he now is banish'd, her own price
Proclaims how she esteem'd him and his virtue;
By her election may be truly read   53
What kind of man he is.
    Sec. Gent.   I honour him,
Even out of your report. But pray you, tell me,
Is she sole child to the king?
    First Gent.   His only child.   56
He had two sons,—if this be worth your hearing,
Mark it,—the eldest of them at three years old,
I' the swathing clothes the other, from their nursery

Were stol'n; and to this hour no guess in know-
ledge   60
Which way they went.
    Sec. Gent.   How long is this ago?
    First Gent. Some twenty years.
    Sec. Gent. That a king's children should be
so convey'd,
So slackly guarded, and the search so slow, 64
That could not trace them!
    First Gent.   Howsoe'er 'tis strange,
Or that the negligence may well be laugh'd at,
Yet is it true, sir.
    Sec. Gent.   I do well believe you.
    First Gent. We must forbear. Here comes
the gentleman,   68
The queen, and princess.   [*Exeunt.*

Enter the QUEEN, POSTHUMUS, *and* IMOGEN.

    Queen. No, be assur'd you shall not find me,
daughter,
After the slander of most step-mothers,
Evil-ey'd unto you; you're my prisoner, but 72
Your gaoler shall deliver you the keys
That lock up your restraint. For you, Posthu-
mus,
So soon as I can win the offended king,
I will be known your advocate; marry, yet 76
The fire of rage is in him, and 'twere good
You lean'd unto his sentence with what patience
Your wisdom may inform you.
    Post.   Please your highness,
I will from hence to-day.
    Queen.   You know the peril: 80
I'll fetch a turn about the garden, pitying
The pangs of barr'd affections, though the king
Hath charg'd you should not speak together.
                           [*Exit.*
    Imo.   O!
Dissembling courtesy. How fine this tyrant 84
Can tickle where she wounds! My dearest hus-
band,
I something fear my father's wrath; but no-
thing,—
Always reserv'd my holy duty,—what
His rage can do on me. You must be gone; 88
And I shall here abide the hourly shot
Of angry eyes, not comforted to live,
But that there is this jewel in the world
That I may see again.
    Post.   My queen! my mistress! 92
O lady, weep no more, lest I give cause
To be suspected of more tenderness
Than doth become a man. I will remain
The loyal'st husband that did e'er plight troth.
My residence in Rome at one Philario's,   97
Who to my father was a friend, to me
Known but by letter; thither write, my queen,
And with mine eyes I'll drink the words you
send,   100
Though ink be made of gall.

             Re-enter QUEEN.

    Queen.   Be brief, I pray you;
If the king come, I shall incur I know not
How much of his displeasure. [*Aside.*] Yet I'll
move him

To walk this way. I never do him wrong, 104
But he does buy my injuries to be friends,
Pays dear for my offences.   [*Exit.*
    Post.   Should we be taking leave
As long a term as yet we have to live,
The loathness to depart would grow. Adieu!
    Imo. Nay, stay a little: 109
Were you but riding forth to air yourself
Such parting were too petty. Look here, love;
This diamond was my mother's; take it, heart;
But keep it till you woo another wife,   113
When Imogen is dead.
    Post.   How! how! another?
You gentle gods, give me but this I have,
And sear up my embracements from a next 116
With bonds of death!—Remain, remain thou
here   [*Putting on the ring.*
While sense can keep it on! And, sweetest,
fairest,
As I my poor self did exchange for you,
To your so infinite loss, so in our trifles   120
I still win of you; for my sake wear this;
It is a manacle of love; I'll place it
Upon this fairest prisoner.
             [*Putting a bracelet on her arm.*
    Imo.   O the gods!
When shall we see again?

    Enter CYMBELINE *and* Lords.

    Post.   Alack! the king! 124
    Cym. Thou basest thing, avoid! hence, from
my sight!
If after this command thou fraught the court
With thy unworthiness, thou diest. Away!
Thou 'rt poison to my blood.
    Post.   The gods protect you 128
And bless the good remainders of the court!
I am gone.   [*Exit.*
    Imo.   There cannot be a pinch in death
More sharp than this is.
    Cym.   O disloyal thing,
That shouldst repair my youth, thou heap'st
instead   132
A year's age on me.
    Imo.   I beseech you, sir,
Harm not yourself with your vexation;
I am senseless of your wrath; a touch more rare
Subdues all pangs, all fears.
    Cym.   Past grace? obedience?
    Imo. Past hope, and in despair; that way,
past grace.   137
    Cym. That mightst have had the sole son of
my queen!
    Imo. O bless'd, that I might not! I chose an
eagle
And did avoid a puttock.   140
    Cym. Thou took'st a beggar; wouldst have
made my throne
A seat for baseness.
    Imo.   No; I rather added
A lustre to it.
    Cym.   O thou vile one!
    Imo.   Sir,
It is your fault that I have lov'd Posthumus;
You bred him as my playfellow, and he is 145
A man worth any woman, overbuys me

Almost the sum he pays.
   Cym.   What! art thou mad?
   Imo. Almost, sir; heaven restore me! Would
   I were   148
A neat-herd's daughter, and my Leonatus
Our neighbour shepherd's son!
   Cym.   Thou foolish thing!

       Re-enter QUEEN.

They were again together; you have done
Not after our command. Away with her, 152
And pen her up.
   Queen.   Beseech your patience. Peace!
Dear lady daughter, peace! Sweet sovereign,
Leave us to ourselves, and make yourself some
   comfort
Out of your best advice.
   Cym.   Nay, let her languish 156
A drop of blood a day; and, being aged,
Die of this folly!
          [*Exeunt* CYMBELINE *and* Lords.
   Queen.   Fie! you must give way:

       Enter PISANIO.

Here is your servant. How now, sir! What
   news?
   Pis. My lord your son drew on my master.
   Queen.   Ha! 160
No harm, I trust, is done?
   Pis.   There might have been,
But that my master rather play'd than fought,
And had no help of anger; they were parted
By gentlemen at hand.
   Queen.   I am very glad on't. 164
   Imo. Your son's my father's friend; he takes
   his part.
To draw upon an exile! O brave sir!
I would there were in Afric both together,
Myself by with a needle, that I might prick 168
The goer-back. Why came you from your
   master?
   Pis. On his command: he would not suffer me
To bring him to the haven; left these notes
Of what commands I should be subject to, 172
When it pleas'd you to employ me.
   Queen.   This hath been
Your faithful servant; I dare lay mine honour
He will remain so.
   Pis.   I humbly thank your highness.
   Queen. Pray, walk awhile.
   Imo. [*To* PISANIO.] About some half-hour
   hence,   176
I pray you, speak with me. You shall at least
Go see my lord aboard; for this time leave me.
            [*Exeunt.*

   SCENE II.—*The Same. A Public Place.*

     Enter CLOTEN *and two* Lords.

   First Lord. Sir, I would advise you to shift a
shirt; the violence of action hath made you reek
as a sacrifice. Where air comes out, air comes
in; there's none abroad so wholesome as that
you vent.   5
   Clo. If my shirt were bloody, then to shift it.
Have I hurt him?

   Sec. Lord. [*Aside.*] No faith; not so much as
his patience.   9
   First Lord. Hurt him! his body 's a passable
carcass if he be not hurt; it is a throughfare
for steel if it be not hurt.   12
   Sec. Lord. [*Aside.*] His steel was in debt: it
went o' the backside the town.
   Clo. The villain would not stand me.
   Sec. Lord. [*Aside.*] No; but he fled forward
still, toward your face.   17
   First Lord. Stand you! You have land
enough of your own; but he added to your
having, gave you some ground.   20
   Sec. Lord. [*Aside.*] As many inches as you
have oceans. Puppies!
   Clo. I would they had not come between
us.   24
   Sec. Lord. [*Aside.*] So would I till you had
measured how long a fool you were upon the
ground.
   Clo. And that she should love this fellow and
refuse me!   29
   Sec. Lord. [*Aside.*] If it be a sin to make a
true election, she is damned.
   First Lord. Sir, as I told you always, her
beauty and her brain go not together; she's a
good sign, but I have seen small reflection of
her wit.
   Sec. Lord. [*Aside.*] She shines not upon fools,
lest the reflection should hurt her.   37
   Clo. Come, I'll to my chamber. Would there
had been some hurt done!
   Sec. Lord. [*Aside.*] I wish not so; unless it
had been the fall of an ass, which is no great
hurt.
   Clo. You'll go with us?
   First Lord. I'll attend your lordship.   44
   Clo. Nay, come, let's go together.
   Sec. Lord. Well, my lord.   [*Exeunt.*

   SCENE III.—*A Room in* CYMBELINE'S *Palace.*

     Enter IMOGEN *and* PISANIO.

   Imo. I would thou grew'st unto the shores of
   the haven,
And question'dst every sail: if he should write,
And I not have it, 'twere a paper lost,
As offer'd mercy is. What was the last   4
That he spake to thee?
   Pis.   It was his queen, his queen!
   Imo. Then wav'd his handkerchief?
   Pis.   And kiss'd it, madam.
   Imo. Senseless linen, happier therein than I!
And that was all?
   Pis.   No, madam; for so long 8
As he could make me with this eye or ear
Distinguish him from others, he did keep
The deck, with glove, or hat, or handkerchief,
Still waving, as the fits and stirs of 's mind 12
Could best express how slow his soul sail'd on,
How swift his ship.
   Imo.   Thou shouldst have made him
As little as a crow, or less, ere left
To after-eye him.
   Pis.   Madam, so I did.   16

Imo. I would have broke mine eye-strings,
    crack'd them, but
To look upon him, till the diminution
Of space had pointed him sharp as my needle,
Nay, follow'd him, till he had melted from 20
The smallness of a gnat to air, and then
Have turn'd mine eye, and wept. But, good
    Pisanio,
When shall we hear from him?
    Pis.   Be assur'd, madam,
With his next vantage.   24
    Imo. I did not take my leave of him, but had
Most pretty things to say; ere I could tell him
How I would think on him at certain hours
Such thoughts and such, or I could make him
    swear   28
The shes of Italy should not betray
Mine interest and his honour, or have charg'd
    him,
At the sixth hour of morn, at noon, at midnight,
To encounter me with orisons, for then   32
I am in heaven for him; or ere I could
Give him that parting kiss which I had set
Betwix two charming words, comes in my father,
And like the tyrannous breathing of the north
Shakes all our buds from growing.

              Enter a Lady.

Lady.   The queen, madam, 37
Desires your highness' company.
    Imo. Those things I bid you do, get them
    dispatch'd.
I will attend the queen.
    Pis.   Madam, I shall. [*Exeunt.*

SCENE IV.—*Rome. A Room in* PHILARIO'S
    House.

Enter PHILARIO, IACHIMO, *a* Frenchman, *a*
    Dutchman, *and a* Spaniard.

Iach. Believe it, sir, I have seen him in
Britain; he was then of a crescent note, expected to prove so worthy as since he hath been
allowed the name of; but I could then have
looked on him without the help of admiration,
though the catalogue of his endowments had
been tabled by his side and I to peruse him
by items.   8
    Phi. You speak of him when he was less
furnished than now he is with that which
makes him both without and within.
    French. I have seen him in France: we had
very many there could behold the sun with as
firm eyes as he.   14
    Iach. This matter of marrying his king's
daughter,—wherein he must be weighed rather
by her value than his own,—words him, I
doubt not, a great deal from the matter.
    French. And then, his banishment.   19
    Iach. Ay, and the approbation of those that
weep this lamentable divorce under her colours
are wonderfully to extend him; be it but to
fortify her judgment, which else an easy battery
might lay flat, for taking a beggar without less
quality. But how comes it, he is to sojourn
with you? How creeps acquaintance?   26

    Phi. His father and I were soldiers together;
to whom I have been often bound for no less
than my life. Here comes the Briton: let him
be so entertained amongst you as suits, with
gentlemen of your knowing, to a stranger of his
quality.   32

            Enter POSTHUMUS.

I beseech you all, be better known to this gentleman, whom I commend to you, as a noble
friend of mine; how worthy he is I will leave to
appear hereafter, rather than story him in his
own hearing.   37
    French. Sir, we have known together in
Orleans.
    Post. Since when I have been debtor to you
for courtesies, which I will be ever to pay and
yet pay still.   42
    French. Sir, you o'er-rate my poor kindness.
I was glad I did atone my countryman and you;
it had been pity you should have been put
together with so mortal a purpose as then each
bore, upon importance of so slight and trivial a
nature.   48
    Post. By your pardon, sir, I was then a young
traveller; rather shunned to go even with what
I heard than in my every action to be guided by
others' experiences; but, upon my mended judgment,—if I offend not to say it is mended,—
my quarrel was not altogether slight.   54
    French. Faith, yes, to be put to the arbitre-
ment of swords, and by such two that would by
all likelihood have confounded one the other, or
have fallen both.
    Iach. Can we, with manners, ask what was
the difference?   60
    French. Safely, I think. 'Twas a contention
in public, which may, without contradiction,
suffer the report. It was much like an argument
that fell out last night, where each of us fell
in praise of our country mistresses; this gentleman at that time vouching—and upon warrant
of bloody affirmation—his to be more fair, virtuous, wise, chaste, constant, qualified, and less
attemptable, than any the rarest of our ladies in
France.
    Iach. That lady is not now living, or this
gentleman's opinion by this worn out.   72
    Post. She holds her virtue still and I my
mind.
    Iach. You must not so far prefer her 'fore
ours of Italy.   76
    Post. Being so far provoked as I was in
France, I would abate her nothing, though I
profess myself her adorer, not her friend.   79
    Iach. As fair and as good—a kind of hand-
in-hand comparison—had been something too
fair and too good for any lady in Britain. If she
went before others I have seen, as that diamond
of yours outlustres many I have beheld, I could
not but believe she excelled many; but I have
not seen the most precious diamond that is, nor
you the lady.   87
    Post. I praised her as I rated her; so do I
my stone.
    Iach. What do you esteem it at?

Post. More than the world enjoys.

Iach. Either your unparagoned mistress is dead, or she's outprized by a trifle.   93

Post. You are mistaken; the one may be sold, or given; or if there were wealth enough for the purchase, or merit for the gift; the other is not a thing for sale, and only the gift of the gods.

Iach. Which the gods have given you?

Post. Which, by their graces, I will keep.   100

Iach. You may wear her in title yours, but, you know, strange fowl light upon neighbouring ponds. Your ring may be stolen, too; so your brace of unprizeable estimations, the one is but frail and the other casual; a cunning thief, or a that way accomplished courtier, would hazard the winning both of first and last.   107

Post. Your Italy contains none so accomplished a courtier to convince the honour of my mistress, if, in the holding or loss of that, you term her frail. I do nothing doubt you have store of thieves; notwithstanding I fear not my ring.   113

Phi. Let us leave here, gentlemen.

Post. Sir, with all my heart. This worthy signior, I thank him, makes no stranger of me; we are familiar at first.   117

Iach. With five times so much conversation I should get ground of your fair mistress, make her go back, even to the yielding, had I admittance and opportunity to friend.   121

Post. No, no.

Iach. I dare thereupon pawn the moiety of my estate to your ring, which, in my opinion, o'ervalues it something; but I make my wager rather against your confidence than her reputation; and, to bar your offence herein too, I durst attempt it against any lady in the world.

Post. You are a great deal abused in too bold a persuasion; and I doubt not you sustain what you're worthy of by your attempt.

Iach. What's that?   132

Post. A repulse; though your attempt, as you call it, deserves more,—a punishment too.

Phi. Gentlemen, enough of this; it came in too suddenly; let it die as it was born, and, I pray you, be better acquainted.   137

Iach. Would I had put my estate and my neighbour's on the approbation of what I have spoke!   140

Post. What lady would you choose to assail?

Iach. Yours; whom in constancy you think stands so safe. I will lay you ten thousand ducats to your ring, that, commend me to the court where your lady is, with no more advantage than the opportunity of a second conference, and I will bring from thence that honour of hers which you imagine so reserved.

Post. I will wage against your gold, gold to it: my ring I hold dear as my finger; 'tis part of it.

Iach. You are afraid, and therein the wiser. If you buy ladies' flesh at a million a dram, you cannot preserve it from tainting. But I see you have some religion in you, that you fear.   154

Post. This is but a custom in your tongue; you bear a graver purpose, I hope.

Iach. I am the master of my speeches, and would undergo what's spoken, I swear.   158

Post. Will you? I shall but lend my diamond till your return. Let there be covenants drawn between's: my mistress exceeds in goodness the hugeness of your unworthy thinking; I dare you to this match. Here's my ring.

Phi. I will have it no lay.   164

Iach. By the gods, it is one. If I bring you no sufficient testimony that I have enjoyed the dearest bodily part of your mistress, my ten thousand ducats are yours; so is your diamond too: if I come off, and leave her in such honour as you have trust in, she your jewel, this your jewel, and my gold are yours; provided I have your commendation for my more free entertainment.   173

Post. I embrace these conditions; let us have articles betwixt us. Only, thus far you shall answer: if you make your voyage upon her and give me directly to understand that you have prevailed, I am no further your enemy; she is not worth our debate: if she remain unseduced,—you not making it appear otherwise, —for your ill opinion, and the assault you have made to her chastity, you shall answer me with your sword.   183

Iach. Your hand; a covenant. We will have these things set down by lawful counsel, and straight away for Britain, lest the bargain should catch cold and starve. I will fetch my gold and have our two wagers recorded.   188

Post. Agreed.

[*Exeunt* POSTHUMUS *and* IACHIMO.

French. Will this hold, think you?

Phi. Signior Iachimo will not from it. Pray, let us follow 'em.   [*Exeunt.*

SCENE V.—*Britain. A Room in* CYMBELINE'S *Palace.*

Enter QUEEN, Ladies, *and* CORNELIUS.

Queen. Whiles yet the dew's on ground, gather those flowers:
Make haste; who has the note of them?

First Lady.   I, madam.

Queen. Dispatch.   [*Exeunt Ladies.*
Now, Master doctor, have you brought those drugs?   4

Cor. Pleaseth your highness, ay; here they are, madam: [*Presenting a small box.*
But I beseech your Grace, without offence,—
My conscience bids me ask,—wherefore you have
Commanded of me these most poisonous compounds,   8
Which are the movers of a languishing death,
But though slow, deadly?

Queen.   I wonder, doctor,
Thou ask'st me such a question: have I not been
Thy pupil long? Hast thou not learn'd me how
To make perfumes? distil? preserve? yea, so   12
That our great king himself doth woo me oft
For my confections? Having thus far proceeded,—

Unless thou think'st me devilish,—is't not
  meet   16
That I did amplify my judgment in
Other conclusions? I will try the forces
Of these thy compounds on such creatures as
We count not worth the hanging,—but none
  human,—   20
To try the vigour of them and apply
Allayments to their act, and by them gather
Their several virtues and effects.
  Cor.   Your highness
Shall from this practice but make hard your
  heart;   24
Besides, the seeing these effects will be
Both noisome and infectious.
  Queen.   O! content thee.

      Enter PISANIO.

[*Aside.*] Here comes a flattering rascal; upon
  him
Will I first work: he's for his master,   28
And enemy to my son. How now, Pisanio!
Doctor, your service for this time is ended;
Take your own way.
  Cor. [*Aside.*] I do suspect you, madam;
But you shall do no harm.
  Queen. [*To* PISANIO.] Hark thee, a word.
  Cor. [*Aside.*] I do not like her. She doth
  think she has   33
Strange lingering poisons; I do know her spirit,
And will not trust one of her malice with
A drug of such damn'd nature. Those she has
Will stupify and dull the sense awhile;   37
Which first, perchance, she'll prove on cats and
  dogs,
Then afterward up higher; but there is
No danger in what show of death it makes, 40
More than the locking-up the spirits a time,
To be more fresh, reviving. She is fool'd
With a most false effect; and I the truer,
So to be false with her.
  Queen.   No further service, doctor, 44
Until I send for thee.
  Cor.   I humbly take my leave.
                        [*Exit.*
  Queen. Weeps she still, sayst thou? Dost
  thou think in time
She will not quench, and let instructions enter
Where folly now possesses? Do thou work: 48
When thou shalt bring me word she loves my
  son,
I'll tell thee on the instant thou art then
As great as is thy master; greater, for
His fortunes all lie speechless, and his name 52
Is at last gasp; return he cannot, nor
Continue where he is; to shift his being
Is to exchange one misery with another,
And every day that comes to decay   56
A day's work in him. What shalt thou expect,
To be depender on a thing that leans,
Who cannot be new built, nor has no friends,
So much as but to prop him?
      [*The* QUEEN *drops the box;* PISANIO
                       takes it up.
  Thou tak'st up 60

Thou know'st not what; but take it for thy
  labour:
It is a thing I made, which hath the king
Five times redeem'd from death; I do not know
What is more cordial: nay, I prithee, take it; 64
It is an earnest of a further good
That I mean to thee. Tell thy mistress how
The case stands with her; do't as from thyself.
Think what a chance thou changest on, but
  think   68
Thou hast thy mistress still, to boot, my son,
Who shall take notice of thee. I'll move the
  king
To any shape of thy preferment such
As thou'lt desire; and then myself, I chiefly, 72
That set thee on to this desert, am bound
To load thy merit richly. Call my women;
Think on my words.   [*Exit* PISANIO.
            A sly and constant knave,
Not to be shak'd; the agent for his master, 76
And the remembrancer of her to hold
The hand-fast to her lord. I have given him
  that
Which, if he take, shall quite unpeople her
Of leigers for her sweet, and which she after, 80
Except she bend her humour, shall be assur'd
To taste of too.

    Re-enter PISANIO *and* Ladies.

      So, so;—well done, well done.
The violets, cowslips, and the prime-roses
Bear to my closet. Fare thee well, Pisanio: 84
Think on my words.
            [*Exeunt* QUEEN *and* Ladies.
  Pis.   And shall do:
But when to my good lord I prove untrue,
I'll choke myself; there's all I'll do for you.
                       [*Exit.*

SCENE VI.—*The Same. Another Room in the
          Palace.*

      Enter IMOGEN.

  Imo. A father cruel, and a step-dame false;
A foolish suitor to a wedded lady,
That hath her husband banish'd: O! that hus-
  band,
My supreme crown of grief! and those repeated
Vexations of it! Had I been thief-stol'n,   5
As my two brothers, happy! but most miser-
  able
Is the desire that's glorious: bless'd be those,
How mean so'er, that have their honest wills, 8
Which seasons comfort. Who may this be?
  Fie!

    Enter PISANIO *and* IACHIMO.

  Pis. Madam, a noble gentleman of Rome,
Comes from my lord with letters.
  Iach.   Change you, madam?
The worthy Leonatus is in safety,   12
And greets your highness dearly.
             [*Presents a letter.*
  Imo.   Thanks, good sir:
You are kindly welcome.
  Iach. [*Aside.*] All of her that is out of door
  most rich!

If she be furnish'd with a mind so rare, 16
She is alone the Arabian bird, and I
Have lost the wager. Boldness be my friend!
Arm me, audacity, from head to foot!
Or, like the Parthian, I shall flying fight; 20
Rather, directly fly.

*Imo. He is one of the noblest note, to whose
kindnesses I am most infinitely tied. Reflect upon
him accordingly, as you value your truest*
LEONATUS.

So far I read aloud;
But even the very middle of my heart 27
Is warm'd by the rest, and takes it thankfully.
You are as welcome, worthy sir, as I
Have words to bid you; and shall find it so
In all that I can do.

Iach. Thanks, fairest lady.
What! are men mad? Hath nature given them
eyes 32
To see this vaulted arch, and the rich crop
Of sea and land, which can distinguish 'twixt
The fiery orbs above and the twinn'd stones
Upon the number'd beach? and can we not 36
Partition make with spectacles so precious
'Twixt fair and foul?

Imo. What makes your admiration?
Iach. It cannot be i' the eye; for apes and
monkeys
'Twixt two such shes would chatter this way
and 40
Contemn with mows the other; nor i' the judg-
ment,
For idiots in this case of favour would
Be wisely definite; nor i' the appetite;
Sluttery to such neat excellence oppos'd 44
Should make desire vomit emptiness,
Not so allur'd to feed.

Imo. What is the matter, trow?
Iach. The cloyed will,—
That satiate yet unsatisfied desire, that tub 48
Both fill'd and running,—ravening first the
lamb,
Longs after for the garbage.

Imo. What, dear sir,
Thus raps you? are you well?
Iach. Thanks, madam, well.
[*To* PISANIO.] Beseech you, sir, 52
Desire my man's abode where I did leave him;
He's strange and peevish.

Pis. I was going, sir,
To give him welcome. [*Exit.*
Imo. Continues well my lord his health, be-
seech you? 56
Iach. Well, madam.
Imo. Is he dispos'd to mirth? I hope he is.
Iach. Exceeding pleasant; none a stranger
there
So merry and so gamesome: he is call'd 60
The Briton reveller.
Imo. When he was here
He did incline to sadness, and oft-times
Not knowing why.
Iach. I never saw him sad.
There is a Frenchman his companion, one, 64
An eminent monsieur, that, it seems, much
loves

A Gallian girl at home; he furnaces
The thick sighs from him, whiles the jolly
Briton—
Your lord, I mean—laughs from 's free lungs,
cries, 'O! 68
Can my sides hold, to think that man, who
knows
By history, report, or his own proof,
What woman is, yea, what she cannot choose
But must be, will his free hours languish for 72
Assured bondage?'
Imo. Will my lord say so?
Iach. Ay, madam, with his eyes in flood with
laughter:
It is a recreation to be by
And hear him mock the Frenchman; but,
heavens know, 76
Some men are much to blame.
Imo. Not he, I hope.
Iach. Not he; but yet heaven's bounty to-
wards him might
Be us'd more thankfully. In himself, 'tis much;
In you,—which I account his beyond all
talents,— 80
Whilst I am bound to wonder, I am bound
To pity too.
Imo. What do you pity, sir?
Iach. Two creatures, heartily.
Imo. Am I one, sir?
You look on me: what wrack discern you in
me 84
Deserves your pity?
Iach. Lamentable! What!
To hide me from the radiant sun and solace
I' the dungeon by a snuff?
Imo. I pray you, sir,
Deliver with more openness your answers 88
To my demands. Why do you pity me?
Iach. That others do,
I was about to say, enjoy your—But
It is an office of the gods to venge it, 92
Not mine to speak on 't.
Imo. You do seem to know
Something of me, or what concerns me; pray
you,—
Since doubting things go ill often hurts more
Than to be sure they do; for certainties 96
Either are past remedies, or, timely knowing,
The remedy then born,—discover to me
What both you spur and stop.
Iach. Had I this cheek
To bathe my lips upon; this hand, whose touch,
Whose every touch, would force the feeler's soul
To the oath of loyalty; this object, which 102
Takes prisoner the wild motion of mine eye,
Firing it only here; should I—damn'd then—
Slaver with lips as common as the stairs 105
That mount the Capitol; join gripes with hands
Made hard with hourly falsehood,—falsehood,
as
With labour;—then by-peeping in an eye, 108
Base and illustrous as the smoky light
That's fed with stinking tallow; it were fit
That all the plagues of hell should at one time
Encounter such revolt.
Imo. My lord, I fear, 112

Has forgot Britain.

Iach. And himself. Not I,
Inclin'd to this intelligence, pronounce
The beggary of his change; but 'tis your graces
That from my mutest conscience to my tongue
Charms this report out.

Imo. Let me hear no more. 117

Iach. O dearest soul! your cause doth strike
my heart
With pity, that doth make me sick. A lady
So fair,—and fasten'd to an empery 120
Would make the great'st king double,—to be
partner'd
With tom-boys hir'd with that self-exhibition
Which your own coffers yield! with diseas'd
ventures
That play with all infirmities for gold 124
Which rottenness can lend nature! such boil'd
stuff
As well might poison poison! Be reveng'd;
Or she that bore you was no queen, and you
Recoil from your great stock.

Imo. Reveng'd! 128
How should I be reveng'd? If this be true,—
As I have such a heart, that both mine ears
Must not in haste abuse,—if it be true,
How should I be reveng'd?

Iach. Should he make me 132
Live like Diana's priest, betwixt cold sheets,
Whiles he is vaulting variable ramps,
In your despite, upon your purse? Revenge it.
I dedicate myself to your sweet pleasure, 136
More noble than that runagate to your bed,
And will continue fast to your affection,
Still close as sure.

Imo. What ho, Pisanio!

Iach. Let me my service tender on your lips.

Imo. Away! I do condemn mine ears that
have 141
So long attended thee. If thou wert honour-
able,
Thou wouldst have told this tale for virtue,
not
For such an end thou seek'st; as base as
strange. 144
Thou wrong'st a gentleman, who is as far
From thy report as thou from honour, and
solicit'st here a lady that disdains
Thee and the devil alike. What ho, Pisanio! 148
The king my father shall be made acquainted
Of thy assault; if he shall think it fit,
A saucy stranger in his court to mart
As in a Romish stew and to expound 152
His beastly mind to us, he hath a court
He little cares for and a daughter who
He not respects at all. What ho, Pisanio!

Iach. O happy Leonatus! I may say: 156
The credit that thy lady hath of thee
Deserves thy trust, and thy most perfect good-
ness
Her assur'd credit. Blessed live you long!
A lady to the worthiest sir that ever 160
Country call'd his; and you his mistress, only
For the most worthiest fit. Give me your par-
don.
have spoken this, to know if your affiance

Were deeply rooted, and shall make your lord
That which he is, new o'er; and he is one 165
The truest manner'd; such a holy witch
That he enchants societies into him;
Half all men's hearts are his.

Imo. You make amends. 168

Iach. He sits 'mongst men like a descended
god:
He hath a kind of honour sets him off,
More than a mortal seeming. Be not angry,
Most mighty princess, that I have adventur'd 172
To try your taking of a false report; which hath
Honour'd with confirmation your great judg-
ment
In the election of a sir so rare,
Which you know cannot err. The love I bear
him 176
Made me to fan you thus; but the gods made
you,
Unlike all others, chaffless. Pray, your pardon.

Imo. All 's well, sir. Take my power i' the
court for yours.

Iach. My humble thanks. I had almost for-
got 180
To entreat your Grace but in a small request,
And yet of moment too, for it concerns
Your lord, myself, and other noble friends,
Are partners in the business.

Imo. Pray, what is 't? 184

Iach. Some dozen Romans of us and your
lord,
The best feather of our wing, have mingled
sums
To buy a present for the emperor;
Which I, the factor for the rest, have done 188
In France; 'tis plate of rare device, and jewels
Of rich and exquisite form; their values great;
And I am something curious, being strange,
To have them in safe stowage. May it please
you 192
To take them in protection?

Imo. Willingly;
And pawn mine honour for their safety: since
My lord hath interest in them, I will keep them
In my bedchamber.

Iach. They are in a trunk, 196
Attended by my men; I will make bold
To send them to you, only for this night;
I must aboard to-morrow.

Imo. O! no, no.

Iach. Yes, I beseech, or I shall short my
word 200
By lengthening my return. From Gallia
I cross'd the seas on purpose and on promise
To see your Grace.

Imo. I thank you for your pains;
But not away to-morrow!

Iach. O! I must, madam: 204
Therefore I shall beseech you, if you please
To greet your lord with writing, do 't to-night:
I have outstood my time, which is material
To the tender of our present.

Imo. I will write. 208
Send your trunk to me; it shall safe be kept,
And truly yielded you. You're very welcome.
[*Exeunt.*

ACT II

SCENE I.—*Britain. Before* CYMBELINE'S *Palace.*

Enter CLOTEN *and two* Lords.

Clo. Was there ever man had such luck! when I kissed the jack, upon an up-cast to be hit away! I had a hundred pound on 't; and then a whoreson jackanapes must take me up for swearing, as if I borrowed mine oaths of him and might not spend them at my pleasure.

First Lord. What got he by that? You have broke his pate with your bowl.   8

Sec. Lord. [*Aside.*] If his wit had been like him that broke it, it would have run all out.

Clo. When a gentleman is disposed to swear, it is not for any standers-by to curtail his oaths, ha?   13

Sec. Lord. No, my lord; [*Aside.*] nor crop the ears of them.

Clo. Whoreson dog! I give him satisfaction! Would he had been one of my rank!   17

Sec. Lord. [*Aside.*] To have smelt like a fool.

Clo. I am not vexed more at any thing in the earth. A pox on 't! I had rather not be so noble as I am. They dare not fight with me because of the queen my mother. Every Jack-slave hath his bellyful of fighting, and I must go up and down like a cock that nobody can match.

Sec. Lord. [*Aside.*] You are cock and capon too; and you crow, cock, with your comb on.

Clo. Sayest thou?   28

Sec. Lord. It is not fit your lordship should undertake every companion that you give offence to.

Clo. No, I know that; but it is fit I should commit offence to my inferiors.   33

Sec. Lord. Ay, it is fit for your lordship only.

Clo. Why, so I say.   36

First Lord. Did you hear of a stranger that's come to court to-night?

Clo. A stranger, and I not know on 't!

Sec. Lord. [*Aside.*] He's a strange fellow himself, and knows it not.   41

First Lord. There's an Italian come; and 'tis thought, one of Leonatus' friends.

Clo. Leonatus! a banished rascal; and he's another, whatsoever he be. Who told you of this stranger?

First Lord. One of your lordship's pages.

Clo. Is it fit I went to look upon him? Is there no derogation in 't?   49

First Lord. You cannot derogate, my lord.

Clo. Not easily, I think.

Sec. Lord. [*Aside.*] You are a fool, granted; therefore your issues, being foolish, do not derogate.

Clo. Come, I'll go see this Italian. What I have lost to-day at bowls I'll win to-night of him. Come, go.   57

Sec. Lord. I'll attend your lordship.

[*Exeunt* CLOTEN *and First* Lord.

That such a crafty devil as is his mother

Should yield the world this ass! a woman that 60
Bears all down with her brain, and this her son
Cannot take two from twenty for his heart
And leave eighteen. Alas! poor princess,
Thou divine Imogen, what thou endur'st   64
Betwixt a father by thy step-dame govern'd,
A mother hourly coining plots, a wooer
More hateful than the foul expulsion is
Of thy dear husband, than that horrid act   68
Of the divorce he'd make. The heavens hold
firm
The walls of thy dear honour; keep unshak'd
That temple, thy fair mind; that thou mays'
stand,
To enjoy thy banish'd lord and this great land
[*Exit*

SCENE II.—*A Bedchamber; in one part of it a Trunk.*

IMOGEN *reading in her bed; a* Lady *attending.*

Imo. Who's there? my woman Helen?

Lady.   Please you, madam

Imo. What hour is it?

Lady.   Almost midnight, madam

Imo. I have read three hours then; mine eyes
are weak;
Fold down the leaf where I have left; to bed:
Take not away the taper, leave it burning,
And if thou canst awake by four o' the clock,
I prithee, call me. Sleep has seized me wholly
[*Exit* Lady
To your protection I commend me, gods!
From fairies and the tempters of the night
Guard me, beseech ye!
          [*Sleeps.* IACHIMO *comes from the trunk*

Iach. The crickets sing, and man's o'er
labour'd sense
Repairs itself by rest. Our Tarquin thus   12
Did softly press the rushes ere he waken'd
The chastity he wounded. Cytherea,
How bravely thou becom'st thy bed! fresh lily
And whiter than the sheets! That I might
touch!   16
But kiss: one kiss! Rubies unparagon'd,
How dearly they do 't! 'Tis her breathing that
Perfumes the chamber thus; the flame of the
taper
Bows toward her, and would under-peep her
lids,   20
To see the enclosed lights, now canopied
Under these windows, white and azure lac'd
With blue of heaven's own tinct. But my design,
To note the chamber: I will write all down: 24
Such and such pictures; there the window; such
Th' adornment of her bed; the arras, figures,
Why, such and such; and the contents o' the
story.
Ah! but some natural notes about her body, 28
Above ten thousand meaner moveables
Would testify, to enrich mine inventory.
O sleep! thou ape of death, lie dull upon her
And be her senses but as a monument   32
Thus in a chapel lying. Come off, come off:—
[*Taking off her bracelet*

As slippery as the Gordian knot was hard!
'Tis mine; and this will witness outwardly,
As strongly as the conscience does within, 36
To the madding of her lord. On her left breast
A mole cinque-spotted, like the crimson drops
I' the bottom of a cowslip: here's a voucher;
Stronger than ever law could make: this
   secret   40
Will force him think I have pick'd the lock and
   ta'en
The treasure of her honour. No more. To what
   end?
Why should I write this down, that's riveted,
Screw'd to my memory? She hath been reading
   late   44
The tale of Tereus; here the leaf's turn'd down
Where Philomel gave up. I have enough:
To the trunk again, and shut the spring of it.
Swift, swift, you dragons of the night, that
   dawning   48
May bare the raven's eye! I lodge in fear;
Though this a heavenly angel, hell is here.
                         [*Clock strikes.*
One, two, three: time, time!
   [*Goes into the trunk. The scene closes.*

SCENE III.—*An Ante-chamber adjoining*
   IMOGEN'S *Apartments.*

Enter CLOTEN *and* Lords.

First Lord. Your lordship is the most patient
man in loss, the most coldest that ever turned
up ace.
   Clo. It would make any man cold to lose. 4
   First Lord. But not every man patient after
the noble temper of your lordship. You are
most hot and furious when you win.
   Clo. Winning will put any man into courage.
If I could get this foolish Imogen, I should have
gold enough. It's almost morning, is't not?
   First Lord. Day, my lord.   11
   Clo. I would this music would come. I am
advised to give her music o' mornings; they say
it will penetrate.

Enter Musicians.

Come on; tune. If you can penetrate her with
your fingering, so; we'll try with tongue too:
if none will do, let her remain; but I'll never
give o'er. First, a very excellent good-con-
ceited thing; after, a wonderful sweet air, with
admirable rich words to it: and then let her
consider.   21

SONG.

   Hark! hark! the lark at heaven's gate sings,
      And Phœbus 'gins arise,
   His steeds to water at those springs   24
      On chalic'd flowers that lies;
   And winking Mary-buds begin
      To ope their golden eyes:
   With every thing that pretty is,   28
      My lady sweet, arise:
        Arise, arise!

So, get you gone. If this penetrate, I will consider your music the better; if it do not, it is
a vice in her ears, which horse-hairs and calves'-

guts, nor the voice of unpaved eunuch to boot,
can never amend.   [*Exeunt* Musicians.
   Sec. Lord. Here comes the king.   36
   Clo. I am glad I was up so late, for that's the
reason I was up so early; he cannot choose but
take this service I have done fatherly.

Enter CYMBELINE *and* QUEEN.

Good morrow to your majesty and to my
gracious mother.   41
   Cym. Attend you here the door of our stern
   daughter?
Will she not forth?
   Clo. I have assail'd her with musics, but she
vouchsafes no notice.   45
   Cym. The exile of her minion is too new,
She hath not yet forgot him; some more time
Must wear the print of his remembrance out, 48
And then she's yours.
   Queen.   You are most bound to the king,
Who lets go by no vantages that may
Prefer you to his daughter. Frame yourself
To orderly soliciting, and be friended   52
With aptness of the season; make denials
Increase your services; so seem as if
You were inspir'd to do those duties which
You tender to her; that you in all obey her 56
Save when command to your dismission tends,
And therein you are senseless.
   Clo.   Senseless! not so.

Enter a Messenger.

   Mess. So like you, sir, ambassadors from
   Rome;
The one is Caius Lucius.
   Cym.   A worthy fellow, 60
Albeit he comes on angry purpose now;
But that's no fault of his: we must receive him
According to the honour of his sender;
And towards himself, his goodness forespent
   on us,   64
We must extend our notice. Our dear son,
When you have given good morning to your
   mistress,
Attend the queen and us; we shall have need
To employ you towards this Roman. Come,
   our queen.   [*Exeunt all but* CLOTEN.
   Clo. If she be up, I'll speak with her; if not,
Let her lie still, and dream. By your leave, ho!
                         [*Knocks.*
I know her women are about her. What
If I do line one of their hands? 'Tis gold   72
Which buys admittance; oft it doth; yea, and
   makes
Diana's rangers false themselves, yield up
Their deer to the stand o' the stealer; and 'tis
   gold
Which makes the true man kill'd and saves the
   thief;   76
Nay, sometime hangs both thief and true man.
   What
Can it not do and undo? I will make
One of her women lawyer to me, for
I yet not understand the case myself.   80
By your leave.   [*Knocks.*

Enter a Lady.

Lady. Who's there, that knocks?
Clo. A gentleman.
Lady. No more?
Clo. Yes, and a gentlewoman's son.
Lady. [*Aside.*] That's more
Than some whose tailors are as dear as yours 84
Can justly boast of. What's your lordship's
pleasure?
Clo. Your lady's person: is she ready?
Lady. Ay,
To keep her chamber.
Clo. There's gold for you; sell me your good
report. 88
Lady. How! my good name? or to report of
you
What I shall think is good?—The princess!

Enter IMOGEN.

Clo. Good morrow, fairest; sister, your sweet
hand.
[*Exit* Lady.
Imo. Good morrow, sir. You lay out too
much pains 92
For purchasing but trouble; the thanks I give
Is telling you that I am poor of thanks
And scarce can spare them.
Clo. Still, I swear I love you.
Imo. If you but said so, 'twere as deep with
me: 96
If you swear still, your recompense is still
That I regard it not.
Clo. This is no answer.
Imo. But that you shall not say I yield being
silent
I would not speak. I pray you, spare me: faith,
I shall unfold equal discourtesy 101
To your best kindness. One of your great know-
ing
Should learn, being taught, forbearance.
Clo. To leave you in your madness, 'twere
my sin: 104
I will not.
Imo. Fools cure not mad folks.
Clo. Do you call me fool?
Imo. As I am mad, I do:
If you'll be patient, I'll no more be mad; 108
That cures us both. I am much sorry, sir,
You put me to forget a lady's manners,
By being so verbal; and learn now, for all,
That I, which know my heart, do here pronounce
By the very truth of it, I care not for you; 113
And am so near the lack of charity,—
To accuse myself,—I hate you; which I had
rather
You felt than make 't my boast.
Clo. You sin against 116
Obedience, which you owe your father. For
The contract you pretend with that base wretch,
One bred of alms and foster'd with cold dishes,
With scraps o' the court, it is no contract,
none; 120
And though it be allow'd in meaner parties—
Yet who than he more mean?—to knit their
souls
On whom there is no more dependancy

But brats and beggary—in self-figur'd knot; 124
Yet you are curb'd from that enlargement by
The consequence o' the crown, and must not soil
The precious note of it with a base slave,
A hilding for livery, a squire's cloth, 128
A pantler, not so eminent.
Imo. Profane fellow!
Wert thou the son of Jupiter, and no more
But what thou art besides, thou wert too base
To be his groom; thou wert dignified enough,
Even to the point of envy, if 'twere made 133
Comparative for your virtues, to be styl'd
The under-hangman of his kingdom, and hated
For being preferr'd so well.
Clo. The south-fog rot him!
Imo. He never can meet more mischance
than come 137
To be but nam'd of thee. His meanest garment
That ever hath but clipp'd his body, is dearer
In my respect than all the hairs above thee, 140
Were they all made such men. How now,
Pisanio!

Enter PISANIO.

Clo. 'His garment!' Now, the devil—
Imo. To Dorothy my woman hie thee pre-
sently,—
Clo. 'His garment!'
Imo. I am sprighted with a fool, 144
Frighted, and anger'd worse. Go, bid my
woman
Search for a jewel that too casually
Hath left mine arm; it was thy master's, 'shrew me
If I would lose it for a revenue 148
Of any king's in Europe. I do think
I saw 't this morning; confident I am
Last night 'twas on mine arm, I kiss'd it;
I hope it be not gone to tell my lord 152
That I kiss aught but he.
Pis. 'Twill not be lost.
Imo. I hope so; go, and search.
[*Exit* PISANIO.
Clo. You have abus'd me:
'His meanest garment!'
Imo. Ay, I said so, sir: 155
If you will make 't an action, call witness to 't.
Clo. I will inform your father.
Imo. Your mother too:
She's my good lady, and will conceive, I hope,
But the worst of me. So I leave you, sir,
To the worst of discontent. [*Exit.*
Clo. I'll be reveng'd. 160
'His meanest garment!' Well. [*Exit.*

SCENE IV.—*Rome. A Room in* PHILARIO'S
House.

Enter POSTHUMUS *and* PHILARIO.

Post. Fear it not, sir; I would I were so sure
To win the king as I am bold her honour
Will remain hers.
Phi. What means do you make to him?
Post. Not any, but abide the change of time,
Quake in the present winter's state and wish 5
That warmer days would come; in these sear'd
hopes,

I barely gratify your love; they failing,
I must die much your debtor.　　　　　　　8
　Phi. Your very goodness and your company
O'erpays all I can do. By this, your king
Hath heard of great Augustus; Caius Lucius
Will do's commission throughly, and I think
He'll grant the tribute, send the arrearages, 13
Or look upon our Romans, whose remembrance
Is yet fresh in their grief.
　Post.　　　　　　I do believe—
Statist though I am none, nor like to be—　16
That this will prove a war; and you shall hear
The legions now in Gallia sooner landed
In our not-fearing Britain, than have tidings
Of any penny tribute paid. Our countrymen 20
Are men more order'd than when Julius Cæsar
Smil'd at their lack of skill, but found their courage
Worthy his frowning at: their discipline,—
Now winged,—with their courage will make known　　　　　　　　　24
To their approvers they are people such
That mend upon the world.
　Phi.　　　　　　See! Iachimo!

Enter IACHIMO.

　Post. The swiftest harts have posted you by land,
And winds of all the corners kiss'd your sails, 28
To make your vessel nimble.
　Phi.　　　　　　Welcome, sir.
　Post. I hope the briefness of your answer made
The speediness of your return.
　Iach.　　　　　　Your lady
Is one of the fairest that I have look'd upon. 32
　Post. And therewithal the best; or let her beauty
Look through a casement to allure false hearts
And be false with them.
　Iach.　　　　Here are letters for you.
　Post. Their tenour good, I trust.
　Iach.　　　　'Tis very like. 36
　Phi. Was Caius Lucius in the Britain court
When you were there?
　Iach.　　　　He was expected then,
But not approach'd.
　Post.　　　　All is well yet.
Sparkles this stone as it was wont? or is't not 40
Too dull for your good wearing?
　Iach.　　　　If I have lost it,
I should have lost the worth of it in gold.
I'll make a journey twice as far to enjoy
A second night of such sweet shortness which 44
Was mine in Britain; for the ring is won.
　Post. The stone's too hard to come by.
　Iach.　　　　Not a whit,
Your lady being so easy.
　Post.　　　　Make not, sir,
Your loss your sport; I hope you know that we
Must not continue friends.
　Iach.　　　　Good sir, we must, 49
If you keep covenant. Had I not brought
The knowledge of your mistress home, I grant
We were to question further, but I now　52
Profess myself the winner of her honour,

Together with your ring; and not the wronger
Of her or you, having proceeded but
By both your wills.
　Post.　　　If you can make't apparent 56
That you have tasted her in bed, my hand
And ring is yours; if not, the foul opinion
You had of her pure honour gains or loses
Your sword or mine or masterless leaves both 60
To who shall find them.
　Iach.　　　　Sir, my circumstances
Being so near the truth as I will make them,
Must first induce you to believe: whose strength
I will confirm with oath; which, I doubt not, 64
You'll give me leave to spare, when you shall find
You need it not.
　Post.　　　Proceed.
　Iach.　　　First, her bedchamber,—
Where I confess I slept not, but profess
Had that was well worth watching,—it was hang'd　　　　　　　68
With tapestry of silk and silver; the story
Proud Cleopatra, when she met her Roman,
And Cydnus swell'd above the banks, or for
The press of boats or pride; a piece of work 72
So bravely done, so rich, that it did strive
In workmanship and value; which I wonder'd
Could be rarely and exactly wrought,
Since the true life on't was—
　Post.　　　This is true; 76
And this you might have heard of here, by me,
Or by some other.
　Iach.　　　More particulars
Must justify my knowledge.
　Post.　　　So they must,
Or do your honour injury.
　Iach.　　　The chimney　80
Is south the chamber, and the chimney-piece
Chaste Dian bathing; never saw I figures
So likely to report themselves; the cutter
Was as another nature, dumb; outwent her, 84
Motion and breath left out.
　Post.　　　This is a thing
Which you might from relation likewise reap,
Being, as it is, much spoke of.
　Iach.　　　The roof o' the chamber
With golden cherubins is fretted; her and-irons—　　　　　　　88
I had forgot them—were two winking Cupids
Of silver, each on one foot standing, nicely
Depending on their brands.
　Post.　　　This is her honour!
Let it be granted you have seen all this,—and praise　　　　　　　92
Be given to your remembrance,—the description
Of what is in her chamber nothing saves
The wager you have laid.
　Iach.　　　Then, if you can,
Be pale: I beg but leave to air this jewel; see!
　　　　　　　　[*Showing the bracelet.*
And now 'tis up again; it must be married 97
To that your diamond; I'll keep them.
　Post.　　　　Jove!
Once more let me behold it. Is it that
Which I left with her?

Iach. Sir,—I thank her,—that: 100
She stripp'd it from her arm; I see her yet;
Her pretty action did outsell her gift,
And yet enrich'd it too. She gave it me, and said
She priz'd it once.

Post. May be she pluck'd it off 104
To send it me.

Iach. She writes so to you, doth she?

Post. O! no, no, no, 'tis true. Here, take this
too; [*Gives the ring.*
It is a basilisk unto mine eye,
Kills me to look on 't. Let there be no honour
Where there is beauty; truth where semblance;
love 109
Where there 's another man; the vows of women
Of no more bondage be to where they are made
Than they are to their virtues, which is no-
thing. 112
O! above measure false.

Phi. Have patience, sir,
And take your ring again; 'tis not yet won:
It may be probable she lost it; or
Who knows if one of her women, being cor-
rupted, 116
Hath stol'n it from her?

Post. Very true;
And so I hope he came by 't. Back my ring.
Render to me some corporal sign about her,
More evident than this; for this was stol'n. 120

Iach. By Jupiter, I had it from her arm.

Post. Hark you, he swears; by Jupiter he
swears.
'Tis true; nay, keep the ring; 'tis true: I am sure
She would not lose it; her attendants are 124
All sworn and honourable; they induc'd to steal
it!
And by a stranger! No, he hath enjoy'd her;
The cognizance of her incontinency
Is this; she hath bought the name of whore thus
dearly. 128
There, take thy hire; and all the fiends of hell
Divide themselves between you!

Phi. Sir, be patient:
This is not strong enough to be believ'd
Of one persuaded well of—

Post. Never talk on 't; 132
She hath been colted by him.

Iach. If you seek
For further satisfying, under her breast,
Worthy the pressing, lies a mole, right proud
Of that most delicate lodging: by my life, 136
I kiss'd it, and it gave me present hunger
To feed again, though full. You do remember
This stain upon her?

Post. Ay, and it doth confirm
Another stain, as big as hell can hold, 140
Were there no more but it.

Iach. Will you hear more?

Post. Spare your arithmetic; never count the
turns;
Once, and a million!

Iach. I'll be sworn,—

Post. No swearing.
If you will swear you have not done 't, you lie;
And I will kill thee if thou dost deny 145
Thou'st made me cuckold.

Iach. I'll deny nothing.

Post. O! that I had her here, to tear her limb-
meal.
I will go there and do 't, i' the court, before 148
Her father. I'll do something— [*Exit.*

Phi. Quite besides
The government of patience! You have won:
Let 's follow him, and pervert the present wrath
He hath against himself.

Iach. With all my heart. 152
[*Exeunt.*

SCENE V.—*The Same. Another Room in the
Same.*

Enter POSTHUMUS.

Post. Is there no way for men to be, but
women
Must be half-workers? We are all bastards; all,
And that most venerable man which I
Did call my father was I know not where 4
When I was stamp'd; some coiner with his tools
Made me a counterfeit; yet my mother seem'd
The Dian of that time; so doth my wife
The nonpareil of this. O! vengeance, venge-
ance; 8
Me of my lawful pleasure she restrain'd
And pray'd me oft forbearance; did it with
A pudency so rosy the sweet view on 't
Might well have warm'd old Saturn; that I
thought her 12
As chaste as unsunn'd snow. O! all the devils!
This yellow Iachimo, in an hour,—was 't not?
Or less—at first?—perchance he spoke not, but
Like a full-acorn'd boar, a German one, 16
Cried 'O!' and mounted; found no opposition
But what he look'd for should oppose and she
Should from encounter guard. Could I find out
The woman's part in me! For there 's no motion
That tends to vice in man but I affirm 21
It is the woman's part; be it lying, note it,
The woman's; flattering, hers; deceiving, hers;
Lust and rank thoughts, hers, hers; revenges,
hers; 24
Ambitions, covetings, change of prides, disdain,
Nice longing, slanders, mutability,
All faults that man may name, nay, that hell
knows,
Why, hers, in part, or all; but rather, all; 28
For even to vice
They are not constant, but are changing still
One vice but of a minute old for one
Not half so old as that. I'll write against them,
Detest them, curse them. Yet 'tis greater skill 33
In a true hate to pray they have their will:
The very devils cannot plague them better.
[*Exit.*

ACT III

SCENE I.—*Britain. A Hall in* CYMBELINE'S
Palace.

Enter at one door CYMBELINE, QUEEN, CLOTEN,
and Lords; *and at another* CAIUS LUCIUS *and*
Attendants.

Cym. Now say what would Augustus Cæsar
with us?

Luc. When Julius Cæsar—whose remembrance yet
Lives in men's eyes, and will to ears and tongues
Be theme and hearing ever—was in this Britain,
And conquer'd it, Cassibelan, thine uncle,— 5
Famous in Cæsar's praises, no whit less
Than in his feats deserving it,—for him
And his succession, granted Rome a tribute, 8
Yearly three thousand pounds, which by thee
    lately
Is left untender'd.
  Queen.   And, to kill the marvel,
Shall be so ever.
  Clo.   There be many Cæsars
Ere such another Julius. Britain is   12
A world by itself, and we will nothing pay
For wearing our own noses.
  Queen.   That opportunity,
Which then they had to take from 's, to resume,
We have again. Remember, sir, my liege, 16
The kings your ancestors, together with
The natural bravery of your isle, which stands
As Neptune's park, ribbed and paled in
With rocks unscaleable and roaring waters, 20
With sands, that will not bear your enemies'
    boats,
But suck them up to the topmast. A kind of
    conquest
Cæsar made here, but made not here his brag
Of 'came, and saw, and overcame:' with
    shame—   24
The first that ever touch'd him—he was carried
From off our coast, twice beaten; and his shipping—
Poor ignorant baubles!—on our terrible seas,
Like egg-shells mov'd upon their surges, crack'd
As easily 'gainst our rocks: for joy whereof 29
The fam'd Cassibelan, who was once at point—
O giglot fortune!—to master Cæsar's sword,
Made Lud's town with rejoicing-fires bright, 32
And Britons strut with courage.
  Clo. Come, there's no more tribute to be paid.
Our kingdom is stronger than it was at that
time; and, as I said, there is no moe such
Cæsars; other of them may have crooked noses,
but to owe such straight arms, none.
  Cym. Son, let your mother end.   39
  Clo. We have yet many among us can gripe
as hard as Cassibelan; I do not say I am one,
but I have a hand. Why tribute? why should
we pay tribute? If Cæsar can hide the sun from
us with a blanket, or put the moon in his pocket,
we will pay him tribute for light; else, sir, no
more tribute, pray you now.
  Cym. You must know,
Till the injurious Romans did extort   48
This tribute from us, we were free; Cæsar's
    ambition—
Which swell'd so much that it did almost stretch
The sides o' the world—against all colour here
Did put the yoke upon 's; which to shake off 52
Becomes a war-like people, whom we reckon
Ourselves to be. We do say then to Cæsar
Our ancestor was that Mulmutius which
Ordain'd our laws, whose use the sword of
    Cæsar

Hath too much mangled; whose repair and
    franchise   57
Shall, by the power we hold, be our good deed,
Though Rome be therefore angry. Mulmutius
    made our laws,
Who was the first of Britain which did put 60
His brows within a golden crown, and call'd
Himself a king.
  Luc.   I am sorry, Cymbeline,
That I am to pronounce Augustus Cæsar—
Cæsar, that hath more kings his servants than
Thyself domestic officers—thine enemy.   65
Receive it from me, then: war and confusion
In Cæsar's name pronounce I 'gainst thee: look
For fury not to be resisted. Thus defied,   68
I thank thee for myself.
  Cym.   Thou art welcome, Caius.
Thy Cæsar knighted me; my youth I spent
Much under him; of him I gather'd honour;
Which he, to seek of me again, perforce,   72
Behoves me keep at utterance. I am perfect
That the Pannonians and Dalmatians for
Their liberties are now in arms; a precedent
Which not to read would show the Britons cold:
So Cæsar shall not find them.
  Luc.   Let proof speak. 77
  Clo. His majesty bids you welcome. Make
pastime with us a day or two, or longer; if you
seek us afterwards in other terms, you shall find
us in our salt-water girdle; if you beat us out of
it, it is yours; if you fall in the adventure, our
crows shall fare the better for you; and there's
an end.   84
  Luc. So, sir.
  Cym. I know your master's pleasure and he
    mine:
All the remain is 'Welcome!'   [*Exeunt.*

SCENE II.—*Another Room in the Same.*

Enter PISANIO, *reading a letter.*

Pis. How! of adultery! Wherefore write you
    not
What monster's her accuser? Leonatus!
O master! what a strange infection
Is fall'n into thy ear! What false Italian—   4
As poisonous-tongu'd as handed—hath prevail'd
On thy too ready hearing? Disloyal! No:
She's punish'd for her truth, and undergoes,
More goddess-like than wife-like, such assaults 8
As would take in some virtue. O my master!
Thy mind to her is now as low as were
Thy fortunes. How! that I should murder her?
Upon the love and truth and vows which I   12
Have made to thy command? I, her? her blood?
If it be so to do good service, never
Let me be counted serviceable. How look I,
That I should seem to lack humanity   16
So much as this fact comes to?—*Do't: the
    letter
That I have sent her by her own command
Shall give thee opportunity:*—O damn'd paper!
Black as the ink that's on thee. Senseless
    bauble,   20
Art thou a feodary for this act, and look'st

So virgin-like without? Lo! here she comes.
I am ignorant in what I am commanded.

Enter IMOGEN.

Imo. How now, Pisanio!   24
Pis. Madam, here is a letter from my lord.
Imo. Who? thy lord? that is my lord, Leonatus.
O! learn'd indeed were that astronomer
That knew the stars as I his characters;   28
He'd lay the future open. You good gods,
Let what is here contain'd relish of love,
Of my lord's health, of his content, yet not
That we two are asunder; let that grieve him,—
Some griefs are med'cinable; that is one of
      them,   33
For it doth physic love,—of his content,
All but in that! Good wax, thy leave. Bless'd be
You bees that make these locks of counsel!
      Lovers   36
And men in dangerous bonds pray not alike;
Though forfeiters you cast in prison, yet
You clasp young Cupid's tables. Good news,
      gods!
*Justice, and your father's wrath, should he
take me in his dominion, could not be so cruel to
me, as you, O the dearest of creatures, would not
even renew me with your eyes. Take notice that
I am in Cambria, at Milford-Haven; what
your own love will out of this advise you, follow. So, he wishes you all happiness, that remains loyal to his vow, and your, increasing in
love,*   LEONATUS POSTHUMUS.
O! for a horse with wings! Hear'st thou,
      Pisanio?   49
He is at Milford-Haven; read, and tell me
How far 'tis thither. If one of mean affairs
May plod it in a week, why may not I   52
Glide thither in a day? Then, true Pisanio,—
Who long'st, like me, to see thy lord; who
      long'st,—
O! let me 'bate,—but not like me; yet long'st,
But in a fainter kind:—O! not like me,   56
For mine's beyond beyond; say, and speak
      thick;—
Love's counsellor should fill the bores of hearing,
To the smothering of the sense,—how far it is
To this same blessed Milford; and, by the way,
Tell me how Wales was made so happy as   61
T' inherit such a haven; but, first of all,
How we may steal from hence, and, for the gap
That we shall make in time, from our hencegoing   64
And our return, to excuse; but first, how get
      hence.
Why should excuse be born or ere begot?
We'll talk of that hereafter. Prithee, speak,
How many score of miles may we well ride 68
'Twixt hour and hour?
Pis.   One score 'twixt sun and sun,
Madam,'s enough for you, and too much too.
Imo. Why, one that rode to's execution,
      man,
Could never go so slow: I have heard of riding
      wagers,   72

Where horses have been nimbler than the sands
That run i' the clock's behalf. But this is foolery;
Go bid my woman feign a sickness; say
She'll home to her father; and provide me presently   76
A riding-suit, no costlier than would fit
A franklin's housewife.
Pis.   Madam, you're best consider.
Imo. I see before me, man; nor here, nor
      here,
Nor what ensues, but have a fog in them,   80
That I cannot look through. Away, I prithee;
Do as I bid thee. There's no more to say;
Accessible is none but Milford way.   [*Exeunt.*

SCENE III.—*Wales. A mountainous Country
      with a Cave.*

Enter from the Cave, BELARIUS, GUIDERIUS,
      and ARVIRAGUS.

Bel. A goodly day not to keep house, with
      such
Whose roof's as low as ours! Stoop, boys; this
      gate
Instructs you how to adore the heavens, and
      bows you
To a morning's holy office; the gates of
      monarchs   4
Are arch'd so high that giants may jet through
And keep their impious turbans on, without
Good morrow to the sun. Hail, thou fair
      heaven!   7
We house i' the rock, yet use thee not so hardly
As prouder livers do.
Gui.   Hail, heaven!
Arv.   Hail, heaven!
Bel. Now for our mountain sport. Up to
      yond hill;
Your legs are young; I'll tread these flats. Consider,
When you above perceive me like a crow,   12
That it is place which lessens and sets off;
And you may then revolve what tales I have
      told you
Of courts, of princes, of the tricks in war;
This service is not service, so being done,   16
But being so allow'd; to apprehend thus
Draws us a profit from all things we see,
And often, to our comfort, shall we find
The sharded beetle in a safer hold   20
Than is the full-wing'd eagle. O! this life
Is nobler than attending for a check,
Richer than doing nothing for a bribe,
Prouder than rustling in unpaid-for silk;   24
Such gain the cap of him that makes 'em fine,
Yet keeps his book uncross'd; no life to ours.
Gui. Out of your proof you speak; we, poor
      unfledg'd,
Have never wing'd from view o' the nest, nor
      know not   28
What air's from home. Haply this life is best,
If quiet life be best; sweeter to you
That have a sharper known, well corresponding
With your stiff age; but unto us it is   32
A cell of ignorance, travelling a-bed,
A prison for a debtor, that not dares

To stride a limit.
Arv.   What should we speak of
When we are old as you? when we shall hear 36
The rain and wind beat dark December, how
In this our pinching cave shall we discourse
The freezing hours away? We have seen no-
     thing;
We are beastly, subtle as the fox for prey, 40
Like war-like as the wolf for what we eat;
Our valour is to chase what flies; our cage
We make a quire, as doth the prison'd bird,
And sing our bondage freely.
Bel.   How you speak! 44
Did you but know the city's usuries
And felt them knowingly; the art o' the court,
As hard to leave as keep, whose top to climb
Is certain falling, or so slippery that   48
The fear's as bad as falling; the toil of the war,
A pain that only seems to seek out danger
I' the name of fame and honour; which dies i'
     the search,
And hath as oft a slanderous epitaph   52
As record of fair act; nay, many times,
Doth ill deserve by doing well; what's worse,
Must curtsy at the censure: O boys! this story
The world may read in me; my body's mark'd
With Roman swords, and my report was once
First with the best of note; Cymbeline lov'd me,
And when a soldier was the theme, my name
Was not far off; then was I as a tree   60
Whose boughs did bend with fruit, but, in one
     night,
A storm or robbery, call it what you will,
Shook down my mellow hangings, nay, my
     leaves,
And left me bare to weather.
Gui.   Uncertain favour! 64
Bel. My fault being nothing,—as I have told
     you oft,—
But that two villains, whose false oaths pre-
     vail'd
Before my perfect honour, swore to Cymbeline
I was confederate with the Romans; so   68
Follow'd my banishment, and this twenty years
This rock and these demesnes have been my
     world,
Where I have liv'd at honest freedom, paid
More pious debts to heaven than in all   72
The fore-end of my time. But, up to the moun-
     tains!
This is not hunter's language. He that strikes
The venison first shall be the lord o' the feast;
To him the other two shall minister;   76
And we will fear no poison which attends
In place of greater state. I'll meet you in the
     valleys.
     [*Exeunt* GUIDERIUS *and* ARVIRAGUS.
How hard it is to hide the sparks of nature!
These boys know little they are sons to the king;
Nor Cymbeline dreams that they are alive. 81
They think they are mine; and, though train'd
     up thus meanly
I' the cave wherein they bow, their thoughts do
     hit
The roofs of palaces, and nature prompts them
In simple and low things to prince it much 85

Beyond the trick of others. This Polydore,
The heir of Cymbeline and Britain, who
The king his father call'd Guiderius,—Jove! 88
When on my three-foot stool I sit and tell
The war-like feats I have done, his spirits fly out
Into my story: say, 'Thus mine enemy fell,
And thus I set my foot on's neck;' even then 92
The princely blood flows in his cheek, he sweats,
Strains his young nerves, and puts himself in
     posture
That acts my words. The younger brother,
     Cadwal,
Once Arviragus,—in as like a figure,   96
Strikes life into my speech and shows much
     more
His own conceiving. Hark! the game is rous'd.
O Cymbeline! heaven and my conscience knows
Thou didst unjustly banish me; whereon, 100
At three and two years old, I stole these babes,
Thinking to bar thee of succession, as
Thou reft'st me of my lands. Euriphile,
Thou wast their nurse; they took thee for their
     mother,   104
And every day do honour to her grave:
Myself, Belarius, that am Morgan call'd,
They take for natural father. The game is up.
     [*Exit.*

SCENE IV.—*Near Milford-Haven.*

Enter PISANIO *and* IMOGEN.

Imo. Thou told'st me, when we came from
     horse, the place
Was near at hand: ne'er long'd my mother so
To see me first, as I have now. Pisanio! man!
Where is Posthumus? What is in thy mind, 4
That makes thee stare thus? Wherefore breaks
     that sigh
From the inward of thee? One, but painted
     thus,
Would be interpreted a thing perplex'd
Beyond self-explication; put thyself   8
Into a haviour of less fear, ere wildness
Vanquish my staider senses. What's the
     matter?
Why tender'st thou that paper to me with
A look untender? If 't be summer news,   12
Smile to 't before; if winterly, thou need'st
But keep that count'nance still. My husband's
     hand!
That drug-damn'd Italy hath out-crafted him,
And he's at some hard point. Speak, man; thy
     tongue   16
May take off some extremity, which to read
Would be even mortal to me.
Pis.   Please you, read;
And you shall find me, wretched man, a thing
The most disdain'd of fortune.   20
*Imo. Thy mistress, Pisanio, hath played the
strumpet in my bed; the testimonies whereof
lie bleeding in me. I speak not out of weak
surmises, but from proof as strong as my grief
and as certain as I expect my revenge. That
part thou, Pisanio, must act for me, if thy faith
be not tainted with the breach of hers. Let
thine own hands take away her life; I shall*

give thee opportunity at Milford-Haven; she
hath my letter for the purpose; where, if thou
fear to strike, and to make me certain it is
done, thou art the pandar to her dishonour and
equally to me disloyal. 33
    Pis. What shall I need to draw my sword?
the paper
Hath cut her throat already. No, 'tis slander,
Whose edge is sharper than the sword, whose
tongue 36
Outvenoms all the worms of Nile, whose breath
Rides on the posting winds and doth belie
All corners of the world; kings, queens, and
states,
Maids, matrons, nay, the secrets of the grave 40
This viperous slander enters. What cheer,
madam?
    Imo. False to his bed! What is it to be false?
To lie in watch there and to think on him?
To weep 'twixt clock and clock? if sleep charge
nature, 44
To break it with a fearful dream of him,
And cry myself awake? that's false to's bed, is
it?
    Pis. Alas! good lady.
    Imo. I false! Thy conscience witness!
Iachimo, 48
Thou didst accuse him of incontinency;
Thou then look'dst like a villain; now methinks
Thy favour's good enough. Some jay of Italy,
Whose mother was her painting, hath betray'd
him: 52
Poor I am stale, a garment out of fashion,
And, for I am richer than to hang by the walls,
I must be ripp'd; to pieces with me! O!
Men's vows are women's traitors! All good
seeming, 56
By thy revolt, O husband! shall be thought
Put on for villany; not born where't grows,
But worn a bait for ladies.
    Pis. Good madam, hear me.
    Imo. True honest men being heard, like false
Æneas, 60
Were in his time thought false, and Sinon's
weeping
Did scandal many a holy tear, took pity
From most true wretchedness; so thou, Posthu-
mus,
Wilt lay the leaven on all proper men; 64
Goodly and gallant shall be false and perjur'd
From thy great fail. Come, fellow, be thou
honest;
Do thou thy master's bidding. When thou seest
him,
A little witness my obedience; look! 68
I draw the sword myself; take it, and hit
The innocent mansion of my love, my heart.
Fear not, 'tis empty of all things but grief;
Thy master is not there, who was indeed 72
The riches of it: do his bidding; strike.
Thou mayst be valiant in a better cause,
But now thou seem'st a coward.
    Pis. Hence, vile instrument!
Thou shalt not damn my hand.
    Imo. Why, I must die; 76
And if I do not by thy hand, thou art

No servant of thy master's. Against self-
slaughter
There is a prohibition so divine
That cravens my weak hand. Come, here's my
heart. 80
Something's afore't; soft, soft! we'll no de-
fence;
Obedient as the scabbard. What is here?
The scriptures of the loyal Leonatus
All turn'd to heresy! Away, away! 84
Corrupters of my faith; you shall no more
Be stomachers to my heart. Thus may poor
fools
Believe false teachers; though those that are
betray'd
Do feel the treason sharply, yet the traitor 88
Stands in worse case of woe.
And thou, Posthumus, thou that didst set up
My disobedience 'gainst the king my father,
And make me put into contempt the suits 92
Of princely fellows, shalt hereafter find
It is no act of common passage, but
A strain of rareness; and I grieve myself
To think, when thou shalt be disedg'd by her 96
That now thou tir'st on, how thy memory
Will then be pang'd by me. Prithee, dispatch;
The lamb entreats the butcher; where's thy
knife?
Thou art too slow to do thy master's bidding,
When I desire it too.
    Pis. O, gracious lady! 101
Since I receiv'd command to do this business
I have not slept one wink.
    Imo. Do't, and to bed then.
    Pis. I'll wake mine eyeballs blind first.
    Imo. Wherefore then
Didst undertake it? Why hast thou abus'd 105
So many miles with a pretence? this place?
Mine action and thine own? our horses' labour?
The time inviting thee? the perturb'd court, 108
For my being absent?—whereunto I never
Purpose return.—Why hast thou gone so far,
To be unbent when thou hast ta'en thy stand,
The elected deer before thee?
    Pis. But to win time 112
To lose so bad employment, in the which
I have consider'd of a course. Good lady,
Hear me with patience.
    Imo. Talk thy tongue weary; speak:
I have heard I am a strumpet, and mine ear, 116
Therein false struck, can take no greater wound,
Nor tent to bottom that. But speak.
    Pis. Then, madam,
I thought you would not back again.
    Imo. Most like,
Bringing me here to kill me.
    Pis. Not so, neither; 120
But if I were as wise as honest, then
My purpose would prove well. It cannot be
But that my master is abus'd; some villain,
Some villain, ay, and singular in his art, 124
Hath done you both this cursed injury.
    Imo. Some Roman courtezan.
    Pis. No, on my life.
I'll give but notice you are dead and send him
Some bloody sign of it; for 'tis commanded 128

I should do so: you shall be miss'd at court,
And that will well confirm it.

Imo.   Why, good fellow,
What shall I do the while? where bide? how
  live?
Or in my life what comfort, when I am   132
Dead to my husband?

Pis.   If you'll back to the court,—

Imo. No court, no father; nor no more ado
With that harsh, noble, simple nothing Cloten!
That Cloten, whose love-suit hath been to me
As fearful as a siege.

Pis.   If not at court,   137
Then not in Britain must you bide.

Imo.   Where then?
Hath Britain all the sun that shines? Day,
  night,
Are they not but in Britain? I' the world's
  volume   140
Our Britain seems as of it, but not in't;
In a great pool a swan's nest: prithee, think
There's livers out of Britain.

Pis.   I am most glad
You think of other place. The ambassador,   144
Lucius the Roman, comes to Milford-Haven
To-morrow; now, if you could wear a mind
Dark as your fortune is, and but disguise
That which, t' appear itself, must not yet be   148
But by self-danger, you should tread a course
Pretty, and full of view; yea, haply, near
The residence of Posthumus; so nigh at least
That though his actions were not visible, yet   152
Report should render him hourly to your ear
As truly as he moves.

Imo.   O! for such means:
Though peril to my modesty, not death on't,
I would adventure.

Pis.   Well, then, here's the point:
You must forget to be a woman; change   157
Command into obedience; fear and niceness—
The handmaids of all women, or more truly
Woman it pretty self—into a waggish courage;
Ready in gibes, quick-answer'd, saucy, and   161
As quarrelous as the weasel; nay, you must
Forget that rarest treasure of your cheek,
Exposing it—but, O! the harder heart,   164
Alack! no remedy—to the greedy touch
Of common-kissing Titan, and forget
Your laboursome and dainty trims, wherein
You made great Juno angry.

Imo.   Nay, be brief: 168
I see into thy end, and am almost
A man already.

Pis.   First, make yourself but like one.
Forethinking this, I have already fit—
'Tis in my cloak-bag—doublet, hat, hose, all 172
That answer to them; would you in their serv-
  ing,
And with what imitation you can borrow
From youth of such a season, 'fore noble Lucius
Present yourself, desire his service, tell him 176
Wherein you are happy,—which you'll make
  him know,
If that his head have ear in music,—doubtless
With joy he will embrace you, for he's honour-
  able,

And, doubling that, most holy. Your means
  abroad,   180
You have me, rich; and I will never fail
Beginning nor supplyment.

Imo.   Thou art all the comfort
The gods will diet me with. Prithee, away;
There's more to be consider'd, but we'll even 184
All that good time will give us; this attempt
I'm soldier to, and will abide it with
A prince's courage. Away, I prithee.

Pis. Well, madam, we must take a short fare-
  well,   188
Lest, being miss'd, I be suspected of
Your carriage from the court. My noble mistress,
Here is a box, I had it from the queen,
What's in't is precious; if you are sick at sea, 192
Or stomach-qualm'd at land, a dram of this
Will drive away distemper. To some shade,
And fit you to your manhood. May the gods
Direct you to the best!

Imo.   Amen. I thank thee. [*Exeunt.*

SCENE V.—*A Room in* CYMBELINE'S *Palace.*

Enter CYMBELINE, QUEEN, CLOTEN, LUCIUS,
  Lords, *and* Attendants.

Cym. Thus far; and so farewell.

Luc.   Thanks, royal sir.
My emperor hath wrote, I must from hence;
And am right sorry that I must report ye
My master's enemy.

Cym.   Our subjects, sir,   4
Will not endure his yoke; and for ourself
To show less sovereignty than they, must needs
Appear unking-like.

Luc.   So, sir: I desire of you
A conduct over land to Milford-Haven.   8
Madam, all joy befall your Grace.

Queen.   And you!

Cym. My lords, you are appointed for that
  office;
The due of honour in no point omit.
So, farewell, noble Lucius.

Luc.   Your hand, my lord. 12

Clo. Receive it friendly; but from this time
  forth
I wear it as your enemy.

Luc.   Sir, the event
Is yet to name the winner. Fare you well.

Cym. Leave not the worthy Lucius, good
  my lords,   16
Till he have cross'd the Severn. Happiness!
                [*Exeunt* LUCIUS *and* Lords.

Queen. He goes hence frowning; but it
  honours us
That we have given him cause.

Clo.   'Tis all the better;
Your valiant Britons have their wishes in it. 20

Cym. Lucius hath wrote already to the em-
  peror
How it goes here. It fits us therefore ripely
Our chariots and horsemen be in readiness:
The powers that he already hath in Gallia   24
Will soon be drawn to head, from whence he
  moves
His war for Britain.

Queen.   'Tis not sleepy business;
But must be look'd to speedily and strongly. 27

Cym. Our expectation that it would be thus
Hath made us forward. But, my gentle queen,
Where is our daughter? She hath not appear'd
Before the Roman, nor to us hath tender'd
The duty of the day; she looks us like 32
A thing more made of malice than of duty:
We have noted it. Call her before us, for
We have been too slight in sufferance.
                [*Exit an* Attendant.

Queen.   Royal sir.
Since the exile of Posthumus, most retir'd 36
Hath her life been; the cure whereof, my lord,
'Tis time must do. Beseech your majesty,
Forbear sharp speeches to her; she's a lady
So tender of rebukes that words are strokes, 40
And strokes death to her.

Re-enter Attendant.

Cym.   Where is she, sir? How
Can her contempt be answer'd?

Atten.   Please you, sir,
Her chambers are all lock'd, and there's no
    answer
That will be given to the loudest noise we make.

Queen. My lord, when last I went to visit her,
She pray'd me to excuse her keeping close,
Whereto constrain'd by her infirmity,
She should that duty leave unpaid to you, 48
Which daily she was bound to proffer: this
She wish'd me to make known, but our great
    court
Made me to blame in memory.

Cym.   Her doors lock'd!
Not seen of late! Grant, heavens, that which
    I fear 52
Prove false!   [*Exit.*

Queen. Son, I say, follow the king.

Clo. That man of hers, Pisanio, her old ser-
    vant,
I have not seen these two days.

Queen.   Go, look after.
                [*Exit* CLOTEN.
Pisanio, thou that stand'st so for Posthumus! 56
He hath a drug of mine; I pray his absence
Proceed by swallowing that, for he believes
It is a thing most precious. But for her,
Where is she gone? Haply, despair hath seiz'd
    her, 60
Or, wing'd with fervour of her love, she's flown
To her desir'd Posthumus. Gone she is
To death or to dishonour, and my end
Can make good use of either; she being down, 64
I have the placing of the British crown.

Re-enter CLOTEN.

How now, my son!

Clo.   'Tis certain she is fled.
Go in and cheer the king; he rages, none
Dare come about him.

Queen.   [*Aside.*] All the better; may 68
This night forestall him of the coming day!
                [*Exit.*

Clo. I love and hate her; for she's fair and
    royal,

And that she hath all courtly parts more ex-
    quisite
Than lady, ladies, woman; from every one 72
The best she hath, and she, of all compounded,
Outsells them all. I love her therefore; but
Disdaining me and throwing favours on
The low Posthumus slanders so her judgment 76
That what's else rare is chok'd, and in that
    point
I will conclude to hate her, nay, indeed,
To be reveng'd upon her. For, when fools 79
Shall—

Enter PISANIO.

Who is here? What! are you packing, sirrah?
Come hither. Ah! you precious pandar. Villain,
Where is thy lady? In a word; or else
Thou art straightway with the fiends.

Pis.   O! good my lord.

Clo. Where is thy lady? or, by Jupiter 84
I will not ask again. Close villain,
I'll have this secret from thy heart, or rip
Thy heart to find it. Is she with Posthumus?
From whose so many weights of baseness can-
    not 88
A dram of worth be drawn.

Pis.   Alas! my lord,
How can she be with him? When was she
    miss'd?
He is in Rome.

Clo.   Where is she, sir? Come nearer,
No further halting; satisfy me home 92
What is become of her?

Pis.   O! my all-worthy lord.

Clo.   All-worthy villain!
Discover where thy mistress is at once.
At the next word; no more of 'worthy lord!' 96
Speak, or thy silence on the instant is
Thy condemnation and thy death.

Pis.   Then, sir,
This paper is the history of my knowledge
Touching her flight.   [*Presenting a letter.*

Clo.   Let's see't. I will pursue her 100
Even to Augustus' throne.

Pis.   [*Aside.*] Or this, or perish.
She's far enough; and what he learns by this
May prove his travel, not her danger.

Clo.   Hum!

Pis. [*Aside.*] I'll write to my lord she's dead.
    O Imogen! 104
Safe mayst thou wander, safe return agen!

Clo. Sirrah, is this letter true?

Pis. Sir, as I think. 107

Clo. It is Posthumus' hand; I know't. Sirrah, if thou wouldst not be a villain, but do me
true service, undergo those employments wherein I should have cause to use thee with a serious
industry, that is, what villany soe'er I bid thee
do, to perform it directly and truly, I would
think thee an honest man; thou shouldst neither
want my means for thy relief nor my voice for
thy preferment. 116

Pis. Well, my good lord.

Clo. Wilt thou serve me? For since patiently
and constantly thou hast stuck to the bare fortune of that beggar Posthumus, thou canst not,

in the course of gratitude, but be a diligent follower of mine. Wilt thou serve me?

Pis. Sir, I will. 123

Clo. Give me thy hand; here's my purse. Hast any of thy late master's garments in thy possession?

Pis. I have, my lord, at my lodging, the same suit he wore when he took leave of my lady and mistress. 129

Clo. The first service thou dost me, fetch that suit hither: let it be thy first service; go.

Pis. I shall, my lord. [*Exit.*

Clo. Meet thee at Milford-Haven!—I forgot to ask him one thing; I'll remember't anon,— even there, thou villain Posthumus, will I kill thee. I would these garments were come. She said upon a time,—the bitterness of it I now belch from my heart,—that she held the very garment of Posthumus in more respect than my noble and natural person, together with the adornment of my qualities. With that suit upon my back will I ravish her: first kill him, and in her eyes; there shall she see my valour, which will then be a torment to her contempt. He on the ground, my speech of insultment ended on his dead body, and when my lust hath dined, —which, as I say, to vex her, I will execute in the clothes that she so praised,—to the court I'll knock her back, foot her home again. She hath despised me rejoicingly, and I'll be merry in my revenge.

Re-enter PISANIO, *with the clothes.*

Be those the garments? 152

Pis. Ay, my noble lord.

Clo. How long is't since she went to Milford-Haven?

Pis. She can scarce be there yet. 155

Clo. Bring this apparel to my chamber; that is the second thing that I have commanded thee: the third is, that thou wilt be a voluntary mute to my design. Be but duteous, and true preferment shall tender itself to thee. My revenge is now at Milford; would I had wings to follow it! Come, and be true. [*Exit.*

Pis. Thou bidd'st me to my loss; for true to thee

Were to prove false, which I will never be, 164 To him that is most true. To Milford go, And find not her whom thou pursu'st. Flow, flow,

You heavenly blessings, on her! This fool's speed

Be cross'd with slowness; labour be his meed! [*Exit.*

SCENE VI.—*Wales. Before the Cave of* BELARIUS.

Enter IMOGEN, *in boy's clothes.*

Imo. I see a man's life is a tedious one; I have tir'd myself, and for two nights together Have made the ground my bed; I should be sick But that my resolution helps me. Milford, 4 When from the mountain-top Pisanio show'd thee,

Thou wast within a ken. O Jove! I think Foundations fly the wretched; such, I mean, Where they should be reliev'd. Two beggars told me 8 I could not miss my way; will poor folks lie, That have afflictions on them, knowing 'tis A punishment or trial? Yes; no wonder, When rich ones scarce tell true. To lapse in fulness 12 Is sorer than to lie for need, and falsehood Is worse in kings than beggars. My dear lord! Thou art one o' the false ones. Now I think on thee,

My hunger's gone, but even before I was 16 At point to sink for food. But what is this? Here is a path to't; 'tis some savage hold; I were best not call, I dare not call, yet famine, Ere clean it o'erthrow nature, makes it valiant. Plenty and peace breeds cowards, hardness ever Of hardiness is mother. Ho! Who's here? If any thing that's civil, speak; if savage, Take or lend. Ho! No answer? Then I'll enter. Best draw my sword; and if mine enemy 25 But fear the sword like me, he'll scarcely look on't.

Such a foe, good heavens! [*Exit to the cave.*

Enter BELARIUS, GUIDERIUS, *and* ARVIRAGUS.

Bel. You, Polydore, have prov'd best woodman, and 28 Are master of the feast; Cadwal and I Will play the cook and servant, 'tis our match; The sweat of industry would dry and die But for the end it works to. Come; our stomachs 32 Will make what's homely savoury; weariness Can snore upon the flint when resty sloth Finds the down pillow hard. Now, peace be here,

Poor house, that keep'st thyself!

Gui. I am throughly weary. 36

Arv. I am weak with toil, yet strong in appetite.

Gui. There is cold meat i' the cave; we'll browse on that,

Whilst what we have kill'd be cook'd.

Bel. [*Looking into the cave.*] Stay; come not in; But that it eats our victuals, I should think 40 Here were a fairy.

Gui. What's the matter, sir?

Bel. By Jupiter, an angel! or, if not, An earthly paragon! Behold divineness No elder than a boy! 44

Re-enter IMOGEN.

Imo. Good masters, harm me not: Before I enter'd here, I call'd; and thought To have begg'd or bought what I have took. Good troth,

I have stol'n nought, nor would not, though I had found 48 Gold strew'd i' the floor. Here's money for my meat;

I would have left it on the board so soon As I had made my meal, and parted

With prayers for the provider.
Gui.   Money, youth? 52
Arv. All gold and silver rather turn to dirt!
As 'tis no better reckon'd but of those
Who worship dirty gods.
Imo.   I see you're angry.
Know, if you kill me for my fault, I should 56
Have died had I not made it.
Bel.   Whither bound?
Imo. To Milford-Haven.
Bel. What's your name?
Imo. Fidele, sir. I have a kinsman who 60
Is bound for Italy; he embark'd at Milford:
To whom being going, almost spent with hunger,
I am fall'n in this offence.
Bel.   Prithee, fair youth,
Think us no churls, nor measure our good
    minds   64
By this rude place we live in. Well encounter'd!
'Tis almost night; you shall have better cheer
Ere you depart, and thanks to stay and eat it.
Boys, bid him welcome.
Gui.   Were you a woman, youth, 68
I should woo hard but be your groom. In
    honesty,
I bid for you, as I do buy.
Arv.   I'll make 't my comfort
He is a man; I'll love him as my brother;
And such a welcome as I'd give to him 72
After a long absence, such is yours: most wel-
    come!
Be sprightly, for you fall 'mongst friends.
Imo.   'Mongst friends.
If brothers. [*Aside.*] Would it had been so, that
    they
Had been my father's sons; then had my prize 76
Been less, and so more equal ballasting
To thee, Posthumus.
Bel.   He wrings at some distress.
Gui. Would I could free 't!
Arv.   Or I, whate'er it be,
What pain it cost, what danger. Gods!
Bel.   Hark, boys.
                                        [*Whispering.*
Imo. Great men,   81
That had a court no bigger than this cave,
That did attend themselves and had the virtue
Which their own conscience seal'd them,—lay-
    ing by   84
That nothing-gift of differing multitudes,—
Could not out-peer these twain. Pardon me,
    gods!
I'd change my sex to be companion with them,
Since Leonatus' false.
Bel.   It shall be so. 88
Boys, we'll go dress our hunt. Fair youth, come
    in:
Discourse is heavy, fasting; when we have
    supp'd,
We'll mannerly demand thee of thy story,
So far as thou wilt speak it.
Gui.   Pray, draw near. 92
Arv. The night to the owl and morn to the
    lark less welcome.
Imo. Thanks, sir.
Arv.   I pray, draw near. [*Exeunt.*

SCENE VII.—*Rome. A Public Place.*

Enter two Senators *and* Tribunes.

First Sen. This is the tenour of the emperor's
    writ:
That since the common men are now in action
'Gainst the Pannonians and Dalmatians,
And that the legions now in Gallia are   4
Full weak to undertake our wars against
The fall'n-off Britons, that we do incite
The gentry to this business. He creates
Lucius pro-consul; and to you the tribunes, 8
For this immediate levy, he commends
His absolute commission. Long live Cæsar!
First Tri. Is Lucius general of the forces?
Sec. Sen.   Ay.
First Tri. Remaining now in Gallia?
First Sen.   With those legions
Which I have spoke of, whereunto your levy 13
Must be supplyant; the words of your commis-
    sion
Will tie you to the numbers and the time
Of their dispatch.
First Tri. We will discharge our duty. 16
                                        [*Exeunt.*

ACT IV

SCENE I.—*Wales. The Forest, near the Cave
    of* BELARIUS.

Enter CLOTEN.

Clo. I am near to the place where they should
meet, if Pisanio have mapped it truly. How fit
his garments serve me! Why should his mistress, who was made by him that made the tailor,
not be fit too? the rather,—saving reverence of
the word,—for 'tis said a woman's fitness comes
by fits. Therein I must play the workman. I
dare speak it to myself,—for it is not vain-glory,
for a man and his glass to confer in his own
chamber,—I mean, the lines of my body are as
well drawn as his; no less young, more strong,
not beneath him in fortunes, beyond him in the
advantage of the time, above him in birth, alike
conversant in general services, and more remarkable in single oppositions; yet this imperceiverant thing loves him in my despite. What
mortality is! Posthumus, thy head, which now
is growing upon thy shoulders, shall within this
hour be off, thy mistress enforced, thy garments
cut to pieces before thy face; and all this done,
spurn her home to her father, who may haply
be a little angry for my so rough usage, but my
mother, having power of his testiness, shall turn
all into my commendations. My horse is tied
up safe; out, sword, and to a sore purpose!
Fortune, put them into my hand! This is the
very description of their meeting-place; and the
fellow dares not deceive me.   [*Exit.*

SCENE II.—*Before the Cave of* BELARIUS.

Enter, from the Cave, BELARIUS, GUIDERIUS,
    ARVIRAGUS, *and* IMOGEN.

Bel. [*To* IMOGEN.] You are not well; remain
here in the cave;

We'll come to you after hunting.
 Arv. [*To* IMOGEN.] Brother, stay here;
Are we not brothers?
 Imo.   So man and man should be,
But clay and clay differs in dignity, 4
Whose dust is both alike. I am very sick.
 Gui. Go you to hunting; I'll abide with him.
 Imo. So sick I am not, yet I am not well;
But not so citizen a wanton as 8
To seem to die ere sick. So please you, leave
me;
Stick to your journal course; the breach of
custom
Is breach of all. I am ill; but your being by me
Cannot amend me; society is no comfort 12
To one not sociable. I am not very sick,
Since I can reason of it; pray you, trust me here,
I'll rob none but myself, and let me die,
Stealing so poorly.
 Gui. I love thee; I have spoke it;
How much the quantity, the weight as much, 17
As I do love my father.
 Bel. What! how! how!
 Arv. If it be sin to say so, sir, I yoke me
In my good brother's fault: I know not why 20
I love this youth; and I have heard you say,
Love's reason's without reason: the bier at
door,
And a demand who is't shall die, I'd say
'My father, not this youth.'
 Bel. [*Aside.*] O noble strain! 24
O worthiness of nature! breed of greatness!
Cowards father cowards, and base things sire
base:
Nature hath meal and bran, contempt and
grace.
I'm not their father; yet who this should be, 28
Doth miracle itself, lov'd before me.
'Tis the ninth hour o' the morn.
 Arv. Brother, farewell.
 Imo. I wish ye sport.
 Arv. You health. So please you, sir.
 Imo. [*Aside.*] These are kind creatures. Gods,
what lies I have heard! 32
Our courtiers say all's savage but at court:
Experience, O! thou disprov'st report.
The imperious seas breed monsters, for the dish
Poor tributary rivers as sweet fish. 36
I am sick still, heart-sick. Pisanio,
I'll now taste of thy drug. [*Swallows some.*
 Gui. I could not stir him;
He said he was gentle, but unfortunate;
Dishonestly afflicted, but yet honest. 40
 Arv. Thus did he answer me; yet said here-
after
I might know more.
 Bel. To the field, to the field!
[*To* IMOGEN.] We'll leave you for this time; go
in and rest.
 Arv. We'll not be long away.
 Bel. Pray, be not sick, 44
For you must be our housewife.
 Imo. Well or ill,
I am bound to you.
 Bel. And shalt be ever.
    [*Exit* IMOGEN.

This youth, howe'er distress'd, appears he hath
had
Good ancestors.
 Arv. How angel-like he sings! 48
 Gui. But his neat cookery! he cut our roots
In characters,
And sauc'd our broths as Juno had been sick
And he her dieter.
 Arv. Nobly he yokes
A smiling with a sigh, as if the sigh 52
Was that it was, for not being such a smile;
The smile mocking the sigh, that it would fly
From so divine a temple, to commix
With winds that sailors rail at.
 Gui. I do note 56
That grief and patience rooted in him, both
Mingle their spurs together.
 Arv. Grow, patience!
And let the stinking-elder, grief, untwine
His perishing root with the increasing vine! 60
 Bel. It is great morning. Come, away!—
Who's there?

    Enter CLOTEN.

 Clo. I cannot find those runagates; that
villain
Hath mock'd me. I am faint.
 Bel. 'Those runagates!'
Means he not us? I partly know him; 'tis 64
Cloten, the son o' the queen. I fear some am-
bush.
I saw him not these many years, and yet
I know 'tis he. We are held as outlaws: hence!
 Gui. He is but one. You and my brother
search 68
What companies are near; pray you, away;
Let me alone with him.
   [*Exeunt* BELARIUS *and* ARVIRAGUS.
 Clo. Soft! What are you
That fly me thus? some villain mountainers?
I have heard of such. What slave art thou?
 Gui. A thing
More slavish did I ne'er than answering 73
A 'slave' without a knock.
 Clo. Thou art a robber,
A law-breaker, a villain. Yield thee, thief.
 Gui. To who? to thee? What art thou? Have
not I 76
An arm as big as thine? a heart as big?
Thy words, I grant, are bigger, for I wear not
My dagger in my mouth. Say what thou art,
Why I should yield to thee?
 Clo. Thou villain base, 80
Know'st me not by my clothes?
 Gui. No, nor thy tailor, rascal,
Who is thy grandfather: he made those clothes,
Which, as it seems, make thee.
 Clo. Thou precious varlet,
My tailor made them not.
 Gui. Hence then, and thank
The man that gave them thee. Thou art some
fool; 85
I am loath to beat thee.
 Clo. Thou injurious thief,
Hear but my name, and tremble.

Gui.   What's thy name?
Clo. Cloten, thou villain.   88
Gui. Cloten, thou double villain, be thy
          name,
I cannot tremble at it; were it Toad, or Adder,
          Spider,
'Twould move me sooner.
Clo.   To thy further fear,
Nay, to thy mere confusion, thou shalt know 92
I am son to the queen.
Gui.   I'm sorry for't, not seeming
So worthy as thy birth.
Clo.   Art not afeard?
Gui. Those that I reverence those I fear, the
          wise;
At fools I laugh, not fear them.
Clo.   Die the death: 96
When I have slain thee with my proper hand,
I'll follow those that even now fled hence,
And on the gates of Lud's town set your heads:
Yield, rustic mountaineer.   [*Exeunt fighting.*

          Re-enter BELARIUS *and* ARVIRAGUS.

Bel. No companies abroad.   101
Arv. None in the world. You did mistake
          him, sure.
Bel. I cannot tell; long is it since I saw him,
But time hath nothing blurr'd those lines of
          favour   104
Which then he wore; the snatches in his voice,
And burst of speaking, were as his. I am abso-
          lute
'Twas very Cloten.
Arv.   In this place we left them:
I wish my brother make good time with him, 108
You say he is so fell.
Bel.   Being scarce made up,
I mean, to man, he had not apprehension
Of roaring terrors; for defect of judgment
Is oft the cease of fear. But see, thy brother. 112

          Re-enter GUIDERIUS, *with* CLOTEN'S *head.*

Gui. This Cloten was a fool, an empty purse,
There was no money in't. Not Hercules
Could have knock'd out his brains, for he had
          none;
Yet I not doing this, the fool had borne   116
My head as I do his.
Bel.   What hast thou done?
Gui. I am perfect what: cut off one Cloten's
          head,
Son to the queen, after his own report;
Who call'd me traitor, mountaineer, and swore,
With his own single hand he'd take us in, 121
Displace our heads where—thank the gods!—
          they grow,
And set them on Lud's town.
Bel.   We are all undone.
Gui. Why, worthy father, what have we to
          lose,   124
But that he swore to take, our lives? The law
Protects not us; then why should we be tender
To let an arrogant piece of flesh threat us,
Play judge and executioner all himself,   128
For we do fear the law? What company

Discover you abroad?
Bel.   No single soul
Can we set eye on; but in all safe reason
He must have some attendants. Though his
          humour   132
Was nothing but mutation, ay, and that
From one bad thing to worse; not frenzy, not
Absolute madness could so far have rav'd
To bring him here alone. Although, perhaps,
It may be heard at court that such as we 137
Cave here, hunt here, are outlaws, and in time
May make some stronger head; the which he
          hearing,—
As it is like him,—might break out, and swear
He'd fetch us in; yet is't not probable   141
To come alone, either he so undertaking,
Or they so suffering; then, on good ground we
          fear,
If we do fear this body hath a tail   144
More perilous than the head.
Arv.   Let ordinance
Come as the gods foresay it; howsoe'er,
My brother hath done well.
Bel.   I had no mind
To hunt this day; the boy Fidele's sickness 148
Did make my way long forth.
Gui.   With his own sword,
Which he did wave against my throat, I have
          ta'en
His head from him; I'll throw't into the creek
Behind our rock, and let it to the sea,   152
And tell the fishes he's the queen's son, Cloten:
That's all I reck.   [*Exit.*
Bel.   I fear 'twill be reveng'd.
Would, Polydore, thou hadst not done't!
          though valour
Becomes thee well enough.
Arv.   Would I had done't 156
So the revenge alone pursu'd me! Polydore,
I love thee brotherly, but envy much
Thou hast robb'd me of this deed; I would re-
          venges,
That possible strength might meet, would seek
          us through   160
And put us to our answer.
Bel.   Well, 'tis done.—
We'll hunt no more to-day, nor seek for danger
Where there's no profit. I prithee, to our rock;
You and Fidele play the cooks; I'll stay   164
Till hasty Polydore return, and bring him
To dinner presently.
Arv.   Poor sick Fidele!
I'll willingly to him; to gain his colour
I'd let a parish of such Clotens blood,   168
And praise myself for charity.   [*Exit.*
Bel.   O thou goddess!
Thou divine Nature, how thyself thou blazon'st
In these two princely boys. They are as gentle
As zephyrs, blowing below the violet,   172
Not wagging his sweet head; and yet as rough,
Their royal blood enchaf'd, as the rud'st wind,
That by the top doth take the mountain pine,
And make him stoop to the vale. 'Tis wonder
That an invisible instinct should frame them
To royalty unlearn'd, honour untaught,
Civility not seen from other, valour

That wildly grows in them, but yields a crop 180
As if it had been sow'd! Yet still it's strange
What Cloten's being here to us portends,
Or what his death will bring us.

Re-enter GUIDERIUS.

Gui.   Where's my brother?
I have sent Cloten's clotpoll down the stream,
In embassy to his mother; his body's hostage
For his return.   [*Solemn music.*
Bel.   My ingenious instrument!
Hark! Polydore, it sounds; but what occasion
Hath Cadwal now to give it motion? Hark! 188
Gui. Is he at home?
Bel.   He went hence even now.
Gui. What does he mean? since death of my
    dear'st mother
It did not speak before. All solemn things
Should answer solemn accidents. The matter?
Triumphs for nothing and lamenting toys 193
Is jollity for apes and grief for boys.
Is Cadwal mad?

Re-enter ARVIRAGUS, *with* IMOGEN, *as dead,*
bearing her in his arms.

Bel.   Look! here he comes,
And brings the dire occasion in his arms 196
Of what we blame him for.
Arv.   The bird is dead
That we have made so much on. I had rather
Have skipp'd from sixteen years of age to sixty,
To have turn'd my leaping-time into a crutch,
Than have seen this.
Gui.   O, sweetest, fairest lily! 201
My brother wears thee not the one half so well
As when thou grew'st thyself.
Bel.   O melancholy!
Who ever yet could sound thy bottom? find 204
The ooze, to show what coast thy sluggish crare
Might easiliest harbour in? Thou blessed thing!
Jove knows what man thou mightst have made;
    but I,
Thou diedst, a most rare boy, of melancholy. 208
How found you him?
Arv.   Stark, as you see:
Thus smiling, as some fly had tickled slumber,
Not as death's dart, being laugh'd at; his right
    cheek
Reposing on a cushion.
Gui.   Where?
Arv.   O' the floor, 212
His arms thus leagu'd; I thought he slept, and
    put
My clouted brogues from off my feet, whose
    rudeness
Answer'd my steps too loud.
Gui.   Why, he but sleeps:
If he be gone, he'll make his grave a bed; 216
With female fairies will his tomb be haunted,
And worms will not come to thee.
Arv.   With fairest flowers
While summer lasts and I live here, Fidele,
I'll sweeten thy sad grave; thou shalt not lack
The flower that's like thy face, pale primrose,
    nor   221

The azur'd hare-bell, like thy veins, no, nor
The leaf of eglantine, whom not to slander,
Out-sweeten'd not thy breath: the ruddock
    would,   224
With charitable bill,—O bill! sore-shaming
Those rich-left heirs, that let their fathers lie
Without a monument,—bring thee all this;
Yea, and furr'd moss besides, when flowers are
    none,   228
To winter-ground thy corse.
Gui.   Prithee, have done,
And do not play in wench-like words with that
Which is so serious. Let us bury him,
And not protract with admiration what 232
Is now due debt. To the grave!
Arv.   Say, where shall's lay him?
Gui. By good Euriphile, our mother.
Arv.   Be't so:
And let us, Polydore, though now our voices
Have got the mannish crack, sing him to the
    ground,   236
As once our mother; use like note and words,
Save that Euriphile must be Fidele.
Gui. Cadwal,
I cannot sing; I'll weep, and word it with
    thee;   240
For notes of sorrow out of tune are worse
Than priests and fanes that lie.
Arv.   We'll speak it then.
Bel. Great griefs, I see, medicine the less, for
    Cloten
Is quite forgot. He was a queen's son, boys, 244
And though he came our enemy, remember
He was paid for that; though mean and mighty
    rotting
Together, have one dust, yet reverence—
That angel of the world—doth make distinc-
    tion   248
Of place 'tween high and low. Our foe was
    princely,
And though you took his life, as being our foe,
Yet bury him as a prince.
Gui.   Pray you, fetch him hither.
Thersites' body is as good as Ajax'   252
When neither are alive.
Arv.   If you'll go fetch him,
We'll say our song the whilst. Brother, begin.
    [*Exit* BELARIUS.
Gui. Nay, Cadwal, we must lay his head to
    the east;
My father hath a reason for't.
Arv.   'Tis true.   256
Gui. Come on then, and remove him.
Arv.   So, begin.

Gui.   Fear no more the heat o' the sun,
        Nor the furious winter's rages;
    Thou thy worldly task hast done,   260
        Home art gone, and ta'en thy wages;
    Golden lads and girls all must,
    As chimney-sweepers, come to dust.

Arv.   Fear no more the frown o' the great,   264
        Thou art past the tyrant's stroke:
    Care no more to clothe and eat;
        To thee the reed is as the oak:
    The sceptre, learning, physic, must   268
        All follow this, and come to dust.

Gui. Fear no more the lightning-flash,
Arv.   Nor the all-dreaded thunder-stone;
Gui. Fear not slander, censure rash; 272
Arv.   Thou hast finish'd joy and moan:
Both. All lovers young, all lovers must
    Consign to thee, and come to dust.

Gui. No exorciser harm thee! 276
Arv.   Nor no witchcraft charm thee!
Gui. Ghost unlaid forbear thee!
Arv.   Nothing ill come near thee!
Both. Quiet consummation have; 280
    And renowned be thy grave!

Re-enter BELARIUS, *with the body of* CLOTEN.

Gui. We have done our obsequies. Come,
lay him down.
Bel. Here's a few flowers; but 'bout mid-
night, more;
The herbs that have on them cold dew o' the
night 284
Are strewings fitt'st for graves. Upon their
faces
You were as flowers, now wither'd; even so
These herblets shall, which we upon you strew.
Come on, away; apart upon our knees. 288
The ground that gave them first has them again;
Their pleasures here are past, so is their pain.
    [*Exeunt* BELARIUS, GUIDERIUS, *and*
    ARVIRAGUS.

Imo. [*Awaking.*] Yes, sir, to Milford-Haven;
which is the way?
I thank you. By yond bush? Pray, how far
thither? 292
'Ods pittikins! can it be six mile yet?
I have gone all night: Faith, I'll lie down and
sleep.
[*Seeing the body of* CLOTEN.] But, soft! no bed-
fellow! O gods and goddesses!
These flowers are like the pleasures of the world;
This bloody man, the care on 't. I hope I
dream; 297
For so I thought I was a cave-keeper,
And cook to honest creatures; but 'tis not so,
'Twas but a bolt of nothing, shot at nothing, 300
Which the brain makes of fumes. Our very eyes
Are sometimes like our judgments, blind. Good
faith,
I tremble still with fear; but if there be
Yet left in heaven as small a drop of pity 304
As a wren's eye, fear'd gods, a part of it!
The dream's here still; even when I wake, it is
Without me, as within me; not imagin'd, felt.
A headless man! The garments of Posthumus!
I know the shape of 's leg, this is his hand, 309
His foot Mercurial, his Martial thigh,
The brawns of Hercules, but his Jovial face—
Murder in heaven? How! 'Tis gone. Pisanio,
All curses madded Hecuba gave the Greeks, 313
And mine to boot, be darted on thee! Thou,
Conspir'd with that irregulous devil, Cloten,
Hast here cut off my lord. To write and read
Be henceforth treacherous! Damn'd Pisanio 317
Hath with his forged letters, damn'd Pisanio,
From this most bravest vessel of the world
Struck the main-top! O Posthumus! alas! 320

Where is thy head? where's that? Ay me!
where's that?
Pisanio might have kill'd thee at the heart,
And left this head on. How should this be?
Pisanio?
'Tis he and Cloten; malice and lucre in them
Have laid this woe here. O! 'tis pregnant, preg-
nant! 325
The drug he gave me, which he said was pre-
cious
And cordial to me, have I not found it
Murderous to the senses? That confirms it
home; 328
This is Pisanio's deed, and Cloten's: O!
Give colour to my pale cheek with thy blood,
That we the horrider may seem to those
Which chance to find us. O! my lord, my lord!
    [*Falls on the body.*

Enter LUCIUS, *a* Captain, *other* Officers, *and a*
Soothsayer.

Cap. To them the legions garrison'd in
Gallia, 333
After your will, have cross'd the sea, attending
You here at Milford-Haven with your ships:
They are in readiness.
Luc.   But what from Rome? 336
Cap. The senate hath stirr'd up the confiners
And gentlemen of Italy, most willing spirits,
That promise noble service; and they come
Under the conduct of bold Iachimo, 340
Sienna's brother.
Luc.   When expect you them?
Cap. With the next benefit o' the wind.
Luc.   This forwardness
Makes our hopes fair. Command our present
numbers
Be muster'd; bid the captains look to 't. Now,
sir, 344
What have you dream'd of late of this war's
purpose?
Sooth. Last night the very gods show'd me a
vision,—
I fast and pray'd for their intelligence,—thus
I saw Jove's bird, the Roman eagle, wing'd 348
From the spongy south to this part of the west
There vanish'd in the sunbeams; which por-
tends,
Unless my sins abuse my divination,
Success to the Roman host.
Luc.   Dream often so, 352
And never false. Soft, ho! what trunk is here
Without his top? The ruin speaks that some-
time
It was a worthy building. How! a page!
Or dead or sleeping on him? But dead rather, 356
For nature doth abhor to make his bed
With the defunct, or sleep upon the dead.
Let's see the boy's face.
Cap.   He's alive, my lord.
Luc. He'll, then, instruct us of this body.
Young one, 360
Inform us of thy fortunes, for it seems
They crave to be demanded. Who is this
Thou mak'st thy bloody pillow? Or who was
he

That, otherwise than noble nature did, 364
Hath alter'd that good picture? What's thy
  interest
In this sad wrack? How came it? Who is it?
  What art thou?
  Imo.   I am nothing; or if not,
Nothing to be were better. This was my master,
A very valiant Briton and a good, 369
That here by mountaineers lies slain. Alas!
There are no more such masters; I may wander
From east to occident, cry out for service, 372
Try many, all good, serve truly, never
Find such another master.
  Luc.   'Lack, good youth!
Thou mov'st no less with thy complaining than
Thy master in bleeding. Say his name, good
  friend. 376
  Imo. Richard du Champ.—[*Aside.*] If I do
  lie and do
No harm by it, though the gods hear, I hope
They'll pardon it.—Say you, sir?
  Luc.   Thy name?
  Imo.   Fidele, sir.
  Luc. Thou dost approve thyself the very
  same; 380
Thy name well fits thy faith, thy faith thy name.
Wilt take thy chance with me? I will not say
Thou shalt be so well master'd, but be sure
No less belov'd. The Roman emperor's letters,
Sent by a consul to me, should not sooner 385
Than thine own worth prefer thee. Go with me.
  Imo. I'll follow, sir. But first, an't please
  the gods,
I'll hide my master from the flies, as deep 388
As these poor pickaxes can dig; and when
With wild wood-leaves and weeds I ha' strew'd
  his grave,
And on it said a century of prayers,
Such as I can, twice o'er, I'll weep and sigh; 392
And, leaving so his service, follow you,
So please you entertain me.
  Luc.   Ay, good youth,
And rather father thee than master thee.
My friends, 396
The boy hath taught us manly duties; let us
Find out the prettiest daisied plot we can,
And make him with our pikes and partisans
A grave; come, arm him. Boy, he is preferr'd
By thee to us, and he shall be interr'd 401
As soldiers can. Be cheerful; wipe thine eyes:
Some falls are means the happier to arise.
                          [*Exeunt.*

SCENE III.—*A Room in* CYMBELINE'S *Palace.*

Enter CYMBELINE, Lords, PISANIO, *and*
Attendants.

  Cym. Again; and bring me word how 'tis
  with her.   [*Exit an* Attendant.
A fever with the absence of her son,
A madness, of which her life's in danger.
  Heavens!
How deeply you at once do touch me. Imogen,
The great part of my comfort, gone; my queen
Upon a desperate bed, and in a time
When fearful wars point at me; her son gone,

So needful for this present: it strikes me, past 8
The hope of comfort. But for thee, fellow,
Who needs must know of her departure and
Dost seem so ignorant, we'll enforce it from
  thee
By a sharp torture.
  Pis.   Sir, my life is yours, 12
I humbly set it at your will; but, for my mistress,
I nothing know where she remains, why gone,
Nor when she purposes return. Beseech your
  highness,
Hold me your loyal servant.
  First Lord.   Good my liege, 16
The day that she was missing he was here;
I dare be bound he's true and shall perform
All parts of his subjection loyally. For Cloten,
There wants no diligence in seeking him, 20
And will, no doubt, be found.
  Cym.   The time is troublesome.
[*To* PISANIO.] We'll slip you for a season; but
  our jealousy
Does yet depend.
  First Lord.   So please your highness,
The Roman legions, all from Gallia drawn, 24
Are landed on your coast, with a supply
Of Roman gentlemen, by the senate sent.
  Cym. Now for the counsel of my son and
  queen!
I am amaz'd with matter.
  First Lord.   Good my liege, 28
Your preparation can affront no less
Than what you hear of; come more, for more
  you're ready:
The want is, but to put those powers in motion
That long to move.
  Cym.   I thank you. Let's withdraw; 32
And meet the time as it seeks us. We fear not
What can from Italy annoy us, but
We grieve at chances here. Away!
                   [*Exeunt all but* PISANIO.
  Pis. I heard no letter from my master since
I wrote him Imogen was slain; 'tis strange; 37
Nor hear I from my mistress, who did promise
To yield me often tidings; neither know I
What is betid to Cloten; but remain 40
Perplex'd in all: the heavens still must work.
Wherein I am false I am honest; not true to be
  true:
These present wars shall find I love my country,
Even to the note o' the king, or I'll fall in them.
All other doubts, by time let them be clear'd; 45
Fortune brings in some boats that are not
  steer'd.   [*Exit.*

SCENE IV.—*Wales. Before the Cave of*
BELARIUS.

Enter BELARIUS, GUIDERIUS, *and* ARVIRAGUS.

  Gui. The noise is round about us.
  Bel.   Let us from it.
  Arv. What pleasure, sir, find we in life, to
  lock it
From action and adventure?
  Gui.   Nay, what hope
Have we in hiding us? this way, the Romans 4

Must or for Britons slay us, or receive us
For barbarous and unnatural revolts
During their use, and slay us after.

Bel.   Sons,
We'll higher to the mountains; there secure us.
To the king's party there's no going; newness 9
Of Cloten's death,—we being not known, not
    muster'd
Among the bands,—may drive us to a render
Where we have liv'd, and so extort from's that
Which we have done, whose answer would be
    death   13
Drawn on with torture.

Gui.   This is, sir, a doubt
In such a time nothing becoming you,
Nor satisfying us.

Arv.   It is not likely   16
That when they hear the Roman horses neigh,
Behold their quarter'd fires, have both their
    eyes
And ears so cloy'd importantly as now,
That they will waste their time upon our note,
To know from whence we are.

Bel.   O! I am known 21
Of many in the army; many years,
Though Cloten then but young, you see, not
    wore him
From my remembrance. And, besides, the king
Hath not deserv'd my service nor your loves 25
Who find in my exile the want of breeding,
The certainty of this hard life; aye hopeless
To have the courtesy your cradle promis'd, 28
But to be still hot summer's tanlings and
The shrinking slaves of winter.

Gui.   Than be so
Better to cease to be. Pray, sir, to the army:
I and my brother are not known; yourself, 32
So out of thought, and thereto so o'ergrown,
Cannot be question'd.

Arv.   By this sun that shines,
I'll thither: what thing is it that I never
Did see man die! scarce ever look'd on blood 36
But that of coward hares, hot goats, and veni-
    son!
Never bestrid a horse, save one that had
A rider like myself, who ne'er wore rowel
Nor iron on his heel! I am asham'd   40
To look upon the holy sun, to have
The benefit of his bless'd beams, remaining
So long a poor unknown.

Gui.   By heavens! I'll go:
If you will bless me, sir, and give me leave, 44
I'll take the better care; but if you will not,
The hazard therefore due fall on me by
The hands of Romans.

Arv.   So say I; amen.

Bel. No reason I, since of your lives you set
So slight a valuation, should reserve   49
My crack'd one to more care. Have with you,
    boys!
If in your country wars you chance to die,
That is my bed too, lads, and there I'll lie: 52
Lead, lead.—[*Aside.*] The time seems long;
    their blood thinks scorn,
Till it fly out and show them princes born.
                                            [*Exeunt.*

ACT V

SCENE I.—*Britain. The Roman Camp.*

Enter POSTHUMUS, *with a bloody handkerchief.*

Post. Yea, bloody cloth, I'll keep thee, for I
    wish'd
Thou shouldst be colour'd thus. You married
    ones,
If each of you should take this course, how
    many
Must murder wives much better than them-
    selves   4
For wrying but a little! O Pisanio!
Every good servant does not all commands;
No bond but to do just ones. Gods! if you
Should have ta'en vengeance on my faults, I
    never   8
Had liv'd to put on this; so had you sav'd
The noble Imogen to repent, and struck
Me, wretch more worth your vengeance. But,
    alack!
You snatch some hence for little faults; that's
    love,   12
To have them fall no more; you some permit
To second ills with ills, each elder worse,
And make them dread it, to the doers' thrift.
But Imogen is your own; do your best wills, 16
And make me bless'd to obey. I am brought
    hither
Among the Italian gentry, and to fight
Against my lady's kingdom; 'tis enough
That, Britain, I have kill'd thy mistress-piece! 20
I'll give no wound to thee. Therefore good
    heavens,
Hear patiently my purpose: I'll disrobe me
Of these Italian weeds, and suit myself
As does a Briton peasant; so I'll fight   24
Against the part I come with, so I'll die
For thee, O Imogen! even for whom my life
Is, every breath, a death: and thus, unknown,
Pitied nor hated, to the face of peril   28
Myself I'll dedicate. Let me make men know
More valour in me than my habits show.
Gods! put the strength o' the Leonati in me.
To shame the guise o' the world, I will begin 32
The fashion, less without and more within.
                                            [*Exit.*

SCENE II.—*Field of Battle between the British
    and Roman Camps.*

Enter, from one door, LUCIUS, IACHIMO, *and the*
Roman Army; *the* British *at another;* LEO-
NATUS POSTHUMUS *following like a poor soldier.*
*They march over and go out. Alarums. Then
enter again in skirmish,* IACHIMO *and* POSTHU-
MUS; *he vanquisheth and disarmeth* IACHIMO,
and then leaves him.

Iach. The heaviness and guilt within my
    bosom
Takes off my manhood: I have belied a lady,
The princess of this country, and the air on't
Revengingly enfeebles me; or could this carl, 4
A very drudge of nature's, have subdu'd me
In my profession? Knighthoods and honours,
    borne

As I wear mine, are titles but of scorn.
If that thy gentry, Britain, go before 8
This lout as he exceeds our lords, the odds
Is that we scarce are men and you are gods.
                               [*Exit.*

The battle continues; the Britons *fly;* CYMBELINE
is taken; then enter, to his rescue, BELARIUS,
GUIDERIUS, *and* ARVIRAGUS.

  Bel. Stand, stand! We have the advantage
    of the ground.
The lane is guarded; nothing routs us but 12
The villany of our fears.
  Gui. ⎫
  Arv. ⎬   Stand, stand, and fight!

Re-enter POSTHUMUS, *and seconds the* Britons;
they rescue CYMBELINE, *and exeunt. Then,
re-enter* LUCIUS, IACHIMO, *and* IMOGEN.

  Luc. Away, boy, from the troops, and save
    thyself;
For friends kill friends, and the disorder's such
As war were hoodwink'd.
  Iach.   'Tis their fresh supplies. 16
  Luc. It is a day turn'd strangely: or betimes
Let's re-inforce, or fly.   [*Exeunt.*

SCENE III.—*Another Part of the Field.*

Enter POSTHUMUS *and a* British Lord.

  Lord. Cam'st thou from where they made
    the stand?
  Post.   I did:
Though you, it seems, come from the fliers.
  Lord.   I did.
  Post. No blame be to you, sir; for all was
    lost,
But that the heavens fought. The king himself 4
Of his wings destitute, the army broken,
And but the backs of Britons seen, all flying
Through a strait lane; the enemy full-hearted,
Lolling the tongue with slaughtering, having
    work 8
More plentiful than tools to do't, struck down
Some mortally, some slightly touch'd, some
    falling
Merely through fear; that the strait pass was
    damm'd
With dead men hurt behind, and cowards living
To die with lengthen'd shame.
  Lord.   Where was this lane? 13
  Post. Close by the battle, ditch'd, and wall'd
    with turf;
Which gave advantage to an ancient soldier,
An honest one, I warrant; who deserv'd 16
So long a breeding as his white beard came to,
In doing this for his country; athwart the lane,
He, with two striplings,—lads more like to run
The country base than to commit such
    slaughter,— 20
With faces fit for masks, or rather fairer
Than those for preservation cas'd, or shame,—
Made good the passage; cried to those that fled,
'Our Britain's harts die flying, not our men: 24
To darkness fleet souls that fly backwards.
    Stand!

Or we are Romans, and will give you that
Like beasts which you shun beastly, and may
    save,
But to look back in frown: stand, stand!' These
    three, 28
Three thousand confident, in act as many,—
For three performers are the file when all
The rest do nothing,—with this word, 'Stand,
    stand!'
Accommodated by the place, more charming 32
With their own nobleness,—which could have
    turn'd
A distaff to a lance,—gilded pale looks,
Part shame, part spirit renew'd; that some,
    turn'd coward
But by example,—O! a sin of war, 36
Damn'd in the first beginners,—'gan to look
The way that they did, and to grin like lions
Upon the pikes o' the hunters. Then began
A stop i' the chaser, a retire, anon, 40
A rout, confusion thick; forthwith they fly
Chickens, the way which they stoop'd eagles;
    slaves,
The strides they victors made. And now our
    cowards—
Like fragments in hard voyages—became 44
The life o' the need; having found the back door
    open
Of the unguarded hearts, Heavens! how they
    wound;
Some slain before; some dying; some their
    friends
O'er-borne i' the former wave; ten, chas'd by
    one, 48
Are now each one the slaughter-man of twenty;
Those that would die or ere resist are grown
The mortal bugs o' the field.
  Lord.   This was strange chance:
A narrow lane, an old man, and two boys! 52
  Post. Nay, do not wonder at it; you are made
Rather to wonder at the things you hear
Than to work any. Will you rime upon't,
And vent it for a mockery? Here is one: 56
'Two boys, an old man twice a boy, a lane,
Preserv'd the Britons, was the Romans' bane.'
  Lord. Nay, be not angry, sir.
  Post.   'Lack! to what end?
Who dares not stand his foe, I'll be his friend;
For if he'll do, as he is made to do, 61
I know he'll quickly fly my friendship too.
You have put me into rime.
  Lord.   Farewell; you're angry. [*Exit.*
  Post. Still going?—This is a lord! O noble
    misery! 64
To be i' the field, and ask, 'what news?' of me!
To-day how many would have given their
    honours
To have sav'd their carcases! took heel to do't,
And yet died too! I, in mine own woe charm'd,
Could not find death where I did hear him
    groan, 69
Nor feel him where he struck: being an ugly
    monster,
'Tis strange he hides him in fresh cups, soft
    beds,
Sweet words; or hath more ministers than we 72

That draw his knives i' the war. Well, I will
find him;
For being now a favourer to the Briton,
No more a Briton, I have resum'd again
The part I came in; fight I will no more,   76
But yield me to the veriest hind that shall
Once touch my shoulder. Great the slaughter is
Here made by the Roman; great the answer be
Britons must take. For me, my ransom's
death;   80
On either side I come to spend my breath,
Which neither here I'll keep nor bear agen,
But end it by some means for Imogen.

Enter two British Captains, *and* Soldiers.

First Cap. Great Jupiter be prais'd! Lucius
is taken.   84
'Tis thought the old man and his sons were
angels.
  Sec. Cap. There was a fourth man, in a silly
habit,
That gave th' affront with them.
  First Cap.   So 'tis reported;
But none of 'em can be found. Stand! who is
there?   88
  Post. A Roman,
Who had not now been drooping here, if seconds
Had answer'd him.
  Sec. Cap.   Lay hands on him; a dog!
A lag of Rome shall not return to tell   92
What crows have peck'd them here. He brags
his service
As if he were of note: bring him to the king.

Enter CYMBELINE, *attended;* BELARIUS, GUIDE-
RIUS, ARVIRAGUS, PISANIO, *and Roman Captives. The* Captains *present* POSTHUMUS *to*
CYMBELINE, *who delivers him over to a* Gaoler;
then exeunt omnes.

    SCENE IV.—*Britain. A Prison.*

    Enter POSTHUMUS *and two* Gaolers.

First Gaol. You shall not now be stol'n, you
have locks upon you;
So graze as you find pasture.
  Sec. Gaol.   Ay, or a stomach.
        [*Exeunt* Gaolers.
  Post. Most welcome, bondage! for thou art
a way,
I think, to liberty. Yet am I better   4
Than one that's sick o' the gout, since he had
rather
Groan so in perpetuity than be cur'd
By the sure physician death; who is the key
To unbar these locks. My conscience, thou art
fetter'd   8
More than my shanks and wrists: you good
gods, give me
The penitent instrument to pick that bolt;
Then, free for ever! Is't enough I am sorry?
So children temporal fathers do appease;   12
Gods are more full of mercy. Must I repent?
I cannot do it better than in gyves,
Desir'd more than constrain'd; to satisfy,
If of my freedom 'tis the main part, take   16

No stricter render of me than my all.
I know you are more clement than vile men,
Who of their broken debtors take a third,
A sixth, a tenth, letting them thrive again   20
On their abatement: that's not my desire;
For Imogen's dear life take mine; and though
'Tis not so dear, yet 'tis a life; you coin'd it;
'Tween man and man they weigh not every
stamp;   24
Though light, take pieces for the figure's sake:
You rather mine, being yours; and so great
powers,
If you will take this audit, take this life,
And cancel these cold bonds. O Imogen!   28
I'll speak to thee in silence.   [*Sleeps.*

Solemn music. Enter as in an apparition SICILIUS
LEONATUS, *father to* POSTHUMUS, *an old man,
attired like a warrior; leading in his hand an
ancient matron, his wife, and mother to* POST-
HUMUS, *with music before them. Then, after
other music, follow the two young* LEONATI,
brothers to POSTHUMUS, *with wounds, as they
died in the wars. They circle* POSTHUMUS *round,
as he lies sleeping.*

  Sici. No more, thou thunder-master, show
    Thy spite on mortal flies:
  With Mars fall out, with Juno chide,   32
    That thy adulteries
      Rates and revenges.
  Hath my poor boy done aught but well,
    Whose face I never saw?   36
  I died whilst in the womb he stay'd
    Attending nature's law:
  Whose father then—as men report,
    Thou orphans' father art—   40
  Thou shouldst have been, and shielded
    him
    From this earth-vexing smart.

  Moth. Lucina lent not me her aid,
    But took me in my throes;   44
  That from me was Posthumus ript,
    Came crying 'mongst his foes,
    A thing of pity!

  Sici. Great nature, like his ancestry,   48
    Moulded the stuff so fair,
  That he deserv'd the praise o' the world,
    As great Silicius' heir.

  First Bro. When once he was mature for man,
    In Britain where was he   53
  That could stand up his parallel,
    Or fruitful object be
  In eye of Imogen, that best   56
    Could deem his dignity?

  Moth. With marriage wherefore was he mock'd,
    To be exil'd, and thrown
  From Leonati's seat, and cast   60
    From her his dearest one,
    Sweet Imogen?

  Sici. Why did you suffer Iachimo,
    Slight thing of Italy,   64

To taint his nobler heart and brain
  With needless jealousy;
And to become the geck and scorn
  O' the other's villany?   68

Sec. Bro. For this from stiller seats we came,
  Our parents and us twain,
That striking in our country's cause
  Fell bravely and were slain;   72
Our fealty and Tenantius' right
  With honour to maintain.

First Bro. Like hardiment Posthumus hath
  To Cymbeline perform'd: 76
Then Jupiter, thou king of gods,
  Why hast thou thus adjourn'd
The graces for his merits due,
  Being all to dolours turn'd?   80

Sici. Thy crystal window ope; look out;
  No longer exercise
Upon a valiant race thy harsh
  And potent injuries.   84

Moth. Since, Jupiter, our son is good,
  Take off his miseries.

Sici. Peep through thy marble mansion; help!
  Or we poor ghosts will cry   88
To the shining synod of the rest
  Against thy deity.

Both Bro. Help, Jupiter! or we appeal,
  And from thy justice fly.   92

Jupiter descends in thunder and lightning, sitting upon an eagle: he throws a thunderbolt. The Ghosts fall on their knees.

Jup. No more, you petty spirits of region low,
  Offend our hearing; hush! How dare you
    ghosts
Accuse the thunderer, whose bolt, you know,
Sky-planted, batters all rebelling coasts? 96
Poor shadows of Elysium, hence; and rest
Upon your never-withering banks of flowers:
Be not with mortal accidents opprest;
  No care of yours it is; you know 'tis ours. 100
Whom best I love I cross; to make my gift,
The more delay'd, delighted. Be content;
Your low-laid son our godhead will uplift:
His comforts thrive, his trials well are spent.
Our Jovial star reign'd at his birth, and in 105
  Our temple was he married. Rise, and fade!
He shall be lord of Lady Imogen,
And happier much by his affliction made. 108
This tablet lay upon his breast, wherein
Our pleasure his full fortune doth confine;
And so, away: no further with your din
Express impatience, lest you stir up mine. 112
Mount, eagle, to my palace crystalline.
                    [Ascends.
Sici. He came in thunder; his celestial breath
Was sulphurous to smell; the holy eagle
Stoop'd, as to foot us; his ascension is 116
More sweet than our bless'd fields; his royal bird
Prunes the immortal wing and cloys his beak,

As when his god is pleas'd.
  All.   Thanks, Jupiter!
Sici. The marble pavement closes; he is
  enter'd   120
His radiant roof. Away! and, to be blest,
Let us with care perform his great behest.
                [The Ghosts vanish.
Post. [*Awaking.*] Sleep, thou hast been a
  grandsire, and begot
A father to me; and thou hast created 124
A mother and two brothers. But—O scorn!—
Gone! they went hence so soon as they were
  born:
And so I am awake. Poor wretches, that depend
On greatness' favour dream as I have done; 128
Wake, and find nothing. But, alas! I swerve:
Many dream not to find, neither deserve,
And yet are steep'd in favours; so am I,
That have this golden chance and know not
  why.   132
What fairies haunt this ground? A book? O
  rare one!
Be not, as is our fangled world, a garment
Nobler than that it covers: let thy effects
So follow, to be most unlike our courtiers, 136
As good as promise.
  Whenas a lion's whelp shall, to himself unknown, without seeking find, and be embraced by a piece of tender air; and when from a stately cedar shall be lopped branches, which, being dead many years, shall after revive, be jointed to the old stock, and freshly grow, then shall Posthumus end his miseries, Britain be fortunate, and flourish in peace and plenty.
'Tis still a dream, or else such stuff as madmen
Tongue and brain not; either both or nothing;
Or senseless speaking, or a speaking such 148
As sense cannot untie. Be what it is,
The action of my life is like it, which
I'll keep, if but for sympathy.

Re-enter Gaolers.

First Gaol. Come, sir, are you ready for
  death?   153
Post. Over-roasted rather; ready long ago.
First Gaol. Hanging is the word, sir: if you
be ready for that, you are well cooked.
Post. So, if I prove a good repast to the
spectators, the dish pays the shot.   158
First Gaol. A heavy reckoning for you, sir;
but the comfort is, you shall be called to no
more payments, fear no more tavern-bills, which
are often the sadness of parting, as the procuring of mirth. You come in faint for want of
meat, depart reeling with too much drink, sorry
that you have paid too much; and sorry that
you are paid too much; purse and brain both
empty; the brain the heavier for being too light,
the purse too light, being drawn of heaviness:
of this contradiction you shall now be quit. O!
the charity of a penny cord! it sums up thousands in a trice: you have no true debitor and
creditor but it; of what's past, is, and to come,
the discharge. Your neck, sir, is pen, book and
counters; so the acquittance follows.   174
Post. I am merrier to die than thou art to live.

First Gaol. Indeed, sir, he that sleeps feels not the toothache; but a man that were to sleep your sleep, and a hangman to help him to bed, I think he would change places with his officer; for look you, sir, you know not which way you shall go.   181

Post. Yes, indeed do I, fellow.

First Gaol. Your death has eyes in 's head, then; I have not seen him so pictured: you must either be directed by some that take upon them to know, or take upon yourself that which I am sure you do not know, or jump the after inquiry on your own peril: and how you shall speed in your journey's end, I think you'll never return to tell one.   190

Post. I tell thee, fellow, there are none want eyes to direct them the way I am going but such as wink and will not use them.

First Gaol. What an infinite mock is this, that a man should have the best use of eyes to see the way of blindness! I am sure hanging's the way of winking.   197

Enter a Messenger.

Mess. Knock off his manacles; bring your prisoner to the king.

Post. Thou bring'st good news; I am called to be made free.   201

First Gaol. I'll be hang'd, then.

Post. Thou shalt be then freer than a gaoler; no bolts for the dead.   204

[*Exeunt all but first* Gaoler.

First Gaol. Unless a man would marry a gallows and beget young gibbets, I never saw one so prone. Yet, on my conscience, there are verier knaves desire to live, for all he be a Roman; and there be some of them too, that die against their wills; so should I, if I were one. I would we were all of one mind, and one mind good; O! there were desolation of gaolers and gallowses. I speak against my present profit, but my wish hath a preferment in't.

[*Exit.*

SCENE V.—CYMBELINE'S *Tent.*

Enter CYMBELINE, BELARIUS, GUIDERIUS, ARVIRAGUS, PISANIO, Lords, Officers, *and* Attendants.

Cym. Stand by my side, you whom the gods have made
Preservers of my throne. Woe is my heart
That the poor soldier that so richly fought,
Whose rags sham'd gilded arms, whose naked breast   4
Stepp'd before targes of proof, cannot be found!
He shall be happy that can find him, if
Our grace can make him so.

Bel.   I never saw
Such noble fury in so poor a thing;   8
Such precious deeds in one that promis'd nought
But beggary and poor looks.

Cym.   No tidings of him?

Pis. He hath been search'd among the dead and living,
But no trace of him.

Cym.   To my grief, I am   12
The heir of his reward; which I will add
[*To* BELARIUS, GUIDERIUS, *and* ARVIRAGUS.
To you, the liver, heart, and brain of Britain,
By whom, I grant, she lives. 'Tis now the time
To ask of whence you are: report it.

Bel.   Sir,   16
In Cambria are we born, and gentlemen:
Further to boast were neither true nor modest,
Unless I add, we are honest.

Cym.   Bow your knees.
Arise, my knights o' the battle: I create you 20
Companions to our person, and will fit you
With dignities becoming your estates.

Enter CORNELIUS and Ladies.

There's business in these faces. Why so sadly
Greet you our victory? you look like Romans, 24
And not o' the court of Britain.

Cor.   Hail, great king!
To sour your happiness, I must report
The queen is dead.

Cym.   Whom worse than a physician
Would this report become? But I consider,   28
By medicine life may be prolong'd, yet death
Will seize the doctor too. How ended she?

Cor. With horror, madly dying, like her life;
Which, being cruel to the world, concluded   32
Most cruel to herself. What she confess'd
I will report, so please you: these her women
Can trip me if I err; who with wet cheeks
Were present when she finish'd.

Cym.   Prithee, say. 36

Cor. First, she confess'd she never lov'd you, only
Affected greatness got by you, not you;
Married your royalty, was wife to your place;
Abhorr'd your person.

Cym.   She alone knew this; 40
And, but she spoke it dying, I would not
Believe her lips in opening it. Proceed.

Cor. Your daughter, whom she bore in hand to love
With such integrity, she did confess   44
Was as a scorpion to her sight; whose life,
But that her flight prevented it, she had
Ta'en off by poison.

Cym.   O most delicate fiend!
Who is 't can read a woman? Is there more?   48

Cor. More, sir, and worse. She did confess she had
For you a mortal mineral; which, being took,
Should by the minute feed on life, and ling'ring,
By inches waste you; in which time she purpos'd,   52
By watching, weeping, tendance, kissing, to
O'ercome you with her show; yea, and in time—
When she had fitted you with her craft—to work
Her son into the adoption of the crown;   56
But failing of her end by his strange absence,
Grew shameless-desperate; open'd, in despite
Of heaven and men, her purposes; repented
The evils she hatch'd were not effected: so, 60
Despairing died.

Cym.   Heard you all this, her women?

First Lady. We did, so please your highness.
Cym.   Mine eyes
Were not in fault, for she was beautiful;
Mine ears, that heard her flattery; nor my
heart,   64
That thought her like her seeming: it had been
vicious
To have mistrusted her: yet, O my daughter!
That it was folly in me, thou mayst say,
And prove it in thy feeling. Heaven mend all!

Enter LUCIUS, IACHIMO, *the* Soothsayer, *and
other Roman Prisoners, guarded:* POSTHUMUS
behind, and IMOGEN.

Thou com'st not, Caius, now for tribute; that 69
The Britons have raz'd out, though with the
loss
Of many a bold one; whose kinsmen have made
suit
That their good souls may be appeas'd with
slaughter   72
Of you their captives, which ourself have
granted:
So, think of your estate.
    Luc. Consider, sir, the chance of war: the
day
Was yours by accident; had it gone with us, 76
We should not, when the blood was cool, have
threaten'd
Our prisoners with the sword. But since the
gods
Will have it thus, that nothing but our lives
May be call'd ransom, let it come; sufficeth, 80
A Roman with a Roman's heart can suffer;
Augustus lives to think on 't; and so much
For my peculiar care. This one thing only
I will entreat; my boy, a Briton born,   84
Let him be ransom'd; never master had
A page so kind, so duteous, diligent,
So tender over his occasions, true,
So feat, so nurse-like. Let his virtue join   88
With my request, which I'll make bold your
highness
Cannot deny; he hath done no Briton harm,
Though he have serv'd a Roman. Save him, sir,
And spare no blood beside.   92
    Cym. I have surely seen him;
His favour is familiar to me. Boy,
Thou hast look'd thyself into my grace,
And art mine own. I know not why nor where-
fore,   96
To say, 'live, boy:' ne'er thank thy master; live:
And ask of Cymbeline what boon thou wilt,
Fitting my bounty and thy state, I'll give it;
Yea, though thou do demand a prisoner, 100
The noblest ta'en.
    Imo.   I humbly thank your highness.
    Luc. I do not bid thee beg my life, good lad;
And yet I know thou wilt.
    Imo.   No, no; alack!
There's other work in hand. I see a thing 104
Bitter to me as death; your life, good master,
Must shuffle for itself.
    Luc.   The boy disdains me,
He leaves me, scorns me; briefly die their joys
That place them on the truth of girls and boys.

Why stands he so perplex'd?
    Cym.   What wouldst thou, boy? 109
I love thee more and more; think more and
more
What's best to ask. Know'st him thou look'st
on? speak;
Wilt have him live? Is he thy kin? thy friend?
    Imo. He is a Roman; no more kin to me 113
Than I to your highness; who, being born your
vassal,
Am something nearer.
    Cym.   Wherefore ey'st him so?
    Imo. I'll tell you, sir, in private, if you please
To give me hearing.
    Cym.   Ay, with all my heart, 117
And lend my best attention. What's thy name?
    Imo. Fidele, sir.
    Cym.   Thou 'rt my good youth, my page;
I'll be thy master: walk with me; speak freely.
        [CYMBELINE *and* IMOGEN *converse apart.*
    Bel. Is not this boy reviv'd from death?
    Arv.   One sand another 121
Not more resembles;—that sweet rosy lad
Who died, and was Fidele. What think you?
    Gui. The same dead thing alive.   124
    Bel. Peace, peace! see further; he eyes us
not; forbear;
Creatures may be alike; were 't he, I am sure
He would have spoke to us.
    Gui.   But we saw him dead.
    Bel. Be silent; let's see further.
    Pis.   [*Aside.*] It is my mistress: 128
Since she is living, let the time run on
To good, or bad.
        [CYMBELINE *and* IMOGEN *come forward.*
    Cym.   Come, stand thou by our side:
Make thy demand aloud.—[*To* IACHIMO.] Sir,
step you forth;
Give answer to this boy, and do it freely,   132
Or, by our greatness and the grace of it,
Which is our honour, bitter torture shall
Winnow the truth from falsehood. On, speak
to him.
    Imo. My boon is, that this gentleman may
render   136
Of whom he had this ring.
    Post.   [*Aside.*] What's that to him?
    Cym. That diamond upon your finger, say
How came it yours?
    Iach. Thou'lt torture me to leave unspoken
that   140
Which, to be spoke, would torture thee.
    Cym.   How! me?
    Iach. I am glad to be constrain'd to utter
that
Which torments me to conceal. By villany
I got this ring; 'twas Leonatus' jewel,   144
Whom thou didst banish, and—which more
may grieve thee,
As it doth me—a nobler sir ne'er liv'd
'Twixt sky and ground. Wilt thou hear more,
my lord?
    Cym. All that belongs to this.
    Iach.   That paragon, thy daughter,—
For whom my heart drops blood, and my false
spirits
                                            149

Quail to remember,—Give me leave; I faint.
  Cym. My daughter! what of her? Renew
    thy strength;
I had rather thou shouldst live while nature
    will   152
Than die ere I hear more. Strive, man, and
    speak.
  Iach. Upon a time,—unhappy was the clock
That struck the hour!—it was in Rome,—
    accurs'd
The mansion where!—'twas at a feast—O,
    would   156
Our viands had been poison'd, or at least
Those which I heav'd to head!—the good Post-
    humus,—
What should I say? he was too good to be
Where ill men were; and was the best of all   160
Amongst the rar'st of good ones;—sitting sadly
Hearing us praise our loves of Italy
For beauty that made barren the swell'd boast
Of him that best could speak; for feature
    laming   164
The shrine of Venus, or straight-pight Minerva,
Postures beyond brief nature; for condition,
A shop of all the qualities that man
Loves woman for; besides that hook of wiving,
Fairness which strikes the eye.
  Cym.   I stand on fire. 169
Come to the matter.
  Iach.   All too soon I shall,
Unless thou wouldst grieve quickly. This Post-
    humus—
Most like a noble lord in love, and one   172
That had a royal lover—took his hint;
And, not dispraising whom we prais'd,—therein
He was as calm as virtue,—he began
His mistress' picture; which by his tongue being
    made,   176
And then a mind put in't, either our brags
Were crack'd of kitchen trulls, or his descrip-
    tion
Prov'd us unspeaking sots.
  Cym.   Nay, nay, to the purpose.
  Iach. Your daughter's chastity, there it be-
    gins.   180
He spake of her as Dian had hot dreams,
And she alone were cold; whereat I, wretch,
Made scruple of his praise, and wager'd with
    him
Pieces of gold 'gainst this, which then he wore
Upon his honour'd finger, to attain   185
In suit the place of his bed, and win this ring
By hers and mine adultery. He, true knight,
No lesser of her honour confident   188
Than I did truly find her, stakes this ring;
And would so, had it been a carbuncle
Of Phœbus' wheel; and might so safely, had it
Been all the worth of 's car. Away to Britain
Post I in this design. Well may you, sir,   193
Remember me at court, where I was taught
Of your chaste daughter the wide difference
'Twixt amorous and villanous. Being thus
    quench'd   196
Of hope, not longing, mine Italian brain
'Gan in your duller Britain operate
Most vilely; for my vantage, excellent;

And, to be brief, my practice so prevail'd,   200
That I return'd with simular proof enough
To make the noble Leonatus mad,
By wounding his belief in her renown
With token thus, and thus; averring notes 204
Of chamber-hanging, pictures, this her brace-
    let;—
Oh cunning! how I got it!—nay, some marks
Of secret on her person, that he could not
But think her bond of chastity quite crack'd, 208
I having ta'en the forfeit. Whereupon,—
Methinks I see him now,—
  Post. [*Coming forward.*] Ay, so thou dost,
Italian fiend!—Ay me, most credulous fool,
Egregious murderer, thief, any thing   212
That's due to all the villains past, in being,
To come. O! give me cord, or knife, or poison,
Some upright justicer. Thou king, send out
For torturers ingenious; it is I   216
That all the abhorred things o' the earth amend
By being worse than they. I am Posthumus,
That kill'd thy daughter; villain-like, I lie;
That caus'd a lesser villain than myself,   220
A sacrilegious thief, to do't; the temple
Of virtue was she; yea, and she herself.
Spit, and throw stones, cast mire upon me, set
The dogs o' the street to bay me; every villain
Be call'd Posthumus Leonatus; and   225
Be villany less than 'twas! O Imogen!
My queen, my life, my wife! O Imogen,
Imogen, Imogen!
  Imo.   Peace, my lord! hear, hear!
  Post. Shall's have a play of this? Thou scorn-
    ful page,   229
There lie thy part.   [*Striking her: she falls.*
  Pis.   O, gentlemen, help!
Mine, and your mistress! O! my Lord Posthu-
    mus,
You ne'er kill'd Imogen till now. Help, help!
Mine honour'd lady!
  Cym.   Does the world go round? 233
  Post. How come these staggers on me?
  Pis.   Wake, my mistress!
  Cym. If this be so, the gods do mean to strike
    me
To death with mortal joy.
  Pis.   How fares my mistress? 236
  Imo. O! get thee from my sight:
Thou gav'st me poison: dangerous fellow,
    hence!
Breathe not where princes are.
  Cym.   The tune of Imogen!
  Pis. Lady,   240
The gods throw stones of sulphur on me, if
That box I gave you was not thought by me
A precious thing: I had it from the queen.
  Cym. New matter still?
  Imo.   It poison'd me.
  Cor.   O gods! 244
I left out one thing which the queen confess'd,
Which must approve thee honest: 'If Pisanio
Have,' said she, 'given his mistress that con-
    fection
Which I gave him for cordial, she is serv'd 248
As I would serve a rat.'
  Cym.   What's this, Cornelius?

Cor. The queen, sir, very oft importun'd me
To temper poisons for her, still pretending
The satisfaction of her knowledge only   252
In killing creatures vile, as cats and dogs,
Of no esteem; I, dreading that her purpose
Was of more danger, did compound for her
A certain stuff, which, being ta'en, would cease
The present power of life, but in short time 257
All offices of nature should again
Do their due functions. Have you ta'en of it?
Imo. Most like I did, for I was dead.
Bel.   My boys, 260
There was our error.
Gui.   This is, sure, Fidele.
Imo. Why did you throw your wedded lady
from you?
Think that you are upon a rock; and now
Throw me again.   [*Embracing him.*
Post. Hang there like fruit, my soul,
Till the tree die!
Cym.   How now, my flesh, my child!
What, mak'st thou me a dullard in this act?
Wilt thou not speak to me?
Imo.   [*Kneeling.*]   Your blessing, sir.
Bel. [*To* GUIDERIUS *and* ARVIRAGUS.] Though
you did love this youth, I blame ye not;
You had a motive for't.
Cym.   My tears that fall 269
Prove holy water on thee! Imogen,
Thy mother's dead.
Imo.   I am sorry for't, my lord.
Cym. O, she was naught; and long of her it
was   272
That we meet here so strangely; but her son
Is gone, we know not how, nor where.
Pis.   My lord,
Now fear is from me, I'll speak troth. Lord
Cloten,
Upon my lady's missing, came to me   276
With his sword drawn, foam'd at the mouth,
and swore
If I discover'd not which way she was gone,
It was my instant death. By accident,
I had a feigned letter of my master's   280
Then in my pocket, which directed him
To seek her on the mountains near to Milford;
Where, in a frenzy, in my master's garments,
Which he enforc'd from me, away he posts 284
With unchaste purpose and with oath to violate
My lady's honour; what became of him
I further know not.
Gui.   Let me end the story:
I slew him there.
Cym.   Marry, the gods forfend! 288
I would not thy good deeds should from my lips
Pluck a hard sentence: prithee, valiant youth,
Deny't again.
Gui. I have spoke it, and I did it.
Cym. He was a prince.   292
Gui. A most incivil one. The wrongs he did me
Were nothing prince-like; for he did provoke
me
With language that would make me spurn the
sea
If it could so roar to me. I cut off 's head; 296
And am right glad he is not standing here

To tell this tale of mine.
Cym.   I am sorry for thee:
By thine own tongue thou art condemn'd, and
must
Endure our law. Thou'rt dead.
Imo.   That headless man 300
I thought had been my lord.
Cym.   Bind the offender,
And take him from our presence.
Bel.   Stay, sir king:
This man is better than the man he slew,
As well descended as thyself; and hath   304
More of thee merited than a band of Clotens
Had ever scar for. [*To the* Guard.] Let his
arms alone;
They were not born for bondage.
Cym.   Why, old soldier,
Wilt thou undo the worth thou art unpaid for,
By tasting of our wrath? How of descent 309
As good as we?
Arv.   In that he spake too far.
Cym. And thou shalt die for't.
Bel.   We will die all three:
But I will prove that two on 's are as good 312
As I have given out him. My sons, I must
For mine own part unfold a dangerous speech,
Though, haply, well for you.
Arv.   Your danger's ours.
Gui. And our good his.
Bel.   Have at it, then, by leave. 316
Thou hadst, great king, a subject who was call'd
Belarius.
Cym. What of him? he is
A banish'd traitor.
Bel.   He it is that hath
Assum'd this age: indeed, a banish'd man; 320
I know not how a traitor.
Cym.   Take him hence:
The whole world shall not save him.
Bel.   Not too hot:
First pay me for the nursing of thy sons;
And let it be confiscate all so soon   324
As I have receiv'd it.
Cym.   Nursing of my sons!
Bel. I am too blunt and saucy; here's my
knee:
Ere I arise I will prefer my sons;
Then spare not the old father. Mighty sir, 328
These two young gentlemen, that call me father,
And think they are my sons, are none of mine;
They are the issue of your loins, my liege,
And blood of your begetting.
Cym.   How! my issue! 332
Bel. So sure as you your father's. I, old
Morgan,
Am that Belarius whom you sometime banish'd:
Your pleasure was my mere offence, my punish-
ment
Itself, and all my treason; that I suffer'd 336
Was all the harm I did. These gentle princes—
For such and so they are—these twenty years
Have I train'd up; those arts they have as I
Could put into them; my breeding was, sir, as
Your highness knows. Their nurse, Euriphile,
Whom for the theft I wedded, stole these children
Upon my banishment: I mov'd her to't,

Having receiv'd the punishment before, 344
For that which I did then; beaten for loyalty
Excited me to treason. Their dear loss,
The more of you 'twas felt the more it shap'd
Unto my end of stealing them. But, gracious
   sir, 348
Here are your sons again; and I must lose
Two of the sweet'st companions in the world.
The benediction of these covering heavens
Fall on their heads like dew! for they are
   worthy 352
To inlay heaven with stars.
   Cym.   Thou weep'st, and speak'st.
The service that you three have done is more
Unlike than this thou tell'st. I lost my children:
If these be they, I know not how to wish 356
A pair of worthier sons.
   Bel.   Be pleas'd awhile.
This gentleman, whom I call Polydore,
Most worthy prince, as yours, is true Guiderius;
This gentleman, my Cadwal, Arviragus, 360
Your younger princely son; he, sir, was lapp'd
In a most curious mantle, wrought by the hand
Of his queen mother, which, for more proba-
   tion,
I can with ease produce.
   Cym.   Guiderius had 364
Upon his neck a mole, a sanguine star;
It was a mark of wonder.
   Bel.   This is he,
Who hath upon him still that natural stamp.
It was wise nature's end in the donation, 368
To be his evidence now.
   Cym.   O! what, am I
A mother to the birth of three? Ne'er mother
Rejoic'd deliverance more. Blest pray you be,
That, after this strange starting from your orbs,
You may reign in them now. O Imogen! 373
Thou hast lost by this a kingdom.
   Imo.   No, my lord;
I have got two worlds by 't. O my gentle
   brothers!
Have we thus met? O, never say hereafter 376
But I am truest speaker: you call'd me brother,
When I was but your sister; I you brothers
When ye were so indeed.
   Cym.   Did you e'er meet?
   Arv. Ay, my good lord.
   Gui.   And at first meeting lov'd; 380
Continu'd so, until we thought he died.
   Cor. By the queen's dram she swallow'd.
   Cym.   O rare instinct!
When shall I hear all through? This fierce
   abridgment
Hath to it circumstantial branches, which 384
Distinction should be rich in. Where? how
   liv'd you?
And when came you to serve our Roman captive?
How parted with your brothers? how first met
   them?
Why fled you from the court, and whither?
   These, 388
And your three motives to the battle, with
I know not how much more, should be de-
   manded,
And all the other by-dependances,

From chance to chance, but nor the time nor
   place 392
Will serve our long inter'gatories. See,
Posthumus anchors upon Imogen,
And she, like harmless lightning, throws her eye
On him, her brothers, me, her master, hitting
Each object with a joy: the counterchange 397
Is severally in all. Let's quit this ground,
[*To* BELARIUS.] Thou art my brother; so we'll
   hold thee ever. 400
   Imo. You are my father too; and did relieve
   me,
To see this gracious season.
   Cym.   All o'erjoy'd
Save these in bonds; let them be joyful too,
For they shall taste our comfort.
   Imo.   My good master, 404
I will yet do you service.
   Luc.   Happy be you!
   Cym. The forlorn soldier, that so nobly
   fought
He would have well becom'd this place and
   grac'd
The thankings of a king.
   Post.   I am, sir, 408
The soldier that did company these three
In poor beseeming; 'twas a fitment for
The purpose I then follow'd. That I was he,
Speak, Iachimo; I had you down and might 412
Have made you finish.
   Iach.   [*Kneeling.*] I am down again;
But now my heavy conscience sinks my knee,
As then your force did. Take that life, beseech
   you,
Which I so often owe, but your ring first, 416
And here the bracelet of the truest princess
That ever swore her faith.
   Post.   Kneel not to me:
The power that I have on you is to spare you;
The malice towards you to forgive you. Live,
And deal with others better.
   Cym.   Nobly doom'd: 421
We'll learn our freeness of a son-in-law;
Pardon 's the word to all.
   Arv.   You holp us, sir,
As you did mean indeed to be our brother; 424
Joy'd are we that you are.
   Post. Your servant, princes. Good my lord
   of Rome,
Call forth your soothsayer. As I slept, me-
   thought
Great Jupiter, upon his eagle back'd, 428
Appear'd to me, with other spritely shows
Of mine own kindred: when I wak'd, I found
This label on my bosom; whose containing
Is so from sense in hardness that I can 432
Make no collection of it; let him show
His skill in the construction.
   Luc.   Philarmonus!
   Sooth. Here, my good lord.
   Luc.   Read, and declare the meaning.

Sooth. Whenas a lion's whelp shall, to him-
self unknown, without seeking find, and be em-
braced by a piece of tender air; and when from

a stately cedar shall be lopped branches, which,
being dead many years, shall after revive, be
jointed to the old stock, and freshly grow: then
shall Posthumus end his miseries, Britain be
fortunate, and flourish in peace and plenty.

Thou, Leonatus, art the lion's whelp;   444
The fit and apt construction of thy name,
Being Leo-natus, doth import so much.
[*To* CYMBELINE.] The piece of tender air, thy
    virtuous daughter,
Which we call *mollis aer;* and *mollis aer*   448
We term it *mulier;* which *mulier*, I divine,
Is this most constant wife; who, even now,
Answering the letter of the oracle,
Unknown to you, [*To* POSTHUMUS.] unsought,
    were clipp'd about   452
With this most tender air.
    Cym.   This hath some seeming.
    Sooth. The lofty cedar, royal Cymbeline,
Personates thee, and thy lopp'd branches point
Thy two sons forth; who, by Belarius stolen,   456
For many years thought dead, are now reviv'd,
To the majestic cedar join'd, whose issue
Promises Britain peace and plenty.
    Cym.   Well;
My peace we will begin. And, Caius Lucius,   460
Although the victor, we submit to Cæsar,
And to the Roman empire; promising
To pay our wonted tribute, from the which

We were dissuaded by our wicked queen;   464
Whom heavens—in justice both on her and
    hers—
Have laid most heavy hand.
    Soth. The fingers of the powers above do
    tune
The harmony of this peace. The vision   468
Which I made known to Lucius ere the stroke
Of this yet scarce-cold battle, at this instant
Is full accomplish'd; for the Roman eagle,
From south to west on wing soaring aloft,   472
Lessen'd herself, and in the beams o' the sun
So vanish'd: which foreshow'd our princely
    eagle,
The imperial Cæsar, should again unite
His favour with the radiant Cymbeline,   476
Which shines here in the west.
    Cym.   Laud we the gods;
And let our crooked smokes climb to their
    nostrils
From our bless'd altars. Publish we this peace
To all our subjects. Set we forward: let   480
A Roman and a British ensign wave
Friendly together; so through Lud's town
    march:
And in the temple of great Jupiter
Our peace we'll ratify; seal it with feasts.   484
Set on there. Never was a war did cease,
Ere bloody hands were wash'd, with such a
    peace.   [*Exeunt.*

PERICLES
PRINCE OF TYRE

DRAMATIS PERSONÆ

ANTIOCHUS, King of Antioch.
PERICLES, Prince of Tyre.
HELICANUS, } two Lords of Tyre.
ESCANES,
SIMONIDES, King of Pentapolis.
CLEON, Governor of Tarsus.
LYSIMACHUS, Governor of Mitylene.
CERIMON, a Lord of Ephesus.
THALIARD, a Lord of Antioch.
PHILEMON, Servant to Cerimon.
LEONINE, Servant to Dionyza.
Marshal.

A Pandar.
BOULT, his Servant.

The Daughter of Antiochus.
DIONYZA, Wife to Cleon.
THAISA, Daughter to Simonides.
MARINA, Daughter to Pericles and Thaisa.
LYCHORIDA, Nurse to Marina.
A Bawd.

Lords, Ladies, Knights, Gentlemen, Sailors, Pirates,
Fishermen, and Messengers.

DIANA.

GOWER, as Chorus.

SCENE.—*Dispersedly in various Countries.*

ACT I

Before the Palace of Antioch.

Enter GOWER.

To sing a song that old was sung,
From ashes ancient Gower is come,
Assuming man's infirmities,
To glad your ear, and please your eyes.   4
It hath been sung at festivals,
On ember-eves, and holy-ales;
And lords and ladies in their lives
Have read it for restoratives: 8
The purchase is to make men glorious;
Et bonum quo antiquius, eo melius.
If you, born in these latter times,
When wit's more ripe, accept my rimes,   12
And that to hear an old man sing
May to your wishes pleasure bring,
I life would wish, and that I might
Waste it for you like taper-light.   16
This Antioch, then, Antiochus the Great
Built up, this city, for his chiefest seat,
The fairest in all Syria,
I tell you what mine authors say: 20
This king unto him took a fere,
Who died and left a female heir,
So buxom, blithe, and full of face
As heaven had lent her all his grace;   24
With whom the father liking took,
And her to incest did provoke.
Bad child, worse father! to entice his own
To evil should be done by none.   28
By custom what they did begin
Was with long use account no sin.
The beauty of this sinful dame
Made many princes thither frame,   32
To seek her as a bed-fellow,
In marriage-pleasures play-fellow:

Which to prevent, he made a law,
To keep her still, and men in awe,   36
That whoso ask'd her for his wife,
His riddle told not, lost his life:
So for her many a wight did die,
As yon grim looks do testify.   40
What now ensues, to the judgment of your
eye
I give, my cause who best can justify. [*Exit.*

SCENE I.—*Antioch. A Room in the Palace.*

Enter ANTIOCHUS, PERICLES, *and* Attendants.

Ant. Young Prince of Tyre, you have at large
receiv'd
The danger of the task you undertake.
Per. I have, Antiochus, and, with a soul
Embolden'd with the glory of her praise,   4
Think death no hazard in this enterprise.
Ant. Bring in our daughter, clothed like a
bride,
For the embracements even of Jove himself;
At whose conception, till Lucina reign'd,   8
Nature this dowry gave, to glad her presence,
The senate-house of planets all did sit,
To knit in her their best perfections.   [*Music.*

Enter the Daughter of ANTIOCHUS.

Per. See, where she comes apparell'd like the
spring,   12
Graces her subjects, and her thoughts the king
Of every virtue gives renown to men!
Her face the book of praises, where is read
Nothing but curious pleasures, as from thence
Sorrow were ever raz'd, and testy wrath   17
Could never be her mild companion.
You gods, that made me man, and sway in love,
That hath inflam'd desire in my breast   20
To taste the fruit of yon celestial tree

Or die in the adventure, be my helps,
As I am son and servant to your will,
To compass such a boundless happiness!   24
     Ant. Prince Pericles,—
     Per. That would be son to great Antiochus.
     Ant. Before thee stands this fair Hesperides,
With golden fruit, but dangerous to be touch'd;
For death-like dragons here affright thee hard:
Her face, like heaven, enticeth thee to view
Her countless glory, which desert must gain;
And which, without desert, because thine eye   32
Presumes to reach, all thy whole heap must die.
Yon sometime famous princes, like thyself,
Drawn by report, adventurous by desire,
Tell thee with speechless tongues and semblance
     pale,   36
That without covering, save yon field of stars,
They here stand martyrs, slain in Cupid's wars;
And with dead cheeks advise thee to desist
For going on death's net, whom none resist.   40
     Per. Antiochus, I thank thee, who hath
     taught
My frail mortality to know itself,
And by those fearful objects to prepare
This body, like to them, to what I must;   44
For death remember'd should be like a mirror,
Who tells us life's but breath, to trust it error.
I'll make my will then; and as sick men do,
Who know the world, see heaven, but feeling
     woe,   48
Gripe not at earthly joys as erst they did:
So I bequeath a happy peace to you
And all good men, as every prince should do;
My riches to the earth from whence they came,
     [*To the Daughter of* ANTIOCHUS.
But my unspotted fire of love to you.   53
Thus ready for the way of life or death,
I wait the sharpest blow.
     Ant. Scorning advice, read the conclusion
     then;   56
Which read and not expounded, 'tis decreed,
As these before thee thou thyself shalt bleed.
     Daugh. Of all say'd yet, mayst thou prove
     prosperous!
Of all say'd yet, I wish thee happiness!   60
     Per. Like a bold champion, I assume the
     lists,
Nor ask advice of any other thought
But faithfulness and courage.

     I am no viper, yet I feed   64
       On mother's flesh which did me breed;
     I sought a husband, in which labour
     I found that kindness in a father.
     He's father, son, and husband mild,   68
     I mother, wife, and yet his child.
     How they may be, and yet in two,
     As you will live, resolve it you.

Sharp physic is the last: but, O you powers!   72
That give heaven countless eyes to view men's
     acts,
Why cloud they not their sights perpetually,
If this be true, which makes me pale to read it?
Fair glass of light, I lov'd you, and could still,
Were not this glorious casket stor'd with ill!   77
But I must tell you now my thoughts revolt;

For he's no man on whom perfections wait
That, knowing sin within, will touch the gate.
You're a fair viol, and your sense the strings,
Who, finger'd to make men his lawful music,
Would draw heaven down and all the gods to
     hearken;
But being play'd upon before your time,   84
Hell only danceth at so harsh a chime.
Good sooth, I care not for you.
     Ant. Prince Pericles, touch not, upon thy
     life,
For that's an article within our law,   88
As dangerous as the rest. Your time's expir'd:
Either expound now or receive your sentence.
     Per. Great king,
Few love to hear the sins they love to act;   92
'Twould braid yourself too near for me to tell it.
Who has a book of all that monarchs do,
He's more secure to keep it shut than shown;
For vice repeated is like the wandering wind,   96
Blows dust in others' eyes, to spread itself;
And yet the end of all is bought thus dear,
The breath is gone, and the sore eyes see clear
To stop the air would hurt them. The blind
     mole casts   100
Copp'd hills towards heaven, to tell the earth is
     throng'd
By man's oppression; and the poor worm doth
     die for't.
Kings are earth's gods; in vice their law's their
     will;
And if Jove stray, who dares say Jove doth ill?
It is enough you know; and it is fit,   105
What being more known grows worse, to
     smother it.
All love the womb that their first being bred,
Then give my tongue like leave to love my head.
     Ant. [*Aside.*] Heaven! that I had thy head;
     he has found the meaning: 109
But I will gloze with him. Young Prince of
     Tyre,
Though by the tenour of our strict edict,
Your exposition misinterpreting,   112
We might proceed to cancel of your days;
Yet hope, succeeding from so fair a tree
As your fair self, doth tune us otherwise:
Forty days longer we do respite you;   116
If by which time our secret be undone,
This mercy shows we'll joy in such a son:
And until then your entertain shall be
As doth befit our honour and your worth.   120
               [*Exeunt all but* PERICLES.
     Per. How courtesy would seem to cover sin,
When what is done is like a hypocrite,
The which is good in nothing but in sight!
If it be true that I interpret false,   124
Then were it certain you were not so bad
As with foul incest to abuse your soul;
Where now you're both a father and a son,
By your untimely claspings with your child,—
Which pleasure fits a husband, not a father;—
And she an eater of her mother's flesh,
By the defiling of her parent's bed;
And both like serpents are, who though they
     feed   132
On sweetest flowers, yet they poison breed.

Antioch, farewell! for wisdom sees, those men
Blush not in actions blacker than the night,
Will shun no course to keep them from the
    light.   136
One sin, I know, another doth provoke.
Murder's as near to lust as flame to smoke.
Poison and treason are the hands of sin,
Ay, and the targets, to put off the shame: 140
Then, lest my life be cropp'd to keep you clear,
By flight I'll shun the danger which I fear.
                                          [*Exit.*

Re-enter ANTIOCHUS.

Ant. He hath found the meaning, for which
    we mean
To take his head.   144
He must not live to trumpet forth my infamy,
Nor tell the world Antiochus doth sin
In such a loathed manner;
And therefore instantly this prince must die, 148
For by his fall my honour must keep high.
Who attends us there?

Enter THALIARD.

Thal.   Doth your highness call?
Ant. Thaliard,
You're of our chamber, and our mind partakes
Her private actions to your secrecy;   153
And for your faithfulness we will advance you.
Thaliard, behold, here's poison, and here's
    gold;
We hate the Prince of Tyre, and thou must kill
    him: 156
It fits thee not to ask the reason why,
Because we bid it. Say, is it done?
Thal. My lord, 'tis done.
Ant. Enough.   160

Enter a Messenger.

Let your breath cool yourself, telling your haste.
Mess. My lord, Prince Pericles is fled. [*Exit.*
Ant.   [*To* THALIARD.] As thou
Wilt live, fly after; and, as an arrow shot
From a well-experienc'd archer hits the mark
His eye doth level at, so thou ne'er return 165
Unless thou say 'Prince Pericles is dead.'
Thal. My lord,
If I can get him within my pistol's length, 168
I'll make him sure enough: so, farewell to your
    highness.
Ant. Thaliard, adieu!   [*Exit* THALIARD.
                  Till Pericles be dead,
My heart can lend no succour to my head. [*Exit.*

SCENE II.—*Tyre. A Room in the Palace.*

Enter PERICLES.

Per. [*To those without.*] Let none disturb us.—
    Why should this change of thoughts,
The sad companion, dull-ey'd melancholy,
Be my so us'd a guest, as not an hour
In the day's glorious walk or peaceful night— 4
The tomb where grief should sleep—can breed
    me quiet?
Here pleasures court mine eyes, and mine eyes
    shun them,
And danger, which I feared, is at Antioch,

Whose arm seems far too short to hit me here;
Yet neither pleasure's art can joy my spirits, 9
Nor yet the other's distance comfort me.
Then it is thus: the passions of the mind,
That have their first conception by mis-dread, 12
Have after-nourishment and life by care;
And what was first but fear what might be done,
Grows elder now and cares it be not done.
And so with me: the great Antiochus,—   16
'Gainst whom I am too little to contend,
Since he's so great can make his will his act,—
Will think me speaking, though I swear to
    silence;
Nor boots it me to say I honour him,   20
If he suspect I may dishonour him;
And what may make him blush in being known,
He'll stop the course by which it might be
    known.
With hostile forces he'll o'erspread the land, 24
And with the ostent of war will look so huge,
Amazement shall drive courage from the state,
Our men be vanquish'd ere they do resist,
And subjects punish'd that ne'er thought
    offence: 28
Which care of them, not pity of myself,—
Who am no more but as the tops of trees,
Which fence the roots they grow by and defend
    them,—   31
Make both my body pine and soul to languish,
And punish that before that he would punish.

Enter HELICANUS *and other Lords.*

First Lord. Joy and all comfort in your
    sacred breast!
Sec. Lord. And keep your mind, till you re-
    turn to us,
Peaceful and comfortable.   36
Hel. Peace, peace! and give experience
    tongue.
They do abuse the king that flatter him;
For flattery is the bellows blows up sin;
The thing the which is flatter'd, but a spark, 40
To which that blast gives heat and stronger
    glowing;
Whereas reproof, obedient and in order,
Fits kings, as they are men, for they may err:
When Signior Sooth here does proclaim a peace,
He flatters you, makes war upon your life. 45
Prince, pardon me, or strike me, if you please;
I cannot be much lower than my knees.
Per. All leave us else; but let your cares o'er-
    look   48
What shipping and what lading's in our haven,
And then return to us.   [*Exeunt* Lords.
                  Helicanus, thou
Hast mov'd us; what seest thou in our looks?
Hel. An angry brow, dread lord.   52
Per. If there be such a dart in prince's frowns,
How durst thy tongue move anger to our face?
Hel. How dare the plants look up to heaven,
    from whence
They have their nourishment?
Per.   Thou know'st I have power 56
To take thy life from thee.
Hel. [*Kneeling.*] I have ground the axe my-
    self;

Do you but strike the blow.
Per.   Rise, prithee, rise;
Sit down; thou art no flatterer: 60
I thank thee for it; and heaven forbid
That kings should let their ears hear their faults
          hid!
Fit counsellor and servant for a prince,
Who by thy wisdom mak'st a prince thy ser-
          vant,   64
What wouldst thou have me do?
Hel.   To bear with patience
Such griefs as you yourself do lay upon your-
          self.
Per. Thou speak'st like a physician, Heli-
          canus,
That minister'st a potion unto me   68
That thou wouldst tremble to receive thyself.
Attend me then: I went to Antioch,
Where as thou know'st, against the face of
          death
I sought the purchase of a glorious beauty, 72
From whence an issue I might propagate
Are arms to princes and bring joys to subjects.
Her face was to mine eye beyond all wonder;
The rest, hark in thine ear, as black as incest;
Which by my knowledge found, the sinful father
Seem'd not to strike, but smooth; but thou
          know'st this,
'Tis time to fear when tyrants seem to kiss.
Which fear so grew in me, I hither fled,   80
Under the covering of a careful night,
Who seem'd my good protector; and, being
          here,
Bethought me what was past, what might suc-
          ceed.
I knew him tyrannous; and tyrants' fears 84
Decrease not, but grow faster than the years.
And should he doubt it, as no doubt he doth,
That I should open to the listening air
How many worthy princes' bloods were shed, 88
To keep his bed of blackness unlaid ope,
To lop that doubt he'll fill this land with arms,
And make pretence of wrong that I have done
          him;
When all, for mine, if I may call't, offence, 92
Must feel war's blow, who spares not innocence:
Which love to all, of which thyself art one,
Who now reprov'st me for it,—
Hel.   Alas! sir.
Per. Drew sleep out of mine eyes, blood from
          my cheeks,   96
Musings into my mind, with thousand doubts
How I might stop this tempest, ere it came;
And finding little comfort to relieve them,
I thought it princely charity to grieve them. 100
Hel. Well, my lord, since you have given me
          leave to speak,
Freely will I speak. Antiochus you fear,
And justly too, I think, you fear the tyrant,
Who either by public war or private treason 104
Will take away your life.
Therefore, my lord, go travel for a while,
Till that his rage and anger be forgot,
Or till the Destinies do cut his thread of life. 108
Your rule direct to any; if to me,
Day serves not light more faithful than I'll be.

Per. I do not doubt thy faith;
But should he wrong my liberties in my ab-
          sence?   112
Hel. We'll mingle our bloods together in the
          earth,
From whence we had our being and our birth.
Per. Tyre, I now look from thee then, and to
          Tarsus
Intend my travel, where I'll hear from thee, 116
And by whose letters I'll dispose myself.
The care I had and have of subjects' good
On thee I'll lay, whose wisdom's strength can
          bear it.
I'll take thy word for faith, not ask thine oath;
Who shuns not to break one will sure crack
          both.   121
But in our orbs we'll live so round and safe,
That time of both this truth shall ne'er convince,
Thou show'dst a subject's shine, I a true prince.
                                    [*Exeunt.*

SCENE III.—*The Same. An Antechamber in
          the Palace.*

Enter THALIARD.

Thal. So this is Tyre, and this the court.
Here must I kill King Pericles; and if I do not, I
am sure to be hanged at home: 'tis dangerous.
Well, I perceive he was a wise fellow, and had
good discretion, that, being bid to ask what he
would of the king, desired he might know none
of his secrets: now do I see he had some reason
for it; for if a king bid a man be a villain, he is
bound by the indenture of his oath to be one.
Hush! here come the lords of Tyre.   10

Enter HELICANUS, ESCANES, *and other* Lords.

Hel. You shall not need, my fellow peers of
          Tyre,
Further to question me of your king's depar-
          ture:
His seal'd commission, left in trust with me, 13
Doth speak sufficiently he's gone to travel.
Thal. [*Aside.*] How! the king gone!
Hel. If further yet you will be satisfied,   16
Why, as it were unlicens'd of your loves,
He would depart, I'll give some light unto you.
Being at Antioch—
Thal.   [*Aside.*] What from Antioch?
Hel. Royal Antiochus—on what cause I
          know not—   20
Took some displeasure at him, at least he judg'd
          so;
And doubting lest that he had err'd or sinn'd,
To show his sorrow he'd correct himself;
So puts himself unto the shipman's toil,   24
With whom each minute threatens life or death.
Thal. [*Aside.*] Well, I perceive
I shall not be hang'd now, although I would;
But since he's gone, the king it sure must
          please: 28
He 'scap'd the land, to perish at the sea.
I'll present myself. [*Aloud.*] Peace to the lords
          of Tyre.
Hel. Lord Thaliard from Antiochus is wel-
          come.

Thal. From him I come,   32
With message unto princely Pericles;
But since my landing I have understood
Your lord hath betook himself to unknown
    travels,
My message must return from whence it came.

   Hel. We have no reason to desire it,   37
Commended to our master, not to us:
Yet, ere you shall depart, this we desire,
As friends to Antioch, we may feast in Tyre.   40
                  [*Exeunt.*

SCENE IV.—*Tarsus. A Room in the Governor's House.*

Enter CLEON, DIONYZA, *and* Attendants.

   Cle. My Dionyza, shall we rest us here,
And by relating tales of others' griefs,
See if 'twill teach us to forget our own?

   Dio. That were to blow at fire in hope to
    quench it;   4
For who digs hills because they do aspire
Throws down one mountain to cast up a higher.
O my distressed lord! even such our griefs are;
Here they're but felt, and seen with mischief's
    eyes,   8
But like to groves, being topp'd, they higher
    rise.

   Cle. O Dionyza,
Who wanteth food, and will not say he wants it,
Or can conceal his hunger till he famish?   12
Our tongues and sorrows do sound deep
Our woes into the air; our eyes do weep
Till tongues fetch breath that may proclaim
    them louder;
That if heaven slumber while their creatures
    want,   16
They may awake their helps to comfort them.
I'll then discourse our woes, felt several years,
And wanting breath to speak help me with tears.

   Dio. I'll do my best, sir.   20

   Cle. This Tarsus, o'er which I have the
    government,
A city on whom plenty held full hand,
For riches strew'd herself even in the streets;
Whose towers bore heads so high they kiss'd
    the clouds,   24
And strangers ne'er beheld but wonder'd at;
Whose men and dames so jetted and adorn'd,
Like one another's glass to trim them by:
Their tables were stor'd full to glad the sight,   28
And not so much to feed on as delight;
All poverty was scorn'd, and pride so great,
The name of help grew odious to repeat.

   Dio. O! 'tis too true.   32

   Cle. But see what heaven can do! By this
    our change,
These mouths, whom but of late earth, sea, and
    air
Were all too little to content and please,
Although they gave their creatures in abun-
    dance,   36
As houses are defil'd for want of use,
They are now starv'd for want of exercise;
Those palates who, not yet two summers
    younger,

Must have inventions to delight the taste,   40
Would now be glad of bread, and beg for it;
Those mothers who, to nousle up their babes,
Thought nought too curious, are ready now
To eat those little darlings whom they lov'd.   44
So sharp are hunger's teeth, that man and wife
Draw lots who first shall die to lengthen life.
Here stands a lord, and there a lady weeping;
Here many sink, yet those which see them fall
Have scarce strength left to give them burial.   49
Is not this true?

   Dio. Our cheeks and hollow eyes do witness
    it.

   Cle. O! let those cities that of plenty's cup
And her prosperities so largely taste,   53
With their superfluous riots, hear these tears:
The misery of Tarsus may be theirs.

Enter a Lord.

   Lord. Where's the lord governor?   56

   Cle. Here.
Speak out thy sorrows which thou bring'st in
    haste,
For comfort is too far for us to expect.

   Lord. We have descried, upon our neigh-
    bouring shore,   60
A portly sail of ships make hitherward.

   Cle. I thought as much.
One sorrow never comes but brings an heir
That may succeed as his inheritor;   64
And so in ours. Some neighbouring nation,
Taking advantage of our misery,
Hath stuff'd these hollow vessels with their
    power,
To beat us down, the which are down already;
And make a conquest of unhappy me,   69
Whereas no glory's got to overcome.

   Lord. That's the least fear; for by the sem-
    blance
Of their white flags display'd, they bring us
    peace,   72
And come to us as favourers, not as foes.

   Cle. Thou speak'st like him's untutor'd to
    repeat:
Who makes the fairest show means most deceit.
But bring they what they will and what they
    can,   76
What need we fear?
The ground's the lowest and we are half way
    there.
Go tell their general we attend him here,
To know for what he comes, and whence he
    comes,   80
And what he craves.

   Lord. I go, my lord.   [*Exit.*

   Cle. Welcome is peace if he on peace consist;
If wars we are unable to resist.   84

Enter PERICLES, *with* Attendants.

   Per. Lord governor, for so we hear you are,
Let not our ships and number of our men,
Be like a beacon fir'd to amaze your eyes.
We have heard your miseries as far as Tyre,   88
And seen the desolation of your streets:
Nor come we to add sorrow to your tears,
But to relieve them of their heavy load;

And these our ships, you happily may think 92
Are like the Trojan horse was stuff'd within
With bloody veins, expecting overthrow,
Are stor'd with corn to make your needy bread,
And give them life whom hunger starv'd half
    dead.   96
    All. The gods of Greece protect you!
And we'll pray for you.
    Per.   Arise, I pray you, rise:
We do not look for reverence, but for love,
And harbourage for ourself, our ships, and men.
    Cle. The which when any shall not gratify,
Or pay you with unthankfulness in thought,
Be it our wives, our children, or ourselves,
The curse of heaven and men succeed their evils!
Till when—the which, I hope, shall ne'er be
    seen—   105
Your Grace is welcome to our town and us.
    Per. Which welcome we'll accept; feast here
    awhile,
Until our stars that frown lend us a smile. 108
                        [Exeunt.

ACT II

Enter GOWER.

Here have you seen a mighty king
His child, I wis, to incest bring;
A better prince and benign lord,
That will prove awful both in deed and word. 4
Be quiet, then, as men should be,
Till he hath pass'd necessity.
I'll show you those in troubles reign,
Losing a mite, a mountain gain.   8
The good in conversation,
To whom I give my benison,
Is still at Tarsus, where each man
Thinks all is writ he spoken can;   12
And, to remember what he does,
Build his statue to make him glorious:
But tidings to the contrary
Are brought your eyes; what need speak I?

DUMB SHOW.

Enter, from one side, PERICLES, *talking with*
CLEON; *all their Train with them. Enter, at*
another door, a Gentleman, *with a letter to*
PERICLES; *who shows the letter to* CLEON; *then*
gives the Messenger *a reward, and knights*
him. Exeunt PERICLES, CLEON, &c., *severally.*

Good Helicane hath stay'd at home,
Not to eat honey like a drone
From others' labours; for though he strive
To killen bad, keep good alive,   20
And to fulfil his prince' desire,
Sends word of all that haps in Tyre:
How Thaliard came full bent with sin
And had intent to murder him;   24
And that in Tarsus was not best
Longer for him to make his rest.
He, doing so, put forth to seas,
Where when men been, there's seldom ease;
For now the wind begins to blow;   29
Thunder above and deeps below
Make such unquiet, that the ship

Should house him safe is wrack'd and split; 32
And he, good prince, having all lost,
By waves from coast to coast is tost.
All perishen of man, of pelf,
Ne aught escapen but himself;   36
Till Fortune, tir'd with doing bad,
Threw him ashore, to give him glad;
And here he comes. What shall be next,
Pardon old Gower, this longs the text. [Exit

SCENE I.—*Pentapolis. An open Place by*
the Sea-side.

Enter PERICLES, *wet.*

    Per. Yet cease your ire, you angry stars of
    heaven!
Wind, rain, and thunder, remember, earthly man
Is but a substance that must yield to you;
And I, as fits my nature, do obey you.   4
Alas! the sea hath cast me on the rocks,
Wash'd me from shore to shore, and left me
    breath
Nothing to think on but ensuing death:
Let it suffice the greatness of your powers   8
To have bereft a prince of all his fortunes;
And having thrown him from your watery
    grave,
Here to have death in peace is all he'll crave.

Enter three Fishermen.

    First Fish. What, ho, Pilch!   12
    Sec. Fish. Ha! come and bring away the nets.
    First Fish. What, Patch-breech, I say!
    Third Fish. What say you, master?
    First Fish. Look how thou stirrest now!
come away, or I'll fetch thee with a wannion. 17
    Third Fish. Faith, master, I am thinking of
the poor men that were cast away before us
even now.   20
    First Fish. Alas! poor souls; it grieved my
heart to hear what pitiful cries they made to us
to help them, when, well-a-day, we could scarce
help ourselves.   24
    Third Fish. Nay, master, said not I as much
when I saw the porpus how he bounced and
tumbled? they say they're half fish half flesh;
a plague on them! they ne'er come but I look to
be washed. Master, I marvel how the fishes live
in the sea.   30
    First Fish. Why, as men do a-land; the great
ones eat up the little ones; I can compare our
rich misers to nothing so fitly as to a whale;
a' plays and tumbles, driving the poor fry before
him, and at last devours them all at a mouthful.
Such whales have I heard on o' the land, who
never leave gaping till they've swallowed the
whole parish, church, steeple, bells, and all. 38
    Per. [*Aside.*] A pretty moral.
    Third Fish. But master, if I had been the
sexton, I would have been that day in the
belfry.
    Sec. Fish. Why, man?   43
    Third Fish. Because he should have swal-
lowed me too; and when I had been in his
belly, I would have kept such a jangling of the
bells, that he should never have left till he cast

bells, steeple, church, and parish, up again. But
if the good King Simonides were of my mind,—

Per. [*Aside.*] Simonides!

Third Fish. We would purge the land of
these drones, that rob the bee of her honey. 52

Per. [*Aside.*] How from the finny subject of
the sea

These fishers tell the infirmities of men;

And from their watery empire recollect

All that may men approve or men detect!   56

[*Aloud.*] Peace be at your labour, honest fishermen.

Sec. Fish. Honest! good fellow, what's that?
if it be a day fits you, search out of the calendar,
and nobody look after it.   60

Per. Y' may see the sea hath cast me on your
coast.

Sec. Fish. What a drunken knave was the
sea, to cast thee in our way!

Per. A man whom both the waters and the
wind,   64

In that vast tennis-court, have made the ball

For them to play upon, entreats you pity him;

He asks of you, that never us'd to beg.

First Fish. No, friend, cannot you beg? here's
them in our country of Greece gets more with
begging than we can do with working.   70

Sec. Fish. Canst thou catch any fishes then?

Per. I never practised it.

Sec. Fish. Nay then thou wilt starve, sure;
for here's nothing to be got now-a-days unless
thou canst fish for't.

Per. What I have been I have forgot to
know,   76

But what I am want teaches me to think on;

A man throng'd up with cold; my veins are
chill,

And have no more of life than may suffice

To give my tongue that heat to ask your help;

Which if you shall refuse, when I am dead, 81

For that I am a man, pray see me buried.

First Fish. Die, quoth-a? Now, gods forbid!
I have a gown here; come, put it on; keep
thee warm. Now, afore me, a handsome fellow!
Come, thou shalt go home, and we'll have flesh
for holidays, fish for fasting-days, and moreo'er
puddings and flap-jacks; and thou shalt be
welcome.   89

Per. I thank you, sir.

First Fish. Hark you, my friend; you said
you could not beg.   92

Per. I did but crave.

Sec. Fish. But crave! Then I'll turn craver
too, and so I shall 'scape whipping.

Per. Why, are all your beggars whipped,
then?   97

Sec. Fish. O! not all, my friend, not all; for
if all your beggars were whipped, I would wish
no better office than to be beadle. But, master,
I'll go draw up the net.   101

[*Exit with Third* Fisherman.

Per. How well this honest mirth becomes
their labour!

First Fish. Hark you, sir; do you know
where ye are?   104

Per. Not well.

First Fish. Why, I'll tell you: this is called
Pentapolis, and our king the good Simonides.

Per. The good King Simonides do you call
him?   109

First Fish. Ay, sir; and he deserves to be
so called for his peaceable reign and good
government.   112

Per. He is a happy king, since he gains from
his subjects the name of good by his government.
How far is his court distant from this shore?

First Fish. Marry, sir, half a day's journey;
and I'll tell you, he hath a fair daughter, and
to-morrow is her birthday; and there are princes
and knights come from all parts of the world to
just and tourney for her love.   120

Per. Were my fortunes equal to my desires,
I could wish to make one there.

First Fish. O! sir, things must be as they
may; and what a man cannot get, he may lawfully deal for his wife's soul,—   125

Re-enter Second and Third Fishermen,
drawing up a net.

Sec. Fish. Help, master, help! here's a fish
hangs in the net, like a poor man's right in the
law; 'twill hardly come out. Ha! bots on't, 'tis
come at last, and 'tis turned to a rusty armour.

Per. An armour, friends! I pray you, let
me see it.

Thanks, Fortune, yet, that after all my crosses

Thou giv'st me somewhat to repair myself; 132

And though it was mine own, part of mine
heritage,

Which my dead father did bequeath to me,

With this strict charge, even as he left his life,

'Keep it, my Pericles, it hath been a shield 136

'Twixt me and death;'—and pointed to this
brace;

'For that it sav'd me, keep it; in like necessity—

The which the gods protect thee from!—'t may
defend thee.'

It kept where I kept, I so dearly lov'd it; 140

Till the rough seas, that spare not any man,

Took it in rage, though calm'd they have given
't again.

I thank thee for't; my shipwrack now's no ill,

Since I have here my father's gift in's will. 144

First Fish. What mean you, sir?

Per. To beg of you, kind friends, this coat
of worth,

For it was sometime target to a king;

I know it by this mark. He lov'd me dearly, 148

And for his sake I wish the having of it;

And that you'd guide me to your sovereign's
court,

Where with it I may appear a gentleman;

And if that ever my low fortunes better, 152

I'll pay your bounties; till then rest your debtor.

First Fish. Why, wilt thou tourney for the
lady?

Per. I'll show the virtue I have borne in
arms.   157

First Fish. Why, do'e take it; and the gods
give thee good on't!

Sec. Fish. Ay, but hark you, my friend; 'twas
we that made up this garment through the

rough seams of the water; there are certain
condolements, certain vails. I hope, sir, if you
thrive, you'll remember from whence you had it.
　Per. Believe it, I will.　　　　　165
By your furtherance I am cloth'd in steel;
And spite of all the rapture of the sea,
This jewel holds his biding on my arm:　　168
Unto thy value will I mount myself
Upon a courser, whose delightful steps
Shall make the gazer joy to see him tread.
Only, my friend, I yet am unprovided　172
Of a pair of bases.
　Sec. Fish. We'll sure provide; thou shalt
have my best gown to make thee a pair, and
I'll bring thee to the court myself.　　176
　Per. Then honour be but a goal to my will!
This day I'll rise, or else add ill to ill. [*Exeunt.*

SCENE II.—*The Same. A public Way. Platform
leading to the Lists. A Pavilion near it, for
the reception of the* KING, *Princess, Ladies,
Lords, &c.*

Enter SIMONIDES, THAISA, Lords, *and* Attendants.

　Sim. Are the knights ready to begin the
triumph?
　First Lord. They are, my liege;
And stay your coming to present themselves.
　Sim. Return them, we are ready; and our
daughter,　　　　　　　　　　4
In honour of whose birth these triumphs are,
Sits here, like beauty's child, whom nature gat
For men to see, and seeing wonder at.
　　　　　　　　　[*Exit a Lord.*
　Thai. It pleaseth you, my royal father, to
express　　　　　　　　　　8
My commendations great, whose merit's less.
　Sim. 'Tis fit it should be so; for princes are
A model, which heaven makes like to itself:
As jewels lose their glory if neglected,　12
So princes their renowns if not respected.
'Tis now your honour, daughter, to explain
The labour of each knight in his device.
　Thai. Which, to preserve mine honour, I'll
perform.　　　　　　　　　　16

Enter a Knight; *he passes over the stage, and
his Squire presents his shield to the Princess.*

　Sim. Who is the first that doth prefer him-
self?
　Thai. A knight of Sparta, my renowned
father;
And the device he bears upon his shield
Is a black Ethiop reaching at the sun;　20
The word, *Lux tua vita mihi.*
　Sim. He loves you well that holds his life of
you. [*The Second* Knight *passes over.*
Who is the second that presents himself?
　Thai. A prince of Macedon, my royal father;
And the device he bears upon his shield　25
Is an arm'd knight that's conquer'd by a lady;
The motto thus, in Spanish, *Piu por dulzura
que por fuerza.*
　　　　　　[*The Third* Knight *passes over.*
　Sim. And what's the third?
　Thai.　　　　The third of Antioch; 28

And his device, a wreath of chivalry;
The word, *Me pompæ provexit apex.*
　　　　　　[*The Fourth* Knight *passes over.*
　Sim. What is the fourth?
　Thai. A burning torch that's turned upside
down;　　　　　　　　　　32
The word, *Quod me alit me extinguit.*
　Sim. Which shows that beauty hath his
power and will,
Which can as well inflame as it can kill.
　　　　　　[*The Fifth* Knight *passes over.*
　Thai. The fifth, a hand environed with
clouds,　　　　　　　　　　36
Holding out gold that's by the touchstone tried;
The motto thus, *Sic spectanda fides.*
　　　[*The Sixth* Knight, PERICLES, *passes over.*
　Sim. And what's
The sixth and last, the which the knight himself
With such a graceful courtesy deliver'd?　41
　Thai. He seems to be a stranger; but his
present is
A wither'd branch, that's only green at top;
The motto, *In hac spe vivo.*　　　44
　Sim. A pretty moral;
From the dejected state wherein he is,
He hopes by you his fortune yet may flourish.
　First Lord. He had need mean better than
his outward show　　　　　　48
Can any way speak in his just commend;
For, by his rusty outside he appears
To have practis'd more the whipstock than the
lance.
　Sec. Lord. He well may be a stranger, for he
comes　　　　　　　　　　52
To an honour'd triumph strangely furnished.
　Third Lord. And on set purpose let his
armour rust
Until this day, to scour it in the dust.
　Sim. Opinion's but a fool, that makes us
scan　　　　　　　　　　56
The outward habit by the inward man.
But stay, the knights are coming; we'll with-
draw
Into the gallery.
　　　　　[*Exeunt. Great shouts, and all cry,
　　　　　　　　　'The mean knight!'*

SCENE III.—*The Same. A Hall of State.
A Banquet prepared.*

Enter SIMONIDES, THAISA, Marshal, Ladies,
Lords, Knights *from tilting, and* Attendants.

　Sim. Knights,
To say you're welcome were superfluous.
To place upon the volume of your deeds,
As in a title-page, your worth in arms,　4
Were more than you expect, or more than's fit,
Since every worth in show commends itself.
Prepare for mirth, for mirth becomes a feast:
You are princes and my guests.　　8
　Thai. But you, my knight and guest;
To whom this wreath of victory I give,
And crown you king of this day's happiness.
　Per. 'Tis more by fortune, lady, than by
merit.　　　　　　　　　　12
　Sim. Call it by what you will, the day is yours;

And here, I hope, is none that envies it.
In framing an artist art hath thus decreed,
To make some good, but others to exceed; 16
And you're her labour'd scholar. Come, queen
o' the feast,—
For, daughter, so you are,—here take your
place;
Marshal the rest, as they deserve their grace.
Knights. We are honour'd much by good
Simonides. 20
Sim. Your presence glads our days; honour
we love,
For who hates honour, hates the gods above.
Marshal. Sir, yonder is your place.
Per.   Some other is more fit.
First Knight. Contend not, sir: for we are
gentlemen 24
That neither in our hearts nor outward eyes
Envy the great nor do the low despise.
Per. You are right courteous knights.
Sim.   Sit, sir; sit.
Per. By Jove, I wonder, that is king of
thoughts, 28
These cates resist me, she but thought upon.
Thai. [*Aside.*] By Juno, that is queen of
marriage,
All viands that I eat do seem unsavoury,
Wishing him my meat. Sure, he's a gallant
gentleman. 32
Sim. He's but a country gentleman;
He has done no more than other knights have
done;
He has broken a staff or so; so let it pass.
Thai. To me he seems like diamond to glass.
Per. Yon king's to me like to my father's
picture, 37
Which tells me in that glory once he was,
Had princes sit, like stars, about his throne,
And he the sun for them to reverence. 40
None that beheld him, but like lesser lights
Did vail their crowns to his supremacy;
Where now his son's like a glow-worm in the
night,
The which hath fire in darkness, none in light:
Whereby I see that Time's the king of men; 45
He's both their parent, and he is their grave,
And gives them what he will, not what they
crave.
Sim. What, are you merry, knights? 48
First Knight. Who can be other in this royal
presence?
Sim. Here, with a cup that's stor'd unto the
brim,
As you do love, fill to your mistress' lips,
We drink this health to you.
Knights.   We thank your Grace.
Sim. Yet pause awhile; 53
Yon knight doth sit too melancholy,
As if the entertainment in our court
Had not a show might countervail his worth. 56
Note it not you, Thaisa?
Thai.   What is it
To me, my father?
Sim.   O! attend, my daughter:
Princes in this should live like gods above,
Who freely give to every one that comes 60

To honour them;
And princes not doing so are like to gnats,
Which make a sound, but kill'd are wonder'd
at.
Therefore to make his entrance more sweet, 64
Here say we drink this standing-bowl of wine to
him.
Thai. Alas! my father, it befits not me
Unto a stranger knight to be so bold;
He may my proffer take for an offence, 68
Since men take women's gifts for impudence.
Sim. How!
Do as I bid you, or you'll move me else.
Thai. [*Aside.*] Now, by the gods, he could not
please me better. 72
Sim. And further tell him, we desire to know
of him,
Of whence he is, his name, and parentage.
Thai. The king, my father, sir, has drunk to
you.
Per. I thank him. 76
Thai. Wishing it so much blood unto your
life.
Per. I thank both him and you, and pledge
him freely.
Thai. And further he desires to know of you,
Of whence you are, your name and parentage.
Per. A gentleman of Tyre, my name, Peri-
cles; 81
My education been in arts and arms;
Who, looking for adventures in the world,
Was by the rough seas reft of ships and men, 84
And after shipwrack, driven upon this shore.
Thai. He thanks your Grace; names himself
Pericles,
A gentleman of Tyre,
Who only by misfortune of the seas 88
Bereft of ships and men, cast on this shore.
Sim. Now, by the gods, I pity his misfortune,
And will awake him from his melancholy.
Come, gentlemen, we sit too long on trifles, 92
And waste the time which looks for other revels.
Even in your armours, as you are address'd,
Will very well become a soldier's dance.
I will not have excuse, with saying this 96
Loud music is too harsh for ladies' heads
Since they love men in arms as well as beds.
            [*The* Knights *dance.*
So this was well ask'd, 'twas so well perform'd.
Come, sir; 100
Here is a lady that wants breathing too:
And I have often heard, you knights of Tyre
Are excellent in making ladies trip,
And that their measures are as excellent. 104
Per. In those that practise them they are,
my lord.
Sim. O! that's as much as you would be
denied
Of your fair courtesy.
            [*The* Knights *and* Ladies *dance.*
                        Unclasp, unclasp;
Thanks, gentlemen, to all; all have done well,
[*To* PERICLES.] But you the best. Pages and
lights, to conduct 109
These knights unto their several lodgings!
            Yours, sir,

We have given order to be next our own.
Per. I am at your Grace's pleasure.   112
Sim. Princes, it is too late to talk of love,
And that's the mark I know you level at;
Therefore each one betake him to his rest;
To-morrow all for speeding do their best. 116
                                        [*Exeunt.*

SCENE IV.—*Tyre. A Room in the Governor's
                House.*

Enter HELICANUS *and* ESCANES.

Hel. No, Escanes, know this of me,
Antiochus from incest liv'd not free;
For which, the most high gods not minding
        longer
To withhold the vengeance that they had in
        store,   4
Due to this heinous capital offence,
Even in the height and pride of all his glory,
When he was seated in a chariot
Of an inestimable value, and his daughter with
        him,   8
A fire from heaven came and shrivell'd up
Their bodies, even to loathing; for they so stunk,
That all those eyes ador'd them ere their fall
Scorn now their hand should give them
        burial.   12
Esca. 'Twas very strange.
Hel.   And yet but just; for though
This king were great, his greatness was no guard
To bar heaven's shaft, but sin had his reward.
Esca. 'Tis very true.   16

        Enter two or three Lords.

First Lord. See, not a man in private con-
        ference
Or council has respect with him but he.
Sec. Lord. It shall no longer grieve without
        reproof.
Third Lord. And curs'd be he that will not
        second it.   20
First Lord. Follow me then. Lord Helicane,
        a word.
Hel. With me? and welcome. Happy day,
        my lords.
First Lord. Know that our griefs are risen
        to the top,
And now at length they overflow their banks. 24
Hel. Your griefs! for what? wrong not the
        prince you love.
First Lord. Wrong not yourself then, noble
        Helicane;
But if the prince do live, let us salute him,
Or know what ground's made happy by his
        breath.   28
If in the world he live, we'll seek him out;
If in his grave he rest, we'll find him there;
And be resolv'd he lives to govern us,
Or dead, give's cause to mourn his funeral, 32
And leaves us to our free election.
Sec. Lord. Whose death's indeed the strongest
        in our censure:
And knowing this kingdom is without a head,
Like goodly buildings left without a roof 36
Soon fall to ruin, your noble self,

That best know'st how to rule and how to reign,
We thus submit unto, our sovereign.
All. Live, noble Helicane!   40
Hel. For honour's cause forbear your suf-
        frages:
If that you love Prince Pericles, forbear.
Take I your wish, I leap into the seas,
Where's hourly trouble for a minute's ease. 44
A twelvemonth longer, let me entreat you
To forbear the absence of your king;
If in which time expir'd he not return,
I shall with aged patience bear your yoke. 48
But if I cannot win you to this love,
Go search like nobles, like noble subjects,
And in your search spend your adventurous
        worth;
Whom if you find, and win unto return, 52
You shall like diamonds sit about his crown.
First Lord. To wisdom he's a fool that will
        not yield;
And since Lord Helicane enjoineth us,
We with our travels will endeavour it. 56
Hel. Then you love us, we you, and we'll
        clasp hands:
When peers thus knit, a kingdom ever stands.
                                        [*Exeunt.*

SCENE V.—*Pentapolis. A Room in the
                Palace.*

Enter SIMONIDES, *reading a letter; the* Knights
        meet him.

First Knight. Good morrow to the good
        Simonides.
Sim. Knights, from my daughter this I let
        you know,
That for this twelvemonth she'll not undertake
A married life.   4
Her reason to herself is only known,
Which yet from her by no means can I get.
Sec. Knight. May we not get access to her,
        my lord?
Sim. Faith, by no means; she hath so strictly
        tied   8
Her to her chamber that 'tis impossible.
One twelve moons more she'll wear Diana's
        livery;
This by the eye of Cynthia hath she vow'd,
And on her virgin honour will not break it. 12
Third Knight. Though loath to bid farewell,
        we take our leaves.   [*Exeunt* Knights.
Sim. So,
They're well dispatch'd; now to my daughter's
        letter.
She tells me here, she'll wed the stranger knight,
Or never more to view nor day nor light. 17
'Tis well, mistress; your choice agrees with
        mine;
I like that well: how absolute she's in't,
Not minding whether I dislike or no!   20
Well, I do commend her choice;
And will no longer have it be delay'd.
Soft! here he comes: I must dissemble it.

        Enter PERICLES.

Per. All fortune to the good Simonides! 24

Sim. To you as much sir! I am beholding
  to you
For your sweet music this last night: I do
Protest my ears were never better fed
With such delightful pleasing harmony. 28
  Per. It is your Grace's pleasure to commend,
Not my desert.
  Sim.   Sir, you are music's master.
  Per. The worst of all her scholars, my good
  lord.
  Sim. Let me ask you one thing. 32
What do you think of my daughter, sir?
  Per. A most virtuous princess.
  Sim. And she is fair too, is she not?
  Per. As a fair day in summer; wondrous fair.
  Sim. My daughter, sir, thinks very well of
  you; 37
Ay, so well, that you must be her master,
And she will be your scholar: therefore look
  to it.
  Per. I am unworthy for her schoolmaster. 40
  Sim. She thinks not so; peruse this writing
  else.
  Per. [*Aside.*] What's here?
A letter that she loves the knight of Tyre!
'Tis the king's subtilty to have my life. 44
O! seek not to entrap me, gracious lord,
A stranger and distressed gentleman,
That never aim'd so high to love your daughter,
But bent all offices to honour her. 48
  Sim. Thou hast bewitch'd my daughter, and
  thou art
A villain.
  Per. By the gods, I have not:
Never did thought of mine levy offence; 52
Nor never did my actions yet commence
A deed might gain her love or your displeasure.
  Sim. Traitor, thou liest.
  Per.   Traitor!
  Sim.   Ay, traitor.
  Per. Even in his throat, unless it be the
  king, 56
That calls me traitor, I return the lie.
  Sim. [*Aside.*] Now, by the gods, I do applaud
  his courage.
  Per. My actions are as noble as my thoughts,
That never relish'd of a base descent. 60
I came unto your court for honour's cause,
And not to be a rebel to her state;
And he that otherwise accounts of me,
This sword shall prove he's honour's enemy. 64
  Sim. No?
Here comes my daughter, she can witness it.

Enter THAISA.

  Per. Then, as you are as virtuous as fair,
Resolve your angry father, if my tongue 68
Did e'er solicit, or my hand subscribe
To any syllable that made love to you.
  Thai. Why, sir, say if you had,
Who takes offence at that would make me
  glad? 72
  Sim. Yea, mistress, are you so peremptory?
[*Aside.*] I am glad on't, with all my heart.
I'll tame you; I'll bring you in subjection,
Will you, not having my consent, 76

Bestow your love and your affections
Upon a stranger? [*Aside.*] who, for aught I
  know,
May be, nor can I think the contrary,
As great in blood as I myself.— 80
[*Aloud.*] Therefore, hear you, mistress; either
  frame
Your will to mine; and you, sir, hear you,
Either be rul'd by me, or I will make you—
Man and wife: 84
Nay, come, your hands and lips must seal it
  too;
And being join'd, I'll thus your hopes destroy;
And for a further grief,—God give you joy!
What! are you both pleas'd?
  Thai.   Yes, if you love me, sir. 88
  Per. Even as my life, or blood that fosters it.
  Sim. What! are you both agreed?
  Thai. }
  Per. } Yes, if 't please your majesty.
  Sim. It pleaseth me so well, that I will see
  you wed; 92
Then with what haste you can get you to bed.
                                        [*Exeunt.*

ACT III

Enter GOWER.

Now sleep yslaked hath the rout;
No din but snores the house about,
Made louder by the o'er-fed breast
Of this most pompous marriage-feast. 4
The cat, with eyne of burning coal,
Now couches fore the mouse's hole;
And crickets sing at the oven's mouth,
E'er the blither for their drouth. 8
Hymen hath brought the bride to bed,
Where, by the loss of maidenhead,
A babe is moulded. Be attent;
And time that is so briefly spent 12
With your fine fancies quaintly eche;
What's dumb in show I'll plain with speech.

DUMB SHOW.

Enter, from one side, PERICLES *and* SIMONIDES,
  with Attendants; *a* Messenger *meets them,*
  kneels, and gives PERICLES *a letter:* PERICLES
  shows it to SIMONIDES; *the* Lords *kneel to*
  PERICLES. *Then enter* THAISA *with child, and*
  LYCHORIDA: SIMONIDES *shows his daughter the*
  letter; she rejoices: she and PERICLES *take leave*
  of her father, and all depart.

By many a dern and painful perch,
Of Pericles the careful search 16
By the four opposing coigns,
Which the world together joins,
Is made with all due diligence
That horse and sail and high expense, 20
Can stead the quest. At last from Tyre,—
Fame answering the most strange inquire—
To the court of King Simonides
Are letters brought, the tenour these: 24
Antiochus and his daughter dead;
The men of Tyrus on the head
Of Helicanus would set on

The crown of Tyre, but he will none: 28
The mutiny he there hastes t' oppress;
Says to 'em, if King Pericles
Come not home in twice six moons,
He, obedient to their dooms,   32
Will take the crown. The sum of this,
Brought hither to Pentapolis,
Yravished the regions round,
And every one with claps can sound,   36
'Our heir-apparent is a king!
Who dream'd, who thought of such a thing?'
Brief, he must hence depart to Tyre:
His queen, with child, makes her desire,—   40
Which now shall cross?—along to go;
Omit we all their dole and woe:
Lychorida, her nurse, she takes,
And so to sea. Their vessel shakes   44
On Neptune's billow; half the flood
Hath their keel cut: but Fortune's mood
Varies again; the grisled north
Disgorges such a tempest forth,   48
That, as a duck for life that dives,
So up and down the poor ship drives.
The lady shrieks, and well-a-near
Does fall in travail with her fear;   52
And what ensues in this fell storm
Shall for itself itself perform.
I nill relate, action may
Conveniently the rest convey,   56
Which might not what by me is told.
In your imagination hold
This stage the ship, upon whose deck
The sea-tost Pericles appears to speak.   60
                   [*Exit.*

SCENE I.

Enter PERICLES, *on shipboard.*

Per. Thou God of this great vast, rebuke
   these surges,
Which wash both heaven and hell; and thou,
   that hast
Upon the winds command, bind them in brass,
Having call'd them from the deep. O! still   4
Thy deafening, dreadful thunders; gently
   quench
Thy nimble, sulphurous flashes. O! how Lycho-
   rida,
How does my queen? Thou stormest venom-
   ously;
Wilt thou spit all thyself? The seaman's whistle
Is as a whisper in the ears of death,   9
Unheard. Lychorida! Lucina, O!
Divinest patroness, and midwife gentle
To those that cry by night, convey thy deity 12
Aboard our dancing boat; make swift the pangs
Of my queen's travails!

Enter LYCHORIDA, *with an Infant.*
               Now, Lychorida!
Lyc. Here is a thing too young for such a
   place,
Who, if it had conceit, would die, as I   16
Am like to do: take in your arms this piece
Of your dead queen.
Per.   How, how, Lychorida!

Lyc. Patience, good sir; do not assist the
   storm.
Here's all that is left living of your queen,   20
A little daughter: for the sake of it,
Be manly, and take comfort.
Per.   O you gods!
Why do you make us love your goodly gifts,
And snatch them straight away? We here
   below,   24
Recall not what we give, and therein may
Use honour with you.
Lyc.   Patience, good sir,
Even for this charge.
Per.   Now, mild may be thy life!
For a more blust'rous birth had never babe: 28
Quiet and gentle thy conditions!
For thou art the rudeliest welcome to this world
That e'er was prince's child. Happy what fol-
   lows!
Thou hast as chiding a nativity   32
As fire, air, water, earth, and heaven can make,
To herald thee from the womb; even at the first
Thy loss is more than can thy portage quit,
With all thou canst find here. Now, the good
   gods   36
Throw their best eyes upon't!

Enter two Sailors.

First Sail. What courage, sir? God save you!
Per. Courage enough. I do not fear the flaw;
It hath done to me the worst. Yet for the love
Of this poor infant, this fresh-new sea-farer, 41
I would it would be quiet.
First Sail. Slack the bolins there! thou wilt
not, wilt thou? Blow, and split thyself.   44
Sec. Sail. But sea-room, an the brine and
cloudy billow kiss the moon, I care not.
First Sail. Sir, your queen must overboard:
the sea works high, the wind is loud, and will
not lie till the ship be cleared of the dead. 49
Per. That's your superstition.
First Sail. Pardon us, sir; with us at sea it
hath been still observed, and we are strong in
custom. Therefore briefly yield her, for she
must overboard straight.
Per. As you think meet. Most wretched
   queen!
Lyc. Here she lies, sir.   56
Per. A terrible child-bed hast thou had, my
   dear;
No light, no fire: the unfriendly elements
Forgot thee utterly; nor have I time
To give thee hallow'd to thy grave, but straight
Must cast thee, scarcely coffin'd, in the ooze; 61
Where, for a monument upon thy bones,
And aye-remaining lamps, the belching whale
And humming water must o'erwhelm thy
   corpse,   64
Lying with simple shells! O Lychorida!
Bid Nestor bring me spices, ink and paper,
My casket and my jewels; and bid Nicander
Bring me the satin coffer: lay the babe   68
Upon the pillow. Hie thee, whiles I say
A priestly farewell to her: suddenly, woman.
                    [*Exit* LYCHORIDA.

Sec. Sail. Sir, we have a chest beneath the hatches, caulk'd and bitumed ready. 72

Per. I thank thee. Mariner, say what coast is this?

Sec. Sail. We are near Tarsus.

Per. Thither, gentle mariner, 76 Alter thy course for Tyre. When canst thou reach it?

Sec. Sail. By break of day, if the wind cease.

Per. O! make for Tarsus. There will I visit Cleon, for the babe 80 Cannot hold out to Tyrus; there I'll leave it At careful nursing. Go thy ways, good mariner; I'll bring the body presently. [*Exeunt.*

SCENE II.—*Ephesus. A Room in* CERIMON'S *House.*

Enter CERIMON, *a Servant, and some Persons who have been shipwracked.*

Cer. Philemon, ho!

Enter PHILEMON.

Phil. Doth my lord call?

Cer. Get fire and meat for these poor men; 'T has been a turbulent and stormy night. 4

Ser. I have been in many; but such a night as this Till now I ne'er endur'd.

Cer. Your master will be dead ere you return; There's nothing can be minister'd to nature 8 That can recover him. [*To* PHILEMON.] Give this to the 'pothecary, And tell me how it works.

[*Exeunt all except* CERIMON.

Enter two Gentlemen.

First Gent. Good morrow, sir.

Sec. Gent. Good morrow to your lordship.

Cer. Gentlemen, Why do you stir so early? 12

First Gent. Sir, Our lodgings, standing bleak upon the sea, Shook as the earth did quake; The very principals did seem to rend, 16 And all to topple. Pure surprise and fear Made me to quit the house.

Sec. Gent. That is the cause we trouble you so early; 'Tis not our husbandry.

Cer. O! you say well. 20

First Gent. But I much marvel that your lordship, having Rich tire about you, should at these early hours Shake off the golden slumber of repose. 'Tis most strange, 24 Nature should be so conversant with pain, Being thereto not compell'd.

Cer. I hold it ever, Virtue and cunning were endowments greater Than nobleness and riches; careless heirs 28 May the two latter darken and expend, But immortality attends the former, Making a man a god. 'Tis known I ever Have studied physic, through which secret art, By turning o'er authorities, I have— 33

Together with my practice—made familiar To me and to my aid the blest infusions That dwell in vegetives, in metals, stones; 36 And can speak of the disturbances That nature works, and of her cures; which doth give me A more content in course of true delight Than to be thirsty after tottering honour, 40 Or tie my treasure up in silken bags, To please the fool and death.

Sec. Gent. Your honour has through Ephesus pour'd forth Your charity, and hundreds call themselves 44 Your creatures, who by you have been restor'd: And not your knowledge, your personal pain, but even Your purse, still open, hath built Lord Cerimon 47 Such strong renown as time shall ne'er decay.

Enter two Servants, *with a chest.*

First Serv. So; lift there.

Cer. What is that?

First Serv. Sir, even now Did the sea toss upon our shore this chest: 'Tis of some wrack.

Cer. Set it down; let's look upon't.

Sec. Gent. 'Tis like a coffin, sir.

Cer. Whate'er it be, 52 'Tis wondrous heavy. Wrench it open straight; If the sea's stomach be o'ercharg'd with gold, 'Tis a good constraint of fortune it belches upon us.

Sec. Gent. 'Tis so, my lord.

Cer. How close 'tis caulk'd and bitumed! 56 Did the sea cast it up?

First Serv. I never saw so huge a billow, sir, As toss'd it upon shore.

Cer. Come, wrench it open. Soft! it smells most sweetly in my sense. 60

Sec. Gent. A delicate odour.

Cer. As ever hit my nostril. So, up with it. O you most potent gods! what's here? a corse!

First Gent. Most strange! 64

Cer. Shrouded in cloth of state; balm'd and entreasur'd With full bags of spices! A passport too! Apollo, perfect me i' the characters!

Here I give to understand, 68 *If e'er this coffin drive a-land,* *I, King Pericles, have lost* *This queen worth all our mundane cost.* *Who finds her, give her burying;* 72 *She was the daughter of a king:* *Besides this treasure for a fee,* *The gods requite his charity!*

If thou liv'st, Pericles, thou hast a heart 76 That even cracks for woe! This chanc'd tonight.

Sec. Gent. Most likely, sir.

Cer. Nay, certainly to-night; For look, how fresh she looks. They were too rough That threw her in the sea. Make fire within; 80 Fetch hither all the boxes in my closet.

[*Exit Second* Servant.

Death may usurp on nature many hours,
And yet the fire of life kindle again
The overpress'd spirits. I heard   84
Of an Egyptian, that had nine hours lien dead,
Who was by good appliances recovered.

Re-enter Servant, *with boxes, napkins, and fire.*

Well said, well said; the fire and cloths.
The rough and woeful music that we have,   88
Cause it to sound, beseech you.
The viol once more;—how thou stirr'st, thou
    block!
The music there! I pray you, give her air.
Gentlemen,   92
This queen will live; nature awakes, a warmth
Breathes out of her; she hath not been entranc'd
Above five hours. See! how she 'gins to blow
Into life's flower again.

First Gent.   The heavens   96
Through you increase our wonder and set up
Your fame for ever.

Cer.   She is alive! behold,
Her eyelids, cases to those heavenly jewels
Which Pericles hath lost,   100
Begin to part their fringes of bright gold;
The diamonds of a most praised water
Do appear, to make the world twice rich. Live,
And make us weep to hear your fate, fair crea-
    ture,   104
Rare as you seem to be!   [*She moves.*
Thai.   O dear Diana!
Where am I? Where's my lord? What world
is this?

Sec. Gent. Is not this strange?
First Gent.   Most rare.
Cer.   Hush, gentle neighbours!
Lend me your hands; to the next chamber bear
her.   108
Get linen; now this matter must be look'd to,
For her relapse is mortal. Come, come;
And Æsculapius guide us!

    [*Exeunt, carrying* THAISA *away.*

SCENE III.—*Tarsus. A Room in* CLEON'S
House.

Enter PERICLES, CLEON, DIONYZA, *and* LYCHO-
RIDA, *with* MARINA *in her arms.*

Per. Most honour'd Cleon, I must needs be
    gone;
My twelve months are expir'd, and Tyrus stands
In a litigious peace. You and your lady
Take from my heart all thankfulness; the gods
Make up the rest upon you!   5
Cle. Your shafts of fortune, though they hurt
    you mortally,
Yet glance full wanderingly on us.
Dion.   O your sweet queen!
That the strict fates had pleas'd you had brought
    her hither,   8
To have bless'd mine eyes with her!
Per.   We cannot but obey
The powers above us. Could I rage and roar
As doth the sea she lies in, yet the end
Must be as 'tis. My gentle babe Marina—
    whom,   12

For she was born at sea, I have nam'd so—here
I charge your charity withal, and leave her
The infant of your care, beseeching you   15
To give her princely training, that she may be
Manner'd as she is born.
Cle.   Fear not, my lord, but think
Your Grace, that fed my country with your
    corn—
For which the people's prayers still fall upon
    you—   19
Must in your child be thought on. If neglection
Should therein make me vile, the common body,
By you reliev'd, would force me to my duty;
But if to that my nature need a spur,
The gods revenge it upon me and mine,   24
To the end of generation!
Per.   I believe you;
Your honour and your goodness teach me to 't,
Without your vows. Till she be married,
    madam,
By bright Diana, whom we honour, all   28
Unscissar'd shall this hair of mine remain,
Though I show ill in 't. So I take my leave.
Good madam, make me blessed in your care
In bringing up my child.
Dion.   I have one myself,   32
Who shall not be more dear to my respect
Than yours, my lord.
Per.   Madam, my thanks and prayers.
Cle. We'll bring your Grace e'en to the edge
    o' the shore;
Then give you up to the mask'd Neptune and   36
The gentlest winds of heaven.
Per.   I will embrace
Your offer. Come, dearest madam. O! no tears,
Lychorida, no tears:
Look to your little mistress, on whose grace   40
You may depend hereafter. Come, my lord.
    [*Exeunt.*

SCENE IV.—*Ephesus. A Room in* CERIMON'S
House.

Enter CERIMON *and* THAISA.

Cer. Madam, this letter, and some certain
    jewels,
Lay with you in your coffer; which are now
At your command. Know you the character?
Thai. It is my lord's.   4
That I was shipp'd at sea, I well remember,
Even on my eaning time; but whether there
Deliver'd, by the holy gods,
I cannot rightly say. But since King Pericles,   8
My wedded lord, I ne'er shall see again,
A vestal livery will I take me to,
And never more have joy.
Cer. Madam, if this you purpose as you
    speak,   12
Diana's temple is not distant far,
Where you may abide till your date expire.
Moreover, if you please, a niece of mine
Shall there attend you.   16
Thai. My recompense is thanks, that's all;
Yet my good will is great, though the gift
    small.
    [*Exeunt.*

ACT IV

Enter GOWER.

Imagine Pericles arriv'd at Tyre,
Welcom'd and settled to his own desire.
His woeful queen we leave at Ephesus,
Unto Diana there a votaress.   4
Now to Marina bend your mind,
Whom our fast-growing scene must find
At Tarsus, and by Cleon train'd
In music, letters; who hath gain'd   8
Of education all the grace,
Which makes her both the heart and place
Of general wonder. But, alack!
That monster envy, oft the wrack   12
Of earned praise, Marina's life
Seeks to take off by treason's knife.
And in this kind hath our Cleon
One daughter, and a wench full grown,   16
Even ripe for marriage-rite; this maid
Hight Philoten, and it is said
For certain in our story, she
Would ever with Marina be: 20
Be't when she weav'd the sleided silk
With fingers, long, small, white as milk,
Or when she would with sharp neeld wound
The cambric, which she made more sound   24
By hurting it; when to the lute
She sung, and made the night-bird mute,
That still records with moan; or when
She would with rich and constant pen   28
Vail to her mistress Dian; still
This Philoten contends in skill
With absolute Marina: so
With the dove of Paphos might the crow   32
Vie feathers white. Marina gets
All praises, which are paid as debts,
And not as given. This so darks
In Philoten all graceful marks,   36
That Cleon's wife, with envy rare,
A present murderer does prepare
For good Marina, that her daughter
Might stand peerless by this slaughter.   40
The sooner her vile thoughts to stead,
Lychorida, our nurse, is dead:
And cursed Dionyza hath
The pregnant instrument of wrath   44
Prest for this blow. The unborn event
I do commend to your content:
Only I carry winged time
Post on the lame feet of my rime;   48
Which never could I so convey,
Unless your thoughts went on my way.
Dionyza doth appear,
With Leonine, a murderer.   [*Exit.*

SCENE I.—*Tarsus. An open Place near the*
Sea-shore.

Enter DIONYZA *and* LEONINE.

Dion. Thy oath remember; thou hast sworn
to do't:
'Tis but a blow, which never shall be known.
Thou canst not do a thing i' the world so soon,
To yield thee so much profit. Let not con-
science,   4
Which is but cold, inflaming love i' thy bosom,
Inflame too nicely; nor let pity, which
Even women have cast off, melt thee, but be
A soldier to thy purpose.   8
Leon. I'll do't; but yet she is a goodly crea-
ture.
Dion. The fitter, then, the gods should have
her. Here
She comes weeping for her only mistress' death.
Thou art resolv'd?
Leon.   I am resolv'd.   12

Enter MARINA, *with a basket of flowers.*

Mar. No, I will rob Tellus of her weed,
To strew thy green with flowers; the yellows,
blues,
The purple violets, and marigolds,
Shall as a carpet hang upon thy grave,   16
While summer days do last. Ay me! poor maid,
Born in a tempest, when my mother died,
This world to me is like a lasting storm,
Whirring me from my friends.   20
Dion. How now, Marina! why do you keep
alone?
How chance my daughter is not with you? Do
not
Consume your blood with sorrowing; you have
A nurse of me. Lord! how your favour's
chang'd   24
With this unprofitable woe. Come,
Give me your flowers, ere the sea mar it.
Walk with Leonine; the air is quick there,
And it pierces and sharpens the stomach.
Come,   28
Leonine, take her by the arm, walk with her.
Mar. No, I pray you;
I'll not bereave you of your servant.
Dion.   Come, come;
I love the king your father, and yourself,   32
With more than foreign heart. We every day
Expect him here; when he shall come and find
Our paragon to all reports thus blasted,   35
He will repent the breadth of his great voyage;
Blame both my lord and me, that we have taken
No care to your best courses. Go, I pray you;
Walk, and be cheerful once again; reserve
That excellent complexion, which did steal   40
The eyes of young and old. Care not for me;
I can go home alone.
Mar.   Well, I will go;
But yet I have no desire to it.   43
Dion. Come, come, I know 'tis good for you.
Walk half an hour, Leonine, at least.
Remember what I have said.
Leon.   I warrant you, madam.
Dion. I'll leave you, my sweet lady, for a
while;   47
Pray you walk softly, do not heat your blood:
What! I must have care of you.
Mar.   My thanks, sweet madam.
[*Exit* DIONYZA.
Is this wind westerly that blows?
Leon.   South-west.
Mar. When I was born, the wind was north.
Leon.   Was 't so?
Mar. My father, as nurse said, did never fear,

But cried 'Good seamen!' to the sailors, galling
His kingly hands haling ropes;
And, clasping to the mast, endur'd a sea
That almost burst the deck. 56
Leon. When was this?
Mar. When I was born:
Never were waves nor wind more violent;
And from the ladder-tackle washes off 60
A canvas-climber. 'Ha!' says one, 'wilt out?'
And with a dropping industry they skip
From stem to stern; the boatswain whistles, and
The master calls, and trebles their confusion. 64
Leon. Come; say your prayers.
Mar. What mean you?
Leon. If you require a little space for prayer,
I grant it. Pray; but be not tedious, 68
For the gods are quick of ear, and I am sworn
To do my work with haste.
Mar. Why will you kill me?
Leon. To satisfy my lady.
Mar. Why would she have me kill'd? 72
Now, as I can remember, by my troth,
I never did her hurt in all my life.
I never spake bad word, nor did ill turn
To any living creature; believe me, la, 76
I never kill'd a mouse, nor hurt a fly;
I trod upon a worm against my will,
But I wept for it. How have I offended,
Wherein my death might yield her any profit,
Or my life imply her any danger? 81
Leon. My commission
Is not to reason of the deed, but do't.
Mar. You will not do't for all the world, I
hope. 84
You are well favour'd, and your looks foreshow
You have a gentle heart. I saw you lately,
When you caught hurt in parting two that
fought;
Good sooth, it show'd well in you; do so now;
Your lady seeks my life; come you between, 89
And save poor me, the weaker.
Leon. I am sworn,
And will dispatch.

Enter Pirates, *whilst* MARINA *is struggling.*
First Pirate. Hold, villain! 92
[LEONINE *runs away.*
Sec. Pirate. A prize! a prize!
Third Pirate. Half-part, mates, half-part.
Come, let's have her aboard suddenly.
[*Exeunt* Pirates *with* MARINA.

Re-enter LEONINE.

Leon. These roguing thieves serve the great
pirate Valdes; 96
And they have seiz'd Marina. Let her go;
There's no hope she'll return. I'll swear she's
dead,
And thrown into the sea. But I'll see further;
Perhaps they will but please themselves upon
her, 100
Not carry her aboard. If she remain,
Whom they have ravish'd must by me be
slain.
[*Exit.*

SCENE II.—*Mitylene. A Room in a Brothel.*

Enter Pandar, Bawd, *and* BOULT.

Pand. Boult.
Boult. Sir?
Pand. Search the market narrowly; Mitylene
is full of gallants; we lost too much money this
mart by being too wenchless. 5
Bawd. We were never so much out of creatures. We have but poor three, and they can
do no more than they can do; and they with
continual action are even as good as rotten. 9
Pand. Therefore, let's have fresh ones, whate-
e'er we pay for them. If there be not a conscience to be used in every trade, we shall never
prosper. 13
Bawd. Thou sayst true; 'tis not the bringing
up of poor bastards, as, I think, I have brought
up some eleven— 16
Boult. Ay, to eleven; and brought them down
again. But shall I search the market?
Bawd. What else, man? The stuff we have
a strong wind will blow it to pieces, they are
so pitifully sodden. 21
Pand. Thou sayst true; they're too unwholesome, o' conscience. The poor Transylvanian is
dead, that lay with the little baggage. 24
Boult. Ay, she quickly pooped him; she made
him roast-meat for worms. But I'll go search
the market. [*Exit.*
Pand. Three or four thousand chequins were
as pretty a proportion to live quietly, and so
give over.
Bawd. Why to give over, I pray you? is it a
shame to get when we are old? 32
Pand. O! our credit comes not in like the
commodity, nor the commodity wages not with
the danger; therefore, in our youths we could
pick up some pretty estate, 'twere not amiss to
keep our door hatched. Besides, the sore terms
we stand upon with the gods will be strong with
us for giving over. 39
Bawd. Come, other sorts offend as well as we.
Pand. As well as we! ay, and better too; we
offend worse. Neither is our profession any
trade; it's no calling. But here comes Boult.

Re-enter BOULT, *with the* Pirates *and* MARINA.

Boult. Come your ways. My masters, you
say she's a virgin? 45
First Pirate. O! sir, we doubt it not.
Boult. Master, I have gone through for this
piece, you see: if you like her, so; if not, I have
lost my earnest. 49
Bawd. Boult, has she any qualities?
Boult. She has a good face, speaks well, and
has excellent good clothes; there's no further
necessity of qualities can make her be refused.
Bawd. What's her price, Boult?
Boult. I cannot be bated one doit of a thousand pieces. 56
Pand. Well, follow me, my masters, you
shall have your money presently. Wife, take
her in; instruct her what she has to do, that she
may not be raw in her entertainment. 60
[*Exeunt* Pandar *and* Pirates.

Bawd. Boult, take you the marks of her, the colour of her hair, complexion, height, age, with warrant of her virginity; and cry, 'He that will give most, shall have her first'. Such a maidenhead were no cheap thing, if men were as they have been. Get this done as I command you.   67

Boult. Performance shall follow.   [*Exit.*

Mar. Alack! that Leonine was so slack, so slow.

He should have struck, not spoke; or that these pirates—

Not enough barbarous—had not o'erboard thrown me

For to seek my mother!   72

Bawd. Why lament you, pretty one?

Mar. That I am pretty.

Bawd. Come, the gods have done their part in you.

Mar. I accuse them not.   76

Bawd. You are lit into my hands, where you are like to live.

Mar. The more my fault

To 'scape his hands where I was like to die. 80

Bawd. Ay, and you shall live in pleasure.

Mar. No.

Bawd. Yes, indeed, shall you, and taste gentlemen of all fashions. You shall fare well; you shall have the difference of all complexions. What! do you stop your ears?

Mar. Are you a woman?

Bawd. What would you have me be, an I be not a woman?   89

Mar. An honest woman, or not a woman.

Bawd. Marry, whip thee, gosling; I think I shall have something to do with you. Come, you are a young foolish sapling, and must be bowed as I would have you.

Mar. The gods defend me!   95

Bawd. If it please the gods to defend you by men, then men must comfort you, men must feed you, men must stir you up. Boult's returned.

Re-enter BOULT.

Now, sir, hast thou cried her through the market?   101

Boult. I have cried her almost to the number of her hairs; I have drawn her picture with my voice.   104

Bawd. And I prithee, tell me, how dost thou find the inclination of the people, especially of the younger sort?

Boult. Faith, they listened to me, as they would have hearkened to their father's testament. There was a Spaniard's mouth so watered, that he went to bed to her very description.

Bawd. We shall have him here to-morrow with his best ruff on.   113

Boult. To-night, to-night. But, mistress, do you know the French knight that cowers i' the hams?   116

Bawd. Who? Monsieur Veroles?

Boult. Ay; he offered to cut a caper at the proclamation; but he made a groan at it, and swore he would see her to-morrow.   120

Bawd. Well, well; as for him, he brought his disease hither: here he does but repair it. I know he will come in our shadow, to scatter his crowns in the sun.   124

Boult. Well, if we had of every nation a traveller, we should lodge them with this sign.

Bawd. [*To* MARINA.] Pray you, come hither awhile. You have fortunes coming upon you. Mark me: you must seem to do that fearfully, which you commit willingly; to despise profit where you have most gain. To weep that you live as ye do makes pity in your lovers; seldom but that pity begets you a good opinion, and that opinion a mere profit.

Mar. I understand you not.   136

Boult. O! take her home, mistress, take her home; these blushes of hers must be quenched with some present practice.

Bawd. Thou sayst true, i' faith, so they must; for your bride goes to that with shame which is her way to go with warrant.

Boult. Faith, some do, and some do not. But, mistress, if I have bargained for the joint,— 144

Bawd. Thou mayst cut a morsel off the spit.

Boult. I may so?

Bawd. Who should deny it? Come, young one, I like the manner of your garments well.

Boult. Ay, by my faith, they shall not be changed yet.   150

Bawd. Boult, spend thou that in the town; report what a sojourner we have; you'll lose nothing by custom. When nature framed this piece, she meant thee a good turn; therefore say what a paragon she is, and thou hast the harvest out of thine own report.   156

Boult. I warrant you, mistress, thunder shall not so awake the beds of eels as my giving out her beauty stir up the lewdly-inclined. I'll bring home some to-night.   160

Bawd. Come your ways; follow me.

Mar. If fires be hot, knives sharp, or waters deep,

Untied I still my virgin knot will keep.

Diana, aid my purpose!   164

Bawd. What have we to do with Diana? Pray you, will you go with us?   [*Exeunt.*

SCENE III.—*Tarsus. A Room in* CLEON'S *House.*

Enter CLEON *and* DIONYZA.

Dion. Why, are you foolish? Can it be undone?

Cle. O Dionyza! such a piece of slaughter The sun and moon ne'er look'd upon.

Dion.   I think

You'll turn a child again.   4

Cle. Were I chief lord of all this spacious world,

I'd give it to undo the deed. O lady!

Much less in blood than virtue, yet a princess

To equal any single crown o' the earth   8

I' the justice of compare. O villain Leonine!

Whom thou hast poison'd too;

If thou hadst drunk to him 't had been a kindness

Becoming well thy fact; what canst thou say 12
When noble Pericles shall demand his child?
  Dion. That she is dead. Nurses are not the
fates,
To foster it, nor ever to preserve.
She died at night; I'll say so. Who can cross it?
Unless you play the pious innocent,   17
And for an honest attribute cry out
'She died by foul play'.
  Cle.   O! go to. Well, well,
Of all the faults beneath the heavens, the gods
Do like this worst.
  Dion.   Be one of those that think 21
The pretty wrens of Tarsus will fly hence,
And open this to Pericles. I do shame
To think of what a noble strain you are,   24
And of how coward a spirit.
  Cle.   To such proceeding
Who ever but his approbation added,
Though not his prime consent, he did not flow
From honourable sources.
  Dion.   Be it so, then;   28
Yet none does know but you how she came dead,
Nor none can know, Leonine being gone.
She did distain my child, and stood between
Her and her fortunes; none would look on her,
But cast their gazes on Marina's face,   33
Whilst ours was blurted at and held a malkin
Not worth the time of day. It pierc'd me
    thorough;
And though you call my course unnatural, 36
You not your child well loving, yet I find
It greets me as an enterprise of kindness
Perform'd to your sole daughter.
  Cle.   Heavens forgive it!
  Dion. And as for Pericles,   40
What should he say? We wept after her hearse,
And even yet we mourn; her monument
Is almost finish'd, and her epitaphs
In glittering golden characters express   44
A general praise to her, and care in us
At whose expense 'tis done.
  Cle.   Thou art like the harpy,
Which, to betray, dost with thine angel's face,
Seize with thine eagle's talons.   48
  Dion. You are like one that superstitiously
Doth swear to the gods that winter kills the flies;
But yet I know you'll do as I advise. [*Exeunt.*

SCENE IV.—*Before the Monument of* MARINA
at Tarsus.

Enter GOWER.

*Thus time we waste, and longest leagues make
    short;*
Sail seas in cockles, have an wish but for't;
Making—to take your imagination—
From bourn to bourn, region to region.   4
*By you being pardon'd, we commit no crime
To use one language in each several clime
Where our scenes seem to live. I do beseech you
To learn of me, who stand i' the gaps to teach
    you,*   8
*The stages of our story. Pericles
Is now again thwarting the wayward seas,
Attended on by many a lord and knight,*

To see his daughter, all his life's delight.   12
*Old Helicanus goes along. Behind
Is left to govern it, you bear in mind,
Old Escanes, whom Helicanus late
Advanc'd in time to great and high estate.*   16
*Well-sailing ships and bounteous winds have
    brought
This king to Tarsus, think his pilot thought,
So with his steerage shall your thoughts grow on,
To fetch his daughter home, who first is gone.* 20
*Like motes and shadows see them move awhile;
Your ears unto your eyes I'll reconcile.*

DUMB SHOW.

Enter at one door PERICLES, *with his Train;* CLEON
and DIONYZA *at the other.* CLEON *shows* PERI-
CLES *the tomb of* MARINA; *whereat* PERICLES
*makes lamentation, puts on sack-cloth, and in
a mighty passion departs. Exeunt* CLEON *and*
DIONYZA.

*See how belief may suffer by foul show!
This borrow'd passion stands for true old woe;
And Pericles, in sorrow all devour'd,*   25
*With sighs shot through, and biggest tears o'er-
    shower'd,
Leaves Tarsus and again embarks. He swears
Never to wash his face, nor cut his hairs;*   28
*He puts on sackcloth, and to sea. He bears
A tempest, which his mortal vessel tears,
And yet he rides it out. Now please you wit
The epitaph is for Marina writ*   32
By wicked Dionyza.
    [*Reads inscription on* MARINA'S *monument.*

THE FAIREST, SWEET'ST, AND BEST LIES HERE,
WHO WITHER'D IN HER SPRING OF YEAR:
SHE WAS OF TYRUS THE KING'S DAUGHTER,
ON WHOM FOUL DEATH HATH MADE THIS
    SLAUGHTER.   37
MARINA WAS SHE CALL'D; AND AT HER BIRTH,
THETIS, BEING PROUD, SWALLOW'D SOME PART
    O' THE EARTH:
THEREFORE THE EARTH, FEARING TO BE O'ER-
    FLOW'D,   40
HATH THETIS' BIRTH-CHILD ON THE HEAVENS
    BESTOW'D:
WHEREFORE SHE DOES, AND SWEARS SHE'LL
    NEVER STINT,
MAKE RAGING BATTERY UPON SHORES OF FLINT.

No visor does become black villany   44
*So well as soft and tender flattery.
Let Pericles believe his daughter's dead,
And bear his courses to be ordered
By Lady Fortune; while our scene must play
His daughter's woe and heavy well-a-day*   49
*In her unholy service. Patience then,
And think you now are all in Mitylen.* [*Exit.*

SCENE V.—*Mitylene. A Street before the
Brothel.*

Enter, from the brothel, two Gentlemen.

  First Gent. Did you ever hear the like?
  Sec. Gent. No, nor never shall do in such a
place as this, she being once gone.

First Gent. But to have divinity preached there! did you ever dream of such a thing? 5

Sec. Gent. No, no. Come, I am for no more bawdy-houses. Shall 's go hear the vestals sing?

First Gent. I 'll do any thing now that is virtuous; but I am out of the road of rutting for ever. [*Exeunt.*

SCENE VI.—*The Same. A Room in the Brothel.*

Enter Pandar, Bawd, *and* BOULT.

Pand. Well, I had rather than twice the worth of her she had ne'er come here.

Bawd. Fie, fie upon her! she is able to freeze the god Priapus, and undo a whole generation; we must either get her ravished, or be rid of her. When she should do for clients her fitment, and do me the kindness of our profession, she has me her quirks, her reasons, her master-reasons, her prayers, her knees; that she would make a puritan of the devil if he should cheapen a kiss of her.

Boult. Faith, I must ravish her, or she'll disfurnish us of all our cavaliers, and make all our swearers priests. 13

Pand. Now, the pox upon her green-sickness for me!

Bawd. Faith, there 's no rather way to be rid on 't but by the way to the pox. Here comes the Lord Lysimachus, disguised.

Boult. We should have both lord and lown if the peevish baggage would but give way to customers. 21

Enter LYSIMACHUS.

Lys. How now! How a dozen of virginities?

Bawd. Now, the gods to-bless your honour!

Boult. I am glad to see your honour in good health. 25

Lys. You may so; 'tis the better for you that your resorters stand upon sound legs. How now! wholesome iniquity, have you that a man may deal withal, and defy the surgeon? 29

Bawd. We have here one, sir, if she would—but there never came her like in Mitylene.

Lys. If she'd do the deed of darkness, thou wouldst say. 33

Bawd. Your honour knows what 'tis to say well enough.

Lys. Well; call forth, call forth. 36

Boult. For flesh and blood, sir, white and red, you shall see a rose; and she were a rose indeed if she had but—

Lys. What, prithee? 40

Boult. O! sir, I can be modest.

Lys. That dignifies the renown of a bawd no less than it gives a good report to a number to be chaste. [*Exit* BOULT.

Bawd. Here comes that which grows to the stalk; never plucked yet, I can assure you.—

Re-enter BOULT *with* MARINA.

Is she not a fair creature? 47

Lys. Faith, she would serve after a long **voyage** at sea. Well, there 's for you; leave us.

Bawd. I beseech your honour, give me leave; a word, and I 'll have done presently.

Lys. I beseech you do. 52

Bawd. [*To* MARINA.] First, I would have you note, this is an honourable man.

Mar. I desire to find him so, that I may worthily note him. 56

Bawd. Next, he 's the governor of this country, and a man whom I am bound to.

Mar. If he govern the country, you are bound to him indeed; but how honourable he is in that I know not. 61

Bawd. Pray you, without any more virginal fencing, will you use him kindly? He will line your apron with gold. 64

Mar. What he will do graciously, I will thankfully receive.

Lys. Ha' you done?

Bawd. My lord, she 's not paced yet; you must take some pains to work her to your manage. Come, we will leave his honour and her together. 71

Lys. Go thy ways. [*Exeunt* Bawd, Pandar, *and* BOULT.] Now, pretty one, how long have you been at this trade?

Mar. What trade, sir?

Lys. Why, I cannot name 't but I shall offend. 76

Mar. I cannot be offended with my trade. Please you to name it.

Lys. How long have you been of this profession? 80

Mar. E'er since I can remember.

Lys. Did you go to 't so young? Were you a gamester at five or at seven?

Mar. Earlier too, sir, if now I be one. 84

Lys. Why, the house you dwell in proclaims you to be a creature of sale.

Mar. Do you know this house to be a place of such resort, and will come into 't? I hear say you are of honourable parts, and are the governor of this place.

Lys. Why, hath your principal made known unto you who I am? 92

Mar. Who is my principal?

Lys. Why, your herb-woman; she that sets seeds and roots of shame and iniquity. O! you have heard something of my power, and so stand aloof for more serious wooing. But I protest to thee, pretty one, my authority shall not see thee, or else look friendly upon thee. Come, bring me to some private place; come, come. 100

Mar. If you were born to honour, show it now;

If put upon you, make the judgment good
That thought you worthy of it.

Lys. How 's this? how 's this? Some more; be sage. 104

Mar. For me,

That am a maid, though most ungentle fortune
Hath plac'd me in this sty, where, since I came,
Diseases have been sold dearer than physic, 108
O! that the gods
Would set me free from this unhallow'd place,
Though they did change me to the meanest bird
That flies i' the purer air!

Lys.   I did not think 112
Thou couldst have spoke so well; ne'er dream'd
thou couldst.
Had I brought hither a corrupted mind,
Thy speech had alter'd it. Hold, here's gold for
thee;
Persever in that clear way thou goest,   116
And the gods strengthen thee!
Mar. The good gods preserve you!
Lys. For me, be you thoughten
That I came with no ill intent, for to me   120
The very doors and windows savour vilely.
Farewell. Thou art a piece of virtue, and
I doubt not but thy training hath been noble.
Hold, here's more gold for thee.   124
A curse upon him, die he like a thief,
That robs thee of thy goodness! If thou dost
Hear from me, it shall be for thy good.

Re-enter BOULT.

Boult. I beseech your honour, one piece for
me.   129
Lys. Avaunt! thou damned door-keeper.
Your house,
But for this virgin that doth prop it, would
Sink and overwhelm you. Away!   [*Exit.*
Boult. How's this? We must take another
course with you. If your peevish chastity,
which is not worth a breakfast in the cheapest
country under the cope, shall undo a whole
household, let me be gelded like a spaniel.
Come your ways.
Mar. Whither would you have me?   139
Boult. I must have your maidenhead taken
off, or the common hangman shall execute it.
Come your ways. We'll have no more gentle-
men driven away. Come your ways, I say.

Re-enter Bawd.

Bawd. How now! what's the matter?   144
Boult. Worse and worse, mistress; she has
here spoken holy words to the Lord Lysimachus.
Bawd. O! abominable.   148
Boult. She makes our profession as it were to
stink afore the face of the gods.
Bawd. Marry, hang her up for ever!
Boult. The nobleman would have dealt with
her like a nobleman, and she sent him away as
cold as a snowball; saying his prayers too.
Bawd. Boult, take her away; use her at thy
pleasure; crack the glass of her virginity, and
make the rest malleable.   157
Boult. An if she were a thornier piece of
ground than she is, she shall be ploughed.
Mar. Hark, hark, you gods!   160
Bawd. She conjures; away with her! Would
she had never come within my doors! Marry,
hang you! She's born to undo us. Will you not
go the way of women-kind? Marry, come up,
my dish of chastity with rosemary and bays! 165
[*Exit.*
Boult. Come, mistress; come your ways with
me.
Mar. Whither wilt thou have me?

Boult. To take from you the jewel you hold
so dear.   169
Mar. Prithee, tell me one thing first.
Boult. Come now, your one thing.
Mar. What canst thou wish thine enemy
to be?   173
Boult. Why, I could wish him to be my
master, or rather, my mistress.
Mar. Neither of these are so bad as thou art,
Since they do better thee in their command. 177
Thou hold'st a place, for which the pained'st
fiend
Of hell would not in reputation change;
Thou art the damned door-keeper to every 180
Coystril that comes inquiring for his Tib,
To the choleric fisting of every rogue
Thy ear is liable, thy food is such
As hath been belch'd on by infected lungs. 184
Boult. What would you have me do? go to
the wars, would you? where a man may serve
seven years for the loss of a leg, and have not
money enough in the end to buy him a wooden
one?   189
Mar. Do any thing but this thou doest.
Empty
Old receptacles, or common sewers, of filth;
Serve by indenture to the common hangman:
Any of these ways are yet better than this; 193
For what thou professest, a baboon, could he
speak,
Would own a name too dear. O! that the gods
Would safely deliver me from this place.   196
Here, here's gold for thee.
If that thy master would gain by me,
Proclaim that I can sing, weave, sew, and dance,
With other virtues, which I'll keep from boast;
And I will undertake all these to teach.   201
I doubt not but this populous city will
Yield many scholars.
Boult. But can you teach all this you speak
of?   204
Mar. Prove that I cannot, take me home
again,
And prostitute me to the basest groom
That doth frequent your house.
Boult. Well, I will see what I can do for thee;
if I can place thee, I will.   209
Mar. But, amongst honest women.
Boult. Faith, my acquaintance lies little a-
mongst them. But since my master and mistress
have bought you, there's no going but by their
consent; therefore I will make them acquainted
with your purpose, and I doubt not but I shall
find them tractable enough. Come; I'll do for
thee what I can; come your ways.   [*Exeunt.*

ACT V

Enter GOWER.

*Marina thus the brothel 'scapes, and chances
Into an honest house, our story says.
She sings like one immortal, and she dances
As goddess-like to her admired lays;*   4
*Deep clerks she dumbs; and with her neeld com-
poses
Nature's own shape, of bud, bird, branch, or berry,*

That even her art sisters the natural roses;
Her inkle, silk, twin with the rubied cherry; 8
That pupils lacks she none of noble race,
Who pour their bounty on her; and her gain
She gives the cursed bawd.   Here we her place;
And to her father turn our thoughts again, 12
Where we left him, on the sea.   We there him lost,
Whence, driven before the winds, he is arriv'd
Here where his daughter dwells: and on this
   coast
Suppose him now at anchor.   The city striv'd 16
God Neptune's annual feast to keep; from whence
Lysimachus our Tyrian ship espies,
His banners sable, trimm'd with rich expense;
And to him in his barge with fervour hies. 20
In your supposing once more put your sight
Of heavy Pericles; think this his bark;
Where what is done in action, more, if might,
Shall be discover'd; please you, sit and hark.
                                  [Exit.

SCENE I.—*On board* PERICLES' *Ship, off Mity-*
lene. A Pavilion on deck, with a curtain before
it; PERICLES *within it, reclined on a couch. A*
barge lying beside the Tyrian vessel.

Enter two Sailors, one belonging to the Tyrian
vessel, the other to the barge; to them HELI-
CANUS.

Tyr. Sail. [*To the* Sailor of Mitylene.] Where's
the Lord Helicanus? he can resolve you.
O! here he is.—
Sir, there's a barge put off from Mitylene,
And in it is Lysimachus, the governor, 4
Who craves to come aboard. What is your will?
  Hel. That he have his. Call up some gentle-
men.
  Tyr. Sail. Ho, gentlemen! my lord calls.

Enter two or three Gentlemen.

  First Gent. Doth your lordship call? 8
  Hel. Gentlemen, there's some of worth would
come aboard;
I pray ye, greet them fairly.
    [Gentlemen *and* Sailors *descend, and go on*
                    board the barge.

Enter from thence, LYSIMACHUS *and* Lords; *the*
Gentlemen *and the two* Sailors.

  Tyr. Sail. Sir,
This is the man that can, in aught you would,
Resolve you. 13
  Lys. Hail, reverend sir! The gods preserve
you!
  Hel. And you, sir, to outlive the age I am,
And die as I would do.
  Lys.   You wish me well. 16
Being on shore, honouring of Neptune's
triumphs,
Seeing this goodly vessel ride before us,
I made to it to know of whence you are.
  Hel. First, what is your place? 20
  Lys. I am the governor of this place you lie
before.
  Hel. Sir,
Our vessel is of Tyre, in it the king;

A man who for this three months hath not
spoken 24
To any one, nor taken sustenance
But to prorogue his grief.
  Lys. Upon what ground is his distempera-
ture?
  Hel. 'Twould be too tedious to repeat; 28
But the main grief springs from the loss
Of a beloved daughter and a wife.
  Lys. May we not see him?
  Hel. You may; 32
But bootless is your sight: he will not speak
To any.
  Lys. Yet let me obtain my wish.
  Hel. Behold him. [PERICLES *discovered.*] This
was a goodly person, 36
Till the disaster that, one mortal night,
Drove him to this.
  Lys. Sir king, all hail! the gods preserve you!
Hail, royal sir! 40
  Hel. It is in vain; he will not speak to you.
  First Lord. Sir,
We have a maid in Mitylene, I durst wager,
Would win some words of him.
  Lys.   'Tis well bethought. 44
She questionless with her sweet harmony
And other chosen attractions, would allure,
And make a battery through his deafen'd ports
Which now are midway stopp'd: 48
She is all happy as the fair'st of all,
And with her fellow maids is now upon
The leafy shelter that abuts against
The island's side. 52
    [*Whispers first* Lord, *who puts off in*
             the barge of LYSIMACHUS.
  Hel. Sure, all 's effectless; yet nothing we'll
omit,
That bears recovery's name. But, since your
kindness
We have stretch'd thus far, let us beseech you,
That for our gold we may provision have, 56
Wherein we are not destitute for want,
But weary for the staleness.
  Lys.   O! sir, a courtesy,
Which if we should deny, the most just gods
For every graff would send a caterpillar, 60
And so afflict our province. Yet once more
Let me entreat to know at large the cause
Of your king's sorrow.
  Hel.   Sit, sir, I will recount it to you;
But see, I am prevented.

Re-enter, from the barge, Lord, *with* MARINA,
and a young Lady.

  Lys.   O! here is 64
The lady that I sent for. Welcome, fair one!
Is 't not a goodly presence?
  Hel.   She 's a gallant lady.
  Lys. She 's such a one, that were I well assur'd
Came of a gentle kind and noble stock, 68
I'd wish no better choice, and think me rarely
wed.
Fair one, all goodness that consists in bounty
Expect even here, where is a kingly patient:
If that thy prosperous and artificial feat 72
Can draw him but to answer thee in aught,

Thy sacred physic shall receive such pay
As thy desires can wish.

   Mar.   Sir, I will use
My utmost skill in his recovery,   76
Provided
That none but I and my companion maid
Be suffer'd to come near him.

   Lys.   Come, let us leave her;
And the gods make her prosperous!   80
                   [MARINA *sings.*

   Lys. Mark'd he your music?
   Mar.   No, nor look'd on us.
   Lys. See, she will speak to him.
   Mar. Hail, sir! my lord, lend ear.
   Per. Hum! ha!   84
   Mar. I am a maid,
My lord, that ne'er before invited eyes,
But have been gaz'd on like a comet; she speaks,
My lord, that, may be, hath endur'd a grief 88
Might equal yours, if both were justly weigh'd.
Though wayward Fortune did malign my state,
My derivation was from ancestors
Who stood equivalent with mighty kings; 92
But time hath rooted out my parentage,
And to the world and awkward casualties
Bound me in servitude.—[*Aside.*] I will desist;
But there is something glows upon my cheek,
And whispers in mine ear, 'Go not till he speak.'

   Per. My fortunes—parentage—good parent-
   age—
To equal mine!—was it not thus? what say you?
   Mar. I said, my lord, if you did know my
   parentage,   100
You would not do me violence.
   Per. I do think so. Pray you, turn your eyes
upon me.
You are like something that—What country-
woman?
Here of these shores?
   Mar.   No, nor of any shores; 104
Yet I was mortally brought forth, and am
No other than I appear.
   Per. I am great with woe, and shall deliver
weeping.
My dearest wife was like this maid, and such a
   one   108
My daughter might have been: my queen's
   square brows;
Her stature to an inch; as wand-like straight;
As silver-voic'd; her eyes as jewel-like,
And cas'd as richly; in pace another Juno; 112
Who starves the ears she feeds, and makes them
hungry,
The more she gives them speech. Where do you
live?
   Mar. Where I am but a stranger; from the
deck
You may discern the place.
   Per.   Where were you bred? 116
And how achiev'd you these endowments, which
You make more rich to owe?
   Mar. Should I tell my history, it would seem
Like lies, disdain'd in the reporting.   120
   Per. Prithee, speak;
Falseness cannot come from thee, for thou
look'st

Modest as justice, and thou seem'st a palace
For the crown'd truth to dwell in. I believe thee,
And make my senses credit thy relation 125
To points that seem impossible; for thou lookest
Like one I lov'd indeed. What were thy friends?
Didst thou not say when I did push thee back,—
Which was when I perceiv'd thee,—that thou
cam'st   129
From good descending?
   Mar.   So indeed I did.
   Per. Report thy parentage. I think thou
saidst
Thou hadst been toss'd from wrong to injury,
And that thou thought'st thy griefs might equal mine,
If both were open'd.
   Mar.   Some such thing
I said, and said no more but what my thoughts
Did warrant me was likely.
   Per.   Tell thy story; 136
If thine consider'd prove the thousandth part
Of my endurance, thou art a man, and I
Have suffer'd like a girl; yet thou dost look
Like Patience gazing on kings' graves, and
   smiling   140
Extremity out of act. What were thy friends?
How lost thou them? Thy name, my most kind
virgin?
Recount, I do beseech thee. Come, sit by me.
   Mar. My name is Marina.
   Per.   O! I am mock'd, 144
And thou by some incensed god sent hither
To make the world to laugh at me.
   Mar.   Patience, good sir,
Or here I'll cease.
   Per.   Nay, I'll be patient.
Thou little know'st how thou dost startle me,
To call thyself Marina.
   Mar.   The name   149
Was given me by one that had some power;
My father, and a king.
   Per.   How! a king's daughter?
And call'd Marina?
   Mar.   You said you would believe me;
But, not to be a troubler of your peace,   153
I will end here.
   Per.   But are you flesh and blood?
Have you a working pulse? and are no fairy?
Motion!—Well; speak on. Where were you
born?   156
And wherefore call'd Marina?
   Mar.   Call'd Marina
For I was born at sea.
   Per.   At sea! what mother?
   Mar. My mother was the daughter of a king;
Who died the minute I was born,   160
As my good nurse Lychorida hath oft
Deliver'd weeping.
   Per.   O! stop there a little.
This is the rarest dream that e'er dull sleep
Did mock sad fools withal; this cannot be. 164
My daughter's buried. Well; where were you
bred?
I'll hear you more to the bottom of your story,
And never interrupt you.
   Mar. You'll scorn to believe me; 'twere best
I did give o'er.   168

Per. I will believe you by the syllable
Of what you shall deliver. Yet, give me leave:
How came you in these parts? where were you
bred?
Mar. The king my father did in Tarsus leave
me, 172
Till cruel Cleon, with his wicked wife,
Did seek to murder me; and having woo'd
A villain to attempt it, who having drawn to do 't,
A crew of pirates came and rescu'd me; 176
Brought me to Mitylene. But, good sir,
Whither will you have me? Why do you weep?
It may be
You think me an impostor; no, good faith;
I am the daughter to King Pericles, 180
If good King Pericles be.
Per. Ho, Helicanus!
Hel. Calls my lord?
Per. Thou art a grave and noble counsellor,
Most wise in general; tell me, if thou canst, 185
What this maid is, or what is like to be,
That thus hath made me weep?
Hel. I know not; but
Here is the regent, sir, of Mitylene, 188
Speaks nobly of her.
Lys. She never would tell
Her parentage; being demanded that,
She would sit still and weep.
Per. O Helicanus! strike me, honour'd sir;
Give me a gash, put me to present pain, 193
Lest this great sea of joys rushing upon me
O'erbear the shores of my mortality,
And drown me with their sweetness. O! come
hither, 196
Thou that begett'st him that did thee beget;
Thou that wast born at sea, buried at Tarsus,
And found at sea again. O Helicanus!
Down on thy knees, thank the holy gods as
loud 200
As thunder threatens us; this is Marina.
What was thy mother's name? tell me but that,
For truth can never be confirm'd enough,
Though doubts did ever sleep.
Mar. First, sir, I pray, 204
What is your title?
Per. I am Pericles of Tyre: but tell me now
My drown'd queen's name, as in the rest you said
Thou hast been god-like perfect; 208
Thou'rt heir of kingdoms, and another life
To Pericles thy father.
Mar. Is it no more to be your daughter than
To say my mother's name was Thaisa? 212
Thaisa was my mother, who did end
The minute I began.
Per. Now, blessing on thee! rise; thou art
my child,
Give me fresh garments. Mine own, Helicanus;
She is not dead at Tarsus, as she should have
been, 217
By savage Cleon; she shall tell thee all;
When thou shalt kneel, and justify in know-
ledge
She is thy very princess. Who is this? 220
Hel. Sir, 'tis the governor of Mitylene,
Who, hearing of your melancholy state,
Did come to see you.

Per. I embrace you.
Give me my robes. I am wild in my beholding.
O heavens! bless my girl. But, hark! what
music? 225
Tell Helicanus, my Marina, tell him
O'er, point by point, for yet he seems to doubt,
How sure you are my daughter. But, what
music? 228
Hel. My lord, I hear none.
Per. None!
The music of the spheres! List, my Marina.
Lys. It is not good to cross him; give him
way. 232
Per. Rarest sounds! Do ye not hear?
Lys. My lord, I hear. [*Music.*
Per. Most heavenly music:
It nips me unto list'ning, and thick slumber
Hangs upon mine eyes; let me rest. [*Sleeps.*
Lys. A pillow for his head. 237
So, leave him all. Well, my companion friends,
If this but answer to my just belief,
I'll well remember you. 240
[*Exeunt all but* PERICLES.

DIANA *appears to* PERICLES *as in a vision.*
Dia. My temple stands in Ephesus; hie thee
thither,
And do upon mine altar sacrifice.
There, when my maiden priests are met together,
Before the people all, 244
Reveal how thou at sea didst lose thy wife;
To mourn thy crosses, with thy daughter's, call
And give them repetition to the life.
Perform my bidding, or thou liv'st in woe; 248
Do it, and happy; by my silver bow!
Awake, and tell thy dream! [*Disappears.*
Per. Celestial Dian, goddess argentine,
I will obey thee! Helicanus!

Enter HELICANUS, LYSIMACHUS, *and* MARINA.
Hel. Sir? 252
Per. My purpose was for Tarsus, there to
strike
The inhospitable Cleon: but I am
For other service first: toward Ephesus
Turn our blown sails; eftsoons I'll tell thee
why. 256
[*To* LYSIMACHUS.] Shall we refresh us, sir, upon
your shore,
And give you gold for such provision
As our intents will need?
Lys. Sir, 260
With all my heart; and when you come ashore,
I have another suit.
Per. You shall prevail,
Were it to woo my daughter; for it seems
You have been noble towards her.
Lys. Sir, lend me your arm. 264
Per. Come, my Marina. [*Exeunt.*

SCENE II.—*Before the Temple of* DIANA *at*
Ephesus.

Enter GOWER.
Now our sands are almost run;
More a little, and then dumb.

This, my last boon, give me,
For such kindness must relieve me,   4
That you aptly will suppose
What pageantry, what feats, what shows,
What minstrelsy, and pretty din,
The regent made in Mitylen   8
To greet the king. So he thriv'd,
That he is promis'd to be wiv'd
To fair Marina; but in no wise
Till he had done his sacrifice,   12
As Dian bade: whereto being bound,
The interim, pray you, all confound.
In feather'd briefness sails are fill'd,
And wishes fall out as they're will'd.   16
At Ephesus, the temple see,
Our king and all his company.
That he can hither come so soon,
Is by your fancy's thankful doom.   [*Exit.*

SCENE III.—*The Temple of* DIANA *at Ephesus;*
THAISA *standing near the altar, as high*
priestess; a number of Virgins *on each side;*
CERIMON *and other Inhabitants of Ephesus*
attending.

Enter PERICLES, *with his Train;* LYSIMACHUS,
     HELICANUS, MARINA, *and a* Lady.

Per. Hail, Dian! to perform thy just command,
I here confess myself the King of Tyre;
Who, frighted from my country, did wed
At Pentapolis the fair Thaisa.   4
At sea in childbed died she, but brought forth
A maid-child call'd Marina; who, O goddess!
Wears yet thy silver livery. She at Tarsus
Was nurs'd with Cleon, whom at fourteen
     years   8
He sought to murder; but her better stars
Brought her to Mitylene, 'gainst whose shore
Riding, her fortunes brought the maid aboard
     us,
Where, by her own most clear remembrance,
     she   12
Made known herself my daughter.
     Thai.   Voice and favour!
You are, you are—O royal Pericles!
     [*She faints.*
Per. What means the nun? she dies! help,
     gentlemen!
Cer. Noble sir,   16
If you have told Diana's altar true,
This is your wife.
Per.   Reverend appearer, no;
I threw her o'erboard with these very arms.
Cer. Upon this coast, I warrant you.
Per.   'Tis most certain.
Cer. Look to the lady. O! she's but o'er-
     joy'd.   21
Early in blustering morn this lady was
Thrown upon this shore. I op'd the coffin,
Found there rich jewels; recover'd her, and
     plac'd her   24
Here in Diana's temple.
Per.   May we see them?
Cer. Great sir, they shall be brought you to
     my house,

Whither I invite you. Look! Thaisa is
Recovered.
Thai.   O! let me look!   28
If he be none of mine, my sanctity
Will to my sense bend no licentious ear,
But curb it, spite of seeing. O! my lord,
Are you not Pericles? Like him you speak, 32
Like him you are. Did you not name a tempest,
A birth, and death?
Per.   The voice of dead Thaisa!
Thai. That Thaisa am I, supposed dead
And drown'd.   36
Per. Immortal Dian!
Thai.   Now I know you better.
When we with tears parted Pentapolis,
The king my father gave you such a ring.
     [*Shows a ring.*
Per. This, this: no more, you gods! your
     present kindness   40
Makes my past miseries sport: you shall do
     well,
That on the touching of her lips I may
Melt and no more be seen. O! come, be buried
A second time within these arms.
Mar.   My heart   44
Leaps to be gone into my mother's bosom.
     [*Kneels to* THAISA.
Per. Look, who kneels here! Flesh of thy
     flesh, Thaisa;
Thy burden at the sea, and call'd Marina,
For she was yielded there.
Thai.   Bless'd, and mine own! 48
Hel. Hail, madam, and my queen!
Thai.   I know you not.
Per. You have heard me say, when I did fly
     from Tyre,
I left behind an ancient substitute;
Can you remember what I call'd the man? 52
I have nam'd him oft.
Thai.   'Twas Helicanus then.
Per. Still confirmation!
Embrace him, dear Thaisa; this is he.
Now do I long to hear how you were found, 56
How possibly preserv'd, and whom to thank,
Besides the gods, for this great miracle.
Thai. Lord Cerimon, my lord; this man,
Through whom the gods have shown their
     power; that can   60
From first to last resolve you.
Per.   Reverend sir,
The gods can have no mortal officer
More like a god than you. Will you deliver
How this dead queen re-lives?
Cer.   I will, my lord. 64
Beseech you, first go with me to my house,
Where shall be shown you all was found with
     her;
How she came placed here in the temple;
No needful thing omitted.   68
Per. Pure Dian! bless thee for thy vision; I
Will offer night-oblations to thee. Thaisa,
This prince, the fair-betrothed of your daughter,
Shall marry her at Pentapolis. And now   72
This ornament
Makes me look dismal will I clip to form;
And what this fourteen years no razor touch'd

To grace thy marriage-day I'll beautify.   76

   Thai. Lord Cerimon hath letters of good
     credit, sir,

My father's dead.

   Per. Heavens make a star of him! Yet there,
     my queen,

We'll celebrate their nuptials, and ourselves 80

Will in that kingdom spend our following
   days;

Our son and daughter shall in Tyrus reign.

Lord Cerimon, we do our longing stay

To hear the rest untold. Sir, lead's the way. 84

                     [*Exeunt.*

       Enter GOWER.

In Antiochus and his daughter you have heard
Of monstrous lust the due and just reward:
In Pericles, his queen, and daughter, seen—

Although assail'd with fortune fierce and
   keen—   88

Virtue preserv'd from fell destruction's blast,

Led on by heaven, and crown'd with joy at last.

In Helicanus may you well descry

A figure of truth, of faith, of loyalty.   92

In reverend Cerimon there well appears

The worth that learned charity aye wears.

For wicked Cleon and his wife, when fame

Had spread their cursed deed, and honour'd
   name   96

Of Pericles, to rage the city turn,

That him and his they in his palace burn:

The gods for murder seemed so content

To punish them; although not done, but
   meant.   100

So on your patience evermore attending,

New joy wait on you! Here our play hath end-
   ing.   [*Exit.*

POEMS

VENUS AND ADONIS

'Vilia miretur vulgus; mihi flavus Apollo
Pocula Castalia plena ministret aqua.'

TO THE RIGHT HONOURABLE HENRY WRIOTHESLY

EARL OF SOUTHAMPTON, AND BARON OF TICHFIELD

RIGHT HONOURABLE,

I KNOW not how I shall offend in dedicating my unpolished lines to your lordship, nor how the world will censure me for choosing so strong a prop to support so weak a burden: only, if your honour seem but pleased, I account myself highly praised, and vow to take advantage of all idle hours, till I have honoured you with some graver labour. But if the first heir of my invention prove deformed, I shall be sorry it had so noble a godfather, and never after ear so barren a land, for fear it yield me still so bad a harvest. I leave it to your honourable survey, and your honour to your heart's content; which I wish may always answer your own wish and the world's hopeful expectation.

Your honour's in all duty,

WILLIAM SHAKESPEARE.

EVEN as the sun with purple-colour'd face
Had ta'en his last leave of the weeping morn,
Rose-cheek'd Adonis hied him to the chase;
Hunting he lov'd, but love he laugh'd to scorn;
  Sick-thoughted Venus makes amain unto him, 5
  And like a bold-fac'd suitor 'gins to woo him.

'Thrice fairer than myself,' thus she began,
'The field's chief flower, sweet above compare, 8
Stain to all nymphs, more lovely than a man,
More white and red than doves or roses are;
  Nature that made thee, with herself at strife,
  Saith that the world hath ending with thy life. 12

'Vouchsafe, thou wonder, to alight thy steed,
And rein his proud head to the saddle-bow;
If thou wilt deign this favour, for thy meed
A thousand honey secrets shalt thou know: 16
  Here come and sit, where never serpent hisses;
  And being set, I'll smother thee with kisses:

'And yet not cloy thy lips with loath'd satiety,
But rather famish them amid their plenty, 20
Making them red and pale with fresh variety;
Ten kisses short as one, one long as twenty:
  A summer's day will seem an hour but short,
  Being wasted in such time-beguiling sport.' 24

With this she seizeth on his sweating palm,
The precedent of pith and livelihood,
And, trembling in her passion, calls it balm,
Earth's sovereign salve to do a goddess good: 28
  Being so enrag'd, desire doth lend her force
  Courageously to pluck him from his horse.

Over one arm the lusty courser's rein,
Under her other was the tender boy, 32
Who blush'd and pouted in a dull disdain,
With leaden appetite, unapt to toy;
  She red and hot as coals of glowing fire,
  He red for shame, but frosty in desire. 36

The studded bridle on a ragged bough
Nimbly she fastens;—O! how quick is love:—
The steed is stalled up, and even now
To tie the rider she begins to prove: 40
  Backward she push'd him, as she would be thrust, [lust.
  And govern'd him in strength, though not in

So soon was she along, as he was down,
Each leaning on their elbows and their hips: 44
Now doth she stroke his cheek, now doth he frown,
And 'gins to chide, but soon she stops his lips;
  And kissing speaks, with lustful language broken,
  'If thou wilt chide, thy lips shall never open.'

He burns with bashful shame; she with her tears
Doth quench the maiden burning of his cheeks;
Then with her windy sighs and golden hairs
To fan and blow them dry again she seeks: 52
  He saith she is immodest, blames her miss;
  What follows more she murders with a kiss.

Even as an empty eagle, sharp by fast,
Tires with her beak on feathers, flesh and bone,
Shaking her wings, devouring all in haste, 57
Till either gorge be stuff'd or prey be gone;
  Even so she kiss'd his brow, his cheek, his chin,
  And where she ends she doth anew begin. 60

Forc'd to content, but never to obey,
Panting he lies, and breatheth in her face;
She feedeth on the steam, as on a prey,
And calls it heavenly moisture, air of grace; 64
  Wishing her cheeks were gardens full of flowers,
  So they were dew'd with such distilling showers.

Look! how a bird lies tangled in a net,
So fasten'd in her arms Adonis lies; 68
Pure shame and aw'd resistance made him fret,
Which bred more beauty in his angry eyes:
  Rain added to a river that is rank
  Perforce will force it overflow the bank. 72

Still she entreats, and prettily entreats,
For to a pretty ear she tunes her tale;
Still is he sullen, still he lowers and frets,
'Twixt crimson shame and anger ashy-pale; 76
  Being red, she loves him best; and being white,
  Her best is better'd with a more delight.

Look how he can, she cannot choose but love;
And by her fair immortal hand she swears, 80
From his soft bosom never to remove,
Till he take truce with her contending tears,
  Which long have rain'd, making her cheeks all wet;
  And one sweet kiss shall pay this countless debt.   84

Upon this promise did he raise his chin
Like a dive-dapper peering through a wave,
Who, being look'd on, ducks as quickly in;
So offers he to give what she did crave; 88
  But when her lips were ready for his pay,
  He winks, and turns his lips another way.

Never did passenger in summer's heat
More thirst for drink than she for this good turn.   92
Her help she sees, but help she cannot get;
She bathes in water, yet her fire must burn:
  'O! pity,' 'gan she cry, 'flint-hearted boy:
  'Tis but a kiss I beg; why art thou coy? 96

'I have been woo'd, as I entreat thee now,
Even by the stern and direful god of war,
Whose sinewy neck in battle ne'er did bow,
Who conquers where he comes in every jar; 100
  Yet hath he been my captive and my slave,
  And begg'd for that which thou unask'd shalt have.

'Over my altars hath he hung his lance,
His batter'd shield, his uncontrolled crest, 104
And for my sake hath learn'd to sport and dance,
To toy, to wanton, dally, smile, and jest;
  Scorning his churlish drum and ensign red,
  Making my arms his field, his tent my bed.

'Thus he that overrul'd I oversway'd,   109
Leading him prisoner in a red-rose chain:
Strong-temper'd steel his stronger strength obey'd,
Yet was he servile to my coy disdain.   112
  O! be not proud, nor brag not of thy might,
  For mastering her that foil'd the god of fight.

'Touch but my lips with those fair lips of thine,—
Though mine be not so fair, yet are they red,—
The kiss shall be thine own as well as mine: 117
What seest thou in the ground? hold up thy head:
  Look in mine eyeballs, there thy beauty lies;
  Then why not lips on lips, since eyes in eyes?   120

'Art thou asham'd to kiss? then wink again,
And I will wink; so shall the day seem night;
Love keeps his revels where there are but twain;
Be bold to play, our sport is not in sight: 124
  These blue-vein'd violets whereon we lean
  Never can blab, nor know not what we mean.

'The tender spring upon thy tempting lip
Shows thee unripe, yet mayst thou well be tasted.   128
Make use of time, let not advantage slip;
Beauty within itself should not be wasted:
  Fair flowers that are not gather'd in their prime   131
  Rot and consume themselves in little time.

'Were I hard-favour'd, foul, or wrinkled-old,
Ill-nurtur'd, crooked, churlish, harsh in voice,
O'erworn, despised, rheumatic, and cold,
Thick-sighted, barren, lean, and lacking juice,
  Then mightst thou pause, for then I were not for thee;   137
  But having no defects, why dost abhor me?

'Thou canst not see one wrinkle in my brow;
Mine eyes are grey and bright, and quick in turning;   140
My beauty as the spring doth yearly grow;
My flesh is soft and plump, my marrow burning;
  My smooth moist hand, were it with thy hand felt,
  Would in thy palm dissolve, or seem to melt.

'Bid me discourse, I will enchant thine ear, 145
Or like a fairy trip upon the green,
Or, like a nymph, with long dishevell'd hair,
Dance on the sands, and yet no footing seen:
  Love is a spirit all compact of fire,   149
  Not gross to sink, but light, and will aspire.

'Witness this primrose bank whereon I lie;
These forceless flowers like sturdy trees support me;   152
Two strengthless doves will draw me through the sky,
From morn till night, even where I list to sport me:
  Is love so light, sweet boy, and may it be
  That thou shouldst think it heavy unto thee?

'Is thine own heart to thine own face affected?
Can thy right hand seize love upon thy left?
Then woo thyself, be of thyself rejected,
Steal thine own freedom, and complain on theft.   160
  Narcissus so himself himself forsook,
  And died to kiss his shadow in the brook.

'Torches are made to light, jewels to wear,
Dainties to taste, fresh beauty for the use, 164
Herbs for their smell, and sappy plants to bear;
Things growing to themselves are growth's abuse:
  Seeds spring from seeds, and beauty breedeth beauty;
  Thou wast begot; to get it is thy duty.   168

'Upon the earth's increase why shouldst thou
feed,
Unless the earth with thy increase be fed?
By law of nature thou art bound to breed,
That thine may live when thou thyself art dead;
  And so in spite of death thou dost survive, 173
  In that thy likeness still is left alive.'

By this the love-sick queen began to sweat,
For where they lay the shadow had forsook
them,   176
And Titan, tired in the mid-day heat,
With burning eye did hotly overlook them;
  Wishing Adonis had his team to guide,
  So he were like him and by Venus' side. 180

And now Adonis with a lazy spright,
And with a heavy, dark, disliking eye,
His louring brows o'erwhelming his fair sight,
Like misty vapours when they blot the sky, 184
  Souring his cheeks, cries, 'Fie! no more of
love:
  The sun doth burn my face; I must remove.'

'Ay me,' quoth Venus, 'young, and so unkind?
What bare excuses mak'st thou to be gone; 188
I'll sigh celestial breath, whose gentle wind
Shall cool the heat of this descending sun:
  I'll make a shadow for thee of my hairs;
  If they burn too, I'll quench them with my
tears.   192

'The sun that shines from heaven shines but
warm,
And lo! I lie between that sun and thee:
The heat I have from thence doth little harm,
Thine eye darts forth the fire that burneth me;
  And were I not immortal, life were done 197
  Between this heavenly and earthly sun.

'Art thou obdurate, flinty, hard as steel?
Nay, more than flint, for stone at rain re-
lenteth.   200
Art thou a woman's son, and canst not feel
What 'tis to love? how want of love tormenteth?
  O! had thy mother borne so hard a mind,
  She had not brought forth thee, but died
unkind.   204

'What am I that thou shouldst contemn me
this?
Or what great danger dwells upon my suit?
What were thy lips the worse for one poor kiss?
Speak, fair; but speak fair words, or else be
mute: 208
  Give me one kiss, I'll give it thee again,
  And one for interest, if thou wilt have twain.

'Fie! lifeless picture, cold and senseless stone,
Well-painted idol, image dull and dead,   212
Statue contenting but the eye alone,
Thing like a man, but of no woman bred:
  Thou art no man, though of a man's com-
plexion,
  For men will kiss even by their own direction.'

This said, impatience chokes her pleading
tongue,   217
And swelling passion doth provoke a pause;
Red cheeks and fiery eyes blaze forth her wrong;
Being judge in love, she cannot right her cause:
  And now she weeps, and now she fain would
speak,   221
  And now her sobs do her intendments break.

Sometimes she shakes her head, and then his
hand;
Now gazeth she on him, now on the ground; 224
Sometimes her arms infold him like a band:
She would, he will not in her arms be bound;
  And when from thence he struggles to be
gone,
  She locks her lily fingers one in one.   228

'Fondling,' she saith, 'since I have hemm'd thee
here
Within the circuit of this ivory pale,
I'll be a park, and thou shalt be my deer;
Feed where thou wilt, on mountain or in dale:
  Graze on my lips, and if those hills be dry, 233
  Stray lower, where the pleasant fountains lie.

'Within this limit is relief enough,
Sweet bottom-grass and high delightful plain,
Round rising hillocks, brakes obscure and
rough,   237
To shelter thee from tempest and from rain:
  Then be my deer, since I am such a park;
  No dog shall rouse thee, though a thousand
bark.'   240

At this Adonis smiles as in disdain,
That in each cheek appears a pretty dimple:
Love made those hollows, if himself were slain,
He might be buried in a tomb so simple;   244
  Foreknowing well, if there he came to lie,
  Why, there Love liv'd and there he could not
die.

These lovely caves, these round enchanting pits,
Open'd their mouths to swallow Venus' liking.
Being mad before, how doth she now for wits?
Struck dead at first, what needs a second strik-
ing?   250
  Poor queen of love, in thine own law forlorn,
  To love a cheek that smiles at thee in scorn!

Now which way shall she turn? what shall she
say?
Her words are done, her woes the more increas-
ing;   254
The time is spent, her object will away,
And from her twining arms doth urge releasing:
  'Pity,' she cries; 'some favour, some re-
morse!'
  Away he springs, and hasteth to his horse.

But, lo! from forth a copse that neighbours by,
A breeding jennet, lusty, young, and proud, 260
Adonis' trampling courser doth espy,
And forth she rushes, snorts and neighs aloud:
  The strong-neck'd steed, being tied unto a
tree,
  Breaketh his rein, and to her straight goes he.

Imperiously he leaps, he neighs, he bounds, 265
And now his woven girths he breaks asunder;
The bearing earth with his hard hoof he wounds,
Whose hollow womb resounds like heaven's thunder; 268
    The iron bit he crushes 'tween his teeth,
    Controlling what he was controlled with.

His ears up-prick'd; his braided hanging mane 271
Upon his compass'd crest now stand on end;
His nostrils drink the air, and forth again,
As from a furnace, vapours doth he send:
    His eye, which scornfully glisters like fire,
    Shows his hot courage and his high desire.

Sometime he trots, as if he told the steps, 277
With gentle majesty and modest pride;
Anon he rears upright, curvets and leaps,
As who should say, 'Lo! thus my strength is tried, 280
    And this I do to captivate the eye
    Of the fair breeder that is standing by.'

What recketh he his rider's angry stir,
His flattering 'Holla,' or his 'Stand, I say?' 284
What cares he now for curb or pricking spur?
For rich caparisons or trapping gay?
    He sees his love, and nothing else he sees,
    Nor nothing else with his proud sight agrees.

Look, when a painter would surpass the life,
In limning out a well-proportion'd steed,
His art with nature's workmanship at strife,
As if the dead the living should exceed; 292
    So did this horse excel a common one,
    In shape, in courage, colour, pace and bone.

Round-hoof'd, short-jointed, fetlocks shag and long,
Broad breast, full eye, small head, and nostril wide, 296
High crest, short ears, straight legs and passing strong,
Thin mane, thick tail, broad buttock, tender hide:
    Look, what a horse should have he did not lack,
    Save a proud rider on so proud a back. 300

Sometimes he scuds far off, and there he stares;
Anon he starts at stirring of a feather;
To bid the wind a base he now prepares,
And whe'r he run or fly they know not whether;
    For through his mane and tail the high wind sings, 305
    Fanning the hairs, who wave like feather'd wings.

He looks upon his love, and neighs unto her;
She answers him as if she knew his mind; 308
Being proud, as females are, to see him woo her,
She puts on outward strangeness, seems unkind,
    Spurns at his love and scorns the heat he feels,
    Beating his kind embracements with her heels.

Then, like a melancholy malcontent, 313
He vails his tail that, like a falling plume
Cool shadow to his melting buttock lent:
He stamps, and bites the poor flies in his fume.
    His love, perceiving how he is enrag'd, 317
    Grew kinder, and his fury was assuag'd.

His testy master goeth about to take him;
When lo! the unback'd breeder, full of fear, 320
Jealous of catching, swiftly doth forsake him,
With her the horse, and left Adonis there.
    As they were mad, unto the wood they hie them,
    Out-stripping crows that strive to over-fly them. 324

All swoln with chafing, down Adonis sits,
Banning his boisterous and unruly beast:
And now the happy season once more fits,
That love-sick Love by pleading may be blest;
    For lovers say, the heart hath treble wrong
    When it is barr'd the aidance of the tongue.

An oven that is stopp'd, or river stay'd,
Burneth more hotly, swelleth with more rage:
So of concealed sorrow may be said; 333
Free vent of words love's fire doth assuage;
    But when the heart's attorney once is mute,
    The client breaks, as desperate in his suit. 336

He sees her coming, and begins to glow,—
Even as a dying coal revives with wind,—
And with his bonnet hides his angry brow;
Looks on the dull earth with disturbed mind,
    Taking no notice that she is so nigh, 341
    For all askance he holds her in his eye.

O! what a sight it was, wistly to view
How she came stealing to the wayward boy;
To note the fighting conflict of her hue, 345
How white and red each other did destroy:
    But now her cheek was pale, and by and by
    It flash'd forth fire, as lightning from the sky.

Now was she just before him as he sat, 349
And like a lowly lover down she kneels;
With one fair hand she heaveth up his hat,
Her other tender hand his fair cheek feels: 352
    His tenderer cheek receives her soft hand's print,
    As apt as new-fall'n snow takes any dint.

O! what a war of looks was then between them;
Her eyes petitioners to his eyes suing; 356
His eyes saw her eyes as they had not seen them;
Her eyes woo'd still, his eyes disdain'd the wooing:
    And all this dumb play had his acts made plain
    With tears, which, chorus-like, her eyes did rain. 360

Full gently now she takes him by the hand,
A lily prison'd in a gaol of snow,
Or ivory in an alabaster band;
So white a friend engirts so white a foe: 364
    This beauteous combat, wilful and unwilling,
    Show'd like two silver doves that sit a-billing.

Once more the engine of her thoughts began:
'O fairest mover on this mortal round,   368
Would thou wert as I am, and I a man,
My heart all whole as thine, thy heart my wound;
  For one sweet look thy help I would assure
    thee,
    Though nothing but my body's bane would
    cure thee.'   372

'Give me my hand,' saith he, 'why dost thou
  feel it?'
'Give me my heart,' saith she, 'and thou shalt
  have it;
O! give it me, lest thy hard heart do steel it,
  And being steel'd, soft sighs can never grave it:
    Then love's deep groans I never shall regard,
    Because Adonis' heart hath made mine hard.'

'For shame,' he cries, 'let go, and let me go;
My day's delight is past, my horse is gone,   380
And 'tis your fault I am bereft him so:
I pray you hence, and leave me here alone:
  For all my mind, my thought, my busy care,
  Is how to get my palfrey from the mare.'   384

Thus she replies: 'Thy palfrey, as he should,
Welcomes the warm approach of sweet desire:
Affection is a coal that must be cool'd;
Else, suffer'd, it will set the heart on fire: 388
  The sea hath bounds, but deep desire hath
    none;
  Therefore no marvel though thy horse be gone.

'How like a jade he stood, tied to the tree,
Servilely master'd with a leathern rein!   392
But when he saw his love, his youth's fair fee,
He held such petty bondage in disdain;
  Throwing the base thong from his bending
    crest,
  Enfranchising his mouth, his back, his
    breast.   396

'Who sees his true-love in her naked bed,
Teaching the sheets a whiter hue than white,
But, when his glutton eye so full hath fed,
His other agents aim at like delight?   400
  Who is so faint, that dare not be so bold
  To touch the fire, the weather being cold?

'Let me excuse thy courser, gentle boy;
And learn of him, I heartily beseech thee,   404
To take advantage on presented joy;
Though I were dumb, yet his proceedings teach
  thee.
  O learn to love; the lesson is but plain,
  And once made perfect, never lost again.'   408

'I know not love,' quoth he, 'nor will not know
  it,
Unless it be a boar, and then I chase it;
'Tis much to borrow, and I will not owe it;
My love to love is love but to disgrace it;   412
  For I have heard it is a life in death,
  That laughs and weeps, and all but with a
    breath.

'Who wears a garment shapeless and unfinish'd?
Who plucks the bud before one leaf put forth?
If springing things be any jot diminish'd,   417
They wither in their prime, prove nothing worth:
  The colt that's back'd and burden'd being
    young
  Loseth his pride and never waxeth strong.   420

'You hurt my hand with wringing; let us part,
And leave this idle theme, this bootless chat:
Remove your siege from my unyielding heart;
To love's alarms it will not ope the gate: 424
  Dismiss your vows, your feigned tears, your
    flattery;
  For where a heart is hard, they make no
    battery.'

'What! canst thou talk?' quoth she, 'hast thou
  a tongue?
O! would thou hadst not, or I had no hearing;
Thy mermaid's voice hath done me double
  wrong;   429
I had my load before, now press'd with bearing:
  Melodious discord, heavenly tune, harsh-
    sounding,
  Ear's deep-sweet music, and heart's deep-sore
    wounding.   432

'Had I no eyes, but ears, my ears would love
That inward beauty and invisible;
Or were I deaf, thy outward parts would move
Each part in me that were but sensible: 436
  Though neither eyes nor ears, to hear nor
    see,
  Yet should I be in love by touching thee.

'Say, that the sense of feeling were bereft me,
And that I could not see, nor hear, nor touch,
And nothing but the very smell were left me,
Yet would my love to thee be still as much;
  For from the still'tory of thy face excelling
  Comes breath perfum'd that breedeth love by
    smelling.   444

'But O! what banquet wert thou to the taste,
Being nurse and feeder of the other four;
Would they not wish the feast might ever last,
And bid Suspicion double-lock the door,   448
  Lest Jealousy, that sour unwelcome guest,
  Should, by his stealing in, disturb the feast?'

Once more the ruby-colour'd portal open'd,
Which to his speech did honey passage yield;
Like a red morn, that ever yet betoken'd   453
Wrack to the seaman, tempest to the field,
  Sorrow to shepherds, woe unto the birds,
  Gusts and foul flaws to herdmen and to herds.

This ill presage advisedly she marketh: 457
Even as the wind is hush'd before it raineth,
Or as the wolf doth grin before he barketh,
Or as the berry breaks before it staineth,   460
  Or like the deadly bullet of a gun,
  His meaning struck her ere his words begun.

And at his look she flatly falleth down,
For looks kill love and love by looks reviveth;
A smile recures the wounding of a frown; 465
But blessed bankrupt, that by love so thriveth!
  The silly boy, believing she is dead,
  Claps her pale cheek, till clapping makes it
    red;   468

And all-amaz'd brake off his late intent,
For sharply he did think to reprehend her,
Which cunning love did wittily prevent:
Fair fall the wit that can so well defend her! 472
  For on the grass she lies as she were slain,
  Till his breath breatheth life in her again.

He wrings her nose, he strikes her on the cheeks,
He bends her fingers, holds her pulses hard, 476
He chafes her lips; a thousand ways he seeks
To mend the hurt that his unkindness marr'd:
  He kisses her; and she, by her good will,
  Will never rise, so he will kiss her still. 480

The night of sorrow now is turn'd to day:
Her two blue windows faintly she up-heaveth,
Like the fair sun, when in his fresh array
He cheers the morn and all the world reliev-
    eth: 484
  And as the bright sun glorifies the sky,
  So is her face illumin'd with her eye;

Whose beams upon his hairless face are fix'd,
As if from thence they borrow'd all their shine. 489
Were never four such lamps together mix'd,
Had not his clouded with his brows' repine;
  But hers, which through the crystal tears gave
    light,
  Shone like the moon in water seen by night.

'O! where am I?' quoth she, in earth or
    heaven,   493
Or in the ocean drench'd, or in the fire?
What hour is this? or morn or weary even?
Do I delight to die, or life desire?   496
  But now I liv'd, and life was death's annoy;
  But now I died, and death was lively joy.

'O! thou didst kill me; kill me once again:
Thy eyes' shrewd tutor, that hard heart of
    thine,   500
Hath taught them scornful tricks and such dis-
    dain
That they have murder'd this poor heart of mine;
  And these mine eyes, true leaders to their
    queen,
  But for thy piteous lips no more had seen. 504

'Long may they kiss each other for this cure!
O! never let their crimson liveries wear;
And as they last, their verdure still endure,
To drive infection from the dangerous year: 508
  That the star-gazers, having writ on death,
  May say, the plague is banish'd by thy breath.

'Pure lips, sweet seals in my soft lips imprinted,
What bargains may I make, still to be sealing?
To sell myself I can be well contented,   513
So thou wilt buy and pay and use good dealing;

Which purchase if thou make, for fear of slips
Set thy seal-manual on my wax-red lips. 516

'A thousand kisses buys my heart from me;
And pay them at thy leisure, one by one.
What is ten hundred touches unto thee?
Are they not quickly told and quickly gone? 520
  Say, for non-payment that the debt should
    double,
  Is twenty hundred kisses such a trouble?'

'Fair queen,' quoth he, 'if any love you owe me,
Measure my strangeness with my unripe
    years: 524
Before I know myself, seek not to know me;
No fisher but the ungrown fry forbears:
  The mellow plum doth fall, the green sticks
    fast,
  Or being early pluck'd is sour to taste. 528

'Look! the world's comforter, with weary gait,
His day's hot task hath ended in the west;
The owl, night's herald, shrieks, 'tis very late;
The sheep are gone to fold, birds to their nest,
  And coal-black clouds that shadow heaven's
    light   533
  Do summon us to part and bid good night.

'Now let me say good night, and so say you;
If you will say so, you shall have a kiss.' 536
'Good night,' quoth she; and ere he says adieu,
The honey fee of parting tender'd is:
  Her arms do lend his neck a sweet embrace;
  Incorporate then they seem, face grows to
    face.

Till, breathless, he disjoin'd, and backward drew
The heavenly moisture, that sweet coral mouth,
Whose precious taste her thirsty lips well knew,
Whereon they surfeit, yet complain on drouth:
  He with her plenty press'd, she faint with
    dearth,   545
  Their lips together glu'd, fall to the earth.

Now quick desire hath caught the yielding prey,
And glutton-like she feeds, yet never filleth; 548
Her lips are conquerors, his lips obey,
Paying what ransom the insulter willeth;
  Whose vulture thought doth pitch the price
    so high,
  That she will draw his lips' rich treasure dry.

And having felt the sweetness of the spoil, 553
With blindfold fury she begins to forage;
Her face doth reek and smoke, her blood doth
    boil,
And careless lust stirs up a desperate courage;
  Planting oblivion, beating reason back, 557
  Forgetting shame's pure blush and honour's
    wrack.

Hot, faint, and weary, with her hard embracing,
Like a wild bird being tam'd with too much
    handling,   560
Or as the fleet-foot roe that's tir'd with chasing,
Or like the froward infant still'd with dandling,
  He now obeys, and now no more resisteth,
  While she takes all she can, not all she listeth.

What wax so frozen but dissolves with temper-
　　ing,　　　　　　　　　　　　　　　565
And yields at last to every light impression?
Things out of hope are compass'd oft with
　　venturing,
Chiefly in love, whose leave exceeds commis-
　　sion:　　　　　　　　　　　　　　568
　　Affection faints not like a pale-fac'd coward,
　　But then woos best when most his choice is
　　froward.

When he did frown, O! had she then gave
　　over,　　　　　　　　　　　　　　571
Such nectar from his lips she had not suck'd.
Foul words and frowns must not repel a lover;
What though the rose have prickles, yet 'tis
　　pluck'd:
　　Were beauty under twenty locks kept fast,
　　Yet love breaks through and picks them all
　　at last.　　　　　　　　　　　　576

For pity now she can no more detain him;
The poor fool prays her that he may depart:
She is resolv'd no longer to restrain him, 579
Bids him farewell, and look well to her heart,
　　The which, by Cupid's bow she doth protest,
　　He carries thence incaged in his breast.

'Sweet boy,' she says, 'this night I'll waste in
　　sorrow,
For my sick heart commands mine eyes to
　　watch.　　　　　　　　　　　　584
Tell me, Love's master, shall we meet to-mor-
　　row?
Say, shall we? shall we? wilt thou make the
　　match?'
　　He tells her, no; to-morrow he intends
　　To hunt the boar with certain of his friends.

'The boar!' quoth she; whereat a sudden pale,
Like lawn being spread upon the blushing rose,
Usurps her cheeks, she trembles at his tale, 591
And on his neck her yoking arms she throws:
　　She sinketh down, still hanging by his neck,
　　He on her belly falls, she on her back.

Now is she in the very lists of love,
Her champion mounted for the hot encounter:
All is imaginary she doth prove,　　　597
He will not manage her, although he mount her;
　　That worse than Tantalus' is her annoy,
　　To clip Elysium and to lack her joy.　600

Even as poor birds, deceiv'd with painted grapes,
Do surfeit by the eye and pine the maw,
Even so she languisheth in her mishaps,
As those poor birds that helpless berries saw.
　　The warm effects which she in him finds
　　missing,　　　　　　　　　　605
　　She seeks to kindle with continual kissing.

But all in vain; good queen, it will not be:
She hath assay'd as much as may be prov'd; 608
Her pleading hath deserv'd a greater fee;
She's Love, she loves, and yet she is not lov'd.
　　'Fie, fie!' he says, 'you crush me; let me go;
　　You have no reason to withhold me so.' 612

'Thou hadst been gone,' quoth she, 'sweet boy,
　　ere this,
But that thou told'st me thou wouldst hunt the
　　boar.
O! be advis'd; thou know'st not what it is
With javelin's point a churlish swine to gore,
　　Whose tushes never sheath'd he whetteth
　　still,　　　　　　　　　　　　617
　　Like to a mortal butcher, bent to kill.

'On his bow-back he hath a battle set
Of bristly pikes, that ever threat his foes; 620
His eyes like glow-worms shine when he doth
　　fret;
His snout digs sepulchres where'er he goes;
　　Being mov'd, he strikes whate'er is in his way,
　　And whom he strikes his crooked tushes
　　slay.　　　　　　　　　　　　624

'His brawny sides, with hairy bristles arm'd,
Are better proof than thy spear's point can
　　enter;
His short thick neck cannot be easily harm'd;
Being ireful, on the lion he will venture: 628
　　The thorny brambles and embracing bushes,
　　As fearful of him part, through whom he
　　rushes.

'Alas! he nought esteems that face of thine,
To which Love's eyes pay tributary gazes; 632
Nor thy soft hands, sweet lips, and crystal eyne,
Whose full perfection all the world amazes;
　　But having thee at vantage, wondrous dread!
　　Would root these beauties as he roots the
　　mead.　　　　　　　　　　　636

'O! let him keep his loathsome cabin still;
Beauty hath nought to do with such foul fiends:
Come not within his danger by his will;
They that thrive well take counsel of their
　　friends.　　　　　　　　　　640
　　When thou didst name the boar, not to dis-
　　semble,
　　I fear'd thy fortune, and my joints did tremble.

'Didst thou not mark my face? was it not
　　white?　　　　　　　　　　　643
Saw'st thou not signs of fear lurk in mine eye?
Grew I not faint? And fell I not downright?
Within my bosom, whereon thou dost lie,
　　My boding heart pants, beats, and takes no
　　rest,
　　But, like an earthquake, shakes thee on my
　　breast.　　　　　　　　　　648

'For where Love reigns, disturbing Jealousy
Doth call himself Affection's sentinel;
Gives false alarms, suggesteth mutiny,
And in a peaceful hour doth cry "Kill, kill!" 652
　　Distempering gentle Love in his desire,
　　As air and water do abate the fire.

'This sour informer, this bate-breeding spy,
This canker that eats up Love's tender spring,
This carry-tale, dissentious Jealousy,　657
That sometime true news, sometime false doth
　　bring,
　　Knocks at my heart, and whispers in mine ear
　　That if I love thee, I thy death should fear:

'And more than so, presenteth to mine eye 661
The picture of an angry-chafing boar,
Under whose sharp fangs on his back doth lie
An image like thyself, all stain'd with gore; 664
  Whose blood upon the fresh flowers being
    shed
  Doth make them droop with grief and hang
    the head.

'What should I do, seeing thee so indeed,
That tremble at the imagination?   668
The thought of it doth make my faint heart
  bleed,
And fear doth teach it divination:
  I prophesy thy death, my living sorrow, 671
  If thou encounter with the boar to-morrow.

'But if thou needs wilt hunt, be rul'd by me;
Uncouple at the timorous flying hare,
Or at the fox which lives by subtilty,
Or at the roe which no encounter dare: 676
  Pursue these fearful creatures o'er the downs,
  And on thy well-breath'd horse keep with thy
    hounds.

'And when thou hast on foot the purblind hare,
Mark the poor wretch, to overshoot his troubles
How he outruns the winds, and with what
  care   681
He cranks and crosses with a thousand doubles:
  The many musits through the which he goes
  Are like a labyrinth to amaze his foes. 684

'Sometime he runs among a flock of sheep,
To make the cunning hounds mistake their
  smell,
And sometime where earth-delving conies keep,
To stop the loud pursuers in their yell, 688
  And sometime sorteth with a herd of deer;
  Danger deviseth shifts; wit waits on fear:

'For there his smell with others being mingled,
The hot scent-snuffing hounds are driven to
  doubt,   692
Ceasing their clamorous cry till they have singled
With much ado the cold fault cleanly out;
  Then do they spend their mouths: Echo re-
    plies,
  As if another chase were in the skies.   696

'By this, poor Wat, far off upon a hill,
Stands on his hinder legs with listening ear,
To hearken if his foes pursue him still:
Anon their loud alarums he doth hear;   700
  And now his grief may be compared well
  To one sore sick that hears the passing-bell.

'Then shalt thou see the dew-bedabbled wretch
Turn, and return, indenting with the way; 704
Each envious briar his weary legs doth scratch,
Each shadow makes him stop, each murmur
  stay:
  For misery is trodden on by many,
  And being low never reliev'd by any.   708

'Lie quietly, and hear a little more;
Nay, do not struggle, for thou shalt not rise:

To make thee hate the hunting of the boar,
Unlike myself thou hear'st me moralize;   712
  Applying this to that, and so to so;
  For love can comment upon every woe.

'Where did I leave?' 'No matter where,' quoth
  he;
'Leave me, and then the story aptly ends: 716
The night is spent,' 'Why, what of that?' quoth
  she.
'I am,' quoth he, 'expected of my friends;
  And now 'tis dark, and going I shall fall.'
  'In night,' quoth she, 'desire sees best of all.'

'But if thou fall, O! then imagine this,   721
The earth, in love with thee, thy footing trips,
And all is but to rob thee of a kiss.
Rich preys make true men thieves; so do thy
  lips   724
  Make modest Dian cloudy and forlorn,
  Lest she should steal a kiss and die forsworn.

'Now of this dark night I perceive the reason:
Cynthia for shame obscures her silver shine, 728
Till forging Nature be condemn'd of treason,
For stealing moulds from heaven that were
  divine;
  Wherein she fram'd thee in high heaven's
    despite,   731
  To shame the sun by day and her by night.

'And therefore hath she brib'd the Destinies,
To cross the curious workmanship of nature,
To mingle beauty with infirmities,
And pure perfection with impure defeature; 736
  Making it subject to the tyranny
  Of mad mischances and much misery;

'As burning fevers, agues pale and faint,
Life-poisoning pestilence and frenzies wood, 740
The marrow-eating sickness, whose attaint
Disorder breeds by heating of the blood;
  Surfeits, imposthumes, grief, and damn'd
    despair,
  Swear nature's death for framing thee so fair.

'And not the least of all these maladies   745
But in one minute's fight brings beauty under:
Both favour, savour, hue, and qualities,
Whereat the impartial gazer late did wonder,
  Are on the sudden wasted, thaw'd and
    done,   749
  As mountain-snow melts with the mid-day
    sun.

'Therefore, despite of fruitless chastity,
Love-lacking vestals and self-loving nuns, 752
That on the earth would breed a scarcity
And barren dearth of daughters and of sons,
  Be prodigal: the lamp that burns by night
  Dries up his oil to lend the world his light.

'What is thy body but a swallowing grave, 757
Seeming to bury that posterity
Which by the rights of time thou needs must have,
If thou destroy them not in dark obscurity? 760
  If so, the world will hold thee in disdain,
  Sith in thy pride so fair a hope is slain.

'So in thyself thyself art made away;
A mischief worse than civil home-bred strife,
Of theirs whose desperate hands themselves do
    slay,   765
Or butcher-sire that reaves his son of life.
    Foul-cankering rust the hidden treasure frets,
    But gold that's put to use more gold begets.'

'Nay then,' quoth Adon, 'you will fall again 769
Into your idle over-handled theme;
The kiss I gave you is bestow'd in vain,
And all in vain you strive against the stream;
    For by this black-fac'd night, desire's foul
    nurse,   773
    Your treatise makes me like you worse and
    worse.

'If love have lent you twenty thousand tongues,
And every tongue more moving than your
    own,   776
Bewitching like the wanton mermaid's songs,
Yet from mine ear the tempting tune is blown;
    For know, my heart stands armed in mine
    ear,
    And will not let a false sound enter there; 780

'Lest the deceiving harmony should run
Into the quiet closure of my breast;
And then my little heart were quite undone,
In his bedchamber to be barr'd of rest.   784
    No, lady, no; my heart longs not to groan,
    But soundly sleeps, while now it sleeps alone.

'What have you urg'd that I cannot reprove?
The path is smooth that leadeth on to danger;
I hate not love, but your device in love,   789
That lends embracements unto every stranger.
    You do it for increase: O strange excuse!
    When reason is the bawd to lust's abuse.   792

'Call it not love, for Love to heaven is fled,
Since sweating Lust on earth usurp'd his name;
Under whose simple semblance he hath fed
Upon fresh beauty, blotting it with blame;   796
    Which the hot tyrant stains and soon be-
    reaves,
    As caterpillars do the tender leaves.

'Love comforteth like sunshine after rain,
But Lust's effect is tempest after sun;   800
Love's gentle spring doth always fresh remain,
Lust's winter comes ere summer half be done.
    Love surfeits not, Lust like a glutton dies;
    Love is all truth, Lust full of forged lies. 804

'More I could tell, but more I dare not say;
The text is old, the orator too green.
Therefore, in sadness, now I will away;
My face is full of shame, my heart of teen: 808
    Mine ears, that to your wanton talk attended,
    Do burn themselves for having so offended.'

With this he breaketh from the sweet embrace
Of those fair arms which bound him to her
    breast,   812
And homeward through the dark laund runs
    apace;

Leaves Love upon her back deeply distress'd.
    Look, how a bright star shooteth from the sky,
    So glides he in the night from Venus' eye; 816

Which after him she darts, as one on shore
Gazing upon a late-embarked friend,
Till the wild waves will have him seen no more,
Whose ridges with the meeting clouds contend:
    So did the merciless and pitchy night   821
    Fold in the object that did feed her sight.

Whereat amaz'd, as one that unaware
Hath dropp'd a precious jewel in the flood, 824
Or 'stonish'd as night-wanderers often are,
Their light blown out in some mistrustful wood;
    Even so confounded in the dark she lay,
    Having lost the fair discovery of her way. 828

And now she beats her heart, whereat it groans,
That all the neighbour caves, as seeming
    troubled,
Make verbal repetition of her moans;
Passion on passion deeply is redoubled: 832
    'Ay me!' she cries, and twenty times, 'Woe,
    woe!'
    And twenty echoes twenty times cry so.

She marking them, begins a wailing note,
And sings extemporally a woeful ditty;   836
How love makes young men thrall and old men
    dote;
How love is wise in folly, foolish-witty:
    Her heavy anthem still concludes in woe,
    And still the choir of echoes answer so.   840

Her song was tedious, and outwore the night,
For lovers' hours are long, though seeming
    short:
If pleas'd themselves, others, they think, delight
In such like circumstance, with such like
    sport: 844
    Their copious stories, oftentimes begun,
    End without audience, and are never done.

For who hath she to spend the night withal,
But idle sounds resembling parasites;   848
Like shrill-tongu'd tapsters answering every call,
Soothing the humour of fantastic wits?
    She says, ''Tis so': they answer all, ''Tis so';
    And would say after her, if she said 'No'. 852

Lo! here the gentle lark, weary of rest,
From his moist cabinet mounts up on high,
And wakes the morning, from whose silver breast
The sun ariseth in his majesty;   856
    Who doth the world so gloriously behold,
    That cedar-tops and hills seem burnish'd gold.

Venus salutes him with this fair good morrow;
'O thou clear god, and patron of all light, 860
From whom each lamp and shining star doth
    borrow
The beauteous influence that makes him bright,
    There lives a son that suck'd an earthly
    mother,
    May lend thee light, as thou dost lend to
    other.'   864

This said, she hasteth to a myrtle grove,
Musing the morning is so much o'erworn,
And yet she hears no tidings of her love;
She hearkens for his hounds and for his horn:
　Anon she hears them chant it lustily,　869
And all in haste she coasteth to the cry.

And as she runs, the bushes in the way
Some catch her by the neck, some kiss her face,
Some twine about her thigh to make her stay:
She wildly breaketh from their strict embrace,
　Like a milch doe, whose swelling dugs do ache,
　Hasting to feed her fawn hid in some brake.

By this she hears the hounds are at a bay; 877
Whereat she starts, like one that spies an adder
Wreath'd up in fatal folds just in his way,
The fear whereof doth make him shake and
　shudder;　880
　Even so the timorous yelping of the hounds
　Appals her senses, and her spirit confounds.

For now she knows it is no gentle chase,
But the blunt boar, rough bear, or lion proud,
Because the cry remaineth in one place,　885
Where fearfully the dogs exclaim aloud:
　Finding their enemy to be so curst,
　They all strain courtesy who shall cope him
　first.　888

This dismal cry rings sadly in her ear,
Through which it enters to surprise her heart;
Who, overcome by doubt and bloodless fear,
With cold-pale weakness numbs each feeling
　part;　892
　Like soldiers, when their captain once doth
　yield,
　They basely fly and dare not stay the field.

Thus stands she in a trembling ecstasy,
Till, cheering up her senses sore dismay'd, 896
She tells them 'tis a causeless fantasy,
And childish error, that they are afraid;
　Bids them leave quaking, bids them fear no
　more:
　And with that word she spied the hunted
　boar,　900

Whose frothy mouth bepainted all with red,
Like milk and blood being mingled both to-
　gether,
A second fear through all her sinews spread,
Which madly hurries her she knows not
　whither:　904
　This way she runs, and now she will no further,
　But back retires to rate the boar for murther.

A thousand spleens bear her a thousand ways,
She treads the path that she untreads again;
Her more than haste is mated with delays, 909
Like the proceedings of a drunken brain,
　Full of respects, yet nought at all respecting,
　In hand with all things, nought at all effect-
　ing.　912

Here kennel'd in a brake she finds a hound,
And asks the weary caitiff for his master,
And there another licking of his wound,
'Gainst venom'd sores the only sovereign plas-
　ter;　916
And here she meets another sadly scowling,
To whom she speaks, and he replies with
　howling.

When he hath ceas'd his ill-resounding noise,
Another flap-mouth'd mourner, black and
　grim,　920
Against the welkin volleys out his voice;
Another and another answer him,
　Clapping their proud tails to the ground
　below,
　Shaking their scratch'd ears, bleeding as they
　go.　924

Look, how the world's poor people are amaz'd
At apparitions, signs, and prodigies,
Whereon with fearful eyes they long have gaz'd,
Infusing them with dreadful prophecies;　928
　So she at these sad sighs draws up her breath,
　And, sighing it again, exclaims on Death.

'Hard-favour'd tyrant, ugly, meagre, lean,
Hateful divorce of love,'—thus chides she
　Death,—　932
'Grim-grinning ghost, earth's worm, what dost
　thou mean
To stifle beauty and to steal his breath,
　Who when he liv'd, his breath and beauty set
　Gloss on the rose, smell to the violet?　936

'If he be dead, O no! it cannot be,
Seeing his beauty, thou shouldst strike at it;
O yes! it may; thou hast no eyes to see,
But hatefully at random dost thou hit.　940
　Thy mark is feeble age, but thy false dart
　Mistakes that aim and cleaves an infant's
　heart.

'Hadst thou but bid beware, then he had spoke,
And, hearing him, thy power had lost his
　power.　944
The Destinies will curse thee for this stroke;
They bid thee crop a weed, thou pluck'st a
　flower.
　Love's golden arrow at him should have fled,
　And not Death's ebon dart, to strike him
　dead.　948

'Dost thou drink tears, that thou provok'st
　such weeping?
What may a heavy groan advantage thee?
Why hast thou cast into eternal sleeping　951
Those eyes that taught all other eyes to see?
　Now Nature cares not for thy mortal vigour,
　Since her best work is ruin'd with thy rigour.'

Here overcome, as one full of despair,　955
She vail'd her eyelids, who, like sluices, stopp'd
The crystal tide that from her two cheeks fair
In the sweet channel of her bosom dropp'd;
　But through the flood-gates breaks the silver
　rain,
　And with his strong course opens them again.

O! how her eyes and tears did lend and bor-
　　row; 961
Her eyes seen in the tears, tears in her eye;
Both crystals, where they view'd each other's
　　sorrow,
Sorrow that friendly sighs sought still to dry;
　　But like a stormy day, now wind, now rain,
　　Sighs dry her cheeks, tears make them wet
　　　again.

Variable passions throng her constant woe,
As striving who should best become her grief;
All entertain'd, each passion labours so, 969
That every present sorrow seemeth chief,
　　But none is best; then join they all together,
　　Like many clouds consulting for foul weather.

By this, far off she hears some huntsman holla;
A nurse's song ne'er pleas'd her babe so well:
The dire imagination she did follow
This sound of hope doth labour to expel; 976
　　For now reviving joy bids her rejoice,
　　And flatters her it is Adonis' voice.

Whereat her tears began to turn their tide,
Being prison'd in her eye, like pearls in glass;
Yet sometimes falls an orient drop beside, 981
Which her cheek melts, as scorning it should
　　pass,
　　To wash the foul face of the sluttish ground,
　　Who is but drunken when she seemeth
　　　drown'd. 984

O hard-believing love! how strange it seems
Not to believe, and yet too credulous;
Thy weal and woe are both of them extremes;
Despair and hope make thee ridiculous: 988
　　The one doth flatter thee in thoughts unlikely,
　　In likely thoughts the other kills thee quickly.

Now she unweaves the web that she hath
　　wrought,
Adonis lives, and Death is not to blame; 992
It was not she that call'd him all to naught,
Now she adds honours to his hateful name;
　　She clepes him king of graves, and grave for
　　　kings,
　　Imperious supreme of all mortal things. 996

'No, no,' quoth she, 'sweet Death, I did but jest;
Yet pardon me, I felt a kind of fear
Whenas I met the boar, that bloody beast,
Which knows no pity, but is still severe; 1000
　　Then, gentle shadow,—truth I must con-
　　　fess,—
　　I rail'd on thee, fearing my love's decease.

''Tis not my fault: the boar provok'd my tongue;
Be wreak'd on him, invisible commander; 1004
'Tis he, foul creature, that hath done thee wrong;
I did but act, he's author of my slander:
　　Grief hath two tongues: and never woman
　　　yet,
　　Could rule them both without ten women's
　　　wit.' 1008

Thus hoping that Adonis is alive,
Her rash suspect she doth extenuate;
And that his beauty may the better thrive,
With Death she humbly doth insinuate; 1012
　　Tells him of trophies, statues, tombs; and
　　　stories
　　His victories, his triumphs, and his glories.

'O Jove!' quoth she, 'how much a fool was I,
To be of such a weak and silly mind 1016
To wail his death who lives and must not die
Till mutual overthrow of mortal kind;
　　For he being dead, with him is beauty slain,
　　And, beauty dead, black chaos comes again.

'Fie, fie, fond love! thou art so full of fear 1021
As one with treasure laden, hemm'd with
　　thieves;
Trifles, unwitnessed with eye or ear,
Thy coward heart with false bethinking grieves.'
　　Even at this word she hears a merry horn,
　　Whereat she leaps that was but late forlorn.

As falcon to the lure, away she flies;
The grass stoops not, she treads on it so light;
And in her haste unfortunately spies 1029
The foul boar's conquest on her fair delight;
　　Which seen, her eyes, as murder'd with the
　　　view,
　　Like stars asham'd of day, themselves with-
　　　drew: 1032

Or, as the snail, whose tender horns being hit,
Shrinks backwards in his shelly cave with pain,
And there, all smother'd up, in shade doth sit,
Long after fearing to creep forth again; 1036
　　So, at his bloody view, her eyes are fled
　　Into the deep dark cabins of her head:

Where they resign their office and their light
To the disposing of her troubled brain; 1040
Who bids them still consort with ugly night,
And never wound the heart with looks again;
　　Who, like a king perplexed in his throne,
　　By their suggestion gives a deadly groan,

Whereat each tributary subject quakes, 1045
As when the wind, imprison'd in the ground,
Struggling for passage, earth's foundation
　　shakes,
Which with cold terror doth men's minds con-
　　found.
　　This mutiny each part doth so surprise 1049
　　That from their dark beds once more leap her
　　　eyes;

And, being open'd, threw unwilling light
Upon the wide wound that the boar had
　　trench'd 1052
In his soft flank; whose wonted lily white
With purple tears, that his wound wept, was
　　drench'd:
　　No flower was nigh, no grass, herb, leaf, or
　　　weed,
　　But stole his blood and seem'd with him to
　　　bleed. 1056

This solemn sympathy poor Venus noteth,
Over one shoulder doth she hang her head,
Dumbly she passions, franticly she doteth;
She thinks he could not die, he is not dead: 1060
  Her voice is stopp'd, her joints forget to bow,
  Her eyes are mad that they have wept till now.

Upon his hurt she looks so steadfastly,
That her sight dazzling makes the wound seem three; 1064
And then she reprehends her mangling eye,
That makes more gashes where no breach should be:
  His face seems twain, each several limb is doubled;
  For oft the eye mistakes, the brain being troubled. 1068

'My tongue cannot express my grief for one,
And yet,' quoth she, 'behold two Adons dead!
My sighs are blown away, my salt tears gone,
Mine eyes are turn'd to fire, my heart to lead:
  Heavy heart's lead, melt at mine eyes' red fire! 1073
  So shall I die by drops of hot desire.

'Alas! poor world, what treasure hast thou lost?
What face remains alive that's worth the viewing?
Whose tongue is music now? what canst thou boast 1077
Of things long since, or anything ensuing?
  The flowers are sweet, their colours fresh and trim;
  But true-sweet beauty liv'd and died with him.

'Bonnet nor veil henceforth no creature wear!
Nor sun nor wind will ever strive to kiss you:
Having no fair to lose, you need not fear;
The sun doth scorn you, and the wind doth hiss you: 1084
  But when Adonis liv'd, sun and sharp air
  Lurk'd like two thieves, to rob him of his fair:

'And therefore would he put his bonnet on,
Under whose brim the gaudy sun would peep;
The wind would blow it off, and, being gone, 1089
Play with his locks: then would Adonis weep;
  And straight, in pity of his tender years,
  They both would strive who first should dry his tears. 1092

'To see his face the lion walk'd along
Behind some hedge, because he would not fear him;
To recreate himself when he hath sung,
The tiger would be tame and gently hear him;
  If he had spoke, the wolf would leave his prey, 1097
  And never fright the silly lamb that day.

'When he beheld his shadow in the brook,
The fishes spread on it their golden gills; 1100
When he was by, the birds such pleasure took,
That some would sing, some other in their bills
  Would bring him mulberries and ripe-red cherries.
  He fed them with his sight, they him with berries. 1104

'But this foul, grim, and urchin-snouted boar,
Whose downward eye still looketh for a grave,
Ne'er saw the beauteous livery that he wore;
Witness the entertainment that he gave: 1108
  If he did see his face, why then I know
  He thought to kiss him, and hath kill'd him so.

''Tis true, 'tis true; thus was Adonis slain:
He ran upon the boar with his sharp spear, 1112
Who did not whet his teeth at him again,
But by a kiss thought to persuade him there;
  And nuzzling in his flank, the loving swine
  Sheath'd unaware the tusk in his soft groin.

'Had I been tooth'd like him, I must confess,
With kissing him I should have kill'd him first;
But he is dead, and never did he bless
My youth with his; the more am I accurst.' 1120
  With this she falleth in the place she stood,
  And stains her face with his congealed blood.

She looks upon his lips, and they are pale;
She takes him by the hand, and that is cold;
She whispers in his ears a heavy tale, 1125
As if they heard the woeful words she told:
  She lifts the coffer-lids that close his eyes,
  Where, lo! two lamps, burnt out, in darkness lies; 1128

Two glasses where herself herself beheld
A thousand times, and now no more reflect;
Their virtue lost, wherein they late excell'd,
And every beauty robb'd of his effect: 1132
  'Wonder of time,' quoth she, 'this is my spite,
  That, you being dead, the day should yet be light.

'Since thou art dead, lo! here I prophesy,
Sorrow on love hereafter shall attend: 1136
It shall be waited on with jealousy,
Find sweet beginning, but unsavoury end;
  Ne'er settled equally, but high or low;
  That all love's pleasure shall not match his woe.

'It shall be fickle, false, and full of fraud, 1141
Bud and be blasted in a breathing-while;
The bottom poison, and the top o'erstraw'd
With sweets that shall the truest sight beguile:
  The strongest body shall it make most weak,
  Strike the wise dumb and teach the fool to speak. 1146

'It shall be sparing and too full of riot,
Teaching decrepit age to tread the measures;
The staring ruffian shall it keep in quiet, 1149
Pluck down the rich, enrich the poor with treasures;
  It shall be raging mad, and silly mild,
  Make the young old, the old become a child.

'It shall suspect where is no cause of fear; 1153
It shall not fear where it should most mistrust;
It shall be merciful, and too severe,
And most deceiving when it seems most just;
  Perverse it shall be, where it shows most toward, 1157
  Put fear to valour, courage to the coward.

'It shall be cause of war and dire events,
And set dissension 'twixt the son and sire; 1160
Subject and servile to all discontents,
As dry combustious matter is to fire:
  Sith in his prime Death doth my love destroy,
  They that love best their love shall not enjoy.'

By this, the boy that by her side lay kill'd 1165
Was melted like a vapour from her sight,
And in his blood that on the ground lay spill'd,
A purple flower sprung up, chequer'd with
    white;   1168
  Resembling well his pale cheeks, and the
    blood
  Which in round drops upon their whiteness
    stood.

She bows her head, the new-sprung flower to
    smell,
Comparing it to her Adonis' breath;   1172
And says within her bosom it shall dwell,
Since he himself is reft from her by death:
  She crops the stalk, and in the breach appears
  Green dropping sap, which she compares to
    tears.   1176

'Poor flower,' quoth she, 'this was thy father's
    guise,
Sweet issue of a more sweet-smelling sire
For every little grief to wet his eyes:
To grow unto himself was his desire,   1180
  And so 'tis thine; but know, it is as good
  To wither in my breast as in his blood.

'Here was thy father's bed, here in my breast;
Thou art the next of blood, and 'tis thy right:
Lo! in this hollow cradle take thy rest,   1185
My throbbing heart shall rock thee day and
    night:
  There shall not be one minute in an hour
  Wherein I will not kiss my sweet love's
    flower.'   1188

Thus weary of the world, away she hies,
And yokes her silver doves; by whose swift aid
Their mistress, mounted, through the empty
    skies
In her light chariot quickly is convey'd;   1192
  Holding their course to Paphos, where their
    queen
  Means to immure herself and not be seen.

THE RAPE OF LUCRECE

TO THE RIGHT HONOURABLE HENRY WRIOTHESLY

EARL OF SOUTHAMPTON AND BARON OF TICHFIELD

THE love I dedicate to your lordship is without end; whereof this pamphlet, without beginning, is but a superfluous moiety. The warrant I have of your honourable disposition, not the worth of my untutored lines, makes it assured of acceptance. What I have done is yours; what I have to do is yours; being part in all I have, devoted yours. Were my worth greater, my duty would show greater; meantime, as it is, it is bound to your lordship, to whom I wish long life, still lengthened with happiness.

Your lordship's in all duty,

WILLIAM SHAKESPEARE.

THE ARGUMENT

LUCIUS TARQUINIUS,—for his excessive pride surnamed Superbus,—after he had caused his own father-in-law, Servius Tullius, to be cruelly murdered, and contrary to the Roman laws and customs, not requiring or staying for the people's suffrages, had possessed himself of the kingdom, went, accompanied with his sons and other noblemen of Rome, to besiege Ardea. During which siege the principal men of the army meeting one evening at the tent of Sextus Tarquinius, the king's son, in their discourses after supper, every one commended the virtues of his own wife: among whom Collatinus extolled the incomparable chastity of his wife Lucretia. In that pleasant humour they all posted to Rome; and intending, by their secret and sudden arrival, to make trial of that which every one had before avouched, only Collatinus finds his wife—though it were late in the night—spinning amongst her maids: the other ladies were all found dancing and revelling, or in several disports. Whereupon the noblemen yielded Collatinus the victory, and his wife the fame. At that time Sextus Tarquinius, being inflamed with Lucrece' beauty, yet smothering his passions for the present, departed with the rest back to the camp; from whence he shortly after privily withdrew himself, and was, according to his estate, royally entertained and lodged by Lucrece at Collatium. The same night he treacherously stealeth into her chamber, violently ravished her, and early in the morning speedeth away. Lucrece, in this lamentable plight, hastily dispatcheth messengers, one to Rome for her father, and another to the camp for Collatine. They came, the one accompanied with Junius Brutus, the other with Publius Valerius; and finding Lucrece attired in mourning habit, demanded the cause of her sorrow. She, first taking an oath of them for her revenge, revealed the actor, and the whole manner of his dealing, and withal suddenly stabbed herself. Which done, with one consent they all vowed to root out the whole hated family of the Tarquins; and, bearing the dead body to Rome, Brutus acquainted the people with the doer and manner of the vile deed, with a bitter invective against the tyranny of the king: wherewith the people were so moved, that with one consent and a general acclamation the Tarquins were all exiled, and the state government changed from kings to consuls.

FROM the besieged Ardea all in post,
Borne by the trustless wings of false desire,
Lust-breathed Tarquin leaves the Roman host,
And to Collatium bears the lightless fire   4
Which, in pale embers hid, lurks to aspire,
    And girdle with embracing flames the waist
    Of Collatine's fair love, Lucrece the chaste.

Haply that name of chaste unhappily set   8
This bateless edge on his keen appetite;
When Collatine unwisely did not let
To praise the clear unmatched red and white
Which triumph'd in that sky of his delight, 12
    Where mortal stars, as bright as heaven's beauties,
    With pure aspects did him peculiar duties.

For he the night before, in Tarquin's tent,
Unlock'd the treasure of his happy state;   16
What priceless wealth the heavens had him lent
In the possession of his beauteous mate;
Reckoning his fortune at such high-proud rate,
    That kings might be espoused to more fame,
    But king nor peer to such a peerless dame. 21

O happiness enjoy'd but of a few!
And, if possess'd, as soon decay'd and done
As is the morning's silver-melting dew   24
Against the golden splendour of the sun;

An expir'd date, cancell'd ere well begun:
    Honour and beauty, in the owner's arms,
    Are weakly fortress'd from a world of harms.

Beauty itself doth of itself persuade   29
The eyes of men without an orator;
What needeth then apology be made
To set forth that which is so singular?   32
Or why is Collatine the publisher
    Of that rich jewel he should keep unknown
    From thievish ears, because it is his own?

Perchance his boast of Lucrece' sovereignty 36
Suggested this proud issue of a king;
For by our ears our hearts oft tainted be:
Perchance that envy of so rich a thing,
Braving compare, disdainfully did sting   40
    His high-pitch'd thoughts, that meaner men should vaunt
    That golden hap which their superiors want.

But some untimely thought did instigate
His all-too-timeless speed, if none of those: 44
His honour, his affairs, his friends, his state,
Neglected all, with swift intent he goes
To quench the coal which in his liver glows.
    O! rash false heat, wrapp'd in repentant cold,
    Thy hasty spring still blasts, and ne'er grows old.   49

When at Collatium this false lord arriv'd,
Well was he welcom'd by the Roman dame,
Within whose face beauty and virtue striv'd 52
Which of them both should underprop her fame:
When virtue bragg'd, beauty would blush for
shame;
    When beauty boasted blushes, in despite
    Virtue would stain that o'er with silver
    white.   56

But beauty, in that white intituled,
From Venus' doves doth challenge that fair
field;
Then virtue claims from beauty beauty's red,
Which virtue gave the golden age to gild   60
Their silver cheeks, and call'd it then their
shield;
    Teaching them thus to use it in the fight,
    When shame assail'd, the red should fence
    the white.

This heraldry in Lucrece' face was seen,   64
Argu'd by beauty's red and virtue's white:
Of either's colour was the other queen,
Proving from world's minority their right:
Yet their ambition makes them still to fight; 68
    The sovereignty of either being so great,
    That oft they interchange each other's seat.

This silent war of lilies and of roses,
Which Tarquin view'd in her fair face's field, 72
In their pure ranks his traitor eye encloses;
Where, lest between them both it should be
kill'd,
    The coward captive vanquished doth yield
    To those two armies that would let him go, 76
    Rather than triumph in so false a foe.

Now thinks he that her husband's shallow
tongue—
The niggard prodigal that prais'd her so—
In that high task hath done her beauty wrong,
Which far exceeds his barren skill to show: 81
Therefore that praise which Collatine doth
owe
    Enchanted Tarquin answers with surmise,
    In silent wonder of still-gazing eyes.   84

This earthly saint, adored by this devil,
Little suspecteth the false worshipper;
For unstain'd thoughts do seldom dream on
evil,
Birds never lim'd no secret bushes fear: 88
So guiltless she securely gives good cheer
    And reverend welcome to her princely guest,
    Whose inward ill no outward harm express'd:

For that he colour'd with his high estate,   92
Hiding base sin in plaits of majesty;
That nothing in him seem'd inordinate,
Save sometime too much wonder of his eye,
Which, having all, all could not satisfy;   96
    But, poorly rich, so wanteth in his store,
    That, cloy'd with much, he pineth still for
    more.

But she, that never cop'd with stranger eyes,
Could pick no meaning from their parling
looks,   100
Nor read the subtle-shining secrecies
Writ in the glassy margents of such books:
She touch'd no unknown baits, nor fear'd no
hooks;
    Nor could she moralize his wanton sight, 104
    More than his eyes were open'd to the light.

He stories to her ears her husband's fame,
Won in the fields of fruitful Italy;
And decks with praises Collatine's high name,
Made glorious by his manly chivalry   109
With bruised arms and wreaths of victory:
    Her joy with heav'd-up hand she doth ex-
    press,
    And, wordless, so greets heaven for his suc-
    cess.   112

Far from the purpose of his coming thither,
He makes excuses for his being there:
No cloudy show of stormy blustering weather
Doth yet in this fair welkin once appear;   116
Till sable Night, mother of Dread and Fear,
    Upon the world dim darkness doth display,
    And in her vaulty prison stows the Day.

For then is Tarquin brought unto his bed, 120
Intending weariness with heavy spright;
For after supper long he questioned
With modest Lucrece, and wore out the night:
Now leaden slumber with life's strength doth
fight,   124
    And every one to rest themselves betake,
    Save thieves, and cares, and troubled minds,
    that wake.

As one of which doth Tarquin lie revolving
The sundry dangers of his will's obtaining; 128
Yet ever to obtain his will resolving,
Though weak-built hopes persuade him to ab-
staining:
Despair to gain doth traffic oft for gaining;
    And when great treasure is the meed pro-
    pos'd,   132
    Though death be adjunct, there's no death
    suppos'd.

Those that much covet are with gain so fond,
For what they have not, that which they possess
They scatter and unloose it from their bond, 136
And so, by hoping more, they have but less;
Or, gaining more, the profit of excess
    Is but to surfeit, and such griefs sustain,
    That they prove bankrupt in this poor-rich
    gain.   140

The aim of all is but to nurse the life
With honour, wealth, and ease, in waning age;
And in this aim there is such thwarting strife,
That one for all, or all for one we gage;   144
As life for honour in fell battles' rage:
    Honour for wealth; and oft that wealth doth
    cost
    The death of all, and all together lost.

So that in venturing ill we leave to be   148
The things we are for that which we expect;
And this ambitious foul infirmity,
In having much, torments us with defect
Of that we have: so then we do neglect   152
  The thing we have: and, all for want of wit,
  Make something nothing by augmenting it.

Such hazard now must doting Tarquin make,
Pawning his honour to obtain his lust,   156
And for himself himself he must forsake:
Then where is truth, if there be no self-trust?
When shall he think to find a stranger just,
  When he himself himself confounds, betrays
  To slanderous tongues and wretched hateful
    days?   161

Now stole upon the time the dead of night,
When heavy sleep had clos'd up mortal eyes;
No comfortable star did lend his light,   164
No noise but owls' and wolves' death-boding
  cries;
Now serves the season that they may surprise
  The silly lambs; pure thoughts are dead and
    still,
  While lust and murder wake to stain and kill.

And now this lustful lord leap'd from his bed,
Throwing his mantle rudely o'er his arm;
Is madly toss'd between desire and dread;
Th' one sweetly flatters, th' other feareth harm;
But honest fear, bewitch'd with lust's foul
  charm,   173
  Doth too too oft betake him to retire,
  Beaten away by brain-sick rude desire.

His falchion on a flint he softly smiteth,   176
That from the cold stone sparks of fire do fly;
Whereat a waxen torch forthwith he lighteth,
Which must be lode-star to his lustful eye;
And to the flame thus speaks advisedly: 180
  'As from this cold flint I enforc'd this fire,
  So Lucrece must I force to my desire.'

Here pale with fear he doth premeditate
The dangers of his loathsome enterprise,   184
And in his inward mind he doth debate
What following sorrow may on this arise:
Then looking scornfully, he doth despise 187
  His naked armour of still-slaughter'd lust,
  And justly thus controls his thoughts unjust:

'Fair torch, burn out thy light, and lend it not
To darken her whose light excelleth thine; 191
And die, unhallow'd thoughts, before you blot
With your uncleanness that which is divine;
Offer pure incense to so pure a shrine:
  Let fair humanity abhor the deed
  That spots and stains love's modest snow-
    white weed.   196

'O shame to knighthood and to shining arms!
O foul dishonour to my household's grave!
O impious act, including all foul harms!
A martial man to be soft fancy's slave!   200
True valour still a true respect should have;
  Then my digression is so vile, so base,
  That it will live engraven in my face.

Yea, though I die, the scandal will survive, 204
And be an eye-sore in my golden coat;
Some loathsome dash the herald will contrive,
To cipher me how fondly I did dote;
That my posterity sham'd with the note, 208
  Shall curse my bones, and hold it for no sin
  To wish that I their father had not been.

'What win I if I gain the thing I seek?
A dream, a breath, a froth of fleeting joy. 212
Who buys a minute's mirth to wail a week?
Or sells eternity to get a toy?
For one sweet grape who will the vine destroy?
  Or what fond beggar, but to touch the crown,
  Would with the sceptre straight be strucken
    down?   217

'If Collatinus dream of my intent,
Will he not wake, and in a desperate rage
Post hither, this vile purpose to prevent? 220
This siege that hath engirt his marriage,
This blur to youth, this sorrow to the sage,
  This dying virtue, this surviving shame,
  Whose crime will bear an ever-during blame?

'O! what excuse can my invention make, 225
When thou shalt charge me with so black a
  deed?
Will not my tongue be mute, my frail joints
  shake,
Mine eyes forego their light, my false heart
  bleed?   228
  The guilt being great, the fear doth still exceed;
  And extreme fear can neither fight nor fly,
  But coward-like with trembling terror die.

'Had Collatinus kill'd my son or sire,   232
Or lain in ambush to betray my life,
Or were he not my dear friend, this desire
Might have excuse to work upon his wife,
As in revenge or quittal of such strife: 236
  But as he is my kinsman, my dear friend,
  The shame and fault finds no excuse nor end.

'Shameful it is; ay, if the fact be known:
Hateful it is; there is no hate in loving: 240
I'll beg her love; but she is not her own:
The worst is but denial and reproving:
My will is strong, past reason's weak removing.
  Who fears a sentence, or an old man's saw,
  Shall by a painted cloth be kept in awe.' 245

Thus, graceless, holds he disputation
'Tween frozen conscience and hot-burning will,
And with good thoughts makes dispensation,
Urging the worser sense for vantage still; 249
  Which in a moment doth confound and kill
  All pure effects, and doth so far proceed,
  That what is vile shows like a virtuous deed.

Quoth he, 'She took me kindly by the hand, 253
And gaz'd for tidings in my eager eyes,
Fearing some hard news from the war-like band
Where her beloved Collatinus lies.   256
O! how her fear did make her colour rise:
  First red as roses that on lawn we lay,
  Then white as lawn, the roses took away.

'And how her hand, in my hand being lock'd,
Forc'd it to tremble with her loyal fear! 261
Which struck her sad, and then it faster rock'd,
Until her husband's welfare she did hear;
Whereat she smiled with so sweet a cheer, 264
    That like Narcissus seen her as she stood,
    Self-love had never drown'd him in the flood.

'Why hunt I then for colour or excuses?
All orators are dumb when beauty pleadeth; 268
Poor wretches have remorse in poor abuses;
Love thrives not in the heart that shadows
    dreadeth:
Affection is my captain, and he leadeth;
    And when his gaudy banner is display'd, 272
    The coward fights and will not be dismay'd.

'Then, childish fear, avaunt! debating, die!
Respect and reason, wait on wrinkled age!
My heart shall never countermand mine eye:
Sad pause and deep regard beseem the sage; 277
My part is youth, and beats these from the stage.
    Desire my pilot is, beauty my prize;
    Then who fears sinking where such treasure
    lies?' 280

As corn o'ergrown by weeds, so heedful fear
Is almost chok'd by unresisted lust.
Away he steals with open listening ear,
Full of foul hope, and full of fond mistrust; 284
Both which, as servitors to the unjust,
    So cross him with their opposite persuasion,
    That now he vows a league, and now invasion.

Within his thought his heavenly image sits, 288
And in the self-same seat sits Collatine:
That eye which looks on her confounds his wits;
That eye which him beholds, as more divine,
Unto a view so false will not incline; 292
    But with a pure appeal seeks to the heart,
    Which once corrupted, takes the worser part;

And therein heartens up his servile powers,
Who, flatter'd by their leader's jocund show,
Stuff up his lust, as minutes fill up hours; 297
And as their captain, so their pride doth grow,
Paying more slavish tribute than they owe.
    By reprobate desire thus madly led, 300
    The Roman lord marcheth to Lucrece' bed.

The locks between her chamber and his will,
Each one by him enforc'd, retires his ward;
But as they open they all rate his ill, 304
Which drives the creeping thief to some regard:
The threshold grates the door to have him heard;
    Night-wandering weasels shriek to see him
    there;
    They fright him, yet he still pursues his fear.

As each unwilling portal yields him way, 309
Through little vents and crannies of the place
The wind wars with his torch to make him stay,
And blows the smoke of it into his face, 312
Extinguishing his conduct in this case;
    But his hot heart, which fond desire doth
    scorch,
    Puffs forth another wind that fires the torch:

And being lighted, by the light he spies 316
Lucretia's glove, wherein her needle sticks:
He takes it from the rushes where it lies,
And griping it, the neeld his finger pricks;
As who should say, 'This glove to wanton
    tricks 320
    Is not inur'd; return again in haste;
    Thou seest our mistress' ornaments are
    chaste.'

But all these poor forbiddings could not stay
    him;
He in the worst sense construes their denial: 324
The door, the wind, the glove, that did delay
    him,
He takes for accidental things of trial;
    Or as those bars which stop the hourly dial,
    Who with a ling'ring stay his course doth let,
    Till every minute pays the hour his debt. 329

'So, so,' quoth he, 'these lets attend the time,
Like little frosts that sometime threat the spring,
To add a more rejoicing to the prime, 332
And give the sneaped birds more cause to sing.
Pain pays the income of each precious thing;
    Huge rocks, high winds, strong pirates,
    shelves and sands,
    The merchant fears, ere rich at home he
    lands.' 336

Now is he come unto the chamber door,
That shuts him from the heaven of his thought,
Which with a yielding latch, and with no more,
Hath barr'd him from the blessed thing he
    sought. 340
So from himself impiety hath wrought,
    That for his prey to pray he doth begin,
    As if the heavens should countenance his sin.

But in the midst of his unfruitful prayer, 344
Having solicited the eternal power
That his foul thoughts might compass his fair
    fair,
And they would stand auspicious to the hour,
Even there he starts: quoth he, 'I must de-
    flower; 348
    The powers to whom I pray abhor this fact,
    How can they then assist me in the act?

'Then Love and Fortune be my gods, my guide!
My will is back'd with resolution: 352
Thoughts are but dreams till their effects be
    tried;
The blackest sin is clear'd with absolution;
Against love's fire fear's frost hath dissolution;
    The eye of heaven is out, and misty night 356
    Covers the shame that follows sweet delight.'

This said, his guilty hand pluck'd up the latch,
And with his knee the door he opens wide.
The dove sleeps fast that this night-owl will
    catch: 360
Thus treason works ere traitors be espied.
Who sees the lurking serpent steps aside;
    But she, sound sleeping, fearing no such
    thing,
    Lies at the mercy of his mortal sting. 364

Into the chamber wickedly he stalks,
And gazeth on her yet unstained bed.
The curtains being close, about he walks,
Rolling his greedy eyeballs in his head: 368
By their high treason is his heart misled;
  Which gives the watchword to his hand full soon,
  To draw the cloud that hides the silver moon.

Look, as the fair and fiery-pointed sun,   372
Rushing from forth a cloud, bereaves our sight;
Even so, the curtain drawn, his eyes begun
To wink, being blinded with a greater light:
Whether it is that she reflects so bright,   376
  That dazzleth them, or else some shame supposed,
  But blind they are, and keep themselves enclosed.

O! had they in that darksome prison died,
Then had they seen the period of their ill;   380
Then Collatine again, by Lucrece' side,
In his clear bed might have reposed still:
But they must ope, this blessed league to kill,
  And holy-thoughted Lucrece to their sight 384
  Must sell her joy, her life, her world's delight.

Her lily hand her rosy cheek lies under,
Cozening the pillow of a lawful kiss;
Who, therefore angry, seems to part in sunder,
Swelling on either side to want his bliss;   389
Between whose hills her head entombed is:
  Where, like a virtuous monument she lies,
  To be admir'd of lewd unhallow'd eyes. 392

Without the bed her other fair hand was,
On the green coverlet; whose perfect white
Show'd like an April daisy on the grass,
With pearly sweat, resembling dew of night. 396
Her eyes, like marigolds, had sheath'd their light,
  And canopied in darkness sweetly lay,
  Till they might open to adorn the day.

Her hair, like golden threads, play'd with her breath;   400
O modest wantons! wanton modesty!
Showing life's triumph in the map of death,
And death's dim look in life's mortality:
Each in her sleep themselves so beautify, 404
  As if between them twain there were no strife,
  But that life liv'd in death, and death in life.

Her breasts, like ivory globes circled with blue,
A pair of maiden worlds unconquered, 408
Save of their lord no bearing yoke they knew,
And him by oath they truly honoured.
These worlds in Tarquin new ambition bred;
  Who, like a foul usurper, went about 412
  From this fair throne to heave the owner out.

What could he see but mightily he noted?
What did he note but strongly he desir'd?
What he beheld, on that he firmly doted, 416
And in his will his wilful eye he tir'd.
With more than admiration he admir'd
  Her azure veins, her alabaster skin,
  Her coral lips, her snow-white dimpled chin.

As the grim lion fawneth o'er his prey,   421
Sharp hunger by the conquest satisfied,
So o'er this sleeping soul doth Tarquin stay,
His rage of lust by gazing qualified;   424
Slack'd, not suppress'd; for standing by her side,
  His eye, which late this mutiny restrains,
  Unto a greater uproar tempts his veins:

And they, like straggling slaves for pillage fighting,   428
Obdurate vassals fell exploits effecting,
In bloody death and ravishment delighting,
Nor children's tears nor mothers' groans respecting,
Swell in their pride, the onset still expecting: 432
  Anon his beating heart, alarum striking,
  Gives the hot charge and bids them do their liking.

His drumming heart cheers up his burning eye,
His eye commends the leading to his hand; 436
His hand, as proud of such a dignity,
Smoking with pride, march'd on to make his stand
On her bare breast, the heart of all her land;
  Whose ranks of blue veins, as his hand did scale, 440
  Left their round turrets destitute and pale.

They, mustering to the quiet cabinet
Where their dear governess and lady lies,
Do tell her she is dreadfully beset, 444
And fright her with confusion of their cries:
She, much amaz'd, breaks ope her lock'd-up eyes,
  Who, peeping forth this tumult to behold,
  Are by his flaming torch dimm'd and controll'd. 448

Imagine her as one in dead of night
From forth dull sleep by dreadful fancy waking,
That thinks she hath beheld some ghastly sprite,
Whose grim aspect sets every joint a-shaking;
What terror 'tis! but she, in worser taking, 453
  From sleep disturbed, heedfully doth view
  The sight which makes supposed terror true.

Wrapp'd and confounded in a thousand fears,
Like to a new-kill'd bird she trembling lies; 457
She dares not look; yet, winking, there appears
Quick-shifting antics, ugly in her eyes:
Such shadows are the weak brain's forgeries;
  Who, angry that the eyes fly from their lights,
  In darkness daunts them with more dreadful sights.

His hand, that yet remains upon her breast,
Rude ram to batter such an ivory wall! 464
May feel her heart,—poor citizen,—distress'd
Wounding itself to death, rise up and fall,
Beating her bulk, that his hand shakes withal.
  This moves in him more rage, and lesser pity, 468
  To make the breach and enter this sweet city.

First, like a trumpet, doth his tongue begin
To sound a parley to his heartless foe;
Who o'er the white sheet peers her whiter chin, 472
The reason of this rash alarm to know,
Which he by dumb demeanour seeks to show;
But she with vehement prayers urgeth still
Under what colour he commits this ill. 476

Thus he replies: 'The colour in thy face,—
That even for anger makes the lily pale,
And the red rose blush at her own disgrace,—
Shall plead for me and tell my loving tale; 480
Under that colour am I come to scale
Thy never-conquer'd fort: the fault is thine,
For those thine eyes betray thee unto mine.

'Thus I forestall thee, if thou mean to chide: 484
Thy beauty hath ensnar'd thee to this night,
Where thou with patience must my will abide,
My will that marks thee for my earth's delight,
Which I to conquer sought with all my might; 488
But as reproof and reason beat it dead,
By thy bright beauty was it newly bred.

'I see what crosses my attempt will bring;
I know what thorns the growing rose defends;
I think the honey guarded with a sting; 493
All this, beforehand, counsel comprehends:
But will is deaf and hears no heedful friends;
Only he hath an eye to gaze on beauty, 496
And dotes on what he looks, 'gainst law or duty.

'I have debated, even in my soul,
What wrong, what shame, what sorrow I shall breed;
But nothing can affection's course control, 500
Or stop the headlong fury of his speed.
I know repentant tears ensue the deed,
Reproach, disdain, and deadly enmity;
Yet strive I to embrace mine infamy.' 504

This said, he shakes aloft his Roman blade,
Which like a falcon towering in the skies,
Coucheth the fowl below with his wings' shade,
Whose crooked beak threats if he mount he dies: 508
So under his insulting falchion lies
Harmless Lucretia, marking what he tells
With trembling fear, as fowl hear falcon's bells.

'Lucrece,' quoth he, 'this night I must enjoy thee; 512
If thou deny, then force must work my way,
For in thy bed I purpose to destroy thee:
That done, some worthless slave of thine I'll slay,
To kill thine honour with thy life's decay; 516
And in thy dead arms do I mean to place him,
Swearing I slew him, seeing thee embrace him.

'So thy surviving husband shall remain
The scornful mark of every open eye; 520
Thy kinsmen hang their heads at this disdain,
Thy issue blurr'd with nameless bastardy:
And thou, the author of their obloquy,
Shalt have thy trespass cited up in rimes, 524
And sung by children in succeeding times.

'But if thou yield, I rest thy secret friend:
The fault unknown is as a thought unacted;
A little harm done to a great good end, 528
For lawful policy remains enacted.
The poisonous simple sometimes is compacted
In a pure compound; being so applied,
His venom in effect is purified. 532

'Then for thy husband and thy children's sake,
Tender my suit: bequeath not to their lot
The shame that from them no device can take,
The blemish that will never be forgot; 536
Worse than a slavish wipe or birth-hour's blot:
For marks descried in men's nativity
Are nature's faults, not their own infamy.'

Here with a cockatrice' dead-killing eye 540
He rouseth up himself, and makes a pause;
While she, the picture of pure piety,
Like a white hind under the gripe's sharp claws,
Pleads in a wilderness where are no laws, 544
To the rough beast that knows no gentle right,
Nor aught obeys but his foul appetite.

But when a black-fac'd cloud the world doth threat,
In his dim mist the aspiring mountains hiding,
From earth's dark womb some gentle gust doth get, 549
Which blows these pitchy vapours from their biding,
Hindering their present fall by this dividing;
So his unhallow'd haste her words delays, 552
And moody Pluto winks while Orpheus plays.

Yet, foul night-waking cat, he doth but dally,
While in his hold-fast foot the weak mouse panteth:
Her sad behaviour feeds his vulture folly, 556
A swallowing gulf that even in plenty wanteth:
His ear her prayers admits, but his heart granteth
No penetrable entrance to her plaining:
Tears harden lust though marble wear with raining. 560

Her pity-pleading eyes are sadly fix'd
In the remorseless wrinkles of his face;
Her modest eloquence with sighs is mix'd,
Which to her oratory adds more grace. 564
She puts the period often from his place;
And midst the sentence so her accent breaks,
That twice she doth begin ere once she speaks.

She conjures him by high almighty Jove, 568
By knighthood, gentry, and sweet friendship's oath,
By her untimely tears, her husband's love,
By holy human law, and common troth,
By heaven and earth, and all the power of both,
That to his borrow'd bed he make retire, 573
And stoop to honour, not to foul desire.

Quoth she, 'Reward not hospitality
With such black payment as thou hast pre-
    tended;   576
Mud not the fountain that gave drink to thee;
Mar not the thing that cannot be amended;
End thy ill aim before thy shoot be ended;
    He is no woodman that doth bend his bow
    To strike a poor unseasonable doe.   581

'My husband is thy friend, for his sake spare
    me;
Thyself art mighty, for thine own sake leave
    me;
Myself a weakling, do not, then, ensnare me; 584
Thou look'dst not like deceit, do not deceive me.
My sighs, like whirlwinds, labour hence to
    heave thee;
    If ever man were mov'd with woman's moans,
    Be moved with my tears, my sighs, my
    groans.   588

'All which together, like a troubled ocean,
Beat at thy rocky and wrack-threatening heart,
To soften it with their continual motion;
For stones dissolv'd to water do convert.   592
O! if no harder than a stone thou art,
    Melt at my tears, and be compassionate;
    Soft pity enters at an iron gate.

'In Tarquin's likeness I did entertain thee; 596
Hast thou put on his shape to do him shame?
To all the host of heaven I complain me,
Thou wrong'st his honour, wound'st his
    princely name.
Thou art not what thou seem'st; and if the
    same,   600
    Thou seem'st not what thou art, a god, a king;
    For kings like gods should govern every thing.

'How will thy shame be seeded in thine age,
When thus thy vices bud before thy spring! 604
If in thy hope thou dar'st do such outrage,
What dar'st thou not when once thou art a king?
O! be remembered no outrageous thing
    From vassal actors can be wip'd away;   608
    Then kings' misdeeds cannot be hid in clay.

'This deed will make thee only lov'd for fear;
But happy monarchs still are fear'd for love:
With foul offenders thou perforce must bear,
When they in thee the like offences prove: 613
If but for fear of this, thy will remove;
    For princes are the glass, the school, the book,
    Where subjects' eyes do learn, do read, do
    look.   616

'And wilt thou be the school where Lust shall
    learn?
Must he in thee read lectures of such shame?
Wilt thou be glass wherein it shall discern
Authority for sin, warrant for blame,   620
To privilege dishonour in thy name?
    Thou back'st reproach against long-living
    laud,
    And mak'st fair reputation but a bawd.

'Hast thou command? by him that gave it
    thee,   624
From a pure heart command thy rebel will:
Draw not thy sword to guard iniquity,
For it was lent thee all that brood to kill.
Thy princely office how canst thou fulfil, 628
    When, pattern'd by thy fault, foul sin may
    say,
    He learn'd to sin, and thou didst teach the
    way?

'Think but how vile a spectacle it were,
To view thy present trespass in another.
Men's faults do seldom to themselves appear; 632
Their own transgressions partially they smother:
This guilt would seem death-worthy in thy
    brother.
    O! how are they wrapp'd in with infamies 636
    That from their own misdeeds askance their
    eyes.

'To thee, to thee, my heav'd-up hands appeal,
Not to seducing lust, thy rash relier:
I sue for exil'd majesty's repeal;   640
Let him return, and flattering thoughts retire:
His true respect will prison false desire,
    And wipe the dim mist from thy doting eyne,
    That thou shalt see thy state and pity mine.'

'Have done,' quoth he; 'my uncontrolled tide
Turns not, but swells the higher by this let.
Small lights are soon blown out, huge fires
    abide,
And with the wind in greater fury fret: 648
The petty streams that pay a daily debt
    To their salt sovereign, with their fresh falls'
    haste
    Add to his flow, but alter not his taste.'

'Thou art,' quoth she, 'a sea, a sovereign
    king;   652
And lo! there falls into thy boundless flood
Black lust, dishonour, shame, misgoverning,
Who seek to stain the ocean of thy blood.
If all these petty ills shall change thy good, 656
    Thy sea within a puddle's womb is hears'd,
    And not the puddle in thy sea dispers'd.

'So shall these slaves be king, and thou their
    slave;
Thou nobly base, they basely dignified;   660
Thou their fair life, and they thy fouler grave;
Thou loathed in their shame, they in thy pride:
The lesser thing should not the greater hide;
    The cedar stoops not to the base shrub's
    foot,   664
    But low shrubs wither at the cedar's root.

'So let thy thoughts, low vassals to thy state'—
'No more,' quoth he; 'by heaven, I will not hear
    thee:
Yield to my love; if not, enforced hate,   668
Instead of love's coy touch, shall rudely tear
    thee;
That done, despitefully I mean to bear thee
    Unto the base bed of some rascal groom,
    To be thy partner in this shameful doom.' 672

This said, he sets his foot upon the light,
For light and lust are deadly enemies:
Shame folded up in blind concealing night,
When most unseen, then most doth tyrannize.
The wolf hath seiz'd his prey, the poor lamb
 cries; 677
 Till with her own white fleece her voice con-
 troll'd
 Entombs her outcry in her lips' sweet fold:

For with the nightly linen that she wears 680
He pens her piteous clamours in her head,
Cooling his hot face in the chastest tears
That ever modest eyes with sorrow shed.
O! that prone lust should stain so pure a bed,
 The spots whereof could weeping purify, 685
 Her tears should drop on them perpetually.

But she hath lost a dearer thing than life,
And he hath won what he would lose again;
This forced league doth force a further strife;
This momentary joy breeds months of pain;
This hot desire converts to cold disdain:
 Pure Chastity is rifled of her store, 692
 And Lust, the thief, far poorer than before.

Look! as the full-fed hound or gorged hawk,
Unapt for tender smell or speedy flight,
Make slow pursuit, or altogether balk 696
The prey wherein by nature they delight;
So surfeit-taking Tarquin fares this night:
 His taste delicious, in digestion souring,
 Devours his will, that liv'd by foul devouring.

O! deeper sin than bottomless conceit 701
Can comprehend in still imagination;
Drunken Desire must vomit his receipt,
Ere he can see his own abomination. 704
While Lust is in his pride, no exclamation
Can curb his heat, or rein his rash desire,
Till like a jade Self-will himself doth tire.

And then with lank and lean discolour'd cheek,
With heavy eye, knit brow, and strengthless
 pace, 709
Feeble Desire, all recreant, poor, and meek,
Like to a bankrupt beggar wails his case:
The flesh being proud, Desire doth fight with
 Grace, 712
 For there it revels; and when that decays,
 The guilty rebel for remission prays.

So fares it with this faultful lord of Rome,
Who this accomplishment so hotly chas'd; 716
For now against himself he sounds this doom,
That through the length of times he stands dis-
 grac'd;
Besides, his soul's fair temple is defac'd;
 To whose weak ruins muster troops of cares,
 To ask the spotted princess how she fares. 721

She says, her subjects with foul insurrection
Have batter'd down her consecrated wall,
And by their mortal fault brought in subjection
Her immortality, and made her thrall 725
To living death, and pain perpetual:

Which in her prescience she controlled still,
But her foresight could not forestall their
 will. 728

Even in this thought through the dark night he
 stealeth,
A captive victor that hath lost in gain;
Bearing away the wound that nothing healeth,
The scar that will despite of cure remain; 732
Leaving his spoil perplex'd in greater pain.
 She bears the load of lust he left behind,
 And he the burden of a guilty mind.

He like a thievish dog creeps sadly thence, 736
She like a wearied lamb lies panting there;
He scowls and hates himself for his offence,
She desperate with her nails her flesh doth
 tear;
He faintly flies, sweating with guilty fear, 740
 She stays, exclaiming on the direful night;
 He runs, and chides his vanish'd, loath'd
 delight.

He thence departs a heavy convertite,
She there remains a hopeless castaway; 744
He in his speed looks for the morning light,
She prays she never may behold the day;
'For day,' quoth she, 'night's 'scapes doth open
 lay,
 And my true eyes have never practis'd how
 To cloak offences with a cunning brow. 749

'They think not but that every eye can see
The same disgrace which they themselves be-
 hold;
And therefore would they still in darkness be,
To have their unseen sin remain untold; 753
For they their guilt with weeping will unfold,
 And grave, like water that doth eat in steel,
 Upon my cheeks what helpless shame I feel.'

Here she exclaims against repose and rest, 757
And bids her eyes hereafter still be blind.
She wakes her heart by beating on her breast,
And bids it leap from thence where it may find
Some purer chest to close so pure a mind. 761
 Frantic with grief thus breathes she forth
 her spite
 Against the unseen secrecy of night:

'O comfort-killing Night, image of hell! 764
Dim register and notary of shame!
Black stage for tragedies and murders fell!
Vast sin-concealing chaos! nurse of blame!
Blind muffled bawd! dark harbour for defame!
 Grim cave of death! whispering conspirator
 With close-tongu'd treason and the ravisher!

'O hateful, vaporous, and foggy Night!
Since thou art guilty of my curseless crime, 772
Muster thy mists to meet the eastern light,
Make war against proportion'd course of time;
Or if thou wilt permit the sun to climb
 His wonted height, yet ere he go to bed, 776
 Knit poisonous clouds about his golden
 head.

'With rotten damps ravish the morning air;
Let their exhal'd unwholesome breaths make
    sick
The life of purity, the supreme fair,   780
Ere he arrive his weary noontide prick;
And let thy misty vapours march so thick,
   That in their smoky ranks his smother'd light
   May set at noon and make perpetual night.

'Were Tarquin Night, as he is but Night's
    child,   785
The silver-shining queen he would distain;
Her twinkling handmaids too, by him defil'd,
Through Night's black bosom should not peep
    again: 788
So should I have co-partners in my pain;
   And fellowship in woe doth woe assuage,
   As palmers' chat makes short their pilgrim-
    age.

'Where now I have no one to blush with me,
To cross their arms and hang their heads with
    mine,   793
To mask their brows and hide their infamy;
But I alone alone must sit and pine,
Seasoning the earth with showers of silver
    brine,   796
   Mingling my talk with tears, my grief with
    groans,
   Poor wasting monuments of lasting moans.

'O Night! thou furnace of foul-reeking smoke,
Let not the jealous Day behold that face   800
Which underneath thy black all-hiding cloak
Immodestly lies martyr'd with disgrace:
Keep still possession of thy gloomy place,
   That all the faults which in thy reign are
    made   804
   May likewise be sepulchred in thy shade.

'Make me not object to the tell-tale Day!
The light will show, character'd in my brow,
The story of sweet chastity's decay,   808
The impious breach of holy wedlock vow:
Yea, the illiterate, that know not how
   To 'cipher what is writ in learned books,
   Will quote my loathsome trespass in my
    looks.   812

'The nurse, to still her child, will tell my story,
And fright her crying babe with Tarquin's name;
The orator, to deck his oratory,
Will couple my reproach to Tarquin's shame;
Feast-finding minstrels, tuning my defame, 817
   Will tie the hearers to attend each line,
   How Tarquin wronged me, I Collatine.

'Let my good name, that senseless reputation,
For Collatine's dear love be kept unspotted: 821
If that be made a theme for disputation,
The branches of another root are rotted,
And undeserv'd reproach to him allotted 824
   That is as clear from this attaint of mine,
   As I ere this was pure to Collatine.

'O unseen shame! invisible disgrace!
O unfelt sore! crest-wounding, private scar! 828

Reproach is stamp'd in Collatinus' face,
And Tarquin's eye may read the mot afar,
How he in peace is wounded, not in war.
   Alas! how many bear such shameful blows,
   Which not themselves, but he that gives them
    knows.   833

'If, Collatine, thine honour lay in me,
From me by strong assault it is bereft.
My honey lost, and I, a drone-like bee,   836
Have no perfection of my summer left,
But robb'd and ransack'd by injurious theft:
   In thy weak hive a wandering wasp hath crept,
   And suck'd the honey which thy chaste bee
    kept.   840

'Yet am I guilty of thy honour's wrack;
Yet for thy honour did I entertain him;
Coming from thee, I could not put him back,
For it had been dishonour to disdain him: 844
Besides, of weariness he did complain him,
   And talk'd of virtue: O! unlook'd-for evil,
   When virtue is profan'd in such a devil.

'Why should the worm intrude the maiden bud?
Or hateful cuckoos hatch in sparrows' nests?
Or toads infect fair founts with venom mud?
Or tyrant folly lurk in gentle breasts?
Or kings be breakers of their own behests? 852
   But no perfection is so absolute,
   That some impurity doth not pollute.

'The aged man that coffers-up his gold
Is plagu'd with cramps and gouts and painful
    fits;   856
And scarce hath eyes his treasure to behold,
But like still-pining Tantalus he sits,
And useless barns the harvest of his wits;
   Having no other pleasure of his gain   860
   But torment that it cannot cure his pain.

'So then he hath it when he cannot use it,
And leaves it to be master'd by his young;
Who in their pride do presently abuse it: 864
Their father was too weak, and they too strong,
To hold their cursed-blessed fortune long.
   The sweets we wish for turn to loathed sours
   Even in the moment that we call them ours.

'Unruly blasts wait on the tender spring; 869
Unwholesome weeds take root with precious
    flowers;
The adder hisses where the sweet birds sing;
What virtue breeds iniquity devours: 872
We have no good that we can say is ours,
   But ill-annexed Opportunity
   Or kills his life, or else his quality.

'O Opportunity! thy guilt is great,   876
'Tis thou that execut'st the traitor's treason;
Thou sett'st the wolf where he the lamb may get;
Whoever plots the sin, thou point'st the season;
'Tis thou that spurn'st at right, at law, at
    reason;   880
   And in thy shady cell, where none may spy
    him,
   Sits Sin to seize the souls that wander by him.

'Thou mak'st the vestal violate her oath;
Thou blow'st the fire when temperance is
   thaw'd;   884
Thou smother'st honesty, thou murder'st troth;
Thou foul abettor! thou notorious bawd!
Thou plantest scandal and displacest laud:
   Thou ravisher, thou traitor, thou false thief,
   Thy honey turns to gall, thy joy to grief! 889

'Thy secret pleasure turns to open shame,
Thy private feasting to a public fast,
Thy smoothing titles to a ragged name,   892
Thy sugar'd tongue to bitter wormwood taste:
Thy violent vanities can never last.
   How comes it, then, vile Opportunity,
   Being so bad, such numbers seek for thee?

'When wilt thou be the humble suppliant's
   friend,   897
And bring him where his suit may be obtain'd?
When wilt thou sort an hour great strifes to end?
Or free that soul which wretchedness hath
   chain'd?   900
Give physic to the sick, ease to the pain'd?
   The poor, lame, blind, halt, creep, cry out for
   thee;
   But they ne'er meet with Opportunity.

'The patient dies while the physician sleeps; 904
The orphan pines while the oppressor feeds;
Justice is feasting while the widow weeps;
Advice is sporting while infection breeds:
Thou grant'st no time for charitable deeds: 908
   Wrath, envy, treason, rape, and murder's
   rages,
   Thy heinous hours wait on them as their
   pages.

'When Truth and Virtue have to do with thee,
A thousand crosses keep them from thy aid: 912
They buy thy help; but Sin ne'er gives a fee,
He gratis comes; and thou art well appaid
As well to hear as grant what he hath said.
   My Collatine would else have come to me 916
   When Tarquin did, but he was stay'd by thee.

'Guilty thou art of murder and of theft,
Guilty of perjury and subornation,
Guilty of treason, forgery, and shift,   920
Guilty of incest, that abomination;
An accessary by thine inclination
   To all sins past, and all that are to come,
   From the creation to the general doom. 924

'Mis-shapen Time, copesmate of ugly Night,
Swift subtle post, carrier of grisly care,
Eater of youth, false slave to false delight,
Base watch of woes, sin's pack-horse, virtue's
   snare;   928
Thou nursest all, and murderest all that are;
   O! hear me, then, injurious, shifting Time,
   Be guilty of my death, since of my crime.

'Why hath thy servant, Opportunity,   932
Betray'd the hours thou gav'st me to repose?
Cancell'd my fortunes, and enchained me
To endless date of never-ending woes?

Time's office is to fine the hate of foes; 936
   To eat up errors by opinion bred,
   Not spend the dowry of a lawful bed.

'Time's glory is to calm contending kings,
To unmask falsehood and bring truth to light,
To stamp the seal of time in aged things, 941
To wake the morn and sentinel the night,
To wrong the wronger till he render right,
   To ruinate proud buildings with thy hours,
   And smear with dust their glittering golden
   towers;   945

'To fill with worm-holes stately monuments,
To feed oblivion with decay of things,
To blot old books and alter their contents, 948
To pluck the quills from ancient ravens' wings,
To dry the old oak's sap and cherish springs,
   To spoil antiquities of hammer'd steel,
   And turn the giddy round of Fortune's
   wheel;   952

'To show the beldam daughters of her daughter,
To make the child a man, the man a child,
To slay the tiger that doth live by slaughter,
To tame the unicorn and lion wild,   956
To mock the subtle, in themselves beguil'd,
   To cheer the ploughman with increaseful
   crops,
   And waste huge stones with little water-drops.

'Why work'st thou mischief in thy pilgrimage,
Unless thou couldst return to make amends?
One poor retiring minute in an age
Would purchase thee a thousand thousand
   friends,
Lending him wit that to bad debtors lends: 964
   O! this dread night, wouldst thou one hour
   come back,
   I could prevent this storm and shun thy wrack.

'Thou ceaseless lackey to eternity,
With some mischance cross Tarquin in his
   flight;   968
Devise extremes beyond extremity,
To make him curse this cursed crimeful night:
Let ghastly shadows his lewd eyes affright,
   And the dire thought of his committed evil
   Shape every bush a hideous shapeless devil.

'Disturb his hours of rest with restless trances,
Afflict him in his bed with bedrid groans;
Let there bechance him pitiful mischances 976
To make him moan, but pity not his moans:
Stone him with harden'd hearts, harder than
   stones;
   And let mild women to him lose their mild-
   ness,
   Wilder to him than tigers in their wildness.

'Let him have time to tear his curled hair, 981
Let him have time against himself to rave,
Let him have time of Time's help to despair,
Let him have time to live a loathed slave, 984
Let him have time a beggar's orts to crave,
   And time to see one that by alms doth live
   Disdain to him disdained scraps to give.

'Let him have time to see his friends his foes,
And merry fools to mock at him resort;   989
Let him have time to mark how slow time goes
In time of sorrow, and how swift and short
His time of folly and his time of sport;   992
   And ever let his unrecalling crime
   Have time to wail the abusing of his time.

'O Time! thou tutor both to good and bad,
Teach me to curse him that thou taught'st this
   ill;   996
At his own shadow let the thief run mad,
Himself himself seek every hour to kill:
Such wretched hands such wretched blood
   should spill;   999
   For who so base would such an office have
   As slanderous deathsman to so base a slave?

'The baser is he, coming from a king,
To shame his hope with deeds degenerate:
The mightier man, the mightier is the thing 1004
That makes him honour'd, or begets him hate;
For greatest scandal waits on greatest state.
   The moon being clouded presently is miss'd,
   But little stars may hide them when they list.

'The crow may bathe his coal-black wings in
   mire,   1009
And unperceiv'd fly with the filth away;
But if the like the snow-white swan desire,
The stain upon his silver down will stay.   1012
Poor grooms are sightless night, kings glorious
   day,
   Gnats are unnoted wheresoe'er they fly,
   But eagles gaz'd upon with every eye.

'Out, idle words! servants to shallow fools, 1016
Unprofitable sounds, weak arbitrators!
Busy yourselves in skill-contending schools;
Debate where leisure serves with dull debaters;
To trembling clients be you mediators: 1020
   For me, I force not argument a straw,
   Since that my case is past the help of law.

'In vain I rail at Opportunity,
At Time, at Tarquin, and uncheerful Night;
In vain I cavil with my infamy,   1025
In vain I spurn at my confirm'd despite;
This helpless smoke of words doth me no right.
   The remedy indeed to do me good,   1028
   Is to let forth my foul-defiled blood.

'Poor hand, why quiver'st thou at this decree?
Honour thyself to rid me of this shame;
For if I die, my honour lives in thee,   1032
But if I live, thou liv'st in my defame;
Since thou couldst not defend thy loyal dame,
   And wast afeard to scratch her wicked foe,
   Kill both thyself and her for yielding so.' 1036

This said, from her be-tumbled couch she start-
   eth,
To find some desperate instrument of death:
But this no slaughter-house no tool imparteth
To make more vent for passage of her breath;
Which, thronging through her lips, so vanisheth
   As smoke from Ætna, that in air consumes,
   Or that which from discharged cannon fumes.

'In vain,' quoth she, 'I live, and seek in vain
Some happy mean to end a hapless life: 1045
I fear'd by Tarquin's falchion to be slain,
Yet for the self-same purpose seek a knife:
But when I fear'd I was a loyal wife: 1048
   So am I now: O no! that cannot be;
   Of that true type hath Tarquin rifled me.

'O! that is gone for which I sought to live,
And therefore now I need not fear to die. 1052
To clear this spot by death, at least I give
A badge of fame to slander's livery;
A dying life to living infamy.
   Poor helpless help, the treasure stol'n away,
   To burn the guiltless casket where it lay? 1057

'Well, well, dear Collatine, thou shalt not know
The stained taste of violated troth;
I will not wrong thy true affection so,   1060
To flatter thee with an infringed oath;
This bastard graff shall never come to growth;
   He shall not boast who did thy stock pollute
   That thou art doting father of his fruit. 1064

'Nor shall he smile at thee in secret thought,
Nor laugh with his companions at thy state;
But thou shalt know thy interest was not bought
Basely with gold, but stol'n from forth thy
   gate.   1068
For me, I am the mistress of my fate,
   And with my trespass never will dispense,
   Till life to death acquit my forc'd offence.

'I will not poison thee with my attaint,   1072
Nor fold my fault in cleanly-coin'd excuses;
My sable ground of sin I will not paint,
To hide the truth of this false night's abuses;
My tongue shall utter all; mine eyes, like
   sluices,   1076
   As from a mountain-spring that feeds a dale,
   Shall gush pure streams to purge my impure
   tale.'

By this, lamenting Philomel had ended   1079
The well-tun'd warble of her nightly sorrow,
And solemn night with slow sad gait descended
To ugly hell; when, lo! the blushing morrow
Lends light to all fair eyes that light will bor-
   row:
   But cloudy Lucrece shames herself to see,
   And therefore still in night would cloister'd
   be.   1085

Revealing day through every cranny spies,
And seems to point her out where she sits weep-
   ing;
To whom she sobbing speaks: 'O eye of eyes!
Why pry'st thou through my window? leave
   thy peeping,   1089
Mock with thy tickling beams eyes that are
   sleeping:
   Brand not my forehead with thy piercing
   light,
   For day hath nought to do what's done by
   night.'   1092

Thus cavils she with everything she sees:
True grief is fond and testy as a child,
Who wayward once, his mood with nought
      agrees:
Old woes, not infant sorrows, bear them mild;
Continuance tames the one; the other wild, 1097
      Like an unpractis'd swimmer plunging still,
      With too much labour drowns for want of skill.

So she, deep-drenched in a sea of care,   1100
Holds disputation with each thing she views,
And to herself all sorrow doth compare;
No object but her passion's strength renews,
And as one shifts, another straight ensues: 1104
      Sometime her grief is dumb and hath no
         words;
      Sometime 'tis mad and too much talk affords.

The little birds that tune their morning's joy
Make her moans mad with their sweet melody:
For mirth doth search the bottom of annoy;
Sad souls are slain in merry company;
Grief best is pleas'd with grief's society:
      True sorrow then is feelingly suffic'd   1112
      When with like semblance it is sympathiz'd.

'Tis double death to drown in ken of shore;
He ten times pines that pines beholding food;
To see the salve doth make the wound ache
      more;   1116
Great grief grieves most at that would do it
      good;
Deep woes roll forward like a gentle flood,
      Who, being stopp'd, the bounding banks o'er-
         flows;
      Grief dallied with nor law nor limit knows.

'You mocking birds,' quoth she, 'your tunes
      entomb   1121
Within your hollow-swelling feather'd breasts,
And in my hearing be you mute and dumb:
My restless discord loves no stops nor rests;
A woeful hostess brooks not merry guests: 1125
      Relish your nimble notes to pleasing ears;
      Distress likes dumps when time is kept with
         tears.

'Come, Philomel, that sing'st of ravishment,
Make thy sad grove in my dishevell'd hair: 1129
As the dank earth weeps at thy languishment,
So I at each sad strain will strain a tear,
And with deep groans the diapason bear; 1132
      For burthen-wise I'll hum on Tarquin still,
      While thou on Tereus descant'st better skill.

'And whiles against a thorn thou bear'st thy part
To keep thy sharp woes waking, wretched I,
To imitate thee well, against my heart   1137
Will fix a sharp knife to affright mine eye,
Who, if it wink, shall thereon fall and die.
      These means, as frets upon an instrument,
      Shall tune our heart-strings to true languish-
      ment.   1141

'And for, poor bird, thou sing'st not in the day,
As shaming any eye should thee behold,
Some dark deep desert, seated from the way,

That knows nor parching heat nor freezing
      cold,   1145
We will find out; and there we will unfold
      To creatures stern sad tunes, to change their
      kinds:
      Since men prove beasts, let beasts bear gentle
      minds.   1148

As the poor frighted deer, that stands at gaze,
Wildly determining which way to fly,
Or one encompass'd with a winding maze,
That cannot tread the way out readily;   1152
So with herself is she in mutiny,
      To live or die which of the twain were better,
      When life is sham'd, and death reproach's
         debtor.   1155

'To kill myself,' quoth she, 'alack! what were it
But with my body my poor soul's pollution?
They that lose half with greater patience bear it
Than they whose whole is swallow'd in con-
      fusion.
That mother tries a merciless conclusion, 1160
      Who, having two sweet babes, when death
         takes one,
      Will slay the other and be nurse to none.

'My body or my soul, which was the dearer,
When the one pure, the other made divine? 1164
Whose love of either to myself was nearer,
When both were kept for heaven and Collatine?
Ay me! the bark peel'd from the lofty pine,
      His leaves will wither and his sap decay; 1168
      So must my soul, her bark being peel'd away.

'Her house is sack'd, her quiet interrupted,
Her mansion batter'd by the enemy;
Her sacred temple spotted, spoil'd, corrupted,
Grossly engirt with daring infamy;   1173
Then let it not be call'd impiety,
      If in this blemish'd fort I make some hole
      Through which I may convey this troubled
         soul.   1176

'Yet die I will not till my Collatine
Have heard the cause of my untimely death;
That he may vow, in that sad hour of mine,
Revenge on him that made me stop my
      breath.   1180
My stained blood to Tarquin I'll bequeath,
      Which by him tainted, shall for him be spent,
      And as his due writ in my testament.

'Mine honour I'll bequeath unto the knife 1184
That wounds my body so dishonoured.
'Tis honour to deprive dishonour'd life;
The one will live, the other being dead:
So of shame's ashes shall my fame be bred; 1188
      For in my death I murder shameful scorn:
      My shame so dead, mine honour is new-born.

'Dear lord of that dear jewel I have lost,
What legacy shall I bequeath to thee?   1192
My resolution, love, shall be thy boast,
By whose example thou reveng'd mayst be.
How Tarquin must be us'd, read it in me:
      Myself, thy friend, will kill myself, thy foe,
      And for my sake serve thou false Tarquin so.

'This brief abridgment of my will I make:
My soul and body to the skies and ground;
My resolution, husband, do thou take;   1200
Mine honour be the knife's that makes my
   wound;
My shame be his that did my fame confound;
And all my fame that lives disbursed be
   To those that live, and think no shame of me.

'Thou, Collatine, shalt oversee this will; 1205
How was I overseen that thou shalt see it!
My blood shall wash the slander of mine ill;
My life's foul deed, my life's fair end shall free it.
Faint not, faint heart, but stoutly say, "So be
   it:"   1209
   Yield to my hand; my hand shall conquer
     thee:
   Thou dead, both die, and both shall victors
     be.'

This plot of death when sadly she had laid, 1212
And wip'd the brinish pearl from her bright
   eyes,
With untun'd tongue she hoarsely call'd her
   maid,
Whose swift obedience to her mistress hies;
For fleet-wing'd duty with thought's feathers
   flies.   1216
   Poor Lucrece' cheeks unto her maid seem so
   As winter meads when sun doth melt their
     snow.

Her mistress she doth give demure good-
   morrow,
With soft slow tongue, true mark of modesty,
And sorts a sad look to her lady's sorrow, 1221
For why her face wore sorrow's livery;
But durst not ask of her audaciously
   Why her two suns were cloud-eclipsed so,
   Nor why her fair cheeks over-wash'd with
     woe.   1225

But as the earth doth weep, the sun being set,
Each flower moisten'd like a melting eye;
Even so the maid with swelling drops 'gan wet
Her circled eyne, enforc'd by sympathy 1229
Of those fair suns set in her mistress' sky,
   Who in a salt-wav'd ocean quench their light,
   Which makes the maid weep like the dewy
     night.   1232

A pretty while these pretty creatures stand,
Like ivory conduits coral cisterns filling;
One justly weeps, the other takes in hand
No cause but company of her drops spilling;
Their gentle sex to weep are often willing, 1237
   Grieving themselves to guess at others'
     smarts,
   And then they drown their eyes or break their
     hearts:

For men have marble, women waxen minds,
And therefore are they form'd as marble will;
The weak oppress'd, the impression of strange
   kinds

Is form'd in them by force, by fraud, or skill:
Then call them not the authors of their ill, 1244
   No more than wax shall be accounted evil
   Wherein is stamp'd the semblance of a devil.

Their smoothness, like a goodly champaign
   plain,
Lays open all the little worms that creep; 1248
In men, as in a rough-grown grove, remain
Cave-keeping evils that obscurely sleep:
Through crystal walls each little mote will peep:
   Though men can cover crimes with bold stern
     looks,   1252
   Poor women's faces are their own faults'
     books.

No man inveigh against the wither'd flower,
But chide rough winter that the flower hath
   kill'd:
Not that devour'd, but that which doth devour,
Is worthy blame. O! let it not be hild   1257
Poor women's faults, that they are so fulfill'd
   With men's abuses: those proud lords, to
     blame,
   Make weak-made women tenants to their
     shame.   1260

The precedent whereof in Lucrece view,
Assail'd by night with circumstances strong
Of present death, and shame that might ensue
By that her death, to do her husband wrong:
Such danger to resistance did belong,   1265
   That dying fear through all her body spread;
   And who cannot abuse a body dead?

By this, mild patience bid fair Lucrece speak
To the poor counterfeit of her complaining:
'My girl,' quoth she, 'on what occasion break
Those tears from thee, that down thy cheeks
   are raining?
If thou dost weep for grief of my sustaining,
   Know, gentle wench, it small avails my
     mood: 1273
   If tears could help, mine own would do me
     good.

'But tell me, girl, when went'—and there she
   stay'd
Till after a deep groan—'Tarquin from
   hence?'—   1276
'Madam, ere I was up,' replied the maid,
'The more to blame my sluggard negligence:
Yet with the fault I thus far can dispense;
   Myself was stirring ere the break of day, 1280
   And, ere I rose, was Tarquin gone away.

'But, lady, if your maid may be so bold,
She would request to know your heaviness.'
'O! peace,' quoth Lucrece; 'if it should be
   told,   1284
The repetition cannot make it less;
For more it is than I can well express:
   And that deep torture may be call'd a hell,
   When more is felt than one hath power to
     tell.   1288

'Go, get me hither paper, ink, and pen:
Yet save that labour, for I have them here.
What should I say? One of my husband's men
Bid thou be ready by and by, to bear   1292
A letter to my lord, my love, my dear:
  Bid him with speed prepare to carry it;
  The cause craves haste, and it will soon be
    writ.'   1295

Her maid is gone, and she prepares to write,
First hovering o'er the paper with her quill:
Conceit and grief an eager combat fight;
What wit sets down is blotted straight with will;
This is too curious-good, this blunt and ill: 1300
  Much like a press of people at a door,
  Throng her inventions, which shall go before.

At last she thus begins: 'Thou worthy lord
Of that unworthy wife that greeteth thee, 1304
Health to thy person! next vouchsafe t' afford,
If ever, love, thy Lucrece thou wilt see,
Some present speed to come and visit me.
  So I commend me from our house in grief:
  My woes are tedious, though my words are
    brief.'   1309

Here folds she up the tenour of her woe,
Her certain sorrow writ uncertainly.
By this short schedule Collatine may know 1312
Her grief, but not her grief's true quality:
She dares not thereof make discovery,
  Lest he should hold it her own gross abuse,
  Ere she with blood had stain'd her stain'd
    excuse.   1316

Besides, the life and feeling of her passion
She hoards, to spend when he is by to hear her;
When sighs, and groans, and tears may grace
    the fashion
Of her disgrace, the better so to clear her 1320
From that suspicion which the world might
    bear her.
  To shun this blot, she would not blot the
    letter
  With words, till action might become them
    better.

To see sad sights moves more than hear them
    told;   1324
For then the eye interprets to the ear
The heavy motion that it doth behold,
When every part a part of woe doth bear:
  'Tis but a part of sorrow that we hear; 1328
  Deep sounds make lesser noise than shallow
    fords,
  And sorrow ebbs, being blown with wind of
    words.

Her letter now is seal'd, and on it writ
'At Ardea to my lord, with more than haste.'
The post attends, and she delivers it,   1333
Charging the sour-fac'd groom to hie as fast
As lagging fowls before the northern blast.
  Speed more than speed but dull and slow she
    deems: 1336
  Extremity still urgeth such extremes.

The homely villein curtsies to her low;
And, blushing on her, with a steadfast eye
Receives the scroll without or yea or no, 1340
And forth with bashful innocence doth hie:
But they whose guilt within their bosoms lie
  Imagine every eye beholds their blame;
  For Lucrece thought he blush'd to see her
    shame: 1344

When, silly groom! God wot, it was defect
Of spirit, life, and bold audacity.
Such harmless creatures have a true respect
To talk in deeds, while others saucily   1348
Promise more speed, but do it leisurely:
  Even so this pattern of the worn-out age
  Pawn'd honest looks, but laid no words to
    gage.

His kindled duty kindled their mistrust,   1352
That two red fires in both their faces blaz'd;
She thought he blush'd, as knowing Tarquin's
    lust,
And, blushing with him, wistly on him gaz'd;
Her earnest eye did make him more amaz'd:
  The more she saw the blood his cheeks re-
    plenish,   1357
  The more she thought he spied in her some
    blemish.

But long she thinks till he return again,
And yet the duteous vassal scarce is gone. 1360
The weary time she cannot entertain,
For now 'tis stale to sigh, to weep, and groan:
So woe hath wearied woe, moan tired moan,
  That she her plaints a little while doth stay,
  Pausing for means to mourn some newer
    way.   1365

At last she calls to mind where hangs a piece
Of skilful painting, made for Priam's Troy;
Before the which is drawn the power of Greece,
For Helen's rape the city to destroy,   1369
Threat'ning cloud-kissing Ilion with annoy;
  Which the conceited painter drew so proud,
  As heaven, it seem'd, to kiss the turrets bow'd.

A thousand lamentable objects there,   1373
In scorn of nature, art gave lifeless life;
Many a dry drop seem'd a weeping tear,
Shed for the slaughter'd husband by the wife:
The red blood reek'd, to show the painter's
    strife;   1377
  And dying eyes gleam'd forth their ashy
    lights,
  Like dying coals burnt out in tedious nights.

There might you see the labouring pioner, 1380
Begrim'd with sweat, and smeared all with dust;
And from the towers of Troy there would appear
The very eyes of men through loop-holes thrust,
Gazing upon the Greeks with little lust: 1384
  Such sweet observance in this work was
    had,
  That one might see those far-off eyes look
    sad.

In great commanders grace and majesty
You might behold, triumphing in their faces;
In youth quick bearing and dexterity;   1389
And here and there the painter interlaces
Pale cowards, marching on with trembling
    paces;
    Which heartless peasants did so well re-
    semble,   1392
    That one would swear he saw them quake and
    tremble.

In Ajax and Ulysses, O! what art
Of physiognomy might one behold;
The face of either cipher'd either's heart;   1396
Their face their manners most expressly told:
In Ajax' eyes blunt rage and rigour roll'd;
    But the mild glance that sly Ulysses lent
    Show'd deep regard and smiling government.

There pleading might you see grave Nestor
    stand,   1401
As 'twere encouraging the Greeks to fight;
Making such sober action with his hand,
That it beguil'd attention, charm'd the sight.
In speech, it seem'd, his beard, all silver white,
    Wagg'd up and down, and from his lips did fly
    Thin winding breath, which purl'd up to the
    sky.

About him were a press of gaping faces,   1408
Which seem'd to swallow up his sound advice;
All jointly listening, but with several graces,
As if some mermaid did their ears entice,
Some high, some low, the painter was so
    nice;   1412
    The scalps of many, almost hid behind,
    To jump up higher seem'd, to mock the mind.

Here one man's hand lean'd on another's head,
His nose being shadow'd by his neighbour's ear;
Here one being throng'd bears back, all boll'n
    and red;   1417
Another smother'd, seems to pelt and swear;
And in their rage such signs of rage they bear,
    As, but for loss of Nestor's golden words,   1420
    It seem'd they would debate with angry
    swords.

For much imaginary work was there;
Conceit deceitful, so compact, so kind,
That for Achilles' image stood his spear,   1424
Grip'd in an armed hand; himself behind,
Was left unseen, save to the eye of mind:
    A hand, a foot, a face, a leg, a head,
    Stood for the whole to be imagined.   1428

And from the walls of strong-besieged Troy,
When their brave hope, bold Hector, march'd
    to field,
Stood many Trojan mothers, sharing joy
To see their youthful sons bright weapons
    wield;   1432
And to their hope they such odd action yield,
    That through their light joy seemed to ap-
    pear,—
    Like bright things stain'd—a kind of heavy
    fear.

And, from the strand of Dardan, where they
    fought,   1436
To Simois' reedy banks the red blood ran,
Whose waves to imitate the battle sought
With swelling ridges; and their ranks began
To break upon the galled shore, and than   1440
    Retire again, till meeting greater ranks
    They join and shoot their foam at Simois'
    banks.

To this well-painted piece is Lucrece come,
To find a face where all distress is stell'd.   1444
Many she sees where cares have carved some,
But none where all distress and dolour dwell'd,
Till she despairing Hecuba beheld,
    Staring on Priam's wounds with her old
    eyes,
    Which bleeding under Pyrrhus' proud foot
    lies.   1449

In her the painter had anatomiz'd
Time's ruin, beauty's wrack, and grim care's
    reign:
Her cheeks with chaps and wrinkles were dis-
    guis'd;   1452
Of what she was no semblance did remain:
Her blue blood chang'd to black in every vein,
    Wanting the spring that those shrunk pipes
    had fed,
    Show'd life imprison'd in a body dead.   1456

On this sad shadow Lucrece spends her eyes,
And shapes her sorrow to the beldam's woes,
Who nothing wants to answer her but cries,
And bitter words to ban her cruel foes: 1460
The painter was no god to lend her those;
    And therefore Lucrece swears he did her
    wrong,
    To give her so much grief and not a tongue.

'Poor instrument,' quoth she, 'without a sound,
I'll tune thy woes with my lamenting tongue,
And drop sweet balm in Priam's painted wound,
And rail on Pyrrhus that hath done him wrong,
And with my tears quench Troy that burns so
    long,   1468
    And with my knife scratch out the angry eyes
    Of all the Greeks that are thine enemies.

'Show me the strumpet that began this stir,
That with my nails her beauty I may tear.   1472
Thy heat of lust, fond Paris, did incur
This load of wrath that burning Troy doth
    bear:
Thy eye kindled the fire that burneth here;
    And here in Troy, for trespass of thine eye,
    The sire, the son, the dame, and daughter
    die.

'Why should the private pleasure of some one
Become the public plague of many moe?
Let sin, alone committed, light alone   1480
Upon his head that hath transgressed so;
Let guiltless souls be freed from guilty woe:
    For one's offence why should so many fall,
    To plague a private sin in general?   1484

'Lo! here weeps Hecuba, here Priam dies,
Here manly Hector faints, here Troilus swounds,
Here friend by friend in bloody channel lies,
And friend to friend gives unadvised wounds,
And one man's lust these many lives confounds:
    Had doting Priam check'd his son's desire,
    Troy had been bright with fame and not with
    fire.'

Here feelingly she weeps Troy's painted woes;
For sorrow, like a heavy-hanging bell,   1493
Once set on ringing, with his own weight goes;
Then little strength rings out the doleful knell:
So Lucrece, set a-work, sad tales doth tell 1496
    To pencil'd pensiveness and colour'd sorrow;
    She lends them words, and she their looks
    doth borrow.

She throws her eyes about the painting round,
And whom she finds forlorn she doth lament:
At last she sees a wretched image bound,   1501
That piteous looks to Phrygian shepherds lent;
His face, though full of cares, yet show'd con-
    tent;
    Onward to Troy with the blunt swains he goes,
    So mild, that Patience seem'd to scorn his
    woes.

In him the painter labour'd with his skill 1506
To hide deceit, and give the harmless show
An humble gait, calm looks, eyes wailing still,
A brow unbent that seem'd to welcome woe;
Cheeks neither red nor pale, but mingled so
    That blushing red no guilty instance gave,
    Nor ashy pale the fear that false hearts have.

But, like a constant and confirmed devil, 1513
He entertain'd a show so seeming-just,
And therein so ensconc'd his secret evil,
That jealousy itself could not mistrust   1516
False-creeping craft and perjury should thrust
    Into so bright a day such black-fac'd storms,
    Or blot with hell-born sin such saint-like
    forms.   1519

The well-skill'd workman this mild image drew
For perjur'd Sinon, whose enchanting story
The credulous old Priam after slew;
Whose words, like wildfire, burnt the shining
    glory
Of rich-built Ilion, that the skies were sorry, 1524
    And little stars shot from their fixed places,
    When their glass fell wherein they view'd
    their faces.

This picture she advisedly perus'd,
And chid the painter for his wondrous skill, 1528
Saying, some shape in Sinon's was abus'd;
So fair a form lodg'd not a mind so ill:
And still on him she gaz'd, and gazing still,
    Such signs of truth in his plain face she spied,
    That she concludes the picture was belied.

'It cannot be,' quoth she, 'that so much guile,'—
She would have said,—'can lurk in such a look;'

But Tarquin's shape came in her mind the
    while,   1536
And from her tongue 'can lurk' from 'cannot'
    took:
'It cannot be,' she in that sense forsook,
    And turn'd it thus, 'It cannot be, I find,
    But such a face should bear a wicked mind:

'For even as subtle Sinon here is painted, 1541
So sober-sad, so weary, and so mild,
And if with grief or travail he had fainted,
To me came Tarquin armed; so beguil'd 1544
With outward honesty, but yet defil'd
    With inward vice: as Priam him did cherish,
    So did I Tarquin; so my Troy did perish.

'Look, look, how listening Priam wets his eyes,
To see those borrow'd tears that Sinon sheds!
Priam, why art thou old and yet not wise?
For every tear he falls a Trojan bleeds:
His eye drops fire, no water thence proceeds;
    Those round clear pearls of his, that move
    thy pity,   1553
    Are balls of quenchless fire to burn thy city.

'Such devils steal effects from lightless hell;
For Sinon in his fire doth quake with cold, 1556
And in that cold hot-burning fire doth dwell;
These contraries such unity do hold,
Only to flatter fools and make them bold:
    So Priam's trust false Sinon's tears doth
    flatter,   1560
    That he finds means to burn his Troy with
    water.'

Here, all enrag'd, such passion her assails
That patience is quite beaten from her breast.
She tears the senseless Sinon with her nails,
Comparing him to that unhappy guest   1565
Whose deed hath made herself herself detest:
    At last she smilingly with this gives o'er;
    'Fool, fool!' quoth she, 'his wounds will not
    be sore.'   1568

Thus ebbs and flows the current of her sorrow,
And time doth weary time with her complain-
    ing.
She looks for night, and then she longs for
    morrow,
And both she thinks too long with her remain-
    ing: 1572
Short time seems long in sorrow's sharp sus-
    taining:
    Though woe be heavy, yet it seldom sleeps;
    And they that watch see time how slow it
    creeps.

Which all this time hath overslipp'd her
    thought,   1576
That she with painted images hath spent;
Being from the feeling of her own grief brought
By deep surmise of others' detriment,
Losing her woes in shows of discontent.   1580
    It easeth some, though none it ever cur'd,
    To think their dolour others have endur'd.

But now the mindful messenger, come back,
Brings home his lord and other company; 1584
Who finds his Lucrece clad in mourning black;
And round about her tear-distained eye
Blue circles stream'd, like rainbows in the sky:
  These water-galls in her dim element   1588
  Foretell new storms to those already spent.

Which when her sad-beholding husband saw,
Amazedly in her sad face he stares:
Her eyes, though sod in tears, look'd red and
  raw,   1592
Her lively colour kill'd with deadly cares.
He hath no power to ask her how she fares:
  Both stood like old acquaintance in a trance,
  Met far from home, wondering each other's
  chance.   1596

At last he takes her by the bloodless hand,
And thus begins: 'What uncouth ill event
Hath thee befall'n, that thou dost trembling
  stand?
Sweet love, what spite hath thy fair colour
  spent?   1600
Why art thou thus attir'd in discontent?
  Unmask, dear dear, this moody heaviness,
  And tell thy grief, that we may give redress.'

Three times with sighs she gives her sorrow fire,
Ere once she can discharge one word of woe:
At length address'd to answer his desire,
She modestly prepares to let them know
Her honour is ta'en prisoner by the foe;   1608
  While Collatine and his consorted lords
  With sad attention long to hear her words.

And now this pale swan in her watery nest
Begins the sad dirge of her certain ending. 1612
'Few words,' quoth she, 'shall fit the trespass
  best,
Where no excuse can give the fault amending:
In me moe woe than words are now depending;
  And my laments would be drawn out too long,
  To tell them all with one poor tired tongue.

'Then be this all the task it hath to say:
Dear husband, in the interest of thy bed
A stranger came, and on that pillow lay   1620
Where thou wast wont to rest thy weary head;
And what wrong else may be imagined
  By foul enforcement might be done to me,
  From that, alas! thy Lucrece is not free. 1624

'For in the dreadful dead of dark midnight,
With shining falchion in my chamber came
A creeping creature with a flaming light,
And softly cried, "Awake, thou Roman dame,
And entertain my love; else lasting shame 1629
  On thee and thine this night I will inflict,
  If thou my love's desire do contradict.

'"For some hard-favour'd groom of thine,"
  quoth he,   1632
"Unless thou yoke thy liking to my will,
I'll murder straight, and then I'll slaughter thee,
And swear I found you where you did fulfil
The loathsome act of lust, and so did kill 1636

The lechers in their deed: this act will be
My fame, and thy perpetual infamy."

'With this I did begin to start and cry,
And then against my heart he set his sword,
Swearing, unless I took all patiently,   1641
I should not live to speak another word;
So should my shame still rest upon record,
  And never be forgot in mighty Rome   1644
  The adulterate death of Lucrece and her
  groom.

'Mine enemy was strong, my poor self weak,
And far the weaker with so strong a fear:
My bloody judge forbade my tongue to speak;
No rightful plea might plead for justice there:
His scarlet lust came evidence to swear
  That my poor beauty had purloin'd his eyes;
  And when the judge is robb'd the prisoner
  dies.   1652

'O! teach me how to make mine own excuse,
Or, at the least, this refuge let me find;
Though my gross blood be stain'd with this
  abuse,
Immaculate and spotless is my mind;   1656
That was not forc'd; that never was inclin'd
  To accessary yieldings, but still pure
  Doth in her poison'd closet yet endure.'

Lo! here the helpless merchant of this loss, 1660
With head declin'd, and voice damm'd up with
  woe,
With sad-set eyes, and wretched arms across,
From lips new-waxen pale begins to blow
The grief away that stops his answer so: 1664
  But, wretched as he is, he strives in vain;
  What he breathes out his breath drinks up
  again.

As through an arch the violent roaring tide
Outruns the eye that doth behold his haste,
Yet in the eddy boundeth in his pride   1669
Back to the strait that forc'd him on so fast;
In rage sent out, recall'd in rage, being past:
  Even so his sighs, his sorrows, make a saw,
  To push grief on, and back the same grief
  draw.   1673

Which speechless woe of his poor she attendeth,
And his untimely frenzy thus awaketh:
'Dear lord, thy sorrow to my sorrow lendeth
Another power; no flood by raining slaketh.
My woe too sensible thy passion maketh 1678
  More feeling-painful: let it then suffice
  To drown one woe, one pair of weeping eyes.

'And for my sake, when I might charm thee so,
For she that was thy Lucrece, now attend me:
Be suddenly revenged on my foe,
Thine, mine, his own: suppose thou dost de-
  fend me   1684
From what is past: the help that thou shalt lend
  me
  Comes all too late, yet let the traitor die;
  For sparing justice feeds iniquity.

'But ere I name him, you, fair lords,' quoth she,—
Speaking to those that came with Collatine,—
'Shall plight your honourable faiths to me,
With swift pursuit to venge this wrong of mine;
For 'tis a meritorious fair design   1692
   To chase injustice with revengeful arms:
   Knights, by their oaths, should right poor
    ladies' harms.'

At this request, with noble disposition
Each present lord began to promise aid, 1696
As bound in knighthood to her imposition,
Longing to hear the hateful foe bewray'd:
But she, that yet her sad task hath not said,
   The protestation stops. 'O! speak,' quoth she,
   'How may this forced stain be wip'd from
    me?   1701

'What is the quality of mine offence,
Being constrain'd with dreadful circumstance?
May my pure mind with the foul act dispense,
My low-declined honour to advance? 1705
May any terms acquit me from this chance?
   The poison'd fountain clears itself again;
   And why not I from this compelled stain?'

With this, they all at once began to say, 1709
Her body's stain her mind untainted clears;
While with a joyless smile she turns away
The face, that map which deep impression bears
Of hard misfortune, carv'd in it with tears. 1713
   'No, no,' quoth she, 'no dame, hereafter
    living,
   By my excuse shall claim excuse's giving.'

Here with a sigh, as if her heart would break,
She throws forth Tarquin's name, 'He, he,' she
   says,   1717
But more than 'he' her poor tongue could not
   speak;
Till after many accents and delays,
Untimely breathings, sick and short assays,
   She utters this, 'He, he, fair lords, 'tis he,
   That guides this hand to give this wound to
    me.'

Even here she sheathed in her harmless breast
A harmful knife, that thence her soul un-
   sheath'd: 1724
That blow did bail it from the deep unrest
Of that polluted prison where it breath'd;
Her contrite sighs unto the clouds bequeath'd
   Her winged sprite, and through her wounds
    doth fly   1728
   Life's lasting date from cancell'd destiny.

Stone-still, astonish'd with this deadly deed,
Stood Collatine and all his lordly crew;
Till Lucrece' father, that beholds her bleed, 1732
Himself on her self-slaughter'd body threw;
And from the purple fountain Brutus drew
   The murderous knife, and as it left the place,
   Her blood, in poor revenge, held it in chase;

And bubbling from her breast, it doth divide
In two slow rivers, that the crimson blood
Circles her body in on every side,

Who, like a late-sack'd island, vastly stood, 1740
Bare and unpeopled in this fearful flood.
   Some of her blood still pure and red remain'd,
   And some look'd black, and that false Tar-
    quin stain'd.

About the mourning and congealed face, 1744
Of that black blood a watery rigol goes,
Which seems to weep upon the tainted place:
And ever since, as pitying Lucrece' woes,
Corrupted blood some watery token shows;
   And blood untainted still doth red abide,
   Blushing at that which is so putrified.

'Daughter, dear daughter!' old Lucretius cries,
That life was mine which thou hast here de-
   priv'd.   1752
If in the child the father's image lies,
Where shall I live now Lucrece is unliv'd?
Thou wast not to this end from me deriv'd.
   If children predecease progenitors,   1756
   We are their offspring, and they none of ours.

'Poor broken glass, I often did behold
In thy sweet semblance my old age now born;
But now that fair fresh mirror, dim and old,
Shows me a bare-bon'd death by time outworn.
O! from thy cheeks my image thou hast torn,
   And shiver'd all the beauty of my glass,
   That I no more can see what once I was. 1764

'O Time! cease thou thy course, and last no
   longer,
If they surcease to be that should survive,
Shall rotten death make conquest of the
   stronger,
And leave the faltering feeble souls alive? 1768
The old bees die, the young possess their hive:
   Then live, sweet Lucrece, live again and see
   Thy father die, and not thy father thee!'

By this, starts Collatine as from a dream, 1772
And bids Lucretius give his sorrow place;
And then in key-cold Lucrece' bleeding stream
He falls, and bathes the pale fear in his face,
And counterfeits to die with her a space; 1776
   Till manly shame bids him possess his breath
   And live to be revenged on her death.

The deep vexation of his inward soul
Hath serv'd a dumb arrest upon his tongue;
Who, mad that sorrow should his use control
Or keep him from heart-easing words so long,
Begins to talk; but through his lips do throng
   Weak words so thick, come in his poor heart's
    aid,   1784
   That no man could distinguish what he said.

Yet sometime 'Tarquin' was pronounced plain,
But through his teeth, as if the name he tore.
This windy tempest, till it blow up rain, 1788
Held back his sorrow's tide to make it more;
At last it rains, and busy winds give o'er:
   Then son and father weep with equal strife
   Who should weep most, for daughter or for
    wife.   1792

The one doth call her his, the other his,
Yet neither may possess the claim they lay.
The father says, 'She's mine.' 'O! mine she is,'
Replies her husband; 'do not take away 1796
My sorrow's interest; let no mourner say
He weeps for her, for she was only mine,
And only must be wail'd by Collatine.'

'O!' quoth Lucretius, 'I did give that life 1800
Which she too early and too late hath spill'd.'
'Woe, woe,' quoth Collatine, 'she was my wife,
I ow'd her, and 'tis mine that she hath kill'd.'
'My daughter' and 'my wife' with clamours
fill'd 1804
The dispers'd air, who, holding Lucrece' life,
Answer'd their cries, 'my daughter' and 'my
wife.'

Brutus, who pluck'd the knife from Lucrece'
side,
Seeing such emulation in their woe, 1808
Began to clothe his wit in state and pride,
Burying in Lucrece' wound his folly's show.
He with the Romans was esteemed so
As silly-jeering idiots are with kings, 1812
For sportive words and uttering foolish
things:

But now he throws that shallow habit by,
Wherein deep policy did him disguise;
And arm'd his long-hid wits advisedly, 1816
To check the tears in Collatinus' eyes.
'Thou wronged lord of Rome,' quoth he, 'arise:
Let my unsounded self, suppos'd a fool,
Now set thy long-experienc'd wit to school.

'Why, Collatine, is woe the cure for woe? 1821
Do wounds help wounds, or grief help grievous
deeds?
Is it revenge to give thyself a blow
For his foul act by whom thy fair wife bleeds?
Such childish humour from weak minds pro-
ceeds: 1825

Thy wretched wife mistook the matter so,
To slay herself, that should have slain her foe.

'Courageous Roman, do not steep thy heart
In such relenting dew of lamentations; 1829
But kneel with me and help to bear thy part,
To rouse our Roman gods with invocations,
That they will suffer these abominations, 1832
Since Rome herself in them doth stand dis-
grac'd,
By our strong arms from forth her fair streets
chas'd.

'Now, by the Capitol that we adore,
And by this chaste blood so unjustly stain'd,
By heaven's fair sun that breeds the fat earth's
store, 1837
By all our country rights in Rome maintain'd,
And by chaste Lucrece' soul, that late com-
plain'd
Her wrongs to us, and by this bloody
knife, 1840
We will revenge the death of this true wife.'

This said, he struck his hand upon his breast,
And kiss'd the fatal knife to end his vow;
And to his protestation urg'd the rest, 1844
Who, wondering at him, did his words allow:
Then jointly to the ground their knees they bow;
And that deep vow, which Brutus made be-
fore,
He doth again repeat, and that they swore.

When they had sworn to this advised doom,
They did conclude to bear dead Lucrece thence;
To show her bleeding body thorough Rome,
And so to publish Tarquin's foul offence: 1852
Which being done with speedy diligence,
The Romans plausibly did give consent
To Tarquin's everlasting banishment.

SONNETS

TO THE · ONLIE · BEGETTER · OF ·
THESE · INSUING · SONNETS,
MR. W. H., ALL HAPPINESSE
AND · THAT · ETERNITIE ·
PROMISED ·
BY ·
OUR EVER-LIVING POET ·
WISHETH ·
THE WELL-WISHING ·
ADVENTURER · IN
SETTING ·
FORTH.

T. T.

I

From fairest creatures we desire increase,
That thereby beauty's rose might never die,
But as the riper should by time decease,
His tender heir might bear his memory:
But thou, contracted to thine own bright eyes,
Feed'st thy light's flame with self-substantial
    fuel,   6
Making a famine where abundance lies,
Thyself thy foe, to thy sweet self too cruel.
Thou that art now the world's fresh ornament
And only herald to the gaudy spring,
Within thine own bud buriest thy content 11
And, tender churl, mak'st waste in niggarding.
  Pity the world, or else this glutton be,
  To eat the world's due, by the grave and thee.

II

When forty winters shall besiege thy brow,
And dig deep trenches in thy beauty's field,
Thy youth's proud livery, so gaz'd on now,
Will be a tatter'd weed, of small worth held:
Then being ask'd where all thy beauty lies,
Where all the treasure of thy lusty days, 6
To say, within thine own deep-sunken eyes,
Were an all-eating shame and thriftless praise.
How much more praise deserv'd thy beauty's
    use,
If thou couldst answer, 'This fair child of mine
Shall sum my count, and make my old excuse,'
Proving his beauty by succession thine! 12
  This were to be new made when thou art old,
  And see thy blood warm when thou feel'st it
  cold.

III

Look in thy glass, and tell the face thou viewest
Now is the time that face should form another;
Whose fresh repair if now thou not renewest,
Thou dost beguile the world, unbless some
    mother,
For where is she so fair whose unear'd womb
Disdains the tillage of thy husbandry? 6
Or who is he so fond will be the tomb
Of his self-love, to stop posterity?

Thou art thy mother's glass, and she in thee
Calls back the lovely April of her prime;
So thou through windows of thine age shalt see
Despite of wrinkles, this thy golden time. 1.
  But if thou live, remember'd not to be,
  Die single, and thine image dies with thee.

IV

Unthrifty loveliness, why dost thou spend
Upon thyself thy beauty's legacy?
Nature's bequest gives nothing, but doth lend
And being frank, she lends to those are free:
Then, beauteous niggard, why dost thou abuse
The bounteous largess given thee to give?
Profitless usurer, why dost thou use
So great a sum of sums, yet canst not live?
For having traffic with thyself alone,
Thou of thyself thy sweet self dost deceive:
Then how, when Nature calls thee to be gone
What acceptable audit canst thou leave? 1
  Thy unus'd beauty must be tomb'd with thee
  Which used, lives th' executor to be.

V

Those hours, that with gentle work did frame
The lovely gaze where every eye doth dwell,
Will play the tyrants to the very same
And that unfair which fairly doth excel;
For never-resting time leads summer on
To hideous winter, and confounds him there
Sap check'd with frost, and lusty leaves quite
    gone,
Beauty o'ersnow'd and bareness every where
Then, were not summer's distillation left,
A liquid prisoner pent in walls of glass,
Beauty's effect with beauty were bereft,
Nor it, nor no remembrance what it was: 1
  But flowers distill'd, though they with winte
  meet,
  Leese but their show; their substance still live
  sweet.

VI

Then let not winter's ragged hand deface
In thee thy summer, ere thou be distill'd:
Make sweet some vial; treasure thou some place
With beauty's treasure, ere it be self-kill'd.

That use is not forbidden usury,   5
Which happies those that pay the willing loan;
That's for thyself to breed another thee,
Or ten times happier, be it ten for one;
Ten times thyself were happier than thou art,
If ten of thine ten times refigur'd thee;
Then what could death do, if thou shouldst
    depart,
Leaving thee living in posterity?   12
  Be not self-will'd, for thou art much too fair
  To be death's conquest and make worms
    thine heir.

VII

Lo! in the orient when the gracious light
Lifts up his burning head, each under eye
Doth homage to his new-appearing sight,
Serving with looks his sacred majesty;
And having climb'd the steep-up heavenly hill,
Resembling strong youth in his middle age,   6
Yet mortal looks adore his beauty still,
Attending on his golden pilgrimage;
But when from highmost pitch, with weary car,
Like feeble age, he reeleth from the day,
The eyes, 'fore duteous, now converted are
From his low tract, and look another way: 12
  So thou, thyself outgoing in thy noon,
  Unlook'd on diest, unless thou get a son.

VIII

Music to hear, why hear'st thou music sadly?
Sweets with sweets war not, joy delights in joy:
Why lov'st thou that which thou receiv'st not
    gladly,
Or else receiv'st with pleasure thine annoy?
If the true concord of well-tuned sounds,
By unions married, do offend thine ear,   6
They do but sweetly chide thee, who confounds
In singleness the parts that thou shouldst bear.
Mark how one string, sweet husband to an-
    other,
Strikes each in each by mutual ordering;
Resembling sire and child and happy mother,
Who, all in one, one pleasing note do sing: 12
  Whose speechless song, being many, seeming
    one,
  Sings this to thee: 'Thou single wilt prove
    none.'

IX

Is it for fear to wet a widow's eye
That thou consum'st thyself in single life?
Ah! if thou issueless shalt hap to die,
The world will wail thee, like a makeless wife;
The world will be thy widow, and still weep
That thou no form of thee hast left behind,   6
When every private widow well may keep
By children's eyes her husband's shape in mind.
Look! what an unthrift in the world doth spend
Shifts but his place, for still the world enjoys it;
But beauty's waste hath in the world an end,
And kept unus'd, the user so destroys it.   12
  No love toward others in that bosom sits
  That on himself such murderous shame com-
    mits.

X

For shame! deny that thou bear'st love to any,
Who for thyself art so unprovident.
Grant, if thou wilt, thou art belov'd of many,
But that thou none lov'st is most evident;
For thou art so possess'd with murderous hate
That 'gainst thyself thou stick'st not to con-
    spire,   6
Seeking that beauteous roof to ruinate
Which to repair should be thy chief desire.
O! change thy thought, that I may change my
    mind:
Shall hate be fairer lodg'd than gentle love?
Be, as thy presence is, gracious and kind,
Or to thyself at least kind-hearted prove: 12
  Make thee another self, for love of me,
  That beauty still may live in thine or thee.

XI

As fast as thou shalt wane, so fast thou grow'st
In one of thine, from that which thou departest;
And that fresh blood which youngly thou be-
    stow'st
Thou mayst call thine when thou from youth
    convertest.
Herein lives wisdom, beauty and increase;
Without this, folly, age and cold decay: 6
If all were minded so, the times should cease
And threescore year would make the world
    away.
Let those whom Nature hath not made for
    store,
Harsh, featureless and rude, barrenly perish:
Look, whom she best endow'd she gave the
    more;
Which bounteous gift thou shouldst in bounty
    cherish: 12
  She carv'd thee for her seal, and meant
    thereby
  Thou shouldst print more, nor let that copy
    die.

XII

When I do count the clock that tells the time,
And see the brave day sunk in hideous night;
When I behold the violet past prime,
And sable curls, all silver'd o'er with white;
When lofty trees I see barren of leaves,
Which erst from heat did canopy the herd,   6
And summer's green all girded up in sheaves,
Borne on the bier with white and bristly beard,
Then of thy beauty do I question make,
That thou among the wastes of time must go,
Since sweets and beauties do themselves forsake
And die as fast as they see others grow;   12
  And nothing 'gainst Time's scythe can make
    defence
  Save breed, to brave him when he takes thee
    hence.

XIII

O! that you were yourself; but, love, you are
No longer yours than you yourself here live:
Against this coming end you should prepare,
And your sweet semblance to some other give:

So should that beauty which you hold in lease
Find no determination; then you were   6
Yourself again, after yourself's decease,
When your sweet issue your sweet form should
     bear.
Who lets so fair a house fall to decay,
Which husbandry in honour might uphold
Against the stormy gusts of winter's day
And barren rage of death's eternal cold?   12
   O! none but unthrifts. Dear my love, you
      know
   You had a father: let your son say so.

XIV

Not from the stars do I my judgment pluck;
And yet methinks I have astronomy,
But not to tell of good or evil luck,
Of plagues, of dearths, or seasons' quality;
Nor can I fortune to brief minutes tell,   5
Pointing to each his thunder, rain, and wind,
Or say with princes if it shall go well,
By oft predict that I in heaven find:
But from thine eyes my knowledge I derive,
And, constant stars, in them I read such art
As 'Truth and beauty shall together thrive, 11
If from thyself to store thou wouldst convert;'
   Or else of thee this I prognosticate:
   'Thy end is truth's and beauty's doom and
      date.'

XV

When I consider every thing that grows
Holds in perfection but a little moment,
That this huge stage presenteth nought but
     shows
Whereon the stars in secret influence comment;
When I perceive that men as plants increase, 5
Cheered and check'd e'en by the self-same sky,
Vaunt in their youthful sap, at height decrease,
And wear their brave state out of memory;
Then the conceit of this inconstant stay
Sets you most rich in youth before my sight,
Where wasteful Time debateth with Decay,   11
To change your day of youth to sullied night;
   And, all in war with Time for love of you,
   As he takes from you, I engraft you new.

XVI

But wherefore do not you a mightier way
Make war upon this bloody tyrant, Time?
And fortify yourself in your decay
With means more blessed than my barren rime?
Now stand you on the top of happy hours,
And many maiden gardens, yet unset,   6
With virtuous wish would bear you living
     flowers
Much liker than your painted counterfeit:
So should the lines of life that life repair,
Which this, Time's pencil, or my pupil pen,
Neither in inward worth nor outward fair,
Can make you live yourself in eyes of men. 12
   To give away yourself keeps yourself still;
   And you must live, drawn by your own sweet
      skill.

XVII

Who will believe my verse in time to come,
If it were fill'd with your most high deserts?
Though yet, heaven knows, it is but as a tomb
Which hides your life and shows not half your
     parts.
If I could write the beauty of your eyes
And in fresh numbers number all your graces,
The age to come would say, 'This poet lies;
Such heavenly touches ne'er touch'd earthly
     faces.'
So should my papers, yellow'd with their age
Be scorn'd, like old men of less truth than
     tongue,
And your true rights be term'd a poet's rage
And stretched metre of an antique song: 12
   But were some child of yours alive that time
   You should live twice,—in it and in my rime

XVIII

Shall I compare thee to a summer's day?
Thou art more lovely and more temperate:
Rough winds do shake the darling buds of May
And summer's lease hath all too short a date
Sometime too hot the eye of heaven shines,
And often is his gold complexion dimm'd:
And every fair from fair sometime declines,
By chance, or nature's changing course un-
     trimm'd;
But thy eternal summer shall not fade,
Nor lose possession of that fair thou ow'st,
Nor shall death brag thou wander'st in his
     shade,
When in eternal lines to time thou grow'st; 12
   So long as men can breathe, or eyes can see,
   So long lives this, and this gives life to thee

XIX

Devouring Time, blunt thou the lion's paws,
And make the earth devour her own sweet
     brood;
Pluck the keen teeth from the fierce tiger's jaws
And burn the long-liv'd phœnix in her blood
Make glad and sorry seasons as thou fleets,
And do whate'er thou wilt, swift-footed Time,
To the wide world and all her fading sweets;
But I forbid thee one most heinous crime:
O! carve not with thy hours my love's fair
     brow,
Nor draw no lines there with thine antique pen
Him in thy course untainted do allow
For beauty's pattern to succeeding men.   1
   Yet, do thy worst, old Time: despite thy
      wrong,
   My love shall in my verse ever live young.

XX

A woman's face with Nature's own hand
     painted
Hast thou, the master-mistress of my passion
A woman's gentle heart, but not acquainted
With shifting change, as is false women'
     fashion;

An eye more bright than theirs, less false in
　　rolling,
Gilding the object whereupon it gazeth;　　6
A man in hue all hues in his controlling,
Which steals men's eyes and women's souls
　　amazeth.
And for a woman wert thou first created;
Till Nature, as she wrought thee, fell a-doting,
And by addition me of thee defeated,
By adding one thing to my purpose nothing.　12
　　But since she prick'd thee out for women's
　　　pleasure,
　　Mine be thy love, and thy love's use their
　　　treasure.

XXI

So is it not with me as with that Muse
Stirr'd by a painted beauty to his verse,
Who heaven itself for ornament doth use
And every fair with his fair doth rehearse,
Making a couplement of proud compare,
With sun and moon, with earth and sea's rich
　　gems,　　6
With April's first-born flowers, and all things rare
That heaven's air in this huge rondure hems.
O! let me, true in love, but truly write,
And then believe me, my love is as fair
As any mother's child, though not so bright
As those gold candles fix'd in heaven's air:　12
　　Let them say more that like of hear-say well;
　　I will not praise that purpose not to sell.

XXII

My glass shall not persuade me I am old,
So long as youth and thou are of one date;
But when in thee time's furrows I behold,
Then look I death my days should expiate.
For all that beauty that doth cover thee
Is but the seemly raiment of my heart,　　6
Which in thy breast doth live, as thine in me:
How can I then, be elder than thou art?
O! therefore, love, be of thyself so wary
As I, not for myself, but for thee will;
Bearing thy heart, which I will keep so chary
As tender nurse her babe from faring ill.　　12
　　Presume not on thy heart when mine is slain;
　　Thou gav'st me thine, not to give back again.

XXIII

As an unperfect actor on the stage,
Who with his fear is put besides his part,
Or some fierce thing replete with too much rage,
Whose strength's abundance weakens his own
　　heart;
So I, for fear of trust, forget to say
The perfect ceremony of love's rite,　　6
And in mine own love's strength seem to decay,
O'ercharg'd with burden of mine own love's
　　might.
O! let my books be then the eloquence
And dumb presagers of my speaking breast,
Who plead for love, and look for recompense,
More than that tongue that more hath more
　　express'd.　　12
　　O! learn to read what silent love hath writ:
　　To hear with eyes belongs to love's fine wit.

XXIV

Mine eye hath play'd the painter and hath
　　stell'd
Thy beauty's form in table of my heart;
My body is the frame wherein 'tis held,
And perspective it is best painter's art.
For through the painter must you see his skill,
To find where your true image pictur'd lies,　6
Which in my bosom's shop is hanging still,
That hath his windows glazed with thine eyes.
Now see what good turns eyes for eyes have
　　done:
Mine eyes have drawn thy shape, and thine for
　　me
Are windows to my breast where-through the
　　sun
Delights to peep, to gaze therein on thee;　12
　　Yet eyes this cunning want to grace their art,
　　They draw but what they see, know not the
　　　heart.

XXV

Let those who are in favour with their stars
Of public honour and proud titles boast,
Whilst I, whom fortune of such triumph bars,
Unlook'd for joy in that I honour most.
Great princes' favourites their fair leaves
　　spread
But as the marigold at the sun's eye,　　6
And in themselves their pride lies buried,
For at a frown they in their glory die.
The painful warrior famoused for fight,
After a thousand victories once foil'd,
Is from the book of honour razed quite,
And all the rest forgot for which he toil'd:　12
　　Then happy I, that love and am belov'd,
　　Where I may not remove nor be remov'd.

XXVI

Lord of my love, to whom in vassalage
Thy merit hath my duty strongly knit,
To thee I send this written ambassage,
To witness duty, not to show my wit:
Duty so great, which wit so poor as mine
May make seem bare, in wanting words to show
　　it,　　6
But that I hope some good conceit of thine
In thy soul's thought, all naked, will bestow it;
Till whatsoever star that guides my moving
Points on me graciously with fair aspect,
And puts apparel on my tatter'd loving,
To show me worthy of thy sweet respect:　12
　　Then may I dare to boast how I do love thee;
　　Till then not show my head where thou mayst
　　　prove me.

XXVII

Weary with toil, I haste me to my bed,
The dear repose for limbs with travel tired;
But then begins a journey in my head
To work my mind, when body's work's expir'd:
For then my thoughts—from far where I
　　abide—
Intend a zealous pilgrimage to thee,　　6
And keep my drooping eyelids open wide,
Looking on darkness which the blind do see:

Save that my soul's imaginary sight
Presents thy shadow to my sightless view,
Which, like a jewel hung in ghastly night,
Makes black night beauteous and her old face
  new.   12
  Lo! thus, by day my limbs, by night my mind,
  For thee, and for myself no quiet find.

XXVIII

How can I then return in happy plight,
That am debarr'd the benefit of rest?
When day's oppression is not eas'd by night,
But day by night, and night by day oppress'd,
And each, though enemies to either's reign,
Do in consent shake hands to torture me, 6
The one by toil, the other to complain
How far I toil, still further off from thee.
I tell the day, to please him thou art bright
And dost him grace when clouds do blot the
  heaven:
So flatter I the swart-complexion'd night;
When sparkling stars twire not thou gild'st the
  even.   12
  But day doth daily draw my sorrows longer,
  And night doth nightly make grief's strength
    seem stronger.

XXIX

When in disgrace with fortune and men's eyes
I all alone beweep my outcast state,
And trouble deaf heaven with my bootless cries,
And look upon myself, and curse my fate,
Wishing me like to one more rich in hope,
Featur'd like him, like him with friends
  possess'd,   6
Desiring this man's art, and that man's scope,
With what I most enjoy contented least;
Yet in these thoughts myself almost despising,
Haply I think on thee,—and then my state,
Like to the lark at break of day arising
From sullen earth, sings hymns at heaven's
  gate;   12
  For thy sweet love remember'd such wealth
    brings
  That then I scorn to change my state with
    kings.

XXX

When to the sessions of sweet silent thought
I summon up remembrance of things past,
I sigh the lack of many a thing I sought,
And with old woes new wail my dear times'
  waste:
Then can I drown an eye, unus'd to flow,
For precious friends hid in death's dateless
  night,   6
And weep afresh love's long since cancell'd
  woe,
And moan the expense of many a vanish'd
  sight:
Then can I grieve at grievances foregone,
And heavily from woe to woe tell o'er
The sad account of fore-bemoaned moan,
Which I new pay as if not paid before. 12
  But if the while I think on thee, dear friend,
  All losses are restor'd and sorrows end.

XXXI

Thy bosom is endeared with all hearts,
Which I by lacking have supposed dead;
And there reigns Love, and all Love's loving
  parts,
And all those friends which I thought buried.
How many a holy and obsequious tear 5
Hath dear religious love stol'n from mine eye,
As interest of the dead, which now appear
But things remov'd that hidden in thee lie!
Thou art the grave where buried love doth live,
Hung with the trophies of my lovers gone,
Who all their parts of me to thee did give,
That due of many now is thine alone: 12
  Their images I lov'd I view in thee,
  And thou—all they—hast all the all of me.

XXXII

If thou survive my well-contented day,
When that churl Death my bones with dust
  shall cover,
And shalt by fortune once more re-survey
These poor rude lines of thy deceased lover,
Compare them with the bettering of the time
And though they be outstripp'd by every pen, 6
Reserve them for my love, not for their rime,
Exceeded by the height of happier men.
O! then vouchsafe me but this loving thought
'Had my friend's Muse grown with this grow
  ing age,
A dearer birth than this his love had brought
To march in ranks of better equipage: 1.
  But since he died, and poets better prove,
  Theirs for their style I'll read, his for hi
  love.'

XXXIII

Full many a glorious morning have I seen
Flatter the mountain-tops with sovereign eye
Kissing with golden face the meadows green,
Gilding pale streams with heavenly alchymy;
Anon permit the basest clouds to ride
With ugly rack on his celestial face,
And from the forlorn world his visage hide,
Stealing unseen to west with this disgrace:
Even so my sun one early morn did shine,
With all-triumphant splendour on my brow;
But, out! alack! he was but one hour mine,
The region cloud hath mask'd him from m
  now.
  Yet him for this my love no whit disdaineth
  Suns of the world may stain when heaven'
  sun staineth.

XXXIV

Why didst thou promise such a beauteous day
And make me travel forth without my cloak
To let base clouds o'ertake me in my way,
Hiding thy bravery in their rotten smoke?
'Tis not enough that through the cloud tho
  break,
To dry the rain on my storm-beaten face,
For no man well of such a salve can speak
That heals the wound and cures not the di
  grace:

Nor can thy shame give physic to my grief;
Though thou repent, yet I have still the loss:
The offender's sorrow lends but weak relief
To him that bears the strong offence's cross. 12
  Ah! but those tears are pearl which thy love
    sheds,
  And they are rich and ransom all ill deeds.

XXXV

No more be griev'd at that which thou hast
  done:
Roses have thorns, and silver fountains mud;
Clouds and eclipses stain both moon and sun,
And loathsome canker lives in sweetest bud.
All men make faults, and even I in this,
Authorising thy trespass with compare,   6
Myself corrupting, salving thy amiss,
Excusing thy sins more than thy sins are;
For to thy sensual fault I bring in sense,—
Thy adverse party is thy advocate,—
And 'gainst myself a lawful plea commence:
Such civil war is in my love and hate,   12
  That I an accessary needs must be
  To that sweet thief which sourly robs from
    me.

XXXVI

Let me confess that we two must be twain,
Although our undivided loves are one:
So shall those blots that do with me remain,
Without thy help, by me be borne alone.
In our two loves there is but one respect,
Though in our lives a separable spite,   6
Which, though it alter not love's sole effect,
Yet doth it steal sweet hours from love's de-
    light.
I may not evermore acknowledge thee,
Lest my bewailed guilt should do thee shame,
Nor thou with public kindness honour me, 11
Unless thou take that honour from thy name:
  But do not so; I love thee in such sort
  As thou being mine, mine is thy good report.

XXXVII

As a decrepit father takes delight
To see his active child do deeds of youth,
So I, made lame by fortune's dearest spite,
Take all my comfort of thy worth and truth;
For whether beauty, birth, or wealth, or wit,
Or any of these all, or all, or more,   6
Entitled in thy parts do crowned sit,
I make my love engrafted to this store:
So then I am not lame, poor, nor despis'd,
Whilst that this shadow doth such substance
    give
That I in thy abundance am suffic'd
And by a part of all thy glory live.   12
  Look what is best, that best I wish in thee:
  This wish I have; then ten times happy me!

XXXVIII

How can my Muse want subject to invent,
While thou dost breathe, that pour'st into my
    verse
Thine own sweet argument, too excellent
For every vulgar paper to rehearse?

O! give thyself the thanks, if aught in me
Worthy perusal stand against thy sight;   6
For who's so dumb that cannot write to thee,
When thou thyself dost give invention light?
Be thou the tenth Muse, ten times more in worth
Than those old nine which rimers invocate;
And he that calls on thee, let him bring forth
Eternal numbers to outlive long date.   12
  If my slight Muse do please these curious
    days,
  The pain be mine, but thine shall be the
    praise.

XXXIX

O! how thy worth with manners may I sing,
When thou art all the better part of me?
What can mine own praise to mine own self
    bring?
And what is 't but mine own when I praise thee?
Even for this let us divided live,
And our dear love lose name of single one,   6
That by this separation I may give
That due to thee, which thou deserv'st alone.
O absence! what a torment wouldst thou prove,
Were it not thy sour leisure gave sweet leave
To entertain the time with thoughts of love,
Which time and thoughts so sweetly doth
    deceive,   12
  And that thou teachest how to make one
    twain,
  By praising him here who doth hence remain.

XL

Take all my loves, my love, yea, take them all;
What hast thou then more than thou hadst
    before?
No love, my love, that thou mayst true love call;
All mine was thine before thou hadst this more
Then, if for my love thou my love receivest,
I cannot blame thee for my love thou usest; 6
But yet be blam'd, if thou thyself deceivest
By wilful taste of what thyself refusest.
I do forgive thy robbery, gentle thief,
Although thou steal thee all my poverty;
And yet, love knows it is a greater grief   11
To bear love's wrong than hate's known injury.
  Lascivious grace, in whom all ill well shows,
  Kill me with spites; yet we must not be foes.

XLI

Those pretty wrongs that liberty commits,
When I am sometimes absent from thy heart,
Thy beauty and thy years full well befits,
For still temptation follows where thou art.
Gentle thou art, and therefore to be won,
Beauteous thou art, therefore to be assail'd; 6
And when a woman woos, what woman's son
Will sourly leave her till she have prevail'd?
Ay me! but yet thou mightst my seat forbear,
And chide thy beauty and thy straying youth,
Who lead thee in their riot even there
Where thou art forc'd to break a twofold
    truth;—   12
  Hers, by thy beauty tempting her to thee,
  Thine, by thy beauty being false to me.

XLII

That thou hast her, it is not all my grief,
And yet it may be said I lov'd her dearly;
That she hath thee, is of my wailing chief,
A loss in love that touches me more nearly.
Loving offenders, thus I will excuse ye:
Thou dost love her, because thou know'st I love her;   6
And for my sake even so doth she abuse me,
Suffering my friend for my sake to approve her.
If I lose thee, my loss is my love's gain,
And losing her, my friend hath found that loss;
Both find each other, and I lose both twain,
And both for my sake lay on me this cross: 12
    But here's the joy; my friend and I are one;
    Sweet flattery! then she loves but me alone.

XLIII

When most I wink, then do mine eyes best see,
For all the day they view things unrespected;
But when I sleep, in dreams they look on thee,
And darkly bright, are bright in dark directed.
Then thou, whose shadow shadows doth make bright,
How would thy shadow's form form happy show   6
To the clear day with thy much clearer light,
When to unseeing eyes thy shade shines so!
How would, I say, mine eyes be blessed made
By looking on thee in the living day,
When in dead night thy fair imperfect shade
Through heavy sleep on sightless eyes doth stay!   12
    All days are nights to see till I see thee,
    And nights bright days when dreams do
    show thee me.

XLIV

If the dull substance of my flesh were thought,
Injurious distance should not stop my way;
For then, despite of space, I would be brought,
From limits far remote, where thou dost stay.
No matter then although my foot did stand
Upon the furthest earth remov'd from thee; 6
For nimble thought can jump both sea and land,
As soon as think the place where he would be.
But, ah! thought kills me that I am not thought,
To leap large lengths of miles when thou art gone,
But that, so much of earth and water wrought,
I must attend time's leisure with my moan; 12
    Receiving nought by elements so slow
    But heavy tears, badges of either's woe.

XLV

The other two, slight air and purging fire,
Are both with thee, wherever I abide;
The first my thought, the other my desire,
These present-absent with swift motion slide.
For when these quicker elements are gone
In tender embassy of love to thee,   6
My life, being made of four, with two alone
Sinks down to death, oppress'd with melancholy;

Until life's composition be recur'd
By those sweet messengers return'd from thee
Who even but now come back again, assur'd
Of thy fair health, recounting it to me: 1
    This told, I joy; but then no longer glad,
    I send them back again, and straight grow
    sad.

XLVI

Mine eye and heart are at a mortal war,
How to divide the conquest of thy sight;
Mine eye my heart thy picture's sight would bar,
My heart mine eye the freedom of that right
My heart doth plead that thou in him dos lie,—
A closet never pierc'd with crystal eyes,—
But the defendant doth that plea deny,
And says in him thy fair appearance lies.
To 'cide this title is impannelled
A quest of thoughts, all tenants to the heart;
And by their verdict is determined
The clear eye's moiety and the dear heart' part: 1
    As thus; mine eye's due is thine outward par
    And my heart's right thine inward love o
    heart.

XLVII

Betwixt mine eye and heart a league is took,
And each doth good turns now unto the other
When that mine eye is famish'd for a look,
Or heart in love with sighs himself dot smother,
With my love's picture then my eye doth feas
And to the painted banquet bids my heart;
Another time mine eye is my heart's guest,
And in his thoughts of love doth share part:
So, either by thy picture or my love,
Thyself away art present still with me;
For thou not further than my thoughts can move,
And I am still with them and they with the
    Or, if they sleep, thy picture in my sight
    Awakes my heart to heart's and eye's deligh

XLVIII

How careful was I when I took my way,
Each trifle under truest bars to thrust,
That to my use it might unused stay
From hands of falsehood, in sure wards trust!
But thou, to whom my jewels trifles are,
Most worthy comfort, now my greatest grief,
Thou, best of dearest and mine only care,
Art left the prey of every vulgar thief.
Thee have I not lock'd up in any chest,
Save where thou art not, though I feel tho art,
Within the gentle closure of my breast,
From whence at pleasure thou mayst come an part;
    And even thence thou wilt be stol'n, I fea
    For truth proves thievish for a prize so dea

XLIX

Against that time, if ever that time come,
When I shall see thee frown on my defects,
When as thy love hath cast his utmost sum,
Call'd to that audit by advis'd respects;
Against that time when thou shalt strangely
    pass,   5
And scarcely greet me with that sun, thine eye,
When love, converted from the thing it was,
Shall reasons find of settled gravity;
Against that time do I ensconce me here
Within the knowledge of mine own desert,
And this my hand against myself uprear,
To guard the lawful reasons on thy part: 12
    To leave poor me thou hast the strength of
      laws,
    Since why to love I can allege no cause.

L

How heavy do I journey on the way,
When what I seek, my weary travel's end,
Doth teach that ease and that repose to say,
'Thus far the miles are measur'd from thy
    friend!'
The beast that bears me, tired with my woe,
Plods dully on, to bear that weight in me,   6
As if by some instinct the wretch did know·
His rider lov'd not speed, being made from
    thee:
The bloody spur cannot provoke him on
That sometimes anger thrusts into his hide,
Which heavily he answers with a groan
More sharp to me than spurring to his side; 12
    For that same groan doth put this in my
      mind:
    My grief lies onward, and my joy behind.

LI

Thus can my love excuse the slow offence
Of my dull bearer when from thee I speed:
From where thou art why should I haste me
    thence?
Till I return, of posting is no need.
O! what excuse will my poor beast then find,
When swift extremity can seem but slow?   6
Then should I spur, though mounted on the
    wind,
In winged speed no motion shall I know:
Then can no horse with my desire keep pace;
Therefore desire, of perfect'st love being made,
Shall neigh—no dull flesh—in his fiery race; 11
But love, for love, thus shall excuse my jade,—
    'Since from thee going, he went wilful-slow,
    Towards thee I'll run and give him leave to
      go.'

LII

So am I as the rich, whose blessed key
Can bring him to his sweet up-locked treasure,
The which he will not every hour survey,
For blunting the fine point of seldom pleasure.
Therefore are feasts so solemn and so rare,
Since, seldom coming, in the long year set,   6
Like stones of worth they thinly placed are,
Or captain jewels in the carconet.

So is the time that keeps you as my chest,
Or as the wardrobe which the robe doth hide,
To make some special instant special blest
By new unfolding his imprison'd pride.   12
    Blessed are you, whose worthiness gives
      scope,
    Being had, to triumph; being lack'd, to hope.

LIII

What is your substance, whereof are you made,
That millions of strange shadows on you
    tend?
Since every one hath, every one, one shade,
And you, but one, can every shadow lend.
Describe Adonis, and the counterfeit
Is poorly imitated after you;   6
On Helen's cheek all art of beauty set,
And you in Grecian tires are painted new:
Speak of the spring and foison of the year,
The one doth shadow of your beauty show,
The other as your bounty doth appear;
And you in every blessed shape we know.   12
    In all external grace you have some part,
    But you like none, none you, for constant
      heart.

LIV

O! how much more doth beauty beauteous
    seem
By that sweet ornament which truth doth give!
The rose looks fair, but fairer we it deem
For that sweet odour which doth in it live.
The canker-blooms have full as deep a dye
As the perfumed tincture of the roses,   6
Hang on such thorns, and play as wantonly
When summer's breath their masked buds dis-
    closes:
But, for their virtue only is their show,
They live unwoo'd, and unrespected fade;
Die to themselves. Sweet roses do not so;   11
Of their sweet deaths are sweetest odours made:
    And so of you, beauteous and lovely youth,
    When that shall vade, my verse distils your
      truth.

LV

Not marble, nor the gilded monuments
Of princes, shall outlive this powerful rime;
But you shall shine more bright in these con-
    tents
Than unswept stone, besmear'd with sluttish
    time.
When wasteful war shall statues overturn,
And broils root out the work of masonry,   6
Nor Mars his sword nor war's quick fire shall
    burn
The living record of your memory.
'Gainst death and all-oblivious enmity
Shall you pace forth; your praise shall still find
    room
Even in the eyes of all posterity
That wear this world out to the ending doom. 12
    So, till the judgment that yourself arise,
    You live in this, and dwell in lovers' eyes.

LVI

Sweet love, renew thy force; be it not said
Thy edge should blunter be than appetite,
Which but to-day by feeding is allay'd,
To-morrow sharpen'd in his former might:
So, love, be thou; although to-day thou fill
Thy hungry eyes, even till they wink with ful-
ness,   6
To-morrow see again, and do not kill
The spirit of love with a perpetual dulness.
Let this sad interim like the ocean be
Which parts the shore, where two contracted
new
Come daily to the banks, that, when they see
Return of love, more bless'd may be the view; 12
    Or call it winter, which, being full of care,
    Makes summer's welcome thrice more wish'd,
    more rare.

LVII

Being your slave, what should I do but tend
Upon the hours and times of your desire?
I have no precious time at all to spend,
Nor services to do, till you require.
Nor dare I chide the world-without-end hour
Whilst I, my sovereign, watch the clock for
you,   6
Nor think the bitterness of absence sour
When you have bid your servant once adieu;
Nor dare I question with my jealous thought
Where you may be, or your affairs suppose,
But, like a sad slave, stay and think of nought,
Save, where you are how happy you make
those.   12
    So true a fool is love that in your will,
    Though you do anything, he thinks no ill.

LVIII

That god forbid that made me first your slave,
I should in thought control your times of
pleasure,
Or at your hand the account of hours to crave,
Being your vassal, bound to stay your leisure!
O! let me suffer, being at your beck,
The imprison'd absence of your liberty;   6
And patience, tame to sufferance, bide each
check,
Without accusing you of injury.
Be where you list, your charter is so strong
That you yourself may privilege your time
To what you will; to you it doth belong
Yourself to pardon of self-doing crime.   12
    I am to wait, though waiting so be hell,
    Not blame your pleasure, be it ill or well.

LIX

If there be nothing new, but that which is
Hath been before, how are our brains beguil'd,
Which, labouring for invention, bear amiss
The second burden of a former child!
O! that record could with a backward look,
Even of five hundred courses of the sun,   6
Show me your image in some antique book,
Since mind at first in character was done!

That I might see what the old world could
say
To this composed wonder of your frame;
Whe'r we are mended, or whe'r better they,
Or whether revolution be the same.   12
    O! sure I am, the wits of former days
    To subjects worse have given admiring
    praise.

LX

Like as the waves make towards the pebbled
shore,
So do our minutes hasten to their end;
Each changing place with that which goes
before,
In sequent toil all forwards do contend.
Nativity, once in the main of light,
Crawls to maturity, wherewith being crown'd, 6
Crooked eclipses 'gainst his glory fight,
And Time that gave doth now his gift con-
found.
Time doth transfix the flourish set on youth
And delves the parallels in beauty's brow,
Feeds on the rarities of nature's truth,
And nothing stands but for his scythe to
mow: 12
    And yet to times in hope my verse shall
    stand,
    Praising thy worth, despite his cruel hand.

LXI

Is it thy will thy image should keep open
My heavy eyelids to the weary night?
Dost thou desire my slumbers should be
broken,
While shadows, like to thee, do mock my sight?
Is it thy spirit that thou send'st from thee
So far from home, into my deeds to pry,   6
To find out shames and idle hours in me,
The scope and tenour of thy jealousy?
O, no! thy love, though much, is not so
great;
It is my love that keeps mine eye awake:
Mine own true love that doth my rest defeat,
To play the watchman ever for thy sake: 12
    For thee watch I whilst thou dost wake else-
    where,
    From me far off, with others all too near.

LXII

Sin of self-love possesseth all mine eye
And all my soul and all my every part;
And for this sin there is no remedy,
It is so grounded inward in my heart.
Methinks no face so gracious is as mine,
No shape so true, no truth of such account;   6
And for myself mine own worth do define,
As I all other in all worths surmount.
But when my glass shows me myself indeed,
Beated and chopp'd with tann'd antiquity,
Mine own self-love quite contrary I read;   12
    'Tis thee, myself,—that for myself I praise,
    Painting my age with beauty of thy days.

LXIII

Against my love shall be, as I am now,
With Time's injurious hand crush'd and o'er-
   worn;
When hours have drain'd his blood and fill'd
   his brow
With lines and wrinkles; when his youthful
   morn
Hath travell'd on to age's steepy night;
And all those beauties whereof now he's king   6
Are vanishing or vanish'd out of sight,
Stealing away the treasure of his spring;
For such a time do I now fortify
Against confounding age's cruel knife,
That he shall never cut from memory
My sweet love's beauty, though my lover's
   life: 12
   His beauty shall in these black lines be seen,
   And they shall live, and he in them still green.

LXIV

When I have seen by Time's fell hand defac'd
The rich-proud cost of outworn buried age;
When sometime lofty towers I see down-raz'd,
And brass eternal slave to mortal rage;
When I have seen the hungry ocean gain
Advantage on the kingdom of the shore,   6
And the firm soil win of the watery main,
Increasing store with loss, and loss with store;
When I have seen such interchange of state,
Or state itself confounded to decay;
Ruin hath taught me thus to ruminate—
That Time will come and take my love away.   12
   This thought is as a death, which cannot choose
   But weep to have that which it fears to lose.

LXV

Since brass, nor stone, nor earth, nor boundless
   sea,
But sad mortality o'ersways their power,
How with this rage shall beauty hold a plea,
Whose action is no stronger than a flower?
O! how shall summer's honey breath hold out
Against the wrackful siege of battering days,   6
When rocks impregnable are not so stout,
Nor gates of steel so strong, but Time decays?
O fearful meditation! where, alack,
Shall Time's best jewel from Time's chest lie
   hid?
Or what strong hand can hold his swift foot
   back?
Or who his spoil of beauty can forbid?   12
   O! none, unless this miracle have might,
   That in black ink my love may still shine
   bright.

LXVI

Tir'd with all these, for restful death I cry
As to behold desert a beggar born,
And needy nothing trimm'd in jollity,
And purest faith unhappily forsworn,
And gilded honour shamefully misplac'd,
And maiden virtue rudely strumpeted,   6
And right perfection wrongfully disgraced,
And strength by limping sway disabled,

And art made tongue-tied by authority,
And folly—doctor-like—controlling skill,
And simple truth miscall'd simplicity,
And captive good attending captain ill: 12
   Tir'd with all these, from these would I be
   gone,
   Save that, to die, I leave my love alone.

LXVII

Ah! wherefore with infection should he live,
And with his presence grace impiety,
That sin by him advantage should achieve,
And lace itself with his society?
Why should false painting imitate his cheek,
And steal dead seeing of his living hue?   6
Why should poor beauty indirectly seek
Roses of shadow, since his rose is true?
Why should he live, now Nature bankrupt is,
Beggar'd of blood to blush through lively
   veins?
For she hath no exchequer now but his,
And, proud of many, lives upon his gains.   12
   O! him she stores, to show what wealth she
   had
   In days long since, before these last so bad.

LXVIII

Thus is his cheek the map of days outworn,
When beauty liv'd and died as flowers do
   now,
Before these bastard signs of fair were born,
Or durst inhabit on a living brow;
Before the golden tresses of the dead,
The right of sepulchres, were shorn away,   6
To live a second life on second head;
Ere beauty's dead fleece made another gay:
In him those holy antique hours are seen,
Without all ornament, itself and true,
Making no summer of another's green,
Robbing no old to dress his beauty new;   12
   And him as for a map doth Nature store,
   To show false Art what beauty was of yore.

LXIX

Those parts of thee that the world's eye doth
   view
Want nothing that the thought of hearts can
   mend;
All tongues—the voice of souls—give thee that
   due,
Uttering bare truth, even so as foes commend.
Thy outward thus with outward praise is
   crown'd;
But those same tongues, that give thee so thine
   own,   6
In other accents do this praise confound
By seeing farther than the eye hath shown.
They look into the beauty of thy mind,
And that, in guess, they measure by thy deeds;
Then,—churls,—their thoughts, although their
   eyes were kind,   11
To thy fair flower add the rank smell of weeds:
   But why thy odour matcheth not thy show,
   The soil is this, that thou dost common grow.

LXX

That thou art blam'd shall not be thy defect,
For slander's mark was ever yet the fair;
The ornament of beauty is suspect,
A crow that flies in heaven's sweetest air.
So thou be good, slander doth but approve
Thy worth the greater, being woo'd of time; 6
For canker vice the sweetest buds doth love,
And thou present'st a pure unstained prime.
Thou hast pass'd by the ambush of young days,
Either not assail'd, or victor being charg'd;
Yet this thy praise cannot be so thy praise,
To tie up envy evermore enlarg'd: 12
  If some suspect of ill mask'd not thy show,
  Then thou alone kingdoms of hearts shouldst
  owe.

LXXI

No longer mourn for me when I am dead
Than you shall hear the surly sullen bell
Give warning to the world that I am fled
From this vile world, with vilest worms to dwell:
Nay, if you read this line, remember not
The hand that writ it; for I love you so, 6
That I in your sweet thoughts would be forgot,
If thinking on me then should make you woe.
O! if,—I say, you look upon this verse,
When I perhaps compounded am with clay,
Do not so much as my poor name rehearse,
But let your love even with my life decay; 12
  Lest the wise world should look into your
  moan,
  And mock you with me after I am gone.

LXXII

O! lest the world should task you to recite
What merit lived in me, that you should love
After my death,—dear love, forget me quite,
For you in me can nothing worthy prove,
Unless you would devise some virtuous lie,
To do more for me than mine own desert, 6
And hang more praise upon deceased I
Than niggard truth would willingly impart:
O! lest your true love may seem false in this,
That you for love speak well of me untrue,
My name be buried where my body is,
And live no more to shame nor me nor you. 12
  For I am sham'd by that which I bring forth,
  And so should you, to love things nothing
  worth.

LXXIII

That time of year thou mayst in me behold
When yellow leaves, or none, or few, do hang
Upon those boughs which shake against the
  cold,
Bare ruin'd choirs, where late the sweet birds
  sang.
In me thou see'st the twilight of such day
As after sunset fadeth in the west; 6
Which by and by black night doth take away,
Death's second self, that seals up all in rest.
In me thou see'st the glowing of such fire,
That on the ashes of his youth doth lie,
As the death-bed whereon it must expire 11
Consum'd with that which it was nourish'd by.

This thou perceiv'st, which makes thy love
  more strong,
To love that well which thou must leave ere
  long.

LXXIV

But be contented: when that fell arrest
Without all bail shall carry me away,
My life hath in this line some interest,
Which for memorial still with thee shall stay.
When thou reviewest this, thou dost review
The very part was consecrate to thee: 6
The earth can have but earth, which is his due;
My spirit is thine, the better part of me:
So then thou hast but lost the dregs of life,
The prey of worms, my body being dead;
The coward conquest of a wretch's knife,
Too base of thee to be remembered. 12
  The worth of that is that which it contains,
  And that is this, and this with thee remains.

LXXV

So are you to my thoughts as food to life,
Or as sweet-season'd showers are to the
  ground;
And for the peace of you I hold such strife
As 'twixt a miser and his wealth is found;
Now proud as an enjoyer, and anon 5
Doubting the filching age will steal his treasure;
Now counting best to be with you alone,
Then better'd that the world may see my
  pleasure:
Sometime, all full with feasting on your sight,
And by and by clean starved for a look;
Possessing or pursuing no delight,
Save what is had or must from you be took. 12
  Thus do I pine and surfeit day by day,
  Or gluttoning on all, or all away.

LXXVI

Why is my verse so barren of new pride,
So far from variation or quick change?
Why with the time do I not glance aside
To new-found methods and to compounds
  strange?
Why write I still all one, ever the same,
And keep invention in a noted weed, 6
That every word doth almost tell my name,
Showing their birth, and where they did pro-
  ceed?
O! know, sweet love, I always write of you,
And you and love are still my argument;
So all my best is dressing old words new,
Spending again what is already spent: 12
  For as the sun is daily new and old,
  So is my love still telling what is told.

LXXVII

Thy glass will show thee how thy beauties wear,
Thy dial how thy precious minutes waste;
The vacant leaves thy mind's imprint will bear,
And of this book this learning mayst thou taste.
The wrinkles which thy glass will truly show
Of mouthed graves will give thee memory; 6
Thou by thy dial's shady stealth mayst know
Time's thievish progress to eternity.

Look! what thy memory cannot contain,
Commit to these waste blanks, and thou shalt find
Those children nursed, deliver'd from thy brain,
To take a new acquaintance of thy mind.   12
   These offices, so oft as thou wilt look,
   Shall profit thee and much enrich thy book.

LXXVIII

So oft have I invok'd thee for my Muse
And found such fair assistance in my verse
As every alien pen hath got my use
And under thee their poesy disperse.
Thine eyes, that taught the dumb on high to sing
And heavy ignorance aloft to fly,   6
Have added feathers to the learned's wing
And given grace a double majesty.
Yet be most proud of that which I compile,
Whose influence is thine, and born of thee:
In others' works thou dost but mend the style,
And arts with thy sweet graces graced be;   12
   But thou art all my art, and dost advance
   As high as learning my rude ignorance.

LXXIX

Whilst I alone did call upon thy aid,
My verse alone had all thy gentle grace;
But now my gracious numbers are decay'd,
And my sick muse doth give another place.
I grant, sweet love, thy lovely argument
Deserves the travail of a worthier pen;   6
Yet what of thee thy poet doth invent
He robs thee of, and pays it thee again.
He lends thee virtue, and he stole that word
From thy behaviour; beauty doth he give,
And found it in thy cheek; he can afford
No praise to thee but what in thee doth live.   12
   Then thank him not for that which he doth say,
   Since what he owes thee thou thyself dost pay.

LXXX

O! how I faint when I of you do write,
Knowing a better spirit doth use your name,
And in the praise thereof spends all his might,
To make me tongue-tied, speaking of your fame!
But since your worth—wide as the ocean is,—   6
The humble as the proudest sail doth bear,
My saucy bark, inferior far to his,
On your broad main doth wilfully appear.
Your shallowest help will hold me up afloat,
Whilst he upon your soundless deep doth ride;
Or, being wrack'd, I am a worthless boat,
He of tall building and of goodly pride;   12
   Then if he thrive and I be cast away,
   The worst was this;—my love was my decay.

LXXXI

Or I shall live your epitaph to make,
Or you survive when I in earth am rotten;
From hence your memory death cannot take,
Although in me each part will be forgotten.
Your name from hence immortal life shall have,
Though I, once gone, to all the world must die: 6
The earth can yield me but a common grave,
When you entombed in men's eyes shall lie.
Your monument shall be my gentle verse,
Which eyes not yet created shall o'er-read;
And tongues to be your being shall rehearse,   11
When all the breathers of this world are dead;
   You still shall live,—such virtue hath my pen,—
   Where breath most breathes,—even in the mouths of men.

LXXXII

I grant thou wert not married to my Muse,
And therefore mayst without attaint o'erlook
The dedicated words which writers use
Of their fair subject, blessing every book.
Thou art as fair in knowledge as in hue,
Finding thy worth a limit past my praise;   6
And therefore art enforc'd to seek anew
Some fresher stamp of the time-bettering days.
And do so, love; yet when they have devis'd
What strained touches rhetoric can lend,
Thou truly fair wert truly sympathized   11
In true plain words by thy true-telling friend;
   And their gross painting might be better used
   Where cheeks need blood; in thee it is abus'd.

LXXXIII

I never saw that you did painting need,
And therefore to your fair no painting set;
I found, or thought I found, you did exceed
The barren tender of a poet's debt:
And therefore have I slept in your report,
That you yourself, being extant, well might show   6
How far a modern quill doth come too short,
Speaking of worth, what worth in you doth grow.
This silence for my sin you did impute,
Which shall be most my glory, being dumb;
For I impair not beauty being mute,   11
When others would give life, and bring a tomb.
   There lives more life in one of your fair eyes
   Than both your poets can in praise devise.

LXXXIV

Who is it that says most? which can say more
Than this rich praise,—that you alone are you?
In whose confine immured is the store
Which should example where your equal grew.
Lean penury within that pen doth dwell   5
That to his subject lends not some small glory;
But he that writes of you, if he can tell
That you are you, so dignifies his story,
Let him but copy what in you is writ,
Not making worse what nature made so clear,
And such a counterpart shall fame his wit,   12
Making his style admired every where.
   You to your beauteous blessings add a curse,
   Being fond on praise, which makes your praises worse.

LXXXV

My tongue-tied Muse in manners holds her
  still,
Whilst comments of your praise, richly com-
  pil'd,
Deserve their character with golden quill,
And precious phrase by all the Muses fil'd.
I think good thoughts, while others write good
  words,
And, like unletter'd clerk, still cry 'Amen'   6
To every hymn that able spirit affords,
In polish'd form of well-refined pen.
Hearing you prais'd, I say, ''Tis so, 'tis true,'
And to the most of praise add something more;
But that is in my thought, whose love to you,
Though words come hindmost, holds his rank
  before.   12
    Then others for the breath of words respect,
    Me for my dumb thoughts, speaking in effect.

LXXXVI

Was it the proud full sail of his great verse,
Bound for the prize of all too precious you,
That did my ripe thoughts in my brain inhearse,
Making their tomb the womb wherein they
  grew?
Was it his spirit, by spirits taught to write
Above a mortal pitch, that struck me dead?   6
No, neither he, nor his compeers by night
Giving him aid, my verse astonished.
He, nor that affable familiar ghost
Which nightly gulls him with intelligence,
As victors of my silence cannot boast;
I was not sick of any fear from thence: 12
    But when your countenance fill'd up his line,
    Then lack'd I matter; that enfeebled mine.

LXXXVII

Farewell! thou art too dear for my possessing,
And like enough thou know'st thy estimate:
The charter of thy worth gives thee releasing;
My bonds in thee are all determinate.
For how do I hold thee but by thy granting?
And for that riches where is my deserving?   6
The cause of this fair gift in me is wanting,
And so my patent back again is swerving.
Thyself thou gav'st, thy own worth then not
  knowing,
Or me, to whom thou gav'st it, else mistaking; 11
So thy great gift, upon misprision growing,
Comes home again, on better judgment making.
    Thus have I had thee, as a dream doth flatter,
    In sleep a king, but, waking, no such matter.

LXXXVIII

When thou shalt be dispos'd to set me light,
And place my merit in the eye of scorn,
Upon thy side against myself I'll fight,
And prove thee virtuous, though thou art for-
  sworn.
With mine own weakness, being best ac-
  quainted,
Upon thy part I can set down a story   6
Of faults conceal'd, wherein I am attainted;
That thou in losing me shalt win much glory:
And I by this will be a gainer too;
For bending all my loving thoughts on thee,
The injuries that to myself I do,
Doing thee vantage, double-vantage me.   12
    Such is my love, to thee I so belong,
    That for thy right myself will bear all wrong.

LXXXIX

Say that thou didst forsake me for some fault,
And I will comment upon that offence:
Speak of my lameness, and I straight will halt,
Against thy reasons making no defence.
Thou canst not, love, disgrace me half so ill,
To set a form upon desired change,   6
As I'll myself disgrace; knowing thy will,
I will acquaintance strangle, and look strange;
Be absent from thy walks; and in my tongue
Thy sweet beloved name no more shall dwell,
Lest I, too much profane, should do it wrong,
And haply of our old acquaintance tell.   12
    For thee, against myself I'll vow debate,
    For I must ne'er love him whom thou dost
      hate.

XC

Then hate me when thou wilt; if ever, now;
Now, while the world is bent my deeds to
  cross,
Join with the spite of fortune, make me bow,
And do not drop in for an after-loss:
Ah! do not, when my heart hath 'scap'd this
  sorrow,
Come in the rearward of a conquer'd woe;   6
Give not a windy night a rainy morrow,
To linger out a purpos'd overthrow.
If thou wilt leave me, do not leave me last,
When other petty griefs have done their spite,
But in the onset come: so shall I taste
At first the very worst of fortune's might;   12
    And other strains of woe, which now seem woe,
    Compar'd with loss of thee will not seem so.

XCI

Some glory in their birth, some in their skill,
Some in their wealth, some in their body's
  force;
Some in their garments, though new-fangled ill;
Some in their hawks and hounds, some in their
  horse;
And every humour hath his adjunct pleasure,
Wherein it finds a joy above the rest: 6
But these particulars are not my measure,
All these I better in one general best.
Thy love is better than high birth to me,
Richer than wealth, prouder than garments'
  cost,
Of more delight than hawks or horses be;
And having thee, of all men's pride I boast: 12
    Wretched in this alone, that thou mayst take
    All this away, and me most wretched make.

XCII

But do thy worst to steal thyself away,
For term of life thou art assured mine;
And life no longer than thy love will stay,
For it depends upon that love of thine.

Then need I not to fear the worst of wrongs,
When in the least of them my life hath end. 6
I see a better state to me belongs
Than that which on thy humour doth depend;
Thou canst not vex me with inconstant mind,
Since that my life on thy revolt doth lie.
O! what a happy title do I find,
Happy to have thy love, happy to die: 12
   But what's so blessed-fair that fears no blot?
   Thou mayst be false, and yet I know it not.

XCIII

So shall I live, supposing thou art true,
Like a deceived husband; so love's face
May still seem love to me, though alter'd new;
Thy looks with me, thy heart in other place:
For there can live no hatred in thine eye,
Therefore in that I cannot know thy change. 6
In many's looks the false heart's history
Is writ in moods, and frowns, and wrinkles
   strange,
But heaven in thy creation did decree
That in thy face sweet love should ever dwell;
Whate'er thy thoughts or thy heart's workings
   be,
Thy looks should nothing thence but sweetness
   tell. 12
   How like Eve's apple doth thy beauty grow,
   If thy sweet virtue answer not thy show!

XCIV

They that have power to hurt and will do
   none,
That do not do the thing they most do show,
Who, moving others, are themselves as stone,
Unmoved, cold, and to temptation slow;
They rightly do inherit heaven's graces,
And husband nature's riches from expense; 6
They are the lords and owners of their faces,
Others but stewards of their excellence.
The summer's flower is to the summer sweet,
Though to itself it only live and die,
But if that flower with base infection meet,
The basest weed outbraves his dignity: 12
   For sweetest things turn sourest by their
     deeds;
   Lilies that fester smell far worse than weeds.

XCV

How sweet and lovely dost thou make the
   shame
Which, like a canker in the fragrant rose,
Doth spot the beauty of thy budding name!
O! in what sweets dost thou thy sins enclose.
That tongue that tells the story of thy days,
Making lascivious comments on thy sport, 6
Cannot dispraise but in a kind of praise;
Naming thy name blesses an ill report.
O! what a mansion have those vices got
Which for their habitation chose out thee,
Where beauty's veil doth cover every blot
And all things turn to fair that eyes can see! 12
   Take heed, dear heart, of this large privilege;
   The hardest knife ill-used doth lose his edge.

XCVI

Some say thy fault is youth, some wantonness;
Some say thy grace is youth and gentle sport;
Both grace and faults are lov'd of more and
   less:
Thou makest faults graces that to thee resort.
As on the finger of a throned queen
The basest jewel will be well esteem'd, 6
So are those errors that in thee are seen
To truths translated and for true things deem'd.
How many lambs might the stern wolf betray,
If like a lamb he could his looks translate!
How many gazers mightst thou lead away,
If thou wouldst use the strength of all thy
   state! 12
   But do not so; I love thee in such sort,
   As, thou being mine, mine is thy good report.

XCVII

How like a winter hath my absence been
From thee, the pleasure of the fleeting year!
What freezings have I felt, what dark days
   seen!
What old December's bareness every where!
And yet this time remov'd was summer's time;
The teeming autumn, big with rich increase, 6
Bearing the wanton burden of the prime,
Like widow'd wombs after their lords' decease:
Yet this abundant issue seem'd to me
But hope of orphans and unfather'd fruit;
For summer and his pleasures wait on thee,
And, thou away, the very birds are mute: 12
   Or, if they sing, 'tis with so dull a cheer,
   That leaves look pale, dreading the winter's
     near.

XCVIII

From you have I been absent in the spring,
When proud-pied April, dress'd in all his trim,
Hath put a spirit of youth in every thing,
That heavy Saturn laugh'd and leap'd with him.
Yet nor the lays of birds, nor the sweet smell
Of different flowers in odour and in hue, 6
Could make me any summer's story tell,
Or from their proud lap pluck them where they
   grew:
Nor did I wonder at the lily's white,
Nor praise the deep vermilion in the rose;
They were but sweet, but figures of delight,
Drawn after you, you pattern of all those. 12
   Yet seem'd it winter still, and, you away,
   As with your shadow I with these did play.

XCIX

The forward violet thus did I chide:
Sweet thief, whence didst thou steal thy sweet
   that smells,
If not from my love's breath? The purple pride
Which on thy soft cheek for complexion dwells
In my love's veins thou hast too grossly dy'd.
The lily I condemned for thy hand, 6
And buds of marjoram had stol'n thy hair;
The roses fearfully on thorns did stand,
One blushing shame, another white despair;

A third, nor red nor white, had stol'n of both,
And to his robbery had annex'd thy breath;
But, for his theft, in pride of all his growth 12
A vengeful canker eat him up to death.
 More flowers I noted, yet I none could see
 But sweet or colour it had stol'n from thee.

C

Where art thou, Muse, that thou forget'st so
 long
To speak of that which gives thee all thy might?
Spend'st thou thy fury on some worthless song,
Darkening thy power to lend base subjects
 light?
Return, forgetful Muse, and straight redeem
In gentle numbers time so idly spent; 6
Sing to the ear that doth thy lays esteem
And gives thy pen both skill and argument.
Rise, resty Muse, my love's sweet face survey,
If Time have any wrinkle graven there;
If any, be a satire to decay,
And make Time's spoils despised every where. 12
 Give my love fame faster than Time wastes
  life;
 So thou prevent'st his scythe and crooked
  knife.

CI

O truant Muse, what shall be thy amends
For thy neglect of truth in beauty dy'd?
Both truth and beauty on my love depends;
So dost thou too, and therein dignified.
Make answer, Muse: wilt thou not haply say, 5
'Truth needs no colour, with his colour fix'd:
Beauty no pencil, beauty's truth to lay;
But best is best, if never intermix'd?'
Because he needs no praise, wilt thou be dumb?
Excuse not silence so; for 't lies in thee
To make him much outlive a gilded tomb
And to be prais'd of ages yet to be. 12
 Then do thy office, Muse; I teach thee how
 To make him seem long hence as he shows
  now.

CII

My love is strengthen'd, though more weak in
 seeming;
I love not less, though less the show appear:
That love is merchandiz'd whose rich esteeming
The owner's tongue doth publish everywhere.
Our love was new, and then but in the spring,
When I was wont to greet it with my lays; 6
As Philomel in summer's front doth sing,
And stops her pipe in growth of riper days:
Not that the summer is less pleasant now
Than when her mournful hymns did hush the
 night,
But that wild music burthens every bough,
And sweets grown common lose their dear
 delight. 12
 Therefore, like her, I sometime hold my
  tongue,
 Because I would not dull you with my song.

CIII

Alack! what poverty my Muse brings forth,
That having such a scope to show her pride,
The argument, all bare, is of more worth
Than when it hath my added praise beside!
O! blame me not, if I no more can write!
Look in your glass, and there appears a face 6
That over-goes my blunt invention quite,
Dulling my lines and doing me disgrace.
Were it not sinful then, striving to mend,
To mar the subject that before was well?
For to no other pass my verses tend
Than of your graces and your gifts to tell; 12
 And more, much more, than in my verse can
  sit,
 Your own glass shows you when you look in
  it.

CIV

To me, fair friend, you never can be old,
For as you were when first your eye I ey'd,
Such seems your beauty still. Three winters
 cold
Have from the forests shook three summers'
 pride,
Three beauteous springs to yellow autumn
 turn'd
In process of the seasons have I seen, 6
Three April perfumes in three hot Junes burn'd,
Since first I saw you fresh, which yet are green.
Ah! yet doth beauty, like a dial-hand,
Steal from his figure, and no pace perceiv'd;
So your sweet hue, which methinks still doth
 stand,
Hath motion, and mine eye may be deceiv'd: 12
 For fear of which, hear this, thou age unbred:
 Ere you were born was beauty's summer
  dead.

CV

Let not my love be call'd idolatry,
Nor my beloved as an idol show,
Since all alike my songs and praises be
To one, of one, still such, and ever so.
Kind is my love to-day, to-morrow kind,
Still constant in a wondrous excellence; 6
Therefore my verse, to constancy confin'd,
One thing expressing, leaves out difference.
'Fair, kind, and true,' is all my argument,
'Fair, kind, and true,' varying to other words;
And in this change is my invention spent,
Three themes in one, which wondrous scope
 affords. 12
 'Fair, kind, and true,' have often liv'd alone,
 Which three till now never kept seat in one.

CVI

When in the chronicle of wasted time
I see descriptions of the fairest wights,
And beauty making beautiful old rime,
In praise of ladies dead and lovely knights,
Then, in the blazon of sweet beauty's best,
Of hand, of foot, of lip, of eye, of brow, 6
I see their antique pen would have express'd
Even such a beauty as you master now.

So all their praises are but prophecies
Of this our time, all you prefiguring;
And, for they look'd but with divining eyes,   11
They had not skill enough your worth to sing:
  For we, which now behold these present days,
  Have eyes to wonder, but lack tongues to praise.

CVII

Not mine own fears, nor the prophetic soul
Of the wide world dreaming on things to come,
Can yet the lease of my true love control,
Suppos'd as forfeit to a confin'd doom.
The mortal moon hath her eclipse endur'd,
And the sad augurs mock their own presage;   6
Incertainties now crown themselves assur'd,
And peace proclaims olives of endless age.
Now with the drops of this most balmy time
My love looks fresh, and Death to me subscribes,
Since, spite of him, I'll live in this poor rime,   11
While he insults o'er dull and speechless tribes:
  And thou in this shalt find thy monument,
  When tyrants' crests and tombs of brass are spent.

CVIII

What's in the brain, that ink may character,
Which hath not figur'd to thee my true spirit?
What's new to speak, what new to register,
That may express my love, or thy dear merit?
Nothing, sweet boy; but yet, like prayers divine,
I must each day say o'er the very same;   6
Counting no old thing old, thou mine, I thine,
Even as when first I hallow'd thy fair name.
So that eternal love in love's fresh case
Weighs not the dust and injury of age,
Nor gives to necessary wrinkles place,
But makes antiquity for aye his page;   12
  Finding the first conceit of love there bred,
  Where time and outward form would show it dead.

CIX

O! never say that I was false of heart,
Though absence seem'd my flame to qualify.
As easy might I from myself depart
As from my soul, which in thy breast doth lie:
That is my home of love: if I have rang'd,
Like him that travels, I return again;   6
Just to the time, not with the time exchang'd,
So that myself bring water for my stain.
Never believe, though in my nature reign'd
All frailties that besiege all kinds of blood,
That it could so preposterously be stain'd,
To leave for nothing all thy sum of good;   12
  For nothing this wide universe I call,
  Save thou, my rose; in it thou art my all.

CX

Alas! 'tis true I have gone here and there,
And made myself a motley to the view,
Gor'd mine own thoughts, sold cheap what is most dear,
Made old offences of affections new;
Most true it is that I have look'd on truth
Askance and strangely; but, by all above,   6
These blenches gave my heart another youth,
And worse essays prov'd thee my best of love.
Now all is done, save what shall have no end:
Mine appetite I never more will grind
On newer proof, to try an older friend,
A god in love, to whom I am confin'd.   12
  Then give me welcome, next my heaven the best,
  Even to thy pure and most most loving breast.

CXI

O! for my sake do you with Fortune chide
The guilty goddess of my harmful deeds,
That did not better for my life provide
Than public means which public manners breeds.
Thence comes it that my name receives a brand,
And almost thence my nature is subdu'd   6
To what it works in, like the dyer's hand:
Pity me, then, and wish I were renew'd;
Whilst, like a willing patient, I will drink
Potions of eisel 'gainst my strong infection;
No bitterness that I will bitter think,
Nor double penance, to correct correction.   12
  Pity me, then, dear friend, and I assure ye
  Even that your pity is enough to cure me.

CXII

Your love and pity doth the impression fill
Which vulgar scandal stamp'd upon my brow;
For what care I who calls me well or ill,
So you o'er-green my bad, my good allow?
You are my all-the-world, and I must strive
To know my shames and praises from your tongue;   6
None else to me, nor I to none alive,
That my steel'd sense or changes right or wrong.
In so profound abysm I throw all care
Of other's voices, that my adder's sense
To critic and to flatterer stopped are.
Mark how with my neglect I do dispense: 12
  You are so strongly in my purpose bred,
  That all the world besides methinks are dead.

CXIII

Since I left you, mine eye is in my mind;
And that which governs me to go about
Doth part his function and is partly blind,
Seems seeing, but effectually is out;
For it no form delivers to the heart   5
Of bird, of flower, or shape, which it doth latch:
Of his quick objects hath the mind no part,
Nor his own vision holds what it doth catch;

For if it see the rud'st or gentlest sight,
The most sweet favour or deformed'st creature,
The mountain or the sea, the day or night,
The crow or dove, it shapes them to your
feature: 12
  Incapable of more, replete with you,
  My most true mind thus maketh mine un-
  true.

CXIV

Or whether doth my mind being crown'd with
you,
Drink up the monarch's plague, this flattery?
Or whether shall I say, mine eye saith true,
And that your love taught it this alchymy,
To make of monsters and things indigest
Such cherubins as your sweet self resemble, 6
Creating every bad a perfect best,
As fast as objects to his beams assemble?
O! 'tis the first, 'tis flattery in my seeing,
And my great mind most kingly drinks it up:
Mine eye well knows what with his gust is
'greeing,
And to his palate doth prepare the cup: 12
  If it be poison'd, 'tis the lesser sin
  That mine eye loves it and doth first begin.

CXV

Those lines that I before have writ do lie,
Even those that said I could not love you
dearer:
Yet then my judgment knew no reason why
My most full flame should afterwards burn
clearer.
But reckoning Time, whose million'd accidents
Creep in 'twixt vows, and change decrees of
kings,   6
Tan sacred beauty, blunt the sharp'st intents,
Divert strong minds to the course of altering
things,
Alas! why, fearing of Time's tyranny,
Might I not then say, 'Now I love you best',
When I was certain o'er incertainty,
Crowning the present, doubting of the rest? 12
  Love is a babe; then might I not say so,
  To give full growth to that which still doth
  grow?

CXVI

Let me not to the marriage of true minds
Admit impediments. Love is not love
Which alters when it alteration finds,
Or bends with the remover to remove:
O, no! it is an ever-fixed mark,
That looks on tempests and is never shaken; 6
It is the star to every wandering bark,
Whose worth 's unknown, although his height
be taken.
Love 's not Time's fool, though rosy lips and
cheeks
Within his bending sickle's compass come;
Love alters not with his brief hours and weeks,
But bears it out even to the edge of doom. 12
  If this be error, and upon me prov'd,
  I never writ, nor no man ever lov'd.

CXVII

Accuse me thus: that I have scanted all
Wherein I should your great deserts repay,
Forgot upon your dearest love to call,
Whereto all bonds do tie me day by day;
That I have frequent been with unknown
minds,
And given to time your own dear-purchas'd
right;   6
That I have hoisted sail to all the winds
Which should transport me furthest from your
sight.
Book both my wilfulness and errors down,
And on just proof surmise accumulate;
Bring me within the level of your frown,
But shoot not at me in your waken'd hate; 12
  Since my appeal says I did strive to prove
  The constancy and virtue of your love.

CXVIII

Like as, to make our appetites more keen,
With eager compounds we our palate urge;
As, to prevent our maladies unseen,
We sicken to shun sickness when we purge;
Even so, being full of your ne'er-cloying sweet-
ness,
To bitter sauces did I frame my feeding;   6
And, sick of welfare, found a kind of meetness
To be diseas'd, ere that there was true needing.
Thus policy in love, to anticipate
The ills that were not, grew to faults assur'd,
And brought to medicine a healthful state, 12
Which, rank of goodness, would by ill be cur'd;
  But thence I learn, and find the lesson true,
  Drugs poison him that so fell sick of you.

CXIX

What potions have I drunk of Siren tears,
Distill'd from limbecks foul as hell within,
Applying fears to hopes, and hopes to fears,
Still losing when I saw myself to win!
What wretched errors hath my heart com-
mitted,
Whilst it hath thought itself so blessed never! 6
How have mine eyes out of their spheres been
fitted,
In the distraction of this madding fever!
O benefit of ill! now I find true
That better is by evil still made better;
And ruin'd love, when it is built anew,   11
Grows fairer than at first, more strong, far
greater.
  So I return rebuk'd to my content,
  And gain by ill thrice more than I have spent.

CXX

That you were once unkind befriends me now,
And for that sorrow, which I then did feel,
Needs must I under my transgression bow,
Unless my nerves were brass or hammer'd steel.
For if you were by my unkindness shaken,
As I by yours, you 've pass'd a hell of time; 6
And I, a tyrant, have no leisure taken
To weigh how once I suffer'd in your crime.

O! that our night of woe might have remember'd
My deepest sense, how hard true sorrow hits,
And soon to you, as you to me, then tender'd   11
The humble salve which wounded bosoms fits!
    But that your trespass now becomes a fee;
    Mine ransoms yours, and yours must ransom
    me.

CXXI

'Tis better to be vile than vile esteem'd,
When not to be receives reproach of being;
And the just pleasure lost, which is so deem'd
Not by our feeling, but by others' seeing:
For why should others' false adulterate eyes
Give salutation to my sportive blood?   6
Or on my frailties why are frailer spies,
Which in their wills count bad what I think
    good?
No, I am that I am, and they that level
At my abuses reckon up their own:
I may be straight though they themselves be
    bevel;
By their rank thoughts my deeds must not be
    shown;   12
    Unless this general evil they maintain,
    All men are bad and in their badness reign.

CXXII

Thy gift, thy tables, are within my brain
Full character'd with lasting memory,
Which shall above that idle rank remain,
Beyond all date, even to eternity:
Or, at the least, so long as brain and heart
Have faculty by nature to subsist;   6
Till each to raz'd oblivion yield his part
Of thee, thy record never can be miss'd.
That poor retention could not so much hold,
Nor need I tallies thy dear love to score;
Therefore to give them from me was I bold,
To trust those tables that receive thee more: 12
    To keep an adjunct to remember thee
    Were to import forgetfulness in me.

CXXIII

No, Time, thou shalt not boast that I do
    change:
Thy pyramids built up with newer might
To me are nothing novel, nothing strange;
They are but dressings of a former sight.
Our dates are brief, and therefore we admire
What thou dost foist upon us that is old;   6
And rather make them born to our desire
Than think that we before have heard them told.
Thy registers and thee I both defy,
Not wondering at the present nor the past,
For thy records and what we see doth lie,
Made more or less by thy continual haste.   12
    This I do vow, and this shall ever be;
    I will be true, despite thy scythe and thee.

CXXIV

If my dear love were but the child of state,
It might for Fortune's bastard be unfather'd,
As subject to Time's love or to Time's hate,
Weeds among weeds, or flowers with flowers
    gather'd.

No, it was builded far from accident;
It suffers not in smiling pomp, nor falls   6
Under the blow of thralled discontent,
Whereto the inviting time our fashion calls:
It fears not policy, that heretic,
Which works on leases of short number'd
    hours,
But all alone stands hugely politic,
That it nor grows with heat, nor drowns
    with showers.   12
    To this I witness call the fools of time,
    Which die for goodness, who have liv'd for
    crime.

CXXV

Were 't aught to me I bore the canopy,
With my extern the outward honouring,
Or laid great bases for eternity,
Which prove more short than waste or ruining?
Have I not seen dwellers on form and favour
Lose all and more by paying too much rent,   6
For compound sweet foregoing simple savour
Pitiful thrivers, in their gazing spent?
No; let me be obsequious in thy heart,
And take thou my oblation, poor but free,
Which is not mix'd with seconds, knows no
    art,
But mutual render, only me for thee.   12
    Hence, thou suborn'd informer! a true soul
    When most impeach'd stands least in thy
    control.

CXXVI

O thou, my lovely boy, who in thy power
Dost hold Time's fickle glass, his sickle hour;
Who hast by waning grown, and therein show'st
Thy lovers withering as thy sweet self grow'st;
If Nature, sovereign mistress over wrack,
As thou goest onwards, still will pluck thee
    back,   6
She keeps thee to this purpose, that her skill
May time disgrace and wretched minutes kill.
Yet fear her, O thou minion of her pleasure!
She may detain, but not still keep, her treasure!
    Her audit, though delay'd, answer'd must be,
    And her quietus is to render thee.   12

CXXVII

In the old age black was not counted fair,
Or if it were, it bore not beauty's name;
But now is black beauty's successive heir,
And beauty slander'd with a bastard's shame:
For since each hand hath put on Nature's
    power,
Fairing the foul with Art's false borrow'd face,   6
Sweet beauty hath no name, no holy bower,
But is profan'd, if not lives in disgrace.
Therefore my mistress' brows are raven black,
Her eyes so suited, and they mourners seem
At such who, not born fair, no beauty lack,
Sland'ring creation with a false esteem: 12
    Yet so they mourn, becoming of their woe,
    That every tongue says beauty should look
    so.

CXXVIII

How oft, when thou, my music, music play'st,
Upon that blessed wood whose motion sounds
With thy sweet fingers, when thou gently
    sway'st
The wiry concord that mine ear confounds,
Do I envy those jacks that nimble leap
To kiss the tender inward of thy hand,   6
Whilst my poor lips, which should that harvest
    reap,
At the wood's boldness by thee blushing stand!
To be so tickl'd, they would change their state
And situation with those dancing chips,   10
O'er whom thy fingers walk with gentle gait,
Making dead wood more bless'd than living
    lips.
    Since saucy jacks so happy are in this,
    Give them thy fingers, me thy lips to kiss.

CXXIX

The expense of spirit in a waste of shame
Is lust in action; and till action, lust
Is perjur'd, murderous, bloody, full of blame,
Savage, extreme, rude, cruel, not to trust;
Enjoy'd no sooner but despised straight;
Past reason hunted; and no sooner had,   6
Past reason hated, as a swallow'd bait,
On purpose laid to make the taker mad:
Mad in pursuit, and in possession so;
Had, having, and in quest to have, extreme;
A bliss in proof,—and prov'd, a very woe;
Before, a joy propos'd; behind, a dream.   12
    All this the world well knows; yet none
    knows well
    To shun the heaven that leads men to this
    hell.

CXXX

My mistress' eyes are nothing like the sun;
Coral is far more red than her lips' red:
If snow be white, why then her breasts are dun;
If hairs be wires, black wires grow on her head.
I have seen roses damask'd, red and white,
But no such roses see I in her cheeks;   6
And in some perfumes is there more delight
Than in the breath that from my mistress reeks.
I love to hear her speak, yet well I know
That music hath a far more pleasing sound:
I grant I never saw a goddess go,—
My mistress, when she walks, treads on the
    ground: 12
    And yet, by heaven, I think my love as rare
    As any she belied with false compare.

CXXXI

Thou art as tyrannous, so as thou art,
As those whose beauties proudly make them
    cruel;
For well thou know'st to my dear doting heart
Thou art the fairest and most precious jewel.
Yet, in good faith, some say that thee behold,
Thy face hath not the power to make love
    groan: 6
To say they err I dare not be so bold,
Although I swear it to myself alone.

And to be sure that is not false I swear,
A thousand groans, but thinking on thy face,
One on another's neck, do witness bear
Thy black is fairest in my judgment's place.   12
    In nothing art thou black save in thy deeds,
    And thence this slander, as I think, proceeds.

CXXXII

Thine eyes I love, and they, as pitying me,
Knowing thy heart torments me with disdain,
Have put on black and loving mourners be,
Looking with pretty ruth upon my pain.
And truly not the morning sun of heaven
Better becomes the grey cheeks of the east,   6
Nor that full star that ushers in the even,
Doth half that glory to the sober west,
As those two mourning eyes become thy face:
O! let it then as well beseem thy heart
To mourn for me, since mourning doth thee
    grace,
And suit thy pity like in every part.   12
    Then will I swear beauty herself is black,
    And all they foul that thy complexion lack.

CXXXIII

Beshrew that heart that makes my heart to
    groan
For that deep wound it gives my friend and me!
Is 't not enough to torture me alone,
But slave to slavery my sweet'st friend must be?
Me from myself thy cruel eye hath taken,
And my next self thou harder hast engross'd: 6
Of him, myself, and thee, I am forsaken;
A torment thrice threefold thus to be cross'd.
Prison my heart in thy steel bosom's ward,
But then my friend's heart let my poor heart bail;
Whoe'er keeps me, let my heart be his guard;
Thou canst not then use rigour in my jail: 12
    And yet thou wilt; for I, being pent in thee,
    Perforce am thine, and all that is in me.

CXXXIV

So, now I have confess'd that he is thine,
And I myself am mortgag'd to thy will,
Myself I'll forfeit, so that other mine
Thou wilt restore, to be my comfort still:
But thou wilt not, nor he will not be free,
For thou art covetous and he is kind;   6
He learn'd but surety-like to write for me,
Under that bond that him as fast doth bind.
The statute of thy beauty thou wilt take,
Thou usurer, that putt'st forth all to use,
And sue a friend came debtor for my sake;
So him I lose through my unkind abuse.   12
    Him have I lost; thou hast both him and me:
    He pays the whole, and yet am I not free.

CXXXV

Whoever hath her wish, thou hast thy *Will*,
And *Will* to boot, and *Will* in over-plus;
More than enough am I that vex thee still,
To thy sweet will making addition thus.
Wilt thou, whose will is large and spacious,
Not once vouchsafe to hide my will in thine?   6
Shall will in others seem right gracious,
And in my will no fair acceptance shine?

The sea, all water, yet receives rain still,
And in abundance addeth to his store;
So thou, being rich in *Will*, add to thy *Will*   11
One will of mine, to make thy large *Will* more.
   Let no unkind 'No' fair beseechers kill;
   Think all but one, and me in that one *Will*.

CXXXVI

If thy soul check thee that I come so near,
Swear to thy blind soul that I was thy *Will*,
And will, thy soul knows, is admitted there;
Thus far for love, my love-suit, sweet, fulfil.
Will will fulfil the treasure of thy love,
Ay, fill it full with wills, and my will one.   6
In things of great receipt with ease we prove
Among a number one is reckon'd none:
Then in the number let me pass untold,
Though in thy stores' account I one must be;
For nothing hold me, so it please thee hold
That nothing me, a something sweet to thee: 12
   Make but my name thy love, and love that still,
   And then thou lov'st me,—for my name is
   Will.

CXXXVII

Thou blind fool, Love, what dost thou to mine
   eyes,
That they behold, and see not what they see?
They know what beauty is, see where it lies,
Yet what the best is take the worst to be.
If eyes, corrupt by over-partial looks,
Be anchor'd in the bay where all men ride,   6
Why of eyes' falsehood hast thou forged hooks,
Whereto the judgment of my heart is tied?
Why should my heart think that a several plot
Which my heart knows the wide world's
   common place?
Or mine eyes, seeing this, say this is not,
To put fair truth upon so foul a face?   12
   In things right true my heart and eyes have
   err'd,
   And to this false plague are they now trans-
   ferr'd.

CXXXVIII

When my love swears that she is made of truth,
I do believe her, though I know she lies,
That she might think me some untutor'd youth,
Unlearned in the world's false subtleties.
Thus vainly thinking that she thinks me young,
Although she knows my days are past the best,   6
Simply I credit her false-speaking tongue:
On both sides thus is simple truth supprest.
But wherefore says she not she is unjust?
And wherefore say not I that I am old?
O! love's best habit is in seeming trust,
And age in love loves not to have years told: 12
   Therefore I lie with her, and she with me,
   And in our faults by lies we flatter'd be.

CXXXIX

O! call not me to justify the wrong
That thy unkindness lays upon my heart;
Wound me not with thine eye, but with thy
   tongue:
Use power with power, and slay me not by art.

Tell me thou lovest elsewhere; but in my sight,
Dear heart, forbear to glance thine eye aside: 6
What need'st thou wound with cunning, when
   thy might
Is more than my o'erpress'd defence can bide?
Let me excuse thee: ah! my love well knows
Her pretty looks have been my enemies;
And therefore from my face she turns my
   foes,   11
That they elsewhere might dart their injuries:
   Yet do not so; but since I am near slain,
   Kill me outright with looks, and rid my pain.

CXL

Be wise as thou art cruel; do not press
My tongue-tied patience with too much dis-
   dain;
Lest sorrow lend me words, and words express
The manner of my pity-wanting pain.
If I might teach thee wit, better it were,
Though not to love, yet, love, to tell me so;—   6
As testy sick men, when their deaths be near,
No news but health from their physicians
   know;—
For, if I should despair, I should grow mad,
And in my madness might speak ill of thee:
Now this ill-wresting world is grown so bad,
Mad slanderers by mad ears believed be.   12
   That I may not be so, nor thou belied,
   Bear thine eyes straight, though thy proud
   heart go wide.

CXLI

In faith, I do not love thee with mine eyes,
For they in thee a thousand errors note;
But 'tis my heart that loves what they despise,
Who, in despite of view, is pleas'd to dote.
Nor are mine ears with thy tongue's tune de-
   lighted;
Nor tender feeling, to base touches prone.   6
Nor taste nor smell desire to be invited
To any sensual feast with thee alone:
But my five wits nor my five senses can
Dissuade one foolish heart from serving thee,
Who leaves unsway'd the likeness of a man,
Thy proud heart's slave and vassal wretch to
   be: 12
   Only my plague thus far I count my gain,
   That she that makes me sin awards me pain.

CXLII

Love is my sin, and thy dear virtue hate,
Hate of my sin, grounded on sinful loving:
O! but with mine compare thou thine own
   state,
And thou shalt find it merits not reproving;
Or, if it do, not from those lips of thine,
That have profan'd their scarlet ornaments   6
And seal'd false bonds of love as oft as mine,
Robb'd others' beds' revenues of their rents.
Be it lawful I love thee, as thou lov'st those
Whom thine eyes woo as mine importune thee:
Root pity in thy heart, that when it grows,
Thy pity may deserve to pitied be.   12
   If thou dost seek to have what thou dost hide,
   By self-example mayst thou be denied!

CXLIII

Lo, as a careful housewife runs to catch
One of her feather'd creatures broke away,
Sets down her babe, and makes all quick dispatch
In pursuit of the thing she would have stay;
Whilst her neglected child holds her in chase,
Cries to catch her whose busy care is bent 6
To follow that which flies before her face,
Not prizing her poor infant's discontent:
So runn'st thou after that which flies from thee,
Whilst I thy babe chase thee afar behind;
But if thou catch thy hope, turn back to me,
And play the mother's part, kiss me, be kind; 12
    So will I pray that thou mayst have thy *Will*,
    If thou turn back and my loud crying still.

CXLIV

Two loves I have of comfort and despair,
Which like two spirits do suggest me still:
The better angel is a man right fair,
The worser spirit a woman, colour'd ill.
To win me soon to hell, my female evil
Tempteth my better angel from my side, 6
And would corrupt my saint to be a devil,
Wooing his purity with her foul pride.
And whether that my angel be turn'd fiend
Suspect I may, but not directly tell;
But being both from me, both to each friend,
I guess one angel in another's hell: 12
    Yet this shall I ne'er know, but live in doubt,
    Till my bad angel fire my good one out.

CXLV

Those lips that Love's own hand did make,
Breath'd forth the sound that said 'I hate',
To me that languish'd for her sake:
But when she saw my woeful state,
Straight in her heart did mercy come,
Chiding that tongue that ever sweet 6
Was us'd in giving gentle doom;
And taught it thus anew to greet;
'I hate', she alter'd with an end,
That follow'd it as gentle day
Doth follow night, who like a fiend
From heaven to hell is flown away. 12
    'I hate' from hate away she threw,
    And sav'd my life, saying—'Not you'.

CXLVI

Poor soul, the centre of my sinful earth,
Fool'd by these rebel powers that thee array,
Why dost thou pine within and suffer dearth,
Painting thy outward walls so costly gay?
Why so large cost, having so short a lease,
Dost thou upon thy fading mansion spend? 6
Shall worms, inheritors of this excess,
Eat up thy charge? Is this thy body's end?
Then, soul, live thou upon thy servant's loss,
And let that pine to aggravate thy store;
Buy terms divine in selling hours of dross;
Within be fed, without be rich no more: 12
    So shalt thou feed on Death, that feeds on
        men,
    And Death once dead, there's no more dying
        then.

CXLVII

My love is as a fever, longing still
For that which longer nurseth the disease;
Feeding on that which doth preserve the ill,
The uncertain sickly appetite to please.
My reason, the physician to my love,
Angry that his prescriptions are not kept, 6
Hath left me, and I desperate now approve
Desire is death, which physic did except.
Past cure I am, now Reason is past care,
And frantic-mad with evermore unrest;
My thoughts and my discourse as madmen's
    are,
At random from the truth vainly express'd; 12
    For I have sworn thee fair, and thought thee
        bright,
    Who art as black as hell, as dark as night.

CXLVIII

O me! what eyes hath Love put in my head,
Which have no correspondence with true sight;
Or, if they have, where is my judgment fled,
That censures falsely what they see aright?
If that be fair whereon my false eyes dote,
What means the world to say it is not so? 6
If it be not, then love doth well denote
Love's eye is not so true as all men's: no.
How can it? O! how can Love's eye be true,
That is so vex'd with watching and with tears?
No marvel then, though I mistake my view;
The sun itself sees not till heaven clears. 12
    O cunning Love! with tears thou keep'st me
        blind,
    Lest eyes well-seeing thy foul faults should
        find.

CXLIX

Canst thou, O cruel! say I love thee not,
When I against myself with thee partake?
Do I not think on thee, when I forgot
Am of myself, all tyrant, for thy sake?
Who hateth thee that I do call my friend?
On whom frown'st thou that I do fawn upon? 6
Nay, if thou lour'st on me, do I not spend
Revenge upon myself with present moan?
What merit do I in myself respect,
That is so proud thy service to despise,
When all my best doth worship thy defect,
Commanded by the motion of thine eyes? 12
    But, love, hate on, for now I know thy mind;
    Those that can see thou lov'st and I am
        blind.

CL

O! from what power hast thou this powerful
    might,
With insufficiency my heart to sway?
To make me give the lie to my true sight,
And swear that brightness doth not grace the
    day?
Whence hast thou this becoming of things ill,
That in the very refuse of thy deeds 6
There is such strength and warrantise of skill,
That, in my mind, thy worst all best exceeds?

Who taught thee how to make me love thee
   more,
The more I hear and see just cause of hate?
O! though I love what others do abhor,
With others thou shouldst not abhor my
   state: 12
   If thy unworthiness rais'd love in me,
   More worthy I to be belov'd of thee.

CLI

Love is too young to know what conscience is;
Yet who knows not conscience is born of love?
Then, gentle cheater, urge not my amiss,
Lest guilty of my faults thy sweet self prove:
For, thou betraying me, I do betray
My nobler part to my gross body's treason; 6
My soul doth tell my body that he may
Triumph in love; flesh stays no further reason,
But rising at thy name doth point out thee
As his triumphant prize. Proud of this pride,
He is contented thy poor drudge to be,
To stand in thy affairs, fall by thy side.   12
   No want of conscience hold it that I call
   Her 'love' for whose dear love I rise and fall.

CLII

In loving thee thou know'st I am forsworn,
But thou art twice forsworn, to me love swear-
   ing;
In act thy bed-vow broke, and new faith torn,
In vowing new hate after new love bearing.
But why of two oaths' breach do I accuse thee,
When I break twenty? I am perjur'd most; 6
For all my vows are oaths but to misuse thee,
And all my honest faith in thee is lost:
For I have sworn deep oaths of thy deep kind-
   ness,
Oaths of thy love, thy truth, thy constancy;
And, to enlighten thee, gave eyes to blindness,

Or made them swear against the thing they
   see;   12
For I have sworn thee fair; more perjur'd I,
To swear against the truth so foul a lie!

CLIII

Cupid laid by his brand and fell asleep:
A maid of Dian's this advantage found,
And his love-kindling fire did quickly steep
In a cold valley-fountain of that ground;
Which borrow'd from this holy fire of Love
A dateless lively heat, still to endure,   6
And grew a seething bath, which yet men prove
Against strange maladies a sovereign cure.
But at my mistress' eye Love's brand new-fired,
The boy for trial needs would touch my breast;
I, sick withal, the help of bath desired,
And thither hied, a sad distemper'd guest,   12
   But found no cure: the bath for my help lies
   Where Cupid got new fire, my mistress' eyes.

CLIV

The little Love-god lying once asleep
Laid by his side his heart-inflaming brand,
Whilst many nymphs that vow'd chaste life to
   keep
Came tripping by; but in her maiden hand
The fairest votary took up that fire   5
Which many legions of true hearts had warm'd;
And so the general of hot desire
Was, sleeping, by a virgin hand disarm'd.
This brand she quenched in a cool well by,
Which from Love's fire took heat perpetual,
Growing a bath and healthful remedy
For men diseas'd; but I, my mistress' thrall, 12
   Came there for cure, and this by that I prove,
   Love's fire heats water, water cools not love.

A LOVER'S COMPLAINT

FROM off a hill whose concave womb re-worded
A plaintful story from a sistering vale,
My spirits to attend this double voice accorded,
And down I laid to list the sad-tun'd tale;   4
Ere long espied a fickle maid full pale,
Tearing of papers, breaking rings a-twain,
Storming her world with sorrow's wind and
   rain.

Upon her head a platted hive of straw,   8
Which fortified her visage from the sun,
Whereon the thought might think sometime it
   saw
The carcass of a beauty spent and done:
Time had not scythed all that youth begun, 12
Nor youth all quit; but, spite of heaven's fell
   rage,
Some beauty peep'd through lattice of sear'd
   age.

Oft did she heave her napkin to her eyne,
Which on it had conceited characters,   16
Laundering the silken figures in the brine
That season'd woe had pelleted in tears,
And often reading what content it bears;
As often shrieking undistinguish'd woe   20
In clamours of all size, both high and low.

Sometimes her levell'd eyes their carriage ride,
As they did battery to the spheres intend;
Sometime diverted, their poor balls are tied 24
To the orbed earth; sometimes they do extend
Their view right on; anon their gazes lend
To every place at once, and nowhere fix'd,
The mind and sight distractedly commix'd. 28

Her hair, nor loose nor tied in formal plat,
Proclaim'd in her a careless hand of pride;
For some, untuck'd, descended her sheav'd hat,

Hanging her pale and pined cheek beside; 32
Some in her threaden fillet still did bide,
And true to bondage would not break from
    thence
Though slackly braided in loose negligence.

A thousand favours from a maund she drew 36
Of amber, crystal, and of beaded jet,
Which one by one she in a river threw,
Upon whose weeping margent she was set;
Like usury, applying wet to wet, 40
Or monarch's hands that let not bounty fall
Where want cries some, but where excess begs
    all.

Of folded schedules had she many a one,
Which she perus'd, sigh'd, tore, and gave the
    flood; 44
Crack'd many a ring of posied gold and bone,
Bidding them find their sepulchres in mud;
Found yet more letters sadly penn'd in blood,
With sleided silk feat and affectedly 48
Enswath'd, and seal'd to curious secrecy.

These often bath'd she in her fluxive eyes,
And often kiss'd, and often 'gan to tear;
Cried 'O false blood! thou register of lies, 52
What unapproved witness dost thou bear;
Ink would have seem'd more black and damned
    here.'
This said, in top of rage the lines she rents,
Big discontent so breaking their contents. 56

A reverend man that graz'd his cattle nigh—
Sometime a blusterer, that the ruffle knew
Of court, of city, and had let go by
The swiftest hours, observed as they flew— 60
Towards this afflicted fancy fastly drew;
And, privileg'd by age, desires to know
In brief the grounds and motives of her woe.

So slides he down upon his grained bat, 64
And comely-distant sits he by her side;
When he again desires her, being sat,
Her grievance with his hearing to divide:
If that from him there may be aught applied 68
Which may her suffering ecstacy assuage,
'Tis promis'd in the charity of age.

'Father,' she says, 'though in me you behold
The injury of many a blasting hour, 72
Let it not tell your judgment I am old;
Not age, but sorrow, over me hath power:
I might as yet have been a spreading flower,
Fresh to myself, if I had self-applied 76
Love to myself and to no love beside.

'But woe is me! too early I attended
A youthful suit, it was to gain my grace,
Of one by nature's outwards so commended, 80
That maidens' eyes stuck over all his face.
Love lack'd a dwelling, and made him her
    place;
And when in his fair parts she did abide,
She was new lodg'd and newly deified. 84

'His browny locks did hang in crooked curls,
And every light occasion of the wind
Upon his lips their silken parcels hurls.
What's sweet to do, to do will aptly find: 88
Each eye that saw him did enchant the mind,
For on his visage was in little drawn
What largeness thinks in Paradise was sawn.

'Small show of man was yet upon his chin; 92
His phœnix down began but to appear
Like unshorn velvet on that termless skin
Whose bare out-bragg'd the web it seem'd to
    wear;
Yet show'd his visage by that cost more dear, 96
And nice affections wavering stood in doubt
If best were as it was, or best without.

'His qualities were beauteous as his form,
For maiden-tongu'd he was, and thereof free; 100
Yet, if men mov'd him, was he such a storm
As oft 'twixt May and April is to see,
When winds breathe sweet, unruly though they
    be.
His rudeness so with his authoriz'd youth 104
Did livery falseness in a pride of truth.

'Well could he ride, and often men would say
"That horse his mettle from his rider takes:
Proud of subjection, noble by the sway, 108
What rounds, what bounds, what course, what
    stop he makes!"
And controversy hence a question takes,
Whether the horse by him became his deed,
Or he his manage by the well-doing steed. 112

'But quickly on this side the verdict went:
His real habitude gave life and grace
To appertainings and to ornament,
Accomplish'd in himself, not in his case: 116
All aids, themselves made fairer by their place,
Came for additions; yet their purpos'd trim
Piec'd not his grace, but were all grac'd by him.

'So on the tip of his subduing tongue 120
All kind of arguments and question deep,
All replication prompt, and reason strong,
For his advantage still did wake and sleep:
To make the weeper laugh, the laugher weep,
He had the dialect and different skill, 125
Catching all passions in his craft of will:

'That he did in the general bosom reign
Of young, of old; and sexes both enchanted, 128
To dwell with him in thoughts, or to remain
In personal duty, following where he haunted:
Consents bewitch'd, ere he desire, have
    granted;
And dialogu'd for him what he would say, 132
Ask'd their own wills, and made their wills
    obey.

'Many there were that did his picture get,
To serve their eyes, and in it put their mind;
Like fools that in the imagination set 136
The goodly objects which abroad they find
Of lands and mansions, theirs in thought
    assign'd;

And labouring in more pleasures to bestow
  them
Than the true gouty landlord which doth owe
  them.   140

'So many have, that never touch'd his hand,
Sweetly suppos'd them mistress of his heart.
My woeful self, that did in freedom stand,
And was my own fee-simple, not in part,   144
What with his art in youth, and youth in art,
Threw my affections in his charmed power,
Reserv'd the stalk and gave him all my flower.

'Yet did I not, as some my equals did,   148
Demand of him, nor being desired yielded;
Finding myself in honour so forbid,
With safest distance I mine honour shielded.
Experience for me many bulwarks builded   152
Of proofs new-bleeding, which remain'd the
  foil
Of this false jewel, and his amorous spoil.

'But, ah! who ever shunn'd by precedent
The destin'd ill she must herself assay?   156
Or forc'd examples, 'gainst her own content,
To put the by-pass'd perils in her way?
Counsel may stop awhile what will not stay;
For when we rage, advice is often seen   160
By blunting us to make our wits more keen.

'Nor gives it satisfaction to our blood,
That we must curb it upon others' proof;
To be forbid the sweets that seem so good, 164
For fear of harms that preach in our behoof.
O appetite! from judgment stand aloof;
The one a palate hath that needs will taste, 167
Though Reason weep, and cry "It is thy last."

'For further I could say "This man's untrue",
And knew the patterns of his foul beguiling;
Heard where his plants in others' orchards
  grew,
Saw how deceits were gilded in his smiling; 172
Knew vows were ever brokers to defiling;
Thought characters and words merely but art,
And bastards of his foul adulterate heart.

'And long upon these terms I held my city, 176
Till thus he 'gan besiege me: "Gentle maid,
Have of my suffering youth some feeling pity,
And be not of my holy vows afraid:
That's to ye sworn to none was ever said; 180
For feasts of love I have been call'd unto,
Till now did ne'er invite, nor never woo.

'"All my offences that abroad you see
Are errors of the blood, none of the mind; 184
Love made them not: with acture they may be,
Where neither party is nor true nor kind:
They sought their shame that so their shame did
  find,
And so much less of shame in me remains, 188
By how much of me their reproach contains.

'"Among the many that mine eyes have seen,
Not one whose flame my heart so much as
  warm'd,
Or my affection put to the smallest teen, 192
Or any of my leisures ever charm'd:
Harm have I done to them, but ne'er was
  harm'd;
Kept hearts in liveries, but mine own was free,
And reign'd, commanding in his monarchy. 196

'"Look here, what tributes wounded fancies
  sent me,
Of paled pearls and rubies red as blood;
Figuring that they their passions likewise lent
  me
Of grief and blushes, aptly understood   200
In bloodless white and the encrimson'd mood;
Effects of terror and dear modesty,
Encamp'd in hearts, but fighting outwardly.

'"And, lo! behold these talents of their hair,
With twisted metal amorously impleach'd, 205
I have receiv'd from many a several fair,
Their kind acceptance weepingly beseech'd,
With the annexions of fair gems enrich'd, 208
And deep-brain'd sonnets, that did amplify
Each stone's dear nature, worth, and quality.

'"The diamond; why, 'twas beautiful and hard,
Whereto his invis'd properties did tend;   212
The deep-green emerald, in whose fresh regard
Weak sights their sickly radiance do amend;
The heaven-hu'd sapphire and the opal blend
With objects manifold: each several stone, 216
With wit well blazon'd, smil'd or made some
  moan.

'"Lo! all these trophies of affections hot,
Of pensiv'd and subdu'd desires the tender, 219
Nature hath charg'd me that I hoard them not,
But yield them up where I myself must render,
That is, to you, my origin and ender;
For these, of force, must your oblations be,
Since I their altar, you enpatron me.   224

'"O! then, advance of yours that phraseless
  hand,
Whose white weighs down the airy scale of
  praise;
Take all these similes to your own command,
Hallow'd with sighs that burning lungs did
  raise;   228
What me your minister, for you obeys,
Works under you; and to your audit comes
Their distract parcels in combined sums.

'"Lo! this device was sent me from a nun, 232
Or sister sanctified, of holiest note;
Which late her noble suit in court did shun,
Whose rarest havings made the blossoms dote;
For she was sought by spirits of richest coat, 236
But kept cold distance, and did thence remove,
To spend her living in eternal love.

"'But, O my sweet! what labour is 't to leave
The thing we have not, mastering what not
strives,   240
Paling the place which did no form receive,
Playing patient sports in unconstrained gyves?
She that her fame so to herself contrives,
The scars of battle 'scapeth by the flight,   244
And makes her absence valiant, not her might.

"'O! pardon me, in that my boast is true;
The accident which brought me to her eye
Upon the moment did her force subdue,   248
And now she would the caged cloister fly;
Religious love put out Religion's eye:
Not to be tempted, would she be immur'd,
And now, to tempt, all liberty procur'd.   252

"'How mighty then you are, O! hear me tell:
The broken bosoms that to me belong
Have emptied all their fountains in my well,
And mine I pour your ocean all among: 256
I strong o'er them, and you o'er me being
strong,
Must for your victory us all congest,
As compound love to physic your cold breast.

"'My parts had power to charm a sacred nun,
Who, disciplin'd, ay, dieted in grace,   261
Believ'd her eyes when they to assail begun,
All vows and consecrations giving place.
O most potential love! vow, bond, nor space,
In thee hath neither sting, knot, nor confine,
For thou art all, and all things else are thine.

"'When thou impressest, what are precepts
worth
Of stale example? When thou wilt inflame,   268
How coldly those impediments stand forth
Of wealth, of filial fear, law, kindred, fame!
Love's arms are peace, 'gainst rule, 'gainst
sense, 'gainst shame,
And sweetens, in the suffering pangs it bears,
The aloes of all forces, shocks, and fears.   273

"'Now all these hearts that do on mine depend,
Feeling it break, with bleeding groans they
pine;
And supplicant their sighs to you extend,   276
To leave the battery that you make 'gainst
mine,
Lending soft audience to my sweet design,
And credent soul to that strong-bonded oath
That shall prefer and undertake my troth."   280

'This said, his watery eyes he did dismount,
Whose sights till then were level'd on my face;
Each cheek a river running from a fount   283
With brinish current downward flow'd apace.
O! how the channel to the stream gave grace;
Who glaz'd with crystal gate the glowing roses
That flame through water which their hue
encloses.

'O father! what a hell of witchcraft lies   288
In the small orb of one particular tear,
But with the inundation of the eyes
What rocky heart to water will not wear?
What breast so cold that is not warmed here?
O cleft effect! cold modesty, hot wrath,   293
Both fire from hence and chill extincture hath.

'For, lo! his passion, but an art of craft,
Even there resolv'd my reason into tears;   296
There my white stole of chastity I daff'd,
Shook off my sober guards and civil fears;
Appear to him, as he to me appears,
All melting; though our drops this difference
bore,   300
His poison'd me, and mine did him restore.

'In him a plenitude of subtle matter,
Applied to cautels, all strange forms receives,
Of burning blushes, or of weeping water,   304
Or swounding paleness; and he takes and
leaves,
In either's aptness, as it best deceives,
To blush at speeches rank, to weep at woes,
Or to turn white and swound at tragic shows:

'That not a heart which in his level came   309
Could 'scape the hail of his all-hurting aim,
Showing fair nature is both kind and tame;
And, veil'd in them, did win whom he would
maim: 312
Against the thing he sought he would exclaim;
When he most burn'd in heart-wish'd luxury,
He preach'd pure maid, and prais'd cold chas-
tity.

'Thus merely with the garment of a Grace   316
The naked and concealed fiend he cover'd;
That the unexperient gave the tempter place,
Which like a cherubin above them hover'd.
Who, young and simple, would not be so
lover'd?   320
Ay me! I fell; and yet do question make
What I should do again for such a sake.

'O! that infected moisture of his eye,
O! that false fire which in his cheek so glow'd,
O! that forc'd thunder from his heart did fly,
O! that sad breath his spongy lungs bestow'd,
O! all that borrow'd motion seeming ow'd,
Would yet again betray the fore-betray'd,   328
And new pervert a reconciled maid.'

THE PASSIONATE PILGRIM

I

WHEN my love swears that she is made of
  truth,
I do believe her, though I know she lies,
That she might think me some untutor'd
  youth,
Unskilful in the world's false forgeries.
Thus vainly thinking that she thinks me young,
Although I know my years be past the best,   6
I smiling credit her false-speaking tongue,
Outfacing faults in love with love's ill rest.
But wherefore says my love that she is young?
And wherefore say not I that I am old?
O! love's best habit is a soothing tongue,
And age, in love, loves not to have years told. 12
  Therefore I'll lie with love, and love with me,
  Since that our faults in love thus smother'd
    be.

II

Two loves I have of comfort and despair,
Which like two spirits do suggest me still;
The better angel is a man, right fair,
The worser spirit a woman, colour'd ill.
To win me soon to hell, my female evil
Tempteth my better angel from my side,   6
And would corrupt a saint to be a devil,
Wooing his purity with her fair pride:
And whether that my angel be turn'd fiend
Suspect I may, but not directly tell;
For being both to me, both to each friend,
I guess one angel in another's hell.   12
  The truth I shall not know, but live in doubt,
  Till my bad angel fire my good one out.

III

Did not the heavenly rhetoric of thine eye,
'Gainst whom the world could not hold argu-
  ment,
Persuade my heart to this false perjury?
Vows for thee broke deserve not punishment.
A woman I forswore; but I will prove,
Thou being a goddess, I forswore not thee: 6
My vow was earthly, thou a heavenly love;
Thy grace being gain'd cures all disgrace in me.
My vow was breath, and breath a vapour is;
Then thou, fair sun, that on this earth dost
  shine,
Exhale this vapour vow; in thee it is:
If broken, then it is no fault of mine.   12
  If by me broke, what fool is not so wise
  To break an oath, to win a paradise?

IV

Sweet Cytherea, sitting by a brook
With young Adonis, lovely, fresh, and green,
Did court the lad with many a lovely look,
Such looks as none could look but beauty's
  queen.

She told him stories to delight his ear;
She show'd him favours to allure his eye;   6
To win his heart, she touch'd him here and
  there,—
Touches so soft still conquer chastity.
But whether unripe years did want conceit,
Or he refus'd to take her figur'd proffer,
The tender nibbler would not touch the bait,
But smile and jest at every gentle offer: 12
  Then fell she on her back, fair queen, and
    toward:
  He rose and ran away; ah! fool too froward.

V

If love make me forsworn, how shall I swear to
  love?
O! never faith could hold, if not to beauty
  vow'd:
Though to myself forsworn, to thee I'll constant prove;
Those thoughts, to me like oaks, to thee like
  osiers bow'd.
Study his bias leaves, and makes his book thine
  eyes,
Where all those pleasures live that art can com-
  prehend.   6
If knowledge be the mark, to know thee shall
  suffice;
Well learned is that tongue that well can thee
  commend;
All ignorant that soul that sees thee without
  wonder;
Which is to me some praise, that I thy parts
  admire:
Thine eye Jove's lightning seems, thy voice his
  dreadful thunder,
Which, not to anger bent, is music and sweet
  fire,   12
  Celestial as thou art, O! do not love that
    wrong,
  To sing heaven's praise with such an earthly
    tongue.

VI

Scarce had the sun dried up the dewy morn,
And scarce the herd gone to the hedge for
  shade,
When Cytherea, all in love forlorn,
A longing tarriance for Adonis made
Under an osier growing by a brook,
A brook where Adon us'd to cool his spleen: 6
Hot was the day; she hotter that did look
For his approach, that often there had been.
Anon he comes, and throws his mantle by,
And stood stark naked on the brook's green
  brim:
The sun look'd on the world with glorious eye,
Yet not so wistly as this queen on him: 12
  He, spying her, bounc'd in, whereas he
    stood:
  'O Jove', quoth she, 'why was not I a flood!'

VII

Fair is my love, but not so fair as fickle;
Mild as a dove, but neither true nor trusty;
Brighter than glass, and yet, as glass is, brittle;
Softer than wax, and yet, as iron, rusty:
    A lily pale, with damask dye to grace her,
    None fairer, nor none falser to deface her. 6

Her lips to mine how often hath she join'd,
Between each kiss her oaths of true love swearing!
How many tales to please me hath she coin'd,
Dreading my love, the loss thereof still fearing!
    Yet in the midst of all her pure protestings,
    Her faith, her oaths, her tears, and all were
      jestings. 12

She burn'd with love, as straw with fire flameth;
She burn'd out love, as soon as straw out-
    burneth;
She fram'd the love, and yet she foil'd the
    framing;
She bade love last, and yet she fell a-turning.
    Was this a lover, or a lecher whether? 17
    Bad in the best, though excellent in neither.

VIII

If music and sweet poetry agree,
As they must needs, the sister and the brother,
Then must the love be great 'twixt thee and me,
Because thou lov'st the one, and I the other.
Dowland to thee is dear, whose heavenly touch
Upon the lute doth ravish human sense; 6
Spenser to me, whose deep conceit is such
As, passing all conceit, needs no defence.
Thou lov'st to hear the sweet melodious sound
That Phœbus' lute, the queen of music, makes;
And I in deep delight am chiefly drown'd
Whenas himself to singing he betakes. 12
    One god is god of both, as poets feign;
    One knight loves both, and both in thee
    remain.

IX

Fair was the morn when the fair queen of love,
    *   *   *   *   *   *   *
Paler for sorrow than her milk-white dove,
For Adon's sake, a youngster proud and wild;
Her stand she takes upon a steep-up hill:
Anon Adonis comes with horn and hounds; 6
She, silly queen, with more than love's good will,
Forbade the boy he should not pass those
    grounds:
'Once,' quoth she, 'did I see a fair sweet youth
Here in these brakes deep-wounded with a boar,
Deep in the thigh, a spectacle of ruth! 11
See, in my thigh,' quoth she, 'here was the sore.
    She showed hers; he saw more wounds than
      one,
    And blushing fled, and left her all alone.

X

Sweet rose, fair flower, untimely pluck'd, soon
    vaded,
Pluck'd in the bud, and vaded in the spring!
Bright orient pearl, alack! too timely shaded;
Fair creature, kill'd too soon by death's sharp
    sting!

Like a green plum that hangs upon a tree,
And falls, through wind, before the fall
    should be. 6

I weep for thee, and yet no cause I have;
For why thou left'st me nothing in thy will:
And yet thou left'st me more than I did crave;
For why I craved nothing of thee still:
    O yes, dear friend, I pardon crave of thee,
    Thy discontent thou didst bequeath to me. 12

XI

Venus, with young Adonis sitting by her
Under a myrtle shade, began to woo him:
She told the youngling how god Mars did try
    her,
And as he fell to her, so fell she to him.
'Even thus', quoth she, 'the war-like god em-
    brac'd me',
And then she clipp'd Adonis in her arms; 6
'Even thus', quoth she, 'the war-like god un-
    lac'd me',
As if the boy should use like loving charms.
'Even thus', quoth she, 'he seized on my lips',
And with her lips on his did act the seizure;
And as she fetched breath, away he skips,
And would not take her meaning nor her
    pleasure. 12
    Ah! that I had my lady at this bay,
    To kiss and clip me till I ran away.

XII

Crabbed age and youth cannot live together:
Youth is full of pleasure, age is full of care;
Youth like summer morn, age like winter
    weather;
Youth like summer brave, age like winter bare.
Youth is full of sport, age's breath is short;
    Youth is nimble, age is lame; 6
Youth is hot and bold, age is weak and cold;
Youth is wild, and age is tame.
Age, I do abhor thee, youth, I do adore thee;
    O! my love, my love is young:
Age, I do defy thee: O! sweet shepherd, hie thee,
    For methinks thou stay'st too long. 12

XIII

Beauty is but a vain and doubtful good;
A shining gloss that vadeth suddenly;
A flower that dies when first it 'gins to bud;
A brittle glass that's broken presently:
    A doubtful good, a gloss, a glass, a flower,
    Lost, vaded, broken, dead within an hour. 6

And as goods lost are seld or never found,
As vaded gloss no rubbing will refresh,
As flowers dead lie wither'd on the ground,
As broken glass no cement can redress,
    So beauty blemish'd once 's for ever lost,
    In spite of physic, painting, pain, and cost. 12

XIV

Good night, good rest. Ah! neither be my
    share:
She bade good night that kept my rest away;
And daff'd me to a cabin hang'd with care,
To descant on the doubts of my decay.

'Farewell,' quoth she, 'and come again to-
morrow':
Fare well I could not, for I supp'd with sorrow.   6

Yet at my parting sweetly did she smile,
In scorn of friendship, nill I construe whether:
'T may be, she joy'd to jest at my exile,
'T may be, again to make me wander thither:
'Wander,' a word for shadows like myself, 11
As take the pain, but cannot pluck the pelf.

Lord! how mine eyes throw gazes to the east;
My heart doth charge the watch; the morning
rise
Doth cite each moving sense from idle rest.
Not daring trust the office of mine eyes,
While Philomela sits and sings, I sit and
mark,
And wish her lays were tuned like the lark; 18

For she doth welcome daylight with her ditty,
And drives away dark dismal-dreaming night:
The night so pack'd, I post unto my pretty;
Heart hath his hope, and eyes their wished
sight;
Sorrow chang'd to solace, solace mix'd with
sorrow;
For why, she sigh'd and bade me come to-
morrow.   24

Were I with her, the night would post too
soon;
But now are minutes added to the hours;
To spite me now, each minute seems a moon;
Yet not for me, shine sun to succour flowers!
Pack night, peep day; good day, of night now
borrow:
Short, night, to-night, and length thyself to-
morrow.   30

SONNETS TO SUNDRY NOTES OF MUSIC

I

It was a lording's daughter, the fairest one of
three,
That liked of her master as well as well might
be,
Till looking on an Englishman, the fair'st that
eye could see,
Her fancy fell a-turning.   4

Long was the combat doubtful that love with
love did fight,
To leave the master loveless, or kill the gallant
knight:
To put in practice either, alas! it was a spite
Unto the silly damsel.   8

But one must be refused; more mickle was the
pain
That nothing could be used to turn them both
to gain,
For of the two the trusty knight was wounded
with disdain:
Alas! she could not help it.   12

Thus art with arms contending was victor of
the day,
Which by a gift of learning did bear the maid
away;
Then lullaby, the learned man hath got the lady
gay;
For now my song is ended.   16

II

On a day, alack the day!
Love, whose month was ever May,
Spied a blossom passing fair,
Playing in the wanton air: 4
Through the velvet leaves the wind,
All unseen, 'gan passage find;
That the lover, sick to death,
Wish'd himself the heaven's breath.   8

'Air,' quoth he, 'thy cheeks may blow;
Air, would I might triumph so!
But, alas! my hand hath sworn
Ne'er to pluck thee from thy thorn: 12
Vow, alack! for youth unmeet:
Youth, so apt to pluck a sweet.
Thou for whom Jove would swear
Juno but an Ethiop were;   16
And deny himself for Jove,
Turning mortal for thy love.'

III

My flocks feed not,
My ewes breed not,
My rams speed not,
All is amiss: 4
Love's denying,
Faith's defying,
Heart's renying,
Causer of this.   8
All my merry jigs are quite forgot,
All my lady's love is lost, God wot:
Where her faith was firmly fix'd in love,
There a nay is plac'd without remove. 12
One silly cross
Wrought all my loss;
O! frowning Fortune, cursed, fickle
dame;
For now I see   16
Inconstancy
More in women than in men remain.

In black mourn I,
All fears scorn I,   20
Love hath forlorn me,
Living in thrall:
Heart is bleeding,
All help needing,   24
O! cruel speeding,
Fraughted with gall.

My shepherd's pipe can sound no deal,
My wether's bell rings doleful knell; 28
My curtal dog, that wont to have play'd,
Plays not at all, but seems afraid;
My sighs so deep
Procure to weep, 32
   In howling wise, to see my doleful plight.
How sighs resound
Through heartless ground,
   Like a thousand vanquish'd men in
     bloody fight! 36

Clear well spring not,
Sweet birds sing not,
Green plants bring not
   Forth their dye; 40
Herds stand weeping,
Flocks all sleeping,
Nymphs back peeping
   Fearfully: 44
All our pleasure known to us poor swains,
All our merry meetings on the plains,
All our evening sport from us is fled,
All our love is lost, for Love is dead. 48
Farewell, sweet lass,
Thy like ne'er was
   For a sweet content, the cause of all my
     moan:
Poor Corydon 52
Must live alone;
   Other help for him I see that there is
     none.

IV

Whenas thine eye hath chose the dame,
And stall'd the deer that thou should'st strike,
Let reason rule things worthy blame,
As well as fancy, partial wight: 4
   Take counsel of some wiser head,
   Neither too young nor yet unwed.

And when thou com'st thy tale to tell,
Smooth not thy tongue with filed talk, 8
Lest she some subtle practice smell;
A cripple soon can find a halt:
   But plainly say thou lov'st her well,
   And set thy person forth to sell. 12

What though her frowning brows be bent,
Her cloudy looks will clear ere night;
And then too late she will repent
That thus dissembled her delight; 16
   And twice desire, ere it be day,
   That which with scorn she put away.

What though she strive to try her strength,
And ban and brawl, and say thee nay, 20
Her feeble force will yield at length,
When craft hath taught her thus to say,
   'Had women been so strong as men,
   In faith, you had not had it then.' 24

And to her will frame all thy ways;
Spare not to spend, and chiefly there
Where thy desert may merit praise,
By ringing in thy lady's ear: 28
   The strongest castle, tower, and town,
   The golden bullet beats it down.

Serve always with assured trust,
And in thy suit be humble true; 32
Unless thy lady prove unjust,
Seek never thou to choose anew.
   When time shall serve, be thou not slack
   To proffer, though she put thee back. 36

The wiles and guiles that women work,
Dissembled with an outward show,
The tricks and toys that in them lurk,
The cock that treads them shall not know. 40
   Have you not heard it said full oft,
   A woman's nay doth stand for nought?

Think, women love to match with men
And not to live so like a saint: 44
Here is no heaven; they holy then
Begin when age doth them attaint.
   Were kisses all the joys in bed,
   One woman would another wed. 48

But, soft! enough! too much, I fear;
For if my mistress hear my song,
She will not stick to ring my ear,
To teach my tongue to be so long: 52
   Yet will she blush, here be it said, .
   To hear her secrets so bewray'd.

V

Live with me, and be my love,
And we will all the pleasures prove
That hills and valleys, dales and fields,
And all the craggy mountains yields. 4

There will we sit upon the rocks,
And see the shepherds feed their flocks,
By shallow rivers, by whose falls
Melodious birds sing madrigals. 8

There will I make thee a bed of roses,
With a thousand fragrant posies,
A cap of flowers, and a kirtle
Embroider'd all with leaves of myrtle. 12

A belt of straw and ivy buds,
With coral clasps and amber studs;
And if these pleasures may thee move,
Then live with me and be my love. 16

LOVE'S ANSWER.

If that the world and love were young,
And truth in every shepherd's tongue,
These pretty pleasures might me move,
To live with thee and be thy love. 20

VI

As it fell upon a day
In the merry month of May,
Sitting in a pleasant shade
Which a grove of myrtles made, 4
Beasts did leap, and birds did sing,
Trees did grow, and plants did spring;
Every thing did banish moan,
Save the nightingale alone: 8
She, poor bird, as all forlorn,
Lean'd her breast up-till a thorn,
And there sung the dolefull'st ditty,
That to hear it was great pity: 12
'Fie, fie, fie!' now would she cry;
'Tereu, Tereu!' by and by;

That to hear her so complain,
Scarce I could from tears refrain;   16
For her griefs, so lively shown,
Made me think upon mine own.
Ah! thought I, thou mourn'st in vain,
None takes pity on thy pain: 20
Senseless trees they cannot hear thee,
Ruthless beasts they will not cheer thee:
King Pandion he is dead,
All thy friends are lapp'd in lead,   24
All thy fellow birds do sing
Careless of thy sorrowing.
Even so, poor bird, like thee,
None alive will pity me,   28
Whilst as fickle Fortune smil'd,
Thou and I were both beguil'd.
   Every one that flatters thee
Is no friend in misery.   32
Words are easy, like the wind;
Faithful friends are hard to find:
Every man will be thy friend
Whilst thou hast wherewith to spend;   36

But if store of crowns be scant,
No man will supply thy want.
If that one be prodigal,
Bountiful they will him call,   40
And with such-like flattering,
'Pity but he were a king.'
If he be addict to vice,
Quickly him they will entice,   44
If to women he be bent,
They have him at commandement:
But if Fortune once do frown,
Then farewell his great renown;   48
They that fawn'd on him before
Use his company no more.
He that is thy friend indeed,
He will help thee in thy need: 52
If thou sorrow, he will weep;
If thou wake, he cannot sleep:
Thus of every grief in heart
He with thee does bear a part.   56
These are certain signs to know
Faithful friend from flattering foe.

THE PHŒNIX AND THE TURTLE

LET the bird of loudest lay,
On the sole Arabian tree,
Herald sad and trumpet be,
To whose sound chaste wings obey.   4

But thou shrieking harbinger,
Foul precurrer of the fiend,
Augur of the fever's end,
To this troop come thou not near.   8

From this session interdict
Every fowl of tyrant wing,
Save the eagle, feather'd king:
Keep the obsequy so strict.   12

Let the priest in surplice white
That defunctive music can,
Be the death-divining swan,
Lest the requiem lack his right.   16

And thou treble-dated crow,
That thy sable gender mak'st
With the breath thou giv'st and tak'st,
'Mongst our mourners shalt thou go.   20

Here the anthem doth commence:
Love and constancy is dead;
Phœnix and the turtle fled
In a mutual flame from hence.   24

So they lov'd, as love in twain
Had the essence but in one;
Two distincts, division none:
Number there in love was slain.   28

Hearts remote, yet not asunder;
Distance, and no space was seen
'Twixt the turtle and his queen:
But in them it were a wonder.   32

So between them love did shine,
That the turtle saw his right
Flaming in the phœnix' sight;
Either was the other's mine.   36

Property was thus appall'd,
That the self was not the same;
Single nature's double name
Neither two nor one was call'd.   40

Reason, in itself confounded,
Saw division grow together;
To themselves yet either neither,
Simple were so well compounded,   44

That it cried, 'How true a twain
Seemeth this concordant one!
Love hath reason, reason none,
If what parts can so remain.'   48

Whereupon it made this threne
To the phœnix and the dove,
Co-supremes and stars of love,
As chorus to their tragic scene.   52

THRENOS

Beauty, truth, and rarity
Grace in all simplicity,
Here enclos'd in cinders lie.   55

Death is now the phœnix' nest;
And the turtle's loyal breast
To eternity doth rest,   58

Leaving no posterity:
'Twas not their infirmity,
It was married chastity.   61

Truth may seem, but cannot be;
Beauty brag, but 'tis not she;
Truth and beauty buried be.   64

To this urn let those repair
That are either true or fair;
For these dead birds sigh a prayer.   67

INDEX OF CHARACTERS

MALCOLM, Macbeth.
MALVOLIO, Twelfth Night.
MAMILLIUS, Winter's T.
MARCADE, Love's L. L.
MARC ANTONY, Ant. & Cleop.
MARCELLUS, Hamlet.
MARCH, EDMUND MORTIMER, EARL OF, 1 Hen. IV, 1 Hen. VI.
MARCH, EDWARD, EARL OF (afterwards EDWARD IV), 2 & 3 Hen. VI, Rich. III.
MARCIUS, YOUNG, Coriolanus.
MARCUS ANDRONICUS, Tit. Andr.
MARCUS ANTONIUS, Jul. Cæs.
MARCUS BRUTUS, Jul. Cæs.
MARDIAN, Ant. & Cleop.
MARGARELON, Troilus.
MARGARET, Much Ado.
MARGARET, QUEEN, 1, 2, & 3 Hen. VI, Rich. III.
MARGARET PLANTAGENET, LADY, Rich. III.
MARIA, Love's L. L.
MARIA, Twelfth Night.
MARIANA, All's Well.
MARIANA, Meas. for Meas.
MARINA, Pericles.
MARK ANTONY, Ant. & Cleop.
MARTEXT, SIR OLIVER, As You Like It.
MARTIUS, Tit. Andr.
MARULLUS, Jul. Cæs.
MECÆNAS, Ant. & Cleop.
MELUN, K. John.
MENAS, Ant. & Cleop.
MENECRATES, Ant. & Cleop.
MENELAUS, Troilus.
MENENIUS AGRIPPA, Coriol.
MENTEITH, Macbeth.
MERCHANT, A, Com. of Err.
MERCUTIO, Rom. & Jul.
MESSALA, Jul. Cæs.
METELLUS CIMBER, Jul. Cæs.
MICHAEL, 2 Hen. VI.
MICHAEL, SIR, 1 Hen. IV.
MILAN, DUKE OF, Two G. of Ver.
MIRANDA, Tempest.
MONTAGUE, Rom. & Jul.
MONTAGUE, LADY, Rom. & Jul.
MONTAGUE, MARQUESS OF, 3 Hen. VI.
MONTANO, Othello.
MONTGOMERY, SIR JOHN, 3 Hen. VI.
MONTJOY, Hen. V.
MOPSA, Winter's T.
MORGAN, Cymbeline.
MOROCCO, PRINCE OF, M. of Ven.
MORTIMER, EDMUND, EARL OF MARCH, 1 Hen. IV, 1 Hen. VI.
MORTIMER, LADY, 1 Hen. IV.
MORTIMER, SIR HUGH, 3 Hen. VI.
MORTIMER, SIR JOHN, 3 Hen. VI.

MORTON, 2 Hen. IV.
MORTON, JOHN, BISHOP OF ELY, Rich. III.
MOTH (a page), Love's L. L.
MOTH (a fairy), Mids. N. Dr.
MOULDY, 2 Hen. IV.
MOWBRAY, THOMAS, DUKE OF NORFOLK, Rich. II.
MOWBRAY, LORD, 2 Hen. IV.
MUSTARD-SEED, Mids. N. Dr.
MUTIUS, Tit. Andr.

NATHANIEL, SIR, Love's L. L.
NERISSA, M. of Ven.
NESTOR, Troilus.
NICANOR, Coriolanus.
NORFOLK, DUKES OF, Rich. II, 3 Hen. VI, Rich. III, Hen. VIII.
NORTHUMBERLAND, EARL OF, 3 Hen. VI.
NORTHUMBERLAND, HENRY PERCY, EARL OF, Rich. II, 1 & 2 Hen. IV.
NORTHUMBERLAND, LADY, 2 Hen. IV.
NORTHUMBERLAND, SIWARD, EARL OF, Macbeth.
NURSE, Rom. & Jul.
NYM, Hen. V, Merry Wives.

OBERON, Mids. N. Dr.
OCTAVIA, Ant. & Cleop.
OCTAVIUS CÆSAR, Jul. Cæs., Ant. & Cleop.
OLIVER, As You Like It.
OLIVIA, Twelfth Night.
OPHELIA, Hamlet.
ORLANDO, As You Like It.
ORLEANS, BASTARD OF, 1 Hen. VI.
ORLEANS, DUKE OF, Hen. V.
ORLEANS, MASTER-GUNNER OF, 1 Hen. VI.
ORSINO, DUKE OF ILLYRIA, Twelfth Night.
OSRIC, Hamlet.
OSWALD, K. Lear.
OTHELLO, THE MOOR, Othello.
OVERDONE, MISTRESS, Meas. for Meas.
OXFORD, EARL OF, 3 Hen. VI, Rich. III.

PAGE, A, All's Well.
PAGE, A, Tam. of Shrew.
PAGE, ANNE, Merry Wives.
PAGE, MR., Merry Wives.
PAGE, MISTRESS, Merry Wives.
PAGE, WILLIAM, Merry Wives.
PANDAR, A, Pericles.
PANDARUS, Troilus.
PANDULPH, CARDINAL, K. John.
PANTHINO, Two G. of Ver.
PARIS, Rom. & Jul.
PARIS, Troilus.
PARIS, GOVERNOR OF, 1 Hen. VI.

PAROLLES, All's Well.
PATIENCE, Hen. VIII.
PATROCLUS, Troilus.
PAULINA, Winter's T.
PEASE-BLOSSOM, Mids. N. Dr
PEDANT, Tam. of Shrew.
PEDRO, DON, Much Ado.
PEMBROKE, EARL OF, K. John, 3 Hen. VI.
PERCY, HENRY, EARL OF NORTHUMBERLAND, Rich. II, 1 & 2 Hen. IV.
PERCY, HENRY (HOTSPUR), Rich. II, 1 Hen. IV.
PERCY, LADY, 1 & 2 Hen. IV.
PERCY, THOMAS, EARL OF WORCESTER, 1 Hen. IV.
PERDITA, Winter's T.
PERICLES, PRINCE OF TYRE, Pericles.
PETER, 2 Hen. VI.
PETER, Rom. & Jul.
PETER (a friar), Meas. for Meas.
PETER OF POMFRET, K. John.
PETO, 1 & 2 Hen. IV.
PETRUCHIO, Tam. of Shrew.
PHEBE, As You Like It.
PHILARIO, Cymbeline.
PHILEMON, Pericles.
PHILIP, KING OF FRANCE, K. John.
PHILIP THE BASTARD, K. John.
PHILO, Ant. & Cleop.
PHILOSTRATE, Mids. N. Dr.
PHILOTUS, Timon.
PHRYNIA, Timon.
PIERCE OF EXTON, SIR, Rich. II.
PINCH, Com. of Err.
PINDARUS, Jul. Cæs.
PISANIO, Cymbeline.
PISTOL, 2 Hen. IV, Hen. V, Merry Wives.
PLANTAGENET, LADY MARGARET, Rich. III.
PLANTAGENET, RICHARD (afterwards Duke of York), 1, 2, & 3 Hen. VI.
PLAYERS, Hamlet.
PLAYERS, Tam. of Shrew.
POINS, 1 & 2 Hen. IV.
POLIXENES, Winter's T.
POLONIUS, Hamlet.
POLYDORE, Cymbeline.
POMPEIUS, SEXTUS, Ant. & Cleop.
POMPEY, Meas. for Meas.
POPILIUS LENA, Jul. Cæs.
PORTIA, Jul. Cæs.
PORTIA, M. of Ven.
POSTHUMUS LEONATUS, Cymbeline.
PRIAM, KING OF TROY, Troilus.
PROCULEIUS, Ant. & Cleop.
PROSPERO, Tempest.
PROTEUS, Two G. of Ver.
PROVOST, Meas. for Meas.
PUBLIUS, Jul. Cæs.

INDEX OF FIRST LINES OF SONGS, ETC.

GLOSSARY

ABATE, *v.t.* to deduct, except, L.'s L.'s L. v. 2. 545; to blunt, take the edge off, Rich. III. v. 4. 48; to deprive, K. Lear, ii. 4. 161.

ABHOR, *v.t.* to reject, Hen. VIII. ii. 4. 79.

ABJECTS, *sub.* servile persons, Rich. III. i. 1. 106.

ABLE, *v.t.* to warrant, K. Lear, iv. 6. 173.

ABODE, *v.t.* to forebode, 3 Hen. VI. v. 6. 45.

ABODEMENTS, *sub.* evil omens, 3 Hen. VI. iv. 7. 13.

ABRAM, *adj.* auburn, Coriol. ii. 3. 21.

ABRIDGMENT, *sub.* a short entertainment, Mid. N. Dr. v. 1. 39; Ham. ii. 2. 448.

ABSEY-BOOK, *sub.* a primer, K. John, i. 1. 196.

ABSOLUTE, *adj.* resolved, Meas. for Meas. iii. 1. 5; perfect, Hen. V. iii. 7. 27; Ham. v. 2. 112; positive, Coriol. iii. 2. 39.

ABY, *v.t.* to pay for, atone for, Mid. N. Dr. iii. 2. 175.

ACCITE, *v.t.* to cite, summon, 2 Hen. IV. v. 2. 141; Tit. Andr. i. 1. 27; to excite, 2 Hen. IV. ii. 2. 67.

ACKNOWN, BE NOT, do not pretend to be cognizant of, Oth. iii. 3. 320.

ACONITUM, *sub.* the plant aconite, or wolf's bane, 2 Hen. IV. iv. 4. 48.

ACTURE, *sub.* performance, Lov. Comp. 185.

ADDICTION, *sub.* inclination, Hen. V. i. 1. 54; Oth. ii. 2. 6.

ADDITION, *sub.* title, Merry Wives of W. ii. 2. 316; Macb. i. 3. 106.

ADDRESSED, *adj.* ready, Mid. N. Dr. v. 1. 106; Jul. Cæs. iii. 1. 29.

ADOPTIOUS, *adj.* given by adoption, not real, All's Well i. 1. 190.

AERY. *see* AIERY.

AFAR OFF, *adv.* indirectly, remotely, Merry Wives of W. i. 1. 215; Wint. Tale, ii. 1. 103.

AFFECT, *sub.* inclination, L.'s L.'s L. i. 1. 150; Oth. i. 3. 265; *v.t.* to love, Two Gent. of Ver. iii. 1. 82.

AFFECTION, *sub.* affectation, L.'s L.'s L. v. 1. 4.

AFFECTIONED, *adj.* full of affectation, Twelfth Night, ii. 3. 162.

AFFEERED, *pt.p.* confirmed, a law term, Macb. iv. 3. 34.

AFFRONT, *v.t.* to confront, to face, Wint. Tale, v. 1. 75; Cymb. iv. 3. 29.

AFFY, *v.t.* to betroth, Tam. of Shrew, iv. 4. 49; 2 Hen. VI. iv. 1. 80; *v.i.* to confide, Tit. Andr. i. 1. 47.

AFTER-SUPPER, *sub.* rere-supper, Mid. N. Dr. v. 1. 34.

AGLET-BABY, *sub.* the figure cut on the tag of a lace [Fr. *aiguillette*], Tam. of Shrew, i. 2. 79.

AGNIZE, *v.t.* to acknowledge, avow, Oth. i. 3. 232.

AGOOD, *adv.* much, a great deal, Two Gent. of Ver. iv. 4. 172.

A-HOLD, *adv.* to lay a ship a-hold = to keep her up to wind, Temp. i. 1. 54.

AIERY, AERY, *sub.* the brood of an eagle, K. John, v. 2. 149; Rich. III. i. 3. 264, 270. 'An aery of children', alluding to a company of young actors, Ham. ii. 2. 362.

AIM, *sub.* a guess, Jul. Cæs. i. 2. 162.

AIM, TO CRY, *v.i.* a phrase borrowed from archery, Merry Wives of W. iii. 2. 47; to give encouragement to, K. John, ii. 1. 196.

ALDERLIEFEST, *adj.* dearest of all, 2 Hen. VI. i. 1. 28.

ALL AMORT, *adj.* quite dejected [Fr. *à la mort*], Tam. of Shrew, iv. 3. 36; 1 Hen. VI. iii. 2. 124.

ALLAY, *sub.* mitigation, Wint. Tale, iv. 1. 9.

ALL HID, *sub.* the game of hide and seek, L.'s L.'s L. iv. 3. 78.

ALLICHOLY, *adj.* Two Gent. of Ver. iv. 2. 28; *sub.* melancholy, Merry Wives of W. i. 4. 160.

ALLOW, *v.* to approve, 2 Hen. IV. i. 3. 5; K. Lear, ii. 4. 194.

ALL-THING, *adv.* in every way, Macb. iii. 1. 13.

ALMS-DRINK, *sub.* liquor drunk to ease another, Ant. & Cleo. ii. 7. 5.

AMES-ACE, *sub.* the lowest throw of dice, All's Well, ii. 3. 85.

ANCHOR, *sub.* an anchorite, a hermit, Ham. iii. 2. 231.

ANCIENT, *sub.* an officer next in rank to a lieutenant, 1 Hen. IV. iv. 2. 26. *Comp.* Ancient Pistol.

ANNEXION, *sub.* addition, Lov. Comp. 208.

ANSWERABLE, *adj.* corresponding, Oth. i. 3. 351.

ANTICK, *sub.* the buffoon of the old plays, Rich. II. iii. 2. 162.

ANTRE, *sub.* a cavern [Fr. *antre*], Oth. i. 3. 140.

APPEACH, *v.i.* to impeach, All's Well, i. 3. 199; *v.t.* Rich. II. v. 2. 79.

APPEAL, *sub.* impeachment, Rich. II. i. 1. 4; i. 3. 21.

APPLE-JOHN, *sub.* a shrivelled up winter apple, 1 Hen. IV. iii. 3. 5; 2 Hen. IV. ii. 4. 3.

APPOINTMENT, *sub.* equipment, K. John, ii. 1. 296.

APPROOF, *sub.* approval, proof, Meas. for Meas. ii. 4. 175; All's Well, ii. 5. 3.

APRICOCK, *sub.* apricot, Mid. N. Dr. iii. 1. 173; Rich. II. iii. 4. 29.

APRON-MAN, *sub.* a mechanic, Coriol. iv. 6. 97.

ARCH, *sub.* chief, master, K. Lear, ii. 1. 61.

ARGOSY, *sub.* a large merchantman, from *Ragusa* in Sicily, Mer. of Ven. i. 1. 9; Tam. of Shrew, ii. 1. 368, 370.

AROINT THEE, *int.* avaunt, stand off, begone, Macb. i. 3. 6; K. Lear, iii. 4. 127.

ARTHUR'S SHOW, *sub.* an archery exhibition by a society of London archers, who assumed the name of Prince Arthur's knights, 2 Hen. IV. iii. 2. 303.

ARTICULATE, *v.i.* to draw up articles for a peace, Coriol. i. 9. 77; *pt.p.* specified, set forth, 1 Hen. IV. v. 1. 72.

ASKANCE, *adv.* awry, with sidelong glance, Ven. and Adon. 342; *v.t.* to make to turn aside, Lucrece, 637.

ASSINEGO, *sub.* an ass, Troil. & Cres. ii. 1. 49.

ATONE, *v.t.* to reconcile, set at one, Rich. II. i. 1. 202; Cymb. i. 4. 44.

ATTAINT, *sub.* stain, disgrace, Com. of Err. iii. 2. 16; Troil. & Cres. i. 2. 26; Lucrece, 825.

AUGUR, *sub.* augury, Macb. iii. 4. 124.

AUNT, *sub.* an old woman, Mid. N. Dr. ii. 1. 51; a loose woman, Wint. Tale, iv. 2. 11.

AVISE, *v.t.* to inform. 'Are you avised?'='Do you know?' Merry Wives of W. i. 1. 171.

BABY, *sub.* a doll, Macb. iii. 4. 106.

BACKARE, *int.* go back! Tam. of Shrew, ii. 1. 73.

BACKSWORDMAN, *sub.* a singlestick player, 2 Hen. IV. iii. 2. 71.

BACK-TRICK, *sub.* a caper backwards in dancing, Twelfth Night, i. 3. 133.

BAFFLE, *v.i.* to disgrace, Twelfth Night, ii. 5. 176; 1 Hen. IV. i. 2. 113.

BALDRICK, *sub.* a belt, Much Ado, i. 1. 252.

BALE, *sub.* evil, mischief, Coriol. i. 1. 169.

BALK, *v.t.* to balk logic = to dispute, chop logic, Tam. of Shrew, i. 1. 34.

BALKED, *pt.p.* heaped up in balks or ridges, 1 Hen. IV. i. 1. 69.

BALLOW, *sub.* a cudgel, K. Lear, iv. 6. 248.

BAN-DOGS, *sub.* fierce dogs, which are kept tied up, 2 Hen. VI. i. 4. 21.

BANDY, *v.t.* to fight, contend; a metaphor taken from striking the balls at tennis, As You Like It, v. 1. 62; Rom. & Jul. ii. 5. 14.

BANK, *v.t.* to land on the banks of, K. John, v. 2. 104.

BANQUET, *sub.* dessert, Tam. of Shrew, v. 2. 9; Rom. & Jul. i. 5. 126.

BARBASON, *sub.* the name of a fiend, Merry Wives of W. ii. 2. 315; Hen. V. ii. 1. 57.

BARBED, *pt.p.* armed; spoken of a horse, Rich. II. iii. 3. 117; Rich. III. i. 1. 10.

BARE, *v.t.* to shave, Meas. for Meas. iv. 2. 188; All's Well, iv. 1. 54.

BARFUL, *adj.* full of difficulties, Twelfth Night, i. 4. 41.

BARM, *sub.* yeast, Mid. N. Dr. ii. 1. 38.

BARN, *sub.* a child, Much Ado, iii. 4. 48; 1 Hen. IV. ii. 3. 6.

BASE, *sub.* a rustic game, Cymb. v. 3. 19; 'To bid a base' = to challenge in the game, Two Gent. of Ver. i. 2. 94; Ven. & Ad. 303

BASE COURT, *sub.* a back yard, the lower court in a castle [Fr. *basse-cour*], Rich. II. iii. 3. 182.

BASES, *sub.* housings worn by knights on horseback, Per. ii. 1. 173.

BASILISCO-LIKE, *adj. Basilisco,* a character in the old play of *Soliman and Perseda,* indulges in iteration as in the text, K. John i. 1. 244.

BASILISK, *sub.* a large cannon, 1 Hen. IV. ii. 3. 58.

BASTA, *int.* enough! [Ital.] Tam. of Shrew, i. 1. 202.

BASTARD, *sub.* a sweet Spanish wine, Meas. for Meas. iii. 2. 4; 1 Hen. IV. ii. 4. 83.

BATE, *v.i.* to flutter as a hawk, Tam. of Shrew, iv. 1. 199.

BATED, *pt.p.* abated, sunk, Mer. of Ven. iii. 3. 32.

BATELESS, *adj.* which cannot be blunted, Lucr. 9.

BAT-FOWLING, *pr.p.* fowling at night by means of a net with torches and poles, Temp. ii. 1. 193.

BATLER, *sub.* a flat piece of wood, with which washer-women beat linen, As You Like It, ii. 4. 48.

BATTEN, *v.t.* to feed coarsely, Coriol. iv. 5. 35; Ham. iii. 4. 67.

BATTLE, *sub.* an army, or division of an army, 1 Hen. IV. iv. 1. 129; Hen. V. iv. 3. 3.

BAUBLE, *sub.* a fool's staff, All's Well, iv. 5. 32.

BAVIN, *adj.* composed of dry waste brushwood, used in contempt, 1 Hen. IV. iii. 2. 61.

BAWBLING, *adj.* insignificant, Twelfth Night, v. 1. 58.

BAWCOCK, *sub.* a term of rude endearment [Fr. *beau coq*], Twelfth Night, iii. 4. 127; Hen. V. iii. 2. 27.

BAY, *sub.* the space between the main timbers of a roof in a building, Meas. for Meas. ii. 1. 261.

BEADSMAN, *sub.* one paid to say prayers for others, Two Gent. of Ver. i. 1. 18; Rich. II. iii. 2. 116.

BEAR A BRAIN, to be intelligent, Rom. & Jul. i. 3. 29.

BEAR HARD, to dislike, Jul. Cæs. i. 2. 318.

BEARING-CLOTH, *sub.* the cloth in which a child was carried to be christened, Wint. Tale, iii. 3. 119; 1 Hen. VI. i. 3. 42.

BEAR IN HAND, to deceive, Macb. iii. 1. 81; Ham. ii. 2. 67.

BEAST, *sub.* an ox, K. Lear, iii. 4. 107.

BEAVER, *sub.* that part of a helmet which covers the face, 1 Hen. IV. iv. 1. 104; Ham. i. 2. 229.

BEDLAM, *sub.* a lunatic, K. John, ii. 1. 183; *adj.* mad, 2 Hen. VI. iii. 1. 51.

BEHESTS, *sub.* commands, Rom. & Jul. iv. 2. 20.

BEING, *conj.* seeing that, Much Ado, v. 1. 61.

BE-LEED, *pt.p.* forced to lee of the wind, Oth. i. 1. 30.

BERGOMASK, *sub.* a dance after the manner of the peasants of *Bergamasco,* a country in Italy, belonging to the Venetians, Mid. N. Dr. v. 1. 361.

BESHREW, *v.t.* to curse (not used seriously), L.'s L.'s L. v. 2. 46; Rom. & Jul. v. 2. 25.

BESLUBBER, *v.t.* to besmear, 1 Hen. IV. ii. 4. 244.

BESMIRCH, *v.t.* to besmear, Hen. V. iv. 3. 110; Ham. i. 3. 15.

BESTRAUGHT, *adj.* mad, distracted, Tam. of Shrew, Ind. 2. 27.

BETEEM, *v.t.* to allow, grant, Ham. i. 2. 141; with a play on the meaning, to pour out, Mid. N. Dr. i. 1. 131.

BEWRAY, *v.t.* to discover, to reveal, K. Lear, iii. 6. 120; Lucrece, 1698.

BEZONIAN, *sub.* a base fellow [Ital. *bisognoso*] 2 Hen. IV. v. 3. 115; 2 Hen. VI. iv. 1. 134.

BIDDY! a call to allure chickens, Twelfth Night, iii. 4. 130.

BIGGIN, *sub.* a nightcap [Fr. *béguin*], 2 Hen. IV. iv. 5. 26.

BILBO, *sub.* a sword-blade of great flexibility, manufactured at *Bilboa,* Merry Wives of W. i. 1. 167; iii. 5. 115.

BILBOES, *sub.* a species of fetters used at sea, Ham. v. 2. 6.

BILL, *sub.* brown-bills = battle-axes painted brown, 2 Hen. VI. iv. 10. 14; K. Lear, iv. 6. 93.

BIRD, *sub.* the young of any bird, 1 Hen. IV. v. 1. 60; Tit. Andr. ii. 3. 12.

BIRD-BOLT, *sub.* a blunt-headed arrow, Much Ado, i. 1. 42; L.'s L.'s L. iv. 3. 25; Twelfth Night, i. 5. 99.

BIRTH-CHILD, *sub.* a child adopted on account of being born in a certain domain, Pericles, iv. 4. 41.

BISSON, *adj.* blear-eyed, dim-sighted, Coriol. ii. 1. 71; 'bisson rheum' = blinding tears, Ham. ii. 2. 537.

BLACKS, *sub.* mourning clothes, suits of mourning, Wint. Tale, i. 2. 133.

BLADED, *pt.p.* (1) adorned with blades or (2) in the blade, Macb. ii. 1. 55.

BLANK, *sub.* the white mark in centre of a target [Fr. *blanc*], Ham. iv. 1. 42; the aim, Oth. iii. 4. 127; *v.t.* to blanch, to make pale, Ham. iii. 2. 232.

BLANKS, *sub.* blank charters sealed by the king, to be filled up at pleasure, Rich. II. ii. 1. 251.

BLENCH, *v.i.* to start, flinch, Ham. ii. 2. 634; to be inconstant, Wint. Tale, i. 2. 333.

BLENCHES, *sub.* inconstancies, Sonnets, cx. 7.

BLENT, *pt.p.* blended, mixed, Twelfth Night, i. 5. 259; Mer. of Ven. iii. 2. 182.

BLISTERED, *adj.* garnished with puffs, Hen. VIII i. 3. 31.

BLOCK, *sub.* the wood on which a hat is made, Much Ado, i. 1. 78; the fashion of a hat, K. Lear, iv. 6. 188.

BLOOD, *sub.* a spirited young man, K. John, ii. 1. 2.

BLOOD-BOLTERED, *adj.* matted with blood, Macb. iv. 1. 123.

BLOOD, WORST IN, in worst condition, Coriol. i. 1. 141.

BLOWSE, *sub.* a coarse beauty, Tit. Andr. iv. 2. 73.

BLUE-BOTTLE, *adj.* an allusion to the blue dress of a beadle, 2 Hen. IV. v. 4. 22.

BLUE-EYED, *adj.* with a dark circle round the eye, Temp. i. 2. 269. *Comp.* BLUE, As You Like It, iii. 2. 398; Lucrece, 1587.

BLURTED AT, *pt.p.* sneered at, Pericles, iv. 3. 34.

BOB, *v.t.* to beat, to drub, Rich. III. v. 3. 335; to cheat, Troil. & Cres. iii. 1. 76; Oth. v. 1. 16; *sub.* a cutting remark, As You Like It, ii. 7. 55.

BODKIN, *sub.* a dagger, Ham. iii. 1. 76.

BOGGLE, *v.i.* to hesitate, All's Well, v. 3. 234.

BOLINS, *sub.* bowlines, Pericles, iii. 1. 43.

BOLLEN, *adj.* swollen, Lucrece, 1417.

BOLT, *v.t.* to sift, refine, Wint. Tale, iv. 3. 377; Troil. & Cres. i. 1. 19, 21.

BOLTER, *sub.* a sieve, 1 Hen. IV. iii. 3. 80.

BOMBARD, *sub.* a leathern drinking vessel, Temp. ii. 2. 21; 1 Hen. IV. ii. 4. 503.

BOMBAST, *sub.* cotton padding, 1 Hen. IV. ii. 4. 364; 'bombast circumstance' = inflated talk, Oth. i. 1. 13.

BONA-ROBA, *sub.* a showily dressed woman of light character, 2 Hen. IV. iii. 2. 26.

BOSKY, *adj.* woody, Temp. iv. 1. 81.

BOTTOM, *sub.* ball of thread, Tam. of Shrew, iv. 3. 137; *v.t.* to wind thread on, Two Gent. of Ver. iii. 2. 53.

BOUND, *v.t.* to make to leap, Hen. V. v. 2. 145.

BOURN, *sub.* a limit or boundary, Temp. ii. 1. 159; Ham. iii. 1. 79; a stream, K. Lear, iii. 6. 28.

Bow, *sub.* a yoke, As You Like It, iii. 3. 85.

BOWGET, *sub.* a leathern pouch, Wint. Tale, iv. 2.

BRABBLE, *sub.* quarrel, Twelfth Night, v. 1. 69.

BRACE, *sub.* armour for the arm, Per. ii. 1. 137; state of defence, Oth. i. 3. 24.

BRACH, *sub.* a female hound, 1 Hen. IV. iii. 1. 240; K. Lear, i. 4. 125.

BRAID, *adj.* deceitful, All's Well, iv. 2. 73; *v.t.* to upbraid, Pericles, i. 1. 93.

BRAIN-PAN, *sub.* the skull, 2 Hen. VI. iv. 10. 13.

BRAVE, *adj.* fine, beautiful, Temp. i. 2. 6; *v.t.* to make fine, Tam. of Shrew, iv. 3. 125.

BRAVERY, *sub.* finery, Meas. for Meas. i. 3. 10; Tam. of Shrew, iv. 3. 57; bravado, Jul. Cæs. v. 1. 10; Ham. v. 2. 79.

BRAWL, *sub.* a French dance, L.'s L.'s L. iii. 1. 9.

BREACH, *sub.* 'breach of the sea' = the surf, Twelfth Night, ii. 1. 23.

BREAST, *sub.* voice in singing, Twelfth Night, ii. 3. 21.

BREATH, *sub.* voice in singing, Twelfth Night, ii. 3. 22.

BREESE, *sub.* the gadfly, Troil. & Cres. i. 3. 48; Ant. & Cleo. iii. 8. 24.

BRIBED BUCK, perhaps stolen buck, perhaps buck given away in presents, Merry Wives of W. v. 5. 27.

BRIEF, *sub.* a short summary, Mid. N. Dr. v. 1. 42; a short account, All's Well, v. 3. 137; a letter, 1 Hen. IV. iv. 4. 1; a list, Ant. & Cleo. v. 2. 137.

BROACH, *v.t.* to pierce through, or transfix, Hen. V. v. Chorus, 32; Tit. Andr. iv. 2. 86.

BROCK, *sub.* a badger (term of reproach), Twelfth Night, ii. 5. 115.

BROGUES, *sub.* shoes made of untanned hide, Cymb. iv. 2. 214.

BROOCH, *v.t.* to adorn, Ant. & Cleo. iv. 13. 25.

BUBUKLES, *sub.* pimples, Hen. V. iii. 6. 111.

BUCK, *v.t.* to wash linen with lye, and afterwards beat it, Merry Wives of W. iii. 3. 165.

BUCKLERSBURY, *sub.* a street in London chiefly inhabited by druggists, Merry Wives of W. iii. 3. 79.

BUCK OF THE FIRST HEAD, one in its fifth year, L.'s L.'s L. iv. 2. 10.

BUG, *sub.* an object of terror, 3 Hen. VI. v. 2. 2.

BUGLE, *sub.* a black bead, As You Like It, iii. 5. 47; Wint. Tale, iv. 3. 224.

BULK, *sub.* projecting part of a building, Coriol. ii. 1. 229; Oth. v. 1. 1; the breast, the trunk, Ham. ii. 1. 95; Lucrece, 467.

BULLY-ROOK, *sub.* a swaggering cheater, Merry Wives of W. i. 3. 2.

BUNG, *sub.* a pickpocket, 2 Hen. IV. ii. 4. 136.

BURGONET, *sub.* a close-fitting helmet, 2 Hen. VI. 200.

BUSH, *sub.* advertisement (a bush of ivy was usually the vintner's sign), As You Like It, Epil. 4.

BUSKY, *adv.* woody, 1 Hen. IV. v. 1. 2.

BUSS, *sub.* a kiss, 2 Hen. IV. ii. 4. 291; *v.t.* to kiss, K. John, iii. 4. 35.

BUTTONS, *sub.* buds, Ham. i. 3. 40.

BUTTONS, IN HIS, within his power to succeed in it, Merry Wives of W. iii. 2. 74.

BY-DRINKINGS, *sub.* occasional drinkings, 1 Hen. IV. iii. 3. 84.

CADDIS, *sub.* a galloon of worsted, Wint. Tale, iv. 3. 208.

CADDIS-GARTER, *adj.* worsted garter (in derision); garters of the time were worn in sight, and naturally were of costly material, 1 Hen. IV. ii. 4. 80.

CADE, *sub.* a cask, a barrel, 2 Hen. VI. iv. 2. 36.

CAGE, *sub.* a prison, 2 Hen. VI. iv. 2. 59.

CAKE, *sub.*' my cake is dough on both sides' = our plans are quite frustrated, Tam. of Shrew, i. 1. 109.

CAKED, *pt.p.* coagulated, inert, Tim. of Ath. ii. 2. 226.

CALIVER, *sub.* a kind of musket, 1 Hen. IV. iv. 2. 21; 2 Hen. IV. iii. 2. 295.

CALL, *sub.* a whistle to lure birds, Tam. of Shrew, iv. 1. 197; K. John, iii. 4. 174.

CALLAT, *sub.* a drab, Wint. Tale, ii. 3. 90; Oth. iv. 2. 121; 2 Hen. VI. i. 3. 86.

CANARY, *sub.* a lively dance, All's Well, ii. 1. 77; *v.i.* to dance the above dance, L.'s L.'s L. iii. 1. 13.

CANDLE-MINE, *sub.* a magazine of tallow, 2 Hen. IV. ii. 4. 328.

CANDLE-WASTER, *sub.* one who sits up late to study, Much Ado, v. 1. 18.

CANKER and CANKER-BLOOM, *sub.* the rose of the sweet-briar, Much Ado, i. 3. 28; 1 Hen. IV. i. 3. 176; Sonnets, liv. 5.

CANKER-BLOSSOM, *sub.* a blossom eaten by the cankerworm, Mid. N. Dr. iii. 2. 282.

CANTLE, *sub.* a small piece, a slice, 1 Hen. IV. iii. 1. 101; Ant. & Cleo. iii. 8. 16.

CANTON, *sub.* a song, Twelfth Night, i. 5. 291.

CANZONET, *sub.* a song, a ditty [Ital. *canzonetta*], L.'s L.'s L. iv. 2. 125.

CAPITULATE, *v.i.* to make an agreement, Coriol. v. 3. 82; to combine, 1 Hen. IV. iii. 2. 120.

CAPOCCHIA, *sub.* a fool,—fem. of *capocchio*,—Troil. & Cres. iv. 2. 32. An Italian word.

CARAWAYS, *sub.* comfits made with caraway seeds, 2 Hen. IV. v. 3. 3.

CARBONADO, *sub.* meat scotched for broiling, Coriol. iv. 5. 199; *v.t.* to hack like a carbonado, Wint. Tale, iv. 3. 267; K. Lear, ii. 2. 41.

CARD, *sub.* 'cooling card' = a stroke which suddenly turns the tables, 1 Hen. VI. v. 3. 84.

CARDECU, *sub.* [*quart d'écu*], quarter of a French crown, All's Well, iv. 3. 314; v. 2. 35.

CARKANET, *sub.* a necklace [Fr. *carcan*], Com. of Err. iii. 1. 4 (Sonnets, liii. 8, CARCONET.)

CARL, *sub.* a clown, peasant, Cymb. v. 2. 4.

CARLOT, *sub.* a peasant, As You Like It, iii. 5. 108.

CARPETS, *sub.* table cloths, Tam. of Shrew, iv. 1. 52.

CARRACK, *sub.* a huge ship of burthen [Ital. *caracca*], Oth. i. 2. 50.

CASE, *v.t.* to strip off the skin, All's Well, iii. 6. 110.

CASQUE, *sub.* a helmet [Fr. *casque*], Rich. II. i. 3. 81; Coriol. iv. 7. 43.

CASSOCK, *sub.* a military cloak, All's Well, iv. 3. 193.

CAST, *v.t.* to dismiss, Oth. i. 1. 150; *pt.p.* emptied out, Meas. for Meas. iii. 1. 91; *adj.* second-hand, cast off, As You Like It, iii. 4. 15.

CATAIAN, *sub.* a Chinaman, a native of Cathay, a cant term, Merry Wives of W. ii. 1. 147; Twelfth Night, ii. 3. 83.

CATLINGS, *sub.* small strings for musical instruments, made of cat-gut, Troil. & Cres. iii. 3. 309.

CAUTEL, *sub.* craft, stratagem, Ham. i. 3. 15; Lov. Comp. 303.

CAUTELOUS, *adj.* crafty, cunning, deceitful, Coriol. iv. 1. 33; Jul. Cæs. ii. 1. 129.

CEASE, *sub.* extinction, Ham. iii. 3. 15; Cymb. iv. 2. 112.

CEINTURE [O. Ed. CENTRE], *sub.* cincture, girdle, K. John, iv. 3. 155.

CENSER, THIN MAN IN A, 'a plate or dish, in which was incense, and at the bottom of which was usually represented in rude carving the figure of some saint' (*Hanmer*), 2 Hen. IV. v. 4. 20.

CENSURE, *sub.* opinion, judgment, Wint. Tale, ii. 1. 36; Ham. iii. 2. 31; judicial sentence, Oth. v. 2. 367.

CEREMENTS, *sub.* the wrappings of an embalmed body, Ham. i. 4. 48.

'CERN, *v.t.* to concern, Tam. of Shrew, v. 1. 76.

CESSE, *v.i.* to cease, All's Well, v. 3. 72.

CHACE, *sub.* a term at tennis [quibbling], Hen. V. i. 2. 266.

CHAMBERS, *sub.* small cannons, 2 Hen. IV. ii. 4. 56.

CHANGEABLE, *adj.* varying in colour, Twelfth Night, ii. 4. 75.

CHANSON, *sub.* a song, Ham. ii. 2. 447.

CHAPE, *sub.* the metal at the end of a scabbard, All's Well, iv. 3. 165.

CHARACTER, *sub.* handwriting, K. Lear, i. 2. 68.

CHARE, *sub.* a turn of work, Ant. & Cleo. v. 2. 230.

CHARGE-HOUSE, *sub* a school-house, L.'s L.'s L. v. 1. 88.

CHARNECO, *sub.* a kind of wine, named from Charneca in Portugal, 2 Hen. VI. ii. 3. 63.

CHAUDRON, *sub.* entrails, Macb. iv. 1. 33.

CHEATOR, *sub.* an escheator, Merry Wives of W. i. 3. 75.

CHERRY-PIT, *sub.* a children's game, Twelfth Night, iii. 4. 131.

CHEVERIL, *sub.* kid-leather, Rom. & Jul. ii. 4. 90; *adj.* yielding, flexible, Twelfth Night, iii. 1. 13; Hen. VIII. ii. 3. 32.

CHEWET, *sub.* a chough [Fr. *chouette*], 1 Hen. IV. v. 1. 29. [There may be an allusion to another word, which means a sort of meat pie.]

CHILDING, *adj.* fruitful, Mid. N. Dr. ii. 1. 112.

CHILDNESS, *sub.* childish disposition, Wint. Tale, i. 2. 170.

CHOPINE, *sub.* a high-soled shoe, Ham. ii. 2. 455.

CHOPPY, *adj.* chapped, Macb. i. 3. 44.

CHRISTOM CHILD, *sub.* a chrisom child, one who died within a month of birth; the chrisom was a white cloth put on the infant at baptism, Hen. V. ii. 3. 12.

CHUFF, *sub.* a churl, 1 Hen. IV. ii. 2. 98.

'CIDE, *v.t.* to decide, Sonnets, xlvi. 9.

CINQUE-PACE, *sub.* a grave dance [Fr. *cinque pas*], Much Ado, ii. 1. 78; Twelfth Night, i. 3. 141.

CIRCUMSTANCE, *sub.* circumlocution, Ham. i. 5. 127.

CITAL, *sub.* a recital, 1 Hen. IV. v. 2. 61.

CITIZEN, *sub.* town-bred, effeminate, Cymb. iv. 2. 8.

CITTERN, *sub.* a guitar, L.'s L.'s L. v. 2. 611.

CLACK-DISH, *sub.* a beggar's dish with a loose cover, by moving which he attracted the notice of passers by, Meas. for Meas. iii. 2. 139.

CLAP, AT A, at a blow, K. Lear, i. 4. 318.

CLAPPER-CLAW, *v.t.* to beat soundly, Merry Wives of W. ii. 3. 67; Troil. & Cres. v. 4. 1.

CLAW, *v.t.* to flatter, Much Ado, i. 3. 19.

CLEPE, *v.t.* to cail, Ham. i. 4. 19; Ven. & Ad. 995.

CLIMATE, *sub.* clime, region, Jul. Cæs. i. 3. 32.

CLIMATURES, *sub.* fellow-countrymen, Ham. i. 1. 125.

CLING, *v.t.* to shrivel up, Macb. v. 5. 40.

CLIP, *v.t.* to embrace, Oth. iii. 3. 465; Ant. & Cleo. v. 2. 360.

CLIPPER, *sub.* a defacer of coin, Hen. V. iv. 1. 249.

CLOUD, *sub.* a spot between the eyes of horses, regarded as a blemish, Ant. & Cleo. iii. 2. 51.

CLOUT, *sub.* piece of canvas in centre of target, L.'s L.'s L. iv. 1. 138; 2 Hen. IV. iii. 2. 52.

CLOUTED, *adj.* hobnailed; or according to some, patched, 2 Hen. VI. iv. 2. 199; Cymb. iv. 2. 214.

CLOY, *v.t.* to stroke with the claw, Cymb. v. 4. 118.

COBLOAF, *sub.* a misshapen loaf of bread, run out in the baking into lumps, Troil. & Cres. ii. 1. 41.

COCK, *sub.* a cock-boat, K. Lear. iv. 6. 20; a weathercock, K. Lear, iii. 2. 3.

COCK-A-HOOP, TO SET, to cast off all restraint, Rom. & Jul. i. 5. 85.

COCKLE, *sub.* a weed in corn, the corn-cockle, *Lychnis Githago*, L.'s L.'s L. iv. 3. 383.

COCKNEY, *sub.* one bred and born in the city, and ignorant of all things out of it, Twelfth Night, iv. 1. 15; K. Lear, ii. 4. 123.

COCK-SHUT TIME, twilight, Rich. III. v. 3. 70.

CODLING, *sub.* an unripe apple, Twelfth Night, i. 5. 168.

COFFIN, the crust of a pie, Tit. Andr. v. 2. 189.

COG, *v.i.* to cheat, Much Ado, v. 1. 95; *v.t.* to filch, Coriol. iii. 2. 133.

COIGN, *sub.* a corner-stone [Fr. *coin*], Coriol. v. 4. 1; Macb. i. 6. 7.

COIL, *sub.* bustle, tumult, Much Ado, iii. 3. 99; Ham. iii. 1. 67.

COLLECTION, *sub.* inference, Cymb. v. 5. 433; Ham. iv. 5. 9.

COLLIED, *adj.* sooty, black, Mid. N. Dr. i. 1. 145; *pt.p.* Oth. ii. 3. 208.

COMMA, *sub.* the smallest break or stop, Ham. v. 2. 42.

COMMODITY, *sub.* profit, advantage, K. Lear, iv. 1. 21.

COMPACT, *pt.p.* made up of, composed, Mid. N. Dr. v. 1. 8; As You Like It, ii. 7. 5.

COMPASSED, *adj.* round, arched, Tam. of Shrew, iv. 3. 139; Ven. & Adon. 272.

COMPETITOR, *sub.* partner, L.'s L.'s L. ii. 1. 82; Ant. & Cleo. v. 1. 42.

COMPTIBLE, *adj.* sensitive, Twelfth Night, i. 5. 188.

CON, *v.t.* to learn, to know, to understand, Twelfth Night, ii. 3. 163; to *con* thanks = to *give* thanks, All's Well, iv. 3. 175; Tim. of Ath. iv. 3. 431.

CONCLUSION, *sub.* an experiment, Ant. & Cleo. v. 2. 356; Cymb. i. 5. 18.

CONCLUSION, STILL, silent inference, or perhaps settled demeanour, Ant. & Cleo. iv. 13. 28.

CONSUL, *sub.* Venetian senator, Oth. i. 1. 25.

CONVENT, *v.i.* to be suitable, Twelfth Night, v. 1. 394.

CONVICTED, *pt.p.* defeated, K. John, iii. 4. 2.

CONVINCE, *v.t.* to overcome, Macb. i. 7. 64; iv. 3. 142; Cymb. i. 4. 109.

CONVIVE, *v.i.* to feast together, Troil. & Cres. iv. 5. 271.

CONY-CATCH, *v.i.* cheat, Merry Wives of W. i. 1. 129; i. 3. 34.

COPATAIN, *adj.* high-crowned and pointed, Tam. of Shrew, v. 1. 69.

COPE, *v.t.* to encounter, As You Like It, ii. 1. 67; Ven. & Adon. 888; to requite, Mer. of Ven. iv. 1. 413.

COPESMATE, *sub.* a companion, Lucrece, 925.

COPPED, *adj.* round-topped, Per. i. 1. 101.

COPY, *sub.* lease, Macb. iii. 2. 38.

CORANTO, *sub.* a quick lively dance, All's Well, ii. 3. 49; Twelfth Night, i. 3. 139.

CORINTHIAN, *sub.* a wencher, 1 Hen. IV. ii. 4. 13.

CORKY, *adj.* shrivelled, K. Lear, iii. 7. 29.

COROLLARY, *sub.* a surplus [Fr. *corollaire*], Temp. iv. 1. 57.

CORROSIVE, *and* { *sub.* an irritant remedy, 2 Hen. VI.
CORSIVE, { iii. 2. 403; *adj.* irritating, giving pain, 1 Hen. VI. iii. 3. 3.

COSTARD, *sub.* the head,—properly an apple,—Merry Wives of W. iii. 1. 14; K. Lear, iv. 6. 248.

COTE, *v.t.* to come up with, and pass on the way, Ham. ii. 2. 338.

COT-QUEAN, *sub.* a man busying himself with the business of women, Rom. & Jul. iv. 4. 6.

COUNTER, *adv.* to run or hunt counter is to follow the game backwards on the scent, Com. of Err. iv. 2. 39; 2 Hen. IV. i. 2. 102 (here a play is intended on the name of the well-known London debtors' prison, the Counter); Ham. iv. 5. 110.

COUNTER-CASTER, *sub.* a reckoner, caster-up of accounts, Oth. i. 1. 31.

COUNTERFEIT, *sub.* a portrait, Mer. of Ven. iii. 2. 115; Ham. iii. 4. 54; a piece of bad money, 1 Hen. IV. ii. 4. 548.

COUNTERPOINT, *sub.* a counterpane, Tam. of Shrew, ii. 1. 345.

COUNTERVAIL, *v.t.* to outweigh, Rom. & Jul. ii. 6. 4.

COUPLET, *sub.* a pair, Twelfth Night, iii. 4. 414; Ham. v. 1. 309.

COURSE, *sub.* a large sail, Temp. i. 1. 55; the onset of dogs in bear-baiting, Macb. v. 7. 2; K. Lear, iii. 7. 54.

COURT-CUPBOARD, *sub.* a sideboard used for the display of plate, Rom. & Jul. i. 5. 8.

COURT HOLY-WATER, *sub.* flattery [Fr. *eau bénite de la cour*], K. Lear, iii. 2. 10.

COWER, *v.i.* to sink or squat down, Per. iv. 2. 115.

COWL-STAFF, *sub.* a pole on which a basket is borne by two persons, Merry Wives of W. iii. 3. 157.

COY, *v.t.* to stroke, to caress, Mid. N. Dr. iv. 1. 2; *v.i.* to disdain, Cor. v. 1. 6.

COYSTRIL, *sub.* a mean fellow, originally a groom, Twelfth Night, i. 3. 44; Per. iv. 6. 181.

COZIER, *sub.* a cobbler, Twelfth Night, ii. 3. 99.

CRACK, *v.i.* to boast, L.'s L.'s L. iv. 3. 268; Cymb. v. 5. 178, 208; *sub.* a pert forward boy, 2 Hen. IV. iii. 2. 34; Coriol. i. 3. 74.

CRACKED WITHIN THE RING, uncurrent [quibbling], Ham. ii. 2. 457.

CRACKER, *sub.* a blusterer, K. John, ii. 1. 147.

CRANK, *sub.* a winding passage, Coriol. i. 1. 143.

CRANTS, *sub.* a garland, a chaplet, Ham. v. 1. 254.

CRARE, *sub.* a small vessel, Cymb. iv. 2. 205.

CRAVEN, *v.t.* to make recreant or cowardly, Cymb. iii. 4. 80.

CREEK, *sub.* a rivulet, a winding part of a rivulet, Cymb. iv. 2. 151.

CRESSET, *sub.* an open lamp set on a beacon, or carried on a pole, 1 Hen. IV. iii. 1. 15.

CRIB, *sub.* a hovel, 2 Hen. IV. iii. 1. 9.

CRISP, *adj.* curled, Temp. iv. 1. 130; Mer. of Ven. iii. 2. 92.

CRITIC, *sub.* a cynic, a carper, Troil. & Cres. v. 2. 128.

CROSS-ROW, *sub.* the Christ-cross Row, the alphabet, Rich. III. i. 1. 55.

CROW-KEEPER, *sub.* the boy, or stuffed figure, to keep away crows, Rom. & Jul. i. 4. 6; K. Lear, iv. 6. 89.

CRUEL, *adj.* crewel, worsted [quibbling], K. Lear, ii. 4. 7.

CRUZADO, *sub.* a Portuguese coin worth about six shillings, Oth. iii. 4. 27.

CRY, *sub.* a pack, Coriol. iii. 3. 118; a company, Ham. iii. 2. 294.

CRY AIM, to encourage, K. John, ii. 1. 196.

CRY YOU MERCY, I beg your pardon, Merry Wives of W. iii. 5. 27; Meas. for Meas. iv. 1. 12.

CUB-DRAWN, *adj.* sucked dry by cubs, made ravenous, K. Lear, iii. 1. 12.

CULLION, *sub.* a mean fellow [Fr. *couillon*, Ital. *coglione*], Hen. V. iii. 2. 23; 2 Hen. VI. i. 3. 43.

CULLIONLY, *adj.* mean, contemptible, K. Lear, ii. 2. 36.

CULVERIN, *sub.* a kind of cannon, 1 Hen. IV. iii. 3. 58.

CURB, *v.t.* to bend [Fr. *courber*], Ham. iii. 4. 155.

CURIOSITY, *sub.* scrupulosity, Tim. of Ath. iv. 3. 303; K. Lear, i. 1. 6.

CURIOUS, *adj.* elegant, Cymb. v. 5. 362; careful, anxious, Cymb. i. 6. 191.

CURRENTS, *sub.* occurrences, 1 Hen. IV. ii. 3. 60.

CURST, *adj.* ill-tempered, Much Ado, ii. 1. 22; K. Lear, ii. 1. 67.

CUSHES, *sub.* cuisses, armour for the thighs, 1 Hen. IV. iv. 1. 105.

CUSTARD-COFFIN, *sub.* the crust of a custard, Tam. of Shrew, iv. 3. 82. *Comp.* COFFIN.

CUSTOMER, *sub.* a loose woman, All's Well, v. 3. 291; Oth. iv. 1. 120.

CUT, *sub.* a horse, Twelfth Night, ii. 3. 206.

CUT AND LONG-TAIL, of every sort, Merry Wives of W. iii. 4. 47.

CUTTLE, *sub.* a bully, 2 Hen. IV. ii. 4. 138.

DAFF, *v.t.* to take off, Lov. Comp. 297; to put by, to turn aside with slight and neglect, Much Ado, iii. 3. 187; 1 Hen. IV. iv. 1. 96.

DAGONET, *sub.* a foolish knight at the court of King Arthur, 2 Hen. IV. iii. 2. 303.

DANCING HORSE, a performing horse, belonging to one Bankes, a Scotchman, L.'s L.'s L. i. 2. 58.

DANGER, *sub.* power, control, according to some debt, Mer. of Ven. iv. 1. 180.

DARE, *v.t.* to terrify, make to couch; larks were caught by small mirrors fastened on scarlet cloth, Hen. V. iv. 2. 36; Hen. VIII. iii. 2. 283.

DARRAIGN, *v.t.* to arrange, or put in order of battle, 3 Hen. VI. ii. 2. 72.

DASH, *sub.* a stigma, Wint. Tale, v. 2. 127; Lucrece, 206.

DAUBERY, *sub.* false pretence, cheating, Merry Wives of W. iv. 2. 190.

DAY-BED, *sub.* a sofa, Twelfth Night, ii. 4. 55; Rich. III. iii. 7. 71.

DAY-WOMAN, *sub.* a dairy woman, L.'s L.'s L. i. 2. 138.

DEAR, *adj.* dear was used for anything powerfully though unpleasantly affecting the feelings, L.'s L.'s L. v. 2. 872; 1 Hen. IV. iii. 2. 123.

DEATH-TOKENS, *sub.* plague spots, Troil. & Cres. ii. 3. 189.

DECENT, *adj.* becoming, Hen. VIII. iv. 2. 146.

DECK, *sub.* a pack of cards, 3 Hen. VI. v. 1. 44; *v.t.* to cover, perhaps to sprinkle, Temp. i. 2. 155.

DEEDLESS, *adj.* inactive, Troil. & Cres. iv. 5. 98.

DEEM, *sub.* a surmise, opinion, Troil. & Cres. iv. 4. 59.

DEFEAT, *v.t.* to disguise, Oth. i. 3. 346.

DEFEND, *v.t.* to forbid, Much Ado, ii. 1. 99; Rich. II. i. 3. 15; Ant. & Cleo. iii. 3. 43.

DELIGHTED, *adj.* framed for delight, Meas. for Meas. iii. 1. 119; delightful, Oth. i. 3. 291; Cymb. v. 4. 102.

DEMERIT, *sub.* desert, Coriol. i. 1. 278; Macb. iv. 3. 225; Oth. i. 2. 22.

DEMURING *pr.p.* looking demure, Ant. & Cleo. iv. 13. 29.

DENIER, *sub.* a very small piece of (French) money, Tam. of Shrew, Induc. 1. 9; Rich. III. i. 2. 253.

DERACINATE, *v.t.* to eradicate, to root up [Fr. *déraciner*], Hen. V. v. 2. 47; Troil. & Cres. i. 3. 99.

DERN, *adj.* dreary, secret, K. Lear. iii. 7. 63; Per. iii. Prol. 15.

DESCENDING, *sub.* lineage, Per. v. 1. 130.

DESIGN, *v.t.* to point out mention before, Rich. II. i. 1. 203; Ham. i. 1. 94.

DEVEST, *v.t.* to undress, Oth. ii. 3. 183.

DEWBERRIES, *sub.* fruit of *Rubus Cæsius*, a large kind of blackberry, Mid. N. Dr. iii. 1. 173.

DICH, *v.t.* do to, happen to, Tim. of Ath. i. 2. 74.

DIET, *sub.* regimen, Two Gent. of Ver. ii. 1. 26; Tim. of Ath. iv. 3. 87.

DIETED, *pt.p.* bound strictly, All's Well, iv. 3. 35.

DIFFUSE, *v.t.* to confuse, K. Lear, i. 4. 2.

DIFFUSED, *adj* wild, irregular, Merry Wives of W. iv. 4. 56; Hen. V. v. 2. 61.

DISAPPOINTED, *pt.p.* unprepared, Ham. i. 5. 77.

DISCANDY, *v.i.* to dissolve, to melt, to thaw, Ant. & Cleo. iii. 11. 165.

DISCLOSE, *v.t.* to hatch, Ham. v. 1. 309; *sub.* the coming forth of the chicken from the shell, Ham. iii. 1. 175.

DISCOVERER, *sub.* scout, 2 Hen. IV. iv. 1. 3.

DISEDGE, *v.i.* to surfeit, Cymb. iii. 4. 96.

DISLIMN, *v.i.* to efface, blot, Ant. & Cleo. iv. 12. 10.

DISME, *sub.* tenth [Old Fr. *disme*], Troil. & Cres. ii. 2. 19.

DISPONGE, *v.i.* to pour down, Ant. & Cleo. iv. 9. 13.

DISPOSE, *sub.* disposition, Troil. & Cres. ii. 3. 176; Oth. i. 3. 403.

DISTANCE, *sub.* hostility, alienation, Macb. iii. 1. 116.

DISVOUCH, *v.t.* to contradict, Meas. for Meas. iv. 4. 1.

DIVE-DAPPER, *sub.* the dab-chick, Ven. & Adon. 86.

DIVISION, *sub.* variation in music, modulation, 1 Hen. IV. iii. 1. 210; Rom. & Jul. iii. 5. 29.

DOCUMENT, *sub.* instruction, Ham. iv. 5. 177.

DOFF, *v.t.* to put off, Tam. of Shrew, iii. 2. 103; Rom. & Jul. i. 2. 47.

DOWLAS, *sub.* coarse linen, 1 Hen. IV. iii. 3. 79.

DOWLE, *sub.* down, the soft plumage of a feather, Temp. iii. 3. 65.

DOWN-GYVED, *adj.* covering the ankles like fetters, Haᴍ. ii. 1. 80.

DOWN-ROPING, *adj.* hanging down in glutinous strings, Hen. V. iv. 2. 48.

DOWN SLEEVES, hanging sleeves, Much Ado, iii. 4. 20.

DOXY, *sub.* a mistress, a canting word [*Comp.* Dekker's 'Bellman of London'], Wint. Tale, iv. 2. 2.

DRAFF, *sub.* dregs, refuse, Merry Wives of W. iv. 2. 112; 1 Hen. IV. iv. 2. 38.

DRAUGHT, *sub.* a privy, Troil. & Cres. v. 1. 84; Tim. of Ath. v. 1. 107.

DRAW DRY-FOOT, follow game by the scent, Com. of Err. iv. 2. 39.

DRAWER, *sub.* a tapster, Merry Wives of W. ii. 2. 167; 1 Hen. IV. ii. 4. 7.

DRAWN, *pt.p.* quaffed, Temp. ii. 2. 158.

DRAWN FOX, a fox turned out of his earth, 1 Hen. IV. iii. 3. 128.

DRIBBLING, *adj.* weakly shot, Meas. for Meas. i. 3. 2.

DROLLERY, *sub.* a puppet show, Temp. iii. 3. 21; a humorous painting, 2 Hen. IV. ii. 1. 160.

DRUMBLE, *v.i.* to be sluggish, Merry Wives of W. iii. 3. 157.

DRY-BEAT, *v.t.* to thrash, cudgel, L.'s L.'s L. v. 2. 264; Rom. & Jul. iii. 1. 84.

DUDGEON, *sub.* the handle of a dagger, Macb. ii. 1. 46.

DUN, *sub.* name for a horse. 'To draw dun from mire', a rustic game played with a log of wood, Rom. & Jul. i. 4. 41.

DUN'S THE MOUSE, a proverbial expression now unintelligible, Rom. & Jul. i. 4. 40.

DUP, *v.t.* to open, Ham. iv. 5. 54.

DURANCE, *sub.* prison dress, Com. of Err. iv. 3. 26. There seems a play on another meaning of durance, which was a kind of durable stuff.

EAGER, *adj.* sour, Ham. i. 5. 69; keen, Sonnets, cxviii. 2; Ham. i. 4. 2.

EAN, *v.t.* to yean, to bring forth young, 3 Hen. VI. ii. 5. 36.

EANLING, *sub.* a young lamb, Mer. of Ven. i. 3. 80.

EAR, *v.t.* to plough or cultivate, All's Well, i. 3. 48; *pr. p.* Ant. & Cleo. i. 2. 120.

ECSTASY, *sub.* a temporary aberration of the mind from joy or grief, Much Ado, ii. 3. 167; Ham. iii. 1. 169.

EGAL, *adj.* equal, Tit. Andr. iv. 4. 4.

ELD, *sub.* old times, old age, Merry Wives of W. iv. 4. 37; Meas. for Meas. iii. 1. 36.

ELF, *v.t.* to entangle hair in so intricate a manner that it is not to be unravelled; supposed to be the work of fairies in the night, K. Lear, ii. 3. 10.

EMBALLING, *pr.p.* being invested with ball and sceptre at coronation, Hen. VIII. ii. 3. 47.

EMBARQUEMENTS, *sub.* hindrances, restraints, Coriol. i. 10. 22.

EMBOSS, *v.t.* to hunt to death, All's Well, iii. 6. 106.

EMBOSSED, *part. adj.* swollen out, As You Like It, ii. 7. 67; 1 Hen. IV. iii. 3. 176; foaming at the mouth from hard running, Tam. of Shrew, Ind. 1. 17; Ant. & Cleo. iv. 11. 3.

EMBOWELLED, *pt.p.* emptied, All's Well, i. 3. 249.

EMPERɪ, *sub.* dominion, Hen. V. i. 2. 226; a country subject to a prince's sway, Cymb. i. 6. 120.

ENDEARED, *pt.p.* bound, 2 Hen. IV. ii. 3. 11; Tim. of Ath. i. 2. 236.

ENGINE, *sub.* an instrument of war, a piece of ordnance, Troil. & Cres. ii. 3. 144; Oth. iii. 3. 356; instrument of torture, K. Lear, i. 4. 292.

ENGLUT, *v.t.* to swallow [Fr. *engloutir*], Oth. i. 3. 57.

ENMESH, *v.t.* to entangle, ensnare, Oth. ii. 3. 371.

ENMEW, *v.t.* to mew up, Meas. for Meas. iii. 1. 89.

ENSCONCE, *v.t.* to cover as with a fort, to shelter, Merry Wives of W. iii. 3. 96; Lucrece, 1515.

ENSEAMED, *part. adj.* filthy, Ham. iii. 4. 92.

ENSEAR, *v.t.* to sear up, to make dry, Tim. of Ath. iv. 3. 188.

ENSHIELD, *part. adj.* shielded, protected, Meas. for Meas. ii. 4. 81.

ENSTEEPED, *part. adj.* lying under water, Oth. ii. 1. 70.

ENTERTAIN, *v.t.* to take into one's service, Jul. Cæs. v. 5. 60; K. Lear, iii. 6. 83; *sub.* reception, Per. i. 1. 119.

ENTREATMENTS, *sub.* invitations, Ham. i. 3. 122.

EPHESIAN, *sub.* a boon companion, Merry Wives of W. iv. 5. 19.

ERINGO, *sub.* the candied roots of sea-holly, Merry Wives of W. v. 5. 23.

ERRING, *part. adj.* wandering, Ham. i. 1. 154; Oth. i. 3. 362.

ESCAPE, *sub.* a freak, Tit. Andr. iv. 2. 114; Oth. i. 3. 136, 197.

ESCOTED, *pt.p.* paid, maintained, Ham. ii. 2. 370.

EVEN CHRISTIAN, *sub.* fellow Christian, Ham. v. 1. 31.

EVEN-PLEACHED, *adj.* evenly interwoven, Hen. V. v. 2. 42.

EVITATE, *v.t.* to avoid, Merry W. of W. v. 5. 253.

EXCEED, *v.i.* to be of surpassing excellence, Much Ado, iii. 4. 17; Per. ii. 3. 15.

EXCREMENT, *sub.* hair, beard, anything growing out of the body, L.'s L.'s L. v. 1. 112; Mer. of Ven. iii. 2. 87; Wint. Tale, iv. 3. 736; Ham. iii. 4. 120.

EXHIBITION, *sub.* a money allowance, K. Lear, i. 2. 25; Oth. i. 3. 239.

EXIGENT, *sub.* extremity, pressing necessity, Jul. Cæs. v. 1. 19; also the end, 1 Hen. VI. ii. 5. 9; Ant. & Cleo. iv. 12. 63.

EXORCISER, *sub.* one who raises spirits, Cymb. iv. 2. 276.

EXORCIST, *sub.* th same, All's Well, v. 3. 309; Jul. Cæs. ii. 1. 323.

EXPEDIENCE, *sub.* expedition, enterpriᵴe, 1 Hen. IV. i. 1. 33; also haste, Rich. II. ii. 1. 287; Hen. V. iv. 3. 70.

EXPEDIENT, *adj.* expeditious, quick, K. John, ii. 1. 60; 2 Hen. VI. iii. 1. 288.

EXSUFFLICATE, *v.i.* inflated, or perhaps contemptible, Oth. iii. 3. 182.

EXTENT, *sub.* seizure, a law term, As You Like It, iii. 1. 17; favour, Ham. ii. 2. 399.

EXTRAVAGANT, *adj.* wandering about, Ham. i. 1. 154; Oth. i. 1. 137.

EYAS, *sub.* a young hawk just taken from the nest, Ham. ii. 2. 363.

EYAS-MUSKET, *sub.* young sparrow-hawk, Merry Wives of W. iii. 3. 22.

EYE, *sub.* a shade of colour, Temp. ii. 1. 58; *v.i.* to look, appear, Ant. & Cleo. i. 3. 19.

FACE, *v.t.* to brave, bully, Tam. of Shrew, iv. 3. 125; to trim a garment, 1 Hen. IV. ii. 3. 65; to lie with effrontery, Com. of Err. iii. 1. 47.

FADGE, *v.i.* to turn out, to suit, L.'s L.'s L. v. 1. 158; Twelfth Night, ii. 2. 34.

FADING, *sub.* burden of song, Wint. Tale, iv. 3. 195.

FAIL, *sub.* failure, omission, Wint. Tale, ii. 2. 41.

FAIRING, *sub.* a present, L.'s L.'s L. v. 2. 2.

FAIRY, *sub.* an enchantress, Ant. & Cleo. iv. 8. 12.

FALL, *sub.* a cadence in music, Twelfth Night, i. 1. 4.

FALLOW, *adj.* yellowish brown, Merry Wives of W. i. 1. 92.

FALSE, *v.t.* to falsify, perjure, Cymb. ii. 3. 74.

FAME, *v.t.* to make famous, Sonnets, lxxxiv. 11.

FANCIES, *sub.* love-songs, or songs in general, 2 Hen. IV. iii. 2. 346.

FANCY, *v.t.* to love, Tam. of Shrew, ii. 1. 12; Twelfth Night, ii. 5. 30; Lucrece, 200.

FANG, *v.t.* to seize, lay hold of, Tim. of Ath. iv. 3. 23.

FANGLED, *adj.* fond of finery, Cymb. v. 4. 134.

FANTASTIC, *sub.* a dandy, *Dram. Per.* of Meas. for Meas. fond of finery, Two Gent. of Ver. ii. 7. 47.

FANTASTICAL, *adj.* imaginary, Macb. i. 3. 53, 139; incredible, Oth. ii. 1. 227; imaginative, Twelfth Night, i. 1. 15.

FANTASTICOES, *sub.* coxcombs, Rom. & Jul. ii. 4. 31.

FAP, *adj.* drunk, Merry Wives of W. i. 1. 184.

FAR, *adv.* further, Wint. Tale, iv. 3. 443.

FARCED, *pt.p.* stuffed out, full, Hen. V. iv. 1. 283.

FARDEL, *sub.* a bundle, a pack [Ital. *fardello*], Wint. Tale, iv. 3. 729, 742, 783; Ham. iii. 1. 76.

FARROW, *sub.* a litter of pigs, Macb. iv. 1. 65.

FARTHINGALE, *sub.* a hooped petticoat, Two Gent. of Ver. ii. 7. 51; Merry Wives of W. iii. 3. 69.

FASHIONS, *sub.* a skin disease in horses, now called *farcy*, Tam. of Shrew, iii. 2. 54.

FAST, *pt.p.* fasted, Cymb. iv. 2. 347.

FAST AND LOOSE, a cheating game, L.'s L.'s L. iii. 1. 109.

FAT, *sub.* a vat, Ant. & Cleo. ii. 7. 122.

FAT, *adj.* heavy, unpleasant, Twelfth Night, v. 1. 113.

FAVOUR, *sub.* countenance, visage, Meas. for Meas. iv. 2. 33; Jul. Cæs. i. 3. 129.

FAVOURS, *sub.* features, As You Like It, iii. 2. 280; 1 Hen. IV. iii. 2. 136; K. Lear, iii. 7. 40.

FEAR, *v.t.* to frighten, Mer. of Ven. i. 1. 9; Tam. of Shrew, i. 2. 214.

FEARFUL, *adj.* timorous, frightened, Rom. & Jul. iii. 3. 1; Ven. & Adon. 677.

FEATURE, *sub.* form, shape, Two Gent. of Ver. iv. 4. 74; Cymb. v. 5. 164; perhaps thing composed, As You Like It, iii. 3. 3.

FEDERARY, *sub.* confederate, Wint. Tale, ii. 1. 89.

FEEDER, *sub.* a shepherd, As You Like It, ii. 4. 100; a servant, Ant. & Cleo. iii. 11. 109; Tim. of Ath. ii. 1. 169 (according to some, a parasite).

FEEDING, *sub.* pasturage, Wint. Tale, iv. 4. 169.

FEE-GRIEF, *sub.* grief not shared by any, Macb. iv. 3. 196.

FELLOWLY, *adj.* companionable, sympathetic, Temp. v. 1. 64.

FEODARY, *sub.* confederate, Meas. for Meas. ii. 4. 123; Cymb. iii. 2. 21.

FERE, *sub.* a spouse, Tit. Andr. iv. 1. 89; Per. Prol. 21.

FERRET, *v.t.* to worry, Hen. V. iv. 4. 30.

FERVENCY, *sub.* eagerness, Ant. & Cleo. iii. 5. 18.

FETCH, *sub.* a trick, a stratagem, Ham. ii. 1. 38; K. Lear, ii. 4. 90.

FETCH OFF, *v.t.* to make away with, Wint. Tale, i. 2. 334.

FETTLE, *v.t.* to get into condition, prepare, Rom. & Jul. iii. 5. 154.

FEWNESS, *sub.* rarity, or brevity, Meas. for Meas. i. 4. 39.

FIELD-BED, *sub.* camp-bed, Rom. & Jul. ii. 1. 40.

FIG, *v.t.* to insult by thrusting the thumb between two fingers, 2 Hen. IV. v. 3. 1.

FIGHTS, *sub.* canvas hung up to screen the crew of a ship during action, Merry Wives of W. ii. 2. 144.

FIGO, *sub.* [*see* FIG], Hen. V. iii. 6. 60.

FIGURE, *sub.* a turn of rhetoric, Two Gent. of Ver. ii. 1. 156; L.'s L.'s L. i. 2. 59; a method of fortune-telling, Merry Wives of W. iv. 2. 189.

FIGURES, *sub.* disquieting fancies, Merry Wives of W. iv. 2. 234; Jul. Cæs. ii. 1. 231.

FILE, *sub.* a list, Macb. iii. 1. 95.

FILE, *v.t.* to defile, Macb. iii. 1. 65.

FILLS, *sub.* shafts, Troil. & Cres. iii. 2. 46.

FILTH, *sub.* term of contempt, Tim. of Ath. iv. 1. 6; Oth. v. 2. 229.

FINELESS, *adj.* without end, Oth. iii. 3. 173.

FINICAL, *adj.* foppish, K. Lear, ii. 2. 19.

FIRE-DRAKE, *sub.* a meteor, fiery dragon, Hen. VIII. v. 4. 46.

FIRK, *v.t.* to beat, Hen. V. iv. 4. 29.

FIST, *v.t.* to grasp, Coriol. iv. 5. 131; Per. iv. 6. 182.

FITCHEW, *sub.* a polecat, Troil. & Cres. v. 1. 67; Oth. iv. 1. 148.

FITTED, *pt.p.* worked as if by fits, Sonnets, cxix. 7.

FIVES, *sub.* inflammation of parotid glands in horses [French *avives*], Tam. of Shrew, iii. 2. 56.

FLAP-DRAGON, *sub.* a small burning body lighted and put afloat in a glass of liquor, to be swallowed burning, snapdragon, L.'s L.'s L. v. 1. 46; 2 Hen. IV. ii. 4. 267; *v.t.* to swallow like a flap-dragon, Wint. Tale, iii. 3. 100.

FLAP-EARED, *adj.* broad hanging ears, Tam. of Shrew, iv. i. 160.

FLAP-JACK, *adj.* a pancake, Per. ii. 1. 88.

FLAP-MOUNTED, *adj.* with broad hanging lips, Ven. & Ad. 920.

FLAT, *sub.* sandbank, Mer. of Ven. i. 1. 26; iii. 1. 5.

FLAT-LONG, *adv.* flat, Temp. ii. 1. 188.

FLAW, *sub.* a crack, K. Lear, ii. 4. 288; *fig.* Ant. & Cleo. iii. 10. 34; *v.t.* to break, crack, Hen. VIII. i. 1. 95.

FLAWS, *sub.* outbursts of passion, Meas. for Meas. ii.3.11; Macb. iii. 4. 63; sudden gusts of wind, Coriol. v. 3. 74; Ven.&Adon.456; small blades of ice,2 Hen. IV. iv.4.35.

FLECKED, *adj.* spotted, Rom. & Jul. ii. 3. 3.

FLEWED, *adj.* 'Flews' are the large hanging chaps of a hound, Mid. N. Dr. iv. 1. 126.

FLICKER, *v.i.* to twinkle, K. Lear, ii. 2. 114.

FLIGHT, *sub.* a long, light arrow, Much Ado, i. 1. 40.

FLIGHTY, *adj.* swift, Macb. iv. 1. 145.

FLIRT-GILLS, *sub.* light wenches, Rom. & Jul. ii. 4. 163.

FLOCK, *sub.* a lock of wool, 1 Hen. IV. ii. 1. 7.

FLOTE, *sub.* wave, Temp. i. 2. 234.

FLOURISH, *sub.* ornament, Rich. III. i. 3. 241; Sonnets, lxix; a sounding of trumpets, Meas. for Meas. iv. 1. 76; Mer. of Ven. iii. 2. 49.

FOBBED, *pt.p.* cheated, 1 Hen. IV. i. 2. 68.

FOIN, *sub.* a thrust, K. Lear, iv. 6. 252; *v.i.* to thrust in fencing, MerryWives of W, ii. 3. 24; Much Ado, v. 1.84.

FOISON, OR FOIZON, *sub.* plenty [Fr. *foison*], Temp. ii. 1. 170; iv. 1. 110; Macb. iv. 3. 88.

FOOT, *v.t.* to kick, Mer. of Ven. i. 3. 119; to seize with the talon, Cymb. v. 4. 116.

FOP, *sub.* a fool, K. Lear. i. 2. 14.

FORBID, *pt.p.* accursed, Macb. i. 3. 46.

FORDO, *v.t.* to lay violent hands upon, to destroy, K. Lear, v. 3. 293; Oth. v. 1. 129.

FORDONE, *pt.p.* exhausted, Mid. N. Dr. v. 2. 4.

FORE-END, *sub.* the first part, Cymb. iii. 3. 73.

FORE-HAND, *sub.* advantage, Hen. V. iv. 1. 300; the best part, the pick, Troil. & Cres. i. 3. 143; *adj.* anticipated, Much Ado, iv. 1. 50.

FORE-HAND SHAFT, an arrow for shooting point blank, 2 Hen. IV. iii. 2. 52.

FORFEND, *v.i.* to forbid, 3 Hen. VI. ii. 1. 190; Oth. v. 2. 32.

FORGETIVE, *adj.* inventive, 2 Hen. IV. iv. 3. 107.

FORK, *sub.* the tongue of a snake, Meas. for Meas. iii. 1. 16; Macb. iv. 1. 16; the head of an arrow, K. Lear, i. 1. 146.

FORSLOW, *v.i.* to delay, 3 Hen. VI. ii. 3. 56.

FORTED, *adj.* fortified, Meas. for Meas. v. 1. 12.

FORTH-RIGHT, *sub.* a straight path, Temp. iii. 3. 3; Troil. & Cres. iii. 3. 158.

FOSSET-SELLER, *sub.* a seller of taps, Coriol. ii. 1. 80.

FOUTRA, *sub.* expression of contempt, 2 Hen. IV. v. 3. 118.

FOX, *sub.* a broadsword, Hen. V. iv. 4. 9.

FOXSHIP, *sub.* cunning and selfishness, Coriol. iv. 2. 18.

FRACTED, *pt.p.* broken, Tim. of Ath. ii. 1. 22.

FRAMPOLD, *adj.* unquiet, quarrelsome, Merry Wives of W. ii. 2. 95.

FRANK, *sub.* a sty, 2 Hen. IV. ii. 2. 160; *v.i.* to shut up in a sty, Rich. III. i. 3. 314; iv. 5. 3.

FRANKLIN, *sub.* a yeoman, Wint. Tale, v. 2. 181; Cymb. iii. 2. 78.

FRAUGHTING, *part. adj.* constituting the freight, Temp. i. 2. 13.

FREE, *adj.* innocent, Wint. Tale. i. 2. 113; Ham. ii. 2. 598.

FRESHES, *sub.* springs of fresh water, Temp. iii. 2. 77.

FRET, *v.t.* to adorn, Jul. Cæs. ii. 1. 104; Cymb. ii. 4. 88.

FRETS, *sub.* the stops of a guitar, Lucrece, 1140.

FRIPPERY, *sub.* an old clothes shop, Temp. iv. 1. 228.

FRONTIER, *sub.* an outwork, fortification, 1 Hen. IV. ii. 3. 57.

FRONTLET, *sub.* a band for the forehead, *fig.* K. Lear, i. 4. 210.

FRUSH, *v.t.* to break, bruise, or crush [Fr. *froisser*], Troil. & Cres. v. 6. 29.

FUBBED OFF, *pt.p.* put off with excuses, 2 Hen. IV. ii. 1. 39.

FULLAMS, *sub.* a kind of false dice, Merry Wives of W. i. 3. 92.

FUMITER *and* FUMITORY, *sub.* the plant *Fumaria*, Hen. V. v. 2. 45; K. Lear, iv. 4. 3.

FUSTILARIAN, *sub.* a term of reproach, 2 Hen. IV. ii. 1. 68.

GABERDINE, *sub.* the coarse frock of a peasant [Ital. *gavardina*], Temp. ii. 2. 41; Mer. of Ven. i. 3. 113.

GAD, *sub.* a sharp-pointed instrument, a goad, Tit. Andr. iv. 1. 103; 'upon the gad' = on the spur of the moment, K. Lear, i. 2. 26.

GAGE, *v.t.* to pledge, Ham. i. 1. 91; Lucrece, 144; *sub.* also a pledge pawned, Rich. II. i. 1. 146.

GAIN-GIVING, *sub.* misgiving, Ham. v. 2. 227.

GAIT, *sub.* proceeding, Ham. i. 2. 31.

GALL, *v.i.* to scoff, to jest bitterly, Hen. V. v. 1. 78.

GALLED, *pt.p.* worn by the action of the waves, Hen. V. iii. 1. 12; Lucrece, 1440; irritated as the eyes are by tears, Rich. III. iv. 4. 53; Ham. i. 2. 155.

GALLIARD, *sub.* the name of a dance, Twelfth Night, i. 3. 139; Hen. V. i. 2. 252.

GALLIASSE, *sub.* a large galley, Tam. of Shrew, ii. 1. 372.

GALLIMAUFRY, *sub.* a medley or jumble of things together, Merry Wives of W. ii. 1. 117; Wint. Tale, iv. 3. 337.

GALLOW, *v.t.* to frighten, K. Lear, iii. 2. 44.

GALLOWGLASSES, *sub.* heavy armed Irish foot-soldiers, 2 Hen. VI. iv. 9. 26; Macb. i. 2. 13.

GALLOWS, *sub.* a knave, one fit for the gallows, L.'s L.'s L. v. 2. 12.

GAPE, *v.i.* to cry out loudly, Hen. VIII. v. 4. 3. *Comp.* 'a gaping pig' (which however may mean a pig prepared for the table with a lemon in its mouth), Mer. of Ven. iv. 1. 47.

GARBOIL, *sub.* disturbance, commotion, Ant. & Cleo. i. 3. 61.

GARDEN-HOUSE, *sub.* a summer-house, Meas. for Meas. v. 1. 223.

GARISH, *adj.* glittering, gaudy, Rich. III. iv. 4. 89; Rom. & Jul. iii. 2. 25.

GARNER, *v.t.* lay up, store up, Oth. iv. 2. 56.

GARNISH, *sub.* equipment, Mer. of Ven. ii. 6. 45.

GASKINS, *sub.* loose breeches, Twelfth Night, i. 5. 27.

GASTED, *pt.p.* frightened, K. Lear, ii. 1. 57.

GASTNESS, *sub.* ghastliness, Oth. v. 1. 106.

GAUDY, *adj.* festive, Ant. & Cleo. iii. 11. 182.

GAWDS, *sub.* toys, nicknacks, Mid. N. Dr. i. 1. 33; K. John, iii. 3. 36.

GECK, *sub.* a dupe, Twelfth Night, v. 1. 355; Cymb. v. 4. 67.

GEMINY, *sub.* a pair, Merry Wives of W. ii. 2. 9.

GENERATION, *sub.* offspring, Wint. Tale, ii. 1. 147; K. Lear, i. 1. 119.

GENEROSITY, *sub.* nobility, Coriol. i. 1. 217.

GENEROUS, *adj.* of noble birth, Meas. for Meas. iv. 6. 13; Oth. iii. 3. 280.

GENTLE, *v.t.* to ennoble, Hen. V. iv. 3. 63.

GENTRY, *sub.* courtesy, Ham. ii. 2. 22; v. 2. 115.

GERMENS, *sub.* seeds, germs, Macb. iv. 1. 59; K. Lear, iii. 2. 8.

GEST, *sub.* a period of stopping in a place, originally the halting-place in a royal progress [Fr. *giste*, *gîte*], Wint. Tale, i. 2. 41.

GESTS, *sub.* acts, exploits, Ant. & Cleo. iv. 8. 2.

GHOST, *v.t.* to visit as a ghost, to haunt, Ant. & Cleo. ii. 6. 13.

GIB, *sub.* an old tom-cat, Ham. iii. 4. 190.

GIB CAT, *sub.* the same, 1 Hen. IV. i. 2. 83.

GIBBER, *v.i.* to speak inarticulately, Ham. i. 1. 116.

GIBBET, *v.t.* to hang, 2 Hen. IV. iii. 2. 285.

GIG, *sub.* a top, L.'s L.'s L. iv. 3. 167; v. 1. 71.

GIGLOT, *sub.* a light wench, Meas. for Meas. v. 1. 347; *adj.* 1 Hen. VI. iv. 7. 41; Cymb. iii. 1. 31.

GILT, *sub.* money, Hen. V. ii. Chor. 26; gilding, fair show, Twelfth Night, iii. 2. 27; Coriol. i. 3. 44.

GIMMAL, *adj.* double, or made with double rings, Hen. V. iv. 2. 49.

GIMMALS [Fol. GIMMORS], *sub.* connecting parts in the mechanism of a clock, 1 Hen. VI. i. 2. 41.

GING, *sub.* a gang, a pack, Merry Wives of W. iv. 2. 126.

GIRD, *sub.* a scoff, sarcasm, Tam. of Shrew, v. 2. 58; 1 Hen. VI. iii. 1. 131; *v.t.* to gibe, taunt, 2 Hen. IV. i. 2. 6; Coriol. i. 1. 262.

GIVE OUT, to report, Coriol. i. 1. 199; to give over, 2 Hen. VI. iv. 8. 27.

GLEEKS, *sub.* scoffs, 1 Hen. VI. iii. 2. 123.

GNARLING, *adj.* snarling, Rich. II. i. 3. 292; *v.i.* 2 Hen. VI. iii. 1. 192.

GOD, *v.t.* to worship, Coriol. v. 3. 111.

GOD 'ILD YOU, God yield you (i.e. reward you), As You Like It, iii. 3. 81.

GOOD, *adj.* wealthy, Mer. of Ven. i. 3. 12; Coriol. i. 1. 16.

GOOD DEED, in very deed, Wint. Tale, i. 2. 42.

GORBELLIED, *adj.* big-bellied, 1 Hen. IV. ii. 2. 97.

GORGE, *sub.* the throat, Wint. Tale, ii. 1. 43.

GORGET, *sub.* armour for the throat, Troil. & Cres. i. 3. 174.

GOSPELLED, *pt.p.* indued with precepts of the gospel, Macb. iii. 1. 88.

GOSS, *sub.* gorse, Temp. iv. 1. 180.

GOSSIP, *sub.* a sponsor, Wint. Tale, ii. 3. 41; *v.t.* to christen, All's Well, i. 1. 191.

GOUJEERS, *sub.* the French disease, K. Lear, v. 3. 24.

GOURDS, *sub.* false dice, Merry Wives of W. i. 3. 92.

GOUT, *sub.* a drop [Fr. *goutte*], Macb. ii. 1. 46.

GRAIN, *sub.* the kermes of which the purple dye was made, a fast colour, Com. of Err. iii. 2. 109; Twelfth Night, i. 5. 257.

GRAINED, *adj.* dyed in grain, Ham. iii. 4. 90; furrowed, rough, Coriol. iv. 5. 114; Lov. Comp. 64.

GRANGE, *sub.* a farm, or lone house in the country, Oth. i. 1. 106.

GRATIFY, *v.t.* to reward, Mer. of Ven. iv. 1. 407; Coriol. ii. 2. 45.

GRATULATE, *adj.* gratifying, Meas. for Meas. v. 1. 531.

GREAT MORNING, broad daylight, Troil. & Cres. iv. 3. 1; Cymb. iv. 2. 61.

GREEK, *sub.* a boon companion, a merry fellow, Twelfth Night, iv. 1. 19; Troil. & Cres. i. 2. 116; iv. 4. 56.

GRIEF-SHOT, *adj.* sorrow-stricken, Coriol. v. 1. 45.

GRIME, *v.t.* to begrime, K. Lear, ii. 3. 9.

GRIPE, *sub.* a griffin, Lucrece, 543.

GRIZE, *sub.* a step, Twelfth Night, iii. 1. 138; Oth. i. 3. 200.

GRIZZLE, *sub.* a tinge of grey, Twelfth Night, v. 1. 169.

GROUND, *sub.* the original air, on which the variations are made, Rich. III. iii. 7. 48.

GROUNDLINGS, *sub.* vulgar spectators, who stood in what is now the pit of the theatre, Ham. iii. 2. 12.

GROW TO, to have a strong flavour, Mer. of Ven. ii. 2. 18.

GROW TO A POINT, to come to the point, Mid. N. Dr. i. 2. 10.

GUARD, *v.t.* to trim, K. John, iv. 2. 10; *pt.p.* trimmed, ornamented, Mer. of Ven. ii. 2. 170.

GUARDS, *sub.* two stars of Ursa Minor were called guards of the pole, Oth. ii. 1. 15; trimmings, Meas. for Meas. iii. 1. 95.

GUILDER, *sub.* a Dutch coin, Com. of Err. i. 1. 8.

GULES, *adj.* red, in heraldry, Tim. of Ath. iv. 3. 59; Ham. ii. 2. 488.

GULF, *sub.* the gullet, Macb. iv. 1. 23.

GULL, *sub.* a young unfeathered bird, 1 Hen. IV. v. 1. 60; Tim. of Ath. ii. 1. 31.

GUMMED VELVET, *sub.* velvet stiffened with gum, 1 Hen. IV. ii. 2. 3.

GUST, *v.t.* to taste, Twelfth Night, i. 3. 34.

GUTTERED, *part. adj.* worn by the action of water, Oth. ii. 1. 69.

HABITUDE, *sub.* condition of body, Lov. Comp. 114.

HACK, *v.i.* to grow common, Merry Wives of W. ii. 1. 52.

HAGGARD, *sub.* a wild hawk, Much Ado, iii. 1. 36; *adj.* Oth. iii. 3. 260.

HAIR, *sub.* nature, texture, 1 Hen. IV. iv. 1. 61.

HALF-CHECKED BIT, mutilated of which only one part remained, Tam. of Shrew, iii. 2. 58.

HALL, *interj.* a hall! a cry to make room for dancers, Rom. & Jul. i. 5. 30.

HAND-FAST, *sub.* a contract, betrothal, Cymb. i. 5. 78; custody, Wint. Tale, iv. 3. 798.

HANDY-DANDY, a game in which an object is passed from one to another, K. Lear, iv. 6. 158.

HANGMAN BOYS, young rascals, Two Gent. of Ver. iv. 4. 61.

HAPPELY, *or* ⎰ *adv.* perchance, Meas. for Meas. iv. 2. 98;
HAPPILY, ⎱ Twelfth Night, iv. 2. 58.

HARDIMENTS, *sub.* feats of arms and valour, 1 Hen. IV. i. 3. 101; Cymb. v. 4. 75.

HARLOT, *adj.* base, Wint. Tale, ii. 3. 4 (harlot king).

HARLOTRY, *sub.* a harlot, Oth. iv. 2. 239; a silly wench, Rom. & Jul. iv. 2. 14.

HARROW, *v.t.* to disquiet, to distract, Ham. i. 1. 44; i. 5. 16.

HARRY, *v.t.* to vex, to harry, Ant. & Cleo. iii. 3. 40.

HATCH, *sub.* a half door, K. John, i. 1. 171; K. Lear, iii. 6. 76.

HAUGHT, *adj.* haughty, Rich. II. iv. 1. 254; 3 Hen. VI. ii. 1. 169.

HAUNCH, *sub.* the rear, latter end, 2 Hen. IV. iv. 4. 92.

HAVOC, *interj.* to cry 'havoc!' signifies to give no quarter, Jul. Cæs. iii. 1. 273; Ham. v. 2. 378.

HAWKING, *adj.* hawk-like, All's Well, i. 1. 106.

HAY, *sub.* a circular dance, L.'s L.'s L. v. 1. 166; an exclamation used by a fencer when he hits his adversary [*It. hai!* 'You have it!'], Rom. & Jul. ii. 4. 28.

HEAD, *sub.* an armed force, 1 Hen. IV. iv. 4. 25; K. John, v. 2. 113; Ham. iv. 5. 101; source, All's Well, i. 3. 180.

HEAD-LUGGED, *part. adj.* dragged by the ears, savage, K. Lear, iv. 2. 42.

HEAP, *sub.* company of persons, Rich. III. ii. 1. 53.

HEARTED, *pt.p.* placed or rooted in the heart, Oth. i. 3. 373; iii. 3. 449.

HEAT, *v.t.* to run over, traverse, Wint. Tale, i. 2. 96.

HEAVES, *sub.* deep sighs, Wint. Tale, ii. 3. 35; Ham. iv. 1. 1.

HEBONA [Fol. HEBENON], *sub.* a word of doubtful meaning; the yew, ebony, and henbane have all been suggested, Ham. i. 5. 62.

HECTIC, *sub.* a fever, Ham. iv. 3. 68.

HEDGE, *v.i.* to skulk, Merry Wives of W. ii. 2. 27; Troil. & Cres. iii. 1. 66.

HEDGE-PRIEST, *sub.* clergyman of the lowest order, L.'s L.'s L. v. 2. 543.

HEEL, *v.t.* to dance, Troil. & Cres. iv. 4. 146.

HEFTS, *sub.* heavings, Wint. Tale, ii. 1. 44.

HELM, *v.t.* to steer, Meas. for Meas. iii. 2. 155.

HELPLESS, *adj.* incurable, Lucrece, 756; useless, unprofitable, Rich. III. i. 2. 13; Ven. & Adon. 604.

HENCHMAN, *sub.* a page, Mid. N. Dr. ii. 1. 121.

HENT, *v.t.* to seize, take, Meas. for Meas. iv. 6. 14; Wint. Tale, iv. 2. 134; *sub.* hold, seizure, Ham. iii. 3. 88.

HERBLETS, *sub.* small herbs, Cymb. iv. 2. 287.

HERB OF GRACE, rue, Rich. II. iii. 4. 105; Ham. iv. 5. 181.

HERCULES AND HIS LOAD, the Globe theatre, from its sign, Ham. ii. 2. 386.

HERMIT, *sub.* a beadsman, Macb. i. 6. 20.

HESTS, *sub.* commands, Temp. i. 2. 274; iii. 1. 37.

HEWGH, *sub.* a sound to represent the whizzing of an arrow, K. Lear, iv. 6. 94.

HIDE FOX, AND ALL AFTER, the game of hide and seek, Ham. iv. 2. 32.

HIGH AND LOW, kinds of false dice, Merry Wives of W. i. 3. 93.

HIGH-BATTLED, *adj.* at the head of a victorious army, Ant. & Cleo. iii. 11. 29.

HIGH-DAY, *adj.* holiday, Mer. of Ven. ii. 9. 98.

HIGH LONE, *adj.* alone on one's own feet; a term of the nursery, Rom. & Jul. i. 3. 36.

HIGHT, is called, L.'s L.'s L. i. 1. 169.

HIGH-VICED, *adj.* conspicuously wicked, Tim. of Ath. iv. 3. 110.

HILDING, *sub.* a menial, All's Well, iii. 6. 4; Cymb. ii. 3. 128; *adj.* base, Hen. V. iv. 11. 29.

HIP, TO CATCH ON, have in one's power; a wrestling or hunting phrase, Mer. of Ven. i. 3. 47; Oth. ii. 1. 317.

HIPPED, *pt.p.* hurt in the hips, Tam. of Shrew, iii. 2. 50.

HIREN, *sub.* Irene, name of the heroine in a lost drama by Peele, 2 Hen. IV. ii. 4. 172.

HIT TOGETHER, *v.* agree or act together, K. Lear, i. 1. 308.

HIVE, *sub.* a kind of bonnet, Lov. Comp. 8.

HOAR, *v.t.* to make white, as with leprosy, Tim. of Ath. iii. 3. 156.

HOBBY-HORSE, *sub.* a principal part in the morris-dance, Ham. iii. 2. 144; a light woman, Much Ado, iii. 2. 75; Oth. iv. 1. 158.

HODGE-PUDDING, *sub.* perhaps a haggis, Merry Wives of W. v. 5. 163.

HOLDING, *sub.* a burthen of a song, Ant. & Cleo. ii. 7. 118; congruity, sense, All's Well, iv. 2. 27.

HOLIDAME, *sub.* halidom, holiness, Tam. of Shrew, v. 2. 100.

HOLY-ALES, *sub.* rural festivals, Per. i. Prol. 6.

HONEYING, *pr.p.* fondling, Ham. iii. 4. 93.

HONEY-STALKS, *sub.* clover, Tit. Andr. iv. 4. 90.

HOODMAN, *sub.* the person blinded in the game of blind man's buff, All's Well, iv. 3. 137.

HOODMAN-BLIND, *sub.* blind man's buff, Ham. iii. 4. 77.

HORN-MAD, *adj.* mad like a savage bull [quibbling], Com. of Err. ii. 1. 57; Merry Wives of W. i. 4. 51.

HOROLOGE, *sub.* a clock, Oth. ii. 3. 136.

HOST, *v.i.* to lodge, Com. of Err. i. 2. 9; All's Well, iii. 5. 94.

HOT AT HAND, not to be held in, Jul. Cæs. iv. 2. 23.

HOT-HOUSE, *sub.* a bagnio, Meas. for Meas. ii. 1. 67.

HOX, *v.t.* to hough, to hamstring, Wint. Tale, i. 2. 244.

HOY, *sub.* a small coasting vessel, Com. of Err. iv. 3. 39.

HUGGER-MUGGER, IN, secretly, with hurried secrecy, Ham. iv. 5. 84.

HULL, *v.i.* to float, Twelfth Night, i. 5. 217; Rich. III. iv. 4. 439.

HULLING, *pr.p.* floating at the mercy of the waves, Hen. VIII. ii. 4. 197.

HUNT, *sub.* game killed in the chase, Cymb. iii. 6. 89.

HUNTS-UP, *sub.* tunes to arouse the huntsman, Rom. & Jul. iii. 5. 34.

HURLY, *and* HURLY-BURLY, *sub.* tumult, uproar, K. John, iii. 4. 169; Macb. i. 1. 3.

HURRICANO, *sub.* waterspout, Troil. & Cres. v. 2. 169; K. Lear, iii. 2. 2.

HURTLESS, *adj.* harmless, K. Lear, iv. 6. 171.

HURTLING, *sub.* a clashing noise, As You Like It, iv. 3 133.

HURTLE, *v.i.* to come together with noise, Jul. Cæs. ii. 2. 22.

HUSBANDRY, *sub.* management, Macb. ii. 1. 4; Tim. of Ath. ii. 2. 165.

HYEN, *sub.* an hyæna, As You Like It, iv. 1. 163.

ICE BROOK, *sub.* supposed to be the river Salo, near Bibilis, in Spain, Oth. v. 2. 252.

IGNOMY, *sub.* ignominy, Meas. for Meas. ii. 4. 112.

ILLUME, *v.t.* to illuminate, Ham. i. 1. 37.

ILLUSTROUS, *adj.* wanting lustre, without brightness, Cymb. i. 6. 109.

IMBAR, *v.t.* to secure, or perhaps to exclude, Hen. V. i. 2. 94.

IMMANITY, *sub.* ferocity, 1 Hen. VI. v. 1. 13.

IMMEDIACY, *sub.* directness, K. Lear, v. 3. 66.

IMMOMENT, *adj.* insignificant, Ant. & Cleo. v. 2. 165.

IMP, *sub.* child, used affectedly, L.'s L.'s L. i. 2. 5; Hen. V. iv. 1. 45; *v.t.* to graft new feathers into a hawk's wing, Rich. II. ii. 1. 292.

IMPASTED, *pt.p.* coagulated, Ham. ii. 2. 490.

IMPERCEIVERANT, *sub.* dull, undiscerning, Cymb. iv. 1. 15.

IMPORTANCE, *sub.* importunity, Twelfth Night, v. 1. 375; Cymb. i. 4. 47.

IMPORTANT, *adj.* urgent, importunate, Com. of Err. v. 1. 138; K. Lear, iv. 4. 26.

IMPOSE, *sub.* command, Two Gent. iv. 3. 8.

IMPOSTHUME, *sub.* an abscess, Troil. & Cres. v. 1. 24.

IMPRESS, *sub.* a device with a motto, Rich. II. iii. 1. 25.

INCARNADINE, *v.t.* to dye red, Macb. ii. 2. 63.

INCH-MEAL, *sub.* piecemeal, Temp. ii. 2. 3.

INCONTINENT, *sub.* immediately, As You Like It, v. 2. 44.

INCONTINENTLY, *adv.* the same, Oth. i. 3. 307.

INCONY, *adj.* delicate, pretty, L.'s L.'s L. iii. i. 142; iv. 1. 146.

INDENT, *v.t.* to make terms, 1 Hen. IV. i. 3. 87.

INDUCTION, *sub.* introduction, and preparation, 1 Hen. IV. iii. 1. 2; Rich. III. i. 1. 32.

INEXECRABLE, *adj.* that cannot be sufficiently execrated, Mer. of Ven. iv. 1. 128.

INFORM, *v.i.* to take shape, Macb. ii. 1. 48; to animate, inspire, Coriol. v. 3. 71.

INFORMAL, *adj.* crazy, Meas. for Meas. v. 1. 230.

INHERIT, *v.t.* to possess, Temp. iv. 1. 154.

INKLE, *sub.* a kind of coarse tape, L.'s L.'s L. iii. 1. 146; Wint. Tale, iv. 3. 208; Per. v. Prol. 8.

INLAND, *adj.* civilized, perhaps living near the capital, As You Like It, iii. 2. 367.

INNOCENT, *sub.* an idiot, All 's Well, iv. 3. 214; Per. iv. 3. 17.

INSANE, *adj.* causing insanity, Macb. i. 3. 84.

INSANIE, *sub.* madness, L.'s L.'s L. v. 1. 28. [Holofernes.]

INSCULPED, *pt.p.* engraved, cut, Mer. of Ven. ii. 7. 57.

INSCULPTURE, *sub.* an inscription cut in stone, Tim. of Ath. v. 4. 67.

INSISTURE, *sub.* persistency, Troil. & Cres. i. 3. 87.

INSTANCE, *sub.* motive, Ham. iii. 2. 194; proof, 2 Hen. IV. iii. 1. 103.

INTELLIGENCER, *sub.* agent, go-between, Rich. III. iv. 4. 71.

INTELLIGENCING, *adj.* going between parties, Wint. Tale, ii. 3. 68.

INTEND, *v.t.* to pretend, Much Ado, ii. 2. 46; Rich. III. iii. 7. 44.

INTENDMENT, *sub.* design purpose, As You Like It, i. 1. 142; Ven. & Adon. 222; aim, Hen. V. i. 2. 144.

INTENIBLE, *adj.* unretentive, All 's Well, i. 3. 210.

INTENTION, *sub.* aim, direction, Merry Wives of W. i. 3. 71; Wint. Tale, i. 2. 139.

INTENTIVELY, *adv.* attentively, or perhaps consecutively, Oth. i. 3. 155.

INTERESSED, *pt.p.* interested [legal sense], K. Lear, i. 1. 87.

INTRINSE, *adj.* hard to untie, K. Lear, ii. 2. 80.

INTRINSICATE, *adj.* the same, Ant. & Cleo. v. 2. 306.

INVECTIVELY, *adj.* reproachfully, As You Like It, ii. 1. 58.

INVINCIBLE, *adj.* invisible [Qy. error], 2 Hen. IV. iii. 2. 340.

INWARD, *adj.* intimate, Rich. III. iii. 4. 8; secret, Much Ado, iv. 1. 12; *sub.* an intimate friend, Meas. for Meas. iii. 2. 142.

INWARDNESS, *sub.* intimacy, Much Ado, iv. 1. 247.

IRON-WITTED, *adj.* unfeeling, insensible, Rich. III. iv. 2. 28.

IRREGULOUS, *adj.* lawless, Cymb. iv. 2. 315.

ITERANCE, *sub.* repetition, Oth. v. 2. 148.

I WIS, *adv.* certainly [Ang.-Sax. ge-wis], Mer. of Ven. ii. 9. 68; Rich. III. i. 3. 102.

JACK, *sub.* the small ball aimed at in the game of bowls, Cymb. ii. 1. 2; a term of reproach, Rich. III. i. 3. 72; 1 Hen. IV. iii. 3. 98; a figure which struck the bell in old clocks, Rich. II. v. 5. 60; Rich. III. iv. 2. 113.

JACK-A-LENT, *sub.* a stuffed figure thrown at during Lent, Merry Wives of W. iii. 3. 27; v. 5. 137.

JACKS, *sub.* the keys of a virginal, Sonnets, cxxviii. 5; a drinking vessel, Tam. of Shrew, iv. 1. 51.

JACK-SAUCE, *sub.* a saucy Jack, Hen. V. iv. 7. 149.

JADE, *v.t.* to drive like a jade, Ant. & Cleo. iii. 1. 34; to treat with contempt, Hen. VIII. iii. 2. 281; to run away with, Twelfth Night, ii. 5. 180.

JADED, *adj.* worn out with work, 2 Hen. VI. iv. 1. 52.

JAR, *sub.* a tick of the clock, Wint. Tale, i. 2. 43; *v.i.* to tick, Rich. II. v. 5. 51.

JAUNCE, *sub.* a wild ramble, Rom. & Jul. ii. 5. 26; *v.i.* to ramble, Rom. & Jul. ii. 5. 53; to spur hard, Rich. II. v. 5. 94.

JAY, *sub.* a loose woman, Merry Wives of W. iii. 3. 44.

JENNET, *sub.* a Spanish horse, Ven. & Ad. 260.

JESSES, *sub.* foot straps, which attached the legs of a hawk to the fist, Oth. iii. 3. 261.

JET, *v.i.* to strut, Twelfth Night, ii. 5. 36; Cymb. iii. 3. 5; to advance insultingly, Rich. III. ii. 4. 51; Tit. Andr. ii. 1. 64.

JIG, *sub.* a ludicrous ballad, Ham. ii. 2. 530; L.'s L.'s L. iii. 1. 12.

JIGGING, *pr.p.* composing jigs, Jul. Cæs. iv. 3. 136.

JOINT-RING, *sub.* a split ring, gimmal-ring, Oth. iv. 3. 74.

JOLTHEAD, *sub.* a blockhead, Tam. of Shrew, iv. 1. 169.

JOURNAL, *adj.* diurnal, daily, Meas. for Meas. iv. 3. 95; Cymb. iv. 2. 10.

JOVIAL, *adj.* like Jove, Cymb. iv. 2. 311.

JOWL, *or* JOLL, *v.t.* to knock, to dash, All 's Well i. 3. 60; Ham. v. 1. 82.

JUDICIOUS, *adj.* judicial, Coriol. v. 5. 128.

JUMP, *v.t.* to risk, Coriol. iii. 1. 153; Cymb. v. 4. 187; to agree, Twelfth Night, v. 1. 262; *adv.* just, exactly, Ham. v. 2. 389; Oth. ii. 3. 395.

JUSTICER, *sub.* a minister of justice, K. Lear, iii. 6. 24; Cymb. v. 5. 215.

KAM, *adj.* crooked, away from the point, Coriol. iii. 1. 302.

KECKSIES, *sub.* hemlock, and other hollow-stalked plants, Hen. V. v. 2. 52.

KEECH, *sub.* a roll of tallow, Hen. VIII. i. 1. 55.

KEEL, *v.t.* to cool, or perhaps to skim, L.'s L.'s L. v. 2. 928.

KEEP, *v.t.* to guard, Wint. Tale, ii. 1. 133; sub. keeping, custody, Tam. of Shrew, i. 2. 120; to dwell, Ham. ii. 1. 8.

KERN, *sub.* a light-armed Irish foot-soldier, Rich. II. ii. 1. 157; Macb. i. 2. 13.

KERSEY, *sub.* cheap woollen cloth, L.'s L.'s L. v. 2. 414.

KETTLE, *sub.* a kettle-drum, Ham. v. 2. 289.

KEY, *sub.* a tuning key, Temp. i. 2. 83.

KEY-COLD, *adj.* stone-cold, cold as a key, Rich. III. i. 2. 5; Lucrece, 1774.

KIBE, *sub.* a chilblain, Temp. ii. 1. 284; a chap on the heel, Ham. v. 1. 152.

KICK AT, *v.t.* to turn away from with loathing and disgust, Coriol. ii. 2. 129.

KICKSHAW, *sub.* a trifle, Twelfth Night, i. 3. 124; 2 Hen. IV. v. 1. 29.

KICKY-WICKY, *sub.* a ludicrous term for a wife, All 's Well, ii. 3. 297.

KILN-HOLE, *sub.* the fireplace of an oven or kiln, Merry Wives of W. iv. 2. 61; Wint. Tale, iv. 3. 247.

KINDLE, *v.i.* to bring forth young, As You Like It, iii. 2. 362; *v.t.* to incite to a thing, K. John, i. 1. 33.

KINDLESS, *adj.* unnatural, Ham. ii. 2. 617.

KISSING-COMFITS, *sub.* sugar-plums perfumed for sweetening the breath, Merry Wives of W. v. 5. 22.

KITCHEN, *v.t.* to entertain in the kitchen, Com. of Err. v. 1. 418.

KNACK, *sub.* a toy, or pretty trifle, Mid. N. Dr. i. 1. 34; Wint. Tale, iv. 3. 361.

KNAP, *v.t.* to snap or break short; to hit or rap smartly, Mer. of Ven. iii. 1. 10; K. Lear, ii. 4. 125.

KNOT-GRASS, *sub.* a herb supposed to have the power of checking growth, Mid. N. Dr. iii. 2. 329.

KNOT-PATED, *adj.* thick-headed, 1 Hen. IV. ii. 4. 79.

LABOURSOME, *adj.* elaborate, Ham. i. 2. 59; Cymb. iii. 4. 167.

LACED, *pt.p.* adorned, embellished, Macb. ii. 3. 119; Cymb. ii. 2. 22.

LACED MUTTON, *sub.* a prostitute, Two Gent. i. 1. 102.

LADE, *v.t.* to empty, to drain, 3 Hen. VI. iii. 2. 139.

LADY-SMOCK, *sub.* the plant *Cardamine pratensis,* L.'s L.'s L. v. 2. 903.

LAG, *sub.* a fragment, thing left, Cymb. v. 3. 92; the lowest class, Tim. of Ath. iii. 6. 91.

LAG END, the last part, the fag end, Hen. VIII. i. 3. 35.

LAID, *pt.p.* waylaid, 'the country is laid' = set on its guard to arrest, 2 Hen. IV. iv. 10. 4.

LAMPASS, *sub.* a disease in a horse's palate, Tam. of Shrew, iii. 2. 53.

LAND, *sub.* lawn Temp. iv. 1. 130; L.'s L.'s L. v. 2. 310.

LAND-DAMN, *v.t.* corrupt word in Wint. Tale, ii. 1. 142.

LANK, *v.i.* to shrink, Ant. & Cleo. i. 4. 71.

LANTERN, *or* LANTHORN, *sub.* a louvre, a window-turret, Rom. & Jul. v. 3. 84.

LAP, *v.t.* to wrap up, Macb. i. 2. 55; Cymb. v. 5. 361.

LAPSED, *pt.p.* surprised, Twelfth Night, iii. 3. 36.

LARD, *v.t.* to ornament, Ham. iv. 5. 38.

LATCH, *v.t.* to catch, lay hold of, Macb. iv. 3. 195; Son. cxiii. 6; to close, or, perhaps, to smear over, Mid. N. Dr. iii. 2. 36.

LATTEN, *adj.* a mixed metal, Merry Wives of W. i. 1. 167.

LAUND, *sub.* lawn, wood opening, 3 Hen. VI. iii. 1. 2. *Comp.* LAND.

LAUNDER, *v.t.* to wash, Lov. Comp. 17.

LAVOLT, *sub.* a kind of waltz, Troil. & Cres. iv. 4. 86.

LEADING, *sub.* the power of leading, generalship, 1 Hen. IV. iv. 3. 17.

LEAGUER, *sub.* a camp, All 's Well, iii. 6. 27.

LEASH, *sub.* a set of three, from the string or thong for leading greyhounds, to which usually three dogs were coupled, 1 Hen. IV. ii. 4. 7.

LEATHER-COAT, *sub.* a kind of apple, the golden russeting, 2 Hen. IV. v. 3. 42.

LEER, *sub.* complexion, colour, As You Like It, iv. 1. 69; Tit. Andr. iv. 2. 120.

LEESE, *v.t.* to lose, Sonnets, v. 14.

LEET, *sub.* a manor court, Tam. of Shrew, Ind. ii. 89, Oth. ii. 3.

LEG, *sub.* a bow, Coriol. ii. 1. 78; Tim. of Ath. i. 2. 241.

LEGERITY, *sub.* lightness, nimbleness, Hen. V. iv. 1. 23.

LEIGER, *sub.* a resident ambassador, Meas. for Meas. iii. 1. 57; Cymb. i. 5. 80.

LENTEN, *adj.* sparing, meagre, Ham. ii. 2. 337; Twelfth Night, i. 5. 9.

LIBERAL, *adj.* licentious, Much Ado, iv. 1. 93; Ham. iv. 7. 171; Oth. ii. 1. 164.

LIBERTY, *sub.* licentiousness, Tim. of Ath. iv. 1. 25; Ham. ii. 1. 32.

LIFTER, *sub.* a thief, Troil. & Cres. i. 2. 127.

LIGHT O' LOVE, *sub.* the name of a tune, Two Gent. i. 2. 80; Much Ado, iii. 4. 44.

LIMBECK, *sub.* an alembic, Macb. i. 7. 67; Son. cxix. 2.

LIMB-MEAL, *adv.* limb by limb, Cymb. ii. 4. 147.

LIMBO, *sub.* the edge or border of hell, All 's Well, v. 3. 264; Tit. Andr. iii. 1. 150.

LIME, *v.t.* to put lime into liquor, Merry Wives of W. i. 3. 14.

LIMIT, *v.t.* to appoint, Meas. for Meas. iv. 2. 175; Macb. ii. 3. 58.

LIMN, *v.t.* to draw in colours, As You Like It, ii. 7. 197.

LINE, *v.t.* to draw, delineate, As You Like It, iii. 2. 98; to strengthen, 1 Hen. IV. ii. 3. 88; Macb. i. 3. 112.

LINE-GROVE, *sub.* probably a grove of lime trees, Temp. v. 1. 10.

LINK, *sub.* a torch, Tam. of Shrew, iv. 1. 137.

LINSEY-WOOLSEY, *sub.* gibberish, jargon, All 's Well, iv. 1,13.

LINSTOCK, *sub.* the stick for holding a gunner's match, Hen. V. iii. Chorus, 33.

LIP, *v.t.* to kiss, Oth. iv. 1. 72; Ant. & Cleo. ii. 5. 30.

LIPSBURY PINFOLD, to have one in; a difficult expression, perhaps to have one between the teeth, K. Lear, ii. 2. 9.

LIQUOR, *v.t.* to moisten with oil, 1 Hen. IV. ii. 1. 94.

LIST, *sub.* wish, desire, Oth. ii. 1. 104; *v.i.* to desire, Ven. & Adon. 564; to attend to, Tam. of Shrew, ii. 1. 357.

LITHER, *adj.* yielding, flexible, 1 Hen. VI. iv. 7. 21.

LITIGIOUS, *adj.* doubtful, precarious, Per. iii. 3. 3.

LITTLE, IN, in miniature, As You Like It, iii. 2. 149; Ham. ii. 2. 392.

LOB, *sub.* a lubber, a heavy fellow, Mid. N. Dr. ii. 1. 16; *v.t.* to hang down, to droop, Hen. V. iv. 2. 47.

LOCKRAM, *sub.* a cheap kind of linen, Coriol. ii. 1. 228.

LODE-STAR, *sub.* the pole-star, Mid. N. Dr. i. 1. 183; Lucrece, 179.

LODGED, *pt.p.* laid flat as corn is by wind and rain, Rich. II. iii. 3. 162; Macb. iv. 1. 55.

LOGGATS, *sub.* a rustic game, something like bowls, Ham. v. 1. 99.

LONG OF, on account of, Mid. N. Dr. iii. 2. 339; Cymb v. 5. 272.

LOOF, *v.t.* to luff, bring close to the wind, Ant. & Cleo. iii. 8. 27.

LOON, *sub.* a base fellow, Macb. v. 3. 11.

LOOPED, *adj.* full of holes, K. Lear, iii. 4. 31.

LOOSE, *sub.* the discharge of an arrow, L.'s L.'s L. v. 2. 750; *v.t.* to let loose, discharge as an arrow, Hen. VIII. v. 4. 60.

LORD'S TOKENS, *sub.* plague spots, L.'s L.'s L. v. 2. 424.

LOTS TO BLANKS, 'any odds,' Coriol. v. 2. 10.

LOUTED, *pt.p.* made a fool of, 1 Hen. VI. iv. 3. 13.

LOVE-DAY, *sub.* a day for the amicable settlement of differences, Tit. Andr. i. 1. 491.

LOVES, OF ALL, for the sake of everything lovely, an adjuration, Merry Wives of W. ii. 2. 119.

LOWN, *sub.* a base fellow, Oth. ii. 3. 96; Per. iv. 6. 19. [*Comp.* LOON.]

LOZEL, *sub.* a worthless fellow, Wint. Tale, ii. 3. 108.

LUCE, *sub.* a pike, Merry Wives of W. i. 1. 17.

LUMPISH, *adj.* dull, heavy, Two Gent. iii. 2. 62.

LUNES, *sub.* freaks of madness, Merry Wives of W. iv. 2. 22 [Fol. LINES]; Wint. Tale, ii. 2. 30.

LURCH, *v.i.* to skulk, Merry Wives of W. ii. 2. 27; to win with great ease, a phrase used at cards, Coriol. ii. 2. 106.

LURE, *sub.* apparatus used by falconers to recall their hawks, Tam. of Shrew, iv. 1. 195; the whistle or call to allure the hawk, Ven. & Ad. 1027; *v.i.* to call, allure a hawk, Rom. & Jul. ii. 2. 159.

LUSH, *adj.* luxuriant, Temp. ii. 1. 55.

LUSTIG, *adj. lustig* is Dutch for merry or cheerful, All 's Well, ii. 3. 47.

LUXURIOUS, *adj.* lascivious, Much Ado, iv. 1. 41; Hen. V. iv. 4. 20.

LUXURY, *sub.* lust, Merry Wives of W. v. 5. 100; Troil. & Cres. v. 2. 53.

LYM, *sub.* a bloodhound, so called because he was held by a lym or leash, K. Lear, iii. 6. 72.

MACULATE, *adj.* stained, impure, L.'s L.'s L. i. 2. 98.

MACULATION, *sub.* stain, the spot of guilt, Troil. & Cres. iv. 4. 64.

MAD, *adj.* wild, untrained, 1 Hen. VI. v. 3. 191.

MADE, *pt.p.* fastened, Com. of Err. iii. 1. 93.

MAGGOT-PIE, *sub.* a magpie, Macb. iii. 4. 125.

MAGNIFICO, *sub.* the title of a Venetian grandee, Mer. of Ven. iii. 2. 281; Oth. i. 2. 12.

MAID MARIAN, a character in the morris-dance, 1 Hen. IV. iii. 3. 128.

MAILED UP, wrapped up, a hawking term, 2 Hen. VI. ii. 4. 31; to mail a hawk was to pinion her, or fasten her wings with a girdle.

MAIN, *sub.* a hand at dice, 1 Hen. IV. iv. 1. 47; the mainland, K. Lear, iii. 1. 6.

MAIN-COURSE, *sub.* a mainsail, Temp. i. 1. 40.

MAINED, *pt.p.* maimed, 2 Hen. VI. iv. 2. 176.

MAKELESS, *adj.* mateless, widowed, Sonnets, ix. 4.

MALKIN, *sub.* a kitchen slut, Coriol. ii. 1. 227.

MALL, *sub.* Mary, Temp. ii. 2. 51; 'Mistress Mall's picture', improbably explained as referring to the picture of the notorious Mary Firth, or Mall Cut-purse, Twelfth Night, i. 3. 137.

MALLARD, *sub.* a wild drake, Ant. & Cleo. iii. 8. 29.

MALLECHO, *sub.* mischief [perhaps Span. *malhecho*], Ham. iii. 2. 148.

MALT-WORM, *sub.* a tippler of ale, 1 Hen. IV. ii. 1. 83; 2 Hen. IV. ii. 4. 366.

MAMMER, *v.i.* to hesitate, Oth. iii. 3. 70 (perhaps to mutter in hesitation).

MAMMET, *sub.* a doll, 1 Hen. IV. ii. 3. 97; Rom. & Jul. iii. 5. 186. Some have suggested *breasts* as its meaning in the first passage.

MAMMOCK, *v.t.* tear in fragments, Coriol. i. 3. 71.

MAN, *v.t.* to tame a hawk, Tam. of Shrew, iv. 1. 196; to direct, to aim, Oth. v. 2. 269.

MANAGE, *sub.* taming of a horse, Temp. i. 2. 70; As You Like It, i. 1. 13; Rich. II. iii. 3. 179; *v.t.* to train, break in a horse, Ven. & Ad. 598.

MANDRAGORA, *sub.* mandrake, Oth. iii. 3. 331; Ant. & Cleo. i. 5. 4.

MANDRAKE, *sub.* the plant *Atropa Mandragora*, the root of which was supposed to bear human shape, and to shriek when pulled out of the ground, causing madness or death to the hearer, 2 Hen. IV. i. 2. 16; 2 Hen. VI. iii. 2. 310; Rom. & Jul. iv. 3. 48.

MANKIND, *adj.* masculine, applied to a woman, Wint. Tale, ii. 3. 67; Coriol. iv. 2. 16.

MANNED, *pt.p.* furnished with a servant, 2 Hen. IV. i. 2. 18, 59.

MANNER, TO BE TAKEN WITH THE, to be caught in the act, L.'s L.'s L. i. 1. 202; Wint. Tale, iv. 3. 775; 1 Hen. IV. ii. 4. 226.

MAN-QUELLER, *sub.* a murderer, 2 Hen. IV. ii. 1. 60.

MANURE, *v.t.* to cultivate, Oth. i. 3. 329.

MAPPERY, *sub.* the study of maps, theory as opposed to real practice in warfare, Troil. & Cres. i. 3. 205.

MARBLED, *adj.* like marble, everlasting, Tim. of Ath. iv. 3. 192.

MARCHPANE, *sub.* confectionery made of a paste of pounded almonds formed into cakes, Rom. & Jul. i. 5. 9.

MARE, *sub.* the nightmare, 2 Hen. IV. ii. 1. 86; 'to ride the wild mare'= to play at see-saw, 2 Hen. IV. ii. 4. 268.

MARK, *sub.* God bless or save the mark = saving your favour, 1 Hen. IV. i. 3. 56; Oth. i. 1. 33.

MARTIAL, *adj.* like Mars, Cymb. iv. 2. 310.

MARTLEMAS, *sub.* 11th of November, supposed to be a time of fair weather, applied to a hale old man, 2 Hen. IV. ii. 2. 112.

MARY-BUDS, *sub.* flowers of the marigold, Cymb. ii. 3. 26.

MASHED, *pt.p.* mixed or beaten into a confused mass, Tit. Andr. iii. 2. 38.

MATE, *v.t.* to confound, to paralyse, Macb. v. 1. 85; Ven. & Ad. 909; 2 Hen. VI. iii. 1. 265; to cope with, to match, Hen. VIII. iii. 2. 275.

MAUGRE, *prep.* in spite of, Twelfth Night, iii. 1. 165; K. Lear, v. 3. 133.

MAUND, *sub.* a basket, Lov. Comp. 36.

MAZZARD, *sub.* a head, Ham. v. 1. 95; Oth. ii. 3. 157.

MEACOCK, *adj.* spiritless, henpecked, Tam. of Shrew, ii. 1. 307.

MEALED, *pt.p.* mingled, Meas. for Meas. iv. 2. 86.

MEAN, *sub.* an intermediate part (alto or tenor) between the treble and bass, Two Gent. of Ver. i. 2. 92; L.'s L.'s L. v. 2. 329; Wint. Tale, iv. 2. 46; poor, humble, Com. of Err. i. 1. 54.

MECHANICAL, *sub.* a handicraftsman, Mid. N. Dr. iii. 2. 9; Jul. Cæs. i. 1. 3.

MEDICINE, *sub.* a physician, All's Well, ii. 1. 75; Macb. v. 2. 27.

MEINY, *sub.* household, attendants, K. Lear, ii. 4. 35.

MELL, *v.i.* to meddle, All's Well, iv. 3. 258.

MERCHANT, *sub.* a fellow, a chap [Ital. *mercatante*], 1 Hen. VI. ii. 3. 57; Tam. of Shrew, iv. 2. 63; Rom. & Jul. ii. 4. 154.

MERE, *adj.* entire, absolute, Oth. ii. 2. 3; Troil. & Cres. i. 3. 111; *adv.* All's Well, iii. 5. 55.

MERED, *adj.* only, entire, Ant. & Cleo. iii. 11. 10.

MERELY, *adv.* entirely, Ham. i. 2. 137.

MESS, *sub.* a set of four, L.'s L.'s L. v. 3. 207; v. 2. 362; 3 Hen. VI. i. 4. 73; a small quantity or fragment, 2 Hen. IV. ii. 1. 106; Oth. iv. 1. 210.

METAPHYSICAL, *adj.* supernatural, Macb. i. 5. 30.

MEW, *v.t.* to pen up, to imprison, Mid. N. Dr. i. 1. 71; Rom. & Jul. iii. 4. 11.

MEW! an interjection of contempt, K. Lear, iv. 2. 68.

MICHER, *sub.* a truant, 1 Hen. IV. ii. 4. 455.

MICHING, *adj.* sneaking, lurking, Ham. iii. 2. 148.

MIDDLE-EARTH, *sub.* the world, Merry Wives of W. v. 5. 86.

MILCH, *adj.* moist, shedding tears, Ham. ii. 2. 548.

MILLINER, *sub.* a man dealing in fancy articles, Wint. Tale, iv. 4. 192; 1 Hen. IV. i. 3. 36.

MILL-SIXPENCE, *sub.* coin that first had milled edge [1561], Merry Wives of W. i. 1. 160.

MILLSTONES, TO WEEP [proverbial], not to weep at all, Rich. III. i. 3. 353; i. 4. 249.

MIND, *sub.* 'put in mind of'= informed, Oth. ii. 3. 138.

MINE, *v.t.* to undermine, to sap, As You Like It, i. 1. 22; Ham. iii. 4. 148.

MINERAL, *sub.* a mine, Ham. iv. 1. 26; a poisonous drug, Oth. i. 2. 74; Cymb. v. 5. 50.

MINIKIN, *adj.* small, pretty, K. Lear, iii. 6. 46.

MINIMUS, *sub.* anything very small, Mid. N. Dr. iii. 2. 329.

MINUTE-JACKS, *sub.* time-servers, Tim. of Ath. iii. 6. 108.

MIRE, *v.i.* to sink as in the mud, Tim. of Ath. iv. 3. 148.

MISER, *sub.* a miserable wretch, 1 Hen. VI. v. 4. 7.

MISPRISED, *adj.* mistaken, Mid. N. Dr. iii. 2. 74.

MISPRISION, *sub.* contempt, mistake, Much Ado, iv. 1. 187.

MISS, *adv.* misconduct, Ven. & Adon. 53.

MISSINGLY, *adv.* with regret, Wint. Tale, iv. 1. 34.

MISSIVE, *sub.* a messenger, Macb. i. 5. 7; Ant. & Cleo. ii. 2. 78.

MIST, *v.t.* to throw a mist upon anything, K. Lear, v. 3. 264.

MISTRESS, *sub.* the jack at the game of bowls, Troil. & Cres. iii. 2. 50.

MOBLED, *pt.p.* having the head closely wrapped up, Ham. ii. 2. 533.

MODERN, *adj.* trite, commonplace, Macb. iv. 3. 170; Oth. i. 3. 109.

MOLDWARP, *sub.* a mole, 1 Hen. IV. iii. 1. 148.

MOME, *sub.* a blockhead, Com. of Err. iii. 1. 32.

MOMENTANY, *adj.* momentary, instantaneous, Mid. N. Dr. i. 1. 143.

MONARCHO, *sub.* name of a crazy Italian, living in London about 1580, who professed to be monarch of the world, L.'s L.'s L. iv. 1. 102.

MONTANT, *sub.* a fencing term, an upward thrust, Merry Wives of W. ii. 3. 27. [*Comp.* 'Mountanto' applied to Benedick in 'Much Ado about Nothing', i. 1. 30].

MONUMENTAL, *adj.* ancestral, memorial, All's Well, iv. 3. 20; Troil. & Cres. iii. 3. 153.

MOOD, *sub.* fit of passion, Two Gent. iv. 1. 51; Rom. & Jul. iii. 1. 13.

MOONISH, *adj.* unconstant, As You Like It, iii. 2. 436.

MOP, *sub.* a grimace, Temp. iv. 1. 47.

MOPPING, *pr.p.* making grimaces, K. Lear, iv. 1. 62.

MORISCO, *sub.* a Morris-dancer, 2 Hen. VI. iii. 1. 365.

MORRIS-PIKE, *sub.* a Moorish pike, Com. of Err. iv. 3. 27

MORT, *sub.* a set of notes sounded at the death of the deer, Wint. Tale, i. 2. 119.

MORTAL, *adj.* deadly, causing death, Com. of Err. i. 1. 11; 2 Hen. VI. iii. 2. 263; Lucrece, 364; perhaps = abounding, excessive; according to some, human, As You Like It, ii. 4. 55.

MOTHER, *sub.* the disease *hysterica passio*, K. Lear, ii. 4. 56.

MOTION, *sub.* a puppet-show, Wint. Tale, iv. 2. 104; Lucrece, 1326; a puppet, Meas. for Meas. iii. 2. 121.

MOTIVE, *sub.* a mover, author, Tim. of Ath. v. 4. 27; Oth. iv. 2. 42.

MOTLEY, *adj.* the particoloured dress of a fool, As You Like It, ii. 7. 13; *sub.* a fool, As You Like It, iii. 3. 84; Sonnets, cx. 2.

MOULD, *sub.* 'men of mould' = earth-born men, Hen. V. iii. 2. 24.

MOULTEN, *adj.* without feathers, 1 Hen. IV. iii. 1. 151.

MOUNTANT, *adj.* lifted up, Tim. of Ath. iv. 3. 136.

MOUSE, *sub.* a term of endearment, Twelfth Night, i. 5. 68; L.'s L.'s L. v. 2. 19.

MOUSE, *v.t.* to tear in pieces, K. John, ii. 1. 354.

MOW, *sub.* a grimace, Temp. iv. 1. 47.

MOY, *sub.* imaginary name of a coin, evolved from a misunderstanding of French *moy*, Hen. V. iv. 4. 14.

MULLED, *adj.* insipid, flat, Coriol. iv. 5. 240.

MURAL [O. Ed. MORAL], *sub.* perhaps wall, Mid. N. Dr. v. 1. 210 (? read 'wall').

MURDERING-PIECE, *sub.* a cannon loaded with chain shot, Ham. iv. 5. 95.

MURE, *sub.* a wall, 2 Hen. IV. iv. 4. 119.

MURRION, *adj.* infected with the murrain, Mid. N. Dr. ii. 1. 97.

MUSCADEL, *sub.* a sweet wine, Tam. of Shrew, iii. 2. 175.

MUSET, *sub.* a gap in a hedge or thicket through which a hare is accustomed to pass, Ven. & Adon. 683.

MUSS, *sub.* a scramble, Ant. & Cleo. iii. 11. 91.

MUTINE, *v.i.* to mutiny, to rebel, Ham. iii. 4. 83.

MUTINES, *sub.* mutineers, K. John, ii. 1. 378; Ham. v. 2. 6.

NAYWARD, TO THE, in the negative direction, towards denial or disbelief, Wint. Tale, ii. 1. 63.

NAYWORD, *sub.* a byword, Twelfth Night, ii. 3. 147; a watchword, word of intelligence, Merry Wives of W. ii. 2. 132; v. 2. 5.

NEAF, *sub.* a fist, Mid. N. Dr. iv. 1. 20. *Comp.* NEIF.

NEAR, *adj.* nearer, Macb. ii. 3. 147; Rich. II. iii. 2. 64; v. 1. 88.

NEAR-LEGGED, *adj.* knock-kneed, Tam. of Shrew, iii. 2. 58.

NEAT, *adj.* foppish, 1 Hen. IV. i. 3. 33; K. Lear, ii. 2. 45.

NEB, *sub.* bill or beak, Wint. Tale, i. 2. 183.

NECESSITIED, *pt.p.* so poor as to urgently need, All's Well, v. 3. 85.

NEEDFUL, *adj.* wanting supplies, 3 Hen. VI. ii. 1. 147.

NEEDLY *adj.* absolutely, Rom. & Jul. iii. 2. 117.

NEELD, *sub.* needle, Per. Prol. iv 23; Mid. N. Dr. iii. 2. 204.

NEEZE, *v.i.* to sneeze, Mid. N. Dr. ii. 1. 56.

NEIF, *sub.* a fist, 2 Hen. IV. ii. 4. 199.

NEPHEW, *sub.* grandchild, Oth. i. 1. 112.

NETHER-STOCKS, *sub.* stockings, 1 Hen. IV. ii. 4. 132.

NICE, *adj.* scrupulous, Two Gent. of Ver. iii. 1. 82; Mer. of Ven. i. 1. 14; trivial, Rom. & Jul. iii. 1. 160; Jul. Cæs. iv. 3. 8; 'makes nice of no vile hold' = is not prudish with respect of &c., K. John, iii. 4. 138.

NICENESS, NICETY, *sub.* coyness, Meas. for Meas. ii. 4. 163; Cymb. iii. 4. 158.

NICHOLAS' CLERKS, ST., highwaymen, 1 Hen. IV. ii. 1. 67 St. Nicholas was also patron of scholars, Two Gent. of Ver. iii. 1. 303.

NIECE, *sub.* granddaughter, Rich. III. iv. 1. 1.

NIGHT-CROW, *sub.* the night-heron, *Ardea nycticorax*, or according to some, the owl; according to others, the night-jar, 3 Hen. VI. v. 6. 45.

NIGHTED, *adj.* dark, K. Lear, iv. 5. 13.

NIGHT-RULE, *sub.* revelry, nightly diversion, Mid. N. Dr. iii. 2. 5.

NILL, will not, Tam. of Shrew, ii. 1. 265; Ham. v. 1. 18.

NINE-FOLD, *sub.* explained 'nine foals', or 'nine familiars', K. Lear, iii. 4. 124.

NINE MEN'S MORRIS, a sort of game played with stones on figures cut in the green turf, Mid. N. Dr. ii. 1. 98. 'Morris' is a corruption of *merrils* [Fr. *merelles*]. '*Le jeu des merelles*, the boyish game called merills, or five-penny morris, played here most commonly with stones, but in France with pawns, ... and termed *merelles*.'—Cotgrave, Fr. Dic.

NINNY, *sub.* a fool, Temp. iii. 2. 73.

NOD, GIVE YOU THE, a term in the game of cards called 'Noddy', Troil. & Cres. i. 2. 209.

NODDY, *sub.* a simpleton, Two Gent. of Ver. i. 1. 120.

NOISE, *sub.* music, Temp. iii. 2. 147; a company of musicians, 2 Hen. IV. ii. 4. 13.

NOOK-SHOTTEN, *adj.* running out into numerous angles or corners, shooting out into capes and necks of land, Hen. V. iii. 5. 14. *Comp.* Cymb. iii. 4. 140, 141.

NOTE, *sub.* stigma, mark of reproach, Rich. II. i. 1. 43.

NOTED, *pt.p.* marked with a stigma, disgraced, Jul. Cæs. iv. 3. 2.

NOUSLE, *v.t.* to nourish delicately, Per. i. 4. 42.

NOVUM, *sub.* a game of dice, L.'s L'.s L. v. 2. 545.

NOWL, *sub.* the head, Mid. N. Dr. iii. 2. 17.

NUMBERED, *part. adj.* having full numbers, richly stored with, Cymb. i. 6. 36.

NUTHOOK, *sub.* a catchpole, Merry Wives of W. i. 1. 173; 2 Hen. IV. v. 4. 8.

NUZZLING, *pr.p.* pushing with the nose, nosing, Ven. & Adon. 1115.

O, *sub.* anything round, Mid. N. Dr. iii. 2. 188; Ant. & Cleo. v. 2. 81; perhaps pit, Hen. V. Chor. 13.

OBSEQUIOUS, *adj.* connected with obsequies, funeral, Tit. Andr. v. 3. 152; Ham. i. 2. 92.

OBSEQUIOUSLY, *adv.* as becomes a funeral, Rich. III. i. 2. 3.

OBSTRUCT, *sub.* an obstacle, Ant. & Cleo. iii. 6. 61.

OCCULTED, *adj.* hidden, Ham. iii. 2. 85.

ODD-EVEN, *sub.* perhaps the interval between twelve at night and one in the morning, Oth. i. 1. 124.

ŒILIADES, *sub.* amorous glances, Merry Wives of W. i. 3. 66; K. Lear, v. 5. 25.

O'ER-CROW, *v.t.* to overcome, Ham. v. 2. 367.

O'ERGROWN, *pt.p.* having long locks, Cymb. iv. 4. 33.

O'ERLOOKED, *pt.p.* bewitched, Mer. of Ven. iii. 2. 15; Merry Wives of W. v. 5. 89.

O'ER-PARTED, *pt.p.* having too difficult a part assigned to one, L.'s L.'s L. v. 2. 585.

O'ER-RAUGHT, *pt.t.* overtook, Ham. iii. 1. 17; *pt.p.* swindled, Com. of Err. i. 2. 96.

O'ER-SIZED, *pt.p.* smeared over as with size, Ham. ii. 2. 493.

OFF-CAP, *v.t.* to take the cap off, Oth. i. 1. 10.

OFFICED, *pt.p.* holding a certain position, Wint. Tale, i. 2. 172; having a certain function, Oth. i. 3. 272.

OFFICES, *sub.* servants' apartments in a great house, Rich. II. i. 2. 69; Macb. ii. 1. 14.

OLD, *adj.* wold, K. Lear, iii. 4. 123.

OLD, *adj.* abundant, plentiful, great, Merry Wives of W. iv. 2. 22; Troil. & Cres. i. 2. 126; Rom. & Jul. iii. 3. 93; Macb. ii. 3. 2.

ON, *prep.* of, Mer. of Ven. ii. 6. 67; Wint. Tale, ii. 2. 31; Macb. v. 1. 74; Ham. iii. 1. 180.

ONEYERS, *sub.* unexplained, 1 Hen. IV. ii. 1. 85.

OPEN, *v.i.* to give tongue, to bark on the scent, Merry Wives of W. iv. 2. 213.

OPERANT, *adj.* active, Tim. of Ath. iv. 3. 25; Ham. iii. 2. 186.

OR, *adv.* before, Cymb. ii. 4. 14.

ORGULOUS, *adj.* proud [Fr. *orgueilleux*], Troil. & Cres. i. Prol. 2.

ORT, *sub.* leaving, refuse, Troil. & Cres. v. 2. 155; Jul. Cæs. iv. 1. 37; Lucrece, 985.

OUGHT, *v.t.* owed, 1 Hen. IV. iii. 3. 151.

OUPHES, *sub.* goblins, Merry Wives of W. iv. 3. 51; v. 5. 63.

OUTFACE, *v.t.* to put out of countenance, Mer. of Ven. iv. 2. 17.

OUT-PEER, *v.t.* surpass, Cymb. iii. 6. 86.

OUT-VIED, *pt.p.* beaten by a higher card, Tam. of Shrew, ii. 1. 379.

OVERBUY, *v.t.* to pay too much for, Cymb. i. 1. 146.

OVER-SCUTCHED, *part. adj.* worn out, 2 Hen. IV. iii. 2. 344.

OVERSEEN, *pt.p.* bewitched, Lucrece, 1206.

OVERSHOT, *pt.p.* put to shame, L.'s L.'s L. i. 1. 141; Hen. V. iii. 7. 139. Perhaps, quibbling with the sense, tipsy.

OVERTURE, *sub.* disclosure, Wint. Tale, ii. 1. 171; K. Lear, iii. 7. 89; declaration, Twelfth Night, i. 5. 226.

OWCHES, *sub.* ornaments, 2 Hen. IV. ii. 4. 52.

OWE, *v.t.* to own, to possess, Temp. i. 2. 404; Rich. II. iv. 1. 185.

OYES, *int.* 'hear ye!' the public crier's word [Fr. *oyez*], Merry Wives of W. v. 5. 47; Troil. & Cres. iv. 5. 142.

PACK, *v.t.* to plot, to shuffle cards unfairly, Tit. Andr. iv. 2. 157; Ant. & Cleo. iv. 12. 19; *sub.* a confederacy, Merry Wives of W. iv. 2. 126.

PACKING, *sub.* plotting, K. Lear, iii. 1. 26.

PADDOCK, *sub.* a toad, Ham. iii. 4. 190; a familiar spirit like a toad, Macb. i. 1. 9.

PAID, *pt.p.* perhaps drunk, Cymb. v. 4. 165.

PAINFUL, *adj.* laborious, Temp. iii. 1. 1; Sonnets, xxv. 9.

PAINTED CLOTH, cloth or canvas hangings, painted with figures and sentences, As You Like It, iii. 2. 291; Troil. & Cres. v. 10. 46.

PAJOCK, *sub.* some term of contempt, explained 'peacock', which is doubtful, Ham. iii. 2. 300. 'Some in Leinster and Ulster are ... grown to be as very patchcockes as the wild Irish' (Spenser, 'A View of the State of Ireland'. Grosart, vol. ix, p. 104, ed. 1882).

PALABRAS, *sub.* words [Span.], Much Ado, iii. 5. 18; 'paucas pallabris' (Sly) = pocas palabras [Span.], few words, Tam. of Shrew, Ind. i. 5.

PALED, *adj.* pale, Lov. Comp. 198.

PALL, *v.t.* to wrap one's self up, Macb. i. 5. 52.

PALLIAMENT, *sub.* a robe, Tit. Andr. i. 1. 182.

PALMY, *adj.* victorious, Ham. i. 1. 113.

PANTALOON, *sub.* an old fool, taken from the Italian comedy, As You Like It, ii. 7. 158; Tam. of Shrew, iii. 1. 37.

PANTLER, *sub.* a servant in charge of the pantry, Wint. Tale, iv. 3. 56.

'PARITOR, *sub.* apparitor, an officer in the bishop's court, L.'s L.'s L. iii. 1. 196.

PARLOUS, *adj.* a vulgar corruption of perilous = mischievous, alarming, As You Like It, iii. 2. 46.

PARMACETI, *sub.* spermaceti, 1 Hen. IV. i. 3. 58.

PART, *v.t.* to quit, to leave, Rich. II. iii. 1. 3; Per. v. 3. 38.

PARTED, *pt.p.* gifted, Troil. & Cres. iii. 3. 96.

PARTIAL, *adj.* 'a partial slander' = the reproach of partiality, Rich. II. i. 3. 241.

PARTI-COATED, *adj.* having a coat of various colours, L.'s L.'s L. v. 2. 774.

PARTLET, *sub.* the name for the hen in *Reynard the Fox*, so called from her ruff, Wint. Tale, ii. 3. 75; 1 Hen. IV. iii. 3. 60.

PASH, *sub.* the head, Wint. Tale, i. 2. 129; *v.t.* to beat, Troil. & Cres. ii. 3. 217; *part. adj.* v. 5. 10.

PASS, *v.t.* to die, K. Lear, v. 3. 315; 2 Hen. VI. iii. 3. 25; *v.t.* to care for, regard, 2 Hen. VI. iv. 2. 140; to exceed bounds, Merry Wives of W. i. 1. 185; Troil. & Cres. i. 2. 180; to pass sentence on, Meas. for Meas. ii. 1. 19; *sub.* 'pass of pate' = sally of wit, Temp. iv. 1. 246.

PASSADO, *sub.* a term in fencing, L.'s L.'s L. i. 2. 188; Rom. & Jul. ii. 4. 27.

PASSES, *sub.* proceedings, Meas. for Meas. v. 1. 371.

PASSY-MEASURE, *sub.* a corruption of the Italian *passamezzo*, a slow and stately dance, Twelfth Night, v. 1. 208.

PATCH, *sub.* a fool, Temp. iii. 2. 73; Macb. v. 3. 15.

PATCHERY, *sub.* roguery, Troil. & Cres. ii. 3. 78; Tim. of Ath. v. 1. 101.

PATH, *v.i.* to walk, Jul. Cæs. ii. 1. 83.

PATINES, *sub.* metal plates, Mer. of Ven. v. 1. 59.

PAUNCH, *v.t.* rip up, Temp. iii. 2. 101.

PAVIN, *sub.* a stately dance, Twelfth Night, v. 1. 209.

PAX, *sub.* a small piece of metal offered to be kissed; but Pistol probably meant 'pix', a box which held the Host, Hen. V. iii. 6. 42.

PEACH, *v.t.* to accuse, turn king's evidence, 1 Hen. IV. ii. 2. 50.

PEACHES, *v.t.* betrays, Meas. for Meas. iv. 3. 12.

PEAK, *v.i.* to grow thin, Macb. i. 3. 23; to mope, Ham. ii. 2. 602.

PEAKING, *adj.* sneaking, Merry Wives of W. iii. 5. 73.

PEARL, *sub.* a cataract in the eye, Two Gent. of Ver. v. 2. 13 [quibbling].

PEARL, *sub.* 'kingdom's pearl' = fine youth, or perhaps choice nobility of the country, Macb. v. 7. 85.

PEAT, *sub.* a pet, a darling, Tam. of Shrew, i. 1. 78.

PECULIAR, *adj.* preserved, guarded, Meas. for Meas. i. 2. 96.

PEDANT, *sub.* a schoolmaster, L.'s L.'s L. iii. 1. 187; Tam. of Shrew, iii. 1. 88.

PEELED, *part. adj.* shaven, 1 Hen. VI. i. 3. 30.

PEER, *v.i.* to appear, Wint. Tale, iv. 3. 3; Ven. & Adon. 86.

PEEVISH, *adj.* silly, foolish, Twelfth Night, i. 5. 321; Rich. III. iv. 2. 96.

PEG, *v.t.* to wedge, Temp. i. 2. 295.

PEGS, *sub.* the pins of an instrument, Oth. ii. 1. 203.

PEISE, *v.t.* to make heavy and so retard, Mer. of Ven. iii. 2. 22; to poise, balance, K. John, ii. 1. 575 [peized] 'peise down' = to weigh down, Rich. III. v. 3. 106.

PELT, *v.i.* to chafe with anger, Lucrece, 1418.

PELTING, *adj.* paltry, Mid. N. Dr. ii. 1. 91; K. Lear, ii. 3. 18.

PENDULOUS, *adj.* impending, K. Lear, iii. 4. 66.

PENETRATIVE, *adj.* affecting the heart, Ant. & Cleo. iv. 12. 75.

PENSIONER, *sub.* gentleman pensioner, gentlemen in the personal service of the sovereign, Merry Wives of W. ii. 2. 81; Mid. N. Dr. ii. 1. 10.

PENSIVED, *adj.* pensive, Lov. Comp. 219.

PENT-HOUSE, *sub.* a shed standing aslope from the main building, Much Ado, iii. 3. 109; *fig.* the eyelid, Macb. i. 3. 20.

PERDU, *sub.* a soldier sent on a forlorn hope, K. Lear, iv. 7. 35.

PERFECT, *pt.p.* fully satisfied, Macb. iii. 4. 21; *adj.* certain, Wint. Tale, iii. 3. 1; Cymb. iii. 1. 73.

PERIAPTS, *sub.* amulets, 1 Hen. VI. v. 3. 2.

PERKED UP, dressed up, adorned, Hen. VIII. ii. 3. 21.

PERNICIOUSLY, *adv.* excessively, or else maliciously, Hen. VIII. ii. 1. 50.

PERPEND, *v.i.* to reflect, consider, Merry Wives of W. ii. 1. 117; Hen. V. iv. 4. 8.

PERSPECTIVELY, *adv.* as through a perspective, Hen. V. v. 2. 347.

PERSPECTIVES, *sub.* glasses cut so as to form an optical delusion, All's Well, v 3. 48; Twelfth Night, v. 1. 227.

PERT, *adj.* lively, L.'s L.'s L. v. 2. 273; Mid. N. Dr. i. 1. 13.

PERTTAUNT-LIKE, a word not yet explained, L.'s L.'s L. v. 2. 67.

PETAR, *sub.* an engine charged with powder to blow up gates, Ham. iii. 4. 207.

PETTISH, *adj.* capricious, Troil. & Cres. ii. 3. 140.

PETTITOES, *sub.* feet, *properly*, pigs' feet, Wint. Tale, iv. 3. 621.

PEW, *sub.* a seat, K. Lear, iii. 4. 53.

PEW-FELLOW, *sub.* companion, Rich. III. iv. 4. 58.

PHANTASIME, *sub.* a fantastical person, L.'s L.'s L. iv. 1. 102; v. 1. 20.

PHANTASMA, *sub.* a vision, Jul. Cæs. ii. 1. 65.

PHILIP AND JACOB, first of May, festival of St. Philip and St. James, Meas. for Meas. iii. 2. 218.

PHRASELESS, *adj.* indescribable, Lov. Comp. 225.

PHYSIC, *v.t.* to heal, to keep in health, Macb. i. 3. 55; Cymb. iii. 2. 34.

PHYSICAL, *adj.* wholesome, Coriol. i. 5. 18; Jul. Cæs. ii. 1. 261.

PIA MATER, the membrane that covers the brain, the brain itself, L.'s L.'s L. iv. 2. 71; Twelfth Night, i. 5. 122.

PICK [O. Ed. PECK], *v.t.* to pitch, Coriol. i. 1. 206; Hen. VIII. v. 4. 96.

PICKED, *adj.* refined, punctilious, L.'s L.'s L. v. 1. 14; K. John i. 1. 193; Ham. v. 1. 150.

PICK-THANKS, *sub.* officious fellows, 1 Hen. IV. iii. 2. 25.

PIECE, *sub.* excellent person, Temp. i. 2. 56; Per. iv. 6. 122; a vessel of wine, Troil. & Cres. iv. 1. 62; a coin, Coriol. iii. 3. 32; a work of art, a statue, Wint. Tale, v. 2. 107.

PIGHT, *pt.p.* pitched, ready, Troil. & Cres. v. 10. 24; K. Lear, ii. 1. 67.

PILCHER, *sub.* a scabbard, Rom. & Jul. iii. 1. 86.

PILL, *v.t.* to plunder, Rich. II. ii. 1. 247; Tim. of Ath. iv. 1. 12.

PIN, *sub.* bull's-eye, centre of a target, L.'s L.'s L. iv. 1. 140; Rom. & Jul. ii. 4. 15; 'a pin' in contempt, in answer to an excuse or evasion, Merry Wives of W. i. 1. 118; Troil. & Cres. v. 2. 21.

PIN AND WEB, a disease of the eye, Wint. Tale, i. 2. 291; comp. K. Lear, iii. 4. 120.

PIN-BUTTOCK, *sub.* narrow buttock, All's Well, ii. 2. 19.

PINFOLD, *sub.* the pound, Two Gent. of Ver. i. 1. 114; K. Lear, ii. 2. 9.

PINKED, *part. adj.* pierced with small holes, Hen. VIII. v. 4. 51.

PINK EYNE, small, or perhaps winking, half-shut eyes, Ant. & Cleo. ii. 7. 121.

PIONED, *p.p.* a doubtful word, 'covered with marsh marigold', or 'dug', Temp. iv. 1. 64.

PIP, *sub.* a spot on cards, Tam. of Shrew, i. 2. 33; 'a pip out' = intoxicated, with reference to a game called 'one-and-thirty', Tam. of Shrew, i. 2. 33.

PIPE-WINE, *sub.* wine from the butt, playing on the other meaning of pipe, Merry Wives of W. iii. 2. 94.

PITCH, *sub.* the height which a falcon soars, Rich. II. i. 1. 109; 2 Hen. VI. ii. 1. 6.

PLACKET, *sub.* opening in a petticoat, or a petticoat, Wint. Tale, iv. 4. 624; K. Lear, iii. 4. 97.

PLAIN, *adj.* mere, nothing else but, Temp. v. 1. 266; K. John, ii. 1. 462; *v.i.* to complain, K. Lear, iii. 1. 39.

PLAIN-SONG, *sub.* the plain melody without variations, Hen. V. iii. 2. 7; Hen. VIII. i. 3. 45.

PLAITS, *sub.* folds, Lucrece, 93.

PLANCHED, *adj.* made of planks, Meas. for Meas. iv. 1. 32.

PLANT, *sub.* the sole of the foot, Ant. & Cleo. ii. 7. 2.

PLANTAGE, *sub.* plants, vegetation, Troil. & Cres. iii. 2. 184.

PLASH, *sub.* a pool, Tam. of Shrew, i. 1. 23.

PLATE, *sub.* a piece of money, Ant. & Cleo. v. 2. 92.

PLATFORMS, *sub.* plans, schemes, 1 Hen. VI. ii. 1. 77.

PLAUSIBLY, *adv.* willingly, or by acclamation, Lucrece, 1854.

PLAUSIVE, *adj.* pleasing, All's Well, i. 2. 53; Ham. i. 4. 30.

PLEACHED, *adj.* folded, interwoven, Much Ado, iii. 1. 7; Ant. & Cleo. iv. 12. 73.

PLIGHTED, *pt.p.* doubtful, intricate, K. Lear, i. 1. 283.

PLUME UP, *v.t.* prank up, to make to triumph, Oth. i. 3. 399.

PLURISY, *sub.* superabundance, Ham. iv. 7. 117.

POINT, *sub.* a signal given by blast of trumpet, 2 Hen. IV. iv. 1. 52; Coriol. iv. 6. 126.

POINT, AT, on the point, Coriol. iii. 1. 193; K. Lear, iii. 1. 33.

POINT, AT A, fully prepared, Macb. iv. 3.135; Ham. i.2. 200.

POINT-DEVISE, *adj.* affectedly nice, finical, L.'s L.'s L. v. 1. 21; *adv.* Twelfth Night, ii. 5. 178.

POINTS, *sub.* tags of laces, Tam. of Shrew, iii. 2. 50; 2 Hen. IV. i. 1. 53.

POKING-STICKS, *sub.* irons for setting out ruffs, Wint. Tale, iv. 3. 228.

POLACK, *sub.* a native of Poland, Ham. ii. 2. 63.

POLE, *sub.* standard, Ant. & Cleo. iv. 13. 65.

POLLED, *pt.p.* laid bare, Coriol. iv. 5. 216.

POMANDER, *sub.* a ball of perfumes, Wint. Tale, iv. 3. 611.

POMGARNET, *sub.* pomegranate, name of a room in a tavern, 1 Hen. IV. ii. 4. 42.

POME-WATER, *sub.* a large kind of apple, L.'s L.'s L. iv. 2. 4.

POOP, *v.t.* to strike fatally, Per. iv. 2. 25.

POOR-JOHN, *sub.* salted and dried hake, Temp. ii. 2. 28.

POPERIN, *sub.* a sort of pear from *Poperinghe*, a town in French Flanders, Rom. & Jul. ii. 1. 38.

POPINJAY, *sub.* a parrot, 1 Hen. IV. i. 3. 50.

POPISH, *adj.* bigoted, Tit. Andr. v. 1. 76.

POPULAR, *adj.* vulgar, Hen. V. iv. 1. 38; Coriol. ii. 1. 233.

POPULARITY, *sub.* vulgarity, 1 Hen. IV. iii. 2. 69.

PORING, *pr.p.* 'poring dark' = darkness which makes one strain his eyes, Hen. V. iv. Chor. 2.

PORPENTINE, *sub.* the porcupine, 2 Hen. VI. iii. 1. 363; Ham. i. 5. 20.

PORTAGE, *sub.* port-hole, Hen. V. iii. 1. 10; port-dues, Per. iii. 1. 35.

POSY, *sub.* motto, Mer. of Ven. v. 1. 151; Ham. iii. 2. 164.

POT, TO THE, to sure destruction, Coriol. i. 4. 47.

POTATO, *sub.* regarded as an exciting dish, Merry Wives of W. v. 5. 21; Troil. & Cres. v. 2. 54.

POTCH, *v.i.* to thrust, Coriol. i. 10. 15.

POTHER, *sub.* turmoil, Coriol. ii. 1. 237; K. Lear, iii. 2. 50.

POTTLE-POT, *sub.* a tankard containing two quarts, 2 Hen. IV. ii. 2. 86.

POULTER, *sub.* a poulterer, 1 Hen. IV. ii. 4. 487.

POUNCET-BOX, *sub.* a perfume box with perforated lid [comp. Fr. *poinçonner*], 1 Hen. IV. i. 3. 38.

POWDER, *v.t.* to salt, 1 Hen. IV. v. 4. 112; Meas. for Meas. iii. 2. 64.

POWDERING-TUB, *sub.* a salting tub, referring to a favourite medical treatment of the time, Hen. V. ii. 1. 79.

PRACTICE, *sub.* treachery, artifice, Meas. for Meas. v. 1. 108; Hen. V. ii. 2. 90.

PRACTISANTS, *sub.* performers of a stratagem, 1 Hen. VI. iii. 2. 20.

PRACTISE, *v.t.* to plot, As You Like It, i. 1. 158.

PRAISE, *v.t.* to appraise, value, Twelfth Night, i. 5. 213; Oth. v. 1. 66.

PRECEDENT, *sub.* rough draft, K. John, v. 2. 3; Rich. III. iii. 6. 7.

PRECEPTIAL, *adj.* instructive, Much Ado, v. 1. 24.

PREGNANCY, *sub.* ready wit, 2 Hen. IV. i. 2. 194.

PREGNANT, *adj.* ready, clever, ingenious, Ham. ii. 2. 216; iii. 2. 66; very probable, Wint. Tale, v. 2. 34.

PRESENCE, *sub.* the presence chamber, Rich. II. i. 3. 289.

PREST, *adj.* ready, Mer. of Ven. i. 1. 161.

PRESTER JOHN, *sub.* a fabulous eastern monarch, Much Ado, ii. 1. 278.

PRETENCE, *sub.* design, Coriol. i. 2. 20.

PRETEND, *v.t.* to assert, 3 Hen. VI. iv. 7. 57.

PRICK, *sub.* point of a dial, Lucrece, 781; the bull's-eye in a target, L.'s L.'s L. iv. 1. 136.

PRICKET, *sub.* a buck of the second year, L.'s L.'s L. iv. 2. 22.

PRICK-SONG, *sub.* music written down, in opposition to plain-song, Rom. & Jul. ii. 4. 22.

PRIG, *sub.* a thief, Wint. Tale, iv. 3. 109.

PRIMAL, *adj.* first, Ham. iii. 3. 37.

PRIME, *adj.* the spring, Lucrece, 332; Sonnets, xcvii. 7.

PRIMERO, *sub.* a game at cards, Hen. VIII. v. 1. 7; Merry Wives of W. iv. 5. 105.

PRIMY, *adj.* early, or perhaps flourishing, Ham. i. 3. 7.

PRINCIPALS, *sub.* the corner beams of a house, Per. iii. 2. 16.

PRINCOX, *sub.* a pert, saucy fellow, Rom. & Jul. i. 5. 90.

PRISER, *sub.* perhaps prize-fighter, As You Like It, ii. 3. 8.

PRIZE, *sub.* value, estimation, Cymb. iii. 6. 76; Ant. & Cleo. v. 2. 182.

PRIZED, *pt.p.* estimated, Much Ado, iii. 1. 90.

PROBAL, *adj.* satisfactory, reasonable, Oth. ii. 3. 347.

PROBATION, *sub.* proof, Cymb. v. 5. 363; trial, Meas. for Meas. v. 1. 157; Twelfth Night, ii. 5. 144.

PRODITOR, *sub.* a traitor, 1 Hen. VI. i. 3. 31.

PROFACE, *interj.* much good may it do you!—an expression addressed to guests by their hosts, 2 Hen. IV. v. 3. 28.

PROLIXIOUS, *adj.* tedious, causing delay, Meas. for Meas. ii. 4. 163.

PROPEND, *v.i.* to incline, Troil. & Cres. ii. 2. 190.

PROPENSION, *sub.* inclination, Troil. & Cres. ii. 2. 133.

PROPER, *adj.* handsome, Oth. iv. 3. 35; Ant. & Cleo. iii. 3. 38; peculiar to one's self, Meas. for Meas. i. 1. 30; own, Meas. for Meas. i. 2. 138; 'proper-false', handsome, but deceitful, Twelfth Night, ii. 2. 30.

PROPERTIED, *pt.p.* endued with qualities, Ant. & Cleo. v. 2. 83.

PROPERTIES, *sub.* stage requisites, Merry Wives of W. iv. 4. 80; Mid. N. Dr. i. 2. 109.

PROPERTY, *v.t.* to make a tool of, Twelfth Night, iv. 2. 101; K. John, v. 2. 79; *sub.* an instrument for one's designs, a tool, Merry Wives of W. iii. 4. 10; Jul. Cæs. iv. 1. 40.

PROPOSE, *v.t.* to speak, to converse, Much Ado, iii. 1. 3.

PROPUGNATION, *sub.* means of opposition, defence, Troil. & Cres. ii. 2. 136.

PUGGING, *adj.* thieving, Wint. Tale, iv. 2. 7.

PUISNY, *adj.* unskilful, As You Like It, iii. 4. 44.

PUKE-STOCKING, *adj.* puke, dark-coloured, perhaps puce, 1 Hen. IV. ii. 4. 79.

PUN, *v.t.* to pound, to beat, Troil. & Cres. ii. 1. 42.

PUNTO, *sub.* a stroke in fencing, Merry Wives of W. ii.3.26.

PUNTO REVERSO, *sub.* a back-handed stroke in fencing, Rom. & Jul. ii. 4. 28.

PURL, *v.i.* to curl, to run in circles, Lucrece, 1407.

PURPLES, LONG, the purple orchis, *Orchis mascula*, Ham. iv. 7. 170.

PUSH, *sub.* an expression of contempt, Much Ado, v. 1. 38; Tim. of Ath. iii. 6. 120.

PUSH-PIN, *sub.* a childish game, L.'s L.'s L. iv. 3. 169.

PUT ON, to instigate, Oth. ii. 3. 360; K. Lear, i. 4. 230.

PUT OVER, to refer, K. John, i. 1. 62.

PUTTOCK, *sub.* a kite, 2 Hen. VI. iii. 2. 191; Cymb. i. 1. 140.

PUZZEL, *sub.* a foul drab, 1 Hen. VI. i. 4. 107.

PYRAMIDES, *sub.* pyramids, Ant. & Cleo. v. 2. 61.

PYRAMIS, *sub.* a pyramid, 1 Hen. VI. i. 6. 21.

QUAINT, *adj.* fine, delicate, Temp. i. 2. 317; Mid. N. Dr. ii. 1. 99.

QUALIFIED, *adj.* excellent, well composed, Cymb. i. 4. 68.

QUALIFY, *v.t.* to moderate, Meas. for Meas. i. 1. 65; Much Ado, v. 4. 67.

QUALITY, *sub.* profession, Ham. ii. 2. 461.

QUANTITY, *sub.* value, Mid. N. Dr. i. 1. 232; Ham. iii. 2. 46.

QUARREL [O. Ed. QUARRY], *sub.* cause, Macb. i. 2. 14.

QUARRELOUS, *adj.* quarrelsome, Cymb. iii. 4. 162.

QUARRY, *sub.* heap of slaughtered game [Fr. *curée*], Macb. iv. 3. 206; Ham. v. 2. 378.

QUARTERED, *pt.p.* slaughtered, Coriol. i. 1. 205.

QUAT, *sub.* a pimple, applied contemptuously to a person, Oth. v. 1. 11.

QUATCH-BUTTOCK, *adj.* squat or flat buttock, All's Well, ii. 2. 19.

QUEASY, *adj.* disgusted, Ant. & Cleo. iii. 6. 20; ticklish, difficult, K. Lear, ii. 1. 19; fastidious, Much Ado, ii. 1. 402.

QUELL, *sub.* a murder, Macb. i. 7. 72.

QUERN, *sub.* a handmill, Mid. N. Dr. ii. 1. 36.

QUESTANT, *sub.* aspirant, All's Well, ii. 1. 16.

QUESTION, *sub.* conversation, As You Like It, iii. 4. 37; v. 4. 168; Mer. of Ven. iv. 1. 73; *v.t.* to talk, converse, Lucrece, 122.

QUESTIONABLE, *adj.* inviting converse, Ham. i. 4. 43.

QUESTRIST, *sub.* searcher, K. Lear, iii. 7. 17.

QUESTS, *sub.* inquiries, Meas. for Meas. iv. 1. 63.

QUICK, *adj.* alive, Merry Wives of W. iii. 4. 90; fresh, Temp. iii. 2. 77; pregnant, L.'s L.'s L. v. 2. 680.

QUIDDITY, *sub.* subtlety, 1 Hen. IV. i. 2. 51; Ham. v. 1. 105.

QUIETUS, *sub.* settlement of an account, Ham. iii. 1. 75.

QUILL, IN THE, in a body, 2 Hen. VI. i. 3. 4.

QUILLETS, *sub.* cavilling, chicanery, 1 Hen. VI. ii. 4. 17; Tim. of Ath. iv. 3. 156.

QUINTAIN, *sub.* a post, block, or dummy figure set up for tilting at, As You Like It, i. 2. 268.

QUIP, *sub.* piece of repartee, Two Gent. of Ver. iv. 2. 12; 1 Hen. IV. i. 2. 51.

QUIRK, *sub.* a sudden turn, an evasion, Per. iv. 6. 8; All's Well, iii. 2. 51; a shallow conceit, Much Ado, ii. 3. 256; Oth. ii. 1. 63.

QUIVER, *adj.* nimble, 2 Hen. IV. iii. 2. 304.

QUOIF, *sub.* a cap, Wint. Tale, iv. 3. 226; 2 Hen. IV. i. 1. 147.

QUOIT, *v.t.* to throw, 2 Hen. IV. ii. 4. 205.

QUOTE, *v.t.* to note, examine, scrutinize, notice, Troil. & Cres. iv. 5. 232; Tit. Andr. iv. 1. 50.

RABATO, *sub.* a kind of ruff, Much Ado, iii. 4. 6.

RABBIT-SUCKER, *sub.* a sucking rabbit, 1 Hen. IV. ii. 4. 486.

RACE, *sub.* a root, Wint. Tale, iv. 2. 51.

RACK, *v.i.* to move above as the clouds do, 3 Hen. VI. ii. 1. 27; *sub.* a cloud, a mass of floating clouds, Temp. iv. 1. 156; Ham. ii. 2. 514; Sonnets, xxxiii. 6.

RAG, *sub.* a beggarly person, Tam. of Shrew, iv. 3. 112; Tim. of Ath. iv. 3. 272.

RAGED, *pt.p.* chafed, Rich. II. ii. 1. 70.

RAGING-WOOD, *adj.* raving mad, 1 Hen. VI. iv. 7. 35.

RAKE UP, *v.t.* to bury, to cover up, K. Lear, iv. 6. 282.

RAMPALLIAN, *sub.* a term of low abuse, 2 Hen. IV. ii. 1. 67.

RAMPING, *prt.p.* rampant, 1 Hen. IV. iii. 1. 152; 3 Hen. VI. v. 2. 13.

RAMPS, *sub.* wanton wenches, Cymb. i. 6. 134.

RANGE, *v.t.* to dispose in order, Ant. & Cleo. i. 1. 34; *sub.* ranks of an army, Ant. & Cleo. iii. 11. 5.

RANK, *sub.* perhaps pace, As You Like It, i. 2. 114.

RANK, *adj.* swollen, Ven. & Adon. 71.

RAP, *v.t.* to transport, Macb. i. 3. 57, 142; Cymb. i. 6. 51.

RAPTURE, *sub.* violent motion, Coriol. ii. 1. 226; Troil. & Cres. iii. 2. 138; plundering, robbing, according to some violent tossing, Per. ii. 1. 167.

RASCAL, *sub.* a deer too lean to be hunted, As You Like It, iii. 3. 60; *adj.* 1 Hen. VI. iv. 2. 49.

RAVEL, *v.t.* to unravel, Rich. II. iv. 1. 228; Ham. iii. 4. 186.

RAVIN, *adj.* ravening, All's Well, iii. 2. 120; *v.t.* to devour greedily, Macb. ii. 4. 28.

RAVINED, *pt.p.* gorged with prey, Macb. iv. 1. 24.

RAYED, *pt.p.* befouled, Tam. of Shrew, iv. 1. 3; afflicted, or perhaps defiled, Tam. of Shrew, iii. 2. 55.

RAZE, *sub.* root, 1 Hen. IV. ii. 1. 27. *Comp.* RACE.

RAZED, *part. adj.* slashed, Ham. iii. 2. 293.

RAZURE, *sub.* erasure, Meas. for Meas. v. 1. 13.

REBATE, *v.t.* to blunt, Meas. for Meas. i. 4. 60.

RECHEAT, *sub.* hunting term, a set of notes sounded to call the dogs off from a wrong scent, Much Ado, i. 1. 251.

RECORD, *v.t.* to sing, Two Gent. of Ver. v. 4. 6; *v.i.* Per. iv. Prol. 27.

RECORDER, *sub.* a kind of flute, Mid. N. Dr. v. 1. 124; Ham. iii. 2. 367.

RECOURSE, *sub.* frequent flowing, Troil. & Cres. v. 3. 55.

RECOVER THE WIND, to get the windward of the game, so as to drive it into a toil, Ham. iii. 2. 368.

REDE, *sub.* advice, counsel, Ham. i. 3. 51.

RED-LATTICE, *sub.* the window of an ale-house, used adjectively, Merry Wives of W. ii. 2. 29.

REDUCE, *v.t.* to bring back, Rich. III. v. 4. 49.

REED, *adj.* piping, Mer. of Ven. iii. 4. 67.

REEKY, *adj.* filthy, Rom. & Jul. iv. 1. 83.

REFELL, *v.t.* to refute, Meas. for Meas. v. 1. 95.

REGIMENT, *sub.* rule, Ant. & Cleo. iii. 6. 95.

REGION, *sub.* the sky, the upper air, Rom. & Jul. ii. 2. 21; Ham. ii. 2. 517; *adj.* Ham. ii. 2. 615; Sonnets, xxxiii. 12.

REJOURN, *v.t.* to adjourn, Coriol. ii. 1. 80.

REMEDIATE, *adj.* medicinal, K. Lear, iv. 4. 17.

REMEMBER, *v.t.* to remind, Temp. i. 2. 243.

REMORSE, *sub.* pity, Meas. for Meas. ii. 2. 54; Merry Wives of W. iii. 5. 10.

REMORSEFUL, *adj.* compassionate, Two Gent. of Ver. iv. 3. 13.

RENDER, *v.t.* to account, Tim. of Ath. iv. 1. 9; *v.i.* to surrender, Macb. v. 7. 24; Ant. & Cleo. iii. 8. 42.

RENDER, *sub.* a surrender, Cymb. v. 4. 17; Sonnets, cxxv 12; account, statement, Tim. of Ath. v. 1. 154; Cymb. iv. 4. 11.

RENEGE, *v.t.* to deny, K. Lear, ii. 2. 83; Ant. & Cleo. i. 1. 8.

RENT, *v.t.* to rend, to tear, Mid. N. Dr. iii. 2. 215.

RENYING, *pr.p.* denying, Son. Sun. Notes of Mus. iii. 7.

REPASTURE, *sub.* food [Armado's verses], L.'s L.'s L. iv. 1. 96.

REPLENISHED, *part. adj.* consummate, Wint. Tale, ii. 1. 78; Rich. III. iv. 3. 18.

REPLICATION, *sub.* echo, reverberation, Jul. Cæs. i. 1. 50; answer, Ham. iv. 2. 13.

REPRISAL, *sub.* prize, 1 Hen. IV. iv. 1. 118.

REPROBATION, *sub.* perdition, Oth. v. 2. 207.

REPUGN, *v.t.* to oppose, 1 Hen. VI. v. 1. 94.

REPUGNANCY, *sub.* opposition, Tim. of Ath. iii. 5. 46.

RERE-MICE, *sub.* bats, Mid. N. Dr. ii. 2. 4.

RESOLVE, *v.t.* to dissolve, Tim. of Ath. iv. 3. 445; Ham. i. 2. 130; to free from doubt, Meas. for Meas. iv. 2. 226; to answer, Tit. Andr. v. 3. 35.

RESPECT, *sub.* consideration, K. John, iii. 1. 58; Ham. iii. 1. 68.

RESPECTIVE, *adj.* careful, Mer. of Ven. v. 1. 156; Rom. & Jul. iii. 1. 129.

RESPECTIVELY, *adv.* particularly, Tim. of Ath. iii. 1. 8.

'REST, *v.t.* to arrest, Com. of Err. iv. 2. 42.

REST, *sub.* 'to set up one's', a phrase in a game at cards, to venture one's final stakes held in reserve, fully make up one's mind, be resolved, Com. of Err. iv. 3. 26; All's Well, ii. 1. 138.

RESTY, *adj.* lazy, slothful, Cymb. iii. 6. 34; Sonnets, c. 9.

REVOLT, *sub.* a rebel, Cymb. iv. 4. 6; K. John, v. 2. 151.

RIBAUDRED, *adj.* ribald, Ant. & Cleo. iii. 8. 20.

RID, *v.t.* to make away with, Temp. i. 2. 364.

RIGGISH, *adj.* wanton, Ant. & Cleo. ii. 2. 248.

RIGOL, *sub.* a circle, 2 Hen. IV. iv. 5. 35; Lucrece, 1745.

RIM [O. Ed. RYMME], *sub.* the abdomen, Hen. V. iv. 4. 15.

RIVAGE, *sub.* shore, Hen. V. iii. Chor. 14.

RIVAL, *sub.* partner, Ham. i. 1. 13.

RIVELLED, *part. adj.* wrinkled, Troil. & Cres. v. 1. 26.

RIVO, *interj.* of doubtful meaning, a bacchanalian exclamation, 1 Hen. IV. ii. 4. 126.

ROAD, *sub.* a prostitute, 2 Hen. IV. ii. 2. 183; a road-stead, Mer. of Ven. i. 1. 19; a journey, Hen. VIII. iv. 2. 17; an incursion, Coriol. iii. 1. 5.

ROBUSTIOUS, *adj.* rough, Ham. iii. 2. 10.

ROCKED, *pt.p.* trembled, shook, Lucrece, 262.

ROGUING, *adj.* vagrant, roaming, Per. iv. 1. 96.

ROISTING, *adj.* bold, bullying, defiant, Troil. & Cres. ii. 2. 208.

ROMAGE, *sub.* bustle, tumultuous hurry, Ham. i. 1. 107.

RONDURE, *sub.* circle, Sonnets, xxi. 8.

RONYON, *sub.* scurvy wretch, Macb. i. 3. 5; Merry Wives, iv. 2. 199.

ROOK, *v.t.* to cower, 3 Hen. VI. v. 6. 45.

ROOKY, *adj.* misty, gloomy, or else full of crows, Macb. iii. 2. 51.

ROOTED, *pt.p.* learned by heart, Coriol. iii. 2. 55.

ROPERY, *sub.* roguery, Rom. & Jul. ii. 4. 155.

ROPE-TRICKS, *sub.* knavish tricks, Tam. of Shrew, i. 2. 113.

ROPING, *part. adj.* dripping, Hen. V. iv. 2. 48. *Comp.* DOWN-ROPING.

ROTHER, *sub.* an ox, Tim. of Ath. iv. 3. 12.

ROUND, *adj.* plain, honest, Hen. V. iv. 1. 219; *sub.* a circle, Macb. iv. 1. 88; Ven. & Adon. 368.

ROUND WITH, BE, speak freely with, Com. of Err. ii. 1. 82; Twelfth Night, ii. 3. 104.

ROUND[1], *v.t.* to surround, Mid. N. Dr. iv. 1. 57; Rich. II. iii. 2. 161; to finish off, Temp. iv. 1. 158; *v.i.* to grow big, Wint. Tale, ii. 1. 16.

ROUND[2], *v.t.* to whisper, Wint. Tale, i. 2. 217; K. John, ii. 1. 566.

ROUNDEL, *sub.* a dance, Mid. N. Dr. ii. 2. 1; rung of a ladder, Jul. Cæs. ii. 1. 24.

ROUNDLY, *adv.* plainly, directly, As You Like It, v. 3. 12.

ROUNDURE, *sub.* circuit, K. John, ii. 1. 259.

ROUSE, *sub.* a free and deep draught, Ham. i. 2. 127; i. 4. 8.

ROUT, *sub.* the crowd, the mob, Com. of Err. iii. 1. 101; Jul. Cæs. i. 2. 78; brawl, Oth. ii. 3. 212.

ROYNISH, *adj.* scurvy, coarse, As You Like It, ii. 2. 8.

RUB, *sub.* a term in the game of bowls, an impediment, Rich. II. iii. 4. 4; *fig.* Hen. V. ii. 2. 188.

RUBIOUS, *adj.* red, ruby-like, Twelfth Night, i. 4. 32.

RUDDOCK, *sub.* the redbreast, Cymb. iv. 2. 224.

RUDESBY, *sub.* rude fellow, Tam. of Shrew, iii. 2. 10; Twelfth Night, iv. 1. 55.

RUFFLE, *v.t.* to be boisterous, K. Lear, ii. 4. 304; stir, bustle, Lov. Comp. 58.

RUG-HEADED, *adj.* rough-headed, Rich. II. ii. 1. 157.

RUINATE, *v.t.* to ruin, 3 Hen. VI. v. 1. 83; Lucrece, 94.

RULE, *sub.* behaviour, Twelfth Night, ii. 3. 133.

RUMP-FED, *adj.* pampered, or else fed on offal, Macb. i. 3. 6.

RUNAGATE, *sub.* vagabond, Rich. III. iv. 4. 465.

RUNNING BANQUET, a hasty refreshment, *fig.* Hen. VIII. i. 4. 12; v. 4. 71.

RUSH ASIDE, push aside, Rom. & Jul. iii. 3. 26.

RUTH, *sub.* pity, Rich. II. iii. 4. 106; Coriol. i. 1. 203.

SABLES, *sub.* rich fur, Ham. iv. 7. 80.

SACKERSON, *sub.* name of a famous bear at Paris Garden on the Bank side, Merry Wives of W. i. 1. 310.

SACRING BELL, a bell rung when the elements are consecrated at Mass, Hen. VIII. iii. 2. 296.

SAFE, *adj.* sure, sound, Cymb. iv. 2. 131.

SAG, *v.t.* to droop, sink, Macb. v. 3. 10.

SAGITTARY, *sub.* a centaur aiding the Trojans against the Greeks, Troil. & Cres. v. 5. 14; residence of the commanding officers at Venice, with figure of an archer over the gates, Oth. i. 1. 159.

SALLET, *sub.* a close-fitting helmet, 2 Hen. VI. iv. 10. 13; a salad, 2 Hen. VI. iv. 10. 9.

SALLETS, (i.e. salads), *sub.* stirring passages, perhaps ribaldries, Ham. ii. 2. 471.

SAMINGO, *sub.* for Saint Domingo, the patron saint of drinkers, 2 Hen. IV. v. 3. 77.

SAND-BLIND, *adj.* half blind, purblind, Mer. of Ven. ii. 2. 37.

SANDED, *adj.* of a sandy colour, Mid. N. Dr. iv. 1. 126.

SARCENET, *sub.* fine silk, Troil. & Cres. v. 1. 36.

SAWN, *pt.p.* sewn, or perhaps seen, Lov. Comp. 91.

SAY, *sub.* a kind of serge, 2 Hen. VI. iv. 7. 27; *v.t.* to try, assay, Pericles, i. 1. 59.

SCALD, *adj.* scabby, mangy, Hen. V. v. 1. 5; Ant. & Cleo. v. 2. 214.

SCALE, *v.t.* to scatter, make clear, make plain, Coriol. i. 1. 97; to weigh, Meas. for Meas. iii. 1. 267; Coriol. ii. 3. 257.

SCAMBLE, *v.i.* to scramble, Much Ado, v. 1. 94; Hen. V. v. 2. 217.

SCAMEL, *sub.* some sort of birds, possibly seamels, sea-mews, Temp. ii. 2. 185.

SCANDAL, *v.t.* to bring into disgrace, defame, Jul. Cæs. i. 2. 76; Cymb. iii. 4. 62.

SCANT, *adv.* scarcely, Rom. & Jul. i. 2. 104; *v.t.* to limit, shorten, K. Lear, ii. 4. 142.

SCONCE, *sub.* a covering for the head, Com. of Err. ii. 2. 37; the head, Hamlet, v. 1. 108; a fort, Hen. V. iii. 6. 78.

SCOT, *sub.* contribution, 1 Hen. IV. v. 4. 115.

SCOTCH, *sub.* a cut, wound, Ant. & Cleo. iv. 7. 10; *v.t.* to notch, scutch, Coriol. iv. 5. 198; Macb. iii. 2. 13.

SCRIMERS, *sub.* fencers, Ham. iv. 7. 100.

SCRIP, *sub.* a written list, Mid. N. Dr. i. 2. 3.

SCROWL, *v.t.* perhaps to scrawl, Tit. Andr. ii. 4. 5.

SCROWLES, *sub.* mangy fellows, K. John, ii. 1. 373.

SCRUBBED, *adj.* stunted, Mer. of Ven. v. 1. 162.

SEAM, *sub.* lard, Troil. & Cres. ii. 3. 197.

SEAR, *v.t.* to brand, Wint. Tale, ii. 1. 72.

SEARED, *adj.* withered, blighted, Cymb. ii. 4. 6.

SECURITY, *sub.* carelessness, Jul. Cæs. ii. 3. 8; Macb. iii. 5. 32.

SEEDNESS, *sub.* sowing of the seed, Meas. for Meas. i. 4. 42.

SEEL, *v.t.* to close up the eyes of a hawk, Oth. i. 3. 271; Macb. iii. 2. 46.

SELD, *adv.* seldom, Troil. & Cres. iv. 5. 149.

SELD-SHOWN, *adj.* rarely given to vulgar eyes, Coriol. ii. 1. 232.

SELF, *adj.* same, Mer. of Ven. i. 1. 149.

SENNET, *sub.* set of notes on a trumpet, frequent in stage directions, K. Lear, i. 1; Coriol. ii. 1, 2, &c.

SERPIGO, *sub.* a sort of skin eruption, Meas. for Meas. iii. 1. 31; Troil. & Cres. ii. 3. 82.

SEWER, *sub.* an officer whose original office was to taste the dishes placed on the royal table, Macb. i. 7, *stage direction*, 2nd line.

SHALES, *sub.* husks, shells, Hen. V. iv. 2. 18.

SHARD-BORNE, *part. adj.* carried through the air on wing-cases, Macb. iii. 2. 42.

SHARDED, *part. adj.* having wing-cases, Cymb. iii. 3. 20.

SHARDS, *sub.* potsherds, Ham. v. 1. 253; wing-cases, Ant. & Cleo. iii. 2. 20.

SHEARMAN, *sub.* one who shears cloth, 2 Hen. VI. iv. 2. 145.

SHEAVED, *part. adj.* made of straw, Lov. Comp. 31.

SHEEP-BITER, *sub.* a malicious and treacherous fellow, Twelfth Night, ii. 5. 6.

SHENT, *pt.p.* rated, reviled, Twelfth Night, iv. 2. 115; Coriol. v. 2. 104; Ham. iii. 2. 423.

SHIP-TIRE, *sub.* a head-dress, Merry Wives of W. iii. 3. 60.

SHIVE, *sub.* a slice, Tit. Andr. ii. 1. 87.

SHOG, *v.i.* to move on, Hen. V. ii. 1. 47.

SHOTTEN HERRING, *sub.* one that has shed its roe, 1 Hen. IV. ii. 4. 145.

SHOUGHS, *sub.* shaggy dogs, Macb. iii. 1. 94.

SHOVE-GROAT SHILLING, one used in the game of shove-groat, 2 Hen. IV. ii. 4. 205.

SHOVEL-BOARD, *sub.* a shilling used in the game of that name, Merry Wives of W. i. 1. 161.

SHREWD, *adj.* mischievous, Jul. Cæs. iii. 1. 158; As You Like It, v. 4. 480.

SICLES, *sub.* shekels, Meas. for Meas. ii. 2. 149.

SIDE SLEEVES, *sub.* long hanging sleeves, Much Ado, iii. 4. 21.

SIEGE, *sub.* a seat, Meas. for Meas. iv. 2. 101; rank, Ham. iv. 7. 76; Oth. i. 2. 22; excrement, Temp. ii. 2. 114.

SIGHTLESS, *adj.* blind, Lucrece, 1013; invisible, Macb. i. 5. 50; ugly, K. John, iii. 1. 45.

SIGN, *v.t.* to mark, stamp, to be a prognostic or omen, K. John, iv. 2. 237; Jul. Cæs. iii. 1. 206; Ant. & Cleo. iv. 3. 14.

SIMPLE, *sub.* a medicinal herb, Merry Wives of W. i. 4. 65; Rom. & Jul. v. 1. 40.

SIMULAR, *adj.* pretended, feigned, Cymb. v. 5. 201; *sub.* simulator, pretender, K. Lear, iii. 2. 54.

SINGLED, *pt.p.* separated, L.'s L.'s L. v. 1. 87.

SISTERING, *part. adj.* neighbouring, Lov. Comp. 2.

SIZES, *sub.* portions, allowances, K. Lear, ii. 4. 178.

SKEINS-MATES, *sub.* a word of doubtful meaning, perhaps messmates, or knavish companions, &c., Rom. & Jul. ii. 4. 163.

SKILLET, *sub.* a little pot, Oth. i. 3. 274.

SKILL-LESS, *adj.* ignorant, Temp. iii. 1. 53; Twelfth Night, iii. 3. 9.

SKILLS NOT, IT, it is of no importance, it matters not, Twelfth Night, v. 1. 298; 2 Hen. VI. iii. 1. 281.

SKIMBLE-SKAMBLE, *adj.* wild, confused, 1 Hen. IV. iii. 1. 153.

SKIPPER, *sub.* a thoughtless fellow, Tam. of Shrew, ii. 1. 333.

SKIRR, *v.i.* to scour or move rapidly, Macb. v. 3. 35.

SLAB, *adj.* slimy, viscous, Macb. iv. 1. 32.

SLAVE, *v.t.* to make a slave of, or perhaps to treat as a slave would, K. Lear, iv. 1. 69.

SLEAVE, *and* } *sub.* floss silk, Troil. & Cres. v. 1. 35;
SLEAVE SILK } Macb. ii. 2. 38.

SLEDDED, *adj.* on sledges, Ham. i. 1. 63.

SLEEVE-HAND, *sub.* a wristband, Wint. Tale, iv. 3. 212.

SLEEVELESS, *adj.* useless, unprofitable, Troil. & Cres. v. 4. 9.

SLEIDED, *pt.p.* untwisted, Pericles, iv. Prol. 21.

SLIP, *sub.* a counterfeit coin, Rom. & Jul. ii. 4. 53; Ven. & Ad. 515.

SLIVER, *sub.* a branch torn off, Ham. iv. 7. 174; *v.t.* to tear off, to break off, Macb. iv. 1. 28; K. Lear, iv. 2. 34.

SLOPS, *sub.* large loose trousers, 2 Hen. IV. i. 2. 33.

SLUBBER, *v.t.* to slur over, Mer. of Ven. ii. 8. 39; to soil, Oth. i. 3. 227.

SMACK, *sub.* a smattering, All's Well, iv. 1. 18.

SMALL, *adj.* shrill-voiced, Coriol. iii. 2. 114; Twelfth Night, i. 4. 32.

SMATCH, *sub.* smack, taste, Jul. Cæs. v. 5. 46.

SMATTER, *v.i.* to prattle, to chatter, Rom. & Jul. iii. 5. 172.

SMOOTH, *v.t.* to flatter, Rich. III. i. 3. 48; Tit. Andr. iv. 4. 95.

SNEAP, *v.t.* to check, to nip, L.'s L.'s L. i. 1. 100; Wint. Tale, i. 2. 13; *sub.* a snub, 2 Hen. IV. ii. 1. 137.

SNECK UP! an expression of contempt, go and be hanged, Twelfth Night, ii. 3. 103.

SNUFF, *sub.* the smouldering wick of a candle, Cymb. i. 6. 87; an object of loathing and contempt, All's Well, i. 2. 59.

SNUFFS, *sub.* quarrels, K. Lear, iii. 1. 26; to take or be in snuff = to take offence at, Mid. N. Dr. v. 1. 256; 1 Hen. IV. i. 3. 41.

SOILED, *adj.* luxuriously fed, high-blooded, K. Lear, iv. 6. 125.

SOLIDARE, *sub.* a small piece of money, Tim. of Ath. iii. 1. 47.

SORE, *sub.* a buck of the fourth year, L.'s L.'s L. iv. 2. 59.

SOREL, *sub.* a buck of the third year, L.'s L.'s L. iv. 2. 60.

SORT, *sub.* company, in contempt, Mid. N. Dr. iii. 2. 21; Rich. III. v. 3. 317; a lot, Troil. & Cres. i. 3. 376.

SOT, *sub.* a fool, Twelfth Night, i. 5. 128.

SOUSE, *v.t.* to swoop down on, as a bird of prey does, K. John, v. 2. 150.

SOUSED, *pt.p.* pickled, 1 Hen. IV. iv. 2. 13.

SOWLE, *v.t.* to pull, or drag, Coriol. iv. 5. 214.

SPAN-COUNTER, *sub.* a boyish game, 2 Hen. VI. iv. 2. 170.

SPANIEL, *v.t.* to follow subserviently, Ant. & Cleo. iv. 10. 34.

SPED, *pt.p.* done for, provided for, Mer. of Ven. ii. 9. 72; Rom. & Jul. iii. 1. 96.

SPERR, *v.t.* to bar, to enclose, Troil. & Cres. Prol. 19.

SPINNER, *sub.* a spider, Rom. & Jul. i. 4. 60; Mid. N. Dr. ii. 2. 21.

SPOT, *sub.* a piece of embroidery, Coriol. i. 3. 57.

SPRAG, *adj.* quick, sharp, Merry Wives of W. iv. 1. 85.

SPRINGHALT, *sub.* a lameness in horses, Hen. VIII. i. 3. 13.

SQUANDERED, *pt.p.* scattered, Mer. of Ven. i. 3. 22.

SQUANDERING, *pr.p.* going at random, As You Like It, ii. 7. 57.

SQUARE, *sub.* 'the most precious square' = most valuable part, K. Lear, i. 1. 76; the embroidery about the bosom of a smock or shift, Wint. Tale, iv. 3. 212; *v.t.* to quarrel, Mid. N. Dr. ii. 1. 30; Ant. & Cleo. ii. 1. 45.

SQUARER, *sub.* brawler, braggart, Much Ado, i. 1. 83.

SQUASH, *sub.* an unripe peascod, Mid. N. Dr. iii. 1. 195; Twelfth Night, i. 5. 167; Wint. Tale, i. 2. 161.

SQUINY, *v.i.* to look asquint, K. Lear, iv. 6. 141.

SQUIRE, *sub.* a square, rule, measure, L.'s L.'s L. v. 2. 475; 1 Hen. IV. ii. 2. 14.

STALE, *sub.* a decoy, Temp. iv. 1. 187; Tam. of Shrew, iii. 1. 91; a dupe, laughing-stock, 3 Hen. VI. iii. 3. 260; a prostitute, Much Ado, ii. 2. 26.

STAMP, *v.t.* give currency to, Coriol. v. 2. 22.

STANDING-BOWL, *sub.* a footed goblet, Per. ii. 3. 64.

STANDING-TUCK, *sub.* a rapier standing on end, 1 Hen. IV. ii. 4. 278.

STANIEL, *sub.* a kestrel hawk, Twelfth Night, ii. 5. 126.

STATE, *sub.* a chair of state, with a canopy, 1 Hen. IV. ii. 4. 423; 3 Hen. VI. i. 1. 168.

STATIST, *sub.* a statesman, Ham. v. 2. 33.

STELLED, *part. adj.* starry, K. Lear, iii. 7. 61; *pt.p.* fixed, Lucrece, 1444; Sonnets, xxiv. 1.

STICKLER, *sub.* one whose duty was to separate combatants, Troil. & Cres. v. 8. 18.

STIGMATIC, *sub.* one bearing a brand of deformity, 2 Hen. VI. v. 1. 215; 3 Hen. VI. ii. 2. 136.

STIGMATICAL, *adj.* marked with deformity, Com. of Err. iv. 2. 22.

STINT, *v.i.* to stop, to cease, Rom. & Jul. i. 3. 48; Per. iv. 4. 42; to check, Tit. Andr. iv. 4. 85; Hen. VIII. i. 2. 76.

STITHY, *sub.* a smithy, or perhaps an anvil, Ham. iii. 2. 89; *v.t.* to forge, Troil. & Cres. iv. 5. 254.

STOCCADO, *sub.* a thrust in fencing, Merry Wives of W. ii. 1. 233; 'a stock', Merry Wives of W. ii. 3. 26. *Comp.* STUCK.

STOCCATA, *sub.* a stockado, Rom. & Jul. iii. 1. 79.

STOCK-FISH, *sub.* dried cod, Meas. for Meas. iii. 2. 118.

STOMACH, *sub.* stubborn courage, Temp. i. 2. 157; 2 Hen. IV. i. 1. 129; pride, Hen. VIII. iv. 2. 34.

STONE-BOW, *sub.* a crossbow, from which stones and bullets were shot, Twelfth Night, ii. 5. 52.

STOOP, *v.t.* to swoop, pounce down on prey, Hen. V. iv. 1. 113; Cymb. v. 3. 42.

STORED, *pt.p.* filled, charged, Per. ii. 3. 49.

STOUP, *sub.* a drinking cup, Twelfth Night, ii. 3. 14.

STOVER, *sub.* fodder for cattle, Temp. iv. 1. 63.

STRAIN COURTESY, to decline to go first, Rom. & Jul. ii. 4. 57; Ven. & Ad. 888.

STRAINED, *pt.p.* forced, constrained, Mer. of Ven. iv. 1. 184.

STRAPPADO, *sub.* a species of punishment; the victim's arms were strapped behind his back, and he was suddenly let fall, 1 Hen. IV. ii. 4. 266.

STRIKE [sail], a naval term, to submit, give way, Rich. II. ii. 1. 267.

STRIKERS, *sub.* dissolute fellows, 1 Hen. IV. ii. 1. 82.

STROSSERS, *sub.* trousers, Hen. V. iii. 7. 60.

'STROY, *v.t.* to destroy, Ant. & Cleo. 9. 54.

STUCK, *sub.* a thrust in fencing, a stock, Twelfth Night, iii. 4. 307; Ham. iv. 7. 161.

STUDIED, *pt.p.* practised, instructed, Mer. of Ven. ii. 2. 211; Macb. i. 4. 9.

STUFFED, *adj.* complete, Much Ado, i. 1. 60; Wint. Tale, ii. 1. 184.

STUFF-O'-THE-CONSCIENCE, essence of, Oth. i. 2. 2.

SUBSCRIBE, *v.t.* to yield, 1 Hen. VI. ii. 4. 44; K. Lear, iii. 7. 65.

SUBSCRIPTION, *sub.* obedience, K. Lear, iii. 2. 18.

SUCCESS, *sub.* succession, Wint. Tale, i. 2. 394; 2 Hen. IV. iv. 2. 47.

SUCCESSANTLY, *adv.* in succession, Tit. Andr. iv. 4. 112.

SUGGEST, *v.t.* to tempt, Rich. II. iii. 4. 75; Oth. ii. 3. 361.

SUGGESTION, *sub.* temptation, Temp. iv. 1. 26.

SUITED, *pt.p.* dressed, Mer. of Ven. i. 2. 78.

SUMMERED, *pt.p.* provided, as cattle are with pasture, Hen. V. v. 2. 334.

SUPERVIZE, *sub.* inspection, Ham. v. 2. 23.

SUR-ADDITION, *sub.* extra title, surname, Cymb. i. 1. 33.

SURCEASE, *sub.* accomplishment, Macb. i. 7. 4; to cease, Lucrece, 1766; Rom. & Jul. iv. 1. 97.

SUR-REINED, *pt.p.* overridden, Hen. V. iii. 5. 19.

SUSPIRE, *v.i.* draw the breath of life, K. John, iii. 4. 80.

SWABBER, *sub.* one whose duty it is to sweep the deck of a ship, Temp. ii. 2. 49; Twelfth Night, i. 5. 217.

SWAG-BELLIED, *adj.* having a loose, hanging belly, Oth. ii. 3. 81.

SWARTH, *sub.* swathe, the grass cut by one sweep of the scythe, Twelfth Night, ii. 3. 164; *adj.* swarthy, black, Tit. Andr. ii. 3. 72.

SWASHER, *sub.* a bully, a braggart, Hen. V. iii. 2. 31.

SWASHING, *adj.* swaggering, dashing, As You Like It, i. 3. 123.

SWATH, *sub.* wrapping, swaddling-clothes, Tim. of Ath. iv. 3. 253.

SWAYED, *pt.p.* strained, Tam. of Shrew, iii. 2. 57.

SWINGE, *v.t.* to beat, Two Gent. of Ver. ii. 1. 91; 2 Hen. IV. v. 4. 23.

SWINGE-BUCKLER, *sub.* a roisterer, 2 Hen. IV. iii. 2. 24.

SWOOPSTAKE, *adv.* wholesale, indiscriminately, Ham. iv. 5. 141.

SWORDER, *sub.* a gladiator, 2 Hen. VI. iv. 1. 135.

SWOUND, *v.i.* to swoon, Rom. & Jul. ii. 2. 56.

SYMPATHY, *sub.* equality, Oth. ii. 1. 233.

TABLE, *sub.* canvas of a picture, K. John, ii. 1. 503; Sonnets, xxiv. 2; the palm of the hand, a term in palmistry, Mer. of Ven. ii. 2. 174.

TABLE-BOOK, *sub.* a memorandum book, or case of tablets, Wint. Tale, iv. 4. 612; Ham. ii. 2. 136.

TABLED, *pt.p.* set down, Cymb. i. 4. 7.

TABLES, *sub.* tablets, Ham. i. 5. 107; the game of backgammon, L.'s L.'s L. v. 2. 327.

TABOURINES, *sub.* drums, Troil. & Cres. iv. 5. 274; Ant. & Cleo. iv. 8. 37.

TACKLED STAIR, *sub.* a rope ladder, Rom. & Jul. ii. 4. 203.

TAFFETA, *sub.* thin silk, L.'s L.'s L. v. 2. 159; Twelfth Night, ii. 4. 76.

TAG, } *sub.* the mob, Coriol. iii. 1. 247; Jul.
TAG-RAG PEOPLE, } Cæs. i. 2. 259.

TAINT, *v.t.* to discredit, Oth. i. 3. 273.

TAKE, *v.i.* to captivate, Temp. v. 1. 313; Wint. Tale, iv. 3. 119; *v.t.* to strike with disease, Merry Wives of W. iv. 4. 33; to take refuge in, Com. of Err. i. 2. 94; to jump over, K. John, v. 2. 138.

TAKE IN, to conquer, Coriol. i. 2. 24.

TAKE ME WITH YOU, make me understand you, Rom. & Jul. iii. 5. 142; 1 Hen. IV. ii. 4. 513.

TAKE OUT, to copy, Oth. iii. 3. 296.

TAKE THOUGHT, to suffer grief, Jul. Cæs. ii. 1. 187.

TAKE UP, to obtain on credit, 2 Hen. VI. iv. 7. 134; to reprove, Two Gent. of Ver. i. 2. 132; to reconcile, Twelfth Night, iii. 4. 323.

TALENTS, *sub.* lockets containing hair, Lov. Comp. 204.

TALLOW KETCH, a vessel filled with tallow, according to some a tallow keech, a round lump of tallow, 1 Hen. IV. ii. 4. 256.

TARRE, *v.t.* to set on dogs to fight, K. John, iv. 1. 117; to urge on, Ham. ii. 2. 379.

TARTAR, *sub.* Tartarus, hell, Hen. V. ii. 2. 123.

TASSEL-GENTLE, *sub.* tercel-gentle, the male goshawk, Rom. & Jul. ii. 2. 159.

TASTE, *v.i.* to act as sewer or server, K. John, v. 6. 28; *v.t.* to try, Twelfth Night, iii. 1. 92.

TAWDRY LACE, *sub.* a necklace worn by country girls, Wint. Tale, iv. 3. 252.

TAX, *v.t.* to accuse, Ham. i. 4. 18; As You Like It, ii. 7. 86.

TAXATION, *sub.* satire, invective, As You Like It, i. 2. 92.

TEEN, *sub.* grief, Temp. i. 2. 64; Rich. III. iv. 1. 96.

TENDER, *sub.* care, regard, 1 Hen. IV. v. 4. 49; K. Lear, i. 4. 233; *v.t.* to regard with tender affection, Two Gent. of Ver. iv. 4. 147; Com. of Err. v. 1. 132.

TENDER-HEFTED, *part. adj.* set in a delicate handle, or perhaps moved by tender emotions, K. Lear, ii. 4. 174.

TENT, *sub.* a roll of lint which was always put into a fresh wound, Troil. & Cres. ii. 2. 16; v. 1. 11.

TENT[1], *v.t.* to lodge, reside, *fig.* Coriol. iii. 2. 116.

TENT[2], *v.t.* to search, probe, Ham. ii. 2. 634; Cymb. iii. 4. 118; to cure, Coriol. i. 9. 31; iii. 1. 235.

TERCEL, *sub.* the male goshawk, Troil. & Cres. iii. 2. 54·

TERMAGANT, *sub.* a supposed Mahomedan female deity, represented in our old plays as a most violent character, Ham. iii. 2. 16; *adj.* 1 Hen. IV. v. 4. 114.

TERMLESS, *adj.* indescribable, Lov. Comp. 94.

TESTER, *sub.* a sixpence, 2 Hen. IV. iii. 2. 299; money in general, Merry Wives of W. i. 3. 94 (Pistol).

TESTERN, *v.t.* to present with a tester, Two Gent. of Ver. i. 1. 155.

TESTRIL, *sub.* sixpence, Twelfth Night, ii. 3. 36.

TESTY, *adj.* fretful, Mid. N. Dr. iii. 2. 358; Coriol. ii. 1. 48.

TETCHY, *adj.* peevish, touchy, Rich. III. iv. 4. 169.

TETTER, *sub.* a cutaneous disease, Ham. i. 5. 71; *v.t.* to affect with tetter, Coriol. iii. 1. 78.

THARBOROUGH, *sub.* a kind of constable, L.'s L.'s L. i. 1. 183. Cf. THIRD-BOROUGH.

THAT, *conj.* because, Two Gent. of Ver. iv. 1. 71.

THEORIC, *sub.* a theory, Oth. i. 1. 24.

THEREAFTER, *adv.* according as, 2 Hen. IV. iii. 2. 56.

THICK, *adv.* close, quick, Lucrece, 1784; 2 Hen. IV. ii. 3. 24; Troil. & Cres. iii. 2. 36.

THICK-EYED, *adj.* dim-eyed, 1 Hen. IV. ii. 3. 51.

THICK-PLEACHED, *pt.p.* thickly intertwined, Much Ado, i. 2. 11.

THICK-SKIN, *sub.* blockhead, Merry Wives of W. iv. 5. 2.

THILL-HORSE, *sub.* shaft-horse, Mer. of Ven. ii. 2. 103.

THINK, *v.i.* to be full of sorrowful thoughts, Ant. & Cleo. iii. 11. 1.

THIRD-BOROUGH [O. Ed. HEAD-BOROUGH], *sub.* a kind of constable, Tam. of Shrew, Ind. 1. 12.

THOUGHT, *sub.* melancholy, Ham. iii. 1. 85.

THOUGHT-EXECUTING, *part. adj.* executing with the quickness of thought, K. Lear, iii. 2. 4.

THRASONICAL, *adj.* boastful, As You Like It, v. 2. 35.

THREE-MAN BEETLE, *sub.* a rammer managed by three men, 2 Hen. IV. i. 2. 259.

THREE-PILE, *sub.* the richest kind of velvet, Wint. Tale, iv. 2. 14.

THREE-PILED, *adj.* having a thick pile, Meas. for Meas. i. 2. 34; superfine [metaphorically], L.'s L.'s L. v. 2. 408.

THRENE, *sub.* a dirge, Phœn. & Turt. 49.

THRICE-REPURED, *adj.* three times refined, Troil. & Cres. iii. 2. 21.

THRID, *sub.* thread, fibre, Temp. iv. 1. 3.

THRUM, *sub.* the tufted end of a thread in weaving, Mid. N. Dr. v. 1. 293.

THRUMMED HAT, *sub.* a hat made of very coarse woollen cloth, Merry Wives of W. iv. 2. 82.

THUNDER-STONE, *sub.* a thunderbolt, Jul. Cæs. i. 3. 49.

THWART, *adj.* perverse, cross, K. Lear, i. 4. 307.

TICKLE-BRAIN, *sub.* strong drink, 1 Hen. IV. ii. 4. 443.

TICK-TACK, *sub.* a sort of backgammon, Meas. for Meas. i. 2. 202.

TILLY-FALLY *or* TILLY-VALLY, *int.* an expression of contempt, Twelfth Night, ii. 3. 86; 2 Hen. IV. ii. 4. 89.

TIMELESS, *adj.* untimely, Rich. II. iv. 1. 5.

TIMELY-PARTED, *adj.* recently dead, 2 Hen. VI. iii. 2. 161.

TINCT, *sub.* the grand elixir sought by alchemists, All's Well, v. 3. 102; colour, Ham. iii. 4. 91.

TIRE, *sub.* a headdress, Merry Wives of W. iii. 3. 61; Much Ado, iii. 4. 13; furniture, Pericles, iii. 2. 22; *v.i.* to feed greedily, 3 Hen. VI. i. 1. 269; Ven. & Ad. 56.

TIRING-HOUSE, *sub.* the dressing-room of a theatre, Mid. N. Dr. iii. 1. 5.

TIRRITS, *sub.* perhaps terrors (Mistress Quickly), 2 Hen. IV. ii. 4. 219.

TISICK, *sub.* a cough, Troil. & Cres. v. 3. 101.

TOAZE, *v.t.* to drag out, Wint. Tale, iv. 3. 763.

TOD, *v.i.* to yield a tod, Wint. Tale, iv. 2. 33; *sub.* 28 lbs. of wool, Wint. Tale, iv. 2. 34.

TOFORE, *adv.* before, L.'s L.'s L. iii. 1. 88; Tit. Andr. iii. 1. 293.

TOGED, *adj.* gowned, robed, Oth. i. 1. 25.

TOKENED, *adj.* marked with plague-spots, Ant. & Cleo. iii. 8. 19.

TOM-BOY, *sub.* a drab, Cymb. i. 6. 122.

TONGUE, *v.t.* to denounce, Meas. for Meas. iv. 4. 28.

TOPLESS, *adj.* supreme, Troil. & Cres. i. 3. 152.

TORCHER, *sub.* a torch-bearer, All's Well, ii. 1. 165.

TORTIVE, *adj.* twisted, turned awry, Troil. & Cres. i. 3. 9.

TOTTERING, *adj.* hanging in tatters or rags, K. John, v. 5. 7.

TOUCH, *v.t.* to wound, Tim. of Ath. iii. 5. 19; Cymb. i. 1. 10; *sub.* a touchstone, 1 Hen. IV. iv. 4. 10; of 'noble touch' = of proved excellence, Coriol. iv. 1. 49.

TOUCH NEAR, to concern deeply, Two Gent. of Ver. iii. 1. 60.

TOUSE, *v.t.* to pull, to tear, Meas. for Meas. v. 1. 309.

TOWARD, *adj.* tractable, Tam. of Shrew, v. 2. 183; bold, 3 Hen. VI. ii. 2. 66.

TOWARD, TOWARDS, *adv.* in preparation, Tim. of Ath. iii. 6. 68; Ham. i. 1. 77; Rom. & Jul. i. 5. 126.

TOWER, *v.i.* to soar as a bird of prey, K. John, v. 2. 149.

TRACT, *sub.* trace, track, Hen. VIII. i. 1. 40; Tim. of Ath. i. 1. 51.

TRADE, *sub.* track, resort, Rich. II. iii. 3. 156; *v.i.* to go in a particular direction, Mer. of Ven. iii. 4. 54.

TRAIN, *sub.* bait, allurement, Macb. iv. 3. 118; *v.t.* to entice, allure, Com. of Err. iii. 2. 45; Tit. Andr. v. 1. 104.

TRAJECT [O. Ed. TRANECT], *sub.* a ferry [It. *tragetto*], Mer. of Ven. iii. 4. 53.

TRAMMEL UP, to catch as in a net, Macb. i. 7. 3.

TRASH, *v.t.* to lop, to cut off high branches, Temp. i. 2. 81; to restrain a dog by a trash, or strap, Oth. ii. 1. 315.

TRAVERSE, *v.t.* to make a thrust, Merry Wives of W. ii. 3. 25.

TRAVERSED, *adj.* crossed, folded, Tim. of Ath. v. 4. 7.

TRAY-TRIP, *sub.* a game of dice, in which success depended on throwing a 'trois', Twelfth Night, ii. 5. 209.

TREACHERS, *sub.* traitors, K. Lear, i. 2. 138.

TREBLE-DATED, *adj.* living for three ages, Phœn. & Turt. 17.

TRENCHER-MAN, *sub.* a good feeder, Much Ado, i. 1. 52.

TREY, *sub.* a three at cards, L.'s L.'s L. v. 2. 233.

TRIBULATION, *sub.* a name applied to Puritans, either to the whole sect, or some particular congregation, Hen. VIII. v. 4. 67.

TRICK, *v.t.* to draw, paint [heraldic term], Ham. ii. 2. 488; *sub.* special peculiarity of look, voice, &c., Wint. Tale, ii. 3. 100; 1 Hen. IV. v. 2. 11; K. Lear, iv. 6. 109.

TRICKSY, *adj.* sportive, Temp. v. 1. 226; Mer. of Ven. iii. 5. 75.

TRIGON, *sub.* a triangle, 2 Hen. IV. ii. 4. 288.

TRILL, *v.i.* to trickle, K. Lear, iv. 3. 14.

TRIPLEX, *sub.* triple-time in music, Twelfth Night, v. 1. 41.

TRISTFUL, *adj.* sorrowful, Ham. iii. 4. 50.

TRIUMPH, *sub.* a trump card, Ant. & Cleo. iv. 12. 20.

TROLL, *v.i.* to sing in rotation, Temp. iii. 2. 129.

TROL-MY-DAMES, *sub.* the French game of *trou-madame*, Wint. Tale, iv. 2. 93.

TROPICALLY, *adv.* figuratively, Ham. iii. 2. 250.

TROTH-PLIGHT, *sub.* betrothal, Wint. Tale, i. 2. 278.

TRUCKLE-BED, *sub.* a low bed, which runs on casters, and can be pushed under another, Merry Wives of W. iv. 5. 7; Rom. & Jul. ii. 1. 39.

TRUE-PENNY, *sub.* an honest fellow, Ham. i. 5. 150.

TRUNDLE-TAIL, *sub.* a long-tailed dog, K. Lear, iii. 6. 73.

TRUNK SLEEVE, *sub.* a full sleeve, Tam. of Shrew, iv. 3. 141.

TRY, BRING TO, to bring a ship as close to the wind as possible, Temp. i. 1. 40.

TUB, *and* } *sub.* refers to a particular process of curing
TUB-FAST, } venereal disease by sweating, Meas. for Meas. iii. 2. 61; Tim. of Ath. iv. 3. 86, 87.

TUCK, *sub.* a rapier, Twelfth Night, iii. 4. 247; 1 Hen. IV. ii. 4. 178.

TUCKET, *adj.* a flourish on a trumpet, Hen. V. iv. 2. 35.

TUFT, *sub.* clump, As You Like It, iii. 5. 75; Rich. II. ii. 3. 53.

TUNE, *sub.* accent, Cymb. v. 5. 239.

TURLYGOOD, *sub.* apparently a name given to Bedlam beggars, K. Lear, ii. 3. 20.

TURN TURK, to become wicked, Ham. iii. 2. 292; Much Ado, iii. 4. 56.

TWIGGEN, *adj.* cased in wicker work, Oth. ii. 3. 153.

TWILLED, *part. adj.* perhaps sedged or covered with reeds, Temp. iv. 1. 64.

TWIRE, *v.i.* to twinkle, Sonnets, xxviii. 12.

TWIST, *sub.* a string, Coriol. v. 5. 96.

UMBER, *sub.* red ochre, As You Like It, i. 3. 115.

UMBER'D, *adj.* darkened, Hen. V. iv. Chor. 9.

UMBRAGE, *sub.* shadow [*Hamlet's* Euphuism], Ham. v. 2. 126.

UNANEL'D, *pt.p.* without extreme unction, Ham. i. 5. 77.

UNBARBED, *part. adj.* bare, without armour, Coriol. iii.2.99.

UNBATED, *pt.p.* unblunted, without the button at the point, Ham. iv. 7. 138; v. 2. 331.

UNBOLT, *v.* to reveal, Tim. of Ath. i. 1. 52.

UNBOLTED, *part. adj.* coarse, or unrefined, K. Lear, ii.2.70.

UNBONNETED, *pt.p.* without saluting, on equal terms, Oth. i. 2. 23.

UNBOOKISH, *adj.* skill-less, foolish, Oth. iv. 1. 102.

UNBRACED, *pt.p.* unbuttoned, Jul. Cæs. i. 3. 48; Ham. ii. 1. 78.

UNCAPE, *v.t.* to uncouple, throw off the hounds, Merry Wives of W. iii. 3. 175.

UNCASE, *v.t.* to undress, L.'s L.'s L. v. 2. 706; Tam. of Shrew, i. 1. 211.

UNCOLTED, *pt.p.* deprived of one's horse, 1 Hen. IV. ii. 2. 45.

UNCROSSED, *pt.p.* not struck out, not cancelled (The tradesman's book was crossed when the account was paid), Cymb. iii. 3. 26.

UNDEAF, *sub.* cure of deafness, Rich. II. ii. 1. 16.

UNDERBEAR, *v.t.* to face, trim, Much Ado, iii. 4. 21.

UNDERCREST, *v.t.* to wear on the crest, Coriol. i. 9. 72.

UNDERSKINKER, *sub.* an underdrawer, tapster, 1 Hen. IV. ii. 4. 26.

UNDERTAKER, *sub.* a surety, or agent for others, Twelfth Night, iii. 4. 353.

UNEARED, *part. adj.* unploughed, Sonnets, iii. 5. *Comp.* EAR, *v.t.*

UNEXPRESSIVE, *adj.* inexpressible, As You Like It, iii. 2. 10.

UNFAIR, *v.t.* to deprive of beauty, Sonnets, v. 4.

UNFOLDING STAR, *sub.* the star that bids the shepherd unfold, Meas. for Meas. iv. 2. 219.

UNHAIRED, *part. adj.* beardless, foolish, K. John, v. 2. 133.

UNHATCHED, *pt.p.* which has not yet taken effect, Oth. iii. 4. 140; unfledged, Ham. i. 3. 65; unhacked, unhurt, Twelfth Night, iii. 4. 260.

UNHOUSELED, *pt.p.* without receiving the sacrament, Ham. i. 5. 77.

UNION, *sub.* a fine pearl, Ham. v. 2. 286.

UNJOINTED, *part. adj.* incoherent, 1 Hen. IV. i. 3. 65.

UNKENNEL, *v.t.* to drive a fox from his earth, Merry Wives of W. iii. 3. 174; to reveal, Ham. iii. 2. 86.

UNMANNED, *adj.* untamed, Rom. & Jul. iii. 2. 14.

UNMITIGABLE, *adj.* implacable, Temp. i. 2. 276.

UNNECESSARY, *adj.* useless, needless, Hen. V. iv. 2. 27; K. Lear, ii. 2. 68.

UNPINKED, *pt.p.* not pierced with eyelet-holes, Tam. of Shrew, iv. 1. 136.

UNPREGNANT, *adj.* dull, without sense, Meas. for Meas. iv. 4. 23.

UNPRIZEABLE, *adj.* invaluable, Cymb. i. 4. 104.

UNPRIZED, unvalued, or perhaps priceless, K. Lear, i. 1. 262.

UNPROPER, *adj.* not one's own, common, Oth. iv. 1. 69.

UNPROVIDE, *v.t.* to unfurnish, to deprive of what is necessary, Oth. iv. 1. 217.

UNRAKED, *pt.p.* not made up for the night, Merry Wives of W. v. 5. 50.

UNRECURING, *adj.* incurable, Tit. Andr. iii. 1. 90.

UNRESPECTIVE, *adj.* unthinking, devoid of respect, Rich. III. iv. 2. 29.

UNRESPECTIVE SINK, the sewer, where worthless things are thrown, Troil. & Cres. ii. 2. 71.

UNROLLED, *pt.p.* struck off the roll, Wint. Tale, iv. 2. 131.

UNROOSTED, driven from the roost, henpecked, Wint. Tale, ii. 3. 74.

UNSCANNED, *adj.* inconsidered, Coriol. iii. 1. 311.

UNSEAM, *v.t.* to rip, Macb. i. 2. 22.

UNSISTING, *adj.* unresting, Meas. for Meas. iv. 2. 92.

UNSTANCHED, *adj.* incontinent, Temp. i. 1. 53.

UNSTATE, *v.t.* to divest of state, K. Lear, i. 2. 111.

UNTENT, *v.t.* to remove out of a tent, Troil. & Cres. ii. 3. 180.

UNTENTED, *adj.* incurable, (1) that which has not been or (2) cannot be tented, K. Lear, i. 4. 324.

UNTHRIFT, *adj.* good for nothing, Tim. of Ath. iv. 3. 311; *sub.* a prodigal, Sonnets, ix. 9.

UNTRUSSING, *pr.p.* unloosing the points of the hose, Meas. for Meas. iii. 2. 194.

UNVALUED, *adj.* mean, Ham. i. 3. 19; invaluable, Rich. III. i. 4. 27.

UNWEIGHED, *adj.* reckless, Merry Wives of W. ii. 1. 23.

UNWEIGHING, *adj.* thoughtless, Meas. for Meas. iii. 2. 151.

UNYOKE, *v.t.* to ease one's labour, or burden, Ham. v. 1. 57.

UP-CAST, *sub.* a throw, or cast, at bowls; perhaps the final throw, Cymb. ii. 1. 2.

UPSHOOT, *sub.* the deciding shot, L.'s L.'s L. iv. 1. 140.

UP-SPRING, *sub.* a boisterous dance, translation of the German *hüpfauf*, Ham. i. 4. 9.

URCHIN, *sub.* a hedgehog, Temp. i. 2. 326; a goblin, Merry Wives of W. iv. 4. 51.

USANCE, *sub.* interest of money, Mer. of Ven. i. 3. 46.

USE, *sub.* usage, Meas. for Meas. i. 1. 40.

UTIS, *sub.* boisterous merriment, 2 Hen. IV. ii. 4. 22.

UTTER, *v.t.* to pass from one to another, L.'s L.'s L. ii. 1. 16; Rom. & Jul. v. 1. 67.

UTTERANCE, TO THE, to the last extremity [Fr. *à outrance*], Macb. iii. 1. 72.

VADE, *v.i.* to fade, Rich. II. i. 2. 20; Pass. Pil. 131.

VAIL, *sub.* a setting, a sinking, Troil. & Cres. v. 8. 7; to lower, let fall, Mer. of Ven. i. 1. 28; Ham. i. 2. 70.

VAILS, *sub.* money given to servants, Per. ii. 1. 163.

VALANCE, *sub.* a fringe of drapery, Tam. of Shrew, ii. 1. 348.

VALANCED, *pt.p.* fringed, Ham. ii. 2. 451.

VALUED FILE, the list in which the good are distinguished from the worthless, Macb. iii. 1. 95.

VANTBRACE, *sub.* armour for the forearm, Troil. & Cres. i. 3. 297.

VAST, *sub.* a dreary stretch of sea, Wint. Tale, i. 1. 33; Pericles, iii. 1. 1.

VAST OF NIGHT, the deep time of night, Temp. i. 2. 327; Ham. i. 2. 198.

VAULTAGES, *sub.* caverns, Hen. V. ii. 4. 124.

VAUNT, *sub.* the van, the opening, Troil. & Cres. prol. 27.

VAUNT-COURIERS, *sub.* forerunners, precursors [Fr. *avant-courriers*], K. Lear, iii. 2. 5.

VAWARD, *sub.* vanguard, the first part (met.) Mid. N. Dr. iv. 1. 111; 2 Hen. IV. i. 2. 202.

VELURE, *sub.* velvet, Tam. of Shrew, iii. 2. 63.

VELVET-GUARDS, *sub.* those who wear velvet linings, 1 Hen. IV. iii. 1. 260.

VENEW, *sub.* a bout at fencing, L.'s L.'s L. v. 1. 63.

VENEY, *sub.* the same, Merry Wives of W. i. 1. 298.

VENT, *sub.* discharge, Ant. & Cleo. v. 2. 350; 'full of vent', (1) effervescent, or (2) full of the scent of game, or (3) full of rumour, Coriol. iv. 5. 239.

VENTAGES, *sub.* apertures, stops in a flute, Ham. iii. 2. 380.

VENTRICLE, *sub.* a cavity, L.'s L.'s L. iv. 2. 70.

VERBAL, *adj.* plain-spoken, or else verbose, perhaps playing with words, Cymb. ii. 3. 111.

VIA, *interj.* a word of encouragement, go forward, away with you, Merry Wives of W. ii. 2. 161; Mer. of Ven. ii. 2. 11.

VICE, *sub.* the buffoon in the old Moral play, Twelfth Night, iv. 2. 138; Rich. III. iii. 1. 82; 2 Hen. IV. iii. 2. 347; *v.t.* to screw (met.), Wint. Tale, i. 2. 416.

VIE, *v.i.* to stake at cards, and so to contend with, Ant. & Cleo. v. 2. 98; Tam. of Shrew, ii. I. 303.

VILLIAGO, *sub.* base, coward [Ital. *vigliacco*], 2 Hen. VI. iv. 8. 49.

VINDICATIVE, *adj.* revengeful, Troil. & Cres. iv. 5. 107.

VINEWEDST, *adj.* musty, mouldy, Troil. & Cres. ii. 1. 15.

VIOL-DE-GAMBOYS, *sub.* a violoncello, Twelfth Night, i. 3. 28.

VIOLENT, *v.i.* to be violent, Troil. & Cres. iv. 4. 4.

VIRGINALLING, *pr.p.* playing with the fingers, as upon the virginal, Wint. Tale, i. 2. 126.

VISITINGS, *pr.p.* fits, attacks, Macb. i. 5. 46.

VOICE, *v.t.* to proclaim, Tim. of Ath. iv. 3. 82; *sub.* a vote, Mid. N. Dr. i. 1. 54; Coriol. ii. 3. 83.

VOIDING-LOBBY, *sub.* ante-room, 2 Hen. VI. iv. 1. 61.

WAFT, *v.t.* to beckon, Com. of Err. ii. 2. 113.

WAFTAGE, *sub.* passage by water, Troil. & Cres. iii. 2. 10.

WAFTURE, *sub.* waving of the hand, Jul. Cæs. ii. 1. 246.

WAGE, *v.t.* to remunerate, Coriol. v. 5. 40; to risk, K. Lear, i. 1. 158; waged equal = were on an equality, Ant. & Cleo. v. 1. 31.

WAIST, *sub.* that part of the ship between the quarter-deck and the forecastle, Temp. i. 2. 197.

WAKE, *sub.* a late revel, Wint. Tale, iv. 2. 110; *v.t.* to keep late revel, Ham. i. 4. 8.

WALL-EYED, *adj.* fierce-eyed, with a large portion of the white visible, K. John, iv. 3. 49.

WALL-NEWT, *sub.* a lizard, K. Lear, iii. 4. 133.

WANNED, *v.i.* turned pale, Ham. ii. 2. 588.

WANNION. In the phrase, 'with a wannion' = 'with a vengeance'. The form 'wenion' is not uncommon in writers of the period, Per. ii. 1. 17.

WAPPENED, *pt.p.* of doubtful meaning, perhaps over-worn, stale, Tim. of Ath. iv. 3. 38.

WARD, *sub.* a guard in fencing, Temp. i. 2. 468; (meta-phorically), Wint. Tale, i. 2. 33; a bolt, Lucrece, 303.

WARDEN, *sub.* a large baking pear, Wint. Tale, iv. 2. 49.

WARDER, *sub.* a truncheon, Rich. II. i. 2. 118.

WARN, *v.t.* to summon to battle, Jul. Cæs. v. 1. 5; Rom. & Jul. v. 3. 207.

WARRENER, *sub.* a gamekeeper, Merry Wives of W. i. 4. 28.

WASSAIL, *sub.* revelry, Macb. i. 7. 64.

WAT, *sub.* term for the hare, Ven. & Ad. 697.

WATCH, *sub.* a watch candle, which marked the hours, Rich. III. v. 3. 54; *v.t.* to tame by keeping awake, Tam. of Shrew, iv. 1. 198; Oth. iii. 3. 23.

WATCH-CASE, *sub.* a sentry box, 2 Hen. IV. iii. 1. 17.

WATER, *sub.* lustre of a diamond, Per. iii. 2. 102; *v.i.* to drink, 1 Hen. IV. ii. 4. 17.

WATER-COLOURS, *sub.* weak fellows, 1 Hen. IV. v. 1. 80.

WATER-GALLS, secondary rainbows, Lucrece, 1588.

WATERISH, *adj.* watery, Oth. iii. 3. 15; watery, or else weak, K. Lear, i. 1. 261.

WATER-RUGS, *sub.* rough water-dogs, Macb. iii. 1. 94.

WATERS, FOR ALL, fit for anything, Twelfth Night, iv. 2. 69.

WATERS, TO RAISE, excite tears, Mer. of Ven. ii. 2. 52.

WATER-WORK, *sub.* a painting in water-colour, 2 Hen. IV. ii. 1. 162.

WATERY, *adj.* eagerly desirous, Troil. & Cres. iii. 2. 20.

WAUL, *v.i.* to cry as an infant, K. Lear, iv. 6. 185.

WAVE, *v.i.* to fluctuate, Coriol. ii. 2. 19.

WAXEN, *v.i.* to grow, to increase, Mid. N. Dr. ii. 1. 56.

WEALS-MEN, *sub.* statesmen, Coriol. ii. 1. 60.

WEALTH, *sub.* prosperity, Mer. of Ven. v. 1. 249.

WEATHER, *sub.* storm, K. John, iv. 2. 109.

WEB AND THE PIN, *sub.* a disease of the eye, perhaps the cataract, K. Lear, iii. 4. 120.

WEEK, TO BE IN BY THE, to be a close prisoner, L.'s L.'s L. v. 2. 61.

WEEPING-RIPE, ready to weep, 3 Hen. VI. i. 4. 172.

WEET, *v.t.* to know, Ant. & Cleo. i. 1. 39.

WEIRD, *adj.* fatal, Macb. i. 3. 32; iii. 1. 2.

WELKIN, *sub.* blue, Temp. i. 2. 4; Twelfth Night, ii. 3. 61; *adj.* Wint. Tale, i. 2. 137.

WELL-GRACED, *adj.* graceful or popular, Rich. II. v. 2. 24.

WELL-SEEN, *adj.* well-skilled, Tam. of Shrew, i. 2. 136.

WELL-WISHED, *adj.* popular, Meas. for Meas. ii. 4. 28.

WELSH HOOK, *sub.* a sort of battle-axe, 1 Hen. IV. ii. 4. 377.

WESTWARD-HO! the cry of watermen on the Thames, Twelfth Night, iii. 1. 148.

WEZAND, *sub.* the windpipe, Temp. iii. 2. 102.

WHEEL, *sub.* the burthen or refrain of a song, or else a spinning wheel at which it was sung, Ham. iv. 5. 171; *v.t.* to roam, Troil. & Cres. v. 7. 2; Oth. i. 1. 137.

WHELK, *sub.* a pimple, Hen. V. iii. 6. 111.

WHELKED, *adj.* covered with knobs, K. Lear, iv. 6. 72.

WHEN, an exclamation of impatience, Temp. i. 2. 316; Jul. Cæs. ii. 1. 5; 'when as', *conj.* when, Sonnets, xlix. 3.

WHE'R, *adv.* whether, Temp. v. 1. 111; Com. of Err. iv. 1. 60.

WHERE, *adv.* whereas, Coriol. i. 1. 106.

WHEY-FACE, *adj.* pale-faced, Macb. v. 3. 17; covered with youthful down, Merry Wives of W. i. 4. 22.

WHIFFLER, *sub.* one who cleared the way in a procession, Hen. V. v. Chor. 12.

WHILE, *adv.* until, Macb. iii. 1. 44; Rich. II. i. 3. 122; 'whiles', Twelfth Night, iv. 3. 29.

WHILE AS, *conj.* while, 2 Hen. VI. i. 1. 226.

WHILE, THE, *adv.* meanwhile, As You Like It, ii. 5. 31.

WHILE-ERE, *adv.* not long ago, Temp. iii. 2. 130.

WHILES, *adv.* while, Temp. i. 2. 343; 'the whiles' = mean-while, Tam. of Shrew, iii. 1. 22.

WHILST, THE, while, Ham. iii. 2. 93; meanwhile, Rich. II. v. 2. 22.

WHIPSTER, *sub.* a term of contempt for a novice, Oth. v. 2. 242.

WHIPSTOCK, *sub.* handle of a whip, Per. ii. 2. 51.

WHIR, *v.i.* to hurry away, Per. iv. 1. 20.

WHIST, *adj.* still, Temp. i. 2. 378.

WHISTLE, WORTH THE, worth notice, regard. *Comp.* the proverb, 'It's a poor dog that is not worth the whist-ling', K. Lear, iv. 2. 29.

WHISTLE HER OFF, dismiss the hawk from the fist, Oth. iii. 3. 262.

WHITE, *sub.* the bull's-eye in a target, Tam. of Shrew, v. 2. 187.

WHITE-LIVERED, *adj.* cowardly, Rich. III. iv. 4. 465. *Comp.* LILY-LIVERED.

WHITING-TIME, *sub.* bleaching-time, Merry Wives of W. iii. 3. 141.

WHITSTER, *sub.* a bleacher, Merry Wives of W. iii. 3. 15.

WHITTLE, *sub.* a clasp-knife, Tim. of Ath. v. 1. 185.

WHOOBUB, *sub.* hubbub, Wint. Tale, iv. 3. 631.

WIDE, *adv.* distracted, astray, Much Ado, iv. 1. 62; K. Lear, iv. 7. 50.

WIGHTLY [O. Ed. WHITELY], *adj.* nimble, L.'s L.'s L. iii. 1. 206.

WILD, *sub.* weald, 1 Hen. IV. ii. 1. 60.

WILDERNESS, *sub.* wideness, Meas. for Meas. iii. 1. 140.

WILD MARE, TO RIDE THE, to play at see-saw, 2 Hen. IV. ii. 4. 268.

WILDNESS, *sub.* distraction, Ham. iii. 1. 40.

WILFUL-BLAME, wilfully incurring blame, 1 Hen. IV. iii. 1. 176.

WIMPLED, *pt.p.* blindfolded, L.'s L.'s L. iii. 1. 189. ('Wimple' was a kerchief, covering the head and neck.)

WIND, *sub.* 'have the wind of' = have the advantage of, Tit. Andr. iv. 2. 134; 'allow the wind', to give air, All's Well, v. 2. 10.

WIND, *v.i.* to scent, Tit. Andr. iv. 1. 97; to blow, Much Ado, i. 1. 251; to manage, 1 Hen. IV. iv. 1. 109.

WINDGALLS, *sub.* swellings in the legs of a horse, Tam. of Shrew, iii. 2. 54.

WINDLASS, *sub.* a circuit, Ham. ii. 1. 65.

WINDOW, *pt.p.* seated in a window, Ant. & Cleo. iv. 12. 72.

WINDOW-BARS, *sub.* lattice-like embroidery, worn by women across the breast, Tim. of Ath. iv. 3. 117.

WINDOWED, *adj.* full of holes, K. Lear, iii. 4. 31.

WINDRING, *pr.p.* winding, Temp. iv. 1. 128.

WINK, *sub.* sleep, Temp. ii. 1. 250; to be blind, to be in the dark, Com. of Err. iii. 2. 58.

WINKING, *pr.p.* blind, Cymb. ii. 4. 89.

WINNOWED, *adj.* wise, sensible, Ham. v. 2. 201.

WINTER-GROUND, *v.t.* to protect a plant from the cold by covering it up with straw, Cymb. iv. 2. 229.

WIPE, *sub.* a brand, mark of disgrace, Lucrece, 537.

WISE-WOMAN, *sub.* a witch, Merry Wives of W. iv. 5. 59; Twelfth Night, iii. 4. 116.

WISP OF STRAW, *sub.* the badge of a scold, 3 Hen. VI. ii. 2. 144.

WISTLY, *adj.* wistfully, Rich. II. v. 4. 7; Ven. & Ad. 343.

WITCH, *sub.* a wizard, Cymb. i. 6. 166.

WITH, *prep.* by, being greeted with, Macb. iii. 6. 40; Ant. & Cleo. v. 2. 170.

WITH HIMSELF = in possession of his faculties, Tit. Andr. i. 1. 368.

WITHAL, COULD NOT DO = I could not help it, Mer. of Ven. iii. 4. 72.

WITHOUT, *adv.* except, Two Gent. of Ver. ii. 1. 38.

WITTOL, *sub.* a contented cuckold, Merry Wives of W. ii. 2. 317.

WITTOLLY, *adj.* wittol-like, Merry Wives of W. ii. 2. 288.

WOMAN, *v.t.* 'woman me to it' = make me show my woman's weakness, All's Well, iii. 2. 53.

WOMAN'D, *adj.* accompanied by a woman, Oth. iii. 4. 194.

WOMAN-QUELLER, *sub.* a murderer of woman, 2 Hen. IV. ii. 1. 60.

WOMAN-TIRED, *adj.* henpecked, Wint. Tale, ii. 3. 74. *Comp.* TO TIRE.

WOMB, *v.t.* to enclose, Wint. Tale, iv. 3. 503.

WOMBY, *adj.* hollow, Hen. V. ii. 4. 124.

WONDERED, *pt.p.* wonder-working, Temp. iv. 1. 123.

WOO, *v.t.* to solicit, Per. v. 1. 174.

WOOD, *adj.* mad, Mid. N. Dr. ii. 1. 192; 1 Hen. VI. iv. 7. 35; Ven. & Ad. 740.

WOODCOCK, *sub.* a simpleton, Tam. of Shrew, i. 2. 164.

WOODEN THING, 'an awkward business, not likely to succeed' [Steevens], 1 Hen. VI. v. 3. 89.

WOODMAN, *sub.* a wencher, Meas. for Meas. iv. 3. 174.

WOOLLEN, IN THE, between blankets, Much Ado, ii. 1. 33.

WOOLWARD, TO GO, to wear wool instead of linen next the skin, as a penance, L.'s L.'s L. v. 2. 716.

WORD, *v.t.* to represent, Cymb. i. 4. 17; to fool with words, Ant. & Cleo. v. 2. 190.

WORK, *sub.* a fortification, Hen. VIII. v. 4. 63; Oth. iii. 2. 3.

WORKY-DAY, *adj.* common, Ant. & Cleo. i. 2. 57. *Comp.* WORKING-DAY, As You Like It, i. 3. 12.

WORLD, *sub.* 'to go to the world' = to be married, Much Ado, ii. 1. 332; All's Well, i. 3. 37; 'woman of the world' = married woman, As You Like It, v. 3. 5; 'a world to see' = a wonder to see, Much Ado, iii. 5. 38; Tam. of Shrew, ii. 1. 305; the microcosm, Lov. Comp. 7; K. Lear, iii. 1. 10.

WORM, *sub.* a serpent, Meas. for Meas. iii. 1. 17; Macb. iii. 4. 29; a creature, Temp. iii. 1. 31; Cymb. iii. 4. 37 (the mole); Merry Wives of W. v. 5. 89.

WRANGLER, *sub.* an adversary, a tennis term, Hen. V. i. 2. 264.

WREAK, *sub.* vengeance, Coriol. iv. 5. 91; to revenge, Rom. & Jul. iii. 5. 102.

WREAKFUL, *adj.* revengeful, Tim. of Ath. iv. 3. 230.

WREST, *sub.* a tuning key, Troil. & Cres. iii. 3. 23.

WRETCH, *sub.* a term of endearment, Rom. & Jul. i. 3. 44; Oth. iii. 3. 90; Ant. & Cleo. v. 2. 305.

WRING, *v.t.* to writhe, Much Ado, v. 1. 28.

WRINGING, *sub.* torture, Hen. V. iv. 1. 256.

WRIT = wrote, claimed, All's Well, ii. 3. 67.

WRITHLED, *pt.p.* wrinkled, 1 Hen. VI. ii. 3. 23.

WRY, *v.i.* to swerve, Cymb. v. 1. 5.

YARE, *adj.* ready, nimble, active, Temp. v. 1. 224; Twelfth Night, iii. 4. 248.

YARELY, *adv.* readily, briskly, Temp. i. 1. 4; Ant. & Cleo. ii. 2. 219.

YAW, *v.t.* to move unsteadily as a ship which does not answer the helm, Ham. v. 2. 121.

YEAR, *sub.* years, Meas. for Meas. ii. 1. 260.

YEARN, *v.t.* to grieve, vex, Merry Wives of W. iii. 5. 45; Hen. V. iv. 3. 26; *v.i.* Jul. Cæs. ii. 2. 129.

YELLOW, *adj.* emblem of jealousy, Wint. Tale, ii. 3. 106.

YELLOWNESS, *sub.* jealousy, Merry Wives of W. i. 3. 109.

YELLOWS, *sub.* jaundice in horses, Tam. of Shrew, iii. 2. 55.

YERK, *v.t.* to lash out, to strike quickly, Hen. V. iv. 7. 84; Oth. i. 2. 5.

YESTY, *adj.* foaming, frothy, Macb. iv. 1. 53; Ham. v. 2. 199.

YOUNG, *adj.* recent, Hen. VIII. iii. 2. 47.

YOUNKER, *sub.* a stripling, 1 Hen. IV. iii. 3. 91; 3 Hen. VI. ii. 1. 24.

ZANY, *sub.* a buffoon, L.'s L.'s L. v. 2. 464; Twelfth Night, i. 5. 95.

SHAKESPEARE'S PLAYS

IN THEIR HISTORICAL ORDER

	Malone (d. 1812) 1821.	Furnivall 1877.	Modern Critics.		
1588		Love's L. L.		1588	
1589	{ 1 Hen. VI	Titus Andr.		} 1589	
		Com. of E.			
1590		Mid. N. D.	Love's L. L.	c. 1590	
1591	2 Hen. VI	Two Gent.	Com. of E.	c. 1591	
	3 Hen. VI				
	Two Gent.				
1592	{ Com. of E.	1 Hen. VI	Two Gent.	c. 1592	Experiment.
		Rom. & Jul.	1 Hen. VI	1592	
			2 Hen. VI	1592?	
			3 Hen. VI	1592?	
1593	Rich. II	2 Hen. VI	Rich. III	c. 1593	
	Rich. III	3 Hen. VI	Rom. & Jul.	c. 1593	
		Rich. II			
1594	Love's L. L.	Rich. III	Tit. Andr.	1594	Development.
	Merch. of V.		Rich. II	c. 1594	
	Mid. N. D.		Mid. N. D.	c. 1594	
			John	c. 1594	
1595		John	Merch. of V.	c. 1595	
1596	Tam. Sh.	Merch. of V.	Tam. Sh.	c. 1596	
	Rom. & Jul.	1 Hen. IV			
	John	Tam. Sh.			
1597	1 Hen. IV	2 Hen. IV	1 Hen. IV	1597?	
1598		M. Wives	2 Hen. IV	1598?	
1599	2 Hen. IV	Hen. V	Hen. V	1599	
	As Y. L.	Much Ado	M. Wives	1599?	
	Hen. V		Much Ado	c. 1599	
			Jul. Cæs.	1599	
1600	Much Ado	As Y. L.	As Y. L.	c. 1600	
	Hamlet		Tw. N.	1600?	
1601	M. Wives	Tw. N.			
		All's W.			
		Jul. Cæs.			
1602	Troilus	Hamlet	All's W.	c. 1602	The Tragedies.
			Troilus	c. 1602	
			Hamlet	c. 1602	
1603	Meas. for M.	Meas. for M.			
	Hen. VIII				
1604	Othello	Othello	Meas. for M.	c. 1604	
			Othello	c. 1604	
1605	Lear	Macbeth	Lear	1605?	
		Lear			
1606	All's W.	Ant. & Cleop.	Macb.	1606?	
	Macb.	Troilus			
1607	Jul. Cæs.	Cor.	Ant. & Cleop.	1607?	
	Tw. N.	Timon			
1608	Ant. & Cleop.	Pericles	Cor.	c. 1608	
			Timon	c. 1608	
			Pericles	c. 1608	
1609	Cymb.				The Romances.
1610	Cor.	Temp.	Cymb.	1610?	
	Timon		Wint. Tale	1610?	
1611	Wint. Tale	Cymb.	Temp.	1611?	
	Temp.	Wint. Tale	Hen. VIII	c. 1611	
1613		Hen. VIII		1613	

(*Titus Andr.* and *Pericles* are not assigned a date by Malone.)

F. MADAN

NOTES ON THE
SEQUENCE OF SHAKESPEARE'S PLAYS

Three representative lists are here printed for comparison: (1) the order suggested by Malone, the first who handled the problem with wide knowledge and with the insight of a scholar, but who lacked much information which we now possess; (2) that adopted from Delius by Furnivall, based to some extent on metrical tests; (3) that of modern critics, so far as the available evidence, when gathered up and carefully considered, leads to definite or probable results.   F. M.

The sources on which scholars draw for their evidence are five in number:—

(1) *The Dates of Performance.* Henslowe's *Diary* records the appearance of 'hary the vj'—i.e. the *First Part of King Henry VI*, as a new play, on March 3, 1592, and of 'titus and ondronicus' on January 23, 1594. John Manningham saw *Twelfth Night* at the Middle Temple on February 2, 1602; the Revels Accounts note court performances of *Othello* at Hallowmas (Nov. 1), 1604, *Measure for Measure* on December 26, 1604, and *The Tempest* at Hallowmas, 1611. Simon Forman saw *Macbeth* on April 20, 1610, *The Winter's Tale* on May 15, 1611, and *Cymbeline* at some intermediate date. A very important date usually ignored is the evidence of a German, Thomas Platter, who saw a play of *Julius Caesar* in London on September 21, 1599, followed by a jig (*Anglia*, Band 22, pp. 456–64); there can be little doubt that this was Shakespeare's play. But even a definite date such as that of the first performance of *Titus Andronicus* causes misgivings. If the text which has come down to us is Shakespeare's, it looks like poor prentice-work—an exaggerated copy of the style of Kyd, such as might have been written at the outset of his career; yet it is difficult to believe that the author of *Richard III* and *Romeo and Juliet* failed completely as an artist, but at once recovered himself with *Richard II*.

(2) *Literary allusions.* The most important is Francis Meres's list in *Palladis Tamia*, 1598, of the plays then written—*The Two Gentlemen of Verona*, *The Comedy of Errors*, *Love's Labour's Lost*, [*Love's Labour Won*,] *A Midsummer Night's Dream*, *The Merchant of Venice*, *Richard II*, *Richard III*, *Henry IV*, *King John*, *Titus Andronicus*, and *Romeo and Juliet*. The famous note of Gabriel Harvey, suggesting that he had seen Shakespeare's *Hamlet* in 1598, raises a problem instead of solving it.

(3) *Allusions in the Plays.* Unfortunately these are few in number, and more often than not prove deceptive. But a clear example is the allusion to Essex in Ireland in the chorus before the last act of *King Henry V*, which fixes the date of the performance between April 15 and September 28, 1599.

(4) *The Date of Publication.* This always gives a downward limit and is sometimes helpful. Thus the licensing of *Troilus and Cressida* for publication in 1603, though no edition earlier than 1609 is now known, is a valuable clue.

(5) *Style and Versification.* These are dangerous tests, but certain broad characteristics of Shakespeare's art emerge from them if they are tactfully used. The comparative frequency of rhyme and of prose is usually an indication of early and late work respectively; so too the change in modulating blank verse from a form so stereotyped at first that it tends to the couplet, to the perfect freedom of the romantic plays. Thus it is a fact of value to note that Shakespeare's use of a weakly stressed ending to the line, carrying over the rhythm to the line which follows, begins as a slight experiment in *Macbeth*, where two lines (II. i. 12, IV. iii. 22) end with 'and'. Again, a blind adherence to the rhyme test would make the *Midsummer Night's Dream* Shakespeare's earliest play; but a sober criticism will note that the fairy setting gave scope for purely poetic writing and justified a lavish use of rhyme.

The chronology of Shakespeare's plays is far from certain, and a heavy proportion of the dates assigned to them is conjectural. Perhaps what may be called a working order has been established, but even then we cannot be certain that the texts handed down to us are those of the first performance. *Love's Labour's Lost* was stated on the title-page of the 1598 Quarto to have been 'Newly corrected and augmented *By W. Shakespere*' and the text exhibits clear traces of revision.

PERCY SIMPSON